READER'S DIGEST ENCYCLOPAEDIA OF
GARDEN PLANTS AND FLOWERS

Edited and designed by The Reader's Digest Association, London

ROY HAY, MBE, VMH (CONSULTANT EDITOR)
KENNETH A. BECKETT (TECHNICAL ADVISER)

Major contributors

Richard C. Barnard, MA (For) Cantab
Alan Bloom, VMH
Audrey V. Brooks, BSc, MIBiol
P. R. Chapman, ARPS
D. L. Clarke, BA, FLS, VMH
O. J. Clayton
John S. Coles, NDH (Hons), MIBiol
H. S. J. Crane, AH, RHS
S. Millar Gault, MBE, FLS, VMH
Richard Gorer
Madge Green
Frank E. Griggs, TD
S. J. Grubb
Denis Hardwicke
Keith M. Harris, BSc
P. Francis Hunt, MSc
H. Raymond Jeffs
Reginald Kaye
Roy Lancaster
M. E. Leeburn

David McClintock
E. W. Macdonald
F. R. McQuown, MA, FLS
Margaret J. Martin, MSc, ARIC
A. F. Mitchell, BA, BAg (For), VMH
H. F. Newsom
G. E. Nicholson
S. A. Pearce, MBE, AH, RHS, FInstPA (late)
Brigadier C. E. Lucas Phillips, OBE, MC
James Platt
F. G. Potter, AH, RHS
G. D. Rowley
H. C. Russell, ARAeS (late)
Peter J. Seabrook, NDH
Fred Shepherd
Peter Temple, LRIBA, MInstRA, FRSA
L. G. Turner
Ian P. C. Unwin
Michael Upward
Humphrey James Welch

W. John Wright, BSc (Hort), NDH (Hons)

Artists and Photographers

Bernard Alfieri
H. R. Allen, ARCA
E. B. Anderson, MSc, VMH (late)
Heather Angel, MSc
D. C. Arminson
A–Z Botanical Collection Ltd
Norman Barber
Richard C. Barnard, MA (For) Cantab
H. E. Bawden
Kenneth A. Beckett
Arthur Boarder
Pamela Booth, FRPS
Leonora Box
Pat Brindley

Janet Browne Associates
Leonard W. Brummitt
H. Bruty, BEM, AH, RHS
Camera Press
P. R. Chapman, ARPS
John K. B. Cowley, NDH
Ernest Crowson, AIIP, FRPS
J. G. Elliott
Roy Elliott, ARPS
Valerie Finnis
H. Castle Fletcher, BSc
Flora-bild
Floraprint Ltd
Christine Foord (NHPA)

R. G. Foord (NHPA)
Alan Fox
Neville Fox-Davies
John Gapp
Ian Garrard
P. Gatehouse
Melvyn Gill, ARCA
Roy Grubb
Brian Halliwell
Peter Harris
Eliot Hodgkin
J. C. W. Houghton
J. K. Hulme
David Hutter
George E. Hyde, FRES
Will Ingwersen, VMH
H. Raymond Jeffs
A. C. Jermy
Reginald Kaye
Gillian Kenny
Mervyn S. Kessell
D. Lambert, NDH
Roy Lancaster
H. Langford, ARPS
A. High Lawson
Patricia Ann Lenander
J. L. MacCombe
Peter and Irene Mace
F. R. McQuown, MA, FLS
David K. Mann
John Markham, FRPS, FZS
Hamilton Marshall
Brian Mathew
Elsa M. Megson
Donald F. Merrett
Frank Naylor

H. Newman
G. E. Nicholson
Maurice Nimmo
L. F. Oland, Dip Hort (Wisley)
The Orchid Society of Great Britain
Sheila Orme
Frances Perry, MBE, VMH, FLS
V. Phipps (NHPA)
Portman Picture Library
Ray Procter, AH, RHS
John Rignall
Kenneth Rittener, FRPS
J. Roberts
Gerald Rodway
J. Roger
G. D. Rowley
Royal Danish Horticultural Society
R. V. G. Rundle
H. C. Russell, ARAeS (late)
David Sander
Dieter Schacht
W. Schacht
Kenneth Scowen, FIIP, FRPS
Donald Smith, NDH
Harry Smith
Kathleen Smith, MSIA
Allan McG. Stirling
W. A. Tait
E. Tattersall
Graham Thomas, VMH
Derek Tilley
Tourist Photo Library
Humphrey James Welch
Dennis Woodland, Dip Hort (Wisley)
Elsie Wrigley, ATD, DA (Man)
Ian Yeomans

MANY OTHER PEOPLE AND ORGANISATIONS ASSISTED IN THE PREPARATION
OF THIS ENCYCLOPAEDIA. THE PUBLISHERS ACKNOWLEDGE THE HELP OF THE FOLLOWING:

J. R. McBain Allan, BSc (Hort), NDH; J. C. Allgrove Ltd; Allwood Brothers; *Amateur Gardening*;
Walter Blom & Son Ltd; William Davidson; Dobies of Chester; The Dutch Bulb Council;
East Malling Research Station; *The Field*; Fisons Limited; G. Fuller; *Gardeners Chronicle*;
E. G. Gilbert, NDH; A. Hall, BSc (Dip); R. Hall; J. L. Harkness; D. R. Hunt, MA;
Will Ingwersen, VMH; Rowland Jackman; P. de Jager and Sons Ltd; Gwen L. Key, Dip Hort;
Laxton & Bunyard Nurseries Ltd; T. R. H. Lebar; S. L. Lord, AH, RHS; Brian Mathew;
Paul R. Miles; John Murphy; Notcutts Nurseries Ltd; E. M. Osborn; P. S. Patrick;
Frances Perry, MBE, VMH, FLS; *Popular Gardening*; *Practical Gardening*; Royal Botanic Gardens;
The Royal Horticultural Society; Frank S. Shackel; Sluis and Groot; The Spalding Bulb Company;
E. Stevens; Sutton Seeds; Thompson & Morgan (Ipswich) Ltd; W. J. Unwin Ltd;
D. H. J. Whitwell, NDH, RHS; James Wood, ARCS, DIC; Denis Woodland, Dip Hort (Wisley)

READER'S DIGEST ENCYCLOPAEDIA OF

GARDEN PLANTS AND FLOWERS

The Reader's Digest Association Limited
London

CONTENTS

PREFACE

This encyclopaedia contains detailed descriptions of
more than 3000 plants, all of which can be grown in Great Britain.
It tells how to identify, cultivate and propagate them, and how to combat
pests and diseases. The plants have been selected for the appeal of their
flowers, foliage or fruits, the ease with which they can be
cultivated and their availability.

HOW PLANTS ARE NAMED

For the gardener, the naming of a plant begins with its genus—roughly the equivalent of a surname. In the system of plant classification which is followed by botanists, a genus (pl. genera) is a group of plants which are physically similar or are closely related through natural evolution and breeding.

A genus is made up of a number of species, which may contain a number of varieties, and several related genera again make up a family.

The name of the plant's genus is followed by that of its species. Thus *Aesculus pavia* belongs to the genus *Aesculus* and to the species *pavia*.

Many of the better known genera also have common or popular names. *Aesculus* is popularly known as horse chestnut. The names of plants are always given in Latin, which is an internationally recognised scientific language.

Species and varieties. Where a species varies, and distinct forms are known, an extra or varietal name is added. Varieties which occur naturally are true or botanical varieties. They, too, are named in Latin and written in italics, for example *Aesculus pavia humilis*.

Varieties which arise in cultivation are known as cultivated varieties (or cultivars); these are distinguished from naturally occurring varieties by having the varietal name written in ordinary type, inside single quotation marks—for example *Aesculus hippocastanum* 'Baumannii'.

Hybrids. The interbreeding of two species belonging to the same genus results in a cross, usually showing characteristics from both parents. Such a plant is given a Latin name, prefixed by a multiplication sign. *Aesculus* × *carnea* is a hybrid species between *Aesculus hippocastanum* and *Aesculus pavia*.

A hybrid name can also be used as a grex or collective name, and covers all the progeny of a particular cross. In particular, the collective or grex name concept is given to seedlings of orchid hybrids before the best seedlings are named separately.

It is also possible for two species belonging to different, but related, genera to be crossed, to produce a hybrid genus. In this case, the multiplication sign precedes the genus name, as for example in × *Cupressocyparis*, a hybrid genus between *Cupressus macrocarpa* and *Chamaecyparis nootkatensis*.

NAME CHANGES AND SYNONYMS

The basic principles, which attempt to create a stable system of naming, are set out in The International Code of Botanical Nomenclature and The International Code of Nomenclature for Cultivated Plants. These have been followed in the encyclopaedia. Botanists frequently, in the light of further research, change the name of a species, and sometimes place it in a different genus. Such changes, however, are slow in becoming accepted.

Where name changes have occurred comparatively recently, the older and more commonly accepted names have been used, and reference is made to the latest, botanically correct name. For example, *Alyssum maritimum* is currently classified as *Lobularia maritima*, but is here described under *Alyssum*.

ORDER OF PLANT NAMES IN THE ENCYCLOPAEDIA

Aesculus	genus name
Horse chestnut	common name
Hippocastanaceae	family name
Aesculus pavia	species
Aesculus pavia humilis	natural variety
Aesculus hippocastanum 'Baumannii'	cultivated variety
Aesculus × *carnea*	hybrid

It also happens that botanists rename species either within a genus or within one closely related. In such cases, the correct name is used, and the older name is given as a synonym as in *Abies procera*, syn. *Abies nobilis*, or *Aechmea chantinii*, syn. *Billbergia chantinii*.

NUMBER OF SPECIES

Botanists are constantly revising their conception of the number of species within a genus. In this encyclopaedia, the conclusions set out in the seventh edition of *A Dictionary of Flowering Plants and Ferns*, by J. C. Willis, have been followed. This work lists every known plant genus with its latest accepted number of species.

PLANT DESCRIPTIONS

The genera described are listed under their Latin botanical names, in alphabetical order. Fruits, vegetables and herbs are described under their common names.

Some genera contain only species of one type. In *Abelia*, for instance, all the species are shrubs. Other genera include various types of plants, such as annuals, biennials, shrubs and succulents. *Euphorbia* is an example of this. The types of plants as well as their hardiness are made clear in the introduction to each entry.

The name of a species is followed, where applicable, by the synonym and common name.

The geographical areas refer to the countries where the species are found growing wild, or from where they were first introduced into cultivation in Great Britain.

Height and spread. The height given is that which a mature plant can be expected to reach under ideal growing conditions. In the case of hardy trees and shrubs, the height and spread are those achieved after 20 years of growth in ideal conditions.

For rock garden and alpine plants, the term 'spread' indicates the amount of surface growth a plant will make at maturity.

Success in growing any plant, however, depends very much on the soil and position, and the care given during the formative years.

Planting distances for herbaceous plants, half-hardy annuals and vegetables indicate the growing space plants require under normal conditions. Where hardy annuals and biennials are sown or planted in the open ground, 'spacing' refers to the distance that should be left between the plants after thinning out the seedlings.

FLOWERS

Unless otherwise stated, flowers are single—that is, they have only one ring (or whorl) of petals. Where no flower size is indicated for a species or variety, this is because the flowers are insignificant, and the plant is generally grown for a different purpose.

The fruits of plants grown for flower or foliage are usually inedible.

CULTIVATION

Most plants thrive in ordinary garden soil—one that is neither too acid nor too alkaline, with a pH content between 5 and 7. It should also contain a reasonable amount of humus-forming material, such as peat, hop manure or garden compost. Where no mention is made of staking and/or dead-heading, these are normally unnecessary.

Definite times of the year are given for setting out hardy plants in their permanent positions. These times refer to nurserymen's stock lifted from the open ground. However, garden centres offer plants already established in containers, and these may be planted at any time of the year. During severe frosts, container-grown plants should be kept in a frost-free shed or heeled in. In periods of drought, ensure that the plants are kept well watered after planting out.

Great climatic variations occur in the British Isles, and it is impossible to be dogmatic about the exact timing of gardening operations, such as seed sowing and planting. The sowing time between Cornwall and the north-east of England or the north of Scotland may vary by as much as a month. The sowing and planting times given are based on the climate in southern England. If severe weather is experienced during early spring, it is wise to delay planting or sowing until the ground has warmed up.

Greenhouse plants. The suggested temperatures for greenhouse and house plants should be adhered to as closely as possible. Unless otherwise stated, these are winter day and night minimum temperatures, below which plants may suffer. Temperatures can rise above these levels by as much as 18–24°C (33–44°F) on summer days without harm to plants, as long as adequate ventilation and shading are provided.

PROPAGATION AND PRUNING

Under each plant entry, information is given about the methods and timing for propagation and pruning. More detailed advice is given, with illustrations, in the chapters beginning on pp. 770 and 782.

PESTS AND DISEASES

The troubles which affect plants are fully described under each genus. Although some pests and diseases occur in almost every garden in every season, many more are only occasionally a nuisance, or they may be restricted to limited areas. All pests and diseases printed in small capitals, as for example APHIDS or GREY MOULD, are further described in the separate chapter beginning on p. 746. In this section, too, control measures are indicated.

ILLUSTRATIONS

More than 2500 different plants are illustrated in the encyclopaedia. The colours of a plant can sometimes vary slightly, according to the time of the day, the intensity of light or the contrast of background. Soils, according to their acidity or alkalinity, also play a part in the colour intensity of a flower.

The black-and-white illustrations are intended to give an overall idea of the growth habit of a mature plant typical of its genus. It may be upright, prostrate, round-headed or bushy. Where the habits of species within a genus differ widely, more drawings are added to show the range of variability.

Abelia

Caprifoliaceae

ABELIA FLORIBUNDA

Abies

Silver fir. *Pinaceae*

ABIES GRANDIS · ABIES KOREANA

A genus of 30 species of semi-evergreen or deciduous shrubs. They are easily grown, bushy plants, hardy in the south and west of Britain; elsewhere they require protection and are best grown as wall shrubs. The tubular or funnel-shaped flowers are borne on the lateral shoots.

A. floribunda. Mexico. Height up to 5 ft (in Cornwall up to 10 ft); spread 4 ft. A tender evergreen shrub requiring wall protection even in mild areas. The glossy mid to deep green leaves are broadly ovate. Narrowly tubular, bright magenta-rose flowers, 1½ in. long, are freely produced from May to July.

A. × grandiflora. Garden origin. Height 5–6 ft; spread 3–4 ft. A semi-evergreen hardy hybrid of spreading habit. It has bright green, ovate-pointed leaves. Pink and white, slightly fragrant and tubular flowers, about 1 in. long, are abundantly borne from July to October.

A. schumannii. Central China. Height up to 8 ft; spread 6–7 ft. A deciduous species of bushy habit, with ovate, dark green leaves. The tubular lilac-pink flowers, 1 in. long, continue in profusion from June to September. The species is slightly tender, and the top growths may be frosted, but the shrub generally recovers.

A. triflora. Himalayas. Height up to 15 ft; spread up to 8 ft. A hardy deciduous shrub or small tree of upright and bushy habit, with dull green lanceolate leaves. Pale pink, sweetly scented, tubular flowers, ¾ in. long, appear in June.

Cultivation. Plant in September and October or in March and April in any ordinary garden soil and in a sunny position, protected from cold winds.

Propagation. Take cuttings, 3–4 in. long, of the current season's wood in July. Insert three or four cuttings in a 3 in. pot of equal parts (by volume) peat and sand; root the cuttings at a bottom heat of 16–18°C (61–64°F), or place the pots in a cold frame. The cuttings should be ready for planting out the following spring.

Pruning. No regular pruning is required. Overgrown shoots may be thinned out occasionally after flowering to encourage new growth. Old and thin wood of evergreen species should be removed after flowering, and of deciduous species in February.

Aaron's beard: see *Hypericum calycinum*

A genus of 50 species of evergreen coniferous trees, native to the northern temperate regions. Nearly all are hardy, but a few of the cultivated species start into growth early in the year and may be damaged by late spring frosts.

These trees are usually conical in shape with attractive needle-like foliage. Most species flower in Great Britain and later bear ovoid cones, generally on the topmost branches only. They ripen on the trees during the first season and disintegrate in the autumn, leaving only a spike and a baseplate.

The species described are all useful as background trees; several make fine specimen trees, and the small-growing *A. koreana* may be grown in a shrub border. The genus contains few dwarf forms, but in several species slow-growing forms have been selected and are suitable for growing on large rock gardens.

See also CONIFERS.

A. balsamea. N.E. America. Height 25 ft; spread 6–8 ft. This species is seldom cultivated, but has given rise to the hardy, dwarf form 'Hudsonia' (height up to 3 ft; spread 4 ft). A round-topped, spreading bush with densely set foliage that is glossy mid-green and with two white bands on the undersides of the leaves.

'Nana' is a small, globe-shaped, slow-growing bush, with the leaves arranged almost radially. 'Prostrata' has flat foliage in two comb-like rows.

A. bracteata (Santa Lucia fir). California. Height 50 ft; spread 10 ft. This species is tender when young and requires protection against late spring frosts until it is about 4 ft tall. The crown is conic with a narrow-spired top; the lower branches droop. Dark green leaves, that are hard and spine-tipped, have bright silver bands beneath. The 3–4 in. long, ovoid cones are remarkable for the 2 in. long protruding spines of the bracts which bear drops of resin.

A. concolor (white fir). Mid-California, Mexico. Height 35 ft; spread 6–9 ft. A species of variable growth; as a young tree it is symmetrical, branched in whorls with an open, rather sparse conic crown. The bark is smooth, often with resin-blisters, and the 2 in. long, sparse grey-green leaves stand almost vertically from the shoots. The green and purple cylindrical cones, up to 5 in. long, are seldom seen.

Abelia × grandiflora

Abies balsamea 'Hudsonia'

Abies koreana (immature cones)

A. c. lowiana (Low's white fir) is a northern form, similar to *A. grandis,* but distinguished by the early development of deeply fissured, corky bark that is brown or nearly black. The long, deep green leaves lie flat in northern forms; in southern forms they are blue-grey and curve upwards. This variety, which is usually a taller, stronger-growing tree than the species, has a narrow, columnar or regularly conic crown.

'Violacea' is smaller and slower-growing than the type species; the young leaves are pale blue-grey, darkening slightly with age.

A. delavayi forrestii: see *A. forrestii*

A. forrestii. S.W. China. Height 50 ft; spread 15 ft. This species is botanically classified as *A. delavayi forrestii.* It is a stiff, formal tree with ascending branches; in ideal conditions it grows as much as 3 ft annually. The stout, bright red or orange shoots are almost hidden by dense dark green leaves that are bright silver on the undersides. Rich purple-blue cones, which are $3\frac{1}{2}$ in. long and $1\frac{3}{4}$ in. wide, with slightly protruding bracts, stand up from the upper branches in lines.

This species grows best in the cooler areas of the north and west, and is usually unreliable on frosty sites in the south and east.

A. grandis (grand fir). British Columbia to California. Height 65 ft; spread 20 ft. A vigorous, shapely species. The young bark, which is smooth and shiny with resin-blisters, turns dull grey with age and develops patches of small, shallowly fissured squares. The shiny, bright green leaves, with two silver bands beneath, are laid flat on either side of the olive-brown shoots. Cones, 2–4 in. long, are sometimes borne.

This species is unsuitable for exposed sites; tall trees tend to lose the top of their crowns, although they quickly grow again, often with five or six leading shoots.

A. homolepis (Nikko fir). Japan. Height 25 ft; spread 10–15 ft. A sturdy, hardy tree of moderate growth, suitable for dry areas susceptible to spring frosts. The crown soon becomes broadly columnar and in time may spread to over 30 ft. The bark is an unusual pink-brown and peels off in fine shreds. The growth buds are globular, white and resinous, the shoots a smooth, shiny pink-buff. Broad, pale green leaves, with bright silver bands beneath, lie thickly on either side of the shoots. Purple cones, 4 in. long and $1\frac{1}{2}$ in. wide, with white resin drops, may be borne quite low on the tree.

A. koreana (Korean fir). Korea. Height 15 ft; spread 10 ft. A small tree or bush, with small, rather sparse dark green leaves having bright silver undersides. It is hardy, but late frosts may destroy the new shoots. The species is chiefly grown for the crimson, pink or green female flowers which are freely borne in May on plants only 5 ft high; they stand in upright lines along the shoots. The male flowers are globular, red-brown opening to yellow, and clustered among the leaves. Blue-green, 3 in. long cones with brown bracts are later produced.

A. nobilis: see *A. procera*

A. nordmanniana (Caucasian fir). Caucasus, Asia Minor. Height 50 ft; spread 15 ft. This species has bright green and white-banded leaves, densely set and lying forwards to cover the shoots. The 6 in. long, dark brown cylindrical cones are borne near the top of mature trees. The species thrives in the west and north, but also grows well, although more slowly, in other parts of the country.

A. procera, syn. *A. nobilis* (noble fir). Washington, California. Height 20–45 ft; spread 8–10 ft. A fine specimen tree, symmetrical when young, wind-tolerant and suitable for high altitudes. Growth is about 12 in. a year in western areas, less elsewhere. The bark of mature trees is silvery-grey, deeply fissured with smooth patches and areas of shallow square plates. The blue-grey foliage varies in brightness; in the form 'Glauca' it is almost silver. The leaves are densely borne, the middle ones rising above the shoots and lying forward. Many trees cone when only 20 ft high; the yellow-brown cones are 6–10 in. long with points on the sharply down-pressed bracts.

Cultivation. Young plants grow well in most well-drained soils, but mature trees require a deep, slightly acid soil, moist but well drained. *A. grandis* will tolerate limestone and chalk soils, provided there is a shallow acid surface soil. In general, avoid exposed positions and entirely alkaline soils. Young trees should preferably be no more than 12 in. high and must have a good, single leading shoot. Plant in November on light soils, in April on wet or heavy soils, preferably in lightly shaded positions which will give protection from late spring frosts.

Maintain a weed-free root-run about a yard across for several years. Thereafter apply a deep mulch and an annual dressing of balanced fertiliser in early May.

Propagation. The species are best raised from seed. Sow in pans of John Innes seed compost in a cold frame in February, or broadcast in outdoor seed beds in March. Prick out the seedlings into a nursery bed, when large enough to handle, and grow on for two to four years before planting out in permanent positions.

Pruning. It is essential to maintain a single dominant leading shoot. If forking or competing side-shoots occur, the shoot further from the main axis must be removed flush with the trunk in March or April. With equal forking, cut out either shoot.

Pests. ADELGIDS, particularly the silver fir adelgid, suck sap and produce tufts of white waxy wool on leaves and branches.

Diseases. A fungus infection causes DIE-BACK; the leaves redden, then turn dark brown and shrivel, often remaining attached to the dead shoots for up to a year after dying.

RUST, due to a number of different fungi, shows as small white blisters on the leaves. One of these rust fungi also causes WITCHES BROOMS.

Abies procera (mature cone)

Abies procera (male catkins)

Abutilon × *hybridum*

Abutilon

Malvaceae

A genus of more than 100 species of half-hardy and tender annuals, perennials, evergreen shrubs and small trees. They generally require greenhouse treatment, but as pot plants they may be used for summer bedding, and a few species can be grown as wall shrubs in sheltered areas in the south and west of Great Britain.

The flowers are widely funnel-shaped; they are generally borne singly from the leaf axils, but occasionally in small clusters.

ABUTILON × HYBRIDUM   ABUTILON VITIFOLIUM

A. × hybridum. Garden origin. Height 6–8 ft; spread 4–6 ft in a greenhouse border; as a pot plant, 2–4 ft high. This hybrid between *A. darwinii* and *A. striatum* is a well-branched shrub with mid-green palmate leaves, three to five-lobed. The pendent flowers, in shades of yellow, orange and red, are 1½ in. long and produced from May to October.

Varieties include: 'Ashford Red', salmon-red; 'Boule de Neige', pure white with orange stamens; 'Canary Bird', yellow; and 'Golden Fleece', rich yellow. 'Savitzii' has small leaves, heavily variegated with white margins.

A. megapotamicum. Brazil. Height and spread 6–8 ft; as a pot plant, 3–4 ft. A slender-stemmed, half-hardy, spreading shrub; the bright green leaves are ovate, toothed and slender-pointed, sometimes three-lobed. The conspicuous pendent flowers appear from May to October. They have yellow petals and red calyces, and are 1½ in. long. 'Variegatum' has leaves mottled with yellow. The species may be grown outdoors in sheltered areas.

A. × milleri. Garden origin. Height and spread 6–8 ft in a greenhouse border; as a pot plant, height 3–4 ft. A hybrid similar to *A. megapotamicum,* but even more tender; it bears large leaves that are mottled with yellow. Orange-yellow flowers, 1½ in. long and with red veins, appear from May to October.

A. striatum. Brazil. Height 6 ft or more; spread up to 4 ft in the greenhouse border; height as a pot plant, 2–4 ft. A tender, slender shrub with palmate mid to deep green leaves that have three to five serrated lobes. The 1½ in. long flowers are orange with crimson veins and open from May to October. The variety 'Thompsonii', sometimes listed as *A. thompsonii,* has slightly smaller leaves, heavily mottled with yellow.

A. thompsonii: see *A. striatum*

A. vitifolium. Chile. Height 8 ft or more; spread 5 ft or more. This near-hardy species is suitable as a wall shrub in all but the coldest areas. It survives the winter in most areas, but only attains full shrubby proportions in the south and west; elsewhere it makes a tall thin shrub and tends to be short-lived. The palmate, three or five-lobed leaves are covered with short white hairs. Stalked, axillary clusters of mauve or lavender flowers are produced from May to October. The flowers, which open out flat when mature, measure 2 in. across.

'Album' is an attractive white form.

Cultivation. Grow abutilons in the greenhouse border or in 6–8 in. pots of John Innes potting compost No. 2. In pots, *A. megapotamicum* and *A. × milleri* will need canes for support. Water freely during the growing season; keep just moist for the rest of the year. Give a dilute liquid feed at 10–14 day intervals from May to September, and shade the glass lightly during the hottest months. Ventilate the greenhouse freely when the temperature exceeds 13°C (55°F).

Pot on annually in March or April if large container plants are required; otherwise discard every two years and replace with new plants grown from cuttings.

A. megapotamicum and *A. vitifolium* grow outdoors in any ordinary, well-drained garden soil. They do best in sun, but will succeed in partial shade provided the site is sheltered and warm. Plant *A. megapotamicum* in May, *A. vitifolium* in May or September, preferably against sheltered and sunny walls; winter protection of both species with straw or bracken is essential in all but the mildest districts.

Propagation. Take 3–4 in. cuttings of half-ripe lateral shoots between May and August, and insert in equal parts (by volume) peat and sand in a propagating frame at a temperature of 15–18°C (59–64°F). Pot the rooted cuttings singly in 3–3½ in. pots of John Innes potting compost No. 1, and grow on until planting out in the border or potting on as necessary. Harden off outdoor plants in a cold frame before planting out in May or September.

All species can also be raised from seeds, but named varieties do not come true; *A. vitifolium* is better grown from seeds, as cuttings are difficult to root. Sow during March or April in pots or pans of seed compost at a temperature of 15–18°C (59–64°F). Prick out the seedlings, when large enough to handle, into boxes and then singly into 3½–4 in. pots of John Innes potting compost No. 1; treat as described for cuttings.

Pruning. In the greenhouse, cut back main stems by half and laterals to 3–4 in. in March. Remove frosted and dead shoots from outdoor plants in March or April.

Pests. Rounded brown scales on the undersides of the leaves and on stems are caused by SCALE INSECTS, particularly soft scale; they make the plants sticky and sooty.

GLASSHOUSE WHITEFLY produce similar symptoms on greenhouse plants.

MEALY BUGS feed on the leaves and stems, producing conspicuous tufts of white waxy wool; the plants are fouled with sticky excretions.

Diseases. Generally trouble-free.

Acacia

Wattle. *Leguminosae*

A genus of about 800 species of tender deciduous and evergreen shrubs and trees. They require little heat but plenty of space, and are suitable for the greenhouse bed or for pot culture. Some species are leafless; what appear to be leaves are modified leaf stalks (phyllodes). The minute petal-less flowers are borne in globular clusters, the numerous long, slender stamens giving the flower heads a fluffy appearance. In sheltered areas, particularly in Cornwall, the Isle of Wight and Isles of Scilly, the species described, all evergreen, can be grown outdoors.

Abutilon megapotamicum

Abutilon vitifolium 'Album'

Acacia armata

Acacia dealbata

Acacia longifolia

Acaena microphylla (fruits)

Acantholimon glumaceum

A. armata. Australia. Height up to 10 ft; spread 4–6 ft. A shrubby species with dark green phyllodes and spine-tipped branches. The yellow flowers, $\frac{1}{3}$ in. wide, are borne singly or in pairs in the crowded upper leaf axils in April.

ACACIA DEALBATA

A. dealbata (mimosa). Australia, Tasmania. Height 25 ft or more; spread 5 ft. The fern-like leaves are grey-green and covered with a silvery down when young. The fragrant yellow flowers are borne in 6–9 in. long panicles from December to March, according to the greenhouse temperature.

A. longifolia. Australia, Tasmania. Height 20 ft; spread 10 ft. A species with willow-like grey-green phyllodes. The flowers open in March; they are golden-yellow and fragrant, and are borne in erect axillary racemes 2–3 in. long.

Cultivation. Plant acacias in the greenhouse border for free-growing specimens, or pot them in John Innes potting compost No. 2 to restrict their size. *A. armata* needs a 6 in. pot; start the other species in 3 in. pots, moving them in stages to 10–12 in. pots or small tubs. Acacias will survive at a winter temperature of 4°C (39°F), but for earlier flowering increase the temperature to 7°C (45°F).

Give the plants plenty of light throughout the year; water moderately in autumn and winter, freely in spring and summer. Provide as much ventilation as possible throughout the year. Pot on as necessary and repot established plants every other year in March. Feed all pot plants with liquid manure at fortnightly intervals from May to August.

Propagation. Sow seeds in April in pans of John Innes seed compost at a temperature of 16°C (61°F). Prick off the seedlings, when large enough to handle, singly into 3 in. pots of John Innes potting compost No. 1; pot on as necessary.

Alternatively, take 2–4 in. cuttings of half-ripe lateral shoots, with a heel, of *A. armata* and *A. longifolia.* Insert the cuttings in equal parts (by volume) peat and sand in a propagating case with a bottom heat of 16–18°C (61–64°F). When rooted, pot the cuttings singly in 3 in. pots and treat as described for seedlings.

Pruning. None is required; large specimens may be cut back up to two-thirds of their height after flowering, to restrict the size.

Pests. Wilting of the foliage may be due to ROOT MEALY BUGS attacking the roots.

TORTRIX CATERPILLARS spin the leaves together and eat the young shoots.

Diseases. Generally trouble-free.

Acacia, common: see *Robinia pseudoacacia*
Acacia, false: see *Robinia pseudoacacia*
Acacia, mophead: see *Robinia pseudoacacia* 'Inermis'
Acacia, rose: see *Robinia hispida*

Acaena
New Zealand burr. *Rosaceae*

A genus of 100 species of hardy herbaceous perennials. The two described are effective ground-cover plants and are also suitable for growing between paving stones and with dwarf bulbs. They form tight mats of densely foliaged branches, with insignificant flowers that appear between June and September and green, red or russet-brown globular burrs from July onwards.

A. buchananii. New Zealand. Height 1–2 in.; spread 24 in. This plant has grey-green pinnate leaves and amber-brown burrs.

A. microphylla. New Zealand. Height 1–2 in.; spread 18–24 in. This species, which is the one most commonly grown, has bronze-green pinnate leaves. The crimson burrs are composed of many small spiny seeds.

Cultivation. Plant between September and March in any well-drained garden soil in full sun. Both species are tolerant of partial shade.

Propagation. Sow the seeds in a cold frame between September and March, and prick off the seedlings into pans or boxes of John Innes potting compost No. 1. Grow them on outdoors and plant out in May. Alternatively, divide and replant between September and March.

Pests and diseases. Generally trouble-free.

Acantholimon
Prickly heath. *Plumbaginaceae*

ACANTHOLIMON VENUSTUM

A genus of 150 species of rather slow-growing hardy evergreen perennials mainly native to desert regions. The species described, which are good rock-garden plants, have mats of needle-like leaves and produce loose spikes of starry flowers between June and September. They can also be grown in alpine houses or cold greenhouses.

A. glumaceum. Armenia. Height 6 in.; spread 12 in. A compact plant with dark green spiky leaves. Mauve to rose-pink flowers, $\frac{1}{2}$ in. across, are borne in 4 in. spikes which each have six to eight florets. This is the most common species and the easiest for general cultivation.

A. venustum. Asia Minor. Height 6–8 in.; spread 12 in. This plant has loose tufts of silver-grey foliage and pale rose-coloured flowers, $\frac{1}{3}$ in. across, appearing well above the leaves. It is variable, less hardy than *A. glumaceum,* and winter damp may retard growth.

Cultivation. Acantholimons thrive on gritty, well-drained soil with limestone chippings added. They are hardy in a well-drained sunny position; in damp districts *A. venustum* is best grown on a dry wall. Plant both species in March or April. Remove the faded flowering stems.

Top dress *A. glumaceum* each March with a mixture of equal parts (by volume) peat, loam and sand, or with John Innes potting compost No. 1; the plants otherwise tend to become leggy and die off in the centre.

For alpine-house or cold-greenhouse cultivation, grow in 8 in. pots or pans using John Innes potting compost No. 1. Repot every second or third year in March.

Propagation. Sow the seeds during February in pans of John Innes seed compost and place in a cold frame. When the seedlings are large enough to handle, prick off into 3 in. pots of equal parts peat and sand. Plant out a year later in March.

Insert 2 in. cuttings of non-flowering basal shoots in July or August in a cold frame containing equal parts (by volume) peat and sand. Pot on rooted cuttings in a mixture of 3 parts John Innes potting compost No. 1 and 1 part limestone chippings (parts by volume) and grow on in a cold frame ready for planting out the following March or April.

Pests and diseases. Generally trouble-free.

Acanthus

Bear's breeches. *Acanthaceae*

ACANTHUS MOLLIS

A genus of 50 species of herbaceous perennials. With their handsome leaves and bold flower spikes, composed of overlapping bracts and tubular flowers, these make striking border plants. The species described are hardy.

A. longifolius. Dalmatia, Balkans. Height 2–3 ft; planting distance 24 in. The long, wavy, dark green leaves are deeply cut. Lilac-coloured flowers appear in 12 in. spikes in June and July.

A. mollis. Italy. Height 3 ft; planting distance 24 in. The ovate, glossy, mid-green leaves have a heart-shaped base and wavy margins. White and purple flowers are produced in 18 in. spikes in July and August. In cultivation, this species is usually represented by the more robust form. *A. m. latifolius.*

A. spinosus. S.E. Europe. Height 3–4 ft; planting distance 3 ft. The dark green lanceolate leaves are deeply cut and spiny. White and purple flowers with green bracts are borne in 18 in. spikes in July and August.

Cultivation. Plant between October and March in a sunny or lightly shaded position in deep, well-drained soil. Leave the plants undisturbed until they become overcrowded. Cut the stems back almost to ground level after flowering.

Propagation. Sow seeds during March in boxes or pans of seed compost in a cold frame. When the seedlings are showing two or three true leaves, prick them out into a nursery bed, 6 in. apart. Grow them on for two years before setting them out in permanent positions.

Take 3 in. long cuttings of the thicker roots between December and February and insert them in boxes of sandy soil in a cold frame. When they are well rooted and showing young leaves, grow the cuttings on outdoors in a nursery bed. Plant out from October onwards.

The plants may also be increased by root division between October and March.

Pests and diseases. Generally trouble-free.

Acer

Maple. *Aceraceae*

A genus of 200 species of generally deciduous trees and shrubs notable for their ornamental foliage. They are widely distributed throughout the Northern Hemisphere, some of the North American and European species being grown chiefly for their timber value. The species native to China and Japan are among the most decorative of foliage trees and shrubs.

The species described here are all deciduous and hardy. The palmate leaves are generally five-lobed and often assume brilliant autumn colours. The inconspicuous flowers are usually green or yellow-green, sometimes flushed with red or purple. They are borne in racemes or corymbs, sometimes pendulous, and are of little decorative value, with the exception of those of *A. platanoides* and *A. circinatum*. The seeds (or keys) have prominent wings. Some species, notably *A. negundo* and *A. rubrum*, have male and female flowers on separate trees.

ACER PALMATUM 'DISSECTUM'

ACER GRISEUM   ACER PSEUDOPLATANUS

A. campestre (hedge maple). Europe, including Great Britain. Height 15–20 ft; spread 10 ft. A round-headed tree with mid-green leaves that are downy beneath; they turn yellow in autumn. This species is common as a hedgerow shrub in the south of Britain.

A. capillipes. Japan. Height and spread 30 ft. A tree of erect habit, with young red growths. The narrow, three-lobed leaves are red-tinted when young; they later become mid-green, and turn crimson in autumn. The green bark is striped white lengthwise.

A. cappadocicum. Caucasus, Asia Minor, Himalayas, China. Height 25–30 ft; spread 10–15 ft.

Acantholimon venustum

Acanthus mollis

Acer davidii

Acer japonicum

Acer griseum

Acer grosseri hersii

Acer pennsylvanicum (trunk)

Acer japonicum 'Aureum'

The five or seven-lobed palmate leaves are glossy dark green and turn rich yellow in autumn. The variety 'Rubrum' has young red leaves; 'Aureum' has young yellow leaves, which turn green and yellow again in autumn.

A. circinatum (vine maple). N.W. America. Height and spread 6–8 ft. The almost circular seven or nine-lobed mid-green leaves turn red and orange in autumn. Sparsely borne clusters of ½ in. wide flowers with purple sepals and white petals appear in April.

A. dasycarpum: see A. saccharinum

A. davidii. Central China. Height 20 ft; spread 10 ft. A variable tree sometimes with horizontal branches. The dark green undivided leaves are tinged red-bronze when unfolding and turn yellow, red and purple in autumn. The grey bark is striated white, particularly if the tree is grown in a semi-shaded position.

A. ginnala. China, Japan. Height up to 20 ft; spread 10 ft. A bushy shrub with three-lobed, slightly heart-shaped, pale to mid-green leaves which turn vivid crimson in autumn. One of the best acers for autumn colour.

A. griseum. S.W. China. Height up to 15 ft; spread 8 ft. A slow-growing tree with mid-green trifoliate leaves which turn red and scarlet in autumn. The buff-coloured bark of the trunk and branches flakes off to reveal light orange-brown bark. This is outstanding for autumn colour.

A. grosseri. China. Height up to 25 ft; spread 15 ft. The three-lobed, glossy, yellow-green leaves assume red autumn tints. The bark is conspicuously striated white. The variety A. g. hersii has longer lateral lobes to the leaves.

A. japonicum. Japan. Height up to 20 ft; spread 8–10 ft. A slow-growing tree of bushy habit with soft green palmate leaves that have seven to eleven lobes; they turn rich crimson in autumn.

Numerous cultivated varieties include the following: 'Aconitifolium', with deeply toothed, long narrow lobes to the leaves, turning crimson in autumn; 'Aureum', slow-growing and with yellow leaves turning rich crimson in autumn; 'Vitifolium', with broad vine-shaped leaves assuming rich crimson tints.

A. lobelii. S. Italy. Height up to 30 ft; spread 10–15 ft. A vigorous tree of narrow columnar habit. The palmate, three to five-lobed leaves are deep green.

A. negundo (box elder). N. America. Height 20–25 ft; spread 15–20 ft. A tree of wide-spreading habit with pinnate pale to mid-green leaves, composed of three to five leaflets. 'Variegatum' is a common white variegated variety. Other forms include 'Aureum', with golden-yellow leaves; A. n. californicum, fast-growing with pink seed-wings and downy young shoots; 'Elegantissimum', with leaves variegated bright yellow.

A. nikoense. Japan. Height up to 15 ft; spread 7–8 ft. A slow-growing tree with mid-green trifoliate leaves on hairy stalks; they assume deep red autumn tints.

A. palmatum (Japanese maple). Japan, Central China. Height up to 15 ft; spread 8 ft. A slow-growing tree of rounded form with five or seven-lobed pale to mid-green leaves.

The Japanese maple is the parent of numerous forms; they all have outstanding autumn colours

and are among the most commonly grown ornamental maples. The following are readily available: 'Atropurpureum' has bronze-red foliage; 'Dissectum' forms a low, rounded bush with finely cut, light green leaves; 'Dissectum Atropurpureum' is similar to 'Dissectum', but with bronze-red leaves.

A. p. heptalobum, syn. A. p. septemlobum 'Elegans' has deeply divided, dark green leaves turning crimson; A. p. heptalobum 'Osakazuki' has mid-green leaves assuming brilliant orange, crimson and scarlet autumn tints; A. p. heptalobum 'Senkaki' has coral-red bark and yellow autumn foliage.

A. pennsylvanicum (snake bark maple, moosewood). Eastern N. America. Height 20 ft; spread 10 ft. A tree of erect habit. The pale to mid-green leaves, with three conspicuous tapering lobes, are pink-tinged on opening; they turn yellow in autumn. The young green bark later becomes striped with white.

A. platanoides (Norway maple). Europe. Height 30–35 ft; spread 15–20 ft. A vigorous tree; the five-lobed leaves are thinner and of a brighter green than those of A. pseudoplatanus, which it resembles. The leaves turn yellow in autumn. Flat heads, 2–3 in. across, of bright green-yellow flowers appear in April before the leaves.

Numerous distinct forms include: 'Crimson King', deep purple-crimson leaves; 'Drummondii', white-margined foliage; 'Laciniatum' (eagle's claw maple), of erect and narrow habit, the lobes of the mid or pale green leaves are reduced to claw-like points; 'Reitenbachii', young red foliage, turning green in summer and deep red in autumn.

A. pseudoplatanus (sycamore). Europe. Height 35 ft; spread 15 ft. A round-headed tree with bright green, five-lobed leaves that turn yellow in autumn. It is suitable for a wind-break, particularly in maritime positions; it seeds itself freely.

Numerous named varieties include: 'Brilliantissimum', slow-growing with shrimp-pink young leaves; 'Corstorphinense', pale yellow young leaves turning golden in summer and finally green; 'Leopoldii', 'Luteo-virens' and 'Simon-Louis Frères' are all forms with leaves mottled with white, cream or cream and purple; 'Worlei' has yellow foliage from spring to July.

A. rubrum (red maple). Eastern N. America. Height 20–25 ft; spread 8–10 ft. A slow-growing, round-headed tree with leaves that are dark green above, blue-white beneath. They are five-lobed, the middle lobe being the longest. Selected forms, such as 'Schlesinger', turn brilliant red in autumn.

A. saccharinum, syn. A. dasycarpum (silver maple). Eastern N. America. Height 25–30 ft; spread 10–15 ft. A fast-growing tree with a round head and pendulous branches. The deeply lobed leaves are bright green above, silvery-white beneath; they occasionally fade to red and yellow.

Named forms include: 'Laciniatum', with deeply divided lobes; 'Pyramidale', syn. 'Fastigiatum', of upright habit.

A. tataricum. S.E. Europe, Asia Minor. Height 15 ft; spread 8 ft. A slow-growing bushy shrub with pale to mid-green, irregularly toothed, broadly ovate leaves which turn yellow in autumn. The wings of the seeds are pale red.

Acer japonicum 'Vitifolium'

Acer palmatum (fruits)

Acer pseudoplatanus

Acer saccharinum

Cultivation. Plant acers from October to March in well-drained but moist and cool soil and in sun or partial shade. *A. rubrum,* although tolerant of chalk, does best in a moist, lime-free soil. The Asiatic species are lime-tolerant; they require protection from cold winds and late frosts followed by early morning sun. Species grown for their autumn colours should be planted in positions sheltered from prevailing autumn winds.
Propagation. Increase the species by seeds sown in October in a cold frame or in open ground.

Named forms, particularly coloured or variegated forms, must be grafted in March on to rootstocks of the type species.
Pruning. None required.
Pests. Most species may be attacked by APHIDS which cause sticky and sooty foliage.

GALL MITES produce conspicuous galls on the leaves, particularly on *A. campestre* and *A. pseudoplatanus.*

RED SPIDER MITES may be troublesome on Japanese maples grown in warm, dry positions.
Diseases. CORAL SPOT causes die-back of shoots, and pink to red cushion-like spore pustules appear at the base of the dead wood.

HONEY FUNGUS causes rapid death of plants.

SCORCHING of the foliage is a common occurrence, particularly in spring; the leaves turn brown at the margins and then shrivel.

TAR SPOT shows on the leaves as large black spots with bright yellow edges during summer.

VERTICILLIUM WILT causes sudden wilting followed by withering of the leaves and die-back of the shoots. Internally affected shoots have brown or green-brown streaks.

Achillea filipendulina
'Coronation Gold'

Achillea millefolium
'Cerise Queen'

Achillea tomentosa

Achillea

Yarrow. *Compositae*

ACHILLEA FILIPENDULINA 'GOLD PLATE'

A genus of 200 species of hardy herbaceous perennials. The dwarf species and varieties described are suitable for rock gardens, the taller ones for mixed borders and for cutting. The tiny flowers are borne in loose clusters or tightly packed heads; with the exceptions of *A. ptarmica* and *A. clavennae,* all the species have fern-like leaves. The flat flower heads of varieties of *A. filipendulina* may be dried for winter decoration.
A. chrysocoma. Greece. Height 4 in.; spread 10 in. A species with deeply cut, grey-green leaves that form a woolly carpet. Mustard-yellow flower heads, 2–3 in. wide, appear in June and July.
A. clavennae. Austria, E. Alps. Height 4 in.; spread 10 in. This rock plant has deeply cut, tufted, silver-green leaves. Single white daisy-like flowers, $\frac{1}{3}$ in. across, are carried in loosely massed heads in May and June.
A. clypeolata. Balkans. Height 18 in.; spread 15 in. This border species has hairy, pinnate,

silver-green leaves. Tightly packed heads, 4–5 in. across, of deep yellow florets are produced from June to August.
A. eupatorium: see *A. filipendulina*
A. filipendulina, syn. *A. eupatorium.* Caucasus. Height and spread 3–4 ft. A border species with mid-green leaves and compact, 4–6 in. wide clusters of lemon-yellow flowers. The flowering season is from July to September. The species is superseded by improved varieties.

'Coronation Gold' (height 3 ft; spread 24 in.) carries flat heads of deep yellow flowers from June to August; 'Gold Plate' (height 4–5 ft; spread 24 in.) also has deep yellow flowers.
A. × 'Kellereri'. Height 6 in.; spread 9–12 in. This attractive rock plant has finely cut grey-green foliage. The white flowers are similar to those of *A. clavennae,* but are carried in larger, tighter clusters in June and July.
A. × 'King Edward', syn. *A. lewisii.* Height 4–6 in.; spread 8 in. This hybrid between *A. clavennae* and *A. tomentosa* is suitable for a rock garden where it forms a hummock of grey-green foliage. Buff-yellow flower heads, $1\frac{1}{2}$–$2\frac{1}{2}$ in. across, are carried from May to September.
A. lewisii: see *A. × 'King Edward'*
A. millefolium (yarrow). Great Britain. Height 2–$2\frac{1}{2}$ ft; spread 15 in. The type plant can be a lawn weed, with deep green leaves and 4 in. wide flattened heads of tiny white to cerise flowers. These appear between June and September. The following varieties are good border plants.

'Cerise Queen', cherry-red flowers in June and July; 'Kelwayi', clear red.

Achillea ptarmica 'The Pearl'

A. ptarmica (sneezewort). Great Britain. Height 2–$2\frac{1}{2}$ ft; spread 15 in. This species has narrowly lanceolate, toothed, mid-green leaves. Daisy-like white flowers open in 2–4 in. wide clusters from June to August. Two good border varieties are 'Perry's White', which carries loose heads of button-shaped white flowers from June to August; and 'The Pearl', with similar but slightly later flowers from July to September.
A. taygetea. Middle East. Height 18 in.; spread 5 in. This border plant is excellent for cut flowers. It has silver-grey pinnate leaves, and its pale yellow flowers are borne in flat heads, 2–4 in. wide, from June to September. 'Moonshine' is slightly taller, with pale sulphur-yellow flowers.

A. tomentosa. Europe, N. Asia. Height 6–9 in.; spread 12 in. This species is suitable as ground cover for a rock garden or a border. It has long, narrow, downy, grey-green leaves and bright yellow densely packed flower heads, 3 in. across; these appear between July and September.

Cultivation. Plant between October and March in any well-drained garden soil in a sunny position. Cut back all tall varieties to ground level in November. Protect *A. chrysocoma* from winter wet with panes of glass or cloches.

Propagation. In March, divide the roots into portions each with four or five young shoots and replant direct in permanent positions.

Alternatively, sow the seeds in pans on the surface of John Innes seed compost in a cold frame or greenhouse during March. Prick off the seedlings into pans or boxes and later transfer them to a nursery bed. Plant in the flowering site between October and March.

Pests and diseases. Generally trouble-free.

Achimenes

Gesneriaceae

ACHIMENES LONGIFLORA

A genus of 50 species of deciduous greenhouse perennials with curious tuber-like scaly rhizomes. The plants are generally bushy in growth, with hairy, ovate to lanceolate, toothed, mid-green leaves. Tubular or trumpet-shaped flowers are borne solitarily or a few together in the upper leaf axils. The species described make useful and attractive pot plants, flowering from July to September.

A. grandiflora. Mexico. Height up to 24 in. An erect plant, with the stems and leaf under-surfaces often flushed red. Although basically tubular, the solitary red-purple flowers expand to flat, pansy-like blooms up to 2 in. wide.

A. heterophylla. Guatemala. Height up to 12 in. The sharply pointed, rough, hairy leaves of this species are sometimes asymmetrical in outline and are borne in whorls of three. Solitary, $1\frac{1}{2}$ in. wide orange flowers are similar in shape to those of *A. grandiflora.*

'Little Beauty' is rather more bushy in habit and has crimson-pink flowers.

A. longiflora. Mexico to Panama. The reclining stems of this plant reach about 12 in. in length and, like the leaf undersurfaces, may be flushed with red. Each solitary 2 in. wide flower is composed of a long, curved tube and rounded petals. In colour the flowers vary from pale red through lavender to deep purple-blue.

The following varieties are available: 'Alba', white; 'Guerrero', pale violet-blue; 'Major', violet-blue flowers, 3 in. across.

Cultivation. Start the tubers into growth in March or April at a temperature of about 16°C

(61°F). Plant them 1 in. deep in a proprietary peat-based compost, or John Innes potting compost No. 2, six to a 5 in. pot, eight to a 6 in. pot. Water sparingly at first, increasing gradually as the plants develop. During the growing season give a liquid feed at intervals of 10–14 days from the time the flower buds show until after flowering. Support the lengthening stems with twiggy sticks or canes and raffia. Shade the plants from strong sunlight and syringe in hot weather. Dry the plants off during September or October.

Propagation. Each planted tuber produces up to six fresh ones during the year. Leave these in the pots after the plants have been dried off. Separate the brittle young tubers in March and pot up and grow on in John Innes potting compost No. 2.

Pests and diseases. Generally trouble-free.

Acidanthera

Iridaceae

ACIDANTHERA BICOLOR

A genus of 20 species of half-hardy and tender bulbous plants. Only one species is generally available; it is suitable only for mild areas and elsewhere is best grown in a greenhouse.

A. bicolor. Abyssinia. Although the hardiest of the genus, this species will not survive outdoors in places where frost can penetrate to the corms. The variety *A. b. murielae* (height 3 ft; planting distance 6–9 in.) is stronger-growing and more generally available. The sword-shaped leaves are mid-green. The fragrant, star-shaped flowers, 2 in. wide and six or eight to a stem, are white with purple centres; they appear in August and September and are good as cut flowers.

Cultivation. Acidantheras will flower in almost any type of soil, provided it is not waterlogged. Plant 4–5 in. deep in April or May in groups of about a dozen in a south-facing position among shrubs or perennials, or close to a south-facing wall. For cut flowers, plant 4 in. apart and 3 in. deep in rows spaced 24 in. apart.

After flowering, and before the first severe frosts, lift the plants whole and dry them thoroughly in a warm room or greenhouse. Remove cormlets and dead roots, stems and scales and store the bulbs and cormlets in a dry, warm place until the following spring.

Corms planted in pots in a greenhouse in February will flower from July onwards. Plant them five or six to a 6 in. pot using John Innes potting compost No. 1. Repot annually in February or March.

Propagation. Each corm planted in good garden soil should produce a new corm every year, but may not do so in poor soil. The corms usually produce many cormlets which should flower two or three years later if planted in May in good soil and kept free from weeds. Cormlets will reach

Achimenes heterophylla 'Little Beauty'

Acidanthera bicolor murielae

flowering size more quickly if grown on in a deep frame or in a greenhouse.

Pests. The young shoots, leaves and stems may be eaten by SLUGS, which leave shiny trails of slime on the plants.

THRIPS may infest the flowers, causing discoloration and distortion.

Diseases. The occurrence of CORE ROT is due to a fungus which attacks the central core of the corms. During storage the damage spreads outwards causing a complete rot of the corms, which become spongy and dark brown or black. If infected corms are planted, they fail to grow or produce weak shoots which eventually die.

HARD ROT and LEAF SPOT cause minute brown spots on both surfaces of the leaves; small black fruiting bodies of the fungus arise on the spots, which later become pale at the centre. On the corms, large black-brown spots develop; these are somewhat sunken and often zoned. In store, infected corms may become hard and shrivelled.

Aconitum napellus

Aconitum wilsonii

Aconite, winter: see *Eranthis hyemalis*

Aconitum

Monkshood. *Ranunculaceae*

ACONITUM WILSONII

A genus of 300 species of hardy herbaceous perennials. The hooded flowers are generally borne in racemes; those described require no support. All parts of these plants are poisonous.

A. carmichaelii: see *A. fischeri*

A. fischeri, syn. *A. carmichaelii*. China. Height 3 ft; planting distance 15 in. The glossy dark green leaves are deeply cut. Racemes of violet-blue flowers, with 1–1½ in. high hoods, are borne in August and September.

A. napellus. Europe, Asia. Height 3½ ft; planting distance 15 in. The dark green leaves are deeply cut and divided into pointed segments. Racemes of deep blue flowers, with 1–1½ in. high hoods, are produced in July and August.

The following forms are more often grown than the species: 'Bicolor' (height 3½ ft, planting distance 15 in.) bears blue and white flowers in spikes in July and August; 'Bressingham Spire' (height 3 ft, planting distance 15 in.) bears violet-blue flowers in tapering spikes in July and August; 'Newry Blue' (height 3 ft, planting distance 15 in.) carries deep blue flowers in closely set spikes in June and July; 'Spark's Variety' (height 4–5 ft, planting distance 18 in.) has dark blue flowers in branching spikes in July and August.

A. wilsonii. China. Height 4–6 ft; planting distance 18 in. The dark green leaves are tripartite. Pyramids of amethyst-blue flowers, with hoods up to 2 in. high, are borne in August and September. 'Barker's Variety' is a deeper blue.

Cultivation. Plant aconitums between October and March in moist, deep soil in partial shade. They will also grow in sun if the soil is not allowed to dry out. Mulch them annually in spring after their second year. Cut back *A. napellus* after flowering to encourage growth of further stems. Cut down the flowering stems of all plants in October.

Propagation. Divide the roots during suitable weather between October and March.

Sow seeds during March or April in boxes or pans of seed compost in a cold greenhouse or frame. Transplant the seedlings into a nursery bed when they are large enough to handle. Plant out from October onwards.

Pests and diseases. Generally trouble-free.

Acroclinium roseum: see *Helipterum roseum*

Actinidia

Actinidiaceae

A genus of 40 species of hardy, deciduous climbing shrubs of twining habit. Those described are all suitable for growing on walls (with additional support), pergolas or old trees.

A. arguta. Japan. Height 50 ft. This vigorous climber is suitable for growing over a tree. The bright green leaves, alternately arranged, are ovate to ovate-oblong. The fragrant, round white flowers, ¾ in. across, have purple anthers and are produced in clusters during June and July. They are followed by green-yellow berries.

A. a. cordifolia is distinguished by its heart-shaped leaves and purple petioles.

A. chinensis (Chinese gooseberry). China. Height 30 ft. This is a vigorous ornamental climber with dark green heart-shaped leaves. Clusters of round cream-white flowers, 1½ in. wide, appear from June to August, and mature to buff-yellow. They are followed by edible egg-shaped fruits covered with brown hairs.

ACTINIDIA KOLOMIKTA

A. kolomikta (Kolomikta vine). China, Japan. Height 6–12 ft. A slender species suitable for a sheltered wall or fence. It is grown for its attractive foliage; each dark green heart-shaped leaf is marked to a varying degree with pink or white at the tip. Round white flowers, ½ in. across, are borne in June.

Cultivation. Actinidias will grow in any soil except those that are chalky, lacking humus or badly drained, but they do best in a rich loam. Plant from November to March in a sunny or partly shaded position, the stronger growers against high walls or trees. The male and female flowers of *A. chinensis* are usually on separate plants, and specimens of each sex should be grown near each other to ensure pollination.

Actinidia chinensis

Actinidia kolomikta

Adiantum pedatum

Pinch out the growing points of *A. arguta* and *A. chinensis* when young, to encourage a spreading habit. *A. kolomikta* has a bushier form of growth. All the species may require some initial training on wall supports.

Propagation. Sow the seeds in a cold greenhouse or frame during October or November, as soon as they are ripe. Prick out the seedlings into pots in the spring when they are large enough to handle.

Insert 3–4 in. cuttings of half-ripened wood in sandy peat in a frame during July or August. Maintain a close atmosphere, ideally with bottom heat and mist propagation. Pot the rooted cuttings into 4–5 in. containers.

Plunge established pot plants, both seedlings and cuttings, into an outdoor nursery bed until they are needed for planting out.

Pruning. If space is restricted, thin out and cut back the growths in February.

Pests. CATS are attracted to some species, particularly *A. kolomikta,* and may damage the stems, occasionally killing the plants.

Diseases. Generally trouble-free.

Adamsia scilloides: see *Puschkinia scilloides*

Adiantum

Maidenhair fern. *Adiantaceae*

A genus of 200 species of ferns. Some of the species are hardy enough for garden cultivation, others are better suited for the cool greenhouse or for growing indoors.

A. capillus-veneris (maidenhair fern). Subtropical and temperate zones, including the British Isles. Height and spread 6–10 in. This species can be grown in the open only in sheltered areas in the south and west, and is generally cultivated as an indoor pot plant. Sometimes it seeds itself in the crevices of a damp, shaded greenhouse wall, where it will flourish without any soil. It is evergreen under glass and in sheltered positions. The light green triangular fronds, on black stalks, are slightly glaucous.

A. cuneatum: see *A. raddianum*

A. formosum. Australia, New Zealand. Height 2–3 ft; spread 24 in. This evergreen species is a vigorous plant for a cool greenhouse. The stalks are purple-black and bear light green, quadripinnate, roughly triangular fronds. The pinnules are small and numerous.

A. microphyllum: see *A. venustum*

ADIANTUM PEDATUM   ADIANTUM RADDIANUM

A. pedatum. N. America, Japan. Height 6–18 in.; spread 12–24 in. This is a hardy outdoor species which dies down soon after the first frosts. The gracefully drooping fronds are pedate, the pinnae springing from a single point at the top of each stem. They are light green, darkening slightly as they mature, and borne on purple stalks. *A. p.* 'Aleuticum', 4–5 in. high, with a spread of 6–9 in., is a fine fern for a rock garden; it will stand more sun than the species and the taller varieties. The pinnules are glaucous green and closely set. *A. p.* 'Japonicum', 18 in. high, with a spread of 12 in., has copper-pink fronds in spring, which turn green as they mature.

Adiantum capillus-veneris

Adiantum venustum

A. raddianum, syn. *A. cuneatum.* Brazil. Height 12–18 in.; spread 15–24 in. This is an evergreen species suitable for indoor or cool greenhouse cultivation, especially in a hanging basket; it is the most widely grown commercial fern. The pale green triangular fronds, erect when young, bend gracefully as they mature. They consist of hundreds of small pinnules. The stalks are purple-black. *A. r.* 'Fragrantissimum' differs from the type in emitting a powerful fragrance when grown in a mass. *A. r.* 'Fritz Luthii' is a handsome variety with longer, narrower fronds.

ADIANTUM VENUSTUM

A. venustum, syn. *A. microphyllum.* Canada, Kashmir. Height 6 in.; spread 9 in. The fronds, carried on purple-black stalks, are narrowly triangular. Each of the numerous pinnules has a convex upper surface. This fully hardy garden species displays a wide colour range in the course of a year, the light green fronds becoming slightly glaucous as they mature, then turning to a warm brown after frost. They remain intact until new pink fronds appear in early spring.

Cultivation. Plant the hardy species during April in semi-shade in a soil enriched with leaf-mould or peat, and with bone-meal (1 oz. per sq. yd) worked in thoroughly. Plant the rhizomes of *A. venustum* no more than ½ in. deep; those of other species no more than 1 in. Apply a top-dressing of bone-meal (1 oz. per sq. yd) each spring. Pot the other species during March in a mixture of 3 parts peat, 1 part loam, 1 part coarse sand and ½ part lime rubble (parts by volume). The pots should be just large enough to contain the roots and have broken crocks or crushed bricks at the base to assist drainage. Maintain a minimum temperature of 7°C (45°F) throughout the year, and always keep the plants away from direct sunlight. Give sufficient water to prevent the compost drying out but do not allow it to become soggy.

Propagation. March is the best month for sowing spores (see entry under FERNS).

Alternatively, increase species and all named varieties by division of the rhizomes. This method is particularly suitable if only a few extra plants are wanted. Division is best done in spring. Shake the plants free of soil in March and cut the rhizomes into pieces which each have a growing point. Pot these pieces in the smallest pots that will contain the roots, using a compost of equal parts (by volume) loam, leaf-mould or peat, and coarse sand. Water them and keep them in shade. Maintain a moist atmosphere afterwards by spraying occasionally between the pots and by damping down the greenhouse floor.

Pests. The roots may be eaten by WOOD LICE, and ROOT MEALY BUGS may infest the root system and check growth.

LEAF-BLOTCH EELWORMS invade the frond tissue and make large black marks on it.

Diseases. Generally trouble-free.

Adonis amurensis

Adonis vernalis

Aechmea chantinii

Adonis
Ranunculaceae

A genus of 20 species of hardy annuals and herbaceous perennials. Those described here are perennial, early spring-flowering plants suitable for the front of a border or for a rock garden. They have deeply dissected fern-like foliage and yellow, somewhat bowl-shaped flowers.

A. amurensis. Manchuria, Japan. Height 9–15 in.; planting distance 12 in. The delicate, matt green leaves are finely cut. In cultivation this species is generally represented by the double form, 'Flore-pleno'. It bears bright yellow flowers, 2 in. across, in February and March.

A. vernalis. Europe, Siberia. Height 9–12 in.; planting distance 12 in. The mid-green leaves are finely dissected. Single yellow flowers, 2 in. across, appear in March and open out flat in bright sun.

Cultivation. Any ordinary garden soil is suitable for these plants, but a light soil, with leaf-mould added to retain moisture, is ideal. Plant in a sunny or partly shaded site between July and October, with the crowns 1 in. below the soil surface. The plants disappear below ground before mid-July.

Propagation. Divide and replant the roots in September or early October.

Sow seeds from June to August in boxes or pans of John Innes seed compost in a cold frame. Germination may be slow. When large enough to handle, prick the seedlings out into boxes and grow them on for a year. Transplant into nursery rows and grow on for a further year before planting out in permanent positions.

Pests and diseases. Generally trouble-free.

Aechmea
Bromeliaceae

AECHMEA FASCIATA

A genus containing some 150 species of evergreen plants. Most species are epiphytic, though some are terrestrial. They have spreading or tubular rosettes of leaves that are heavily or lightly spined and sheathed at the base to form a water-holding vase.

Most aechmeas are easy to cultivate as greenhouse and house plants; there are a large number of hybrids.

See also BROMELIADS.

A. chantinii, syn. *Billbergia chantinii.* Amazon region of Brazil and Peru. Height up to 3 ft. The funnel-shaped rosette of dark green spined leaves is banded with silver scales. An oval, 4–6 in. long flower panicle usually rises well above the leaves, with orange to salmon-coloured recurved bracts and a closely branched head of

Aechmea fasciata

yellow to red flowers. The colour of leaves, bracts and flowers are variable. The plant spreads by stolons, sometimes many inches long.

A. fasciata, syn. *Billbergia rhodocyanea*. Brazil. Height 24 in. The green or grey-green leaves form an open vase-shaped rosette; they have black spines and are cross-banded with silver scales. The tubular flowers, blue at first, later turning to rose, are crowded in a compact conical head, up to 6 in. long, of pale pink spined bracts; they appear in August. It is the easiest grown of all bromeliads and needs little attention. It is easily increased by detaching and rooting the stolons or side-shoots.

A. fulgens. Brazil. Height 15 in. The broad, dusty green leaves are minutely spined and form an open rosette. An erect oval panicle, 4–6 in. long, carries numerous stalked, branched and waxen blue flowers in August and September. Vermilion, long-lasting berries follow.

A. f. discolor is a variety more common than the type; the undersides of the leaves are purple, covered with white powdery scales.

Cultivation. Plant firmly during late spring and early summer in any open-textured, lime-free mixture. Finish the plants off in 5 in. pots. Minute doses of liquid fertiliser may be given by leaf spray or applied to the soil. Keep the rosette moist or filled with water. Water the soil freely during the growing period, but do not allow waterlogging. When growth slows down, keep the rosette and the soil just moist. In a dry atmosphere it is necessary to mist-spray throughout the year to maintain a constant high humidity.

Propagation. Remove stolons or side-shoots attached to the mother plant when they are one-third to half the size of the full-grown parent. Sever with a sharp knife as close as possible to the base and allow the cut surface to dry for a day or two. Plant firmly but not too deeply in the same compost as the parent plant. Stake until roots are well formed, which can be ascertained by giving the plant a gentle pull.

Propagation by seeds is possible, but seed-raised plants generally take up to five years to reach flowering size.

Pests and diseases. Generally trouble-free.

Aërangis
Orchidaceae

A genus of 70 species of tropical, perennial, evergreen, epiphytic orchids from Africa and Madagascar. They have erect stems which occasionally produce one or more basal shoots. These plants require a warm greenhouse.

The following three species have sometimes been listed in the genus *Angraecum*. They usually have thick, strap-shaped, blue-green leaves unequally bi-lobed at the tips and arranged on a short stem. The long-spurred flowers, which are borne on spikes, are basically white or cream, shaded with green or salmon.

See also ORCHIDS.

A. biloba. Tropical Africa. The flowers, 1½–2 in. across, which are carried on pendulous stems, 6–12 in. long, are fragrant at night. They are white, occasionally flushed with pink and with salmon-orange spurs; they appear from October to December.

AËRANGIS KOTSCHYANA

A. kotschyana. Tropical Africa. This species is often sold under the erroneous name of *A. kotschyi*. It has pendulous flower stems up to 18 in. long, each carrying up to 15 fragrant flowers. They appear from July to September and are 1–1½ in. wide, pure white with 6–9 in. long spirally-twisted salmon-pink spurs.

A. kotschyi: see *A. kotschyana*

A. rhodosticta. Tropical Africa. A popular species, bearing up to 12 cream-white flowers with orange-red central columns on each 9 in. long stem. The 1 in. wide flowers have green-tinged spurs; they appear from April to August.

Cultivation. Grow aërangis in a compost made up of equal parts (by volume) osmunda fibre and sphagnum moss, and in perforated pans or baskets, 5–6 in. across.

These plants thrive in some shade, but full winter light, in a warm greenhouse. A humid atmosphere should be maintained by frequent damping down. Give an occasional liquid feed from May to September and ventilate the greenhouse daily between April and October. Between October and April open the ventilators only on mild days. Maintain a minimum winter temperature of 16°C (61°F). During the growing season, water copiously but decrease the quantity in winter during the period of minimum growth.

Propagation. The lower part of each stem usually produces basal shoots which may be used as cuttings when they reach a length of 3–4 in., usually in April or May.

Insert the cuttings in 2 in. pots of the growing compost and place in a propagating case at a temperature of 18–21°C (64–70°F). When rooted, pot on the cuttings as necessary.

Pests and diseases. Generally trouble-free.

Aechmea fulgens (berries)

Aërangis biloba

Aërangis rhodosticta

21

Aërides

Orchidaceae

A genus of 40 species of tropical, perennial, evergreen, epiphytic orchids from Asia. These plants have erect stems which may each produce one or a few basal shoots. Aërides are fairly free-flowering and thrive in an intermediate greenhouse.

The leaves are oblong-obovate to narrowly strap-shaped, and usually mid-green. Long arching down-curved flower stems carry dense spikes of fleshy blooms all along the stem; they are long-lasting and fragrant, in various shades of mauve, pink, purple and white. They all have horn-like spurs of varying lengths.

See also ORCHIDS.

A. crispa. India, Ceylon. The upright stem is often red-brown, with strap-shaped leaves. Curving flower stems, 12–18 in. long, carry numerous white flowers, 2 in. across and suffused with purple-rose, from June to August.

A. falcata. Burma, Thailand. This miniature species has cylindrical leaves on a short stem. White flowers, heavily suffused blue and with purple lips, are carried on 20 in. long stems between April and July; each flower measures up to 1½ in. across.

A. japonica. Japan. This requires cooler but brighter winter conditions than the others. It has a few linear or oblong leaves. The 1 in. wide flowers are green-white barred with brown-purple towards the base; the lips are white and spotted with violet. The flowering season is generally from May to July.

Aërides falcata

Aërides odorata

Aeschynanthus lobbianus

AËRIDES ODORATA

A. odorata. Burma to Malesia and China. The upright stems of this species bear numerous oblong-ovate, dark green leaves. Pendulous flower stems, 12–18 in. long, bear flowers that are 1 in. across, and white to cream and red-tinged at the tips; the lips are white with purple spots. Flowering is from June to August.

Cultivation. Grow these orchids in equal parts (by volume) osmunda fibre and sphagnum moss in perforated pans or baskets 5–6 in. across. Protect them from excessive sunlight and keep them shaded from early spring to late autumn. Water freely from May to October and keep the plants just moist from October to April; they may be given a monthly weak liquid feed from May to October. Ventilation should be given daily from May to September, but only on mild days from October to April. During winter provide a minimum night temperature of 10°C (50°F). For *A. japonica* lower the temperature a few degrees in winter, and provide more ventilation and less shade during summer.

Propagation. The lower parts of the stems often produce basal shoots which may be used as cuttings when they reach a length of 3–4 in., usually in April or May. Insert the cuttings in 2 in. pots of the growing compost and place in a propagating case at a temperature of 18–21°C (64–70°F). When well rooted, pot the cuttings on as necessary.

Pests. Generally trouble-free, although MEALY BUGS and SLUGS may cause damage to developing shoots and leaves.

Diseases. Generally trouble-free.

Aeschynanthus speciosus

Aeschynanthus

Gesneriaceae

AESCHYNANTHUS LOBBIANUS

A genus of 80 species of perennial trailing and climbing evergreen greenhouse plants grown for their showy flowers. The ovate pointed leaves are usually arranged in opposite alternate pairs. They are suitable for growing in hanging baskets.

A. lobbianus. Java. Height and spread 18–24 in. A prostrate or feebly climbing species with glossy deep green leaves. Clusters of crimson, hooded flowers, each 1½ in. long and with a conspicuous purple-brown tubular calyx, are borne terminally from May to June.

A. marmoratus (habitat uncertain). Height 24 in.; spread 12 in. The leaves of this trailing plant are up to 3½ in. long, red-purple beneath, with a lacy network of yellow veins on the pale green upper sides. Green tubular flowers, about 2 in. long, with chocolate-brown blotches, appear from the upper leaf axils from June to September.

A. pulcher. Java. Height 24 in.; spread 12 in. A climbing or trailing plant, with mid-green leaves. The tubular flowers, which appear in June, are about 1½ in. long, scarlet with yellow throats.

A. speciosus, syn. *Trichosporum speciosum.* Indonesia. Height 6–24 in.; spread 12–18 in. A species with pale green leaves. Clusters of tubular, bright orange, dark-lipped flowers, 2–2½ in. long, appear from July to September.

Aesculus indica

Aesculus × carnea

Aesculus hippocastanum
(flowers)

Aesculus hippocastanum
(fruits)

Cultivation. Plant in March in a compost of 3 parts fibrous peat and 1 part dried moss (parts by volume) in 8–10 in. hanging baskets. The ideal minimum winter temperature is 13°C (55°F), but the plants will survive at 7°C (45°F) if kept dry.

Syringe the plants frequently in hot weather and lightly shade from June to August. Give established plants an occasional liquid feed during summer. Keep the compost moist, except from November to February when watering should be only slight.

Repot every three years in March or April.

Propagation. Take tip cuttings, 3 in. long, of non-flowering shoots in May or June. Insert the cuttings in a mixture of equal parts (by volume) peat and sand at a temperature of 18–21°C (64–70°F). Alternatively, layer the trailing growths by pegging them in moist compost at any time from April to July.

Pests. Generally trouble-free.

Diseases. White spots of variable size on the leaves are caused by LEAF SPOT.

Aesculus

Horse chestnut. *Hippocastanaceae*

A genus of 13 species of deciduous flowering trees or shrubs. The majority are easy to cultivate and hardy in most areas of Britain. The palmate leaves are composed of five to seven generally toothed leaflets. Prominently borne, erect and narrowly conical panicles of white or pink flowers are a striking feature of these trees in spring.

A. × carnea (red horse chestnut). Origin unknown. Height 15–20 ft; spread 8–10 ft. This is a hybrid between *A. hippocastanum* and *A. pavia.* The mid-green leaves emerge from gummy leaf buds. Rose-pink flowers, borne in 6–8 in. long panicles, appear from May to June. This hybrid comes true from seed. The variety 'Briotii' has deeper pink flowers in larger panicles.

AESCULUS HIPPOCASTANUM

A. hippocastanum (common horse chestnut). Balkans. Height up to 30 ft; spread 10–15 ft. A fast-growing, wide-spreading tree with prominent sticky brown leaf buds and mid to dark green leaves. White flowers, blotched red at the base, are borne in erect panicles, 8–12 in. long, in May. The prickly green fruits contain shiny, mahogany-brown seeds or conkers.

Due to its eventual size and far-reaching surface roots this species is more suitable for avenues and parks than small gardens. 'Baumannii', syn. 'Flore-pleno' has long-lasting double white flowers. It does not set seed.

A. indica (Indian horse chestnut). N. India. Height up to 30 ft; spread 10–15 ft. The winter leaf buds are large and resinous, and unfold to glossy mid to dark green leaves. White flowers, tinged pale pink and blotched yellow and red, appear in erect 8–12 in. long panicles in June or July. The seeds or conkers are shiny black.

A. parviflora. S. United States. Height and spread 7–8 ft. A bushy, upright shrub spreading by means of suckers from the base. The leaves are smooth, mid-green above, paler green beneath; the foliage sometimes assumes autumn colours. Erect, 8–12 in. panicles of white flowers with long, pale pink stamens, are produced in July.

Aethionema grandiflorum

Aethionema pulchellum

Aethionema × 'Warley Rose'

Agapanthus orientalis

A. pavia (red buckeye). N. America. Height up to 10 ft; spread 6–8 ft. A round-headed shrub or small tree with mid-green leaves. Bright red flowers in erect, 3–6 in. long panicles open in June. The variety 'Atrosanguinea' has darker red flowers; *A. p. humilis*, with red flowers, is low-growing, sometimes prostrate.

Cultivation. Plant aesculus between October and March in any fertile garden soil and in a sunny or partially shaded position.

Propagation. The species are easily raised from seeds, sown in a nursery bed outdoors during September or October. Grow the seedlings on for two or three years before transplanting to permanent positions.

Hybrids and selected forms do not breed true and must be increased by grafting on to stocks of *A. hippocastanum* or the type species, in March.

Pruning. None normally required. Old specimens of the bushy *A. parviflora* may be thinned out in February by cutting the oldest stems down to ground level.

Pests. Generally trouble-free, but SCALE INSECTS may form conspicuous colonies on *A. hippocastanum* in south-east England.

Diseases. LEAF SPOT shows as small, irregular, discoloured spots on the foliage in spring. The spots later become brown and coalesce so that the whole affected leaf withers.

Aethionema
Cruciferae

A genus of 70 species of hardy evergreen perennials originating in the Mediterranean regions. Those described are dwarf sub-shrubs, some with a spreading habit. They form thick mats of leaves, with cross-shaped flowers that are generally rose-pink. Aethionemas are good rock-garden plants.

A. grandiflorum. Lebanon, Turkey. Height 6 in.; spread 12–18 in. The grey-green leaves of this loosely branched species are ovate-oblong. The flowers, in a delicate shade of pink, are arranged in $1\frac{1}{2}$–2 in. wide domed heads; these are carried profusely between May and July.

A. iberideum. Mediterranean areas. Height 6 in.; spread 12 in. This species has ovate blue-green leaves. White flowers are freely produced in 2 in. terminal racemes from May to July.

A. pulchellum. Asia Minor. Height 6–9 in.; spread 15 in. This species is like a more compact form of *A. grandiflorum.* It has smaller leaves and shorter flower stalks. Its numerous flowers are a darker pink and open from May to July.

A. × 'Warley Rose'. Height 4–6 in.; spread 15 in. This hybrid has glaucous or grey-green linear leaves. Deep rose flowers appear in broad spikes, 2–3 in. long, in April and May.

Cultivation. Any well-drained garden soil in a sunny position is suitable for aethionemas. Plant between September and March; remove the stems after the flowers have faded.

Propagation. Sow the seeds in a cold frame or greenhouse in March. Prick out the seedlings when they are large enough to handle. Pot on in May and June, and plant out in the flowering positions between October and March.

The hybrid *A. × 'Warley Rose'* is best increased in June or July by 2 in. soft cuttings of non-flowering shoots. Insert in a closed cold frame in equal parts (by volume) peat and sand. Pot the rooted cuttings individually and grow on in the frame for planting out the following April.

Pests and diseases. Generally trouble-free.

Aethiopappus pulcherrimus: see *Centaurea pulcherrima*

Agapanthus
African lily. *Liliaceae*

AGAPANTHUS CAMPANULATUS

A genus of hardy and half-hardy perennial plants which grow in compact clumps and have fleshy roots. About ten species are botanically recognised, but classification is confused. Most of the species in cultivation, and particularly the hybrids, are hardier than generally supposed and can be grown outdoors in the south and west. Elsewhere they require a sheltered sunny border and winter protection. They provide handsome cut flowers and the long-stemmed seed heads can be dried for winter decoration.

The species described here have strap-shaped mid-green leaves which may be evergreen or deciduous. The widely to narrowly funnel-shaped flowers are 1–3 in. long and are produced in rounded umbels. Flowering begins in June under glass, outdoors in July and continues until August or September.

A. africanus, syn. *A. umbellatus*. Cape Province. Height 2–$2\frac{1}{2}$ ft; planting distance 15–18 in. A half-hardy evergreen species with crowded umbels of deep blue or blue-violet flowers.

A. campanulatus. Natal. Height 2–$2\frac{1}{2}$ ft; planting distance 15–18 in. This almost hardy deciduous species is sometimes incorrectly known as *A. mooreanus,* a name which has been applied to hybrids of *A. campanulatus.* Crowded umbels of pale blue flowers are borne in late summer.

The variety 'Isis' bears large heads of clear lavender-blue flowers.

A. caulescens. Swaziland. Height 2–$2\frac{1}{2}$ ft; planting distance 15–18 in. An almost hardy deciduous species with crowded umbels of bright to deep blue flowers. There are several sub-species whose flowers vary in shades of blue. White forms are also known.

A. inapertus. S. Africa. Height 4 ft; planting distance 15–18 in. This hardy species has deciduous leaves and few-flowered loose umbels of deep blue to violet-blue flowers.

A. mooreanus: see *A. campanulatus*

A. orientalis. Cape Province. Height 2–$2\frac{1}{2}$ ft; planting distance 15–18 in. A half-hardy evergreen plant, now classified as a sub-species of *A. praecox.* It is fairly reliable outdoors except

Agapanthus campanulatus 'Isis'

Agapanthus 'Headbourne Hybrid'

during unusually cold winters. It bears densely packed blue flower heads, and white and double blue forms are available.

A. praecox, syn. *A. umbellatus.* E. Cape Province, Natal. Height 2–2½ ft; planting distance 15–18 in. This variable half-hardy evergreen species is probably the most widely grown. Dense umbels of bright to pale blue 2–3 in. long flowers are produced from July onwards. White-flowered forms are known. The sub-species *A. p. orientalis* is often listed as a separate species.

A. umbellatus: see *A. africanus, A. praecox*

HYBRIDS These include the popular 'Headbourne Hybrids' which are generally hardier than the species. Height 2–2½ ft; planting distance 15–18 in. Erect stems carry spherical umbels of deep violet-blue to pale blue flowers.

Cultivation. These plants thrive in any fertile, well-drained soil; choose a sunny and sheltered position, particularly in cold areas. Plant hardy species and hybrids outdoors in April, setting the crowns about 2 in. below ground level; do not disturb after planting. Water well during the growing season and cut back the stems to ground level after flowering, unless seeds are required for propagation or as dried winter decoration. In cold districts or known frost pockets, protect from October to April with a 6–9 in. deep layer of bracken, weathered ashes or coarse sand.

The half-hardy species are better planted in 7–8 in. pots of John Innes potting compost No. 2, in March or April. After two years they may be divided and placed in similarly sized containers or potted on into 12 in. containers or small tubs. Stand the pots in a sunny, sheltered position outdoors from May until September or October, then move to a frost-free greenhouse for the winter. During the resting period keep the plants just moist, but increase watering as growth is restarted in spring. After flowering, remove the stems as near to the base as possible; remove yellow leaves during the winter.

Propagation. Divide and replant, or pot up the fleshy roots in April or May.

Seeds germinate readily, but seedlings may take two or three years to reach flowering size. Sow during April in pots of seed compost at a temperature of 13–15°C (55–59°F). When large enough to handle, prick off the seedlings into boxes. Transfer the young plants to 3½ in. pots of John Innes potting compost No. 1 and later into 5 in. pots. Overwinter the plants in a frost-free greenhouse or frame and plant out the following spring when danger of frost is over.

Pests and diseases. Generally trouble-free.

Agathaea coelestis: see *Felicia amelloides*

Agave
Agavaceae

AGAVE AMERICANA

A genus of 300 species of greenhouse perennials. These succulents are grown for their sword-shaped leaves, which are arranged in rosettes, usually on short stems. At maturity, which the plant may not reach for 50 years or more, a flower-spike arises from the centre of the rosette in summer. The spike, which in the species described consists of panicles of tubular or bell-shaped flowers, supplants the growing point, and the rosette usually dies after flowering. However, with the exception of *A. americana*, agaves seldom flower in Great Britain.

See also CACTUS.

The following species can be grown as house plants if given plenty of light; in frost-free districts they may survive outdoors.

Agave americana 'Marginata'

Agave victoriae-reginae

A. americana. Mexico. Height 4 ft. The rosettes of spine-tipped, narrow, grey-green leaves may reach 3 ft in the wild. It can be used as a bedding plant during the summer and will even survive the winter outside in the Isles of Scilly. Here it may produce 10 ft long spikes of yellow-green flowers on 15–20 ft flowering stems in late summer. After flowering the rosette dies.

A. a. 'Marginata', syn. 'Variegata', has yellow leaf margins.

A. filifera. Mexico. Height 10 in. The stiff tapering leaves, 1 in. wide, of the spherical rosette are shiny green, marked with two or three white lines on the upper surface. They are edged with horny tissue which breaks up into threads. The flower-spike, when it occurs, is $5\frac{1}{2}$ ft long and is carried on an 8 ft high stem.

A. parviflora. Mexico. Height 4 in. The leaves, $\frac{1}{2}$ in. wide, are similar to those of *A. filifera.* They are marked above with a few white lines. White threads split off from the horny upper margins of the leaf, and the lower margins are toothed.

A. stricta. Mexico. Height 14 in. The closely packed, slender, dark green leaves, about $\frac{1}{2}$ in. wide, end in a spine 1 in. long. They are arranged in a rosette, which does not die after flowering. The flower-spike, $2\frac{1}{2}$ ft long, is carried on a 6 ft long stem.

A. victoriae-reginae. Mexico. Height 6 in. This species needs a higher winter temperature than the other species, preferably 10°C (50°F). The leaves are dark green marked with white stripes. They are keeled at the tips and end in a spine; the margins show a white line of horny tissue. The flowering spike may reach a height of 12 ft.

Cultivation. Agaves grow well in John Innes potting compost No. 2. The smallest specimens described need 3 in. pots, the largest 12 in. During the summer, place them in a sunny position outdoors; large specimens can be bedded out. In winter, keep the plants at a temperature of 5°C (41°F); large specimens can be stored under the greenhouse staging, with their roots plunged in ashes. Water freely during the growing period. Repot annually in April.

Propagation. All the species described here, with the exception of *A. victoriae-reginae*, produce a number of offsets round the rosettes. Remove the offsets from the parents and leave them to dry for several days before potting up in John Innes potting compost No. 2. Agaves are also easily raised from seeds sown in April at a temperature of 21°C (70°F).

Pests. Conspicuous tufts of white waxy wool on the plants are caused by MEALY BUGS. ROOT MEALY BUGS may infest the roots and check growth.

Diseases. Generally trouble-free.

Ageratum houstonianum 'Fairy Pink'

Aglaonema pictum (flowering spathes)

Aglaonema treubii

Ageratum
Compositae

A genus of 60 species of half-hardy annuals and biennials. The species described are grown chiefly for summer bedding. The taller-growing varieties are useful for cutting; the shorter varieties are also grown in pots under glass. The neat flower heads, which resemble shaving brushes, are carried in clusters.

A. conyzoides. Tropical America. Height 24 in.; planting distance 18 in. An annual of bushy, long-branching habit, especially suitable for cutting. The leaves are mid-green and ovate, with toothed edges. Blue or white flower clusters, 2 in. across, appear from July to October.

A. houstonianum, syn. *A. mexicanum.* Mexico. Height 5–12 in.; planting distance 6–12 in. A dwarf, compact species represented by many excellent garden varieties. The leaves are heart-shaped, mid-green and hairy. The tetraploid and F_1 hybrids are recommended for their large heads of flowers and their vigour. They bloom from early summer until the first severe frosts. The flowers, in 3–4 in. trusses, are usually bright blue or white, but a few pink varieties, such as 'Fairy Pink', are also available. Of the tetraploids, 'Blue Mink' is recommended, while 'Blue Chip' is an early and long-flowering F_1 hybrid. 'Blue Cap' is not an F_1 hybrid, but is recommended as a good dwarf variety.

A. mexicanum: see *A. houstonianum*

Cultivation. A sheltered, sunny site and soil that retains moisture give the best results. Dry soils reduce plant vigour and shorten the flowering period. Set out the plants in their flowering positions in late May or June, when danger of frost has passed.

Plants for early spring flowering should be potted on into 5 in. pots of John Innes potting compost No. 1 in September or October, grown through the winter months at 10°C (50°F) and watered sparingly.

Dead-head all plants regularly to prolong the flowering period.

Propagation. Sow the seeds under glass at 16–18°C (61–64°F) in March and April for summer flowering, and in August for winter flowering. Prick off the seedlings 2 in. apart into boxes, or pot into $3\frac{1}{2}$ in. pots. Harden off bedding plants in a cold frame before transplanting to the flowering site in late May or early June.

Pests. Generally trouble-free.

Diseases. A FOOT and ROOT ROT sometimes causes plants to collapse at ground level.

Aglaonema
Araceae

A genus of 50 species of evergreen perennial greenhouse and house plants. They are cultivated for their arum-like flowering spathes and for their variegated ornamental leaves. They thrive in warm, moist, shaded conditions.

A. commutatum. Philippines, Malaya. Height 6 in.; spread 9–12 in. The dark green lanceolate leaves have silver-grey markings. White spathes, 2 in. long, appear in July, followed by heads of dark red berries.

A. costatum. Malaya. Height 6 in.; spread 9 in. A species with round mid-green leaves with ivory-coloured mid-ribs. The white spathes, up to 1 in. long, are borne in July.

A. oblongifolium. Malaya. Height up to $3\frac{1}{2}$ ft; spread 12–15 in. *A. o. curtisii* is the largest cultivated species of aglaonema. The 9 in. long leaves are dark green with silvery markings; the green-white spathes, 2–4 in. long, appear in July.

A. pictum. Malaya, Sumatra. Height 6 in.; spread 9 in. The leaves are stippled in three shades of green, from dark to silvery. Yellow-green spathes, 2 in. long, are produced in August.

A. treubii. Indonesia. Height 9 in.; spread 12 in. The leaves, flowers and berries are similar to those of *A. commutatum.* Small and compact, it makes a good house plant.

Cultivation. Pot in March in a rich, well-drained compost, such as John Innes potting compost No. 2 or 3, or in a proprietary peat-based mixture. Grow house plants in 5–6 in. pots placed in larger containers filled with damp peat, moss or vermiculite. Keep away from gas-appliance fumes, which can cause loss of leaves. The minimum winter temperature needed is 10°C (50°F); 16°C (61°F) is ideal. *A. costatum* and *A. pictum* need a little more heat than the other species. In summer, provide ventilation when 21°C (70°F) is reached.

Repot or, if larger plants are wanted, pot on every second or third year in April. In years when the plants are not repotted they may need a liquid feed once a month during the growing season.

Propagation. Sow seeds at a temperature of 27°C (81°F) in spring; the resulting seedlings may be inferior in leaf colours.

In April or May, take basal shoots or suckers with several leaves attached and root in pots of the growing compost in a propagating case at a temperature of 18–21°C (64–70°F).

Plants may be divided and replanted in April.

Pests and diseases. Generally trouble-free.

Agrostemma coronaria: see *Lychnis coronaria*

Ajuga
Labiatae

A genus of 40 species of hardy annuals and herbaceous perennials that form useful ground-cover plants. The perennial species described have deep green, oblong-ovate leaves and tubular flowers with protruding lips.

A. genevensis. Europe. Height 6–12 in.; planting distance 6 in. The leaves are coarsely toothed. Blue, rose-pink or white flowers in 2 in. long spikes appear in June and July. *A. g.* 'Brockbankii' is a dwarf form with deep blue flowers.

A. pyramidalis. Europe. Height 9 in.; planting distance 6 in. The leaves, which appear at the base, are toothed. Spikes, 4–6 in. long, of blue flowers with purple bracts, appear in May.

A. reptans (bugle). Europe. Height 4–12 in.; planting distance 12–18 in. Whorls of blue flowers, $\frac{1}{2}$–$\frac{3}{4}$ in. long, are borne on erect shoots in June and July. 'Atropurpurea' is a purple-leaved form; 'Multicolor', syn. 'Rainbow', has bronze, pink and yellow variegated foliage; 'Variegata' has grey-green leaves with cream variegations.

Cultivation. Plant in ordinary soil at any time when the ground is not frozen or waterlogged. *A. pyramidalis* and *A. reptans* need a moist, partially shaded position, *A. genevensis* a well-drained sunny site.

Propagation. Divide the plants at any time when the ground is in workable condition.

Pests and diseases. Generally trouble-free.

Alchemilla
Lady's mantle. *Rosaceae*

A genus of 250 species of hardy herbaceous perennials. The plants described have handsome foliage and are suitable for floral arrangements.

A. alpina. Europe, Greenland, N. Asia. Height 6 in.; planting distance 9–12 in. The light green palmate leaves are divided into narrow leaflets. Star-shaped green flowers, about $\frac{1}{6}$ in. across, are borne in corymbs from June to August.

ALCHEMILLA MOLLIS

A. mollis. Carpathians to Asia Minor. Height 12–18 in.; planting distance 15 in. The light green, hairy and palmate leaves have shallow rounded lobes with serrated edges. The star-shaped flowers, $\frac{1}{8}$ in. across, have yellow-green calyces in place of petals. They appear in intricately branched heads from June to August.

Cultivation. Plant alchemillas between October and March in a sunny or partially shaded position in any moist but well-drained garden soil. Provide twiggy sticks for support. Cut back the stems to 1 in. above the ground after flowering.

Propagation. The seeds germinate readily, producing masses of self-sown seedlings.

Sow seeds during March in pans of seed compost in a cold frame. Prick off the seedlings into boxes and later into a nursery bed. Plant out between October and March.

Alchemillas can be divided and replanted at any time between October and March when the weather is suitable.

Pests and diseases. Generally trouble-free.

Allamanda
Apocynaceae

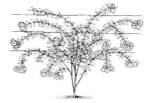

ALLAMANDA CATHARTICA

A genus of 15 species of evergreen greenhouse climbers and shrubs with large showy flowers. The climbers are the most attractive, but need plenty of space.

A. cathartica. S. America. Height 10–15 ft; spread 6–10 ft. In cultivation the species is represented by *A. c.* 'Grandiflora' and *A. c.* 'Hendersonii'. They have lanceolate mid-green leaves arranged in pairs or in whorls of three or four along each stem. 'Grandiflora' bears pale yellow trumpet-shaped flowers, about 3 in.

Ajuga pyramidalis

Ajuga reptans 'Multicolor'

Alchemilla mollis

Allamanda cathartica 'Grandiflora'

Allium aflatunense

Allium albopilosum

Allium giganteum

Allium narcissiflorum

across; 'Hendersonii' is similar, but the flowers are orange-yellow. Both varieties flower from July to September. Although natural semi-climbers, these plants can be bush-trained.

A. neriifolia. S. America. Height 3–6 ft; spread 18–24 in. The lanceolate mid-green leaves of this shrubby plant are in whorls of three or four. Tubular yellow flowers, 1½ in. across, are borne from June to August.

Cultivation. Pot the plants in February or March in John Innes potting compost No. 3 or in a mixture of 3 parts loam, 2 parts leaf-mould or peat and 1 part sharp sand (parts by volume). Keep the plants almost dry during winter, but water plentifully in summer. Give a liquid feed at ten-day intervals from May to September.

Stop climbers when the desired height is reached by pinching out the leaders, and train to wires attached to the roof. If the plants are grown as shrubs, pinch out all growing points when the shoots reach a length of 9–12 in. Shrubs require frequent stopping. The plants have a vigorous root system and should be potted on annually in April into larger pots. Finish the varieties of *A. cathartica* in 18 in. tubs; *A. neriifolia* should finish in a 10–12 in. pot. The required winter temperature is 13°C (55°F).

Propagation. Take 3 in. long tip or lateral cuttings of non-flowering shoots in April or May. Root in equal parts (by volume) peat and sand at a temperature of 21–24°C (70–75°F). Pot on the rooted cuttings as necessary.

Pruning. In February, shorten the previous year's growths to within one or two nodes of the old wood of both climbers and shrubs.

Pests and diseases. Generally trouble-free.

Allium

Alliaceae

A genus of bulbous plants with 280 species, many found wild all over the Northern Hemisphere. Those selected for garden cultivation have terminal umbels of brightly coloured flowers, and are hardy and easy to grow. The foliage varies from the rolled-round leaves of garden onions and chives to the broad, oval leaves of wild garlic. Most species have the typical onion smell.

A. aflatunense. Central Asia. Height 2½ ft; planting distance 9 in. The strap-shaped leaves are a glaucous grey-green. The star-shaped pinkish flowers, which appear in 3–4 in. wide umbels during May and June, are good for cutting.

A. albopilosum. Middle East. Height 18 in.; planting distance 4–5 in. The leaves are strap-shaped, slightly glaucous and hairy underneath. The umbels, up to 6 in. across, produce as many as 80 lilac-pink star-shaped flowers in June.

A. ascalonicum: see Shallot

A. azureum: see *A. caeruleum*

A. beesianum. W. China. Height 15–18 in.; planting distance 6 in. The slightly glaucous leaves are linear and sparse. Bright blue or purple bell-shaped flowers are borne during July and August in umbels up to 2 in. wide. This species has a leek-like stem instead of a bulb.

A. caeruleum, syn. *A. azureum.* Siberia. Height 24 in.; planting distance 6 in. The mid-green

Allium moly

leaves are linear and angled. Deep blue star-shaped flowers are produced during June and July in umbels up to 3 in. wide.

A. cepa: see Onion

A. fistulosum: see Onion, Welsh

A. giganteum. Himalayas. Height 4 ft; planting distance 9–12 in. The leaves are glaucous and broadly strap-shaped. Deep lilac star-shaped flowers are produced in 4 in. wide umbels in June.

A. moly. S. Europe. Height 12 in.; planting distance 4 in. The leaves are grey and lanceolate. Bright yellow star-shaped flowers appear in 2 in. wide umbels during June and July.

A. narcissiflorum. Alps, Caucasus. Height 9 in.; planting distance 12 in. One of the most distinctive ornamental onions, with linear grey-green leaves and deeply bell-shaped pink flowers. It is represented in cultivation by *A. n. insubricum,* which bears nodding clusters of four to eight flowers, ½ in. long, in June and July.

A. neapolitanum. Mediterranean. Height 12 in.; planting distance 4 in. The mid-green leaves are narrowly strap-shaped and spreading. Star-shaped white flowers are carried from March to May in umbels 2–2½ in. wide. This species is hardy only in the mildest parts of the country.

A. oreophilum: see *A. ostrowskianum*

A. ostrowskianum, syn. *A. oreophilum.* Turkestan. Height 12 in.; planting distance 3 in. The linear, drooping leaves are slightly glaucous. Star-shaped rose-coloured flowers are borne in 1½–2 in. wide umbels in June.

A. porrum: see Leek

A. rosenbachianum. Bokhara. Height 24 in.; planting distance 6–9 in. The mid-green leaves are linear-lanceolate. In May and June the plant produces many rich purple star-shaped flowers, tightly packed in umbels 5–6 in. across.

A. roseum. W. Mediterranean. Height up to 12 in.; planting distance 4 in. The leaves are mid-green, broadly linear and spreading. Bright pink star-shaped flowers appear in 3–4 in. wide umbels during June.

A. sativum: see Garlic

A. schoenoprasum: see Chives

A. schubertii. E. Mediterranean. Height up to 24 in.; planting distance 6–9 in. The mid-green, strap-shaped, slightly wavy leaves spread to 12 in. The plant carries 4–6 in. wide umbels of star-shaped rose-red flowers in June and July.

A. siculum. Sicily. Height 2–4 ft; planting distance 9 in. The mid-green linear-lanceolate leaves are keeled. Bell-shaped green-white flowers, marked with purple, appear during May and June in umbels up to 4 in. wide.

A. triquetrum. S. Europe, Great Britain. Height 12 in.; planting distance 4 in. The leaves are mid-green, strap-shaped and keeled. The three-sided flower stems produce 1½–2 in. wide umbels of bell-shaped white flowers in April and May. The plant is not fully hardy.

A. zebdanense (sometimes incorrectly spelt as *zebadense*). Lebanon, Turkey. Height 18 in.; planting distance 6 in. Only two or three leaves, mid-green and linear-lanceolate, sheathe the lower flower stem. A few bell-shaped white flowers appear in 2 in. wide umbels during May.

Cultivation. Alliums do best in well-drained soil, open to the sun. Plant the smaller types among alpine plants, the others between low-growing shrubs or herbaceous plants. Plant in September or October, covering the bulbs to three or four times their own depth—for instance 3–4 in. of soil above a 1 in. bulb—and leave untouched for several years until the clumps are so thick that flowering is stifled. Large plants may need staking, especially on exposed sites. Dead-head the flowers, leaving the stems to feed the bulbs, and remove dead leaves and stems in the autumn.

Some dwarf species, such as *A. moly* and *A. ostrowskianum*, can be grown as pot plants if kept in a cold greenhouse or frame until nearly in flower, and then brought indoors. Plant in 6 in. pans of John Innes potting compost No. 1, setting about half a dozen bulbs in each pan.

Propagation. Many species set seeds. Soon after ripening, sow these in pots in a cold greenhouse or frame to produce flowering bulbs after two to four years. Sow bought seeds at any time between October and April. Sow the seeds thinly and leave for a year. Then either space them further apart in pots or boxes or set them in nursery rows outdoors.

Species which multiply rapidly can be split in the autumn or as growth starts in the spring. Replant both spring and autumn-divided bulbs immediately and keep the soil moist.

Pests. The young shoots, leaves and stems may be eaten by SLUGS.

Diseases. WHITE ROT may cause the leaves to turn yellow and die back; the roots rot and the base of the bulb becomes covered with a white fluffy fungus growth.

Almonds, ornamental: see Prunus

Aloe
Liliaceae

A genus of 275 species of greenhouse perennials. New species are still being discovered. These succulents are grown chiefly for their rosettes of thick, tapering leaves. The plants bear a superficial resemblance to the agaves, but their rosettes do not die after flowering. Long-stemmed racemes of bell-like or tubular flowers are produced from the leaf axils.

See also CACTUS.

A. aristata. Cape Province. Height 4–6 in. This species is almost hardy outdoors if sheltered from excess rain. The stemless rosette often has densely clustered leaves; these are grey-green, covered with white tubercles, and have horny white edges. The flowers are orange and appear in 12 in. high racemes in May or June. The plant forms offsets freely.

A. ferox. Natal. Height up to 12 ft. A slow-growing species. The margins and surfaces of the glaucous leaves are covered with brown spines. The 2–3 ft long racemes of red flowers are borne in terminal clusters in March.

ALOE VARIEGATA

A. variegata (partridge-breasted aloe). Cape Province. Height 12 in. This species often grows better in the dry air of a living-room than in a greenhouse. The erect, 5 in. long leaves are keeled towards the base and arranged in three closely overlapping ranks. They are dark green marked with irregular bands of white, and have white toothed edges. Orange flowers in a loose raceme about 12 in. high are produced in March and April. The plant forms offsets freely.

Cultivation. Grow aloes in 3–12 in. pots, according to the size of the plant. They grow well in John Innes potting compost No. 2 and make good pot plants for sunny window-ledges, though some species grow too tall for indoor cultivation. In summer, place them outdoors in a sunny position and give them plenty of water in hot weather. In winter aloes require a minimum temperature of 5°C (41°F) and only enough water to keep the plants just moist.

Repot annually in April.

Propagation. Remove offsets during the summer, leave them to dry for about two days, then pot them up in John Innes potting compost No. 2.

Aloes are also easily raised from seeds, which should be sown in March at a temperature of 21°C (70°F).

Pests. Tufts of white waxy wool on plant stems are caused by MEALY BUGS. ROOT MEALY BUGS infest root systems and check growth.

Diseases. Generally trouble-free.

Aloe, partridge-breasted: see *Aloe variegata*

Alonsoa
Mask flower. *Scrophulariaceae*

A genus of six species of half-hardy perennials. Those mentioned flower well in the first year from seed and are treated as annuals. They can be used in borders, for formal bedding and as pot plants under glass. As cut flowers they are attractive but short-lived. Although these are easy plants to grow, prolonged periods of wet weather are detrimental to flowering.

Allium ostrowskianum

Allium siculum

Aloe variegata

A. acutifolia, syn. *A. myrtifolia.* Peru. Height 2–3 ft; planting distance 6–9 in. A bushy plant with broad, pointed leaves that are mid-green and toothed along their margins. Deep red saucer-shaped flowers, ¾ in. wide, are produced from June to October. This makes an excellent pot plant for winter flowering under glass.

A. compacta: see *A. warscewiczii*

A. myrtifolia: see *A. acutifolia*

ALONSOA WARSCEWICZII

A. warscewiczii, syn. *A. compacta.* Peru. Height 12–24 in.; planting distance 15 in. This is the most popular species, being compact and well-branched, with red stems. The ovate leaves are dark green, and heart-shaped at the base. The spurred flowers, 1 in. across, are a brilliant scarlet and produced from July to October.

Cultivation. A rich, well-drained loam in a sunny situation is required. Set out the plants in their flowering position in May.

Grow pot plants for summer or winter flowering under glass in 5 in. containers, using John Innes potting compost No. 1. Stop the plants, to encourage bushy growth, by removing the growing tips when they are 2–3 in. high.

Propagation. Sow the seeds in boxes of seed compost, just covering them, at a temperature of 15°C (59°F). Sow in February or March for outdoor plants, in early February for summer-flowering pot plants, and in August for winter flowering. After pricking out, harden off outdoor plants in a cold frame before planting out in May.

Pests. APHIDS may infest stems and leaves, particularly on winter-flowering pot plants.

Diseases. Generally trouble-free.

Aloysia citriodora: see *Lippia citriodora*

Alstroemeria

Peruvian lily. *Alstroemeriaceae*
(formerly *Amaryllidaceae*)

ALSTROEMERIA AURANTIACA

A genus of 50 species of South American herbaceous perennials with fleshy, tuberous roots. The hardy and half-hardy plants described can be grown in borders or in cool greenhouses. They have twisted lanceolate leaves that are glaucous; irregularly trumpet-shaped flowers are borne on slender leafy stems from June to September and are long-lasting when cut.

A. aurantiaca. Chile. Height 3 ft; planting distance 12–15 in. This is the hardiest of the species. The flowers are 1½–2 in. wide and rich yellow to orange-scarlet, with the two upper petals veined with red.

Good garden varieties include: 'Dover Orange', slightly taller than the type, with orange-red flowers; 'Lutea', bright yellow with carmine markings; and 'Moerheim's Orange', a taller and more vigorous form.

A. chilensis. Chile. Height 2–3 ft; planting distance 9–12 in. This hardy species carries up to a dozen open, red or pink flowers, 1½–2 in. wide, on branched stalks at the top of the stem; the two upper petals are lined with yellow.

A. ligtu. Chile. Height 24 in.; planting distance 12 in. A half-hardy species producing 1½–2 in. wide flowers in several shades of lilac, pink or purple; the upper petals have purple stripes.

Ligtu hybrids are taller and more hardy than the parents and are available in a wide range of colours, including white, pink, scarlet, flame, orange and yellow.

A. pelegrina. Chile. Height and spread 12–15 in. This half-hardy species has erect stems clad in grey-green leaves. The widely funnel-shaped, 2 in. wide flowers may be borne singly or in a small terminal cluster. They range from near white through rose-lilac to crimson, flushed pale yellow and flecked red-purple on the upper pair of lateral petals. The form 'Alba', known as Lily of the Incas, is pure white.

A. pulchella. Brazil. Height 3 ft; planting distance 9–12 in. A half-hardy species, bearing red and green flowers, 1½–2 in. wide, with red-brown spots. Each stem carries four to six flowers.

A. violacea. Chile. Height 24 in.; planting distance 9–12 in. A half-hardy species; each stem carries a dozen or more bright lilac flowers, each measuring 1½–2 in. across.

Cultivation. Plant in March or early April, using young pot-grown specimens and taking care not to disturb the roots. Plant them in groups, to a depth of 4–6 in., in any well-drained fertile soil; choose a sheltered position and preferably one where they can be left untouched for years.

Occasionally, no top growth is made during the first year. Until the clumps are established, remove only a few flower stems for indoor use. When necessary, use twiggy sticks for support.

Dead-heading is recommended, particularly for *A. aurantiaca*, unless seeds are required. Cut the stems down to ground level in the autumn when the leaves have died. Except in the milder areas of the south and west, protect all species but *A. aurantiaca* from winter frosts with a layer of bracken, coarse sand, peat or weathered ashes.

For greenhouse plants, transfer young plants from their 3½ in. pots directly into the greenhouse border; or pot up in final 6–8 in. containers of John Innes potting compost No. 2. Use twiggy sticks for support. Give fortnightly feeds from June to September and provide light shade during the hottest months. Water freely during the growing period, but keep the soil barely moist from late October until March. In winter maintain a minimum greenhouse temperature of 5–7°C (41–45°F).

Propagation. Sow seeds in March in pots or pans of seed compost and place in a cold frame

Alonsoa warscewiczii

Alstroemeria aurantiaca

Alstroemeria pelegrina

or greenhouse. Prick out the seedlings into $3\frac{1}{2}$ in. pots and plunge in peat in a cold frame. Plant in the flowering site the following spring.

Alternatively, break up established clumps into 4–6 in. clusters between March and early April and replant immediately without removing any soil. To obtain a greater number of plants, carefully separate individual roots, also in March or April. Pot them up into 4–6 in. pots and plunge in peat in a cold frame; plant out in permanent positions about one year later.

Pests. Early growth can be severely checked by SLUGS, which eat young shoots, leaves and stems.

Caterpillars of the SWIFT MOTH may feed on the roots and damage the growing points.

Diseases. Plants are stunted by a VIRUS disease; the leaves show a yellow mottling and are sometimes distorted.

Althaea

Hollyhock. *Malvaceae*

ALTHAEA ROSEA

A genus of 12 hardy annual, biennial and perennial species, well known for their tall spikes of widely funnel-shaped flowers. Single and double-flowering forms, in a wide range of colours, including deep crimson, scarlet, pink, yellow, white and violet, are available. They are suited to cottage gardens and the backs of annual and herbaceous borders, and are at their best when grown as biennials.

A. chinensis: see *A. rosea*

A. ficifolia. Siberia. Height up to 6 ft; planting distance 24 in. A strong-growing perennial, moderately rust-resistant. The mid-green leaves have seven lobes and the single or double yellow flowers, up to 4 in. in diameter, are produced in June, 12 months after sowing. Many of the modern hybrids listed under *A. rosea* are in part derived from this species.

A. frutex: see *Hibiscus syriacus*

A. rosea, syn. *A. chinensis.* China. Height $4\frac{1}{2}$ ft when grown as an annual, 9 ft as a biennial; planting distances 15 in. and 24 in. The leaves are light green, rough and hairy, with five or six lobes. Single and double flowers, 4 in. or more across and in shades of pink, are carried on rigid stems from July to September. Many varieties are listed, in shades of yellow, red, pink and white. These include 'Chater's Double', with paeony-shaped double flowers, available in separate colours or as a mixture; 'Begonia Flowered Crested Mixed'; 'Single Mixed'; and 'Double Triumph Mixed', the best of the annual forms.

Cultivation. A heavy, rich soil and a sheltered site are ideal; plants in exposed positions, and also tall varieties, require staking. Water freely during dry weather and apply an annual mulch of well-rotted manure or compost.

Where more than a year's growth is required, cut down the plants to 6 in. after flowering. Dead-heading is unnecessary, unless self-seeding has to be prevented. The best flowers come from young plants, however, and retention of plants into the second year of flowering encourages the spread of rust.

Protection with cloches is advisable during periods of extreme cold, and in exposed gardens.

Propagation. To grow plants as perennials or biennials, sow the seeds outdoors in shallow drills, 9 in. apart, in June or July. Thin out or transplant the seedlings to 24 in. apart in September or October. In cold districts, sow the seeds in boxes and prick out into 6 in. pots for overwintering in a cold frame. Plant out in April.

For annuals, sow seeds in February in a temperature of 13°C (55°F). Prick out the seedlings into pots and harden in a cold frame before planting out in April. Alternatively, sow directly in the site in April and thin to 15 in. apart.

Pests. CATERPILLARS of various species of moth eat the leaves and stems.

CAPSID BUGS sometimes feed on young growth, causing tattering of the leaves.

Diseases. RUST shows on the leaves and stems as raised, spore-bearing pustules which are at first orange, but later turn brown. In severe cases, shrivelling of the leaves or even of the whole plant may occur.

Aluminium plant: see *Pilea cadierei*

Alyssum

Cruciferae

ALYSSUM MARITIMUM

A genus of 150 species of hardy annuals, herbaceous perennials and evergreen sub-shrubs. The species described are suitable for rock gardens and on dry walls, the larger species for the front of herbaceous borders. Alyssums have roughly cross-shaped flowers.

A. argenteum. S.E. Europe. Height 12–18 in.; spread 9–12 in. The oblong leaves of this shrubby perennial are grey-green. Bright yellow flowers, in heads 2–3 in. across, are borne in profusion from June to August.

A. maritimum, now botanically known as *Lobularia maritima.* Europe, W. Asia. Height 3–6 in.; spread 8–12 in. A densely branched bushy annual with linear, somewhat grey-green leaves. Short rounded racemes, 1–2 in. long, of white, lilac or purple flowers, are borne profusely from June to September.

The species is usually represented in cultivation by improved varieties, of which the following are recommended: 'Lilac Queen', deep lilac; 'Little Dorrit', syn. 'Little Gem', pure white; 'Minimum', syn. 'Snow Carpet' (3–4 in. high),

Althaea rosea

Althaea rosea
(double-flowered)

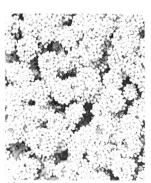

Alyssum maritimum
'Minimum'

Alyssum maritimum
'Rosie O'Day'

pure white; 'Rosie O'Day' (3–4 in. high), deep rose-pink; 'Royal Carpet' (3–4 in. high), violet-purple; and 'Violet Queen', bright violet-purple.

A. montanum. Europe. Height 4–6 in.; spread 12 in. This is a low-growing sub-shrubby perennial with obovate to oblong grey-green leaves. Loose racemes, 2 in. long, of bright yellow flowers appear in May and June.

A. saxatile (gold dust). E. Europe, Balkans, Russia. Height 9–12 in.; spread 12–18 in. An evergreen shrubby perennial with lanceolate grey-green leaves. Golden-yellow flowers in dense corymbs, 4–6 in. long, are borne from April to June.

Named varieties include: 'Citrinum', bright lemon-gold; 'Compactum' (6 in. high), golden-yellow; 'Dudley Neville', an unusual biscuit-yellow; and 'Plenum', syn. 'Flore-pleno', double and golden-yellow.

A. serpyllifolium. S.W. Europe. Height 2 in.; spread 12 in. This prostrate sub-shrub is not reliably hardy. It has grey ovate leaves; numerous heads, 1 in. across, of clear yellow flowers are borne in June.

Cultivation. Alyssums thrive in any ordinary, well-drained garden soil, in full sun. Plant annuals in April, perennials and shrubby species between September and March; cut the perennials back hard after flowering to prolong their life and make them more compact. Dead-head the annual species regularly by trimming lightly with scissors.

Propagation. Take 2–3 in. long cuttings of perennial species and varieties in June; insert in equal parts (by volume) peat and sand in a cold frame. When the cuttings are rooted, pot them singly into 3 in. pots of John Innes potting compost No. 1, and grow them on in a cold frame. Plant out in permanent flowering positions the following March.

All species can be raised from seeds. Sow seeds of perennials in boxes or pans of John Innes seed compost in a cold frame during March. Pot the seedlings singly in 3 in. pots of John Innes potting compost No. 1, when they are large enough to handle, and plant out in flowering positions from September onwards.

Sow seeds of annual species in pans or boxes of seed compost in February or March at a temperature of 10–13°C (50–55°F). Prick off the seedlings into boxes of John Innes potting compost No. 1 and harden them off in a cold frame before planting out in April.

Alternatively, sow the annuals thinly in the flowering site in March or April; thin out the seedlings to the required spacings. A further sowing in May prolongs the flowering period for several months.

Pests. Young plants may be eaten by SLUGS.

FLEA BEETLES may eat small holes in seedling leaves.

Diseases. Small blisters covered with white down on the undersides of the leaves reveal DOWNY MILDEW. This stunts the plants and often distorts the leaves or makes them curl.

WHITE BLISTER produces swellings full of white powdery spores on leaves and stems.

Amaracus dictamnus: see *Origanum dictamnus*
Amaranth, globe: see *Gomphrena globosa*

Alyssum saxatile

Alyssum serpyllifolium

Amaranthus tricolor

Amaranthus caudatus

Amaranthus

Amaranthaceae

AMARANTHUS CAUDATUS

A genus of 60 species of half-hardy annuals, some grown for their brightly coloured foliage, others for their tassel or plume-like flowers. Those mentioned are excellent for summer borders or as pot plants for greenhouse decoration. They last well in water when cut. If carefully dried, they hold their colour for a considerable time.

A. caudatus (love-lies-bleeding). Tropics. Height 3–4 ft; planting distance 18 in. This is the most popular species, with ovate leaves that are entire and light green. It is grown mainly for its drooping racemes, 18 in. and more long, of crimson flowers that appear from July to October. The stems turn crimson in the autumn.

The variety 'Viridis' has attractive pale green flowers which are particularly popular for flower arrangements.

A. hybridus. America. Height 3–4 ft; planting distance 12–18 in. A tall, thin-growing plant, similar to *A. caudatus* but with erect plumes of blood-red flowers from August to October. The foliage is flushed with copper.

A. hypochondriacus (prince's feather). Tropical America. Height 4–5 ft; planting distance 3 ft. A species similar to *A. caudatus*, but with erect rather than pendulous spikes.

A. tricolor (Joseph's coat). India. Height 2–3 ft; planting distance 12–18 in. A strong-growing, bushy plant, with hybrid forms grown for their attractive foliage. The ovate, pointed leaves are scarlet or crimson, overlaid with yellow, bronze and green. The racemes of flowers are dense, erect and brush-like, 6 in. and more high, deep red in colour and often fasciated. They appear in August and September.

All the varieties make striking bedding plants. 'Molten Fire' is particularly recommended, having deep copper-crimson leaves; it makes an excellent pot plant for a cool greenhouse. The variety 'Salicifolius' has drooping, willow-shaped leaves of orange, carmine and bronze.

Cultivation. A deeply cultivated soil, enriched with manure, and a sunny situation are ideal, although *A. caudatus* will grow moderately well even in poor soil. Set out plants in May.

For pot culture, transplant the seedlings into 5 in. or 6 in. pots of John Innes potting compost No. 1, and grow on at 13–15°C (55–59°F). A close, humid atmosphere and regular watering deepen the leaf colour of pot plants.

Propagation. Sow the seeds in seed compost under glass in March, at a temperature of 15°C (59°F). Prick out the seedlings into pots or boxes and harden off outdoor plants in a cold frame before planting out in May. Alternatively, sow directly in the flowering site in April, thinning out to the required spacing.

Pests. APHIDS sometimes infest plants.
Diseases. Generally trouble-free.

Amaryllis

Amaryllidaceae

AMARYLLIS BELLADONNA

A genus of a single bulbous species. It produces attractive flowers, suitable for cutting. Amaryllis can be grown in the open in an unsheltered position only in the south-west peninsula and the Scilly Isles and Channel Islands; elsewhere they need the protection of a south or west wall.

A. belladonna, syns. *Hippeastrum equestre, Callicore rosea.* S. Africa. Height 2–2½ ft; planting distance 12 in. Strap-shaped mid-green leaves, which appear after the flowers, last from early in the year until mid-summer. Three to four pale pink trumpet-shaped flowers, 4–5 in. across, appear on bare stems in September and October; they are sweetly scented. 'Hathor' is pure white with a yellow throat; 'Parkeri' is deep pink with a yellow throat and up to 12 flowers to a stem.

A. formosissima: see *Sprekelia formosissima*
Cultivation. Plant in June or July, with 6–8 in. of well-drained soil covering the bulb tops. Amaryllis do best at the foot of a south-facing wall; they need maximum warmth from summer sunshine and protection for the young leaves which appear in late winter and early spring.

If left undisturbed, new bulbs will develop and form clumps of plants over a period of years. Stakes are unnecessary; remove flowers as they die, and stems and leaves when they die down.

Propagation. During March sow seeds 1 in. deep in 4 in. pots of seed compost. Place these in a greenhouse at a temperature of 16°C (61°F). The seedlings will take up to eight years to flower and the blooms are likely to be variable in size, number and colour.

Lift mature plants when the leaves begin to turn yellow in summer; divide the bulbs and replant immediately.

Pests. Tunnels are sometimes hollowed out in the bulbs by NARCISSUS FLY MAGGOTS, causing the destruction of growing points.

BULB SCALE MITES infest the bulb scales, causing red discoloration and distortion of the leaves and flowers.
Diseases. Generally trouble-free.

Amaryllis, pot: see Hippeastrum

Amelanchier

Snowy mespilus, June berry. *Rosaceae*

A genus of 35 species of deciduous trees and shrubs distributed in N. America, Europe and N. Asia. They are hardy, easily grown trees, outstanding for their freely borne white flowers in spring and for their bright autumn foliage. Edible berries are produced and may be used in desserts.

A. canadensis (shadbush). Eastern N. America. Height and spread up to 10 ft. A suckering shrub with mid-green leaves, woolly on both sides; they are ovate, sharply toothed, and assume soft red or yellow tints in autumn. A profusion of pure white star-shaped flowers is borne in erect or curved racemes, 3–4 in. long, in April. They are followed by round, black, sweet-tasting berries which ripen in June.

Cultivation. Plant amelanchiers from November to early March, in any good garden soil that does not dry out; they thrive in a sunny or partially shaded position.

Propagation. Sow seeds from June to August in pots of John Innes seed compost in a cold frame. Line out the seedlings, when large enough to handle, in nursery rows outdoors and grow on for two or three years.

Alternatively, layer branches in September and separate from the parent plant the following autumn. Rooted suckers may be separated from October to March.

Pruning. None required.
Pests. Generally trouble-free.
Diseases. FIREBLIGHT causes a blackening and shrivelling of the flowers.

Anacyclus

Mount Atlas daisy. *Compositae*

A genus of 25 species of hardy evergreen perennials from the Atlas Mountains. The plants described have finely cut fern-like leaves which form neat mats. The flowering stems are prostrate for most of their length, becoming erect

Amaryllis belladonna

Amelanchier canadensis
(flowers)

Amelanchier canadensis
(autumn foliage)

at the tips, with white-yellow daisy-like flowers. The reverse sides of the petals are dull red, so that the plants are attractive in bud as well as in flower. These are good rock garden plants.

A. depressus. Morocco. Height 2 in.; spread 12 in. This species has grey-green leaves and the flowers measure 2 in. across. The flowering season lasts from June to August.

Cultivation. A well-drained soil is required and, ideally, a position in full sun. Plant in September or April; remove faded flower stems. The plants may be harmed if the soil is excessively wet and not sharply drained. Protection can be given against winter rain by raised panes of glass.

Propagation. If the seeds are fresh, sow them in October in gritty seed compost in a greenhouse at a temperature of 7–10°C (45–50°F). Pot up the seedlings individually in March. Over-watering will spoil them, but they must not be allowed to dry out. Plant out in September or April.

When using stored seeds, sow thinly in February and allow them to freeze for at least two nights, then bring into a temperature of 7–10°C (45–50°F) for germination. The seeds may take up to three years to germinate.

To propagate from cuttings, remove non-flowering side-shoots, 3 in. long, during March, April, July or August and insert them in equal parts (by volume) peat and sand in a cold frame. Pot up the rooted cuttings into 3 in. pots of John Innes potting compost No. 1. Plant out March and April cuttings in September, July and August cuttings in April of the following year.

Pests. APHIDS occasionally infest foliage, sucking the sap and making plants sticky and sooty.

Diseases. Generally trouble-free.

Anacyclus depressus

Anagallis arvensis

Anagallis tenella 'Studland'

Anagallis
Primulaceae

A genus of 31 species of hardy and half-hardy annuals and evergreen perennials. Those described are suitable for edging borders or for rock gardens and alpine houses. They also make attractive pot plants for cold greenhouses.

A. arvensis (scarlet pimpernel). Europe. Height 1–2 in.; planting distance 6 in. A hardy annual of low-spreading or prostrate habit, with ovate light green leaves. Saucer-shaped scarlet flowers, $\frac{3}{8}$ in. across, are produced from July to October.

This plant is a familiar weed in fields and gardens, but the cultivated varieties are well worth growing. *A. a. caerulea* is the most popular, producing a mass of dark blue flowers.

A. grandiflora: see *A. linifolia*

A. linifolia, syn. *A. grandiflora.* W. Mediterranean. Height 12 in.; spread 12–15 in. Though a perennial, this species should be treated as an annual as it is not reliably hardy in cultivation. If it is particularly well sited, it will seed itself. The leaves are dark green and narrowly lanceolate; the saucer-shaped flowers, resembling those of the scarlet pimpernel, are gentian-blue with red-purple undersides, and are 1–1$\frac{1}{4}$ in. across. The flowering season is from June to September.

Several garden forms, available in varying shades of blue and red, make excellent pot plants.

A. tenella (bog pimpernel). W. Europe, including

Anagallis linifolia

Great Britain. Height 1 in.; spread 12–15 in. A half-hardy perennial species with spoon-shaped mid-green leaves; the frail, prostrate stems are studded with upturned bell-like flowers, $\frac{1}{3}$ in. long, from May to July. These are usually pale pink, sometimes with deeper pink veins. A particularly fine form of this species is 'Studland', with deeper pink flowers.

This species requires the protection of an alpine house in dry, cold areas.

Cultivation. Outdoors, plant anagallis where they can benefit from full sun, *A. tenella* in April, *A. arvensis* and *A. linifolia* in May. The latter two species require ordinary, well-drained soil, but for *A. tenella* it should be moist at all times.

For summer flowering of *A. arvensis* under glass, set six or seven plants in a 12 in. pan of John Innes potting compost No. 1. Shade the plants from excessively hot sunshine and ventilate the greenhouse freely. For winter flowering, grow single plants in 5 in. pots and maintain a temperature of 7–10°C (45–50°F).

In the alpine house, grow *A. linifolia* and *A. tenella* in 8–10 in. pans of John Innes potting compost No. 1; repot annually in March.

Propagation. Increase *A. tenella* by division and replanting in April or May.

Sow seeds of *A. linifolia* under glass at a temperature of 16°C (61°F), and of *A. arvensis* in the flowering positions in March or April. Sow in July or August for winter-flowering pot plants.

Prick out the seedlings of *A. linifolia* into pots or boxes, and harden off outdoor plants in a cold frame before setting them out in May.

Pests. APHIDS may infest plants under glass.

Diseases. Generally trouble-free.

Ananas
Bromeliaceae

A genus of five species of evergreen plants. All species are terrestrial; one is the edible pineapple. They are suitable as greenhouse ornamental plants, but warm greenhouse cultivation is needed to produce edible pineapples.

See also BROMELIADS.

A. comosus, syn. *A. sativus.* Brazil and Colombia. Height 3 ft. This is the commercial pineapple, grown in tropical countries. The pineapple was first introduced into Britain at Richmond, Surrey, and edible fruit was produced there in 1715.

The pointed and strap-shaped arching grey-green serrated leaves form a dense rosette, 3–5 ft across. The flower stem is short and stout, with inconspicuous pink bracts and an ovoid head, 3 in. long of three-petalled blue blossoms. Fleshy succulent fruits develop which coalesce to form the typical pineapple.

A. c. 'Variegatus' has leaves with longitudinal bands of cream to white near the margins, and red spines. The whole centre of the plant turns bright rose at flowering time.

ANANAS COMOSUS

A. sativus: see *A. comosus*
Cultivation. Plant in late spring or early summer in a mixture of 2 parts fibrous loam, 1 part leaf-mould or peat, and 1 part sand (parts by volume). Water freely during growth, but allow to dry out between waterings. Repot annually in March; final pot size should be 6–8 in.
Propagation. Slips or shoots form at the base of the plants and may be detached at any time, preferably in March or April. The crown of leaves on top of the fruit will also develop into a new plant if potted up and grown on. Remove the shoots or crown leaves with a sharp knife and leave for a few days to dry. Pot the cuttings in coarse sand; after about a month repot in the final compost. Strong bottom heat of 23°C (74°F) is advisable during the rooting period.
Pests and diseases. Generally trouble-free.

Anaphalis

Pearl everlasting. *Compositae*

ANAPHALIS NUBIGENA

A genus of 35 species of hardy, erect herbaceous perennials. The attractive grey foliage and white everlasting flat flower heads of these species make them popular plants for floral arrangements, either when freshly cut or when dried for winter decoration.
A. margaritacea. N. America, E. Asia. Height and planting distance 12–18 in. The leaves are grey-green and tapering. Pearly white flowers, 3 in. across, are freely produced in August.
A. nubigena. Himalayas. Height up to 8 in.;

planting distance 9–12 in. The lanceolate silver-grey leaves are woolly. Off-white flowers, ½ in. across, appear in close terminal clusters in August and September. This species does well in dry places on a rock garden.
A. triplinervis. Himalayas. Height 12 in.; planting distance 12–15 in. The undersides of the silver-grey leaves are covered with white woolly hairs. White flowers are borne in small bunched heads, 3–4 in. across, in August.
A. yedoensis. Japan. Height up to 24 in.; planting distance 12–15 in. The grey-green leaves are lanceolate. It bears closely bunched white flowers, 3–4 in. across, from July to September.
Cultivation. Plant between September and April in a sunny position and in well-drained soil. The plants will also grow in dry shade. If the plants become untidy in autumn, cut them hard back.
Propagation. Divide during suitable weather between September and April.

Take 2–3 in. long cuttings of basal shoots in April or May and root in equal parts (by volume) peat and sand, in a cold frame. Plant them out in a nursery bed when they are well rooted.

Sow seeds in a box or pan of seed compost in March or April and place them in a cold frame. Prick the seedlings out into boxes when they are large enough to handle and then into a nursery bed; plant out from October to March.
Pests and diseases. Generally trouble-free.

Anchusa

Boraginaceae

ANCHUSA AZUREA

A genus of 50 species of hardy biennials and herbaceous perennials, including plants suitable for rock gardens. They provide a vivid display of colour if planted in groups, and some can be grown in pots or pans in an alpine house.
A. angustissima. E. Europe. Height 9–12 in.; planting distance 6–9 in. A perennial species suitable for a rock garden and the front of a herbaceous border. It has tough hairy stems and long, narrow, dark green leaves. Gentian-blue flowers, salver-shaped and ⅓–½ in. across, are borne in dense cymes from May to July. If cut down after flowering, the plants usually bloom again in the autumn.
A. azurea, syn. *A. italica.* Caucasus. Height 3–5 ft, planting distance 12–18 in. This herbaceous perennial is the most widely grown species. The mid-green leaves are lanceolate. Salver-shaped bright blue flowers, ⅓ in. across, are produced in large panicles from June to August.

Popular varieties are: 'Dropmore', 5–6 ft, with rich deep blue flowers; 'Loddon Royalist', 3 ft, gentian-blue; 'Morning Glory', 4–5 ft, deep blue; 'Opal', 4 ft, sky-blue; and 'Royal Blue', 3–4 ft, an intense gentian-blue.

Ananas comosus 'Variegatus'

Anaphalis triplinervis

Anaphalis yedoensis

Anchusa azurea
'Loddon Royalist'

Anchusa azurea 'Royal Blue'

Anchusa caespitosa

Androsace chamaejasme

Anchusa azurea 'Dropmore'

A. caespitosa. Crete. Height 2–3 in.; spread 9 in. A rock garden or alpine house perennial species, with deep green, bristly, linear leaves that form prostrate rosettes. Salver-shaped flowers, up to $\frac{1}{3}$ in. across, appear from May to July in dense clusters in the centres of the rosettes. They are vivid deep blue with a white eye.

A. capensis. Africa. Height 18 in.; spacing 6–9 in. A biennial species of bushy habit, usually grown as an annual. It is a good plant for a mixed border and is also suitable for growing as a pot plant. The mid-green leaves are rather hairy, narrow and pointed; the flowers, blue and saucer-shaped, are $\frac{1}{4}$ in. across and produced in elongated panicles from July to August. 'Blue Bird' is a striking variety, producing sprays of flowers similar to forget-me-nots throughout the summer.

A. italica: see A. azurea

A. myosotidiflora: see Brunnera macrophylla

Cultivation. Plant A. angustissima and A. azurea outdoors between October and March. These deep-rooted plants will grow in any fertile garden soil, given a sunny position. Add sand or weathered ashes to heavy soil to improve the drainage. Support the plants with twiggy sticks; further flowers may result if the upper halves of the stems are removed after flowering. In any case, cut down old stems in October.

A. caespitosa is not easy to grow outdoors, though it will sometimes last for a number of years if planted on a raised bed or in a limestone scree in a sunny position. Generally it is best grown in an alpine house in a 6–8 in. pan of John Innes potting compost No. 1. Plant in September or April and repot in March every other year.

Any well-cultivated soil in a sunny position is suitable for A. capensis. Plants sown in June and treated as biennials require winter protection under cloches in all but the most sheltered areas.

For flowering under glass in April and May, pot on January-sown seedlings into final 5 in. pots of John Innes potting compost No. 2.

Propagation. Increase A. azurea by root cuttings taken in January or February; A. angustissima by basal cuttings, 2 in. long, taken in March or April. Insert both types of cuttings in boxes of John Innes seed compost in a cold frame and set them out in a nursery bed during April or May. Plant in their flowering positions from October onwards.

To increase A. caespitosa, take 2 in. root cuttings in March or April and insert them into equal parts (by volume) peat and sand. When four or five leaves are showing, set the plants in 3 in. pots of John Innes potting compost No. 1. Pot on as necessary until they are in their final 6–8 in. pans. If they are to be planted outdoors, do this in September or the following April.

To grow A. capensis as an annual, sow the seeds in the open ground in April, thinning out the seedlings to the required spacing. Sow in June if they are to be grown as biennials, again thinning to the required spacing.

For flowering under glass, sow seeds in January at a temperature of 13–16°C (55–61°F). Pot the seedlings singly in 3 in. pots of John Innes potting compost No. 1 and pot on as necessary.

Pests. Generally trouble-free.

Diseases. CUCUMBER MOSAIC VIRUS produces mosaic symptoms of yellow spots on the leaves.

Andromeda floribunda: see *Pieris floribunda*
Andromeda formosa: see *Pieris formosa*
Andromeda japonica: see *Pieris japonica*

Androsace

Rock jasmine. *Primulaceae*

A genus of over 100 species of hardy perennials. Some are suitable for alpine houses; others, protected from winter moisture, will grow on rock gardens. The high-alpine species, which are indicated in the species descriptions, produce hummocks of tiny rosettes of leaves and myriads of flowers. The compact form is modified in the lower-growing species, which have looser clumps of foliage and flowers borne in umbels.

Unless otherwise stated, all the species described have linear to narrowly lanceolate, mid-green leaves, often covered with silky white hairs, and small primrose-like flowers.

A. alpina, syn. A. glacialis. Europe. Height 1 in.; spread 6 in. This high-alpine species has loosely tufted rosettes that form a flat cushion. Pale to rose-pink flowers, $\frac{1}{3}$ in. wide, appear from May to June in thick clusters which hide the leaves. The plant is difficult to cultivate and is best grown in an alpine house.

A. carnea. Europe. Height 3 in.; spread 6–9 in. The rosettes of this species are elongated; pale pink flowers, about $\frac{1}{4}$ in. across, are borne in umbels in June and July. The variety 'Laggeri', a little smaller than the type, is easier to grow and self-seeds readily. The flowers, slightly larger than the type species, are deep rose-pink with a golden eye. Both plants are best grown in an alpine house.

A. chamaejasme. Mountains of Northern Hemisphere. Height 1–2 in.; spread 6 in. A high-alpine species with loose mats of rosettes; it is best grown in an alpine house. Hairy flowering stems carry white flowers, $\frac{1}{4}$ in. wide, in June.

A. glacialis: see A. alpina

A. helvetica. Switzerland. Height 2 in.; spread 4–6 in. A high-alpine species that makes a tufted

Androsace helvetica

dome of leaves encasing the almost sessile solitary white flowers, $\frac{1}{4}$ in. wide, which appear in April and May. It needs alpine-house conditions, but is comparatively easy to grow.

A. imbricata. Alps and Pyrenees. Height 1 in.; spread up to 4 in. A congested high-alpine species, with silvery rosettes. The tiny white flowers, $\frac{1}{5}$ in. across, are borne during May. Although hardy, this plant does best in an alpine house where it can be protected from winter wet.

A. lanuginosa. Himalayas. Height up to $1\frac{1}{2}$ in.; spread 12–18 in. The trailing, mat-forming habit of this species distinguishes it from the rosette-forming kinds. It grows satisfactorily outdoors. The leaves are ovate and silver-green. Pinkish flowers, $\frac{1}{3}$ in. wide, open between June and October. The variety 'Leichtlinii' has white flowers with a red eye.

A. pyrenaica. Pyrenees. Height $1\frac{1}{2}$–2 in.; spread 4 in. The rosettes of this high-alpine species, which are smaller than those of others in the genus, form densely tufted domes. Sessile white flowers, $\frac{1}{6}$ in. across, are borne in May and June. It grows best in an alpine house.

A. sarmentosa. Himalayas. Height 4 in.; spread up to 24 in. This species is easy to grow on a rock garden. The rosettes vary in width from 1 in. in winter to 3 in. in summer. The foliage is predominantly mid-green in summer, but in winter the outer leaves wither to reveal a button of woolly grey-green leaves. Dome-shaped heads of $\frac{1}{4}$ in. wide rose-pink flowers are borne on 2–4 in. stems from April to June.

The variety *A. s. chumbyi* has a more compact habit and is more robust. *A. s. yunnanensis* has leaves that are more woolly, and deep rose flowers on 3–4 in. stems.

A. sempervivoides. Kashmir, Tibet. Height 2 in.; spread 9–12 in. This species, which is suitable for a rock garden, has flat rosettes of bright green leaves; it bears umbels of bright pink flowers, each $\frac{1}{5}$ in. across, in May and June.

A. villosa. European Alps, Asia. Height 2–3 in.; spread 9–12 in. This species has compact silver-green rosettes. The flowers are pure white or pink with a yellow eye, measure $\frac{1}{3}$ in. across, and appear between May and June. The plant is

suitable for an alpine house or for growing outdoors on a sunny scree.

The variety *A. v. arachnoidea* is more hairy and bears a profusion of pure white flowers on 1 in. long stems. The small yellow eye on each flower changes to crimson.

Cultivation. Plant androsaces in March or April in a sunny position in sharply drained soil, preferably with limestone grit or coarse sand added. In the alpine house, pot them in 3 in. pots between March and June in a mixture of 3 parts sifted leaf-mould and 1 part finely crushed grit (parts by volume). Top off with coarse chippings and stand the pots in a partially shaded site from May to September. Repot in March when the pots become congested, generally after three years.

Propagation. Sow the seeds in January or February in pans of John Innes seed compost. Allow them to freeze for about a fortnight, then bring the pans into a temperature of 7°C (45°F).

If the seeds do not germinate the first spring, keep the pans until the following spring. Prevent moss from growing on top by covering the compost with fine grit.

Pot the seedlings up in 3 in. pots when four true leaves are showing and keep in a partially shaded frame. Water from below, giving little or no water in winter.

Alternatively, except for *A. lanuginosa*, detach single rosettes from the plants in June. Insert them in sand and place in a cold frame. Overwinter in pots until planting out the following April. For *A. lanuginosa*, take 2 in. basal shoots and treat as described for rosettes.

Pests. APHIDS infest leaves in summer, sucking the sap and causing severe damage.

ROOT MEALY BUGS and ROOT APHIDS infest roots and check growth.

GLASSHOUSE RED SPIDER MITES infest leaves, causing a fine light mottling of the upper surfaces which is followed by bronzing and death.

BIRDS will also attack plants and tear the rosettes to pieces.

Diseases. Generally trouble-free.

Anemone

Windflower. *Ranunculaceae*

ANEMONE × HYBRIDA

A genus of 150 species of hardy herbaceous, perennials. The summer and autumn-flowering herbaceous species are fibrous-rooted, long-lived plants, suitable for growing in a border; they have branching stems. The spring-flowering species are generally tuberous-rooted and suitable for rock gardens, for naturalising in open woodland and for providing cut flowers.

Anemone flowers are cup or bowl-shaped, composed of from five to twenty petaloid sepals, sometimes opening out flat when mature.

Androsace imbricata

Androsace lanuginosa

Androsace sarmentosa

Androsace sarmentosa chumbyi

Anemone coronaria St Brigid

Anemone × *hybrida* 'Queen Charlotte'

Anemone × *fulgens*

Anemone hupehensis

Anemone blanda

The leaves are generally three or five-lobed, deeply cut and mid to deep green; on the stems they are borne in whorls of three.

SUMMER AND AUTUMN-FLOWERING SPECIES

A. × elegans: see A. × hybrida

A. hupehensis. China. Height 2½–3 ft; planting distance 24 in. This tufted species is one parent of A. × hybrida. Sprays of 2 in. wide mauve-pink flowers open from August to October.

A. × hybrida (sometimes listed as A. japonica or A. × elegans). Height 2–3 ft; planting distance 12–18 in. A group of hybrids that are free-flowering once established although they rarely make strong growth during the first year. The flowers, 2–3 in. wide, are produced from August to October.

Recommended named forms include: 'Honorine Jobert' (4 ft high), with white flowers, popularly known as A. japonica. 'Lorelei', delicate rose-pink; 'Louise Uhink', pure white; 'Max Vogel', pink; 'Queen Charlotte', semi-double, pink; and 'September Charm', clear pink flowers.

A. japonica: see A. × hybrida

A. × lesseri. Height 12–18 in.; planting distance 12 in. This garden hybrid bears rose-red flowers, 1½–2 in. across, on erect stems in May and June. There are purple, yellow and white forms, but these are not readily available.

SPRING-FLOWERING SPECIES

A. blanda. Greece. Height up to 6 in.; planting distance 4 in. The blue flowers, 1–1½ in. across, are borne from February to April. Pale blue, mauve, pink and white forms are available.

A. coronaria. E. Mediterranean regions. Height 6–12 in.; planting distance 3–4 in. The 1½–2 in. wide flowers, produced in March and April, are white or in several shades of blue and red. Descended from this species are the two most popular strains of florists' anemones:

De Caen. Height 6–12 in.; planting distance 4–6 in. This is the florists' single anemone, with the same colour range as A. coronaria. Each plant may produce 20 or more flowers over a long flowering season (see CULTIVATION). The best varieties include: 'Hollandia', syn. 'His Excellency', scarlet; 'Mr Fokker', blue; 'Sylphide', magenta; and 'The Bride', white. There are also various mixed strains of De Caen anemones.

St Brigid. Height 6–12 in.; planting distance 4–6 in. A double or semi-double strain, with colours similar to those of De Caen but with fewer flowers to each plant. Three good varieties are: 'Lord Lieutenant', blue; 'The Admiral', magenta; and 'The Governor', scarlet.

A. × fulgens. Height 12 in.; planting distance 4–6 in. This hybrid has scarlet 2 in. wide flowers with narrow sepals. The flowers are produced from March to May.

A. narcissiflora. Alps, Pyrenees and Apennines. Height and planting distance 12 in. A tufted species bearing 1–1½ in. wide white or cream flowers, sometimes flushed pale purple in bud; they are borne in terminal leafy umbels from May to July.

A. nemorosa. Europe, including Great Britain. Height 6–8 in.; planting distance 6 in. This native wood anemone is useful for naturalising in open woodland. The flowers are 1 in. across and appear in March and April. They are white, sometimes flushed with pink. 'Robinsoniana' has lavender-blue flowers, slightly larger than the type; 'Vestal', is similar to the type but has a boss of white petaloids.

A. sulphurea: see *Pulsatilla alpina* 'Sulphurea'

Cultivation of summer and autumn-flowering species. Plant between October and March in any fertile, well-drained but moisture-retentive soil, in partial shade. These plants, and particularly *A.* × *hybrida*, are best left undisturbed for several years after planting. Cut the stems down to ground level after flowering.

Cultivation of spring-flowering species. Grow these in any good, well-drained soil, in sun or partial shade; varieties of *A. coronaria* and *A.* × *fulgens* do best in full sun. Plant at a depth of 1½–2 in. during September or October.

A. coronaria can be flowered almost all the year round by successive planting. Large corms take about three months to flower, smaller corms up to six months. For winter-flowering, protect with cloches from October onwards.

Varieties of *A. coronaria* and *A.* × *fulgens* quickly deteriorate and should be replaced every two or three years.

Propagation of summer and autumn-flowering species. Divide and replant during suitable weather between October and March.

Take root cuttings of *A.* × *hybrida* between November and January; insert in boxes of equal parts (by volume) peat and sand in a cold frame. When about three leaves have developed, line out the young plants in nursery rows and plant out in October of the following year.

Propagation of spring-flowering species. Separate the offsets or divide the rhizomes after the top growth has died down in late summer.

Sow seeds when ripe, or during August and September, in pots or pans of seed compost and place in a cold frame or greenhouse. Prick off the seedlings, when large enough to handle, into boxes; line out the young plants in nursery rows at the end of the first growing season and grow on for one or two years before planting out in permanent positions.

Pests. Seedlings may be attacked by FLEA BEETLES which eat small holes in the leaves.

CATERPILLARS and various CUTWORMS eat leaves, flower buds and stems of older plants.

APHIDS may infest stems and leaves, making the plants sticky and sooty.

SLUGS may attack tubers and young shoots.

Diseases. Several virus diseases, such as ARABIS MOSAIC and CUCUMBER MOSAIC VIRUSES, may affect anemones. General symptoms are stunting of plants; yellowing of foliage, which is sometimes twisted and distorted; and flowers of poor size and colour. One virus causes browning and withering of the foliage.

CLUSTER CUP RUST causes a malformation of the leaves, which become thickened and less divided, with long, thick leaf stalks. Yellow cups bearing fungus spores form on the affected leaves and also on the stems. Severely diseased plants do not flower.

Angelica

Angelica archangelica. Umbelliferae

ANGELICA

A hardy biennial or short-lived perennial herb, which is longer-lived if the flowers are removed.

Height 6–10 ft; planting distance 3 ft. Europe. The stems are ridged and the aromatic leaves deeply dissected. Yellow-green flowers appear in clusters of rounded umbels, 3 in. across, in July and August. Stems and leaves are light green.

Angelica is used in confectionery, the candied young flower stems, leaf-stalks and leaf-midribs being used for cake and trifle decoration, and also in liqueurs. The roots and leaves may be cooked fresh, with rhubarb and apples to reduce the acidity. Fresh or dried leaves may be infused to make tea, and dried leaves can be included in an aromatic *pot-pourri.*

Cultivation. Plant angelicas in March in a moist, sunny or partially shady position where the soil is rich in humus. To encourage the growth of strong foliage, remove the flower heads as soon as they appear in July of the following year or a year later. The plants usually die after flowering and producing seeds, but if they are not allowed to flower, they will live for an extra year or two.

Propagation. Sow seeds outdoors in March or April in shallow drills 12 in. apart; prick out the seedlings to 12 in. spacings as soon as they are large enough to handle. Keep the seed bed clean and free from weeds until the following March; lift the plants carefully and transplant them to their final quarters.

Alternatively, allow plants not needed for harvesting to flower and seed themselves. These seeds germinate quickly, and will produce plenty of seedlings for planting out the following spring.

Harvesting and storing. Cut the main stems of angelica for candying in May or June, while they are tender, or the side-growths in August. Remove leaflets from stems and leaf stalks.

Harvest leaves for drying, picking them before flowering-time while they are still a fresh green. For methods of drying see entry under HERBS.

If the roots are to be used, dig them up in their first autumn before they become woody.

Pests and diseases. Generally trouble-free.

Angel's fishing rod: see Dierama
Angel's tears: see *Billbergia nutans* and *Narcissus triandrus albus*
Angel's trumpet: see *Datura cornigera*

Anemone coronaria De Caen

Anemone narcissiflora

Anemone nemorosa 'Robinsoniana'

Angelica

Angraecum
Orchidaceae

A genus of 220 species of tropical African and Madagascan evergreen epiphytic orchids. Erect stems take the place of a pseudobulb and sometimes have one or more basal shoots. These plants generally require a warm greenhouse.

The leaves are carried in two opposite rows along the stems, or are borne as flattened tufts; they are lanceolate, ovate, strap-shaped or needle-like, and vary greatly in size. The green or white star-like flowers are borne on wiry stems. They vary in size, but are always spurred.

See also ORCHIDS.

A. distichum. Tropical Africa. This species does well in intermediate conditions. The bright green, flattened, ovate leaves are neatly arranged on a 12 in. high stem. White flowers, $\frac{2}{4}$ in. across, on short, down-curving stems, are freely produced from August to October.

A. eburneum. Madagascar. A widely cultivated large-flowered species with light green strap-shaped leaves on a stem up to 3 ft high. Arching or pendulous flower stems, 2–3 ft long, bear pale green, short-stalked flowers, 3–4 in. wide, from December to March.

Angraecum sesquipedale

ANGRAECUM SESQUIPEDALE

A. sesquipedale. Madagascar. A large, robust species, with short, strap-shaped, glaucous dark green leaves. Each flower stem is up to 6 in. long and from March to May bears two to four flowers that measure 5–6 in. across and have spurs up to 12 in. long. They have a thick, wax-like texture and are ivory-cream, occasionally tinged with pale green.

Cultivation. Grow these orchids in well-crocked pans or baskets containing a compost of equal parts (by volume) osmunda fibre and sphagnum moss. Maintain a minimum winter temperature of 14°C (57°F), although *A. distichum* will tolerate 10°C (50°F).

There is no resting phase, and the plants should be ventilated daily between May and October, from October to April only on mild days. Shade the greenhouse on sunny days from April to October, and give an occasional liquid feed from May to October. Water freely from May to October, but reduce the amount of water from November to April.

Propagation. Remove strong new growths about 12 in. long from the top of old stems in May and use them as cuttings.

Insert the cuttings in 4 in. pots of the growing compost and place in a propagating case at a temperature of 18–21°C (64–70°F). Pot on the rooted cuttings as necessary.

Alternatively, detach basal shoots in April or May and treat as described for cuttings.

Pests and diseases. Generally trouble-free.

Antennaria
Compositae

ANTENNARIA DIOICA

A genus of 100 species of hardy evergreen perennials. Those described are grey-leaved mat-forming plants, with small tufted flowers which vary in colour from white to deep rose. They are suitable for rock gardens and alpine houses.

A. dioica. Europe, Asia, N. America. Height 2–12 in.; spread 18 in. The spathulate grey-green leaves form a dense creeping mat which roots where it spreads. White, pink-tipped flowers, about $\frac{1}{4}$ in. across, are borne in terminal clusters during May and June.

A. d. 'Aprica' has bright silver-grey foliage; 'Minima' (height 2 in.) is smaller in all its parts than the type; 'Nyewood' (height 3–4 in.) bears crimson flowers. The flowers of 'Rosea' (height 4–6 in.) are deep pink.

Cultivation. Plant well-rooted purchased plants in light, well-drained soil in a sunny position between September and March.

Propagation. Divide in March or April and replant direct in final positions.

Pests and diseases. Generally trouble-free.

Antennaria dioica 'Aprica'

Anthemis
Compositae

ANTHEMIS TINCTORIA

A genus of 200 species of hardy annuals, biennials and herbaceous perennials, only a few of which are of decorative value. Those described here are perennials, with attractively cut leaves and daisy-like flowers. *A. nobilis* may be used as a substitute for grass in forming a lawn.

A. cupaniana. Italy. Height 6–12 in.; planting distance 12–15 in. A spreading, cushion-forming plant, with grey, aromatic, finely dissected leaves. White flowers, 2–2$\frac{1}{2}$ in. across, are borne on short, erect stems from June to August.

A. nobilis (common chamomile). Europe, including Great Britain. The currently correct name of this plant is *Chamaemelum nobile*. Height 6–9 in.; planting distance 12–15 in. A mat-forming species with finely dissected, aromatic, mid-green foliage that has a mossy appearance. Daisy-like flowers, 1$\frac{1}{2}$ in. across, are borne on sparingly branched stems from June to August. Provided it is not subject to hard wear, common

Anthemis cupaniana

chamomile can be used to form small fragrant lawns. For this purpose it is advisable to obtain the vigorous non-flowering variety 'Treneague', which needs little mowing.

A. sancti-johannis. Bulgaria. Height 18 in.; planting distance 12–15 in. The deeply lobed and toothed leaves are grey-green and hairy. Bright orange flowers, 2–2½ in. across, are borne from June to August.

A. tinctoria (ox-eye chamomile). Europe. This species has been superseded by its hybrids with *A. sancti-johannis.* The following recommended varieties (height 2½ ft; planting distance 15–18 in.) have mid-green leaves that are deeply lobed and toothed. Flowers, 2–2½ in. wide, are borne from June to August.

'E. C. Buxton', lemon-yellow; 'Grallagh Gold', deep golden-yellow; 'Wargrave Variety', cream.

Cultivation. Plant decorative anthemis between September and March in a sunny situation in any ordinary, well-drained soil. On exposed sites, tall plants may need supporting with twiggy sticks. Cut down the old flower stems in October.

To grow *A. nobilis* for a lawn, set young plants in well-drained soil in an open position, 6 in. apart each way, in March or April. It may be necessary to mow the plants carefully once or twice a year to remove long stems.

Propagation. Increase the non-flowering variety of *A. nobilis* from cuttings of lateral shoots, 3 in. long, taken between May and August. Insert them in a mixture of equal parts (by volume) peat and sand in a cold frame; plant the rooted cuttings out in September or the following March.

Propagate decorative anthemis from cuttings of young basal shoots, 2–3 in. long, taken in April or May. Insert the cuttings in sandy soil in a cold frame; transfer them to nursery beds when they are well rooted, and set them out in their flowering positions in September or October.

Alternatively, divide and replant the roots between September and March.

Pests and diseases. Generally trouble-free.

Anthericum

St Bernard's lily. *Liliaceae*

A genus of 300 species of herbaceous perennials. The two hardy species described are the only ones in general cultivation; they are decorative garden plants with slender spikes of starry white flowers that may be used for floral arrangements.

A. graminifolium: see *A. ramosum*

A. liliago. S. Europe. Height 18–24 in.; planting distance 12–15 in. The grass-like mid-green leaves grow in tufts, and 1½ in. wide flowers are produced in May and June.

A. ramosum, syn. *A. graminifolium.* S. Europe. Height 2–3 ft; planting distance 12–15 in. The leaves are similar to those of *A. liliago.* White flowers, ¾ in. across, open from June to August.

Cultivation. Plant between October and March in partial shade in light, loamy soil that does not dry out in summer. Mulch in early March with well-rotted manure or garden compost. Cut the stems back to ground level after flowering unless seeds are required.

Propagation. Sow seeds in March in a box or pan

of seed compost in a cold frame. Prick off the seedlings into 3 in. pots and grow them on in an open frame, or in a plunge bed of peat or soil, ready for planting out from October onwards.

Plants can also be divided during suitable weather between October and March, but as disturbance is harmful it is best to divide only overcrowded plants.

Pests and diseases. Generally trouble-free.

Anthriscus cerefolium: see Chervil

Anthurium

Araceae

ANTHURIUM SCHERZERIANUM

A genus of 550 species of evergreen greenhouse plants. Some are grown for their striking flowering spathes, others for their ornamental leaves. Apart from *A. scherzerianum*, the following species require warmth and a humid atmosphere.

A. andreanum (painter's palette). Colombia. Height 18 in.; spread 12 in. A foliage plant with dark green, heart-shaped leaves up to 8 in. long. The waxy red or white flower spathes are 4 in. long and 3 in. wide with a cylindrical 3 in. long spadix; they appear from May to September.

A. crystallinum. Colombia. Height 18 in.; spread 12 in. A foliage plant with dark green, heart-shaped, velvety leaves, up to 24 in. long and 12 in. across. They are violet when young, maturing to deep green, with the midribs and veins ivory above and pale pink beneath. Insignificant green flower spathes appear from May to September.

A. scherzerianum. Guatemala. Height 9 in.; spread 12–18 in. This species has lanceolate dark green leaves up to 7 in. long. From April to October it bears 3–4 in. long, waxy, palette-shaped spathes of brilliant scarlet with a spiral, orange-red spadix. Suitable as a house plant.

Cultivation. Anthuriums do best when kept at a constant temperature. The minimum winter temperature for *A. andreanum* and *A. crystallinum* is 13°C (55°F), although at this level the leaves of the latter may yellow at the edges; the ideal is 16°C (61°F). For *A. scherzerianum*, 10°C (50°F) is the minimum, 13°C (55°F) the ideal. Pot in March in a compost of 3 parts peat to 1 part chopped sphagnum moss (parts by volume), mixed with a little loam and charcoal. The pots should be one-third full of drainage material; pot greenhouse plants in 6–8 in. pots or on 8–10 in. rafts. House plants can be grown in 4–5 in. pots. Keep the growing point well clear of the compost.

Water the plants moderately from October to March; during the growing season and whenever the temperature exceeds 16°C (61°F) the plants should be freely watered.

In the greenhouse, maintain a high humidity by damping down twice a day and syringing the

Anthemis tinctoria 'Grallagh Gold'

Anthericum liliago

Anthurium andreanum

Anthurium scherzerianum

Antirrhinum majus
'Apple Blossom'

Antirrhinum majus
'Sunlight'

Antirrhinum majus 'Harrison's Rust Resistant'

leaves daily during hot weather. In the home, stand the pots on trays of pebbles, kept moist.

New roots appear from the growing point, and these should be covered with sphagnum moss. Apply liquid manure or a foliar feed once a fortnight from May to August. Provide deep shade for *A. crystallinum* during summer; lightly shade the other two species.

Repot every third year in April; top-dress raft-grown plants annually with compost.

Propagation. Remove plants from their pots in March or April and clean off the compost. Divide the fibrous roots so that each piece retains a growing point. Pot in fresh compost, and keep in humid conditions until established.

Germinate seeds of *A. andreanum* and *A. crystallinum* in peaty compost in a propagating case heated to 21–24°C (70–75°F).

Pests. Colonies of APHIDS, particularly mottled arum aphid, infest flowers and foliage, extracting sap and fouling the plants with sticky excretions.

Diseases. Dead brown spots on the leaves are caused by LEAF SPOT.

Antirrhinum

Snapdragon. *Scrophulariaceae*

A genus of 42 species of annuals, perennials and a few sub-shrubs. The most valuable garden species is the short-lived, woody-based hardy perennial *A. majus,* with its numerous varieties in a wide range of colours.

Usually treated as annuals, these plants are excellent for bedding and for growing in pots. The taller forms are suitable for cutting and the dwarf varieties for edging borders and for rock gardens. The fragrant flowers, in spikes, are tubular and end in rounded upper and lower lips.

Rust may be troublesome in some areas, and the rust-resistant types should be grown.

ANTIRRHINUM MAJUS

A. majus. Mediterranean regions. Height $\frac{3}{4}$–4 ft; planting distance 9–18 in. The leaves are ovate, mid-green and glossy. The pink flowers are produced from July to the first frosts.

The garden varieties, which have almost completely replaced the type, can be divided into three groups according to height:

A. m. Maximum. Height 3–4 ft; planting distance 18 in. Many named forms are available. Tip Top is a strain of large, base-branching plants; the pink 'Apple Blossom' is particularly recommended. Rust-resistant varieties include 'Harrison's Rust Resistant' a mixed-colours strain with compact spikes.

Among the F_1 hybrids, the Rocket group produces plants of great vigour, while the Supreme F_1 doubles, including the mixture 'Glamour Shades', are good as cut flowers.

The F_1 varieties bred for cut flowers include 'Lavender Lady' and 'Pink Ice'.

The Sentinel group produces strong-growing plants with well-shaped spikes up to 3 ft high. 'Cavalier', orange flushed with rose; 'Majorette' is pink; 'Sunlight', bright pale yellow; and 'White Spire', pure white.

The Tetraploids or Tetra Snaps are outstanding for the size of their flowers and flower spikes, as well as their colour combinations. In the Penstemon-flowered group, a recent addition, the flowers have an open, trumpet-like form. These plants are particularly suitable for cutting; especially recommended are the F_1 'Bright Butterflies' mixture; and 'Innovation Mixed', in red, pink, yellow and orange shades, and white.

A. m. Nanum. Height 18 in.; planting distance 10–12 in. These intermediate or semi-dwarf varieties are widely used for summer bedding. Recommended are 'Black Prince', deep crimson and dark bronze leaves; 'Nelrose', pink; and 'Welcome', brilliant crimson. Rust-resistant varieties include 'Orange Glow', 'Scarlet Monarch' and 'Yellow Monarch'.

F_1 hybrids are represented by the 'Carioca Hybrids', height 16–18 in.; 'Regal Hybrids', 18 in.; and 'Sprite Hybrids', 14–16 in. These are available in mixtures and in separate colours, and are recommended for their reliability.

'Hyacinth Flowered', 18 in., is another group for bedding. The stems branch freely from the base and carry dense spikes of large flowers.

A. m. Pumilum, syn. *A. m.* Nanum Compactum. Height 6 in.; planting distance 9 in. In this dwarf group, 'Tom Thumb Mixed', 8 in., and 'Magic Carpet', 4 in., are popular; F_1 'Floral Carpet Mixed', 8 in., is also recommended.

Cultivation. Any well-cultivated garden soil is suitable, but a well-drained light to medium soil, enriched with well-rotted manure, gives the best results. A sunny position is best. With the exception of single-stem plants grown close together for cutting, encourage bushy growth by pinching out the growing points, either when the plants are 3–4 in. high or when they are established in their flowering position.

Staking is required only for tall varieties grown in exposed situations. Remove faded spikes to prolong the flowering period. Young plants, set out in September for early-summer flowering, need winter cloche protection on exposed sites.

Antirrhinums grown as pot plants can be flowered at any time of the year under glass by varying the sowing dates. Grow single plants in 5 in. pots or set two or three plants in an 8–9 in. pot. A minimum temperature of 4–7°C (39–45°F) is recommended for winter flowering, although antirrhinums can also be grown in cold greenhouses. Do not pinch out pot plants, but remove the side-shoots to produce finer flower spikes.

Propagation. Although it is possible to root cuttings, antirrhinums are best grown from seeds sown in pots or pans in February or March, at a temperature of 16–18°C (61–64°F).

Damping-off of seedlings, often caused by excess ammonia in sterilised compost, can be a problem. To avoid this, sow the seeds thinly in a compost of equal parts (by volume) sand and moss peat, with no nutrient. Water the seeds in gently, using a fine rose, or just cover with fine sand or grit. The seedlings germinate in 10–20 days; thereafter water with dilute liquid feed.

Alternatively, sow in a proprietary peat seed compost; feeding is then unnecessary.

When the seedlings are large enough to handle, prick them out into boxes of John Innes potting compost No. 1, and grow on at 10–12°C (50–54°F). Pot up into 3½ in. pots for greenhouse flowering, or harden off in a cold frame before planting outside from March to June.

For earlier flowering, sow the seeds in July or August, potting them in September or planting out in a sheltered and well-drained position.

For pot plants to flower in late winter or early spring, choose F_1 varieties suitable for growing under glass and make successive sowings from July to September, either without heat or, to speed flowering, at 10°C (50°F).

Pests. APHIDS may infest young growths.

BUMBLE BEES sometimes pierce the bases of the flowers to reach the nectar.

Diseases. DAMPING-OFF, due to various fungi, causes the collapse of seedlings at ground level.

DOWNY MILDEW affects young plants, causing a severe check to growth. The leaves become curled and dull and the undersurfaces develop a grey, mealy fungal growth.

FOOT and ROOT ROT, due to various fungi, show as a blackening of the tissues at the base of the main stems and of the roots. Affected plants wilt. The same symptoms can occur as a result of VERTICILLIUM WILT.

GREY MOULD may affect the flowers and flower stalks in a wet season. The tissues rot and become covered with a grey velvety fungal growth.

LEAF SPOT and STEM ROT show as pale brown, circular spots on the leaves, flowers and fruits. Dark spots develop on the stems and on these can be seen the pin-point black fruiting bodies of the fungus. Girdling of the stems may occur.

RUST shows on the leaves and stems as dark brown spore pustules. In severe cases the plants look brown and scorched.

Antirrhinum majus Pumilum 'Floral Carpet Mixed'

Aphelandra squarrosa 'Louisae'

Aphelandra

Acanthaceae

APHELANDRA SQUARROSA

A genus of 200 species of evergreen greenhouse shrubs. *A. squarrosa*, grown as a house plant, is the most popular species with its ornamental leaves and attractive flowers.

A. squarrosa. Brazil. Height 9–24 in.; spread 12 in. The pointed lanceolate leaves, up to 9 in. long, are dark green, often with ivory veins, and borne in opposite alternate pairs. The angular cone-shaped flower spike is borne terminally. It is 3–4 in. long and is composed of closely overlapping yellow bracts. Tubular yellow flowers, 1½ in. long, emerge from the bracts from July to September.

A. s. 'Louisae' has narrower leaves boldly veined with white.

Cultivation. Pot in March in 5 or 6 in. pots using John Innes potting compost No. 2. During the growing period the plants need frequent watering; from October to March they should be kept just moist. They must not be allowed to dry out.

In summer, lightly shade plants grown in the greenhouse; house plants should have plenty of light at all times. Feed weekly with a liquid manure in summer, fortnightly for the rest of the year. The minimum winter temperature required is 10°C (50°F). Repot annually in March.

Propagation. After flowering, cut the main stem back to a pair of good leaves to encourage the production of side-shoots from the leaf axils below. Detach these shoots when they are 3–4 in. long and use them as cuttings. Insert in equal parts (by volume) peat and sand at 21°C (70°F) in a propagating frame and when rooted set in 3 in. pots. Pot on as necessary.

Pests. SCALE INSECTS, particularly hemispherical scale, form brown excrescences on leaves and stems and make the plants sticky and sooty.

Diseases. Brown blotches on the leaves and premature leaf fall usually indicate a PHYSIOLOGICAL DISORDER.

Aponogeton distachyus

Aponogeton

Aponogetonaceae

APONOGETON DISTACHYUS

A genus of 30 species of perennial aquatic plants from the tropics and sub-tropics. Stems growing from a tuberous rootstock carry floating leaves and flowers. Only one species, *A. distachyus,* is hardy throughout the British Isles; it is widely grown in ornamental pools and lakes.

A. distachyus (water hawthorn). S. Africa. Water depth 9–24 in.; surface spread 18 in.; planting distance 6 in. A fleshy stemmed species; the elongated ovate leaves are light green, sometimes with maroon-brown markings.

Forked, deeply lobed flower clusters rise just above water level. They have a thick waxy texture, are up to 4 in. across and heavily scented. When first open they are pure white with black anthers, but after four or five days they become cream-coloured or green-white and subsequently turn completely green as they fade. As cut flowers they last for several days. The flowering season extends from June to October (sometimes until December in mild weather), with occasional rest periods of 10–21 days.

Cultivation. Grow in neutral or slightly acid soil covered with still or slowly moving water. This plant will grow in partial shade, although it flowers more freely in full sun.

Plant between mid-April and June. If planting in containers, set one tuber in a 5 in. pot or three in a 10–12 in. pot. The pot soil must be rich to avoid the need for frequent replanting; a mixture

Aporocactus flagelliformis
(hybrid)

Aporocactus flagelliformis

of equal parts (by volume) heavy loam and well-decayed manure is suitable. Soak it thoroughly before pushing in the tubers.

If planting without containers, push the tubers into the mud on the base of the pool. Alternatively, wrap each in a small piece of turf, weight with a stone and drop into position.

Propagation. Seeds are freely produced on established plants. Sow under glass as soon as they are ripe at a temperature of 13–16°C (55–61°F). Place a layer of loam, 2–3 in. thick, on the bottom of a watertight vessel; cover the loam with 4–6 in. water and broadcast the seeds. Protect the seedlings from frost during the winter.

When the tubers have grown to about the size of peas they are ready for planting out. Small flowers may be produced the year after sowing.

A. distachyus can also be increased in May by division of old tubers which have several crowns, but the plants are slow to become established.

Pests and diseases. Generally trouble-free.

Aporocactus

Cactaceae

A genus of six species of greenhouse perennials. These much-branched cacti consist of slender, pendent stems; they are rapid growers and flower freely. They are suitable for hanging baskets and will also succeed on sunny window-ledges.

See also CACTUS.

A. flagelliformis (rat's tail cactus). Mexico. Length up to 3 ft. The stems, about $\frac{1}{2}$ in. thick, have 8–12 ribs, are mid-green and covered with short brownish spines. Magenta funnel-shaped flowers, about 3 in. long, are formed profusely along the stems; they open in April and May.

A hybrid between *A. flagelliformis* and *Heliocereus speciosus* is frequently listed as *A. mallisonii* although its correct name is × *Heliaporus smithii.* The stems are shorter, stiffer and more deeply ribbed than those of *A. flagelliformis,* and the red flowers are slightly larger but less profuse. The blooms appear in March and April on older stems only.

A. mallisonii: see *A. flagelliformis*

Cultivation. These cacti need a rich soil, preferably one containing leaf-mould. Grow them in 5–6 in. pots or in 9 in. baskets. In the growing period give the plants plenty of water and use a high-potassium liquid feed once a fortnight. Bring the plants into a greenhouse for the winter and keep them at a temperature of 5°C (41°F) and slightly moist. Repot annually, after flowering.

Propagation. The true species can be grown from seeds sown in March at a temperature of 21°C (70°F). The plants are also easily propagated by cuttings taken between April and July. Remove a stem and allow it to dry for three days before potting it up in a mixture of 2 parts John Innes potting compost No. 2 and 1 part leaf-mould (parts by volume).

Pests. Conspicuous tufts of white waxy wool on the plants are caused by MEALY BUGS. ROOT MEALY BUGS infest root systems and check growth. GLASSHOUSE RED SPIDER MITES may infest the stems, causing discoloration and webbing.

Diseases. Generally trouble-free.

APPLE

Malus sylvestris, syn. *M. pumila. Rosaceae*

Apple blossom

These hardy, deciduous, spring-flowering trees are grown extensively for the dessert and culinary fruits which they bear in late summer and autumn. Most varieties are directly related to *Malus sylvestris*, sub-species *mitis*, which grows wild in Europe, western Asia and the Himalayas. There may have been crossings with *M. pruni-folia* and, in the case of the crab apple, *M. baccata*. With cool storage, the many varieties give a continuous supply of fruits from late July to the following spring.

Crab apple: see *Malus*

The most suitable areas for growing apples in Great Britain are those south of the Trent below altitudes of about 400 ft and not exposed to wind or salt-laden spray. North of the Trent the growing season is too short for the best results; roughly west of the line Liverpool–Taunton it is too cool and wet. Apples grown in these areas are generally of poorer quality and there is an increased risk of disease.

For the greatest chance of success in cold northern areas avoid the choicest varieties, such as 'Cox's Orange Pippin', and plant instead late-flowering culinary or dessert frost-resistant varieties. In western areas, except Cornwall and west Wales, 'Laxton's Superb' and 'James Grieve' will tolerate damp conditions.

The height and spread of an apple tree depends on the variety, the rootstock and the type of soil. Average figures are:

Dwarf bush, 8–10 ft × 8–10 ft; trunk 2–3 ft high. Bush, 10–12 ft × 10–12 ft; trunk 2–3 ft high. Half-standard, 12–15 ft × 12–15 ft; trunk 4 ft high. Standard, 15–20 ft × 15–20 ft; trunk 6 ft high.

Half-standards and standards are not recommended for general planting; their height and spread make management difficult. Trees grown in trained or restricted form occupy the least space and are usually supported on a framework of posts and wires. However, they require more attention than free-growing forms. Approximate heights and widths are:

Cordons (oblique), 10–12 ft long on supports 7 ft tall. Espalier, 8 ft high × 10–15 ft wide. Dwarf pyramid, 8–10 ft high × 3–6 ft wide.

Cropping is improved by cross-pollination. Varieties intended to pollinate one another must have simultaneous flowering periods and the

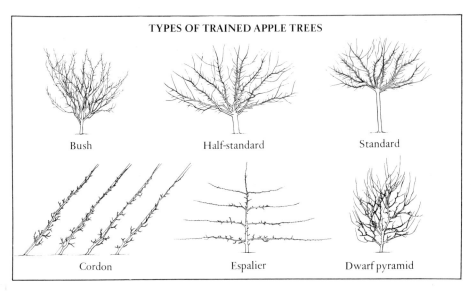

TYPES OF TRAINED APPLE TREES

Bush

Half-standard

Standard

Cordon

Espalier

Dwarf pyramid

Apple 'Bramley's Seedling'

Apple 'Cox's Orange Pippin'

Apple 'Egremont Russet'

varieties must be compatible. A few well-known apples, known as triploids, are poor pollinators. A notable example is 'Bramley's Seedling'.

In choosing varieties to give a succession of fruits, it should be remembered that early-ripening varieties have only a short season of use. All varieties listed are recommended for flavour. The months given are those in which the fruits can be used, for dessert (D) or cooking (C).

'Bramley's Seedling' (C). October to March. The best all-purpose cooker. Large green fruits, sometimes flushed with red. Growth too vigorous for small gardens. Flowers susceptible to frost. Poor pollinator. Flowers mid-season.

'Cox's Orange Pippin' (D). November to January. Doyen of dessert varieties. Dull red with russet skin; flesh firm and juicy. Susceptible to diseases; succeeds best in well-drained fertile soils on sites not subject to late frosts. Flowers mid-season.

'Egremont Russet' (D). October to December. A good garden variety. Hardy; regular cropper; compact growth; resistant to scab. Flesh firm and of distinctive flavour. Flowers early.

'Ellison's Orange' (D). September and October. Yellow, variously striped and flushed with red; flesh soft, of good flavour and aroma. Inclined to biennial bearing. Flowers mid-season.

'George Cave' (D). Mid to late August. Promising early variety. Bright red-yellow fruits; firm, juicy, sweet. Regular cropper. Flowers early.

'Golden Noble' (C). September to January. Clear yellow skin with slight roughness; yellow, soft flesh. Regular and prolific cropper. Flowers late.

'Grenadier' (C). First early, August and September. Large green-yellow fruits; crisp and acid. Reliable, scab resistant. Flowers mid-season.

'James Grieve' (D). A good September apple, but liable to bruise. Pale yellow with red streaks; crisp and juicy. Frost resistant, but susceptible to diseases. Flowers mid-season.

'Lane's Prince Albert' (C). November to March. Yellow-green with red streaks; acid soft flesh, of good flavour. A regular cropper, but susceptible to lime sulphur spray damage. Flowers mid-season.

'Laxton's Fortune' (D). September and October. Yellow with red flush; crisp and juicy. Regular cropper. Frost resistant. Flowers mid-season.

'Lord Lambourne' (D). October and November. Succeeds where 'Cox's Orange Pippin' will not grow well. Green-yellow fruits with red stripes and flush; juicy, sweet. Flowers early.

'Merton Russet' (D). December to February. Golden-yellow, heavily suffused with russeting; flesh crisp, with a good, somewhat acid, aromatic flavour. A regular, heavy cropper, with rather small fruits. Flowers mid-season.

'Merton Worcester' (D). September and October. A cross between 'Cox's Orange Pippin' and 'Worcester Pearmain'. Yellow fruits with bright crimson flush; sweet, slightly aromatic. Inclined to biennial bearing. Flowers mid-season.

'Newton Wonder' (C, D). November to March. Large yellow-green fruits with crimson flush and stripe; firm, crisp, acid. Inclined to biennial bearing. Flowers late.

'Orleans Reinette' (D). January and February. A good late variety. Golden yellow with russet patches; crisp, sweet, juicy. Tends to shrivel if storage is unsatisfactory. Hardy, prolific, but subject to canker. Flowers late.

'Peasgood's Nonsuch' (D, C). October to November. Yellow-green, sometimes flushed or streaked with orange or red; flesh soft and juicy, of moderate flavour and cooking to a froth. Moderate cropper. Flowers mid-season.

'St Edmund's Pippin' (D). September and October. Orange-yellow, heavily russeted; flesh tender and juicy, of fine aromatic flavour. Heavy cropper, with rather small fruits. Flowers early.

'St Edmund's Russet' (D). September and October. A good early russet. Small fruits completely covered with russet. Flesh pure yellow, juicy. Produces fruit at tips of shoots. Flowers early.

'Sunset' (D). October to December. Yellow with orange-red flush and some thin russeting. Regular cropper; fine flavour. Will often succeed where 'Cox's Orange Pippin' does not. Flowers mid-season.

'Tydeman's Early' (D). Late August to early September. Yellow-green, suffused bright red; flesh firm and juicy, of moderate flavour, with tough skin. Moderate to heavy cropper; inclined to tip bearing. Flowers mid-season.

Apple 'Ellison's Orange'

Apple 'Peasgood's Nonsuch'

Apple 'George Cave'

Apple 'Golden Noble'

Apple 'Grenadier'

Apple 'James Grieve'

'Worcester Pearmain' (D). August to September. Golden-yellow, heavily suffused and streaked with scarlet-crimson; flesh crisp and juicy, with a pleasant sweet flavour. A good, regular cropper, but inclined to tip bearing. Susceptible to scab. Flowers early.

Cultivation. The best results are obtained on well-drained, deep soils that do not dry out seriously in summer. Where necessary, improve the soil by adding bulky organic matter, such as compost. Choose a sunny position, but avoid exposed situations if possible; otherwise, plant windbreaks or reduce the distances between trees to provide mutual protection.

Apples will not succeed near coasts because of damage from salt-laden winds. Avoid sites subject to spring frosts, such as those at the bottoms of slopes or where buildings or walls interrupt the flow of cold air to lower ground.

Choose a tree form to suit the available space, allowing adequate room for the ultimate size. The nurseryman will match rootstock type to tree form in producing the young tree but should be told of any extreme soil conditions, such as deep, fertile soil that will cause vigorous growth.

The normal season for planting is between November and March. November planting gives the following year's growth a better start. Plant container-grown trees at any time.

Maiden trees (a single stem comprising one season's growth) transplant better than older ones. For quicker results, or to allow the nurseryman to do the initial training of trees grown in restricted form, plant older trees but make sure a minimum of roots is broken off when planting; ideally the root ball and its soil should be planted intact.

Wider spacings than average are required for vigorous varieties, such as 'Bramley's Seedling', and on deep, fertile soils which encourage vigorous growth. The following is a general guide to planting distances, the first figures in each case being the spacing between trees, the second between rows:

DWARF BUSH	10–12 ft;	10–12 ft
BUSH	12–15 ft;	12–15 ft
HALF-STANDARD	20–25 ft;	30–40 ft
STANDARD	30–35 ft;	35–40 ft
CORDON	$2\frac{1}{2}$–3 ft;	6–10 ft
ESPALIER	12–15 ft;	8–10 ft
DWARF PYRAMID	$3\frac{1}{2}$–5 ft;	7–10 ft

Do not plant when the soil is either frozen or saturated, though a thin surface crust of frost does no harm. If planting cannot be carried out as soon as the trees are available, store them in a frost-free shed and protect the roots from drying out.

Before planting cordons, construct a supporting framework of posts, 10 ft apart, with 7 ft above ground and 3 ft below soil level (18 in. if set in concrete). Fix wires 3 ft and 6 ft above ground level, with adjustable straining bolts at the ends of the row. Attach bamboo canes at an angle of 45 degrees to span the wires at the points where the trees will be planted.

Set the first tree 6 ft in from an end post, planting this and subsequent trees at an angle of 45 degrees, with the scion uppermost. This will prevent the union being forced open if the tree is bent lower when it reaches the top of the framework. Plant the last tree in the row next to the other end post. Tie the trees to the canes.

For espaliers, erect a supporting framework of posts and wires, the wires corresponding with the number of tiers it is planned to grow. Four to six is usual, with 12–15 in. between wires.

During the winter, firm any trees that have been lifted by frost. Watch for drying out after bud-burst and water the soil if necessary; mulch with straw or rotted manure after the soil has warmed up in the spring and before it dries out, especially if the trees have been planted in grass.

Watering may be required to help the trees to become established. Drought may also retard the growth of mature trees, though they may show no immediate signs of being affected. During prolonged dry weather, water the ground around trees from May to July, giving 4 gal. per sq. yd at each application. Give annual dressings of nitrogen and potash in January or February to the rooting area—a circle 6 in. from the trunk extending to 12 in. beyond the tips of the branches. If the soil has been adequately prepared before planting, there is no need for extra fertiliser in the first year; start in the second winter.

Apple 'Newton Wonder'

Apple 'Merton Worcester'

Apple 'Lane's Prince Albert'

Apple 'Laxton's Fortune'

For established bush and standard trees in cultivated soil, the basic rate for nitrogen, applied as sulphate of ammonia, is 1 oz. per sq. yd—up to 2 oz. for trees in grass. Apply up to 4 oz. per sq. yd of hoof and horn for trained trees if growth has to be stimulated. Mix with sand to assist even spreading and vary the rate according to the condition of the tree—giving less if growth is vigorous, with fruits that are too large and poorly coloured, and more to encourage growth.

To improve fruit quality, apply sulphate of potash at $\frac{3}{4}$ oz. per sq. yd. Maintain the phosphate level by applying superphosphate of lime every third winter at $1\frac{1}{2}$–2 oz. per sq. yd.

Mulch trained trees with farmyard manure. Avoid excessive feeding as this reduces the quality of the fruits and may induce too-vigorous growth, with increased risk of disease.

Disturbing the soil deeply around trees will damage the roots, so control weeds by shallow hoeing or by chemical sprays. For an improved working surface, better fruit colour, and to conserve the organic matter in the soil, grass down orchard trees after they have been planted for two to four years, provided they are growing satisfactorily—that is, if the leading shoots are making at least 18 in. of new growth each year.

Either sow grass seed, preferably in late summer, or level the surface and allow wild grasses, such as annual meadow grass, to establish themselves. Regular mowing helps to kill most annual weeds and the remainder can be controlled with selective herbicides.

If the grass is established by late summer, trim it once or twice during the autumn with a lawnmower set to give good ground clearance. Start regular mowing in the following year, keeping the growth especially short at flowering time to reduce frost risk, and in dry weather to prevent trees suffering from lack of water.

It is possible to plant trees direct into grass, but they may suffer from competition with the grass. Reduce this risk by mulching around newly planted trees, watering during dry spells and feeding more generously during the early years.

Bird damage is an increasing problem, especially to fruit buds. Protection can be given by means of scarers, protective sprays and by spreading fine rayon webbing on trees. Alternatively, grow trained trees in cages or under nets. If fruits are grown for exhibition, prevent damage by covering individual apples with muslin bags or perforated polythene sleeves.

Established trees can be allowed to carry a light crop in the second season after planting, but earlier cropping than this diverts too much energy from growth. Early fruiting tends to open up trees by pulling down young branches.

Horizontal shoots are more fruitful than those that grow upright; they can be encouraged by tying down a proportion of shoots each August.

Light crops may be due to inadequate growth in the early years after planting, to the variety, the situation, inadequate pollination, lack of feeding or to attacks by pests or diseases. Occasionally light cropping years may be due to weather conditions or to the natural biennial-bearing habit of varieties such as 'Newton Wonder'.

Support heavily laden branches to prevent them being broken. Tie them to stout poles or prop them up with forked stakes. Narrow angles between branches are liable to split and should be eliminated where possible when pruning.

Heavy crops are often made up of small fruits. When pruning old trees with many spurs, reduce the number of fruit buds so that they bear fewer but larger apples. Remove damaged and misshapen fruits and 'king' fruits (the central fruit of each cluster) which keep badly. Thin out the remaining fruits while they are small, allowing for a further natural fall in late June to early July and aiming at a final spacing of 4–6 in. apart for dessert apples, 6–9 in. for cookers.

Pick apples as they become ready; when the fruit is lifted and twisted lightly, the stalk should part easily. It is often necessary to pick over a crop several times, taking first the apples on the top of the tree, then those on the sides, and finally those on inner branches.

Harvest early varieties before they are ripe but leave the late ripeners (which will not ripen on the tree anyway) for as long as autumn gales, birds and frost allow.

Take care not to bruise the apples. Leave the stalks intact if the fruits are to be stored.

Store in a cool, moist atmosphere—a temperature of 2–4°C (36–39°F) is ideal—and examine the fruits regularly to remove any that are rotting. To store for a prolonged period, wrap the apples in newspaper or proprietary oiled wraps; or keep them in unsealed polythene bags.

Cool storage slows ripening; a moist atmosphere prevents shrivelling in store. These conditions are more often found in cellars than in attics or box rooms. Protect stored fruits against slugs and mice.

Depending on the cause of blemishes, damaged fruits can be stored for a short time but should be used first. If the skin is broken, brown rot may quickly set in. Slightly scabbed apples will often keep as long as perfect fruits.

Propagation. Seedling apples are not usually an improvement on the parent, especially if they result from natural crossing. Instead, for propagation purposes, material from desirable varieties is budded or grafted on to apple rootstocks, of which there are a number of known performance. These, together with a range of tree forms and pruning methods, provide types to meet most requirements, from quick-bearing trees requiring limited space to standard trees which need more room and are slow to start cropping, but continue over several decades.

The more vigorous stocks are not recommended for garden purposes. The large trees they produce are difficult to manage and may well create serious problems by outgrowing their allotted space. Only on notoriously poor soils should such stocks be used to produce trees of medium size.

It is possible to buy rootstocks, which should be planted in winter 9 in. apart in rows 3 ft apart, for budding in the following July or August, or for grafting in the following March or April. Completely virus-free trees can be assured only when both stock and scion (variety) have been properly tested and found to be clean and healthy. Virus-tested scions and rootstocks are being used increasingly and should be specified.

Bud as for roses (see chapter headed PROPAGATION), but 9–12 in. above soil level. Cut the head of the rootstock back to the bud in the following February; if a bud has failed, cut the stock back to below the bud and graft on the chosen variety. Young trees transplant well as maiden trees in winter after one year, when they will have made up to 4 ft of growth from the bud.

Graft at a similar height to budding as the rootstock starts into growth, using dormant shoots of the chosen variety from a virus-tested tree if the rootstock is also virus-tested.

Some nurserymen sell 'family trees', consisting of three or four different varieties of equal vigour budded on a single tree.

Pruning. See chapter headed PRUNING.

Pests. BIRDS peck holes in ripe fruits, causing these to rot.

CODLING MOTH and APPLE SAWFLY larvae burrow into the core of the fruits, rendering them inedible.

APHIDS of various species infest young shoots, leaves and fruits, and WOOLLY APHIDS infest branches and twigs, covering them with conspicuous tufts of white waxy wool; they also encourage the growth of disfiguring galls.

CAPSID BUGS pierce the tissues of young buds, fruits and leaves, causing distortions and a characteristic tattering of the leaves.

CATERPILLARS of many different species of moth eat the leaves and young buds.

FRUIT TREE RED SPIDER MITES infest the undersides of the leaves which, in severe infestations, become bronzed, wither and die.

Diseases. APPLE CANKER shows as an elliptic diseased area on the bark, which shrinks in concentric rings as the canker grows. The affected area may girdle the branch so that all parts above die back. In summer, white pustules of fungus spores develop on the cankered areas, and later small red bodies bearing the winter-resting spores are formed in the cracked bark.

APPLE MILDEW first appears when the buds break in spring and shows as a white powdery deposit on the emerging growths. It spreads to later developing leaves. In severe cases, diseased blossoms and leaves wither and fall.

APPLE SCAB produces brown or black scabs of varying sizes on the fruits. In a severe infection these may be numerous and coalesce, almost covering the fruits. Later, they become somewhat corky and the fruits crack. Olive-green blotches are produced on the leaves, which may fall prematurely. On the shoots, small blister-like pimples develop and these later burst the bark and show as ring-like cracks or scabs.

BITTER PIT is a disorder of the fruits which shows first as shadowy spots underneath the skin, later becoming more pronounced and

Apple 'Lord Lambourne'

Apple 'Merton Russet'

Apple 'St Edmund's Pippin'

Apple 'Sunset'

Recommended rootstocks

NAME	TYPE OF TREE PRODUCED	NOTES
'Malling IX'	Dwarf to very dwarf	Roots brittle; trees need staking throughout their life
'Malling IXA'	Dwarf to very dwarf	As above, but virus-tested
'Malling-Merton 106'	Semi-dwarf	In common with other MM rootstocks, resists woolly aphids
'Malling II'	Semi-vigorous	Widely used. Gives small trees on poor soils
'Malling-Merton III'	Semi-vigorous	Resistant to drought. May replace 'Malling II'
'Malling XXV'	Very vigorous	For standard trees where ample room is available

showing on the surface as slightly sunken pits. Small brown areas of tissue are found beneath the skin and scattered throughout the flesh.

BROWN ROT causes a rapid decay of the fruits, either on the tree or in store. They turn brown and are covered with white raised cushions of fungus spores, often arranged concentrically. Diseased fruits shrivel and dry up. Cankers may develop on the spurs and kill them.

COX SPOT, though most common on 'Cox's Orange Pippin', may occur on other varieties. It shows as tan-coloured spots on the leaves.

EYE ROT may affect the fruits. This shows first as a rotting of the tissues at the eye end, extending until much or all of the fruit is rotten.

FIREBLIGHT may attack apple trees, causing a blackening and shrivelling of flowers and a progressive die-back of branches. These bear brown and withered leaves which do not fall.

FROST DAMAGE can cause a crinkling of the young leaves, and they often have a blistered appearance as the epidermis (outer layer of cells) becomes separated from the inner tissues and is raised in irregular patches. Flower trusses may turn brown or the petals remain untouched, but the stamens turn black.

HONEY FUNGUS may attack apple trees and cause rapid death. Die-back of trees can also be due to wind rocking or waterlogged soil.

MINERAL DEFICIENCIES cause varying types of leaf discoloration, such as scorching of the leaf margins (lack of potash); orange-brown spots between the veins (magnesium deficiency); light green-yellow or red leaves which fall early (nitrogen deficiency); yellowing between the veins (iron and/or manganese deficiency) known as CHLOROSIS.

RUSSETTING of the skin may occur if young fruits are damaged, or the developing fruits may become pear-shaped.

Apple 'Tydeman's Early'

Apple 'Worcester Pearmain'

Apricot 'Moorpark'

Apple of Peru: see *Nicandra physaloides*

Apricot

Prunus armeniaca. Rosaceae

APRICOT

A hardy, deciduous, early-flowering tree bearing edible plum-like fruits. It is native to China. In Great Britain, apricots may be grown as bush trees in the open in warm sheltered areas in the south and west, but the best fruit crops are produced on fan-trained trees against warm, sheltered walls. Even so, reliable cropping can only be expected south of the River Trent; north of there apricots require greenhouse cultivation.

The blossoms appear as early as February, and apricots therefore require protection from spring frosts and winds. The trees usually bear their first crop when about four years old; they are self-fertile, but to ensure adequate pollination it is advisable to hand-pollinate the flowers with a camel-hair brush.

Height of bush trees, 12 ft; spread 10 ft; height of fan-trained trees, 8 ft; spread 12 ft.

The saucer-shaped, five-petalled flowers, 1 in. across, are white, sometimes flushed pink; they are borne in clusters on short spurs on the naked branches from February to March. The broadly ovate leaves are glossy mid to deep green and shallowly toothed. Clusters of round fruits, about 1½ in. wide, yellow and faintly tinged with red, ripen in August.

The variety in general cultivation is 'Moorpark', with juicy, sweet fruits that are brown-orange with a brown-red flush and darker spots.

Cultivation. Plant the trees during October or November in any fertile, well-drained garden soil. Too rich soil encourages unnecessary growth.

In the open, plant bush trees 15 ft apart. Against south-facing walls, set fan-trained trees at intervals of 15–18 ft and 6–9 in. out from the base, with the stems inclined towards the wall. Tie the shoots in place to wires stretched between vine eyes.

A south-facing wall provides ideal conditions in the southern counties and in the Midlands. Protect the flowers outdoors against spring frosts by covering them with muslin or fine close-mesh netting. This may be left on the trees until the fruits appear. Water freely during dry summers.

Avoid disturbing the roots of the trees, and keep the soil free from weeds; mulch annually with well-rotted manure or compost in late spring. During April and May, when the fruits have formed stones and are about 1 in. wide, thin them out so that they are at least 4 in. apart each way. Leave them on the trees to ripen, and handle carefully when picking. The fruits will store for about a month if kept in a cool place.

In winter, apply 4 oz. bone-meal and 1 oz. sulphate of potash per sq. yd. Growth may also be stimulated with an additional feed of 1 oz. sulphate of ammonia per sq. yd in June.

In the greenhouse, grow apricots fan-trained, setting them in the border at intervals of 15–18 ft. Water plentifully during summer and syringe the leaves daily. Ventilate freely in summer and provide a winter temperature of 1–4°C (34–39°F).

Propagation. Increase stocks by budding in July or August, or by grafting in March, on to plum rootstock, preferably 'St Julien A'. See also chapter headed PROPAGATION.

Pruning. No pruning is required for established bush trees except to remove dead and weak wood during winter. Build up the framework of bush and fan trees by shortening the leading shoots to 15–20 in. above the union in March.

In May and June, pinch back the laterals of fan-trained trees to 3 in. and the sub-laterals to one leaf. Thin out crossing branches.

When the desired height is reached, little pruning is necessary except to remove fruited shoots in autumn. Tie in replacement shoots from the base of the laterals.

Pests. GLASSHOUSE RED SPIDER MITES infest the undersides of leaves, particularly on greenhouse trees and in warm, dry situations outdoors. They cause a fine speckling on the upper surfaces of the leaves; the foliage turns bronze, withers and dies.

quilegia discolor

Aquilegia flabellata pumila

SCALE INSECTS and APHIDS infest young shoots
d older stems and leaves, making the plants
icky and sooty.

BIRDS and WASPS may damage the fruits.

iseases. APRICOT DIE-BACK causes shoots or large
anches to die back.

RUST affects the leaves in late summer and
ows on the lower surfaces as powdery orange
 brown pustules of spores. Premature leaf fall
ay occur.

SILVER LEAF shows as a silvering of the foliage
lowed by die-back of infected branches.

Aquilegia

Columbine. *Ranunculaceae*

AQUILEGIA FLABELLATA PUMILA

genus of 100 species of hardy herbaceous
rennials. The smaller of the plants described
e suitable for rock gardens, although they are
t always easy to grow; the remainder may be
own in borders. All have a basic tripartite leaf
rm, with an overall appearance of a large-
ved maidenhair fern. The distinctive flowers
e funnel-shaped with a prominent spur to each
 the five petals. Some species have particularly
ng spurs. Aquilegias are fairly short-lived
nts, but they produce an abundance of seeds.

PINE SPECIES

akitensis: see *A. flabellata pumila*

alpina. Switzerland. Height and spread 12 in.
is species has dissected grey-green leaves and
ep blue or blue and white flowers, 2 in. long,
t appear in May.

A. bertolonii. Italy. Height and spread 6 in. This
is an attractive dwarf species with grey-green
leaves that are less deeply cut than those of *A.
alpina*. It has rich blue-purple flowers, 2 in. long,
in May and June.

A. discolor. Spain. Height 4 in.; spread 6 in. This
species can be grown on a rock garden, but is
better suited to an alpine house. The leaves are
similar to those of *A. bertolonii*. Pale blue and
white flowers, 1½ in. long, are borne on 4–6 in.
high stems in June.

A. ecalcarata, syn. *Semiaquilegia adoxioides*. W.
China. Height 8–12 in.; spread 9 in. The
dissected fern-like leaves are mid-green, tinged
bronze-red when young. Graceful stems bear
small panicles of red-purple spur-less flowers, 1 in.
long, between May and July.

A. flabellata. Japan. Height 6–10 in.; spread 6–8
in. The dissected ovate leaves are grey-green.
Flowers in shades from white to violet-blue, 1½–2
in. long, appear from May to July. 'Nana Alba', a
white form, is more compact than the type; *A. f.
pumila*, syn. *A. akitensis*, is a pinkish-mauve
dwarf form rarely exceeding 4 in. in height.

A. scopulorum. Rocky Mountains. Height and
spread 6 in. The blue-grey leaflets are deeply cut.
The 1½ in. long flowers, which vary in colour from
pale lavender to deep violet, have spurs in a
darker shade and are produced from May to July.
Plants raised from seeds grown near other species
may well be hybrids and vary considerably.

BORDER SPECIES

A. caerulea. United States. Height 12–24 in.;
planting distance 12 in. The leaves are light
green. White long-spurred flowers, 2–3 in. across
and tinted light blue and yellow, are borne from
April to July. The variety 'Crimson Star' has red
and white flowers.

A. canadensis. Canada, U.S.A. Height 18–24 in.;
planting distance 12 in. This species, which has
light green leaves, bears 1½ in. wide lemon-yellow
flowers, with bright red spurs, in May and June.

A. longissima. S. United States, Mexico. Height
2–3 ft; spread 12–18 in. A graceful species

Aquilegia bertolonii

Aquilegia longissima

with leaflets that are pale green above and glaucous beneath. Slender branched stems bear pale yellow, 1–1½ in. long flowers with narrow spurs that may reach 3 in. or more in length. The flowers appear from June to September, provided the plants are regularly dead-headed. It is one of the parents of the long-spurred hybrids.

A. vulgaris (granny's bonnet). Europe. Height 18–24 in.; planting distance 12 in. The leaves are grey-green. This species is variable in colour, producing blue, pink or white flowers. The short-spurred flowers, 1–1½ in. across, open in May and June. *A. v. atrata* has dark violet flowers.

The long-spurred *A. vulgaris* hybrids are more popular than the type species. Among the best are 'McKana Hybrids' and 'Mrs Scott-Elliot's Strain'. Both are 3 ft high and have pale green leaves. They bear cream, yellow, pink, red, crimson or blue flowers, each 2–3 in. wide, in May and June.

Cultivation of alpine and border species. Plant aquilegias outdoors between September and March in a moist but well-drained leafy soil in a sunny or partially shaded position. Cut the flower stems of border plants down to ground level after flowering, and dead-head the alpine species.

All alpine species may be grown in an alpine house. Use 8–10 in. pans of John Innes potting compost No. 1, setting three or four plants in each pan; repot every other year in March.

Propagation of alpine and border species. Sow seeds when ripe, in July and August, or during March in boxes of seed compost and place in a cold frame. Prick out the seedlings, when large enough to handle, into boxes of John Innes potting compost No. 1. Plants to be grown in an alpine house should later be potted in 3 in. pots and eventually transferred to pans; those to be grown outdoors should be transferred to a nursery bed where they can grow on until planted out from September onwards, up to 14 months after sowing.

Seeds gathered from mixed plantings of species or varieties will not come true to type, as the species inter-hybridise easily.

Aquilegias may also be propagated by division between October and March.

Pests. The larvae of LEAF MINERS tunnel into leaves. APHIDS infest stems and leaves, making the plants sticky and sooty.

Diseases. Fungi may cause LEAF SPOT; it shows as brown-rimmed, white or grey-brown spots.

CLUSTER CUP RUST appears in spring as small orange patches on the undersides of the leaves.

CUCUMBER MOSAIC VIRUS produces yellow mottling on the leaves and turns the veins yellow; older leaves may become brown, and growth is often stunted; flowering is reduced or ceases.

Aquilegia vulgaris (long-spurred hybrids)

Arabis albida 'Flore Pleno'

Araucaria araucana (cone and foliage)

Arabis
Cruciferae

A genus of 120 species of hardy annuals and evergreen perennials. Some are invasive weeds; others, including the two described, are choice cushion-like plants for growing on rock gardens or in alpine houses. The flowers are white or pink, cross-shaped and with rounded petals.

A. albida, syn. *A. caucasica*. Height 9 in.; sprea up to 24 in. The obovate leaves are grey-gree and hoary. White flowers, ½ in. in diameter, a produced throughout the long flowering seaso from February to June. The plant is too invasiv for a normal rock garden and is more suitable fo a dry wall or bank, in company with alyssum and aubrietas. Less invasive varieties are 'Co cinea', crimson; 'Flore Pleno', double white; an 'Snowflake', large, single white.

A. blepharophylla. California. Height 3–4 in spread 9 in. The leaves are spathulate an mid-green. This plant has purple-pink flower ½ in. across, which open from March to Ma Severe winters can kill it, and it is best grown i an alpine house.

A. caucasica: see *A. albida*

Cultivation. If grown outdoors, both speci require well-drained soil in partial shade. Plant i September, October or March. Peg down *albida*, to keep it tidy; remove dead flower stem of both species unless seeds are required.

To grow arabis in an alpine house, use 8–10 i pans of John Innes potting compost No. Repot every other March.

Propagation. Cut *A. albida* back hard afte flowering and lift and divide in September.

Sow seeds of *A. blepharophylla* in pans of see compost in a cold frame in July. Prick th seedlings out into 3 in. pots when two true leave appear, as they resent being moved once roots a developed. Set out pot-grown plants in April.

Alternatively, insert cuttings of non-flowerin rosettes in June or July in equal parts (by volum peat and sand, and place in a cold frame. Pot in 3 in. pots when rooted and plant out th following March.

Pests. GALL MIDGE larvae attack growing point causing them to swell into large galls. Growth checked and flowering may be prevented.

Diseases. WHITE BLISTER shows as swellings white powdery spores on leaves and stems.

CLUB ROOT causes roots to develop irregul swellings: plants become stunted or the folia becomes discoloured.

DOWNY MILDEW may attack leaves and cau yellow blotches which show as a grey fur coating on the underside.

ARABIS MOSAIC VIRUS and TURNIP MOSAIC VIR cause mottling of foliage and stunting of plan

---

Aralia: see Dizygotheca
Aralia japonica: see *Fatsia japonica*
Aralia sieboldii: see *Fatsia japonica*

Araucaria
Araucariaceae

A genus of 18 species of evergreen conifero trees, native to the Southern Hemisphere. Or one species, *A. araucana* (monkey puzzle), generally hardy outdoors. This is a win resistant tree of highly distinctive habit wh may eventually reach a height of 60–70 ft and i suitable specimen tree only for a large garden.

See also CONIFERS.

The other species described is tender a requires greenhouse treatment except in the Is

f Scilly. It is usually grown as a pot plant; once it
reaches a height of 4 ft or more it generally
becomes bare at the base and is best replaced.

OUTDOOR SPECIES
. araucana, syn. *A. imbricata* (Chile pine,
monkey puzzle). Chile, Argentina. Height 20 ft;
spread 10 ft. This species is broadly columnar
with a conical top in the young stage; it later
becomes broadly domed. Growth is usually about
12 in. a year once the plant has reached a height of
5 ft, which may take ten years. Shape and spread
range from narrow columns with no low
branches, to trees with branches that sweep to the
ground. The dark green leaves are closely
overlapping, rigid and spine-tipped.

ARAUCARIA ARAUCANA

The species is dioecious; male trees produce
terminal clusters of two to six catkins like small
bananas, which shed pollen in June and then
turn dark brown. Female trees produce globular
cones, 4–7 in. long and 3–5 in. wide, on the
upper sides of some top branches. When mature,
after 2½ years, the cones are covered in golden
spikes, and each contains up to 200 large seeds.
Flowering begins after about 30 years.
. imbricata: see *A. araucana*

GREENHOUSE SPECIES
. excelsa (Norfolk Island pine). Norfolk Island.
Height 3–6 ft; spread 2–3 ft. This species is
pyramidal in outline with tiered whorls of
branches. The slender, tapering needles are
awl-shaped and bright green.

ARAUCARIA EXCELSA

Cultivation of outdoor species. These trees thrive
in most soils and conditions, but should not be
grown in badly drained areas. Plant in October or
early November on light soils, and in March on
heavier ground. Use plants less than 12 in. high.
Cultivation of greenhouse species. Pot *A. excelsa*
in John Innes potting compost No. 2, finishing
the plant in an 8–10 in. pot. Provide a minimum
winter temperature of 5°C (41°F). Water freely in
spring and early summer, keeping the plant just
moist during winter. It needs a well-ventilated
buoyant atmosphere in a well-lit position; in the
greenhouse shade lightly in summer. The plant
may be stood outdoors from June to August.
Pot on every other year in March until the final
pot size is reached; thereafter repot every other
year. Give a liquid feed at fortnightly intervals
from May to August.
Propagation of outdoor species. Sow seeds singly

in 3½ in. pots of John Innes seed compost in a cold
frame in March. Pot on the seedlings as necessary
using John Innes potting compost No. 1. After
about three years the seedlings should be ready to
plant out. Fertile seeds are rarely set in Great
Britain, being found only where a male and a
female tree are in close proximity.

Alternatively, take 3–4 in. long cuttings from
the tips of vertical shoots in July and insert in
equal parts (by volume) peat and sand in a cold
frame. When rooted, but no earlier than April, pot
singly in 3–4 in. pots of John Innes potting
compost No. 1, and grow on for three years
before planting out in permanent positions.
Propagation of greenhouse species. Sow the
seeds in March, singly in 2½–3 in. pots of John
Innes potting compost No. 1, at a temperature of
10–13°C (50–55°F). Pot the seedlings on as
described under CULTIVATION.

Alternatively, cut leggy plants back to within
6 in. of the base in January to promote young
growths for cuttings. When the shoots are 3 in.
long remove those close to the base and insert in
equal parts (by volume) peat and sand in a
propagating case at a temperature of 13–16°C
(55–61°F). When rooted, pot the cuttings singly.
Pruning. None required.
Pests. Generally trouble-free.
Diseases. HONEY FUNGUS may kill plants.

Arbor-vitae: see Thuja

Arbutus

Strawberry tree. *Ericaceae*

ARBUTUS × HYBRIDA

A genus of 20 species of hardy and half-hardy
evergreen trees and large shrubs. They are grown
for their handsome foliage, pitcher or urn-shaped
flowers and edible, but insipid, red fruits. In
addition, some species have attractive bark. The
majority of species flower when still young.
A. andrachne. S.E. Europe, Asia Minor. Height
up to 15 ft; spread 8 ft. This species is tender
when young, but with care it will mature into a
hardy shrub. The peeling bark is smooth and
cinnamon-red. The dark green leathery leaves,
light green beneath, are ovate to oblong; some
are serrate while others on the same branch
are entire. The white flowers are borne in
terminal panicles, 2–3 in. long, in March and
April; the strawberry-like fruits are orange-red.
A. andrachnoides: see *A.* × *hybrida*
A. × **hybrida,** syn. *A. andrachnoides*. S.E. Europe,
Asia Minor. Height up to 10 ft; spread 7–8 ft. A
natural hybrid between *A. andrachne* and *A.
unedo*, with attractive cinnamon bark; hardy in
all but the coldest areas. The dark green, ovate,
slightly leathery leaves are serrate. Ivory-white
flowers are borne in nodding terminal panicles,

Arbutus andrachne

Arbutus unedo 'Rubra' (flowers)

Arbutus unedo (fruits)

Arctostaphylos uva-ursi (fruits)

Arctotis acaulis

Arctotis × *hybrida*

3 in. or more long, during March and April. The red strawberry-like fruits are rarely produced.

A. menziesii (madroña). California to British Columbia. Height 15–20 ft; spread 8–10 ft. This species, with smooth, terracotta bark, is hardy in southern gardens. The dark green leaves, glossy above, glaucous beneath, are ovate, sometimes serrate but chiefly with entire margins. White flowers are borne in erect terminal panicles, 9 in. long, in April and May; they are followed by orange-red globular fruits.

The species requires shelter from cold north and east winds.

A. unedo. S. Europe, S.W. Ireland and Asia Minor. Height 15–20 ft; spread 10 ft or more. A shrub with rough and shreddy bark; it is hardy in southern areas. The glossy, dark green, serrate leaves are elliptic to obovate. White or pink flowers are borne in pendent terminal panicles, 3 in. long, from October to December, often at the same time as the orange-red strawberry-like fruits from the previous year's flowers.

The variety 'Rubra', syn. 'Croomei', is of bushy habit with soft red flowers.

Cultivation. Plant these trees in October or from March to May in good, lime-free loam in a sunny position, sheltered from cold north and east winds. *A. unedo* and its forms are lime-tolerant. Young plants are tender and in winter require protection with bracken or straw. Once established they will withstand greater cold and exposure.

Propagation. Sow seeds when ripe, usually in March, in pans of 2 parts peat and 1 part sand (parts by volume); place the pans in a cold frame. Prick off the seedlings when large enough to handle, singly into 3 in. pots of John Innes potting compost No. 2. Grow on in a cold frame for one or two years, potting on as necessary. Transplant the young plants to their permanent positions from March to May.

Alternatively, take heel cuttings, 3–4 in. long, of half-ripened wood in July; insert the cuttings in equal parts (by volume) peat and sand in a propagating frame at a bottom heat of 16–18°C (61–64°F). When rooted, treat the cuttings as described for seedlings.

Pruning. None required; straggly shoots may be cut back to main stems in April. Remove the lower branches on established specimens of *A. menziesii* to expose the bark.

Pests. Generally trouble-free.

Diseases. LEAF SPOT shows as small brown spots on the foliage.

Arctostaphylos

Bearberry, manzanita. *Ericaceae*

ARCTOSTAPHYLOS UVA-URSI

A genus of 70 species of deciduous and evergreen plants ranging from small trees to creeping shrubs. Only two species are in general cultivation in Great Britain; these are hardy berrying shrubs, useful for ground cover.

A. nevadensis (pine-mat manzanita). California and Oregon. Height up to 9 in.; spread 6–10 ft. An evergreen procumbent and mat-forming shrub with downy grey leaves, obovate and with a short point. The urn-shaped white or red-tinged white flowers are borne in April and May in compact racemes or panicles about 2 in. long. They are followed by globose red berries.

A. uva-ursi. Cool regions of the N. Hemisphere, including Britain. Height 4–6 in.; spread 4 ft. A prostrate evergreen shrub of rapidly spreading habit, similar to *A. nevadensis*. The glossy, mid to dark green, obovate leaves are leathery. Pendent 1–1½ in. long racemes of white, flushed pink, urn-shaped flowers appear in April and May; these are followed by glossy red globose berries.

Cultivation. Plant in September and October or in March and April. Arctostaphylos dislike lime and should be grown in a peaty moist soil and in sun or partial shade.

Propagation. Layer long branches in March and separate from the parent plant after one or two years. Take heel cuttings, 2–3 in. long, of lateral shoots in July and August; insert in equal parts (by volume) peat and sand in a cold frame. When rooted, pot the cuttings singly in 3 in. pots of 4 parts lime-free loam, 2 parts peat and 1 part coarse sand (parts by volume). Plunge outdoors and grow on until September when the young plants may be set in permanent positions.

Sow seeds in September or October in pans of 2 parts peat and 1 part sand (parts by volume); place the pans in a cold frame. When the seedlings are large enough to handle, prick them out in boxes of 2 parts lime-free loam, 2 parts peat and 1 part coarse sand (parts by volume). Later place in 3–3½ in. pots of the same compost and plunge outdoors, or plant direct in a nursery bed. Grow the young plants on for one or two years before setting them in their permanent sites.

Pruning. None required.

Pests and diseases. Generally trouble-free.

Arctotis

Compositae

ARCTOTIS BREVISCAPA

A genus of 65 species of half-hardy annuals and perennials. The following species, although perennial, are invariably grown as annuals because they flower in the first year from seeds. The leaves and stems are woolly, giving a silver-green appearance. The flowers are daisy-like, with the outer petals long, tubular and light-coloured and the central disc brown, purple or violet.

These plants are excellent for borders and for growing in pots. They are also suitable for cutting, although they last only a few days in water. The flowers tend to close in the early afternoon and during dull, overcast weather.

A. acaulis, syn. *A. scapigera.* Africa. Height 6–9 in.; planting distance 12 in. This dwarf plant is suitable for edging borders and for window-boxes. The leaves, which are cut or lobed, carry a mass of white hairs on the undersides. The single flowers, $3\frac{1}{2}$ in. across, are borne on smooth stems in July and August. Varieties are available in colours from orange to deep red.

A. breviscapa. Africa. Height 6 in.; planting distance 9 in. This compact plant, which has deeply cut leaves, is suitable for edging borders. The flowers, 2 in. across and vivid orange with a black central disc, are produced from July to the first frosts. The variety *A. b. aurantiaca* is orange-yellow with a metallic-purple disc.

A. × *hybrida.* Height 12–24 in.; planting distance 12 in. This name includes the many interspecific hybrids listed by seedsmen. They are popular plants for the border and for bedding out and their flowers are longer-lasting than the species when cut. The leaves are narrow and grey-green. Long-stemmed flowers, up to 4 in. across, are produced from July to the first frosts and are available in brilliant shades of red, yellow, orange, apricot, carmine, cream and white, many attractively zoned with a contrasting colour.

A. scapigera: see *A. acaulis*

A. stoechadifolia. Africa. Height $2\frac{1}{2}$–3 ft; planting distance 12 in. A quick-growing plant, best grown in bold groups at the back of a border. The thick, ribbed stems carry grey-green leaves which are narrow and toothed. The flowers, produced from July to the first frosts, are 3 in. across and pearl-white with a blue central disc surrounded by a narrow golden zone. The variety *A. s. grandis* has larger flowers and is available in colours from white to primrose.

Cultivation. These plants grow well in most soils, preferably in an open sunny site. Stop young plants when 5 in. high by pinching out the growing tips, to encourage a bushy habit. Support tall, large-flowered varieties with twiggy sticks. Dead-head to extend the flowering period.

Move plants which are to flower under glass into 5 in. pots of John Innes potting compost No. 1 in April, and grow on at a temperature of 13°C (55°F). Avoid over-watering young plants; heavy, wet soil encourages basal rotting.

Propagation. Sow the seeds in March in boxes or pans of seed compost, just covering them. A temperature of 18°C (64°F) is required. Prick out the seedlings into boxes and harden off well before planting out in May (or April in sheltered spots in the south and west).

Alternatively, sow directly in the flowering site in April, later thinning out the seedlings to the required planting distance.

Pests. APHIDS infest young growths.

Diseases. GREY MOULD may cause rotting of the tissues in wet conditions; the affected areas become covered with a grey velvety fungal growth.

Ardisia

Myrsinaceae

A genus of 400 species of evergreen trees and shrubs. They are chiefly grown for their bright red berries which last from autumn until the following June. Only one species is in general cultivation; it requires greenhouse treatment or it may be grown as a house plant.

A. crispa. E. Indies. Height 2–3 ft; spread 12–18 in. A shrub of upright habit, with shining dark green leaves; they are up to 4 in. long, oblong-lanceolate with wavy margins, and are arranged alternately. Sweet-scented, cream-white, star-shaped flowers, tinged with red and $\frac{1}{2}$ in. across, appear in axillary umbels in June; they are followed by round scarlet berries which may persist until the next crop of flowers appears.

ARDISIA CRISPA

Cultivation. Grow ardisias in 5–6 in. pots containing John Innes potting compost No. 2. They require a minimum winter temperature of 7°C (45°F). Keep the plants well ventilated in summer, and water freely; during winter keep them just moist. Feed weekly with a liquid manure from April until the berries colour; in summer lightly shade the greenhouse.

Pot on in April for one or two years, after which the plants deteriorate and are best discarded. Cut-back plants can be repotted when the new shoots are about 3 in. long.

Propagation. Sow ripe seeds in pans of seed compost in March at a temperature of 18°C (64°F). When the seedlings are large enough to handle, prick out singly in 3 in. pots of John Innes potting compost No. 1; pot on as necessary.

Alternatively, take heel cuttings, 3 in. long, of lateral shoots from May to August. Insert in equal parts (by volume) peat and sand at a bottom heat of 16–18°C (61–64°F). Treat the rooted cuttings as advised for seedlings.

Pruning. Leggy plants can be pruned hard back in February. Cut down to within 3–4 in. of the base; when the cuts stop bleeding, restart growth by watering the compost and keeping the plants at 10°C (50°F). Remove all but the strongest shoots.

Pests and diseases. Generally trouble-free.

Arenaria

Caryophyllaceae

A genus of 250 species of hardy or half-hardy annual and sub-shrubby evergreen plants. The following low-growing plants are creeping or mat-forming; they are hardy and suitable for rock gardens or alpine houses.

A. balearica. Balearic Isles, Corsica. Height 1 in.; spread 18 in. The minute leaves of this plant are ovate and mid-green. White star-like flowers, $\frac{1}{3}$ in. across, open between March and July. The species grows best when covering the shady sides of rocks. It is apt to invade nearby plants, but may be partially destroyed in severe winters.

A. grandiflora. European Alps, N. Africa. Height 2–3 in.; spread up to 12 in. This species carries a

Ardisia crispa (fruits)

Arenaria balearica

Arenaria montana

dense growth of bright green pointed leaves. Shallowly funnel-shaped white flowers, $\frac{3}{4}$ in. across, open from May to August.

A. montana. France, Spain. Height up to 6 in.; spread up to 18 in. A dense, mat-forming species with mid or dark green, narrowly lanceolate leaves. The glistening white, $\frac{1}{2}$–$\frac{3}{4}$ in. wide, saucer-shaped flowers are borne on slender branched stems during May and June.

A. purpurascens. Pyrenees, Spain. Height 2–3 in.; spread 12 in. This prostrate plant has lanceolate mid-green leaves with slender points. Star-shaped purple flowers, $\frac{1}{2}$–$\frac{3}{4}$ in. across, appear in clusters of two or three on 2 in. stalks in July and August. 'Elliott's Variety' is a particularly free-flowering form with clear pink flowers.

Cultivation. Arenarias require sharply drained gritty soil. *A. balearica* needs shade and *A. montana* will grow in partial shade, but the others do best in full sun. Plant in March. Dead-head if seeds are not required.

Propagation. Divide and replant *A. balearica* and *A. purpurascens* in March or April.

Take 1–2 in. non-flowering basal shoot cuttings of *A. grandiflora* and *A. montana* between June and August, and insert in equal parts (by volume) peat and sand in a cold frame. Pot up when rooted and grow on in the frame until March, when they can be planted out.

Pests and diseases. Generally trouble-free.

Argemone grandiflora

Arisaema candidissimum

Aristolochia elegans

Argemone
Papaveraceae

ARGEMONE PLATYCERAS

A genus of ten species of annuals and perennials. The following are treated as hardy annuals and make unusual border plants, being strong-growing, with deeply cut, prickly leaves and showy, poppy-like flowers. When broken, the stem exudes a bright yellow sap.

A. grandiflora. Mexico. Height 3 ft; planting distance 12 in. The glaucous-green thistle-like leaves are smooth and white-veined. White flowers, 4 in. across, are produced in clusters of three to six in June and July.

A. mexicana (devil's fig, prickly poppy). Tropical America. Height 24 in.; planting distance 12 in. Sprawling stems carry pinnate glaucous leaves, blotched with white. Scented orange or yellow flowers, $3\frac{1}{2}$ in. across, appear from June onwards.

A. platyceras (crested poppy). N. and S. America. Height 2–4 ft; planting distance 15 in. A strong-growing plant with spiny, glaucous leaves. The flowers are white or purple, 2–3 in. across, and appear in August and September.

Cultivation. A light, dry soil and a sunny position are required. Staking is generally unnecessary and may damage the succulent stems. Dead-heading improves subsequent flowers.

Propagation. Sow seeds in boxes of seed compost in March at 18°C (64°F). Prick out the seedlings into $3\frac{1}{2}$ in. pots and harden off in a cold frame before planting out in May. Alternatively, sow directly in the open ground in April, thinning out the seedlings to the required distances.

Pests and diseases. Generally trouble-free.

Arisaema
Araceae

ARISAEMA CANDIDISSIMUM

A genus of 150 species of herbaceous perennials. The hardy species described is the most frequently grown; it is ideal for growing in a woodland garden in company with small hardy ferns. It has hooded flower-like spathes and a bulky tuberous root.

A. candidissimum. China. Height 6 in.; planting distance 9–12 in. The broad, glossy pale green leaves are trifoliate. A white spathe, veined green and sometimes tinged rose, up to 3 in. long, is borne in June.

Cultivation. Plant the tubers in October in a shady position. Set them 6 in. deep in moist soil containing plenty of leaf-mould or peat.

Propagation. Remove and replant offsets when new growth starts in March or early April.

Pests and diseases. Generally trouble-free.

Aristolochia
Dutchman's pipe. *Aristolochiaceae*

ARISTOLOCHIA DURIOR

A genus of 350 species of tender and hardy, evergreen and deciduous perennials, including climbing and herbaceous plants. The few species in cultivation are climbers, suitable for walls, trellis and arbours, or for greenhouse borders.

Each curiously shaped flower has a curved tubular corolla with an inflated base and expanded into a hood above. They are borne solitarily from the upper leaf axils.

OUTDOOR SPECIES

A. altissima. Sicily, Algeria. Height 8–10 ft. This evergreen species is not reliably hardy, except in the south and west. It has bright green heart-shaped leaves, with pointed tips. Bright yellow flowers, 1–$1\frac{1}{2}$ in. long and striped with brown, appear in June and July.

A. durior, syns. *A. macrophylla, A. sipho.* N. America. Height 20 ft or more. A hardy deciduous species of vigorous growth; given support for its twining stems it provides good wall covering. The large and handsome mid-green leaves are broadly heart-shaped. Yellow, brown and green flowers, 1–1½ in. long and shaped like an old Dutch pipe, are borne in June.

A. macrophylla: see *A. durior*

A. sipho: see *A. durior*

GREENHOUSE SPECIES

A. elegans. Brazil. Height 10 ft or more. A tender evergreen climber with broadly heart-shaped, pale to mid-green leaves. The 3–4 in. wide flowers, which appear from July to September, consist of a 1½ in. long yellow tube and a purple-brown, white-veined hood.

Cultivation of outdoor species. Hardy aristolochias thrive in any fertile garden soil where good drainage can be provided. Plant *A. altissima* in April or May, *A. durior* during suitable weather between September and April. Both species do well in sun or partial shade. Provide temporary winter protection, particularly for *A. altissima,* until the plants are well established.

These climbers tend to grow vertically unless the shoots of the young plants are stopped; pinch out the growing points once or twice to encourage branching. The twining stems need tying in to trelliswork if they are grown against walls.

Cultivation of greenhouse species. *A. elegans* is best grown in the greenhouse border, although it may also be grown in a 7–9 in. pot of John Innes potting compost No. 3. A minimum winter temperature of 10°C (50°F) is needed. Train the plants up wires or twiggy sticks.

Admit plenty of light in winter, but shade the greenhouse in summer. Keep the plants just moist from October to March, and water freely when in full growth.

Pot on annually in March or April until the plants are in 10–12 in. pots, thereafter repot annually. Give a liquid feed at intervals of seven to ten days from May to September.

Propagation of outdoor species. Take 3 in. cuttings from terminal growths during July, and insert in equal parts (by volume) peat and sand in a propagating case with a temperature of 18°C (64°F). When rooted, transfer the cuttings singly to 3 in. pots of John Innes potting compost No. 2, later potting on into 4 in. pots. Harden off in a cold frame before planting out, *A. durior* in September, *A. altissima* the following May.

Shoots may also be layered during September or October; the layers should root and be ready for severing and replanting one year later.

Both species may also be increased from seeds sown in pots or pans of seed compost during March, at a temperature of 13–16°C (55–61°F). Prick off the seedlings when they are large enough to handle, one to a 3 in. pot, and grow on as described for cuttings. Support the young plants by tying them to canes.

Propagation of greenhouse species. Take 3–4 in. long cuttings of lateral shoots in May and June; insert the cuttings in equal parts (by volume) peat and sand in a propagating case with a temperature of 21–24°C (70–75°F). When rooted, pot the cuttings singly in 3 in. pots of John Innes potting compost No. 2 and pot on as necessary.

Alternatively, increase *A. elegans* by seeds sown in April in pans of John Innes seed compost at a temperature of 21–24°C (70–75°F). When the seedlings are large enough to handle, prick off and treat as described for cuttings.

Pruning. Where space is restricted, the plants should be thinned out and have superfluous growths shortened by a third in February.

Cut back lateral shoots of pot plants to 2–3 in. long spurs from December to February. Plants grown in the greenhouse border should have the leading shoots tipped and the lateral growths reduced by two-thirds.

Pests. Infestations of APHIDS may check the growth of young plants.

GLASSHOUSE RED SPIDER MITES cause a fine mottling of the foliage, and premature leaf fall.

Diseases. Yellow mottling of the foliage is caused by CUCUMBER MOSAIC VIRUS.

Armeria

Thrift. *Plumbaginaceae*

ARMERIA MARITIMA

A genus of 80 species of hardy evergreen perennials, suitable for the front of borders and for rock gardens. They form hummocks of grass-like leaves; small flowers are packed into long-lasting globose heads on slender stems.

A. arenaria: see *A. plantaginea*

A. caespitosa. Spain. Height 2–3 in.; spread 6–9 in. This species may also be grown in an alpine house. It bears slightly grey-green leaves and ½–¾ in. heads of stemless pink flowers in May.

'Bevan's Variety' has deeper pink flower heads on 1–2 in. long stems.

A. maritima. Europe. Height 6–12 in.; spread 12 in. This species forms a mid to grey-green hummock of leaves. Pink flower heads, 1 in. across, are borne from May to July.

'Alba' is a good white form; 'Merlin' is rich pink; and 'Vindictive' is rich rose-red.

A. plantaginea, now known as *A. arenaria.* Central and S. Europe. Height up to 24 in.; spread 12 in. A species with mid to deep green foliage. It is mainly represented in cultivation by 'Bees Ruby', with bright ruby-red flower heads, 1–1½ in. across, from June to August.

Cultivation. Plant armerias between September and April in ordinary, well-drained garden soil, in full sun. Remove the faded flower heads to make the tufts of leaves look neater.

In the alpine house, plant *A. caespitosa* between September and April in 6–8 in. pans of John Innes potting compost No. 1. Repot or pot on every two or three years in April.

Propagation. Divide and replant the roots in March or April.

Sow seeds during March or April in boxes of seed compost in a cold frame. Prick off the

Armeria caespitosa 'Bevan's Variety'

Armeria maritima 'Vindictive'

seedlings into 3 in. pots of John Innes potting compost No. 1 and plunge outside. Transplant to the flowering site from September onwards.

Take 2 in. long basal cuttings during July or August and insert them in a mixture of equal parts (by volume) peat and sand, in a cold frame. Pot the rooted cuttings singly in 3–3½ in. pots of John Innes potting compost No. 1 and plunge outdoors until the following autumn, when they can be planted out. Larger cuttings may be planted *in situ* in March or September.

Pests. Generally trouble-free.

Diseases. In spring, RUST may show on leaves and stems as small white pustules that burst open, releasing yellow spores. Later, purple spots with light brown pustules develop.

Arnebia echioides

Artemisia gnaphalodes

Artemisia lactiflora

Arnebia

Boraginaceae

ARNEBIA ECHIOIDES

A genus of 25 species of tender and hardy annuals and herbaceous perennials. Only one species is readily available and in general cultivation; this is a hardy perennial, suitable for growing at the front of mixed and herbaceous borders or on large rock gardens.

A. echioides, syn. *Macrotomia echioides* (prophet flower). N.E. Turkey. Height 9–12 in.; planting distance 9 in. A tufted species with basal, hoary-green leaves, lanceolate to linear-oblong. Erect, branching stems carry terminal clusters of bright primrose-yellow flowers from April to June or sometimes later. Each tubular flower has five rounded, spreading petals, and measures ½–¾ in. across; the petals are marked with five purple blotches which later fade and disappear entirely.

Cultivation. Plant in September and October or in March and April, in any ordinary, well-drained soil and in a sunny position.

Propagation. Divide and replant multiple-crowned plants in March or April.

Alternatively, cut 1–1½ in. long sections of thick roots during February or March, and insert in equal parts (by volume) peat and sand in a propagating case at a temperature of 13–16°C (55–61°F). When three or four young leaves appear, pot the cuttings singly into 3–3½ in. pots of John Innes potting compost No. 1, and later plunge outside until setting out in permanent positions in autumn of the same year.

Seeds may be sown during March, in pots or pans of seed compost in a cold frame. Prick off the seedlings, when large enough to handle, into 3 in. pots of John Innes potting compost No. 1 and treat as described for root cuttings.

Pests and diseases. Generally trouble-free.

Arrowhead: see Sagittaria

Artemisia ludoviciana

Artemisia

Compositae

A genus of 400 species of hardy and half-hardy herbaceous perennials, and evergreen and semi-evergreen shrubs and sub-shrubs. The plants are suitable as wall shrubs, for shrub and mixed borders, for rock gardens and alpine houses.

The small, ray-less, button-shaped yellow flowers are generally insignificant. Apart from a few herbaceous species, artemisias are grown for their silver-grey, aromatic, feathery foliage.

ARTEMISIA LUDOVICIANA

HERBACEOUS PERENNIAL SPECIES

A. dracunculus: see Tarragon

A. gnaphalodes. W. Canada, south to Mexico. Height 2–4 ft; planting distance 15–18 in. A hardy species now considered to be a variety of *A. ludoviciana*. It has woolly, white, obovate and entire leaves. Panicles, up to 8 in. long, of silver-white, brown-tipped flowers, are produced in September and October.

A. lactiflora (white mugwort). China, India. Height 4–5 ft; planting distance 15–18 in. This hardy species has pinnately lobed, mid-green leaves that are deeply cut. Pyramidal plumes, 6–8 in. long, of fragrant cream-white flowers are borne in August and September.

A. ludoviciana (white sage). N. America. Height 2–4 ft; planting distance 15–18 in. This hardy species closely resembles *A. gnaphalodes*, but some of the lower leaves are deeply divided.

A. stelleriana (dusty miller, old woman, beach wormwood). N. America, E. Asia. Height 18–24 in.; planting distance 12–15 in. A hardy species with ovate, deeply lobed, almost white leaves. Panicles, 4–6 in. long, of yellow flowers appear in August and September. This plant has become naturalised in coastal areas in the south-west

SHRUBBY SPECIES

A. abrotanum (southernwood, lad's love, old man). S. Europe. Height and spread 2–4 ft. A hardy, erect and deciduous or semi-evergreen shrub of bushy habit. The downy hoary-green leaves are doubly or trebly pinnate with narrow divisions. Dull yellow globose flowers are borne in elongated panicles from July to September.

ARTEMISIA ABROTANUM

A. absinthium (common wormwood). Europe, including Great Britain. Height and spread 3 ft. A hardy sub-shrubby deciduous species with silver-grey leaves, deeply dissected into slender filaments. Globose yellow flowers are borne in slender leafy panicles in July and August. 'Lambrook Silver' is a selected silvery form.

A. arborescens. S. Europe. Height and spread 3½ ft. This deciduous or semi-evergreen species is not reliably hardy in cold districts and may not survive severe winters. Grown against a sunny wall in mild areas, it reaches a height of 6 ft or more. The silver-white leaves are doubly or trebly divided into very narrow filaments. Yellow globose flowers are carried in terminal leafy panicles during June or July.

A. brachyloba. Mongolia. Height 1 in.; spread 6 in. A hardy, prostrate species with deeply dissected silver-white leaves. Erect, 4–5 in. high racemes, rising above the mat of evergreen foliage, bear yellow flowers from August to September.

A. lanata, syn. *A. pedemontana.* Mountains of Central Europe. Height 1–2 in.; spread 9 in. This hardy, prostrate species forms evergreen cushions of glistening grey-green leaves, dissected into fine segments. Yellow flowers are carried in 8 in. high racemes from July to September.

A. nutans. Sicily. Height 24 in.; spread 18–24 in. This is a hardy evergreen bushy plant with silver-grey leaves divided into linear segments. The pale yellow flowers, which are borne in August and September, are of little merit and are best removed before they develop.

'Silver Queen' (height 2½ ft; planting distance 15 in.) is an outstanding hybrid with narrow, willow-like grey leaves.

A. pedemontana: see *A. lanata*

A. schmidtiana. Japan. This hardy species is represented in cultivation by its dwarf form 'Nana'. Height 3 in.; spread 9–12 in. The finely divided silver-grey leaves form a compact evergreen dome. The drooping, dull yellow flowers are completely encased in silver woolly bracts; they are borne along the stems like tiny balls, towards the end of September.

Cultivation of herbaceous perennial species. Plant at any time during suitable weather between October and March. These species thrive in light, well-drained soil and in full sun, but *A. lactiflora* requires a moisture-retentive soil and will tolerate partial shade. Cut the plants down almost to ground level in October.

Cultivation of shrubby species. Grow these species in any ordinary, well-drained garden soil, in a sunny position. Plant in March or April, except for *A. arborescens* which should be planted during April or May. Remove faded flower stems and protect dwarf, woolly-leaved species from winter damp with raised panes of glass.

In the alpine house, grow prostrate and dwarf species in 6–10 in. pans of John Innes potting compost No. 1. Pot on or repot every second year in March or April.

Propagation of herbaceous perennial species. Divide and replant between October and March.

A. stelleriana may also be increased from 2–3 in. long heel cuttings taken in July and August and treated as cuttings of shrubby species.

Propagation of shrubby species. Take 3–4 in. long semi-hardwood cuttings, preferably with a heel, during August. Insert in equal parts (by volume) peat and sand in a cold frame. The following March, pot the rooted cuttings in 3–3½ in. containers of John Innes potting compost No. 1 and plunge outdoors in a sheltered bed. Plant out in permanent positions in September. Cuttings of *A. arborescens* should not be plunged outdoors until May; they are best overwintered in a cold frame the first year and set out in May.

Pruning. Cut back *A. absinthium* annually in April to within 6 in. of ground level. The other shrubby species need no pruning, other than to keep them in good shape by removing leggy or frosted growths in early spring.

Pests. Colonies of cream-coloured ROOT APHIDS may develop on the leaves.

Diseases. The leaves may be attacked by RUST which shows on the undersurfaces; pale brown spots with cinnamon-brown spores develop and later turn into almost black pustules.

Artichokes: see Globe artichoke and Jerusalem artichoke
Artillery plant: see *Pilea muscosa*
Arum lily: see *Zantedeschia aethiopica*
Arum, pink: see *Zantedeschia rehmannii*

Aruncus

Goat's beard. *Rosaceae*

ARUNCUS SYLVESTER

A genus of 12 species of hardy herbaceous perennials, formerly included in the genus *Spiraea*. These are handsome plants which look especially effective near a pool.

A. sylvester, syn. *Spiraea aruncus.* N. Hemisphere. Height 4–6 ft; planting distance 24 in. The attractive light green leaves are composed of several lanceolate leaflets. Narrow, erect, 8–10 in. long plumes of cream-white flowers, $\frac{1}{8}$ in. across, are borne in June. The form 'Kneiffii' has deeply cut leaflets and is only about 24 in. high.

Artemisia abrotanum

Artemisia absinthium

Artemisia schmidtiana 'Nana'

Aruncus sylvester

Arundinaria variegata

Arundinaria japonica

Asclepias curassavica

Cultivation. Plant between October and March in partial shade, in deep, moist, loamy soil. Cut the stems down in October.

Propagation. Divide and replant in October.

Pests. The larvae of a SAWFLY species eat holes in leaves, often reducing them to skeletons of veins.

Diseases. Generally trouble-free.

Arundinaria

Bamboo. *Gramineae*

A genus of 150 species of hardy evergreen bamboos. Many of these are tall-growing plants, generally too large for small gardens; *A. japonica* can be invasive.

Certain species, notably *A. murielae* and *A. nitida*, have never been known to flower in cultivation. In other species flowering occurs only at prolonged intervals—up to 50 or more years apart—and may then be followed by a moribund, leafless period; flowered branches may die, and occasionally the whole plant. *A. japonica* flowers regularly, but the insignificant grass-like spikes are hidden by the leaves.

A. japonica, syn. *Bambusa metake*. Japan. Height 10–15 ft; planting distance 6–8 ft. A vigorous species with oblong-lanceolate, sharp-pointed leaves that are dark glossy green above, somewhat glaucous beneath. This species forms thickets and is not suitable for a small garden.

A. murielae. China. Height 6–8 ft; planting distance 3 ft. A clump-forming species with rigid persistent stems bearing dark green, narrowly oblong-lanceolate leaves. When fully established the stems arch slightly outwards.

A. nitida. China. Height 9–10 ft; planting distance 4 ft. This fast-growing species requires plenty of space. The purple stems, with a waxy bloom, carry narrowly oblong-lanceolate leaves with bristly margins; they are bright green above, glaucous beneath.

A. variegata. Japan. Height up to 4 ft; planting distance 6 ft. A dense thicket-forming bamboo, with zigzagged dark green canes. The narrowly oblong-lanceolate leaves are rich mid-green, striped with white.

Cultivation. Plant arundinarias in April or May in ordinary, moist garden soil. The roots should not be allowed to dry out, and the plants should be set in a position sheltered from cold winds. Arundinarias do well in sun or in partial shade; *A. nitida* is more tolerant of shade than the other species.

Propagation. Divide and replant the tough roots in April.

Pests and diseases. Generally trouble-free.

Asclepias

Milkweed. *Asclepiadaceae*

A genus of 120 species of hardy and tender herbaceous perennials, shrubs and sub-shrubs. Those described are herbaceous or sub-shrubby perennials of vigorous habit, ideal for wild gardens, sheltered borders or cool greenhouses.

A. curassavica (blood flower). Tropical America. Height up to 3 ft; planting distance 18 in. This woody-based half-hardy perennial has slender-pointed mid-green lanceolate leaves arranged in opposite alternate pairs. The $\frac{3}{4}$ in. wide crown-shaped flowers are bright orange-red and borne in dense, erect, 2 in. wide umbels that emerge from the upper leaf axils from June to October.

A. incarnata (swamp milkweed). N. America. Height 2–4 ft; planting distance 24 in. The mid-green leaves of this hardy plant are lanceolate. Crown-like flesh-pink flowers, $\frac{1}{4}$ in. across, are carried in 2 in. wide umbels during July and August.

ASCLEPIAS TUBEROSA

A. tuberosa. N. America. Height 12–24 in.; planting distance 9–12 in. A hardy species with oblong mid-green leaves that are alternate. Broad heads of waxy, bright orange flowers are borne on erect downy stems in July and August. The flowers are crown-like and $\frac{1}{4}$ in. wide. It resents disturbance and is difficult to establish.

Cultivation. The half-hardy *A. curassavica* may be grown in a sunny, sheltered border, preferably at the foot of a wall, but is better treated as a greenhouse plant with a winter temperature of 7–10°C (45–50°F). Grow mature plants in 6–8 in. pots of John Innes potting compost No. 2.

Plant the hardy species in sunny but moist positions between October and March. *A. incarnata* requires soil containing leaf-mould or peat; *A. tuberosa* needs deep, sandy, peaty soil, with little or no lime. In exposed sites the plants may need supporting with twiggy sticks. The top growth dies down in autumn and is not renewed until late spring; care must be taken not to damage the roots when forking the soil over.

Propagation. Sow seeds of *A. curassavica* during February or March in John Innes seed compost at a temperature of 16–18°C (61–64°F). When the seedlings are large enough to handle, prick them off singly into 3 in. pots of John Innes potting compost No. 2. Pot them on successively and finish off in 6–8 in. pots or plant out in a greenhouse border.

Divide and replant the roots of *A. incarnata* between October and April.

Sow seeds of *A. tuberosa* under glass in March in boxes or pans of John Innes seed compost at a temperature of 15°C (59°F). When the seedlings are large enough to handle, prick them out into boxes; harden the young plants off during April or May before transferring them to an outdoor nursery bed. Plant out from October to March.

Pests. Generally trouble-free.

Diseases. Plants may be stunted by CUCUMBER MOSAIC VIRUS, which mottles the leaves with yellow-green and distorts them

Ash, weeping: see *Fraxinus excelsior* 'Pendula'
Ash, white: see *Fraxinus americana*

Asparagus, culinary

Asparagus officinalis. Liliaceae

A hardy perennial vegetable that requires thorough soil preparation to obtain a good crop. The young, light green, sometimes purple-flushed shoots with closely scaled terminal tips are a choice early-summer vegetable with a distinctive flavour. Asparagus is chiefly grown commercially as it occupies the soil and site permanently but crops for only a few weeks each year. Plants raised from seeds take three or four years before reaching harvesting size; two, three or even four-year-old crowns are sometimes recommended for planting in prepared beds, but one-year-old crowns generally establish themselves best with less risk of losses. Once established, a bed will continue to produce crops for many years, and the size and quality of the shoots improve each year.

VARIETIES

A number of heavy-cropping, easily grown varieties are available, most being of the purple-tinged type. 'Connovers Colossal' has plump shoots with slender tips; 'Martha Washington' and 'Mary Washington', recent introductions from America, are outstanding for the size and quality of the individual shoots which appear abundantly over a long season. 'Purple Argenteuil' has fine-textured shoots with large tips.

'White Cap' is a white-tinged variety, ready for cutting slightly earlier than purple varieties.

Cultivation. If plants are to be raised from seeds, prepare a seed bed in autumn. Dig the bed a spit deep and incorporate plenty of well-rotted manure or compost. In April, sow the seeds thinly in drills $\frac{1}{2}$ in. deep. When the seedlings are about 6 in. high, thin to 12 in. apart.

Hoe the topsoil to keep it loose and free of weeds; water liberally throughout summer. In autumn, when the ferny foliage begins to change colour, it should be cut close to ground level and burnt to prevent berries of female plants from producing unwanted inferior seedlings. The following April, transplant the young plants to the permanent bed, but it will be another two or three seasons before shoots can be harvested.

It is preferable to purchase one-year-old male crowns, if possible, as these produce a more uniform crop; plant in a permanent bed during late March or early April. Cropping can usually begin in the second year after planting.

Choose a site protected from north-east winds. A hedge, fence or a temporary shelter of sacking on 4 ft high poles will give adequate protection.

The best crops are produced on light, sandy soils; heavy, well-drained soil can be lightened by working in plenty of well-rotted compost, and will generally yield successful crops a week or two later than on light soils. On heavy soils that tend to be waterlogged, asparagus is better grown in a raised bed.

Prepare the bed in autumn by digging manure into the topsoil at the rate of a bucket per sq.

yd. In spring, level the bed and dress with 4 oz. of general fertiliser per sq. yd. A 4 ft wide bed will accommodate two rows; alternatively, set the crowns in single rows, 24 in. apart.

Avoid exposing the thick, succulent roots to the air. Make holes 6–8 in. deep at 15 in. intervals along the rows. Place the young plants in the holes with the crowns 4 in. below the surface; spread out the roots evenly and firm the surface.

Mulch with well-rotted manure or compost annually in autumn and cut back the foliage to within 1 in. of ground level. In spring, dress rows annually with a general fertiliser at the rate of 2 oz. per sq. yd. Some authorities recommend drawing a ridge of soil 5 in. up over the crowns in spring, when cropping size is reached, so that longer, blanched stems will develop. Level out the ridge again when cutting back the foliage.

Harvesting. In the first year of cropping, harvest only two or three shoots from each plant over a short period about mid-May. When the bed is well established, harvesting can be extended from early May to mid-June. Cut the shoots when 4–6 in. high, 4 in. below the normal surface level or about 9 in. below the ridge tip, using a sharp, serrated knife and taking care not to damage any other stems. After mid-June leave any further stems to develop until autumn.

Forcing. Crowns may be forced to extend the season or for exhibition purposes. Lift four-year-old or older crowns in autumn and place them under the greenhouse staging in good, light soil reaching 2 in. above their crowns. Keep the crowns at a temperature of 16°C (61°F), and in moist soil. Although best discarded, the forced crowns may be replanted in the permanent bed after harvesting; they generally take a year or two to produce worthwhile crops again.

Pests. Both adults and larvae of the ASPARAGUS BEETLE feed on the young shoots and foliage; they make the plants sticky and black.

Diseases. FROST DAMAGE blackens the tips of the shoots, or they become withered and often slightly pinched at soil level.

VIOLET ROOT ROT causes the top growth to turn to yellow and die. The roots are covered with purple-violet web-like strands of fungus.

Asparagus 'White Cap'

Asparagus plumosus

Asparagus sprengeri

Asparagus, ornamental

Liliaceae

ASPARAGUS PLUMOSUS

A genus of 300 species of foliage plants, including hardy and tender shrubs, climbers, tuberous and fibrous-rooted perennials. The species described here are suitable for a living-room or a greenhouse. They are grown for their attractive feathery foliage which consists of modified branchlets (phylloclades) with the appearance of leaves. Mature plants bear green-white star-shaped, but inconspicuous flowers in small axillary clusters in June and July. The flowers may be followed by clusters of berries.

A. medeoloides (smilax). S. Africa. Height up to 10 ft; spread 9 in. A climbing species which needs to be trained up strings. The thin wiry stems bear bright green, broadly ovate phylloclades. This species may bear globular purple berries.

A. officinalis: see Asparagus, culinary

A. plumosus (asparagus fern). S. Africa. Height 10 ft; spread 12–24 in. This species is non-climbing in its juvenile stage when it is grown as a pot plant. Mature plants are climbing, the main stems throwing out horizontal frond-like branches covered with clusters of bright green thread-like phylloclades. Red globular berries are sometimes produced. 'Compactus' is a non-climbing dwarf variety about 24 in. high.

A. sprengeri. Natal. Height 12 in.; spread 3–4 ft. An arching semi-prostrate species usually grown in a hanging basket. The wiry stems, bearing small hooked prickles, are covered with yellow to mid-green, stiff, linear-oblong phylloclades. Red globular berries sometimes appear. The dwarf variety, 'Compactus', is up to 18 in. long.

Cultivation. Grow these foliage plants in 5–6 in. pots of John Innes potting compost No. 2; set *A. sprengeri* in a 9 in. hanging basket. Maintain a minimum temperature in winter of 7°C (45°F). Water freely in summer and keep the plants just moist in winter. Train the climbing species on canes, or plant them out in the greenhouse border and train up strings or wires. Shade the greenhouse in summer; in the home, place the plants in a well-lit position, out of direct sunlight.

Pot on annually in April until the plants are in their final pots; thereafter repot every other year in April. Give a liquid feed at 10–14 day intervals from May to September.

Propagation. Divide the plants in March or April and pot up in the growing compost.

Alternatively, sow seeds in pots or pans of seed compost during April, at a temperature of 16°C (61°F). When the seedlings are large enough to handle, pot up singly in 3 in. pots of John Innes potting compost No. 1 and pot on as necessary.

Pruning. Mature fronds that show yellow phylloclades, particularly on *A. sprengeri*, should be removed at the base to encourage new shoots.

Pests. Light mottling and bleaching of the leaves are caused by GLASSHOUSE RED SPIDER MITES.

SCALE INSECTS, particularly hemispherical scale, form brown excrescences on the stems and make the plants sticky and sooty.

Diseases. Generally trouble-free.

Asparagus pea

Asperula suberosa

Asperula orientalis

Asparagus pea

Tetragonolobus purpureus. Leguminosae

A little-known half-hardy annual, grown for its edible seed pods. It forms a loose bush about 12 in. high and bears small, sweet-pea-like, scarlet flowers. These are followed by cylindrical green seed pods with four wavy-margined flanges or wings. The pods will reach a length of about 3 in., but should be gathered when about half this length and cooked whole.

Cultivation. Asparagus peas thrive in any fertile, well-drained soil, enriched with a dressing of compost in the top spit. Sow seeds in April or May, setting them 4 in. apart in rows 18 in. apart. Support the plants with 12 in. high twiggy pea sticks in exposed areas.

Harvesting. Gather the young pods for use when they are no more than 1½ in. long.

Pests and diseases. Asparagus peas may suffer from the same disorders as described under PEA.

Aspen: see *Populus tremula*

Asperula
Rubiaceae

ASPERULA SUBEROSA

ASPERULA ODORATA

A genus of 200 species of hardy annuals and perennials. Most are of dwarf habit and suitable for rock gardens, alpine houses or the fronts of borders. The annual species may be grown as spring-flowering pot plants.

ALPINE SPECIES

A. lilaciflora. E. Mediterranean. This species is represented in cultivation by the variety *A. l. caespitosa* (height 2–3 in.; spread 4–6 in.). Awl-shaped bright green leaves form a low compact carpet. Tubular deep carmine flowers, ½ in. long, are borne in June and July.

A. suberosa. Asia Minor, Greece. Height 2–3 in.; spread 6 in. This species forms a semi-trailing tuft of linear, white, hairy leaves and carries a profusion of shell-pink flowers in June and July. Each ½ in. long flower is tubular, with four slender spreading lobes.

ANNUAL SPECIES

A. azurea-setosa: see *A. orientalis*

A. orientalis, syn. *A. azurea-setosa*. Syria. Height 12 in.; spacing 3–4 in. The leaves are mid-green, narrowly lanceolate and hairy. Scented, pale blue, tubular flowers are borne in terminal clusters, ¾ in. across, in July. Good for cutting.

HERBACEOUS SPECIES

A. hexaphylla. Italy. Height 9–12 in.; planting distance 12 in. This perennial species has lanceolate mid-green leaves arranged in whorls. Dense terminal heads of round pink flowers, ¼ in. across, are borne in June and July.

A. odorata (woodruff). Europe, Siberia. Height 6–9 in.; planting distance 12–18 in. The linear mid-green leaves are carried in whorls; sweetly fragrant flowers, ¼ in. across, appear on slender stems in May and June. They are cross-shaped and pure white. In the wild, woodruff is found in woods; in gardens it is best used as ground cover for moist patches beneath trees.

Cultivation of alpine species. Plant between October and March in a sunny position in any sharply drained, gritty soil. The woolly leaves of *A. suberosa* may be harmed by excessive wetness n winter, and should be protected with raised panes of glass or open cloches.

In the alpine house, set the plants in 6 in. pans of John Innes potting compost No. 1. Repot in March every two or three years.

Cultivation of annual species. Outdoors, the plants do best in moist soil, in partial shade. For flowering under glass in April, set five plants to a 5 in. pot of John Innes potting compost No. 1 and overwinter them at 4–7°C (40–45°F).

Cultivation of herbaceous species. Plant between October and March in sun or partial shade in light but moist soil.

Propagation of alpine species. Take soft cuttings of non-flowering basal shoots, 1–1½ in. long, in April or May. Insert them in pots or pans of sand in a cold frame. Pot the rooted cuttings singly in 2–2½ in. pots of 2 parts John Innes potting compost No. 1 to 1 part limestone grit (parts by volume). Grow on in an outdoor plunge bed, and plant out in March or April of the following year.

Propagation of annual species. Broadcast seeds in the flowering site in April and rake them gently into the soil. Thin out to the required spacing.

To grow annuals as pot plants, sow the seeds in September in a cool greenhouse; when the seedlings are large enough to handle, prick them off at the rate of five to a 5 in. pot.

Propagation of herbaceous species. Divide and replant between October and March.

Pests and diseases. Generally trouble-free.

Aspidistra

Liliaceae

A genus of eight evergreen species of greenhouse and house plants. They are all extremely easy to grow as they will tolerate most living-room conditions and are not averse to gas fumes, bad light and extremes of temperature.

A. elatior. China. Height 12 in.; spread 24 in. The dark green oblong-lanceolate leaves, up to 20 in. long, narrow to a stalk. Inconspicuous, fleshy, dull purple, cup-shaped flowers, about 1 in. across, are produced at soil level in August. 'Variegata' has white to cream striped leaves.

Cultivation. Plant in March in 6 in. pots in a rich compost such as John Innes potting compost No. 2. Water freely in summer and wash the leaves occasionally. In winter, keep the compost just moist. The ideal temperature is 7–10°C (45–50°F), but the plants will tolerate short periods of lower temperatures. Aspidistras do best in light shade.

Repot every second or third year in March or April. If large plants are wanted, pot on in larger size pots, up to 10 in. During the years when plants are not being repotted give a monthly feed of weak liquid manure in summer.

Propagation. Divide and replant the roots in March or April.

Pests. Infestations of GLASSHOUSE RED SPIDER MITES occur on the undersides of leaves and cause a fine light mottling of the upper surfaces.

SCALE INSECTS, especially aspidistra scale, form small brown scales on leaves and stems.

Diseases. Browning of the leaf tips and splitting of leaves indicate a PHYSIOLOGICAL DISORDER.

Asplenium

Spleenwort. *Aspleniaceae*

A genus of 650 species of evergreen ferns. Three are suitable for rock gardens; the others are greenhouse or house plants.

A. adiantum-nigrum (black spleenwort). Temperate zones of N. Hemisphere. Height and spread 9 in. or more. A hardy and variable species suitable for a rock garden or a dry wall. It has glossy, black-stemmed, bipinnate leaves that are triangular in outline. The individual toothed pinnae are pale to mid-green, and may be ovate, lanceolate, obovate or wedge-shaped.

A. bulbiferum. Australia, New Zealand. Height 18–24 in.; spread 2–3 ft. This is a plant for greenhouse and indoor cultivation. The lanceolate mid-green fronds are finely cut. Young ferns arise from the bulbils on them and these gradually weigh down the fronds.

A. flabellifolium (necklace fern). Australia, New Zealand. Height 3 in.; spread 12 in. This species is ideal for a hanging basket in a cool greenhouse. The pale green, linear, pinnate fronds are long and straggling with small, fan-shaped pinnae; they root at the tips.

ASPLENIUM NIDUS

A. nidus (bird's-nest fern). Tropical Asia, Pacific Islands. Height 2–4 ft; spread 12–24 in. This is becoming a popular house plant. The glossy, bright green fronds, which are entire and lanceolate, form a shuttlecock-shaped rosette. In the wild the species is an epiphyte and resembles a bird's nest.

ASPLENIUM TRICHOMANES

A. trichomanes (maidenhair spleenwort). Temperate zones. Height and spread 3–9 in. This hardy species, which requires lime, makes an attractive rock-garden or pot plant. The bright green fronds are pinnate; the midribs of the pinnae are glossy black. *A. t.* 'Cristatum' has branching, crested frond-tips.

Cultivation. Outdoors, plant the hardy species in vertical or sloping crevices in the rock garden, using a compost of equal parts (by volume) leaf-mould, loam and mortar rubble. Plant in damp weather between April and September.

Pot-grown plants of all species require a well-drained compost. For all except *A. nidus* use equal parts (by volume) loam, leaf-mould or peat, and coarse sand; *A. nidus* needs 2 parts fibrous

Aspidistra elatior 'Variegata'

Asplenium adiantum-nigrum

Asplenium nidus

Aster amellus 'King George'

Aster novi-belgii 'Jenny'

Aster novi-belgii 'Winston S. Churchill'

Aster acris

Aster amellus 'Rudolph von Goethe'

peat, 1 part fibrous loam, and 1 part coarse sand (parts by volume). Final pot size should be 5–6 in.

A. bulbiferum and *A. flabellifolium* will survive slight frost. *A. nidus* needs a winter temperature of 13°C (55°F).

Water freely during the growing season, and for the rest of the year just sufficiently to keep the soil moist. Shade is essential for all species.

Propagation. Sow spores, preferably in March, July or August (see entry under FERNS). The hardy species can also be divided in spring. Cut the crowns carefully with a sharp knife.

A. bulbiferum and *A. flabellifolium* are easily increased by detaching the tiny plants from their fronds when they show three or four leaves. Prick off into boxes, and later pot up.

Pests. The roots may be eaten by WOODLICE, and SLUGS may eat the fronds and stalks.

TARSONEMID MITES sometimes infest crowns of ferns, causing stunted, distorted growth.

Diseases. Generally trouble-free.

Aster

Michaelmas daisy. *Compositae*

A genus of 500 species of hardy herbaceous perennials, ranging greatly in height, flower-size and colour. The following are suitable for growing in rock gardens or borders, where they look best planted in bold groups of one colour. They are excellent as cut flowers.

The flowers are daisy-like and, unless otherwise stated, have yellow centres.

A. acris, now known as *A. sedifolius*. S. Europe. Height 2–2½ ft; planting distance 15 in. A bushy species with lanceolate hoary-green leaves. Clear lavender-blue flowers, 1 in. across and with golden centres, are densely borne on erect stems in August and September. 'Nanus' (height and planting distance 12 in.) is recommended.

ASTER ALPINUS

A. alpinus. Europe. Height 6 in.; spread 12–18 in. This dwarf species of spreading habit is a variably coloured plant with grey-green spathulate leaves. Purple-blue flowers, 1–1½ in. wide and with orange-yellow centres, appear in July. Red-purple and lilac forms are known.

'Albus', a less vigorous form, has white flowers; 'Beechwood', mauve-blue flowers. 'Wargrave Variety', pale pink tinged purple.

A. amellus. Italy. Height 18–24 in.; planting distance 15 in. This species has rough-textured obovate, grey-green leaves. The flowers, 2–2½ in. across, are borne on woody stems in August and September. It is represented in cultivation by

Aster novi-belgii 'Crimson Brocade'

Aster novi-belgii 'Chequers'

Aster novae-angliae 'Barr's Pink'

Aster alpinus 'Wargrave Variety'

Aster × *frikartii*

Aster novi-belgii 'Fellowship'

Aster novi-belgii 'The Cardinal'

several varieties, including: 'King George', violet-blue; 'Lady Hindlip', deep rose-pink; 'Nocturne', lilac-lavender; 'Rudolph von Goethe', pale mauve-blue; and 'Sonia', rose-pink.

A. ericoides. E. United States, Canada. Height 2–3 ft; planting distance 24 in. A species with linear-lanceolate, mid-green leaves. Slender erect stems, much branched above, bear numerous tiny flowers, $\frac{1}{3}$–$\frac{1}{2}$ in. across, in September and October. They are white or tinged with pink.

Varieties include 'Blue Star', palest blue; 'Delight', white; 'Ringdove', pale rose-mauve.

A. farreri. Tibet. Height 18 in.; planting distance 12 in. The dull green lanceolate leaves are rough-textured. Gold-centred violet flowers, 2 in. across, appear in June.

A. flaccidus: see *A. tibeticus*

A. × frikartii. Height 2½ ft; planting distance 15 in. This hybrid between *A. amellus* and *A. thomsonii* has rough, dark green, oblong leaves. Orange-centred blue flowers, 2 in. across, are freely borne from August to October.

A. linosyris, syn. *Crinitaria linosyris* (goldilocks). Europe. Height 18–24 in.; planting distance 12 in. The leaves are lanceolate and dull green. Bright yellow flowers, $\frac{1}{2}$ in. across, are borne during August and September in compact clusters at the ends of slender stems. The variety 'Gold Dust' is slightly earlier and brighter.

A. novae-angliae (Michaelmas daisy). N. America. Height 4–5 ft; planting distance 18 in. The dull green leaves are lanceolate and stem-clasping. Clusters of flowers, 1–2 in. wide, are

produced in early autumn. The species is represented in cultivation by such varieties as 'Barr's Pink', bright pink, September; 'Harrington's Pink', clear pink, September; 'Lye End Beauty', lavender, September and October; 'September Ruby', rich rose-crimson, September.

ASTER NOVI-BELGII

A. novi-belgii (Michaelmas daisy). N. America. The species has been superseded by numerous varieties (planting distance 15 in.). The mid to deep green leaves are slender-pointed and stem-clasping; the flowers are 1½–2 in. across and appear in September and October. The following varieties are recommended:

'Ada Ballard' (3 ft), double, mauve-blue; 'Blandie' (4 ft), double, cream-white; 'Chequers' (2½ ft), rich purple-violet; 'Crimson Brocade' (3 ft), double, red, particularly free-flowering; 'Eventide' (3 ft), semi-double, violet-blue; 'Fellowship' (4 ft), semi-double, pink; 'Freda Ballard' (3 ft), semi-double, deep carmine; 'Gayborder Royal' (24 in.), bright crimson; 'Marie Ballard' (3 ft), double, light blue; 'Orlando' (3½ ft), semi-double, pink; 'Patricia

Aster novi-belgii 'Patricia Ballard'

Aster novi-belgii (mixed varieties)

Aster novi-belgii 'Orlando'

Aster novi-belgii 'Professor Kippenburg'

Aster yunnanensis

Ballard' (3 ft), semi-double, rose-pink; 'Royal Velvet' (3½ ft), amethyst-purple; 'The Cardinal' (4 ft), deep rose-red; 'Winston S. Churchill' (2½ ft), double, glowing ruby-red.

The dwarf varieties, which are particularly free-flowering, are suitable for the fronts of borders and for small town gardens.

'Audrey' (12 in.), semi-double, pale blue; 'Blue Bouquet' (15 in.), bright blue; 'Jenny' (18 in.), double, rose-red; 'Lady in Blue' (10 in.), semi-double, rich blue; 'Little Pink Baby' (15 in.), double, pink; 'Little Red Boy' (15 in.), deep rose-red; 'Professor Kippenburg' (9 in.), semi-double, light purple-blue; 'Snow Sprite' (12 in.), semi-double, white.

A. pappei: see *Felicia pappei*

A. sedifolius: see *A. acris*

A. tibeticus. Himalayas. Height 6 in.; spread 12–15 in. This slender rock-garden plant is correctly known as *A. flaccidus.* It has sparse foliage, composed of lanceolate, narrowly spathulate mid-green leaves. Single blue-purple flowers, 1–2 in. wide, open in June.

A. thomsonii. Himalayas. Height and planting distance 15 in. This dwarf species is represented in cultivation by the form 'Nana'. The ovate, toothed, stem-clasping leaves are grey-green and hairy. Pale lavender-blue flowers, 1½–2½ in. across, are produced from August to October.

A. tongolensis: see *A. yunnanensis*

A. yunnanensis. China. Height 15–18 in.; planting distance 12 in. The plant in cultivation under this name is correctly *A. tongolensis.* The leaves are dark green and lanceolate. Orange-centred, bright blue-mauve flowers, 2½ in. across, open in June and July. 'Napsbury' is a deep blue variety with larger flowers.

Cultivation. Grow asters in any fertile garden soil in a sunny open position; they need a well-drained soil that does not dry out in late summer and autumn when most of them flower. Plant between October and March.

Most of the taller species and varieties need staking with twiggy supports. Dig up and burn plants which die off before the flowers mature, as this helps to keep the stock free from pests and diseases. Remove the inflorescences from early-flowering plants after flowering. Cut down the stems of all plants from late October onwards. Varieties of *A. novi-belgii* deteriorate after two or three years and should be divided regularly; replant only healthy pieces with young shoots from the outside of each clump.

Propagation. Divide and replant the roots during suitable weather between October and March, preferably in March. To raise large numbers of plants, pull the clumps apart into single shoots in March or April and set these 6 in. apart each way. Divide *A. novi-belgii* like this annually.

Pests. Asters may be attacked by TARSONEMID MITES, which stunt or scar stems, infest young buds and kill or distort flowers. Severe infestations may curtail or even prevent flowering.

SLUGS eat young plants, and CATERPILLARS feed on the leaves of older plants, sometimes killing the terminal growing points.

Diseases. Rotting of the roots, and sometimes the crown, may be caused by BLACK ROOT ROT and RHIZOCTONIA. The leaves become discoloured and the shoots may die back. POWDERY MILDEW shows as a white powder on the leaves.

ASTER WILT (VERTICILLIUM WILT), which occurs in both wet and dry seasons, affects many species and varieties, particularly *A. novi-belgii.* The stems and leaves may turn brown and wither, but the leaves do not fall. The shoots wilt and die. Affected plants may die after two or three years. However, *A. novae-angliae* seems to be immune.

Aster, China: see Callistephus
Aster, Stokes': see Stokesia

Astilbe

Saxifragaceae

A genus of 25 species of hardy herbaceous perennials. They are suitable for growing in herbaceous borders or on rock gardens, and are particularly effective when planted in groups beside a pool, where they associate well with irises and primulas. They have mid to deep green, deeply divided foliage which has coppery tints when young, and colourful plume-like heads of tiny flowers.

. × **arendsii.** Height 2–3 ft; planting distance 2–18 in. A garden hybrid with deep green ern-like foliage. The minute flowers are borne a loose, pyramidal panicles, 12–15 in. long, etween June and August. Recommended varieties include 'Bressingham Beauty' (2½–3 ft igh), clear pink; 'Deutschland' (24 in.), white; 'anal' (24 in.), dark red; 'Federsee' (2½ ft), ose-red; 'Hyacinth' (2½–3 ft), rose-pink; 'Red entinel' (2½ ft), brick-red; 'Rhineland' (2½ ft), ink; 'White Gloria' (24 in.), white.

. **chinensis pumila.** China. Height 9–12 in., pread 12 in. This dwarf plant has fern-like id-green leaves. Spikes of small rose-purple owers, densely arranged in erect 6 in. panicles, e borne from July to October.

. × **crispa.** Height and spread 6–8 in. The aves of this group of dwarf hybrids are slightly arser than those of A. chinensis pumila. They e ovate, deeply cut and mid-green, and have a ightly crinkled appearance. Minute flowers, arying from white through pink to pale red, en in 6 in. long plume-like heads between ly and August. There are several varieties, cluding 'Gnome', rose-pink, and 'Peter Pan', eep pink.

. **davidii.** China. Height 5–6 ft; planting dis-nce 24 in. The feathery, coarsely toothed aves of this species are bronze-green when oung, turning dark green. Minute rose-purple owers are borne in erect, slender panicles, up to 4 in. long, in August.

. **glaberrima,** syns. A. japonica terrestris, A. xatilis. China, Japan. Height and spread 4–6 . The much-dissected leaves of this dwarf ecies are mid-green with bronze highlights. he pale pink and cream flowers are borne in ½–3½ in. long spikes from June to August.

. **grandis.** China. Height 4–6 ft; planting dis-nce 24 in. The dark green, pinnately divided aves are slightly hairy. Minute white flowers e produced in July; they are borne in spreading anicles up to 3 ft long.

. **japonica terrestris**: see A. glaberrima

. **saxatilis**: see A. glaberrima

ASTILBE SIMPLICIFOLIA

. **simplicifolia.** Japan. Height 6 in.; spread 6–9 . The mid-green ovate leaves are deeply cut. iny pale pink or white flowers are crowded to plume-like 4 in. high panicles, which are roduced in August. This species is represented cultivation by hybrid forms such as 'Atro-osea' (height and spread 18 in.), with branching right pink spikes from June to August.

ultivation. Astilbes require a permanently oist soil and thrive in sun or shade. Plant from ctober to March. Water freely during hot dry ummers, and apply a mulch of decayed manure, af-mould or peat in April on poor soil. Cut own the plants to ground level in October and ft and divide every three years.

The shorter varieties make good pot plants. Lift and pot them in 5–6 in. pots containing John Innes potting compost No. 2 during September or October. Plunge the pots in a cold frame until December; move to a greenhouse with a temperature of 10–13°C (50–55°F), gradually raising this to 15°C (59°F), to encourage early flowering.

Propagation. Divide and replant astilbes in March or April; shade newly planted divisions during hot spells and water freely in dry weather during spring and summer.

Pests and diseases. Generally trouble-free.

Astrantia

Masterwort. *Umbelliferae*

ASTRANTIA MAJOR

A genus of ten species of hardy herbaceous perennials. The species described are suitable for mixed borders or informal planting in sun or shade. Their flowers last well when cut.

A. carniolica. Europe. Height 24 in.; planting distance 12–15 in. The attractive mid-green leaves are slender-pointed and much-divided. Tiny, star-like, white flowers, tinged with pink and surrounded by white bracts, appear in July and August. They measure 1 in. across and are long-lasting in water.

A. c. 'Rubra', 12 in. high and requiring a planting distance of 9–12 in., bears clusters of purple-red flowers and bracts in July.

A. helleborifolia: see A. maxima

A. major. Europe. Height 24 in.; planting distance 15 in. This species has ovate-lanceolate leaves that are mid-green and tripartite. Star-like greenish-pink flowers, with similarly coloured narrow bracts, are produced in June and July. They measure 1 in. across.

A. maxima, syn. A. helleborifolia. E. Caucasus. Height 18–24 in.; planting distance 15 in. The three-lobed leaves are bright green. Star-like shell-pink flower heads, 1–1½ in. across, are borne in June and July.

Cultivation. Plant astrantias between October and March in any ordinary garden soil. A partially shaded position is generally best, but a sunny spot will do if the soil stays reasonably moist in summer. In an exposed position the plants may need supporting with twiggy sticks. Cut down the stems in late summer.

Propagation. Divide and replant the roots between October and March.

Sow seeds in boxes of seed compost in September and place in a cold frame. The following spring, prick out the seedlings into boxes; plant out in a nursery bed in June or July and grow on. Plant in permanent positions the following spring.

Pests and diseases. Generally trouble-free.

Astilbe × arendsii 'Hyacinth'

Astilbe × arendsii 'Rhineland'

Astilbe simplicifolia (hybrid)

Astrantia major

Astrophytum myriostigma

Astrophytum asterias

Astrophytum capricorne

Astrophytum
Cactaceae

A genus of six species of greenhouse perennials with several varieties and hybrids. These globular, ribbed cacti are grown for their white-scaled bodies and magnificent flowers. These are produced singly or in numbers from the top of the plant body and may last four or five days.

The plants are usually solitary, producing offsets only occasionally on old specimens. All are fairly easy to grow.

See also CACTUS.

ASTROPHYTUM MYRIOSTIGMA

A. asterias (sea urchin cactus, sand dollar cactus). Mexico. Height up to 1¼ in.; spread 3 in. The apple-green stem is a flattened sphere with eight broad, shallow ribs marked with white scales. It is spineless, but bears white woolly tufts in the widely spaced rows of areoles. The daisy-like flowers are about 1¼ in. across, yellow, and usually produced freely from June to August even on young plants. The species is slow-growing and does not produce offsets.

A. capricorne (goat's horn cactus). Mexico. Height up to 10 in.; spread up to 5 in. The stem is globular, becoming cylindrical with age. It is ligh green, marked with white woolly scales and ha seven or eight sharply crested ribs bearin depressed areoles. From the areoles sever; curved, flattened, brown-black spines develop The daisy-like or star-shaped flowers are yellow with a red centre, and about 2 in. across. They ar produced from June to August and occur even o young plants.

A. myriostigma (bishop's cap cactus). Mexic Height up to 6 in.; spread 5 in. A globular plar becoming columnar-cylindrical with age. It ha five or six prominent ribs, usually spineless bu occasionally producing a few short spines. Th grey plant body is often covered almost com pletely with dense white scales.

The daisy-like flowers, about 1½ in. across, ar pale yellow with a silken sheen in sunlight. Th plant flowers freely from an early age, usuall from June to August. *A. m. quadricostatur* (bishop's mitre cactus) has only four ribs.

A. ornatum. Mexico. Height up to 12 in.; spread in. A globular plant, becoming cylindrical wit age. The plant body is grey with darker marking and has copious bands of white scales. Th areoles bear 5–11 stout spines, 2 in. long an yellow at first, later becoming black. The pal yellow daisy-like flowers are 2–3½ in. across they usually appear from June to August o mature plants growing in full sun.

Cultivation. Astrophytum species need a porou soil consisting of 2 parts loam, 1 part decaye leaf-mould and 1 part coarse sand (parts b volume), with 1 oz. bone-meal added to each gal. bucket of soil. Pot the plants in March c April and stand them in maximum light and fu sun, allowing them plenty of air. In winter, th plants need a temperature not lower than 5° (41°F).

Water the plants only from the beginning c March to the end of October, whenever the so becomes dry. Pot on the plants at the beginnin of each growing season if the pots are full of root. until the plants are finally in 5 in. pots.

Propagation. These plants are usually raised fror seeds sown in spring at a temperature of 21° (70°F). On rare occasions offsets are produce on old plants, though never on *A. asterias*. Th offsets may be detached during summer and s(in sand. They should have rooted in 2–3 month. when they can be potted in the growing medium

Pests. The roots may be infested by ROOT MEAL BUGS; these cause a check to growth.

Diseases. Generally trouble-free.

Athyrium
Athyriaceae

A genus of 180 species of ferns. Of the tw described, one is suitable for growing outdoor: and the other is best grown in a cool greenhouse

A. filix-femina (lady fern). Temperate zone. Height and spread 1½–3 ft. The dainty, fres green fronds of this hardy native fern ar bipinnate. *A. f-f.* 'Plumosum' has finely divide golden-green fronds. *A. f-f.* 'Victoriae' is a outstanding variety, its deep green frond having a criss-cross pattern and crested border

goeringianum 'Pictum' (Japanese painted fern). Japan. Height and spread 12–18 in. This species is hardy, but may not withstand severe winter weather and is therefore better grown under glass. The lanceolate to triangular bipinnate fronds are sage green, variegated with silver-grey. The midribs are purple.

ATHYRIUM FILIX-FEMINA 'VICTORIAE'

Cultivation. Plant A. filix-femina during April or September in light shade in a humus-rich soil. Give an annual top-dressing of leaf-mould or peat, enriched with bone-meal. Do not allow the plants to dry out at any time. Lift and replant them every third or fourth year, as the rootstock gradually rises out of the ground and causes the young roots to dry out.

The top growth of A. filix-femina may be cut down to ground level in autumn.

Plant A. goeringianum 'Pictum' in a 5 or 6 in. pot, using a compost of equal parts (by volume) loam, leaf-mould or peat, and coarse sand. Maintain a minimum temperature of 7–10°C (45–50°F). Water freely during the growing period, moderately in winter.

Propagation. Both the species and A. filix-femina 'Plumosum' breed fairly true from spores; A. f-f. 'Victoriae' usually produces interesting forms. Sow the spores at any time (see entry under FERNS), later discarding indifferent variations.

The plants may also be divided and replanted in April once a few crowns have formed.

Pests and diseases. Generally trouble-free.

---

tragene alpina: see Clematis alpina

Aubergine: see Egg plant

Aubrieta

Cruciferae

A genus of 15 species of low-growing hardy evergreen perennials. Any of the following plants will make a colourful show on dry walls, on rock banks or in a sunny position on rock gardens. All thrive in soils containing lime.

A. deltoidea. Sicily to Asia Minor. Height 3–4 in.; spread 18–24 in. This is a spreading, matforming species. The hoary green leaves are obovate with a few large teeth. Cross-shaped flowers, $\frac{1}{2}$–$\frac{3}{4}$ in. wide and with rounded petals in shades of purple to rose-lilac are borne in short terminal spikes between March and June. The variety 'Aurea' has gold-edged leaves, 'Variegata' white-edged leaves. Both have purple flowers.

There are several varieties with larger flowers in varying shades of red and purple: 'Barker's Double' has long-lasting, rose-purple, double flowers; 'Dr Mules' is an old favourite with violet-purple flowers; 'Godstone' has bright purple flowers; 'Gurgedyke' is bright purple;

'Magician' is deep red-purple; 'Riverslea', mauve-pink, is later-flowering; 'Tauricola' bears deep purple-blue flowers.

Cultivation. Plant between September and March in well-drained garden soil, preferably containing lime, in a sunny position. After flowering, cut back rock-garden plants to encourage a neat habit of growth, but do no more than remove old flowering stems from plants grown to trail over dry walls.

Propagation. Sow seeds in boxes or pans of John Innes seed compost in a cold frame or greenhouse during February or March; prick off the seedlings into boxes containing John Innes potting compost No. 1. When they are well rooted, pot them individually into 3 in. pots and plunge them outside. Plant out in September or October.

Aubrietas may also be increased by cuttings taken from established cut-back plants in June or July. Mound peat and sand over the crowns, and use the new shoots that appear as cuttings.

In August or September take 2 in. basal cuttings, inserting them in equal parts (by volume) peat and sand in a cold frame. The following March, pot the rooted cuttings singly in 3 in. pots of John Innes potting compost No. 1 and grow on ready for planting out between September and March.

Divide established plants in September and replant direct in permanent positions.

Pests. Generally trouble-free.

Diseases. WHITE BLISTER causes blisters or swellings full of white powdery spores on the leaves and sometimes on the stems.

DOWNY MILDEW may cause yellow blotches on the leaves; it shows as a grey furry coating on the undersides of the foliage.

Aucuba

Cornaceae

AUCUBA JAPONICA

A genus of three species of hardy evergreen shrubs, native to China, the Himalayas and Japan. They are unisexual, and plants of both sexes need to be planted to produce berries. They are easy to grow and will tolerate dense shade and atmospheric pollution. Aucubas are suitable subjects for planting in urns or other containers in shady courtyards; they may also be grown as house plants in halls and patios.

A. japonica (spotted laurel). Japan. Height 6–12 ft; spread 5–7 ft. A rounded bushy shrub with shiny dark green leaves that are leathery, narrowly ovate, and usually widely toothed towards the apex. Olive-green star-shaped flowers appear in erect panicles, 2–4 in. long, in March and April. Small clusters of bright scarlet ovoid berries on female plants often persist from autumn to the following spring.

Athyrium filix-femina 'Plumosum'

Athyrium goeringianum 'Pictum'

Aubrieta deltoidea

Numerous forms are in cultivation, and include the following: 'Crotonoides', a female plant with broad leaves barred and mottled with gold; 'Fructu-albo', yellow-white berries; 'Longifolia', with narrower and longer leaves than those of the species; they are bright green in both forms, and the female plant is one of the most prolific fruit-bearing aucubas.

'Maculata', syn. 'Variegata', is the common female variegated form with yellow-spotted leaves; 'Nana Rotundifolia', syn. 'Rotundifolia', is low-growing with rich green leaves in both male and female forms; 'Salicifolia' is a female form with narrow, willow-like leaves.

Cultivation. Aucubas are among the most easily grown evergreen shrubs. Plant in September and October or in March and April, in ordinary garden soil and in a sunny or partially shaded position; they thrive in town and seaside gardens. To obtain berries, plant one male form to three female forms to ensure cross-pollination.

Aucubas grown in containers should be planted in John Innes potting compost No. 2; they may be given a weak liquid feed at intervals of two to three weeks from May to September.

Aucuba japonica

Aucuba japonica 'Maculata'

Ballota pseudo-dictamnus

House plants are grown in 6–8 in. pots of John Innes potting compost No. 2. They should be kept in a cool room, shaded from direct sunlight, and kept moist at all times. Repot or pot on annually in March.

Propagation. Seeds may be sown in September or October, but this is a slow method of propagation.

Take cuttings, 4–6 in. long, preferably with a heel, of lateral shoots in August and September; insert in equal parts (by volume) peat and sand in a cold frame. The following April, line the rooted cuttings out in nursery rows and grow on for two years before setting in permanent positions.

Pruning. None required; old stems may be cut back to within 2–3 ft in April.

Pests. Generally trouble-free.

Diseases. A PHYSIOLOGICAL DISORDER shows as black blotches on the leaves; it is usually the result of unsuitable soil conditions.

Aunt Eliza: see *Curtonus paniculata*
Avena candida: see *Helictotrichon sempervirens*
Avens: see Geum
Avens, water: see *Geum rivale*
Azalea: see Rhododendron

B

Baby's tears: see *Helxine soleirolii*
Bachelor's buttons: see *Kerria japonica* 'Pleniflora'
Balloon flower: see Platycodon

Ballota

Labiatae

BALLOTA PSEUDO-DICTAMNUS

A genus of 35 species of herbaceous perennials and deciduous sub-shrubs, occurring in the Mediterranean regions and N. Africa. It includes several weeds, and only one species is in general cultivation. The dead-nettle-like flowers are insignificant; the plant is grown for its foliage.
B. pseudo-dictamnus. Eastern Mediterranean. Height 12–24 in.; spread 24 in. A low-growing, much-branched, fairly hardy shrub with spreading white woolly growths. The heart-shaped woolly-grey leaves are opposite; tubular, two-lipped white flowers, spotted with purple and about ½ in. long, are borne in whorls in July.
Cultivation. Plant in April or May in poor or ordinary, well-drained garden soil and in full sun. Ballotas are susceptible to winter wet, and in damp areas need the protection of open cloches.

Propagation. Take cuttings, about 3 in. long, of non-flowering lateral shoots in July and August; insert the cuttings in equal parts (by volume) peat and sand in a cold frame. Plant out the rooted cuttings the following April or May.
Pruning. Cut back the growths by half in April.
Pests and diseases. Generally trouble-free.

Balm

Melissa officinalis. Labiatae

BALM

This is a hardy herbaceous perennial, grown as a herb for its lemon-scented leaves or as a decorative plant in herbaceous borders.

Height 2–4 ft; planting distance 12–18 in. Central S. Europe, Great Britain. A bushy clump-forming plant, with branching hairy stems bearing wrinkled and toothed, nettle-like pale green leaves. Tiny, white, tubular flowers are borne in leafy racemes during June and July.

Balm leaves and young shoots are used fresh for flavouring fruit salads and iced drinks. The dried leaves retain their fragrance and are suitable as an ingredient of *pot-pourri*.

The variety *M. o.* 'Aurea' (golden balm) is equally suitable as a herb and as a decorative herbaceous plant; the gold-green colour of the leaves often fades as flowering time approaches.
Cultivation. Plant balm in October or March in ordinary, well-drained garden soil, preferably in full sun. Cut plants with variegated foliage back to 6 in. above ground level in June to encourage the production of fresh young shoots. In October, cut all growths hard back to just above ground level, and cover the roots with straw or bracken in the coldest areas.
Propagation. Divide and replant the roots in October or March.

Alternatively, sow seeds outdoors in late April or early May, where the plants are to grow. Thin the seedlings to 12–18 in. apart.
Harvesting and storing. Gather the young shoots and leaves throughout summer and use fresh. Leaves for drying should preferably be picked before flowering begins; for drying methods see entry under HERBS.
Pests and diseases. Generally trouble-free.

Balm, bee: see *Monarda didyma*
Balm of Gilead: see *Populus candicans*
Balsam: see *Impatiens balsamina*
Bamboo: see Arundinaria
Bamboo, Chinese sacred: see Nandina
Bambusa metake: see *Arundinaria japonica*
Banana, Canary Islands: see *Musa cavendishii*

Baptisia
False indigo. *Leguminosae*

BAPTISIA AUSTRALIS

A genus of 35 species of erect hardy herbaceous perennials suitable for mixed borders or informal planting. Only the species described is in general cultivation.
B. australis. N. America. Height 2–4 ft; spread 18–24 in. This species has attractive trifoliate mid-green leaves composed of obovate notched leaflets. Indigo-blue spikes of sweet-pea-like flowers, $\frac{1}{2}$–$\frac{3}{4}$ in. long, are borne in June.
Cultivation. Plant between October and March in deep, moist soil in full sun. In exposed positions, the plants may need the support of twiggy sticks. Cut the flowering stems back to ground level after flowering.
Propagation. Sow seeds during April in the open or in pans of seed compost in a cold frame. Prick off the seedlings into boxes or singly into 3 in. pots, using John Innes potting compost No. 2, then into a nursery bed. Grow on and plant out where they are to flower 18 months or two years after sowing.

Divide the woody roots during suitable weather between October and March.
Pests and diseases. Generally trouble-free.

Barberry: see Berberis
Barrenwort: see Epimedium
Bartonia aurea: see *Mentzelia lindleyi*

Basil
Ocimum basilicum. Labiatae

A half-hardy annual grown as a culinary herb.

Height 2–3 ft; planting distance 12 in. Tropical Asia. A plant with four-sided stems and stalked, ovate, aromatic leaves that are bright green above and grey-green, sometimes tinged with purple, beneath. Small, white, tubular flowers, carried in whorls from the leaf axils, are produced in August.

The leaves have a strong, clove-like flavour and are used fresh or dried in soups, omelettes, salads, fish dishes, and minced meat.

BASIL

Cultivation. Grow basil in a warm, sheltered position in light, well-drained soil. Water the plants during dry weather, but let the soil dry out between waterings. Pinch off the flowers as early as possible to promote foliage growth.
Propagation. Sow seeds in March in pots or pans of seed compost at a temperature of 13°C (55°F). When the seedlings are large enough to handle, prick them out in trays and grow on at the same temperature. Harden the young plants off in mid-May, and at the end of the month plant them out 12 in. apart in rows 15 in. apart.

Alternatively, sow seeds $\frac{1}{2}$ in. deep in May in seed drills 15 in. apart. Thin out the seedlings gradually until they are 12 in. apart.
Harvesting and storing. Fresh leaves may be picked from July to September. They may also be dried or deep-frozen for winter use. See entry under HERBS.
Pests and diseases. Generally trouble-free.

Bay, laurel: see Laurus
Bay, sweet: see *Laurus nobilis*

Beans
Leguminosae

These extensively cultivated vegetables are divided into three groups: broad beans, French beans and runner beans.
Broad bean (*Vicia faba*). A hardy, easily grown annual cultivated for the edible seeds contained in its pods and used as a summer vegetable. Except for one or two dwarf varieties, the plants grow to a height of 3 ft or more. Autumn-sown crops can be useful in giving protection the following spring to early crops of more tender vegetables planted among them.

Golden balm

Baptisia australis

Basil

Broad bean Longpod 'Exhibition'

French bean 'Blue Coco'

French bean 'Carmine King'

The pendent pods, which mature from May to July, are 6–12 in. long and contain large, green-white or darker green seeds. There is little difference in flavour between the white and green-seeded forms, but the latter are more suitable for deep-freezing.

VARIETIES

These are of two types, Longpods and Windsors. Longpods have kidney-shaped seeds in long, slender pods, while Windsors have almost round seeds in shorter, broader pods. Reliable varieties among the white-seeded Longpods include: 'Bunyards', 'Colossal', 'Exhibition' and 'Imperial'. Among the green-seeded Longpods, 'Green Giant', 'Green Longpod' and 'Masterpiece' are recommended.

White-seeded Windsors include: 'Broad Windsor' and 'Giant White Windsor'; green-seeded Windsors are 'Harlington' and 'Unrivalled'. These varieties are suitable for spring sowing only. For sowing in November, December and January in the south and in particularly sheltered areas the hardy Longpod types 'Aquadulce Claudia' and 'Seville' are suitable.

'Sutton's Dwarf' is a Longpod dwarf variety which branches freely and grows to a height of 10–12 in. It is excellent for a small garden and for growing under cloches as an early crop. It may be sown in succession until July.

Cultivation. Broad beans can be grown on any fertile, well-drained garden soil, but medium to heavy soils give the best results for spring sowing, and light soils for autumn and winter sowings. Dress acid soils with lime. Prepare the seed bed by digging the ground two spits deep and working well-rotted manure into the bottom spit at the rate of a bucket per sq. yd. Before sowing, add fish manure at 3 oz. per sq. yd.

For an early crop, sow in open ground in November or December, or under cloches in January. Seedlings may also be raised in a greenhouse or frame and transplanted in March. For main crops, sow outdoors in early April and at the beginning of May.

Sow the seeds 6 in. apart in 3 in. deep drills. Maximum use is made of the space available if double rows are sown 6 in. apart, with the seeds staggered in the rows, and 2½ ft between the rows. Or sow in single rows 24 in. apart. Dwarf varieties need 24 in. between double rows and 15 in. between single rows.

Start picking the pods as soon as the seeds are about ¾ in. across. After harvesting, cut the tops down, and leave the roots in the soil to release their nitrogen.

French, dwarf or kidney bean (*Phaseolus vulgaris*). An annual grown for its edible pods, which generally mature from July to October. It is tender, but early sowings under glass and late-spring sowings outdoors under cloches ensure early crops. By successional sowings, under glass or outdoors, supplies can be had from early June to mid-November.

The pods are pale to mid-green, narrow and up to 5 in. long; they are generally flat, but plump, pencil-podded, stringless types are also available. Besides the familiar green French beans, there are excellent yellow varieties.

Haricot beans and flageolet beans are types of French beans, but only the dried seeds are eaten, not the whole pod. Flageolets should be harvested while the beans in the pods are soft and green; haricots, when the seeds have ripened to white or light brown, according to variety.

VARIETIES

Flat-podded, free-cropping varieties include: 'Canadian Wonder', 'Masterpiece' and 'The Prince'. 'Masterpiece' is also suitable for forcing to give the earliest crop of the season.

Reliable pencil-podded, stringless varieties are: 'Phoenix Claudia', 'Sprite' and 'Tendergreen', all of which are also excellent for canning and freezing. 'Mont d'Or' is a well-flavoured, yellow-podded bean.

A good haricot variety is 'Comtesse de Chambord', which produces large numbers of small, white-seeded pods. 'White Leviathan' is a well-flavoured flageolet bean.

There are coloured-podded varieties of ornamental value. 'Blue Coco' has well-flavoured, bright blue-purple pods which turn green when cooked; 'Carmine King' has pods heavily marked with carmine red.

Cultivation. French beans crop best on a light, well-drained soil; improve heavy soil by forking in plenty of humus, and add lime if the soil is acid. Dig the ground deeply in autumn, working in a bucket of well-rotted manure per sq. yd. Three weeks before sowing, apply a dressing of fish manure at the rate of 3 oz. per sq. yd.

For an early June crop, sow seeds under cloches in mid-March and keep them covered until the end of May. For main crops make the first sowing outdoors about the third week of April in the south, in early May in northerly districts. Make successional sowings once a month until mid-July.

Sow the seeds 2–3 in. apart in 2 in. deep drills drawn 18 in. apart. When the young plants are showing the first pair of leaves, thin them out to 6 in. apart. The non-climbing forms are self-supporting, but in exposed positions they need the support of twiggy sticks. Tall pea sticks will be needed for climbing varieties.

At the beginning of October put cloches over the latest sowings to protect the plants and keep them cropping into November.

Pick the pods when they are young and tender. If they are left too long on the plants they become stringy in texture and the plants stop producing new pods. Cut the tops down when the crop is finished, but leave the roots in the ground to release nitrogen.

Runner bean, scarlet runner bean (*Phaseolus multiflorus*). A tender perennial twining plant, usually grown as an annual. It bears edible seed pods which are used as a late-summer vegetable.

The pods are 12 in. or more long and up to 1 in. wide; they have a more distinct flavour than French beans, but are of a coarser texture. Given the right conditions runner beans are easily grown and produce prolific crops of tender pods from July to September, and even into November when the weather is favourable. A large number of varieties is available.

VARIETIES

For early crops, grow semi-dwarf varieties such as 'Kelvedon Marvel', 'Kelvedon Wonder' and 'Princeps'. Alternatively, grow a non-climbing variety such as 'Hammond's Dwarf'. Such varieties do not need supports; they crop two or three weeks before twining varieties.

For main crops over a long season, grow 'Best of All', 'Challenge' or 'Streamline'. These need training up poles or strings.

'Mammoth White', a white-flowered and white-seeded variety, is best grown for a late crop; 'Painted Lady' has bi-coloured, crimson and white flowers.

Cultivation. Most types of soil are suitable provided they are properly prepared for the deep, moist root-run which runner beans need. On heavy soil or deep loam, dig the ground deeply in winter, working in plenty of well-rotted manure. On light or sandy soil, take out trenches, 18–24 in. wide and two spits deep. Place a thick layer of well-rotted manure or compost in the bottom, cover with 6 in. of soil, and add another layer of manure before replacing the topsoil.

Avoid excessive use of fertilisers on runner beans at any stage of growth, as this results in lush rank growth, and a poor crop of beans.

For early crops, sow seeds in a cold greenhouse or frame at the beginning of May for planting out in June, or sow outdoors in mid-April under cloches that have been in position for a month.

Sow the seeds 2 in. deep and 9 in. apart. For semi-dwarf varieties grown as bushes, make the rows 24 in. apart; pinch out the growing tips to promote bushy growth and to prevent climbing stems from developing.

Grow twining types in double rows, and support with a pair of 8 ft long poles set 12 in. apart and crossed and tied together 6 in. from the top. Allow 12–15 in. between each pair of poles in the row and place a pole horizontally along the top where the poles cross; tie securely to make a firm structure. Sow one seed at each pole and a few extra ones at the end of the row to replace seeds that do not germinate. Allow a space of 5 ft between double rows.

Alternatively, grow runner beans in single rows. Support the plants with a stout, 8 ft tall pole at each end of the row, and stretch wires between the two at the top and near the bottom; tie strings between the top and bottom wires for each individual plant to climb. Allow a distance of 3 ft between single rows.

In small gardens where space is restricted, erect a strong centre pole and fix strings from it in maypole fashion. Sow eight to ten seeds in a circle round the pole, about 12 in. away.

Water the plants well during dry spells; a mulch of peat or grass clippings, 1 in. deep, helps to preserve moisture. Spray the plants with water when they are in flower to help the flowers to set, and pinch out the growing points when the plants have reached the top of their supports. Pick the pods before the seeds begin to swell. The more pods that are picked, the more the plants will produce.

Pests. The seeds may be eaten by SLUGS, MILLEPEDES and the maggots of BEAN SEED FLY.

APHIDS, especially the bean aphid, infest the terminal shoots of young and established plants. CAPSID BUGS feed on young tissues, causing tattering of the leaves and BLINDNESS of buds.

In dry weather, GLASSHOUSE RED SPIDER MITES may infest leaves, which bronze and wither in severe infestations.

Diseases. Brown spots on leaves and stems may be due to ANTHRACNOSE OF DWARF BEAN, which also causes brown sunken areas on the pods.

FOOT and ROOT ROT may be caused by several fungi including RHIZOCTONIA and BLACK ROOT ROT fungus. The roots die and often show black patches; the stem-bases become discoloured and may decay. The foliage turns yellow and withers.

FUSARIUM WILT causes the leaves to turn yellow and the plants to wilt. The stem-bases and roots show red marks.

GREY MOULD attacks the pods in wet seasons and in poorly drained soil; the pods are covered with a grey fungal growth and rot.

A PHYSIOLOGICAL DISORDER, due to lack of moisture at the roots and/or cold night temperatures, prevents the flowers from setting.

RUST shows on the leaves as scattered pustules bearing first brown, then black spores.

VIRUS DISEASES cause stunting of plants which bear distorted pods and leaves, mottled with dark and pale green or green-and-yellow areas.

Runner bean 'Streamline' (in flower)

Bean tree, Indian: see *Catalpa bignonioides*
Bearberry: see *Arctostaphylos uva-ursi*
Bear's breeches: see Acanthus
Beauty bush: see *Kolkwitzia amabilis*
Beaver-tail: see *Sedum morganianum*
Beech: see Fagus
Beech, common: see *Fagus sylvatica*
Beech, common purple: see *Fagus sylvatica* 'Purpurea'
Beech, copper: see *Fagus sylvatica* 'Cuprea'
Beech, Dawyck: see *Fagus sylvatica* 'Fastigiata'
Beech, fernleaf: see *Fagus sylvatica* 'Laciniata'
Beech, weeping: see *Fagus sylvatica* 'Pendula'

Beet, Beetroot

Beta vulgaris Crassa. *Chenopodiaceae*

A biennial root vegetable grown as an annual. It is hardy except in the severest winters, when some protection should be given with a covering of straw or cloches. The tender, dark crimson flesh is suitable for pickling and as an accompaniment to cold meats and salads; it can also be used to make soup. Crops can be pulled throughout the year or harvested and stored.

VARIETIES
The two main types are the long and the globe-rooted beetroots. The globe type are the most popular; they are less prone to bolting than other varieties and can be sown several weeks earlier, to provide roots from June onwards. 'Avonearly', 'Boltardy' and 'Early Bunch' are recommended. For later sowings to provide roots for autumn and early winter use, sow the small-rooted, quick-growing 'Little Ball'.

The long-rooted types are still frequently used for a main crop which is allowed to mature in the ground before being harvested and stored in early winter. 'Cheltenham Green Top' is a good variety.

Cultivation. Beetroots thrive on light soils, but will grow successfully on most fertile, well-cultivated soils. Heavy soils may be lightened by incorporating liberal amounts of sedge peat, decayed compost or well-rotted manure.

Runner bean 'Streamline'

Beet 'Boltardy'

Dig the ground over in early winter and apply a top-dressing of 2 oz. per sq. yd of general-purpose fertiliser prior to sowing. Break the soil down to a fine tilth to promote the rapid growth essential for the production of tender roots.

Make successional sowings of early globe varieties to ensure a continuity of young roots. Make the first sowing in late March or early April and continue until early July in the north and the third week of July in the south. Sow a main crop of long-rooted beets in late May.

Sow the seeds thinly in $\frac{3}{4}$ in. deep drills. Allow 12 in. between rows of the globe type and 18 in. between rows of the long-rooted varieties. Thin the seedlings to leave globe beets $4\frac{1}{2}$ in. apart and long-rooted beets 8 in. apart.

Harvesting and storing. Pull early globes as required, as soon as they are large enough. Main crops for winter use can be left in the ground until required if they are covered with straw or bracken to protect them from frost. Alternatively, lift in November and store the beetroots in boxes of sand or peat in a frost-proof shed or outdoors in a clamp. Cut the tops off roots for storing, being careful not to cut too close to the crown or the root will bleed. Lift all roots with great care, using a fork and putting it into the ground to the side of the row. Damaged roots bleed freely.

Pests. The leaves may be tunnelled through by MANGOLD FLY maggots which cause extensive mines and check the growth of young plants.

Older plants may be damaged by infestations of SWIFT MOTH caterpillars.

Diseases. CROWN GALL occasionally produces large warty outgrowths on the roots.

DAMPING-OFF causes the collapse of seedlings.

LEAF SPOT, due to several fungi, shows as brown spots on the leaves. The diseased tissues often fall away, leaving holes.

MINERAL DEFICIENCIES cause various symptoms: BORON DEFICIENCY results in heart rot which shows as a browning of the crowns; the roots sometimes turn black. MAGNESIUM DEFICIENCY shows as pale areas between the veins followed by browning of the tissues. MANGANESE DEFICIENCY causes a trouble known as speckled yellows, in which the leaves show yellow blotches between the veins and roll inwards.

SCAB shows on the roots as small marks or sunken pits or as raised knob-like scabs.

VIOLET ROOT ROT causes slight yellowing and stunting of the leaves; affected roots are covered with a web of felt-like purple fungal growth.

Beet, spinach: see Spinach
Beetroot: see Beet

Begonia
Begoniaceae

A genus of 900 species of tender perennial evergreen and deciduous plants grown for their flowers and foliage. They range in size from a few inches to bamboo-like shrubs 10 ft or more high; there are also a few climbers. All are suitable for a greenhouse, and some can be used for outdoor bedding schemes and as house plants. Begonias

Begonia evansiana

Begonia socotrana
'Van de Meer's Glory'

Begonia × tuberhybrida
(mixed)

are unisexual, male and female flowers being borne on the same plant; the male flowers are the more showy, the female can be distinguished by the prominent, winged ovaries. The latter bear triangular, often winged seed capsules.

Begonias are here divided into three groups: tuberous, rhizomatous and fibrous-rooted. The flower shape is characteristic of all three groups, varying only in size. Male flowers generally have four ovate-oblong petals, two of which are shorter than the others; female flowers have four or five similar petals, more equal in size.

Tuberous begonia hybrids and varieties are generally deciduous; they bear single female and double male flowers. Rhizomatous begonias are evergreen, the majority being grown for their foliage, which is borne on a creeping rootstock. Fibrous-rooted begonias are also evergreen; they have tall, erect, sometimes shrubby stems and are chiefly grown for their flowers.

Unless stated otherwise, the leaves are ear-shaped, though varying greatly in proportions.

BEGONIA × TUBERHYBRIDA   BEGONIA × 'GLOIRE DE LORRAINE'

TUBEROUS BEGONIAS
B. evansiana. China, Japan. Height up to 18 in.; spread 12 in. A half-hardy species which, in a sheltered position, will survive outdoors. The leaves are glossy mid-green above, flushed red beneath. Flesh-pink flowers, $1-1\frac{1}{2}$ in. across, borne in axillary branched panicles, appear from June to September. Bulbils form in the leaf axils.
B. Hiemalis: see *B. socotrana*
B. Lorraine: see *B. socotrana*
B. Pendula: see *B. × tuberhybrida*
B. socotrana. Island of Socotra. Height and spread 12-18 in. This is a rare, seldom-cultivated species which has been superseded by the hybrid strain popularly known as Lorraine begonias. The mid-green leaves are rounded in outline and depressed in the centre. Massed deep pink flowers, $\frac{3}{4}-1$ in. wide, are produced in December and January. Among the most outstanding are: 'Ege's Favourite', 'Gloire de Lorraine', 'Marina' and 'Mrs Lionel de Rothschild'; they all bear abundant pink flowers which open from November to January.

The Hiemalis or large winter-flowered group resemble Lorraine begonias, but with larger flowers in a wider colour range. Varieties include: 'De Ridder's Yellow', double, yellow; 'Eveleen's Orange', deep orange; 'Exquisite', pink; 'Thought of Christmas', double, white; 'Van de Meer's Glory', salmon-orange.
B. × tuberhybrida. Height 12-24 in.; spread 12-15 in. This name is applied to the popular race of tuberous hybrids with mid-green leaves and large, rose-like flowers. The few single female flowers are overshadowed by the double male flowers, 3-6 in. across, which are borne from June to September. They are chiefly grown as bedding or pot plants.

Begonia boweri

Begonia × tuberhybrida
Pendula 'Golden Shower'

Begonia × tuberhybrida
'Diana Wynyard'

Begonia × tuberhybrida
'Festiva'

Varieties include: 'Diana Wynyard', with large white flowers; 'Festiva', rich yellow; 'Harlequin', white, edged with bright pink; 'Jamboree', compact blooms with ruffled petals of yellow and orange-red; 'Olympia', bright crimson; 'Mary Heatley', soft orange; 'Rhapsody', rose-pink; 'Rosanna', rose-pink; 'Seville', yellow, edged with bright pink.

The hybrid strain listed as Pendula has similar origins to that of *B.* × *tuberhybrida*, but the growths are more slender and pendulous. The double male flowers are smaller, 2–3 in. wide, but are more freely borne, from June to September. Named varieties include: 'Dawn', pale yellow; 'Golden Shower', golden-yellow; 'Lou-Anne', rose-pink; 'Red Cascade', scarlet; and 'Rose Cascade', rose-pink.

RHIZOMATOUS BEGONIAS

B. boweri. Mexico. Height and spread 6–9 in. A foliage plant with hairy leaves, emerald green with a broken chocolate-brown margin. Pale pink or white, $\frac{1}{2}$ in. wide flowers are borne in short panicles from February to May.

B. daedalea. Mexico. Height and spread 12 in. This foliage plant has mid-green leaves with a red network that turns mahogany brown. White, pink-tinged flowers appear in summer.

B. × *feastii.* Height and spread 9 in. A hybrid foliage plant with mid-green leaves, red underneath and edged with long white hairs. The leaf stalks are covered with red hairs. Panicles of $\frac{1}{2}$ in. wide, pale pink flowers are borne on 9 in. long stems from January to May. In cultivation it is usually represented by 'Bunchii' which has crested and frilled leaf margins.

B. manicata. Mexico. Height and spread up to 18 in. A winter-flowering species with large mid-green leaves that have narrow red margins and tufts of red hairs on their undersides. There is an umbrella-like collar of red scales at the top of the red-spotted leaf stalks. Pink flowers, $\frac{1}{3}-\frac{1}{2}$ in. across, are borne in much-branched panicles from January to March.

B. masoniana (iron cross). S.E. Asia. Height 9 in.; spread 12 in. This is an outstanding, seldom-flowering foliage plant; the mid-green hairy leaves have corrugated surfaces. The common name refers to the pattern of four or five deep bronze-purple bars that radiate from the centre of the leaf, forming a cross.

BEGONIA MASONIANA

B. rex. Assam. Height up to 12 in.; spread up to 18 in. This species is the principal parent of the foliage hybrids known as Rex begonias. The species, with dark green wrinkled leaves and a silvery zone close to the margin, is rarely seen, but several named and unnamed varieties are available. The leaf colour of these ranges from silver patterns or zones on dark green to forms variously zoned or patterned with cream, red or purple. Pale pink flowers, $\frac{1}{2}$ in. across, are sometimes produced on mature plants, in panicles just above the foliage, from June to September.

FIBROUS-ROOTED BEGONIAS

B. albo-picta. Brazil. Height 4 ft or more; spread 12–18 in. An erect shrubby species, grown for its narrow leaves which are bright green and covered with silver spots. Green-white flowers, $\frac{1}{2}$ in. wide, are borne in short panicles throughout summer.

Begonia × *tuberhybrida* 'Mary Heatley'   Begonia *rex* (hybrids)

Begonia × *tuberhybrida*
'Jamboree'

Begonia × *tuberhybrida*
'Rosanna'

B. coccinea. Brazil. Height 6 ft or more; spread 3 ft. This shrubby, bamboo-like species bears pale to mid-green leaves with red margins. Bright coral-red, 1 in. wide flowers are borne in large panicles from May to October.

'President Carnot' is a hybrid of similar appearance, but more vigorous, with paler flowers and with silver-spotted leaves that are red-purple beneath.

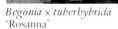

BEGONIA COCCINEA 'PRESIDENT CARNOT'

B. corallina. Brazil. Height up to 7 ft; spread 1½–2½ ft. A branching shrub with mid-green leaves, speckled with white above and flushed red beneath. Bright coral-pink, ¾ in. wide flowers are borne in panicles from May to December.

B. fuchsioides. Mexico. Height up to 4 ft; spread 18–24 in. This compact shrub bears glossy mid to deep green, ovate and toothed leaves. Bright red or pink flowers, ¾ in. across, are carried in short axillary panicles from October to March.

B. haageana. Brazil. Height up to 4 ft; spread 24 in. A shrubby species with hairy leaves that are deep green above, purple-red beneath; the stems and leaf stalks are red and hairy. The white, pink-tinged, 1 in. wide flowers are borne in panicles from June to September.

B. × 'Lucerna'. This hybrid is probably derived from *B. corallina*, which it resembles. The olive-green leaves are spotted with silver and flushed red beneath. Pendulous clusters, up to 12 in. across, of pink flowers occur at any time of the year, but particularly in spring and summer.

B. metallica. Brazil. Height 3 ft; spread 24 in. A species with branched stems carrying lustrous metallic green leaves with crimson veins beneath. The white, flushed pink, ½–¾ in. wide flowers are borne in short panicles in September.

B. semperflorens. Brazil. Height and spread 6–9 in., but often larger. A much-branched dwarf species with glossy, bright green or dark purple leaves. Red, pink or white flowers, ¾–1 in. across, are borne in few-flowered panicles from June to September or October.

The named hybrids of this species are among the most popular summer bedding plants. Green-foliaged forms include: 'Flamingo', white flowers, edged with deep pink; 'Organdy', a mixture of red, pink and white; 'Pandy', blood-red flowers. Purple-brown foliage forms include: 'Carmen', rose-pink flowers; 'Coffee and Cream', pure white; 'Indian Maid', deep scarlet flowers.

Cultivation. A light soil mixture is essential for the fine root system of begonias. They do well in a proprietary peat compost, or in John Innes potting compost No. 2. The plants thrive in moist conditions, but the compost should always be well drained; most species do best under glass, placed in partial shade.

Cultivation of tuberous begonias. Start the tubers of *B.* × *tuberhybrida* into growth in March or April at a temperature of 18°C (64°F), embedding them hollow side uppermost in 3 in. deep boxes of moist peat. As the leafy shoots are produced, pot on in 4–5 in. pots of the growing compost, finishing off in 6–8 in. pots. If large flowers are wanted for exhibition purposes, restrict each plant to one growth with only two or three side-shoots; the other growths can be used as cuttings for propagation. Four to six weeks after the plants have been moved into their final pots, give a liquid feed every two weeks until the flowers fade. When these begonias are grown as house plants they should be protected from cold draughts, or bud-drop may occur.

For bedding schemes outdoors, plant in any good, well-drained garden soil, preferably enriched with peat or leaf-mould, in sun or partial shade. Harden the plants off in a cold frame in May and bed them out at the end of the month or in early June. Lift in early October before the first frosts. If the plants are lifted earlier, they should be boxed in moist peat and kept growing in the greenhouse until natural leaf-fall occurs.

Begonia fuchsioides

Begonia × 'Lucerna'

Begonia manicata

Begonia masoniana

Begonia coccinea

Begonia haageana

When the leaves are turning yellow, dry off the plants by gradually withholding water; over-winter the tubers at a temperature of 7°C (45°F), covering them with dry peat or old soil. Lightly water the peat or soil occasionally during winter to prevent the tubers from shrivelling.

Plant tubers of the half-hardy *B. evansiana* outdoors in any good, well-drained soil, enriched with peat. Set the tubers 2–3 in. deep in a sheltered position, preferably at the foot of a south or west wall. In mild districts, the tubers may be left in the ground for the winter; cover with a protective layer of peat or weathered ashes. To grow these begonias in a cool greenhouse, start the tubers into growth in March or April; set one tuber to a 3½–4 in. pot or three in a 5–6 in. pot of the growing compost, at a temperature of 10°C (50°F). Ventilate and lightly shade the green-house during summer, and feed fortnightly with a liquid manure until the flowers fade.

As the leaves turn yellow, gradually withhold water and dry the tubers off in their pots; over-winter at a temperature of 2–4°C (35–40°F).

The Lorraine and other winter-flowering begonias are usually raised annually from cut-tings. Start pruned plants into growth in March or April by raising the temperature to 10–13°C (50–55°F). When the young shoots are 2–3 in. long, sever at the base and pot up singly in 2½ in. pots containing equal parts (by volume) peat and sand. Root the cuttings at 18°C (64°F); pot on successively until the plants are in their final 5–6 in. pots. Ventilate the greenhouse during summer and provide light shading; syringe the plants in hot weather. Give the plants a liquid feed at 10–14 day intervals about a month after moving into their final pots; pinch out the growing tips two or three times in the early stages to promote bushy plants. Insert canes at each potting stage to support the slender leafy growths.

Flower buds that appear before the end of September should be carefully removed to delay flowering until November. From late autumn until after flowering maintain a temperature of 10–13°C (50–55°F). After flowering, gradually withhold water, although the plants must never be allowed to dry out. When the leaves turn yellow, cut the plants back to within 6 in. of the base and keep them barely moist at 7°C (45°F).

Cultivation of rhizomatous and fibrous-rooted begonias. These are grown in the green-house or as house plants; set in 6–8 in. pots of the growing compost, although sub-shrubby species such as *B. coccinea* and *B. corallina* do better in larger pots or tubs, or planted out in the greenhouse border. Provide a winter temperature of 10°C (50°F), except for *B. boweri, B. masoniana* and *B. rex,* which require 13°C (55°F). During summer, keep the plants humid and shaded, but ventilate the greenhouse when the temperature exceeds 18°C (64°F); syringe the foliage frequently. In winter, reduce watering but keep the plants just moist.

In the home, keep the plants in a well-lit position, but out of direct sunlight. Plunge the pots in peat or vermiculite, kept moist, or stand on pebbles in a tray of water. The plants will not thrive in rooms with gas heating.

Pot on or repot established plants annually in April; give a liquid feed at fortnightly intervals from May to September.

To raise bedding or pot plants of *B. semper-florens,* sow seeds in pans or boxes of John Innes seed compost in February or March at a temperature of 16°C (61°F). Prick off the seedlings when the first true leaf is visible; set the seedlings in boxes of the growing compost. Harden off plants to be used for bedding and set in their flowering sites from late May. For pot culture, pot up in 3½ in. pots, later moving to 5 in. pots. Discard after flowering.

Propagation. Species can be raised from seeds as described under cultivation of *B. semperflorens.*

Tuberous begonias may be propagated by stem cuttings or by division of the tubers when young growths are visible. Take 3–4 in. cuttings in April from basal shoots preferably with a heel of the parent tuber attached; insert the cuttings in equal parts (by volume) peat and sand in a propagating case at a temperature of 18–21°C (64–70°F). When rooted, pot the cuttings in 3½ in. pots of the growing compost and pot on as necessary.

At potting time, cut large tubers into pieces each retaining at least one healthy shoot.

B. evansiana can also be increased from bulbils, taken from the dying stems in autumn. Store in barely moist peat and pot up the following spring; they will usually produce flowering plants the same year.

Lorraine and winter-flowering begonias are increased as described under CULTIVATION.

Rhizomatous begonias are increased by division in April at potting time. Ensure that each piece retains a healthy growing point.

Propagate fibrous-rooted or sub-shrubby begonias by stem cuttings taken from May to August. Detach 2–4 in. long, non-flowering shoots and insert in equal parts (by volume) peat and sand in a propagating case at a temperature of 18–21°C (64–70°F). When rooted, pot the cuttings in 3–3½ in. pots of the growing compost and pot on as necessary.

Many species and varieties, particularly the large-leaved rhizomatous begonias such as *B. masoniana* and *B. rex*, are increased by leaf cuttings in May and June. Sever newly matured leaves with a portion of stem and insert in pans or boxes of equal parts (by volume) peat and sand in such a manner that the leaf rests on the surface of the compost. Nick the intersecting main veins on the underside of the leaf before placing on the compost; wrinkled or waved leaves should be kept in contact with the compost by placing pebbles near the intersections. Keep the compost moist. Place in a propagating case at a temperature of 18–21°C (64–70°F); when the plantlets have produced two or three leaves, detach from the parent leaf and pot up in 3 in. pots of the growing compost; pot on as necessary.

Alternatively, cut the leaf into 1 in. squares and place on the rooting medium; treat the resulting plantlets as described above.

Pruning. Remove old flowered shoots of sub-shrubby, fibrous-rooted species at the base, in March prior to potting on or repotting.

Cut out two or three-year-old stems of *B. coccinea* and *B. corallina*. Occasionally pinch out young plants of vigorous-growing species, such as *B. haageana* and *B. metallica*, to prevent them becoming leggy.

Pests. Roots and tubers are damaged by WEEVILS which feed on the roots and tunnel into tubers; in severe attacks, the plants may die.

LEAF-BLOTCH EELWORMS invade the leaves, causing blotchy discoloration and dying-off.

ROOT KNOT EELWORMS infest roots and form contorted galls; leaves show signs of nutrient deficiency and the plants may collapse.

TARSONEMID MITES feed on young growths, killing the flower buds and making the leaves distorted and brittle.

Diseases. Brown blotches on the leaves and flowers are caused by GREY MOULD. The affected areas become covered with grey spore masses.

POWDERY MILDEW causes white powdery spots or patches on the leaves and stems. BLACK ROOT ROT causes the roots to turn black and to decay; the foliage becomes discoloured and may die.

DAMPING-OFF fungi attack seedlings and young plants, causing them to collapse at ground level. BACTERIAL WILT and LEAF SPOT of winter-flowering begonias show as small blister-like

translucent spots on the leaves; these enlarge and coalesce, and the leaves turn brown and rot.

CUCUMBER MOSAIC and TOMATO SPOTTED WILT viruses produce chlorotic rings and mottling on the leaves which may become distorted.

Bell, Canterbury: see *Campanula medium*
Bellflower: see Campanula
Bellflower, Chilean: see *Lapageria rosea*
Bellflower, chimney: see *Campanula pyramidalis*
Bellflower, nettle-leaved: see *Campanula trachelium*

Bellis

Daisy. *Compositae*

A genus of 15 species of hardy perennials, often grown as biennials. The most common species, *B. perennis*, a lawn weed, has given rise to many garden varieties which are excellent plants for edging borders and for carpet bedding. They are also suitable for cutting and can be grown in window-boxes and in pots for winter-flowering.

BELLIS PERENNIS MONSTROSA

B. perennis (common daisy). Europe, Asia Minor. Height 1–4 in.; planting distance 3–5 in. This tufted hardy perennial, usually grown as a biennial, has orbicular-ovate mid-green leaves. The flowers measure ½–1 in. across and consist of white ray-like florets, sometimes tinged with pink, encircling a yellow disc. They are borne from March until October.

The large-flowered varieties are generally listed under *B. p.* Monstrosa (height 5–6 in.; planting distance 6–9 in.). Like the type, these perennial plants are generally treated as biennials. They include plants with double flowers, 2 in. or more across, in colours ranging from white through pink to crimson, and flower from May to July. 'Giant Double' is available in either mixed or separate colours.

The double miniature varieties have button-shaped flowers, ½–1 in. across. Among the better-known varieties are: 'Dresden China', pink; 'Lilliput', crimson; 'Pomponette', white to crimson, with small quilled petals; 'Quilled Mixed', with slightly larger flowers; 'Red Buttons', carmine-red; and 'Rob Roy', red.

Cultivation. Plant in October or November in any fertile garden soil, in sun or partial shade. Regular dead-heading prevents inferior seedlings sowing themselves.

Grow pot plants in 3½–4 in. containers, using John Innes potting compost No. 1. Keep them in a cold frame throughout summer and early autumn and move them into a cool greenhouse in October for winter flowering. Maintain a temperature of 4–7°C (39–45°F).

Begonia semperflorens

Bellis perennis Monstrosa

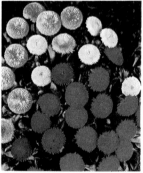

Bellis perennis (miniature)

Propagation. Divide 'Dresden China' and 'Rob Roy', neither of which produces seeds, in March.

Sow the seeds of other varieties in June in shallow drills in an outdoor seed bed. Transplant the seedlings for growing on when they are large enough to handle, and set them in the flowering site, 6–9 in. apart, in September.

For pot plants, grow on the seedlings until they are large enough to be put into containers.

Pests and diseases. Generally trouble-free.

Bells of Ireland: see *Moluccella laevis*

Beloperone
Acanthaceae

BELOPERONE GUTTATA

A genus of 60 species of tropical evergreen shrubs and sub-shrubs, only one species of which is in general cultivation. This is suitable for cool greenhouse conditions, and as a house plant.

B. guttata (shrimp plant). Mexico. Height 18–24 in.; spread 12–18 in. The ovate leaves are soft green and overlapping. Inconspicuous white flowers, produced almost continuously on mature plants from April until December, are protected by attractive overlapping brown-pink bracts. The whole inflorescence forms a pendent spike up to 6 in. long, resembling somewhat the body of a shrimp.

Cultivation. Pot in March in 5–6 in. pots containing John Innes potting compost No. 2 or 3. In summer, keep the plants cool and ventilate well; this produces long-lasting flowers. Shade greenhouse plants against strong sunlight and water freely from March to November; in winter, give just enough water to prevent the plants drying out. Water house plants as for greenhouse plants, but copious watering should be delayed until April. Feed all plants weekly with a liquid manure from May to September.

The minimum winter temperature needed is 7°C (45°F). Remove the first bracts of young plants to encourage sturdy, free-flowering plants.

Plants grown in 5–6 in. pots are usually raised annually from cuttings. Plants that are over-wintered and cut back may be potted on in March to produce large specimen plants.

Propagation. Take 2–3 in. long stem cuttings of half-ripe shoots in March or April. Insert the cuttings in individual pots of equal parts (by volume) peat and sand at a temperature of 18°C (64°F); pot on as necessary.

Pruning. In February, cut the main stems back lightly to maintain shape; or halve all growths if cuttings are required.

Pests. Generally trouble-free.

Diseases. Brown or yellow blotches may develop on the leaves, and a PHYSIOLOGICAL DISORDER will cause them to drop.

Berberis
Barberry. *Berberidaceae*

A genus of 450 species of deciduous and evergreen, usually spiny shrubs with leaves in rosette-like clusters. With the exception of a few S. American species they are hardy and easy to cultivate. The evergreen species are grown for their handsome glossy foliage and, in a few species such as *B. darwinii* and *B.* × *stenophylla*, for the abundantly borne flowers. Deciduous species are chiefly grown for their autumn colours and clusters of brightly coloured berries that usually persist well into the winter.

BERBERIS × STENOPHYLLA

The pendent flowers are globular or cup-shaped, usually borne in small clusters, occasionally singly. Some species and their hybrids make excellent hedges, and many of the dwarf species are well suited to small gardens.

The species are often difficult to identify as they hybridise freely if grown together, and seedlings seldom come true to type.

BERBERIS × RUBROSTILLA   BERBERIS VERRUCULOSA

B. aggregata. W. China. Height and spread 5 ft or more. A deciduous shrub of bushy habit, with lanceolate to obovate, pale to mid-green leaves that are toothed. The foliage turns red and orange in autumn. Panicles, 1 in. long, of yellow flowers appear in July and are followed by round coral-red berries with a waxy bloom.

Good varieties include: 'Barbarossa', vigorous grower, up to 6 ft, with scarlet berries in such profusion that the branches are weighed down and arch; 'Buccaneer', of erect habit and with long-lasting, brilliant red berries.

B. buxifolia. S. America. Height and spread up to 6 ft. A hardy evergreen shrub, with leathery, obovate, dark green leaves that are grey beneath. Yellow flowers, in 1 in. long clusters, appear in March and April and are followed by globular blue-black berries with a waxy bloom. 'Nana', is a dwarf form, tufted and mound-like; it rarely exceeds 18 in. in height and seldom flowers.

B. calliantha. S.E. Tibet. Height and spread up to 3 ft. A compact and hardy evergreen shrub with young stems tinged red. The dark green, narrow, holly-like leaves are conspicuously waxy-white beneath. Soft-yellow flowers are borne in clusters, ¾–1 in. long, in May; they are followed by round blue-black berries.

Beloperone guttata

Berberis aggregata (fruits)

Berberis aggregata
'Barbarossa' (fruits)

Berberis darwinii (flowers)

Berberis darwinii (fruits)

Berberis thunbergii
(autumn colour)

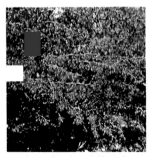

Berberis thunbergii (fruits)

B. candidula. W. Hupeh, China. Height and spread 24 in. This dwarf evergreen shrub is allied to *B. calliantha*. It is of dome-shaped habit, with glossy, dark green, elliptic leaves that are blue-white beneath. Yellow $\frac{1}{3}$–$\frac{1}{2}$ in. wide flowers are borne singly or in twos or threes in May and June. Ovoid blue-black berries appear in late summer.

B. chillanensis: see *B. montana*

B. darwinii. Chile. Height and spread 8–10 ft. A hardy evergreen shrub of bushy habit, with small, dark green, glossy, holly-like leaves. Clusters, 1–1$\frac{1}{2}$ in. long, of rich yellow—or orange tinged with red—flowers appear during April and May; they are followed by blue berries. This is one of the most outstanding spring-flowering berberis and makes a good hedge plant. 'Firefly' has rich orange-red flowers; 'Prostrata' is a dwarf form.

B. dictiophylla. China. Height up to 7 ft; spread 3–4 ft. A deciduous shrub of upright growth; the young shoots are covered with a waxy, glaucous bloom. The elliptic pale to mid-green leaves, glaucous beneath, turn rich red in autumn. Short-stalked yellow flowers, $\frac{3}{4}$ in. long, are carried in ones or twos in the leaf axils during May and are followed by ovoid red berries with a white waxy bloom.

B. gagnepainii. China. Height up to 6 ft; spread 4–5 ft. An evergreen shrub of dense erect habit. In cultivation it is represented by *B. g. lanceifolia*. This has mid to deep green narrowly lanceolate leaves with crinkled, coarsely toothed edges. Clusters, up to 1 in. long, of yellow flowers appear in May; they are followed by ovoid black berries. This species is suitable for a hedge.

B. hookeri, syn. *B. wallichiana*. Himalayas. Height up to 5 ft; spread 4–5 ft. An evergreen shrub of dense compact habit with glossy, dark green, holly-like leaves that are glaucous beneath. Pale yellow flowers are borne in 1 in. long clusters in April and May; they are followed by ovoid black berries. 'Nana' is a dwarf form, 2–3 ft high; 'Viridis' is the most common form in cultivation; the leaves are green beneath.

B. linearifolia. Chile. Height up to 10 ft; spread 3–4 ft. A slow-growing evergreen shrub of erect habit; once established it may make upright growths, often 2–4 ft long. The linear spineless leaves are glossy deep green above, glaucous beneath. Rich orange flowers, in 1 in. long clusters of four to six, are borne in April; the ovoid berries are black with a blue-white waxy bloom.

The species is not generally hardy throughout Great Britain and is best grown in the south or in other mild areas. 'Orange King' is an outstanding form with orange and apricot flowers.

B. × lologensis. Chile. Height and spread 8–10 ft. A natural, evergreen hardy hybrid between *B. linearifolia* and *B. darwinii*. It is slower growing than *B. darwinii*, to which it is similar in foliage and habit. Rich apricot-yellow flowers are freely borne in clusters up to 1 in. long in March and April. Ovoid purple berries later appear.

B. montana, syn. *B. chillanensis*. Chile. Height up to 6 ft; spread 4–6 ft. A deciduous shrub with somewhat angular branches and fresh green obovate leaves. The solitary flowers, up to 1 in. across, are borne on slender drooping pedicels in April and May; they are yellow and orange, and resemble the Tazetta narcissi; ovoid black berries are later produced.

Berberis × *rubrostilla*

B. × rubrostilla. Garden origin. Height 4 ft or more; spread 6–8 ft. This hardy hybrid between *B. wilsonae* and *B. aggregata* is a deciduous shrub of compact habit and with arching branches. The oblanceolate leaves are toothed and glaucous; they assume brilliant ruby tints in autumn. Yellow flowers are borne in racemes, up to 1 in. long, in May, and are followed by sprays of ovoid, coral-red berries.

B. sieboldii. Japan. Height and spread 3–4 ft. A deciduous shrub of compact habit, suckering from the base. The bright green oblong-elliptic leaves are borne on dark red shoots; they turn rich carmine in autumn. Yellow flowers appear in May in 1$\frac{1}{2}$ in. long clusters; they are followed by globose shining red berries.

B. × stenophylla. Height 8–10 ft; spread 10–12 ft. This is an evergreen hardy hybrid of *B. darwinii* and *B. empetrifolia*. It forms a thick mass of arching branches carrying linear-lanceolate deep green leaves, glaucous beneath. Golden-yellow flowers in 1 in. long racemes are freely produced during April. Globular purple berries with a bloom are generally sparsely borne. It is suitable as a specimen shrub, planted on banks, or grown as a hedge.

Numerous dwarf varieties include: 'Coccinea', with red buds and coral flowers; 'Corallina', with coral buds and yellow flowers.

B. thunbergii. Japan. Height 4 ft or more; spread up to 6 ft. A rounded and compact deciduous shrub with obovate leaves that are pale to mid-green above, glaucous beneath; they turn brilliant red in autumn. Pale-yellow flowers are borne freely in $\frac{1}{2}$–$\frac{3}{4}$ in. long clusters; they are followed by small, ovoid, scarlet berries.

Striking varieties include 'Atropurpurea', with rich purple-red leaves throughout spring and summer; 'Atropurpurea Nana'. a dwarf form (12–18 in. high) with similarly coloured leaves; 'Erecta', compact, but fastigiate in habit. Both the species and the varieties form good hedges.

B. verruculosa. W. China. Height and spread 3–5 ft. A slow-growing evergreen shrub of compact habit, with elliptic spine-toothed leaves, glossy dark green above, white beneath. Yellow flowers, up to $\frac{1}{2}$ in. across, appear singly or in pairs, in May or June; they are followed by ovoid black berries.

B. wallichiana: see B. hookeri

B. wilsonae. W. China. Height and spread 2–4 ft. A dwarf deciduous shrub of semi-prostrate and spreading habit. The small lanceolate leaves are soft green above, glaucous grey beneath; they turn brilliant red in autumn. Yellow flowers are borne in 1 in. long clusters in July and are followed by coral-red berries which blend well with the autumn foliage. It is a useful species for ground cover on banks.

Cultivation. Plant the deciduous berberis species from October to March, the evergreen and more tender species in September and October or in March and April. Berberis, with the exception of a few S. American species and varieties, are easy to grow and tolerate shallow and thin soils.

Deciduous species grown for their autumn berries and colour should be planted in sunny positions; the evergreen species do well in sun or light shade.

For hedges, use 12–15 in. high plants, setting them at intervals of 18–24 in. After planting, remove the upper quarter of all shoots to promote bushy growth.

Propagation. All species are easily raised from seeds, sown in the open in November, but resulting seedlings may not come true.

Alternatively, take cuttings, 3–4 in. long, of lateral shoots with a heel in August and September; insert the cuttings in equal parts (by volume) peat and sand in a cold frame. The following April or May, line out the rooted cuttings in nursery rows outdoors and grow on for one or two years before transplanting to permanent positions. It is an advantage to place cuttings of evergreen species in 4 in. pots of John Innes potting compost No. 2 and plunge outdoors until planting time.

Suckering species may be divided and re-planted at any time from October to March.

Pruning. No regular pruning is required, but remove old stems from ground level or cut them back to healthy young shoots. Shorten long straggly growths to maintain well-shaped plants. Prune deciduous species in February, evergreens after flowering.

Trim established hedges to the required shape once a year; evergreen hedges after flowering, and deciduous hedges in August or September.

Pests. Generally trouble-free.

Diseases. HONEY FUNGUS may cause the rapid death of these shrubs.

Bergamot, sweet: see Monarda didyma
Bergamot, wild: see Monarda fistulosa

Bergenia

Saxifragaceae

A genus of six hardy herbaceous perennials, formerly known as Saxifraga or Megasea. The plants have glossy, mid-green, leathery leaves that sometimes change to shades of red in autumn. Being evergreen and large-leaved, the plants are useful for ground cover.

B. beesiana: see B. purpurascens

Bergenia stracheyi 'Silberlicht'

B. cordifolia. Siberia. Height 12 in.; planting distance 12–15 in. The leaves are rounded with a heart-shaped base. Drooping heads of lilac-rose, bell-shaped flowers, each 1 in. long, appear in March and April. B. c. purpurea has pink-purple flowers and purple-tinged leaves.

BERGENIA CRASSIFOLIA

B. crassifolia. Siberia. Height and planting distance 12 in. A species with ovate leaves. Panicles of pale pink, bell-shaped flowers, 1 in. long, are borne from January to April.

B. delavayi: see B. purpurascens

B. purpurascens, syns. B. beesiana, B. delavayi. Height 15 in.; planting distance 24 in. A species somewhat similar to B. crassifolia, but with narrower elliptic leaves, often slightly convex. Bell-shaped flowers, $\frac{3}{4}$–1 in. long, with purple-brown calyces and purple-red to pink petals, are borne well above the leaves in loose panicles during April and May.

The hybrid 'Ballawley', syn. 'Delbees' is derived from the plants originally known as B. delavayi and B. beesiana, probably crossed with B. cordifolia. It is larger in growth than its parents, with broader leaves and larger fuchsia-red flowers.

B. stracheyi. Himalayas. Height 9–12 in.; planting distance 9 in. This species has relatively small obovate leaves and is less successful as ground cover. Sprays of pale pink to white flowers are produced in March and April. They are bell-shaped and $\frac{1}{2}$–$\frac{3}{4}$ in. long.

The following hybrids are more free-flowering than the species; they are available in a wider colour range.

'Abendglut', syn. 'Evening Glow'. Height and planting distance 9 in. Some of the heart-shaped

Bergenia cordifolia

Bergenia purpurascens

Bergenia purpurascens 'Ballawley'

leaves may turn to red-bronze. Red-purple bell-shaped flowers, 1 in. long, are borne in March and April; they appear almost phosphorescent at sunset.

'Silberlicht', syn. 'Silver Light'. Height 12–15 in.; planting distance 12 in. The broad, heart-shaped leaves may turn red-bronze. White bell-shaped flowers appear in April; they are $\frac{3}{4}$ in. long and have attractive pale pink calyces.

Cultivation. Bergenias grow in almost any soil, including those containing lime. Plant well-rooted plants between October and March in sun or partial shade. Leave undisturbed until overcrowding makes lifting and dividing necessary. Remove the stems after flowering.

Propagation. Divide and replant during September, October or March.

Pests. Generally trouble-free.

Diseases. Large brown blotches on the leaves are symptoms of LEAF SPOT fungus.

Berry, silver: see *Elaeagnus commutata*
Beta vulgaris: see Spinach
Beta vulgaris Crassa: see Beet
Betonica grandiflora: see *Stachys macrantha*
Betonica macrantha: see *Stachys macrantha*

Betula pendula (bark)

Betula pendula

Billbergia nutans

Betula

Birch. *Betulaceae*

BETULA PENDULA

A genus of 60 species of deciduous trees and shrubs occurring throughout the temperate and Arctic zones of the Northern Hemisphere. The majority of these ornamental trees are hardy; with their graceful habit and beautiful bark they make attractive specimen trees. All the species described bear female and male catkins in April and May, the male being $1\frac{1}{2}$–$2\frac{1}{2}$ in. long and pale yellow; the much smaller, insignificant female catkins are in shades of green and vary in shape and size from species to species.

B. alba: see *B. pendula*

B. albo-sinensis var. *septentrionalis*. China. Height 18–20 ft; spread 8–10 ft. The bark is orange to orange-brown or red and is particularly attractive in winter. The broadly ovate, mid-green leaves are covered in silky hairs.

B. ermani. China, Korea, Japan. Height 18–25 ft; spread 8–12 ft. This species has orange-brown branches and beautiful peeling bark, which is orange-brown changing to cream-white. The ovate mid-green leaves are 2–3 in. long. It starts into growth early in the year and is liable to damage from spring frosts.

B. papyrifera (paper birch, canoe birch). N. America. Height 20–30 ft; spread 10–15 ft. The gleaming white bark peels away in large strips on old trees. It bears triangular, slender-pointed, mid-green leaves.

B. pendula, syns. *B. alba, B. verrucosa* (silver birch). Europe, including Great Britain; Asia Minor. Height 20–30 ft; spread 8–12 ft. A tree of graceful habit, with silvery bark which, in mature trees, becomes rough at the base. The broadly ovate leaves are mid-green.

Numerous forms include *B. p.* 'Dalecarlica' (Swedish birch), with graceful drooping branches and deeply cut mid-green leaves; 'Fastigiata', of slender, erect habit; 'Tristis', a symmetrical tree with pendulous branches; 'Youngii' (Young's weeping birch), a dome-shaped tree with weeping branches, excellent as a specimen for a lawn.

B. verrucosa: see *B. pendula*

Cultivation. Although native trees are often found on thin acid or sandy soils, betulas thrive in good loamy soil and in sun or shade. Plant from October to March. Those species which come into growth early should be planted in positions sheltered from winds and frost. The trees have wide-spreading surface roots and should not be planted close to borders or fences.

Propagation. Sow seeds in pans or boxes when ripe, or in March, in John Innes seed compost in a cold frame. Prick off the seedlings, when large enough to handle, into boxes and later into nursery rows outdoors. Grow on for two or three years before planting out in permanent positions.

Graft varieties of *B. pendula* on to seedling stocks of the type species in March.

Pruning. None required.

Pests. The leaves may be infested with APHIDS which suck the sap and excrete large quantities of honey-dew, making the foliage sticky.

CATERPILLARS of various moths and the larvae of SAWFLIES eat leaf tissues and may cause extensive defoliation.

WEEVILS also feed on the leaves, cutting and rolling parts of the leaves into cylindrical cases.

Diseases. BRACKET FUNGI of various types, in particular BIRCH POLYPORE, may enter dead wood and cause rotting of the heart wood.

HONEY FUNGUS may cause the death of trees.

A PHYSIOLOGICAL DISORDER shows as brown blotches or yellowing of the leaves followed by premature leaf-fall; the disorder is due to unsuitable soil conditions.

RUST shows on the leaves as bright red-yellow spots, and powdery masses of orange spots are released from the undersurfaces. Premature defoliation may occur.

WITCHES' BROOMS show as dense masses of shoots; many twigs in the brooms die, but others remain alive, and the brooms gradually increase.

Bignonia stans: see *Tecoma stans*
Bilberry: see *Vaccinium myrtillus*

Billbergia

Bromeliaceae

A genus containing 50 species and countless hybrids of evergreen greenhouse plants. Most of these are epiphytic, but a few grow on the ground. Each rosette seldom has more than eight strap-shaped leaves. The plants are easy to grow as house or greenhouse plants.

See also BROMELIADS.

3. chantinii: see *Aechmea chantinii*

3. nutans (angel's tears, queen's tears). Brazil, Uruguay, Paraguay, Argentina. Height 18 in. The erect, narrow, serrated, dark green leaves are about 18 in. long. The 3–4 in. long drooping flower cluster has large pink bracts and 1–1½ in. long tubular green flowers, edged with blue. The petals reflex to show golden-yellow stamens. This species will survive short periods at temperatures as low as 2°C (35°F).

BILLBERGIA NUTANS

3. pyramidalis. Brazil. Height 12–15 in. A vase-shaped rosette of broad apple-green leaves surrounds a narrow erect panicle rising slightly higher. The woolly flower stem is enclosed by pink bracts from which the closely packed globular flower cluster, 4–6 in. long, extends. The red flowers arc tipped with blue.

3. rhodocyanea: see *Aechmea fasciata*

3. × 'Windii'. Height 18 in. A hybrid of *B. nutans*. The rigid grey-green leaves with a covering of moisture-holding grey scales give the plant a floury look. The flower stem is partly enclosed by large pink bracts and terminates in a cluster of pendent, 1–1½ in. long tubular flowers with pink sepals and green-blue margined petals. The petals curve back to reveal the long pale yellow stamens.

Cultivation. Plant firmly in 4–5 in. pots during late spring or early summer in any open-textured lime-free mixture. Give small doses of liquid fertiliser as a foliage spray or applied to the soil during the growing period. Keep the rosettes moist or filled with water. Water the soil freely during the growing period, but do not allow waterlogging. When growth slows down, keep the rosette and soil just moist. Provide a humid atmosphere throughout the year.

Propagation. Remove suckers or side-shoots attached to the parent plant when they are half the size of the full-grown plant. Allow cut surfaces to dry for a day or two and then plant firmly but not too deeply in the same compost as that for the parent plant. Stake until roots are well formed, which can be ascertained by giving the plant a gentle pull.

Pests and diseases. Generally trouble-free.

Blackberry

Rubus fruticosus. Rosaceae

The cultivated blackberry, grown for its fruits, has been developed from forms of *R. fruticosus*, or related species, some of which are native to Great Britain. It is a hardy, woody perennial, usually with spines, and self-fertile. It fruits in late summer on growths produced the previous season and can be grown in all parts of the country. The stems reach a height of 6–8 ft and a spread of 8–10 ft; they need the support of posts or a permanent framework.

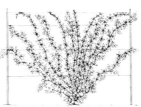

BLACKBERRY

Recommended varieties are:

'**Himalaya Giant**'. September and October. The large, round black fruits are sweet when fully ripe and have a good flavour. This vigorous variety is good for cooking and bottling.

'**Merton Early**'. August and September. The firm, shiny berries of this dessert variety have a good flavour. It is moderately vigorous.

'**Merton Thornless**'. August. Firm, sweet berries of good flavour. Requires a rich soil.

'**Oregon Thornless**'. August and September. Similar to 'Merton Thornless', but with deeply cut ferny leaves.

Cultivation. Blackberries grow best in soil that is well-drained but retains moisture (moisture retention can be improved by incorporating organic matter in the soil), and is either slightly acid or at least free from lime. As they do not flower until June, they can be grown in frost hollows. Site in sun or partial shade.

Planting is best done in November, but can be carried out until March if necessary. Cut the canes down to 9 in. above ground level immediately after planting. Blackberries can be grown on wires, either in the open or against walls, or grown as single plants up supporting posts. If wires are used, these should be 10–12 gauge and set 3 ft, 4 ft and 5 ft above ground level, with a thinner wire at 6 ft for attaching new growths temporarily. Use vine eyes to secure wires to walls. Allow 12–16 ft between plants. Tie the fruiting shoots to the wires with string or twists of plastic-covered wire.

For single posts, use 9–10 ft lengths of 4 in. × 4 in. timber. Insert them so that 7 ft is above ground level and tie the shoots to the post. Allow 5–6 ft between plants.

Water during dry spells from June to August, before the fruits ripen. Give annual dressings of 1 oz. sulphate of potash in winter and ½ oz. sulphate of ammonia in March, both per sq. yd.

Propagation. Blackberries increase readily by tip layering. Peg the shoots down in August or September; sever from the parent plant and plant out the following April. The canes will usually fruit the following year.

Billbergia pyramidalis

Billbergia × 'Windii'

Blackberry 'Oregon Thornless'

Pruning. Immediately after fruiting, cut out the old canes which have borne fruit. This will provide more space for the new shoots which have been growing up during the summer and will continue to do so into the autumn. The amount of old wood cut out will depend on the quantity and form of the new shoots that will replace it; with 'Himalaya Giant', a proportion of old wood may be left in.

Pests. RASPBERRY BEETLE maggots tunnel in the ripening fruits, making them inedible.

Diseases. CROWN GALL may occur at ground level, when a gall about the size of a walnut develops at the crown. It can also occur higher up the canes, producing numerous smaller galls.

GREY MOULD causes a rotting of the berries, which become covered with a fluffy brown-grey growth.

RUBUS STUNT is a virus disease which causes affected plants to produce numerous small stunted shoots with distorted leaves. No fruit is formed and diseased plants eventually die.

RUST produces dark red spots on the upper sides of the leaves; pustules on the under surface contain spores which are orange-yellow in early summer, black later in the year.

Black-eyed susan: see *Rudbeckia hirta* and *Thunbergia alata*

Black locust: see *Robinia pseudoacacia*

Blackthorn: see *Prunus spinosa*

Bladder senna: see Colutea

Blanket flower: see Gaillardia

Blazing star: see Liatris

Bleeding heart: see *Dicentra spectabilis*

Bletia hyacinthina: see *Bletilla striata*

Bletilla striata

Borage

Bletilla

Orchidaceae

BLETILLA STRIATA

A genus of nine species of terrestrial orchids from E. Asia, only one of which is in general cultivation. This is a tufted plant with underground pseudobulbs that resemble flattened, globular tubers. It requires a cool greenhouse, but may also be grown as a house plant; in mild areas it may be planted outdoors in sheltered borders or against a south or west-facing wall.

See also ORCHIDS.

B. striata, syn. *Bletia hyacinthina*. China and Japan. This deciduous and almost hardy plant produces tufts of slender, lanceolate and pleated leaves, mid-green in colour; they are long and erect, arching over slightly at the tips. From the centre of each tuft arises an arching stem, 12 in. or more in length, carrying six or more 2 in. wide flowers; the petals are rich mauve-pink and the lip purple with a crisped margin and five shallow ribs. The flowers appear in May.

Cultivation. In the greenhouse or indoors, grow bletillas in 5–6 in. pots of equal parts (by volume) loam, leaf-mould, peat, sphagnum moss and coarse sand. Shade the greenhouse lightly between May and September. Water freely during the growing period, but keep the compost just moist while the plants are dormant. Give a weak liquid feed at fortnightly intervals from late May to August, and ventilate the greenhouse or room freely when the temperature exceeds 13°C (55°F). The temperature in winter should not fall below 5°C (41°F).

Repot or pot on every other year in March.

Outdoors, grow bletillas in any ordinary well-drained garden soil, enriched with peat or leaf-mould. The site may be in sun or partial shade, but should be sheltered from north and east winds. Plant during September or October in cold districts, protect throughout winter with bracken, coarse sand or weathered ashes.

Propagation. Divide and replant the pseudobulbs in March or April.

Pests. Young shoots may be damaged by SLUGS.

Diseases. Generally trouble-free.

Blood flower: see *Asclepias curassavica* and *Haemanthus katherinae*

Blood root: see Sanguinaria

Bluebell, common: see *Endymion nonscriptus*

Bluebell, Scottish: see *Campanula rotundifolia*

Blueberry: see Vaccinium

Blueberry, high bush: see *Vaccinium corymbosum*

Blueberry, swamp: see *Vaccinium corymbosum*

Blue-eyed mary: see *Omphalodes verna*

Blue lace flower: see *Didiscus caerulus*

Bluets: see Houstonia

Bocconia cordata: see *Macleaya cordata*

Bocconia microcarpa: see *Macleaya microcarpa*

Borage

Borago officinalis. Boraginaceae

BORAGE

This is a hardy annual culinary herb with a flavour similar to that of cucumber.

Height 1½–3 ft; spacing 9–12 in. Europe including Great Britain. Borage has hollow stems bearing corrugated ovate leaves, covered with rough silvery hairs. The pendent flowers are in the form of five-petalled blue stars; they are ¾–1 in. wide and borne from June to September. Pink and white-flowered forms are known.

Use the young leaves and flowers to flavour salads and fruit cups. The flowers can also be candied for decorating confectionery and the leaves infused to make a refreshing drink.

Cultivation. Borage will grow in almost any type of soil, but thrives in well-drained ground in a sunny position. The attractive flowers are seen to their best advantage when the plants are grown in clumps at the top of a sunny bank or high on a large rock garden.

Propagation. Sow seeds in April in shallow drills 12 in. apart where the plants are to grow, later thinning the seedlings to 12 in. apart. The plants are ready for use about eight weeks after sowing. Make further sowings from May to July to provide a long supply of young leaves, and again in September to provide fresh leaves for the following spring.

Borage seeds itself freely, and unwanted seedlings should be removed to keep the plants under control.

Harvesting and storing. For culinary purposes use only the young leaves, even for drying. The leaves are succulent and difficult to dry; they will turn black if the ventilation is inadequate or the temperature too high. For drying methods see entry under HERBS.

Pests and diseases. Generally trouble-free.

Borago officinalis: see Borage
Borecole: see Kale
Bottle brush: see Callistemon

Bougainvillea

Nyctaginaceae

BOUGAINVILLEA SPECTABILIS

A genus of 18 species of shrubby climbing deciduous greenhouse plants. The flowers are insignificant, but they are surrounded by brilliantly coloured papery bracts that persist on the plants for a long time.

B. × buttiana. A hybrid of *B. glabra* and the seldom-cultivated *B. peruviana*. It is similar in vigour and appearance to *B. glabra*. The best-known form is 'Mrs Butt', with rose-crimson bracts that fade to magenta. Mutants with orange bracts are known; these include 'Brilliant', with coppery-orange bracts maturing to cerise-red; and 'Kiltie Campbell', with orange bracts that shade to a deeper colour as they age.

B. glabra. Brazil. Height 5–8 ft in a pot, 20 ft or more in a greenhouse border. Although a strong climber, this is the best species for growing in a pot as it will flower when quite small. The mid-green leaves are ovate. Terminal and axillary panicles, 6–9 in. long, appear in late summer and early autumn. The insignificant white flowers are surrounded by spectacular bracts in various shades of red and purple.

B. spectabilis. Brazil. Height 5–8 ft in a pot, 30 ft or more in a greenhouse border. A vigorous climber with spiny growths and dark green elliptic leaves. The flower panicles, 9–12 in. long, with magenta bracts, are produced from June to September. There are cerise, scarlet and deep pink varieties in cultivation.

Cultivation. The plants may be grown in 6–8 in. pots, although they are more effective if planted out in the greenhouse border. For pot-grown plants use John Innes potting compost No. 3. Plant or pot in February. Train pot-grown plants up canes or sticks; plants in the border may be trained along wires or strings up and under the greenhouse roof. During summer, give established pot plants weekly feeds of liquid manure and water all plants frequently.

When flowering ceases, gradually dry off the plants and keep them just moist until March when they can be restarted into growth. A winter temperature of 7°C (45°F) is sufficient for *B. × buttiana* and *B. glabra*, but *B. spectabilis* needs a minimum of 10°C (50°F).

Maintain slightly higher temperatures when growth restarts in March. Give the plants ample light, and syringe them frequently in hot weather. Good drainage is essential.

Repot or, when necessary, pot on annually in February or March.

Propagation. Take 3 in. long cuttings of half-ripe young wood in summer and set them in a sandy mixture in 2 in. pots. Place in a propagating case and maintain a bottom heat of 21–24°C (70–75°F). The cuttings should root in about three weeks. Cuttings, 6 in. long, can also be taken of mature pieces of dormant shoots in January and rooted in the same manner at a temperature of 18°C (64°F).

Pruning. Shorten the main growths in February by about one-third, and spur-prune all laterals back to the main growths. Cut out and discard all weak growths.

Pests and diseases. Generally trouble-free.

Bouvardia

Rubiaceae

BOUVARDIA LONGIFLORA

A genus of 50 species of greenhouse evergreen shrubs with fragrant, showy flowers that are produced over a long period. Only one species is in general cultivation, and hybrids are more easily available from nurseries.

B. × domestica. Height up to 24 in.; spread 18 in. This shrub has ovate mid-green leaves, arranged in opposite pairs. Terminal clusters, up to 6 in. across, of pink, white or red flowers, are freely produced from June to November. The individual flowers are tubular and have four spreading petals. The variety 'President Cleveland' has bright crimson-scarlet flowers.

B. longiflora. Mexico. Height up to 3 ft; spread 24 in. This species has ovate leaves that are glossy and mid-green. Loose clusters, up to 4 in. across, of fragrant, white, tubular flowers appear from October to December.

Cultivation. Pot the plants in March in 5–6 in.

Bougainvillea × buttiana 'Mrs Butt'

Bougainvillea spectabilis

Bouvardia × domestica 'President Cleveland'

pots containing John Innes potting compost No. 2. Maintain a temperature of about 13°C (55°F) during summer and winter, although *B. longiflora* will survive at a winter temperature of 7–10°C (45–50°F). The plants can be stood outside in a shaded and sheltered position from June until August.

Stop established plants twice, between April and the end of May, to obtain flowers in July and August; autumn-flowering plants should be pinched out several times until the end of August.

During the growing season, give the plants ample water, maintain a moist atmosphere and feed weekly from May to September with a weak liquid manure. If they are kept in the greenhouse throughout the summer, the glass should be lightly shaded. Let the plants have all the light possible during autumn and winter. After flowering, keep the plants barely moist until growth is restarted in February or March.

Repot or pot on annually in March.

Propagation. Take cuttings of young growths in spring when these are about 3 in. long. Insert the cuttings in equal parts (by volume) peat and sand and keep them shaded and moist, but do not allow water to rest on the leaves. If a temperature of 21°C (70°F) can be maintained, the cuttings will root in about three weeks. When rooted, pot the cuttings in 3 in. pots and pot on as necessary.

Pruning. After flowering, keep the plants just moist for about six weeks, then cut the main lateral growths back hard to within 1 in. of the base. This is generally done at the beginning of February. After pruning, give the plants more water to encourage fresh growth. Plants in pots often deteriorate after two years, and they are best raised annually from cuttings.

Pests. Colonies of MEALY BUGS produce white waxy wool on the stems and leaves, and make the plants sticky.

SCALE INSECTS, particularly hemispherical scale, form brown excrescences on leaves and stems, and make the plants sticky and sooty.

Diseases. Generally trouble-free.

Box: see *Buxus*
Box, common: see *Buxus sempervirens*
Box elder: see *Acer negundo*
Box, ground: see *Polygala chamaebuxus*

Brachycome

Compositae

BRACHYCOME IBERIDIFOLIA

A genus of 75 species of annual and perennial plants. The species described here resembles a cineraria and is suitable for borders, for edging and as a summer-flowering pot plant.

B. iberidifolia (Swan River daisy). Australia. Height up to 18 in.; planting distance 15 in. A half-hardy annual with slender stems carrying deeply cut pale green leaves. The fragrant flowers are daisy-like, 1¼ in. across and range in colour from white to pink, lilac and blue-purple. They bloom from late June to September. The variety 'Purple Splendour' has rich blue-purple flowers.

Cultivation. Brachycomes thrive in rich loamy soil, in a sunny sheltered position. Set the young plants out in May and support with twiggy sticks. Pinch out the growing tips to encourage the formation of side-shoots.

Under glass, set the plants in 5 in. pots of John Innes potting compost No. 1; water freely in summer, but keep winter-flowering plants just moist. Maintain a minimum winter temperature of 10°C (50°F).

Propagation. For outdoor plants, sow the seed under glass in March, just covering them with compost. Maintain a temperature of 18°C (64°F until the seedlings are established, reducing this to 16°C (61°F) after pricking out. Harden off in a cold frame before planting out in May. Alternatively, sow directly in the flowering site in April and thin out to the required spacing.

A March sowing also provides plants suitable for summer flowering in pots; for winter pot plants, sow in September.

Pests and diseases. Generally trouble-free.

Brassica cernua : see Cabbage, Chinese
Brassica oleracea Botrytis: see Cauliflower
Brassica oleracea Bullata: see Cabbage, Savoy
Brassica oleracea Capitata: see Cabbage
Brassica oleracea Costata: see Cabbage Portuguese
Brassica oleracea Gemmifera: see Brussels sprouts
Brassica rapa : see Turnip
Brassica rutabaga : see Swede

× **Brassolaeliocattleya**

Orchidaceae

× BRASSOLAELIOCATTLEYA

A group of trigeneric hybrids between *Brassavola*, *Laelia* and *Cattleya*. The general growth habit, foliage and flowers are similar to those of *Cattleya*. Flowering is usually between October and March.

See also ORCHIDS.

Named forms, with flowers up to 6 in. across include the following:

'Melrose', a hybrid between × *Brassolaeliocattleya* Alfred Mollett and × *Laeliocattleya* Mrs T. Ward; several forms, in shades of magenta-purple and lavender-pink, are available.

'Norman's Bay', a hybrid between × *Brassocattleya* Hartland and × *Laeliocattleya* Ishtar; it has rose-magenta flowers, with a darker lip and gold veining in the throat.

Brachycome iberidifolia

× *Brassolaeliocattleya* 'Melrose'

× *Brassolaeliocattleya* 'Norman's Bay'

'Nuggett', a hybrid between × *Brassolaelio-cattleya* Palmyre and × *Laeliocattleya* Luminosa, with yellow petals and sepals; outstanding varieties have been bred from this form.

'Gomari', a hybrid between × *Brassolaelio-cattleya* Nigoma and × *Laeliocattleya* Sori, with light mauve-pink flowers, a dark pink lip and yellow throat.

Cultivation, propagation, pests and diseases. See entry under CATTLEYA.

Bridal wreath: see *Spiraea* × *arguta*

Briza
Gramineae

BRIZA MAXIMA

A genus of 20 species of hardy annual and perennial flowering grasses. They are grown for their ornamental panicles of pearly or purple-brown spikelets which dangle on thread-like stalks. They are useful in flower arrangement or dried for winter decoration.

B. maxima (pearl grass). Mediterranean regions. Height 15–20 in.; planting distance 6–9 in. An annual species which forms a small tuft of erect stems. The narrow, pointed leaves are bright green. The upper part of each stem carries a loose panicle of pendent, heart-shaped or ovate spikelets, ½–1 in. long, from May to July.

B. media (quaking grass). Europe, Siberia. Height 12–18 in.; planting distance 6 in. A slow-creeping perennial species with erect slender stems. The light green leaves are flat and tapering. Heart-shaped, purple-brown spikelets, ⅓–¼ in. long, are borne from May to August.

Cultivation. Plant in April in ordinary, well-drained garden soil and in a sunny position. Cut the flower stems for drying in sunny weather when the spikelets are fully developed, and before they set seeds. Hang to dry in a cool place.

Propagation. Divide and replant roots of *B. media* in March or April.

Sow seeds of *B. maxima* thinly in the flowering site during September or March and April. Thin the seedlings to the required planting distances, when large enough to handle.

Pests and diseases. Generally trouble-free.

Broad bean: see Beans
Broccoli: see Cauliflower

Brodiaea
Alliaceae

A genus of 40 species of cormous and bulbous plants. They come from N. and S. America, where they inhabit regions of hot dry summers and wet, frost-free winters. Some of the species have recently been placed in separate genera, but the species available in Great Britain are retained under the more familiar *Brodiaea* heading.

The species described are typified by narrow, strap-shaped, mid-green leaves and terminal clusters of starry or tubular flowers borne on erect, leafless stems. All are reasonably hardy if grown in a sunny site, preferably at the foot of a south wall.

BRODIAEA GRANDIFLORA

B. coronaria: see *B. grandiflora*
B. grandiflora, syns. *B. coronaria, Hookera coronaria.* U.S.A. Height up to 18 in.; planting distance 2–3 in. Starry, blue-purple flowers, 1½ in. wide, are borne in loose clusters of seven or more in May and June.
B. ida-maia, syn. *Dichelostemma ida-maia.* California. Height 24 in.; planting distance 4–6 in. Slender stems carry up to 20 tubular flowers in June. Each flower has a crimson tube, and the yellow petals are banded with green.
B. laxa, syn. *Triteleia laxa.* California. Height up to 24 in.; planting distance 2–3 in. The loose, many-flowered clusters are made up of blue-purple, widely tubular flowers, 1½ in. across. The flowering period is in July.
B. × *tubergenii*, syn. *Triteleia* × *tubergenii.* Height 18 in.; planting distance 2–3 in. This hybrid has 1–1½ in. wide blue-mauve flowers. They are borne in open umbels, 3–4 in. across, during May and June.
B. uniflora: see *Ipheion uniflorum*
Cultivation. Plant the corms in September in groups of five or six in any well-drained garden soil and in a sunny position, preferably with the protection of a south wall.

The plants can also be grown in a greenhouse with a minimum temperature of 5–7°C (41–45°F), either in pots or in the border. Place five or six corms in a 5–6 in. pot of John Innes potting compost No. 1, or grouped together in the border, in August or September. Give them a good soaking after planting, then water sparingly until the leaf shoots appear. Water regularly once growth is well developed. After flowering, reduce watering until the foliage turns yellow, then dry off completely. Store the pots in a warm, dry place; repot or plant the corms the following late summer. In August or September, at intervals of two or three years, lift and divide bulbs grown in borders outdoors or under glass.
Propagation. Remove offsets at planting time and grow them on separately for two or three years until they reach flowering size.

Alternatively, sow seeds in March in pans of John Innes seed compost, at a temperature of 13–16°C (55–61°F). One-year-old seedling corms can be grown on as for offsets, but will take three to five years to reach maturity.
Pests and diseases. Generally trouble-free.

Briza maxima

Brodiaea ida-maia

Brodiaea laxa

Brodiaea × *tubergenii*

BROMELIADS

Tillandsias growing wild on a branch

The botanical name for the bromeliad or pineapple family of plants is *Bromeliaceae*. There are 60 genera containing some 1400 different species.

Bromeliads grow within a wide area in southern U.S.A., Central and South America: from the Atlantic Ocean in the east to the Pacific Ocean in the west and including the islands of the West Indies and the Caribbean.

This family is among the most versatile of the whole plant kingdom, for its members grow in almost every kind of habitat. Numerous bromeliads grow on trees and enormous cacti, and even on telephone wires. Some species that grow high in trees are often called air plants or air pines because they appear to take their nourishment solely from the atmosphere.

In fact, they subsist on the nourishment provided by the rains and the accumulation of decayed plant and animal remains. Those species found growing on tree trunks and branches derive only support from their hosts.

Other bromeliads are terrestrial, growing on the ground, in scrub desert or in thick jungle leaf-mould. They are found in marshes, on salt-saturated beaches and on rocks, and in altitudes from sea level to many thousands of feet high.

The leaves are arranged spirally in rosettes. Many species have watertight bases to the leaves which form reservoirs able to hold rain-water and detritus to nourish the plants. Others, such as the tillandsias, have moisture-absorbing scales and are not adapted to hold water.

This intriguing family of plants varies greatly in size: the smallest species, a Tillandsia, is less than 2 in. high, and among the largest is an Aechmea with leaves 9 ft long. But the majority of species available are moderate in size and suitable for pot culture.

Many different plant shapes are found in this family. Some genera are bulbous or bottle-shaped, others have spreading rosettes or are formed like open vases; yet others are grass, moss or lichen-like. The Spanish moss of south-eastern U.S.A. is, in fact, a species of Tillandsia. The leaves may be strap or sword-like, lanceolate or spoon-shaped; some are semi-succulent or fleshy; they may be toothed or spined, or completely smooth edged. Added to these decorative forms are the varieties of colours and designs brought about by the combinations of leaves, bracts and inflorescences. The leaves may be green, grey, cream, red or purple, sometimes with longitudinal stripes. They may be spotted or mottled, cross-banded or reticulated.

When flowering time approaches, which can be at any time of the year but is usually between spring and autumn, the inner leaves of many species assume brilliant colours of different hues. Only after flowering do the leaves gradually regain their normal colour. The inflorescences may carry both coloured bracts and flowers. The berries or capsules which follow are brightly coloured in some species, and remain so for several months. Some species have fragrant flowers. One of the most important fruit crops of tropical areas, the pineapple, is included in the family.

In nature, bromeliads have the singular characteristic of supporting many different kinds of fauna and flora within the reservoirs formed by the enclosing leaf bases. The complete life cycle of microscopic and larger animals and aquatic plants takes place in these reservoirs.

Since bromeliads are mainly tropical and sub-tropical they do best in a heated and humid greenhouse. Temperatures should not fall below 16–18°C (61–64°F) for most species, though some kinds will tolerate lower values. Maintain a humidity of 65–70 per cent. During the winter months the humidity should be reduced to avoid excess moisture which can cause rotting.

Water and spray the plants with rain-water. Tap water often contains lime which is detrimental to many bromeliads. Water the plants towards evening from June to September. In late autumn, winter and spring, spray or water in the morning, gradually reducing humidity and water during the dullest and coldest months.

Avoid cold draughts; a closed greenhouse admits enough air for the requirements of bromeliads during the winter months. In summer, open the ventilators.

Bromeliads thrive in good light and sunshine; in summer provide shading to filter the sun's rays. Pot in late spring and summer. Bromeliads do not require much root-room, and 3–5 in. pots are usually large enough. They should be repotted as necessary, but even the largest species will thrive in 7 in. pots.

Bromeliads may be induced to flower at a pre-determined date by the application of chemical stimulants, such as calcium carbide solutions, ethylene gas or naphthalene acetic acid.

The seeds of bromeliads are contained in succulent, juicy berries or dry capsules which form after flowering.

Plants with dry capsules produce tiny seeds which are dispersed by the winds in their natural habitats. It may take 3–30 years for a bromeliad seed to grow to flowering size. Vegetative reproduction is a quicker and surer way of increasing the species.

Bromeliad seeds lose vigour quickly but fresh seeds will usually germinate within days if given the right conditions. Sow the cleaned and dry seeds in pans containing an open, moisture-retaining mixture of equal parts (by volume) leaf-mould, sand, grit and pumice granules. A mixture of 2 parts moss peat and 1 part coarse sand is also suitable. Do not cover the seeds; germinate at a temperature of 27°C (80°F) and in a continuously humid atmosphere.

When the seedlings have produced three or four leaves, remove the cover from the container for increasing periods so that the seedlings will become acclimatised. Prick out about 1 in. apart into well-drained pots or pans when the plants have six or more leaves.

Broom: see Cytisus, Genista, Ruscus and Spartium
Broom, Butcher's: see *Ruscus aculeatus*
Broom, common: see *Cytisus scoparius*
Broom, Dalmatian: see *Genista dalmatica*
Broom, Madeira: see *Genista virgata*
Broom, Mt Etna: see *Genista aetnensis*
Broom, purple: see *Cytisus purpureus*
Broom, Spanish: see Spartium
Broom, Warminster: see *Cytisus × praecox*
Broom, white: see *Cytisus albus*

Browallia
Solanaceae

A genus of six species of half-hardy annuals with tubular, violet-shaped flowers, generally grown as flowering pot plants under glass. In mild areas they can also be grown in the open.

B. speciosa. Colombia. Height up to 4 ft. This species is best grown as a pot plant, the new hybrids being particularly recommended. Pinching out produces a compact plant 18–24 in. high, but unpinched plants are more suitable for cutting. The leaves are bright green, pointed and ovate. The flowers, 2 in. across and violet-blue, are carried from June to September.

B. s. major, the most commonly listed variety and recommended for winter flowering, has deep blue flowers; 'Silver Bells' is white.

BROWALLIA VISCOSA

B. viscosa. Colombia. Height 12 in.; planting distance 6 in. A compact plant, suitable both for bedding and for growing in pots. The leaves are ovate, mid-green and slightly sticky. The flowers, 1 in. across and bright blue with white centres, are produced from July to September. The variety 'Sapphire', 6–9 in., is the most commonly listed.

Cultivation. A good loam is ideal, but browallias also grow reasonably well on poor, dry soils. Set in a sunny position. Staking is unnecessary, provided the taller species are pinched out to encourage branching.

For pot plants, transplant the young seedlings into 3 in. containers of John Innes potting compost No. 1. When well established, transfer to the final 5 in. pots. Plants to flower in winter require a minimum temperature of 13–16°C (55–61°F).

Propagation. Sow the seeds in pans of seed compost at 18°C (64°F), in March. Sowings can also be made in August for winter flowering in pots, and in February for early-summer flowering. Prick out the seedlings into pots or boxes. Plants for bedding out must be hardened off in a cold frame before planting out in late May.

Pests and diseases. Generally trouble-free.

Brugmansia: see Datura

Brunfelsia
Solanaceae

A genus of 30 species of greenhouse evergreen shrubs. They have attractive flowers which are borne solitarily in the upper leaf axils, sometimes in abundance on vigorous shoots. Each flower is salver-shaped with a long tube.

BRUNFELSIA CALYCINA

B. calycina. Brazil, Peru. Height up to 24 in.; spread 12 in. The mid-green, shining leaves are lanceolate. Fragrant flowers, 2 in. across, open violet-purple and fade to near white, from April to August. Flowering will continue throughout most of the year at a temperature of 13–16°C (55–61°F). The variety *B. c. macrantha* has flowers up to 3 in. wide.

B. undulata. West Indies. Height up to 4 ft; spread 24 in. A species with mid or deep green lanceolate leaves. White or deep cream flowers are borne from June to October; the tube is up to 3 in. long and the petals spread to 1½ in. across.

Cultivation. Pot in late summer or early autumn in John Innes potting compost No. 2 or in a proprietary peat mixture. Grow the plants in 6–8 in. pots. Provide a moist atmosphere during the summer, and shade the plants from hot sun. Keep the plants fairly dry during winter, but give them all the light available. Although a winter temperature of 10°C (50°F) is preferable, the plants will survive at 5°C (41°F) for short periods.

If the plants become pot-bound, pot on after flowering or in March or April.

During the growing period, keep the plants well watered, and syringe the leaves in hot weather. The plants do not like excessive heat in summer, and the greenhouse should be ventilated whenever possible. Give a weak liquid feed once a month from June to September.

Propagation. Take cuttings, 3 in. long, from February to August. The cuttings should be firm but less woody than half-ripe cuttings. Insert singly in 2½ in. pots, or four to a 3½ in. pot, in a compost of equal parts (by volume) coarse sand and peat; at a temperature of 21°C (70°F) the cuttings will root in about four weeks.

Pruning. *B. calycina* seldom needs pruning. Cut back *B. undulata* moderately in February to make compact and shapely plants. Pinch out the tips of the shoots when these are about 6 in. long.

Pests and diseases. Generally trouble-free.

Brunnera
Boraginaceae

A genus of three species of hardy herbaceous perennials. They are suitable for growing under trees, and make good ground cover.

Browallia speciosa

Brunfelsia calycina macrantha

B. macrophylla, syn. *Anchusa myosotidiflora.* W. Caucasus. Height 12–18 in.; planting distance 18 in. The matt-green leaves are rough and heart-shaped. Sprays of blue, forget-me-not-like flowers, $\frac{1}{4}$ in. across, appear in May and June. *B. m.* 'Variegata' has cream and green leaves, which colour more effectively in shade.

BRUNNERA MACROPHYLLA

Cultivation. Plant brunneras between October and March in any ordinary garden soil. They can be grown in sun, provided the soil does not dry out in summer, but do best in light shade. Remove any shoots of *B. m.* 'Variegata' that revert to green foliage, but take care not to cut into the roots, as this encourages new green growths. Remove the stems after flowering.

Propagation. Divide and replant the roots in October or March.

Take root cuttings in October or November and insert in boxes of equal parts peat and sand in a cold frame. Plant out the rooted cuttings in a nursery bed in May or June, when the leaves are well developed, and grow on until they are ready for planting out in the autumn.

Pests and diseases. Generally trouble-free.

Brussels sprouts

Brassica oleracea Gemmifera. *Cruciferae*

This green vegetable, thought to have originated in Belgium, is a descendant of the wild cabbage. It is cultivated as a hardy biennial and grown for the small, tight-leaved, cabbage-like buds which cluster thickly, one to each leaf axil, on the tall stem below a loose head of large leaves. This popular vegetable matures during autumn and winter, and numerous varieties are available.

VARIETIES

The newer varieties bear smooth solid sprouts about the size of large walnuts, evenly distributed up the stem. On light soils and in windy and exposed positions, dwarf-growing varieties such as 'Cambridge Special' and 'Dwarf Gem' are recommended. These mature in October and last until Christmas, as does 'Sutton's Fillbasket', a vigorous variety producing large solid sprouts. 'Seven Hills' and 'Vremo Inter' mature later.

On medium to heavy soils, the best varieties include the F_1 hybrid 'Avoncross', maturing in October and November; 'Early Half Tall', maturing in September and October; 'Market Rearguard', maturing from December to March, and 'Winter Harvest', ready for use in November and December.

The F_1 hybrid 'Thor' is particularly suitable for deep-freezing; it bears small to medium-sized sprouts which mature in November. F_1 hybrids should not be allowed to set seeds as they do not come true to type.

Brunnera macrophylla

Brussels sprouts
'Sutton's Fillbasket'

Cultivation. Brussels sprouts should not be grown in soil that grew a brassica crop the previous year. Prepare the bed in autumn by digging it deeply and by incorporating 1½ buckets of manure per sq. yd. If manure is not available, add the same amount of well-rotted compost in autumn, and in spring rake in 3 oz. of a complete fertiliser per sq. yd. Shoddy makes an excellent alternative to manure if dug in during the autumn.

If a greenhouse is available, make the first sowings in January and February to produce autumn crops for domestic use or exhibition purposes. Sow seeds in pots or pans of seed compost, and germinate at a temperature of 10–13°C (50–55°F). As soon as the seedlings are showing the first pair of leaves, prick them out into boxes of John Innes potting compost No. 1, setting them 2 in. apart either way. Harden off the young plants in a cold frame before transplanting to the permanent bed from April to May.

In the south and in sheltered northern areas seeds may be sown in mid-September, in a warm spot outdoors, to produce seedlings for early transplanting and harvesting the following year. Sow the seeds thinly in drills up to $\frac{1}{2}$ in. deep and 6 in. apart.

A few days before transplanting the young plants, level the permanent bed. Transplant and firm in the young plants in batches between mid-May and mid-June to give a succession of crops. Choose a showery spell for transplanting, or water the plants lightly and often until they are established. Transplant only healthy, 4–6 in. high plants with a growing point at the centre, and space them out 2½–3 ft apart each way.

To advance the maturing time, the terminal buds may be removed when the plants have made good growth, but the buttons still lack solidity, usually in October; the sprouts will be ready three weeks after stopping. Batches of plants may be stopped in succession.

Remove the large, lower leaves of the plants in autumn as they turn yellow. Leave the main head of leaves on the plants until the end of February, to protect the buttons beneath it from the most severe frosts and to encourage the rise of sap to feed them.

Harvesting. Pick the sprouts from the stem as they ripen. They gradually mature from the bottom of the stem upwards and should be harvested in this order. A second crop of sprout greens will develop at the bottom of the stem and are useful in small gardens and when a bad winter makes green vegetables scarce.

Pests. APHIDS may infest the button sprouts, and CABBAGE WHITEFLY attack the undersides of leaves, even during winter.

Maggots of CABBAGE ROOT FLY feed on the roots, and young plants suddenly wilt and die.

FLEA BEETLES eat small circular holes in the foliage of seedlings, and CATERPILLARS of various species of butterfly and moth eat large holes out of the leaves.

Diseases. Brussels sprouts are infected with the same diseases as commonly seen on CAULIFLOWER, with the exception of whiptail. They are, however, also liable to SPRAY DAMAGE due to the effects of hormone weedkillers. Affected plants show rough wart-like outgrowths at the stem-bases; this should not be confused with CLUB ROOT. The leaves may become narrowed; the plants remain stunted and may fail to crop.

Buckeye, red: see *Aesculus pavia*
Buckthorn, sea: see *Hippophae rhamnoides*

Buddleia

syn. **Buddleja**. *Buddlejaceae*

BUDDLEIA ALTERNIFOLIA

A genus of 100 species of deciduous and evergreen shrubs and small trees, distributed in America, Africa and Asia. Many of the species make decorative garden plants; some are hardy and easily grown; others are half-hardy and should be grown against a wall or in a cool greenhouse. In mild areas, half-hardy species will often survive outdoors. Buddleias are grown for their profusion of flowers; these are slender and tubular with four spreading lobes and are arranged in globular or plume-shaped clusters.

B. alternifolia. China. Height 12–20 ft; spread 15–20 ft. A hardy deciduous shrub or small tree with long arching branches. The narrowly lanceolate pale green leaves are glaucous beneath. Sweet-scented, lavender-blue flowers are borne in rounded clusters, 1 in. wide, all along the previous year's growths, in June. This wide-spreading species is suitable for growing on banks; it can also be trained as a standard tree, when it is even more effective. The form 'Argentea' has hairy, silvery leaves.

B. colvilei. Himalayas. Height 10–18 ft; spread 6–10 ft. A half-hardy semi-evergreen shrub, developing into a wide-spreading tree. The dark green ovate-lanceolate leaves are finely toothed. Rose-pink flowers are borne on the previous year's growths in drooping terminal panicles, 6–8 in. long, in June and July. It is hardy in the south and west of Britain if grown against a wall. 'Kewensis' has rich rose-red flowers.

B. crispa, syn. *B. paniculata.* N. India. Height 6–10 ft; spread 4–8 ft. A half-hardy deciduous shrub of bushy habit. The growths and the ovate-lanceolate, coarsely toothed leaves are covered in white felt, giving a silvery appearance. Fragrant lilac-pink flowers with an orange eye are borne in plume-shaped clusters, 3–4 in. long, on the current year's shoots in July.

B. davidii (butterfly bush). China. Height and spread 9 ft or more. A hardy deciduous shrub, strong-growing and wide-spreading. The mid-green leaves are lanceolate and toothed. Fragrant, lilac-purple flowers are borne in slightly arching, dense, plume-shaped clusters, 10–20 in. long, from July to October on growths of the current year. Butterflies are much attracted to the flowers. Among numerous varieties are 'Black Knight', dark violet-purple flowers; 'Empire Blue', blue flowers with an orange eye; 'Fortune', pure lilac flowers with an orange eye; 'Harlequin', a sport of 'Royal Red', with attractively variegated leaves; 'Royal Red', rich red-purple flowers; 'White Cloud' and 'White Profusion', pure white flowers in dense spikes.

BUDDLEIA DAVIDII

B. fallowiana. China. Height 5–10 ft; spread 4–6 ft. A half-hardy deciduous shrub of bushy habit. The lanceolate leaves are grey above and silvery beneath. Sweet-scented lavender flowers are produced in terminal plume-shaped clusters, 6–10 in. long, on the current season's growths from July to September. 'Alba' is hardier than the species and has cream-white flowers.

B. globosa. Chile, Peru. Height 10–12 ft; spread 10 ft. An almost hardy evergreen or semi-evergreen shrub of vigorous, upright habit. The dark green lanceolate leaves are tawny beneath and have wrinkled surfaces. Scented orange-yellow flowers are borne in globular heads which are arranged in terminal, tapering clusters, 6–8 in. long. They appear in May and June on the previous season's wood.

B. paniculata: see *B. crispa*

Cultivation. Plant buddleias in October and November or in March and April in good loamy soil and in full sun; they are tolerant of lime. The half-hardy species and varieties are best grown against a warm, west-facing wall.

Propagation. Take cuttings, 4–5 in. long with a heel, of half-ripe lateral shoots in July and August; insert the cuttings in equal parts (by volume) peat and sand in a cold frame. Line out the rooted cuttings in nursery rows the following May and transplant to permanent positions in October or the following March.

B. davidii may also be increased by hardwood cuttings, 9–12 in. long, taken in October and inserted in a nursery bed outside.

Pruning. No regular pruning is required, but vigorous growers, such as *B. davidii* and in particular its varieties, can be kept at a manageable size by pruning in March. Cut all the previous year's growths back to within 2–3 in. of the old wood; this produces strong, erect stems and large flower clusters.

Species such as *B. globosa,* which flower on the previous season's growths, should be lightly pruned after flowering by removing faded clusters with 2–3 in. of stem. *B. alternifolia* may be kept neat and bushy by removing two-thirds of all stems after flowering.

Pests. Generally trouble-free.

Diseases. CUCUMBER MOSAIC VIRUS causes the leaves to become distorted and mottled.

Bugbane: see Cimicifuga
Bugle: see Ajuga

Buddleia alternifolia

Buddleia colvilei

Buddleia crispa

Buddleia davidii 'White Cloud'

Buddleia globosa

POT CULTUR

Crocus vernus 'Little Dorrit'   *Narcissus* 'Queen of Bicolors'   *Lachenalia bulbifera*

Winter and spring flowering bulbs

Two distinct kinds of bulbs are used for growing indoors: those that are bought afresh each year for forcing and afterwards either planted in the garden or discarded, and the longer-lived, tender kinds that will flower in succession throughout the year and survive indoors indefinitely.

Forcing bulbs. Hyacinths, single early and double early tulips, narcissi or daffodils, large-flowered crocuses, scillas, dwarf irises and chionodoxas are the most popular bulbs for planting in bowls from late August to October to flower from mid-December onwards.

Specially prepared bulbs are best for this winter forcing. When purchased from a reputable supplier they will have been well grown, lifted at the right time, and thoroughly dried to prevent disease or premature rooting. They will also have been stored at carefully controlled temperatures to induce the proper development of the flower buds inside the bulb for flowering at the desired time. Such bulbs already contain immature flowers and leaves and do not immediately need fertiliser or other plant foods. However, they must have a medium to root in—compost, a water-retaining fibre or water being most suitable.

A correctly balanced compost, such as John Innes potting compost No. 2, is the best medium for growing all bulbs in containers, including glazed bowls which do not have drainage holes. Bulb fibre is quite satisfactory and is cleaner and easier to handle. Bulbs grown in compost

and subsequently planted out in the garden will usually flower again the following year, whereas those in fibre often take a year to recover.

Place a layer of compost or moistened fibre in each bowl. Set the bulbs as close as possible; it does not matter if they touch. Fill the spaces with compost.

The noses of large bulbs such as hyacinth and daffodil bulbs may be left exposed, but cover all other bulbs completely. The surface of the rooting medium should be well below the rim of the bowl.

Put the bowls in the coolest, darkest place available. If they are stood outdoors, place them against a north-facing wall and underneath at least 6 in. of ashes or peat. Cover the ash or peat surface with slates, asbestos sheeting or black polythene.

The purpose of preliminary forcing in a cool, dark environment is to encourage root and leaf formation. Every two or three weeks check that the bowls have not dried out. Well-dampened fibre or compost in deep bowls does not normally need more than an occasional watering, if any at all during this stage.

When the tips of the leaves are showing 1–2 in., move the bowls to a greenhouse or to the window-sill of a cool room. A temperature of 10°C (50°F) is ideal. When the leaves are about 4 in. high, raise the temperature gradually to 18°C (64°F).

Narcissi, hyacinths and tulips may need support; tie string round the stems or stake each separately.

The first early narcissi, 'Soleil d'Or' and 'Paper White', will flower in November if planted in August; the first early hyacinths and early tulips will flower by Christmas.

Do not bring all the bowls in at once if a succession of flowers is wanted. Even if they show the necessary leaf development at the same time, a delay of four or five weeks will do no harm if they are in the cold. If brought indoors in succession, bulbs of a single variety may flower from before Christmas until Easter.

Remove flowers as they fade, but not the leaves and stems. Move the bowls to a light, cool place; a greenhouse kept at a temperature between 4°C (39°F) and 7°C (45°F) is suitable.

Keep the bowls watered. In March or April remove the bulbs and rooting medium, without separating them, from the containers and plant them in the garden. If set in clumps among shrubs, in a herbaceous border or in a rock garden, the bulbs usually recover and will flower for several years. Plant them 8 in. deep. Forced bulbs can rarely be brought to flower indoors again.

Hyacinths and the tazetta narcissi can also be grown in containers of water. Choose a container in which the roots will have space to grow and in which the bulbs will rest without falling into the water. Special glass bulb jars, 6–9 in. tall and with constricted necks, are available.

Start the bulbs into growth from August to November. Fill the jars with tap water to $\frac{1}{2}$ in. above the neck; fill other containers, such as vases, to near the rim. Place one bulb in each jar, making sure that only the base is in water. The bulb will rot if it is completely immersed.

Place the bulbs in their jars in a cool, frost-free place until the roots are 3–4 in. long and the leaves showing at least 1 in. out of the bulb. Keep hyacinths in the dark

F INDOOR BULBS

Tulipa 'Peach Blossom'

Hyacinthus orientalis 'Queen of the Blues'

during this period, but stand tazetta narcissi on a window-sill. Make sure that the base of each bulb remains in water until the roots emerge, topping up if necessary, and that afterwards the roots are always in water.

Bulbs grown in this way with no food to draw on will be shrivelled and poor at the end of the season, and are less likely than other forced bulbs to recover if planted outdoors.

Growing tender bulbs. Tender or half-hardy bulbs that can be grown indoors or in the greenhouse include hippeastrums (usually sold as amaryllis), vallotas, clivias, freesias, nerines and lachenalias.

These bulbs should be grown in well-drained pots containing a good compost. They do not need a period in the dark after potting up.

Large bulbs, such as hippeastrums, are best grown singly; others, such as freesias and lachenalias, are best grown six or more to a 5 in. pot. Do not plant as close as forced bulbs.

Wash or scrub any pots that are being re-used and dry them well. If using clay pots, place crocks (pieces of broken clay pot) over the drainage holes, concave side downwards, to prevent soil clogging the hole or being washed out through it. It is advisable, though not essential, to place a layer of coarse turf or peat over the crocks. In the case of plastic pots with several small drainage holes in the base, crocks are unnecessary provided a layer of turf or peat is included.

Next put a layer of John Innes potting compost No. 2 in each pot. Press the compost gently with the tips of the fingers and place the bulbs on it. Position large

bulbs so that their tips are level with the soil surface; place smaller bulbs with their tips about an inch below the soil.

Add more compost between the bulbs, and firm it well until the surface is an inch below the rim of the pot, then give a sharp tap on the side of the pot to settle the compost and leave a level surface.

Water each pot at once, filling the space between the soil surface and the rim carefully. If the compost was very dry, a second watering will be necessary when the first has soaked in.

The correct time of the year for potting, the temperatures and details of management vary from one kind of bulb to another. They are explained in the entries for each bulb genus.

In general, give only a little water immediately after potting, but increase the amounts gradually as the flower stems and leaves emerge and grow.

All the tender bulbs do best in a greenhouse where light and a steady temperature can be maintained, but they will also grow in the house if kept in the light at the appropriate temperatures.

Even when grown in a greenhouse, the pots can be moved indoors at any time after the stems begin to lengthen. They will come to no harm if stood in a relatively dark part of the room for the week or two they are in bloom. As the flowers fade, cut off each single bloom where it joins the top of the main stalk. The stalk will later die down gradually; when it is yellow and collapsed, cut it off at the top of the bulb. Watering should be increased at this stage, for the leaves are needed to feed the bulbs in preparation for flowering again the following year.

Some bulbs have evergreen leaves; they continue to produce new leaves at intervals while shedding the older ones. These bulbs should be kept moist at all times.

Deciduous bulbs, such as lachenalias and freesias, produce a number of leaves at, or before, flowering time; the leaves reach their full growth some weeks later and then die back in late summer or autumn. Dry these bulbs off by withholding water as the leaves begin to yellow.

Most of the deciduous bulbs can be flowered in succession over several months if watering and temperatures are regulated as follows:

For early flowering and to ensure good bulb growth the following year, start watering early and provide more than the minimum necessary warmth. If later flowering is wanted, start watering later and give lower temperatures. However, a late start may allow the bulbs insufficient time to recover for the following year, leading to fewer flowers or even none at all until another year has passed.

All long-lived tender bulbs except freesias and lachenalias can remain untouched in the same pot and compost for two years; vallotas and nerines can stay even longer. Even freesias and lachenalias, at their best if repotted annually, will grow and flower for a couple of years without repotting. These bulbs produce a large number of small offsets which, if left more than two years, will so crowd the pot that flowering will be severely restricted.

Bulbs such as nerines and vallotas, which do best when undisturbed, can be kept in the same compost for an extra year or two if the top inch is removed and replaced by new material, ideally John Innes potting compost No. 3.

Eventually all composts become exhausted and the bulbs need a fresh supply. They are best repotted during the period of least growth, when the leaves of deciduous bulbs are gone and the evergreen bulbs are not producing new leaves.

Invert the pot over one hand and tap the edge on a firm surface. The whole ball of bulbs and compost should then come out in one piece. If it does not, dislodge it by pressing a finger or stick through the drainage hole.

Clean the bulbs and remove old roots by crumbling them away, together with the old compost; the roots of most corms will need removing. Roots that are perennial and alive, such as those of vallotas, and others that are white and fleshy, should not be broken or removed; hold the whole ball of roots and compost under a running tap and wash away the old soil.

Separate the bulbs where necessary and repot them as before, using larger pots where single bulbs and their roots have increased in size. Remove offset bulbs and pot or box them separately in John Innes potting compost No. 1 to grow on to flowering size.

Bulrush: see Scirpus
Burning bush: see Dictamnus and *Kochia scoparia* 'Trichophylla'
Burr, New Zealand: see Acaena
Burro's tail: see *Sedum morganianum*
Busy lizzie: see *Impatiens holstii* and *I. sultanii*
Buttercup: see Ranunculus
Buttercup, Bermuda: see *Oxalis cernua*
Butterfly bush: see *Buddleia davidii*
Butterfly flower: see Schizanthus
Butterwort: see Pinguicula

Buxus sempervirens

Buxus

Box. *Buxaceae*

BUXUS SEMPERVIRENS

A genus of 70 species of hardy evergreen shrubs and small trees. Only one species is in general cultivation, and this is widely grown as low edgings to borders, for hedging and as clipped specimen plants.

B. sempervirens (common box). Europe, W. Asia, N. Africa. Height up to 10 ft; spread 4–6 ft. A slow-growing species of bushy habit, with ovate to oblong, glossy dark green leaves; these are opposite on the square stems and notched at the apex. Inconspicuous, pale green, honey-scented flowers, with yellow anthers, are borne in April.

Numerous varieties include: 'Elegantissima', of dense habit, with grey-green leaves edged silver; 'Handsworthensis', of upright growth, suitable for hedges and screens; 'Latifolia Maculata', a compact bush (height 3–6 ft) with broad leaves variegated yellow; 'Pyramidalis', of erect habit and suitable as a clipped bush; 'Suffruticosa', the dwarf form used for edging.

Cultivation. Plant in September and October or in March and April in any ordinary garden soil, and in sun or light shade.

For hedges, space 9–12 in. high plants at intervals of 12–15 in.; remove the upper third of the leading shoots after planting or in April to promote bushy growth.

Propagation. Take cuttings, 3–4 in. long, in August and September and insert in equal parts (by volume) peat and sand in a cold frame. Line the rooted cuttings out in nursery rows the following April or May and grow on for two years before setting out in permanent positions.

Pruning. Clip hedges and topiary specimens to required shape in August and September.

Pests. Occasionally BOX SUCKERS feed on the sap of young leaves which fail to expand; the affected shoots become cabbage-like in appearance.

Diseases. LEAF SPOT due to different fungi shows as pale brown spots.

A PHYSIOLOGICAL DISORDER shows as browning or yellowing of whole leaves.

RUST produces small, dark brown, powdery masses of spores on both leaf surfaces.

Cabbage 'January King'

Cabbage 'Wheeler's Imperial'

C

Cabbage

Brassica oleracea Capitata. *Cruciferae*

A biennial vegetable cultivated as an annual for its tight-centred head of leaves which is used for cooking and in salads and pickles. The original wild cabbage has been highly developed to produce round-headed and pointed culinary types and varieties with dark green, light green, near-white, pink, or purple-red leaves. Some varieties are principally ornamental. For culinary purposes, varieties are available at any time of year, but although winter-maturing types are reasonably hardy, they do not withstand the same severe frosts as the savoy cabbage.

This group of cabbages also includes Chinese cabbages, coleworts, spring greens, Couve Tronchuda (Portuguese cabbage) and ornamental cabbages.

VARIETIES
There are two main types of cabbage, those with round heads such as 'Primo' and 'Christmas Drumhead', and those with conical heads, such as 'Greyhound' and 'Winnigstadt'.

'Greyhound', 'May Express', 'Pride of the Market' and 'Primo' are quick-growing varieties. Sow under glass in February ready for cutting in late May and early June. Sown outdoors in April and transplanted in June, they are ready for use in August and September. They may also be sown in mid-July on ground from which early peas, broad beans or lettuces have been cleared; they will be ready for cutting in October.

Spring-sown drumhead varieties, such as 'Webb's Favourite', and the dwarf 'Delicatesse', with ball-like heads, are ready from August to October; 'Christmas Drumhead', sown in spring, matures in October or November; and 'January King' from December to February. 'Winnigstadt' is an outstanding exhibition variety; it is a compact grower with a solid, pointed head of rather grey-green leaves.

For autumn sowing to produce spring crops, it is important to choose varieties which have been bred specially to resist bolting in spring. The earliest to mature is 'Harbinger', with a small, dark green head. 'April', 'Durham Elf', and 'Wheeler's Imperial' are small early varieties, slightly later than 'Harbinger'.

'Early Giant' and 'Early Offenham' are early-maturing varieties with larger heads.

Red cabbages, which are chiefly grown for pickling, are usually sown in spring, but an autumn sowing can be made, especially for large-growing varieties such as 'The Lydiate'. This is an extremely hardy variety, suitable for growing in northern gardens.

'Blood Red', 'Dwarf Dutch' and 'Ruby Red' are quick-maturing, compact varieties which should be sown in spring. 'Niggerhead' is a dark purple-red, early-maturing variety of medium size, suitable for a spring-sowing.

Chinese cabbage (*Brassica cernua*). A quick-growing cabbage, similar to a cos lettuce. 'Michihli' and 'Pe-tsai' are two popular varieties.

Sow the seeds in June where the plants are to mature; Chinese cabbages should never be transplanted. Sow in rows 15 in. apart and thin the seedlings to 12 in. apart. Keep the plants well watered during dry spells. They are ready for cutting in late summer and early autumn.

Coleworts, collards, spring greens. These are the popular descriptions of some of the small-growing cabbages that are grown for cutting, while still young, from November to April. 'Early Giant' and 'First Early Market 218' are particularly suitable for growing in this way.

Sow seeds in the last week in July where the plants are to grow. Use ground that was well manured for an early-maturing vegetable crop; hoe the surface lightly and sow the seeds thinly. Thin the subsequent seedlings to 4–5 in. apart.

Couve Tronchuda, Portuguese cabbage (*Brassica oleracea* Costata). This is a loose-centred cabbage which forms a large, leafy, mid-green edible plant with prominent white midribs. Sow seeds in a seed bed in April and transplant the young plants in June or July. They are ready for cutting in September and October.

Ornamental cabbages. There are four kinds of these plants: white plain-leaved, pink plain-leaved, white fringe-leaved and pink fringe-leaved. They are round-headed cabbages with crinkly leaves, variegated with pink and white. Seeds are usually bought as a mixture. 'Sekito' is bright green, suffused with red.

Savoy cabbage (*Brassica oleracea* Bullata). This is a round-headed, rather flat-topped cabbage with densely wrinkled leaves. It is easily grown and is especially valuable as a fresh green autumn and winter vegetable; its flavour is considered to be improved by a touch of frost.

Many varieties are available which mature from September onwards, but since Brussels sprouts, cabbages and cauliflowers all mature at the same time, it is advisable to grow late-maturing savoy varieties such as 'New Year', 'Ormskirk Extra Late' and 'Rearguard'. The latter two are suitable for use until early April.

Cultivation. Cabbages do well on any ordinary, well-drained garden soil, but those which are to stand through the winter for spring use should be grown on a light soil.

Prepare the growing bed for January and spring-sown plants early in winter by digging it over and working in a bucket of well-rotted manure or compost per sq. yd. Unless the soil is already limy, rake in 4 oz. of carbonate of lime per sq. yd in spring.

Make sowings under glass in mid or late January. Sow the seeds in pots or pans of seed compost and cover lightly with more compost. Germinate the seeds at a temperature of 10°C (50°F). When the seedlings are large enough to handle, prick them out into boxes and grow on at the same temperature. When the young plants are growing strongly, harden them off in a cold frame, before setting them out, 18 in. apart either way, in their final quarters in early April.

For spring sowings in the open, draw $\frac{3}{4}$ in. deep drills, 6 in. apart, in a seed bed in April. Thin the seedlings as they grow; during June, when they have developed into strong young plants, transplant them to the final bed, setting them 18 in. apart either way. Keep the rows free of weeds. If growth seems slow, hoe in nitro-chalk or nitrate of soda at 1 oz. to the yd run.

Make autumn sowings in the first week of August in the same way as for spring sowings. Transplant the young cabbages to the final bed during the second half of September; in the north, the young plants may be left in the seed bed through the winter and transplanted in spring. Set the young plants in a bed that was well manured for a summer crop. Make the rows 18 in. apart and set smaller-growing varieties 12 in. apart, larger-growing 15 in. apart.

Sow seeds of savoy cabbage thinly in $\frac{1}{2}$ in. deep drills drawn 8 in. apart. Sow during the first week in May, or a little later in southern districts. Transplant the seedlings in mid-July to the prepared bed, setting them in rows 20 in. apart with 15–18 in. between the plants. Early varieties required for autumn can be sown in late March and transplanted in June.

Harvesting. In summer and autumn, cut cabbages as soon as they have developed a good head. Varieties that mature during winter can be left in the bed for a longer period.

Pests. APHIDS, particularly the cabbage aphids, infest leaves and make the plants sticky.

BIRDS, especially wood-pigeons, strip the leaves and uproot young plants.

Maggots of the CABBAGE ROOT FLY feed on the roots, and young plants may wilt and collapse.

FLEA BEETLES eat small circular holes in the leaves of seedlings, and CATERPILLARS of various species of butterfly and moth eat large holes out of the leaves and tunnel into the hearts of plants.

Diseases. CLUB ROOT causes thickened, swollen and distorted root masses; the plants become stunted, and the foliage discoloured.

DAMPING-OFF of seedlings and WIRE STEM of established plants are caused by the fungus RHIZOCTONIA. The stems of seedlings collapse at ground level; in established plants, the bases of the stems are hard, brown and shrunken.

FROST DAMAGE may injure the tissues of plants which have been grown soft; the damaged areas may suffer from a SOFT ROT or GREY MOULD.

LEAF SPOT due to several different fungi shows on the leaves as round brown spots.

SPRAY DAMAGE shows as rough, wart-like outgrowths at the stem-base; these should not be confused with club root. The leaves become narrow and the plants remain stunted.

Cabbage 'Niggerhead' (red)

Cabbage Couve Tronchuda

Cabbage 'Sekito' (ornamental)

Cabbage, Portuguese: see Cabbage
Cabbage, skunk: see *Lysichiton americanum*

An echinocereus growing among rocks in the wild

CACTUS

Cacti belong to the family *Cactaceae*, and have several features not possessed by members of other plant families. The chief characteristic of cacti is the areole, which is a growth, rather resembling a minute pincushion, from which wool, spines, flowers and new shoots develop. Although many succulent plants from other families, such as some euphorbias, resemble cacti, they can be distinguished by the fact that, although they may possess spines, these do not come from an areole but arise like rose thorns.

Contrary to popular opinion, cacti flower regularly, although those that reach a height of 20–40 ft in nature are unlikely to bloom in a small greenhouse. There are, however, many smaller species which will flower freely; the flowers have no stalks, so are unsuitable as cut blooms.

With the exception of the genus *Pereskia* all cacti are succulent: they are able to store water in their tissues to carry them through periods of drought. Since most cacti have no permanent leaves, the storage tissue is the stem of the plant. This is known as the plant body, and is usually either globose (globular or spherical) or cylindrical in shape. Most

opuntias and all epiphyllums have flattened stems that are composed of jointed segments. Epiphyllum segments are sometimes incorrectly called leaves. Opuntia segments are known as pads.

Succulent plants are not all members of the *Cactaceae* family, but belong to many other plant families. Some succulents store their water in stems, in the same way as cacti, and have few, if any, leaves. Others are leaf succulents, having fleshy leaves, full of water-storage tissue. The flowers of these other succulents vary in shape from genus to genus.

Most cylindrical and globular cacti have 'ribs', a term used to describe the pleats or ridges on the plant body. Other cacti have tubercles, which are swollen parts of the plant body, usually arranged spirally around the plant.

Cacti are noted for their spines, although some, such as lophophoras, are spineless. Spines may be stout and sharp in some species, bristle or hair-like in others; barbed species may occur with either. Typical spines are divided into two types: central and radial. Central spines arise from the central part of an areole and are usually stronger and larger than the radial spines. These rise from the outer part of an areole, and are inferior to the central spines. Opuntias also have minute barbed bristles (glochids) on each areole.

It is generally known that most cacti are desert plants. However, deserts vary. At one extreme, where little or no rain falls, they are quite arid and no cacti are found. Other deserts are characterised by heavy, but infrequent, rainfall. Most cacti and other succulents are found in this type of desert, taking in water when they get the chance, and storing it until the rains come again. There are some cacti, the epiphyllums and their relatives, which come from rain-forest areas. These are chiefly epiphytes: plants obtaining support from other plants, usually trees, but not depending on them for nourishment.

With one possible exception, *Rhipsalis baccifera*, all cacti are native to the American continent. Those cacti growing in the wild in Europe and Africa have been introduced at some time in the past. Many of the other succulents are native to African deserts, notably the Karroo.

Many cacti and other succulents are easy plants to cultivate in a good, well-drained soil, but they usually require some heat in winter. Apart from the shade-loving forest types, cacti and succulents require plenty of sun. They will survive short periods of neglect far better than most greenhouse plants, but appreciate plenty of water during the growing period. Most can be grown from seeds, obtainable from specialist nurseries.

Caladium

Araceae

CALADIUM BICOLOR

A genus of 15 species of greenhouse perennials. The roots are tuberous, and the plants die down in autumn. Although these plants require special attention, they are outstanding for their brilliantly coloured ornamental foliage.

C. bicolor. Tropical S. America. Height 9–15 in.; spread 12 in. This variable species has arrow-head-shaped leaves of varying sizes on long leaf stalks. The leaf colours are in shades of white and red, with combinations between those colours and green. Some leaves are entirely coloured, others are mid-green with markings and veins of white, cream, red or crimson.

The white-leaved 'Candidum' has a network of green veins; 'John Peel' is heavily veined with metallic red; 'Macahyba' has scarlet veins and lilac blotches; 'Pink Cloud' is mottled with pink; 'Seagull' is dark green with prominent broad white veins; 'Stoplight' is suffused with crimson and has narrow green margins.

Cultivation. Start the tubers into growth in March at a temperature of 21°C (70°F). Place the tubers in boxes of damp peat or moss, and syringe them twice daily.

When growth has started, pot the tubers, 1 in. deep, in John Innes potting compost No. 2 or in a proprietary peat mixture. Good drainage is essential. The size of the pot is determined by the size of the tuber: small tubers are put in 4 in. pots, large ones in 6–8 in. pots.

Keep the compost just moist and maintain a humid atmosphere and a temperature of 21°C (70°F) until the roots are well developed. When the leaves are emerging, and until they wither, the plants require frequent watering. Begin to feed the plants with a liquid fertiliser once a week when the pot is full of roots. During the summer, the greenhouse should be damped down frequently; syringe the leaves daily. Give light shading; too heavy shading will prevent the leaves acquiring their brilliant colourings.

When the plants are well developed, gradually harden them to lower temperatures and drier conditions. They can be brought into the house, but must be protected from draughts at all times.

In autumn, the leaves begin to fade, and watering should be reduced. Eventually the foliage dies down and the tubers should be rested in a semi-dry state for the winter. Overwinter the tubers in their pots and keep these underneath the greenhouse staging during the winter, at a temperature of 13°C (55°F). Give just enough water to keep the soil barely moist. A light watering once a month should be sufficient.

Propagation. Detach the offsets from the tubers when repotting in March. Grow on as for adult plants; the offsets should produce good-sized tubers in one or two years.

Pests and diseases. Generally trouble-free.

Calamondin: see *Citrus mitis*

Calandrinia

Portulacaceae

A genus of 150 species of annuals and perennials. The following species are semi-prostrate plants bearing a profusion of short-lived but attractive flowers. They are suitable for borders and rock gardens; for the best results choose a sheltered, sunny site. Under warm conditions seeds set freely and produce self-sown plants in great numbers the following year.

C. discolor. Chile. Height 15–18 in.; planting distance 12 in. Though strictly a perennial, this plant is usually grown as an annual. The leaves are spathulate, grey-green above and purple beneath. The bowl-shaped flowers, in August, are 2 in. across and pale purple with contrasting yellow stamens.

C. umbellata. Peru. Height 4–6 in.; planting distance 9–12 in. This perennial is usually grown as an annual but can also be grown as a biennial in the south and west. It is the best of the species, a compact plant that thrives in dry situations and is recommended for edging paths and for rock gardens. It can also be grown in pots in a cold greenhouse. The leaves are narrow and linear, grey-green and hairy, forming a bushy mat of ground cover. The cup-shaped flowers, $\frac{3}{4}$ in. across and borne in clusters from July to September, are vivid crimson-purple.

Cultivation. A light, sandy soil is required, in an open sunny site.

Grow pot plants under glass in $3\frac{1}{2}$ in. pots of John Innes potting compost No. 1. Water sparingly; shading is unnecessary, even in hot sun.

Propagation. Except in the case of *C. umbellata*, grown as a biennial, sow the seeds in pans or pots of seed compost, in March or April, at 18°C (64°F). Prick out the young seedlings into boxes, grow on at a temperature of 13°C (55°F) and harden off in a cold frame before planting out in May. Alternatively, sow directly in the flowering site in April and thin out to the required spacing.

To grow *C. umbellata* as a biennial, sow the seeds in June, either in the site or in boxes, to plant out in September. Protect with cloches.

Pests and diseases. Generally trouble-free.

Caladium bicolor

Caladium bicolor (mixed)

Calandrinia umbellata

Calanthe

Orchidaceae

Calanthe masuca

Calanthe vestita

A variable genus of 120 species of orchids, widely distributed from Africa and Asia to tropical Australia and the Pacific Islands. The genus includes epiphytic and terrestrial species; the two described are terrestrial and should be grown in an intermediate greenhouse. They have prominent single-jointed pseudobulbs, each with a basal cluster of mid-green lanceolate leaves.

The flowers are carried on spikes arising from the base of the pseudobulbs and range from violet through pink-purple to white. They are approximately 2 in. across, and the lip has three clefts, giving the flower a four-lobed appearance.

See also ORCHIDS.

CALANTHE VESTITA

C. masuca. Tropical Asia. This evergreen species has erect arching flower stems that are 2–3 ft long. Numerous closely set flowers appear from June to October; they are violet-purple.

C. vestita. Malesia. This deciduous species has large silver-green pseudobulbs. The erect flower stems are up to 3 ft long, and each carries up to 25 blooms. The flowers are white and 1½–2 in. across; the lip is white or flushed pale rose and with a red or yellow crest. They appear from October to February, after the foliage has died down.

Cultivation. *C. masuca* requires a compost of 3 parts fibrous loam and 1 part of a mixture comprising equal parts leaf-mould, sand and chopped sphagnum (parts by volume). Grow in 6 in. pots and keep moist all year.

C. vestita needs a similar compost but with 1 extra part fibrous loam and 1 part well-decayed manure. Set three pseudobulbs to a 7 in. pot, or one to a 5 in. pot. This species has a resting period and should be kept completely dry until growth restarts. *C. masuca* and *C. vestita* both require a minimum winter temperature of 13°C (55°F). Shade calanthes on sunny days between April and September and ventilate from May to October. Feed *C. vestita* with weak liquid manure every ten days or so, from the time the leaves are half grown until they are fully developed. When the foliage turns yellow in late summer, cease watering completely until the new season's growth appears in March or April. It may be advisable to give the plant one or two moderate waterings during the flowering period.

Repot *C. vestita* annually after flowering; separate the pseudobulbs and repot singly.

Propagation. After flowering, detach the offsets from the parent pseudobulbs and pot up singly in the growing compost in 3–4 in. pots.

Pests. Small circular or elongated semi-transparent scales on leaves and stems are caused by SCALE INSECTS.

Diseases. Generally trouble-free.

Calathea insignis

Calathea makoyana

Calathea

Marantaceae

A genus of 150 species of greenhouse evergreen perennials. They have attractive foliage, and are suitable as house plants. The species are sometimes offered under the name *Maranta.*

C. insignis. Brazil. Height and spread 9 in. The lanceolate mid to dark green leaves, about 6 in. long, are marked with dark green blotches at intervals along the midrib on the upper leaf surfaces. The undersides are maroon.

C. lindeniana. Brazil. Height 9–12 in.; spread 12–18 in. The oblong or ovate leaves, about 6 in. long, are dark green on the upper side, with an emerald-green zone around the midrib. The leaf margins are edged with a narrow band of the same emerald-green. On the undersides, the leaves are maroon with dark markings where the light green zones appear on the upper sides.

C. louisae. Brazil. Height 9–12 in.; spread 12–18 in. The lanceolate leaves, up to 7 in. long, are mid-green with irregular olive-green or grey blotches spreading from the veins. The undersides are green-purple with green margins.

C. makoyana (peacock plant). Brazil. Height 18–24 in.; spread 12–18 in. The leaves are oblong, usually 6 in. long, though larger in mature plants. They are silvery-green above, edged with mid-green, and have the principal veins marked with irregular dark green blotches. On the undersides, the zones are red or purple.

C. ornata. Colombia. Height and spread 18 in. or more. A variable species with dark green leaves, about 7 in. long. From the midribs the veins in young leaves are variegated with thin rose-pink stripes. As the foliage matures the pink stripes fade to ivory. The undersides of the leaves are dark purple.

C. zebrina. Brazil. Height and spread 18 in. or more. The narrow, oblong leaves are up to 18 in. long; they are soft emerald-green with horizontal bands of dark green that show purple beneath.

Cultivation. With the exception of *C. ornata* and *C. zebrina*, which require warm greenhouse treatment, calatheas are suitable as house plants and will also do well in bottle gardens.

Pot the plants in March in John Innes potting compost No. 2, or in a proprietary peat compost. Grow the house plants in 4–5 in. pots; *C. ornata* and *C. zebrina* are grown in 6–8 in. pots or planted out in the greenhouse border if large plants are wanted. Provide ample drainage, and shade the plants at all times. Bright sunlight is likely to change the colouring of the leaves. During the growing season, water freely and maintain a moist atmosphere; syringe with rain-water, as tap water may cause a white spotting of the leaves. In the home, place the pots in an absorbent material such as sphagnum moss to maintain a moist atmosphere.

The species will survive at a minimum winter temperature of 10°C (50°F), but a temperature of 13–16°C (55–61°F) is preferable. Water to keep the plants just moist in winter.

The plants quickly exhaust the compost; they need annual potting on in June or July. Give a weak liquid feed at intervals of 10–14 days from June to September.

Propagation. Divide the rhizomatous crowns so that each piece retains a few leaves and sturdy roots. As a temperature of 16–18°C (61–64°F) is necessary after division to encourage new root growth, plants should be divided in late June.

Pests and diseases. Generally trouble-free.

Calceolaria
Scrophulariaceae

A genus of about 400 species of hardy, half-hardy and tender annuals, biennials, perennials and sub-shrubs, grown for their freely produced, rounded or ovoid, pouch-shaped flowers. The species described here are suitable for growing in rock gardens or alpine houses, for bedding schemes and as pot plants.

CALCEOLARIA TENELLA

ALPINE SPECIES

C. biflora. Chile. Height 6–12 in.; spread 12–18 in. This near-hardy, perennial species forms a basal rosette of ovate, pale to mid-green leaves. Yellow flowers, 1 in. long, are carried in pairs on stems up to 12 in. high in July and August.

C. darwinii. Magellan Straits. Height 2–4 in.; spread 6–9 in. A half-hardy perennial species with ovate, mid-green leaves. The bright yellow flowers, 1–1½ in. long, are spotted chestnut-brown and have a pure white horizontal band across the top of the lower lip. They open in June and July.

C. × 'John Innes'. Height 4–6 in.; spread up to 12 in. This hybrid between *C. plantaginea* and *C. polyrrhiza* is a hardy plant, with lanceolate pale to mid-green leaves. Slender erect stems bear one or more bright yellow flowers, 1½ in. long, in May.

C. polyrrhiza. Patagonia. Height 3–4 in.; spread 12 in. This creeping plant is an almost hardy perennial; it has lanceolate mid-green leaves. Yellow flowers, 1 in. long, open in June and July.

C. tenella. Chile. Height 3–4 in.; spread 9–12 in. This perennial mat-forming species has ovate, fresh green leaves. Bright yellow flowers, 1½ in. long, appear on 2 in. stalks between May and September. The plant spreads freely in light, sandy soil and is hardy in sheltered positions.

BEDDING AND POT-GROWN SPECIES

C. gracilis. Ecuador. Height 12–18 in.; planting distance 6 in. This half-hardy annual is suitable for growing in borders or in pots. The leaves are mid-green, deeply cut, hairy and sticky. Lemon-yellow flowers, up to ½ in. long, are produced in great profusion from July to September.

C. × herbeo-hybrida. Height 8–18 in. This name covers a group of half-hardy biennial hybrids, best grown as pot plants under glass. The ovate leaves are soft, mid-green and slightly hairy. The flowers are 2–2½ in. long, in shades of yellow, orange and red, either spotted or blotched with

Calceolaria × herbeo-hybrida

crimson; they are produced under glass from May to July, outdoors from June to August.

The Monarch strain, in a range of colours, has flowers which are 2½ in. across, and exquisitely marked; 'Multiflora Nana' is a dwarf plant up to 8 in. high; it bears masses of 1½ in. wide flowers in shades of red and yellow, spotted with crimson.

CALCEOLARIA × HERBEO-HYBRIDA   CALCEOLARIA INTEGRIFOLIA

C. integrifolia, syn. *C. rugosa.* Chile. Height 18–24 in.; planting distance 12–15 in. A half-hardy sub-shrubby perennial of upright bushy habit, suitable for pot culture. It can be grown against a wall in sheltered areas or in a greenhouse border where it may reach a height of 4 ft. It bears matt, mid-green leaves, oblong to lanceolate and finely wrinkled; the foliage is usually evergreen. The yellow flowers, ½–1 in. long, are freely produced from July to September.

C. mexicana. Mexico. Height 9–10 in.; planting distance 6 in. A half-hardy bushy annual, suitable for bedding. The mid-green leaves are laciniated. Pale yellow flowers, ½ in. long, are carried in spikes above the leaves from July to September.

C. rugosa: see *C. integrifolia*

C. scabiosifolia. Peru. Height up to 24 in.; planting distance 6 in. A half-hardy annual, suitable for bedding out. The hairy leaves are

Calceolaria darwinii

Calceolaria × 'John Innes'

mid-green and deeply divided. Pale yellow flowers, $\frac{1}{2}$ in. long, are carried in dense clusters from May to October.

Cultivation of alpine species. These dwarf calceolarias require an ordinary, well-drained, but moisture-retentive soil; *C. darwinii* and *C. tenella* do best in a rich leafy lime-free soil. Flowering is most profuse in full sun, but the plants will tolerate partial shade.

Plant in April or May and remove dead or faded flower stems after flowering. Place a raised sheet of glass over the plants in winter to protect them from excessive dampness.

In the alpine house, grow in 6–8 in. pans containing John Innes potting compost No. 1 or in equal parts (by volume) peat loam, leaf-mould and sand. Repot every second year in April.

Cultivation of bedding and pot plants. A light, moderately rich and acid soil is best for these half-hardy calceolarias. Plant outdoors in May or June; *C. integrifolia* requires the protection of a south or west-facing wall, in sun or partial shade. Most ordinary garden soils give reasonable results. Twiggy support may be needed for the taller varieties.

Under glass, pot the plants in final 5–7 in. pots in May for summer flowering. Water freely in summer, moderately throughout the winter, increasing the amount in February, and raising the temperature to 13°C (55°F).

Propagation of alpine species. Sow seeds in July, as soon as they are ripe, on the surface of John Innes seed compost, and place the containers in a cold frame or greenhouse. When the seedlings are large enough to handle, prick them off into pots or boxes. Pot the young plants for outdoor planting, singly into 3 in. pots of John Innes potting compost No. 2 and grow on in a frost-free frame; they should be ready for planting out in their permanent positions the following April.

Plants for the alpine house are set three or four to an 8 in. pan as described under CULTIVATION.

Seeds may also be sown in March and treated similarly, but they will germinate less quickly than fresh seeds.

Divide and replant hardy plants in April.

Propagation of bedding and pot plants. Annual species can be sown in the flowering site in April and thinned to the appropriate distance.

Alternatively, sow seeds of annual, biennial and perennial species under glass. Sow *C. gracilis*, *C. mexicana* and *C. scabiosifolia* in February or March, *C.* × *herbeo-hybrida* in June, and *C. integrifolia* in March or April. Sow in pots or pans of seed compost at a minimum temperature of 18°C (64°F). The seeds are tiny and require careful handling; sow thinly on the surface of the compost, and shade the germinating seeds and young seedlings from strong sun. When large enough, prick off the seedlings into boxes.

Harden off the annuals in a cold frame and plant out in May. Pot up biennial and perennial plants, intended for growing outdoors, in 3 in. pots of John Innes potting compost No. 1 or plant directly in a frame. Overwinter *C. integrifolia* in a frost-free frame and plant out in May or June of the following year. *C.* × *herbeo-hybrida* needs a winter temperature of 7–10°C (45–50°F); grown as a pot plant it should be placed in its final pot in February or March.

Calceolaria tenella

Calceolaria integrifolia

Calendula officinalis
'Kelmscott Giant Orange'

Treat biennial or perennial pot plants a described under CULTIVATION.

The perennial *C. integrifolia* may also b increased from cuttings. Take 3 in. long latera shoots, preferably with a heel, in August o September; insert in equal parts (by volume) pea and sand in a propagating frame at a temperatur of 15°C (59°F). When rooted, pot the cutting singly in 3 in. pots of John Innes potting compos No. 1 or 2 and treat as described for seedlings.

Pruning. Shorten all growths of *C. integrifolia* by half in April to maintain bushy plants.

Pests. Outdoors, leaves and flowers are infeste by APHIDS which suck the sap and foul the plant with sticky honey-dew and sooty mould.

SLUGS may be troublesome.

In the greenhouse GLASSHOUSE LEAFHOPPER feed on the undersides of leaves causing a coars mottling on the upper surfaces.

GLASSHOUSE WHITEFLY may also infest th undersides of leaves, making plants sticky an sooty; the small white adults fly off the plant when disturbed.

Diseases. Outdoors, the plants are generall trouble-free, but under glass several fungi ma cause FOOT ROT and ROOT ROT; the leaves becom yellow and wilt and the plants may collapse.

TOMATO SPOTTED WILT VIRUS causes sever stunting, and the affected plants have a rosette appearance. The leaves become distorted with large, pale, irregular blotches, and the gree tissue between may be raised in blisters.

Calendula
Marigold. *Compositae*

CALENDULA OFFICINALIS

A genus of 20–30 species of sub-shrubs an annual herbaceous plants. The most commonly grown species, described here, is excellent fo borders and for cutting. It can also be grown i pots under glass for cutting in winter. Th flowers last well in water. The leaves and stem have a pungent aroma. This plant reproduce itself freely from self-sown seeds.

C. officinalis (pot marigold). S. Europe. Heigh 24 in.; spacing 12–15 in. A hardy annual of bush habit, erect and self-supporting if not crowded The obovate-lanceolate leaves are light green long and narrow. Daisy-like flowers, up to 4 in across and bright orange or yellow, are freely produced from May to the first frosts.

The many varieties include: 'Art Shades', mixture of bright and pastel shades; 'Creste Mixed', with two outer rows of plain petals sur rounding a quilled centre; 'Geisha Girl', recently introduced fully double form, red orange, with incurving petals; 'Kelmscott Gian Orange', with fully double, bright orang flowers; 'Pacific Beauty', available as a mixture o n separate colours, including apricot, cream and delicate pink shades; and 'Radio', with curled and quilled petals in deep orange and golden yellow.

Cultivation. These plants thrive with little or no attention on the poorest soils and under the worst possible conditions. For the best results, however, and a high percentage of fully double flowers, a well-drained, medium garden soil is required. If the plants are grown for cutting, pinch out the terminal buds to encourage lateral shoots. Dead-heading prolongs flowering and prevents self-sown seedlings, which can grow to weed proportions the following year.

Seedlings from a September sowing can be potted up into 5–6 in. pots of John Innes potting compost No. 2, to flower in winter under glass. Autumn-sown seedlings, left outdoors to flower in spring, need cloche protection in cold areas.

Propagation. Sow the seeds in the flowering site, covering them with $\frac{1}{2}$ in. of soil, in March for summer flowering or in September for late spring flowering. Thin out to the required spacing.

Pests. CATERPILLARS, particularly CUTWORMS, eat the stems and lower leaves.

Diseases. CUCUMBER MOSAIC VIRUS causes mottling and distortion of the leaves; the flowers are small and misshapen.

POWDERY MILDEW shows as a white powdery deposit on the leaves and on the stems.

RUST develops on the undersides of the leaves and shows as pustules bearing orange spores.

SMUT shows on the leaves as dark, irregular spots which spread rapidly in wet weather.

Calico bush: see *Kalmia latifolia*

Callicarpa
Verbenaceae

A genus of 140 species of deciduous shrubs and small trees. Most of the species are tropical, but those described are hardy enough to be grown outdoors in the south of Great Britain or in a cool greenhouse elsewhere. Their attraction lies in the large clusters of violet or lilac berries in autumn; the leaves often assume shades of yellow, pink or lilac in October. The flowers are insignificant, borne in small axillary clusters.

CALLICARPA RUBELLA (IN WINTER)

C. bodinieri giraldii, syn. *C. giraldiana.* China. Height up to 6 ft; spread 5–6 ft. The narrow, pale green leaves are lanceolate, downy and toothed. They assume yellow and red autumn tints. Lilac flowers are freely produced in July; they are borne in rounded clusters, $\frac{3}{4}$–$1\frac{1}{2}$ in. wide, and are followed by round, violet-purple berries.

C. giraldiana: see *C. bodinieri giraldii*

C. japonica. Japan. Height and spread 5 ft. The ovate-lanceolate, slender-pointed leaves are pale

to mid-green and turn yellow in autumn. Pink flowers, in rounded clusters, 1–1$\frac{1}{2}$ in. across, appear in August; the berries are lilac-purple.

C. rubella. China, Burma, Assam. Height 7–10 ft; spread 5–6 ft. The pale to mid-green leaves are lanceolate to ovate-oblong, and toothed. Clusters, 1 in. across, of numerous small pink flowers are borne in July and are followed by a profusion of brilliant red-purple, rounded berries which persist for as long as seven months. It can be grown outdoors only in mild western areas.

Cultivation. Plant hardy callicarpas from October to March, in any good garden soil and in a sunny sheltered position, preferably against a south wall. Berries are more freely produced when several plants are grown together. Cover the lower parts of young plants with bracken or straw in winter.

Under glass, grow callicarpas in the greenhouse border or in 10–12 in. pots or small tubs of John Innes potting compost No. 2. Provide a winter temperature of 4°C (39°F); pot plants may be stood outdoors from May to September.

Propagation. Take cuttings, 3–4 in. long, of lateral shoots, preferably with a heel, in June and July. Insert the cuttings in equal parts (by volume) peat and sand at a bottom heat of 16–18°C (61–64°F). Pot when rooted in 3 in. pots of John Innes potting compost No. 1.

Pruning. Cut the previous year's growths back to young wood in February.

Pests and diseases. Generally trouble-free.

Callicore rosea: see *Amaryllis belladonna*

Callicarpa rubella

Callirhoe
Malvaceae

CALLIRHOE INVOLUCRATA

A genus of ten species of annuals and perennials; the two species described are excellent for rock gardens, banks and borders, and have long flowering periods. They thrive on dry soils.

C. involucrata. California. Height 6 in.; spacing 12 in. A dwarf hardy perennial of trailing habit. The leaves are mid-green, narrow and toothed. Crimson bowl-shaped flowers, up to 2 in. across, are produced from July to August.

C. pedata. Texas. Height 24 in.; spacing 12 in. This species flowers well from seed in the first season and is generally listed as an annual, although in sandy soil the roots will survive a mild winter. Erect stems carry lobed or dissected mid-green leaves. Bowl-shaped crimson flowers, 2 in. across, are produced from June to August.

Cultivation. An open, sunny position and light soil are required. *C. pedata* needs staking in all but the most sheltered sites. Cut back the dead stems of both species in spring.

Propagation. Sow the seeds in the flowering site in March, just covering them, and thin out

Callirhoe involucrata

the seedlings to the required spacing when they are large enough to handle. These plants do not transplant well and sowing under glass is not recommended.

Pests and diseases. Generally trouble-free.

Callistemon
Bottle brush. *Myrtaceae*

CALLISTEMON SALIGNUS

A genus of 25 species of evergreen trees and shrubs occurring in Australia and Tasmania. Many species are outstanding for their bottle-brush-like scarlet flower spikes. The following species are half-hardy and require cool greenhouse cultivation except in the mildest areas.

C. citrinus. Australia. Height 5–6 ft; spread 4–5 ft. A shrub or small tree of graceful, open habit. The grey-green leaves are linear to lanceolate. Small flowers with numerous brilliant red stamens are borne in cylindrical spikes, 2–4 in. long, in July. 'Splendens' is an outstanding form.

C. linearis. New South Wales. Height 3–5 ft; spread 3–4 ft. A shrub of open habit, with light-green, narrow linear leaves. The flowers, with bright red stamens, are borne in densely packed cylindrical spikes, 3–5 in. long, in July. This species is hardy in the south of Britain.

C. salignus. Australia. Height 5–8 ft; spread 4–5 ft. This near-hardy species is of bushy habit. The linear-lanceolate leaves are mid-green. Yellow flowers with pale yellow stamens are borne in cylindrical spikes, 1½–3 in. long, in June.

Cultivation. Plant outdoors in April or May in any ordinary, well-drained soil and in a sunny sheltered position, preferably against a south or west-facing wall.

Under glass, grow these shrubs in 10–12 in. pots or in large tubs of John Innes potting compost No. 2, or planted out in the greenhouse border. Overwinter at a temperature of 7–10°C (45–50°F); admit as much light as possible and water freely during summer. Repot mature plants every second or third year in April; feed monthly from May to September.

Propagation. Take cuttings, 3–4 in. long, of lateral shoots of half-ripened wood with a heel from June to August; insert the cuttings in equal parts (by volume) peat and sand at a bottom heat of 18–21°C (64–70°F).

Alternatively, sow seeds in pans of John Innes seed compost in March; germinate at a temperature of 16–18°C (61–64°F); prick off the seedlings into pots or boxes, when large enough to handle. Pot singly into 3 in. pots and overwinter at a temperature of 7°C (45°F). Pot on into 5 in. pots the following March and grow on for a further year before planting out.

Pruning. None required.

Pests and diseases. Generally trouble-free.

Callistephus chinensis 'Chater's Erfurt'

Callistephus
China aster. *Compositae*

CALLISTEPHUS CHINENSIS

A single species of half-hardy annual which ha given rise to a large number of varieties. These ar popular plants for growing in borders, in pots an for cutting. To help prevent wilt disease, do no grow china asters in the same ground for tw consecutive years.

C. chinensis. China and Japan. Height 18 in. planting distance 12 in. An erect plant with ovate mid-green, coarsely toothed leaves. The daisy like flowers are solitary and dark purple. Th species has been superseded by its varieties which flower from July to the first frosts. The are in shades of pink, red, purple and white. Th following are recommended:

Ball Type strain, height 2½ ft, planting distanc 18 in. (mid-season), is wilt-resistant and ideal fo cutting, with long, clean stems and fully double incurved flowers. Bouquet Powder Puffs strain height 18–24 in., planting distance 18 in. (earl to mid-season), is wilt and weather-resistant, an bears large, fully double flowers with quille centres in a good range of colours. 'Miss Europe is a clear pink form.

Chrysanthemum Flowered strain, height 9–1 in., planting distance 12 in. (early), is compac and ideal for formal bedding, with tight-petalled

Callistemon citrinus

Callistephus chinensis
Bouquet Powder Puffs

Callistephus chinensis
'Miss Europe'

Callistephus chinensis 'Fire Devil'

Callistephus chinensis
Lilliput (mixed)

Callistephus chinensis Ostrich
Plume (mixed)

Callistephus chinensis
Peony Flowered

Callistephus chinensis 'Pirette'

...lly double flowers; 'Chater's Erfurt' is a good ...ose-pink form. Duchess strain, height 24 in., ...lanting distance 18 in. (late-flowering), is a ...ecently introduced wilt-resistant type with ...hick, incurving petals. The flowers are heavy and ...ome support may be needed; the form 'Fire ...Devil' has bright red flowers.

Giants of California strain, height 2½ ft. ...lanting distance 24 in. (mid to late-season), is of ...preading habit, with large ruffled flowers. ...illiput strain, height 15 in., planting distance 12 ...n. (mid-season), forms pyramidal plants with a ...nass of quilled, button-like flowers. It is ...veather-resistant and available in a wide range of ...olours, ideal for cutting and for growing in pots.

Ostrich Plume strain, height 15 in., planting ...istance 18 in. (early), is the best-known double ...ariety, with large, ostrich-feather flowers; wilt-...esistant. This is a popular bedding variety in a ...ull range of colours.

Peony Flowered strain, height 24 in., planting ...istance 15–18 in., has shell-pink flowers with ...road and incurving petals.

Pompon strain, height 15 in., planting distance ...2 in. (mid-season), is weather-resistant and has ...eat, button-like flowers, some with contrasting ...entres; they are excellent for cutting. ...Pirette' is cerise-scarlet with a white centre.

Queen of the Market strain, height 15 in., ...lanting distance 12 in. (early), is compact and ...opular for cutting and for growing in pots. It has ...arge, fully double flowers. Single Sinensis strain, ...eight 24 in., planting distance 18 in. (mid-...eason), is wilt-resistant and bears single flowers ...ith clear yellow central discs and long, graceful ...urrounding petals.

'Unicum Mixed' (spider aster), height 24 in., ...lanting distance 18 in. (mid-season), has large ...ouble flowers with slender quilled petals.

'Waldersee Mixed', height 12 in., planting distance 9 in. (early or mid-season), is an upright bushy plant carrying a profusion of small, star-shaped flowers.

Cultivation. A medium loam is best, although any well-drained garden soil gives reasonable results. Choose an open, sunny position, with protection from the wind for the large-flowered varieties. The latter may require light staking. Removal of the first dead flowers improves the flowers carried on side-shoots.

Plants from a late sowing in May or June can be placed in 5 in. pots of John Innes potting compost No. 2, grown in frames during the summer and flowered in a frost-free greenhouse from October to December.

Propagation. Sow the seeds under glass in March, at a temperature of 16°C (61°F). Transplant the seedlings into boxes, grow them on, and then harden them off in a cold frame before planting out in May. For pot plants, sow in May or June.

Seeds may also be sown thinly in a cold frame in March or April and the seedlings planted out in May; or sown directly in the flowering site in April, and thinned to the required spacing.

Pests. APHIDS infest young plants and check growth. CATERPILLARS eat stems and leaves.

Diseases. CALLISTEPHUS WILT may attack plants, usually just as they are about to flower. A pinkish growth of fungus can often be found on the stems just above ground level.

CUCUMBER MOSAIC VIRUS causes a yellow mottling or complete CHLOROSIS of the leaves. The flowers are small, misshapen and more numerous than is usual on a healthy plant.

TOMATO SPOTTED WILT VIRUS distorts the central leaves, giving the plant a rosetted habit; dark green mottling or streaking develops on the leaves. The flowers are distorted.

Calluna vulgaris 'Foxii Nana'

Calluna vulgaris 'Gold Haze'

Calluna vulgaris 'Hammondii'

Calluna vulgaris 'Peter Sparkes'

Caltha palustris 'Alba'

FOOT and ROOT ROT due to several different fungi, including RHIZOCTONIA and BLACK ROOT ROT fungus, may cause the collapse of seedlings or more mature plants. The tissues at ground level may be blackened and shrunken.

Calluna

Ling, heather. *Ericaceae*

A genus containing only one hardy evergreen species, but with hundreds of named varieties. These are suitable as specimen plants or for ground cover, and may also be used for cut flowers. All are easy to grow in any but limy soils.

C. vulgaris. N.W. Europe, naturalised in E. United States. Height and spread vary from 3 in. to 2½ ft. The scale-like stubby leaves range in colour from green and grey through shades of orange and red. Flowering period extends from July to November, or later, depending on the variety, and most remain in flower for at least two months. Single or double flowers, in shades of white, pink or purple, are arranged in terminal spikes that may be 12 in. or more long.

Unless otherwise stated, the following varieties have heights and spreads of 12–18 in., mid-green leaves and bear single flowers from August to September.

'Alba Plena', white double flowers; 'Alba Pumila', the smallest white-flowering ling; 'Alba Rigida', prostrate with stiff branches, white flowers; 'Barnett Anley', thick spikes of petunia-purple flowers; 'Beoley Gold', golden-yellow leaves, white flowers; 'Blaze-away', golden foliage turning red in winter, purple flowers.

'Co. Wicklow' (height 9 in.), compact with shell-pink double flowers; 'Elsie Purnell' (height 24 in.), strong racemes of silver-pink double flowers; 'Foxii Nana', compact mounds of mid-green leaves, flowers are rarely produced; 'Golden Feather', heavily branched, golden to orange feathery foliage, purple flowers.

'Gold Haze' (height 24 in. or more), yellow leaves and massed white flowers; 'Hammondii', dark green leaves, white flowers; 'H. E. Beale', double pink flowers; 'Hirsuta Typica' (height 9 in.), silver-grey leaves, mauve flowers; 'J. H. Hamilton' (height 6–8 in.), double pink flowers; 'Joan Sparkes' (height 9 in.), double purple flower racemes.

'Mrs Ronald Gray', prostrate with purple flowers, useful as ground cover; 'Peter Sparkes', similar to 'H. E. Beale', but with deeper pink flowers; 'Robert Chapman', an outstanding foliage variety with gold, orange and red-tinted leaves and purple flowers; 'Ruth Sparkes', compact, with yellow leaves and double white flowers; 'Sister Anne', syn. 'Hirsuta Compressa' (height 6 in.), compact with grey-green leaves, purple flowers.

Cultivation, propagation, pruning: see entry under HEATHS AND HEATHERS.

Pests. Generally trouble-free.

Diseases. HEATHER DIE-BACK is caused by a fungus and shows first as a grey discoloration of the foliage. This is followed by the death of some or all of the shoots.

HONEY FUNGUS often attacks callunas.

Caltha

Marsh marigold, kingcup.
Ranunculaceae

CALTHA PALUSTRIS

A genus of 20 species of hardy herbaceous perennials that are suitable for growing in marshy ground, around pool margins or in shallow water. Most are free flowering, providing a splendid display in spring. The apparent petals of the flowers are, in fact, petaloid sepals.

C. leptosepala. N. America. Height 6–8 in. planting distance 9–12 in. A scarce species, less vigorous than the others and best sited just above water level. The rounded or heart-shaped light green leaves are held in an upright position. Star-like flowers, about 1 in. across, with narrow silver-white sepals surrounding yellow stamens, appear in April and May.

C. palustris. Europe, including Great Britain. Water depth up to 6 in.; height 12–15 in. planting distance 9–12 in. The deep green rounded leaves, lightly toothed at the edges, sometimes have a purple sheen. Cup-shaped flowers, 1 in. across and varying from light to deep golden-yellow, are borne in profusion in April and May.

The variety 'Alba', from the Himalayas, is smaller than the type; it is less free-flowering and does not grow so well in water. The flowers are white and flat, with yellow stamens. They appear in April and May, and again in autumn.

The garden variety 'Plena' is one of the showiest water or waterside plants. It is smaller than the type, but planted in groups it provides a fine display in April. Short branching stems bear numerous fully double flowers which have several rows of deep yellow petals. The green centres eventually turn gold. This variety will grow in water up to 6 in. deep but usually does better with the crown barely submerged.

C. polypetala. Caucasus, Turkey. Water depth up to 6 in.; height up to 24 in.; planting distance 12–18 in. This species has stems sprawling over an area 2–3 ft across after a few seasons, and is especially suitable for a large pool. In a small ornamental pool allow one plant to a 10–12 in. container or to 1 sq. ft of marginal shelf; for lakeside planting, space 18 in. apart.

The deep green leaves are almost heart-shaped and thick stems support saucer-shaped deep golden-yellow flowers, 2 in. across. After flowering in April and May, the flower stems become increasingly decumbent, rooting at the nodes.

Cultivation. Plant from March to September. *C. leptosepala* requires slightly acid soil with a high humus content, in sun or light shade. Keep the plants cool and moist at all times. The other species and varieties thrive in loamy soil, neutral or slightly acid, in sun or partial shade. If planted above water level the ground must be kept continuously moist. For plants that will grow in water, use containers at least 6 in. deep.

The leaves of most plants deteriorate in late summer and may be removed if unsightly.

Propagation. Divide and replant the roots in May or early June after flowering. Lift the plants and wash the soil from their roots. The crowns usually part easily into separate pieces; shorten the roots on these to make planting easier. Where the stems of *C. polypetala* have rooted into the surrounding soil, cut through on either side of the newly formed plant and transplant.

Except on *C. palustris* 'Plena', seeds are plentifully produced. Sow seeds when ripe, during summer or the following March, in plain loam or John Innes seed compost. Stand the pots or boxes in water in a lightly shaded cold frame. When large enough to handle, prick out the seedlings into deeper boxes of soil; immerse in water and grow on until they are ready to plant out, the following September or October.

Pests. Generally trouble-free.

Diseases. Two different RUST fungi may develop on *C. palustris*. These show in spring as small yellow spots with a white halo. They appear on the undersides of the leaves as elongated swellings on the stems, or grouped in scattered rounded clusters with irregular rims on the lower leaf surfaces or leaf stalks. Later, small scattered spots erupt to show brown powdery spores.

Camassia

Quamash. *Liliaceae*

CAMASSIA CUSICKII

A genus of five or six species of bulbs. The genus name and the common name are derived from the American-Indian word for one of the species, which is used as a food. All species are hardy as garden plants and can be left to flower year after year. They provide early splashes of blue in perennial borders or among widely spaced dwarf shrubs. The leaves of all the species described are strap-shaped, pointed and mid-green. The flowers are star-shaped and borne in terminal racemes during June and July.

C. cusickii. N.W. United States. Height 3–4 ft; planting distance 9 in. The tall flower stem carries pale lavender flowers, 1½ in. across. The bulbs weigh up to ½ lb. each and multiply freely.

C. esculenta: see *C. quamash*

C. fraseri: see *C. scilloides*

C. howellii. Oregon. Height 24 in.; planting distance 4–6 in. The stout flower stem bears many pale purple, 1 in. wide flowers, which open at midday.

C. leichtlinii. Oregon. Height 3 ft; planting distance 6 in. One of the best species, with erect stems and spires of 1½ in. white or blue flowers. *C. l.* 'Atrocoerulea' is deep blue-purple.

C. quamash, syn. *C. esculenta.* Western Canada to California. Height 2½ ft; planting distance 4–6 in. Large, edible bulbs. The top 4–8 in. of the flower stems are thickly covered with 1–1½ in. wide flowers ranging in colour from white to purple and blue. A variable species, with several sub-species and named varieties.

C. scilloides, syn. *C. fraseri.* Central U.S.A. Height 12–18 in.; planting distance 4–6 in. Oval bulbs produce pale blue flowers, 1 in. across.

Cultivation. Camassias grow best in heavy, moist soils which do not dry out during the spring and early summer. Plant in September or October, 3–4 in. deep, and leave for several years until they become crowded. Remove dead flower heads unless seeds are required for increasing stock.

Propagation. In September, remove the offsets produced on the main bulbs and replant them immediately. These will grow on to flower in one to three years, depending on their size.

The seeds ripen during the summer. Sow at once in a frame or pot, keeping the seed compost moist at all times. Plant out the seedling bulbs in a nursery bed in the autumn of the following year. The bulbs take from three to five years to reach flowering size.

Pests and diseases. Generally trouble-free.

Camellia

Theaceae

A genus of 82 species of generally hardy evergreen trees and shrubs. They are native to India, China and Japan and are eminently suitable for outdoor cultivation, in greenhouse borders or as pot plants. They are easily grown shrubs in lime-free soil.

Camellias are among the most popular evergreen shrubs, valued for their handsome, usually glossy foliage and for their cup or bowl-shaped flowers. These may be single, semi-double or double, and come in a wide range of shades of white, pink and red in late winter or spring. There are a number of varieties in cultivation of which the double forms are the most popular

C. 'Cornish Snow'. Height and spread 8–10 ft. This hybrid between *C. cuspidata* and *C. saluenensis* is a graceful shrub with slender arching growths. The glossy, rich green leaves are elliptic, tapering to a point; they are tinged with purple when young. The almost stemless flowers, 1–1½ in. across, are pink in bud and open white with yellow stamens. They are freely borne along the branches from February to April. Hardy in a sheltered position in most of Britain.

CAMELLIA JAPONICA

C. japonica (common camellia). Japan, Korea. Height and spread 6–12 ft. The glossy, dark green, leathery leaves are normally broadly ovate,

Caltha palustris 'Plena'

Camassia leichtlinii 'Atrocoerulea'

Camassia quamash

Camellia japonica 'C. M. Wilson'

Camellia japonica 'Adolphe Audusson'

Camellia japonica 'Donckelarii'

Camellia japonica 'Contessa Lavinia Maggi'

Camellia japonica 'Jupiter'

tapering to a small point. The flowers, which are borne at the ends of the branchlets, vary in colour from white through pink to red and purple. They also vary in size from 3 to 5 in. across, occasionally larger. They are generally divided into the following categories: single, semi-double, anemone-flowered, paeony-flowered, double, and formal double with numerous small, neatly overlapping petals.

This species was formerly considered to be suitable only as a greenhouse plant. It is, however, generally hardy, but as it comes into flower as early as February and continues into May, the flowers are easily damaged by frost. In cold districts it is advisable to grow it in a cold greenhouse. The white and pink-flowered varieties are generally more susceptible to frost damage than the red.

Among the numerous varieties the following are recommended: 'Adolphe Audusson', of erect habit with semi-double, 5 in. wide, crimson-scarlet flowers with golden stamens, early; 'Alba Simplex', single white flowers opening flat, with conspicuous yellow stamens, mid-season; 'Anemonaeflora', dark crimson flowers of anemone form, mid-season; 'Arejishi', of upright habit, with long, narrow leaves and dark salmon-rose flowers of paeony form, early.

'Chandleri', bright red flowers with an occasional white blotch, semi-double to anemone form, mid-season; 'C. M. Wilson', light pink flowers of anemone form, early to mid-season; 'Contessa Lavinia Maggi', formal double, white flowers flushed with pink and streaked with crimson, mid-season.

'Donckelarii', semi-double, red flowers often marbled white, mid-season; 'Elegans', of slow-spreading habit, with rose-pink flowers, 5 in. across, of anemone to paeony form, early to

mid-season; 'Fred Sander', of upright habit, with semi-double, crimson flowers with fimbriated and curled petals, mid-season; 'Furoan', single soft pink with yellow stamens, mid-season.

'Gloire de Nantes', of erect habit, with large semi-double, rose-pink flowers, early to mid-season; 'Jupiter', of vigorous erect growth, with carmine flowers, varying from single to semi-double; 'Kelvingtoniana', large semi-double to loose paeony-form flowers of crimson, striped and blotched white, mid-season or late.

'Lady Buller': see 'Nagasaki'; 'Lady Clare', of vigorous, but low and pendulous growth, with large, semi-double, rose-pink flowers, early to mid-season; 'Lady Vansittart', wavy-margined leaves and semi-double flowers with wavy-edged, white petals, striped rose-pink, mid to late season; 'Magnoliaeflora', of slow compact growth, with semi-double, palest blush-pink flowers, best grown under glass, mid-season.

'Mathotiana', vigorous shrub with double rose-formed red flowers; this hybrid and its forms are best grown under glass, mid to late season. 'Mathotiana Alba', white flowers; 'Mathotiana Rosea', clear pink; 'Mathotiana Rubra', rose-red to purple; 'Mathotiana Supreme', rose-red, suitable for growing in the open.

'Nagasaki' syn. 'Lady Buller', of slow-spreading habit, large, semi-double, rose-red flowers, flecked white, mid-season; 'Nobilissima', white flowers, of paeony form, with yellow shading, best grown under glass, early; 'Professor Charles S. Sargent', of upright, compact habit with dark red flowers of full paeony form, mid-season; 'White Swan', single, pure white flowers with a boss of golden stamens.

C. × 'Leonard Messel'. Height 8–15 ft, spread 5–10 ft. This hybrid between *C. reticulata* and *C.* × *williamsii* 'Mary Christian' is a free-flowering and hardy shrub in southern gardens. The leathery, glossy, dark green leaves are oblong. Semi-double, bright rose-pink flowers, 4–5 in. across with prominent yellow stamens, are borne in March and April.

C. reticulata. W. China. Height 10–15 ft; spread 8–12 ft. A shrub or small tree of open, lax habit with leathery, dark green, broadly elliptic and reticulate leaves which are variable in size. The single flowers, 6 in. wide, are soft rose or pink in the wild form and deeper pink to turkey-red in the garden forms; they are borne from February to April.

The wild form is half-hardy but does well in the south-west, especially if grown against a wall. It is variable in flower. In cultivation, the species is generally represented by named varieties which include the following.

'Captain Rawes', syn. *C. r. semiplena,* with semi-double turkey-red flowers, 8 in. across, and 'Robert Fortune', syn. *C. r. flore-pleno,* with double rose-red flowers, are two beautiful and early-flowering shrubs. They can be grown in a cool greenhouse or as wall shrubs in the south; they were introduced to Britain long before the wild species was known. 'Mary Williams' is a selected seedling of *C. reticulata*; it has large, single, deep pink flowers and golden stamens.

Several other garden forms have been imported from China via America since the Second World War. They have large semi-double or double flowers and appear unsuitable for cultivation outdoors. Recommended forms for growing in a cool greenhouse include: 'Buddha' (height 15 ft), of weeping habit, with single to semi-double, rose-pink flowers; 'Noble Pearl' (height 6–8 ft), of compact habit, with semi-double, turkey-red flowers similar to those of 'Captain Rawes'; 'Shot Silk' (height 15 ft), of stiff, upright habit, with large semi-double flowers with wavy, brilliant pink petals.

C. saluenensis. W. China. Height 10–15 ft; spread 6–12 ft. A much-branched, freely flowering shrub of upright or spreading habit. The deep green reticulate leaves are oblong to elliptic, toothed and leathery. Single flowers, 1–2 in. wide with conspicuous yellow stamens, appear in March and April. They vary in colour from white to deep rose. The species is hardy, except in cold, exposed areas, but should be given the shelter of a wall. It is one of the parents of *C. × williamsii.*

C. sasanqua. China. Height and spread 10–15 ft. A bushy shrub or small tree with thin, leathery, dark green and elliptic or oblong-elliptic leaves. The flowers are 1–2 in. wide and generally single. They vary in colour from white to rose-pink and are borne from November to February. The species requires more sun than is usually available in winter to produce abundant flowers.

The variety 'Narumi-Gata' can often be brought to flower in the south if planted in a sunny position against a sheltered wall. The leaves are glossy green, and the sweet-scented, single, white flowers open from pink buds in November. Other varieties which may succeed in the south include: 'Crimson King', with mahogany-red fragrant flowers; 'Duff Alan', with single, white flowers; 'Hugh Evans', with deep pink, scented flowers; and 'Rosea Plena', with double, pink flowers.

Camellia japonica 'Furoan'

C. × williamsii. Height 6–8 ft; spread 4–6 ft. This outstanding group of hybrids between *C. saluenensis* and *C. japonica* was originally raised in Cornwall. They are generally hardy in woodland conditions or as wall shrubs. The glossy foliage resembles that of *C. japonica.* Flowers are freely produced even on small plants and these, unlike other camellia varieties, are shed as they fade. The flowers, generally 2–3 in. across, vary from single, with prominent yellow stamens, to semi-double, and range in colour from white and pale shell-pink to rich rose-purple. Flowering begins in November and continues to April.

Varieties include: 'Caerhays', of upright habit, bright mauve-pink, semi-double; 'Charles Michael', single, blush-pink, funnel-shaped; 'Citation', pale pink, semi-double; 'Coppelia', single, flat, pale pink; 'Donation', of upright almost tree-like habit, with semi-double, silver-pink flowers, up to 4 in. across, one of the finest of the camellias.

'Francis Hanger', of erect habit, with single white blooms; 'Hiraethlyn', of upright habit, pale pink, single, funnel shaped flowers; 'J. C. Williams', one of the original seedlings, of spreading growth, with matt-green leaves and single blush-pink flowers and golden stamens.

'Mary Christian', of erect habit, with single, bright pink flowers; 'November Pink', of bushy habit, bright pink, single flowers from November to March; 'St Ewe', of upright habit, single, bright purple-pink, funnel-shaped flowers.

C. × 'Salutation'. Height 6–8 ft; spread 4–6 ft. A hybrid of *C. saluenensis* and *C. reticulata* 'Captain Rawes', with ovate, slightly glossy, mid to deep green leaves. Semi-double, rose-pink flowers, 3–4 in. across, are borne from February to April. This shrub is best grown against a wall in the open or in a cool greenhouse.

Camellia japonica 'Kelvingtoniana'

Camellia japonica 'White Swan'

Camellia japonica 'Mathotiana'

Camellia japonica 'Lady Vansittart'

Camellia × 'Leonard Messel'

Camellia reticulata 'Mary Williams'

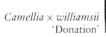

Camellia × *williamsii* 'Donation'

Cultivation. Camellias are easily grown in any good, lime-free soil; light soils should be enriched with leaf-mould. They give the best results in a position with a westerly or sheltered northerly aspect, against a wall, or in woodland where the high canopy of trees will give them protection from frost and early-morning sun. Plant in September and October or in March and April. In an east-facing position the morning sun after frost may damage the blooms. Camellias thrive in sun, provided they have a cool root run, and a southern aspect should therefore be avoided.

They do not tolerate windy and exposed positions or waterlogged conditions. Young plants may need staking until they are well established. In April, give a good mulch, about 2 in. deep, of old farmyard manure, leaf-mould or a lime-free compost.

Dead-head all camellias, with the exception of C. × *williamsii*, after flowering.

Early-flowering varieties in particular are best grown in 8–12 in. pots and small tubs containing a compost of 4 parts lime-free loam, 2 parts peat or leaf-mould, 1 part coarse sand (parts by volume) and 4 oz. of bone-meal per bushel. Stand the pots or tubs outdoors in a sheltered, partially shaded position from May to October, then bring into a cold greenhouse and maintain a temperature of 4–7°C (40–45°F) until May.

If earlier flowers are wanted under glass, increase the temperature by 5°C (10°F) from early December.

Camellias may also be grown under glass throughout the year, planted out in the border.

Propagation. Take cuttings, 3–4 in. long, of half-ripe lateral shoots from June to August; root the cuttings in equal parts (by volume) peat and sand at a bottom heat of 13–16°C (55–61°F). C. *reticulata* and its varieties do not root easily, although they may succeed under mist propagation. Layering is the best method.

To obtain large numbers of plants take leaf-bud cuttings from June to August and root in boxes under the same conditions as recommended for cuttings.

Alternatively, layer large specimens in September; the layers should be sufficiently rooted to be separated about 18 months later.

Pruning. None required, but straggly shoots may be shortened in April.

Pests. Outdoors, BIRDS, particularly blue-tits, may damage the flowers.

Under glass, SCALE INSECTS and APHIDS infest leaves and buds, making the foliage sticky and encouraging sooty moulds.

MEALY BUGS often infest stems and buds, producing conspicuous tufts of white waxy wool.

Diseases. BUD DROP is usually due to too dry soil conditions or frost damage.

FROST DAMAGE causes a distortion of the leaves and browning of the buds.

HONEY FUNGUS occasionally causes the rapid death of the shrubs.

OEDEMA shows on the leaves as corky growths.

PHYSIOLOGICAL DISORDERS of various types occur: cold night temperatures may cause a bronzing of the leaves; too alkaline soil conditions cause small dark brown or black spots to develop on the leaves, which may be a poor shade of green, and slightly puckered round the spots.

Campanula

Bellflower. *Campanulaceae*

A genus of 300 species of hardy and half-hardy annuals, biennials and herbaceous perennials and sub-shrubs. Of the species described, two are biennials, the others perennials and, unless otherwise stated, all are hardy.

They are suitable plants for growing in borders or rock gardens or for edging paths and borders. They are most effective when grown in bold groups of one variety, and several are good for cut flowers. The biennials may also be used in bedding schemes or grown as spring-flowering pot plants. C. *isophylla* makes a good plant for the home or a cool greenhouse.

In the following descriptions, planting distances are given for species and varieties usually grown in groups. The term 'spread' applies to the annual surface spread of plants grown as specimens on rock gardens or used for edging.

CAMPANULA CARPATICA

There are two distinct basic flower forms in this genus: star-like, as in C. *poscharskyana* and C. *garganica*; and bell-shaped, ranging from the wide bells of C. *carpatica* to the tubular or bottle-shaped flowers of C. *zoysii*.

C. **alliariifolia.** Caucasus, Asia Minor. Height 18–24 in.; planting distance 12 in. The leaves of this perennial species are heart-shaped and grey-green. Spikes of nodding, bell-like, cream-white flowers, 2 in. long, are produced in June and July. The variety 'Ivory Bells' has flowers that are slightly larger.

C. **allionii.** French Alps, Piedmont. Height 2–3 in.; spread 6 in. This dwarf perennial is not an easy plant to cultivate; it will flourish only in scree conditions or in an alpine house. It has lanceolate mid-green leaves; single, pale purple, bell-shaped flowers, 1–1½ in. long, open from early June to July. This plant increases by underground stolons.

C. **arvatica.** N. Spain. Height 2 in.; spread 12 in. A dwarf perennial species with mid-green leaves that are rounded and heart-shaped at the base of the plant, ovate and shallowly toothed on the trailing stems. It bears star-like blue flowers, 1 in. wide, in July. 'Alba' has white flowers.

C. **aucheri.** E. Caucasus. Height 2 in.; spread 4 in. This dwarf, tufted perennial has oblong or ovate, crenately toothed, mid-green leaves. It is conspicuous for its 1 in. long, deep purple, bell-like flowers.

C. **barbata.** European Alps, Norway. Height 3–18 in.; spread 6–12 in. A dwarf perennial forming a cluster of rosettes each producing one stem bearing a few lanceolate mid-green leaves. One-sided, sparsely flowered panicles appear in June. The nodding bell-shaped flowers, 1–1½ in. long and with long woolly hairs protruding from

Camellia reticulata 'Shot Silk'

Camellia sasanqua

Camellia × *williamsii* 'J. C. Williams'

Campanula alliariifolia

Campanula allionii

Campanula arvatica 'Alba'

Campanula aucheri

Campanula carpatica

their mouths, vary from blue-purple to white.
C. × burghaltii. Height 18–24 in.; planting
distance 9–12 in. This perennial border hybrid
has ovate mid-green leaves which are formed in
tufts. The bell-shaped, blue-grey flowers, 2–2½
in. long and deep purple in bud, are drooping;
they are borne on wiry stems in June.
C. carpatica. Carpathian Mountains. Height
9–12 in.; planting distance and spread 12–15 in.
A perennial species suitable for the front of a
border or for a large rock garden. It is clump-
forming, with ovate-cordate, toothed, mid-green
leaves. The cup-shaped flowers are 1–1⅓ in. wide
and vary from shades of blue and purple to
white. They are produced in July and August.

There are several named forms including
'Ditton Blue' (6 in. high), indigo-blue; 'Isobel'
(9 in. high), bright violet; 'Turbinata' a more
compact form with distinctive grey hairy foliage; and 'White Star' (12 in. high), pure white.
C. cochlearifolia, syn. **C. pusilla.** European Alps.
Height 4–6 in.; spread 12 in. This dwarf perennial species is one of the most easily grown
campanulas. The thin roots spread freely, producing a mat of small tufts of round mid-green
shallowly toothed leaves. Wiry stems carry bell-
shaped flowers, ½ in. long, from July to
September. The many colour forms of this free-
flowering species include 'Alba', pure white.
C. excisa. Switzerland. Height 3–4 in.; spread
6–12 in. A somewhat difficult species of dwarf
perennial best grown on a granite scree or in a
small trough. It has thin, wiry stems and spreads
by underground stolons. The leaves are linear
and mid-green. Each bell-shaped blue flower is
up to 1 in. long, and has a circular hole at the
junction of each petal lobe. The flowers are
borne in June.
C. garganica. Greece, Italy. Height 5–6 in.;
spread up to 12 in. This dwarf perennial species

has kidney-shaped mid-green leaves with
rounded teeth. The foliage is almost hidden
from May to September by a profusion of 6 in.
long panicles of star-shaped blue flowers.
'Hirsuta' has grey hairy leaves; 'W. H. Paine'
has rich blue flowers with a white eye.

CAMPANULA GARGANICA

C. glomerata. Europe, including Great Britain;
temperate Asia. Height 4–18 in.; spread 12–24
in. A variable species with ovate, toothed, mid-
green leaves. Dense heads of erect, purple bell-
like flowers, ¾–1 in. long, are borne on rigid
leafy stems from May to October.

C. g. acaulis is a dwarf, almost stemless form;
C. g. 'Alba' has white flowers on 15–18 in. tall
stems; **C. g. dahurica** the most common form in
cultivation, has rich violet flowers on 18–24 in.
tall stems.
C. grandis: see C. latiloba
C. isophylla. N. Italy. Height 6 in.; spread
12–18 in. A dwarf perennial, hardy only in the
south and west of England; elsewhere it is best
grown as a house plant or in a cold greenhouse.
The heart-shaped, toothed, mid-green leaves
grow on a tangle of stems from a thick rootstock. In August and September the foliage is
almost concealed by 1 in. wide star-shaped
blue flowers. 'Alba' is a white form; 'Mayii' has
variegated, slightly hairy leaves.
C. lactiflora. Caucasus. Height 3–5 ft; planting
distance 15–18 in. This perennial border plant

Campanula glomerata

Campanula isophylla

has light green ovate leaves. Light lavender-blue, open bell-shaped flowers, 1½ in. across, are borne on the branching stems in June and July.

Good varieties include: 'Loddon Anna' (up to 4 ft high), soft mushroom-pink; 'Pouffe' (9 in. high), spreading dome shape, with light lavender flowers, June to September; 'Pritchard's Variety' (3 ft high), deep lavender-blue flowers.

C. latifolia, syn. *C. macrantha* (giant bellflower). Europe, Asia. Height 4–5 ft; spread 15–18 in. The mid-green ovate-oblong leaves of this perennial border species are borne on long stalks. Tubular purple-blue flowers, 2¼ in. long, are carried on erect stems in July. 'Alba' is a white form; 'Brantwood' is rich violet-purple; and 'Gloaming' pastel-blue.

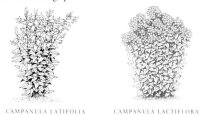

CAMPANULA LATIFOLIA   CAMPANULA LACTIFLORA

C. latiloba, syn. *C. grandis.* Siberia. Height 1–3 ft; planting distance 18 in. A perennial border plant with long, lanceolate, mid-green leaves having serrated edges. Broadly bell-shaped, violet-blue flowers, 2 in. across, are borne in June. 'Alba' is a white form; 'Percy Piper' (3 ft high) has deep blue, bowl-shaped flowers.

C. macrantha: see *C. latifolia*

C. medium (Canterbury bell). S. Europe. Height 1¼–3 ft; planting distance 12 in. A biennial species of sturdy upright habit. The long, bright green leaves are hairy and wavy-toothed. White, blue, pink or violet, bell-shaped flowers, 1–1½ in. long, are borne singly from May to July.

The most popular form is Calycanthema, the so-called cup and saucer variety, which produces bell-like flowers, 2–3 in. long, surrounded by a conspicuous calyx of the same colour. There are double and single-flowered strains. A recent introduction is the dwarf mixed strain 'Bells of Holland' (height 15 in.), which is of conical habit and has flowers 1¼ in. long.

C. morettiana. Dalmatia, S. Tyrol. Height 2–3 in.; spread 6 in. This is a half-hardy dwarf perennial species, best grown in an alpine house, in pans of tufa. It forms a tuft of heart-shaped mid-green leaves. Upright bell-shaped flowers, deep blue and 1 in. long, open in June.

C. muralis: see *C. portenschlagiana*

C. nitida: see *C. persicifolia* 'Planiflora'

C. persicifolia (peach-leaved campanula). Europe, Siberia. Height 1–3 ft; planting distance 12–15 in. An evergreen perennial border plant. The long, narrow, mid-green, leathery leaves grow in rosettes. Clusters of 1 in. wide saucer-shaped flowers are produced close to the main stem from June to August. They are white or in shades of blue and purple-blue. 'Telham Beauty' has large, rich blue flowers. 'Planiflora', syn. *C. nitida*, is a dwarf form, 9–12 in. high; 'Planiflora Alba' has white flowers.

CAMPANULA PERSICIFOLIA

C. portenschlagiana, syn. *C. muralis.* S. Europe. Height 6 in.; spread 18–24 in. This dwarf perennial is a long-lived, invasive species that

Campanula carpatica 'Ditton Blue'

Campanula cochlearifolia 'Alba'

Campanula garganica

Campanula lactiflora
'Pritchard's Variety'

Campanula latifolia

Campanula latiloba

does best in a lightly shaded position in wall and path crevices. The rounded heart-shaped, sharply toothed, mid-green leaves form a dense mass. Deep blue-purple, bell-shaped flowers, ¾ in. long, appear between June and November.

CAMPANULA PORTENSCHLAGIANA

C. poscharskyana. Dalmatia. Height up to 12 in.; spread 2–3 ft. A perennial even more rampant than *C. portenschlagiana.* The rounded, sharply toothed leaves are mid-green. Long sprays of lavender-blue, star-like flowers, 1 in. across, are borne from June to November.

C. pulla. E. Europe. Height 3–4 in.; spread 9–12 in. This dwarf perennial is best grown in partial shade. The leaves, which are ovate with rounded teeth, form broad tufts of shiny mid-green rosettes. Pendulous, rich purple, bell-shaped flowers, ¾ in. long, are borne in June.

C. × pulloides. Height 6 in.; spread 6–9 in. This hybrid perennial is similar to *C. pulla,* but of more vigorous growth and with hairy leaves.

C. pusilla: see *C. cochleariifolia*

C. pyramidalis (chimney bellflower). S. Europe. Height 4 ft; planting distance 18 in. A half-hardy border perennial usually grown as a biennial, as it often deteriorates in the second year of flowering. The leaves are almost heart-shaped and rich green. Blue or white bell-shaped flowers, 1–1½ in. long, are borne in broad spires during July. It may be grown as a May-flowering pot plant.

C. raineri. Italy, Switzerland. Height 3–4 in.; spread 4–6 in. This dwarf perennial forms tufts of grey-green leaves that are ovate to obovate and toothed. Solitary, bell-shaped, blue flowers, 1–1½ in. across, are produced in June.

C. rotundifolia (harebell; also known as bluebell in Scotland). N. Hemisphere. Height 6–12 in.; spread 9–18 in. This perennial species has rounded, heart-shaped basal leaves which are sharply toothed and mid-green; the sparse stem leaves are linear-lanceolate. The bell-shaped flowers, ¾ in. long, slate-blue to blue-purple, are carried from June to August.

'Alba', has pure white flowers.

C. × 'Stansfieldii'. Height 5 in.; spread 9–12 in. A perennial hybrid forming a spreading cushion of triangular-ovate, pale green, slightly hairy leaves. Violet bell-shaped flowers, 1 in. long, are borne in branched sprays from June to August.

C. zoysii. Italian Alps. Height 3 in.; spread 6 in. A dwarf perennial species, best grown in an alpine house. The numerous rosettes of ovate mid-green leaves arise from creeping stolons; the stem leaves are linear. The distinctive ½ in. long, light blue flowers, which appear in July, are oval in outline, pinched at the mouth, then expanded to form a puckered ruff.

Cultivation. Campanulas thrive in any well-drained, fertile garden soil, though *C. allionii* and *C. excisa* do better in lime-free soil. For the

Campanula persicifolia 'Planiflora Alba'

Campanula zoysii

most part, the species and their varieties grow equally well in sun or partial shade.

Plant between September and April. Avoid exposed sites for the taller varieties, which need the support of twiggy sticks. Remove faded flower spikes unless seeds are required; in the case of *C. persicifolia,* dead-heading encourages the growth of subsidiary flower spikes.

Rock-garden plants with soft or hairy leaves are best protected from winter damp by placing them in an alpine house or cold greenhouse, or by covering them with raised sheets of glass or open cloches. Protect the rosettes of *C. pyramidalis* with cloches in cold districts.

Indoors and in the alpine house, grow campanulas in 4–8 in. pans (depending on the vigour of the plant) of John Innes potting compost No. 1 to which has been added ⅓ part grit. *C. morettiana* may also be grown in tufa.

The biennials, *C. medium* and *C. pyramidalis,* may be flowered in pots under glass; lift young plants in September and pot in 6 in. and 8–10 in. containers respectively, filled with John Innes potting compost No. 2. Overwinter in a cold frame and move the plants into the greenhouse in February and grow on at 7–10°C (45–50°F).

Propagation. Sow seeds in October, March or April in pots or pans of seed compost, and place in a cold frame or greenhouse. When large enough to handle, prick off the seedlings into

ans or boxes. Transfer the smaller species to 3
n. pots of John Innes potting compost No. 1,
nd grow on until they are ready for planting
ut in March or April, September or October,
epending on the time of sowing. The biennials
nd taller herbaceous species should be lined out
n nursery rows and planted out in October.

Plants with more than a single crown can be
divided and replanted in October, March or
April; C. persicifolia hybrids are best increased
y this method as they do not breed true to type
om seeds.

Campanulas, with the exception of biennial
pecies, can also be propagated from 1–2 in.
uttings of non-flowering basal shoots taken in
April or May. Insert these in equal parts (by
olume) peat and sand in a cold frame. When
ooted, pot the cuttings individually into 3 in.
ots of John Innes potting compost No. 1 and
eat as advised for seedlings.

Pests. Serious damage may be caused to leaves
nd shoots by SLUGS and SNAILS.

FROGHOPPERS suck sap, producing 'cuckoo-
oit'; the infested shoots may wilt.

Diseases. Certain species, in particular C.
nedium and C. persicifolia, may be affected by a
LEAF SPOT fungus. This shows as irregularly
haped spots, up to $\frac{1}{2}$ in. across, coloured green-
rown with purple-brown edges.

RUST may develop on certain species, particu-
rly C. carpatica, C. lactiflora, C. persicifolia and
. trachelium; orange spore masses develop on
he leaves and may overwinter on the basal
aves of C. persicifolia.

SCLEROTINIA DISEASE attacks C. medium and
. pyramidalis and possibly other species when
rown under glass. The stems become dis-
oloured and subsequently collapse. If the stems
re cut open, numerous large black resting
odies are visible, embedded in a white fluffy
ungal growth.

TOMATO SPOTTED WILT VIRUS shows as yellow
ng spots and wavy lines on the leaves; the
lants are stunted.

---

ampanula, peach-leaved: see *Campanula persicifolia*
ampion: see Lychnis and Silene
ampion, moss: see *Silene acaulis*
ampion, sea: see *Silene maritima*

Campsis

Trumpet creeper, trumpet vine. *Bignoniaceae*

CAMPSIS RADICANS

genus of two species of deciduous climbing
hrubs, one hardy, the other not reliably so, and
oth of vigorous, somewhat vertical habit. They
re usually grown for display on walls, where
ney are self-clinging, on fences or on pergolas.

C. chinensis: see *C. grandiflora*
C. grandiflora, syn. *C. chinensis*. China. Height
up to 30 ft, given a warm site. The mid-green
leaves are pinnate. Trumpet-shaped flowers, 3 in.
long, and deep orange and red, are borne in
August and September. It is the less hardy of the
two species.
C. radicans. U.S.A. Height up to 40 ft, given a
warm site. This hardy species is more common
than *C. grandiflora*. The stems produce plenty of
self-clinging aerial roots. The light green
leaves are pinnate; scarlet and orange trumpet-
shaped flowers, up to 3 in. long and with wide,
spreading lobes, appear in August and September. They are more tubular and less wide at the
mouth than those of *C. grandiflora*.
C. × tagliabuana. This is a hybrid between *C.
grandiflora* and *C. radicans*. Height up to 30 ft.
The light green leaves are pinnate and opposite.
The finest variety is 'Madame Gallen', which is
hardy; in August and September it produces
salmon-red flowers the same size and shape as
those of *C. radicans*.
Cultivation. Plant between November and March
in well-drained soil, enriched with manure. All
plants need a sheltered site in full sun. Mulch the
roots and protect the growth with brushwood
until the plants are well established. Tie the
growths to supports until the aerial roots appear.
Propagation. Insert 3–4 in. cuttings of firm young
shoots in equal parts (by volume) peat and sand;
place on a mist propagation bench or in a
propagating frame at 16–21°C (61–70°F) during
July or August. Pot on and grow in a frost-free
greenhouse or frame.

Hardwood cuttings of *C. radicans* and *C. ×
tagliabuana*, 10–12 in. long and taken during
October or November, will root in a cold frame.

Root cuttings can be taken in March and
inserted in pots of equal parts (by volume) sand
and peat; place in a frame at a temperature of
13–16°C (55–61°F). Pot up during the summer
and overwinter in a cold greenhouse or frame.
Plant out in March.

To raise plants from seeds, sow under glass
during March in pans of seed compost at a
temperature of 10–13°C (50–55°F). Prick out the
seedlings singly into 3 in. pots and grow on in a
frame. Transfer to 5 in. pots and plunge in a
nursery bed. Support the young growths with
canes; plant out the following spring.

Alternatively, layer long branches in October
or November. They should have rooted by the
following autumn.
Pruning. Cut back newly planted specimens to
within 6 in. of ground level to encourage basal
growth. Hard-prune established plants in February, cutting back the previous year's shoots to
within a few inches of their bases.
Pests. APHIDS may infest young growth, causing
distortion and loss of flowers.

GLASSHOUSE RED SPIDER MITES may infest the
undersides of leaves.

SCALE INSECTS, particularly brown scale, form
rounded brown excrescences on the stems.
Diseases. BUD-DROP may occur, due to low
temperatures at night or dryness at the roots.

Canary creeper: see *Tropaeolum peregrinum*
Candytuft: see Iberis

Campanula medium
Calycanthema (mixed varieties)

Campanula portenschlagiana

Campsis radicans

Canna
Cannaceae

There are 55 species of these most attractive tender herbaceous plants from tropical and sub-tropical America. They are cultivated in greenhouses and conservatories, and may also be used in the open for summer bedding schemes. Their broad leaves and bright flowers provide a striking note among smaller plants. Although the species are rarely commercially available, several fine varieties which were bred from the best have taken their place and can be purchased under the general name of *C. hybrida*.

CANNA HYBRIDA

Canna hybrida 'President'

Canna hybrida 'Lucifer'

C. edulis. S. America, West Indies. Height 6 ft or more; planting distance 2–3 ft. A robust greenhouse perennial with large ovate-oblong leaves, deep green above, red-purple beneath. The leafy flower stems are strongly flushed with red-purple and bear terminal racemes of tubular flowers from June to September. Each flower is about 3 in. long, with pale red sepals, yellow petals and brick-red staminodes. Canna starch is obtained from the tuberous roots.

C. hybrida. Height up to 4 ft; planting distance 12–18 in. There are two main types: green-leaved and brown or purple-leaved. The broad leaves are ovate-lanceolate, 24 in. or more in length and up to 12 in. wide. The flowers are orange, red or rich yellow in colour, gladiolus-like in appearance and 2–3 in. long. The following varieties are recommended:

Green-leaved. 'Bonfire', 3 ft, orange-scarlet; 'Evening Star', 3 ft, carmine-pink; 'J. B. van der Schoot', 3 ft, yellow speckled with red; 'Orange Perfection', 2½ ft, soft orange; 'President', 3 ft, vivid scarlet.

Brown or purple-leaved. 'America', 3 ft, deep red; 'Di Bartolo', 3 ft, deep pink; 'Lucifer', 3–3½ ft, red with irregular yellow margins; 'Wyoming', 4½ ft, bronze-yellow.

Cultivation. Plant the fleshy rhizomes in pots or boxes in February or March, just covering them with rich, peaty compost. Place in a greenhouse at a minimum temperature of 16°C (61°F). If more than one shoot appears on a rhizome, divide the rhizome into sections, each with a shoot and some new roots, and pot into 4–5 in. pots, again using a rich, peaty compost. In April, move the growing plants into 6–7 in. pots or into tubs and grow on at a temperature of 13–16°C (55–61°F). In late May, tubs can be moved to a sunny, sheltered position outdoors.

Alternatively, set the plants outdoors in a sheltered bed or border, after all risk of frost has passed. Bring the plants under cover again before the autumn frosts.

Plants lifted from beds or borders should be partially dried before the leaves and roots are cut off in readiness for storing through the winter. Store in moist, but not wet, peat or leaf-mould in a frost-free place. If kept too dry, the rhizome will shrivel and die; if too wet, they will rot.

Propagation. Divide the rhizomes when shoots are visible, as described under CULTIVATION.

Cannas can be raised from seeds but do not come true to variety. The seed coats are hard, so either soak the seeds in warm water for 24 hours or file a small nick in each seed to allow water to enter. Sow during January or February, either in pans or boxes or singly in 3 in. pots. Use a peat compost and provide a minimum temperature of 21°C (70°F). When the seedlings are filling their pots or boxes with roots, pot on in the same way as plants raised from rhizomes.

Pests. The rhizomes may be eaten by SLUGS, LEATHERJACKETS and CUTWORMS.

Diseases. Generally trouble-free.

Cantaloupe melon: see Melon
Caper spurge: see *Euphorbia lathyrus*

Capsicum
Solanaceae

CAPSICUM

A genus of 50 species of half-hardy and tender annuals, short-lived perennials, evergreen and deciduous shrubs and sub-shrubs. Capsicums are chiefly grown for their glossy, round, ovoid or conical, brightly coloured fruits. They make decorative pot plants, and the large-fruiting varieties are popular for culinary purposes.

In warm sheltered areas in the south and west culinary varieties may be grown outdoors. Pot plants may be stood outside during the summer.

The pendent flowers measure ½–¾ in. across and are somewhat bowl-shaped with a central cone of yellow stamens. They are white to green-white and appear singly in the upper leaf axils from June to August.

C. annuum (red pepper, green pepper, chilli). Tropics. A variable, sub-shrubby, short-lived perennial species, usually grown as an annual. It has mid-green oblong to ovate leaves. Several varieties are in cultivation, differing mainly in the shape of the fruits, which may be erect or pendulous. They range from spherical through oblong to slenderly conical, some being twisted or wrinkled, and are red, yellow or green.

In cultivation, the species is generally represented by the following two forms, which may be grown outdoors, but do best under glass.

C. a. acuminatum. Height 1½–3 ft; planting distance 15–18 in. A shrubby perennial with red slenderly conical, often twisted fruits that measure 4–12 in. in length. This form includes the chilli, cayenne and paprika fruits, used in curries, pickles and sauces; the unripe fruits are

Capsicum annuum

sed in chilli vinegar. Recommended culinary
arieties include: 'Californian Wonder',
Cayenne Chilli' and 'World Beater'.

A number of decorative varieties, some of
which may be hybrids with *C. frutescens,* are
available: 'Christmas Greeting' (height 18 in.),
with cone-shaped fruits, 1–1½ in. long, ranging
om green, violet and yellow to red; 'Coral
orn' (height 7 in.), with slenderly conical,
omewhat twisted fruits; 'Fiesta' (height 9 in.), a
ushy plant with slenderly conical 2 in. long
uits that change colour from green through
ory to red; and 'The Rising Sun' (height 18 in.),
with globular tomato-like fruits.

C. a. grossum. Height 12–18 in.; planting
istance 15–18 in. This shrubby perennial is
milar in habit to *C. a. acuminatum,* but with
dged, almost oblong, blunt-pointed fruits 3–5
. long; they are generally used green but may
ventually ripen to red or yellow. Two popular
ulinary varieties are 'Bull-nosed Red' and
Bull-nosed Yellow'.

. *frutescens.* Tropics. Height 1½–6 ft; planting
istance 18–24 in. A bushy perennial species,
sually grown as an annual. The dwarf types are
uitable as pot plants, while the taller varieties
ay be grown outdoors. Branching stems carry
blong-ovate, slender-pointed leaves. The edible
uits are erect, generally bluntly conical,
though in the variety 'Baccatum' they are
pherical to shortly ovoid. They have an ex-
emely hot and acrid flavour; in Great Britain
is species and its varieties are mainly grown for
rnamental purposes.

'Chameleon' (height 12 in.) bears fruits that
hange from green to white, purple and finally
ed. The recently introduced 'Fips' (height 7 in.)
 compact; the fruits, borne well above the
oliage, turn from green to yellow and finally red.

'Friesdorfer' (height 3 ft) is a less common
ecorative variety with long, stiff stems bearing
onical red and yellow fruits. The fruiting stems
re attractive and long-lasting in water; they
hould be cut after frost has removed the leaves.
ultivation. Outdoors, grow culinary varieties of
. *annuum* and *C. frutescens* 'Friesdorfer' in
ertile, well-drained soil, enriched with well-
otted compost or manure. Plant in late May or
arly June, after danger of frost has passed, in a
heltered sunny position against a south wall.

The fruits should be ready for picking in
ugust or September and should be eaten fresh.

Decorative varieties of both species are best
rown indoors, in the greenhouse border or as pot
ants. Grow the dwarf forms in final 4–5 in. pots,
e taller varieties in 7–9 in. pots of John Innes
otting compost No. 2. Use canes for support of
ll varieties, and lightly shade the glass during
e hottest months.

Syringe the leaves daily during the flowering
eriod to assist fruit-setting. Give a dilute liquid
ed at ten-day intervals when the fruits first
ppear and until they show colour.
ropagation. Sow seeds in pots of seed compost
uring March, at a temperature of 15–18°C
9–64°F). When the seedlings are large enough
 handle, prick them out individually into 3 in.
ots of John Innes potting compost No. 1 and pot
 as necessary. Harden off outdoor plants in a
ld frame before planting out in May or June.

Pests. Infestations of GLASSHOUSE RED SPIDER
MITES may occur on the leaves, particularly on
plants under glass. A fine mottling on the upper
leaf surfaces is followed by bronzing of the
foliage, which falls.

CAPSID BUG cripples and distorts the growing
points and leaves.
Diseases. Generally trouble-free.

Caraway
Carum carvi. Umbelliferae

CARAWAY

This hardy biennial herb is used in cooking and
for flavouring.

Height 3 ft; planting distance 12 in. Europe.
An aromatic plant, with ferny, mid-green leaves,
similar to those of cow parsley; minute green
flowers are carried in umbels in June and July.

Dried caraway seeds are used for flavouring in
cakes and breads, salads and cheeses; they may
also be sprinkled on lamb and pork for roasting.
Commercially, caraway seeds are used to flavour
the liqueur Kümmel and several cordials; they
are also distilled for use in cosmetics.
Cultivation. These herbs thrive in any fertile,
well-drained soil, preferably in full sun. As the
plants are grown only to produce seeds they
should not be fed or given any top-dressing.
Propagation. For the largest plants, sow seeds in
September to secure a seed crop the following
year; alternatively, sow in March for a crop the
same year.

Sow seeds where the plants are to flower, in
shallow drills 12 in. apart, later thinning the
seedlings to 6 in. apart, and finally to 12 in. apart.
Harvesting and storing. When the seeds are ripe,
cut the plants at ground level and tie the stalks in
small bundles. Hang the bundles in a dry, airy
place, until the seeds are dry, when they will drop
off easily. Place a sheet of paper under the
bundles to catch the seeds.

A simple method of gathering large quantities
is to put the dried bundles in a canvas bag and
beat it with a stick. Put the seeds through a fine
sieve to remove the dust, and pick out any
remaining pieces of stalk by hand. For drying
methods, see also entry under HERBS.

Store the seeds in airtight jars.
Pests and diseases. Generally trouble-free.

Cardiocrinum
Giant lily. Liliaceae

A genus of three species of hardy bulbous
perennials, closely related to the genus *Lilium,*
but the bulbs die after flowering. These plants are
distinguished from true lilies in having dark

Capsicum annuum grossum

Capsicum annuum grossum

Caraway

Cardiocrinum giganteum

Carpenteria californica

Carpinus betulus (fruits)

green, broadly ovate, heart-shaped leaves, borne in rosettes at or near the base of the stems. The scented flowers are slenderly trumpet-shaped and carried on robust stems in a many-flowered terminal, spire-like raceme. They are followed by smooth, oblong-ovoid, pale green seed capsules that turn yellow.

C. cordatum. Japan. Height 4–6 ft; planting distance 3 ft. This species comes into growth early in the year, and the young shoots require protection from spring frosts. The young leaves are bronze-crimson, later turning dark green with a coppery lustre. The main basal leaves are arranged in a whorl-like rosette, 12–24 in. above ground. Cream-white flowers, up to 6 in. long, streaked with yellow and with purple-red markings within, are borne in large terminal racemes in August.

CARDIOCRINUM GIGANTEUM

C. giganteum. Himalayas, Tibet. Height 6–10 ft; planting distance 3–4 ft. This species is similar to *C. cordatum*, but is hardier, larger in all its parts and the leaves are arranged in a spiral from ground level to just below the first flower. The fragrant flowers, 6 in. or more long, are cream or green-white, streaked with purple or crimson-brown within the trumpet. The flowering period is July and August.

The variety *C. g. yunnanense* (height 7 ft) has pure white flowers with red markings; the foliage is bronze-green when young.

Cultivation. Cardiocrinums are monocarpic plants dying after flowering, but leaving behind small offset bulbs which will reach flowering size after three to five years. Plant mature bulbs in October, in moisture-retentive, but well-drained soil enriched with leaf-mould or well-rotted manure. Choose a sheltered site in light shade and set the bulbs with the nose just below soil level. Bulbs are sometimes offered in sets of four different sizes so that a continued flowering cycle can be established.

Water freely during dry spells and apply an annual mulch of well-rotted compost or manure in spring. Staking is not required.

Propagation. Remove the offsets in October and replant direct in the flowering site; they generally take three to five years to flower, depending on size and culture.

Alternatively, sow seeds when ripe, usually in October, in pots or pans of John Innes seed compost and place in a cold frame. When the seedlings are large enough to handle, prick off into a cold frame or a sheltered nursery bed outdoors. Grow on for three or four years before transplanting to the flowering site. Plants raised from seeds take up to seven years to reach flowering size.

Pests and diseases. Generally trouble-free.

Carnation: see *Dianthus caryophyllus*

Carpenteria
Philadelphaceae

CARPENTERIA CALIFORNICA

A genus of a single species. This is an almo— hardy evergreen shrub, grown chiefly for i— attractive flowers.

C. californica. California. Height up to 10 ft spread 6–8 ft. A bushy shrub with lanceola— leaves that are rich glossy green above an glaucous beneath. The single anemone-shaped scented flowers are glistening white; they are 2– in. across and are borne in June and July.

Cultivation. Carpenterias are tolerant of lime an— thrive in any good garden soil and in full sun. Th— plants need protection from cold winds in wint— and early spring, and are best grown against south or south-west wall. Plant in April or May.

Propagation. Sow seeds in March or April in par— of John Innes seed compost and germinate at temperature of 16–18°C (61–64°F). Prick o— into pans or boxes when seedlings are larg— enough to handle; later place in 3 in. pots of Joh— Innes potting compost No. 1 in a cold fram— Pot on as necessary into 4–5 in. pots during th— summer; overwinter the young plants in frost-free cold frame and plant out in May.

Pruning. None required; straggly shoots may l— shortened after flowering.

Pests and diseases. Generally trouble-free.

Carpinus
Hornbeam. *Betulaceae*

CARPINUS BETULUS 'PYRAMIDALIS'

A genus of 35 species of deciduous trees and, le— frequently, shrubs distributed throughout th— Northern Hemisphere. They make handsom— specimen trees and are excellent for hedgin— retaining their old leaves until the followi— spring. The flowers are borne in pendulou— separately sexed catkins, the male being yellov— green, up to 4 in. long, and the female green an— up to 2 in. long.

C. betulus (common hornbeam). Europe, inclu— ing Great Britain; Asia Minor. Height 15–25 f— spread 10–15 ft. A hardy, large-headed speci— with an attractive grey trunk. The mid-gree— ovate leaves are prominently veined and doubl— toothed. The catkins appear in April and Ma— and female catkins are followed by pendulo—

lusters of winged nutlets. This handsome tree makes an excellent hedge, similar to beech.

Numerous varieties include: 'Fastigiata', of pyramidal form; 'Incisa', with small, deeply toothed leaves; 'Purpurea', with purple leaves when young; 'Pyramidalis', a slow-growing, densely conical form useful as a specimen tree where space is limited.

C. caroliniana (American hornbeam). Eastern N. America. Height 15–20 ft; spread 10–15 ft. This graceful tree has fluted grey bark and carries ovate mid-green leaves that assume orange to red autumn tints. Catkins are borne in April and May and are followed by winged nuts.

C. japonica. Japan. Height 10–20 ft; spread 10–15 ft. A small tree or large shrub of spreading habit. The oblong mid-green leaves are prominently corrugated. Catkins in April and May are followed by winged nuts.

Cultivation. Plant from November to March in any ordinary garden soil and in a sunny or partially shaded position.

Plant hedges of *C. betulus* from October to March, spacing the young plants 15–20 in. apart. Fork in a general fertiliser prior to planting, at the rate of 4 oz. per sq. yd. The young hedging plants must never be allowed to dry out, and benefit from an annual mulch of leaf-mould, well-rotted manure or compost.

Propagation. Sow seeds in nursery rows outdoors in September and October; transplant the seedlings the following autumn to a nursery bed and grow on for three or four years before moving to permanent positions.

Pruning. None required. Hedges should be clipped annually in July, lightly to the required shape on young hedges, and fairly hard on established hedges.

Pests. Generally trouble-free.

Diseases. HONEY FUNGUS may cause the rapid death of trees.

Carrion flower: see Stapelia

Carrot

Daucus carota. Umbelliferae

A hardy biennial vegetable cultivated as an annual. It is grown for its orange-red tap-roots which are used mainly as a vegetable, but also raw in salads. By successive sowings in the open and by the use of cloches and frames, young tender carrots can be harvested throughout the year. Large, well-developed roots from a main-crop sowing may be stored for winter use.

VARIETIES
There are three main groups of carrots: short-rooted, with a cylindrical or almost spherical root; intermediate-rooted, with a medium-length, blunt-ended, cylindrical or tapering root; and long-rooted, with a long, tapering, sharply pointed root.

Short-rooted varieties are best used for an early or forced crop. They are ready for pulling about 14 weeks after sowing. Recommended varieties include 'Amsterdam Forcing', with slender, 5 in. long, cylindrical, coreless roots; 'French Forcing' is an almost spherical variety.

Intermediate-rooted varieties are larger and more slow-growing, suitable for outdoor sowing from early April onwards to provide the main crop. 'Autumn King', 'Favourite' and 'Redcored Chantenay' are reliable varieties.

Long-rooted varieties are grown as a late-maturing main crop; their perfectly symmetrical large roots also make them particularly suitable for exhibition purposes. 'New Red Intermediate' and 'St Valery' are outstanding, with large, well-coloured roots, excellent for storing for winter use.

Cultivation. Carrots grow best in a deep, light loam, in sun or partial shade, a position in full sun being advisable for early crops. Good crops of main-crop varieties can be grown on heavier, well-prepared soils. Dig the soil deeply in autumn and leave it rough through the winter for frost to break it down. No manure should be added as this may cause the roots to fork. Where possible, grow carrots on a plot that was well manured the previous season. Shortly before sowing, rake in a complete fertiliser at the rate of 4 oz. per sq. yd.

Make the first outdoor sowing in early March if soil and weather conditions are suitable. Cloches may be placed, about a month before sowing, where the drills are to be made, so that the soil is warmed up; leave the cloches in position until the seeds have germinated.

Draw ½ in. deep drills 9–12 in. apart and sow the seeds thinly, mixing them with dry sand or soil. Thin crowded seedlings, when large enough to handle, to 1 in. apart, thinning later to final 2–3 in. intervals.

Make successional sowings of early varieties at fortnightly intervals until the middle of April. From April until mid-July make fortnightly sowings of intermediate and long-rooted main-crop varieties. Sow the seeds in ½ in. deep drills, 12 in. apart, and thin the seedlings as they grow until they are 6 in. apart. Later thinnings are usually large enough for kitchen use.

Sow seeds of early-maturing varieties from October to January in a cold frame. Broadcast the seeds thinly or sow in rows 6 in. apart.

Harvesting and storing. Pull short-rooted early varieties as they are required, once they have reached the desired size. Harvesting can continue over several weeks.

Dig up main-crop roots from the middle of October. Use any split or damaged roots as soon as possible and store healthy roots for use through the winter. Clean off the soil and cut off the leaves about ½ in. above the crown; pack the roots in an outdoor clamp or in layers in deep boxes of sand, kept in a dry, cool, frost-proof shed or cellar.

Exhibition. Main-crop carrots grown for show purposes should be given special care. Bore holes about 2½ ft deep and 4 in. wide at the top, tapering to a point at the base. Space the holes 12 in. each way. Prepare a mixture of equal parts (by volume) fertile soil, leaf-mould and well-decayed manure. Pass this through a fine sieve and add ¼ lb. of bone-meal to every bushel of the mixture. Fill the holes with the planting mixture, pressing it down firmly with a stick, and sow three or four seeds in each hole. When the seedlings appear, remove the three weaker ones.

Carpinus betulus (flowers)

Carrot 'Amsterdam Forcing'

Carrot 'New Red Intermediate'

Keep the bed free of weeds and give an occasional thorough watering.

Pests. APHIDS infest the leaves, which become stunted, weakened and discoloured; these pests also transmit virus diseases.

Maggots of CARROT FLY tunnel into roots; the first indication of attack is a red discoloration of the foliage.

Diseases. The foliage of young seedlings may turn yellow and collapse due to DAMPING-OFF.

MOTLEY DWARF DISEASE is a virus disease which shows as a twisting of the petioles and CHLOROSIS of the foliage which later turns red. Affected plants are stunted and, on lifting, the root tips and root hairs will be seen to be dead.

SCLEROTINIA DISEASE may develop during the growing period or on stored roots. The roots are rapidly destroyed by a white fluffy fungus which later forms hard, black, resting bodies on the diseased tissues.

SOFT ROT due to a bacteria occurs in storage on injured roots, or where storage conditions are too damp. Affected roots are rapidly destroyed by a soft, watery rot.

SPLITTING of roots is due to an irregular supply of moisture in the soil.

VIOLET ROOT ROT shows as a violet or purple-coloured web of fungus threads over part of the roots, which may shrink.

Carrot 'Redcored Chantenay'

Caryopteris × *clandonensis*

Cassia corymbosa

Cartwheel flower: see *Heracleum mantegazzianum*
Carum carvi: see Caraway
Carum petroselinum: see Parsley

Caryopteris
Verbenaceae

CARYOPTERIS × CLANDONENSIS

A genus of 15 species of hardy and half-hardy deciduous shrubs, native to E. Asia. They are grown for their aromatic grey-green foliage and for their clusters of blue flowers, which appear in late summer and autumn. The species in cultivation are not strong growers, and have been superseded by hybrids which are hardier.

C. × *clandonensis.* Height and spread 2–4 ft. This hybrid between *C. incana* and *C. mongholica* is of bushy habit. The narrow grey-green leaves are aromatic and may be toothed or entire. Clusters, 1–2 in. wide, of bright blue, tubular flowers are borne in the leaf axils and at the ends of the shoots during August and September.

Named varieties include 'Ferndown', deep blue or mauve flowers; 'Heavenly Blue', of more erect, compact habit than the type, and with deeper blue flowers; 'Kew Blue', of compact habit, with rich blue flowers.

Cultivation. These shrubs will thrive in ordinary, well-drained garden soil; plant in September and October or in March and April in a sunny position; in cold areas they require the protection of a wall or a fence.

Propagation. Take cuttings, 3–4 in. long, of half-ripened lateral shoots in August or September; insert the cuttings in a cold frame in equal parts (by volume) peat and sand. The following spring pot the rooted cuttings singly into 3½ in. pots of John Innes potting compost No. 2. Plunge outdoors and set in permanent positions in September or October.

Pruning. Cut the previous year's growths hard back in March; strong growths should be pruned to young healthy buds, and weak stems may be cut to ground level or removed altogether.

Pests and diseases. Generally trouble-free.

Casaba melon: see Melon

Cassia
Leguminosae

CASSIA CORYMBOSA

A genus of more than 500 species, mainly tropical, of hardy annuals and perennials, hardy and half-hardy evergreen shrubs and trees. The following ornamental species require greenhouse cultivation, although *C. corymbosa* may be grown outdoors in the mildest areas.

C. australis. Australia. Height and spread up to 6 ft. A shrubby species with mid-green pinnate leaves, composed of 9–12 pairs of linear-oblong leaflets. The flat, five-petalled, saucer-shaped flowers are produced in May and June in axillary clusters of from three to six golden-yellow flowers, each 1 in. across.

C. corymbosa. Tropical America. Height and spread up to 6 ft. This shrubby species bears pinnate, pale to mid-green leaves composed of two or three pairs of ovate leaflets. The saucer-shaped flowers, 1–1¼ in. wide, are borne in axillary and terminal racemes of up to eight flowers. They are rich yellow and appear from August to September.

Cultivation. Grow cassias in John Innes potting compost No. 2 or 3; the plants require 8–12 in. pots, but will do better planted out in the greenhouse border. Admit as much light as possible and water freely during the growing period; water moderately in winter, keeping the plants just moist. Ventilate the greenhouse whenever the temperature exceeds 13°C (55°F). A temperature of 7°C (45°F) is sufficient during the winter months.

Repot the plants annually in March before new growth starts, and give a weak liquid feed at intervals of two weeks from May to September.

In mild areas, *C. corymbosa* may be grown in the open in well-drained garden soil against a south or west-facing wall.

Propagation. Sow seeds in March or April in pans of John Innes seed compost at a temperature of 16°C (61°F). Prick off the seedlings, when large enough to handle, into 3 in. pots of John Innes potting compost No. 2; pot on as necessary.

Alternatively, take cuttings, 3–4 in. long, of half-ripened wood with a heel in July or August; insert in equal parts (by volume) peat and sand in a propagating frame with a bottom heat of 16–18°C (61–64°F). Pot the rooted cuttings in 3 in. pots of John Innes potting compost No. 1 and overwinter at a temperature of 4–7°C (40–45°F). Pot on as necessary.

Pruning. Shorten the new growths by one-third to a half in March or April; to keep the shrubs within bounds prune all growths back to within 12–18 in. of ground level in March or April.

Pests. The root systems of pot plants may be infested by ROOT MEALY BUGS which cause wilting of the top growth.

Diseases. Generally trouble-free.

Cassiope
Ericaceae

A genus of 12 species of hardy evergreen, heath-like shrubs, native to the Arctic regions and mountains of the Northern Hemisphere. They are dwarf shrubby or mat-forming plants suitable for cool peaty soils on banks or rock gardens. They bear scale-like, overlapping leaves and solitary bell-shaped flowers on thin stems.

C. lycopodioides. N.E. Asia. Height 2–3 in.; spread 12–18 in. A prostrate shrub with spreading, slender and wiry branchlets and tiny dark green leaves. White flowers, $\frac{1}{4}$ in. long, are borne in April and May on 1 in. long stems.

C. tetragona. Europe, Asia, N. America. Height and spread up to 12 in. A small shrub of upright tufted habit, with tiny deep green leaves. White flowers, $\frac{1}{4}$ in. long, are borne in April and May.

C. wardii. Assam, S.E. Tibet. Height and spread 6–9 in. An erect shrub with mid-green leaves fringed with long white hairs. White flowers, $\frac{1}{4}$ in. long, appear during May.

Cultivation. Plant from March to May in peaty, acid soil with plenty of humus and in a cool, moist position. Cassiopes grow naturally in open situations and should not be planted under trees or in dense shade. They are excellent plants for a peat wall garden which is facing north or west.

Cassiopes are at their best in Scotland and the north and west of Great Britain; in the south, unless they can be grown in a cool, north-facing position, they are best grown in pans of equal parts (by volume) peat, lime-free leaf-mould, loam and sand.

Propagation. Take cuttings, $1\frac{1}{2}$–2 in. long, of non-flowering shoots in August and September; insert the cuttings in equal parts (by volume) peat and sand in a cold frame. Grow on the rooted cuttings for a year before planting out.

The erect-growing species may be layered in September; the layers should be sufficiently rooted to be separated from the parent plants the following autumn.

Pruning. None required.

Pests and diseases. Generally trouble-free.

Castanea
Sweet chestnut. *Fagaceae*

A genus of 12 species of hardy deciduous trees and shrubs, distributed over the northern temperate regions. They have ribbed bark, toothed leaves and flowers in catkins. Few of the exotic species are cultivated in Great Britain except in botanic gardens and collections.

CASTANEA SATIVA

C. sativa (sweet or Spanish chestnut). S. Europe, Asia Minor, N. Africa. Height 25–30 ft; spread 15–20 ft. This species bears oblong-lanceolate, mid-green, prominently veined and toothed leaves. Erect, pale green-yellow catkins, 3–5 in. long, are borne in July; they are followed by spiny burrs which contain edible, red-brown nuts, about 1 in. wide.

Cultivation. Castaneas thrive in any good garden soil. Plant from October to March in an open sunny position.

Propagation. Sow seeds, as soon as ripe, usually in October, in nursery rows outdoors; transplant the seedlings the following autumn and grow on for three or four years before moving to permanent positions.

Named varieties do not breed true to type and must be grafted on to rootstocks of *C. sativa* in March or April.

Pruning. None required.

Pests and diseases. Generally trouble-free.

Castor oil plant: see Ricinus

Catalpa
Bignoniaceae

CATALPA BIGNONIOIDES

A genus of 11 species of hardy deciduous trees occurring in E. Asia and N. and S. America. They are vigorous growers, and eventually become large trees of rounded shape with handsome foliage and foxglove-like flowers. They are excellent trees for town gardens, but succeed best in the south of Britain.

C. bignonioides (Indian bean tree). E. North America. Height and spread 15–20 ft. The bright green heart-shaped leaves are opposite; they have a pungent smell when crushed. Upright flower panicles, 8–10 in. long, are borne in July. The

Cassiope tetragona

Cassiope wardii

Castanea sativa (fruits)

flowers are $1\frac{1}{2}$ in. long, white with yellow and purple markings and slightly frilled at the mouth. They are followed by slender seed pods, shaped like narrow beans, and up to 15 in. long. 'Aurea' is a yellow-leaved form.

Cultivation. Plant catalpas from October to March, during suitable weather, in any good garden soil and in a sunny, sheltered position.

Propagation. Take cuttings, 3–4 in. long, of half-ripened wood with a heel in July or August; insert the cuttings in equal parts (by volume) peat and sand at a temperature of 18°C (64°F). Pot the rooted cuttings in John Innes potting compost No. 1 and overwinter in a cold frame. Set out in nursery rows the following April and grow on for two or three years before planting out.

Pruning. None required.

Pests. Generally trouble-free.

Diseases. A PHYSIOLOGICAL DISORDER due to unsuitable soil conditions shows as brown blotching or yellowing of the leaves.

Catalpa bignonioides

Catananche caerulea 'Major'

Cattleya dowiana

Catananche
Cupid's dart. *Compositae*

CATANANCHE CAERULEA

A genus of five species of hardy herbaceous perennials and annuals. The short-lived perennial species described is suitable for the front of a border. The flowers are good for cutting and may be dried for winter decoration.

C. caerulea. W. Mediterranean. Height $1\frac{1}{2}$–$2\frac{1}{2}$ ft; planting distance 15–18 in. The grey-green leaves are narrowly lanceolate. Purple-blue, somewhat cornflower-like flowers with strap-shaped florets and papery bracts are borne on wiry stems. They measure $1\frac{1}{2}$ in. across. 'Major' is a vigorous variety with larger, deep lavender-blue flowers which last well when cut; 'Perry's White' is the best white variety; 'Bicolor' is blue and white.

Cultivation. Plant catananches from September to April in a sunny position in light, well-drained garden soil. In exposed positions they may need supporting with twiggy sticks. Cut down the dead flower stems in October.

Propagation. Sow seeds during April or May in pans of seed compost in a cold frame. Prick off the seedlings into boxes, then into a nursery bed, and grow them on until they are ready for their permanent positions. Seeds sown in February or March under glass at a temperature of 13°C (55°F) will flower the same year if pricked out into boxes, hardened off in a cold frame and planted out in May.

To ensure that named varieties come true to type, increase by root cuttings taken in March and inserted in boxes of John Innes seed compost in a cold frame. Plant out in a nursery bed when the leaves are well developed.

Pests and diseases. Generally trouble-free.

Catchfly: see Silene
Catharanthus: see *Vinca rosea*
Cathedral bell: see *Cobaea scandens*

Cattleya
Orchidaceae

CATTLEYA BOWRINGIANA

A genus of 60 species of epiphytic orchids distributed from Mexico to S. Brazil. These are warm or intermediate greenhouse plants with elongated pseudobulbs, one or two-jointed; they grow erect from a short, branching rhizome.

Each pseudobulb carries at its tip one or two oblong-ovate to shortly strap-shaped evergreen leaves, mid to deep green in colour. One arching flower stem bearing several flowers rises from the top of each pseudobulb. The flowers are characterised by a broad, tongue-shaped lip that is often frilled or fringed.

The species of cattleya have been crossed with each other and with those of other genera to produce a large number of hybrids. These often bear larger, more highly coloured flowers.

See also ORCHIDS.

C. bowringiana. British Honduras. This species has a two-leaved pseudobulb up to 24 in. high. The 8 in. long flowering stem carries between five and ten flowers, each about 4 in. across, which open between September and December. They are light rose-purple with dark purple margins on the lips and yellow-white throats with faint purple veins. This is an intermediate greenhouse orchid; it should be grown in bright light, but out of direct sun.

C. dowiana. Costa Rica. A handsome species with a 12 in. high, one-leaved pseudobulb. The flowers, on a 5 in. long stem, are 6–8 in. across and clear golden-yellow. The lip is reddish with yellow veins; five or six blooms appear between October and December. The variety 'Aurea' has brighter yellow veins on the lip. Grow this species in a warm greenhouse.

C. intermedia. Brazil. The pseudobulbs of this species are 12 in. high, each with two leaves. The flowering stem, up to 9 in. long, produces 5–12 flowers, each about 5 in. across. The sepals and petals are pale lilac-pink; the lip is strongly three-lobed, with a deep rose-purple mid-lobe, a narrow pink margin and purple-veined throat. Flowering is from May to June. This species needs bright conditions, but not full sun in summer, in an intermediate greenhouse.

C. labiata. Brazil. A one-leaved species with pseudobulbs 5–10 in. high. The flowering stem is up to 6 in. long and carries two to five flowers, each 5–7 in. across, between September and November. The petals and sepals are a pale pink-mauve, sometimes yellow. The lip is large with frilled edges and has a yellow throat and a mid-lobe with a large purple patch; the margins are pink. 'Candida' has white petals and sepals. Grow in an intermediate greenhouse.

C. loddigesii. Brazil, Paraguay. This species has two leaves on a 12 in. high pseudobulb. The flowering stem is up to 11 in. long and carries three to six, pale rose-lilac flowers, 4 in. across. The lip is three-lobed, the mid-lobe being yellow with wavy white margins; the throat is also yellow. Flowering is from August to September. This plant requires bright light, out of direct sun, in an intermediate greenhouse.

C. mossiae. Venezuela. Each pseudobulb is 5–10 in. high and produces one leaf. Three to six pale lavender flowers, 4–7 in. wide, appear on the 6 in. long flowering stem in May and June. Each flower has a large lip with wavy margins; the mid-lobe is rich purple, mottled and veined with paler shades, and the throat is yellow. Grow in an intermediate greenhouse.

C. skinneri. Guatemala. A two-leaved species with a 9 in. high pseudobulb. The 6 in. long flowering stem bears five to nine flowers, about 3 in. across, from March to June. The petals and sepals are pale pink-purple; the lip has smooth margins and is deep pink-purple with a pure white throat. This plant needs bright light, but not full sun in summer; it should be grown in an intermediate greenhouse.

C. trianaei. Colombia. The pseudobulb is 5–10 in. high and has one leaf. Two or three flowers, up to 7 in. across, appear on a 9 in. long flowering stem. They are pale pink, with a deep purple mid-lobe on the lip and an orange-yellow throat. This species is winter-flowering. Grow in an intermediate greenhouse.

Cultivation. Grow cattleyas in 3–10 in. pots (depending on the size of the plants), preferably with large holes in the sides to allow air to get to the roots, and drainage holes in the bottom. The perforated-type pots or open woodwork baskets are especially suitable for large plants.

Use a compost of 2 parts osmunda fibre and 1 part sphagnum moss (parts by volume) and pot so that the plant is firmly anchored, with the rhizome resting on the surface wholly exposed to the air. Cattleyas have alternate phases of growth and rest. They need a humid atmosphere and plenty of water during the growing period. In the resting period after flowering they require 2·5°C (5°F) lower temperatures and less water, although the pseudobulbs should not be allowed to shrink. Ventilation should be given when the greenhouse temperature reaches 24°C (75°F); provide light or moderate shading on sunny days from April to September. Summer growths should be encouraged by higher temperature, but only if extra humidity can be provided. Winter growths do not produce such strong flowers.

Species grown in an intermediate greenhouse require a minimum winter temperature of 10°C (50°F), in a warm greenhouse 14°C (57°F). Repot every two or three years when a new bud or growing point begins to develop roots.

Propagation. When a plant branches into two or more rhizomes it may be divided at the time of repotting with a growing point to each piece. Set the back end of the rhizome near the edge of the pot containing the growing compost, with the growing point to the middle.

Alternatively, cut through one large rhizome while still in the pot; when the basal part starts growing the two separate pieces can be repotted.

Pests. The undersides of leaves and the stem bases may be infested by SCALE INSECTS, which cause yellow blotching and make the plants sticky and sooty.

APHIDS, especially the orchid aphids, infest plants and produce similar symptoms.

Diseases. Black and often sunken spots on the leaves or bulbs are due to a PHYSIOLOGICAL DISORDER, usually caused by water remaining on the leaves and/or low night temperatures.

One or more VIRUS DISEASES may also cause sunken brown or black leaf patterns. These vary in form, but often appear as elongated streaks. One virus causes a breaking of flower colour.

Cauliflower

Brassica oleracea Botrytis. *Umbelliferae*

CAULIFLOWER

A half-hardy biennial plant, grown as an annual vegetable. It bears large clusters of thick-stalked, unopened white flowers, known as curd, which develop at the centre of the large leaves.

There are four distinct groups of summer and autumn cauliflowers, and by choosing suitable varieties, these vegetables may be gathered from May to December.

Also described under this heading is the closely related broccoli.

VARIETIES OF CAULIFLOWER

These are divided into four groups according to their maturity.

GROUP 1. This early-maturing quick-growing group, developed in Germany, Holland and Denmark, includes in order of maturity: 'Classic', 'Delta', 'Snowball', 'Erfurt', 'Polaris', 'Walcheren' and 'Dominant'. They can be harvested in late May or June. These cauliflowers are of dwarf habit with pale to mid-green small leaves that give little protection to the curds. The solid, fine-flavoured heads are pure white.

GROUP 2. The following varieties, of French origin, mature later than those in Group 1, being ready for harvesting in late June and July. 'All the Year Round' and 'Le Cerf' mature in that order. They are of dwarf habit, but more vigorous than Group 1 and have darker leaves.

A cauliflower crop can be obtained in August, by sowing varieties of Group 2 outdoors in April and later transplanting to the main bed. This method of cultivation is also suitable for exhibition cauliflowers for August shows.

GROUP 3. The varieties mentioned provide cauliflowers from September well into December. The plants are quite distinct from those in Groups 1 and 2; they are taller, and have large blue-green leaves, affording excellent

Cattleya dowiana 'Aurea'

Cattleya labiata 'Candida'

Cattleya loddigesii

protection to the ripening curds. Recommended varieties, of Italian development, include: 'Conquest', 'Majestic', 'Veitch's Autumn Giant', 'Superlative', 'Novo', 'Veitch's Self-protecting' and 'Morse's January', maturing in this order.

Recently a sub-group known as 'Flora Blanca' has become popular. 'Beacon' and 'White Chief' are outstanding September varieties. They are useful for exhibition and table use.

GROUP 4. This late-maturing group, originating in Australia, produces curds ready for cutting from September to December. They mature over the same period as those in Group 3, but the plants are small and extremely reliable, bearing pure white solid curds free from bracts which can often occur in Group 3. Some of the best varieties are 'Boomerang', 'Kangaroo', 'South Pacific', 'Barrier Reef', 'Canberra' and 'Snowcap', which mature in that order.

Broccoli, winter cauliflower. This hardy vegetable matures between November and June, depending on variety. There are two types of broccoli: curding and sprouting. The curding type (better known as winter cauliflower) is practically identical to cauliflower, but the curd is of slightly coarser texture and a duller white. Sprouting broccoli has a shoot bearing a small head of white or purple unopened flowers rising from each leaf axil.

Cauliflower 'Polaris'

Cauliflower 'All the Year Round'

Cauliflower 'Superb Early White'

BROCCOLI 'PURPLE SPROUTING'

VARIETIES OF BROCCOLI

Until the end of the last century, only the yellow-headed type was grown in Great Britain. The curding, white-headed varieties of today bear little resemblance to the types from which they were bred.

The Peerless or Feltham strains are the most suitable for cultivation in southern England. Good varieties, listed in order of maturity, include: 'Superb Early White' or 'Extra Early Feltham', January and February; 'Westmarsh Early' or 'Early Feltham', February and March; 'Snow White' or 'Mid-Feltham', March and April; 'Satisfaction' or 'Late Feltham', April and May; 'Late Queen', 'Whitsuntide' or 'Extra Late Feltham', May and June.

The Peerless strain is prone to leaf spot in the humid climate of the extreme south-west, and is superseded by the Roscoff strain. The following varieties, in order of maturity, are particularly suitable for cultivation in Cornwall, Devon, Pembroke, and Kent: 'Trevean First' or 'Saint Gwithian', November and December; 'Trevean Second' or 'Saint Agnes', December and January; 'Trevean Third' or 'Saint Hilary', January and February; 'Trevean Fourth' or 'Saint David', February and March, 'Trevean Fifth' or 'Saint Keverne', March and April; and 'Trevean Sixth', April and May.

The hardy white-headed strains were developed for growing in the colder Midlands,

and northern and Scottish areas. Curding broccoli varieties, listed in order of maturity, include: 'Reading Giant' or 'Saint George', March and April; 'Continuity' or 'Thanet', April; 'Mayfare', 'White Cliffs' or 'May Blossom', May; and 'Progress', 'June Market', 'Manston' or 'Midsummer', May and June.

Sprouting broccoli include such excellent varieties as the green-headed 'Italian Sprouting' and 'Calabrese', for use in September and October; 'Christmas Purple' or 'Early Purple', January and February; 'Purple Sprouting', also known as 'Midseason', or 'White Sprouting', March and April; and 'Late Purple' or 'Late White', ready for harvesting in April and May.

The multi-headed type known as perennial broccoli produces a dozen or more small, cream-white curds annually in May over several years. 'Bouquet' and 'Nine Star Perennial' are recommended varieties.

Cultivation of cauliflowers and broccoli. A sunny position is essential for cauliflowers. They thrive in rich, loamy soils, but light or sandy soils will produce successful crops, if well-rotted manure or compost at the rate of a large bucket per sq. yd is dug in during winter. In spring, give all soils, unless already limy, a top-dressing of carbonate of lime at 4 oz. per sq. yd. A fortnight before setting out the young plants, hoe in a dressing of general fertiliser at 3 oz. per sq. yd.

Sow seeds of varieties in Groups 1 and 2 at the end of September or January. Sow the seeds in pots or pans of seed compost and germinate at a temperature of 10–16°C (50–61°F). When the seedlings show their first pair of true leaves, prick them out 2–3 in. apart each way in trays of the seed compost and grow on at the same temperature, in a light position. Harden off strong young plants in a cold frame and transplant to their final quarters from early April onwards. Set the plants, with the soil-ball intact, in shallow holes, 18 in. apart each way. Give the young plants a thorough soaking.

Sow seeds of broccoli and intermediate crops of cauliflower varieties in Groups 3 and 4 in outdoor seed beds from March to May. Sow the seeds in ½ in. deep drills, 9–12 in. apart. Thin the seedlings as they grow to prevent overcrowding and to allow healthy plants to develop. Transplant to the main bed in the same way as described for greenhouse-raised plants, but allow 24 in. each way between the tall-growing plants of Group 3.

Keep the plants well watered. A light dressing of nitrate of soda or nitro-chalk once or twice during the growing season is beneficial and improves the quality of the curds.

Harvesting of cauliflowers. Cut cauliflowers early in the morning while the dew is still on them. If too many curds mature at the same time, break the ribs of a few of the inner leaves so that the leaves fall over the curds. This will keep a cauliflower in good condition in the bed for a few days. Whole plants, roots included, may be pulled up, the curds covered with tissue-paper, and suspended upside-down in a cool shed; the curds will keep fresh for one to three weeks. This storing method is particularly useful for exhibition plants that reach prime condition before the show date approaches.

Harvesting of broccoli. Treat curding varieties as described under cauliflower. Cut sprouting broccoli when the flowering shoots in the leaf axils are about 9–12 in. long, and before the flowers open. Cut the shoots about 2 in. from their base. A second crop of shoots usually follows. The leaves should be left on the plants to protect the growing flowering shoots, and may also be used as a vegetable when the crop of shoots is finished.

Pests. BIRDS, particularly wood-pigeons, strip the leaf tissues from the veins.

Maggots of the CABBAGE ROOT FLY may attack the roots and cause wilting and collapse of plants.

FLEA BEETLES eat small circular holes in the leaves of seedlings; CATERPILLARS of various species also feed on the leaves.

Diseases. Cauliflowers and broccoli are affected by the same diseases as CABBAGE. In addition they are sometimes prone to the following:

DOWNY MILDEW commonly occurs on seedlings and shows as a white mealy or furry fungal growth on the undersides of the leaves.

CLUB ROOT causes the roots to become a thickened, swollen, distorted mass; the plants become stunted, and the foliage discoloured. Affected plants wilt quickly on hot days.

DAMPING-OFF of seedlings and WIRE STEM of mature plants are caused by the fungus RHIZOCTONIA. The seedlings collapse at ground level; in older plants, the bases of the stems become hard, brown and shrunken.

FROST DAMAGE may injure the tissues of plants which have been grown soft. The damaged areas may be entered by SOFT ROT and GREY MOULD.

LEAF SPOT, due to several different fungi, shows on plants grown too soft; round brown spots appear on the leaves and later fall out.

SPRAY DAMAGE, due to the effects of hormone weedkillers, shows as rough wart-like outgrowths at the stem-bases; these should not be confused with CLUB ROOT. The leaves become narrow, and the plants remain stunted.

WHIPTAIL causes the leaves to become ruffled, thin and strap-like; the curds may not develop.

Ceanothus

Rhamnaceae

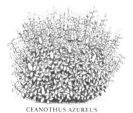

CEANOTHUS AZUREUS

A genus of 55 species of evergreen and deciduous shrubs or small trees, native to N. America, chiefly California. Some of the evergreen spring-flowering species are hardy in the open in southern areas, but require the protection of sunny walls elsewhere. The deciduous summer-flowering hybrids are hardy throughout the country. Numerous hybrids have been obtained from the evergreen species, and most of these are hardy when grown against a sheltered wall.

These plants are among the most outstanding and popular of flowering shrubs, well worth the effort of providing them with suitable conditions. The tiny, star-shaped, usually blue flowers are carried in dense panicles or simple umbels.

C. austromontanus: see *C.* × 'Edinensis'

C. × 'Autumnal Blue', height 8–10 ft; spread 6–10 ft. A vigorous hardy evergreen hybrid of branching habit. The large, glossy green leaves are ovate. Panicles, 3–4 in. long, of small, soft blue flowers appear from July until autumn.

C. azureus. Mexico. Height and spread 4–6 ft. This deciduous shrub needs the protection of a sheltered sunny wall. It has ovate-lanceolate, mid-green leaves, and bears 3 in. long fluffy panicles of numerous, tiny, deep blue flowers that open from July to September.

C. × 'Brilliant': see *C.* × *veitchianus*

C. × *burkwoodii*. Height 6–10 ft; spread 6–8 ft, or more when planted against a wall. A hardy evergreen hybrid of branching habit, with ovate shiny green leaves that are grey underneath. Bright blue flowers, in panicles up to 2 in. long, are borne from July to October.

C. × 'Cascade'. Height and spread 10 ft or more against a wall. An evergreen half-hardy hybrid shrub with arching branches. The glossy green leaves are narrowly ovate. Panicles, up to 2½ in. long, of small, rich blue flowers are carried on long stems in May.

C. × 'Delight'. Height and spread 10 ft or more. This hardy evergreen hybrid carries deep green ovate leaves. Panicles, 2–3 in. long, of small, bright blue flowers appear in May.

C. dentatus. Height and spread 10 ft or more on a wall. Evergreen shrub of bushy, erect habit; it is hardy in the open in mild areas. The dark green leaves are ovate, resinous, and grey beneath. Small blue flowers are borne in round clusters up to 1¾ in. across in May and June.

'Floribundus' has larger leaves and a greater profusion of flowers; 'Russellianus' has smaller, glossy green leaves and bright blue flowers.

C. × 'Edinensis', syn. *C. austromontanus*. Height 4–5 ft; spread 5–6 ft or more on a wall. A half-hardy evergreen shrub, low-growing and bushy. The ovate leaves are light to olive green. Small powder-blue flowers open in axillary clusters, 1–2 in. long, in May and June.

C. × 'Gloire de Versailles'. Height and spread 6–8 ft. This hardy deciduous shrub of strong, open habit has ovate, mid-green leaves, larger than those of most of the genus. Panicles, up to 8 in. long, of soft powder-blue, fragrant flowers are borne on long stems from June to October. It is often used in formal planting as it can be kept to a required height by hard pruning in spring.

C. impressus. Height and spread 10 ft or more. Half-hardy, evergreen species of bushy, twiggy habit, usually grown as a wall shrub. The small, deep green leaves are glossy above and downy beneath; they are crowded on the rigid stems. Clusters, up to 1¼ in. long, of small, deep-blue flowers are freely borne in April and May.

C. × *lobbianus*. Height and spread up to 10 ft. This hybrid between *C. thyrsiflorus* and *C. dentatus* is a half-hardy evergreen shrub, similar to *C. dentatus*, with which it is often confused. Bright blue flowers are borne in May and June.

C. × 'Marie Simon'. Height and spread 5–6 ft. A

Cauliflower 'Late Queen'

Broccoli 'Calabrese'

Ceanothus × 'Delight'

hardy deciduous hybrid with ovate, mid-green leaves. It is similar to *C.* × 'Gloire de Versailles'. Pale pink flowers in terminal panicles, 6 in. or more long, are borne from July to September.

C. rigidus. Height and spread 4–6 ft. A half-hardy evergreen shrub of stiff, compact habit, suitable for a restricted space against a wall. The small, dark green, leathery leaves are wedge-shaped. Clusters, ¾–1 in. wide, of small violet flowers, are freely borne from March to May.

C. thyrsiflorus. Height and spread 10 ft or more. This is one of the hardiest evergreen species and may be grown as a small tree. The shiny dark green leaves are oblong. Small, light blue flowers are borne in axillary panicles, 3 in. long, during May and June.

'Repens' is a more compact mound-forming shrub (height 4–5 ft; spread 5–6 ft), ideal for a large rock garden or a sunny bank.

CEANOTHUS THYRSIFLORUS

C. × 'Topaz'. Height and spread 4–5 ft. A hardy deciduous shrub, similar to *C.* × 'Gloire de Versailles', but less vigorous. Rich indigo-blue flowers are borne in panicles, 4–6 in. long, from June to October.

C. × *veitchianus*, syn. 'Brilliant'. Height and spread 10 ft or more. A hardy and vigorous evergreen hybrid between *C. rigidus* and *C. thyrsiflorus*. It is of upright branching habit and carries ovate and toothed, shiny dark green leaves. Panicles, 1–2 in. long, of small, bright blue flowers, are borne profusely in May and June.

Cultivation. Plant ceanothus in September or April and May in good, light garden soil. Some species and hybrids show signs of chlorosis when grown in soils with a high lime content. The hardy varieties may be grown in an open sunny position in the south, but these shrubs are best trained against south or west-facing walls and fences.

Propagation. Take cuttings, 3–4 in. long with a heel, of firm lateral shoots in July; insert in a propagating frame at a temperature of 16°C (61°F) and in equal parts (by volume) peat and sand. Pot the rooted cuttings in 3 in. containers of John Innes potting compost No. 2 and overwinter in a cold frame. Pot on into 4–5 in. pots the following May and plunge outdoors; transplant to permanent positions the following September.

Pruning. The evergreen species require no regular pruning, but shorten the previous year's growths of summer-flowering shrubs such as 'Autumnal Blue' in April. Cut the deciduous varieties back hard in April by shortening the previous year's shoots to 3 in. of the old wood.

Pests. The stems may be infested with brown and mussel SCALE INSECTS.

Diseases. Alkaline soil conditions may cause CHLOROSIS, which shows as a yellowing between the veins, or the leaves may be almost white.

FROST DAMAGE results in die-back of the shoots; HONEY FUNGUS may cause death of the shrubs.

Ceanothus × 'Gloire de Versailles'

Ceanothus thyrsiflorus

Cedrus atlantica 'Glauca'

Cedar: see Cedrus
Cedar, Atlas: see *Cedrus atlantica*
Cedar, blue Atlas: see *Cedrus atlantica* 'Glauca'
Cedar, incense: see *Libocedrus decurrens*
Cedar, Japanese: see Cryptomeria
Cedar of Lebanon: see *Cedrus libani*
Cedar, pencil: see *Juniperus virginiana*
Cedar, western red: see *Thuja plicata*
Cedar, white: see *Thuja occidentalis*

Cedrus

Cedar. *Pinaceae*

A genus of four species of evergreen coniferous trees. They are hardy and long-lived, and make suitable specimen trees on extensive lawns. Growth is rapid after a few years on any well-drained soil. The young shoots bear slender, spirally arranged, needle-like leaves; on second-year and older shoots, tufts of 20–50 shorter needles are produced from short woody spurs. The cones are barrel-shaped; they are only produced on mature trees and take more than two years to ripen and disintegrate on the trees.

See also CONIFERS.

CEDRUS ATLANTICA   CEDRUS ATLANTICA 'PENDULA'

C. atlantica (Atlas cedar). Atlas Mountains. Height 50 ft; spread 15 ft. The leading shoot of this species is nearly erect, with ascending terminal branches in all but the oldest trees. The crown is narrowly conic, becoming broader with age but usually retaining a pointed tip. Bunches of 20 or more short, dark green leaves grow on old shoots; the young shoots have single, longer needle-like leaves.

Flowering is in September, when numerous small, erect male flowers appear on the upper sides of branches. The 3–4 in. long cones are composed of closely overlapping, flat-topped scales that are pale blue-green until ripe. In cultivation, this species is generally represented by the form 'Glauca' (blue Atlas cedar), with blue-green to bright glaucous foliage; the cones have a blue, glowing sheen.

'Fastigiata' (height 40 ft; spread 8 ft) is a narrowly columnar form with short, strongly ascending branches and grey-blue foliage. 'Pendula', a rare form, has an arching stem and long shoots reaching the ground. Young plants are slow-growing, but mature trees make imposing specimens.

C. deodara (deodar). Western Himalayas. Height 40 ft; spread 10 ft. A species of pendulous habit, with drooping branches; many trees remain narrow and single-stemmed at the top. The leaves are blue-grey when young, maturing to dark green. Cylindrical, erect male flowers are borne in October and shed pollen in November. The female flowers, borne high up in the crown are infrequent. They mature to 3–4 in. long, pale brown cones, with numerous closely overlapped leathery scales. Trees less than 40 years old seldom bear cones.

'Pendula' (height up to 3 ft; spread 6 ft) is a low-growing weeping form.

CEDRUS DEODARA   CEDRUS LIBANI

C. libani (cedar of Lebanon). Syria, S.E. Turkey. Height 40 ft; spread 25 ft. In its young stages this species is of narrowly conic habit, with an erect leader and horizontal branches. The foliage and cones are similar to those of *C. atlantica,* but the leaves are shorter and dark green or banded with silver-blue. This cedar grows best in warm, dry eastern regions; heavy snowfalls may break the lower branches of mature specimens. 'Aurea' is a rare, slow-growing variety, with golden foliage, brightest in spring and summer.

'Nana' is a dwarf variety, forming a squat, dense bush (height and spread up to $3\frac{1}{4}$ ft); its appearance is improved by thinning out the branches and foliage to expose the trunk. 'Sargentii' is a slow-growing, pendulous form, suitable for a prominent spot on the rock garden, cultivated in a large pot or in a deep sink garden; it is prostrate unless the leader is staked to the required height.

Cultivation. These trees thrive in any ordinary, well-drained soil, particularly in maritime gardens. Plant in November or April, choosing small plants, 12–18 in. high, with a single, well-developed leading shoot. Plants up to this height do not require support, but plants up to about 3 ft high will need staking. Incorporate leaf-mould, damp peat and bone-meal when planting, and firm the soil well; apply a general fertiliser in late April for a few years.

In frost-prone areas, *C. deodara* does best in a lightly shaded position; the other species should be grown in a sunny position.

Propagation. Sow seeds of the species in pans of John Innes seed compost under glass in March, or in the open in April. Prick off the seedlings when about 3 in. high into nursery rows outdoors and grow on for three or four years before transplanting to permanent positions. *C. a.* 'Glauca' is best raised from seedlings selected for colour. Although named varieties do not breed true to type, a batch of seedlings will usually yield one or two as good as the variety.

Pruning. Maintain a single leading shoot until the required height is reached. On evenly forked trees, remove one branch at the end of the growing season. No other pruning is advisable until the lowest branches begin to deteriorate, when they should be cut off flush with the bole; this is best done from February to April.

Pests. Generally trouble-free.

Diseases. HONEY FUNGUS occasionally causes the death of trees, but this may also be the result of a PHYSIOLOGICAL DISORDER.

Celastrus

Staff vine, climbing bittersweet. *Celastraceae*

A genus of 30 species of hardy deciduous shrubs, of twining habit. All those described require supports when grown on walls. They are valuable for clothing arbours, tall fences, walls or tree stumps. The starry green-yellow flowers, $\frac{1}{4}$ in. across and appearing in axillary cymes or terminal panicles during June and July, are inconspicuous. The freely produced fruits which follow are the plants' main attraction. These are pea-sized and brilliantly coloured. After ripening, they split into three sections to reveal scarlet seeds. They often persist well into winter.

CELASTRUS ORBICULATUS

C. angulatus, syn. *C. latifolius.* China. Height up to 20 ft. A vigorous plant which requires plenty of space; it can spread as much as 30 ft. It is unisexual, so it is essential to place at least two plants of different sexes together to ensure cross-pollination. Consult a nurseryman when buying the plants. The round mid-green leaves are bluntly serrated. The fruits are orange.

C. articulatus: see *C. orbiculatus*

C. hypoglaucus: see *C. hypoleucus*

C. hypoleucus, syn. *C. hypoglaucus.* China. Height up to 30 ft. Another vigorous climber. It is bisexual and can be planted singly. The leaves are oblong, mid-green above and glaucous beneath. The fruits are yellow and red. This species is distinct from the others in having a purple-pink waxy bloom on its young shoots.

C. latifolius: see *C. angulatus*

C. orbiculatus, syn. *C. articulatus.* N.E. Asia. Height up to 30 ft. This is the finest species and even more vigorous than *C. angulatus.* It is bisexual and can be planted singly. The variably shaped mid-green leaves have a wedge-shaped base and are edged with shallow teeth. Orange and scarlet fruits are massed on the branches.

Cultivation. Plant young specimens from November to March. Celastrus will grow in any soil that is not waterlogged, excessively dry or chalky, and in any position not exposed to north or east winds. Prepare the soil well, particularly if planting at the base of an old tree. Once established, the plants require little attention.

Propagation. To grow from seeds, sow these in boxes of seed compost in November and place in a cold frame. Prick out the seedlings into boxes.

Take cuttings either from half-ripe growths (4 in.) in July, or from ripe wood (9 in.) in October or November. Insert both types in pots containing equal parts (by volume) sand and peat in a propagating frame heated to 13–16°C (55–61°F).

Pot both seedlings and cuttings singly, then plunge the pots in an outdoor nursery bed.

One-year-old growths layered during October will usually have rooted a year later.

Cedrus deodara 'Pendula'

Cedrus libani (cones)

Cedrus libani 'Nana'

Celastrus orbiculatus (fruits)

125

Celeriac 'Giant Prague'

Celery 'Giant Red'

Celery (specimen head)

Pruning. None is needed when the plants are growing freely on old trees. When they are grown on pergolas or walls, thin out unwanted growths and cut back the main shoots to about half their length during February.

Pests. SCALE INSECTS sometimes infest the stems.

Diseases. Generally trouble-free.

Celeriac

Apium graveolens Rapaceum. *Umbelliferae*

A hardy biennial plant, usually grown as an annual. It is a recent introduction to Great Britain and is cultivated for its thick roots that are used as an autumn and winter vegetable. The plant resembles celery, but at ground level develops a swollen root similar to a turnip. Apart from the edible roots, which have a celery flavour, the leaves can also be used fresh to flavour soups and stews.

VARIETIES

Only a few are available; these include: 'Claudia', with smooth non-branching roots virtually without side-shoots; 'Giant Prague', large well-flavoured roots each weighing up to 4 lb.; and 'Marble Ball', a disease-resistant variety, excellent for storage.

Cultivation. Grow celeriac in fertile, well-drained soil that has been improved during the winter months by digging in liberal amounts of well-rotted manure or compost.

Sow seeds thinly in March in pots or pans of seed compost, and germinate in a greenhouse at a temperature of 16°C (61°F). As soon as the seedlings are large enough to handle, prick them out into boxes of seed compost and, when well-established, harden off in a cold frame.

Alternatively, sow seeds in boxes of seed compost, placed in a cold frame or under cloches, in late March or early April. When the seedlings are large enough to handle, prick them out 2 in. apart each way in a prepared bed enriched with well-decayed manure. Keep the plants covered with cloches until they are well-established and then harden them off.

Outdoors, seeds may be broadcast thinly in April in a sheltered, sunny seed bed. Thin the seedlings as necessary.

In June, plant out the seedlings, setting them 12–15 in. apart each way, and handling the root-balls carefully. Keep the plants well-watered in the early stages. Remove any side-growths that appear during September and October, when the roots begin to swell.

Harvesting. The roots may be lifted as required from mid-September onwards, but they are seldom large enough for use until November. Draw soil round the swelling roots in November to keep the tops blanched if the leaves are wanted. Lift the remainder in December, remove the foliage and store the roots in boxes of sand or soil in a cool, dry shed.

Pests. Maggots of the CARROT FLY sometimes tunnel into the roots.

Diseases. Stunting of the plants may be caused by ARABIS MOSAIC VIRUS and CUCUMBER MOSAIC VIRUS; the leaves may be distorted and show yellow and green mottling.

CELERY LEAF SPOT shows on the leaves as small brown spots with minute black fruiting bodies of the fungus.

DAMPING-OFF causes young plants to wither; the roots show a red-brown discoloration.

A PHYSIOLOGICAL DISORDER, usually due to poor soil and/or lack of moisture at the roots, may result in the plants going to seed.

Celery

Apium graveolens. Umbelliferae

A hardy biennial vegetable, cultivated as an annual for its tight cluster of crisp, 12–18 in. long, crescent-sectioned stalks. These may be used raw from autumn to spring in salads, or blanched and cooked as a vegetable and as flavouring for soups and stews. The pale green, deeply divided leaves at the top of the stalks may also be used, fresh or dried, for flavouring and in *bouquets garnis*.

The most commonly grown varieties are white, pink or red. The white matures first, followed by the pink, and lastly the red, which is the hardiest. These must all be grown in trenches and earthed up.

Self-blanching white or green types that do not require earthing up are less hardy and have a milder flavour; they must be cleared from ground outdoors before frosts begin.

VARIETIES

The following white varieties are recommended: 'Clandon White' and 'Solid White' are both excellent for table use and for exhibition; 'Wareing's Dwarf White' is early-maturing, of compact growth and with a firm heart.

'Ideal Pink' and 'Unrivalled Pink' are pink-tinged, well-flavoured varieties; they are strong-growing and outstanding for show purposes.

'Giant Red' and 'Standard Bearer Red' are late-maturing, extremely crisp varieties.

Self-blanching varieties include: 'Golden Self-blanching' and 'Lathom Self-blanching', both firm-hearted varieties that mature from August onwards. 'Greensleeves' and 'Utah' are green varieties with crisp heads of good flavour. These do not require earthing up and are ready for harvesting from August to October.

Cultivation. Grow celery in an open, sunny position, and in well-drained but moisture-retentive soil. Prepare the bed in late winter or early spring; take out trenches 12 in. deep by 18 in. wide and 3 ft apart. Pile the soil from the trenches alongside and use this for growing catch crops such as lettuces, radishes or dwarf beans, which will be cleared before celery has to be earthed up. Fork over the base of each trench and add a 6 in. layer of well-rotted manure or compost; cover with 3–4 in. of soil.

For self-blanching white and green varieties, it is sufficient to dig the plot one spit deep. Work in two buckets of well-rotted manure or compost per sq. yd.

Young plants may be purchased or raised from seeds. For crops of white, pink and red varieties, sow seeds during the second half of March in pots or boxes of seed compost placed in a greenhouse at a temperature of 13–16°C (55–61°F). When the seedlings are large enough to handle, prick them out into trays of John Innes potting compost No. 1, setting them 2 in. apart each way. Grow on the young plants in the greenhouse until well-established, then harden them off; plant out in late May or early June.

Seeds may also be sown thinly in an outdoor seed bed where the soil has been warmed for a month under cloches. Thin the seedlings as they grow to prevent overcrowding, and keep the cloches in place until transplanting.

Raise seedlings of self-blanching white and green varieties in the same manner, but delay sowing until early April. This usually prevents bolting, to which these varieties are prone.

In late May or early June, transplant the young 3–4 in. high plants to their final quarters, keeping the soil-balls intact. White, pink and red varieties should be spaced 9 in. apart in a single row along the centre of the prepared trench; firm the roots and water thoroughly to settle the soil. Plant self-blanching white and green varieties in the prepared flat bed, setting them in a square block and spacing them 9 in. apart.

Keep the beds well watered, and remove any side-growths that appear from the base.

Earth up the trenches when the plants are 12–15 in. high, probably in mid-August and at a time when the soil is reasonably dry. Tie the stems loosely with raffia just below the leaves, and fork soil from the ridges into the trenches round each plant to form a slope reaching about halfway up the stem. Three weeks later draw more earth round the plants, to the base of the leaves. Make the final earthing up three weeks later. Soil must not be allowed to fall between the stems, and the earthed-up slopes should be firm and smooth to carry away rain.

In December, place dry straw or bracken over late-maturing plants left in the bed as protection against frost and rain.

Harvesting. The heads of trench-grown celery are not usually blanched sufficiently for use until at least eight weeks after the first earthing up.

Varieties grown at ground level are ready for use from the end of August. When a plant is removed, fill in the gap with soil to prevent too much light reaching the remaining plants.

Pests. Maggots of CARROT FLY may damage roots and stems.

CELERY FLY maggots tunnel into the leaves, causing blotch mines and checking growth of young plants.

SLUGS may feed on the leaf stalks, particularly after earthing up.

Diseases. Stunting of plants may be caused by several fungi, in particular ARABIS MOSAIC VIRUS and CUCUMBER MOSAIC VIRUS; the leaves, which may be distorted, show a yellow and green mottling.

BORON DEFICIENCY leads to poor growth with yellowing and withering of the leaves, and brown cracking across the stalks.

CELERY HEART ROT causes the centres of plants to decompose into a slimy, brown mass.

CELERY LEAF SPOT shows on the leaves, and sometimes the stalks, as small brown spots with minute black fruiting bodies of the fungus.

DAMPING-OFF fungi cause seedlings and young plants to wither or droop; the roots usually show a red-brown discoloration.

PHYSIOLOGICAL DISORDERS, due to lack of moisture, cause the plants to go to seed and the stalks to split. The same symptoms may be due to excess nitrogen in the soil.

Celosia
Amaranthaceae

CELOSIA ARGENTEA CRISTATA

A genus of 60 annual species, mostly suitable for summer flowering under glass or occasionally for summer bedding outdoors. They produce showy heads of plumed or crested flowers, predominantly red or yellow. Given adequate warmth they are easy to grow, provided there is no check to cause premature flowering.

C. argentea. Tropical Asia. Height 24 in.; planting distance 12 in. A compact plant with pale green lanceolate leaves. Erect or drooping feathery plumes of silver-white flowers, 3 in. across, are produced from July to September. The many cultivated varieties now available have flowers in shades of red, orange and yellow; they are listed under the following headings:

C. a. Cristata (cockscomb). Tropical Asia. Height up to 12 in.; planting distance 9 in. A dwarf, compact plant with slender, ovate, light green leaves. Crested heads, 3–5 in. across, of red, orange or yellow flowers are produced from July to September. The variety 'Jewel Box' is recommended; it is available in a wide colour range.

CELOSIA ARGENTEA PYRAMIDALIS

C. a. Pyramidalis, syn. Plumosa. Tropical Asia. Height up to 24 in.; planting distance 9–12 in. The leaves are mid-green and ovate. A feathery flower plume, 3–6 in. high, is carried from July to August. This species is grown as a pot plant and for bedding; the tall forms are used for cutting. The Lilliput strain is particularly suitable for growing in pots; it includes the forms 'Golden Feather', 'Fiery Feather' and 'Lilliput Mixed'. The 24 in. high 'Thompson's Magnifica Mixed' has a wide range of colours and is recommended for cutting; the flowers of this strain may also be dried and used for winter decoration.

Cultivation. For outdoor cultivation, choose a rich, well-drained soil in a sheltered, sunny position. Under glass, a temperature of 16°C (61°F), good ventilation and regular watering are required. Grow pot plants in John Innes potting compost No. 1, using $3\frac{1}{2}$ in. containers for the

Celery 'Greensleeves'

Celosia argentea Cristata

Celosia argentea Pyramidalis

compact varieties and 5 in. containers for the remainder. Spray the foliage of plants under glass to encourage growth and increase flower size. Once the roots fill the pots, apply liquid fertiliser at 14-day intervals.

Propagation. Sow the seeds in pans of seed compost in February at a temperature of 18°C (64°F); prick off the seedlings into boxes and grow on at 15°C (59°F). Outdoor plants must be hardened off in a cold frame before planting out in a border in late May. For indoor pot plants, pot on the seedlings as described under CULTIVATION.

Pests. Generally trouble-free.

Diseases. FOOT and ROOT ROT, due to one or more fungi, cause rotting of the roots and of the collar portion of the plants. They eventually wilt or collapse completely.

Centaurea cyanus 'Polka Dot'

Centaurea gymnocarpa

Centaurea hypoleuca

Centaurea
Compositae

CENTAUREA CYANUS

A genus of 600 species of annual, biennial and perennial herbaceous plants. With the exceptions of *C. gymnocarpa* and *C. pulchra*, the species described are hardy. All are suitable for growing in borders, and for providing cut flowers; the annuals may also be grown in pots under glass, and *C. gymnocarpa* may be used in bedding schemes.

The flowers are composed of a globular base from which arise numerous slender tubular florets; many of the species have attractive silvery foliage.

C. cyanus (cornflower). Great Britain. Height ¾–3 ft; spacing 9–15 in. An erect, branched annual with narrowly lanceolate, grey-green leaves and branched sprays of pink, red, purple, blue or white flowers. These are 1–2 in. across and are produced from June to September. The many garden varieties are divided into two groups according to their heights:

Tall varieties (2–3 ft), ideal for cutting, include the Ball strain, available as a mixture and in separate colours. 'Blue Diadem' is a new variety with extra-large flowers.

The compact varieties (height up to 12 in.), are best for bedding and for growing in pots. They include 'Dwarf Rose Gem', rose-red; 'Jubilee Gem', blue; and the 'Polka Dot' strain in a range of colours.

C. dealbata. Caucasus, Persia. Height 18–24 in.; planting distance 24 in. A perennial species with deeply cut pinnate leaves that are grey-green above, silvery beneath. Rose-pink flowers, 2½–3 in. across, are borne on branching stems in June and July and again in September. The variety 'John Coutts' has glowing rose-pink flowers with pale yellow centres; and 'Stenbergii' bears deep pink flowers.

Centaurea macrocephala

C. gymnocarpa. Caprera Island, Sardinia. Height and planting distance 18–24 in. A sub-shrubby perennial, not reliably hardy. The fern-like, deeply dissected foliage is thickly felted with white hairs. Small clusters of 1 in. wide, rose-purple flowers are borne in August; they are usually partly hidden by the leaves.

C. hypoleuca. Armenia. Height and planting distance 18 in. A compact but vigorous perennial species with deeply cut, grey-green leaves. The pink flowers measure 2 in. across and are borne in succession from May to August. The variety *C. h. simplicicaulis* (height 10 in.) has lilac-pink flowers in May and June.

C. macrocephala. Armenia, Caucasus. Height 3–5 ft; planting distance 24 in. A perennial species with rough, light green, oblong leaves. The stout stems bear yellow flowers, 3–4 in. across, in June and July. This is a most effective border plant, and the flowers are long-lasting when cut.

C. montana. Pyrenees, Alps, Carpathians. Height 18–24 in.; planting distance 12 in. This perennial species of lax growth has mid to deep green, white-hairy, oblong-lanceolate leaves. Blue flowers, 2½–3 in. across, are borne in profusion during May and June.

'Alba', 'Rosea' and 'Violetta' are recommended forms with, respectively, white, pink and deep blue-purple flowers.

CENTAUREA MONTANA

C. moschata (sweet sultan). Orient. Height 24 in.; spacing 9 in. An annual species with thin, willowy stems and narrow grey-green leaves, marginally toothed. The scented flowers, 3 in. across, are white, yellow, pink or purple. They are produced from June to September.

C. pulcherrima, syn. *Aethiopappus pulcherrimus.* Caucasus. Height 24 in.; planting distance 12 in.

pinnate leaves. Bright pink flowers, 2½ in. across, are freely borne in June and July.

C. pulchra. Kashmir. A perennial species; the variety *C. p. major* is more widely grown than the type. Height 24 in.; planting distance 12 in. It has smooth, silvery, pinnate leaves. Rose-pink flowers, 2 in. across, are borne in August. This plant is not reliably hardy in cold districts.

C. ruthenica. E. Europe; Siberia. Height 3–4 ft; planting distance 18–24 in. A perennial species with deeply cut, glossy dark green leaves. Sulphur-yellow thistle-like flowers, 1½ in. across, are borne on slender stems in July and August.

Cultivation. Grow centaureas in any fertile, well-drained garden soil, in a sunny position. Plant perennial species from October to March; lift and divide every third or fourth year.

In exposed positions staking with twiggy sticks may be needed, especially for taller plants. Dead-heading is recommended for all species and may prolong flowering of the annuals.

In all but the most sheltered districts, use cloches to protect autumn-sown annuals intended for early-summer flowering outdoors; overwinter *C. gymnocarpa* under glass at a temperature of 5–7°C (41–45°F). Seedlings from an autumn sowing can be grown on in John Innes potting compost No. 1, three to a 6 in. pot, and overwintered in a cold greenhouse for flowering in May or June.

Extra-large specimens may be obtained by lifting plants of *C. gymnocarpa* in September and growing on in pots until the next season.

Propagation. Sow seeds of the annual species in the flowering site in September, March or April. A succession of sowings in spring extends the flowering season. Thin out the seedlings to the required spacing. September-sown plants grow larger and require a slightly wider spacing.

Divide and replant perennial species between October and March.

Alternatively, sow seeds of perennial species, except *C. gymnocarpa*, during April. Sow in boxes or pans of seed compost in a cold frame. Prick off the seedlings, when large enough to handle, into boxes, then grow on in nursery rows. Pot seedlings of *C. dealbata*, *C. hypoleuca* and *C. pulchra* singly in 3–3½ in. pots of John Innes potting compost No. 1 and plunge outdoors. Move the plants from nursery rows to flowering sites in October; overwinter pot-grown species in a cold frame; plant out the following April.

Increase *C. gymnocarpa* from 3–4 in. cuttings of lateral shoots taken in August or September. Insert in a mixture of equal parts (by volume) peat and sand in an open propagating case at a minimum temperature of 15°C (59°F). When rooted, pot the cuttings singly in 3–3½ in. pots of John Innes potting compost No. 1 and overwinter at a temperature of 5–7°C (41–45°F). Pot on to 4–5 in. pots in March and harden off in a cold frame before planting out in late May.

Pests. Generally trouble-free.

Diseases. *C. cyanus* is affected by PETAL BLIGHT which causes oval, water-soaked spots on the outer florets; these spread rapidly.

POWDERY MILDEW shows as a white powdery coating on leaves, stems and flowers.

RUST affects *C. cyanus*; it appears as brown spore masses on the undersides of the leaves.

Centranthus

Valerian. *Valerianaceae*

A genus of 12 species of annuals and hardy herbaceous perennials. The perennial described is easily grown, colourful and long-flowering.

CENTRANTHUS RUBER

C. ruber, syn. *Kentranthus ruber.* Europe. Height 1½–3 ft; planting distance 12 in. The ovate glaucous leaves emit an unpleasant smell when bruised. Panicles of red or deep pink, star-shaped flowers, ¼ in. across, are borne on erect stems from June to late summer. *C. r.* 'Albus' is a white form.

Cultivation. Plant in March or April in a sunny site. They thrive in poor, well-drained soil and especially on chalk or limestone. Cut down dead growth from October onwards.

Propagation. Sow seeds between April and June, either where the plants are to flower or in a seed bed. If the seeds are sown in the flowering site, thin the seedlings to the required distance; if in a seed bed, transplant them to the flowering positions while the plants are quite small.

Pests and diseases. Generally trouble-free.

Cerastium

Caryophyllaceae

CERASTIUM TOMENTOSUM

A genus of 60 species of hardy annuals and herbaceous perennials. All but a few are too invasive and weedy for garden cultivation, but those described can be grown on rock gardens.

C. alpinum. European Alps, Great Britain. Height 2–4 in.; spread 9 in. This mat-forming perennial has grey to pale green lanceolate leaves and bears a few white, star-shaped flowers, ¾ in. across, from May to August. These have deeply cut petals and are carried in clusters. The form 'Lanatum' makes attractive woolly silver tufts, but the flowers are insignificant.

C. biebersteinii (snow-in-summer). Crimea. Height 4–6 in.; spread 24 in. or more. A dense, mat-forming, invasive species which should be grown only on rough banks or on large rock gardens well away from smaller, choice species. It produces spreading plants with woolly, silver-grey, linear to narrowly lanceolate leaves. White, cup-shaped flowers, ¾–1 in. across, are borne on slender-branched stems in May and June.

Centranthus ruber

Cerastium alpinum (in the wild)

Cerastium tomentosum

C. tomentosum (snow-in-summer). S. and E. Europe. Height 4–6 in.; spread 24 in. or more. This species closely resembles *C. biebersteinii* in habit and size, but the leaves are less woolly and silvery. The flowers also are similar, but they are rarely more than ¾ in. across and have narrower petals, thus giving a starry appearance. It is possible that many plants listed under this name are hybrids between it and *C. biebersteinii*.

Cultivation. Plant in March, April or September in gritty, well-drained soil. Set the plants in a sunny position and protect them from winter dampness with raised sheets of glass.

C. alpinum 'Lanatum' grows best in an alpine house as it does not tolerate mild wet winters outdoors. Plant in March or April in 6–8 in. pans in a mixture of equal parts (by volume) loam, peat and coarse sand or grit. Repot every other year in March or April.

Propagation. Divide in March or April and replant direct in permanent positions.

Pests and diseases. Generally trouble-free.

Cerastium tomentosum (in winter)

Ceratostigma willmottianum

Cercidiphyllum japonicum (autumn foliage)

Ceratostigma
Plumbaginaceae

CERATOSTIGMA WILLMOTTIANUM

A genus of eight species of half-hardy low-growing shrubs and herbaceous perennials. Those described here are suitable for growing in sheltered shrubberies or mixed borders; they are not recommended for north-eastern gardens. The slender tubular flowers are bright blue and open to five spreading lobes at the mouth; the foliage may take on attractive red tints in autumn.

C. griffithii. Himalayas, China. Height and spread 3–4 ft. A bushy, much branched, ever-green shrub with obovate, dull green leaves, covered in bristles; the foliage turns scarlet in autumn. Bright blue flowers, ½–¾ in. across, are borne in terminal clusters from August into the autumn. The species is tender and only suitable for a mild garden or against a wall.

C. plumbaginoides. China. Height up to 12 in.; spread 15 in. This sub-shrubby perennial is suitable for a rock garden, a dry wall or as ground cover. The obovate-lanceolate, mid-green leaves take on red tints in autumn. Small terminal clusters of blue flowers, ¾ in. across, are carried from July to November.

C. willmottianum. W. China. Height and spread about 3 ft. A half-hardy deciduous shrub with dark green, diamond-shaped and pointed, stalk-less leaves. In autumn, the foliage may turn red. Small, rich blue flowers are borne in terminal clusters, 2½ in. wide, and in the upper leaf axils; they appear in July. Hardy when established.

Cultivation. Plant in April or May in light loamy soil and in full sun. All species do better if given the protection of a warm wall.

Propagation. Take cuttings, 3 in. long, preferably with a heel, of half-ripe lateral shoots in July; root in equal parts (by volume) peat and sand in a propagating frame with a bottom heat of 16–18°C (61–64°F). Pot the rooted cuttings in 3–3½ in. pots of John Innes potting compost No. 1 and overwinter in a frost-free frame or green-house. Plant out in permanent positions in April.

C. plumbaginoides may be divided and re-planted in April; rooted suckers may be removed, potted up and treated as described for cuttings.

Pruning. No regular pruning is required, but old or damaged shoots should be cut back to ground level in March.

Pests and diseases. Generally trouble-free.

Cercidiphyllum
Cercidiphyllaceae

CERCIDIPHYLLUM JAPONICUM

A genus of only two species of deciduous trees, native to China and Japan. They are grown for their elegance of form and foliage which often colours richly in autumn.

C. japonicum. Japan. Height 20–25 ft; spread 15–20 ft. A hardy species, although the young growths may be caught by late frosts. The young unfolding leaves are red but soon become rich green; they are round, toothed and grey-green beneath. The foliage often assumes beautiful red and yellow autumn tints. Small clusters of petal-less male and female flowers appear on separate trees in March and April before the leaves. The male flowers consist of a tuft of slender stamens with red anthers. Female flowers form a cluster of ⅝ in. long green follicles (ovaries) with thread-like rose-purple styles.

Cultivation. Plant in any good moisture-retentive soil from October to March in a position sheltered from early-morning frosts and cold winds; woodland conditions are ideal. These shrubs will tolerate lime, but autumn colours will often be less pronounced on limy soils.

Propagation. Sow seeds in March in pans of John Innes seed compost and place in a cold frame; prick off seedlings, when large enough to handle, later transferring to a nursery bed. Transplant to permanent sites two or three years later.

Pruning. None required.

Pests and diseases. Generally trouble-free.

Cercis
Leguminosae

A genus of seven species of deciduous trees, native to China, N. America and S. Europe. The following two species are hardy. They flower on the naked stems in late spring.

C. *racemosa.* China. Height and spread 20 ft or more. A deciduous tree or shrub with ovate leaves that are bright green above and downy beneath. Rose-pink, pea-shaped flowers, in pendulous 4 in. long racemes, appear in May; they are followed by seed pods 3–5 in. long. The species does not flower until it is eight to ten years old.

CERCIS SILIQUASTRUM

C. *siliquastrum* (Judas tree). S. Europe, Orient. Height 15–20 ft; spread 10–15 ft. A wide-spreading tree or shrub with rounded, somewhat glaucous-green leaves. Rich rose-purple, pea-shaped, $\frac{1}{4}$–$\frac{1}{2}$ in. long flowers are borne in clusters of three to six on the naked stems in May. They are followed by flat, green seed pods, freely set; these are 3–4 in. long and red-tinted when fully ripe in late summer.

Cultivation. Large cercis plants resent root disturbance; young plants should be set in any good garden soil and in full sun, in late September and October or in April and May. The flowers of *C. siliquastrum* are sometimes damaged by late spring frosts, and the shrub is best grown in a sheltered position; in northern gardens give the protection of a south wall.

Propagation. Sow seeds of the species in March in pans of John Innes seed compost, and germinate at a temperature of 13–18°C (55–64°F); pot the seedlings, when large enough to handle, in 3 in. pots of John Innes potting compost No. 1 and plunge outdoors. Pot on as necessary into 4 or 5 in. containers of John Innes potting compost No. ?, and set the young plants in their permanent sites when two years old.

Pruning. None required.

Pests. Generally trouble-free.

Diseases. CORAL SPOT causes die-back of shoots, and pink to red cushion-like pustules appear towards the base of the dead wood. Large branches may be killed.

Cereus

Cactaceae

CEREUS JAMACARU

A genus of 50 greenhouse perennial species. These columnar cacti have cylindrical stems which branch from the upper part in mature specimens. In the wild some species reach a height of at least 30 ft. The plants are vigorous and easy to cultivate.

Cereus seeds are often one of the main constituents of packets of mixed cactus seed. These plants rarely flower in pots, but large specimens planted out in greenhouse beds will bloom. The 2–3 in. wide flowers are funnel-shaped, usually white, and often scented. They appear in June and July and open at night.

See also CACTUS.

C. *caerulescens.* Argentina. Height 2–3 ft. The stem is deep blue-green changing to green with age. It is up to $1\frac{1}{2}$ in. thick and has eight ribs, with areoles about $\frac{1}{2}$ in. apart. The areoles are covered with white wool and bear 10–15 strong black spines. The flowers are readily produced; they are white or rose, 8 in. long, and scaly on the outside.

C. *jamacaru.* S. America. Height 2–3 ft. In the wild the deeply ribbed main stems are up to 24 in. across and 30 ft tall. Cultivated as a background plant in a large greenhouse, the stem will reach a diameter of about 6 in. This is green and has between five and eight ribs bearing eight yellow spines on each areole. The flowers are white.

C. *peruvianus.* S.E. Brazil, W. Argentina. Height 2–3 ft. Similar to *C. jamacaru,* but with thicker ribs and brown spines. These two species are the ones most frequently seen in cultivation.

Cultivation. Cerei are easy to cultivate in pots or greenhouse borders. The first pots should be 3–6 in., according to the size of the plants. Plant them in John Innes potting compost No. 2, with extra grit or fine gravel added. Give them plenty of water during the summer, but keep them dry in winter. Overwinter the plants at a temperature of 5°C (41°F). Repot annually in March.

Keep these cacti within bounds when they become too tall by restarting them from cuttings taken in spring or early summer. Cut off the top 12 in. of the plant, allow it to dry for a week, and then pot it up in sandy compost. It should root quickly. By this means, stout-stemmed cerei can be grown successfully in a 10 in. pot. The original stem will send out new branches.

Propagation. The plants can be raised from seeds sown in April at a temperature of 21°C (70°F).

Alternatively, propagation by cuttings is easy. The branches sent out by the main stem, after beheading as described under CULTIVATION, can be removed when 3–4 in. long. Leave the cuttings, taken in spring or summer, to dry for a few days, then pot up in a sandy compost.

Pests. Conspicuous tufts of white waxy wool are caused by MEALY BUGS. ROOT MEALY BUGS sometimes infest the root systems, but cerei generally withstand attacks by pests.

Diseases. Generally trouble-free.

Cestrum

Solanaceae

A genus of 150 species of deciduous and evergreen shrubs occurring from Mexico to S. America. These shrubs, with their rather rambling growth, are chiefly suitable for conservatories and cool greenhouses, but a few may succeed outdoors in the south and west of Great Britain on warm sheltered walls. In severe winters, they may be cut back by frost, but will usually break again from the base.

Cercis siliquastrum

Cereus jamacaru

Cestrum aurantiacum

Cestrum fasciculatum

Cestrum × newellii

Chaenomeles japonica 'Brilliant'

Chaenomeles speciosa 'Apple
Blossom'

C. aurantiacum. Guatemala. Height up to 8 ft;
spread 5–6 ft. This is a semi-evergreen shrub
requiring greenhouse cultivation except in mild
southern and western areas. The ovate leaves are
pale to mid-green. Tubular, bright orange flowers
are borne in terminal and axillary panicles, 6–8 in.
long, from June to September.
C. elegans: see *C. purpureum*
C. fasciculatum. Mexico. Height 5–8 ft; spread
4–7 ft. Evergreen shrub with slender arching
growths. The ovate, lanceolate leaves are light
green and slightly downy. Salmon-red,
pitcher-shaped flowers, crowded in terminal and
axillary clusters, 2–3 in. wide, are borne from
April and continue until early summer. The
species is hardier than the similar *C. purpureum*
and makes a good wall shrub.
C. × newellii. Height up to 10 ft; spread 8 ft. This
evergreen seedling is of unrecorded parentage,
but is thought to be a hybrid between *C.
purpureum* and *C. fasciculatum*. It resembles *C.
purpureum*, but has larger, bright orange-
crimson flowers, each about 1 in. long. A fine wall
shrub for the mildest areas.
C. parqui. Chile. Height and spread 3–4 ft, often
considerably more on a sheltered wall. A half-
hardy deciduous shrub of bushy habit, bearing
narrow, lanceolate, tapering and glabrous leaves.
Green-yellow flowers, fragrant at night, appear in
terminal and axillary panicles, up to 6 in. long,
from July to September.

CESTRUM PURPUREUM

C. purpureum, syn. *C. elegans*. Mexico. Height
up to 10 ft when trained on a wall; spread 4–5 ft.
An evergreen shrub of graceful, rambling habit
and with lanceolate, dark green, downy leaves.
Small, bright purple-red, tubular flowers are
carried in dense pendulous clusters, up to 4 in.
long, from May to late summer. These are
sometimes followed by small, round, purple-red
berries. This species makes a fine wall shrub in
mild gardens in the south and west; elsewhere it
is suitable for growing in a cool greenhouse.
Cultivation. Cestrums thrive in any ordinary
garden soil, but for best results grow them in a
rich loamy soil. Plant during April and May in a
sunny, sheltered position, trained against a south
or west-facing wall. These shrubs are not suitable
for outdoor cultivation in the north and east.

For cultivation under glass, grow cestrums in
10–12 in. pots or tubs of John Innes potting
compost No. 2 or 3; better results are achieved by
growing the shrubs in the greenhouse border.
Overwinter at a temperature of 7–10°C
(45–50°F). Grow the shrubs in a well-lit position,
but lightly shade the greenhouse from May to
September. Ventilate and water freely; during
winter keep the plants just moist.

Pot on or repot annually in March or April;
from May to September give a weak liquid feed at
intervals of two weeks.

Propagation. Take cuttings, 3–4 in. long, o
half-ripened lateral shoots in July and August
insert the cuttings in equal parts (by volume) pea
and sand at a bottom heat of 21–24°C (70–75°F)
When rooted, pot the cuttings singly in 3 in. pot
of John Innes potting compost No. 2 and pot o
as required. Overwinter at a temperature o
7–10°C (45–50°F); harden off the following Ma
and plant out in permanent positions in June. I
the greenhouse, pot on as necessary.
Pruning. To keep the shrubs within bounds, thi
out two or three-year-old stems from the base i
February and March. Spur back all laterals to 6 in
annually at the same time.
Pests and diseases. Generally trouble-free.

Chaenomeles

Japanese quince, japonica or cydonia. *Rosaceae*

CHAENOMELES SPECIOSA

A genus of three species of deciduous spring
flowering shrubs occurring in China and Japar
They are closely related to *Cydonia* (the tru
quince) in which genus they were formerl
included, but differ in having toothed leaves an
several flowers in a cluster. They are hardy an
grow well on banks or on walls. In autumn the
bear edible fruits, used for preserves.
C. japonica (Maule's quince). Japan. Heigh
about 3 ft; spread 5–7 ft. A dwarf shrub
wide-spreading habit. The mid-green, ovate t
round leaves are downy. Orange-red, apple
blossom flowers, 1–1½ in. across, are borne singl
or in clusters of twos or threes on the previou
year's growths from March to May. These ar
sometimes followed by fragrant, apple-shape
yellow fruits.

C. j. alpina is smaller, with bright orang
flowers; 'Brilliant' has clear scarlet flower.
'Versicolor Lutescens' has pale yellow flower
flushed pink.
C. lagenaria: see *C. speciosa*
C. speciosa, syn. *C. lagenaria* (japonica, Japanes
quince). China. Height up to 6 ft, or more on
wall; spread 4–6 ft. This is the best-know
species; it has dark green glossy leaves that ar
ovate to oblong. The bowl-shaped flowers, borr
two to four in a cluster and up to 2 in. wide, are i
various shades of red. In mild weather flowerin
may begin in January and continue to April. Th
fruits are fragrant and green-yellow.

Numerous garden forms have been raised an
include: 'Apple Blossom', with single and semi
double white flowers, flushed pink; 'Aurora
with rose flowers, slightly tinged yellow; 'Crim
son and Gold' with flowers having red petals an
yellow stamens; 'Crown of Gold', rich crimso
flowers with prominent golden stamens; 'Etna
large crimson-scarlet flowers; 'Fascination', wit
vivid orange-red flowers.

Chaenomeles speciosa (fruits)

'Kermesina Semi-Plena' with semi-double, velvety, red flowers; 'Moerloesii', pink and white flowers; 'Nivalis', pure white flowers; 'Phylis Moore', double, salmon-pink flowers; 'Pink Lady', of compact habit, with pure rose-pink flowers; 'Rowallane', of upright habit, with semi-double, clear red flowers; 'Rosea Plena', double rose-pink flowers; 'Rubra Grandiflora', of low, spreading habit, with large crimson flowers; Simonii', of dwarf, almost prostrate and spreading habit, with red flowers; 'Spitfire', deep crimson-red flowers.

C. × *superba*. Height up to 6 ft; spread 4–6 ft. This is a group of free-flowering hybrids between C. *japonica* and C. *speciosa*, similar in habit to that of C. *speciosa*. Recommended forms, which flower from March to May, include: 'Fire Dance', of spreading habit, glowing signal-red flowers; 'Hever Castle', shrimp-pink flowers; 'Knap Hill Scarlet', with large orange-scarlet flowers.

Cultivation. These shrubs thrive in any ordinary garden soil, and do best in a sunny position or trained against a wall of any aspect. Plant from October to March.

Propagation. Take cuttings, 4 in. long, of lateral shoots with a heel in July and August; insert in equal parts (by volume) peat and sand in a propagating frame with a bottom temperature of 16°C (61°F). Pot up the rooted cuttings in 3 in. pots of John Innes potting compost No. 1 and overwinter in a cold frame.

Alternatively, layer long shoots in September; the layers may be slow to root, but should be ready for separating from the parent plant one or two years later.

Sow seeds when ripe, in September or October, in boxes or pans of John Innes seed compost; place the boxes in a cold frame. Prick out the seedlings, when large enough to handle, into a nursery bed outdoors. They will take three to five years to reach flowering size; named varieties do not breed true to type.

Pruning. When grown as a bush, little pruning is required except to thin out crowded branches after flowering. Trained on a wall, these shrubs

should be pruned after flowering in May by cutting back the previous season's growths to two or three buds.

Pests. Sometimes BIRDS attack the flowers.

Diseases. Extreme alkaline soil conditions may cause CHLOROSIS which shows as a yellowing between the veins; sometimes the leaves are almost white.

FIREBLIGHT causes a shrivelling of flowers and a progressive die-back of branches, which bear brown and withered leaves that do not fall.

Chamaecyparis

Cypress. *Cupressaceae*

A genus of six species of hardy evergreen coniferous trees native to North America, Japan and Formosa. They are of slow or moderate growth and differ from the majority of the related cypresses (*Cupressus*) by having the foliage arranged in sprays flattened into one plane, and in bearing smaller cones.

The leaves, in the form of small flat, overlapping scales are borne in pairs on either side of the shoots. Globular cones are freely produced after a few years' growth, except on some permanently juvenile forms; they are composed of a few circular scales with a central spike.

The shape of these trees varies from narrowly conic to broad-crowned specimens. There are numerous dwarf and large-growing forms, all easy to grow, and suitable for a variety of purposes, from rock gardens to lawn specimens or screening and other large-scale planting.

See also CONIFERS.

CHAMAECYPARIS LAWSONIANA

C. *lawsoniana* (Lawson cypress). S.W. Oregon, N.W. California. Height 40 ft; spread 10 ft. This species grows 12–24 in. a year; it is narrowly conic, with a pointed top and drooping leading shoots. The dense crown is often pendulous, and the smooth bark eventually peels off in large strips. The tiny leaves, dark green above with grey marks beneath, show translucent spots; when crushed, they have a parsley-like scent.

Ovoid, dark red male flowers cluster along the tips of the sprays and shed pollen in April; the cones, $\frac{1}{3}$ in. wide, are often profusely borne.

'Allumii' (height 20 ft; spread 5 ft), is a narrowly conic, upright, dull blue-grey form; with age it broadens at the base. It is suitable for formal planting.

'Columnaris', sometimes listed as 'Columnaris Glauca' (height 15 ft; spread 24 in.), a slender, pale grey form of upright habit; good in mixed plantings or as a single, formal dot plant. 'Erecta', syn. 'Erecta Viridis' (height 30 ft; spread 5 ft), a tall, rather broad, pointed-topped column of bright green, with upright branches.

Chaenomeles speciosa
'Crown of Gold'

Chamaecyparis lawsoniana
'Allumii'

Chamaecyparis lawsoniana
'Fletcheri'

'Fletcheri' (height 20 ft; spread 6 ft), usually a multiple column of blue-green, dense fuzzy foliage; 'Green Pillar', syn. 'Jackman's Erecta' is slower and of better shape; more dense and paler in colour. 'Lanei' (height 30 ft; spread 6 ft), a golden form of conic outline; 'Lutea' (height 30 ft; spread 6 ft), a bright golden form with pendulous foliage and a columnar crown; a steady grower in most conditions.

'Pottenii' (height 25 ft; spread 5 ft), a pale green form with feathery foliage, the tips of which stand out level from the upright branches; good for small formal plantings; 'Stewartii' (height 30 ft; spread 8 ft), a bright golden form with distinct, narrow sprays of foliage, green towards the inside and slightly ascending, forming a conic crown.

'Triomphe de Boskoop' (height 45 ft; spread 10 ft), a vigorous grey-blue, open-crowned form with a good, single bole; 'Winston Churchill' (height 25 ft; spread 8 ft), a brilliant, dense golden seedling of 'Lutea' with a rather rounded conic crown.

Dwarf forms include 'Ellwoodii' (height 10 ft; spread 12 in), a grey-green columnar tree; it is extremely slow-growing and suitable for several years in a rock garden; its growth may be retarded by annual lifting and replanting in autumn. Restrict growth to a single leader.

'Ellwood's Gold' (height 6 ft; spread 18 in.) is yellow-green in spring and early summer, becoming dull green later; 'Ellwood's White' has white variegation.

'Minima' (height and spread 3 ft) and 'Nana' (height 4 ft; spread 3 ft) are both reliable dwarf forms, usually represented in cultivation by the blue-green forms 'Minima Glauca' and 'Nana Glauca'; 'Minima' forms a globose or round-topped plant, while 'Nana' is broadly conic.

C. nootkatensis (Nootka cypress). Alaska to Oregon. Height 30 ft; spread 15 ft. An extremely hardy, steadily growing species which maintains a neat, broad, regularly conic shape at all ages. It bears pendulous, dark green and resinous foliage, with an unpleasant smell when crushed, and blue-grey $\frac{1}{2}$ in. wide cones.

This species is useful on cold elevated sites. The variety 'Pendula' has more widely spaced branches curving upwards at the ends with vertically hanging branchlets.

C. obtusa (Hinoki cypress). Japan. Height up to 25 ft; spread 10 ft. An attractive slow-growing species of broadly conic shape. The straight bole has red-brown bark, with regular, shallow, parallel fissures; the branches, with cones about $\frac{1}{3}$ in. across, grow horizontally, then sweep upwards. It bears bright green leaves with silvery marks on the undersides; they have a sweet, resinous smell when crushed. This species is least tolerant of lime or dry soil and grows best in western regions.

'Crippsii' (height 15 ft; spread 8 ft), a bright golden form, particularly good when young. 'Filicoides' (height 10 ft; spread 5 ft), a form with sparse branches having long, hanging, fern-like flat sprays; 'Gracilis', smaller-growing than the type, with slender branchlets, pendent at the tips; 'Lycopodioides' (height 15 ft; spread 5 ft), a variety with bunched, fasciated, nodding and silver-marked foliage.

Chamaecyparis lawsoniana (male flowers)

Chamaecyparis lawsoniana (cones)

Chamaecyparis obtusa 'Crippsii'

Chamaecyparis obtusa 'Nana Aurea'

'Nana Gracilis' (height 8 ft; spread 6 ft), semi-dwarf form with upright flat fans of rich shiny green foliage; 'Tetragona Aurea' (height 1 ft; spread 8 ft), a form with upswept branches carrying dense tufts of bright golden foliage, gaunt and spiky as a young plant.

The species has provided numerous dwarf forms, including some of the smallest conifer known: 'Kosteri' (height 3 ft; spread 24 in.), with foliage in twisted sprays; left untrained it forms a spreading bush and is best grown with the central stem trained as a leader. 'Nana' (height and spread 24 in.) is one of the best dwarf conifers with dense, dull, dark green foliage in tight rounded sprays. 'Nana Aurea' is an attractive golden dwarf form of similar size.

'Pygmaea' (height up to 12 in.; spread up to ft), a flat-topped form with tight, fan-like sprays of horizontal foliage.

CHAMAECYPARIS PISIFERA 'PLUMOSA'

C. pisifera (Sawara cypress). Japan. Height 30 ft; spread 15 ft. A conic species with a nodding leading shoot. The bright green foliage is borne in fern-like sprays, pungently resinous when crushed, and marked with fine silver lines beneath. The bark is bright brown with parallel ridges, and the $\frac{1}{4}$ in. wide cones cluster along the sprays. The type species is rare in cultivation and is largely represented by the following varieties.

'Aurea', similar to the species, but with bright golden new growths, which fade in winter; 'Cyaneoviridis' (height up to 15 ft; spread 10 ft) also known as 'Boulevard', a bright, blue-silver and green feathery plant, brightest in light shade

'Filifera' (height 20 ft; spread 15 ft), a sparsely branching bush with dark grey-green foliage hanging in long threads with few divisions; 'Filifera Aurea', a bright golden form, available as a domed bush or a slender small tree.

'Plumosa' (height 30 ft; spread 15 ft), broadly conic at first, becoming a broad column and usually forking at 6 ft; the pale green foliage is fluffy from the protruding points of the fine scales. 'Plumosa Aurea' is bright gold when young; it sometimes reverts to green.

'Squarrosa' (height 30 ft; spread 20 ft), a slow-growing tree, broadly conic with horizontal branches upswept at the ends; the dense blue-grey foliage is suitable for cutting.

The species has given rise to a large number of slow-growing dwarf forms: 'Compacta' (height 24 in.; spread 4 ft), a compact, low-growing, bun-shaped bush bearing wholly adult, grey-green foliage, arranged in closely set, somewhat recurved sprays. This plant increases in size more rapidly than the variety 'Nana' (height and spread 18 in.) which has tighter and more closely set leaves. Both forms are grey-green; variegated forms also exist.

'Plumosa Aurea Nana' (height 3 ft; spread 24 in.) forms a conical bush; good plants retain their golden colour throughout the year. 'Plumosa Pygmaea' is a similar but slower-growing form; unlike the previous form it is fully hardy.

Cultivation. These conifers thrive in any ordinary, well-drained garden soil and in an open position or in moderate shade. The golden varieties are best grown in full sun, to preserve their colour.

Plant in October on light soils or in April on heavy soils. Large plants may be used but plants of 18 in. or less grow more rapidly and require no staking. Fertilisers are seldom necessary, but a light dressing of a nitrogenous type in April may improve the leaf colour.

Propagation. Sow seeds of the species in pans of John Innes seed compost under glass in February or outside in March or April. Prick out the seedlings, when about 3 in. high, into nursery rows and grow on for two years before transplanting to permanent sites. Named varieties do not come true and must be raised from cuttings.

Select strong new shoots about 4 in. long, preferably with a heel, in May or January. Insert the cuttings in equal parts (by volume) peat and sand in a cold frame for spring cuttings, and in a propagating case at a temperature of 16–18°C (61–64°F) for winter cuttings. Pot the rooted cuttings singly in 3–3½ in. containers of John Innes potting compost No. 2 and plunge outdoors. In autumn, line out in nursery rows and grow on for three years before planting out.

Pruning. None is necessary, except to maintain a single leading shoot when forking occurs. Such pruning may be required in March or April, particularly for some forms of C. lawsoniana. Watch C. pisifera 'Squarrosa' and 'Plumosa' for forking when 5–6 ft tall.

Pests. Generally trouble-free.

Diseases. HONEY FUNGUS may cause death of trees.

Chamaemelum nobile: see *Anthemis nobilis*
Chamaerops excelsa: see *Trachycarpus fortunei*
Chamomile, common: see *Anthemis nobilis*

Chamomile, ox-eye: see *Anthemis tinctoria*
Checkerberry: see *Gaultheria procumbens*

Cheiranthus
Wallflower. *Cruciferae*

CHEIRANTHUS × ALLIONII

A genus of ten species of hardy sub-shrubby perennials; they are short-lived and usually grown as biennials, but valued for their freely produced flowers. The dwarf species are often listed under *Erysimum*.

Wallflowers are among the most popular late spring and early summer-flowering plants and may be grown in beds and borders. The dwarf types are suitable for rock gardens, and the taller varieties make good cut flowers.

The flowers are cross-shaped with rounded oblong petals; they are sometimes fragrant.

C. × allionii (Siberian wallflower). Height 15 in.; planting distance 12 in. This hybrid should properly be included in *Erysimum*, but is described here as it has for long been classified as a true wallflower. The mid-green lanceolate leaves form a rounded ground-covering mound. Terminal spikes of ½ in. wide orange flowers appear from May to July. Recommended varieties include 'Orange Queen', rich deep orange, and 'Golden Bedder', orange-gold.

C. alpinus: see *Erysimum alpinum*
C. capitatus: see *Erysimum capitatum*
C. cheiri. Europe. Height 8–24 in.; planting distance 10–12 in. for dwarf wallflowers, 12–15 in. for tall varieties. A showy plant of erect habit with dark green lanceolate leaves. The ½–1 in. wide flowers are usually yellow, and are carried in dense spikes from April to June.

Numerous varieties are available in colours that include white, yellow, orange, scarlet, crimson and purple. Taller varieties (height 15–18 in.) include: 'Blood Red', deep red; 'Carmine King', carmine; 'Cloth of Gold', golden-yellow; 'Eastern Queen', salmon red; 'Feltham Early', mahogany; 'Fire King', rich orange-red.

'Persian Carpet', a mixture of subtle shades; 'Primrose Monarch', primrose-yellow; 'Ruby Gem', velvety ruby-red; 'Scarlet Emperor', brilliant red; and 'Vulcan', deep velvet-crimson.

Dwarf varieties (height 9–12 in.), include: 'Golden Bedder', 'Orange Bedder', 'Primrose Bedder' and 'Scarlet Bedder'. 'Harpur Crewe' is a fully double, yellow sterile variety. The strain 'Tom Thumb Mixed' comes in a range of colours.

C. mutabilis: see *C. semperflorens*
C. semperflorens, syn. *C. mutabilis*. Morocco. Height 12 in.; planting distance 6–8 in. This species has downy mid-green and lanceolate leaves. The fragrant cream-coloured flowers turn purple; they measure ½–¾ in. across and are freely produced in racemes from May to August.

Chamaecyparis pisifera 'Cyaneoviridis'

Cheiranthus × allionii 'Orange Queen'

Cheiranthus cheiri 'Orange Bedder', 'Scarlet Bedder' and 'Primrose Bedder'

Cultivation. Plant during October in any well-drained garden soil and in a sunny position. Acid soils should be dressed with 4 oz. ground limestone or hydrated lime per sq. yd. Erect a windbreak on exposed sites during exceptionally cold weather. When the plants are 5–6 in. high, pinch out the tips to encourage branching.

Propagation. Sow seeds thinly in an open seed bed during May or June. When the seedlings are large enough to handle, set them 6–9 in. apart in nursery rows and grow on until planting out in the flowering site in October.

C. cheiri 'Harpur Crewe' can only be increased from cuttings. Select 1½–2 in. long lateral shoots with a heel during June and July; insert in equal parts (by volume) peat and sand in a cold frame. When rooted, place the cuttings singly in 3 in. pots of John Innes potting compost No. 1 and plunge outdoors until the following March.

Pests. The roots may be destroyed by CABBAGE ROOT FLY maggots, causing the plants to wilt.

Diseases. Irregular swellings on the roots are caused by CLUB ROOT; the plants become stunted.

CROWN GALL sometimes produces a swelling of the stems at soil level; LEAFY GALL shows as a mass of abortive shoots at soil level.

DOWNY MILDEW produces yellow blotches on the leaves and a grey furry coating on the undersurfaces; it may stunt the plants.

RHIZOCTONIA may cause roots and stems to rot.

STEM ROT, due to a fungus, may also occur; this shows on the stems as decayed areas bearing pin-point, black, spore-producing bodies.

WHITE BLISTER produces powdery white spores on the leaves and sometimes on stems.

WINTER INJURY causes branches and occasionally whole plants to wither.

Chelone obliqua

Cherry 'Merton Bigarreau'

Chelone
Turtle-head. *Scrophulariaceae*

CHELONE OBLIQUA

A genus of four species of hardy herbaceous perennials. The flowers are snapdragon-like and borne on erect stems. The plants described are suitable for herbaceous and mixed borders.

C. barbata: see *Penstemon barbatus*

C. lyonii. N. America. Height 2–3 ft; planting distance 18–24 in. A species with dark green leaves that are broadly ovate and borne in opposite pairs. Terminal clusters of pink flowers, 1 in. long, open from July to September.

C. obliqua. N. America. Height up to 24 in.; planting distance 12–18 in. Prominent veining is a feature of the broad, dark green, lanceolate leaves. Terminal spikes of deep rose flowers, 1 in. long, are borne in August and September.

Cultivation. Plant chelones during suitable weather between September and March in a sunny or partially shaded position in deep light

soil. In an exposed position they may need supporting with twiggy sticks. Cut down the dead stems in October.

Propagation. Sow seeds in boxes or pans of John Innes seed compost, either under glass in March at a temperature of about 15°C (59°F), or in a cold frame in April. Prick out the seedlings into boxes in May or early June, and later into a nursery bed. Plant out in permanent positions, 18 months to two years after sowing.

Divide and replant the roots between September and March.

Pests and diseases. Generally trouble-free.

Cherries, Japanese: see Prunus
Cherries, ornamental: see Prunus

Cherry
Prunus avium, P. cerasus. Rosaceae

CHERRY

These hardy deciduous trees are grown for their edible, single-seeded fruits. Cultivated cherries originated from two species, both of which now occur wild in Great Britain but were probably introduced from Asia Minor by the Romans. They are *Prunus avium,* the sweet cherry, and *P. cerasus,* the acid cherry. Neither thrives at more than 500 ft above sea-level, nor in frost pockets.

Sweet cherries are usually grown as standard and half-standards. As there are no dwarfing rootstocks commercially available, bush trees are hardly practical and sweet cherries are therefore unsuitable for small gardens. They are self-sterile, and to ensure pollination more than one variety needs to be planted.

Ideally, sweet cherries should be grown only in areas where the normal summer rainfall provides a steady water supply for the swelling fruits, ensuring good size without splitting.

Acid cherries can be grown as bushes or be fan-trained. They do not require such fertile soil as sweet cherries, but need equally good drainage. They bear fruit after six to ten years.

The following measurements are the average heights and spreads: sweet cherry, standard or half-standard, 40 × 30 ft; acid cherry, bush 20 × 15 ft, fan-trained 15 ft. Planting distances: sweet cherry, standard or half-standard, 35–45 ft; acid cherry, bush 18–20 ft, fan-trained 15–18 ft.

Treat all varieties of sweet cherries as self-sterile; 'Early Rivers' will pollinate the 'Merton' varieties 'Frogmore Early', 'White Heart', and vice versa. The acid cherry 'Morello' is self-fertile; it will pollinate sweet cherries that flower at the same time.

SWEET CHERRIES

'Bigarreau Napoleon'. Late July. Large, pale yellow, mottled dark red, good-flavoured fruit. Moderately vigorous and spreading. Flowers late

Early Rivers'. Mid to late June. Juicy, red-black fruits of delicious flavour. Vigorous growth. Flowers early.

Frogmore Early'. Late June. Large, pale yellow, marbled light red, soft and juicy, fine-flavoured fruits. Vigorous, spreading tree. Flowers late.

Merton Bigarreau'. Mid to late July. Red to black, rich flavour. Vigorous and spreading. Flowers mid-season.

Merton Bounty'. Late June to early July. Purple juicy fruits with soft skins. Vigorous growth. Flowers mid-season.

Merton Favourite'. Early July. Black, large, good-flavoured fruits. Vigorous and spreading. Flowers early to mid-season.

White Heart'. Late July. Pale yellow, flushed and mottled red, medium-sized, tender and good-flavoured fruits. Moderately vigorous, of spreading and arching growth. Flowers late. The name 'White Heart' is sometimes used to describe other cherry varieties of similar appearance.

ACID CHERRY

Morello'. July and August. Round, deep red to black fruits. Prolific. Self-fertile. Suitable for a north wall. Flowers late.

Cultivation. Plant fan-trained trees when they are four years old, bush trees, standards and half-standards when they are two years old. Cherries can be planted at any time from November to February, but November is the best month.

Sweet cherries require a deep, well-drained, fertile loam and will not thrive on poorer soils. For preference, the soil should contain some lime. Acid cherries grow satisfactorily on most ordinary soils provided they are well drained. An open site is needed for all cherries, preferably on a slope so that frost danger is minimised.

Once sweet cherries become established they can be grassed down. Grow acid cherries in bare soil kept free of weeds by shallow hoeing or chemical weed-killers.

Birds attack the flower buds in winter and the developing fruits in summer, particularly those of sweet cherries. Where only a few trees are grown, protect them with nets if possible.

Mulch sweet cherries with well-rotted manure in spring and feed with $\frac{1}{2}-\frac{3}{4}$ oz. sulphate of potash per sq. yd. Every third year give an application of 2–3 oz. superphosphate per sq. yd.

Apply sulphate of ammonia at $1\frac{1}{2}-2$ oz. per sq. yd and sulphate of potash at $\frac{1}{2}$ oz. per sq. yd, both in spring, to all acid cherries. Apply superphosphate every two or three years at $1\frac{1}{2}-2$ oz. per sq. yd. Give slightly smaller amounts of fertiliser to fan-trained trees, where less growth is required. Ensure regular water supplies in summer to acid cherries growing on walls.

Light crops of sweet cherries may be due to poor pollination, because of bad weather or because compatible varieties are too far apart.

Leave the fruits on the trees until fully ripe, unless they start to split, but use them quickly after picking. Splitting may be caused by intermittent heavy rain in summer.

Acid cherries are best cut off the tree, using scissors to prevent tearing the bark and so giving entry to diseases.

Propagation. This is usually done by budding or grafting. There are no dwarfing rootstocks generally available, though these are being developed, and the wild cherry has been widely used as a rootstock for sweet and acid cherries. To overcome bacterial canker a resistant rootstock, 'Malling F 12/1', is used to build up the trunk and branches, the buds being inserted at the base of the lateral branches.

Pruning. Shorten the leaders of all young trees by half in winter. As the trees mature, pruning of sweet cherries can be less severe and after four years entails only the removal of dead wood and unwanted branches. Prune acid cherries annually throughout their life. The method is explained in the chapter headed PRUNING.

Pests. BIRDS, particularly bullfinches, eat buds during the winter and others, notably blackbirds, eat the ripening fruits.

APHIDS, especially cherry blackfly, infest the tips of young shoots, distorting leaves and checking growth.

Diseases. BACTERIAL CANKER either prevents the buds of infected branches from opening in the spring or causes unfolding leaves to turn yellow and become narrow and curled; they wither and die during the summer. Towards the base of an affected limb and usually on one side, will be found an elongated shallow lesion which enlarges, and the diseased branch shows a characteristic flattening along one side. Copious gum exudes from the lesion.

CHLOROSIS shows on the leaves as a yellowing between the veins and is a common trouble on trees growing in soils that are too alkaline.

HONEY FUNGUS may kill trees rapidly. They can also die fairly quickly as a result of waterlogging.

SHOT HOLE, due to a fungus, causes numerous brown rounded spots on the leaves. The tissues fall away, leaving holes in the leaves.

SILVER LEAF causes a silvering of the foliage on one or more branches, which die back, eventually killing the tree. Flat purple fruiting bodies of the fungus appear on dead wood. A purple-brown stain appears in the inner tissues of diseased stems; a cross-section of a branch with silvered leaves should be examined for such signs.

Chervil

Anthriscus cerefolium. Umbelliferae

This hardy biennial herb, generally grown as an annual, is used for flavouring.

Height 12–18 in.; spacing 9–12 in. S.E. Europe, W. Asia. The ridged stems of chervil are hollow and strongly aromatic. The leaves are bright green and ferny, somewhat similar to

Cherry 'Morello'

Chervil

Chicory (chicons)

Chicory (flowers)

Chimonanthus praecox

those of parsley; there are both smooth-leaved and curly varieties. White flowers in umbels, 3 in. across, are borne from June to August in the plant's second year.

CHERVIL

Use the leaves fresh, dried or frozen in the same way as parsley, for flavouring salads, soups and sauces, and as *fines herbes* for omelettes. The dried leaves can also be used in stuffings.

Cultivation. Chervil is easy to grow on all types of soil, in sun or partial shade. Fresh leaves are ready for use six to eight weeks after sowing. Pinch out the flower buds as soon as they appear if the seeds are not required.

Chervil is hardy, and fresh leaves are often available all year round. In severe winters, protect the plants with cloches.

Propagation. For a succession of fresh leaves, sow seeds outdoors where the plants are to grow, at monthly intervals from March to August in rows 12 in. apart. Thin the seedlings to 6 in. apart at first, then to 12 in.

The seeds remain viable for only about a year and should be sown as soon as possible after they are ripe. Alternatively, allow some plants to seed themselves and transplant the seedlings when they are large enough to handle.

Seeds can also be sown in boxes or trays of seed compost from September onwards and grown in the greenhouse for winter use. Maintain a temperature of 7–10°C (45–50°F) from the time of sowing onwards. Space the seeds well apart and grow the plants on in the boxes, or prick out the seedlings singly into 3–4 in. pots containing John Innes potting compost No. 2.

Harvesting and storing. Use fresh leaves whenever possible as these have the best flavour. For drying, cut the leaves between six and eight weeks after sowing or, if the plants are left to grow on, before flowering in the second year. For methods of drying and deep-freezing, see entry under HERBS.

Pests and diseases. Generally trouble-free.

Chestnut, common horse: see *Aesculus hippocastanum*
Chestnut, horse: see Aesculus
Chestnut, Indian horse: see *Aesculus indica*
Chestnut, red horse: see *Aesculus × carnea*
Chestnut, Spanish: see *Castanea sativa*
Chestnut, sweet: see Castanea

Chicory

Cichorium intybus. Compositae

A hardy perennial plant grown as an annual for its hearted head of leaves which are used in winter and spring salads. The hearts, known as chicons, are white, crisp and slightly bitter.

Chicory is sometimes grown as a decorative plant in mixed or herbaceous borders. Sky-blue dandelion-like flowers, 1–1½ in. across, appear in succession from July to October on erect branched stems up to 3 ft high. There is also a pink-flowered variety.

VARIETIES
Few varieties are available, but 'Witloof of Brussels' is a reliable form with long chicons.

CHICORY

Cultivation. Chicory requires careful cultivation over two stages; first to produce large, healthy tap-roots, and second to force these roots from which the chicons develop.

Grow chicory on ground that was well manured for a previous crop. In early spring dig the plot deeply, and apply a top-dressing of 6 oz of carbonate of lime per sq. yd, except on lime or chalky soil.

Sow seeds during late April or early May in ½ in. deep drills, 15 in. apart. When the seedlings show their third leaf, thin them to 9 in. apart.

Forcing and harvesting. In November, when the leaves are dying down and the roots are fully grown, lift these carefully. They should be 2–3 in. thick at the top and up to 12 in. long. Trim them to 8 in. and cut off their foliage just above the crown; store in a frost-proof but cool place.

Force a few roots at a time to keep up a succession of chicons through the winter. Pack the roots upright, 2–3 in. apart, in boxes or pots containing sand or light soil. Cover with boxes or pots to shut out all light and place at a temperature of 7–10°C (45–50°F). Cut the hearted chicons when they are 5–6 in. long.

Pests. The roots may be eaten by caterpillars of SWIFT MOTHS, and SLUGS may be troublesome.
Diseases. Generally trouble-free.

Chilean fire bush: see Embothrium
Chili: see *Capsicum annuum*

Chimonanthus

Winter sweet. *Calycanthaceae*

CHIMONANTHUS PRAECOX

A genus of four species of deciduous and evergreen shrubs, native to China. Only one species is in general cultivation; this is grown for its scented flowers in winter.

C. fragrans: see *C. praecox*

C. praecox, syn. *C. fragrans.* Height up to 10 ft, or more on a wall; spread 8–10 ft. A deciduous shrub of bushy habit and twiggy growth. The shiny, mid-green, willow-like leaves are lanceolate. The cup-shaped flowers, ¾–1 in. wide, are borne singly or in pairs from the joints on the naked twigs. They have yellow outer petals and shorter, purple inner ones and appear from December to February. They have a heavy spicy scent. The species is hardy, but takes several years to reach flowering size. 'Grandiflorus' has larger, deeper yellow flowers with red centres; 'Luteus' has pure yellow flowers.

Cultivation. Plant in any good garden soil from October to March. These shrubs do best in full sun and preferably grown against a south or west-facing wall.

Propagation. Sow seeds when ripe, in September or October, in a cold frame or greenhouse; prick the seedlings out, when large enough to handle, into 3½ in. pots and plunge outdoors. Plant out in nursery rows in October and transplant to their flowering positions three or four years later. Plants raised from seeds usually take five to ten years to reach flowering size.

Alternatively, layer long shoots in September; sever from the parent plant two years later.

Pruning. Bush-grown shrubs require little pruning except to thin out old and crowded wood after flowering. Wall-trained shrubs should be pruned in March by cutting hard back all flowered shoots to within a few inches of the base.

Pests. Generally trouble-free.

Diseases. A PHYSIOLOGICAL DISORDER due to unsuitable soil conditions shows as brown blotches or yellowing on the leaves.

Chincherinchee: see *Ornithogalum thyrsoides*
Chinese cabbage: see Cabbage
Chinese lantern: see *Physalis alkekengii*

Chionodoxa

Glory of the snow. *Liliaceae*

CHIONODOXA LUCILIAE

A genus of six species of hardy bulbous perennials. These early spring-flowering plants are suitable for growing on rock gardens, at the front of borders and in short grass. The species described bear strap-shaped and blunt-tipped, mid-green leaves, often with bronze margins when young. The star-shaped, six-petalled flowers are carried in loose racemes.

C. gigantea, syn. *C. grandiflora.* Asia Minor. Height 8 in.; planting distance 3–4 in. This species is thought by botanists to be a large form of *C. luciliae.* The flower-spike carries several pale violet-blue flowers, 1½ in. across, each with a small white centre. Flowering is from late February to April.

C. grandiflora: see *C. gigantea*
C. luciliae. Crete, Asia Minor. Height 6 in.; planting distance 2–4 in. This species bears light blue, white-centred flowers, up to 1 in. across, from February to March. *C. l.* 'Alba' is a white form of this species; *C. l.* 'Rosea' and 'Pink Giant' are pink forms.

C. sardensis. Asia Minor. Height 4–6 in.; planting distance 2–4 in. The small bulb produces two folded leaves. Slender stems carry nodding sky-blue flowers, ¾ in. across, with tiny white centres. Flowering is from March to early May.

Cultivation. Plant in autumn, in ordinary well-drained garden soil and in full sun. Set the bulbs 2–3 in. deep in large groups. Once established little attention is required except to lift and divide overcrowded plants, preferably as the foliage is dying down.

Propagation. The seeds set freely under good conditions. Remove the round seed pods in late spring, when the seeds are ripe (black) but before the capsules have opened. Sow the seeds in a frame or border at once and leave until the foliage dies down the following year. Transplant the seedlings to their flowering positions during the second summer.

Pests. The leaves and flowers may be eaten by SLUGS.

Diseases. The anthers and, less frequently, the ovaries are sometimes converted into masses of black powdery spores by SMUT.

Chittam wood: see *Cotinus americanus*

Chives

Allium schoenoprasum. Alliaceae

CHIVES

This hardy perennial herb is used for flavouring. It is easy to grow and increases rapidly.

Height 6–10 in.; planting distance 12 in. Europe, including Great Britain; N. Asia. The grass-like tubular leaves are mid-green. Starry, rose-pink flowers, arranged in dense globular heads, 1–1½ in. across, appear in June and July.

The leaves are mainly used fresh to give their mild, onion-like flavour to salads, soups and egg and cheese dishes. They are also used in *sauce tartare* and as *fines herbes.*

Cultivation. Chives thrive in medium, loamy soil and in sun or semi-shade; they can be grown in any fertile, well-drained garden soil and do well in window-boxes. They need frequent watering during dry spells. Pinch off the flower heads.

The plants die down completely in winter and reappear the following spring, producing leaves ready for use by early May. Clumps protected by cloches throughout the winter produce leaves by March or April. Give the plants a top-dressing of well-rotted compost in March or April.

Chionodoxa gigantea

Chionodoxa luciliae

Chionodoxa sardensis

Clumps lifted for propagation in September or October may be grown indoors in pots to provide fresh leaves for winter use. Place them in John Innes potting compost No. 1; keep them well watered and harvest the leaves regularly so as to maintain steady growth.

Propagation. Sow seeds outdoors in March in drills ½ in. deep and 12 in. apart. Thin the seedlings to 6 in. apart and transplant to permanent positions in May. Thereafter, increase the stock by division.

Every four years lift the clumps in September or October, divide them with a sharp knife into bunches of about half a dozen shoots and replant them about 12 in. apart in fresh ground that has been dressed with well-rotted compost.

Harvesting and storing. Cut the leaves close to the ground when they have reached their normal height. They are generally used fresh, but the leaves can be dried or deep-frozen. For methods of drying, see entry under HERBS. A clump may also be lifted and grown indoors for winter use.

Pests. Generally trouble-free.

Diseases. On the leaves, RUST shows as elongated yellow or red-yellow pustules.

Chives (flowers)

Chlorophytum elatum 'Variegatum'

Chlorophytum

Liliaceae

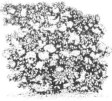

CHLOROPHYTUM ELATUM 'VARIEGATUM'

A genus of 215 species of evergreen greenhouse plants. Only one species is in general cultivation. It is easy to grow and makes an attractive foliage plant for the greenhouse or a living-room.

C. capense: see *C. elatum*

C. comosum: see *C. elatum*

C. elatum 'Variegatum', syn. *C. comosum*. S. Africa. Height 10 in. The narrow, linear leaves, which may reach 12 in., are pale to mid green, banded with white. In some forms the margins are white and the centre band green, in others the margins are green and the centre white. In summer the plant produces flowering stems up to 24 in. long, the upper third of which branches to form a diffuse panicle. The white star-shaped flowers, 1 in. wide, are mixed with small plantlets which can be pegged down to root. The plant is now more correctly listed as *C. capense*.

Cultivation. Grow chlorophytums in John Innes potting compost No. 2 or in a proprietary peat mixture. Keep the compost moist in spring and summer; give less water from October to March, but do not let the plants dry out completely. Maintain a minimum winter temperature of 7°C (45°F), although the plants can survive for short periods in lower temperatures if kept dry.

Give the plants as much light and air as possible in summer.

Large specimens give the best effect, and the plants may be potted on annually in March or April until they are in 6–8 in. pots. Browning at the leaf tips is common if potting on or feeding is neglected; give the plants liquid manure once a week from June to September. Keep house plants in a well-lit, draught-proof position.

Propagation. Peg the young plantlets at the ends of the inflorescence into small pots containing the growing compost. Ensure that they are well rooted before separating from the parent.

Large plants can be divided and replanted during March and April.

Pests. Generally trouble-free.

Diseases. A PHYSIOLOGICAL DISORDER causes the leaf tips to turn brown or the leaf blades to split.

Choisya

Mexican orange. *Rutaceae*

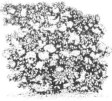

CHOISYA TERNATA

A genus of six species of evergreen flowering shrubs, native to Mexico. Only one species is in general cultivation; it is hardy, but in the north is best grown as a wall shrub.

C. ternata. Height 5–6 ft, or more in mild gardens or on sheltered walls; spread 6–8 ft. A shrub of wide-spreading and rounded, bushy habit. The trifoliate glossy green leaves are highly aromatic when crushed. Sweet-scented orange-blossom-like white flowers, 1–1½ in. across, are borne in corymbs in the leaf axils at the ends of the shoots; they appear in April and May, and intermittently until the winter.

Cultivation. Choisyas thrive in any well-drained garden soil. Plant in April and May in a sheltered position, preferably in full sun, although the shrubs are tolerant of partial shade. In cold northern gardens, they do best against a south wall as the foliage is liable to frost damage.

Propagation. Take cuttings, 3 in. long, of half-ripened lateral shoots in August; insert in equal parts (by volume) peat and sand at a temperature of 16–18°C (61–64°F). Pot the rooted cuttings in 3 in. containers of John Innes potting compost No. 2 and overwinter in a cold frame. Pot on into 4 in. pots the following May and plunge outdoors. Alternatively, in mild areas line the cuttings out in nursery rows and grow on until May of the next year. In cold areas, overwinter the young pot plants in a cold frame.

Pruning. No regular pruning is required, but shorten and thin out straggly shoots immediately after the main flowering. Frost-damaged shoots should be removed entirely in March; new shoots will appear from the base.

Pests. Generally trouble-free.

Diseases. FROST DAMAGE may kill the shoots; and HONEY FUNGUS has been known to cause the rapid death of shrubs.

Choisya ternata

Christmas tree: see *Picea abies*

Chrysanthemum 'Bronze Rayonnante' (Thread-petalled)

Chrysanthemum 'Catena' (Anemone-flowered)

Chrysanthemum hosmariense

Chrysanthemum alpinum

Chrysanthemum carinatum

CHRYSANTHEMUM
Compositae

A genus of more than 200 species of hardy annuals, hardy and half-hardy sub-shrubs and herbaceous and greenhouse perennials. Botanically, the genus now includes *Pyrethrum* and *Tanacetum* which are described separately.

These plants are suitable for growing on rock gardens, in mixed borders and as pot plants outdoors, in the greenhouse or in the home.

For ease of reference, chrysanthemums have here been divided into alpine, annual and perennial species, followed by the large group popularly known as florists' chrysanthemums.

ALPINE SPECIES
These hardy dwarf or sub-shrubby species have deeply cut, ovate to obovate leaves and single, daisy-like flowers.

C. alpinum. European Alps. Height 6 in.; spread up to 12 in. This species forms tufts of deep green foliage, and bears neat white flowers, 1–1¼ in. across, in July and August.

C. haradjanii: see *Tanacetum densum* 'Amani'

C. hosmariense, syn. *Leucanthemum hosmariense*. Asia Minor. Height 6–8 in.; spread 12 in. or more. A sub-shrubby species with silver-grey leaves. White flowers, 1½ in. across, appear from March to November.

C. weyrichii. Kamchatka. Height 4–6 in.; spread 6–9 in. This plant has a woody rootstock from which rise the shiny light green leaves. The handsome flowers are nearly 2 in. across and have pink ray florets and bright yellow discs. They are borne in late September.

ANNUAL SPECIES
The following species are all free-flowering and hardy in the open. They are well-branched, bushy plants with much-divided ovate leaves and daisy-like flowers. They are suitable as edgings to borders, for informal bedding, as pot plants and as cut flowers.

CHRYSANTHEMUM CARINATUM

C. carinatum, syn. *C. tricolor.* N. Africa. Height 24 in.; planting distance 12 in. An erect plant with stiff, bright green leaves. The single flowers

141

Chrysanthemum parthenium 'Snowball'

Chrysanthemum parthenium 'Gold Star'

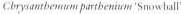

Chrysanthemum coronarium

Chrysanthemum coronarium
'Flore-plenum'

are borne on long stiff stems from June to September. They are $2\frac{1}{2}$ in. across and have purple discs surrounded by ray petals banded with different colours.

Numerous named varieties are available: 'Merry Mixed' and the recently introduced 'Monarch Court Jesters' are recommended for their large, attractively zoned, single flowers in a wide range of colours; they are suitable for growing outdoors or in pots. 'Dunnett's Mixed' bears a profusion of double flowers in a wide range of colours; 'Northern Star' has large, pure white, yellow-zoned single flowers.

C. coronarium. Mediterranean areas. Height 1–4 ft; planting distance 15 in. A species of erect and branching habit, with pale green leaves. Double, semi-double or single flowers, produced from July to August, range from white to golden-yellow; they are $1\frac{1}{2}$–2 in. across.

Recommended varieties include: 'Flore-plenum', $2\frac{1}{2}$ ft, with semi or fully double flowers in shades of golden-yellow and white; 'Golden Crown', up to 4 ft, of upright growth with silver-green foliage and single, deep yellow flowers; 'Golden Gem', 12 in., a compact plant, excellent for pot cultivation, with golden-yellow double flowers; 'Golden Glory', 24 in., with deep yellow, single flowers.

C. frutescens. Canary Islands. Height and spread 12–18 in. This sub-shrubby plant is a perennial species which is usually grown as an annual pot plant in a greenhouse or in summer bedding schemes. The leaves are pale to glaucous-green; white or pale yellow flowers, 2 in. across, are borne from May to October, sometimes longer.

The species may be grown as a perennial in a greenhouse border where it will reach shrubby proportions, up to 3 ft, and be in flower for much of the year.

C. multicaule. Algeria. Height 6–12 in.; planting distance 9 in. A compact, bushy plant, excellent for window-boxes, pots, rock gardens and for edging borders. The leaves are blue-grey, rather

fleshy and coarsely toothed. Single, bright golden-yellow flowers, 1 in. across, are borne from July to August.

CHRYSANTHEMUM PARTHENIUM 'SNOWBALL'

C. parthenium, syn. *Matricaria eximia.* Great Britain. Height and planting distance 9–18 in. A bushy, hardy but short-lived perennial species that is usually grown as an annual. It has pungently aromatic light green leaves. White flowers, $\frac{3}{4}$ in. across, are freely produced from July to September.

Several varieties are available; they all flower the first year from seed. The flowers are long-lasting and the plants are ideal for beds, pots and window-boxes. 'Aureum', 18 in., has golden-green foliage and single white flowers; 'Golden Ball', 10 in., is compact, with clusters of ball-shaped, golden-yellow flowers; 'Gold Star', 8 in., has a row of white ray petals surrounding the yellow centre; 'Snowball', 12 in., has ivory-white pompon-like flowers; 'White Bonnet', $2\frac{1}{2}$ ft, has double, pure white flowers.

C. segetum. Great Britain. Height 18 in.; planting distance 12 in. This species is suitable for growing in a border and for cutting. The oblong leaves are grey-green; single flowers, $2\frac{1}{2}$ in. across and usually yellow, are borne from July to September. Two good varieties are: 'Eastern Star', primrose-yellow with a brown disc; and 'Evening Star', bright golden-yellow.

C. × spectabile. Height 3–4 ft; planting distance 18 in. A hybrid between *C. carinatum* and *C. coronarium,* ideal for cutting and for border cultivation. The leaves are somewhat grey-green

Chrysanthemum 'Cossack' (Medium exhibition)

Chrysanthemum 'Charles Shoesmith' (Large exhibition)

nd deeply toothed. Single, variously coloured flowers, 3–4 in. wide, are produced from June to September. 'Cecilia', $2\frac{1}{2}$ ft, is a tetraploid form with long-stemmed flowers; these are white, banded yellow and with a bright yellow disc.

C. tricolor: see *C. carinatum*

PERENNIAL SPECIES.

Those described are hardy and free-flowering, with ovate, deeply lobed and cut foliage, and single or double daisy-like flowers. They are excellent as cut flowers.

C. coccineum: see *Pyrethrum roseum*

C. corymbosum, syns. *Pyrethrum corymbosum*, *Tanacetum corymbosum*. Europe, Caucasus, Asia Minor. Height $2\frac{1}{2}$–3 ft; planting distance 12–15 in. This species has mid-green leaves and branching heads of single white flowers, $1\frac{1}{2}$–2 in. across, on erect stems. They flower in July.

C. erubescens: see *C. rubellum*

C. frutescens: see ANNUAL SPECIES

CHRYSANTHEMUM MAXIMUM

C. maximum (Shasta daisy). Pyrenees. Height $2\frac{1}{2}$–3 ft; planting distance 12–18 in. This is a coarse species, with dark green leaves that are lanceolate and toothed. Single white flowers, $2\frac{1}{2}$–3 in. across and with a golden eye, are borne on strong stems from June to August.

The type species has been superseded by numerous named varieties: 'Aglaia', $2\frac{1}{2}$ ft high, semi-double white flowers; 'Esther Read', $2\frac{1}{2}$ ft, double white; 'Horace Read', 3 ft, double cream-white; 'H. Seibert', $2\frac{1}{2}$ ft, single white, frilled petals; 'Wirral Pride', 3 ft, semi-double white; 'Wirral Supreme', 3 ft, double white.

C. parthenium: see ANNUAL SPECIES

C. rubellum. Japan. Height $1\frac{1}{2}$–$2\frac{1}{2}$ ft; planting distance 12–18 in. A species with mid-green leaves and with terminal heads of single, pink, fragrant flowers, $1\frac{1}{2}$–2 in. across. These are borne from August to October. Also known as *C. erubescens,* this plant should correctly be listed as *C. zawadskii latilobum.*

The following are good varieties: 'Clara Curtis', clear pink; 'Duchess of Edinburgh', bright crimson; 'Mary Stoker', soft yellow; 'Royal Command', semi-double, purple-red.

C. uliginosum, syn. *Pyrethrum uliginosum* (moon daisy). Hungary, E. Europe. Height up to 6 ft; planting distance 18 in. This tall-growing species has deeply cut, slightly grey-green foliage. Single white flowers, 2 in. across, with sulphur-green centres, are borne on erect branching stems in October and November.

C. zawadskii latilobum: see *C. rubellum*

FLORISTS' CHRYSANTHEMUMS

The following large group comprises half-hardy border perennials and hardy greenhouse plants. They are all derived from the rarely grown *C. indicum* and *C. morifolium* and possibly from other wild species native to China and Japan.

These varieties all have deep green and obovate leaves, clefted into rounded lobes. They are suitable for growing in borders or as pot plants, outdoors or in the greenhouse. Some varieties are also suitable as house plants and all provide excellent cut flowers.

The varieties are classified as early-flowering (outdoor) or late-flowering (indoor), according to their natural flowering time.

These chrysanthemums are further classified under seven main groups, according to the type of bloom:

1. INCURVED; blooms with close, firm petals forming a perfect globe.

2. REFLEXED; blooms with petals falling outwards and downwards, and overlapping like feathers on a bird.

Chrysanthemum maximum 'Wirral Pride'

Chrysanthemum 'Audrey Shoesmith' (Exhibition incurved)

143

3. INTERMEDIATE (formerly Incurving); similar to Group 1, but the petals incurve loosely and irregularly.

4. SINGLE; blooms with five or less rows of petals round a central disc or daisy eye.

5. ANEMONE CENTRED; similar to Group 4, but the central disc consists of tubular florets forming a raised cushion.

6. POMPONS; small globular or button-shaped blooms with tightly packed petals.

7. OTHER TYPES; chiefly thread-petalled or spidery blooms with long, tubular or spoon-shaped petals. This also includes the spray types and the cascade chrysanthemums.

Because of the wide diversity of size of bloom and flowering time within these seven groups, varieties have been further divided. There are hundreds of varieties within each subdivision; here only one example is given for each:

Late-flowering (indoor) varieties which bloom in the greenhouse from October to December (height 2½–6 ft). Large exhibition: 'Charles Shoesmith', light bronze, 8–9 in., November. Medium exhibition: 'Cossack', crimson, 8–9 in., November. Exhibition incurved, large-flowered: 'Audrey Shoesmith', pink, 6–7 in., November. Exhibition incurved, medium-flowered: 'Maylen', cream-white, 6–7 in., November.

Reflexed decorative, large-flowered: 'Firecracker', brilliant crimson, 6–7 in., November. Reflexed decorative, medium-flowered: 'Rose Harrison', pink, 4–5 in., December. Intermediate decorative, large-flowered: 'Yellow Fred Shoesmith', yellow, 6–7 in., November to December. Intermediate decorative, medium-flowered: 'Loveliness', lilac, 4–5 in., November. Anemone, large-flowered: 'Marion Stacey', purple-red, 5–6 in., November to December. Anemone, medium-flowered: 'Denebola', pink to white, 4–5 in., November.

Single, large-flowered: 'Preference', pink, 6–7 in., November. Single, medium-flowered: 'Mason's Bronze', 3–4 in., November. Pompon: 'Forty Niner', yellow, 1 in., November. Spray: 'Portrait', pink, 1–2 in., November. Thread-petalled: 'Bronze Rayonnante', bronze, 5–6 in., October to November. Spidery: 'Honeysuckle', yellow, 4–5 in., October.

October-flowering, intermediate decorative, large-flowered: 'Gold Plate', golden reflexed, 7–8 in. October-flowering, large: 'Fantastic', white to pale pink, 8–9 in. October-flowering, spray: 'Mermaid', pink, 1–2 in. Other types: 'Sweet Seventeen', pink reflexed, 3–4 in., October. Cascade: 'Charm', yellow, bronze, red, violet or pink, 1½ in., October.

Early-flowering (outdoor) varieties which bloom in the open without protection from August to late September (height 3–5 ft, pompons 1–2 ft): Incurved decorative, large-flowered: 'Primrose Evelyn Bush', yellow, 4–5 in., September. Incurved decorative, medium-flowered: 'Martin Riley', yellow, 3–4 in., September. Reflexed, large-flowered: 'Tracey Waller', pink, 6–7 in., September. Reflexed, medium-flowered: 'Pinksmoor', pink, 4–5 in.

Intermediate decorative, large-flowered: 'Escort', red, 5–6 in., September. Intermediate decorative, medium-flowered: 'Claret Glow', cerise, 4–5 in., August. Anemone: 'Catena', buff,

Chrysanthemum 'Maylen'
(Exhibition incurved)

Chrysanthemum 'Firecracker'
(Reflexed decorative)

Chrysanthemum 'Loveliness'
(Intermediate decorative)

Chrysanthemum 'Yellow Fred Shoesmith'
(Intermediate decorative)

Chrysanthemum 'Marion Stacey'
(Anemone-flowered)

Chrysanthemum 'Preference'
(Single- flowered)

Chrysanthemum 'Pinksmoor' (Reflexed medium-flowered)

Chrysanthemum 'Gold Plate' (Intermediate decorative)

3–4 in., August. Single, large-flowered: 'Daphne', pink, 3–4 in., August. Single, medium-flowered: 'Doreen Woolman', pink, 3–4 in., September.

Pompon (true): 'Fairie', pink, 1 in., August. Pompon (semi): 'Denise', yellow, 1–2 in., August. Spray: 'Golden Orfe', golden-yellow, 2–3 in., September. Other types: 'Orchid Spoon', pink 1–2 in., September.

Cultivation of alpine species. Plant from September to April in well-drained, gritty soil, and in a sunny position. If planted in too rich soil these plants lose their compact habit.

Cultivation of annual species. The annual chrysanthemums grow and flower freely in all soils, but give the best results in fertile, light, well-drained soil, in a sunny position. On exposed sites staking with twiggy pea sticks may be necessary for tall varieties. Pinch out the first flower buds on plants grown for cutting to encourage longer-stemmed side-shoots.

Autumn-sown seedlings may be potted into 5 in. pots of John Innes potting compost No. 1 and grown on in a cold greenhouse to flower in late spring and early summer.

C. frutescens is grown from cuttings; plants raised for bedding purposes should be grown in 4–5 in. pots of John Innes potting compost No. 1. Bed out when danger of frost is past, usually in late May.

At the end of the summer discard all plants except those that are to be used for propagation in February. Lift these plants in September and pot in 5–6 in. pots of John Innes potting compost No. 2; cut the plants back by half to promote lateral growths for cuttings, and keep the plants growing throughout the winter at a temperature of 7–10°C (45–50°F).

Cultivation of perennial species. Plant from September to April in a sunny position and in well-drained, fertile soil, preferably containing lime. *C. uliginosum* does best in moist soil and will tolerate partial shade. Every third year lift, divide and replant in March or April.

Varieties of *C. rubellum* often produce such large flower clusters that the plants need supporting with short pea sticks. Cut the stems of all perennials back to ground level in December.

Cultivation of florists' chrysanthemums. Outdoor varieties may be grown in the open ground, or in containers such as pots or boxes. The soil should be well drained with ample supplies of organic material. Prepare the ground in spring with a dressing of a complete base fertiliser, 6 oz. per sq. yd. For outdoor pot plants, use John Innes potting compost No. 2, or a proprietary loamless mixture.

Plant out in early May, or in late April in milder areas. The soil should be moist, but not wet and sticky. It is essential to plant shallowly, or the young shoots may not develop.

Firm the plants enough to keep them in an upright position, but be careful not to damage the young roots. Set out the plants at intervals of 12–18 in., and insert supporting canes or stakes. Tie the stems loosely to the stakes, which should be about 4 ft tall. Continue tying in the plants with raffia or soft twine as they grow, or support with welded wire mesh fastened to wooden battens, secured to strong upright stakes. Raise the wire mesh as the plants grow.

Water well immediately after planting and not again for three or four days. After this, an adequate supply of water is essential for steady growth; plants will require a thorough soaking every seven days in all but rainy weather.

Feed with liquid manure every seven to ten days from mid-June until the buds begin to show colour, usually in early August.

The greenhouse (late-flowering) varieties are grown in pots. The best results are obtained from plants which are given three pottings. In March, pot up young plants into 3 in. pots; after four or five weeks pot on into 5 in. pots, and finally in mid-May into 8 or 9 in. pots.

As with planting, potting must be shallow, and the compost not too wet. The first potting, using John Innes potting compost No. 2, should

Chrysanthemum 'Denebola' (Anemone-flowered)

Chrysanthemum 'Mason's Bronze' (Single-flowered)

be done loosely, no attempt being made to compress the compost. Successive pottings should be progressively firmer, although care must be taken to avoid breaking the ball of soil. Use John Innes potting compost No. 3 for the final potting.

At the final potting the soil level should be 1 in. below the rim of the pot. Water thoroughly and then withold water for about seven days. Insert three 5 ft long canes in each pot and tie the stem loosely to the supports.

The greenhouse varieties may also be planted in the open ground, in the same manner as the outdoor types. They may also be stood outside in their pots for the summer. Lift greenhouse varieties and bring them indoors again by the end of September.

Place varieties already in pots on the greenhouse floor. Varieties lifted from the open ground should be potted up in 9 in. pots of John Innes potting compost No. 3, or planted straight into the greenhouse border.

Train cascade chrysanthemums by restricting each plant to two or three leading shoots. Stand the pots on a raised surface 4–5 ft above ground level, and train the shoots downwards to canes or wires sloping up from the ground. Stop the lateral shoots at three leaves and again at the next three leaves to promote bushy growth down the leaders. The last stopping should be by mid-September. The form 'Charm', which makes a bush 3 ft wide and 24 in. high, does not require training.

Supplementary feeding will be necessary from the end of June until the buds show colour. Use a liquid fertiliser that contains all the ingredients needed in a complete fertiliser, otherwise lank growth will be produced. Take care to avoid over-feeding; the dose recommended by the makers should never be exceeded. Cascade varieties should be fed once a week.

The compost in pots must never be allowed to dry out completely; fully grown plants will need water every 48 hours, and in hot dry weather more frequently.

Disbudding. Unless plants are grown to produce sprays, it is a mistake to allow too many stems to develop and produce flowers. Reduce outdoor varieties to six flowering stems as soon as these are large enough to be easily handled. At the end of July remove flowering stems from greenhouse varieties until only four stems are left on each plant. Exhibition incurved and reflexed decorative varieties should be reduced to three flowering stems per plant.

For the production of large flowers it is essential that each flower stem should be disbudded. This consists of removing all buds and side-shoots except the central bud on each stem. Start to disbud outdoor varieties at the end of July. Remove the side-shoots when they are about ¾ in. long. Greenhouse and October-flowering varieties should be disbudded from the end of August until late October.

Stopping. A chrysanthemum plant, when left to grow naturally, will continue to grow taller until a bud is produced at the tip of the main stem. This is known as the break bud. When the break bud has formed, side-shoots will develop in most of the leaf axils. This development is

Chrysanthemum 'Portrait'
(Spray)

Chrysanthemum 'Fantastic'
(Intermediate decorative)

Chrysanthemum 'Charm'
(Cascade)

Chrysanthemum 'Tracey Waller'
(Reflexed large-flowered)

Chrysanthemum 'Primrose Evelyn Bush'
(Incurved decorative)

known as the natural break, after which the break bud will shrivel and disappear. The side stems which develop from the natural break shoots will elongate and form flowering stems; the buds which form at the tips of the natural break stems are known as first crown buds.

When a plant is 6–8 in. tall, pinch out or break off the growing tip. Shoots will then appear in the leaf axils earlier than if the plants were allowed to make a natural break. This is known as stopping and is purely a means of hastening the process of the production of lateral shoots. More crown buds can be produced by pinching out the growing tip of the first laterals thereby causing the formation of second lateral shoots, which will develop a bud at their tips.

Flowers from second crown buds are usually smaller than those from first crowns, although the colours are often more intense.

Stop all outdoor varieties not later than June 21, or the flowers will be of poor quality and may be damaged by autumn frosts. Greenhouse varieties are stopped from April until mid-June according to their rate of growth.

After flowering, cut the stems of greenhouse varieties back to 6 in. This allows light and air to reach the crowns and encourages new basal growth from which cuttings will later be taken.

Outdoor varieties may be overwintered in the ground in southern England during an average winter. Clear all rubbish and dead leaves from around the plants, but do not cut down the stems until the following spring. Then cut the stems back to about 6 in. from ground level.

brysanthemum 'Fairie' (Pompon)

Chrysanthemum 'Martin Riley' (Incurved decorative)

Chrysanthemum 'Escort' (Intermediate decorative)

Chrysanthemum 'Claret Glow' (Intermediate decorative)

Alternatively, lift and store the chrysanemum stools (or crowns) for overwintering in cold frame or a greenhouse. Cut the flowering ems back to 6 in. and remove all green shoots ground level. Label the stools before lifting, en wash the soil away from the roots with ater. Box the stools 3 in. deep in John Innes tting compost No. 1 or in a loamless compost. ace the boxes in a greenhouse or in a cold st-free frame. In the greenhouse, place the xes in a position where they will get the aximum light and air; water the stools in.

All chrysanthemums are best grown from wly rooted cuttings. Ideally, the stools should t be planted out again, but used only to oduce the young basal growths from which ttings are taken.

ntrolled flowering. It has become standard actice to have chrysanthemums in flower all ar round. The flowering of many chrysanemums can be advanced or delayed by reguting the amount of light and/or darkness to nich they are subjected. Lighting or darkeng to control bud initiation can be carried out in electrically lit greenhouse.

As a general rule, bud initiation takes place hen the period of continuous darkness exceeds hours. Bud forming can therefore be delayed providing a short period of light during the iddle of the night. The length of this period of ght obviously depends on the time of year, nging from about two hours in August and ptember to five hours in December and nuary. The light intensity required can be provided by 100-watt lamps placed 6 ft apart and suspended 4 ft above the plants.

During the summer months, on the other hand, there is insufficient darkness for autumn and winter-flowering varieties to initiate their buds. Bud formation may be induced by giving the plants in the greenhouse artificial darkness so as to extend the night beyond the necessary $9\frac{1}{2}$ hours. The artificial darkness must be absolute; dense black polythene is suitable.

One of the most common uses of an artificial lighting programme is to delay the flowering of natural November varieties until the Christmas period. This is done by planting freshly rooted plants in the greenhouse border in late July and providing them with light every night from 11 p.m. to 1 a.m. until the end of September.

Some differences in cultivation apply to delayed flowering varieties: the plants must never be allowed to become woody and hard. The temperature must be kept at around 15°C (59°F) until the buds are well formed, and then lowered to 10°C (50°F); only two blooms should be carried on each plant.

Chrysanthemums as house plants. Due to their wide range of colour and their excellent keeping qualities in centrally heated homes, small pot chrysanthemums are popular as house plants.

The production of these plants is highly specialised and to some extent artificial. In many cases the flowering is regulated by the use of light and/or shade as previously described under CONTROLLED FLOWERING. The plants have further been treated with a growth regulator. The

Chrysanthemum 'Daphne'
(Single-flowered)

Chrysanthemum 'Doreen
Woolman' (Single-flowered)

Chrysanthemum 'Denise'
(Semi-pompon)

purpose of such chemicals is not to retard or suppress growth, but to compress it by shortening the internodes. In this way sturdier, more luxuriant plants are produced. Many of the varieties used for indoor cultivation grow naturally to 4–5 ft. If such house plants are grown on for a second year they may well become too tall to manage indoors.

There are few differences between the cultivation of these pot plants and any other greenhouse-flowering chrysanthemum. They are usually potted up in a loamless compost, and each pot may have three to five plants.

Propagation of alpine species. Take cuttings, 2–3 in. long, with or without a heel, in June or July; insert in a well-ventilated frame in a mixture of equal parts (by volume) peat and sand. Pot up singly in 3 in. pots of John Innes potting compost No. 1 in September; overwinter in the frame and plant out the following April.

Propagation of annual species. Sow the seeds in the flowering site in March or April, just covering them. Thin out the seedlings to the required distance. In mild districts and with cloche protection in winter, a September sowing gives larger plants and earlier flowers. It also provides plants for growing in pots in a cold greenhouse.

Alternatively, sow the seeds under glass in February, at a temperature of 13°C (55°F); prick out the seedlings into boxes and harden off in a cold frame before planting out in April.

Take cuttings, 2–3 in. long, of non-flowering side-shoots of *C. frutescens* in September or February. Autumn cuttings provide larger plants for bedding out the following spring.

Propagation of perennial species. Take 2–3 in. long cuttings of basal shoots in March or April and insert them in equal parts (by volume) peat and sand in a cold frame. Plant out when the cuttings are well rooted.

Lift and divide established clumps in March or April.

Propagation of florists' chrysanthemums. Take cuttings of outdoor varieties in March; of large-flowered greenhouse varieties in January and February; of early-flowering greenhouse types in April and May; and of late-flowering types in June. The cuttings should be 2–2½ in. long and close-jointed.

As a general rule, take basal cuttings from stools. In the case of varieties which do not produce basal growths, take cuttings of growths coming from low down on the old stems. Remove the cuttings just below a leaf joint and trim off the lower leaves, retaining about 1 in. for insertion in the rooting compost.

Insert the cuttings 1 in. deep and 2 in. apart either way in trays of equal parts (by volume) peat and sand. One thorough watering is necessary to settle the cuttings in, but do not water again until they show signs of having rooted, after two to three weeks. The cuttings may be sprayed with clean water, to keep them from becoming too limp.

Place the trays in a propagator or in a box covered with glass. A gentle bottom heat gives quicker results, but is not essential. In a cold greenhouse, a soil-warming cable under the trays is a great advantage, although at no time should the temperature rise above 15°C (59°F).

Transfer the cuttings singly to 3–3½ in. pc containing John Innes potting compost No. 1 a proprietary loamless compost. Be careful n to damage the fine roots when potting u Stand the pots in a cool airy position; only und adverse weather conditions do they need prote tion. Cuttings taken during April and May c be planted straight into their flowering quarte

When the young plants have filled the pc with roots, after about four or five weeks, pot into 5 in. pots and finally into 8–9 in. pots.

Cascade chrysanthemums are raised fro seeds, sown in pots or boxes of seed compost January or February, at a temperature 13–16°C (55–61°F). Pot the seedlings in 3 containers of John Innes potting compost No. Seed-raised plants of 'Charm' have been know to carry as many as 1000 sweetly scente brightly coloured flowers on one plant.

Pests. CHRYSANTHEMUM EELWORM invades le tissues and produces characteristic dark brov discolorations of the triangular areas betwe the leaf veins. The lower leaves turn brown, w and die; the pests gradually spread up the plar and eventually kill them.

Maggots of CHRYSANTHEMUM LEAF MIN tunnel into the leaf tissues and produce narrc mines which disfigure and weaken the plants.

CHRYSANTHEMUM STOOL MINER maggots fe on the roots and tunnel into stems. They m cause severe injury to plants grown under glass.

CAPSID BUGS suck sap from young tissues a cause stunted and tattered growth of termir shoots and flowers. EARWIGS feed on t petals, giving the blooms a ragged appearance.

Stems, leaves and flowers may be attacked APHIDS, CATERPILLARS and CUTWORMS.

GLASSHOUSE RED SPIDER MITES, THRIPS a WHITEFLIES may be troublesome on plants grov under glass. All these cause stunted growth.

Outdoors, SLUGS and SNAILS feed on leave stems and flowers and leave trails of shiny slim

Diseases. CHRYSANTHEMUM VIRUS DISEAS caused by different viruses may be serious und glass. Aspermy, a virus spread by aphids, caus stunted blooms broken by pale streaks or flec the florets may be twisted, tubular or of unev length. Stunt is characterised by a reduction growth and early flowering.

Other symptoms of virus infection in chrysa themums include mottling, dwarfing and d tortion of leaves and flowers.

GREY MOULD causes rotting of flowers, bu leaves and stems, characterised by a grey flu fungal growth on the affected tissues. T disease is encouraged by a moist atmosphere the greenhouse and is often found on flow previously attacked by petal blight.

LEAF SPOT appears on the leaves as circu black or brown spots, up to 1 in. in diameter is usually more severe in badly ventilated gree houses and where growth is soft following cessive nitrogenous manuring. Outdoors, *parthenium* in particular may be infected; t lower leaves are attacked first, and the dise gradually spreads upwards, causing the folia to wither and fall.

LEAFY GALL takes the form of numerous she thickened or distorted buds at the base of ea stem. This is due to a bacterial infection eas read when handling the plants. The disease usually occurs on greenhouse plants only, but it may occasionally attack *C. maximum* outdoors.

PETAL BLIGHT or flower scorch can be damaging, particularly outdoors in wet weather. Pink-brown pin-point spots on the ray florets gradually increase in size, becoming oval and brown in colour. In damp weather there is a dull white bloom on the affected areas. Infection spreads rapidly until the flowers are completely brown.

POWDERY MILDEW forms a white mealy covering on the upper surface of the leaves, and also on stems and flower buds. There may be a premature dropping of the lower leaves. The disease is encouraged by high temperatures in the greenhouse and dryness at the roots.

RAY BLIGHT begins at the centre of the flowers. A dark brown or black discoloration gradually extends to the base of the petals, causing the blooms to break apart. The disease, which is serious only in the greenhouse, may attack stems and leaves, 'Shoesmith' varieties being the most susceptible. It may also be troublesome on cuttings, killing the growing points.

ROOT ROT caused by several soil-borne fungi may result in poor growth; it occurs under bad soil conditions, such as waterlogging.

RUST shows as red-brown powdery pustules, the size of a pinhead, on the undersides of leaves. The disease spreads rapidly.

VERTICILLIUM WILT may develop from infected roots or be picked up from the soil. The leaves turn yellow and wilt from the base upwards.

WHITE RUST is a rare disease. It shows as yellow spots on the upper leaf surfaces and as buff or pink pustules on the undersides.

Ciboul: see Onion, Welsh
Cichorium intybus: see Chicory
Cigar flower: see *Cuphea ignea*

Cimicifuga

Bugbane. *Ranunculaceae*

A genus of 15 species of hardy herbaceous perennials. The species described are tall, graceful plants with wand-like spikes of small cream or white flowers. All are suitable for herbaceous borders or informal planting among trees or shrubs. The leaves are somewhat fern-like, being divided into many ovate mid-green leaflets.

C. *americana*, syn. *C. cordifolia*. N. America. Height 2–4 ft; planting distance 18–24 in. Tiny, fluffy, cream-white flowers are produced during August and September in erect, slender, branched spikes, 24 in. or more in length.

C. *cordifolia*: see *C. americana*

C. *dahurica*. Japan. Height 4–5 ft; planting distance 1½–3 ft. Slender spikes of star-like cream-white flowers, ¼ in. across, are borne in August and September.

C. *foetida*. Europe, Siberia. Height 4–5 ft; planting distance 18–24 in. Erect branched spikes of star-shaped green-yellow flowers, ¼ in. across, appear in July and August. 'Elstead Variety', 4 ft high, produces feathery racemes of white flowers in September and October. The variety *C. f. intermedia*, syn. *C. simplex*, is similar to the type

but the flowering stem tips are usually unbranched. 'White Pearl' is a purer white and flowers in September and October.

CIMICIFUGA FOETIDA INTERMEDIA

C. *japonica*. Japan. Height 3–4 ft; planting distance 2–3 ft. Racemes of round white flowers, ¼ in. across, appear in August and September.

C. *racemosa* (black snake-root). N. America, Canada. Height 4–5 ft; planting distance 24 in. Graceful spikes of feathery white flowers, ¼ in. across, appear in July and August.

C. *ramosa*. Japan. Height 5–6 ft; planting distance 24 in. Tapering spikes of feathery white flowers, ¼ in. across, are borne in September.

C. *simplex*: see *C. foetida*

Cultivation. Plant during suitable weather from October to March. Cimicifugas do best in a lightly shaded position in moist, leafy soil. In exposed positions provide support for the stems. Once planted, they should not be disturbed except to divide the roots for propagation. Give a top-dressing of leaf-mould every March. Cut down the stems in November.

Propagation. Divide and replant the roots between October and March.

Pests and diseases. Generally trouble-free.

Cineraria

Compositae

CINERARIA CRUENTA

The following species and its varieties are botanically included in the genus *Senecio,* but popularly they are better known as cinerarias. These winter and spring-flowering pot plants produce compact masses of daisy-like flowers in a range of bright colours.

C. *cruenta*, syn. *Senecio cruentus*. Canary Islands. Height up to 18 in. A half-hardy perennial, usually grown as a greenhouse biennial. The mid to dark green leaves are ovate to palmate and marginally toothed. The flowers, ¾–3 in. across, are produced from December to June.

The numerous varieties, often listed as *Cineraria hybrida*, are popular as winter-flowering pot plants. They vary in height and flower size, and colours include white, lavender, blue, mauve, red, pink and various bicolours. Several distinct selections, differing in habit and height, are available from seedsmen. The selections, all in mixed colours, are classified as follows:

Chrysanthemum 'Golden Orfe' (Spray)

Cimicifuga foetida 'White Pearl'

Cineraria cruenta 'Gem Mixed'

Hybrida Grandiflora (height 18–21 in.), of compact habit, with large, broad-petalled flowers; varieties include 'Brilliant', 'Exhibition Mixed' and 'Monarch'.

Double Flowered (height 12–18 in.), of compact habit, with double or semi-double flowers. Recommended varieties include 'Double Duplex' and 'Gubler's Double Mixed'.

Multiflora Nana (height 12–15 in.), compact and with broad-petalled flowers. Varieties include 'Berlin Market'; 'Dwarf Large-flowered Mixed'; 'Gaytime Mixture'; and 'Gem Mixed'.

Stellata (height 18–30 in.), usually open-branched, graceful plants, with narrow-petalled, star-shaped flowers. The varieties 'Feltham Beauty' and 'Mixed Star' are recommended.

C. hybrida: see *C. cruenta*

C. maritima: see *Senecio maritima*

Cultivation. Cinerarias require cool greenhouse conditions. Grow them in John Innes potting compost No. 2 in final 6–7 in. pots. From October, maintain a temperature of 8°C (46°F); after the flower buds have formed, the temperature may be raised to 16°C (61°F) to speed flowering. However, cool conditions and liquid feeding every 14 days once the flower buds have formed give the best results. Water regularly but carefully; over-watering may cause premature collapse of the plants.

Propagation. Sow seeds in pots or pans of John Innes seed compost between April and August at a temperature of 13°C (55°F). Prick off the seedlings into boxes or singly into 3 in. pots of John Innes potting compost No. 1 and grow on through the summer in a cold frame with the lights removed. Light shading with muslin or hessian is necessary during hot spells. Move the plants to a cool greenhouse in September or October. Spring-sown plants flower in December or January, those sown during summer, the following May or June.

Pests. Cinerarias are attacked by many of the pests which attack chrysanthemums.

In particular, APHIDS often infest leaves and stems, making the plants sticky and checking or distorting growth.

THRIPS infest flowers and leaves, causing a light flecking and other discolorations.

CHRYSANTHEMUM LEAF MINER maggots tunnel into the leaves.

Diseases. CROWN and ROOT ROT, due to several different fungi, may cause the plants to collapse, particularly if they are over-watered.

GREY MOULD may cause rotting of plant tissues if the atmosphere is cold and damp; affected areas become heavily covered with a grey, velvety fungal growth.

LEAF SPOT may occur, showing first as pinpoint black specks on the leaves, increasing in size until they are up to $\frac{1}{2}$ in. across. They may then coalesce, and badly affected leaves are killed.

POWDERY MILDEW shows as a powdery white coating on the leaves.

RUST shows on the leaves as spore-bearing pustules, orange at first, red later.

TOMATO SPOTTED WILT VIRUS causes severe mottling of the leaves followed by brown streaks along the veins, particularly on the undersides. Affected plants are stunted and flower production is poor or non-existent.

Cineraria cruenta 'Gem Mixed'

Cineraria cruenta Stellata

CIRRHOPETALUM

Cinquefoil: see Potentilla
Cinquefoil, spring: see *Potentilla verna*

Cirrhopetalum
Orchidaceae

A genus of 70 evergreen species of epiphyt orchids, found in Africa, Asia and the Pacif Islands. The single-leaved pseudobulbs are ovo or oblong with dark green leaves that are short strap-shaped. The flowers usually have elongate and fused lateral sepals, giving a tubular effec the lip is joined to the petals by a delicate hing They are borne on erect flower stems rising fro the base of the bulbs. Most species bear a termin umbel of from two to more than 50 flowers; a fe have solitary flowers. The flowering peric extends from April to June.

The species described here should be grown an intermediate greenhouse.

See also ORCHIDS.

C. fascinator. Himalayas. A species closely relate to *C. ornatissimum*. The pseudobulb is about 2 i high. Each 5 in. long stem bears a solitary flowe of light green, striped, marbled and flushed wit purple. The flower is 6–9 in. long with the dors sepals and petals purple-fringed.

C. longiflorum: see *C. umbellatum*

C. medusae. Malesia. This species has a 2 i high pseudobulb. Each umbel is a mop-like hea of 50 or more flowers on a 6 in. long flower ster These consist of narrow lateral sepals, up to 5 i long, that are cream-white, spotted with pin large, cream-coloured bracts surround th umbels. The outstanding variety 'Alba' h pure white flowers.

C. ornatissimum. Himalayas. A robust speci with a 1–1¼ in. high pseudobulb. The flowe stems are 6 in. long and carry two to five flowe in each umbel. The lateral sepals are up to 6 i long and dull yellow-green with bold lengthwi stripes of maroon.

C. thouarsii: see *C. umbellatum*

C. umbellatum. E. Africa, Madagascar to Ne Guinea and Tahiti. This variable but free flowering species is often listed under th erroneous names of *C. longiflorum* or *C thouarsii*. The pseudobulb is 2 in. high. Eac umbel carries up to ten flowers on a 7 in. lon stem. The lateral sepals are up to 2 in. long an the much smaller cup-shaped dorsal sepal bea an upright hair-like antenna at its apex. Th colour varies from pure yellow, through pa yellow-buff variously spotted and flushed wi red, to almost pure red.

C. vaginatum. Malesia. A free-flowering specie basically similar to *C. medusae* but smaller an with only about 15 flowers in each umbel. Th lateral sepals are up to 4 in. long and pale yellow

Cultivation. Grow these orchids in 4–10 in. pans, on pieces of tree fern or on rafts of wood, preferably suspended. Use a mixture of 2 parts osmunda fibre and 1 part sphagnum moss (parts by volume). Water freely from May to October, moderately from October to April. Give light shade on sunny days from April to October, and ventilate on mild days. During winter, provide a minimum night temperature of 10°C (50°F).

Repot or pot on from March to June.

Propagation. Divide and pot up the rhizomes when repotting.

Pests. MEALY BUGS occasionally cause damage.

Diseases. Generally trouble-free.

Cissus

Vitidaceae (Vitaceae)

CISSUS ANTARCTICA

A genus of 350 species of mainly woody evergreen climbers and including ten species of stem succulents. The latter rarely flower in cultivation, but climbing species bear insignificant tiny yellow or green-tinted flowers in starry axillary clusters. The species described are suitable for greenhouse cultivation or as house plants, the succulents being grown chiefly for their weird shapes, the climbing species for the beauty of their foliage.

SUCCULENT SPECIES (see also CACTUS)

C. bainesii. South-west Africa. Height and spread up to 24 in. The single, bottle-shaped stem may reach a height of 6 ft in the wild, but in cultivation it seldom exceeds 24 in.; the stem is up to 10 in. thick. It is yellow-brown and often partly covered by the previous year's papery bark, which peels off gradually.

The large mid-green trifoliate leaves are deeply serrated or notched round the edges and are cabbage-like in texture. They are produced in summer and drop off in late autumn, when the plant becomes dormant. Mature plants occasionally bear star-shaped yellow flowers, $\frac{1}{4}$ in. across, on a branched inflorescence. Red, grape-like fruits are sometimes produced.

C. cactiformis. East Africa. Height up to 10 ft, spread 3–4 ft if trained against a greenhouse wall. The green climbing and branching stems are three or four-angled and have brown, crenated, horny edges. Aerial roots develop at the nodes. Ovate mid-green leaves appear in autumn when new growth starts; they last only during the two months of the growing season. Flowers and subsequent fruits are rarely produced.

C. juttae. South-west Africa. A species similar to *C. bainesii,* but with less serrated, glaucous leaves; the stems are often lobed and convoluted.

C. quadrangularis. Southern and tropical Africa. Height 7–8 ft. This species is similar to *C. cactiformis,* but its clambering stems are less

stout, four-angled, and not crenated on their rough, horny edges. Aerial roots develop at the nodes. The plant bears palmate mid-green leaves which last for a short growing season of about two months in September and October.

CLIMBING SPECIES

C. antarctica (kangaroo vine). Australia. Height 15–20 ft. This species tolerates smoky atmospheres and is suitable as a house plant or in a cool greenhouse. The shining dark green leaves are ovate with sharply toothed margins. They are oblong-ovate and up to 4 in. long. As a house plant in a 6 in. pot the species seldom exceeds 6–8 ft.

C. discolor. East Indies. Height 15–20 ft; as a pot plant up to 8 ft. This species is one of the most spectacular of all foliage plants, but it requires warm conditions. It is semi-evergreen and in winter sheds many of the leaves and loses the delicate colours of the remaining foliage. The triangular leaves, up to 6 in. long and wide, are vivid green marbled with white and purple; the undersides are deep crimson.

C. sicyoides. S. America. Height 15–20 ft; as a pot plant up to 10 ft. A vigorous climber for a greenhouse or a warm room. Each leaf is composed of five elliptic leaflets, about 2 in. long and 1 in. wide; they are dark green with bright crimson leaf stalks.

Cultivation of succulent species. Grow in a soil consisting of equal parts (by volume) loam, peat and crushed brick or gravel. Keep the plants in full sun all year round and provide a winter temperature not lower than 5°C (41°F).

The climbing species, such as *C. cactiformis* and *C. quadrangularis,* may be trained against a greenhouse wall or twisted round three or four canes inserted in each pot.

As these succulents are drought resistant, water is only required during the growing season. Begin watering as soon as new leaves develop, but allow the soil to dry out between waterings. Repot or pot on annually in March or April; final pot size should be 8–10 in.

Cultivation of climbing species. Grow greenhouse climbers in John Innes potting compost No. 2, in 6 in. pots or planted out in the greenhouse border. Maintain a winter temperature of 7–10°C (45–50°F). Water freely during spring and summer, keeping the compost just moist in winter; *C. discolor* tends to lose its leaves at low winter temperatures and through over-watering.

Place the plants in a well-lit position, providing light shading and ventilation in the greenhouse during summer. Insert twiggy sticks or canes to support pot-grown plants; in the greenhouse border train the shoots up strings or wires.

C. discolor may be grown as a trailing plant; set one plant to a 10 in. basket suspended from the greenhouse roof.

Pot on or repot annually in March or April; give a weak liquid feed at fortnightly intervals from May to September.

Propagation of succulent species. Increase *C. cactiformis* and *C. quadrangularis* by 3–4 in. long stem cuttings taken between April and June. Allow the cut surfaces to heal before setting the cuttings singly in $2\frac{1}{2}$ in. pots of the growing compost. Propagate *C. bainesii* and *C. juttae* by seeds, which can be extracted from the ripe,

Cissus juttae

Cissus antarctica

Cissus discolor

grape-like fruits. Sow seeds in spring in pans of John Innes seed compost and germinate at a temperature of 21°C (70°F). Transplant the seedlings when these are 1–2 in. high into the usual growing compost.

Propagation of climbing species. Take cuttings, 3–4 in. long, in June and July of lateral shoots; insert in equal parts (by volume) peat and sand in a propagating case at a temperature of 16–18°C (61–64°F). When rooted, set the cuttings in 3 in. containers of John Innes potting compost No. 2 and pot on as necessary.

Pruning. No pruning is required for the succulent species. Climbers, such as *C. antarctica* and *C. sicyoides* need no regular cutting back, although the growing points of young plants should be pinched out to promote branching growth. Cut leggy plants back hard to 6 in. of the base in April.

Shorten the main growths of pot-grown plants of *C. discolor* by two-thirds at the end of February and spur back all laterals to 6 in. unless they are required for cuttings.

Pests. The foliage may be infested by GLASSHOUSE RED SPIDER MITES, APHIDS and MEALY BUGS.

Diseases. The succulent species are generally trouble-free, but a PHYSIOLOGICAL DISORDER may cause leaf-drop and brown blotches on the leaves of climbing species.

Cistus × aguilari

Cistus ladaniferus

Cistus × purpureus

Cistus

Rock rose, sun rose. *Cistaceae*

CISTUS × PURPUREUS

A genus of about 20 species of evergreen shrubs occurring in the Iberian Peninsula and the Mediterranean regions. Rock roses are conspicuous shrubs with their single rose-like flowers borne in profusion in April and May. They vary from low shrubs 12 in. high to upright bushes of 8 ft. They are not fully hardy throughout Britain, but those described do well in the south.

Apart from a few species, most of the cistus in cultivation are natural or garden hybrids. The saucer-shaped flowers, of a thin, papery texture, with five petals and often with conspicuous stamens, open in the morning and shed their petals in the afternoon, but so many buds are set that a long succession of flowers is kept up in sunny weather for two or three months. For the greatest effect, a number of plants should be grown together.

C. × aguilari. Height and spread 4–5 ft. This hybrid between *C. populifolius* and *C. ladaniferus* is a shrub of upright bushy habit. The lanceolate, shiny, light green leaves have wavy margins. Pure white flowers, about 3 in. across, appear in profusion in June and July. The variety 'Maculatus' has purple-crimson blotches at the base of each petal.

C. × corbariensis. Height 3–4 ft; spread 6–9 ft. Hybrid between *C. salvifolius* and *C. populifolius*. A low, spreading shrub of bushy habit with ovate dull green leaves with wavy margins. The white flowers, 1½ in. across, have a yellow stain at the base of each petal; they are freely borne from May to June. The buds are tinged red. This is one of the hardiest of the rock roses.

C. × cyprius. Height 6–8 ft; spread 7–9 ft. A hybrid between *C. ladaniferus* and *C. laurifolius*. The olive-green leaves are oblong-lanceolate and sticky to the touch. White flowers, 3 in. wide, with crimson-maroon blotches, appear in clusters of three to six in June and July.

C. ladaniferus. S.W. Europe, Mediterranean regions. Height up to 6 ft or more; spread 4 ft. A hardy shrub of stiff, erect habit and with open branches. The dull green leathery leaves are narrowly ovate-lanceolate. White flowers, 2½ in. across, with conspicuous bright yellow stamens and a maroon blotch at the base of the petals, appear in clusters of up to eight in May and June.

C. × lusitanicus. Height and spread 12–24 in. A dwarf hybrid between *C. ladaniferus* and *C. hirsutus*. The narrowly lanceolate leaves are dark green. White flowers, about 2 in. across, with a distinctive crimson blotch at the base of each petal, appear in terminal clusters in June and July. The variety 'Decumbens' is wide-spreading, up to 4 ft across; it has dark green foliage.

C. palbinhaii. Portugal. Height and spread 3 ft. A compact, low-growing bush with glossy, dark green, obovate and sticky leaves. The solitary white flowers, nearly 4 in. across, have crinkled petals and appear in May and June.

C. populifolius. S.W. Europe. Height up to 6 ft; spread 4–5 ft. A hardy species of erect, open habit, with broadly ovate light green leaves. White flowers, 2 in. wide, with a yellow stain at the base of each petal, appear in clusters of two to five in June. *C. p. lasiocalyx* has larger flowers.

C. × purpureus. Height 4–5 ft; spread 4 ft. Hybrid between *C. ladaniferus* and *C. villosus*, and a vigorous bush of upright habit. The lanceolate leaves are grey-green. Rose to purple flowers, 2–3 in. across, with a dark maroon blotch at the base of each petal, appear from May to July.

C. salvifolius. S. Europe, Aegean. Height 12–24 in.; spread 24 in. This species, hardy in the south, carries grey-green sage-like leaves. The white flowers, about 1½ in. across, with yellow basal stains, appear in ones or threes in June. It makes good ground cover on poor soil in mild areas.

C. 'Silver Pink'. Height and spread 2–3 ft. A hardy hybrid between *C. laurifolius* and *C. villosus*. The thick-textured lanceolate leaves are dark green above, grey beneath. Clear pink flowers, each with a central bunch of yellow stamens, and 3 in. across, are carried on erect stems well above the foliage in June and July.

C. × skanbergii. Greece. Height and spread 3–4 ft. This natural hybrid is a bush of upright habit, with linear-lanceolate, grey-green leaves. Clear pink flowers, 1½ in. wide, are carried in clusters of six in the leaf axils and at the ends of the shoots during June and July.

C. villosus. Mediterranean regions. Height up to 4 ft; spread 3–4 ft. A half-hardy, much branched, compact bush with grey-green, ovate-oblong leaves that are covered with down on both sides.

he flowers are 2–2½ in. across and are borne in
erminal clusters of three to five during June and
uly. The species hybridises freely, and the
owers vary from pale to deep rose-purple.

Cultivation. Cistus do not transplant well and
hould be planted from pots during April and
May. They do well on most soils, but are at their
est on poor, well-drained soils; they require as
much sun as possible, in an open position but
heltered from east and north winds. They make
admirable plants for hot, dry banks and will
olerate seaside exposure. Young plants appear to
withstand frost better than older specimens.

Propagation. Sow seeds, which generally set
reely, in March in pans of John Innes seed
ompost; place in a cold frame and prick off
he seedlings singly, when large enough to
andle, into 2½ in. pots. Pot on into 4 in. pots and
overwinter in a cold frame; plant out the
ollowing April or May.

The hybrids do not breed true from seeds; take
uttings, 3–4 in. long, of half-ripened non-
flowering shoots with a heel in July and August.
nsert the cuttings in equal parts (by volume)
eat and sand in a propagating frame with a
emperature of 16°C (61°F). When rooted, place
the cuttings singly in 3 in. pots of John Innes
potting compost No. 1 and overwinter in a cold
rame. Pot on into 4 in. containers the following
May and plunge outdoors or in an open frame.
Overwinter in a cold frame before planting out
n permanent positions in April or May.

Pruning. No pruning is required, and older plants
eldom recover from being cut back. On young
plants, straggly growths may be lightly trimmed
o provide bushy growth in March. Remove all
dead and frost-damaged wood.

Pests. Generally trouble-free.

Diseases. The shoots may die back because of
FROST DAMAGE.

Citrus

Rutaceae

CITRUS SINENSIS

A genus of about 12 species of evergreen spiny
trees and shrubs originating in eastern Asia.
Several species, such as the orange, tangerine,
lemon, lime and grapefruit, are grown commercially in Mediterranean and many sub-
tropical countries, for their edible thick-skinned
fruits. In Great Britain, the species may be grown
from seeds as house plants; under favourable
greenhouse conditions flowers may be produced,
but a temperature of 18–24°C (64–75°F) is
required for fruits to mature.

These shrubs bear lustrous dark green, ovate to
elliptic leaves and clusters of fragrant, usually
white flowers with five oblong petals that curve
outwards, and with prominent stamens.

The species described here require greenhouse
cultivation; young plants are suitable for growing
in a living-room.

C. aurantium (sour orange, Seville orange).
Tropical Asia. Height 3–4 ft. This species has
ovate, slender-pointed leaves on spiny branches.
The clusters of fragrant white flowers, 1 in.
across, are borne from April to June. In a large
greenhouse, with sufficient heat, this species may
be grown as a fruiting tree, but it is more
commonly grown as a foliage house plant.

C. a. sinensis: see *C. sinensis*

C. limon (lemon). E. Asia. Height up to 4 ft. An
ornamental species with elliptic leaves; fragrant,
white, red-flushed flowers, about ¾ in. across, are
borne from April to June. Under favourable
conditions fruits are borne which usually take a
year to ripen.

C. mitis (calamondin). Philippines. Height 18 in.
This is the best of the species for pot culture,
flowering and fruiting freely while still small. It
has lanceolate, mid to deep green leaves and
clusters of three or four fragrant white flowers,
½ in. across. These are followed by round orange-
yellow fruits, 1–1½ in. wide.

C. nobilis: see *C. reticulata*

C. paradisi (grapefruit). E. Asia. Height 3–4 ft. As
an ornamental plant this species forms a well-
branched bush with glossy, mid to dark green
ovate leaves. White, solitary flowers, 1 in. or
more across, are occasionally borne between
April and June. It is less easy to cultivate indoors
than the other citrus species.

C. reticulata, syn. *C. nobilis* (mandarin, tangerine,
king orange). China. Height 3–4 ft as an
ornamental species. This is the hardiest of the
fruit-bearing species. It bears narrowly ovate to
elliptic or lanceolate leaves; clusters of white
flowers, about 1 in. wide, are produced between
April and June. The round orange fruits, with
wrinkled loose skins, are 2–3 in. wide.

C. sinensis, syn. *C. aurantium sinensis* (sweet
orange). China. Height 3–4 ft as a house plant. A
round-headed, slightly spiny plant with ovate-
oblong, dark green leaves. Fragrant white
flowers, 1 in. across, may be borne between April
and June. Well-known edible varieties of this
species include blood oranges such as 'Maltese'
and 'Ruby'; the large 'Jaffa' and the 'Washington
Navel' oranges.

Cultivation. Grow citrus plants in 8–10 in. final
pots or small tubs of John Innes potting compost
No. 2. The plants dislike root disturbance, and
potting on should be carried out during the
winter months. Once the plants are in their final
containers, remove the top 2 in. of compost
annually in April and replace with a mixture of
equal parts (by volume) loam and manure.

Keep the plants just moist in winter, and water
more freely in summer; syringe the leaves daily
in hot weather and shade the glass lightly.

During summer ventilate the house freely and
stand the plants in a well-lit position; they may
also be plunged outdoors ·in full sun from
mid-June until late September.

Provide an average winter temperature of 7°C
(45°F), although *C. limon* does better at 10°C
(50°F), and *C. mitis* at 13°C (55°F). The other
species will withstand occasional short periods of
frost provided they are in a draught-free position.

Cistus salvifolius

Citrus limon (fruits)

Citrus mitis (fruits)

Citrus sinensis
(flowers and fruits)

Propagation. Sow seeds in pots or pans of John Innes seed compost in March, at a temperature of 16°C (61°F). Prick off the seedlings, when large enough to handle, into 3–3½ in. pots of John Innes potting compost No. 2 and grow on at the same temperature. Pot on as necessary.

Alternatively, take 3–4 in. long cuttings of half-ripe wood in July and August; insert the cuttings in equal parts (by volume) peat and sand in a propagating case with a temperature of 16–18°C (61–64°F). Pot the rooted cuttings as described for seedlings.

Pruning. No regular pruning is required, but all growths may be shortened by two-thirds every two or three years in early March to keep the plants shapely.

Pests. SCALE INSECTS, particularly soft scale, may infest the undersides of the leaves which become fouled with sticky honeydew; thick growths of sooty mould may develop.

MEALY BUGS cause conspicuous masses of white waxy wool on the leaves and stems, and make the plants sticky and sooty.

Diseases. A PHYSIOLOGICAL DISORDER may cause the leaves to turn yellow; leaf-drop may occur.

Cladanthus arabicus

Clarkia pulchella

Clary

Cladanthus

Compositae

CLADANTHUS ARABICUS

A genus of four species of annuals. The hardy annual described is generally grown as a border plant. Both the flowers and foliage are scented; a profusion of blooms appears from June until the first autumn frosts.

C. arabicus. Spain. Height 2½ ft; spacing 12 in. This plant forms a steadily increasing mound of growth, producing four or five new side-shoots beneath each flower. Pale green feathery foliage partially submerges the daisy-like flowers, which are 2 in. across, single and golden-yellow.

Cultivation. Cladanthus grow well under a wide range of conditions, but a light soil and a sunny position are recommended. Removal of dead flower heads extends the flowering season.

Propagation. Sow the seeds in the flowering site in March or April, thinning out the seedlings to the required spacing when they become large enough to handle.

Pests and diseases. Generally trouble-free.

Clarkia

Oenotheraceae

A genus of 36 species of hardy annuals. The following are of erect and branching habit and are used mainly for border decoration, but can also be grown for cutting or as pot plants.

C. elegans. syn. *C. unguiculata.* California. Height up to 24 in.; spacing 12 in. A popular garden plant with ovate mid-green leaves. Double flowers, up to 2 in. across and on 9–12 in. spikes are produced from July to September. Numerous varieties are listed by seedsmen, including 'Mixed' which is made up of white, lavender, purple, scarlet, salmon and orange flowers. Separate colours are also available, such as 'Enchantress', salmon pink; and 'Firebrand', bright scarlet flowers.

CLARKIA ELEGANS

C. pulchella. N. America. Height 18 in.; spacing 12 in. An erect, branching plant with slender stems and ovate mid-green leaves. Lavender semi-double flowers, 1½ in. across, are massed on 6–9 in. spikes, forming dainty sprays. They bloom from July to September. Garden varieties are generally listed as mixtures, in shades of white, violet and rose.

C. unguiculata: see *C. elegans.*

Cultivation. A medium to light, slightly acid loam, in a sunny situation, gives the best results. Avoid heavy feeding, which delays and reduces flowering and encourages too much leaf growth.

Grow pot plants in 5 in. containers of John Innes potting compost No. 1. Place these in a cool greenhouse at 7°C (45°F) from October until they flower in February or March.

Propagation. Sow the seeds in the flowering site in March, thinning out the seedlings to the required spacing. In sheltered areas or where winter protection with cloches can be provided, a September sowing brings flowering forward to May or June. This sowing also provides seedlings to pot up for early spring-flowering under glass.

Pests. Generally trouble-free.

Diseases. GREY MOULD attacks the base of the stems, covering these with a grey velvety fungal growth and causing plants to wilt.

FOOT and ROOT ROT cause the collapse of seedlings or older plants, but no fungal growth is seen on the stems.

Clary

Salvia sclarea. Labiatae

This hardy biennial plant, usually grown in Great Britain as an annual, is occasionally used as a culinary herb to flavour soups and casseroles. Clary is used commercially in perfumery.

Height 2½ ft; spacing 12 in. Mediterranean region. Clary is sufficiently decorative to be grown in the flower border. Large, hairy, triangular-ovate leaves appear early in the year; tubular blue-white flowers, 1 in. long and with striking purple-blue or yellow bracts, are borne in August. The pungently aromatic leaves may be used fresh, dried or deep-frozen.

Cultivation. Clary grows best in reasonably fertile, well-drained soil, in full sun.

Propagation. Sow seeds in April in shallow drills 15 in. apart where the plants are to grow. As soon as the seedlings are large enough, thin them out to 12 in. apart.

Harvesting and storing. The leaves are generally used fresh, but they may be dried or deep-frozen. See entry under HERBS.

Pests and diseases. Generally trouble-free.

Cleistocactus

Cactaceae

CLEISTOCACTUS STRAUSII

A genus of 30 species of slow-growing greenhouse perennials. These columnar cacti have slender stems, which are erect or rambling with many shallow ribs and numerous spines. The flowers are borne singly from upper areoles and last four or five days; they do not open fully, hence the plant's name, which is derived from the Greek *cleistos*, meaning closed.

See also CACTUS.

C. baumannii. Argentina, Paraguay, Uruguay. Height up to 6 ft. The narrow, light green stem, usually branched, has 12–16 shallow ribs. The areoles are close together and bear brown-black felt, and 15–20 white to brown needle-like spines up to 1 in. long.

The orange-scarlet tubular flowers appear in June; they are 1–2 in. long and curve down at the tip. They are produced profusely on well-established plants.

C. smaragdiflorus. Argentina. Height up to 4 ft. The cylindrical stem, with 12–14 low ribs, is unbranched and densely spined. Each areole bears numerous thin radial spines and several stronger, dark brown central spines up to $\frac{3}{4}$ in. long. The tubular flowers, in July, are green outside, orange inside, and 2–2$\frac{1}{2}$ in. long.

C. strausii. Argentina, Bolivia. Height up to 6 ft. The light green, erect stem, which sometimes branches from the base, is 2–3 in. in diameter, with up to 25 shallow ribs. The areoles bear white wool and 30 or more bristly white spines, which are often so dense that the plant body can scarcely be seen. Older plants may produce a few pale yellow central spines up to 2 in. long. The dark red tubular flowers, up to 3 in. long, appear near the top of the stems in July and August. This is the most attractive and popular species of the genus, but it does not flower freely in Britain. *C. s. jujuyensis* has dark red-brown central spines.

C. tominensis. Bolivia. Height up to 6 ft. The unbranched, light green stem is erect and with 18–20 ribs. From the areoles rise eight or nine $\frac{1}{2}$ in. long radial spines and three 1 in. long central spines. The tubular light red flowers, 1 in. long, appear from June until August.

Cultivation. Cleistocacti do best in a soil consisting of 4 parts loam, 3 parts leaf-mould, 2 parts sand and 1 part gravel (parts by volume), with 1 oz. bone-meal added to each 2 gal. bucket of soil. Pot the plants in March or April in pots up to 9 in. across, and place them in a position where they will get the maximum light and sun. Water generously from February to November but keep them dry in winter, when the temperature should not be less than 5°C (41°F). Move the plants into larger pots at the beginning of the growing season.

Propagation. Sow seeds in March at a temperature of 21°C (70°F). Take stem cuttings from June to August. Let the cut surfaces heal before potting the cuttings in the growing compost.

Pests and diseases. Generally trouble-free.

Clematis

Ranunculaceae

A genus of 250 species of tender and hardy, deciduous and evergreen woody flowering climbers. They are among the most popular climbers and may, according to the species and variety, flower throughout the year. They cling by means of twining leaf stalks and are suitable for growing on walls or trellis-work, pergolas and posts, and for covering old tree stumps. The climbing species, as well as the several hybrid groups described here, are all hardy enough to be grown in the open. The genus also includes a number of hardy herbaceous perennials which make excellent border plants.

Generally, the flowers are composed of four ovate petal-like sepals forming a pendent cup, bell, or urn-shaped flower. In some species, notably *C. macropetala* and some hybrids, staminodes (petal-like stamens) are present, thus giving a double or semi-double appearance to the flowers.

CLEMATIS MONTANA

CLIMBING SPECIES

C. alpina, syn. *Atragene alpina.* S. and Central Europe. Height up to 6 ft. A charming but weak-growing deciduous species, of bushy habit and best grown on stakes against a wall or over an old bush or tree stump. The dark green, compound leaves consist of nine ovate-lanceolate, coarsely serrated leaflets. Pendulous, cup-shaped, violet-blue flowers, 1–1$\frac{1}{2}$ in. wide and with pale grey staminodes, are produced in April and May. 'Siberica', syn. 'Alba', is a white-flowered form.

C. armandii. China. Height up to 30 ft; spread 25–60 ft. This is a vigorous evergreen species with strong lateral growths. The glossy dark green leaves are trifoliate with ovate-lanceolate, prominently veined leaflets. Saucer-shaped white flowers, 2–2$\frac{1}{2}$ in. wide, are borne in April.

Cleistocactus baumannii

Cleistocactus strausii

Clematis alpina

Clematis chrysocoma

Clematis flammula

Clematis macropetala
'Markhamii'

Clematis orientalis

'Apple Blossom' has pink and white flowers, more highly coloured on their undersides; 'Snow Drift' has pure white flowers which are larger than those of the species.

C. chrysocoma. Yunnan, China. Height up to 10 ft. This deciduous species resembles *C. montana*, but is less vigorous. The trifoliate leaves are covered with brown-yellow felt. Single, white, saucer-shaped flowers, 1¾–2 in. wide and tinged with pink, are produced on pedicels in the leaf axils. They appear during June and July, but flowering often continues on new growths well into late summer or early autumn. The species has been used in hybridisation with *C. montana*.

C. c. sericea, syn. *C. spooneri*, produces white flowers in May; it is more vigorous.

C. fargesii. China. Height 20 ft. This vigorous deciduous climber is sometimes known as *C. f. souliei*. The dark green compound leaves are 9 in. long and consist of 15 ovate-acuminate leaflets. Pure white, saucer-shaped flowers, up to 2 in. across and composed of six petal-like sepals, appear from June to September.

C. flammula. S. Europe. Height 10 ft. Most of the growth of this bushy, deciduous species is borne in a tangled mass at the top. Bright green leaves composed of three to five broadly ovate to lanceolate leaflets set off perfectly the small, pure white, sweetly scented flowers; these appear from August to October in panicles 10–12 in. long.

C. florida. China. Height 10 ft. A deciduous, sometimes semi-evergreen, shrubby climber of rather sparse habit. The dark green biternate leaves are composed of nine leaflets. The saucer-shaped white flowers, borne singly on downy stalks during April and May, are 2½–3 in. across; each petal has a central green stripe. *C. f.* 'Sieboldii', syn. *C. f. bicolor* (Japan) has double flowers with purple staminodes.

C. macropetala. Siberia, N. China. Height up to 12 ft. This slender deciduous species of bushy habit is related to *C. alpina*. The stems have swollen nodes which produce dark green biternate leaves. Light and dark blue, nodding, bell-shaped flowers, 2–3 in. across, with centres of paler blue staminodes, appear on slender pedicels in May and June. Named varieties include 'Maidwell Hall', deep blue; and 'Markhamii', rose-pink.

C. montana. Himalayas. Height up to 40 ft; spread 15–20 ft. This deciduous and vigorous species is one of the easiest flowering climbers to cultivate. It tends to grow straight up at first but branches at the top. The dark green leaves are trifoliate. Pure white flowers, 1½–2 in. across, are produced in large clusters from the leaf axils in May. 'Elizabeth', soft pink; 'Rubens', bronze-green foliage and pale pink flowers; 'Tetra-rose', lilac-pink; and *C. m. wilsonii*, large white flowers in July and August.

C. orientalis. Caucasus, Iran, Himalayas, China, Manchuria. Height up to 20 ft. A vigorous, deciduous, well-branched species. The light green ferny leaves are deeply dissected. This species varies from form to form, but at its best produces a spectacular display of nodding, scented, yellow, star-like flowers, 1½ in. wide, from August to October. The silky seed heads, in early autumn, are silvery-grey.

C. rehderiana. China. Height up to 25 ft. This bushy, deciduous species is a vigorous grower and should be planted where it can ramble over a small tree, bush, low wall or fence. The pale to mid-green leaves are bipinnate, consisting of seven to nine leaflets. Cowslip-scented, primrose-yellow, bell-shaped flowers appear in panicles, 6–9 in. long, from August to October.

C. spooneri: see *C. chrysocoma sericea*

C. tangutica. China. Height 15–20 ft. A deciduous species, similar to *C. orientalis* and once thought to be a variety of it. It is one of the finest yellow-flowered clematis, a slender vigorous plant, seen at its best when allowed to ramble freely. The leaves are grey-green and pinnately divided, each leaflet sometimes deeply trilobed. Rich yellow, lantern-shaped flowers, 1½–2 in. wide, appear singly on 6 in. stems from August to October. They are followed by attractive silvery seed heads; these consist of small ovoid seeds each bearing a long awn.

C. × violacea. Height up to 12 ft. A deciduous hybrid between *C. flammula* and *C. viticella*. The dark green leaves are pinnate or bipinnate. Fragrant, pale violet-mauve flowers, 1¼ in. across, are freely produced in terminal panicles during August and September. 'Rubro-marginata' has white flowers fringed violet-red.

C. viticella. S. Europe. Height 9–12 ft. A slender, deciduous, semi-woody species of moderately bushy habit. The growths tend to die back in winter and require pruning to within 24 in. of ground level in February or March. The dark green leaves are divided into a number of ovate leaflets. Violet or purple-red, widely bell-shaped, nodding flowers, 2–2½ in. across, are borne singly on 3–4 in. stems from July to September. There are several fine varieties: 'Abundance', soft purple; 'Alba Luxurians', white, mauve-flushed; 'Kermesina' red-purple; 'Royal Velours', rich purple.

HYBRIDS

FLORIDA GROUP. This deciduous group contains many fine double-flowered varieties. Height and spread vary considerably according to district, soil and cultivation, but the plants can be grown successfully on supports of every kind. The dark green leaves vary in shape, depending on variety. Double rosette-shaped flowers, 3–6 in. across, are borne in May and June on short lateral growths from the previous year's wood. Train the main growths to prevent overcrowding. Remove flower stems after flowering. Cut out dead and weak shoots annually in March.

'Belle of Woking', pale mauve; 'Countess of Lovelace', violet-blue; 'Duchess of Edinburgh', pure white.

JACKMANII GROUP. This group of deciduous hybrids contains many of the most spectacular varieties, all suitable for growing against various supports. Height and spread are variable. The dark green leaves are usually trifoliate or more or less biternate, and the saucer-shaped flowers measure 5–7 in. across. Prune during February, cutting back the previous year's growth to within 6 in. of the base. This also encourages new strong growths and free flowering during the following summer and autumn. Plants grown over trees and pergolas require no pruning except for the removal of dead and weak shoots.

Clematis florida 'Sieboldii'

Clematis × 'Jackmanii Superba'

Clematis × 'Vyvyan Pennell'

Clematis × 'Lasurstern'

Clematis montana 'Rubens'

'Comtesse de Bouchaud', soft rose-pink, June to August; 'Gipsy Queen', dark velvety purple, July to September; 'Jackmanii', rich violet-purple, July and August; 'Jackmanii Superba', dark violet-purple, July to September; 'Madame Edouard André', bright velvety red, and 'Perle D'Azur', light blue, both June to August; and 'Vyvyan Pennell', double, deep violet-blue flushed carmine.

LANUGINOSA GROUP. This deciduous group contains many excellent large-flowered varieties and is suitable for growing on supports of every kind. Height and spread vary. The mid-green leaves are usually trifoliate but sometimes simple. The flowers are flat, with spreading sepals, and 6–8 in. wide. Prune these plants in the same way as those of the Jackmanii group. To obtain earlier flowers, prune secondary growths only, to within a few inches of the base, and train the main growth over its support.

'Beauty of Worcester', violet-blue, May to August; 'Blue Gem', soft pale blue, June to September; 'Daniel Deronda', deep violet-blue, June to September; 'King George V', light pink with deep pink stripe, May to June; 'Lady Northcliffe', lavender-blue, May to June or August to September.

'Marie Boisselot', pure white, May to October; 'Mrs Cholmondeley', light blue, May to August; 'Prins Hendrick', syn. 'Prins Henry', sky-blue, June to August; 'W. E. Gladstone', pale lavender, June to September; 'William Kennett', deep lavender-blue, May to August.

MONTANA GROUP. The average height and spread of this group of deciduous hybrids is 20 ft, up to 40 ft on tall buildings and trees. They are ideal for rambling over archways, pergolas, trees and large shrubs. They bear dark green trifoliate leaves and saucer-shaped flowers, 2–3 in. across. The varieties listed flower in April and May. Prune hard back the first February after planting, cutting back to plump buds within 6 in. of ground level. Thereafter prune lateral growths to shape annually in March.

'Elizabeth', soft pink, large, sweetly scented; 'Grandiflora', white; 'Pink Perfection', deep pink.

CLEMATIS × 'NELLIE MOSER'

PATENS GROUP. Deciduous hybrids growing to a height of 12 ft with a spread of 6 ft, although these measurements vary according to site and conditions. The dark green leaves are composed of three to five ovate-lanceolate leaflets. The flowers are flat, circular and 5–7 in. across; they appear in May and June on short side-growths from the previous year's wood. Prune after flowering by reducing all laterals to about 6 in. of the old wood.

'Barbara Jackman', soft rose-pink with deeper stripe; 'Edouard Desfosse', violet-blue with darker blue stripe; 'Lady Londesborough', soft mauve; 'Lasurstern', deep purple-blue; 'Nellie

Clematis tangutica
(seed heads)

Clematis × 'The President'

Clematis × 'Ernest Markham'

Clematis × 'Nellie Moser'

Moser', palest mauve with pink stripe; 'The President', deep violet-purple.

TEXENSIS GROUP. This is a group of deciduous weak-growing hybrids which do best in sheltered positions. Height 4–6 ft; spread 24 in. The glaucous or silvery-green pinnate leaves are borne on long petioles. Nodding pitcher-shaped flowers, 1–1½ in. long, appear from July to September. Prune during February, cutting back to live wood just above ground level.

'Duchess of Albany', bright rose-pink; 'Gravetye Beauty', deep rich red; 'Sir Trevor Lawrence', carmine.

VITICELLA GROUP. A small group of deciduous, vigorous hybrids. Height 8–12 ft; spread 3–4 ft. The dark green leaves may be trifoliate, or more or less biternate. Saucer-shaped, 1½ in. wide flowers are freely borne from the leaf axils from July to September. Prune the plants during February in the same way as those of the Jackmanii group.

'Duchess of Sunderland', purple-red; 'Ernest Markham', glowing red, large flowers; 'Huldine', white inside, mauve outside; 'Lady Betty Balfour', violet-blue; 'Mrs Spencer Castle', pale purple; 'Ville de Lyon', carmine.

HERBACEOUS SPECIES

C. heracleifolia, syn. *C. tubulosa.* China. Height up to 3 ft; planting distance 18 in. The coarsely trifoliate dark green leaves are slightly downy. Purple-blue tubular flowers, up to 1 in. long, are borne in clusters during August and September. The tips of the sepals are recurved, like those of a large hyacinth. Although usually grown as a herbaceous border plant this species is really a sprawling sub-shrub, and may be grown on supports in a shrub border.

The variety 'Davidiana', up to 3½ ft high, has light violet-blue flowers, larger than those of the species; 'Wyevale', 3–4 ft high, has fragrant flax-blue flowers.

C. integrifolia. S.E. Europe, W. Asia. Height 24 in.; planting distance 12 in. The ovate mid-green leaves are prominently veined. Bell-shaped indigo-blue flowers, 1–1½ in. across, open from June to September. *C. i. hendersonii* has larger, deep blue flowers.

C. recta. Europe, E. Asia. Height 3–4 ft; planting distance 18 in. A species with slender climbing stems and dark green leaves that are pinnately divided. Pure white fragrant flowers are borne profusely in June and July. They are star-shaped and ¾ in. across, and are followed by silky fluffy seed heads. The young leaves of *C. r. purpurea* are purple.

CLEMATIS HERACLEIFOLIA   CLEMATIS INTEGRIFOLIA

C. tubulosa: see *C. heracleifolia*

Cultivation of climbing species. Plant during suitable weather between October and May, preferably in an alkaline soil. These species in an open position but one which shades the base of the main stem and the roots from strong sun. Shade can be provided by planting low-growing shrubs on the south side of the plants.

The young growths of restricted wall-trained plants may need tying in from time to time, otherwise they are self-supporting. An annual mulch, in spring, of well-rotted manure, compost or peat is beneficial.

Cultivation of herbaceous species. Plant these species in a sunny border, between October and May; they do well in any ordinary garden soil, but thrive in alkaline conditions.

C. recta and its varieties require support; plant near low-growing shrubs up which they can climb. *C. integrifolia* is weak-stemmed and needs the support of twiggy sticks.

All herbaceous clematis benefit from an annual mulch in spring of compost, peat or well-rotted manure. Cut back the stems of *C. heracleifolia* and *C. recta* to about 6 in. above ground, and the remaining species to ground level, in November or March.

Propagation of climbing species. Take stem cuttings, 4–5 in. long, of half-ripened wood in July, with two buds at the base. Insert in a mixture of equal parts (by volume) peat and sand in a frame with a bottom heat of 15–18°C (59–64°F). Pot the rooted cuttings singly into 3 in. pots of John Innes potting compost No. 1. Overwinter in a frost-free frame or greenhouse; in spring pot on into 4–5 in. pots, and plunge outdoors. Transplant to permanent sites from October onwards.

The species can be raised from seeds sown in October in pots or pans of John Innes seed compost; place these in a cold frame or greenhouse until they have germinated, usually by the following spring. Prick out the seedlings singly into 3½ in. pots of John Innes potting compost No. 1 and plunge outdoors. Plant in permanent positions from October onwards.

Plants layered in March will usually have rooted within a year.

Propagation of herbaceous species. Take 3 in. basal cuttings in April or May and insert in a mixture of equal parts (by volume) peat and sand in a cold frame. When rooted, pot the cuttings singly in 3½ in. containers of John Innes potting compost No. 1 and plunge in an outdoor nursery bed. The young plants will be ready for planting in their permanent positions from October onwards of the same year.

Alternatively, divide and replant the roots between October and March.

Pruning of climbing species. Species clematis should not be pruned unless they are in positions where it is necessary to restrict their spread. In this case, remove or shorten surplus growths by up to two-thirds; early-flowering species, such as *C. alpina, C. armandii* and *C. montana* should be pruned after flowering; summer and autumn-flowering species in February or March. The pruning of hybrids is explained under each of the group headings.

Pests. Young shoots may be eaten by SLUGS.

APHIDS may infest growing points.

EARWIGS hide in crevices and eat ragged holes out of petals and leaves.

Diseases. Shoots may wilt and die very rapidly, often down to the base, due to CLEMATIS WILT. Usually new shoots develop later in the season or the following spring.

POWDERY MILDEW shows as a white powdery coating on leaves and sometimes on flowers.

Yellow mottling of the foliage and distortion of flowers are caused by a VIRUS DISEASE.

Cleome

Spider flower. *Capparidaceae*

CLEOME SPINOSA

A genus of 150 annual herbaceous species and, in a few cases, shrubs. The species described here is a half-hardy plant of strong, almost bushy growth. It is suitable for borders, as a dot plant to provide contrast in formal bedding schemes, and for growing under glass in pots. The unusual, spider-like flower heads are scented.

C. pungens: see *C. spinosa*

C. spinosa, syn. *C. pungens*. Tropical America. Height 3–4 ft; planting distance 18 in. An erect plant with hairy stems, and thorns at the base of each leaf stalk. The mid-green leaves are divided into five to seven oblong leaflets. The white, flushed pink flowers have narrow petals and long stamens; they measure 4 in. across and are borne from July to the first frosts.

The best-known varieties are 'Helen Campbell', white, and 'Pink Queen'. A new yellow, 'Golden Sparkler', 12 in., is also recommended.

Cultivation. Grow cleomes in a fertile, well-drained soil enriched with humus. A position in full sun is essential.

Grow plants for summer flowering under glass in 6 in. pots of John Innes potting compost No. 2.

Propagation. Sow the seeds under glass in March at 18°C (64°F). When the seedlings are large enough to handle, prick them off into 3½ in. pots. Harden off outdoor plants in a cold frame before planting out in May.

Pests. APHIDS may infest young growths.

Diseases. Generally trouble-free.

Clematis × 'Ville de Lyon'

Clematis heracleifolia 'Wyevale'

Clematis integrifolia

Cleome spinosa

Clerodendrum
Verbenaceae

A genus of about 400 species of flowering trees, shrubs and climbers distributed in Africa and Asia. Climbing species are generally tender and require greenhouse cultivation; two shrubby species, *C. bungei* and *C. trichotomum* may be grown outdoors in sheltered positions.

C. bungei. China. Height and spread 6–8 ft. A deciduous, semi-woody, suckering shrub with tall slender stems. The heart-shaped leaves are dark green. Fragrant, rose-pink, star-shaped flowers are borne in flattened terminal heads, 4–5 in. across, during August and September. The species is slightly tender and is best grown in a sheltered position. It may be cut down by frost, but established plants throw up new shoots in spring.

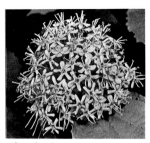

Clerodendrum bungei

Clerodendrum speciosissimum

Clerodendrum thomsonae

Clerodendrum trichotomum
(fruits)

CLERODENDRUM SPECIOSISSIMUM

C. fallax: see *C. speciosissimum*

C. speciosissimum, syn. *C. fallax*. Java. Height 3 ft or more; spread 18–24 in. An evergreen shrubby species requiring greenhouse cultivation. It has heart-shaped, mid-green leaves, up to 12 in. long. Tiered, erect panicles of flowers are produced from July to September; each scarlet flower is 1½ in. across and the panicle may be 10 in. long.

C. thomsonae. W. Africa. Height up to 12 ft. An evergreen tender climber with ovate, pointed, deep green leaves. The flowers are borne in terminal and axillary pendulous panicles, up to 6 in. long, from June to September. The individual flower consists of a white lantern-shaped calyx and a crimson starry corolla.

CLERODENDRUM TRICHOTOMUM

C. trichotomum. Japan, E. China. Height and spread 10–15 ft. Slow-growing deciduous shrub of bushy but open habit. The mid-green, ovate leaves are downy beneath; when crushed they have an unpleasant foetid odour. Scented, star-shaped, pink-white flowers are borne in erect inflorescences, 6–9 in. wide, in August and September. They are followed by turquoise-blue berries surrounded by persistent dark red calyces. The variety *C. t. fargesii* has smooth leaves and lighter blue berries usually produced in greater profusion.

Cultivation. Grow the tender species in John Innes potting compost No. 2 or 3, in 6–8 in. pots; the best results are obtained by planting direct in the greenhouse border. Provide a temperature

Clerodendrum trichotomum fargesii

in winter of 13°C (55°F) and keep the plants jus moist. During spring and summer, water freel and ventilate when the temperature exceeds 18° (64°F); give light shading on hot days.

Pot on or repot annually in April; give a wea liquid feed at intervals of 10–14 days from Ma to September.

Plant hardy species in any fertile, well-draine garden soil in September and October or i March and April; set in a sunny, sheltered site.

Propagation. Increase hardy species by detachin rooted suckers in September and October or i March. Line out in a sheltered nursery bed or in cold frame. Plant out the following October.

Take cuttings, 5 in. long, of lateral shoots preferably with a heel, in August and September insert in equal parts (by volume) peat and sand i a cold frame. Line out the rooted cuttings in nursery bed the following spring and grow on fo one or two years before transplanting to th flowering positions.

Tender species are also increased by cuttings 3–4 in. long, of lateral shoots taken from April t June. Insert the cuttings in equal parts (b volume) peat and sand in a propagating case at temperature of 18–21°C (64–70°F). Whe rooted, pot the cuttings singly in 3 in. pots of Joh Innes potting compost No. 1 and pot on a required or plant in the greenhouse border.

Pruning. No regular pruning is required, bu frost-damaged shoot-tips of hardy shrubb species should be removed in March or April Large specimens outdoors may be cut hard bac to within 12 in. of the base in April.

Cut *C. speciosissimum* hard back after flower ing, usually to about 6 in. from the base. Th climbing *C. thomsonae* needs no regular pruning but remove untidy growths and shorten latera shoots by half or two-thirds in April.

Pests and diseases. Generally trouble-free.

Clethra
Clethraceae

A genus of 120 species of deciduous an evergreen shrubs and small trees occurring i America, China, Japan and Madeira. Most of th evergreen species are tender and grow well onl in the mildest localities in Great Britain; the deciduous species are hardy.

C. alnifolia (sweet pepper bush). E. United States. Height and spread 6 ft or more. A deciduous shrub of erect, bushy habit, with mid-green obovate to oblong leaves, having serrated margins. Fragrant, bell-shaped cream-white flowers in terminal racemes, 2–6 in. long, are borne from August to October. *C. a. paniculata* has arching branches with narrow leaves and larger flowers in terminal panicles. 'Rosea', with glossy leaves and buds, has pink-tinged flowers.

CLETHRA ALNIFOLIA

C. arborea. Madeira. Height 10–18 ft; spread 6–12 ft. A tender evergreen tree or tall shrub. The rich dark green leaves are oblanceolate and serrated. The young growths, the leaf and flower stalks, and the undersides of the leaves are all covered with rust-coloured hairs. White, cup-shaped, sweet-scented flowers are borne in terminal panicles, up to 6 in. long, from August to October. This species can be grown outdoors only in the mildest parts of Great Britain, but is admirable for a cool greenhouse.

Cultivation. Clethras require a lime-free soil with plenty of humus and moisture. Plant in September and October or in March and April in a sunny or lightly shaded position, such as a shrubbery or woodland.

C. arborea is best planted in the greenhouse border or in 18–24 in. tubs of 2 parts lime-free loam, 2 parts peat and 1 part sand (parts by volume). Provide a winter temperature of 4–7°C (39–45°F); pot-grown plants may be stood outdoors during the summer.

Propagation. Take cuttings, 3–4 in. long, of lateral shoots, preferably with a heel, during July and August; insert in equal parts (by volume) peat and sand in a propagating frame with a bottom heat of 16°C (61°F). Pot the rooted cuttings in 3 in. pots containing a lime-free compost as recommended for tub-grown plants; overwinter in a frost-free frame or greenhouse.

Alternatively, layer long shoots in September; sever from the parent one or two years later.

Pruning. None required.

Pests and diseases. Generally trouble-free.

Clianthus

Leguminosae

A genus of two species of evergreen climbing shrubs or sub-shrubs. They are suitable for greenhouse cultivation, although *C. puniceus* can be grown outdoors in mild districts.

C. dampieri: see *C. formosus*

C. formosus, syn. *C. dampieri* (glory pea). Australia. A prostrate sub-shrub that may spread to 24 in. The pinnate leaves, like the rest of the plant, are covered with silver-grey hairs. The claw-shaped flowers appear in clusters of from four to six, from March to June. They are 2–2½ in. long, brilliant, glossy crimson-scarlet with a black blotch at the base of the ovate-pointed standard.

CLIANTHUS PUNICEUS

C. puniceus (parrot's bill). New Zealand. Height up to 12 ft. This climber needs support as it tends to spread rather than to ascend. The pinnate mid-green leaves are composed of from 12 to 24 leaflets. Crimson-scarlet, claw-shaped flowers appear in May and June in axillary clusters, about 4 in. long, of six or more flowers. There is a white form, *C. p.* 'Albus'.

Cultivation. Grow *C. formosus* in hanging baskets or 5–6 in. pots containing a sandy compost, such as John Innes potting compost No. 3 with an additional part of grit. This species is often difficult to cultivate, and is unlikely to flower more than once. Water the plants from below by immersing the pots in a bucket. Keep water off the leaves except in extremely hot weather, when they may be syringed lightly early in the day. A winter temperature of 7°C (45°F) is sufficient, provided a dry atmosphere is maintained. Raise the temperature to 10–13°C (50–55°F), during spring and summer, and give full ventilation.

C. puniceus is an easier plant than *C. formosus*. It is best planted out in the greenhouse border in a position where it can be trained to wires or trellis on a wall. In mild districts, it will often survive for many years outdoors if given wall protection; in winter cover the base of the plants with a 12 in. mound of bracken, ashes or coarse sand. In severe frosts, straw mats may be hung to protect the branches.

If grown in the greenhouse border or in the house, a minimum winter temperature of 5°C (41°F) is required, or early flower production will be inhibited.

Throughout winter, keep *C. puniceus* on the dry side; in spring and summer, give ample water and syringe the leaves frequently to discourage red spider mites. Maintain a moist atmosphere in summer; allow full ventilation at all times, except during fog or in low temperatures.

Propagation. *C. formosus* can be grown only from seeds; it is intolerant of root disturbance and is short-lived. Sow the seeds separately in February in 2 in. pots of John Innes seed compost at a temperature of 13–16°C (55–61°F); pot on as soon as three or four true leaves have fully developed.

Sow seeds of *C. puniceus* in March in pots or pans of John Innes seed compost; germinate at a temperature of 13–16°C (55–61°F). Prick out the seedlings, when large enough to handle, into 3 in. pots; pot on into 5 in. pots and eventually plant out in the greenhouse border. The plants will flower in two or three years.

Clethra alnifolia

Clianthus formosus

Clianthus puniceus

Take 3 in. long heel cuttings of lateral shoots in June or July and root singly in 2½ in. pots of John Innes seed compost. Place in a propagating case at a temperature of 16–18°C (61–64°F).
Pruning. No pruning should be attempted with *C. formosus*. Prune *C. puniceus* only if the plants become too large; cut back the main growths to the desired height or thin them out at the base after flowering in June.
Pests. GLASSHOUSE RED SPIDER MITES infest the leaves and cause mottling and bleaching.
Diseases. Generally trouble-free.

Clivia × cyrtanthiflora

Clivia miniata

Clivia nobilis

Cobaea scandens

Clivia
Amaryllidaceae

CLIVIA MINIATA

A genus of three species of leek-like plants, formerly known as *Imantophyllum*. They are not hardy but make attractive pot plants for a greenhouse or conservatory. The leaves are strap-shaped, dark green and glossy, and up to 24 in. long; new ones appear each summer while an equal number die off each autumn and winter. The stout flower stems produce 10–60 flowers in terminal umbels.

The flowers of the species described are trumpet-shaped and 2–3 in. long.
C. × cyrtanthiflora. Height 12–19 in. A garden hybrid between *C. miniata* and *C. nobilis*, with light flame-coloured flowers in March and April, occasionally later. There are many unnamed varieties with yellow, orange and red flowers.
C. miniata. Natal. Height 18 in. A species with widely spreading leaves. The flowering stems carry 10–20 erect orange to red flowers from March through to August.
C. nobilis. S. Africa. Height 12 in; spread 18 in. This species bears orange-red, green-tipped drooping flowers in May.
Cultivation. When they become available in spring, plant the crowns singly in 5 in. pots of John Innes potting compost No. 2, at a temperature of 16°C (61°F). Keep the plants warm and watered, but not too wet, through the summer. From autumn until spring, water only if the soil dries out completely. Protect from frost. Strong plants will produce new shoots and whole plants should be potted after flowering into 7–8 in. pots; a year or two later pot on, in spring, into 10–12 in. pots, without dividing, if really handsome displays are wanted.

When a 10–12 in. pot is completely full of roots, and therefore overcrowded, knock the plant out of the pot and wash the old soil away carefully from the fleshy roots, which are easily damaged. Pull the shoots apart and pot them singly into 4–5 in. pots, just burying the base of the stems. Use John Innes potting compost No. 1 and maintain a temperature of 16°C (61°F).

Propagation. Seeds can be produced by pollinating the open flowers. The seed-raised plants will have flowers that are variable in size and shade. Sow home-produced seeds when ripe (when the fruit is red) and bought seeds as soon as they can be obtained. Sow the seeds singly in 3 in. pots of John Innes potting compost No. 1, at a temperature of 16°C (61°F). Pot on into 5 in. pots.
Pests. The plants may be infested by MEALY BUGS; conspicuous tufts of white waxy wool appear.
Diseases. Generally trouble-free.

Clover, white: see *Trifolium repens*

Cobaea
Cobaeaceae (Polemoniaceae)

A genus of 18 species of half-hardy perennial climbers. The single species described is usually grown as an annual and provides quick decorative cover for pergolas, trelliswork and other forms of support. The bell-shaped flowers are popular for flower arrangements.

This plant tends to grow vertically at first, but it spreads at the top. As a perennial the species may be grown in a greenhouse, but it is too vigorous for a small house.

COBAEA SCANDENS

C. scandens (cathedral bell, cup and saucer plant). Mexico. Height 20 ft or more; planting distance 24 in. This vigorous climber supports itself by means of pea-like branched tendrils that grow from the ends of the leaf stalks. The leaves are mid to dark green and pinnate, with three pairs of leaflets. Each flower has a purple bell-shaped corolla embraced by a green saucer-like calyx. They are 2½–3 in. long and are freely borne from May to October.

The variety 'Alba' has green-white flowers.
Cultivation. Plant in any ordinary, well-drained soil in early June; rich soil produces excessive growth at the expense of flowers. Choose a sunny, sheltered position.

Provide support for the plant's tendrils, using pea sticks, wire mesh or netting, or trelliswork. During dry sunny weather, water plentifully, particularly on quick-draining soils.

For flowering under glass, grow cobaeas in 8 in. pots of John Innes potting compost No. 2 or 3. Support with canes or twiggy sticks. These plants make excellent perennial evergreen climbers if the winter temperature does not fall below 5–8°C (41–46°F). Planted in the greenhouse border and trained on wires or strings up under the greenhouse roof, the rampant growth provides useful cover for plants requiring shade.
Propagation. Sow the seeds under glass in March or April at a temperature of 18°C (64°F). Place one seed to each 3 in. pot of John Innes potting

ompost No. 1. Pot the seedlings on as necessary,
r harden off plants before planting outdoors.

runing. Prune only to control excessive growth
under glass, preferably in September and October,
r in March.

ests. Plants under glass may be attacked by
LASSHOUSE RED SPIDER MITES, THRIPS, MEALY BUGS
nd SCALE INSECTS.

APHIDS infest plants under glass and outdoors.

iseases. Generally trouble-free.

---

ob-nut: see *Corylus avellana*

ochlearia armoracia: see Horseradish

ockscomb: see *Celosia argentea cristata*

Cocos
Palmae

A genus which now contains only one species, *C.
ucifera*, the coconut palm. The species described
orrectly belongs to the genus *Syagrus*. However,
: is described under *Cocos* because this is
he generic name by which it is still commonly
nown. It is a dwarf palm suitable for greenhouse
ultivation; young specimens are sometimes
rown as house plants.

COCOS WEDDELIANA

. weddeliana, botanically known as *Syagrus
weddeliana*. S. America. Height 6 ft; spread 2–
ft. The plant takes at least 20 years to reach its
aximum height and spread, and is usually seen
s a small plant about 12 in. high and wide. The
rching, pinnate leaves are composed of long, thin
eaflets, dark green above, glaucous beneath.

ultivation. Grow in 4–6 in. pots of John Innes
otting compost No. 1. The minimum tempera-
ure in winter should be 16°C (61°F) and in
ummer 21°C (70°F). Ventilate well and main-
ain a moist atmosphere by frequently damping
own the staging and floor of the greenhouse.
ightly shade the greenhouse from early May
ntil late August. Water the plants freely from
May to September, moderately in October, and
paringly from November to April. Repot or pot
n every second or third year in May; give a
weak liquid feed every two or three weeks from
May to September.

Propagation. Sow seeds in February or March.
prinkle the seeds on the surface of a peat
ompost and keep the pots or pans in a humid
tmosphere at a temperature of 24–27°C
75–81°F). Germination is erratic; as the seeds
erminate prick the seedlings off singly into 3 in.
ots and grow on in the same humid conditions.
When two or three leaves have developed,
ansfer the pots to the greenhouse staging and
row on until the following spring, when the
lantlets should need potting on into 4 in. pots.

ests and diseases. Generally trouble-free.

Codiaeum variegatum 'Reidii'

Codiaeum
Croton. *Euphorbiaceae*

CODIAEUM VARIEGATUM

A genus of 15 species of evergreen shrubs. Only
one species is in general cultivation in Great
Britain. It is an ornamental foliage plant, suitable
for a greenhouse or as a house plant.

C. variegatum. Malaysia. Height as a pot plant
up to 24 in.; spread 12–18 in.; vigorous plants
under ideal greenhouse conditions may reach
a height of 4–10 ft. This species is represented
in cultivation by *C. v. pictum* and its varieties.
There are wide variations in the colourful leaves,
which range from linear to ovate and are
variously lobed, and from green with white or
yellow spots or blotches to combinations of pink,
red, orange and near black.

Recommended varieties include 'Carrierei',
with oblong-elliptic leaves that are yellow-
green when young, later maturing to dark green
with a red centre. 'Disraeli' has lanceolate-
spathulate, mid-green leaves, heavily blotched
with cream-yellow above and flushed red beneath. 'Reidii' bears oblong-ovate, slightly
recurved and wavy mid-green leaves with a
distinct ladder-like pattern of cream veins;
as they age, they become suffused with pale red.

Cultivation. Pot the plants in March or April in
5–7 in. pots of John Innes potting compost No. 2.

The plants require a humid atmosphere and
good light to bring out the leaf colours. In the
greenhouse, give only light shading from May to
September. They are susceptible to draughts and
sudden changes in temperature which may cause
the leaves to drop. The best winter temperature is
16°C (61°F); if this cannot be maintained
constantly, a temperature of 13°C (55°F) or even
10°C (50°F) is sufficient for short periods. The
plants will be slightly checked at the lower
temperature, but this is preferable to leaf-drop
due to changing temperatures.

Cocos weddeliana

Codiaeum variegatum pictum

Codiaeum variegatum 'Carrierei'

163

Codiaeum variegatum 'Disraeli'

Codonopsis clematidea

Codonopsis ovata

Codonopsis vinciflora

In winter, apply water sparingly; it should be heated to about 16°C (61°F). In summer, water frequently and syringe the leaves in hot weather. Give a liquid feed to young plants every two or three weeks from June to September. Established plants need a weekly feed during the summer. Pot on annually in March or April.

During summer the plants can be moved from the greenhouse to the living-room. They must be hardened off gradually for the lower temperatures they will get in the home.

For permanent room culture, give the plants a well-lit, draught-proof situation where the temperature does not drop below 10–13°C (50–55°F) at night.

Propagation. Take tip cuttings, 3 in. long, of strong shoots of lateral growths from March to June and root these in warm, close conditions. The plant stems are filled with a white, milky latex which gushes out as soon as the plant tissue is cut. To stop the bleeding, dip the cuttings in powdered charcoal before inserting in 2½ in. pots of equal parts (by volume) peat and sand.

Place the cuttings in a propagating case and root at a temperature of 24°C (75°F).

Pruning. If the plants are doing well, or if large bushy specimens are required, no pruning is necessary. Leggy or sparse-leaved specimens can be hard pruned in March. Cut the top growth down to within a few inches of the soil and dust the cut ends with powdered charcoal. Under moist and warm conditions the plants should soon start into growth again.

Pests. SCALE INSECTS form rounded brown scales under the leaves and on stems, and make the plants sticky and sooty.

GLASSHOUSE RED SPIDER MITES infest the undersides of leaves and cause a light mottling of the upper leaf surfaces.

MEALY BUGS form conspicuous tufts of white waxy wool on leaves and stems, and make the plants sticky and sooty.

Diseases. Generally trouble-free.

Codonopsis
Campanulaceae

CODONOPSIS OVATA

A genus of about 30 species of climbing herbaceous perennials and annuals. The flowers are bell or star-shaped and in some species are beautifully marked inside; the plants are at their best growing at the top of a bank or rock garden. Those described are hardy perennials.

C. clematidea. Asia. Height 12–24 in.; planting distance 12 in. The light green leaves are ovate with a slender point. Blue-tinged white flowers, with brown-gold and black markings inside, are produced in June and July. They are deeply bell-shaped and 1–1½ in. long.

C. convolvulacea. China. Height 3–4 ft; planting distance 24 in. This slender, twining plant has smooth, light green leaves that are ovate and alternate. Lavender-blue, star-shaped flowers 1½–2 in. across, open in July.

C. ovata. Himalayas, Kashmir. Height 6–12 in. planting distance 12 in. This plant is of low spreading habit and has ovate, hairy, light green leaves. Pale blue, bell-shaped flowers appear July and August. They have orange and purple markings inside and are 1–1½ in. long.

C. vinciflora. Tibet. Height 3–4 ft; spread up to 24 in. A twining plant with pale green lanceolate to ovate leaves. The blue-purple flowers are periwinkle-like, 1½–2 in. across and with wide spreading elliptic petals. They are borne singly in the upper leaf axils in July.

Cultivation. Plant at any time between October and April. Choose a sunny or lightly shaded position in well-drained loamy soil. *C. convolvulacea* and *C. vinciflora* need pea sticks up which to twine, or may be allowed to climb through a shrub. Do not disturb the plants once they are established. Dead stems may be cut down from October onwards.

Propagation. Sow seeds during March in boxes or pans of seed compost and place them in a cold frame. Prick out the seedlings into boxes, then into a nursery bed. Plant out in October.

Take cuttings of basal shoots in April or May and insert in equal parts (by volume) peat and sand in a cold frame. Pot them when well rooted. Plant out from October onwards.

Pests and diseases. Generally trouble-free.

Coelogyne
Orchidaceae

COELOGYNE CRISTATA

A genus of 200 species of tropical epiphytic orchids confined to Asia and the Pacific Islands. They are evergreen with erect or pendulous flower stems. The often fragrant flowers are borne in spikes of from one to more than 30 flowers; they vary from pure white and pale green-yellow to shades of brown and dusky salmon-pink. The single-jointed pseudobulbs are variously shaped, from rounded to elongated flask-shaped, and up to 6 in. high by 1 in. or more wide. They bear one or two leaves which are strap-shaped, and vary considerably in size.

Coelogynes are tolerant plants, but do best under the correct conditions, which vary from species to species. The cool-house species, *C. cristata*, can be grown as a house plant and will flower for long periods.

See also ORCHIDS.

C. asperata. E. Malesia. The prominently ribbed pseudobulbs are up to 6 in. high and bear two pale green leaves. Pendulous flower stems, up to 8 in.

ong, carry spikes of 15 flowers, each 3 in. across. The sepals and petals are pale buff-green to cream-white, with a conspicuous membranous bract at the base. The lip is white or cream, heavily shaded with deep rust-red and spotted with patches of yellow and occasional red flecks and streaks. The flowers open one at a time, usually from April to June. This species thrives in a warm greenhouse, and should be given ample shade from April to September. It has no marked resting period.

. cristata. Himalayas. This easily grown species is suitable for cultivation in a living-room, as it thrives in cool conditions. The wrinkled pseudobulbs, 2–3 in. high, carry leathery dark green leaves. Each pendulous spike, about 6 in. long, is composed of up to seven pure white fragrant flowers, 2–3 in. wide, shaded pale orange in the centre of the lip and on the prominent crests. The flowers open successively from December to March. Water freely from early April to October, but keep just moist during winter.

. massangeana. India, W. Malesia. The pseudobulbs, 3–4 in. high, carry two lanceolate, mid-green, strongly veined leaves and drooping flower stems up to 24 in. long. The flowers, 2 in. across, are arranged in two rows of up to 30 flowers; they are pale yellow-buff, with a sepia-brown lip that has white veins and bright yellow crests. They open from January to August. Grow in an intermediate greenhouse with moderate shade in summer.

. speciosa. Malesia. A species with a 1–3 in. high, single-leaved pseudobulb. Each leaf is oblong-lanceolate and dark green. The flower spikes carry two or three flowers each; these are about 3 in. across and range in colour from buff-green to pale salmon-pink; the keeled lip is marked with crimson and brown, with deep chocolate or yellow crests. The flowers open singly at any time from January to December. 'Alba' is a pure white variety. This species can be grown in an intermediate or cool greenhouse, and needs shading from April to October.

Cultivation. Grow coelogynes in 3–5 in. pots or 8–10 in. pans of 2 parts fine osmunda fibre, 1 part sphagnum moss and 1 part leaf-mould (parts by volume). All species thrive in a humid atmosphere, and ventilation should be given on warm days from April to October. Water *C. massangeana* moderately from April to September, and the other species more freely. Reduce watering from November to March for all species. Repot every two or three years from March to May; *C. cristata* will flower more freely in an overcrowded pot.

Propagation. Divide and pot up the plants at potting time from March to May.

Pests and diseases. Generally trouble-free.

Coix
Gramineae

A genus of five species of half-hardy annual broad-leaved grasses. They are chiefly grown for their attractive bead-shaped seeds which are grey and pearly and may be used for stringing. These grasses are not suitable for drying.

Coelogyne speciosa

C. lacryma-jobi (Job's tears). India, China. Height 18–24 in.; planting distance 6–9 in. A tufted species with short, broad, pale to mid-green leaves. Numerous arching stems carry small, pendulous clusters of grey-green, woody seeds from July to September.

COIX LACRYMA-JOBI

Cultivation. Grow these grasses in any well-drained garden soil, enriched with humus, and set in a sunny, south-facing position.

Propagation. Sow seeds during February or March in pots or pans of John Innes seed compost at a temperature of 13–16°C (55–61°F). Transplant the seedlings to their flowering positions at the end of May when danger of frost is past.

Seeds may also be sown outdoors in April where the plants are to grow.

Pests. Generally trouble-free.

Diseases. Plants may be attacked by POWDERY MILDEW, especially after heavy applications of nitrogenous manure. White or brown patches of fungal growth appear, first on the lower leaves which turn yellow and shrivel.

Coelogyne cristata

Coix lacryma-jobi

Colchicum
Autumn crocus. *Liliaceae*

A genus of some 65 bulbous species with crocus-like flowers, few of which are in cultivation. Both colchicums and crocuses produce their stemless flowers direct from the corms, the flower stalk being a tubular extension of the petals.

Colchicum agrippinum

Colchicum autumnale
'Roseum-plenum'

Colchicum speciosum
'Atrorubens'

Colchicum byzantinum

Differences between the two genera are found in the corms, those of the colchicum being oval in shape, whereas crocus corms are flat or round. Colchicums have longer, broader leaves than crocuses.

The species described are completely hardy. The flowers are coloured pink or lilac to pale purple, with some white varieties, and are borne from September to November. The one exception is the February-flowering *C. luteum*, which has yellow flowers. The leaves are glossy, ovate-lanceolate and mid to dark green unless otherwise stated.

Colchicums make an attractive splash of colour in shrub borders or rough grass and may be left for many years. A disadvantage is the rapid growth of their large leaves, which may smother smaller plants and which look untidy while withering and dying.

COLCHICUM SPECIOSUM (LEAVES)

C. agrippinum, syn. *C. variegatum*. Origin unknown. Height of flowers, 3–4 in., leaves 4–6 in.; planting distance 6 in. The pointed, semiprostrate leaves that appear in spring are barely

glossy. This species produces many tessellate reddish-purple flowers from each corm. Th flower tube is pale and longer than the flowe which it supports.

C. autumnale. Europe, including Great Britai Height of flowers, 6 in., leaves 8–10 in.; plantin distance 9 in. Several lilac-coloured flowers a produced from each corm. *C. a.* 'Album' is a whit form; *C. a.* 'Roseum-plenum' is a double rose pink, easily grown variety.

C. byzantinum. Asia Minor. Height of flower 6–8 in., leaves 12–16 in.; planting distance 9 ir The folded leaves are 4 in. across. This is free-flowering species bearing pale lilac-pink, 4– in. deep flowers. It does not appear to set seeds.

C. luteum. Kashmir, Himalayas and north int Russia. Height of flowers, 3–4 in., leaves 10–1 in.; planting distance 4–6 in. The leaves appea with the flowers, staying short until flowerin finishes and then increasing in length befor yellowing and dying in June. This is the onl spring-flowering species generally available, an the only one with yellow flowers. It is mor curious than beautiful.

C. speciosum. Widely distributed north, east an south from Asia Minor. Height of flowers, 6 in leaves 12–16 in.; planting distance 9–12 in. Th flowers of this species are in shades of mauv *C. s.* 'Album' has fine white flowers; *C. s. born muelleri* has lilac-rose flowers with white centre and pale green tubes.

C. speciosum has been crossed with tesse lated species, with chequerboard colouring, t

Coleus
Labiatae

A genus of 150 species of evergreen perennial plants. They are suitable for cultivation in the greenhouse or the home, and are grown for their ornamental foliage or winter flowers. Only the following two species are in general cultivation.

C. blumei. Java. Height 18 in. or more; spread 12 in. or more. The species is a perennial sub-shrubby foliage plant; it is usually raised annually from cuttings. The ornamental, nettle-like leaves are in varied shades of green, yellow, red and maroon. The small blue and white, tubular, two-lipped flowers should be pinched out before they develop, to maintain a bushy, leafy plant. Numerous varieties are known, with different types of leaf patterning in red, bronze, brown, purple, yellow and white and shades of green.

COLEUS BLUMEI

C. thyrsoideus. Central Africa. Height up to 3 ft; spread 18–24 in. The mid-green leaves are roughly heart-shaped. Tubular, bright blue flowers are produced in large numbers in a terminal branched panicle, 9 in. long. They appear from November to March.

Cultivation. Plant in March or April in John Innes potting compost No. 3; a proprietary peat compost can also be used for *C. blumei*. Provide a winter temperature of 13°C (55°F) for both species. During winter, *C. thyrsoideus* will need enough water to keep the flowers in good condition, but *C. blumei* should be kept on the dry side. In winter, the leaf colours of *C. blumei* fade somewhat but they deepen again as the hours of daylight lengthen.

The plants can be continuously potted on if large specimens are required; final potting for *C. blumei* should be 6 or 7 in. pots, for *C. thyrsoideus* 7–10 in. pots. Pinch out the growing tips at regular intervals of two or three weeks to encourage the production of side-shoots. Both species are rarely grown on for a second year, but can be overwintered for cuttings to be taken the following spring.

Feed the plants weekly with liquid manure from June to September.

Propagation. Sow seeds of *C. blumei* in January in order to obtain large plants.

The best forms are preserved by means of 3 in. long tip cuttings of non-flowering shoots, taken in August or March. Root the cuttings singly in 2½ in. pots of John Innes potting compost No. 1, at a temperature of 16–18°C (61–64°F). Pot the cuttings on successively until they are in their final 6–7 in. pots.

Take cuttings, 3 in. long, of young shoots from cut-back plants of *C. thyrsoideus* in March or April. Treat the cuttings as those of *C. blumei*, but pot on until the plants are in 7–10 in. pots.

Colchicum speciosum 'Album'

Colchicum speciosum 'The Giant'

produce a number of hybrids: 'Atrorubens', crimson-purple; 'Autumn Queen', violet-purple; 'Lilac Wonder', deep lilac-pink with white stripes; 'The Giant', large mauve flowers with white base; 'Violet Queen', deep mauve with a thin white stripe on each petal; and 'Waterlily', large mauve double flowers.

C. variegatum: see *C. agrippinum*

Cultivation. Plant colchicums 3–4 in. deep, either as soon as the corms can be bought in August or September, or when the leaves are dead and the corms can be lifted in June or July.

Arrange small clumps of six or more corms in sites where the flowers can be seen to advantage in the autumn, and the leaves will not be too obtrusive or smothering in spring.

Propagation. The species, except for *C. byzantinum*, can be raised from seeds. Sow seeds when ripe (June or July), in a cold frame in 6–8 in. pots or pans, using John Innes seed compost. Germination may take 18 months. Plant out the small corms in a nursery bed a year after germination. They take from three to six years, occasionally longer, to reach flowering size.

All, however, increase steadily by the production of offsets. Separate these when the corms are lifted in June or July, and either replant in the flowering site or grow them on for a year or two in a spare piece of ground.

Pests. The corms and leaves may be eaten by SLUGS; these pests are particularly troublesome on *C. luteum*.

Diseases. Generally trouble-free.

Colchicum speciosum bornmuelleri

Coleus blumei

Coleus thyrsoideus

Coleus blumei (mixed varieties)

Collinsia bicolor

Cultivation. A moist but well-drained soil in partial shade is ideal, although most soils give good results. Insert twiggy sticks for support.

Plants from a September sowing can be lifted in April and put into 5 in. pots of John Innes potting compost No. 1 for summer-flowering in a cold greenhouse.

Propagation. Sow the seeds in the flowering site, just covering them, in September, March or April. Thin out the seedlings to the required spacing, leaving autumn-sown seedlings until spring before thinning. A succession of sowings in the spring will extend the flowering period.

Pests and diseases. Generally trouble-free.

Columbine: see Aquilegia

Columnea

Gesneriaceae

COLUMNEA MICROPHYLLA

A genus of 200 species of tender, evergreen, epiphytic sub-shrubs and perennial climbers. They are grown as basket plants, chiefly for their showy hooded flowers, which are produced close together from the leaf axils, singly and successively, as growth extends. The lanceolate to elliptic leaves are slightly fleshy.

C. × banksii. Garden origin. A sub-shrubby hybrid with pendulous stems, 2–3 ft long, bearing glossy dark green leaves. The flowers, $2\frac{1}{2}$–3 in. long, are orange-red with a few orange markings in the throat. They are produced between November and April and are sometimes followed by white berries tinged with violet.

C. gloriosa. Costa Rica. The slender, 2–4 ft long, pendulous stems of this sub-shrub are covered with pale to mid-green hairy leaves. Bright scarlet flowers, 2–$2\frac{1}{2}$ in. long, with a small yellow patch in the throat, are borne profusely between October and April. 'Purpurea' has deep purple-flushed leaves.

C. microphylla. Costa Rica. A species with pendulous stems up to 6 ft long. The light green, broadly ovate leaves are covered with purple hairs. Bright orange-scarlet flowers, $1\frac{1}{2}$–2 in. long, are borne between November and April.

C. schiedeana. Mexico. A climbing or pendulous species with stems 3–4 ft long. These have swollen nodes and are lightly covered with pale to mid-green leaves. Scarlet flowers, up to 2 in. long and mottled with yellow and brown, are borne from May to July.

Cultivation. Columneas are best grown in 10 in. wide hanging baskets containing a proprietary peat compost or a mixture of 2 parts John Innes potting compost No. 2 and 1 part sphagnum moss (parts by volume).

For winter-flowering species, maintain a minimum winter temperature of 13–16°C (55–61°F);

Pruning. If *C. blumei* is being grown on for a second year, shorten all growths by two-thirds in February. Cut back all growths of *C. thyrsoideus* to within 3–4 in. of the base after flowering.

Pests. ROOT KNOT EELWORMS invade roots and form swollen, contorted galls. LEAF EELWORMS infest leaves, causing discoloration and leaf-drop.

MEALY BUGS form white waxy wool on the stems and leaves. Scales develop under leaves attacked by GLASSHOUSE WHITEFLY.

Diseases. Generally trouble-free.

Collinsia

Scrophulariaceae

COLLINSIA BICOLOR

A genus of 20 species of hardy annuals. The species described is suitable for borders, for bedding out and as pot plants under glass.

C. bicolor. California. Height up to 24 in.; spacing 6 in. Slender growths carry pairs of lanceolate mid-green leaves. The showy flowers are 1 in. long, their upper lips white, their lower lips lilac. They are produced from June to September. The variety 'Salmon Beauty' has flowers of pure salmon-rose; a multicoloured mixture is also available in shades of white, lilac, rose and purple.

Columnea gloriosa 'Purpurea'

Columnea microphylla

Colutea arborescens
(flower and fruit)

keep the plants moist to ensure continuous flowering. Summer-flowering species should be overwintered at 10–13°C (50–55°F).

In summer, water freely; ventilate the house when the temperature exceeds 18°C (64°F), and lightly shade the glass from late April to October. Provide a humid atmosphere by frequent damping down.

Repot or pot on winter-flowering species every other year in June; summer-flowering species in September or March. Give all established plants a weak liquid feed at intervals of seven to ten days from May to September.

Propagation. Take 3 in. long cuttings of non-flowering stems from March to May. Insert in equal parts (by volume) peat and sand in a propagating case, at a temperature of 18–21°C (64–70°F). When well rooted, pot the cuttings singly into 3 in. pots containing the growing compost. When the plants are well established, pinch out the growing points to encourage bushy development. Transfer the plants from pots to baskets, setting three plants to a 10–12 in. basket.

Pruning. Cut out entirely dead and weak shoots, and remove faded flowers. Bare stems may be cut back to base at the same time.

Pests and diseases. Generally trouble-free.

Colutea

Bladder senna. *Leguminosae*

A genus of 26 species of tender and hardy deciduous flowering shrubs. Only one species is in general cultivation, and is grown chiefly for its attractive seed pods.

C. arborescens. S. Europe, Mediterranean regions. Height and spread 8 ft. A hardy species of bushy, open growth. The light green leaves are pinnate. Yellow pea-shaped flowers, ¾ in. long, are carried in racemes from June to September; they are followed by 3 in. long, inflated pods, pale green heavily flushed red or copper.

COLUTEA ARBORESCENS

Cultivation. Plant in ordinary garden soil in a sunny position from October to March.
Propagation. Sow seeds in the open in March, transplanting the seedlings to their permanent positions in October.

Alternatively, take cuttings, 3–4 in. long, of ripe lateral shoots with a heel in September; insert the cuttings in equal parts (by volume) peat and sand in a cold frame. Pot the rooted cuttings in 4 in. containers of John Innes potting compost No. 2 the following April or May; plunge outdoors until planting out in October.
Pruning. Remove weak and thin shoots in March, and cut back strong branches to within a few buds of the old wood.
Pests and diseases. Generally trouble-free.

Comfrey: see Symphytum
Coneflower: see Rudbeckia
Coneflower, purple: see Echinacea

Cones: laterally borne clusters of *Picea glauca*, and terminal single cones of *Picea smithiana* and *Picea abies*

CONIFERS

This group of primitive plants, nearly all trees, is generally taken to include just over 600 species in the three orders, *Coniferales, Taxales* and *Ginkgoales,* although only those in the first order actually bear cones. Apart from a few genera which are deciduous or have lanceolate leaves, conifers are characterised by tough evergreen, scale-, awl-, needle-like or linear leaves, often closely overlapping. The maidenhair tree (*Ginkgo*), often classified as a conifer but botanically distinct, bears fan-shaped leaves. Characteristic also of conifers, although not of universal occurrence, is the erect habit. This is typified among the firs and pines which have a single leading stem and whorls of branches marking each season's growth. The presence of resin canals (resin-bearing tissues within the stems), is another feature common to most conifers.

Although a few conifers are bushes less than 3 ft high, many of the tree forms are immensely tall; several have reached a height of 300 ft, and one specimen of coast redwood, *Sequoia sempervirens,* is the tallest known tree, 366 ft high. The closely related giant redwood, *Sequoia gigantea,* is the largest of all organisms, one specimen weighing about 4000 tons. A small tree, the bristlecone pine (*Pinus aristata*), is the oldest living organism, one being about 4860 years old.

Conifers are a major source of the world's timber supply and are found throughout the temperate zones: in vast forests across the northern plains of Asia and America, and on the mountain ranges to the south and in the Southern Hemisphere. In the Tropics they are restricted to a few high mountains. The timbers are mainly light and easily worked and are widely used for construction work, roofs, joists, floors and doors, and also in heavier work like railway sleepers. Smaller trees are used for pulp production and are the chief source of newsprint, packing paper, cardboard and boxes. Conifers also provide much of the world's supply of resin and turpentine.

Conifers are useful in the designing of gardens. They give shelter, solidity and colour in winter, and make outstanding specimen trees.

Their great variation in foliage textures and colour has been immensely increased by garden varieties of diverse forms and bright colours. They generally thrive on poorer soils than many other trees, and some are well suited to deep peaty or shallow rocky soils. In gardens, however, conifers usually succeed better in fertile soil. They do best in damp and slightly acid soils and, in general, their growth is markedly better in the west and the north, and in Ireland, than in the drier east. However, some species grow well on chalk or limestone soils, and some are drought-tolerant, especially the true cedars and certain junipers and cypresses.

DWARF CONIFERS. Many of the coniferous genera have dwarf forms, which are becoming increasingly popular for small gardens. They are suitable for rock gardens, as isolated groups on a lawn or in any open space; they associate particularly well with heathers. Because of their slow growth they also make good specimens for window-boxes, sink and trough gardens; as pot plants they will tolerate cool indoor conditions for short periods.

The term dwarf is relative and does not truly apply to height, since many dwarf conifers in time become quite large. These forms are more accurately described as slow-growing, and those listed under the various genera are all so slow-growing that they may safely be used as dwarf plants for many years.

Unless otherwise stated in the generic descriptions of conifers, dwarf forms are identical with their larger relatives in respect of hardiness, soil, climatic and cultural requirements. In dry eastern localities, dwarf conifers may succeed better since local environments, such as shelter from drying winds or special pockets of soil, can easily be provided. Generally, dwarf forms cone less freely than the large specimens or not at all.

Most conifer species are readily increased from seeds, and are best raised in this way. Named varieties must be propagated by cuttings or by grafting, and several species, such as those of *Thuja* and *Sequoia,* grow well from cuttings. No seeds of *Metasequoia* nor of Leyland cypress are available and these too must be increased from cuttings.

The unisexual flowers of conifers are of the simplest form, consisting of tiny leaf-like scales bearing either clusters of pollen cells or naked ovules. They are generally borne in a short thick spike known botanically as a strobilus (-li). In female strobili, each scale is closely associated with a bract, which in some genera, notably *Pinus* and *Cryptomeria,* are partially or wholly fused to it. Generally, female strobili are round or barrel-shaped; the male strobili are more elongated, being catkin-like in such genera as *Abies* and *Cedrus.*

After pollination, which is effected by the wind carrying the light pollen, the scales of the female strobili enlarge and become woody, forming the characteristic cones of *Abies, Araucaria, Larix, Picea, Pinus* and *Pseudotsuga.* In some species, notably *Pseudotsuga menziesii* and *Abies bracteata,* the bracts enlarge to slender appendages and protrude from between the cone scales. These cones, when ripe, carry the seeds, usually in the form of ovoid nutlets, each bearing a papery wing. On dry days, the cone scales gape open to release the seeds, which are then borne off by the wind.

Although the majority of conifers are cone-bearing, there are a number of exceptions. Genera such as *Taxus* and *Juniperus* bear berry-like, somewhat fleshy fruits which appear to have no affinity with cones. In these genera, however, the ovule-bearing scales are reduced to one or a few only. After pollination, scales and bracts fuse together around the developing seeds and become fleshy. Thus the 'berries' of junipers are really small fleshy cones. In the yew (*Taxus*), where only one ovule develops, the outer seed coat forms a sticky fleshy cup in which the polished nut-like seed is carried.

Conophytum

Aizoaceae

A genus of 270 species of succulent greenhouse perennials, formerly included in the genus *Mesembryanthemum*. All the species are native to S. and S.W. Africa. Like *Lithops*, they are mimicry plants, resembling the stones among which they grow in nature.

Conophytums grow in clumps of succulent plant bodies composed of pairs of fused leaves. Some look like bunches of small grapes, some are speckled and marked and others are distinctively two-lobed.

Few species are over 2 in. high or more than 3 in. in diameter. The flowering period is from August to November; the daisy-like flowers range in colour from white, cream, yellow and pink to purple-red.

See also CACTUS.

CONOPHYTUM NOTABILE

C. albescens. Height $1\frac{1}{2}$ in.; spread $\frac{3}{4}$ in. The grey-green plant body is divided into two lobes at the top, and is marked with thin red lines on the crown. Yellow flowers, $\frac{1}{2}$ in. across, appear in September. This is a clump-forming species.

C. bilobum. Height 2 in.; spread 1 in. The two-lobed grey-green plant body gradually turns red. The yellow flowers, 1 in. wide, are borne in September and October. With age, several plant bodies are formed, all joined to one stem.

C. calculus. Height 2 in.; spread 3 in. This species has a spherical pale green body up to $\frac{3}{4}$ in. in diameter, with a shallow, $\frac{1}{4}$ in. long fissure across the top. The petals of the deep yellow daisy-like flowers, $\frac{1}{2}$ in. across, which appear in October and November, are tipped with brown.

C. concavum. Height 2 in.; spread 1 in. The individual globular body of this clump-forming species is slightly concave on the upper surface. It is green-purple, with a shallow fissure in the centre. White flowers, $\frac{1}{2}$ in. across, are borne during October.

C. ernianum. Height up to 1 in.; spread $\frac{3}{4}$ in. Each plant body is grey-green with numerous dark green dots. It is split at the top. Pink flowers, each measuring $\frac{1}{2}$ in. across, are produced during August and September.

C. frutescens. Height 1 in.; spread $\frac{1}{2}$ in. A clump-forming species. Each dark green plant body is divided into two lobes. Orange-yellow flowers, measuring $\frac{1}{2}$ in. across, are borne from July to September.

C. globosum. Height up to $1\frac{1}{2}$ in.; spread 3 in. The almost globular body, up to $\frac{3}{4}$ in. in diameter, is smooth glossy green, tinged grey. There is a small fissure at the top. Pink flowers, $\frac{1}{2}$ in. wide, are produced in September.

C. halenbergense. Height $\frac{1}{2}-\frac{3}{4}$ in.; spread 3 in. The heart-shaped body of this clump-forming species has a fissure across the top; it is blue-green with darker speckles. The flowers, $\frac{1}{2}$ in. across, are yellow; they are borne in October and November.

C. meyerae. Height $\frac{3}{4}-1\frac{1}{2}$ in.; spread 3 in. The plant body is divided into two flat lobes. It is dark grey-green, faintly marked with darker lines and dots. Yellow flowers, $\frac{1}{2}$ in. wide, appear in October and November.

C. mundum. Height up to $1\frac{1}{2}$ in.; spread $\frac{1}{2}-\frac{3}{4}$ in. The globular body, with a flattened top, is dull green with darker green dots. There is a shallow fissure at the crown. The yellow flowers, $\frac{1}{2}$ in. across, are produced in September and October.

C. notabile. Height 2 in.; spread 1 in. Similar to *C. bilobum*, but red-pink flowers appear from April to June. It is one of the first conophytums to come into growth, and watering may be started as early as April.

C. obcordellum. Height $1\frac{1}{2}$ in.; spread $\frac{1}{2}-\frac{3}{4}$ in. Each globular plant body of this clump-forming species is flat at the top. They are grey-green, with darker dots and a minute fissure in the centre. Cream flowers, $\frac{1}{2}$ in. wide, appear in October.

C. pillansii. Height $1\frac{1}{2}$ in.; spread 1 in. The body is globular, bright yellow-green and with a $\frac{1}{4}$ in. deep cleft. Purple-red flowers, $\frac{1}{2}$ in. across, are borne in September and October.

C. praegratum. Height 1 in.; spread $\frac{3}{4}$ in. The pear-shaped body is dark blue-green, with olive-green dots and a shallow oval fissure. Pink flowers, up to $\frac{1}{2}$ in. across, appear in October.

C. quaesitum. Height up to 2 in.; spread $\frac{1}{2}-\frac{3}{4}$ in. The pear-shaped plant body has a minute fissure at the crown. It is blue-green with darker dots. White flowers, $\frac{3}{4}$ in. across, are produced during October and November.

C. scitulum. Height up to 2 in.; spread $\frac{1}{2}-\frac{3}{4}$ in. Each plant body is cone-shaped, grey-green tinged with red, and marked with prominent, broken red-brown lines. There is a narrow fissure on the top. White flowers, $\frac{3}{4}$ in. across, appear in October and November.

C. sitzlerianum. Height $1\frac{1}{2}$ in.; spread $\frac{1}{2}$ in. The blue-green plant body has two blunt lobes with red tips. Golden-yellow flowers, $\frac{3}{4}$ in. across, appear in September and October.

C. taylorianum. Height and spread $\frac{3}{4}-1$ in. The heart-shaped body has a slight fissure in each lobe. The dark grey-green skin is speckled with red. Pink flowers, up to $\frac{1}{2}$ in. across, are produced during October.

C. truncatellum. Height $\frac{3}{4}$ in.; spread up to 6 in. Each globular plant body of this clump-forming species is cleft at the crown. They are grey-green with darker minute spots. Cream-white flowers, $\frac{1}{4}$ in. across, appear in October.

C. uviforme. Height $\frac{3}{4}$ in.; spread up to 6 in. The globular bright green plant body has darker green speckles and a cleft top. The yellow-white flowers are $\frac{1}{2}$ in. wide and appear in October. A clump-forming species.

C. wiggettae. Height up to $\frac{3}{4}$ in.; spread up to 6 in. Each flat globular body of this clump-forming species has a fissure at the top. They are grey-green, with dark red-brown dots. The flowers, in October, are white and $\frac{1}{2}$ in. wide.

Cultivation. Conophytums are easily grown under the right conditions. The soil must be porous, and should consist of equal parts (by volume) loam, sharp sand and small granite

Conophytum bilobum

Conophytum notabile

Convallaria majalis

Convolvulus tricolor

Convolvulus tricolor
(mixed varieties)

Convolvulus althaeoides

chips. Keep the plants on a greenhouse shelf where they will receive plenty of light and sun. They flower most freely in small pots or pans, 4–6 in. wide.

The plants rest from December until July, with the exception of *C. notabile,* which comes into growth in April. Give them one good watering in March to prevent shrivelling. From July until they finish flowering, water them whenever the soil is dry. Cease watering all species at the end of October when the plant bodies will divide and start to shrivel.

New growth appears through the old skin, which should be removed with tweezers when it becomes brown and peels off easily.

Do not allow the winter temperature to fall below 5°C (41°F). The plants tolerate heat in summer, but need plenty of air.

Move every three years, in July, into larger pots if big specimens are wanted.

Propagation. Increase by seeds, sown in May at a minimum temperature of 21°C (70°F); sprinkle the dust-fine seeds on top of John Innes seed compost and do not cover with soil. Alternatively, divide the clumps in summer.

Take cuttings in July as closely as possible to the base of the plant body, keeping a small piece of the older tissue attached. Insert in 2½ in. pots of coarse sand and root at 18–21°C (64–70°F). Pot the rooted cuttings in the growing compost.

Pests. Conspicuous tufts of white waxy wool on the plants are caused by MEALY BUGS. ROOT MEALY BUGS infest root systems and check growth.

Diseases. Rotting of the plants may be due to a PHYSIOLOGICAL DISORDER.

Convallaria

Lily of the valley. *Liliaceae*

A genus of only one species of hardy herbaceous perennial. This well-known plant grows from a branched, creeping, horizontal rhizome and spreads quickly under suitable conditions.

In Britain, lily of the valley is spring-flowering and is excellent for wild gardens or for planting in massed clumps in cool shady corners. The plants may also be forced under glass to provide flowers during winter.

CONVALLARIA MAJALIS

C. majalis. Europe, Asia, N. America. Height 6–8 in.; spread 24 in. or more. The elliptic mid-green leaves grow in pairs. Arching stems carry from five to eight white waxy flowers in April and May; they are bell-shaped, ¼ in. long and have a characteristic sweet scent.

'Fortin's Giant' is a large-flowered white variety, often used for forcing; 'Rosea' is a form with pink flowers.

Cultivation. Grow convallarias in partial shade in ordinary garden soil containing plenty of leaf-mould or compost. They will thrive in the open or in the partial shade of buildings, but they grow best under not-too-dense deciduous trees. They need ample moisture at the roots. Plant the crowns singly in September or October, about 3–4 in. apart, with their pointed ends uppermost and just below the surface of the soil; or plant small clumps of crowns 6–8 in. apart.

For flowering under glass or indoors, plant a dozen plump single crowns during October or November in a 6 in. pot of compost consisting of equal parts (by volume) loam and leaf-mould, with some sharp sand added to ensure good drainage. Stand the pot in a cold greenhouse or frame until January; then bring it into a warm greenhouse or living-room with a temperature of about 20°C (68°F). Frequent watering is necessary for rapid growth.

Propagation. Lift and divide the rhizomes with a fork at any time from October to March. Divide and replant the individual crowns 3–4 in. apart just below the surface; give a top dressing of compost or leaf-mould, and water well.

Sow seeds when ripe, and before October, in boxes or pans of John Innes seed compost. Transfer the young plants to a nursery bed and grow on for two or three years before setting in permanent positions.

Pests. Rhizomes of established plants may be damaged by SWIFT MOTH CATERPILLARS.

Diseases. In wet situations a GREY MOULD fungus shows as grey spots and scorched areas on the leaves. The stalks may decay at the base, causing the plants to topple. A velvety mould covers the diseased tissue, and later black resting bodies of the fungus develop.

Convolvulus

Convolvulaceae

CONVOLVULUS CNEORUM

A genus of 250 species of tender, half-hardy and hardy annuals and herbaceous erect and climbing perennials, deciduous and evergreen shrubs and sub-shrubs. The species described are suitable for growing in mixed and annual borders, on banks and on large rock gardens. *C. cneorum* may also be grown in an alpine house.

The widely funnel-shaped flowers are borne in the upper leaf axils, singly or in small clusters. They generally open in the early morning and fade during the afternoon; they are not suitable for cutting.

ANNUAL SPECIES

C. major: see *Ipomoea purpurea*

C. minor: see *C. tricolor*

C. tricolor, syn. *C. minor.* S. Europe. Height 12–15 in.; planting distance 6–9 in. A hardy species of erect, bushy growth, with dark green, ovate-lanceolate to spathulate leaves. Solitary, 1½ in. wide flowers appear profusely from the upper leaf axils from July to September; they are rich blue, ranging from white to yellow at the throat.

Several available varieties include: 'Crimson Monarch', cherry-crimson; 'Dark Blue'; 'Royal Ensign', deep blue with white centre and yellow throat; and 'Sky Blue'.

SHRUBBY AND PERENNIAL SPECIES

C. althaeoides. S. Europe. Height 2–3 in.; spread 2–3 ft or more. A hardy, prostrate or semi-climbing plant with grey-green foliage. The lower leaves are ovate to triangular, the upper leaves are deeply dissected. Pink to purple flowers, 1 in. wide, are borne along the upper stems from July to September.

The species tends to be invasive, but the stems die away completely during winter.

C. cneorum. S.E. Europe. Height and spread 2–3 ft. A half-hardy evergreen shrub of compact bushy habit. The narrow, lanceolate leaves are covered with silky, silvery hairs. Pink buds open to white flowers; they are borne in terminal clusters, 1 in. across, from May to September.

C. mauritanicus. N. Africa. Height 2–3 in.; spread 18–24 in. or more. A tufted, mat-forming plant with a woody rootstock; hardy only in sheltered areas. The leaves are ovate to obovate and mid-green. Satiny, purple-blue flowers, 1 in. across, are borne singly from June to September.

Cultivation of annual species. Grow these plants in any ordinary, well-drained garden soil, in a sunny position. Remove the seed heads regularly to ensure a succession of flowers.

Cultivation of shrubby and perennial species. Plant during April or May in any ordinary, well-drained garden soil, in a sunny and sheltered position. In wet areas protect the hairy foliage of *C. cneorum* in winter with panes of glass or open-ended cloches.

C. cneorum can also be grown in an alpine house, in 6–8 in. pans of John Innes potting compost No. 1. Repot annually in March.

Propagation of annual species. Sow seeds under glass during March, in pots or pans of John Innes seed compost at a temperature of 15–18°C (59–64°F). Prick out the seedlings, when large enough to handle, into boxes; harden off in a cold frame before planting out in May.

Alternatively, sow directly in the flowering site in April, and thin out the seedlings to the required distance. A September sowing, protected with cloches in winter, gives larger plants.

Propagation of shrubby and perennial species. Take 1½–3 in. heel cuttings of basal shoots or lateral growths between June and August; insert in equal parts (by volume) peat and sand in a cold frame. Pot the rooted cuttings singly into 3 in. pots of John Innes potting compost No. 2; overwinter in a frost-free frame and plant out the following May. Overwinter a few rooted cuttings or young plants every year, to replace any plants killed during the winter.

C. althaeoides may be divided and replanted in April.

Pests. Plants under glass may be infested by GLASSHOUSE RED SPIDER MITES which cause fine, light mottling of the leaves, and bronzing.

Diseases. Generally trouble-free.

Coral berry: see *Symphoricarpos orbiculatus*
Coral flower: see Heuchera
Coral tree, common: see *Erythrina crista-galli*

Cordyline
Cabbage palm. *Liliaceae*

A genus of 15 species of evergreen palm-like shrubs and trees grown for their handsome foliage. They are tender or half-hardy plants and require greenhouse cultivation; the tender types will survive in a warm living-room. *C. australis* and *C. indivisa* may also be grown outdoors in mild areas in the south and west.

CORDYLINE TERMINALIS

C. australis. New Zealand, Australia. Height up to 25 ft; spread 6–10 ft; as a pot plant, height 2–3 ft. A slow-growing species with an erect stem that branches after flowering. The narrow, lanceolate to strap-shaped, grey-green leaves are borne in dense arching clusters at the top of the branches. The form 'Lentiginosa', syn. 'Purpurea', has leaves flushed with purple.

In mild areas outdoors, eight to ten-year-old trees may bear plume-like panicles, up to 3 ft long by 24 in. wide, of fragrant cream-white flowers in June and July. The flowers may be followed by clusters of round white berries.

C. indivisa. New Zealand. Height up to 20 ft; spread 6 ft; as a pot plant, height 3–4 ft. This species produces a single, unbranched stem. The lanceolate, long-pointed and narrow leaves are mid-green with red or yellow midribs. Outdoors, loose pendulous panicles, 24 in. long by 18 in. wide, of off-white flowers flushed purple, appear in June and July. Clusters of round purple berries are produced in autumn.

C. terminalis. S.E. Asia. Height 1½–3 ft. This is the most tender species and requires pot culture under warm conditions. It is often listed as *Dracaena terminalis*. The leaves develop on young plants from a central growing point; only with age is the palm-like trunk revealed. The lanceolate leaves are mid to deep green, variously flushed with cream, red or purple.

In cultivation, the species is generally represented by variegated forms, such as 'Eugène André', with bright red young foliage, fading to dark bronze; 'Guilfoylei', with leaves striped red and pink or white; 'Tricolor', red and purple.

Cultivation. Grow cordylines in 6–8 in. pots of John Innes potting compost No. 2 or a proprietary peat compost. Provide a winter temperature of 4–7°C (39–45°F) for *C. australis* and *C. indivisa*; *C. terminalis* requires a temperature of 10–13°C (50–55°F).

C. australis and *C. indivisa* should be grown in full light throughout the year; for *C. terminalis* lightly shade the greenhouse in summer.

Convolvulus cneorum

Convolvulus mauritanicus

Cordyline australis

Cordyline indivisa

Coreopsis drummondii 'Golden Crown'

Coreopsis verticillata

Pests. Generally trouble-free.

Diseases. LEAF SPOT shows on the leaves as brown irregular spots with purple margins; pinpoint black dots are scattered over the spots.

Coreopsis
Compositae

COREOPSIS GRANDIFLORA

A genus of 120 species of hardy annuals and herbaceous perennials, the annuals sometimes being listed under the genus *Calliopsis*. The species described are free-flowering, upright, bushy plants with deeply cut leaves and colourful daisy-like flowers, excellent in borders and for cutting. They thrive in smoky industrial areas and are most effective when planted in bold groups of one variety. The annuals also make good spring and summer-flowering pot plants.

ANNUAL SPECIES

C. bicolor: see *C. tinctoria*

C. drummondii. Texas. Height 24 in.; spacing 12 in. A species of erect and branching habit, with dark green leaves. The flowers measure 2 in. across and are bright yellow with a deep purple central disc and a red-brown blotch at the base of each ray floret. They appear from July to September. Single colour strains in yellow, crimson and crimson-scarlet are obtainable.

'Golden Crown' is deep golden-yellow with a chestnut-brown centre.

C. tinctoria, syn. *C. bicolor.* N. America. Height 2–3 ft; spacing 6–9 in. This is the most popular of the annuals. The leaves are mid to dark green; stiff stems carry a profusion of bright yellow flowers, 2 in. across, from July to September.

Garden varieties include: 'All Double Mixed', $2\frac{1}{2}$ ft, with double and semi-double flowers in a variety of yellow to chestnut colour combinations; 'Dwarf Mixed', 9 in., a free-flowering variety suitable for growing in pots and for bedding; and 'Single Mixed', 3 ft, with single yellow or rich chestnut flowers, blotched with maroon or dark crimson.

PERENNIAL SPECIES

C. grandiflora. U.S.A. Height 12–18 in.; planting distance 18 in. This robust species has light to mid-green leaves that are narrow and deeply toothed. Bright yellow flowers, up to $2\frac{1}{2}$ in. across, are borne on long stems from June to August; they are excellent for cutting.

The following are good varieties: 'Badengold', 3 ft high, with golden-yellow flowers larger than the type, but less free-flowering; 'Goldfink' syn. 'Goldfinch', 6–8 in., bright yellow; 'Mayfield Giant', 3 ft, orange-yellow; and 'Sunburst', $2\frac{1}{2}$ ft, rich yellow, double.

C. verticillata. U.S.A. Height 18–24 in.; planting distance 12–18 in. A long-lived species of erect bushy growth, with bright green, finely divided,

Coreopsis grandiflora

Ventilate the greenhouse for all species when the temperature exceeds 16°C (61°F), or stand *C. australis* and *C. indivisa* outdoors in summer.

Water freely during summer, but keep the plants just moist during winter. Give a liquid feed at intervals of ten days from May to September, and repot or pot on every second or third year in March.

Outdoors, grow *C. australis* and *C. indivisa* in fertile, well-drained garden soil. They are tolerant of exposure to strong winds in maritime areas, and do well in full sun or partial shade.

Propagation. Detach suckers in March and April and pot in 4 in. containers of John Innes potting compost No. 2. Grow on in a greenhouse at a temperature of 10–13°C (50–55°F) for 12 months before potting on or planting out.

Alternatively, cut stems of old leggy plants into 3 in. sections in May or June. Insert the sections vertically, just burying them, in equal parts (by volume) peat and sand in a propagating frame with a temperature of 18–21°C (64–70°F). When top growth shows, pot the cuttings singly into $3\frac{1}{2}$–4 in. pots of John Innes potting compost No. 2 and pot on as necessary. The first leaves of *C. terminalis* varieties are usually green, but after one or two years coloured foliage is produced.

Sow seeds, when available, in pots or pans of seed compost in April at a temperature of 16–18°C (61–64°F). Pot the seedlings, when large enough to handle, individually into 3 in. containers of John Innes potting compost No. 1. Pot on as necessary.

Pruning. None is required, but leggy plants may have their tops cut off, and the subsequent suckers used for propagation purposes.

ern-like leaves that are distinct from those of other species. Clear yellow flowers, 1½ in. across, are borne profusely from June to September.

Cultivation of annual species. Any fertile, well-drained garden soil in an open sunny site is satisfactory, but the best results are obtained on light soils. Tall plants require staking. Cut back early-sown plants after they have carried their first flush of flowers to encourage a second flowering. They seed themselves freely if the surrounding soil remains undisturbed.

For flowering under glass in spring and summer, set five plants in a 6 in. pot containing John Innes potting compost No. 2.

Cultivation of perennial species. Plant between October and March. The perennial plants require the same cultural conditions as previously described for annuals. Additionally, *C. grandiflora* should be supported at an early stage with pea sticks. The variety 'Sunburst' is short-lived if not cut back after flowering.

Propagation of annual species. For a succession of flowers, sow the seeds in the flowering site from March to June, and thin out the seedlings to the required spacings. Seeds may also be sown in September, but the seedlings require cloche protection in cold areas.

For pot plants to flower in spring and summer, sow seeds in pans of seed compost under glass at a temperature of 16°C (61°F), in September and March respectively. Prick out the seedlings and pot up as soon as they are well rooted.

Propagation of perennial species. Divide the plants in October or March, making sure that each portion has a number of shoots. Replant directly in permanent positions.

Alternatively, sow seeds in open ground in April; prick out the seedlings into a nursery bed and grow on, before transferring them to the flowering site from October onwards.

Pests. FROGHOPPERS suck sap and produce 'cuckoo-spit'; young shoots are weakened and may wilt.

Flowers may be eaten by SLUGS.

Diseases. Generally trouble-free.

Cornel: see Cornus
Cornflower: see *Centaurea cyanus*
Corn, Indian: see Sweet corn
Corn-on-the-cob: see Sweet corn

Corn salad

Valerianella locusta. Valerianaceae

A hardy annual cultivated for its leaves which can be used, when young and crisp, in winter and spring salads. The plant is also known as lamb's lettuce.

Height 6–9 in. Europe, including Great Britain. This plant resembles off-white forget-me-nots; it should not be allowed to flower unless seeds are required.

Cultivation. Corn salad grows in autumn and winter, and therefore requires a sunny, sheltered position. Well-drained garden soil that was well manured for a summer vegetable crop is ideal.

Propagation. Sow seeds thinly in ½ in. deep drills, 6 in. apart, or broadcast in finely raked soil.

Cornus florida (autumn foliage)

Thinning is unnecessary. Make sowings every fortnight from early August to the end of September and again in March and April.

Harvesting and storing. When the plants have developed three or four pairs of leaves, pull them whole, taking care not to damage the tender leaves. Cut off the roots and use the fresh leaves.

Pests and diseases. Generally trouble-free.

Corn salad

Cornus

Cornel, dogwood. *Cornaceae*

This genus has been divided into several separate genera on the strength of differences in the arrangement of fruit and flowers. As the proposed names are not yet in general usage, the original classification of the genus has been retained here. It contains 40 species of mainly deciduous small trees, shrubs and herbaceous perennials. The species described are all hardy and grown for their flowers, decorative foliage or coloured bark.

The flowers are small and star-shaped, usually white, yellow or yellow-green. They are borne on the previous season's growths in rounded or flattened clusters, which in some species are surrounded by large petal-like bracts.

The following species are deciduous unless otherwise noted:

C. alba. Siberia to Manchuria, N. Korea. Height 8–10 ft; spread up to 10 ft. This species is now placed in the genus *Swida*. It is a suckering foliage shrub of vigorous, upright habit with the current season's stems red in winter. The ovate mid-green leaves are grey beneath; they often turn red or orange in autumn. Inconspicuous

Cornus alba 'Spaethii'

Cornus alba 'Westonbirt' (in winter)

Cornus florida 'Rubra'

Cornus kousa (fruits)

Cornus nuttallii

Cornus canadensis

Cornus controversa 'Variegata'

yellow-white flowers are borne in flattened clusters, 1–2 in. across, in May and June; they are followed by white globular berries. Good forms include: 'Elegantissima', with red stems and leaves margined and mottled with white; 'Sibirica', with shiny coral-red stems; 'Spaethii', golden variegated leaves and red bark in winter; 'Westonbirt', brilliant red stems in winter.

CORNUS CANADENSIS

C. canadensis. N. America. Height 4–6 in.; spread 24 in. or more. A herbaceous perennial with an extensively creeping rootstock. It is now placed in the genus *Chamaepericlymenum*. The mid-green ovate leaves are crowded together, sometimes up to six, at the top of the stems. Pure white ovate bracts, about ½ in. long, surround the flattened clusters of tiny green-purple flowers which are borne terminally in June. They are followed by clusters of red globose berries. Suitable for ground cover in peaty or woodland soils; the young shoots are susceptible to spring frosts.
C. capitata. Himalayas. Height 15–20 ft; spread 10–18 ft. This species is now in the genus *Dendrobenthamia*. It is a tender evergreen tree with dull, grey-green, ovate-lanceolate leaves. Tiny flowers, in crowded flattened clusters surrounded by four to six cream-yellow bracts, 1½–2 in. long, appear in June and July.
C. controversa. China, Japan. Height and spread 15–20 ft. The mid-green leaves of this species are alternate and ovate. White flowers are freely

borne in broad, flat clusters, 2–3 in. wide, during June and July. They are followed in autumn by blue-black globose berries. The form 'Variegata' has leaves variegated with white.
C. florida (flowering dogwood). E. United States. Height 10–15 ft; spread 20 ft or more. A well-branched shrub or small tree now listed in the genus *Cynoxylon*. The dark green leaves are opposite, broadly ovate, and glaucous beneath; they turn brilliant orange and scarlet in autumn. The rounded clusters of inconspicuous green flowers in May are surrounded by four white petal-like bracts, 1½–2 in. long. Globular, strawberry-like fruits are borne from late summer onwards. *C. f.* 'Rubra' has pink and white bracts.

CORNUS KOUSA CHINENSIS

C. kousa. Japan, Korea. Height up to 10 ft; spread 8–10 ft. A shrubby species of spreading growth. The ovate, narrowly pointed, mid to dark green leaves have wavy margins. Four white, ovate slender-pointed bracts, 1–1½ in. long, surround the rounded purple-green flower clusters. Flowering is in June; strawberry-like fruits ripen in September.

C. k. chinensis is more upright and has larger bracts; the foliage turns crimson in autumn.
C. mas (cornelian cherry). Europe. Height 8–12 ft; spread 6–10 ft. This shrub of bushy, twiggy habit has dark green, ovate leaves. Small golden yellow flowers are borne in rounded clusters, ½–1 in. across, on the naked stems of the previous

ear's growth, from February to April. They are sometimes followed by red, semi-translucent oval berries. There are several forms: 'Aurea', which has foliage suffused with yellow; 'Elegantissima', with yellow and pink variegations; and 'Variegata', with white margins.

C. nuttallii. Western N. America. Height 15–20 ft; spread 8–10 ft. A free-flowering species, now in the genus *Cynoxylon*, with dull green, ovate or obovate leaves. The rounded flower clusters, $\frac{3}{4}$ in. across, are surrounded by four to eight spreading bracts, $1\frac{1}{2}$–3 in. long, which open cream-white in May and become white, flushed pink. They are followed by strawberry-like fruits.

C. stolonifera. N. America. Height up to 8 ft; spread 7–10 ft. This species, now in the genus *Swida*, is a vigorous shrub of suckering habit, with dull red bark in winter. The leaves and flowers resemble those of *C. alba.* It is usually represented in cultivation by 'Flaviramea' which has bright green-yellow winter bark.

Cultivation. Plant the tree species from September to November in any good garden soil and in a position with plenty of sun to ripen the wood. Plant the vigorous, bushy species, grown for their decorative bark and foliage, in March or April in moist soil, in sun or partial shade.

C. alba and its varieties are best grown as isolated specimens.

Propagation. Sow seeds of *C. capitata, C. florida, C. kousa, C. nuttallii* and *C. mas* when ripe, in August or September, in pots or pans of John Innes seed compost and place in a cold frame. The seeds may take 18 months to germinate. When the seedlings are large enough to handle, set them singly in 3 in. pots of John Innes potting compost No. 2 and later plant out in nursery rows. Grow on for two or three years before planting out.

Alternatively, all species may be propagated by half-ripe cuttings, 3–4 in. long, preferably with a heel, taken in July or August. Insert the cuttings in equal parts (by volume) peat and sand in a propagating case or under mist at a temperature of 16°C (61°F). Pot the rooted cuttings in 3 in. containers of John Innes potting compost No. 2 and overwinter in a cold frame. Set out in nursery rows the following May and grow on for two or three years before transplanting to permanent positions.

Increase suckering species by removing and replanting rooted suckers in November.

Layer long shoots of all species in September; sever *C. alba* and *C. stolonifera* the following October; other species will usually require a further year.

Pruning. Tree species require no regular pruning; shrubby species grown for their bark, notably *C. alba* and its varieties, should be cut hard back to within a few inches of the ground in early April.

Pests and diseases. Generally trouble-free.

Cortaderia

Pampas grass. *Gramineae*

A genus of 15 species of perennial evergreen grasses. They make fine specimen plants, particularly when their silky, silvery flowering plumes stand out against a dark background. The hardy plants described are suitable for herbaceous or shrub borders or as specimen plants for lawns.

C. argentea: see *C. selloana*

CORTADERIA SELLOANA

C. selloana, syns. *C. argentea, Gynerium argenteum.* Argentina. Height 6–9 ft; planting distance 5–6 ft. Slender, arching leaves, which are glaucous and rough-edged, form a dense mass on the erect stems. The stems carry 15–18 in. long silvery plumes. The plumes of female plants are more silky than those of male plants.

'Pumila', 4–6 ft high, is a more compact form; 'Rendatleri', 6–8 ft, has pale, silver-purple plumes; 'Sunningdale Silver', 8–10 ft, has loose white plumes, larger than those of the species.

Cultivation. Plant cortaderias in April in any well-drained fertile soil. For the best results choose a reasonably sheltered sunny site, either on a lawn or among shrubs. Tidy the plants in spring by removing the dead leaves. Wear gloves for this operation as the leaf edges are sharp.

Propagation. Plants are best increased by division and replanting in April.

Pests and diseases. Generally trouble-free.

Corydalis

Papaveraceae

CORYDALIS CASHMERIANA

A genus of 320 species of hardy perennials with delicate fern-like foliage and quaint, tubular, spurred flowers. The species described are suitable for rock gardens or alpine houses.

C. cashmeriana. Kashmir. Height 6 in.; spread up to 9 in. This species requires cool, humid conditions and is difficult to cultivate outdoors in the south of England. The dissected blue-green foliage is surrounded by racemes of $\frac{3}{4}$–1 in. long, brilliant clear blue flowers from May to August. Each raceme is 2–3 in. long. This plant is best grown in an alpine house.

C. lutea. Europe, including Great Britain. Height 6–8 in.; spread 12 in. The fern-like leaves of this species are slightly glaucous. Yellow flowers, similar to those of *C. cashmeriana,* appear from April through to November. This is the common yellow corydalis often seen on old walls, where it self-seeds in profusion. Keep it in check by frequently uprooting the self-sown plants.

Cultivation. Plant corydalis in March in a sunny position. Grow *C. cashmeriana* in a cool leafy

Cornus mas

Cortaderia selloana

Corydalis cashmeriana

soil that is completely free from lime; it does better outdoors in Western Scotland than elsewhere in Great Britain. In an alpine house, plant in 6–8 in. pans of John Innes potting compost No. 1. Repot annually in March.

C. lutea grows satisfactorily in any fertile, well-drained garden soil, in sun or shade.

Propagation. Sow seeds in pans of seed compost in a cold frame, in February or March or in September or October. Prick out the seedlings when the first true leaf appears, as the root is extremely brittle on older seedlings. Pot them individually in 2½–3 in. pots of John Innes potting compost No. 1, overwinter in a cold frame, and plant out in March or April. *C. lutea* can also be sown *in situ.*

Pests and diseases. Generally trouble-free.

Corydalis lutea

Corylopsis pauciflora

Corylopsis willmottiae

Corylus avellana (nuts)

Corylopsis
Hamamelidaceae

CORYLOPSIS PAUCIFLORA (IN FLOWER)

A genus of 20 species of hardy, deciduous, flowering shrubs or small trees, native to China and Japan. They flower early in the year on the naked wood, bearing fragrant bell-shaped flowers in catkin-like, drooping racemes. The leaves often colour well in autumn.

C. glabrescens, syn. *C. gotoana.* Japan. Height up to 10 ft; spread 6–8 ft. A shrub or small tree of upright but open habit and with twiggy growths. The broadly ovate, glaucous-green leaves are bristle-toothed. Pale yellow flowers are borne in racemes, 1–1½ in. long, in March and April.

C. gotoana: see *C. glabrescens*

C. pauciflora. Japan. Height up to 6 ft; spread 6–10 ft. A densely branched shrub of wide-spreading habit with slender twiggy growths. The bright green leaves are ovate and pointed with a few teeth. Pale yellow flowers are produced in short drooping racemes, 1 in. long; they are scented like cowslips and are freely borne in March and April. This ornamental shrub requires shelter from cold winds.

C. platypetala. Central China. Height 6–9 ft; spread up to 6 ft. A species with young purple shoots. The mid-green leaves are broadly ovate and toothed. Pale primrose fragrant flowers are carried in pendent racemes, 2–3 in. long, in April.

C. spicata. Japan. Height and spread 5–6 ft. A shrubby species with both spreading and erect branches. The rounded or heart-shaped leaves are glaucous-green and toothed. Narrow, green-yellow, cowslip-scented flowers are borne in racemes, 1–1¼ in. long, in March and April.

C. willmottiae. W. China. Height up to 10 ft; spread 5–8 ft. This shrub of upright open habit has bright green, broadly ovate leaves. The racemes, 2–3 in. long, of pale yellow sweetly scented flowers, open in March and April.

Cultivation. Plant these shrubs from October to March in any ordinary garden soil, preferably lime-free although lime is tolerated if the soil is enriched with peat or leaf-mould. They thrive in sun or partial shade; as they flower and come into growth early they may be damaged by spring frosts, and are therefore best given the protection of a south or west-facing wall, or grown among other shrubs or under open woodland conditions.

Propagation. Layer shoots in October and separate from the parent plant one or two years later.

Alternatively, take cuttings, 3–4 in. long, of lateral shoots with a heel in July or in August and September. Insert the cuttings in equal parts (by volume) peat and sand in a propagating case with a bottom heat of 16°C (61°F). Pot the rooted cuttings in 3 in. pots of John Innes potting compost No. 1 and overwinter in a cold frame. Line out in nursery rows outdoors the following May and grow on for a further two years before transplanting to permanent positions.

Pruning. None required. Old or weak wood may be removed near ground level after flowering.

Pests and diseases. Generally trouble-free.

Corylus
Corylaceae

CORYLUS AVELLANA 'CONTORTA' (IN WINTER)

A genus of 15 species of hardy deciduous nut-bearing trees and shrubs. Several species cultivated for their nuts, also produce decorative forms. The male flowers, borne in catkins, are ornamental in spring; they are cylindrical and pendulous, moving in the wind. The plants are unisexual and the small inconspicuous female flowers appear at the same time. They are followed by the nuts, which mature in September and October.

C. avellana (hazel, cob-nut). Europe, W. Asia, N. Africa. Height up to 20 ft; spread 15 ft or more. The mid-green leaves are broadly ovate and prominently serrated. Yellow male catkins, up to 2½ in. long, are produced in February. The ovoid nuts grow in clusters of two to four and are enclosed in a sheath-like cup of lobed, toothed bracts (the husk).

The variety 'Aurea' is an unusual form with soft yellow leaves; 'Contorta' (corkscrew hazel) is slower-growing, reaching a height of about 8 ft, and has curiously twisted branches. 'Cosford' bears thin-shelled nuts with a good flavour.

C. colurna (Turkish hazel). S.E. Europe, W. Asia. Height 25–30 ft; spread 20–25 ft. A stately tree of symmetrical habit, with attractive grey corrugated bark. The dark green leaves are broadly ovate; yellow male catkins, 2–3 in. long, appear in February or March. Each ovoid nut, borne in clusters of three to six, is completely enclosed in a flask-shaped sheath of bracts.

C. maxima (filbert). S. Europe, W. Asia. Height and spread 10 ft. This shrub is similar to *C. avellana*, but is more robust and has larger leaves. The catkins are 3–4 in. long; the ovoid nuts have a flask-like sheath of bracts and appear singly or in groups of two or three.

The variety 'Kentish Cob' produces large, glossy, well-flavoured nuts; 'Purpurea' has rich purple leaves.

Cultivation. Plant between October and March in any well-drained soil. Corylus trees do best in an open sunny site that is protected from east winds, but they will grow in partial shade.

Plant young specimens that have been pruned to a height of about 18 in. These will develop into bushes with up to six main branches.

Keep weeds in check during the growing season. Gather the nuts when the husks are beginning to turn brown, and spread them out to dry in an airy shed for a few days before storing.
Propagation. Peg down layers in the autumn; sever the layers when well rooted—usually after a year—and grow them on in a nursery bed for one or two years before transplanting.

During October or November, sow the seeds singly in 4 in. pots of John Innes potting compost No. 1 and place in a cold frame. Set out the young plants in a nursery bed one year later and grow them on for one or two years before planting in their permanent positions. Purple-leaved varieties do not always come true from seeds.
Pruning. In the early years after planting, cut back the previous year's growths by half to build up the bush and encourage production of side branches. When flowering starts on these, after four or five years, shorten old growths in March after flowering, cutting back to a strong shoot. This will stimulate the production of new shoots.

Leave unpruned twiggy laterals from the previous year, as these will carry the crop. In late summer, remove any strong shoots that have grown in the centre of the bush; cut these out at ground level or as near to the base as possible.
Pests. The leaves may be eaten by CATERPILLARS.

SQUIRRELS feed on the nuts, destroying whole crops in woodland areas.

WEEVILS bore holes in the shells and eat the kernels; they also attack the leaves.
Diseases. Following an attack by weevils, BROWN ROT fungus may develop, causing the nuts to fall in July and August.

GREY MOULD is a wound parasite which causes die-back of shoots; the fruiting bodies of the fungus appear towards the base of the dead wood as grey-brown, cushion-like, velvety pustules.

HONEY FUNGUS causes rapid death of trees.

POWDERY MILDEW attacks the young leaves and flowers, producing white powdery patches which may cover the undersides of the leaves.

Cosmea : see Cosmos

Cosmos

syn. Cosmea. *Compositae*

A genus of 25 species of annuals and perennials. The two half-hardy annuals described are showy and free-flowering, excellent for growing in borders, in pots and for cutting. The single, dahlia-like flowers are produced in quantity over a long period, right up to the first autumn frosts.

COSMOS BIPINNATUS

C. bipinnatus. Mexico. Height up to 3 ft; planting distance 24 in. This popular garden plant has finely cut mid-green leaves. The flowers are up to 4 in. across, white, crimson, rose or pink, and appear from August to September.

Recommended varieties include 'Sensation Mixed', 3 ft, an early and large-flowering strain; and 'Radiance', 2½ ft, with deep rose and crimson bicoloured flowers.
C. sulphureus. Mexico. Height 24 in.; planting distance 18 in. This species resembles *C. bipinnatus* but has more coarsely cut leaves of a darker green, and yellow flowers borne on long stems well above the foliage. 'Klondyke' is a fully double, golden-orange variety; 'Sunset', 2½ ft, a recent introduction, carries a profusion of brilliant vermilion-red semi-double flowers.
Cultivation. These plants prefer a light, rather poor soil and do best in hot, dry seasons. Rich soils tend to produce excessive foliage and to delay flowering. Staking is usually required when the plants are at full height. Dead-head to ensure a succession of large flowers.

Grow plants for summer flowering under glass in final 6 in. pots of John Innes potting compost No. 1. Keep the greenhouse well ventilated and on the dry side.
Propagation. Sow the seeds under glass at a temperature of 16°C (61°F) in February or March. Prick out the seedlings into boxes and pot into 3½ in. pots for flowering under glass, or harden off in a cold frame before planting out in May.
Pests. APHIDS may infest young plants.

GLASSHOUSE RED SPIDER MITES can be troublesome under glass.
Diseases. Generally trouble-free.

Cotinus

Smoke tree. *Anacardiaceae*

COTINUS COGGYGRIA

A genus of three species of hardy, deciduous trees and shrubs, previously included in the genus *Rhus*. The two species in cultivation are grown principally for their brilliant autumn colours.
C. americanus, syn. *Rhus cotinoides* (chittam wood). S.E. United States. Height 10 ft or more;

Corylus avellana (male catkins)

Corylus avellana 'Contorta'

Cosmos bipinnatus

Cosmos sulphureus 'Klondyke'

Cotinus coggygria 'Foliis Purpureis'

spread 7–8 ft. This species grows as an upright, twiggy shrub, or less commonly as a small tree with a rounded head. The glaucous-green leaves are ovate to obovate. They turn from brilliant red to claret and orange in autumn. The inconspicuous green-white flowers are borne in terminal panicles, 6–12 in. long, in July.

C. coggygria, syn. *Rhus cotinus* (smoke tree). Europe to the Caucasus. Height and spread 8 ft or more. A rounded shrub with light green, round to ovate or obovate leaves which colour brilliantly in autumn. Loose, feathery panicles, 6–8 in. long, of small purple flowers are borne in July. Part of the inflorescence is often covered in silky hairs.

There are a number of named varieties: 'Atropurpureus', bearing pink-purple inflorescences; 'Foliis Purpureis' and 'Royal Purple', with dark plum-purple foliage which assumes light red autumn tints.

Cultivation. These colourful shrubs are easily grown in ordinary, well-drained garden soil and in a sunny position. Plant from October to March. In rich, manured soil these plants will not assume autumn tints.

Propagation. Layer long shoots in September and sever from the parent plants after approximately one year.

Alternatively, take cuttings, 4–5 in. long, of lateral shoots, preferably with a heel, in August or September; insert the cuttings in equal parts (by volume) peat and sand in a cold frame. Line out the rooted cuttings in a nursery bed in May or pot in 4 in. pots of John Innes potting compost No. 2 and plunge outside. Transplant to permanent positions the following spring.

Pruning. None is required, but straggly growths may be shortened or removed in March.

Pests. Generally trouble-free.

Diseases. POWDERY MILDEW frequently occurs on purple-leaved forms of *C. coggygria*; it shows as a powdery white deposit on the leaves, which may be distorted.

VERTICILLIUM WILT is the probable cause of sudden die-back of branches; it does not kill the shrubs immediately.

Cotinus coggygria (autumn foliage)

Cotinus coggygria (fruiting plumes)

Cotoneaster × 'Cornubius' (flowers)

Cotoneaster

Rosaceae

COTONEASTER HORIZONTALIS

A genus of about 50 species of hardy evergreen and deciduous shrubs, ranging from prostrate mat-forming types and dwarf hummocks to large bushes and trees. Many of the deciduous species have rich autumn tints, and the evergreen species and hybrids are useful for hedging and screening; creeping forms are suitable for ground cover. All the species have five-petalled, white or pink, flattened or cup-shaped flowers, usually followed by conspicuous berries in autumn.

Cotoneaster conspicuus

C. adpressus. W. China. Height 12–18 in.; spread 5–6 ft. A spreading deciduous shrub with dull green ovate leaves which turn scarlet in autumn. Inconspicuous white flowers, tipped with pink, appear in June, singly or in pairs, and are followed by globose bright red berries. This is a suitable plant for a rock garden or border edge.

C. a. praecox is a taller variety; it grows up to 24 in. high and has arching branches and large orange-red berries.

C. bullatus. W. China. Height 8–12 ft; spread 8–10 ft. A deciduous shrub with dark green glossy, ovate leaves that have a corrugated surface. Clusters, 1½–2 in. across, of small pink-white flowers are borne in June, followed by bright red ovoid to globose berries.

C. congestus. Himalayas. Height 2–6 in.; spread 1–3 ft. A dwarf or creeping evergreen shrub which forms a dense mound or a carpet of tightly packed branches bearing ovate bright green leaves. Small pink flowers, singly or in clusters of two or three, are borne in June and are followed by clusters of globose red berries. This shrub is suitable even for a small rock garden.

C. conspicuus. S.E. Tibet. Height 6–7 ft; spread 5–6 ft. An evergreen shrub which forms a dense mound of arching stems. The ovate, shining mid-green leaves are hidden in June by ½–1 in. wide clusters of white flowers which crowd the stems. Bright red globose berries ripen in September and October.

C. c. 'Decorus' (height and spread 2–3 ft) is a free-berrying form suitable for a large rock garden or a bank. When purchasing plants of this form, make sure these have been vegetatively propagated, as seedlings vary considerably.

C. × 'Cornubius'. Height and spread 20 ft. A vigorous semi-evergreen shrub, probably a cross between *C. frigidus* and *C. henryanus*; it has dark green lanceolate leaves. Clusters, 2–3 in. across, of cream flowers appear in June. In autumn the long branches are borne down by the weight of large bunches of red globose fruits which often last well into the winter. This is a handsome shrub which is excellent for screening.

. dammeri. China. Height 2–3 in.; spread 5–7 ft. prostrate evergreen shrub with ovate, dark reen and glossy leaves. White flowers appear in une, singly or in pairs, and are followed by lobose sealing-wax-red berries. This is a vigorus shrub, ideal for carpeting banks and bare round beneath taller shrubs and trees.

. franchetii. China. Height 6–8 ft; spread 5–6 ft. n evergreen shrub of graceful arching habit. he ovate leaves are grey-green. Clusters, $\frac{1}{2}$–1 in. cross, of white and pink flowers are borne in une, and are followed by bunches of ovoid range-red berries. This species is particularly uitable for hedging.

C. f. sternianus, sometimes sold as *C. wardii,* is variety with sage-green leaves and numerous range-red berries.

. frigidus. Himalayas. Height 12–15 ft; spread 0–15 ft. A fast-growing semi-evergreen or eciduous shrub or small tree, with mid to dark reen, oblong leaves. Clusters, 2–4 in. wide, of hite flowers are produced in June; they are ollowed by globose crimson berries in large, eavy bunches which last well into the winter.

C. f. 'Xanthocarpus', syn. *C. f.* 'Fructu-luteo', is striking form with cream-yellow berries.

. horizontalis. China. Height 24 in.; spread 6–7 :. A deciduous shrub with branches arranged in n attractive herring-bone fashion. The broadly vate, glossy dark green leaves turn red in utumn. Pink flowers, $\frac{1}{3}$–$\frac{1}{2}$ in. across, appear ingly or in pairs in June, and are followed by lobose red berries thickly clustered along the ranches. A useful shrub for covering unsightly anks and bare rocks, and particularly attractive rown against a north or east-facing wall, when it ay reach a height of up to 8 ft.

C. h. 'Variegatus' is a slower-growing form /ith smaller cream-white variegated leaves, nged pink.

. × hybridus-pendulus. Of garden origin. leight 2–3 in.; spread 6–7 ft. An evergreen arpeting shrub with ovate leaves that are hining green. Clusters, 1–1$\frac{1}{2}$ in. across, of white owers are borne in June, and are followed by an bundance of bright red globose berries. When rown on its own roots and allowed to spread, it akes excellent ground cover. It may also be rafted on to a stem of *C. frigidus* to form a veeping shrub or miniature tree with branches eaching to the ground.

. lacteus. China. Height 10–15 ft; spread 8–12 :. An evergreen shrub with ovate, leathery, deep reen leaves, grey and hairy beneath. Corymbs, –3 in. wide, of cream-white flowers are borne in une and July; these are followed by dense lusters of red obovoid berries which are late in pening and last well into the winter. This pecies is an excellent hedging shrub.

. microphyllus. Himalayas. Height 6 in.; spread –8 ft. An evergreen dwarf shrub with wide-preading branches. The glossy dark green, ovate eaves are grey and hairy beneath. White flowers, in. across, appear in May and June, singly or in vos or threes; they are followed by globose carlet berries which often crowd the branches. n extremely robust shrub, useful for covering are banks, walls and unsightly ground.

C. m. cochleatus is a completely prostrate form /ith broader leaves; suitable for ground cover.

C. × rothschildianus. Garden hybrid between *C. salicifolius* and *C. frigidus* 'Xanthocarpus'. Height 6–10 ft; spread 10–15 ft. A semi-evergreen wide-spreading shrub, with lanceolate leaves that are mid-green above, grey beneath at first, later changing to pale green. Flattened clusters, 2–3 in. across, of small white flowers appear in June; cream-yellow globose berries are borne in abundance and ripen in September.

COTONEASTER SALICIFOLIUS

C. salicifolius. China. Height and spread 12–15 ft. An evergreen shrub, with glossy green, narrow, willow-like leaves that are grey-white and hairy beneath. Corymbs, 2–3 in. wide, of white flowers are borne in June and are followed by globose, bright red berries in dense clusters.

The variety *C. s. floccosus* has more glossy and narrower green leaves, white woolly beneath, and large bunches of small, bright red berries on the arching branches. *C. s.* 'Repens' (height 12 in.) is suitable for ground cover.

C. simonsii. Assam. Height 6–8 ft; spread 4–5 ft. A semi-evergreen shrub of erect habit, with dark green ovate leaves. Clusters, 1$\frac{1}{2}$–$\frac{3}{4}$ in. across, of white flowers are produced in June and are followed by clusters of small, obovoid, orange-red berries. This species is frequently used for informal hedging.

C. wardii. S.E. Tibet. Height 5–8 ft; spread 3–7 ft. A spreading evergreen shrub, with ovate leaves that are dark green and glossy above, grey-white and felted beneath. Clusters, 1–1$\frac{1}{2}$ in. across, of small, white, pink-tinted flowers are borne in June; they are followed by orange-red obovoid berries which ripen in September. This species is often confused with *C. franchetii sternianus,* but is distinguished by the glossy upper leaf surfaces.

C. × watereri. Garden hybrid between *C. henryanus* and *C. frigidus.* Height and spread 12–15 ft. Semi-evergreen shrub or small tree with lanceolate leaves that are dark green above, pale green beneath. White flowers in 2–3 in. wide clusters are borne in June. In autumn, large bunches of globose red berries are freely borne and often last well into winter.

Cultivation. Cotoneasters are easy to grow in ordinary garden soil, preferably in a sunny position. Plant from October to February; seed-grown plants are notoriously variable, and named forms should be vegetatively propagated to ensure that they come true to type. This applies particularly to *C. conspicuus* 'Decorus'.

For hedges, set young plants of *C. franchetii* and *C. simonsii* 12–15 in. apart; *C. frigidus, C. lacteus* and *C. × watereri* should be spaced 2–3 ft apart, for a screen 4–6 ft or more apart. After planting, remove the upper quarter of all shoots to promote bushy growth.

Propagation. Collect the berries as soon as ripe (in September or October). Remove the seeds and sow in pans of John Innes seed compost; place in a

Cotoneaster × 'Cornubius' (fruits)

Cotoneaster franchetii

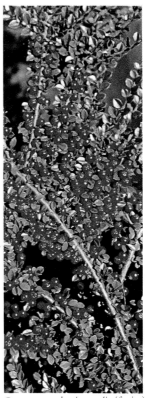

Cotoneaster horizontalis (fruits)

cold frame. In some cases germination may take up to 18 months. Prick the seedlings off into boxes and later into nursery rows outdoors. Grow on for two or three years before transplanting to permanent positions.

Take heel cuttings, 3–4 in. long, of ripened shoots of evergreen species in late August or September, and of semi-mature shoots of deciduous species in July or August. Insert both types of cuttings in equal parts (by volume) peat and sand in a cold frame; when rooted, line out in nursery rows outdoors the following April or May and grow on for two years before planting in permanent positions

Layering in October or November provides another method of propagation. The layers will usually root within a year.

Pruning. No regular pruning is required, but vigorous forms may be pruned hard back in late winter or early spring when they have outgrown their allotted space. Deciduous species should be cut back in February, evergreen species in April.

When grown as a hedge, evergreen species may need the vigorous shoots and side-growths pruned back immediately after flowering. Cut the current season's shoots back to the nearest berry cluster. Trim the deciduous hedge species in August or September.

Pests. In summer, stems and leaves may be infested with APHIDS and SCALE INSECTS, making the plants sticky and sooty. BIRDS often take the berries in winter.

Diseases. FIREBLIGHT causes blackening and shrivelling of flowers, and a progressive die-back of branches bearing brown and withered leaves.

HONEY FUNGUS causes plants to die quickly.

SILVER LEAF may result in die-back of shoots, and the foliage takes on a silvery tinge.

Cotoneaster lacteus (fruits)

Cotoneaster × rothschildianus (fruits)

Cotoneaster × watereri (fruits)

Cotyledon orbiculata dinteri

Cottonwood: see *Populus deltoides*
Cottonwood, black: see *Populus trichocarpa*

Cotyledon

Crassulaceae

COTYLEDON PANICULATA

A genus of 40 species of succulent plants suitable for cool greenhouse treatment. These are shrubby succulents, many of them with attractively coloured foliage. The flower panicles in most species are pendulous and do not appear until the plants are two or three years old, or even later. The opposite pairs of leaves are arranged crosswise one above another; in some species they are evergreen and slightly fleshy, in others they are deciduous and produced in winter.

See also CACTUS.

The following species are easily grown if given full sun. They can be grown as house plants if kept on a sunny window-ledge.

C. barbeyi. E. Africa. Height up to 24 in.; spread 18–24 in. A branched evergreen shrub with slightly fleshy, obovate and glossy light green leaves about 4 in. long. The tubular flowers, up to 1 in. long, are orange-red with fine hairs. They appear in November.

C. ladismithensis. S. Africa. Height up to 6 in. spread up to 12 in. This species is a compact evergreen shrub. It has fleshy, dark green leaves which are hairy and slightly sticky. They are rounded at the top and tapering at the base. It has not yet flowered in cultivation.

C. orbiculata. S. and S.W. Africa. Height 3–4 ft spread up to 24 in. A branched evergreen shrub bearing round, grey-green fleshy leaves with thin red edges. The yellow and red tubular flowers $\frac{1}{2}$–$\frac{3}{4}$ in. long, appear in July and August. There are several varieties and forms of this species: *C. o. dinteri* is of compact habit, with almost cylindrical glaucous leaves; *C. o. oophylla* has round fleshy leaves with a white waxy sheen.

C. paniculata. S. and S.W. Africa. Height up to 9 in.; spread 12–15 in. This extremely slow growing deciduous plant has a fleshy brown stem, greatly swollen at the base. The branches are devoid of leaves except at the ends. The leaves, produced in late autumn, are light green narrowly spoon-shaped, and about 1 in. long. The dark red tubular flowers, 1 in. long, are streaked with green; they appear in July and August, but the species does not flower freely.

C. reticulata. S. Africa. Height up to 9 in.; spread 12–15 in. Similar to *C. paniculata,* but branches near the base. The narrow deciduous leaves are produced in October. The erect tubular flowers $\frac{1}{2}$ in. long, are green-yellow and appear from June to August.

C. teretifolia. S. Africa. Height and spread 4–6 in. A bushy, branched plant with narrow glaucous green leaves. These are evergreen and marked with a distinctive groove along the upper surface. The tubular yellow flowers are produced during December.

C. undulata. S. Africa. Height up to 24 in.; spread up to 4 in. This is one of the most popular species Its single stem bears rounded, white-grey, waxy evergreen leaves which are thick and fleshy, with prominent wavy margins. In bright sunshine the leaves take on shades of purple. Orange-yellow tubular flowers, $\frac{3}{4}$ in. long, are produced from June to August.

Cultivation. Cotyledons require a light, sandy soil consisting of equal parts (by volume) loam, sand and well-decayed leaf-mould. Grow them in 7–9 in. pots, in full sun. Water whenever the soil is dry, except for the deciduous species *C. paniculata* and *C. reticulata.* These have a long resting period during summer and must be kept dry until the leaves appear.

During the dry period the plants live on water stored in their thick stems, and bear their flowers Do not water *C. undulata* from above, or the leaves will be marked. In March or April, pot on the plants into larger pots if necessary

Propagation. Softwood cuttings, 2–3 in. long, are the best method of propagation as they root quite readily. Take the cuttings during summer. As older plants become leggy and bare, restart them from cuttings. Let the cut surfaces heal before inserting the cuttings in the growing compost

Pests. Conspicuous tufts of white wax on the young growths are caused by MEALY BUGS.
Diseases. Generally trouble-free.

Courgette: see Marrow
Couve Tronchuda: see Cabbage
Cowberry: see *Vaccinium vitis-idaea*
Cowslip, blue: see *Pulmonaria angustifolia*
Cowslip, giant: see *Primula florindae*
Cowslip, Himalayan: see *Primula sikkimensis*
Cowslip, Jerusalem: see *Pulmonaria officinalis*
Cowslip, Virginian: see *Mertensia virginica*
Crambe maritima: see Sea kale
Cranberry: see *Vaccinium oxycoccus*
Cranberry, mountain: see *Vaccinium vitis-idaea*
Crane's bill: see Geranium
Crane's bill, bloody: see *Geranium sanguineum*
Crane's bill, meadow: see *Geranium pratense*

Crassula

Crassulaceae

CRASSULA SARCOCAULIS

A genus of 300 species of succulent herbaceous plants and shrubs, and evergreen rock-garden plants. The following species are mostly greenhouse or house plants, but three are suitable for rock gardens in sheltered areas of the south and west, provided the soil is sharply drained.

The thickened leaves are often covered with hair or 'meal'; the small flowers are generally starry and borne in terminal panicles.

See also CACTUS.

C. arborescens, syn. *C. cotyledon*. Cape Province. Height and spread 2–3 ft. A well-branched, shrubby greenhouse plant with rounded to shortly obovate grey-green leaves, often margined with red. The flowers, which are seldom produced in Britain, are white maturing to red; they are borne in terminal panicles, 2–3 in. across, during May and June.

C. cooperi. Cape Province, Transvaal. Height 3 in.; spread up to 12 in. A tufted or mat-forming species with narrowly lanceolate mid-green leaves that are flushed and dimpled with red. Pale pink flowers appear from May to July in sparsely flowered clusters, $\frac{1}{2}$–$\frac{3}{4}$ in. across. This is a half-hardy species which may be grown outside in sheltered situations.

C. cotyledon: see *C. arborescens*

C. deceptrix. Cape Province, Namaqualand. Height 2 in.; spread up to 6 in. The stems of this plant, which branches from the base, are covered with closely packed, rounded triangular leaves that have a white mealy covering. Minute, white, bell-shaped flowers are produced from October to November in clusters, $1\frac{1}{2}$–$2\frac{1}{2}$ in. long.

This is a winter-growing plant for the greenhouse; during the growing season it should be kept a few degrees warmer than other species.

C. falcata. Cape Province. Height up to 24 in.; spread 9–12 in. A shrubby plant with a thick, fleshy stem and numerous laterally flattened, sickle-shaped, fleshy, blue-green leaves which are horizontal near the stem but twisted at the tip. Rounded, 3 in. wide heads of bright orange-red flowers are borne from June to August. This is a species to grow under glass or as a house plant, though indoors it may need cutting back to keep it to a manageable size.

C. milfordae, syn. *C. sedifolia*. Basutoland. Height 1 in.; spread 12–15 in. This evergreen species forms dense cushions of tiny grey-green rosettes which bear 1 in. heads of white flowers, opening from crimson buds, in June and July. It is hardier than *C. sarcocaulis*, but seldom blooms in Britain. The true species may no longer be in cultivation and has been replaced by an allied plant which is usually listed either as *C.* sp. Basutoland or as *C. sediformis*.

C. sarcocaulis. S. Africa. Height up to 9 in. though generally less; spread 6 in. This dwarf shrubby plant will survive mild winters outside, but is more reliable when grown in an alpine house. Woody stems produce small, pointed green leaves that are flushed with red, especially in summer. The flower heads, each $\frac{1}{2}$ in. across, are formed of clusters of minute pink flowers that open from attractive crimson buds between July and September.

C. sedifolia: see *C. milfordae*

C. sediformis: see *C. milfordae*

C. socialis. Cape Province. Height about 1 in.; spread 2–3 in. This species branches freely from the base to form mats of rosettes. The leaves in the rosettes are bright green and triangular, with horny, slightly toothed edges. Tiny panicles, $\frac{1}{2}$ in. across, of minute bell-like white flowers are produced from the centres of the rosettes during March and April. This is a winter-growing greenhouse plant or house plant and should be given some shade in summer.

C. teres. S.W. Africa. Height up to 3 in.; spread 2–3 in. A species for growing under glass or indoors. On each branch the rounded green leaves are packed in four close rows to form a column. Terminal minute, stemless and bell-shaped white flowers, in $\frac{1}{2}$–1 in. wide clusters, usually open in September.

Cultivation. Crassulas need a sharply drained soil, such as 2 parts John Innes potting compost No. 2 and 1 part coarse sand or grit (parts by volume). Grow them in 3–6 in. pots or pans according to the size of the plant. Water the plants described throughout the year, giving a little extra when the flowers appear and a little less after flowering. They do best on a sunny window-ledge, and in winter require a minimum temperature of 7°C (45°F). Repot every second year in April.

Outdoors, in sheltered areas of the south and west, plant *C. cooperi*, *C. sarcocaulis* and *C. milfordae* during May in sharply drained soil in a sunny position.

Propagation. Crassulas can be grown from leaf cuttings taken in spring and summer. Pull a leaf from the main stem, leave it to dry for a day, then place it on the surface of the growing compost. The leaf will form roots and eventually a small rosette will appear at the base. Remove and pot up the new plant when well rooted.

Crassula arborescens

Crassula deceptrix

Crassula falcata (flowers)

Plants can also be raised from seeds scattered on the surface of John Innes seed compost in a pan during April or May. Germinate the seeds at 15–18°C (59–64°F). Prick out the seedlings into pots or pans and pot up as necessary.

Stemmed species, particularly *C. arborescens* and *C. falcata*, can be increased from 2–3 in. stem cuttings, taken between May and July. Let them dry for a few days before potting singly in 2–3 in. containers of the growing compost. Grow on under the same conditions as for mature plants.

C. cooperi and *C. sedifolia* may be divided after flowering or in May.

Pests. Conspicuous tufts of white waxy wool on plants are caused by MEALY BUGS.

ROOT MEALY BUGS and WEEVIL grubs may attack the roots and check growth.

Diseases. Bad drainage or over-watering can cause GREY MOULD to develop on the tufted species. The leaves become covered with a grey velvety fungal growth.

Waterlogging may also cause a PHYSIOLOGICAL DISORDER in all species; the roots rot and subsequently the top growth wilts. Excessively dry soil may cause brown, sunken, shrivelled patches to develop on the leaves.

Crataegus × lavallei

Crataegus oxyacanthoides 'Coccinea Plena'

Crataegus × prunifolia

Crataegus

Ornamental thorn. *Rosaceae*

CRATAEGUS OXYACANTHOIDES

A genus of 200 species of deciduous trees and shrubs, normally with thorny branches. The majority are extremely tough and hardy, being tolerant of industrial pollution and exposure to coastal winds.

White, pink or red clusters of saucer-shaped five-petalled flowers are followed in autumn by bunches of colourful fruits (haws). The leaves of some species have rich autumn tints, and they all make ideal specimen trees for a lawn. The common hawthorn, *C. monogyna*, is used almost exclusively for hedging.

C. × carrierei: see *C. × lavallei*

C. coccinea (scarlet haw). N. America. Height and spread 15–20 ft. A small tree with a wide-spreading head of thorny branches. The dark green leaves are usually ovate, shallowly lobed and toothed; they turn red in autumn. Clusters, 2–3 in. across, of white flowers are borne in May and are followed by scarlet haws in large drooping bunches.

C. crus-galli (cockspur thorn). E. North America. Height 15 ft; spread 15–20 ft. This wide-spreading tree with viciously thorny branches carries glossy green, ovate leaves that are toothed in the upper half; they turn brilliant scarlet in autumn. Clusters, 2–3 in. wide, of white flowers are borne in June and are followed by red haws which usually last well into the New Year.

C. × lavallei, syn. *C. × carrierei*. Garden hybrid between *C. crus-galli* and *C. pubescens stipulacea*. Height 15–20 ft; spread 10–15 ft. A densely branched, almost thornless tree with glossy, dark green, ovate leaves, coarsely toothed, and downy beneath. They often remain on the tree until December. Erect clusters, 2–3 in. across, of white flowers appear in June; orange-red haws ripen in September and October and are long-lasting.

C. laevigata: see *C. oxyacanthoides*

C. monogyna (common hawthorn, quick, may). Europe, including Great Britain. Height 25–30 ft; spread 15–20 ft. This thorny, densely branched species is extensively used throughout Britain for hedging or screening. The glossy dark green leaves are lobed and toothed. Clusters, 2–3 in. across, of white, heavily scented flowers smother the branches in May, and are followed in autumn by clusters of small crimson haws.

C. m. 'Biflora', syn. *C. m.* 'Praecox', (Glastonbury thorn), is an unusual form which produces a second, smaller crop of flowers between November and March during mild spells; *C. m.* 'Stricta', syn. *C. m.* 'Fastigiata', is an extremely hardy tree with erect branches.

C. oxyacanthoides, correctly *C. laevigata* (hawthorn, may). Europe, including Great Britain. Height 15–20 ft; spread 15–18 ft. This species is less common than the closely related *C. monogyna*. It has more rounded, shallower-lobed, mid-green leaves. Clusters, 2–3 in. wide, of sweetly scented white flowers with two or three styles are borne in May and are followed in autumn by crimson ovoid haws.

The species is represented in gardens by the following forms, several of which are probably hybrids between this species and *C. monogyna*: 'Coccinea Plena' ('Paul's Double Scarlet Thorn'), double scarlet flowers; 'Plena', double white; 'Punicea', syn. 'Coccinea', single scarlet; 'Rosea', single pink; 'Rosea Pleno-flore', double pink. All these forms (height 15–20 ft; spread 15–18 ft) make excellent single specimen trees.

C. × prunifolia. Of garden origin and possibly a hybrid between *C. crus-galli* and *C. macracantha*. Height and spread 15–20 ft. This plant has a broad compact head of spiny branches. The ovate, finely toothed leaves are glossy green above and somewhat downy beneath; they turn orange and scarlet in autumn. Round, 2–3 in. wide clusters of white flowers are borne in June and are followed by large red haws persisting into winter.

Cultivation. Plant ornamental thorns at any time during winter when weather permits; they thrive in ordinary garden soil and, though tolerant of partial shade, do better in an open, sunny position. They withstand exposure and periods of drought and waterlogging.

When planting *C. monogyna* as a hedge, use 12–18 in. high plants, spacing these at intervals of 12–15 in. For a screen, use plants 3–4 ft high and plant at intervals of 2–3 ft.

Propagation. Increase species by seeds, which usually take 18 months or more to germinate. Gather the seeds as soon as ripe, stratify for 18 months and sow outdoors in February or March.

C. coccinea, *C. × lavallei* and *C. × prunifolia* may be budded in July or grafted in February or March on to *C. crus-galli* or *C. oxyacanthoides*.

Named forms of *C. monogyna* and *C. oxyacanthoides* may be budded or grafted on to stocks of *C. monogyna* in spring.

Pruning. No regular pruning is required. Trim hedges or screens of *C. monogyna* at any time between July and March. Large hedges and screens, particularly if they have been neglected, will tolerate heavy pruning in July or August.

Pests. CATERPILLARS of various moths may feed on the leaves.

Diseases. FIREBLIGHT causes blackening and shrivelling of flowers and a progressive die-back of branches bearing brown and withered leaves.

HONEY FUNGUS causes the rapid death of trees.

LEAF SPOT due to various fungi shows as small brown or black spots on the foliage.

POWDERY MILDEW appears as a white powdery deposit on the leaves; badly affected shoots may be distorted at the tips.

RUST shows as yellow or orange swellings on young shoots, leaves and fruits in early summer.

Cream cups: see *Platystemon californicus*

Creeping jenny: see *Lysimachia nummularia*

Crepis
Compositae

A genus of 200 species of hardy annuals, biennials and herbaceous perennials. Only three species are generally available; they are suitable for rock gardens or for the front of borders. All have dandelion like flowers.

C. aurea. European Alps. Height 4–6 in.; planting distance 9–12 in. A perennial species with light green dandelion-like leaves. The 1 in. wide orange or copper-red flowers are borne from July to September.

C. incana. Greece. Height 9 in.; planting distance 12 in. This perennial forms a clump of grey-green, broadly ovate leaves. Soft pink flowers, 1–1½ in. across, are produced in July and August.

C. rubra. Italy, Greece. Height 12 in.; spacing 6 in. An annual species with a rosette of pale green, toothed, lanceolate leaves surrounding the flower stems. The flowers are 1 in. or more across, white or rose-red, and appear in August.

Cultivation. These plants thrive and remain compact in most well-drained garden soils, including poor soils, provided the site is sunny. *C. rubra* should be dead-headed to prevent self-seeding. Plant the perennial species in August or September; *C. rubra* should be raised in March or September.

Propagation. Sow seeds of the perennial species during April in pans or boxes of seed compost in a cold frame. Prick off the seedlings into boxes, or singly into 3 in. pots of John Innes potting compost No. 1; transplant to permanent positions in August or September.

Alternatively, divide and replant in April.

Sow seeds of *C. rubra* in the flowering site during September, or March and April, and thin out the seedlings to the required spacing.

Pests and diseases. Generally trouble-free.

Cress: see Mustard and cress

Crinitaria linosyris: see *Aster linosyris*

Crinodendron
Elaeocarpaceae

A genus of two species of evergreen trees and shrubs occurring in S. America. One species only is sufficiently hardy to be cultivated in the open in Britain, and then only in mild areas.

C. hookerianum, syn. *Tricuspidaria lanceolata* (lantern tree). Chile. Height 10–15 ft; spread 6–10 ft. A half-hardy shrub of upright and dense bushy growth. The dark green elliptic leaves are leathery and toothed. Waxy, crimson, urn-shaped flowers, 1–1¼ in. long, are borne on 2–3 in. long pendent stalks from the upper leaf axils of the branchlets. The flowering period extends from April to June. A striking and beautiful shrub and fairly easy to cultivate, but only for sheltered gardens or walls in the south and west.

CRINODENDRON HOOKERIANUM

Cultivation. This shrub does best in a rich, moist and lime-free soil. Plant in April or May in a partially shaded position, and ideally in the shelter of a wall.

Propagation. Take cuttings, 3–4 in. long, of half-ripe shoots with a heel during July and August; insert in equal parts (by volume) peat and sand in a propagating case at a temperature of 16°C (61°F). Pot the rooted cuttings in 3 in. containers of John Innes potting compost No. 1 (minus lime) or in a mixture of 3 parts lime-free loam, 1 part peat, 1 part leaf-mould and 1 part coarse sand (parts by volume).

Overwinter the cuttings in a frost-free frame or greenhouse. Pot on as required into 4–5 in. pots and plunge in a well-ventilated cold frame. Leave the young plants in the cold frame for another winter before planting out.

Pruning. None required.

Pests. Generally trouble-free.

Diseases. HONEY FUNGUS causes death of plants.

Crinum
Amaryllidaceae

CRINUM × POWELLII

A genus of more than 100 species of mainly tender bulbous plants. The few that are grown in Britain are suitable for outdoor planting only in sheltered sites of the south and west. Elsewhere, they do best in a frost-free greenhouse border.

Crepis incana

Crinodendron hookerianum

Crinum moorei

Crinum × powellii

Crocosmia × crocosmiiflora

Crocosmia × crocosmiiflora
'Solfatare'

Crocosmia masonorum

The species described have strap-shaped, pointed, mid-green leaves and trumpet-shaped flowers, 3–6 in. long.

C. bulbispermum, syn. *C. longifolium.* S. Africa. Height 12–18 in. The large bulbs, which have long necks growing out of the ground, produce spreading leaves which remain evergreen. The stems carry wide-open white flowers, sometimes flushed with red, in September and October.

C. longifolium: see *C. bulbispermum*

C. moorei. S. Africa. Height 18–24 in. The bulbs and foliage are like *C. bulbispermum;* the stems have as many as ten flowers, with white and pink petals and green tubes. They are borne from July to September.

C. × powellii. Height 18 in. A garden hybrid raised from crossing *C. bulbispermum* and *C. moorei.* Flowers, varying from pink to white, are borne from July to September.

Cultivation. Outdoors, set the bulbs 12–18 in. apart and 10–12 in. deep. Plant in April or May in rich, well-drained soil, at the foot of a south-facing wall. Water freely in summer. Protect the emerging shoots with bracken, coarse sand or ashes during frost.

Alternatively, plant the bulbs in the greenhouse border or three to an 8–10 in. pot of John Innes potting compost No. 2. Move the containers outdoors in late May and bring them back into the greenhouse by early October. Repot every third year in March.

Propagation. Sow the large seeds singly, as soon as ripe, in 3–4 in. pots of John Innes seed compost. Germinate at a temperature of 21°C (70°F). Pot the seedlings on as necessary; keep them moist throughout the year if a temperature of 16°C (61°F) can be maintained. Little water is needed in the winter if the temperature is lower.

Remove offsets in March. Pot these singly and grow on in the same way as the seedlings. The offsets may reach flowering size in three years; the seedlings need a year or two longer.

Pests. Unhealthy bulbs are sometimes infested by BULB MITES.

Diseases. Generally trouble-free.

Crocosmia

Iridaceae

A genus of six species of bulbs from tropical and southern Africa, closely related to *Tritonia* and *Montbretia* with which they are often confused. They grow from small corms which produce upright, sword-shaped, mid-green leaves. The stems grow up to 3 ft and bear double ranks of tubular flowers in various shades of orange and red from midsummer onwards. *C. masonorum* is hardy; the other species and their hybrids usually survive all but the most severe winters if planted in a well-drained soil; they are excellent as cut flowers.

C. aurea, syn. *Tritonia aurea.* S. Africa. Height 3 ft; planting distance 4 in. The leaves of this species grow in a fan shape to $2\frac{1}{2}$ ft. The pale orange or rich yellow flowers, $1\frac{1}{2}$–2 in. long, are produced during July and August.

C. × crocosmiiflora, syn. *Montbretia crocosmiiflora.* Height up to 24 in.; planting distance 4–6 in. The botanical name covers a wide range of seedlings produced from crosses of *C. aurea* and *C. pottsii,* some of them raised almost 100 years ago, but many others produced and named since then. They are popularly known as montbretias. Hardier than the other crocosmias or tritonias, some have become naturalised on banks, in hedges and in rough ground in south-west England, west Wales, Ireland and the western islands of Scotland. The flowers are trumpet-shaped, $1\frac{1}{2}$ in. long, and borne from July to September on 3 ft stems; they range in colour from yellow to deepest red.

Numerous varieties are available and include: 'Earlham Hybrids', large flowers in mixed orange and red shades; 'Emily McKenzie', orange flecked with brown; 'His Majesty', bright scarlet with orange centre; 'Solfatare', apricot-yellow flowers and bronze-flushed leaves; and 'Star of the East', open orange flowers.

CROCOSMIA MASONORUM

C. masonorum. S. Africa. Height $2\frac{1}{2}$ ft; planting distance 6–9 in. New corms are often produced on long underground stems. The leaves have a pleated appearance. Widely expanded orange flowers, 1 in. long, are closely packed on arching stems during July and August.

C. pottsii. S. Africa. Height 4 ft; planting distance 4–6 in. A broad-leaved species. The flowers, $1\frac{1}{4}$ in. long and light orange and red in colour, appear in August. New corms are produced on short underground stems, by which the plant spreads.

Cultivation. Crocosmias need open, sandy, well-drained soil and plenty of water in the summer. Plant 4–6 in. apart and 2–3 in. deep in the early spring in clumps. Place them on the south side of a sheltering wall, or among groups of shrubs or herbaceous perennials. The flowers are useful for cutting; otherwise, remove the flowering stems when the last flowers have died and gather seeds for propagation.

In cold areas, lift the corms in October unless they are in a position where frosts are unlikely to penetrate to them; plants left in the ground should have the dead leaves cut to ground level in early March before the new foliage appears.

Store lifted corms in a frost-free place, removing the soil and leaves when the latter are quite brown. Storage can be difficult; corms kept damp will rot, but if allowed to dry out completely they may shrivel and die.

Propagation. Collect any seeds produced in the autumn and sow at once in pots placed in a cool greenhouse or frame. Seeds should germinate by the spring. They should flower one or two years later, producing variations in colour and perhaps shape of flower.

Clumps may be lifted and divided every three or four years either just after flowering or before growth starts in the spring.

Pests and diseases. Generally trouble-free.

Crocus aureus

CROCUS
Iridaceae

This genus of bulbous plants contains more than 70 species and numerous varieties that flower in the open between August and April. These dwarf plants are remarkably hardy, coming from the higher ground of countries north and east of the Mediterranean regions.

Most crocus species and varieties require a well-drained soil and a sunny position. They are particularly suitable for rock and sink gardens and do well in the alpine house. Robust species, such as *C. aureus*, *C. speciosus* and *C. vernus*, thrive in short grass, provided it is not mowed before their leaves turn yellow in late spring. Species which flower in autumn before their leaves appear are particularly effective planted among low ground cover.

The crocus flower consists of a slender corolla tube springing direct from the corm and expanding into six ovate petals. Of this structure almost half is underground. Flower sizes given are the height of the flower above ground.

The leaves of all the plants described are linear, and mid to dark green with a central white stripe.

Crocuses grow from small corms. The spacing and depth of planting of these corms depends on their flowering date and the situation in which they are planted. These details are dealt with in the section headed CULTIVATION.

C. ancyrensis (often listed as 'Golden Bunch'). Turkey. A species with rich yellow flowers, 2–2½ in. high, rounded and long-lasting. They appear in February and March. The medium-sized corms produce up to 20 flowers each.

C. angustifolius: see *C. susianus*

C. asturicus. N. Spain. Leaves develop only when the flowers have finished. Mauve flowers, 3½–4 in. high with pointed petals, appear in September and October. The variety *C. a. atropurpureus* has a deeper and more uniform colour.

C. aureus, syn. *C. luteus.* Yugoslavia and south-eastwards into Turkey. The leaves grow taller than the 4 in. orange-yellow flowers, which appear in March and form a neat cup shape. *C. a. lacteus* is a milk-white form.

'Dutch Yellow' is a hardy and reliable form, more compact than the species.

C. balansae. Asia Minor. Bright orange 3 in. flowers, with dark markings outside, open wide in early March. 'Zwanenburg' has flowers with a deep bronze-red exterior.

C. banaticus, syns. *C. iridiflorus* and *C. byzantinus.* Hungary. The only crocus with the three outer petals twice as tall and broader than the inner ones. The outer petals are deep purple and often reflexed when fully open, while the inner ones are pale and remain erect. The flowers are 3–4 in. high and appear in October before the foliage has developed.

C. biflorus (Scotch crocus). Italy and eastwards to the Crimea. This species bears 4 in. white flowers with a purple-blue flush, during February and early March.

C. b. adamii, syn. *C. b. adamicus.* Causasus Mountains. A variety with pale or deep lilac colouring and darker veining outside; *C. b. argenteus* is smaller than the species, with more

Crocus ancyrensis

Crocus chrysanthus 'Advance'

Crocus biflorus weldenii

Crocus chrysanthus
'E. A. Bowles'

Crocus chrysanthus
'Zwanenburg Bronze'

pronounced stripes outside and with a yellow base inside the flower.

C. b. weldenii, from Yugoslavia and Bulgaria, is paler than the species, with pale blue flecks on the outside. *C. b. w.* 'Albus' is a pure white form.

C. byzantinus: see *C. banaticus*

C. cancellatus, syns. *C. nudiflorus* and *C. schimperi.* Greece, Asia Minor, Palestine, Iran. The leaves of this variable species develop after the flowers fade. The rounded, $3\frac{1}{2}$–5 in. flowers, borne in September and October, are basically white, with varied amounts of purple veining and flushing, yellow anthers and scarlet stigma. *C. c. cilicicus* is rose-lilac; the flowers have longer petals and white anthers.

C. candidus. W. Turkey. The leaves grow with the spring flowers, which often persist into April. This is a variable plant—originally white, now with flowers from pale yellow to orange; they are 3 in. high. *C. c. subflavus* is a pale yellow variety with bronze markings.

C. chrysanthus. Greece, Turkey. Short, narrow, hoary-green leaves appear with the flowers. The golden-yellow flowers are 3 in. high. This February-flowering species is the parent of numerous varieties and, with other species, of many hybrids. It is suitable for growing in pots or pans in a cold greenhouse, but does equally well in the open.

Some of the hybrids are: 'Advance', pale yellow with bronze-mauve streaks on the outside; 'Blue Bird', mauve-blue outside, pale cream margins and cream-white inside—a large and free-flowering variety; 'Blue Pearl', pale blue outside, white within; 'E. A. Bowles', rich yellow with bronzed base; 'Goldilocks', deep yellow with rich purple base; 'Ladykiller', purple-blue flowers edged with white, clear white inside; 'Princess Beatrix', clear blue with yellow base; 'Snow Bunting', white marked with deep purple outside, and with an orange base; 'Zwanenburg Bronze', dark bronze outside and rich yellow inside.

C. corsicus. Corsica. One of the later species to flower, it produces 2 in. blooms, pale lilac flecked with purple, in April.

C. dalmaticus. Yugoslavia. A vigorous species. The pointed lavender flowers, $2\frac{1}{2}$ in. high, have a yellow base; they appear in February and March.

C. etruscus. N.W. Italy. Mauve, 3 in. flowers with lilac veins, sometimes bronzed on the outer petals, appear in March. The variety 'Zwanenburg' has blue flowers.

C. fleischeri. Asia Minor. Narrow leaves appear first. The 3 in. flowers are white and star-shaped, with bright scarlet stigmas, and are produced in February and March.

C. 'Golden Bunch': see *C. ancyrensis* and *C. suterianus*

C. imperati. Naples and S. Italy. Cup-shaped, 3–4 in. high flowers appear on a long tube from December to February. The outside petals are buff streaked with purple, the inner ones bright satin-purple.

C. iridiflorus: see *C. banaticus*

C. korolkowii. Turkestan, Afghanistan. The large corm produces 3 in. star-shaped flowers, which are yellow inside and flushed with deep purple outside. March-flowering.

C. kotschyanus, syn. *C. zonatus.* Lebanon. Leaves follow the flowers, which are 3 in. high, lilac-blue, with bright orange spots at the base; they appear in September and October.

C. laevigatus. Greece. Strongly scented, $2\frac{1}{2}$ in. high flowers appear from October to December. The colour varies from pale lavender to near white, veined with rich purple and with an orange throat. *C. l. fontenayi* is a variety with purple flowers with buff exteriors; they appear later in the winter.

C. longiflorus, syn. *C. odorus.* Italy, Sicily. One of the most strongly scented crocuses. The flowers are 3 in. high, with a deep lilac exterior; the purple-blue interior has an orange throat. October and November-flowering. *C. l. melitensis* is prominently feathered with purple. Both the species and its variety are hardy plants for growing outside or in pots or pans under glass.

C. luteus: see *C. aureus*

C. medius. Mountains of S.E. France and N.W. Italy. Lightly scented $3\frac{1}{2}$ in. high flowers, which are lilac with a purple base and deep orange stigmas, appear in October and November. Leaves follow the flowers. It needs a sunny place and is also good for an alpine house.

C. minimus. Corsica, Sardinia. One of the smallest of the crocuses generally available. The 2 in. high flowers are dull yellow marked with purple; they open in April.

C. niveus. Greece. Mid-green leaves appear with the flowers, which are 3 in. high and pure white with orange throats, scarlet stigmas and yellow anthers. A hardy species, but the flowers, which open in November, are often spoilt by the weather; it is better grown in a frame or under cloches.

C. nudiflorus: see *C. cancellatus*

C. ochroleucus. Syria. Ivory-white flowers, 3 in. high, with some orange at the base open during October and November; the leaves appear with the later flowers. Pure white forms are also known in cultivation.

C. odorus: see *C. longiflorus*

Crocus chrysanthus 'Snow Bunting'

Crocus kotschyanus

C. olivieri. Greece, Rumania. Broad leaves and rounded, $2\frac{1}{2}$ in. high flowers of a rich orange colour. This March-flowering species is suitable for a rock garden but can also be grown in pots or pans in a cool greenhouse.

C. pulchellus. Greece, Turkey. Lavender flowers, 4 in. high, with a bright yellow throat appear from September to November. The leaves are produced after the flowers.

C. sativus (saffron crocus). Leaves appear first. October-flowering, with rich red-purple flowers, 4 in. high, opening to display the large red stigmas and orange anthers. Once open, the flowers do not close again, unlike most other crocuses. This crocus has been cultivated for centuries to produce saffron dye from the dried stigmas. It is not easy to grow in Great Britain, and is rarely available, as it needs a warm summer to ripen its corms.

C. s. cartwrightianus. Greece. A slightly larger variety, rose-lilac in colour, with similar red stigmas and yellow anthers; it flowers in the autumn and succeeds better than the species.

C. schimperi: see *C. cancellatus*

C. sieberi. Crete. The 3 in. flowers of this species are pale mauve, yellow at the base; they appear in February and March. The more common form is *C. s. atticus*, from the mainland of Greece, a variety that flowers earlier than the Cretan form. Both have rich red stigmas and are vigorous-growing plants.

'Hubert Edelsten' is a garden hybrid with rose-lilac flowers; 'Violet Queen' has rounded, violet-blue flowers.

C. speciosus. S.E. Europe, Asia Minor, Iran. One of the easiest crocuses to grow. It has 4–5 in. bright lilac-blue flowers, with yellow anthers and scarlet stigmas; these open in October. Many forms are grown as garden hybrids, including *C. s. aitchisonii*, which has larger pale blue flowers in November. 'Albus' is a pure white form; and the variety 'Artabir' has pale blue flowers marked with darker lines.

C. susianus, syn. *C. angustifolius.* S.W. Russia. A dwarf species flowering in February. This is the cloth of gold crocus, one of the oldest in cultivation. The star-shaped $2\frac{1}{2}$–3 in. flowers are bronze outside, golden-yellow inside. A good garden plant, also excellent for alpine houses. *C. s. minor* has deeper colouring.

C. suterianus. Asia Minor. A rich yellow species, with 3 in. flowers that appear in February and March. It is also known as 'Golden Bunch'.

C. tomasinianus. E. coast of the Adriatic. Narrow buds appear in late winter, displaying only the pale mauve exterior of the outer petals. The 3 in. high flowers open in February and March to show the inner lilac petals.

Flower colours are variable, but the following varieties are a deeper mauve than the type: 'Barr's Purple', and 'Whitewell Purple'.

C. vernus. Mountain areas from the Pyrenees to the Carpathians, particularly the Alps. This is the parent of the numerous varieties of large Dutch crocuses which have supplanted the wild species in gardens. The species and its wild varieties flower in March.

They may be planted in a border or in grass where, undisturbed, they will increase into dense-flowering clumps and remain almost indefinitely. The flowers of the species are 3–4 in. high, those of the varieties 4–5 in.

Of the numerous garden varieties to choose from, the following represent the chief colourings generally available:

'Joan of Arc', large, white; 'Little Dorrit', large, silvered lilac; 'Queen of the Blues', long and large, lavender-blue; 'Pickwick', large and pale lilac, with deep lilac stripes and purple base; 'Negro Boy', glossy deep red-purple; 'Purpureus Grandiflorus', large, shining purple-blue—one of the best, it also grows well in pots; 'Striped Beauty', silvery white, with deep mauve stripes and a violet-purple base; and 'Vanguard', flowers a fortnight ahead of the others and is grey-blue outside, pale blue inside.

Crocus chrysanthus 'Blue Pearl'

Crocus imperati

Crocus sieberi

Crocus tomasinianus

Crocus ochroleucus

Crocus speciosus

Crocus tomasinianus 'Whitewell Purple'

C. versicolor. S. France. A vigorous March-flowering species, with flowers 4 in. high in various shades of mauve. One commonly found variety is 'Picturatus', also known as 'Cloth of Silver' or 'Zilverlakense'. This is white or pale mauve, with darker markings.

C. zonatus: see *C. kotschyanus*

Cultivation. Crocuses may be planted in almost any soil, provided it is well drained. They are best grown in rock gardens but can be used as edgings to flower or shrub borders; alone, with other dwarf bulbs such as snowdrops; or between and beneath creeping plants such as aubrietas. Some species, such as *C. speciosus, C. vernus* and the varieties of the latter, are effective when naturalised in short grass.

Small groups of all kinds are invaluable for providing spots of colour in rock gardens. Here, a few bulbs irregularly spaced are usually sufficient for a pleasing display.

At their best in groups beneath deciduous shrubs or trees, or entirely in the open, crocuses benefit from any available warmth and protection from wind to encourage the flowers to open as soon and as often as possible.

The winter and early spring-flowering kinds may be grown in lawns, where they will flower and make some leaf growth to build up new corms before the grass needs cutting in the spring. Mowing may remove some of the leaves before they die and thus reduce the vigour of the corms, but these will usually survive for a few years and can easily be replaced if they fail.

The smallest species and varieties, particularly those that flower in winter, make admirable plants for pans in a cool greenhouse or alpine house and may be brought indoors when first in flower. Plant them seven or eight to a 6 in. pan of John Innes potting compost No. 1.

All crocuses are best planted as soon as the corms are available, but *C. vernus* varieties may be left until November if time or space for planting is not available. As a general rule set the corms 2–3 in. deep; in light soils deeper planting to 6 in. is advantageous where summer cultivation might disturb shallow corms. Space the corms 3–4 in. apart.

For planting a limited number of corms in cultivated ground, use a trowel or dibber; when planting in grass and in large numbers, the use of a crowbar avoids stooping.

Do not remove the flowers as they die and do not tie the leaves into bunches or cut them before they are dead; wait until they are yellow and can be pulled off.

Propagation. The small cormlets which are produced in varying quantities by the different species and varieties soon grow to flowering size if removed and planted separately. Lift the corms as soon as the leaves are turning brown, and dry the offsets in shallow trays in a warm greenhouse or shed for a few days.

Remove leaves, dead roots, skins and old corms, then grade the offsets into two or three sizes. Replant the largest for flowering the following year and the remainder in drills far enough apart for a narrow hoe to be used to keep down weeds. Take out the drills in well-drained soil and in a sunny position. Set these smaller cormlets 2–3 in. deep and 1–2 in. apart.

Keep the drills free of weeds throughout the growing season. The smaller corms should reach flowering size in two years.

Seeds are freely produced by some species, giving plants that are reasonably true to type unless cross-pollination has taken place. Seeds from garden hybrids are likely to give extremely varied seedlings.

Crocus seed capsules are thrust up quickly on short stalks, during June and July. Collect the capsules when they begin to split open and sow the seeds in boxes or pots of John Innes seed compost. Cover with $\frac{1}{2}$ in. of compost and place in a cold frame or cold greenhouse. Leave the seedlings in their pots or boxes for two years, then plant them out in their flowering positions or transplant to an outdoor nursery bed and grow on for a further year.

Seedlings usually take two to four years to reach flowering size.

Pests. Corms in the soil may be eaten by MICE and LEATHERJACKETS.

BIRDS, particularly sparrows, damage the young flowers.

APHIDS feed on corms in store, and on young unfolding leaves.

Diseases. GLADIOLUS DRY ROT shows on the corms as numerous small black lesions, which coalesce to large black areas. The corms may then suffer from a DRY ROT and shrivel.

GLADIOLUS SCAB causes round sunken craters to develop towards the base of the corms. Each crater has a prominent raised rim and may be covered with a shiny, varnish-like coating.

A PHYSIOLOGICAL DISORDER, due to a check in growth, shows as crinkling of the leaves.

STORAGE ROT, due to a BLUE MOULD, affects the corms, which bear buff-coloured or pink resting bodies of the fungus. Under moist conditions the blue mould develops on the lesions, and the corms decay rapidly.

Crocus, Chilean: see *Tecophilaea cyanocrocus*
Crocus, saffron: see *Crocus sativus*
Crocus, Scotch: see *Crocus biflorus*

Crossandra

Acanthaceae

CROSSANDRA UNDULIFOLIA

A genus of 50 species of tropical evergreen sub-shrubs. They have long-lasting flowers, and are suitable for greenhouse cultivation.

C. nilotica. East Africa. Height up to 24 in.; spread 15 in. This species will flower when only a few inches high. It has elliptic, dark green, glossy leaves up to 4 in. long. Terminal spikes, $2\frac{1}{2}$–3 in. long, of brick-red flowers open over a six-week period from early spring to late autumn. Each flower is about 1 in. wide, and consists of a long

Crocus medius

Crocus susianus

Crossandra nilotica

slender tube at the end of which are five petal-like lobes; the lower three petals form a lip.

C. undulifolia. East Indies. Height up to 3 ft; spread up to 24 in. The wavy-edged elliptic leaves are dark green. Flower spikes, up to 4 in. long, are composed of orange-red flowers, similar to but slightly larger than those of *C. nilotica.* Flowering begins in April and may continue until autumn.

Cultivation. These plants require winter greenhouse treatment to survive. Grow them in 4½–5 in. pots of John Innes potting compost No. 3, and for large specimens pot on successively until they are in 7 or 8 in. pots. Grown as house plants and discarded after flowering, a proprietary soilless compost and 4½–5 in. pots give good results.

The plants require warm conditions and a winter temperature of not less than 13°C (55°F). Give only enough water during winter to prevent the plants drying out; when signs of new growth appear, water more freely and, as flowering approaches, keep the plants continuously moist.

Provide light shading in summer, but between September and May admit as much light as possible. Give a liquid feed once a week from June to September.

Propagation. Take 2–3 in. long softwood cuttings from March to June. Root in equal parts (by volume) peat and sand at a temperature of 21°C (70°F). When rooted, pot up in 3 in. pots of John Innes potting compost No. 2 and grow on.

The plants can also be raised from seeds sown in March and germinated at a temperature of 16°C (61°F). Prick the seedlings off into pans or boxes when large enough to handle. Later, pot up in 3 in. pots and grow on.

Pruning. Shorten all flowering growths by two-thirds after flowering.

Pests and diseases. Generally trouble-free.

Croton: see Codiaeum
Crowfoot, common water: see *Ranunculus aquatilis*
Crown Imperial: see *Fritillaria imperialis*
Crown of thorns: see *Euphorbia splendens*

Cryptanthus acaulis 'Rubra'

Cryptanthus bivittatus

Cryptanthus zonatus

Cryptanthus

Earth star, starfish. *Bromeliaceae*

A genus of 22 species of dwarf evergreen plants native to Brazil. Unlike other bromeliads, the leaves of this genus do not have the watertight bases that form reservoirs for holding water and nourishment. The succulent leaves of some species are highly and variously coloured. The small three-petalled flowers are white; they may occur at any time of year, but are generally insignificant. These are excellent foliage plants for the home, greenhouse or bottle garden.

See also BROMELIADS.

C. acaulis. Height 3 in. The wavy, spined, mid-green leaves are white, scaly beneath, and arranged in a rosette. The variety 'Argenteus' (4 in. high) has leaves covered with silver scales on both surfaces, giving them a powdery appearance. 'Rubra' is coloured purple-brown overlying green. The species may form offshoots several inches high, but care must be taken not to knock the plant, or the plantlets will fall off.

C. × 'Apple Blossom'. Height 5 in. A recent hybrid. The smooth-edged leaves flare outwards from scaly mauve leaf stalks; the leaves are cream-white at the base, edged and mottled with bright green.

CRYPTANTHUS BIVITTATUS

C. bivittatus. Height 3 in. The narrow toothed leaves lie flat to form a small wavy rosette, 6 in. across, usually with two larger leaves up to 9 in. long. Each leaf is striped dark green on light green and is tinged with rosy red, particularly at the base. Like *C. acaulis,* offshoots will fall off if the plant is accidentally knocked.

C. bromelioides. Height 12–14 in. An upright plant with mid-green, finely spined leaves that are borne on slender stalks; they are asymmetrically arranged.

'Tricolor' is of more spreading habit and has longitudinal stripes of white, cream-yellow, rose and green.

C. fosterianus. Height 3 in. The long, succulent thick leaves lie flat, forming rosettes up to 18 in. across. They are dark copper-brown, cross-barred with irregular bands of grey scales, and are wavy and toothed.

C. zonatus. Height 4 in. Similar to *C. fosterianus,* but with thinner green leaves forming a rosette 9 in. across. *C. z. fuscus* has red-brown leaves.

Cultivation. Pot the plants during April and May in 3–4 in. pots or 4–6 in. pans. Any open-textured soil mixture with added leaf-mould is satisfactory, such as 3 parts John Innes potting compost No. 1 and 1 part leaf-mould, coarse peat or sphagnum moss (parts by volume). Water the plants well during the growing season, but reduce watering when growth stops. During winter keep the soil barely moist.

Propagation. Offshoots will appear between the leaves or from the base. These are easily removed preferably in April, when quite small. Grow on by firming these plantlets into 2–2½ in. pots of the usual potting mixture.

Pests and diseases. Generally trouble-free.

Cryptomeria

Japanese cedar. *Taxodiaceae*

A genus containing a single species. This is an evergreen coniferous tree with awl-shaped leaves and globular cones. There are several smaller decorative varieties in cultivation.

See also CONIFERS.

C. japonica. China and Japan. Height 50 ft; spread up to 15 ft. A hardy, fast-growing tree with a narrow conic crown and a spreading base; it is excellent as a specimen tree. The bright orange-brown bark is soft and stringy, tending to shred. The leaves are wide-spreading and yellow-green in the Chinese form, bent closer and dark green in the Japanese form. The foliage is borne in long and sparse, or dense and short, bunches on the cord-like shoots.

Cylindrical clusters of small, ovoid male flowers appear at the ends of all minor shoots; they shed pollen in February. The rosette-like female flowers are produced behind the male flowers and develop into ¾ in. wide cones.

CRYPTOMERIA JAPONICA

'Elegans' (height 15 ft; spread 10 ft) is a permanently juvenile-foliaged form, grown for its winter colour. It has branches sweeping to the ground and the leaves are blue-green in summer, purple or bronze-red in winter.

The species has given rise to a number of dwarf forms which include the following: 'Bandai-sugi' (height 3 ft; spread 18 in.), a small irregular bush with closely set and irregular foliage.

'Compressa' (height and spread 3 ft), a neat, globose plant with spreading, short and densely set juvenile foliage that is rich red-bronze during winter.

'Elegans Nana', syn. 'Elegans Compacta' (height and spread 3 ft or more), a slow, compact-growing form of 'Elegans' with crowded twigs and leaves.

'Globosa Nana' (height 3 ft; spread 5 ft), a form with no apparent trunk, and sometimes disappointing as a young plant; it matures to a broad, round-topped bush with densely held, pendulous, mid-green foliage. Suitable as a specimen on a lawn.

'Jindai-sugi' (height 5 ft; spread 3 ft), a conical bush with regular mid-green foliage; the short, stiff, straight leaves point forward over the shoots at a narrow angle.

'Spiralis', sometimes known as granny's ringlets, with mid-green foliage twisted spirally round the branches. Some plants grow to tree-like proportions, but others are extremely slow-growing and dense, and can be treated as dwarf conifers.

'Vilmoriniana', a form similar to 'Compressa', but with less spreading foliage of a duller bronze hue in winter.

Cultivation. These conifers, although tolerant of most soils, grow best in slightly acid, deep, damp but well-drained soil. They are slow-growing in light shade, and the best results are obtained in a sunny sheltered position.

Plant in October or November on light soils, in April on heavier soils.

Small plants up to 24 in. high are the easiest to establish. Apply an annual dressing of 3–4 oz. of general fertiliser over the root-run in May to improve growth and colour. Young plants must never be allowed to dry out, and they must be kept clear of weeds.

Propagation. Sow seeds in pans of John Innes seed compost under glass in February, or outside in April. Prick out the seedlings, when about 3 in.

high, into a nursery bed; they should be ready to plant out in two or three years.

Named varieties should be increased by 2–4 in. long cuttings taken in September; insert the cuttings in equal parts (by volume) peat and sand in a cold frame. When rooted, pot the cuttings singly in 3½ in. pots of John Innes potting compost No. 2 and plunge outdoors. In autumn, line out in nursery rows and grow on for a further year or two before planting out.

Pruning. None required except to maintain a single bole by cutting out any forking of the main shoot, preferably in April.

Pests. Generally trouble-free.

Diseases. GREY MOULD can be troublesome on seedlings, showing as a sparse web of grey fungal growth over the affected parts of the plants.

Cucumber, gherkin

Cucumis sativus. Cucurbitaceae

A half-hardy annual trailing plant grown for its long, green-skinned fruits which are best matured under glass. The fruits vary from 6–12 in. long and from 1½–2½ in. in diameter; they mature in summer and early autumn. The white, crisp and succulent flesh, which surrounds a core of seeds, has a distinctive, delicate flavour. Most varieties are chiefly used in salads, but gherkins, the small-growing types, are also pickled.

Varieties, known as glass or greenhouse cucumbers, generally produce the best crops under glass where a temperature of 21°C (70°F) can be maintained. Some varieties will grow satisfactorily in a cool greenhouse or a cold frame, but cropping is generally less prolific.

Ridge cucumbers and gherkins are suitable for cultivation outdoors.

VARIETIES

Reliable house cucumbers include 'Butcher's Disease Resister' and 'Telegraph', the latter being excellent for exhibition and for table use. Recently a number of F₁ hybrids have been developed. The fruits of these do not usually reach the size of the above varieties, but the plants are resistant to gummosis and give a heavy crop. Good varieties are 'Rocket' and 'Simex', which bear all-female flowers.

'Rochford's Market', a short-fruited variety, is one of the most suitable for frame cultivation.

Recommended ridge cucumbers for cultivation in the open are: 'Long Green', 'King of the Ridge' and 'Perfection Ridge'.

'Venlo Pickler' is a vigorous and free-fruiting gherkin variety.

Cultivation of greenhouse cucumbers. Sow seeds in late February or early March, singly in 3 in. pots of seed compost. Place the pots in a part of the greenhouse where a temperature of 18°C (64°F) can be maintained. The seeds usually germinate after four or five days, and the pots should be placed on the staging where they will get the maximum light.

When the seedlings have three true leaves, pot them singly into 5 in. sterilised pots of John Innes potting compost No. 2; set the seedlings so that the lower part of the stem is covered. Provide a humid atmosphere.

Cryptomeria japonica (cones)

Cryptomeria japonica 'Elegans' (in winter)

Cryptomeria japonica 'Elegans Nana' (in autumn)

Cryptomeria japonica 'Spiralis'

Prepare the growing bed at least two weeks before planting out; it should measure $2\frac{1}{2}$ ft across and 20 in. in depth. As a base, use a 4 in. deep layer of strawy manure, followed by an equally thick layer of chopped turfy loam, a further layer of manure, and a 4 in. deep equal layer of chopped loam. Cover this compost thinly with well-rotted manure, topped by 3 in. of fine, sterilised soil. Sprinkle the bed with carbonate of lime and a little bone-meal or hoof and horn. Soak the bed with water and raise the greenhouse temperature to 21°C (70°F).

When the young plants are three or four weeks old and well established, move them to the bed, setting them 3 ft apart; water thoroughly to settle the soil around the roots.

The plants grow rapidly. They should be trained to wires fastened horizontally to the glazing bars at 6 in. intervals. Tie the main and lateral stems securely but loosely to the wires. Pinch out the growing tip of the main stem when a plant reaches the fifth wire. Stop the lateral, fruit-bearing growths at the second leaf joint, and any sub-laterals at the first joint.

Remove tendrils and all male flowers as they appear; allow only two female flowers on each lateral. Female flowers are distinguished from male flowers by the tiny immature cucumber behind the flower.

Water regularly, and keep the atmosphere humid at all times; ventilate the house on hot days so as to keep the air circulating. Give a fortnightly feed of dried blood or fish meal to provide the nitrogen that cucumbers require. Place a thin mulch of mixed soil and peat from time to time to cover the white root fibres which appear on the surface.

As the fruits develop, make sure that they are hanging clear of ties and wires. Shade the house from late April to September.

Frame cultivation. Excellent summer crops can be produced in a frame or under Dutch lights. Raise the seedlings as described under GREENHOUSE CULTIVATION, sowing the seeds in late May and germinating in a frame or under cloches.

Make the bed at the highest point of the frame or light. Cover a mound of well-rotted manure with 4–5 in. of fine loam. When the seedlings are growing well, plant them out in the bed, 3 ft apart.

As soon as the plants have made their third leaf, pinch out the growing tips and, as the lateral growths develop, train them into the space available. When the laterals have four or five leaves, pinch out the growing tips. Remove any male flowers and allow only one female flower to set on each lateral. It may be necessary to thin out further growth from time to time.

Shade the glass when necessary to prevent direct sunlight from scorching the plants. Throughout the growing season water freely, but ventilate only on very hot days, closing the frame or lights at night.

Cultivation of ridge cucumbers and gherkins. These thrive on any ordinary, well-drained soil, in full sun. Light, well-drained soils that quickly warm up give the best results. Prepare the bed in autumn, by deep digging. During May, take out a trench about 12 in. deep; place a 6 in. layer of farmyard manure or well-rotted compost in the

Cucumber (greenhouse)

Cucumber (ridge)

bottom and cover with soil to form a ridge over the trench. If more than one trench is needed, leave 4 ft between trenches.

At the end of May sow two seeds every 24 in. along the ridge and cover with a glass jar until the seedlings are established. Keep the strongest plant of each pair and discard the other.

Pinch out the growing tip of a plant when seven leaves have formed; male flowers need not be removed. Keep the plants well watered, but use a fine spray so that the soil is not washed away from the fibrous roots near the surface. When the fruits reach a length of about 3 in., give a feed of liquid manure once a week.

Harvesting. Cut cucumbers while they are young and have the best flavour, and to encourage further cropping. Fruits left on the plants go to seed and cause cropping to cease.

Exhibition. For show purposes choose fruits that are young and of a good length. Cut them with a length of stem by which they can be handled so that the bloom on the skin is not spoilt, and leave the remains of the flower on the end of the fruit. Fruits to be shown together should be of uniform size.

Pests. Under glass, the undersides of the leaves may be infested by GLASSHOUSE RED SPIDER MITES which cause a fine light mottling on the upper surfaces. Severe infestations cause bronzing, wilting and collapse of plants; the stems and leaves are covered with a silk webbing.

WOODLICE, under glass and outdoors, eat holes in the leaves and may also feed on the surface of young cucumbers.

Diseases. ANTHRACNOSE OF CUCUMBER shows on the leaves as pale green spots which quickly become red-brown and enlarge until the whole leaf withers. Stems and fruits may also become infected.

Sunken spots on house cucumbers, caused by GUMMOSIS OF CUCUMBER, exude a gummy liquid which becomes covered with dark green spore masses. Affected fruits are often distorted. Small pale brown spots may appear on the leaves and stems.

CUCUMBER MOSAIC VIRUS causes a yellow mottling of the leaves, which are distorted. Affected plants are stunted and have a bushy non-climbing habit; the fruits are light yellow-green, often distorted, and with spots or raised warts of dark green.

GREY MOULD shows as a grey velvety growth on stems, fruits and leaves.

PHYSIOLOGICAL DISORDERS may arise under glass as a result of faulty cultural conditions: over-watering causes withering of the fruits, commencing at the blossom end. Excess nitrogen in the soil can cause bitterness of the fruit; however, this may also be due to pollination.

POWDERY MILDEW shows as a white powdery coating on the leaves and stems.

ROOT ROT can be due to several fungi, including RHIZOCTONIA and BLACK ROOT ROT fungus. The rotting of the roots leads to discoloration of stems and foliage, chiefly of young plants, followed by the collapse of plants.

SCLEROTINIA DISEASE causes brown wet lesions on the stems, leaves and occasionally fruits. Later, white fluffy growths appear, in which develop large black resting bodies of the fungus.

VERTICILLIUM WILT causes the leaves of green-house cucumbers to turn yellow from the base upwards; the plants wilt.

Cucumis melo: see Melon
Cucumis sativus: see Cucumber
Cucurbita maxima: see Pumpkin
Cucurbita moschata: see Pumpkin
Cucurbita pepo ovifera: see Marrow
Cup and saucer plant: see *Cobaea scandens*

Cuphea
Lythraceae

CUPHEA IGNEA

A genus of some 250 species of annuals, evergreen perennials and sub-shrubs from Mexico south to Peru. They are suitable as greenhouse plants, but a few species, particularly *C. ignea,* can be used as bedding plants.

C. cyanea. Mexico. Height up to 18 in.; spread 10 in. This sub-shrub with hairy, ovate, mid-green leaves has a clammy feel. Tubular flowers, 1 in. long, are produced in terminal racemes through-out the summer. The calyx is yellow with a scarlet base, and the barely protruding petals are violet-blue.

C. ignea (cigar flower). Mexico. Height and spread about 12 in. An evergreen sub-shrub with lanceolate, smooth, mid-green leaves. The tubu-lar, 1 in. long, bright scarlet flowers are borne singly in the leaf axils at the ends of the shoots. The mouth of the tube is purple-black and white. Flowering period is from April to the end of November; well-grown plants flower through most of the year. This species may be used as a bedding plant outdoors during summer.

C. miniata. Mexico. Height and spread up to 24 in. This evergreen sub-shrub has ovate mid-green leaves, slender-pointed and lightly covered with white bristles. Tubular, $1\frac{1}{2}$ in. long, pale scarlet flowers appear from the upper leaf axils from June until September.

Cultivation. Grow the plants in John Innes potting compost No. 2. Plants raised from cuttings should be potted on during the summer until they finish in 5 or 6 in. pots. Thereafter give a weekly feed of liquid manure until September.

Maintain a humid atmosphere and give the plants ample light, but apply light shading to the greenhouse in summer. The plants can be put outdoors from May to September. In winter, keep them barely moist and maintain a tem-perature of 7°C (45°F).

Propagation. Take cuttings of lateral shoots, 2–3 in. long, in March or April. Root in equal parts (by volume) peat and sand in a propagating case at a temperature of 16–18°C (61–64°F). When the cuttings are rooted, pot up into 3 in. pots of John Innes potting compost No. 1 and grow on.

Sow seeds of all species in January or February in pans of John Innes seed compost and germi-nate at a temperature of 13–16°C (55–61°F). When the seedlings are large enough to handle, prick out into boxes, then pot on during the summer into 3, 5 and finally 6 in. pots.

Pruning. Cut back all species by two-thirds in late autumn or early winter. They are seldom grown on for more than two seasons.

Pests and diseases. Generally trouble-free.

Cupid's dart: see Catananche

× Cupressocyparis
Leyland cypress. *Cupressaceae*

A hybrid genus of one hybrid species and two or three varieties. The species described is a vigorous, hardy evergreen coniferous tree with triangular scale-like leaves and globular cones. It is a cross between *Cupressus macrocarpa* and *Chamaecyparis nootkatensis.*

See also CONIFERS.

× CUPRESSOCYPARIS LEYLANDII

× *C. leylandii.* Height 50 ft; spread 15 ft. A species which is excellent as a specimen tree; it may also be used for hedging or screening. The habit is columnar with a characteristic kink at the base of the leading shoot. The leaves are grey-green or hoary, and the cones are $\frac{1}{2}-\frac{3}{4}$ in. across. Tall trees are columnar with a narrow conic top, and the crown is always dense.

Two forms are generally available: 'Hagger-ston Grey' has angular shoots arising at all angles and is clothed with small, dark grey-green leaves. It rarely cones.

'Leighton Green' has long branchlets or rows of flat triangular shoots in a lacy pattern; this form is brighter and paler green than the type and cones freely. It is suitable for hedging, but difficult to propagate.

Cultivation. Plant these conifers in April or May in any ordinary, well-drained soil that allows deep rooting, and in sun or partial shade. On shallow soils, these trees may rapidly develop a dense crown which renders them unstable after a few years. Pull back such trees to the vertical and stake or guy for two years.

Plants 18–24 in. high are the easiest to establish, but plants up to 8 ft can be used if they are firmly staked. For hedges, space young plants 18–24 in. apart. On poor soils an annual dressing of general fertiliser aids maximum growth.

Propagation. Take 4 in. long cuttings of lateral shoots in September and October; insert the cuttings in equal parts (by volume) peat and sand in a cold frame. When rooted, pot the cuttings singly in $2\frac{1}{2}$ in. pots of John Innes potting compost No. 2 and plunge outdoors, or line the cuttings

Cuphea ignea

× *Cupressocyparis leylandii*

× *Cupressocyparis leylandii*
(foliage and cones)

Cupressus arizonica (foliage and cones)

Cupressus macrocarpa 'Donard Gold'

Cupressus macrocarpa (cones)

out in a nursery bed. They should be ready for planting out the following autumn.

Pruning. None is necessary unless a clean bole is required. Clip established hedges annually in September. Hedge tops become straggly if first trimmed to the required height. To prevent this, allow the leading shoots to exceed the desired height by 12 in., then cut these at 12 in. below the ultimate height. Side-shoots will develop and grow to form a solid top.

Pests and diseases. Generally trouble-free.

Cupressus

True cypress. *Cupressaceae*

A genus of about 20 species of evergreen coniferous trees of moderate size, differing from *Chamaecyparis* in having their cylindrical shoots arranged in plume-like branchlets, and in their larger cones. Most are dense and columnar in shape, of medium or rapid growth. The foliage consists of closely pressed, rather fleshy scales, clothing the shoots. Juvenile leaves are slender and pointed, spreading level, usually with down-curved tips. In most cases, globular cones with a spine to each scale are freely borne from an early age. Several species are too tender for general planting, but *C. macrocarpa* is suitable for screening and hedging. The species described here are useful as decorative specimen trees where space is limited.

See also CONIFERS.

C. arizonica (Arizona cypress). Arizona. Height 35 ft; spread 15 ft. Plants generally offered under this name or as *C. a.* 'Bonita' are *C. glabra*. Old and established trees of *C. arizonica* can be distinguished by their green-grey foliage and brown, finely fissured, stringy bark.

C. glabra. Arizona. Height 35 ft; spread 12 ft. A hardy conic tree, often offered as *C. arizonica* 'Bonita'. The bark is smooth, purple and blistered until large flakes peel away to reveal pale yellow patches. Small, blunt, closely pressed, blue-grey leaves, many with a small white spot, cover the twigs. The pale yellow male flowers cluster at the tips of the shoots after August; they become bright yellow as they shed pollen in April. The cones are purple-brown and 1 in. across.

C. macrocarpa (Monterey cypress). California. Height 50 ft; spread 15 ft. A vigorous tree, hardy in all but the coldest winters when young trees may be damaged. Younger trees are columnar with conic tops, but broaden with maturity and become spreading and flat-topped, resembling *Cedrus libani.* The species is suitable for shelter-trees in coastal and western regions, but liable to be browned by cold, dry winds in the east.

The red-brown bark is criss-crossed with shallow ridges, and the densely bunched shoots are clothed in rich, dark green, blunt-ended leaves which give off an aromatic fragrance when crushed. Golden male flowers are scattered in terminal clusters; the shiny brown cones are 1–1½ in. across and clustered along the shoots. The variety 'Donard Gold' is a fast-growing golden conifer.

C. sempervirens (Mediterranean or Italian cypress). France to Iran. Height 25 ft; spread

5–10 ft. A hardy species, pointed when young but forming a square-topped column when mature. It has dull, dark green foliage. The cones, about 1 in. across, are freely scattered over the crown and become dull and grey with age.

Cultivation. These conifers thrive in any ordinary, well-drained soil. Plant in September and October or in April in a sunny position; the less-hardy species should be sheltered from north and east winds. Seedlings under 24 in. high are the easiest to establish.

Propagation. Sow seeds in pans of John Innes seed compost under glass in March. Prick off the seedlings, when large enough to handle, singly into 3½ in. pots of John Innes potting compost No. 2 and plunge outdoors. Transplant to permanent positions in autumn.

Named varieties do not come true to type, and must be increased from cuttings. Take 3–4 in. long cuttings of lateral shoots with a heel in September and October; insert the cuttings in equal parts (by volume) peat and sand in a cold frame. When rooted, pot the cuttings as advised for seedlings.

Pruning. None required except to reduce forked trees to a single leading shoot in March or April.

Pests. APHIDS, particularly the cypress aphid, suck sap from leaves; bronzing and premature leaf fall occur. MITES cause similar symptoms and cover affected parts with a fine silk webbing.

Diseases. GREY MOULD may be troublesome on one-year-old seedlings of *C. macrocarpa* and *C. sempervirens.* It shows as a sparse web of grey fungal growth over the affected parts.

HONEY FUNGUS has been known to kill cypresses; another fungus may attack and destroy branches of *C. macrocarpa.*

Currant

Ribes. Grossulariaceae, syn. *Saxifragaceae*

BLACK CURRANT

Black, white and red currants are hardy deciduous shrubs grown extensively in cool, temperate areas for their juicy, acid fruits in summer. They thrive in all parts of the British Isles.

Black currants are grown as bushes but red and white currants are also satisfactory as cordons, against walls or, with support, for hedging. When grown as bushes in exposed places they may be subject to wind damage. Red and white currants may also be grown as standards, about 4 ft high, allowing a low vegetable crop such as lettuce to be grown underneath.

The black currant originates from *Ribes nigrum*, and carries the greater part of its crop on growths produced the previous year. Culture and pruning is aimed at encouraging this annual replacement growth, some of which may come from below ground level.

The average height and spread of black currants is 5 ft × 4 ft. Planting distances: 5–6 ft between both rows and bushes, or 6–8 ft between rows, 3–4 ft between bushes.

Modern varieties of red and white currants originated from *Ribes sativum* and *R. petraeum,* which occur in western Central Europe. They fruit on short spurs carried on the old wood and the lower parts of the previous year's growth. Training is aimed at producing a clear stem of about 9 in. and a framework of established branches bearing the fruiting spurs.

The average height and spread of bushes is 5 ft × 4 ft; of cordons, 6 ft × 12 in. Planting distances: bush, as for black currants; cordons, 15 in. between each, in rows 5–6 ft apart.

All varieties of black, red and white currants are self-fertile.

BLACK CURRANTS

'Baldwin'. A late variety that bears medium to large berries possessing a high vitamin C content. It forms a compact bush.

'Boskoop Giant'. An early variety, that bears long bunches of large, well-flavoured berries. It makes a large bush.

'Laxton's Giant'. An early variety, with very large juicy fruits that ripen evenly. A vigorous, somewhat spreading bush.

'Wellington XXX'. This mid-season variety carries large, sweet berries of good flavour. It forms a vigorous, spreading bush.

'Westwick Choice'. A late-fruiting variety with medium to large berries. It is compact, and a heavy cropper.

RED CURRANTS

'Laxton's No. 1'. An early variety with medium or large, bright red berries. It is a regular and heavy cropper, with strong upright growths.

'Red Lake'. This variety fruits mid to late season, bearing large, good-quality berries. It is moderately vigorous and makes upright growths.

WHITE CURRANTS

'White Versailles'. An early cropper with large, semi-translucent, richly flavoured berries of the palest yellow. It is a prolific and strong grower.

Cultivation. Currants can be grown in a wide range of moisture-retentive soils, but they will not tolerate bad drainage. Red currants may be short-lived on dry, sandy soils. All types do best in open, sunny positions which are not subject to late spring frosts; they grow well in partial shade.

Plant between October and March, preferably in autumn. Plant black currants deeply—a little deeper than they were in the nursery.

Insert stakes for red and white currants, grown as cordons. Stakes for individual cordons should be 2 in. × 2 in. and 8 ft tall, with about 5–6 ft above ground. A row of cordons needs 4 in. × 4 in. end posts, 10 ft apart, between which are stretched wires at 3 ft and 5 ft above soil level. Tie the cordons to canes fastened to these wires.

Firm the bushes after frost; mulch during spring with rotted manure or compost. Pull out any red or white currant suckers that grow up from below ground. Water during dry spells, especially black currants.

In March, feed black currants with sulphate of ammonia at 1–1½ oz. per sq. yd, spread evenly over the root area. A dressing of ½ oz. sulphate of potash per sq. yd is also advisable.

Red and white currants respond to applications of sulphate of potash at ½–1 oz. per sq. yd in February and March.

Currants are shallow rooting, and deep disturbance of the soil should be avoided, particularly round black currants. Keep weeds under control by mulching or by using weedkillers.

Ripening fruits, and the buds on red and white currants, are liable to attacks by birds. Protect with netting and pick the fruits as they ripen.

Propagation. Take hardwood cuttings from healthy wood in autumn, 8–10 in. long for black currants and 12–14 in. for red and white currants. Set them 6 in. apart in rows.

Encourage black currants to produce new shoots from below ground by inserting the cuttings with all buds intact and with only two showing above soil level.

Red and white currants are usually grown with a 7–9 in. single stem, or leg, beneath the branches, and all buds except the upper three or four should be removed; insert only half of each cutting in the soil.

After a year, transplant the cuttings to wider spacings or set them in their fruiting positions.

To produce red and white currant standards, root the cuttings as already described and tie the plants to canes. As side-shoots appear, shorten these to three or four leaves. When the stem is about 4 ft high, remove the growing point to encourage side-shoots to form near the top. The following spring remove all side-shoots from the main stem below the head of branches.

Pruning. After planting, cut black currants down to 3 in. above ground level to establish the root system. If growth has been good on mature bushes, remove the majority of the old, dark wood that has fruited; otherwise, cut out about one-third of the branches in autumn, leaving in as much as possible of the new, light brown growths.

Cut back the previous season's growths of red and white currants by half during the winter of planting. In subsequent winters shorten the shoots by about one-third. Prune established standard currants by shortening the shoots by a third of their length.

The pruning of currants is dealt with more fully in the chapter headed PRUNING.

Pests. BLACK CURRANT GALL MITES cause the condition known as big-bud and also transmit reversion virus disease.

BIRDS, particularly bullfinches, eat the currant buds during the winter, and blackbirds attack ripening fruits.

APHIDS infest young shoots and leaves, causing blisters and other distortions and making plants sticky and sooty.

Diseases. AMERICAN GOOSEBERRY MILDEW infects the tips of the shoots late in the season, producing a white powdery coating on the leaves and shoots and often causing distortion.

CORAL SPOT commonly infects red currants, causing die-back of branches and occasionally complete death of affected plants. The dead stems bear numerous pink to red cushion-like spore pustules.

GREY MOULD causes the berries to rot and they become covered with a brown-grey fluffy fungal growth.

HONEY FUNGUS causes death of plants.

Black currant 'Laxton's Giant'

Red currant 'Red Lake'

REVERSION IS A VIRUS DISEASE of black currants which causes a reduction in cropping. The infected leaves are narrow and have less than five pairs of veins on the main lobe.

SILVER LEAF affects red and black currants, producing a silvering of the leaves on one or more branches, which later die back.

Currant, buffalo: see *Ribes aureum*
Currant, flowering: see *Ribes*
Currant, golden: see *Ribes aureum*
Currant, Indian: see *Symphoricarpos orbiculatus*
Curry plant: see *Helichrysum angustifolium*

Curtonus
Iridaceae

CURTONUS PANICULATUS

A genus of one species of cormous plant, often included in *Antholyza* and sometimes in *Montbretia*. It can be treated as a hardy herbaceous perennial once it is established, and is also suitable for naturalising.

C. paniculatus, syn. *Antholyza paniculata* (aunt eliza, pleated leaves). S. Africa, particularly Natal and the Transvaal. Height 4 ft; planting distance 9 in. The pleated, mid-green, sword-shaped leaves are 2½ ft long. Deep orange-red tubular flowers, up to 2 in. long, are carried in August and September on the zigzagged upper third of the tall stems. One flower is borne at each angle.

Cultivation. Set out newly divided plants or purchased corms in September or October, planting them 6 in. deep. Group three or five plants in each clump, setting these among herbaceous plants or dwarf shrubs, or along the foot of a south-facing wall. The plants will survive in almost any soil but do best in well-drained soils that are rich in humus. Cut the stems below the lowest flower when the last flower dies in the autumn and cut back the old leaves in spring just before the new ones appear.

Propagation. These plants can be increased by division of larger clumps either in the autumn after flowering or in March before much growth is visible. In the spring it is important to replant the divided pieces, which should each consist of a small corm, roots and a cluster of leaves, as soon as possible after they are separated. Ensure that the ground remains moist until new leaves, growing strongly, show that the plants have established themselves.

Alternatively, increase by seeds sown when ripe (September) in pots of John Innes seed compost in a cold frame or greenhouse, or in open ground the following March. Prick out seedlings raised under glass into a nursery bed the following May or June. Plant out in October, 18 months or two years after sowing.

Pests and diseases. Generally trouble-free.

Curtonus paniculatus

Cyananthus lobatus

Cyananthus lobatus 'Albus'

Cyananthus microphyllus

Cyananthus
Campanulaceae

A genus of about 30 species of hardy herbaceous perennials related to campanulas and suitable for rock gardens. Their upturned bell or funnel-shaped flowers have a somewhat gentian-like character and make an attractive display in the early autumn.

C. integer: see *C. microphyllus*
C. lobatus. Himalayas. Height 4 in.; spread 12–15 in. The prostrate stems are set with pale green ovate leaves and carry at their tips bright blue, funnel-shaped flowers, each about 1 in. across. These are encased in hairy calyces and appear in August and September. 'Albus' has ivory-white flowers.

C. microphyllus, syn. *C. integer.* N. India, Nepal. Height 3 in.; spread up to 12 in. This is the easiest species to grow. The tufted trailing stems rise from a woody rootstock and have narrow, elliptic, mid-green leaves. Blue-purple terminal flowers, produced in September, are narrow funnel-shaped and about 1 in. across; the five petals open out flat.

C. sherriffii. Bhutan, S. Tibet. Height 2 in.; spread up to 18 in. The stems are prostrate and spread from a woody rootstock. This plant is covered with soft hairs and, although hardy, may be harmed by winter moisture; it should be given protection by a raised pane of glass. The mid-green leaves are broadly ovoid, and the plant bears bright blue bell-shaped flowers, 1 in. across, in September.

Cultivation. Plant in March or April in a sunny position. The fleshy roots need constant moisture but good drainage, and the plants are best grown in a lime-free soil that contains peat or leaf-mould. Incorporate sand to assist drainage.

Propagation. The plants are easy to propagate from 1½–2 in. cuttings of basal shoots taken between April and June, and inserted in equal parts (by volume) peat and sand in a cold frame. When rooted, pot the cuttings in 3 in. pots of equal parts (by volume) loam, leaf-mould, peat and coarse sand. Pinch out the growing tips when the plants are established, and overwinter in a well-ventilated cold frame. Water moderately during the winter; plant out in March or April.

Pests and diseases. Generally trouble-free.

Cyclamen
Primulaceae

CYCLAMEN COUM   CYCLAMEN NEAPOLITANUM

A genus of 15 species of tuberous plants found wild in the Mediterranean countries and islands. The flowers are basically shuttlecock-shaped, with sharply reflexed petals. Several species are

Cyclamen × *atkinsii* 'Roseum'

Cyclamen coum

Cyclamen coum (mixed)

Cyclamen europaeum

hardy and thrive in the open or under the shelter of trees and large shrubs. They flower from late summer to May and provide attractive foliage for the rest of the year; some are sweetly scented. Tender strains of *C. persicum* are popular as winter-flowering pot plants.

The naming within this genus has recently been undergoing change. The following names are those in general use.

C. × atkinsii. Height 4 in.; planting distance 4–6 in. A hardy hybrid, unknown in the wild; it has been classified as a hybrid between various species, including two forms of *C. coum*. There are three forms, all with rounded, mid to deep green leaves, marbled with silver. They produce $\frac{1}{2}$–$\frac{3}{4}$ in. long flowers from December to March. *C. × atkinsii* is crimson-purple; 'Album', white with pink base; 'Roseum', pink.

C. cilicium. Asia Minor. Height 4 in.; planting distance 4–6 in. A half-hardy species, with rounded-cordate, mid-green leaves with a silver zone. The flowers are borne in October and November, usually before the leaves appear; they are pale pink, with a red spot near the petal base, and $\frac{3}{4}$–1 in. long.

C. coum, syns. *C. ibericum*, *C. orbiculatum* and *C. vernum*. S.E. Europe into Asia. Height 3 in.; planting distance 4–6 in. A hardy species. The rounded-cordate, mid-green leaves are dark red below and sometimes marbled with silver above. The flowers, up to $\frac{3}{4}$ in. long, appear from December to March; pointed buds open to rounded flowers with broad petals in shades of pink or carmine, occasionally white.

C. cyprium. Cyprus. Height 4 in.; planting distance 4–6 in. This half-hardy species bears velvety rounded leaves that are dark green with yellow-green markings above and crimson beneath; the foliage appears together with the

flowers in October. The flowers are scented, 1 in. long, and pale pink or white with a deep pink spot at the base of each petal.

C. europaeum. Hungary, south to Italy. Height 4 in.; planting distance 4–6 in. This is one of the hardiest species. The rounded-cordate to kidney-shaped leaves are mid-green, with indistinct silvery markings on the upper surfaces. Strongly scented, rich carmine flowers, $\frac{3}{4}$ in. long, are borne from July to September.

C. ibericum: see *C. coum*

C. libanoticum. Lebanon. Height 6 in.; planting distance 4–6 in. This half-hardy species does best in a shaded, cool greenhouse. The toothed, ivy-shaped leaves are red beneath, and deep green above with a white zone. Pale pink 1–1$\frac{1}{2}$ in. long flowers appear in February and March.

C. neapolitanum. Italy, Greece. Height 4 in.; planting distance 4–6 in. A hardy species whose variable leaves persist until May; they are deep green with silvery markings above and red beneath. Usually in flower from August to November, the species can be brought to flower in July by prolonged wet weather or by thorough watering. The flowers are 1 in. long and colours vary from mauve to pale pink; there is a white form, 'Album'. The species is long-lived in good conditions, and produces numerous flowers from older tubers.

C. orbiculatum: see *C. coum*

C. persicum. E. Mediterranean regions. Height and planting distance 6–9 in. This is the progenitor of winter-flowering pot cyclamens; it flowers in sheltered places in the open during March and April. The dark green, rounded-cordate to ovate leaves are marbled with silver. Fragrant, 1–1$\frac{1}{2}$ in. long flowers are borne well above the foliage; the petals, in shades of pink, are narrower than those of the florists' varieties.

Cyclamen neapolitanum

Cyclamen persicum

Cyclamen persicum
(wild species)

Cyclamen persicum 'Triumph White'

Cyclamen persicum 'Silberstrahl'

Cyclamen persicum 'Rex'

Less hardy garden varieties with superior flowers, up to 2½ in. long, have been developed in a wide range of colours, from purple and red through pink and pale mauve to white. The marbling of the leaves varies considerably, and the size and shape of the flowers, some of which are scented, differ from strain to strain.

The following tender varieties are often listed under the name Giganteum: 'Butterfly', salmon-pink, frilled petals; 'Cardinal', cerise-scarlet, silvery marbled foliage; 'Cattleya', orchid-purple; 'Grandia', large spreading, salmon-pink blooms with strongly waved and ruffled petals; 'Perfection Mixed', shades of red, pink, mauve and white; 'Rex', a mixed strain selected for its silver-patterned foliage; 'Ruffled Hybrids', fringed and ruffled flowers in shades of pink, red and lilac.

'Silberstrahl', red flowers, each petal having a narrow silvery-white margin; 'Triumph White', profusely borne, large white flowers; 'Victoria' (Krause), bicoloured red and white, with fringed or crested margins; 'White Swan', an outstanding white variety.

C. repandum. France to Greece and nearby islands. Height up to 6 in.; planting distance 6–8 in. This species is half-hardy and does best in a cool greenhouse or frame. The rounded-cordate, shallowly lobed leaves are mid-green, marbled silver above and red beneath. Scented red, pink or white flowers, 1 in. long and with narrow twisted petals, are borne in April.

C. vernum: see *C. coum*

Cultivation. All species thrive in well-drained soil containing ample organic matter; they need shade from hot sun and shelter from winds. Plant hardy types in late summer and early autumn, setting them in clusters and 6 in. apart. Barely cover the corms of *C. neapolitanum* with soil, but add 1 in. of leaf-mould annually after the flowers have finished and the leaves have died. The other species may be planted 1–2 in. deep, or more on light soils.

Many hardy kinds do best in woodland conditions where they can remain undisturbed the year round. Removal of the dead leaves is generally unnecessary.

The half-hardy species may be grown as pot plants, setting one corm to a 4–6 in. pot or pan, or five to a larger pan, containing equal parts (by volume) loam, leaf-mould, peat and sand plus ¼ lb. John Innes base fertiliser per bushel. Keep the plants cool, moist and shaded.

The tender strains of *C. persicum* are widely sold during autumn and winter and with a little care can be grown successfully. They are usually grown successively in 2½ in., 3½ in. and 5–6 in. pots, using John Innes potting compost No. 1 for the smaller size pots and John Innes potting compost No. 2 for the final potting.

No artificial heat is required during the summer in a frame or a greenhouse, but maintain a temperature of 10–13°C (50–55°F) during the winter. When the plants are in their final pots, from about the end of May onwards, allow at least a pot space between each pot, e.g. 5 in. between 5 in. pots, so that the increasing numbers of leaves can spread. Plants grown in a frame during the summer should be housed in a greenhouse from September.

Indoors during the winter, the plants will not continue to flower and thrive in an unheated room for long; maintain a temperature of 13–15°C (55–59°F) and place in full light. They suffer in the high temperature and dry air of central heating. To counteract this, stand the pots on 1 in. of gravel placed in bowls or saucers containing ½ in. of water. If the compost dries out, water from the top but avoid pouring water into the centre of the plant.

After flowering, move the plants to a cool greenhouse, frame or north-facing window. Feed with liquid fertiliser, give less water, and when they stop producing new leaves, generally about June, stop watering altogether. In mid-August, knock the soil and corms out of the pots, remove old soil, dead leaves and roots from the corms. Provided the corms are sound and firm, pot up into 5 in. pots of John Innes potting compost No. 1 or in the growing mixture, with the tops of the corms just showing.

Replace in the frame or greenhouse, and water well. Flowering may be expected again from

eptember onwards, but the plants should not
e taken indoors until there are at least six
owers on each plant.

ropagation. The corms of cyclamens do not
ivide or produce offsets, and propagation by
eeds is the only means by which these plants
an be increased.

Collect the seeds of hardy and half-hardy
ypes when they ripen in summer. The pot plant
arieties do not seed readily, but can be induced
o do so by transferring pollen from stamens to
tigma with the tip of a knife or a small brush.
eliable seeds can also be bought.

Sow the seeds of hardy and half-hardy types
ot later than September. Seeds of pot-plant
arieties may be sown in August or September,
o produce large plants for flowering about 15
nonths later. Alternatively, sow seeds in
anuary or February to raise smaller plants for
lowering the following winter.

Sow all seeds in pots or pans of John Innes
eed compost. Sow thinly, but space the larger
eeds of the florists' varieties of *C. persicum* 1 in.
part. Place January and February sowings in a
reenhouse heated to 13–16°C (55–61°F).

Autumn sowings can be germinated in a
vell-ventilated, shaded cold frame or the con-
ainers may be placed outside against a north
vall. The latter method produces the sturdiest
eedlings. Prick off the seedlings into 2½ in. pots
of John Innes potting compost No. 1, when the
econd leaves have appeared, and grow on at
temperature of 16°C (61°F).

Overwinter the hardy species in a cold frame,
nd plant out in their flowering positions in May
r late summer.

In May, pot on plants for indoor flowering
nto 3½ in. pots of John Innes potting compost
No. 2, transferring them later into the 5–6 in.
ots in which they will flower. Plants of the
lorists' varieties should produce their first
lowers in late October or November. If flower-
ng plants are wanted for Christmas, remove the
irst flower buds. In December, when several
lowers appear together, take the plants indoors.

Pests. The corms may be eaten by MICE and the
vhite maggots of VINE WEEVILS.

TARSONEMID MITES infest leaf and flower buds,
ausing severe distortion.

APHIDS and THRIPS may also be troublesome.

Diseases. BLACK ROOT ROT kills the roots, which
urn black and fail to anchor the corms. The
oliage of affected plants becomes discoloured
nd wilts.

CUCUMBER MOSAIC VIRUS may cause mottling
nd distortion of the foliage; the flowers show
olour breaking.

GREY MOULD commonly attacks pot plants,
ausing spotting of the petals and rotting of the
eaves and leaf stalks. Diseased leaf tissues be-
ome covered with a grey velvety fungus.

PHYSIOLOGICAL DISORDERS, due to unsuitable
ultural conditions, show as leaf discolorations,
uch as yellowing or brown blotching. Affected
issues may be entered by SOFT ROT.

RHIZOCTONIA may kill the roots of seedlings,
ausing these to collapse.

Cymbidium
Orchidaceae

A genus of about 50 species of orchids that in the
wild grow terrestrially or as epiphytes, but in
cultivation are all grown terrestrially. The species
described here are evergreen. These plants are
found from Ceylon to India and Japan, and
throughout Malaysia to Australia. The pseudobulbs are usually stout and about 6 in. high,
unless otherwise stated. Long, narrow, curved,
mid-green leaves cover the pseudobulbs with
their sheathing bases. The sprays of flowers arise
from the base of the pseudobulb and may be erect
or pendulous, 6 in. long in the miniatures and up
to 4 ft in the large hybrids. The flowers are 1–5½
in. across and can be of almost any colour except
blue and black. They are long-lasting, both on the
plant and when cut.

Cymbidiums are generally easy to grow,
require cool or intermediate temperatures, and
are ideal for newcomers to orchid culture. The
species have been crossed to produce a large
number of hybrids, and these have mainly
superseded the species.

See also ORCHIDS.

CYMBIDIUM EBURNEUM

C. aloifolium, sometimes listed as *C. simulans.*
India, Ceylon. The pseudobulb is about 3 in. high,
with narrow strap-shaped leaves. It has several
pendulous stems, up to 18 in. long, with
numerous 1½ in. wide, pale brown-yellow
flowers, which open in July and August. Grow
this species in an intermediate greenhouse in a
semi-shaded position and preferably suspended.

C. dayanum. India, Malesia. The flower stems
are pendulous, about 12 in. long, and carry several
sweet-scented flowers, each 3 in. across. The
white sepals and petals have a central purple
streak; the lip is white, purple and yellow, and the
column is almost black. This species flowers in
October, and thrives in a cool greenhouse.

C. eburneum. India. A somewhat difficult species.
The flower sprays, 8–12 in. long, carry two or
three fragrant flowers in April and May. These
are erect and up to 4 in. across, pure ivory-white
with a yellow band on the centre of the lip. It
has been much used in hybridisation. Grow
in semi-shade in an intermediate greenhouse.

C. elegans. India. A species producing numerous
curving leaves and arched 6–18 in. long flower
stems. The bell-like flowers, 1½ in. long, are a
delicate pale ochre yellow, with two bright
orange keels on the lip, and are crowded close
together. Flowering is in October and November.
This species needs an intermediate greenhouse.

C. giganteum. India. A species with 6 in. high
pseudobulbs and long, sword-like leaves. The
arching flower stems are 2–3 ft long, with up to a
dozen fragrant flowers each about 4 in. across.

Cyclamen persicum
'Victoria' (Krause)

Cyclamen repandum

Cymbidium dayanum

Cymbidium eburneum

The sepals and petals are yellow-green with purple streaks; the lip is yellow with purple or red-brown blotches. This species is in flower from September to February; it should be grown in a cool greenhouse.

C. lowianum. Burma. Pendulous 18 in. long flower stems each bear up to 40 flowers between March and May. These are 4–5 in. across and have green-yellow sepals and petals with red-brown veins, and a yellow lip with a purple-red mid-lobe.

This species requires a cool greenhouse. It is often used in hybridisation and has many varieties, including *C. l. concolor* which has flowers with clear yellow petals and sepals and an orange patch on the lip.

C. simulans: see *C. aloifolium*

C. tigrinum. Burma. This is a miniature species with 1 in. high, nearly round pseudobulbs. The flowers, borne on 6–9 in. stems, are about 2 in. across and there are two to four on each inflorescence. They open in May and June. The sepals and petals are olive-green, the lip white with red veins on the side-lobes and red spots on the mid-lobe. Grow this species in an intermediate greenhouse.

C. tracyanum. Burma. The inflorescences, on 24 in. stems, are composed of five to fifteen flowers, each 5–6 in. across. The sepals and petals are green-yellow with bold brown stripes; the lip is pale yellow with purple veins and spots and an unusual white fringed margin. The flowers appear between November and January. A cool greenhouse is suitable for this species.

HYBRIDS These are derived from several different species, and have to a great extent superseded the species in cultivation. The flowers measure 3–5 in. across and are freely produced from February to June. These hybrids require an intermediate greenhouse. Named varieties include: *C.* × 'Alexanderi Westonbirt', pink; Babylon 'Castle Hill', deep pink; 'Balkis', white, 'Baltic', green; 'Cariga', bright yellow; 'Miretta', green; *C.* × *pauwelsii* 'Comte de Hemptirne', russet; Pearl 'Magnificum', yellow; 'Prince Charles', light pink; 'Princess Elizabeth', white; Rosanna 'Pinkie', pink; 'Vieux Rose', rose-pink.

Cultivation. Grow cymbidiums in an open neutral or alkaline compost of 1 part loam, 2 parts osmunda fibre and 1 part sphagnum moss (parts by volume), plus a little bone-meal; add some charcoal and finely broken crocks for drainage. Start single pseudobulbs in 4–5 in. containers and pot on successively every second year after flowering. Large, vigorous varieties may be finished off in tubs or in deep boxes up to 18 in. in diameter.

Cool greenhouse species should be kept at about 16°C (61°F) day and night in summer; in winter they require 7–10°C (45–50°F) at night and 13–16°C (55–61°F) during the day. The Malayan species need the warmer conditions of 18°C (64°F) of the intermediate house in summer. Make sure shading is in place for all species by the end of February for the spring and summer; remove it in autumn. Open the ventilators whenever possible, even at night when it is warm enough, but avoid draughts. Water frequently when the compost becomes moderately dry, but less often in cold, damp weather.

Cymbidium lowianum

Cymbidium tracyanum

Cymbidium Rosanna 'Pinkie'

There is no resting phase, but the period of least activity is from October to February. Repot after flowering, when the new growths are about 3 in. high. Cut away all dead roots, and thin out the remainder if there are too many.

Propagation. Divide the old plants from March to May with a new growth to each part, and add a little bone-meal to the growing compost. Do not water for three or four days after potting, but syringe the leaves and the tops of the pots. If potted in February or March, withhold water for seven to ten days.

Pests. Leaves and stems may be infested by SCALE INSECTS, especially cymbidium scale, making the plants sticky and sooty.

APHIDS, particularly the orchid aphid, produce white-fringed black scales on the undersides of leaves. Greenfly often appear on the flowers.

Diseases. Unsuitable cultural conditions produce PHYSIOLOGICAL DISORDERS. These result in black spots on the foliage or a general discoloration of the leaves.

One or more VIRUS DISEASES may cause various symptoms. The most usual produces yellow-green spots, rings or streaks, with a distinct contrast between the light and dark areas. Later the markings become brown.

Cynoglossum
Hound's tongue. *Boraginaceae*

CYNOGLOSSUM AMABILE

A genus of 50–60 species of herbaceous perennials and biennials. The common name alludes to the shape of the leaves. The species described here are all hardy.

C. amabile. China. Height 18–24 in.; planting distance 12 in. This biennial plant has grey-green, downy, lanceolate leaves. Turquoise-blue, drooping, funnel-shaped flowers, $1\frac{1}{2}$ in. long, are produced in July and August.

C. nervosum. Himalayas. Height 18–24 in.; planting distance 12 in. A perennial with narrow, mid-green leaves that are rough and hairy. Intensely blue flowers, $\frac{3}{8}$ in. across and resembling forget-me-nots, are borne on branching stems in June and July.

Cultivation. Plant between October and March in a sunny or lightly shaded position in moderately rich, well-drained soil. Support *C. nervosum* with twiggy sticks. Cut down the stems of both species in October.

Propagation. Sow seeds of *C. amabile* in an outdoor nursery bed in May or June. Thin out the seedlings, or prick them off into rows, and plant out from October onwards. Alternatively, for flowering the same year, sow at a temperature of 13–16°C (55–61°F) during February or March. Prick off into boxes, harden off in a cold frame and plant out in May.

Sow seeds of *C. nervosum* in March or April in a cold frame. Prick out into a nursery bed and grow on for planting out in the autumn. Plants of this species may also be divided and replanted between October and March.

Pests. Generally trouble-free.

Diseases. In *C. amabile* the TOBACCO MOSAIC VIRUS may cause a mottling of the leaves and a certain amount of malformation and stunting.

Cyperus
Cyperaceae

CYPERUS ALTERNIFOLIUS

A genus of 550 species of moisture-loving, rush-like plants of graceful habit. Flower spikelets are borne in symmetrical heads with leaf-like bracts. The tender species, including the papyrus of biblical fame, are grown as pot plants and to decorate pools under glass; some may be moved outdoors during the summer. The hardy species may be grown at the margins of pools and lakes and present no problems in cultivation.

C. alternifolius (umbrella grass). Africa. Water depth up to 6 in.; height up to 3 ft; spread up to 24 in. A tender evergreen perennial species, usually grown as a pot plant. It forms a compact clump of stiff, dark green stems with insignificant leaves around the base. The stems are bare and carry at the top long, arching, green leaf-like bracts arranged like the ribs of an umbrella, with a span of 6–12 in.

Small inflorescences form at the base of the bracts from July to September. They are fluffy and yellow at first while bearing pollen, then turn through green to light brown as the seeds ripen. This plant may be stood permanently in shallow water in a sunny position under glass or used for the decoration of outside pools during the summer months. The form 'Variegatus' has leaves and stems striped with white.

The variety 'Gracilis', height 12–18 in., is quite distinct, although grown in the same way as the type. This is a stiff and formal plant with dark green, round, rigid stems which carry slightly arching, rather stiff green bracts. The tiny green-white inflorescences are not showy. The stems are produced in great profusion to form dense tufts on mature plants.

C. haspan viviparus. Africa. Water depth up to 6 in.; height 18–24 in.; spread 15–18 in. A variety of a tender evergreen species which forms a dense thicket of short smooth stems. These carry linear leaves that sheathe the lower part of the light green feathery flower heads from June to September. It grows best in an open bed beside a greenhouse pool but can also be grown as a pot plant. For the latter, stand a 6 in. pot or 7–8 in. pan filled with loamy soil in shallow water; alternatively, three-quarters fill a watertight bowl, 8–10 in. across and 6–8 in. deep, with soil, then cover the soil with 1 in. of water.

If a flower head is bent over and pinned down in another bowl containing soil and water, roots will develop to form new plants.

C. longus (sweet galingale). Europe, including Great Britain. Water depth up to 18 in.; height 18–24 in.; spread 12–15 in. A rather invasive and strong-growing hardy perennial with a tough creeping rootstock. It is best planted as marginal shelter and decoration at a large pool or lake, but may also be grown as a single specimen in a small pool if the roots are restricted in a container.

This plant has wide, ribbed, dark olive-green leaves. Heads of red-brown plumes, with three exceptionally long, pendulous, shiny green bracts, are borne in August and September.

C. papyrus (Egyptian paper rush). N. and E. Africa. Height 8–10 ft; spread 2–4 ft. A tender, evergreen plant for a large greenhouse. Triangular, smooth, dark green stems, which are 2–3 in. thick at the base, rise from a thick woody rootstock. They are crowned with globular heads, up to 12 in. across, of thread-like pendulous stems, each terminating in a fluffy, sulphur-green inflorescence. Flowering is from July to September. The leaves are insignificant. The pithy insides of the stems were dried and compressed by the ancient Egyptians to make paper.

C. vegetus. Chile. Water depth up to 6 in.; height 18–24 in.; spread 9–12 in. A compact hardy perennial much like *C. alternifolius* but less densely tufted. The grass-like leaves are light glossy green in colour. Tough stems carry heads of tightly packed green plumes, 6 in. or more across, which later turn to brown. Flowering is in August and September. A good marginal rush, non-invasive, provided it is not allowed to seed. It is useful for flower decoration.

Cultivation. To grow tender species (except *C. papyrus*) as pot plants, use John Innes potting compost No. 1 for young plants and No. 2 for the final potting into 5 in. pots; water freely. Alternatively, pot in plain loam and stand the pots in shallow water. Plant from May to September; maintain a minimum temperature of 13°C (55°F). Give occasional liquid feeds, and remove old stems as they turn yellow.

C. papyrus requires a temperature of 18–21°C (64–70°F). Pot young plants in John Innes potting compost No. 2 or No. 3 and water freely until they are growing well. Plant finally in half tubs or similar containers, 18–24 in. across and 8–12 in. deep. Place a layer of turves over the bottom, then fill the tub to within 2 in. from the top with good fibrous loam mixed with well-decayed manure. Stand in a tray of water, and remove old flower heads as they die off.

Plant the hardy varieties between April and June in the margin of a pond or in perforated containers filled with 6–8 in. of rich soil. The site may be sunny or partially shaded. Cover with up to 6 in. of water—up to 18 in. for *C. longus*. Remove old flower heads before the seeds ripen. Clean up and remove old foliage in autumn, or in spring if the plants are to provide winter shelter for birds.

Propagation. Lift old plants of the hardy species in April or May, detach young growths and replant these in the pool margin.

Cynoglossum nervosum

Cyperus alternifolius 'Variegatus'

Cyperus papyrus

Cypripedium calceolus

Cypripedium reginae

Cytisus battandieri

Cytisus × beanii

Divide the old crowns of greenhouse species between April and August, removing and discarding woody material. Plant the divided pieces in 3 in. pots of John Innes potting compost No. 2; water sparingly until they are established.

The variety *C. haspan viviparus* can also be increased either by detaching the heads with a short length of stem and inserting into wet soil, or by bending the stems over and inserting the heads in wet soil. Roots and shoots are quickly produced in a temperature of 16°C (61°F). Pot the plants as soon as they are large enough to handle. *C. alternifolius* may also be treated in this way but does not root quite so readily.

Sow the seeds of hardy varieties in April in boxes of loam, standing these in shallow water. Prick out the seedlings into boxes, also in water, and grow on until large enough to plant out.

C. alternifolius, *C. vegetus* and *C. papyrus* produce seeds freely. Sow from March to May in John Innes seed compost at a temperature of 18–21°C (64–70°F). Prick out the seedlings into boxes, then into 3 in. pots before final potting.

Pests and diseases. Generally trouble-free.

Cypress: see Chamaecyparis
Cypress, Arizona: see *Cupressus arizonica*
Cypress, bald: see Taxodium
Cypress, Hinoki: see *Chamaecyparis obtusa*
Cypress, Italian: see *Cupressus sempervirens*
Cypress, Lawson's: see *Chamaecyparis lawsoniana*
Cypress, Leyland: see × Cupressocyparis
Cypress, Mediterranean: see *Cupressus sempervirens*
Cypress, Monterey: see *Cupressus macrocarpa*
Cypress, Nootka: see *Chamaecyparis nootkatensis*
Cypress, Sawara: see *Chamaecyparis pisifera*
Cypress, summer: see *Kochia scoparia*
Cypress, swamp: see Taxodium
Cypress, true: see Cupressus

Cypripedium

Lady's slipper. *Orchidaceae*

CYPRIPEDIUM REGINAE

A genus of 50 species of terrestrial, hardy or tender, clump-forming orchids from the temperate zones. Certain species of *Paphiopedilum* are sometimes, but erroneously, listed as cypripediums. These rhizomatous, generally deciduous plants are not difficult to grow under the right soil conditions. They are suitable for planting beneath trees, on rock gardens or in mixed borders. The flowers are usually borne singly on erect stems, and are composed of fused lateral sepals, a relatively large dorsal sepal and a conspicuous pouch or slipper-like lip.

See also ORCHIDS.

C. calceolus. Europe, Asia, N. America. Height 12–18 in.; planting distance 9–12 in. A hardy species suitable for a sheltered rock garden. The ovate-lanceolate, prominently ribbed leaves are mid-green. From one to three flowers, 3 in. across, are borne on 12 in. long stems in July; they have maroon petals and sepals and a pale yellow lip.

C. reginae. N. America. Height 1½–3 ft; planting distance 12 in. This hardy species bears longitudinally pleated, pale green, lanceolate to ovate leaves. The flower spikes, which appear in June and July, often bear four flowers, up to 4 in. wide. The petals and sepals are pure white; the large balloon-like lip is heavily flushed and mottled bright rose-purple.

Cultivation. These plants thrive in deep to light shade. The soil should be well drained and contain plenty of leaf-mould; *C. reginae* needs a more moist situation in peaty, lime-free soil. Plant so that the crowns are 2–3 in. deep, in March or April.

Propagation. Divide and replant the clumps in March or April.

Pests. Leaves and stems may be infested by APHIDS and SCALE INSECTS of various species, making the plants sticky and sooty.

Diseases. Unsuitable cultural conditions result in PHYSIOLOGICAL DISORDERS which produce various types of leaf spotting or general discoloration. Sometimes the affected areas are entered by secondary fungi which cause rotting.

Cyrtomium falcatum: see *Polystichum falcatum*

Cytisus

Broom. *Leguminosae*

CYTISUS SCOPARIUS

A genus of 25–30 species of mainly deciduous and a few evergreen shrubs, which vary from prostrate plants to bushes 10 ft or more high. They are related to *Genista*, and are native to Europe, Asia Minor and N. Africa. A few species are tender and require greenhouse cultivation. Those described here are hardy, unless otherwise stated; with their numerous hybrids they make excellent garden plants.

The flowers are sweet-pea-shaped and generally carried in great profusion. In many species the leaves are only present on the branches for a few months of the year. They are suitable for ground cover, on rock gardens and as wall shrubs.

C. albus, syn. *C. multiflorus* (white broom). Spain, Portugal, N.W. Africa. Height and spread up to 6 ft. A bushy species of upright habit with long arching branches. The foliage is grey-green, the upper leaves being simple and almost insignificant, and the lower leaves trifoliate.

Cytisus × praecox

Numerous white flowers, ½ in. long, are borne singly or in clusters of two or three at the joints along the previous year's growths. Flowering is in April and May, and the feathery sprays are excellent for cutting.

C. ardoinii. Maritime Alps. Height 2–4 in.; spread 12 in. or more. This is a mat-forming, usually decumbent, alpine shrub. The tiny, trifoliate, grey-green leaves are hairy. Bright yellow flowers, ½ in. long, are borne in April and May in clusters of two and three, sometimes up to six, and almost cover the plant. Suitable for ground cover and excellent on a rock garden.

C. battandieri. Morocco. Height up to 15 ft; spread 8–12 ft. A shrub of upright, almost tree-like habit with large, silvery, trifoliate leaves. Golden-yellow, pineapple-scented flowers are freely produced along the lateral shoots in May and June. They are borne in erect or recurving cylindrical racemes, up to 4 in. long. It makes a fine wall shrub, but requires protection in northern gardens.

C. × beanii. Height 18–24 in.; spread 3 ft. A dwarf hybrid between *C. ardoinii* and *C. purgans*. The mid-green, hairy, linear leaves are undivided. Golden-yellow flowers, ½ in. long, are borne singly or in clusters of up to three on the previous year's growths in May. A good rock-garden plant.

C. canariensis (genista). Canary Islands. Height up to 6 ft; spread 4–5 ft; as a pot plant, height 12–18 in.; spread 12 in. A tender, well-branched and green-stemmed evergreen shrub with hoary-green trifoliate leaves. Fragrant yellow flowers are borne in short terminal spikes, 2 in. long, from April to July.

C. × 'Gold Spear'. Height and spread 4 ft. This is a floriferous seedling of *C. × praecox* 'Allgold'. Its numerous upright shoots are covered with bright yellow, long-lasting flowers in May.

C. × kewensis. Height 12–24 in., spread 4 ft. A hybrid between *C. albus* and *C. ardoinii* and of spreading, procumbent habit, with trifoliate, mid-green leaves. Pale yellow flowers, ½ in. long, appear during May in great profusion, singly or in twos or threes in the joints of the previous year's shoots. Suitable for a large rock garden or on a sunny ledge.

C. multiflorus: see *C. albus*

C. nigricans. Central and S.E. Europe. Height 3–4 ft; spread 3 ft. This species, of erect growth, has trifoliate, mid-green leaves. Yellow flowers, 1 in. long, in slender, erect racemes, are borne at the ends of the current year's growths; they appear in June and continue to September.

C. × 'Porlock'. Height up to 10 ft; spread 4 ft. A semi-evergreen, half-hardy hybrid between *C. monspessulanus* and *C. × racemosus*. It is of upright habit and bears light green, trifoliate leaves. Sweet-scented, butter-yellow flowers, ½ in. long, are carried freely in racemes or clusters at the ends of the young growths in April and May. It is hardy in mild areas; in cold and northern gardens it requires wall protection.

C. × praecox (Warminster broom). Height and spread 5–6 ft. This hybrid between *C. albus* and *C. purgans* is of bushy, vigorous habit, with arching growths bearing ovate grey-green leaves. Cream-white flowers, ½ in. long, with an acrid smell, are borne in great profusion during April and May. The form 'Allgold' has rich sulphur-yellow flowers.

C. purgans. S.E. France, Spain, N. Africa. Height and spread up to 4 ft. A species of dense, bushy and erect habit; it is rigid and the branches are usually leafless. Fragrant, rich golden-yellow flowers, ½ in. long, are produced singly or in pairs in the joints of the previous year's wood during April and May.

C. purpureus (purple broom). Central and S.E. Europe. Height 12–24 in.; spread 4–5 ft. The trifoliate leaves are dark green. Axillary, purple flowers, ½–¾ in. long, are borne singly or in twos or threes on the previous year's shoots in May and June. 'Albus' is a white form; 'Atropurpureus' has darker purple flowers than the type species.

C. × racemosus. Garden hybrid. Height 6–8 ft; spread 5–6 ft; as a pot plant, height 18 in.; spread 12 in. This twiggy evergreen shrub with grey-green trifoliate leaves is a tender species. Fragrant, bright yellow flowers are borne from March to May in terminal racemes measuring up to 4 in. long.

C. scoparius (common broom). W. Europe, including Great Britain. Height and spread 8 ft. This species is of upright habit with erect, bright green branches which give it an evergreen appearance in winter. The tiny mid-green leaves are trifoliate at the base of the shoots, but simple above. Rich yellow flowers, 1 in. long, in pairs or singly, are freely produced in the joints of the previous year's growths during May and June.

Among the numerous hybrids and varieties are: 'Andreanus', yellow and chocolate flowers; 'Burkwoodii', rich crimson-red flowers; 'Cornish Cream', cream and white flowers; 'Donard Seedling', vigorous, with purple-rose and orange flowers, suffused pink; 'Firefly', yellow flowers with bronze-crimson wings.

'Golden Sunlight', rich yellow flowers; 'Goldfinch', purple flowers with yellow and red wings; 'Johnson's Crimson', free-flowering, of arching habit, with clear crimson blooms; 'Killiney Red', bright red flowers; 'Killiney Salmon', salmon-red flowers with orange wings; 'Lord Lambourne', bicoloured flowers of cream-yellow and maroon-crimson; 'Maria Burkwood', light rose flowers; 'Sulphureus', syn. 'Pallidus', deep cream flowers; 'Windlesham Ruby', of bushy habit, and with ruby-red flowers.

Cytisus × kewensis

Cytisus nigricans

Cytisus × racemosus

Cytisus scoparius 'Johnson's Crimson'

Cytisus scoparius
'Lord Lambourne'

Daboecia cantabrica

Daboecia cantabrica
'Globosa Pink'

Daboecia cantabrica 'Praegerae'

Cultivation. All brooms are easily grown, but they resent root disturbance and pot-grown specimens should be used for planting in September and October or in March and April. They thrive in ordinary, well-drained garden soil, poor rather than rich, and in full sun. Most species are lime-tolerant, but then often short-lived, particularly *C. albus* and the hybrids of *C. scoparium*.

Grow the tender *C. canariensis* and *C.* × *racemosus* in John Innes potting compost No. 2 in 5–8 in. pots or planted out in the greenhouse border. Overwinter at a temperature of 7–10°C (45–50°F), which will cause *C.* × *racemosus* to flower from February onwards. During spring and summer, water freely and shade the glass lightly; pot-grown plants may be stood outdoors from June to September. In winter, keep the plants just moist.

Pot on or repot annually in October; give a weak liquid feed at two-week intervals from April to August.

Propagation. The species are easily raised from seeds sown in pots or pans during April, and placed in a cold frame; prick out the seedlings singly into 3–4 in. pots of John Innes potting compost No. 1 or 2 and plunge outdoors. Transplant to permanent sites in September.

Named varieties and *C.* × *racemosus* do not breed true from seeds and should be vegetatively propagated. Take cuttings, 3–4 in. long, of lateral shoots with a heel in August or September. Insert the cuttings of hardy species in equal parts (by volume) peat and sand in a cold frame. When rooted, pot the cuttings in 3–4 in. pots of John Innes potting compost No. 2; plunge the pots outdoors and transplant to final quarters in September or October.

Increase *C. canariensis* and *C.* × *racemosus* by 3 in. long cuttings of lateral shoots, preferably with a heel, taken in July. Insert the cuttings in equal parts (by volume) peat and sand in a propagating case at a temperature of 16–18°C (61–64°F). When rooted, pot the cuttings singly in 3 in. pots of John Innes potting compost No. 1 and pot on as required.

Pruning. Many of the species and hybrids require no regular pruning but, when necessary, prune those which flower on the previous season's shoots immediately after flowering by removing up to two-thirds of all growths. Those species which flower on the current year's shoots may be cut hard back just before they come into growth in spring.

C. scoparius and its hybrids tend to become bare at the base and leggy with age; once they are established, prune them annually after flowering by cutting off most of the previous summer's growths, taking care not to cut into the old wood. Mature plants that have become hard-wooded and leggy do not respond to hard pruning and should be discarded.

Remove all flowered shoots of pot-grown specimens of *C. canariensis* and *C.* × *racemosus* after flowering, to keep them compact.

Pests. Disfiguring growths caused by GALL MITES may occur on the stems.

Diseases. Generally trouble-free.

D

Daboecia

Ericaceae

A genus of two species of evergreen sub-shrubs, one of which is hardy. The 6 in. long racemes bear the largest flowers of any heath (up to ½ in. long), but the faded corollas drop and do not, like those of the ericas, provide winter decoration. They are attractive plants for a rock garden or for ground cover over large areas.

D. azorica. Azores. Height and spread 6 in. Tender in most parts of Britain. Of compact habit with narrow leaves that are dark green above, silver beneath. Bell-like rich ruby flowers appear in June. The species is thought to be interfertile with *D. cantabrica*, and hardy azoricas may be hybrids from this cross. Some of these presumed hybrids have been named and differ chiefly in the size and colour of their flowers: 'Bearsden', deep garnet-red; 'William Buchanan', syn. 'Seedling No. 1', deep rose-red.

D. cantabrica, syn. *D. polifolia* (St Dabeoc's heath). Ireland, France, Iberian Peninsula. Height and spread up to 3 ft. The hard-pointed, dark green leaves are silvery beneath. Purple-pink

flowers are produced from May until early winter. Some may come more or less true from seed; these hardy species and varieties hybridise easily if planted in close proximity.

The following varieties are recommended: 'Atropurpurea', rich purple flowers; 'Bicolor', flowers white, pink, purple or variously streaked with these colours, any of which may be on the same raceme; 'Globosa Pink', similar to 'Alba Globosa' but with pink-purple flowers; 'Porter's Variety' (height 6 in.), crimson-purple flowers; 'Praegerae' (height 12 in.; spread 24 in.), deep pink flowers.

Several white-flowered forms are known: 'Alba Globosa' has broader flowers than the species; 'David Ross' is an erect and strong-growing variety.

D. polifolia: see *D. cantabrica*

Cultivation, propagation, pruning: see entry under HEATHS AND HEATHERS.

Pests and diseases. Generally trouble free.

Daffodil: see Narcissus

Daffodil, Tenby: see *Narcissus pseudonarcissus obvallaris*

Daffodil, wild: see *Narcissus pseudonarcissus*

DAHLIA

Compositae

Dahlia 'Klankstad Kerkrade' (Small cactus)

A genus of 20 species of half-hardy tuberous perennials. Modern garden dahlias, whose widely ranging forms and colours make them outstanding plants for garden decoration and as cut flowers, are derived from three Mexican species, *D. pinnata*, *D. coccinea* and *D. rosea*, which may themselves all originate from one species, *D. variabilis*.

Dahlias are divided into two groups: border dahlias which, although suitable for mixed borders, should ideally be grown on their own; and bedding dahlias, which are grown as annuals from seeds.

All dahlias have pinnate leaves with ovate leaflets. These, except for a few bronze-foliaged varieties such as 'Bishop of Llandaff' and 'David Howard', are mid to dark green.

Border Dahlias

All those described flower freely from the time stated until cut down by frost. They are classified into the following groups:

SINGLE-FLOWERED. Height $1\frac{1}{2}$–$2\frac{1}{2}$ ft; planting distance 18–24 in.; diameter of bloom up to 4 in. Each flower consists of a single outer ring of florets, which may overlap, and a central disc. Flowering starts in early August.

Varieties include: 'Nellie Geerlings', scarlet; 'Orangeade', flame; 'Princess Marie Jose', lilac-pink; 'Sion', bronze.

ANEMONE-FLOWERED. Height 2–$3\frac{1}{2}$ ft; planting distance 24 in.; diameter of bloom up to 4 in. The double flowers have flat outer florets surrounding a densely packed group of shorter tubular florets, often of a contrasting colour. Flowering is from early August.

'Asahi Chohje', red and white outer petals, white centre; 'Bridesmaid', white outer petals, lemon centre; 'Comet', maroon; 'Lucy', purple outer petals, yellow centre.

COLLERETTE. Height $2\frac{1}{2}$–4 ft; planting distance 2–$2\frac{1}{2}$ ft; diameter of bloom up to 4 in. These dahlias have blooms with a single ring of flat ray florets, sometimes overlapping, an inner ring (or collar) of smaller florets and a central disc. Flowering is from early August.

'Can-Can', pink petals, yellow collar; 'Mrs H. Brown', orange and flame petals, yellow collar; 'Nonsense', cream-white petals, orange collar; 'Ruwenzori', scarlet petals, yellow collar.

PAEONY-FLOWERED. Height up to 3 ft; planting distance 24 in.; diameter of bloom up to 4 in. The flowers consist of two or more rings of flat ray florets and a central disc. Flowering is from early August.

'Bishop of Llandaff', scarlet; 'Fascination', purple; 'Grenadier', scarlet; 'Oranje Flora', syn. 'Orange Flora', orange.

DECORATIVE. The blooms are fully double, without a central disc. They consist of broad, flat ray florets, slightly twisted and usually bluntly pointed. The group is divided into five sections, according to the size of blooms.

GIANT. Height 4–5 ft; planting distance 4 ft; diameter of bloom 10 in. or more. Flowering is

Dahlia 'Can-Can' (Collerette)

Dahlia 'Nonsense' (Collerette)   *Dahlia* 'Comet' (Anemone-flowered)

Dahlia 'Princess Marie Jose' (Single-flowered)

Dahlia 'Ruwenzori' (Collerette)

Dahlia 'Crossfield Festival' (Giant decorative)

Dahlia 'Holland Festival' (Giant decorative)

Dahlia 'Betty Russell' (Medium decorative)

from August. 'Burgess Ray', yellow; 'Crossfield Festival', bicoloured, light red and white; 'Hamari Girl', pink; 'Holland Festival', rich orange with white-tipped petals; 'Jocondo', purple; 'Liberator', crimson.

DAHLIA (LARGE DECORATIVE)

LARGE. Height 3½–5 ft; planting distance 4 ft; diameter of bloom 8–10 in. Flowering is from August. 'Bunratty', purple; 'Dutch Triumph', pink, yellow centre; 'Enfield Salmon', pink; 'Robert Damp', yellow.

MEDIUM. Height 3½–4 ft; planting distance 3 ft; diameter of bloom 6–8 in. Flowering is from August. 'Betty Russell', syn. 'Yellow Terpo', yellow; 'Breckland Joy', bronze; 'First Lady', yellow; 'Golden Turban', shades of yellow-orange; 'Sterling Silver', white; 'Terpo', crimson.

SMALL. Height 3½–4 ft; planting distance 2½ ft; diameter of bloom 4–6 in. Flowering is from August. 'Dedham', shades of pink and mauve; 'Glorie Van Heemstede', yellow; 'Millbank Inferno', shades of red and orange; 'Snow Queen', white; 'That's It', flame; 'Towneley Class', white, flushed with lavender.

MINIATURE. Height 3–4 ft; planting distance 2½ ft; diameter of bloom up to 4 in. Flowering is from August. 'David Howard', orange; 'Doris Duke', pink; 'Jo's Choice', scarlet; 'Newby', peach.

BALL. These dahlias have fully double, ball-shaped blooms, sometimes flattened on top. The sides of the ray florets curve inwards for more than half their length, have blunt or round tips and are arranged spirally. The group is divided into two sections.

BALL. Height 3–4 ft; planting distance 2½ ft; diameter of bloom 4–6 in. Flowering is from August. 'Bernard Colwyn Hayes', deep pink; 'Doreen Hayes', scarlet; 'Esmonde', yellow; 'Gloire de Lyon', white.

MINIATURE BALL. Height 3–4 ft; planting distance 2½ ft; diameter of bloom up to 4 in. Flowering is from August. 'Dr John Grainger', orange; 'Florence Vernon', lilac; 'Nelly Birch', scarlet; 'Sulphurea', yellow; 'Swiss Miss', shades of crimson-purple and dark pink.

POMPON. Height 3–4 ft; planting distance 2½ ft; diameter of bloom up to 2 in. The flowers are similar to those of ball dahlias but are much smaller and more globular; the florets curve inwards along their whole length. Flowering is from August.

'Andrew Lockwood', lilac; 'Little Conn', dark red; 'Moor Place', purple; 'Pom of Poms', scarlet; 'Rhondda', lilac, white centre.

CACTUS (c) AND SEMI-CACTUS (s-c). The blooms are fully double, with pointed ray florets. In cactus dahlias these are rolled back, or quilled, for over half their length; in semi-cactus they are broader and quilled for half their length or less. The group is divided into five sections.

Dahlia 'Golden Turban' (Medium decorative)

Dahlia 'Dedham' (Small decorative)

Dahlia 'Glorie Van Heemstede' (Small decorative)

Dahlia 'Millbank Inferno' (Small decorative)

Dahlia 'Doris Duke'
(Miniature decorative)

Dahlia 'Bernard Colwyn
Hayes' (Ball)

Dahlia 'Swiss Miss'
(Miniature ball)

Dahlia 'Little Conn' (Pompon)

Dahlia 'Frontispiece' (Giant semi-cactus)

GIANT. Height 4–5 ft; planting distance 4 ft; diameter of bloom 10 in. or more. Flowering is from early September. 'Cocorico' (s-c), scarlet; 'Danny' (c), pink; 'Frontispiece' (s-c), cream-white; 'Gladys M. Reynolds' (c), bronze; 'Hamari Boy' (s-c), yellow; 'Polar Sight' (c), cream-white; 'Respectable' (s-c), yellow.

LARGE. Height 4–5 ft; planting distance 4 ft; diameter of bloom 8–10 in. Flowering is from late August. 'Cum Laude' (c), deep pink; 'Drakenburg' (c), purple; 'General Mourer' (s-c), purple; 'Irish Visit' (c), crimson; 'Nantenan' (s-c), yellow; 'Royal Highness' (c), pink; 'Royal Sceptre' (s-c), orange to deep yellow; 'Royal Wedding' (s-c), flame, with yellow centre; 'Soest Vooruit' (c), orange.

MEDIUM. Height 3½–4½ ft; planting distance 3 ft; diameter of bloom 8–10 in. Flowering is from mid-August. 'Apache' (s-c), bright red; 'Authority' (c), shades of bronze and orange; 'Autumn Fire' (s-c), apricot-yellow, tinged with flame at floret tips; 'Countess Dunraven' (s-c), pink; 'Hamari Bride' (s-c), white; 'Priscilla' (c), flame; 'Rotterdam' (s-c), crimson; 'Sure Thing' (c), red; 'Sweet Secret' (s-c), blended dark pink and yellow; 'Topaz' (c), yellow; and 'Tornado' (c), orange-red flowers.

SMALL. Height 3½–4 ft; planting distance 2½ ft; diameter of bloom 4–6 in. Flowering is from early August. 'Doris Day' (c), crimson; 'Hoek's Yellow' (s-c), yellow; 'Klankstad Kerkrade' (c), yellow; 'Marilyn' (s-c), pink; 'Paul Chester' (c), orange, with yellow centre; 'Rothesay Red' (s-c), crimson; 'White Swallow' (s-c), white; 'Wortor Sally Ann' (c), lilac.

MINIATURE. Height 3–4 ft; planting distance 2½ ft; diameter of bloom up to 4 in. Flowering is from August. 'Charmer' (c), purple; 'Chasamay' (c), pink; 'Happy Mood' (s-c), yellow; 'Hazel' (c), lilac, fading to white; 'Little Ann' (s-c), pink; 'Lynne Bartholomew' (s-c), cherry-purple; 'Pirouette' (c), yellow; 'Poppet' (c), blended salmon and yellow; 'Snip' (s-c), bronze, tinged with orange; 'Yellow Mood' (s-c), yellow.

Bedding Dahlias

Height 12–20 in., planting distance 12–24 in. The flowers, which may be single, semi-double or double, are white or in shades of yellow, pink, red or lilac. They measure 2–3 in. across and appear from July to the first severe frosts.

'Fascination' is a dwarf, paeony-flowered variety with flowers of pink or purple; 'Princess Marie Jose' bears single, lilac-pink flowers.

Dahlia 'Nantenan' (Large semi-cactus)

Dahlia 'Polar Sight' (Giant cactus)

Dahlia 'Apache' (Medium semi-cactus)

Dahlia 'Cum Laude' (Large cactus)

Dahlia 'Royal Sceptre' (Large semi-cactus)

Dahlia 'Authority' (Medium cactus)

Dahlia 'Autumn Fire' (Medium semi-cactus)

There are also many seed strains and mixtures obtainable. 'Coltness Hybrids' is the best-known group; mixtures and separate colours are available. 'Pink Radiance' has single, rose-pink flowers with a bold crimson zone.

DAHLIA (DWARF BEDDING)

'Unwin's Dwarf Hybrids' produces semi-double flowers in a wide range of bright colours, including yellow, orange, pink and crimson. 'Early Bird' is a selected dwarf form, seldom exceeding 12 in. in height, with flowers in a similar colour range.

Cultivation of border dahlias. Plant the unsprouted tubers in mid-April, at least 4 in. deep. Plant rooted cuttings and sprouted tubers during the third week in May, but if the weather is cold and wet, wait until conditions improve. Any soil will give reasonable results provided it is well drained and enriched with peat, compost or manure. Regardless of the type of soil, rake in 4 oz. of bone-meal per sq. yd at planting time.

Dahlias do best in an open, sunny position, and preferably in a bed of their own.

All border dahlias need support; insert stout stakes, 12 in. shorter than the final height of the plants, in each planting hole before placing the tuber or young plant in position. Tie the stems loosely to the stakes, and as the plants grow make additional ties.

Stop all plants by pinching out the leading shoots three or four weeks after planting.

If large flowers on long stems are wanted for cutting or exhibition purposes, disbud the plants regularly by removing the young flower buds. Each main stem carries a terminal flower bud and two smaller buds below; remove the small buds and leave only the terminal bud. Dead-head the plants as the flowers fade.

Lift and store the tubers each autumn. A week after frosts have blackened the foliage, cut the stems down to 6 in. above ground. Make a cut of one spade's depth around each plant, 12 in. from the main stem. Holding the stems, gently ease the tubers from the soil with the spade. Take care not to damage the point above the stems from

Dahlia 'Doris Day' (Small cactus)

Dahlia 'Hoek's Yellow' (Small semi-cactus)

Dahlia 'Lynne Bartholomew' (Miniature semi-cactus)

Dahlia 'Yellow Mood' (Miniature semi-cactus)

Dahlia 'Sure Thing' (Medium cactus)

Dahlia 'Sweet Secret' (Medium semi-cactus)

where the tubers grow and from where new growths will begin. Discard any broken tubers. Place the tubers upside-down for a week, under cover, to drain off the water in the hollow stems.

Place the tubers in shallow boxes and barely cover them with slightly damp peat; do not allow the peat to cover the crowns. Store the boxes in a frost-proof place at a temperature of 5°C (41°F).

During the winter, inspect the tubers every few weeks for signs of shrivelling and diseases. Shrivelled tubers may be placed overnight in a bucket of water, to plump them up; dry the tubers thoroughly before replacing in their storage. Cut away any damaged parts and dust the wounds with flowers of sulphur.

Cultivation of bedding dahlias. These grow best in a medium to heavy soil and in an open, sunny position. Enrich poor soil by digging in well-rotted manure some weeks before planting; avoid excessive feeding, however, as this will encourage foliage at the expense of flowers. Water freely in hot weather and remove dead flowers to encourage continuous flowering. No staking, stopping or disbudding is required.

Propagation of border dahlias. Division of the tubers and basal cuttings are the best propagation methods, and will produce plants identical to the parents. Plants raised from seeds do not breed true to the type.

Division is the simplest method, as this does not require heat to start the plants into growth, and blooms will be produced two or three weeks earlier than plants raised from cuttings.

In March, place the tubers in shallow boxes containing a mixture of equal parts (by volume) peat and sand, leaving the crowns clear. Put the boxes in a frost-proof place and keep the mixture moist, but avoid watering the crowns. In two or three weeks, the eyes on the crowns of the tubers will swell.

Divide the tubers with a sharp knife, ensuring that each division has an undamaged eye. After division, dust the cut parts with flowers of sulphur, to prevent possible fungus attack. They can now be planted not less than 4 in. deep.

If the ground is not ready, pot the tubers singly in John Innes potting compost No. 2 and place in a frost-proof frame until frosts are over.

Take cuttings from tubers started into growth in a greenhouse or frame from mid-February onwards. The ideal temperature is 15–18°C (59–64°F); the minimum practicable temperature is 7°C (45°F), but growth will be slow.

Discard any damaged tubers and remove old fibrous roots from the others. Place the tubers in moist peat, either in 4–6 in. deep boxes or directly on the covered staging. Ensure that the crowns are completely clear of the compost. Water the compost, avoiding the crowns, and give more water from time to time if the compost dries out.

When the young growths are 3 in. long, cut them off with a sharp knife at least ¼ in. from the crown, thus leaving small stumps from which new growths will appear. Remove the lower part of leaves from each cutting and dip the base in hormone rooting powder. Insert the cuttings around the edges of 3 in. pots, four to a pot, using a compost of equal parts (by volume) loam, peat and sharp sand.

Water the compost thoroughly and place the pots in a propagating frame or on the greenhouse staging at a temperature of 15–18°C (59–64°F). Keep the compost moist and shade the plants from bright sunshine.

Three or four weeks later, when the cuttings are well rooted, pot them singly into 3 in. pots and place them in a frost-proof frame until they are wanted for planting out.

Alternatively, insert the cuttings, 2 in. apart in rows 3 in. apart, directly into a soil-based propagating frame, using a similar compost. When rooted, pot on as already described.

Propagation of bedding dahlias. Sow seeds under glass during February or March in boxes or pans of John Innes seed compost; germinate at a temperature of 16°C(61°F).

Prick off the seedlings, when large enough to handle, first into boxes and later into 3 in. pots. Harden the young plants off in a cold frame from mid-April onwards, then plant out in late May, or when danger of frost is over.

Pests. Dahlias may be infested by APHIDS of many different species at almost any stage of growth. Severe infestations cause distortion of young growths and loss of sap, which weakens the plants. Aphids also transmit virus diseases.

CATERPILLARS of various species of moths eat large, rounded holes in the leaves and sometimes tunnel in stems or spin the young leaves together.

CAPSID BUGS inject toxic saliva into young tissues, killing buds, distorting shoots, and causing a characteristic tattering of the leaves.

EARWIGS eat ragged holes in leaves and petals and often hide in the flowers.

Diseases. Dahlias are commonly infected by CUCUMBER MOSAIC, TOMATO SPOTTED WILT and occasionally by other viruses. Affected plants are stunted; yellow or brown rings and spots, often concentric in shape, develop on the leaves, which may be distorted.

DAMPING-OFF can cause the collapse of cuttings.

GREY MOULD may damage cuttings, but is more troublesome on flower stalks, buds and older flowers in wet summers. Affected tissues decay and eventually become covered with a grey mass of fungus spores.

LEAFY GALL shows as a mass of abortive shoots at ground level.

PETAL BLIGHT occasionally infects the flowers, and shows as small, brown, water-soaked spots, which develop on the outer petals and then spread inwards until the whole bloom becomes affected. The disease is usually followed by an attack of grey mould.

SCLEROTINIA DISEASE produces a decay of the stems, so that they collapse. The diseased stems contain a fluffy, white fungal growth, in which are large, black resting bodies. The fungus may also cause tubers to rot.

VERTICILLIUM WILT causes plants to wilt, even when there is no drought.

Daisy: see Bellis
Daisy, African: see Dimorphotheca
Daisy bush: see Olearia
Daisy, common: see *Bellis perennis*
Daisy, gloriosa: see *Rudbeckia hirta* Tetra 'Gloriosa'
Daisy, kingfisher: see *Felicia bergeriana*
Daisy, Livingstone: see Mesembryanthemum
Daisy, michaelmas: see *Aster novae-angliae*
Daisy, moon: see *Chrysanthemum uliginosum*
Daisy, Mount Atlas: see Anacyclus
Daisy, Shasta: see *Chrysanthemum maximum*
Daisy, Swan river: see *Brachycome iberidifolia*

Daphne
Thymelaeaceae

A genus of 70 species of evergreen and deciduous shrubs, native to Europe and Asia. They have sweetly scented flowers that are tubular at the base, expanding at the mouth into four lobes. These dwarf or medium-sized shrubs are handsome plants for a rock garden or the front of a shrub border. Those described are all hardy and, with the exception of a few species, notably *D. genkwa*, are easy to grow.

D. arbuscula. Hungary. Height up to 6 in.; spread up to 12 in. A rounded evergreen species with dark green, shiny, linear-oblanceolate leaves that are crowded at the ends of the branchlets. The rose-purple flowers appear in June in terminal clusters, 1–1½ in. across.

Daphne blagayana

D. blagayana. E. Europe. Height up to 6 in.; spread 6 ft. A mat-forming species with narrow, obovate, mid-green leaves, crowded towards the ends of shoots, giving a sparse appearance. Cream-white flowers, about ½ in. across, are borne in dense terminal heads of 20 or more during April and May.

D. × burkwoodii. Height and spread 3–4 ft. A semi-evergreen hybrid between *D. cneorum* and *D. caucasica.* The leaves are oblanceolate and light green. Soft pink flowers are borne in May and June in dense terminal clusters, up to 2 in. across. This hybrid is largely represented in cultivation by the form 'Somerset'.

DAPHNE CNEORUM

D. cneorum (garland flower). C. and S. Europe. Height 6 in.; spread 2–3 ft. An evergreen shrub of prostrate growth. The slender stems are clothed with deep green, narrowly oblong leaves and carry dense terminal clusters of six or more flowers. These are ½ in. wide, rose-pink and highly scented, appearing in May and June. The pure white-flowered form 'Alba' is less vigorous; 'Eximia' is larger than the type species and considered to be the finest form; 'Pygmaea' is fully prostrate and free-flowering.

D. collina. Italy, Asia Minor. Height and spread 2½–3 ft. An evergreen species of compact, bushy and branching habit. The glossy dark green leaves are oblanceolate. Rose-purple flowers, 1½ in. across, are borne in terminal heads of 10 to 15, during May and June.

D. genkwa. China. Height 2–3 ft; spread 12–24 in. A deciduous species of upright, sparse habit with slender branches. The light green lanceolate leaves are usually opposite. Lavender-blue flowers, ½ in. wide, appear in clusters of three to seven along the naked branches in April and May. They are only slightly scented.

Dahlia 'Poppet' (Miniature cactus)

Dahlia 'Fascination' (Bedding)

Daphne arbuscula

Daphne cneorum

213

Daphne mezereum

Daphne odora

Daphne petraea

Daphne retusa

Although hardy, this species can be difficult to establish and grow outdoors. Plants on their own roots are preferable to those grafted on to stock of *D. mezereum* and may be tried in light shade in lime-free soil. It makes a good pot plant in the alpine house or planted out in a cold greenhouse.
D. laureola (spurge laurel). Europe, including Great Britain; W. Asia. Height 2–4 ft; spread 3–5 ft. An evergreen shrub of bushy habit with shiny, deep green, oblong to ovate-lanceolate leaves. The green-yellow flowers, $\frac{1}{4}$ in. across, are in short racemes of five to ten. They are borne in the leaf axils of the upper parts of the previous year's growths in February and March. The ovoid berries are black when ripe. This species is grown chiefly for its handsome foliage.

DAPHNE MEZEREUM (IN FLOWER)

D. mezereum (mezereon). Europe, Asia Minor, Siberia. Height up to 5 ft; spread 2–4 ft. A deciduous bush of erect, rounded habit. The oblanceolate leaves are dull, light green above and pale grey-green beneath. The $\frac{1}{2}$ in. wide flowers appear from February to April; they are borne in dense clusters of twos or threes on the uppermost portion of the previous year's leafless stems. They vary from pale purple-pink to violet-red and are followed by scarlet berries.
'Alba' is a white-flowered form with yellow fruits; 'Grandiflora' has larger, bright purple flowers and often begins to flower in autumn.
D. odora. China, Japan. Height and spread 5–6 ft. A bushy evergreen shrub of lax habit with narrowly ovate or oblong, shiny, mid-green leaves. The pale purple flowers, $\frac{1}{2}-\frac{3}{4}$ in. wide, in crowded terminal heads, open in January or February and carry on to April. This species is not quite hardy and requires wall protection in cold areas.
'Aureomarginata' is a hardier form with leaves having narrow cream-white margins.

DAPHNE PETRAEA 'GRANDIFLORA'

D. petraea. N. Italy. Height 3–6 in.; spread up to 12 in. A slow-growing evergreen alpine shrub with twiggy growths. The glossy, dark green, leathery leaves are narrow and oblong, and crowded on the twigs. Rose-pink flowers, $\frac{1}{3}-\frac{1}{2}$ in. across, appear in May and June in terminal clusters of two or three. This shrub is usually grown in pans in an alpine house. 'Grandiflora' has larger flowers.
D. retusa. W. China. Height up to 3 ft; spread $1\frac{1}{2}$–3 ft. An evergreen alpine shrub of rounded bushy habit with stout shoots. The lustrous, dark

green leaves are oblong-obovate. They are thick in texture and are borne densely towards the end of the shoots. The $\frac{3}{4}$ in. wide flowers, which are crowded in terminal clusters, are rose-purple, paler inside. They appear in May and June and are followed by bright red, shortly ovoid berries.
Cultivation. Plant in September or March and April in ordinary garden soil, including soil containing chalk; daphnes thrive in sun or partial shade in a well-drained site. When buying plants ensure that these are not grafted.
In the alpine house, set the plants in 6–8 in. pots or 8–10 in. pans of John Innes potting compost No. 2. Pot on every two or three years in February or March and give a dilute liquid feed once a month from May to September.
Propagation. Take cuttings, 2–4 in. long, of lateral non-flowering shoots, preferably with a heel, from July to September. Insert the cuttings in equal parts (by volume) peat and sand in a cold frame; the following spring place the rooted cuttings in 3 in. pots of John Innes potting compost No. 1. Plunge the pots outdoors and later pot on into 4 or 5 in. containers. Transplant the cuttings to their permanent positions one or two years later.
Alternatively, sow seeds when ripe (not later than October) in pots or boxes of seed compost in a cold frame; pot the seedlings when large enough to handle and grow on as for cuttings.
Pruning. None required, but straggly growth may be removed in March.
Pests. Infestations of APHIDS on young shoots and leaves may cause a check to growth.
Diseases. Severe mottling and distortion of leaves may be caused by CUCUMBER MOSAIC VIRUS; the plants may be stunted and flower poorly.
HONEY FUNGUS causes the death of shrubs.
LEAF SPOT shows as small brown spots on the leaves, particularly at the base and on the leaf stalks. Premature defoliation occurs.

Datura

Solanaceae

A genus of ten species of half-hardy annuals and tender shrubby or tree-like perennials. The shrubby species are sometimes listed as a separate genus, *Brugmansia*. Those described have trumpet-shaped flowers, often heavily scented.
The two shrubby species described are tender and require greenhouse treatment. The annual may be grown as border plants or for summer flowering in a cool greenhouse.

DATURA METELOIDES

ANNUAL SPECIES
D. ceratocaula. Tropical America. Height 3 ft; planting distance 24 in. This species has thick, strong stems with mid-green, ovate and deeply

cut leaves. The white flowers, which appear in July and August, are tinged with blue and sweetly scented. They are 6 in. long.

D. metel. India. Height 2–4 ft; planting distance 24 in. A shrubby species with red stems bearing ovate dark green leaves. Cream-white flowers, 8 in. long, are rather sparingly produced in June. 'Fastuosa' has double red-purple flowers.

D. meteloides. Texas. Height 3 ft; planting distance 2½ ft. A bushy, short-lived shrubby species, usually listed and grown as an annual. The grey, hairy, ovate leaves have a pungent smell. The flowers, which appear in July, are pleasantly fragrant; they are white or pale rose-lavender and 6 in. long.

SHRUBBY SPECIES

D. cornigera, syn. *Brugmansia knightii* (angel's trumpet). Mexico. Height and spread 6–8 ft. This species is naturally evergreen, but may be deciduous if overwintered in cool conditions. The mid-green leaves are ovate with an elongated point. Pendulous flowers are produced from June to August; they are white or cream, about 6 in. long, and heavily fragrant.

The species is usually represented in cultivation by the semi-double form 'Knightii'.

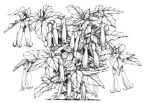

DATURA SANGUINEA

D. sanguinea. Peru. Height 4–6 ft; spread 3–5 ft. An evergreen species with oblong mid-green leaves; they have wavy margins and are covered with soft white hairs. The orange-red flowers, about 8 in. long, appear in July and August.

Cultivation of annual species. Grow in any ordinary garden soil, preferably enriched with well-decayed manure or compost, and in a sunny position. Plant out when danger of frost is past.

Under glass, the plants may be grown in a greenhouse border or in 6 in. pots of John Innes potting compost No. 2; shade the greenhouse lightly and ventilate on hot days.

Cultivation of shrubby species. These plants are easily grown in John Innes potting compost No. 2. They do best planted out in a greenhouse border, but may also be grown in pots and potted on until they finish in 10–12 in. pots or tubs. They are best grown as shrubs pruned hard back annually, but may also be trained as small standards; let them reach the required height before pinching out the growing tips to encourage branching. A trunk of 4 ft is ideal.

During winter, keep the plants cool and just moist at a temperature of 7°C (45°F). In spring and summer, ventilate freely and keep the compost well watered. Pot-grown plants may be stood outdoors in sheltered positions between June and September. In the greenhouse, give light shading, and syringe the leaves.

Pot on until the plants are in their final containers; thereafter repot annually in March or April. Give a liquid feed at 10–14 day intervals from May to September.

Propagation of annual species. Sow seeds under glass in March at a temperature of 16°C (61°F). Prick off the seedlings, when large enough to handle, into 3½ in. pots of John Innes potting compost No. 1 and grow on. Harden off outdoor plants before planting out in late May.

D. meteloides may also be increased from 3–4 in. cuttings of one-year-old growths taken in August. Insert these in a mixture of equal parts (by volume) peat and sand in a propagating frame at a temperature of 15–18°C (59–64°F). When rooted, place the cuttings in 3½ in. pots, later in 5 in. pots of John Innes potting compost No. 1. Overwinter in a frost-free greenhouse or frame and plant out in late May.

Propagation of shrubby species. Take 4–6 in. cuttings of young shoots, preferably with a heel, in May; insert in equal parts (by volume) peat and sand in a propagating case at a temperature of 15–18°C (59–64°F). When rooted, set the cuttings in 3½ in. pots of John Innes potting compost No. 2; pot on as required.

Pruning. In February, cut all growths of shrubby greenhouse species back to within 6 in. of the base; young shoots may be used for cuttings in May. Established standards should be pruned to shape annually in February.

Pests. In the greenhouse, the leaves may be infested with GLASSHOUSE RED SPIDER MITES. These cause mottling of the leaf surfaces.

Diseases. Yellow concentric markings on the leaves of shrubby species are caused by TOMATO SPOTTED WILT VIRUS.

Daucus carota : see Carrot

Datura cornigera 'Knightii'

Davallia

Davalliaceae

A genus of 40 species of ferns. The two described grow from creeping surface rhizomes. Though one is hardy, both are best grown under glass or indoors where, with year-round warmth, they are evergreen.

D. canariensis (hare's-foot). Spain, Canary Isles, N. Africa. Height 12–18 in. The most popular species, it can be grown as a house plant or in the greenhouse. Its leathery mid-green fronds are triangular and quadripinnate. The stout rhizomes are covered with pale brown scales and resemble a hare's foot; when grown in a pot or basket, they hang down over the sides.

D. mariesii. Japan. Height 6–10 in. This species, although hardy, is usually grown in a cool greenhouse. It has light green fronds that are triangular and quadripinnate. The slender rhizomes, which are covered with red-brown scales, may be intertwined to form fern-balls, fern-crosses and other ornamental shapes.

Cultivation. Grow the plants in 6 in. pans or in baskets containing a compost of fibrous peat, a little chopped sphagnum moss, and enough coarse sand to maintain good drainage. Mould the surface of the compost into the shape of a dome, embedding the roots in it but leaving the rhizomes exposed. Secure the rhizomes to the compost with hooks of soft wire to steady them until they are rooting freely.

Datura sanguinea

Davallia mariesii

Davidia involucrata

Delphinium 'Butterball'

Delphinium 'Cressida'

Delphinium 'Mullion'

Delphinium 'Purple Ruffles'

D. canariensis needs a minimum temperature of 10°C (50°F). *D. mariesii* is fully hardy.

Water davallias liberally in summer, sparingly in winter. Never allow the compost to dry out.

Propagation. For a large number of plants, sow spores in March (see entry under FERNS). Otherwise, divide the rhizomes in April.

Pests and diseases. Generally trouble-free.

Davidia

Pocket-handkerchief tree, dove tree, ghost tree. *Davidiaceae*

DAVIDIA INVOLUCRATA

A genus of a single species, native to W. China. This is a hardy deciduous tree, grown for its ornamental foliage and attractive floral bracts. The pendent inflorescence consists of inconspicuous flowers surrounded by large, glistening white bracts of unequal size.

D. involucrata. Height 18–25 ft; spread 10–18 ft. A species with upright or ascending branches; it may be grown with a single stem, but is apt to branch from the base. The alternate pale to mid-green leaves are broadly ovate, terminating in a slender point; they are downy beneath, toothed and prominently veined. Pendent globose clusters of green-yellow flowers, about $\frac{3}{4}$ in. across, appear in May on long stalks from among the young leaves. The flowers are totally obscured by a pair of ovate cream-white bracts of unequal size, the largest being up to 7 in. long. The fruits, which are frequently set, are broadly ovoid, $1\frac{1}{2}$ in. long and green with a pattern of russet spots or netting.

In cultivation the species is frequently represented by *D. i. vilmoriniana*, sometimes considered a distinct species. It has smooth leaves of a paler green.

Cultivation. These plants thrive in any good garden soil with ample moisture. Plant from October to March in sun or partial shade; they make excellent specimen trees for a lawn.

Propagation. Layer long shoots in October and sever from the parent plant two years later.

Take cuttings, 4–5 in. long, of lateral shoots, preferably with a heel, in July and August. Insert the cuttings in equal parts (by volume) peat and sand in a cold frame; the following spring, pot the rooted cuttings in $3\frac{1}{2}$ in. pots of John Innes potting compost No. 2. Plunge the pots outdoors and transfer the young plants to a nursery bed in October, transplanting to permanent positions two or three years later.

Alternatively, increase by seeds sown in October in pots of seed compost in a cold frame; germination usually takes $1\frac{1}{2}$–$2\frac{1}{2}$ years. Treat resulting seedlings as recommended for cuttings.

Pruning. None required.

Pests. Generally trouble-free.

Diseases. Trees may be killed by HONEY FUNGUS. Young leaves may be scorched or killed by late frosts in spring.

David's harp: see *Polygonatam* × *hybridum*

Delphinium

Ranunculaceae

DELPHINIUM BELLADONNA

A genus of 250 species of hardy and half-hardy annuals and herbaceous perennials with spurred flowers. They are largely represented in gardens by the annual larkspurs and the race of perennial hybrids derived from *D. elatum.* The hybrids are popular as border plants, with their stately, showy spires of true blue, purple or white flowers. Recent experimental breeding work should make other varieties in shades of red and yellow available.

D. ajacis (rocket larkspur). Mediterranean regions. Height 1–3 ft; spacing 9–12 in. A hardy annual with upright, sparsely branching stems, and finely cut, fern-like, mid-green leaves. Loose racemes, up to 24 in. long, of blue or violet flowers are carried from June to August.

Garden hybrids, probably derived from this species, include the Hyacinth-flowered group, which bears double flowers in thickly set, blunt-ended spikes with less tendency to branch than the type species. The petals are more weather-resistant. These early-flowering plants are excellent for cutting and for growing in pots under glass. There are both tall and dwarf forms, 24 in. and 12 in. high respectively.

D. consolida (larkspur). Europe, including Great Britain. Height up to 4 ft; spread 12–15 in. An erect-growing hardy annual, usually well-branched from the base. The mid-green leaves are cut into several linear segments, giving a ferny appearance. Racemes, 9–15 in. long, of blue, purple, red, pink or white flowers, more densely borne than those of *D. ajacis*, open from June to August. The species is largely represented in cultivation by the following strains and varieties.

The Giant Imperial strain (height 4 ft), is a base-branching type grown for cutting and for annual and mixed borders. The strain is available in a wide range of colours, such as 'Blue Spire', and 'Dazzler', carmine scarlet.

The Stock-flowered group is the most popular for cut flowers. They flower slightly earlier than the Giant Imperial strain, and grow up to 3 ft high. 'Rosamund' is bright rose.

D. cardinale. California. Height $1\frac{1}{2}$–$2\frac{1}{2}$ ft; spread 12 in. A hardy, short-lived perennial with palmate, deeply dissected, mid-green leaves. Loose racemes, 9–12 in. long, of bright red cup-shaped flowers, shaded yellow in the centre, are borne on slender stems in July and August.

Delphinium 'Xenia Field'

Delphinium 'Baby Doll'

Delphinium 'Blue Tit'

Delphinium 'Mighty Atom'

Delphinium Pacific Hybrids

Delphinium 'Blue Jade'

The species may be flowered the same year from seeds sown under glass in February.

D. elatum. Pyrenees to Siberia. Height 3–5 ft; spread 18–24 in. This hardy erect perennial has deeply cut and toothed palmate, mid-green leaves. Spikes, 12 in. or more long, of blue, cupped flowers, each with a brown eye and a wrinkled spur, appear in June and July.

The true species is now seldom cultivated, being represented by a race of hybrids derived from crosses with *D. grandiflorum* and other species. These are classified into two main groups: Large-flowered or Elatum varieties and Belladonna varieties.

The Elatum varieties are of stiffly erect habit with large flat florets, often semi-double or double. Well-grown plants may reach a height of 8 ft, with a spread of 2½–3 ft. This group is further sub-divided into tall and dwarf varieties, the latter ranging from 3–4½ ft and having sturdy stems, less prone to wind damage.

Tall varieties (height 4½–6 ft) include: 'Betty Hay', pale blue with a white eye; 'Butterball', rich cream with a yellow eye; 'Cressida', pale sky-blue, white eye; 'Daily Express', bright sky-blue with a black eye.

'Mullion', late-flowering, cobalt-blue with a black-brown eye; 'Purple Ruffles', fully double, deep purple flushed deep blue; 'Purple Triumph', violet-blue with a black and gold eye; 'Royal Marine', deep purple; 'Silver Moon', silver-mauve with a white eye; 'Swanlake', pure white with a velvety brown eye; and 'Xenia Field', palest lavender-white with a cream-white eye.

Also grouped under tall varieties are the Pacific Hybrids. This is a race of mainly seed-grown varieties, with good spikes of semi or double flowers on strong 4–6 ft high stems. They range in colour from white, through pink and purple, to blue. Several single-colour strains are available:

'Astolat', shades of lilac and pink; 'Black Night', deep violet; 'Galahad', white; and 'Summer Skies', true blue.

Dwarf varieties (height 3–4½ ft) include: 'Baby Doll', pale mauve, yellow-white eye; 'Blue Tit', indigo-blue with a small black-brown eye; 'Blue Jade', sky-blue with a brown eye; 'Cinderella', mauve-heliotrope.

'Mighty Atom', large florets of deep lavender; 'Page Boy', low-growing, with brilliant mid-blue, white-eyed florets.

The Belladonna varieties (height 3½–4½ ft) are smaller, more branched and graceful plants with wiry stems and looser spikes of cupped florets. Well-grown plants rarely exceed 5 ft with a spread of 18–24 in.

Recommended varieties include: 'Blue Bees', bright pale blue; 'Bonita', gentian-blue; 'Loddon Blue', royal blue; 'Lamartine', deep violet-blue; 'Moerheimii', pure white; 'Pink Sensation', pink; 'Wendy', gentian-blue, flecked purple.

D. grandiflorum. Siberia, China. Height 1–2½ ft; planting distance 12 in. This hardy perennial species has deeply cut, palmately divided, mid-green leaves. The violet-blue, widely funnel-shaped, long-spurred flowers are borne in 9–12 in. long racemes on branching stems in July and August. The variety 'Blue Butterfly' (height 12 in.) has bright blue flowers.

D. nudicaule. California. Height 12 in. or more; planting distance 6–9 in. This tufted, short-lived perennial bears long-stalked, somewhat fleshy, mid-green leaves; each is divided into three toothed or notched leaflets. The red or orange-red flowers are cup-shaped and spurred, up to 1¼ in. long; they are borne in loose panicles from April to July.

D. tatsiense. China. Height 9–15 in.; planting distance 6 in. A short-lived perennial species, suitable for a rock garden. The palmate light

217

Delphinium 'Page Boy'

Delphinium 'Wendy'

Delphinium nudicaule

Delphinium tatsiense

green leaves are deeply cut. Loose branching panicles, about 6 in. long, of deep purple-blue, long-spurred and widely funnel-shaped flowers are produced in June and July.

Cultivation. Plant the perennial species and hybrids from September to March in deep, rich soil. Choose a sunny position, preferably sheltered from prevailing winds.

Stake the plants in April; tall varieties with large flower spikes need stout canes; the dwarf varieties and annuals need only twiggy pea-sticks or in sheltered gardens no support at all. Cut the stems back to the nearest healthy leaf below the raceme after flowering. In favourable summers a second flower crop may occur. Cut all stems back to ground level in autumn.

Set out annual species and varieties in April, or for large, early-flowering plants, sow seeds in the flowering sites in autumn and protect with cloches during winter.

Propagation. The Elatum and Belladonna groups are best increased from basal cuttings, 3–4 in. long, in April. These should be taken close to the rootstock and inserted in equal parts (by volume) peat and sand in a cold frame. When rooted, line the cuttings out in nursery rows and transplant to permanent positions in September.

Alternatively, divide and replant the hybrids in March or April.

All perennial species may be raised from seeds sown in the flowering site in March, April or September; thin the resulting seedlings to the required planting distances.

Delphinium seeds are short-lived and should be sown as soon as possible. If this is not practicable, store the seeds at a temperature of 2–5°C (36–41°F) until sowing.

Seeds of *D. grandiflorum* and *D. tatsiense* may also be sown in pots or pans of seed compost in February at a temperature of 13°C (55°F). Prick off the seedlings into boxes, and harden off in a cold frame. Plant out in permanent positions in April for flowering the same year.

Sow seeds of the annual *D. ajacis* in the flowering site in September, or March and April; thin the seedlings, when large enough to handle, to the necessary planting distances.

Pests. Early growth can be checked by SLUGS which eat the young shoots; they also eat holes in the leaves of older plants.

SNAILS cause similar damage.

Diseases. CROWN ROT and ROOT ROT are caused by several different fungi, including the BLACK ROOT ROT fungus. The roots and crown tissues become black and rotten and the top growth dies away. A similar disease, of unknown origin, sometimes occurs; in this case the inner tissues of the crown also become black and rot away, and the top growth wilts and dies. A hollow centre can be seen if the crown is cut longitudinally.

CUCUMBER MOSAIC and TOMATO SPOTTED WILT VIRUS cause stunting of plants and distortion of the leaves. These show brilliant yellow ring and line patterns, in concentric rings or variable areas of mottling.

POWDERY MILDEW shows as a white powdery coating on leaves, stems and flowers.

STEM ROT can be due to several different fungi, including GREY MOULD. This shows as a grey velvety fungal growth at the base of the stem.

Dendrobium

Orchidaceae

DENDROBIUM NOBILE

One of the largest genera of orchids, with 900 species, widely distributed in tropical Asia from Ceylon to the Samoan and Tongan islands and across to Japan in the north, and to New Zealand in the south. Most are deciduous epiphytes, but the more tropical species are evergreen.

There is great diversity of form in this genus ranging from tiny pseudobulbous plants with one or two flowers to enormous non-bulbous plants with rod-like stems several feet long bearing hundreds of flowers. The flowers are of the same structure, with sepals of equal length, the two lateral ones being joined to the foot of the column to form a chin, or mentum. The petals are usually the same length as the sepals, but may be broader. The lip is extremely variable; it can be fringed, lobed or simple, but is usually keeled

The leaves are mid to dark green and generally oblong to ovate. Dendrobiums from the tropical lowlands up to intermediate altitudes are easy to grow in a warm greenhouse, with plenty of moisture during the growing season and a definite resting period. The species from tropical highlands and temperate regions need a cool greenhouse. A number of hybrids are known.

See also ORCHIDS.

D. aphyllum: see *D. pierardii*

D. aureum, syn. *D. heterocarpum*. N. India to Ceylon and throughout Malesia to the Philippines. A deciduous species with slender, leafy pseudobulbs up to 12 in. high. In January and February flowers, 2 in. across, are produced in groups of two or three from the upper nodes of old leafless stems. They consist of spreading and pointed sepals and petals which are cream-white or yellow; the pointed golden-yellow lip is streaked with red-purple and has a velvety texture. They have a fragrance reminiscent of primroses. Grow in a warm greenhouse.

D. bigibbum. Australia. This evergreen species is the state flower of Queensland. The erect pseudobulbs are slender, up to 18 in. long, with narrow, fleshy, mid-green leaves on the upper half. The inflorescence is a graceful spray at the top of the stem, with five to ten bright rose-purple flowers, about 2 in. across. The sepals are narrow and pointed, the petals broad and rounded. The deep rose-purple lip has a pure white crest. Flowering is during September and October.

The variety *D. b. phalaenopsis* has flowers about 3 in. across, white to rose-purple with a darker red lip. It flowers from August to December and needs no resting phase. Grow these plants in a warm greenhouse at a temperature of 27–29°C (81–84°F) and in a humid atmosphere. Keep them in bright light, but shaded from April to September.

D. brymerianum. Burma. An evergreen species with 12–24 in. high pseudobulbs, slightly swollen in the middle, with two rows of light green leaves. Near the top of each stem arises, from February to March, a few-flowered inflorescence with blooms 3 in. across, on 2 in. stalks. They have narrow, spreading sepals and petals that are golden-yellow with a waxy texture. The side-lobes of the lip are orange with fringed margins. The margin of the mid-lobe is conspicuous, consisting of finely branched filaments, almost as long as the lip itself, giving a gold filigree-like appearance. The column is very short. This plant needs a winter resting phase and warm greenhouse conditions.

D. densiflorum. Himalayas. A deciduous species with club-shaped, four-angled pseudobulbs, up to 12 in. high. Each has about five dark green leaves near the top and a showy drooping inflorescence with 50–100 flowers encircling the stem. The flowers open from March to May; they measure 2 in. across and have broad sepals and petals that are pure golden-yellow with a sparkling, crystalline texture. The lip is almost circular, slightly concave and velvety within, coloured a deeper gold than the petals. Grow this species in a warm greenhouse, moving to cool dry conditions during the resting period.

D. d. albo-lutea: see *D. thyrsiflorum*

D. fimbriatum. Nepal to Burma. This deciduous species has pendulous slender pseudobulbs up to 4 ft long with two rows of mid-green leaves along the entire length. The flowers are borne from March to May on two or three-year-old stems, in pendulous sprays of 12–20 flowers, each 2 in. across. The broad, rounded sepals and petals are light orange-yellow. The lip is nearly circular, of a crystalline texture, deep orange-yellow with pale yellow lacerated margins.

D. f. oculatum has a large maroon patch at the centre of the lip; it is free-flowering.

Grow both plants in a warm greenhouse.

D. gouldii: see *D. veratrifolium*

D. heterocarpum: see *D. aureum*

D. kingianum. New South Wales, Queensland. A dainty evergreen species with club-shaped pseudobulbs, 2–4 in. high, which narrow towards the apex. Each bears about five dark green leathery leaves at its tip. The inflorescence is apical with two to six flowers, nearly 1 in. across; they are produced in April and May. The sepals and petals are tinged with rose-red or purple, and the petals are narrower than the sepals. The mentum is yellow at the top, and the lip is deep violet with white margins and green-white keels.

D. k. album has pseudobulbs 6–12 in. long, with pure white flowers. The species and its variety thrive in a cool greenhouse.

D. loddigesii, syn. *D. pulchellum.* China. This deciduous species can be grown as an indoor basket plant in a bright, not too sunny window. It has slender, pendulous pseudobulbs with numerous oblong dark green leaves. The delicate flowers are solitary, 1½ in. across, and borne at intervals along the stem from February to April. The petals are broader than the sepals; both are pale rose-lilac to bright rose-red. The lip is orbicular, white with an orange-yellow throat and purple-fringed margins. Warm or intermediate greenhouse conditions are necessary.

Dendrobium fimbriatum oculatum

D. moschatum. India, Burma. Erect, slender and leafy pseudobulbs, up to 5 ft high, bear leathery evergreen leaves. A pendulous inflorescence arises from the upper part of each of the previous year's stems; it appears from May to July and is composed of 7–15 flowers, each up to 3 in. across. They have a strong musky scent. The sepals and petals are pale yellow or light orange with light purple veins; the petals are broader than the sepals. The cup-shaped lip is downy, pale yellow with two maroon patches at the base and with five yellow, fringed keels.

D. m. cupreum has light orange flowers without purple veining. These plants need ample light in a warm greenhouse.

D. nobile. N.E. India to S. China. This evergreen species needs plenty of light and can be grown on a window-sill if given warmth. The bright green leaves grow on cylindrical pseudobulbs which are swollen at the nodes and up to 18 in. high. The flowers measure 2–3 in. across and appear in profusion from January to March at most of the nodes in groups of two or three. The sepals are narrow and pointed, the petals broader and rounded, white at the base, then grading to mauve at the tips. The lip is broad and downy with a dark maroon throat surrounded by a white or yellow zone which ends in a purple patch.

There are more than 80 varieties: 'Album' is a pure white form with a deep purple throat. These plants require an intermediate greenhouse, but do better if extra heat can be given until the pseudobulbs have matured. Thereafter move to a cooler greenhouse and water sparingly.

D. pierardii, syn. *D. aphyllum.* N.E. India to Malesia. A species with slender pendulous pseudobulbs, 24 in. or more long, covered with sheaths of dark green, ovate, deciduous leaves. The flowers are borne on old stems after the leaves have fallen, usually in April and May. The

Dendrobium brymerianum

Dendrobium densiflorum

short-stemmed, three-flowered inflorescences are produced at the nodes along almost the whole length of the stem. The flowers are 2 in. across, and both sepals and petals are broad and a delicate translucent mauve-pink. The lip is cup-shaped, downy inside, cream-white or pale yellow with fine purple veins at the base. This species requires a warm greenhouse, a humid atmosphere and a moderate resting period.

D. primulinum. Himalayas. The pseudobulbs of this deciduous species may be erect or drooping, 12–18 in. long; they are stout and leafy. Fragrant flowers, 2–3 in. across, appear in February and March at the upper nodes, either singly or in pairs. They have narrow, waxy, pale mauve-lilac sepals and petals. The lip is downy, flat and nearly circular, pale primrose-yellow with some purple streaks in the throat.

D. p. giganteum is larger in all its parts. Grow these plants in an intermediate greenhouse.

D. pulchellum: see *D. loddigesii*

D. speciosum. Coastal regions of E. Australia. A robust evergreen species with spindle-shaped pseudobulbs, 1–1½ in. thick and up to 18 in. high. At the top grow three or four leathery, glossy, dark green leaves and a 24 in. long spike of densely set, fragrant flowers. They are borne from February to April and are ¾–1½ in. across with narrow cream-yellow sepals and petals. The lip is white with purple spots. Grow this species in a cool to intermediate greenhouse.

D. thyrsiflorum, syn. *D. densiflorum albo-lutea.* Burma. This deciduous species resembles *D. densiflorum* but has narrower pseudobulbs, up to 18 in. high, with more numerous oblong deep green leaves. The flowers, 1½–2 in. across, have white translucent sepals and petals and orange-yellow lips; they are borne in large pendulous trusses of up to 100 flowers from March to May. Grow in an intermediate greenhouse.

D. veratrifolium, botanically known as *D. gouldii.* New Guinea, Solomon Islands and New Hebrides. This species has evergreen leaves on slender pseudobulbs about 12 in. high, with erect 2–3 ft long inflorescences at their tips. The flowers, with a keeled lower lip and spathulate sepals, are about 1½ in. wide and appear in various numbers, from September to November.

The name *D. gouldii* is given to the brown and yellow-flowered forms whilst *D. veratrifolium* is restricted to the mauve and white-flowered plants. They all need a warm greenhouse.

D. victoriae-reginae. Philippines. This evergreen species grows well on a raft, but can be grown upright with staking. The slender 6–12 in. long pseudobulbs are pendulous, wiry at the base and swollen above. The upper half is covered with sheaths of dark green leaves.

Two to five-flowered inflorescences are produced laterally from the older leafless stems at the same time as the new leafy shoots, from April to October. The flowers are more than 1 in. across with broad purple-blue sepals and petals shading to white at the base. The mentum is dark violet; the violet-blue lip has a white, purple-streaked throat. Grow in an intermediate greenhouse.

D. wardianum. Assam, Burma. The pseudobulbs of this species are about 24 in. long and swollen at the nodes. They bear deciduous leaves. Smooth waxy flowers, 3–4 in. across, are produced in

May in pairs at the upper nodes, 30 or 40 to a pseudobulb; the sepals and petals are white with purple tips, the petals twice as broad as the sepals. The concave lip is white with a bright yellow throat, two deep maroon spots at the base and a deep purple tip.

'Album' is a pure white form with a yellow throat. Grow in an intermediate greenhouse.

Cultivation. Grow dendrobiums in 2½–5 in. pots or in 3–5 in. pans, depending on size of plant; use a compost of 3 parts osmunda fibre and 1 part sphagnum moss (parts by volume).

After mid-March shade all dendrobiums. At first, shade only at mid-day but gradually increase this to six or seven hours on hot days in mid-summer; decrease from August and remove the shading altogether before October. Adjust the ventilation to allow a gentle but not draughty circulation of air night and day when the outside temperature is above freezing.

Warm-house species require a minimum winter temperature of 16°C (61°F); intermediate 13°C (55°F), cool 5°C (41°F). Dendrobiums need a resting period from November to March, with temperatures lowered by 2·5°C (5°F) and just enough water to keep the surface compost moist; water freely in the growing season. Damp down the greenhouse floor and staging three or four times a day in hot weather.

Propagation. Divide and repot when the new growths are starting to put out roots, usually shortly after flowering.

Pests. Leaves may be infested by APHIDS, particularly the orchid aphid. These produce white-fringed black scales and make the plants sticky and sooty. Other aphids infest the flowers.

Diseases. Unsuitable cultural conditions cause PHYSIOLOGICAL DISORDERS which result in various types of leaf spotting or general discoloration. Affected areas may be entered by secondary fungi which cause rotting of the tissues.

Denmoza rhodacanthus: see *Echinopsis rhodocantha*

Deodar: see *Cedrus deodara*

Desfontainea
Loganiaceae

DESFONTAINEA SPINOSA

A genus of one species of evergreen shrub from S. America. It is moderately hardy, and suitable for cultivation outdoors in all but the coldest areas.

D. spinosa. Chile, Peru. Height and spread 5 ft or more. A dense, compact shrub of slow growth. The shiny, dark green, holly-like leaves are borne on erect stems. The 1½ in. long, scarlet and yellow waxy flowers appear in June and July and are borne singly from the leaf axils; they are slender, trumpet-shaped and pendulous.

Dendrobium loddigesii

Dendrobium nobile

Dendrobium victoriae-reginae

Dendrobium wardianum

Cultivation. Plant in September or April in a cool, peaty soil. These shrubs do best in partial shade, in a sheltered position or against a wall.

Propagation. Take cuttings, 3–4 in. long, of lateral non-flowering shoots, with a heel, during July and August; insert the cuttings in equal parts (by volume) peat and sand in a propagating frame with a bottom heat of 16–18°C (61–64°F). Pot when rooted in 3 in. pots of John Innes potting compost No. 1 and overwinter in a frost-free frame or greenhouse; pot on into 4–5 in. pots during summer and grow on for a further year before planting out in permanent positions.

Pruning. None required.

Pests and diseases. Generally trouble-free.

Deutzia

Philadelphaceae, syn. *Saxifragaceae*

DEUTZIA × ELEGANTISSIMA

A genus of about 50 species of deciduous flowering shrubs, native to China, Japan, the Himalayas and Mexico. The leaves are alternate and the bark is usually brown, eventually peeling. These shrubs, with their freely borne, white, pink or purple flowers, make handsome garden plants. They are fully hardy, although young growths may be damaged by late spring frosts.

D. × elegantissima. Height and spread 4–5 ft. A hybrid between *D. purpurascens* and *D. sieboldiana.* This shrub, of upright, bushy habit, is suitable for a small garden. The lanceolate leaves are slender-pointed, and matt green. Fragrant, star-shaped, pink to pale rose-purple flowers, 2–3 in. wide, are borne in panicles on the arching branches in May and June. 'Fasciculata' has bright rose-pink flowers.

D. gracilis. Japan. Height 3–4 ft; spread 4–6 ft. A bushy shrub with mid-green lanceolate leaves that are toothed and end in slender points. The pure white, star-shaped flowers are borne in erect racemes or panicles, about 3 in. long, in June. This species is the parent of many hybrids.

D. × hybrida. Height 4–6 ft; spread 4–8 ft. Many fine hybrids have been grouped under this name, particularly those derived from *D. longifolia.* They are of bushy habit with lanceolate, pale to mid-green leaves. They usually flower in June and July, the round clusters of star-shaped flowers being 2–3 in. across.

'Contraste' has loose panicles, rich purple on the outside and delicate lilac-pink within; 'Jaconde' is a strong-growing form with large rose-purple flowers; 'Magician' is tall-growing and has large mauve-pink flowers edged with white and tinged purple on the reverse; 'Mont Rose' is vigorous with erect arching stems, the open, rich rose-purple flowers have dark shadings and become paler as they fade; 'Perle Rose' is a graceful form with panicles of soft rose flowers.

D. × kalmiiflora. Height 5–6 ft; spread 4–6 ft. A hybrid between *D. parviflora* and *D. purpurascens,* with graceful arching branches. The mid to deep green leaves are ovate-oblong to ovate-lanceolate. Clusters of 5–12 starry flowers, ¾–1 in. across, white inside and deep rose on the reverse, are borne in June.

D. × magnifica. Height up to 8 ft; spread 6–8 ft. A vigorous hybrid between *D. scabra* and *D. vilmorinae,* with upright stems and ovate-oblong grey-green leaves that are rough to the touch. White, double, pompon-like flowers appear in June, packed in broad, erect panicles, 3 in. high.

D. monbeigii. China. Height 4–6 ft; spread 4–5 ft. The ovate-lanceolate leaves are dull green above, white and hairy beneath. Star-shaped white flowers, in round panicles 2–3 in. wide, are produced in June.

D. × rosea. Height and spread 3 ft. This hybrid between *D. gracilis* and *D. purpurascens* is of compact habit, with arching branches. The dull green leaves are ovate-lanceolate to ovate-oblong. Open bell-shaped, soft rose flowers are borne in rounded clusters, 2–3 in. across, in June and July. 'Campanulata' has white flowers with purple calyces; 'Carminea' has rose-pink flowers.

D. scabra. China, Japan. Height 6–10 ft; spread 4–6 ft. A bushy species with erect branches and attractive, peeling, brown bark. The ovate to ovate-lanceolate leaves are pale to mid-green. The cup-shaped flowers are in erect panicles, 3–6 in. long, usually white but sometimes flushed pink outside; they appear in June and July. The species has produced a number of forms, of which the following are recommended: 'Candidissima', double white flowers; 'Codsall Pink', double purple-pink flowers; 'Plena', double white flowers suffused with rose-purple.

D. setchuenensis. China. Height up to 6 ft; spread 3–4 ft. A graceful shrub with brown peeling bark and dull green ovate-lanceolate leaves that are finely toothed and have downy undersides. The star-shaped white flowers, which are borne in June and July, are in corymbs, 2–3 in. across. The variety *D. s. corymbiflora* has 4 in. wide corymbs; each flower is more than ½ in. across.

Cultivation. Plant deutzias from October to February during suitable weather in any ordinary well-drained garden soil. They grow well in full sun, but also under light woodland conditions where the varieties with coloured flowers retain their colour better. Avoid planting in open positions with northerly aspects.

Propagation. Take cuttings, 3–4 in. long, of semi-ripe lateral shoots in July and August; insert the cuttings in equal parts (by volume) peat and sand in a cold frame. The following April or May line out the rooted cuttings in nursery rows outdoors and grow on until the following autumn when they may be planted out.

Alternatively, take hardwood cuttings, 10–12 in. long, of lateral shoots in October; insert the cuttings in a nursery bed outdoors and plant out one year later.

Pruning. Remove old flowering stems at ground level in July to encourage new growths.

Pests. Generally trouble-free.

Diseases. The flowers may develop poorly because of a PHYSIOLOGICAL DISORDER which may be due to cold weather or lack of vigour.

Desfontainea spinosa

Deutzia × elegantissima

Deutzia gracilis

Deutzia × hybrida 'Magician'

Dianthus 'Charles Musgrave' (Old-fashioned pink)

Dianthus 'London Poppet' (Modern pink)

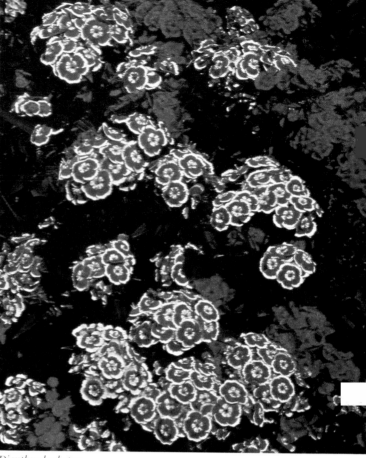

Dianthus barbatus

Dianthus 'Sweet Wivelsfield'

Dianthus caesius

DIANTHUS
Pinks and carnations. *Caryophyllaceae*

A genus of 300 species of annuals and evergreen perennials, the latter mainly low-growing sub-shrubs. The genus, which includes the well-known carnations, pinks and sweet williams, is generally characterised by tufted, cushion-forming mats with linear or narrowly lanceolate leaves. These are usually pointed and often blue or grey-green in colour. The salver-shaped flowers, which rise from tubular calyces, are excellent for cutting.

Most of the forms of hardy dianthus, grown in annual and herbaceous borders and beds, are of hybrid origin. Several hardy dwarf species, with their compact cushion-forming growth, are ideal for rock gardens and dry walls.

The perpetual-flowering carnations—the double-flowered florists' forms—are tender perennials and require greenhouse cultivation.

Dianthi have been famous since classical times for the beauty of their flowers and, in many cases, for their scent. The grey-green foliage of many perennials is attractive in winter, but some species and varieties tend to be short-lived. This necessitates frequent propagation, generally every three or four years.

The plants are tolerant of alkaline soils, and lime was once thought to be a necessity. Although this has been proved wrong, dianthus should be grown in soil that is not too acid. They are tolerant of salt spray and a smoke-polluted atmosphere.

Most species hybridise easily, and there are numerous cultivated forms. These include garden pinks, annual and border carnations, and the perpetual-flowering carnations.

SPECIES
These hardy perennials are suitable for growing on rock gardens or at the front of herbaceous borders. For detailed advice on cultivation and propagation see also GARDEN PINKS.

D. × allwoodii: see MODERN PINKS

D. alpinus. Austrian Alps. Height 4 in.; planting distance 6 in. This species forms mid to deep green mats of foliage and bears 1–1½ in. wide flowers from late May to August. The colour varies from pale pink to purple, with a white eye and purple spots. 'Albus' has white flowers.

This short-lived species is variable, and should be raised from seeds. Propagate good forms from cuttings every two years.

**. *arenarius*. N. Europe. Height 8–12 in.; plant-
ng distance 6 in. A dense mat-forming species
with green or grey-green leaves. The fragrant
owers, about 1 in. across, are white with
ringed petals and a green eye; they are borne
rom June to August. The plant will grow in
partially shaded position.

**. × *arvernensis*. Auvergne, France. Height and
lanting distance 6 in. This plant resembles a
ompact-growing *D. caesius*, and is probably a
ybrid or form of that species. Numerous pink,
ragrant flowers appear from May to August.

Another hybrid is frequently listed under the
ame name; it has large purple flowers on stems
2–20 in. high. Height and colour of the plant
hould be checked before buying.

DIANTHUS BARBATUS

. *barbatus* (sweet william). E. Europe. Height
2–24 in.; planting distance 8–10 in. Although a
hort-lived perennial, this well-known border
lant is often grown as a hardy biennial from
eeds. It bears densely packed flattened heads,
3–5 in. across, of single or double flowers during
une and July. These are in various colours from
vhite to red, or marked with other colours;
hose known as annulatus, or auricula-eyed, are
oloured in concentric zones.

The species has been crossed with *D. × all-
voodii* to produce the hybrid strain 'Sweet
Wivelsfield', which has looser and larger flower
heads, sometimes 7–8 in. across. It has a greater
ange of colour than the sweet william.

This species and its hybrids are best grown in
roups in a herbaceous border. They thrive in a
unny position, in any ordinary, well-drained
oil; acid soils should be dressed with lime.
taking is unnecessary unless the soil is rich or
he position windy. If the flower stems are
emoved immediately after flowering the plants
vill bloom again the following year.

Sow seeds thinly in the open ground and
ransplant the seedlings to the flowering positions in October. Alternatively, for flowering the
ame year, sow under glass in March at a
emperature of 13°C (55°F). Prick out the seed-
ings 3 in. apart in boxes of John Innes potting
compost No. 1 and grow on at a temperature of
10°C (50°F). Harden off and plant out in May.

. *caesius* (Cheddar pink). Europe, including
Great Britain. Height 4–12 in.; planting distance
9–12 in. This variable native species is now
correctly known as *D. gratianopolitanus*. It
makes an excellent plant for a rock garden and is
onger-lived than most other dianthus species.
The creeping rooting stems may ultimately form
a mat up to 24 in. across.

The leaves are grey-green, and the fragrant,
ringed flowers, 1 in. or more across, are pink.
They are freely borne from May to July. 'La
Bourboulle' and the double 'Flore-pleno' have
horter flower stems and clear pink flowers.

Dianthus alpinus

D. × *calalpinus*. Garden origin. Height 3 in.;
planting distance 6 in. An easily grown hybrid
between *D. alpinus* and the rare and difficult *D.
callizonus*. In habit and leaf form it resembles *D.
alpinus*. The fragrant flowers, up to 1½ in. across,
are pink with a white dotted zone in the centre;
they open from June to August.

D. *chinensis*, syn. *D. sinensis* (Indian pink). E.
Asia. Height 9 in.; planting distance 6 in. The
true species is seldom grown, but there are
several cultivated annuals and short-lived perennials derived from it. The leaves are pale to
mid-green and there are single and double-
flowered strains, self-coloured or in mixtures.
Individual flowers, 1½ in. or more across, may
have intricate markings on the petals. Flowering
is from July until the first autumn frosts.

Good established forms include: 'Bravo',
bright red; 'Fireball', double scarlet; 'Gaiety'
and 'Gaiety Double', mixed colours; 'Heddewigii', single or double mixed; and 'Snowball',
large double white. 'Baby Doll', a new dwarf
strain of mixed colours, grows up to 6 in.

Indian pinks thrive in a sunny position in
well-drained alkaline or neutral soil. Remove the
dead flowers to ensure a long flowering period.

These hardy plants are usually raised annually
from seeds. Sow the seeds thinly outdoors in
mid-April where the plants are to flower and
thin the seedlings to 6 in. apart.

Dianthus chinensis 'Bravo'

Dianthus chinensis
'Heddewigii'

For earlier blooming, sow in boxes of seed compost in September and overwinter the seedlings in a frost-free frame. Alternatively, sow under glass in March at a temperature of 13°C (55°F), and plant out in May.

D. carthusianorum. Central Europe. Height 1–3 ft; planting distance 12 in. A border plant with lanky stems and sparse mid-green foliage. The magenta-pink flowers, usually $\frac{1}{2}$–$\frac{3}{4}$ in. across, are borne in dense rounded terminal clusters which appear from June to September. *D. c. multiflorus* reaches a height of 2–3 ft and bears up to 70 flowers in each head.

D. caryophyllus (carnation, gilliflower, clove-pink). W. and S. France. Height 9 in.; planting distance 18 in. This species is the main progenitor of the border and perpetual-flowering carnations and has the typical bright grey-green foliage. The flowers are about 1–$1\frac{1}{2}$ in. across, usually dull purple; they are borne in July on 24 in. high stems which need staking. They have a strong, sweet, clove fragrance.

D. deltoides (maiden pink). Europe. Height 6–9 in.; planting distance 4 in. This species is suitable for a rock garden and for crevices in paving. The narrow leaves are mid to deep green, sometimes with a red or purple flush. The flowers, $\frac{1}{2}$–$\frac{3}{4}$ in. across, are freely produced from June to autumn, with colours varying from red through pink to white.

The plant will thrive in any well-drained soil or site, except in complete shade. It seeds itself freely, but unwanted seedlings are easily pulled out. Cultivated varieties come fairly true from seeds, unless they are grown near other varieties, in which case they may hybridise.

Good cultivated varieties include: 'Albus', white; 'Brilliant', bright rose-pink; 'Flashing Light', bright crimson; and 'Wisley Variety', carmine-red with dark green foliage.

D. gratianopolitanus: see *D. caesius*

Dianthus deltoides

Dianthus 'Dad's Favourite' (Old-fashioned pink)

Dianthus 'Inchmery' (Old-fashioned pink)

Dianthus haematocalyx

D. haematocalyx. Greece. Height 6–12 in.; planting distance 4 in. A species with grey-green leaves which form a cushion 3 in. high. Branching, 6–9 in. stems bear flowers about $\frac{3}{4}$ in. across, over an extended period from July onwards. The calyx is larger than in most species and blood-red in colour; the petals are rose-purple above with a yellow reverse.

The dwarf variety *D. h. alpinus* (height 3–4 in.) should probably correctly be listed as *D. pindicola*. It is easy to grow and usually comes true from seeds.

D. knappii. Hungary. Height 10–15 in.; planting distance 4 in. This is an unusual species suitable for a rock garden or a border. The leaves are pale or slightly grey-green. The flower colour, bright sulphur-yellow with a mauve spot at the base of each petal, is rare in the genus.

The flowers are about $\frac{1}{2}$ in. across and are borne in clusters in June at the end of long stems which may need staking in exposed situations. The plant may die after flowering, but it comes true from seeds and is best treated as a biennial.

Dianthus neglectus

D. neglectus. S.W. Europe. Height 4–9 in.; planting distance 6 in. This species is extremely variable both in the wild and in cultivation; the better forms make attractive rock-garden plants. They form dense grey-green tufts and flower in July and August; they vary from pale pink to deep crimson with a buff reverse.

In the best forms the flowers are $1\frac{1}{4}$ in. across with overlapping petals of a good clear pink or crimson on stems only about 1 in. long. Plants should be obtained from a reliable nursery or grown from seeds, the inferior seedlings being rejected. Propagate good forms from cuttings.

D. noeanus. Bulgaria, Turkey. Height 8–12 in.; planting distance 6–8 in. This long-lived species is sometimes listed as *Acanthophyllum spinosum*. It forms a dense hummock of sharp-pointed, grass-like, mid-green leaves, and is suitable for wall crevices or a rock garden. The $\frac{1}{2}$ in. wide, deeply fringed white flowers are borne from July onwards on arching stems in clusters of between two and five. The scent is exceptionally strong in hot weather.

D. pindicola: see *D. haematocalyx alpinus*

D. plumarius (pink). S.W. Europe. In the wild form this species resembles *D. caesius*, but the petals are more deeply fringed. The true wild *D. plumarius* is seldom seen and may prove difficult to obtain. It is mentioned because it is a parent of the garden pinks.

D. sinensis: see *D. chinensis*

D. superbus. Europe, N. Asia to Japan. Height 9–18 in.; planting distance 6 in. This tufted species has mid-green leaves. The shorter forms are suitable for a rock garden; the taller ones which require staking, for a herbaceous border.

The strongly fragrant flowers, $1\frac{1}{2}$ in. or more across, are pale to deep lilac, occasionally white and are produced from July onwards on branching stems. The petals have a green spot at the base and are deeply fringed. The species is short-lived and develops straggly stems; it is best treated as a biennial and raised as described for *D. barbatus*.

The hybrid 'Loveliness', the result of a cross with *D.* × *allwoodii*, is a better plant, having stronger stems, a wider colour range and a stronger fragrance. This hybrid, too, is best treated as a biennial. Both species and hybrid will tolerate more shade and thrive in a damper soil than most other dianthus species.

GARDEN PINKS

The hybrids described here are believed to be descended, at least in part, from *D. plumarius*. They have grey-green leaves and single or double flowers, 1–2 in. across, with smooth or fringed edges to the petals. The main colour groups are: 1. Selfs (one colour only); 2. Bi-colours (an outer zone of one colour and a central zone or eye of another colour); 3. Laced pinks (the central zone extended to form a loop round each petal); and 4. Fancies (with irregular markings). These flower types are found in all groups of pinks.

Old-fashioned pinks. Height 10–15 in.; planting distance 9–12 in. This group of border plants includes some old favourites and also some newer ones with the same habit of growth, which is slower than that of modern pinks. They need propagating only every four or five years and should not normally be stopped. Those listed flower in June only and, except where stated, are double.

'Charles Musgrave' (syn. 'Musgrave's Pink'), single, white with a green eye; 'Dad's Favourite', white ground, laced purple; 'Emil Paré', deep pink, long-flowering; 'Excelsior' (syn. 'Pink Mrs Sinkins'), carmine with a darker eye; 'Inchmery', pale pink; 'Ipswich Crimson', deep crimson; 'Isolde', palest pink, irregularly laced purple; 'Mrs Sinkins', white; and 'Whiteladies', a better, stronger-growing white.

Modern pinks. Height 10–15 in.; planting distance 9–12 in. By crossing an old-fashioned pink with a perpetual-flowering carnation, the hybrid *D.* × *allwoodii* was produced. This became the parent of modern pinks.

These border plants are faster-growing than the old-fashioned pinks; they produce many more blooms, mainly during June and July, and usually flower again in September and October. They must be propagated more often, normally every two or three years. Except where stated, those listed are double.

Good border varieties, which are also suitable for exhibition, include: 'Cherryripe', bright cherry-pink; 'Daphne', single, pale pink with a crimson eye; 'Diane', salmon-red; 'Doris', palest salmon-pink; 'Freckles', silver-pink with red flecks; 'London Poppet', palest pink with a ruby-red eye and lacing; 'Prudence', palest pink with a crimson eye and lacing; 'Show Beauty', deep rose-pink with a maroon eye; 'Show Pearl', almost pure white; and 'Show Portrait', crimson.

Good miniature hybrids (height 3–6 in.; planting distance 6–9 in.) for the rock garden include: 'Bombardier', red; 'Fay', single mauve; 'Little Jock', pink; 'Mercury', cyclamen-pink with a maroon eye; 'Pluto', white with a purple eye; 'Spencer Bickham', single pink; and 'Wisp', single white with a purple eye.

Cultivation of species and garden pinks. When grown on rock gardens, the species and miniature hybrids require the sunniest positions available and good drainage. Cultivation is as for pinks grown in borders, but in less-rich soil. Feeding is not advisable.

In a border, the species and garden pinks should be in a sunny position. Dig the soil one spit deep, and work in a light dressing of well-rotted farmyard manure or compost. Raise the bed 6 in. above the level of the surrounding soil if the drainage is poor. Make a soil test and apply lime if the pH is below 6·5.

Rake bone-meal at 4 oz. per sq. yd into the surface just prior to setting out the plants in March or from September to November. Plant firmly and, to avoid stem rot, bury as little as possible of the stems. If the plants tend to sway when first planted, secure them temporarily to 6 in. stakes with thin wire rings.

With spring planting, water the plants during dry spells. With autumn planting, ensure that leaves or rubbish do not collect round the base of the plants during winter. In spring, apply sulphate of potash at 2 oz. per sq. yd to young plants and water it in. Apply a proprietary high-potash fertiliser to old plants in March at the rate recommended by the manufacturers.

In March or April, stop any young pinks that run to flower without making good side-shoots, by breaking off the top of the main shoots just above a joint.

Tops snap off best in the early morning during damp weather. Stopping delays flowering in modern pinks, and may prevent old-fashioned pinks from flowering for a season; but it is essential to build up good side-growths before flowers are produced.

Old plants seldom require stopping, as they usually make good side-shoots. If they do not produce such growths, remove one-third of the flower stems.

Large pinks sometimes need staking. Insert branched twigs in the soil in April or May so that they are 4–6 in. above the plants. The flower stems will grow through them.

For cut flowers, pinks should be picked early in the morning and stood up to their necks in water for four hours before being arranged.

After flowering, remove old flower stems completely, water the plants thoroughly, and apply a proprietary high-potash fertiliser.

Pinks generally need less water than most plants; in excessively dry weather, unless they are in bloom, give them a good soaking at 5 gal. per sq. yd. Do not use organic mulches, as these may cause stem rot.

Modern pinks may bloom up to Christmas in mild weather. After Christmas, remove all bud-bearing stems or they will produce poor blooms in early spring and retard summer flowering.

Propagation of species and garden pinks. The species plants generally come true from seeds, but named varieties and most pinks show great variation from seminal propagation. However, raising plants from seeds is an easy and cheap

Dianthus 'Mrs Sinkins' (Old-fashioned pink)

Dianthus 'Whiteladies' (Old-fashioned pink)

Dianthus 'Daphne' (Modern pink)

Dianthus 'Diane' (Modern pink)

method of obtaining numbers of plants, the best of which can later be propagated vegetatively.

Between mid-April and July—the earlier the better—sow seeds thinly in boxes of seed compost in a cold greenhouse or frame. When the first true leaves appear, prick out the seedlings, in boxes of John Innes potting compost No. 1 and grow on. When the young plants are well-developed, set in the flowering site.

Increase named varieties and good forms by cuttings taken between June and early August. Select vigorous side-shoots, 3–4 in. long, and insert in equal parts (by volume) peat, loam and sand in a shaded cold frame. Pot the rooted cuttings individually into 3½ in. pots of John Innes potting compost No. 1, or plant directly in the flowering sites.

Layer side-shoots between June and August as described under BORDER CARNATIONS.

BORDER CARNATIONS

Height 2–3 ft; planting distance 15–18 in. These hardy perennial border plants have grey-green leaves and double, often scented flowers with smooth-edged petals about 2 in. across. The main divisions are selfs (one colour only), fancies (more than one colour) and picotees (a ground of pale colour with an edge of a darker colour). These divisions are further sub-divided for exhibition purposes.

The flowering period is during July in the south and during August in the north; the plants flower only once in the season. Firm staking is needed. The plants are short-lived, and are best discarded and replaced after two years.

DIANTHUS (BORDER CARNATION)

The following is a representative selection: 'Beauty of Cambridge', yellow; 'Catherine Glover', yellow, flecked scarlet; 'Consul', apricot; 'Eva Humphries', white-ground picotee with dark wine-red edging; 'Fiery Cross', scarlet; 'Harmony', grey, flecked cerise; 'Imperial Clove', violet-carmine, scented; 'Lavender Clove', lavender, scented; 'Leslie Rennison', purple overlaid rose, scented; 'Merlin Clove', white, marked crimson, scented; 'Perfect Clove', deep crimson, scented; 'Robin Thain', white, marked crimson, scented; 'Santa Claus', yellow-ground picotee, heavy purple edge; 'Thomas Lee', pale-yellow ground picotee, edged and flecked with scarlet; and 'Zebra', maize-yellow, marked crimson.

ANNUAL CARNATIONS

Height 18 in.; planting distance 12 in. These are half-hardy perennials, grown as annuals; they are not recommended for cold areas in the north. They bear grey-green leaves and double flowers, 1½–2 in. across, and make excellent bedding plants, flowering from July to the autumn frosts.

Most seedsmen offer special selections, in mixed and a range of single colours. 'Chabaud' and 'Grenadin' are recommended strains.

Dianthus 'Doris'
(Modern pink)

Dianthus 'Prudence'
(Modern pink)

Dianthus 'Show Beauty'
(Modern pink)

Dianthus 'Show Pearl'
(Modern pink)

Dianthus 'Merlin Clove' (Border carnation)

Dianthus 'Thomas Lee' (Border carnation)

Cultivation of border and annual carnations. These plants thrive in the same type of soil and under the same conditions as described for SPECIES and GARDEN PINKS. Plant hardy perennials in March or in September and October and annual carnations in May.

In May, insert a 3 ft bamboo cane along each border carnation and secure the single stems of first-year plants with thin wire rings; older plants need proprietary wire rings, which clip on to the stakes and encircle the whole plant, or loops of string tied round the stems.

Do not stop these carnations, but disbud the flower stems in June. The main stem of young border carnations has a crown bud at the top and side-shoots with buds at their tips. Older plants with several main stems may not have side-shoots. Retain the crown bud and the end buds on the side-shoots, but remove all other buds.

Do not apply fertilisers to border carnations after flowering. Feeding may encourage an inferior second crop of flower stems in autumn.

Propagation of border and annual carnations. Sow seeds of border carnations from April to June as for SPECIES and GARDEN PINKS.

Sow seeds of annual carnations thinly in pans or boxes of John Innes seed compost in January or February and maintain a temperature of 15°C (59°F). After germination, reduce the temperature to 10°C (50°F). Prick out in boxes of John Innes potting compost No. 1, harden off in a cold frame and plant outdoors in May.

Increase border carnations by layering in July and August. Young plants provide the best layers, but should not be spoilt by using too many shoots as layers. After six weeks, sever the layers from the parent plants, cutting close to the layers; after a further three or four weeks, the plantlets may be lifted for planting out.

PERPETUAL-FLOWERING CARNATIONS

The familiar double-flowered, often fragrant, and grey-green-leaved carnations seen in florists' shops are grown as greenhouse perennials to provide cut flowers throughout the year.

The production of flowers in winter is determined by the minimum temperature in the greenhouse. At 1°C (34°F), the plants survive but make no growth and are late starting in the spring. At 5°C (41°F), the plants will grow, but produce only a few blooms; at 7°C (45°F), a fair number of good winter blooms are produced. At 10°C (50°F), flower production is prolific.

The following varieties provide a good colour range. White: 'Fragrant Ann' or 'Northwood'; cream: 'Allwood's Cream'; pink: 'Paris' or 'Bailey's Splendour'; cerise: 'Viking' or 'Canup's Pride'; salmon: 'Tetra' or 'Laddie Sim'; scarlet: 'Majestic' or 'Jumbo Sim'; crimson: 'Aleck Sparkes' or 'Joker'; yellow: 'Brigadoon'; mauve-purple: 'Margaret'. Fancy varieties include 'Arthur Sim', white, marked red, and 'Zuni', cerise, flecked crimson-maroon.

Cultivation of perpetual-flowering carnations. In the greenhouse, these plants require full light and adequate ventilation.

Ideally the staging should be 3 ft from the ground on one side to take first-year plants, and a few inches from the ground on the other side to take second-year plants. Maintain a minimum winter temperature of 7°C (45°F).

Start young plants or rooted cuttings into growth in February or March, using 2½ in. pots of John Innes potting compost No. 1. When the roots are through to the sides of the pots, pot on into 4 in. pots and later into 6 in. pots using John Innes potting compost No. 2.

Pinch out the growing points when the young plants have made 10–12 pairs of leaves and stop the resulting side-shoots in the same way, leaving five or seven joints on each. A third stopping, up to the middle of June, will result in autumn flowers; stopping from mid-June to mid-July produces winter flowers; and stopping from mid-July to the end of August ensures early spring flowers. If the plants are not ready for a third stopping by mid-July, they can be left to flower in autumn if desired.

The plants should not be allowed to dry out nor to be permanently wet. Damp down the greenhouse staging in hot weather, and apply light shading to the glass from June to September. As the plants increase, support them with wire rings, clipped to stakes.

No feeding is needed until the first flower buds develop; thereafter, apply a proprietary fertiliser, at the rate recommended by the maker, every seven or ten days in summer, once

a month in winter if a temperature of 7°C (45°F) or above is maintained. Overhead spraying once a week in the warmer months is beneficial.

When flower buds develop, remove all but the crown bud on each stem, and on all side-shoots down to the seventh joint from the top. Cut the blooms when they are about three-quarters open. Stand the flowers in deep water for 24 hours before arranging them.

Pot second-year plants that have finished flowering into 8 in. pots in spring, using John Innes potting compost No. 2. Stand the pots on the low staging to bloom for the second year; thereafter plant out in a sheltered place in the garden to flower until the first frosts.

Propagation of perpetual-flowering carnations. Take cuttings of side-shoots from December to February. Choose young healthy plants and detach side-shoots 6–8 in. long, with six or seven fully developed pairs of leaves.

Space the cuttings, 1 in. apart, in pans of sharp sand, inserting them nearly up to the lowest pair of leaves. Place the pans in a closed propagating frame with a temperature of 16–18°C (61–64°F).

When the tops of the cuttings begin to grow, gradually admit more air and reduce the temperature to 10°C (50°F) over a period of a week. During the next fortnight, remove the glass altogether and allow the temperature to fall to that of the greenhouse. Pot the rooted cuttings in 3 in. containers of John Innes potting compost and pot on as necessary.

Sow seeds thinly in pans or boxes of seed compost during January and February, at a temperature of 15°C (59°F). Prick out the seedlings into 3 in. pots and thereafter treat as advised under CULTIVATION. Stop the young plants once only to ensure early blooms.

Pests. APHIDS infest stems, leaves and flower stalks, fouling the plants with honeydew and checking growth; ROOT APHIDS may infest the root systems.

Maggots of the CARNATION FLY tunnel into leaves and stems, particularly on outdoor plants. In severe attacks the plants wilt and die.

BIRDS sometimes peck out the tips of shoots in winter; CATERPILLARS may feed on the leaves.

Under glass, GLASSHOUSE RED SPIDER MITES infest leaves and stems, causing a light mottling, bleaching and, in severe cases, a webbing.

THRIPS infest flowers, under glass and outdoors, and the damaged petals become marked with unsightly flecks.

TORTRIX CATERPILLARS spin the leaves of perpetual-flowering carnations together.

Diseases. CARNATION RING SPOT may infect D. barbatus and border carnations. Circular grey spots erupt into pustules of black-brown spores; the disease may cause leaves to wither, stems to snap and the flowers to be deformed.

CARNATION STEM-ROT AND DIE-BACK occurs on plants under glass; it frequently starts at the cut end of a stalk, which shrivels and turns dark purple-brown. The stem dies back, and the shoots and leaves wither. A pink growth of fungal threads and spores develops on the affected tissues. Internal tissues are not discoloured. Occasionally BASAL ROT of cuttings is caused by the same fungus.

Dianthus 'Show Portrait' (Modern pink)

Dianthus 'Perfect Clove' (Border carnation)

Dianthus 'Zebra' (Border carnation)

Dianthus 'Arthur Sim' (Perpetual carnation)

Dianthus 'Jumbo Sim' (Perpetual carnation)

Dianthus 'Fragrant Ann' (Perpetual carnation)

Dianthus 'Laddie Sim' (Perpetual carnation)

Dianthus 'Zuni' (Perpetual carnation)

Diascia barberae

Dicentra cucullaria

DAMPING-OFF and FOOT ROT cause seedlings and cuttings to collapse.

DIANTHUS LEAF SPOT chiefly affects *D. barbatus*, causing brown spots, frequently with purple margins.

FUSARIUM WILT affects carnations under glass and occasionally outdoor plants, particularly pinks. The leaves become yellow, and the plants wilt; browning of the inner tissues occurs.

GREY MOULD sometimes causes rotting of the blooms of perpetual-flowering carnations; these become covered with a grey mass of spores.

LEAF ROT on species and pinks shows as grey or brown patches on leaves and stems; the leaf bases may be similarly discoloured and may bear small raised bodies of the fungus.

LEAF SPOT shows as brown or white spots, often with purple margins.

LEAFY GALL frequently occurs under glass and shows as a mass of abortive and often fasciated shoots at ground level.

POWDERY MILDEW appears as a white powder on the leaves and occasionally on the calyces of perpetual-flowering carnations.

RHIZOCTONIA commonly causes a collar rot of cuttings in unsterilised compost.

RUST attacks the leaves and stems, producing pustules with dark brown powdery masses of spores; *D. barbatus* and plants under glass are particularly susceptible.

SMUT affects greenhouse plants. The anthers become filled with black spore masses, giving the flowers a sooty appearance. Affected flower buds are shorter and fatter than normal, and diseased plants produce numerous side-shoots.

STEM ROT develops after damping-off, causing the tissues of seedlings to shrink; it shows as a white growth with black spores. On mature plants, white or brown-yellow spots with dark margins develop on stems, leaves and buds.

VERTICILLIUM WILT causes rapid wilting under glass. The foliage turns grey-green at first, but the plants soon dry out and turn straw-coloured. A brown discoloration can be seen in the inner tissues of affected stems.

Diascia

Scrophulariaceae

DIASCIA BARBERAE

A genus of 42 annual and perennial species. The half-hardy annual described here is recommended for edging borders and paths and also as a summer-flowering pot plant, although it is listed by only a few seedsmen.

D. barberae. S. Africa. Height up to 12 in.; planting distance 6 in. A slender, low-growing plant with glossy, dark green, ovate and toothed leaves. The rose-pink flowers, $\frac{3}{4}$ in. across, are shell-like with two spurs. They appear from May to July.

Cultivation. Any light soil in a sunny situation is satisfactory. To encourage branching, pinch out the centres of young plants when they are 2 in. high. When the first flush of flowers is fading, cut back the plants to a height of about 2 in. to encourage the production of new growth and a second flush of flowers. Repeat this treatment after subsequent flushes to prolong flowering until late October.

For flowering under glass, set five or six plants in a 5 in. pot of John Innes potting compost No. 1.

Propagation. Sow the seeds under glass in February or March at a temperature of 16°C (61°F), just covering them. Prick out the seedlings into boxes and then either transplant into 5 in. pots for flowering under glass, or harden off in a cold frame before planting out in May.

Pests and diseases. Generally trouble-free.

Dicentra

syn. **Dielytra**. *Fumariaceae*
(formerly *Papaveraceae*)

DICENTRA FORMOSA   DICENTRA SPECTABILIS

A genus of 20 species of hardy herbaceous perennials. They are graceful plants with arching sprays of pendulous flowers that are basically flattened and bi-lobed, widely to narrowly heart-shaped. They have dissected fern-like foliage, often grey-green.

These are excellent border plants, although *D. spectabilis* dies down completely soon after midsummer; the smaller species also do well on rock gardens.

D. cucullaria. N. America. Height and planting distance 3–6 in. This species has somewhat fleshy, pale to mid-green leaves. Elongated heart-shaped, yellow-tipped flowers, up to 1 in. long, of white or pale rose-purple are borne in nodding racemes from April to June.

D. eximia N. America. Height 12–18 in.; planting distance 12 in. This species has grey-green foliage. Bright rose-pink, narrowly heart-shaped flowers, $\frac{3}{4}$–1 in. long, are borne in drooping racemes from May to September. 'Alba' has pure white flowers.

D. formosa. N. America. Height 12–18 in.; planting distance 18 in. The leaves of this species are bright green. Pink, narrowly heart-shaped flowers, $\frac{3}{4}$–1 in. long, are produced in arching racemes during May and June.

'Bountiful' bears plump, deep pink flowers from April to June and usually has a smaller display again in autumn.

D. spectabilis (bleeding heart). China, Japan. Height $1\frac{1}{2}$–$2\frac{1}{2}$ ft; planting distance 18 in. A species with grey-green leaves. The rose-red heart-shaped flowers, 1 in long, have glistening white protruding inner petals. The flowers are borne in arching racemes in May and June.

Dicentra eximia

Cultivation. Plant between October and March in any well-drained garden soil enriched with peat, leaf-mould or compost, and in a position sheltered from late spring frosts and strong winds. Once planted, leave the brittle roots undisturbed.

Propagation. Divide and replant the roots during suitable weather between October and March.

Sow seeds in March, in boxes or pans of seed compost at a temperature of 15°C (59°F). Prick the seedlings out into boxes and harden them off in a cold frame before planting them out in their flowering positions a year after sowing.

Alternatively, take 3–4 in. long root cuttings in March and insert in equal parts (by volume) peat and sand in a cold frame. When young leaves are well developed, line the cuttings out in nursery rows outdoors; transplant to permanent positions in October.

Pests and diseases. Generally trouble-free.

Dichelostemma ida-maia : see *Brodiaea ida-maia*

Dictamnus
Burning bush. *Rutaceae*

DICTAMNUS ALBUS

A genus of six species of hardy herbaceous perennials. The species described is a handsome, usually long-lived plant for a sunny border. It should not be confused with the hardy annual *Kochia scoparia trichophylla*, known by the same common name.

D. albus, syn. *D. fraxinella*. S. Europe, Asia. Height 24 in.; planting distance 18 in. This is a strongly aromatic plant. The old flower heads in particular are rich in oil; on a warm, still evening one can sometimes ignite the halo of volatilised oil—hence the common name. The glossy, dark green, compound leaves are finely toothed.

Sturdy 9–12 in. spikes of fragrant white spider-like flowers are borne in June and July. *D. a.* 'Purpurea' is a pink, red-striped form.

D. fraxinella: see *D. albus*

Cultivation. Plant dictamnus between October and March. Choose a sunny position where the soil is well drained and, ideally, contains lime. If the soil is acid, add lime at 2–4 oz. per sq. yd. Do not disturb the plants, particularly the large ones, once they are established. Cut the stems back to their base in October or November.

Propagation. Sow freshly gathered seeds thinly in a seed bed outdoors in August or September. Transplant the seedlings to their flowering positions from October onwards, two years later.

Pests and diseases. Generally trouble-free.

Didiscus
Umbelliferae

DIDISCUS CAERULEA

The single half-hardy annual species described, now included in the genus *Trachymene*, is suitable for planting in groups among other annuals, for cutting and for growing in pots for summer-flowering in a greenhouse.

D. caeruleus (blue lace flower). Australia. Height 18 in.; planting distance 9 in. A bushy plant with light green, deeply divided leaves. Both the young stems and the foliage are sticky to touch. Long stems carry umbels, 1–2 in. across, of slightly scented lavender-blue flowers. These are rounded and rather like small annual scabious in appearance; they appear from July to August.

Cultivation. Grow in any well-cultivated garden soil in a sheltered sunny position. Staking with bushy twigs may be required.

Grow pot plants in final 5 in. containers, using John Innes potting compost No. 1. Water freely in hot weather, shade lightly from hot sun and give a liquid feed, to increase flower size, when the flower buds have formed.

Propagation. Sow the seeds under glass in March at a temperature of 15°C (59°F), just covering them. As soon as they are large enough to handle, prick off the seedlings into 3 in. pots or seed boxes. Plants in boxes should be hardened off in a cold frame before planting out in May.

Pests and diseases. Generally trouble-free.

Dieffenbachia
Araceae

A genus of 30 species of evergreen perennials, grown for their striking leaves. They are suitable for greenhouse cultivation and for homes with central heating, or where regular heat can be maintained throughout the winter.

Dicentra formosa 'Bountiful'

Dicentra spectabilis

Dictamnus albus 'Purpurea'

Didiscus caeruleus

Dieffenbachia picta

Dieffenbachia picta 'Exotica'

Dieffenbachia picta 'Roehrsii'

Dierama pulcherrimum
'Windhover'

D. amoena. Tropical America. Height 2–4 ft. The leaves of this species are oblong and emerge in succession from a central stem that may become trunk-like in time. They are dark green with white and cream marbling along the lateral veins. Leaves on mature plants may be 18–24 in. long and 8 in. or more wide.

DIEFFENBACHIA PICTA

D. picta. Brazil, Colombia. Height 1½–4 ft. The oblong leaves may be up to 12 in. or more long; they vary considerably in colour and size.

The type species has a basic leaf colour of dark green and large cream blotches between the lateral veins. 'Bausei' has the main leaf in two shades of green with silver spots. 'Exotica' has leaves heavily suffused with pale yellow, with a contrasting green midrib and margin. 'Roehrsii' has pale yellow-green leaves with the lateral veins picked out in ivory.

Cultivation. Grow in John Innes potting compost No. 3. Dieffenbachias require warm, humid conditions and a winter temperature not lower than 16°C (61°F), but will survive at 13°C (55°F). A temperature as low as 7°C (45°F) is tolerated for a short period, but the plants will lose some of their lower leaves. In cool conditions, water sparingly during winter as the main stems are susceptible to rotting.

In adequate warmth the plants grow all year round without any resting period. In winter, admit as much daylight as possible, but during the rest of the year provide some shading, quite heavy in summer. In a room, give the plants a reasonably well-lit position, but out of direct sunlight; avoid draughts.

A humid atmosphere is essential. If the plant are grown in the home, plunge the pots in a absorbent material, such as peat, and keep thi moist. Water the compost only when necessary In the greenhouse, during hot weather, syring the leaves twice a day; when the temperatur reaches 21°C (70°F) admit air.

Pot on in April or May; manageable plant should finish in 6 in. pots. If large specimens ar wanted, pot on each year and finish off in 12 ir pots or small tubs. All parts of the plants ar poisonous if freshly cut surfaces or sap ar brought in contact with eyes or mouth.

Propagation. Strip a plant of its lower leave from April to June and detach the tip or growing point with a portion of stem about 3 in. i length. This can be rooted as a cutting in equa parts (by volume) peat and sand at a temperatur of 21–24°C (70–75°F). Cut the rest of the sten into sections, 2–3 in. long and just cover with similar compost; root the stem cuttings in propagating case at 21–24°C (70–75°F).

After the cuttings have rooted, harden them of on the greenhouse bench before potting up int 3–4 in. pots containing John Innes pottin compost No. 1. Pot on as they increase in size Once the cuttings have rooted, the original plan can be discarded although it will usually brea again from the base.

Pests and diseases. Generally trouble-free.

Dielytra: see Dicentra

Dierama

Wand flower, angel's fishing rod.
Iridaceae

A genus of 25 species of evergreen or semi evergreen perennials with congested bulbou rootstocks. The two described are suitable fo borders in all but the coldest areas. They hav wiry, graceful, arching stems that bear narrow trumpet-shaped pendent flowers, 1 in. or mor long, on thread-like pedicels. The tufted leave are mid-green and grass-like.

DIERAMA PULCHERRIMUM

D. pendulum. S. Africa. Height 3 ft; plantin distance 9–18 in. Pink-purple flowers appear i June and July. 'Album' has pure white flowers 'Pumilum' (height 18–24 in.) is similar to th type species, but more suitable for a rock garde or the front of a herbaceous border.

D. pulcherrimum. S. Africa. Height 6 ft; plantin distance 12–24 in. This species is considered b some authorities to be a more vigorous form c *D. pendulum.* It is larger in all its parts, the dee red flowers appearing from August to October.

Named forms include: 'Album', white; 'Heron', deep wine-red; 'Kingfisher', pale pink; 'Port Wine', wine-purple; 'Skylark', deep violet; and 'Windhover', rose-pink.

Cultivation. Grow dieramas in any ordinary, well-drained soil enriched with peat or leaf-mould. If possible, choose a sunny but sheltered site, although they will also grow in partial shade.

Plant the corms in September or April 4–6 in. deep. Except in cold districts, do not lift the plants unless they become overcrowded or unless they are wanted for propagation. Cut off stems when flowering ceases in the autumn, and cut back damaged or dying leaves before growth begins in spring. In cold districts, plant the corms in April; lift in October or November and clean off old stems, leaves and roots, then store in a dry, frost-free greenhouse or shed.

Propagation. Variations in colour and height can be obtained from seed-raised plants. Sow in pots or boxes of seed compost in a cold frame during March or April. Prick off the seedlings singly into 3 in. pots of John Innes potting compost No. 1; transplant to flowering sites in September or October. In cold districts, overwinter the young plants in a frame and plant out the following April. Flowers can be expected after one or two years.

To increase stocks of existing plants, lift them in October and separate the small offsets. Plant these in a nursery bed and grow on until the corms reach flowering size, generally the following September or October.

Pests and diseases. Generally trouble-free.

Diervilla florida: see *Weigela florida*
Diervilla middendorfiana: see *Weigela middendorfiana*

Digitalis

Foxglove. *Scrophulariaceae*

DIGITALIS PURPUREA

A genus of about 30 species of hardy biennial and perennial plants. With their tall, one-sided spikes of tubular flowers, they are a familiar sight in woodlands and wild gardens. Many species, including the common foxglove, are best treated as biennials since they tend to deteriorate after the second year from seeds, especially on heavy soils. They can be grown in borders, where they are useful for cutting, or as pot plants.

D. ambigua: see *D. grandiflora*

D. ferruginea. S. Europe. Height up to 5 ft; planting distance 18 in. A biennial with leafy spikes arising from a rosette of lanceolate mid-green leaves that are smooth or fringed with hairs. Brown-red flowers, in spikes 24 in. long and covered with fine, soft hairs, open in July.

D. grandiflora, syn. *D. ambigua*. Europe, Caucasus, Siberia. Height 2–3 ft; planting dis-

Digitalis purpurea

tance 12 in. A perennial species with lanceolate mid-green leaves that are toothed and hairy. The sulphur-yellow flowers, netted with brown, are 2 in. long and are borne on spikes up to 24 in. long in July and August.

D. lutea. S.W. Europe, N.W. Africa. Height 1–3 ft; planting distance 12 in. The glossy, mid-green, lanceolate leaves of this perennial are finely serrated. Yellow flowers, $\frac{3}{4}$ in. long, are borne on erect tapering stems from May to July.

D. × mertonensis. Height 2–3 ft; planting distance 12 in. A perennial hybrid with mid-green lanceolate leaves. The 1 in. long flowers are a crushed strawberry shade; they appear from June to September.

D. purpurea. W. Europe, including Great Britain. Height 3–5 ft; planting distance up to 24 in. This is the common English foxglove, normally biennial but often perennial under ideal conditions. The oblong rich green leaves form a rosette. From this rise spikes, up to 3 ft high, of purple, red or maroon, spotted flowers; they are produced from June to July.

Of the many garden varieties, the 'Excelsior' strain, (5 ft), is outstanding. The flowers, carried all round the spikes, are held horizontally and thus show the markings in the tubular florets. The large spikes bear white, cream, or pink to purple flowers. It is excellent for growing in borders and for cut flowers.

The recently introduced 'Foxy' is similar to the 'Excelsior' strain, but is not as tall ($2\frac{1}{2}$ ft). It flowers, in a range of colours, as an annual, although it is a true biennial. The leading flower spike is surrounded by up to nine side-shoots, all suitable for cutting.

'Shirley Hybrids' are closer to the type, but up to 7 ft in height. The flowers range from white to shades of red and purple.

Cultivation. Plant digitalis between October and April in partial shade in any ordinary garden soil that does not dry out in summer.

Digitalis purpurea 'Excelsior'

Digitalis purpurea 'Foxy'

Remove the central spike when it has flowered to encourage flowering side-shoots to increase in size. Cut down the whole plant of perennial species in October.

For spring-flowering pot plants, lift young plants in September, transfer them to 7 in. containers of John Innes potting compost No. 2 and keep in a cold greenhouse throughout the winter. Discard after flowering.

Propagation. Sow the seeds, which are very fine, outside in May or June, scattering them on the surface and gently raking them in. A thin covering of damp peat improves germination. Space out the seedlings 6 in. apart in a nursery bed, and move to the flowering positions or into pots in September.

'Foxy' may be sown under glass in February or March and hardened off in a cold frame before planting out in April to flower in July and August.

Pests. Generally trouble-free.

Diseases. Plants growing in over-wet soil may develop CROWN ROT and ROOT ROT in winter.

Dill

Dimorphotheca aurantiaca

Dill

Peucedanum graveolens. Umbelliferae

DILL

The leaves and seeds of this hardy annual herb are used for flavouring.

Height 3 ft; spacing 9–12 in. Europe. The erect, hollow, ridged stem is striped dark green and white and bears fine, thread-like, blue-green leaves. Minute, starry yellow flowers are carried in umbels, 2–3 in. across, from June to August.

The leaves can be used fresh or dried to garnish salads and to give their rather anise-like flavour to potatoes, beans, peas, soups, poultry, hors d'oeuvres and fish. The dried seeds have a stronger taste than the leaves and are often used to flavour vinegar for pickling, especially of gherkins. The seeds can also be used as a condiment to add to sauces.

Cultivation. Grow dill in any well-drained, fertile soil, in a sunny position.

Propagation. For a constant summer supply of fresh leaves make successional monthly sowings from March to July. The plants are ready for use six to eight weeks after sowing. For a crop of seeds, sow before April to give the crop plenty of time to ripen at the end of the season.

Sow the seeds outdoors in shallow drills 9–12 in. apart; thin the seedlings to 9–12 in. apart and keep the rows well weeded and watered.

Dill seeds itself readily, often resulting in stronger plants than those produced by hand sowing. Do not grow dill near fennel as they may prove difficult to identify.

Harvesting and storing. The leaves may be dried or deep-frozen, but it is difficult to retain a good leaf colour. See entry under HERBS.

For winter use, once the supply of fresh leaves has ceased, it is generally more satisfactory to dry the seeds and store them in airtight containers. Cut the plants when the seeds are turning brown, usually in August. Spread them on paper and dry until the seeds shake loose easily.

Pests and diseases. Generally trouble-free.

Dimorphotheca

Cape marigold, African daisy. *Compositae*

DIMORPHOTHECA BARBERIAE 'COMPACTA'

A genus of seven species of half-hardy annual and perennial plants. The species described here are suitable for herbaceous borders, for bedding out, and for growing as pot plants. They require a sunny position, as the bright daisy-like flowers do not open in shade or on dull days. Seed-raised plants flower the same season, and the perennial species are usually treated as annuals.

D. annua, syn. *D. pluvialis*. S. Africa. Height 9–12 in.; planting distance 6 in. An attractive annual with short branching stems and oblong, dark green, hairy leaves. The flowers have cream-white ray petals, which are purple on the underside, surrounding a deep golden-brown central disc. They are 2 in. across and appear from June to August. Both leaves and flowers are scented. The variety 'Ringens' has blue markings on each ray petal.

D. aurantiaca (star of the veldt). S. Africa. Height 12–18 in.; planting distance 12 in. This perennial has mid-green leaves that are narrowly oblong and alternate. Bright orange flowers, 2 in. across and with a dark brown disc tipped with metallic blue, are borne from June to September.

The following varieties are recommended: 'Glistening White', 6–9 in. high, with silver-white flowers; 'Goliath', 12–15 in., rich orange flowers with green-black centres; 'Salmon Beauty', 12–15 in., orange-salmon.

D. barberiae. S. Africa. Height 18–24 in.; planting distance 12 in. The lanceolate, downy, mid-green leaves of this perennial are aromatic. Bright purple-pink flowers, dull purple beneath and 2–2½ in. across, are produced from June to September. 'Compacta' is more compact and slightly hardier than the type species.

D. calendulacea. S. Africa. Height up to 12 in.; planting distance 6 in. An attractive annual with slender stems and dark green leaves that are oblong and wavy-toothed. Pale yellow to white flowers, with steely-blue centres and measuring 2½ in. across, appear from July to September.

D. ecklonis, syn. *Osteospermum ecklonis*. S. Africa. Height 24 in.; planting distance 12 in. A vigorous, bushy perennial with erect stems and clusters of mid-green lanceolate leaves. The flowers, in July and August, have purple-pink ray petals and deep blue discs; they are 3 in. across.

Dimorphotheca barberiae

D. pluvialis: see *D. annua*

Cultivation. Plant in May in a warm, sunny position in light, well-drained loam. Dead-heading encourages repeat flowering.

All species are generally grown as annuals, but if the perennials are to be grown on for a further year, the old stems should be cut down in October. Use cloches to protect the plants from excessive dampness in winter.

For flowering under glass from April to July, grow three plants in each 6 in. pot of John Innes potting compost No. 1. Maintain a winter temperature of 7°C (45°F) and water sparingly.

Propagation. For outdoor plants, sow seeds of both annual and perennial species in the flowering site in May, and thin out the seedlings to the required planting distance. In favourable weather, they will grow quickly and may flower within six weeks of sowing. Alternatively, sow seeds under glass in March at a temperature of 18°C (64°F); prick off the seedlings into boxes, and harden off in a cold frame before planting out when danger of frost is past.

For spring and summer-flowering pot plants, sow seeds between January and March in 6 in. pots of John Innes potting compost No. 1. Thin out the seedlings to three plants per pot.

Named varieties of *D. aurantiaca* can be increased by 3 in. half-ripe cuttings taken in July or August, rooted in equal parts (by volume) peat and sand in a cold frame. Overwinter in 3 in. pots of John Innes potting compost No. 1 in a cold frame or greenhouse. Plant out in May.

Pests. Generally trouble-free.

Diseases. Rotting of the tissues, which become covered with a grey velvety fungal growth in wet weather, may be caused by GREY MOULD.

Dipelta
Caprifoliaceae

DIPELTA FLORIBUNDA

A genus of four species of hardy or near-hardy deciduous shrubs, native to China. They are grown for their showy foxglove-like flowers and attractive peeling bark.

D. floribunda. Height up to 15 ft; spread 7–10 ft. A shrubby species of upright, open habit and with attractive, peeling, light brown bark. The mid-green ovate-lanceolate leaves are long-pointed and veined. The sweet-scented flowers are 1 in. long, pale pink, flushed yellow in the throat; they are borne in May and June, singly or in clusters of two to six, on the previous year's growths.

D. ventricosa. Height 6–8 ft; spread 5–7 ft. This is similar to *D. floribunda,* but the rose-lilac flowers are more inflated and slightly longer.

D. yunnanensis. Height 6–8 ft; spread 5–7 ft. A shrub of similar habit to the two preceding species, but rather more graceful. The narrow leaves are dark green, glossy, slender-pointed and with marked veins. The funnel-shaped flowers, which appear in May and June, have rounded lobes; they are ¾–1 in. long and cream-coloured, flushed with pink.

Cultivation. These shrubs are easy to grow in any good garden soil. Plant in October and November or in March in a sheltered, sunny or partially shaded position.

Propagation. Take cuttings, 3–4 in. long, of semi-ripe lateral shoots in July and August; insert the cuttings in equal parts (by volume) peat and sand in a cold frame. The following April or May line out the rooted cuttings in nursery rows outdoors; grow on until the following autumn when they are ready for planting out.

Alternatively, take hardwood cuttings, 12 in. long, of strong current-season stems in October; insert the cuttings in a nursery bed outdoors and plant out one year later.

Pruning. After flowering, remove one or two old stems at ground level to keep the bushes shapely and within bounds.

Pests and diseases. Generally trouble-free.

Diplacus
Scrophulariaceae

DIPLACUS GLUTINOSUS

A small genus of six or seven species of evergreen shrubby perennials, sometimes included in the genus *Mimulus.* They are suitable for greenhouse cultivation and for planting outdoors in summer.

D. glutinosus, syn. *Mimulus glutinosus.* California. Height in cultivation 18 in. with a 15 in. spread. The sticky, lanceolate leaves are mid to dark green. Trumpet-shaped flowers, about 2 in. across, appear from April to November from the upper leaf axils; they are orange, salmon, crimson or pale buff. Plants grown outdoors in sheltered sunny positions often remain in flower from July until the first frosts.

Cultivation. Grow diplacus in John Innes potting compost No. 2. High temperatures are not required at any time, and the plants may be stood outdoors for the summer months. Maintain a winter temperature of 5°C (41°F). Keep the plants barely moist during the winter and give moderate amounts of water throughout the growing season. At no time should the compost become waterlogged.

Ample light is required at all times, but light shading may be necessary in summer if the plants are kept in a greenhouse.

Repot or pot on in March or April; the plants are usually finished in 6 in. pots, but potting on into larger pots will result in larger plants.

Propagation. Take heel cuttings, 2–3 in. long, of firm young growths in April or in July. Insert the cuttings in equal parts (by volume) peat and sand

Dimorphotheca ecklonis

Dipelta yunnanensis

Diplacus glutinosus

at a temperature of 16–18°C (61–64°F); pot up in 3 in. and later 5 in. containers. Cuttings taken in spring will flower the same year; cuttings taken in summer should be grown on during winter to flower the following year.

Pruning. Reduce all growths by half during the winter months. The plants break naturally, and apart from an initial pinching out when the cuttings are first potted, no stopping is necessary.

Pests and diseases. Generally trouble-free.

Dipladenia splendens

Disanthus cercidifolius
(autumn foliage)

Dizygotheca elegantissima

Dipladenia
Apocynaceae

DIPLADENIA SPLENDENS

A genus of 30 species of twining, evergreen, greenhouse shrubs. The one species in general cultivation, *D. splendens*, is sometimes classified under the genus *Mandevilla*. It is suitable for growing in a greenhouse or, during summer, in a living-room.

D. splendens. Brazil. Height up to 15 ft; in cultivation it is usually twined round cane supports as a pot plant or trained on strings or wires against a greenhouse wall. It will flower when only about 9 in. high. The elliptic leaves are shining mid-green. Flower spikes, 6–8 in. long, consisting of rose-pink, trumpet-shaped flowers, are borne from June to September.

This plant is sometimes used for indoor decoration during the summer. Although it is often discarded after flowering it can be over-wintered under the correct conditions.

Cultivation. Dipladenias are best grown in a well-drained rich soil; John Innes potting compost No. 3 is suitable. Maintain a temperature of 13°C (55°F) throughout the winter and increase this to a minimum of 16°C (61°F) when growth begins in March. Keep the plants on the dry side in winter, giving only enough water to prevent the plants from flagging. Water freely from the beginning of the growing season until the flowers have dropped. Gradually withhold water, but do not let the plants dry out completely.

The plants require a humid atmosphere in summer; damp down the greenhouse floor and syringe the leaves daily.

When flowering begins, admit air when possible. Pot on annually in March; the plants may be finished off in 12 in. pots; plants grown in the home do well finished off in 6 in. pots. Give a weekly liquid feed from June to September.

Propagation. Take 3 in. long heel cuttings in March or April of young lateral shoots, or pieces of the older stems with two leaves in June or July. Insert the cuttings in equal parts (by volume) peat and sand in a propagating frame at a temperature of 16–18°C (61–64°F). When rooted, pot up the cuttings singly in 3 in. pots of John Innes potting compost No. 2.

Pruning. After flowering, cut the current year's growth hard back unless an extension of the plant is required. Normally only about 2 in. of a year's growth is retained. If cuttings are to be taken prune lightly after flowering and cut the growths hard back after propagation the following spring.

Pests and diseases. Generally trouble-free.

Disanthus
Hamamelidaceae

A genus consisting of a single species. This is a hardy deciduous shrub from Japan, related to *Hamamelis* (witch hazel). It is chiefly grown for its magnificent autumn foliage.

D. cercidifolius. Japan. Height 6–10 ft; spread 7–8 ft. A species of upright, bushy habit, with slender growths. The round or heart-shaped leaves have a blue-green cast and prominent veins; in autumn the foliage assumes brilliant shades of red and scarlet. Insignificant, starry, $\frac{1}{2}$ in. wide dark purple flowers are borne in pairs in the leaf-axils during October after leaf-fall.

DISANTHUS CERCIDIFOLIUS

Cultivation. These shrubs are not tolerant of lime and should be grown only in neutral or acid, peaty and moist soils. Plant from October to March in sun or partial shade in a sheltered position. They thrive in semi-woodland conditions. Young plants require protection with bracken or straw in winter. Once established these shrubs are fully hardy.

Propagation. Layer long shoots in September or October and sever from the parent plants one or two years later.

In July, take half-ripe cuttings, 4 in. long, of lateral shoots with a heel. Insert the cuttings in equal parts (by volume) peat and sand in a propagating case with a temperature of 16–18°C (61–64°F). Pot when rooted into 3 in. pots of John Innes potting compost No. 1 (minus lime) and overwinter in a cold frame. Line the rooted cuttings out in nursery rows the following April or May and grow on for two or three years before transplanting to permanent positions.

Pruning. None required, except the removal of untidy shoots in February.

Pests and diseases. Generally trouble-free.

Dizygotheca
Araliaceae

A genus of 17 species of evergreen trees and shrubs from Australasia. They were formerly included in the genus *Aralia*. The species in cultivation is an ornamental foliage plant, suitable for a greenhouse or as a house plant.

D. elegantissima. New Hebrides. Height up to ⁵ ft; spread 18 in. The appearance of this shrub or small tree changes markedly as the plant matures. In its young state, up to 4 ft high, the species bears graceful, palmate leaves composed of seven to ten linear leaflets, which may be 3 in. long but barely ½ in. wide. The leaves, as they emerge, are coppery red, but change to very dark green as they mature. The juvenile form is grown as a house plant. Mature leaves develop on plants 4–5 ft high, and by that time most of the fine foliage has been shed.

Cultivation. The plants can be grown in John Innes potting compost No. 2 or 3, or in a proprietary loamless compost. The winter temperature should be not less than 13°C (55°F); during summer the plants will thrive in high greenhouse temperatures provided a humid atmosphere is maintained by daily syringing and damping down.

In the home, place the plants in a well-lit situation, but out of direct sunlight. In the greenhouse, provide moderate shading during spring and summer; admit as much light as possible in autumn and winter.

Pot the plants on every one or two years in May and finish off in 9–10 in. pots. When they are not being potted on, give fortnightly liquid feeds from May until the end of August.

Propagation. Sow seeds 1½ in. apart in boxes of seed compost from February to April. A temperature of 21°C (70°F) is necessary for germination. Pot the seedlings in 2½ in. pots of John Innes potting compost No. 1 when they have developed two true leaves. Pot on into 4 in. pots.

Pruning. None is necessary, but overgrown plants with substantial trunks can be cut hard back to a few inches in March. Juvenile foliage will sprout from the hard stump.

Pests and diseases. Generally trouble-free.

Dodecatheon

Shooting star. *Primulaceae*

DODECATHEON MEADIA

A genus of 52 species of hardy herbaceous perennials. The nodding flowers, which resemble those of cyclamen, are borne in terminal heads on smooth, leafless stems.

D. integrifolium. British Columbia. Height 9–12 in.; planting distance 12 in. The light green leaves are erect and spathulate. Rose-purple flowers, ¾ in. long, are produced in May and June. This species is similar to *D. meadia*, but distinguished from it by its fleshy bracts.

D. jeffreyi. N. America. Height 18–24 in.; planting distance 12 in. The light green leaves are erect and spathulate. Red-purple flowers, ¾ in. long, appear in May and June. The petals are reflexed, the stamens dark purple.

D. meadia. N. America. Height 12–18 in.; planting distance 12 in. The light green, ovate-oblong, toothed leaves appear in rosettes near the ground. Rose-purple flowers, ¾ in. long, with reflexed petals and bright yellow anthers, are produced in May and June.

D. pauciflorum. W. United States. Height 8–10 in.; planting distance 4–6 in. A tufted species with mid-green, lanceolate-spathulate leaves. Umbels of lilac-purple flowers, 1 in. long, are borne during April and May.

Cultivation. Plant dodecatheons between September and March in partial shade in moist, leafy soil. Leave them undisturbed to form a clump. Top-dress with leaf-mould or old manure annually in February.

Propagation. Sow seeds during September or March in pans of seed compost in a cold frame. When the seedlings are large enough to handle, grow them on in a nursery bed for two years before planting out in their permanent positions.

Divide established plants in autumn.

Pests and diseases. Generally trouble-free.

Dogwood: see Cornus
Dogwood, flowering: see *Cornus florida*

Doronicum

Leopard's bane. *Compositae*

DORONICUM PARDALIANCHES

A genus of 35 species of hardy herbaceous perennials. These early-flowering plants, if regularly dead-headed, often produce a second show of their daisy-like flowers in autumn. They are excellent as cut flowers.

Doronicum cordatum

D. austriacum. Central Europe. Height 18–24 in.; planting distance 12 in. The bright green heart-shaped leaves are rough and toothed. Single yellow flowers, about 2½ in. across, are borne in April and May.

Dodecatheon meadia

Dodecatheon pauciflorum

Doronicum austriacum

Doronicum plantagineum

Draba aizoides

Drába mollissima

Draba rigida

D. cordatum, syn. *D. columnae.* Balkans, Asia Minor. Height 8–12 in.; planting distance 9 in. The bright green kidney-shaped leaves clasp the stem. Single golden-yellow flowers, 2 in. across, are produced in April and May.

D. pardalianches (great leopard's bane). Europe, naturalised in Great Britain. Height up to 3 ft; planting distance 12–15 in. This robust species has tufts of long-stalked, broadly ovate-cordate, pale green basal leaves. The flowering stems bear smaller, ovate leaves with winged stalks. Bright yellow flowers, up to 3 in. across, open from May to July.

D. plantagineum. S.W. Europe. Height 24 in.; planting distance 12–18 in. The bright green leaves are heart-shaped, slightly toothed and hairy. Single golden-yellow flowers, 2½ in. across, are borne from April to June. 'Excelsum', syn. 'Harpur Crewe', has golden-yellow flowers up to 3 in. across; 'Miss Mason', height 18 in., has bright yellow flowers 2½ in. across.

Cultivation. Plant between October and March in sun or partial shade in deep, moist soil. Plants in exposed positions may need supporting. Dead-head regularly, and cut stems down in autumn.

Propagation. Divide and replant the roots between October and March.

Pests. Generally trouble-free.

Diseases. On the leaves, POWDERY MILDEW shows as a white powdery coating.

Dorotheanthus bellidiflorus: see *Mesembryanthemum criniflorum*

Dorotheanthus gramineus: see *Mesembryanthemum tricolor*

Dove tree: see Davidia

Draba

Whitlow grass. *Cruciferae*

A genus of 300 species of hardy perennial herbaceous plants which are attractive on rock gardens or in an alpine house. The species described form regular domes of closely packed rosettes, from which rise thin wiry stems bearing short racemes of yellow flowers.

D. aizoides. Middle European mountains. Height 4 in.; spread 6–9 in. This is a showy species with rigid, linear, grey-green leaves and clusters of lemon-yellow cross-shaped flowers, each about $\frac{1}{4}$ in. in diameter. These are borne on 2–4 in. stems in April.

D. bryoides, syn. *D. rigida bryoides.* Caucasus. Height 2 in.; spread up to 3 in. This plant forms a dense green cushion of small, oblong, rigid leaves. A few golden-yellow, cross-shaped flowers, $\frac{1}{5}$ in. across, are borne on wiry 2 in. stems in April. *D. b. imbricata,* syn. *D. imbricata* is a smaller and more compact plant, with a surface spread of only 1 in.

D. imbricata: see *D. bryoides imbricata*

D. mollissima. Caucasus. Height 1 in.; spread 6 in. or more. The lanceolate hairy, pale grey-green leaves are packed into numerous tiny, tightly crowded rosettes. Bright yellow, cross-shaped flowers, $\frac{1}{3}-\frac{1}{2}$ in. across, are borne in terminal racemes during May and June.

D. polytricha. Armenia. Height 2 in.; spread 6–9 in. This plant forms hard cushions of grey-green, oblong-lanceolate leaves covered with small white hairs. Pale yellow, cross-shaped flowers, $\frac{1}{5}$ in. across, open in April.

D. rigida. Armenia. Height 3–4 in.; spread 3–6 in. Compact mid-green cushions are formed by the minute rosettes of linear leaves. In April, corymbs of dainty, golden-yellow, cross-shaped flowers, each $\frac{1}{4}$ in. across, open on short stems.

D. rigida bryoides: see *D. bryoides*

Cultivation. Plant drabas in March or April in a sunny position. They grow well in a mixture of loam and coarse sand, with good drainage. Keep them moist during the growing period and during flowering; water sparingly at other times. Avoid pouring water over the cushions and in winter protect the woolly foliage from the wet with raised panes of glass.

In the alpine house, grow drabas in 6–8 in. pans, in a mixture of 2 parts John Innes potting compost No. 1 and 1 part limestone grit (parts by volume). Ideally, wedge the young plants between tufa, limestone or other porous rock in the pans. Repot annually in March.

Propagation. Detach non-flowering rosettes in June or July and treat them as cuttings, setting them to root in pots of sand in a cold frame. When they are well rooted, grow on in 2½ in. pots containing 2 parts John Innes potting compost No. 1 and 1 part limestone grit (parts by volume). Plant out 12 months later.

All species increase readily from seeds sown in March and April in a cold frame. Prick off the seedlings into boxes and later pot them up individually in 2½ in. pots of John Innes potting compost No. 1. Overwinter in a cold frame and plant out the following spring.

Pests and diseases. Generally trouble-free.

Dracaena

Agavaceae

A genus of 40 species of evergreen shrubby plants, grown for their ornamental foliage. They are mainly palm-like and will assume tree-like forms. The species require greenhouse cultivation, and may also be grown as house plants.

DRACAENA FRAGRANS

D. deremensis. Tropical Africa. Height 4 ft or more; spread 15 in. This species has a tuft of sword-like leaves, up to 18 in. long. They are glossy dark green with two longitudinal silver stripes. In the variety 'Bausei', the leaf margin is dark green and the centre white; 'Warneckii' has white stripes.

D. draco (dragon tree). Canary Islands. Height 3 ft or more; spread 24 in. The hard, sword-like leaves, 18 in. long, are mid-green. The species is long-lived; there is a well-known specimen at La Orotava, in the Canary Islands, which is said to be more than 1000 years old.

D. fragrans. Guinea and W. Africa. Height 4 ft or more; spread 2–2½ ft. This species is similar to *D. deremensis,* but the mature leaves may be up to 3 ft long; they are broader and rounded at the tips. The leaf colour is variable. The variety 'Massangeana' has wide green margins and a gold centre; 'Lindenii' has broad gold margins and a narrow green and gold centre.

D. godseffiana. Congo. Height 24 in. or more; spread 15 in. A branching shrub with thin wiry stems which carry whorls of two or three laurel-like leaves at intervals along the stems. The leaves are obovate, about 3 in. long, and dark green spotted with cream. In the variety 'Florida Beauty', the spots coalesce.

D. sanderiana. Congo. The usual height of this species is 18 in.; spread 15 in. Large specimens up to 6–7 ft can be obtained by finishing off in 10 in. pots. This species branches from the base and carries its leaves densely along the stems. The 8 in. long, slightly wavy leaves are usually grey-green with silver or ivory margins.

D. terminalis: see *Cordyline terminalis*

Cultivation. Grow dracaenas in John Innes potting compost No. 3.

The minimum winter temperature varies according to the species: *D. deremensis* and *D. fragrans* require 13°C (55°F); *D. godseffiana* and *D. sanderiana* 10°C (50°F); *D. draco* 7°C (45°F). During spring and summer, encourage the growth of greenhouse specimens with humid conditions and a night temperature of 16°C (61°F). *D. godseffiana* and *D. sanderiana* tolerate the drier conditions of the home.

Ensure that the leaves fully develop their colours by giving the plants ample light. During winter, keep the plants on the dry side; water generously from May until September, sparingly

Dracaena deremensis 'Warneckii'

between September and early November and between March and May. Grow *D. deremensis* and *D. fragrans* in 6–7 in. pots for as long as possible; feed them every fortnight with liquid manure from June to September.

D. godseffiana and *D. sanderiana* will make good specimens in 5 in. pots. *D. draco* usually makes a larger plant than the other species and may need to be potted on to a 9 or 10 in. pot. Repotting is best done in April.

Give light shading in the greenhouse during the hottest summer months; in rooms allow as much light as possible to the plants at all times.

Propagation. Take basal shoots or tip cuttings of mature growths with 3 in. of stem in March and April. Older, leafless stems may be cut into 2–3 in. sections and just covered with compost. If leaves are present, strip these away first. Place the cuttings in equal parts (by volume) peat and sand, in a propagating case at a temperature of 21–24°C (70–75°F).

The first leaves on the rooted cuttings will be true green, but within a few months coloured leaves are produced. Set the cuttings in 3 in. pots of John Innes potting compost No. 1 and pot on as necessary.

Pests. ROOT MEALY BUGS invade the roots and may check growth. SCALE INSECTS, form round white or pearl-grey scales on the leaves and stems.

Diseases. LEAF SPOT fungus attacks the leaves, producing pale brown irregular spots with a purple border and pinpoint-sized black dots.

Dracaena godseffiana

Dracaena sanderiana

Dracocephalum virginianum: see *Physostegia virginiana*

Dragon tree: see *Dracaena draco*

Dried oak leaves and hydrangea flowers are used in this winter arrangement.

DRIED FLOWERS

At one time, arrangements of dried flowers for winter decoration, when fresh flowers are scarce and expensive, were confined to the silver-cream pampas-grass (*Cortaderia*) and the orange-red Chinese lanterns (*Physalis alkekengii*). However, by employing various preservation methods, a wide variety of plants can be induced to maintain their colours, and the exact shape of flowers and leaves.

The various preserving methods all involve quick drying; many flowers with non-succulent stems can have the heads preserved in drying agents, such as silver sand mixed with borax, or silica gel crystals or powder (the crystals can be bought in small quantities from most chemists). After drying, the flower heads may be provided with false stems made from florists' wire, drinking straws or pipe cleaners. Spread a ½ in. deep layer of the drying agent in a box and place the flower heads, small sprays of berries and single leaves which are to be preserved on top, taking care that they do not touch each other. Sprinkle more of the drying agent carefully over the flowers, ensuring in particular that it falls between the petals. Leave in an airing cupboard or over a radiator, until the plant material feels crisp and dry. This usually takes three days. Single-petalled flowers, without thickened centres, are most suitable.

Clear red and orange roses keep their colours particularly well, while pink-petalled roses are less successful; white varieties, although tending to turn cream, are still attractive. Pansies (*Viola*), geranium (*Pelargonium*) florets, sprigs of delphinium, gentians (*Gentiana*) and sprays of fuchsia dry extremely well and preserve their natural colours; they are attractive arranged with dried sprigs of lavender, the grey-silver leaves of *Stachys lanata* or whitebeam (*Sorbus*).

Several flowers can be easily and quickly dried by hanging them upside-down in small bunches in a dry and airy place. Flowers particularly suitable for drying in this manner include the well-known everlastings, such as *Eryngium, Helichrysum* and *Helipterum.* Long-stemmed annual and perennial delphiniums, onion and leek flower heads, most varieties of corn and other cereals, and seed heads of hollyhock (*Althaea*) and foxglove (*Digitalis*) may be dried in the same manner. Also recommended for drying are *Astilbe,* lavender-pink heathers (*Erica*), flowers and seed heads of bugbane (*Cimicifuga*) and statice (*Limonium*).

The flowers and seed heads should be gathered on long stems during dry weather after the dew has disappeared from the plants. They should be picked just as the flowers open or when the seed heads begin to ripen and turn brown; full-blown flowers do not preserve well.

The lantern-shaped seed heads of *Physalis* may be similarly preserved; strip the leaves off the stems before hanging them up to dry. Afterwards arrange with preserved leaves of beech (*Fagus*).

Hydrangea flower heads are ideal for winter decoration; they should be picked towards the end of September when they feel dry and thick to the touch. Stand the cut stems in bottles of water and leave in an airing cupboard for a few days until the flowers feel crisp.

Dried pampas-grass often turns fluffy and dull cream-white. If the plumes are picked when they are only just emerging from their sheaths, they maintain their immature and grass-like shape and indoors open into filmy silvery plumes. The large plumes may be broken up into small pieces and arranged with other preserved flowers, such as pink and smoke-blue hydrangeas, or with preserved green wheat and fresh scarlet *Ranunculus.* When arrangements are made up of dried and fresh flowers that require water in the containers, it is worth varnishing the dried stem ends or dipping them in candle-wax to prevent rotting.

Sprays of foliage can be preserved by standing the stems in a solution of 1 part glycerine to 2 parts water (parts by volume); the glycerine mixes best with warm water. The colours of the leaves change considerably, depending upon the time of year they are picked and preserved as well as on the type of leaf. Some leaves become cream-white, others change to a warm chestnut-brown, tan or green-bronze. Beech leaves are possibly the easiest and most popular to preserve; select perfect sprays from June to early September for a variety of shades.

One of the most attractive foliage subjects for drying in this way is Mexican orange blossom (*Choisya ternata*), the leaves of which pale to a soft warm cream colour. Leaves of oak (*Quercus*), horse chestnut (*Aesculus*), water iris and aspidistra, as well as sprays of wild or cultivated clematis, *Elaeagnus* and *Eucalyptus,* generally preserve well. In damp seasons when growth is soft and flabby, the leaves may fail to absorb the glycerine. Colour-perfect, undamaged leaves and foliage sprays should always be gathered when fully mature and during dry and settled weather. *Eucalyptus* foliage assumes a pearly grey-blue colour if hung upside-down to dry.

Sprays and individual leaves of beech *Crocosmia,* ferns, iris and whitebeam may also be preserved by pressing them under a heavy weight for a short time. Some will even maintain their shape and colour if picked in early autumn, placed in shallow containers of water and allowed to dry out slowly.

Generally, there are no hard and fast rules for drying and preserving flowers foliage and seed heads, and different drying methods often achieve a wide variety of colour.

Dryas
Rosaceae

A genus of two species of hardy prostrate evergreen sub-shrubs. The one described is suitable for rock gardens and for growing in association with bulbs.

D. octopetala. N. and W. Europe, including Great Britain; N. America. Height 3–4 in.; spread 24 in. This mat-forming plant has prostrate woody stems that bear lustrous mid to deep green oblong-ovate, shallowly lobed leaves that are grey-green beneath. White saucer-shaped flowers, eight-petalled and 1 in. across, appear in June and July; in the early autumn they are followed by graceful fluffy seed heads.

Cultivation. Plant dryas from September to March in any well-drained garden soil in a sunny position. The plants resent root disturbance and should not be moved once established.

Propagation. Take 1½–2 in. heel cuttings of side-shoots in August or March and insert them in sand in a cold frame. When rooted, pot them individually into 3 in. pots of John Innes potting compost No. 1. Grow on in the frame and plant out the following spring or autumn.

Sow seeds in September or October in a cold frame; prick off the seedlings first into pans and then into 2½–3 in. pots. Grow them on in the frame, and plant out the following September.

To propagate by division, lift the plants in March. Sever the self-rooted stems and replant direct in their final positions. They root especially well in sandy soil.

Pests and diseases. Generally trouble-free.

Dryopteris
Buckler fern. *Aspidiaceae*

A genus of 150 species of ferns deriving their name from the shape of the scales protecting the spore capsules. Those described are perennials.

D. aemula (hay-scented buckler fern). W. Europe, Azores, Madeira. Height and spread 18–24 in. A hardy species. The bright green, triangular, bipinnate fronds are crinkly and covered with minute glands. The plant smells of new-mown hay.

D. borreri, syn. *D. pseudomas* (golden-scaled male fern). Temperate zones. Height and spread 2–3 ft. The lanceolate fronds of this hardy species are golden-green, the stalks thickly clothed with golden-brown scales. *D. b.* 'The King' and *D. b.* 'Ramosissima' are crested forms.

D. cristata (crested buckler fern). N. Hemisphere. Height and spread 24 in. or more. A species similar to *D. filix-mas*, but with more spreading, pale or yellow-green fronds. It does well in moist or boggy soils.

D. dilatata (broad buckler fern). Circumpolar, N. Hemisphere. Height and spread 2–4 ft. This hardy plant has deep green, triangular, tripinnate fronds which arch gracefully. They are used as background foliage for exhibition dahlias.

D. erythrosora. China, Japan, Philippines. Height and spread 18–24 in. This species is hardy in sheltered areas. Under glass it remains evergreen.

Dryopteris erythrosora

The broadly triangular, pinnate-pinnatifid fronds are a light copper colour when young, maturing to deep green.

D. filix-mas (male fern). Temperate zones, N. Hemisphere. Height and spread 2–4 ft. A hardy plant with deep green, lanceolate fronds that are almost bipinnate. This is the most common native fern in gardens, where it often springs up from wind-borne spores, and sometimes assumes weed proportions.

D. pseudomas: see *D. borreri*

D. villarsii (rigid buckler fern). Europe. Height and spread 15–18 in. This neat, hardy rock-garden plant is found in the wild in Britain in the limestone districts of Yorkshire and Lancashire and occasionally in N. Wales. The narrowly triangular, bipinnate fronds are a dull sage green, and have tiny glands which give out a fragrant smell.

Cultivation. Plant dryopteris during March or April in shade in a loamy soil. *D. aemula* requires acid or neutral soil; the other species will grow in alkaline or acid soil.

The top growth may be cut down in autumn.

Propagation. March is the best time to sow spores (see entry under FERNS). The crowns may be divided and replanted in April.

Pests. Generally trouble-free.

Diseases. Sometimes RUST develops on *D. dilatata* and *D. filix-mas*. It shows as scattered or loosely grouped brown spore pustules on the undersurface of the fronds.

Dryas octopetala

Dryopteris borreri

Dryopteris cristata

Duck potato: see *Sagittaria latifolia*
Dusty miller: see *Artemisia stelleriana*
Dutchman's pipe: see Aristolochia
Dwarf beans: see Beans (French)

Earth star: see Cryptanthus

Eccremocarpus

Chilean glory flower. *Bignoniaceae*

A genus of five species of evergreen climbing plants. They are half-hardy in Great Britain, and except in the mildest areas, are usually cut to the ground by frosts. They are suitable for covering pergolas, walls and fences.

E. scaber. Chile. Height 8–10 ft. A species with slender stems and dark green pinnate leaves. It tends to grow upright at first, branching later. The main stalk of each leaf ends in a tendril, which attaches itself to any support. The 1 in. long orange-scarlet flowers are tubular and appear freely from June to October in racemes of 10–12. Red and yellow forms are known.

ECCREMOCARPUS SCABER

Cultivation. Plant seedlings in late May, in groups of three as raised in their pots, in pockets of loamy, well-drained soil at the base of a sheltered south or south-west wall. Provide twiggy sticks for early support, with trellis-work, wires or string thereafter. Water copiously during dry weather. Remove old flower heads unless the seeds are wanted.

Propagation. Sow the seeds in seed compost during February or early March, placing the pots or boxes in a greenhouse or frame heated to 13–16°C (55–61°F). Prick out the seedlings into 4 in. pots, three to a pot, and grow them on in a frost-free greenhouse or frame. Provide support for the rapid-growing shoots and gradually harden them off before planting out.

Pruning. If grown as short-lived perennials, cut out all frosted growths in April.

Pests. Plants may be infested by APHIDS or GLASS-HOUSE RED SPIDER MITES.

Diseases. Generally trouble-free.

Echeveria

Crassulaceae

A genus of 200 species of house plants and greenhouse perennials. These easily grown succulents are cultivated chiefly for their beautiful coloured leaves, which often have a white waxy sheen. The leaves are arranged in rosettes.

The plants usually spread to form a thick carpet. They need a light position, because the colouring of the leaves depends on the strength of the light. They can be kept outdoors in summer. The bell-shaped flowers are produced in loose sprays on arching stems.

See also CACTUS.

ECHEVERIA SETOSA

E. derenbergii. Mexico. Height 2–3 in. The broad, spathulate, concave leaves are tightly arranged in a stemless rosette about 3 in. across. The leaves are pale green with red edges and covered with a white bloom. The orange flowers are carried on a stem about 3 in. high in June. Offsets are freely produced.

E. gibbiflora 'Carunculata'. Mexico. Height 24 in. or more. A shrubby plant with broad, spathulate, slightly concave leaves up to 12 in. long. The bottom leaves tend to die off. The leaves are a beautiful pale mauve and have, on their upper surfaces, protuberances which are most apparent in autumn. The red flowers open in autumn and are carried on a stem about 18 in. long.

E. runyonii. Mexico. Height 3 in. The leaves are arranged in a loose, short-stemmed, flattened rosette. They are spathulate and blue-green. The white flowers are borne in September. Water moderately in the growing season, otherwise the leaves become lush and tinged with green. The plant forms offsets freely.

E. setosa. Mexico. Height 3 in. The leaves, densely covered with white hairs, are arranged in an almost stemless rosette. Red flowers on 3–4 in. long stems are produced throughout summer. This species only occasionally forms offsets.

Cultivation. Echeverias are among the easiest of succulent plants to cultivate. Grow them in 3–4 in. pots, using John Innes potting compost No. 2. Water generously during summer and keep just moist in winter and at a temperature of 5°C (41°F). Be careful to keep water off the foliage as the waxy coating on the leaves is easily marked. For the same reason, handle them carefully. Stand the plants outdoors in summer in a sunny position. Move the pots into the house or the greenhouse for the winter, giving them as much light as possible.

During the winter a plant often loses its bottom leaves and becomes leggy. When this happens, cut the top of the plant off in March. Let the leafy top dry for two days, and then pot it up in John Innes potting compost No. 2. It will root easily. The old stem can be kept for propagation. Repot annually in April.

Propagation. Old stems that have been cut down will usually send out new shoots from the leaf

Eccremocarpus scaber

Echeveria derenbergii

Echeveria setosa

ars. Remove these shoots in March and pot
em up in John Innes potting compost No. 2
ter they have been left to dry for two days.
ffsets formed round the plants can also be
moved in March and potted up after drying.

Many species can be propagated from leaf
ttings in spring or early summer. Remove
ump, healthy leaves, place them in a seed tray
sandy compost, and keep them slightly moist.
aintain a minimum temperature of 16°C
1°F). New plantlets will appear; when the old
af has withered away, pot up the plantlets
dividually in the growing compost.

Echeverias can also be raised from seeds sown
March at a temperature of 21°C (70°F).

ests. Colonies of MEALY BUGS cover the bases of
aves with tufts of white waxy wool. ROOT MEALY
JGS infest root systems, checking growth.

iseases. Generally trouble-free.

Echinacea

Purple cone flower. *Compositae*

ECHINACEA PURPUREA

genus of three species of hardy herbaceous
erennials, closely related to *Rudbeckia*. The
pecies described, which has daisy-like flowers, is
eal for a sunny border.

purpurea. N. America. Height 3–4 ft; planting
stance 18–24 in. The mid-green leaves are
nceolate, rough and slightly toothed. The
urple-crimson flowers, about 4 in. across, have
one-shaped orange centres and are produced
om July to September. Of the named varieties,
obert Bloom' is purple-rose, larger than the
ype and more free-flowering; 'The King' is
imson-pink with a mahogany centre; 'White
ustre' is white with a deep orange centre.

ultivation. Plant echinaceas between October
nd March in a sunny position in any fertile,
ell-drained soil. The flowering period of the
lants can be prolonged by cutting off stems
arrying faded flowers. Cut down all remaining
ems in October.

ropagation. Divide and replant the roots between
ctober and March.

Take root cuttings in February; insert in
qual parts (by volume) peat and sand in a cold
ame. Plant them out in a nursery bed when
oung leaves appear, and then into their flower-
g positions from October onwards.

Sow seeds in boxes or pans of seed compost
March under glass at a temperature of 13°C
5°F). Prick the seedlings out into boxes and
arden them off before setting outdoors in a
ursery bed in June or July. Plant out from
ctober onwards. Alternatively, sow in a sunny
ed outdoors in April, prick the seedlings out into
nursery bed and finally plant out in the autumn.
ests and diseases. Generally trouble-free.

Echinocactus

Cactaceae

A genus of ten species of greenhouse perennials.
These slow-growing, globular or cylindrical cacti
may reach 3 ft in diameter in the wild. They
are cultivated for their beautiful spines; most
species are unlikely to flower in cultivation.

The rare *E. horizonthalonius* is the easiest to
flower, but it is difficult to obtain. Echinocacti
need full sunlight to produce good spine
formation and so are unsuitable as house plants.

See also CACTUS.

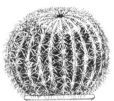

ECHINOCACTUS GRUSONII

E. grusonii. Central Mexico. Height up to 6 in. A
solitary, globular plant that may reach a diameter
of 3 ft in old specimens. A good pot plant would
take many years to reach 6 in. The green plant
body has numerous ribs and radiating groups of
golden-yellow spines arching back from the
areoles and completely covering the body.

The tubular yellow flowers, about 2 in. across,
are produced during May in a circle on the woolly
crown of large plants.

E. horizonthalonius. Mexico, southern U.S.A.
Height 10 in. This solitary, globular, blue-grey
plant has 7–13 ribs, and thick yellow spines. The
tubular, 2 in. wide flowers are pink and occur
even on young plants. Water this species with
extreme care, making sure that the compost dries
out between waterings.

Cultivation. Grow echinocacti in 6–12 in. pots,
according to the species, using an open compost,
such as 1 part sand to 2 parts John Innes potting
compost No. 2 (parts by volume). Place the plants
in full sunlight in the greenhouse. Ventilate freely
during summer, and give them a dry resting
period from October to March. Keep the plants at
a minimum winter temperature of 5°C (41°F).
Water *E. grusonii* freely in summer. Repot
annually in March.

Propagation. Sow seeds in April at a temperature
of 21°C (70°F). Cover them only lightly with soil.

Pests. Conspicuous tufts of white waxy wool on
plants are caused by MEALY BUGS. ROOT MEALY
BUGS infest root systems, checking growth.

Diseases. Generally trouble-free.

Echinocereus

Cactaceae

A genus of 75 species of greenhouse perennials.
These cacti are hardy if kept completely dry from
October to March. They are easily grown and are
cultivated for their vivid, funnel-shaped, 2 in.
wide flowers which are produced in June and July
and last about a week.

See also CACTUS.

Echinacea purpurea 'The King'

Echinocactus grusonii

Echinocereus knippelianus

Echinocereus pectinatus

Echinocereus pentalophus

Echinops banaticus

The slower-growing *E. knippelianus* and *pectinatus* need an open compost; 2 parts John Innes potting compost No. 2 and 1 part grit sharp sand (parts by volume), is suitable. Water these species with more caution than the sprawling species, allowing them to dry out between waterings. Both types of echinocerei need full sun. Overwinter all species in a light position and at a temperature not above 5°C (41°F).

Propagation. Echinocerei can be raised easily from seeds scattered on the surface of pans of John Innes seed compost in early spring. Germinate the seeds under glass at a temperature 21°C (70°F).

Branching species can also be propagated by stem cuttings taken at any time between the end of April and the beginning of August. Remove the stems, dry them for three or four days, and then pot them up in equal parts (by volume) peat and coarse sand.

Pests. Conspicuous tufts of white waxy wool on plants are caused by MEALY BUGS. ROOT MEALY BUGS infest root systems and check growth.

Diseases. A PHYSIOLOGICAL DISORDER due to bad drainage shows as a rotting of the roots and discoloration or complete collapse of the top growth.

Echinocerei can be roughly divided into two types: rapid-growing species that form sprawling branches from the base; and slow-growing, upright species with single stems that usually have beautiful spines.

E. knippelianus. Central Mexico. Height 2 in. A spherical, single-stemmed plant. The stem is dark green, about 2 in. across, and divided into five prominent ribs. It is slow-growing and seldom branches. In mature plants the woolly areoles bear from one to three short spines round a $\frac{1}{2}$ in. long central spine. The pale pink flowers are only $1\frac{1}{2}$ in. long; they are produced in clusters during April and May.

E. pectinatus. Central Mexico. Height 8 in. This is a cylindrical plant, occasionally branching. The green stem has 25 ribs, which are closely covered with small, comb-like white spines, 16 of which radiate from each areole. The vivid cerise-pink flowers are about 3 in. long and open into wide bells in June.

E. pentalophus. Mexico. Height 6 in. An easily grown, sprawling, vigorous plant with branching pale green stems about 1 in. across. Each stem has five ribs with prominent tubercles and slightly woolly areoles, each bearing white marginal spines and one central spine about $\frac{3}{4}$ in. long. The deep pink bell-shaped flowers, produced in mid-summer, are about 4 in. long.

E. procumbens. Mexico. Height 4–6 in. A sprawling, vigorous, easily grown plant similar to *E. pentalophus* but with darker central spines and purple flowers.

Cultivation. The spreading echinocerei need a rich soil, such as John Innes potting compost No. 2. They require plenty of root room and ideally should be grown in 6–8 in. pans, so that their roots can spread outwards; they may, however, be grown in 3–6 in. pots. Keep them dry between October and March, but water freely in summer.

Echinops

Globe thistle. *Compositae*

ECHINOPS BANATICUS

A genus of 100 species of hardy herbaceous biennials and perennials. The handsome spherical flowers have a metallic lustre and may be cut and dried for winter decoration. The perennial species described here have thistle-like leaves.

E. banaticus. Hungary, Balkans. Height 3–4 ft; planting distance 24 in. The slender, spiny, dark green leaves are downy on the underside. Globular heads of blue flowers, 1–1$\frac{1}{2}$ in. across, are borne on the branching stems during June and August.

E. humilis. Asia. Height 3–5 ft; planting distance 24 in. The dark green leaves have wavy edges and are almost spineless; the upper sides are cobwebby. Blue flowers, about 1 in. across, appear in August and September. 'Blue Cloud' and 'Taplow Blue', both with soft blue flowers, are two recommended varieties.

E. ritro. S. Europe, Balkans. Height 3–4 ft; planting distance 24 in. The deep grey-green leaves, which are without spines, are downy beneath. This compact species produces globular steel-blue flowers, 1$\frac{1}{2}$–2 in. across, during July and August.

Cultivation. Plant echinops from October to March in a sunny position in any ordinary well-drained garden soil. No staking is required. Cut the stems to ground level in October.

Propagation. Divide the roots during suitable weather between October and March.

Insert root cuttings in a box of sandy soil in November or December and overwinter them in a cold frame. In the spring, transplant the cuttings to a nursery bed when they have well-developed shoots; plant out in autumn.

Sow seeds outdoors during April in a sunny position. Prick out the seedlings into nursery rows, finally setting them out in their permanent positions in the autumn.

Pests and diseases. Generally trouble-free.

Echinopsis

Cactaceae

A genus of 35 species of greenhouse perennials. These cacti are hardy if kept completely dry during winter. They are grown for their freely produced, sweetly scented flowers, which open during the evening and last for about two days. The pink or white flowers are funnel-shaped and about 4–8 in. long.

See also CACTUS.

E. × 'Green Gold'. Garden origin. Height up to 6 in. This hybrid has a globular to shortly ovoid body, rich mid-green, with about 12 prominent ribs. Golden-yellow flowers, 4 in. or more long, appear near the top of the plant during summer.
E. multiplex. Brazil. Height 6 in. The globular green plant body branches freely from any point. It has about 12 sharp ribs which carry stout brown spines. The scented pink flowers have tubes 8 in. long and are 6 in. across; they are produced during summer.
E. rhodacantha, syn. *Denmoza rhodacantha.* Argentina. Height 6 in. or more. A globular species when young, but eventually becoming cylindrical. The plant body is dark, matt green, with about 15 prominent ribs. Young spines are blood-red, ageing to rust-red and then grey. Red flowers, up to 3 in. long, appear from the top of the plant at any time during the summer.
E. rhodotricha. Argentina, Paraguay. Height up to 2½ ft. This is one of the larger-growing species, with a mid-green cylindrical body. It has 8–13 ribs which bear yellow-brown spines, four to seven radials and one central spine from each areole. It blooms when about 6 in. high. The white, unscented flowers are 3 in. across with 6 in. long tubes, and bloom in early summer. The flowers open in the evening and last through the following day.
Cultivation. These cacti are best grown in a rich soil, such as John Innes potting compost No. 2; they should be given a generous amount of water in summer. Grow them in 4–6 in. pots. Once the flower buds are forming, feed the plants fortnightly with a high-potassium liquid fertiliser. To ensure that they flower well, keep them cool, 2°C (36°F), and dry in winter. Always place them where they will receive the maximum light. Repot annually in April.
Propagation. The plants are easily increased by removing offsets, which may already have roots. Pot up in 3 in. containers of the growing compost. Echinopsis may also be raised from seeds sown in early spring at a temperature of 21°C (70°F).

Pests. Colonies of MEALY BUGS and ROOT MEALY BUGS may infest the root systems and subsequently check growth.
Diseases. Generally trouble-free.

Echium

Boraginaceae

A genus of 40 species of hardy and half-hardy annuals and biennials, the biennials flowering from seed in their first year if sown in early spring. With one exception, the species and varieties described are particularly suitable for borders. *E. wildpretii* requires the protection of a greenhouse in all but the mildest areas.
E. bourgeanum: see *E. wildpretii*
E. plantagineum. Mediterranean and Great Britain. Height 3 ft; planting distance 18 in. A bushy, hardy annual, with oblong mid-green leaves. Blue or pale purple tubular flowers are carried in 9 in. long branching spikes from June to August.

Garden hybrids sometimes listed under this species produce clusters of upward-facing bell-shaped flowers in white, pink, carmine, mauve, blue and purple. 'Blue Bedder', 12 in. and 'Dwarf Hybrids', 12 in., are particularly recommended.
E. rubrum. Europe. Height 3 ft; planting distance 12 in. A bushy, hardy biennial suitable for a herbaceous or mixed border. This species will often live for more than two years. The mid-green leaves are narrower and more pointed than those of *E. plantagineum.* Bright red tubular flowers, ½ in. long, with protruding yellow stamens, are produced from May to July. The variety 'Burgundy' has long spikes of dark red flowers.
E. vulgare. Europe, including Great Britain. Height 24 in.; planting distance 9 in. A hardy biennial, usually grown as an annual, of compact, bushy habit. The leaves are dark green and lanceolate. The flowers, purple in bud, changing to violet, are tubular, ⅓ in. long, and carried in short, dense spikes. They bloom in great profusion from June to August and are attractive to bees.
E. wildpretii. Canary Islands. Height up to 10 ft; planting distance 3–4 ft. The plant listed under this name is correctly *E. bourgeanum.* It is a tender woody-stemmed biennial. In the first year it forms a short stem bearing mid-green lanceolate leaves covered with silvery hairs. The following season the flowering stem appears and rapidly grows to a height of 6 ft or more. The slender spire is composed of many side-branches, closely packed with pink or mauve tubular flowers that open from May to July.
Cultivation. Most soils and sites give reasonable results, but a light, dry soil in an open, sunny position encourages free flowering.

E. wildpretii, grown in the greenhouse, requires a winter temperature of 7–10°C (45–50°F). Water freely during the growing season and ventilate the greenhouse when the temperature exceeds 13°C (55°F). Pot on to a final 10 or 12 in. container filled with John Innes potting compost No. 3.
Propagation. Sow the seeds in the flowering site in March or September, thinning out the seedlings in April. Alternatively, sow under glass in

Echinopsis × 'Green Gold'

Echinopsis rhodotricha

Echium plantagineum 'Dwarf Hybrids'

Edraianthus serpyllifolius

Edraianthus pumilio

Edraianthus graminifolius

Egg plant 'Long Purple'

February or March at a temperature of 13–16°C (55–61°F); prick out the seedlings into boxes and harden off in a cold frame before planting out in permanent positions in May.

Sow the seeds of *E. wildpretii* in April at 16°C (61°F). Prick off the seedlings into 3 in. pots.
Pests. GLASSHOUSE RED SPIDER MITES may be troublesome on *E. wildpretii* under glass.
Diseases. Generally trouble-free.

Edelweiss: see Leontopodium

Edraianthus
Campanulaceae

EDRAIANTHUS PUMILIO

A genus of ten species of herbaceous perennial plants closely related to *Campanula* and somewhat similar in appearance. The plants are hardy and suitable for rock gardens, but they are generally short-lived. All species bear clusters of upturned bell-shaped flowers.

E. graminifolius. Dalmatia. Height 3 in.; spread 9 in. This species forms rosettes of bristly, needle-shaped, grey-green leaves. Purple flowers, $\frac{3}{4}$ in. long, are borne from May to July.

E. pumilio. Dalmatia. Height 2–3 in.; spread 6–9 in. A clump-forming, compact species with linear grey-green leaves. Purple-blue flowers, 1 in. long, appear from May to July. It needs the protection of raised panes of glass or of open-ended cloches during winter.

E. serpyllifolius. Balkan Peninsula. Height 1 in.; spread 6–9 in. A mat-forming species with lanceolate deep green leaves. Glowing purple flowers, $\frac{3}{4}$–1 in. long, are carried on the tips of prostrate stems in June. The flowers of 'Major' are larger and in a deeper shade of purple.

Cultivation. Plant *E. graminifolius* and *E. pumilio* between September and March in a sunny position. They need deep, well-drained soil for their stout roots and grow particularly well in a mixture of 3 parts fibrous loam to 2 parts limestone grit (parts by volume).

Plant *E. serpyllifolius* between September and March, in a well-drained scree or lime-filled trough in full sun. It does well in rock gardens made with tufa.

Propagation. Take cuttings of non-flowering basal shoots, $1\frac{1}{2}$–2 in. long, in July or August, and insert in equal parts (by volume) peat and sand in a cold frame. When rooted, pot the cuttings singly in $2\frac{1}{2}$ in. pots of John Innes potting compost No. 1; grow on in a plunge bed for a further year before setting the plants out in permanent positions between September and March.

All species may also be propagated from seeds sown in March, in pots or pans of John Innes seed compost, and placed in a cold frame. Prick out the seedlings individually into $2\frac{1}{2}$ in. pots of John Innes potting compost No. 1 when they are large enough to handle; thereafter treat as described for cuttings.
Pests. SLUGS sometimes eat holes in young leaves and flowers.
Diseases. Generally trouble-free.

Egg plant (Aubergine)
Solanum melongena ovigerum. Solanaceae

This tender annual plant is extensively grown as a vegetable in America and Europe. In Great Britain it is best grown under glass, although during warm summers it may also be grown in the open after hardening off.

Egg plants are grown for their fruits which

ary, according to variety, from the size of a large plum or egg to oblong shapes about 6 in. long. The skin is smooth and glossy with a slight bloom and the flesh is similar to that of young marrows. Egg plants may be cooked and served in the same way as marrows.

EGG PLANT

VARIETIES

These differ in shape and colour and may be round, ovoid or oblong, and with white or purple skins. Well-flavoured purple varieties include 'Long Purple' and 'New York'.

Cultivation. Grow egg plants in well-drained soil enriched with decayed manure. Choose a sheltered sunny site, preferably against a wall. Sow seeds in boxes of seed compost in early February at a temperature of 18°C (64°F). As soon as the seedlings are large enough to handle, prick them out into 3 in. pots of John Innes potting compost No. 1. Harden off during May and plant out in early June.

For pot culture under glass, place the young plants in 8 in. containers of John Innes potting compost No. 2 or 3. When the plants are 5–6 in. high, pinch out the growing tips to encourage two leading shoots. Remove any side-shoots as they appear and give a liquid feed at two or three-week intervals. Allow only four fruits to form on each plant. Let the fruits ripen before picking them from July onwards and use as soon as possible after harvesting.

Good crops can be produced in frames or under cloches; the fruits mature later than those grown in a greenhouse.

Pests and diseases. Generally trouble-free.

Eglantine: see *Rosa rubiginosa*

Egyptian onion: see Onion

Eichhornia

EICHHORNIA SPECIOSA

A genus of seven species of tropical evergreen aquatic plants with attractive orchid-like flowers. Only one species, *E. speciosa*, is widely grown; it is used as a decorative floating plant in outside pools and occasionally in aquaria.

E. crassipes: see *E. speciosa*

E. speciosa, syn. *E. crassipes* (floating water hyacinth). Tropical America. Water depth 6–18 in.; height above water 6–9 in.; spread 6–12 in. A tender perennial aquatic, principally floating but which also grows in mud where the water depth is insufficient to allow floating. Under glass, in a heated pool or in cramped conditions, the leaves may be 18–24 in. high.

This plant has short thick stems which carry 3–4 in. long spikes of flat, lavender-blue flowers, each with a conspicuous yellow eye on the uppermost petal. The glossy dark green leaves, roughly heart-shaped, are attached to the plant by inflated petioles. These are built up of spongy tissue, and with their tough outer skins act as buoys and enable the plant to float.

Stolons are freely produced, and young plants rapidly develop on these. Great chains and colonies of plants become established even in the relatively low summer temperatures of the British climate. In addition, the dense feathery roots, often brilliant purple in colour, extend 12–18 in. into the water.

Cultivation. This is a floating plant but the bottom soil should be fertile and at least 2 in. deep, so that the water contains the necessary nutrient minerals. Site in full sun.

No planting is necessary; merely place the plants on the surface of the water, between May and September. For outdoor pools, wait until early June, a little later in cold districts.

Bring outdoor plants into the greenhouse by the end of September and overwinter them in wet soil, though not in water. Keep in full light and in a temperature of 13–16°C (55–61°F).

Propagation. New plants are produced on the stolons between May and September. When a young plant is showing several well-formed leaves it is ready to be detached.

Pests and diseases. Generally trouble-free.

Elaeagnus

Elaeagnaceae

ELAEAGNUS UMBELLATA

A genus of about 45 species of hardy evergreen or deciduous shrubs grown for their attractive foliage. They bear clusters, $\frac{1}{2}-\frac{3}{4}$ in. wide, of sweetly scented but inconspicuous bell-shaped flowers. The majority of species are fast-growing and suitable for most soils and aspects; the evergreen species, which are tolerant of shade, wind and seaside exposure, make useful hedges or screens.

E. angustifolia (oleaster). S. Europe, W. Asia. Height and spread 10–15 ft. A deciduous wide-spreading shrub or small tree. The branches are occasionally spiny, white when young, and carry narrow, willow-like, silver grey-green leaves. The silvery flowers are borne in June and are followed by edible, oval, silvered-amber fruits. This species is suitable only for a large

Eichhornia speciosa

Elaeagnus macrophylla

garden; the silvery foliage contrasts effectively with purple-leaved plants.

E. argentea: see *E. commutata*

E. commutata, syn. *E. argentea* (silver berry). N. America. Height and spread 6–8 ft. A slow-growing deciduous shrub of suckering habit. The erect, scaly and red-brown stems carry ovate deep silver-green leaves. Silver flowers in May are followed by edible, silvery, egg-shaped fruits.

E. × ebbingei. Garden origin. Height and spread 10–15 ft. This hybrid between *E. macrophylla* and *E. pungens* is a fast-growing evergreen shrub with leathery, silver-grey, broadly ovate leaves. Silvery flowers are borne in October and November and are followed by small, egg-shaped, red or orange fruits. This hybrid is ideal for hedges and screens, especially near the sea.

E. glabra. China, Korea, Japan. Height and spread 10–12 ft. An evergreen shrub. The elliptic-ovate leathery leaves are silver-grey. Silvery flowers are produced in October and November; the egg-shaped fruits are orange or red when ripe. It is similar to *E. × ebbingei* but less vigorous.

E. macrophylla. Korea, Japan. Height and spread 6–10 ft. Spreading evergreen shrub with scandent stems when well established. The broad, ovate, leathery leaves are a silver grey-green when young, becoming shining mid-green when mature. Silvery flowers appear in October and November, and are followed by red oval fruits.

E. multiflora. Japan, China. Height 8–10 ft; spread 10–12 ft. A wide-spreading deciduous shrub with ovate leaves that are dark green above, silvery beneath. Yellow-white flowers are produced with the new shoots in April and May. Edible oblong red fruits ripen in July.

E. pungens. Japan. Height and spread 8–12 ft. Vigorous, spreading, evergreen shrub occasionally with spiny stems. The ovate leathery leaves are glossy green above, dull white beneath. Silvery flowers are borne in October and November and are sometimes followed by small, oval, red or orange fruits. A strong-growing shrub, excellent for hedging.

The variety 'Dicksonii' is a slower-growing form with broad, irregular, yellow margins to the leaves; 'Maculata' has leaves splashed with gold and is slower-growing than the species; 'Variegata' is a vigorous form with narrow cream-yellow margins to the leaves.

E. umbellata. China, Korea, Japan. Height 10–15 ft; spread 10–18 ft. A vigorous, wide-spreading deciduous shrub, with narrowly ovate leaves that are pale green above and silvery beneath. Cream-white flowers crowd the branches in May and are followed by round red fruits. This is suitable only for a large garden where it makes an excellent specimen tree for a lawn.

Cultivation. Plant deciduous species from October to December, evergreen species in April or September. All species will grow in ordinary, even poor and shallow chalk soils. *E. angustifolia* and *E. commutata*, in particular, thrive on sandy soils. Deciduous species require a position in full sun, evergreen species do equally well in sun or in partial shade.

For hedges, space young plants at intervals of 15–18 in., for screens space at 2–3 ft. After planting, remove the upper third of all shoots to promote bushy growth.

Propagation. Evergreen species are increased by cuttings, 3–4 in. long, taken in late August and September; insert the cuttings in equal parts (by volume) peat and sand in a cold frame. The following spring, pot the rooted cuttings in 3½–4 in. pots of John Innes potting compost No. 2, plunge outdoors or in an open frame and transplant to permanent positions in October.

Increase deciduous species by seeds sown in pans of John Innes seed compost when ripe (July to September) and place in a cold frame; prick the seedlings off when large enough to handle, into 3 in. pots, later transferring to nursery beds. Grow on for one or two years before planting out.

Pruning. No regular pruning is needed, but long straggling shoots may be shortened during April and May. The variegated forms of *E. pungens* tend to produce green-leaved shoots; these should be removed immediately they appear.

Trim established hedges in June and, if necessary, again in September.

Pests. Generally trouble-free.

Diseases. Irregular brown blotches on the leaves are due to LEAF SPOT.

Elaeagnus pungens 'Maculata'

Elaeagnus umbellata (fruits)

Embothrium coccineum lanceolatum

Embothrium

Chilean fire bush. *Proteaceae*

EMBOTHRIUM COCCINEUM

A genus of eight species of evergreen trees and shrubs from S. America and W. Australia. Only one species is in general cultivation; it is tender, although the varieties are hardier than the type. It is grown for the freely borne scarlet flowers, but is suitable for outdoor cultivation only in the south and west of Great Britain.

E. coccineum. Chile. Height 15–20 ft; spread 7–10 ft. A suckering tree of upright habit and stiff growths. The leathery ovate-lanceolate leaves are shiny mid-green. Brilliant scarlet flowers are borne in terminal or axillary cemes, 3–4 in. long, during May and June. The flowers are tubular at first, but later the arrow lobes expand and recurve.

E. c. lanceolatum makes a slender, graceful ree and is hardier than the species; the leaves re linear-lanceolate. The form 'Norquinco 'alley' is extremely free-flowering; *E. c. ongifolium* has longer leaves. Both are hardier han the type species.

Cultivation. Embothriums do well on neutral nd acid soils; they do not tolerate limy or halky soils. Plant in April or May in full sun ear a south or west-facing wall. During winter, rotect the shrubs with straw or bracken until stablished.

Propagation. Sow imported seeds in March or April in pots or pans of John Innes seed compost under glass at a temperature of 13–16°C 55–61°F). Prick out, when large enough to handle, in 3 in. pots of John Innes potting ompost No. 1, excluding lime. Pot on as re-quired and grow on in a frost-free frame or greenhouse for two years; harden off and plant ut in permanent positions in May.

Alternatively, detach suckers from the base nd establish in pots. Propagation by cuttings is xtremely difficult.

Pruning. None required, but straggly growths nay be shortened after flowering.

Pests and diseases. Generally trouble-free.

Endive

Cichorium endivia. Compositae

A half-hardy annual, grown as a salad plant. Endive somewhat resembles lettuce and is an excellent alternative in late autumn and early winter. The pale green, crisp and usually deeply dissected leaves are bitter, and the plants should be blanched before use.

VARIETIES

Two groups are available: those with curled eaves, sometimes known as Staghorns, and hose with plain leaves, known as Batavians. Recommended varieties are 'Moss Curled' for an early sowing, 'Extra Fine Green Curled' for use n summer and 'Broad-leafed Batavian' for use n autumn and winter.

Cultivation. Endives thrive on light, well-drained soils, but heavy soils will give satis-factory crops if the ground is kept lightened by he addition of strawy manure. On fertile soils, apply a dressing of a general-purpose fertiliser at 2 oz. per sq. yd before sowing. Later sowings are deal on ground where an early crop, such as otatoes, has been grown. Dress poor soils liber-lly with decayed manure.

Sow seeds where the plants are to grow, to avoid a possible check to growth after trans-planting. Sow the seeds thinly, in ½ in. deep drills drawn 15 in. apart. Thin the seedlings as hey grow until they are 12–15 in. apart. Water he bed thoroughly at least once a week and keep it free of weeds.

Make the first sowing in April and, for a continuous supply, make further sowings at ntervals of three or four weeks until mid-August. Unless late-sown plants are grown in a

sheltered and sunny position, they are better grown in cold frames or under Dutch lights. If the frames are carefully ventilated and covered with mats in frosty weather, plants should last well into the New Year.

Blanching and harvesting. Plants are generally ready for blanching about three months after sowing. Gather the leaves together when they are dry, and tie with raffia round the plant so that light is kept from all except the outer leaves. Alternatively, cover the plants with inverted boxes or pots, in which the drainage holes have been blocked. Blanching takes seven to ten days in summer, up to three weeks in autumn and winter. Prepare a few plants at a time, as they do not keep well after blanching.

Pests and diseases. Generally trouble-free.

Endymion

Liliaceae

This is the current botanical name for a genus of ten species of bulbous plants formerly included in the genus *Scilla*. It includes the English bluebell and similar plants found growing wild in western Europe and in African countries bordering the western Mediterranean. The Scottish bluebell is *Campanula rotundifolia*, and the English bluebell is known as wild hyacinth in Scotland.

Two hardy species are generally available in Great Britain. They have strap-shaped, pointed, glossy, mid-green leaves. Bell-shaped purple-blue flowers, $\frac{1}{2}$–$\frac{3}{4}$ in. long, are borne from April to June. The native plant, *E. nonscriptus*, is well known for the expanses of colour that it provides in open woodland, and also in the hedgerows and grassy seaward slopes of the West Country.

The two species described hybridise readily when grown side by side, and the resulting progeny usually combine the characteristics of both parents.

E. campanulatus: see *E. hispanicus*
E. hispanicus, syns. *E. campanulatus, Scilla campanulata* and *S. hispanica.* W. and S. Europe and N. Africa. Height 12 in.; planting distance 4–6 in. This species thrives in the open and will persist untended for many years. The leaves and flowers are broader than those of the English bluebell and the erect stems are only slightly inclined at the tip. Many coloured varieties have been named, including 'Excelsior', large, deep blue flowers; 'Myosotis', clear blue; 'Queen of the Pinks', deep pink; and 'White Triumphator', tall, pure white.
E. nonscriptus, syns. *Scilla nonscripta, S. nutans, S. festalis* and *Hyacinthus nonscriptus* (English bluebell, wild hyacinth). Great Britain and W. Europe. Height up to 12 in.; planting distance 4 in. This species thrives equally well in sun or in partial shade. The leaves are erect at first but spread later. The flowering stems are reflexed at the tips until the last flowers open, when they gradually straighten. White and pink varieties exist and are sometimes offered for sale.
Cultivation. Endymion bulbs have no outer skin to protect them from drying and damage; they soon shrivel or go mouldy if storage is too dry or too damp. They should therefore be planted as

Endive 'Broad-leafed Batavian'

Endive 'Moss Curled' (blanched)

Endymion hispanicus

soon as available. Both species are best planted 4–6 in. deep. They need moist but not water-logged soil containing ample organic matter.

Propagation. Leave the seeds to ripen, fall and grow; or collect the seeds and scatter them where new plants are wanted, preferably in semi-shade on decayed fallen leaves in a place where they will not be disturbed by cultivation. If this is not possible, sow the collected seeds in shallow drills, again in semi-shade; lift and plant out two or three years later. Flowering-sized bulbs take from four to six years to develop.

Stocks can be built up by lifting annually and replanting at once, giving the small offsets space to increase in size. Plant the larger bulbs more deeply and at wider spacings, and strew the smaller ones an inch or so apart in shallow drills.

Pests. Generally trouble-free.

Diseases. An attack of RUST shows on both sides of the leaves as yellow spots which produce powdery masses of dark brown spores.

A VIRUS DISEASE causes yellow mottling of the foliage and stems.

Enkianthus campanulatus
(autumn foliage and seeds)

Enkianthus campanulatus
(flowers)

Epidendrum brassavolae

Enkianthus

Ericaceae

ENKIANTHUS CAMPANULATUS

A genus of ten species of hardy deciduous or partially evergreen shrubs with alternate leaves. They are grown for their profusion of small flowers, usually bell-shaped, and for their brilliant autumn foliage.

E. campanulatus. Japan. Height 8 ft or more; spread 3–5 ft. An upright deciduous shrub with erect whorled branches and smooth red shoots. The leaves, usually in clusters at the ends of the shoots, are dull green, obovate or elliptic and finely toothed; they turn brilliant red in autumn. Cream-yellow flowers with red veins are freely carried in terminal pendulous racemes, about 3 in. long, in May.

E. cernuus. Japan. Height up to 6 ft; spread 3–4 ft. A well-branched deciduous shrub of upright habit. The leaves are dull green, elliptic or oblong, pointed or blunt; they assume orange and red autumn tints. White flowers, frilled at the mouth, appear in May in pendulous racemes up to 3 in. long. *E. c. rubens* has deep red flowers and shorter and broader leaves, which assume red autumn colours.

E. perulatus. Japan. Height up to 6 ft; spread 3–4 ft. A slow-growing, compact deciduous species, densely leaved, with red young growths. The neat ovate to obovate leaves are clustered towards the ends of the shoots; they are sharply pointed and finely toothed; in autumn they turn rich red. The urn-shaped white flowers are profusely borne in May in 2 in. long racemes at the ends of the shoots.

Cultivation. These shrubs require an acid or neutral soil; they will grow in ordinary lime-free soil and benefit from added peat or leaf-mould. Light woodland conditions are ideal. Plant in October and November or in March in a sunny sheltered position.

Propagation. Take cuttings, 3 in. long, in August or September, of lateral shoots with a heel; insert in equal parts (by volume) peat and sand in a cold frame. The following April or May line out the rooted cuttings in nursery rows outdoors and grow on for two or three years before planting in permanent positions.

Pests and diseases. Generally trouble-free.

Epidendrum

Orchidaceae

EPIDENDRUM PRISMATOCARPUM

A genus of about 400 species of orchids extending from Florida to Brazil. All the species are epiphytic and most are deciduous with considerable differences in plant form. Many are pseudobulbous with a few apical leathery leaves of various sizes and shapes, whilst others have thin cane or reed-like, many-leaved stems of varying lengths.

The flower spikes are always terminal and erect or arching, carrying a single or numerous flowers. The lip is usually larger than the sepals and petals, and it is always more or less fused to the column. Epidendrums are relatively easy to grow; some require warm conditions, others are intermediate or a cool greenhouse or even a warm window-sill or a well-lit shelf. A great many hybrids have been raised between the species and with other closely related genera such as *Cattleya* and *Laelia*.

See also ORCHIDS.

E. brassavolae. Guatemala. A species with flattened pear-shaped pseudobulbs 4–6 in. high carrying two shortly strap-shaped, mid-green leaves. The sweetly scented inflorescence is 12–24 in. long; it emerges from a 3 in. sheath at the top of the pseudobulb, and bears up to 30 flowers, each 4 in. across. The sepals and petals are long, narrow and curving, light yellow and tinged purple on the backs. The purple lip is heart-shaped, pale yellow or white at the base, and the column is green with purple spots. This plant flowers from July to August; it requires intermediate greenhouse temperatures.

E. ciliare. C. America, W. Indies, Brazil. This species has short, slender pseudobulbs with two strap-shaped mid-green leaves at the tip. The flower stem is about 10 in. long, and bears up to eight yellow-green and blue flowers, 4 in. across in December and January. These have long narrow and spreading sepals and petals. The white lip is deeply three-lobed, the side lobes

Epidendrum fragrans

finely lacerated and the mid-lobe long and very narrow. Grow in an intermediate greenhouse.

E. cochleatum. Florida to Colombia and Venezuela. The pseudobulbs are about 4 in. high and thickened in the middle, with two mid-green strap-shaped leaves. The erect flower spike increases gradually to 12 in. and produces a succession of flowers, about 1½ in. wide, with four or five open at one time; the flowering period is from January to July or often all year round. The pale green sepals and petals are narrow and hang downwards because of the twisted flower stalks. The shell-shaped lip is upward-facing and erect; it is deep purple, yellow at the base with purple veins. This species should be grown in an intermediate greenhouse.

E. crassilabium: see *E. variegatum*

E. endresii. C. America. The slender pseudobulbs of this species are up to 12 in. high and bear two rows of elliptic, fleshy light or olive green leaves, their bases almost encircling the pseudobulb. The erect inflorescence is up to 12 in. long and has about 15 flowers, each 1 in. across, that appear from January to May, or intermittently throughout the year. They are waxy white, and have spreading sepals and petals, the petals being narrower than the sepals. The four-lobed lip is marked with violet and orange. Grow in an intermediate greenhouse.

E. fragrans. W. Indies, Guianas, Venezuela, Brazil. A species with pseudobulbs 3–4 in. high, each carrying one lanceolate, mid-green leaf and a 9 in. long flower spike of two to five flowers that measure 2 in. across. These have cream-yellow sepals and petals and a concave, almost circular lip which is white with purple stripes. They are produced during summer and autumn and have a spicy scent.

This species requires intermediate to warm greenhouse conditions.

E. falcatum: see *E. parkinsonianum*

E. ibaguense, syn. *E. radicans*. C. and S. America. A species with a cane-like stem, growing to a height of 3 ft or more; it bears fleshy, oblong, pale to mid-green leaves in two ranks throughout its length. The slender, wiry flowering stem, which can attain a height of up to 4 ft, has a round head of brilliantly coloured flowers each 1 in. or more across; they appear from October to January. The colours range from pink and lilac to red, orange and yellow; they are usually self-coloured, but the labellum may be differently coloured from the sepals. The sepals and petals are narrow and spreading; the lip is four-lobed and fringed.

Many hybrids have been produced, including the popular Rainbow range, with every shade between yellow and red. This species and its hybrids should be grown under intermediate greenhouse conditions.

E. nocturnum. W. Indies, C. America to Peru. This species has pseudobulbs up to 3 ft high and linear or oblong-lanceolate mid-green leaves at the top. The flower stem, 12–24 in. high, arises from a large compressed sheath; it carries a single fragrant 4 in. wide flower; the scent is stronger at night. The sepals and petals are narrow and yellow-green; the three-lobed lip is white, with a long and narrow mid-lobe. The flowers appear from March to May, or intermittently throughout the year. Grow in a warm greenhouse.

E. parkinsonianum, syn. *E. falcatum*. C. America, Panama. A pendulous plant best grown on a raft, with mid-green, fleshy, lanceolate, tapering leaves produced singly at 1–2 in. intervals from the rhizome. The 3 in. wide flowers, in groups of two to five, appear on stems up to 12 in. long from January to September. The 2½ in. long narrow petals are pale green, the lip yellow, with wide side-lobes and a long narrow mid-lobe. Grow this species in an intermediate greenhouse.

E. prismatocarpum. Costa Rica. A showy species with narrow pseudobulbs about 9 in. high, each carrying two mid-green, shortly strap-shaped leaves. The flower stems are erect and bear 10–20 waxy flowers, 2 in. across, from May to August. These have narrow, pale green-yellow sepals and petals with dark purple spots. The lip is narrow and pointed, light purple with a yellow tip and a white border. This species requires intermediate greenhouse temperatures.

E. radicans: see *E. ibaguense*

E. variegatum, syn. *E. crassilabium*. Tropical and C. America, W. Indies. This species, which is botanically known as *E. vespa*, has pseudobulbs that vary from orbicular to long and narrow. They are usually compressed and measure from 2½ in. by 2 in. to ¾ in. by 9 in. Each bears two or three thin but rigid leaves. Erect stems up to 12 in. long carry numerous flowers 1 in. across. They have thick rigid sepals and petals that are green with purple-brown spots. The lip is white, tinged with green and has a few pink-purple streaks. Flowering is during the winter months.

It is best grown in an intermediate greenhouse.

E. vespa: see *E. variegatum*

Cultivation. Grow epidendrums on slabs of tree fern, or in baskets or pots, fitting the size of the plants. Use a compost of 3 parts osmunda fibre and 1 part sphagnum moss (all parts by volume). The stem-rooting species can be grown

Epidendrum ciliare

Epidendrum cochleatum

Epidendrum nocturnum

in a mixture of equal parts (by volume) John Innes potting compost No. 1 and moss. Plants for a warm greenhouse need a minimum winter temperature of 16°C (61°F); those for an intermediate house need 13°C (55°F). Ventilate the greenhouse when the day temperature exceeds 21–24°C (70–75°F).

The species with hard pseudobulbs require a definite resting period from November to March, with only sufficient water to stop them shrivelling. Water freely during the growing season. Those with softer pseudobulbs, the cane-stemmed plants, need to be kept moist throughout the year. Shade the greenhouse on sunny days from April to October.

Propagation. Divide the plants from March to May and repot them or fasten to fresh slabs of tree fern. Cuttings of the cane-stemmed plants may be taken from March to May; insert in pots of sphagnum moss and place in an intermediate greenhouse.

Pests. Leaves and stems may be infested by SCALE INSECTS which give the plants a sooty scurfy appearance.

Diseases. Generally trouble-free.

Epidendrum prismatocarpum

Epilobium glabellum

Epimedium × rubrum

Epilobium

Willow-herb. *Onagraceae*

A genus of 215 species of hardy herbaceous perennials and sub-shrubs. The dwarf herbaceous species described here are not straggly and invasive like the common willow-herb and are suitable for rock gardens. They have shallow funnel-shaped flowers and lanceolate leaves.

E. dodonaei, syn. *E. fleischeri.* Europe. Height and spread up to 12 in. To keep this species neat and compact, grow the plants on a scree where their stolons can thread among the stones. The linear to narrowly lanceolate leaves are mid-green; four-petalled deep rose flowers, about 1 in. across, appear from June to August.

E. fleischeri: see *E. dodonaei*

E. glabellum. New Zealand. Height 9 in.; spread 12–15 in. The leaves are mid-green; cream-white flowers, 1 in. wide, are produced on leafy stems from June to September.

E. kai-koense Japan. Height 4 in.; spread 12 in. This neat plant has purple-green leaves and carries a succession of rose-pink flowers, ¾ in. across, from June to September. It is not a long-lived species, but self-sown seedlings may occasionally appear.

Cultivation. Plant between September and March in any ordinary, well-drained garden soil in a sunny position.

Propagation. Sow seeds in February or March in boxes or pans of John Innes seed compost, and place them in a cold frame. Prick off the seedlings when large enough to handle, and pot on into 3 in. containers of John Innes potting compost No. 1. Plant out from September to March.

Alternatively take 1½–2 in. cuttings of basal shoots in April or May; set them in equal parts (by volume) peat and sand in a cold frame. Pot into 3 in. pots when well rooted and plant out between September and March.

Pests and diseases. Generally trouble-free.

Epimedium

Barrenwort, bishop's hat. *Berberidaceae*

A genus of 21 species of hardy semi-evergreen or evergreen perennials. They retain their leaves throughout the winter and are attractive ground-cover plants for positions in partial shade. In spring the fresh green of the young leaves is tinted with pink or red; in summer the leaves turn a deeper green and are beautifully veined, in autumn they are richly tinted with yellow, red and bronze. The leaves are divided, being composed of lopsided heart-shaped leaflets, often sharply serrated.

The flowers are saucer-shaped and, in some species, spurred. Both the foliage and flowers are useful for decorative arrangements.

E. grandiflorum, syn. *E. macranthum.* Japan. Height and planting distance 9–12 in. White, carmine-pink, violet or yellow spurred flowers, 1 in. long, are borne in June. The crimson-carmine 'Rose Queen' is a good variety.

E. macranthum: see *E. grandiflorum*

E. perralderianum. Algeria. Height 12 in.; planting distance 15 in. The young leaves of this evergreen plant are bright green with bronze-red markings, gradually turning to copper-bronze in winter. Sprays of yellow flowers, ½–¾ in. long and with short spurs, appear in June.

E. pinnatum. Iran, Caucasus. Height 9–12 in.; planting distance 12 in. An evergreen species with mid-green hairy leaves that take on red tints in autumn. Bright yellow flowers, ½–¾ in. long with short spurs and red nectar-bearing glands, are borne from May to July on slender arching stems. *E. p. colchicum* is more free-flowering than the type, and the flowers are larger.

E. × rubrum. Height and planting distance 12 in. The mid-green leaves are tinged red when young, and turn orange and yellow in autumn. Crimson flowers, ¾–1 in. long, are produced in May.

Epimedium × rubrum
(young foliage and flowers)

E. × versicolor 'Sulphureum'. Height and planting distance 12 in. The mid-green leaves have prickly teeth. This hybrid bears pendulous pale yellow flowers, ¾ in. long, in May.

E. × warleyense. Height and planting distance 9 in. The leaves are mid-green, with red markings when young, and have prickly teeth. Copper-red owers, ¾ in. long, appear in April and May; they ave short spurs.

E. × *youngianum.* Japan. Height up to 6–8 n.; planting distance 12 in. The mid-green leaves re marked with red when young and have prickly teeth; they are flushed orange-red in utumn. Pink flowers, ½–¾ in. long, are borne in April and May. 'Niveum' is a white form.

Cultivation. Plant between September and March in partial shade in moist sandy loam. Epimediums grow well under trees provided the soil does not dry out. Give them a top dressing of peat or leaf-mould in early spring. Removal of the old leaves in March, just prior to formation of the flower spikes, is advisable.

Propagation. Divide and replant the rhizomatous roots between September and March.

Sow seeds when ripe during July or August in pans of seed compost in a cold frame. Prick off the seedlings into an outdoor bed when they are large enough to handle, transferring them to their final positions the following spring.

Pests and diseases. Generally trouble-free.

Epiphyllum
Cactaceae

EPIPHYLLUM × ACKERMANNII

A genus of 21 species of perennial house plants and greenhouse plants. These large-flowering cacti will survive at a minimum winter temperature of 5°C (41°F), but their large, showy flowers are produced more freely if the plants are kept a few degrees warmer. The bell-shaped flowers, may be as much as 6 in. across.

The plants have flattened stems with wavy or notched edges. The appearance of the stems has led to the plants being called, erroneously, leaf cacti. They are easy to grow and there are hundreds of hybrids, often listed as *E.* × *ackermannii.* Species epiphyllums are more difficult to flower, and are seldom seen.

See also CACTUS.

Red hybrids. Height 2–3 ft. The scarlet flowers may be 4–6 in. across and are carried along the edges of the fleshy stems. These are dark green with wavy edges, and are flattened or triangular in section.

The flowers appear in May and June and open in the daytime. Even young plants, in a 4 in. pot, flower well. 'London Glory' is a vigorous variety with crimson-scarlet flowers, shaded purple.

White and yellow hybrids. Height up to 3 ft. There are several pale-flowered epiphyllums; the most popular is *E. cooperi.* Many of these have heavily scented, 4 in. wide flowers, which open in the evening during May and June. White and yellow epiphyllums tend to produce their buds at the base of the stems and do not

Epiphyllum 'London Glory'

flower as freely as the red hybrids. They are vigorous growers. 'London Sunshine' is a good yellow variety with a white centre.

Cultivation. Although epiphyllums are cacti, they are not desert plants. They are natives of the forests of tropical America, and do not need full sun. They do well on an east-facing window-sill or where they can receive good, diffused light. Grow them in 6–9 in. pots, using a compost containing plenty of leaf-mould and bone-meal, or a proprietary peat compost.

Never allow the plants to become completely dry at the roots, even in winter. Once the flower buds start to develop, give the plants a fortnightly liquid feed with a high-potassium fertiliser. Protect the plants from full sun in summer. Repot annually, after flowering. If the stems become shrivelled, cut the top off the plant. Leave to dry off for a few days, before potting up in John Innes potting compost No. 2.

Propagation. Epiphyllums can be raised from seeds sown in April at a temperature of 21°C (70°F). As these plants are hybrids, they do not breed true. Good forms can be increased vegetatively from May to July. Remove healthy side shoots and dry these for a few days before potting up in John Innes potting compost No. 2.

Pests. Tufts of white waxy wool on plants are caused by MEALY BUGS. ROOT MEALY BUGS and ROOT KNOT EELWORMS attack the roots.

Diseases. A physiological disorder, CORKY SCAB OF CACTI, shows as irregular rusty or corky spots on the stems.

A VIRUS DISEASE causes yellow or sometimes purple spots to develop, and the flower colour may be broken.

Epiphyllum cooperi

Epiphyllum 'London Sunshine'

Eranthis
Ranunculaceae

A genus of hardy tuberous-rooted, spring-flowering perennials with seven known species, of which two are generally available. A more vigorous hybrid race between these two species has been raised in Holland.

The plants flower in early spring and die away by early summer. The naked stems produce a terminal ruff or collar of divided leaves beneath a solitary yellow buttercup-like flower.

These plants are useful for growing beneath deciduous trees and between shrubs.

E. cilicica. Asia Minor. Height 2–3 in.; planting distance 3 in. Bronze-green narrowly segmented foliage and deep yellow, 1 in. wide flowers appear in March; the stems are pink.

Eranthis hyemalis

Eremurus elwesii 'Albus'

Eremurus robustus

E. hyemalis (winter aconite). Europe, naturalised in parts of Great Britain. Height 4 in.; planting distance 3 in. This is the most common species; it bears deeply cut, pale green leaves. Lemon-yellow flowers, $\frac{3}{4}$–1 in. across, appear from February onwards, or earlier in mild seasons and districts.

E. × tubergenii. Garden origin. Height 4 in.; planting distance 3–4 in. This hybrid combines the characteristics of E. cilicica and E. hyemalis, but is more robust. Rich yellow flowers, $1\frac{1}{4}$ in. across, are produced in March.

Two named selections are available: 'Glory', yellow, slightly fragrant flowers and bronze-tinted young foliage, February and March. 'Guinea Gold', deep yellow, fragrant flowers, and bronze leaves and stems, March and April.

Cultivation. Plant the small tubers as soon as available in late summer, setting them 1 in. deep and 3 in. apart in groups.

Eranthis thrive in well-drained but moisture-retentive soil, preferably in heavy loam. They do well beneath deciduous trees or between shrubs, in sun or partial shade. They are sometimes difficult to establish permanently due to lack of moisture during the growing season in spring.

Propagation. Lift the tubers as the plants begin to die down, cutting or breaking them into separate sections and replanting these at once.

Alternatively, sow seeds of the species as soon as ripe, generally in April and May. Sow in pans or boxes of seed compost and place in a cold frame. Leave the boxes in a cold frame for two complete growing seasons before setting out the young tubers in their flowering positions. It will probably be another one or two years before they reach flowering size.

Pests. The opening flowers are sometimes damaged by BIRDS.

Diseases. Leaves and leaf stalks infected by SMUT have blister-like swellings, which burst open to release a mass of black, soot-like spores.

Eremurus

Foxtail lily. *Liliaceae*

FREMURUS ELWESII

A genus of 50 species of hardy herbaceous perennials with majestic spikes of star-shaped flowers. They are suitable as cut flowers.

E. bungei: see E. stenophyllus bungei

E. elwesii. Origin uncertain. Height 6–10 ft; planting distance 2–3 ft. The light green leaves are strap-shaped. Fragrant, soft pink flowers are borne in 3–4 ft long spikes in May. E. e. 'Albus' is a pure white variety.

E. himalaicus. Himalayas. Height 2–4 ft; planting distance 2–3 ft. The light green leaves are strap-shaped. Pure white flowers with orange anthers are produced in 24 in. spikes in May.

E. olgae. Turkestan. Height 4–5 ft; planting distance 24 in. The light green leaves are narrowly strap-shaped and recurved. Densely packed white flowers, tinted pale pink, are produced in 18–24 in. spikes in June and July.

E. robustus. Turkestan. Height 8–10 ft; planting distance 4 ft. The narrow, strap-shaped, bright green leaves are up to 4 ft long. Peach-yellow flowers open in May and June in 2–4 ft spikes.

E. 'Shelford Hybrids'. Height 5–7 ft; planting distance 2–3 ft. The light green leaves are strap-shaped. Flowers ranging from pale pink to glowing copper-orange are borne in 2–3 ft spikes in June and July.

E. stenophyllus bungei, syn. E. bungei. Iran, Afghanistan, Turkestan. Height 2–3 ft; planting distance 24 in. The narrow strap-shaped leaves are light green. Golden-yellow flowers with orange anthers appear in 18 in. spikes in June.

Cultivation. Plant in September or October, with the crown of the plants 6 in. deep, in well-drained loam. Choose a sunny position, though preferably not one exposed to early-morning sun. Leave the plants undisturbed until they become overcrowded. Mulch annually with old manure in September or October. Unless seeds are wanted, cut down the stems after flowering.

Propagation. Divide and replant the roots in September or October.

Sow seeds when ripe or when obtainable, preferably not later than March, under glass at a temperature of 15°C (59°F). Grow the seedlings on singly in 3–4 in. pots in a cold frame for two years before planting out in a nursery bed. Seeds may be slow to germinate, and fresh seeds usually germinate the quickest.

Pests and diseases. Generally trouble-free.

Erica carnea 'Springwood'

Erica cinerea 'C. D. Eason'

ERICA

Heath, heather. *Ericaceae*

A genus of more than 500 species of evergreen shrubs and sub-shrubs. Most species are native to South Africa, but only one of these is hardy in Britain. Those species originating from W. Europe and the Mediterranean areas are, with a few exceptions, hardy. Ericas range in height from miniatures, 2–3 in. high, to tree heaths which in sheltered places in Cornwall and S.W. Ireland may reach 20 ft.

These plants are chiefly grown for their flowers, although there are some attractive foliage varieties. The needle-like leaves are in whorls and usually mid-green; in a few varieties they are orange, red or yellow. The bell-shaped white, pink, purple or bi-coloured flowers are carried in terminal racemes.

Ericas are suitable as specimen plants, for hedging or for ground cover. They are easy to grow; the winter-flowering species tolerate chalk.

In addition to the hardy species, two tender species, *E. gracilis* and *E. hyemalis* are in cultivation. They are popular as winter-flowering greenhouse plants and are widely grown commercially for the Christmas trade.

ERICA MEDITERRANEA

E. arborea. Mediterranean area and N.E. Africa. Height up to 12 ft; spread 6–8 ft. A hardy species which in Cornwall and S.W. Ireland may grow to 20 ft in height. Ash-white, slightly fragrant flowers appear in 2–4 in. long racemes in March and April. 'Alpina' is hardier and bushier, the leaves are fresh green; 'Gold Tips' has young golden growths.

E. australis. Iberian Peninsula. Height up to 6 ft, but given support or tied against a wall it may be twice as high; spread 4 ft. Hardy. The tubular flowers, which are rich rose-pink, are carried profusely in 2–3 in. long racemes from April to June. 'Mr Robert' is hardier, with white flowers.

E. carnea, syn. *E. herbacea.* European Alps. Prostrate or up to 12 in. in height; spread up to 24 in. A fully hardy species, excellent as ground cover. The leaves are usually light green, but may be bronze or dull yellow. The flowers, in terminal racemes 3–6 in. long, are white or in varying shades of pink; they appear from November to May. This species will grow on chalky soils.

Varieties include: 'Aurea', golden-yellow leaves, pink flowers; 'Carnea', compact, pink flowers freely borne from February onwards; 'Cecilia M. Beale', white flowers from December; 'Eileen Porter', carmine, November onwards; 'King George', compact, rose-pink flowers.

'Loughrigg', dark green leaves turning bronze, pink flower buds open to rose-purple in February; 'Praecox Rubra', prostrate, deep rich pink flowers from December onwards; 'Snow Queen', white flowers from December; 'Springwood', spreading, with white flowers; 'Winter Beauty', of compact growth, rich pink flowers.

E. ciliaris (Dorset heath). Morocco and W. Europe, including Great Britain. Height 12–18 in.; spread 24 in. or more. This hardy species remains in flower from July until the winter. The leaves are pale green. Bell-shaped flowers, in

Erica arborea

Erica arborea 'Gold Tips'

Erica australis

Erica carnea 'Winter Beauty'

Erica cinerea 'Cevennes'

Erica carnea 'Praecox Rubra'

Erica cinerea 'Alba Minor'

Erica cinerea 'Golden Drop'

Erica cinerea 'Pallida'

Erica × darleyensis

terminal racemes 2–4 in. long, range in colour from white through shades of pink to rose-purple.

Varieties include: 'Aurea', golden leaves and pink flowers; 'Corfe Castle', deep cherry-pink flowers; 'David McClintock', leaves turn bronze in winter, white flowers with pink tips, late-flowering; 'Globosa', soft pink flowers; 'Maweana', robust, purple-pink flowers; 'Mrs C. H. Gill', dark green leaves, cerise flowers; 'Stoborough' (height 24 in.), white flowers.

E. cinerea (bell heather). W. Europe from Norway to Madeira, naturalised in E. United States. Height and spread 9–12 in. Hardy. The leaves are deep green. The flowers, which are borne from June to October in terminal racemes 3–6 in. long, are white or in striking shades of deep pink, red, maroon and mahogany. The flowers fade to russet-brown bells.

Varieties include: 'Alba Minor', compact habit, white flowers; 'Atrorubens', ruby-red long-lasting flowers; 'Carnea', rich pink flowers; 'C. D. Eason', glowing rose-red flowers; 'Cevennes', pale lavender flowers; 'C. G. Best', milky pink flowers; 'Coccinea' (height up to 6 in.), deep carmine-red flowers.

'Golden Drop', prostrate, copper-red leaves, especially in winter, flowers sparsely; 'Hookstone White', white flowers; 'Joyce Burfitt', maroon flowers; 'Pallida', large spikes of pale pink flowers; 'Velvet Night', purple-black flowers.

E. codonodes: see E. lusitanica
E. corsica: see E. terminalis
E. × darleyensis. A garden hybrid between E. carnea and E. mediterranea. Height up to 24 in.; spread up to 3 ft or more. A fully hardy plant which grows well in limy soils. The leaves are mid-green. Terminal 3–6 in. long racemes of white, pink or purple flowers appear from December to May, and are at their best in March and April. The young growths are often cream white or pink in May.

'Arthur Johnston', slender racemes of rose flowers, fast grower; 'George Rendall', pale green leaves, pink flowers.

'Silberschmelze', syns. 'Molten Silver' and 'Silver Bells', vigorous, white flowers.
E. erigena: see E. mediterranea
E. gracilis. S. Africa. Height 12–18 in.; spread 12 in. A winter-flowering greenhouse species with pale green leaves. The numerous side-shoots are tipped with clusters of three or four globe-shaped flowers, ⅓ in. long. These are rose-purple and appear in profusion from October to January. There is also a white form which is sometimes listed as E. nivalis.
E. herbacea: see E. carnea
E. hibernica: see E. mediterranea
E. hyemalis. Origin unknown, possibly a garden hybrid. Height up to 24 in.; spread 12–15 in. An erect greenhouse shrub. The thread-like leaves are mid-green. The tubular, ¾ in. long flowers are white with a pink flush; they are produced in terminal racemes from November to January.
E. lusitanica, syn. E. codonodes. France, Iberian Peninsula. Height up to 10 ft; spread up to 3 ft. A fairly hardy species which usually recovers well when cut by frost. Bright apple-green leaves. Pink flower buds are produced in early winter, and the abundant white flowers, borne in 2–3 in. long racemes, last until May or later.
E. mackaiana. Ireland and Spain. Height and spread 6–9 in. Hardy. The leaves are mid-green. Terminal 2–3 in. long racemes of purple-pink flowers are produced from July to September. The young shoots are sometimes red.

Varieties include: 'Dr Ronald Gray', white flowers; 'Lawsoniana', pale pink flowers; 'Plena', syn. 'Crawfordii', pink double flowers.

E. mediterranea, syns. *E. erigena*, *E. hibernica*. Ireland, Spain, France. Height 10 ft or more; spread up to 4 ft, though most varieties are smaller. This species will flower as early as December and last until June. It is not fully hardy in cold districts, such as the east coast. The mid-green leaves are arranged in whorls of four on woody, brittle stems. The flowers, usually purple-pink, are carried in 3–6 in. long terminal leafy and branched racemes. It tolerates limy soils and does well provided it is not too dry.

Varieties (height and spread 3–4 ft) include: 'Alba', white flowers; 'Brightness', bronze-green leaves, bronze-red buds opening to rose-purple flowers; 'Superba' (height 10 ft or more; spread 3–4 ft), pink-purple flowers, suitable as a hedging plant; 'W. T. Rackliff', of dense growth, with cream-white flowers.

E. nivalis: see *E. gracilis*
E. stricta: see *E. terminalis*
E. terminalis, syns. *E. stricta*, *E. corsica*. S.W. Mediterranean, naturalised in N. Ireland. Height up to 8 ft; spread up to 4 ft. Generally hardy. The dark green leaves, which are closely arranged in whorls along the stems, are bright green when young. Pink or purple flowers, in 1–2 in. wide clusters, appear in profusion during June and may continue until winter. The faded russet-brown flowers remain attractive. It is a good hedging plant and will tolerate lime in the soil.
E. tetralix (cross-leaved heath). W. Europe, naturalised in E. United States. Height and spread 9–12 in. A hardy species which in the wild prefers boggy places, but does well in ordinary, non-limy garden soil. The grey-green leaves are hairy and often glandular. Soft pink flowers, usually in terminal clusters up to 1–2 in. wide, are produced from late June to August.

Varieties include: 'Con Underwood', crimson flowers; 'L. E. Underwood', terracotta buds opening to apricot-pink flowers; 'Mollis', silver-grey glandular leaves and white flowers.
E. vagans (Cornish heath). W. Europe, including Great Britain, naturalised in E. United States. Height up to 4 ft; spread up to 8 ft. A hardy species with mid-green leaves. The pale purple or pink flowers are borne in 6–9 in. long racemes from July to winter, when they turn an attractive brown. This is the most vigorous native heath; it will tolerate mildly alkaline soils. The stems may be split by hard frosts but will rapidly sprout again from the base.

Varieties include: 'Diana Hornibrook', glowing red flowers; 'Grandiflora', strong grower, soft pink flowers; 'Lyonesse', pure white flowers; 'Mrs D. F. Maxwell', deep cherry-pink flowers; 'St Keverne', rose-pink flowers; 'Viridiflora', flowers resembling small pale green leaves.
E. × *veitchii*. A garden hybrid between *E. arborea* and *E. lusitanica*. Height up to 8 ft; spread 3 ft. Fully hardy only in S.W. England. 'Exeter' is the only known form. The leaves are mid-green. Pure white scented flowers are produced in 3–6 in. long racemes from January to March.
E. × *watsonii*. S.W. England, France. A hybrid between *E. ciliaris* and *E. tetralix*. Height up to 9 in.; spread 24 in. or more. Mid-green leaves. Pink bell-shaped flowers are carried in 3–4 in. long terminal racemes from July to September.

Varieties include: 'Dawn' (height 6 in.),

Erica × watsonii 'Dawn'

Erica vagans 'Lyonesse'

Erica hyemalis

Erica tetralix

Erica tetralix 'Mollis'

Erica vagans 'Mrs D. F. Maxwell'

yellow-tipped leaves in spring, rose-pink flowers; 'H. Maxwell' (height 12 in.), pink flowers.
Cultivation, propagation, pruning of hardy species: see entry under HEATHS AND HEATHERS.
Cultivation of greenhouse species. Grow *E. gracilis* and *E. hyemalis* in well-crocked 5–6 in. pots and in a compost of 2 parts peat and 1 part sharp sand (parts by volume). Overwinter the plants at a temperature of 5°C (41°F); higher artificial temperatures should be avoided. When the outside temperature in winter exceeds 5°C (41°F), ventilate the greenhouse and reduce or discontinue artificial heat.

Provide a dry, airy atmosphere and water carefully, preferably with rainwater. The plants should not be allowed to dry out at any time, but should be kept evenly moist throughout the year. In summer, provide as much air as possible or stand the pots outside. Feeding is generally not required, though a weak liquid feed applied at fortnightly intervals from May to September will ensure fine plants.

Repot the plants annually in March. Firm potting is essential.
Propagation of greenhouse species. Take cuttings, about 1 in. long, of young shoots in March. Insert the cuttings closely in peat and sand in shallow boxes, pans or pots two-thirds filled with crocks. Root the cuttings in a close atmosphere at a temperature of 16°C (61°F), under mist or in polythene bags, turning these daily. Water with lime-free water.
Pruning of greenhouse species. Cut off the racemes and trim the plants lightly after flowering. Do not cut the current growths back more than one-third.
Pests. Hardy species are generally trouble-free. Under glass, SCALE INSECTS, particularly oleander scale, may infest the plant stems.

Diseases. A grey discoloration of the foliage on hardy species is due to a fungus which causes HEATHER DIE-BACK. Greenhouse species are generally trouble-free.

Erigeron

Fleabane. *Compositae*

A genus of over 200 species of hardy herbaceous annuals, biennials and perennials. All the plants described are perennial. The varieties have larger, more colourful flowers than the species and are more suitable for garden display. The mid-green leaves are spathulate to lanceolate and the daisy-like flowers, which are borne from June to August, measure 2–2½ in. across. They are excellent as cut flowers.

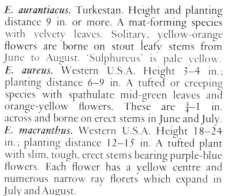

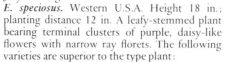

ERIGERON SPECIOSUS

E. aurantiacus. Turkestan. Height and planting distance 9 in. or more. A mat-forming species with velvety leaves. Solitary, yellow-orange flowers are borne on stout leafy stems from June to August. 'Sulphureus' is pale yellow.
E. aureus. Western U.S.A. Height 3–4 in.; planting distance 6–9 in. A tufted or creeping species with spathulate mid-green leaves and orange-yellow flowers. These are ¾–1 in. across and borne on erect stems in June and July.
E. macranthus. Western U.S.A. Height 18–24 in.; planting distance 12–15 in. A tufted plant with slim, tough, erect stems bearing purple-blue flowers. Each flower has a yellow centre and numerous narrow ray florets which expand in July and August.
E. speciosus. Western U.S.A. Height 18 in.; planting distance 12 in. A leafy-stemmed plant bearing terminal clusters of purple, daisy-like flowers with narrow ray florets. The following varieties are superior to the type plant:
'Darkest of All', 18–24 in. high, violet-blue; 'Felicity', 18–24 in., light pink; 'Foerster's Liebling', 18 in., deep pink, semi-double; 'Gaiety', 18–24 in., bright pink; 'Prosperity', 18 in., blue, semi-double; 'Quakeress', 18–24 in., light mauve-pink.
Cultivation. Plant between October and March in a sunny position in moist but well-drained soil. In exposed positions support the plants with twiggy sticks. Removal of dead flowers encourages further flowering later in the season. Cut the stems down to ground level in autumn.
Propagation. Divide and replant the roots between October and March.
Sow seeds during April or May in pots or boxes of seed compost and place in a cold frame. Prick out the seedlings into boxes and subsequently into a nursery bed; in the autumn transfer the young plants to their final positions.
Pests and diseases. Generally trouble-free.

Erigeron macranthus

Erigeron speciosus 'Felicity'

Erigeron speciosus 'Foerster's Liebling'

Erinus alpinus

Erigeron aurantiacus 'Sulphureus'

Erinus

Scrophulariaceae

ERINUS ALPINUS

A genus containing one variable dwarf and hardy evergreen perennial species, suitable for rock gardens. It will thrive on a drystone wall. Though not a long-lived plant, it seeds freely.
E. alpinus. Mountains of W. Europe. Height 3 in.; spread 6 in. Spathulate mid-green leaves, deeply toothed, form evergreen tufts of low mounds. A profusion of bright pink starry flowers, ¼ in. across, are borne from March to August.
'Albus' is a white variety; 'Dr Hanele' is bright carmine; 'Mrs Charles Boyle' is deep pink.
Cultivation. Plant between September and March in any well-drained garden soil in a sunny position on a rock garden, scree or paved area.
Propagation. In April, scatter fresh seeds where the plants are wanted. The different varieties come true from seeds.
Pests and diseases. Generally trouble-free.

Erodium

Stork's bill. *Geraniaceae*

This genus of 90 species of annuals, herbaceous perennials and sub-shrubs is closely related to *Geranium,* and includes many attractive compact-growing types suitable for rock gardens and alpine houses. They are generally hardy.
E. chamaedryoides, syn. *E. reichardii.* Majorca. Height 1–2 in.; spread about 9 in. This perennial forms a flat mat of mid-green crenate foliage.

from June to August it produces rounded pink-veined white flowers, each about $\frac{1}{3}$ in. across, which are carried on $\frac{1}{2}$ in. high stems.

The variety usually grown is 'Roseum', which bears clear pink flowers from April to June.

E. chrysanthum. Greece. Height 4–6 in.; spread 12–15 in. This perennial species forms tufts of deeply divided fern-like silver foliage. The sprays of $\frac{3}{4}$ in. wide, saucer-shaped flowers are sulphur-yellow and appear from June to September.

E. corsicum. Corsica, Sardinia. Height 8 in.; spread about 9 in. A short-lived perennial, similar in habit to *E. chamaedryoides.* The downy, soft grey leaves are ovate with rounded teeth, and form small tufts. Almost stemless saucer-shaped flowers, $\frac{3}{4}$ in. across and clear pink, veined with red, open from April to June. This plant is particularly susceptible to winter moisture and should be given protection outdoors with raised panes of glass.

'Rubrum' has rich red flowers.

ERODIUM MACRADENUM

E. macradenum. Pyrenees. Height 9 in.; spread 9–12 in. A perennial species with mid-green, deeply divided, fern-like foliage. The lilac flowers, about 1 in. in diameter and saucer-shaped, have dark violet blotches on the two upper petals and are borne in sprays well above the foliage from June to August.

'Roseum' has rose-coloured flowers with darker veinings.

E. reichardii: see *E. chamaedryoides*

Cultivation. These plants do better in limy soils than in acid ones, and grow particularly well on tufa. Plant them in April in a well-drained soil in full sun. *E. corsicum* does best at the foot of a sheltered wall. In the alpine house, grow *E. corsicum* in 6–8 in. pans of John Innes potting compost No. 1; repot in March, annually or every other year.

Propagation. For all species except *E. chamaedryoides*, take 2 in. cuttings from basal shoots of the old wood in April. Insert the cuttings in equal parts (by volume) peat and sand in boxes or pans and place them in a cold frame. Pot when rooted into 3 in. containers of John Innes potting compost No. 1. They can be planted out in September or October, or overwintered in a cold frame and planted out in permanent positions the following March or April.

Increase *E. chamaedryoides* by taking 1–2 in. root cuttings in March from the thickest pieces of root. Set them in boxes or pans of equal parts (by volume) peat and sand in a cold frame; pot up when three or four leaves have formed, in 3 in. pots of John Innes potting compost No. 1. Grow on in the frame and plant out the following March or April.

Pests. Plants may be infested by APHIDS, particularly when grown under glass.

Diseases. Generally trouble-free.

Eryngium
Umbelliferae

A genus of 230 species of hardy and tender herbaceous perennials. The following species are hardy and are suitable for growing in borders. They have spiny leaves and teasel-like heads of flowers with a collar of conspicuous, narrow, often spine-toothed bracts; some species have a glistening metallic sheen and make attractive winter decoration when cut and dried.

ERYNGIUM BOURGATII

E. alpinum. Europe. Height 18–24 in.; planting distance 15 in. The dark green-blue basal leaves are heart-shaped, the stem leaves are deeply cut. Steel-blue flower heads, 1 in. long and surrounded by prominent bracts of the same colour, are produced from July to September.

E. bourgatii. Pyrenees. Height 18 in.; planting distance 12 in. The glaucous tripartite leaves have grey markings and are deeply cut. Silver-blue flower heads, $1\frac{1}{2}$ in. long and surrounded by long silvery bracts, are borne in July and August.

E. bromeliifolium. Mexico. Height 3–4 ft; planting distance 18–24 in. A rosette-forming species with mid-green, strap-shaped, toothed leaves. Green flower heads, 1 in. long, appear in July.

E. giganteum. Caucasus, Iran. Height 3–4 ft; planting distance 24 in. The stems and the heart-shaped, round-toothed leaves are blue, tinged ivory. Silver-blue flower heads, $1\frac{1}{2}$–2 in. long, open in August and September. It dies after flowering and should be grown as a biennial.

E. maritimum (sea holly). Europe, including Great Britain. Height and planting distance 12–18 in. This well-branched species bears silver-green, rounded basal leaves and palmate, deeply cut stem leaves. Cone-shaped heads, $\frac{3}{4}$–1 in. long, of metallic-blue flowers mature in succession from July to September.

E. × oliverianum. Height 3–4 ft; planting distance 24 in. A hybrid with round blue-green leaves that are deeply cut. Deep blue flower heads, 1 in. long, appear from July to September.

E. planum. E. Europe, Asia. Height 24 in.; planting distance 18 in. This species has dark green heart-shaped leaves. Globular deep blue flowers, $\frac{1}{2}$ in. across, are borne in July and August.

E. tripartitum. Mediterranean regions. Height $2\frac{1}{2}$ ft; planting distance 18 in. The smooth, dark green, wedge-shaped leaves are coarsely toothed and less spiny than those of the other species described. Globular grey-blue flower heads, $\frac{1}{2}$ in. long, are carried from July to September.

E. variifolium. N. Africa. Height 2–$2\frac{1}{2}$ ft; planting distance 12–15 in. Glossy, dark green, oblong-orbiculate leaves, marbled with white, radiate from the rootstock of this evergreen tufted species. Round blue flower heads, $\frac{3}{4}$ in. across, are borne in July and August.

Erodium chamaedryoides 'Roseum'

Erodium corsicum

Eryngium alpinum

Eryngium × oliverianum

Eryngium maritimum

Eryngium tripartitum

Erysimum alpinum 'Moonlight'

Erythrina crista-galli

Cultivation. Plant eryngiums between October and April in a sunny position and in ordinary, well-drained soil. Slender plants, such as *E. tripartitum*, need twiggy sticks for supports in exposed positions. Cut the stems almost to ground level after flowering. For winter decoration, cut the flowers before they fade.

Propagation. Take root cuttings during February and insert in boxes of equal parts (by volume) peat and sand in a cold frame. When young leaves are well developed, set the plants in nursery rows and plant out in their flowering positions from October to April.

Sow seeds during March or April in boxes of John Innes seed compost and place in a cold frame. Prick out the seedlings, when large enough to handle, preferably singly into 3 in. pots of John Innes potting compost No. 1. Plant out in permanent positions from October onwards.

Tufted species, such as *E. alpinum* and *E. tripartitum* may be divided and planted out in permanent sites in March.

Pests and diseases. Generally trouble-free.

Erysimum
Cruciferae

ERYSIMUM RUPESTRE

A genus of 100 species of hardy annuals, biennials and sub-shrubby perennials. The plants resemble small wallflowers and, although short-lived, are attractive on rock gardens and at the front of borders. The species described are perennials.

E. alpinum, syn. *Cheiranthus alpinus.* Scandinavia. Height 6 in.; planting distance 4–6 in. A species with lanceolate dark green leaves; fragrant sulphur-yellow flowers, $\frac{1}{2}$ in. across, are produced in May.

'K. Elmhurst' (height 18 in.; spread up to 12 in.) is a bushy variety with pale mauve flowers. 'Moonlight' has primrose-yellow flowers.

E. capitatum, syn. *Cheiranthus capitatus.* California. Height 8–10 in.; planting distance 6 in. This sub-shrubby species has dark green lanceolate leaves. Large heads of scented cream-white flowers, 1 in. across, are borne in April and May; occasionally flowers are produced at other times of the year.

E. rupestre. Asia Minor. Height and planting distance up to 12 in. A variable, tufted species with mid-green leaves that are spathulate to oblong-ovate. Cross-shaped, sulphur-yellow flowers, opening from April to June, are borne in ovoid heads 2–4 in. across.

Cultivation. Plant erysimums between September and March in ordinary, well-drained soil and in full sun. They thrive on poor soils.

Propagation. Take heel cuttings, 2–2$\frac{1}{2}$ in. long, in July or August. Insert in equal parts (by volume) peat and sand in a cold frame and, when rooted, pot the cuttings singly in 3 in. containers of John Innes potting compost No. 1. Overwinter the cuttings in a cold frame and plant out in permanent positions in April.

Pests and diseases. Generally trouble-free.

Erythrina
Leguminosae

ERYTHRINA CRISTA-GALLI

A genus of 100 species of half-hardy herbaceous perennials and deciduous trees and shrubs. One shrubby, flowering species can be cultivated outdoors in sheltered areas in the south and west. Elsewhere it requires cool greenhouse conditions.

E. crista-galli (common coral tree). Brazil. Height 3–8 ft; spread 3–4 ft. This shrubby species grows from a stout, woody rootstock, producing annual herbaceous stems. The trifoliate, glaucous-green leaves, which are widely spaced on the stems, consist of ovate, leathery leaflets. Pea-shaped flowers, 1$\frac{1}{2}$–2 in. long, waxy and deep red, are freely borne in June and July at the tips of the shoots. *E. c. compacta* is a dwarf form.

Cultivation. Outdoors, these shrubs should be grown at the foot of a warm, preferably south-facing wall. Plant in April or May in good loamy soil enriched with peat or well-decayed manure. Protect the roots in winter with a thick layer of leaves, peat, bracken or weathered ashes. Alternatively, lift the roots in October and overwinter in a frost-free greenhouse; plant out again when growth begins in May.

In the greenhouse, grow erythrinas in 8–10 in. pots or small tubs of John Innes potting compost No. 2. Overwinter at a temperature of 4–7°C (40–45°F); when growth restarts in spring, raise the temperature to 13°C (55°F). Keep the plants just moist in winter, but water freely during spring and summer. Admit as much air as possible during summer; on hot days lightly shade the greenhouse and syringe the foliage. Pot plants may be stood outdoors in summer.

Pot on until the plants are in their final pots; thereafter repot annually in March. Give a liquid feed at fortnightly intervals from May to August.

Propagation. Take cuttings, 3–4 in. long, of young shoots with a heel in April; insert the cuttings singly in $2\frac{1}{2}$ in. pots of equal parts (by volume) peat and sand and root at a bottom heat of 21–24°C (70–75°F). When rooted, pot the cuttings in $3\frac{1}{2}$ in. pots of John Innes potting compost No. 1 and pot on as required.

Pruning. Cut all stems close to the rootstock in October prior to covering the roots or lifting them for storing. Shrubs grown under glass should be cut hard back to within 6 in. of the base in February or March.

Pests. Outdoors, these shrubs are generally trouble-free. In the greenhouse, GLASSHOUSE RED SPIDER MITES may cause mottling, bronzing and falling of the leaves. The foliage and stems of severely infested plants are covered with a fine silken webbing.

Diseases. Generally trouble-free.

Erythronium

Liliaceae

Few of the 25 species of this hardy bulb genus are generally available, but most have been grown in gardens in the past and are still maintained in various botanical gardens.

The species described have narrow to broad, lanceolate mid-green leaves, often marbled or blotched with grey or maroon. The nodding flowers have six petals, lanceolate, pointed and reflexed like a Turk's-cap lily; they are 2–3 in. across and appear in April and May.

ERYTHRONIUM TUOLUMNENSE

E. dens-canis (dog's-tooth violet). Central Europe through Asia to Japan. Height 6 in.; planting distance 4–6 in. A variable species with several named varieties. The leaves are usually blotched with grey or brown. The flowers are pink-purple.

Varieties include: 'Lilac Wonder', pale purple with brown blotches at the base of the flowers; 'Pink Perfection', clear pink; 'Purple King', rich purple with a spotted and striped brown and white centre; 'Rose Beauty', deep pink, leaves mottled; and 'White Splendour'.

E. revolutum (American trout lily). British Columbia to N. California. Height 12 in.; planting distance 4–6 in. The leaves are lightly mottled with white and brown. The flowers are all more or less mottled, changing as they age. There are many forms, some named as separate varieties, ranging in colour from near-white with purple mottling to pink or purple with still deeper markings. 'White Beauty' is a white form with a yellow centre and with heavily mottled leaves.

E. tuolumnense. California. Height 9–12 in.; planting distance 4–6 in. A species with bright green leaves and yellow flowers.

Hybrids of *E. revolutum* and *E. tuolumnense* include: 'Kondo', which has pale yellow flowers with a brown basal ring and lightly mottled leaves; 'Pagoda' (height up to 18 in.), which also has yellow flowers with a central brown ring, and bronze leaves.

Cultivation. A moist, but not waterlogged soil is essential for erythroniums; deep planting in soil rich in organic matter is suitable. A north slope or some shade also helps to prevent drying out and encourages growth.

Plant the fleshy corms in the late summer, in groups of a dozen or more. Once planted, leave undisturbed for years, but if a move is necessary this is best done as the leaves die down after flowering.

Propagation. The species and some of the varieties can be raised from seeds but may produce variable seedlings. Sow the seeds in a shaded frame when ripe (not later than September), either in pots plunged in peat or direct in the frame bed. In neither case allow the soil to dry out. The plants may take five or more years to reach flowering size. After two years, prick the seedlings out 2 in. apart.

Offsets, when they occur, may be removed when the leaves die down in summer. Grow the offsets on in a nursery bed outdoors until they reach flowering size usually after three years.

Pests and diseases. Generally trouble-free.

Escallonia

Escalloniaceae

A genus of about 60 species of evergreen and deciduous shrubs or trees from S. America. Although most of the species are slightly tender, they grow well in the southern and western counties including Scotland, particularly by the sea, where they are much used for hedging. Elsewhere they must be given wall protection. Generally, the leaves are lanceolate to oblanceolate and mid to deep green, often glossy. The flowers, which are borne in terminal and lateral panicles, 2–4 in. or more long, are shortly tubular, with widely expanded rounded lobes.

A number of hybrids have been raised from the hardier species and these have generally superseded the species. The species and hybrids described here are evergreen.

E. × 'Edinensis'. Height and spread 8–12 ft. This semi-evergreen hybrid has a cascading habit, with slender arching branches. The foliage is small and bright green. Rose-pink flowers are carried profusely in June and July.

Erythronium dens-canis

Erythronium revolutum (hybrid)

Erythronium tuolumnense

Escallonia macrantha

Escallonia 'Donard Seedling'

Escallonia 'Donard Star'

Escallonia 'Glory of Donard'

Escallonia 'Apple Blossom'

E. × iveyi. Height up to 10 ft; spread 6–8 ft. This hybrid makes a vigorous, rounded shrub, when grown in the open. The ovate leaves are glossy deep green. White flowers appear in July and August and are crowded in terminal panicles 5–6 in. long. The shrub is slightly tender, but may be grown in the open in mild western areas and as a wall shrub elsewhere.

ESCALLONIA × IVEYI

E. macrantha. S. America. Height 6–10 ft; spread 6 ft. This species forms a rounded leafy bush. The glossy deep green leaves are ovate to obovate and doubly toothed. Terminal racemes, of rose-crimson flowers are borne from June to September. This species is only hardy in the west; it is resistant to sea-gales and is much used as a hedging plant.

E. rubra. Chile. Height up to 15 ft; spread 6 ft. A quick-growing species of loose habit and with rich, glossy green leaves that are obovate to lanceolate. The red flowers are produced in loose terminal panicles in July and August. The type species has been superseded by the named

hybrids, but the variety *E. r.* 'Pygmaea' is frequently planted in rock gardens, where it may reach a height of 12–24 in. with a considerably wider spread.

GARDEN VARIETIES:

'Apple Blossom'. Height and spread 5 ft. A hybrid of stiff, compact and bushy habit, with light green leaves. The cup-shaped flowers are pale pink and freely borne from June to October.

'C. F. Ball'. Height up to 8 ft; spread 5 ft. This hybrid has upright stems which arch at the tips; the foliage is dark green. Tubular red flowers appear from May to October. This is thought to be the hardiest variety.

'Donard Brilliance'. Height and spread 6 ft. This bushy hybrid is of graceful habit with pendulous branches and shiny green foliage. The bright rose-red flowers appear in June and bloom intermittently until September.

'Donard Seedling'. Height 6–8 ft; spread 5–6 ft. This hybrid has long, arching branches and glossy dark green leaves. Sprays of apple-blossom-pink flowers appear in June and July. This is a suitable hedging plant.

'Donard Star'. Height 5–6 ft; spread 5 ft. A compact hybrid of fairly upright habit. The foliage is dark green and glossy; rose-pink flowers are borne from June onwards.

'Glory of Donard'. Height and spread 5–6 ft. A recently introduced hybrid with glossy mid to deep green leaves. Large deep carmine flowers are borne from June onwards.

Cultivation. Escallonias grow well in any ordinary, well-drained garden soil, including one containing lime. In cold gardens, the more tender species should be grown on south-facing walls, but in the south they thrive in an open sunny position. Plant in October or March and April.

For hedges, use 12 in. high plants and set in trenches at intervals of 18 in. in September and October or in March and April. After planting, remove the top quarter of all shoots to promote bushy growth.

Propagation. Take cuttings, 3–4 in. long, of half-ripe non-flowering shoots with a heel in August and September; insert the cuttings in equal parts (by volume) peat and sand in a cold frame or, if available, at a bottom heat of 13–16°C (55–61°F). Pot the rooted cuttings singly in 3 in. containers of John Innes potting compost No. 2 and overwinter in a cold frame. Plunge outdoors in May and pot on when necessary into 4 in. pots before planting out the following April.

Pruning. No regular pruning is required, but it is advisable to remove flowering growths when these are over. Established hedges may be pruned fairly hard after flowering, but flower more freely if trimmed only lightly.

The dwarf form of *E. rubra* tends to produce suckering shoots of a vigorous habit; these should be removed at base.

Pests. Generally trouble-free.

Diseases. SILVER LEAF may cause the die-back of branches which bear leaves tinged with silver.

Eschscholzia

Papaveraceae

A genus of ten annual and perennial species with bright, poppy-like flowers which tend to close in cool, dull weather. The following species are particularly recommended for growing in borders and on sunny slopes. They produce self-sown seedlings in succeeding years.

E. caespitosa. California. Height 5 in.; spacing 6 in. A hardy annual, dwarf in habit, excellent for edging and for a rock garden. The blue-green leaves are finely divided, almost thread-like. Yellow flowers, 1 in. across, are carried in profusion from June to September. 'Sundew', lemon yellow, is a popular variety.

E. californica (Californian poppy). W. America. Height 12–15 in.; spacing 6 in. This popular hardy annual has finely cut blue-green leaves. Masses of bright orange-yellow, saucer-shaped flowers, 3 in. across, appear from June to October. They are followed by 3–4 in. long, cylindrical blue-green seed pods.

Several varieties are listed by seedsmen: 'Monarch Art Shades', 12 in., with semi-double flowers, and the compact 'Mission Bells', 9 in., are both mixtures with an excellent range of colours—scarlet, orange, white, yellow, crimson and rose-carmine.

Cultivation. Poor, sandy soils and sunny sites give the greatest quantity of flowers and intensity of colour. Removal of the seed pods encourages further flowers but this is an arduous job, better replaced by successive sowings. Gather cut flowers at the bud stage. September-sown plants need cloche protection to overwinter unless the site is sheltered and well drained.

Propagation. Sow the seeds, just covering them, in the flowering site in September or March. Thin out the young plants to the required spacing.

Pests and diseases. Generally trouble-free.

Eucalyptus

Gum tree. *Myrtaceae*

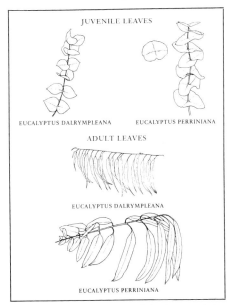

JUVENILE LEAVES

EUCALYPTUS DALRYMPLEANA EUCALYPTUS PERRINIANA

ADULT LEAVES

EUCALYPTUS DALRYMPLEANA

EUCALYPTUS PERRINIANA

A genus of evergreen trees and shrubs, containing some 660 species, varieties and hybrids. They occur naturally only in Australia and Tasmania.

Of all plant genera, this genus shows the greatest variation in size at maturity, ranging from shrubs often under 10 ft to the tallest known broad-leaved tree in the world (*E. regnans*, 373 ft). There are species adapted to almost every climatic condition, from tropical rain-forests to arid deserts and freezing alpine regions. The hardy eucalypts grow well in gardens as trees, pruned shrubs and stooled plants (cut back to base annually). Less hardy species are excellent in bedding schemes, and as foliage pot plants.

The form of a mature tree is characteristic: a sparsely branched crown with a thin covering of pendulous sickle-shaped leaves. The partial shade cast by eucalypts is excellent for rhododendrons and other woodland shrubs and plants. The young twigs and branches have white or coloured bark. The smooth outer bark on the bole and older branches is deciduous in most species. It is shed partly or completely each year after they reach an age of four or five years, to expose the pale cream or white bark beneath. This darkens in time, and causes a striking mottled effect.

Prolific flowering begins, in hardy species, when these are from four to six years old. The flower buds occur in umbels from the leaf axils in early summer and open about a year later into tufts of stamens with white or cream-coloured filaments. The individual flowers are $\frac{1}{2}$–1 in. across and all are sweet scented.

Eschscholzia californica

Eschscholzia californica 'Monarch Art Shades'

Eucalyptus dalrympleana (patterned trunk)

261

Eucalyptus dalrympleana
(young and adult foliage)

Eucalyptus globulus (flowers
and adult foliage)

Eucalyptus globulus (juvenile
foliage)

As pruned shrubs or stooled plants, eucalypts are outstanding for the unusual shape, colour and texture of their foliage. The juvenile leaf is often completely different in shape, size, colour, arrangement and attachment from the adult leaf (heterophylly). The juvenile leaves, usually sessile and in opposite pairs, may be present for a few pairs only, or continue for several years' growth. The change from juvenile to adult leaves, which are usually petiolate and alternately arranged, may be sudden or gradual over a year or more, and occurs as the leaves develop in succession on the growing shoots.

In the species which, as seedlings, produce the juvenile form of leaves for one or more years, annual stooling, pollarding or overall pruning of a bush will result in the annual shoots always bearing juvenile foliage.

Eucalypts have an unusual indefinite habit of growth from naked growing points. They continue in growth from early spring until autumn, or throughout the year in mild climates with well-distributed rainfall. Eucalypts do not form resting buds in July, when extension growth normally ceases on most other trees and shrubs. Unless otherwise stated the height and spread given refer to mature trees about 20 years old.

In its infinite variety, eucalyptus foliage is excellent for flower arrangement. Cut in winter when dormant, it has a useful life of several weeks, and the colourful young summer growths will last several days if the stems are charred or scalded for about 15 seconds after cutting.

E. coccifera (Mount Wellington peppermint). Tasmania. Height 30–40 ft; spread 10–30 ft. A sub-alpine, wind-resistant species, hardy if originating from exposed and high altitudes. Suitable as a pruned shrub or for a screen. The juvenile leaves are elliptic, green or blue-green; they are produced on warty twigs and persist for one or two years. The thick adult leaves are lanceolate, green or glaucous. The shoots are glaucous-white, and the smooth bark on the trunk is mottled pale grey or white when newly exposed. White flowers in clusters of three to seven are freely produced in May and June.

The seeds of this species require cold wet stratification before sowing.

E. coriacea: see *E. pauciflora*

E. dalrympleana (broad-leaved kindling-bark). New South Wales, Victoria, Tasmania. Height in ten years up to 45 ft; spread 10 ft. A fast-growing species, reasonably hardy. The juvenile leaves, which persist for two or three years, are ovoid, dark green or blue-green. Adult leaves are light green and pendulous. The young shoots and foliage are coloured bright orange or scarlet, with pink or red bark on the stems. The bark on branches and trunk is white or pale cream when first exposed, but later changes to salmon-pink or light brown. The white flowers open in clusters of three in October and November. It may be grown as a tree for its attractive trunk and older branches, or as a stooled or annually pruned shrub for its juvenile foliage.

E. divaricata: see *E. gunnii*

E. glaucescens. Victoria, New South Wales. Height in eight years 25 ft; spread 12 ft; stooled plants, height and spread 5 ft. Extremely hardy. The round juvenile leaves, up to $1\frac{1}{2}$ in. long and wide, are brilliant blue-green. A gradual change to the adult glaucous or sub-glaucous leaves begins in the second year. These develop from round, through lanceolate to oblong, falcate leaves, up to 6 in. long and 1 in. wide; the young adult leaves are sometimes tinged with pink. The young bark is smooth, green or covered with a blue-white bloom. The bark becomes red-brown on four or five-year-old wood and sheds to expose smooth white bark ageing to grey. Flowers in clusters of three, appear in October.

It is a fast-growing species, though not windfast on exposed sites. It makes a handsome tree in a sheltered position, or it may be grown as an annually stooled foliage shrub. The seeds need cold wet stratification.

E. globulus (Tasmanian blue gum). Tasmania. Height 50 ft; spread 20 ft. A tender species. It is the most common eucalypt raised for summer bedding purposes.

The juvenile leaves are cordate-ovate, stem-clasping and glaucous. They persist to the second or third year. Adult leaves are mid-green and falcate lanceolate; they are up to 20 in. long, with gradually tapering points. The old bark is smooth and bluish-white when newly exposed.

E. gunnii, syn. *E. divaricata* (cider gum). Tasmania. Height in ten years 45 ft; spread 15 ft; stooled plants, height 5–6 ft; spread 3–4 ft. A sub-alpine species with several hybrids and closely related species. It is hardy, and the eucalypt most commonly grown in Britain. The round, juvenile leaves, up to $2\frac{1}{2}$ in. in diameter, vary from blue-green to brilliant silvery-white. They persist into the second year, and then gradually change to adult lanceolate leaves which may be dark green or blue-green. The young shoots are glaucous-pink or green.

The bark on the bole and older branches is smooth, pale green or cream at first, darkening with age to grey or grey-brown. On twigs and young branches the bark varies from yellow-green to pink, red-brown or, rarely, glaucous. White flowers appear in clusters of three in July and August. This species is fast-growing (18 ft has been recorded during three years), and requires staking and tying for the first four or five years. In smaller gardens the species is best grown as an annually stooled shrub for its outstanding juvenile foliage.

E. nicholii. New South Wales. Height in five years up to 20 ft; spread 7 ft; stooled plants, height 5 ft; spread 4 ft. Tender to moderately hardy, depending on provenance. The narrow-linear juvenile leaves, 2 in. long and $\frac{1}{4}$ in. wide, are deep green or glaucous. The young leaves and growing points are, at the juvenile stage, purple with a white hoary bloom. Adult leaves are dark green, up to 4 in. long. The species is best grown as a foliage or bedding plant, or as an annually pruned shrub.

E. niphophila (alpine snow gum). New South Wales, Victoria. Height and spread in ten years up to 20 ft. An ornamental tree, extremely hardy and wind resistant. It is slow-growing for the first few years, after which it increases in height by 3–4 ft annually.

It has lanceolate adult leaves, thick and glossy green or glaucous, and only a few pairs of juvenile leaves. The growing points and young leaves are range to light mahogany. In winter, branchlets nd twigs are glossy red, but when growth starts in spring they turn blue-white and become covered with a blue-white glaucous loom. This glaucous exudation is also apparent n flower buds and fruits. Clusters of 7–15 white owers appear in June.

The bark is an outstanding feature of this pecies. It is blue-white on a young tree; at the ge of four or five years the bark begins shedding nnually in autumn. The newly exposed bark is ale cream, ageing through grey to red-brown. he result is a mottled bark in several shades and olours at the same time.

The seeds need cold wet stratification.

. parviflora. New South Wales. Height 30 ft or nore; spread 15 ft; stooled plants, height 6 ft; pread 4 ft. Hardy and fast-growing. The ovate, uvenile leaves, 1 in. long and $\frac{3}{4}$ in. wide, are green r sub-glaucous and borne on branching shoots iving a feathery foliage. After one or more years, here is a gradual change to the stalked, sub-pposite adult leaves, 3 in. long and $\frac{1}{2}$ in. wide. he smooth bark is dull grey, ageing to brown. White flowers in clusters of up to seven appear in ate July. This species does well on chalky soils.

. pauciflora, syn. *E. coriacea* (cabbage gum). New South Wales, Victoria, Tasmania. Height 0–40 ft; spread 20 ft; stooled plants, height 7 ft; pread 5 ft. A hardy species. It is similar to *E. iphophila,* but the glossy, dark red to orange-ellow twigs do not turn blue-white. It is rarely overed with a glaucous bloom. Clusters of five to inc white flowers open in June.

E. p. nana (height 20 ft; spread 7 ft; stooled lants, height and spread 4 ft) is of slender habit. The light green leaves are narrowly lanceolate. White flowers in clusters of 5–12 are borne in profusion in early June.

E. perriniana (round-leaved snow gum). New South Wales, Victoria, Tasmania. Height in three years, 18 ft; spread 6 ft; stooled plants, height and spread 3–6 ft. A fully hardy species, best grown as a pollarded tree or an annually stooled shrub. The paired juvenile leaves are joined to form a disc with the stems growing through the middle (per-foliate). They are glaucous and persist for about two years. The glaucous adult leaves are long and pendulous. Young, juvenile and adult leaves have an attractive lavender-purple colour.

The bark is smooth, glaucous or green, often showing the leaf scars of the juvenile leaves. It is shed from about the fourth year, the blotches turning brown with age. White flowers in clusters of three are freely produced on quite young plants in July and August.

E. pulverulenta. New South Wales. Height in four years up to 18 ft; spread 5 ft; stooled plants, height 7 ft; spread 6 ft. A hardy species of stiff angular habit. Oval juvenile and adult leaves are stem-clasping, up to $2\frac{1}{2}$ in. long and wide. They are glaucous, covered in a brilliant silvery-white bloom, which is washed off in time. Smooth white bark peels after a few years to reveal cream to light brown patches. Pale cream flowers, 1 in. across, appear in clusters of three in April and May. The plant is most spectacular when grown as an annually stooled specimen.

E. urnigera (urn-fruited gum). Tasmania. Height in four years up to 18 ft; spread 10 ft. A hardy

Eucalyptus gunnii (juvenile foliage)

and vigorous species. The leaves are similar to those of *E. gunnii* in shape and arrangement, but they are larger. Juvenile leaves have crenulate margins. Both juvenile and adult leaves are dark glossy green. The bark is pale green or cream; with age, red-brown blotches appear. Cream flowers, 1 in. across, in clusters of three, appear in July and August. They are followed by urn-shaped glossy green fruits.

E. u. glauca has blue-grey juvenile leaves and glaucous or dark green adult leaves.

Cultivation. Eucalypts require full sunshine and a well-drained soil of moderate fertility which must be kept moist in summer until the plants are established. It is not yet known whether all species tolerate calcareous soils, but they will all grow in acid and neutral soils. Avoid very dry sites, unless copious watering by hose is possible, and sites liable to waterlogging. Choose a site sheltered from freezing winds and gales, and in full light.

Plant in June or July. Eucalypts are sensitive to root damage and restriction; the best results are obtained by using young plants 6–12 in. tall.

Eucalypts are fast growers, and many species will reach a height of 15 ft over three years if left unpruned. In poor soils, add moist peat and some slow-acting fertiliser such as John Innes base fertiliser or bone-meal. Plant the seedlings 2 in. deep so that the swollen root (lignotuber) is well covered. Keep the ground moist and do not let the young plants wilt.

Young plants must be securely staked for the first five or six years to prevent wind rocking. Drive three strong, durable stakes into the ground, about 15 in. from the seedling; tie the seedling to a cane and the cane to the three stakes. After two or three years remove the cane and tie

Eucalyptus gunnii (flowers and adult foliage)

Eucalyptus nicholii (young foliage)

the sapling itself to the stakes. Renew ties as the plant grows and check monthly during summer to see that there is no constriction.

Protection of the basal stem is recommended during the first winter in cold areas, particularly for the less hardy species. During the first winter place straw or sacking round the stem or stand two barn cloches on end around the plant and tie together, or erect a wind screen of hessian or clear polythene. Do not give overhead cover.

If a plant appears to be dead after the winter do not dig it up immediately. If the lignotuber and roots are alive, new shoots will appear from the base during May.

The less hardy and tender species are suitable for focal points in summer bedding schemes or for foliage pot plants. These are best grown from seeds sown in July or August. Pot the seedlings in 6–9 in. pots containing John Innes potting compost No. 3. Stand them in full sun outdoors until the first frosts are likely, then move to a cool greenhouse with a minimum winter temperature of 4°C (39°F). The following spring harden off the plants before setting them out.

Propagation. All eucalypts are raised from seeds. In Great Britain the best plants will grow from the seeds of hardy strains which have been established here. Furthermore, the seeds should have come from trees growing in localities subject to similar or more severe frosts than are liable to occur at the planting site. Seeds may be bought from a number of seedsmen and nurserymen, but not all suppliers give sufficient detail regarding the seed provenance.

The small woody capsules of the eucalyptus fruits do not mature until a year after flowering. Pick the one-year-old and older fruits at flowering time and leave in a dry room to open. It is not necessary to separate the seeds from the chaff. Most seeds germinate within a fortnight but seeds of certain species such as *E. coccifera*, *E. niphophila* and *E. pauciflora* should be subjected to cold wet stratification for six to eight weeks. The seeds should then be sown at once.

Sow the seeds of hardy species in February or early March at a depth of ⅛ in. in finely sifted compost, such as John Innes seed compost or any proprietary soil-less compost. Cover the seed pan with glass and a single thickness of newspaper, and germinate the seeds at a soil temperature of 13–16°C (55–61°F) if soil warming is available, and at a minimum air temperature of 4°C (39°F). Remove the covering as soon as germination has started and move the seed box off bottom heat and to full light. Keep the compost moist at all times, watering from below.

Pot when the first pair of seedling leaves (above the cotyledons) has expanded and the second pair is showing. Pot in 4 in. or 'long-tom' fibre, paper or peat pots, using John Innes potting compost No. 1 or an equivalent soil-less compost. The lifting, separating and transplanting must be done carefully but quickly to avoid drying of the roots. Water the pots immediately. Shade the seedlings from direct sunlight for about a week, then place in full light. Keep them moist and dampen overhead from a fine rose in sunny periods. As soon as the seedlings have recovered from transplanting, move them to an open cold frame, using the lights only during heavy or prolonged rain, gales or frost. Inspect for roots growing through the pots and prune these off.

When the seedling stem is strong enough, it should be tied to a small split cane, inserted 1 in from the stem. Sweet-pea rings may be used for subsequent ties.

By June most seedlings will be 6 in. tall and ready for planting out in their permanent positions, or for potting-on for pot culture. Growth is rapid during June and July. If planting out is delayed beyond this time the young plants may never recover from the root check. If larger plants are required for planting out, pot into 12 in. deep fibre or paper pots, using John Innes potting compost No. 3.

In the case of pot-grown plants saturate the ball of soil before planting. During dry periods water as necessary until the plants become dormant in late autumn.

Remove the top edge and all unrotted parts of paper, fibre or peat pots before planting and take care not to disturb the roots in any way.

Pruning. Cut back eucalypts annually or periodically. By correct pruning they can be grown in almost any form and kept to any desired size.

The characteristic of apical dominance is strongly developed. The normal form of an unpruned tree in the sapling stage is a single stem with a fast-growing leading shoot and a narrow crown of branches. If the end of the leading shoot is damaged or pruned off, a side-shoot will rapidly form a new leader. This growth habit makes it difficult to form the framework needed for a shrub, bush or standard tree by the usual pruning techniques.

To form a seedling into a low-branching bush, half-standard or standard type of tree, prune in mid or late June. Cut back the leading shoot to the

Eucalyptus niphophila (flowers and adult foliage)

Eucalyptus niphophila (white trunk)

Eucalyptus pauciflora nana (flowers)

Eucalyptus perriniana (standard with juvenile foliage)

start of the current season's growth just above the whorl of close-spaced side-shoots persisting from the previous autumn growth. This should be done in the second, third or fourth year, depending on the length of clear bole required. The side-shoots in the whorl below the cut will then grow vigorously. One or a few shoots will soon become dominant and must be pinched out or cut back so that growth on the other shoots is not suppressed. Side-shoots on the stem may be pruned off later to form a clear bole; do not reduce the crown of branches to less than half the total height.

Trees planted on exposed sites may be cut back to 1 in. above ground level in early spring after planting. The following summer, thin the numerous shoots which develop from the base to one stem for a tree, or several stems for a bush. This cutting back allows the roots to become well developed and provide a firm anchorage.

If a tree becomes top-heavy or unstable, it may be cut back to base, topped or lopped to reduce wind pressure on the stem. This should be done in early spring before growth starts. If lopping has to be done early in winter to reduce wind pressure, or if pruning is carried out to obtain cut foliage, always leave a few leafy branches. This inhibits the development of adventitious shoots until spring when pruning must be completed.

To keep a plant at the juvenile leaf stage, as a foliage plant or for cut foliage, all annual growths must be cut off. This should be done in early spring, after the danger of severe frosts has passed, but before new growth begins. To form stooled (coppiced) plants, seedlings planted the previous summer should be cut back to 1 in. above the ground level in early spring. Every following spring, cut all shoots off as near as possible to the base.

Eucalypts are often grown as pollarded trees on short legs or stems. Cut back the sapling to 6 in. above the desired height of stem in early spring. Prune off all side-shoots flush with the stem. New shoots will soon appear all up the stem; they should be rubbed off at once except for those on the top 6 in. Every subsequent spring, cut off the shoots retained at the top of the stem as close to their base as possible. On bush-type and pollarded trees, one or a few shoots will rapidly start outgrowing the others; these dominant shoots must be pinched out or cut back to a pair of side-shoots in late May and June.

Foliage plants in pots can be shaped into branching leafy bushes by frequent pinching out of the growing points of the upper strong-growing shoots. If the plants become too large, or if the leaves start changing to the adult form, they can be cut back to just above the roots. Pot plants can then be treated as stooled plants and cut back in early spring, annually or biennially.

Alternatively, well-branched plants can be cut back to leave the branches, in outline, forming the shape of an inverted bowl. In a cool greenhouse, cut back during January as the plants will start into growth in February. Plants which are too large can be partially pruned before moving them into the house in autumn.

Pests. SUCKERS, in particular the blue gum psyllid, feed on the young shoots and exude silky white wax. They may seriously attack the juvenile foliage of the glaucous species and cause distortion or die-back. No harmful pests of mature trees are known in Britain.

Diseases. Newly germinated seedlings are susceptible to DAMPING-OFF, and BOTRYTIS may attack young shoots following wilting or frost damage.

SILVER LEAF occasionally attacks mature trees.

Eucalyptus pulverulenta (juvenile foliage)

Eucryphia
Eucryphiaceae

EUCRYPHIA GLUTINOSA

A genus of five or six species of evergreen and deciduous trees and shrubs, native to S. America, Australia and Tasmania. The following species and their hybrids, which are usually hardy only in the south and west, are among the most attractive summer-flowering shrubs available. They bear large, cup-shaped flowers.

E. cordifolia. Chile. Height 10 ft or more; spread 6–8 ft. An evergreen tree of upright habit, hardy in the most southerly counties and westwards. The leathery dull green leaves are oblong-ovate with wavy margins. Solitary white flowers, $2\frac{1}{2}$ in. across, are produced in August and September in the terminal leaf-axils. The stamens are numerous and conspicuous, with rust-brown anthers.

E. glutinosa. Chile. Height 10 ft or more; spread 6–8 ft. A deciduous or partially evergreen species. It is slow-growing and of erect, open habit, and the hardiest of the species. The glossy rich green leaves are pinnate, with three to five ovate leaflets. The foliage assumes shades of orange-red in autumn. White flowers, $2\frac{1}{2}$ in. wide, with numerous stamens and yellow anthers, are borne singly or in pairs at the ends of the shoots in July and August.

Eucryphia glutinosa

E. × intermedia. Height 10 ft or more; spread 6–8 ft. This evergreen hybrid between *E. glutinosa* and *E. lucida* occurred in a garden in N. Ireland. It is an erect, quick-growing shrub, hardy in the south, with simple or trifoliate dark green leaves that are grey beneath. The flowers, $1\frac{1}{2}$–2 in. across, are pure white with a central boss of golden stamens, and are borne at the apex of the shoots in August and September.

E. lucida. Tasmania. Height 10 ft or more; spread 6–8 ft. A tender, evergreen, densely leafy shrub, with oblong, dark green glossy leaves that are glaucous beneath. The pure white flowers are fragrant, $1\frac{1}{2}$–2 in. across, and borne on short stalks from the leaf axils. They appear in June and July. This species, although tender, grows well in the west. It has a mountain form, *E. l. billardieri*, which is hardier and grows 4–6 ft high, with smaller leaves and flowers.

E. × nymansensis. Height 15 ft or more; spread 6–8 ft. This natural evergreen hybrid between *E. cordifolia* and *E. glutinosa* is a quick-growing

Eucryphia × nymansensis

vigorous tree, generally hardy in the south. The erect branches are covered with lustrous green leaves that are simple, or pinnate with three to five leaflets. The cream flowers, $2\frac{1}{2}$ in. across, with overlapping petals, are borne singly or in clusters of two or three during August and September, sometimes later.

Cultivation. All eucryphias do well on light, neutral or acid soils with a cool root run. The species and hybrids described, with the exception of *E. glutinosa*, are tolerant of lime and chalk. Plant the hardier species in September and October, more tender species in April and May. They require a sheltered position in sun or partial shade. The protection of light woodland or a west-facing wall is ideal. In winter, protect young plants from frost with a covering of straw mats or bracken.

Propagation. Take cuttings, 3–4 in. long, of lateral non-flowering shoots, preferably with a heel, during August and September. Insert the cuttings in equal parts (by volume) peat and sand in a propagating case at a temperature of 16–18°C (61–64°F). When rooted, pot the cuttings singly in 3 in. pots of John Innes potting compost No. 1. and overwinter in a frost-free frame or greenhouse. The following April or May plunge the pots outdoors and pot on during the summer into 4 in. pots. Leave in a sheltered position or put in a cold frame for the winter and plant out in permanent positions in April.

Pruning. None required, but pinch out leading shoots of young plants to encourage branching.

Pests and diseases. Generally trouble-free.

Eulalia japonica: see *Miscanthus sinensis*

Euonymus alata

Euonymus europaea (fruits)

Euonymus fortunei 'Silver Queen'

Euonymus
Spindle tree. *Celastraceae*

EUONYMUS ALATA

A genus of 176 species of deciduous and evergreen trees and shrubs. The flowers are inconspicuous, and the deciduous species are grown chiefly for the autumn colour of their foliage, and for their distinctive fruits which are usually composed of four or five lobes, each of which contains a number of orange-red seeds.

The deciduous species described are hardy, while evergreen species are suitable for cultivation only in mild southern and western areas. The evergreen species and their forms are valuable for hedging and ground cover.

E. alata. China, Japan. Height and spread 6–8 ft. A slow-growing deciduous shrub of stiff but open habit, and with corky wings on the branches. The narrowly ovate to obovate dark green leaves are tapered at both ends; in autumn they turn crimson to rose-scarlet. The small, insignificant, green-yellow flowers, which appear in May or June, are followed by purple fruits with scarlet seeds.

E. europaea (common spindle tree). Europe including Great Britain. Height 6–10 ft; spread 4–10 ft. A deciduous species forming a shrub or small tree, often naked towards the ground but with a bushy head. The narrowly ovate mid-green leaves are slender pointed. Inconspicuous green-white flowers appear in May, and are followed by a profusion of rose-red capsules which open to reveal the orange seeds.

Several named varieties include: 'Alba', syn. 'Fructu-albo', with white seed capsules; 'Atropurpurea', with dull purple leaves, turning bright red in autumn; and 'Red Cascade', with abundant large rose-red seed capsules.

E. fortunei, syn. *E. radicans.* Japan. Height up to 10 ft against a wall; spread 4–6 ft. A prostrate, creeping or climbing evergreen shrub. It appears to have a juvenile, prostrate form and an adult form when the growths become erect and bushy. The leaves are glossy dark green, ovate and toothed; in the creeping form they are $\frac{1}{2}$–$1\frac{1}{2}$ in. long, but up to $2\frac{1}{2}$ in. long in the adult form. The insignificant, small, green-white flowers are borne in cymes in May and June on adult plants. The fruits are $\frac{1}{3}$ in. wide, with orange seeds enclosed in a pink capsule. This species makes admirable ground cover and good wall climbers in the juvenile form.

A number of forms are in cultivation, including: 'Carrierei' (height $2\frac{1}{2}$–3 ft; spread 6 ft or more), of spreading, bushy habit; 'Colorata', a good ground-cover plant with leaves tinged rose-purple in winter; 'Minima', syn. 'Kewensis', prostrate with tiny leaves; 'Silver Queen', syn. 'Variegata' (height and spread 6 ft), slow-growing with broad leaves edged with white; and 'Vegeta' (height 24 in.; spread 8 ft), free-fruiting and bushy.

E. japonica. Japan. Height 10–15 ft; spread 5 ft or more. A densely leafy evergreen shrub of upright bushy habit, and with obovate to narrowly ovate shallow-toothed leaves that are leathery and glossy dark green. Cymes, 2 in. long, of green-white flowers, appear in May and June. The pink and orange fruits are seldom seen in cultivation. Although not reliably hardy in cold eastern areas, this species is hardy in the south and west and is suitable for hedging. It is recommended for coastal districts, being tolerant of salt spray.

Numerous forms have been raised and include: 'Albo-marginata', with narrow white-margined leaves; 'Aureo-picta', with a bright yellow blotch in the centre of each leaf; 'Macrophylla Alba', with large grey-green leaves with broad white margins, a handsome wall shrub.

'Microphylla' has small, lanceolate, dark green leaves; this and the following forms are slow-growing and of dense, compact habit (height 12–36 in.; spread 12 in.); 'Microphylla Pulchella', syn. 'Aurea', with yellow leaves; and 'Microphylla Variegata', with white margins to the leaves.

E. latifolia. Europe. Height 10 ft or more; spread 5–8 ft. A deciduous species with a loose, spreading head of branches. The mid-green leaves are ovate to obovate, finely toothed and pointed; they assume brilliant red autumn tints.

Insignificant, small green flowers appear in May and are followed as early as August by persistent, pendulous fruits, $\frac{3}{4}$ in. wide. These are rich rose-red and contain orange seeds.

E. planipes: see *E. sachalinensis*

E. radicans: see *E. fortunei*

E. sachalinensis, syn. *E. planipes*. Japan. This deciduous species closely resembles *E. latifolia* in all aspects. However, the leaves are coarsely toothed, and the fruits are conical at the top with the lobes scarcely winged.

E. yedoensis. Japan. Height 10–20 ft; spread 8–10 ft. A deciduous species of strong-growing, upright habit, forming a shrub or small tree. The shiny mid-green leaves are ovate to obovate, strongly veined beneath and with minute teeth; they turn red and yellow in autumn. Numerous cymes of insignificant, small white flowers are borne in May. The subsequent fruits are pink, $\frac{1}{2}$–$\frac{3}{4}$ in. across and contain orange-red seeds, which remain long after the leaves have fallen.

Cultivation. These shrubs and trees are easily grown in ordinary garden soil and in sun or partial shade. The evergreen species tolerate a considerable amount of shade, but require a sheltered position; variegated forms are usually less hardy and are best grown against walls, by sheltered banks or with the overhead protection of trees. Plant evergreen species in September and October or in April and May, the deciduous species from October to March.

For evergreen hedges, use young plants about 12 in. high, placed at intervals of 15–18 in. Plant in September or October and pinch out the growing points to encourage bushy growth; during the first year of growth pinch out the leading shoots to promote further branching.

Propagation. Take cuttings, 3–4 in. long, of lateral shoots, with a heel, in August or September; insert in equal parts (by volume) peat and sand in a cold frame. When rooted the following spring, line the cuttings out, in April or May, in nursery rows and grow on for one or two years before planting out.

Alternatively, sow seeds when ripe (usually in September) in pots or pans of John Innes seed compost placed in a cold greenhouse or frame. The seeds often take 18 months to germinate; when large enough to handle, prick the seedlings off into boxes and later into nursery rows outdoors. Grow on as for cuttings.

Pruning. Deciduous species require no regular pruning, but the shoots may be thinned out and shortened in February to maintain a shapely form. Established hedges of *E. japonica* should be clipped to shape in April and trimmed, if necessary, from mid-August to mid-September.

Pests. Leaves and stems, particularly of *E. europaea*, may be infested by APHIDS, especially the black bean aphid.

SCALE INSECTS infest the stems of *E. japonica*, and make the plants sticky and sooty. CATERPILLARS may eat the leaves.

Diseases. HONEY FUNGUS may cause the rapid death of shrubs.

Several different fungi cause LEAF SPOT which shows as brown, irregular spots on the leaves.

POWDERY MILDEW is common on *E. japonica*, and shows as a powdery white coating on the leaves and the shoots.

Eupatorium

Hemp agrimony. *Compositae*

A genus of 1200 species of hardy, half-hardy and tender herbaceous and shrubby plants. The hardy herbaceous perennials described are suitable for growing in large borders or wild gardens where the soil is moist.

EUPATORIUM PURPUREUM

E. ageratoides: see *E. rugosum*

E. cannabinum. Europe, N. Africa, Asia. Height 2–4 ft; planting distance 24 in. The mid-green broadly lanceolate leaves are opposite. Rounded terminal heads, 4–5 in. across, of small red-purple flowers are borne from July to September. *E. c.* 'Plenum', with double purple-pink flowers, is more widely grown than the type species.

E. fraseri: see *E. rugosum*

E. purpureum. N. America. Height 4–6 ft; planting distance 3 ft. The slender, pointed, mid-green leaves are in whorls. Heads, 4–5 in. wide, of rose-purple flowers open on branching stems in August and September.

E. rugosum, syns. *E. ageratoides*, *E. fraseri*. N. America. Height 2–4 ft; planting distance 24 in. The oval mid-green leaves are opposite. Flat fluffy heads, 3–4 in. across, of white flowers are produced during July and August on slender branching stems.

Cultivation. Plant between October and March in sun or partial shade in any average soil that is reasonably moist. Cut the stems almost to ground level after flowering.

Propagation. Divide and replant between October and March.

Pests and diseases. Generally trouble-free.

Euphorbia

Euphorbiaceae

A widely distributed genus of 2000 species of annuals, herbaceous biennials, perennials and sub-shrubs, and deciduous and evergreen shrubs, many of which are succulent. The herbaceous and sub-shrubby species described here are generally hardy; the shrubby species and the succulents require indoor or greenhouse cultivation.

The herbaceous euphorbias are suitable for borders with poor soil and some, such as *E. characias* and *E. wulfenii* are good for cutting. The tender shrubby species include the well-known *E. pulcherrima* (poinsettia).

Euphorbia flowers are small and insignificant, but are often surrounded by conspicuous bracts with a petal-like appearance. The succulents, however, are chiefly grown for their interesting forms which resemble those of cacti and are often spined (see also CACTUS). These succulents have

Euonymus japonica (in flower)

Euonymus japonica 'Aureo-picta'

Eupatorium purpureum

Euphorbia polychroma

Euphorbia marginata

Euphorbia fulgens

Euphorbia pulcherrima

insignificant separate male and female flowers and are unisexual or bisexual according to the species. The seed pods explode when ripe and scatter their contents widely.

Euphorbias all contain a white milky sap which is highly irritant to sensitive skins.

ANNUALS AND BIENNIALS

E. heterophylla (fire on the mountain, annual poinsettia). Central America. Height 24 in.; spacing 12 in. A half-hardy annual which forms a neat bush. The dark green leaves vary in shape from ovate to lanceolate, sometimes with lobes. Each shoot terminates in a 4 in. wide whorl of fiery scarlet bracts and crimson-orange flowers, borne from July to September.

EUPHORBIA LATHYRUS

E. lathyrus (caper spurge). Europe. Height 3 ft; spacing 18 in. A biennial species suitable for a wild garden. The roots of mature plants are said to secrete a substance disliked by moles, but its effectiveness seems to vary in different districts. Erect stems carry green, linear leaves symmetrically arranged. Insignificant yellow flowers, in 2 in. umbels, are produced in leafy heads during June and July. This species often reproduces itself from self-sown seedlings.

E. marginata (snow on the mountain). N. America. Height 24 in.; spacing 12 in. This annual species of bushy growth has ovate, bright green leaves that become edged and veined with white as the plant matures. Small clusters of insignificant white flowers appear in September. The variegated foliage is used in flower arrangements; to stop the flow of milky sap, scald the freshly cut stems in hot water.

GREENHOUSE SHRUBS

E. fulgens. Mexico. Height 4 ft; spread 12–15 in. A slender deciduous shrub with thin branches bearing elliptic-lanceolate, mid-green leaves.

Conspicuous scarlet bracts are borne in recurved wand-like terminal sprays, up to 12 in. long, from November to February.

E. milii: see *E. splendens*

EUPHORBIA PULCHERRIMA

E. pulcherrima (poinsettia). Mexico. Height 4–5 ft; spread 12–15 in. This deciduous species is a popular house plant for Christmas decoration. The elliptic bright green leaves are entire or shallowly lobed. Flowers, surrounded by numerous elliptic bracts that may be 6 in. long, are borne from November to February; the whole inflorescence may be 12 in. across. The bracts are usually deep crimson, but scarlet, pink and white forms have been raised.

E. splendens, now known as *E. milii* (crown of thorns). Madagascar. Height and spread 12–24 in. This is a semi-prostrate, spiny, semi-succulent shrub with a woody base. The tips of the shoots bear lanceolate-obovate and mid-green leaves. The 2–3 in. wide inflorescences are branching cymes borne on long stalks from the upper parts of the stem. Two kidney-shaped crimson bracts extend beneath the flowers. The plant may flower at any time, but most freely during winter.

PERENNIALS AND SUB-SHRUBS

EUPHORBIA BIGLANDULOSA

E. biglandulosa (now correctly known as *E. rigida*). Greece. Height and spread 12–18 in. A perennial of erect or semi-erect habit, with lanceolate grey-green leaves. Terminal heads, 3–4 in. wide, of bright green-yellow bracts and flowers appear in late January and continue until April or May. The bracts often take on an orange hue as they age.

EUPHORBIA CHARACIAS

E. characias. Europe. Height and planting distance 3–4 ft. A herbaceous perennial with dark blue-grey oblong leaves that are evergreen in mild winters. Sulphur-yellow inflorescences, ½ in. across and with paper-like bracts, are formed in large terminal heads in May and June.

E. cyparissias. Europe. Height 12 in.; planting distance 24 in. This perennial is a dense, leafy species, useful for ground cover, although invasive. The pale green leaves are linear. Heads, 2 in. across, of round green-yellow flowers are produced in April and May.

E. epithymoides: see *E. polychroma*

EUPHORBIA GRIFFITHII

E. griffithii. Himalayas. Height 2–2½ ft; planting distance 24 in. A perennial with lanceolate mid-green leaves with pale pink midribs. Flame-coloured bracts are borne in round inflorescences, 2–4 in. across, in May and June. As these fade, the plant becomes an attractive green-leaved bush. 'Fireglow' has brilliant flame-orange bracts.

EUPHORBIA MYRSINITES

E. myrsinites. S. Europe, Asia Minor. Height 6 in.; planting distance 15 in. A perennial suitable for the front of a border. Obovate blue-grey leaves clothe the trailing stems. Terminal heads, 2–4 in. wide, of sulphur-yellow bracts are borne in March and April.

E. palustris. Europe, W. Asia. Height 3 ft; planting distance 24 in. This is a sturdy, bushy perennial with yellow oblong-lanceolate leaves. Terminal heads, 4–6 in. wide, of sulphur-yellow bracts are produced in June and July.

E. polychroma, syn. *E. epithymoides*. E. Europe. Height 18 in.; planting distance 24 in. A bushy evergreen sub-shrubby species with bright green ovate leaves. Bright yellow, 3 in. wide heads of bracts are borne during April and May.

Euphorbia griffithii

E. rigida: see *E. biglandulosa*

E. robbiae. N.W. Asia Minor. Height 18 in.; planting distance 24 in. The obovate leaves of this perennial are dark green and leathery. Pale yellow-green bracts are borne in 2–3 in. wide heads in June and July. Thrives in shade.

E. sikkimensis. Himalayas. Height 3–4 ft; planting distance 24 in. A perennial species with mid-green lanceolate leaves; in March and April the young growths and leaf veins are bright red. Round, 2–3 in. wide inflorescences of chrome-yellow bracts are produced in July and August.

E. veneta: see *E. wulfenii*

E. wulfenii, syn. *E. veneta*. Europe. Height and spread up to 4 ft. This bushy evergreen sub-shrub has blue-green lanceolate leaves and rounded bright yellow-green flower bracts. These are densely arranged in terminal columnar panicles about 9 in. long and mature from May to July.

SUCCULENTS

E. bubalina. South Africa. Height 12 in. An easily grown plant, similar to a miniature palm. The green stem is about ¾ in. thick and marked with leaf scars; it bears 4 in. long, lanceolate green leaves on its top section. These leaves fall during winter. Minute, bell-shaped green flowers appear in July and often set seeds.

E. echinus. Morocco. Height up to 3 ft. A heavily branched, leafless species. Its green stems are six or seven-sided, with wavy ridges that bear pairs of grey spines. The small, green, bell-shaped flowers of this bisexual species are borne in July.

E. obesa. Cape Province. Height 6 in. An almost spherical plant which becomes cylindrical with age. It consists of a leafless, spineless stem having eight broad ribs. The stem is grey-green, striped and banded with brown-purple which gives it a chequered appearance. Bell-shaped male and female flowers are borne on the top of separate plants during summer; the green inflorescence is minute, but sweetly scented.

E. valida. Cape Province. Height 3 in. This spherical plant broadens and flattens with age. It is dark green and has eight to ten ribs with lateral markings. Small, sweetly scented green flowers are borne on male and female plants between May and September. The flower stalks become woody and persist for years.

Euphorbia splendens

Euphorbia characias

Euphorbia robbiae

Euphorbia wulfenii

Euphorbia echinus

Euphorbia palustris

Cultivation of annuals and biennials. All species grow well in ordinary garden soil, in sun or partial shade. The colour of the foliage is intensified on poor dry soils. September-sown plants need cloche protection in cold districts.

Cultivation of greenhouse shrubs. Grow these plants in 5–6 in. pots of John Innes potting compost No. 2. Maintain a winter temperature of 13–16°C (55–61°F). *E. fulgens* and *E. pulcherrima* should be gradually dried off after flowering. These species are generally raised annually from cuttings, and the temperature should be increased to 18°C (64°F) from April onwards.

During summer, provide a humid atmosphere for *E. fulgens* and *E. pulcherrima* and shade the glass to prevent the young leaves becoming scorched. Water freely during the growing period; in winter and until after flowering keep the plants just moist. Give a weak liquid feed at intervals of seven to ten days from June to September. Ventilate the house freely when the temperature exceeds 18°C (64°F). *E. pulcherrima* may be stood outdoors in a sheltered sunny position from June to early September.

E. splendens thrives in a drier atmosphere, in full sun and good ventilation; water freely from May to August and keep just moist for the rest of the year. Give a fortnightly feed from June to August. Repot every second year in March.

When the plants are in flower, they may be brought into a living-room with a temperature not lower than 13°C (55°F). Place in a well-lit position away from cold draughts and keep the compost just moist.

Cultivation of perennials and sub-shrubs. Plant between September and April in a sunny position and in any ordinary, well-drained soil.

Set out only small plants of *E. characias* and *E. wulfenii*, as large specimens resent root disturbance. Grow *E. wulfenii* near a wall or fence, as it is susceptible to east winds in spring. The faded flower stems of all plants may be cut to ground level to keep the plants bushy.

Cultivation of succulents. The succulent euphorbias need a well-drained compost such as 2 parts John Innes potting compost No. 2 and 1 part grit or sharp sand (parts by volume). Grow the plants in 3–6 in. pots, in full sun, and water generously during summer and early autumn. In winter and early spring keep the plants dry and at 5°C (41°F). Repot annually in May.

Propagation of annuals and biennials. Sow seeds in the flowering site in March or April; the biennials may also be sown in September. When large enough to handle, thin out the seedlings to the required spacing. Alternatively, sow in pans of seed compost under glass in March at a temperature of 16°C (61°F); prick out the seedlings into boxes and harden off in a cold frame before planting out in May.

Propagation of greenhouse shrubs. Remove young shoots from cut-back plants of *E. fulgens* and *E. pulcherrima* when these are 3–4 in. long, during April and May. The cuttings may be dipped in powdered charcoal to check the flow of latex; insert singly in 2½–3 in. pots of equal parts (by volume) peat and sand in a propagating case at a temperature of 18–21°C (64–70°F). Pot on the rooted cuttings as necessary and start feeding when the plants are in their final pots.

To increase *E. splendens*, take tip cuttings, 3–4 in. long, in July; let the cuttings dry for a couple of days before inserting singly in 2½–3 in. pots of equal parts (by volume) peat and sand. Root in a ventilated propagating case at a temperature of 16–18°C (61–64°F) or on a shaded greenhouse bench. When rooted, pot the cuttings on.

Propagation of perennials and sub-shrubs. Sow seeds during March in pans of John Innes seed compost and place in a cold frame. Prick out the seedlings into nursery rows and transplant to their final positions in the autumn.

Alternatively, insert 3 in. long cuttings of basal shoots in equal parts (by volume) peat and sand in a cold frame during April or May. Plant out when the cuttings are well rooted.

These species can also be propagated by division between September and April.

Propagation of succulents. These euphorbias germinate freely from seeds, provided they are fresh. Seeds collected from growing plants can be sown immediately. Since male and female flowers often occur on separate plants it is usually necessary to cross-pollinate using a brush. To prevent the seeds from being lost when they are released from the pods, place a muslin cover over the plants before the pods ripen.

Cuttings are difficult to root. In June, remove a branch and dry the cutting for at least a week before potting it up in a compost of 2 parts coarse sand and 1 part peat (parts by volume). If rotting occurs, cut out the damaged tissue and dry the branch again before repotting.

Pruning. Only greenhouse shrubs require pruning. Cut back the current season's growths of *E. fulgens* and *E. pulcherrima* to within 6 in. of the base after flowering. The cut-back plants may be used for propagation or they may be potted on and grown for two or three years. No pruning is needed for *E. splendens*.

Pests. Generally trouble-free.

Diseases. Greenhouse species may suffer from a PHYSIOLOGICAL DISORDER; the leaves show yellow or brown discoloration and premature leaf-drop may occur.

BLACK ROOT ROT makes the roots rotten and black, and the leaves become discoloured.

On outdoor plants, shoots damaged by cold winds or frost may be infected by GREY MOULD which causes further DIE-BACK. The affected tissues show a grey velvety fungal growth.

Eutoca viscida: see *Phacelia viscida*
Everlasting flower: see Helichrysum
Everlasting pearl: see Anaphalis

Exacum
Gentianaceae

A genus of 40 species of evergreen annuals, biennials and perennials, and sub-shrubby plants. Only one species is in general cultivation;

this is a greenhouse annual or biennial that may also be grown as a house plant.

E. affine. Island of Socotra. Height and spread 9–12 in. A compact bushy plant with ovate, shining, mid to deep green leaves. The shallowly saucer-shaped, purple flowers, $\frac{1}{2}-\frac{3}{4}$ in. across, with conspicuous yellow stamens, are fragrant; they are solitary and are freely borne from the leaf axils from July to September.

EXACUM AFFINE

Cultivation. Grow exacums in 5 in. pots of John Innes potting compost No. 2. Provide a constant temperature of not less than 13–16°C (55–61°F). Ventilate the greenhouse when the temperature exceeds 16°C (61°F), and give light shading to the glass during the hottest months. Keep the compost moist at all times, and give a dilute liquid feed at 10–14 day intervals from May to August.

Propagation. Sow the fine seeds thinly on the surface of seed compost during March, and germinate at a temperature of 18°C (64°F). If a minimum winter temperature of 16°C (61°F) can be assured, a sowing in late August gives larger plants for flowering the following year.

Place the seed boxes in polythene bags or under sheets of glass to preserve humidity, and position them in light shade; water from below. Prick out the seedlings, when large enough to handle, into boxes of John Innes potting compost No. 1 or a proprietary peat compost; move into 3 in. pots. Pot on as necessary.

Pests and diseases. Generally trouble-free.

Euphorbia obesa

Exacum affine

Fagus sylvatica (fruits or mast)

F

Fagus
Beech. *Fagaceae*

FAGUS SYLVATICA

A genus of ten species of deciduous trees, native to Europe, E. Asia and N. America. They have smooth grey trunks and alternate ovate leaves, and are valued for their timber. Several exotic species are in cultivation in botanic collections,

but none is distinctive enough to be planted generally. The species described here is the common beech, extensively used in woodlands and parks. It is suitable for a tall hedge, and while it is generally too large for the average garden, the weeping and coloured varieties make handsome specimen trees.

F. sylvatica (common beech). Europe, including Great Britain. This native tree eventually has a thick grey trunk and a wide-spreading head of branches. The leaves are broadly ovate, pointed and wavy-margined, with five to nine pairs of veins. The young foliage is bright green, turning mid to deep green as it matures; in autumn the leaves assume yellow and russet tints.

The inconspicuous green flowers are unisexual; the males are crowded in globose heads, while the female flowers are in clusters of two or three. They are borne in May and in autumn are succeeded by woody fruits which contain two triangular brown nuts (mast). The species is excellent for a tall-growing hedge which will retain the russet leaves until the following spring if trimmed in late summer.

Numerous varieties have occurred; among the best are: 'Asplenifolia', syns. 'Heterophylla', 'Laciniata' (fernleaf beech), with narrow deeply cut leaves; 'Cuprea' (copper beech), with dark, copper-red foliage; 'Fastigiata', (Dawyck beech), of columnar habit; 'Pendula' (weeping beech), with pendulous branches; 'Purpurea' (common purple beech), with purple-red leaves; 'Purpurea Pendula', a weeping form of 'Purpurea'.

'Riversii', syn. 'Rivers' Purple', the deepest coloured purple beech; 'Rohanii', similar to 'Asplenifolia' but with purple leaves; 'Rotundifolia', with rounded leaves; 'Tricolor', with purple leaves edged with pink and white; and 'Zlatia', with young golden-yellow leaves that gradually become light green.

Cultivation. These trees grow well on all except heavy, wet soils. Plant from October to March in an open sunny position.

For hedges, use plants about 18 in. high and space 18–24 in. apart. Remove the upper quarter of all shoots after planting to encourage branching; repeat this tipping the following year and thereafter trim the hedge to shape.

Propagation. Sow seeds of *F. sylvatica* outdoors in October and transplant the seedlings to permanent sites two or three years later.

Coloured or variegated varieties do not breed true from seeds and should be grafted in March on to seedlings of *F. sylvatica*.

Pruning. None required for specimen trees; established hedges should be trimmed to the required shape in July or August.

Pests. Trunks and branches may be infested by SCALE INSECTS, notably the beech scale, which produce tufts of white wax; beech APHIDS produce similar tufts of white wax on the undersides of leaves and excrete large quantities of sticky honey-dew.

WEEVIL larvae may tunnel into the leaf tissues.

Diseases. Sunken cankers on branches and stems of young trees may be caused by APPLE CANKER or other closely related fungi; shoots girdled by cankers die back.

BRACKET FUNGI may enter dead wood and cause rotting of the heartwood; later, large bracket-shaped fruiting bodies develop on the trunk or branches if the tree is neglected.

CORAL SPOT may develop on dead shoots and then cause further die-back; pink to red cushion-like pustules of spores appear towards the base of dead wood.

FROST DAMAGE shows as browning of the foliage, as die-back of the young shoots, and sometimes as cankers on the stems.

HONEY FUNGUS causes rapid death of trees.

SCORCHING of the foliage occurs on copper beeches, particularly in spring. The leaves turn brown, especially round the margins; they curl and shrivel, giving a scorched appearance.

× *Fatshedera lizei* 'Variegata'

Fatsia japonica (flowers)

Fair maids of France: see *Ranunculus aconitifolius* and *Saxifraga granulata*
False indigo: see Baptisia

× Fatshedera
Araliaceae

This unusual bigeneric hybrid is a hardy evergreen foliage plant suitable for growing as ground cover, on banks and on walls. It may also be grown in a cold greenhouse or in the home.

× FATSHEDERA LIZEI

× *F. lizei.* Height 4–8 ft; spread 3–4 ft. A bigeneric hybrid between *Fatsia japonica* 'Moseri' and *Hedera helix* 'Hibernica'. This is a sprawling shrub with stout shoots which tend to grow erect and then flop. The shiny deep green leaves are leathery and palmate with five deep lobes. Pale green flowers are borne in October and November but seldom open outdoors. They are carried in terminal panicles, 8–10 in. long, and are composed of numerous round umbels.

The form 'Variegata' has cream-white markings on the leaves.

Cultivation. Plant these shrubs in September and October or in March and April in ordinary, well-drained garden soil and in sun or shade.

Grow pot plants in 6–8 in. pots of John Innes potting compost No. 2; provide a winter temperature of 4–7°C (39–45°F). Pot on or repot annually in March.

Propagation. Take cuttings, 4–5 in. long, in July and August of tip or side-shoots; insert the cuttings in equal parts (by volume) peat and sand in a cold frame. When the cuttings are rooted the following spring, pot up in 4 in. pots of John Innes potting compost No. 2 or line out in nursery rows outdoors; pot on as required for pot culture. Plants in the open should be transplanted to their permanent positions a year later.

Pruning. No regular pruning is required, but lateral growths may be shortened in March or April. When grown for ground cover, the upright growths should be pegged down into the soil when they are about 18 in. long.

Pests and diseases. Generally trouble-free.

Fatsia
Araliaceae

FATSIA JAPONICA

A monotypic genus consisting of an evergreen species, native to Japan and Formosa. It is grown for its handsome foliage and white autumn

owers; it is frequently grown as a pot plant. It
hardy outdoors in the south; elsewhere it
quires wall protection.

japonica, syns. _Aralia japonica, Aralia
eboldii._ Japan. Height and spread 8–15 ft. An
ect shrub with strong growths that produce
w branches. The large leaves are rich and
ossy, mid to deep green above, paler beneath;
ey are palmate, with seven to nine coarsely
othed oblong-lanceolate lobes. White flowers
ppear in October, in panicles 9–18 in. long,
omposed of rounded umbels 1–1½ in. wide.

Cultivation. Fatsias thrive in any good garden
oil and in a sheltered position in sun or shade;
ney grow well in city gardens. In cold areas
lant fatsias against a south or west-facing wall.
lant in September and October, or in April.

For pot culture, grow fatsias in 5–7 in. pots,
r small tubs, of John Innes potting compost No.
or a proprietary peat compost. Provide a
vinter temperature of 2–4°C (36–39°F); pot on
r repot annually in March.

Propagation. Sow seeds in April in pots or pans
f John Innes seed compost at a temperature of
0–13°C (50–55°F). Prick out the seedlings,
vhen large enough to handle, into 3 in. pots of
ohn Innes potting compost No. 1 and grow on
a cold frame; pot on as necessary into 5 in.
ots and plant out the following April.

Sucker shoots can be detached in March or
pril and used as cuttings; pot singly in 3 in.
ots of John Innes potting compost No. 1 and
oot in a cold frame. Thereafter treat the rooted
uttings as advised for seedlings.

Pruning. None required, but straggly growths
nay be shortened in April.

Pests. Generally trouble-free.

Diseases. FROST DAMAGE shows as distortion of
he leaves, which often have small holes.

Faucaria

Aizoaceae

FAUCARIA TIGRINA

genus of 36 species of greenhouse perennials.
hese small succulents of the vast _Mesembry-
nthemum_ group of plants consist of several pairs
f leaves arranged crosswise, one above the other.
he leaves are broad at the base, keeled under-
eath and toothed along the edges. The flowers,
n autumn, are daisy-like and chiefly yellow, with
ne or two white-flowered varieties.

See also CACTUS.

. tigrina. Cape Province. Height 2 in. An almost
temless plant with four or five pairs of leaves.
hese are grey-green and covered with white
ots; their nine or ten recurved teeth terminate in
ong bristles. The plant grows during summer
nd autumn and soon forms a cluster. The
olden-yellow flowers are about 2 in. across.

F. tuberculosa. Cape Province. Height up to 3 in.
An almost stemless plant with three or four pairs
of leaves. They are dark green with white
wart-like tubercles on their upper surfaces and
from three to five teeth on each edge. The yellow
flowers are about 1½ in. wide. The plant gradually
forms a clump up to 6 in. across.

Cultivation. Faucarias do best in an open compost, such as 2 parts John Innes potting compost
No. 2 and 1 part sharp sand or grit (parts by
volume). Grow them in 3–6 in. pots in a sunny
position. Water generously during late summer
and autumn, but keep them dry during winter.
Overwinter the plants at a temperature of 5°C
(41°F). Give water again from about May,
sparingly at first, increasing gradually.

The plants need repotting every third year in
April. Divide and replant the clumps when the
stems become prominent.

Propagation. Faucarias are easily raised from
seeds, but the results are variable. Sow the seeds
in spring at 21°C (70°F) and keep the seedlings
moist during their first winter.

Propagation by cuttings is easy. Remove a
head and short piece of stem from the clump and
dry it for two days before potting it up in the
growing compost. The best time for taking
cuttings is from June to August.

Pests. Tufts of white waxy wool on plants are
caused by MEALY BUGS. Root systems may be
infested with ROOT MEALY BUGS which cause a
check to growth.

Diseases. A PHYSIOLOGICAL DISORDER which
shows as rotting of the tissues is usually due to
over-watering during the resting period.

Felicia

Compositae

FELICIA PAPPEI

A genus of 60 species of half-hardy annuals and
perennials or evergreen sub-shrubs with simple,
daisy-like flowers. The half-hardy species described are suitable for bedding out, for edging
borders and for growing in window-boxes and in
pots under glass.

F. amelloides, syn. _Agathaea coelestis_ (blue
marguerite). S. Africa. Height 18 in.; planting
distance 9 in. A perennial species of bushy habit
which may be overwintered outdoors in mild
areas but is usually grown as an annual. The
mid-green leaves are round to ovate. Sky-blue
flowers, 1½ in. across, are carried well above the
foliage from June to August; they remain closed
in dull weather.

F. bergeriana (kingfisher daisy). S. Africa. Height
and planting distance 6 in. A half-hardy annual
forming a dense mat of ovate, grey hairy leaves.
The flowers are ¾ in. across, with a central yellow
disc and steel-blue ray petals; they are carried

Faucaria tuberculosa

Felicia amelloides

from June to September. The petals curl back in dull weather and open again in the sun.

F. pappei, syn. *Aster pappei*. Africa. Height 15 in.; planting distance 12–15 in. This true perennial species forms a neat bushy sub-shrub with linear, pale green, slightly succulent leaves. China-blue flowers, 1 in. across, first appear in July and sometimes continue until December.

Cultivation. Grow felicias in any ordinary, well-drained garden soil, in a sunny, sheltered position. Plant perennials in May and protect them during winter with open cloches. In subsequent years, shorten the growths in April by $\frac{1}{2}$–$\frac{3}{4}$ in. and remove all frosted shoots. Plant out the annuals in April or May and dead-head by shearing over after the first flush of flowers to ensure a second crop of blooms.

For flowering under glass, set the plants in 3 in. pots of John Innes potting compost No. 1, moving them later to 5 in. pots of No. 2 compost. A minimum winter temperature of 5–7°C (41–45°F) is required.

Propagation. Sow seeds of annuals in pots or pans of John Innes seed compost under glass in February or March, at a temperature of 16°C (61°F). Prick out the seedlings into pots or boxes of John Innes potting compost No. 1 and grow on at 10°C (50°F). After hardening off, they can be planted out in April or May.

A succession of sowings from February to September will provide pot plants to flower under glass all the year round.

Increase perennial species by softwood cuttings, 2–2$\frac{1}{2}$ in. long, taken between June and August. Insert the cuttings in equal parts (by volume) peat and sand in a cold frame and, when rooted, pot up singly into 3 in. pots of John Innes potting compost No. 1. Pinch out the tips when the plants are 3 in. high to promote bushy growth; overwinter in a frost-free frame or greenhouse. Plant out in flowering positions the following April.

Pests and diseases. Generally trouble-free.

Fennel

Foeniculum vulgare. Umbelliferae

FENNEL

The two plants described are quite distinct, *Foeniculum vulgare* being a hardy perennial herb used for flavouring, while *F. v. dulce,* grown as an annual, is primarily used as a vegetable.

Fennel (*F. vulgare*). Europe. Height 5–8 ft; planting distance 12–24 in. This is an aromatic perennial plant of striking appearance with a haze of thread-like, blue-green leaves on polished stems. Tiny golden-yellow flowers are borne in flat umbels, 3–4 in. across, in July and August.

The leaves may be used fresh or dried to flavour fish, cheese dishes, sauces, pickles and

Fennel (in flower)

Fennel (foliage)

Florence fennel

chutney. They may also be used to make fennel tea. Cook the thick stalks as celery or shred them raw into salads. The ribbed, cigar-shaped seeds, which are strongly anise-flavoured, may be used in soups, bread and cakes.

Florence fennel, finocchio (*F. v. dulce*). Italy. Height 24 in.; spacing 9–12 in. This annual plant is similar in general appearance to the common fennel, but is smaller, with a bulbous stem base.

Use the swollen stems raw in salads, or simmer them in a stock. They have a sweet anise-like taste. When the stem bases are harvested, the leaves can be used in the same way as those of the perennial fennel. A warm summer is needed to produce a good crop.

Cultivation of common fennel. The plants grow best in a warm sunny position; they do well in any ordinary, well-drained garden soil. Pinch off the flower stems as soon as they form, unless the seeds are to be harvested.

To provide fresh fennel through the winter, lift some clumps in October and place them in boxes of peat to force in a cool greenhouse at a temperature of 13°C (55°F).

Cultivation of Florence fennel. Grow Florence fennel in a sunny position. The best results are obtained on light, sandy soils, but any fertile, well-drained soil is satisfactory. As the stem bases of young plants begin to swell, they should be earthed up in trenches or covered with paper collars to blanch the bulbs.

Propagation of common fennel. When raising fennel for seeds, sow in March so that the slow-maturing seeds can be gathered in late September or October just before they are ripe. Otherwise, sow in April or May. Sow outdoors in shallow drills 15 in. apart, subsequently thinning the seedlings to 12 in.

Divide established plants in spring. As soon as shoots show above the ground, usually in March, lift the plants, divide them into portions, and replant them to stand 12 in. apart in rows 15 in. apart.

Propagation of Florence fennel. Work a light dressing of complete fertiliser into the soil before sowing Florence fennel in April. Sow the seeds in shallow drills 20 in. apart; when the seedlings are large enough to handle, thin them to 9–12 in. apart. Water well during dry spells.

Harvesting and storing common fennel. Fennel leaves are difficult to dry; it is better to lift some clumps in October and grow them in pots indoors to provide a supply of fresh leaves through the winter months.

From June onwards, leaves can be gathered for deep freezing. See entry under HERBS.

If fennel seeds are to be dried, gather the flower heads in late September or October just before the seeds are ripe. Spread the seed heads on paper and let them dry slowly indoors without artificial heat, turning them frequently, as the seeds transpire and may develop mould. If the seeds do not shake out easily from the heads when they are dry, comb them out with a metal comb. Store the dried seeds in airtight containers.

Harvesting Florence fennel. Gather the swollen stem bases for cooking as required. The leaves may be used in the same way as those of common fennel.

Pests and diseases. Generally trouble-free.

SPORE PROPAGATION OF FERNS

A mature *Adiantum* frond; the close-up of pinnae shows marginal groups of spore capsules

A mature *Dryopteris* frond with pinnae. The spore capsules are arranged in groups between the veins

A young prothallus measuring about $\frac{1}{8}$ in. across and bearing male and female organs

A mature prothallus, measuring about $\frac{1}{3}$ in. in diameter, from which a young plantlet has been produced

FERNS

There are about 10,000 species of ferns, found in every part of the world that can support vegetation; but the greatest number grow in the tropics. Detailed descriptions of the more important genera will be found under the following entries: *Adiantum, Asplenium, Athyrium, Davallia, Dryopteris, Nephrolepis, Onoclea, Osmunda, Phyllitis, Platycerium, Polypodium, Polystichum* and *Pteris*.

Ferns are foliage plants which, in cultivation, need shady positions, whether they are grown in the garden, in a greenhouse or in a window-box. They vary greatly in form, stature and habit; as well as being attractive in their own right, they serve as foils for flowering plants.

Ferns are neuter plants, producing neither flowers nor seeds. They reproduce in the following unique manner.

The fern frond bears on its undersurface tiny heaps of capsules, each containing powdery spores. When sown, these spores produce small, flat, heart-shaped growths called prothalli, which have male and female organs. Each male organ contains mobile cells which swim across the surface moisture on the prothallus to fertilise the female organ's egg cells. Fertilisation produces a tiny new fern.

The prothalli, which in no way resemble the original fern, may grow for years as independent plants before they form their sexual organs. But generally they live for only one season.

In this way, one generation alternates with another: neuter fern, sexual prothalli, neuter fern, and so on.

Propagation from spores. Collect spores by folding a mature frond, on which the spore heaps have begun to turn brown, in a sheet of clean white paper. In two or three days the frond will have released a fine dust of spores.

Make a compost of equal parts (by volume) loam, leaf-mould or peat, and coarse sand, and sieve it finely. Sterilise a seed-pan (preferably earthenware) and half-fill it with the compost, placing the rougher sievings at the bottom of the pan to assist drainage and then firming the surface. Sterilise the compost by pouring boiling water through it until the seed-pan is too hot to handle. When the pan has cooled, cover it with clean glass to exclude fungus spores and moss spores.

Collect a tiny portion of spores on the tip of a knife and, lifting the glass, sow them thinly over the compost. Replace the glass immediately and put the pan in a shady part of the greenhouse. For genera requiring additional warmth, the temperature is given under PROPAGATION.

Four to twelve weeks later a green film of minute prothalli will appear. Keep the glass in place and moisten the prothalli from below by standing the pan in water.

When they have grown into tiny plants, prick them off into boxes or pans of compost and keep them in a close atmosphere. After a time they will form fronds. When these young ferns are large enough to handle, harden them off and pot them singly in small pots. Do not adopt the common practice of standing the pots in saucers of water: this causes sour compost and loss of roots.

Young plants of greenhouse species require the winter temperatures recommended for mature ferns.

Some species may also be vegetatively propagated as explained under the various generic entries.

Fern, asparagus: see *Asparagus plumosus*
Fern, bird's-nest: see *Asplenium nidus*
Fern, broad buckler: see *Dryopteris dilatata*
Fern, Christmas: see *Polystichum acrostichiodes*
Fern, crested buckler: see *Dryopteris cristata*
Fern, flowering: see *Osmunda regalis*
Fern, golden-scaled male: see *Dryopteris borreri*
Fern, hard shield: see *Polystichum aculeatum*
Fern, hay-scented buckler: see *Dryopteris aemula*
Fern, Japanese holly: see *Polystichum falcatum*
Fern, Japanese painted: see *Athyrium goeringianum*
Fern, lady: see *Athyrium filix-femina*
Fern, maidenhair: see *Adiantum capillus-veneris*
Fern, male: see *Dryopteris filix-mas*
Fern, necklace: see *Asplenium flabellifolium*
Fern, ostrich feather: see *Matteuccia struthiopteris*
Fern, ribbon: see *Pteris cretica*
Fern, rigid buckler: see *Dryopteris villarsii*
Fern, royal: see *Osmunda regalis*
Fern, sensitive: see *Onoclea sensibilis*
Fern, shuttlecock: see *Matteuccia struthiopteris*
Fern, soft shield: see *Polystichum setiferum*
Fern, staghorn: see Platycerium
Fern, sword: see *Nephrolepis cordifolia* and *Polystichum munitum*

Ferocactus

Cactaceae

A genus of 35 species of greenhouse perennials. These barrel-shaped, sharply ribbed cacti are grown for their coloured, and usually curved, spines. To develop these spines the plants need full sunlight, which makes them unsuitable as house plants. They are easy to grow but do not often produce their apical funnel-shaped flowers in cultivation.

See also CACTUS.

FEROCACTUS ACANTHODES

F. acanthodes. S. California. Height up to 3 ft. The plant body is solitary, glaucous-green, and has 13–23 ribs. The grey woolly areoles bear eight yellow radial spines and a long, flattened central spine, red in colour and hooked at the tip. The central spine has been known to reach lengths of 4–5 in. The 2 in. long yellow flowers are borne in June and July.

F. melocactiformis. E. Mexico. Height up to 24 in. The plant body is solitary in cultivation, but forms offsets in the wild. It is blue-green, with up to 25 ribs on an adult plant. The areoles bear nine recurved radial spines and three or four central spines, each yellow and up to $2\frac{1}{2}$ in. long. The 2 in. long pale yellow flowers are produced in June and July.

Cultivation. Grow ferocacti in 3–8 in. pots, depending on the size of the plants. Use an open compost, such as 1 part sand to 2 parts John Innes potting compost No. 2 (parts by volume). Let the plants dry out between waterings, and from the end of October to the beginning of March cease watering. They need full sun, and if the greenhouse is in a shady position the plants may be stood outdoors during summer. In winter, keep the plants at a temperature of 5°C (41°F). Repot annually in April.

Propagation. Sow seeds in April and cover with a dusting of soil. Germinate the seeds at a temperature of 21°C (70°F). The seedlings grow slowly during their first year and should be kept slightly moist during their first winter.

Pests. Colonies of MEALY BUGS produce conspicuous tufts of white waxy wool on the plants. ROOT MEALY BUGS infest roots and check growth.

GLASSHOUSE RED SPIDER MITES may be troublesome if the atmosphere is dry.

Diseases. Generally trouble-free.

Festuca

Gramineae

A genus of 80 species of hardy perennial ornamental grasses. The species described are suitable for growing on sunny banks; the attrac-

tive tufts of slender leaves are sometimes used for edging purposes. They are also effective planted in groups among hardy heathers.

F. alpina. European Alps. Height 4–6 in. planting distance 6 in. The bright green thread-like leaves form a dense tuft. Slender, 1 in. long pale green flower panicles, sometimes tinged with violet, are produced in July and August.

F. amethystina. Alps, S.E. Europe. Height 12 in. planting distance 9–12 in. This evergreen plant forms a dense tuft of spreading, glaucous bristle-like leaves. Dark violet panicles, $1\frac{1}{2}$–2 in. long, appear in May and June.

F. glacialis. Pyrenees. Height 3–6 in.; planting distance 4–6 in. The species forms a neat tuft of thread-like silver-blue leaves. Blue-grey, 1–$1\frac{1}{2}$ in. long panicles, sometimes tinged with violet, are borne in July and August.

FESTUCA GLAUCA

F. glauca. Europe. Height 6–9 in.; planting distance 6 in. The bristle-like blue-grey leaves form a thick tuft. Oval purple spikelets, $\frac{1}{4}$ in. long, appear in June and July.

Cultivation. Plant between September and April in a sunny position. Light, well-drained soil suits these plants best. *F. alpina* grows well on chalk. In late spring the developing flower heads may be cut off if the plants are being grown primarily for their leaves. If left on, remove the dead flowers before they can shed seeds.

Propagation. Sow seeds during April in light soil in the open. Prick off the seedlings, when large enough to handle, in small tufts of three or four into nursery rows. Plant out in September.

Festucas may be divided and replanted during suitable weather between September and April.

Pests and diseases. Generally trouble-free.

Ficus

Moraceae

FICUS PUMILA

A genus of 800 species of hardy and tender deciduous and evergreen trees and shrubs, including creeping and climbing plants. The genus includes the ornamental rubber trees and the edible fig. The following evergreen species are grown for their attractive foliage and are popular as house plants.

F. benjamina. India. Height up to 6 ft. This species, which grows to tree-like proportions in

Ferocactus acanthodes

Festuca glauca

Ficus benjamina

Ficus radicans 'Variegata'

he wild, has slender, slightly pendulous side-branches and elliptic, slender-pointed leaves. The young foliage is soft green; as the leaves mature they turn dark green.

F. carica: see Fig

F. deltoidea: see *F. diversifolia*

F. diversifolia (mistletoe fig). India, Malaysia. Height 12–24 in. In the wild, this species forms a large shrub or small tree. Now correctly known as *F. deltoidea*, this slow-growing bushy species has broadly ovate to obovate leaves, dark green above, pale green or fawn beneath. Long-stalked, dull red or yellow, berry-like fruits, $\frac{1}{2}$–$\frac{3}{4}$ in. long, are freely borne in the upper leaf axils throughout the year.

F. elastica (India-rubber plant). Tropical Asia. Height up to 4 ft. This species, which as a pot plant has a single unbranched stem, is variable, and a number of forms are known.

The type is rarely obtainable and has been superseded by the variety *F. e. decora*. This has shiny dark green and oblong-ovate leaves which may reach 12 in. in length. They are arranged spirally along the stem and are borne on short leaf stalks. The prominent midrib shows red on the underside of young leaves. Young leaf buds are covered with a bronze-red sheath, which is pale green in the type.

There are various variegated forms. The young leaves of 'Doescheri' are pale green, tinted with pink, and have broad ivory margins; with age the green portions darken, the pink variegations disappear and the cream-coloured leaf margins become narrower.

'Schryveriana' has rectangular variegated cream patches on the leaves, and 'Tricolor' is variegated with cream, sometimes flushed pink.

F. lyrata, syn. *F. pandurata* (fiddle-back fig). W. Africa. Height 4 ft. A sparingly branched species bearing large glossy, dark green, fiddle-shaped leaves with wavy margins.

F. pandurata: see *F. lyrata*

F. pumila. China. Height and spread on a wall 4–5 ft or more. A climber which can also be grown as a trailing pot plant or trained up supports (height 18–24 in.). It has two types of

foliage, but mature leaves are very rarely seen on cultivated plants. The juvenile leaves are ovate and pointed, dark green with prominent veins.

F. radicans. East Indies. Height 3–4 in. The species is mainly represented in cultivation by the variegated form 'Variegata'. This is a trailing plant, suitable for a hanging basket or as edging to a greenhouse bench. The elliptic-lanceolate leaves are slender-pointed and mid-green with slightly wavy margins; they have conspicuous cream-white edges.

Cultivation. The various species of ficus require different winter temperatures, but they all grow in 4–12 in. pots, according to size, containing John Innes potting compost No. 2 or a proprietary peat compost.

In winter, provide a temperature of 16–18°C (61–64°F) for *F. elastica* and *F. lyrata*; for *F. benjamina* and *F. radicans* give 13–16°C (55–61°F); and for *F. diversifolia* and *F. pumila* provide a temperature of 7–10°C (45–50°F). The latter species will survive outdoors, in ordinary, well-drained soil, against a sheltered wall or in a shrub border in the south and west.

Water all species freely during the summer, keeping them just moist in winter. Place in a well-lit position but out of direct sunlight; *F. diversifolia*, *F. pumila* and *F. radicans* will tolerate shade. Maintain a humid atmosphere in summer by damping down, and ventilate the greenhouse when the temperature reaches 5°C (10°F) above the minimum temperatures.

Sponge the leaves to remove dust.

Pot on every other year in April, and give a weak liquid manure at 10–14 day intervals from May to September.

Propagation. Increase by cuttings or air-layering. Take 2–4 in. cuttings of lateral shoots of *F. benjamina*, *F. diversifolia*, *F. pumila* and *F. radicans* from April to June. Insert the cuttings in equal parts (by volume) peat and sand in a propagating frame at a temperature of 16–18°C (61–64°F); when rooted, pot the cuttings singly into 3 in. pots of the growing compost and pot on as necessary.

Increase *F. elastica* and *F. lyrata* by taking 4–6 in. cuttings of lateral shoots from April to June and rooting them at a temperature of 21–24°C (70–75°F). Treat the cuttings as already described. *F. elastica* may also be propagated from leaf-bud cuttings taken at the same time and treated as described above.

Alternatively, propagate *F. benjamina*, *F. elastica* and *F. lyrata* by air-layering from May to July. See chapter on PROPAGATION.

Pruning. None normally required. *F. diversifolia*, *F. radicans* and *F. pumila* branch naturally, but they can be encouraged to make more bushy growth by pinching out the growing tips in the early stages.

Pests. Conspicuous tufts of white waxy wool on the stems and leaves are caused by MEALY BUGS, which also make the plants sticky.

SCALE INSECTS form rounded brown scales on the stems and leaves.

Diseases. Yellow or brown discolorations of the foliage, followed by leaf-drop, is due to a PHYSIOLOGICAL DISORDER.

BLACK ROOT ROT causes the roots to rot and turn black; the leaves become discoloured.

Ficus elastica decora

Ficus elastica 'Tricolor'

Ficus lyrata

Ficus pumila

277

Fig

Ficus carica. Moraceae

Fig trees grow in the wild from Syria to Afghanistan and are cultivated in temperate and sub-tropical areas. They are deciduous and not completely hardy, although frost-damaged plants usually regenerate from suckers.

FIG

Figs can be grown successfully as bush trees in southern and western areas of Great Britain; further north they are more reliable when fan-trained against a south-facing wall, or grown against a wall in a cold lean-to greenhouse. Outdoors, ripe fruit is not usually obtained north of the Trent. Both bush and fan-trained trees need sunny positions; ideally, bush trees should have protection on the north and east sides.

Fig trees tend to produce an abundance of fruits near the tips of shoots, most of which fail to mature without protection. With outdoor trees, it is important to remove the obvious fruits during the autumn, leaving tiny fruits to develop and mature the following season. On trees under glass, fruits are borne on both overwintered shoots and those of the current season.

The average height and spread for a regularly pruned fig on a wall outdoors or under glass is 8–10 ft × 12–15 ft; for a free-growing bush outdoors, 12–15 ft × 8–10 ft. Planting distances: up to 15 ft for fan-trained wall trees; 10–15 ft for bush types.

The variety most commonly grown in Britain is 'Brown Turkey', which bears brown-green fruits. It is more suitable for cultivation under glass or against a wall outdoors than as a bush. 'White Marseilles', the best bush tree, bears pale green fruits which are nearly white when ripe.

Both are prolific mid-season varieties with sweet-flavoured fruits.

Cultivation. To get good crops in the British Isles it is necessary to restrict the roots, both in the open and under glass. This results in short, well-ripened shoots. Dig a hole 3 ft square and 3 ft deep in the planting position and line the sides and base with concrete or bricks. Provide drainage holes in the bottom. Fill the planting hole with fertile garden soil or fibrous loam to which 2 lb. of bone-meal has been added. Plant the trees at any time during the dormant period from November to March.

Alternatively, set the plants in 12 in. pots and sink in the growing position in March. Ensure that each pot projects slightly above the soil; it will then retain water and the roots will be prevented from growing over the top. Check up on the root growth every other year by digging down around the pot during the winter months. Prune away any roots which have grown through the drainage holes of the pot.

Fig 'White Marseilles'

Filipendula camtschatica rosea

Support fan-trained trees with horizont[al] wires at intervals of 12 in. from ground level up [to] 10 ft. Ensure that there is adequate space f[or] training in the developing shoots.

Mulch newly planted outdoor trees and wat[er] throughout the summer as necessary. Water wit[h] care under glass, giving generous amounts whe[n] the fruits are swelling but reducing supplies whi[le] they are ripening.

Feeding is unnecessary during the first three o[r] four years while the main framework is bein[g] built up. Later, feed carefully with liquid manur[e] to avoid long, unfruitful shoots, but give suffic[i]ent to swell the crop. Mulch with rotted manur[e] in April or May, and if the plants are in need o[f] stimulation dress the soil with 1 oz. of bone-mea[l] per sq. yd in spring.

Leave the fruits to ripen on the tree (usuall[y] mid-August to October). When they are ripe, th[e] stalk softens and the fruit hangs down.

Except in the south and west, give fros[t] protection to fan trees from December to March. Untie the branches from the framework, pu[ll] them close to the ground and wrap them wit[h] thick bundles of straw. Tie the branches back o[n] the framework in spring.

Propagation. The best results are obtained fro[m] layering in summer, severing the layers fro[m] the parent plant 12 months later.

Alternatively, take 4–6 in. heel cuttings o[f] semi-ripe wood in August and September; inser[t] singly in 3 in. pots of equal parts (by volume) pea[t] and sand in a cold frame. Pot the rooted cutting[s] on as necessary, planting out in the sprin[g] 18 months after taking the cuttings.

Pruning. Remove all frost-damaged, bent an[d] crowded shoots from established trees in lat[e] March. Surplus shoots can also be removed i[n] summer. Stop young, fruit-bearing growths a[t] four leaves in June.

Pests. Generally trouble-free.

Diseases. CORAL SPOT causes a die-back of shoots[;] pink to red cushion-like spore pustules appea[r] towards the base of the dead wood.

GREY MOULD attacks the young shoots, causin[g] them to die back for a distance of up to 12 in. o[r] more. The fruiting bodies of the fungus appea[r] towards the base of the dead wood as brown-gre[y] cushion-like pustules. The fungus can also attac[k] the fruit, causing it to rot or fall before it is rip[e;] sometimes the fruit dries up and hangs on the tre[e] in a mummified condition.

An irregular supply of moisture at the root[s] may cause a PHYSIOLOGICAL DISORDER resulting i[n] premature fruit-drop.

Fig, devil's: see *Argemone mexicana*
Fig, fiddle-back: see *Ficus lyrata*
Fig, mistletoe: see *Ficus diversifolia*
Filbert: see *Corylus maxima*

Filipendula

Rosaceae

A genus of ten species of hardy herbaceou[s] perennials, closely related to *Spiraea*. They thriv[e] in moist soil and associate well with *Lythrum* an[d] *Lysimachia*. The following species are useful fo[r]

orders and for cutting; apart from the variety of
hexapetala, they are also excellent for waterside planting. They bear large fluffy heads of tiny
red, pink or white flowers.

FILIPENDULA HEXAPETALA

F. camtschatica, syns. *Spiraea camtschatica*, *S.
gigantea*. Manchuria. Height 4–8 ft; planting
distance 24 in. This species has mid-green
palmate leaves. Tiny, fragrant, fleecy white
flowers are borne in 6–8 in. wide plumes during
July and August. *F. c. rosea* has red-pink flowers.

F. hexapetala, syn. *Spiraea filipendula* (drop-
wort). Europe, including Great Britain; Asia
Minor; Siberia. Height 2–3 ft; planting distance
18 in. The mid-green pinnate leaves are deeply
cut and fern-like. During June and July small
cream-white flowers, sometimes tinged with
pink, appear in flattened panicles 4–6 in. across.

In cultivation the species is usually represented
by the more freely available variety 'Flore Pleno',
which is 18–24 in. high and bears dense heads of
double white flowers. It is less suitable for moist
soils than the type species.

F. palmata, syn. *Spiraea digitata*. Siberia. Height
2–3 ft; planting distance 18 in. The five-lobed
leaves are dark green, with white hairs beneath.
Tiny rose-pink flowers, fading to pale pink and
white, are borne in 6 in. wide plumes during July.

F. rubra, syns. *Spiraea lobata*, *S. venusta* (queen
of the prairie). E. United States. Height 3–7 ft;
planting distance 24 in. Strong stems carry
mid-green leaves which have seven to nine lobes
with a large terminal leaflet. Heads, 6–9 in.
across, of peach-pink flowers appear on branching
stems in July and August.

F. r. venusta, with deep pink flowers, is the
form most common in cultivation.

F. ulmaria, syn. *Spiraea ulmaria* (meadow sweet,
queen of the meadows). Europe, N. Asia. Height
2–3 ft; planting distance 18 in. The pinnate,
coarsely serrated leaves are dark green above,
white hairy on the underside. Branching, flattened heads, up to 6 in. across, of cream-white
fragrant flowers are borne from June to August.
The young leaves of 'Aurea' (height 18 in.;
planting distance 12 in.) are golden-green.

Cultivation. Plant between October and March.
F. hexapetala thrives in full sun and will grow in
any ordinary, well-drained soil, preferably
alkaline. *F. ulmaria* 'Aurea' needs moist soil and
partial shade. The other species and varieties
described do well in sunny or partly shaded
positions in any ordinary soil that does not dry
out in summer. Mulch all plants with compost or
old manure in April or May, and cut the stems
down in October.

Propagation. Filipendulas are usually increased
by dividing and replanting the crowns during
suitable weather between October and March.

Sow seeds in pans or pots of seed compost in
February or March at a temperature of 10–13°C

Filipendula hexapetala

(50–55°F). Prick off the seedlings into boxes
when they are large enough to handle. In
June or July, set the young plants in a nursery
row; they should be large enough to plant out in
their permanent positions that autumn or the
following spring. Seedlings usually take three
years to reach flowering size.
Pests. Generally trouble-free.
Diseases. A white powdery coating on the leaves
is caused by POWDERY MILDEW.

Finger-nail plant: see *Neoregelia spectabilis*
Fir: see Abies and Picea
Fir, Caucasian: see *Abies nordmanniana*
Fir, Douglas: see Pseudotsuga
Fir, grand: see *Abies grandis*
Fir, Korean: see *Abies koreana*
Fir, Low's white: see *Abies concolor lowiana*
Fir, Nikko: see *Abies homolepis*
Fir, noble: see *Abies procera*
Fir, Santa Lucia: see *Abies bracteata*
Fir, silver: see Abies
Fir, white: see *Abies concolor*
Fire on the mountain: see *Euphorbia hetero-
phylla*
Firethorn: see Pyracantha

Filipendula rubra

Fittonia

Acanthaceae

A genus of two or more species of creeping
perennial plants with ornamental foliage. They
are suitable for cultivation in a warm greenhouse,
and although they are sometimes grown as house
plants, they are not easy to cultivate under most
room conditions.

F. argyroneura. Peru. The ovate leaves, up to 4 in.

Fittonia argyroneura

Fittonia verschaffeltii

Forsythia × intermedia 'Spectabilis'

Forsythia × intermedia 'Lynwood'

long, are dark green with the veins picked out in ivory, so that the leaf appears to be netted. The inconspicuous flowers, often cream or bordering on yellow, appear in terminal spikes. They are seldom produced and should be pinched out.

F. verschaffeltii. Peru. This species is similar to *F. argyroneura,* but is easier to cultivate and is more suitable for room culture. The dark green leaves are larger, and the veins are brilliant carmine.

Cultivation. Grow fittonias in John Innes potting compost No. 2, or in a proprietary peat mixture. The plants require warm, humid and shady conditions. A winter temperature of 13°C (55°F) is necessary, and *F. argyroneura* does better at 16°C (61°F). High temperatures will do no harm in summer. Keep the compost drier during cold weather and short daylight periods, but never allow it to dry out completely.

Set rooted young plants in 4 in. pans from May onwards; pot on successively as required and finish in 8–10 in. pans. Re-potting is seldom necessary, as the plants are usually discarded after about three years. In the second year of growth give a weekly feed of liquid manure from June to September.

During the growing season, give ample water, syringe the plants liberally, and frequently damp down the greenhouse. In winter, give the plants all the light available, but shade the glass heavily from spring to autumn.

Propagation. Divide the plants or separate rooted offsets from April onwards. Pot the plantlets in 4 in. pans of the growing compost and place in a propagating case at a temperature of 21°C (70°F) until established.

Pruning. Fittonias, particularly *F. argyroneura,* tend to spread and become untidy. Trim the creeping stems back to vigorous young growths when required, to keep the plants in shape.

Pests and diseases. Generally trouble-free.

Flageolet beans: see Beans (French)
Flame creeper: see *Tropaeolum speciosum*
Flax: see Linum
Flax, common: see *Linum usitatissimum*
Flax, New Zealand: see *Phormium tenax*
Flax, scarlet: see *Linum grandiflorum* 'Rubrum'
Fleabane: see Erigeron
Flower-of-an-hour: see *Hibiscus trionum*
Foam flower: see *Tiarella cordifolia*
Foam of May: see *Spiraea × arguta*
Foeniculum vulgare: see Fennel
Forget-me-not: see Myosotis
Forget-me-not, giant: see *Myosotidium hortensia*
Forget-me-not, water: see *Myosotis scorpioides*

Forsythia
Oleaceae

A genus of seven species of deciduous shrubs, native to E. Asia and S.E. Europe. These hardy, easily grown shrubs are among the most popular and best-known spring-flowering shrubs; some varieties also make good hedging plants. The flowers, in shades of yellow, are tubular at the base with four expanding oblong lobes; they usually appear before the leaves.

Forsythia × 'Beatrix Farrand'

F. × 'Beatrix Farrand'. Height and spread 8 ft. This is a tetraploid hybrid between *F.* 'Arnold Giant' and *F. ovata.* The mid-green leaves are ovate and prominently toothed. Rich yellow flowers, 1½ in. across with orange markings in the throat, are freely borne during March and April.

FORSYTHIA × INTERMEDIA 'SPECTABILIS'

F. × intermedia. Height 8 ft or more; spread 7–8 ft. A vigorous shrub of stiff and compact habit. It is a hybrid between *F. suspensa* and *F. viridissima.* The dark green leaves are lanceolate and toothed. Golden-yellow flowers, 1–1¼ in. across, are borne in abundance during March and April in clusters of one to six on the previous year's growths. This hybrid is mainly represented in gardens by the form 'Spectabilis'; with bright yellow flowers. It is suitable for hedging.

Several forms are available; 'Lynwood' is extremely free-flowering, with the largest rich yellow flowers of the group.

F. ovata. Korea. Height and spread 4–5 ft. A species of spreading, bushy habit and with dull green leaves that are ovate to almost orbicular and either coarsely toothed or entire; they sometimes turn yellow in autumn. The primrose-yellow flowers, ½ in. long, open as early as February. They appear in ones or twos at each joint, often carried on short growths on the old wood. This species is less floriferous than other forsythia species but flowers earlier.

F. suspensa. China. Height and spread 8–10 ft or more against a wall. A rambling shrub with drooping branches and broadly ovate, often tri-foliate, mid-green leaves. The bright yellow pendulous flowers, 1 in. across, are borne in March and early April in clusters of two and four all along the previous year's shoots.

F. s. atrocaulis has black-purple stems and lemon-yellow flowers; *F. s. fortunei* is the most vigorous form, with arching branches; *F. s. sieboldii*, with pendulous or trailing stems, is excellent for covering banks.

FORSYTHIA SUSPENSA (IN FLOWER)

F. viridissima. China. Height up to 8 ft; spread 6–8 ft. This species is of upright habit, with stiff erect branches. The dark green leaves are lanceolate and sometimes toothed in the upper half; they often become purple-tinted in autumn. Bright yellow flowers, $\frac{1}{2}$–$\frac{3}{4}$ in. across, are borne in April, singly or in clusters of three.

Cultivation. Forsythias thrive in ordinary garden soils and grow well in city gardens. Plant from October to March in sun or partial shade; as a wall shrub, *F. suspensa* does well in any aspect. *F. s. sieboldii* is particularly suitable for an east or north-facing wall.

Plant informal hedges of *F.* × *intermedia* 'Spectabilis' in October and November, spacing young plants, 18–24 in. high, at intervals of 18 in. After planting, remove the upper third of all shoots; when the growths are 6 in. long, pinch out the tips to promote bushy growth.

Propagation. Take cuttings, 10–12 in. long, in October, of strong shoots of the current season's growth; insert the cuttings in a nursery bed outdoors. The rooted cuttings should be ready for planting out one year later.

F. suspensa and its varieties often root themselves where the drooping branches touch the soil; separate the rooted layers from the parent plant in October and plant in nursery rows or in permanent positions if large enough. Alternatively, layer suitable branches in October and separate the following autumn.

Pruning. As soon as flowering is over, usually in April, remove old and damaged wood and shorten vigorous flowering shoots to keep the shrubs tidy. *F. suspensa* and its varieties, if grown against a wall, should have the lateral growths cut hard back, immediately after flowering, to one or two buds of the old wood.

Clip established hedges of *F.* × *intermedia* 'Spectabilis' lightly in April, after flowering. No further trimming should be done until the following April.

Pests. BIRDS may destroy the young flower buds.
Diseases. HONEY FUNGUS may kill the shrubs.

Fothergilla

Hamamelidaceae

A genus of four species of hardy, deciduous, low-growing shrubs, native to S.E. North America. These shrubs, which are related to *Hamamelis* (witch-hazel), are notable for their brilliant autumn colours. The flowers have no

Fothergilla monticola (flowers)

petals but consist of numerous long, cream-white stamens in bottle-brush-like spikes.

F. gardenii. S.E. America. Height 2–3 ft; spread 3–4 ft. A species of slender, upright growth with mid-green ovate or obovate leaves that are coarsely toothed on the upper part; they turn red and crimson in autumn. The sweet-scented flowers are carried in catkin-like spikes, $1\frac{1}{2}$ in. long, on the naked wood in April and May.

FOTHERGILLA MAJOR

F. major. Allegheny Mountains, U.S.A. Height 6–8 ft; spread 4–6 ft. This species has broadly ovate leaves, glossy dark green above and glaucous beneath; in autumn they assume orange-yellow or red tints. The erect spikes of sweet-scented flowers are 1–2 in. long and appear in May before the leaves.

F. monticola. S.E. United States. Height 6–8 ft; spread 5–8 ft. This species is similar to *F. major*, but of more spreading habit, and the leaves are not glaucous beneath. The autumn colour is in various shades of red and orange.

Cultivation. These shrubs require a light, moist, lime-free soil with plenty of peat or humus. Plant in October and November or in March in light shade or full sun.

Propagation. Layer long shoots in September; it usually takes two years for the layers to root, after which they should be separated from the parent plant and set in their permanent sites.

Pruning. None required.

Pests and diseases. Generally trouble-free.

Fothergilla monticola (autumn foliage)

Four o'clock plant: see *Mirabilis jalapa*
Foxglove: see Digitalis
Foxglove, Chinese: see *Rehmannia angulata*
Fragaria × **ananassa**: see Strawberry

Fraxinus excelsior 'Aurea'

Fraxinus ornus

Freesia 'Aurora'

Freesia 'Ballerina'

Fraxinus

Ash. Oleaceae

A genus of about 70 species of hardy deciduous trees, distributed over the cooler regions of the Northern Hemisphere. The leaves are usually pinnate and opposite, but are occasionally seen in whorls of three. Several species are in general cultivation; they make good specimen trees for parks and large gardens.

FRAXINUS ORNUS

With the exception of *F. mariesii* and *F. ornus*, the flowers are inconspicuous and consist of yellow-green filaments and brown stamens; they are borne in April and are followed by winged fruits, known as keys.

F. americana (white ash). E. United States. Height 25–35 ft; spread 10–15 ft. A fine specimen tree suitable for moist soil, with stout green-grey twigs and pinnate leaves composed of seven leaflets. These are ovate, slender-pointed and mid-green with pale, almost glaucous undersides. The foliage may assume autumn tints of amber, yellow and purple. The species is dioecious, with insignificant petal-less green flowers borne in tufts, about 1 in. long, during May. They are followed, on female trees, by narrow winged fruits or keys, each containing a cylindrical seed.

F. angustifolia. S. Europe, N. Africa. Height 20–30 ft; spread 10–18 ft. A fast-growing species with mid-green pinnate leaves, composed of seven to thirteen lanceolate toothed leaflets. The single-seeded fruits with narrow, flattened wings, 1 in. long, are green turning to light brown.

FRAXINUS EXCELSIOR 'PENDULA'

F. excelsior (common ash). Europe, including Great Britain; Asia Minor. Height 20–30 ft; spread 12–15 ft. This native species is quick-growing with wide-spreading surface roots; it should not be grown near buildings or fences.

The dark green leaves are composed of seven to eleven oblong-lanceolate leaflets. The winged fruits are in pendent clusters, 1½ in. long, green at first, becoming brown. The species may eventually reach a height of 100 ft and is generally too large for the average garden. The following garden forms are recommended: 'Aurea', with golden-yellow young shoots and clear yellow autumn colour; 'Diversifolia', syn.

'Monophylla', an unusual form with leaves having only one, occasionally three, jaggedly toothed leaflets; 'Pendula' (weeping ash), with pendulous branches.

F. ornus (manna ash). S. Europe, Asia Minor. Height and spread 10–18 ft. A species of bushy habit, with dull green leaves, composed of five to seven ovate to obovate leaflets. The flowers are cream-white, heavily and pleasantly scented. They are borne in May in panicles 3–4 in. long. The green fruits, 1 in. long, ripen to brown.

F. oxycarpa. S. Europe to Asia Minor and Iran. Height 15–25 ft; spread 8–15 ft. This species is closely related and similar to *F. angustifolia*, with equally attractive foliage. 'Raywood' is of more upright habit, with blue-green leaves which turn plum-purple in autumn.

Cultivation. These trees thrive in any ordinary garden soil. Plant from October to March in a sunny or partially shaded position. They are wind-resistant and suitable for growing in towns and maritime districts.

Propagation. Sow seeds when ripe, usually in October, in pots or pans of John Innes seed compost, and place in a cold frame. When large enough to handle, prick the seedlings out into nursery rows and grow on for three or four years before transplanting to permanent positions. The seeds may take 18 months to germinate.

Named varieties do not come true from seeds, but must be grafted on to stock of the type species in March.

Pruning. None required.

Pests. Generally trouble-free.

Diseases. ASH CANKER is due to the APPLE CANKER fungus and other organisms. Damage varies from small warts on the bark to large black cankers which cause extensive die-back.

BRACKET FUNGI may enter dead wood and cause rotting of the heartwood. Later, large bracket-shaped fruiting bodies may develop on the trunks and branches.

FROST DAMAGE may prevent the development of terminal shoots, and frequent forking in young trees results.

HONEY FUNGUS may cause the death of trees.

A PHYSIOLOGICAL DISORDER due to an irregular supply of moisture in the soil causes die-back of shoots or extensive crown die-back.

Freesia

Iridaceae

FREESIA × HYBRIDA

A genus of South African bulbous plants with 20 species. The beautiful, sweetly scented freesias, widely grown for the flower trade and in garden greenhouses, are the progeny of two species which are not now in general cultivation. One of the forms of *F. refracta*, a pale cream species, was

Freesia (mixed varieties)

crossed with *F. armstrongii,* a pink and white species with yellow streaks, and from these a new race of multi-coloured hybrids was developed.

These hybrids are sometimes listed under the name *F. × hybrida,* but are correctly known as *F. × kewensis.* They have mid-green, narrowly lanceolate leaves and grow to a height of 18–24 in. Thin branching stems bear one-sided spikes of flowers set among short bracts. The fragrant flowers are funnel shaped and 1–2 in. long.

None is really hardy, although some varieties flower for many years in mild areas such as the Scillies and the Channel Islands. In the main, they are grown in a cool greenhouse. However, specially prepared corms that can be planted outside in April to flower in July and August are now available. They will flower outdoors only for the first season.

The following are a few of those available: 'Apotheose', mauve-lilac with white centre; 'Aurora', clear buttercup-yellow; 'Ballerina', pure white; 'Buttercup', light yellow; 'Celeste', soft blue and lilac; 'Elder's Giant White'; 'Fantasy', cream-yellow; 'Madame Curie', red; 'Nieuw Amsterdam', magenta; 'Romany', double, mauve; 'Rose Marie', rose-pink with white throat; and 'Souvenir', yellow.

Cultivation. Outdoors, freesias require a light, rich, sandy soil and a sunny, sheltered site. Indoors, grow them in John Innes potting compost No. 2, or in equal parts (by volume) sand, loam, leaf-mould and well-rotted manure.

Plant prepared corms in April. Unless the site is particularly sheltered, provide twiggy sticks for support. Lift after the foliage has turned yellow, and thereafter treat as unprepared corms.

For growing outdoors in the mild areas mentioned, plant ordinary (unprepared) corms in August or September. They will flower in April or May and may be left in the ground to flower in subsequent seasons.

For plants to flower under glass from January to April, plant ordinary corms from August to December. Set them 2–3 in. apart in boxes, beds or in pots, in either a greenhouse or frame; or, in the case of August plantings, in a sheltered site outdoors. Just cover the tops with compost and add a 1 in. layer of fine peat. Give little water until

growth begins. Freesias started outdoors must be brought into the greenhouse by October.

From October onwards, maintain a minimum temperature of 5°C (41°F). Gradually increase the water supply and apply a dilute liquid feed at fortnightly intervals once the flower buds show. To support freesias grown in pots or boxes, insert small pea sticks or light canes and stretch strings between them; for plants grown in beds, use 4–6 in. mesh netting suspended from posts, raising the netting gradually as the plants grow.

Water freely while the plants are in flower, easing off as they begin to die down. Allow the plants to become completely dry, and leave them until July or early August. Then lift and dry the corms, remove the offsets and store both in a dry, frost-free place, ready for replanting. Avoid excessive warmth if they are to be replanted after October, or growth may start prematurely.

Propagation. Offsets removed when the corms are lifted in late summer can be grown on in the same way as mature corms. Most will flower the following year.

Plants can also be raised from seeds, to flower from October to March and to provide future corms. The seeds are hard-coated and should be soaked in water for 24 hours to ensure even germination. Make successive sowings from March to June, in pots, boxes or beds, in a cool greenhouse or frame. Seeds sown after mid-May will germinate in the open.

Sow the seeds sparingly, afterwards thinning to leave five or six seedlings to a 5 in. pot or a spacing of 1½–2 in. each way in boxes and beds. Plants in pots and boxes may be grown on during summer in a sheltered site outdoors.

Pests. APHIDS infest the stems and leaves and transmit virus disease.

GLASSHOUSE RED SPIDER MITES infest plants under glass, and CATERPILLARS sometimes attack plants grown outdoors.

Diseases. Freesias grown in large numbers under glass are liable to attacks of GLADIOLUS DRY ROT FUNGUS, a FUSARIUM WILT and a VIRUS DISEASE specific to freesias.

Fremontia

Sterculiaceae

FREMONTIA CALIFORNICA

A genus of two species of deciduous flowering trees or shrubs, native to California and Mexico. Only one species is cultivated to any extent; it is slightly tender and is suitable as a wall shrub in mild districts.

F. californica. California. Height 8–12 ft; spread 6–8 ft. A deciduous or semi-evergreen species of upright habit. The young growths are covered with a soft brown down; the palmate leaves are dull green above, brown and hairy beneath, and

Freesia 'Fantasy'

Freesia 'Romany'

Freesia 'Rose Marie'

Freesia (mixed varieties)

Fremontia californica

Fritillaria latifolia aurea

Fritillaria meleagris 'Alba'

Fritillaria imperialis

Fritillaria imperialis 'Aurora'

usually composed of three to seven irregular lobes. The golden-yellow waxy flowers are five-petalled, cup-shaped and 2 in. across. They are borne singly from May to October.

Cultivation. Grow fremontias in well-drained sandy soil and in full sun. Set out pot-grown young plants in April or May, preferably training them against a trellis on a south or west-facing wall; tie in the trunk and main branches.

Propagation. Sow seeds in pots of John Innes seed compost at a temperature of 16°C (61°F) during March or April. When large enough to handle, prick off the seedlings separately into 3 in. pots of John Innes potting compost No. 1; plant out in late summer or, preferably, pot on into 5–6 in. pots and plant out in the flowering sites the following April or May.

Pruning. None required except the removal in early April of any weather-damaged shoots.

Pests and diseases. Generally trouble-free.

French beans: see Beans

Fritillaria

Liliaceae

A genus of 85 species of hardy bulbous plants found wild in the northern temperate zone. Most are cultivated in botanical centres and private collections, a few in domestic gardens. Many species are not easily established or maintained in the soils and climate of Great Britain, but under the right cultural conditions they will grow either outdoors or in pots in a cool greenhouse.

F. acmopetala. Asia Minor. Height 15–18 in.; planting distance 4–8 in. This is one of the more successful species in Britain; it bears mid-green linear stem leaves and two or three bell-shaped flowers, $1\frac{1}{2}$ in. long. Three pale green outer petals

surround three somewhat smaller inner petals, which are purple-brown outside and yellow-green, veined with brown, inside. The flowers appear in April.

FRITILLARIA IMPERIALIS

F. imperialis (crown imperial). Himalayas. Height 2–3 ft; planting distance 9–15 in. Narrowly lanceolate, glossy green leaves are carried in whorls along the stem. The tulip-shaped flowers, about 2 in. long, open in April; they are yellow to rich red in colour and borne in a terminal pendent cluster.

Named varieties include 'Aurora', orange-yellow; 'Lutea', lemon-yellow; 'Orange Brilliant', orange-brown; and 'Rubra', red.

FRITILLARIA LATIFOLIA

F. latifolia. Caucasus, Turkey and Silicia. Height 4–8 in.; planting distance 4 in. This species is similar to *F. meleagris* but is shorter and with fewer leaves. The flowers vary from maroon-purple to yellow. *F. l. aurea* has chrome-yellow flowers, chequered brown; those of *F. l. nobilis* are maroon-purple outside, with deeper chequering, and yellow-green within.

F. meleagris (snake's head). Great Britain, N. and Central Europe to the Caucasus. Height 12–18 in.; planting distance 4–6 in. Found wild in meadows, often near rivers. The linear, mid-green, slightly glaucous leaves ascend the stem, and the bell-shaped flowers grow in pairs or singly at the top. Each blossom, white with purple-chequered markings, is about 1½ in. long and appears in April and early May.

Recommended varieties include 'Alba', white, veined green; 'Aphrodite', white; 'Artemis', purple-grey with darker chequering; 'Charon', dull deep purple; 'Poseidon', purple spotted with brown; and 'Saturnus', violet-red.

FRITILLARIA MELEAGRIS

F. pallidiflora. S. Siberia. Height 12–15 in.; planting distance 4–8 in. A stout stem carries grey-green leaves, oblong on the lower part but lanceolate on the upper part. Yellow bell-shaped flowers, 1½ in. long, appear from the axils of the upper leaves in clusters of up to six during April.

F. pontica. S.E. Europe and Turkey. Height 18 in.; planting distance 4–8 in. The narrow, lanceolate, deep green leaves grow on the upper stem, the topmost in a whorl below the green and purple flowers. These are solitary and bell-shaped, about 1½ in. long, and are produced in May and June.

Cultivation. Grow in fertile, well-drained soil. *F. imperialis* does best in an undisturbed border in full sun or partial shade. *F. meleagris* grows well in short turf as well as in borders; it thrives in moist conditions. The other species, which are less hardy, need well-drained sites in sunny borders or on rock gardens, or they may be grown in a frame or cool greenhouse.

Handle all bulbs carefully. They are composed of a few fleshy scales and most are intolerant of bruising or prolonged exposure to air. Plant them on their sides so that the hollow crowns do not retain water, or surround them with coarse sand.

Outdoors, plant from September to November, 4–6 in. deep; 8 in. deep for *F. imperialis.* Leave undisturbed, not transplanting for at least four years. Stems may be cut down to ground level when they die off during summer.

Plants in pots require John Innes potting compost No. 2, or equal parts (by volume) loam, sand, peat and leaf-mould. Pot the bulbs singly in 5–8 in. pots in September or October and place in a greenhouse heated to 5–7°C (41–45°F). Water sparingly until growth begins, then moderately, decreasing gradually after flowering. When the leaves are dead, allow the compost to dry out.

Many fritillarias produce small offsets, which may be separated from the parent bulb after the foliage has died down in summer, and replanted.

Propagation. Seeds can be bought, or collected from the plants when ripe. It is important to use fresh seeds, ideally sowing them in July or August directly after harvesting. Sow them in 4–5 in. pots in a cool greenhouse or frame, and just cover with compost, coarse sand or grit. Keep well shaded until the autumn. Overwinter at a temperature of 5°C (41°F).

Seedlings will appear in spring. Except for *F. imperialis*, prick these out, eight or ten to a 5 in. pot, being careful to avoid root damage. Keep in a cold frame for at least one year and then set the bulbs and soil ball in the flowering site, avoiding root disturbance as much as possible. Prick out the largest *F. imperialis* seedlings into frames or outdoor beds and plant out the bulbs when they are nearly large enough to flower. Seedlings do not flower until they are four to six years old.

The bulbils or offsets from parent bulbs are best treated as seedlings and grown on in pots or frames until they reach flowering size.

Pests and diseases. Generally trouble-free.

Fuchsia
Onagraceae

FUCHSIA MAGELLANICA 'GRACILIS'

A genus of about 100 species of deciduous trees and shrubs, native to Central and South America and New Zealand. Few species are in general cultivation, having been superseded by numerous hardy and slightly tender hybrids. In mild areas fuchsias are fully hardy and are often used as hedging plants; the tender varieties are suitable for cool greenhouse cultivation; they may also be used for outdoor summer bedding.

The upright species and varieties may be grown as bushes, standards or against walls, as pot plants in a cool greenhouse, or outdoors; trailing and prostrate forms make attractive plants for hanging baskets.

Fuchsias are chiefly grown for their attractive pendulous flowers, which consist of a tube terminating in four spreading sepals and four overlapping petals, forming a bell, often in a contrasting colour to the waxy sepals.

F. corymbiflora. Peru. Height 4–6 ft; spread 2–3 ft. A tender shrub with arching stems carrying oblong-lanceolate, pale to mid-green and pink-veined leaves. Crimson flowers, 3–4 in. long, are borne in pendulous corymbs from June to September. It is best grown as a pot or border plant in a cool greenhouse.

F. fulgens. Mexico. Height 3–4 ft; spread 2–3 ft. A tender shrubby species with soft red stems. The ovate or heart-shaped leaves are toothed and pale to mid-green. The flowers, which are borne in terminal panicles from July to October, are 2–3 in. long. The tube is scarlet, the short lobes tipped with green, and the petals may be scarlet or green. This species is a parent of several hybrids. It may be grown as a pot plant in a cool greenhouse; in very mild districts it can also be grown outdoors, preferably against a wall.

Fritillaria meleagris

Fuchsia fulgens

Fuchsia magellanica 'Gracilis'

Fuchsia 'Brilliant'

Fuchsia 'Jack French'

Fuchsia 'Mission Bells'

Fuchsia 'Mrs Popple'

Fuchsia 'Tennessee Waltz'

Fuchsia 'Citation'

F.macrostemma: see *F. magellanica*

F. magellanica, syn. *F. macrostemma*. Mexico, Peru, Chile, Falkland Islands. Height 4–6 ft; spread 2–4 ft. This bushy shrub is the hardiest of the fuchsias, and is much used for hedging in Cornwall and Eire, where it may reach a height of 8–10 ft. The lanceolate mid-green leaves are in opposite pairs or in whorls of three. Pendent flowers, 1½–2 in. long, are borne on slender stems from the leaf axils. They have a crimson tube and sepals and purple petals with protruding stamens. The flowering period extends from July to October. In cold districts the species may be cut down by frost, but they usually recover.

Numerous varieties, hardy in the south, are available: 'Alba' has bright green leaves and palest pink flowers; 'Conica' has red and purple flowers; 'Mrs P. Wood' is similar to 'Alba', but with larger, deep pink flowers.

'Gracilis' has narrower leaves and more slender flowers than the type species; 'Gracilis Variegata' has red and purple flowers and leaves margined with cream.

'Pumila' is a miniature variety, 6 in. or more high, with red and purple flowers ¾ in. long; 'Riccartonii' is a vigorous erect grower with flowers having red sepals and purple petals.

'Versicolor' bears flowers similar to those of 'Gracilis'; the foliage is strikingly variegated with grey-green and white or yellow, with rose-pink tinting.

F. procumbens. New Zealand. Height 2 in.; spread 24 in. or more. A prostrate plant, suitable for a hanging basket, with heart-shaped, pale to mid-green leaves. It is generally hardy and will survive most winters outdoors. The axillary flowers, ¾ in. long, have no petals but consist of a yellow tube with reflexed green and purple sepals. Flowering is from June to September.

The plant's main attraction lies in the 1 in. long red ovoid berries that follow the flowers.

F. triphylla. West Indies. Height 24 in. or more; spread 18 in. A compact downy sub-shrub with lanceolate leaves in whorls of three or four; they are mid-green above, heavily suffused with purple-red beneath. The brilliant orange-scarlet flowers, 1½–2 in. long and with short petals, are borne in dense terminal clusters from July to October. This species is tender and is best grown as a pot plant in a cool greenhouse.

HYBRIDS

Fuchsia hybrids are derived chiefly from crosses between *F. fulgens* and forms of *F. magellanica*, and probably from other species. Half-hardy or garden varieties will survive outdoors for a number of years, particularly if they are planted deeply and given a mulch in autumn.

The height and spread of fuchsia hybrids vary considerably, depending on the method of training and whether they are grown in pots or in borders. Height is also determined by the individual variety. Except where otherwise stated, varieties grown as standards or pyramids in pots under glass can attain a height of 3–5 ft with a spread of 1½-2½ ft. Specimens grown as bushes rarely exceed a height of 24 in. with a similar spread. However, several varieties grown as shrubs in sheltered gardens in the south and west may reach 6 ft or more with a spread of 4–6 ft. Even in less-favoured areas, where top growth

Fuchsia 'Cascade'

is cut to ground level by frost each winter, annual height and spread may exceed 24 in.

The following named varieties, with flowers 2–4 in. long, are suitable for growing outdoors: 'Alice Hofman', carmine sepals and double white petals; 'Brilliant', bushy, with large scarlet and magenta flowers; 'Charming', red sepals, red-purple petals, yellow-green foliage; 'Madame Cornelissen', red sepals, clear white petals; 'Margaret', vigorous grower, semi-double, crimson sepals, violet-purple petals; 'Mission Bells', vigorous and bushy, red sepals and rich purple petals; 'Mrs Popple', strong grower of arching habit, red sepals and purple petals.

FUCHSIA HYBRID (BUSH)   FUCHSIA HYBRID (STANDARD)

'Princess Dollar', low dense habit, reflexed carmine sepals and double, frilled, deep violet petals; 'Tennessee Waltz', compact and erect with rose-pink sepals and semi-double lilac petals; 'Thompsonii', compact and erect with scarlet sepals and purple petals; 'Tom Thumb' (height and spread usually less than 12 in.), cherry-red sepals, mauve petals.

The following hybrid varieties are more tender and require greenhouse cultivation; they may be grown in pots or baskets, as bushes, standards or pyramids, and many can be used for summer bedding schemes in the open.

'Achievement', cerise sepals, magenta petals, not suitable as a basket plant; 'Avocet', vigorous

Fuchsia 'Avocet'

Fuchsia 'Checkerboard'

Fuchsia 'Miss California'

Fuchsia 'Ting-a-ling'

Fuchsia 'Lyes Unique'

Fuchsia 'Marin Glow'

and free-flowering with red sepals and white petals; 'Bon Accord', of bushy habit, with erectly held flowers having waxy white sepals and pale purple petals.

'Cascade', of drooping habit, ideal for a hanging basket, single flowers with white sepals flushed carmine and deep red petals; 'Checkerboard', suitable for bedding, red sepals changing to white, deep red petals; 'Citation', of upright bushy habit, suitable for bedding, rose-pink sepals, white petals; 'Constellation', double ivory-white flowers.

FUCHSIA HYBRID (PYRAMID)   FUCHSIA (PENDULOUS)

'Falling Stars', a hanging-basket variety with light red sepals and turkey-red petals; 'Fascination', of bushy habit, suitable as a standard, double flowers with waxy red sepals and rose-pink petals; 'Flying Cloud', pendulous and of bushy habit, double flowers with white petals lightly veined red, and white corolla; 'Forget-me-not', pale flesh-pink sepals, light blue petals.

'Gartenmeister Bonstedt', suitable for bedding, olive-green foliage with red-purple veins, rich orange-red flowers; 'Golden Marinka', vigorous grower suitable for a hanging basket, golden foliage, red flowers; 'Jack French', of well-branched habit, suitable for pot cultivation, large flowers with rich red sepals and royal-purple petals.

'Lyes Unique', suitable for summer bedding, white tube and sepals, pale orange-red petals; 'Marin Glow', suitable for summer bedding, white sepals, petunia-purple petals; 'Marinka',

similar to 'Golden Marinka', but with green foliage; 'Miss California', slow-growing, with pink flowers.

'National Velvet', of upright habit, suitable for summer bedding, double flowers with cherry-red sepals and purple petals; 'Rose of Castile Improved', strong-growing and almost hardy, flesh-pink sepals, purple petals; 'Royal Purple', suitable for summer bedding, turkey-red sepals, purple petals; 'Rufus the Red', suitable for summer bedding, deep salmon-red flowers.

'Snowcap', suitable for summer bedding, semi-double flowers with cherry-red sepals and white petals; 'Swingtime', a good hanging-basket plant with shiny red sepals, milky-white petals; 'Texas Longhorn', for pot cultivation, large double flowers with bright red sepals and white petals; 'Thalia', suitable for bedding, dark green leaves, red beneath, orange-red flowers; 'Ting-a-ling', well-branched and free-flowering with shapely white flowers; and 'White Spider', with pure white flowers.

Cultivation. The garden fuchsias will grow in almost any well-drained soil with the addition of humus, such as peat or leaf-mould, and a little bone-meal. Set out well-hardened plants in May or June, when the danger of night frost is over, in full sun or light shade. Water frequently during dry spells. In mild areas, hardy fuchsias make shrubs, but in colder regions they grow like herbaceous plants and are cut to the ground by the first severe frost. Cut the plants down to base at the beginning of November, and cover the roots with a deep mulch of bracken, ashes or peat.

Tender fuchsias for greenhouse cultivation or for summer bedding should be grown in 6–9 in. pots of John Innes potting compost No. 3 or, if they are to be kept for one season only, in a proprietary soil-less compost. In March, trim the plants lightly, water and start them into growth at a temperature of 10°C (50°F). As the plants break, take the young shoots for cuttings.

Fuchsia 'Thalia'

Fuchsia 'Rufus the Red'

Fuchsia 'Snowcap'

Fuchsia 'Swingtime'

Pot the rooted cuttings in 3 in. pots of the growing compost, and later pot on into 5 or 6 in. pots in which the plants will flower. Pinch out the leading shoots and the laterals several times to encourage bushy plants.

If large specimens are wanted, keep the plants growing throughout the winter at a temperature of 13°C (55°F). Pot on the following spring and summer until they are in 8–9 in. pots. Stop the leading shoot at 6 in. intervals, and all lateral shoots at every second leaf until six weeks before flowering is wanted. In this way, pyramids of flowers 4–5 ft high can be obtained.

Standards are formed by letting the main growing point ascend and removing all laterals, until a trunk of the desired height is obtained. A stouter main stem may be achieved by leaving a number of shortened laterals on the stem until it is established. The leading shoot is then pinched out. For a weeping standard attach the laterals to a wire framework.

Varieties with low or arching growth habit, such as 'Marinka', should be grown in 10 in. hanging baskets.

In the greenhouse, provide a cool, humid but airy atmosphere during the growing season and lightly shade the glass. In winter the plants require a temperature of 4–7°C (39–45°F); they should be kept barely moist.

Repot established plants annually in March and give them a liquid feed once a week from June to September; feed young plants at intervals of three weeks.

Pot plants raised for summer bedding may be stood outside or planted out from mid-June. Keep them moist or the flower buds may drop. After flowering gradually withhold water, and after leaf-fall give no more water until growth is restarted in spring. In October, lift and move to a frost-free greenhouse.

Propagation. Take tip cuttings, 3–4 in. long, from shoots without flower buds in March. Insert the cuttings singly in 2 in. pots of equal parts (by volume) peat and sand at a temperature of 16°C (61°F); pot on as described under CULTIVATION.

Sow seeds in March or April at a temperature of 16°C (61°F). Prick off the seedlings, when large enough to handle, into boxes of John Innes potting compost No. 2 and then singly into 3 in. pots. Thereafter treat as described for cuttings. Plants raised from seeds of named hybrids do not come true to type.

Pruning. Cut hardy species and hybrids down to ground level in November or in March or April except where the climate is sufficiently mild to grow fuchsias as deciduous shrubs. Remove dead or diseased wood in March or April.

Trim back greenhouse species and varieties lightly in February; overgrown plants may be cut hard back at the same time.

Pests. Hardy species and varieties are generally trouble-free.

APHIDS infest leaves and stems, sucking sap from young growths and excreting honeydew.

GLASSHOUSE RED SPIDER MITES infest the undersides of leaves, causing mottling, bronzing and premature leaf drop.

In the greenhouse, GLASSHOUSE WHITEFLY may form large colonies on the undersides of the leaves and make the plants sticky and sooty.

Diseases. Hardy species and their varieties are generally trouble-free.

In the greenhouse, RUST shows as pale orange powdery pustules on the leaves, predominantly on the undersurfaces.

BLACK ROOT ROT turns the roots black and rotten; the leaves become discoloured

A PHYSIOLOGICAL DISORDER results in purple or yellow blotches on the leaves, which later fall.

Fuchsia, Californian: see Zauschneria
Funkia: see Hosta
Funkia longipes: see *Hosta rectifolia*
Furze: see Ulex

G

Gaillardia aristata 'Wirral Flame'

Gaillardia pulchella 'Lollipops'

Galanthus nivalis

Gaillardia aristata 'Mandarin'

Gaillardia

Blanket flower. *Compositae*

GAILLARDIA ARISTATA

A genus of 28 species of hardy annual and perennial herbaceous plants. Those described are suitable for growing in herbaceous borders and provide a good choice of bright red and yellow daisy-like flowers for cutting.

G. aristata, syn. *G. grandiflora*. S. United States. Height 2–2½ ft; planting distance 18 in. The grey-green lanceolate leaves of this perennial species are alternate; the flowers have yellow ray-florets and red disc-florets. They are 3 in. wide and are borne from June to October.

This variable plant is less widely grown than the many striking hybrids of which it is one parent. These include: 'Burgundy', deep wine-red; 'Dazzler', bright orange-yellow with maroon-red centre; 'Goblin' (9 in. high), yellow and red; 'Ipswich Beauty', orange and brown-red; 'Mandarin', flame-orange and red; 'Wirral Flame', deep red with gold-tipped petals. The flowers of these varieties are 3–4 in. across.

G. grandiflora: see *G. aristata*

G. pulchella. C. and S. United States. Height 18 in.; planting distance 12 in. An annual with leaves that are spathulate, grey-green and hairy. Single flowers, 2 in. across, appear from July to October.

Garden varieties vary in form, having enlarged ray-florets with quilled central discs or ball-shaped flower heads. 'Lollipops' (12 in.), is weather-resistant and free-flowering, with raspberry-red or red and yellow flowers; 'Picta Lorenziana' (18 in.), has double flowers and bright colours ranging from yellow through bronze to red.

Cultivation. Gaillardias thrive in light, well-drained soil and a sunny site, although they will grow reasonably well in most soils and shaded positions. Plant them between March and May, depending on when the seeds were sown. Provide twiggy supports where necessary, especially for the taller plants with large flower heads. Remove dead flowers to prolong the flowering period.

Propagation. Sow seeds of annual gaillardias in the flowering site in April and thin the seedlings to the required planting distance.

Seeds of perennial species may also be sown outdoors in May or June, the seedlings pricked off into a nursery bed and grown on for planting out in March or April of the following year.

Seeds of annual and perennial species may also be sown in pots or pans of seed compost under glass during February or March, at a temperature of 15°C (59°F). Prick off the seedlings into boxes and after hardening off in a cold frame plant out in May for flowering the same summer.

Pests. Generally trouble-free.

Diseases. DOWNY MILDEW causes yellowing of the leaves; the undersurfaces develop a white, downy fungal growth.

Galanthus

Snowdrop. *Amaryllidaceae*

GALANTHUS NIVALIS

The drooping white flowers of the common snowdrop are familiar to most. Less well known are the dozen or more related hardy species and the many varieties. Only minute details distinguish these, and all are so similar as to be easily recognisable as belonging to the same genus.

Snowdrops should not be confused with leucojums (snowflakes), their spring and summer-flowering relatives. Snowdrops have three long outer and three short inner petals, while all six snowflake petals are the same size. Also, snowflakes are generally taller and bear two or more flowers to each stem. Snowdrops flower earliest in the mildest parts of the country, the time of flowering depending on the weather.

G. elwesii. Asia Minor and neighbouring islands. Height 6–10 in.; planting distance 4–8 in. The strap-shaped leaves are broad and glaucous; the $1\frac{1}{4}$ in. long flowers are deep green on the inner petals. They are borne in February and March.

G. nivalis (common snowdrop). Europe, including parts of Great Britain. Height 3–8 in.; planting distance 3–6 in. Many apparently wild plants have been naturalised from gardens. The species is variable, especially in height, growing tallest in rich soil in partial shade. The slightly glaucous leaves are flat and strap-shaped. The flowers, from January onwards, are white with green markings on the inner petals, and about 1 in. long. The sub-species *G. n. reginae-olgae*, flowers in October before the leaves. Named varieties include the following:

G. n. 'Flore-plena' has double flowers with the stamens converted to petals; these, with the six normal petals, give the flower a less elegant form. 'S. Arnott' is a vigorous hybrid, taller than the species and with $1\frac{1}{2}$ in. long flowers. 'Viridapicis' has flowers with a green spot on the outer as well as the inner petals.

Cultivation. Snowdrops are not easy to establish, but once started need little attention. They will survive in most soils and weather but grow best in heavy loams with plenty of moisture, and with some shade. Competition from other plants is not harmful as long as the leaves receive good light from January to April. They do well in open woodland and in grass under trees, provided the lower branches are clear of the ground.

The bulbs dry out rapidly if left out of the ground too long; it is better, therefore, to move plants just after flowering than to plant dry bulbs in the autumn. When it is necessary to plant dry bulbs, order them early, do not expose to the air and plant them as soon as possible. The first year's results may be disappointing but they will recover and eventually start to increase.

Propagation. Seeds of most species and of single varieties can be collected; sow as soon as possible in pots or direct in a frame and keep shaded and watered. Where the plants are doing well, the seeds may be left to fall and grow. Sow purchased seeds as soon as they are available, between autumn and March. Seedlings take up to five years to reach maturity.

Snowdrops can also be increased by dividing the clustered plants at or just after flowering time. Lift and divide carefully so that each bulb is separated with its roots and leaves intact; keep from drying out during this process. Replant at the same depth as before, either with the old plants or in shaded beds for further increase and subsequent division.

Pests. The bulbs are sometimes invaded by STEM AND BULB EELWORMS, causing discoloration, rotting and death.

NARCISSUS FLY MAGGOTS tunnel in the tissues of bulbs and eventually kill the growing points.

Diseases. The occurrence of GREY MOULD affects the leaves and flower stalks, which are soon destroyed and become covered with a grey velvety fungal growth. Small black resting bodies develop on the bulbs, which decay.

Galega
Goat's rue. *Leguminosae*

A genus of six species of hardy herbaceous perennials. They are of bushy, vigorous growth and are suitable for growing at the back of a border or for a wild garden.

G. officinalis. Italy, Balkans, Asia Minor. Height 3–5 ft; planting distance 2–2$\frac{1}{2}$ ft. The light green leaves are short-stalked and pinnate. Globular white or pale lilac flowers are produced in 1$\frac{1}{2}$ in. long spikes during June and July. *G. o.* 'Alba' is pure white; 'Her Majesty' is soft lilac-blue; 'Lady Wilson' is mauve and cream.

G. orientalis. Caucasus. Height 3 ft; planting distance 24 in. The light green oblong leaves have hairy stems. Blue-mauve, pea-like flowers are borne in 1$\frac{1}{2}$ in. long spikes in June.

Cultivation. Plant galegas between October and March in sun or light shade in well-drained soil. They look best when planted in groups of three or more. In rich soil the growth may sprawl, and the plants should be supported with twiggy pea sticks. Cut the flowered stems down almost to ground level when they have faded.

Propagation. Sow seeds during April in a sunny position in the open. Prick out the seedlings into a nursery bed when they are large enough to handle. Plant out from October onwards.

Galegas can also be propagated by dividing the tough roots in suitable weather between October and March.

Pests and diseases. Generally trouble-free.

Galtonia
Summer hyacinth. *Liliaceae*

GALTONIA CANDICANS

A genus of four bulbous species. Only one, probably the hardiest, is readily available. It produces tall spires of slightly scented white flowers in late summer. They make an attractive display when other plants are past their best, and they are also suitable for pot culture.

G. candicans, syn. *Hyacinthus candicans.* Africa. Height 4 ft; planting distance 6–8 in. Large round bulbs produce narrow-pointed, semi-erect, slightly glaucous leaves up to 2$\frac{1}{2}$ ft long. From July to September the single erect flower stem carries a dozen or more bell-shaped white flowers, 1$\frac{1}{2}$ in. long, on stalks 1 in. or more in length. Each flower has pale green markings at the base and on the tips of the petals.

Cultivation. Plant at least 6 in. deep in March or early April, setting three or five together or

Galanthus nivalis reginae-olgae

Galanthus nivalis 'Flore-plena'

Galega officinalis

Galega officinalis 'Alba'

scattering the bulbs among early-flowering herbaceous plants or annuals.

Galtonias can also be planted in October for flowering in a greenhouse in May and June; set three to five bulbs in a 6 in. or 8 in. pot of John Innes potting compost No. 1. Provide a temperature of 4–7°C (39–45°F). Keep the bulbs in their pots through the winter and then plant out as a group in the following spring. Leave undisturbed once established in a permanent bed or border. Remove the flower stems when tidying the border during the autumn.

Propagation. Seeds are produced in favourable summers and may be sown in pots or directly into the bed of a frame during March. The seedlings take four or five years to flower.

Offsets, which are not plentiful, can be removed from the parent bulbs in September or October, replanted immediately, and grown on in the same way as seedlings.

Pests and diseases. Generally trouble-free, although GREY MOULD may sometimes weaken or kill newly planted bulbs.

Gardener's garters: see *Phalaris arundinacea*
Garden pea: see Pea

Galtonia candicans

Gardenia jasminoides 'Florida'

Garlic

Gardenia

Rubiaceae

GARDENIA JASMINOIDES

A genus of 250 species of tender evergreen or semi-evergreen flowering shrubs or, more rarely, small trees. Only one species is in general cultivation and this requires greenhouse treatment. The strongly fragrant double forms provide excellent cut flowers for table decoration or button-holes. Sever them, on long stems, just as the centre petals are about to open.

G. jasminoides (Cape jasmine). China. Height and spread 2–4 ft. The species is represented in cultivation by the double-flowered 'Florida'; the plants generally seen are superior forms of this, and 'Fortuniana' is the most outstanding. This shrub bears dark green, glossy, lanceolate leaves in whorls of three. Solitary, white, waxen, heavily scented flowers, 3 in. across, are borne from the leaf axils at the top of the shoots. The main flowering period is from June to August. The similar variety 'Veitchiana' flowers in winter.

Cultivation. Grow gardenias in 6–8 in. pots of John Innes potting compost No. 2 or a proprietary peat compost. In winter, provide a temperature of 12°C (54°F) for summer-flowering plants, 16–18°C (61–64°F) for winter-flowering plants. Keep summer-flowering plants just moist in winter, but water 'Veitchiana' freely.

In summer, water the plants freely and feed with a liquid manure at 10–14 day intervals from May to October. Established plants may be plunged in peat in a sunny position outdoors from late June to mid-September.

In the greenhouse, ventilate when the temperature exceeds 18°C (64°F), and lightly shade the glass from late April to September. Provide a humid atmosphere by frequent damping down in hot weather.

Repot or pot on annually in April.

Propagation. Take 3 in. long cuttings of lateral non-flowering shoots, preferably with a heel, in February or March; insert in equal parts (by volume) peat and sand in a propagating frame, at a temperature of 18–21°C (64–70°F). Pot the rooted cuttings singly into 3 in. containers of the growing compost. Grow them on at a temperature of 18°C (64°F) and shaded from strong sunlight. Pot on as necessary.

Pruning. Shorten all growths of established plants by half or two-thirds after flowering. Pinch out the tips of shoots on young plants from cuttings in summer, to induce bushy growth.

Pests. APHIDS infest young shoots and make the plants sticky and sooty.

GLASSHOUSE RED SPIDER MITES infest the undersides of leaves and cause a light mottling and discoloration of the upper leaf surfaces.

MEALY BUGS infest stems, forming conspicuous colonies covered in white waxy wool.

Diseases. BUD DROP is generally caused by unsuitable cultural conditions.

Garland flower: see *Daphne cneorum*

Garlic

Allium sativum. Alliaceae

A hardy perennial herb of the onion family, grown for its strong flavour and aroma.

Height 1–3 ft; planting distance 9–12 in. Central Asia. This plant has linear grey-green leaves and carries globular heads, 1–1½ in. across, of small, white, red-tinged flowers in June.

The bulb is a compound mass of bulblets or cloves which are used to flavour salads, soups, fish and meat dishes. They have a penetrating flavour, similar to onions, and should be used sparingly. Garlic also has antiseptic and disinfectant properties.

Cultivation. Garlic does best in a light soil that has been well manured and dug in early winter, to allow the bed to settle by early spring. Choose a position that is sunny but moist. Pinch off the flower heads as early as possible so that all the nourishment is diverted to the bulbs, which are ready for lifting by late July or early August. An additional planting in October will provide bulbs for early use before the main crop is ready.

Propagation. Buy bulbs from a reliable source in January in readiness for planting in February. Plant them whole or broken down into cloves. If cloves are used, set them in drills 3 in. deep. Whole bulbs should be planted with the nose just below soil level. In both cases set them 6 in. apart in rows spaced 12–15 in. apart. Keep the best bulbs each year to provide the next season's cloves for planting.

Harvesting and storing. When the foliage turns yellow, usually in August, lift the bulbs and allow

them to dry thoroughly in the sun. Tie the dried
bulbs into bundles and store them in a dry, cool,
frost-proof place.

Pests. Generally trouble-free.

Diseases. A yellowing and dying-back of the
leaves is caused by WHITE ROT; the roots rot and
the base of the bulb becomes covered with a
white fluffy fungal growth.

Garrya
Garryaceae

GARRYA ELLIPTICA

A genus of 18 species of hardy and tender
evergreen shrubs, of which only one species is in
general cultivation. These shrubs are grown for
their attractive pendulous catkins, male and
female flowers being borne on separate plants.
Some nurserymen offer plants of both sexes, but
male plants are the most ornamental and are
most frequently seen.

G. elliptica. California, Oregon. Height 8–15 ft;
spread 6–12 ft. A quick-growing shrub of bushy
habit. Generally hardy, but in cold or exposed
areas it is best given the protection of a wall. The
ovate, thick and leathery leaves are grey-green.
The male flowers grow in decorative, drooping,
grey-green catkins, 6–9 in. long, which drape the
branches during February and March, or earlier
in mild districts. The female catkins are smaller,
less attractive and silver-grey; they are followed
by round clusters of silky purple-green fruits
containing a deep purple juice. Plants of both
sexes are required for fruits to be produced.

Cultivation. Garryas do not transplant easily;
they resent root disturbance and are normally
grown and supplied in containers by nurserymen.
Plant young plants in April and give protection
during the first winter with bracken, or erect a
polythene screen until established. Large specimen shrubs should not be moved. The shrubs are
easy to grow in all well-drained garden soils; they
thrive in sun or shade although they flower better
in full sun. Where possible, plant against a south
or west-facing wall.

Propagation. Take cuttings, 3–4 in. long, of
semi-ripe side-shoots with a heel, in August and
September. Insert the cuttings in equal parts (by
volume) peat and sand and root in a cold frame.
The following spring, pot the rooted cuttings in
3½ in. pots of John Innes potting compost No. 2;
plunge the pots outdoors and transplant to
permanent positions the following spring.

Layer long shoots in September and sever from
the parent plants one or two years later.

Pruning. No regular pruning is required; straggly
growths may be shortened after flowering.

Pests. Generally trouble-free.

Diseases. Purple blotches or blackening of the
leaves are due to FROST DAMAGE.

Gasteria
Liliaceae

A genus of 70 species of greenhouse perennials.
These succulents are small, clump-forming
plants, almost stemless and with their tough,
glossy leaves usually arranged in two ranks. They
are grown for their attractively marked leaves.

The red tubular flowers, 1 in. long, are widest at
the base, and are carried on a 12 in. long arching
stem; they are produced at any time during the
growing period. Gasterias make easily-grown
house plants.

See also CACTUS.

G. liliputana. S. Africa. Height 2–3 in. This is the
smallest species. The leaves, 2 in. long, are keeled
underneath and arranged spirally on a short stem.
They are dark green, heavily flecked with white.

G. maculata. S. Africa. Height 8 in. The strap-
shaped leaves are 8 in. long and have a horny
terminal spine. They are dark green, marked with
white flecks.

GASTERIA VERRUCOSA

G. verrucosa. S. Africa. Height 6 in. The tapering
4–6 in. long leaves are arranged in pairs, one
above the other. They are dark green, heavily
marked with grey tubercles.

Cultivation. Gasterias are summer-growing
plants; during their growing period water them
freely and keep them in a sunny position, though
they will tolerate some shade. During winter
keep the plants dry if they are being grown in a
greenhouse; in the drier atmosphere of a
living-room they should be kept moist to prevent
excess shrivelling. The winter temperature
should not be allowed to fall below 5°C (41°F).
Plant in 4 in. pots, using John Innes potting
compost No. 2.

Propagation. Gasterias can be raised from seeds
sown in spring, but the plants hybridise freely
and the seedlings may well be inferior.

Increase existing plants by splitting up the
clumps or by taking leaf cuttings during summer,
drying them off for two or three days and potting
them up in John Innes potting compost No. 2.

Pests. Infestations of MEALY BUGS produce conspicuous tufts of white waxy wool on plants. ROOT
MEALY BUGS may infest root systems and cause
a check to growth.

Diseases. Generally trouble-free.

Gaultheria
Ericaceae

A genus of 200 species of evergreen flowering
shrubs. The following are suitable for growing in
lime-free soil in rock gardens, wild gardens, peat
beds or mixed borders, and also provide useful

Garrya elliptica

Gasteria maculata

ground cover. They bear urn-shaped flowers followed by attractive berries. All are hardy, although the young growths may be nipped by spring frost.

G. antipoda. New Zealand. Height 4 ft; spread 2–3 ft. This species is variable and forms either an erect or a prostrate shrub. The leaves are mid-green, ovate to obovate or oblong, thick, leathery and toothed. White flowers, up to $\frac{1}{8}$ in. long, are borne during June and July. They are followed by white or red globose berries. The species is suitable for a rock garden.

G. miqueliana. Japan. Height 12 in.; spread 3–4 ft. This species has toothed, dark green leaves that are ovate to obovate. Small white flowers appear in May and June; they are borne in racemes, 1–2 in. long, from the upper leaf axils. The white globose berries are often flushed pink.

G. procumbens (partridge-berry, winter-green, checkerberry). N.E. America. Height 3–6 in.; spread 3 ft or more. A creeping species, useful for ground cover. The shiny, dark green leaves, which are clustered at the ends of the shoots, are obovate or ovate and toothed. White or pink flowers, about $\frac{1}{4}$ in. long, are carried in short terminal racemes in July and August. They are followed by bright red globose berries.

G. shallon. Western N. America. Height and spread 4–6 ft. This species spreads by suckers to form wide thickets with upright growths. The mid to dark green leaves are broadly ovate. Axillary racemes, 2–3 in. long, of pale pink or white flowers, are borne in May and June. The globose berries are purple-black. This species increases rapidly and is useful where bold ground cover is required, growing well under trees in moist soil.

G. sinensis. Upper Burma. Height 4–6 in.; spread 6 in. A compact, prostrate shrub with ovate, minutely bristled, deep green leaves. White flowers, $\frac{1}{4}$ in. long, are borne singly in the upper leaf axils during April and May and are followed by globose berries; these are usually blue, but may be pink or white.

Gaultheria shallon

Gazania × hybrida 'Hazel'

GAULTHERIA TRICHOPHYLLA

G. trichophylla. Himalayas. Height 3 in.; spread 12 in. This species forms a tuft of wiry stems covered with glossy, dark green, elliptic leaves. Solitary deep pink flowers, $\frac{1}{6}$ in. long, are produced in the leaf axils in May and June; ovoid blue berries follow in August and September.

Cultivation. Gaultherias require a moist, acid soil with added peat or lime-free leaf-mould. Plant in September and October, or in April and May, in partial shade, and in a position away from drips from overhead trees which they will not tolerate. The dwarf species thrive in peat beds.

Propagation. Take cuttings, 2–3 in. long, of lateral shoots, preferably with a heel, in July or August; insert in equal parts (by volume) peat and sand in a cold frame. Pot the rooted cuttings the following spring in 3–3½ in. pots of 2 parts peat, 2 parts lime-free loam and 1 part coarse sand (parts by volume); plunge outdoors until the autumn when they may be planted out.

G. shallon may be increased by detaching and replanting rooted suckers in September.

Extract seeds from the berries, mix with fine sand and sow on the surface of peat in pots or pans in October. Place these in a cold frame and prick off the seedlings, when they are large enough to handle, into boxes of a lime-free compost, such as 2 parts lime-free loam, 2 parts peat and 1 part sand (parts by volume). Pot singly into 3 in. pots of the same type of compost and plunge outdoors. Grow on in nursery rows for one or two years before planting out in permanent positions in spring or autumn.

Pruning. None required, but *G. shallon* may be cut hard back in April or May to control growth.

Pests and diseases. Generally trouble-free.

Gayfeather: see Liatris

Gazania

Compositae

GAZANIA SPLENDENS

A genus of perennial herbaceous plants with 40 species. Except in the mildest areas they must be grown as annuals. These low-growing plants are cultivated for their daisy-shaped flowers, which close in the evening. They are useful as pot plants, for cut flowers and for bedding out.

G. × hybrida. Height 9 in.; planting distance 12 in. A hybrid bred from *G. splendens* and other species. The dark green foliage is lanceolate, toothed and grey on the underside. The flowers, 2–3 in. wide and in a range of colours but predominantly orange, are produced from July to the first frosts. 'Monarch Mixed' includes yellow, orange, brown, red, pink and ruby flowers, all strikingly zoned.

Other named varieties include: 'Bridget', orange-yellow, zoned with maroon; 'Hazel', mahogany-crimson, tipped orange-yellow and zoned with purple-brown; and 'Snuggle Bonnie', glowing maize-yellow, paling towards the tips.

G. splendens. S. Africa. Height 9 in.; planting distance 12 in. The spathulate leaves are dark green on top, silky white on the underside. The flowers are 3 in. across, with bright orange ray florets and black and white spots at the base. They bloom from July to September.

Cultivation. Gazanias need well-drained soil and full sun; they make good subjects for seaside gardens. For cultivation as pot plants under glass, grow them in 5 in. pots containing John Innes potting compost No. 1. Keep the plants on the dry side from September to March, and at a temperature of 5–7°C (41–45°F).

Gazania × hybrida 'Snuggle Bonnie'

Gazania × hybrida 'Bridget'

Propagation. Sow the seeds under glass in January or February at a temperature of 16°C (61°F). Prick out the seedlings into 3 in. pots and harden off before planting out in June.

Cuttings can be taken in July or August and rooted in equal parts (by volume) peat and sand. Pot them individually into 3 in. containers, and overwinter at a temperature of 7–10°C (45–50°F). Plant out in June.

Pests. Generally trouble-free.

Diseases. GREY MOULD causes rotting of the tissues in wet weather; the affected areas become covered with a grey velvety fungal growth.

Gean: see *Prunus avium*

Genista

Broom. *Leguminosae*

A genus of 75 species of deciduous or almost leafless shrubs. They are hardy, easily grown plants, valuable for their profusion of pea-shaped flowers in late spring and early summer. The leaves are alternate on the branches which are sometimes spined. Some species make fine specimen plants, others are excellent for ground cover or on a rock garden. See also *Cytisus*.

G. aetnensis. (Mt Etna broom). Sardinia, Sicily. Height 15–20 ft; spread 15–18 ft. A shrub of loose, open habit, with light green, rush-like, spineless branches. The few mid-green leaves are linear, with silky hairs. Golden-yellow flowers, about $\frac{1}{2}$ in. long, are borne during July and August in loose terminal racemes, 3–4 in. long.

G. cinerea. Italy, Spain, N. Africa. Height 10 ft; spread 5–8 ft. This species has slender, slightly arched, grey branches bearing linear-lanceolate, grey-green leaves. The sweet-scented yellow flowers, $\frac{1}{2}$ in. long, are profusely borne in loose terminal racemes, 3 in. long, in June and July.

G. dalmatica, syn. *G. sylvestris pungens* (dalmatian broom). W. Balkans. Height 6 in.; spread 2–3 ft. A dwarf shrub of compact hummock-forming habit. The dark green leaves are linear. Bright yellow flowers are borne in June and July, in densely set terminal racemes, 1–1$\frac{1}{2}$ in. long. This species is suitable for a rock garden or as ground cover on dry banks.

G. delphinensis. S. France. Height 1–2 in.; spread 3–4 ft. The most prostrate broom in cultivation, and excellent for a rock garden. The rich green branches are winged and rather zigzagged, with a few bright green ovate leaves. The bright yellow flowers are carried in 2 in. long terminal or axillary racemes in June and July.

G. hispanica (Spanish gorse). S.W. Europe. Height 2–4 ft; spread up to 8 ft. A much-branched, densely spined species with deep green upright growths. It is hardy only in the south. It bears deep green, linear-lanceolate leaves and golden-yellow flowers. These are carried in terminal clusters, 1 in. across, in June and July. The flowers are usually borne so profusely that the shrub takes on a golden hue.

Genista aetnensis

Genista cinerea

Genista hispanica

Genista hispanica
(growth habit)

Genista lydia

Genista pilosa

G. lydia. S.E. Europe, Syria. Height 2–3 ft; spread up to 6 ft. A dwarf species, with numerous arching or prostrate grey-green branches. The leaves are grey-green and linear. Bright yellow flowers are freely borne in racemes, 3 in. long, on spine-tipped shoots in May and June. Suitable for training over walls, for covering banks or on a large rock garden.

G. pilosa. S. Europe, including S.W. England. Height as a shrub 18 in.; spread 2–3 ft; height as a creeper, 3 in.; spread 3–4 ft. A variable species, growing as a prostrate shrub with a tangled mass of whip-like shoots, or as a bush with erect shoots. The prostrate form is more common, but both forms do well on a sunny bank or a rock garden. The narrow, obovate, mid-green leaves are alternate on the upper part of the stems, but clustering below. Small yellow flowers are borne in great profusion from May to July in terminal racemes, 1 in. long.

G. sylvestris pungens: see *G. dalmatica*

G. tinctoria (dyer's greenweed). Europe, including Great Britain; W. and N. Asia. Height 6 in.–3 ft; spread up to 6 ft. This is a variable species ranging from a prostrate shrub to an erect bush with slender, grooved stems. The linear-lanceolate leaves are dark green. It blooms from June to August, bearing its deep yellow flowers in erect, 3–4 in. long, terminal racemes on stems which often branch near the top and form a panicle of flowers.

Forms include: 'Humifusa' (height 3–4 in.; spread 18–24 in.), prostrate, with deep yellow flowers; 'Plena' (height 6–9 in.; spread 6–8 ft), prostrate, with 6 in. long flowering stems of double deep yellow flowers; and 'Royal Gold', with dense racemes of rich yellow flowers.

G. virgata (Madeira broom). Madeira. Height and spread 12 ft. A shrub with erect, slightly pendent, grey-green branches. The grey-green leaves are variable and may be elliptic or obovate, narrowly oblong or lanceolate. The flowers, which are bright yellow and scented, appear in June and July in terminal racemes 1–2 in. long.

Cultivation. Brooms are easy to cultivate in ordinary, light and well-drained soil. They require a position in full sun with the exception of *G. virgata,* which will tolerate some shade. Do not feed or mulch these shrubs, as most of them, especially the dwarf species, succeed best on poor, sharply drained soils. Established plants do not transplant well; young pot-grown plants should be set out from October to April.

Propagation. Take cuttings, 2–4 in. long, of lateral shoots with a heel in August; insert the cuttings in equal parts (by volume) peat and sand in a cold frame. The following spring, pot the rooted cuttings in 3–3½ in. pots of John Innes potting compost No. 1 or 2; plunge outdoors and set in permanent sites from October to April.

Sow seeds in March in pans of John Innes seed compost and place in a cold frame; prick out the seedlings, when large enough to handle, into 3 in. pots of John Innes potting compost No. 1 or 2 and treat as for rooted cuttings.

Pruning. No regular pruning is required; encourage bushy growth by pinching out the growing points on young plants after flowering. Thin out crowded shoots of mature bushes after flowering to keep the plants open.

Pests and diseases. Generally trouble-free.

Gentian: see Gentiana
Gentian, marsh: see *Gentiana pneumonanthe*
Gentian root: see *Gentiana lutea*
Gentian, spring: see *Gentiana verna*
Gentian, trumpet: see *Gentiana acaulis*
Gentian, willow: see *Gentiana asclepiadea*
Gentian, yellow: see *Gentiana lutea*

Gentiana

Gentian. *Gentianaceae*

A genus of 400 species of annuals and herbaceous perennials of great variety, together with several hybrids. Those described are all hardy perennials and, unless otherwise stated, have trumpet-shaped flowers. The smaller gentians are suitable for rock gardens and alpine houses; *G. lutea,* the largest gentian in cultivation, is more suitable for mixed borders or as a specimen plant at the edge of a lawn or in a shrubbery.

G. acaulis (trumpet gentian). Europe. Height 3 in.; spread up to 18 in. This is a variable plant and the name embraces a number of species with only superficial differences. The more common names

...re *G. kochiana*, *G. angustifolia* and *G. clusii*, of which the first is most usually seen in cultivation. They are easy to grow, forming mats of sturdy, glossy mid-green, ovate leaves, but they are sometimes unpredictable in their flowering pattern. They flower only under certain conditions, which appear to vary from plant to plant; a clump which produces a profusion of blooms one year may never do so again. The flowers are brilliant deep blue, 2–3 in. long, and appear in May and June.

GENTIANA ACAULIS

G. angustifolia: see *G. acaulis*

G. asclepiadea (willow gentian). Europe. Height 15–24 in.; spread 12–18 in. The slender arching stems, with willow-like mid-green leaves, bear deep blue flowers, 1–1½ in. long, in July and August. This species is best planted in a mixed border or among shrubs in a damp, partially shaded site.

GENTIANA ASCLEPIADEA

G. clusii: see *G. acaulis*

G. farreri. N.W. China, Tibet. Height 4 in.; spread 9–12 in. This is one of the few Asiatic gentians that will tolerate lime in the soil. The central tuft of foliage, with narrowly lanceolate, pale green leaves, produces slender shoots each bearing an upturned deep flower of shining Cambridge blue, shading to white at the throat. Each flower is 1½–2 in. across. This is a good late-summer or autumn-flowering species, continuing to bloom from August until October.

G. gracilipes. China. Height 6–9 in.; spread 12–15 in. This plant forms a central tuft of lanceolate, narrow, mid-green leaves from which emerge branching stems. Each stem tip bears a narrow funnel-shaped purple flower, with green stripes on the outside. The flowers are about 1½ in. long and appear in July and August.

G. kochiana: see *G. acaulis*

G. lutea (yellow gentian, gentian root). Europe. Height 3–5 ft; spread 15 in. A robust, erect species with ovate, mid-green, prominently veined leaves. The 1 in. long yellow flowers have a starry appearance and are unlike the usual gentian. They open in July and August and are arranged in whorls in the upper leaf axils, forming long spires up to half the plant's height.

G. × macaulayi. Height 6 in.; spread 12–18 in. This is one of the best hybrids for flowering in September and October. The narrowly lanceolate, pale to mid-green foliage is similar to that of

Gentiana farreri

G. farreri, one of its parents; it bears deep blue flowers, each about 2⅓ in. long. It will grow in a partially shaded position.

G. × 'Kidbrooke Seedling' and *G.* × 'King-fisher' are vigorous forms of *G.* × *macaulayi*, with deep violet-blue flowers appearing in September and October.

G. pneumonanthe (marsh gentian). Northern Hemisphere. Height 6–18 in.; spread 12 in. This is one of the gentians native to Great Britain, although rare. It has slender stems of variable height and narrowly lanceolate mid-green leaves. Blue flowers, 1½ in. long, of varying shades and spotted with green inside are borne singly or in few-flowered racemes in August and September.

G. saxosa. New Zealand. Height 4 in.; spread 6 in. The dark green glossy leaves of this species are spathulate and form neat tufts from which rise deep purple-green stems bearing white bell-shaped flowers, 1 in. wide, in August and September. This species is a particularly good plant for an alpine house.

G. septemfida. Asia Minor to Iran. Height 9–12 in.; spread 12 in. This is the easiest gentian to grow. The lanceolate mid-green leaves form compact tufts. Terminal clusters of 1½ in. long, deep blue flowers are produced in July and August. This plant is best chosen while in flower as the seedlings are not always true to type.

G. sino-ornata. W. China, Tibet. Height 6 in.; spread 12–15 in. This is considered to be the finest autumn-flowering gentian, and is extremely easy to grow in acid soil. It produces linear-lanceolate mid-green leaves, and sheets of brilliant blue flowers which are striped with deep blue and green-yellow. They are 2 in. long and open from September to November.

G. × 'Stevenagensis'. Height 4 in.; spread 12–15 in. This is a vigorous, prostrate hybrid. The flowering shoots arise from a rosette of mid-green narrowly lanceolate leaves and produce upturned 2 in. long trumpet-shaped flowers of rich deep blue from September to November. 'Midnight' is a similar hybrid, with deep indigo-blue flowers that open in August and September.

G. verna (spring gentian). Europe, including Great Britain. Height 3 in.; spread 6 in. This species is represented in cultivation by the variety 'Angulosa', which forms close tufts of mid-green

Gentiana asclepiadea

Gentiana acaulis

Gentiana lutea

Gentiana sino-ornata

Gentiana gracilipes

Gentiana saxosa

ovate-lanceolate leaves. Intense blue, star-like, 1 in. long flowers are borne in May and June. This variety thrives in well-drained soil containing leaf-mould and lime.

Cultivation. In general, the European species flower in spring, and the Asiatic, which are easier to grow if given suitable conditions, in autumn.

Plant the European species in a sunny position in leafy soil, or in pans in an alpine house, between September and March. *G. lutea* may be planted in partial shade; it requires a moisture-retentive soil.

Plant the Asiatic species outdoors or in the alpine house in March or April. They thrive in deep soil, enriched with plenty of leaf-mould or peat, which should not be allowed to dry out in the summer. *G. sino-ornata* and its hybrids require lime-free soil, otherwise the leaves will turn yellow.

In the alpine house, grow gentians in 4–8 in. pans depending on vigour and spread, and repot annually at the time recommended for planting. Grow *G. acaulis, G. gracilipes, G. septemfida* and *G. verna* in a mixture of 2 parts John Innes potting compost No. 1 and 1 part grit (parts by volume). Grow *G. asclepiadea* in John Innes potting compost No. 1 and the remaining species in a compost made of 2 parts lime-free loam to 1 part each of sand, peat and leaf-mould.

Propagation. *G. asclepiadea, G. gracilipes, G. lutea, G. pneumonanthe, G. saxosa* and *G. septemfida* may all be raised from seeds. Sow ripe seeds in pans of seed compost before October and place in a cold frame. Freezing after sowing will often hasten germination.

Prick out the seedlings when they are large enough to handle. When the plants are well developed pot them up singly, using 4 in. pots of John Innes potting compost No. 2 for *G. lutea* and 3 in. pots of John Innes potting compost No. 1 for the others. Keep the young plants in the frame, or plunge them outdoors, until they are ready for planting out in September.

Except for *G. acaulis,* which is best divided in June, all gentians may be divided in March.

All species can be increased from 1–2 in. cuttings taken from the basal shoots in April or May and inserted in a mixture of equal parts (by volume) peat and sand in a cold frame. When rooted, pot singly into 3 in. pots of John Innes potting compost No. 1; grow on in the frame and plant out in March of the following year.

Pests. Generally trouble-free.

Diseases. Several fungi may cause ROOT ROT, particularly on waterlogged soils.

Geranium

Crane's-bill. *Geraniaceae*

A genus of 400 species of hardy herbaceous perennials. They should not be confused with the bedding and pot varieties described under their correct botanical name, *Pelargonium.*

The species vary greatly in stature and in habit; some are suitable for herbaceous borders or as ground cover, others for rock gardens. Most are free-flowering, with saucer-shaped blooms that range from pink through purple to blue.

Geranium grandiflorum

In the descriptions that follow, planting distance applies to border perennials which are usually set in groups; spread applies to the surface spread of prostrate or alpine species.

G. armenum: see *G. psilostemon*

G. × 'Ballerina'. Height 6–9 in.; spread 12 in. This vigorous hybrid, suitable for a rock garden, has palmate, deeply lobed, grey-green leaves. The flowers are 1 in. wide and pink, heavily veined with deeper red-pink. They appear from June to September.

G. cinereum. Balkans. Height 4–6 in.; spread 9–12 in. An alpine species with round to kidney-shaped, grey-green leaves that are cut into five or seven wedge-shaped lobes. Crimson-magenta flowers, 1 in. across, with almost black centres, are freely borne from May to October.

The variety *G. c. subcaulescens* is often listed as a separate species. It is described here under *G. subcaulescens.*

G. dalmaticum. Dalmatia. Height 6 in.; spread 9–12 in. This species forms dense, low cushions of palmately lobed, mid-green, glossy leaves that are tinted red and orange in the autumn. The dainty clusters of light pink flowers, each about 1 in. across, appear from June to August. 'Album' is a pure white form.

G. endressii. W. Pyrenees. Height 12–18 in.; planting distance 18 in. A species with mid-green, palmate and deeply lobed leaves. Pale pink flowers, 1 in. across, open from May to August; they are lightly veined with red. This is a good ground-cover plant for a lightly shaded position.

'A. T. Johnson' (height 12 in.) has silver-pink flowers; 'Rose Clair' (height 18 in.) is salmon-rose with purple veining; 'Wargrave Pink' (height 18 in.) has clear pink flowers.

Named hybrids include the attractive 'Claridge Druce' (height and planting distance 18 in.), with palmate mid-green and deeply lobed leaves and lilac-pink flowers, 2 in. across.

G. farreri: see *G. napuligerum*

G. grandiflorum. Central Asia. Height 12 in.; planting distance 18–24 in. A spreading, bushy species, with round, mid-green, long-stalked leaves. Blue-purple flowers, 1½–2 in. across, appear in June and July.

Gentiana septemfida

Gentiana verna 'Angulosa'

Geranium endressii 'Claridge Druce'

Geranium ibericum

Geranium dalmaticum

Geranium psilostemon

G. ibericum, syn. *G. platypetalum*. Caucasus, Iran. Height 18–24 in.; planting distance 18 in. The plant offered under this name is now known to be a sterile hybrid of *G. ibericum*; it is correctly classified as *G. × magnificum*. The five to seven-lobed mid-green leaves are erect. Glossy violet-blue flowers, 1 in. across, are produced in July and August.

G. macrorrhizum. S.E. Alps, Balkans. Height 12–15 in.; planting distance 15–18 in. A species with five-lobed mid-green leaves that are aromatic when crushed. Pale magenta-pink flowers, 1 in. across, are borne from May to July. 'Walter Ingwersen' has clear pink flowers.

G. × magnificum: see *G. ibericum*

G. napuligerum, syn. *G. farreri*. Yunnan. Height 6 in.; spread 12 in. A slow-growing species, suitable for a scree. The palmate, deeply lobed, mid-green leaves form a close mat. Clear pale rose flowers, ¾ in. across, appear from May to August. 'Album' is a white variety.

G. platypetalum: see *G. ibericum*

G. pratense (meadow crane's-bill). N. Europe, including Great Britain. Height 1½–2½ ft; planting distance 24 in. This species has mid-green, long-stalked leaves which are five to seven-lobed and deeply divided. Blue or violet-blue flowers, 1½ in. across and with crimson veins, are borne from July to September. 'Album' is white; 'Flore-pleno' has double blue flowers; 'Mrs Kendall Clarke' has single, clear blue flowers.

The hybrid 'Johnson's Blue' (height and planting distance 15 in.) has dark green, deeply lobed, palmate leaves. The light blue, 2 in. wide flowers are produced from July onwards.

G. psilostemon, syn. *G. armenum*. Armenia. Height 2½ ft; planting distance 24 in. A border species with palmate, five-lobed, mid-green leaves. Vivid magenta flowers, 1½ in. across and with a black central spot, are produced during June and July.

G. pylzowianum. Kansu. Height 3 in.; spread 6–9 in. This low-growing species makes excellent light ground cover in a rock garden as it spreads rapidly unless grown in poor soil. The mid-green leaves are rounded and deeply cut. Clear pink flowers, ¾ in. across, appear in June and July; they are usually sparsely produced.

G. renardii. Caucasus. Height 9 in.; spread up to 12 in. A clump-forming species, suitable for a rock garden, with rounded, handsomely veined, grey-green leaves. Pale lavender flowers, about 1 in. across, and with purple veins on the petals, appear from May to July.

GERANIUM SANGUINEUM

G. sanguineum (bloody crane's-bill). Europe, including Great Britain. Height 6–9 in.; spread 18 in. or more. A good ground-cover plant with mid-green, deeply lobed leaves. The crimson-magenta flowers, about 1½ in. across, open from June to September. A slightly smaller variety, 'Album', has white flowers; the dwarf form *G. s. lancastrense* (height 3–4 in.; spread 12–15 in.) forms mats of soft, dark green leaves and has 1 in. wide pale pink flowers with darker veins.

G. subcaulescens. Balkans. Height 4–6 in.; spread 12 in. or more. This rock-garden plant has grey-green, orbicular and lobed leaves. Masses of 1 in. wide, bright crimson-magenta flowers with almost black centres are borne from May to October. The variety 'Splendens' is paler, but with larger flowers.

'Russell Prichard' (height 6–8 in.; planting distance 18 in.) is a hybrid, excellent for ground cover; it has palmate pale grey leaves and trailing flower stems. These bear a profusion of magenta-cerise flowers, 1½–2 in. across.

G. sylvaticum. Europe. Height 18–24 in.; planting distance 18 in. A species with rounded seven-lobed silver-green leaves. Purple flowers, 1–1½ in. across, are borne in loose terminal clusters in May and June. 'Album' is pure white; 'Mayflower', lavender-blue; 'Wanneri', pink.

G. wallichianum. Himalayas. Height 6–9 in.; planting distance 24 in. This species, suitable for the front of a border, has silky, light green, hairy-stemmed leaves that are wedge-shaped and deeply toothed. Purple-blue flowers, 1–1½ in. across, open from July to September. 'Buxton's Blue' has clearer blue flowers with white centres.

G. wlassovianum. Siberia, Manchuria. Height 15 in.; planting distance 24 in. This is a spreading plant, with loose, branching stems and kidney-shaped leaves that are dark green and lobed. Lavender-blue flowers, 1½ in. across, are produced from June to September.

Geranium napuligerum 'Album'

Geranium wallichianum

Cultivation. Plant geraniums between September and March in any ordinary, well-drained soil, in sun or partial shade. *G. cinereum* is best planted in March unless the site is sheltered and sunny. Tall-growing species, such as *G. pratense* and *G. psilostemon*, may need the support of twiggy sticks, particularly in exposed or shady sites.

Cut back old flowering stems almost to ground level to encourage new compact growth and a second flush of flowers.

Propagation. Divide the plants between September and March and replant *in situ.*

Sow seeds from September to March, in pots or pans of seed compost in a cold frame. Prick off the seedlings, when large enough to handle, into boxes of John Innes potting compost No. 1; set the seedlings in nursery rows for the summer. Plant in permanent positions from September to March. The smaller species such as *G. cinereum* and *G. pylzowianum* are best potted into 3 in. containers and plunged outside.

Pests. Young plants may be eaten by SLUGS.

Diseases. Yellow spots on the upper surfaces of the leaves are caused by RUST; large numbers of red-brown dusty pustules appear on the lower surfaces. The disease is more prevalent on wild geranium species in Great Britain and is only occasionally found on cultivated species.

Geranium, ivy-leaved: see *Pelargonium peltatum*

Geranium, oak-leaved: see *Pelargonium quercifolium*

Geranium, peppermint: see *Pelargonium tomentosum*

Gerbera
Compositae

A genus of 70 species of half-hardy and tender perennial flowering plants. The lanceolate, hairy, mid-green leaves are prominently lobed and arranged in rosettes. The daisy-like flowers come in a wide range of colours, including yellow, orange, cream, white, pink, crimson and purple; they are excellent as cut flowers. In Great Britain these plants require greenhouse cultivation, although in mild, sheltered areas of the south and west they may survive outdoors.

GERBERA JAMESONII

G. jamesonii. Transvaal. Height 12–15 in.; spread up to 24 in. The lobed leaves are hairy throughout, the older ones becoming woolly beneath as they age. Numerous solitary orange-scarlet flowers, 3–5 in. or more across, are borne from May to August. Single or double-flowered varieties and hybrids in attractive pastel colours are generally available.

Cultivation. In the greenhouse, grow gerberas in the border, or in 6–8 in. pots of John Innes potting compost No. 2. Overwinter at a temperature of 5–7°C (41–45°F), keeping the plants just moist at all times.

In summer, water and ventilate freely, giving light shade to the greenhouse from May to September. Feed pot plants at 10–14 day intervals with a weak liquid manure.

Pot on pot-grown plants annually in March when they are being divided.

Outdoors, grow gerberas in ordinary, well-drained garden soil, in a sunny sheltered position at the foot of a wall. Cut faded flower stems down to ground level.

Propagation. In March, divide established plants into single crowns and pot up in 4 in. containers of the growing compost or set out in the greenhouse border. Pot on as necessary.

Alternatively, sow seeds in pots or pans of seed compost in February or March, at a temperature of 16–18°C (61–64°F). Prick off the seedlings, when large enough to handle, into boxes, later transferring singly to $3\frac{1}{2}$–4 in. pots of the growing compost, or plant out in flowering positions.

Pests. Young growths may become infested with TARSONEMID MITES, which also distort the stems and the foliage.

APHIDS may also infest plants.

Diseases. The collapse of seedlings and larger plants may be due to DAMPING OFF and ROOT ROT.

LEAF SPOT, caused by a fungus, is particularly common in south-west England. It shows as large brown spots covered with minute pin-point dots, and with a thin purple border; the spots later coalesce, and the leaves shrivel up.

Germander: see *Teucrium chamaedrys*

Geranium renardii

Geranium subcaulescens

Gerbera jamesonii

Geum chiloense
'Lady Stratheden'

Geum chiloense
'Mrs Bradshaw'

Geum reptans

Geum chiloense 'Prince of Orange'

Geum

Avens. *Rosaceae*

A genus of 40 species of hardy herbaceous perennials, suitable for growing in borders or on rock gardens. The mid-green leaves are pinnate with a large terminal leaflet, and the long-lasting, bright flowers are saucer to bowl-shaped.

The term planting distance applies to border perennials which are usually grown in groups of three or more; for rock-garden plants, which are generally set singly, the term spread denotes the surface spread of mature plants.

GEUM REPTANS

G. × *borisii*. Height and planting distance 12 in. This hybrid bears bowl-shaped orange-scarlet flowers, 1 in. across, on its branching stems in May, and intermittently until September. The plant is suitable for the front of a border.
G. bulgaricum. Bulgaria. Height 12–18 in.; planting distance 12 in. A border species with drooping, bell-like flowers. These are bright yellow and measure 1 in. across; they appear from June to August.
G. chiloense. Chile. This border species has been superseded by varieties (height 18–24 in.; planting distance 12–18 in.). Bowl-shaped flowers, 1½ in. across, are borne from June to September. The following are recommended: 'Fire Opal', semi-double flame flowers; 'Lady Stratheden', double yellow; 'Mrs Bradshaw', semi-double scarlet; and 'Prince of Orange', orange.
G. montanum. European Alps. Height 6–12 in.; spread 9–12 in. An alpine species with golden-yellow saucer-shaped flowers, 1 in. wide; they are produced from May to July and are followed by fluffy silver-grey seed heads.

G. reptans. European Alps. Height 9–12 in.; spread 12–15 in. This alpine species is similar to *G. montanum*, differing only in size and in having conspicuous red runners.
G. rivale (water avens). Europe, Asia, N. America. Height and planting distance 12–18 in. A border species with nodding, bell-like flowers, 1¼ in. across; they appear from May throughout the summer and have red-purple calyces and yellow-pink petals veined with red-purple. A good variety is 'Leonard', with copper and gold flowers.
G. rossii. Alaska. Height and planting distance 12 in. Sprays of bright yellow bowl-shaped flowers, 1 in. across, are borne in May and June. This species is suitable for the front of a border.
Cultivation. Plant geums between September and March in any ordinary garden soil, preferably enriched with leaf-mould or peat. *G. rivale* also thrives in moist soil. These plants all grow equally well in sun or partial shade.

In exposed positions *G. chiloense* and its varieties may need supporting with twiggy sticks. Cut the stems almost to ground level after flowering. Lift and divide the plants every second or third year in March or April.
Propagation. Sow ripe seeds in pots or pans of seed compost from June to August, or in February or March, and place in a cold frame. Prick off the seedlings, when large enough to handle, into boxes of John Innes potting compost No. 1. Seedlings of *G. montanum* and *G. reptans* are best set in 3 in. pots of John Innes potting compost No. 1, and plunged outdoors. For the other species, summer-sown plants should be over-wintered in a cold frame and transferred to nursery rows in the spring. Grow on through the summer and plant out from September onwards. Plants from a spring sowing will be ready for nursery rows that summer and can be planted out from September of the same year.

Named varieties are best increased by division in March or April. The small plants borne on runners of *G. reptans* may be detached during summer and treated as seedlings.
Pests and diseases. Generally trouble-free.

Gherkin: see Cucumber
Ghost tree: see Davidia

Gilia

Polemoniaceae

GILIA TRICOLOR

A genus of 120 species of annual, biennial and perennial herbaceous plants grown for their showy flowers and attractive foliage. The hardy annuals described are easy to raise, and the dwarf ones are good for growing on rock gardens.
G. achilleifolia. California. Height 24 in.; spacing 9 in. A hardy annual of bushy habit with finely

Gilia capitata

divided mid-green leaves covered with soft, sticky hairs. Clusters of mid-blue funnel-shaped flowers, 1 in. across, are carried at the tops of the erect stems from July to August. The variety 'Major' has flowers larger than the type.

G. capitata. California. Height 18 in.; spacing 9 in. A hardy annual with mid-green, fern-like foliage and carrying 'pincushion' heads of lavender-blue flowers, ½ in. across, from June to September. This is a good species for cutting and for massing in borders.

G. coronopifolia: see *G. rubra*

G. lutea, syn. *Leptosiphon hybridus.* California. Height 4–6 in.; spacing 4 in. A hardy annual with mid-green leaves, deeply divided into pointed lobes, clustered on the stems. Brightly coloured, long-tubed, star-shaped flowers, ½ in. across, appear from June to September. The mixed garden varieties, for example 'French Hybrids', 6 in., are yellow, orange, red and pink. This plant can be used for edging borders or for sowing in paving cracks.

G. rubra, syn. *G. coronopifolia.* California. Height 3–5 ft. A half-hardy biennial species with rosettes of finely cut mid-green leaves beneath erect stems. Spikes of 1½ in. wide trumpet-shaped scarlet flowers, each spike 2–4 ft long, open in July. This is a good pot plant for flowering from late winter to spring in a cool greenhouse.

G. tricolor. California. Height 24 in.; spacing 9 in. A hardy annual with deeply cut mid-green foliage. Slender stems carry clusters of bell-shaped ¾ in. wide flowers in June. These are pale violet ringed with maroon at the base.

Cultivation. Gilias thrive in a sunny position. They do especially well in light, well-drained soil, but most are easily grown in any average soil. On exposed sites the tall species require twiggy support. On heavy soils and in cold districts, September-sown plants need cloche protection during the winter.

For flowering under glass, grow in John Innes potting compost No. 1 in 5 in. pots and overwinter at a temperature of 7–10°C (45–50°F).

Propagation. Sow annual species in the flowering site in September or March, to flower respectively in early or late summer. Thin out the seedlings to the required spacing, leaving autumn-sown seedlings until the spring.

Sow *G. rubra* under glass at 15°C (59°F) in May or June. Prick out the seedlings into 3½ in. pots and grow them on in a cold frame through the summer. Pot on into 5 in. pots and grow on in the greenhouse until the plants flower.

Pests and diseases. Generally trouble-free.

Gilliflower: see *Dianthus caryophyllus*
Ginger-wort: see Hedychium

Ginkgo
Maidenhair tree, *Ginkgoaceae*

GINKGO BILOBA

A genus of a single species. It is distantly allied to conifers but is a more primitive, deciduous tree with fan-shaped leaves, rather like the leaflets of maidenhair fern. It is hardy, but requires warm summers for vigorous growth; it is suitable only for a large garden.

See also CONIFERS.

G. biloba. China. Height 30 ft; spread 10 ft. Growth and shape of this species vary; some specimens are like flagpoles with small, sparse and irregularly placed branches, others are broadly columnar like an elm, and yet others form wide, many-stemmed trees. In winter, the branches are knobbed with the leaf spurs. The bark is dark grey, becoming fissured and fluted.

The leathery, fan-shaped leaves are partially divided in the middle; they are fresh pale green in colour, darken through the summer, then turn bright golden in autumn. The male flowers, rarely seen, are thick, short, yellow catkins; they appear at the same time as the leaves. Female flowers are borne on separate trees, but are only produced after hot summers; they grow in pairs on long stalks. The subsequent green fruits are plum-shaped, 1 in. or more long; they turn yellow when ripe and give off a rancid smell.

Cultivation. These trees thrive in a warm sunny position, although they will tolerate moderate exposure. Any ordinary garden soil is suitable, preferably enriched with leaf-mould or well-rotted compost. Plant in early April, using 2–3 ft high trees which seldom require staking.

Propagation. Ginkgos are always raised from imported seeds. Sow as soon as ripe, preferably not later than October, in a cold frame or greenhouse in pans of John Innes seed compost. Pot into 4 in. pots when the seedlings are large enough to handle, and plant out in nursery bed from the following October to March. Grow on for three or four years before planting out in their permanent positions.

Pruning. These trees resent pruning and shortened shoots will die further back.

Pests and diseases. Generally trouble-free.

Gilia lutea 'French Hybrids'

Gilia tricolor

Ginkgo biloba (autumn foliage)

Gladiolus byzantinus

Gladiolus tristis

Gladiolus 'Albert Schweitzer'
(Large-flowered)

Gladiolus 'Flowersong'
(Large-flowered)

Gladiolus 'Picardy' (Large-flowered)

GLADIOLUS

Sword lily. *Iridaceae*

A genus of 300 species of half-hardy bulbous flowering plants. The original species have largely been superseded by cultivated hybrids, whose colours range over almost the whole spectrum. Gladioli are good plants for the border and excellent as cut flowers.

GLADIOLUS PRIMULINUS

The dark green leaves are slender, prominently ribbed, and narrow to a point. The florets, arranged on a thick flower stem and forming a spike, all face one way. Each floret is slightly alternate to its neighbour, and the spacing of the florets is generally even. In some varieties the florets overlap each other, in others they are loosely arranged.

Each individual floret is composed of six petals.

The upper central petal is extended forward; the three lower petals, the falls, are of equal size and slightly reflexed; the two wing petals are behind the lower and upper petals.

G. blandus. S. Africa. Height 18 in.; planting distance 4–6 in. White, red and yellow blotched flower spikes, 12 in. long, are produced in June. The florets, $2\frac{1}{2}$ in. across, are loosely arranged on the flower spike.

G. byzantinus. Asia Minor. Height 24 in.; planting distance 4–6 in. A fully hardy species which may be left in the ground undisturbed. The flower spikes, 15 in. long, are composed of loosely arranged wine-red florets, $2\frac{1}{2}$ in. across. They appear in June.

G. × colvillii. Height 12–24 in.; planting distance 4–6 in. The flower spikes, 10 in. long, consist of daintily and loosely arranged rose-red, yellow-throated florets, 3 in. across. They are borne in June and July.

G. tristis. Natal. Height 18 in.; planting distance 4–6 in. Scented yellow-white flowers, tinged with red on the reverse, are produced in July. The spikes are 10 in. long, with the 2 in. wide florets loosely arranged along them.

Gladiolus 'Melodie' (Butterfly)

Gladiolus 'Forgotten Dreams' (Large-flowered)

HYBRIDS

LARGE-FLOWERED HYBRIDS These are vigorous growers and reach a height of 2–4 ft; planting distance 4–6 in. The strong, erect stems terminate in a 20 in. long flower spike. The individual florets, in a vast range of colours, are 4–7 in. across and roughly triangular. These hybrids flower from late July until September; they are best grown for general garden display or for exhibition purposes.

'Albert Schweitzer', salmon-orange, deepening to fiery orange at the edges; the throats are marked with orange-scarlet. 'Aristocrat', velvety garnet-red with slightly darker throats.

'Bishop', lavender with violet and crimson throats. 'Blue Conqueror', deep violet-blue with lighter blue centres.

'Dr Fleming', glistening light salmon-pink with cream throats. 'Eurovision', deep vermilion. 'Flowersong', frilled, bright golden-yellow. 'Forgotten Dreams', primrose; the falls are yellow with carmine picotee edges.

'Gold Standard', golden-yellow. 'Green Woodpecker', green-lemon; the throats are wine-red and the falls deep yellow. 'Grock', light mauve-pink with deeper pink throats.

'Jo Wagenaar', glowing blood-scarlet with a velvety sheen to the petals. 'Life Flame', vivid cochineal-red, tinged with orange. 'Little Rock', velvety maroon.

'Mabel Violet', violet-purple, with deeper purple, slightly ruffled edges. 'Maria Goretti', silver-white. 'Musical', rose-lilac, with cream throats. 'Picardy', salmon-apricot.

'President Kennedy', salmon-orange with crimson throats. 'Rosy Frills', flesh-pink, with rose-coloured frilled edges. 'Rotterdam', vivid scarlet-vermilion. 'Sweepstake', shell-pink, with carmine and cream throats; a good show variety.

'Toulouse Lautrec', deep apricot-salmon, with bright yellow, chestnut-marked throats. 'Uhu', ash-grey and salmon, with mahogany-brown marks; the throats are yellow. 'White Angel', pure white.

PRIMULINUS HYBRIDS These are free-flowering, but less vigorous than the large-flowered hybrids. Height 1½–3 ft; planting distance 4–6 in. The flower spike, 15 in. long, is composed of loosely arranged florets. These appear in July and August; most are 2–3 in. across, and the top petal of each floret is hooded. They are ideal as cut flowers, and include the following:

'Ivory and Mauve', ivory-cream flushed with carmine; mauve throats. 'Joyce', soft cherry-rose, yellow throats. 'Red Star', star-shaped, brilliant orange-scarlet florets, lighter in the centre; the falls are crimson-scarlet with gold stripes. 'Richard Unwin', velvety chestnut-crimson, with broad cream stripes on the falls. 'Rosy Maid', rich apricot-salmon, with yellow falls.

Gladiolus 'Toulouse Lautrec' (Large-flowered)

Gladiolus 'Joyce' (Primulinus)

Gladiolus 'Salmon Star'
(Primulinus)

Gladiolus 'Greenbird' (Miniature)

'Salmon Star', star-shaped, orange-salmon florets, paler at the edges; deep crimson-scarlet falls with prominent gold stripes. 'Scarlet Knight', brick-red, with narrow cream stripes.

MINIATURE HYBRIDS The florets of these are similar in arrangement to those of the primulinus types, but smaller. Height 1½–3 ft; planting distance 4–6 in. The florets, which are usually ruffled or frilled, are 1½–2 in. across and closely arranged in a 15 in. long flower spike. The flowering period is July and August. These hybrids make excellent cut flowers.

'Bo Peep', lightly frilled apricot-salmon florets, deeper apricot at tips, and freckled with primrose. 'Dancing Doll', frilled cream florets flushed with salmon and with scarlet blotches.

'Graceful', lightly frilled orange-salmon florets with deep orange flecks and scarlet and yellow blotches. 'Greenbird', lightly frilled sulphur-green florets with crimson throats; there are up to ten florets in each spike.

'Southport', ruffled ivory flowers, cream throats. 'Zenith', shell-pink deeply frilled flowers.

BUTTERFLY HYBRIDS These hybrids are larger than the miniature types. Height 2–4 ft; planting distance 4–6 in. The florets, 2–4 in. across, are closely spaced on a thick stem, and often have striking throat markings and blotches. The flower spikes, in July and August, are 18 in. long. They are ideal for indoor decoration.

'Daily Sketch', sulphur-yellow with buff throats and crimson lines. 'Donald Duck', lemon-yellow with orange-scarlet blotches. 'Ice Follies', delicate ivory-white with cream throats.

'Mme Butterfly', pearly shell-pink with salmon and violet throats. 'Melodie', salmon-pink, deeper pink towards the wavy edges, and with vivid scarlet throats.

'Summer Fairy', salmon-red, red towards the edges, and with maroon throats; the falls are cream. 'Walt Disney', soft sulphur-lemon with blood-red blotches.

Cultivation. Gladioli do best in well-drained soil in a sunny position. As soon as the soil is workable, prepare it for planting. Cover the soil thinly with well-rotted manure and dig this in. Rake bone-meal into the surface at the rate of 3–4 oz per sq. yd. Improve heavy or too-light soil by working in plenty of peat.

Plant the corms 4 in. deep in heavy soil, 6 in. deep in light soil, from mid-March to mid-April. Make sure that the base of each corm is settled firmly in the soil; in heavy soil set them on a base of sharp sand to aid drainage. Three or four fortnightly plantings of the same variety will provide blooms throughout the summer. Do not plant shallowly, or the plants may topple over when in full bloom.

Gladioli grown for cutting purposes should be planted in single or double rows or drills, 12–15

ladiolus 'Graceful' (Miniature)

cases, leave at least four leaves intact after cutting the flower spike, in order to maintain the development of the new corm and cormlets.

Lift gladioli with a fork when the foliage begins to turn yellow-brown, generally in mid-October, and before the first frost. Take care not to bruise the corms. Remove any soil sticking to them, and cut off the main stem $\frac{1}{2}$ in. above each corm. Dry off the corms for seven to ten days in a dry, airy place. When quite dry, store the corms in trays or shallow boxes in a cool but frost-proof place.

The corms can be cleaned at the time of storing or later. Break away and discard the old shrivelled corms at the base of the new corms as soon as they will come away easily in the fingers. Pull off the tough outer skin on large corms, and also remove the small cormlets and store these separately if they are wanted for propagation. Check the corms occasionally during the winter and discard any that show signs of disease.

Plump, high-necked corms with a small root scar produce better plants than the larger, flatter corms with a broad root scar.

To obtain earlier flowers, place the corms in a well-lit position in a greenhouse in February or early March. Stand them in empty trays at a temperature of 12°C (54°F). The corms will soon sprout and can then be planted out during March in the usual way. In the greenhouse, watch out for aphids infesting the young sprouts.

Propagation. Gladioli can be increased from cormlets or from seeds. Cormlets, which take one to three years to reach flowering size, are produced at the base of the new corm and are generally the size of a large sweet-pea seed. Plant the cormlets in mid-March in the same type of soil as for corms. Set them close together in drills 2–3 in. deep and place a layer of sand below and above to help growth and to ease lifting. Provide at least 12 in. of clearance between the drills.

When the plants appear above ground, they need little attention; simply keep them weed-free and well watered. In the autumn, when the leaves become discoloured, lift the cormlets and store them in the same way as adult corms. The following spring plant out and tend them as before. Most cormlets reach flowering size during the second year, otherwise carry out the previous storing and growing cycle for another year.

Seeds take the same time as cormlets to produce flowers but, unlike cormlets, they do not breed true to colour and often not true to type.

Sow seeds in February or early March. Sow in boxes containing a mixture of 5 parts loam, 4 parts well-decayed leaf-mould and 1 part well-rotted compost (parts by volume), or in John Innes Potting compost No. 1, or in one of the new soil-less composts. Add a generous sprinkling of bone-meal and just enough sand to make the mixture porous. Sow the seeds thinly and shallowly. Germinate in the greenhouse at 7–13°C (45–55°F). The seedlings generally appear four or five weeks after sowing.

After germination remove the boxes to a cold frame. During the first fortnight in June remove the boxes from the frame, and sink them to their rims in a sheltered position in the ground outside. Partial shade will not harm them. Keep their roots moist, and feed moderately with liquid

. apart. Draw out the deep drills with the point a hoe. For exhibition purposes plant the corms single or double rows. Allow at least 18–24 in. tween single rows, 12 in. between double ws, with a path, 2–3 ft wide, separating each ir of double rows. For display in the mixed rder, plant gladioli in clumps, setting the rms 4–6 in. apart.

Do not hoe or apply fertiliser until the young oots appear; then hoe shallowly and often to eck weed growth and to aerate the soil. Apply a ght top-dressing of fish manure around the ung shoots.

Withhold water until secondary roots have rmed, eight to ten weeks after planting. After at, water generously, particularly during dry riods after the flower spike has appeared.

Staking is usually unnecessary, except for the rge-flowered hybrids or if the plants are grown exposed positions. Strings stretched between akes alongside each row usually provide equate support. Plants grown for exhibition rposes should be supported with canes, inrted on the side opposite to that of the developg flower spike. Secure the stem to the cane with ffia or wire rings.

For indoor decoration cut the gladiolus spikes hen the first floret is just opening. With exbition plants, timing of cutting depends on the riety, and on judgment and experience. In all

Gladiolus 'Scarlet Knight' (Primulinus)

Gladiolus 'Donald Duck' (Butterfly)

manure during the summer to help the developing corms. Lift the cormlets from the boxes in autumn, when the foliage has withered. Dry off, store and replant them the following spring. Some may reach flowering size late in the first year, others will take two or more years.

Pests. THRIPS and APHIDS may infest corms in store, producing rough brown patches. Thrips also infest the growing plants, causing a light mottling of leaves and flowers. The flowers may eventually die.

SWIFT MOTH CATERPILLARS and other soil pests feed on the corms of growing plants.

Diseases. CORE ROT is due to a fungus which attacks the central core of the corm in store. The disease spreads outwards, causing a complete rot of the corm, which becomes spongy and dark brown or black. If affected corms are planted, they will fail to grow or will produce weak shoots which turn yellow and die. The leaves from less badly diseased corms show small brown spots with red margins. In wet weather decayed areas bear grey mould, and flowers become spotted.

CUCUMBER MOSAIC VIRUS causes white blotches on the flowers and sometimes chlorotic streaks on the leaves. Other virus diseases can also affect gladioli, causing slight chlorotic spotting, or prominent yellow rings or ring-and-line patterns.

GLADIOLUS DRY ROT causes premature yellowing and death of the foliage, and decay of the leaf-sheaths at ground level. Small black resting bodies of the fungus are produced in large numbers on the decayed bases. The corms may also be affected and at first show numerous small black lesions which coalesce to form larger black areas.

GLADIOLUS SCAB shows on the leaves as red-brown specks which enlarge to become dark brown spots. In most seasons no further damage occurs, but in wet weather the tissues at ground level may decay, causing the plant to topple. Round, sunken, shiny craters develop towards the base of the corm.

GLADIOLUS YELLOWS shows as a yellowing of the leaves, usually starting as stripes between the veins, but later the leaves die back.

HARD ROT and LEAF SPOT cause minute brown spots on both surfaces of the leaves. Small black fruiting bodies of the fungus appear on the spots, which later become pale at the centre. Large black-brown spots, frequently zoned and sunken, develop on the corms. In store, affected corms may become hard and shrivelled.

STORAGE ROT due to a blue mould shows on the corms as two or three sunken lesions, $\frac{1}{2}$ in. or more across, irregular in shape and red-brown in colour. Each lesion bears a number of buff-coloured or pink resting bodies of the fungus. Under moist conditions the blue mould develops on the lesions and the corms decay.

Glaucium flavum

Gleditschia triacanthos
(fruits and foliage)

Gleditschia triacanthos
'Sunburst'

Glaucium

Horned poppy. *Papaveraceae*

A genus of 25 species of hardy annuals and herbaceous biennials and perennials. The biennial species described make outstanding plants for mixed borders and for wild gardens, although the flowers are short-lived.

G. corniculatum. Europe. Height 9 in.; planti distance 12 in. A hardy biennial that can also grown as an annual. The downy leaves a oblong, mid-green and deeply cut. Poppy-shap crimson flowers, 2 in. across, with a black spot the base of each petal, open in June.

GLAUCIUM CORNICULATUM

G. flavum. W. Europe, including Great Britai N. Africa. Height 12–24 in.; planting distance 1 in. A biennial or short-lived perennial whic frequently flowers in its first year from seeds. has pale grey-green, ovate, lobed leaves, an flowers freely from June to September. Th flowers, about 3 in. across, are bright yellow an cup-shaped, each with four petals.

Cultivation. If glauciums are grown as biennial plant them between October and March. The require an open sunny position and ordinar well-drained garden soil.

Propagation. As glauciums do not always trans plant well, they are best grown as annuals fro seeds sown in March or April in the flowerin site. Cover the seeds lightly and thin the seedling to the required planting distance.

To grow as biennials, sow the seeds in May June in pots or boxes of seed compost, and plac in a cold frame. When the seedlings are larg enough to handle, prick them off into 3 in. pots John Innes potting compost No. 1. Grow on in cold frame and plant out in flowering position from October onwards.

Pests and diseases. Generally trouble-free.

Glechoma hederacea: see *Nepeta hederacea*

Gleditschia

Leguminosae

GLEDITSCHIA TRIACANTHOS

A genus of 11 species of deciduous trees native t Iran, Asia and N. America. Most of them a armed with simple or branched spines whic become smaller as the trees age. They mak handsome specimen trees for a lawn and a chiefly grown for their ornamental pinna foliage. The green flowers are small and insign ficant, being borne in short racemes in July.

G. triacanthos (honey locust). N. Americ Height 18–30 ft; spread 12–15 ft. A hardy tre having the trunk and branches armed with spine which are either simple or branched and 3–12 i ng. The leaves are light green, pinnate or ▯ubly pinnate with 20–32 oblong-lanceolate ▯aflets. The foliage turns clear yellow in autumn. ▯wisted dark brown seed pods remain on the ▯ees all winter; they contain a sweet-tasting pulp ▯ which the seeds are embedded.

Named varieties include: 'Elegantissima', com-▯ct, slow-growing and with fern-like foliage; ▯unburst', with young golden-yellow foliage.

▯ultivation. These trees thrive in any good ▯rden soil; plant during suitable weather from ▯ctober to March in a sunny position.

▯ropagation. Sow seeds in March in containers of ▯hn Innes seed compost and place in a cold ▯ame; prick out the seedlings, when large ▯ough to handle, into 3 in. pots of John Innes ▯tting compost No. 1. Line out in nursery rows ▯d grow on for two or three years before ▯ansplanting to permanent positions.

▯runing. None required except to remove dead ▯ood in March.

▯ests and diseases. Generally trouble-free.

Globe artichoke

Cynara scolymus. Compositae

GLOBE ARTICHOKE

▯ perennial plant, chiefly grown as a summer ▯egetable but decorative enough to be grown in ▯erbaceous borders. The plant is short-lived, not ▯lly hardy and should be given winter protec-▯on. It reaches a height of 5 ft and resembles the ▯cotch thistle. The grey-green, tightly over-▯pping floral bracts form a rounded or conical ▯ead up to 5 in. across, from which small, pale ▯urple florets emerge.

The edible flower heads should be removed ▯hile still in the bud stage. They may be boiled ▯nd served hot or cold. The edible parts of the ▯ower head are the fleshy base of each scale and ▯e artichoke heart, which is the bottom of the ▯ower and has the finest flavour. The hearts may ▯e extracted and served on their own.

The young leaf shoots, known as chards, are ▯so edible and may be used as celery. After ▯arvesting the heads, cut down the foliage to ▯romote new growth. When these shoots are ▯bout 24 in. high, tie them together and blanch ▯r five or six weeks with black polythene or ▯rown-paper collars or lengths of drainpipe.

▯ARIETIES

▯ew are available but 'Gros Camus de Bretagne' ▯nd 'Gros Vert de Laon' have fine-flavoured, ▯rge heads.

▯ultivation. Globe artichokes should be grown ▯ a sheltered, sunny position, and in fertile, ▯ell-drained and well-cultivated soil. During ▯inter, dig in liberal amounts of well-decayed ▯anure and leave the ground rough. Before ▯anting, fork over and level the plot; rake the soil

to a fine tilth and add a dressing of a general fertiliser at 3 oz. per sq. yd.

Propagation. Increase by detaching rooted suckers. Remove the 9 in. long suckers, or side-growths, in April or November, and pot up in 4–5 in. containers of John Innes potting compost No. 1. Overwinter suckers taken in November in a frost-free frame or greenhouse; spring-potted suckers can be planted out as soon as well-rooted.

Plant out the suckers in mid-April in the south, about a fortnight later in the north. Set the plants at intervals of 3 ft.

The plants will survive up to six years, but for the best results they should be renewed every three years. Maintain a succession of crops by planting a fresh bed each year, using suckers from established plants.

Two and three-year-old plants produce mature heads first, one-year-old plants will give a late supply of heads in autumn.

In early November discard three-year-old plants, having detached the long suckers for propagation. Cut the stems down to about 18 in. during November on one and two-year-old plants. Draw soil up to the stems and cover the area with a 12 in. layer of straw or bracken; do not cover the top of the ridges. The covering may need replacing during winter.

As soon as the danger of frost is over, remove the protection, fork in a light dressing of well-rotted manure and remove any suckers that are not required for propagation.

Harvesting. Cut the heads from late June onwards, removing first those at the tops of the stems. Lateral heads mature slightly later.

Pests. Generally trouble-free.

Diseases. PETAL BLIGHT may cause pale brown circular blotches on the heads, which often rot.

Globe flower: see Trollius

Gloriosa

Glory lily. Liliaceae

GLORIOSA ROTHSCHILDIANA

A genus of five species of tender tuberous-rooted perennial climbers, related to the genus *Lilium*. In Great Britain, these plants require greenhouse cultivation except in the mildest and most sheltered areas. They are cultivated for their succession of flowers which resemble those of Turk's-cap lilies, having six narrow reflexed petals that are crisped and curled at the margins. The species described have glossy, mid-green lanceolate leaves, the upper ones tipped with hooked tendrils.

G. rothschildiana. Tropical Africa. Height 6 ft. The flowers of this species are produced in succession from late June to August, and are

Globe artichoke

Globe artichoke (flowers)

Gloriosa rothschildiana

borne singly on long stalks from the axils of the upper leaves; they are 3–4 in. across, crimson, edged with yellow, and have wavy-edged petals.

G. superba. Asia and Africa. Height 6 ft. This species is similar to *G. rothschildiana*, but the flowers are yellow, turning through orange to red, and the edges of the petals are more crimped.

Cultivation. Plant the tubers in February or March in the greenhouse border or set one tuber to a 6–7 in. pot or three to a 10 in. pot of John Innes potting compost No. 2. Start the tubers into growth at a temperature of 16–19°C (61–66°F) and maintain a humid atmosphere; keep the plants just moist.

Each tuber may produce from one to three stems, and as these emerge they require staking. Insert canes or trelliswork for pot-grown plants and train border plants along wires or string stretched up pillars and along the greenhouse roof. Give a well-diluted liquid feed weekly during the growing season, and water freely. After flowering, when the stems die back, dry off the tubers and store them under the staging at a temperature of 10–13°C (50–55°F).

Gloriosas may be planted outdoors in June for flowering in August. They need full sun in a position sheltered from winds; the brittle stems should be trained against trelliswork for support. After flowering, dry off the tubers and store as previously described until growth is restarted the following February.

Propagation. Sow seeds singly in 3 in. pots of John Innes seed compost during February or March. Maintain a temperature of 21–24°C (70–75°F) for germination, then lower to the normal growing temperature for adult plants. Pot on the seedlings into 3½–4 in. pots of John Innes potting compost No. 1 and grow on during summer; dry off in September or October for winter storing. Repot the young tubers in 5 in. pots of John Innes potting compost No. 2 the following spring and repeat the cycle. The plants take two to four years to flower.

Gloriosas produce offsets, or small tubers, during the growing season; these may be detached from the parent plants when growth is restarted in February and potted up and grown on as recommended for seedlings, but at a temperature of 16–19°C (61–66°F).

Pests. Generally trouble-free.

Diseases. A PHYSIOLOGICAL DISORDER, due to over-watering, causes yellow, brown or khaki-coloured patches to develop on the leaves, which often fall prematurely.

Glory flower, Chilean: see Eccremocarpus
Glory of the snow: see Chionodoxa
Gloxinia: see *Sinningia speciosa*
Goat's beard: see Aruncus

Godetia

Onagraceae

A genus of 20 species of hardy annuals, now included under *Clarkia*. The following are popular border plants, of bushy growth, with brightly coloured single or double flowers. They can also be grown as pot plants or for cutting.

Godetia grandiflora
'Azalea-flowered Mixed'

Godetia grandiflora 'Crimson Glow'

Godetia grandiflora 'Dwarf Mixed'

Godetia grandiflora 'Sybil Sherwood'

G. amoena. N. America. Height 24 in.; spacin 12 in. A species with mid-green lanceolate leave and slender stems. Loose spikes of lilac c red-pink funnel-shaped flowers, 2 in. acros appear in July. The form correctly called *C a. whitneyi* is widely known as *G. grandiflora*.

G. grandiflora, syn. *G. amoena whitneyi*. Cal fornia. Height 12–15 in.; spacing 6 in. This is th most popular species, forming a compact plar with mid-green, oblong and pointed leaves. Th rose-purple funnel-shaped flowers, 2 in. acros are carried in clusters from June to August. Ther are many garden varieties, with single or doubl flowers and colours ranging from red throug lilac to white.

'Azalea-flowered Mixed', 12 in., has sem double flowers with waved, frilled petals. 'Crim son Glow', 9 in., is a dwarf plant with intens colouring. 'Dwarf Mixed', 12–15 in., is a mixtur of the best dwarf named varieties, includin shades of crimson, pink, salmon, cherry-red an white. 'Kelvedon Glory', 15 in., is a dee salmon-orange. 'Sybil Sherwood', 18 in., bea flowers of salmon-pink.

Cultivation. A light, moist soil and a sunny si are best for godetias. Excessively rich so encourage foliage at the expense of flower Plants raised from autumn sowings need cloch protection in cold, exposed areas.

September-sown plants can be potted into 5 i pots of John Innes potting compost No. 1 an kept in a cool greenhouse for winter flowering.

Propagation. Sow the seeds in the flowering sit just covering them with soil, in Septembe March or April. Thin to the required spacin leaving autumn-sown plants until the spring.

Pests. Generally trouble-free.

Diseases. The plants may be attacked by FOO STEM and ROOT ROT, which are due to sever different fungi, including GREY MOULD; in eac case they wilt or collapse completely.

Gold dust: see *Alyssum saxatile*
Golden chain: see Laburnum
Golden rain: see Laburnum
Golden rod: see Solidago
Goldilocks: see *Aster linosyris*

Gomphrena

Amaranthaceae

GOMPHRENA GLOBOSA

A genus of 100 species of half-hardy annuals, biennials and herbaceous perennials. Only one species with its varieties is in general cultivation; it is suitable for outdoor bedding and is also an easily grown pot plant for a greenhouse. The colourful, everlasting, clover-like flower heads may be cut and dried for winter decoration.

G. globosa (globe amaranth). India. Height 12 in.; planting distance 6–9 in. A bushy annual with erect stems and hairy, light green leaves that are oblong-ovate, tapering towards the base. Orange, yellow, purple, pink or white ovoid flower heads, $\frac{1}{2}$–$1\frac{1}{2}$ in. long, appear from July to September.

Selected single colour strains are available; the dwarf form 'Buddy' (height and spread 6 in.) is a compact plant with long-lasting vivid purple flowers. Tall-growing mixed strains produce flowers in various colours.

Cultivation. Outdoors, grow gomphrenas in any ordinary, well-drained garden soil, in a sunny position, setting the young plants out in May when danger of frost is past. For everlasting flowers, cut the blooms just before they are fully open and hang them in bunches upside-down in a cool airy place to dry.

In the greenhouse, grow gomphrenas in 5 in. pots of John Innes potting compost No. 2. Keep the plants in a sunny position and ventilate the greenhouse freely. Avoid over-watering, but keep the compost just moist at all times.

Propagation. Sow seeds in pots or pans of seed compost during March, under glass at a temperature of 15–18°C (59–64°F). When they are large enough to handle, prick off the seedlings into boxes and harden off bedding plants in a cold frame before planting out in May. For greenhouse plants, pot the seedlings into $3\frac{1}{2}$ in. pots of John Innes potting compost No. 2, later transferring to 5 in. pots.

Pests and diseases. Generally trouble-free.

Gooseberry

Grossularia uva-crispa, syns. *Ribes uva-crispa* and *R. grossularia.*
Grossulariaceae, syn. *Saxifragaceae*

This hardy, deciduous, fruit-bearing shrub occurs wild in temperate and cool areas of Europe and can be grown in all parts of the British Isles. The branches are heavily thorned.

Gooseberries are normally grown as bushes with a 9 in. leg, or clear stem, beneath the branches, but they can also be cultivated as cordons. The latter are particularly easy to look after; they also save space as they can be grown on a fence or as a boundary between plots. However, because of bird damage to the buds in winter, both bushes and cordons give the best results when grown under netting. The flavour of gooseberries develops particularly well under cool growing conditions.

The height of bushes is 4–5 ft, height of cordons 4–6 ft. Planting distances for bushes, 5–6 ft in each direction or, for easy access, 8 ft × 4 ft; for cordons, up to 24 in. apart in rows 5 ft apart.

All the commonly cultivated varieties produce good crops from late May to August.

GOOSEBERRY

'Careless'. A mid-season variety with large, oval, downy, yellow-green berries of fine flavour. A spreading bush of moderate vigour. Culinary.
'Keepsake'. This early variety bears large, green, ovoid berries of good flavour. Spreading habit. Dessert or culinary.
'Lancer'. Late-cropping with round to ovoid, medium-sized, yellow-green berries of good flavour. Spreading habit. Dessert or culinary.
'Langley Gage'. A mid-season variety with green-white berries of good flavour. Compact, upright habit. Dessert.
'Leveller'. A mid-season variety with large, ovoid, green-yellow berries of good flavour. Spreading growth; needs extra-good growing conditions. Dessert or culinary.
'Whinham's Industry'. A mid-season variety, with large, oval, hairy, red berries of sweet flavour. Of vigorous, arching habit, but prone to mildew. Dessert or culinary.
'Whitesmith'. This mid-season variety carries large white berries of excellent flavour. Vigorous growth. Dessert or culinary.
Cultivation. Plant two or three-year-old bushes between November and March, if possible before the end of the year, ideally in a well-drained but moisture-retentive loam. Shallow soils that dry out in summer give fruits of poor size and the bushes will generally be short-lived.

Gooseberries can be grown in full sun, but they also thrive in partial shade. Avoid sites liable to late spring frosts and strong summer winds. Firm the roots well and support cordons at planting time with 2 in. × 2 in. stakes which stand 6 ft above ground level. Check the plants from time to time during the winter, firming any that have been lifted by frost.

Apply a mulch of well-rotted compost in spring to prevent the soil drying out. During dry spells between May and July, water newly planted bushes to help them become established, and water mature bushes to swell the fruits.

Feed annually in winter with sulphate of potash at $\frac{1}{2}$–1 oz. per sq. yd to satisfy the high need for potassium. In addition to the compost mulch, apply nitrogen in March, in the form of sulphate of ammonia at up to 1 oz. per sq. yd.

Gomphrena globosa

Gooseberry 'Whinham's Industry'

Avoid digging near bushes. Control weeds by mulching, shallow hoeing or by using paraquat. Remove suckers as they form if the bushes are growing on a leg.

Damage to buds by birds in winter may eventually spoil the shape of the bushes. If they are not grown in fruit cages, net them and delay pruning until bud-break, then cut back to undamaged buds.

Light crops can result from frost damage in spring. To reduce the risk, cover the bushes in April with muslin or fine netting, keep the soil moist, and move mulches to one side during flowering and while the berries are small. When the fruits are large enough, from late May, thin them out and use the immature berries for cooking or bottling. Leave the remainder of the fruits to ripen and use them for dessert purposes when they show their red or yellow colour.

It is possible to pick over a bush a number of times, leaving the last fruits to develop the full dessert quality. Careful pruning, to keep the growths well spaced, makes picking easier.

Propagation. Gooseberries are prone to virus diseases and should be obtained from reputable nurseries. Existing stock may be increased from hardwood cuttings in October. Take 12–15 in. long cuttings, removing all but the top four or five buds and inserting them 6 in. deep in a nursery bed outdoors. Grow on the cuttings for about one year; plant out the rooted cuttings in permanent positions the following November to March.

Pruning. If new bushes have not been pruned before delivery, delay pruning until bud-burst in spring so as to assess bird damage to the buds.

Aim to build up the shape of the bushes and, once the framework is established, to maintain a supply of young growths that will form fruiting spurs while allowing room for picking. Hard pruning of cordons or bushes improves fruit size and maintains vigour in older bushes.

See also chapter on PRUNING.

Pests. BIRDS, especially bullfinches, eat the buds during the winter.

GOOSEBERRY SAWFLY larvae attack the leaves in early summer and quickly reduce whole bushes to a skeleton of veins.

Diseases. AMERICAN GOOSEBERRY MILDEW produces a white powdery deposit on the fruits, leaves and shoots; the shoots are often distorted at the tips.

CLUSTER CUP RUST may infect the leaves, shoots or fruits and produce red or orange-coloured blotches which become thickened and covered with small warts or pimples. The warts soon burst and the blotch then shows as a cluster of cup-like structures producing yellow spores.

GREY MOULD causes a die-back of the bush, branch by branch, until the whole plant is killed. The bark becomes cracked irregularly and the fruiting bodies of the fungus then appear in the cracks as grey, velvety, cushion-like pustules of spores; they often arise from hard black masses of fungal threads embedded in the bark.

HONEY FUNGUS may kill bushes rapidly.

Gooseberry 'Careless'

Gourds (Ornamental mixed)

Gooseberry, Barbados: see *Pereskia aculeata*
Gooseberry, Chinese: see *Actinidia chinensis*
Gorse: see Ulex
Gorse, Spanish: see *Genista hispanica*

Gourds (ornamental)

Cucurbita pepo. Cucurbitaceae

These half-hardy annual plants, native to tropical America, are grown for their attractive ornamental fruits which are used for winter decoration. The plants bear pale to mid-green, stiffly hairy heart-shaped, five-lobed leaves. The orange-yellow bell-shaped flowers, 4–5 in. across, expand widely at the mouth. They are borne singly from the upper leaf axils from July to September. Hand pollination is generally required, the female flower being distinguished by the bulbous ovary. The smooth or knobbly fruits, in a wide range of shapes, and in shades of green yellow and orange, are borne in early autumn.

GOURDS

VARIETIES

These differ in shape and colour and are usually bought as a mixture, such as 'Sutton's Ornamental'. Single selections include 'Apple-shaped', 'Egg-shaped', 'Pear-shaped', 'Hercules Club' and 'Small Warted'.

Cultivation. Grow ornamental gourds in any ordinary, well-drained soil and in full sun. Sow seeds in early May in pots of seed compost, placed in a cold frame, and plant out at the end of May. Seeds may also be sown in the open, in late May, where the plants are to grow. Train the plants up fences or trelliswork, setting them at intervals of 3 ft; they may also be grown up tripods, one plant to each support.

Harvesting. Allow the fruits to ripen on the plants until they are quite hard and the foliage begins to die. Cut the fruits with a sharp knife, wipe them clean and leave them to dry out for a few weeks. A coat of clear varnish helps to preserve the attractive colours.

Pests and diseases. Generally trouble-free.

Granadilla: see *Passiflora quadrangularis*
Granny's bonnet: see *Aquilegia vulgaris*

Grape

Vitis vinifera. Vitaceae

GRAPE VINE

The grape-vine is found growing wild in the temperate regions of S. Europe and parts of N. Africa and W. Asia. It is thought to have originated in Asia Minor around the Caspian Sea, and records of its cultivation go back several thousand years.

The grape, or vine, was introduced to Great Britain by the Romans, and vast vineyards existed through the Middle Ages, principally around the monasteries. After the Dissolution, vineyards ceased to exist on a commercial scale in Britain.

It is a hardy deciduous climber, cultivated commercially on a large scale for its edible fruits, used for wine-making and for table desserts.

The mid-green maple-like leaves are palmate and three to five-lobed; in autumn they assume shades of red and purple. Yellow-green flowers are borne in pendent panicles and appear outdoors during May, under glass in March or April. They are followed by globular to ovoid fruits in clusters, and ripen to golden-green or red-purple according to variety.

Although hardy, grapes need a long warm summer to ripen the fruits, and they are seldom successful in Britain without some sort of glass protection. Outdoors, they do best in the southern half of England and Wales, preferably on a south-facing slope free from spring frosts.

Vines are self-fertile, but cross-pollination is desirable; any two varieties which flower at the same time are suitable. Under glass, artificial pollination is sometimes necessary.

OUTDOOR VARIETIES

On suitable sites, the following varieties, chiefly suitable for wine-making, can be trained against a wall, where they may reach a height and spread of 10–15 ft in the open, or as cordons (height 24 in.; spread 4 ft):

'Riesling Sylvaner'. Light tawny-yellow grapes ripen in October; usually a good cropper for wines of the Alsatian type.

'Siegerrebe'. Large golden berries of fine muscat flavour, ripening in October.

GREENHOUSE VARIETIES

These may be grown in greenhouse borders or in pots. Some are also suitable for outdoor cultivation under cloches, while others require high night temperatures during flowering.

Trained on a framework of wires against a greenhouse wall and up under the roof, single rods or cordons may reach a height of 20 ft with a 3 ft spread. The fruits ripen from July to October, depending on the heat available.

'Black Hamburgh'. A soft-fleshed, sweet, blue-black variety ripening in mid-season. Hardy and prolific, it may also be grown on walls and under cloches outdoors.

'Buckland Sweetwater'. Medium to large green juicy berries, early. Also suitable for a south or south-west wall.

'Madresfield Court'. An early black grape of excellent flavour. It needs warm conditions and is suitable for pot culture.

'Muscat of Alexandria'. Large, ovoid, amber berries of superior flavour. It requires high night temperatures during flowering, and ripens late in the season.

Cultivation and pruning. For grapes grown in greenhouse borders, make up a bed of a mixture of 3 parts loam and 1 part rotted manure (parts by volume). Set out pot-grown plants in late autumn or winter, preferably in late October, at intervals of 3–4 ft. Train the plants against wires running the length of the greenhouse and attached to the greenhouse by eye bolts every 10 ft. The wires should be 12 in. apart, and be set 6 in. from the glass. Water the young plants liberally to encourage them to make as much growth as possible during the first season, but allow only one stem (cordon or rod) to develop. If only one plant is being grown, train two or three rods from it.

See also chapter headed PRUNING.

In the autumn, when the leaves have changed colour, but before they fall, remove half to two-thirds of the growth of first-year rods, cutting back to a bud on well-ripened wood. The following spring, train the leading shoot up, and the laterals horizontally along the wires on alternate sides. After flowering, stop the laterals at two leaves beyond the fruit clusters and stop subsequent shoots (sub-laterals) at one leaf. Rub out all other shoots and allow only two or three fruit bunches to set in the first cropping year.

In the autumn, remove one-third to half of the new growth, and back to well-ripened wood on the leading rod; cut the selected laterals back to two buds. The lateral shoots will form the basis of the subsequent fruiting spurs. Cut back the main rod and lateral shoots each autumn, for one or two more years, to fill the available space and to build up a strong rod and fruit spurs.

Rest the vines in winter by giving full ventilation and allowing some frost into the house. Apply a 5 per cent tar-oil winter wash to the rods while they are dormant and renew the top inch of border soil. Untie the rods in late January and let their tops arch over to encourage even breaking of shoots along their length.

Close the greenhouse down in February when growth restarts and tie the rods into place. Most grapes require no artificial heat, but varieties such as 'Madresfield Court' and 'Muscat of Alexandria' need a long growing season and do best at a temperature of 10–13°C (50–55°F). Syringe the rods before mid-day to encourage growth. In unheated houses, ventilate freely on warm days to delay growth while there is still a risk of frost damage to the young shoots.

When the young shoots are about 1 in. long, reduce them to two per spur, and when these are 3–4 in. long, remove the weaker of the two.

Maintain a humid atmosphere, especially on sunny days, until flowering begins; thereafter ventilate the house freely. Pollinate the flowers by hand or with a soft brush.

Thin the fruit bunches to one per 12 in. of lateral stem, allowing a maximum of three on strong mature vines. As the berries begin to swell, cut out small and overcrowded fruits in the centre of each bunch, to improve its shape. Maintain a minimum temperature of 18°C (64°F), and a moist atmosphere by frequent damping down. Give a proprietary liquid feed or water-in dried blood at ½ oz. per sq. yd every ten days until the fruits have ripened.

When about half grown, the fruits cease swelling temporarily during seed maturation; fluctuations in temperature and humidity during this time should be avoided. As the fruits ripen, increase ventilation and reduce humidity.

After harvesting, reduce watering and give maximum ventilation. Remove all sub-laterals to help ripen the laterals.

Grape 'Riesling Sylvaner'

Grape 'Black Hamburgh'

Cultivation under glass. Plant two-year-old vines from October to February in 10–12 in. pots of John Innes potting compost No. 3. Build up the plants as previously described, training them on a wire framework in the greenhouse or on four or five canes, 4–6 ft high, inserted around the edge of each pot. When the plants are fully established they may produce about six bunches each.

Repot every winter into fresh compost.

Cultivation on outside walls. Plant between October and February in ordinary, well-drained soil, enriched with decayed manure or compost, and against a sheltered sunny wall that will afford protection against late-spring frosts. Set the plants 4–5 ft apart and train as vines under glass, allowing one rod to develop on each plant, three or four if only one vine is grown. After the first season's growth remove two-thirds of the main stems, and in subsequent years repeat this treatment in September until the stems fill the allotted space.

The plants should not be allowed to fruit until they are three years old. Thereafter, each lateral should carry one bunch of grapes only.

On first-year plants allow lateral shoots to reach a length of 24 in. before pinching out; tie the shoots into place fan-wise. On mature plants stop the laterals at two leaves after the flower clusters, sub-laterals at one leaf.

Keep the plants watered, and mulch established vines annually in March with well-rotted compost or manure.

Cultivation in open ground. Plant outdoor vines during suitable weather from October to February, setting the plants at intervals of $4\frac{1}{2}$ ft and allowing 3 ft between the rows. They require a fertile, well-drained soil in a sunny, sheltered position, preferably on a south-facing slope. At planting time, insert stout canes to each plant and stretch string or wire along the rows.

First-year plants should be pruned to 24 in. When the shoots begin to break, rub out all lower shoots and leave the top three or four to train along the wires. Later remove the weaker of these to leave one or two main fruiting rods, depending on whether the vine is trained as an inverted L or as a T shape. Lateral shoots should be trained as described for fan-trained vines.

On two-armed or T cordons, set the plants at intervals of 6 ft and train one main stem on either side of the stakes.

Prune established cordon-grown plants just before leaf-fall, cutting all laterals back to two or three buds. Pinch out laterals and sub-laterals as for wall-grown plants to allow one bunch of grapes to each lateral shoot.

Cloches are generally necessary to ripen the crop and to give protection against birds. They should be placed in position in August and may consist of side panels only.

Propagation. Take eye-cuttings, $1\frac{1}{2}$–2 in. long, from ripe stems in February; each cutting should have one bud or eye. Place the cuttings singly in 3 in. pots of John Innes potting compost No. 1 at a temperature of 13–16°C (55–61°F); bury the cuttings horizontally in the compost so that only the buds show. When rooted, pot the cuttings in 5 in. pots of John Innes potting compost No. 2.

For pot culture, pot on as necessary and insert canes for support; in the greenhouse border set the young plants in their permanent positions in June. For outdoor culture grow the young plants on in their 5 in. pots and set out in October.

Alternatively, take 9–12 in. long hardwood cuttings in October or November; insert the cuttings in their growing positions outdoors.

Pests. GLASSHOUSE RED SPIDER MITES infest leaves which may turn bronze, wither and die.

MEALY BUGS · produce conspicuous tufts of white waxy wool on the stems.

SCALE INSECTS may infest stems and make plants sticky and sooty.

Diseases. GREY MOULD affects berries which have split; they become covered with a brown-grey fluffy growth. HONEY FUNGUS may kill plants.

MAGNESIUM DEFICIENCY frequently shows between the veins of the leaves as yellow-orange blotches, which later turn brown.

OEDEMA, which chiefly occurs on indoor vines, is due to excessive heat and humidity. It shows on the leaves, and sometimes stems and berries, as water-soaked spots which erupt in corky growths.

PHYSIOLOGICAL DISORDERS, due to neglect, result in irregular brown blotches on the leaves; premature yellowing or leaf-fall may follow.

POWDERY MILDEW shows on the leaves, shoots and fruits as a white powdery deposit.

SCALD shows on the berries as discoloured sunken patches.

SHANKING first shows as a dark spot along the stalk of each grape and finally girdles it so that the grape fails to ripen. Fruits of black varieties turn red, whilst those of the golden-green varieties remain green and translucent.

SPLITTING of healthy berries is due to irregular supply of moisture at the roots.

SPRAY DAMAGE, due to the effects of hormone weedkillers, commonly occurs on vines. The leaves become narrow and fan-shaped, are frequently cupped, and the shoots twist spirally.

Grape 'Muscat of Alexandria'

Grevillea alpina

Grape, Amurland: see *Vitis amurensis*
Grape, fox: see *Vitis labrusca*
Grapefruit: see *Citrus paradisi*
Grape, Oregon: see *Mahonia aquifolium*
Grape, riverbank: see *Vitis riparia*
Grape, Teinturier: see *Vitis vinifera* 'Purpurea'
Grapevine: see Vitis
Grape, wine: see *Vitis vinifera*
Graptopetalum weinbergii: see *Sedum weinbergii*
Grass, blue-eyed: see *Sisyrinchium angustifolium*
Grass, feather: see Stipa
Grass, fountain: see *Pennisetum setaceum*
Grass, hare's tail: see *Lagurus ovatus*
Grass, pearl: see *Briza maxima*
Grass, quaking: see *Briza media*
Grass, umbrella: see *Cyperus alternifolius*
Grass, whitlow: see Draba
Greenweed, dyer's: see *Genista tinctoria*

Grevillea

Proteaceae

A genus of 190 species of evergreen trees and shrubs. In Great Britain, these plants are tender and require cool greenhouse cultivation, although those described may be grown outdoors in the south and west. With the exception of *G. robusta*, grevilleas are grown for their conspicuous petal-less flowers; these consist of a tubular calyx and a prominent curved style.

GREVILLEA SULPHUREA

G. alpestris: see *G. alpina*

G. alpina, syn. *G. alpestris*. Australia. Height and spread 1–3 ft. A dwarf shrub of open, bushy habit. The dark green leaves are downy, narrowly oblong to ovate with recurved margins. Terminal clusters of about five flowers, each $\frac{3}{4}$ in. long, are borne from March to June. The swollen calyx is red at the base and fading into yellow above; the prominent protruding styles are red.

G. robusta. New South Wales. Height 3–6 ft; spread 18 in. This foliage shrub is best grown as a pot plant in a cool greenhouse or used in summer bedding schemes outdoors. In young, vigorous plants the mid to deep green pinnate leaves may be 12–18 in. long. They are covered with silky hairs and are pale bronze when young. The species seldom flowers in cultivation.

G. rosmarinifolia. New South Wales. Height and spread 6 ft. This shrubby species is hardy in mild south and south-west districts. It has linear-oblong leaves that are mid to deep green above, and pale green beneath. Rose-red flowers, about 1 in. long, and crowded in terminal racemes, are produced from May to September.

G. sulphurea. New South Wales. Height and spread 6 ft. This shrub of open bushy habit is the hardiest of the species and is suitable for outdoor cultivation in mild maritime areas and in the south and south-west. The pale green leaves are linear-oblong. Clusters of up to 12 flowers are borne from May to September; the yellow calyx is about $\frac{1}{2}$ in. long, with a protruding yellow style 1 in. long.

G. thyrsoides. W. Australia. Height 4–6 ft; spread 2–4 ft. A bushy species, hardy in mild districts. The mid-green leaves are pinnate and divided into several linear segments. Racemes of rose-pink flowers, each with a $\frac{1}{4}$ in. long calyx and a 1 in. long style, appear from March to June.

Cultivation. Grevilleas dislike chalky and limy soils; they thrive in a neutral or acid soil, preferably enriched with peat or leaf-mould. Outdoors, plant in April or May in a sheltered, sunny position, against a warm, sunny wall. In winter, cover the roots with straw or bracken.

In the greenhouse, grow the smaller species in 5–7 in. pots, the larger species in 9–12 in. pots or tubs of John Innes potting compost No. 2 or in a mixture of 2 parts lime-free loam, 1 part peat and 1 part coarse sand (parts by volume). Overwinter the plants at a temperature of 4–7°C (39–45°F) and stand the pots outdoors from May to October. Water freely during spring and summer, but in winter keep the compost just moist. Give a weak liquid feed at fortnightly intervals from May to September. Repot or pot on in March every other year.

Propagation. Take 2–3 in. long cuttings of lateral shoots, preferably with a heel, in July. Insert in equal parts (by volume) peat and sand in a propagating case with a bottom temperature of 15–18°C (59–64°F). Pot when rooted into 3 in. pots of the growing compost and pot on as necessary. Grow on outdoor plants under glass until the following spring and harden off in a cold frame before planting out in May.

G. robusta is generally grown from seeds. Sow these in March in pots or pans of equal parts (by volume) peat, lime-free loam and sand, and germinate at a temperature of 13–16°C (55–61°F). Prick off the seedlings, when large enough to handle, singly into 3 in. pots and treat as described for cuttings.

Pruning. None is required except to remove untidy and frost-damaged wood in April.

Pests. Generally trouble-free, but young plants under glass may be infested by TORTRIX CATERPILLARS which spin the leaves together.

Diseases. Generally trouble-free.

Griselinia

Cornaceae

A genus of six species of slightly tender evergreen trees or shrubs. Only a few species are in general cultivation, and these are used for hedging in mild and maritime areas.

GRISELINIA LITTORALIS

G. littoralis. New Zealand. Height 10–25 ft; spread 6–15 ft. A slow-growing species, subject to frost damage and fully hardy only in mild localities or sheltered gardens. It has ovate-oblong, leathery, lustrous yellow-green leaves. The green flowers, which are unisexual and produced on separate plants in April or May, are inconspicuous and of no garden merit. In southern and western areas, particularly by the sea, it is an excellent plant for hedging or screening.

G. l. 'Variegata' is a less hardy form with conspicuous white variegated leaves.

G. lucida. New Zealand. This tender species is similar in growth to *G. littoralis*, but with larger leaves that are mid-green and glossy. It is suitable only for the mildest areas or for a conservatory.

Cultivation. Plant griselinias in October and November, or in March and April; young plants are best planted in spring. The shrubs thrive in any ordinary garden soil, and in sun or shade. They are tolerant of salt spray and gales, but, in all but the mildest areas, young plants require winter protection during the first few years until established. Erect wattle fencing, a canvas screen or a cane or chicken-wire framework, packed with bracken or straw.

Grevillea robusta

Grevillea sulphurea

Griselinia lucida

For hedges, set young plants at intervals of 18 in.; for screens, space at 2–3 ft intervals. After planting remove the growing tips of all shoots to promote bushy growth.

Propagation. Take heel cuttings, 3–4 in. long, of side-shoots in August or September; insert in equal parts (by volume) peat and sand in a cold frame. The following spring, pot up the rooted cuttings in 3½ in. pots of John Innes potting compost No. 2. Plunge outdoors for the summer, overwinter in a cold frame and transplant to permanent positions the following April.

Pruning. No regular pruning is required, but loose, straggly growths should be shortened to shape in April or August. Trim hedges annually in June or July.

Pests. Generally trouble-free.

Diseases. A PHYSIOLOGICAL DISORDER which shows as blackening of the shoots is due to unsuitable cultural conditions.

Gunnera manicata (flowers)

Gunnera manicata (foliage)

Guzmania monostachya

Gum, alpine snow: see *Eucalyptus niphophila*
Gum, cabbage: see *Eucalyptus pauciflora*
Gum, cider: see *Eucalyptus gunnii*
Gum, round-leaved snow: see *Eucalyptus perriniana*
Gum, sweet: see *Liquidambar styraciflua*
Gum, Tasmanian blue: see *Eucalyptus globulus*
Gum tree: see Eucalyptus
Gum, urn-fruited: see *Eucalyptus urnigera*

Gunnera

Gunneraceae syn. *Haloragidaceae*

GUNNERA MANICATA (IN FLOWER)

A genus of 50 tender and near-hardy herbaceous perennials varying from dwarf spreading species to majestic plants that form great foliage clumps suitable for growing beside a lake or pool. *G. manicata* is the most common of these and is the easiest species to obtain. The young leaves of gunnera may be blackened by late frosts, but new growth soon appears. The spire-like green flower spikes are hidden by the leaves.

G. chilensis, syn. *G. scabra*. Chile. Height up to 6 ft; planting distance 5 ft. The palmate, lobed and toothed dark green leaves measure 4–5 ft across. Green-brown flower spikes, 18 in. high, are borne in July and August.

G. magellanica. S. America. Height 4 in.; planting distance 9–12 in. A mat-forming plant with dark green kidney-shaped leaves. Green flower spikes, 3 in. high, appear in July and August.

G. manicata. Brazil. Height 6–10 ft; planting distance 10–15 ft. Enormous, dark green, kidney-shaped, lobed and toothed leaves, sometimes up to 10 ft across, are borne on stout prickly stems, and make this a most striking plant. Insignificant green flowers form dense, cone-shaped panicles, 24 in. high and 12 in. wide at the base. These first

flowers appear with the young leaves in April and develop slowly, changing through red to brown. Pollen is shed in May or June, and the seeds ripen in October.

G. scabra: see *G. chilensis*

Cultivation. Plant during April or May in sun or light shade in deep, moist soil, preferably with shelter to prevent summer winds tearing the foliage. *G. chilensis* will grow in a drier soil than the other two species. Do not disturb after planting. Protect the crowns of *G. chilensis* and *G. manicata* in winter by covering them with their own leaves weighted down with soil. Draw this aside in spring and pack it down around the base of the plant to act as a mulch.

Propagation. Sow seeds thinly in March or April in boxes or pans of seed compost at a temperature of 16°C (61°F). Grow the seedlings on until they are large enough to transfer to 3 in. pots of John Innes potting compost No. 1 or 2. Pot finally into 5–6 in. pots and overwinter in a frost-free greenhouse or shed, or in a cold frame with straw protection. Plant out in April or May.

Alternatively, increase by division, using the small crowns that form round the sides and base of old plants. In late April or May remove those that have already rooted, and plant in appropriate-sized pots of John Innes potting compost No. 2. Keep them shaded until growth is well established, then plunge the pots into an ash or peat bed. Treat in the same way as described for seedlings during the first winter.

Pests and diseases. Generally trouble-free.

Gunpowder plant: see *Pilea muscosa*

Guzmania

Bromeliaceae

A genus of 110 species of evergreen perennials suitable for cultivation in the greenhouse or the home. The genus is predominantly epiphytic, with a few terrestrial species. The species vary in diameter from 7 or 8 in. to 3 or 4 ft. The rosettes of glossy smooth-edged leaves form water-holding vases.

The floral bracts are often brilliant and last for many months; they range from yellow through orange to flame-red. The white or yellow, tubular, three-petalled flowers, which appear either on a stem or sunk in the leaf rosette, are short-lived.

See also BROMELIADS.

G. lingulata. W. Indies, Guyana, Colombia, Brazil, Bolivia, Ecuador. Height 12 in. This species has leaves up to 18 in. long; they are shiny, bright green, narrow and ridged. The flowering stem, up to 12 in. high, is surmounted by crimson bracts, 2½ in. long; they are triangular and outstretched and have a cluster of yellow-white flowers at the centre. The bracts remain in colour for weeks, but the flowers are short-lived.

G. monostachya, syn. *G. tricolor*. S. Florida, W. Indies, Brazil. Height 16 in. The narrow green leaves, slightly arched, form a rosette often 2½ ft in diameter. The cylindrical flower spike, 15 in. high, has a stem clasped by small green bracts that are tipped with white and striped vertically with brown-purple. Towards the apex of the spike the bracts change colour to vermilion. The white flowers barely emerge from the bracts.

G. picta: see *Nidularium fulgens*

G. sanguinea. Colombia. Height 12 in. Lanceolate, out-curving, red-tinged leaves form a dense rosette with a central boss of pale yellow or white, 2½ in. long, tubular flowers.

G. tricolor: see *G. monostachya*

Cultivation. As guzmanias come from the tropical rain forests, they need a high humidity and free circulation of warm air. Plant in 3–4 in. pots during late spring or early summer in a potting mixture of equal parts (by volume) coarse sand, leaf-mould and osmunda fibre. Place the plants in a partially shaded position. Water freely in summer, and keep just moist in winter.

Guzmanias require considerable root aeration and acidity; always water with rainwater.

Propagation. Leave the offshoots produced by the plants until they are rooted. Then detach the plantlets, usually in April, from the mother plant and pot up in the growing mixture.

Pests and diseases. Generally trouble-free.

Gynerium argenteum: see *Cortaderia selloana*

Gynura

Compositae

GYNURA SARMENTOSA

A genus of 100 species of evergreen perennial plants cultivated for their attractive leaves and stems. Only two species are in general cultivation and these require greenhouse treatment, or they may be grown as house plants.

The flowers have a heavy pungent smell which may be unpleasant to some people.

G. aurantiaca. Java. Height up to 3 ft; spread 18 in. The stems and leaves are thickly covered with bright violet-purple hairs. The dark green leaves are roughly triangular, up to 6 in. long, and may be entire or shallowly lobed. Small clusters of orange, groundsel-like flower heads, about 1 in. long, are borne on erect stems in February.

G. sarmentosa. India. Height 4–5 ft or more. This is similar to *G. aurantiaca* but it is a twining or trailing species that eventually requires support. Pale orange flower heads, about ½ in. long, are borne in terminal panicles in March and April.

Cultivation. Gynuras are more attractive as small plants and should be replaced at least every second year. Grow in John Innes potting compost No. 2 or in a proprietary peat compost, setting young plants in 5–6 in. pots in March or April. They will survive a winter temperature of 10°C (50°F), but 13°C (55°F) is more satisfactory. In winter, give the plants as much light as possible and keep them barely moist.

During spring and summer, the plants will need some shading; the compost should be kept moist, and the greenhouse should be frequently damped down. Keep water off the foliage, particularly during hot, bright spells.

If gynuras are being kept for more than one season, pot on in April or May into the next pot size; give them a liquid feed at fortnightly intervals from June to September.

G. sarmentosa can be grown in hanging baskets; set three plants to a 10 in. basket. In pots, this species may be grown as a trailing plant or be trained up a support of twiggy sticks or canes.

Propagation. Take cuttings, 3 in. long, of firm young shoots in April. Insert the cuttings, four to a 3 in. pot of equal parts (by volume) peat and sand, at a temperature of 18–21°C (64–70°F). As soon as the cuttings are well rooted, pot up singly in 3 in. pots containing John Innes potting compost No. 1, and keep them at the same temperature for a week or two until established. Grow on at 16°C (61°F) until the plants have filled their pots with roots. Pot on and gradually expose the plants to more airy conditions.

Pruning. Cut all lateral growths back to 3 in. in March or April and use the shoots for cuttings. The plants can be grown on for a second year if wanted. To avoid leggy plants of *G. aurantiaca*, pinch the growing points out two or three times at intervals while the plants are still young.

Pests and diseases. Generally trouble-free.

Gypsophila

Caryophyllaceae

A genus of 125 species of hardy annuals and herbaceous and evergreen perennials, including alpine species, with tiny, star-like flowers.

The annuals, with their delicate stems, are suitable for growing in mixed borders where they serve as a foil to other plants; they also make good cut flowers. The herbaceous border perennials form bushy dome-shaped plants with numerous slender flower stems that are good for cutting. They associate well with such perennials as coreopsis, erigerons, heleniums and phlox. As they develop deep fleshy roots they should be planted in a position where they can be left undisturbed for years.

The alpine species described here are suitable for rock gardens or dry walls. *G. arietioides* is better grown in an alpine house.

GYPSOPHILA PANICULATA

BORDER SPECIES

G. elegans. Caucasus. Height 24 in.; planting distance 12 in. An easily grown annual species with narrow, linear, glaucous leaves. Numerous white, pink or carmine flowers, ½ in. across, appear from May to September in branched panicles. 'Alba Grandiflora' and 'Covent Garden' both have white flowers; 'Rosea' is bright rose.

Guzmania sanguinea

Gynura sarmentosa

Gypsophila elegans

G. paniculata. S.E. Europe, Caucasus, Siberia. Height 3 ft; planting distance 2–3 ft. This perennial species has grey-green grass-like leaves; it is covered with loose panicles of numerous white flowers from June to August. 'Bristol Fairy' has double white flowers.

'Compacta-plena' (height 18 in.), double white; 'Pink Star', double pink; 'Rosy Veil', double pink, slightly paler than 'Pink Star'.

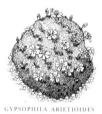

GYPSOPHILA ARIETIOIDES

ALPINE SPECIES

G. arietioides. Iran. Height 2 in.; spread 6–9 in. This forms a tight hard cushion of minute ovate, grey-green leaves. Stemless white or pale pink flowers, $\frac{1}{8}$ in. across, are freely borne in June.

G. cerastioides. Himalayas. Height 3 in.; spread 12–18 in. This species forms tufts of elliptic grey leaves. Numerous short clusters of clear white flowers, about $\frac{1}{3}$ in. across and marked with purple veins, are borne from June to October.

G. fratensis: see *G. repens*

G. prostrata: see *G. repens*

G. repens, syn. *G. prostrata*. Europe. Height up to 6 in.; spread up to 24 in. A mat-forming species of many-branched wiry stems and linear grey-green leaves. The flowers, $\frac{1}{3}$ in. across, vary from white to deep pink and appear from June to August.

G. r. 'Fratensis' (height 3–4 in.; spread 18–24 in.) has lanceolate grey-green leaves and carries a mass of pink flowers in June and July. It is sometimes listed as *G. fratensis*.

Cultivation of border species. These thrive in any well-drained garden soil in a sunny position. Acid soils should be dressed with 2–4 oz. lime per sq. yd. Use twiggy sticks for supports.

Plant perennials between October and March, and sow annuals in September or March.

Cultivation of alpine species. *G. arietioides* is best grown in an alpine house, in a 6–8 in. pot or pan containing 2 parts John Innes potting compost No. 1 to 1 part limestone grit (parts by volume). Repot in March every second or third year.

Plant *G. cerastioides* and *G. repens* in March or September in well-drained soil, preferably with some brick rubble added to it, and in a sunny position. *G. repens* and its forms are best planted where they can hang over rocks and walls.

Propagation of border species. Sow seeds of annual species in the flowering site in September or March; thin out the seedlings to the required planting distances.

Sow seeds of perennial species in pans or boxes of seed compost in a cold frame during March. Prick off the seedlings into boxes of John Innes potting compost No. 1 and later transfer to nursery rows outdoors; grow on until planting out from October to March.

Perennials can also be increased from cuttings, taken in April or May; select 3 in. long basal shoots and insert in equal parts (by volume) peat and sand in a cold frame. Alternatively, take lateral shoots, 2–3 in. long, in July and root in the same manner. In either case, pot the rooted cuttings into 3 in. pots of John Innes potting compost No. 1. Cuttings taken in spring can be set in nursery rows during summer and will be ready for planting out that autumn or the following spring. Summer cuttings should be overwintered in a cold frame.

Propagation of alpine species. Take young shoots, $\frac{1}{2}$–1 in. long, of *G. arietioides* in March; insert in coarse sand in boxes or pans and place in a cold frame. When rooted, pot the cuttings in 2–2$\frac{1}{2}$ in. pots of the growing compost; pot on as necessary.

Divide *G. cerastioides* in March or September and plant direct in permanent positions.

Take 2 in. cuttings from basal shoots or small lateral shoots of *G. repens* in April or May. Insert them in equal parts (by volume) peat and sand in a cold frame; place the cuttings in 3 in. pots of John Innes potting compost No. 1 when they are rooted, and plant out in September.

Pests and diseases. Generally trouble-free.

Gypsophila paniculata

Gypsophila repens 'Fratensis'

Haberlea rhodopensis

H

Haberlea

Gesneriaceae

A genus of two species of hardy, tufted herbaceous plants. They are related to *Ramonda*, and are suitable for growing in north-facing crevices or in shady corners of rock gardens.

H. ferdinandi-coburgii. Balkans. Height 4–6 in.; spread 6–9 in. Each plant forms a rosette of thick, dark green, obovate leaves. The primrose-shaped lilac-purple flowers have frilled lobes and are about 1 in. across. They are carried, three or four to a spray, on 4–6 in. stems in May.

H. rhodopensis. Thrace. Height 3 in.; spread 6–9 in. This is similar to *H. ferdinandi-coburgii* but is smaller in all respects. 'Virginalis' is pure white.

Cultivation. Plant in September or March in well-drained soil, preferably enriched with peat or leaf-mould, and in a shaded position. Haberleas are best placed in rock crevices to prevent rain getting into the rosettes.

Propagation. The most rapid method of propagation is from leaf cuttings. Gently remove, with a sideways pull, entire newly mature leaves from the rosettes in June or July and insert one-third of their length in a mixture of equal parts (by volume) peat and sand in a box or pan in shaded cold frame. Pot into 3 in. pots in March in equal parts (by volume) loam, peat and sand, and keep in the frame. Plant out in September.

Alternatively, sow seeds in September, March or April in boxes or pans of John Innes seed compost and place them in a cold frame where they can become chilled during the winter. Bring them into a temperature of 10–13°C (50–55°F) in February. Prick off the seedlings into boxes or pans and subsequently pot on into 3 in. pots containing 2 parts loam to 1 part each peat and sand (parts by volume). Overwinter in a cold frame and plant out in March.

Pests. SLUGS eat leaves and flower stems.
Diseases. Generally trouble-free.

Haemanthus

Blood lily. *Amaryllidaceae*

HAEMANTHUS KATHERINAE

A genus of 50 species of tender evergreen and deciduous bulbous plants, which in Great Britain require greenhouse cultivation. They bear thick-textured, ovate or oblong leaves and a single stout stem topped by a dense umbel of small star-shaped flowers with long stamens. In some species the umbel is spherical; in others it has a shaving-brush-like appearance and the flower head is enclosed in coloured bracts.

H. albiflos. S. Africa. Height 9–12 in. An evergreen species with oblong mid-green leaves that curve horizontally. The 2 in. long heads of white flowers and bracts appear in June.
H. coccineus. S. Africa. Height 9–12 in. The elongated-oblong mid-green leaves of this deciduous species are prostrate and only develop fully after the flowers have died. Each stem carries a 2–3 in. long head of red flowers and bracts in August and September.
H. katherinae (blood flower). Natal. Height 12 in. A deciduous species with mid-green, lanceo-late, wavy-edged leaves; these are erect and unite at the base to form a short stem. Salmon-red flowers are borne in 6 in. wide heads in July.
H. multiflorus. Central Africa. Height 18 in. or more. This deciduous species has erect, oblong-lanceolate, mid-green leaves that are joined at the base like those of *H. katherinae*. The flower stem, up to 3 ft high, bears a 6 in. wide spherical head of red flowers in April.
Cultivation. The bulbs of haemanthus may be 3 in. wide and deep; they need 6–8 in. pots or tubs in which to thrive. Pot in March, just covering the necks of the bulbs with John Innes potting compost No. 2; once potted, do not disturb for several years, but give a weak liquid manure feed at fortnightly intervals from May to August.

Keep the plants moist from February until the leaves begin to yellow, then dry off in their pots until growth is restarted the following spring.

Provide a temperature of 16°C (61°F) during the growing season, and overwinter at a temperature of 10°C (50°F). Repot every third year, in February or March.
Propagation. Remove offsets when the plants are being repotted. Pot these in 3–4 in. pots, depending on the size of the offsets, of John Innes potting compost No. 2, and treat as for mature plants, potting on as necessary. The young plants generally take two years or more to reach flowering size.
Pests. Conspicuous tufts of white waxy wool on the leaves are produced by MEALY BUGS.
Diseases. Generally trouble-free.

Halesia

Snowdrop tree. *Styracaceae*

A genus of six species of hardy, deciduous trees or shrubs, native to N. America and China. The American species only are in general cultivation, and make attractive spring-flowering plants.
H. carolina, syn. *H. tetraptera.* S.E. United States. Height 15–20 ft; spread 25 ft or more. This shrubby species has wide-spreading branches, carrying light green, ovate to obovate and pointed leaves. The bell-shaped silver-white flowers, $\frac{1}{2}$ in. long, are usually freely borne; they are carried in pendent clusters of five or six in May on the previous year's growths. They are followed by cigar-shaped four-winged fruits, often up to $1\frac{1}{2}$ in. long.

HALESIA MONTICOLA

H. monticola. Mountains of S.E. United States. Height 15–20 ft; spread 10–25 ft. A tree-like species with leaves similar to those of *H. carolina*. The bell-shaped white flowers, $\frac{3}{4}$–1 in. long, are borne in clusters of two to five during May. The winged, cigar-shaped fruits are up to 2 in. long. The variety 'Rosea' has pale pink flowers; *H. m. vestita* is a vigorous grower with leaves that are downy beneath.
H. tetraptera: see *H. carolina*
Cultivation. Halesias do well in moist, lime-free soils and in sunny, slightly sheltered positions; light woodland conditions are ideal. Plant in suitable weather from October to March.
Propagation. Layer long shoots in September and sever from the parent plants when rooted, one or two years later.

Alternatively, sow seeds when ripe, usually in October, in pots of seed compost in a cold frame; prick off the seedlings, when large enough to handle, into nursery rows outdoors, and grow on for two or three years.
Pruning. No regular pruning is required, but long shoots may be shortened after flowering to maintain the bushy shape.
Pests and diseases. Generally trouble-free.

Haemanthus coccineus

Haemanthus katherinae

Halesia carolina (flowers)

Halesia carolina (fruits)

Halimium ocymoides

Halimium lasianthum formosum

Hamamelis × intermedia 'Jelena' (flowers)

Halimium

Cistaceae

HALIMIUM OCYMOIDES

A genus of 14 species of half-hardy and hardy evergreen shrubs, distributed in the Mediterranean regions. They are related to *Cistus* and *Helianthemum* and are suitable for growing on large rock gardens, particularly near the sea. They are valued for their yellow flowers, similar to small single roses, with red or mahogany blotches at the base of each petal.

H. lasianthum formosum. Portugal. Height 1½–3 ft; spread 2–4 ft. This shrub is hardy in the south and west. It bears grey-green oblong to obovate leaves. The flowers, appearing from May to July, are 1½ in. wide and golden-yellow with a purple-brown blotch at the base of each petal. The variety 'Concolor' lacks the basal blotches.

H. libanotis. Mediterranean regions. Height 2–3 ft; spread 1½–2½ ft. A hardy species of erect habit, with slender shoots. The linear smooth leaves are mid-green above, white beneath. Yellow flowers, 1 in. wide, are carried in June in twos or threes at the ends of axillary shoots.

H. ocymoides, syn. *Helianthemum algarvense.* Spain, Portugal. Height 2–3 ft; spread 3–4 ft. A hardy compact shrub of branching habit, with narrowly obovate or oblong grey leaves. The flowers, up to 1 in. wide, are bright yellow with chocolate blotch at the base of each petal; they are borne in June in panicles.

Cultivation. Halimiums are easily grown in any light, well-drained soil and in full sun. Plant in September or April in a sheltered position.

Propagation. Take cuttings, 2–3 in. long, of lateral shoots with a heel in July and August; insert the cuttings in equal parts (by volume) peat and sand in a propagating case with a bottom heat of 13–16°C (55–61°F). When rooted, pot the cuttings in 3 in. pots of John Innes potting compost No. 1, and overwinter in a frost-free frame. The following May, pot on into 4 in. pots and plunge outdoors until transplanting to permanent positions in September or April.

Pruning. None required.

Pests and diseases. Generally trouble-free.

Hamamelis

Witch hazel. *Hamamelidaceae*

A genus of six species of hardy deciduous free-flowering shrubs, suitable as specimen trees, for shrub borders and woodland planting. Most will tolerate mild air pollution in industrial areas. In most species the flowers are produced in winter and early spring, which makes them valuable plants for a winter garden. The flowers, which are produced in axillary clusters, are sometimes fragrant and have a spidery appearance with long strap-shaped petals; the colours range from yellow through copper to red. Cut branches keep well in water. The foliage is often richly coloured in autumn.

H. × intermedia. Garden origin. Height and spread 6–10 ft. A strong-growing variable hybrid between *H. japonica* and *H. mollis.* The leaves are broadly ovate to obovate, mid-green and turning yellow in autumn. The flowers open in February and are 1–1¼ in. across, with twisted and crimped, yellow or copper-tinted petals.

Several varieties are available: 'Carmine Red' has shiny dark green leaves and copper-red flowers that generally open in March. 'Hiltingbury' is one of the best forms for autumn colour; the foliage turns yellow, copper, scarlet and red; the flowers are pale copper, suffused with red. The leaves of 'Jelena', syn. 'Copper Beauty', turn orange, bronze and red in autumn; the flowers are yellow, suffused with rich copper and are carried in dense clusters. 'Ruby Glow' has bright copper-red flowers and leaves that turn yellow, flushed with red in autumn.

H. japonica (Japanese witch hazel). Japan. Height and spread 8–10 ft. A large shrub or small spreading tree with ovate, glossy, mid-green leaves; the autumn foliage is yellow, sometimes flushed with red. The flowers measure ¾–1 in. across and open in February or March; the twisted and crimped petals are yellow, sometimes tinged with red.

H. j. arborea is a taller-growing variety of wide-spreading habit (height up to 20 ft); the flowers, with rich yellow petals and claret-red calyces, open in early March. 'Flavopurpurascens' is of similar habit, but rarely as large; the pale sulphur-yellow flowers are suf-

Hamamelis mollis 'Pallida'

Hamamelis japonica arborea

Hamamelis mollis 'Brevipetala'

Hamamelis mollis (autumn foliage)

fused with red and open slightly earlier. 'Zuc-cariniana' also resembles *H. j. arborea,* but is more erect; the flowers, with sulphur-yellow petals and green-tinted calyces, often have a strong pungent scent; they open in late March.

HAMAMELIS MOLLIS

H. mollis (Chinese witch hazel). Central China. Height and spread 6–8 ft or more. A large shrub or small tree with ascending branches and mid-green, felted leaves that are broadly obovate; they turn yellow in autumn. The flowers are 1–1¼ in. wide, with broad, flat petals of a rich golden-yellow, flushed red at the base; they are sweetly scented and thickly clustered along the twigs in January or earlier.

'Brevipetala' is a form with leaves that are glaucous beneath; the small flowers have short, blunt, deep yellow petals, and are borne in dense clusters. 'Pallida' has paler yellow flowers, faintly flushed with claret-red at the centre and densely packed on the twigs.

H. vernalis (Ozark witch hazel). Central United States. Height and spread 4–6 ft. An erect suckering shrub, of denser habit than the other species. The leaves are obovate and mid-green, slightly grey-green beneath; they assume yellow autumn tints. Clusters of ¼–½ in. wide flowers, with a pleasantly pungent scent, thickly clothe the stems in January or February; the tiny,

crimped petals range from pale to tawny-yellow and the calyces are dark red.

This species tolerates fairly moist soils and is particularly suitable beside lakes and streams.

H. virginiana (common witch hazel). E. United States and Canada. Height 8–10 ft or more; spread 6–8 ft or more. A large shrub or small tree of spreading habit, with obovate, mid-green leaves that turn yellow in autumn. The insignificant flowers are ¾–1 in. across, with twisted and crimped yellow petals; they generally unfurl in September or October.

This species is especially suitable for woodland gardens. It withstands cold and adverse conditions better than the large-flowered hybrids and garden varieties, and is extremely vigorous as a young plant.

Cultivation. Plant during suitable weather between October and March, in a neutral or acid, moisture-retentive soil. In heavy soils, incorporate liberal amounts of peat, leaf-mould or well-decayed manure before planting. For all species except *H. virginiana,* choose a sunny or semi-shaded site sheltered from cold winds.

Propagation. Layer suitable long shoots in September; they are usually ready to be severed and replanted after two years.

Take 4 in. long heel cuttings of lateral shoots in September and insert them in equal parts (by volume) peat and sand in a cold frame. Only a small percentage of these may root and these will be slow. If available, a mist propagating unit or propagating frame with a bottom heat of 16°C (61°F) gives faster and more reliable results if cuttings are taken in July and August.

When rooted, pot the cuttings singly into 3½ in. pots containing lime-free John Innes compost No. 1, or a compost of 3 parts lime-free

Hamamelis virginiana

Haworthia limifolia

Haworthia maughanii

Haworthia truncata

loam, 1 part peat and 1 part sand (parts by volume), and plunge outdoors (overwinter heat-raised cuttings in a frost-free frame). In the autumn, transfer the young plants to nursery rows and grow on for two or three years before planting out in permanent positions.

Sow seeds when ripe in October, in pots or pans of lime-free seed compost, or in a mixture of equal parts (by volume) lime-free loam, peat and sand. Place the containers in a cold frame. Germination may take 18–30 months. Prick off the seedlings, singly into 3 in. pots, and treat as described for cuttings.

Named varieties should be propagated by grafting on to rootstocks of *H. virginiana* in early April under glass, at a temperature of 13–16°C (55–61°F).

Pruning. Cut back straggly branches on large established specimens after flowering.

Pests and diseases. Generally trouble-free.

Harebell: see *Campanula rotundifolia*
Hares-foot: see *Davallia canariensis*
Haricot bean: see Beans (French)
Harlequin flower: see *Sparaxis tricolor*
Hart's-tongue: see *Phyllitis scolopendrium*
Haw, scarlet: see *Crataegus coccinea*

Haworthia

Liliaceae

A genus of 150 species of greenhouse perennials. These small succulents are grown for their thickened, attractively marked leaves. These are thick, stiff and tapering, and usually arranged in rosettes, which in some species are elongated. The flowers, which are produced during summer, are borne in loose, 4 in. long racemes of small bells on long straggling stalks. Those of the species described are green-white.

These easily grown succulents make good house plants for a window ledge.

See also entry under CACTUS.

H. limifolia. S. Africa. Height 2 in. A slow-growing, short-stemmed species with triangular leaves in a rosette. The leaves are dark green marked with glossy transverse lines of tubercles. The flowers are produced from June onwards. This species forms many offsets or stolons.

H. margaritifera. S. Africa. Height 3 in. This species holds its lanceolate leaves in broad rosettes. The leaves are initially erect, but spread outwards with age. They are dark green, and heavily marked with conspicuous white tubercles. The flowers appear from June onwards. Offsets are formed freely.

H. maughanii. S. Africa. Height 1 in. One of the rarer and choicer haworthias. A slow-growing species with cylindrical mid-green leaves held almost vertically and arranged in rosettes. The ends of the leaves are flat, as if cut off. These truncated ends are almost transparent and act as windows, allowing light to reach the inner tissues of the plant. The flowers are borne in August. In the wild, the whole plant except the transparent leaf tips is buried. Offsets are not usually formed in cultivation.

H. truncata. S. Africa. Height 1 in. A rare, choice plant, related to *H. maughanii*. It is slow-growing and has similarly truncated and transparent leaves. The short, cylindrical, mid-green leaves are arranged in two rows. The flowers appear in August. Offsets are not usually formed.

Cultivation. Haworthias need a porous soil, such as equal parts (by volume) John Innes potting compost No. 2 and grit. They do equally well in full sun or partial shade. Keep the plants moist during summer and gradually dry them off in late autumn. Keep them dry through winter if they are in a greenhouse, but give them a little water if they are being grown as house plants. The minimum winter temperature should be 5°C (41°F). Repot annually in spring.

Propagation. Sow seeds in spring at a temperature of 21°C (70°F). Those species which form offsets can be propagated by removing the young rosettes and drying them for about two days, before potting them up in June. Use the compost recommended for cultivation.

Pests. Infestations of MEALY BUGS produce conspicuous tufts of white waxy wool on the plants. ROOT MEALY BUGS check growth.

Diseases. Generally trouble-free.

Hawthorn, common: see *Crataegus monogyna* and *C. oxyacanthoides*
Hawthorn, water: see *Aponogeton distachyus*
Hazel: see *Corylus avellana*
Hazel, corkscrew: see *Corylus avellana* 'Contorta'
Hazel, Turkish: see *Corylus colurna*
Heartsease: see *Viola tricolor*
Heath: see Erica
Heath, Cornish: see *Erica vagans*
Heath, cross-leaved: see *Erica tetralix*
Heath, Dorset: see *Erica ciliaris*
Heath, St Dabeoc's: see *Daboecia cantabrica*
Heather: see Calluna and Erica
Heather, bell: see *Erica cinerea*
Heath, prickly: see Acantholimon

The heath garden at the Royal Horticultural Society's Garden, Wisley, Surrey

HEATHS AND HEATHERS

These plants are evergreen shrubs and sub-shrubs of the *Ericaceae* family. Probably no group of plants is of greater ornamental value throughout the year. Those described are nearly all hardy and, apart from a general susceptibility to honey fungus, are largely free from pests and diseases. Most species remain in bloom for many weeks, or even months.

Strictly speaking, the term heath is applicable only to ericas; heathers, only to callunas. In practice, and in the comments that follow, the terms are used loosely for both genera and also for such genera as *Daboecia* and *Phyllodoce*.

An increasing number of heathers, notably among the newer varieties and especially among the callunas, have remarkably coloured foliage. The colours range from glowing reds, russets, oranges, yellows and bronzes to greens and greys. Most of these varieties are at their best in late winter and spring, and the colours often vary on each plant with the seasons.

Individual heath and heather flowers are small, in shades of pink, purple, red or white, occasionally bi-coloured, and single or double. The flowers nearly all grow in terminal racemes; in young plants of some varieties, such as *Calluna* 'Elsie Purnell', these may exceed 12 in. in length.

Apart from their use in rock gardens, heaths make good ground-cover plants, and several varieties are suitable for hedging. Others are good as cut flowers, and those with double flowers may be dried for winter decoration. Heathers may also be grown in pots as specimen plants in the cool greenhouse.

There are specialist heath nurseries, and most general nurserymen stock a range of species and varieties.

Cultivation. Although heaths and heathers are best grown in peaty, acid soils, they will tolerate many others. Heavy soils may be lightened with the addition of sharp sand, peat or hop manure. Peat added to light soils improves the water-holding capacity, but no heathers should be planted in pure peat.

The showiest winter-flowering ericas, such as *E. carnea*, *E. mediterranea* and *E. × darleyensis* also grow well in chalky soils; *E. terminalis* and *E. vagans* will tolerate a small amount of lime.

Heathers need an open position in full sun; they should be kept free of fallen leaves. Dig the ground thoroughly. Add a top dressing of peat, at least 2 in. thick, and apply bone-meal at the rate of 4 oz. per sq. yd, mixed thoroughly with the topsoil. An annual top-dressing of peat helps to conserve moisture.

Plant from March until May, or during October and November. Set the plants deeply so that the whole of the stem is buried and the foliage rests on the soil. On dry soil, add moist peat round the roots.

Watering is essential on all soils during spring and dry spells, and during establishment in the first year after planting. No staking is needed, except for some aged specimens of tree heaths such as *Erica australis* and *E. terminalis*.

The spacing of plants depends on the varieties and the rapidity with which they spread. As a guide, set the smaller kinds at intervals of 12 in., the taller, spreading varieties at 18 in. Heaths are best planted in groups of at least six; the broader the drift, the more striking the result. Wide spacing requires fewer plants but leads to increased weed growth.

Propagation. The most usual and satisfactory method is by cuttings which should be taken from July to October. Use young side-shoots, 1–2 in. long, with or without a small heel of old wood. Insert the shoots a third of their length in pots or pans of a moist, well-drained rooting medium, such as 2 parts sharp sand and 1 part acid peat (parts by volume). Root the cuttings in a mist propagator. Hormone rooting compounds are unnecessary.

When the cuttings have rooted, grow on in a nursery bed, a cold greenhouse or a cold frame. Transplant the cuttings to their flowering quarters when they are about 3 in. high.

Large plants may also be propagated by layering. In March, select healthy stems from the outside of the plants; bend these down to soil level and bury under the soil with only the tips showing. Keep the layers in position with stones or bent wire pegs. After a year the layers should have rooted; they can then be severed from the parent plants and set out in their permanent positions. Prostrate varieties may root themselves naturally.

Pruning. The dead flowers on callunas and summer-flowering ericas are ornamental in their varying buffs and browns, and may be left on the plants during winter. In spring, clip off the dead flower stems close to the foliage. Cut back winter and spring-flowering heaths after flowering. Trim tall-growing varieties lightly with shears either in late autumn or before new growth starts, to prevent legginess.

Hebe × *andersonii*
'Variegata'

Hebe 'Carl Teschner'

Hebe 'Pagei'

Hebe armstrongii

Hebe
Scrophulariaceae

HEBE 'PAGEI'

This genus of about 100 species of evergreen flowering shrubs was formerly included in the genus *Veronica*. Grown for their decorative flowers and foliage, hebes are generally half-hardy and are best suited to frost-free maritime districts or sheltered areas inland. They are resistant to exposure and salt-laden gales. Some have closely overlapping, scale-like leaves and resemble a cypress. They are known as whipcord or cupressoid hebes. Each flower has four petals of unequal size and may be rounded or pointed.

H. albicans. New Zealand. Height and spread 24 in. A hardy, dense, rounded shrub suitable as a foliage plant. The lanceolate leaves are glaucous; white flowers are borne in racemes 2 in. long in June and July.

H. × andersonii 'Variegata'. Height 3 ft; spread 2–3 ft. A tender hybrid shrub with wavy, oblong-lanceolate, mid-green leaves, variegated with cream. Lavender flowers are borne in dense spikes, 3–5 in. long, from July to October.

H. armstrongii. New Zealand. Height 3 ft; spread 2–3 ft. A moderately hardy whipcord species of rounded habit with tiny, rounded-ovate and closely overlapping, deep golden-green leaves. Terminal, 1 in. long clusters of white flowers appear from June to August.

H. 'Autumn Glory'. Height and spread 2–3 ft. A moderately hardy hybrid shrub with dark green ovate leaves on purple stems. Spikes, 1–1½ in. long, of violet-blue flowers are freely produced from July well into the autumn.

H. 'Bowles' Hybrid'. Height up to 24 in.; spread 18–24 in. This moderately hardy hybrid has lanceolate mid-green leaves. The 2 in. long spikes of mauve flowers first appear in May and continue until September.

H. brachysiphon, syn. *H. traversii*. New Zealand. Height up to 6 ft; spread 4–6 ft. A hardy shrub of bushy habit, with dark green, narrowly ovate leaves. The white flowers, borne in racemes 2 in. long, are produced in June and July.

H. buchananii 'Minor'. New Zealand. Height 2 in.; spread 6 in. A hardy, dwarf evergreen, cushion-forming species of dense wiry twigs with light green rounded leaves. Small, stemless, white flowers appear somewhat sparsely in June.

H. 'Carl Teschner'. Height up to 12 in.; spread 2–2½ ft. This hybrid forms a dense and spreading moderately hardy shrub. Slightly grey-green ovate leaves are borne on dark wiry stems. Spikes, 1 in. long, of violet-blue flowers appear in June and July. Suitable for ground cover.

H. catarractae. Garden origin. Height 9 in.; spread 1½–2½ ft. This sub-shrub bears mid-green ovate-lanceolate leaves and produces masses of pale purple-white flowers, ⅓ in. across, from July to September.

H. colensoi 'Glauca'. New Zealand. Height up to 3 ft; spread 2–3 ft. A dense-growing, moderately hardy foliage shrub with small, stiff, obovate-oblong leaves that are waxy and glaucous. The white flowers are borne in dense, 1 in. long racemes during July and August.

H. cupressoides. New Zealand. Height 3–5 ft; spread 2–4 ft. A hardy species with tiny cypress-like leaves that are grey-green. Short spikes, ½–1 in. long, of pale blue flowers are borne in June.

H. 'Edinensis'. Height and spread 12–18 in. A perfectly hardy hybrid shrub forming a hummock. The bright green overlapping leaves are triangular-ovate. The plant rarely flowers.

H. × franciscana 'Blue Gem'. Height and spread 4 ft. A compact, almost hardy, shrubby hybrid with rounded rich green leaves. The violet flowers are borne intermittently in 2–3 in. long racemes throughout the year.

'Latifolia' is a form much planted in exposed maritime gardens; the flowers are mauve. 'Variegata', with cream margins to the leaves and mauve-blue flowers, is less vigorous; it is suitable for window-boxes and bedding schemes.

H. 'Great Orme'. Height up to 4 ft; spread 3–4 ft. A hardy hybrid of upright and bushy habit, and resistant to salt-laden winds. The dark green leaves are lanceolate. Pink flowers are borne in erect spikes, 4 in. long, from May to July.

H. hulkeana. New Zealand. Height up to 4 ft; spread 2–4 ft. This tender species of upright habit is best grown against a wall. The shiny pale green leaves are broadly ovate. Pale lavender-blue flowers are borne in May and June in terminal panicles up to 12 in. long.

. macrantha. New Zealand. Height 24 in., spread 18 in. A tender shrubby species requiring protection in cold areas. The shiny, light green leaves are broadly ovate and toothed. Glistening white blooms, ¾ in. across, are borne in short few-flowered racemes in June.

. pageana: see *H.* 'Pagei'

. 'Pagei', syns. *H. pageana, H. pinguifolia* 'Pagei'. New Zealand. Height 6–9 in.; spread 3 ft. A hardy bushy shrub, probably a variety or hybrid of *H. pinguifolia* and often listed under that name. The small obovate leaves are glaucous. Spikes, ¾–1 in. long, of white flowers are borne in May and June.

. pimeleoides var. 'Glauco-caerulea'. New Zealand. Height up to 12 in.; spread 24 in. This moderately hardy shrub has ovate deeply glaucous leaves. Dark purple flowers are produced in 1 in. long spikes from June to August.

. pinguifolia 'Pagei': see *H.* 'Pagei'

. salicifolia. New Zealand. Height and spread 8–10 ft. A moderately hardy shrub, frequently grown in maritime districts. The slenderly pointed lanceolate leaves are pale green. Racemes, up to 6 in. long, of white, lilac-tinted flowers are borne from June to August.

. speciosa. New Zealand. Height up to 5 ft; spread 4–5 ft. A tender species with large oblong leaves that are glossy dark green. The purple-red or blue-purple flowers are borne in 4 in. long racemes from July onwards.

This species has produced numerous hybrids and forms which make good plants for a cool greenhouse or for pot culture. They include: 'Gloriosa', bright pink; 'La Seduisante', bright carmine-red; and 'Simon Deleaux', rich red.

. traversii: see *H. brachysiphon*

. 'Waikiki'. Height up to 24 in.; spread 18–24 in. A moderately hardy variety of bushy habit. The ovate leaves are copper-red when young and become shiny mid-green. Violet-blue flowers in 2 in. long racemes are borne in June and July.

Cultivation. Plant hebes in September and October or in April and May; they thrive in most well-drained garden soils, including chalk, and in full sun. The tender species require wall protection in inland gardens.

Prostrate species are generally hardy and make excellent ground cover; they can even be grown successfully in urban gardens. Dead-head all species as soon as flowering is over.

Under glass, grow hebes in 6–8 in. pots of John Innes potting compost No. 2. Overwinter at a temperature of 5–7°C (40–45°F). Repot or pot on annually in March or April.

Propagation. Take cuttings, 2–4 in. long, of non-flowering growths during July and August; insert the cuttings in equal parts (by volume) peat and sand in a cold frame. Varieties of *H. speciosa* are best rooted in a cool greenhouse or a frame which can be kept frost-free. The following April, pot the rooted cuttings in 3–3½ in. pots of John Innes potting compost No. 1. Plunge the pots outdoors and transplant the hardy species and varieties to their flowering positions in September; tender plants should be potted on and overwintered in a cold frame.

Pruning. No regular pruning is required, but leggy shrubs may be pruned hard back in April; new shoots break freely from the base.

Hebe macrantha

Pests. Generally trouble-free.

Diseases. In the south-west, or under cool greenhouse conditions, particularly in winter, DOWNY MILDEW may show as a grey mould in pale blotches on the leaves.

HONEY FUNGUS may sometimes cause the rapid death of these shrubs.

LEAF SPOT shows as white spots with brown margins on the leaves; the disease is most troublesome in the south-west and in Wales.

Hedera
Araliaceae

HEDERA HELIX 'GLACIER'

A genus of 15 species of hardy evergreen climbers. Two forms of growth are produced: juvenile or runner growth, with lobed leaves and aerial roots which attach themselves to any surface; and adult or arborescent growth, which has entire leaves with wavy margins and no aerial roots, and which bears flowers and fruits. This arborescent growth is produced from the summit of the runner growth when it reaches the top of its support. Cuttings taken from the arborescent growth will retain the adult form and develop

Hedera colchica 'Variegata' (flowering shoot)

Hedera canariensis 'Variegata'

Hedera helix 'Conglomerata'

Hedera helix 'Goldheart'

into rounded, bushy shrubs which flower and fruit freely. These are known as 'tree ivies'.

All ivies, and in particular, *H. helix* and its many varieties, make excellent house plants for unheated rooms.

H. amurensis: see *H. colchica*

H. canariensis (Canary Island ivy). Canary Islands, N. Africa. Height 15–20 ft. A handsome, rapidly growing species, which thrives in sun or shade. It is rather more erect than *H. helix* and ideal growing on a trellis. The growth may be cut back by severe winters. The leathery leaves are lobed and broadly ovate with a heart-shaped base. They are bright green in summer, turning bronze-green in winter. *H. c. azorica* is a vigorous variety with shallowly lobed light green leaves. When young, stems and leaves are covered with thick brown felt.

H. c. 'Variegata', syn. 'Gloire de Marengo', has leaves which are dark green in the centre, merging through silver-grey to a white border.

H. colchica, syn. *H. amurensis* (Persian ivy). Persia. Height 20–30 ft. This species is a rapid climber. The dark green ovate or heart-shaped leaves are 8–10 in. long and 6 in. wide. The young growth is covered with yellow down.

H. c. dentata has thin, widely toothed, dark green, sometimes purple-tinted leaves. It is an excellent wall plant. *H. c.* 'Variegata' has leaves marked with cream-yellow and pale green.

H. helix (common ivy). Europe. Height 50–100 ft. This is a species native to Britain. It is one of the hardiest and most useful of all climbing plants, good for ground and wall cover. The leaves are glossy dark green, often with silver markings along the veins.

The named varieties of this species, especially the smaller-leaved forms, are suitable for indoor pot culture. Recommended forms include: 'Aureo-variegata', syn. 'Chrysophylla', with leaves variegated with soft yellow, often reverting to green. 'Buttercup', also known as 'Golden Cloud' or 'Russell's Gold', is one of the finest golden ivies. 'Conglomerata' (height up to 24 in., spread 3 ft) is a bushy, non-climbing form, with small wavy leaves densely set along rigid stems.

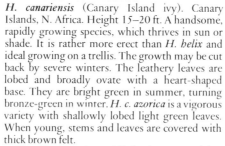

'Deltoides' has distinctively shaped leaves, the two basal lobes being round and overlapping. 'Digitata' (finger-leaved ivy) has broad leaves divided into five narrow, finger-like lobes.

'Discolor' (marble-leaved ivy) is a neat small-leaved plant mottled with red-tinged cream. 'Glacier' has small leaves variegated with silver-grey and edged with white. 'Goldheart', also known as 'Jubilee', has small, tapering, dark green leaves with a gold centre.

'Sagittaefolia' has arrow-shaped leaves with five lobes, the central one long and triangular. 'Silver Queen', syn. 'Marginata', has leaves with a grey and blue-green centre and broad, cream-white margin tinged with pink in winter. 'Tricolor', syn. 'Marginata-rubra' has pale green leaves with a white border which turns deep rose-red in late autumn. This is a beautiful but slow-growing plant.

Cultivation. All the ivies thrive in any soil and almost any situation. Plant them in mild weather at any time between September and March. The variegated forms colour best in a south or west facing position.

For pot culture, grow ivies in 4–6 in. pots of John Innes potting compost No. 2, or in a proprietary peat compost. Train the plants up thin canes. Place in full light, but out of direct sun in summer; they will tolerate semi-shade. Keep the plants just moist throughout the year; feed with weak liquid manure at monthly intervals from April to September. Repot or pot on every other year in March. Ivies will survive the winter in unheated rooms.

Propagation. Increase all ivies by cuttings. Take 3–5 in. cuttings from the tips of shoots in July or August. If a bush is wanted, take the cuttings from adult growth; if a climber, take them from runner growth. Root in equal parts (by volume) peat and sand in a closed frame or under mist propagation. Pot the rooted cuttings one to a 3 in. pot, and grow them on in a cold frame or greenhouse until needed for planting in their permanent positions. Pot on house plants as necessary, in March.

Alternatively, take 6 in. cuttings from ripe shoots in October or November, removing the soft tips. Insert them in a prepared bed of sandy soil in a sheltered position outdoors.

Pruning. When ivy is grown on walls or fences, cut it back close to its support during February or March each year. Prune again in summer to remove excessively long runners or other unwanted growth. Prevent top growth from rambling over roofs or gutters. Even where unlimited growth is wanted, prevent it from becoming too matted and heavy, or it may break away from its support.

Arborescent growth may need occasional pruning to maintain shape. Do this with secateurs in March and July.

Overgrown leggy pot plants may be cut back by about half in March or April.

Pests. SCALE INSECTS, especially soft scale, infest the undersides of leaves and make the plant sticky and sooty.

BRYOBIA MITES cause a fine light mottling of the upper leaf surfaces.

Diseases. LEAF SPOT shows on the leaves as brown spots which become white in the centre, but retain purple-brown margins.

HEDGES

apart from being attractive features in themselves, hedges serve to define boundaries, provide privacy and shut out unsightly views; they also form windbreaks and screens, sheltering areas of the garden from the prevailing wind.

The type of hedge required and the climatic and soil conditions are the governing factors when choosing hedging or screening plants. They should be able to withstand regular trimming or, in the case of informal hedges, retain their shape with a minimum of pruning.

Small-growing compact shrubs, such as *Buxus sempervirens* 'Suffruticosa' and *Lavandula*, are excellent for dwarf hedges. Many decorative shrubs, including *Berberis, Cotoneaster, Forsythia, Fuchsia* and *Rhododendron*, make attractive informal hedges, requiring only occasional pruning. Evergreen hedging plants such as *Euonymus japonicus, Ligustrum ovalifolium, Lonicera nitida, Prunus lusitanica* and *Taxus baccata* eventually form dense, wall-like barriers that may be close-clipped to the desired shape. Plants for windbreaks and shelter hedges include *Chamaecyparis lawsoniana,* × *Cupressocyparis leylandii, Griselinia littoralis, Ilex aquifolium* and *Pinus radiata*

Many hedging plants do not thrive in the windy and salt-laden conditions of seaside districts, but shrubs such as *Escallonia, Griselinia, Hebe* and *Olearia* are among those which are suitable.

Good, deeply cultivated soil is essential for the establishment of hedges. Prepare the site for a new hedge thoroughly, removing all perennial weed roots; if the site is very wet, raise the soil level to a slight ridge about 12 in. high and 24 in. across. Incorporate a layer of well-decayed manure or compost about 12 in. below the surface. For spring planting, which is recommended for most evergreens, the ground should be prepared in autumn and winter; sites for deciduous hedges to be

Ilex aquifolium

Prunus lusitanica

× *Cupressocyparis leylandii*

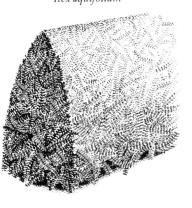

Lonicera nitida

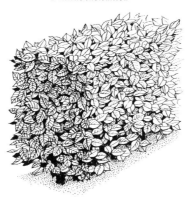

Fagus sylvatica

Taxus baccata

Buxus sempervirens

Ligustrum ovalifolium

Rosmarinus officinalis

planted in the autumn are best prepared in spring and kept weed-free during the summer. Shortly before planting, fork a complete fertiliser, at 2 oz. per yd run, into the soil over a 12 in. wide area along the hedge line.

Planting times and distances are given in the table below. But, in fact, most deciduous hedges may be planted when the weather and soil conditions permit, from October to March, preferably in October or early November. Evergreens can also be planted in April or early May.

The ideal age of young specimens for planting varies, but as a general rule they should be small enough to make handling easy and staking unnecessary. Plant in a single row against a garden line to ensure a straight hedge, or along a guide-line for a curved hedge. Set the young plants to the same depth as in the nursery, indicated by the soil mark on the stems. Ease fine soil around the roots, and firm well; more shrubs die from loose planting than from any other cause.

Young plants will need watering during dry spells in spring and early summer. Allow at least 2 gal. to soak in around each plant daily. Syringing, preferably with rainwater, is also beneficial. Keep the hedge bottom free of weeds, and do not allow any other plants to grow within 12 in. on either side of a new hedge.

Regular applications of fertiliser are generally unnecessary, but all young hedges benefit from a dressing of complete fertiliser in February, one year after spring planting, 18 months after an autumn planting. Apply 1 oz. to each yd run on each side of the hedge. Repeat this dressing annually if growth is poor.

Staking is usually not required. On exposed sites, however, they may need the shelter of a temporary fence or screen until they become established. Alternatively, support each plant individually, or erect a line of stakes with wires or strings stretched between them to support the intervening hedging plants.

For all types of hedge, early training is important. Side branching must be encouraged, to promote thick bushy growth from base to apex. Hedges which are allowed to reach the desired height before being pruned, quickly become bare and straggly at the base. At planting time or in spring, cut back all growths to half or two-thirds of their length.

Informal hedges may be left to grow freely after the initial tipping at planting time, but if lateral branching is poor it is advisable to sacrifice the second year's flush of flowers in favour of a second pruning. Formal hedges should be allowed to reach the desired height in stages, the leading shoots being pruned regularly when they are 9–12 in. long.

An established hedge should preferably be widest at the bottom with a rounded or broadly sloping top. This encourages better growth of the lower branches and provides the best shelter from winds.

The ideal times for pruning or clipping full-grown hedges are advised under individual entries; for informal hedges it is necessary only to remove untidy or flowered growths, using secateurs. Formal hedges with dense growth should be close-clipped to a clear outline, using shears or a mechanical trimmer. Broad-leaved hedges may look unsightly with leaves sliced through and are better trimmed with secateurs.

The following table lists some of the more popular hedging plants; the rates of growth given are those generally achieved on average soils.

Plants for hedges	Foliage	Growth rate	Planting months	Spacing	Trim
Berberis darwinii	Evergreen	Medium	Oct.–Nov. or Mar.	18 in.	May–June
Berberis × stenophylla	Evergreen	Medium	Oct.–Nov. or Mar.	18 in.	May–June
Buxus sempervirens	Evergreen	Slow	Oct.–Nov. or Mar.–Apr.	15 in.	June
Buxus sempervirens 'Suffruticosa'	Evergreen	Slow	Oct.–Nov. or Mar.–Apr.	9 in.	June
Carpinus betulus	Deciduous (winter brown)	Medium	Oct.–Mar.	24 in.	July–Aug.
Chamaecyparis lawsoniana	Evergreen	Fast	Oct.–Mar.	18 in.	June and Sept.
Crataegus monogyna	Deciduous	Medium	Oct.–Mar.	12 in.	June–Aug.
Crataegus oxyacanthoides	Deciduous	Medium	Oct.–Mar.	12 in.	June–Aug.
× *Cupressocyparis leylandii*	Evergreen	Fast	Oct.–Nov. or Apr.–May	2–3 ft	May–June
Escallonia macrantha	Evergreen	Medium	Oct.–Nov. or Apr.	18 in.	June
Euonymus japonicus	Evergreen	Slow	Mar.–Apr. or Sept.–Oct.	18 in.	July
Fagus sylvatica	Deciduous (winter brown)	Slow for 2 years then medium	Oct.–Mar.	18 in.	July–Aug.
Fuchsia magellanica	Deciduous	Fast	Apr.–May	12 in.	Oct. or Mar.
Griselinia littoralis	Evergreen	Medium	Mar.–May	2–3 ft	June–July
Ilex aquifolium	Evergreen	Slow	Apr.–May or Sept.–Oct.	18 in.	July
Lavandula spica	Evergreen	Slow	Oct.–Nov. or Mar.–Apr.	9–12 in.	Sept.
Ligustrum ovalifolium	Evergreen	Fast	Oct.–Apr.	15 in.	May–June & July–Aug.
Lonicera nitida	Evergreen	Fast	Oct.–Apr.	9–12 in.	Apr.–Sept.
Prunus cerasifera	Deciduous	Medium	Oct.–Mar.	18 in.	July
Prunus lusitanica	Evergreen	Slow	Mar.–May or Sept.–Oct.	18 in.	June–July
Rosa eglanteria	Deciduous	Medium	Oct.–Mar.	15 in.	July and Mar.
Rose 'Queen Elizabeth'	Deciduous	Fast	Oct.–Mar.	18 in.	Oct. or Mar.
Rosmarinus officinalis	Evergreen	Medium	Sept.–Oct. or Mar.–Apr.	15 in.	July–Aug.
Taxus baccata	Evergreen	Slow	Mar.–May or Sept.–Oct.	18 in.	June–July
Thuja plicata	Evergreen	Medium	Mar.–May or Sept.–Oct.	18 in.	June–July

Hedychium

Ginger-wort. *Zingiberaceae*

A genus of 50 species of herbaceous perennials. The stout, reed-like stems carry lanceolate sheathing leaves in two parallel ranks; the stems are topped with spikes of orchid-like, often fragrant flowers. Hedychiums require greenhouse cultivation, except in the mildest areas.

H. coccineum. India. Height 4 ft or more; spread 3–4 ft. The stems of this species are covered throughout their length with narrow lanceolate mid-green leaves up to 18 in. long. The red flowers, borne in terminal spikes from July to September, are up to 2 in. wide. Forms are known with pale red or pink flowers.

H. coronarium. India. Height 3 ft; spread 2–3 ft. The stems are clad with mid-green leaves that are up to 24 in. long and slightly downy beneath. Terminal spikes of fragrant white flowers, up to 3 in. wide appear from June to August.

H. flavum. N. India. Height up to 5 ft; spread 3–4 ft. The oblong-lanceolate mid-green leaves are up to 12 in. long. Fragrant flowers, 3 in. across, are densely borne in terminal spikes from July to September; they are yellow with an orange blotch in the centre.

HEDYCHIUM GARDNERIANUM

H. gardnerianum. N. India. Height 6 ft or more; spread up to 5 ft. This species will survive outdoors in mild districts. The lanceolate mid-green leaves are about 10 in. long. The yellow flowers, about 2 in. across, open in spikes from July to September to disclose brilliant red stamens.

H. greenei. Bhutan. Height 4 ft; spread 3–4 ft. The mid-green lanceolate leaves are 8 in. long. The flowers, composed of rather thin petals, are about 3 in. wide, bright red, and appear in dense terminal spikes from July to September.

H. spicatum. India. Height 3 ft; spread 3–4 ft. This species has lanceolate to oblong-lanceolate mid-green leaves, varying in length from 4–15 in. Loose spikes of yellow, 2 in. wide flowers are produced in October.

Cultivation. Hedychiums should be grown in 9–12 in. pots or in small tubs. They require a rich compost, such as John Innes potting compost No. 3. Maintain a temperature of 7°C (45°F) in winter; during late autumn and winter, keep the plants barely moist.

Water sparingly at first in March, and increase the amount of water as growth progresses. During the growing period, feed with liquid manure at 10–14 day intervals.

If space allows, hedychiums do well planted out in the greenhouse border. Otherwise, repot plants every other year in March.

Propagation. Divide and replant the rhizomes when repotting in March or April.

Pruning. Cut down flowering stems to within a few inches of the base from October onwards. Non-flowering stems can be retained, but there is little value in doing so.

Pests and diseases. Generally trouble-free.

Hedysarum

Leguminosae

HEDYSARUM CORONARIUM

A genus of 150 species of hardy annuals, biennials and herbaceous perennials, and deciduous shrubs and sub-shrubs. Few species are in general cultivation, although they are easy to grow in mixed borders, shrubberies or on sunny banks. The spikes of small pea-like flowers are good for cutting.

H. coronarium. Europe. Height 3–4 ft; planting distance 18–24 in. A shrubby biennial or short-lived perennial that may also be grown as an annual. The pale green leaves are pinnate and composed of elliptic leaflets. Fragrant red flowers are borne in dense spikes, 3 in. long, from August to September.

H. multijugum. Mongolia. Height and spread 4–5 ft. This is a deciduous shrub of sparse, lax habit and with zigzag branchlets. The pinnate mid-green leaves are composed of up to 20 pairs of ovate-oblong leaflets. Rose-purple flowers are borne on the current year's growths in erect axillary racemes, 6–12 in. long; they appear from June to September.

Cultivation. Grow hedysarums in any ordinary, well-drained garden soil, in a sunny position. Staking of *H. coronarium* may be necessary on exposed sites.

Plant pot-grown specimens of *H. multijugum* in September or in March and April; once established the plants should not be disturbed. Young plants of *H. coronarium* should be set out in September. Cut back *H. coronarium* to just above ground level in November.

Propagation. Sow seeds of *H. coronarium* during May or June in a nursery bed, and transplant the seedlings to the flowering site in September.

Alternatively, sow directly in the flowering site in September or March and treat as annuals, thinning out the seedlings to the appropriate planting distances.

Sow the seeds of *H. multijugum* in March or April in pans of seed compost and place in a cold frame. Prick out the seedlings, when large enough to handle, singly into 3½ in. pots of John Innes potting compost No. 1 or 2. Plunge outdoors and transplant to permanent positions in September or the following spring.

Alternatively, layer long shoots in September and sever from the parent plant one year later.

Pruning. Thin out old and weak wood on *H. multijugum* and shorten straggly shoots of the previous year in February.

Pests and diseases. Generally trouble-free.

Hedychium coccineum

Hedychium gardnerianum

Hedysarum coronarium

HELENIUM

Helenium autumnale 'Golden Youth'

Helenium autumnale 'Latest Red'

Helenium autumnale
'Baudirektor Linne'

Helenium autumnale
'Mahogany'

Helenium autumnale
'Wyndley'

Helenium
Compositae

HELENIUM AUTUMNALE

A genus of 40 species of hardy herbaceous annuals and perennials. They are free-flowering and provide long-lasting cut blooms. The daisy-like flowers have prominent central discs.

H. autumnale. Canada, United States. Height 4–6 ft; planting distance 12–18 in. A hardy perennial with winged stems and mid-green lanceolate leaves. Yellow flowers, 1–1½ in. across, are borne from August to October. It is superseded by colourful hybrids and varieties:

'Baudirektor Linne', height 4 ft, orange and mahogany-red, August and September; 'Bruno', 3–3½ ft, mahogany, July to September; 'Butterpat', 3 ft, rich yellow, August and September; 'Coppelia', 3–3½ ft, rich orange and copper-red, July and August; 'Golden Youth', 2½ ft, pure yellow, June and July; 'July Sun', 3 ft, golden-orange, July and August; 'Latest Red', syn. 'Spatrot', 3½ ft, rich bronze-red, August and September; 'Mahogany', 2½ ft, red and golden-brown, July and August; 'Moerheim Beauty', 3 ft, bronze-red, July to September; 'Pumilum Magnificum', 24 in., deep yellow, and 'Wyndley', 24 in., yellow and copper, June to August.

Cultivation. Plant between October and April in a sunny position in any ordinary soil. In exposed positions support the plants with canes or stout pea sticks. Some early-flowering varieties produce a second crop of flower heads if cut back as soon as the first flush has finished. In any case cut down dead stems in November. Dividing and replanting every three years improves flowering.

Propagation. Divide and replant the roots between October and April.

Pests. Stems, leaves and flowers may be eaten by SLUGS. TORTRIX CATERPILLARS spin the leaves together and eat them.

Diseases. A VIRUS DISEASE turns the flowers green.

Helianthemum
Rock rose. *Cistaceae*

HELIANTHEMUM NUMMULARIUM

A genus of 100 species of hardy evergreen shrubs, sub-shrubs and herbaceous plants that provide a blaze of colour throughout the summer. They are suitable for rock gardens, but need careful siting as they may swamp less vigorous plants.

H. alpestre, syn. *H. oelandicum,* sub-species *italicum.* Mountains of Central and Southern Europe. Height 3–4 in.; spread 12 in. This low-growing sub-shrubby plant has elliptic mid-green leaves. The bright yellow saucer-shaped flowers, ¾ in. across, appear in profusion during June and July.

The variety 'Serpyllifolium', syn. *H. serpyllifolium glabrum* (height 2–3 in.; spread up to 24 in.) is almost prostrate with grey-green leaves, smaller than those of the type species.

H. chamaecistus: see *H. nummularium*

H. lunulatum. Italy. Height 9 in.; eventual spread up to 12 in. A neat shrubby species with grey elliptic leaves. It is covered with bright golden saucer-shaped flowers, ½ in. wide, in June and July; it often blooms again in late summer.

H. nummularium, syns. *H. chamaecistus, H. vulgare.* Europe, including Great Britain. Height 4–6 in.; spread 24 in. This species is the well-known rock rose, which has elliptic leaves that are deep green above, paler beneath. The saucer-shaped flowers are ½–1 in. across, and numerous colour forms are available. They all flower profusely in June and July.

Among the named varieties, the 'Ben' series are particularly good garden plants, including 'Ben Afflick', orange and buff, and 'Ben Heckla', deep bronze-gold. Other good varieties include: 'Beech Park Scarlet', crimson-scarlet; 'The Bride', white; 'Wisley Pink', pink; and 'Wisley Primrose', yellow. All have grey foliage. 'Jubilee' has bright yellow double flowers.

H. oelandicum italicum: see *H. alpestre*

H. serpyllifolium glabrum: see *H. alpestre* 'Serpyllifolium'

H. vulgare: see *H. nummularium*

Cultivation. Plant helianthemums between September and March in any ordinary, well-drained garden soil in a sunny position. *H. nummularium* and its varieties spread profusely and should be cut hard back with shears after flowering, to maintain a neat shape. Trimming of all species after flowering induces further flowering between August and November.

Propagation. Take 2–3 in. cuttings of non-flowering lateral shoots with a heel between June and August. Insert in pots or pans of equal parts (by volume) peat and sand and place in a cold frame. When rooted, pot the cuttings singly in 3 in. pots of John Innes potting compost No. 1 and overwinter in a cold frame. Pinch out the growing tips to promote bushy growth. The following April set out in permanent positions.

Pests. Generally trouble-free.

Diseases. In hot summers, POWDERY MILDEW may coat the leaves with white meal.

LEAF SPOT causes minute white circular spots with purple margins on the foliage.

Helianthus

Sunflower. *Compositae*

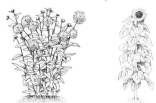

HELIANTHUS DECAPETALUS   HELIANTHUS ANNUUS
'LODDON GOLD'

A genus of 55 species of hardy annuals and perennials. Most are tall enough for planting in clumps at the back of wide borders. All the species described bear yellow daisy-like flowers, *H. salicifolius* in September and October, the remainder from late July to September.

Helianthus decapetalus 'Soleil d'Or'

H. annuus (sunflower). U.S.A. Height 3–10 ft; planting distance 12–18 in. An annual with mid-green heart-shaped leaves that are coarsely toothed. The flowers, 12 in. or more across, have large brown or purple discs and are borne singly. *H. a.* 'Flore Pleno' has double flowers.

Among a number of garden varieties, the following are recommended: 'Autumn Beauty', 3 ft, sulphur-yellow with a copper-bronze stain; 'Italian White', 4–5 ft, pale primrose; 'Mars', 5–6 ft, yellow with a dark brown disc; 'Russian Giant', 8–10 ft, large yellow.

H. atrorubens, syn. *H. sparsifolius.* U.S.A. Height 4–7 ft; planting distance 2–2½ ft. This perennial species has rough, hairy leaves that are mid-green and ovate. The flowers are 2 in. across; they have dark red discs, and are borne on purple stems. 'Monarch', 4–6 ft, bears semi-double golden flowers up to 6 in. across, in September.

H. cucumerifolius: see *H. debilis*

H. debilis, syn. *H. cucumerifolius.* N. America. Height 3 ft; planting distance 18 in. A bushy annual species with marginally toothed, ovate, glossy green foliage. The bright yellow flowers are 3 in. or more across. The variety 'Excelsior' is a mixed strain in shades of deep and pale yellow zoned with red and bronze. 'Sunburst' is a multi-hued strain derived from *H. annuus* crossed with *H. debilis*; the plants, which reach a height of 4 ft, bear 4–6 in. wide flowers in shades of yellow, red and purple, with darker basal zones.

H. decapetalus. U.S.A. Height 4–6 ft; planting distance 18–24 in. The mid-green, broadly ovate leaves of this perennial are rough and sharply toothed; the light yellow flowers are 2–3 in. wide.

Recommended varieties include: 'Capenoch Star', 4 ft, single, lemon-yellow; 'Loddon Gold', 5 ft, double, golden-yellow; 'Soleil d'Or', 4–5 ft, semi-double, golden-yellow; 'Triomphe de Gand', 4 ft, semi-double, golden-yellow.

Helianthemum nummularium 'Beech Park Scarlet'

Helianthemum nummularium 'Jubilee'

Helianthus annuus

Helianthus annuus 'Flore Pleno'

Helichrysum bracteatum 'Dwarf Spangle Mixed'

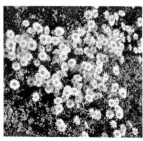

Helichrysum bellidioides

Helichrysum coralloides

H. orgyalis: see *H. salicifolius*

H. salicifolius, syn. *H. orgyalis*. U.S.A. Height 6–8 ft; planting distance 18–24 in. Long mid-green leaves, like those of a willow, cover the erect stems of this perennial. The golden-yellow flowers, 1½ in. across, are borne in sprays.

H. sparsifolius: see *H. atrorubens*

H. tuberosus: see Jerusalem artichoke

Cultivation. Both the annual and perennial species require well-drained garden soil in a sunny position. Support tall plants with stout canes or stakes; remove the dead flowers to prevent self-seeding.

Plant perennials in October, November or April. Cut down flowering stems almost to ground level in October or after flowering. Divide double varieties every third year, or they may revert to single forms.

Propagation. Sow seeds of both annuals and perennials during March or April in a sunny position outdoors. Sow annuals where the plants are to flower, setting two or three seeds in each station, later thinning to one seedling. Sow seeds of perennials in a nursery bed, pricking off the seedlings 6 in. apart and transplanting to their permanent positions in October.

Seeds of annuals may also be sown under glass in February or March at a temperature of 16°C (61°F). Grow the seedlings on in 3½ in. pots of John Innes potting compost No. 1; harden off in a cold frame and plant out in May.

Divide perennials between October and April and replant direct in permanent positions.

Pests. Generally trouble-free.

Diseases. GREY MOULD causes a rotting of the flowers in wet weather, the blooms becoming covered with a grey, velvety fungal growth.

SCLEROTINIA DISEASE causes a discoloration of the stems, which subsequently collapse. If cut open, the stems are seen to contain numerous large black resting bodies embedded in the white fluffy fungal growth.

Heliaporus smithii: see *Aporocactus flagelliformis*

Helichrysum

Everlasting or straw flower.
Compositae

HELICHRYSUM BRACTEATUM

A genus of 500 species of hardy and half-hardy shrubs, sub-shrubs, herbaceous perennials and annuals. These plants are suitable for sunny rock gardens and sheltered borders, preferably at the foot of a south wall. The shrubby and true alpine species are mainly cultivated for their attractive grey-green or white woolly foliage, the flowers being small and groundsel-like. Several of the alpines are best grown in an alpine house.

The annual species and a few of the perennial are suitable for borders. The showy daisy-like flowers of the annual species, with persistent chaffy bracts, are everlasting and much used i winter-flower arrangements.

ANNUAL SPECIES

H. bracteatum, syn. *H. macranthum*. Australia Height 3–4 ft; planting distance 12 in. A half-hardy annual, with mid-green lanceolat leaves. The orange, yellow or pink flowers, up t 2 in. across, are produced from July to September Varieties are available in a wide colour range including red, pink, yellow, white and orange

'Monstrosum' has larger, double flowers 'Nanum' is a dwarf form. 'Monstrosum Doubl Mixed' (height 2½ ft), and 'Dwarf Spangle Mixed (height 12 in.) are recommended forms, th latter being useful for troughs and window-boxe as well as for bedding out.

H. macranthum: see *H. bracteatum*

PERENNIAL AND SHRUBBY SPECIES

H. alveolatum: see *H. splendidum*

H. anatolicum: see *H. plicatum*

H. angustifolium (curry plant). S. Europe. Heigh 8–15 in.; spread 12–24 in. A half-hardy perennia or sub-shrubby species, grown for its foliage o silver-grey, narrow, needle-like leaves. It i covered with down and gives off a strong smell o curry. Small mustard-yellow flowers are borne ir clusters, 1–2 in. across, from June to August.

H. bellidioides. New Zealand. Height 3 in. spread 12 in. A half-hardy alpine species, suitable for a sunny rock garden, with matted, slende branching stems that form a prostrate shrublet It bears ovate leaves, dark green above, whit woolly beneath. Clusters, ¾ in. across, of white everlasting flowers appear from May to July.

H. coralloides. New Zealand. Height up to 10 in. spread up to 6 in. This half-hardy, upright branched shrublet is suitable for growing in ar alpine house. It is a striking foliage plant with small, scale-like, closely overlapping leaves. These are grey-green and woolly when young, glossy grey-green in the adult form. The tiny white flowers, which are rarely produced ir cultivation, are borne terminally.

H. marginatum: see *H. milfordiae*

H. milfordiae, syn. *H. marginatum*. S. Africa Height 2 in.; spread about 9 in. This half-hardy alpine species does not tolerate winter wet and i best grown in an alpine house. The soft silve oblong leaves form dense cushions. Crimson flower buds open to white flowers, 1 in. across, ir May and June.

H. orientale. S.E. Europe. Height and spread 12 in. A half-hardy foliage species, susceptible to winter wet and suitable for growing in an alpine house. It forms a mound of grey-felted obovate leaves and bears terminal clusters, 1½ in. wide of lemon-yellow flowers. These appear in Augus and September.

H. plicatum, syn. *H. anatolicum*. S.E. Europe Height 2–2½ ft; spread 2–3 ft. This half-hardy species forms a dense evergreen sub-shrub with slender, erect growths. It bears silver-grey, linea leaves and golden-yellow flowers crowded ir terminal clusters, 1½–2 in. wide. The flowers usually appear in July.

H. rosmarinifolium, syn. *Ozothamnus rosmarinifolium* (snow-in-summer). Victoria, Tasmania eight 6–9 ft; spread 2–5 ft. An erect evergreen shrub, of almost fastigiate habit and with white-felted stems; it is hardy only in the mildest areas. The linear leaves, which are closely set, are dark green above, white beneath. Round corymbs, up to 1 in. across, of small, white flowers, are borne in profusion at the ends of short lateral growths during June and July.

H. selago. New Zealand. Height and spread 6–9 in. This half-hardy, compact and wiry shrublet has closely overlapping, scale-like, silver-grey leaves. Off-white flowers, in clusters about 1 in. across, appear from June to August.

H. splendidum, syns. *H. alveolatum, H. triniatum.* S. Africa. Height at least 15 in.; spread up to 3 ft. This half-hardy shrub is generally too large for a rock garden, but it may be cut hard back each spring to form a neat mound of silver-grey, linear and downy foliage. Tiny yellow flowers are borne in closely packed globose terminal clusters, 1–1½ in. wide. They appear in July and August.

H. triliniatum: see *H. splendidum*

H. virgineum. Balkans. Height 9 in.; spread up to 9 in. A half-hardy shrubby species, best grown in an alpine house or on a sunny scree. The leaves are similar to those of *H. orientale,* but are densely coated with silvery wool. Cream-white flower clusters, of groundsel-like appearance and 1 in. across, open from silver-pink buds in May.

Cultivation of annual species. A light, well-drained soil in an open, sunny situation is recommended; rich soil encourages more flowers but reduces the strength of their colour. Plants from seeds sown in the open require cloche protection until frost is over. Dead-head to encourage flowering on side-shoots.

Flowers for winter decoration should be cut before they are fully open and showing the central disc. Tie them in bunches and hang them upside-down in a cool room or shed until they are dry. They become brittle if dried in bright sunshine.

Cultivation of perennial and shrubby species. These thrive in any ordinary, sharply drained soil in a sunny position; in areas subject to high rainfall, *H. milfordiae, H. orientale* and *H. virgineum* are best grown in pans in the alpine house. Plant all outdoor species between August and September or April and May in sheltered positions or at the foot of a south-facing wall. In severe winters, protect the roots with straw or bracken, and cover low-growing species with panes of glass or open-ended cloches.

Plants for the alpine house should be potted in September. Use 5–6 in. pots or 6–8 in. pans of 2 parts John Innes potting compost No. 1 and 1 part fine grit or coarse sand (parts by volume). Repot every second or third year in September.

Propagation of annual species. Sow seeds in pans of seed compost under glass in February or March at a temperature of 18°C (64°F). Prick out the seedlings into boxes and harden off in a cold frame before setting out in the flowering site in April or May.

Propagation of perennial and shrubby species. Take 1½–2 in. cuttings of lateral shoots of *H. coralloides* and *H. selago* and detach the small shoots of *H. milfordiae* and *H. bellidioides,* from April to July. Insert the cuttings or shoots in a mixture of 3 parts coarse sand and 1 part peat (parts by volume) in a cold frame. Pot when rooted, using 2½ in. containers of the growing mixture used for alpine-house culture. Overwinter in a cold frame and pot on or plant out the following April or May.

The shrubby species can be propagated from lateral shoots, 3 in. long and preferably with a heel, taken in July and August. Insert in the rooting mixture recommended for *H. coralloides* and pot, when rooted, into 3–3½ in. containers. Overwinter in a cold frame. Pot on into 4–5 in. pots the following May and plunge outdoors until transplanting to permanent positions in August or September.

Pruning. No pruning is necessary for *H. rosmarinifolius*; trim other shrubby species back to old wood in April.

Pests. Generally trouble-free.

Diseases. Patches of white fungal growth on the undersides of the leaves are caused by DOWNY MILDEW; yellowing of the leaves also occurs.

Helichrysum splendidum

Helictotrichon

Gramineae

A genus of 94 species of tender and hardy evergreen perennial grasses. One species only is in general cultivation and is suitable for planting in herbaceous and mixed borders.

H. sempervirens, syns. *Avena candida, A. sempervirens.* S.W. Europe. Height and spread 12–18 in. A hardy, densely tufted species with linear, somewhat arching leaves of an intense blue-grey. Loose panicles, about 6 in. long, of drooping, oat-like spikelets are produced in June and July on slender stems, up to 4 ft tall.

Cultivation. Plant at any time between October and April, in any ordinary, well-drained garden soil and in an open, sunny position. Remove faded flower stems in autumn.

Propagation. Divide and replant large plants between October and April.

Pests and diseases. Generally trouble-free.

Heliocereus

Cactaceae

A genus of three or four species of greenhouse perennials. These are branching and jointed, slender-stemmed, columnar cacti with crenated ribs bearing bristly spines. The large showy flowers are borne one at a time at any point on the stem; each flower lasts two or three days.

The following species are easy to cultivate; they can be grown as house plants if placed on a sunny window-ledge.

See also CACTUS.

H. amecaensis. Mexico. Height and spread 3 ft. The light green stems are up to 2 in. thick and prostrate or clambering. They have three to five ribs bearing short, white, bristle-like spines. The funnel shaped flowers are about 4–5 in. in diameter and have green outer petals and white inner petals. They appear from April to June.

H. cinnabarinus. Guatemala. Height and spread

Helictotrichon sempervirens

Heliocereus amecaensis

3 ft. The erect and spreading stems, about $\frac{3}{4}$ in. thick, branch from the base and produce aerial roots. The three or four ribs each bear ten white bristle-like spines at each areole. The funnel-shaped flowers, borne from April to June, are 6–7 in. in diameter; they have green outer petals, white inner petals and a rose-pink style.

H. speciosus. Mexico, Central America. Height and spread 3 ft. The clambering or prostrate stems are up to 2 in. thick and branch from the base. They are red when young, but later become bright green. The three to five ribs are markedly undulating. The felted areoles are about $1\frac{1}{2}$ in. apart and bear numerous needle-like yellow spines $\frac{1}{2}-\frac{3}{4}$ in. long.

The open funnel-shaped, scarlet flowers, which are 8 in. long and up to 6 in. across, remain open for several days; they appear in April and May. This species is often hybridised with *Epiphyllum.*

Cultivation. Heliocerei require a richer soil than desert cacti. Grow them in a compost of equal parts (by volume) loam, sand and well-decayed leaf-mould. Feed the plants with a liquid manure when the buds begin to develop. Never allow the soil to dry out entirely, but do not give much water in winter.

Pot the plants in March or April in 9–10 in. pots. They require the support of canes or they may be trained against the greenhouse wall.

Keep the plants in a bright, warm position all the year round; they require a winter temperature of 7–10°C (45–50°F). Move into larger pots at the beginning of the growing season if the roots fill the pots.

Propagation. Sow seeds in March at a temperature of 21°C (70°F). Alternatively, take 3–4 in. long softwood cuttings from June to August. Let the cut surfaces heal for a few days before potting the cuttings in the growing compost.

Pests. Tufts of white wax on young growths are due to MEALY BUGS.

Diseases. Generally trouble-free.

Heliopsis
Compositae

HELIOPSIS SCABRA

A genus of 12 species of annuals and herbaceous perennials. The perennials are border plants which associate well with monardas, phloxes, salvias, *Chrysanthemum maximum,* and the late-flowering delphiniums. The flowers are carried on erect branching stems.

H. scabra. N. America. Height 3–4 ft; planting distance 18–24 in. Both the stems and the mid-green lanceolate leaves of this hardy perennial are rough. The single, daisy-like yellow flowers, borne in July and August, are 3 in. wide. The following are good varieties:

'Gigantea', height 4–5 ft, semi-double,

Heliocereus speciosus

Heliopsis scabra 'Golden Plume'

Heliotropium × *hybridum*

golden-yellow flowers; 'Golden Plume', $3\frac{1}{2}$ ft double, rich yellow; 'Goldgreenheart', $3\frac{1}{2}$ ft double, lemon-yellow tinged with green in the centre; 'Incomparabilis', 3 ft, double, zinnia-like orange-yellow.

Cultivation. Plant between October and March in a sunny position in any ordinary garden soil. Cut down the flowering stems to ground level in October or November.

Propagation. Divide and replant the roots between October and April.

Pests and diseases. Generally trouble-free.

Heliotrope: see Heliotropium

Heliotropium
Heliotrope, cherry pie. *Boraginaceae*

HELIOTROPIUM × HYBRIDUM

A genus of 250 species of half-hardy and tender annuals and shrubs. Only a few shrubby species are in general cultivation and are represented by the evergreen hybrid race derived from *H. corymbosum* and *H. peruvianum.* They require cool greenhouse cultivation and may also be used in summer bedding schemes.

H. × hybridum. Garden origin. Height as a pot plant 12–18 in.; as a standard, 24 in. or more; spread 12–15 in. The oblong-lanceolate leaves are mid to dark green and finely wrinkled.

Fragrant, forget-me-not-like, small flowers are borne in corymbs, 3 in. or more across; they vary in colour from dark violet through lavender to white. The plants can be brought to flower at any time of year, but the usual flowering period is from May to October. There are a number of named forms, including 'Florence Nightingale', pale mauve; and 'Marina', violet-blue flower clusters up to 6 in. wide.

Recommended seed strains, which come true to type, are: 'Lemoine's Giant', a vigorous, large-flowered form with purple flowers, and 'Marguerite', with large heads of dark blue-purple flowers having a white eye.

Cultivation. Grow these plants in John Innes potting compost No. 2, in 4–6 in. pots or planted out in the border. Overwinter at a temperature of 7–10°C (45–50°F); for early flowering provide a temperature of 16°C (61°F) during winter. In the greenhouse, grow heliotropes in a well-lit position, lightly shaded in summer. Ventilate freely when the temperature exceeds 13°C (55°F). The atmosphere should be kept relatively humid by damping down during hot weather. Water freely during the summer and keep the plants just moist in winter. Repot or pot on annually in March; give a weak liquid feed at intervals of ten days from May to September.

In the border, large specimens of heliotrope may require the support of canes.

For outdoor bedding schemes, set out young plants grown as annuals or one-year-old standards. They thrive in any fertile, well-drained garden soil in full sun. Raise low-growing plants from 3–4 in. long cuttings, taken in September or the following February; insert in equal parts (by volume) peat and sand in a propagating frame with a temperature of 16–18°C (61–64°F). When rooted, box or pot up the cuttings singly into 3–3½ in. pots of John Innes potting compost No. 1 and plant out in late May.

For standard specimens, take 3–4 in. long cuttings in July and root as described for low-growing bedding plants. Place the rooted cuttings in 3½ in. pots of John Innes potting compost No. 1 and finish off in 5–6 in. containers. Begin training the young plants while they are still in their 3½ in. pots; stake each plant individually with a cane and pinch out all lateral shoots. Grow the plants to the desired stem height and then pinch out the growing tip at three to four leaves above the stem height to provide the main branches of the head. Pinch out the lateral branches when they have four or five leaves, to promote bushy growth. Harden off in a cold frame and plant out in late May.

Standards may be lifted in October, potted up in 5–6 in. pots or larger of John Innes potting compost No. 2 and grown on for a further year.

Propagation. Increase greenhouse plants by rooting cuttings as described for bedding plants under CULTIVATION.

Alternatively, sow seeds for bedding plants in February in pots or pans of John Innes seed compost. Germinate at a temperature of 16–18°C (61–64°F) and prick out the seedlings, when large enough to handle, into boxes of John Innes potting compost No. 1. Pinch out when 3 in. high to promote bushy growth; finer plants are obtained if potted up in 4 in. pots before hardening off and planting out.

Pruning. Cut free-standing shrubs in the greenhouse border back by half or two-thirds in February and March.

Standards, lifted in October, should have all growths shortened by half at potting time; lateral growths produced the following spring may need pinching out to promote branching.

Pests. In the greenhouse, GLASSHOUSE WHITEFLY may infest the undersides of leaves, making the plants sticky.

Diseases. Generally trouble-free.

H. manglesii, syn. *Rhodanthe manglesii*. Australia. Height 15 in.; spacing 6 in. This hardy annual is suitable for a herbaceous border and for a rock garden. The leaves are oblong and glaucous. Each stem carries a single red or white flower, 1½ in. across, with a yellow centre. The flowering period is from July to September. Good double-flowered varieties come in mixed colours from white to pink.

HELIPTERUM ROSEUM

H. roseum, syn. *Acroclinium roseum*. Australia. Height 15 in.; spacing 6 in. A hardy annual with narrow, pointed, grey-green leaves. Slender stems carry semi-double, rose-coloured flowers, 1 in. across, during July and August. Varieties, with larger flowers than the type, include 'Large Flowered Mixed', syn. 'Grandiflorum', with rose-pink and white flowers.

Cultivation. Helipterums are easy to grow on most soils, but do best on poor, sharply drained soil and in a sunny site.

Cut the flowers for drying before the petals are fully expanded and hang them upside-down in a cool, airy place.

Grow pot plants in John Innes potting compost No. 1, five to a 5 in. container.

Propagation. Sow the seeds in the flowering site in April and thin the seedlings to the required spacing. Direct sowing is preferable as helipterums do not always transplant well. However, seeds sown under glass in March, at a temperature of 16°C (61°F), may be grown on in boxes and hardened off in a cold frame before planting out in the flowering positions in May.

To raise plants for flowering under glass from May to July, sow the seeds in February or March in 5 in. pots containing John Innes potting compost No. 1; thin to leave five plants to a pot.

Pests. Young plants may be attacked by APHIDS.

Diseases. Generally trouble-free.

Hellebore, green: see *Helleborus viridis*
Hellebore, stinking: see *Helleborus foetidus*

Heliotropium × hybridum 'Marguerite'

Helipterum manglesii

Helleborus argutifolius

Helipterum

Compositae

A genus of 90 species of annual and perennial herbaceous plants, shrubs and sub-shrubs. Those described are annuals with daisy-like, straw-textured, everlasting flowers. They are suitable for borders or for growing in pots under glass.

H. humboldtianum. Australia. Height 18 in.; spacing 6 in. A hardy annual, useful for edging borders. This plant has narrow pointed leaves which are near-white and woolly-textured. The erect stems carry 3 in. clusters of fragrant yellow flowers from July to September. After drying, the flowers turn green.

Helleborus

Ranunculaceae

A genus of 20 species of hardy evergreen and deciduous perennials. These winter-flowering plants, suitable for mixed borders, are excellent for long-lasting cut flowers.

H. abchasicus. Caucasus. Height 12–18 in.; planting distance 18 in. The evergreen leaves are smooth, dark green, lanceolate and toothed. Cup-shaped purple flowers, green inside, and up to 3 in. across, open from January to March.

H. argutifolius, syn. *H. corsicus*. Corsica, Sardinia. Height and planting distance 24 in. The evergreen leaves are three-lobed, mid to pale

Helleborus atrorubens

Helleborus niger

Helleborus orientalis

Helxine soleirolii

green, and thick and spiny. Cup-shaped yellow-green flowers, up to 2 in. across, open in March and April.

H. atrorubens. S.E. Europe. Height 10 in.; planting distance 18 in. The deciduous leaves are dark green, broadly lanceolate and deeply lobed. Deep plum-purple, cup-shaped flowers, up to 2 in. across and with yellow anthers, open from January to March or April.

H. corsicus: see H. argutifolius

H. foetidus (stinking hellebore). Europe. Height and planting distance 24 in. An evergreen species with leaves that are narrowly lanceolate, dark shiny green and deeply cut. Crowded panicles of $\frac{1}{2}$–1 in. wide yellow-green flowers, often rimmed with purple, are borne from March to May.

H. niger (Christmas rose). Central and S. Europe. Height 12–18 in.; planting distance 18 in. This popular plant has evergreen leaves which are leathery and dark green and have seven to nine lobes. Saucer-shaped white flowers, $1\frac{1}{2}$–2 in. across, are produced from December to March. They have golden anthers. 'Potter's Wheel', 12 in. high, bears glistening white flowers, up to 5 in. across and with broad, overlapping sepals, from January to March. The leaves are glossier than those of the type species.

H. orientalis (lenten rose). Greece, Asia Minor. Height 18–24 in.; planting distance 18 in. In mild districts the broad, dark green leaves are evergreen. In February and March the slightly branched stems carry saucer-shaped cream flowers, freckled crimson within, and $1\frac{1}{2}$–2 in. across. This variable plant often produces flowers in shades of crimson, purple, pink and white.

H. purpurascens. Hungary. Height 9–12 in., spread 12–15 in. A deciduous species with mid-green palmate leaves cleft into five wedge-shaped, deeply lobed leaflets. The 2 in. wide bowl-shaped flowers, dull purple outside and green-purple inside, open during March and April.

H. viridis (green hellebore). Europe. Height 12 in.; planting distance 18 in. The deciduous leaves are pedate and dull green. Cup-shaped yellow-green flowers, up to 2 in. across, are produced during February and March.

Cultivation. Plant during October in partial shade and in deep, well-drained but moist soil. H. foetidus, in particular, thrives in shade. Once planted, hellebores should not be disturbed. Protect the opening blooms of H. niger with cloches from December onwards.

Propagation. Sow seeds when ripe, usually in June or July, in boxes or pans of sandy soil, and place them in a cold frame. Prick off the seedlings into a nursery bed; they will be ready for planting out in their permanent positions in the autumn of the following year and should flower when they are two to three years old.

Divide the roots of H. atrorubens in October, those of H. niger and H. orientalis in March.

Pests. Generally trouble-free.

Diseases. The leaves are prone to LEAF SPOT which shows as round or elliptical black blotches. Diseased leaves wither and die.

Helxine

Urticaceae

A genus containing only one species. This is a creeping, half-hardy perennial foliage plant, suitable as ground cover. It may also be grown in a cool greenhouse or as a house plant.

H. soleirolii (mind your own business, baby's tears). Corsica. This species is correctly known as *Soleirolia soleirolii*. It is a prostrate plant with pink stems that root as they grow. The densely set, rounded leaves are pale to mid-green.

H. s. 'Argentea' is silver-variegated; *H. s.* 'Aurea' has golden-green foliage.

Cultivation. Grow in ordinary garden soil and in sunny or moist and shady conditions where waterlogging will not occur. Outdoors it may be scorched by frost, and may be killed in extremely severe winters, although some parts usually survive. In a cool greenhouse it is evergreen. It grows wild in many parts of the British Isles.

Grow in a greenhouse or in the home, setting the plants in 4–6 in. or larger pans containing John Innes potting compost No. 1. Overwinter at a temperature of 4–7°C (39–45°F) in the greenhouse; provide slight shading during summer. Water freely from April to September, less frequently during winter. The plants may be potted on in April, but they are best raised and treated as annuals.

Propagation. Detach rooted stem pieces at any time from April to September, preferably in the first two months of that period. Set the plantlets directly into their growing positions outdoors or in pans of the growing compost.

Pests and diseases. Generally trouble-free.

Hemerocallis

Day lily. *Liliaceae*

HEMEROCALLIS FULVA

A genus of 20 species of hardy herbaceous perennials. They form clumps of arching, strap-shaped, pale to mid-green leaves and, in summer

Hemerocallis 'Cartwheels'

ear lily-like trumpet-shaped flowers. Numerous
ybrids are available in a wide range of colours.

. citrina. China, Japan. Height 3½ ft; planting
istance 2–3 ft. Lemon-yellow flowers, 4–5 in.
ide at the mouth, appear in July and August.
hey are slightly fragrant.

. fulva. Japan, Siberia. Height 3 ft; planting
istance 2–3 ft. Red, apricot-tinged flowers,
½ in. across, are borne from June to August.

. thunbergii. Japan. Height 3 ft; planting dis-
ance 2–3 ft. Sulphur-apricot flowers, 3–4 in.
cross, are produced in July and August.

ARDEN HYBRIDS These are 2½–3 ft high
nd require a planting distance of 18 in. The
owers, borne from June to August, measure
–7 in. across. Good forms include:

'Black Magic', ruby-purple with a yellow
hroat; 'Cartwheels', large, bright golden-yellow
owers which open out almost flat; 'Golden
Orchid', orange-yellow; 'Hornby Castle', dull
rick-red; 'Hyperion', large, pure yellow;
Marion Vaughn', pale yellow with a green
hroat; 'Morocco Red', maroon-red with a yellow
hroat; 'Pieces of Eight', rich tan-yellow; 'Pink
Damask', warm pink with a yellow throat; 'Pink
relude', pink; 'Stafford', bright red.

ultivation. Plant between October and April in a
unny or lightly shaded position in good soil.
fter planting, leave them undisturbed. Cut the
tems almost to ground level after flowering.

ropagation. Divide and replant the roots be-
ween October and April.

ests and diseases. Generally trouble-free.

---

emlock: see Tsuga
emlock, eastern: see *Tsuga canadensis*
emlock, mountain: see *Tsuga mertensiana*
emlock, western: see *Tsuga heterophylla*
emp, African: see *Sparmannia africana*
emp agrimony: see Eupatorium

Hepatica

Ranunculaceae

 genus of ten species of hardy, woodland,
artially evergreen herbaceous plants, formerly
lassified under *Anemone*. They flower in early
pring, and are especially suited to shady corners
n rock gardens. All the species described have
i-lobed mid-green leaves.

H. angulosa: see *H. transsilvanica*

H. × media 'Ballard's Variety'. Height 6 in.;
spread 6–10 in. This hybrid between *H. triloba*
and *H. transsilvanica* carries anemone-like soft
lavender-blue flowers, each 1 in. across, from
February to April.

H. nobilis: see *H. triloba*

H. transsilvanica, syn. *H. angulosa*. Rumania.
Height 4 in.; spread up to 12 in. The saucer-
shaped flowers, 1 in. across, are a pale mauve-
blue and open from February to April.

H. trifolia: see *H. triloba*

H. triloba, syns. *H. nobilis, H. trifolia*. Europe,
Asia, America. Height 3–4 in.; spread up to 12 in.
This is the common hepatica which flowers from
February to April. It bears single anemone-like
flowers, ¾–1 in. across. The plant is variable
and has several named colour forms, including
plants in shades of white, red and purple. The
double forms are attractive and there is also a rare
white form in cultivation.

Cultivation. Plant hepaticas in September,
October or after flowering, either in sun or,
preferably, in partial shade. They thrive in soil
that contains lime, provided it has peat or
leaf-mould added to it.

Propagation. Divide the plants in August or
September and replant directly in soil that
contains leaf-mould or peat.

Pests. Generally trouble-free.

Diseases. Two fungi may cause LEAF SPOTS; tiny
black pin-head structures may be seen on
affected areas.

Heracleum

Umbelliferae

HERACLEUM MANTEGAZZIANUM

A genus of 70 species of hardy herbaceous
biennials and perennials. The one described is a
large, coarse plant, unsuitable for herbaceous
borders but ideal for growing beside large ponds
or in wild gardens.

H. mantegazzianum. Caucasus. Height 10–12 ft;
planting distance 4–6 ft. A biennial or short-lived
perennial species with mid-green leaves, 3 ft
long, that are unequally lobed and deeply cut.
The stout fluted stem is spotted and blotched
with purple-red. White starry flowers are borne
in numerous spherical umbels, up to 18 in. wide,
during July and August.

Cultivation. Plant during suitable weather
between October and March in a sunny or
partially shaded position in deep, moist soil. Cut
the stems to ground level after flowering.

Propagation. Sow seeds in the open in March or
April. Transplant the seedlings into a nursery bed
in May or June and plant out in permanent
positions from October onwards.

Pests and diseases. Generally trouble-free.

Hemerocallis 'Marion Vaughn'

Hemerocallis 'Pink Damask'

Hemerocallis 'Pink Prelude'

Hepatica triloba

Heracleum mantegazzianum

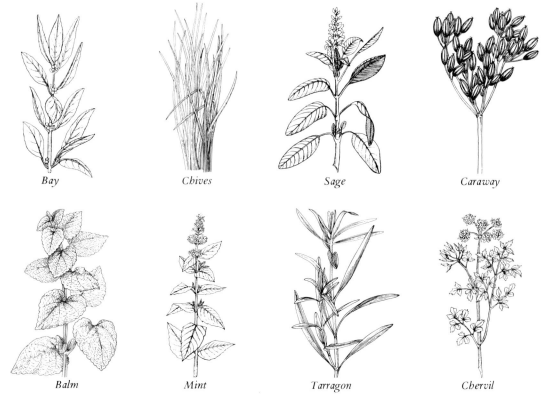

Bay   Chives   Sage   Caraway

Balm   Mint   Tarragon   Chervil

Clary

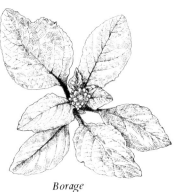

Borage

HERBS

These annual, perennial and shrubby plants are chiefly grown for their culinary uses, although they often make attractive specimen plants in mixed borders. In most gardens, a small plot can be set aside for growing a few choice herbs.

Generally, herbs need a light, fertile, well-drained soil and full sun. They can be grown in odd corners in the garden but, if space allows, a herb garden is a convenient and attractive way of grouping them.

Ideally, the site should be in a south-facing position and on a slight slope. Beds should be planned so as to make access easy to each group of plants, placing tall-growing varieties at the back where they do not overshadow smaller ones; keep herbs which thrive in moist soil at the base of the slope.

Many herbs can also be grown in window-boxes, and in pots on outside window-sills. Use John Innes potting compost No. 1 or 2, with a layer of crocks at the bottom to ensure good drainage. Keep the compost just moist during the growing season. The window-sill should preferably face south or west so that the plants receive direct sunshine for the greater part of the day.

The culinary uses of herbs are mentioned under the individual entries. Generally, the best flavour is imparted by using fresh herbs, which will keep for a limited period in completely dry and airtight containers. For winter use, herbs must be dried or frozen. Certain evergreen herbs, such as chives and dill, are not suitable for drying and should be frozen or the plants potted up for growing indoors.

The time of harvesting varies according to whether the herbs are being grown for their leaves, flowers, seeds or stems. Plants grown for their leaves and stems should be gathered in the young leaf stage before flowering begins. Harvest flower heads when in full bloom, and seeds when the pods ripen and begin to turn yellow or brown.

Choose a dry day for harvesting the herbs, and gather them early in the day before the sun becomes hot, but after morning dew has vanished. Handle the sprigs of leafy shoots carefully to avoid bruising. Large leaves may be stripped off the stems before drying, but small leaves are better left on the sprigs. Discard all damaged and discoloured leaves and, if necessary, wash the remainder gently in cool water. Spread the leaves or sprigs thinly in flat shallow containers, ideally on cheesecloth-covered frames which will allow air to circulate. Place the containers in a dry, warm and airy place, out of sunshine. An airing cupboard or the warming drawer of a cooker is suitable if there is reasonable ventilation. Leave for at least four or five days, turning the herbs once a day. They are ready for storing when they have become brittle and rattle slightly when touched.

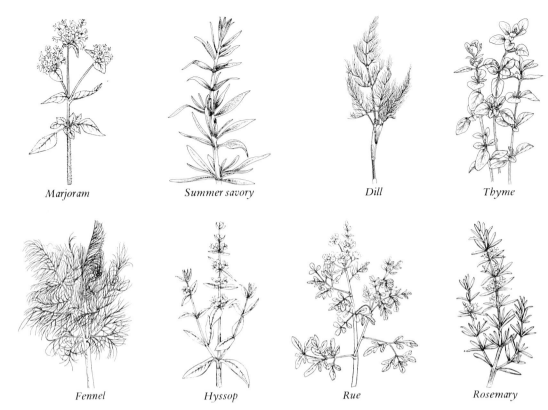

Marjoram *Summer savory* *Dill* *Thyme*

Fennel *Hyssop* *Rue* *Rosemary*

Alternatively, tie sprigs into small bunches and hang upside-down in a shaded, dry, warm and airy place. These will take a little longer to dry out completely. It is possible to dry herbs more quickly in front of a fire or in the oven at low heat, but some of the flavour and aroma will be lost.

The leaves should be completely dry before storing permanently. Check this by keeping them in clear glass containers for a week and examining them daily for signs of moisture on the glass. If this occurs, turn the leaves out on trays and dry for a few more days.

When completely dry, large-leaved herbs should be stripped from the stems. Small-leaved, fine-stemmed herbs, such as rosemary and thyme, retain their flavour better when stored whole and crumbled before use. Discard as much chaff as possible and pack the leaves or sprigs into small, preferably opaque containers; clear jars should be stored in a dark place. Seal and label each container immediately.

Herbs, both dried and frozen, may be stored separately according to variety, or mixed in suitable combinations. It is often time and labour-saving to make up herb bouquets, tied in muslin bags, at the time of drying.

The procedure for drying flower heads and seed pods is the same. Loosen the seeds by rubbing the dried heads or pods between the palms of the hands until the seeds drop out. If possible, do this out-doors in a slight breeze which will blow off some of the chaff. Dry the seeds for another week or so, stirring them gently once a day. Check for moisture as before and store in the same way as leaves.

Freezing is an excellent method of preserving herbs such as chervil and parsley, which have tender leaves unsuitable for drying. Gather and wash the herbs and place them in an enamel colander. Blanch the herbs by immersing the colander in boiling water for one minute, then plunge into cold water. Leave until thoroughly cold, drain well and freeze immediately, storing them in small plastic bags, kitchen foil or waxed cartons.

Frozen herbs need not be thawed for use in soups and stews, and can be chopped more easily while still frozen. Once thawed, they lose their crispness and are better used for flavouring than for garnishing. Do not refreeze.

Apart from their culinary uses, dried herbs may be used to make sachets, *pot-pourris* and pomanders, which give off a long-lasting fragrance in rooms, airing cupboards, drawers and linen closets. Lavender sachets are well known, but many other herbs and flowers make pleasant mixtures. Particularly fragrant mixtures include: lemon thyme with verbena; any fragrant-leaved geranium with rosemary; lavender, rosemary and a few cloves with a piece of orange or lemon zest; and equal parts of peppermint, lemon verbena, lemon balm, rose geranium and rose petals.

Angelica

Garlic

Hesperis
Cruciferae

A genus of 30 species of hardy herbaceous biennials and perennials. The perennial species described tends to be short-lived.

HESPERIS MATRONALIS

H. matronalis (damask violet, sweet rocket). S. Europe, W. Asia. Height 2–3 ft; planting distance 18 in. A species with dark green lanceolate leaves and 18 in. long spikes of white, mauve or purple flowers, which give off a fragrance in the evening. The flowers are cross-shaped, with oblong petals, and open in June. 'Candidissima', 15 in., is a dwarf white variety; 'Purpurea', 2–3 ft, is purple.

Cultivation. Plant between October and March in a sunny position in moist, sandy loam. Remove the flowering spikes after flowering.

Propagation. Sow seeds thinly during April in a sunny position in open ground. Prick off the seedlings into a nursery bed in May or June.

Plant out in the autumn. Divide the roots during suitable weather between October and March. If left undisturbed, *H. matronalis* and its varieties will usually increase by self-sown seedlings, but the varieties will not breed true.

Pests and diseases. Generally trouble-free.

Heuchera
Coral flower. *Saxifragaceae*

HEUCHERA SANGUINEA

A genus of 50 species of hardy herbaceous perennials. They provide good edging for borders, ground cover beneath deciduous trees, and decorative cut flowers.

H. sanguinea. Mexico, Arizona. Height 12–18 in.; planting distance 18 in. The dark green heart-shaped or round leaves are evergreen. Slender stems carry 6–9 in. panicles of tiny, bright red, bell-shaped flowers from June to September. The species is less attractive than the modern hybrids and varieties, of which the following are recommended:

'Bressingham Blaze', deep coral-flame; 'Pretty Polly', rose-pink; 'Pearl Drops', white; 'Red Spangles', blood-red; 'Scintillation', pink, tipped with coral; 'Splendour', salmon-scarlet; 'Sunset', bright red. All these are 18–24 in. high, and need a planting distance of 9–12 in.

Cultivation. Plant between October and April in either a sunny or partially shaded position in light, well-drained soil. Avoid heavy clay. Remove the stems after flowering. Should the crowns of old plants tend to rise out of the ground, either mulch them or, in March or April every third year, lift, divide and replant them more deeply.

Propagation. Sow seeds during March or April in seed compost in a cold frame. When the seedlings are large enough to handle, prick them off into boxes, later into a nursery bed. Plant out in permanent positions from October onwards.

Divide and replant roots of named varieties between October and April.

Pests. Generally trouble-free.

Diseases. A mass of abortive and often split shoots at ground level is caused by LEAFY GALL.

Hibiscus
Malvaceae

A genus of 300 species of hardy and tender annuals, evergreen and deciduous shrubs and small trees. Three tender evergreen species are in general cultivation and in Great Britain require greenhouse treatment; they may also be grown as house plants. The hardy species described are suitable for annual or mixed borders.

The flowers are widely funnel-shaped; they are showy but short-lived.

ANNUAL SPECIES

H. trionum (flower-of-an-hour). Africa. Height 2½ ft; spacing 12 in. A hardy species with dark green, ovate, coarsely toothed leaves. The flowers measure up to 3 in. across and are cream-white to pale yellow with bright maroon-chocolate centres. They appear continuously from August to September, and each flower is followed by an inflated bladder-like calyx bearing the seed capsule. The flowers open for only a few hours in the morning, but seeds now offered by some seedsmen produce plants with blooms that remain open most of the day.

GREENHOUSE SPECIES

H. mutabilis. China. Height and spread 6 ft or more. A shrub or small tree with angular, heart-shaped, mid-green and slightly downy leaves. The flowers, which last for one day only, are produced singly from the upper leaf axils on slender 2 in. stems. They are 4 in. across, white or pale pink on opening and change to deep red as the day advances. As a pot plant the species reaches a height of 3 ft.

H. rosa-sinensis. China. Height and spread 6 ft. This species bears dark green, broadly ovate, coarsely toothed and sometimes shallowly lobed, pointed leaves. The 5 in. wide flowers are borne from June to September in the upper leaf axils; they are short-lived, but produced in great numbers. In the type species they are single and deep crimson, but double and semi-double forms of hybrid origin with yellow, pink and salmon flowers are available.

The variety 'Cooperi' has smaller crimson flowers and narrower leaves, variegated with cream and crimson.

H. schizopetalus. E. Africa. Height up to 10 ft

Hesperis matronalis

Heuchera sanguinea

Hibiscus trionum

spread 8 ft. A weak-branched shrub, best grown against a wall or trained up under the greenhouse roof. It has elliptic to ovate mid-green leaves. The pendulous flowers, 3 in. across, are orange-red; the petals are reflexed and cut into a deep fringe.

SHRUBBY SPECIES

HIBISCUS SYRIACUS

H. syriacus, syn. *Althaea frutex*. Syria. Height 6–10 ft; spread 4–6 ft. This hardy, deciduous species forms a much-branched shrub with erect growths. The rich green ovate leaves have rounded teeth and are usually three-lobed. The flowers, 3 in. across, are borne singly in the upper axils of the young shoots. They are produced in succession from July to October and vary from white, through pink and red, to purple.

Named forms include: 'Ardens', double flowers, rose, tinted violet; 'Blue Bird', mid-blue with large red centre; 'Coeleste', deep blue; 'Dorothy Crane', pure white with crimson centre; 'Elegantissimus', double, white with maroon centre; 'Hamabo', blush-white with crimson centre; 'Jeanne d'Arc', compact, double, white.

'Mauve Queen', mauve with maroon centre; 'Monstrosus', white with maroon centre; 'Violaceus Plenus', double, wine-red; 'Woodbridge', rich rose-pink deepening at the centre; and 'W. R. Smith', white with crinkled petals.

Cultivation of annual species. Grow in any ordinary, well-drained garden soil, in a sunny site. If the plants are allowed to seed and the soil is left undisturbed, self-sown plants may appear the following year.

Cultivation of greenhouse species. Under glass, grow hibiscus in John Innes potting compost No. 2 or 3, or in a proprietary peat compost, preferably in the greenhouse border or in 8–12 in. pots or tubs. The smaller-growing *H. rosa-sinensis* 'Cooperi' may be grown in a 5 in. pot and kept in the home. Overwinter the plants at a temperature of 7–10°C (45–50°F); *H. schizo-petalus* does better at 10–13°C (50–55°F).

The plants, and particularly the variegated types, retain their foliage and remain colourful throughout the winter months if the compost is kept moist, and if a temperature of about 16°C (61°F) can be maintained.

If high temperatures cannot be maintained, keep the plants just moist in winter; they will probably lose most of their leaves. When growth restarts in March, give water in increasing amounts. Place in full light, but shade the glass lightly on hot summer days; ventilate the house when the temperature exceeds 21°C (70°F).

Repot or pot on annually in March or early April, and give a weak liquid feed at fortnightly intervals from May to September.

Cultivation of shrubby species. The species *H. syriacus* and its varieties thrive in any well-drained, fertile soil. Plant from October to

Hibiscus rosa-sinensis

March in a sheltered border in full sun. As these shrubs are late-flowering, it is advisable to give them wall protection in northern gardens.

Propagation of annual species. Sow the seeds in the flowering site in April, and thin out the seedlings to the appropriate spacing.

For larger and earlier-flowering plants, sow under glass in pots or pans of seed compost during March, at a temperature of 13–16°C (55–61°F). Prick off the seedlings, when large enough to handle, into boxes and harden off in a cold frame before planting out in early May.

Propagation of greenhouse species. Take 3–4 in. cuttings of firm lateral shoots, preferably with a heel, at any time between April and August. Insert in equal parts (by volume) peat and sand in a propagating case at 18°C (64°F). When rooted, pot the cuttings singly in 3–3½ in. pots of John Innes potting compost No. 2, and pot on as necessary. Pinch out the growing points of the young plants two or three times to encourage bushy growth.

Propagation of shrubby species. Take heel cuttings, 3–4 in. long, of half-ripe lateral, non-flowering shoots in July. Insert the cuttings in equal parts (by volume) peat and sand in a propagating case at a temperature of 16°C (61°F). When rooted, pot the cuttings singly in 3 in. containers of John Innes potting compost No. 1 and overwinter in a cold frame. The following May, pot on into 4 in. pots and plunge outdoors until planting out in October.

Pruning. In March, prune pot-grown specimens hard back to 6 in. Plants grown in the greenhouse border should be kept within bounds by shortening all lateral shoots to within 3 in. of the old wood and removing the upper third of leading shoots in early spring.

Hibiscus syriacus 'Dorothy Crane'

No regular pruning of outdoor shrubs is needed, but long shoots may be shortened immediately after flowering.

Pests. Young shoots, flower buds and flowers may be infested with APHIDS which foul them with sticky excretions.

MEALY BUGS form conspicuous tufts of white waxy wool on the stems and leaves of greenhouse plants.

Diseases. Too-dry soil conditions or low night temperatures may cause BUD DROP.

Yellowing of the leaves of greenhouse plants is due to a PHYSIOLOGICAL DISORDER. Small black spots appear on the leaves and premature leaf-fall may occur.

Hippeastrum 'American Express'

Hippeastrum 'Bouquet'

Hippeastrum (hybrid)

Hippeastrum

Amaryllidaceae

HIPPEASTRUM AULICUM

A genus of tropical and sub-tropical bulbs with 75 species which are related to, and often sold as, *Amaryllis*. Hippeastrums are less hardy than amaryllis and require the protection of a greenhouse, conservatory or warm room. They are excellent plants for growing indoors and, with careful timing, a succession of bulbs can provide colour for most of the year.

All grow from large bulbs, with strap-shaped mid to deep green leaves. The one or two stout flower stems carry one or more large trumpet or funnel-shaped flowers.

The numerous varieties that have been raised by many years of breeding are among the boldest of greenhouse flowers.

H. × ackermannii. Height 18–24 in. An old hybrid probably raised from a cross between *H. aulicum* and another hybrid. Deep red, 5–6 in. long flowers appear in winter and spring.

H. aulicum. Brazil, Paraguay. Height 18 in. A winter-flowering species producing usually two, sometimes three or four, flowers. Each is 5–6 in. long, and red with a green base and purple blotch.

H. candidum. Argentina. Height 2–3 ft. The drooping, scented flowers, 5–6 in. long, are white tinged with green or yellow. The leaves grow at the same time as the flowers, in the summer.

H. equestre. S. America and naturalised in other tropical regions. Height 1½–2½ ft. The leaves develop fully after flowering. This is a variable species, with 4–5 in. long flowers in many shades of red, appearing in winter and spring. It is sometimes confused with *Amaryllis belladonna*.

H. reticulatum. Brazil. Height 12–24 in. This plant has white-striped leaves; pink-striped flowers, 3 in. long, appear in the autumn. It requires rather warm conditions.

H. rutilum. Brazil, Venezuela. Height 12 in. Several flowers, up to 4 in. long, appear in spring. They are in shades of red, with green streaks.

Hippeastrum 'Candy Cane'

Hippeastrum 'Nivalis'

H. vittatum. Peru. Height 2½–3 ft. The leaves are 24 in. long, appearing after the flowers. In the spring it produces 5 in. long white flowers with red stripes.

HYBRIDS

These hippeastrums (height 12–18 in.) can be bought in un-named mixtures or as named varieties in true colours, including white, pink, red and near orange; also with striped or frilled flowers and large overlapping petals. They carry three or four flowers on one or two stout stems.

Recommended named varieties include 'American Express', deep lustrous crimson-scarlet; 'Bouquet', salmon-pink, eyed and veined with scarlet; 'Candy Cane', white, flushed and streaked with crimson; 'Nivalis', white with a yellow-flushed throat; 'Prima Donna', crimson flushed with white in bud.

Cultivation. Bulbs of the winter and spring-flowering group planted in September or October will flower from February onwards, depending on the temperature at which they are grown. They need a minimum temperature of 13–16°C (55–61°F). Specially treated bulbs can be bought and will flower in the New Year after November planting. Pot the summer and autumn-flowering pecies in early spring and grow at the same emperature. All need a cycle of watering and eeding before flowering, and a rest period of three months before watering and growth is restarted.

Plant one bulb in a 5–7 in. pot of John Innes potting compost No. 2, leaving half the bulb exposed. Give a little water until signs of growth appear at the top of the bulb; the flower bud shows either before or soon after the leaves, at which time water more freely. Feed weekly with liquid manure during the growing season. The leaves continue to develop after flowering and require more water and liquid manure until they begin to turn yellow. Then withhold water until the leaves die off, and keep the bulb and soil dry until restarting growth.

Repotting is not necessary each year, although the surface soil may be replaced just before watering recommences.

Propagation. Seeds saved from the hybrids produce mixed results, but the species come true to type unless cross-pollination occurs. Sow seeds when ripe, or in March, in pots or boxes, with the seeds spaced 1 in. apart; just cover with fine compost and keep shaded at a temperature of 16–18°C (61–64°F) until germination begins.

Keep the seedlings warm and well watered until large enough to prick out singly into 2½ in. pots. Pot on as the roots fill the pots and do not let the plants dry out until after the first flowering; this will be in three or more years, according to the amount of warmth and plant food given.

Pests. The bulbs may be infested by TARSONEMID MITES, feeding between the scales and causing severe malformation of the flowers, combined with extensive scarring and red discoloration of the leaves.

THRIPS and GLASSHOUSE RED SPIDER MITES may cause similar symptoms.

MEALY BUGS may infest bulbs and leaves.

Diseases. A PHYSIOLOGICAL DISORDER due to unsuitable cultural conditions may cause a check to growth; red blotches may develop on the leaves, flower stalks and bulbs.

TOMATO SPOTTED WILT VIRUS causes numerous pale yellow or white spots, either isolated or coalesced into pale patches on the leaves. Numerous blood-red spots and pale spots may appear along the leaf edges. Leaves turn yellow.

Hippophae
Elaeagnaceae

HIPPOPHAE RHAMNOIDES

A genus of three species of hardy deciduous shrubs, chiefly grown for their attractive berries.

H. rhamnoides (sea buckthorn). Europe, temperate Asia. Height and spread 8–10 ft. A bushy shrub which may sometimes attain tree proportions, up to 30 ft. The brown-scaled branches are clothed with sharp spines and linear silvery leaves. Inconspicuous yellow flowers are borne in April on separate plants. If male and female plants are grown together, the female plants bear small, round, bright orange berries which thickly cluster the branches during autumn and winter. The berries contain an intensely acrid juice and are generally shunned by birds.

Cultivation. These are easily grown plants in any well-drained, ordinary garden soil. They thrive in sandy areas by the sea and make excellent coastal shrubs or suitable windbreaks in exposed areas. Plant in a sunny or partially shady position from October to February in groups that include both sexes. One male plant can pollinate six or more female plants.

For hedges, set young plants 18–24 in. apart; for windbreaks, 4–5 ft apart. After planting, remove the upper third of all shoots to promote bushy growth.

Propagation. Sow seeds as soon as ripe, generally in October, in pans of John Innes seed compost, and place in a cold frame. Prick off the seedlings, when large enough to handle, into boxes and later into nursery rows. Grow on until the autumn and transplant to permanent positions.

Pruning. No regular pruning is required, but cut back long straggly growths during July and August. Trim hedges in August.

Pests and diseases. Generally trouble-free.

Hoheria
Malvaceae

HOHERIA GLABRATA

A genus of five species of evergreen and deciduous shrubs, native to New Zealand. These flowering plants are not generally hardy, but the following species will survive most winters in the south and west of Great Britain. The broadly funnel-shaped flowers are usually freely borne.

H. glabrata, syn. *Plagianthus lyallii.* Height 10–15 ft; spread 8–10 ft. A deciduous species of upright habit, with dull green cordate-ovate leaves having jagged teeth. The pure white sweet-scented flowers, 1½ in. across, are borne in June and July in axillary clusters.

H. lyallii, syn. *Plagianthus lyallii ribifolia.* This deciduous species is almost identical to *H. glabrata,* but the leaves are grey and downy, and the flowers appear in August.

H. sexstylosa. Height 10–15 ft; spread 6–10 ft. An evergreen species of upright habit and with slender growths, hardier than the other species described. The shiny leathery leaves are grey-green, sometimes yellow-green, lanceolate and prominently toothed. White flowers, 1 in. across, with conspicuous stamens, are freely borne in axillary clusters during July and August. 'Pendula' is a weeping form.

Hippeastrum 'Prima Donna'

Hippophae rhamnoides
(berries)

Hoheria glabrata

Holodiscus discolor

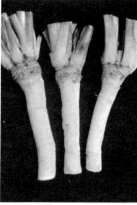

Horseradish

Hosta elata

Cultivation. Hoherias thrive in any good, well-drained garden soil. Plant in April or May in sun or partial shade and in a position sheltered from cold winds. Hoherias make good wall shrubs on south or south-west facing walls.

Propagation. Sow seeds in March or April in pans of seed compost and germinate at a temperature of 13–16°C (55–61°F). Prick off the seedlings, when large enough to handle, singly into 3 in. pots of John Innes potting compost No. 1; pot on as necessary into 4–5 in. pots during the summer. Overwinter the young plants in a cold frame and plant out the following April or May.

Alternatively, layer long shoots in September and sever from the parent plants one year later.

Pruning. Cut out dead and damaged wood and shorten straggly growths in March or April. At the same time thin out overgrown wall shrubs.

Pests and diseases. Generally trouble-free.

Holly: see Ilex
Holly, common: see *Ilex aquifolium*
Holly, English: see *Ilex aquifolium*
Holly, hedgehog: see *Ilex aquifolium* 'Ferox'
Hollyhock: see Althaea
Holly, Maori: see *Olearia ilicifolia*
Holly, sea: see *Eryngium maritimum*
Holly, weeping: see *Ilex aquifolium* 'Pendula'

Holodiscus

Rosaceae

HOLODISCUS DISCOLOR

A genus of eight species of hardy deciduous flowering shrubs, formerly included in *Spiraea*. Only one species is in general cultivation.

H. discolor. W. North America. Height 6–12 ft; spread 4–8 ft. This species, of spreading graceful habit, has arching branches with broadly ovate, almost lobed leaves that are mid-green above, downy white beneath. The minute, cream-white, star-shaped flowers, borne in wide, arching panicles, 8 in. long, appear in July. The form most commonly seen is *H. d. ariaefolius*, which has grey-green leaves.

Cultivation. These shrubs are easily grown in any ordinary garden soil which does not dry out during summer. Plant in a sunny position during October and November or in March.

Propagation. Take cuttings, 3–4 in. long, of lateral shoots, preferably with a heel, in August; insert the cuttings in equal parts (by volume) peat and sand in a cold frame. The following May, line out the rooted cuttings in nursery rows outdoors and grow on until October when they can be planted out in their flowering positions.

Pruning. None required.

Pests and diseases. Generally trouble-free.

Honesty: see Lunaria

Honey locust: see *Gleditschia triacanthos*
Honeysuckle, common: see *Lonicera periclymenum*
Honeysuckle, giant: see *Lonicera hildebrandiana*
Honeysuckle, goat-leaf: see *Lonicera caprifolium*
Honeysuckle, Japanese: see *Lonicera japonica*
Honeysuckle, scarlet trumpet: see *Lonicera × brownii*
Hookera coronaria: see *Brodiaea coronaria*
Hornbeam: see Carpinus
Hornbeam, American: see *Carpinus caroliniana*
Hornbeam, common: see *Carpinus betulus*
Horse chestnut: see Aesculus
Horsemint: see Monarda

Horseradish

Cochlearia armoracia. Cruciferae

A hardy long-lasting perennial, grown for its edible roots. It reaches a height of 24 in. and has large, rough, dark green leaves. In early summer small, white, four-petalled, cross-shaped flowers are produced. The long tap root has a pungent peppery flavour and is used grated and mixed with cream as a condiment to meat, fish and salads or for flavouring sauces.

Cultivation. Horseradish thrives in any ordinary well-drained garden soil and in sun or partial shade. The long roots are difficult to eradicate and horseradish should be grown as a perennial in a corner where it can be left undisturbed, or as an annual.

Dig and manure the bed during winter. In February purchase roots (known as thongs), about 9–12 in. long and finger-thick. Plant vertically 12 in. apart in rows at intervals of 18 in. the top of the thong should be about 2 in. below the soil surface. Lift the roots as required during the summer; in early winter lift the remainder and store in boxes of soil or sand for winter use.

Pests. Generally trouble-free.

Diseases. ARABIS MOSAIC VIRUS causes brown spots on the leaves of old plants. A different virus may show as a severe mosaic on the leaves of plants which become stunted.

LEAF SPOT is due to several fungi. It most often shows as pale white spots on the leaves; affected tissues fall out, giving a SHOTHOLE appearance.

WHITE BLISTER shows as glistening white pustules on the leaves.

Hosta

syn. **Funkia**. Plantain lily. *Liliaceae*

A genus of 20 or more species of hardy herbaceous perennials. Hostas are grown for their attractive foliage and racemes of nodding trumpet-like flowers; they are suitable for shady borders, in woodland and for waterside planting. They provide excellent ground cover and, once established, can be left undisturbed for years.

H. albomarginata. Japan. Height and planting distance 15–18 in. This species resembles *H. lancifolia* in habit, but bears somewhat smaller leaves, margined white. The funnel-shaped, 2 in.

Hosta undulata

Hosta crispula

tance 18 in.) has pale green young leaves that are broadly variegated with buff-yellow; they turn glaucous-green by flowering time. 'Aureomarginata' resembles the type species, but each leaf has a narrow gold margin.

H. f. gigantea: see *H. elata*

H. glauca: see *H. sieboldiana*

H. lancifolia. China, Japan. Height and planting distance 24 in. The narrow, lanceolate, glossy mid-green leaves of this species grow in neat mounds. Pale lilac flowers, 1½ in. long, are produced from July to September.

H. plantaginea. China, Japan. Height 18–24 in.; planting distance 2–2½ ft. A species with heart-shaped, glossy yellow-green leaves. Fragrant white flowers, 4–5 in. long, open during August and September.

H. rectifolia, syn. *Funkia longipes*. Japan. Height 3–3½ ft; planting distance 2–2½ ft. The broadly lanceolate, dark green leaves are carried erect. Violet-mauve flowers, 2 in. long, are freely borne on slender spikes in July.

HOSTA SIEBOLDIANA

H. sieboldiana, syn. *H. glauca*. Japan. Height and planting distance 24 in. The broadly lanceolate to ovate leaves of this species are glossy and mid-green and strongly veined. Off-white flowers, tinged with purple and 1½ in. long, are produced in August. 'Elegans' bears pale lilac-coloured flowers in July and August, and has glaucous leaves.

H. undulata. Japan. Height and planting distance 24 in. This species bears wavy oblong leaves that are mid-green with white or silvery markings. Pale lilac-coloured, funnel-shaped flowers, 2 in. long, are carried in August.

H. u. erromena has slightly darker flowers and plain mid-green leaves. 'Medio-variegata' has light green leaves variegated with yellow in the centre; mauve flowers are carried in 12 in. spikes.

H. ventricosa. E. Asia. Height 3 ft; planting distance 24 in. A vigorous reliable species with broadly ovate, glaucous leaves. The violet-mauve funnel-shaped flowers, 1½–2 in. long, are freely produced in July and August.

H. v. 'Variegata', slightly shorter than the type species, has dark green leaves strikingly variegated with yellow.

Cultivation. Plant hostas at any time during suitable weather from October to March, in sun or partial shade in any well-drained but moisture-retentive soil enriched with leaf-mould, peat or well-rotted compost. Variegated plants retain their colouring better when grown in partial shade.

Propagation. Hostas may be raised from seeds, but those with variegated foliage do not come true. Division is the best method. Divide and replant the crowns in March as growth begins.

Pests. SLUGS may feed on the leaves.

Diseases. Generally trouble-free.

long flowers, which appear in July and August, are lilac with violet stripes.

H. crispula. Japan. Height and planting distance 24 in. A species with broadly lanceolate, long-pointed, dark green leaves with prominent white margins. Lilac-purple flowers, up to 2 in. long, are borne in August.

HOSTA CRISPULA

H. elata, syn. *H. fortunei gigantea*. Japan. Height up to 3 ft; planting distance 18 in. A robust species that forms mounds of dark green, somewhat glossy foliage; each leaf is ovate-elliptic and wavy-margined. Racemes of white to pale blue-violet flowers, each 2–2½ in. long, are carried on slender, rigid stems, well above the foliage, in June and July.

H. fortunei. Japan. Height 2–3 ft; planting distance 18 in. The long-stalked, grey-green, boldly veined leaves are ovate with a heart-shaped base. Lilac flowers, 1½ in. long, are produced in July.

'Albopicta' (height 18–24 in.; planting dis-

Hosta fortunei 'Albopicta'

Hosta fortunei 'Aureomarginata'

Hosta sieboldiana

Hound's tongue: see Cynoglossum
Houseleek: see Sempervivum

Houstonia

Bluets. *Rubiaceae*

HOUSTONIA CAERULEA

A genus of 50 species of hardy evergreen perennial plants suitable for growing in cool, moist corners of rock gardens.

H. caerulea. Virginia. Height 3 in.; spread 12–18 in. The true species is seldom seen; the plant in cultivation listed under this name is correctly *H. serpyllifolia*. It resembles chickweed, forming bright green carpets of lanceolate-spathulate leaves. Numerous milk-blue, star-shaped, four-petalled flowers, $\frac{1}{3}$–$\frac{1}{2}$ in. across, are borne from April to July. 'Millard's Variety', a sturdier plant, has deeper blue flowers.

H. serpyllifolia: see *H. caerulea*

Cultivation. Plant in March or April in moist, lime-free soil, preferably in a semi-shaded, north-facing position.

Propagation. Divide the plants in March or April, or immediately after flowering, and replant direct in permanent positions.

Pests and diseases. Generally trouble-free.

Houstonia caerulea

Houttuynia cordata 'Plena'

Howea forsteriana

Houttuynia

Saururaceae

HOUTTUYNIA CORDATA

The genus consists of a single species of hardy herbaceous perennial which thrives in any cool, moist soil in light shade and will also grow in wet soil or shallow water. In ideal conditions it may be invasive.

H. cordata. China and Japan. Water depth 1–2 in.; height 12–18 in.; planting distance 9–12 in. The branching stems of this species are produced singly from underground runners and eventually cover a wide area. Erect bright red stems bear pointed heart-shaped leaves, blue-green and rather metallic in appearance.

The terminal flower heads are erect cones, $\frac{1}{2}$–$\frac{3}{4}$ in. high, with four rounded pure white bracts held horizontally at the base. The whole plant has a tangy aroma.

The variety 'Plena' has double flower heads composed of numerous white bracts.

Cultivation. Choose a soft moist soil in dapple shade. Plant in March, April, September or October. If planting dormant runners, place these horizontally 3 in. deep; put in plants from pots a pot depth only. No other attention is required but keep the plants within bounds if they spread too rapidly.

Propagation. Increase by division during March, April, September or October. Pot pieces of the underground stem, each with a growing point or developed shoot, into 3–4 in. pots of John Innes potting compost No. 1 and grow on until well rooted. Alternatively, plant the pieces directly in new growing positions.

Pests and diseases. Generally trouble-free.

Howea

Palmae

A genus of two species of palms grown as greenhouse and house plants. The genus was formerly known as *Kentia* and the species may be listed as such in catalogues. The height and leaf sizes given here are those common under greenhouse or home cultivation.

H. belmoreana. Lord Howe Islands. Height up to 10 ft; spread 6–8 ft. The dark green pinnate leaves, carried on 18 in. long stems, are 18 in. long and 12 in. across. They consist of numerous linear-lanceolate leaflets.

H. forsteriana. Lord Howe Islands. Height up to 10 ft; spread 6–8 ft. This is the species most frequently seen in cultivation. The leaves differ from those of *H. belmoreana* only in having drooping, and fewer, leaflets.

Cultivation. Grow the plants in John Innes potting compost No. 3. The ideal winter temperature is 10–12°C (50–54°F), the minimum 7°C (45°F). In the greenhouse, give full light in winter, moderate shade in summer. Water sparingly between November and March, plentifully from April to July and moderately from July to October.

Give house plants as much light as possible in winter. Pot on every second year in April or early May, finishing house plants in 8–10 in. pots; in the greenhouse they may be continued in tubs. Feed the plants once a fortnight with liquid manure from April to September in years when they are not potted on.

Propagation. In February, place the large seeds on the surface of pans filled with peat; germinate at a temperature of 27°C (81°F). Pot the seedlings singly, when the first leaf is fully developed, in $2\frac{1}{2}$–3 in. pots of John Innes potting compost No. 1, and keep at a temperature of 18°C (64°F) until they are well established.

Pruning. Cut out all dead leaves.

Pests and diseases. Generally trouble-free.

Hoya

Asclepiadaceae

A genus of 200 species of evergreen, chiefly climbing or trailing plants. They are grown for their ornamental foliage and attractive flowers.

hey are suitable for greenhouse cultivation, and variegated forms of *H. carnosa* are also popular as house plants.

H. bella. India. Height 9–12 in.; spread 15–18 in. A twiggy sub-shrub with slightly pendulous branches. The fleshy ovate leaves are pale green, sometimes with silvery spots. The white waxy flowers, in 2 in. wide umbels that emerge from the leaf axils, are fragrant and star-shaped with a rose-crimson or purple centre. The plant may flower at any time from May to September.

HOYA CARNOSA

H. carnosa. Queensland. Height up to 20 ft. A vigorous climber that adheres by means of aerial roots. The ovate fleshy leaves are mid-green.

The species has a curious habit of forming the whole stem of the new growth before any leaves develop. Fragrant, white to flesh-pink, star-shaped flowers are borne in axillary umbels, 3 in. or more wide; they appear from May to September. Often a second crop of flowers will follow on the same flower stalk. The plant rarely blooms before it is two years old.

There are two variegated-leaf forms: one has pink margins that fade to cream, the other gold centres and dark green margins.

Cultivation. Hoyas grow best in a compost containing plenty of peat, such as John Innes potting compost No. 2 or in a proprietary peat mixture. *H. bella* will survive at a winter temperature of 10°C (50°F), but will be stronger at 13°C (55°F). *H. carnosa* requires 10°C (50°F), but will tolerate 7°C (45°F). Give both species a minimum temperature of 16°C (61°F) in spring and summer. Shade the glass lightly in summer for *H. carnosa*, heavily for *H. bella*.

During winter, keep the plants on the dry side, but give them all the light available. Place *H. bella* in a raised position or in a hanging basket so that the pendulous flowers can be appreciated.

Maintain a humid atmosphere throughout spring and summer, and admit fresh air whenever possible. Syringe the leaves in hot weather. Repot in late spring. Give the plants a feed of liquid manure at three-weekly intervals in summer.

H. bella will grow and flower in a 5 in. pot, but is better grown in a 10 in. hanging basket; *H. carnosa* should be in a 10–12 in. pot, but it will do better if planted out in the greenhouse border. Grown in the house it should be in a 5–6 in. pot and trained round a support of canes or wire.

Propagation. Take cuttings, 2–3 in. long, of young shoots of *H. bella* in June. Insert the cuttings in equal parts (by volume) peat and sand and root at a temperature of 16–18°C (61–64°F).

Propagate *H. carnosa* by cuttings, 3–4 in. long, of mature stems in June or July and treat as *H. bella*. This species may also be increased by layering in April or May.

Pruning. No pruning is necessary. Pinch out the growing tips as soon as the young plants are established to promote branching. Overgrown plants of *H. carnosa* can be cut back, but are slow to recover and they are better replaced.

Pests. Generally trouble-free.

Diseases. A PHYSIOLOGICAL DISORDER, usually due to over-watering, causes the leaves to turn brown.

Humble plant: see *Mimosa pudica*

Hyacinth, common: see *Hyacinthus orientalis*

Hyacinth, feather: see *Muscari comosum* 'Monstrosum'

Hyacinth, floating water: see *Eichhornia speciosa*

Hyacinth, grape: see Muscari

Hyacinth, Roman: see *Hyacinthus orientalis albulus*

Hyacinth, summer: see Galtonia

Hyacinth, tassel: see *Muscari comosum* 'Monstrosum'

Hyacinth, water: see Eichhornia

Hyacinth, wild: see *Endymion nonscriptus*

Hyacinthus

Liliaceae

HYACINTHUS ORIENTALIS

The hyacinths grown in such numbers in homes, gardens and nurseries every winter have all sprung from one hardy species, the tall and elegant *Hyacinthus orientalis*. Some 30 other species are found growing around the eastern Mediterranean and in Africa, but few are in general cultivation and these are more suitable for rock gardens or alpine houses.

However, the species described are available from specialist nurserymen. They have strap-shaped mid-green leaves, and spikes of bell-shaped flowers. The spikes are compact, one to a bulb, except those of the Roman hyacinths, which are loose and grow two or three to a bulb.

H. amethystinus. Spain, France, Yugoslavia. Height 8 in.; planting distance 3–8 in. The stem carries up to 12 drooping flowers, pale blue with violet bracts, in a 1½–2 in. high spike in April and May. It seeds freely. 'Albus' is a white form.

H. azureus. Asia Minor. Height 8 in.; planting distance 3–8 in. The tightly packed, 1–1½ in. high spike of pale blue flowers is produced in February and March. This species is sometimes mistaken for *Muscari* (grape hyacinth).

H. candicans: see *Galtonia candicans*

H. orientalis (common hyacinth). E. Europe, W. Asia. This species is no longer generally grown, but is represented in cultivation by its larger-flowered hybrids commonly known as Dutch hyacinths. Height and planting distance 6–9 in. The flower spikes are 4–6 in. long. Several varieties are in cultivation in a wide range of colours. Skilled production and special storage conditions enable most of these to flower from

Hoya carnosa

Hyacinthus orientalis albulus

Hyacinthus orientalis 'City of Haarlem'

Hyacinthus orientalis 'Jan Bos'

Hyacinthus orientalis 'Delft Blue'

Hyacinthus orientalis 'Queen of the Blues'

before Christmas until May. The following list includes some of the best for forcing and for outdoor bedding:

White: 'Carnegie'; 'L'Innocence'; 'Madam Sophie', double.

Yellow: 'City of Haarlem', primrose; 'Prince Henry', cream-yellow; 'Yellow Hammer', cream; 'Orange Boven', salmon-orange.

Pink and red: 'Amsterdam', salmon-red; 'Chestnut Flower', double pale pink; 'Eclipse', double dark red; 'Jan Bos', cerise-pink; 'Lady Derby', shell-pink; 'Pink Pearl', pink; 'Princess Irene', pink; 'Tubergen's Scarlet', deep pink.

Blue: 'Amethyst', lilac-mauve; 'Bismark', clear blue; 'Delft Blue', soft blue; 'General Kohler', double lavender-blue; 'Myosotis', sky-blue; 'Ostara', deep purple-blue; 'Queen of the Blues', pale azure-blue.

H. o. albulus (Roman hyacinth). Height 6 in.; planting distance 6–9 in. White, pink and blue-flowered varieties are available. They can be flowered from December to May.

Cultivation. The production and preparation of hyacinths has become so specialised that gardeners and non-specialist nurserymen do best to purchase bulbs from specialist nurseries. Treat the bulbs as recommended.

Potted in August or September, the treated bulbs of the smaller Roman hyacinths and of the large-flowered varieties will flower before Christmas. Untreated bulbs will flower later; pot in succession from August to October and bring into warmth and light as they are ready.

For details of growing hyacinths and other bulbs in bowls and pots, see entry under BULBS, INDOOR. After flowering, forced hyacinths can be planted 6 in. deep outside during March or April in odd corners, and can be expected to recover and flower again. Keep the ground free of weeds and remove the dead stalks and foliage at the end of the season. If left undisturbed they will continue to flower year after year.

For a spring bedding display, plant hyacinths 5–6 in. deep in the autumn after the summer-flowering plants have been removed. Plant the bulbs 6 in. apart if they are to flower alone, a few inches further apart if they are sharing the ground with other plants. Dig up after flowering and replant in a position where they can remain untouched to flower again, in the same way as the forced potted bulbs.

The small species, such as *H. amethystinus* and *H. azureus,* may be grown in a rock garden or at the front of a border, or in pans in the alpine house. Plant them in September or October, 2–3 in. deep and apart.

Propagation. All hyacinths can be raised from seeds sown soon after they ripen. Sow thinly in boxes of John Innes seed compost in a cold frame or cold greenhouse. Leave the seedlings undisturbed for the first year; then space them out in boxes or plant them out in nursery rows.

The species will usually come true and flower in two or three years. The large-flowered varieties will not come true and will take from three to six years to flower, the chances of obtaining a plant better than existing varieties being slight. All the named varieties are raised from bulbils, obtained by a special technique carried out by professional growers.

Pests. The tissues are sometimes invaded by STEⱯ AND BULB EELWORMS, which cause discoloratio and rapid decay of the leaves and flowers.

NARCISSUS FLY MAGGOTS tunnel in the tissues the bulbs. APHIDS may infest leaves and flowers.

Diseases. The bulbs may be affected at the nos by GREY BULB ROT, causing a dry grey rot whic prevents the shoots getting far above ground. dense fungal growth soon destroys the bulbs an quickly produces large resting bodies, whic contaminate the soil and infect other bulbs th following year.

PHYSIOLOGICAL DISORDERS of many types occu particularly on forced bulbs. Incorrect lifting storing or forcing can cause browning of one more florets; complete fracturing of the stem below the flower truss, known as LOOSE BUD at a comparatively early stage of growth; poo development of roots or even complete lack roots; and irregular growth.

Discoloration of the foliage and poor develop ment of the flowers are usually due t unsuitable cultural conditions.

SOFT ROT, due to bacteria, shows as a soft, slim and evil-smelling rot of the leaves and bulbs it often begins in the inflorescences when floret have withered due to a physiological disorder.

STORAGE ROT infects the bulbs. The scales, sometimes complete bulbs, rot and becom covered with a blue mould.

A VIRUS DISEASE shows as pale chlorotic spot and stripes on the leaves, which may b crumpled, twisted and drooping. Few flowers ar formed, and these are smaller than those healthy plants.

Hydrangea
Hydrangeaceae

A genus of 80 species of deciduous and evergree flowering shrubs and climbers. The specie described, with the exception of *H. integerrima* are all deciduous. They are hardy in the south an west and make admirable shrubs for tow gardens and mild maritime areas; elsewhere the may require greenhouse cultivation. The decidu ous climbing species are generally hardier.

The small star-shaped flowers are borne i wide terminal corymbs or panicles on th previous year's growths; the inner fertile floret are usually surrounded by sterile outer florets.

The climbing species are of branching habit and attach themselves to walls, fences or tre trunks by aerial roots.

H. acuminata: see *H. macrophylla serrata*

H. altissima: see *H. anomala*

H. anomala, syn. *H. altissima*. Himalayas, China Height 35 ft or more. This vigorous climber bear smooth, ovate to elliptic, mid-green leaves. Fla 7–8 in. wide corymbs of white flowers ar produced in June. It needs a south or west wall a similarly sheltered position.

H. arborescens. N.E. America. Height and sprea 4–6 ft. A fully hardy shrub of loose habit, wit bright green leaves that are ovate and pointed The dull white flowers are borne in flat corymbs 4–6 in. across, from July to September; they fade to bronze-brown. The variety 'Grandiflora' ha

rge pure white flowers, all sterile, borne in solid
ounded clusters that often cause the stems to
oop by their weight.

This species, with its varieties, is a good
ubstitute for *H. macrophylla* in areas where the
tter is not hardy.

H. aspera. China, Himalayas. Height and spread
p to 8 ft. A shrubby species occasionally
eaching tree-like proportions. It comes into
rowth early in the year and is not suitable for
ardens subject to late spring frosts. The leaves
re variable in shape, from lanceolate to ovate,
nely toothed and rich dull green above, grey
owny beneath. Corymbs, 4–12 in. across, are
omposed of inner fertile porcelain-blue florets
nd outer sterile lilac-pink florets. They appear in
une and July.

H. hortensis: see *H. macrophylla*

H. integerrima. Chile. Height 20 ft or more;
pread 6 ft or more. A self-clinging evergreen
limber with glossy, dark green, broadly ovate
eaves. Lateral stems, often pendulous in old
pecimens, bear dense domed panicles, 2–3 in.
vide, of cream-white flowers in June and July.

In colder parts of the country this species
hould be grown against a sheltered south or
vest-facing wall.

H. involucrata. Japan. Height and spread 4–6 ft.
A spreading shrub with broadly ovate, slender-
pointed, mid-green leaves. The broadly dome-
haped flower heads are 3–5 in. across; they are
omposed of numerous, tiny, fertile florets of blue
or pink, and larger sterile florets of white or palest
blue. Immature flower heads are surrounded by
ip to six ovate, leafy bracts. Flowering is in
August and September.

HYDRANGEA MACROPHYLLA
HORTENSIA (POTPLANT)

H. macrophylla, syns. *H. hortensis*, *H. opuloides*
(common hydrangea). China, Japan. Height and
spread 4–6 ft, in mild areas up to 12 ft. This
species forms a rounded shrub with broadly
ovate, coarsely-toothed leaves that are shiny and
ight green. The flowers are borne in flat corymbs,
6 in. or more wide. They appear from July to
September and vary in colour from pink to blue.

The variety *H. m. serrata*, syn. *H. acuminata*, is
smaller (height and spread 3–5 ft). The slender
upright shoots bear ovate or lanceolate slender-
pointed mid-green leaves which often take on
purple or wine-coloured shades in autumn. The
corymbs, 2–2½ in. across, are composed of pink,
lilac or white fertile florets surrounded by usually
blue sterile florets.

Garden forms of this variety include 'Blue
Bird', with blue fertile and sterile florets; 'Grays-
wood', with blue fertile florets and white sterile
florets that become rose-pink and finally crimson;
'Intermedia', with pink sterile florets; and
'Rosalba', with blue fertile florets and white
sterile florets, turning crimson.

Hydrangea macrophylla serrata 'Intermedia'

There are numerous named varieties of the
type species, divided into two groups: the
Hortensia group with round corymbs or mop
heads, 5–8 in. wide, composed chiefly of sterile
single or double florets; and the Lacecap (or
Normalis) group with flat heads, 4–6 in. across,
of inner fertile florets surrounded by sterile
florets. On some soils, particularly those of an
alkaline nature. almost all the blue varieties turn
pink or red-purple, while on acid or neutral soils
pink varieties may turn blue or purple.

HYDRANGEA MACROPHYLLA HORTENSIA

HORTENSIA: 'Altona', large cherry-pink or
mid-blue; 'Ami Pasquier', dwarf habit, deep red
or light blue; 'Deutschland', deep rose-pink or
mid-blue; 'Domotoi', double pale pink or blue;
'Europa', large serrated petals, deep pink or pale
blue; 'Générale Vicomtesse de Vibraye', bright
rose-pink or sky-blue; 'Goliath', small heads
with large florets, clear pink or purple-blue;
'Hamburg', deep rose or deep blue.

'Kluis Superba', compact habit, light rose-red
or deep blue; 'Madame E. Mouillière', tender,
white becoming pink-tinted; 'Niedersachsen',
pink or pale blue; 'Parsifal', deep rose-red or
violet-purple; 'Westfalen', rich crimson-red or
deep purple-blue.
LACECAPS: 'Blue Wave', vigorous grower, pink
or blue; 'Lanarth White', compact habit, white
with blue or pink centres; 'Mariesii', rich pink or

Hydrangea integerrima

Hydrangea involucrata

Hydrangea macrophylla
'Générale Vicomtesse
de Vibraye'

Hydrangea macrophylla 'Deutschland'

Hydrangea macrophylla 'Blue Wave'

Hydrangea paniculata
'Grandiflora'

Hydrangea petiolaris

blue; 'Tricolor', foliage variegated in shades of green, silver and cream, pink or blue flowers; 'White-Wave', large white.

H. opuloides: see *H. macrophylla*

H. paniculata. China, Japan. Height and spread 12–15 ft. This species is a hardy shrub with arching, flowering shoots. The mid-green leaves are ovate and pointed. The flowers are freely produced in erect, pyramidal, terminal panicles, 6–8 in. long, during August and September; they are white, ageing to pink.

The species is largely represented by the variety 'Grandiflora', which produces massive panicles up to 18 in. long; 'Praecox' is a smaller shrub, flowering six weeks earlier; the cream-white panicles are up to 10 in. long.

HYDRANGEA PETIOLARIS

H. petiolaris, syn. *H. scandens* (Japanese climbing hydrangea). Japan. A hardy vigorous climber which may reach a height of 60 ft or more when planted at the base of a tree with rough bark. It does well on a north or north-east wall or as a screening plant. The serrated leaves are ovate with a pointed apex; they are rich dark green above, pale green and downy beneath. Flat corymbs, 7–10 in. across, of cream-white flowers are freely produced in June.

H. quercifolia. S.E. United States. Height up to 6 ft; spread 4–6 ft. A shrub of loose habit, with broadly ovate dark green leaves that have three to seven sharp lobes. The foliage often assumes autumn tints. The flowers are white and appear in erect terminal panicles, 4–12 in. long, in July. The sterile outer florets often turn purple as they fade.

H. sargentiana. China. Height and spread up to 10 ft. A shrub of upright, sparse habit and with shoots that are densely covered with stiff bristly hairs. The ovate, pointed leaves are deep green above, pale green and bristly beneath. Flat corymbs, 6–10 in. across, of rose-lilac florets are borne in July and August; they are surrounded by sterile white florets tinged with pink.

H. scandens: see *H. petiolaris*

H. villosa. China. Height 6–9 ft; spread 6–12 ft. A rounded shrub with hairy, angular shoots. The ovate to oblong-lanceolate leaves are long and slender-pointed, dull green and bristly above, grey and downy beneath. The pale purple corymbs, which appear in August, are 6 in. across; they are borne terminally and in the leaf axils.

Cultivation. Plant hydrangeas in October and November or in March and April in good loamy soil that is moisture-retentive and previously enriched with well-decayed manure, compost or peat. They are best grown in a sheltered position, against a wall or hedge or beneath a canopy of high trees. The tender young growths are easily damaged by late spring frosts, and hydrangeas should not be grown in positions where morning sun after night frost may damage the growths.

Hydrangeas thrive in sun or partial shade with the exception of *H. sargentiana*, which does best in deep shade, and *H. villosa* which is best in partial shade. Young climbing plants take two or three years to become established.

The blue garden varieties of *H. macrophylla* will not produce good blue flowers on alkaline soils. Dress the soil liberally with peat and apply substances such as sequestrene or aluminium sulphate annually. Pink varieties of the same species tend to be less clear or take on purple hues when grown on acid soils; dress the roots with 2 oz. of ground limestone per sq. yd annually to preserve the pink colours.

All hydrangeas, particularly *H. paniculata* benefit from an annual mulch of well-decayed manure, applied in April.

For pot culture, grow well-branched specimens in 6 in. pots of John Innes potting compost No. 2 or 3 (a single-stemmed plant may be grown in a 4 in. pot); omit lime in the compost for blue varieties. Start the plants into growth in January or February at a temperature of 7–10°C (45–50°F); keep them moist until they are in full leaf, then water liberally. Pot-grown hydrangeas are seldom kept for more than one season; after flowering, plant out in a sheltered position in the garden. If they are to be grown on, cut all shoots back to two good pairs of leaves and pot on into an 8 in. container. Stand the pot plants in a cold frame until growth is restarted.

Propagation. Increase climbing species by 3 in. cuttings from vigorous young side growths taken during June or July; insert the cuttings in equal parts (by volume) peat and sand in a cold frame or greenhouse. When rooted, pot the cuttings singly in 3½ in. pots of John Innes potting compost No. 2 and plunge outdoors until planting out in October.

Propagate hardy shrubby species by 4–6 in. cuttings of strong non-flowering shoots taken in August or September. Insert the cuttings in peat and sand, preferably in a propagating case with a bottom heat of 13–16°C (55–61°F), although they may be rooted in a cold frame. When rooted, pot the cuttings singly in 3½ in. pots of John Innes potting compost No. 2 and overwinter in a cold frame. The following April or May line the young plants out in nursery rows and grow on until planting out in the autumn.

For pot-grown specimens pot on the cuttings successively until they are in the final 6 in. pots; pinch out the growing points when three pairs of leaves have formed, to promote bushy growth. Single-headed plants are increased by tip cuttings, 4 in. long, taken in September and rooted and potted on as already described.

Pruning. Most species require no regular pruning except to remove dead flower heads after flowering or in March. Remove weak and damaged shoots in February or March.

Cut back the previous year's flowering shoots of *H. arborescens* and *H. paniculata* by half in February or March. Thin out at ground level two or three-year-old flowered shoots of *H. macrophylla* to promote new shoots.

Pests. Generally trouble-free, but APHIDS may feed on stems and foliage.

Plants under glass may be infested by GLASSHOUSE RED SPIDER MITES.

Diseases. Very alkaline soil conditions cause CHLOROSIS, which shows as a yellowing between the veins, or the leaves may be almost white.

HONEY FUNGUS may cause the death of shrubs.

Hydrangea, common: see *Hydrangea macrophylla*

Hydrangea, climbing: see *Hydrangea petiolaris*

Hymenocallis

Amaryllidaceae

A genus of 50 species of tender and half-hardy, evergreen and deciduous, bulbous-rooted perennials, sometimes confused with *Pancratium*.

The species described here are best grown as greenhouse pot plants; their times of flowering vary according to the temperatures available. *H. × festalis* is hardy enough to overwinter outdoors in sheltered sites in the south and west, but must be protected against frosts.

The scented flowers are somewhat daffodil-like, the cup or trumpet, sometimes with fringed or toothed margins, being formed of the stamen filaments which have become flattened and fused. Each bulb produces a clump of arching, mid-green, strap-shaped leaves, and a single sturdy leafless stem terminating in a flower umbel.

HYMENOCALLIS HARRISIANA

H. amancaes, syn. *Pancratium amancaes*. Chile and Peru. Height 18–24 in. A deciduous species with cream-white to yellow flowers, 4–5 in. across; these appear in April if raised in a warm greenhouse, in late summer in a cool house.

H. calathina, syn. *Pancratium calathinum*. Peru. Height 24 in. or more. This deciduous species is now correctly known as *H. narcissiflora*. White flowers, 4–6 in. across, are borne in March and April in a warm house, during June and July in a cool greenhouse.

H. × festalis. Garden origin. Height 18 in.; planting distance 12–15 in. This strong-growing, deciduous and half-hardy species is strictly a bigeneric hybrid between *H. calathina* and *Elisena longipetala*; it is usually included in *Hymenocallis*. It may be planted outdoors in sheltered spots in the south and west. White, 4–5 in. wide flowers with long, narrow, reflexed petals are borne from April to June under heated glass, a month or two later outdoors.

H. harrisiana. Mexico. Height 9–12 in. This species is deciduous, with arching, oblong-lanceolate, mid-green leaves. Erect flowering stems bear umbels of 6–8 in. wide pure white flowers during June and July.

H. × macrostephana. Garden origin. Height 12–18 in. A semi-evergreen hybrid between *H. calathina* and *H. speciosa*. The flowers are white and measure 5–7 in. across; they appear during April and May in a warm greenhouse, during July and August in an unheated house. 'Advance' is a slightly larger form with more thickly textured, pure white flowers.

H. narcissiflora: see *H. calathina*

Cultivation. Plant from November to January in 6–8 in. pots of John Innes potting compost No. 2. The neck of each bulb should be just above the surface of the compost. For early flowers, maintain a temperature of 13–16°C (55–61°F); for later flowering the greenhouse need only be kept frost-free, at 3–5°C (37–41°F).

Give a dilute liquid feed at fortnightly intervals from April to August and shade the greenhouse lightly during the hottest months of the year. Water freely during the growing season; in winter keep the compost just moist except for the

Hydrangea quercifolia

Hydrangea villosa

Hymenocallis amancaes

Hymenocallis × festalis

evergreen *H. × macrostephana*, which should be kept moist at all times. Remove the leaves of the deciduous and evergreen species as they die.

Repot or pot on every second or third year in April; in other years, top-dress with compost.

Outdoors, plant *H. × festalis* from pots during late May, in any ordinary, well-drained garden soil; choose a sheltered site in full sun. Protect in winter with a layer of bracken, coarse sand or weathered ashes.

Propagation. Remove any offsets at repotting time, and pot them singly in 3 in. pots of the growing compost. Pot on as necessary; they will reach flowering size in two or three years.

Pests. Conspicuous tufts of white, waxy wool on the leaves are produced by MEALY BUGS.

Diseases. Generally trouble-free.

Hymenocallis × macrostephana

Hypericum calycinum

Hypericum

St John's wort. *Hypericaceae*

HYPERICUM POLYPHYLLUM

A genus of 400 species of herbaceous perennials and deciduous and evergreen shrubs and sub-shrubs. The following species are mainly ever-green; they are suitable for a shrubbery, as ground cover in borders and on banks or rock gardens. The dwarf species, such as *H. coris* and *H. olympicum*, are also suitable for growing in an alpine house. Although hardy, they may be short-lived in cold areas, but are valued for their late-summer and autumn flowers. These are in shades of yellow, cup-shaped, often opening out flat, and have a central boss of golden stamens.

H. calycinum (rose of Sharon, Aaron's beard). S.E. Europe, Asia Minor. Height 12–18 in.; spread indefinite. A vigorous erect sub-shrub, forming a dense carpet by means of stolons. The ovate-oblong leaves are bright green above, somewhat glaucous beneath. Golden-yellow flowers, up to 3 in. across with conspicuous stamens, are borne singly, occasionally in pairs, at the ends of the shoots from June to September.

H. coris. S. Europe. Height 6 in.; spread 12 in. This perennial species is suitable for a rock garden and grows best in poor soil. The foliage is grey-green and heather-like. Clear golden flowers, $\frac{1}{2}$–$\frac{3}{4}$ in. across, are carried in July.

H. elatum. Canary Islands. Height 3–4 ft; spread 4–6 ft. A semi-evergreen shrubby species with angled branching stems. It is hardy in the south where it has become naturalised in mild areas. The deep green ovate leaves are aromatic when bruised. Yellow flowers, 1 in. wide, are carried profusely in the terminal leaf axils from July to October; they are followed by ovoid, red berries.

The berrying branches are much used in flower arrangements and last well in water. The variety 'Elstead' is an outstanding form with large clusters of salmon-red berries in autumn.

Hypericum elatum 'Elstead' (autumn foliage and fruits)

Hypericum patulum 'Hidcote'

H. × moserianum. Height 1–2$\frac{1}{2}$ ft; spread 3–4 ft. This evergreen hybrid between *H. calycinum* and *H. patulum* forms a low-spreading bush, admirable as ground cover. The ovate leaves are deep green, glaucous beneath. Rich yellow flowers, 2–2$\frac{1}{2}$ in. across, are freely produced from July to October; they are carried in clusters of one to five at the ends of the shoots.

The variety 'Tricolor' is less vigorous than the type plant, with green-and-white variegated leaves, margined red.

H. olympicum. S.E. Europe, Asia Minor. Height 9–12 in.; spread 12 in. This species forms a small shrub with grey-green ovate leaves. Golden-yellow flowers, up to 1$\frac{1}{2}$ in. across, are borne in profusion at the tips of the shoots in July and August. 'Citrinum' has lemon-yellow flowers.

H. patulum. Himalayas, China, Japan. Height 3–6 ft; spread 4–5 ft. A deciduous or semi-evergreen species with ovate to ovate-lanceolate deep green leaves that are glaucous beneath. The golden-yellow flowers, 1$\frac{1}{2}$–2 in. wide, are borne in terminal cymes from July to September.

There are a number of named forms including 'Hidcote', with larger flowers produced in great profusion; and *H. p. forrestii*, with overlapping petals forming bowl-shaped flowers.

H. polyphyllum. S.W. Asia Minor. Height 6 in.; spread 12 in. This shrubby species forms a dense carpet of elliptic, glaucous leaves. The golden flowers, sometimes flushed red in bud, are 1$\frac{1}{2}$ in. wide and borne from July to September. The form 'Sulphureum' has paler yellow flowers.

H. reptans. Sikkim. Height 3 in.; spread 12–18 in. A mat-forming species with rounded, light green leaves that turn red-brown in autumn. Scarlet buds open to 1$\frac{1}{2}$ in. wide orange-yellow flowers from July to September.

H. 'Rowallane Hybrid'. Height 4–5 ft; spread 5–7 ft. This hybrid shrub can be grown as a wall shrub in the south; in cold areas it should be treated as an annually stooled plant and cut back to base each autumn. The ovate-lanceolate leaves are rich green above, glaucous beneath. The well-formed flowers are golden-yellow and up to 3 in. across; they are borne in terminal clusters from April to October or November.

Cultivation. Grow hypericums in any fertile and well-drained garden soil, in a sunny position; *H. calycinum* will tolerate dry shade, but flowering is more profuse in full sun. Plant between October and April, preferably in spring for *H. coris, H. olympicum* and *H.* 'Rowallane Hybrid'.

In the south, grow *H.* 'Rowallane Hybrid' against a west-facing wall. Elsewhere, protect the roots in winter with a layer of bracken, weathered ashes or coarse sand.

In the alpine house, grow hypericums in 6–8 in. pans of John Innes potting compost No. 1, and repot annually in March.

Propagation. For the smaller species, take 2 in. cuttings of soft basal growths in May or June. Insert these in a mixture of equal parts (by volume) peat and sand, in a cold frame. When rooted, pot singly into 3 in. pots of John Innes potting compost No. 1 and overwinter in a frost-free frame or greenhouse. Transplant to flowering positions the following April.

H. calycinum can also be increased by division of the roots between October and April.

For the taller shrubs, take cuttings, 4–5 in. long, of lateral non-flowering shoots, preferably with a heel, between July and September. Insert the cuttings in a cold frame as previously described; in April or May line the young plants out in nursery rows. In cold districts, cuttings of *H* 'Rowallane Hybrid' are best potted singly in 3 in. pots of John Innes potting compost No. 1 and overwintered in a frost-free frame or greenhouse before lining out.

Pruning. Cut *H. calycinum* back to within a few inches of the base in March every few years to keep it compact; in other years trim to shape in March and through the year when necessary. Unless it is grown as a larger shrub, *H. elatum* should be cut hard back in the same manner, annually in March, to encourage the production of strong flowering shoots.

H. patulum and wall-grown specimens of *H.* 'Rowallane Hybrid' should have the previous year's shoots shortened to within a few buds of the old wood in March; stooled plants of *H.* 'Rowallane Hybrid' are cut down to ground level in October or November.

Pests. Generally trouble-free.

Diseases. Small orange or yellow spots on the leaves are caused by RUST; later, orange and brown clusters of spores appear.

Hyssopus

Hyssop. *Labiatae*

A genus of one species of hardy herbaceous perennial. It is an erect bushy plant, partially evergreen, which is best grown in a sunny border. It may be used for an ornamental low hedge or as a culinary herb.

The young leaves have a bitter minty flavour;

they may be used fresh in salads, and fresh or dried in soups or in stuffings for meat and game. The aromatic leaves may also be used dried in *pot-pourri*.

H. officinalis. Mediterranean regions to Central Asia. Height 18 in. or more; planting distance 12 in. The aromatic mid-green leaves are narrowly lanceolate and arranged in alternate opposite pairs. Purple-blue, two-lipped, tubular flowers, $\frac{1}{2}$–$\frac{3}{4}$ in. across, are borne from July to September in terminal whorled spikes. 'Albus' is a white form; 'Roseus' is pale pink.

Cultivation. Plant during suitable weather at any time between September and March. Any ordinary, well-drained garden soil is suitable, preferably in a sunny position. Remove the faded flower stems unless seeds are required.

For hedges, set the young plants at intervals of 9–12 in.; pinch out the growing points to promote bushy growth.

For flavouring, the fresh leaves may be picked all year round, although they are at their best just before the flowers open. For drying, pick the leaves when young (for methods of drying see entry under HERBS).

Propagation. Sow seeds in March in pans of seed compost in a cold frame or in the open ground in April. Prick off the seedlings into boxes, then singly into 3 in. pots of John Innes potting compost No. 1. Set the young plants in their permanent positions in September.

Alternatively, take 2–3 in. basal cuttings in April or May and insert in equal parts (by volume) peat and sand in a cold frame. When rooted, pot the cuttings in 3 in. containers of John Innes potting compost No. 1 and grow on until planting out in the autumn.

Pruning. Lightly trim established hedges in March or April and cut specimen plants back to within 3 in. of ground level to keep them shapely.

Pests and diseases. Generally trouble-free.

Hypericum polyphyllum 'Sulphureum'

Hyssopus officinalis

I

Iberis

Candytuft. *Cruciferae*

A genus of 30 species of hardy and half-hardy annuals and evergreen sub-shrubs. The annuals are suitable for growing in borders and for cutting, while the dwarf sub-shrubs described here are recommended for rock gardens and dry walls. These plants are excellent for town gardens as they are tolerant of smoke and grime. The flowers are roughly cross-shaped and borne in broad racemes or corymbs.

In the descriptions that follow, planting distance refers to border species which are usually set in groups; spread equals the leaf area covered by mature plants of the perennial species.

I. amara. Great Britain. Height 15 in.; planting distance 6 in. An upright hardy annual with

lanceolate mid-green leaves and 2 in. racemes of fragrant flowers, ranging in colour from white through pink to red-purple.

'Giant Hyacinth Flowered White' is a recommended variety with dense white racemes.

I. gibraltarica. Gibraltar. Height up to 12 in.; spread 12–18 in. This evergreen sub-shrub is not reliably hardy, but is easily replaced as it seeds itself freely. The dark green, narrowly oblong leaves are thick-textured. Lilac flowers in dense flattened corymbs, $1\frac{1}{2}$–2 in. across, are produced in April and May.

I. saxatilis. S. Europe. Height 3 in.; spread about 12 in. A hardy perennial alpine species, forming a neat dark green bush of linear fleshy leaves. Flat terminal heads, about 2 in. across, of white flowers appear from May to July.

I. sempervirens. S. Europe. Height 9 in.; spread 18–24 in. This hardy perennial evergreen is

Iberis amara

represented in cultivation by a spreading bushy form, with dark green, narrow, oblong leaves. Dense 1½ in. wide heads of white flowers are borne in May and June.

'Little Gem' (height 4 in.; spread 6–9 in.) is a neat erect form with white flowers; 'Snowflake' (height 6–9 in.) is a more spreading, mat-forming plant with pure white flowers. There is also a double form, 'Plena'.

I. umbellata. S. Europe. Height 6–15 in.; planting distance 9 in. A hardy annual, with narrow, pointed mid-green leaves. The white and pale purple flowers are borne in 2 in. clusters; with successive sowings, flowers can be obtained from June to September.

Recommended varieties include: 'Dwarf Fairy Mixed' (height 10 in.), of dome-shaped habit with white, lavender, rose-pink and red flowers; 'Red Flash' (height 12 in.), vivid carmine; 'Rose Cardinal' (height 10 in.), rose-scarlet; and 'Vulcan' (height 15 in.), a tetraploid with large carmine flowers.

Cultivation. These plants all thrive in ordinary, well-drained garden soil, in a sunny position. They do well on poor soils. Dead-head regularly species grown for their flowers, to extend the flowering period.

Plant perennial species during suitable weather between September and March and sow annuals from September to May.

Propagation. Sow seeds of annual species successively in the flowering site during September, March, April and May in order to extend the flowering season. Thin out the seedlings to the appropriate planting distances.

Alternatively, sow seeds in pots or boxes of seed compost under glass in February, at a temperature of 16°C (61°F). Prick off the seedlings into boxes of John Innes potting compost No. 1 and harden off in a cold frame before planting out in April.

Increase perennial species by 2 in. long soft-wood cuttings taken from non-flowering shoots between June and August. Insert the cuttings in a cold frame in equal parts (by volume) peat and sand. Pot the rooted cuttings in 3 in. pots of John Innes potting compost No. 1 and overwinter in a cold frame. The following March or April, set the young plants out.

Pests. FLEA BEETLES eat small holes in the leaves.
Diseases. Generally trouble-free.

Ilex

Holly. *Aquifoliaceae*

A genus of 300 species of tender and hardy deciduous and evergreen trees and shrubs. The most commonly grown species is *I. aquifolium* which, with its numerous garden varieties, is extensively used for hedging or as single specimen trees in parks and gardens. All species have inconspicuous, five-petalled, white or green flowers, $\frac{1}{4}-\frac{1}{3}$ in. across, during April and May, male and female flowers usually being borne on separate trees. Where male and female plants are grown together, brightly coloured berries are produced which last throughout the winter.

The following are hardy evergreen species:

I. × altaclarensis. Garden origin. Height 18–30 ft; spread 10–15 ft. A hybrid between *I. aquifolium* and *I. perado*, with ovate, dark green, spiny leaves that are sometimes almost spineless on old trees. This is a variable tree; the form most commonly grown is 'Hodginsii', a non-berrying male tree with purple twigs and large spiny leaves. Excellent for hedging, particularly in maritime and industrial areas.

Other forms, which in catalogues are often listed as varieties of *I. aquifolium*, include: 'Balearica' (height 18–30 ft; spread 8–12 ft), a vigorous tree, with deep green leathery leaves that are quite smooth or have only a few spiny teeth; it is a female form bearing large regular crops of bright orange-red berries. 'Camelliifolia' (height 15–25 ft; spread 6–8 ft), a female tree of columnar habit, with glossy, dark green, almost spineless leaves and large red berries.

ILEX × ALTACLARENSIS

'Golden King' (height 18–25 ft; spread 8–15 ft) is a female tree bearing golden-margined leaves and large red berries; it is a sport or mutant from 'Hendersonii'. 'Hendersonii' (height 15–25 ft; spread 8–12 ft) is a female tree with spineless dark green leaves and large red berries.

'Lawsoniana' (height 12–25 ft; spread 8–12 ft) is a sport of 'Hendersonii'. The dark green leaves with a conspicuous splash of bright yellow often revert to green; clusters of large orange-red berries are borne throughout winter. 'Mundayi' (height 15–25 ft; spread 8–15 ft) is a male non-berrying tree with attractively deep green-veined leaves, margined with neat, spreading, spiny teeth. 'Wilsonii' (height 18–30 ft; spread 8–15 ft) is a female tree with broad, spiny, dark green leaves and large clusters of red berries.

I. aquifolium (English or common holly). Europe including Great Britain; N. Africa to Asia. Height 18–25 ft; spread 8–12 ft. This native species is the holly found in woods and hedgerows. The glossy dark green leaves are strongly wavy and margined with sharp spines. Female trees bear heavy crops of bright red berries in autumn and winter, usually only when a male tree is close by. This species is possibly the most popular evergreen tree, much used for hedging and for Christmas decoration.

I. aquifolium is extremely variable and has given rise to numerous forms, differing in leaf shape and colour, growth habit and colour of berries. Among the more ornamental forms are: 'Angustifolia' (height 12–20 ft; spread 6–10 ft), a slow-growing female tree of conical habit with narrow, lanceolate, neatly spined, dark green leaves and tiny red berries. 'Argenteo-marginata' (height 18–25 ft; spread 10–15 ft), male and female trees both have oval, spiny, silver-edged leaves, and female trees bear large crops of red berries. 'Argenteo-marginata Pendula' (height 8–12 ft; spread 10–15 ft), sometimes known as

Iberis sempervirens 'Little Gem'

Ilex aquifolium 'Aureo-marginata'

Ilex aquifolium 'Argenteo-marginata'

Perry's Silver Weeping', is a female tree forming large dome, with long weeping branches clothed with ovate spiny, silver-edged leaves; bright red berries are produced.

'Aureo-marginata' (height 15–18 ft; spread 8–10 ft), male and female trees have gold-margined leaves and female trees bear clusters of red berries, 'Bacciflava', syn. *I. a.* 'Fructu-luteo' (height 12–18 ft; spread 15–20 ft) is a dense, conical female tree with ovate, spiny, dark green leaves and abundant crops of bright yellow berries. 'Ferox' (hedgehog holly), (height 8–15 ft; spread 5–8 ft), is a bushy, slow-growing, male tree with ovate dark green leaves, densely covered with short, sharp, pale green spines; 'Ferox Argentea' has cream-white spines to the leaves.

'Golden Queen' (height 10–18 ft; spread 6–10 ft) is a broadly columnar male tree with gold-margined ovate leaves. 'Handsworth New Silver' (height 10–15 ft; spread 5–8 ft) is a broadly columnar female tree with narrowly oblong, silver-margined leaves and red berries. 'J. C. van Tol', syn. 'Polycarpa' (height 10–18 ft; spread 6–10 ft), a female columnar tree having ovate, shiny, dark green, spineless leaves and large red berries freely produced. 'Pendula' (weeping holly) is a spreading tree (height 8–12 ft; spread 10–15 ft), forming a large dome with long weeping branches clothed with shining, dark green, ovate leaves and crowded with clusters of bright red berries.

'Pyramidalis' (height 15–20 ft; spread 6–10 ft) is a strong, erect-growing, female tree with spiny and spineless, ovate, dark green leaves on the same plant; heavy crops of bright red berries are produced each year. 'Silver Queen' (height 12–18 ft; spread 6–10 ft) is a male conical tree with silver-margined, broadly ovate leaves.

I. cornuta. China. Height 5–8 ft; spread 5–6 ft. This is a dense, slow-growing bush. The leaves are rectangular, glossy dark green and usually with five spine-tipped teeth. Female plants bear bright red berries in winter.

I. crenata. Japan. Height 8–10 ft; spread 6–8 ft. A densely branched shrub, completely unlike the prickly-leaved native species. The ovate or lanceolate mid-green leaves are shallowly toothed. Female plants bear tiny black berries in autumn and winter. This small-leaved holly is excellent as a low hedge plant.

The variety 'Convexa' (height 3–4 ft; spread 2–3 ft) is a compact small shrub with tiny, convex, glossy mid-green leaves and large quantities of tiny black berries; it is particularly suitable for a dwarf hedge. 'Golden Gem' (height 12–24 in.; spread 2–4 ft) is a non-berrying form with ovate golden leaves in spring and summer which turn yellow-green in autumn and winter. 'Mariesii' is a dwarf, non-berrying form with neat, rounded, dark green leaves; it is suitable for a rock garden or as a miniature tree.

Cultivation. Plant hollies in sun or shade and in ordinary garden soil, though a moist loamy soil is preferable. Variegated forms should be grown in a sunny position; in heavy shade the leaf colouring is usually poor. The hardy evergreen species and their forms are tolerant of atmospheric pollution and are ideal for planting in industrial areas, on exposed sites and in coastal districts, as specimen trees or as screens.

The variegated forms of *I. aquifolium* are slow to become established and the plants need careful treatment after planting. Always use young plants, as large specimens resent root disturbance and are difficult to transplant. Set the young plants in their planting holes with the soil ball intact, and water frequently during dry weather to prevent leaf drop. Specimen plants in exposed areas require winter protection in the form of screens of sacking, hessian or wattle on the windward side, until established.

Plant hollies preferably in late April or May, or in September or October; they may be planted at any time during winter when the soil is neither frozen nor waterlogged. Plant male and female forms together to assist pollination and to ensure the production of berries. *I. aquifolium* 'J. C. van Tol' and 'Pyramidalis' will produce berries when no male tree is close by.

For hedges, young plants about 18 in. high should be planted in April or May. Set the plants at intervals of 24 in., and water copiously in dry weather. No trimming is required until the following spring, then pinch out the growing tips to promote bushy growth.

Propagation. Increase the species and their forms by cuttings, 2–3 in. long, taken in August. Select well-ripened shoots, preferably with a heel, of the current year's growth. Insert the cuttings in equal parts (by volume) peat and sand in a cold frame; the following April or May plant the rooted cuttings out in nursery rows and grow on for two years before transplanting to permanent sites.

Named forms of *I. aquifolium* may be budded or grafted on to stocks of *I. aquifolium* in June or August; the roots, however, are prone to suckering, and propagation by cuttings is more reliable.

Topwork weeping forms on 6 ft high trained stems of *I. aquifolium* in January and February; alternatively, allow them to grow on their own roots. They will develop into large low mounds, ideal for banks and bare spaces.

Species and their forms may be layered in October and separated from the parent plants two years later.

Pruning. No regular pruning is required, but specimen trees should be clipped to shape in July or August. Hedges should be trimmed annually in April; old hedges may be cut hard back to the old wood if necessary.

Variegated hollies sometimes revert to green if neglected or if they are grown in dense shade; remove all green shoots immediately from the base with a sharp knife or secateurs. Forms with marginal variegations rarely revert to green; the reverted branches bear all yellow or all white leaves which eventually die. Forms with central leaf variegations such as *I.* × *altaclarensis* 'Lawsoniana' often produce shoots with completely green leaves.

Pests. Maggots of HOLLY LEAF MINERS tunnel into leaves and cause unsightly blotches.

In cold winters, HARES may nibble young plants, and BIRDS feed on the berries.

Diseases. HONEY FUNGUS can cause the rapid death of trees.

LEAF SPOT shows as grey spots with dark brown edges or as white spots on the leaves.

Imantophyllum: see Clivia

Ilex aquifolium

Ilex aquifolium 'Bacciflava'

Ilex aquifolium 'Silver Queen'

Impatiens
Balsaminaceae

A genus of about 700 species of hardy, half-hardy and tender annuals and evergreen sub-shrubs. The tender species require greenhouse cultivation and are also popular as house plants. They may also be bedded out in sheltered areas. The plants commonly sold as busy lizzies are hybrids between *I. holstii* and *I. sultanii*; they are particularly suitable for outdoor bedding. The hardy and half-hardy annuals are suitable for annual and mixed borders and the taller species for shrub borders.

These plants bear a profusion of spurred flowers which may be cup-shaped or may open flat; they are sometimes solitary and sometimes in racemes or panicles.

IMPATIENS HOLSTII

GREENHOUSE PERENNIALS

I. holstii, syn. *I. walleriana* (busy lizzie). E. Africa. Height 24 in. or more. A well-branched sub-shrubby species, usually grown as a short-lived perennial. It has bright green elliptic leaves and light green, slightly translucent, succulent stems. Flat, five-petalled, bright scarlet flowers, 1–1½ in. across, are borne from the upper leaf axils from April to October.

I. petersiana. W. Africa. Height up to 3 ft. This well-branched species has bronze-red fleshy stems with bronze-red elliptic leaves. The flat, five-petalled flowers are carmine and 1–1½ in. across; they appear from the upper leaf axils throughout the summer. This species is now considered to be a form of *I. holstii*.

I. sultanii (busy lizzie). Zanzibar. Height 24 in. This species is now considered to be a form of *I. holstii*, which it resembles. The flowers have curved spurs and are up to 2 in. across. They are borne from April to October and may be white, orange, magenta, crimson or scarlet.

I. walleriana: see *I. holstii*

HYBRID VARIETIES. These plants are derived from *I. holstii* and *I. sultanii* and are particularly suitable for outdoor bedding. They include the Imp Strain (height 9 in.; planting distance 9–12 in.) which consists of single-colour varieties in white, rose, carmine, orange, scarlet and violet. 'Orange Baby' and 'Scarlet Baby', both 6 in. high, should be planted 6–9 in. apart.

HARDY AND HALF-HARDY ANNUALS

I. balsamina (balsam). Asia. Height 2½ ft; planting distance 18 in. This half-hardy annual is a compact plant, suitable for growing in beds and in pots under glass. The leaves are pale green and lanceolate; pink flowers, 1½ in. wide, appear in the upper leaf axils from June to September.

This is the parent of several named varieties, including pink, white, crimson and purple forms, single or double. 'Camellia Flowered Mixed'

Impatiens petersiana

Impatiens sultanii

Impatiens roylei

Impatiens 'Scarlet Baby'

(height 18 in.), and 'Tom Thumb Mixed' (height 10 in.) both have large double flowers.

I. biflora. N. America. Height 3 ft; planting distance 24 in. A hardy annual, suitable for moist shade, with toothed, ovate, mid-green leaves. Panicles of 1 in. long orange flowers, spotted with red-brown, appear from July to October.

I. glandulifera: see *I. roylei*

IMPATIENS ROYLEI

I. roylei, syn. *I. glandulifera* (Himalayan touch-me-not). Himalayas. Height 3–5 ft; planting distance 24 in. A hardy annual naturalised in Britain, with thick, succulent branching stems and light green, ovate leaves. The flowers, 2 in. long, are carried in terminal and axillary panicles from August to September; they are purple, rose or yellow, spotted with crimson.

Cultivation of greenhouse perennials. Grow impatiens in 5 in. pots containing a proprietary peat compost or John Innes potting compost No. 1. Provide a winter temperature of 13°C (55°F) to keep the plants flowering throughout the year; they will survive at 7°C (45°F) if kept just moist, but they may lose most of their leaves.

When growth is restarted in March, give water more freely. In the home, keep the plants in well-lit positions, out of direct sunlight; in the greenhouse, shade lightly on hot days.

Repot annually every other year in April. Give a weekly liquid feed from May to September. Discard the plants when they grow too leggy.

Plants raised from seeds and used for summer bedding schemes should be set out in late May, in sun or partial shade.

Cultivation of hardy and half-hardy annuals. Outdoors, grow in any ordinary, well-drained and fertile garden soil, in full sun or partial shade. *I. roylei* is suitable for damp sites.

As a pot plant grow *I. balsamina* in 5 in. containers of John Innes potting compost No. 1.

Propagation of greenhouse perennials. Take 3–4 in. long tip cuttings from vigorous shoots at any time from April to September. Insert in equal parts (by volume) peat and sand and root at a temperature of 16°C (61°F). When rooted, pot the cuttings singly in 3 in. containers of John Innes potting compost No. 2 and pot on as necessary. Pinch out the growing points to encourage bushy growth.

Alternatively, sow seeds in pots or pans of seed compost in March, at a temperature of 16–18°C (61–64°F). Prick out the seedlings, when large enough to handle, into boxes and later into 3½ in. containers of John Innes potting compost No. 2. For bedding plants, harden off in a cold frame and plant out in late May; for pot plants, treat as described for cuttings.

Propagation of hardy and half-hardy annuals. Sow seeds of the hardy species in the flowering site in March or April, and thin out the seedlings to the required planting distances.

Sow seeds of the half-hardy *I. balsamina* as described for greenhouse perennials, but pot the seedlings only if they are to be grown as pot plants; do not pinch out the growing tips. Otherwise, harden off and plant out in late May.

Pruning. Cut back old greenhouse perennial plants in March to within 3 or 4 in. of the base.

Pests. Infestations of APHIDS on leaves and stems weaken the plants, making them sticky and encouraging sooty moulds.

SLUGS may attack seedlings.

GLASSHOUSE RED SPIDER MITES cause mottling and bronzing of the leaves, which may drop.

Diseases. Yellowing of the leaves and premature leaf-fall is due to a PHYSIOLOGICAL DISORDER.

Incarvillea

Bignoniaceae

A genus of about 14 species of herbaceous perennials. The following species have showy, pink, foxglove-like flowers and are suitable for growing in a sunny herbaceous border.

I. delavayi. W. China, Tibet. Height 24 in.; planting distance 15 in. The deep green incised leaves develop after the flowers. Rich rose-pink flowers, 2–3 in. long and wide, are held at right angles to the stem on short stalks. The first flowers open in May or June, a few inches above ground; as the erect stems grow, flowering continues well into July.

I. grandiflora. W. China. Height 9–12 in.; planting distance 12 in. The toothed foliage is dark green; 3 in. long, cerise-pink flowers appear from late May until the end of July.

Cultivation. Plant in March or April, setting the fleshy-rooted crowns just below the soil surface. Incarvilleas require a rich, well-drained soil and a sunny, open position. Renewed growth begins in late spring, and to prevent damage from cultivation in the border, mark established plants with sticks when the dead foliage is removed in autumn. A light mulch, 1 in. deep, of peat or compost applied in autumn is beneficial and also helps to indicate old plants.

Incarvillea delavayi

Propagation. Established plants may be divided and replanted in autumn, but the crowns are tough and difficult to split.

Sow seeds thinly in shallow drills outdoors in March or April; leave the seedlings *in situ* until the second spring, then transplant to their permanent positions.

Pests and diseases. Generally trouble-free.

India-rubber plant: see *Ficus elastica*

Incarvillea grandiflora

Indigofera

Leguminosae

A genus of 700 species of herbaceous perennials and deciduous and evergreen shrubs. Only a few shrubby species are in general cultivation; some of these require greenhouse cultivation, but those described here are generally hardy when grown in the open or as wall shrubs. They are distinguished by their fern-like foliage and pea-like pink or purple flowers.

INDIGOFERA GERARDIANA

I. gerardiana. Himalayas. Height 5–6 ft; spread 4–5 ft. This deciduous species is not reliably hardy and is best grown as a wall shrub. The grey-green pinnate leaves, which are composed of numerous ovate leaflets, do not appear until May or June. Racemes, 3–5 in. long, of rose-purple flowers are carried in the leaf axils from July to October.

I. potaninii. China. Height and spread 6–8 ft. A hardy deciduous species with mid-green pinnate leaves of up to nine ovate leaflets. The axillary racemes, 2–5 in. long, of rose-pink flowers are freely borne during June and July.

Indigofera gerardiana

Indigofera potaninii

Cultivation. Grow indigoferas in a sunny position and in good, well-drained, but not too rich soil; plant in September and October or in April. *I. gerardiana* should preferably be trained against a south-facing wall.

Propagation. Sow seeds in March and April in pans of seed compost in a cold frame; prick off the seedlings, when large enough to handle, into 3 in. pots of John Innes potting compost No. 1. Pot on into 4 in. pots during the summer and over-winter in a cold frame before planting out in permanent positions the following April.

Pruning. No regular pruning is required, but strong shoots of the previous season may be shortened by half in April; remove all weak and frosted shoot tips at the same time. *I. gerardiana* may be cut hard back to a few inches above ground level in April to keep the shrubs within bounds; they break freely from the base.

Pests and diseases. Generally trouble-free.

Inula hookeri

Ionopsidium acaule

Ipheion uniflorum

Inula
Compositae

INULA ROYLEANA

A genus of 200 species of hardy herbaceous perennials. The showy flowers are daisy-like, with numerous narrow ray-florets. The species described are suitable for rock gardens or borders.

I. acaulis. Asia Minor. Height 2–4 in.; spread up to 12 in. This plant forms a flat mat of spathulate mid-green leaves on which rest almost stemless golden daisy-like flowers, each 1½–2 in. wide. These appear in April and May.

I. hookeri. Himalayas. Height and spread 18–24 in. A bushy species with clustered stems set with mid-green oblong-lanceolate leaves. The slightly fragrant, pale yellow flowers are 2½–3½ in. across and open in August and September.

I. royleana. Himalayas. Height 24 in. or more; spread 18–24 in. Clumps of unbranched stems bear ovate mid-green leaves with winged stalks. From August to October, black-green buds expand to 3½–4½ in. wide golden-yellow flowers.

Cultivation. Plant inulas from October to March in any moisture-retentive fertile garden soil in a sunny position.

Propagation. Divide between March and October and replant direct in permanent positions.

Pests and diseases. Generally trouble-free.

Ionopsidium
Cruciferae

A genus of one hardy annual species. This little plant is suited to rock gardens and crevices in paving, and may also be grown as a pot plant in a shaded greenhouse or indoors.

I. acaule (violet cress). Portugal. Height 2–3 in. A tufted, low-growing plant with rounded, glabrous, mid-green leaves on long stems. Single flowers appear from June to September. They are ¼ in. across, four-petalled, and coloured mauve or white tinged with violet.

Cultivation. These plants are easy to grow if planted in moist soil and partial shade; strong sunlight may scorch them. Grow as indoor or greenhouse plants in 4 in. pans of John Innes potting compost No. 1 and overwinter at a temperature of 4–7°C (39–45°F).

Propagation. Sow the seeds thinly, just covering them with soil, in the flowering site from April to July. Thinning is unnecessary. In mild districts seeds may be sown in September, provided the plants are given cloche protection in winter.

For flowering indoors or in a greenhouse in early spring, sow seeds thinly in 4 in. pans of John Innes potting compost No. 1 in September. Thin the seedlings to 2 in. apart each way.

Pests and diseases. Generally trouble-free.

Ipheion
Liliaceae

A genus of about 20 species of hardy bulbs from Mexico, and south to Chile. Like several similar bulb genera, ipheions have recently been undergoing reclassification. The plants described have grass-like leaves and a six-petalled, star-shaped flower on each stem. They are useful for massing in rock gardens or at the front of borders.

I. uniflorum, syns. *Brodiaea uniflora, Milla uniflora* and *Triteleia uniflora.* Peru, Argentina. Height 6–8 in.; planting distance 2–3 in. The bulbs and pale green leaves have a garlic-like smell. The 1½–2 in. wide flowers, produced in April and May, are scented, white to violet-blue. Named varieties include 'Wisley Blue', violet-blue, and 'Caeruleum', pale blue.

Cultivation. Plant plump bulbs 1–2 in. deep in September or October; keep free from weeds and remove dead leaves and flower stems in late summer. Ipheions need a sheltered position in sun or partial shade and well-drained soil.

Propagation. Offsets are freely produced. Lift the bulbs as the leaves die, separate and, if possible, replant at once. If the bulbs must be kept until the autumn before planting, keep them cool and do not allow them to dry out or to become wet. Divide and replant every two or three years.

Pests and diseases. Generally trouble-free.

Ipomoea
Morning glory. *Convolvulaceae*

A genus of 500 species of tender and half-hardy annuals and perennials, including climbers and shrubs. Two of the plants listed below are now classified in the genera *Quamoclit* and *Mina.* They are climbers, popular for their attractive trumpet or claw-shaped flowers. Ipomoeas are fairly easy to grow, but the half-hardy species described here need warm, sheltered sites; they also make excellent pot plants.

Ipomoea quamoclit

Ipomoea purpurea

I. lobata, syn. *I. versicolor.* Mexico. Height 6–10 ft; planting distance 12 in. This plant is now correctly known as *Mina lobata.* It is a half-hardy perennial usually grown as a tender annual, with climbing stems and dark green three-lobed leaves. Up to 12 flowers are carried on slender spikes, suitable for cutting from June to September. Each flower is 2 in. long, crimson when opening but changing through orange and yellow to white as it ages.

I. purpurea, syn. *Convolvulus major.* Tropical America. Height 10 ft or more; planting distance 12 in. A half-hardy annual and a vigorous climber. The leaves are heart-shaped and mid-green. The flowers, 3 in. across, are borne singly or in small clusters from the axils of the leaves from July to September. Their purple colour fades as the flowers age.

'Major Mixed' is a mixture of single and double flowers ranging from white through mauve to blue-pink and rose-purple. 'Scarlett O'Hara' has deep crimson flowers.

IPOMOEA QUAMOCLIT

I. quamoclit, syn. *Quamoclit pennata* (cypress vine). Tropics. Height 6 ft or more; planting distance 12 in. A half-hardy annual suitable for growing outdoors in sheltered sites in the south. The leaves are light green and finely divided. Red and yellow, curved tubular, somewhat claw-like flowers are produced in 1½ in. long racemes in the leaf axils from July to September.

I. rubro-caerulea: see *I. tricolor*
I. tricolor, syn. *I. rubro-caerulea.* Mexico. Height 8 ft or more; planting distance 12 in. A half-hardy perennial, usually grown as an annual. The thin, twining stems carry pale green heart-shaped leaves. This species flowers freely, producing blooms up to 5 in. across from July to September. The red-purple to blue flowers open out in the morning and fade during the afternoon.

The variety 'Flying Saucers' has striped blue and white flowers; 'Heavenly Blue' has flowers in two shades of pale blue.

I. versicolor: see *I. lobata*

Cultivation. Outdoors, grow these plants in light but rich soil, in a sheltered, sunny position. An unshaded wall or fence is an ideal site. Alternatively, grow on poles or pea-sticks in a sheltered border or bed. Dead-heading prolongs the flowering period.

For flowering under glass, grow three plants in an 8 in. pot of John Innes potting compost No. 1, and train them up canes. Later, provide wires or strings for support.

Propagation. Sow seeds under glass in March or April at a temperature of 18°C (64°F). Soak the seeds of *I. tricolor* in water for 24 hours, or file a small notch in the hard seed coat, before sowing. Move the seedlings to 5 in. pots of John Innes potting compost No. 1 and harden off those for growing outdoors before planting out in late May or June. In a late spring, do not plant out until the weather has warmed up. Seeds may also be sown in the flowering site in late May.

Pests. The foliage of young plants may be infested with APHIDS, GLASSHOUSE RED SPIDER MITES, THRIPS and LEAFHOPPERS.

Diseases. Whitened and sometimes malformed young foliage is caused by a PHYSIOLOGICAL DISORDER, due either to low night temperatures or magnesium deficiency.

Ipomoea lobata

Ipomoea tricolor

Iris danfordiae (Bulbous Reticulata)

Iris susiana (Bearded Oncocyclus)

IRIS
Iridaceae

A genus of 300 monocotyledonous plants found throughout the Northern Hemisphere. No irises grow wild in the Southern Hemisphere. Their habitat extends from the Arctic Circle to the Tropic of Cancer, and a large proportion of the species can be grown in Great Britain if cultivated with care and grown in full sun.

The leaves are generally sword-shaped and are usually carried in a fan-like arrangement. The colour of the foliage varies from grey-green to deep glossy green.

The typical iris flower is arranged in multiples of three. The three outer petals are known as the falls, the three inner petals as the standards. Projecting between the falls and standards are the three style arms, which have the appearance of strap-shaped petals. On the hafts of the falls many iris species have fleshy hairs, known as the beard.

As the genus is complex, the brief summary that follows may be used as a guide to the subsequent descriptions. It is divided into four

sections, three of which have sub-sections al with their own characteristics.

The species and hybrids described in the fou iris sections are only a small proportion of thos in general cultivation. They are, however, th most easily grown.

Bearded (Pogoniris) section
Flowers have hairy beards on the falls. Root rhizomatous; leaves flat.
ARILLATE GROUP Rhizomes are stoloniferous growing 1–3 in. under the surface of the soil.
EUPOGON SUB-SECTION Thick rhizomes on th surface of the soil; glaucous leaves.

Beardless iris (Apogon) section
Flowers are beardless, the falls are smooth rhizomatous rootstock; flat and slender leaves.
CALIFORNICAE SUB-SECTION Foliage usually ever green; slender long rhizomes with sparse roots.
HEXAGONA SUB-SECTION Foliage usually ever green; flower stems zigzag; long, slender an creeping rhizomes.

LAEVIGATAE SUB-SECTION Foliage deciduous; slender rhizomes; may be grown in water or bog conditions or in ordinary soil.

SIBIRICAE SUB-SECTION Foliage deciduous; short rhizomes, 1 in. deep, with numerous roots.

SPURIA SUB-SECTION Foliage evergreen; thick, fibrous rhizomes, 2–3 in. deep.

Crested iris section
Flowers have fleshy crests on the falls instead of beards; slender rhizomes on or just below the soil surface; leaves flat, broad and glossy.

Bulbous iris section
Bulbous rootstock; foliage short-lived.

JUNO SUB-SECTION Bulbs are small with fat storage roots attached to the base; leaves channelled in cross-section; flowers produced in the leaf axils.

RETICULATA SUB-SECTION Bulbs are small and covered with a netted skin or tunic; tubular leaves are four or eight-sided.

XIPHIUM SUB-SECTION Medium-sized bulbs with smooth tunic; leaves are channelled in cross-section and comparatively sparse.

Iris pumila (Dwarf bearded)

Iris 'Bee Wings' (Dwarf bearded)

Iris 'Blue Doll' (Dwarf bearded)

'Techny Chimes' (bearded tall hybrid)
tectorum (crested)
tenax (beardless californicae)
'Thor' (bearded regelia hybrid)
tingitana (bulbous xiphium)
'Total Eclipse' (bearded tall hybrid)
'Tricuspis' (beardless miscellaneous, *I. setosa*)
unguicularis (beardless miscellaneous)
'Valimar' (bearded tall hybrid)
'Variegata' (beardless laevigatae, *I. laevigata* and *I. pseudacorus*)
'Variegata' (beardless miscellaneous, *I. foetidissima*)
'Vera' (bearded regelia hybrid)
'Veri Bright' (bearded dwarf hybrid)
versicolor (beardless laevigatae)
'Violet Flare' (beardless sibiricae hybrid)
'Wedgwood' (bulbous xiphium, Dutch hybrid)
'Wentworth' (bulbous reticulata hybrid)
'Wheelhorse' (beardless hexagona hybrid)
'White Swirl' (beardless sibiricae hybrid)
winogradowii (bulbous reticulata)
xiphioides (bulbous xiphium)
xiphium (bulbous xiphium)

Iris 'Orchid Flare' (Dwarf bearded)

Iris 'Bronze Babe' (Intermediate bearded)

Iris 'Circlette' (Intermediate bearded)

Bearded irises (Pogoniris)

ARILLATE Group These members of the bearded irises are distinguished by the prominent white collar (or aril) which adheres to the seed coat. The aril usually develops from the seed stalk which joined it to the pod.

There are two sub-sections in this group: Oncocyclus and Regelia. These hybridise freely, and the hybrids have inherited the spectacular flowers of the oncocyclus species and the easier cultivation of the regelias. All arillate irises have a stoloniferous manner of growth: the new rhizomes form on the ends of thin stolons that vary in length according to the species.

ONCOCYCLUS This group of species contains some of the most fascinating of all irises. Most of them are difficult to grow, however, and should not be attempted without previous study of specialist literature.

Sometimes known as cushion irises, because of the broad diffuse beard, often with a dark patch under it, oncocyclus irises have only a single flower, up to 6 in. across, on each stem. The domed standards curl inwards and overlap and the sharply recurved falls are typical of the flowers of most of the group. The foliage is falcate (sickle-shaped) and often glaucous-green in colour. The only species easily available is *I. susiana*, which flowers in May or June.

I. gatesii. Kurdistan. Height 24 in.; planting distance 12 in. One of the largest iris flowers, the standards and falls often exceed 5 in. in width. The colour is grey-white, with a fine netting of purple-brown veins.

I. susiana. Lebanon. Height 15 in.; planting distance 12 in. This species has been in cultivation since 1573, and is known as the Mourning Iris. The flowers, 4–5 in. across, are pale grey, veined and dotted with purple-black, lightly on the standards and heavily on the falls, where there is also a black patch.

It is easy to obtain, but will usually not last more than one season unless cultivated with care.
Cultivation. Plant the rhizomes in October in a well-raised bed (about 24 in.) covered by the kind of frame that will keep out rain but allow easy ventilation. The soil should be an open mixture of half sharp sand and half good soil. Place the rhizomes on this mixture and cover with 1 in. of sharp sand. Keep the frame open throughout October for the rain to moisten the soil, after which the frame should be closed. During the winter, water sparingly; keep the foliage dry, and maintain full ventilation except in the most severe frosts and fogs.

The leaves appear soon after planting. In early spring, give a liquid feed between the plants monthly from March onwards until the flower spikes appear, and one further application after flowering. From then on keep the plants dry until growth is resumed in October.

Propagation. After the foliage has died down, divide the rhizomes if they are overcrowded.

REGELIA Named after the Russian botanist Regel, they have several general characteristics: the foliage is bright green, narrow and upright, and emerges in January. The flowers, 3–5 in. in diameter, tend to be long, the falls hang close to the stem and the standards are nearly vertical. There are beards on both standards and falls which account for another group name—Hexapogon. The stems generally have two buds, occasionally three, in a terminal spathe. The skin of the rhizomes is usually red.

I. hoogiana. Turkestan. Height up to 20 in.; planting distance 12 in. This species, which flowers in May, has a satiny texture. The colour of standards and falls is blue with a lavender tint and the elongated flowers are 3–4 in. wide. There are two colour forms, 'Bronze Beauty', light bronze shot with violet, and 'Purpurea', which is royal purple.

I. stolonifera. Turkestan. Height 18–24 in.; planting distance 12 in. The flowers, 3 in. wide, are brown, shot with electric blue and with a blue beard. They appear in May. The stolons after which this iris is named are often 6–8 in. long.

HYBRIDS Known as either Oncogelias or Regeliocyclus, these are hybrids between the Oncocyclus and Regelia species. They have been raised mainly in Holland and are readily available. The diameter of the flowers is 3–5 in. Popular varieties (height 12–18 in.; planting distance 12 in.) which flower in May include:

'Chione', standards veined blue on white, falls lightly veined brown with a large blotch under the beard. 'Clara', standards veined black on white ground, falls heavily netted with black-brown. 'Mercurius', violet standards and bronze falls.

'Thor', dull purple veins on grey ground, purple veins on falls. 'Vera', brown flushed with purple, bright blue beard.

Cultivation. Plant the rhizomes in October in the sunniest position available and ensure good drainage. They do best in a rich light soil with some lime. Although unaffected by cold, the hybrid varieties do not thrive in persistent damp; cloche protection will help to prevent losses from this cause. After flowering, use cloches to assist ripening of the rhizomes. Provided the plants are

ris 'Blue Denim' (Intermediate bearded)

Iris 'Green Spot' (Intermediate bearded)

ept dry, they may be left in the ground; otherwise, lift and store the rhizomes from mid-July to October, taking care not to damage the roots when lifting.

Propagation. Divide the rhizomes after the foliage has died down. Store and replant the sections in October.

THE EUPOGONS This sub-section of the bearded irises includes the enormous number of garden hybrids which are added to annually by breeders all over the world. The majority of the true species in the section have little garden value.

All irises in this section are distinguished by a hairy beard that is narrow and elongated, in the centre of the upper part of the falls. The flowers are sweetly scented. The sword-shaped leaves are glaucous with a grey bloom; they die down to form a small over-wintering fan. The thick roots are rhizomatous. All are hardy, but need as much sunshine as they can be given, for the species from which they originate come from the Mediterranean region and the Middle East. For the sake of convenience, the section has been divided into three groups by height: Dwarf bearded irises, Intermediate bearded irises and Tall bearded irises.

DWARF BEARDED IRISES The species and hybrids are all fully hardy. Height from 3–10 in.; planting distance 6–8 in. The flowers, 3–4 in. across, appear from mid-April to early May and are usually stemless.

chamaeiris. S.E. France and N.W. Italy. Height 6–10 in. A variable species with flowers, 3–4 in. wide, in white, purple or yellow. It is often incorrectly called *I. pumila,* but is distinguished from that species by having a real stem and sometimes more than one flower on a stem.

I. pumila. S.E. Europe, eastwards to S. Russia. Height up to 4 in. Most forms of this species are stemless. The flowers, 2–3 in. across, have recurved falls and are in shades of purple, white, yellow and yellow with brown tints. Some Russian forms have flared falls and have been used to improve the dwarf and intermediate hybrids. It is the first bearded species to flower, in early April. As it grows naturally in mountainous terrain, it is best cultivated in the alpine house or

rock garden. Good drainage and division every second year are recommended.

I. p. attica, a slightly smaller form, has straw-yellow flowers tinged with jade-green. HYBRIDS The following dwarf irises (height 4–8 in.) have proved satisfactory and should be obtainable from specialist nurseries.

'Bee Wings', yellow with brown spots on the falls; 'Blue Doll', medium blue; 'Blue Frost', pale blue, one of the earliest; 'Bright White', clear white; 'Orchid Flare', orchid-pink; 'Spring Glade', white standards, pale lime-yellow falls; 'Veri Bright', yellow standards, brown falls.

INTERMEDIATE BEARDED IRISES In this section of the bearded irises, the hybrids have been divided into two groups: short and tall. All are hardy. Flowering during the whole of May, the short varieties come into bloom first. Size of flower varies, but is usually 3–5 in. across.

I. florentina. S. Europe. This is a pale blue-white form of *I. germanica.*

I. germanica (purple flag, London flag). S. Europe. Height 2–3 ft; planting distance 14–16 in. The scented flowers, 3–4 in. across, appear in early May. These have rich blue-purple falls with a white beard and light purple standards. The foliage is evergreen.

HYBRIDS These are vigorous and free-flowering, with well-shaped and flaring flowers throughout May. Those mentioned are only a selection of the many named varieties offered.

Short group (height 10–18 in.; planting distance 10–12 in.; flowers 3–5 in. across): 'Blue Denim', pale blue; 'Brannigan', deep blue-purple; 'Bronze Babe', deep yellow standards, bronze falls; 'Carilla', cream-yellow, blue beard; 'Circlette', white with violet plicata markings; 'Golden Fair', deep yellow; 'Green Spot', pale cream with green thumb marks on falls; 'Meadow Court', yellow standards and red-brown falls.

Taller group (height 18–28 in.; planting distance 10–12 in.; flowers 4–5 in. across): 'Chiltern Gold', medium yellow; 'Langport Smoke', pale blue; 'Langport Star', white; 'Piona', brilliant purple; 'Scintilla', old ivory; 'Solent Breeze', yellow with brown markings.

Iris 'Golden Fair' (Intermediate bearded)

Iris 'Scintilla' (Intermediate bearded)

363

Iris 'Benton Cordelia' (Tall bearded)

Iris 'Blue Drift' (Tall bearded)

Iris 'Allegiance' (Tall bearded)

Iris 'Brass Accents'
(Tall bearded)

Iris 'Dancer's Veil'
(Tall bearded)

TALL BEARDED IRISES Fully hardy. Height 2½–5 ft; planting distance 12–15 in. for rhizomes of the same variety, 18 in. between different varieties. The sword-shaped leaves are usually glaucous. Flowers, 4–6 in. across, appear from late May and through most of June.

IRIS (TALL BEARDED HYBRID)

I. pallida. Adriatic coast. Height 3 ft. The glaucous leaves can be used effectively in the border, or in flower arrangements. The flowers, 4–5 in. wide, are lavender-blue. Two variegated forms exist: 'Aureo-variegata', with yellow striped foliage, and 'Argenteo-variegata', with white stripes. These are good, though not vigorous, foliage plants for the front of the border. The flowers of both are of poor quality.

HYBRIDS There are thousands of named varieties, and many inferior ones are still offered by non-specialist nurseries. There has been tremendous progress since 1940, and few varieties before that date are worthy of consideration. Performance varies from garden to garden, but the following selection of varieties (average height 2 ft 10 in. to 3 ft 4 in.) can be generally recommended. A variety which does consistently badly should be replaced by another in the same colour class. Flowers vary in size from 4–6 in., and are produced from late May until late June.

'Allegiance', deep indigo-blue with yellow beard; 'Benton Cordelia', mauve-pink; 'Benton Evora', magenta; 'Black Taffeta' (height 2½ ft), black; 'Blue Drift', clear mid-blue with yellow beard; 'Blue Eyed Brunette', brown standards and brown falls marked with blue flash; 'Braithwaite',

pale lavender standards and blue-purple fall 'Brass Accents', velvety coffee-brown.

'Carnton', red-brown flowers, 8 in. acros 'Dancer's Veil', white with violet plicata mark ings; 'Desert Song', pale yellow, early flowering 'Eleanor's Pride', pale blue.

'Frost and Flame', white, slightly blue-tinte with red beard; 'Harbour Blue', pale to mid blue; 'Harriet Halloway', mid-blue, earl flowering; 'Immortal Hour', pure white.

'Jane Phillips', pale blue; 'Juliet', coppery-tar 'Muriel Neville', crimson; 'Olympic Torch golden-bronze; 'Pale Primrose', pale yellow, la flowering; 'Party Dress', flamingo-pink wit tangerine beard, late flowering; 'Patrician', whi with golden hafts to the falls and golden bear 'Pink Plume', orchid-pink; 'Silver Tide', whi slight blue tint on opening; 'Staten Island', go standards, red-brown falls.

'Techny Chimes', deep yellow with orang red beard; 'Total Eclipse', blue-black; 'Valimar apricot, well-branched and reliable.

Cultivation. All bearded irises of the Eupogo group require an open sunny position. Althoug they will grow in any good, not too acid, garde soil, they do best in a neutral soil. Plant th rhizomes in late June and early July (earl planting), or in early September (late planting The beds should have been well prepared wit old manure and compost, and bone-meal adde at the rate of 4 oz. per sq. yd. Plant the rhizome facing the same way, in such a position that eac rhizome receives the maximum sunshine. Plar firmly, but shallowly, with the top of th rhizomes just showing, and do not allow th plants to dry out for two to three week Late-planted irises should have the roots we spread out; if these are lifted by frost, do not pres them down, as this will break the roots. Build u around the plants with sand or light soil.

To prevent wind rocking and excessive trans piration, trim the leaves by about half.

Peel off dead leaves and keep the weeds dow as these take nourishment from the soil an

Iris 'Desert Song' (Tall bearded)

Iris 'Eleanor's Pride' (Tall bearded)

Iris 'Harbour Blue' (Tall bearded)

shade the rhizomes. In winter, cut the leaves back for neatness and to discourage slugs. In March, fork in an annual dressing of a general fertiliser which is not too rich in nitrogen, at the rate of 2–4 oz. per sq. yd. During the flowering season the appearance of the beds is improved by the daily removal of dead flower heads.

DWARF BEARDED IRISES Pay extra attention to good drainage. The best position is in a rock-garden pocket or at the edge of a raised border. Plant the rhizomes in small clumps, about 9 in. apart. Keep clear of weeds and replant every two to three years.

INTERMEDIATE BEARDED IRISES Suitable positions include the fronts of beds of bearded irises, the fronts of herbaceous borders and large pockets in the rock garden. They quickly form colourful clumps, but these need replanting every third year, 12 in. apart.

TALL BEARDED IRISES Plant rhizomes singly or in groups, with 18 in. between the plants and 24 in. between the groups. The stems of first year plants should be staked with thin bamboo canes, 3 ft high. After the first year only exceptionally large varieties require staking.

Propagation. Divide the rhizomes after flowering or in September if the clumps are crowded, usually every three years. Early division is recommended as this will allow them to ripen. When dividing the rhizomes cut off pieces from the outer part of the clump and discard the centre. Each piece must have one or two strong fans.

Beardless irises (Apogon)

The rhizomes of these irises are generally more slender than those of the bearded section, and they do not show on the soil surface. The falls are perfectly smooth, without crest or beard, hence the word apogon—beardless.

There are five sub-sections in this group: Californicae, Hexagona, Laevigatae, Sibiricae and Spuria, and also a miscellaneous group.

CALIFORNICAE This sub-section is known as the Pacific Coast irises. All of them come from that area of North America and share many common features. The species and hybrids described here are hardy. The foliage is narrow, tough, dark green and usually evergreen. Flowering season is early May to mid-June.

These irises make good companions for rhododendrons, and they are useful as cut flowers.

I. douglasiana. California. Height 12–18 in.; planting distance 24 in. The coarse, deep green foliage, often with a red tinge at the base of the leaves, spreads out to a diameter of 24 in. Each branched stem carries four or five flowers, 3 in. across. The colour is variable, but usually in shades of blue-purple and lavender with veining on the falls. It is tolerant of lime.

I. innominata. Oregon. Height up to 6 in.; planting distance 9 in. The narrow leaves are evergreen. Each stem carries one flower, occasionally two. The flowers, 2–2½ in. wide, have broad segments and are cream, buff, yellow or orange, with rich brown veins. The species is variable, and forms have been collected with

Iris 'Frost and Flame' (Tall bearded)

Iris innominata (Beardless Californicae)

Iris kaempferi (Beardless Laevigatae)

flowers in orchid-pink and blue-purple. It does best in a soil with plenty of peat and leaf-mould, where it forms small clumps.

I. tenax. Washington, Oregon. Height 12–15 in.; planting distance 12 in. The deciduous leaves are light green. It is free-flowering in shades of blue-purple. There are also rare forms in white, cream and yellow. The stems, each with one or two flowers, 3 in. across, are usually a little shorter than the leaves.

HYBRIDS Californian hybrids are usually raised from mixed seeds. A few named varieties exist and must be increased by division, but the seedlings obtained from a good mixed strain give an excellent range of colours and forms.

The hybrids were originally crosses between *I. douglasiana* and *I. innominata,* and combined the shape and size of bloom of *I. innominata* with the vigour of *I. douglasiana.* Other species were later used for hybridisation, and the modern hybrids are branching and free-flowering. Height 9–18 in.; planting distance 12 in. The smaller hybrids resemble *I. innominata* in growth habit, the taller are like *I. douglasiana.* The flowers, 2–3½ in. across, vary in colour from white through most shades of yellow and orange, and from palest blue to deep purple, some of them with dark thumb-prints on the falls.

When plants are raised from seed, discard young plants without flowers or with poor ones, and of bad growth. This will maintain the quality of the strain. Plant the seedlings out in their flowering positions when they are 3 in. high, singly or in groups.

Cultivation. Plant the rhizomes in October in a sunny or partially shaded position. They dislike lime, with the exception of *I. douglasiana* which will tolerate a certain amount. A neutral or acid soil is best for *I. innominata,* with added peat or leaf-mould. Cut off the deciduous foliage of *I. tenax* when this turns yellow.

Propagation. As these irises are short-lived, save seeds from the best forms to keep the stock going. They grow freely from seeds. Sow from October to April in boxes of seed compost, at a temperature of 7–10°C (45–50°F).

Plant the seedlings out in their final positions when they are small, as they resent disturbance. They will frequently flower the following year. To increase a particular form, detach and replant a rhizome when the new roots start to grow, usually in September. Do not allow the rhizome to dry out in its new position.

HEXAGONA This is the most recently discovered sub-section of the genus and is named for the six-ribbed seed pod. The hardy species and hybrids come from the Louisiana area of the U.S.A. where they grow along waterways in the delta area of the Mississippi. The slender, evergreen foliage is light green. The distinctive seeds have a corky covering and are carried in large pods up to 4 in. long. Flowers, 3–4 in. wide, appear in late June and July.

I. fulva. New Orleans. Height 18 in.; planting distance 12 in. This species has terminal flowers, 3–4 in. wide, as well as flowers in the leaf axils. Both standards and falls, which are terracotta, droop to about 45 degrees and give the flower a wilting look. It is the first of the hexagonas to flower, usually in mid-June.

I. × *fulvala.* A garden hybrid. Two forms are known in cultivation; one of these has red-purple, the other deep blue-purple flowers, 4 in. across. The stems are 24 in. high and both forms flower in late June.

HYBRIDS These are either collected natural hybrids or from controlled breeding. Height 2–3 ft; planting distance 15 in. The stems have a zigzag shape and carry a leaf and flower bud at each change of direction. Several flowers, in various colours, are produced on each stem in late June and early July.

Of the numerous named varieties only the following two have so far proved to grow well in Great Britain: 'Wheelhorse' and 'Dixie Deb'. The rose-red flowers of 'Wheelhorse' are up to 8 in. across, while 'Dixie Deb' has cream-yellow flowers, up to 5 in. across.

Cultivation. These irises require drier positions in Britain than in their homeland. Plant the rhizomes singly in July, just below the surface. A moist, but not wet position and a fairly rich soil with abundant humus is ideal. In winter give a protective covering of humus.

Propagation. Divide and replant the long slender rhizomes after flowering.

LAEVIGATAE Within this sub-section of the beardless irises are all those which thrive in moist conditions. The large range of hardy garden varieties have come from within each species and not from hybridisation between them.

I. albo-purpurea: see *I. laevigata* 'Monstrosa'

I. kaempferi. Manchuria, Korea, Japan. Height 2–3 ft; planting distance 12–18 in. The slender deciduous leaves are ribbed and deep green; each stem has a terminal spathe and one branch carrying three or four flowers. The flowers consist of short standards and broad falls which emerge from slender hafts; where the bearded iris has a beard, this species and all its garden forms have a yellow streak. The flowering season is from June to July.

Japanese gardeners have evolved several strains and numerous named varieties of this iris; the colour range covers shades of blue and red-purple, pink, lavender and white. Some forms are self-coloured, others are netted with white or coloured veins and others again have blended colours.

The flowers, 4–8 in. across, may be single or double, flat or double paeony-shaped. Most nurseries carry good stocks of garden varieties, but these can also be raised from seed; 'Higo' is a particularly good strain, with flowers 8–10 in. across and in a wide range of colours.

I. laevigata. Manchuria, Korea, Japan. Height 18–24 in.; planting distance 9–18 in. This species is a true water and waterside plant, and it grows best in a water depth of up to 6 in. The deciduous, pale green leaves are smooth and unribbed. Each stem carries three flowers, 4–6 in. across, borne in a terminal spathe in early June. These are deep royal blue; the standards and falls are of equal length, and the falls have a white streak.

Recommended varieties include: 'Alba', with flat, pure white flowers; 'Monstrosa', syn. *I. albo-purpurea,* white with deep blue blotches; *I. l. semperflorens,* deep blue flowers in June and again in September; and 'Variegata', silver-striped leaves and soft blue flowers.

Iris pseudacorus (Beardless Laevigatae)

Iris pseudacorus 'Variegata' (Beardless Laevigatae)

Iris sibirica (Beardless Sibiricae)

I. pseudacorus. Europe, Asia. Height 3–4 ft; planting distance 2–3 ft. An extremely hardy, true water iris. It adapts readily to ordinary border conditions, but it will then reach a height of up to 24 in. only. In garden pools, planted at a water depth of up to 18 in., and beside lakes and streams, the species may reach a height of 5 ft. The deciduous blue-green leaves are ribbed and similar to those of *I. kaempferi.* Branching shiny stems carry five or more yellow flowers, 3–3½ in. across and sometimes with brown veins, in late May and early June.

The following forms are suitable for growing in water up to 6 in. deep: 'Bastardii', primrose; 'Golden Queen', yellow; 'Variegata', yellow flowers and yellow-striped foliage—the stripes fade after flowering.

Varieties do not come true from seeds and should be dead-headed after flowering.

I. versicolor. U.S.A. Height 24 in. in water, 15 in. in a border; planting distance 9 in. A hardy species, similar in growth habit to *I. laevigata.* It is suitable for lakeside planting where it quickly forms compact clumps. The broad leaves are blue-green and stiffly erect. The well-branched stems have violet-blue flowers, 3 in. wide, in late May and early June. 'Kermesina' is wine-red.

Cultivation. These plants do well at the margins of streams, ponds and lakes; *I. laevigata* and *I. pseudacorus,* with their forms, are true water irises, suitable for the garden pool. *I. kaempferi* will not tolerate lime, and requires rich feeding and added humus in the soil.

Plant in March and April or in August and September in full sun. *I. laevigata* will grow in water up to 6 in. deep; *I. pseudacorus* in a water depth of 18 in. and its varieties in 6 in. *I. versicolor* will grow in water up to 3 in. deep. Divide and replant the clumps every three years.

Propagation. Divide the rhizomes immediately after flowering, or at any time when growth is active. At this time the rhizomes are easily extracted from the boggy soil and should be replanted immediately.

I. kaempferi and *I. pseudacorus* are easily raised from seeds sown in March or April. Stand the seed boxes outdoors in partial shade. Prick out the seedlings, when large enough to handle, singly into 3 in. pots; plant in the flowering site in September.

SIBIRICAE This sub-section includes many worthwhile species and hybrids. They are all hardy and easy to grow and do well in the herbaceous border, provided the soil is not excessively dry. They may also be grown as marginal plants at the edges of pools. Size of flower, 2½–3½ in. in diameter. They are excellent as cut flowers. The grassy, slender, mid-green foliage dies down in winter.

I. bulleyana. W. China. Height 2–3 ft; planting distance 18 in. This is thought to be a natural hybrid of *I. forrestii,* as it gives variable results from seeds. Good forms are well-branched and have two flowers, 3 in. across, in each spathe, in mid-June. The spreading standards are lilac, and the drooping falls veined and blotched with blue-purple on a light yellow ground.

I. chrysographes. S.W. China. Height 18–24 in.; planting distance 12 in. A variable species; the standards are at an angle of 45 degrees to the stem and the falls droop. The flowers, 2½ in. wide, appear in mid-June; they are deep blue or red-purple with gold veins on the falls. The unbranched stem carries one, two or three flowers. There is an almost black form as well as many paler ones.

I. forrestii. N.W. China. Height up to 24 in. in boggy conditions; planting distance 18 in. This species requires plenty of moisture, particularly in spring, or it may not exceed 15 in. in height. The unbranched stem carries two terminal flowers, 3 in. across, in mid-June. The pale yellow flowers have standards at an angle of 45 degrees to the stem, and drooping falls; the falls sometimes have brown veins.

I. sibirica. Central Europe, Russia. Height 2–3¾ ft; planting distance 24 in. The original species is difficult to obtain as it hybridises freely with other species of the sub-section. It has a well-branched stem with flowers, 2½ in. across, borne above the foliage from early to mid-June. The colour is in varying shades of blue, with white veining on the hafts of the falls.

HYBRIDS These hybrids have the well-branched habit of *I. sibirica.* Height up to 3 ft; planting distance 18–24 in. All are hardy and flower in early and mid-June. The flowers are 3–4 in. across with broad, slightly flared falls and upright standards.

'Blue Cape', royal blue with white veining on the falls; 'Gatineau', light blue with gold markings on the hafts; 'Helen Astor', orchid-pink, slow growing; 'Purple Mere', deep blue-purple; 'Violet Flare', medium violet; 'White Swirl', pure white flaring flowers.

'Margot Holmes' (height 15 in.) is a cross between *I. chrysographes* and *I. douglasiana*; it has deep claret flowers with an orange blotch.

Cultivation. Plant after flowering in late autumn or in April. Set the rhizomes 1 in. deep in good, not too dry, garden soil and in a sunny position. They also do well near water, planted about 6 in. above water level. Avoid hoeing or cultivating round the plants, as the roots are near the surface and easily damaged; in spring use a top-dressing of manure, peat or compost to discourage weeds. Where space permits, set the rhizomes in groups, 24 in. apart.

Propagation. Large clumps tend to grow hollow in the centre and should be divided about every fifth year. Cut the clumps into four to eight pieces. Replant the rhizomes 1 in. deep after flowering, in late autumn after the foliage has died down, or in April when growth restarts.

SPURIA This sub-section of the beardless irises is distinguished by the tough and fibrous rhizomes and by the double ridges at the angles of the seed pods. The foliage is mid-green, narrow and reedy. In autumn the old leaves die down but the new foliage lasts through the winter. The species are hardy, and the tall ones especially are suitable for the herbaceous border. The flowers are 2½–3½ in. across. Within each species there is considerable variation, and unless a proven form can be obtained, the best result is achieved by raising plants from seeds and selecting the best seedlings when they flower. Named hybrid varieties are being raised in the U.S.A.; these are less hardy than the species and are not yet recommended for outdoor cultivation in Great Britain.

Iris ochroleuca (Beardless Spuria)

Iris foetidissima (seeds) (Bearded miscellaneous)

Iris unguicularis (Bearded miscellaneous)

I. graminea. S. and Central Europe. Height 8 in.; planting distance 9–12 in. The grassy leaves are up to 12 in. long. Each flower stem carries a leaf well above the single flower, which appears in early June. The flowers, 2 in. wide, are sweetly scented with a strong perfume resembling ripe plums, and are good for cutting. The standards and style arms are red-purple, and the falls are veined blue-purple on a white ground.

I. ochroleuca (butterfly iris). Asia Minor. Height 4 ft; planting distance 3 ft. The leaves are over 3 ft long, glaucous and slightly twisted. A succession of flowers, 3–4 in. wide, with cream-white standards and falls with a bold yellow blotch, are carried in late June. The standards are open, and the falls vary from flaring to recurved. The plant is vigorous and eventually forms a clump.

There are several forms of this species: *I. o. aurea,* rich yellow; *I. o. monnieri,* soft yellow self-colour; 'Shelford Giant' (height up to 7 ft), yellow and white flowers, 4–5 in. across.

I. spuria. Europe, Middle East. Height 2½–3 ft; planting distance 18–24 in. Similar in growth, habit and flowering to *I. ochroleuca.* The flowers are blue-purple. 'Notha' has deep purple flowers, and is a good form for the herbaceous border.

Cultivation. Plant the fibrous rhizomes in clumps, 2 in. deep, in late October. Any fertile garden soil is suitable, given a sunny position. All the species resent disturbance; if this is unavoidable, autumn lifting is preferable.

Propagation. Divide the rhizomes after the old foliage has died down in autumn. The replanted pieces may take some time to become established, and will not usually flower until the second season after replanting.

MISCELLANEOUS GROUP (APOGON IRISES) There are a number of smaller beardless sub-sections of the genus with only a few species in each. As many of these species are rare, difficult or insignificant they have been excluded.

I. ensata. Kashmir, Tibet, China. Height 12 in.; planting distance 12–15 in. A hardy and deep-rooting species, with deciduous leaves that are mid-green and grassy. The form usually offered is *I. e. lactea.* The flaring falls are cream with a network of lavender veins, and the open standards are soft lavender. Several flowers, 2½ in. wide, are borne terminally in late May.

Plant the rhizomes 2 in. deep in clumps, in late October. Any fertile garden soil is suitable, given a warm sunny position. Increase by division in autumn after the foliage has died down.

I. foetidissima (stinking iris, gladdon or gladwyn iris). Europe. Height 20 in.; planting distance 12–18 in. This hardy plant gives off a rank smell from the leaves when bruised. The dark green glossy foliage is evergreen. Insignificant pale purple flowers, 2–2½ in. across, several to each stem, are carried in June.

The beauty of the plant lies in its seed pods, which split open and peel back to reveal scarlet seeds in autumn. The flower stems may be picked and hung upside-down to dry and then used as winter decoration. *I. f. lutea* is a yellow form with brown veining. There is also a variegated form, 'Variegata'. Both have orange-red seeds.

Plant in autumn, in moist soil rich in humus. Set the rhizomes 1½ in. deep in clumps. This species does well in shade, but is slow growing

and takes more than a year to settle down and flower. Increase by dividing and replanting the rhizomes in October.

I. ruthenica. Transylvania. Height and planting distance 6 in. A dwarf, early-flowering species of variable performance; sometimes it smothers itself in flowers, in other years it produces none. The deep green deciduous leaves are thin and grassy and tend to be carried at an angle to the ground. The flowers are 2 in. across and flaring with falls veined deep blue-purple on a white ground; the standards and crests are blue-purple.

It is suitable for the front of the border or the rock garden. Plant in any good garden soil and in a sunny position in summer or early autumn. Set the rhizomes in clumps, ½ in. deep. Propagate by division of the rhizomes after flowering.

I. setosa. Siberia, Alaska. Height ½–2½ ft; planting distance 9–18 in. This fully hardy species has light green, grassy, deciduous leaves. Well-branched stems carry several flowers, 2½ in. wide, in shades of mauve or slate-grey, in early June. The standards exist only as tiny bristles, but the falls are broad and the style crests conspicuous. 'Tricuspis' (height 2½ ft; planting distance 24 in.) is a vigorous form with royal-purple flowers.

Plant during September, in moist garden soil and in a sunny position. Set the rhizomes in clumps, 1 in. deep. Increase by division and replanting in September.

I. stylosa: see *I. unguicularis*

I. unguicularis, syn. *I. stylosa* (Algerian iris). Algeria. Height 9 in.; planting distance 15 in. The dark green strap-shaped foliage is evergreen; the leaves are about 24 in. long and can be cut back in October to 12 in. for neatness. This winter-flowering iris has soft lavender or lilac flowers 2½–3 in. across, with a yellow blaze on the falls. Flowering begins in October and continues until March; after a poor summer flowering may not begin until February.

Plant the rhizomes 1 in. deep in September, in small clumps rather than singly. In a sunny position, any well-drained soil, even poor soil, is suitable; they will tolerate lime. The plants may take time to settle down and start flowering.

When picking the flowers for indoor decoration gently pull them when they are at the bud stage. They will open indoors in a few minutes.

Increase by division in September.

Crested irises (Evansia)

The irises in this section are characterised by a linear crest, rather like a cock's comb, on the falls. This crest replaces the hairy beard of the Pogoniris. Most of the species are hardy, but the plants are often attacked by slugs and snails. The flowers, 1½–2½ in. across, are delicately coloured and dainty, and the standards lie in the same plane as the falls. The broad leaves, mid to dark green and glossy, are evergreen. Hybrid varieties are few, and these are difficult to obtain.

I. cristata. N. America. Height and planting distance 6 in. This is a hardy species, suitable for the rock garden or a cold greenhouse. Lavender flowers, 2–2½ in. across, with a white patch and a white crest tipped with orange, are produced

Iris japonica (Crested)

Iris tectorum (Crested)

Iris bucharica (Bulbous Juno)

gly in late April and early May. Odd flowers
ay appear at almost any time during the
mmer. *I. c. lacustris* is similar, though only 3 in.
gh and of a more compact habit.

gracilipes. Japan. Height 9 in.; planting
stance 6 in. A hardy species, suitable for a
ck-garden pocket; it requires acid soil. The dark
een glossy leaves are slender and narrow.
anched stems bear flat lavender-pink flowers,
2 in. across, in late April and early May.

japonica. Central China, Japan. Height 24 in.;
anting distance 18 in. An almost hardy species.
short bamboo-like stem carries a fan of broad,
ossy leaves 12–18 in. long. The flat, pale lilac
wers, 2 in. across, are spotted with a deeper
ac shade; they open in late April and early May.
otect the evergreen foliage from damage by
ow with polythene sheeting or glass. Prevent
mage by morning sunshine after frost by
anting in a sheltered position. The most easily
tained form is 'Ledger's Variety', which is
entical to, but hardier than, the species.

ectorum (roof iris). China. Height and planting
stance 12–18 in. In late May and early June
ch stem carries two or three flowers, 3 in.
ross, in lavender with deeper spots and a jagged
ite crest. *I. t.* 'Alba' is a white form. Both forms
e hardy and suitable for the front of the border.

ultivation. Plant the slender rhizomes in May or
ne, just below the soil level. Set the rhizomes
gly or in groups. The species all require a
ghtly moist soil with plenty of leaf-mould, and
cept for *I. tectorum* they do not tolerate lime.
ant in semi-shaded and sheltered positions.
p-dress with leaf-mould in spring.

opagation. Divide and replant the rhizomes
mediately after flowering, except for *I.
acilipes.* This should be divided in spring.

Bulbous irises

JNO SUB-SECTION This is a little known, but
tractive and fairly hardy sub-section. The
otstock consists of a bulb; to this are attached
ick storage roots from which feeding roots
velop during the growing season. If these are
oken, the bulbs take time to recover, and they
ould therefore be handled gently. The manner
growth is similar to that of a sweet corn plant,
th flower buds in the leaf axils. The lanceolate
aves are shiny mid-green above, glaucous
neath and deeply channelled in cross-section.
e foliage is short-lived.

The flowers, 2½–3 in. wide, have standards
d falls, but the standards are little more than
istles; they often hang down at a sharp angle.

IRIS BUCHARICA

bucharica. Turkestan. Height 18 in.; planting
stance 6 in. This is the most easily grown
ecies of the Juno sub-section. Up to seven

sweet-scented flowers, 2½ in. across, are carried
on each stem in April and early May. The
prominent style arms and crests are cream-white;
the falls are bright yellow. It grows well in deep
pots and in sheltered spots in the garden.

I. graeberiana. Turkestan. Height up to 18 in.;
planting distance 9 in. Each stem carries four or
six flowers, 2½ in. across, in late March and early
April. Style arms and crests are pale silver-
mauve; the falls are light cobalt-blue.

I. orchioides. Turkestan. Height up to 12 in.;
planting distance 6–9 in. Similar to *I. bucharica*,
but the flowers, 2½ in. wide, are self-coloured
golden-yellow, and there are four to each stem in
April and May. It is not always hardy, and is best
grown in deep pots.

Cultivation. Plant the bulbs in September in light,
well-drained soil containing humus and some
lime. Set the bulbs 2 in. deep, singly or in clumps.
Outdoors, the best position is where shrubs or
trees will shelter the plants and keep them as dry
as possible in summer.

They can also be grown in pots and given the
protection of an alpine or cool greenhouse.

In September, plant one bulb to a 5 in. pot, in
John Innes potting compost No. 1. Keep the
compost just moist throughout the winter, but
increase the amount of water after flowering and
as the foliage expands. The leaves turn yellow and
die down in June. From then on the bulbs should
be kept dry until growth is restarted in early
autumn. Repot every two or three years.

Propagation. Increase by division and replanting
after the foliage dies down. Allow the plants to
dry out so that the storage roots become limp and
less likely to break. Gently remove the surrounding soil and divide and replant the bulbs.

RETICULATA This group of small bulbous
irises is characterised by the tunic of the bulb,
which is netted (or reticulated) with fibres. The
deep green leaves are tubular, with four or eight
ribs. Each leaf terminates in a pale green sharp
point. Species and garden hybrids are nearly all
hardy and bear early flowers, 2½–3 in. wide.
They are suitable for rockery pockets, the fronts
of borders and for greenhouse pot culture.

IRIS DANFORDIAE

I. danfordiae. E. Turkey. Height 4 in.; planting
distance 2–4 in. The leaves, which are barely
developed at flowering time, are square in
section. Honey-scented flowers, 2½–3 in. across,
in late January and February, are vivid lemon-
yellow and have a distinctive shape. The standards are greatly reduced in size; the hafts of
the falls tilt steeply upwards, while the black
spotted falls stand out horizontally.

Mature bulbs usually flower well, but after
flowering once they often break up into bulblets
of varying sizes. The largest of these take one or
two years to attain flowering size, and the
smallest may take twice as long.

Iris reticulata (Bulbous
Reticulata)

Iris 'Joyce' (Bulbous Reticulata)

I. histrioides 'Major'. Asia Minor, Turkey, N. W. Persia. Height 4 in.; planting distance 2–4 in. This is among the first of the reticulatas to flower. It often starts at Christmas and will survive all weathers, even snow. The leaves are only 1 in. high at flowering time, but will grow to 18 in. during the summer. The flowers are bright royal blue and about $3\frac{1}{2}$ in. across. Suitable for rock gardens and ideal for pan culture.

I. reticulata. Russia, Caucasus, N. Persia. Height 6 in.; planting distance 2–4 in. The best known and most easily grown species of the sub-section. The four-ribbed leaves extend above the flowers at flowering time. In late February and early March, the flowers appear; these are $2\frac{1}{2}$–3 in. across and are deep blue-purple; the falls have an orange blaze.

I. winogradowii. U.S.S.R., Transcaucasia. Height 4 in.; planting distance 3–4 in. This species is closely allied to, and much resembles *I. histrioides* 'Major', but has lemon-yellow flowers opening during February and March.

HYBRIDS These are easily grown, inexpensive to purchase and fully hardy. Height 4–8 in.; planting distance 2–4 in. The following are either colour forms of *I. reticulata* or hybrids between *I. reticulata* and *I. histrioides* 'Major'. The flowers are 3–$3\frac{1}{2}$ in. wide:

'Cantab', pale blue flowers; 'Clairette', pale blue standards, deep blue falls; 'Harmony', deep royal blue; 'Joyce', similar to 'Harmony' but with more contrast between standards and falls; 'J. S. Dijt', purple-red, vigorous grower; 'Wentworth', deep blue-purple.

Cultivation. Plant the bulbs in clumps, 2–3 in. deep in September or October. They are best grown in a light, well-drained and chalky or limestone soil. Outdoors, plant them in pockets in the rockery, in the alpine bed or at the front of herbaceous borders. Avoid planting in heavy soils as they need additional drainage and may not come up a second year. After flowering, feed with a general liquid fertiliser about three times at monthly intervals. This will ensure good bulbs for the following year.

If the bulbs are grown in pans or pots, do not bring them into a warm room before the buds show colour. Otherwise the buds will dry out and fail to open. The moist atmosphere of a greenhouse will usually prevent bud-drying. Plant six bulbs in a 5 in. pot, 1 in. deep, in John Innes potting compost No. 1.

XIPHIUM The species of this sub-section of bulbous irises all come from the hot areas around the Mediterranean. In Britain the species are tender and short-lived. The hybrids known as Dutch, Spanish and English irises, usually do well the first year, and if planted in the correct soil and position will persist and increase.

All the species and hybrids have medium-sized bulbs with no storage roots. The sparse deep green leaves, channelled in cross-section, sometimes have a light grey bloom. They make good cut flowers, but the bulbs take time to recover after the first flower stems have been cut.

I. tingitana. Tangier, Morocco. Height up to 24 in.; planting distance 4–6 in. Not reliably hardy outdoors as the leaves are formed early in the year and both leaves and buds are liable to be damaged by frost. The stems carry two or three flowers,

Iris winogradowii (Bulbous Reticulata)

Iris xiphioides (Bulbous Xiphium)

4 in. across; these are pale blue-purple with yellow patch on the falls. The natural flowering time outdoors is late April and early May, but it unlikely to flower more than once, as it require an extremely hot summer for the bulbs to ripen.

This iris is often used for forcing and can be brought into flower as early as the end of January if grown in a cool greenhouse. Do not subject the plants to excessive heat or the buds will fail to open. After forcing, the bulbs are best discarded as they will not produce flowers again the following year.

I. xiphioides. Pyrenees. Height up to 24 in.; planting distance 6–8 in. A hardy species. The leaves, unlike those of most other irises in this sub-section, do not overwinter, but appear in February. Each flower stem carries two or three flowers in a terminal spathe in July. These are up to 5 in. across, and the colour is deep royal blue with a golden blaze on the falls.

I. xiphium. S. France, Portugal, S. Spain, N.W. Africa. Height up to 24 in.; planting distance 4– in. A half-hardy or hardy species. The flowers 4–$4\frac{1}{2}$ in. wide, one or two to each stem, appear in late June or early July. The colour is in varying shades of purple with a central yellow streak on the falls. There is a self-coloured yellow form.

HYBRIDS The bulbous hybrids fall into three groups: Dutch, Spanish and English. They are hardier than most of the Xiphium species.

DUTCH IRISES These are the first of the hybrids to flower, from early to mid-June. The flowers are 4–5 in. in diameter. Remove the seed pods after flowering to help the bulbs recover. All named varieties available (height 15–24 in.; planting distance 4–6 in.) grow well and should be chosen from their colour description in nursery catalogues. Colours range through white, yellow, blue and purple. Mixed varieties raised from seeds are also available in unusual colour combinations. The most popular variety is the pale blue 'Wedgwood'.

SPANISH IRISES These hybrids (height 12–18 in.; planting distance 3–6 in.) are forms of *I. xiphium* and flower about two weeks later than the Dutch irises, in late June. The bulbs, leaves and flowers, the latter $3\frac{1}{2}$–$4\frac{1}{2}$ in. across, are all smaller than those of the Dutch irises. All named varieties are well worth growing and are available in a range of colours, which includes smoky shades.

ENGLISH IRISES These are the last of the bulbous irises to flower, in July. They are forms and hybrids of *I. xiphioides*. The English irises (height $1\frac{1}{4}$–$2\frac{1}{4}$ ft; planting distance 6–8 in.) have the largest flowers of the group, 5 in. across, but the smallest colour range—there are no yellows. The flowers may be white, blue, pink or purple and, on named varieties, tend to be flecked; mixtures from seeds are often clean and unflecked.

Cultivation. Plant the bulbs 4–6 in. deep in September or October. The tender *I. tingitana* should be grown in pots in a cool greenhouse, but even so will not usually flower a second season. Pot the bulbs in John Innes potting compost No. 2 or 3, six bulbs to a 6 in. container. Place in full sun. *I. xiphioides* requires the same conditions as the English irises, while *I. xiphium* needs a well-drained and sunny position, with some winter protection if in an exposed site. Plant Dutch irises in light fertile soil, in full sun

A hard winter may damage the young leaves produced during the autumn, and although this will not prevent flowering during the first growing season, subsequent blooming may be affected. Winter protection with cloches is recommended. The bulbs may be left in the ground after the foliage dies down; in wet and heavy soils lifting and storing of the bulbs in late summer is advisable.

Dutch irises may be grown in pots for gentle forcing; the pots should never be brought in from the greenhouse until the buds show colour. Spanish irises require a light soil, and a warmer and drier position than Dutch irises. Lift the bulbs when the foliage has died down, to assist the ripening of the bulbs, and replant in September.

The English irises are the easiest of the garden hybrids to cultivate; in rich soil and damp positions they will establish themselves as good perennials. They do not require lifting and the soft bulbs may quickly deteriorate if left out of the ground for long.

Propagation. Increase the species and hybrids by division after the foliage has died down. Most bulbs split into two naturally, with a number of smaller offsets. The largest bulbs will flower the following year, but the smaller offsets should be set aside and grown to maturity in a nursery bed.

Pests. Bulbs in store may be attacked by APHIDS, particularly tulip bulb aphids; they may also infest growing plants. STEM AND BULB EELWORM may cause internal discoloration and rotting of the bulbs and rhizomes, followed by distortion and stunting of stems and leaves. Bulbs may also be attacked by small NARCISSUS FLY larvae. Leaves, stems and flowers, particularly those of *I. unguicularis,* are eaten by SLUGS and SNAILS; the blue-grey larvae of the IRIS SAWFLY feed on the leaves of *I. pseudacorus* and *I. laevigata.* SWIFT MOTH caterpillars damage the rhizomes of bearded irises.

Diseases. All rhizomatous irises may be damaged by the following diseases:

ARABIS MOSAIC VIRUS and CUCUMBER MOSAIC VIRUS, either alone or together, cause a disease which shows as chlorotic streaks and spots on the leaves and flowers. Severely affected plants are stunted, and growth is poor.

LEAF SPOT due to a fungus may appear in spring or autumn, depending on the locality. It is more likely to be troublesome in wet weather. Brown oval-shaped spots develop on the leaves and coalesce until the whole leaf may be killed.

RHIZOME ROT causes a soft rot of the rhizomes, which decay into an evil-smelling, yellow and slimy mass. The leaves turn brown at the tips, then die, and the fan collapses at ground level.

RUST occasionally occurs on *I. foetidissima, I. germanica* and *I. pseudacorus,* and on some other cultivated species. It shows as small red-brown covered pustules, either solitary or in groups on the leaves.

Diseases of bulbous irises:

BLUE MOULD is common on stored bulbs and causes a rotting of the scales, and sometimes of the whole bulbs. The affected tissues become covered with blue-green spore masses.

GREY BULB ROT attacks the bulbs at the neck, causing a dry grey decay, and thus preventing the shoots from getting far above ground. A dense fungal growth soon destroys the bulbs, and then produces large black resting bodies on the debris.

INK DISEASE may cause black spots on the leaves in wet seasons, but is more serious when it occurs on the bulbs. Black crusty patches or streaks appear on the outer scales.

IRIS MOSAIC VIRUS causes chlorotic streaks and spots on the young leaves. Affected plants may be stunted; the flowers often show darker streaks on the normal ground colour.

LEAF SPOT is usually seen only in the second year, when brown oval-shaped spots appear on the leaves, which soon wither.

Iron cross begonia: see *Begonia masoniana*

Ixia

Iridaceae

IXIA VIRIDIFLORA

A genus of about 40 species of bulbs from S. Africa, some of which have recently been reclassified. The six-petalled star-shaped flowers are borne on tall, wiry stems. The species are not hardy in most parts of Britain, but survive outdoors in the mildest parts of the country. They are suitable for cutting or for growing in pots for flowering indoors. Only two species are in cultivation, but a large number of garden hybrids in mixed strains and named varieties are available. The leaves of species and hybrids are narrowly sword-shaped and mid-green.

I. viridiflora. S. Africa. Height 12 in.; planting distance 3–4 in. The 1½ in. wide flowers are an unusual blue-green with a dark centre, and appear in May and June.

The hybrids (height 18 in.; planting distance 4 in.) are more vigorous and reproductive than *I. viridiflora.* Their flowers, 1–1½ in. across, include many shades of yellow, red, purple and blue, usually with dark or light centres.

'Afterglow' is buff-orange with a dark centre; 'Bridesmaid', white flushed with red; 'Conqueror', yellow within, orange-red without; 'Hogarth', pale yellow with a dark eye; 'Uranus', dark yellow with a dark eye; 'Vulcan', scarlet suffused with orange.

Cultivation. In mild areas, plant the corms during October or November, 2–3 in. deep, in a sunny position, in ordinary well-drained garden soil. Plant in rows 15–18 in. apart for cutting, or in groups for garden decoration. Protect from frost with bracken, coarse sand or ashes.

For indoor flowering, in October or November place half-a-dozen corms in a 4–5 in. pot or a dozen in a 7–8 in. pot; cover with 1–2 in. of John Innes potting compost No. 2, and water in. Do not water again until the plants are showing some growth. Maintain a temperature of 4–7°C (39–45°F).

Iris xiphium (Bulbous Xiphium)

Ixia (hybrids)

If the flowers are not cut for indoor decoration, dead-head just below the lowest flower when all have died, leaving the lower part of the stem. Lift or shake the plant out of its pot when the leaves are dead, and store in a warm, dry place until it is time to replant.

Propagation. Most varieties produce offsets or cormlets, and these may be saved and planted separately at the time of planting the flowering-size corms. Seeds may be saved and sown during March in pots or boxes under glass, at a temperature of 16°C (61°F). The seedlings, which should reach flowering size after two or three years, are usually in mixed colours.

Pests and diseases. Generally trouble-free.

Ivy: see Hedera
Ivy, Canary Island: see *Hedera canariensis*
Ivy, common: see *Hedera helix*
Ivy, finger-leaved: see *Hedera helix* 'Digitata'
Ivy, ground: see *Nepeta hederacea*
Ivy, Italian: see *Hedera chrysocarpa*
Ivy, marble-leaved: see *Hedera helix* 'Discolor'
Ivy, Persian: see *Hedera colchica*

Jacobinia carnea

Jacobinia pauciflora

J

Jacobinia

Acanthaceae

A genus of 50 species of evergreen sub-shrubs which in Great Britain require greenhouse cultivation. Some of these are occasionally offered under the name *Justicia*. The slender, tubular, two-lipped flowers are borne in profusion. In

JACOBINIA CARNEA

some species they are carried in dense terminal cone-like spikes, in others they appear in small clusters from the leaf axils.

J. carnea, syn. *Justicia carnea*. Brazil. Height up to 6 ft; spread 3 ft. The opposite dark green leaves are elliptic with a slender point. The flesh-pink flowers appear in terminal heads, 4–6 in. long, in August and September.

J. chrysostephana. Mexico. Height about 4 ft; spread 24 in. Ovate slender-pointed mid-green leaves have the principal veins on the underside picked out in bright red. The yellow flowers, 1–1½ in. long, are produced in terminal heads from November to February.

J. coccinea, syn. *Justicia coccinea*. Brazil. Height 5 ft; spread 3 ft. This species has elliptic mid-green leaves; the terminal heads of scarlet flowers, 2 in. long, appear in February.

J. pauciflora, syn. *Libonia floribunda*. Brazil. Height 12–24 in.; spread 18 in. A twiggy sub-shrub with elliptic mid-green leaves. The flowers, 1 in. long, are produced singly from the leaf axils. They are scarlet with yellow tips and appear from October until the following summer.

J. suberecta. Uruguay. Height and spread 18 in. The grey velvety stems carry ovate, grey, soft-hairy leaves. Orange-scarlet flowers, 1¼ in. long, appear in terminal cymes from July to September. This species can be grown as a basket plant.

Cultivation. The various species require different treatments and are best considered in groups:

J. carnea, *J. chrysostephana* and *J. coccinea* require a winter temperature of 10–13°C (50–55°F). In early spring, increase the temperature gradually to a maximum of 21°C (70°F) and admit air whenever possible. If this is not done the plants will grow lanky.

Grow these species in John Innes potting compost No. 2. In April, place three cuttings to 3 in. pot and pot on the whole group in stages, finishing off in 8–10 in. pots.

Give water freely at all times, although less is required when the plants have been cut back after flowering. During warmer months, syringe the plants regularly. Provide only light shading during the hottest months.

JACOBINIA PAUCIFLORA

J. pauciflora needs a similar winter temperature. Grow this species in John Innes potting compost No. 2. Pot the cuttings singly in 3 in. pots and finish off in 5–6 in. pots. From June to September the plants may be stood outdoors in a sunny position; keep them just moist to encourage the stems to ripen. Take the plants back into the greenhouse at the end of September and water freely until after flowering. Thereafter, keep the plants just moist until growth restarts.

J. suberecta is grown in a similar compost and pot sizes as *J. pauciflora*, but requires a winter temperature of 13°C (55°F). It will tolerate more heat in summer but needs shadier conditions. Once flowering is over, gradually withhold water. Keep the plants just moist in winter and water them freely from April to September.

Propagation. Increase all species by cuttings, 2–3 in. long, of young shoots, taken in April from stooled plants. Pot the cuttings as described under cultivation and root at a temperature of

18–21°C (64–70°F). Stop *J. carnea, J. chryso-stephana* and *J. coccinea* once or twice during summer to encourage branching growth; *J. pauciflora* and *J. suberecta* need pinching out two or three times to produce bushy growth.

Pruning. The species are usually grown as annuals, but may be grown on as stooled plants for several years by cutting them back annually to 4 in., after flowering or in February or March. Cut-back plants can be used for cuttings or may be repotted and grown on.

Pests and diseases. Generally trouble-free.

Jasminum

Jasmine. *Oleaceae*

JASMINUM NUDIFLORUM   JASMINUM POLYANTHUM

A genus of 300 species of tender and hardy, deciduous and evergreen shrubs and climbers. They are suitable as ground cover on rock gardens, for training against walls or fences, or for twining over arbours, trellises and pergolas or to cover old tree stumps. Most of the species described are sufficiently hardy for outdoor planting, but two require greenhouse treatment in all but the mildest districts.

Jasmine flowers are tubular, opening out salviform; they are usually borne in terminal and axillary clusters, sometimes forming panicles. Some species are strongly fragrant. The leaves are opposite and, in most cases, pinnate with a varying number of leaflets.

J. nudiflorum (winter-flowering jasmine). China. Height up to 10 ft. A hardy deciduous scandent shrub that needs support. It will thrive in almost any position, even on a cold, sunless, north wall. The smooth dark green leaves are trifoliate. Bright yellow flowers, $\frac{3}{4}$–1 in. across, are produced from November to April singly or in small clusters in the axils of the previous season's leaves. The flowers are susceptible to cold winds.

J. officinale (common white jasmine). Persia, India, China. Height 30 ft. A vigorous, hardy and deciduous twining climber with mid-green leaves consisting of five, seven or nine leaflets. Pure white flowers are borne profusely in 2–3 in. long axillary clusters from June to October. The

variety 'Affine' has larger flowers, tinged with pink; 'Aureo-variegatum', syn. 'Aureum', has leaves blotched with cream-yellow.

J. parkeri. N.W. India. Height 8–12 in.; spread up to 24 in. A hardy, dense, hummock-forming evergreen shrub with pinnate leaves composed of three to five ovate mid-green leaflets. Yellow, $\frac{1}{2}$ in. wide flowers are borne singly from the upper leaf axils in June.

J. polyanthum. China. Height 5–10 ft. A half-hardy climbing species which thrives outdoors only in sheltered areas in the south and west, where it is sometimes semi-evergreen. In colder areas it should be grown in a cool greenhouse. Growth tends to be vertical at first, branching later. The dark green pinnate leaves have five to seven leaflets. White and pale pink flowers appear in axillary and lateral panicles, 2–5 in. long, from April to June outdoors, from November to April under glass.

J. primulinum (primrose jasmine). China. Height up to 10 ft. A scandent evergreen shrub, hardy only in sheltered gardens in the south and west, preferably on a south or south-west wall. The dark green leaves are trifoliate. Solitary, semi-double yellow flowers, 2 in. across, are produced from March to May.

J. revolutum (Himalayan jasmine). Himalayas, Afghanistan. Height 6–8 ft; spread 4–5 ft. An evergreen non-twining shrub which may be grown free-standing or trained on a wall. Plant in a site sheltered from north and east winds. The dark green leathery leaves consist of three to seven leaflets. Small, fragrant yellow flowers are produced in axillary and terminal clusters, up to 6 in. long, from June to August.

J. × stephanense. Height 10–15 ft. This vigorous hybrid climber may be semi-evergreen in mild winters. It is a twining plant suitable for covering archways or pergolas. The leaves, dull green above and light green below, vary from simple ovate-lanceolate to pinnate, with five leaflets. Lateral and terminal clusters, 2–3 in. long, of fragrant pale pink flowers appear during June.

Cultivation. Outdoors, grow jasminums in any ordinary, well-drained garden soil. With the exceptions of *J. nudiflorum* and *J. officinale* the species all need warm sheltered positions. Plant *J. polyanthum* and *J. primulinum* in April or May, the other species from October to April. Protect *J. polyanthum* and *J. primulinum* in winter with wattle hurdles or wire netting thatched with bracken or straw.

In the greenhouse, *J. polyanthum* and *J. primulinum* do best if planted in the border, but may also be grown in 10–12 in. pots of John Innes potting compost No. 2. The plants are generally trained up wires or strings under the greenhouse roof, or up supporting pillars. Those in pots may be supported with canes or tall bean-sticks. During winter, maintain a minimum temperature of 5°C (41°F); a temperature of 10–13°C (50–55°F), will bring *J. polyanthum* into flower earlier. Keep the compost moist at all times, and water freely in summer; admit as much fresh air as possible.

J. polyanthum can be grown as small pot plants from cuttings taken in March. Pot the cuttings into 3 in. and then 5 in. pots and provide canes, twiggy sticks or wire hoops as support.

Jasminum nudiflorum

Jasminum officinale

Jasminum parkeri

Jasminum polyanthum

Jasminum primulinum

Jeffersonia dubia

Jerusalem artichoke

Pinch out the growing points once, just before the plants are put into 5 in. pots.

During summer, stand pot plants outside in full sun, and avoid over-watering young plants to ensure that the wood is well ripened. Re-house the plants at the end of September and keep them just moist until the flower buds begin to expand; thereafter water more freely.

Propagation. Take nodal cuttings, 3–4 in. long, of semi-ripe wood during August or September. Insert in equal parts (by volume) peat and sand in a frame and overwinter at a temperature of 7–10°C (45–50°F). Cuttings of *J. polyanthum* and *J. primulinum* are best taken with a heel and given bottom heat of 16°C (61°F). When rooted, pot the cuttings singly into 3–3½ in. pots of John Innes potting compost No. 2.

Shoots layered in September or October usually root within a year.

The hardy species may be raised from seeds; sow in pots or pans of seed compost during September or October in a cold frame. Prick out the seedlings when they are large enough to handle; pot into 3–3½ in. pots and treat as described for cuttings.

Pruning. After flowering, cut back the flowering growths of *J. nudiflorum* and *J. primulinum* to within 2 or 3 in. of the base. Cut out completely old and weak wood and tie in the growths.

Thin out the shoots of *J. officinale* after flowering, but do not shorten. No regular pruning is required for the other species, except occasional thinning out of overgrown plants.

Pests. APHIDS may infest young shoots, and tufts of white waxy wool on stems and leaves are caused by MEALY BUGS.

Diseases. Generally trouble-free, but GREY MOULD may cause die-back after frost damage.

Jeffersonia

Podophyllaceae (formerly *Berberidaceae*)

A genus of two species of hardy herbaceous perennials suitable for rock gardens and alpine houses. They are sometimes listed under the synonym *Plagiorhegma*. They bear solitary bowl-shaped flowers in March and April and die down completely during autumn.

J. diphylla. E. United States. Height 4–6 in.; spread 6 in. This species has mid-green leaves divided into two ear-shaped lobes; the white flowers are up to 1 in. across.

J. dubia. Manchuria. Height 4–6 in.; spread 6–9 in. The leaves of this species are circular in outline, deeply cleft at the base and bi-lobed at the tip. They are copper-purple when young, maturing to mid-green above, glaucous beneath. The lavender-blue flowers are 1–1¼ in. across.

Cultivation. Plant jeffersonias in September or October in any ordinary soil enriched with peat or leaf-mould; a position in partial shade or in woodland conditions is ideal.

In the alpine house, grow the plants in 5–6 in. pots of John Innes potting compost No. 1 and repot every two or three years in autumn.

Propagation. Divide the plants in autumn or spring and replant direct in permanent positions.

Jeffersonias can also be raised from seeds, but germination may take as long as 18 months; the resultant plants will take three to five years to reach flowering size. Sow the seeds, directly they ripen, thinly in boxes or pans of John Innes seed compost and place in a cold frame or greenhouse. Leave the seedlings in the boxes or pans for the first year after germination; pot into 3 in. pots of John Innes potting compost No. 1 in September and plunge the pots outside or in a cold frame for another year. Transplant to permanent positions in September or October.

Pests and diseases. Generally trouble-free.

Jerusalem artichoke

Helianthus tuberosus. Compositae

A hardy perennial, grown for its edible tubers which are used as winter vegetables. This is an easily grown plant, which may reach a height of 7–12 ft; it makes a good summer screen.

The freely produced tubers have white flesh under the knobbly, purple skin. They may be served peeled and boiled, accompanied by a white sauce; they may also be used in soups.

VARIETIES

Only two varieties are in general cultivation. The purple-skinned 'Fuseau' has smooth tubers; 'New White' is a white-skinned variety.

Cultivation. Jerusalem artichokes thrive in any ordinary, well-drained soil, in sun or partial shade. No feeding or manuring is required as this will encourage the growth of foliage at the expense of tubers. The bed should be away from other crops as the tall plants overshadow and restrict growth of nearby crops. The plants are easier to keep under control if they are treated as an annual crop, and if all tubers are removed from the ground at the end of the season.

Plant the tubers in late February or early March, 15 in. apart in 5 in. deep drills, 3 ft apart. Small tubers, with at least one eye, are most suitable for planting. In exposed positions, support the plants by stretching wires between posts at a height of about 6 ft.

Harvesting and storing. In late October, when the tubers have matured and the top growth begins to brown, cut the haulms to 12–24 in. above ground level. The tubers may be lifted and stored in a clamp, but they keep their flavour and firm texture better if left in the ground until required. Save the small tubers for spring planting.

Pests. SLUGS and SWIFT MOTH caterpillars eat holes in the tubers.

Diseases. The stems and tubers may be attacked by SCLEROTINIA DISEASE, which shows as a white fluffy fungus on the rotting tissues; large black resting bodies appear.

Juncus

Bog rush. *Juncaceae*

A genus of 300 species of aquatic and bog plants, which have become adapted to growing in poor, acid soils. They are mostly worthless as garden plants, but the two described here make handsome foliage plants at the margins of pools, lakes and streams.

JUNCUS EFFUSUS 'SPIRALIS'

J. effusus 'Spiralis' (corkscrew rush). Origin doubtful but thought to be Japan. Water depth up to 3 in.; height 15–18 in.; planting distance 12–15 in. This variety of the widely distributed *J. effusus* is a hardy evergreen aquatic perennial which grows equally well in shallow water or in wet soil. Its habit is sprawling and untidy, but the dark green cylindrical leaves, in shapes varying from tight curls to perfect corkscrews and extended spirals, are curious and interesting. Insignificant pale brown flower clusters are produced in June and July.

J. glaucus. Europe, including Great Britain. Water depth up to 3 in.; height up to 3 ft; planting distance 18–24 in. A hardy evergreen perennial plant, best suited to large pools and lakes. It slowly forms clumps of foliage which are erect and stiff when young but gradually arch over as the plant gets larger.

The needle-like leaves are at their most attractive when young, being grey-blue in colour and with a fine corrugated texture. The flowers appear in August and September, forming small green tufts at the tips of the leaves.

J. zebrinus: see *Scirpus tabernaemontani* 'Zebrinus'

Cultivation. Any soil is suitable, either saturated or covered with up to 3 in. of water. Plant in April or May, in a sunny position; they also tolerate partial shade. Remove old foliage from time to time and also any straight leaves which appear on *J. effusus* 'Spiralis'.

Propagation. Increase by division in April or May, using a sharp knife to sever the tough rootstock. Replant the divided pieces immediately at the margin of the pool.

Pests and diseases. Generally trouble-free.

Juniperus

Juniper. *Cupressaceae*

A genus of 60 species of evergreen, bushy coniferous trees and shrubs, widely distributed in the Northern Hemisphere. Some of the species are columnar or irregular in shape, others are spreading or prostrate. The foliage is of two distinct types: juvenile, awl shaped; and adult, scale-like or linear leaves. In some species both adult and juvenile leaves are present at the same time on the shoots, but generally only one type of leaf is borne. Some species retain their juvenile foliage permanently. The fleshy ovoid or globular, berry-like cones are black or blue-white.

These are hardy, slow-growing trees and will tolerate dry and alkaline soils. Those of columnar habit make moderate specimen trees while the dwarf spreading species are excellent for ground cover on sunny banks or in rock gardens.

See also CONIFERS.

JUNIPERUS CHINENSIS

J. chinensis (Chinese juniper). China, Mongolia, Japan. Height 20 ft; spread 5 ft. A narrowly or broadly conic and bushy species with brown and stringy bark. The dull, dark green foliage is composed of small, closely pressed, pale-edged adult leaves, dominant on the outer shoots, and bigger, prickly, flat and slender juvenile leaves with two blue lines. The juvenile leaves are borne in whorls of three.

Male flowers, $\frac{1}{4}$ in. wide, are borne on separate trees; the insignificant female flowers develop into bright blue-black fruits about $\frac{1}{3}$ in. across.

'Aurea' is a slow-growing columnar form, the foliage being bright yellow in full light; it is one of the best golden conifers for town gardens. 'Keteleerii' has brighter foliage than the species; it is entirely adult, and of narrowly conic habit.

Dwarf forms and colour variants of the species include the following: 'Japonica' (height 3 ft; spread 4 ft), a spreading bush with two or three ascending main branches bearing adult foliage at their tips, but otherwise densely covered with prickly juvenile foliage; 'Stricta' (height 5 ft; spread 24 in.), of stiffly conic outline and with glaucous-grey juvenile foliage. Numerous spreading, dwarf forms, which are thought to be natural hybrids and which are frequently listed as *J. × media*, include: 'Blaauw' (height up to 4 ft; spread 2$\frac{1}{2}$ ft), a strong-growing and upright form with a few sturdy main branches rising at a steep angle and bearing rich blue-grey foliage. 'Globosa' and 'Globosa Cinerea' (height and spread 4 ft) are similar in habit to 'Blaauw', the former bearing light green foliage and the latter with yellow-green tips to the shoots.

'Pfitzeriana' (height 3 ft; spread 5 ft) has pendulous growing tips and predominantly semi-juvenile foliage; 'Pfitzeriana Aurea' is similar, but

Juncus effusus 'Spiralis'

Juniperus chinensis 'Aurea'

Juniperus communis (fruits)

Juniperus sabina 'Tamariscifolia'

Juniperus chinensis
'Pfitzeriana'

Juniperus communis
'Compressa'

of flatter habit with branchlets and leaves that are bright golden-yellow in summer, becoming yellow-green during autumn and early winter.

J. communis (common juniper). Europe, including Great Britain, and across Asia to N. America. Height up to 10 ft; spread 6 ft. A shrubby bush or small tree suitable for exposed sites with thin soils over chalk. This species has a wide natural range, occurring on both chalk and acid peats. The foliage is entirely juvenile; the leaves are light grey-green below, with a single broad white band above. The fruits are berry-like, green for about a year, then turning blue or black with a grey-white bloom. 'Stricta' (Irish juniper) is of dense, narrow, columnar form, and grey-blue.

Numerous dwarf forms include: 'Compressa' (height 24 in.; spread 6 in.), a slow-growing version of the Irish juniper ('Stricta'), excellent for a small rock garden and for window-boxes; it is particularly effective planted in groups of three or five. 'Hornibrookii' (height 12 in.; spread up to 6 ft), of prostrate wide-spreading habit.

J. horizontalis (creeping, prostrate juniper). N.E. America. Height up to 12 in.; spread 5–6 ft or more. A variable mat-forming species useful for ground cover, with blue-green awl-shaped leaves that are wholly adult; the long main branches rest and often root on the ground. Available forms are: 'Douglasii', with thin, blue-green foliage turning rich purple in autumn; and 'Glauca', a flat-growing form with dense, rich blue-green foliage and long whipcord-like terminal growths. No fruits are produced on any of these forms.

J. × media: see *J. chinensis*

J. procumbens (procumbent juniper). Japan. A spreading prostrate species superseded by the form 'Nana'. This makes a dense mat of grey-green, awl-shaped, closely overlapping adult leaves; it is useful for ground cover. No fruits are borne in cultivation.

J. recurva (drooping juniper). Himalayas, Burma, China. Height 15 ft; spread 10 ft. A spreading bush or conic tree with grey-green pendulous adult foliage that has spreading tips. The old leaves are dull brown and remain on the shoots for some years. The cones, which are about ½ in. long, take two years to ripen and then become purple-black.

J. r. coxii (coffin juniper) (height 20 ft; spread 6 ft) is a tall-growing variety with long, drooping shoots of a brighter green. The leaves are more

widely spaced, and the orange-brown bark hang in papery strips.

J. rigida. Japan, Korea and Manchuria. Height 1 ft or more; spread 6 ft or more. A small tree o pyramidal habit, with slender, pendent branch lets clad in needle-like, yellow-green leaves. The black, white-bloomed cones are $\frac{1}{4}$–$\frac{1}{3}$ in. across.

JUNIPERUS RIGIDA

J. sabina (savin). S. Europe, Asia. Height 12–1 ft; spread 8 ft. A shrubby variable species which seldom reaches tree-like proportions. In cultiva tion it is generally represented by 'Tamariscifolia (height $2\frac{1}{2}$ ft; spread 5 ft). This is a spreading form, with horizontal shoots bearing crowded branchlets lying forward at a narrow angle to the stem. It chiefly carries juvenile leaves, white above and with a gland on the back of each leaf

This shrub is suitable for a formal or wild garden; heavy pruning will limit its size.

J. squamata (scaly-leaved Nepal juniper). Asia Height 24 in.; spread 6 ft. A variable, shrubby species of little garden value. It is the origin o several dwarf garden plants: 'Meyeri' (height 5 ft; spread 6–8 ft) is the strongest form and has the bluest foliage of any juniper; the colour is most intense on vigorous shoots.

J. virginiana (pencil cedar). N. America. Height up to 25 ft; spread 15 ft. A branching, broadly conic, slow-growing species. The pale to mid-green foliage, sometimes with a hoary cast, is a mixture of juvenile and adult leaves, and is similar to that of *J. chinensis*. The adult leaves are more pointed, finer and in thinner arrangements frequently with juvenile shoots at the tips.

'Glauca' (height up to 20 ft; spread 4–5 ft) is a columnar, erect-branched form with pale grey foliage and $\frac{1}{4}$ in. wide fruits which ripen in a year when young, the more vigorous shoots have pink-purple bark.

Selected dwarf forms include: 'Globosa (height and spread 3 ft), a neat, rounded bush requiring no pruning; 'Skyrocket' (height 8–10 ft; spread 6 in.), a narrowly columnar form.

Cultivation. These conifers thrive in ordinary, well-drained garden soil and in full sun or light shade. Coloured forms look best in sunny positions. Plant in April, using seedlings 2–3 ft high. No staking is required.

Propagation. Extract the seeds from ripe berries in September and October and sow immediately in pots or pans of John Innes seed compost in a cold frame. Prick out the seedlings, when large enough to handle, singly into 3½ in. pots of John Innes potting compost No. 2 and plunge outdoors; alternatively, line the seedlings out into nursery rows outdoors. Grow on for one or two years before setting in permanent sites.

Coloured and named forms should be increased from cuttings taken in September and October. Take 2–4 in. long cuttings of lateral shoots, preferably with a heel, and insert in equal parts (by volume) peat and sand in a cold frame. When rooted, pot up and treat the cuttings as advised for seedlings.

Pruning. None required.

Pests. SCALE INSECTS, especially juniper scale, encrust stems and leaves.

CATERPILLARS of the juniper webber moth eat the leaves and spin the foliage together.

Diseases. RUST, caused by several different fungi, may produce gelatinous horn-like masses of yellow-orange spores in April or May.

Justicia carnea : see *Jacobinia carnea*
Justicia coccinea : see *Jacobinia coccinea*

Juniperus squamata 'Meyeri'

K

Kalanchoe

Crassulaceae

A genus of 200 species of greenhouse perennials. These easily grown succulents are cultivated for their beautifully marked leaves, as well as for the clusters of tubular flowers. They are vigorous, shrubby plants with fleshy stems; the leaves are borne in pairs, alternate and opposite.

See also CACTUS.

K. beharensis. Madagascar. Height 24 in. This branching shrub has leaves 5–8 in. long; they are heart-shaped, brown and covered with tiny hairs which make them feel like velvet. The plant tends to lose its lower leaves and become leggy. It rarely flowers in a pot; when it does, it produces small pink blossoms in March and April.

K. blossfeldiana. Madagascar. Height and spread 12 in. or more. An erect bushy species with broadly ovate, pale to mid-green fleshy leaves, each with a prominently scalloped margin. The tubular, ½–1 in. long, scarlet flowers are borne in dense clusters on short leafless stems arising from the upper leaf axils. Flowers may be produced throughout most of the year, but February to May is the usual period of blooming. This species is much used as a winter-flowering pot plant and has been hybridised with other species to produce flowers in pink, red, white or yellow.

K. marmorata. Abyssinia. Height 10–12 in. A small, branching shrub with stalkless ovate leaves about 4 in. long, and indented round the edges. The leaves are blue-green, mottled with chocolate brown. White flowers, about 3 in. long, are sometimes produced from March to May.

K. pumila. Madagascar. Height 8 in. A semi-prostrate plant which looks well in a hanging basket. The lanceolate leaves are less than 1 in. long and coarsely toothed. They, and the stems, are completely covered with white meal and tinged with pink. Pale pink flowers, about 1 in. long, appear in January or February.

Cultivation. Kalanchoes can be grown successfully in John Innes potting compost No. 2. They need 4–6 in. pots. Give them plenty of water in summer. In winter keep them slightly moist, in a light position, and as warm as possible; the minimum temperature should be 5°C (41°F), and preferably a few degrees warmer. They may be grown as house plants on a sunny window-ledge. Repot annually in April.

Propagation. Sow seeds in March, in boxes of seed compost, scattering them on the surface. Germinate at a temperature of 21°C (70°F). Prick out the seedlings, when large enough to handle, into pans or boxes of John Innes potting compost No. 1, and later singly into 2½–3 in. pots. Pot on the seedlings as necessary.

Alternatively, take 3–4 in. stem cuttings from May to August; dry them for two days before potting up in John Innes potting compost No. 1.

Pests. Colonies of MEALY BUGS produce conspicuous tufts of white waxy wool. ROOT MEALY BUGS infest root systems and check growth.

Diseases. Generally trouble-free.

Kalanchoe beharensis

Kalanchoe blossfeldiana

Kale (borecole) and rape kale

Brassica oleracea Acephala, *B. napus. Cruciferae*

These hardy biennial plants are grown as annual winter-green vegetables. They are developed from the wild cabbage and are valued for their edible leaves, produced from January to April when few green vegetables are in season.

VARIETIES

There are two forms of kale: curled-leaved or Scotch, and plain-leaved. 'Extra Curled Scotch' is a popular variety of medium height and has dark green curled leaves. In exposed areas and on light soils, 'Dwarf Curled' is preferable. Reliable plain-leaved varieties include 'Cottager's' with crimped-edged, purple-tinged leaves and 'Hardy Sprouting' with green leaves.

Kale 'Dwarf Curled'

Recommended varieties of rape kale (similar in appearance to curled-leaved kale) include 'Asparagus Kale', 'Favourite', 'Hungry Gap', 'Ragged Jack' and 'Russian'.

Cultivation. Kales are best grown on well-drained, medium or heavy loam, which was well manured for a previous crop. A plot which has produced early potatoes or peas and has been cleared by July is ideal. Do not dig the plot, but dress the surface with 2 oz. per sq. yd of a general-purpose fertiliser.

Sow seeds outdoors in a seed bed, in mid-May in the south, about a month earlier in the north. Thin the seedlings as they grow, to give them enough room to form sturdy, healthy young plants. Transplant to their final quarters in July, setting them 24 in. apart each way.

Varieties of rape kale seldom recover from transplanting; they should be sown where the plants are to grow, in mid-July. Sow in shallow drills, 15 in. apart, and thin the seedlings to final spacings of 12 in.

Harvesting. The leaves are ready for picking from Christmas onwards. Harvest the centre of each plant first to allow the side-growths to produce tender shoots until well into April.

Pests. CATERPILLARS of the diamond-back moth and other species eat holes in the leaves; FLEA BEETLES eat small circular pits in the leaves of young seedlings.

Diseases. DAMPING-OFF causes seedlings to become soft and collapse at ground level.

WIRE STEM of older plants is caused by the fungus RHIZOCTONIA; the bases of the stems become hard, brown and shrunken.

VIOLET ROOT ROT produces a violet web of fungal threads over the roots at ground level.

Kale 'Hungry Gap'

Kalmia latifolia

Kerria japonica

Kerria japonica 'Pleniflora'

Kalmia

Ericaceae

A genus of eight species of hardy evergreen summer-flowering shrubs. They are easily grown in lime-free soil and are particularly suited to light, semi-shaded woodland conditions; they associate well with rhododendrons. The bowl or saucer-shaped flowers are carried in large clusters at the ends of the previous season's shoots.

KALMIA LATIFOLIA

K. angustifolia (sheep laurel). N. America. Height and spread 3–4 ft. A species with lanceolate mid-green leaves. Rose-red flower clusters, 2 in. across, are borne at the ends of the shoots in June. The variety *K. a. ovata* has broader, bright green leaves; 'Rubra' has deep green foliage and deep rose-red flowers.

K. latifolia (calico bush, mountain laurel). E. North America. Height 6–10 ft; spread 8 ft. This shrub bears lanceolate leathery leaves that are glossy mid to dark green; they are poisonous to cattle. Bright pink flower clusters, 3–4 in. wide, with conspicuous stamens, are borne in June. The variety 'Clementine Churchill' is rich rose-red.

Cultivation. Plant kalmias during September and October or April and May; they require a moist peaty, lime-free soil and do best in a partially shaded position.

Propagation. Layer shoots of the current season during August or September; the layers will usually have rooted sufficiently to be severed from the parent plant the following autumn.

Alternatively, take cuttings, 4–5 in. long, of semi-ripe lateral shoots of the current year, in August. Insert the cuttings in equal parts (by volume) peat and sand in a cold frame. Line out the rooted cuttings in a nursery bed outdoors in April, or place in 3½ in. pots of John Innes potting compost No. 2 (minus lime) and plunge outdoors. Grow the young plants on in the nursery bed or pot on into 4 in. pots; transplant to permanent positions two years later in autumn.

Pruning. None required, but trim off the faded flower clusters.

Pests and diseases. Generally trouble-free.

Kentia: see Howea
Kentranthus: see *Centranthus ruber*

Kerria

Jew's mallow. *Rosaceae*

KERRIA JAPONICA

A genus containing only one species; this is a deciduous, spring-flowering shrub, native to China and much cultivated in Japan. The double-flowered form is more frequently seen in cultivation than the type species.

K. japonica. Height and spread 4–6 ft. A hardy, bushy species with slender, glossy green branches. The bright green leaves are ovate-lanceolate and doubly toothed. Solitary yellow-orange flowers, like single roses 1½ in. across, are borne at the ends of the previous season's shoots during April and May.

The variety 'Pleniflora' (bachelor's buttons) is a well-known double form with orange-yellow flowers, 2 in. wide; it is of taller, upright habit and may reach a height of 12 ft; 'Variegata' is a half-hardy dwarf shrub with white-edged foliage, and single yellow flowers.

Cultivation. Kerrias thrive in ordinary garden soil; plant during suitable weather from October to March in a semi-shaded or sunny position. In cold areas they may be grown against walls or fences, the variegated forms preferably against south or west-facing walls.

Propagation. Take cuttings, 4–5 in. long, of lateral growths in August or September; insert the cuttings in equal parts (by volume) peat and

Kniphofia 'Springtime'

Kniphofia uvaria

and in a cold frame. The following April or May
ne the rooted cuttings out in nursery rows and
transplant to flowering positions in October.

Plants composed of numerous stems may be
divided and replanted during suitable weather
from October to March.

Pruning. After flowering, all flowered shoots
may be cut back to strong new growths; thin out
the shoots of 'Pleniflora' entirely to encourage
the production of vigorous young basal shoots.

Pests and diseases. Generally trouble-free.

Kidney bean: see Beans (French)

Kindling-bark, broad-leaved: see *Eucalyptus
dalrympleana*

Kingcup: see Caltha

King of bromeliads: see *Vriesia hieroglyphica*

Kleinia: see Senecio

Kleinia herreiana: see *Senecio herreianus*

Kleinia radicans: see *Senecio radicans*

Kleinia repens: see *Senecio repens*

Kleinia tomentosa: see *Senecio haworthii*

Kniphofia

Torch lily, red hot poker. *Liliaceae*

KNIPHOFIA RUFA

A genus of about 75 species of hardy herbaceous
perennials. They make excellent focal points in a
border, associated with shrubs or as isolated
groups. A selection of named varieties will
provide flowers in a wide range of colours from
June until October. The smooth flower stems rise
erectly above the foliage and terminate in

poker-like spikes of closely set tubular flowers
with the open ends pointing obliquely down.

A few species are in cultivation, but these are
outnumbered by the hybrids; the following
hybrids and species are divided into three groups
according to their flowering periods.

GROUP 1 Height 2–3½ ft; planting distance 24
in. The following species and varieties have
narrow, rush-like, mid-green leaves which become dull to glaucous green later in summer.
They all flower in June and July: 'Alcazar' (height
3 ft), orange flower spikes; 'Bee's Sunset' (height
3 ft), flame-orange; 'Gold Else' (height 2½ ft), soft
yellow; *K. modesta* (height 24 in.), ivory-white,
tipped rose; 'Springtime' (height 3½ ft), yellow,
tipped red; *K. tubergenii* (height 2½ ft), primrose.

GROUP 2 Height up to 5 ft; planting distance 24
in. These hybrids all have broad-spreading, deep
or glaucous green leaves. The flower spikes appear
from July to September: 'Bee's Lemon' (height 3½
ft), rich lemon-yellow spikes; 'Goldmine' (height
3½ ft), deep orange-yellow; 'Maid of Orleans'
(height 2½ ft), ivory-cream; 'Samuel's Sensation'
(height 5 ft), bright scarlet-red; and *K. uvaria*
(height 3 ft), red, orange and yellow.

GROUP 3 Height 1½–2½ ft; planting distance
20–24 in. These species and varieties are slow-
growing; they have grass-like, bright to mid-
green leaves and dainty flower spikes in
September and October: *K. galpinii* (height 20
in.), soft orange-yellow flower spikes; *K.
macowanii* (height 2½ ft), deep orange-red; *K.
nelsonii major* (height 2½ ft), bright flame-red; *K.
rufa* (height 24 in.), yellow, tipped red.

'Bressingham Torch' is a hybrid of *K. galpinii*
(height 2½–3 ft; planting distance 24 in.). Grass-
like pale green leaves, and orange-yellow flower
spikes are borne in June and July.

Cultivation. Kniphofias grow best in full sun and
are adaptable to almost any garden soil; they can
be left undisturbed for years provided the soil is
well drained, particularly in winter. The plants
will not thrive in wet or poorly drained soils, and
they do not require richly manured soils.

Kniphofia macowanii

Kniphofia 'Bee's Lemon'

Kochia scoparia trichophylla
(summer foliage)

Kochia scoparia trichophylla
(autumn foliage)

Koelreuteria paniculata

Koelreuteria paniculata (fruits)

Plant in September and October or in April, making the planting holes sufficiently deep and wide to accommodate the spread-out roots; do not allow the roots to dry out while the plants are establishing themselves. On heavy soils, and in cold, wet districts, the plants will require a 6 in. deep covering of straw or bracken during the first winter, to protect the fleshy crowns from frost.

In early summer, apply a light organic fertiliser or a mulch of peat. In spite of their height, kniphofias do not require staking; faded flower spikes should be removed close to the basal growth to encourage continued flowering. In November or December tie up the remaining leaves to protect the crowns against moisture.

Propagation. Divide and replant established plants in April.

Seeds are available of true species and mixed varieties, and may be sown outdoors in drills, ½ in. deep, in April. Grow the seedlings on in a nursery bed and transplant to their flowering positions the following April.

Pests. The leaves and flowers may be infested with THRIPS, which cause a fine mottling, distortion and discoloration.

Diseases. Generally trouble-free.

Knotweed: see Polygonum

Kochia

Chenopodiaceae

KOCHIA SCOPARIA TRICHOPHYLLA

A genus of 90 species of annual and perennial herbaceous plants and sub-shrubs. The species described is grown for its decorative foliage. It is effective as a specimen plant in bedding schemes, for forming a low temporary hedge, and as a pot plant for a cold greenhouse.

K. scoparia (summer cypress). S. Europe. Height 3 ft; spacing 24 in. A half-hardy annual with a profusion of narrow, pointed, pale green leaves. The flowers are small, green and insignificant. There are two varieties commonly listed: *trichophylla* (burning bush), with light green foliage that turns deep red in autumn; and 'Childsii', which is compact and neater in habit than *trichophylla*.

Cultivation. These plants grow well in all soils and situations, but a fairly light soil and an open sunny site are best. Staking is required only on exposed sites.

Grow pot plants in 5 or 7 in. pots, using John Innes potting compost No. 2. The larger pot encourages larger plants.

Propagation. Sow the seeds under glass in March at a temperature of 16°C (61°F), and harden off the seedlings before planting out in May. Alternatively, sow in the site in April and thin out.

Pests and diseases. Generally trouble-free.

Koelreuteria

Sapindaceae

A genus of eight species of deciduous flowering trees, native to E. Asia. Only one species is in general cultivation and is grown for its handsome foliage and star-shaped flowers.

KOELREUTERIA PANICULATA

K. paniculata. N. China. Height 10–18 ft; spread 8–10 ft. A hardy species, sparsely branched when young but becoming more compact with age and developing a fine head. The pinnate mid-green leaves are up to 14 in. long and are composed of ovate, deeply toothed leaflets; they often assume yellow autumn tints. The yellow flowers, which appear in July, are carried in terminal panicles 6–12 in. long; they are sometimes followed by bladder-like green fruits, flushed with red.

Cultivation. Plant koelreuterias from October to March in good loamy soil and in full sun.

Propagation. Sow seeds when ripe, usually in October, or in March in pans of seed compost in a cold frame. Prick off the seedlings, when large enough to handle, into 3 in. pots of John Innes potting compost No. 1. When they have filled their pots with roots, plant out in nursery rows and grow on for two or three years before transplanting to flowering positions.

Pruning. None required.

Pests and diseases. Generally trouble-free.

Kohleria

Gesneriaceae

KOHLERIA ERIANTHA

A genus of 50 species of tender evergreen and herbaceous rhizomatous plants suitable for greenhouse cultivation. They are grown for their attractive tubular, often foxglove-like flowers that expand at the mouth to five rounded petals. The flowers are generally borne in small clusters from the leaf axils.

K. amabilis. Colombia. Height 12–24 in.; spread 12 in. This deciduous species has semi-procumbent hairy stems. The ovate, dark green leaves are bluntly serrated and have black-purple markings along the veins. Deep rose, hairy, pendent flowers, 2½ in. long and heavily spotted with deep purple on the petals, are borne singly in the leaf axils between June and August.

K. *bogotensis.* Colombia. Height 12–24 in.; spread 12 in. A deciduous species with erect, slightly hairy stems. The velvety, ovate, dark green leaves, that are sometimes borne in whorls of three, are mottled with silver-green and flushed with red beneath. The 1½ in. long flowers are borne singly or in small clusters from June to August; the tube and two upper petals are orange, and the three lower petals are yellow spotted with red.

K. *elegans.* Mexico to Panama. Height up to 2½ ft; spread 15 in. This deciduous species has erect and hairy stems. The mid to deep green, ovate leaves are hairy. Orange-red flowers, ¾ in. long, are borne in small clusters in the upper leaf axils from July to September.

K. *eriantha.* Colombia. Height 2–3 ft; spread 12–18 in. A deciduous species with reddish erect stems. These and the dark green, elliptic leaves are densely covered with purple-brown hairs. Scarlet flowers, 1½–2 in. long, with deep red and yellow spots on the three lower petals, are produced from June to August. The species can be brought to flower all year round by successive propagation from tip shoots.

Cultivation. Start the rhizomes into growth in February by placing them in shallow boxes of peat at a temperature of 21°C (70°F). When the growths are 2 in. high, pot the plants three to a 5 in. pot or five to a 7 in. pot containing John Innes potting compost No. 2 or a proprietary peat compost. *K. amabilis* may also be grown in a hanging basket.

Water moderately until the plants become established; then water freely and reduce the temperature to 18°C (64°F). When the pots have filled with roots, feed the plants with a weak liquid manure at 10–14 day intervals. Provide a humid atmosphere by frequent damping down; ventilate when the temperature exceeds 18°C (64°F), and lightly shade the glass throughout the growing period.

When the leaves begin to yellow, gradually cease watering. Remove dead flowers and leaves and store the pots of resting rhizomes in a dry place at a minimum temperature of 12°C (54°F). Kohlerias can be kept in flower throughout the year by cuttings taken at intervals.

Propagation. Divide the rhizomes at potting time in February or March, ensuring that each piece retains a growing point.

Alternatively, take 3 in. long stem cuttings from June to August. Insert in equal parts (by volume) peat and sand in a propagating case at a temperature of 16–18°C (61–64°F). When rooted, pot the cuttings three to a 4 in. pot, or singly in 3 in. pots of the growing compost. Pot on as required. Cuttings may also be taken in September for plants to flower in late winter.

Pests and diseases. Generally trouble-free.

Kohl-rabi

(turnip cabbage). *Brassica oleracea* Caulorapa. *Cruciferae*

A biennial vegetable grown as an annual. The culinary part, which appears above ground level, is a swollen stem, similar to a leafy turnip. The flavour also resembles that of a turnip.

Two forms are in cultivation, a small, tender, quick-growing edible form and a larger, coarser, slower-growing form used for cattle fodder.

In Great Britain, the small form may be grown as a quick-growing catch crop. Three varieties are available: 'Earliest Purple', 'Earliest White' and 'Purple Delicatesse'.

Cultivation. Kohl-rabi thrives in any fertile, well-drained soil. Sow seeds in shallow drills drawn 15 in. apart, and as soon as the seedlings show the third leaf, thin them to 6 in. apart. Make successional sowings at three-week intervals from March to the end of August to ensure a continuous supply.

Pull the roots when they are about the size of a tennis ball; a March sowing will produce a crop ready for use in June.

Pests. Generally trouble-free.

Diseases. CLUB ROOT causes the true roots to become thickened, swollen and distorted; the foliage looks unhealthy.

Kolkwitzia

Caprifoliaceae

KOLKWITZIA AMABILIS

This genus contains only one species. It is a hardy deciduous shrub, grown for its showy flowers in mid-summer and for its attractive winter bark.

K. *amabilis* (beauty bush). W. China. Height 6–12 ft; spread 4–10 ft. An upright shrub with arching branches and peeling brown bark. The matt dark green leaves are broadly ovate and pointed, hairy and widely toothed. The flowers, which are borne in 2–3 in. wide corymbs, appear in May and June at the ends of short lateral twigs; they are pink with yellow throats and resemble small foxgloves, with a wide, five-lobed mouth.

Cultivation. Plant these shrubs in October and November or in March in ordinary, well-drained garden soil and in full sun.

Propagation. Take cuttings, 4–6 in. long, of firm, lateral, non-flowering shoots, preferably with a heel, in July and August. Insert the cuttings in equal parts (by volume) peat and sand in a cold frame. Line out the rooted cuttings in a nursery bed the following April or May and grow on for one year before transplanting to permanent positions in October.

Pruning. After flowering, remove entirely some of the older flowering stems to keep established bushes vigorous.

Pests. Generally trouble-free.

Diseases. DIE-BACK of the shoots is usually due to cold weather.

Kowhai: see *Sophora microphylla* and *S. tetraptera*

Kohleria amabilis

Kohl-rabi 'Purple Delicatesse'

Kolkwitzia amabilis

L

Laburnum alpinum

Laburnum anagyroides

Laburnum × watereri 'Vossii'

Laburnum

Golden chain or golden rain tree. *Leguminosae*

A genus of six species of hardy, deciduous, spring-flowering trees and shrubs. Two species and their hybrids are in general cultivation. The leaves are trifoliate, with ovate-elliptic leaflets. Yellow, slightly fragrant, pea-like flowers are borne in numerous dense, pendulous racemes which drape the branches throughout late May and early June.

All parts of the trees are highly poisonous, the pale green, bean-like seed pods being particularly dangerous when green and succulent. In gardens where children play, the seed pods should be collected and burnt as soon as they appear.

LABURNUM × WATERERI 'VOSSII'

L. alpinum (Scotch laburnum). South and C. Europe. Height 15–20 ft; spread 10–15 ft. A broad-headed tree that often assumes a picturesque gnarled appearance with age. The leaves are glossy and mid-green. Flowers, in tapering racemes 10 in. or more long, appear from late May to late June. 'Pyramidalis' is a form with erect branches.

L. anagyroides, syn. *L. vulgare* (common laburnum). South and C. Europe. Height 10–18 ft; spread 8–12 ft. A small tree, spreading with age; the leaves are dull green and slightly hairy. The flowers are borne in 6–10 in. long racemes which open from late April to early June.

'Aureum' is a form with soft yellow leaves that turn green as autumn approaches; it may sometimes revert to green. 'Autumnale', syn. 'Semperflorens', frequently produces a second crop of flowers in the autumn.

'Pendulum' is a small weeping form which is usually grafted on to stocks of the type species and trained as a single stem; it is particularly suitable for small gardens.

L. × watereri. Garden origin. A hybrid between *L. alpinum* and *L. anagyroides*. It is intermediate in stature and in the colour and texture of the leaves between those of the parents. Slender flower racemes, 10–12 in. long, appear in late May.

'Vossii', sometimes known as *L. × vossii*, is a free-flowering form with longer racemes.

L. × vossii: see *L. × watereri*

L. vulgare: see *L. anagyroides*

Cultivation. Plant laburnums at any time between October and March, in ordinary, well-drained garden soil, and in sun or partial shade. Young trees need staking until established.

Propagation. Sow seeds in October in pots or pans of seed compost, placed in a cold frame. Prick off the seedlings, when large enough to handle, into boxes and then into nursery rows outdoors. Set the young plants in their flowering positions the following autumn.

The hybrids and the named varieties do not come true from seeds and must be grafted on to seedling stocks of either species in March.

Pruning. None required.

Pests. LEAF CUTTER BEES sometimes cut out circular pieces of leaf tissue. Blotch mines are eaten in the leaves by LEAF MINERS.

Diseases. Trees are rapidly killed by HONEY FUNGUS. The flowers fail to open fully in spring, and this is followed by premature browning of the leaves, leaf-fall and die-back of branches.

SILVER LEAF may cause similar symptoms to those of honey fungus, over a longer period.

Laburnum, common: see *Laburnum anagyroides*
Laburnum, evergreen: see *Piptanthus laburnifolius*
Laburnum, Scotch: see *Laburnum alpinum*

Lachenalia

Liliaceae

LACHENALIA ALOIDES

A genus of 65 species of tender bulbous perennials. The few species in cultivation require greenhouse treatment, and although chiefly grown as pot plants, they are also suitable for growing in hanging baskets; they may be brought into the living-room when in flower.

These plants have erect, strap-shaped leaves, reflexed at the tips and coloured pale green, often flecked or blotched with pale purple. The leaves appear before the racemes of flowers, which are tubular or narrowly bell-shaped and often tri-coloured.

L. aloides, syn. *L. tricolor*. S. Africa. Height 9–12 in. The 1 in. long flowers are borne in nodding racemes from late December to March, depending on the temperatures provided. They are yellow with green edgings and red markings.

Varieties include: 'Aurea', orange-yellow, without markings; 'Lutea', deep yellow; and 'Nelsonii', sometimes listed as *L. nelsonii*, a vigorous and widely grown hybrid with red bulbs and yellow and green flowers.

L. bulbifera, syn. *L. pendula*. S. Africa. Height 6–10 in. The stout stems carry a few flowers,

1 in. long, from December to February; these are deep purple, red or yellow, and red and green at the tips.

L. glaucina. S. Africa. Height 3–6 in. The flowers are white, flushed with yellow or red. They are ½ in. long and are borne horizontally in great numbers from February to March.

L. mutabilis. S. Africa. Height 4–8 in. Slender stems carry ½ in. long flowers in February; these are blue, fading to yellow-green with purple-brown blotches near the tips.

L. nelsonii: see L. aloides

L. orchioides. S. Africa. Height 6–9 in. The fragrant, semi-erect flowers are white or pale yellow, flushed with red or blue. They measure ¼ in. in length and are closely set in a raceme on a stout spotted stem. The main flowering period is in April. The variety 'Atroviolacea' has hyacinth-blue flowers.

L. pendula: see L. bulbifera

L. tricolor: see L. aloides

Cultivation. Pot lachenalias in August or September, setting five to seven bulbs in a 5–6 in. pot. Use John Innes potting compost No. 2 and cover the bulbs with 1 in. of the compost. Keep in a well-ventilated greenhouse or frame at a temperature of 10–13°C (50–55°F), and in maximum light. Plants from bulbs potted in early August and kept at 15–18°C (59–64°F) have a longer flowering season.

Thoroughly soak the compost immediately after potting and then withhold water until the first shoots appear. Water moderately until the plants are in full growth, thereafter freely during the growing period. Give a weak liquid feed at 10–14 day intervals when in full growth.

After flowering, gradually decrease the water supply until the leaves begin to turn yellow; cease watering and let the bulbs dry off. They can be left in the pots until August and then repotted in fresh compost; they must not be stored during winter.

Propagation. Detach the bulbils at repotting time in August and grow them on in the same way as mature bulbs. They should reach flowering size in one or two years.

Pests. Generally trouble-free.

Diseases. A fungus causes BASAL ROT; the roots and bases of young bulbs rot, and growth ceases when the leaves are only a few inches high.

INK DISEASE shows on the leaves as small distinct brown spots. Severely affected plants look unsightly.

Lactuca sativa: see Lettuce
Lad's love: see Artemisia abrotanum
Lady's mantle: see Alchemilla
Lady's slipper: see Cypripedium

Laelia

Orchidaceae

A genus of about 30 species of tropical epiphytic orchids, widely distributed throughout Mexico and Central America to Brazil. The variously jointed pseudobulbs are oblong and elongated, with one or two tough, leathery, oblong lanceolate, mid to dark green leaves. These are evergreen and almost succulent and are borne at the apex of the pseudobulbs. The erect flower spikes, one at the tip of each pseudobulb, each bear up to five large showy flowers.

Laelias are closely related to cattleyas, and the two genera hybridise readily. Numerous hybrids have also been produced with other genera. The species and varieties described here all thrive in an intermediate greenhouse.

See also ORCHIDS

Laelia anceps

L. anceps. Mexico. A species with pseudobulbs about 5 in. high, each bearing one or occasionally two large leaves. The erect flower stems, up to 24 in. long, arch at the tips and carry two to five flowers, each about 4 in. across, in December and January. They have spreading sepals and petals of a deep rose-lilac, and the lip is rich velvety purple with a purple-veined yellow throat.

There are numerous varieties: 'Alba' is pure white with a yellow throat; 'Barkeriana' has deep rose sepals and petals and a crimson-purple yellow-throated lip; 'Hilliana' is pure white with a shell-pink lip and yellow keels; 'Schroederae' has dark maroon or purple sepals and petals which darken at the tips, and a bright crimson-maroon lip with two yellow blotches.

L. autumnalis. Mexico. This species has two, occasionally three-leaved, 4–8 in. high pseudobulbs. The flower stems are about 30 in. long with up to six flowers, each 4 in. across. Their sepals and petals are rose-lilac, deeper at the tips and fading at the base. The lip is a pale rose-lilac, with a deep purple tip and yellow keels. The blooms are scented and appear from November to January. 'Atrorubens' has larger flowers with brilliant deep purple sepals and petals, and cream margins on the lip.

L. harpophylla. Brazil. The pseudobulbs are slender and up to 15 in. high; each carries a single mid-green leaf. Flower stems, up to 12 in. long, bear three to nine flowers, each about 2 in. across, from January to March. The narrow-pointed sepals and petals are deep bright orange; the lip is also orange with bright yellow margins to the mid-lobe.

L. pumila. S. Brazil, Guyana. A dwarf, compact plant with 2 in. high pseudobulbs, each bearing a single mid-green leaf. The inflorescences are up to 6 in. long with one or, rarely, two flowers up to

Lachenalia aloides

Lachenalia bulbifera

Laelia pumila

Laelia purpurata

4 in. across. These have bright rose-purple sepals and petals and a deep crimson-purple lip with yellow keels. The flowers appear during September and October.

L. purpurata. S. Brazil. This species has club-shaped pseudobulbs up to 15 in. high, each carrying a single dark green leaf. Up to nine flowers, each about 7 in. across, are borne on 15 in. long flowering stems from May to July. The sepals are long and narrow, the petals broader with crinkly margins, both white flushed with rose. The lip is large, sometimes up to 3 in. long, and has a yellow throat with fine purple veins; the broad mid-lobe is deep purple with a fine white crinkly margin.

'Atropurpurea' has dark rose sepals and petals and a deep magenta-purple lip.

Cultivation. Grow laelias in relatively small pots for the size of the plants, with large air-holes in the sides and drainage holes in the bottom. Large plants grow well in open woodwork baskets. Use a compost of equal parts (by volume) osmunda fibre and sphagnum moss; the rhizomes should rest on the surface. These plants need good light, but not strong sun; water freely and provide a warm humid atmosphere during the growing season. Ventilate the house on warm days and nights. During the resting period, from November to March, lower the temperature by 2·5°C (5°F) and water sparingly, giving just enough water to prevent shrivelling.

Propagation. Divide the plants when the new growing points begin to develop roots, between February and May. Ensure that each division has a growing point; repot every two or three years with the new shoot to the centre of the pot so that it has room to develop.

Pests and diseases. Generally trouble-free.

× *Laeliocattleya* 'Marietta'

Lagurus ovatus

Lamium galeobdolon 'Variegatum' (foliage)

× **Laeliocattleya**

Orchidaceae

× LAELIOCATTLEYA

A group of bigeneric hybrids between *Laelia* and *Cattleya*. The general growth habit, foliage and flowers are similar to those of *Cattleya*. Flowering is usually between October and March.

See also ORCHIDS.

Named forms include: 'Aconcagua', a hybrid between × *Laeliocattleya* Schroderae and *Cattleya* 'Maggie Raphael'. The white flowers, about 6 in. across, have purple lips with white markings to the edges.

'Edgard van Belle' is a hybrid between × *Laeliocattleya* Cloth of Gold and × *Laeliocattleya* Gallipoli. The flowers, about 5½ in. across, are bright yellow with a vivid deep red lip fringed with white and some yellow deep in the throat. This is one of the greatest potential hybrids for breeding yellow varieties.

'Marietta' is a cross between × *Laeliocattleya* Lustre and *Cattleya* 'C. van Houtte', with 5 in. wide flowers having red-purple sepals and petals; the lip is deep purple with a pair of yellow spots in the throat.

'Queen Mary' is a hybrid between × *Laeliocattleya* Lustre and *Cattleya* 'Peetersii'. The well-shaped flowers, up to 6 in. across, are lavender with darker yellow-throated lips.

Cultivation, propagation, pests and diseases. See descriptions under CATTLEYA.

Lagurus

Gramineae

A genus of one species only. This is a hardy annual grass, sometimes grown in mixed borders for its ornamental value. It may also be dried and used for winter decoration.

L. ovatus (hare's tail grass). Europe. Height 12 in.; planting distance 6 in. The narrow linear leaves are hairy and grey-green. Slender stems terminate in fluffy, white, ovoid inflorescences, 1–1½ in. long, from June to September.

Cultivation. Grow these grasses in a loamy, well-drained soil and in a sunny position. The inflorescences can be gathered in dry weather in August for drying.

Propagation. Sow seeds in August or September, in pots or pans of John Innes seed compost; overwinter in a cold frame or a cool greenhouse. The following April, set the seedlings out in their growing positions.

Pests. Generally trouble-free.

Diseases. Plants may be attacked by POWDERY MILDEW, especially on ground that has been heavily dressed with nitrogenous manure. White or brown patches of fungal growth appear on the lower leaves, which turn yellow and shrivel; the whole plant is gradually affected.

Lamb's lettuce: see Corn salad
Lamb's tongue: see *Stachys lanata*
Lamiastrum galeobdolon: see *Lamium galeobdolon*

Lamium

Dead nettle. *Labiatae*

LAMIUM MACULATUM

A genus of 40–50 species of annuals and herbaceous perennials. Some of the hardy perennial species described here are useful in shady sites and easy to grow in poor soil. The spreading species, such as *L. galeobdolon,* make excellent ground cover. They all tend to be invasive and are difficult to eliminate from sticky soils, as pieces of root left behind will grow again.

These plants have tubular flowers, usually with a hooded upper lip; the leaves are heart-shaped at the base.

L. galeobdolon (yellow archangel). Europe, including Great Britain. Height 6–18 in.; planting distance 12–24 in. This perennial, which is correctly known as *Lamiastrum galeobdolon* and formerly as *Galeobdolon luteum*, is suitable only for the wild garden. Its variety *L. g.* 'Variegatum' (height 6–12 in.) is useful, though rampant, as ground cover. It has silver-flushed evergreen leaves that assume bronze tints in winter. Whorled spikes of yellow flowers, each 1–1¼ in. long, are produced in June and July.

Lamium galeobdolon 'Variegatum' (flowers)

L. garganicum. S. Europe. Height 6 in.; planting distance 12 in. A neat perennial for the front of the border or as ground cover. It bears mid to deep green leaves; pink to red flowers, 1–1¼ in. long, are produced in June and July. It is best grown in moist shade.

L. maculatum. Europe, including Great Britain; N. Africa, W. Asia. Height 12 in.; planting distance 12–24 in. The mid-green leaves of this border plant have a central silver stripe. Pink-purple flowers, 1 in. long, appear in May.

The variety *L. m.* 'Album' has white flowers. 'Aureum' (planting distance 9 in.) has golden foliage; this is a slow-growing variety which requires shade for full effect. 'Roseum' has shell-pink flowers.

L. orvala (giant dead nettle). Italy, France. Height 24 in.; planting distance 12 in. This border perennial does not spread and will tolerate deep shade if the soil is not too dry. The leaves are mid-to deep green; the deep pink to purple flowers, 1¼–1½ in. long, are produced during May and June.

Cultivation. Poor or ordinary garden soil and any situation from sun to full shade is suitable for *L. orvala*, while *L. maculatum* 'Aureum' needs moisture and rich soil. The other species and varieties do well in any soil and in shady places. Plant from October to March. No dead-heading is required; when used for ground cover the plants should be sheared over after flowering to maintain a dense leaf cover.

Propagation. Divide the roots in October or March and replant.

Pests and diseases. Generally trouble-free.

Lampranthus

Aizoaceae

A genus of 100 species of half-hardy perennial plants. These dwarf, shrubby succulents belong to the large *Mesembryanthemum* group of plants. They are popular because of the ease and speed with which they grow and because of their silky, brilliantly coloured, daisy-like flowers. These are produced over a long period, from June to October. Once the danger of frosts is past, many species can be used for summer bedding, for window-boxes or to follow spring-flowering bulbs in rock gardens.

They are densely branched plants with numerous flowers borne singly, or more than one at a time, at the ends of the branches. Each flower may last a week. The flowers usually open only in sunshine, but this varies according to locality.

See also CACTUS.

L. amoenus. S. Africa. Height up to 9 in.; spread 12 in. The semi-cylindrical, tapering leaves are bright green, and become red in bright sunshine. The brilliant purple flowers are about 3 in. across.

L. aurantiacus. S. Africa. Height up to 15 in.; spread 12 in. A sparingly branched plant with tapering, semi-cylindrical, glaucous-green leaves. The bright orange flowers are 1½ in. across.

L. brownii. S. Africa. Height and spread 12 in. The grey-green leaves are tapering and triangular in cross-section. The flowers, ¾ in. wide, are bright tangerine-orange at first; they mature to deep red.

L. coccineus. S. Africa. Height up to 15 in.; spread 12 in. The dull grey-green leaves are triangular in cross-section. The brilliant carmine flowers are 1½ in. in diameter.

L. conspicuus. S. Africa. Height up to 18 in.; spread 12 in. The bright green, red-tipped leaves are incurved, semi-cylindrical or three-angled. The purple-red flowers are 2 in. across.

L. elegans. S. Africa. Height up to 15 in.; spread 12 in. The grey-green leaves are semi-cylindrical. The rose-red flowers measure 1½ in. across.

L. roseus. S. Africa. Height up to 15 in.; spread 12 in. The bright green tapering leaves are triangular in cross-section. The cerise-pink flowers are 1½ in. in diameter.

L. spectabilis. S. Africa. Height and spread up to 12 in. The leaves are bright green, 2½–3 in. long, tapering and triangular in cross-section. The vivid purple flowers are 2–3 in. across.

L. zeyberi. S. Africa. Height up to 15 in.; spread 12 in. The bright green leaves are cylindrical. The purple-violet flowers are 3 in. in diameter.

Cultivation. The plants flower most profusely in poor soil and are therefore best suited to a hot, arid position in full sun. Pot the plants in March or April in 4–5 in. pots. Too rich a soil will cause a lush growth of leaves and only a few flowers. Bed the plants out towards the end of May, when the danger of severe frosts is over. They can be bedded out in their pots so that they can be easily lifted again in autumn.

The plants will have grown too big to bed out again the following spring, and new plants should be raised from cuttings in the autumn. For pots or window-boxes, use a poor soil consisting of 1 part loam, 3 parts sand, and 1 part peat (parts by

Lamium maculatum 'Aureum'

Lamium maculatum 'Roseum'

Lampranthus roseus

Lantana camara 'Cloth of Gold'

Lantana camara
'Spreading Sunset'

Lantana selloviana

Lapageria rosea

volume). Water only when the leaves become limp, and then give a good soaking. Remove flowers as they fade.

Propagation. Sow seeds at any time during spring at a temperature of 21°C (70°F); prick out the seedlings when they are about 1 in. high.

Alternatively, take stem cuttings, about 2 in. long, in late summer or early autumn. Trim the cuttings and leave to dry for a day before inserting them in pots or pans of pure sand. When they have rooted, transfer them, in the growing compost, to 4–5 in. pots, and keep them in a cool, frost-proof frame or greenhouse until May.

Pests. Young growths may be infested with APHIDS, making plants sticky and sooty.

Diseases. Generally trouble-free.

Lantana
Verbenaceae

LANTANA CAMARA

A genus of 150 species of evergreen shrubs, only two of which are in general cultivation. They can be grown in a greenhouse or treated as tender bedding plants.

L. camara. W. Indies, naturalised throughout the Tropics. Height 1½–4 ft; spread 1–3 ft. The elliptic leaves are mid to deep green. Tubular flowers are borne from the leaf axils in domed heads, about 2 in. across. They are produced from May to October and range in colour from white through yellow to brick-red. The flowers often darken as they age, so that two or more colours can be seen in one head.

The variety 'Cloth of Gold' has bright yellow flowers; 'Rose Queen' has pink flowers, salmon-yellow in bud; 'Snow Queen' is pure white; and 'Spreading Sunset' is of prostrate habit, with orange-yellow flowers.

L. montevidensis: see *L. selloviana*

L. selloviana, syn. *L. montevidensis*. Uruguay. Height up to 6 in.; spread 3 ft. A procumbent evergreen shrub with ovate, toothed, mid-green leaves that are covered with a fine down. The compact and slightly domed flower heads, 1–1¼ in. across, are formed of many small tubular florets, bright rose-lilac and yellow-eyed. Flowering may take place at any time of year but is most abundant during the summer months.

Cultivation. John Innes potting compost No. 3 is best for plants that are to be grown for several seasons; a proprietary peat compost is ideal for plants grown for bedding purposes. Grow bedding plants in 5 in. containers, pot plants in 6–8 in. pots. For larger specimens, plant in 10–12 in. pots, small tubs or in the greenhouse border.

Provide a winter temperature of 7°C (45°F) and increase this to 10–13°C (50–55°F) in March and April. Keep the plants barely moist during winter, but water freely in spring and summer.

Allow full light to reach the plants and, if kept in the greenhouse in the summer, give ample ventilation. Shading is not necessary, but the greenhouse should be kept damped down. The pot plants may be stood outside in June and taken in again before autumn frosts can damage them. Plants for bedding should be hardened off in May and planted out in late May or early June.

Give the pot plants a liquid feed at 10–14 day intervals from June to September. Repot or pot on old plants annually in March.

Propagation. Sow seeds during February, in pans or boxes of seed compost, at a temperature of 16°C (61°F). Prick out the seedlings, when large enough to handle, singly into 2½–3 in. pots; pot on as necessary.

Take cuttings, 3 in. long, of young shoots in August and root in equal parts (by volume) peat and sand in a propagating case at a temperature of 16–18°C (61–64°F). Overwinter the rooted cuttings in boxes or singly in 3 in. pots of John Innes potting compost No. 2. Pot on the following spring into final pots. Stop the young plants once or twice in February and March to encourage the formation of side-shoots.

Pruning. If plants are grown on, prune the main shoots back to 4 in. in February.

Pests and diseases. Generally trouble-free.

Lantern tree: see *Crinodendron hookerianum*

Lapageria
Liliaceae

LAPAGERIA ROSEA

A genus of only one species. This is a half-hardy evergreen climbing shrub that can be grown outdoors on a sheltered wall in the south and west, but elsewhere should be treated as a greenhouse climber.

L. rosea (Chilean bell-flower). Chile. Height up to 15 ft. This climber is of slender erect habit. The leathery, dark green, ovate-pointed leaves are borne on twining stems. The pendent, bell-shaped, waxy, rose-crimson flowers measure 3 in. in length; they are usually solitary, although sometimes carried in clusters of two or three, from July to October. The variety 'Albiflora' has pure white flowers.

Cultivation. Lapagerias are intolerant of lime. Outdoors, grow in an acid to neutral, well-drained but moisture-retentive soil, enriched with leaf-mould and fibrous peat. Plant during April or May, against a warm, sheltered wall with partial shade during the hottest part of the day.

Provide wires or trellis as a support for the stems, and tie in the young growths until they become self-attaching. Winter protection is essential in all but the most sheltered districts of southern and western Britain. Use a light covering that lets in air, such as bracken or straw draped loosely among the growths.

In the greenhouse, lapagerias do best planted in the border, but may also be grown in 8–10 in. pots; prepare a compost of 3 parts acid to neutral loam, 2 parts peat or leaf-mould and 1 part coarse sand (parts by volume). Provide strings or wires for support; canes may be used for pot plants.

A minimum winter temperature of 7°C (45°F) is required. Keep the compost moist at all times, and water freely during the growing period. Lightly shade the glass from April to September and ventilate the house on hot summer days.

Propagation. Sow seeds during March or April, in pots or pans of seed compost in a frame or greenhouse; germinate at a temperature of 16–19°C (61–66°F). Prick out the seedlings, when large enough to handle, into pots or boxes of John Innes potting compost (minus lime) and grow them on in a shaded frame or greenhouse. Pot the plants as necessary; outdoor plants will be ready for planting out after two years.

Alternatively, layer strong shoots in April or May, or during November; these generally take up to two years to root.

Pruning. None is required, except to thin out weak growths after flowering.

Pests. Young basal shoots may be eaten by SLUGS.

Colonies of APHIDS infest young shoots and cripple new growths.

Diseases. Generally trouble-free.

Larch: see Larix
Larch, European: see *Larix decidua*
Larch, Japanese: see *Larix leptolepis*
Larch, western: see *Larix occidentalis*

Larix

Larch. *Pinaceae*

LARIX DECIDUA

A genus of about 12 species of deciduous coniferous trees from northern temperate regions. They are graceful trees with open conic crowns; the lower branches point downwards and curve outwards and upwards. The foliage persists for a long time, starting bright green in March and turning golden or russet in November. The needle-like leaves are set spirally on the young shoots; in whorls on spurs on older growths. From an early age small woody, ovoid cones are produced annually.

The species described here are hardy and are of exceptionally rapid early growth. They make suitable specimen trees for a lawn and are attractive to birds.

See also CONIFERS.

L. decidua (European larch). C. Europe. Height 55 ft; spread 20 ft. A robust and wind-tolerant species, narrowly conic for many years, and maturing into a huge tree with a spreading crown and heavy, low branches. The red or pale green 1 in. long female flowers are cylindrical; they are borne on strong branches after a few years. The cones are 1–1½ in. long and ¾ in. wide. The pale yellow male flowers are borne in small, downward-pointing, domed discs; they shed pollen in late March.

L. × *eurolepis.* Height 65 ft; spread 25 ft. A hybrid derived from *L. decidua* and *L. leptolepis*, it is generally more vigorous in all its forms than either parent, and is recommended where rapid growth is required, or on poor soils.

Flowering begins when the tree is quite young and is more dense than in *L. decidua*; the autumn colour of the foliage is a deeper russet. The female flowers may be red, cream, green or a mixture of these colours; they mature to cones that have distinctly out-turned scales and are 1½ in. long and ¾ in. wide.

L. gmelinii. E. Asia. Height 20 ft or more; spread 10 ft or more. A variable species, liable to frost damage, and mainly represented in cultivation by the hardier form, *L. g. japonica*. This has downy twigs and bright green leaves. The small globose male flowers are yellow; the females are ovoid, ½–1 in. long, with pale pink scales. Both types appear in April. Mature cones are brown, about ¾ in. long, with truncated or shallowly notched scales.

L. kaempferi: see *L. leptolepis*

L. leptolepis, syn. *L. kaempferi* (Japanese larch). Japan. Height 60 ft; spread 25 ft. This species, usually more heavily branched and broader than *L. decidua*, is sturdier as a young tree, and more vigorous on poor soils, although less tolerant of dry conditions. It has dark red, red-brown or purple shoots, sometimes with a grey bloom. The leaves are broader and paler green beneath than those of *L. decidua*. The pale yellow male flowers are globular; the females are ovoid, red and cream, and mature to squat cones, ¾ in. long and 1 in. across, with recurved scales.

L. occidentalis (western larch). United States. Height 50 ft; spread 20 ft. This species, which is the tallest-growing of the larches, is variable in Great Britain, probably depending on the origin of the seeds. A good tree is robust and narrow, with pale orange-brown shiny shoots. The slender leaves are glossy, bright grass-green on both sides. The flowers, in April and May, are similar to those of *L. decidua*. The cones, up to 1½ in. long, have the fine points of the bracts protruding from between the scales; they are purple-brown when ripe.

Cultivation. All larches thrive in an open sunny position and in any ordinary moist garden soil. Their rapid early growth makes it essential to use young seedlings, 15–24 in. tall, for planting in November or March.

For the first few years keep the surrounding area clear of weeds, especially grasses; apply a general fertiliser and mulch in March or April.

Propagation. Sow seeds in March in an outdoor nursery bed; transplant the seedlings to permanent positions after two years or line out in nursery rows for one year.

Cuttings are difficult to root and often make poor trees. Take 3 in. long tip cuttings of strong shoots in early July and insert in a mist unit or

Larix decidua (cones)

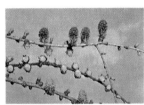

Larix leptolepis (female and male flowers)

Larix leptolepis (cones)

Lathyrus 'Gertrude Tingay'

Lathyrus 'Carlotta'

Lathyrus 'Noel Sutton'

propagating case with a bottom heat of 16°C (61°F). When rooted, pot the cuttings in 4 in. pots of John Innes potting compost No. 1 and plant out in a nursery bed the following April. Grow on for one or two years before transplanting to permanent positions.

Pruning. None is required, except to reduce a forked leading shoot to a single leader as soon as seen. A specimen tree is more graceful if the lowest whorls of strong branches are cut off flush with the trunk to give a clean bole of at least 3 ft.

Pests. ADELGIDS feed on leaves and stems and produce conspicuous tufts of white waxy wool. Severe infestations check growth.

SAWFLY larvae feed on the tips of strong shoots, eventually killing them.

Diseases. HONEY FUNGUS may kill trees.

Several RUST fungi are common on the leaves, producing small bladder-like pustules of yellow spores; these are relatively harmless.

Larkspur: see *Delphinium consolida*
Larkspur, common: see *Delphinium ajacis*

Lathyrus

Sweet pea, everlasting pea. *Leguminosae*

A genus of 130 species of hardy annuals, sub-shrubs and herbaceous perennials; most are climbing plants that support themselves by means of leaf tendrils.

The annual sweet pea, *L. odoratus*, is the best known species; it has numerous garden varieties all easy to grow from seeds. It may also be grown to flower under glass in late spring.

Of the non-climbing perennials described, *L. vernus* is suitable for rock gardens. The remainder are climbers which, though easily grown, are not always readily obtainable from nurseries. Because the roots grow long and deep transplanting of any but young plants is not always successful.

Lathyrus flowers all have the characteristic pea-flower shape, with large wing (standard) petals and central keel petals. They are excellent as cut flowers. The leaves are pinnate, the number of leaflets varying from species to species.

LATHYRUS ODORATUS

ANNUAL SPECIES

L. odoratus (sweet pea). Italy. Height up to 10 ft planting distance 6–10 in. This well-known plant has single pairs of smooth, mid-green, ovate leaflets, the leaf stalk ending in a tendril. The scented flowers, pink, white or purple and 1 in. across, open from June to September.

The many varieties are divided into groups according to height and time of flowering:

The Cuthbertson Floribunda varieties are 8 ft high and flower from late May onwards. They are suitable for growing in a greenhouse and bear five to seven flowers on each stem. A mixture is available and also separate colours: 'Jenny', white, and 'Robert', mid-blue.

Multiflora Gigantea, 8 ft, which is especially recommended for growing under glass, flowers in April. Long vigorous stems carry from six to ten 2 in. blooms. It is available in named varieties, including 'Ramona', orange, and 'Colorama', a balanced mixture.

The Spencer varieties, the most popular of all, flower from June to September and are excellent both for garden and exhibition purposes. They grow from 6–10 ft high, depending on growing conditions, and carry four or five blooms on each long stem. Of the many varieties in this group, the following are recommended for their range of colour, abundance of flowers for cutting and exhibition quality:

'Air Warden', cerise-scarlet; 'Carlotta', carmine; 'Gertrude Tingay', deep lavender; 'Leamington', deep lilac; 'Noel Sutton', rich blue-purple; 'Princess Elizabeth', salmon-pink on cream; 'Royal Flush', rich cream-pink; 'Sonata', soft salmon-pink; 'Spotlight', ivory, flushed with pink; 'Stylish', mid-blue; 'Swan Lake', pure white; 'Tell Tale', white, edged with pink.

There are three main groups of dwarf sweet peas generally available:

Bijou, 18 in., is a recently introduced large-flowered bush type, bearing flowers up to 2 in. across from June to September. These plants are particularly weather-resistant and may often be

Lathyrus Bijou

Lathyrus grandiflorus

grown without supporting sticks. They are available in a mixture and in separate colours.

Knee-hi, 2–4 ft, flowers from June to September, each long stem producing five to ten blooms. This type is more vigorous than the Bijou varieties; with slight support, autumn-sown plants will produce a flowering hedge 4 ft high and 4 ft across. Plants from a spring sowing are generally shorter.

The variety 'Colour Carpet', 8–10 in., of low-spreading habit, is suitable for a rock garden, window-boxes and for edging borders. The flowers are ½–1 in. across and generally carried three to a stem from June to September. This type is rather shy-flowering in wet weather.

L. tingitanus. Mediterranean. Height 6 ft; planting distance 12 in. This species is suitable for a cool greenhouse. The mid-green leaflets, borne in pairs, are lanceolate. The flowers are bi-coloured, deep purple and bright red; they are 1–1½ in. across and are carried in two-flowered racemes at the end of 6 in. stems from June to July.

PERENNIAL SPECIES

L. cirrhosus. Pyrenees. Height 5–6 ft; planting distance 15–18 in. This vigorous plant has narrow, dark green leaves, each with two or three pairs of leaflets. Rose-purple flowers, ¾ in. across, are freely borne from June to August on many-flowered, 9–12 in. long stems.

L. grandiflorus. S. Europe. Height 4–6 ft; planting distance 15–18 in. The mid-green leaves each have one pair of ovate leaflets. Spectacular rose-red flowers, 1½ in. across, are freely produced

from June to September, two or three on each 9–12 in. long peduncle.

L. latifolius (everlasting pea). Europe. Height 6–10 ft; planting distance 18 in. This vigorous plant, widely grown in cottage gardens, is suitable for training to supports in various positions. The dull green leaves consist of two elliptic leaflets. The 1 in. wide flowers are usually rose-purple, but there are red to violet forms and also a white one, *L. l.* 'White Pearl'. Flowering is from June to September on many-flowered peduncles 10–12 in. long.

L. rotundifolius (Persian everlasting pea). E. Europe, Asia Minor. Height 6 ft; planting distance 18 in. This vigorous plant is easily distinguished from other species by its round, dark green leaflets, carried in pairs. Rose-pink flowers ¾–1 in. across, are borne from June to August in crowded clusters at the ends of the 8–10 in. long stems.

LATHYRUS VERNUS

L. vernus, syn. *Orobus vernus*. Europe. Height and spread 9–12 in. This is a non-climbing species; it has deep roots and produces a dense mass of shoots each spring. The pale to mid-green leaves have two or three pairs of ovate leaflets. Purple and blue flowers, ½ in. across, are borne in 2 in. long racemes in April and May. The foliage dies down after the plant has flowered.

The variety 'Albo-roseum' has rose-pink and white bi-coloured flowers.

Cultivation of annual species. Any normal garden soil will give good results, but a well-drained medium loam, slightly alkaline, is ideal. Sweet peas benefit from a cool, deep root run and it is helpful to add bulky organic matter to the soil. For best results, trench or double-dig the land in the autumn, incorporating well-rotted manure in the lower spit.

Pinch out the tips of young plants when they are 4 in. high to encourage the development of strong lateral shoots.

For exhibition purposes, space the plants 10 in. apart in double rows 18 in. apart, inserting an 8 ft cane alongside each plant. Select one side-shoot just above ground level on each plant; tie this single stem to the cane and train cordon fashion. To do this, remove all tendrils and side-shoots, supporting the growing plant by tying in at every other leaf joint. Plants grown in borders and in rows for cutting, but not cordon trained, need support with bushy sticks or netting.

Dead-head, and gather any seed pods from the plants, to encourage continuous flowering through the summer. A dilute liquid feed at weekly intervals is beneficial.

September-sown seedlings, potted into 3–5 in. or 6–8 in. containers of John Innes potting compost No. 2, will flower in May under glass. Maintain an even temperature of 10°C (50°F) and give fortnightly dilute liquid feeds.

Lathyrus 'Royal Flush'

Lathyrus 'Sonata'

Lathyrus 'Spotlight'

Lathyrus Knee-hi (mixed)

Lathyrus latifolius

Lathyrus latifolius 'White Pearl'

Cultivation of perennial species. Plant between October and March in any fertile, well-drained garden soil. They thrive in full sun, trained against fences or walls, arbours and pergolas; they may be allowed to ramble among tall shrubs or may be supported by twiggy pea-sticks. *L. vernus* does not need support.

Dead-head unless seeds are required, and cut down all the current year's growths to ground level in October or November.

Propagation of annual species. Sow the seeds in boxes or pans of seed compost in September or March, at a temperature of 16°C (61°F). Pot the seedlings singly into 3 in. pots of John Innes potting compost No. 1; grow on and pinch out the young plants when 4 in. high. Harden off in a cold frame before planting out; September-sown plants in April, March-sown plants in early May. The seeds of many varieties have thick coats; these should be nicked, or the seeds soaked in water for 12 hours, to speed germination.

Alternatively, sow directly in the flowering site in September, October or March, and thin out in April. Autumn sowings give the best results, but in cold areas the young plants need cloche protection. Stop October-sown plants in February and remove the cloches in April.

Propagation of perennial species. As with annual species, nicking or soaking the seeds speeds germination. Sow in March, in pots or boxes in a cold frame or greenhouse. Prick out the seedlings individually into 3–3½ in. pots of John Innes potting compost No. 1 and plant in the flowering site in October.

Division of the rootstock is also possible, in March, but is a less successful method for species other than *L. latifolius* and *L. vernus*.

Pests. Growth of seedlings can be severely checked in winter and early spring by SLUGS, which eat the stems and leaves.

Established plants may be infested with APHIDS, some of which transmit virus diseases.

The flowers may be damaged by BIRDS; or infested with THRIPS, which cause a fine, light mottling on the petals and leaves.

Diseases. BUD-DROP may occur, due to fluctuations in temperature or to over-dry soil.

DAMPING-OFF fungi may rot seeds sown in the open; it may also cause the collapse of seedlings after germination.

DOWNY MILDEW shows as grey furry patches on the undersides of leaves of young plants.

FOOT ROT and ROOT ROT can be caused by several fungi, including RHIZOCTONIA and BLACK ROOT ROT fungus. The roots die and often show black patches; the stem bases also become discoloured and may decay. The foliage turns yellow and withers, and diseased plants collapse.

FUSARIUM WILT also causes the leaves to turn yellow and plants to wilt. The stem bases show chocolate brown or black marks, and there is poor development of root nodules. If stems and roots are slit open lengthways, a red discoloration of the inner tissues can be seen.

GREY MOULD causes spotting and rotting of the flowers in wet seasons, but the fungal growth is not necessarily seen.

LEAFY GALL shows as a mass of abortive and often fasciated shoots at ground level.

Lathyrus vernus

POWDERY MILDEW produces a white powdery coating on the leaves and stems.

VIRUS DISEASES cause a variety of symptoms, such as bleaching of the veins; mottling and discoloration of the leaves; dead patches on the leaves; brown streaks on the leaves and stems; die-back of some shoots; breaking of the flower colour; distortion of flowers; stunting of plants; and occasionally a rapid death of affected plants.

Laurel, bay: see Laurus
Laurel, cherry: see *Prunus laurocerasus*
Laurel, common: see *Prunus laurocerasus*
Laurel, mountain: see *Kalmia latifolia*
Laurel, ornamental cherry: see Prunus
Laurel, Portugal: see *Prunus lusitanica*
Laurel, sheep: see *Kalmia angustifolia*
Laurel, spotted: see *Aucuba japonica*
Laurel, spurge: see *Daphne laureola*

Laurus
Bay laurel, sweet bay. *Lauraceae*

LAURUS NOBILIS

A genus of two species of unisexual, hardy evergreen shrubs. They thrive in coastal gardens, though the leaves may be seared by persistent cold winds. The species described is often grown as a standard or half-standard in tubs. The leaves are used either freshly picked or in a *bouquet-garni*, for flavouring fish and other dishes.

L. nobilis (sweet bay). Mediterranean region. Height and spread (unrestricted) 10–18 ft. The aromatic leaves are lanceolate and glossy mid to dark green. Both male and female plants have inconspicuous yellow-green flower clusters which open in April. Female plants bear ½ in. long purple-black berries.

Cultivation. Plant in March or April in any ordinary garden soil in a sunny, sheltered position. A 15–18 in. tub containing John Innes potting compost No. 3 is suitable for growing a standard or half-standard specimen.

Propagation. During August or September, take 3 in. heel cuttings of lateral shoots; insert in equal parts peat and sand in a cold frame. In April, pot the rooted cuttings in 3½ in. pots of John Innes potting compost No. 1 and pot on successively as required. The following October, set the young plants out in a nursery bed and grow them on for a year or two before planting out in March or April.

Low-growing shoots layered in July or August will be ready for severing from the parent plant and potting up a year later.

Pruning. No pruning is necessary for shrubs grown in the open garden, but tub-grown specimens should be trimmed to shape twice or more during the summer. Remove sucker shoots from the stems of standards as they appear.

To develop a young tree as a standard, allow the leading shoot to grow to the desired height, pinching back all lateral shoots to two or three leaves. When the leading shoot is 6 in. taller than the desired height of the stem, pinch out the tip. When the lateral shoots have four or five leaves, pinch them again and repeat this process until the basis of the head is formed. Thereafter use secateurs for pruning to shape.

Pests. The stems and the undersides of leaves may be infested with SCALE INSECTS, which make the plants sticky and sooty.

Diseases. Generally trouble-free.

Laurustinus: see *Viburnum tinus*

Lavandula

Lavender. *Labiatae*

A genus of 28 species of hardy evergreen shrubs. The plants described, which are suitable for low-growing short-lived hedges, are widely cultivated for their fragrant flowers and aromatic foliage. The flowers may be dried for use in sachets and *pot-pourris*.

Lavenders tend to grow leggy with age, and the plants are best discarded or replaced after five or six years.

LAVANDULA SPICA

L. nana atropurpurea: see *L. spica* 'Hidcote'
L. spica (old English lavender). Mediterranean regions. Height and spread 3–4 ft. A species with silver-grey, linear-oblong leaves. The tubular, pale grey-blue flowers are borne in terminal spikes up to 2½ in. long, from July to September.

'Hidcote', syn. *L. nana atropurpurea* (height 12–24 in.; spread 18–24 in.) is a compact plant with deep purple-blue flowers in 2 in. spikes. 'Twickle Purple' (height and spread 2–3 ft) has slender purple flower spikes up to 4½ in. long.
L. stoechas (French lavender). Mediterranean regions. Height and spread up to 24 in. A species

with grey-green linear-oblong leaves; dark purple tubular flowers in 1–2 in. long spikes are carried from May to July. The most prominent feature of this species is the tuft of purple ovate bracts that tops each flower spike and persists after the flowers have faded.
L. vera (Dutch lavender). S. Europe. Height 18 in.; spread 2–3 ft. This plant, which is generally considered to be a more compact form of *L. spica*, has grey-green linear-oblong leaves. The blue-purple flowers are borne in 2½ in. spikes from July to September. 'Nana Alba' (height and spread 12–15 in.) has silver-grey foliage and 1½–2 in. long white flower spikes.

Cultivation. Plant lavender between September and March in any ordinary, well-drained soil in a sunny position. For hedges, set the young plants 9–12 in. apart.

If the flowers are required for drying, pick the blooms when they are showing colour but before they are fully open. Cut the whole flower stalks and hang these, tied in bunches, in a cool, airy place to dry. In any case, remove the flower stems as the blooms fade.

Propagation. Take 3–4 in. cuttings of ripe, non-flowering shoots in August and insert in equal parts (by volume) peat and sand in a cold frame. Overwinter the cuttings in the cold frame and transplant to their flowering positions in March or April.

Cuttings, 6–9 in. long, may also be taken in September and inserted *in situ* outdoors.

Pruning. Remove dead flower stems and lightly trim the plants in late summer. Straggly plants may be cut hard back in late March or April to promote bushy growth and to encourage new growths from the base.

Clip established hedges to shape during March or April.

Pests. The stems may be infested with FROG-HOPPERS, which produce cuckoo spit.

Diseases. Shoots injured by FROST DAMAGE may die back, or infected tissues may be attacked by GREY MOULD, which shows as a grey velvety growth on dead shoots. This fungus may also attack the flowers in a wet season, causing them to wilt or turn brown prematurely.

HONEY FUNGUS may kill plants.

LEAF SPOT appears as small spots on the leaves.

SCAB shows as wilting of the shoots, followed by DIE-BACK or death of the whole plant.

Lavatera

Mallow. *Malvaceae*

A genus of 25 species of annual, biennial and perennial herbaceous plants and sub-shrubs, of bushy habit and with open trumpet-shaped, hibiscus-like flowers. The annual species described is suitable for growing in borders, the biennial for wild gardens or shrubberies.
L. arborea (tree mallow). Britain. Height 4–6 ft; planting distance 18 in. A biennial species of stout erect habit, not fully hardy in cold areas, but commonly found naturalised in coastal districts. The leaves are soft, mid-green, velvety and lobed. The flowers are 2 in. across, pale purple with dark veins, and produced in leafy pyramidal panicles,

Laurus nobilis (in flower)

Lavandula spica

Lavandula stoechas

2–3 ft long, from July to August. The variety 'Variegata' has white-mottled leaves and deep red flowers.

L. rosea: see *L. trimestris*

LAVATERA TRIMESTRIS

L. trimestris, syn. *L. rosea*. S. Europe. Height 2–3 ft; spacing 18 in. A hardy annual of erect and bushy habit. This widely grown species is a popular border plant, also suitable for cutting. The lobed, ovate leaves are pale green. Rose-coloured flowers, 4 in. across, are freely produced from the axils of the upper leaves from July to September. The variety 'Loveliness' has deep rose flowers; 'Splendens Alba' has large white flowers.

Cultivation. Most soils are suitable, but over-rich soils should be avoided as these encourage excessive leaf growth. A sunny and sheltered site is ideal. Winter protection with cloches is needed for *L. arborea* in cold districts.

Both species seed themselves freely and produce great numbers of plants the following season if the soil is not disturbed through cultivation.

Propagation. Sow annual lavateras directly in the flowering site in September or April, just covering them with soil. Thin out the seedlings in May. Sow biennials outdoors in May or June; move the young plants to the flowering site in September.

Pests. Generally trouble-free.

Diseases. LEAF SPOT affects leaves, leaf stalks and stems, showing as yellow-brown spots which bear bristle-like fungal structures.

RUST shows on the stems and leaves as raised, spore-bearing pustules which are orange at first, later turning brown. In severe cases, shrivelling of the leaves or even of the whole plant may occur.

Lavender: see Lavandula
Lavender, cotton: see Santolina
Lavender, Dutch: see *Lavandula vera*
Lavender, French: see *Lavandula stoechas*
Lavender, old English: see *Lavandula spica*
Lavender, sea: see Limonium

Lavatera trimestris

Layia elegans

Leek 'Musselburgh'

Layia
Compositae

LAYIA ELEGANS

A genus of 15 species of hardy annuals, suitable for growing in borders and on sunny banks. The bright, daisy-like flowers are abundant and are long-lasting when cut.

L. elegans (tidy tips). California. Height 18 in spacing 10 in. A bushy, well-branched specie with soft, lanceolate leaves that are grey-green i colour, and pleasantly scented. The flowers, 2 ir across, have yellow ray florets, tipped with white surrounding a bright yellow central disc. The bloom from June to October. There is a whit variety, 'Alba', but this is not commonly listed.

Cultivation. All garden soils give reasonabl results but a light, well-drained, sandy soil in sunny site is ideal. These plants stand up well t adverse weather conditions, but in cold district overwintered seedlings need cloche protection.

Propagation. Sow the seeds in the flowering sit in March or April, just covering them with soi and thin out the seedlings to the required spacing In sheltered areas of the south and west, September sowing provides flowers in May.

Pests and diseases. Generally trouble-free.

Leek
Allium porrum. Alliaceae

An easily grown, hardy biennial vegetable cul tivated as an annual for use in autumn an winter. The thick, white, stem-like portion i composed of tightly concentric, succulent layer of leaf bases, each of which parts at the top t form a large, grooved, strap-shaped, grey-greer leaf. The stems, which have a mild onion-lik flavour, are best blanched before harvesting.

VARIETIES
The numerous varieties are divided into thre groups, early, mid-season and late, according t their time of maturing.

'Early Giant', 'Prizetaker' and 'The Lyon' ar reliable early varieties, ready for use from Sep tember to November.

'Musselburgh' and 'Walton Mammoth' ar excellent mid-season varieties for use from November to January. Late-maturing, hardy var ieties that withstand the winter outdoors are 'Empire', 'Royal Favourite' and 'Winter Crop'.

Leeks are popular as exhibition vegetables early-maturing varieties are best grown for thi purpose as most vegetable shows are held be tween August and November; 'Prizetaker' is an outstanding exhibition variety.

Cultivation. Leeks thrive in any ordinary, well-drained soil. It is usually most convenient t grow them where early peas, potatoes and sala crops have been harvested. For best results, dig the ground deeply, incorporating a bucketful o decayed manure or compost per sq. yd. Apply a top-dressing of fish manure at the rate of 3 oz. per sq. yd two or three weeks before planting out the seedlings. On acid soils, give a top-dressing of carbonate of lime at 4 oz. per sq. yd.

Sow seeds in shallow drills in a seed bed in March. At the end of June or early in July lift the seedlings, taking care not to break the roots. Trim off the tips of the foliage to promote stronger root action. Transplant the seedlings to their growing positions, on level ground or in trenches. Level-ground cultivation requires the least labour and produces excellent, short thick leeks. Leeks grown in trenches have longer, well-blanched stems.

On level ground, make 6 in. deep holes with a ubber and drop the seedlings in. Water them in o that soil is washed over the roots. Allow 6 in. etween plants of early and mid-season var-ties, 9 in. for later-maturing types. Space the ows 15 in. apart.

For deep cultivation, take out trenches 12 in. eep and wide and 18 in. apart, heaping the soil etween them. Bury well-rotted manure about in. deep in the bottom of each trench. Set the eedlings 1 in. deep and 9 in. apart in a single ow along each trench; about a month after lanting, draw an inch or two of soil back into he trench around the stems. Repeat this process ach month until there is a ridge of soil on either ide of the stems reaching to just below the base f the leaves. Tie corrugated-cardboard collars ound the stems before earthing up, to keep grit ff the leeks.

xhibition. Prepare the ground as early as pos-ible in late autumn or early winter by digging it wo spits deep and manuring liberally. Sow eeds, preferably of 'Prizetaker', under glass in arly January. Sow in pans of seed compost and erminate at a temperature of 10°C (50°F).

As soon as the seedlings are large enough to andle, prick them off singly into 3 in. pots of eed compost. If necessary, pot on into 5 in. ontainers. Harden the plants off in a cold frame efore planting out in the prepared bed.

Take out shallow trenches about 3 in. deep nd 15 in. wide; set the seedlings 20 in. apart in single line along the centre of the trench and take with thin canes. Every 10–14 days give a iquid feed of 1 oz. nitrate of soda and 1 oz. uperphosphate to each gallon of water.

As soon as the plants have stems 4–5 in. long, ie a 4 in. deep collar of corrugated cardboard ound each. When the stems outgrow these ollars, cover them with 12 in. long pieces of rainpipe, 4 in. across. Pack a small quantity of vood shavings or wool inside the pipe to pre-ent the foliage being damaged.

Lift the plants carefully and wash the roots lean; remove one or two outer skins from the tems if they are marked. Exhibit only stems of niform size, selecting firm specimens which are erfectly straight.

Pests. ONION FLY maggots may attack the roots nd infest the bases of plants, causing wilting nd collapse.

Diseases. WHITE ROT causes the leaves to turn ellow and die back; the roots rot and the bases f the plants become covered with a white uffy fungal growth.

egousia speculum-veneris: see *Specularia speculum*
Lemon: see *Citrus limon*
Lemon thyme: see Thyme

Leontopodium

Edelweiss. *Compositae*

A genus of 30 species of hardy herbaceous erennials. The species described grows readily from seeds and is suitable for rock gardens.
L. alpinum. European Alps. Height 8 in.; spread up to 9 in. This plant has lanceolate, basal, grey-green leaves. The flower stems and the undersides of the leaves are covered with dense white woolly hairs. The small groundsel-like flowers are white and closely surrounded by petal-like woolly white bracts, forming a 2 in. wide flower-like head. The flowering period is during June and July.

LEONTOPODIUM ALPINUM

Cultivation. Plant in March in an open sunny site in firm but well-drained sandy soil.
Propagation. Sow seeds in February or March in boxes or pans containing 2 parts John Innes potting compost No. 1 and 1 part grit (parts by volume), and place in a cold frame. Prick off the seedlings into boxes in April and transfer to 3 in. pots when the plants are well developed; grow on in the frame and plant out the following March.
Pests and diseases. Generally trouble-free.

Leopard's bane: see Doronicum
Lepidium sativum: see Mustard and cress
Leptosiphon hybridus: see *Gilia lutea*

Leptospermum

Myrtaceae

LEPTOSPERMUM SCOPARIUM

A genus of 50 species of slightly tender, evergreen flowering shrubs which are suitable for sheltered and coastal gardens in mild areas. They do well against south-facing walls and also make fine conservatory or cool-greenhouse shrubs.
L. humifusum, syn. *L. scoparium prostratum.* Tasmania. Height up to 6 in.; spread 3 ft. This prostrate, mat-forming shrub is the hardiest species and will survive all but the coldest winters. The dark green leaves are narrowly oblong and pointed. White flowers, saucer-shaped and ¾ in. across, are borne in profusion during May and June.
L. scoparium (Manuka or tea tree). New Zealand. Height 6–10 ft, or more against a wall; spread 4–6 ft. The narrowly oblong and pointed leaves are dark green. Star-shaped white flowers, up to 1 in. across, are freely borne in May and June.

Varieties include: 'Chapmanii', with bright rose-red, saucer-shaped flowers; 'Flore Pleno', double white; 'Keatleyi', large saucer-shaped pink flowers which are paler at the edges; 'Nicholsii', crimson; 'Red Damask', double deep

Leontopodium alpinum

Leptospermum scoparium 'Nichollsii'

red, long-lasting; and 'Roseum Multipetalum', double rose-pink.

L. scoparium prostratum: see *L. humifusum*

Cultivation. Leptospermums can be grown without protection in mild coastal districts. Inland they require a sheltered garden or the protection of a south-facing wall. Plant pot-grown plants in April or May in well-drained light soil, and set in a sunny position.

Propagation. In June or July, take 2–2½ in. cuttings of half-ripe shoots and insert them in pans of equal parts (by volume) peat and sand in a propagating frame at a temperature of 16°C (61°F). Set the rooted cuttings in 3 in. pots of John Innes potting compost No. 1 and over-winter them in a frame or greenhouse with enough heat to keep the frost out. Grow on for a further year in 5–6 in. pots before planting out in the flowering sites in April or May.

Pruning. No pruning is necessary except to remove straggly branches in April.

Pests and diseases. Generally trouble-free.

Lettuce 'Continuity'

Lettuce 'Susan'

Lettuce 'Webb's Wonderful'

Lettuce

Lactuca sativa. Compositae

A half-hardy and hardy annual grown as a salad plant. Fresh lettuce may be had throughout the year by growing varieties that mature outdoors from May to late October. In winter, lettuces can be grown under glass.

VARIETIES

There are two main types, cabbage and cos. The cabbage lettuces are further divided into the early maturing, flattened globular butterheads which have smooth leaves, and the curled-leaf cabbage lettuces, with crimped leaves and globular heads.

Cos lettuces are generally oblong, with crisper leaves and a sweeter flavour than the cabbage type. They withstand drought better, but require a longer growing season. Some cos varieties, known as self-folding, form a close heart on their own, while others must be induced to produce tight centres. Place a rubber band or piece of string round each plant about two weeks before it matures.

Less popular is the so-called leaf or chicken lettuce. This does not produce a compact head, but a loose bunch of leaves. The varieties 'Grand Rapids', 'Oak Leaved' and 'Salad Bowl' are generally recommended.

All lettuce varieties differ in time of maturity and in colour. There are almost-white to grass-green varieties, bronze-tinged and purple-tinged varieties, and some with red-edged leaves.

Reliable varieties for successional sowings include the cabbage types: 'Cobham Green', 'Continuity', 'Susan' and 'Unrivalled', and the curled-leaved 'Webb's Wonderful' and 'Windermere'. These mature in summer.

Recommended cos types are the large, self-folding 'Lobjoit's Green Cos', 'Paris Green', 'White Heart', and the smaller 'Little Gem' and 'Nonsuch' (dwarf cos).

For growing in the open during winter, to mature in spring, use hardy butterheads, such as 'Arctic King', 'Imperial' and 'Valdor', or 'Winter

Density', an intermediate variety between cabbage and cos types. 'Delta', 'Kloek', 'Kwiek' and 'May King' are compact plants suitable for growing under glass.

Lettuce 'Kwiek'

Mixed seeds of up to half-a-dozen varieties are also available; these mature at different times so that lettuces from one sowing can be cut over a month or more.

Cultivation. Successful lettuce crops can be produced on any fertile, well-drained soil. Grow summer crops on ground that was well manured for the previous crop, and apply a general-purpose fertiliser at 2 oz. per sq. yd. If no well-manured ground is available, dig in two bucketfuls of well-rotted manure or compost per sq. yd in autumn.

For winter crops, a well-drained soil is essential; lighten heavy soils by adding peat or well-decayed compost. Do not apply fresh bulky manure for a winter crop, but give a top-dressing of fish manure at 3 oz. per sq. yd or a mixture of 2 parts wood ash to 1 part bone-meal (parts by volume) at 9 oz. per sq. yd.

Sow the seeds thinly in shallow drills where the plants are to grow. Lettuces bolt easily and any check to growth such as transplanting, over-crowding or shortage of water should be avoided. They must be grown quickly to be crisp and tender, and watering is essential. Sow summer varieties in rows 15 in. apart and thin the seedlings to 12 in. apart; dwarf cos varieties need only 9 in. between rows and 6 in. between plants. Maintain a continuous supply by making successional sowings at two or three week intervals from early April until early August.

Lettuces grown in the open during winter for early spring use will be less vigorous in growth than summer lettuces. Sow the seeds in September in rows 12 in. apart and thin the seedlings to 9–12 in. apart. Seeds may also be sown in a seed bed and the seedlings transplanted to their final quarters in November in sheltered southern districts; in exposed areas do not transplant until February or March. Handle all seedlings with care as the leaves bruise easily, and the tap roots may snap off during transplanting.

Under glass. For a winter crop, grow lettuces in a cold frame or greenhouse. Sow seeds in pots or pans of seed compost in August. When large enough to handle, prick out the seedlings into a cold frame or greenhouse border, setting them 9 in. apart each way. Water the soil well before transplanting the seedlings, but thereafter water only when necessary. During mild weather, admit as much air as possible.

Sowings made in August will produce mature plants for use in November and December. Plants raised from seeds sown in January or February will be ready for cutting in April and early May. In greenhouses, heated to 10°C (50°F), or in soil-warmed frames, sowings made during October produce mature plants for January, February and March.

Harvesting. Cut lettuces early in the day while the dew is still on them. Sever them with a sharp knife just below the bottom leaves and use first any plants that are beginning to bolt.

Pests. Roots may be attacked by ROOT APHIDS; other species of APHIDS may infest the leaves.

SLUGS and SNAILS feed on leaves and stems, fouling the plants with their slimy trails. CUT-WORMS and other CATERPILLARS also feed on leaves and stems.

Diseases. DAMPING-OFF may be due to different fungi including RHIZOCTONIA; the seedlings collapse and rot at soil level.

Yellow blotches on the upper leaf-surfaces, and mealy patches on the undersurfaces, are caused by DOWNY MILDEW.

GREY MOULD causes the plants to collapse or wilt; a grey velvety fungal growth appears on the leaves.

LETTUCE VIRUS DISEASES cause a number of different symptoms, including dwarfing of plants, distortion of leaves, mottling, and spotting or bronzing of the leaves, which turn black and shrivel up.

PHYSIOLOGICAL DISORDERS arise as a result of drought and cause the leaves to become tough, rubbery, light in colour and bitter; the plants bolt. High summer temperatures may result in browning of the margins of most of the leaves.

SCLEROTINIA DISEASE affects plants near ground level and shows on rotting tissues as a white fluffy fungal growth in which are embedded large black resting bodies.

Leucanthemum hosmariense: see *Chrysanthemum hosmariense*

Leucojum

Snowflake. *Amaryllidaceae*

Three of the 12 species of this bulbous genus are in general cultivation. The flowers resemble snowdrops (*Galanthus*) but the snowflake flower has a more rounded appearance; all six petals of the snowflake are the same size, whereas the inner three of the snowdrop are smaller than the outer three. All the species described are hardy; they have mid to dark green leaves.

L. aestivum (summer snowflake). Central and S.E. Europe. Height 24 in.; planting distance 6–8 in. This species has strap-shaped, mid-green leaves. White flowers, 1 in. long, with green-tipped petals cluster at the tops of erect stems in April and May. The variety 'Gravetye Giant' is more robust than the species. Both do best in moist soil and tolerate some shade.

L. autumnale. Iberian Peninsula, Mediterranean islands, N. Africa. Height 8–10 in.; planting distance 3–4 in. The leaves of this species are linear and mid-green. White flowers, ½ in. long and with a pink flush, appear from July to September. This species is best grown in sun.

LEUCOJUM VERNUM

L. vernum. Central Europe. Height 8 in.; planting distance 3–4 in. This species has strap-shaped leaves. White, green-tipped, ¾ in. long flowers appear in February and March. It does best in moist conditions and will tolerate some shade. *L. v.* 'Carpathicum' is identical, except that the petals are tipped with yellow.

Leucojum vernum 'Carpathicum'

Cultivation. Plant fresh bulbs as soon as available in late summer or early autumn; plant *L. aestivum* and *L. vernum* 3–4 in. deep in moisture-retentive soil; *L. autumnale* 2 in. deep in free-draining soil. Leave undisturbed for several years. When the groups appear overcrowded, producing too many leaves and too few flowers, lift as the leaves die down, divide and replant at once at the same spacing and depths as recommended for fresh bulbs. No attention is needed during intervening seasons.

Propagation. The offsets produced by leucojums soon become established and flower alongside the older bulbs. Division every few years, as already described, is the normal method of increase. Seeds of *L. aestivum* and *L. vernum* can be saved (*L. autumnale* rarely sets seeds in Great Britain) when they ripen between July and September, and sown in John Innes seed compost in a cold greenhouse or frame. Plant out in nursery rows and leave the seedlings to grow on there until they reach flowering size in four to six years.

Pests and diseases. Generally trouble-free.

Lettuce 'White Heart'

Leucojum aestivum

Leucojum autumnale

Lewisia cotyledon heckneri

Lewisia

Portulacaceae

LEWISIA COTYLEDON

A genus of 20 species of herbaceous and evergreen semi-succulent perennials, some having attractive or showy flowers. They are suitable for rock gardens and alpine houses. With the exception of *L. rediviva,* all those described are evergreen and bear a profusion of widely funnel-shaped flowers.

L. brachycalyx. N.W. America. Height 2–3 in.; spread 6–9 in. Narrow, fleshy, glaucous leaves form a flat rosette from which emerge 1½ in. wide flowers borne singly on short stems. The flowers are satin-white, sometimes tinged with pink, and open flat in bright sunlight during May.

L. columbiana. British Columbia, Cascade Mountains. Height 6–12 in.; spread 3 in. Rosettes of linear-spathulate leaves produce wiry flowering stems with 1½ in. wide heads of magenta or white flowers, with red veining, in May and June.

'Rosea', similar in habit to *L. columbiana* and probably a hybrid, bears purple-red flowers.

L. cotyledon. California. Height up to 12 in.; spread 6 in. This plant forms a dense rosette of mid-green obovate fleshy leaves sometimes with undulate margins. The flowers are pink with white veins, about 1½ in. across, and are carried on 8 in. stems in May and June. The following two varieties were formerly given specific rank:

L. c. heckneri. California. Height and spread about 6–10 in. A rosette-forming plant with ovate-oblong to spathulate mid-green leaves. Branched clusters of deep rose-pink flowers, 1½–2 in. across, appear from April to July.

Lewisia cotyledon

Lewisia cotyledon howellii

L. c. howellii. Oregon. Height and spread about 6 in. The rosettes of this species spread out flat, with oblong-ovate, mid-green leaves which have finely crested margins. Racemose clusters of 1½–2 in. wide flowers open from April to June. The petals are pink, striped with carmine.

There are many hybrids with colours ranging from pale pink to apricot. 'George Henley' is a good form with brick-red flowers.

L. nevadensis, syn. *L. pygmaea nevadensis.* Nevada. Height and spread 3 in. A species closely related to *L. rediviva,* with tufted rosettes of linear fleshy leaves that die away at flowering time. White, ¾–1¼ in. wide flowers appear singly from the leaf axils, from June to August.

L. × 'Phyllellia'. Height 3–6 in.; spread 6–9 in. This hybrid combines the dwarf habit of *L. brachycalyx* with the bright colouring of *L. cotyledon.* Oblong-spathulate mid-green leaves form fleshy rosettes; the flowers, 1–2 in. across and varying from white to pink with a deeper pink veining, are carried from May to July.

L. pygmaea nevadensis: see *L. nevadensis*

L. rediviva (bitter root). U.S.A. Height 3 in.; spread 6 in. Narrow red-green leaves form a rosette which dies down in June when the single stemless flowers appear. Each is 2 in. or more across, rose-pink or white, and resembles a small water-lily.

L. tweedyi. Washington and British Columbia. Height 6 in.; spread 9 in. This is outstanding among the evergreen lewisias. It has wide mid-green leaves formed into a loose rosette which grows more erect than those of the other species. The 2 in. wide flowers vary from palest pink to soft apricot and have a satin sheen.

'Rosea' has vivid pink buds opening to rose-pink flowers with darker petal tips.

Cultivation. Plant lewisias in March or April. Outdoors, set them in a well-drained sunny position on the rock garden, in rich soil containing plenty of gravel. The necks of the thick roots are susceptible to winter wet and should be banked up with a thick layer of chippings for additional drainage.

In the alpine house, grow lewisias in 6–9 in. pans of equal parts (by volume) rich garden soil and chippings; for best results add a handful of well-rotted manure at the base of each pot. Repot annually in March. Water the plants regularly during the growing season, but keep them barely moist once flowering has finished.

Propagation. Detach offsets in June and plant them in a mixture of equal parts (by volume) peat and sand in boxes or pans and place them in a cold frame. When rooted, pot into 3 in. containers of John Innes potting compost No. 1; overwinter them in the frame, and plant out in April.

Alternatively, sow seeds in March in boxes or pans and place them in a cold frame. Prick out the seedlings when they are large enough to handle; pot up into 3 in. pots of John Innes potting compost No. 1, overwinter in the frame and plant out in April.

Lewisias hybridise readily and plants raised from seeds seldom come true to type unless the seed plants are isolated from other species.

Pests. Young seedlings may be eaten by SLUGS.

Diseases. A PHYSIOLOGICAL DISORDER which shows as COLLAR ROT is due to excessive moisture.

Leycesteria

Caprifoliaceae

LEYCESTERIA FORMOSA

A genus of six species of hardy, deciduous flowering shrubs. The two species described have erect bamboo-like growth and pendent racemes of tubular flowers.

L. crocothyrsos. Assam. Height 6–8 ft; spread 4–6 ft. An erect shrub with ovate, slender-pointed leaves, mid to pale green above and glaucous beneath. The fleshy-textured golden flowers, ¾ in. long, have five spreading, rounded, petal-like lobes. They are borne in 2–4 in. long pendent racemes from the previous season's growths, in May and June. Although this species will stand a temperature of –5°C (23°F), it must be sited in a position sheltered from east and north winds.

L. formosa. Himalayas. Height 6 ft; spread 5 ft. The heart-shaped leaves are mid-green with a glaucous sheen. White, funnel-shaped flowers with claret bracts are borne in 2–4 in. long racemes at the apex of the current season's growths in July and August. These are followed, in October, by purple-black ovoid fruits. The hollow stems of this plant may be damaged in a severe winter, but new shoots appear each spring.

Cultivation. These shrubs are especially suitable for seaside districts and will grow in any normal well-drained soil. They are shade-tolerant, but flower most freely in full sun. *L. formosa* may be planted during suitable weather between October and March; *L. crocothyrsos* should not be set outdoors until April or May.

Propagation. Sow seeds in a cold frame in February or March. When the seedlings are large enough to handle, prick them off into pans or boxes, then into 4 in. pots. Grow them on for a year before planting out, overwintering *L. crocothyrsos* in a cold frame.

Alternatively, take 9 in. hardwood cuttings of *L. formosa* in October and insert them in a nursery bed. Grow on for a year before planting them out in September or October.

Semi-hardwood cuttings of lateral shoots of *L. crocothyrsos,* taken with a heel, can be rooted in a cold frame in July. Pot when rooted and overwinter as for seedlings.

Pruning. In March, remove at ground level the shoots which bore flowers the previous year.

Pests and diseases. Generally trouble-free.

Liatris

Blazing star, gayfeather. *Compositae*

A genus of about 40 species of hardy tuberous herbaceous plants. The following are suitable for growing in borders and as cut flowers. The individual flower heads are thistle-like, but are densely borne on wand-like spikes. The leaves are linear and mid-green in colour.

L. callilepis. United States. Height 3 ft; planting distance 18 in. This species has bright carmine flower spikes, up to 12 in. long, on leafy stems from July to September. One of the most reliable species, particularly in poor soils. 'Kobold' (height 24 in.; planting distance 12 in.), is a similar but smaller variety.

L. graminifolia. E. United States. Height 2–3 ft; planting distance 12–18 in. The 12 in. long flower spikes are purple and are carried on slender, nearly leafless stems in August and September. The sparse leaves are spotted with white. This species is suitable for dry soils.

LIATRIS SPICATA

L. spicata. E. and S. United States. Height 2–3 ft; planting distance 12–18 in. This plant has pink-purple flowers in dense spikes 6–15 in. long, borne in September on stout leafy stems. It will tolerate heavier soil than the other species and likes moist conditions; it does well as a bog plant.

Cultivation. Plant firmly in a sunny open position in September and October, or March and April. These plants are easily grown in most soils, but too-heavy soils may lead to rotting in winter. Mulching with well-rotted manure or compost is helpful. Water freely in dry spells.

Remove the fading flowers from the top of the spikes. As the plants disappear below ground in winter, mark their positions to avoid damage by digging or hoeing.

Propagation. Divide and replant the roots in March or April every three or four years.

Most species come true from seeds which are readily obtained. Sow seeds in March in a cold frame or greenhouse and, when large enough to handle, prick out the seedlings into boxes. Grow on in nursery rows, ideally until the autumn of the following year, before planting out.

Pests. Young shoots may be eaten by SLUGS.

Diseases. Generally trouble-free.

Libocedrus

Cupressaceae

This genus has recently been separated into three separate genera of evergreen coniferous trees: *Libocedrus*, with five species; *Austrocedrus* with one species; and *Calocedrus* with three species. Although the species described is now botanically correctly listed under the genus *Calocedrus*, the older classification has been retained here. It makes a handsome specimen tree, but is most effective when planted in close groups.

See also CONIFERS.

L. decurrens, syn. *Calocedrus decurrens* (incense cedar). California, Oregon. Height 25 ft; spread

Leycesteria formosa (fruiting clusters)

Liatris callilepis

Liatris spicata

10–15 ft. A hardy species forming a broadly conic bright green tree, with a rounded top. The pale red-brown bark is fissured into long vertical plates, but the bole is often hidden by close, short, upcurving branches. The dense, fan-like shoots are clothed in scale-like rich dark green leaves. The 1 in. long, narrow, ovoid and smooth cones are yellow; they are borne in clusters.

The type species is rare in cultivation. It is commonly represented by 'Fastigiata' (height 25–30 ft; spread 3–4 ft), a columnar form with perpendicular sides and a blunt crown.

LIBOCEDRUS DECURRENS 'FASTIGIATA'

Cultivation. These trees grow best in fertile, damp, but well-drained garden soil, in a sunny, sheltered position. They grow adequately for years on shallow or heavy soils in exposed sites, but later the trees tend to lose foliage over much of their crowns and become tufted.

Plant in October and November or in March and April using young plants up to 24 in. high. No staking is required.

Propagation. Sow seeds in October in pans of John Innes seed compost in a cold frame or greenhouse. Line out the seedlings in a nursery bed the following April, and grow on for two or three years before setting in permanent sites.

Take 3 in. long tip cuttings from July to September of *L. d.* 'Fastigiata' which does not come true from seeds. Insert in equal parts (by volume) peat and sand in a cold frame. When rooted, but not before the following April, transplant the cuttings to outdoor nursery beds, and grow on for at least a year before planting out in permanent positions.

Pruning. None is required, except to reduce forking main shoots to a single leader.

Pests and diseases. Generally trouble-free.

Libonia floribunda : see *Jacobinia pauciflora*

Ligustrum

Privet. *Oleaceae*

LIGUSTRUM OVALIFOLIUM

A genus of about 45 species of hardy deciduous and evergreen flowering shrubs and small trees, grown extensively as hedging plants.

L. japonicum (Japanese privet). Japan, Korea. Height 6–8 ft; spread 4–6 ft. This evergreen shrub, of dense and compact habit, is hardy in all but the coldest districts. The ovate leaves are a lustrous dark green; tubular white flowers are borne in 4–6 in. panicles during August.

L. lucidum. China, Korea, Japan. Height 10–18 ft; spread 6–10 ft. An evergreen tree which needs protection from cold north and east winds. The ovate glossy leaves are dark green; cream-white tubular flowers are borne in 6–8 in. panicles during August and September.

L. ovalifolium. Japan. Height and spread 12–15 ft. This shrub, which is evergreen except in the severest winters, has glossy, ovate, mid-green leaves. Plants grown as flowering shrubs produce 1½–3 in. panicles of cream flowers in July; they have a heavy fragrance disliked by some people. The flowers are tubular with cross-shaped lobes; they are followed by black berries.

'Aureo-marginatum' (golden privet) has glossy, mid-green, ovate leaves, each with a wide irregular yellow border. This variety is a little more compact than the type plant.

'Variegatum' has leaves edged with pale yellow or cream-white.

Cultivation. Plant in any ordinary garden soil, in either sun or shade.

For growing as a hedge, use plants 1–3 ft high and space them 12–18 in. apart. If the soil is poor, prepare the ground by working in manure or compost and add a general fertiliser at 4 oz. per sq. yd. Plant between October and April and cut back all shoots by one-half or two-thirds of their length in April.

A year later cut back all growths by half again. To promote a good strong bushy base, keep cutting all new growth back by half its length in September each successive year until the desired height is reached.

Propagation. Take 4–6 in. hardwood cuttings of *L. japonicum* and *L. lucidum* in September or October and insert them in a cold frame in equal parts (by volume) peat and sand. The following April or May, plant out the rooted cuttings in a nursery bed sheltered from north and east winds. Set the plants in their final positions from October onwards, or for more robust plants wait a further year (18 months in the nursery bed) before planting out.

Take 12 in. hardwood cuttings of *L. ovalifolium* and insert them in ordinary garden soil in a sheltered border in October. Plant the rooted cuttings out in their permanent positions a year later, between October and April.

Pruning. No pruning is necessary, except to clip established hedges at least twice a year, in May and September.

Pests. LEAF MINERS tunnel into the leaves which become covered with brown blotches.

THRIPS feed on the leaves, causing mottling, silvering and premature leaf-fall.

Diseases. Privets in hedges are frequently killed by HONEY FUNGUS. The plants die fairly rapidly, with the trouble gradually spreading along the whole hedge. LEAF SPOT shows as discoloured patches with brown or red edges.

Libocedrus decurrens

Ligustrum ovalifolium 'Aureo-marginatum'

Lilium 'Enchantment'

Lilium 'Marhan'

LILIUM
Lily. *Liliaceae*

A genus of 80 species of bulbous plants that are generally hardy; only a few choice species require the protection of a greenhouse. In the wild, lilies are found in a broad zone encircling the Northern Hemisphere and roughly coinciding with the Temperate Zone. A few species, such as the madonna lily (*L. candidum*) have been cultivated for 3500 years, but not until the 20th century did the lily become developed on a commercial scale. Since then, numerous species have been introduced, and with the ever-increasing number of hardy hybrids available, lilies are becoming popular garden flowers.

They may be massed together in mixed borders, placed among shrubs and on large rock gardens, or grown as pot plants. Several are suitable for a wild or woodland garden if the planting site is well prepared and is protected from pests and vermin. The shapely blooms and erect stems make them excellent for cutting.

A lily bulb is composed of thick and overlapping scales which are leaves modified for the storage of food. In a fresh dormant bulb the scales are pressed tightly round the bud from which the stems will emerge. Thick roots grow from the basal plate and, in some species and hybrids, roots also grow from the stems just above the bulbs. They are known as stem-rooting bulbs and should be planted deeper than basal-rooting bulbs which produce roots from the basal plate only. Some species have rhizomatous bulbs in which one or more small flattened bulbs grow closely together along a tough basal-rooting horizontal stem.

The leaves are pale to dark green; in some plants the foliage is grass-like and crowded along the stems; in others the leaves are broadly lanceolate and set in whorls at intervals.

The typical lily flower has six petals, or perianth segments, often with prominent stamens; flowers are available in most colour ranges, except blue. They vary in size and shape from 1 in. wide Turk's-caps, named after their recurved and rolled petals, to long trumpets and huge bowl-shaped blooms up to 10 in. across. The flowers are arranged in a loose inflorescence at the top of the stem; they are often fragrant, but in a few species they give off an unpleasant scent that makes them unsuitable for planting near a house or path.

Most lilies are easy to grow, given a well-drained position and reasonable care, while a few are decidedly exacting in their requirements.

The introduction of numerous robust hybrids, notably from the Oregon Bulb Farm, has led to a classification of lilies into nine divisions, with several sub-divisions. This classification has been adopted by the Royal Horticultural Society and the North American Lily Society; it is particularly used for exhibition purposes and by specialist nurserymen.

1. Asiatic hybrids.
2. Martagon hybrids.
3. Candidum hybrids.
4. American hybrids.
5. Longiflorum hybrids.
6. Trumpet and Aurelian hybrids.
7. Oriental hybrids.
8. All hybrids not belonging to any other division.
9. All true species and their botanical forms and varieties.

Lilium × *hollandicum*

Lilium 'Destiny'

In the following descriptions, the lilies are grouped according to the nine divisions, but the index below also lists, in alphabetical order, the lilies described.

INDEX OF SPECIES, VARIETIES AND HYBRIDS

Lilium Citronella

Lilium Harlequin

Lilium × *testaceum*

DIVISION 1 This section contains hybrids and garden forms derived from Asiatic species and hybrid groups. The division is further sub-divided into three groups.

SUB-DIVISION 1 (a). This group contains lilies with upright flowers, borne singly or in umbels in June. They are hardy, stem-rooting plants suitable for ordinary, well-drained soil and in full sun or partial shade. Height 3–4 ft; planting distance 6–9 in.; planting depth 4–6 in.

L. × *elegans* : see *L.* × *maculatum*

L. fortunei : see *L.* × *maculatum*

L. × *hollandicum*, formerly known as *L.* × *umbellatum*. A hybrid group thought to be a cross between *L. bulbiferum croceum* and *L.* × *maculatum*. The upright, cup-shaped flowers, $3–3\frac{1}{2}$ in. across, range from brilliant yellow through orange to dark crimson. They are borne in terminal umbels on strong and erect leafy stems during June and July.

L. × *maculatum*, syns. *L.* × *elegans*, *L. fortunei*, *L.* × *thunbergianum*. Height 12–24 in. An easily grown hybrid group between *L. dauricum* and *L. concolor*. The cup-shaped flowers, in various shades of lemon-yellow, orange and dark red, are $3\frac{1}{4}–4$ in. wide and borne in umbels. Plant in lime-free soil enriched with peat.

Mid-Century Hybrids. This group is mainly produced from crossing hybrids of *L.* × *hollandicum* and *L. tigrinum*. The flowers are borne singly or in umbels, and each may be 4–5 in. wide, outward-facing, upright, or pendent. The colours range from lemon-yellow through shades of orange to crimson and red, speckled with maroon or brown. These hybrids are also excellent for pot culture, and by gentle forcing may be brought into flower at almost any time.

Outstanding named forms include: 'Cinnabar' (height 24 in.), with single, well-spaced, bright maroon-red and upright flowers; it is easily forced, and excellent for a cool greenhouse.

'Croesus', with up to ten single, orange or yellow, cup-shaped flowers with black spots.

'Destiny', the single lemon-yellow flowers are spotted brown, with reflexed tips; up to ten flowers are borne on each stem.

'Enchantment', a vigorous healthy form with umbels of up to 16 bright nasturtium-red flowers; these are cup-shaped and outward-facing and up to 6 in. across.

L. × *thunbergianum*: see *L.* × *maculatum*
L. × *umbellatum*: see *L.* × *hollandicum*

SUB-DIVISION 1 (b). A group with outward-facing reflexed flowers, borne in large umbels. Flowering is in July. They are hardy, mainly stem-rooting plants with the same soil and aspect requirements as those in Sub-division 1 (a).

Preston Hybrids. Height 2–5 ft; planting distance 10 in.; planting depth 6 in. A group of lilies derived from *L. davidii willmottiae*, *L. dauricum* and *L.* × *maculatum*. They are easily grown in lime-free soil and partial shade, and produce numerous stem bulbils. They are divided into the Stenographer Group and the Fighter Group. The freely produced, 4–5 in. wide flowers are borne in branched panicles; the colours vary from golden-orange to bright red.

SUB-DIVISION 1 (c). This group includes lilies with pendent Turk's-cap flowers borne in dense or loose terminal clusters. The flowering period is July, and they are excellent for cutting. Plant in ordinary, well-drained soil, in full sun or partial shade. Height 3–5 ft; planting distance 9–12 in.; planting depth 4–6 in.

Citronella. This group is derived from the Fiesta Hybrids. The bright, pure citron-yellow flowers are recurved and spotted with small black dots; they are about 3 in. wide and borne singly, crowded along the stems.

Fiesta Hybrids. These lilies are crosses between *L. amabile*, *L. a. luteum*, *L. davidii* and other related species. They increase quickly from bulbs and are resistant to most virus diseases. The recurved flowers range in colour from straw-yellow to vivid damson-red, spotted maroon-black. They are 3 in. wide, and up to 30 single flowers may be borne on each stem.

Harlequin. A recently introduced selection of vigorous free-flowering lilies. The recurved flowers, up to 4 in. across, are in shades of pink, pale lilac, old rose, red, purple, cream-white and yellow, with intermediate shades of salmon-buff, tangerine and amber-pink. They are borne on short stalks with up to 20 flowers on each stem.

DIVISION 2 This section contains all hybrids and forms derived from the species of *L. martagon* and *L. hansonii*. They are easily grown, hardy and mainly stem-rooting lilies, thriving in semi-woodland conditions or in garden soil with partial shade. The Turk's-cap flowers are pendent and appear in June and July. Height 4–5 ft; planting distance 9–12 in.; planting depth 4–6 in.

Backhouse Hybrids. A group of basal-rooting hybrids with mid-green, broadly lanceolate leaves arranged in whorls. The flowers, up to $1\frac{1}{2}$ in. long, are in shades of white, ivory, yellow, orange and dark wine-red. Some are marbled and freckled with pink, or have a pink reverse to the petals. These lilies are lime-tolerant.

L. × *dalhansonii*. This hardy lily is a hybrid between *L. hansonii* and *L. martagon dalmaticum*. Brown-red flowers, about $1\frac{1}{4}$ in. long, are orange-spotted and have an unpleasant scent.

'Marhan'. A vigorous plant, originating in Holland from *L. hansonii* and *L. martagon* 'Album'. The 2–3 in. wide flowers are bright yellow, deeply spotted with purple-brown, or orange with red-brown spots. Several forms are available; they are all tolerant of lime.

DIVISION 3 This division contains hybrids and forms derived from European species, notably *L. candidum* and *L. chalcedonicum*, but excluding *L. martagon* (see Division 2).

L. excelsum: see *L.* × *testaceum*

L. × *testaceum*, syn. *L. excelsum*. Height 4–6 ft; planting distance 9 in.; planting depth 4 in. This is one of the oldest garden hybrids. It is basal-rooting. The $2\frac{1}{2}$–3 in. long pendent flowers with recurved petals are borne singly along the stem and open in July and August; the flowers are sweetly scented and are maize or apricot-yellow with red pollen and a few raised red spots. Plant in autumn, in ordinary soil and full sun.

DIVISION 4 The hybrids and garden forms in this division are all of American origin. They are easily grown rhizomatous lilies that produce few or no stem roots.

Bellingham Hybrids. Height 5–7 ft; planting distance 9 in.; planting depth 5–6 in. This strain of complex American lilies gives best results in light shade, in well-drained lime-free soil enriched with leaf-mould. Top-dress annually with leaf-mould and cover with bracken in cold areas during winter. The long pendent buds open to deeply reflexed, $2\frac{1}{2}$–3 in. wide flowers, borne closely along the stem; they are in shades of orange-yellow, red, and blended bi-colours, all intensely spotted with brown; they make excellent long-lasting cut flowers.

'Shuksan', one of the best-known forms, has light orange, pendent Turk's-cap flowers, flushed red at the tips and with a few maroon-black spots inside. It increases rapidly in ideal conditions.

DIVISION 5 A section that contains hybrids and forms derived from *L. longiflorum* and *L. formosanum*. These half-hardy and disease-prone trumpet lilies are not generally available.

DIVISION 6 This section includes trumpet and Aurelian hybrids of Asiatic species not included in Division 1. These are mainly derived from *L.* × *aurelianense*. The division is sub-divided into 4 groups according to flower shape.

L. × *aurelianense* (Aurelian lily). Height 4–7 ft; planting distance 12 in.; planting depth 6–9 in. This hardy and variable stem-rooting lily is a hybrid between *L. sargentiae* and *L. henryi*. Several strains have been selected, and seedlings fall into three main groups: those with long, narrow, strap-shaped petals (a group fairly tolerant of lime); those with large, trumpet-shaped flowers (decidedly not lime-tolerant); and those with bowl-shaped, sometimes bi-coloured flowers (a group which may or may not tolerate lime, depending on the parentage).

Lilium × Golden Splendor

Lilium × Golden Clarion

Lilium 'Green Emerald'

Lilium 'Limelight'

Lilium × *aurelianense*

Lilium × *imperiale*

Lilium Olympic Hybrids

The flowers, up to 5 in. across, are generally pleasantly scented; they are borne in August or September, in successions of two or three. These lilies are usually in shades of white or ivory to apricot; pink forms are also available. The bowl-shaped group often have a contrasting centre of a deeper colour. Plant in ordinary, well-drained soil, in a sunny position with some ground shade for the roots.

SUB-DIVISION 6 (a). This sub-division includes lilies with trumpet or funnel-shaped flowers borne in candelabra umbels at the top of stems in July and August. They are hardy and stem-rooting, requiring a rich, well-drained soil and partial shade. Height 5–6 ft; planting distance 9–10 in.; planting depth 4 in.

Black Magic Strain. These hybrids have fragrant flowers, $6\frac{1}{2}$–$7\frac{1}{2}$ in. long; they are pure white inside, with purple-black on the reverse, and with deep orange pollen.

L. × *creelmannii*: see *L.* × *imperiale*

× **Golden Clarion.** A vigorous strain with funnel-shaped, 5 in. wide flowers that vary from clear bright buttercup-yellow to deep gold; some have distinct brown or wine-red stripes on the reverse of the petals.

× **Golden Splendor.** This strain was developed from selected forms of × Golden Clarion and is similar in vigour and habit. The 6 in. wide flowers are deep gold with a distinct maroon stripe on the reverse of each petal.

'**Green Emerald**'. A hybrid with near-white flowers, about 5 in. across, flushed with emerald-green. The green shade gradually disappears as the funnel-shaped flowers expand.

L. × *imperiale*, syns. *L.* × *princeps*, *L.* × *sargale* and *L.* × *creelmannii*. This hybrid group is derived from *L. regale* and *L. sargentiae*. In cultivation, they are largely superseded by named hybrid strains. The white flowers are broad-petalled and recurved.

'**Limelight**'. This vigorous lily freely produces stem bulbils. The fragrant, narrowly funnel-

shaped flowers are up to 8 in. across. They are borne singly on long, slightly pendent stalks up the stems and are lime-yellow in colour.

Olympic Hybrids. These vigorous and lime-tolerant lilies belong to one of the best-known of the Oregon strains. The fragrant, waxy, trumpet flowers, 6–8 in. across, are white outside, variously coloured cream, pale green, or fuchsia-pink inside and often tinted with brown-green or wine-pink. They are excellent as cut flowers.

'Black Dragon' is an outstanding form of this strain; the 6 in. wide flowers are pure white inside, rich purple-red with white margins on the outside of the petals.

L. × *princeps*: see *L.* × *imperiale*
L. × *sargale*: see *L.* × *imperiale*

SUB-DIVISION 6 (b). A group including lilies with bowl-shaped flowers, generally outward facing. They are borne in clusters at the top of the stem in late July and August. The plants are generally hardy, although some are better suited for pot culture; they are stem-rooting and thrive in loamy, well-drained soil and partial shade. Height 4–7 ft; planting distance 12 in.; planting depth 6 in.

× **First Love.** A hybrid strain of hardy lilies developed in Oregon. The slightly scented flowers are 6–8 in. across, golden with pink edges and pale green throats.

× **Heart's Desire.** A hardy strain of vigorous growth. The widely flaring flowers, about 6 in. across, are in shades of white, cream, yellow and orange; several forms have bright orange throats fading towards the tips of the strap-shaped petals.

SUB-DIVISION 6 (c). This sub-division encompasses lilies with pendent, trumpet or bowl-shaped flowers. These are produced in August and September on sturdy, tall-growing stems. They are hardy, stem-rooting lilies thriving in good loamy soil and in full sun or partial shade. Height 4–6 ft; planting distance 9–12 in.; planting depth 5–6 in. Few varieties are as yet available in Great Britain.

SUB-DIVISION 6 (d). Included in this group are the Asiatic hybrids with flat, star-shaped flowers. These are usually borne singly along the tops of the stems and make excellent cut flowers. The plants are hardy and stem-rooting, giving best results in loamy soil in partially shaded positions. Height 4–6 ft; planting distance 8–10 in.; planting depth 6 in.

'**Bright Star**'. The broad-petalled flowers open nearly flat to reveal 5 in. wide white flowers with a contrasting light orange star in the centre.

× **Golden Sunburst.** A vigorous strain of Oregon development. The flowers are borne during July and August in clusters of up to eight at the top of the stem. They are bright golden-yellow, green veined on the reverse and with prominent brown anthers; the petals recurve as they mature and expand to a diameter of 8 in. These lilies often produce secondary buds.

DIVISION 7 In this section are contained hybrids and forms of oriental species, including *L. henryi*. The division is in four groups, according to flower shape.

SUB-DIVISION 7 (a). This sub-division contains oriental hybrid lilies with trumpet-shaped flowers. These are rare in cultivation, and no forms are generally available.

ilium × First Love

Lilium × Heart's Desire

SUB-DIVISION 7 (b). A group with bowl-shaped flowers arranged symmetrically along the upper half of sturdy stems. Flowering usually begins in July and extends well into August. The plants are stem-rooting, hardy or half-hardy, and eminently suitable for pot culture in a cool greenhouse. In sheltered areas they may be grown outdoors in well-drained gritty soil enriched with leaf-mould and in a position in full sun. Height 3–5 ft; planting distance 12 in.; planting depth 5–6 in.

Empress of China'. This hybrid is not fully hardy and is best grown as a pot plant in a cool greenhouse; in sheltered areas it may be grown outdoors in neutral soil and in sun or partial shade. It bears pure chalk-white flowers, heavily marked with dark red or maroon-purple spots inside; only the tips of the curling petals are unspotted. The sweetly fragrant flowers are up to 7 in. across.

Empress of India'. This strain of half-hardy stem-rooting lilies is suitable for pot culture or outdoor cultivation in sheltered areas. The deep crimson-red flowers are up to 10 in. across.

Empress of Japan'. This strain is similar to 'Empress of India', but the fragrant flowers are pure white, with deep maroon spots and golden bands on the crinkled, 3 in. long petals.

Parkmannii. A strain of half-hardy or tender hybrids that require lime-free soil. They are suitable for pot culture. The fragrant flowers, measuring about 8 in. across, and usually rose-crimson, are recurved with wavy, pure white edges to the petals.

SUB-DIVISION 7 (c). In this sub-division are grouped lilies with flowers that open flat and star-shaped, with the tips of the petals slightly recurved. The flowers are borne in August along the upper parts of strong stems. These stem-rooting hybrids are hardy and have the same soil and growth requirements as those in Division 7 (b). Height 5–7 ft; planting distance 12–15 in.; planting depth 4–6 in.

× **Imperial Crimson**. A hybrid with fragrant flowers, up to 8 in. across; these are deep crimson with white edges to the twisted petals.

× **Imperial Gold**. A strain with slightly twisted petals of heavy texture. The fragrant flowers have the characteristics of the true *L. auratum*, being pure white with a distinct golden band on each petal and dotted with maroon. They measure up to 10 in. across.

SUB-DIVISION 7 (d). This sub-division lists hybrids with recurved blooms. These hardy stem-rooting lilies are generally easy to grow in rich, well-drained soil in full sun. They are also excellent for pot culture.

× **Jamboree**. Height 5–6 ft; planting distance 9–12 in.; planting depth 6 in. A disease-resistant, vigorous strain; the 7 in. wide flowers are borne during August in large loose clusters. The colour is crimson and silver, and the deeply recurved petals are heavily spotted with crimson.

DIVISION 8 This section contains hybrids and forms that are not botanically listed in any of the previous hybrid divisions.

DIVISION 9 This lists all true species and their forms; there are eight sub-divisions, but the species are here listed alphabetically.

L. amabile. Korea. Height 4 ft; planting distance 18 in.; planting depth 5 in. A hardy stem-rooting species best grown in light shade. The nodding Turk's-cap flowers, with recurved petals, are bright red, spotted with black within; they are borne in June and July and measure 3 in. across. The scent is unpleasant to some people.

L. a. luteum is a golden-yellow form.

L. auratum (golden-rayed lily). Japan. Height 5–8 ft; planting distance 12 in.; planting depth 6–12 in. This stem-rooting lily, suitable for pot and tub culture, has fragrant, bowl-shaped flowers, up to 12 in. across. The flowers, borne in August and September, are brilliant white with a golden-yellow ray or band and with raised, deep purple wine-coloured spots on the inner surface of each petal. Although easy to grow, it is a

Lilium 'Bright Star'

Lilium 'Empress of India'

Lilium × Imperial Gold

Lilium amabile

Lilium auratum rubrum

Lilium auratum 'Tom Thumb'

Lilium auratum rubro-vittatum 'Apollo'

short-lived species requiring lime-free soil in a sunny position that affords shade to the lower part of the stem. It is subject to virus diseases.

Recommended varieties include: *L. a. pictum*, heavily marked with crimson spots and broad yellow and crimson bands on each petal; *L. a. platyphyllum* (height 4–6 ft), large wax-white flowers with a golden band on each petal; it is more disease-resistant than the type species. *L. a. rubrum* has red-banded petals.

L. a. rubro-vittatum 'Apollo', pure white flowers with crimson bands; 'Tom Thumb' is a dwarf form (height up to 16 in.), best grown in a cool greenhouse.

L. bulbiferum. Europe. Height up to 3 ft; planting distance 6–8 in.; planting depth 4–6 in. A hardy stem-rooting species usually represented in cultivation by the variety *L. b. croceum* (orange lily). The trumpet-shaped, $2\frac{1}{2}$ in. long flowers are borne in loose umbels during June and July; they are bright tangerine-orange spotted with purple. This vigorous variety needs replanting every four years, in ordinary soil, in sun or shade.

L. canadense (Canada lily). N. America. Height 3–6 ft; planting distance 9 in.; planting depth 4–6 in. A basal-rooting species, easily grown in lime-free soil enriched with leaf-mould and in light shade; woodland conditions are ideal. It

bears pendent, recurved, bell-shaped flowers i July; these are $2–2\frac{1}{2}$ in. long, yellow or re orange, spotted with purple-red or brown.

LILIUM CANDIDUM

L. candidum (madonna lily). Asia Minor. Heig 4–5 ft; planting distance 9 in.; planting dep 2 in. This well-known basal-rooting lily is hard but sometimes difficult to establish. It resen disturbance and is prone to botrytis disease. Pla in ordinary, slightly alkaline soil in full su preferably in October; during warm, dam weather, spray fortnightly against botryt disease. It bears pale green leaves, and after th stems have died down in autumn, it produces winter rosette of basal leaves. Trumpet-shape fragrant flowers, $3–3\frac{1}{2}$ in. long, are borne in Jun and July. They are white with golden pollen.

L. c. cernuum has narrower petals; *L. salonikae* bears earlier and smaller flowers.

ilium candidum

Lilium hansonii

Lilium canadense

ilium auratum

Lilium japonicum

Lilium cernuum

. cernuum. Korea, Manchuria. Height 18 in.; planting distance 7–9 in.; planting depth 4 in. A slender, stem-rooting lily with linear to narrowly lanceolate mid-green leaves. The fragrant Turk's-cap flowers appear in June and July; they are pale pink with red-purple spots, and measure 2 in. across. Plant in any well-drained soil, preferably enriched with peat or leaf-mould, in sun or partial shade.

. dauricum. Asia. Height 18–24 in.; planting distance 8 in.; planting depth 4 in. This hardy species is stem-rooting with spreading underground stems. Bright red, brown-spotted, cup-shaped flowers, up to 2½ in. across, are borne in July. Grow in lime-free soil, in full sun.

. davidii. China. Height 4–6 ft; planting distance in.; planting depth 6 in. A hardy, stem-rooting species that requires staking. A profusion of bright orange-red Turk's-cap flowers are borne in July and August; they are 3–4 in. across, and have black spots and red pollen. Plant in ordinary soil, in sun or light shade. This short-lived species is easily raised from seed, some of which should be saved and sown annually.

The species is the parent of several hybrids listed under Division 1.

. formosanum. Taiwan. Height 4–6 ft; planting distance 12 in.; planting depth 6 in. This

half-hardy stem-rooting species is susceptible to virus diseases. It is easily raised from seeds and may be treated as a biennial. Narrowly trumpet-shaped flowers, up to 6½ in. long, are produced in August and September. They are white, sometimes marked with red-purple or chocolate on the outside. Plant in lime-free soil.

L. giganteum: see *Cardiocrinum giganteum*

L. hansonii. Korea. Height 5 ft; planting distance 10 in.; planting depth 6–8 in. The leaves of this hardy, stem-rooting species are arranged in whorls; these and the flowers have a waxy sheen. The fragrant Turk's-cap flowers, 1½ in. long, are borne in crowded nodding umbels during June and July; they are pale orange-yellow with brown spots. Plant in lime-free soil enriched with leaf-mould, and in light shade.

L. henryi. China. Height up to 8 ft; planting distance 12 in.; planting depth 8 in. A hardy, stem-rooting and lime-tolerant lily with glossy, lanceolate leaves on arching stems that require staking. In August and September, this species bears 3–3½ in. long recurved flowers that are pale apricot-yellow with red spots. Plant in light shade, in ordinary soil.

L. japonicum. Japan. Height 3 ft; planting distance 9 in.; planting depth 6 in. Suitable for a sheltered, shaded position or pot cultivation in a

Lilium leichtlinii

Lilium martagon

Lilium pardalinum

cool greenhouse. It is stem-rooting, and susceptible to virus diseases. The fragrant white flowers, borne in July, open from pink buds; they are trumpet-shaped with slightly recurved petals, and 6–7 in. long. Grow in sandy, lime-free soil and in partial shade.

L. leichtlinii. Korea. A species with one or two yellow flowers, marked with purple. Usually represented by *L. l. maximowiczii.* Height 4–6 ft; planting distance 9–12 in.; planting depth 5 in. A hardy and stem-rooting lily with a many-flowered inflorescence of Turk's-cap flowers in August; these are cinnabar-red with purple spots, and 2½–3 in. long. Plant in loamy, lime-free soil, in sun or partial shade; it increases quickly from seed.

L. longiflorum (Easter lily). Japan. Height up to 3 ft; planting distance 9 in.; planting depth 6 in. A half-hardy stem-rooting species, excellent for pot culture. The heavily fragrant, 5–7 in. long, white, trumpet-shaped flowers with golden pollen are borne in July and August. It is lime-tolerant and quickly raised from seed.

L. mackliniae. Manipur. Height 9–36 in.; planting distance 8 in.; planting depth 4 in. This hardy stem-rooting species has widely bell-shaped flowers, 2 in. across. They are white within, rose-purple on the outside and are borne on strong pedicels along the upper part of the stem in June and July. Plant in semi-shade in moist, well-drained, humus-rich soil. The species is easily raised from seed.

LILIUM MARTAGON

L. martagon (Turk's-cap lily). Albania, E. Europe. Height 5 ft; planting distance 9 in.; planting depth 4 in. A hardy, basal-rooting species, the parent of numerous hybrids (see Division 2). The spathulate leaves are arranged in whorls of six to nine at regular intervals on the stem. The recurved flowers, 1¼–1½ in. long, open in July; they are rose-purple with darker spots and have an unpleasant scent. This is a slow-growing, lime-tolerant species, easily increased from seed.

L. m. 'Album' is a vigorous, free-flowering white form; *L. m. cattaniae* has larger, dark purple, unspotted flowers.

Named forms include 'Blush', with white buds that turn pale pink before opening to ruby-red flowers; 'Gleam', pale pink buds and black-spotted red flowers.

L. monadelphum. Caucasus. Height up to 3 ft; planting distance 9 in.; planting depth 4–5 in. This hardy species is stem-rooting; it bears pendent pale canary or deep yellow Turk's-cap flowers, lightly dotted with purple, and tinged red round the base of each petal. The flowers are fragrant, 2½–3½ in. long and open in June or July. The species is lime-tolerant and is best grown in a partially shaded position.

L. m. szovitsianum, syn. *L. szovitsianum,* is similar to the type species.

Lilium longiflorum

Lilium mackliniae

Lilium monadelphum szovitsianum

. pardalinum (panther lily). California. Height
–7 ft; planting distance 12 in.; planting depth 5
n. A hardy, easily grown, basal-rooting lily with
:aves arranged in whorls. The 2½ in. wide flowers
re orange-red Turk's-caps, light orange-yellow
t the centre and dotted with orange-brown or
urple. They open in July. Plant in a sunny
osition in lime-free soil.

L. p. giganteum, syns. 'Red Giant' and 'Sunset',
s larger and more robust, with deep golden
entres and vermilion petals.

.. pumilum, syn. *L. tenuifolium*. Siberia, China.
Height 2–4 ft; planting distance 6 in.; planting
depth 4 in. This dainty, stem-rooting species is
hort-lived, but is quickly and easily raised from
eed. The nodding, bright red, Turk's-cap
lowers, 1½–2 in. across, are borne in June. Plant
n a sunny position in ordinary garden soil.

LILIUM PYRENAICUM

L. pyrenaicum. Europe. Height 2–3 ft; planting
distance 9 in.; planting depth 5 in. The leaves of
this hardy, basal-rooting lily grow densely along
the stems. The tightly recurved Turk's-cap
flowers are 1½–2 in. long, and are produced in
loose clusters in June. They are bright green-
yellow with purple-black spots and orange-red
pollen; the scent is unpleasant. The species
is lime-tolerant and requires a sunny position.

L. regale. China. Height 4–6 ft; planting distance
12 in.; planting depth 6–9 in. This hardy
stem-rooting species is one of the more popular
lilies. Fragrant, white, funnel-shaped flowers, up
to 5 in. long, are borne, usually in loose clusters,
in July. The centres of the flowers are sulphur-
yellow, and the backs of the petals are shaded
rose-purple. Plant in full sun and in ordinary soil;
the bulbs increase quickly.

L. rubellum. Japan. Height 12–30 in.; planting
distance 9 in.; planting depth 6 in. A stem-
rooting lily, best suited to pot culture in a cool
greenhouse. The bell-shaped, sweetly scented
flowers are up to 3 in. wide; they are clear
rose-pink with golden-yellow anthers. The
flowering period is May and June. Grow in
lime-free soil in partial shade.

LILIUM SARGENTIAE

L. sargentiae. China. Height 4–5 ft; planting
distance 12 in.; planting depth 6–9 in. This
stem-rooting lily is similar to *L. regale*, but less
hardy. In July, it bears loose clusters of white,
trumpet-shaped flowers, 4–5 in. wide, shaded
purple-brown on the reverse of the petals; the

pollen is brown. The species is best grown in full
sun and in lime-free soil. Increase by stem bulbils.

L. speciosum. Japan. Height 4–6 ft; planting
distance 12 in.; planting depth 6 in. A half-hardy
stem-rooting species, ideal for pot culture in a
cool greenhouse. The fragrant, bowl-shaped
white flowers are 3–5 in. long; they have
recurved, wavy petals, heavily shaded with
crimson. The nodding blooms are borne in
wide-spreading racemes in August and
September. Grow in lime-free soil.

Named varieties in shades of crimson or white
are available. 'Gilrey' is ruby-red.

L. superbum. E. North America. Height 4–7 ft;
planting distance 9–12 in.; planting depth 6–8 in.
This stem-rooting species is hardy and easily
grown in fertile soil and partial shade. It needs
frequent watering in summer. The recurved
flowers, 3–4 in. long, are borne in broad panicles
during July and August. They are orange, with
red-spotted centres and red-tipped petals.

L. szovitsianum: see *L. monadelphum szovitsianum*

L. tenuifolium: see *L. pumilum*

L. tigrinum (tiger lily). China, Korea, Japan.
Height 3–6 ft; planting distance 9 in.; planting
depth 6 in. A hardy, stem-rooting species subject
to various virus diseases. Strongly recurved
Turk's-cap flowers, 2½–4 in. long, are borne in
loose racemes in August and September; they are
bright orange-red, spotted with purple-black, and
have prominent anthers with dark red pollen.
Plant in lime-free soil in full sun. The species is
easily increased by freely produced stem bulbils.

The varieties *L. t. fortunei* and *L. t. fortunei
giganteum* have woolly stems and buds; they are
taller and later-flowering than the type species.

L. tsingtauense. China. Height 1½–3 ft; planting
distance 9 in.; planting depth 4 in. Grow this
hardy stem-rooting lily in lime-free soil. In July,
it bears few-flowered clusters of 2 in. long, widely
funnel-shaped, bright orange flowers.

L. wardii. Tibet. Height 3–5 ft; planting distance
12 in.; planting depth 5 in. A small-bulbed,
stem-rooting and hardy species. It bears pink,
purple-spotted Turk's-cap flowers, 2½ in. wide, in
July and August. The flowers are pleasantly
scented. Plant in lime-free soil and light shade.

Cultivation. Outdoors, plant the bulbs between
October and March; basal-rooting lilies do best
when planted in autumn. Purchased bulbs may
have shrivelled in storage and should be plumped
up in trays of moist peat before planting out.

The ideal position is on a south-facing, slightly
sloping site, protected from strong winds. Lilies
thrive in sun or partial shade; the individual
requirements are given under each description.

Most lilies give good results in ordinary,
well-drained garden soil, but some species and
their hybrids do not thrive where lime is present,
and others have a slight preference for lime in the
ground. A soil reading of pH 6·5 is generally safe
for all kinds. All soils should be enriched with
leaf-mould, well-rotted compost or peat. Heavy
soils should also have coarse sand or grit worked
into the top spit.

During the growing season water freely, and
mulch annually in spring with well-rotted
manure, compost or leaf-mould. Artificial
manure should be of a type suitable for root

Lilium pumilum

Lilium pyrenaicum

Lilium regale

407

vegetables with a larger proportion of potash and phosphates than of nitrogen. For lime-hating lilies avoid manures that are alkaline.

Stem-rooting lilies, which produce roots from the stem just above the bulb as well as from beneath it, require deeper planting than basal-rooting types. It is usually safe to plant the bulbs at a depth of two and a half times the height of the bulb. An exception to this rule is *L. candidum*, which should be planted with the nose of the bulb just below the soil surface. This species should also be transplanted, if necessary, when the stems have died down in August or September.

Young lily bulbs have contractile roots, and can pull themselves down to the correct soil depth if they have been planted too near the surface. It is safer to plant shallowly, particularly on heavy soil.

Many lilies have strong, wiry stems and need no staking, but species with arching stems and heavy flower heads, such as *L. henryi*, should be loosely tied to bamboo canes. Late-flowering lilies also require staking to protect them against autumn gales. In spring, cover emerging young shoots with cloches until danger of frost is past.

Pot culture of lilies. Set the bulbs, as soon as available in autumn, singly in 6–8 in. pots or three to a 10 in. pot containing John Innes potting compost No. 1 or a mixture of 1 part well-rotted manure, 1 part loam and $\frac{1}{2}$ part coarse sand (parts by volume). Set stem-rooting lilies well down in the pots, to leave plenty of room for the accommodation of the stem roots.

After potting up, keep the lilies in a cool place to promote good root action; they may be plunged outdoors and covered with ashes or kept in a dark, airy shed or cellar.

When top growth appears, gradually bring the plants into full daylight; keep the compost moist and grow the lilies on to flowering in a cool greenhouse or living-room. After flowering, plunge the pots outdoors in a shaded spot until growth naturally dies down; keep well watered at all times to prevent the bulbs drying out. Repot annually or plant outdoors.

L. longiflorum, L. auratum, L. speciosum and the Mid-Century Hybrids may be gently forced. Bring the pots indoors when top growth appears and maintain a temperature of 16°C (61°F). When buds have formed, increase the temperature to 18–21°C (64–75°F) and feed at 10–14 day intervals with a dilute liquid manure. As soon as the buds show colour, reduce the heat to 16°C (61°F) and stop feeding. Most lilies forced at these temperatures flower six weeks after the buds appear; under cooler conditions flower development is slowed down. With careful regulation of light and heat, it is possible to have *L. longiflorum* and Mid-Century Hybrids in flower at any time of the year. Store the bulbs, until required for forcing, in a refrigerator at 4–7°C (40–45°F). After flowering, the pots of bulbs can be plunged outside or planted out in the garden; they should not be forced again.

Propagation. For all propagation methods, virus-free stock plants should be used. Some lilies increase quite naturally by producing two or more good bulbs every year; congested clumps should be separated and replanted every three or four years between October and March. Tangled

masses of roots and stems of the rhizomatous types of lilies can be divided and replanted at the same time, ensuring that each division has a strong growing point.

Most lilies produce seeds, but named hybrids and varieties do not come true to type. Sow seeds when ripe, usually in September and October, in boxes, 6–9 in. deep, of John Innes seed compost and place in a cold frame.

When the seedlings are large enough to handle, prick them out, 2 in. either way, into boxes of John Innes potting compost No. 1. Transfer the seedlings later into nursery rows outdoors and grow on for one to three years, depending on species, before transplanting to flowering positions.

L. formosanum usually flowers within six months of sowing when grown under glass.

Some lily seeds, such as *L. regale*, produce growth above ground some two to four weeks after sowing. This is called immediate epigeal germination. Seeds of other species, for example *L. pardalinum*, produce small bulbs underground with no top growth. This is known as delayed hypogeal germination. Keep apparent failures of lily sowings for at least 18 months, as old seeds sometimes remain dormant for up to two years.

Alternatively, increase all species and hybrids by scale propagation.

In September and October, or March and April, gently pull off healthy undamaged scales from dormant bulbs. It is not necessary to dig up the bulb; the earth may be scraped away and afterwards replaced. Insert the scales to half their depth, at an oblique angle, into boxes containing equal parts (by volume) peat, and sand. If possible, provide a bottom heat of 10–13°C (50–55°F); otherwise place in a cold frame. Tiny new bulbs will form at the base of the scales. When these bulbs show top growth, pot or box up in John Innes potting compost No. 1. Plunge in an open frame or sheltered bed outdoors and grow on for one to three years, before transplanting to permanent positions.

Several species, such as *L. bulbiferum, L. sargentiae* and *L. tigrinum* produce small black-purple or green bulbils in the leaf axils. These may be detached when the leaves turn yellow and set in nursery rows outdoors or potted up singly in 3 in. pots of John Innes potting compost No. 1 and treated as described for seedlings.

Some stem-rooting lilies also produce small bulbs on the stem just below ground level. If the soil is carefully removed around the stem in early autumn, these offset bulblets can be detached and replanted in fresh ground. They will reach flowering size after one to three years.

Broken-off stems that have not yet flowered should not be discarded; they may be buried horizontally, only just covered by a mixture of equal parts (by volume) peat and sand at a temperature of 16°C (61°F). Bulbils may appear at the base of the stems or in the leaf axils.

Pests. APHIDS may infest bulbs in store; they also attack growing plants and transmit virus diseases.

LEATHERJACKETS may feed on roots and bulbs.

Larvae of the LILY BEETLE may cause severe damage, particularly in southern England, to leaves, stems and flower buds, and foul the plants with black slimy excrement.

Lilium rubellum

Lilium superbum

Lilium tigrinum

MICE, RABBITS and SQUIRRELS may feed on bulbs and young shoots.

Roots, bulbs, stems, leaves and flowers may be damaged by SLUGS; seedlings, in particular, may suffer severe damage. The damage is often extended by MILLEPEDES.

Diseases. BASAL ROT, due to one or more fungi, including RHIZOCTONIA, may cause rotting of the roots and tissues at the base of the bulbs; top growth ceases and the foliage eventually becomes discoloured.

MOSAIC VIRUS causes irregular chlorotic streaks or slight mottling on the leaves, and the flowers are spotted, crumpled and poor. Other VIRUS DISEASES can also cause mottling of the foliage, stunting of plants and rosetting of leaves.

LILY DISEASE (botrytis) shows on the leaves as oval-shaped water-soaked spots which spread rapidly in humid weather and become brown. The fungus may spread from the leaves and cause toppling of the flower stems with disfigured and tattered blooms.

PHYSIOLOGICAL DISORDERS, resulting from too-dry soil conditions or cold night temperatures, show as a yellowing or purpling of the foliage.

STORAGE ROT, due to a BLUE MOULD, found more frequently on imported bulbs, shows as small sunken brown spots on the scales. As these increase in size they become covered with a white fungal growth that turns blue-green. The rot may extend from the scales into the basal plate.

Lily: see Lilium
Lily, African: see Agapanthus
Lily, American trout: see *Erythronium revolutum*
Lily, arum: see *Zantedeschia aethiopica*
Lily, Aurelian: see *Lilium × aurelianense*
Lily, blood: see Haemanthus
Lily, Canada: see *Lilium canadense*
Lily, Cuban: see *Scilla peruviana*
Lily, day: see Hemerocallis
Lily, foxtail: see Eremurus
Lily, giant: see Cardiocrinum
Lily, glory: see Gloriosa
Lily, golden-rayed: see *Lilium auratum*
Lily, Guernsey: see *Nerine sarniensis*
Lily, Jacobean: see *Sprekelia formosissima*
Lily, Kaffir: see *Schizostylis coccinea*
Lily, lent: see *Narcissus pseudonarcissus*
Lily, madonna: see *Lilium candidum*
Lily of the Valley: see Convallaria
Lily, orange: see *Lilium bulbiferum croceum*
Lily, panther: see *Lilium pardalinum*
Lily, Peruvian: see Alstroemeria
Lily, plantain: see Hosta
Lily, St Bernard's: see Anthericum
Lily, Scarborough: see Vallota
Lily, sea: see Pancratium
Lily, sword: see Gladiolus
Lily, tiger: see *Lilium tigrinum*
Lily, torch: see Kniphofia
Lily, Turk's-cap: see *Lilium martagon*
Lily, water: see Nymphaea
Lime: see Tilia
Lime, broad-leaved: see *Tilia platyphyllos*
Lime, common: see *Tilia × europaea*
Lime, silver: see *Tilia petiolaris* and
    T. tomentosa
Lime, small-leaved: see *Tilia cordata*

Limnanthes

Limnanthaceae

A genus of ten species of annuals. The plant described is grown as an edging to paths and borders and as a pot plant to flower under glass in winter and early spring. The flowers are attractive to bees.

LIMNANTHES DOUGLASII

L. douglasii (poached egg flower). N.W. America. Height 6 in.; spacing 4 in. A quick-growing hardy annual with glossy, pale green, deeply cut leaves. The delicately scented flowers, widely funnel-shaped and measuring 1 in. across, are white with a yellow centre. They open from June to August.

Cultivation. An open sunny situation and a cool root run give the best results; these conditions are often found along paths and between rocks and paving. September-sown plants require cloche protection in cold districts. The seeds set freely, and self-sown plants are often produced in succeeding seasons.

Five plants in a 6 in. pan of John Innes potting compost No. 1 will flower in winter and early spring in a frost-free greenhouse.

Propagation. Sow the seeds in the flowering site in September or March, just covering them with soil. Thin out the seedlings as required.

For flowering under glass, a succession of sowings from June to September in 6 in. pans in a cold frame is recommended. Use John Innes potting compost No. 1. Thin out the seedlings to five per pan and move them to a frost-free greenhouse in October.

Pests and diseases. Generally trouble-free.

Limonium

Sea lavender, statice. *Plumbaginaceae*

LIMONIUM SINUATUM

A genus, formerly known as *Statice,* of 300 species of herbaceous annual and perennial plants and deciduous shrubs and sub-shrubs. The perennial species are not all hardy, and some are best treated as annuals.

The following species are suitable for borders, for cutting and pot culture, and for drying as everlasting flowers. The individual flowers are tiny and narrowly funnel-shaped; they are crowded on spikes or in panicles.

Lilium tsingtauense

Lilium wardii

Limnanthes douglasii

409

Limonium sinuatum 'New Art Shades'

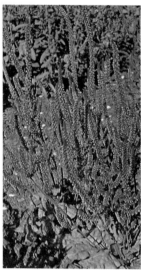

Limonium suworowii

Limonium latifolium

ANNUAL SPECIES

L. bonduellii. Algeria. Height and planting distance 12 in. This species is strictly a perennial, but is best treated as a half-hardy annual. It is excellent for cutting and for drying. The pale green leaves are ovate, deeply lobed and borne in a basal rosette. Erect stems carry loose clusters, 3 in. across, of yellow flowers from July onwards.

L. sinuatum. Mediterranean area. Height 18 in.; planting distance 12 in. A perennial species, generally grown as a half-hardy annual. This is one of the most popular species and the dried flowers are much used as everlastings; it may also be grown in pots to flower under glass. The mid to dark green obovate-lanceolate leaves have deeply waved and lobed margins. Broadly winged stems carry 3–4 in. long clusters of blue and cream flowers surrounded by green bracts; these are produced from late July to September.

Numerous garden varieties are listed, including 'New Art Shades', a blend of colours with salmon, orange, yellow, rose-pink, red, carmine, blue and lavender.

L. suworowii. W. Turkestan. Height 18 in.; planting distance 12 in. A half-hardy annual, much grown for cut flowers or as an early-flowering pot plant under glass. The oblanceolate mid-green leaves, which form a basal rosette, have wavy margins. Rose-pink flowers, densely packed in narrow plume-shaped panicles up to 18 in. long, are produced from July to September.

PERENNIAL SPECIES

L. incanum. Siberia. Height 12–18 in.; planting distance 12 in. A hardy perennial with narrowly elliptic mid-green leaves, mostly close to the ground. Erect, branched spikes, about 9 in. long, of small flowers with a white calyx and red corolla, give a pink effect from June to August. The variety *L. i. dumosum* is a good pink form.

L. latifolium. Bulgaria, S. Russia. Height 24 in; planting distance 18 in. This hardy perennial, with a woody rootstock, forms a rosette of elliptic, mid-green, downy leaves. Lavender-blue flowers, in diffuse panicles up to 9 in. long, appear from July to September. The varieties 'Blue Cloud', light lavender-blue flowers, and 'Violetta', violet, are recommended.

LIMONIUM LATIFOLIUM

Cultivation of annual and perennial species. Limoniums thrive in any ordinary, well-drained soil in an open, sunny situation.

Plant hardy perennial species in March or April, half-hardy annuals in May. Cut down the perennial plants in October or November.

To flower *L. sinuatum* and *L. suworowii* in spring under glass, pot autumn-sown seedlings into 5 in. containers of John Innes potting compost No. 1 and overwinter at 8°C (46°F).

For drying, cut the flower stems just before the flowers are fully opened. Tie the stems in bundles and hang these upside-down in a shady, airy shed.

Propagation of annual species. Sow the seed clusters thinly in pots or pans of seed compost under glass in February or March, at a temperature of 13–16°C (55–61°F). Prick off the seedlings, when large enough to handle, into boxes. Harden off the plants in a cold frame before planting out in the flowering site in May.

Alternatively, sow directly in the flowering site in April and thin out to the required planting distances. This delays flowering, and some blooms may be damaged by autumn frosts and damp.

For pot plants to flower in spring under glass, sow the seeds in a cold frame in September and pot as described under CULTIVATION.

Propagation of perennial species. Sow the seeds in boxes of John Innes seed compost in March at a temperature of 13–16°C (55–61°F). Prick out the seedlings, when large enough to handle, into boxes and harden off in a cold frame before planting out in nursery rows. Grow on the young plants until the autumn of the following year before transplanting to the flowering site.

Division of the roots, though not easy, may be carried out in March or April. It is better to take root cuttings in February or March and insert these in sandy soil in a cold frame to root. When the cuttings have developed three or four leaves, set them out in a nursery bed; grow on and plant out in the autumn of the following year.

Pests. Generally trouble-free.

Diseases. GREY MOULD may cause rotting of the stems and flowers, the affected tissues becoming covered with a grey velvety fungal growth.

POWDERY MILDEW shows as a white powdery coating on leaves and stems.

Linaria

Toadflax. *Scrophulariaceae*

LINARIA MAROCCANA

A genus of 150 species of hardy and half-hardy annuals, herbaceous perennials and sub-shrubs. Those described are suitable for annual and mixed borders, for rock gardens, dry walls or as an edging to paths; *L. maroccana* may also be grown as a pot plant. The perennial species are generally short-lived, but readily seed themselves. The colourful flowers are borne in spikes and resemble small, spurred antirrhinums.

Planting distance refers to border plants, which are usually set in groups, while spread applies to the surface spread of single mature rock-garden plants.

L. alpina. European Alps. Height 3–6 in.; spread 6–9 in. A hardy perennial rock-garden species that forms compact mats of frail stems with linear blue-grey leaves. Numerous sprays of violet flowers appear from June to August; each flower has the lower lip striped with glowing orange, and measures $\frac{1}{2}$ in. in length.

L. cymbalaria, now classified as *Cymbalaria muralis* (ivy-leaved toadflax). S. Europe. Height 2 in.; spread 18 in. This hardy perennial species is too invasive for most rock gardens, but the compact varieties 'Globosa' and 'Globosa Rosea' make neat tufts, 6–8 in. across. The kidney-shaped leaves are pale to mid-green and have five to nine rounded lobes. These varieties carry a succession of pale purple and light pink flowers, $\frac{1}{2}$–$\frac{3}{4}$ in. long, from May to September.

L. dalmatica. S.E. Europe. Height 3–4 ft; planting distance 18 in. A hardy perennial border species with narrowly lanceolate, mid-green leaves. The pale yellow flowers, up to $1\frac{1}{2}$ in. long, are loosely arranged at the tips of the stems; they appear from June to September.

L. macedonica. Macedonia. Height 3–4 ft; planting distance 18 in. This hardy perennial species is similar to *L. dalmatica*, but with grey-green leaves and more numerous flowers, $\frac{3}{4}$–1 in. long. 'Canary Bird' is deep yellow.

L. maroccana. Morocco. Height 8–15 in.; planting distance 6 in. A hardy annual species of bushy habit, suitable for a border and for flowering in pots in a cold greenhouse. The leaves are linear and light green. Each flower has a pointed spur and a white or yellow blotch on the lower lip. They are $\frac{1}{2}$ in. long and open in June and July.

Many varieties are listed in a wide range of colours: 'Fairy Bouquet' (height 8 in.) has $\frac{3}{4}$ in. flowers in distinct shades; 'Excelsior Mixed' (height 12 in.) includes dark violet, blue, crimson, pink and yellow flowers.

L. purpurea. S. Europe, naturalised in Great Britain. Height 2–4 ft; planting distance 12–15 in. This hardy perennial species has narrowly lanceolate to linear mid-green leaves. The flowers are $\frac{1}{3}$–$\frac{1}{2}$ in. long, purple-blue touched with white, and are freely produced in slender spires from July to September. The variety 'Canon Went' has pink flowers; it comes true from seed.

L. reticulata. Portugal. Height 2–3 ft; planting distance 9 in. A hardy annual species with narrow, pointed, pale green leaves. The $\frac{3}{4}$ in. long flowers are purple with an orange or yellow blotch on the lower lip. They are borne from May to July. 'Aureo-purpurea' is dark purple.

L. triornithophora. Portugal, Spain. Height 1–3 ft; planting distance 18 in. This perennial species is hardy except in severe winters; in cold areas or on heavy soils it is best treated as an annual. It has narrow to broadly lanceolate grey-green leaves and rose-purple, 1 in. long flowers marked with yellow or orange on the lower lip. Flowering is from June to September. Commercial seed strains contain a colour range in pink, mauve and purple.

Cultivation. Linarias will grow in any ordinary, well-drained garden soil, in a sunny position. On heavy soil add plenty of grit to aid drainage. *L. cymbalaria* is suitable for dry walls and rock crevices, and will thrive in partial shade. Staking of the taller species is required only in windy places; cut down to ground level in autumn.

Plant perennial species between October and March; protect *L. triornithophora* with bracken or straw throughout the winter in all but the mildest districts.

Sow annual species in March or April. For spring-flowering pot plants of *L. maroccana*, set three or five September-sown seedlings to a 5 in. pot of John Innes potting compost No. 1. Overwinter in a frost-free greenhouse, or ideally at a temperature of 5–7°C (41–45°F).

Propagation. Most species increase readily by self-sown seeds.

Sow purchased seeds thinly during February or March in pans or boxes of seed compost in a cold frame. When the seedlings are large enough to handle, prick them off into boxes of John Innes potting compost No. 1 and plant out in permanent positions in April and May.

Alternatively, sow directly in the flowering site during March or April and thin out the seedlings to the planting distances. This is particularly recommended for the annual species and for *L. alpina*. Annuals may also be sown in the open in September; these generally produce larger and earlier flowers. For spring-flowering pot plants of *L. maroccana* sow seeds in boxes of seed compost in a cold frame; treat the seedlings as described under CULTIVATION.

Take cuttings of good forms of *L. alpina* in May, using 1–$1\frac{1}{2}$ long basal shoots. Insert the cuttings in a cold frame in equal parts (by volume) peat and sand. When the cuttings are well rooted, plant them out in their final positions or pot into 3 in. pots of John Innes potting compost No. 1 and plant out in September.

Take $1\frac{1}{2}$–2 in. softwood cuttings of *L. cymbalaria* 'Globosa' in August or September; insert in a cold frame in equal parts (by volume) peat and sand. Pot the rooted cuttings into $2\frac{1}{2}$ in. pots of John Innes potting compost No. 1; overwinter in the frame, and plant out in May.

Pests and diseases. Generally trouble-free.

Ling: see Calluna

Linnaea

Twin flower. *Caprifoliaceae*

A genus of three species of prostrate hardy evergreen sub-shrubs, named after the Swedish botanist Carl von Linné. The one described is suitable for shady corners in rock gardens.

L. borealis. N. Europe. Height 2–3 in.; spread up to 24 in. This is an attractive ground-cover plant with pairs of small ovate mid to deep green leaves. Slender stems bearing twin trumpet-shaped pendent flowers, flesh pink and $\frac{1}{3}$ in. long, rise from the axils of the leaves; they appear from May to July. This species is represented in cultivation by the more vigorous *L. b. americana*.

Cultivation. Plant during suitable weather between September and March in a cool peaty or leafy soil. These plants thrive in shade.

Propagation. In the spring, plant one or two specimens in a pan containing John Innes potting compost No. 1 and place in a shaded cold frame to encourage fast growth. Give plenty of water during the summer and peg down the runners to encourage rooting. These rooted runners can then be potted up for planting out between September and March, or planted direct in their permanent positions.

Pests and diseases. Generally trouble-free.

Linseed: see *Linum usitatissimum*

Linaria alpina

Linaria maroccana 'Fairy Bouquet'

Linnaea borealis

Linum

Flax. *Linaceae*

A genus of 230 species of hardy and tender annuals, biennials, herbaceous perennials and sub-shrubs. Some of the species described here are suitable for rock gardens, others for herbaceous or mixed borders. The annual species may also be grown in pots to flower under glass.

Shallowly funnel or salver-shaped flowers are carried in terminal branched clusters and produced in great numbers throughout the summer. These are easily grown short-lived plants.

LINUM PERENNE

L. arboreum. Crete. Height and planting distance 12 in. A shrubby perennial chiefly grown as a rock-garden plant or at the front of a herbaceous border. It needs warmth and shelter and is not hardy in cold districts. The narrowly triangular leaves are mid-green. Golden-yellow flowers, 1½–2 in. across, are produced in May and June.

L. austriacum. Austrian Alps. Height 12–24 in.; planting distance 12 in. A hardy border perennial with a woody rootstock from which the linear-lanceolate mid-green leaves grow each season. Arching flower stems carry soft blue, 1 in. wide flowers with shallowly notched petals; they appear in June and July. 'Album' is a white form.

L. campanulatum. S. Europe. Height and planting distance 12 in. A hardy perennial border plant with grey-green oblong-lanceolate leaves. The yellow flowers are ¾ in. across and appear from June to August.

L. flavum. Mid-Europe, eastwards to Russia. Height 12–18 in.; planting distance 9 in. This hardy, sub-shrubby perennial bears narrowly lanceolate, somewhat glaucous-green leaves. Golden-yellow, 1 in. wide flowers are borne from June to August.

L. grandiflorum. Algeria. Height 15–18 in.; spacing 5 in. This is a hardy annual species, with slender stems and narrow, pointed, pale green leaves. The single saucer-shaped flowers are 1½ in. across, of a clear rose colour, and produced from June to August. Several varieties are listed, including 'Bright Eyes' (height 15 in.), with 2 in. wide white flowers and a contrasting carmine eye; 'Rubrum' (scarlet flax), height 12 in., with brilliant crimson flowers.

L. narbonense. S. Europe. Height 12–24 in.; planting distance 12 in. A widely grown hardy border perennial with grey-green narrowly lanceolate leaves. Panicles of rich blue flowers, each 1–1¼ in. across, are produced from late May or early June onwards, sometimes until September. In mild districts it may be evergreen, but it usually dies back in winter.

L. perenne. Europe. Height 12–18 in.; planting distance 12 in. A hardy perennial border plant with leaves that are narrowly lanceolate and grey-green in colour. Abundant sky-blue flowers, each 1 in. across, are borne from June to August. The plant usually lives only two or three years, but is easily raised from seed.

L. trigynum: see *Reinwardtia trigyna*

L. usitatissimum (common flax, linseed). S.W. Asia. Height 24 in.; spacing 5 in. A hardy annual species, now naturalised in Great Britain. The linear-lanceolate leaves are pale green. Slender stems carry single, pale blue, saucer-shaped flowers, ½ in. across, in June and July.

Cultivation. Grow linums in any ordinary, well-drained soil, with or without lime, in an open site; full sun is necessary to obtain the maximum effect from the brilliant flowers.

Plant perennial species in October, November, March or April; cut down dead growth in October or November.

L. grandiflorum may be grown as a spring-flowering pot plant, setting five or six seedlings from a September sowing in a 5 in. container of John Innes potting compost No. 1. In October, move the pot to an unheated greenhouse.

Propagation. Sow the annual species in the flowering site in September or March, and thin out the seedlings to the required spacing. For pot culture, sow seeds of *L. grandiflorum* in a cold frame during the first half of September. Prick out the seedlings, five or six to a 5 in. pot, as described under CULTIVATION.

The perennials are short-lived and require frequent propagation. All grow easily from seeds, although named varieties do not come completely true to type. Sow during March or April in pots or boxes of John Innes seed compost in a cold frame; prick out the seedlings, when large enough to handle, into nursery rows. Grow on until October, then transfer to the flowering site. Some flowers can be expected in the first year.

Take 2 in. cuttings of soft basal shoots of named varieties in April or May. Insert the cuttings in equal parts (by volume) peat and sand in a cold frame. When rooted, transfer the cuttings to nursery rows and grow on until October, when they can be planted out.

Pests and diseases. Generally trouble-free.

Lippia

Verbenaceae

LIPPIA CITRIODORA

A genus of 220 species of tender and half-hardy herbaceous perennials and deciduous flowering shrubs. Only one species is in general cultivation and, except in the south and west, this requires cool greenhouse culture.

L. citriodora, syn. *Aloysia citriodora* (lemon-scented verbena). Chile. Height 5 ft; spread 4 ft. The pale to mid-green lanceolate leaves of this deciduous shrub have a strong lemon scent when

Linum flavum

Linum grandiflorum 'Rubrum'

Linum narbonense

crushed. Tiny, pale mauve, tubular flowers are borne in August in panicles, 3–4 in. long.

Cultivation. Plant in late May in any ordinary, well-drained garden soil, in full sun and in a sheltered position, preferably against a south-facing wall.

In cold areas lippias should be grown in a well-lit position in a greenhouse. Plant the shrubs in March in the greenhouse border or in 6–8 in. pots of John Innes potting compost No. 2. Water freely from March to October and ventilate the house on hot days. In winter, keep the plants just moist and at 7–10°C (45–50°F).

Repot or pot on annually in March.

Propagation. In July, take 3 in. cuttings of lateral shoots or 3 in. stem sections; insert in equal parts (by volume) peat and sand in a propagating frame at a temperature of 16–18°C (61–64°F). Pot the rooted cuttings in 3–3½ in. containers of John Innes potting compost No. 1 and overwinter in a frost-free frame or greenhouse. Plant out in permanent positions the following May.

Pruning. Where conditions are sufficiently mild or sheltered for the shrubs to establish a permanent framework, prune the main growths back to within 12 in. of ground level and lateral shoots to within two or three buds of the old wood in April.

The shrubs may be cut back by frost, but new growths will usually appear from the base again.

On greenhouse shrubs reduce the previous season's shoots by half in April.

Pests and diseases. Generally trouble-free.

Liquidambar

Altingiaceae (formerly *Hamamelidaceae*)

LIQUIDAMBAR STYRACIFLUA

A genus of six species of hardy deciduous trees, with maple-like alternate leaves that usually assume attractive autumn tints. The name is derived from the amber-coloured resin exuded from the trees. Only one species is available.

L. styraciflua (sweet gum). N. America. Height 18–25 ft; spread 8–12 ft. A slender, pyramidal tree with shiny dark green, lobed, palmate leaves. These turn brilliant orange and scarlet in October and November. Inconspicuous green-yellow flowers are produced in March. Deeply fissured corky outgrowths develop on old trees.

Cultivation. Liquidambars thrive in well-drained moist loam in sheltered positions and in full sun or partial shade. Plant between November and March, with the soil ball around the fleshy roots left undisturbed.

These trees are frequently grown as standards with a straight main stem. When the desired height has been reached, cut off the tip of the leading shoot, to induce branch development and formation of the head. The following year, reduce

all new growths by one-third and remove any feathers or side-growths on the main stem.

Propagation. Sow seeds in October in pans or boxes of John Innes seed compost in a cold frame. Seeds may take two years to germinate. Prick off the seedlings, when large enough to handle, into boxes of John Innes potting compost No. 1. Line the seedlings out in nursery rows and grow on for four or five years before planting out.

Alternatively, increase by layering. Peg long branches down in March, and leave for at least two years before severing and replanting.

Pruning. Remove unwanted and crossing branches in November.

Pests and diseases. Generally trouble-free.

Liriodendron

Tulip tree. *Magnoliaceae*

LIRIODENDRON TULIPIFERA

A genus of two species of hardy deciduous flowering trees of imposing stature. The leaves are unusual in shape, having a broad apex which is cut off almost squarely, or with a shallow notch; they turn butter-yellow in autumn. Tulip-shaped flowers are borne by trees that are more than 15 years old.

L. tulipifera. E. United States. Height 18–25 ft; spread 10–15 ft. The light to mid-green leaves turn clear yellow in October and November. Yellow-green, 2 in. long flowers appear in July, followed by slender cone-shaped fruits.

Cultivation. Plant in any well-drained garden soil in a sunny position or in light shade, between October and March.

Propagation. Sow seeds in October or November in pans containing moist sandy loam and place in a cold frame or greenhouse. The following May or June, pot the seedlings singly into 3½ in. containers of John Innes potting compost No. 1. Set out the young plants in a nursery bed in April of the following year; leave them there for three or four years before planting out.

Branches layered in March or April will be ready for severing and planting two years later.

Plants can also be produced by air-layering in a polythene sleeve containing equal parts (by volume) sphagnum moss, peat and sand.

Pruning. None required.

Pests and diseases. Generally trouble-free.

Liriope

Liliaceae

A genus of six species of hardy evergreen perennials, suitable for the front of a border.

L. muscari. Japan, China. Height 12–18 in.; planting distance 15 in. This species forms a

Lippia citriodora

Liquidambar styraciflua
(autumn colours)

Liriodendron tulipifera

compact clump of broad grassy leaves; they are deep green and glossy, and spread to give long-lasting ground cover. Flower spikes, 3–5 in. long, are borne on 9–12 in. long wiry stems. The mauve-lilac flowers are bell-shaped and resemble a grape hyacinth (*Muscari*); they appear from August to November. The species is now correctly known as *L. platyphylla.*

L. platyphylla: see *L. muscari*

L. spicata. Japan, China. Height 15 in.; planting distance 18 in. The leaves are similar to those of *L. muscari*, but are narrower and more erect. Bell-shaped bright lilac-mauve flowers in 2–3 in. long spikes appear from August to October.

Cultivation. Plant in March or April in light sandy soil with low lime content and in sun or partial shade. The plants are drought-resistant as the roots have numerous small storage nodules or tubers. After flowering cut off the flower spikes; the leaves are attractive throughout the year.

Propagation. Lift, divide and replant the fibrous matted roots in March or April.

Pests and diseases. Generally trouble-free.

Liriope muscari

Lithops alpina

Lithops optica rubra

Lithops

Pebble plant, living stone. *Aizoaceae*

A genus of 50 species of greenhouse perennials. The naming of this genus is being reconsidered, and many of the species are being combined or reduced to varieties of other species.

Lithops belong to the huge group of mesembryanthemums. They are small, highly succulent plants consisting of a single pair of thickened, mottled leaves united to form an unbranched body with a slit across the top. The leaves are attached to a short stem which is buried in the soil. Their markings closely resemble the stones of their native desert.

The daisy-like flowers emerge through the slit on top of the body. They are either yellow or white and about 1 in. across. In most species they are produced in September or October, opening in the afternoons of sunny days.

A few species form clumps, but many never form more than two bodies and some take years to produce more than one. Lithops should be placed in full light in the greenhouse.

See also CACTUS.

L. alpina. Namaqualand. Height 1 in. The leaves are light brown, mottled with darker brown. This species is one of the easiest to flower, the yellow blooms appearing in June.

L. erniana. Namaqualand. Height 1 in. The grey plant body is covered with a network of red-brown lines. The white flowers open in September.

L. mundtii. Namaqualand. Height 1 in. The plant body is grey-brown marked with green dots and brown lines. The yellow flowers are produced in September and October.

L. optica. Namaqualand. Height ¾ in. This species has a grey-green plant body. Unlike other lithops, it has a deep cleft between the leaves, which have translucent tips through which light reaches the interior tissues of the plant. White flowers appear in December. It forms clumps readily. The variety *L. o. rubra* is similar to the species, but the plant body is purple-red.

Cultivation. Grow the plants in 3 in. pots, using a mixture of equal parts (by volume) of John Innes potting compost No. 2 and grit or sharp sand. Lithops have a definite resting period from the middle of October until April, during which they should not be watered. Provide a minimum winter temperature of 5°C (41°F), and maximum light throughout the year. The leaves will start to wrinkle and a new pair will eventually appear between the old ones. These new leaves will increase in size as the old ones shrivel. Do not start watering again until the old leaves have completely dried up.

It is important not to over-water, as the bodies then become bloated and may rot. Repot every third year in April.

Propagation. Scatter seeds on the surface of seed compost in April, at a temperature of 21°C (70°F). Alternatively, divide clump-forming species in June. Remove one of the plant bodies with a small piece of stem attached; dry for three or four days, then pot up in the mixture used for cultivation. It will root easily. This is a useful method for dealing with old plants when the stem has become woody and the plant seems to be deteriorating.

Pests. Infestations of MEALY BUGS produce conspicuous tufts of white waxy wool on plants. ROOT MEALY BUGS may infest roots and cause a check to growth.

Diseases. A PHYSIOLOGICAL DISORDER, which shows as a discoloration or collapse of the top growth, is due to over-watering or watering at the wrong time.

Lithospermum

Boraginaceae

LITHOSPERMUM DIFFUSUM

A genus of 60 species of mat-forming, hardy and near-hardy, perennial plants and sub-shrubs notable for their freely produced funnel-shaped blue flowers. They make good ground cover on rock gardens. The species described can all be regarded as hardy.

L. diffusum. S. Europe. Height 4 in.; spread up to 24 in. This sub-shrubby species has spreading prostrate stems with ovate dark green leaves. The deep blue flowers, ½ in. across, have five rounded spreading lobes.

There are two selected colour forms: 'Grace Ward', with slightly larger flowers that are a more intense shade of blue; and 'Heavenly Blue', with an abundance of deep blue flowers. They bloom from June to October.

L. doefleri. Balkans. Height 12–15 in.; spread 12 in. This sub-shrubby species has lanceolate dark green leaves and clusters of nodding blue flowers, each up to ½ in. long, borne on leafy stems during May and June.

L. oleifolium. Pyrenees. Height 6 in.; spread 12 in. This striking sub-shrubby species has rounded grey-green leaves and clusters of sky-blue flowers that open from pink buds from May to August. The flowers are ½ in. long and are carried at the ends of leafy stems.

Cultivation. Plant lithospermums in April, in full sun and in a sandy soil which has had peat or leaf-mould added to it. *L. diffusum* and its forms will not tolerate lime.

L. oleifolium makes an effective alpine-house plant when grown in an 8–10 in. pan of John Innes potting compost No. 1. Repot every other April.

Propagation. Increase lithospermums from soft cuttings of lateral shoots, 1½–2½ in. long, preferably taken with a heel. Take those of *L. diffusum* from mid to late July, others in July or August. Insert all cuttings in a mixture of equal parts (by volume) peat and sand in pans or boxes and place them in a cold frame. Water *L. diffusum* generously to prevent flagging; keep the others just moist. Pot the rooted cuttings into 3 in. pots of John Innes potting compost No. 1, overwinter them in the frame and plant out in April.

Pests and diseases. Generally trouble-free.

Living stone: see Lithops

Lobelia

Campanulaceae

A genus of 200 or more species of hardy and half-hardy annuals, herbaceous perennials and sub-shrubs. The annual species are much used in hanging baskets, for edging, and as summer bedding plants. Some of the perennial species are suitable for herbaceous borders; others, which flower freely the first year when grown from seeds, are normally grown as annuals.

The flowers are basically tubular, flattening out to a broad three to five-lobed lip.

LOBELIA SYPHILITICA

L. cardinalis. N. United States. Height 2½ ft; planting distance 12 in. A short-lived, unreliably hardy border perennial, quite distinct from the bedding lobelias. Erect and branching stems carry oblong-lanceolate mid-green leaves. Leafy racemes of scarlet, five-lobed flowers, about 1 in. across, appear in July and August.

The specific name is frequently applied, erroneously, to named varieties of *L. fulgens.*

L. erinus. S. Africa. Height 4–9 in.; planting distance 4 in. This half-hardy perennial, invariably grown as an annual, is a dwarf spreading bedding plant. The light green leaves are ovate at the base of the plant, longer and narrower on the stems. Pale blue and white flowers, each ¼ in. across, are produced in great numbers from May until the first frosts.

The many garden varieties are usually grouped under two headings: compact and trailing. The most popular compact varieties are 'Cambridge Blue', with pale blue flowers and light green foliage; and 'Crystal Palace', with dark blue flowers and bronze foliage. Also recommended are 'Mrs Clibran', bearing brilliant blue flowers with a conspicuous white eye; 'Rosamund', carmine-red with a white eye; and 'Snowball', a large-flowered white variety which usually includes a few blue-flowered plants.

Of the trailing or Pendula varieties, 'Blue Cascade' is a true Cambridge blue; 'Sapphire' is bright blue with a white eye.

Lobelia erinus

L. fulgens. Mexico. Height 1–3 ft; planting distance 15 in. A half-hardy border perennial which forms a rosette of mainly purple, ovate and toothed leaves. Tapering flower spikes, up to 12 in. long, on thick branching stems, open in August and continue until late October. Each spike is composed of 1 in. long scarlet flowers with a prominent lobed lip.

The variety 'Bee's Flame' has larger, bright scarlet flowers on full, 18 in. long spikes; 'Queen Victoria' has deep red flower spikes and is a popular bedding plant. There are pink varieties in cultivation, but these are less vigorous than the type species, and not easily obtainable from nurseries.

L. syphilitica. E. United States. Height 2–3 ft; planting distance 12 in. A hardy border perennial with lanceolate light green leaves. Spikes, up to 2½ ft long, of clear blue flowers, each 1 in. long, appear from July to September. There is a white variety, 'Alba'. The species is short-lived.

L. tenuior. W. Australia. Height 12 in.; planting distance 6 in. A tender perennial, generally grown as a half-hardy annual; it makes an excellent pot plant for flowering under glass in winter, spring and early summer, and is also suitable for hanging baskets and for bedding. Erect, slender stems carry ovate, light green leaves and a profusion of single bright blue flowers, ¾ in. across, with three lobes. The variety 'Compacta' grows to a height of only 9 in.

Lithospermum diffusum

Lobelia cardinalis

Lobelia erinus 'Rosamund'

Lobelia syphilitica

L. × *vedrariense.* Garden origin. Height 4 ft; planting distance 15 in. This hardy perennial, with lanceolate dark green leaves, is a vigorous hybrid. Purple spikes, up to 4 ft long, of trumpet-shaped flowers are produced from August to October.

Cultivation. Plant *L. erinus* and *L. tenuior* in May, the other species in April, in rich, moist soil and in a sheltered and partially shaded position.

The half-hardy perennials need winter protection, especially in cold, exposed positions. Cover the roots with leaves or bracken, or lift the root-balls carefully with ample soil in late November. Place in boxes in a cold frame or a cold greenhouse. When new growth begins, in late March, separate the rosettes and pot or box in peaty soil until new growing and feeding roots have formed. Plant out when renewed growth is well established.

The taller plants, especially *L.* × *vedrariense*, sometimes require staking.

For flowering under glass, grow plants of *L. erinus* and *L. tenuior* in 4–5 in. pots of John Innes potting compost No. 1.

Propagation. Sow seeds of the bedding varieties, *L. erinus* and *L. tenuior*, in February in pans of seed compost, at a temperature of 16–18°C (61–64°F). Prick out the seedlings in groups of three or four—they are too small to prick out individually—and grow on at a temperature of 10°C (50°F); harden off and plant out in May.

Sow seeds of the taller herbaceous species in March at a temperature of 13–16°C (55–61°F), harden off and prick out into a nursery bed. Lift *L. cardinalis* from the bed and overwinter in a cold frame, but leave the other herbaceous species to grow on in the nursery bed. Plant out in their permanent sites the following April.

The herbaceous species may also be increased by division in March.

Successive sowings of *L. erinus* and *L. tenuior* from February to April will produce plants to flower under glass from May throughout the summer. Sow in September for winter flowering.

Pests. Generally trouble-free.

Diseases. Damping-off and root rot are commonly caused by RHIZOCTONIA; infected plants usually collapse.

STEM ROT shows as pale spots on the leaves of seedlings, often giving these a scorched appearance. The disease may also cause DAMPING-OFF of seedlings.

A VIRUS DISEASE affects *L. cardinalis*; it causes a pronounced mottling in the form of a patchy mosaic of dark green with paler spots on the foliage. All leaves become distorted and the older leaves turn brittle.

Lobivia

Cactaceae

A genus of 75 greenhouse perennial species. These are medium-sized, round or cylindrical cacti with ribs divided into tubercles and bearing conspicuous spines and bristly hairs. The plants form offsets round the base.

They are grown for their highly coloured, open bell-shaped flowers which, although lasting for only a day or so, are freely produced during the summer. The flowers are usually red or yellow.

See also CACTUS.

L. allegraiana. Peru. Height 6 in. This is particularly easy plant to grow and flower. The plant body is bright green with 6–11 ribs. The areoles bear straw-coloured spines, seven of them radial spines and one a 2 in. long central spine. The flowers, 1½–2 in. across, are pink or red.

L. hertrichiana. Peru. Height 4 in. A freely clustering dark green plant similar to *L. allegraiana*, with an almost globular stem. The profuse flowers are scarlet and measure 2 in. across.

L. jajoiana. Argentina. Height 6 in. A cylindrical plant that may be solitary or form only one or two offsets. The green body has 12–15 ribs divided into large tubercles. The woolly areoles bear 9–11 short, pale red marginal spines and a black central spine, about 2 in. long and hooked. The flowers are claret or tomato-coloured with a black throat and measure about 2 in. across.

Cultivation. Lobivias grow well in John Innes potting compost No. 2 with extra grit added. *L. allegraiana* and *L. jajoiana* require 3–4 in. pots; the clustering *L. hertrichiana* needs a 6 in. pot. They require a sunny position and plenty of water in summer. In winter, keep the plant completely dry and rest them at a temperature of 2°C (36°F). Repot them annually when they start to make new growth in spring.

Propagation. Sow seeds in March at a temperature of 21°C (70°F); or detach offsets between May and October. Some offsets will be already rooted, and simply need digging up and repotting in the growing medium. Otherwise dry the offsets for three days before potting.

Pests. Colonies of MEALY BUGS produce conspicuous tufts of white waxy wool on plants. ROOT MEALY BUGS infest roots and check growth.

Diseases. Generally trouble-free.

Lobularia maritima: see *Alyssum maritimum*

Loganberry

Rubus loganobaccus. Rosaceae

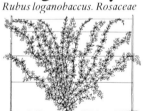

LOGANBERRY

This hardy fruit-bearing perennial is thought to be a cross between the cultivated blackberry and the raspberry. It first occurred in California in the late 19th century and is now widely cultivated for its edible fruits.

The loganberry is a vigorous, scrambling perennial plant, similar in habit to the blackberry. Oblong, dull claret-coloured fruits like elongated raspberries are produced in July and August on shoots of the previous season's growth. The spiny stems reach an average height of 6 ft and spread to 8 ft; they require the support of wires or a timber framework.

Lobivia allegraiana

Lobivia hertrichiana

Lobivia jajoiana

Thornless varieties are known; these generally bear smaller crops of fruit.

Cultivation. Grow loganberries in any ordinary, well-drained soil, preferably enriched with well-rotted manure or compost. Ideally the soil should be slightly acid or neutral. Plant from October to March in a sheltered sunny or partially shaded position. Give annual dressings of 1 oz. sulphate of potash per sq. yd in winter, and $\frac{1}{2}$ oz. sulphate of ammonia in March. During dry spells between June and August, water the plants freely.

Loganberries require training to wires, either in the open or against walls. Secure 10–12-gauge wires to stout supports and set the wires at 3 ft, 4 ft and 5 ft above ground level, with a thinner wire at 6 ft for attaching new growths temporarily. On walls, secure the wires with vine eyes. Set the plants at intervals of 8–10 ft and tie the shoots to the wires with string or twists of paper-covered wire.

After planting, cut back the canes to 12 in. above ground level; no fruits can be expected during the first season, but the shoots should be tied to the supporting wires. The following and subsequent years cut back the fruiting canes after fruiting. It is advisable to keep the young basal shoots away from fruiting canes by tying them in sheaves and then training along the wires after the old canes have been cut away.

Propagation. Loganberries increase readily by tip layering. Peg the shoots down in July or August; sever from the parent plants and plant out in permanent positions the following March.

Pruning. Immediately after fruiting, cut out the old canes which have borne fruit to a few inches above ground level. This will provide more space for the new shoots which have been growing up during the summer and will continue to do so into the autumn.

Pests. Maggots of RASPBERRY BEETLE tunnel into the ripening fruits, making them inedible.

Diseases. CANE SPOT shows as small, circular purple spots on the canes in May or June. They enlarge to elliptic white blotches with purple borders. Later the spots split to form shallow pits or small cankers, giving the fruiting canes a rough and cracked appearance. In severe cases the tips of the canes may be killed. Leaves and fruits sometimes become distorted.

CROWN GALL may occur at ground level, when a gall about the size of a walnut develops at the crown. It can also occur as numerous smaller galls higher up the canes.

GREY MOULD causes a rotting of the berries, which are covered with a grey fluffy growth.

RUBUS STUNT is a virus disease which causes affected plants to produce numerous small stunted shoots with distorted leaves. No fruit is formed and diseased plants eventually die.

RUST produces dark red spots on the upper leaf surfaces; pustules on the undersides contain spores which are at first orange-yellow, later turning black.

SPUR BLIGHT shows at first as dark purple blotches around the bases of the leaves; the patches turn silvery and are studded with black, pin-point, fruiting bodies. Buds at the affected nodes die, as do subsequent shoots.

London pride: see *Saxifraga × urbicum*

Lonicera

Honeysuckle. *Caprifoliaceae*

A genus of 200 species of evergreen and deciduous flowering shrubs and woody climbers. Two of the species described are tender climbing plants and require cool greenhouse treatment, although *L. hildebrandiana* is too vigorous for any but a large greenhouse or conservatory. The outdoor species described are hardy twining climbers, ideal for walls, fences, archways and pergolas, or shrubs, suitable for mixed and shrub borders and against walls.

Lonicera flowers are basically tubular with diverging lips; they are borne in close pairs, the pairs themselves being carried singly, doubly or in small clusters. In the shrubby species particularly, the pairs are often fused, as are the subsequent berries. The flowers, especially those of the climbers, are often fragrant.

GREENHOUSE SPECIES

L. hildebrandiana (giant honeysuckle). Burma. Height 60 ft or more. An evergreen climber with ovate, mid to deep green lustrous leaves. The slightly fragrant flowers are produced in pairs from June to August, two or three pairs forming a cluster. Each flower, up to 6 in. long, is cream-white fading to orange-brown.

L. sempervirens (trumpet vine). S. United States. Height 20 ft or more. An evergreen or partly deciduous climbing shrub, with ovate mid-green leaves. The 2–3 in. long flowers are borne from June to August in slender terminal clusters. They are scarlet outside and orange-yellow inside.

HARDY SPECIES

L. × brownii (scarlet trumpet honeysuckle). Height 10–15 ft. This is a moderately strong-growing semi-evergreen climber. The ovate-oblong leaves are mid-green with a blue tinge above, downy and glaucous beneath. Terminal whorls of slender scarlet flowers, 1–2 in. long, provide an excellent display from June to September, sometimes later.

L. caprifolium (goat-leaf honeysuckle, perfoliate woodbine). Europe, naturalised in Great Britain. Height up to 20 ft. A vigorous deciduous climbing species found wild in south-east England. It is easily distinguished from *L. periclymenum*, the native honeysuckle or woodbine, by its topmost leaves which are perfoliate; the lower leaves are stalked. The leaves are obovate to ovate and light green. Fragrant flowers, 1$\frac{1}{2}$–2 in. long, appear profusely from June onwards, in whorls from the upper leaf axils. They are cream-white, tinged with pink.

L. fragrantissima. China. Height and spread 6 ft. A partially evergreen shrub, with ovate mid-green leaves. The $\frac{3}{4}$ in. long, cream-white flowers are strongly fragrant; they are produced from December to March.

L. involucrata. Canada, W. United States. Height and spread 6–8 ft. This deciduous shrub, of open habit, is tolerant of atmospheric pollution, and is suitable for hedging. The leaves are ovate to oblong and bright green. Yellow flowers, surrounded by prominent green bracts, are borne in axillary pairs from May to July. The red-bracted form is correctly named *L. i. ledebourii*, and is sometimes classed as a distinct species.

Loganberry

Lonicera hildebrandiana

Lonicera sempervirens

Lonicera tatarica

Lonicera × tellmanniana

display throughout the season. 'Belgica' (early Dutch honeysuckle) is of more bushy habit than the species and produces its purple-red and yellow flowers during May and June. 'Serotina' (late Dutch honeysuckle) blooms from July to October; the flowers are red-purple on the outside and cream-white inside.

L. pileata. China. Height 2–3 ft; spread 4–6 ft. This semi-evergreen shrub may lose many of its leaves in a severe winter. Its spreading habit makes it ideal for ground cover, and it will grow in heavy shade under trees. The leaves are pale to mid-green and ovate-oblong. Inconspicuous yellow-green flowers, $\frac{1}{3}$ in. long, are borne on the underside of shoots in April and May and are followed by fruits similar to those of *L. nitida*.

L. × purpusii. Height and spread up to 6 ft. This deciduous hybrid has ovate mid-green leaves. Fragrant, cream-white flowers, $\frac{1}{2}$–$\frac{3}{4}$ in. long, open from December to March.

L. standishii. China. Height and spread 4–5 ft. This deciduous shrubby species is similar to *L. fragrantissima*, but grows more compactly and flowers more freely. The leaves are mid-green and ovate. Cream-white flowers, $\frac{1}{2}$–$\frac{3}{4}$ in. long, open from November to March.

L. syringantha. China. Height and spread 6–8 ft. A dense deciduous shrub, with grey-green oblong leaves. Lilac-pink, sweetly scented, $\frac{1}{2}$ in. long, flowers are freely borne in axillary clusters during May and early June.

LONICERA TATARICA

L. tatarica. S. Russia, Turkestan. Height and spread 6–10 ft. This deciduous shrub is of erect habit. The ovate leaves are dark green above, blue-green beneath. Pink, 1 in. long flowers, in small clusters of pairs, cover the branches in May or early June. Red globular berries follow the flowers in July or August.

L. × tellmanniana. Height 15 ft. This strong-growing, deciduous climber, suitable for a south-west wall is a hybrid between *L. tragophylla* and *L. sempervirens*. The upper pairs of dark green ovate leaves are stalkless. Whorls of red and yellow flowers, 2 in. long, open in June and July.

L. tragophylla (Chinese woodbine). China. Height up to 20 ft. A vigorous deciduous climbing species which needs a shaded position and its roots kept shaded and moist. The ovate leaves, which taper at both ends, are dark green above, glaucous-white beneath. They provide a fine background for the terminal whorls of spectacular golden-yellow flowers; these are 2–3$\frac{1}{2}$ in. long, and appear in June and July.

Cultivation of greenhouse species. Grow loniceras in the greenhouse border, training the stems up wires or strings and along the roof. Provide a winter temperature of 5–7°C (41–45°F); ventilate freely during spring, summer and autumn. Keep the plants just moist in winter, but water freely during the growing season.

L. japonica (Japanese honeysuckle). Japan, Korea, China. Height 25–30 ft. A strong-growing, evergreen, twining plant, which becomes a tangled mass of slender growths. The light green ovate to oblong leaves are lightly downy on both sides. From June to October fragrant, white to pale yellow flowers, 1–1$\frac{1}{2}$ in. long, are produced from the leaf axils on the young growths.

The species is generally represented by 'Aureoreticulata' which has leaves veined and netted with yellow; it is susceptible to frosts and may lose its leaves, but is seldom killed.

L. ledebourii: see *L. involucrata ledebourii*

L. nitida. China. Height and spread 5–6 ft. This dense evergreen shrub makes a fine hedge and will grow satisfactorily in shade. The leaves are ovate and glossy dark green. Insignificant yellow-green flowers, $\frac{1}{4}$ in. long, open in April and May. They are followed by semi-translucent violet or amethyst globular berries.

'Baggesen's Gold' is a golden-leaved variety; it should be planted in full sun.

LONICERA PERICLYMENUM

L. periclymenum (woodbine, honeysuckle). Great Britain, Asia Minor, the Caucasus, W. Asia. Height 15–20 ft. This deciduous climber is one of the best-known and best-loved of the native hedgerow and woodland plants. The ovate to obovate leaves are dark green, the upper ones stalkless and the lower ones stalked. Terminal whorls of 1$\frac{1}{2}$–2 in. long flowers, pale yellow flushed with purple-red, open from July to August. They are followed by bright red berries.

Varieties are grown more widely than the species; they have the advantage of earlier and later flowering and can provide a continuous

Lonicera × purpusii

Mulch annually in March with a light dressing of well-rotted compost on poor soils. Overseeding results in leaf and stem growth at the expense of flower production.

Cultivation of hardy species. Grow loniceras in any ordinary, well-drained soil, enriched with humus in the case of the climbing species. All will grow in sun or partial shade, but the climbers do better in light shade; apart from *L. × tellmanniana* and *L. tragophylla,* climbing species should be sited in such a way that their roots are in shade and their tops in sun.

Plant evergreen climbers during April or May, deciduous species and shrubby species during suitable weather from September to March. Mulch lightly with leaf-mould or well-rotted compost, annually in spring. For hedging, set young plants of *L. nitida* at intervals of 9–12 in.

Propagation of greenhouse species. Take 3–4 in. long stem sections in July or August; insert in equal parts (by volume) peat and sand at a temperature of 16°C (61°F). When rooted, pot the cuttings singly in $3\frac{1}{2}$ in. containers of John Innes potting compost No. 2 and pot on as necessary until they are planted out in the greenhouse border.

Propagation of hardy species. Take 4 in. long stem sections in July or August and insert them in equal parts (by volume) peat and sand in a cold frame. Plant out rooted shrub cuttings in a nursery bed the following April or May. The cuttings of climbing species are better potted into $3\frac{1}{2}$–4 in. pots of John Innes potting compost No. 2 and plunged outside. In both cases grow on until September or October before planting out.

Take 9–12 in. hardwood cuttings in September or October and insert in a sheltered nursery bed. Transfer to the flowering site one year later.

Branches layered between August and November can usually be severed a year later.

Sow the seeds of climbing species when ripe, in September or October, in pots or pans of seed compost and place in a cold frame or greenhouse. Prick out the seedlings, when large enough to handle, into 3 in. pots of John Innes potting compost No. 1 or 2, and then into 4 in. pots. Plunge outdoors until the following autumn, when they may be planted in the flowering site. Plants raised from seeds take several years to reach flowering size.

Pruning. Overgrown and straggly greenhouse plants may be thinned out and lateral shoots spurred back to 6 in. in March or April; too-heavy pruning results in loss of flowers.

Thin out old wood on outdoor plants occasionally, after flowering. Newly planted hedges should have the young growths reduced by half or two-thirds at planting time; tip the young shoots two or three times during the following summer to promote a bushy habit. Cut all new growths back by half each year until the hedge reaches the desired height. Thereafter shear hedges in May and September to maintain shape.

Pests. Young shoots and flower trusses may be infested with APHIDS, which distort them and make the leaves sticky and sooty.

GLASSHOUSE RED SPIDER MITES may attack plants under glass, causing mottling of the leaves and premature leaf-fall.

Diseases. LEAF SPOT, due to one or more fungi, shows as small green spots or larger round brown spots. These later turn pale and dry up. Brown blotches may appear on the foliage.

A PHYSIOLOGICAL DISORDER due to unsuitable cultural conditions shows as yellowing or browning of the leaves, and sometimes as DIE-BACK.

POWDERY MILDEW may show as a white powdery deposit on the leaves.

SILVER LEAF has been known to cause the die-back of shoots bearing silvery leaves.

Loosestrife, purple: see *Lythrum salicaria*

Lophophora
Cactaceae

A genus of possibly three species of greenhouse perennials. Only one species is in general cultivation. These highly succulent, slow-growing cacti have a globular body and a fleshy rootstock. The short, daisy-like flowers are composed of numerous narrow petals. They appear singly from the crown, each lasting two or three days. Fruits often follow the flowers. The plants are easy to grow and, if kept in a sunny window, can be grown as house plants.

See also CACTUS.

L. williamsii (dumpling cactus, mescal button). Mexico, Texas. Height 3 in.; spread up to 6 in. The plant is solitary when young, but later develops offsets. The stem is round, with a slightly depressed centre. There are up to 12 glaucous-grey ribs divided into tubercles, each bearing an areole that is spineless, but produces prominent tufts of white wool. The pale pink or cream flowers, about 1 in. across, appear from April to July and are followed by red oval fruits.

Cultivation. Lophophoras do well in a soil composed of equal parts (by volume) loam, sand and coarse grit or fine gravel. Pot the plants into 5 in. pots, in March or April; do not press the soil too firmly round them, or the fleshy rootstock will be unable to develop properly.

Water from March to October whenever the soil becomes dry. Slight shrinkage may occur in winter, but this is normal. The plants require a minimum winter temperature of 5°C (41°F). Move into larger pots at the start of the growing season if the pots are full of roots.

Propagation. Sow seeds in spring at a temperature of 21°C (70°F). Detach offsets during winter and pot up in the growing compost.

Pests. Young growths at the centres of plants may be attacked by MEALY BUGS.

Diseases. Generally trouble-free.

Love-in-a-mist: see *Nigella damascena*
Love-lies-bleeding: see *Amaranthus caudatus*

Luculia
Rubiaceae

A genus of five species of evergreen shrubs that in Great Britain require cool greenhouse treatment. They have fragrant tubular flowers.

Lonicera standishii

Lonicera × tellmanniana

Lophophora williamsii

L. grandifolia. Bhutan. Height and spread 10 ft or more. A large shrub or small tree with ovate to broadly elliptic mid-green leaves, up to 15 in. long. Fragrant, pure white flowers, 2–2½ in. across, are borne in 6–8 in. wide terminal clusters from May to July.

LUCULIA GRATISSIMA

L. gratissima. Himalayas. Height up to 6 ft; spread 4–5 ft. The ovate-oblong mid-green leaves are up to 8 in. long and are arranged in opposite pairs. Fragrant mauve-pink flowers are borne from November to February in terminal clusters, up to 9 in. across. The individual flower, 1 in. wide, consists of a slender tube which terminates in five rounded lobes, opening out flat.

L. pinceana. Khasia Mountains, India. Height 4–6 ft; spread 4 ft. Similar to *L. gratissima*, but with lanceolate mid-green leaves, up to 6 in. long. The white flower cluster is similar in shape and size to *L. gratissima*, but the individual, strongly fragrant flowers are 1½–2 in. across; they are borne from May to September.

Cultivation. Luculias are best planted out in the greenhouse border, but they can be grown in 10–12 in. pots or small tubs of John Innes potting compost No. 3. They require a winter temperature of 7°C (45°F), but will tolerate 5°C (41°F). After flowering, keep the plants just moist until new growth begins in April. Water should then be given, sparingly at first and then in increasing quantities; in summer, water freely and syringe the leaves daily. Give established plants a weak liquid feed at fortnightly intervals from June to September.

Pot on young plants as required until they are in their final pots. Thereafter, established plants should be repotted every second or third year in April. In the years when they are not repotted, renew the top 2 in. of compost in April.

Let the plants have ample light at all times, but provide light shading from strong sunlight. Ventilate the greenhouse as much as possible during the summer and autumn months.

Propagation. Sow seeds of *L. gratissima* in March or April and germinate at a temperature of 13–16°C (55–61°F). The plants take about three years to reach flowering size.

Take heel cuttings, 3–4 in. long, in May, preferably from stooled plants. Insert the cuttings in equal parts (by volume) peat and sand at a temperature of 16°C (61°F), preferably in a mist propagator. Pot the rooted cuttings in 3½–4 in. containers of John Innes potting compost No. 1 or 2; pot on as necessary.

Pruning. Cut the flowered shoots of established plants back hard to 3 in. as soon as the flowers have faded. For propagation purposes, cut all lateral growths of two or three-year-old plants back to 2–3 in. and bring these plants into a temperature of 16°C (61°F).

Pests and diseases. Generally trouble-free.

Luculia grandifolia

Luculia gratissima

Lunaria rediviva

Lunaria annua

Lunaria

Honesty. *Cruciferae*

A genus of three species of biennial and herbaceous perennial plants. The two hardy species described bear four-petalled flowers opening from April to June; they are followed in summer by silvery seed pods that can be used for indoor decorations. These should be cut in August before they are damaged by autumn gales.

L. annua, syn. *L. biennis.* Europe. Height 2½ ft planting distance 12 in. A quick-growing biennial plant with mid-green, coarsely toothed, heart-shaped leaves. The fragrant purple flowers are cross-shaped and ½ in. across.

Most catalogues list a mixture of different colours; purple and white forms are also available. The form 'Variegata' has crimson flowers and variegated foliage.

L. biennis: see *L. annua*

L. rediviva. Europe. Height 3–3½ ft; planting distance 24 in. A bushy, short-lived perennial species of erect habit with deep green, ovate leaves with serrated edges. The pale, almost white, flat flowers are fragrant and borne in branched racemes, 12 in. or more long.

Cultivation. Lunarias grow best in light soil in a partially shaded position. Plant during suitable weather from September to March.

Propagation. Sow seeds of *L. annua* outdoors in nursery bed in May or June; those of *L. rediviva* in April. Thin out the seedlings, or transplant them to 6 in. spacings, and grow on for planting out in September.

Pests. Generally trouble-free.

Diseases. CLUB ROOT may cause a distortion of the roots, but the top growth is not affected and no symptoms are seen until the plants are lifted.

A VIRUS DISEASE causes white streaks to develop on the flowers, which may be distorted.

WHITE BLISTER causes swellings full of white powdery spores on the leaves and stems.

Lungwort: see Pulmonaria
Lupin: see Lupinus
Lupine: see Lupinus
Lupin, tree: see *Lupinus arboreus*

Lupinus arboreus

Lupinus 'Josephine' (Russell)

Lupinus 'Mrs Micklethwaite' (Russell)

Lupinus

Lupin, lupine. *Leguminosae*

A genus of 200 species of hardy and half-hardy annuals, herbaceous perennials and sub-shrubs. Few species are now grown, but the following with their varieties are generally hardy and excellent for planting in groups in beds or borders. The flowers of the perennial species may be used for cutting.

Lupin flowers are basically shaped like those of peas, but the upper petal or standard is folded back and the lower petals are laterally compressed to form a keel. They are carried densely in slender, spire-like racemes.

Herbaceous perennial varieties are usually classified under *L. polyphyllus* although they are hybrids with various other species.

LUPINUS POLYPHYLLUS

L. arboreus (tree lupin). California; also naturalised in Europe, including Great Britain. Height and spread 2–4 ft. A shrubby species, usually short-lived, with pale green digitate leaves composed of six to nine lanceolate leaflets. The fragrant flowers vary from yellow through shades of lilac and purple to blue. They are borne in racemes, up to 6 in. or more long, from June to August. This is a good species for seaside gardens.

L. hartwegii. Mexico. Height 3 ft; spacing 9–12 in. An annual species of bushy growth with leaves that are divided into seven or more hairy, soft green leaflets. The 12 in. long spikes of bright blue, pink-flushed flowers appear from July to October. Varieties listed include mixtures and separate colours of dark blue, sky-blue and white. The dwarf form 'Pixie Delight' (height 18 in.) is a mixture in shades of red, pink, purple and blue.

L. polyphyllus. Western N. America. Height 3–5 ft; planting distance 24 in. The leaves of this perennial species are digitate, composed of 10–17 lanceolate mid-green leaflets. Blue or red flowers in 24 in. long spikes appear from May to July.

The true species is seldom grown, and the named varieties are a highly selected race of hybrid origin, popularly known as Russell lupins.

In the early years of this century, James Kelway crossed *L. arboreus* (tree lupin) with *L. polyphyllus.* Further breeding work by G. R. Downer and John Harkness, using this hybrid and colour forms of *L. polyphyllus,* produced the modern border lupin as it is known today. Finally, George Russell, by rigorous selection of seed-raised plants, produced the Russell strain.

These varieties often have the keel and standard petals in different colours. In the following list the keel colour is indicated by K., and the standard by S.

Varieties (average height 3 ft, planting distance 2–2½ ft) include: 'Blue Jacket', K. deep blue, S. white; 'Blushing Bride', K. ivory-white, S. white;

Lupinus hartwegii 'Pixie Delight'

Lupinus 'Elsie Waters' (Russell)

Lupinus (mixed Russell varieties)

'Cherry Pie', K. cherry-red, S. carmine marked yellow; 'Elsie Waters', K. bright pink, S. cream-white edged pink; 'Freedom', K. sky-blue, S. white; 'George Russell', K. and S. pink paling to cream at margins; 'Guardsman', self-coloured orange-red; 'Jane Eyre', K. violet-blue, S. white marked blue.

'Josephine', K. slate-blue, S. lemon-yellow; 'Lady Fayre', K. deep pink, S. deep pink marked ivory; 'Lilac Time', K. rose-lilac, S. white with rose flush; 'Limelight', self-coloured rich yellow; 'Mrs Micklethwaite', K. bronze-pink, S. gold; 'Serenade', K. orange-red, S. crimson marked gold; 'Wheatsheaf', K. golden-yellow overlaid pink, S. golden-yellow.

L. pubescens, syn. *L. tricolor.* Mexico. Height 24 in.; spacing 9 in. A free-flowering annual species. The leaves are divided into seven or more velvety, mid-green leaflets. The stems carry 12 in. spikes of well-spaced flowers from June to September; they are violet-blue, marked white.

There are numerous garden varieties in colours from white to crimson, but mixtures are the most commonly listed. 'Rose Queen' (height 18 in.) is a well-known rose-pink variety.

L. tricolor: see *L. pubescens*

Cultivation. Grow lupins in sun or partial shade, in neutral or acid soil. The plants last longer on light soil, although they grow well on heavy soil for a time. Over-rich soil encourages soft growth and makes the stems so heavy that they require staking with twiggy sticks.

Plant from October to March. Remove the flowering part of faded flower stems to prevent self-seeding and to encourage a second flowering later in the year. Cut down all flowering stems to ground level in November.

Propagation. Sow seeds of annual species in the flowering site in September or March and thin out the seedlings to the required spacing. Autumn-sown plants flower earlier than those from a spring sowing.

Seeds of *L. polyphyllus* usually produce plants of mixed colours. Sow the seeds thinly in boxes or pots of John Innes seed compost in a cold frame in March; prick out the seedlings when large enough to handle, to stand 6 in. apart in nursery rows. Transfer to the flowering site in October. Remove flower spikes for the first year.

Named varieties do not come true from seeds and should be propagated by cuttings, in March or April; take 3–4 in. long cuttings close to the rootstock, preferably with a small piece of rootstock attached. Insert these in sandy soil in a cold frame and, when rooted, set in 4 in. pots of John Innes potting compost No. 2 or transfer to nursery rows in May or June; plant out in the flowering positions in October.

Pests. Generally trouble-free.

Diseases. Annual lupins are generally trouble-free, but *L. polyphyllus* and its varieties can be affected by several diseases.

CROWN ROT and ROOT ROT may be due to a number of different fungi, including the BLACK ROOT ROT fungus. The roots and crown tissues become black and rotten, and the top growths wilt or die back completely.

A slight mottling of the leaves, progressive browning of the leaf stalks and finally the death of plants may be caused by CUCUMBER MOSAIC VIRUS.

Lycaste brevispatha

Lycaste cruenta

Lycaste deppei

Other VIRUS DISEASES cause variable symptom The leaflets may show dark green banding, wit light green or yellow areas between the vein yellowing may occur along the veins with tin light green or chlorotic spots becoming brown i older leaves. Leaflets may be upcurled an twisted. Brown streaks may develop on the lea stalks. The flower colour may be broken.

HONEY FUNGUS may kill plants.

POWDERY MILDEW shows as a white powder coating on the leaves.

Lycaste
Orchidaceae

LYCASTE DEPPEI

A genus of 45 species of tropical epiphyti American orchids. Many grow in rock crevices i the mountains. All species have well-defined usually hard, conical pseudobulbs. These bea oblong-lanceolate, much-veined, deep green tough, deciduous leaves at their apices.

The flowers are wax-like and fragrant. Flower ing stems arise from the base of the pseudobulbs often in considerable quantity; each produces single flower. The sepals are usually larger than the petals, the lip smaller. Colours range from pure white and blush-pink, through apple-green and brown-green to deep chrome-yellow. Some species make good house plants if grown on a draught-free window-sill with ample light. A res period is necessary after the pseudobulbs have fully developed.

See also ORCHIDS.

L. brevispatha, syn. *L. candida.* Central America A vigorous species with pseudobulbs up to 3 in high. The flowers on 4 in. stems are about 3 in across and have pale apple-green sepals that are spotted and suffused with rose-pink. The petals are pure white suffused with pink and the lip is white, lightly spotted with deeper pink. They open from January to April. An intermediate greenhouse is ideal for this species.

L. candida: see *L. brevispatha*

L. cruenta. Central America. This species makes an ideal house plant; it is relatively hardy and tolerant of varying conditions of humidity and temperature, including a cool greenhouse. The pseudobulbs are 1½–3 in. high. Each 6 in. long stem carries a single 2–2½ in. wide flower, deep golden-orange to chrome-yellow, of a waxy texture and with a spicy fragrance. The flowers can appear at any time of year, but they usually open in March and April.

L. deppei. Mexico, Guatemala. A robust species with 2½–3½ in. high pseudobulbs. The single flowers are borne on 5 in. long stems from April to June. They have pale green sepals, lightly flushed and mottled with red, and pure white petals. The mid-lobe of the lip is bright chrome-yellow and the side-lobes white; all three lobes are spotted and marked with red. Grow this species in an intermediate greenhouse.

L. macrophylla. Tropical America. This species has pseudobulbs up to 5 in. high. The flowers, on 4–5 in. stems, are similar to those of *L. brevispatha*, but measure up to 5 in. across. They are borne from July to November. This species should be grown in a cool greenhouse.

L. skinneri, syn. *L. virginalis.* Central America. A robust species with pseudobulbs up to 8 in. high. The wax-like fragrant flowers, on stems up to 10 in. long, measure 6 in. across. They have white sepals flushed with pink, and pure white petals flushed or occasionally spotted with deep rose-pink. The white lip is spotted with rose-red and crimson. They appear at any time throughout the year. 'Alba' is pure white. Grow in an intermediate greenhouse.

L. virginalis: see *L. skinneri*

Cultivation. Pot lycastes from March to May in 5–5 in. pots or 5–9 in. pans, or fix them to pieces of tree fern or blocks of wood. A suitable compost is 2 parts turfy loam, 1 part osmunda fibre, 1 part sphagnum moss and 1 part leaf-mould (parts by volume). Lycastes should be kept fairly cool and shaded from April to September, when they may be given full light. Water plentifully during the growing period from May to September, reducing the amount of water when the leaves have dried off. Allow only sufficient moisture to prevent shrinkage of the pseudobulbs during the resting period from October to April. Ventilate the house on mild days throughout the year, and repot every two or three years in spring.

Propagation. Divide and pot up in the growing mixture from March to May.

Pests. Generally trouble-free.

Diseases. Mosaic patterns of light green against a darker background are caused by a VIRUS DISEASE.

Lychnis
Campion. *Caryophyllaceae*

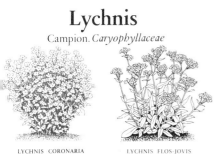

LYCHNIS CORONARIA   LYCHNIS FLOS-JOVIS

A genus of 12 species of hardy and half-hardy annuals and herbaceous perennials. The following hardy perennials are suitable for growing at the front of borders and for cutting; the smaller species are excellent for rock gardens or as edgings. The flowers are salver-shaped with inflated or tubular calyces.

L. alpina. Europe, Siberia, Labrador. Height and planting distance 4 in. This true alpine species is now classified as *Viscaria alpina*. It forms a tuft of dark green linear leaves from which the flowers rise in oblong heads, about 2 in. long, from May to July. These are usually deep rose, but the colour is variable.

'Alba' is a white form; 'Rosea' is deep pink.

Lychnis flos-jovis

L. × arkwrightii. Height 12 in.; planting distance 9–12 in. A hybrid between *L. chalcedonica* and *L. × haageana*. The mid-green leaves are variable in shape, mainly oblong-lanceolate and sometimes tinted purple. Brilliant scarlet-orange flowers, 1½–2 in. across, appear from June to August.

L. chalcedonica. East Russia. Height 2–3 ft; planting distance 12–15 in. This species, possibly one of the most brilliant scarlet herbaceous plants, has mid-green lanceolate leaves. Small bright scarlet flowers shaped like a Maltese cross are borne in dense flattened heads, 3–5 in. across, in July and August.

L. coeli-rosa: see *Silene coeli-rosa*

L. coronaria, syn. *Agrostemma coronaria.* S. Europe. Height up to 24 in.; planting distance 9–12 in. A short-lived perennial with branching stems and silver-grey, woolly, ovate to lanceolate leaves. Single bright crimson-magenta or white flowers, 1½ in. across, are freely produced from July to September.

L. flos-jovis. Europe. Height up to 24 in.; planting distance 9–12 in. The stems and the lanceolate thick leaves of this perennial species are silvery or grey. Purple or red flowers, ½ in. across, appear from June to August and are borne in a loose rounded inflorescence.

L. × haageana. Height 9–12 in.; planting distance 8 in. A hybrid with ovate, lanceolate, mid-green leaves that are sometimes flushed with purple. Orange or scarlet flowers, 2 in. across, appear in June and July.

L. viscaria. Europe, Siberia, Japan. Height 12 in.; planting distance 12–15 in. This species is now known as *Viscaria vulgaris*. It bears ¼–¼ in. wide carmine flowers in an ovoid spike in May and June. The double form 'Splendens Plena' is more frequently grown.

Cultivation. Lychnis will grow in any ordinary, well-drained garden soil, in sun or light shade. Plant from October to March, or in May if raised from seeds sown early in the year. Taller plants in exposed positions may need the support of twiggy sticks. Dead-head all species, particularly *L. coronaria,* to prevent self-seeding. Remove dead stems in autumn or spring, and mulch annually in March with peat or manure.

Lychnis chalcedonica

Lychnis coronaria

Lychnis × haageana

Lychnis viscaria
'Splendens Plena'

Lysichiton americanum

Lysichiton camtschatcense

Lysimachia ephemerum

Propagation. Sow seeds in pots or boxes of seed compost in a cold frame during May or June. With the exception of *L. alpina*, prick off the seedlings, when large enough to handle, directly into nursery rows, and plant out from October onwards. Pot the seedlings of *L. alpina* into 3 in. containers of John Innes potting compost No. 1, and plunge outdoors until October. ·

The short-lived *L. coronaria* may be treated as an annual; sow the seeds in February in a greenhouse at a temperature of 13–16°C (55–61°F). Prick off the seedlings into boxes of John Innes potting compost No. 2; harden off in a cold frame and plant out in the flowering positions in May. Alternatively, sow seeds in the flowering site in August or September and thin to the required planting distances.

Basal cuttings, $1\frac{1}{2}$–3 in. long, can be taken during April or May from all species and hybrids. Insert in equal parts (by volume) peat and sand in a cold frame and line out in nursery rows when rooted. *L. alpina* is best potted and treated as recommended for seedlings.

Pests. APHIDS and FROGHOPPERS may attack flowering shoots.

Diseases. Mottling of the leaves of *L. chalcedonica* may be caused by a VIRUS DISEASE.

Lycopersicon esculentum: see Tomato

Lysichiton

Araceae

LYSICHITON AMERICANUM

A genus, sometimes called *Lysichitum,* of two species of hardy herbaceous perennials. They are plants for growing in wet ground alongside natural ponds or in the margins of artificial pools. They both flower between March and early May, producing arum-like flowers with striking spathes. The massive foliage appears later. Specialist growers usually stock two or three-year-old specimens, which normally commence flowering two or three years later.

L. americanum (skunk cabbage). Canada and N. United States. Height 2–4 ft; planting distance 24 in. A completely hardy and long-lived perennial which slowly forms a large clump of several fleshy rootstocks. These may be 24 in. long, and are mostly below soil level. The massive leaves, $1\frac{1}{2}$–3 ft long, are elongated ovate in shape, with pointed tips and long sheath-like stalks. The leaf blade is grass green, leathery in texture and with a light sheen, while the stalk is soft, rubbery and white to brown. The flowers consist of a clear deep golden-yellow open spathe, 9–18 in. high, enclosing a thick green spadix.

Seeds are freely set. Mature seed heads may be 6–9 in. long and 2–3 in. thick, the seeds ripening by July or early August.

L. camtschatcense. Kamchatka. Height 2–3 ft; planting distance 18–24 in. Similar in general form and habit to *L. americanum*, but smaller. The leaves are glaucous green, and the flower spathes are pure white; they do not seed freely.

Cultivation. These plants do best in deep soil which is rich in humus and well provided with moisture. If planted in the margin of an artificial pool, rich loam should be used to prepare the planting position. This must have a total depth of at least 12 in. and be built up to water level. Plant lysichitons in full sun or partial shade.

Plant out two or three-year-old specimens between April and June, preferably from pots as the roots are harmed by disturbance and frequently die if they are severed. No other cultivation is required for plants grown in pools.

Propagation. Sow the seeds when ripe or as soon as purchased. Sow $\frac{1}{4}$ in. deep in boxes of John Innes seed compost, kept saturated by standing in water. Prick out the seedlings into a nursery bed in wet soil; or prick out into 3 in. pots containing a rich loamy compost, and pot on as necessary. The plants should be ready for planting in their permanent positions in two or three years. Alternatively, sow in the open ground in a lightly shaded position in rich moist soil, spacing the seeds 1 in. apart. Transplant to the permanent site when the rootstock is about a finger's thickness.

It is also possible to propagate by division: remove the young plants which form around the base of old rhizomes and pot these into 4–6 in. pots using a rich loamy compost. Keep watered and shaded until planting out.

Pests and diseases. Generally trouble-free.

Lysichitum: see Lysichiton

Lysimachia

Primulaceae

A genus of 200 species of mainly herbaceous perennials, but including a few sub-shrubs. The herbaceous perennials described here are hardy plants suitable for borders with moist soil; *L. nummularia* is useful for covering old stonework, unsightly wet banks and the edges of ornamental pools. They are all easy to grow, but with the exception of *L. ephemerum* can be invasive.

LYSIMACHIA CLETHROIDES

L. clethroides. China, Japan. Height 3 ft; planting distance 18 in. The leaves are lanceolate and usually mid-green, often turning orange or red in autumn. Small, white, star-shaped flowers are carried from July to September, massed in 4–6 in. long arching spikes.

L. ephemerum. S.W. Europe. Height 3 ft; planting distance 18 in. A species with narrowly oblong-lanceolate, smooth, grey-green leaves

Lysimachia nummularia

Lysimachia clethroides

Small, star-shaped, white flowers, often tinged with purple, are carried in spikes about 12 in. long in July and August.

LYSIMACHIA NUMMULARIA

L. nummularia (moneywort, creeping jenny). Europe, including Great Britain. Planting distance 9–18 in. A vigorous trailing waterside plant, adaptable to growing in dry soil. It is evergreen and provides excellent ground cover. The prostrate stems bear rounded, mid-green leaves; single, bright yellow cup-shaped flowers, ¾ in. across, appear in June and July. 'Aurea' is similar to the type, but with yellow leaves.

LYSIMACHIA PUNCTATA

L. punctata. S.E. Europe. Height 2–3 ft; planting distance 18 in. A long-lived invasive species with broadly lanceolate, mid-green leaves. Whorls of bright yellow, cup-shaped flowers, are borne in 6–8 in. spikes from June to August.
Cultivation. Plant from October to April in ordinary, moist garden soil, in sun or partial

shade. A soil depth of 2 in. is sufficient for *L. nummularia* grown in the margins of ornamental pools; for edging a pool, set the plants a few inches from the pool's rim with the shoots growing towards the water.

Staking is not usually required, but in rich soils the lower stems of tall species may need support with twiggy sticks. Cut down in late autumn.
Propagation. Divide and replant at any time between October and March.

L. nummularia may also be increased from 3–4 in. lengths of stem taken in April or September and planted directly in the flowering site.
Pests and diseases. Generally trouble-free.

Lythrum

Lythraceae

LYTHRUM SALICARIA

A genus of about 35 species, mainly herbaceous perennials but including some annuals and small shrubs. Two hardy herbaceous perennials, *L. salicaria* and *L. virgatum*, though seldom grown, have given rise to varieties that are extremely adaptable to a wide range of conditions and will grow almost anywhere except in full shade. The small flowers are roughly star-shaped and densely carried in spire-like racemes.
L. salicaria (purple loosestrife). Northern temperate zones, including Great Britain; Australia. Height 2–5 ft; planting distance 18 in. The leaves are mid-green and lanceolate. Small red-purple flowers are closely packed in 9–12 in. long spires, from June to September.

Recommended varieties include: 'Dropmore', purple; 'Lady Sackville', bright rose-pink; 'Robert', bright rose-red; 'The Beacon', deep rose-crimson in very dense spikes.
L. virgatum. E. Europe. Height 2–3 ft; planting distance 18 in. This species closely resembles *L. salicaria*, but is a more slender plant. Two good garden varieties are 'Rose Queen', rose-pink and 'The Rocket', deep rose-pink.
Cultivation. Plant in ordinary garden soil in sun or semi-shade in October, or from February to April. These plants thrive in a damp or wet position in semi-shade near water, but they grow well in ordinary garden soil. Cut back in autumn.
Propagation. Divide the roots in October or April.

Named varieties do not come true from seed, but mixed seed is usually available. Sow in April in a cold frame or greenhouse at a temperature of 16°C (61°F). Prick off the seedlings when large enough to handle. Grow on the young plants in nursery rows until the following autumn.

Insert 2–3 in. long basal cuttings, in April, in equal parts (by volume) peat and sand in a cold frame. When rooted, treat as seedlings.
Pests and diseases. Generally trouble-free.

Lysimachia punctata

Lythrum salicaria 'Lady Sackville'

Lythrum virgatum 'Rose Queen'

M

Macleaya
Plume poppy. *Papaveraceae*

A genus of two species of hardy herbaceous perennials, formerly included in *Bocconia*. These can be invasive plants, spreading by means of underground suckers. They are not recommended for small borders but can be useful at the back of a large border or in beds. They produce tiny flowers in large, plume-like panicles.

M. cordata, syn. *Bocconia cordata*. China, Japan. Height 5–8 ft; planting distance 3 ft. The lower part of the stem has large, deeply lobed leaves, bronze above and grey beneath. Plumes, 3 ft long, of small pearly white flowers cover the top half of the stem from June to August. This species is often confused with *M. microcarpa*.

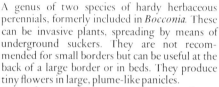

MACLEAYA CORDATA

M. microcarpa, syn. *Bocconia microcarpa*. China. Height 5–8 ft; planting distance 3 ft. This species is similar to *M. cordata*, but the flowers are smaller, pink outside and bronze inside, they are produced two or three weeks earlier. 'Coral Plume' is pinker than the species.

Cultivation. Plant from October to March in a sunny but sheltered position and in deep loamy soil. Support the stems with twiggy sticks when about half-grown, although this is seldom necessary for *M. cordata*. Remove the flower heads after blooming and cut down the stems in autumn.

Propagation. Divide and replant the roots from October to March.

Detach and replant the outer shoots, each with a root attached, in April; or take cuttings, 2–3 in. long, of basal shoots and root in April in a cold frame in a mixture of equal parts (by volume) peat and sand. In both cases grow the plants on in a nursery bed before planting out in October.

Pests and diseases. Generally trouble-free.

Macrotomia echioides: see *Arnebia echioides*
Madroña: see *Arbutus menziesii*

Magnolia
Magnoliaceae

A genus of 80 species of hardy evergreen and deciduous flowering trees and shrubs. It contains some of the most spectacular specimen trees and shrubs, *M. denudata* and *M.* × *soulangeana* being particularly outstanding. The spring-flowering species may have the blooms damaged by frost, and should be planted in sheltered sites. They are frequently grown as wall shrubs.

M. conspicua: see *M. denudata*
M. denudata, syn. *M. conspicua*. China. Height and spread 10–15 ft. This deciduous, slow-growing tree has mid-green ovate leaves that are white and downy beneath. Fragrant, white chalice-shaped flowers, 5–6 in. across, are borne in profusion from March to May.

MAGNOLIA GRANDIFLORA

M. grandiflora. Bull Bay in S.E. United States. Height 10–15 ft; spread 6–10 ft. The mid to dark green glossy leaves of this evergreen tree are ovate and leathery, with a rust-coloured felt beneath that is particularly noticeable on young foliage. Cream-white fragrant flowers, bowl-shaped and 4–8 in. across, appear from July to September. Best grown as a wall shrub.

M. kobus: see *M. stellata*
M. liliiflora, syn. *M. obovata*. Japan. Height 6–8 ft; spread 5–7 ft. The ovate deciduous leaves are mid-green above, paler beneath. Red-purple chalice-shaped flowers, 3–4 in. across, open from April to July. 'Nigra', syn. *M.* × *soulangeana* 'Nigra', has slightly darker and larger flowers.

M. × *loebneri*. Height 15–20 ft; spread 6–12 ft. This deciduous hybrid tree has lanceolate leaves that are mid-green above, paler beneath. White fragrant, star-shaped flowers, 3–4 in. across, are produced profusely during March and early April.

M. obovata: see *M. liliiflora*
M. parviflora: see *M. sieboldii*
M. salicifolia. Japan. Height up to 20 ft; spread up to 10 ft. The lanceolate, deciduous leaves are mid-green above, paler beneath. Star-shaped white flowers, 3–4 in. across, open in April before the leaves expand. One of the fastest-growing magnolias, of erect pyramidal habit.

M. sieboldii, syn. *M. parviflora*. Japan, Korea. Height and spread 10–15 ft. The deciduous, dark green leaves are lanceolate and downy underneath. The pendent, bowl-shaped flowers, 3 in. across, are white with conspicuous claret stamens, and are carried from May to August. The pink seed capsules are decorative and open in October to show orange-coloured seeds. This shrub or small tree is not lime-tolerant.

M. × *soulangeana*. Height 10–15 ft; spread 10–18 ft. This deciduous hybrid tree has mid-green leaves that are broadly lanceolate, and somewhat downy underneath. White, chalice-shaped flowers, 5–6 in. across and stained rose-purple at the base, open in April before the

Macleaya microcarpa

Magnolia grandiflora

Magnolia liliiflora 'Nigra'

Magnolia salicifolia

Magnolia sieboldii

leaves unfurl. There are several named varieties, including: 'Alexandrina', with erect flowers flushed claret-rose at the base; 'Lennei', with more rounded, rose-purple flowers that are white within; and 'Picture', of Japanese origin, with purple flowers, 6 in. across.

M. × soulangeana 'Nigra': see *M. liliiflora* 'Nigra'.

MAGNOLIA STELLATA

M. stellata, now known to be a dwarf mutant form of *M. kobus*. Japan. Height 8–10 ft; spread 8–12 ft. A slow-growing deciduous tree with pale to mid-green lanceolate leaves. The white, star-shaped, fragrant flowers are 3–4 in. across and appear in March and April. 'Rosea' has pink flowers and 'Royal Star' has larger blooms with more petals.

Cultivation. Plant in March or April in well-drained loamy soil in a site sheltered from north and east winds. Support the plants with stakes for the first few years and during this time top-dress each April with leaf-mould, peat or compost.

Propagation. Sow seeds in October, as soon as they ripen, in pans containing a peaty compost and place these in a cold frame. Germination may take 12–18 months. When the seedlings are large enough to handle, plant them directly into a nursery bed outdoors, or pot them singly into 3 in. containers of John Innes potting compost No. 1 and keep in the frame or in a plunge bed. Grow on for three or four years before planting them out in their final positions.

Take 4 in. heel cuttings of half-ripened shoots in July and insert them in coarse sand in a propagating frame at a temperature of 21°C (70°F). Pot the rooted cuttings in 3 in. pots and overwinter them in a cold frame. Plant in a

nursery bed the following April or May and leave them there for two or three years before planting out in permanent positions.

Magnolias may be layered in March or April. It takes up to two years for the layers to root.

Pruning. No pruning is necessary. However, if *M. grandiflora* is being trained against a wall, remove forward-facing shoots from the base in April.

Pests. Generally trouble-free.

Diseases. The buds may turn brown because of FROST DAMAGE, which causes the shoots to die back. Affected tissues are frequently attacked by GREY MOULD, which shows as a brown-grey coating, and which may cause further die-back.

HONEY FUNGUS causes the death of plants.

LEAF SPOT shows as irregular pale spots on the leaves of *M. grandiflora*.

Mahonia

Berberidaceae

A genus of 70 species of hardy evergreen shrubs, grown for their attractive foliage and yellow bell-shaped or globular flowers, which are borne in late winter or early spring. All species produce purple or blue-black berries, those of *M. aquifolium* and *M. japonica*, with their hybrids, being particularly effective. They may be grown as specimen shrubs, and certain dwarf species are useful as ground cover, especially in shade. The foliage may be used for winter decoration.

MAHONIA AQUIFOLIUM

M. aquifolium (Oregon grape). W. North America. Height 3–5 ft; spread 5–6 ft. A suckering shrub with glossy, dark green, leathery

Magnolia × soulangeana

Magnolia stellata

Mahonia aquifolium

Mahonia lomariifolia

Malcolmia maritima 'Dwarf Mixed'

leaves. Each leaf is composed of five to nine spine-toothed leaflets. Fragrant rich yellow flowers are borne in numerous dense clusters, 3–5 in. across, in March and April, and are followed by tight bunches of blue-black berries. This species is useful for ground cover in sun or shade; it is tolerant of wind and suitable for an exposed site. The variety 'Atropurpurea' has leaves which turn rich red-purple in winter.

M. bealei. China. Height and spread 6–8 ft. An upright shrub whose leaves consist of broad-based leathery leaflets; they are grey-green above, yellow-green beneath. Lemon-yellow flowers in stiffly erect racemes, 4–6 in. long, are produced in clusters at the tips of the stems from December to February.

Mahonia × 'Charity'

M. × **'Charity'.** Garden origin. Height 8–10 ft; spread 6–8 ft. A hybrid between *M. japonica* and *M. lomariifolia.* The leaves comprise numerous lanceolate, spine-toothed, dark green leaflets. Fragrant deep yellow flowers are borne in ascending racemes, 9–12 in. long, at the tips of the stems from November to February.

M. japonica. China. Height 8–10 ft; spread 8–12 ft. The glossy, dark green, pinnate, oblong leaves comprise numerous leathery leaflets, ovate to oblong and spine-toothed. Lemon-yellow flowers, with lily-of-the-valley scent, are borne in drooping racemes, 6–9 in. long, from the tips of the stems from January to March. This reliable, winter-flowering shrub is often incorrectly offered as *M. bealei.*

MAHONIA LOMARIIFOLIA

M. lomariifolia. China and Formosa. Height 10–12 ft; spread 6 ft. This species is suitable only for sheltered gardens in the south and west. The dark green, pinnate, oblong leaves, up to 24 in. long, are composed of 15–20 pairs of narrow rigid leaflets. Deep yellow fragrant flowers appear in dense erect racemes, 6–10 in. high, from January to March.

M. pinnata. S.W. United States. Height 8–10 ft; spread 6–8 ft. A vigorous species best grown in an open site. The sea-green, oblong pinnate leaves comprise several strongly spined leaflets. Rich yellow, slightly fragrant flowers are borne in clusters, 2–4 in. across, in March and April.

Cultivation. Plant mahonias, preferably during September and October or April and May, in sun or partial shade and in any good garden soil. The large-leaved species thrive in a moist, leafy soil with a little light shade. Many species take some time to settle down after planting, but once established need little attention.

Propagation. For ground cover, the species are best raised from seeds; collect the seeds as soon as ripe (usually in August) and sow in pans of John Innes seed compost and place in a cold frame. The seeds should have germinated by the following April; when large enough to handle, prick off the seedlings into boxes and later into nursery rows. Grow on for another year or two before moving to permanent positions.

Alternatively, increase species and named forms by cuttings. Take tip cuttings, 3–4 in. long, of leading shoots or of strong lateral growths in July, or take leaf cuttings of the large-leaved species in October or November. Root the cuttings in equal parts (by volume) peat and sand in a propagating case with a bottom heat of 16–18°C (61–64°F). When rooted, pot the cuttings in 3½ in. pots of John Innes potting compost No. 2 and overwinter in a frost-free frame. Pot on as necessary and grow on for a further year before transplanting.

Pruning. No regular pruning is required, but *M. aquifolium* may be pruned hard back annually in April if it is grown as low ground cover.

Pests. Generally trouble-free.

Diseases. LEAF SPOT shows as brown spots in which pin-point black fruiting bodies can be seen.

POWDERY MILDEW produces a white powdery covering on young leaves and shoots.

RUST shows as small red spots on the upper leaf surfaces; on the undersides, powdery masses of brown spores appear.

Maidenhair tree: see Ginkgo
Maize: see Sweet corn

Malcolmia

Cruciferae

MALCOLMIA MARITIMA

A genus of 35 species of herbaceous plants, mostly annual. The most common species is Virginian stock, a low-growing plant used in drifts in borders and for edging.

M. maritima (Virginian stock). S. Mediterranean. Height 8 in. A showy hardy annual with blunt, elliptic, grey-green leaves. The red, lilac, rose or white cross-shaped flowers are $\frac{1}{2}$ in. across and carried on slender stems; they are sweetly scented. Flowering begins about four weeks after sowing and continues for six to eight weeks.

Many varieties are listed, including 'Dwarf Mixed', 6 in., and separate colours such as 'Red', 12 in., and 'Yellow', 10 in.

Cultivation. These plants will grow in practically any soil and site, but an open sunny position gives the best results. Self-sown plants occur in great numbers if the soil is left undisturbed.

Propagation. Sow the seeds thinly in the flowering site, making successional sowings from March to late July, and again in September for plants to flower in April. Rake the seeds into the soil so that they are just covered.

Pests and diseases. Generally trouble-free.

Mallow: see Malva and Lavatera
Mallow, jew's: see Kerria
Mallow, musk: see *Malva moschata*
Mallow, tree: see *Lavatera arborea*

Malope
Malvaceae

MALOPE TRIFIDA

A genus of four species of annual plants. The species described is popular for general garden planting in annual and mixed borders; it is free flowering and lasts well in water when cut.

M. trifida. Spain. Height 3 ft; spacing 9 in. A hardy annual of bushy growth, with erect, branching stems. The mid-green leaves are slightly lobed. The widely trumpet-shaped flowers, 2–3 in. across, are rose-purple with petals attractively veined in a deeper colour. They are borne in clusters from June to September.

This species is usually represented in cultivation by the large-flowered and more free-flowering *M. t. grandiflora* and its varieties 'Alba', white, and 'Rosea', pink.

Cultivation. A light soil and sunny situation are best, although nearly all soils give satisfactory results. Self-sown seedlings occur if the surrounding soil is left undisturbed.

Propagation. Sow the seeds in the flowering site in March or April, just covering them. Thin out the seedlings to the required spacing.

Pests and diseases. Generally trouble-free.

Malus
Crab apple. Rosaceae

A genus of 35 species of hardy deciduous flowering and fruit-bearing trees or shrubs, which include the parents of the great range of edible apples (see entry under APPLE).

The species and varieties described here are those commonly known as crab apples; although they are chiefly grown for ornamental purposes, the fruits may be used for making preserves. These trees are normally grown as standards on $3\frac{1}{2}$–6 ft stems; as bushes they are less effective and require too much space for the average suburban garden.

Although self-fertile, pollination and consequently heavier cropping is more assured if several varieties with overlapping flowering periods are grown together. The trees are suitable for growing in shrub borders or as specimen trees.

The bowl-shaped, five-petalled and slightly fragrant flowers, with golden stamens, are borne in clusters at the ends of lateral spurs. They appear at the same time as the young foliage expands. As they mature, the flowers gradually fade in colour. The round or shortly ovoid apple-like fruits, 1–2 in. long, which ripen in September and October, range in colour through green and yellow, flushed with red or purple.

The species are largely superseded in cultivation by hybrids, which unless otherwise stated, are of garden origin.

MALUS × PURPUREA

M. × atrosanguinea. Height 12–15 ft; spread 10–15 ft. This is a round-headed, densely branched, spreading tree with ovate mid-green leaves. Single bright carmine flowers, 1 in. across, are borne in mid-May. The small yellow fruits have a red flush.

M. coronaria 'Charlottae'. N. America. Height 15–18 ft; spread 10–20 ft. A broad-headed variety with ovate, serrated, mid-green leaves that are attractively tinted with orange and yellow in autumn. Semi-double, delicately scented, flesh-pink flowers, $1\frac{1}{2}$–2 in. across, are borne at the end of May, when the foliage is fully developed. The globular and ribbed fruits, green to yellow, are acid and not particularly attractive.

M. 'Dartmouth'. Height 15–20 ft; spread 8–10 ft. This variety bears ovate mid-green leaves and pure white flowers, $1\frac{1}{2}$ in. across. The large plum-shaped fruits are deep crimson-purple.

M. 'Echtermeyer', syn. *M. × purpurea pendula*. A weeping variety, whose drooping branches reach to ground level; it makes a fine specimen tree. The ovate leaves are mid-green, flushed with purple. Single pale pink flowers, 1 in. across, appear in May. The fruits are purple.

M. × eleyi. Height 20–25 ft; spread 15–20 ft. A broad-headed hybrid with dark red to purple ovate leaves. Clusters of single flowers, 1 in. wide, are deep red-purple and appear in April. The conical fruits are red-purple.

M. floribunda. Japan. Height 12–15 ft; spread 10–15 ft. A round-headed, densely branched, spreading species with mid-green, narrowly ovate and coarsely toothed leaves. Single flowers, 1 in. wide, are freely borne in May; the bright

Malope trifida grandiflora

Malus × eleyi

Malus floribunda

Malus 'John Downie'

Malus × lemoinei

Malus 'Golden Hornet'

Malus hupehensis

carmine buds fade to pale pink soon after opening. They are followed by yellow fruits.

M. 'Golden Hornet'. Height 15–18 ft; spread 10–15 ft. A strong-growing, open, erect tree, with pale green ovate leaves. Single, $\frac{3}{4}$ in. wide, white flowers appear in May. Outstanding crops of bright yellow fruits persist long after the foliage has fallen. This is one of the best of the yellow-fruiting crab apples.

M. × **hillieri**. Height 15–20 ft; spread 8–10 ft. A late-flowering tree with ovate, glossy mid-green leaves. The buds, freely produced on the arching branches in May, open to bright pink semi-double flowers, 1 in. wide. The fruits are scarlet.

M. hupehensis, syn. *Pyrus theifera*. China, Japan. Height 25–30 ft; spread 15–20 ft. A vigorous species, with stiff, spreading branches that carry thick, deep green, ovate and sharply serrated leaves. Single, white, fragrant flowers, tinged with rose-pink and 1–1$\frac{1}{4}$ in. wide, are borne in May and June. Red-tinted yellow fruits are freely produced. 'Rosea' has pink flowers.

M. 'John Downie'. Height 25–30 ft; spread 15–25 ft. An erect tree, wide-spreading with age. The bright mid-green leaves are ovate. Single white flowers, 1–1$\frac{1}{4}$ in. wide, open in May. They are followed by conical yellow fruits, flushed with crimson, which are excellent for preserves. This variety is susceptible to apple scab.

M. 'Katherine'. Height 10–15 ft; spread 6–10 ft. This variety is an erect tree that spreads slightly with age. The leaves are ovate and mid-green. A profusion of semi-double 1$\frac{1}{2}$–2 in. wide flowers appear in mid-May; they are deep pink in bud opening to near white. The fruits are bright red, flushed yellow.

M. × **lemoinei**. Height 15–20 ft; spread 12–20 ft. A broad-headed hybrid with ovate purple leaves that take on a bronze tinge in late summer and autumn. Massed single flowers, purple-crimson

and 1–1$\frac{1}{2}$ in. across, are freely produced in April and May. The fruits are purple-bronze.

M. 'Profusion'. Height 15–20 ft; spread 8–15 ft. An upright variety of open habit. The ovate leaves are mid-green, tinted with purple. Single flowers, 1–1$\frac{1}{2}$ in. across, are borne profusely in mid-May; they are deep red in bud, opening to purple-red with a light pink centre. The small, oval, red fruits are freely produced.

M. pumila 'Niedzwetzkyana'. Caucasus. Height 25–30 ft; spread 15–25 ft. A vigorous open-branched tree with deep green ovate leaves that are flushed with purple. Single purple-red flowers, 1 in. wide, are produced in early May, followed by conical red to dull purple fruits. This form has been much used in hybridisation, producing some of the finest shades of red in foliage, flowers and fruit.

M. × **purpurea**. Height 20–25 ft; spread 10–18 ft. An upright, early-flowering hybrid, slightly spreading with age; the ovate mid-green leaves are flushed with purple. Single purple flowers, 1 in. wide, are borne profusely in late April. The ovoid fruits are small and dull purple.

M. × *p. pendula*: see *M.* 'Echtermeyer'.

M. 'Red Sentinel'. Height 10–15 ft; spread 8–13 ft. This tree has slightly arching branches with ovate mid-green leaves. The single, white, 1 in. wide flowers are produced in mid-May. Large crops of glossy, bright scarlet fruits persist on the tree until March.

M. sargentii. Japan. Height 6–8 ft; spread 8–10 ft. This small species bears glossy mid-green leaves that are ovate to three-lobed. The flowers are single, $\frac{3}{4}$ in. wide, and appear in mid-May; the pink-tinted buds open to white blossoms with overlapping petals and yellow stamens. The small fruits have a bright red flush.

M. tschonoskii. Japan. Height 30–35 ft; spread 6–10 ft. An erect species of pyramidal shape. The

Malus 'Yellow Siberian'

broadly ovate mid-green leaves are felted with grey hairs beneath, and the shoots are downy. Single, white, pink-tinted flowers, 1 in. wide, appear in May. The dull red fruits, flushed yellow, are not showy and soon fall off, but the red and yellow autumn foliage is attractive.

MALUS TSCHONOSKII

M. 'Yellow Siberian'. Height 10–15 ft; spread 8–12 ft. A variety with mid-green ovate leaves; single white flowers, about 1½ in. across, appear in April and May. Cherry-like, bright deep yellow fruits are borne on long stalks. They often persist well into winter.

Cultivation. Crab apples thrive in any ordinary, well-drained garden soil, preferably enriched with well-rotted compost or manure. Plant during suitable weather from October to March in sun or partial shade; standard trees require staking in the early years until established.

No feeding is required, but a light annual mulch in April of well-rotted manure is beneficial in the first years of growth. Specimen trees grown in lawns should have a grass-free root run of 3–4 ft for several years until well established.

Propagation. The species usually come true from seeds, but seed-raised trees take up to ten years or more to reach flowering size.

All hybrids and varieties must be budded in July and August, or grafted in March, on to seedling apple stocks or rootstocks of 'Malling II', 'Malling-Merton III' or 'Malling XXV'

Pruning. No regular pruning is required; dead and straggly shoots should be removed in February. Maiden trees need formative pruning: the leading shoot of a bush tree should be cut back to within 18–24 in. of ground level in March; the following March cut back all lateral shoots to 12 in., after which little or no pruning should be necessary.

To create a standard tree, cut the main stem back to 6 in. above the desired trunk height in March. The resulting three or four shoots should be cut back to 12 in. the following March. Any shoots that arise on the stem below the top branches should be pinched back to three or four leaves. Any further feathering shoots should be pinched back during the summer. Do not remove these spurs for at least two years, as they help to thicken the trunk.

Pests. APHIDS of various species may infest young shoots, leaves and fruit; WOOLLY APHIDS may infest branches and twigs, covering them with conspicuous tufts of white waxy wool and encouraging the growth of disfiguring galls.

CAPSID BUGS pierce the tissues of young buds, leaves and fruit, causing distortions and a characteristic tattering of the leaves; the buds may fail to develop.

CATERPILLARS of several different species of moth feed on the leaves and young buds.

FRUIT TREE RED SPIDER MITES attack the undersides of the leaves which, in severe infestations, turn bronze, wither and fall.

The larvae of CODLING MOTH and APPLE SAWFLY sometimes burrow into the core of fruits.

Diseases. With the possible exception of bitter pit, crab apples are subject to the same diseases as cultivated apples. The following are the ones most likely to occur on ornamental species:

At bud-break in spring, APPLE MILDEW may appear; it shows as a white powdery deposit on the emerging growths and spreads to later-developing leaves; severely diseased foliage withers and falls.

APPLE SCAB produces brown or black scabs on the fruits. Olive-green blotches appear on the leaves, which frequently fall prematurely. On the shoots, small blister-like pimples develop; these later crack the bark and show as ring-like scabs.

HONEY FUNGUS may cause trees to die rapidly.

Malva

Mallow. *Malvaceae*

MALVA ALCEA

A genus of 40 species of annuals and perennials, closely allied to *Lavatera*. Most species are too coarse for general cultivation, but the following border perennials are hardy, easily grown, and excellent on poor soils. They bear broadly funnel-shaped flowers in spire-like racemes.

Malus sargentii

Malva alcea 'Fastigiata'

Malva alcea

Mammillaria erythrosperma (fruits)

Malva moschata 'Alba'

Mammillaria bocasana

Mammillaria densispina

M. alcea. Europe. Height 4 ft; planting distance 18–24 in. The light green leaves are lobed and toothed. Spikes of mauve-pink flowers, 1½–2 in. across, appear from July to October. The variety *M. a.* 'Fastigiata' is more upright, reaching only 3 ft, with satin-pink flowers.

M. moschata (musk mallow). Europe, including Great Britain. Height 24 in.; planting distance 18 in. The deeply cut and lobed mid-green leaves give off a musky smell when crushed. Spikes of rose-pink flowers, 2 in. across, open from June to September. *M. m.* 'Alba' has white flowers.

Cultivation. Plant from October to March in sun or in a partly shaded position in ordinary garden soil. On rich, moist soil, staking with twiggy sticks may be needed. The plants are long-lived in poor, dry soils. Cut down the stems in autumn.

Propagation. Sow seeds in March or April in a cold frame or greenhouse at a temperature of 16°C (61°F). Prick out the seedlings and grow the young plants on in a nursery bed before planting in the flowering site in October.

Alternatively, take 3 in. long cuttings of basal shoots and insert in sandy soil in a cold frame in April. Plant the rooted cuttings out in their flowering positions from October to March.

Pests. Generally trouble-free.

Diseases. The leaves, stems and fruits are affected by RUST which shows as raised spore-bearing pustules, orange at first, later turning to brown.

Mammillaria

Cactaceae

A genus of more than 200 species of greenhouse perennials. These cacti are grown not only for their flowers but also for their beautiful spines. The flowers are chiefly purple-red or cream, the cream-flowered species blooming at an earlier age than the red. The open, bell-shaped flowers are small, about ½ in. across, and grow in a ring on the top of the plant from the axils of the tubercles. Cylindrical fruits sometimes occur.

The globular or cylindrical spiny bodies are small, and the tubercles are arranged spirally, not in ribs. In some species, such as *M. elegans*, the sap is milky. Many species form offsets or spread into clumps, but a few are solitary.

See also CACTUS.

M. bocasana. Mexico. Height 6 in. This is one of the easiest species to grow and flower. It is a clustering blue-green plant, with a body about 2 in. across, covered with fine white spines and silky hairs. A longer yellow or red hooked spine from the centre of each areole projects beyond the white covering. Cream flowers are produced in June followed by purple berries. If left undisturbed, this cactus will eventually form cushion-like clumps, 5–6 in. across.

M. densispina. Mexico. Height 6 in. A dark green round or cylindrical plant, easy but slow growing. The prominent, cone-shaped tubercles bear 25 yellow radial spines which cover the body. Each areole bears two larger, brown central spines. Purple-red flowers are borne in summer.

M. elegans. Mexico. Height up to 8 in. A slow-growing species; the young plants are solitary, older ones may branch. The plant body is cylindrical and pale green with close-set tubercles. From each areole, 20 short white spines grow radially to cover the body. Two longer central spines, white with brown tips, project from each areole beyond the white covering. The flowers are violet-red and produced in July and August.

M. erythrosperma. Mexico. Height 2 in. A freely clustering plant, which soon forms a cushion. The individual globular plant bodies have glossy spines and three or four yellow central spines, one of which is hooked. Deep pink flowers, produced in summer, are followed by red fruits, which resemble tiny, slender figs.

M. gracilis. Mexico. Height 2 in. A freely clustering plant branching at the top. The slender cylindrical stems are bright green and covered with a network of short white radial spines and longer, brown-tipped central spines. White flowers are produced during summer.

M. plumosa. Mexico. Height 2–3 in. This attractive, slow-growing plant clusters freely.

he deep green globular bodies are completely idden by feathery white spines.

It is a difficult plant to flower and is grown for ts feathery spines. The small white flowers nay be produced in December.

M. umbrina. Mexico. Height 4 in. One of the few ed-flowered mammillarias that will bloom when quite young. As a young plant it is solitary, but it orms clusters with age. The cylindrical dark green body is depressed at the crown. The areoles on the long, conical tubercles bear 25 white lender radial spines and at least four thick central pines which are deep red. The plant bears armine flowers in June and July.

M. zeilmanniana. Mexico. Height 2 in. A cluster-ng plant with pale green, glossy and globular oodies. The tubercles are closely set and their areoles bear 18 white marginal spines and four prown central spines, one of which is hooked. A large number of deep violet-red flowers, about $\frac{3}{4}$ in. across, are borne in June and July.

Cultivation. Mammillarias need an open com-post, such as 2 parts John Innes potting compost No. 2 and 1 part grit or sharp sand (parts by volume). Grow them in 3–6 in. pots, according to their size. During summer, water freely, but do not let water accumulate on the plants; this may cause them to rot from the centre. They thrive n full sun. In winter, withhold water complete-y and keep at a minimum temperature of 5°C 41°F). Repot annually in April.

Propagation. Sow seeds in April or May at a emperature of 21°C (70°F). Clustering species an also be increased by removing individual plant bodies between May and August. Dry them or two or three days, and then pot the pieces up n the growing compost.

Pests. Colonies of MEALY BUGS produce conspicu-ous tufts of white waxy wool on plants. ROOT MEALY BUGS may infest roots and check growth.

Diseases. A PHYSIOLOGICAL DISORDER due to bad drainage or careless watering shows as a dis-coloration of the top, or collapse of the plants.

Mandarin: see *Citrus reticulata*
Mandevilla: see Dipladenia
Mangetout: see Pea, garden
Manuka: see *Leptospermum scoparium*
Manzanita: see Arctostaphylos
Manzanita, pine mat: see *Arctostaphylos nevadensis*
Maple: see Acer
Maple, eagle's claw: see *Acer platanoides* 'Laciniatum'
Maple, hedge: see *Acer campestre*
Maple, Japanese: see *Acer palmatum*
Maple, Norway: see *Acer platanoides*
Maple, red: see *Acer rubrum*
Maple, silver: see *Acer saccharinum*
Maple, snake bark: see *Acer pennsylvanicum*
Maple, vine: see *Acer circinatum*

Maranta

Marantaceae

A genus of 25 species of evergreen perennial plants grown for their ornamental foliage. One species with its varieties is in cultivation;

they are suitable for a greenhouse or as house plants and do well in bottle gardens.

M. leuconeura. Brazil. Height 6–8 in.; spread 12 in. or more. A prostrate species with ovate leaves which stand upright at night. The young leaves are emerald-green with brown-purple blotches between the lateral veins. As the leaves mature, they become grey and the blotches darken.

M. l. massangeana has smaller leaves, about 4 in. long. These have pale green margins and darker green centres; the midribs and principal lateral veins are ivory.

M. l. erythrophylla, syn. *M. l. tricolor,* has less rounded leaves, which may reach a length of 6 in. This variety is more erect than the others. The leaves have yellow-green margins and dark green centres with dark crimson midribs and veins.

Cultivation. Grow marantas in John Innes pot-ting compost No. 2, or in a proprietary peat mixture. They will survive at a winter tempera-ture of 10°C (50°F), but do better at 13°C (55°F).

Marantas are rapid growers and need potting on several times; finish off in 5–6 in. pots or 6–8 in. pans. Repot established plants annually in April and give a liquid feed once a fortnight from May to September.

During the growing season maintain a humid atmosphere and syringe the foliage daily with rain water. Shade the plants from April to October; water freely from March to September, moderately for the remainder of the year.

Propagation. The plants are rhizomatous and may be divided and replanted in April.

Alternatively, take cuttings of basal shoots with two or three leaves attached, from May to August. Insert three cuttings to a 3 in. pot containing equal parts (by volume) peat and sand at 21°C (70°F); pot on as required.

Pruning. None is necessary, but straggly growths on mature plants can be removed at any time.

Pests and diseases. Generally trouble-free.

Marguerite, blue: see *Felicia amelloides*
Marigold: see Calendula and Tagetes
Marigold, African: see *Tagetes erecta*
Marigold, Cape: see Dimorphotheca
Marigold, French: see *Tagetes patula*
Marigold, marsh: see Caltha
Marigold, pot: see *Calendula officinalis*

Marjoram

Origanum. Labiatae

MARJORAM

These hardy perennial herbs and sub-shrubs are used for flavouring. Sweet marjoram is generally considered to have the finest flavour.

See also ORIGANUM.

Common marjoram, wild marjoram (*O. vulgare*). Europe, including Great Britain. Height 12–18

Mammillaria elegans

Mammillaria plumosa

Maranta leuconeura

in.; planting distance 12 in. This hardy perennial has rounded, ovate, mid-green leaves in alternate pairs. Tiny, tubular, rose-purple flowers are borne in dense terminal panicles, 3–4 in. long, in July and August. 'Aureum' is an attractive variety with leaves that are golden-yellow when young.

Common marjoram is used for flavouring soups, stews, omelettes and *bouquets garnis*.

Pot marjoram (*O. onites*). S.E. Europe. Height and planting distance 12 in. The red, four-sided stems of this hardy perennial sub-shrub, with their ovate, bright green, aromatic leaves, form sprawling mounds. Whorls of mauve to white tubular flowers, about $\frac{1}{3}$ in. long, are carried on long stems in July and August.

The leaves are used fresh or dried with veal, in stuffings, omelettes and sausage meat.

Sweet marjoram, knotted marjoram (*O. majorana*). Europe. Height 24 in.; planting distance 12 in. A hardy, bushy, perennial sub-shrub with slender, four-sided, red stems bearing ovate grey opposite leaves. The clusters of tubular white, mauve or pink flowers, $\frac{1}{3}$ in. long, which open from June to September, appear from grey-green knot-like bracts from which the plant gets one of its common names. The whole plant is slightly hairy and sweetly aromatic.

The leaves and flowers are used, fresh or dried, to flavour all types of meat, poultry and game before roasting, to impart a sweet but spicy flavour. They can also be used in stuffings for meat, for flavouring omelettes and in *bouquets garnis*. Sweet marjoram has a strong aroma when dried and is excellent for *pot-pourri*.

Cultivation. Grow marjoram in any ordinary, well-drained garden soil, in a sunny position. The plants spread and may need trimming back occasionally; cut back by two-thirds before they die down in winter.

They are generally hardy, but in cold districts cover pot marjoram in winter with a protective layer of peat, leaf-mould or straw. For a winter supply of fresh leaves, insert 2–3 in. long cuttings of non-flowering side-shoots in equal parts (by volume) peat and sand and place in a cold frame during August. Pot the rooted cuttings individually in 3–4 in. pots of John Innes potting compost No. 1 and grow on at about 10°C (50°F).

Propagation. To obtain leaves early in the year sow seeds in February or March in pots or pans of seed compost, at a temperature of 10–13°C (50–55°F). Harden off the young plants before transplanting them outdoors in May. Set the plants 12–18 in. apart each way.

Seeds can also be sown outdoors in late April in drills 9–12 in. apart, the seedlings later thinned to the appropriate spacings.

Increase established plants by taking 2–3 in. cuttings of basal shoots in April or May. Insert them in equal parts (by volume) peat and sand in a cold frame; plant outdoors when rooted.

Harvesting and storing. Pick shoots fresh as required. They are at their best just before the flowers open, and this is when they should be gathered for drying and freezing. A second harvesting may be made in late September or October if a larger crop is required. For drying or freezing, cut the shoots 2 in. above ground and treat as described in the entry for HERBS.

Pests and diseases. Generally trouble-free.

Marjoram, common

Marjoram (common) 'Aureum'

Marrow 'Long Green'

Marrow
Cucurbita pepo ovifera. Cucurbitaceae

A half-hardy annual of bushy or trailing habit bearing large, ovoid or cylindrical, sometime ribbed, edible fruits. They are 12 in. or mor long when mature, with green, cream-white or bi-coloured striped skins and succulent fles which is cooked as a vegetable. The fruits ar produced from July until the end of Septembe and are used fresh or stored for winter use.

VARIETIES

Large-fruiting varieties are being superseded i popularity by smaller varieties. These are pro lific, early-maturing croppers, with firm textured, well-flavoured flesh. 'Improved Gree Bush' has dark green fruits striped with pal green. Similarly coloured fruits are produced b 'Long Green', a prolific trailing type.

Less common but reliable are the round fruited bush types: 'Custard White', 'Custar Yellow', 'Tender and True' and 'White Bush'.

Bush types mature two or three weeks earlie than the trailing types, and they take up les space in small gardens.

'Courgette' is a dwarf bush variety; the fruit should be harvested when they are 4–6 in. long.

Cultivation. Marrows can be grown on any fertile and well-drained soil, rich in organi material. A sheltered, sunny position gives bes results. If the marrow crop can follow an early season crop for which the ground was manure previously, little preparation is required. O unmanured soil work large amounts of well rotted compost or manure into the soil; a mix ture of equal parts (by volume) manure and dead leaves applied at the rate of two bucket per sq. yd is ideal. The organic material may b packed in 9 in. deep trenches, 12 in. wide, wit the soil from the trenches heaped back on top o it. Prepare the bed in early May.

Raise young plants under glass in late April o early May. Sow one or two seeds in 3 in containers of John Innes seed compost, at a temperature of 16–18°C (61–64°F). When th seedlings have developed two rough leaves harden them off in a cold frame, gradually increasing the ventilation. In late May, set th plants out in their growing positions and cove them with cloches for a few days.

Seeds may also be sown in the prepared bed about the end of April. Place the seeds 1 in deep in pairs 3 ft apart and cover with cloches When the seedlings are well through, remove the weaker of the two.

If more than one row of marrows is being grown, allow 4 ft between rows of bush types and 6 ft between rows of trailing marrows.

Water the plants freely; in dry spells wate with an overhead sprinkler for at least an hour week, or thoroughly soak the soil surrounding each plant. Apply a $\frac{1}{2}$ in. deep mulch of compost damp sedge peat, or lawn cuttings.

Nip out the growing tips of the main shoot of trailing types when they are 18 in. long, t encourage the growth of lateral shoots, which bear most of the female flowers. If the fruits ar not setting well, pollinate the plants by hand Use a camel-hair brush to transfer pollen from

e male flowers to the female or pull off male
owers and rub off the pollen on to the stigma of
e female. The female flowers are characterised
y a swelling just behind the bloom.

Harvesting and storing. Cut fruits as they are
equired for use during summer; they should be
arvested when young, preferably when no
ore than 8 in. long, when their flavour is best.
utting also encourages the plants to produce
ore fruits; up to 24 fruits can be harvested
om one plant if they are picked when 12 in.
ng. Leave the last two or three fruits on the
ants until October, when they will be fully
rown and well ripened. Harvest and store
em in an airy, frost-proof place.

Pests. Generally trouble-free.

Diseases. CUCUMBER MOSAIC VIRUS causes stunt-
ng of plants; the leaves are puckered and
ottled yellow or light and dark green. Fruits
re mottled, reduced in size and may die.

GREY MOULD may attack fruits subjected to too
uch watering; the fruits turn yellow, and be-
ome covered with a grey fungal growth.

POWDERY MILDEW shows as a white powdery
ngal growth on the leaves.

Marvel of Peru: see *Mirabilis jalapa*
Mask flower: see Alonsoa
Masterwort: see Astrantia
Matricaria eximia: see *Chrysanthemum parthenium*

Matteuccia

Aspidiaceae

 genus of three species of ferns, only one of
which is in general cultivation. This is a hardy
nd moisture-loving fern of elegant, arching
abit, ideal for waterside planting.

See also FERNS.

M. struthiopteris, syns. *Onoclea germanica*,
struthiopteris germanica (ostrich feather fern,
huttlecock fern). N. Hemisphere. Height 3–5 ft;
pread 2–3 ft. A circle of golden-green sterile
ronds surrounds an inner circle of shorter, dark
rown, fertile fronds; both types of frond are
lliptic-lanceolate and pinnately lobed. The
rown produces several black stolons which form
ubsidiary crowns.

Cultivation. Plant these ferns from October to
April, in any ordinary, moisture-retentive soil; on
ree-draining soils incorporate heavy amounts of
rganic materials. These plants do best in partial
hade, although they will tolerate sun. They need
lenty of room for root development and for best
esults should be planted 4 ft or more apart.

Propagation. Remove offsets and replant in April.

Pests and diseases. Generally trouble-free.

Matthiola

Stock. *Cruciferae*

 genus of 55 species of annual, biennial and
erennial herbaceous plants and sub-shrubs. The
pecies described are popular garden plants for
eds and borders, for growing as pot plants and

for cutting. The heavily scented flowers, in pastel
shades or rich colours, are massed in spikes.

M. bicornis (night-scented stock). Greece.
Height 15 in.; planting distance 9 in. A hardy,
bushy annual with long, narrow, grey-green
leaves. The single four-petalled flowers are a dull
lilac, $\frac{3}{4}$ in. across and carried in 9 in. spikes in July
and August; they open at night, giving out a
heavy scent. During the day the plant has an
untidy appearance and is best grown either in
out-of-the-way spots or with *Malcolmia maritima*
(Virginian stock) to combine the colour and
fragrance of the two.

MATTHIOLA INCANA

M. incana. S. Europe. Height 12–24 in.; planting
distance 12 in. A hardy biennial or short-lived
perennial of bushy habit. The leaves are long and
narrow, of felty texture and grey-green in colour.
Compact 6–9 in. spikes of pale purple flowers
appear in June and July.

Most of the garden hybrids have originated
from this species, the many varieties being
divided into the following six main groups.

The first, the Ten Week stocks, is sub-divided
into several strains, all treated as annuals: Dwarf
Large Flowering, height up to 12 in., are compact
plants, ideal for bedding; they are obtainable in
yellow, pink, crimson, lavender and white.
Excelsior, or Column, height up to $2\frac{1}{2}$ ft, are
plants of upright habit, each producing one
densely flowered stem; they are good for cutting.
The colours are similar to those in the Dwarf
Large Flowering strain, excluding yellow.

Giant Imperial plants, height up to 24 in., are
good for cutting and for bedding; they are
available mainly in shades of copper, gold and
yellow. The Giant Perfection strain, height up to
$2\frac{1}{2}$ ft, is similar and particularly good for
exhibition purposes; popular varieties include
'Queen of the Belgians', with silver-lilac flowers,
and 'Princess Alice', white.

The Mammoth, or Beauty, strain, height up to
18 in., produces plants of erect and bushy habit; it
is mainly represented by such varieties as 'Beauty
of Nice', pink; 'Crimson King', deep crimson;
'Heatham Beauty', rose-mauve; 'Mont Blanc',
white; 'Parma Violet', purple; and 'Yellow of
Nice', pale yellow.

The second main group consists of the Perpetual Flowering, or All the Year Round, stocks.
These are vigorous dwarf plants, height 15 in.,
with wallflower-like foliage; they bear dense
spikes of large, white double flowers and are
suitable for cutting or for growing in pots. Treat
as annuals, sowing in spring, or in September for
spring flowering.

The third group, the Brompton stocks, height
18 in., are upright bushy plants, bearing both
single and double flowers; they are obtainable in
shades of red, pink, purple, yellow and white.
These should be treated as biennials.

Matteuccia struthiopteris

Matthiola bicornis

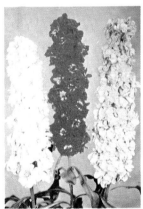

Matthiola incana Excelsior

The East Lothian, or Intermediate, group, height 15 in., may be grown as biennials or as annuals. These are dwarf bushy plants, available in the same shades as the Brompton group.

The last two groups, the Trysomic and the All Double, are similar. These are dwarf bushy plants, 12 in. tall, grown as annuals. Trysomic stocks produce 85 per cent double flowers and are available in all the colours previously mentioned. All Doubles produce 100 per cent double flowers; they are obtainable in all colours except yellow, and in a mixture, 'Dwarf Double Mixed'.

Cultivation. These plants thrive in any good garden soil in full sun, and will tolerate partial shade. The soil should be a fertile medium loam, preferably slightly alkaline. If the soil is poor, it may be enriched with well-rotted organic matter, such as animal manure or compost. Staking is necessary only for tall plants in exposed positions and for leggy plants in shady sites.

When planting out, use only seedlings that are healthy; those that have suffered root damage or have been allowed to dry out will produce premature and dwarfed flower spikes. In the spring, apply a pinch of dried blood or a similar fast-acting nitrogenous fertiliser around each established plant to improve growth and flower size. Biennials overwintered outside need cloche protection from cold drying winds on exposed sites during the coldest months.

For pot plants to flower under glass, place the seedlings in 3 in. pots of John Innes potting compost No. 1, later moving to the final 6 in. containers and No. 2 compost. Plants to flower in winter require a temperature of 10–13°C (50–55°F). Water regularly, and when the flower buds appear give a liquid feed to improve bloom quality.

Excelsior stocks are recommended for cut flower production under glass; plant in the greenhouse border 6–8 in. apart. Good results can be obtained in cold greenhouses, but slight heat induces earlier flowering. If the leaves of young plants under glass look yellow, water the soil with sequestrene iron to improve the leaf colour and to stimulate growth.

Propagation. For plants required to flower under glass in winter, sow the seeds outside in nursery rows in July. Transplant the seedlings to stand 6 in. apart for the summer; pot them in 6 in. containers in September and grow on in a greenhouse at about 7°C (45°F). For a second batch of flowering plants, overwinter some of them in a cold frame.

For summer-flowering annuals, sow the seeds under glass in February or March at a temperature of 13–15°C (55–59°F); prick out into boxes and harden off in a cold frame before planting out in April or May. Alternatively, and for later flowering, sow directly in the flowering site in April, just covering the seeds, and thin out the seedlings to the required spacing.

For all double-flowered plants of the Trysomic strain, grow the seedlings on at 13–15°C (55–59°F), and lower the temperature to 10°C (50°F) for a couple of days before pricking out. The drop in temperature exaggerates the difference in seedling leaf colour which occurs between the yellow double plants and the green singles. Discard the latter.

Matthiola incana 'Dwarf Double Mixed'

Matthiola incana All Double

Maurandia barclaiana

Pests. Seedlings may be attacked by FLEA BEETL which eat small holes in the leaves.

CATERPILLARS may feed extensively on t leaves of older plants.

APHIDS may infest young shoots and cau a check to growth.

Diseases. Irregular swellings on the roots are d to CLUB ROOT; the plants remain stunted.

DAMPING-OFF, FOOT ROT and ROOT ROT can caused by several different fungi, includi RHIZOCTONIA. Affected seedlings or older plan wilt or collapse completely.

DOWNY MILDEW produces yellow blotches the leaves and a grey furry coating on t undersides. Affected plants may be stunted.

GREY MOULD causes withering of one or even of the shoots, which become covered with a gr furry mould.

STEM ROT shows on the stems as decayed are bearing minute, black, spore-producing bodies.

Maurandia

Scrophulariaceae

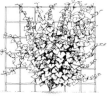

MAURANDIA BARCLAIANA

A genus of ten species of tender and half-hard evergreen climbing perennials. Those describe may be grown outdoors as half-hardy annuals sheltered sites in the south and west, but are mo suitable for greenhouse cultivation as annuals perennials. Like clematis, maurandias climb t twining their leaf stalks round supports; they ca be grown on trelliswork, or on walls with string or wires provided. The species described hav snapdragon-like flowers, borne singly in th upper leaf axils.

M. barclaiana. Mexico. Height up to 15 ft unde glass, 5–7 ft outdoors. A species with dark gree triangular leaves. The 2 in. long, rose-purp flowers are produced from May to Novemb under glass, from July to September in a fir summer outdoors. Deep purple, pink and whi forms are known, but rarely available.

M. erubescens. Mexico. Height up to 15 ft unde glass, 5–7 ft outdoors. The light green leaves a more distinctly triangular than those of *M barclaiana,* and the flowers are 3 in. long. Th inside of the white corolla tube is spotted wit rose-pink and the lobes are also pink. Flowerin is from May to November under glass, from Ju to September outdoors.

Cultivation. Maurandias are best grown in th greenhouse border or in 6–8 in. pots of Joh Innes potting compost No. 2. A minimum winte temperature of 7°C (45°F) is required. Train th plants over strings or wires or, for pot plants, o twiggy sticks. Water freely during the growin season and keep the compost just moist in winte If the plants are grown as perennials, pot them c annually in March or April.

Outdoors, grow maurandias in a fertile and well-drained soil, preferably enriched with well-decayed manure or compost. A sunny and sheltered site is essential. Plant out young specimens from pots in late May, providing small twiggy sticks for support until the growths can attach themselves to the trelliswork.

Propagation. Sow seeds in pots or pans of seed compost during February or March. Germinate under glass at a temperature of 16–19°C (61–66°F). Prick out the seedlings into 3 in. pots of John Innes potting compost No. 1 when they are large enough to handle, and grow on in the greenhouse, potting on as necessary. Harden off plants for outdoor sites before planting them out in late May.

Alternatively, take 2–3 in. cuttings from short leafy shoots in August or February and insert them in equal parts (by volume) peat and sand in a greenhouse at a temperature of 16–19°C (61–66°F). When rooted, transfer the cuttings to 3 in. pots and treat as seedlings.

Pruning. To keep greenhouse perennials within bounds, cut the stems back to within 6 in. of the base in February.

Pests. Young growths may be infested by APHIDS.

Diseases. Generally trouble-free.

Maxillaria
Orchidaceae

There are about 300 evergreen species in this genus of epiphytic and terrestrial orchids, which are found from Florida through the American tropics to Argentina. All species have pseudobulbs, these being evenly spaced out on a creeping or climbing rhizome, or clustered in tufts. The mid-green leaves are leathery, generally strap-shaped and arranged in basal tufts or on the pseudobulbs. The flowers are borne singly on erect stems arising from the base of the pseudobulbs. In some species the flowers are large and showy, in others they are inconspicuous.

See also ORCHIDS.

M. nasuta. Tropical America. An epiphytic species with flattened pseudobulbs about 3 in. high, each carrying one leaf. The single, star-like flowers, 1–1½ in. across, are borne from March to September on erect stems up to 4 in. long; the sepals and petals are pale yellow-green, suffused maroon on the back, and the lip is deep maroon with a bright yellow tip. The column is a contrasting white. This species flowers best in an intermediate greenhouse and benefits from a weak liquid feed during the growing season.

M. nigrescens: see **M. rufescens**

M. picta. Tropical America. This epiphytic species has clustered pseudobulbs 2–3 in. high, each bearing two dark green leaves. The single 2 in. wide flowers are carried on an erect 4 in. long stem during winter; they are yellow with a pattern of red and purple marks. Grow in a shady position in a cool greenhouse.

M. rufescens, often listed as **M. nigrescens**, and allied to **M. picta**. Trinidad. The clustered pseudobulbs of this epiphytic species reach a height of 2½ in., and each bears one leaf. The short, 4–5 in. flowering stems carry solitary, 1½

in. wide flowers, with red-brown sepals and yellow petals. The lip is yellow, heavily spotted with red. This species, which flowers between winter and spring, does best in an intermediate greenhouse and is suitable for raft culture.

M. sanderiana. Tropical America. A robust epiphytic species with single-leaved clustered pseudobulbs, 2–6 in. high. The flowers, on 3–6 in. stems, are up to 6 in. wide and usually white, sometimes with a pale yellow lip. There are red-purple markings on the lip, and the petals and sepals have a deep red base. The flowering times vary with individual plants, but may be at any time between May and October. Cool greenhouse conditions are best for this species.

M. tenuifolia. Central America. This species has 2 in. high pseudobulbs set at intervals along the ascending rhizome, and bears linear dark green leaves. Yellow flowers, 1½–2 in. wide and heavily barred with crimson, are carried on 1½–2 in. long scapes in March.

M. variabilis. Central America. An epiphytic species with single-leaved pseudobulbs up to 1 in. high, borne at intervals along a more or less upright rhizome. The solitary flowers are borne on a 24 in. long stem; they are up to 1 in. across and deep red-purple. There are several colour variants in cultivation. They open from spring to autumn. Grow in an intermediate greenhouse.

Cultivation. Grow maxillarias in 3–5 in. pots or 5–9 in. pans of 2 parts osmunda fibre and 1 part sphagnum moss (parts by volume), or in baskets or on fibre rafts for large specimen plants. They may be fixed to pieces of tree fern or to blocks of wood. Pot from March to May after flowering, and repot every two or three years. Shade the greenhouse on sunny days from April to September, thereafter giving full light. Ventilate on mild days throughout the year; water freely between May and September, thereafter moderately, keeping the plants just moist to prevent the pseudobulbs from shrinking.

Propagation. Divide and pot up in the growing compost from March to May.

Pests and diseases. Generally trouble-free.

May: see *Crataegus monogyna* and *C. oxyacanthoides*

Mazus
Scrophulariaceae

A genus of 20 species of creeping hardy herbaceous perennials suitable for rock gardens. The two species described have pale to mid-green leaves, sometimes bronze-tinted; the flowers resemble flattened snapdragons.

M. radicans, syn. *Mimulus radicans.* New Zealand. Height 2 in.; spread 12 in. or more. This plant forms a flat mat of ovate and coarsely toothed foliage and is studded with white flowers blotched with violet. They are ½ in. long and open from June to August.

M. reptans. Himalayas. Height 1–2 in.; spread 12 in. or more. This species forms a creeping mat of lanceolate, toothed leaves. Lilac flowers, ½–¾ in. long, open from June to August; the lower lips are speckled gold and white.

Maxillaria picta

Maxillaria sanderiana

Mazus reptans

Meconopsis integrifolia

Meconopsis quintuplinervia

Meconopsis betonicifolia

Meconopsis cambrica
(double form)

Cultivation. Plant in March or April in a sunny position in any ordinary soil that does not dry out. The plants are inclined to become straggly over the years and should then be replaced.

Propagation. Divide and replant the roots in April or September.

Pests and diseases. Generally trouble-free.

Meadow-rue: see Thalictrum
Meadowsweet: see *Filipendula ulmaria*

Meconopsis

Papaveraceae

A genus of 43 species of hardy herbaceous perennial plants with poppy-like flowers. The blue-flowered species can prove disappointing as many die after flowering only once; some plants are purple or mauve, rather than blue.

M. baileyi: see *M. betonicifolia*

MECONOPSIS BETONICIFOLIA

M. betonicifolia, syn. *M. baileyi* (Himalayan blue poppy). Tibet, Yunnan, Upper Burma. Height 3–5 ft; planting distance 12–18 in. The leaves are mid-green, oblong and cordate at the base.

Sky-blue to purple flowers, $2\frac{1}{2}$–3 in. across, which open in June and July, are borne in groups of three or four at the top of the stems. They have white filaments and yellow anthers. 'Alba' is white.

This plant often dies after flowering if allowed to flower the first year. Cutting off the stems before flowering in the first year usually establishes it as a short-lived perennial.

MECONOPSIS CAMBRICA

M. cambrica (Welsh poppy). Western Europe including Great Britain. Height and planting distance 12 in. This species is short-lived, but seeds itself freely. The deeply dissected mid-green leaves are slightly hairy and form basal tufts. Yellow or orange flowers, $1\frac{1}{2}$–2 in. across, are freely borne from June to September. There are double forms in yellow and orange.

M. chelidonifolia. Western Szechwan. Height 3 ft; planting distance 24 in. A species with mid-green, deeply pinnately lobed leaves. Pale yellow flowers, 1 in. across, tip the branching red stems in June and July. This species is long-lived if divided and replanted every two or three years.

M. grandis. Nepal, Tibet, Sikkim, Bhutan. Height and planting distance 24 in. The oblong-lanceolate leaves are mid-green. Rich blue to purple flowers, 4–5 in. across, appear in May and

une. The colour usually has a red tinge, but some
plants are close to a deep blue.

M. integrifolia. Tibet, Upper Burma, W. China.
Height up to 24 in.; planting distance 12–18 in.
This border plant is best treated as monocarpic. It
has oblong-lanceolate, pale green and hairy
leaves. The 5 in. wide, yellow flowers are borne
singly on each stem in July.

MECONOPSIS NAPAULENSIS

M. napaulensis, syn. *M. wallichii.* Nepal to
Szechwan. Height 4–6 ft; planting distance 2–3
ft. A border plant best treated as monocarpic,
bearing deeply lobed mid-green leaves with a
covering of red-brown hairs. The 3 in. wide
flowers, borne in June and July, are purple, red,
pink or occasionally white.

M. quintuplinervia (harebell poppy). Tibet, W.
China. Height 9–12 in.; planting distance 12 in.
A dwarf perennial species which spreads underground by rhizomes when established. The obovate to oblanceolate, mid-green leaves are covered
with yellow bristly hairs. Nodding, lavender-
blue or purple flowers, 2 in. across, are borne
on slender leafless stems during May and June.

M. regia. Nepal. Height 3–5 ft; planting distance
24 in. A monocarpic border plant with a rosette of
large elliptic leaves that are densely covered with
gold or silver hairs. Yellow flowers, 4–5 in. wide,
are produced in June and July.

M. wallichii: see *M. napaulensis*

Cultivation. Plant in March or April. *M. cambrica*
does well in any garden soil and in any position.
Other species require a light rich soil that is moist
but quick-draining, in a semi-shaded and
sheltered position. Unlike most monocarpic
plants, which are usually annuals or biennials, the
species of this genus usually take two to four
years before they flower and die.

Plenty of water is needed in summer, but as
little as possible in winter. Staking with twiggy
sticks may be needed in exposed positions, and
dead-heading is recommended to prolong
flowering. Cut down the perennial species in
autumn. In wet regions, place open cloches or
panes of glass over the wintergreen forms of *M.
napaulensis* and *M. regia.*

Propagation. Sow seeds as soon as ripe or in
August and September, in a cold frame or
greenhouse; prick the seedlings out into boxes
and overwinter in a well-ventilated greenhouse
or cold frame. Germination is slower in spring,
but seeds may be sown in March or April at a
temperature of 13–16°C (55–61°F). Prick out the
seedlings, and grow on the young plants in
nursery rows until September or October, when
they can be transferred to their permanent site.
Varieties do not come true to type.

Pests. Generally trouble-free.

Diseases. The undersurfaces of the leaves, flower
stalks and seed pods are affected by DOWNY
MILDEW, which shows as furry grey patches.

Medlar

Mespilus germanica. Rosaceae

A hardy, deciduous, fruit-bearing tree, native to
S.E. Europe and Asia Minor. It is frequently
grown as much for its ornamental appearance as
for its edible fruits. These may be eaten raw when
over-ripe, but are more often used in preserves
and jellies.

The medlar (height 20–25 ft; spread 20 ft) is a
much-branched, spreading tree, usually grown as
a standard. The dull green, oblong-ovate leaves
are finely toothed and often assume russet and
yellow autumn colours. Saucer-shaped flowers,
1–1½ in. across, appear in May or June; they are
white or pink with red anthers and are borne
singly at the tips of the shoots. The round green
fruits each have five leafy pointed calyx segments.
They are hard when harvested, but after storing
for about three weeks the flesh turns soft
and brown, and the fruits are then edible.

Varieties generally available are: 'Notting-
ham', of erect habit, with small, richly flavoured
fruits; and 'Dutch', of more spreading habit and
with larger fruits.

MEDLAR

Cultivation. Plant from October to March, but
preferably just after leaf-fall. Medlars require an
open sunny position; they do well in ordinary,
well-drained garden soil, preferably enriched
with decayed manure. Standard trees require
staking for the first few years until established;
they benefit from an annual mulch in spring
of peat or well-rotted manure.

Pick the fruits on a dry day about early
November and store them in trays, in single
layers, with the eyes downwards, until they are
ready for eating or jelly-making.

Propagation. Sow ripe seeds in September or
early October in pots or boxes of John Innes seed
compost and place in a cold frame. Germination
is erratic. Between April and June, when the
seedlings are large enough to handle, pot them
individually in 3 in. containers of John Innes
potting compost No. 2 or plant directly into a
nursery bed outdoors. Grow on for three or four
years before transplanting to permanent sites.

Named varieties do not come true from
seeds and must be grafted or budded in July
on to seedling medlars or hawthorn stock
(*Crataegus monogyna* or *C. oxyacanthoides*).

Pruning. Little pruning is needed for standard
trees after the initial training, which consists of
cutting all lateral shoots back to two or three
leaves between October and March. When the
tree has reached the desired height, pinch out
the leading shoot to induce growth of the laterals
that will form the main branches.

Remove weak and crossing branches on
established bush and standard trees in March.

Meconopsis grandis

Meconopsis napaulensis

Meconopsis regia

Medlar

Pests. APHIDS and CATERPILLARS of various species may infest the foliage.

Diseases. APPLE MILDEW may appear when the buds break in spring; it shows as a white powdery deposit on the emerging growths. The disease spreads and affected leaves fall prematurely.

Megasea: see Bergenia
Melissa officinalis: see Balm

Melon

Cucumis melo. Cucurbitaceae

Melon 'Sweetheart'

Melon 'Tiger'

Mentha rotundifolia 'Variegata'

A tender annual, grown for its large edible fruits. These are juicy and sweet-flavoured with slightly soft flesh when fully ripe. Greenhouse varieties require a temperature of 16°C (61°F) to produce a satisfactory crop. Some varieties can also be grown in frames or under cloches.

VARIETIES
Of the four main groups into which melons are classified, only two, Cantaloupe and Casaba, are commonly grown in Great Britain. The Cantaloupe groups generally have small rounded fruits, often with heavily white-netted skins and broad ribs that give them a segmented appearance. Recommended varieties with good flavour include: 'Charentais', with orange flesh; 'Ogin', green-fleshed; 'Sweetheart', an F₁ hybrid with scarlet flesh; and 'Tiger', early maturing, with orange flesh.

Casaba melons are larger and oval in shape, generally with green, finely ridged skins. Recommended varieties include the orange-fleshed 'Blenheim Orange', 'King George' and 'Superlative'; the green-fleshed 'Emerald Gem', 'Honeydew' and 'Ringleader'; and the white-fleshed 'Hero of Lockinge'.

Greenhouse cultivation. Raise plants for cropping from May onwards by sowing seeds at monthly intervals from January to May. Sow the seeds ½ in. deep, singly in 3 in. pots of seed compost, pressing them in edgeways. Keep the pots moist and at a temperature of 18°C (64°F) until the seeds have germinated. Lower the temperature to 16°C (61°F), and place the young plants as near the glass as possible. Pot on into 5 in. containers of the seed compost before the smaller pots are filled with roots.

When the plants have formed their fifth leaf, transplant them to their growing quarters, preferably in the greenhouse border. This should have been well prepared with one or two buckets of well-rotted manure to the sq. yd, covered with about 9 in. of fibrous loam. Space the plants 3 ft apart. Alternatively, grow the plants singly in 9 in. pots or large deep boxes of John Innes potting compost No. 3.

Insert a cane at each plant up which the main stem will grow. Fasten horizontal wires to the glazing bars at 12 in. intervals and tie in the lateral growths. When the main stem has reached the top wire, pinch out the growing tip; lateral shoots should be pinched out when they have formed five leaves. Male and female flowers develop on the secondary laterals, the female being distinguished by a swelling like a miniature melon just beneath the bloom.

During early growth a humid atmosphere is essential; provide this by frequent damping down and syringing of the leaves. When the fruits have reached their full size less humidity is required. On hot sunny days, lightly shade the glass; at other times let the plants have as much light as possible.

Artificial pollination is necessary to set fruits: strip the petals off a male flower and push the exposed centre into a female flower. Midday is the best time for pollination. Do not allow more than four fruits to develop on each plant, and not more than one on a single side-shoot.

When the fruits are about the size of a tennis ball, start feeding the plants once a week with a liquid manure; water freely with tepid water every morning. Cease feeding and watering as soon as the fruits are fully grown and start to ripen, but give a little tepid water now and then to prevent the soil from drying out. As the fruits become heavy, support them with nets attached to the greenhouse wires.

Frame cultivation. Excellent fruits can be produced under frames, Dutch lights or cloches, provided the Cantaloupe varieties are grown.

Prepare the beds in frames, Dutch lights or under cloches as for greenhouse cultivation and set plants out in May. Adjust ventilation and watering according to the weather so that the soil is kept permanently moist, and the air, after leaf growth has been made, is dry. Stop the main shoots when they have made five leaves and the side-shoots at three leaves. When the flowers have opened, cease watering but lightly syringe the plants in the evenings before closing the frames. Pollinate the flowers as previously described; when the fruits have set and are about the size of a walnut, begin watering again and continue until the fruits are fully grown and start to ripen. Place a tile or flat stone under each fruit to keep it off the soil.

Harvesting. The fruits should not be cut until they are completely ripe. The best test of ripeness is to press the thumb gently against the end of the fruit furthest from the stalk; if the fruit gives to this pressure, it is ripe. The skins of ripe fruits of some varieties crack away from the stalks and give off a noticeable aroma.

Pests. Generally trouble-free.

Diseases. CUCUMBER MOSAIC VIRUS causes the leaves to curl and become mottled; as they mature they turn yellow. The young fruits are mottled and show dark green warts.

VERTICILLIUM WILT causes the leaves to turn yellow from the base upwards and the whole plant wilts and remains stunted.

Mentha

Mint. Labiatae

A genus of 25 species and numerous natural hybrids of aromatic-leaved, hardy and half-hardy perennials. Although known mainly for their culinary use (see MINT), there are a number of ornamental foliage plants suitable for growing in borders, rock gardens or between paving.

M. × gentilis. Height up to 18 in.; spread 2–3 ft. This hardy garden hybrid has red-purple stems

Mentha × gentilis 'Variegata'

and ovate-lanceolate mid-green leaves. The pale purple tubular flowers are borne in spikes, 4–5 in. long, from July to September. It is represented in cultivation mainly by the form 'Variegata', which has leaves boldly splashed with yellow.

M. requienii. Corsica. Height 1 in.; spread 12 in. or more. A prostrate carpeting species, with tiny, orbicular, bright pale green leaves that give off an aroma of peppermint. The tubular pale purple flowers are borne in ½ in. long spikes from June to August. The species is not reliably hardy during severe winters, but it is seldom killed.

M. rotundifolia (apple mint). N. and W. Asia, N. Africa, Europe, including Great Britain. Height 2–3 ft; spread up to 4 ft. This species is generally considered the best-flavoured culinary mint. As an ornamental plant it is represented by 'Variegata', with cream-white margins to the leaves.

Cultivation. The ornamental mints will grow in any ordinary garden soil, preferably one that does not dry out in summer. A sunny or partially shaded site is suitable for all except *M. requienii*, which does best in partial shade. Plant at any time from October to March; *M. requienii* is best planted in March or April.

M. × gentilis and *M. rotundifolia* are invasive plants and should have their creeping rhizomes confined by slates or tiles embedded vertically around them.

Propagation. With the exception of *M. requienii*, divide the roots at any time from October to March. Choose vigorous 6–9 in. long rhizomes and replant directly in permanent positions. Divide *M. requienii* during March or April.

Pests. Generally trouble-free.

Diseases. In spring, the shoots may become infected with MINT RUST, causing them to become swollen, distorted and covered with orange-coloured spore pustules. Later, the leaves show pale coloured spots, and brown pustules develop on the lower surfaces. Affected leaves dry up.

Mentzelia

Loasaceae

A genus of 70 species of annual, biennial and perennial herbaceous plants. The bushy annual described has showy flowers and makes an attractive plant for annual or mixed borders.

M. lindleyi, syn. *Bartonia aurea.* California. Height 18 in.; spacing 9 in. A hardy annual with succulent stems and rich green, narrow, roughly notched leaves. The chalice-like golden-yellow flowers, 2½ in. across, are sweetly scented and have a central mass of slender stamens. They are produced from June to August.

MENTZELIA LINDLEYI

Cultivation. A light fertile soil in a sunny position is ideal, although any ordinary garden soil gives reasonably good results.

Propagation. Sow the seeds in the flowering site in March or April, just covering them with soil. Thin out the seedlings to stand 9 in. apart.

Pests and diseases. Generally trouble-free.

Menziesia

Ericaceae

MENZIESIA CILIICALYX

A genus of seven species of hardy, deciduous, slow-growing flowering shrubs. They are particularly suitable for peat gardens and associate well with rhododendrons.

M. ciliicalyx. Japan. Height 3–6 ft; spread 18 in. The edges of the obovate, pale green leaves are bristly. Nodding pink to pale purple flowers, which are urn-shaped and up to ¾ in. long, are carried in umbels in May and June.

M. purpurea. Japan. Height 4–5 ft; spread 2–3 ft. The pale to mid-green obovate leaves are sparingly bristled on both surfaces. Clusters of nodding deep red to purple flowers appear in May. They are bell-shaped and up to ¾ in. long.

M. taxifolia: see *Phyllodoce caerulea*

Cultivation. Plant between October and February in lime-free peaty soil in sun or partial shade. Mulch with peat or lime-free leaf-mould in April.

Propagation. Sow seeds in February in pans containing well-drained sand and peat, at a temperature of 13°C (55°F). When the seedlings are large enough to handle, prick them off into pans or boxes containing equal parts (by volume) peat, lime-free loam and sand. Overwinter them in a cold frame; during the following June or July pot up singly into 3 in. pots. Set the plants out in a nursery bed in October of the following year and grow on for two or three years before planting out in final positions between October and February.

Alternatively, in July take 2–2½ in. heel cuttings of lateral shoots and insert them in equal

Mentzelia lindleyi

Menziesia ciliicalyx

parts (by volume) peat and sand in a propagating frame at a temperature of 16°C (61°F). Pot the rooted cuttings singly into 3 in. pots containing equal parts (by volume) peat, lime-free loam and sand. Plant out in a nursery bed the following September or October and grow on there for at least two or three years before planting out in their final positions during frost-free weather between October and February.

Pruning. None required.

Pests and diseases. Generally trouble-free.

Mertensia virginica

Mesembryanthemum criniflorum

Mertensia
Boraginaceae

MERTENSIA VIRGINICA

A genus of 50 species of hardy herbaceous perennials of which four or five are cultivated. They have tubular or bell-like flowers, and are easily grown in borders or rock gardens.

M. ciliata. Rocky Mountains. Height 1–3 ft; planting distance 18 in. A species with ovate glaucous leaves. Clusters of narrow, sky-blue, bell-shaped flowers, $\frac{1}{2}$–$\frac{2}{3}$ in. long, are borne in May and June. It will tolerate a more sunny position than most of the other species, although this reduces height.

M. echioides. Himalayas. Height 12 in.; planting distance 18 in. Its creeping habit makes this species suitable for ground cover in a border. The leaves are oblong to spathulate and mid-green. Clusters of blue flowers, each up to $\frac{1}{2}$ in. long, appear from June to July; a second flush is sometimes produced in September.

M. primuloides is similar to *M. echioides* and commercial stocks appear to be the same plant.

M. virginica (Virginian cowslip). E. United States. Height 12–24 in.; planting distance 12 in. This plant bears blue-grey lanceolate-ovate leaves; drooping terminal racemes of 1 in. long purple-blue flowers appear in May. It disappears completely below ground from July to February.

Cultivation. Plant in October and November or in March and April. A rich loamy soil in a moist shady position is ideal, but all species are fairly adaptable. Cut down in autumn. For best results replant in new positions every four or five years.

Propagation. Divide and replant the roots in October or March.

Alternatively, sow seeds as soon as ripe, or in July and August, in a cold frame or greenhouse. The seeds should germinate the following spring; prick out the seedlings when large enough to handle and grow the young plants on in nursery rows, preferably until the autumn of the second year. Thereafter they can be transplanted to the permanent site.

Pests and diseases. Generally trouble-free.

Mescal button: see *Lophophora williamsii*

Mesembryanthemum
Aizoaceae

A genus of 350 species of succulent plants. Formerly this genus contained about 1000 species, but recent research has resulted in many of these being assigned to new genera, including *Conophytum* and *Faucaria*. *Dorotheanthus* is the currently correct name for the plants described here. They are suitable for banks, rock gardens and the edges of borders, and thrive in dry sunny sites. The colourful daisy-like flowers open only in bright sunshine.

M. criniflorum, syn. *Dorotheanthus bellidiflorus* (Livingstone daisy). S. Africa. Height 6 in.; planting distance 12 in. Although usually grown as a half-hardy annual, this plant is quite hardy. It has a low, spreading habit, with narrow, almost cylindrical, light green leaves which have a glistening, sugary appearance. Given adequate sunshine it carries a mass of brightly coloured and zoned flowers, 1 in. across, from June to August. The wide colour range includes white, crimson to pink, and orange-gold to buff.

M. tricolor, syn. *Dorotheanthus gramineus.* S. Africa. Height 3 in.; planting distance 12 in. A hardy annual species with dark green, narrow, cylindrical leaves. The flowers, deep rose and white with dark centres, are 1$\frac{1}{2}$ in. across and produced from June to August.

Cultivation. These plants require a position in full sun. They do well in any well-drained garden soil, and thrive on light sandy soils.

Propagation. Sow the seeds under glass in March at a temperature of 15°C (59°F). Prick out the seedlings into boxes and harden off before planting out in May. Alternatively, sow directly in the flowering site in April, thinning out the seedlings to the required distance.

Pests. Generally trouble-free.

Diseases. Plants may collapse at ground level due to FOOT ROT, caused by a fungus.

Mespilus germanica: see Medlar

Metasequoia
Dawn redwood. *Taxodiaceae*

METASEQUOIA GLYPTOSTROBOIDES

A genus of a single species. This is a hardy deciduous conifer, suitable as a specimen tree.

See also CONIFERS.

M. glyptostroboides. China. Height 40–45 ft; spread 10–15 ft. A species with a narrowly conic crown that becomes open and sparse if grown in shade; the bark is orange with red-brown flakes peeling off. The mid-green, linear, bluntly tipped leaves, closely set along the shoots, appear in late March and are at first light green. They gradually change through pink to deep red or brown before falling in mid-November. Long-stalked, pendulous, roughly globular cones, 1 in. across, may be borne after hot summers; male flowers have not been produced in cultivation and no fertile seeds are set.

Cultivation. Grow these trees in any fertile, moist soil. Light woodland conditions, or the edge of a pool, are ideal. In such sheltered sites young trees may grow at the rate of 3–4 ft a year. Plant from November to March, using plants 1–3 ft tall. Keep the soil round the base free from weeds for several years, and apply a scattering of Nitro-chalk over the root-run three times annually during the growing season to encourage vigorous growth.

Propagation. Seeds are not yet available. Take 3–4 in. long tip cuttings in June and July or 5–6 in. tip cuttings in November. Insert summer cuttings in equal parts (by volume) peat and sand in a propagating case, preferably under mist, at a temperature of 16–18°C (61–64°F). Cuttings taken in November should be inserted in a similar compost in a cold frame. When rooted, pot the cuttings singly in 3–3½ in. pots of John Innes potting compost No. 2. Plunge outdoors and line out in nursery rows in October; grow the young plants on for one or two years before planting out in permanent positions.

Pruning. A single main stem must be maintained; if the top does not survive early hard frosts, cut back to the strongest of the two or three competing lower shoots in April. No other pruning is necessary.

Pests. Generally trouble-free.

Diseases. HONEY FUNGUS may kill the trees.

Mezereon: see *Daphne mezereum*
Mignonette: see Reseda
Milkweed: see Asclepias
Milkweed, swamp: see *Asclepias incarnata*
Milkwort: see *Polygala calcarea*
Milla uniflora: see *Ipheion uniflorum*

Miltonia

Orchidaceae

A genus of about 25 species of epiphytic orchids from Tropical America, with short-lived but handsome flat pansy-like flowers. These plants have single-jointed pseudobulbs bearing one to three evergreen, narrow and flat leaves which are sometimes pale silvery-green. The flowers have a large flat lip, and range in colour from pure white through pink to deep brick-red, and from yellow through brown and purple to magenta. They are borne on erect or arching stems from the base of the pseudobulb.

These orchids need intermediate or cool greenhouse conditions; there is no marked resting period. Many miltonia hybrids are known and certain species have also been crossed with other related genera.

See also ORCHIDS.

M. × 'Aurora'. A distinctive hybrid between *M.* Belgica and *M.* Memoria 'F. Sander'. The two-leaved pseudobulbs are about 4 in. high. Each flower stem carries up to eight flowers from July to October; the flowers, 3–4 in. across,

are white, blotched with dark purple. The wide lip has a yellow throat. Grow this plant in an intermediate greenhouse.

M. candida. Tropical America. This species has ovate pseudobulbs up to 4 in. high, each with two narrow dark green leaves. Up to five flowers, 3½ in. across, are borne on erect 18 in. long spikes from August to November. They have green-yellow sepals, the petals being brighter yellow with red-brown markings; the lip is white with purple blotches and shading towards the base. This species needs an intermediate greenhouse.

M. regnellii. Tropical America. A free-flowering and fast-growing species with 2 in. high pseudobulbs that bear two leaves. Each spike, up to 18 in. long, carries about six flowers, 2 in. across, with white petals and sepals. The pale rose lip is streaked with deep rose-purple, and has a pale yellow crest. The flowers open from July to October. 'Purpurea' has a darker-coloured lip of rich rose-purple. These plants are best grown in a cool greenhouse.

M. spectabilis. Tropical Brazil. A robust plant with two-leaved pseudobulbs up to 3 in. high; the 8 in. tall stems bear single flowers up to 3 in. across. They open from July to September and have oblong sepals and petals that are white to cream, and tinged with pink towards their bases. The large lip is bright rose-purple with deeper coloured veins and pale rose margins.

'Moreliana' is more commonly grown than the type species; it has maroon-purple sepals and petals. They are suitable for an intermediate or a cool greenhouse.

M. vexillaria. Tropical America. A species with pseudobulbs up to 2½ in. high, bearing four or five leaves. Each 18 in. high stem carries up to ten fragrant flowers that are about 3½ in. across. They appear from May to June and are usually pale rose-mauve, occasionally pure white, with bright yellow veining on the large lip. Grow in an intermediate greenhouse.

Cultivation. Grow miltonias in well-crocked pots or baskets suited to the size of the plants. Use a well-drained compost consisting of 2 parts finely chopped osmunda fibre to 1 part sphagnum moss (parts by volume), with a little sharp sand added.

These plants need cool, airy conditions and should be freely ventilated throughout the year; damp down the greenhouse and spray the plants two or three times a day in summer. Keep them in full light from November to February, shading only on hot summer days from March to October. Keep the plants moist all year round.

Propagation. Divide and repot the plants every two or three years in August and September or in March and April.

Pests. Leaves and stems may be infested by SCALE INSECTS, making the plants sticky and sooty.

Diseases. Generally trouble-free.

Miltonia × 'Aurora'

Miltonia spectabilis 'Moreliana'

Miltonia vexillaria

Mimosa

Leguminosae

A genus of 450–500 species of tender and half-hardy annual and perennial herbaceous plants, and deciduous and evergreen sub-shrubs, shrubs, trees and climbers. Those grown in Great

Britain require greenhouse treatment, and only one species is in general cultivation. It is usually raised as an annual and grown as a pot plant. The leaves are sensitive to touch and movement, the sensitivity being most pronounced at temperatures above 24°C (75°F).

The tree known as mimosa is *Acacia dealbata*.

MIMOSA PUDICA

M. pudica (humble plant, sensitive plant). Brazil. Height 24 in. or more. A short-lived tender sub-shrub, usually grown as an annual. The light green leaves are bipinnate, composed of numerous narrowly elliptic leaflets. When touched during daylight hours these fold together and the leaf stalks droop; they resume their former position after a short period if left undisturbed. Small, pink, tufted, ball-like flowers are borne in axillary clusters, 2–3 in. long, in July and August.

Cultivation. Grow mimosas in final 5 in. pots of John Innes potting compost No. 1, preferably with a cane for support. Keep the plants moist at all times, and give a weak liquid feed at intervals of two weeks from June to September. Keep the plants in a well-lit position, but give light shading during the hottest months. Ventilate the house whenever the temperature exceeds 18–21°C (64–70°F); keep the atmosphere humid by frequent damping down.

Propagation. Sow seeds in pots or pans of seed compost in February or March, at a temperature of 18–21°C (64–70°F). When they are large enough to handle, prick out the seedlings individually into 3 in. pots of John Innes potting compost No. 1; pot on as necessary until they are in their final pots.

Pests and diseases. Generally trouble-free.

Mimulus

Monkey flower. *Scrophulariaceae*

MIMULUS CARDINALIS

A genus of 100 species of hardy annuals and herbaceous perennials. In their natural environment the plants grow in bog conditions, but all the species mentioned do well in ordinary moist garden soil. The species described here are short-lived perennials, suitable for borders, rock gardens or poolside planting; several may also be grown in pots. They have snapdragon-like, open-mouthed flowers.

M. bartonianus: see *M. lewisii*

M. × burnettii. Garden origin. Height 9–12 in.; planting distance 9 in. A hybrid between *M. cupreus* and *M. luteus*, with the mat-forming habit of the latter. The leaves are oblong-ovate and mid-green. Copper-yellow flowers, 1½ in. long, with yellow throats, are carried from May to August. The variety 'A. T. Johnson' (height 15 in.) has yellow flowers blotched with maroon, produced from June to September.

M. cardinalis. Oregon to Mexico. Height 18–24 in.; planting distance 9–12 in. The hairy mid-green leaves are ovate and sharply toothed. The flowers are 1–1½ in. long, and red with a yellow throat; they appear from June to September. This species will stand drier soil than most, but requires a sheltered position.

M. cupreus. Chile. Height 9–12 in.; planting distance 9 in. This plant is suitable for the front of a border or a rock garden. It has oblong-ovate mid-green leaves. The 1½–2 in. wide flowers are produced from June to September; they open yellow, later changing to coppery orange and spotted with brown.

Good cultivated varieties include: 'Red Emperor' (6 in.), bright crimson-scarlet; 'Scarlet Bee' (6 in.), deep scarlet; and 'Whitecroft Scarlet' (4 in.), bright orange-scarlet.

M. glutinosus: see *Diplacus glutinosus*

M. langsdorfii: see *M. luteus guttatus*

M. lewisii, syn. *M. bartonianus*. Central U.S.A. Height 12–24 in.; planting distance 12 in. A floppy species with mats of lanceolate, toothed, hairy pale green leaves that grow from thick fleshy underground stems. The rose-pink flowers are 1–1½ in. long and appear from July to September or later. Plants raised from seeds often include white-flowered forms.

M. luteus (monkey musk). Alaska to New Mexico; naturalised in Great Britain. This species varies in height, occasionally forming a mat as low as 4 in. or growing as tall as 24 in. The leaves are similar to those of *M. cupreus*. Yellow flowers, 1–2 in. long, are variably marked with maroon or crimson-brown spots; they are produced from May to August.

The variety *M. l. alpinus* forms a densely matted growth with stems only a few inches high and is more suitable for a rock garden. 'Duplex' is a hose-in-hose form with a petal-like calyx that gives the appearance of one flower within another.

M. l. guttatus, syn. *M. langsdorfii*, is smaller than the type plant, but with larger flowers, prominently blotched with brown-purple.

M. moschatus. British Columbia to California; naturalised in Great Britain. Height and planting distance 9 in. Suitable for the rock garden and for ground cover in a shady border. The ovate leaves are pale green with white woolly hairs. It flowers freely from June to September, bearing yellow flowers, about ¾ in. long, dotted or splashed with brown.

M. radicans: see *Mazus radicans*

M. ringens (lavender water musk). N. America. Water depth up to 6 in.; height up to 2½ ft; planting distance 6–9 in. A true aquatic species suitable for a small garden pool; it will also grow in ordinary moist soil. It is a decorative, late-flowering marginal plant of erect and almost shrubby habit, with dark green, narrow and

Mimosa pudica

Mimulus × burnettii

Mimulus × burnettii 'A. T. Johnson'

Mimulus cardinalis

Mimulus cupreus 'Whitecroft Scarlet'

Mimulus variegatus 'Queen's Prize'

pointed leaves. Lavender-blue flowers, ¾ in. long, are borne on short pedicels in the axils of the leaves from August to September.

M. variegatus. Chile. Height and planting distance 12 in. This species is similar to *M. luteus*, but usually bears larger flowers, up to 2 in. long, in varying mixtures of yellow and purple. 'Bonfire' is rich orange-scarlet; 'Queen's Prize' is a large-flowered dwarf strain with variously coloured blotches. The flowering period extends from June to September.

Cultivation. Plant between March and May in sun or light shade and in any ordinary garden soil that can be kept continuously moist. *M. luteus* will grow in water up to 3 in. deep; *M. ringens* in a water depth up to 6 in. Cut down old flower stems in November; in cold districts overwinter the plants under cloches.

M. × *burnettii*, *M. cupreus*, *M. luteus*, *M. moschatus* and *M. variegatus* can also be grown as pot plants on a window-sill or in a cold greenhouse. Set the plants singly in 5–6 in. pots of John Innes potting compost No. 2.

Propagation. Divide and replant in March or April. Alternatively, take 2 in. cuttings in April and insert them in a mixture of equal parts (by volume) peat and sand in a cold frame. When rooted, set the cuttings in 3 in. pots of John Innes potting compost No. 1 and plant out in permanent positions during May or June.

Sow seeds of *M. cupreus*, *M. luteus* and *M. variegatus* in February under glass at a temperature of 13–16°C (55–61°F). When large enough to handle, prick out the seedlings into boxes; set the young plants singly in 3 in. pots of John Innes potting compost No. 2 and grow on as pot plants, or harden off the young plants in a cold frame before planting out in May or June to flower the same year.

Sow seeds of other species in April or May in a cold frame or greenhouse. Prick out the seedlings, when large enough to handle, and grow on in nursery rows outdoors before transplanting to flowering positions the following April.

Pests and diseases. Generally trouble-free.

Mina lobata: see *Ipomoea lobata*
Mind-your-own-business: see *Helxine soleirolii*

Mint

Mentha. Labiatae

The two hardy aromatic perennial herbs described here are species grown primarily for flavouring and culinary use. Species with ornamental foliage are described under *Mentha*.

The leaves of both types may be used fresh or dried to make sauce and jelly to serve with lamb, or to make a refreshing tea. Sprigs may be added to iced drinks, fruit salads and vegetables.

Mint is commercially used in chewing-gum, hair tonics, *pot-pourris*, and the liqueurs Créme de Menthe, Chartreuse and Benedictine.

Apple mint, round-leaved mint (*M. rotundifolia*). N. and W. Asia, N. Africa; Europe, including Great Britain. Height 2–3 ft; planting distance 12 in. This is a white-hairy plant, with broadly ovate, strongly fragrant, pale green leaves. Pale

Mimulus cupreus 'Scarlet Bee'

Mimulus luteus

Mimulus moschatus

purple flowers are borne in densely whorled, 2–4 in. long spikes from July to September.

This plant is particularly good for mint sauce.

Common mint, spearmint (*M. spicata*). Europe, including Great Britain. Height 24 in. or more; planting distance 12 in. The ovate-lanceolate leaves are mid-green and prominently veined. Tiny pale purple flowers are carried in whorled leafy spikes, 4–6 in. long, from July to September. This is the common culinary mint.

Cultivation. Plant mints in March or April in a warm, sheltered, shady position. A rich, moist soil is ideal but most types of soil, even heavy clay, will produce satisfactory plants. Dig in a liberal dressing of manure when preparing the bed in early spring.

Mint spreads extensively unless the creeping rhizomes just below the surface are confined. The roots may be restricted by setting the plants in a bottomless bucket sunk into the ground. A surround of vertical slates or tiles below ground level is also effective.

The plants are usually trouble-free; they die down each winter and reappear at the end of March, producing leaves for picking by June.

During early spring, clean the surface of the bed and top-dress with manure or compost. Make a fresh bed every third year, as the plants soon exhaust the soil.

Lift some two or three-year-old roots in October and place them in pots or boxes of good soil for gentle forcing in the greenhouse at a temperature of up to 13°C (55°F). This will provide fresh leaves for use during winter.

Propagation. Take 3–4 in. cuttings of basal shoots in April or May, or of lateral shoots between June and August. Insert in a cold frame in equal parts (by volume) peat and sand and plant out as soon as the cuttings are rooted.

Alternatively, lift and divide the plants in March and replant direct in permanent positions. Water well until they are established.

Harvesting and storing. Pick and use the leaves fresh whenever they are available. For methods of drying, see entry under HERBS.

Pests. Generally trouble-free.

Diseases. In the spring, MINT RUST may infect the shoots. They become swollen, distorted and covered with orange-coloured spore bodies. Later, brown particles develop on the lower leaf surfaces; affected leaves dry and drop off.

Apple mint (left) and Common mint

Mirabilis jalapa

Miscanthus sinensis 'Variegatus'

Mirabilis

Nyctaginaceae

A genus of 60 species of annual and perennial herbaceous plants. The two species described, grown as annuals, are suitable for borders and for growing in pots under glass.

M. jalapa (marvel of Peru, four o'clock plant). Tropical America. Height 24 in.; planting distance 12 in. A tender perennial grown as an annual, with erect stems and mid-green heart-shaped leaves. The fragrant, trumpet-shaped flowers, 1½ in. across, are in various colours, including yellow, red, crimson, rose and white. They open during mid to late afternoon and fade the following morning. During cool or dull weather, the flowers usually open earlier, and stay fresh longer the next day. The flowering season is from July to September. This species is rather too large as a pot plant, but 'Pygmea', 18 in., is more compact.

MIRABILIS JALAPA

M. multiflora. S. United States. Height 3 ft; planting distance 12 in. This tender perennial is grown as a half-hardy annual; it has strong bushy growth and is suitable for a mixed border. The leaves are grey-green and lanceolate. The 2 in. long, purple, trumpet-shaped flowers are produced in clusters from July to September. They remain open in full sun.

Cultivation. A sheltered, sunny site and light, moderately rich soil are required. Tubers stored in a frost-free room during the winter may be planted in April, but generally new plants are raised each year from seed. For flowering under glass, set the plants in 6 in. pots of John Innes potting compost No. 2.

Propagation. Sow the seeds under glass in February or March at a temperature of 18°C (64°F). Prick out the seedlings into boxes; those for planting outdoors must be hardened off in a cold frame before being planted out in late May.

Pests. Young growths may be infested by APHIDS.

Diseases. Generally trouble-free.

Miscanthus

Gramineae

MISCANTHUS SINENSIS

A genus of 20 species of giant grasses that are hardy and perennial. They are suitable as unsupported windbreaks, and with their graceful habit they are among the most popular ornamental foliage grasses as specimen plants in lawns or in mixed borders. They may be dried and used for winter decoration. Flowers are seldom produced in Great Britain.

M. japonicus: see *M. sinensis*

M. sacchariflorus. N. China, S.E. Siberia. Height 9–10 ft; planting distance 3 ft. A species suitable for a windbreak or for providing shade. The narrow arching leaves are mid-green with paler midribs. 'Variegatus' has white-striped leaves.

M. sinensis, syns. *M. japonicus*, *Eulalia japonica*. China, Japan. Height 3–5 ft; planting distance 3 ft. A strong-growing species with narrow blue-green leaves each with a white midrib.

Varieties include: 'Gracillimus' (height 12–30 n.; spread 18–24 in.), with narrower sage-green leaves, a good specimen plant; 'Variegatus' (height 3–4 ft; spread 18–24 in.), with green and buff-yellow variegated leaves; and 'Zebrinus' (height 3–4 ft; spread 24 in.) which has yellow crossbanding at intervals on the arching leaves.

Cultivation. Plant in March or April in any ordinary, moist garden soil and in a sunny position. Despite their height these grasses require no staking; the foliage may be cut during dry weather in August and hung up to dry.

Cut all dead stems down to ground level in late March before new growth begins.

Propagation. Divide and replant the roots during March and April.

Pests. Generally trouble-free.

Diseases. On the lower leaves, POWDERY MILDEW first appears as white or brown patches of fungal growth. The leaves turn yellow and shrivel, and the trouble gradually spreads over the whole plant so that there is a grey-white coating on leaves and stems. Towards the end of the season, small black fruiting bodies develop on the diseased areas. Heavy nitrogenous manuring makes the plants more susceptible to mildew and should therefore be avoided.

Mistletoe: see Viscum

Molucella

Labiatae

MOLUCELLA LAEVIS

A genus of four species of annual and perennial plants. The species described makes an unusual plant for borders and for cutting. The attractive flowers can be dried for winter decoration.

M. laevis (bells of Ireland, shell-flower). W. Asia. Height 24 in.; planting distance 9 in. A half-hardy annual with light green rounded leaves that are carried in a tuft above and below the 9–12 in. long flower spike. The spikes are made up of white fragrant flowers, each surrounded by a large, shell-like, pale green calyx.

Cultivation. Any normal garden soil gives reasonable results but, ideally, molucellas should be grown in light rich soil and in an open, sunny site.

Propagation. Sow the seeds under glass in March, at a temperature of 15°C (59°F), just covering them with compost. Prick off the seedlings into boxes and harden off in a cold frame before planting out in May. As these plants are moderately hardy, seeds may be sown directly in the flowering site in April and the seedlings thinned to the required distance.

Pests and diseases. Generally trouble-free.

Monarch of the veldt: see *Venidium fastuosum*

Monarda

Bergamot, horsemint. *Labiatae*

A genus of 12 species of hardy annuals and perennials with aromatic leaves. In the wild, they inhabit woodland and watersides, but hybrids of *M. didyma* are suitable for growing in borders. The showy flowers are tubular with a prominent hood; they attract bees and butterflies.

MONARDA DIDYMA

M. didyma (Oswego tea, bee balm, sweet bergamot). E. United States, Canada. Height 2–3 ft; planting distance 15 in. A perennial border plant. The mid-green leaves are ovate-lanceolate and hairy; they are sometimes dried and used in tea. Dense whorled heads, 2½–3 in. across, of bright scarlet flowers, are produced from June to September.

Recommended garden varieties include: 'Adam', scarlet; 'Blue Stocking', syn. 'Prairie Night', violet-purple; 'Cambridge Scarlet', bright scarlet; 'Croftway Pink', rose-pink; 'Melissa', pale pink; 'Pale Ponticum', soft lavender; 'Pillar Box', bright red; 'Snow Maiden', white.

Garden forms with purple or mauve coloration are probably hybrids with or forms of *M. fistulosa* (wild bergamot).

Cultivation. Plant in groups of four to six plants in October, March or April. Grow in moist soil in sun or half-shade, and mulch with well-rotted manure or compost in spring.

For dried leaves, gather these just before the flowers open and dry as quickly as possible. Cut down the stems in autumn. Established plants spread from the roots and can be invasive.

Propagation. Divide the roots in March and plant out 2 in. wide tufts from the outer part of the clump, discarding the centre. Growth is quick, and division is advised every two or three years.

Named varieties do not come true from seed. Mixed seeds may be sown in a cold frame or greenhouse in March; prick out the seedlings and grow on the young plants in nursery rows; transplant to the flowering site in October.

Pests and diseases. Generally trouble-free.

Moneywort: see *Lysimachia nummularia*
Monkey flower: see Mimulus
Monkey puzzle: see *Araucaria araucana*
Monkshood: see Aconitum

Monstera

Araceae

A genus of 50 species of evergreen climbers that cling to their supports by aerial roots produced at each node. The species described is characterised by its curiously perforated leaves. The

Molucella laevis

Monarda didyma 'Cambridge Scarlet'

Monarda didyma 'Croftway Pink'

447

perforations are absent in the juvenile leaves, which are entire and heart-shaped. Later, the leaf edges become incised, and finally the perforations appear. Monsteras require greenhouse treatment and are frequently grown as house plants.

Monstera deliciosa (flowering spathe)

Monstera deliciosa (young plant)

Morina longifolia

M. deliciosa. Mexico. Height eventually 20 ft or more. This species has dark green, deeply notched leaves which have numerous perforations. In full-grown plants the leaves may reach a length of 4 ft and be 24 in. wide.

Mature plants produce cream-yellow, arum-like spathes 4–6 in. long, usually borne singly or in groups of two or three. They may occur at any time of year and are followed by club-shaped green-white fruits. The seeds are embedded in a succulent pulp tasting of pineapple.

M. leichtlinii: see *Philodendron leichtlinii*

Cultivation. Grow monsteras in a rich compost such as John Innes potting compost No. 3 or in a proprietary peat compost. The plants require a winter temperature of 10°C (50°F), but will come to little harm at 7°C (45°F) for short periods, provided they are kept fairly dry.

Growth starts as soon as the temperature reaches 18°C (64°F). The plants will then require more water and a humid atmosphere. Provide this by damping down and by syringing the leaves. Shade the glass in summer.

In the greenhouse, grow the plants in the border or in 12 in. pots or small tubs. Train the stems up string or wire. The aerial roots may be packed with moss, kept constantly moist; this encourages more vigorous growth.

House plants should be sunk in their pots in an absorbent material such as peat, which must be kept moist, and the leaves should be sprayed in hot weather. In the home the plants will grow in shady conditions, but will then produce only small leaves. In deep shade the leaves may revert to the juvenile heart shape.

Provide a stake for all plants more than 12 in. high, and train the aerial roots down to enter the soil in the pot. When the plants become too large for this, leave the aerial roots to grow naturally or pack them with moss.

Feed the plants every 10–14 days from April to September with a weak liquid fertiliser; the roots

are easily damaged by a strong fertiliser. Pot o annually in April; final pot size should be 10–1 in. Thereafter repot every two or three years.

Propagation. Remove the growing tip with on mature leaf and insert, in June, in a 4 in. po containing equal parts (by volume) peat an sand. Root at a temperature of 24–27°C (75–81°F). A new plantlet will eventually appea from the next leaf axil on the parent plant.

If several new plants are wanted, remove th top part of a stem, from June to August, and cu into several joints, about 3 in. long, and eac containing one leaf. Root the cuttings as de scribed for tip cuttings.

Monsteras occasionally produce lateral shoots these may be removed when they are 6 in. long and treated as cuttings.

Pests. Generally trouble-free.

Diseases. A PHYSIOLOGICAL DISORDER due to incorrect watering results in brown or yellow blotches developing on the leaves.

Montbretia crocosmiiflora: see *Crocosmia × crocosmiiflora*

Moosewood: see *Acer pennsylvanicum*

Morina
Dipsacaceae

MORINA LONGIFOLIA

A genus of 17 species of hardy herbaceou perennials. Only one is easily available; it i suitable for growing in borders.

M. longifolia. Nepal. Height 2½ ft; planting distance 18 in. This plant has a thistle-lik appearance; the basal, spiny leaves are mid-green and the stems bear similar but smaller leaves The leaf axils carry whorls of numerous narrow and tubular flowers, each 1 in. long with widely expanded petals. The colour is white on opening, rapidly turning pink and finally crimson-purple. The main flowering perioc is June and July, but flower stems occasionally appear until late autumn.

Cultivation. Plant in September and October o in March and April in deep, well-drained garder soil. A sunny position is best, although the plant will thrive in partial shade. Avoid sites that are exposed to wind. Cut the stems down in autumn and protect the roots with litter or bracken in cold districts from November to March.

Propagation. Sow seeds in September, March or April in a cold frame; prick out the seedlings when large enough to handle, and grow the young plants on in a nursery bed. Transplant to the flowering site in spring or autumn of the following year.

Morinas form thick tap roots, and division is therefore seldom practicable.

Pests and diseases. Generally trouble-free.

Morisia

Cruciferae

A genus of a single species of herbaceous perennial. It can be grown in troughs or on rock gardens, and is also suitable for an alpine house.

M. hypogaea: see *M. monanthos*

M. monanthos, syn. *M. hypogaea*. Sardinia and Corsica. Height 1 in.; spread 6 in. The dark green, jaggedly toothed, lanceolate leaves form prostrate rosettes. Clusters of golden-yellow cross-shaped flowers, about $\frac{1}{2}$ in. across, are borne on short stems from March to May.

Cultivation. Plant in September or October. On rock gardens grow morisias in a light, sharply drained soil in full sun. In troughs, use a mixture of 2 parts John Innes potting compost No. 1 and 1 part grit (parts by volume); in the alpine house grow morisias in 6 in. pans in a similar mixture and repot every second or third year in September.

Propagation. Take 1–2 in. long cuttings from the thickest roots in February or March. Insert in equal parts (by volume) peat and sand in a pan and place this in a cold frame. Pot the cuttings singly into $2\frac{1}{2}$ in. pots when small rosettes have formed and grow on in the frame before planting out in September.

Pests and diseases. Generally trouble-free.

Morning glory: see Ipomoea
Morus nigra: see Mulberry
Mother-in-law's tongue: see *Sansevieria trifasciata*
Mother of thousands: see *Saxifraga stolonifera*
Mugwort, white: see *Artemisia lactiflora*

Mulberry

Morus nigra. Moraceae

MULBERRY

These hardy, deciduous, slow-growing trees are cultivated both for their fruits and for their ornamental appearance. Mulberries are of Asiatic and North American origin but have been grown in Britain since 1550. They are self-fertile.

At one time *Morus alba* was cultivated for its leaves, on which silkworms were fed, but *M. nigra* is the species to grow for edible fruits. This is the common or black mulberry, originating in western Asia. Height 15–20 ft; spread 10–15 ft. It is a bushy, round-headed tree with coarse dark green foliage. Each leaf is broadly ovate and toothed, sometimes with two lateral lobes. The small green-yellow flowers are borne in $\frac{1}{2}$ in. long catkins during May and June. They are followed by dark red berry-like fruits which fuse together to form an ovoid, multiple fruit. The berries ripen in August and September; they resemble loganberries and have a pleasant, slightly acid flavour.

Cultivation. Mulberry trees need deep, well-drained, rich loams with adequate supplies of moisture. When grown for fruit production, they are most likely to succeed on sites protected from north and east winds; in northern England and Scotland they need a warm, south-facing wall. Plant in November.

Harvest the fruits in late August and early September by spreading a cloth under the tree and shaking the branches.

Propagation. In autumn or early spring take 12 in. long cuttings that have some two-year-old wood at the base. Plant them deeply so that only two or three buds are above ground. Larger branches will also root and may be planted *in situ*. On a 6–8 ft long shoot trim off the laterals and bury it 2–4 ft deep. Grow smaller cuttings on for two or three years before planting out.

Pruning. Mulberries are liable to bleed when cut, and pruning should be avoided. It is necessary only to remove dead wood and crossing branches from established trees.

Pests. Generally trouble-free.

Diseases. CANKER and DIE-BACK are due to a fungus which produces cankers on the young shoots during summer. Girdling occurs.

Mullein: see Verbascum
Mullein, purple: see *Verbascum phoeniceum*

Musa

Musaceae

MUSA CAVENDISHII

A genus of 35 species of tender evergreen perennials. It includes the edible banana and plantain. Several of the smaller ornamental species are suitable for greenhouse cultivation, but require ample room.

M. acuminata: see *M. cavendishii*

Musa cavendishii (young fruits)

M. cavendishii (Canary Islands banana). East Indies. Height up to 7 ft; spread 6 ft. The bright mid-green elliptic leaves are 2–3 ft long and 12 in. wide. The drooping inflorescence consists of

Morisia monanthos

Mulberry

Musa cavendishii

Musa cavendishii
(flowering spike)

Muscari armeniacum

Muscari botryoides

dark purple leathery bracts, which enclose the hand-shaped clusters of 2 in. long flowers. These appear in June or July and are followed by edible, seedless fruits.

This plant is now known to be a dwarf mutant of *M. acuminata*, which is one of the parents of the bananas of commerce. The correct botanical name is *M. acuminata* 'Dwarf Cavendish'.

M. ensete. Abyssinia. Height and spread as a pot plant 6 ft. The green elliptic leaves, 3 ft long and 12 in. across, have red midribs. Flowers and fruit are rarely borne in cultivation.

M. velutina. Assam. Height 4 ft; spread 5 ft. This slender, pink-stemmed species has elliptic leaves, 3 ft long and 12 in. across; they are mid-green, sometimes blotched with maroon, especially when young. The erect inflorescence appears from June to August; the red bracts enclose hand-shaped clusters of yellow flowers, 2 in. long. They are followed by non-edible, red velvety, oval fruits.

Cultivation. Grow musas in the greenhouse border or in 10–12 in. pots or large tubs of John Innes potting compost No. 3. Minimum winter temperatures are 10°C (50°F) for *M. cavendishii* and *M. ensete*; 16°C (61°F) for *M. velutina*. In summer, ventilate whenever the temperature exceeds 21°C (70°F).

Shade the glass lightly from mid-May to mid-August, when the new leaves are emerging. Water the plants sparingly from October to March, plentifully from April to September.

Pot on young plants twice a year as necessary until they are in their final containers. After fruiting, the fruit-bearing growth of *M. cavendishii* dies and is replaced by suckers, which should be removed and grown on.

M. ensete should be repotted annually or every other year in March or April; it may be used as a bedding plant outdoors from June to late September and overwintered in a cool greenhouse. In mild areas in the south and west it may survive the winter outdoors.

M. velutina is a clump-forming species, whose flowering growths die and should be removed. Numerous sucker shoots replace the old growths. Mature plants may be divided and repotted in March if they have outgrown their containers.

Feed all pot plants with a weak liquid manure at 10–14 day intervals from May to September.

Propagation. Increase *M. ensete* by seeds. These are imported and should be sown in April at a temperature of 21°C (70°F). Prick out the seedlings, when large enough to handle, and pot on as necessary.

Increase the other species by detaching the rooted suckers in April. Pot up individually and grow on. *M. velutina* may be divided as described under CULTIVATION.

Pruning. Remove flowered and fruited stems.

Pests and diseases. Generally trouble-free.

Muscari

Grape hyacinth. *Liliaceae*

This genus of bulbous plants, related to *Hyacinthus*, includes 60 species, of which at least one is considered native to Britain. Several others have long been in cultivation. These hardy dwarf plants are useful as cut flowers and for growing in rock gardens, in clumps at the front of borders or for edging beds.

The species described have mid-green linear leaves, with a channelled inner surface. Their upper flowers are sterile and do not open; with the exception of *M. comosum* they are paler than the lower urn-shaped ones, and ¼ in. long.

M. armeniacum. S.E. Europe, W. Asia. Height 8–10 in.; planting distance 3–4 in. The leaves spread and separate as the flowers appear. The densely packed flowers, borne in April and May, are deep blue with white rims. Named varieties include 'Cantab', which is paler than the species, and 'Heavenly Blue', which is brighter blue.

M. atlanticum: see *M. racemosum*

M. botryoides. Central Europe. Height 6–8 in.; planting distance 3–4 in. The deep sky-blue flowers appear from March to May. *M. b.* 'Album' is a white form.

M. comosum. Central and W. Europe and Mediterranean regions. Height 18 in.; planting distance 4 in. The lower flowers are olive-green, the upper ones purple; they appear in May and June. *M. c.* 'Monstrosum', syn. 'Plumosum' (feather hyacinth, tassel hyacinth) is a variety consisting entirely of sterile, branched blue filaments; since no seeds are set, these filaments are long-lasting.

M. latifolium. Turkey. Height 9–12 in.; planting distance 4 in. The flowers are purple, and appear in April and May.

M. macrocarpum. Turkey. Height 6–9 in.; planting distance 4–6 in. A robust species with semi-prostrate, somewhat glaucous leaves. The fragrant flowers are bright rich yellow with a brown mouth. They are borne in terminal racemes, up to 3 in. long, in April and May.

M. moschatum. W. Turkey. Height 6–9 in.; planting distance 4–6 in. This species is closely related to and resembles *M. macrocarpum*, but the flowers open pale purple and age to ivory.

M. neglectum. N. and S. Mediterranean regions. Height 9 in.; planting distance 3–4 in. The scented, densely packed flowers are dark blue; they appear in April.

M. paradoxum, syn. *Bellevalia paradoxa.* Caucasus, west into Europe. Height 12–15 in.; planting distance 4–5 in. The dark purple flowers have a green interior. Flowering time is in May.

M. racemosum, syn. *M. atlanticum.* Europe, including Great Britain. Height 8 in.; planting distance 3–4 in. The scented flowers, dark blue with a white mouth, appear from March to April. This plant spreads easily in good conditions.

M. tubergenianum (Oxford and Cambridge). Persia. Height 8 in.; planting distance 3–4 in. The name is derived from the dark and pale blue densely packed flowers that open in March.

Cultivation. Any ordinary well-drained soil is suitable for these bulbs. Plant 3 in. deep from August to November, setting the bulbs in groups, in single rows for cutting, or to form an edge to a border or path. Muscaris require full sun; shade increases leaf growth but reduces flowering. Lift and divide the plants every three years.

Muscari bulbs may also be grown in pots or pans of John Innes potting compost No. 1, placing up to 12 bulbs in a 5–6 in. container.

Propagation. Many species spread readily on their own by means of self-sown seeds and bulbils. For planting elsewhere, save seeds in June and sow from July to September in pans or boxes of John Innes seed compost in a cold frame or greenhouse. Plant out the seedlings in nursery rows after a year. The plants will flower two to four years later.

Divide congested clumps after three or four years, waiting until the leaves are yellow before lifting. Replant at once.

Pests. Generally trouble-free.

Diseases. The anthers and, less frequently, the ovaries may be converted into masses of black, soot-like spores by SMUT.

Mushroom

Psalliota campestris. Agaricaceae.

An edible fungus widely grown on a commercial scale. Mushrooms grow rapidly and require little attention once the special compost that they need has been prepared. They can be grown in grass outdoors in summer, but for crops throughout the year mushrooms are best grown in cold frames, in boxes under the greenhouse staging, in outhouses or in cellars.

The distinctive succulent flavour is most pronounced in fresh mushrooms; they quickly become limp and tough. Both the stalk and the cap are edible; young, short-stalked button-mushrooms are nearly spherical with pink gills. As the mushrooms mature the caps expand and flatten at the edges, and the gills become brown. There are white, cream and brown types, the last being most resistant to disease. There is no difference in flavour between the various types, but mature mushrooms are tastier than the young buttons.

Cultivation. For an indoor crop, choose a clean site, free from cold draughts. It should be dark or only dimly lit with good ventilation and a steady temperature of 10–13°C (50–55°F).

Prepare the compost outdoors. Use fresh damp horse manure if available, mix it thoroughly, pile it into a broad heap, and leave it to generate heat. After about a week, moisten the heap if necessary and turn it, so that the material on the outside is moved to the inside. Repeat this process three or four times at intervals of three days after the first turning. The manure is suitable for use when it has lost its smell and is brown and friable. Do not use horse manure that contains wood shavings, sawdust or chemicals. If horse manure is not available, buy a ready-made mushroom compost or treat wheat straw with one of the proprietary chemicals available for making mushroom compost.

When the compost is ready, move it to the chosen site and pack it down firmly to a depth of 10–12 in. The temperature of the compost at first rises to 38°C (100°F) or more; it then falls after a few weeks' interval. When the temperature of the bed is at 24°C (75°F), insert walnut-sized pieces of mushroom spawn to a depth of 1½–2 in., setting them 10–12 in. apart either way. A bed measuring 15–20 sq. ft will take one block of spawn.

After a few days, the spawn will spread fine threads through the compost; ten days later the bed should be covered with sterile sub-soil to preserve heat and prevent loss of moisture.

Mushrooms generally appear eight to ten weeks after the bed was spawned and continue to appear for about three months. If button-mushrooms are required, cut them just before the membrane between the cap and the stalk separates and reveals the gills.

An outdoor crop of mushrooms can be grown in a lawn or field that has not been dressed with hormone weed-killers, and in an open position. Lift small squares of turf about 12 in. apart and 2 in. thick, and insert under each a walnut-sized piece of spawn; replace the turf firmly.

Pests. Maggots of various MUSHROOM FLIES tunnel into the stalks and caps of mushrooms, making them maggoty and inedible.

Diseases. Unhygienic growing conditions cause MUSHROOM DISEASES to develop; the mushrooms may be distorted, blotched or pitted.

Musk, lavender water: see *Mimulus ringens*
Musk, monkey: see *Mimulus luteus*

Mustard and cress

Sinapis alba and *Lepidium sativum. Cruciferae.*

These annuals are usually grown together and used in their seedling stage as salad vegetables and for sandwich fillings. The small, bright green leaves, borne at the top of the 3–4 in. long white stems, have a pungent spicy taste.

VARIETIES

Only one mustard variety, 'White', is commonly grown; it is sometimes substituted by rape (*Brassica napus*) which is considered of superior flavour. Two cress varieties, 'Curled' and 'Plain' are in general cultivation.

Cultivation. Mustard and cress may be grown in the open, but are more successful under glass, as the plants must be grown rapidly to produce tender leafy growth. The seeds may be grown in very fine soil or John Innes seed compost, or on any moisture-retentive medium, such as pads of cotton wool, flannel or pieces of sacking. The latter methods are preferable as no soil adheres to the seedlings.

Place the growing medium in a small seed tray or similar container. Spread the seeds thickly and evenly on top, and press the seeds down lightly, but do not cover with soil. Water with lukewarm water and cover the tray with brown paper or black polythene. Place the tray in a cold frame, under a cloche or, in winter, in a greenhouse with a temperature of 7°C (45°F).

When the seeds have germinated, remove the cover from the tray and keep the growing medium moist, watering with lukewarm water through a fine rose.

Cress will be ready 11–14 days after sowing; if grown together with mustard or rape, sow cress three days before mustard or rape so that the two crops will mature at the same time.

Pests. Adults and larvae of the MUSTARD BEETLE eat holes in leaves and stems.

Diseases. Generally trouble-free.

Muscari macrocarpum

Mushroom

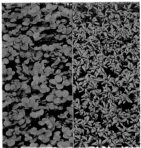

Mustard (left) and cress

451

Myosotidium

Boraginaceae

A genus of one evergreen herbaceous perennial. It is not easy to grow as it needs a cool, damp and sheltered position. It is hardy only in mild districts, preferably near the sea.

M. hortensia, syn. *M. nobile* (giant forget-me-not). Chatham Islands. Height 18 in.; planting distance 15–18 in. This border plant has ovate-cordate, prominently ribbed leaves, glossy mid-green in colour. A profusion of $\frac{1}{2}$ in. wide, white-margined blue flowers, similar to those of forget-me-nots, appears in April and May.

M. nobile: see *M. hortensia*

Cultivation. Plant in September or October in any ordinary garden soil, in a damp, sheltered and sunny position. Protect with bracken, leaves, straw or peat in winter. Mulch in summer with seaweed; cut the stems down in autumn.

Propagation. Sow seeds in March or April in a cold frame or greenhouse. Prick out the seedlings, when large enough to handle, and grow on in a nursery bed before planting out in the flowering site in autumn.

Pests and diseases. Generally trouble-free.

Myosotidium hortensia

Myosotis alpestris

Myosotis alpestris 'Blue Ball'

Myosotis

Forget-me-not. *Boraginaceae*

A genus of 50 species of annual and perennial herbaceous plants, including a number of garden varieties that are usually grown as biennials. The perennials are all rather short-lived and may not last more than two or three years.

These plants have small salver-shaped flowers with bell-shaped calyces. Some are suitable for growing in beds and borders or under glass; others are better sited in rock gardens, while *M. scorpioides* is a moisture-loving plant.

M. alpestris. Europe, including Great Britain. Height 3–8 in.; planting distance 6 in. A bushy hardy perennial, excellent for a rock garden. It has hoary green, oblong-lanceolate leaves, and bears dense spikes of azure-blue flowers with distinctive yellow eyes. The flowers are fragrant, about $\frac{1}{3}$ in. across, and open from April to June.

There are many garden hybrids thought to have originated from this species, including 'Blue Ball', 6 in., which makes a compact ball-shaped plant with rich indigo-blue flowers. 'Carmine King', 9 in., is an erect plant with deep rose-carmine flowers; and 'Alba', 6 in., has white flowers. Mixtures are also available.

M. oblongata: see *M. sylvatica*

M. palustris: see *M. scorpioides*

M. rupicola. European Alps. Height up to 2 in.; spread 4–6 in. This is similar to *M. alpestris*, but smaller. It is suitable for a rock garden, and forms a tightly packed cluster of bright blue flowers in May and June.

M. scorpioides, syn. *M. palustris* (water forget-me-not). Europe, including Great Britain. Water depth up to 3 in.; height 9 in.; planting distance 6–9 in. A hardy evergreen perennial aquatic with a long flowering period in summer. The leaves are elongated, spoon-shaped and covered with rough hairs. Tall stems arise bearing cymes of numerous pale blue, yellow-eyed flowers, $\frac{1}{4}$ in. across, from April to July.

Two varieties are recommended: 'Mermaid' with thick stems and dark green foliage; the flowers are a deep blue, with a deep yellow eye. 'Semperflorens' is more compact than the type, although somewhat variable.

M. sylvatica, syn. *M. oblongata*. Great Britain. Height 12 in. or more; planting distance 6 in. A hardy biennial or short-lived perennial of bushy growth. It is suitable for growing outdoors in borders, under glass to provide cut flowers or for naturalising in woodland. The oblong-lanceolate leaves are mid-green and hairy. Fragrant blue flowers, $\frac{1}{3}$ in. across, are carried in open sprays from May to June.

'Blue Bird', 12 in., has deep blue flowers.

Cultivation. Apart from *M. scorpioides*, these plants grow in any garden soil and position. For best results, however, plant in partial shade and in a soil which retains moisture and contains a fair amount of such organic matter as leaf-mould or compost. In poorly drained soil, plants tend to die off during the winter; cloche protection is helpful under such conditions.

Outdoors, plant in September or October; in the greenhouse, plant the seedlings during October. Under glass, plant in the border, allowing 12 in. between the rows and 6 in. between plants, or in 5–6 in. pots or pans of John Innes potting compost No. 1. They need no heat during winter. Repot annually in March. Plants grown under glass will generally flower a month to six weeks earlier than those grown outdoors.

Plant *M. scorpioides* in April, May, September or October in heavy fertile loam, at water level or covered by up to 3 in. of water. It thrives in full sun or partial shade. Trim off old flower heads occasionally.

Propagation. Sow seeds of all species in April or May, in boxes or pans in a cold frame or in seed beds outside. Prick out the seedlings into a nursery bed. Transfer plants to flower under glass into 3 in. pots of John Innes potting compost No. 1, or grow on and plant out in September.

M. scorpioides can also be increased by taking 2–5 in. basal cuttings in March, or in August or September after flowering. Insert these in boxes of equal parts (by volume) peat, loam and sand kept permanently moist. When rooted, plant the cuttings out in permanent positions.

Pests. Generally trouble-free.

Diseases. In cold, wet conditions GREY MOULD may cause rotting of flowers; the blooms become covered with a grey furry mould.

POWDERY MILDEW shows as a white powdery coating on stems and leaves.

Myrtle: see Myrtus
Myrtle, common: see *Myrtus communis*

Myrtus

Myrtle. *Myrtaceae*

A genus of 100 species of tender and half-hardy evergreen shrubs and, rarely, trees, with aromatic foliage. In Great Britain, these shrubs

quire greenhouse cultivation, although in
eltered areas in the south and west the species
escribed may survive outdoors. The fragrant
hite flowers are saucer-shaped and five-
etalled; they are borne singly from the upper
af-axils and are outstanding for their promin-
it boss of thin stamens.

MYRTUS COMMUNIS

1. bullata. New Zealand. Height up to 10 ft;
pread 6 ft; as a pot plant, 3–4 ft high and 18 in.
vide. A species with ovate-elliptic, heavily cor-
ugated deep green leaves. The $\frac{3}{4}$ in. wide
owers are borne during May and June; they
nay be followed in autumn by purple-black,
rn-shaped fruits.

1. communis (common myrtle). Mediterranean
egions. Height and spread 8–10 ft; as a pot
lant, 2–3 ft high and wide. This species bears
lossy mid to deep green, ovate to lanceolate
eaves, more aromatic than those of *M. bullata*.
he 1 in. wide flowers are produced from June
) August; they are sometimes followed by
urple-black ovoid fruits.

'Tarentina', syn. 'Jenny Reitenbach', is a
mall-growing, compact variety with smaller

leaves and flowers; 'Variegata' has cream-
white variegations to the leaves.

M. luma. Chile. Height and spread up to 10 ft.
This large shrub or small tree has ovate to
elliptic dark green leaves, and bears white
flowers, $\frac{3}{4}$–1 in. across, in September. A feature
of this species is the handsome trunk, which
on older specimens is cinnamon-brown, flaking
to show pale green patches.

Cultivation. In the greenhouse, grow myrtus in
the border or, where space is limited, in 8–10 in.
pots of John Innes potting compost No. 2.
Provide a winter temperature of 5°C (41°F) and
keep the plants just moist. In summer, water
and ventilate freely; pot plants may be stood
outdoors from late May to late September.

Pot on every other year in March or April;
feed established plants with weak liquid manure
at fortnightly intervals from May to September.

Outdoors, plant myrtus in late May in ordinary, well-drained soil and in a sunny sheltered
position, preferably against a wall.

Propagation. Take 2–3 in. cuttings of lateral
non-flowering shoots with a heel in June or July.
Insert in equal parts (by volume) peat and sand
in a propagating frame at a temperature of 16°C
(61°F). When rooted, pot the cuttings singly in
3 in. containers of John Innes potting compost
No. 1 and pot on as necessary.

Pruning. None required except to remove
straggly shoots from the base in March and
April. Frosted shoots on outdoor shrubs should
be removed at the same time.

Pests and diseases. Generally trouble-free.

Myrtus communis

Myrtus luma (patterned trunk
with flaking bark)

N

Nandina

Chinese sacred bamboo.
Nandinaceae, syn. *Berberidaceae*

genus of a single species. In habit this
alf-hardy evergreen shrub somewhat resembles
amboo, but the leaves become red and purple
nted in October and November.

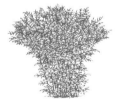

NANDINA DOMESTICA

V. domestica. China. Height 4–6 ft; spread 2–3
t. The pinnate leaves are pale to mid-green when
nature, but stained with red when young. In
)ctober or November the leaves take on shades
f purple. White flowers appear in 6–15 in. wide
anicles during July and may be followed by
carlet or white fruits which ripen in August and

persist through the winter. This shrub, which is a
close relative of *Berberis*, is grown mainly for its
autumn tints.

Cultivation. Plant in rich, moist, well-drained soil
in a sunny sheltered position between March and
May. In severe winters the foliage may be
scorched and the tips killed by frost, but the
shrubs usually recover.

Propagation. Sow seeds in October in a cold
frame or greenhouse. When the seedlings are
large enough to handle, prick them off individually into 3 in. pots of John Innes potting
compost No. 1. Transfer them to a nursery bed
the following September and grow on for two or
three years, planting out in April or May in
permanent positions.

In September take 3–4 in. cuttings of lateral
shoots with a heel and insert them in equal parts
(by volume) peat and sand in a cold frame.
Transfer the rooted cuttings to a nursery bed the
following May and grow on for two or three
years before planting them out in March in their
permanent positions.

Pruning. Thin out dead wood and weak shoots
after flowering.

Pests and diseases. Generally trouble-free.

Nandina domestica

Narcissi (naturalised)

Narcissus bulbocodium

Narcissus cyclamineus

NARCISSUS
Amaryllidaceae

From the earliest days of gardening daffodils and narcissi have heralded the spring, and they are still among the most popular of spring-time bulbs. Most are hardy but some, such as certain forms of *N. tazetta*, 'Soleil d'Or' and 'Paper White', may have their flowers spoilt by frost.

With one exception (see Division 11) all flowers in this large genus have the characteristic cup or corona, and six stamens attached to the perianth tube. However, the species vary in the proportions and relative sizes of the cup and the petals. (Botanically, the latter are perianth segments but are often referred to as petals.)

The species in this genus are all botanically classed as narcissi, although the trumpet narcissi, which have a central trumpet as long as, or longer than, the surrounding petals, are usually known as daffodils.

In addition to white, narcissi flowers are coloured in many shades of yellow, pink, scarlet and orange. The parent species of all these bulbs are chiefly natives of Europe, especially Spain and Portugal, France, Switzerland and Yugoslavia, and North Africa; the exceptions are the tazetta (bunch-flowered) narcissi which are found across Europe, through Asia and into China and Japan.

Having been sought after for centuries, probably all species are now known. About 60 are recognised as true species, with about half the number of natural hybrids. Over 100 wild varieties and their forms exist. The Royal Horticultural Society has grouped narcissi into 11 divisions (described later in this entry), with all garden hybrids and wild forms included in these divisions. In addition, the R.H.S. Classified List and International Register contains about 8000 named cultivated varieties, most of which have been raised in the last 100 years and which are being added to yearly.

In describing the species and varieties, average heights and flower sizes have been given. In cultivation, plant heights and flower sizes depend on soil and climate and, in the case of newly planted bulbs, on the climate where they were grown and the conditions under which they were stored. When planting, the spacing of narcissus bulbs is governed by a number of factors which are dealt with under CULTIVATION.

Dates of flowering vary considerably in different parts of the country. In the Scilly Isles the earliest bloom outdoors in November and the latest in May; in the Midlands the whole narcissus season, from the earliest to the latest varieties, lasts eight weeks at most. Times given here are therefore averages.

The flowering dates of bulbs can be influenced by complicated techniques, which include the advancement of flowering by closely controlled cool storage (to simulate an artificial early winter) and the retardation of flowering by equally careful warm storage; exceptions to this treatment are the tazetta narcissi, which need warm storage for early flowering.

These storage methods are beyond the scope of most amateur gardeners, but treated bulbs can be purchased for especially early or late flowering.

The species of wild daffodils provide a wider range of shapes and sizes than the garden varieties. They are at their best when left to grow and flower for many years in the same place. Their flowering dates are governed by the climate; the dates given here are averages for most of Britain.

Generally, the flat or linear leaves are grey-green while the cylindrical leaves are a glossy deep green. Nearly all the smaller plants do well in pots, but most can also be grown outside.

N. asturiensis, syn. *N. minimus.* Spain. Height 3 in. Linear leaves. A tiny yellow trumpet narcissus, 1 in. long, that grows on rather weak stems and flowers in February in most districts. It needs good drainage and does well in a sunny rock garden or in pots or pans under glass. Similar in shape to the garden varieties in Division 1.

N. bulbocodium (hoop petticoat). S.W. France, Spain, Portugal, N.W. Africa. Height 2–6 in. The variable leaves are cylindrical. This is an all-yellow species with numerous varieties which have a confusing nomenclature. The wide-open 1 in. long trumpets dominate the narrow petals; the stamens and style are curved. It flowers in February and March. Dissimilar to any garden varieties listed in the R.H.S. divisions.

N. b. monophyllus: see *N. cantabricus.*

N. b. obesus is a deep yellow form, 1½ in. long, with thicker leaves; it flowers in March and April. *N. b. romieuxii* is a pale yellow form which flowers from December to February and does best under glass. *N. b. vulgaris citrinus* is lemon-yellow, and *N. b. vulgaris conspicuus* a deep yellow, both flowering in March and April.

N. calcicola. Portugal. Height 6 in. The leaves are linear. This is a sweet-scented jonquil-like species, with several deep yellow flowers on each stem, appearing in March and April; each is ¾ in. across and has a flattened corona. It is sometimes regarded as a taller form of *N. juncifolius.* It is not vigorous and is best grown in pots or pans under glass. Similar in shape to, but smaller than, the garden varieties in Division 7.

N. cantabricus, syn. *N. bulbocodium monophyllus.* Spain and N.W. Africa. Height 3–4 in. A white species resembling *N. bulbocodium,* but with a widely expanded cup or corona; it is best grown in pots or pans in a greenhouse. Flowers in December and January.

N. cyclamineus. Spain and Portugal. Height 6–8 in. This dwarf species, which has dark green linear leaves, flowers in February and March. The rich gold pendent flowers have 1½–2 in. long trumpets, and petals that sweep up and back.

The flower shape is reminiscent of a cyclamen. This species grows well either in the open or in partial shade; it does best in moist soil, where it will seed and increase freely. It is the parent of many hybrids and similar to the garden varieties described in Division 6.

N. × gracilis. Not found in the wild. Height 12–15 in. This cross between a jonquil and *N. poeticus* is related to the garden varieties in Division 7. The linear leaves are mid-green. Scented pale yellow flowers, 1½–2 in. wide and with short cups, appear in May.

N. jonquilla (wild jonquil). S.W. Europe and N.E. Africa. Height 12 in. A species with cylindrical leaves and stems, and strongly scented deep yellow flowers, each 1½–2 in. wide and with a small central cup. The garden varieties in Division 7 are related to it.

A double form is known as 'Queen Anne's Jonquil'. All flower in April and are at their best in a warm, sheltered spot.

N. juncifolius. S.W. Europe. Height 3–6 in. Cylindrical leaves. Deep yellow flowers, ¾ in. across and with a flattened cup, are borne in May. It is suitable for a rock garden or a cool greenhouse. Similar to varieties in Division 7.

N. minimus: see *N. asturiensis*

N. minor. Portugal. Height 8 in. The leaves are narrowly strap-shaped. This variable species, flowering in March, has pale petals with slightly deeper yellow, 1½ in. long trumpets; similar proportions to the varieties in Division 1.

N. × odorus (campernelle jonquil). Height 15–18 in. Linear leaves. An April-flowering hybrid between a trumpet narcissus and a jonquil, this tall plant has two or three pale yellow flowers on each stem. They are scented, 2½ in. wide and have bell-shaped cups. Though known since the 16th century it has not been found growing wild. *N. × o.* 'Campernelli Plenus' is a double form. Similar to the garden varieties in Division 7.

N. poeticus (the poet's narcissus). N. Mediterranean from Spain to Greece. Height 15–18 in. Narrowly strap-shaped leaves. This is a variable species, with many named varieties that are often regarded as separate species; it is found in the wild on mountain ranges. All forms have white petals and flat, bright red cups that are usually frilled. The flowers are 2–3 in. across and appear in April. *N. p. ornatus* is one of the stronger-growing wild forms.

N. pseudonarcissus (wild daffodil, lent lily). Europe, including Great Britain. Height 6–12 in. The leaves are strap-shaped. This species has pale, near-white petals and lemon-yellow 2–2½ in. long trumpets. The flowers are borne in April. It thrives in damp meadowlands.

Many of its varieties were formerly regarded as separate species. *N. p. moschatus* is a white form; *N. p. obvallaris* (Tenby daffodil) is a uniform yellow, but neither is as vigorous nor as self-increasing from seed as the species. Related to the garden varieties in Division 1.

N. rupicola. Spain, Portugal. Height 3–5 in. A dwarf species with clear yellow colouring and a nearly flat six-lobed cup. Similar to the garden varieties in Division 7, but having only one flower, ¾ in. across, on each stem. These open in April and May.

N. scaberulus. Portugal. Height 3–5 in. The leaves are cylindrical and slightly glaucous. Similar to *N. rupicola,* this species has smaller flowers (½ in. across) and slightly deeper colouring. It is best grown in a cold greenhouse. Related to the garden varieties in Division 7.

N. tazetta (bunch-flowered narcissus). Canary Islands, S. Europe, N. Africa, Persia, Kashmir, China and Japan. Height 12–18 in. Strap-shaped leaves. A variable species, distinguished by the many flowers on each stem. The forms in Division 8 are related to this species.

Narcissus jonquilla

Narcissus minor

Narcissus triandrus albus

Narcissus 'Dutch Master' (Div. 1a)

Narcissus 'Golden Harvest' (Div. 1a)

Narcissus 'Foresight' (Div. 1b)

Narcissus 'Trousseau' (Div. 1b)

Narcissus 'Cantatrice' (Div. 1c)

The flowers, which are 1–1½ in. across, have white petals and short, cup-shaped, lemon-yellow coronas; they are strongly scented and are among the earliest to flower (January and February). They are half-hardy only, and the varieties grown in Great Britain do best in bowls or pots under glass, except in the mildest districts.

The species and many older varieties are not now in general cultivation. *N. tazetta* and *N. poeticus* varieties have been much crossed to produce the poetaz varieties listed in Division 8.

N. t. papyraceus ('Paper White'). S. France across to Dalmatia. Height 18–21 in. Strap-shaped leaves. This all-white scented form, 1½ in. across and with a short, cup-shaped corona, is the earliest-blooming narcissus. Cut flowers come in huge quantities from the south of France and the Channel and Scilly Isles before Christmas and in the New Year. It will not survive outdoors for long in cold districts; grown outside it flowers in March but raised in pots or bowls under glass it will flower at Christmas.

N. triandrus. Spain. The type species is not known in cultivation and is represented by its varieties. These all have linear leaves. Related garden varieties are listed in Division 5.

N. t. albus (angel's tears). Spain, Portugal. Height 3–4 in. The drooping, cream-white flowers, borne in March and April, have cup-shaped coronas, ½ in. long, and reflexed, back-swept petals.

N. t. concolor. Spain, Portugal. A golden-yellow, sweetly scented version of *N. t. albus.*

N. watieri. N. Africa. Height 6 in. Narrowly strap-shaped leaves. This species has a single, pure white, ¾ in. wide flower, with an almost flat cup, on each stem. Sweet scented and April flowering; it is not hardy and does best as a pot plant in a cold greenhouse. Rather similar to the garden varieties in Division 7.

Garden varieties

The following selection of garden narcissus is described in the divisions and sub-divisions established by the Royal Horticultural Society. Unless otherwise stated, these plants have strap-shaped, glaucous leaves. The flowers, 2–3 in. across, appear between late March and mid-May.

In the divisions, the varieties are in order of flowering; this index lists them alphabetically.

'Actaea' (Div. 9)
'Ahoy' (Div. 11)
'April Tears' (Div. 5b)
'Aranjuez' (Div. 2a)
'Arbar' (Div. 2b)
'Ardour' (Div. 3a)
'Armada' (Div. 2a)
'Ave' (Div. 2c)
'Baby Doll' (Div. 6a)
'Beersheba' (Div. 1c)
'Beryl' (Div. 6b)
'Blarney' (Div. 3b)
'Broughshane' (Div. 1c)
'Camellia' (Div. 4)
'Cantabile' (Div. 9)
'Cantatrice' (Div. 1c)
'Carlton' (Div. 2a)
'Cheerfulness' (Div. 4)
'Chérie' (Div. 7b)
'Chinese White' (Div. 3c)
'Chungking' (Div. 3a)
'Coverack Perfection' (Div. 2b)
'Cragford' (Div. 8)
'Cushendall' (Div. 3c)
'Duke of Windsor' (Div. 2b)
'Dutch Master' (Div. 1a)
'Eddy Canzony' (Div. 2b)
'Evolution' (Div. 11)
'February Gold' (Div. 6a)
'Fermoy' (Div. 2b)
'Flower Record' (Div. 2b)
'Foresight' (Div. 1b)
'Fortune' (Div. 2a)
'Galway' (Div. 2a)
'Geranium' (Div. 8)
'Gold Collar' (Div. 11)
'Goldcourt' (Div. 1a)
'Golden Ducat' (Div. 4)
'Golden Harvest' (Div. 1a)
'Golden Orchid' (Div. 11)
'Golden Sceptre' (Div. 7a)
'Golden Torch' (Div. 2a)
'Green Island' (Div. 2b)
'Ice Follies' (Div. 2c)
'Irene Copeland' (Div. 4)
'Irish Luck' (Div. 1a)
'Jack Snipe' (Div. 6a)
'John Evelyn' (Div. 2b)
'Joli-Coeur' (Div. 11)
'Jonquil' (Div. 7)
'Kilworth' (Div. 2b)
'Kingscourt' (Div. 1a)
'La Riante' (Div. 3b)
'Mary Copeland' (Div. 4)
'Moonstruck' (Div. 1a)
'Mount Hood' (Div. 1c)
'Orange Queen' (Div. 7b)
'Paper White' (Div. 8)
'Parisienne' (Div. 11)
'Peeping Tom' (Div. 6a)
'Polar Ice' (Div. 3c)
'Polindra' (Div. 2b)
'Preamble' (Div. 1b)
'Queen of Bicolors' (Div. 1b)
'Rippling Waters' (Div. 5a)
'Roseworthy' (Div. 2b)
'St Keverne' (Div. 2a)
'Sarchedon' (Div. 9)
'Scarlet Elegance' (Div. 2a)
'Seraglio' (Div. 3a)
'Sonata' (Div. 9)
'Spellbinder' (Div. 1d)
'Sweetness' (Div. 7a)
'Telemonius Plenus' (Div. 4)
'Tenedos' (Div. 2c)
'Thalia' (Div. 5a)
'Tresamble' (Div. 5a)
'Trevithian' (Div. 7b)
'Trousseau' (Div. 1b)
'Truth' (Div. 2c)
'Tudor Minstrel' (Div. 2b)
'Van Sion' (Div. 4)
'Varna' (Div. 3a)
'Verger' (Div. 3b)
'Yalta' (Div. 3b)
'Yellow Cheerfulness' (Div. 4)

Narcissus 'Irish Luck' (Div. 1a)

Narcissus 'Mount Hood' (Div. 1c)

Narcissus 'Queen of Bicolors' (Div. 1b)

DIVISION 1. Trumpet narcissi or daffodils of garden origin, with only one flower to a stem. The trumpet or corona is as long as, or longer than, the petals.
SUB-DIVISION 1 (a). Height 14–18 in. Trumpet and petals self-coloured or petals paler. 'Dutch Master', clear yellow, broad smooth petals; 'Golden Harvest', deep yellow, with petals twisted slightly; 'Irish Luck', petals and trumpet deep golden-yellow; 'Moonstruck', lemon-yellow; 'Kingscourt', lemon-yellow, smooth and well-shaped; 'Goldcourt', deep lemon-yellow with deeper yellow trumpet.
SUB-DIVISION 1 (b). Height 13–19 in. Trumpet coloured, petals white (Bicolour trumpets). 'Foresight', cream-white petals, mimosa-yellow trumpet; 'Queen of Bicolors', white petals, canary-yellow trumpet; 'Preamble', smooth white petals and bright yellow trumpet; 'Trousseau', white petals and yellow trumpet fading to cream-pink.
SUB-DIVISION 1 (c). Height 13–18 in. Petals and trumpet white, the latter opening cream or yellow (White trumpets). 'Beersheba', pure white, narrow trumpet flower; 'Cantatrice', pure white, narrow trumpet, well-proportioned flower; 'Mount Hood', broad, rounded flower

with cream-white trumpet; 'Broughshane', cream becoming white later.
SUB-DIVISION 1 (d). Height 16–18 in. Any other colour combination in trumpet narcissi (Reversed bicolour trumpets). 'Spellbinder', flowers open clear yellow, the trumpet later turning white.
DIVISION 2. Large-cupped narcissi of garden origin, with one flower to a stem. The cup or corona is more than one-third the length of the petals or perianths.
SUB-DIVISION 2 (a). Height 14–22 in. Petals coloured in shades of yellow, red and orange; corona or cup coloured and usually a darker shade than the petals.
YELLOW-CUPPED FORMS: 'St Keverne', rich gold throughout; 'Carlton', soft yellow self-colour, with broad, frilled cup; 'Galway', deep yellow with brighter cup almost trumpet length; 'Golden Torch', deep golden-yellow, trumpet-like.
ORANGE OR RED-CUPPED FORMS: 'Fortune', yellow petals, cup colours varying from orange to red; 'Scarlet Elegance', deep yellow petals, rich orange-red cup; 'Armada', stiff stem, flat clear yellow petals and uniform orange cup; 'Aranjuez', smooth, soft yellow petals, golden cup with bright red rim.

Narcissus 'Spellbinder' (Div. 1d)

Narcissus 'Carlton' (Div. 2a)

457

Narcissus 'Arbar' (Div. 2b)

Narcissus 'Duke of Windsor'
(Div. 2b)

Narcissus 'John Evelyn' (Div. 2b)

Narcissus 'Polindra' (Div. 2b)

Narcissus 'Eddy Canzony' (Div. 2b)

Narcissus 'Fermoy' (Div. 2b)

Narcissus 'Armada' (Div. 2a)

Narcissus 'Galway' (Div. 2a)

Narcissus 'Tudor Minstrel' (Div. 2b)

SUB-DIVISION 2 (b). Height 13–20 in. Petals white, cup coloured in varying shades of yellow and orange.

YELLOW-CUPPED FORMS: 'Coverack Perfection', cream-white star-shaped petals, rich yellow open cup turning pale as it ages; 'Duke of Windsor', pure white petals, apricot-orange cup ageing to yellow; 'Polindra', cream-white petals, mimosa-yellow cup; 'Tudor Minstrel', white overlapping petals, orange-yellow frilled cup; 'Green Island', cream-white petals, variable green-yellow cup.

ORANGE OR RED-CUPPED FORMS: 'Arbar', broad white petals, open orange-red cup; 'Eddy Canzony', white petals, flat bright orange cup with yellow centre; 'Fermoy', pure white petals, bright orange-red cup; 'Flower Record', white petals, deep red cup; 'John Evelyn', white petals, widely expanded apricot-orange cup; 'Rose-worthy', white petals, rich pink cup; 'Kilworth', cream petals with yellow bases, deep red cup.

SUB-DIVISION 2 (c). Height 14–18 in. Petals white, cup white but not paler than the petals. 'Truth', rounded, slightly frilled; 'Ice Follies', pure white with a wide, flattened cup; 'Tenedos', cream petals, cup yellow becoming cream-white; 'Ave', clear white with broad, pointed petals and rounded cup.

DIVISION 3. Small-cupped narcissi of garden origin, with one flower to a stem. The cup or corona is not more than one-third the length of the petals.

SUB-DIVISION 3 (a). Height 17–18 in. Petals and cup coloured. 'Ardour', soft yellow petals with paler tips, orange-scarlet cup; 'Chungking', almost circular flower, deep yellow with bright orange-red cup; 'Varna', pale lemon-yellow petals, orange-red cup darker at tip than at base; 'Seraglio', pale yellow petals, green-yellow cup with red rim.

SUB-DIVISION 3 (b). Height 14–18 in. Petals white, cup coloured. 'Verger', petals slightly yellow at the base, flat orange-red cup, resembles *N. poeticus*; 'La Riante', pure white petals, vivid, rich orange cup; 'Yalta', cream petals, orange-yellow cup with red rim; 'Blarney', pointed cream-white petals, open fluted cup rich apricot in colour.

SUB-DIVISION 3 (c). Height 14–16 in. All white with a short cup. 'Chinese White'; 'Cushendall'; 'Polar Ice'.

DIVISION 4. Height 12–18 in. These narcissi of garden origin are distinguished by double flowers. 'Van Sion', syn. 'Telemonius Plenus', the common early golden-yellow double, a variable plant with or without a complete trumpet; 'Golden Ducat', deep yellow throughout, no trumpet showing; 'Irene Copeland', camellia-like flowers, with white and yellow interspersed petals; 'Mary Copeland', similar to 'Irene Copeland', but with orange and white petals; 'Camellia', soft yellow throughout, no trumpet visible; 'Cheerfulness', one to three flowers on a stem, cream-white outer petals and orange-rimmed cup filled with more cream petals, late flowering; 'Yellow Cheerfulness' is a pure yellow form of this variety.

DIVISION 5. Height 8–15 in. Triandrus narcissi of garden origin, distinguished by triandrus characteristics (see *N. triandus*); the pendent flowers have reflexed, back-swept petals.

Narcissus 'Ice Follies' (Div. 2c)

Narcissus 'Ardour' (Div. 3a)

Narcissus 'La Riante' (Div. 3b)

Narcissus 'Polar Ice' (Div. 3c)

Narcissus 'Cheerfulness'
(Div. 4)

Narcissus 'Irene Copeland'
(Div. 4)

Narcissus 'Mary Copeland'
(Div. 4)

Narcissus 'Rippling Waters'
(Div. 5a)

Narcissus 'Thalia' (Div. 5a)

SUB-DIVISION 5 (a). Cup or corona not less than two-thirds the length of the petals. 'Rippling Waters', pure white, with two or three flowers per stem; 'Thalia', pale cream petals, white cup; 'Tresamble', cream-white, tall-growing.

SUB-DIVISION 5 (b). Cup or corona less than two-thirds the length of the petals. 'April Tears', deep yellow hybrid with a jonquilla narcissus.

DIVISION 6. Height 8–15 in. Cyclamineus narcissi of garden origin, distinguished by pendent flowers having long trumpet-shaped cups and petals that sweep up and then back (see *N. cyclamineus*).

SUB-DIVISION 6 (a). Cup or corona not less than two-thirds the length of the petals. 'February Gold', yellow petals and a slightly deeper yellow cup; 'Peeping Tom', bright yellow; 'Jack Snipe', slightly reflexed cream-white petals and straight-sided, orange-yellow cup with a pale margin; 'Baby Doll', all yellow with cup of a deeper shade.

SUB-DIVISION 6 (b). Cup or corona less than two-thirds the length of the petals. 'Beryl', a cross between a cyclamineus and a poeticus narcissus; cream petals and orange cup.

DIVISION 7. Height 11–17 in. Jonquil narcissi of garden origin, distinguished by jonquilla characteristics (see *N. jonquilla*). The leaves are mid to dark green.

SUB-DIVISION 7 (a). Cup or corona not less than two-thirds the length of the petals. 'Sweetness', neat, richly scented, canary-yellow petals and short, deep yellow cup; 'Golden Sceptre', sweetly scented, rich golden-yellow flowers with a long cup.

SUB-DIVISION 7 (b). Cup or corona less than two-thirds the length of the petals. 'Orange Queen', 8 in. high, rich yellow, three or four flowers; 'Trevithian', clear buttercup-yellow; 'Chérie', petals pale cream, cup opening a dull yellow then turning pink.

DIVISION 8. Height 15–17 in. Tazetta narcissi of garden origin, distinguished by tazetta characteristics (see *N. tazetta*). The leaves are mid to dark green.

There are two sub-groups in this division: true tazettas, which are often known as polyanthus narcissi, and poetaz narcissi, which were produced by crossing *N. tazetta* with *N. poeticus*.

True tazettas do not thrive outdoors except in the mildest districts, but can be forced in bowls for winter flowering. Outdoors they vary in time of flowering more than any other group. In the warmer parts some will flower before Christmas.

Poetaz narcissi flower later than true tazettas, being influenced by their late-flowering parent, *N. poeticus*; they are hardy.

The only tazetta bulbs generally available are 'Paper White'. Poetaz varieties include: 'Cragford', white petals, deep red cup; 'Geranium', pale cream petals, bright orange cup.

DIVISION 9. Height 14–17 in. Poeticus narcissi of garden origin, distinguished by the pure characteristics of *N. poeticus* without admixture of any others. 'Actaea', the earliest and most widely grown of this group, has white petals and a yellow, crimson-margined cup; 'Sarchedon', white petals with yellow base, yellow cup with broad red edge; 'Sonata', white petals, green-yellow flat cup with faint red edge; 'Cantabile', pure white petals, cup green with red edge.

DIVISION 10. The R.H.S. has placed all species, wild forms and wild hybrids in this division. These are described under the species headings.

DIVISION 11. Miscellaneous narcissi, including all those not falling into any other division. The recently produced Collar and Split-Corona groups belong in this division.

The appearance of these is different from all others. The cup is split into petal-like lobes which lie parallel to the petals.

Collar varieties include: 'Ahoy', white petals, pale yellow cup; 'Evolution', white petals, lemon-yellow cup; 'Gold Collar', yellow petals, deep golden cup.

Split-Corona varieties include: 'Golden Orchid', pale yellow petals, overlaid by the golden-yellow trumpet split into six petal-like segments. 'Joli-Coeur', white petals, ruffled orange cup; 'Parisienne', white petals, large, reflexed, ruffled orange cup.

Cultivation. Narcissi can be grown in many ways. Some are suited to informal planting in rough grass in the open or in partial shade, where they may be left to flower for years without any attention. Some do well in hedge banks; other more formal varieties are suited to borders of shrubs or perennials where they provide early colour before the summer-flowering plants commence. These, too, may remain undisturbed for several years.

Home gardeners can easily grow narcissi under glass or indoors to enjoy their blooms from November to May, with some extra trouble (see BULBS, INDOOR).

For bedding purposes, narcissi planted in the autumn after summer flowers have finished will make a fine display the next spring. They may then be removed to make way for summer bedding and replanted elsewhere to become established and keep on flowering undisturbed for years.

All types of narcissi will provide attractive cut flowers for the home: many thousands of acres are grown commercially for this purpose, including plants grown under glass to produce forced winter-flowering narcissi.

The choice of species or varieties for naturalising in grass or borders depends on various factors. In fine grass or among dwarf plants the *N. bulbocodium* or *N. cyclamineus* groups are most suitable. In tall, rough grass, beneath trees or on hedge banks, *N. pseudonarcissus* and its varieties, or older garden varieties such as

'Beersheba', 'Dutch Master' and 'Golden Harvest' look well. Use some of the less expensive bulbs, such as 'Actaea', 'Fortune' or 'Golden Harvest', for planting beneath shrubs and between herbaceous plants.

Many of the smallest species and varieties fit well into rock gardens and will also fill small gaps between other plants. If planted under dwarf or creeping plants they generally flower and die down before these come into bloom.

In all cases, let narcissus leaves die down completely, or at least become yellow, before removing them. This is necessary so that the foliage can feed the bulbs, thus ensuring flower production in subsequent years.

The practice of knotting leaves for the sake of tidiness is not recommended: it weakens the bulbs by reducing the leaf surface exposed to sun, thus preventing the full formation of food reserve in the bulbs.

Narcissus bulbs thrive in rich, well-manured soil protected by slight shade cast by trees, hedges or taller plants. Apply a 2–3 oz. dressing of complete fertiliser per sq. yd, or one containing potash and phosphate only, at planting time. Potash improves the colour of the flowers. Fresh manure should not be dug in before planting but if available may be added to the soil when digging in winter, i.e. about nine months before the bulbs are planted, to improve fertility.

Soil condition is another important factor in narcissus cultivation. Waterlogged soil can cause rotting, while drought in late spring, between flowering and the time the foliage dies, retards regrowth of the bulbs and leads to smaller flowers and possibly fewer flowers.

Plant the bulbs as soon as they are available, in August or September or even earlier if possible. It is best to aim at a natural look, planting in irregular groups rather than in precise circles or squares on regular lines.

Scatter the bulbs at random on their planting site and plant them exactly where they fall, without altering the spacing. Use a dibber for small bulbs and a trowel or special bulb planter for bigger ones, making the holes flat at the bottom so that the bulbs rest on the soil.

In ground which will not otherwise be cultivated, the hole should be three times the depth of the bulb: place a 2 in. deep bulb into a 6 in. hole and cover with 4 in. of soil. However, bulbs planted in cultivated borders which will be hoed in summer and forked over in winter must be planted a few inches deeper.

The spacing of narcissus bulbs depends on the purpose for which they are being grown, the frequency of lifting and the size of the bulb. For naturalising, scatter the bulbs where they are required and plant them where they fall; in permanent beds or borders, space them 4–8 in. apart. For producing cut flowers, which entails lifting every two to three years, plant in rows 1½–2½ ft apart, setting the bulbs 4–6 in. apart in the rows, depending on their size. The more frequently the bulbs are lifted the closer they may be planted. Small species, such as *N. triandrus*, *N. cyclamineus* and *N. bulbocodium*, should be planted 2–3 in. apart in groups of a dozen.

Plant bulbs of large-flowered varieties in the autumn for a spring bedding display—which

Narcissus 'February Gold' (Div. 6a)

Narcissus 'Peeping Tom' (Div. 6a)

Narcissus 'Beryl' (Div. 6b)

461

Narcissus 'Geranium' (Div. 8)

Narcissus 'Actaea' (Div. 9)

Seed-raised plants are usually poor in quality and differ greatly from the parent plant.

Pests. The microscopic STEM AND BULB EELWORM invades bulb tissues and causes an internal discoloration of the bulb scales. This shows as a brown ring-rot when affected bulbs are cut across. In severe infestations, the stems, leaves and flowers are discoloured and distorted, and the plants are weakened and killed.

TARSONEMID MITES may also infest bulbs. They live in the cavities between the bulb scales, and cause discoloration, scarring and distortion of bulbs, stems and leaves. Severe infestations check growth; damage is often worst on forced bulbs.

NARCISSUS FLY maggots also attack the bulbs. They tunnel into them and eat out extensive galleries in the tissues. Affected bulbs often fail to flower but produce numerous thin leaves.

SLUGS may feed on the bulbs.

Diseases. Among the many NARCISSUS VIRUS DISEASES are ARABIS MOSAIC and CUCUMBER MOSAIC VIRUSES. Varying symptoms are produced, depending on which virus or viruses are present. In general there is a gradual decline in bulb and flower production and affected plants may show yellow striping and mottling of the foliage, particularly early in the season.

BLINDNESS, in which the flower buds appear and then turn brown is a common trouble with double narcissi, grown in pots, such as 'Van Sion' or 'Golden Ducat'. It is usually due to the soil being excessively dry early in the season.

NARCISSUS FIRE, which affects plants in humid weather, at first causes a light brown spotting and rotting of the flowers, followed by rapid decay of the leaves. A GREY MOULD develops on the affected tissues.

Narcissus, bunch-flowered: see *Narcissus tazetta*
Nasturtium: see *Tropaeolum majus*
Nasturtium officinale: see Watercress
Navelwort: see Omphalodes
Nectarine: see Peach
Needle, Adam's: see *Yucca filamentosa*

Nemesia

Scrophulariaceae

A genus of 50 species of annual and perennial herbaceous plants and sub-shrubs. The bushy half-hardy annual described is suitable for formal summer bedding and for mixed borders. Cut flowers last well in water. Nemesias are also effective in pots in a cool greenhouse. Hybrids are available in a wide colour range.

NEMESIA STRUMOSA

N. strumosa. S. Africa. Height 8–18 in.; planting distance 4–6 in. An erect, branching plant with light green, lanceolate, coarsely toothed leaves.

normally entails lifting immediately after flowering—and space them evenly 3–12 in. apart. The precise spacing depends on the type of display wanted and on whether other spring bedding plants are to be planted among them.

Plant either in drills made with a large hoe or spade or in holes made with a trowel. Leave spaces between adjacent bulbs equivalent to the width of two or three bulbs: space 2 in. wide bulbs 4–6 in. apart, and 1 in. bulbs 2–3 in. apart.

In general, the time to lift narcissi is when they become congested and flower less freely. If possible do this between July and September, replanting them immediately.

Lifting and replanting in well-cultivated soil every three or four years is generally advisable for narcissi grown especially for cutting or for exhibition. The finest flowers are usually obtained in the second year after planting, the largest number of flowers in the third year.

If possible, lift the bulbs when the leaves turn yellow but have not died down; it is easier to find each bulb and bulb flies will not have had time to attack. Dry off the bulbs in a warm shed; remove the leaves, skins and roots as soon as the leaves are dry and brittle. Discard any damaged or decayed bulbs at this time.

This is also the time to divide any bulbs that can be separated without tearing the skins. If desired, the various-sized bulbs may be sorted into containers for planting separately later.

Propagation. Increase narcissi by removing the bulb offsets after lifting; replant them separately to grow into flowering size in one or two years.

Narcissi can also be raised from seeds saved in June or July and sown within a few weeks, but bulbs produced by this method will take from three to seven years to reach flowering size.

The obliquely funnel-shaped flowers, with pouched bases, are up to 1 in. across. They are white, yellow or purple, often with spotted and bearded throats, and are borne in terminal clusters from June to August.

Cultivated varieties of this plant are in shades of cream, yellow, blue, orange, scarlet, crimson and pink. They include 'Carnival Mixed', 9 in., with large flowers on dwarf compact plants; 'Sutton's Mixed', 12 in., with large flowers in a wide range of colours; and 'Blue Gem', 8 in., bearing smaller flowers that are sky-blue.

Cultivation. All normal garden soils and sites give reasonable results but, ideally, grow nemesias in a sunny position and in a medium to light, slightly acid soil that contains plenty of organic matter. Water well in hot, dry weather; any check to growth will result in poor, spindly plants. A second flush of flowers may be obtained by cutting back the stems after the first flush.

For flowering under glass in May, grow three plants in a 5 in. pot of John Innes potting compost No. 2; pinch out the growing tips of each plant at a height of 3 in. to encourage bushy growth.

Propagation. Sow the seeds under glass in March, at a temperature of 15°C (59°F), just covering them with compost. Prick off the seedlings into boxes and harden off before planting out in May.

Pests. Generally trouble-free.

Diseases. Plants may collapse at ground level due to FOOT ROT and ROOT ROT, caused by several different fungi.

Nemophila
Hydrophyllaceae

NEMOPHILA MACULATA

A genus of 13 species of hardy annuals of bushy habit. The two species described are suitable for growing at the fronts of borders, for edging paths and for flowering in pots in a cold greenhouse.

N. insignis: see *N. menziesii*

N. maculata. California. Height and spacing 6 in. The spreading stems carry light green lobed leaves. The many saucer-shaped flowers, 1 in. across, are white with purple veins and have a purple blotch on the tips of the petals. They are produced from June to August.

N. menziesii, syn. *N. insignis* (baby blue eyes). California. Height up to 9 in.; spacing 6 in. This plant is also of spreading habit; it has feathery, deeply cut, light green leaves, and carries a profusion of white-centred sky-blue flowers from June to August. The flowers are saucer-shaped and up to 1¼ in. across. A pure white form, 'Alba', is often available.

Cultivation. These plants grow well in any ordinary garden soil but thrive in moist soils, especially sandy loams enriched with compost or similar organic matter. Plant in sun or partial shade.

Neoregelia carolinae 'Tricolor'

Grow pot plants three to a 5 in. container of John Innes potting compost No. 1, and move to a cold greenhouse in October. Water sparingly through the winter.

Propagation. Sow the seeds in the flowering site in September or March, just covering them with soil; thin out the seedlings in April to the required spacing. For pot plants to flower from April to June, sow the seeds in 5 in. pots in September in a cold frame and thin out the seedlings to three per pot.

Pests. Young shoots may be infested by APHIDS.

Diseases. Generally trouble-free.

Neoregelia
Bromeliaceae

A genus of about 40 species of evergreen greenhouse perennials. About 20 species with their varieties and hybrids are in cultivation. Generally terrestrial, a few species are epiphytic on the lower branches of trees. The species described usually have spiny, strap-shaped leaves growing in rosettes or tubular forms with water-holding reservoirs.

The three-petalled, upright flowers grow in the heart of the plant; they are blue, violet or white, and may occur at any time of year. In some species, the floral bracts change colour when flowering begins.

See also BROMELIADS.

N. carolinae, syn. *Nidularium meyendorfii.* Brazil. Height 12 in. The shiny, bright green leaves fold around the base of the rosette, then narrow and flatten out to pointed tips. At flowering time, the centre changes colour to

Nemesia strumosa 'Blue Gem'

Nemesia strumosa 'Sutton's Mixed'

Nemophila menziesii

bright red or purple, the leaves open out, and the packed flower head rises through a circular, 2 in. wide opening. The violet-blue flowers, 1 in. across, in a rounded sessile cluster, open one to three at a time.

N. c. 'Tricolor' has bright green leaves striped with ivory-white. The entire plant turns pink at flowering time and remains so for many months.

N. marechalii. Brazil. Height 12 in. This species is similar to *N. carolinae,* but the lower half or more of each leaf is red, and the flowers are violet.

N. spectabilis (fingernail plant). Brazil. Height 12 in. The leathery leaves are dark green and have strong white bands on their undersurfaces. They are about 12 in. long, forming a rosette 24 in. across. There is a large red spot at the tip of each leaf. At flowering time the heart of the plant turns rose-red, and a dense head of 1 in. wide blue flowers emerges from the circular nest formed by the purple-brown bracts.

Cultivation. Neoregelias do best in an open compost of equal parts (by volume) coarse sand, grit or leaf-mould, and medium loam. Plant during late spring or early summer. Water well when the plants are growing; reduce water and keep the soil just moist from late autumn to early spring. Full light with partial sun will bring out the colours of the leaves and aid flowering.

Pot on or repot every three or four years in April; final potting should be in 6 in. pots.

Propagation. The stolons or offshoots are easy to grow on. Allow them to root while still attached to the mother plant, then sever in June or July. After the offshoots have been removed, fix them securely with stakes so that the roots are just in contact with the growing mixture. Keep the plantlets in a humid atmosphere but, to prevent rotting, water sparingly until new root growth has started. Neoregelias may also be increased from seeds.

Pests and diseases. Generally trouble-free.

Neoregelia carolinae (central leaves)

Nepeta × *faassenii*

Nepeta × *faassenii* 'Six Hills Giant'

Nepeta
Labiatae

A genus of about 250 species of annuals and herbaceous perennials. The perennials described here are hardy and suitable for rock gardens or borders. They bear small tubular and hooded flowers. One species, *N. hederacea,* the ground ivy, may develop into an invasive weed.

NEPETA × FAASSENII

N. × **faassenii.** Garden origin. Height 12–18 in.; planting distance 12 in. This hybrid, often listed as *N. mussinii,* is useful as an edging plant. It bears narrowly ovate grey-green leaves. The 6 in. spikes with whorls of lavender-blue flowers are produced from May to September. The variety 'Six Hills Giant' grows to about 24 in.

N. glechoma: see *N. hederacea*

N. hederacea, syn. *N. glechoma* and currently known as *Glechoma hederacea* (ground ivy) Europe, including Great Britain. Height 4 in. planting distance 12–18 in. or more. A vigorous perennial, ideal for ground cover under trees and shrubs. The leaves are pale to mid-green, kidney-shaped with rounded teeth. Lilac-blue flowers, in. long, are produced in whorls in the upper leaf axils from March to June and sometimes later.

In cultivation the species is generally represented by *N. h.* 'Variegata' with white-marked leaves. This form is useful in hanging baskets and in window-boxes.

N. mussinii: see *N.* × *faassenii*

N. nervosa. Kashmir. Height 12–24 in.; planting distance 12 in. This species, of rounded and bushy habit, is suitable for a border or a rock garden. The mid-green leaves are narrowly lanceolate and prominently veined. Clear blue flowers appear from July to September, closely packed on cylindrical spikes, 6–9 in. long.

Cultivation. Plant in a sunny or half-shaded position in ordinary, well-drained garden soil from October to March. Cut down in autumn.

Propagation. All plants may be divided and replanted in March or April.

N. nervosa and *N.* × *faassenii* can also be increased by cuttings in April; take 2–3 in. cuttings of basal growth and insert in equal parts (by volume) peat and sand in a cold frame. When rooted, pot into 3–3½ in. pots of John Innes potting compost No. 1 and plunge outside. Plant in the flowering site the following March or April.

Sow seeds of *N. nervosa* in March or April in a cold frame or greenhouse at a temperature of 16°C (61°F). Prick out the seedlings, when large enough to handle, and grow the young plants on in nursery rows or in 3½ in. pots until planting out the following spring.

Pests. Generally trouble-free.

Diseases. A white powdery coating on the leaves is caused by POWDERY MILDEW.

Nephrolepis
Oleandraceae

A genus of 30 species of ferns, which increase rapidly by producing numerous stolons. Only three or four species are generally cultivated, but these are among the most important of commercial greenhouse ferns. They are also suitable as house plants.

See also FERNS.

N. cordifolia (sword fern). New Zealand to Japan. Height 2–2½ ft; spread indefinite. Evergreen. The light green fronds are narrowly pinnate on short stalks, the pinnae closely set. *N. c.* 'Plumosa' has almost pinnate leaflets.

N. exaltata. Tropics. Height 1½–2¼ ft; spread indefinite. Evergreen. The pale green fronds are pinnate. *N. e.* 'Bostoniensis' (Boston fern) has wider fronds and grows more rapidly than the type. *N. e.* 'Elegantissima' produces bright green, compact, tripinnate to quadripinnate fronds, the pinnae closely set and overlapping. It reverts occasionally to the pinnate form. *N. e.* 'Hillii' has crinkled, light green, bipinnate fronds. *N. e.*

Nephrolepis exaltata 'Hillii'

Nephrolepis exaltata 'Marshallii'

'Marshallii' has pale green, broad, densely crested fronds. *N. e.* 'Todeoides' has feathery, pale green, finely divided fronds.

NEPHROLEPIS EXALTATA

Cultivation. Plant nephrolepis in March in hanging baskets containing equal parts (by volume) fibrous peat, loam and chopped sphagnum.

If they are grown as house plants, pot the plants in April in 4 or 5 in. pots, using a compost of 3 parts fibrous peat, 2 parts loam, and 1 part sharp sand (parts by volume). These ferns stand up well to room conditions if kept moist and protected from draughts. Maintain a minimum temperature of 10°C (50°F).

Propagation. Separate the young plants from their stolons and pot them in 2 in. pots containing a compost of equal parts (by volume) fibrous peat and sand. Place these in the greenhouse at 13°C (55°F) and pot on as required.

Pests and diseases. Generally trouble-free.

Nerine

Amaryllidaceae

A genus of 30 species of generally half-hardy bulbous plants. With the exception of one species, *N. bowdenii*, these require greenhouse cultivation in Great Britain. The species have been crossed to produce a wide range of hybrids.

The species described have linear to narrowly strap-shaped, mid-green leaves, which usually appear just after the flowers. The strikingly iridescent flowers are borne from August to November on 12–24 in. high stems. They are composed of six narrow, strap-shaped petals that are often crimped and twisted; they are borne in loose umbels on top of the leafless stems and range from rich red through pink to white.

N. bowdenii. Cape Province. Height up to 24 in.; planting distance 6 in. This species is hardy except during very severe winters, but even then it is rarely completely killed. Flower umbels, 4–6 in. across, of up to eight flowers, are carried on each stem from September to November. 'Fenwick's Variety' is larger and more vigorous than the species, with deeper pink flowers.

N. crispa: see *N. undulata*

NERINE FLEXUOSA

N. flexuosa. S. Africa. Height up to 24 in. A tender species with thin stems carrying up to a dozen pink flowers in each 4–6 in. wide umbel. The few leaves appear with the flowers from September to November. 'Alba' is pure white.

N. sarniensis (Guernsey lily). Table Mountain, Cape Province. Height 24 in. A tender species long cultivated in the Channel Islands. The few leaves appear with the flowers. The species is variable, and the flower umbels, up to 6 in. across, range in colour from pale pink to red. The flowering period is from September to November under glass.

N. s. corusca is a scarlet-orange variety.

N. undulata, syn. *N. crispa*. S. Africa. Height 12 in. This tender species bears pink flower umbels, 3 in. across, in October and November.

Cultivation. Outdoors, plant *N. bowdenii* in August or April, in any ordinary, well-drained garden soil. Set the bulbs 4 in. deep, preferably in a sharply drained sunny border against a wall. Leave undisturbed until the plants become crowded and produce fewer flower stems. Lift, divide and replant the clumps, generally every four or five years.

Bulbs exposed on the soil surface may be protected during winter with a 12 in. layer of straw or bracken.

Pot all other species in August, setting one to three bulbs in a 3½–6 in. pot of John Innes potting compost No. 2, with the neck of the bulbs just showing. Begin watering when the flower buds appear and keep the compost just moist through

Nerine bowdenii 'Fenwick's Variety'

Nerine flexuosa (hybrid)

Nerine sarniensis

the winter. Maintain a minimum temperature of 10–13°C (50–55°F) during winter.

When the foliage is well developed, provide a weekly liquid feed for about two months; withhold water from the time the leaves turn yellow until the next flowers appear. Keep the plants in a sunny position.

Offsets generally appear after one or two years; the plants should be repotted every three or four years to maintain strong healthy flowering bulbs. The surface compost in the pots may be replaced if necessary.

Propagation. Divide and replant *N. bowdenii* as described under CULTIVATION.

Remove and repot the offsets of pot-grown plants when they are fully detached from the parent bulbs.

The soft, fleshy seeds, which cannot be stored, should be sown when ripe, usually in May. Sow the seeds singly in 3 in. pots of John Innes seed compost, barely covering them, and keep the plants growing as already described.

Pests. MEALY BUGS sometimes infest the leaves and bulbs of plants grown under glass.

Diseases. A VIRUS DISEASE may cause yellow mottling of the foliage.

Nerine sarniensis corusca

Nerium oleander

Nicandra physaloides

Nerium
Apocynaceae

A genus of three species of tender evergreen flowering shrubs. They may be grown as wall shrubs outdoors in the extreme south-west of Great Britain and in the Channel Islands, but elsewhere they need greenhouse conditions.

NERIUM OLEANDER

N. oleander (oleander). Mediterranean regions. Height 6–15 ft; spread 10–15 ft. A species with mid-green, leathery, narrowly lanceolate leaves. Terminal clusters of single white flowers appear from June to October; the individual flowers, which measure 1–1½ in. across, are tubular with five petal-like lobes that spread out flat. Single and double forms with white, cream, pink and red flowers are available.

Cultivation. Plant during March in the greenhouse border, in small tubs or in 10–12 in. pots of John Innes potting compost No. 2. Water freely during the growing period and keep the plants just moist in winter when a minimum temperature of 7°C (45°F) is required. Pot plants may be stood outdoors during summer; in the greenhouse, place neriums in full light and ventilate freely at all times except in frosty weather.

Repot or pot on annually or every other year in March. Give established plants a weak liquid feed at fortnightly intervals from May to September. Outdoors, plant at the end of May in ordinary garden soil and against a sheltered sunny wall.

Propagation. Take 3–4 in. cuttings of half-ripened shoots in June or July and insert in equal parts (by volume) peat and sand in a propagating frame at a temperature of 16–18°C (61–64°F). Pot the rooted cuttings in 3 in. containers of John Innes potting compost No. 1 and grow on in a greenhouse at a temperature of 13–16°C (55–61°F). Pot on successively as required, and finish off in 10–12 in. pots. Harden off outdoor plants in a cold frame before planting out in late May of the following year.

Alternatively, sow seeds during April, in pots or pans of seed compost, and germinate under glass at a temperature of 18–21°C (64–70°F). Prick off the seedlings, when large enough to handle, into 3 in. pots of John Innes potting compost No. 1 and treat as described for cuttings.

Pruning. Shorten flowering shoots by half after flowering; at the same time, lateral shoots may be cut back to within 4 in. of their base.

Pests. Conspicuous tufts of white waxy wool on the leaves and stems are caused by MEALY BUGS. The plants become sticky and sooty.

SCALE INSECTS, particularly oleander scale, form rounded white or brown scales under the leaves and make the plants sticky and sooty.

Diseases. A PHYSIOLOGICAL DISORDER results in discoloration of the foliage and in leaf-fall.

Nettle, dead: see Lamium
Nettle, giant dead: see *Lamium orvala*

Nicandra
Solanaceae

A genus of a single hardy annual species. This is an unusual and interesting border plant with attractive flowers, foliage and fruit. It is supposed to repel flies.

N. physaloides (shoo-fly, apple of Peru). Peru. Height up to 3 ft; planting distance 12 in. A vigorous plant with spreading branches and ovate, mid-green, toothed and waved leaves. The bell-shaped flowers, 1½ in. or more across, are pale violet with white throats. They are produced from July to September, but open for only a few hours daily at midday. The globular fruits, 1½–2 in. in diameter, are enclosed by bright green and purple calyces. They are carried from August to October. The fruiting branches may be dried for winter decoration.

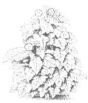

NICANDRA PHYSALOIDES

Cultivation. Grow in a deep, moist, rich soil, in a sunny situation.

Propagation. Sow the seeds under glass in March at a temperature of 15°C (59°F), and prick out the seedlings into 3 in. pots. Harden off in a cold frame before planting out in May.

Pests and diseases. Generally trouble-free.

Nicotiana

Tobacco plant. *Solanaceae*

NICOTIANA × SANDERAE

A genus of 66 species of half-hardy or tender annual and herbaceous perennial plants. Those described are usually grown as annuals in borders or pots. The flowers of most species and hybrids open in the evening, and have a heavy fragrance. *N. tabacum* is used for the production of tobacco.

N. affinis, syn. *N. alata.* S. America. Height 2–3 ft; planting distance 12 in. A half-hardy perennial with erect branches and mid-green oblong leaves. Loose clusters of white tubular flowers, 3 in. long, are produced from June to September. The whole plant is sticky to the touch.

There are numerous garden varieties, all sweetly scented, but the flowers of most of them open only in the evening, unless they are grown in shade. One of the most popular is 'Sensation Mixed', 3 ft, a compact plant with white, cream, pink, crimson and yellow flowers that remain open during the day. 'Lime Green', 2½ ft, has attractive yellow-green flowers which are popular for flower arrangements.

N. alata : see *N. affinis*

N. gigantea : see *N. tabacum*

N. × sanderae. Height 1¼–2½ ft; planting distance 9–12 in. A half-hardy garden hybrid grown outdoors in beds and also in pots under glass. The leaves are mid-green, ovate and pointed. The tubular flowers are 3 in. long, pale yellow tinged with carmine-rose, and produced from June to September. Garden varieties include: 'Crimson Bedder', 15 in., of dwarf, compact habit, and 'White Bedder', 15 in., the flowers of which remain open during the day.

N. suaveolens. Australia. Height up to 24 in.; planting distance 12 in. An erect half-hardy annual which will flourish in partial shade. The leaves are sticky, mid-green and ovate. Sweetly scented, trumpet-shaped, white flowers, 2 in. long and 1 in. across, are carried on loose terminal spikes from July to September.

N. sylvestris. Argentina. Height up to 5 ft; planting distance 24 in. This half-hardy plant can be grown as a biennial or a short-lived perennial in warm, sheltered sites, but elsewhere usually dies off during the winter. Stout stems carry lyre-shaped mid-green leaves and spikes of fragrant white trumpet-shaped flowers, 3½ in. long. These close in full sun but remain open on dull days. They are produced in August.

N. tabacum, syn. *N. gigantea.* S. America. Height 4–6 ft; planting distance 3 ft. A half-hardy annual with mid-green leaves up to 3 ft long, which are oblong-ovate and pointed. Funnel-shaped flowers, pale red or rose coloured, are carried in loose clusters in August. They are 2–3 in. long.

A number of varieties suitable for the production of home-grown tobacco are listed.

Nicotiana affinis 'Sensation Mixed'

Cultivation. Grow nicotianas in rich, well-drained soil and a warm sunny site. Where large leaves are required from smoking varieties, the soil should be heavily manured. Staking is required only for tall varieties on exposed sites. Removal of dead flower heads maintains the flower size on bedding varieties.

For flowering in pots under glass from May to August, grow the plants in John Innes potting compost No. 2 and use a final 7 in. container. Shade from strong sun, water regularly and give an occasional liquid feed.

Propagation. Sow the seeds under glass in February or March, at a temperature of 18°C (64°F), sprinkling them on the surface of the compost. Prick off the seedlings into boxes, or into pots for the larger types; harden off in a cold frame before planting out in May.

Pests. Young plants may be infested by APHIDS.

Diseases. Generally trouble-free.

Nicotiana affinis 'Lime Green'

Nicotiana tabacum

Nidularium

Bromeliaceae

A genus of 22 species of evergreen greenhouse plants, native to Brazil. About 12 species with their varieties and hybrids are in cultivation. In the wild these plants grow in rain forests on rotting tree stumps and the lower branches of trees. All species grow in rosette form and hold water in the reservoirs formed by the leaves.

The leaves are strap-shaped with serrated or spined edges and are green, sometimes with darker flecks, or purple overlying green. The bracts, which at flowering time may be pink,

Nidularium fulgens

Nidularium innocentii var. *innocentii*

Nierembergia caerulea 'Purple Robe Improved'

Nierembergia repens

scarlet or red-purple, occur as a raised inflorescence with the flower branches between the bracts. They usually appear in the centre of the leaf rosette as a distinctive and separate arrangement from the true leaves.

The tubular flowers are white, blue, violet or, rarely, yellow.

See also BROMELIADS.

NIDULARIUM FULGENS

N. fulgens, syns. *N. pictum, Guzmania picta.* Height about 12 in. The shiny, light green, arching leaves are flecked with darker green and the edges are indented rather than toothed. The inflorescence is about 3 in. wide and consists of red bracts, tipped with green, and three-petalled violet-blue flowers, 1–2 in. across.

N. innocentii var. *innocentii.* Height 18 in. The compact rosette is formed of linear, finely toothed leaves, which are green and overlaid with purple-brown on the upper surfaces, wine-red on the undersides. Orange-red bracts, about 4 in. across, sometimes with green tips, surround the ¾ in. wide white flowers. Flowering usually occurs in autumn.

This plant is more commonly named *N. innocentii.* It has six varieties, of which the most decorative is 'Striatum' with wide yellow stripes on the leaves, and rose-red bracts.

N. meyendorfii: see *Neoregelia carolinae*

N. pictum: see *N. fulgens*

Cultivation. Pot nidulariums during late spring or early summer in a light, porous potting mixture; equal parts (by volume) coarse sand, leaf-mould and osmunda fibre or very fibrous loam is suitable. They like a bright position, but not too much direct sun. Give plenty of heat and moisture during the growing season from April to September. The air should be humid, and the roots must not dry out. During late autumn and winter keep the soil just moist. Repot annually in April; final pot size should be 5 or 6 in.

Propagation. Offshoots growing from the base of the plant may be severed when they are about half grown and placed in 2½–3 in. pots of the potting compost. Detach the offshoots of *N. fulgens* carefully as they grow very close to the parent plant. Allow the offshoots to dry for a few days before potting up in the growing mixture. A humid atmosphere and if possible some bottom heat will hasten growth of roots. Nidulariums may also be increased from seeds.

Pests and diseases. Generally trouble-free.

Nierembergia
Solanaceae

A genus of 35 species of perennial herbaceous plants. Two of the species described are half-hardy and usually treated as annuals; they are suitable for bedding and for edging border and can also be flowered in pots. The third species, *N. repens,* is hardy and excellent for rock gardens or for growing in pans in alpine houses.

The plants all bear widely funnel or cup shaped flowers.

SPECIES GROWN AS ANNUALS

N. caerulea, syn. *N. hippomanica.* Argentina Height and planting distance 6–8 in. A sub shrubby plant with slender branching stems that form a hummock. It can be grown as an annual or a perennial, but is unreliably hardy. The fine linear foliage is mid-green; 1 in. wide flowers, pale lavender with a yellow throat, are freely borne from June to September.

The variety 'Purple Robe' has deep violet purple flowers; 'Purple Robe Improved' has deeper violet-purple flowers and is of more compact habit.

NIEREMBERGIA CAERULEA

N. frutescens. Chile. Height 18 in.; planting distance 12 in. A bushy plant with light green linear leaves. The flowers, 1 in. across, are blue or white with a yellow throat; they appear from June to August.

N. hippomanica: see *N. caerulea*

SPECIES GROWN AS PERENNIALS

N. caerulea: see under ANNUALS

N. repens, formerly *N. rivularis.* Argentina Height 2 in.; spread 18–24 in. This hardy species forms a mat of rooting stems with light green spathulate leaves; it bears white flowers, 1 in. wide, in June and July.

NIEREMBERGIA REPENS

N. rivularis: see *N. repens*

Cultivation of species grown as annuals. These plants are easy to grow in any ordinary garden soil, although a moist, but well-drained soil is best. Choose a sunny, sheltered position; the flowers are easily damaged in rough weather. Overwintered plants of *N. caerulea* should be cut to ground level in October or November and protected during winter with panes of glass.

For pot plants to flower in May, grow under glass in 5 in. containers of John Innes potting compost No. 1.

Cultivation of species grown as perennials. Plant in any ordinary, moisture-retentive garden soil in March or April, choosing a sunny position.

Propagation of species grown as annuals. For outdoor and pot plants, sow seeds in pots or pans of seed compost under glass in February or

March, at a temperature of 15°C (59°F). Prick out the seedlings into boxes; if the plants are to be grown outdoors, harden off in a cold frame before planting out in May. Pot-grown plants should be set singly in 5 in. pots of John Innes potting compost No. 1 and grown on under glass.

Alternatively, increase *N. caerulea* by cuttings. Take 2 in. soft cuttings between June and August, choosing lateral growths with a heel and inserting them in sandy soil in a cold frame. Set the rooted cuttings in 3 in. pots of John Innes potting compost No. 1 and pinch them out when established to encourage bushy growth. Overwinter in the frame and plant out in March or April.

Propagation of species grown as perennials. Divide *N. repens* in March or April and replant directly in permanent positions.

Pests and diseases. Generally trouble-free.

Nigella

Ranunculaceae

NIGELLA DAMASCENA

A genus of 20 species of hardy annuals of bushy growth. Those described are excellent border and cut-flower plants, with saucer-shaped flowers, feathery foliage and striking seed pods.

N. damascena (love-in-a-mist). S. Europe. Height 24 in.; spacing 9 in. Erect stems carry bright green finely cut foliage. The showy blue or white flowers, 1½ in. across, are surrounded by a leafy crown of thread-like bracts. They are produced from June to August. The ripe fruit is an inflated, pale brown seed pod, 1 in. long, with red bars and similar leafy bracts.

There are several garden varieties, the most popular being 'Miss Jekyll', with large bright blue semi-double flowers. The more recently introduced 'Persian Jewels Mixed' contains flowers in various shades, from blue, mauve and purple to rose-pink and white.

N. hispanica. Spain. Height 24 in.; spacing 9 in. A vigorous plant with dark green deeply divided leaves. The deep blue flowers, 2½ in. across, are faintly scented and have a cluster of bright red stamens. They are produced from July to September. The seed pods are less inflated than those of *N. damascena*, and have a crown of horn-like projections at the top.

Cultivation. These plants thrive in any well-cultivated soil, in a sunny position. Self-sown plants occur if the soil is left undisturbed. Dead-head to increase the size of later flowers.

Propagation. Sow the seeds in the flowering site during March, just covering them with soil, and thin out the seedlings to 9 in. apart. Alternatively, in sheltered areas or if cloche protection is available, sow in September to secure larger plants and earlier flowers the following year.

Pests and diseases. Generally trouble-free.

Nomocharis

Liliaceae

A genus of 16 species of hardy bulbs which closely resemble *Lilium*. They are native to the Himalayas and the neighbouring mountains of W. China. Though rewarding plants when grown successfully, they seldom do well in the open, except in the cooler moister areas of the west and north. The bulbs are easily damaged and resent transplanting or other disturbance.

The species described have narrow to broad lanceolate, mid-green leaves, which are often glossy. The bowl to saucer-shaped flowers, up to 4 in. across, open in July and August.

N. aperta. China, Tibet. Height 1–3 ft; planting distance 12–15 in. The leaves are chiefly borne near the top of the thin flower stem. The flowers, first nodding then semi-erect, are pale pink spotted with crimson. One to six flowers are produced on each stem, depending on the vigour of the plant.

N. × *finlayorum* (sometimes known as *N. hybrida*). This name covers a hybrid race involving *N. pardanthina*, *N. farreri* and *N. mairei*. Plants raised from seeds of this race show a blend of characteristics from the species involved.

N. hybrida: see *N.* × *finlayorum*

N. mairei. China. Height 2–4 ft; planting distance 12–15 in. A species bearing one to four flowers, which are white flushed with purple and spotted purple inside.

N. oxypetala. Himalayas. Height 18–24 in.; planting distance 12–15 in. The short stem carries a few yellow flowers with purple throats.

N. pardanthina. China. Height 2–3 ft; planting distance 12–15 in. Probably the most widely grown species. It has whorled leaves and up to ten flowers. The flowers are open and pendent, with fringed petals, and coloured pink with deeper pink spots.

NOMOCHARIS SALUENENSIS

N. saluenensis. China, Tibet, Upper Burma. Height 2–4 ft; planting distance 12–15 in. The stout stems carry up to six open flowers, coloured white or pink and flushed with purple.

Several of the species cross freely and garden hybrids have been raised; they are now more generally grown than many of the species. They are often offered as *Nomocharis* × *hybrida*, few having been named.

Cultivation. Moist, deep soil is essential for these plants. Plant them during March, preferably as one or two-year-old seedlings, in light shade in the shelter of trees and shrubs. If bulbs are available, plant them 3–4 in. deep in a similar situation. Take care to avoid damage when hoeing or weeding, as the seedlings are small and will not produce a flower stem until they are two or three years old. They should not need staking, but if

Nigella damascena

Nomocharis aperta

Nomocharis saluenensis

grown in too shady a site may become drawn and then need support. Water generously during long dry spells. Mulch each spring with peat, leaf-mould or well-decayed compost. Dead-head unless seeds are required to increase the stock or to produce new hybrids.

Propagation. Seeds germinate freely if sown thinly in pans of John Innes seed compost at a temperature of 7–10°C (45–50°F), in either October or March. After a year, transplant the seedlings to a nursery bed or grow on in pots or pans until planting out the following spring.

Pests. Stems, leaves and bulbs may be eaten by SLUGS and SNAILS.

Diseases. Generally trouble-free.

Notocactus leninghausii

Notocactus ottonis

Notocactus

Cactaceae

A genus of 15 species of greenhouse perennials. These easily grown cacti are usually solitary and spherical, and have attractively coloured spines and beautiful flowers. The flowers are widely trumpet-shaped; the narrow petals open out flat at the top. They appear singly or two or three at a time from near the crown of the plant; individual flowers may last about a week.

See also CACTUS.

N. apricus. Uruguay. Height up to 3 in.; spread 2–2½ in. This species eventually forms a clump. The light green globular stem has 15–20 almost flattened ribs. From the areoles arise 18–20 grey, bristly spines, curved and radial, and four larger central spines which are red-yellow. The flowers, up to 4 in. long, appear in May and June; they are yellow, tinged with red on the outer petals.

N. concinnus. Brazil, Uruguay. Height 3 in.; spread 4 in. The light green stem is broadly globular, and slightly depressed at the top. It has about 18 notched ribs divided into tubercles. The white woolly areole on each tubercle bears 10–12 bristly yellow spines, and four stronger central spines arranged crosswise.

The flowers are up to 4 in. long and open freely during spring and summer; they have sulphur-yellow inner petals and red outer petals.

N. graessneri. Brazil. Height and spread 4–5 in. The stem is globular, flattened and depressed on top. It is pale green covered with yellow spines. The areoles, on 50–60 spiralling, notched ribs, bear yellow wool, numerous bright yellow radial spines and three to six stouter, central spines. The green-yellow flowers, ¾ in. across, occur from June to September.

N. haselbergii. Brazil. Height up to 6 in.; spread 4–5 in. The globular or cylindrical stem is flattened and slightly depressed at the apex. It is bright green, covered with white-yellow spines. There are 30 or more low, spiralling ribs. The white woolly areoles bear about 20 white radial spines and from three to five pale yellow central spines. Bright orange-red flowers, 1½–2 in. across, occur in spring and early summer.

N. leninghausii. Brazil. Height up to 3 ft; spread 4–5 in. The cylindrical stem is light green, clothed with white wool at the apex, and divided into about 30 low ribs with areoles close together. The areoles bear up to 15 pale yellow radial spines and three or four golden-yellow central spines. The flowers, 1 in. across, are lemon yellow with green outer petals; they appear from June to August. This is an attractive species, but slow growing and shy-flowering.

N. mammulosus. Argentina, Uruguay. Height 5 in.; spread 3–4 in. The globular stem is dark green, and depressed and spineless at the top centre. The 18–20 ribs are deeply notched, and have a small protuberance under each areole. The areoles bear 10–13 yellow-brown radial spines and two to four brown-tipped central spines, one of which is erect and the others downward-pointing. The flowers, from June to August, are yellow with a red stripe on the outer petals.

N. ottonis. Brazil, Argentina, Paraguay, Uruguay. Height 4 in.; spread 3–7 in. The plant may be single or form clumps. The bright green stem is globular or cylindrical and flattened at the top. It is divided into 10–12 broad, rounded ribs. The areoles bear white wool, 10–18 yellow-brown radial spines, and three or four red-brown central spines. The yellow flowers, from May to July, are up to 4 in. long.

N. scopa. Brazil, Uruguay. Height up to 7 in.; spread 3 in. The stem is globular at first, later cylindrical or club-shaped. It is pale green with 30–40 low ribs almost concealed by soft white spines. The areoles contain white wool when young, and later produce 40 or more radial spines and three or four stronger red-brown central spines. The yellow, 2 in. wide flowers appear in April and May.

N. tabularis. Brazil, Uruguay. Height up to 4 in.; spread 4–6 in. The glaucous-green stem is globular or semi-cylindrical, and divided into 16–23 rounded, notched ribs. The areoles contain white wool and produce 16–18 white radial spines and four red central spines. The flowers appear in May and June; they are yellow, tinged red at the base of the petals.

Cultivation. Notocacti do best in a light, porous soil; a mixture of equal parts (by volume) loam, sand and decayed leaf-mould is ideal. In March or April pot the plants in 5–6 in. pots in a position where they will receive the maximum sunshine.

During the growing season water whenever the soil dries out, but keep the plants dry from the end of November until early spring. In winter they require a minimum temperature of 5°C (41°F). Move the plants into larger pots at the beginning of the growing season, March or April, if the roots fill the pots.

Propagation. Sow seeds in spring at a temperature of 21°C (70°F). Alternatively, divide and pot the clump-forming species in early summer.

N. leninghausii can be topped if it becomes too tall: remove the top 6 in. in early summer and treat this as a cutting. The truncated portion will produce secondary growths which can also be treated as cuttings in early summer.

Make sure that any cut surfaces are thoroughly dry before the cuttings are inserted in sand. Pot in the growing compost when the cuttings have rooted, usually after 2–3 months.

Pests. Conspicuous tufts of white waxy wool are caused by infestations of MEALY BUGS.

Diseases. Generally trouble-free.

Notonia: see Senecio

Nymphaea

Water lily. *Nymphaeaceae*

NYMPHAEA ALBA

A genus of 50 species of hardy and tender perennial water plants. Only a few are cultivated, but these and their numerous forms and hybrids are widely grown in pools, ponds and lakes.

Hardy water lilies, which flower over a long period in summer, have elegant blooms and are sometimes sweetly scented. Their large floating leaves provide shade for fish and help to inhibit the growth of algae. Most varieties are extremely long-lived and require little attention.

Although the tender or tropical water lilies are not well known in Great Britain, they are as easy to grow as the hardy forms, provided that the necessary water temperatures are maintained.

The leaves and flowers of water lilies rise from a thick rootstock held securely in the mud by long tough roots. The leaves are round to heart-shaped with a shiny, leathery upper surface.

The flowers are basically cup-shaped with several rows of petals, the outer ones lying almost flat as the flower opens. Shape varies little between varieties but some have more pointed petals than others, giving them a starry appearance. A few are almost completely double; nearly all have conspicuous golden or orange stamens.

HARDY SPECIES AND VARIETIES

Most can be grown almost anywhere in Britain, though a few, such as *N. odorata* 'Sulphurea', grow and flower well only in a warm season and situation.

All have rounded floating leaves, except where overcrowding forces them above the water surface. The colour of the leaves ranges from pale to deep green, some being splashed or flushed with maroon. Leaf size varies considerably according to variety, and in general is proportional to the size and vigour of the plant.

Hardy nymphaeas vary considerably in size and vigour, and in the list that follows they are described as large, medium, small or miniature. It is impossible to give specific figures for each plant since much depends on methods of cultivation. Lilies planted directly in the mud in large pools or lakes may attain a spread several times greater than container-grown plants of the same type.

However, the following figures provide a rough guide to the size of container-grown plants after two or three years' growth:

Large water lilies have leaves 10–18 in. across and a surface spread of $3\frac{1}{2}$–$4\frac{1}{2}$ sq. ft.

Medium: leaves 7–10 in., spread $2\frac{1}{2}$–$3\frac{1}{2}$ sq. ft.
Small: leaves 4–7 in., spread 1–$2\frac{1}{2}$ sq. ft.
Miniature: leaves 2–3 in., spread 12–18 sq. in.

The vigour and size of a plant indicate the depth of water in which it grows best. The strongest thrive in water up to 6 ft deep, while the smallest are limited to 15 in. or less.

Varieties are often catalogued according to their vigour and spread, but nearly all will grow in very much less water than stated, although the leaves and stems will then become congested more quickly.

In general, established plants begin flowering between May and July and continue until late September. Lilies in small, shallow pools, where the water heats up rapidly, flower earlier.

The quantity of blooms fluctuates from season to season, but as many as 20 may be borne at one time; each lasts from three to five days only, the bud opening at about 10 a.m. and closing at about 4 p.m. each day, except in dull or rainy weather when it remains closed. Colours include pure white, blush-white, pink, rose, deep red, yellow, and the so-called copper or changeable varieties; these are straw-yellow flushed with pink on opening, changing to apricot-pink and copper-red as the flower ages.

The rootstock varies from species to species. In the case of the *tuberosa* and *odorata* types it extends for several feet, bearing tubers at intervals. The leaves, flowers and young plants emerge rather sparsely from various points along the length of the root.

Most of the other types have a rather stout branching rhizome, sometimes up to 24 in. long, which is black outside and yellow within. This grows more or less horizontally, usually with the upper surface of the rhizome above mud level but securely held by the true roots beneath. The leaves and flowers emerge from a single upward-facing growing point or crown. Some hybrids combine the characteristics of both types.

Between 40 and 50 varieties are commonly available from specialist growers.

N. alba. Europe, including Great Britain. Large. Water depth 2–4 ft. This is the only native species; it is found in ponds and slow-flowing streams, but is seldom grown in ornamental pools. The leaves are light green; the flowers white with yellow stamens. Each flower measures 4–6 in. across.

N. odorata. N. America. The original wild species, which has bright green leaves and fragrant white flowers, is probably not available.

The variety *N. o.* 'Minor' is obtainable, although scarce. This is a small variety for pools and tubs; water depth 12–15 in. It has dark green leaves and narrow-petalled white flowers, 2–3 in. wide, which are faintly scented. The variety 'Rosea' (Cape Cod lily) is of similar habit. It requires a water depth of 1–$2\frac{1}{2}$ ft and produces fragrant pale pink flowers. Both these varieties are rather shy-flowering and 'Rosea' does better in warm conditions.

The following varieties, although usually catalogued with the prefix *odorata*, are almost certainly hybrids rather than cultivated varieties of the species. They can be grown in small pools but require space to spread their long rootstocks.

N. o. 'Sulphurea'. Medium. Water depth 12–15 in. The mid-green leaves are freely spotted with red. The slightly fragrant, primrose-yellow flowers measure 3 in. across; their narrow petals stand well out of the water.

N. o. 'Sulphurea Grandiflora' is a stronger-growing form with larger flowers, up to 6 in. across, which are more heavily fragrant.

Nymphaea alba

Nymphaea 'Escarboucle'

Nymphaea 'Helvola'

Nymphaea × laydekeri
'Fulgens'

Nymphaea × marliacea
'Albida'

Nymphaea × marliacea 'Rosea'

N. o. 'Turicensis'. Small. Water depth 12 in. The leaves are mid-green and sparse. The pale pink flowers, 3–4 in. wide, are sweetly scented.
N. tuberosa. N.E. United States. Large. Water depth 2–4 ft. The plant grows from a tuberous rootstock and produces deep green leaves. The white flowers, 4–7 in. across, have broad petals.

The variety 'Richardsonii', water depth 2–3 ft, is less vigorous than the type but more free-flowering. It has pure white flowers and bright green glossy leaves. 'Rosea', water depth 2–4 ft, has leaves that are deep green above, pink or red on the undersides, and pale pink flowers.

HARDY HYBRIDS The majority of hardy nymphaea hybrids were raised in the late 19th and early 20th centuries by a Frenchman, Joseph Bory Latour-Marliac, and several now bear his name or that of his son-in-law, Maurice Laydeker. The hybrids are mostly more free-flowering than the species and in a wider range of colours. Several have larger flowers.

Because of uncertainty about their origin, *N. odorata* hybrids are described under HARDY SPECIES AND VARIETIES.

'Aurora'. Small. Water depth 12–24 in. This changeable hybrid is vigorous and free-flowering, especially in a warm season.

The leaves are mid-green, splashed with maroon. The pale yellow flowers measure 2–3 in. across and change to copper and deep rose.

'Conqueror'. Medium. Water depth 1½–2½ ft. A strong-growing variety of elegant habit. Thin stems support the dark green leaves and bright rose-crimson flowers, about 6 in. across. The outside petals and sepals are white, stained and streaked with red.

'Escarboucle'. Medium. Water depth 18–24 in. This is the most brilliant red water lily, although less free-flowering than others. The leaves are dark green, the flowers an open starry shape, 6–8 in. in diameter. The first blooms each season are sometimes white, or white and red.

'Firecrest'. Medium. Water depth 18–24 in. This hybrid bears deep green leaves and faintly scented flowers that measure 4–5 in. across. These are pale pink, changing to deep pink, with fiery red stamens.

'Froebelii'. Small to medium. Water depth 1–2½ ft. A free-flowering lily with deep green leaves that are splashed with maroon. The flowers are 4 in. across, slightly fragrant and deep wine-red.

'Gladstoniana'. Large. Water depth 4–6 ft. This splendid plant is probably the largest-growing water lily. It has mid-green leaves and pure white flowers, 8–10 in. across.

'Graziella'. Small. Water depth 6–24 in. A changeable hybrid with mid-green leaves that are splashed with maroon. The yellow flowers, about 3 in. across, are flushed with pink at first, deepening to copper-red.

'Helvola'. Miniature. Water depth 6–12 in. This is particularly free-flowering, especially in warm pools. Cover the pool with boards and sacking in winter, or at least the part where one of these miniatures is planted, if it is in less than 6 in. of water. Alternatively, move container-grown plants to deeper water. It has olive-green leaves lightly speckled with red. The flowers, which measure 2–2½ in. across, are soft cream with yellow stamens.

'James Brydon'. Small to medium. Water depth ½–3 ft. A very adaptable hybrid with leaves that are glossy maroon when young, turning dark green splashed with maroon. The 4–5 in. wide flowers are deep pink to rose-crimson.

N. × laydekeri. Hybrids with this prefix are small to medium-growing. Water depth ¾–2½ ft. These plants are particularly free-flowering.

N. × l. 'Fulgens' has dark green leaves. The flowers, 4 in. across, are brilliant red-pink to carmine with bright orange-red stamens.

N. × l. 'Lilacea' has mid-green leaves and pale pink to deep rose flowers, 3–4 in. across. These are freely produced, even on young plants.

N. × l. 'Purpurata' has mid to dark green leaves. The flowers, 3–4 in. across, are deep pink to bright rose-crimson; they are produced abundantly throughout the summer.

N. × marliacea. The following hybrids are of medium size and have a particularly leafy habit. If grown in small pools they require frequent lifting and division; they are outstandingly reliable, producing a steady succession of flowers annually.

N. × m. 'Albida'. Water depth 1½–3 ft. An easily grown and prolific plant with abundant light green leaves. The pure white flowers are 4–6 in. in diameter.

N. × m. 'Carnea'. Water depth 1½–3 ft. The maroon leaves age to deep red-green; deep pink buds open into 4–5 in. wide flowers which fade gradually to cream-white. This is the most widely grown water lily, although generally too prolific for a small pool.

N. × m. 'Chromatella'. Water depth 2–4 ft. This is the hardiest and most free-flowering yellow form but, like all yellow and copper forms, it is sometimes difficult to establish. It has light green leaves, splashed with maroon. The flowers, 4–6 in. across, are a deep primrose-yellow with deeper yellow stamens.

N. × m. 'Rosea'. Water depth 24 in. This hybrid is similar to *N. × m.* 'Carnea', but has larger flowers of a pale, lustrous pink. Newly divided plants may produce very pale or white flowers until fully established.

'Masaniello'. Medium to large. Water depth 1½–3 ft. Thick stems carry robust mid-green leaves. The flowers, 4–5 in. across, are rose-pink overlaid with crimson at the base of the petals.

'Rose Arey'. Medium to small. Water depth 12–15 in. This fragrant and beautiful form has mid-green leaves. The flowers, 4–6 in. across, are a deep clear pink with yellow stamens and are borne several inches above water level. The lower petals and sepals reflex as the flower ages. It gives its best display during a warm season.

'Sunrise'. Medium. Water depth 12–18 in. This strong-growing American variety is free-flowering in warm localities. It has mid-green leaves, spotted with maroon, and deep primrose-yellow flowers. These are held above the water surface and are composed of numerous long narrow petals surrounding floppy stamens and deep yellow petaloids. The outer petals reflex.

'William Falconer'. Medium. Water depth 12–18 in. This variety is coloured a deeper red than any others; it is not always freely available. The leaves are maroon. The flowers are a deep beetroot shade and measure 4–6 in. across; the stamens glitter with a dusting of golden pollen.

ROPICAL SPECIES AND VARIETIES

These colourful free-flowering plants are as easy to grow as the hardy varieties, provided the necessary water temperatures can be maintained. These are 21°C (70°F) in summer and 10°C (50°F) in winter; the dormant tubers may also be lifted and stored during the winter in moist sand kept at the above winter temperature.

Those cultivated include a few species, mostly blue-flowered, and a number of hybrids with white, yellow, deep blue, pink or red flowers.

The foliage of tropical lilies is particularly decorative; leaves are rounded to heart-shaped and frequently scalloped at the edges. They may be maroon, green flushed with pink, or green spotted with purple or maroon. The leaves of some varieties have raised, intricate veining on the undersides; a few are viviparous—young plants being formed in the centre of the leaf where the stem terminates.

Generally, the flowering season extends from June to September. The flowers are borne several inches above the water surface on stiff, fleshy stems, the buds opening between 10 a.m. and 12 noon and closing between 4 and 7 p.m. The exceptions are the night-blooming varieties, whose blooms open at dusk and close at some time between dawn and midday.

The flowers frequently have a metallic sheen. They last for between three and five days on the plant or when cut, and are often strongly fragrant. Many varieties produce enormous blooms, a measurement of 6–8 in. across being common. In sub-tropical conditions a few may be over 12 in.

The growth in most cases emanates from a small, nut-like tuber which is cream-white inside and with a hard, almost black outer skin. Young tubers are smooth and egg-shaped; they form round the old tuber, which is usually wrinkled and more or less egg-shaped. Growth emerges from the top, which is the widest part of the tuber. True roots emerge from the growing plant only, not from the tuber.

The following are some of the species and hybrids available from specialist growers. They are all similar in habit, requiring 9–15 in. of water above the roots and spreading over 3–5 sq. ft.

N. capensis (Cape blue water lily). S. Africa. The undersides of the smooth mid-green leaves are red or pink. The fragrant star-shaped flowers, 4–5 in. across, stand 5–10 in. above water and are a uniform light blue.

N. lotus (Egyptian lotus). Egypt. A night-flowering species. Thick, succulent roots and stems bear deep green leaves with slightly ruffled edges. Long, narrowly conical buds with striated sepals open into 6–8 in. wide flowers; the outer petals are horizontal, the inner ones semi-erect. These blooms are pure white and matt, not glistening as in other tropical species.

N. stellata. India and S.E. Asia. A strong, easily grown species which forms tubers freely. Young tubers are sometimes planted in tropical aquaria, where the young underwater leaves are decorative. Surface leaves are smooth and light green.

The star-shaped flowers are heavily fragrant; they are 4–6 in. across, and have narrow petals symmetrically arranged. These are lavender-blue surrounding a golden centre and stamens; the sepals are glossy green speckled with black.

Nymphaea 'Sunrise'

TROPICAL HYBRIDS All have star-shaped flowers. The following are day-flowering:

'Director G. T. Moore'. The deepest 'true blue' tropical form, with mid-green leaves and fragrant flowers of blue-purple. The centre of the flower is bright golden-yellow with a dense boss of blue stamens.

'Mrs Edward Whitaker'. This fine hybrid has rich green foliage flecked with maroon, and pale lavender flowers, 6–8 in. across.

'Mrs G. H. Pring'. A free-flowering hybrid with mid-green leaves; the cream-white fragrant blooms, 4–6 in. across, are splashed with maroon.

'Panama Pacific'. A vigorous free-flowering hybrid with pale to mid-green leaves. The rich rose-purple flowers stand well above the water.

'St Louis'. A reliable variety, with pale green leaves. The pale lemon flowers measure 4–6 in. across, and have deep golden-yellow stamens.

Nymphaea stellata

The following two hybrids are night-flowering:

'Missouri'. The leaves are deep green flushed with red and have scalloped edges. The flowers, measuring 6–12 in. across, have many broad, rounded, clear white petals surrounding a yellow centre and stamens.

'Mrs G. C. Hitchcock'. A large-flowering variety bearing maroon-coloured leaves with scalloped edges. The flowers measure 6–12 in. across. Their rather narrow deep pink petals are white at the centre, and surround deeper pink stamens.

Cultivation of hardy species and hybrids. Plant in ornamental pools, in fertile loamy soils which seldom require additional fertiliser. If the soil is light or a poor-quality clay, either incorporate a layer of decayed cow manure or mix in an organic fertiliser at 1–2 oz. per bushel. Coarse bone-meal is suitable for this purpose.

Nymphaea 'Director G. T. Moore'

Water lilies may be planted either directly in the base of the pool or in perforated containers, as sold by water garden specialists. In either case, large plants require soil 8–12 in. deep (in containers at least 18 in. sq.); medium types need 6–8 in. of soil (in containers at least 12 in. sq.); small varieties need 4–6 in. of soil (in containers 9–12 in. sq.); and miniatures need 3–4 in. of soil (in containers 9–12 in. sq.). Saturate the soil before planting.

Plant the tubers or rhizomes between mid-April and early June, setting them so that the soil is level with the young growing part of the rootstock. Keep the water as clear as possible to allow light and warmth to penetrate.

In natural ponds and lakes, plant the lilies either directly into the soil or mud on the base, or in temporary containers such as baskets or boxes which will rot in due course when the plants are fully established.

Choose a sunny position and plant in shallower water than the maximum that the particular variety will grow in. Nearly all varieties tend to grow towards deeper water.

When planting direct, reach down through the water and push the rootstock into the soft mud. Alternatively, strip the grass from a suitably sized piece of turf, roll the rootstock inside with the crown exposed, secure with string and lower carefully into position.

Water lilies require little attention after planting. However, excessively large leaves may be removed from established plants if desired; prolific varieties and those in small pools may need thinning from time to time.

April or May are the best months for thinning. After draining off the water or lifting the containers, examine the rootstock and select one of the strongest rhizomes or tubers. Using a strong, sharp knife, sever this 6–8 in. back from the growing part and trim off the true roots beneath. Replant the pieces of rhizome.

If the pool is being cleaned at this time, store the rhizomes temporarily in a box covered with wet sacking or paper, and place in shade.

Cultivation of tropical species and hybrids. A tank at least 4 ft sq. is required to produce blooms of a reasonable size, though a water depth of 12 in. is sufficient. Maintain a water temperature of 21°C (70°F) during the growing season. This is especially important when the plants are started into growth. The most practical method of heating the water is to run the existing greenhouse heating pipes, or a lead from them, through the pool, forming a loop. Alternatively, use an immersion heater, though this raises the cost considerably. In greenhouses in mid-summer, sun heat may be sufficient.

The best times to plant are in late May or in June. Cover the base of the tank with 3 in. of good loam and in the centre make a raised mound 3 in. high and 15 in. in diameter. Fill the tank until the mound is just covered with water. Allow the water to heat up, then plant the water lilies in the top of the mound. As growth progresses, increase the water depth to a maximum of 15 in.

When growth stops in the autumn, gradually reduce the water level to allow the tubers to ripen; finally dry them off and store in moist sand warmed to 10°C (50°F). Alternatively, leave the plants where they are and maintain a water temperature of 10°C (50°F).

Propagation of hardy species and hybrids Divide the plants, following the thinning procedure described under CULTIVATION, or use the young offsets produced on the main rootstock.

To remove offsets, lift the plants in April or May and wash them thoroughly. Detach the offsets with a sharp knife. The rootstock can then be replanted. Insert the offsets in small pots of plain loam and stand these in a bowl or tank with the water $\frac{1}{2}$–$\frac{3}{4}$ in. over the pot rims. Keep in full sun and plant out in their permanent positions when well rooted.

Propagation of tropical species and hybrids Increase tropical water lilies by division of overwintered tubers in April. Place the plants separately in 3 in. pots of sand and stand these in a shallow tray of water in full light; maintain a temperature of 18–21°C (64–70°F). When growth starts, one or more thin shoots appear from which tiny arrow-shaped leaves and roots develop, followed fairly quickly by surface leaves. At this stage detach the young plant just above the tuber and plant as already described. Alternatively, pot into a 3 in. pot of the growing medium, stand in shallow warm water and plant out later.

The tuber may produce a second plantlet which can be taken off and potted in the same way. It is possible to obtain three or even four new plants from some tubers if needed.

Viviparous water lilies may also be increased by detaching the plantlets which form in the centres of leaves. Insert these in 3 in. pots placed in shallow warm water. Plant finally when three or four new leaves have appeared.

Pests. APHIDS, particularly water lily aphids, infest foliage and flowers.

WATER LILY BEETLE adults and larvae eat numerous narrow strips out of the leaves.

CATERPILLARS of the brown china mark moth also feed on the leaves and protect themselves by constructing oval cases out of pieces of leaf tissue.

Diseases. LEAF SPOT, due to a fungus, shows as circular pale brown spots with dark edges; small wart-like pustules, producing yellow spores, appear on the upper sides of the spots.

STEM ROT blackens and destroys the stem; the leaves and flowers subsequently collapse.

Nymphaea 'Mrs Edward Whitaker'

Nymphaea 'Panama Pacific'

Nyssa sylvatica (autumn foliage)

Nyssa

Tupelo. *Nyssaceae*

NYSSA SYLVATICA

A genus of ten species of hardy deciduous trees that are remarkable for the brilliant scarlet colour of their leaves in early autumn. The species described, which is of pyramidal form when young, is the only one in general cultivation.

N. sylvatica. E. United States. Height 15–18 ft; spread 8–10 ft. The lustrous mid-green, pointed, ovate leaves turn brilliant scarlet, red or orange in October or November. Insignificant yellow-green flowers open in June.

Cultivation. Plant between October and March in moist, lime-free soil in sun or partial shade. It is especially effective when grown near water where the autumn colouring can be reflected.

Propagation. Sow seeds in October in pans of John Innes seed compost and place in a cold frame. The following May or June, pot the seedlings in 3 in. containers of John Innes potting compost No. 1. Line out in a nursery bed the following March or April and grow on for four or five years before planting out in permanent positions.

Branches layered in September or October will have formed their own roots after one or two years and can be severed.

Pruning. None required.

Pests and diseases. Generally trouble-free.

O

× *Odontioda* 'Mazurka'

Oak: see Quercus

Obedient plant: see *Physostegia virginiana*

Ocimum basilicum: see Basil

× **Odontioda**

Orchidaceae

A group of bigeneric hybrids between *Cochlioda* and *Odontoglossum*. The growth habit and arrangement of foliage and flowers are similar to those of *Odontoglossum*.

See also ORCHIDS.

× ODONTIODA

Named forms, with 2½–3½ in. wide flowers from October to May, include: 'Mazurka', a hybrid between *Odontoglossum* Margin and × *Odontioda* Zorke, with bright red flowers.

'Florence Stirling', a hybrid between × *Odontioda* Astoria and × *Odontioda* Melina, has flowers in a wide colour range from dark magenta to light mauve on a white background.

'Connosa', a hybrid between × *Odontioda* Cornelia and × *Odontioda* Mimosa, bears clear yellow flowers with occasional brown spots.

Cultivation, propagation, pests and diseases. See entry under ODONTOGLOSSUM.

× **Odontocidium**

Orchidaceae

A group of bigeneric hybrids between *Odontoglossum* and *Oncidium*. The growth habit of these orchids is similar to those of *Odontoglossum* and *Oncidium*. The flowering period is from November to May; the individual flowers measure 1½–2½ in. across.

See also ORCHIDS.

Outstanding named forms include: 'Selsfield Gold', a hybrid between *Oncidium tigrinum* and *Odontoglossum* 'Sunbelle'; the flowers have brown bars to the rich lemon-yellow sepals and petals, and a pale cream-yellow lip.

× ODONTOCIDIUM

'Hebe', a cross between *Odontoglossum cirrhosum* and *Oncidium incurvum*, has plum-purple flowers with white edging to the lip.

'Revinum', a hybrid between *Odontoglossum* 'Rêve d'Or' and *Oncidium tigrinum*, bears flowers with pale cream sepals and petals; these have dark brown blotches; the white lip has yellow markings.

Cultivation, propagation, pests and diseases. See entry under ODONTOGLOSSUM.

× *Odontocidium* 'Selsfield Gold'

Odontoglossum

Orchidaceae

A genus of 200 species of tropical epiphytic orchids, found in Central and South America. The pseudobulbs vary in shape and are one or two-leaved. The evergreen leaves are strap-shaped to lanceolate and mid-green; they emerge from the sides and the apex of the pseudobulbs. Erect flower sprays, usually only one to each bulb, arise from the base of the leading pseudobulb and arch over with the weight of the flowers. These have a flat appearance caused by their wide-open sepals and petals, which may be narrow and pointed, or broad and rounded. The lip varies in shape; it differs in colour from the petals, and is often conspicuously marked.

Many natural hybrids occur, and numerous artificial hybrids have been made from crosses between this and related genera. Odontoglossums are usually high-altitude plants and

Odontoglossum × 'Alport'

475

thrive in a cool moist greenhouse. They must be protected from draughts and hot sunny weather.

See also ORCHIDS.

O. × 'Alport'. A hybrid between *O. Alorcus* and *O. Portheron*. It has 4 in. high ovate pseudobulbs each carrying two leaves. The flowers, 3 in. or more across, are borne, 15 to a stem, from October to May; the lip, sepals and wavy-margined petals are white, irregularly blotched with rose or crimson.

O. bictoniense. Central America. This species has ovate, flattened pseudobulbs up to 4 in high, each with two leaves. Each flower spike, up to 2½ ft, bears several or many flowers, about 1½ in. across. They have yellow-green sepals and petals with chestnut-brown blotches, and a pale rose lip with yellow or white markings. Flowering is from October to April.

'Album' has red-brown sepals and petals, and a pure white lip; 'Sulphureum' has yellow sepals and petals, and a white lip; 'Superbum' is a large-flowered form, with dark chocolate-brown sepals and a purple lip.

O. citrosmum, syn. *O. pendulum*. Mexico. A species with orbicular two-leaved pseudobulbs, 3–5 in. high. The leaves are broad and leathery. A pendulous inflorescence, 12–24 in. long, carries, in May and June, as many as 30 fragrant flowers about 2½ in. across. They have broad white sepals and petals sometimes flushed with rose; the lip is rose-red with a yellow, red-spotted crest. 'Album' is pure white with a yellow crest; 'Sulphureum' is yellow-buff with a pink lip.

Odontoglossum bictoniense

Odontoglossum crispum

× *Odontonia* Areta 'Lydart'

ODONTOGLOSSUM CRISPUM

O. crispum. Colombia. This species has sturdy, ovate, two-leaved pseudobulbs about 4 in. high. The arched inflorescence is about 24 in. long and bears numerous flowers, up to 4 in. across; these are white often flushed with pink and have red spots and a yellow crest. The petals have wavy margins and are broader than the sepals. This species is in flower all year round, but the main flowering period is from February to April. There is a vast number of varieties, the basic colours being white, pink or pale yellow, with varying degrees of spotting in shades of red or brown.

O. grande. Guatemala. This species can be grown on a window-sill indoors. The 4 in. high pseudobulbs are broad and ovate, each with two leaves. The flowers are up to 7 in. wide; four to seven are carried on each 12 in. flower spike from August to November. The sepals and petals are bright yellow, barred with chestnut-brown. The short round lip is cream or pale yellow, brown-red at the base with an orange crest.

The variety 'Magnificum' has larger and brighter flowers, produced in greater quantity than the species; 'Sanderae' has shining lemon-yellow flowers.

O. nobile: see *O. pescatorei*

O. pendulum: see *O. citrosmum*

O. pescatorei, syn. *O. nobile*. Colombia. Thi[s] species has ovate two-leaved pseudobulbs abou[t] 4 in. high. The flower scapes are about 24 in[.] long, branching and carrying up to 100 flower[s] from March to May.

The flowers are about 3 in. across, with broa[d] white sepals and petals that are sometimes tinge[d] with rose and blotched with light brown. The li[p] is narrow at the base and then broadly rounded[;] it is white with purple blotches and has [a] yellow, red-streaked crest.

'Schroederianum' is pure white with a rose[-] purple spot in the centre of each sepal and petal[;] the lip is white with rose-purple side-lobes and [a] yellow crest. 'Veitchianum' has large whit[e] flowers that are irregularly blotched with ric[h] magenta-purple.

Cultivation. Grow odontoglossums in well crocked pots or baskets fitted to the size of th[e] plants. Use a well-drained compost consisting o[f] 2 parts finely chopped osmunda fibre to 1 par[t] sphagnum moss (parts by volume) with a littl[e] sharp silver sand added.

These plants need cool, airy and moist conditions, and should be ventilated day and nigh[t] throughout the year except in foggy or frost[y] weather. Damp down the greenhouse and spra[y] the plants two or three times a day in summer[,] once or twice daily in winter. Keep them in ful[l] light from November to February, but shad[e] on hot days from March to October. Keep th[e] plants moist. No resting phase is required, bu[t] *O. grande* needs less water after its pseudobulb[s] have matured.

Propagation. Every two or three years, divide an[d] repot the plants in August and September or i[n] March and April.

Pests. Leaves and stems may be infested by SCAL[E] INSECTS, making the plants sooty and sticky.

APHIDS produce similar symptoms and THRIPS may damage the flowers.

Diseases. One or more fungi or a PHYSIOLOGICAL DISORDER may cause LEAF SPOT; brown or black spots appear on the leaves or the bulbs.

× Odontonia

Orchidaceae

× ODONTONIA

This is a group of bigeneric orchid hybrid[s] between *Miltonia* and *Odontoglossum*. They ar[e] similar in all respects to the latter genus, flowering from November to May.

See also ORCHIDS.

The following are among several outstanding forms: 'Olga', a cross between × *Odontoni[a]* Thisbe and *Odontoglossum crispum*, with 3–4[?] in. wide flowers composed of pure white sepal[s] and petals; the broad lip may occasionally b[e] marked dark red.

Areta 'Lydart', a cross between × *Odontonia* aguna and *Odontoglossum* Clonius, bears 3–4 n. wide, vivid red flowers; the lip has a ellow throat.

'Opilgay', a hybrid between × *Odontonia* vril Gay and *Odontoglossum* 'Opheon' has nid-red, 3 in. wide flowers with white flecking n the edges of sepals and petals.

'Torphea' is a hybrid between × *Odontonia* mphea and *Odontoglossum* 'Palmyrator'; the owers are about 3 in. across, white with straw-erry to deep plum blotches; the white lip s ringed by the same colours.

Cultivation, propagation, pests and diseases. See ntry under ODONTOGLOSSUM.

Oenothera

Onagraceae

A genus of about 80 species of annuals, biennials, herbaceous perennials and sub-shrubs. The following species are all hardy and make excellent plants for borders or wild gardens; *O. acaulis* and *O. missouriensis* are suitable for rock gardens.

The faintly scented flowers are widely funnel-shaped, sometimes opening out nearly flat. They are produced in profusion, but are short-lived.

O. acaulis, syn. *O. taraxifolia*. Chile. Height 6 in.; planting distance 12 in. This deep-rooting peren-nial can be unreliable in cold, wet areas, and is there better treated as a biennial. It forms rosettes of jaggedly toothed, mid-green leaves like a dandelion and, eventually, prostrate zigzag branches. Stemless 3 in. wide flowers arise at ground level from May to September. They are white, turning rose, and open in the evening.

O. biennis. N. America. Height 3 ft; planting distance 12 in. A hardy biennial which will flower the first year from seeds; if allowed to set seed, it will increase to weed-like proportions. The lanceolate leaves are mid-green, forming sub-stantial rosettes. The erect stems carry a pro-fusion of pale yellow flowers, $1\frac{1}{2}$–2 in. across, from June to October.

O. cinaeus. N. America. Height 15 in.; planting distance 12 in. The leaves of this border perennial are lanceolate to ovate; they appear in March and are variously coloured pink, purple, buff or red. By June, when the flower stems are growing, the plant becomes green tinged with purple. Rich yellow flowers, about $1\frac{1}{4}$ in. across, are produced from reddish buds from June to August.

O. erythrosepala: see *O. lamarckiana*

O. fruticosa, syn. *O. glauca*. N. America. Height 6–24 in.; planting distance 12 in. A border perennial that is sometimes confused with the allied *O. tetragona*. It bears mid-green ovate-lanceolate leaves; yellow flowers, 1–$1\frac{1}{2}$ in. across, are produced from June to August.

The species is superseded by the following varieties: *O. f. angustifolia*, syn. *O. linearis*, height 15 in., with sprays of yellow flowers; and 'Yellow River', height 18 in., also yellow.

O. glauca: see *O. fruticosa*

O. lamarckiana. N. America. Height 4 ft; planting distance 15 in. This hardy biennial, similar in habit to *O. biennis*, is now correctly known as *O. erythrosepala*. The mid-green leaves are

Oenothera missouriensis

lanceolate; the flowers, which measure 2–$3\frac{1}{2}$ in. across, are produced in dense spikes from June to September.

OENOTHERA LAMARCKIANA

O. linearis: see *O. fruticosa angustifolia*

O. missouriensis. South Central U.S.A. Height 4–6 in.; planting distance 18 in. An excellent perennial for the border or rock garden, with lanceolate mid-green leaves. The main stems usually lie flat on the ground. Buds, often red-spotted on the outside, open into yellow flowers, $2\frac{1}{2}$–3 in. wide. These are produced from June to August; they open in the evening and persist for several days.

OENOTHERA MISSOURIENSIS

O. perennis, syn. *O. pumila*. Eastern N. America. Height 18 in.; planting distance 12 in. A border perennial bearing pale to mid-green lanceolate leaves; loose leafy spikes, about 6 in. long, of small yellow flowers appear in July.

O. pumila: see *O. perennis*

O. taraxifolia: see *O. acaulis*

O. tetragona. East N. America. Height 1–3 ft; planting distance 12 in. This perennial border species is similar to *O. fruticosa*; it has ovate mid-green leaves. Dense but sparsely flowered spikes of yellow blooms, 1–$1\frac{1}{4}$ in. across, appear from June to September.

Oenothera acaulis

Oenothera biennis

Oenothera fruticosa

477

Olearia macrodonta

Olearia gunniana

Olearia haastii

Olearia × scilloniensis

The following varieties, all with yellow flowers, are more garden worthy than the species: *O. t. fraseri*, with flowers 1½–2½ in. across; 'Fireworks', free flowering with red buds; 'Highlight', free flowering and bright yellow; and 'Riparia', height 9–15 in., with twiggy growths rising from a small rootstock to form a grey-green mound of foliage.

O. trichocalyx. N. America. Height 18 in.; planting distance 6 in. A hardy biennial or short-lived perennial which may be grown as a half-hardy annual. The leaves are grey and deeply cut. The flowers are 2½ in. across, white and sweetly scented; they are produced in June.

Cultivation. Grow oenotheras in any ordinary, well-drained garden soil, in an open sunny site. Plant from October to April. Water freely in dry weather. Cut down perennial species to ground level in October or November.

Propagation. Sow seeds in pots or pans of seed compost in a cold frame during April. Prick out the seedlings and grow them on in nursery rows until October when they can be planted out in permanent positions.

Named varieties do not come true from seeds. Divide and replant the roots in March or April.

Pests. Young shoots may be invaded by STEM AND BULB EELWORMS, causing the tissues to become twisted and distorted.

Diseases. A white powdery coating on the leaves is caused by POWDERY MILDEW.

ROOT ROT may occur on heavy wet soils.

Old man: see *Artemisia abrotanum*
Old woman: see *Artemisia stelleriana*
Oleander: see *Nerium oleander*

Olearia

Daisy bush. *Compositae*

A genus of 100 species of hardy and slightly tender evergreen flowering shrubs, suitable for sheltered districts and for coastal gardens.

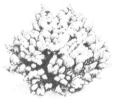

OLEARIA GUNNIANA

O. gunniana. Tasmania. Height 4–5 ft; spread 3–4 ft. This species is hardy in all but severe winters. The narrowly oblong, grey-green leaves have white felted undersides. The 1 in. wide daisy-like white flowers are borne in dense terminal panicles, up to 12 in. long, from May to July. There are pink and purple varieties.

O. haastii. New Zealand. Height 6–8 ft; spread 8–10 ft. This hardy plant tolerates atmospheric pollution and is frequently grown in town gardens. The broadly ovate, glossy mid-green leaves have grey-white felt beneath. White daisy-like flowers, ⅓ in. across, are produced in great profusion, in terminal clusters 2–3 in. wide, during July and August.

O. ilicifolia (Maori holly). New Zealand. Height and spread 8–10 ft. A hardy species with leathery leaves, resembling narrow holly leaves, that are sharply toothed. They are a lustrous mid-green with grey-white felt on the undersides. In June tiny white daisy-like flowers, with a musky fragrance, appear in clusters 2–4 in. across.

OLEARIA MACRODONTA

O. macrodonta. New Zealand. Height 8–12 ft; spread 6–8 ft. This hardy shrub, which has a musky odour, stands up well to wind in mild coastal districts. The holly-like narrowly ovate leaves are mid-green, with white felted undersides. Tiny, white, daisy-like flowers appear in clusters up to 6 in. across in June and July.

O. × scilloniensis. Height and spread 4–5 ft. This hybrid closely resembles *O. gunniana*, but the leaves are a brighter grey-green and the brilliant white daisy-like flowers, from May to July, are even more abundant.

O. semidentata. Chatham Islands. Height and spread 6–9 ft. This tender shrub is suitable only for mild areas of the British Isles. The lanceolate grey-green leaves are white and woolly beneath. The solitary, daisy-like, pale purple flowers, up to 2 in. across, have deeper purple centres; they open in June or July.

Cultivation. Plant *O. semidentata* in May, other species in October, March or April. Well-drained loam in a sunny, sheltered position is ideal, though these shrubs will withstand a greater degree of exposure if grown by the sea.

Propagation. For all species except *O. semidentata*, take 4 in. half-ripe cuttings of lateral shoots in late August and insert them in sandy soil in a cold frame. When they have rooted, pot into 3 in. containers of John Innes potting compost No. 1 and grow on in the frame. Transfer to a nursery bed in May, and plant out in permanent positions the following October.

To increase *O. semidentata*, take 4 in. half-ripe cuttings of lateral shoots in July, and insert them in a propagating frame at a temperature of 16°C (61°F). When they have rooted, pot into 3 in. containers of John Innes potting compost No. 1 and overwinter them in a greenhouse with a minimum temperature of 7–10°C (40–45°F). Pot on into 5–6 in. pots and plant out a year later.

Pruning. Remove any dead shoots in April.

Pests and diseases. Generally trouble-free.

Oleaster: see *Elaeagnus angustifolia*

Omphalodes

Navelwort. *Boraginaceae*

A genus of 28 species of hardy annual and perennial herbaceous plants. Only a few perennial species are in general cultivation; they are

itable for woodland planting and for growing
n rock gardens and at the front of borders.
he five-petalled flowers are similar to large
orget-me-nots.

. cappadocica. Turkey. Height 6–9 in.; spread
4 in. A clump-forming species with basal,
ong-stalked, ovate, bright green leaves; the stem
eaves are hairy above. Sprays of azure-blue
owers, $\frac{2}{3}$ in. across, appear in May and June.

O. luciliae. Greece, Asia Minor. Height 4–6 in.;
spread 18 in. This tufted species has ovate to
blong grey-green leaves and stems that have a
lue-grey pearly sheen. Few-flowered, loose
prays of soft blue flowers, $\frac{1}{2}$–$\frac{2}{3}$ in. across, are borne
rom May to September, occasionally later.

O. verna (blue-eyed mary). S. Europe. Height 6
n.; spread 12 in. A species that spreads by means
f runners. The mid-green, ovate-cordate and
ong-stalked leaves terminate in a short point.
prays of bright blue, white-throated flowers,
ach measuring $\frac{1}{2}$ in. across, are freely produced
rom February to May.

Cultivation. Plant in April. *O. cappadocica* and *O.
erna* thrive in peaty soil, in woodland or in a partly
haded position on a rock garden. *O. luciliae*
hould be planted in well-drained soil, containing
lenty of mortar rubble or tufa, and in full sun.
Water all species freely during hot weather.
Remove faded flower stems to prolong the
lowering period.

Propagation. Divide and replant *O. cappadocica*
nd *O. verna* in March or April, or after flowering
n July and August. Well-established clumps of
O. luciliae may be divided in June and July.

Alternatively, sow seeds of all species in pots or
oxes of John Innes seed compost in July, and
lace in a cold frame. When the seedlings are
arge enough to handle, pot up singly in 3 in. pots
of John Innes potting compost No. 1. Overwinter
n a cold frame and plant out in permanent
ositions the following April or May.

Pests and diseases. Generally trouble-free.

Oncidium

Orchidaceae

ONCIDIUM VARICOSUM

A large genus of 350 species of epiphytic
evergreen orchids widespread throughout the
American sub-tropics. These plants vary considerably in structure: some have pseudobulbs
with one or two large leaves growing from the
apex, while others have stems rising from a
rhizome and carrying large fleshy leaves. Still
others may have variably shaped leaves in a
fan-like arrangement, much like a small iris.

The branched flower stems arise from the base
of the pseudobulbs or from the leaf axils and may
be erect, arching or pendent. The flowers vary in
shape, size and colour. Common characteristics

are the petal-like wings on the column, a bump
below the stigma and a large and many-toothed
crest at the base of the lip. They are usually
yellow or brown and, although small, are bright
and showy. Many of the species have been used
in hybridisation.

Oncidiums are easy to grow, although their
requirements vary according to their native
habitat. They all need a definite resting period.

See also ORCHIDS.

O. altissimum. West Indies. This species has
smooth, compressed, dark green pseudobulbs
about 4 in. high, each with one mid-green
strap-shaped leaf. The flower stems, borne in
August and September, may be up to 7 ft long;
they branch near the tips and carry numerous
flowers, $1\frac{1}{2}$ in. across. These have narrow spreading sepals and petals, pale yellow with large
olive-brown blotches, and with wavy margins.
The lip is sulphur-yellow with a broad chestnut
band across it and around the crest. Grow in an
intermediate greenhouse.

O. cheirophorum. Colombia, Costa Rica. A dwarf
species with 1 in. high pseudobulbs, and lanceolate
mid-green leaves. The branching flower spike is
6 in. or more long and between October and
December bears numerous bright yellow fragrant
flowers up to $\frac{3}{4}$ in. across. The lip is comparatively
large and has a white crest. This species requires a
shady position in a cool greenhouse.

O. ornithorhynchum. Mexico, Guatemala. The
pseudobulbs of this species are about 2 in. high
with two strap-shaped to lanceolate mid to dark
green leaves. The branched pendulous flower
scapes measure up to 24 in. and bear numerous
sweetly scented flowers, nearly 1 in. across. The
sepals and petals are soft rose-lilac, and the darker
rose-lilac lip has a yellow crest. This species
flowers from October to December.

The variety 'Album' is pure white with a
yellow crest. Grow in a cool greenhouse, giving
plenty of light.

O. papilio (butterfly orchid). West Indies. A
species with round pseudobulbs 2 in. high. The
leaves, one on each pseudobulb, are elliptic-
oblong and heavily marked with dark green. A
succession of 3–7 in. wide flowers open one at a
time on inflorescences that are up to 4 ft long. The
crimson sepals and petals are barred with yellow;
the lip is orbicular, canary-yellow with a broad
red margin. This species may flower in any
month of the year. It needs light shade and
warm greenhouse conditions.

O. varicosum. Brazil. The oblong, flattened
pseudobulbs are 3–4 in. high, each with two
lanceolate mid-green leaves. The branching
flower spike is up to 5 ft long, with up to 90
flowers, the individual blooms measuring about
$1\frac{1}{4}$ in. across. The small sepals and petals are
yellow-green with pale red-brown bars, and the
large lip is bright golden-yellow with a dark red
blotch in front of the crest. Flowering is between
September and November. Grow in moderate
shade in a cool to intermediate greenhouse.

Cultivation. Grow oncidiums in pots or baskets
fitted to the size of the plants. They need a
well-drained compost of 2 parts finely chopped
osmunda fibre to 1 part sphagnum moss (parts by
volume) with a little sharp silver sand added.
O. cheirophorum can be grown in hanging

Omphalodes cappadocica

Omphalodes luciliae

Omphalodes verna

Oncidium ornithorhynchum

479

baskets from the roof. Shade the house from April to October and give plenty of water; maintain a moist atmosphere by ventilating and by damping down the greenhouse while the new shoots are growing.

Mature plants should be watered sparingly throughout the year, but should not be allowed to shrivel. The resting phase after flowering is usually from November to March, and temperatures should be lowered by 2·5°C (5°F); keep the plants just moist until growth is restarted in the spring.

Propagation. Divide the plants when the new shoots appear in March or April and repot them every two or three years. Set the old bulbs and the divisions at the edge of a pot containing the growing mixture, with the new growth towards the centre to allow room for it to develop.

Pests. Leaves and flowers may be infested by THRIPS, causing mottling and discoloration.

RED SPIDER MITES cause the same symptoms.

Diseases. Unsuitable cultural conditions produce PHYSIOLOGICAL DISORDERS which result in spotting of the leaves. The affected areas sometimes take on an olive-green appearance, due to the development of a secondary fungus which causes rotting of the tissues.

Oncidium papilio

Oncidium varicosum

Onion 'Ailsa Craig'

Onion

Allium cepa. Alliaceae

ONION

A hardy biennial bulbous plant cultivated as an annual vegetable. The white bulbs are popular for salads, as flavouring, in pickles and by themselves. These bulbs are susceptible to a number of pests and diseases, but with the use of chemicals these can fairly readily be overcome.

VARIETIES

Four main groups of onions are grown: a main crop sown in spring for harvesting in autumn and storing for winter use; a summer crop raised from an autumn sowing or from sets planted in spring; salad onions, also known as spring onions, sown in autumn or spring and pulled when green to be used raw; and pickling onions, small, quick-growing bulbs, sown thickly in spring and ripe by July.

For a main crop 'Ailsa Craig', 'Bedfordshire Champion' and 'Up To Date' are recommended. They produce firm, large bulbs which keep well.

For autumn sowing, select non-bolting varieties specially bred to withstand winter weather. Suitable varieties include 'Autumn Triumph', 'Reliance' and 'Solidity', with large long-lasting bulbs. Varieties planted as sets include 'Rynsburger' and 'Stuttgarter Giant', both with solid, brown-skinned, long-lasting bulbs.

'White Lisbon' is the most popular salad onion variety; it is quick-growing and has clear, white skin. For pickling onions, 'Small Par Silverskin' and 'White Queen' are suitabl 'White Portugal' can be used for pickling and as salad onion; left to mature, it produces firm, fl white bulbs.

Egyptian onion (*Allium cepa aggregatum*). Th is a perennial clustering form of onion wit small, elongated bulbs. The plant is grown for i shallot-like, onion-flavoured clusters of bulbi borne in place of flowers on 3 ft high stem Grow from bulbils set out in August c September in ordinary, well-drained soil; set th bulbils 9–12 in. apart each way. The onions wi be ready for use the following June t September. Established clumps may be divide and replanted in March.

Potato onion. This is a form of the ordinar onion; it forms a cluster of small, shallot-lik bulbils just below the surface of the soil. Th bulbs are mildly onion-flavoured and store wel Grow as advised for onion sets.

Welsh onion (*Allium fistulosum*). This hardy non-bulbous perennial is also known as ciboul o onion green. It grows to a height of 12 in. an resembles a multi-stemmed salad onion. Th pencil-thick shoots grow together in close tuft or clumps. The shoots can be used as sala onions, and the leaves as chives.

Cultivation. Grow the main crop of onions i full sun. A well-drained, light, friable loam previously enriched with plenty of manure, give the best results. Onions may be grown in th same site year after year. Dig the ground deepl in autumn and work in two bucketfuls of well rotted manure or compost per sq. yd; on cla soils, drainage can be improved by double dig ging and by adding a dressing of coarse sand an grit or peat. Sprinkle 5 oz. of carbonate of lim per sq. yd over all but limy soils. Leave th ground rough during winter; two weeks befor sowing, level the plot, raking it to a fine tilth Apply a top-dressing of a general-purpos fertiliser at 4 oz. per sq. yd.

Sowings can be made at any time from mid February to the end of March, provided th surface soil is dry and friable. Sow the seed thinly in rows 12 in. apart to avoid unnecessar thinning later. As soon as the seedlings are larg enough to handle, thin them to about 2 in. apart later to 4 in.; use the thinnings as salad onions Water freely during dry spells, but not when th bulbs begin ripening.

Make an autumn sowing in early August i the north and in late August or early Septembe in the south. Grow in beds manured for previous crop, and top-dress the soil as advise for the main crop. Sow the seeds closer than i spring to allow for winter losses. The following spring, thin the seedlings as for main-cro onions. Autumn-sown onions will be ready fo use about a month before the earliest spring sown onions.

Plant onion sets and potato onions out in March or April in soil manured for a previou crop; top-dress as advised for a main crop. Space the sets 6 in. apart in rows 12 in. apart, and plan so that only the neck is above soil level. If th sets rise out of the soil during the first week afte planting, push them back and firm them i again. Onion sets require a shorter growing season than plants raised from seeds and give better results in cold, wet areas.

Salad onions do well in soil that has been well prepared for previous onion crops. Sow the seeds thickly in $\frac{1}{2}$ in. deep drills, about 6 in. apart. No thinning is required. Sow during July in the north and August in the south for harvesting the following March to May; make further sowings in February or March to continue supplies until the end of June.

Pickling onions do best on light, poor soil. Sow seeds in March or April, either by broadcasting or in shallow drills 6–8 in. apart. No thinning is necessary; the crop will be ready for harvesting in July.

Set young plants of Welsh onion 9–12 in. apart in March or April. They thrive in any fertile, well-drained soil and require little attention. For best results, lift and divide the clumps annually in March.

Harvesting and storing. Pull and use salad onions as they are required. Other onion crops are ready for harvesting when the leaves turn yellow. Bend the leaves over at the necks of the bulbs to admit more sun; the foliage gradually dries off, and the skin of the bulbs turns yellow. At this stage lift the bulbs carefully with a fork and lay them out along the rows to ripen, turning them once or twice; large bulbs usually take up to a month to ripen fully.

Store only healthy bulbs. Tie them up a length of rope arranging them spirally, or place them in crumpled wire netting in boxes. Store the onions in a dry, airy place.

Harvest whole clumps of Welsh onions from June onwards.

Exhibition. For show purposes, sow seeds in early January. 'Ailsa Craig', with large, pale, globe-shaped bulbs, is an outstanding exhibition variety. Sow the seeds thinly and evenly in boxes of John Innes seed compost, cover lightly with the compost, and water thoroughly. Place the boxes under the greenhouse staging at a temperature of 18°C (64°F). As the seedlings appear, place the boxes in a well-lit position in the greenhouse. Ventilate the house except during frosty and foggy weather. When the seedlings are about $1\frac{1}{2}$ in. high, prick them out into boxes containing firmly packed John Innes potting compost No. 1, setting them 3 in. apart either way, and watering in well. Keep the boxes in a light and airy position. During the third week in March, move the boxes to a cold frame and harden off the seedlings prior to planting out in the prepared bed during showery weather in mid-April.

Keep as large a soil ball as possible round the roots, setting the seedlings shallowly but firmly at intervals of 9–12 in. and 15 in. between rows. Water the plants in well. Thereafter treat the plants as described under CULTIVATION for a main crop sown in early spring.

Pests. Maggots of ONION FLY tunnel into bases of young plants and the bulbs of mature plants. These pests are more prevalent on light soils.

STEM and BULB EELWORMS invade leaf and bulb tissues which become swollen and distorted.

Diseases. DOWNY MILDEW causes the leaves to turn grey and fall over. In wet weather they may be covered with a purple coating.

ONION SMUT shows on the leaves of young plants as lead-coloured, swollen, blister-like stripes which release black powdery spores.

SOFT ROT causes stored onions to become soft, slimy and evil-smelling.

STORAGE ROT is due to BLUE MOULD and similar fungi; it shows as blue-green growths between the outermost scales.

A VIRUS DISEASE shows first as yellow streaks at the leaf bases, followed by complete yellowing of the leaves, which become crinkled.

WHITE ROT causes the leaves to turn yellow and die back; the roots rot and the bases of the bulbs are covered with a fluffy fungal growth.

Onion, Egyptian: see Onion
Onion, potato: see Onion
Onion, Welsh: see Onion

Onoclea

Athyriaceae

ONOCLEA SENSIBILIS

A genus of one hardy species of fern. It is suitable for garden cultivation and grows well in wet soil. It is often grown as ground cover to stabilise the banks of streams.

O. sensibilis (sensitive fern). N. America, N. Asia. Height 12–24 in.; spread indefinite. The long-stemmed, pale glaucous-green fronds are pinnate and triangular. They are sensitive to cold and turn brown at the first frost—hence the common name. Sterile fronds appear first, followed in midsummer by fertile fronds which have pinnules resembling masses of small beads.

Cultivation. Plant the rhizomes during April, in sun or shade, just below the soil surface. Any soil is suitable provided it can be kept permanently moist; on dry gravelly soils, add plenty of moisture-retaining humus.

Propagation. If a large number of plants is wanted, sow spores from July to September (see entry under FERNS). Once gathered, the spores remain viable for only a few days.

For a small number of plants, divide the rhizomes in March or April, ensuring that there is a growing point on each piece before replanting.

Pests and diseases. Generally trouble-free.

Ononis

Leguminosae

A genus of 75 species of hardy annuals, herbaceous perennials and deciduous and evergreen sub-shrubs. They are suitable for growing on sunny banks and rock gardens; they tend to be short-lived but are easily replaced. The plants have trifoliate leaves and pea-like flowers.

Onion 'White Portugal'

Onion, Egyptian

Onoclea sensibilis

Ononis aragonensis

Ononis fruticosa

Onopordum acanthium

Onosma tauricum

O. aragonensis, syn. *O. dumosa.* Spain, French Pyrenees, Algeria. Height and spread up to 24 in. A bushy deciduous sub-shrub with grey-green leaves and yellow flowers, $\frac{1}{2}-\frac{3}{4}$ in. long, with red-brown veins. These are borne in short terminal racemes in June and July.

O. cenisia. French Alps, S. Europe, N. Africa. Height 1–2 in.; spread 8–10 in. This prostrate perennial species forms a mat of almost woody stems with mid-green leaves. It bears rich rose-pink flowers, $\frac{3}{4}$ in. long, from June to August.

O. dumosa: see *O. aragonensis*

O. fruticosa. S.E. France, Spain, Algeria. Height and spread up to 24 in. The leaves of this deciduous shrubby species are hoary mid-green. Purple-pink flowers, $\frac{1}{2}-\frac{3}{4}$ in. long, appear from June to August.

O. rotundifolia. Central and S. Europe. Height and spread up to 18 in. A deciduous rounded sub-shrub bearing mid-green leaves. Rose-pink flowers, up to $\frac{3}{4}$ in. long, are borne in clusters of two or three from June to August.

Cultivation. Plant during September and October, or March and April, in any ordinary, well-drained garden soil and in a sunny position.

Propagation. Sow seeds in pans or boxes of seed compost during March in a cold frame or greenhouse. When large enough to handle, prick off the seedlings into boxes and later singly in 3 in. pots of John Innes potting compost No. 1. Care should be taken to prevent the long tap-root from breaking. Plant out in flowering positions in autumn or spring.

Alternatively, take 2–2$\frac{1}{2}$ in. long cuttings of half-ripened shoots with a heel in July; insert in equal parts (by volume) peat and sand in a cold frame. Set the rooted cuttings individually in 3 in. pots of John Innes potting compost No. 1. Transfer the young plants to their permanent positions the following April or May.

Pruning. None required.

Pests and diseases. Generally trouble-free.

Onopordum

Compositae

A genus of 40 species of annual, biennial and perennial herbaceous plants. The two described are thistle-like plants with oblong-lanceolate silver leaves which are jaggedly lobed and spined. They are best planted at the rear of borders, in large shrubberies and in wild gardens. In some gardens they will increase to almost weed-like proportions if allowed to self-seed.

ONOPORDUM ACANTHIUM

O. acanthium (Scotch thistle, cotton thistle). Great Britain. Height 6 ft; planting distance 2$\frac{1}{2}$ ft. A hardy biennial with erect, branching and winged stems. The broad silver-grey leaves are covered with white cobweb-like hairs. Pale purple thistle-like flowers, 2 in. across, appear in July and August. In spite of its spiny leaves, this plant is popular for flower arrangements.

O. arabicum, syn. *O. nervosum.* S. Europe. Height 8 ft; planting distance 2$\frac{1}{2}$ ft. A hardy biennial with thick, branching, prominently winged stems and silvery leaves. Thistle-like flowers, bright purple-red and 2 in. across, are produced in July.

O. nervosum: see *O. arabicum*

Cultivation. These plants grow well in any normal soil, in full sun or in partial shade, but a rich soil is required for producing plants of maximum size. Remove dead flower heads to prevent self-seeding.

Propagation. Sow the seeds in a nursery bed in May, and transplant to the flowering site in September. Seeds may also be sown directly in the flowering site and the seedlings thinned to 2$\frac{1}{2}$ ft apart. A third method is to sow under glass in March at 15°C (59°F) and harden the plants off in a cold frame before setting them out in their flowering positions in April or May.

Pests and diseases. Generally trouble-free.

Onosma

Boraginaceae

ONOSMA ECHIOIDES

A genus of 150 species of evergreen, tender and hardy perennial sub-shrubs with rough, hairy foliage and tubular almond-scented flowers. The two described are hardy and suitable for growing on sunny rock gardens.

O. echioides. S. Europe. Height 6–8 in.; spread up to 12 in. This species has grey-green, hairy, narrow spathulate leaves. Pendent racemes of golden flowers, each $\frac{3}{4}$ in. long, are carried from June to August.

O. tauricum. S.E. Europe. Height 8 in.; spread 9 in. or more. This species is similar to *O. echioides,* but the flowers are a deep yellow and are borne on longer pedicels. It has a particularly long flowering period from April to August.

Cultivation. Plant in April in the sunniest position possible, in light, well-drained soil. The ideal situation is a rock crevice or a dry wall.

Propagation. Take 2 in. softwood cuttings in July or August after flowering and set them in a cold frame in equal parts (by volume) peat and sand. The cuttings will root quickly; pot them in September singly in 3 in. containers of John Innes potting compost No. 1 and keep them in the frame during the winter, giving a minimum of water. Plant out in April.

Sow seeds in March in pans or boxes of seed compost in a cold frame; they are rather slow to germinate. When the seedlings are large enough to handle, set them in 3 in. pots of John Innes

otting compost No. 1 and grow on in the cold frame until planting out the following April.
Pests and diseases. Generally trouble-free.

Opuntia

Prickly pear. *Cactaceae*

OPUNTIA MICRODASYS

A genus of 250 species of greenhouse perennials. They are found all over the Americas and some of the larger species have been introduced into the warmer parts of Europe, where they have become naturalised. These cacti vary in size from coarse, tree-like plants to small species that do well in 4 in. pots.

Opuntias have jointed stems which may be cylindrical or globular, or flattened into round pads. The number of spines varies, but all species bear tufts of glochids (barbed bristles) on each areole. The glochids easily pierce the skin and are difficult to remove.

Few species flower in Britain unless they are planted out in a large greenhouse. The flowers are produced from the areoles on the edges of the joints and are usually red or yellow, broadly bell-shaped; they are up to 3 in. across and are produced in June and July. The species vary considerably in their cultural requirements, but all need plenty of root room and a sunny position. They are not suitable as house plants.

See also CACTUS.

O. microdasys. Mexico. Height up to 3 ft. A much-branched, slow-growing, bushy species. The oval pads are 3–6 in. long and pale green with no spines, but dotted closely with small groups of deep yellow glochids.

The flowers are yellow, but the plant rarely flowers in cultivation.

There are several varieties, all with yellow flowers: *O. m. albispina* has white glochids and is particularly slow-growing. *O. m. minima* is a dwarf variety with pads about 2 in. long and dark yellow glochids. *O. m. pallida* has pale yellow glochids. *O. m. rufida* has thick grey-green pads and dark red-brown glochids.

O. ovata. Argentina. Height 4–6 in. This plant consists of pale green, thick, oval pads about 2 in. long, which spread out to form a clump. The glochids are pale yellow, sometimes with grey spines. This is a high-altitude plant, and is hardy outdoors in winter, if kept dry. It has never flowered in Britain; presumably it needs the intense ultra-violet light of its mountain home to stimulate bud formation.

O. robusta. Mexico. Height up to 24 in. This plant is of tree size in its own country, with almost circular blue-green pads, up to 12 in. across. The widely spaced areoles bear brown glochids and, in some forms, yellow spines. It is grown for its edible fruits in Mexico.

In Britain it is suitable only for growing in a large greenhouse. There is also an unnamed form of *O. robusta* that is hardy in the south of England, provided it is in a well-drained situation. The flowers are yellow.

O. salmiana. Brazil, Paraguay, Argentina. Height 18 in. This species can usually be brought to flower annually, in a 3 in. pot. It is a sprawling plant that usually needs staking with canes. The cylindrical stems, $\frac{1}{2}$ in. in diameter, are glossy dark green. They carry short spines and yellow glochids.

The plant branches freely, and in its native country may be 3 ft high. Numerous white flowers, about 1 in. across, are freely produced during summer. They are followed by dark red spiny fruits that drop off and root.

O. scheeri. Mexico. Height in cultivation 2–3 ft. In the wild this slow-growing species reaches tree-like proportions. The oblong joints are up to 8 in. long, blue-green, and covered with a network of golden spines and hairs. The glochids are yellow-brown. The flowers are yellow, but the plant is unlikely to flower in cultivation.

O. verschaffeltii. Bolivia. Height 12 in. This slow-growing, spreading cactus flowers readily in cultivation. The cylindrical jointed stems are 6 in. long and $\frac{3}{4}$ in. thick. They are dull green, often covered with white, thread-like spines, and bear small, persistent leaves. Red flowers are produced during the summer.

Cultivation. All species need a rich soil, such as John Innes potting compost No. 2, and plenty of water during summer. Grow them in 6 in. pots or larger, according to the size of the species. Repot annually, in March or April. *O. robusta* requires a minimum winter temperature of 3°C (37°F), *O. salmiana* and *O. verschaffeltii* need 5°C (41°F), while *O. microdasys* and *O. scheeri* both need at least 7°C (45°F). *O. ovata* is hardy if kept dry.

Opuntias are not as succulent as many cacti and, with the exception of globular-jointed species such as *O. ovata*, they should be given water during winter—enough to prevent the soil drying out completely.

Propagation. Increase by cuttings taken in June or July. Remove pads, dry them for two or three days and then pot them in John Innes potting compost No. 2, when they will root easily. Many plants have loosely attached joints which may fall off and root.

Opuntia seeds are hard-coated, and may take weeks to germinate. Soaking them in water for a day before sowing may help germination. Most seeds may be sown in early spring at a temperature of 21°C (70°F), but those of some of the high-altitude plants need to be stratified.

Pests. Colonies of MEALY BUGS produce conspicuous tufts of white waxy wool on plants. ROOT MEALY BUGS infest roots and check growth.

Diseases. CORKY SCAB OF CACTI may show as irregular rusty or corky spots on the stems.

Opuntia microdasys rufida

Opuntia salmiana

Opuntia scheeri

Leafy stem-like pseudobulbs (above), and single-jointed pseudobulbs (below), growing in simulated natural conditions in a warm greenhouse.

ORCHIDS
Orchidaceae

This plant family, distributed throughout the world, contains 750 genera and almost 20,000 species. These are perennial herbaceous plants with highly specialised and often bizarre flowers.

Despite their exotic reputation and seemingly rigid requirements, many orchids are remarkably tolerant plants and can withstand considerable neglect. The amateur gardener can grow orchids successfully with a little extra care and a certain degree of automation in the greenhouse. Some species also do well in a well-lit living-room, although a dormant period for a few months in the greenhouse may be necessary.

Almost half the species are terrestrial (growing on the ground), the remainder are epiphytic (living on branches of trees or on rocks, not as parasites, but obtaining their nourishment from the air, rainwater and from humus in bark crevices by means of specially adapted roots). The epiphytic species are more easily grown by the amateur than the terrestrial species.

Generally, an epiphytic orchid plant consists of a horizontal rhizome from which arise, at intervals, erect, usually swollen stems or pseudobulbs. In some genera, such as *Calanthe, Coelogyne* and *Maxillaria,* the pseudobulb is a single swollen internode, bulb-like in appearance, which produces a tuft or fan of strap-shaped or elongated lanceolate leaves. In other genera, such as *Cattleya, Dendrobium* and *Epidendrum,* the pseudobulb is stem-like with few to many joints, sometimes swollen, sometimes barely so; the leaves are strap-shaped or lanceolate to oblong and usually carried one to each joint.

The *Vanda* group of epiphytes (*Aërangis, Aërides, Angraecum, Phalaenopsis* and *Vanda*) do not have pseudobulbs but elongated stems, usually with thick, strap-shaped leaves and pendulous aerial roots.

Terrestrial orchids, such as *Cypripedium,* and all native British orchids, have either a tuft of fleshy roots at the base of the plant or underground tubers. The leaves, which are in basal tufts, are generally strap-shaped and more lax than those of the epiphytic species. Colour varies from pale to dark green but is frequently yellow-green, sometimes spotted or mottled with maroon, dark or light green.

Orchid flowers are composed of three sepals and three petals. They are characterised by having the third petal transformed into a lip, often larger than the other petals. This lip varies from genus to genus, but is often spurred and variously lobed, pouched or keeled. Another unusual characteristic is the form of the reproductive organs which are combined into a single organ, the column, bearing the pollen at the top and the ovary just below. The pollen is not powdery, but remains as two, four, six or eight spherical masses, or pollinia, which are easily carried to the ovary by insects.

Orchids hybridise easily, and up to five genera can be combined into a single hybrid plant. In this way commercially desirable characteristics can be developed and improved. Hybridisation is carried out in many parts of the world, and the International Register of Orchid Hybrids now lists all artificially produced hybrids.

The following notes on cultivation and propagation apply to orchids in general. Additional information may be found in the entries on individual genera.

Cultivation. Depending on their country of origin, orchids are grown in cool, intermediate or warm greenhouses. The minimum temperatures required on winter nights are, respectively: 7°C (45°F); 10°C (50°F); and 14°C (57°F). Minimum summer night temperatures needed are: 14°C (57°F); 18°C (64°F); 22°C (72°F).

Orchids can tolerate a good deal of additional heat and the temperature can safely be allowed to rise by about 11°C (20°F) over the minimum given. Temperatures higher than this should be controlled by ventilating the greenhouse. This also prevents the atmosphere from becoming stagnant; an electric fan blowing continuously helps to distribute heat and prevents pockets of extreme temperatures. The temperature of the warm house can be allowed to rise to 32°C (90°F) or more during the summer growing season with great benefit to the new growths provided the humidity in the greenhouse is around 100 per cent. Otherwise, the moisture will be insufficient, and red spider mites may cause extensive damage.

Shading of the greenhouse also controls temperature and prevents too much direct sunlight which can injure plants that are naturally shade-loving. An orchid greenhouse is best fitted with wooden slatted blinds or plastic netting.

Most orchids require a certain amount of atmospheric humidity. This is best supplied by spraying or damping down the greenhouse. Warm houses require this more frequently than cool houses, and in summer damping down may be needed two or three times a day.

Compost requirements vary and are described under the separate genera; generally most epiphytic orchids thrive in a mixture of 2 parts osmunda fibre and 1 part sphagnum moss (parts by volume). To prepare the compost, cut up the blocks of fibre into pieces about 2–3 in. in diameter and mix thoroughly with the well-shredded moss.

Osmunda fibre is expensive, and the fibrous bark of fir trees or dried bracken is often used as a substitute, either by itself or mixed with moss. Some specialist orchid nurseries supply ready-made composts containing shredded plastic waste. Various wood mosses can be used instead of sphagnum moss, and enriched with dead leaves, preferably beech or oak, that have been kept dry.

Terrestrial species need a more loamy compost; equal parts (by volume) coarse peat or rough leaf-mould, fibrous loam, sand and moss make a suitable mixture.

TYPES OF PSEUDOBULBS AND LEAF FORMS

Single pseudobulb on long rhizome

Multi-jointed evergreen pseudobulb

Succulent cylindrical leaf form

Folded triangular leaf form

Leaf fan on elongated stem

Young fleshy aerial roots

ORCHIDS

The finer material from a bale of osmunda fibre can be incorporated, but the compost must be open and easily drained.

Most terrestrial orchids can be grown in ordinary flower pots; these should be well-drained and crocked. Epiphytes generally do better in specially perforated pots or in wooden baskets, or they may be grown directly on pieces of tree trunk, bark, on rafts of osmunda fibre or on sections of tree-fern stem. Fix the plants with wires or staples and suspend the rafts or pieces of bark in a suitable place.

Potting and repotting should be done when a plant has outgrown its container, preferably just after flowering or during the period when new growth and new roots appear. When potting on young plants of the epiphytic species, stand the rhizome on the drainage material and firmly pack the compost around it, using a strong, blunt stick. The crown of the plant should be level with or slightly above the rim of the pot.

To finish off, place small bundles of compost on the surface, radiating from the centre of the pot, with the ends overlapping the pot rim. With the potting stick, work round the edge of the pots, pressing each bundle down into a U-shape, so that the fibres are packed vertically around the perimeter. This aids rapid drainage, without which the compost would become stagnant and the roots would rot away. Trim off the ragged ends to give a neat appearance. If moss is used, it should be kept growing; it is a good indication of when a plant needs water, as dry moss turns a pale bleached green.

To repot an established epiphytic plant, remove it from the container and tease away the soft, rotted compost; if necessary wash it out in a bucket of water, and remove all dead roots. Hold the rhizome upside-down and pack new compost into the root bases; build this up into a ball larger than the pot size, then squeeze it together and press the ball firmly into the new container. Firm the top by pressing in more compost between the root ball and the pot rim, as already described. If a plant needs dividing, treat each division in the same way as for whole plants.

This treatment also applies when using specially perforated pots or baskets. With plants grown on pieces of tree trunk or bark, pack fresh fibre and/or moss under their crowns to allow the new roots to penetrate; secure by wires or staples. Plants on large pieces of osmunda fibre are wired or stapled directly, with perhaps a little moss under the crown.

Terrestrial species also require firm potting, but a stick will not be required. Leave a $\frac{1}{2}$ in. gap between the top of the compost and the pot rim for watering.

Orchids should not be watered for seven to ten days after potting. Then water sparingly for about two weeks until the young new roots are well established.

FLORAL PARTS

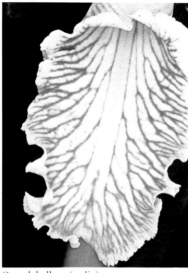

Open labellum (or lip)

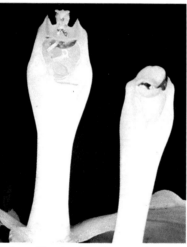

Column (fused style and stamens)

Close-up of pollinia and stigma

During the growing season, from April to September, all plants must be kept moist. With the epiphytes, submerge each pot in a bucket of water for a few minutes. In hot weather do this at least twice a week; in spring and autumn once a week should be enough. Terrestrial species may be watered by can *in situ*; fill up the gap between the compost surface and pot rim each time watering is necessary.

Though not strictly necessary, some plants respond to feeding during the growing season; when buying plants, the nurseryman should be consulted on this point, as many orchids are easily killed by over-feeding.

Some orchid species have a distinct resting phase, usually in autumn. During this period they may lose their leaves; some shed all vegetative parts, leaving only the pseudobulb to continue growth next season. During the rest phase, curtail watering and reduce the atmospheric humidity to the minimum.

Stems of taller orchids need the support of a cane inserted in the pot, and the flower spikes of many hybrids require additional cane support during flowering. As they fade, remove the flowers from the stems.

Propagation. Orchids can be propagated by division, offsets, cuttings or seeds, but division is the simplest method. Cut the rhizome of a well-established plant in two, making sure there are a number of growing points on each half. Alternatively, the rhizome may be cut up into single pieces, each with two or three pseudobulbs. If a large number of plants is needed, the rhizome can be cut into single pseudobulb sections, the older ones of which may produce new growth.

Long-climbing, stem-like pseudobulbs may be cut into lengths of 4–6 in.; treat them as cuttings and insert in the potting medium, keeping them at a high humidity until well rooted.

Other genera, such as *Pleione*, produce small bulbils or offsets. These may be detached and grown on; they should flower within two or three years.

Orchid seeds are extremely small and require the presence of a symbiotic fungus to germinate and thrive. Research has revealed that high germination rates can be obtained by sowing the seeds in glass flasks of agar and mineral nutrients under sterile conditions. Laboratory conditions are needed for this, and the practice is not recommended to amateurs.

Seeds may also be sown by sprinkling them around the base of a mature plant of the same or an allied species, where the essential root fungus naturally occurs. Generally, only the strongest seedlings survive, and only a small percentage, if any, of the seeds sown in this way will germinate. When the seedlings have three or four leaves, gently prise them out of the compost and place singly in $1\frac{1}{2}$–2 in. pots, using a well-chopped compost.

Orchid, slipper: see Paphiopedilum

Origanum
Labiatae

A genus of 15–20 species of aromatic half-hardy shrubs, sub-shrubs and herbaceous plants, suitable for rock gardens and alpine houses.

See also MARJORAM.

O. amanum. Greece. Height 2–4 in.; spread 6 in. This plant forms a low-growing mat of slender stems with close, light green, cordate-ovate leaves. From July to September it bears deep rose flowers that are tubular with five rounded lobes, and $1\frac{1}{2}$ in. long.

O. dictamnus, syn. *Amaracus dictamnus.* Crete. Height and spread 12 in. This species makes a rounded plant with orbicular leaves covered in dense white wool. The tubular pink flowers, largely hidden by rounded rose-purple bracts, are borne from June to August in hop-like heads, $1\frac{1}{2}$–2 in. long.

O. hybridum. Levant. Height 10 in.; spread 18 in. The neat, soft, grey-green, ovate leaves are topped from June to August by rounded hop-like clusters of bracts and lilac-pink flowers. The latter are about $\frac{1}{2}$ in. long.

O. laevigatum. Anatolia. Height up to 4 in.; spread up to 24 in. This plant forms a neat mat of dark green ovate leaves and bears a profusion of tubular red-purple flowers, $\frac{1}{2}$ in. long, in August and September.

Cultivation. Plant origanums in March or April. In the rock garden site them in a sunny sheltered position in ordinary, well-drained soil. As these plants are not reliably hardy, protect them in winter with panes of glass or open cloches.

In the alpine house, grow origanums in 6–8 in. pans of equal parts (by volume) loam, sand and peat, taking particular care to provide free drainage. Water generously during the growing period, but keep the plants just moist in winter. Repot every other year in March.

Propagation. Take 1–2 in. cuttings of non-flowering basal shoots between July and September; insert in equal parts (by volume) peat and sand in boxes or pans and place in a cold frame. Pot the rooted cuttings into 3 in. containers of John Innes potting compost No. 1 and overwinter in a cold frame. Plant out the following March or April.

Pests and diseases. Generally trouble-free.

Ornithogalum
Star of Bethlehem. *Liliaceae*

The 150 species of this bulbous genus are found over most of the temperate zones of Europe, Africa and Asia. Many are tender and only a few are in general cultivation.

The leaves of the species described are basal, mid to dark green, and linear to narrowly strap-shaped. The flowers, except for *O. nutans*, are star-shaped and 1 in. or more across.

O. arabicum. Mediterranean region. Height 18 in.; planting distance 6–8 in. This species needs a sunny, sheltered border. The stout flower stem carries 8–12 scented white flowers, with a black ovary and yellow stamens in the centre of each, in May and June. Imported bulbs flower freely at first, but do not maintain this habit in the British climate. This species is better grown as a pot plant; planted in the autumn it flowers the following spring.

O. balansae. Asia Minor. Height 4–6 in.; planting distance 4 in. The flowers of this hardy dwarf species, borne in March and April, are white with green stripes. It mixes well with the later-flowering crocuses and scillas.

O. nutans. Europe, including Great Britain. Height 15–18 in.; planting distance 6 in. The 10–12 nodding, bell-shaped, 1 in. long flowers appear on erect stems in April and May; they are white and pale green. A hardy species, it thrives and opens out its flowers in semi-shade.

ORNITHOGALUM THYRSOIDES

O. thyrsoides (chincherinchee). S. Africa. Height 18 in. Erect stems carry 20–30 white, cream or yellow flowers from May to July; the fleshy leaves are 12 in. long. It is grown widely in Africa to provide cut flowers, which will travel to Britain and still last for weeks in water. It is not hardy in Great Britain and should be grown as a pot plant in a cool greenhouse or frame for early spring flowering.

Ornithogalum umbellatum

O. umbellatum (star of Bethlehem). Asia and N. Africa through Europe to S. England. Height 12 in.; planting distance 4–8 in. The stout stem carries a corymb of many white flowers, with

Origanum amanum

Ornithogalum nutans

Ornithogalum thyrsoides

green outer stripes. This hardy plant blooms in April and May. Offsets are readily produced.

Cultivation. Ornithogalums will grow in ordinary, well-drained garden soil. Plant the hardy species, *O. balansae*, *O. nutans* and *O. umbellatum*, during October, setting them 2–3 in. deep in irregular groups in narrow borders, short grass or rock gardens. *O. balansae* needs sun, but the other two species will thrive in partial shade. All three can remain undisturbed for years.

Plant the less hardy species, *O. arabicum* and *O. thyrsoides*, in October in 6–8 in. pots of John Innes potting compost No. 2 to flower the following spring.

Dead-head all species regularly unless seeds are wanted for propagation.

Propagation. Seeds, if available, germinate readily. Sow thinly as soon as collected or in the early autumn, in pots of John Innes seed compost. Keep them in a cold frame or cold greenhouse for two years. Dry them off in summer, when the leaves turn yellow; commence rewatering in October. Lift the resulting small bulbs and plant at once in their flowering positions or in nursery rows. In order to remove and replant the bulbils separately, bulbs may also be lifted as the leaves die down in the summer. Bulbils will grow into flowering bulbs a year or two later.

Pests. Generally trouble-free.

Diseases. Sooty spots on the leaves are a symptom of HETEROSPORIUM. In severe cases, the foliage is blackened and killed by the fungus.

Orobus vernus : see *Lathyrus vernus*

Osmanthus
Oleaceae

OSMANTHUS DELAVAYI

A genus of 15 species of evergreen flowering shrubs of graceful habit and slow growth. The species described are hardy and the only ones in general cultivation.

O. aquifolius: see *O. heterophylla*

O. delavayi, syn. *Siphonosmanthus delavayi.* China. Height and spread 6–8 ft. The dark green glossy leaves are ovate and sharply toothed. Clusters of fragrant, white, $\frac{1}{2}$ in. long, tubular flowers are freely produced in April.

O. heterophylla, syns. *O. aquifolius*, *O. ilicifolius.* Japan. Height and spread 6–10 ft. This rounded, spreading shrub is sometimes grown for hedging, though in this case it bears few flowers. The mid-green leaves are variable, some being prickly and holly-like and others, on the same plant, ovate and spine-tipped only. White, $\frac{1}{4}$ in. long, tubular, scented flowers are borne along the branches in dense axillary clusters, 1 in. across, during September and October.

O. ilicifolius: see *O. heterophylla*

Osmanthus delavayi

× *Osmarea burkwoodii*

Cultivation. Plant in sun or partial shade in any well-drained garden soil between October and March. Choose a position sheltered from north and east winds. To grow *O. heterophylla* as a hedge, set the plants 18 in. apart.

Propagation. Take 4 in. cuttings of half-ripe shoots in July and insert them in equal parts (by volume) peat and sand in a propagating frame at a temperature of 18°C (64°F). When rooted, set the cuttings in 3 in. pots of John Innes potting compost No. 1 and overwinter them in a cold frame. Line out in a nursery bed the following April and grow on there for up to two years before planting them in their permanent positions between October and March.

Branches layered in September will be ready for severing one or two years later.

Pruning. No pruning is necessary, except for *O. heterophylla* which needs clipping in April when grown as a hedge.

Pests and diseases. Generally trouble-free.

× Osmarea
Oleaceae

× OSMAREA BURKWOODII

This hardy evergreen flowering shrub is a cross between species of two different genera, *Osmanthus delavayi* and *Phillyrea decora*. It is compact and suitable for hedging.

× *O. burkwoodii*. Height and spread 6–10 ft. The glossy, pointed leaves are ovate and mid to dark green. Clusters of fragrant, tubular, white flowers, $\frac{1}{2}$ in. long, appear in April and May.

Cultivation. This shrub is easily grown in any ordinary garden soil in sun or partial shade. Plant between October and March, spacing hedging plants 18 in. apart.

Propagation. Take 4 in. cuttings of half-ripe shoots in August or September, and insert in equal parts (by volume) sand and peat in a shaded cold frame. The following April or May pot the rooted cuttings in 3 in. containers of John Innes potting compost No. 1, and either grow on in the frame or in a nursery bed. Set the young plants out between October and March.

Pruning. When grown as a hedge, clip the plants to shape in May after flowering. Otherwise, no pruning is needed.

Pests and diseases. Generally trouble-free.

Osmunda
Royal fern. *Osmundaceae*

A genus of ten species of large ferns, the one described being a hardy garden plant. It seldom reaches in cultivation the height of up to 10 ft that it can attain in the wild.

O. regalis (flowering fern, royal fern). Global, except Australasia. Height and spread in cultivation 4–5 ft. The pea-green fronds are broadly lanceolate and bipinnate. The outer ones are sterile; the inner ones have barren lower pinnae and fertile upper pinnae. These fertile pinnae have no pinnules, and their veins are covered with spore capsules which turn brown when ripe and resemble the dead flowers of an astilbe. The plant gradually builds up a mass of crowns and matted black roots 2–3 ft above the ground. These roots are used in orchid compost under the name of osmunda fibre.

OSMUNDA REGALIS

O. r. 'Cristata', height and spread 3–4 ft, has crested pinnae. *O. r.* 'Purpurascens', height and spread 4–5 ft, is a fine waterside plant, with young fronds that are deep copper-pink, maturing to copper-green, with purple midribs.

Cultivation. Plant during March or April, in sun or partial shade, in any humus-rich soil, with the crowns at soil level. Top-dress with humus annually in spring.

The top growth may be cut down in autumn.

Propagation. Sow spores from June to August (see entry under FERNS). They remain viable for only three days after being gathered unless kept in a deep-freeze cabinet.

Divide well-separated, multiple crowns in March or April. If closely set crowns are cut they are unlikely to survive.

Pests and diseases. Generally trouble-free.

Oswego tea: see *Monarda didyma*

Ourisia

Scrophulariaceae

A genus of 20 species of low-growing perennial plants suitable for moist sites on rock gardens. The two species described are hardy enough to survive all but the most severe winters.

O. coccinea. Chilean Andes. Height 6–12 in.; spread up to 24 in. The mid-green, shallowly toothed, ovate leaves form dense mats. Erect stems bear scarlet tubular flowers, 1½ in. long, from May to September.

O. macrophylla. New Zealand. Height 8–12 in.; spread up to 18 in. This is a robust plant with rounded, dentate, mid-green leaves. White tubular flowers, 1 in. long, are borne in spikes in July.

Cultivation. Plant in March or April in a position in partial shade, and in fertile, moist, but well-drained garden soil.

Propagation. Divide the plants in April, and replant direct in permanent positions.

Alternatively, sow seeds in April in pots or pans of John Innes seed compost and place them in a cold frame. When the seedlings are large enough to handle, prick them out into boxes; later, transfer singly to 3 in. pots containing John Innes potting compost No. 1. Overwinter in the frame and plant out in March or April.

Pests and diseases. Generally trouble-free.

Oxalis

Oxalidaceae

OXALIS LACINIATA

A genus of 800 species of tender perennials and shrubs, half-hardy and hardy annuals, and bulbous plants. The leaves are compound palmate, with 3–12 leaflets. Some are weeds, but the hardy perennials described are suitable for rock gardens or for growing in alpine houses. The tender, bulbous *O. cernua* also does well in a cool greenhouse. The species are non-bulbous unless otherwise stated.

Oxalis acetosella

O. acetosella (wood sorrel). N. Temperate region. Height 2 in.; spread 12 in. This species naturalises well in shady woodland corners, where it will seed freely. It forms neat tufts of shamrock-like pale-green leaves. Pearl-white funnel-shaped flowers, each about ½ in. long, appear from March to May, or even later. 'Rosea' has pink flowers with purple veins.

O. adenophylla. Chile. Height 3 in.; spread about 6 in. This species has a curious fibre-coated bulb-like rhizome which produces a rosette of crinkled grey foliage that dies down in winter. The long-stemmed flowers are cup-shaped and satin-pink; they are 1 in. across and appear from May to July.

O. cernua (Bermuda buttercup). S. Africa. Height and spread 9–12 in. This decorative bulbous species can be a troublesome weed in mild areas of the south-west. Elsewhere it needs alpine-house or cool greenhouse treatment. It produces mats of bright mid-green, slightly succulent foliage. Slender flowering stems carry drooping umbels of buttercup-yellow, funnel-shaped flowers, 1 in. long, from April to September.

Osmunda regalis

Ourisia coccinea

Ourisia macrophylla

Oxalis cernua

Oxalis enneaphylla 'Rosea'

Pachysandra terminalis

Paeonia emodi

mat of light green trifoliate leaves, and produces bright pink funnel-shaped flowers, ¾ in. long from June until August.

O. laciniata. Patagonia. Height 2–4 in.; spread 12 in. This species has grey-green leaves composed of 9–12 wavy-margined leaflets borne on thin stalks from fleshy underground rhizomes. The fragrant flowers, borne singly, are shallowly funnel-shaped, about 1 in. across and vary from deep lavender-blue to palest purple with darker veins. They appear from May to August. The plant dies down completely after flowering.

O. magellanica. S. America. Height 2 in.; spread 12 in. This species forms a carpet of bronze shamrock-like leaves. Short-stalked white flowers, cup-shaped and ½ in. long, are produced during May and June.

Cultivation. Plant in March or September. O. chrysantha is not as hardy as other species and should be planted in sun or partial shade in loose gritty soil where the roots can spread under a rock; the roots are then more likely to persist if the top-growth is killed by cold weather.

Plant the remaining species in sun or partial shade in any well-drained soil, preferably enriched with peat or leaf-mould.

In the alpine house, grow the plants in 6–10 in. pans of John Innes potting compost No. 1; repot every other October.

Propagation. Divide the bulbous species and O. chrysantha after they have finished flowering; all other species in March. Replant direct in permanent positions.

Pests and diseases. Generally trouble-free.

Oxford and Cambridge grape hyacinth: see *Muscari tubergenianum*

Oxycoccus palustris: see *Vaccinium oxycoccus*

Ozothamnus rosmarinifolium: see *Helichrysum rosmarinifolium*

O. chrysantha. Brazil. Height 2 in.; spread 12 in. This species forms mats of pale green trifoliate leaves. Funnel-shaped golden flowers, ½ in. across, appear freely from June to September.

O. enneaphylla. Falkland Isles, Patagonia. Height 3 in.; spread 6 in. This bulbous-rooted species produces distinctive, partially folded grey leaves. White funnel-shaped flowers, 1 in. across, are borne singly in June and July. The variety 'Minutaefolia' (height 2 in.) has miniature leaves and bright rose-pink flowers; 'Rosea' has flowers of pale rose-pink.

O. inops. South Africa. Height 4 in.; spread 6 in. This is an attractive but invasive bulbous plant of comparatively recent introduction. It forms a

P Q

Pachysandra

Buxaceae

A genus of four species of hardy evergreen, creeping plants suitable for shady sites and grown principally as ground cover.

P. terminalis. Japan. Height up to 12 in.; spread 18 in. This spreading, sub-shrubby plant has obovate to rhomboid, mid to deep green leaves. Tiny petal-less flowers appear in spikes, 1–2 in. long, in April; they have prominent white stamens, sometimes tinged with purple.

The form 'Variegata' has white-edged leaves and is slightly less vigorous than the type.

Cultivation. Plant between October and March in any fertile soil. Partial shade is ideal, and pachysandras will also thrive in deep shade.

Propagation. Lift, divide and replant in March.

Pests and diseases. Generally trouble-free.

Paeonia

Paeony or Peony.
Paeoniaceae, formerly *Ranunculaceae*

PAEONIA MLOKOSEWITSCHII

A genus of 33 species of hardy herbaceous and shrubby perennials. They are grown for their handsome flowers and attractive foliage, and are suitable for herbaceous, mixed or shrub borders. The shrubby species are best planted in a position shaded from early-morning sun after

Paeonia lactiflora 'Globe of Light'

Paeonia lactiflora 'Augustus John'

Paeonia lactiflora 'Aureole'

Paeonia lactiflora 'Bower of Roses'

night frost. The herbaceous perennials take several years to become established and resent root disturbance. They may remain undisturbed for 50 years or more.

The leaves are composed of several leaflets of irregular size and shape, which may themselves be lobed or unlobed. The large, showy flowers are globular to bowl-shaped, often opening out flat when fully mature; they are excellent for cutting. The seed pods of many species open wide in autumn, revealing glossy blue-black seeds.

P. albiflora: see *P. lactiflora*

P. arietina. S.E. Europe. Height up to 2½ ft; planting distance 24 in. A herbaceous perennial with mid-green leaves that are smooth above, hairy and glaucous beneath. The hairy stems carry single pink flowers, 3–5 in. across, with yellow stamens, in May and June.

P. emodi. N.W. India. Height 1½–2½ ft; planting distance 3 ft. The leaves of this perennial species are dark green with paler undersides. White single flowers, 3–5 in. wide, with yellow stamens, appear in June and July.

P. laciniata: see *P. × smouthii*

P. lactiflora, syn. *P. albiflora*. Siberia, Mongolia. Height 24 in.; planting distance 3 ft. A herbaceous perennial with mid to deep green leaves. The scented, pure white, single flowers, 3–4 in. across, have yellow stamens and are produced in May and June.

The true species is rarely grown and has been superseded by hardy garden forms and hybrids; these hybrids grow to a height of 2½–3½ ft, and produce their double, often scented flowers, 4–7 in. across, between late May and July.

Recommended varieties include: 'Albert Crousse', fully double, scented, bright pink flowers flaked carmine at the centre; 'Augustus John', single, deep cherry-rose; 'Aureole', single, rose-purple with a prominent crown of cream petaloids; 'Baroness Schroeder', double, scented, flesh-coloured flowers turning white; 'Bower of Roses', double, rose-crimson; 'Bowl of Beauty', semi-double, soft pink with conspicuous golden stamens.

'Globe of Light', single, pale rose-pink with a prominent boss of yellow petaloids; 'Karl Rosenfeld', double, rich wine-red; 'La Cygne', double, pure white; 'Lady Alexandra Duff', double, scented, soft pink; 'Lovely', double, carmine; 'Madame Calot', double, scented, pink shading to white; 'Madame Ducel', double, pale flesh-pink.

'President Roosevelt', double, deep red flowers; 'Sarah Bernhardt', double, scented, apple-blossom pink; 'Solange', double, scented, cream-buff fading to white; 'White Wings', single, white with a prominent yellow centre; and 'Whitleyi Major', syn. 'The Bride', single and pure white with yellow stamens.

P. lobata, syn. *P. peregrina*. Portugal, Spain. Height and planting distance 24 in. The deeply cut leaves of this herbaceous perennial are shiny and mid-green above, glaucous and slightly hairy beneath. Deep red single flowers, 3–4 in. across, appear in May and June. The variety 'Sunshine' is brilliant salmon-scarlet.

PAEONIA LUTEA

P. lutea. China, Tibet. Height and spread 4–6 ft. A deciduous shrub with deeply segmented pale green leaves. Yellow single flowers, 2 in. wide and with a lily-like fragrance, appear in June.

'Chromatella' is a hybrid between *P. lutea* and *P. suffruticosa*, and has double sulphur-yellow flowers; 'L'Esperance' is of similar parentage and has semi-double, primrose-yellow flowers with a carmine-red blotch at the base of each petal.

P. l. ludlowii is a more robust form than the type species and has larger flowers less hidden by the pale green foliage.

P. mlokosewitschii. Caucasus. Height 18–24 in.; planting distance 3 ft. This perennial species has

Paeonia lactiflora 'Bowl of Beauty'

Paeonia lactiflora 'Lovely'

Paeonia lactiflora 'White Wings'

Paeonia lactiflora 'Whitleyi Major'

Paeonia mlokosewitschii

pale glaucous-green leaves that deepen with age and sometimes turn yellow or orange in autumn. Single lemon-yellow flowers, 4–5 in. across, with numerous golden stamens, appear in April and May. The seed pods of this species are particularly striking in autumn.

P. moutan: see *P. suffruticosa*

P. obovata. Siberia, China. Height 20–24 in.; planting distance 24 in. Only one form of this perennial, 'Alba', is available. It has dark green deeply divided foliage and single, glistening white flowers, 3–4 in. across. Flowering usually occurs in May, but sometimes continues into early June.

P. officinalis. France to Albania. Height 24 in.; planting distance 3 ft. A herbaceous perennial with deeply cut mid-green leaves that are sometimes hairy beneath. Single crimson flowers, up to 5 in. across, are produced during May and June.

The true species is rarely obtainable and has been superseded by several garden forms or hybrids. These grow to a height of 2½ ft (planting distance 3 ft). The best, all with double 5 in. wide flowers, include: 'Alba-plena', pale pink, fading to white; 'Rosea-plena', deep pink fading with age; and 'Rubra-plena', crimson-red.

P. peregrina: see *P. lobata*

P. × smouthii, syn. *P. laciniata.* Garden origin. Height 20–24 in.; planting distance 24 in. This herbaceous hybrid between *P. lactiflora* and *P. tenuifolia* has lacy dark green leaves; the single crimson flowers, each 3 in. across, are produced during May and June.

P. suffruticosa, syn. *P. moutan.* China, Tibet. Height and spread 5–6 ft. A deciduous shrub with pale to mid-green leaves. The white single flowers, about 6 in. across, have a blotch at the base of each petal that may vary from magenta-purple to rose-pink. They open in May.

Recommended varieties include the following, all semi-double: 'Duchess of Kent', clear bright pink; 'King George V', scarlet, flecked with white; 'Montrose', pale lilac; and 'Mrs William Kelway', pure white. 'Rock's Variety' has white flowers with a prominent maroon-crimson blotch at the base of each petal; they may be single or semi-double.

Cultivation. Grow paeonies in any moist but well-drained garden soil, in sun or half shade; choose a site that is shaded from early-morning sun. Before planting, dig the ground at least one spit deep and incorporate a liberal amount of well-decayed manure or compost.

Paeonia lutea ludlowii

Paeonia lutea 'L'Esperance'

Paeonia officinalis 'Rubra-plena'

Plant between September and March during mild weather. Set the crowns of herbaceous perennials no more than 1 in. deep or they may fail to flower. The union of stock and scion of shrubby paeonies should be about 3 in. below the soil surface. Hoe bone-meal at the rate of 4 oz. per sq. yd into the top 4 in. of soil after planting, taking care not to damage the roots.

Mulch annually with well-rotted manure or compost in April, if the soil is light and sandy or chalky. Water freely in dry weather. Avoid disturbing the plants unless absolutely necessary. Dead-head as the flowers fade, and cut down the foliage of herbaceous perennials in October.

The taller herbaceous species, especially varieties of *P. lactiflora*, may need twiggy sticks for support in exposed positions.

To prevent flowers used for cutting from dropping their petals, cut the blooms as they begin to open and lay them flat in a dry, cool place indoors for 24 hours. Then trim $\frac{1}{2}$ in. from the stems and place deeply in water.

Propagation. All paeonies can be raised from seeds, although named varieties and hybrids do not come true. Sow during September, in pots or pans of seed compost in a cold frame. The seedlings should be large enough to prick out directly into a nursery bed the following May. Grow on in the nursery rows for three or four years before setting out in permanent positions between September and March.

The plants may also be divided and replanted during September. Cut the tough crowns with a sharp knife and ensure that each piece has roots and dormant buds. Great care must be taken when dividing shrubby species and varieties, which have only one or two stems, to ensure that they are well rooted. It is preferable to remove rooted suckers from these plants and replant.

Shrubby species may also be increased by layering; branches pegged down in March will take at least two years to form their own roots.

Take 6–9 in. hardwood cuttings from the shrubby species in October or November and insert them in a shaded nursery bed or cold frame. Grow on for at least two years before planting out in permanent positions. Usually only a small percentage of the cuttings is likely to root.

Graft named varieties on to herbaceous stocks between mid-July and August.

Pruning. None required except to cut out dead wood of shrubby species in March or April.

Pests. Roots and crowns of established plants may be eaten by SWIFT MOTH caterpillars.

Paeonia lutea 'Chromatella'

Diseases. HONEY FUNGUS can cause the rapid death of shrubby paeonies.

LEAF SPOT shows on the leaves as small, light brown spots with grey centres and purple edges; it may also cause spots on the stems.

PAEONY WILT affects the bases of the shoots, which turn brown and die. Brown angular patches form on leaves of other shoots, and the flower buds may turn brown and die. A grey velvety fungal growth may show on the flower buds and stem bases. When similar symptoms occur late in the season they are often caused by GREY MOULD fungus.

A PHYSIOLOGICAL DISORDER, which causes the flower buds to remain small and hard and fail to open, may be due to frost damage, too dry soil conditions, malnutrition, too deep planting or root disturbance.

A VIRUS DISEASE shows as a yellow mosaic of irregularly shaped patches or rings on the leaves.

Paeony: see Paeonia
Pagoda tree, Japanese: see *Sophora japonica*
Painter's palette: see *Anthurium andreanum*
Palm, cabbage: see Cordyline
Palm, Chusan: see Trachycarpus
Palm, date: see *Phoenix dactylifera*
Palm, fan: see Trachycarpus
Pampas-grass: see Cortaderia

Paeonia mlokosewitschii (fruits)

Paeonia officinalis 'Rosea-plena'

Paeonia suffruticosa 'Rock's Variety'

Pancratium

Sea lily. *Amaryllidaceae*

PANCRATIUM MARITIMUM

A genus of 15 species of bulbous plants, only two of which are generally available in Great Britain. These are half-hardy and thrive outdoors only in sheltered sites in the south and west. Elsewhere, they are best grown in a frost-free greenhouse.

The leaves are strap-shaped and grey-green. The fragrant, white, 3 in. wide flowers have six narrow petals, which are sometimes twisted, and an inner narcissus-like cup.

P. amancaes: see *Hymenocallis amancaes*
P. calathinum: see *Hymenocallis calathina*
P. illyricum. S. Italy and some neighbouring islands. Height 18 in.; planting distance 9 in. The flowers appear in May and June, carried in umbels of up to 12, at the top of the stem.
P. maritimum (sea lily). Mediterranean region. Height 12 in.; planting distance 9–12 in. This species is similar to *P. illyricum*, but has narrower leaves, some of which usually persist through the winter. The flowers are strongly scented and open from July to September.
Cultivation. Outdoors, pancratiums need well-drained soil and a position sheltered from north and east winds. Plant deeply, with at least 8 in. of soil above the bulbs. Protect the plants in winter with a thick layer of bracken, coarse sand or weathered ashes.

Both species do better under glass at a temperature of 4–7°C (39–45°F). Grow them in John Innes potting compost No. 3 in 5–7 in. pots. Plant in the autumn as soon as the bulbs are available and give little water during the winter. As the leaves begin to grow, increase the amount of water and continue to water generously during flowering. Remove the flowers and leaves as they die. Water sparingly as the leaves die back or, in the case of *P. maritimum*, when new leaves no longer appear. Pancratiums need repotting every two or three years in autumn.

Pancratium illyricum

Propagation. Sow in John Innes seed compost in March, just covering the seeds, at a temperature of 16–18°C (61–64°F). Pot the seedlings individually in 3 in. pots after a year and repot as necessary. The seedlings take three to five years to reach flowering size.

Remove offsets when the foliage has died down in late summer. Place them singly in 3 or 4 in. pots (depending on the size of the offsets). Pot on each year until they reach flowering size.
Pests and diseases. Generally trouble-free.

Pandanus

Screw pine. *Pandanaceae*

A genus of 600 species of tropical evergreen shrubs. The plants are grown for their ornamental foliage which resembles that of the pineapple (*Ananas*); they require greenhouse treatment. Young plants of *P. sanderi* and *P. veitchii* may be grown as house plants. The common name is derived from the corkscrew-like trunks and leaves of mature plants.
P. candelabrum. W. Africa. Height up to 5 ft; spread up to 4 ft. The form in cultivation is 'Variegatus', with sword-like leaves having spiny edges. The leaves are bright green with two longitudinal white stripes.
P. sanderi. New Guinea. Height up to 3 ft; spread 2–2½ ft. This species forms no apparent trunk. In large specimens the leaves, which are arranged in a rosette, may attain a length of 24 in. The narrow

mid-green leaves are slightly spiny and longitudinally striped with narrow golden bands.

P. veitchii. Polynesia. Height and spread 24 in. Although this species will eventually make a trunk, it is rarely seen in cultivation as more than a stemless rosette. The leaves, which may eventually reach a length of 24 in., are dark green with silver margins.

Cultivation. Grow these plants in John Innes potting compost No. 2, or in a proprietary peat compost. The plants require warm conditions and a winter temperature of 13°C (55°F), although *P. veitchii* will survive at 10°C (50°F).

During winter, keep the compost just moist and take care to prevent water lodging between the leaves in cold periods. In spring and summer, provide ample water and a humid atmosphere; ventilate the greenhouse when the temperature reaches 18–21°C (64–70°F). Lightly shade the glass in summer.

If the plants are grown in a room, plunge the pots in an absorbent material, such as moist peat, or stand them on pebbles above water, to provide a moist atmosphere. Good light is necessary. Pot on young plants annually in April, until they are in their final 10–12 in. pots. Mature plants require repotting when the roots begin to push the plants out of their pots; this should be done in April or May.

Potting on, when necessary, should be done in April. Feed mature plants in the years when they are not repotted, with a weak liquid manure at 10–14 day intervals from May to September.

Propagation. Mature plants produce off-shoots at their base and these may be detached. Pot them up in April in 4 in. pots of John Innes potting compost No. 1. Place the pots in a propagating case at a temperature of 24°C (75°F) until the plantlets are well rooted.

Pruning. None required.

Pests and diseases. Generally trouble-free.

Pansy, garden: see *Viola × wittrockiana*

Papaver

Poppy. *Papaveraceae*

PAPAVER ALPINUM

A genus of 100 species of annual, biennial and perennial herbaceous plants. Those described are suitable for mixed and herbaceous borders, and for rock gardens.

Poppy flowers generally have four broad, overlapping petals which taper towards the base to form a characteristic cup or bowl shape.

ANNUAL SPECIES

P. alpinum (alpine poppy). Height and spread 4–10 in. This rock-garden species is a short-lived perennial, usually raised annually from seeds. It forms low mounds of deeply dissected grey-

Papaver somniferum 'Pink Chiffon'

green leaves from which the slender, leafless flower stems arise. The flowers are 1–2 in. across and range in colour from white and yellow to red and orange.

The following subspecies are now classified as separate species, but apart from colour are distinguished by small botanical features only: *P. a. sendtneri* and *P. a. burseri*, white; *P. a. kerneri*, yellow; *P. a. rhaeticum*, yellow, red or white; and *P. a. suaveolens*, yellow or red.

P. burseri: see *P. alpinum*

P. glaucum (tulip poppy). Syria. Height 18 in.; spacing 12 in. A hardy species with upright stems. The leaves are grey-green, smooth, and cut or lobed. The tulip-like flowers are up to 4 in. across and crimson-scarlet in colour. They appear from May to July.

P. kerneri: see *P. alpinum*

P. nudicaule (Iceland poppy). Northern sub-Arctic regions. Height 1½–2½ ft; spacing 12–18 in. A short-lived perennial, usually grown as a biennial but which can also be treated as a half-hardy annual. This is the only species suitable for cut flowers. The smooth, soft green leaves are deeply lobed and form a basal rosette. Slender, leafless stems carry white or yellow fragrant flowers, 2½ in. across, with petals of tissue-paper-like texture. They appear from June to August.

There are numerous garden varieties, including 'Kelmscott Strain', 2¼ ft, a long-stemmed mixture of pastel shades including pink, salmon, apricot, orange, golden-yellow and scarlet; and 'Champagne Bubbles', 24 in., an F₁ hybrid with large flowers in similar colours.

P. rhaeticum: see *P. alpinum*

P. rhoeas (field poppy). Great Britain. Height 24 in.; spacing 12 in. A hardy species with upright, slender stems, commonly seen in the wild. The leaves are pale green and deeply lobed. The flowers, red with a black centre, are 3 in. across and appear from June to August.

Pandanus veitchii

Papaver alpinum rhaeticum

Papaver nudicaule 'Kelmscott Strain'

Papaver rhoeas 'Shirley Double Mixed'

Papaver orientale 'King George'

Papaver orientale 'Mrs Perry'

Papaver alpinum sendtneri

Most popular of the numerous garden varieties are 'Shirley Single Mixed', 24 in., in attractive shades of pink and white, rose, salmon and crimson; and 'Shirley Double Mixed'.

P. sendtneri: see *P. alpinum*

P. somniferum (opium poppy). Greece and the Orient. Height 2½ ft; spacing 12 in. A hardy species with deeply lobed, smooth, pale grey-green leaves. White, red, pink or purple flowers, up to 4 in. across, are produced from June to August, followed by bulbous, flat-capped seeds.

The most popular garden variety is 'Paeony-flowered Mixed', with fully double flowers; 'Pink Chiffon' has double, clear pink flowers.

P. suaveolens: see *P. alpinum*

PERENNIAL SPECIES

PAPAVER ORIENTALE

P. orientale (oriental poppy) Armenia. Height 2–3 ft; planting distance 24 in. A hardy and spreading border plant which forms clumps of coarse, hairy, deeply cut, mid to deep green leaves. Scarlet flowers, 3½–4 in. or more across, and usually with a black blotch at the base of the petals, appear during late May or early June.

There are numerous garden varieties including: 'Enchantress', carmine-pink; 'Goliath', blood red; 'King George', vivid scarlet, frilled; 'Marcus Perry', bright orange-scarlet; 'Mrs Perry', soft salmon-pink; 'Perry's White', white; 'Salmon Glow', double, salmon-orange; and 'Storm Torch', fiery red.

P. pilosum. Asia Minor. Height 3 ft; planting distance 12 in. The mid-green leaves of this hardy species are oblong and irregularly toothed. Pale scarlet to bright orange flowers, 4 in. wide, are borne in loose clusters and open in June and July.

Cultivation of annual species. Grow in ordinary well-drained soil in a sunny position. Staking is not generally necessary. Biennials and winter-sown annuals require cloche protection during the winter. Most species self-seed; dead flower heads should be removed to prevent this.

When cutting Iceland poppies, select buds just showing colour and scald the stems immediately after cutting to seal the ends.

Cultivation of perennial species. Plant in October, March or April in ordinary well-drained soil and in a sunny position. The plants need staking as they grow. Dead-head after flowering.

In mild weather, *P. orientale* and its varieties sometimes produce a few more flowers in the autumn, if the first flower stems are cut down.

Propagation of annual species. Sow the seeds of annual poppies in the flowering site in March, April or September, just covering them with soil.

ow biennials in the flowering site in May or
ne. In both cases thin out the seedlings to the
quired spacing. If transplanting is necessary,
sturb the roots as little as possible.

ropagation of perennial species. Divide and
plant the roots in March or April. Root cuttings
P. orientale may also be taken and inserted in a
ld frame in winter.

Sow *P. orientale* and *P. pilosum* in pots or pans
seed compost and place in a cold frame or
reenhouse in April. Prick out in nursery rows,
hen the plants are big enough to handle, and
lant out from October to April.

Named varieties do not come true from seeds.

ests. Generally trouble-free.

iseases. Yellow blotches on the leaves are
aused by DOWNY MILDEW; the undersurfaces
evelop a grey fungal growth.

Paphiopedilum

Slipper orchid. *Orchidaceae*

PAPHIOPEDILUM INSIGNE

genus of 50 species of evergreen tropical Asiatic
rchids. They are tufted plants without pseudo-
ulbs, mostly terrestrial and are often listed as
ypripedium. The species fall into two groups:
nose which are uniformly pale to dark green-
aved, and those with grey or blue-green leaves,
nottled or tessellated with darker or lighter
nes. The leaves are strap-shaped to ovate.

The flowers are 2–3½ in. across, often waxy-
extured and borne singly, or sometimes several
ogether on stems arising from the centre of leafy
noots. They are characterised by a wide dorsal
epal, two conspicuous, often warted petals and a
rge slipper or helmet-shaped lip. The lateral
epals are fused, and a rudimentary stamen
staminode), usually shield-shaped, takes the
lace of the more usual column. Colours vary
om yellow, green and brown to violet, purple
nd deep crimson; some species are basically
hite or cream, delicately flushed or heavily
potted with crimson-mauve.

Paphiopedilums have been widely hybridised
o give an extensive range of forms and shades.
Most of the species and nearly all the hybrids are
elatively easy to grow in suitable temperatures.
ome can be successfully flowered in a well-lit
om if kept moist and protected from draughts.
See also ORCHIDS.

. appletonianum. Thailand. This species is often
old under the erroneous names of *P. siamense* or
sublaeve. The stem and leaves together reach a
eight of 18 in. The leaves are blue-green and
essellated. Single flowers, 3 in. across, are borne
n 12 in. stems from January to June. They have a
ale green dorsal sepal, mauve-tipped petals and
brown lip. This species should be grown in a
ol to intermediate greenhouse.

Paphiopedilum insigne

P. barbatum. S.E. Asia. A species with pale green
tessellated leaves, spotted with dark green. One
or two 2½ in. wide flowers are borne on 12 in.
stems from January to June. The large, almost
circular dorsal sepal is white to pale green with
longitudinal purple stripes. The petals are pale
green with shiny crimson hairy warts along the
margins; the lip is deep purple-brown. This plant
grows best in an intermediate greenhouse.

P. callosum. Indo-China. This species is similar in
most respects to *P. barbatum*, but has a pure
white dorsal sepal striped with purple and green,
and green striped petals.

P. fairieanum. India. A pale green-leaved species
with 9 in. high stems. The crimson-striped
solitary flowers, 2–2½ in. across, are borne from
August to October. The white or cream-white
petals are curved almost into an S-shape; the
large lip is brown-green and heavily marked with
crimson. Both the lip and the petals have wavy
crinkled edges. Grow in a cool greenhouse.

P. insigne. North India. This species has stems up
to 10–12 in. long, bearing uniformly pale to
mid-green leaves. The waxy flowers are carried
singly or very occasionally in pairs, between
September and February. They measure up to 5
in. across, and vary in details of colour. The dorsal
sepal is oval, apple-green with numerous dull
purple-brown ·longitudinal veins, and the lip is
yellow-green flushed with brown. This species
does best in a cool, airy position and may be
grown as a house plant.

Paphiopedilum barbatum

Paphiopedilum callosum

Paphiopedilum rothschildianum

Paphiopedilum venustum

Parochetus communis

Parrotia persica (autumn foliage).

P. Maudiae. This hybrid between *P. callosum* and *P. lawrenceanum* was introduced in 1900 and is one of the first so-called green orchids. The pale green leaves are sometimes spotted with black. A few flowers, up to 4 in. across, are borne on stems, 8–12 in. long, from January to June. The dorsal sepal and the petals are white striped with green; the large pale green lip is sometimes suffused with light brown. Grow in a warm greenhouse.

P. rothschildianum. Borneo. A robust species up to 3 ft high, with dark green strap-shaped leaves. The flower spike is approximately 24 in. long and bears up to five flowers, 6 in. or more wide, in May and June. These have pale yellow-white sepals with longitudinal stripes of brown-purple, and yellow-green petals with a brown-yellow lip. The staminode is like a large spider's leg, about $2\frac{1}{2}$ in. long, bent at the elbow and hairy. Grow this species in a shaded warm greenhouse.

PAPHIOPEDILUM ROTHSCHILDIANUM

P. siamense : see *P. appletonianum*
P. sublaeve : see *P. appletonianum*
P. tonsum. Sumatra. A tessellated, deep green-leaved species. Solitary waxy flowers, 3 in. across, are borne at the top of stems, 18 in. high, in September and October. The dorsal sepal is green-white and the petals are similar, but spotted dark brown and flushed with purple; the lip is brown-green. Grow in a warm greenhouse.
P. venustum. Himalayas. A species with tessellated mid-green leaves. Single flowers, $2\frac{1}{2}$–3 in. across, are borne on 10 in. high stems from October to January. The dorsal sepal and the petals are white striped with green; the petals have black-brown warts along the edges. The lip is green-yellow with a network of green veins giving a sculptured effect. This plant thrives in a cool or intermediate greenhouse.
Cultivation. Grow paphiopedilums in 3–6 in. pots, using a mixture of equal parts (by volume) osmunda fibre, sphagnum moss and fibrous loam.

Maintain a high degree of humidity for all species and keep the plants well shaded from March to October. Water freely throughout the year and feed fortnightly with a weak liquid manure from May to September. In mild weather and on sunny days in winter, ventilate the greenhouse. Warm greenhouse species require a minimum winter temperature of 16°C (61°F); intermediate 13°C (55°F); cool 5°C (41°F).

Repot annually or every other year between February and May.
Propagation. Divide and pot up in the growing compost between February and May.
Pests. Generally trouble-free.
Diseases. Unsuitable cultural conditions cause PHYSIOLOGICAL DISORDERS, showing as various types of leaf spotting or general discoloration; the affected areas may be entered by secondary fungi which cause rotting of the tissues.

Parochetus
Leguminosae

A genus of a single species. This is a prostrate herbaceous perennial suitable for ground cover on shady rock gardens. It is generally hardy only in sheltered parts of the country; elsewhere it needs the protection of an alpine house.
P. communis. Himalayas, E. India, E. Africa. Height 3 in.; spread 24 in. This plant has bright green clover-like leaves; vivid blue sweet-pea-shaped flowers, $\frac{1}{2}$–$\frac{3}{4}$ in. across, are borne from October to February, and often through into the summer.
Cultivation. Plant in March or April in moisture-retentive but well-drained soil in sun or partial shade. In the alpine house, grow in John Innes potting compost No. 1 in 8–10 in. pans; repot annually in March.
Propagation. Divide the plants in March or April and replant direct in permanent positions.

Alternatively, insert small rooted pieces in 2 in. pots of John Innes potting compost No. 1 in July; overwinter them in a cold frame and plant out in March or April.
Pests and diseases. Generally trouble-free.

Parrotia
Hamamelidaceae

PARROTIA PERSICA

The single species in this genus is a hardy deciduous shrub or tree. It has wide-spreading branches and is notable for its autumn foliage tints of amber, crimson and gold. It is slow growing, and the foliage colours may vary from year to year, in some gardens merely taking on dull yellow shades.
P. persica. Iran, Caucasus. Height 10–18 ft; spread 10–15 ft. The mid-green leaves are ovate to obovate with a rounded base. The tiny inconspicuous flowers, which have red stamens but no petals, appear in dense 1 in. wide clusters in March and April. The bark on old trees flakes away in patches, resulting in a patterned effect which is shown to best advantage if the lower branches are removed.
Cultivation. Plant in well-drained loamy soil in sun or light shade between October and March. The species is lime-tolerant.
Propagation. Sow seeds in pans of John Innes seed compost in September or October and overwinter them in a cold frame. Germination is erratic and may take 18 months. When the seedlings are large enough to handle, pot them up individually in 3 in. pots of John Innes potting compost No. 1 and grow on in a nursery bed for at least four or five years before planting out in permanent positions.

Branches layered in September may be severed from the parent plant after two years.

Pruning. None required.

Pests and diseases. Generally trouble-free.

Parrot's bill: see *Clianthus puniceus*

Parsley

Carum petroselinum, syns. *Petroselinum crispum, P. sativum. Umbelliferae*

Two distinct varieties of this hardy biennial herb are in cultivation, one used for flavouring and garnishing, the other as a root vegetable. The species is native to Central and S. Europe.

Parsley (*C. p.* Crispum). Height 12–24 in.; spacing 9 in. This herb is usually grown as an annual as its leaves are best in their first year. Hollow branching stems bear mid-green leaves that are densely curled and moss-like. Green-yellow flowers are borne in umbels on stems 2–3 ft high in the second summer; these should be removed as soon as they show.

Recommended varieties include: 'Champion Moss Curled'; 'Giant Curled'; 'Imperial'; and 'Suttons Curly Top'.

Parsley has a distinctive, mildly spicy flavour and is rich in vitamins A and C. The leaves are used to garnish salads and savoury dishes, to flavour sauces and stuffings, and as *fines herbes* and in *bouquets garnis*.

Hamburg parsley, turnip-rooted parsley (*C. p. fusiformis*). Height 12–24 in.; spacing 9 in. This variety is grown as a root vegetable. The long tap roots are smooth and conical like parsnips, and are cooked and used in the same way. The flavour resembles that of celeriac. The leaves, though edible, are coarser and of poorer flavour than those of *C. p.* Crispum.

Cultivation of parsley. Parsley needs a well-drained, fertile soil in a sunny or partially shaded position. Prepare the soil by working in dressings of well-decayed manure or compost. To ensure winter supplies, grow in a sheltered position with a southern aspect.

In September, cut down the plants and water them to encourage fresh growth. Protect September-sown plants and, ideally, established plants, with cloches during the winter.

Cultivation of Hamburg parsley. These plants will grow in well-drained fertile garden soil, preferably enriched with manure or compost.

Propagation of parsley. Sow seeds outdoors, thinly in drills drawn 10 in. apart, between February and June, thinning the seedlings first to 3 in. and then to 9 in. If the weather is severe when a February sowing is to be made, sow in boxes of seed compost under glass at a temperature of 10–15°C (50–55°F); plant the seedlings outdoors in April at distances of 9 in. after hardening off in a cold frame.

Propagation of Hamburg parsley. Sow seeds in March in drills drawn 12 in. apart. Thin the seedlings to 9 in. spacings.

Harvesting and storing. Keep a fresh supply of parsley available all the year round, as it is difficult to dry. For drying, gather in summer early in the day. Wash the leaves well and dry quickly, preferably in an oven kept at about 93°C (200°F) with the door left slightly ajar. Alternatively, dip the leaves in boiling water, spread on baking trays, and put in a very hot oven for one minute. In either case, immediately the leaves are dry, store in airtight, lightproof containers.

From June onwards, leaves can be gathered and deep-frozen. See entry under HERBS.

Lift the roots of Hamburg parsley from September onwards, as required for cooking.

Pests. Maggots of the CARROT FLY sometimes attack roots and stems; CELERY FLY maggots may tunnel into the leaves.

Hamburg parsley is generally trouble-free.

Diseases. On the leaves of parsley, LEAF SPOT shows as small spots which are first brown and then become nearly white.

A VIRUS DISEASE, which stunts growth, is the probable cause of yellow, orange and red tints which sometimes develop on the foliage.

On Hamburg parsley, PARSNIP CANKER shows as red-brown or black cankers in the shoulder of the tap roots.

Parsley

Parsnip

Pastinaca sativa. Umbelliferae

A hardy biennial root vegetable grown as an annual. The roots are long and tapering with pale yellow, sweet-tasting flesh. Parsnips need little attention, but they require a long growing season and occupy the ground for almost a year. The roots are ready for harvesting during autumn and winter.

VARIETIES

These include: 'Avonresister', a small-rooted, good-flavoured variety, resistant to canker; 'Dobie's Exhibition', a long, shapely rooted variety with white skin and of excellent flavour; 'Improved Hollow Crown', a heavy cropper with long, smooth roots; 'Lisbonnais', with fine-textured flesh. 'Offenham' is a short-rooting variety, thick at the top and sharply tapering; it is particularly suitable for shallow soils. 'Tender and True' has long, smooth roots with white flesh and skin.

Cultivation. Parsnips will grow in any soil, but do best in a deep, rich, fairly light soil and in an open sunny position. Use ground which was manured the previous season, as newly manured ground may cause the roots to fork. Dig the plot deeply and rake in a complete fertiliser at 3 oz. per sq. yd prior to sowing.

Sow the seeds in February or March, as soon as the soil can be broken down to a fine tilth. Sow in 1 in. deep drills, 18 in. apart. As soon as the seedlings are visible, thin them slightly and continue thinning until the plants are 9–12 in. apart in the rows. Hoe the bed regularly to keep down weeds.

The roots are ready to harvest when the leaves begin to die down in autumn. Lift them as they are required for use, or lift all the roots in December and store in a clamp.

The flavour is thought to be improved if the roots are not lifted until after frost. Roots left in the bed until March should be lifted or they will start making new growth.

Parsnip 'Dobie's Exhibition'

Parsnip 'Tender and True'

Pests. Maggots of the CELERY FLY tunnel into leaf tissues, causing the leaves to shrivel; in severe infestations, plants suffer check to growth. EAR-WIGS sometimes feed on the leaves.

Diseases. PARSNIP CANKER may show as red-brown or black lesions on the top of the roots.

SPLITTING of roots is generally due to an irregular supply of moisture.

Parthenocissus henryana

Parthenocissus henryana
(autumn foliage)

Parthenocissus tricuspidata
'Veitchii' (autumn foliage)

Parthenocissus

Virginia creeper. *Vitaceae*

PARTHENOCISSUS INSERTA

A genus of ten species of deciduous climbers. They are related to *Ampelopsis* and *Vitis*, but differ from these in having leaves partly three-lobed or divided into leaflets, tendrils usually tipped with sticky discs or hooks, and flowers borne in compound cymes. All species of parthenocissus are suitable for pergolas, walls, fences and rough-barked trees, where they will attach themselves without additional support. They are particularly attractive in autumn, with their brilliantly coloured foliage. Small, often minute, flowers are produced between May and July.

P. henryana (Chinese Virginia creeper). China. Height 25–30 ft. This is an attractive self-clinging species with smooth, angled stems and forked tendrils. It is a vigorous, fairly well-branched plant, capable of covering a large wall rapidly if the young growths are pinched out to encourage spreading. It needs a sheltered site as it is not reliably hardy. The dark green leaves consist of three or five leaflets, attractively variegated with white and pink along the midrib and main veins. The variegation becomes more pronounced when the green turns brilliant red in autumn, and also when the foliage is protected from full sun. Minute green flowers are produced in branched cymes, 6–7 in. long.

P. himalayana, syn. *Vitis semicordata* (Himalayan Virginia creeper). Himalayas. Height 25–30 ft. A self-clinging climber of vigorous habit, erect at first but spreading later. It is not reliably hardy and needs a sheltered site. The young growths and leaf petioles are red and the leaves trifoliate. The foliage becomes rich crimson in autumn. Minute green-yellow flowers are borne in branched cymes, 4–5 in. across. Deep blue fruits are borne in loose clusters.

P. inserta, syn. *Vitis vitacea* (common Virginia creeper). N. America. Height or spread up to 40 ft. This hardy species is similar to *P. quinquefolia* (true Virginia creeper), but is distinguishable by having no adhesive pads at the ends of its tendrils. It is an effective creeper on a tree or pergola, but is at its best trained to horizontal supports, when it produces a curtain of hanging growth. The foliage turns bright red in autumn. The cymes of green-white flowers are 3–4 in. wide.

P. quinquefolia, syn. *Vitis hederacea* (true Virginia creeper). N. America. Height up to 70 ft. This hardy, self-clinging species, of branching habit, is seen at its best growing to the tops of lofty trees. When grown on walls or fences it needs attention to keep the growth within limits. The leaves consist of three or five coarsely serrated leaflets, which turn brilliant crimson in autumn. Inconspicuous green-yellow flowers are produced during May and June in forked umbels $2\frac{1}{2}$ in. across. They are followed by tiny, globular blue-black berries.

P. thomsonii. China, Himalayas. Height up to 20 ft. A slender, hardy, self-clinging species with ornamental foliage that is best displayed on a wall or pillar. The habit is fairly upright. The leaves are compound, usually consisting of five leaflets borne on slender, downy petioles. These are wine-red in spring, deepening to purple-crimson in autumn. Small green flowers are borne during May and June in slender-stalked cymes, 2–3 in. across. They are followed by tiny black fruits.

P. tricuspidata 'Veitchii', syns. *Ampelopsis veitchii, Vitis inconstans.* Japan, China. Height up to 50 ft. This hardy species is self-supporting, branching, and is usually grown against a flat surface, where it grows rapidly once established. The leaves are variable but are usually three-lobed; on younger plants they are sometimes composed of three leaflets. Small yellow-green flowers are produced during June and July in 1–2 in. wide cymes on the short side-shoots. The tiny dark blue fruits, covered with a silvery bloom, are produced freely only during a hot season.

PARTHENOCISSUS TRICUSPIDATA 'VEITCHII'

Cultivation. Dig a planting pocket 24 in. square and 18 in. deep, preferably at the base of a wall or large tree. Fill this with moist, loamy soil and a dressing of rotted manure or compost. Plant out pot-grown specimens (young plants with bare roots do not transplant readily) in mild weather from November to March. Pinch out the growing points of species with a vertical habit, and support the young growths of all species with twiggy sticks until they become self-clinging. *P. henryana* and *P. himalayana* need sheltered sites, but aspect is not important for the others.

Propagation. Take 4–5 in. nodal cuttings of half-ripened growths during August or September and insert them singly in pots of sandy soil. Place these in a propagating frame at a temperature of 13–16°C (55–61°F). When rooted, grow on in a frame, later repotting them in loamy soil.

Hardwood cuttings, 10–12 in. long, can be taken in November. Insert them to half their length in a sheltered border outdoors.

Sow seeds during October or November in boxes of seed compost placed in a cold greenhouse or frame. When the seedlings have produced several true leaves, place them singly in 3 in. pots and grow them on in a frame.

The following spring, plunge potted half-ripe cuttings and seedlings into a nursery bed outdoors, until they are needed for planting in their permanent quarters. Tie each plant securely to a cane or stake.

Layer long shoots in October or November; sever one year later.

Pruning. Remove unwanted or overcrowded growths during the summer.

Pests. SCALE INSECTS of various species infest the stems and make the plants sticky and sooty.

WEEVILS eat the stems below the soil.

APHIDS infest young growths.

GLASSHOUSE RED SPIDER MITES may attack the leaves, causing a fine light mottling and, in severe infestations, bronzing and wilting.

Diseases. HONEY FUNGUS may kill the plants.

Partridge-berry: see *Gaultheria procumbens*
Pasque flower: see *Pulsatilla vulgaris*

Passiflora

Passion flower. *Passifloraceae*

PASSIFLORA CAERULEA

A genus of about 500 species of vigorous, evergreen flowering climbers. They are generally tender and are best given greenhouse treatment, although *P. caerulea* and *P. umbellicata* may be grown outdoors, on trelliswork, arbours or against walls, in sheltered areas of the south and west. The top growth is often killed by frost, but new stems arise from the base except after very severe winters.

The flowers consist of a short tube which expands to a saucer-shaped flower composed of numerous ovate petals; a corona of slender filaments surrounds the stalked ovary and short stamens. The flowers are generally borne singly from the upper leaf axils.

P. × *allardii.* Garden origin. Height 20 ft. This hybrid has three to five-lobed, pale to midgreen, palmate leaves. The flowers, which appear from June to October, are 3 in. across, white, shaded pink and with a blue corona.

P. caerulea (common passion flower). Brazil. Height 20–30 ft. This species has palmate, light to mid-green leaves. The flowers are about 3 in. across and produced from June to September; between the white petals and the stamens is a blue-purple corona. 'Constance Elliott' is pure white and hardier than the species. The species sometimes produces ovoid yellow fruits.

P. × *caponii* 'John Innes'. Garden origin. Height 25 ft. A hybrid between *P. quadrangularis* and *P. racemosa*, resembling the former in habit, but having mainly tri-lobed mid-green leaves, and slightly larger, bowl-shaped, purple, blue, white and green flowers.

P. edulis. Tropical S. America. Height 20 ft. The three-lobed leaves are mid to deep green. White flowers, 3 in. across and with a purple corona, appear in late June. The species produces the well-known passion fruits, which are egg-shaped and purple or yellow; they generally ripen in August and September.

P. mollissima, syn. *Tacsonia mollissima.* S. America. Height 15–20 ft. This species has tri-lobed, mid-green leaves covered with white hairs. Rose-pink, long-tubed flowers, 3 in. across and with a sparse, inconspicuous corona, are borne from June to October. They are sometimes followed by yellow egg-shaped fruits, about 3 in. long.

P. quadrangularis (granadilla). S. America. Height 25 ft. A species with oblong-ovate mid-green leaves. The flowers are white, flushed pale purple and with a prominent long corona of white, blue and purple wavy filaments. The flowers measure 3–4 in. across and are borne from June to September. They are followed by ovoid yellow fruits, 8 in. long. This species is grown commercially in the West Indies and elsewhere for its edible fruits. Under glass, fruits are seldom set.

P. umbellicata. Brazil. Height 15–20 ft. This species has tri-lobed dark green leaves. Attractive purple-brown flowers, 3–4 in. across, are borne from July to September.

Cultivation. Passifloras are best planted out in the greenhouse border, but may also be grown in 10–12 in. pots or tubs of John Innes potting compost No. 3. Train them up strings or wires. No feeding is required, but a light annual mulch in March of well-rotted compost or manure is beneficial. In winter, keep the plants just moist, but water freely in spring and summer. Most species will survive at a winter temperature of 7°C (45°F), but *P. edulis, P. mollissima* and *P. quadrangularis* do better at 10°C (50°F).

Give light shading to the glass in summer, and ventilate freely when the temperature exceeds 21°C (70°F). Keep the atmosphere humid by frequent damping down, and syringe the flowers to encourage the fruits to set.

Outdoors in the south or west, plant *P. caerulea* and *P. umbellicata* during May in any ordinary, well-drained garden soil; choose a sheltered site in sun or partial shade. For at least

Passiflora caerulea (flowers)

Passiflora caerulea (fruits)

Passiflora × *caponii* 'John Innes'

Passiflora edulis

the first year or two, protect the plants during winter with brushwood, cloches or polythene sheeting. Trellis or wire mesh is the best support, and it is advisable to tie in the young growths until the tendrils have taken hold.

Propagation. Take 3–4 in. long stem sections in July or August and insert in equal parts (by volume) peat and sand in a propagating frame at a temperature of 16–18°C (61–64°F). When rooted, pot the cuttings singly in 3½ in. containers of John Innes potting compost No. 2, and pot on as necessary until the plants are in their final pots or planted out in the greenhouse border. Harden off plants for outdoor sites in a cold frame before planting out in May.

Alternatively, sow seeds in pots or pans of seed compost and germinate at a temperature of 18–21°C (64–70°F). Prick out the seedlings, when large enough to handle, into 3 in. pots and treat as described for cuttings.

Pruning. In February or March, thin out overgrown plants at ground level or back to the main stem; spur lateral shoots back to 6 in. at the same time.

Plants grown outdoors are often cut down by frost, but should otherwise be treated in the same manner as greenhouse plants.

Pests. Generally trouble-free.

Diseases. A variable leaf-mottling and distortion, with chlorotic flecks along the lateral veins, is caused by CUCUMBER MOSAIC VIRUS. The symptoms may disappear during the summer and reappear in winter or spring; affected plants look unsightly.

Passiflora quadrangularis

Paulownia tomentosa

Passion flower: see Passiflora
Pastinaca sativa: see Parsnip

Paulownia

Scrophulariaceae

PAULOWNIA TOMENTOSA

A genus of 17 species of hardy deciduous flowering trees of open, rounded habit. The brown-felted flower buds are conspicuous throughout the winter but in exposed gardens may be damaged by frost. The foxglove-like flowers in erect panicles are outstanding, but are not produced until the plants are well established.

P. fargesii. China. Height 15–30 ft; spread 10–20 ft. The heart-shaped slender-pointed leaves are mid-green. Fragrant pale lilac flowers, up to 2½ in. long, and with purple-speckled throats, are borne during June.

P. imperialis: see *P. tomentosa*

P. tomentosa, syn. *P. imperialis.* China. Height 15–25 ft; spread 10–15 ft. The heart-shaped mid-green leaves unfurl after the flowers, which are 1½–2 in. long and open in May. They are lavender-blue and fragrant.

Cultivation. Plant in a sunny, sheltered position in deep, well-drained, loamy soil between October and March. Paulownias are sometimes grown as stooled specimens for dot or accent plants in summer bedding schemes.

Propagation. Sow seeds in equal parts (by volume) peat and sand in a cold frame in March or April; when the seedlings are large enough to handle, prick them off into pans or boxes and later pot them individually in 4 in. containers of John Innes potting compost No. 1. Between October and March set the plants out in a nursery bed and grow on for at least two or three years before planting them out in their final positions.

Take 3–4 in. cuttings of lateral shoots with a heel in July and insert them in sandy soil in a cold frame. The following spring, set them out in a nursery bed. Grow on for two or three years before transferring them to their permanent positions in spring.

Pruning. Normally, no pruning is necessary. However, if grown as dot plants, paulownias must be cut down to ground level every year in March. This will encourage vigorous shoots clad with exceptionally large leaves; stooled plants produce no flowers.

Pests. Generally trouble-free.

Diseases. Rapid death of plants may be caused by HONEY FUNGUS.

LEAF SPOT shows as irregular yellow-brown lesions which later turn grey, or as spots with dark margins.

Peach and nectarine

Prunus persica. Rosaceae

PEACH

The peach is a hardy deciduous tree which bears fruits with rough, hairy skins and single, deeply fissured stones. Its natural habitat is China. The nectarine, a smooth-skinned mutant (sport) of the peach, is slightly less hardy. Because they flower early, both need protection against spring frosts and should be sited in a frost-free position.

Peaches and nectarines can be grown under glass or, as far north as Yorkshire, as fan-trained trees outdoors on south or west-facing walls. Nectarines, in particular, need sheltered sites if they are to grow successfully outdoors. In mild areas that escape spring frosts, peaches can be grown outdoors as bush or half-standard trees. Average heights and spreads are as follows:

On 'St Julien A' stock, bush and half-standard 18 ft × 12 ft, fan 7 ft × 18 ft; on a vigorous rootstock or myrobalan plum, bush and half-standard 20 ft × 15 ft, fan 8 ft × 20 ft.

Planting distances: on 'St Julien A', bush, half-standard and fan 15–18 ft; on a vigorous rootstock or myrobalan plum, bush and half-standard 18–24 ft, fan 16–20 ft.

Peach (flowers)

Although peaches and nectarines are self-fertile, the pollination of both is improved by close planting of different varieties that flower at the same time. Trees on 'St Julien A' semi-dwarfing rootstock are recommended for garden use. Plants raised from seeds will have slightly larger measurements than those given.

PEACHES

'**Duke of York**'. Mid-July. Large yellow fruits, heavily flushed with crimson. Soft, green-yellow flesh of excellent flavour. Grows equally well outdoors and under glass.

'**Hale's Early**'. Late July, early August. Medium-sized, apricot-yellow fruits, flushed and mottled with red. Soft yellow flesh of good flavour. Hardy, but forces well.

'**Peregrine**'. Early August. Large, juicy fruits with crimson skins and good flavour. A favourite variety for growing outdoors.

'**Rochester**'. Mid-August. Large, yellow-fleshed fruits. Particularly suitable for growing outdoors.

NECTARINES

'**Early Rivers**'. Mid-July. Large, green-yellow fruits with a scarlet flush. Tender, good-flavoured flesh. More usually grown under glass.

'**Lord Napier**'. Early August. Large, pale yellow fruits with deep brown flush. Good flavour. More usually grown under glass than outdoors.

Cultivation. Peaches and nectarines grow best in medium loam with good drainage.

Plant either maiden trees, or older, partially trained trees, in late October or November. When planting against a wall, set the stem 6–9 in. out from the base and inclined slightly towards the wall. Allow adequate space for wall-trained trees, which require a framework at least 6–8 ft high, of horizontal wires set 9–12 in. apart.

Erect temporary windbreaks for bushes and half-standards planted outdoors in exposed positions. As well as reducing the force of the wind, this will encourage pollinating insects.

A greenhouse with a minimum span of 8–10 ft, or with a rear wall of this height if it is a lean-to, is needed for growing peaches under glass. They can be planted against the rear wall of a lean-to and fan-trained, or planted close to a side wall of a span house and grown as espaliers on wires attached to the underside of the roof glazing bars. In both cases the wires should be fastened 12 in. apart every 3–4 ft along the length of the house, using vine eyes to hold them 4–6 in. from the glass or wall.

Protect the flowers of outdoor trees against frost by covering with small-mesh netting or hessian, which can be left to give protection against damage by birds.

Pollination is essential for good crops. Trees outside will be pollinated by insects but those under glass must be pollinated artificially. Do this with a camel-hair paint brush or rabbit's tail at about noon each day throughout the flowering period, damping the floor of the greenhouse afterwards and closing the door for a short time to raise the temperature.

Water trees under glass throughout the growing season, starting in February, and syringe daily after the fruits have set. Watch the ground around wall-trained trees for signs of drying out and water as necessary, especially in June and July when the fruits are swelling.

Give a weak liquid fertiliser when watering trees under glass, monthly from June to August. Outdoors, maintain the young growths on bush or wall-trained trees by mulching with rotted manure or compost in spring and applying dried blood at $\frac{1}{2}$ oz. per sq. yd in May.

Avoid disturbing the roots of peaches and nectarines, but keep the soil around the trees clear of weeds by shallow hoeing or by treating with paraquat. Where bush trees are grown in grass, keep this short during the summer. Mulch round all outdoor trees with well-rotted manure.

For trees under glass, remove the top 1 in. of soil in winter and replace it with fibrous loam to which has been added 3 lb. bone-meal and 1 lb. sulphate of potash per cu. yd.

Maintain the size of fruits on all trees by thinning them out to a final spacing of 9 in., starting when they are the size of hazel nuts. Tie back or cut out any shoots that are shading the fruits. Pick the fruits when the flesh starts to soften slightly round the stalk and store in a cool place until required.

Propagation. Peaches are among the few fruits that may give good results when grown from seeds, including those of imported fruits. Sow in September or October, setting the stones singly in 5 in. pots of John Innes potting compost No. 1 in a cold frame or greenhouse. Slight artificial heat, to maintain a night temperature of 7–10°C (45–50°F) in winter, will hasten germination. Repot as necessary and treat as a maiden tree after it has made one season's growth. Seeds may also be sown direct where trees are required.

However, budding is necessary if a named variety of known performance is required. This is done in July or August; suitable rootstocks are seedling peach, 'St Julien A' or myrobalan plum. The method is further explained in the chapter headed PROPAGATION.

Pruning. The fruits of peaches and nectarines are carried on shoots produced the previous season. In the early years of building up a fan-shaped tree, aim to produce a balanced shape by cutting back to buds pointing in the required direction in February. Rub out unwanted shoots in early summer.

In April or May, shorten by about one-third the leading growths of other trees planted as maidens. Subsequently, thin out the growths by removing crowding or crossing branches in summer. Remove tips of any branches that have died by cutting back to a good bud in April.

Where growth is excessive and fruit yield small, root prune in early winter.

For further details on training fan-shaped trees see the chapter headed PRUNING.

Pests. GLASSHOUSE RED SPIDER MITES infest the undersides of leaves and are particularly troublesome under glass and in warm, dry situations outdoors. They cause a fine, light speckling on the upper surface of the leaves which may later turn bronze, wither and die.

SCALE INSECTS and APHIDS infest the stems and leaves, making plants sticky and sooty.

BIRDS and WASPS may damage the fruits.

Diseases. BACTERIAL CANKER is seen during the summer as brown spots on the leaves, which fall out and leave shot holes. Cankers develop and show as elongated, flattened lesions along the

Peach 'Peregrine'

Peach 'Rochester'

Pea 'Dwarf Greensleeves'

Pea 'Kelvedon Wonder'

Pea 'Onward'

branches, from which exudes copious gum. The following spring the buds of an infected branch fail to open, or if leaves do develop they turn yellow and become narrow and curled, soon withering and dying. The branch dies back.

BROWN ROT FUNGUS causes fruits to turn brown and rot. They may remain on the tree, but more frequently fall at maturity.

CHLOROSIS shows on the leaves as a yellowing between the veins, or the leaves may turn almost white. This is a common trouble on trees growing in soils that are too alkaline.

HONEY FUNGUS may kill trees rapidly.

PEACH LEAF CURL causes large blisters to develop on the leaves. They are at first red, but they later swell up and turn white. Many leaves may be affected and they fall quickly.

PEACH MILDEW first appears when the buds break in the spring, and shows as a white powdery deposit on the emerging growth. It then spreads to later-developing foliage, and diseased leaves may fall prematurely. The fruits too, may be attacked. Because of the fruit hairs the disease is not very obvious at first, but later it shows as brown patches on the ripening fruits.

A PHYSIOLOGICAL DISORDER causes the fruits to fall prematurely; this is usually due to an irregular supply of moisture at the roots.

SHOT HOLE, due to a fungus, causes numerous brown, round spots to develop on the leaves. The tissues fall away, leaving holes in the leaves which have a ragged appearance.

SILVER LEAF causes a silvering of the foliage on one or more branches, which then die back. Later, flat purple fruiting bodies of the fungus appear on dead wood. A purple-brown stain is produced in the inner tissues of diseased stems; a cross-section of a branch bearing silvered leaves should be examined for signs of this stain to confirm the presence of the disease.

Peaches, ornamental: see Prunus
Peacock plant: see *Calathea mackoyana*
Peacock tiger flower: see *Tigridia pavonia*
Pea, everlasting: see *Lathyrus latifolius*

Pea, garden

Pisum sativum. Leguminosae

A hardy, climbing annual, grown as a summer vegetable for the round green immature seeds contained in pods. The plants, which vary in height from 15 in. to 6 ft, include round-seeded and wrinkle-seeded types. Round-seeded types have a lower sugar content; they are hardier than wrinkle-seeded peas and are suitable for autumn, winter and early-spring sowings.

VARIETIES

A careful choice of varieties will produce crops from early May to October. For early varieties, ready for picking in May and June, the round-seeded 'Feltham First' and 'Meteor', and the wrinkle-seeded 'Kelvedon Wonder', are recommended. These are dwarf varieties, reaching a height of 18 in., and can easily be covered by cloches in severe weather. The round-seeded 'Improved Pilot' is an early, tall-growing variety, up to 3 ft high.

Good early varieties for picking in June include wrinkle-seeded varieties (height 2½ ft) such as 'Duplex' with pods hanging in pairs, and 'Onward', reliable and heavy-cropping.

Main-crop wrinkle-seeded varieties for harvesting during July and August include 'Dwarf Greensleeves' (height 3–3½ ft), a heavy cropper producing exceptionally long, curved pods; 'Raynes Park' (height 3 ft); and 'Stratagem' (height 24 in.).

For a late crop, ready for picking from September onwards, small-growing, quick-maturing, wrinkle-seeded varieties are recommended: 'Kelvedon Wonder', 'Pioneer' and 'Progress No. 9' (all 18–24 in. high) mature in about 12 weeks; they are less prone to mildew than most varieties. The tall-growing 'Gladstone' (height 4 ft) is outstanding for a late crop as it tolerates drought.

Among the less-common wrinkle-seeded varieties, which should be treated as main-crop varieties, are the 5 ft high purple-podded pea, the seeds of which turn green when cooked. The edible-podded or sugar peas, also known as Mangetout, have broad, fleshy, stringless young pods that should be cooked whole; 5 ft high 'Carouby de Mausanne' is a good variety.

Cultivation. All peas require a rich soil; for early-maturing varieties it is particularly important that it is well drained and well aerated. Dig the plot deeply, preferably three or four months before sowing. Work two bucketfuls of well-rotted manure or compost per sq. yd into the top spit. A week before sowing, rake in a top dressing of general fertiliser at 2–3 oz. per sq. yd.

Take out flat drills, 4–6 in. wide and 3 in. deep. The distance between rows depends on the final height of the variety grown. Varieties up to 18 in. high should be sown in drills 24 in. apart; for 4 ft high varieties space the rows at 3½ ft, and for 6 ft varieties at 5 ft.

Scatter the seeds for winter-growing crops thinly along the drills, but for other crops sow the seeds 2–3 in. apart, setting them alternately at either side of the drill. Sow early varieties in November or February and March, second-early varieties in March, and the main crop during April and May.

As soon as the seedlings are through, hoe along the rows to kill weeds. Insert twiggy pea sticks at each side of the row, sloping them outward to form a V; this encourages open growth and allows light and air to circulate round the plants. Keep the plants well watered during dry spells; in summer apply a ½ in. deep mulch of lawn-mowings, peat or leaf-mould to conserve moisture.

Harvesting. Pick the pods as soon as they are ready; cropping will be reduced if ripe pods are left unpicked. When a row has finished cropping, cut the haulms and add them to the compost heap; leave the roots in the ground to enrich it with nitrogen.

Exhibition. Most exhibition varieties require 11 or 12 weeks from sowing to maturity. Sow seeds in trays or small pots of seed compost in March or April; when large enough to handle, transplant the seedlings to a well-prepared plot. Grow exhibition peas in single rows, allowing 9–12 in. between plants and supporting each with a bamboo cane. Cut out the tendrils and tie each plant to its cane. Allow only the leading shoot to develop and pinch off all side-shoots as they appear.

Do not allow the flowers to set until 21 days before the date of the show, and pinch out the growing tip when six flowers have set on each plant. As the flowers open, spray with insecticide to prevent pea thrips. Water in a liquid feed once a fortnight. When cutting exhibition pods, handle them by the stem only.

Pests. APHIDS infest young shoots and leaves, causing a check to growth, and making the plants sticky and sooty.

Germinating seeds may be eaten by MILLEPEDES, and MICE may eat the seeds in the ground before they have a chance to germinate.

Caterpillars of the PEA MOTH tunnel into maturing pods and feed on the ripening peas, making them maggoty and useless.

PEA THRIPS sometimes appear in large numbers and produce a characteristic silvering of developing pods, as well as damaging flowers and leaves.

Diseases. DAMPING-OFF may cause early-sown peas to rot.

DOWNY MILDEW shows as grey furry patches on the undersides of leaves of young plants.

FUSARIUM WILT and FOOT ROT cause the leaves to yellow and the plants to wilt. The stem-bases show chocolate-brown or black marks; development of root nodules is poor. Stems and roots show a red discoloration of the inner tissues. The plants eventually collapse and die.

GREY MOULD attacks the stems and pods in wet weather, covering them with a grey velvety fungal growth.

MANGANESE DEFICIENCY affects seeds, producing dark rusty-red spots inside, which are seen only when the seeds are split open.

POWDERY MILDEW produces a white powdery coating on leaves and stems.

ROOT ROT can be caused by several different fungi, including RHIZOCTONIA and BLACK ROOT ROT. The roots die and often show black patches; the stem bases become discoloured and may decay and the foliage turns yellow and withers. Diseased plants collapse.

VIRUS DISEASES cause various symptoms, such as mottling and distortion of leaves; dead patches on the foliage; brown streaks on leaves and stems. They may also cause, DIE-BACK of shoots and stunting of plants; the pods may be rough, ridged and distorted.

Pea, glory: see *Clianthus formosus*

Pear

Pyrus communis. Rosaceae

These hardy, deciduous trees bear flowers in spring, edible fruits in late summer and autumn, and often develop attractive autumn leaf colours. *Pyrus communis*, the parent of modern European varieties, is a native of temperate Europe and western Asia as far as the Himalayas.

Although pear trees require much the same care as apple trees, they are generally easier to

bring to fruit-bearing, given adequate cross-pollination. However, they need a warmer site as they flower earlier than apples. Fruit quality is much improved by warm conditions.

The most suitable areas for growing pears are more restricted than those for apples, being mainly in the east and south-east of England. They are not usually successful north of the Trent unless they have a favoured site or are grown on walls. Generally, pears are more tolerant than apples of poor drainage, but less tolerant of drought. They grow best on fertile loams that retain moisture; on soils with a high lime content they are likely to develop chlorosis of the leaves.

Standard trees, which are grafted on vigorous seedling pear rootstocks and are slow to come into cropping, are not recommended for garden use. Bush trees are the best choice.

The height and spread of a pear tree depend on the variety, the rootstock and the type of soil. Average measurements (height and spread) are:

Bush, 10–12 ft; trunk 2–3 ft high. Half-standard, 12–15 ft; trunk 4 ft high. Standard, 15–20 ft; trunk 6 ft high.

Trees grown in trained or restricted form occupy the least space and are usually supported on a framework of posts and wires. They require more attention than free-growing forms.

Typical heights and widths of established trained trees are as follows:

Cordon (oblique), 10–12 ft long on supports 7 ft tall. Espalier, 8 ft high, 10–15 ft wide. Dwarf pyramid, 8–10 ft high, 3–6 ft wide.

The many varieties of pear give a season of use from August to the New Year if cool conditions for storage are available. Late-maturing varieties are rarely successful in Great Britain unless grown against a sunny wall or in a similarly favoured position.

All varieties should be regarded as self-sterile, since even self-fertile varieties crop better after cross-pollination. Any choice of variety outside the following, which with one exception are all dessert fruits, should be made with this pollination factor in mind:

'Conference'. A reliable cropper, even when late frosts occur. Pick in September for eating in October and November. Dark green, tapering fruits flushed with russet; sweet and juicy. Pollinated by 'William's Bon Chrétien' and 'Joséphine de Malines'. Flowers mid-season.

'Doyenné du Comice'. This is more exacting in its requirements than other varieties, needing a sheltered position, rich soil and regular mulching, but it has a particularly good flavour. Pick in early October for eating from late October to early December. Pale yellow fruits with red flush and some russet; white, juicy flesh. Pollinated by 'William's Bon Chrétien' and 'Conference'. Flowers late.

'Dr Jules Guyot'. A heavy cropper. Fruits ready for picking and eating in September. They are large, pale yellow, covered with russet patches and sometimes flushed with red. Flesh cream-yellow, juicy and slightly aromatic. Pollinated by 'Conference', 'Doyenné du Comice' and 'Fertility'. Flowers late.

'Fertility'. A heavy cropper. Pick in September for eating in October. Fruits dull yellow, heavily flushed with russet; flesh yellow, crisp and

Pear 'Conference'

Pear 'Doyenné du Comice'

Pear 'Dr Jules Guyot'

TYPES OF TRAINED PEAR TREES

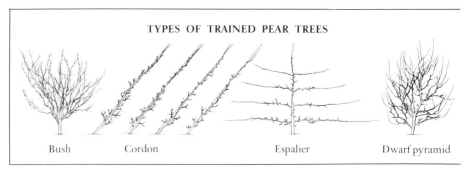

Bush   Cordon   Espalier   Dwarf pyramid

Pear 'Joséphine de Malines'

Pear 'Louise Bonne of Jersey'

Pear 'William's Bon Chrétien'

juicy. Pollinated by 'Doyenné du Comice', 'Dr Jules Guyot' and 'Winter Nelis'. Flowers late.

'Joséphine de Malines'. A good late pear. Pick in October and ripen at a temperature of 16°C (61°F) during December or January. Small, green-yellow fruits; sweet and perfumed. Tends to weak growth. Pollinated by 'Louise Bonne of Jersey', 'William's Bon Chrétien' and 'Conference'. Flowers mid-season.

'Louise Bonne of Jersey'. A regular cropper. Pick in late September for eating in October. Green-yellow fruits flushed with deep red. White, sweet flesh. Pollinated by 'Joséphine de Malines'. Early-flowering.

'Packham's Triumph'. A vigorous-growing, good cropper. Pick in September for eating in November and December. Fruits green, changing to clear yellow when ripe, with a fine golden flush; white flesh, very juicy and sweet. Pollinated by 'Joséphine de Malines' and 'William's Bon Chrétien'. Flowers mid-season.

'Pitmaston Duchess'. A culinary variety and a regular cropper; it can be grown on soil unsuitable for dessert varieties. Pick in September or October for use in October or November. The large yellow fruits, irregularly mottled with russet, have soft, juicy, cream-yellow flesh of medium flavour. Best pollinated by 'Conference'. Flowers mid-season; it is not suitable as a pollinator for other varieties.

'William's Bon Chrétien'. The best September pear, though with a short season. Pick in late August and ripen off the tree. Large, golden-yellow fruits with dots of russet. White, sweet, juicy flesh. Susceptible to scab. Pollinated by 'Conference' and 'Joséphine de Malines'. Flowers mid-season.

'Winter Nelis'. Harvest in mid-October, ripen at a temperature of 16°C (61°F) in December. Dull green russeted fruits; sweet, juicy flesh with a good flavour. Pollinated by 'Doyenné du Comice'. Late-flowering.

Cultivation. The best results are obtained on well-drained deep soils that do not dry out seriously in summer. Improve thin soils by adding bulky organic matter, such as compost. Avoid exposed situations if possible; otherwise, plant windbreaks or close up the distances between trees to provide mutual protection.

Pears will not succeed near coasts, because of damage from salt-laden winds. Avoid sites subject to spring frosts, such as those at the bottoms of slopes or where obstacles interrupt the flow of cold air to lower ground.

The normal season for planting is November to March. November planting gives the following year's growth a better start. Maiden trees transplant better than older ones. If older trees are planted, either for quicker results or to allow the nurseryman to do the initial training of trees grown in restricted form, care must be taken not to break up the root-ball when planting.

The following measurements may be used as a general guide to planting distances, the first figure being the spacing between trees, the second between rows:

BUSH	12–15 ft;	12–15 ft
HALF-STANDARD	18–20 ft;	20–25 ft
STANDARD	20–25 ft;	30–35 ft
CORDON	2½–3 ft;	6–10 ft
ESPALIER	12–15 ft;	8–10 ft
DWARF PYRAMID	3½–5 ft;	7–10 ft

Do not plant when the soil is frozen or saturated, although a thin surface crust of frost does no harm. If planting cannot be carried out as soon as the trees are available, store them in a frost-free shed.

When planting oblique cordons, set the first tree 6 ft in from the end of the row to allow for its ultimate length, and plant at 45 degrees, with the graft union uppermost. This will prevent the union being forced open if the tree is bent lower when it reaches the top of the framework.

Construct a supporting framework of posts 10 ft apart, with 7 ft above ground and 3 ft below soil level (18 in. if set in concrete). Fix wires 3 ft and 6 ft above ground level, with adjustable straining bolts at the ends of rows. Attach bamboo canes to span the wires and tie the trees to them.

During the winter, firm any trees that have been lifted by frost. Watch for drying out after bud burst and water the soil if necessary; mulch with straw or rotted manure after the soil has warmed in spring and before it dries out.

Watering may be required to help the trees become established. Drought can also retard the growth of mature trees, although they may not show immediate signs of being affected. During prolonged dry weather, water the ground around trees from May to July, giving 4 gal. per sq. yd.

Pears need no feeding during the first year. After this, give annual dressings of fertilisers in January or February, keeping them clear of the trunk and applying over an area slightly larger than that covered by the tree's branches.

Give 1½ oz. sulphate of ammonia per sq. yd (up to 2 oz. for trees in grass) and ¾ oz. sulphate of potash per sq. yd. Trees benefit from an annual light dressing of farmyard manure or compost.

Digging around the trees is likely to damage the roots. Control weeds by mulching, shallow hoeing or by spraying with paraquat.

Under suitable conditions, once cropping has started pears usually give regular, heavy crops, even to the extent of branches breaking and growth practically ceasing. Provide supports for heavily laden branches to prevent damage.

Usually, less fruit thinning is necessary than with apples and should be carried out at the end of June. Aim at one fruit per spur, or two per spur on trees that are not bearing heavily. On trees which have some branches heavily laden with fruit and others bare, thin the fruits on cropping branches lightly.

Picking. Most varieties ripen off the tree; even so, the fruits of all except early varieties should be left to mature for as long as possible on the tree. Test by lifting the fruit and twisting slightly: harvest when the fruit parts easily from the tree. Early varieties, such as 'William's Bon Chrétien', are best picked before they have ripened completely on the tree.

Store pears in a cool room or shed: a temperature of 2–4°C (36–39°F) is ideal. They should not be wrapped, but laid out in a single layer for easy inspection. The atmosphere need not be moist, as for apples.

Check frequently for approaching maturity, shown by a slight softening of the flesh close to the stalk, and then bring into a temperature of 16°C (61°F) for two or three days.

Propagation. All pear trees are budded or grafted on to rootstocks of pear or quince. The latter are in more general use and produce a medium-sized and easily managed tree.

Using special budding or grafting techniques, the nurseryman has to overcome incompatibility between some quince rootstock and variety combinations. This is done by using a short length of an intermediate, mutually compatible variety. Two recommended rootstocks are: 'Malling Quince A', a semi-vigorous and good all-round stock; 'Malling Quince C', a moderately dwarfing stock for use with strong-growing varieties on fertile soils.

Pruning. Generally, pears need little pruning in the early years; established trees need more attention. See the chapter headed PRUNING.

Pests. BIRDS peck ripening fruits and attack flower buds during the winter.

APHIDS sometimes infest young growths, making the trees sticky and sooty and distorting young leaves.

PEAR LEAF BLISTER MITES invade leaf tissues and young fruits, causing characteristic yellow or brown blisters.

Diseases. APPLE CANKER shows as an elliptic diseased area on the bark which shrinks in concentric rings as the canker grows. The infected area may girdle the branch so that all parts above die back.

BROWN ROT causes a rapid decay of the fruits, either on the tree or in store. They turn brown and are covered with white raised cushions of fungus spores, often arranged concentrically. Diseased fruits mummify.

CRACKING of fruits which are otherwise healthy is usually due to an irregular supply of moisture in the soil.

EYE ROT may affect the fruits; this shows first as a rotting of the tissues at the eye end, and extends until much or all of the pear is rotten.

FIREBLIGHT affects the flowers, which become blackened and shrivelled; the disease spreads to the young shoots and limbs, killing them. The die-back is progressive, a canker being visible in the autumn at the base of the dead wood. Leaves on affected branches wither and turn brown, but do not fall.

FROST DAMAGE can cause cracking of the bark, particularly at the crotch of the tree. Flower trusses may turn brown, or the petals may remain untouched, but the stamens turn black. If young leaves and very young fruits are blackened, the latter will fall prematurely.

HONEY FUNGUS frequently attacks pear trees, causing their sudden death; rapid die-back of trees can also be due to wind-rocking or waterlogging of the soil.

MINERAL DEFICIENCIES cause varying types of leaf discoloration, such as scorching of the leaf margins (lack of potash); orange-brown spots between the veins (magnesium deficiency); light green-yellow or red leaves which fall early (nitrogen deficiency); and yellowing between the veins (iron and/or manganese deficiency) known as chlorosis.

PEAR SCAB produces brown or black scabs on the fruits. These may be numerous and may almost cover the fruits which are likely to crack. Olive-green blotches are produced on the leaves which may fall prematurely. On the shoots, small blister-like pimples develop and these later burst the bark and show as ring-like cracks or scabs.

A PHYSIOLOGICAL DISORDER causes older leaves to turn black and often fall prematurely.

RUSSETTING of the skin may occur if slightly older fruits are injured; the developing fruit may be distorted.

Pear, prickly: see Opuntia
Pea, sweet: see *Lathyrus odoratus*
Pebble plant: see Lithops

Pelargonium
Geraniaceae

PELARGONIUM CRISPUM

A genus of 250 species of mainly tender sub-shrubs, some of which may be used for outdoor bedding schemes. They are deciduous or evergreen, including succulent species. Those described here are tender evergreen plants, suitable for greenhouse cultivation, as house plants and for summer bedding.

The common zonal pelargoniums are frequently known as geraniums and should not be confused with the genus *Geranium*.

The flowers are five-petalled, the upper two petals often being larger and contrastingly veined or suffused with a darker colour. In some species, and particularly in the hybrid *P.* × *hortorum*, the

Pear 'Winter Nelis'

Pelargonium crispum 'Variegatum'

Pelargonium graveolens

Pelargonium peltatum 'La France'

Pelargonium 'Aztec' (Regal)

Pelargonium 'Lavender Grand Slam' (Regal)

bears triangular to triangular-oblong, deeply lobed and toothed, mid-green aromatic leaves with wavy margins. The pink flowers, 1 in. across, are veined with deep purple; the upper petals each have a central deep purple blotch. The flowers are borne in three to seven-flowered umbels from the upper leaf axils from April to June or even later.

P. tomentosum (peppermint geranium). S. Africa. Height 12–24 in. This semi-prostrate hummock-forming species may be trained as a low climber and may reach a height of 4–5 ft. The palmate, shallowly lobed, pale green leaves are densely, softly hairy; they emit a strong peppermint aroma when bruised. Inconspicuous, narrow-petalled white flowers, $\frac{1}{2}$–$\frac{3}{4}$ in. across, are produced in umbels from the tips of the shoots from June to September.

REGAL PELARGONIUMS. This hybrid group, also known as *P.* × *domesticum*, mainly derives from *P. cucullatum*, *P. fulgidum* and *P. grandiflorum*. Height 15–24 in. The shrubby, erect branching plants bear broadly ovate to palmate toothed and mid-green leaves. The flowers, 1$\frac{1}{2}$–2 in. across, are borne in umbels from the upper leaf axils and range in colour from pink to purple; they are usually veined or blotched with darker shades. They appear in profusion from May to October or the first frosts.

Named varieties include: 'Aztec', bright red, veined with red-purple and margined with white; 'Black Knight', black-purple with white picotee edges to the petals; 'Caprice', deep cherry-red; 'Carisbrooke', large rose-pink flowers frilled and blotched with maroon; 'Grand Slam' rose-red shading to violet-red; 'Lavender Grand Slam', silvery-mauve with a light maroon blotch; 'Nomad', large white flowers, blotched and feathered with crimson on the upper waved and crimped petals.

PELARGONIUM (ZONAL)

ZONAL PELARGONIUMS. A hybrid race, also known as *P.* × *hortorum*, and largely derived from *P. zonale*. Height up to 6 ft. These branching shrubs are distinguished by their rounded, pale to mid-green leaves with a conspicuous zone of bronze or maroon. The flowers $\frac{1}{2}$–1 in. across, are borne in dense rounded umbels from the upper leaf axils from May to October colours include white, pink, red and orange.

Outstanding named varieties include the following: 'Belvedere', mauve-pink; an F_1 hybrid seed strain that includes 'Deep Salmon', 'Light Pink' and 'Scarlet'. 'Cleopatra', soft pink; 'Coronation', rich pink; 'Du Barry', salmon-pink.

'Delight', vermilion-red; 'Gustav Emich' semi-double, vermilion-red; 'Hermione', vigorous, pure white double flowers. The Irene seed strain includes 'Electra', with crimson semi-double flowers. 'King of Denmark', semi-double salmon-pink; 'Maxim Kovaleski', clear orange.

petals are of even size, forming a saucer-shaped flower, generally self-coloured.

P. crispum. S. Africa. Height 24 in. or more. A slender, erect, much-branched shrub. It bears densely arranged, small, fan or wedge-shaped mid-green leaves that are finely crisped and toothed and with a balm-like fragrance. The pink narrow-petalled flowers, 1 in. across, are sparingly borne in clusters of up to three in the upper leaf axils from May to October.

The form 'Variegatum' has foliage margined with cream-white.

P. × domesticum: see REGAL PELARGONIUMS

P. graveolens. S. Africa. Height up to 3 ft. This is a spreading, branching species with palmate, deeply lobed and toothed hoary-green aromatic leaves. Rose-pink flowers, 1 in. across, with a dark purple spot on each of the upper two petals, are carried in five to ten-flowered terminal umbels from June to October.

P. × hortorum: see ZONAL PELARGONIUMS

P. peltatum (ivy-leaved geranium). S. Africa. A trailing species with stems 3 ft or more long. The mid-green fleshy leaves are similar to those of the common ivy. Carmine-pink flowers, up to 1 in. across, are produced in five to seven-flowered umbels from May to October.

Named forms include: 'Blue Peter', mauve; 'La France', double mauve flowers flecked with maroon above; 'L'Elegante', white flowers and cream-edged leaves that turn purple, particularly in autumn; 'Madame Crousse', double, bright pink; 'Sir Percy Blakeney', vigorous, with single crimson flowers.

P. quercifolium (oak-leaved geranium). S. Africa. Height up to 3 ft. This erect, well-branched shrub

Pelargonium 'Carisbrooke' (Regal)

Pelargonium 'Black Knight' (Regal)

Pelargonium Irene 'Electra' (Zonal)

A number of seed strains are now available, of which Carefree can be recommended. This strain includes 'White', 'Bright Pink', 'Deep Salmon' and 'Scarlet', and is also obtainable as a mixed colour range.

Foliage varieties, with flowers chiefly in shades of pink or red, include: 'Caroline Schmidt', green and pale yellow leaves; 'Flower of Spring', margined with white; 'Golden Harry Hieover', golden-flushed; 'Henry Cox', leaves splashed and zoned with maroon, red, green and cream.

Miniature varieties (6–12 in. high) are: 'Red Black Vesuvius', leaves heavily flushed with black-purple, bright scarlet flowers; 'Carolyne', clear pale pink flowers and dark green foliage; 'Dick's White', double white flowers; 'Mme Salleron', leaves flushed with silvery-white.

Cultivation. Grow pelargoniums in 4–6 in. pots of John Innes potting compost No. 2. Maintain a winter temperature of 7–10°C (45–50°F), and keep the plants just moist. Water freely during the growing period; if kept in the greenhouse ventilate freely when the temperature exceeds 13°C (55°F), and give light shade during the hottest months.

Alternatively, plant out pelargoniums from late May onwards in bedding schemes, setting them in ordinary, well-drained garden soil and in full sun. In October, overwinter young plants raised from cuttings or cut back older plants and pot up in John Innes potting compost No. 2.

Plant *P. tomentosum* in the greenhouse border and train the stems up canes, strings or wires.

Zonal pelargoniums may be trained as standards or half-standards from cuttings taken in July. Keep the plants growing through the winter,

pinching out all laterals to three or four leaves above the desired stem height. Thereafter, pinch the growing tip out to create the branching head, subsequently pinching out the laterals when these have made three or four leaves.

Repot or pot on annually in March, and give a weak liquid feed at intervals of ten days from May to September.

Propagation. Take 3 in. long tip cuttings in July for standards, in September for large bush types. Smaller plants can be obtained from cuttings taken from the overwintered plants in March. Insert the cuttings individually in 2½ in. pots of equal parts (by volume) peat and sand or in John Innes seed compost on the open greenhouse bench, covered with paper, for seven to ten days. When rooted, pot the cuttings on as necessary.

Pinch out the growing tips of plants grown as bushes when about 6 in. high.

Alternatively, sow seeds in February in pots or pans of seed compost at a temperature of 16–18°C (61–64°F). Prick out the seedlings into boxes, later transferring to 4 in. pots of John Innes potting compost No. 2.

Pruning. Mature bushy plants grown in the greenhouse may be cut back by one-third or a half in March. Bedding plants, lifted in October for overwintering, should have the upper third of all growths removed before potting up.

Pests. GLASSHOUSE LEAFHOPPERS feed on the leaves and cause conspicuous white flecks.

GLASSHOUSE WHITEFLIES form colonies of small green scales on the undersides of leaves; small white adults fly off when the plants are disturbed.

Grubs of the VINE or CLAY-COLOURED WEEVILS may feed on the roots.

Pelargonium 'Nomad' (Regal)

Pelargonium 'Gustav Emich' (Zonal)

509

Pelargonium 'Golden Harry Hieover' (Zonal)

Pelargonium Carefree (Zonal)

Pennisetum setaceum

Diseases. Cuttings, and sometimes older plants, are destroyed by BLACK LEG which causes a blackening and softening of the stem bases.

BLACK ROOT ROT results in rotting of the roots, which turn black; the foliage becomes discoloured and the leaves may fall prematurely.

GREY MOULD causes cuttings, or even leaves of mature plants, to decay; the affected tissues are covered with a solid grey-brown mass of fungus spores.

LEAFY GALL shows as a mass of abortive and often fasciated shoots at ground level.

OEDEMA is frequent, particularly on *P. peltatum*; it shows on stems and leaves, first as water-soaked spots which break out into small, corky growths. Later, these may burst and appear as blisters full of white powder.

PHYSIOLOGICAL DISORDERS result in discoloration of the foliage; cold night temperatures cause a reddening of the tissues; and too dry soil conditions show as brown blotches on the leaves, which may turn yellow.

RUST shows on the undersurfaces of leaves as brown, powdery, ring-like spore masses.

A VIRUS DISEASE shows as pale chlorotic spots, often in the form of rings, on the leaves which frequently become crinkled and puckered.

Pennisetum

Gramineae

PENNISETUM ORIENTALE

A genus of 130 species of half-hardy perennial grasses with bottle-brush-like flower heads. They are grown in mixed borders for their ornamental value, and are suitable for flower arrangements or in the dried state for winter decoration.

P. alopecuroides. Argentina. Height 3 ft; planting distance 24 in. This long-lived species with its grey-green narrow leaves, up to 18 in. long, forms a tight dense clump. Feathery tawny-yellow plumes, 2–8 in. long, are produced in September and October. The species is most effective when grown as a specimen plant.

P. longistylum: see *P. villosum*

P. orientale. Abyssinia. Height and planting distance up to 12 in. A perennial species best grown as an annual. It has narrow, blue-grey, slightly hairy leaves. The bristly, brown-green flower spikes, 2–5 in. long, appear from July to October; they take on a bronze hue in autumn.

P. ruppelii: see *P. setaceum*

P. setaceum, syn. *P. ruppelii* (fountain grass). Tropical Africa, Arabia and S.W. Asia. Height 2–3 ft; planting distance 18 in. This half-hardy perennial grass produces tufts of mid-green, rough-textured, linear leaves. Stiff slender stems bear narrow feathery heads, up to 12 in. long, composed of numerous silky spikelets. They are cream-green in colour,

Pelargonium 'Du Barry' (Zonal)

often tinged with purple, and appear from July to September.

P. villosum, syn. *P. longistylum*. Abyssinia. Height 18–24 in.; planting distance 12 in. A perennial species, grown as an annual. The narrow, arching, mid-green leaves are borne on slender hairy stems. Terminal white or purple flower spikes, up to 4½ in. long, are produced in June and July.

Cultivation. Plant in April in ordinary, well-drained garden soil and in a sunny sheltered position. Plumes wanted for winter decoration should be cut and hung up to dry in a cool, airy place when fully developed.

None of the species are hardy except in warm, sheltered areas, and even then they usually require winter protection. The plants should be mounded with bracken, coarse sand or weathered ashes. In colder areas, lift the plants in late October, place in pots of John Innes potting compost No. 1 and overwinter in a cool greenhouse. Plant out the following April or May when the danger of frost is past.

Propagation. Divide and replant the roots of perennial species in April.

Annual species are increased by seeds sown in March or April, in pots or pans of John Innes seed compost. Germinate under glass at a temperature of 15–17°C (59–63°F). Prick off the seedlings, when large enough to handle, into boxes of John Innes potting compost No. 1; plant out in May when danger of frost is over.

Pests and diseases. Generally trouble-free.

Penstemon

Scrophulariaceae

A genus of 250 species of hardy and half-hardy herbaceous perennials and sub-shrubs. The hardy alpine species described are suitable for rock gardens or the front of borders; half-hardy tall border plants may survive severe winters under suitably sheltered and well-drained conditions, but they are usually grown as annuals. The genus is short-lived and intolerant of wet conditions.

Penstemons have snapdragon-like, open-mouthed flowers, borne in racemes.

ALPINE SPECIES

P. davidsonii. California. Height 3 in.; spread 9 in. or more. A low-spreading sub-shrub with small, broadly obovate, mid-green leaves. Ruby-red flowers, 1–1¼ in. long, are borne in short racemes during May and June.

P. heterophyllus. California. Height and spread up to 18 in. This species has narrowly lanceolate grey-green leaves on sturdy, woody-based stems. Blue, often pink-flushed flowers, 1 in. long, are borne in spike-like racemes during June and July. 'True Blue' is a pure blue variety.

P. menziesii. N.W. United States. Height 9 in. or more; spread 15 in. or more. A semi-erect sub-shrub with mid-green, obovate to oblong-ovate leaves. Racemes of pale violet-purple flowers, 1–1½ in. long, appear in June.

P. newberryi. W. United States. This species closely resembles *P. menziesii*, but has ovate leaves and pink or rose-purple flowers.

P. pinifolius. S.W. United States. Height 6–9 in.; spread 9–12 in. A distinctive sub-shrub with small linear to narrowly lanceolate grey-green leaves. The ½–¾ in. long orange-red flowers are narrowly tubular; they are borne in short terminal racemes from June to September.

P. roezlii. W. United States. Height 4–9 in.; spread 12 in. or more. This spreading sub-shrub has narrowly lanceolate mid-green leaves. The lavender to violet-blue flowers are ¾ in. long and borne in terminal panicles during July.

P. rupicola. Washington State. Height 3–4 in.; spread 12 in. A prostrate sub-shrub with mid-green ovate leaves. Rose-carmine, 1 in. long flowers are borne in short racemes during May.

P. scouleri. N.W. United States. Height up to 12 in.; spread 18 in. This species is similar to *P. menziesii*, but has lanceolate mid-green leaves and rose-purple flowers borne in June and July.

BORDER SPECIES

P. barbatus, syn. *Chelone barbata*. Colorado. Height 3 ft; planting distance 24 in. The leaves are lanceolate and mid-green; the 1 in. long flowers, produced from June to August, vary from pink to carmine. Lighter and darker-flowered forms exist, and also a form with white flowers.

P. × gloxinioides: see *P. hartwegii*

PENSTEMON HARTWEGII

P. hartwegii. Mexico. Height 24 in.; planting distance 12–18 in. A species with lanceolate to ovate-lanceolate mid-green leaves. Drooping, 2 in. long, scarlet or blood-red flowers appear in June and July. The species is rare, but is an important parent of the race of garden hybrids known as *P. × gloxinioides*. These are not fully hardy and are chiefly used as bedding plants. Recommended varieties include: 'Garnet', deep red; 'King George', crimson-scarlet, banded with white in the throat; 'Myddleton Gem', light crimson; 'Pennington Gem', cerise-crimson, with full white throat; and 'Schonholzeri', syn. 'Firebird', scarlet. All have flowers 1½–2 in. long.

P. ovatus. U.S.A. Height and planting distance 18 in. A species with a sub-shrubby base that will last three or four years without attention. The mid-green, ovate to ovate-lanceolate leaves are often sharply toothed. Purple flowers, ¾ in. long, appear in July. 'Alba' is a white form.

Cultivation of alpine species. Plant from October to March in any ordinary, well-drained garden soil and in full sun. No winter protection is necessary for these hardy plants.

Cultivation of border species. All species do well in any ordinary, well-drained garden soil and in a sunny position. Plant in March and April. If grown as perennials, cut the plants down to just above ground level in October and protect them with cloches during winter.

Propagation of alpine species. Take 1½–2½ in. cuttings of non-flowering side-shoots in July or August; insert in equal parts (by volume) peat and sand in a cold frame. Pot the rooted cuttings individually into 3 in. containers of John Innes potting compost No. 1 and overwinter in a cold frame. Plant out the following April or May.

Sow seeds in pans or boxes of seed compost in a cold frame, during March or April. When the seedlings are large enough to handle, prick them out into boxes, then individually into 3 in. pots of John Innes potting compost No. 1 and plunge outdoors until the autumn when they can be planted in the flowering sites.

Propagation of border species. Take 3 in. long cuttings of non-flowering lateral shoots during August or September, and insert them 3–4 in. apart in a mixture of 2 parts loam, 1 part peat and 1 part sand (parts by volume), in a cold frame. Plant out the rooted cuttings in their permanent positions the following April or May.

Named varieties do not come true from seeds, but good mixed seed is available. Sow under glass during February or March, in boxes or pans of seed compost at a temperature of 13–18°C (55–64°F). Prick out the seedlings into boxes, when they are large enough to handle, and harden them off in a cold frame before planting out in permanent positions in May.

Pests and diseases. Generally trouble-free.

Peony: see Paeonia

Peperomia

Piperaceae

A genus of more than 1000 species of evergreen tufted and climbing plants. Many of these have attractive foliage, and they are popular and easily grown as house plants or used in bottle gardens. Small white or yellow flowers are borne in short spikes, like mice tails; in a few species the flowers are ornamental.

P. argyreia, syn. *P. sandersii*. Brazil. Height and spread 6–9 in. The leaves of this species are thick and smooth, broadly ovate, and up to 4 in. long; the main colour is silver-grey, but with dark green bands along the principal veins. The leaf stalks are usually red.

Penstemon newberryi

Penstemon hartwegii 'King George'

Penstemon hartwegii 'Pennington Gem'

Peperomia caperata

Peperomia hederaefolia

Peperomia magnoliaefolia
'Green Gold'

Pereskia aculeata

P. caperata. Tropical America. Height 3–10 in.; spread 5–6 in. Numerous heart-shaped leaves with deeply corrugated surfaces arise from a central growing point. They rarely exceed a length of 1¼ in. and are dark green with a purple tinge in the valleys of the corrugation and a grey sheen on the peaks. The leaf stalks are pale pink. Pure white flower spikes, 5–6 in. high, which appear from April to December, are often branched, giving them an antler-like appearance.

P. hederaefolia. Brazil. Height about 6 in.; spread 6–8 in. Similar to *P. caperata*, with leaves up to 2½ in. long. The main colour is olive-grey and the principal veins are marked in dark green. The leaf surface undulates to give a quilted effect.

P. magnoliaefolia. San Domingo. Height 6 in.; spread 9 in. or more. A branched shrubby plant with ovate, glossy, mid-green leaves, 2 in. long. The type plant is seldom grown, but two variegated forms are available. The variety 'Variegata' is almost entirely cream-coloured when young; as the leaves mature, the cream variegation becomes light green. The stems are red at first, changing to green with red spots as the plant matures. 'Green Gold' has larger leaves with wide cream margins; much of the cream is retained in mature leaves.

P. obtusifolia. Tropical S. America. Height 6–8 in.; spread 12 in. One of the hardiest species. It is a much-branched plant with purple stems; the thick fleshy leaves, 4–6 in. long, are broadly ovate or rounded and dark green with purple edges. Numerous white flower spikes, up to 2 in. long, are produced from June to September.

P. sandersii: see *P. argyreia*

P. scandens. S. America. Height up to 4 or 5 ft. Only the variegated form is commercially available. This is a climbing or trailing plant; the shoots, up to 5 ft long, can be trained upwards, when they will spread up to 12 in., or be allowed to hang. The leaves are heart-shaped and about 2 in. long; they are almost entirely cream when young, but become pale green with a cream margin in maturity. The main stems are pale green, and the leaf stalks pale pink.

Cultivation. Peperomias have a small root system, and in the wild are practically epiphytic. Plant in John Innes potting compost No. 1 or in a proprietary soil-less compost. They seldom need pots larger than 3½ in., but *P. obtusifolia* and *P. scandens* may eventually need 6 in. pots.

During winter, keep the plants almost dry at a temperature of 10°C (50°F), although for *P. argyreia* and *P. scandens* a temperature of 13°C (55°F) or more is preferable.

Peperomias should never be over-watered; allow the compost to dry out between waterings, in summer and winter, but provide a humid atmosphere from April to September and syringe the leaves twice daily in hot weather. During spring and summer, give moderate shading; in winter they require as much light as possible. In the home, place the plants in a well-lit position that does not receive much direct sunlight, and plunge the pots in a moisture-retentive material.

Repot mature plants annually in April. An occasional feed, once a month, from May to September, is beneficial.

P. scandens is difficult in its early stages; excessive damp during cold periods frequently leads to leaf-drop, but established plants are easier to maintain. Use tepid water for any watering that may be necessary during the winter; a temperature of 16°C (61°F) is satisfactory. This species may be grown as a trailing plant in a hanging basket or trained up a trellis inserted in the pot. Let the plants have fresh air during warm spells and, if possible, keep the air circulating.

Propagation. Increase all species by cuttings, taken between April and August; insert in pots of equal parts (by volume) peat and sand at a temperature of 18°C (64°F) to root.

P. magnoliaefolia, P. obtusifolia and *P. scandens* are propagated by stem cuttings, which should be about 3 in. long. Take leaf cuttings of newly matured leaves of *P. caperata* and *P. hederaefolia* and insert the stalks shallowly in the propagating compost.

Take leaf cuttings of *P. argyreia*; use either the whole leaf or cut the leaf into four squares and insert the cut edges in the compost. Young plantlets will appear at the ends of the main veins.

Pruning. Pinch out the growing points of species with upright stems, such as *P. magnoliaefolia, P. obtusifolia* and *P. scandens,* in early summer to encourage bushy growth.

Pests. Generally trouble-free.

Diseases. OEDEMA is fairly frequent and shows on the leaves, first as water-soaked spots that break out into small wart-like growths. Later, these may burst open and then have a blister-like or white powdery appearance.

Pepper, green: see *Capsicum annuum*
Pepper, red: see *Capsicum annuum*
Peppermint, Mount Wellington: see *Eucalyptus coccifera*

Pereskia

Cactaceae

PERESKIA ACULEATA

A genus of 20 species of greenhouse perennials. These are non-succulent, shrubby cacti with erect or rambling stems and branches covered with spines. Only one species is in general cultivation in Great Britain.

See also CACTUS.

P. aculeata (Barbados gooseberry). Florida, W. Indies, Mexico, Argentina. Height up to 30 ft. This semi-evergreen, rambling shrub has green climbing stems. The young branches bear one to three recurved prickles beneath each leaf which enable the young growths to cling to supports. On older branches numerous straight spines develop from the areoles in the leaf axils.

The ovate mid-green leaves appear in spring and sometimes fall in late autumn. White, pale yellow or pink scented flowers open in October. They are saucer-shaped and 1–1½ in. across.

Cultivation. Grow this woody climber in a soil consisting of 5 parts loam, 2 parts leaf-mould and 1 part sand (parts by volume), with 1 oz. bone-meal and 2 oz. charcoal added to each 1 gal. bucket of soil. Plant in March or April in an 8–10 in. pot and place in a sunny situation. It may also be planted out in the greenhouse border where it will make rampant growth. Wire, cane or string supports are necessary. A minimum winter temperature of 10°C (50°F) is required.

Give plenty of water during the growing season. When the leaves have fallen, give just enough water to prevent the stems from shrivelling. Growing pereskias in pots restricts their size; when a plant has filled its pot with roots, pot on at the beginning of the growing season.

Propagation. Sow seeds in spring at a temperature of 21°C (70°F). Take cuttings of semi-ripe shoots in summer. Insert the cuttings in equal parts (by volume) peat and sand; pot up, when rooted, in the growing compost.

Pruning. After leaf-fall, cut back all side-growths to 1 in. from the main stems.

Pests. Infestations of MEALY BUGS produce conspicuous tufts of white waxy wool on the plants.

Diseases. Generally trouble-free.

Perilla
Labiatae

A genus of between four and six species of annual plants. The one described is grown for its attractive leaves, and as a specimen plant in formal beds where its dark foliage contrasts with bright summer flowers. It can also be grown in pots under glass.

P. frutescens, syn. *P. nankinensis*. China. Height 24 in.; planting distance 12 in. A half-hardy annual with strong, rather coarse growths. The red-purple leaves are ovate, pointed and deeply toothed, and have a spicy smell when bruised. White flowers, ¼ in. across, appear in 4 in. spikes in July and August. The variety 'Foliis Atropurpurea Laciniata' is particularly attractive, having crumpled, deeply cut leaves.

P. nankinensis: see *P. frutescens*

Cultivation. Any well-cultivated soil in an open sunny site will give good results. Pinch out the growing tips of young plants when they are 4 in. high. Under glass, grow the plants in 5–6 in. pots of John Innes potting compost No. 2.

Propagation. Sow seeds during February or March, in pots or pans of seed compost at a temperature of 18°C (64°F). Prick off the seedlings, when large enough to handle, into boxes. Pot as required, or harden off outdoor plants in a cold frame before planting out in May.

Pests and diseases. Generally trouble-free.

Peristrophe
Acanthaceae

A genus of 30 species of greenhouse perennials and sub-shrubs. Only one species is in general cultivation; this is an attractive winter-flowering plant for a cool greenhouse.

P. speciosa India. Height and spread up to 24 in. An evergreen sub-shrub usually raised annually from cuttings. It has ash-grey stems and elliptic mid-green leaves about 4 in. long. The narrow tubular flowers, about 1½ in. long, are produced in clusters from the upper leaf axils, and form large terminal corymbs. They are purple-violet and appear from October to February.

PERISTROPHE SPECIOSA

Cultivation. Grow in John Innes potting compost No. 3. The plants require a winter temperature of 10–13°C (50–55°F); in early spring this should be gradually increased to 21°C (70°F).

Ventilate the greenhouse freely in summer, and water copiously from April to August, moderately from September to March. In warm months, syringe the plants regularly once a day, and provide only light shading from the sun.

Plants raised from cuttings, taken in April, should be potted on successively and finished off in 6 in. pots. Pinch out the growing points two or three times during the growing season to promote bushy growth; the last stopping should be in July. Feed the plants weekly with liquid manure from June to September.

Although the plants are usually discarded after cuttings have been taken in April, they may be grown on, potted into 8–9 in. pots.

Propagation. Take cuttings, 3 in. long, from lateral shoots in April and insert individually in 2½ in. pots containing a mixture of equal parts (by volume) peat and sand, at a bottom heat of 16–18°C (61–64°F). When rooted, pot on the cuttings as described under CULTIVATION.

Pruning. After flowering, usually in February, cut back all growths to 6 in. above soil level to provide young lateral shoots for propagation.

Pests and diseases. Generally trouble-free.

Periwinkle, greater: see *Vinca major*
Periwinkle, lesser: see *Vinca minor*

Pernettya
Ericaceae

PERNETTYA MUCRONATA

A genus of 20 species of hardy, low-growing evergreen shrubs, useful as ground cover in sun or shade. Only one species is in cultivation; it is grown for its colourful fruits. The fruiting branches may be used for winter decoration.

Perilla frutescens

Peristrophe speciosa

Pernettya mucronata (flowers)

Pernettya mucronata (fruits)

Perovskia atriplicifolia 'Blue Spire'

Petunia 'Apple Blossom'

Petunia 'Brass Band'

P. mucronata. S. America. Height and spread 2–3 ft, reaching 5 ft in shade. A species of dense habit when young, becoming leggy with age. The small, sharp-pointed, glossy dark green leaves thickly clothe the erect, often red stems. White heath-like flowers, $\frac{1}{8}$ in. long, are borne in abundance from the leaf axils in late May and early June. Clusters of globular fruits, varying in colour from white through pink and rose to purple and red, are produced in autumn and last throughout the winter. The species is unisexual, and male and female plants must be grown together to ensure fruiting.

There are numerous named forms which include the following: 'Alba', white fruits; 'Atrococcinea', red-purple fruits; 'Bell's Seedling', bright cherry-red fruits; 'Lilacina', lilac fruits; 'Rosea', pink fruits; 'Thymifolia' (height 9–12 in., spread 2–3 ft), a male form of neat habit with tiny, ovate, glossy dark green leaves.

Cultivation. Plant pernettyas in a lime-free soil, preferably in moist peaty loam, at any time between September and May. They are adaptable to shade, but are more compact and fruitful in full sun. Set the plants in groups of three or five to assist pollination and to ensure fruiting; alternatively plant a proven male form, such as *P. m.* 'Thymifolia' with a female form or forms.

Propagation. Named varieties do not come true from seeds and should be increased by cuttings, 2 in. long, taken in September or October. Insert the cuttings in equal parts (by volume) peat and sand in a cold frame. Pot the rooted cuttings in 3 in. pots of John Innes lime-free potting compost No. 1 and plunge outdoors. Line out in nursery rows for a further one or two years before planting out in permanent positions.

The species is easily raised from seeds, and in suitable situations will seed itself freely. Sow seeds of *P. mucronata* in October in a lime-free seed compost in a cold frame. Prick off the seedlings, when large enough to handle, into boxes and later into nursery beds. Grow on for two years before planting out in September.

Pruning. No regular pruning is required. Old plants tend to grow tall and leggy and can be cut back hard into the old wood in late winter or early spring. This will encourage new growths.

Pests and diseases. Generally trouble-free.

Perovskia

Labiatae

PEROVSKIA ATRIPLICIFOLIA

A genus of seven species of hardy shrubby perennials. Only one species is in general cultivation; it is suitable for chalky soils and thrives especially in maritime areas.

P. atriplicifolia. Afghanistan to Tibet. Height 3–5 ft; planting distance 18 in. This herbaceous border plant has grey-green rhomboidal to slightly obovate leaves, which are coarsely toothed and smell of sage. In August and September it produces tubular, two-lipped, violet-blue flowers, $\frac{1}{3}$ in. long, which are borne in panicles up to 12 in. long.

'Blue Mist' has light blue flowers in 12–18 in. long panicles, a few weeks earlier than the species; 'Blue Spire' has deep violet-blue flowers.

Cultivation. Plant from November to March, except in frosty weather, in a sunny position in any well-drained light soil. Leave the old stems during winter, then cut down to 12–18 in. above ground level in spring.

Propagation. Take 3 in. long cuttings of lateral shoots with a heel in July; root the cuttings in equal parts (by volume) peat and sand in a cold frame. Pot the rooted cuttings in 3 in. pots of John Innes potting compost No. 1 and overwinter in a cold frame. Plant in permanent sites in March.

Pests and diseases. Generally trouble-free.

Petroselinum crispum: see Parsley
Petroselinum sativum: see Parsley

Petunia

Solanaceae

PETUNIA HYBRIDA NANA COMPACTA

A genus of 40 species of annual or perennial herbaceous plants. Most of the petunias now grown are garden hybrids; they are half-hardy perennials which flower the first season from seed and are usually grown as half-hardy annuals. These popular plants are also used for edging beds, in window-boxes, tubs and hanging baskets and for pot culture under glass.

P. hybrida. Garden hybrid. Height 9–15 in., planting distance 12 in. Numerous garden varieties are listed under this name. These are colourful, somewhat sticky plants with ovate, mid to dark green leaves. The trumpet-shaped flowers, which open from June until the first severe autumn frosts, are 2–5 in. across in both the single and double forms. Colours include cream, white, pink, red, mauve and blue; a number of bicoloured forms are also available. The F_1 hybrids are rather more expensive, but produce more vigorous and uniform plants.

The varieties fall into four main groups:

The first group, Multiflora, consists of bushy plants, 6–12 in. high, bearing large numbers of comparatively small flowers, 2 in. across. 'Single Mixed' is the most widely grown strain.

Several F_1 varieties are available, including 'Plum Crazy', a mixture of pink, lavender, purple and yellow, variously veined and centred with darker shades. Single colour F_1 varieties include: 'Apple Blossom', pale pink; 'Brass Band', deep cream; 'Dream Girl', deep rose to

Petunia 'Plum Crazy'

Petunia 'Dream Girl'

Petunia 'Sugar Plum'

Petunia 'Cascade'

Petunia 'Pan American All Double Mixed'

pink; 'Polaris', deep blue with white star; 'Red Satin', vivid scarlet; and 'Sugar Plum', orchid-pink with mauve veining.

All these varieties are weather resistant, as are the F_1 doubles in this group which includes 'Cherry Tart', with carnation-like flowers of cherry-pink and white, and a mixture.

The second group, Grandiflora, are plants of similar size but with fewer and larger flowers, 3–4 in. across. These tend to be less weather-resistant, however, and may spot badly after rain. 'Cascade', an F_1 variety, available as a mixture and in red, pink, white and blue, is strongly recommended. 'Fluffy Ruffles' has large flowers, elaborately ruffled and frilled, in shades of crimson, pink, lavender, purple and white, veined with darker shades. 'Superbissima Mixed' is the largest of all the petunias, with 5 in. wide flowers that have deeply ruffled petals and veined throat markings. The double form 'Pan American All Double Mixed' also has large ruffled flowers.

The third group, Nana Compacta, contains dwarf varieties, 6 in. high, with 2 in. flowers; it includes many established strains. The mixtures are popular; separate colours include 'Alderman', indigo-violet; 'Blue Bedder', blue; 'Fire Chief', scarlet; and 'Rose of Heaven', pink.

The fourth group, Pendula varieties, are plants of long trailing habit. They may be used as summer ground cover (height 6 in., spread 2–3 ft), or in tubs and hanging baskets. The flowers are 2 in. across and are available in the same colours as the third group, excluding red. 'Balcony Blended Mixed' is a popular strain.

Cultivation. Grow in light, well-drained soil in a sheltered, sunny site. An over-rich soil, or excessive shade and moisture, encourages leaf growth at the expense of flowers. The flowers are also damaged by wind and heavy rain; for exposed beds choose weather-resistant varieties. Dead-head the plants regularly.

To grow petunias in pots for flowering from May onwards under glass, transplant the seedlings into $3\frac{1}{2}$ in. pots and subsequently move to a final 5 in. pot, using John Innes potting compost No. 1 at both stages.

Propagation. Sow the seeds under glass in March at a temperature of 15°C (59°F) and prick off the seedlings into seed boxes. Harden off outdoor plants in a cold frame before planting them out in late May or early June.

Pests. The leaves and stems of young plants may be infested with APHIDS, checking growth.

Diseases. Several different VIRUS DISEASES, including CUCUMBER MOSAIC VIRUS and TOMATO SPOTTED WILT VIRUS, can infect petunias. Plants may be severely stunted; the leaves are usually distorted and show either mottling or browning of the veins, or brown rings. Flowering may be reduced and blooms only partially developed, or they may open normally but be mottled with streaks.

FOOT ROT and ROOT ROT can be due to several different fungi, including RHIZOCTONIA. The plants wilt or collapse completely, often just as they are about to flower.

Peucedanum graveolens: see Dill

Phacelia

Hydrophyllaceae

A genus of 200 species of annuals. Those described are suitable for borders, for edging beds and for growing in pots under glass. The blue flowers are attractive to bees.

Phacelia campanularia

Phacelia tanacetifolia

Phalaenopsis amabilis

Phalaenopsis lueddemanniana

P. campanularia. California. Height 9 in.; spacing 6 in. A hardy annual of dwarf, bushy habit which makes a showy border plant or an early spring-flowering pot plant for a cold greenhouse. Branching stems carry dark green, ovate, irregularly toothed leaves which are fragrant when crushed. The bell-shaped flowers are upturned, and 1 in. across. They are gentian-blue in colour and produced from June to September.

PHACELIA CAMPANULARIA

P. tanacetifolia. California. Height to over 24 in.; spacing 12 in. A hardy annual with erect stems and finely cut dark green leaves. Crowded spikes of lavender coloured bell-shaped flowers, $\frac{1}{3}$ in. long, appear in July. The whole plant is hairy.

P. viscida, syn. *Eutoca viscida.* California. Height to over 24 in.; spacing 9 in. A hardy annual of upright habit. The pale green leaves are almost heart-shaped, deeply cut around the margin, and smell of formalin when crushed. Spikes, 4–8 in. long, of vivid blue bell-shaped flowers are produced in July. The flowers, 1 in. across, have white centres, speckled with blue, and contrasting white stamens.

Cultivation. These plants will grow on most well-cultivated ground, but for the best results *P. campanularia* requires a well-drained sandy soil, the other two species a damper, heavier soil. All are best in a sunny situation. September-sown plants require cloche protection during the winter. Tall plants need staking.

To grow *P. campanularia* under glass, plant in $3\frac{1}{2}$ in. pots of John Innes potting compost No. 1. In October, move to final 5 in. pots and overwinter in a cold greenhouse.

Propagation. Sow the seeds in the flowering site in March or April, just covering them, and thin out the seedlings to the required spacing. A September sowing in a sheltered site produces earlier-flowering plants and is also best for seedlings to be grown on as pot plants.

Pests. Seedlings are often eaten by SLUGS.

Diseases. Generally trouble-free.

Phalaenopsis

Moth orchid. *Orchidaceae*

PHALAENOPSIS LUEDDEMANNIANA

A genus of about 35 species of epiphytic evergreen orchids, distributed from India and Indonesia to the Philippines, New Guinea and northern Australia. These plants lack pseudo-bulbs and have instead a short rhizome with two rows of large, broad, succulent leaves, densely arranged; they are oblong-lanceolate to shortly strap-shaped and generally mid-green in colour. The aerial roots are long and cling tightly to the sides of the pot or basket.

The inflorescences are lateral and may be short or long, erect or pendulous. They are sometimes branched and vary in shape from moth-like to the typical orchid flower. Some of the flowers are excellent for cutting and are long-lasting. Many beautiful hybrids have been produced. These orchids are easy to grow in a warm, humid greenhouse; they require a resting period during the winter months.

See also ORCHIDS.

P. amabilis. Malesia. The large leaves of this species are arranged on a 1 in. high stem. One or more arching, sometimes branched flower stems, up to $2\frac{1}{2}$ ft long, bear up to 15 flowers, each nearly 4 in. across. The flowers, which appear from October to January have white waxy sepals and petals, the latter being broad and spread flat. The lip is white with large side-lobes which are yellow at the base and red-spotted; the mid-lobe is spear-shaped and ends in two long, backward-curving tendrils.

P. equestris: see *P. rosea*

P. lueddemanniana. Philippines. This species has a 6 in. high stem. The pendulous flower spike, up to 24 in. long, bears a few flowers in May and June. They are 2 in. across and have white sepals and petals marked with bars of amethyst on the lower halves and with cinnamon-brown bars above. The lip is white with narrow side-lobes and a bright amethyst-purple mid-lobe which has a paler margin.

P. rosea, syn. *P. equestris.* Philippines. The bright green leaves are up to 8 in. long. The flower stem, up to 24 in. high is branched with many brightly coloured flowers, $1\frac{1}{2}$ in. across. They have white sepals and petals that are flushed with rose; the side-lobes of the lip are a light rose-purple with darker streaks, and the mid-lobe is bright rose-purple, brown at the base. The flowers are produced at various times of the year, but usually between February and October.

Cultivation. These orchids grow best tied to rafts of wood or osmunda fibre. Alternatively, plant in wooden baskets which should be almost filled with a mixture of 2 parts osmunda fibre and 1 part sphagnum moss (parts by volume).

Keep the greenhouse warm and humid; the minimum winter temperature should be 16°C (61°F). Water frequently during the growing season and feed monthly with liquid manure in spring and summer. Shade the greenhouse from direct sunlight and ventilate on mild days from April to October. No shading is needed during the winter resting period from November to March; the compost should be kept just moist during this period.

Repot every two or three years in May.

Propagation. In May, divide the plants and pot up in the growing compost. Keep the new plants well shaded and water sparingly until new roots appear; they may then be moved to a less shaded position and watered regularly.

Pests and diseases. Generally trouble-free.

Phalaris

Gramineae

PHALARIS ARUNDINACEA

A genus of 20 species of hardy annual and perennial ornamental grasses. The perennial species described here spreads rapidly from a creeping rhizome and is suitable for growing only where the spread can be confined.

P. arundinacea. Northern Hemisphere, including Great Britain. In cultivation, this species is generally represented by *P. a* 'Picta' (gardener's garters). Height and planting distance 24 in. This variety has narrow leaf blades, variegated with cream and bright green longitudinal stripes. Numerous insignificant green or purple flower panicles are produced in June and July.

Cultivation. Plant from October to April in ordinary, well-drained garden soil and in a sunny or partially shaded position. Restrict the spreading rhizomes by replanting every two or three years.

Propagation. Divide and replant the roots from October to April during suitable weather.

Pests and diseases. Generally trouble-free.

Phaseolus multiflorus: see Beans (runner)
Phaseolus vulgaris: see Beans (French)

Philadelphus

Mock orange.
Philadelphaceae, syn. *Saxifragaceae*

PHILADELPHUS × LEMOINEI

A genus of 75 species of hardy deciduous flowering shrubs, often erroneously called *Syringa*. These popular free-flowering plants, which are easily grown, have ovate, mid-green, prominently veined leaves. The white, cup-shaped flowers, which open in June and July, are $\frac{3}{4}$–2 in. across and have a strong fragrance reminiscent of orange blossom.

P. coronarius. N. and Central Italy, Austria, Rumania. Height 6–9 ft; spread 6–8 ft. This dense, bushy shrub is particularly suitable for dry soils. The young foliage of 'Aureus' is bright golden-yellow, becoming green-yellow in summer. This variety retains its colour best when grown in shade or semi-shade.

P. × lemoinei. Height up to 6 ft; spread 4–5 ft. This hybrid between *P. coronarius* and *P.*

microphyllus has leaves that are slightly hairy.
P. microphyllus. S.W. United States. Height and spread 2–3 ft. This neat shrub, with pointed ovate leaves, is suitable for rock gardens. It bears fragrant 1 in. wide flowers either singly or in groups of two or three.

Philadelphus 'Belle Etoile'

In addition to these species there are numerous named hybrids, including the following:

'Avalanche'. Height 3–5 ft; spread 4–6 ft. A loose-growing shrub, whose arching branches bear an abundance of single flowers. 'Beauclerk'. Height 6–8 ft; spread 5–6 ft. The single broad-petalled flowers are milk-white with a light maroon-cerise blotch. 'Belle Etoile'. Height 8–10 ft; spread 10–12 ft. This has single white flowers with faint purple blotches at the base of the petals. 'Burfordiensis'. Height 8–10 ft; spread 10–12 ft. The single white flowers have a prominent boss of yellow stamens.

'Etoile Rose'. Height 5–7 ft; spread 5–6 ft. This plant has single flowers with elongated petals which are white with a carmine-rose basal blotch. 'Sybille'. Height 4 ft; spread 3 ft. Single white flowers with purple markings are borne on arching branches. 'Virginal'. Height 8–9 ft; spread 6–8 ft. A shrub with widely expanding double white flowers.

Cultivation. Plant in any ordinary, well-drained garden soil in full sun or partial shade between October and March.

Propagation. Take 4 in. cuttings of half-ripe lateral shoots in July or August and insert them in equal parts (by volume) peat and sand in a cold frame. Set out the rooted cuttings in a nursery bed during the following April or May and transfer them to their permanent positions from October onwards.

Alternatively, take 12 in. hardwood cuttings in October or November and root these in an outdoor nursery bed or sheltered border. Plant out a year later.

Pruning. Thin out old wood after flowering. Take care to retain young shoots, which will flower the following year.

Pests. Generally trouble-free.

Diseases. Circular yellow blotches with darker edges are caused by LEAF SPOT.

Phalaris arundinacea 'Picta'

Philadelphus 'Burfordiensis'

Philadelphus 'Virginal'

Philesia
Liliaceae

A genus of a single species. This is a half-hardy evergreen dwarf flowering shrub. It is related to *Lapageria* and has similar, but much smaller, bell-like rose-red flowers. This shrub is particularly suitable for growing in the south and west, and will succeed in sheltered positions elsewhere.

P. buxifolia: see *P. magellanica*

P. magellanica, syn. *P. buxifolia.* S. Chile. Height 6–24 in.; spread 1–3 ft. The rigid, glossy dark green leaves are alternate and narrowly lanceolate. Narrowly bell-shaped, 2 in. long, waxy flowers hang at the ends of spreading branches in May and June.

Cultivation. Plant in April or May in lime-free, moist, but well-drained soil containing peat or leaf-mould. Choose a site in partial shade. These shrubs require ample lime-free water during the growing season, and should be top-dressed with peat or leaf-mould in April. Philesias are also suitable for growing in semi-shaded frames in pans containing equal parts (by volume) peat, loam, leaf-mould and sand.

Propagation. Remove suckers in April and plant them direct in their flowering positions.

Take 3 in. cuttings of young shoots in July and insert them in equal parts (by volume) peat and sand in a shaded cold frame. When the cuttings have rooted, the following spring, move them into 3 in. pots containing equal parts (by volume) peat, loam, leaf-mould and sand. Grow them on in the frame for a year or two, repotting when necessary, before planting out in April or May.

Pruning. None required.

Pests and diseases. Generally trouble-free.

Philesia magellanica

Philodendron andreanum

Philodendron bipinnatifidum

Philodendron
Araceae

A genus of 275 species of South American evergreen plants, grown in the greenhouse or as house plants. Most of the species are vigorous climbers, producing aerial roots at every node. They are easily grown and are cultivated for their attractive foliage, which in some species differs in the juvenile form from the adult leaves. The heights given below refer to pot-grown house plants; in the greenhouse border the species will greatly exceed these measurements. They rarely flower in cultivation.

P. andreanum, syn. *P. melanochryson.* Colombia. Height up to 6 ft. A climbing plant with pendulous, arrow-shaped leaves up to 24 in. long. They are dark green with a coppery sheen and ivory veins.

The species is rarely seen; the plant listed as *P. melanochryson* is the juvenile form of *P. andreanum.* This form (height 4–6 ft) has heart-shaped leaves up to 6 in. long, with velvety dark green surfaces. The undersides are purple-pink giving a coppery sheen to the leaf below.

P. bipinnatifidum. Brazil. Height up to 4 ft. This is a compact, non-climbing species. The deep green leaves, which all rise from a central growing point, are borne at the ends of long stalks; they

Philodendron erubescens 'Burgundy'

are three-lobed and deeply incised. Mature leaves, which appear after about two years, may be 24 in. long and 18 in. across. The juvenile leaves are entire and heart-shaped.

P. erubescens. Colombia. Height up to 6 ft. A vigorous climber with roots at each leaf joint. The arrowhead-shaped leaves, about 9 in. long, are dark glossy green with a coppery tinge. The stems and leaf stalks are purple and the leaves, when they emerge, are rose-pink. 'Burgundy' has copper-red young foliage.

P. hastatum. Brazil. Height up to 5 ft. This moderately vigorous climber has mid-green entire leaves, 7 in. long, and shaped like a spear-head. They are borne on broad, fleshy leaf stalks.

P. imbe. Brazil. Height up to 6 ft. A vigorous climber with green stems and leaf stalks dotted with purple. The elongated arrowhead-shaped leaves are bright green and up to 12 in. long. It is too vigorous a plant for the home and is best grown in the greenhouse.

P. leichtlinii: see *Monstera leichtlinii*

P. melanochryson: see *P. andreanum*

P. sagittifolium. Mexico, Central America. Height 5 ft. This species is similar to *P. imbe*, but with smaller leaves, and the stems and leaf stalks lack the purple spots. It is a more moderate grower, and is suited for room cultivation.

P. scandens. Panama. Height up to 6 ft. This is the most widely grown species. It is a climber with slender stems and heart-shaped, mid to dark green leaves tapering to long, slender points. It is a hardy, easily-grown species, tolerant of gas and oil fumes.

Cultivation. Grow philodendrons in a proprietary peat compost in 6–10 in. pots depending on the size of plant required.

The plants grow best in a light position, but out of direct sunlight; in the greenhouse, give light shading from April to October. Provide a winter temperature of 13–16°C (55–61°F), although the plants will survive short periods of temperatures 5°C lower.

Keep philodendrons moist throughout the year, watering freely from April to October, sparingly for the rest of the year. They should never be allowed to dry out completely, but over-watering may lead to rotting of the roots.

Provide a humid atmosphere whenever possible; in the greenhouse syringe the leaves twice daily during hot weather; in the home stand the pots on trays of pebbles kept moist.

Pot-grown climbing species require the support of trellis-work or twiggy sticks; in the greenhouse border, train the plants up wires, strings or trellis-work, padded with moss and kept moist at all times.

Repot house plants every second year in April; in the years when the plants are not being repotted, give a liquid feed at fortnightly intervals from May to September.

Propagation. Increase climbing species in May or June by tip cuttings, 4–6 in. long, taken with a mature leaf. Insert the cuttings singly in 3–4 in. pots of peat, and root in a close atmosphere at a temperature of 21–24°C (70–75°F).

Pieces of stem, consisting of one, two or three joints, may be taken in May or June and rooted under the same conditions as tip cuttings.

Non-climbing species can be increased from seeds or by division. Sow seeds in April at a temperature of 24–27°C (75–80°F). When the seedlings are large enough to handle, prick out into boxes, later potting up in 2½–3 in. pots of the growing compost.

For division, remove the growing point in May or June and when lateral shoots are big enough (about 12 months later), split the parent stem so that each lateral shoot has a piece of parent stem attached. Pot the shoots singly in the growing compost; keep the divided plants at a temperature of 24°C (75°F) until well established.

Pruning. No pruning is required, but stop *P. scandens* regularly to encourage lateral growths, or bend it down and secure the tip to the base of the plant. It will ascend again up the support.

Pests. Generally trouble-free.

Diseases. A PHYSIOLOGICAL DISORDER may cause brown or khaki-coloured blotches to develop on the leaves; they turn yellow and fall prematurely.

Phlomis
Labiatae

A genus of more than 100 species of herbaceous perennials and evergreen sub-shrubs and shrubs. They are not all hardy, and only a few are garden-worthy. The hairy foliage is produced in abundance; the upper parts of the stems carry whorls of sparse tubular flowers with hooded upper lips. The following species are suitable for a herbaceous border.

PHLOMIS FRUTICOSA

P. fruticosa (Jerusalem sage). Mediterranean region. Height 3–4 ft; spread 24 in. A shrubby evergreen species with ovate wedge-shaped leaves that are grey-green and woolly. Whorls of

yellow flowers, 1–1¼ in. long, appear in the upper leaf axils in June and July.

P. russelliana: see *P. viscosa*

P. samia. N. Africa. Height 2–3 ft; planting distance 24 in. A true herbaceous perennial species. The almost heart-shaped leaves are mid-green above and grey and hairy beneath. Whorls of 1 in. long cream-yellow flowers, sometimes marked with green and pink inside, appear in May and June.

PHLOMIS VISCOSA

P. viscosa, syn. *P. russelliana*. Syria. Height 2½–4 ft; planting distance 18 in. or more. This herbaceous perennial has large, wrinkled, mid-green basal leaves, broadly ovate-cordate. Tiers of yellow flowers, each 1–1½ in. long, are borne during June and July.

Cultivation. Plant from October to April in a sunny position. Ordinary garden soil suits *P. samia* and *P. viscosa*, but *P. fruticosa* requires a light, well-drained loam. Cut back untidy plants and cut down *P. samia* in October.

Propagation. Sow seeds in April in a cold frame or greenhouse at a temperature of 15–18°C (59–64°F).

Take cuttings in August and September of *P. fruticosa* and insert in equal parts (by volume) peat and sand in a cold frame. Plant out in nursery rows in April for a further year before transplanting to permanent positions in April.

Divide and replant the roots of *P. samia* and *P. viscosa* in October or March.

Pests and diseases. Generally trouble-free.

Phlox
Polemoniaceae

A genus of 66 species of hardy herbaceous perennials, half-hardy and hardy sub-shrubs and annuals. The tall herbaceous perennials and annuals are suitable for mixed borders and for cutting; the annual *P. drummondii* may also be used in bedding schemes or as spring-flowering pot plants under glass. The sub-shrubs and dwarf perennials are mainly evergreen and ideal for rock gardens and dry walls.

The freely borne flowers are basically salver-shaped, sometimes with notched or cleft petals. They are carried in dense clusters and occur in shades of pink, red, purple and white.

In the following descriptions, the species are grouped under alpine, annual and herbaceous border species.

ALPINE SPECIES
P. adsurgens. California, Oregon. Height and spread 12 in. A perennial species with loose tufts of shining, mid-green, ovate leaves. Heads of soft salmon-pink flowers, 1–1½ in. across, are borne during June and July.

Philodendron scandens

Phlomis fruticosa

Phlomis samia

Phlox douglasii 'Mabel'

Phlox adsurgens

Phlox nana ensifolia

Phlox subulata 'Betty'

Phlox maculata 'Alpha'

P. amoena. S.E. United States. Height 9 in.; spread 12 in. This variable perennial species has short tufts of slightly hairy, lanceolate, mid-green leaves. Clusters of rose-purple flowers, about 1 in. across, are produced in May and June. 'Rosea', is a pink form; 'Variegata' has leaves variegated with silver.

P. douglasii. Western N. America. Height 2–4 in.; spread 18 in. A sub-shrubby species which forms a dense prostrate mat of awl-shaped mid-green leaves. Profusely borne pale lavender flowers, $\frac{1}{2}$–$\frac{3}{4}$ in. across, open in May and June.

Recommended garden forms include: 'Boothman's Variety', clear mauve; 'Eva', small, round, pink flowers; 'Mabel', clear lilac-mauve, free-flowering; and 'Snow Queen', pure white.

P. nana. Texas, Mexico. Height 4 in.; spread 6 in. In cultivation, this shrubby species is generally represented by the variety *P. n. ensifolia*. It has linear mid-green leaves and wiry stems carrying small terminal heads of flowers, each about 1 in. across. These are clear pink with a central white zone and appear in May and June.

P. subulata (moss phlox). E. United States. Height 2–4 in.; spread up to 18 in. There are several named forms of this sub-shrubby species. They form spreading mats of mid-green and linear leaves. In April and May, the purple or pink flowers, about $\frac{1}{2}$–$\frac{3}{4}$ in. wide, appear.

Recommended varieties include: 'Apple Blossom', pale pink; 'Bonita', lavender-blue; 'Betty', soft lavender-mauve with a dark eye; 'G. F. Wilson', clear lilac; 'Sensation', deep pink; and 'Temiscaming', brilliant magenta-red.

ANNUAL SPECIES

P. drummondii. Texas. Height 15 in.; planting distance 9 in. A half-hardy annual with erect stems and lanceolate, light green leaves. The flowers are borne in dense heads, 3 in. across, from July to September and are in varying shades of pink, purple, lavender, red and white.

There are three groups of garden varieties: Stellaris, syn. Cuspidata, has star-shaped flowers with slender pointed petals. It includes the strain 'Twinkle' (height 6 in.), a compact plant with variously coloured flowers.

The large-flowered group, Grandiflora (height 12 in.), is the most popular. It is available as a mixture and in separate colours, including cream, rose, red, crimson and violet.

PHLOX DRUMMONDII

The third group, Nana Compacta (height 9 in.), is comprised of compact plants available as mixtures and in separate colours.

HERBACEOUS BORDER SPECIES

P. decussata: see *P. paniculata*

P. maculata. E. United States. Height 2–3 ft; planting distance 18 in. A border plant with maroon spots on the stems. The mid-green leaves are lanceolate. Tapering, 6 in. long, narrow panicles of purple flowers, $\frac{3}{4}$–1 in. wide, are freely produced from July to September. Recommended named varieties include: 'Alpha', pink; and 'Miss Lingard', pure white.

PHLOX MACULATA

P. paniculata, syn. *P. decussata*. E. United States. Height $1\frac{1}{2}$–4 ft; planting distance 18–24 in. This species has mid-green lanceolate leaves. Dense, ovoid panicles, 4–6 in. long, of purple flowers, which are 1 in. across, are borne from July to September. The species is now superseded by numerous garden varieties (height $2\frac{1}{2}$–$3\frac{1}{2}$ ft) which include the following:

'Border Gem', violet-blue; 'Brigadier', bright salmon-scarlet; 'Dodo Hanbury Forbes', pink; 'Fairy's Petticoat', pale mauve with dark mauve centres; 'Graf Zeppelin', white with red centres; 'Harlequin', vigorous grower, variegated foliage and bright purple flowers.

'Mother of Pearl', white, flushed pink; 'Norah Leigh', variegated foliage of light green and primrose, and panicles of purple-pink flowers, usually 4–5 in. long; 'Olive Symons-Jeune', pink with bright cerise centres; 'Rembrandt', white; 'Russian Violet', violet-purple; 'Signal', glowing scarlet; 'Sir John Falstaff', salmon-pink; 'Starfire', brilliant red; 'Vintage Wine', rich claret-red.

Cultivation of alpine species. Plant all species between September and March. Grow *P. adsurgens* in peaty soil in partial shade, near the base of large rocks; *P. amoena* in a more open position in moist soil; *P. douglasii* in any fertile garden soil and in full sun. *P. nana ensifolia*, although growing well in peaty, well-drained soil in full sun, is best grown in a trough or in an alpine house in an open, lime-free compost; *P. subulata* and its varieties thrive in any fertile garden soil in full sun.

Phlox drummondii

Cultivation of annual species. Grow these plants in any fertile, well-drained garden soil. Plant out seedlings in May in an open sunny site. Dead-heading extends the flowering period. On poor soil, an occasional liquid feed is beneficial.

For spring-flowering plants under glass, pot September-sown seedlings in 3 in. pots of John Innes potting compost No. 1. Pot on into 5 in. containers and overwinter in a greenhouse at a temperature of 7–10°C (45–50°F). Flowering usually begins in March.

Cultivation of herbaceous border species. Plant in a sunny or partially shaded position in October, February or March. The soil should be fertile and moisture-retentive, but well-drained. Mulch with well-rotted manure or compost annually in April to preserve moisture round the roots. Water freely on light soils during dry spells, or the plants will droop and flower poorly.

Older plants produce numerous shoots, and the weaker of these should be thinned out in spring. Staking or support with pea-sticks is usually necessary. Cut the dead flower stems down in October to just above ground level.

Propagation of alpine species. Take $2-2\frac{1}{2}$ in. cuttings in July from basal shoots of all species except *P. nana ensifolia*; insert the cuttings in a cold frame in equal parts (by volume) peat and sand. When well-developed shoots are formed, pot the rooted cuttings in 3 in. pots of John Innes potting compost No. 1 and grow on in the frame for planting out the following March and April.

Take root cuttings of *P. nana ensifolia* in August and place in a cold frame in equal parts (by volume) peat and sand. Pot into 3 in. containers of John Innes potting compost No. 1 the following summer when the plants are an inch or so high. Overwinter the young plants in a cold frame, and plant out in permanent positions the following March or April.

Propagation of annual species. For outdoor plants and for summer-flowering bedding plants, sow seeds in pots or boxes of John Innes seed compost during March. Germinate at a temperature of 15°C (59°F). Prick off the seedlings into boxes of John Innes potting compost No. 1 and later pot up in 3 in. containers, or harden off in a cold frame before planting out in May.

For spring-flowering pot plants under glass, sow the seeds in September.

Propagation of herbaceous border species. Stem cuttings, 3–4 in. long, taken from the base of the plants in March will usually root readily in equal parts (by volume) peat and sand in a cold frame. If stem eelworms are present on the parent plants the pests will often be carried over on cuttings. Root cuttings are free of infestation and may be taken at any time, preferably in February and March. Place $\frac{1}{2}$ in. pieces of the thicker roots in boxes of John Innes seed compost at a temperature of 13°C (55°F). When the shoots are 2–3 in. high, harden off the cuttings in a cold frame and later line out in nursery rows. Cuttings taken in February and March will be ready for setting in their permanent positions after 18 months.

Divide old, healthy clumps in October or March. Discard woody parts and replant sections from the sides of the clump only.

The crown of the plants may be sliced off in late winter or early spring, leaving only the roots in the soil. In spring or early summer, dig up and replant the young plantlets which appear from the roots.

Sow seeds in boxes of seed compost in a cold frame during March or April. Prick out the seedlings, when large enough to handle, into boxes of John Innes potting compost No. 1. Grow on in a nursery bed and plant out in the flowering sites in October of the following year. Named varieties do not come true from seeds.

Pests. Tissues are invaded by STEM EELWORMS and BULB EELWORMS, and shoots become twisted and distorted. Young shoots are killed and older shoots bear long narrow leaves.

SLUGS feed on young stems and leaves.

Diseases. On the leaves, LEAF SPOT shows as brown spots with pale centres which eventually coalesce, giving a scorched effect.

LEAFY GALL may show as a mass of abortive and often fasciated shoots at ground level.

A PHYSIOLOGICAL DISORDER, usually due to an irregular supply of moisture in the soil, causes a yellowing or browning of the leaves.

POWDERY MILDEW shows as a white powdery coating on the leaves.

Phlox, moss: see *Phlox subulata*

Phoenix

Palmae

A genus of 17 species of palms with feathery leaves; a few are small enough for growing in a greenhouse. The species, which include the edible date palm, are unisexual, and fruits are not produced unless plants of each sex are available.

P. canariensis. Canary Islands. Height 15 ft or more; spread 8–10 ft. This species somewhat resembles the familiar date palm, but the crown is more densely leafy. The slender, mid-green, pinnate leaves may reach a length of 10 ft or more; they arch outwards and downwards. Dense panicles, 3 ft or more long, of tiny brown-yellow flowers hang from between the

Phlox paniculata 'Norah Leigh'

Phlox paniculata 'Olive Symons-Jeune'

Phoenix canariensis

leaves during April. They are seldom produced in Great Britain, except in such favoured areas as the Isles of Scilly. Ovoid, golden-brown, date-like fruits, 1 in. long, follow the flowers in favourable seasons. This species is hardy only in the most sheltered parts of southern and western Britain.

P. dactylifera (date palm). N. Africa. Height 15 ft or more; spread 10–12 ft. This species is the commercial date palm; it has pinnate, mid-green leaves up to 6 ft long.

P. robelinii. E. Asia. Height and spread 4–6 ft. This almost stemless palm has dark green leaves 24 in. long, consisting of many narrow leaflets.

Cultivation. Grow in John Innes potting compost No. 2; *P. canariensis* needs a winter temperature of 7°C (45°F); the other two species require 10–13°C (50–55°F). Ventilate whenever the temperature exceeds 18–21°C (64–70°F). Water sparingly during the resting period from November to mid-March, moderately until May, plentifully between May and September, and moderately again until November.

Lightly shade the glass in summer; provide full light for the rest of the year. Final pot size should be 10–12 in., but large specimen plants will require 2–3 ft wide tubs. Repot every two or three years in April; in the years when the plants are not repotted give a liquid manure at 10–14 day intervals from May to September.

Propagation. Remove rooted sucker growths from *P. robelinii* in May, and pot them up singly in the growing compost.

All three species may also be increased by seeds. Sow seeds (date stones) in February or March and germinate at a temperature of 18–21°C (64–70°F). The seeds should germinate within two months; pot seedlings individually into 3 in. pots of John Innes potting compost No. 1 and pot on as required.

Pruning. None required; *P. robelinii* is a suckering plant and should be restricted to a single rosette by cutting out the suckers as they appear, unless these are wanted for propagation.

Pests. Stems and leaves may be infested by SCALE INSECTS and MEALYBUGS.

Diseases. Yellow spotting on the leaves may be caused by SMUT, and small black scabs or warts develop. The outer part is horny, but the inner part protrudes, giving the appearance of sprouting yellow hairs.

Phoenix dactylifera (fruits)

Phormium tenax 'Purpureum'

Phormium tenax 'Variegatum'

Phygelius capensis

Phormium

Agavaceae

A genus of two species of half-hardy evergreen perennials, grown for their foliage although they produce tubular flowers. They thrive in ordinary fertile soil, but can usually be grown outdoors only in south and south-west England. Even there they may be killed in severe winters.

P. tenax (New Zealand flax). New Zealand. Height up to 10 ft; planting distance 4–5 ft. This species is suitable as a border plant and is hardy in all but the coldest districts; it bears leathery, strap-shaped, mid to deep green leaves up to 9 ft long and 4–5 in. wide. Dull red flowers, about 2 in. long, are carried in 3 ft long branched panicles from July to September.

P. t. 'Purpureum' has bronze-purple foliage and *P. t.* 'Variegatum' has leaves striped with green and yellow.

Cultivation. Plant in April or May in deep moist soil and in a sunny position. Protect the plants in winter with straw or bracken. Remove dead flower stems in August or September.

Propagation. Sow seeds in sandy soil in March or April in a greenhouse or frame at a temperature of 15–18°C (59–64°F). Prick off into boxes when the seedlings are large enough to handle, then harden off. Transplant to nursery rows preferably in a cold frame, until March or April of the following year.

Named varieties do not come true from seed. Divide and replant in April, making sure that each piece has at least three or four leaves.

Pests and diseases. Generally trouble-free.

Phygelius

Scrophulariaceae

PHYGELIUS CAPENSIS

A genus of two species of half-hardy evergreen shrubs, usually treated as herbaceous perennials. As shrubs they can only be grown in mild districts and even then require wall protection. They are best grown as border plants, and as such they are generally hardy and drought-resistant. The flowers, which appear in diffuse panicles, are tubular and slightly curved, with five short spreading lobes at the mouth.

P. aequalis. S. Africa. Height 2–2½ ft; planting distance 24 in. A non-shrubby border plant with mid-green leaves that are toothed and lanceolate. Panicles, 6–9 in. long, of orange-buff flowers, are produced from July to October.

P. capensis. S. Africa. Height 2½–3 ft; planting distance 24 in. A sparsely branched border plant with mid to dark green ovate leaves; it may also be grown as a wall shrub. Height against a wall, 6 ft or more. Rust-red to scarlet flowers, 1½ in. long, are produced in panicles, up to 12 in. long, from July to October.

P. c. 'Coccineus' has bright scarlet flowers.

Cultivation. Plant in April in a sunny sheltered position and preferably in light soil. No staking is required if the plants are grown as border plants, but *P. capensis* should be secured to a trellis or similar support if grown as a wall shrub.

In April, trim back herbaceous plants to ground level; remove dead growth from shrubs and cut back to shape.

Propagation. Divide and replant the roots during March or April.

Seeds may be sown in a cold frame in April; prick out seedlings when they are large enough to handle. Pot singly in 4 in. containers of John Innes potting compost No. 1 or plant out in nursery rows until October of the same year. Lift

and overwinter the plants in a cold frame until they are transplanted to permanent positions the following April.
Pests and diseases. Generally trouble-free.

Phyllitis
Aspleniaceae

PHYLLITIS SCOLOPENDRIUM

A genus of eight species of ferns. The single species described is suitable for both garden and indoor cultivation.

P. scolopendrium, syn. *Scolopendrium vulgare* (hart's-tongue). Circumpolar, N. Hemisphere. Height 12–24 in.; spread 10–20 in. Evergreen. The bright green fronds are entire and strap-shaped. *P. s.* 'Crispum' has frond margins which are crisped and waved. It is a sterile variety which can be increased only by vegetative means. *P. s.* 'Cristatum', of which there are several dwarf forms, has fronds which are branched and crested at the tips.

Cultivation. Plant during April in shade in a humus-rich, preferably limy soil.

The best position for indoor plants is a shady window. Pot in 5 or 6 in. pots containing a well-drained compost of equal parts (by volume) loam, leaf-mould or peat, and coarse sand. Water freely during the growing season, at other times just sufficiently to keep the soil moist.

Propagation. Sow spores in March (see entry under FERNS), or divide the plants in April.

To propagate the sterile *P. s.* 'Crispum', first remove the old frond bases. Clean them and plant them in sterilised compost in pots or boxes, covering this with glass to maintain humidity. These bases will form bulbils within a few weeks, eventually growing into small plants. Prick these off into 2 in. pots and grow them on.

Pests. Small notches may be eaten in the leaf margins by WEEVILS.

Diseases. Sometimes RUST develops on young, sterile fronds, showing on their undersurface as brown spore pustules.

Phyllodoce
Ericaceae

A genus of seven species of hardy evergreen heath-like sub-shrubs. They are natives of the mountainous areas of the Northern Hemisphere. The narrow, heath-like leaves are pale to dark green and arranged in whorls. The flowers generally appear from April to June, and sometimes again in the autumn. These plants are suitable for cool, moist, lime-free rock gardens, especially in areas of high rainfall. They may also be grown in an alpine house.

Phyllitis scolopendrium 'Crispum'

P. aleutica. N.E. Asia and Alaska. Height 3–12 in.; spread 12 in. or more. Green-yellow globe-shaped flowers are produced in 1–2 in. long terminal heads.

P. amabilis: see *P. nipponica*

P. breweri. California. Height up to 9 in.; spread 12 in. The deep pink, cup-shaped flowers are deeply lobed and have conspicuous stamens. They appear in 2–3 in. long terminal heads.

PHYLLODOCE CAERULEA

P. caerulea, syn. *Menziesia taxifolia.* N. Europe. Height 3–12 in.; spread 12 in. or more. The urn-shaped flowers are purple-pink and are borne in 1–2 in. long terminal heads.

P. empetriformis. Rocky Mountains. Height 3–12 in.; spread 12 in. or more. The rose-red flowers appear in June and July; they are borne in 1–2 in. long terminal heads and are five-lobed. This species is more tolerant than the others of dry conditions.

P. nipponica, syn. *P. amabilis.* Japan. Height and spread 4–6 in. A dwarf, compact plant. The dark green leaves are grey beneath. The flowers, borne in 1–2 in. long terminal heads, are white, often tinged with pink.

Cultivation, propagation, pruning: see entry under HEATHS AND HEATHERS.

Pests and diseases. Generally trouble-free.

Phyllodoce aleutica

Physalis alkekengii (flowers)

Physalis
Solanaceae

A genus of about 100 species of hardy and tender annuals and herbaceous perennials. They are invasive plants with widely expanded bell-shaped flowers, and only two of the hardy perennials are garden-worthy. They are grown for the brilliant colour of the inflated lantern-like calyx which surrounds the fruit in August and September. The colour persists well, and the dried fruits are useful for winter decoration.

PHYSALIS ALKEKENGII

P. alkekengii (bladder cherry, Chinese lantern). Caucasus to China. Height 12–15 in.; planting distance 18 in. This hardy species has unbranched stems and mid-green, deltoid to ovate leaves. White, $\frac{1}{2}$ in. wide flowers are borne in the upper leaf axils during July and August; they are followed by bright red calyces, 2 in. long, enclosing an edible orange-red berry.

Physalis alkekengii (fruits)

P. franchetii. Japan. Height and planting distance 24 in. A hardy border perennial. The mid-green leaves are deltoid to ovate, narrowing towards the stalk. White flowers, $\frac{1}{2}$–$\frac{3}{4}$ in. long, appear in July and are followed by globular orange fruits, enclosed in an orange-red papery calyx, 2–2$\frac{1}{2}$ in. long. They ripen in September.

P. f. 'Gigantea' grows to a height of 3 ft; P. f. 'Nana' is a dwarf variety.

Cultivation. Plant in March or April in a sunny, well-drained border and in any ordinary garden soil. In autumn, cut off the invasive underground runners with a spade and dig them out.

Cut the fruiting stems when the calyces begin to show colour and hang them in bunches upside-down in a light, airy shed to dry. When the stems and fruits are dry, remove the withered leaves.

Propagation. Lift and divide the roots in March or April; replant the separated pieces immediately.

Sow seeds in a cold frame or outdoors in April, transplanting the seedlings to a nursery bed when they are large enough to handle. In autumn, set the plantlets in their flowering sites. The varieties come fairly true from seeds.

Pests and diseases. Generally trouble-free.

Physostegia
Labiatae

A genus of about 15 species of hardy herbaceous perennials with pink or mauve snapdragon-like flowers. Only one species with its varieties is in general cultivation.

P. virginiana, syn. *Dracocephalum virginianum* (obedient plant). N. America. Height 1–4 ft; planting distance 24 in. The irregular, sharply toothed leaves are lanceolate and mid-green. Closely set, pink or mauve flowers are produced in July and August on spikes about 5 in. long. If the individual flowers are pushed to one side they remain in that position, hence the common name.

The following are all good varieties for the border: 'Rose Bouquet', rose-pink; 'Summer Snow', pure white; 'Summer Spire', deep lilac-purple; and 'Vivid', deep pink. They grow to a height of 2$\frac{1}{2}$–4 ft, depending on the richness and moisture of the soil.

PHYSOSTEGIA VIRGINIANA

Cultivation. Plant in October, March or April in a sunny or half-shaded position and in ordinary garden soil. Mulch in spring and water copiously during dry spells in summer to prevent the roots from drying out. Staking with twiggy sticks may be needed on rich soils. Cut down in November.

Propagation. Divide in October or March, replanting only the outer vigorous roots.

Alternatively, take 2–3 in. cuttings of young shoots in March or April; root the cuttings in pots of sandy soil in a cold frame and transplant to the flowering sites in October.

Pests and diseases. Generally trouble-free.

Phyteuma
Campanulaceae

A genus of 40 species of hardy perennial herbaceous plants. They are suitable for growing on rock gardens, and one species, *P. comosum*, makes an attractive plant in an alpine house. The tiny individual flowers are tubular and form dense globular heads.

P. comosum. Dolomites. Height 2–4 in.; spread 6 in. In its natural habitat this spectacular species grows in limestone crevices. It forms a tuft of

Physalis franchetii (fruits)

Physostegia virginiana

Physostegia virginiana 'Summer Snow'

coarsely toothed, ovate, pointed, mid-green leaves, in the centre of which nestle dense clusters of distinctive purple, flask-shaped flowers. These appear on short stems in July, and each flower head is 1½ in. across.

Phyteuma comosum

P. hemisphaericum. European Alps. Height 4–6 in.; spread 9 in. This plant has grass-like, linear, mid-green leaves and, in June, bears short-stemmed globular flower heads, each head about 1–1½ in. across. The tubular flowers may range from clear blue to almost white.

P. orbiculare. Europe, including Great Britain. Height 12 in.; spread 12–18 in. This species is too tall for a small rock garden but can be grown in a border. It makes an attractive plant, with lanceolate mid-green leaves that are cordate at the base. Dense round heads, 1½ in. across, of bright blue flowers are borne in June.

P. scheuchzeri. European Alps. Height and spread about 12 in. The mid-green leaves of this species are ovate-lanceolate. Bright blue flowers, similar to those of *P. orbiculare*, are borne profusely in May and June.

Cultivation. Outdoors, plant *P. comosum* in March on a scree or dry wall in sun or partial shade. In the alpine house, grow it in 4–6 in. pots of 2 parts John Innes potting compost No. 1 and 1 part limestone grit (parts by volume).

Plant the other species in March in reasonably fertile light soil which is sharply drained or on a scree. They will grow in sun or partial shade.

Propagation. Divide and replant after flowering, or during March or April.

Pests. Stems and leaves may be eaten by SLUGS, which are particularly attracted to *P. comosum*.

Diseases. Generally trouble-free.

Phytolacca

Phytolaccaceae

A genus of 35 species of tender and hardy trees, shrubs and herbaceous perennials. The following perennial species is in general cultivation. It bears dense spikes of tiny star-shaped flowers, but is mainly grown for the foliage and fruit. It is an easily-grown border plant, but the roots and berries are poisonous.

P. americana, syn. *P. decandra* (poke weed, red-ink plant). E. United States. Height 3–10 ft;

planting distance 3 ft. A hardy border plant with ovate mid-green leaves which are tinted red and purple in September or October. The 3–4 in. long erect spikes of white flowers appear from June to September, and are followed by dark purple berries containing a crimson juice.

PHYTOLACCA AMERICANA

P. decandra: see *P. americana*

Cultivation. Plant in October, March or April in ordinary, moist garden soil and in a sunny or shady position. Staking with canes may be needed on exposed and windy sites. Cut the stems down in November.

Propagation. Sow seeds outdoors in March or April; prick out the seedlings, when large enough to handle, into a nursery bed. Plant out in the flowering site, preferably in October of the following year.

Divide and replant the large, fleshy roots from October to March.

Pests and diseases. Generally trouble-free.

Picea

Spruce or fir. *Pinaceae*

A genus of 50 species of hardy evergreen coniferous trees, found in most of the northern temperate regions, particularly on mountain ranges. They are mainly tall and narrowly conic trees and many have pendulous branches. The needle-like leaves are hard and grow from small pegs which remain when the needles are shed, leaving the shoots rough. The pendulous, ovoid or cylindrical cones have pliable woody brown scales; all ripen in their first season. The following species make fine specimen trees and many are useful for shelter belts. The dwarf forms are excellent for rock gardens.

See also CONIFERS.

P. abies, syn. *P. excelsa* (Norway spruce). Europe, W. Russia and Scandinavia. Height 50 ft; spread 20 ft. This species is the Christmas tree, with a narrow-spired crown when young. The crown becomes domed and broader in older trees, which are useful for screens and shelter belts.

The orange-brown bark flakes finely when young, later cracking into dark purple-grey squares. The brown shoots bear four-sided, stiff, mid to deep green needles lying on the upper sides only, the middle ones pointing forwards. The 6 in. long cones are borne when the tree is about 40 years old, appearing near the top at first, but becoming more widely spread as the tree ages. The brown scales are leathery and overlap like semicircular tiles.

The Norway spruce has given rise to numerous dwarf forms, including the following:

'Clanbrassiliana'. Height and spread 3 ft. This form eventually reaches tree-like proportions, but

Phytolacca americana (single flower spike)

Phytolacca americana (fruits)

Picea abies (cone)

Picea abies 'Pumila'

Picea breweriana (cone)

Picea glauca 'Albertiana Conica'

Picea likiangensis (cones)

as it is extremely slow-growing it may be regarded as reliably dwarf. In the early stages, it is a low, rounded bush with a crowded branch system, conic red-brown buds and wiry-looking foliage; each needle appears curved and tapers from the centre. It slowly matures to a round-topped bush.

'Nidiformis'. Height 12 in.; spread 3 ft. This is a reliable spreading form with dark green, wiry foliage. The main branches rise at first at a steep angle and curve over as they grow. This growth habit creates a cone-shaped depression in the centre of a young plant, but the effect is usually lost in older plants.

'Pumila'. Height and spread 24 in. or more. A flat-topped, globose bush, with the branchlets arranged in plate-like layers.

P. alba: see *P. glauca*

PICEA BREWERIANA

P. breweriana (Brewer's spruce). S.W. Oregon. Height 25 ft; spread 10–15 ft. A broadly columnar species with long curtains of shoots that hang from branches which bend slightly down, then arch upwards. Growth is slow, but the girth increases rapidly after about 20 years. Although hardy, this species does best in a sheltered position.

The flattened needles are dark grey-green with two narrow white bands beneath, carried all round the shoot and curving gently.

The centre of the crown may bear large male flowers at the ends of the shoots, but the female flowers are confined to the top, and are borne from about the 30th year. These mature to 5 in. long green cones, pointed at each end, which turn purple-brown in autumn.

P. engelmannii 'Glauca'. N.W. America. Height 25 ft; spread 10 ft. This blue-grey variety of the rare *P. engelmannii* has a narrow outline and pendulous shoots. The bark is orange, peeling off in papery scales. The needles, each with two blue-grey bands, lie forward above the shoots and spread on either side beneath. When crushed, the foliage gives off an aroma of balsam. The cones are up to 3 in. long.

P. excelsa: see *P. abies*

P. glauca, syn. *P. alba* (white or Canadian spruce). Canada, N.E. United States. Height 20 ft; spread 6–8 ft. A moderately slow-growing species of narrowly conic habit. The long thick branches bear slender glaucous shoots covered with narrow grey-green needles; the needles surround the shoot but are densest at the top and sides. They have an unpleasantly pungent smell when bruised. The trunk is covered with grey-brown scaly bark. The cones are pale brown, cylindrical and up to 2½ in. long.

In cultivation, this species is generally represented by the dwarf form 'Albertiana Conica' (height 4 ft; spread 2½ ft), a dense conic bush with fine, soft, grass-green foliage.

'Nana' (height up to 3 ft; spread 2½ ft) is a rigid bush-like form with grey-blue needles.

P. likiangensis. S.W. China. Height 45 ft; spread 25 ft. A variable species, usually broadly conic with strong, slightly ascending lower branches and an open crown. The bark is pale grey with a few shallow fissures. The pale blue-green needles are short, slender and flattened, the upper ones pointing forward; they have white bands, narrow above, broader and brighter on the undersides. Abundant crimson male and female flowers are borne in late May, the latter producing cones up to 3¼ in. long with wavy edges to the scales.

'Purpurea' has a dense crown with numerous vertical shoots near the top; the foliage is dark green; it is less spectacular in flower than the type species.

P. mariana (black spruce). Canada, N.E. United States. Height 15 ft; spread 10 ft. A slow-growing tree with a dense, pointed and narrowly conic crown. The hairy shoots are densely set with small blue needles which emit a pleasant smell of menthol when crushed. Cones, 1½ in. long, are freely borne; they ripen to red-brown.

The dwarf variety 'Nana' (height 12 in.; spread 24 in.) forms a neat, rounded bush with fine, blue-grey foliage densely borne on numerous shoots radiating outwards all over the plant. It is suitable for even the smallest garden or for an alpine house.

P. omorika (Serbian spruce). Yugoslavia. Height 45 ft; spread 10 ft. A narrow, columnar species suitable for city gardens. It tolerates polluted air, and will grow on limestone and in the most acid peat. Broader forms of the species are known, and it is advisable to plant three or four young plants and later discard any that are badly shaped.

The young bark is orange-brown, shredding into fine flakes and later cracking into hard squares. The branches may be short, dense and level, or longer and more widely spaced, curving down then sweeping up at the tips. They carry flat, slightly curving needles, shiny dark green above, with two broad white bands beneath. The bright red female flowers, borne near the top of the tree, mature to 2 in. long, spindle-shaped, dark purple cones; these are often produced within five years of planting. Male flowers are globular and borne on hanging shoots lower in the crown.

PICEA OMORIKA

P. orientalis (Caucasian, Oriental spruce). Caucasus, Asia Minor. Height 45 ft; spread 20 ft. A slow-growing tree for about 15 years, after which growth is rapid; it is sometimes short-lived on dry and shallow soils. The young bark is grey and rough with minute speckles turning pink-brown with age and cracking deeply into circular plates. The short, blunt, shiny dark green needles lie close to the hairy, pale shoots. The upper shoots are long with a spiky appearance, while the lower shoots are densely borne. Cones, up to 4 in. long, are often carried in profusion after about 20 years; they are ashy-brown and narrow at both ends. The male flowers are pointed, and turn deep red when mature.

P. pungens (Colorado spruce). Wyoming to New Mexico. This species is mainly represented in cultivation by the varieties 'Argentea' and 'Glauca'. Colour forms of these are listed under such names as 'Kosteri', 'Kosteriana', 'Koster's', 'Moerheim Blue', 'Moerheimii' and 'Vuykii'. Height 20–25 ft; spread 10 ft.

'Glauca Pendula', height and spread up to 10 ft, is a weeping form.

The shape is narrowly conic with a crown varying from dense, in slow-growing grafted forms, to fairly open in large seedling trees. The stiff, prickly needles radiate from stout shoots, the youngest being grey-blue or nearly white, the inner ones shading to dark blue-green. Cones, 4 in. long, are borne after about 20 years, and ripen to a shiny pale brown; the leathery scales narrow to a toothed point.

P. sitchensis (Sitka spruce). Coasts from Alaska to California. Height 65 ft; spread 15 ft. This species, which is suitable as a specimen tree on a lawn, grows vigorously on poor, acid soils in exposed positions. Young trees have spire-like tops or conic crowns, while old trees are less pointed and broadly columnar with large upward and outward-arching branches.

The flat, sharply pointed needles are rich green above, blue-white beneath and borne on white or buff hairless shoots. The leaves are aromatic when crushed. The red female flowers occur sporadically near the top of the tree; they develop into white, 3 in. long cones with distinctively crinkled toothed scales. Male flowers, sparsely borne, are globular, and borne on short shoots lower in the crown; they shed pollen in early May, when the large leaf buds expand.

P. smithiana (West Himalayan spruce). Nepal to Afghanistan. Height 50 ft; spread 20 ft. An imposing species suitable for an open position where the pendulous branchlets can develop fully. As a seedling it is not fully hardy. Young trees are narrowly conic, but older specimens have large, low branches; usually the branches are horizontal, with hanging curtain-like branchlets.

The slender needles are dark glossy green with faint white lines; they are nearly square in cross-section, forward-lying and sharply pointed. The cones, 6 in. long, are tapered at each end and are borne at the tops of old trees only.

Cultivation. Spruces thrive in deep, moist soil; most species dislike alkaline soils and do better on soils with a moderate or high acid content. Plant during suitable weather from November to March or April in sun or partial shade, and preferably in sheltered positions. On heavy soils delay planting until spring. Young trees are easily damaged by late spring frosts and should not be planted in frosty hollows.

For rapid and shapely growth, use young plants 2–3 ft tall; large plants suffer a check to growth during transplanting which may interfere permanently with the pattern of the lower branches. Apply phosphate when planting and a sprinkling of general or nitrogenous fertiliser each May, and again in June on sandy soils. Protect tender young plants with evergreen branches stuck in the ground; tie the branch tops together well clear of the top of the plants.

Propagation. Sow seeds thinly in March in pots or deep boxes of John Innes seed compost in a cold frame. The following spring, line out the seedlings in nursery rows and grow on for two or three years before planting out in final positions.

Pruning. None is required, except to reduce forked trees to a single leader as soon as possible.

Pests. ADELGIDS, particularly the spruce gall adelgid, feed on the needles and stems and produce pineapple-like galls on young shoots. These check growth and disfigure trees.

APHIDS, particularly the spruce aphid, also feed on the foliage, causing yellowing of the needles.

Premature defoliation and similar symptoms are caused by MITES, *P. glauca* 'Albertiana Conica' being particularly susceptible to attacks by RED SPIDER MITES.

Diseases. Most species may suffer from DIE-BACK of young shoots following FROST DAMAGE.

HONEY FUNGUS may kill trees, those of *P. omorika* being particularly susceptible.

GREY MOULD can be a troublesome disease on seedlings, particularly those of *P. sitchensis*; it shows as a sparse web of grey fungal growth over the affected parts of the trees. When succulent shoots are attacked they collapse and wither.

RUST is caused by two different fungi but is of only local importance; it shows as golden-yellow pustules on the needles in spring and may cause some defoliation.

STEM CANKER may be caused by several different fungi, most of which follow frost damage. It shows first as dead, slightly sunken patches; these girdle the boles, causing die-back.

Pickerel weed: see *Pontederia cordata*

Pieris

Ericaceae

A genus of ten species of hardy evergreen flowering shrubs of compact habit. They require lime-free soil. In spring they bear racemes of waxy, lily of the valley-like flowers.

P. floribunda, syn. *Andromeda floribunda*. S.E. United States. Height and spread 4–6 ft. The narrow, dark green, leathery leaves are elliptic-oblong. Drooping, pitcher-shaped, white flowers are borne in erect terminal panicles, 3–4 in. across, in April and May.

PIERIS FORMOSA 'FORRESTII'

P. formosa, syn. *Andromeda formosa*. Yunnan, E. Himalayas. Height 6–12 ft; spread 10–15 ft. These measurements may be greater in mild districts; elsewhere the plant may be damaged by severe winters. The lanceolate-oblong leaves are copper-red when young, turning green later.

Picea likiangensis (flowers)

Picea mariana (cones and foliage)

Picea orientalis (male flowers)

Picea pungens 'Glauca'

White flowers are carried in drooping panicles, 3–5 in. wide, during April and May.

'Forrestii', a Chinese variety which retains its colour longer than that of the type, has brilliant red young foliage. In April and May, it bears abundant panicles of white flowers.

P. japonica, syn. *Andromeda japonica.* Japan. Height and spread 6–10 ft. The oblong-obovate leaves are copper-red when young, mid-green when mature. In March and April, drooping racemes, 3–4 in. across, of white flowers are produced in terminal clusters. 'Variegata' is a slow-growing form with yellow-white edged leaves that are narrower than those of the type.

Cultivation. Plant in October, March or April in moist, lime-free loam, choosing a sheltered position in partial shade. Top-dress the plants annually with leaf-mould or peat in April and do not allow the soil to dry out during the summer months.

Propagation. Take 3–4 in. cuttings of half-ripe shoots in August and insert them in sandy soil in a cold frame. In April or May transfer the rooted cuttings singly to 3 in. pots containing equal parts (by volume) peat, loam, leaf-mould and sand. Move the plants to a nursery bed in October and grow them on for two or three years before planting out in their permanent positions.

Sow seeds in pans containing equal parts (by volume) sand and peat, in November or March and place in a cold frame. When the seedlings are large enough to handle, prick them off into pans or boxes and later transfer them to 3 in. pots. Set the plants out in a nursery bed in October of the following year and grow on for two or three years before planting in their final positions.

P. formosa can be increased by layering in September. Allow at least two years before severing and planting out.

Pruning.. After flowering, remove the faded flower heads and at the same time lightly cut back any straggling shoots.

Pests and diseases. Generally trouble-free.

Pig-a-back plant: see *Tolmiea menziesii*

Pilea

Urticaceae

PILEA CADIEREI

A genus of 400 species of tender evergreen perennial plants. Only a few are in general cultivation and these are grown in the greenhouse or in the home as foliage plants.

P: cadierei (aluminium plant). Vietnam. Height up to 12 in. A branched species. The oblong-ovate leaves, up to 3 in. long, are opposite; they are dark green with silvery patches between the veins.

The original type plant tends to become leggy as it ages; it is largely represented in cultivation by *P. c.* 'Nana' which stays compact and rarely exceeds 9 in. in height.

P. microphylla: see *P. muscosa*

P. muscosa, syn. *P. microphylla* (gunpowder plant, artillery plant). Tropical America. Height up to 9 in. This is a bushy species. The much-branched stems are densely covered with thyme-like, small, pale to mid-green leaves that give the plant a ferny appearance. When the inconspicuous tufts of yellow-green flowers are mature, from May to September, puffs of pollen are expelled from the anthers.

Cultivation. Grow pileas in 5 in. pots of John Innes potting compost No. 2 or in a proprietary peat compost. A winter temperature of 10–13°C (50–55°F) is required, although occasional lower temperatures will do no harm over short periods. Give full light during the shortest days, but provide moderate shade in spring and summer. Even in the home, pileas do not require such well-lit situations as many other house plants, although too heavy shade is not advisable. Water freely during the growing season, from April to September, moderately until March. Do not let the plants dry out at any time.

Pinch out the growing points of *P. cadierei* in spring to encourage side-shoots.

Repot annually in April, and give a feed of dilute liquid manure at intervals of two weeks from June to September.

Propagation. As pileas are seldom worth growing for more than three years, they should be regularly propagated by cuttings in May. Take stem cuttings, 3–4 in. long, and insert three or four round the rim of a 3 in. pot containing equal parts (by volume) peat and sand. Place in a propagating case at a temperature of 18–21°C (64–70°F); when rooted, pot the young plants on as required.

Pests and diseases. Generally trouble-free.

Pieris formosa 'Forrestii'

Pilea cadierei

Pilea muscosa

Pinguicula

Butterwort. *Lentibulariaceae*

A genus of 35 species of hardy or tender herbaceous perennials of insectivorous habit. Two
of the following species require cool greenhouse
treatment; the pots can be brought into a living-
room during the flowering season. *P. grandiflora*
is a hardy plant which will flourish outdoors in
wet soil, or in pans in an alpine house.

Pinguiculas have fleshy, pale to yellow-green
leaves that rise from a fleshy rootstock to form a
rosette; they are covered with a sticky excretion
that traps insects. The solitary flowers are violet-
shaped, usually with a long slender spur.

P. bakeriana, syn. *P. caudata.* Mexico. Height
5–7 in.; spread 4–5 in. A tender species with
obovate pale green leaves close to the ground.
Rich carmine-pink flowers, 1 in. across, are
produced from July to October.

P. caudata: see *P. bakeriana*

P. grandiflora. W. Europe. Height 6 in.; planting
distance 9 in. This hardy species has ovate to
oblong yellow-green leaves in a flattened
rosette. The flowers appear from May to July;
they are blue-purple and 1–1½ in. across.

P. gypsicola. Mexico. Height and spread 3–4 in.
A tender species with a winter rosette of short,
pale to yellow-green, spathulate leaves that give
way to longer and linear leaves in summer. The
flowers are about 1 in. across, rosy-violet with a
white spur; they are borne from July to October.

Cultivation. In the greenhouse or the alpine
house, grow pinguiculas in a compost of equal
parts (by volume) chopped sphagnum moss and
peat. Set three or four plants in a 6–8 in. pan and
stand this permanently in a shallow tray of
water. Give light shading to the glass during the
summer months and ventilate freely when the
temperature exceeds 10°C (50°F). The greenhouse species require a minimum winter temperature of 7°C (45°F).

Repot every other year in March or April.

Outdoors, plant *P. grandiflora* during March
or April, in boggy ground and ideally in
sphagnum moss. The plants thrive in sun or
partial shade.

Propagation. Sow seeds in pans or pots during
September and October, February and March, at
a temperature of 13°C (55°F). Sprinkle the seeds
thinly on the surface of a mixture of equal parts
(by volume) chopped sphagnum moss and peat;
stand the containers in a shallow tray of water
and cover with glass or polythene. When the
seedlings are large enough to handle, prick them
out into pans or boxes of the growing compost
and treat as described under CULTIVATION.

P. grandiflora seedlings should be hardened
off in a frame before planting out in April.

The multiple crowns of established plants
may be divided at repotting time.

Pests and diseases. Generally trouble-free.

Pinus

Pine. *Pinaceae*

A genus of about 100 species of evergreen
coniferous trees found in almost all forest areas in
the Northern Hemisphere. They vary from
semi-prostrate shrubs to trees up to 250 ft high,
but the majority are moderate to large. Hardiness
varies considerably.

The taller species have long, straight boles and
level or ascending, usually stout branches. The
leaves are needle-like and in groups of two, three
or five bound at the base in a sheath. The cones
are woody, broad and squat or long and
banana-shaped; occasionally they are the size and
shape of pineapples.

These trees are useful in landscaping, as shelter
trees and as single specimens; the dwarf forms
are suited to smaller-scale planting or on rock
gardens where their shape, bark or cones can be
better appreciated.

See also CONIFERS.

P. ayacahuite (Mexican white pine). Mexico to
Guatemala. Height 40 ft; spread 20 ft. A hardy,
fast-growing, five-needled species. The dense
crown is narrow and pointed at the top, broad at
the base, and the finely hairy shoots bear long
blue-green needles in fives. Banana-shaped cones
are freely borne after about 15 years; they may be
up to 15 in. long, and taper to a point with the
basal scales bent backwards. They ripen in the
second year and are orange, then dark brown
with a covering of white resin.

P. bungeana (lacebark pine). China. Height
10–15 ft; spread 6–10 ft. Although hardy, this
species does not establish easily in Great Britain
and usually forms a broadly conical bush. It bears
matt, dark green needles in groups of three. The
brown globose or egg-shaped cones are 2–2½ in.
long, each scale tipped with a reflexed spine. The
trunk of older specimens is attractively patterned
with patches of flaking bark.

P. cembra (arolla pine). Alps, Carpathians.
Height 25 ft; spread 10 ft. A hardy, slow-growing
tree, dense and columnar. The needles, in groups
of five, are set densely on shoots that are thickly
clothed in brown hairs; the outer surfaces of the
needles are dark green, the inner blue-white.
Cones are borne on older trees only; they are 2 in.
long, egg-shaped and green, with rounded, closed
scales. As they mature they turn purple-brown.

P. contorta (lodgepole pine). Western N.
America. A species composed of three distinct
geographical varieties. The most prevalent in
Great Britain is *P. c. contorta* (beach pine).
Height 45 ft; spread 20 ft. An extremely
fast-growing, hardy tree, suitable for shelter or
screening. Strong branches spread from the base,
and the crown is narrow and spire-shaped. The
short, bright or dark green needles lie in pairs
close along the shoots. Pendent, dull brown,
ovoid cones, which may be borne on 3-year-old
trees, are 1½–2 in. long. Male flowers may appear
on some young trees; they form small, yellow,
globular catkins in clusters.

P. c. latifolia (height 35 ft; spread 15 ft) is the
northern and eastern inland form, generally
slower-growing and with longer, more spreading
needles of a duller green.

Pinguicula grandiflora

Pinguicula gypsicola

Pinus ayacahuite (cones)

Pinus bungeana (cone)

Pinus mugo pumilio

Pinus pinaster (cones)

Pinus radiata (cones)

P. c. murrayana (height 30 ft; spread 15 ft) is the southern and western inland form, of neat and compact habit, and slow-growing.

P. coulteri (Coulter's pine, big-cone pine). S.W. California. Height 40 ft; spread 25 ft. A sturdy three-needle pine with a broad, open crown and attractive cones and foliage. It is reliably hardy only in the west and south. The stout glaucous shoots bear long, cylindrical, chestnut-coloured buds and hard, thick, grey-green needles, up to 12 in. long. The pale orange-brown, pineapple-shaped cones are 10–14 in. long and 6 in. wide, weighing up to 5 lb. They have some 200 scales, each terminating in a stout, upcurved, shiny spike; they take two years to ripen. Trees of 12–15 years begin to produce a pair of cones on the main stem; lateral shoots take even longer before they are strong enough to bear the weight of the cones.

P. excelsa: see *P. wallichiana*
P. griffithii: see *P. wallichiana*
P. laricio: see *P. nigra*
P. leucodermis (Bosnian pine). N. Italy, Balkans. Height 30 ft; spread 15 ft. A hardy slow-growing species that grows in the wild on limestone and withstands drought well. The crown is narrow and neatly conic, and the smooth branches bear pairs of dark green needles. The bark of older trees is pale dull-grey, smooth and marked with a lacework of fine cracks. Hard, straight needles are densely set except for a bare length at the base of each year's shoots. The pointed cones are ovoid, 3 in. long and bright blue-purple when young; they ripen to a dull brown in their second summer.

P. mugo (mountain pine). Central and S.E. Europe. Height and spread 6–15 ft. This mountain pine is somewhat variable in habit, but is usually a large shrub of gnarled appearance. The mid-green needles are borne in pairs, and the 2 in. long brown cones are ovoid to broadly top-shaped.

P. m. pumilio (dwarf mountain pine) is an even smaller form, often prostrate and rarely exceeding 6 ft in height. The cones are smaller, globose to ovoid.

P. muricata (bishop pine). W. United States. Height 40 ft; spread 20 ft. This hardy species, which is allied to *P. radiata*, is particularly suitable for seaside planting; it is fast-growing on poor soils. The usual form has a low, domed crown and branches encrusted in cones. Pairs of dark grey-green needles are massed in distinctive whorls around the shoots.

The rarer, northern form is a neater, more narrowly columnar tree with a pointed crown and dark blue-green needles. Both forms have dark grey bark marked with parallel ridges and deep fissures. The oblique, egg-shaped cones, which mature in their second year, are 3 in. long with spines on the swollen tips of the scales. They may adhere in light whorls for over 60 years.

P. nigra (black pine). Mountains of S. Europe. A complex species of which two forms are in general cultivation. *P. n. maritima*, syns. *P. n. calabrica*, *P. laricio* (Corsican pine). Height 40 ft; spread 20 ft. A hardy tree, requiring summer warmth for best growth; it will grow on shallow soils over chalk, and tolerates limestone. It also withstands atmospheric pollution better than most pines. The bole is long and straight, the branches horizontal, forming a tall, narrowly columnar, finally flat-topped crown. Brown-ridged shoots carry pairs of grey-green needles, 6 in. long and often twisted, particularly on young plants. The broad-based, narrowly pointed 3 in. long cones are dull brown, turning pale brown, with rough, flat scales.

P. n. nigra, syns. *P. n. austriaca*, *P. n. nigricans* (Austrian pine). Height 35 ft; spread 20 ft. This variety is suitable for shelter belts on dry, exposed sites, especially on chalk or limestone. It is fast-growing in the early stages. Deeply dark green needles, straight and rigid, are arranged in pairs. The cones are similar to those of *P. n. maritima*, but are broader and yellow in colour before they ripen.

P. parviflora (Japanese white pine). Japan. Height 25 ft; spread 15 ft. A hardy species whose low crown is formed of wide-spreading horizontal branches. The purple bark has patches of black scales curling away from the stem. Blue-grey to white, short and twisted needles are borne in groups of five on the upper sides of the shoots. The squat, ovoid cones, 2 in. long and standing erect from the shoots, are pale brown; they have few but thick scales.

P. peuce (Macedonian pine). Balkans. Height 35 ft; spread 15 ft. A sturdy, hardy tree, neatly conic at first, becoming more columnar in form. The bark is purple, smooth for many years, flaking finely with age. Dark blue-green needles are densely borne in groups of five on smooth, bright green shoots. The cylindrical, curved cones, up to 6 in. long, ripen to brown and become covered with white resin.

P. pinaster (maritime pine). W. Mediterranean. Height 45 ft; spread 20 ft. A hardy tree, fast-growing on the poorest soils. Young trees are oad, strongly branched and have open crowns; d trees have long, straight boles and high omed crowns. The bark is deeply cleft by orange ssures; with age it becomes purple, red and own in small prominent squares. Pale green, ick and rigid needles are sparsely borne in pairs n stout, pale brown shoots. The pointed, shining own cones, 8 in. long, which are produced on ees about ten years old, are arranged in groups f two, three or more. They mature in their econd year and may remain attached to the anches for several years.

PINUS PINEA

. *pinea* (stone pine). Mediterranean regions. Height 25 ft; spread 20 ft. A hardy species that vithstands drought well. The bark of old trees is ed to orange and deeply fissured vertically. The ower branches sweep upwards, while the higher nes radiate to support the spreading low-omed crown of shoots bearing dense, dark reen pairs of needles. Cones are not borne until he tree is about 30 years old; they are nearly pherical, slightly pointed, 6 in. long and overed with tight, smooth, shiny, convex scales; ney mature to light brown in their second year.

. *radiata* (Monterey pine). California. Height 50 ; spread 20 ft. This hardy and fast-growing tree as dark grey, deeply ridged bark which is ssured vertically. The dense, domed crown ppears almost black from a distance, but ne needles, borne in groups of three, are bright rassy green. Cones are produced after 20 years r more and are broad, egg-shaped and 6 in. long. They mature to rich brown in their second year nd may stay on the tree indefinitely, clustered at ntervals along the branches. They are lop-sided, ne lower scales on the outer side having thick, ounded protuberances. Male flowers are borne 12 in. long, pale yellow clusters at the base of ew shoots and are prominent when shedding ollen in April and May.

PINUS RADIATA

. *strobus* (Weymouth pine). Eastern N. America. Height 50 ft; spread 15 ft. A hardy pine f early rapid growth, and with a shapely, arrowly conic and open crown in the young tages. Most old trees are heavily branched with a hin, poor crown. The short, dark blue-green eedles, in groups of five, lie close to the shoots in ong whorls. Thin-scaled, curved, cylindrical, 6 in. ong cones taper to a point; they are pale green, listening with resin and are borne in bunches

on trees about ten years old. They ripen to dark brown, crusted with white.

P. sylvestris (Scots pine). Europe, including Great Britain; Asia. Height 35 ft; spread 15 ft. This is the most widespread species of all pines. Young trees usually have regular conic crowns; as growth slows with age the crown becomes irregular and spreading. The grey-green needles, in pairs, are short and twisted, longer on strong young shoots.

Pale brown conic cones, about 2 in. long, are borne terminally from about the tenth year, taking two years to mature. Male yellow flowers are not borne until several years later; they cluster at the base of new shoots.

'Aurea' is a slow-growing form, seldom reaching 20 ft in height; the new needles and the crown are blue-green, in summer faintly yellow, and turn golden in winter.

'Fastigiata' is a rare small, narrow and erect-branched variety.

The dwarf form 'Beuvronensis' (height 3 ft; spread 4 ft) is a low, broad, rounded bush, slow-growing, with conspicuous brown-red winter buds and short grey leaves. It is most effective planted on the high part of a rock garden, and with the lower foliage cut away to expose the trunk and main branches.

PINUS SYLVESTRIS

P. wallichiana, syns. *P. excelsa, P. griffithii* (Bhutan pine). W. Himalayas. Height 40–45 ft; spread 20 ft. A hardy species suitable as a specimen tree or for background in a sheltered position. In the open, older trees produce heavy branches and often die back at the top. The crown of young trees is regularly conic; in old specimens it is irregular and broad. The sinuous branches retain a smooth bark for many years, but on old trees the bark is orange-brown with shallow, scaly fissures.

The long drooping needles are soft and bright blue-grey; they are borne in groups of five on smooth glaucous shoots. Cones are produced on trees about 15 years old; they are banana-shaped and borne in bunches of two or three at the ends of strong shoots. They are purple-green and grey, encrusted in places with white resin, and mature to dark brown at the end of the second year.

Cultivation. Pines do best in full light; they thrive on well-drained acid soils, and some, notably *P. leucodermis* and *P. sylvestris*, grow equally well on alkaline soils. All, except the coastal form of *P. contorta*, will tolerate some degree of drought once they are well established.

Most species, especially those with needles in twos or threes, do well in exposed positions.

Plant in November, or during spells of suitable weather until the end of March, using seedlings up to 24 in. high. No staking is required. The more vigorous species respond to a general fertiliser applied before growth starts in May.

Pinus strobus (cones)

Pinus sylvestris 'Aurea'

Propagation. Sow seeds of all species thinly, in March, in pots or boxes of John Innes seed compost in a cold frame. The following spring, line the seedlings out in nursery rows outdoors and grow on for two or three years before transplanting to permanent positions. Seedlings of *P. radiata* do not transplant well and should be potted, when large enough to handle, in 3½ in. pots of John Innes potting compost No. 2; at the end of the year plant out in permanent positions.

Varieties and named forms do not breed true from seeds and should be grafted in March on to rootstocks of the type species.

Pruning. Generally none is required but where the leading shoot has been damaged, a whorl of shoots arises from the base of the central shoot. These should be removed, except for one, as soon as possible after damage has occurred. Leave only the straightest or strongest shoot.

Pests. ADELGIDS feed on stems and foliage, producing tufts of white waxy wool.

CATERPILLARS of the pine shoot moth tunnel in the terminal shoots and kill young growths.

SAWFLY larvae may feed in dense clusters on the leaves, especially on *P. contorta*.

Diseases. CANKER and DIE-BACK can be caused by a number of different fungi. They usually follow injuries or occur on trees lacking in vigour due to some PHYSIOLOGICAL DISORDER.

HONEY FUNGUS may kill pines.

GREY MOULD may be troublesome on *P. contorta* seedlings, attacking the lower needles which become covered with a sparse web of grey fungal growth.

RUST attacks the shoots of two-needled pines, causing them to become twisted and then die.

Pinus wallichiana (cones)

Piptanthus laburnifolius

Piptanthus
Leguminosae

PIPTANTHUS LABURNIFOLIUS

A genus of eight species of slightly tender evergreen flowering shrubs that require sheltered sites. The quick-growing species described is sometimes called the evergreen laburnum, but it is apt to lose its leaves in severe winters. It is not always long-lived.

P. laburnifolius, syn. *P. nepalensis*. Himalayas. Height and spread 8–12 ft. The lanceolate leaflets of this shrub, which are covered with silver hairs when young, are dark green above and glaucous beneath. Bright yellow, sweet-pea-like flowers are borne in 2–3 in. erect racemes in May.

P. nepalensis: see *P. laburnifolius*

Cultivation. Plant in a sheltered, sunny position in well-drained sandy loam in October or in March and April.

Propagation. Sow seeds in a mixture of equal parts (by volume) sand and peat in March in a cold greenhouse or frame. Pot the seedlings when they are large enough to handle, setting them singly in 3 in. pots of John Innes potting compost No. 1. Plant them out in a nursery bed in August or September, moving the plants to their final positions a year later in October.

Alternatively, take 3–4 in. cuttings of half-ripe lateral shoots with a heel in July or August and insert them in sandy soil in a cold frame. Transfer the rooted cuttings to 3 in. pots the following April or May and treat them in the manner described for seedlings.

Branches layered in September or October can be severed a year later.

Pruning. Cut out any dead wood between October and February.

Pests and diseases. Generally trouble-free.

Pisum sativum: see Pea
Pitcairnia feliciana: see Bromeliads

Pittosporum
Pittosporaceae

PITTOSPORUM TENUIFOLIUM

A genus of 150 species of tender and half-hardy evergreen flowering shrubs and small trees which have attractive foliage. Most of them are native to Australasia. The flowers are roughly bell-shaped or shortly tubular, with spreading or reflexed petals; those of some species are fragrant.

P. crassifolium. New Zealand. Height 10–15 ft; spread 6 ft. This shrubby species has leathery obovate leaves that are dark green above but off-white or russet-felted beneath. Maroon flowers, in terminal clusters up to 2 in. wide, in April and May, are followed by white, ovoid seed capsules. This species is used for hedges in the Isles of Scilly and Cornwall. Elsewhere, it requires wall protection.

P. dallii. New Zealand. Height and spread 8–10 ft. The mid-green leaves of this near-hardy tree are ovate-lanceolate and leathery. The glossy young shoots are red. In July, sweetly scented white flowers, up to ½ in. wide, may be borne in terminal clusters up to 1½ in. wide. However, flowers are rarely produced in Great Britain.

P. daphniphyllum. China. Height 6–10 ft; spread 6–8 ft. This is a tender shrub, suitable only for mild areas. The dark green leaves are narrowly oblong to narrowly obovate. In May and June massed clusters, up to 1½ in. wide, of small green-yellow flowers with reflexed petals, are produced in terminal panicles, 4–6 in. long. They may be followed by a crop of red globose berries which ripen in August and September.

P. nigricans: see *P. tenuifolium*

P. tenuifolium, syn. *P. nigricans*. New Zealand. Height up to 15 ft; spread 5–7 ft. This almost hardy tree has pale green oblong to obovate leaves with prominently waved margins; they are

orne on almost black stems. The vanilla-
scented, chocolate-purple flowers, $\frac{1}{3}$ in. wide, are
borne in the leaf-axils in May. The flowers are
followed by $\frac{1}{2}$ in. wide globose fruits, which ripen
in August or September. This species makes an
admirable hedging plant in mild localities. 'Silver
Queen' has silver-grey variegated foliage.

P. tobira. Japan, China. Height 8–12 ft; spread
6–10 ft. This shrub is hardy only in sheltered
areas in the south and west, requiring wall
protection elsewhere. The lustrous, dark green
leaves are obovate and leathery. Cream-yellow, $\frac{1}{2}$
in. wide flowers with an orange fragrance are
borne from April to July in terminal clusters, 2–3
in. across. 'Variegatum' is an attractive silver
variegated form.

Cultivation. Plant young pot-grown plants in late
April or May in well-drained fertile soil in a
position sheltered from north and east winds.

To grow *P. tenuifolium* as a hedge, set the
plants 18 in. apart. Tip all the leading growths at
least twice in the first growing season; when the
hedge is large enough, shear to shape annually in
April and July.

Propagation. Separate the seeds from the viscous
substance which surrounds them by rubbing
them through dry sand. In March, sow the seeds
in John Innes seed compost in a cold frame; prick
off the seedlings into 3 in. pots of John Innes
potting compost No. 2. Most species require
potting on in 4–5 in. pots later in the year. Grow
the plants on in their pots in a cold frame for two
years before planting out in permanent positions
in May or June.

In July, take 3–4 in. cuttings of half-ripe lateral
shoots with a heel and insert them in a
propagating frame with bottom heat of 16–18°C
(61–64°F). When rooted, place the cuttings
singly in 3 in. pots of John Innes potting compost
No. 2 and overwinter them in a frost-free frame
or greenhouse.

Fast-growing plants such as *P. tenuifolium*
will be large enough to plant out the following
late April or May. Other species need potting on
in 4–5 in. pots and growing on in a plunge bed or
cold frame; plant them out in late May or June
a year later.

Pruning. Shorten straggly shoots in April or May
to maintain shapely plants. Trim established
hedges annually in April and June.

Pests and diseases. Generally trouble-free.

Plagianthus lyallii : see *Hoheria glabrata*
Plagianthus lyallii ribifolia : see *Hoheria lyallii*
Plagiorhegma : see Jeffersonia
Plane : see Platanus
Plane, London : see *Platanus × acerifolia*
Plane, oriental : see *Platanus orientalis*

Platanus

Plane. *Platanaceae*

A genus of ten species of hardy deciduous trees
which eventually may grow to a height of 100 ft
or more and are tolerant of industrial atmospheric
pollution. Although the leaves resemble those of
maples, they are larger and alternate instead of
opposite. The unisexual flowers produce seed

heads, resembling prickly balls, on pendulous
stalks. Large patches of bark flake off in winter.

P. × acerifolia, now correctly known as *P. ×
hispanicus* (London plane). Height 25–30 ft;
spread 15 ft. This hybrid is a round-headed tree
with lobed leaves and a strong, straight trunk.
The young mid-green leaves and shoots are
covered with fawn hairs which disappear with
maturity. Separate male and female flowers
appear in April and May in spherical clusters, $\frac{1}{4}$–$\frac{1}{3}$
in. across. They are pale green, the females
showing red styles and the males pale yellow
stamens. They are followed by pendulous
globular seed heads, borne singly or in clusters of
two to four. These ripen in September and
October, turning from mid-green to brown.

P. × hispanicus : see *P. × acerifolia*

PLATANUS ORIENTALIS

P. orientalis (oriental plane). S.E. Europe, Asia
Minor. Height 20–30 ft; spread 15–25 ft. A
long-lived tree with a rounded head and short,
broad trunk. The deeply lobed, dark green, glossy
leaves have downy undersides; the flowers are
insignificant and similar to those of *P. acerifolia.*
The globular seed heads, which ripen in
September, are borne in clusters of from two to
six and persist throughout the winter.

Cultivation. Plant between October and March
in well-drained loamy soil, in a sunny position.

Propagation. Seeds of *P. × acerifolia* must be
sown in great quantity as less than 1 per cent
germinate. The resultant plants vary in leaf form
and vigour. Sow them in April in pans or boxes
of John Innes seed compost in a cold frame. Prick
off the seedlings singly into 3 in. pots of John
Innes potting compost No. 2. Subsequently, set
them out in a nursery bed and grow on for three
or four years before planting them out from
October to March in permanent positions.

Take 8–10 in. cuttings of the current season's
wood in October and insert them in a cold frame
or sheltered border. Transfer them to a nursery
bed in October of the following year and grow
on for three or four years before planting out.

Branches pegged down for layering in
September can be severed after one or two years.

Pruning. Cut out crowded shoots and shape the
trees between November and February. They are
tolerant of hard pruning and severe lopping.

Pests. Generally trouble-free.

Diseases. The leaves may wither as a result
of a PHYSIOLOGICAL DISORDER.

Platycerium

Staghorn fern. *Polypodiaceae*

A genus of 17 species of epiphytic ferns. The
species described thrive in a cool greenhouse.

P. alcicorne : see *P. bifurcatum*

Pittosporum crassifolium
(fruits)

Pittosporum tobira

Platanus orientalis

Platycerium bifurcatum

Platycodon grandiflorum

Platystemon californicus

Plectranthus oertendahlii

P. bifurcatum, syn. *P. alcicorne.* Temperate Australia. Height and spread 1½–2½ ft. Evergreen. The round, wavy-edged, barren fronds lie flat against their support. Projecting, antler-like fertile fronds bear the plant's spores near their tips. Both types are mid-green. The fern puts out stolons which gradually develop into a colony of new plants firmly attached to the stock. *P. b.* 'Majus' is a stronger-growing variety with leathery fronds, the fertile ones less divided than those of the type.

PLATYCERIUM BIFURCATUM

P. grande. Malaya, N. Australia. Height and spread 6 ft or more. This evergreen species is similar to *P. bifurcatum* but is larger and more vigorous, and the fronds have deeper lobes. It also bears an additional, upper set of barren fronds which stand erect and fan-like.

Cultivation. Wire the plants to pieces of bark padded with sphagnum moss and hang up in the greenhouse. Alternatively, grow them in hanging baskets containing 2 parts fibrous peat, 1 part sphagnum moss, 1 part fibrous loam (parts by volume). Give established plants a top dressing of 2 parts peat and 1 part fibrous loam, with bone-meal added, each spring.

Good drainage for basket plants is essential. In hot weather spray plants with rainwater each day. During the winter keep the compost just moist and maintain a minimum temperature of 10°C (50°F).

Propagation. Sowing spores in March (see entry under FERNS) is the only means of raising a large number of plants, but it often results in failure.

A more certain method is to detach young plants from the stolons and attach them to fresh bark or plant them in baskets.

Pests and diseases. Generally trouble-free.

Platycodon

Balloon flower. *Campanulaceae*

PLATYCODON GRANDIFLORUM

A genus containing a single species. This is a hardy herbaceous perennial, suitable for growing in a border or on a large rock garden. The common name refers to the inflated shape of the flower buds.

P. grandiflorum. China, Manchuria, Japan. Height 12–24 in.; planting distance 15 in. A long-lived species with broadly ovate glaucous leaves. The balloon-shaped buds open to light blue, saucer-shaped flowers. These are about 1 in. across and are borne in terminal clusters from June to August.

P. g. 'Album' is a white-flowered form. *P. g.* 'Plenum' has semi-double, light blue flowers; two forms of this variety exist: 'Snowflakes', with white semi-double flowers, and 'Mother of Pearl', syn. *P. g.* 'Plenum Roseum', with pale pink flowers.

P. g. mariesii is a dwarf, less-erect variety, suitable for a rock garden or the front of a border. Height 9–12 in.; planting distance 12 in. The saucer-shaped flowers, 2 in. across, are in varying shades from pale to deep blue.

Cultivation. Plant in October or in February or March in ordinary, well-drained soil and in a sunny position. The white fleshy roots are slow-growing and, once established, resent disturbance. Renewed growth begins in late spring and the position of the plants should be marked to avoid damage during spring cultivation.

Propagation. In March, divide and replant any plants more than three or four years old. The divided plants are slow to re-establish themselves; propagation by seeds is preferable.

Sow seeds in March, in boxes under glass or in shallow drills outdoors. The seedlings are fragile and should be handled with care when pricking out. Transplant to flowering sites before the fleshy roots have formed, or delay transplanting until the plants are dormant during winter.

Pests and diseases. Generally trouble-free.

Platystemon

Papaveraceae

A genus of one hardy annual species. This is an attractive plant for edging borders and for planting in drifts on a rock garden. It is not particularly common, but is easy to grow.

P. californicus (cream cups). California. Height 12 in.; spacing 4 in. A compact plant with linear grey-green leaves that form a low cluster. The stems carry a mass of pale yellow or cream saucer-shaped flowers, 1 in. across, during July.

Cultivation. Medium to light soil is ideal, but any ordinary, well-drained soil gives reasonable results. Choose a sunny position.

Propagation. Sow the seeds in the flowering site in March or April, just covering them with soil. Thin out the seedlings to 4 in. apart. In sheltered sites with light soils, a September sowing produces early spring-flowering plants.

Pests and diseases. Generally trouble-free.

Pleated leaves: see *Curtonus paniculata*

Plectranthus

Labiatae

A genus of 250 species of evergreen perennial or sub-shrubby plants. Only a few species are in cultivation, and only one, *P. oertendahlii*, is readily available. It is suitable for cultivation in the greenhouse or the home.

P. oertendahlii. S. Africa. Height up to 6 in. This prostrate foliage plant, which roots from the nodes, is suitable for a hanging basket. The leaves are nearly circular, about 2 in. across, and bronze-green with silvery zones along the main veins. The inflorescence is 4–6 in. long and is composed of a loose panicle of tubular white-purple flowers, about ¾ in. long. The flowering period extends from June to October.

Cultivation. Grow these plants in any loam-based compost, such as John Innes potting compost No. 2, and overwinter at a temperature of 7–10°C (45–50°F). Water freely during spring and summer, but keep the plants just moist in winter.

In the home, stand the plants in a well-lit position; in the greenhouse, give light shading during the summer months, but allow all available light to the plants in winter.

Repot annually in April; set the plants singly in 4–5 in. pots or allow three plants to a 9 in. hanging basket.

Propagation. Detach rooted portions from April to June and pot them up separately in 3 in. pots of the growing compost.

Pests and diseases. Generally trouble-free.

Pleione
Orchidaceae

PLEIONE FORMOSANA (IN FLOWER)

A genus of about ten species of deciduous terrestrial or semi-epiphytic orchids. In the wild, these free-flowering pseudobulbous plants often grow on mossy rocks, tree trunks and branches. Those described here are suitable for an alpine or cool greenhouse, or for growing as house plants. In mild areas some species, notably *P. formosana* and its varieties, will usually survive outdoors in sheltered rock gardens.

The leaves generally appear after the flowers, rising from the bases of the short, squat pseudo-bulbs; they are mid-green, elliptic to lanceolate and prominently ribbed. The flowers, with lanceolate spreading petals and a tubular or trumpet-shaped labellum fringed at the mouth, are borne singly or occasionally in pairs on stems rising from the pseudobulbs. They are in shades of white, yellow, pink or mauve, often heavily marked with other colours.

See also ORCHIDS.

P. bulbocodioides: see *P. formosana*

P. formosana. Tibet to Formosa. This is the most common species, now correctly known as *P. bulbocodioides*; it is almost hardy and is suitable for growing on a sheltered rock garden, in a living-room or in a cold frame. The pseudobulbs are 1 in. high. Flower stems, 6 in. high, carry solitary or paired 3–4 in. wide flowers from January to May; outdoor flowering is in April and May. The long narrow petals and sepals vary from pure white to

Pleione formosana

deep mauve-pink; the fringed and crested lip is usually paler and spotted with brick-red, ginger or yellow.

'Alba' is an attractive pure white form; *P. f. limprichtii* is a richly coloured purple-red form with slightly smaller flowers than the species; 'Oriental Splendour', syn. *P. pricei*, has dark purple pseudobulbs, and the flowers are of a deeper purple colour.

P. humilis. Nepal, N. India. A half-hardy dwarf species with pseudobulbs 1–1½ in. high. The solitary flowers, about 3 in. wide, are borne on 4 in. high stems from January to May; outdoors in April and May. The petals and sepals vary from white to pale mauve, and the fringed and white-keeled lip is heavily spotted with rows of purple, crimson or yellow-brown spots.

P. praecox. Nepal, China, India. This somewhat tender species has barrel-shaped, deep green, 1½ in. high pseudobulbs which are spotted with maroon. Each 6 in. high flowering stem carries a single 3 in. wide flower between November and January. The petals and sepals are deep rose-pink, and the lip, which has a pale yellow disc and five keels, is pale pink.

P. pricei: see *P. formosana*

Cultivation. Indoors or under glass, grow pleiones in a mixture of 2 parts John Innes potting compost No. 1 and 1 part sphagnum moss (parts by volume). Plant in April or May, setting three to five pseudobulbs in a 4–6 in. pan with the basal third of each embedded in the compost. Shade the plants from direct sun between April and September, and ventilate the greenhouse daily except in frosty and foggy weather.

Pleione formosana 'Alba'

Pleione formosana limprichtii

Pleione formosana 'Oriental Splendour'

Pleione humilis

Pleione praecox

Plum 'Cambridge Gage'

Apply a weak liquid feed fortnightly from June to September. Do not over-water, or bring the bulbs into direct contact with water too early in the season, or brown tips and blotches may form on the leaves. Water the plants generously when they are in full growth, using an overhead spray during hot spells; withhold the water supply as the foliage turns yellow and dies away. When the plants are dormant, plunge them in a shaded frame. Repot every two years in April or May.

Outdoors, plant pleiones in April or May in light, well-drained soil enriched with leaf-mould or peat. Choose a sheltered and partially shaded position. In all but the most sheltered positions cover the plants with open-ended cloches from October to April and, ideally, to help ripen the pseudobulbs, place the cloches in position as soon as the leaves begin to turn yellow.

Propagation. Detach the offsets from the base of the parent pseudobulbs at repotting time, and pot them singly in $2\frac{1}{2}$–3 in. pots of the growing compost or several together in a 4 in. pan. Grow on in a cool greenhouse, potting on as necessary.

In addition to offsets, each pseudobulb produces at its top a number of pseudobulbils. These drop off at the end of the growing season and may be collected. In April or May, place them in pans of the growing compost to half their depth and grow on for two seasons. At the end of the first season they should be ready to pot up as described for offsets.

Pests. Young shoots and flowers may be attacked by SLUGS.

GLASSHOUSE RED SPIDER MITES infest plants under glass, causing a mottling and premature yellowing of the foliage.

Diseases. A PHYSIOLOGICAL DISORDER, due to over-watering, shows as browning of the leaf tips and brown blotches on the foliage.

Plum and damson

Prunus domestica and *P. insititia. Rosaceae*

PLUM (FAN-TRAINED)

A group of hardy trees and shrubs, generally deciduous, which bear edible fruits. The plum cultivated in Great Britain is possibly a hybrid between *Prunus spinosa*, the sloe, and *P. cerasifera*, the myrobalan plum.

Gages are a type of plum which produce better-flavoured fruits, but which require more favourable growing conditions. Damsons, which are grown for cooking and jam-making, are generally smaller than plums; they are often tapered at both ends and are usually produced in abundance.

A few varieties can be grown on their own roots, but plums are usually budded or grafted on to a rootstock of known performance and grown as bush, half-standard, standard or fan trees.

There are no really dwarfing rootstocks available for plums, and the trees often take from four to six years to commence cropping. They are not therefore, ideal where space is limited; nor are they suitable for growing as trained trees other than fans.

Because of their early flowering, plums should not be planted in cold or exposed positions. The most satisfactory areas for their cultivation are those in the south and east of England and the West Midlands, with annual rainfalls of 20–35 in. They can be interplanted successfully with black currants.

Gages need a site that is warm and dry in summer; they produce the best-quality fruits when grown against a wall.

Damsons succeed in areas with higher rainfall and less sun than plums. Their hardiness and late flowering make them suitable as windbreaks.

Average height and spread of all three types of trees are as follows: bushes, 15 ft × 12 ft; half-standards, 20 ft × 15 ft; standards, 25 ft × 20 ft; fans, 8 ft × 5 ft.

Planting distances: bushes, 15 ft; half-standards, 18 ft; standards, 20 ft; fans 15–18 ft.

Some varieties are self-fertile but even these usually crop more consistently when pollinators are present.

PLUM (STANDARD)

PLUMS AND GAGES

'Cambridge Gage'. Mid to late August. This greenish-yellow round gage is good for both dessert and bottling. It sets a poor crop with its own pollen and associates best with 'Czar', 'Golden Transparent', 'Laxton's Gage' or 'Oullin's Golden Gage'. Flowers late.

'Coe's Golden Drop'. Late September to early October. An amber-yellow plum with red spots. It is sweet and rich, but not a heavy cropper. It does not set fruit without a pollinator and is best associated with 'Denniston's Superb' or 'Early Transparent Gage'. This is a good dessert plum that requires a sheltered site for consistently good results. Flowers early.

'Czar'. Early August. A rounded ovoid plum, dull red when ripe with a waxy blue bloom. This is a good cooking plum with golden flesh and red juice. It is self-fertile and a good cropper, but is susceptible to silver leaf disease. Flowers late.

'Denniston's Superb'. Mid-August. A broadly ovoid dessert plum, greenish-yellow when ripe. The golden flesh has a gage-like flavour. One of the best varieties for a small garden; it is self-fertile and crops well. Flowers early.

'Early Transparent Gage'. Mid-August. An apricot-yellow gage with carmine spots. It has a good flavour as a dessert fruit, but will not hang long before splitting. It is self-fertile, setting a good crop with its own pollen. Flowers early.

'Golden Transparent'. Early October. A yellow plum, flecked with red. The firm, sweet flesh is of

Plum 'Kirke's'

Plum 'Victoria'

excellent flavour. This is one of the largest dessert plums, but it is a poor to medium cropper. Self-fertile. Flowers late.

'Jefferson's Gage'. Early September. This golden-yellow gage with red spots is a juicy dessert fruit with a rich flavour. It does not set fruit without a pollinator and is best associated with 'Denniston's Superb' or 'Early Transparent Gage'. Flowers early.

'Kirke's'. Mid-September. A purple-black plum with a blue bloom and good flavour. Though not a heavy cropper it is one of the finest dessert plums. Best grown on a wall. It does not set fruit without a pollinator and is best associated with 'Czar', 'Golden Transparent' or 'Laxton's Gage'. Flowers mid-season.

'Laxton's Gage'. August. A large, ovoid, golden-yellow gage with juicy flesh of moderate flavour; suitable for table use. It is a self-fertile, free-cropping gage that flowers late.

'Oullin's Golden Gage'. Mid-August. A green to golden-yellow gage with green dots and lines, and a slight bloom. This sweet but mild-flavoured dessert fruit is also good for bottling. It sets a poor crop with its own pollen and associates best with 'Czar', 'Golden Transparent' or 'Laxton's Gage'. Flowers late.

'Victoria'. Late August. A bright red plum, with darker speckling, sometimes flushed yellow. It is recommended for bottling and jam-making, and has a good flavour for dessert use. The growth is brittle and there is a risk of branches splitting. Susceptible to silver leaf. It is self-fertile and sets a good crop. Flowers mid-season.

DAMSONS

'Farleigh Damson'. Mid-September. The small oval fruits are mainly used for cooking. The black skin is thickly overlaid with a white waxy bloom; the firm green-yellow flesh has a good flavour. A prolific cropper when associated with 'Cambridge Gage', 'Czar' or 'Golden Transparent'. Flowers late.

'Merryweather'. Late August and September. The large, black, fine-flavoured fruits are good for dessert and bottling. Self-fertile and needs no pollinator. Flowers mid-season.

Cultivation. Nurseries usually supply suitable combinations of rootstock and tree forms to suit the space available.

When planting fan-trained trees against a wall, choose 'Oullin's Golden Gage' or 'Victoria' for a north-facing wall; 'Coe's Golden Drop' or 'Victoria' for east-facing; 'Early Transparent Gage', 'Jefferson's Gage' or 'Victoria' for west-facing walls. The most favoured south-facing positions should be reserved for the gages and 'Coe's Golden Drop'.

Plums, gages and damsons do best in deep, well-drained heavy loams, and will tolerate slightly acid soils.

Plant maiden trees (two or three-year-olds if the trees are to be trained) in the autumn, and stake at planting time. For the best results, plant in bare soil so that grass and weeds do not compete for moisture in summer.

Do not bury the union between rootstock and scion, otherwise the variety will form its own roots and the effect of the rootstock will be lost.

Firm any trees that are lifted by frost during the months after planting. Watch for drying out early in the first season after planting; water if necessary or mulch with well-rotted manure, compost or peat to retain moisture.

Plums benefit from dressings of nitrogen and also from applications of bulky organic manures. Give established trees a dressing of sulphate of ammonia or its equivalent annually at $1\frac{1}{2}$–2 oz. per sq. yd (reduced to about half that amount if bulky organic manures are also given) and $\frac{1}{2}$ oz. sulphate of potash. Apply superphosphate every two or three years at $1\frac{1}{2}$–2 oz. per sq. yd. Vary applications according to tree growth and cropping; give less to fan-trained trees, where little extension growth is required.

Plum 'Coe's Golden Drop'

Plum 'Denniston's Superb'

Plum 'Merryweather' (damson)

Plumbago capensis

three weeks in a cool place if picked when under-ripe and wrapped in paper.

Propagation. Most varieties are budded in July and August or grafted in March on to plum rootstocks; a few, including 'Cambridge Gage' are grown on their own roots. See also chapter headed PROPAGATION.

Pruning. Due to the risk of silver leaf disease which attacks through wounds, the timing of pruning is important. To ensure speedy healing of cuts, prune young trees in early spring, established trees in summer. The method is explained in the chapter headed PRUNING.

Pests. BIRDS, especially bullfinches, eat flower buds during the winter.

APHIDS infest young shoots and older leaves, fouling the plants and checking growth.

PLUM SAWFLY larvae tunnel into young fruits.

Diseases. BACTERIAL CANKER is seen during the summer as brown spots on the leaves. The spots fall out, leaving holes. Cankers develop and show as elongated flattened lesions along the branches, with copious gum exuding from them. The following spring the buds of an infected branch either fail to open, or if leaves do develop they turn yellow, become narrow and curled and soon wither and die. The whole branch dies back.

BROWN ROT causes a rapid decay of the fruits while still on the tree, so that they turn brown and are covered with white raised cushions of fungus spores. Diseased fruits shrivel and dry up.

HONEY FUNGUS may kill trees rapidly.

PHYSIOLOGICAL DISORDERS of various types result in gumming of the fruits, discoloration of the leaves and DIE-BACK of the shoots.

SHOT HOLE, due to a fungus, causes numerous brown rounded spots to develop on the leaves; the tissues fall away, leaving holes.

SILVER LEAF causes a silvering of the foliage on one or more branches, which die back. Later, flat purple fruiting bodies of the fungus appear on dead wood. A purple-brown stain is produced on the inner tissues of diseased stems; a cross-section of a branch bearing silvered leaves should be examined for signs of this stain to confirm the presence of the disease. It should not be confused with false silver leaf, a physiological disorder which produces silvering on most leaves, but will not cause die-back.

For trees in cultivated soil, apply fertilisers early in March; for those in grass, apply in December or January.

Plums are shallow-rooted and can be harmed by deep cultivation. Control weeds by shallow hoeing or by spraying with paraquat. If trees are growing in grass, keep it close cut, especially during dry weather in summer.

Remove suckers as they form, pulling them out with as little root disturbance as possible.

If possible, protect the flower buds against bird damage in winter by covering the trees with netting or by spraying with a deterrent.

Reduce the risk of silver leaf attack by avoiding branch splitting and breakage caused by heavy crops, especially on brittle-branched varieties such as 'Victoria'. Support individual branches with stakes, wrapping the branch to avoid chafing, or use a tall central post and tie the branches to it. Thin the crop to 2–3 in. apart (rather more for varieties with large fruits) to improve size, colour and flavour. Start early in June but do not complete thinning until after the natural fall.

Leave dessert fruits to ripen on the tree and pick them carefully when ready; it may be necessary to go over the tree several times. Fruits for jam, bottling or cooking, particularly gages, are best picked before they ripen.

Normally, plums will not store after picking, but 'Coe's Golden Drop' can be kept for two or

Plumbago

Plumbaginaceae

PLUMBAGO CAPENSIS

A genus of 12 species of evergreen flowering shrubs or climbers. They have a wide distribution on all continents except Australia. Two species are in general cultivation; they are ornamental plants which may be grown as pot plants or as climbers in a conservatory or greenhouse.

P. capensis. S. Africa. Height up to 15 ft. A climbing species, best grown in the greenhouse border where the weak, floppy stems need tying to supports. It may also be grown as a pot plant when it will attain a height of 4–6 ft. It has elliptic mid-green leaves about 3 in. long. Panicles, 9–12 in. long, of pale blue flowers are produced from April to November. Each slender-tubed, primrose-like flower is 1 in. across.

P. rosea. East Indies. Height up to 3 ft; spread up to 24 in. The elliptic leaves, 3 in. long, are mid-green. Primrose-like scarlet flowers are borne in 6–9 in. spikes from June to August.

Cultivation. Grow plumbagos in John Innes potting compost No. 3. Both species can be grown in 6–8 in. pots, but *P. capensis* is best planted out in the greenhouse border and trained to wires, string or trellis. A winter temperature of 7°C (45°F) is sufficient for *P. capensis*; if a temperature of 13–16°C (55–61°F) can be given up to December, the flowering period will be prolonged. *P. rosea* needs a winter temperature of 13°C (55°F).

Water freely from April until after flowering or until October. During winter, keep the plants just moist, increasing the amounts of water as new growths appear.

Place in a well-lit position, but in summer provide light shading, particularly for *P. rosea*. Pot plants of *P. capensis* can be stood outdoors in a sunny spot from June to September.

Repot annually in March or April and feed with liquid manure at intervals of two weeks from May to September.

Propagation. Take heel cuttings, 3–4 in. long, of firm non-flowering lateral shoots from *P. capensis* in June or July. Insert the cuttings, three or five to a 3 in. pot in equal parts (by volume) peat and sand, and root at a temperature of 16–18°C (61–64°F).

Increase *P. rosea* by 3–4 in. long cuttings of young basal shoots in April or May. Root the cuttings in the manner described for *P. capensis*, but at a temperature of 18–21°C (64–70°F).

Pruning. Cut back *P. capensis* after flowering, shortening all growths by two-thirds. Cut back *P. rosea* to within 6 in. of the base when it has finished flowering.

Pests. ROOT KNOT EELWORMS invade the roots and form swollen contorted galls. Severe infestations will check growth.

Diseases. A PHYSIOLOGICAL DISORDER results in the leaves turning yellow.

Plum, cherry: see *Prunus cerasifera*
Plums, ornamental: see Prunus
Poached egg flower: see *Limnanthes douglasii*
Pocket-handkerchief tree: see Davidia

Podophyllum
Podophyllaceae

A genus of ten species of hardy herbaceous perennials. They are useful for a shady border with moist soil, rich in humus. The creeping rootstocks and thick fibrous roots are poisonous.
P. emodi. India. Height 12 in.; planting distance 18 in. A species with mid-green orbicular leaves,

deeply lobed and sharply toothed, usually marbled with copper-brown when young. White saucer-shaped flowers, up to 1½ in. across, appear in June and are followed by 1–2 in. long red elliptic fruits. *P. e.* 'Majus' is a larger variety, up to 18 in. high; *P. e. chinensis* is smaller-growing, with more boldly patterned leaves, and flowers delicately flushed with pink.

Cultivation. Plant in March or April in a partly shaded position and in moist soil containing plenty of decayed vegetable matter. Cut the stems down in November.

Propagation. Divide and replant the roots in March or April.

Seeds may be sown in a cold frame in March, or as soon as ripe in summer. Prick out the seedlings when large enough to handle, and grow the young plants on in a nursery bed. Transplant to their permanent positions in March of the second year.

Pests and diseases. Generally trouble-free.

Poinsettia, annual: see *Euphorbia heterophylla*
Poinsettia, Christmas: see *Euphorbia pulcherrima*
Poke weed: see *Phytolacca americana*

Polemonium
Polemoniaceae

A genus of about 50 species of herbaceous perennials. They are hardy and easily grown plants for a border, with bowl or saucer-shaped flowers in shades of blue or purple. The delicate feathery pinnate foliage is composed of lanceolate to ovate leaflets.

P. carneum. W. United States. Height and planting distance 15–20 in. or more. This species produces many-branched spreading stems to form a dome-shaped mound. It bears mid-green pinnate leaves with narrow lanceolate leaflets. A profusion of wide bowl-shaped flowers, ¾–1 in. across, are borne in succession from April to July. The flowers are pink in the type species, but pale yellow and blue forms are known.

P. coeruleum (jacob's ladder, Greek valerian). N. Hemisphere, including England. Height up to 24 in.; spread 12 in. This variable species produces tufts of arching mid-green leaves, composed of slender-pointed lanceolate leaflets. Branched racemes of blue or white, ½ in. wide flowers are borne from April to July, or later.

P. foliosissimum. Rocky Mountains, U.S.A. Height 3 ft; planting distance 18 in. The erect stems of this species carry abundant dark green, pinnate leaves. Clustered heads of bowl-shaped, deep mauve-blue flowers, ½ in. across, are produced from early June to September.

P. humile. Siberia. Height 18–24 in.; planting distance 18 in. The species is rarely available and has been superseded by the more vigorous variety 'Sapphire'. This forms long-lived tufts of pale green foliage, and carries clustered sprays of light blue saucer-shaped flowers, ½ in. across, during May and June.

P. reptans. North America. Height 6–12 in.; planting distance 15 in. This species, which is suitable for a rock garden, forms spreading

Plumbago rosea

Podophyllum emodi

Podophyllum emodi chinensis

Polemonium carneum

matted clumps of deep green leaves. Sprays of bright blue, saucer-shaped, ½ in. wide flowers are borne from May to June. 'Blue Pearl' is the variety most frequently available.

Cultivation. Plant from October to March or April in ordinary garden soil, in sun or in partial shade. Polemoniums will grow in any soil, but flower more profusely in rich, loamy soil as the fibrous roots quickly exhaust the soil.

Cut faded flower stems back to basal growths as soon as flowering is over.

Propagation. Divide and replant older plants from October to March.

Pests and diseases. Generally trouble-free.

Polemonium foliosissimum

Polianthes tuberosa 'The Pearl'

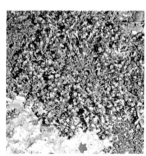

Polygala calcarea

Polianthes

Agavaceae, syn. *Amaryllidaceae*

A genus of 13 species of tender, tuberous-rooted perennials. Only one species is in cultivation. It is grown as a greenhouse pot plant which can be brought into a well-lit living-room during the summer. It produces its heavily scented flowers in late summer in an unheated greenhouse, but with sufficient heat can be induced to flower at almost any season.

POLIANTHES TUBEROSA

P. tuberosa (tuberose). Mexico. Height 2–4 ft. The strap-shaped mid-green leaves grow at ground level. Pure white flowers, about 1 in. long, are borne in erect spikes. Each flower has six open petals growing from a funnel-shaped tube. 'The Pearl' is a double variety.

Cultivation. Plant 1 in. deep in well-moistened John Innes potting compost No. 1 in the autumn as soon as the rhizomes are available, setting them singly in 5 in. pots or three together in 6–7 in. pots. To get a succession of flowers, plunge some of the pots in peat and keep at a minimum temperature of 18°C (64°F). Place others in a cool but frost-free greenhouse or frame.

When planted in moist compost, watering is unnecessary until the first leaves appear; then begin regular watering. In a cool greenhouse water the pots only if the compost becomes dust dry, and then lightly. Do not shade the plants, otherwise they will become tall and thin-stemmed and may need staking. By bringing successive batches into the warmth, flowers can be obtained from spring to late summer.

Propagation. Numerous offsets are produced. These may be removed and replanted in autumn, but in Great Britain they are seldom ripened satisfactorily, and few will produce flowers. It is better to buy a fresh batch of imported tubers each year.

Pests and diseases. Generally trouble-free.

Polyanthus: see *Primula vulgaris*

Polygala myrtifolia grandiflora

Polygala

Polygalaceae

A genus of about 600 species of hardy and tender annuals, perennials, shrubs and sub-shrubs. One of the following species requires greenhouse treatment; the other two are hardy dwarf plants for rock gardens or for growing in pans in an alpine house. The flowers are somewhat pea-like, with wing petals and a keel; they are borne in terminal racemes.

ALPINE SPECIES

P. calcarea (milkwort). Europe, including Great Britain. Height 2–3 in.; spread 12 in. This perennial species forms a mid to dark green mat of spreading branches covered with small ovate-spathulate leaves. It carries a profusion of bright blue racemes, 1–2 in. long, from May to August; each raceme is composed of 6–12 small flowers. The plant is sometimes short-lived.

P. chamaebuxus (ground box). Mountains of Europe. Height 6 in.; spread 9–12 in. A dwarf evergreen shrub forming spreading clumps of dark green oblong-lanceolate leaves. Cream and yellow flowers, tipped with purple, appear from April to June; they are carried in racemes 1–2 in. long, of up to six flowers. The variety 'Purpurea' has flowers tipped with carmine-purple.

GREENHOUSE SPECIES

P. myrtifolia. S. Africa. The only form in cultivation is *P. m. grandiflora*. Height 4 ft or more; spread 2–3 ft. A tender evergreen shrub with pale green obovate leaves. Rich rose-purple flowers, 1–1½ in. long, are produced in short terminal racemes from May to October.

Cultivation of alpine species. Plant these polygalas between September and March. Both species thrive in ordinary, well-drained garden soil, but *P. chamaebuxus* does best in soil enriched with leaf-mould or peat. Plant *P. calcarea* in full sun, *P. chamaebuxus* in partial shade.

In the alpine house, grow polygalas in 6–8 in. pans. *P. calcarea* does well in John Innes potting compost No. 1; for *P. chamaebuxus*, use a mixture of 2 parts John Innes lime-free potting compost No. 1 and 1 part leaf-mould (parts by volume). Repot every two years, after flowering.

Cultivation of greenhouse species. Grow *P. myrtifolia* in the greenhouse border or in 6–8 in. pots of John Innes potting compost No. 2 or a proprietary peat compost. Water freely during summer; in winter keep the compost just moist, never allowing the plants to dry out completely. From May to September give a dilute liquid feed at fortnightly intervals; provide light shade, and ventilate the greenhouse freely when the temperature exceeds 13°C (55°F). In winter, maintain a minimum night temperature of 4–7°C (39–45°F). Repot annually in April.

Propagation of alpine species. Take 1½–2 in. softwood cuttings of lateral or basal shoots, preferably with a heel, between June and August; insert in a cold frame in equal parts (by volume) peat and sand. When rooted, pot the cuttings into 2½–3 in. pots. Overwinter in the frame or plunge outdoors in a sheltered site. They will be ready for planting out in permanent sites the following April or May.

P. chamaebuxus may also be divided and replanted during March.

Propagation of greenhouse species. In April or May, take heel cuttings, about 3 in. long, of young lateral shoots. Insert the cuttings in equal parts (by volume) peat and sand in a propagating frame at a temperature of 16°C (61°F). When rooted, pot the cuttings singly into 3 in. containers of John Innes potting compost No. 1 and pot on as necessary. Pinch out the growing tips at least twice during the early stages to encourage bushy growth.

Pruning of greenhouse species Shorten the growths of *P. myrtifolia grandiflora* by half to two-thirds in late February if the plants are getting too large or leggy.

Pests. Plants under glass may be infested by GLASSHOUSE WHITEFLIES and by GLASSHOUSE RED SPIDER MITES, either of which can cause mottling of the leaves and premature leaf-drop.

Diseases. Generally trouble-free.

Polygonatum

Solomon's seal. *Liliaceae*

POLYGONATUM × HYBRIDUM

A genus of 50 species of herbaceous perennials. They are mainly hardy and are suitable for shady borders and as cut flowers; one dwarf species is excellent for rock gardens or for growing in pans in the alpine house.

The taller species of these easily-grown plants have arching stems with small pendulous clusters of tubular flowers borne from the upper leaf axils.

P. biflorum. Eastern U.S.A. Height 1–3 ft; planting distance 12–18 in. This species has pale to mid-green leaves that are ovate to lanceolate-oblong in shape. Green and white flowers, ½ in. long and usually in pairs, appear in May.

P. commutatum, syn. *P. giganteum* (giant Solomon's seal). U.S.A. Height up to 7 ft; planting distance 2½ ft. In rich, moist soil this species grows extremely tall. The pale to mid-green leaves are ovate to lanceolate-oblong. White flowers, ¾–1¼ in. long, are borne in axillary clusters of three to eight in May.

P. giganteum: see *P. commutatum*

P. hookeri. W. Szechwan, Tibet, Sikkim. Height 2–4 in.; spread 12 in. A dwarf species for the rock garden or alpine house. The mid-green ovate leaves and the ½–¾ in. long, lilac-pink flowers appear together as the plant emerges in May.

P. × *hybridum* (Solomon's seal, David's harp). Europe, including Great Britain; N. Asia. Height 2–4 ft; planting distance 12–18 in. Although 'Solomon's seal' is usually listed under the specific name of *P. multiflorum* the plant is a hybrid between *P. multiflorum* and the rare *P. odoratum.* It is extremely hardy and grows in any soil and almost any aspect. The mid-green leaves are oblong and clasp the stems. White flowers, slightly waisted and up to 1 in. long, are produced in June in clusters of two to five.

P. japonicum. Japan. Height 12–18 in.; planting distance 12 in. A border plant with oblong mid-green leaves. The flowers are white, ⅓–¾ in. long, with green teeth at the end of the corolla tube. They appear in clusters of two or three during April and May.

P. multiflorum: see *P.* × *hybridum*

Cultivation. Plant between September and March in well-drained soil. *P.* × *hybridum* will grow in almost any soil and in a sunny position, provided the roots are protected from sunlight. The other species do best in peaty soil or leaf-mould, preferably under the partial shade of trees or shrubs; otherwise mulch annually in March with peat to prevent the roots drying out in summer. Cut down all species except *P. hookeri* in November.

Grow *P. hookeri* in a shaded part of the rock garden; or in the alpine house, in 6–8 in. pans of John Innes potting compost No. 1. Repot every second or third year in September.

Propagation. Divide and replant the spreading roots in October or March.

Seeds should be sown when ripe, before October, in John Innes seed compost in a cold frame. It may be 18 months before seedlings appear. Prick out the seedlings, when they are large enough to handle, and grow on in a nursery bed for two or three years.

Pests. Considerable damage may be caused by the larvae of SAWFLIES, which feed on the leaves.

Diseases. Generally trouble-free.

Polygonum

Knotweed. *Polygonaceae*

A genus of about 300 species of hardy annuals, herbaceous perennials and deciduous shrubby climbers. All bear an abundance of tiny bell-shaped flowers. Some of the perennial species are weedy or short-lived, but those described are suitable for growing in borders or rock gardens. *P. baldschuanicum* is one of the most rampant and vigorous of all climbers.

Polygala chamaebuxus

Polygonatum hookeri

Polygonatum × *hybridum*

Polygonum tenuicaule

Polygonum affine 'Donald Lowndes'

Polygonum baldschuanicum

Polygonum vaccinifolium

Polygonum amplexicaule
atrosanguineum

ALPINE SPECIES

P. tenuicaule. Japan. Height 4 in.; spread 12–18 in. This plant has ovate mid-green leaves. White flowers are produced in March and April, before the leaves expand, in spikes 1–2 in. long. The species is suitable for an alpine house.

P. vaccinifolium. Himalayas. Height 6 in.; spread up to 3 ft. This widely grown species makes a close mat of shining, evergreen, ovate to elliptic leaves. It produces a clump of erect spikes, $2\frac{1}{2}$–4 in. long, of pale rose-red flowers from August to October. It trails well over a wall.

HERBACEOUS SPECIES

P. affine. Nepal. Height 6–9 in.; planting distance 18 in. This variable species is usually represented in cultivation by the following two varieties, which are valuable for ground cover and for growing on a rock garden:

'Darjeeling Red' spreads rapidly to form a dense mat. The narrow, lanceolate, dark green leaves remain russet-brown in winter until they are replaced in spring by young bright green leaves. Deep pink spikes, 6 in. long, of tiny close-set flowers appear from July to September.

'Donald Lowndes' is more compact and has larger lanceolate leaves which are bright green when young, but darken with age and remain brown until new leaves appear in spring. Bright rose-red flower spikes, 6–8 in. long, are borne in June; young plants flower over a longer period.

POLYGONUM AMPLEXICAULE

P. amplexicaule. Himalayas. Height 3–4 ft; planting distance 2–$2\frac{1}{2}$ ft. A variable species which forms stout bushy clumps that require ample space. The heart-shaped pointed leaves are deep green. The forms most readily available are *P. a. atrosanguineum*, with red flower spikes, and 'Firetail', with scarlet spikes. Both varieties begin flowering in June when the new growths are only 18–24 in. high and continue to produce numerous spikes, 6 in. long, throughout the summer and into autumn.

P. bistorta (snakeweed). Europe, including Great Britain. The true species is rarely cultivated, but the variety 'Superbum' is suitable for a herbaceous border. Height up to 3 ft; planting distance 24 in. A vigorous, mat-forming plant with ovate, light green leaves. In May and June, 6 in. spikes of close-set clear pink flowers are produced; a second crop may follow in late summer.

P. campanulatum. Himalayas. Height $2\frac{1}{2}$–$3\frac{1}{2}$ ft; planting distance $2\frac{1}{2}$ ft. A leafy bushy species which rapidly forms spreading colonies. The growths, which bear ovate, pointed, mid-green leaves, become dense and are profusely set with 2–3 in. wide heads of shell-pink flowers from mid-June to September.

P. macrophyllum: see *P. sphaerostachyum*

P. millettii. Nepal. Height 12–18 in.; planting distance 12 in. A choice, slow-growing species with narrow oblong-lanceolate, deep green leaves. Glowing, deep red flower spikes, 2–3 in. long, appear from June to September.

P. sphaerostachyum, syn. *P. macrophyllum.* Himalayas. Height and planting distance 18 in. The small rootstock produces masses of branching stems to form a dense bushy plant bearing linear, pointed, bright green leaves. Bright pink flower spikes, 2–3 in. long, appear in profusion from June to October.

SHRUBBY CLIMBERS

P. aubertii: see *P. baldschuanicum*

P. baldschuanicum (Russian vine). Bokhara. This species is invaluable for screening purposes. It is useful for twining over an old tree, and is also suitable for growing on wires or a trellis. It may grow 10–15 ft in a year and reach an eventual eight of 40 ft. The pale, bright green leaves are ovate. Pale pink or white flowers, in panicles 0–18 in. long, are borne in great profusion from July to September.

POLYGONUM BALDSCHUANICUM

White-flowered plants may be of the closely allied species *P. aubertii*, from Szechwan.

P. multiflorum. China, Japan. Height 6–10 ft. This species is less vigorous and hardy but makes an attractive twining wall plant. It requires a position facing south or south-west. The light green leaves are ovate, the young stems an attractive red. White or pink-tinted flowers are borne in 8–12 in. long panicles during August and September.

Cultivation of alpine species. Plant between October and March in any ordinary garden soil in a sunny position. Choose the site carefully, as the plants tend to be invasive. *P. tenuicaule* does best in moist soil and in partial shade.

In the alpine house grow *P. tenuicaule* in 6–8 in. pans of John Innes potting compost No. 1. Repot annually between September and March.

Cultivation of herbaceous species. Plant between October and March in rich moist soil in sun or partial shade. *P. campanulatum* is best grown in light shade. In October or November, cut down the flowering stems to ground level.

Cultivation of shrubby climbers. *P. baldschuanicum* thrives in any type of soil, including chalk. Aspect is unimportant, although a little shelter is advisable for young plants. *P. multiflorum* needs a prepared soil pocket of 1 part each of loam, leaf-mould and peat, and $\frac{1}{2}$ part sand (parts by volume) at the base of a wall. Plant out young pot-grown plants of both species during late March or early April, and support the young growths with twiggy sticks, after pinching out the growing points to promote branching. Pinch the plants out two or three times during summer.

In cold areas, protect *P. multiflorum* during the winter by covering the rootstock with bracken or leaves.

Propagation of alpine and herbaceous species. Divide alpine species in March, herbaceous species in October or March; replant direct into permanent positions.

Propagation of shrubby climbers. Take heel cuttings, 3–4 in. long, from half-ripe wood during July or August and insert in a cold frame in equal parts (by volume) sand and peat or sand and soil. Pot up when rooted.

Hardwood cuttings, about 10 in. long, can be rooted in the open ground. Insert them during October or November in a trench, with a layer of sand at the base, preferably in a sheltered position under a wall or hedge. Alternatively, insert the cuttings directly in the flowering site.

Except for cuttings inserted in their permanent sites, all young plants should be potted singly in 4–5 in. containers of John Innes potting compost

Polypodium vulgare 'Macrostachyon'

No. 2. Plunge outdoors until the following spring when the plants may be transplanted to their flowering positions.

Pruning of shrubby climbers. Cut back *P. multiflorum* to 12 in. above ground level in April. *P. baldschuanicum* generally does not require any pruning.

Pests. Young growths of the flowering climbers may be distorted and infested by APHIDS.

Diseases. Generally trouble-free.

Polypodium
Polypodiaceae

A genus of 75 species of ferns with fleshy, creeping rhizomes. The species described is a hardy, evergreen, ornamental garden plant.

See also FERNS.

P. vulgare (polypody). Circumpolar, N. Hemisphere. Height 6–15 in.; spread indefinite. The mid-green fronds are pinnatifid and elegantly drooping; they retain their colour until late winter. *P. v.* 'Cornubiense', which is usually infertile, is a finely cut variety which produces tripinnate, quadripinnate and pinnatifid fronds on the same plant. The pinnatifid fronds are not typical and should be removed.

P. v. 'Macrostachyon' is similar to the type species but is more robust, with broad full fronds that taper to a long point.

P. v. 'Pulcherrimum' is a robust variety with deeply pinnatifid fronds, similar to *P. v.* 'Cornubiense' but fully fertile. The varieties are usually a lighter green than the type species.

Cultivation. Plant the rhizomes during April or May, in sun or partial shade, when the new fronds are just appearing. Set them on or just beneath the surface of the soil—preferably one containing plenty of stones—to which humus has been added. Anchor the rhizomes with staples of bent wire or with stones.

Polygonum bistorta 'Superbum'

Polygonum campanulatum

Polypodium vulgare

Polystichum falcatum

Polystichum setiferum

Polystichum setiferum
'Divisilobum'

If growing the plants under glass, plant them in shallow pans containing a compost of equal parts (by volume) leaf-mould, loam, and gravel or coarse sand or pea-sized mortar rubble. Water freely during the growing season; for the rest of the year keep the soil just moist.

Propagation. Divide and replant the rhizomes in April or May.

Pests. Generally trouble-free.

Diseases. Sometimes RUST develops on the undersurface of the fronds, showing as scattered or loosely grouped brown spore pustules.

Polypody: see *Polypodium vulgare*

Polystichum

Aspidiaceae

A genus of 135 species of hardy ferns. All those described are evergreen. Some are suitable for the garden, others for growing under glass.

P. acrostichioides (Christmas fern). N. America. Height 3 ft; spread 24 in. The deep green fronds of this garden fern are narrowly pinnate and retain their colour throughout the winter. In the U.S.A. they are used for Christmas decoration. The new fronds are covered with glistening white scales. The spore-heaps gradually join together as they ripen, eventually covering the backs of the upper fronds.

P. aculeatum (hard shield fern). Europe, N. America, S.W. Asia, China, Japan. Height 2–3 ft; spread 1–2½ ft. This is an attractive garden fern, found chiefly in the wetter parts of Britain. The lanceolate, pinnate fronds are deep green, glossy and leathery, with deeply dissected pinnules. Stalks and midribs are covered with brown scales.

P. a. 'Gracillimum', height and spread 3 ft, i one of the most beautiful of British ferns. The delicate fronds have almost hair-like pinnules Although hardy, it thrives best in shade in a col greenhouse. *P. a.* 'Pulcherrimum', height and spread 3 ft, has graceful, silky fronds with elongated divisions and terminal pinnae running together to form a tail. They remain green unti early spring. This is a sterile variety but freely produces offsets. It will grow successfully in the garden. Both varieties are a paler green than the type species.

P. falcatum, syn. *Cyrtomium falcatum* (Japanese holly fern). China, Japan, Himalayas. Height and spread 2–3 ft. This is an excellent house plant standing up to the most adverse conditions, and is widely grown commercially. Its deep green polished, pinnate fronds have toothed, sickle-shaped pinnae.

P. f. 'Rochfordianum', height and spread 12–18 in., has pinnae that are twice as big as those of the type species.

P. munitum (sword fern). N. America. Height and spread 3 ft. A garden fern with linear, toothed pinnae. In colour and appearance it is similar to *P. acrostichioides*, the main difference being that its spore-heaps do not join when they ripen.

P. setiferum (soft shield fern). Temperate and tropical regions. Height 2–3 ft; spread 3–5 ft The mid-green fronds of this garden fern are bipinnate. They are more divided than those of the hard shield fern, *P. aculeatum*, of softer texture, and not glossy. They retain their colour throughout the winter. The young fronds are covered with pale brown and white scales. This handsome fern is common in the wetter parts of Britain, except Scotland.

P. s. 'Acutilobum' has pointed pinnules with bristles at the ends. The fronds tend to be prostrate, particularly in winter; the frond midrib often produces bulbils. *P. s.* 'Divisilobum', spread 4–6 ft., has immense fronds, bipinnate at the top, tripinnate lower down. They arch when young but become prostrate in winter.

P. s. 'Plumoso-divisilobum', height 12–24 in., spread 2–4 ft, is a fine form of this variety. The fronds are quadripinnate, so finely divided and overlapping that the pinnae can hardly be seen in the mass of beautifully cut greenery. *P. s.* 'Proliferum' is characterised by the presence of numerous plantlets on the upper surfaces of mature fronds; it is of more spreading habit.

Cultivation. Plant hardy species and varieties during April in shade, in a humus-rich, non-acid soil, preferably containing lime or chalk.

To grow polystichums indoors, plant them in 6 or 7 in. pots, using a compost of equal parts (by volume) leaf-mould or peat, loam and coarse sand. Overwinter greenhouse ferns at a temperature of 7–10°C (45–50°F). Repot them every two or three years and give them a liquid feed at monthly intervals from May to September.

Water freely during the growing season, and for the rest of the year just sufficiently to keep the soil moist.

Propagation. Sow spores in March at a temperature of 10°C (50°F) (see entry under FERNS).

Divide the multiple crowns in March or April. Another method is to detach the bulbil-bearing fronds in September or October. Fill boxes with equal parts (by volume) peat and sand, and peg the fronds on to the surface of this mixture. Pot up the young plants when well rooted.

Pests and diseases. Generally trouble-free.

Pomegranate: see Punica

Pontederia

Pontederiaceae

PONTEDERIA CORDATA

A genus of four species of aquatic perennials, including both hardy and tender types. The hardy *P. cordata* is widely grown as a marginal plant in ornamental pools and lakes.

P. cordata (pickerel weed). N. America. Water depth up to 9 in.; height 1½–2½ ft; planting distance 9–12 in. A strong-growing and compact hardy herbaceous species. Rigid stems grow from almost woody branching rhizomes. The heart-shaped leaves are deep glossy green, sometimes veined and often with maroon-brown patches.

In August and September the plants carry 2–4 in. terminal spikes of closely set purple-blue flowers; each has a yellow eye on the uppermost petal. The buds and flowers are surrounded by soft white hairs.

Cultivation. Plant pontederias between April and June in a 4–6 in. layer of loam and cover with 3–9 in. of water. Position in full sun, at the margins of a pond, lake or slow-flowing stream.

Propagation. Divide in April or May. Lift the plants and cut off side branches with a sharp knife; replant as described under CULTIVATION, pushing the rootstock 2 in. into the soil. Do not cover with more than 3 in. of water until the plants are well established.

Pests and diseases. Generally trouble-free.

Poplar: see Populus
Poplar, balsam: see *Populus balsamifera*
Poplar, Berlin: see *Populus × berolinensis*
Poplar, black: see *Populus nigra*
Poplar, Lombardy: see *Populus nigra* 'Italica'
Poplar, Manchester: see *Populus nigra* 'Betulifolia'
Poplar, Ontario: see *Populus candicans*
Poplar, white: see *Populus alba*
Poppy: see Papaver
Poppy, alpine: see *Papaver alpinum*
Poppy, Californian: see *Eschscholzia californica*
Poppy, crested: see *Argemone platyceras*
Poppy, field: see *Papaver rhoeas*
Poppy, harebell: see *Meconopsis quintuplinervia*
Poppy, Himalayan blue: see *Meconopsis betonicifolia*
Poppy, horned: see Glaucium
Poppy, Iceland: see *Papaver nudicaule*
Poppy, opium: see *Papaver somniferum*
Poppy, oriental: see *Papaver orientale*

Poppy, plume: see Macleaya
Poppy, prickly: see *Argemone mexicana*
Poppy, tree: see Romneya
Poppy, tulip: see *Papaver glaucum*
Poppy, Welsh: see *Meconopsis cambrica*

Populus

Poplar. *Salicaceae*

A genus of 35 species of fast-growing hardy deciduous trees that are effective as tall screens and windbreaks. They are tolerant of wet soil, salt-laden winds and atmospheric pollution; however, their roots may damage building foundations and drainage systems. The flowers are carried in pendulous catkins, with the male and female catkins borne on separate trees.

P. alba (white poplar). Central and S. Europe to W. Siberia and W. Asia. Height 30–40 ft; spread 15–25 ft. The leaves of this suckering species are broadly ovate and usually shallowly lobed. They are grey-green above, white and woolly beneath, and turn yellow in September.

P. balsamifera, syn. *P. tacamahaca* (balsam poplar). N. America. Height 35–45 ft; spread 18–30 ft. The buds of this erect-branched tree are up to 1 in. long and are covered with a yellow gum. The ovate leaves, which are white and net-veined beneath, give off a strong smell of balsam while unfolding.

P. × berolinensis (Berlin poplar). Height 30–40 ft; spread 10–18 ft. This broadly columnar hybrid tree is planted extensively in continental cities. The broadly ovate leaves are bright green above, paler beneath.

POPULUS CANDICANS

P. candicans, syn. *P. × gileadensis* (Ontario poplar or balm of Gilead). N. America. Height 30–40 ft; spread 18–25 ft. The pale green leaves with paler undersides are broadly ovate and emit a strong smell of balsam while unfolding. The heart-shaped leaves of 'Aurora' are cream-white when young and splashed with pink, later becoming a pale green but sometimes still splashed with pink or white. They are most colourful when the plant is stooled or pollarded, which entails cutting back annually in March.

P. deltoides, syn. *P. monilifera* (cottonwood). Eastern N. America. Height 30–40 ft; spread 18–30 ft. The heart-shaped leaves are a glossy dark green. This vigorous, broad-headed tree has been largely superseded by hybrids such as *P. × serotina* and *P. × marilandica*.

P. × gileadensis: see *P. candicans*

P. lasiocarpa. China. Height 18–25 ft; spread 10–15 ft. The massive heart-shaped leaves are mid-green, with conspicuous red leaf stalks and red veins. This species is the largest leaved poplar. It seldom thrives in Great Britain.

Pontederia cordata

Populus alba (catkins)

Populus candicans 'Aurora'

P. × marilandica. Height 35–45 ft; spread 20–35 ft. This fast-growing hybrid, of open spreading habit, has bright green triangular-ovate leaves.

P. monilifera: see *P. deltoides*

P. nigra (black poplar). Europe, W. Asia. Height 45–50 ft, eventually up to 100 ft or more; spread 20–30 ft. The pale to mid-green leaves of this broad-headed tree are triangular-ovate.

    P. n. 'Betulifolia' (Manchester poplar). Height 30–45 ft; spread 15–30 ft. The glossy mid-green leaves are broadly rhomboid. This bushy-headed tree tolerates atmospheric pollution.

    P. n. 'Italica' (Lombardy poplar). Italy. Height 30–50 ft; spread 5–8 ft. The broadly rhomboid leaves are pale to mid-green. This variety has a narrow columnar habit and is often used for screens and windbreaks.

P. × robusta. Height 30–50 ft; spread 10–18 ft. The ovate leaves of this hybrid are copper-red when young, turning shiny bright green.

P. × serotina. Height 35–50 ft; spread 20–40 ft. This fast-growing hybrid is one of the most commonly planted poplars. It has ovate, glossy dark green leaves that are copper-red when young. The leaves of the form 'Aurea' are a bright golden-yellow when opening in April and May. In summer they become yellow-green, then turn bright yellow in autumn.

P. tacamahaca: see *P. balsamifera*

P. tremula (aspen). Europe, Asia, N. Africa. Height 20–30 ft; spread 10–15 ft. The rounded leaves, which are prominently toothed, are grey-green during the summer but turn yellow in autumn. The leaf stalks are long and flattened, and the leaves tremble in the slightest breeze.

P. trichocarpa (black cottonwood). Western N. America. Height 40–50 ft; spread 20–35 ft. The ovate leaves are dark lustrous green above, pale and net-veined beneath; they turn yellow in autumn. The buds are large and sticky; the bark of young trees peels easily, giving off a strong balsam scent.

Cultivation. Poplars are easily grown in any ordinary garden soil, including heavy, cold soils where few other trees will grow. Plant in a sunny open position between November and March, at least 60 ft away from buildings and drains. Stake the young trees until they are well established, particularly in exposed sites. For windbreaks plant *P. nigra* 'Italica' 8–10 ft apart.

Propagation. Insert 10–12 in. leafless hardwood cuttings of one-year-old shoots in a nursery bed between October and December. Plant out in permanent positions one year later.

    Alternatively, remove suckers in October or February and plant direct in permanent positions.

Pruning. None required.

Pests. The leaves may be eaten by CATERPILLARS and POPLAR BEETLE larvae.

    APHIDS produce conspicuous purse-shaped galls on the leaf stalks.

Diseases. Many species, excluding *P. nigra*, may be infected by BACTERIAL CANKER OF POPLARS. Unsightly erupting cankers, ¼–6 in. long, develop on shoots, branches and sometimes the trunk. Young shoots may die back in early summer.

    A BRACKET FUNGUS may enter dead wood and cause rotting of the heartwood if the tree is neglected. Later, the large bracket-shaped fruiting bodies develop on the trunk or branches.

DIE-BACK and CANKER can be due to many different fungi. Dead patches or cankers appear on the shoots and, if girdling occurs, the shoots eventually die back.

HONEY FUNGUS can kill poplars rapidly.

LEAF SPOT shows as irregular black-brown spots on the leaves, which fall prematurely.

PHYSIOLOGICAL DISORDERS, due to adverse cultural conditions, show as black spots on the leaves. Alternatively, the foliage may turn yellow, then brown and fall prematurely.

RUST, due to several different fungi, shows as yellow-orange spore pustules on the lower leaf surfaces. Leaves may fall prematurely.

SILVER LEAF fungus commonly occurs on poplars, and the flat purple fruiting bodies appear on dead branches.

Populus × serotina

Portulaca grandiflora

Potato 'Sutton's Foremost'

Portulaca
Portulacaceae

A genus of 200 species of often succulent annual and perennial herbaceous plants. The half-hardy annual described is suitable for borders and rock gardens and for growing under glass.

P. grandiflora (sun plant). Brazil. Height 6–9 in.; planting distance 6 in. A succulent plant with semi-prostrate red stems. The narrow leaves are cylindrical in cross-section and bright green. The saucer-shaped flowers, 1 in. across, have a central boss of bright yellow stamens. They are red, purple or yellow and are carried in profusion from June to September.

    Varieties listed include 'Double Mixed' and 'Single Mixed', each in a wide range of colours including yellow, white, pink, rose, crimson, purple, orange and scarlet. The doubles have rose-like flowers, but the strain usually contains a few single-flowered plants.

Cultivation. Plant portulacas outdoors in May in any well-drained garden soil; they thrive in full sun, and named strains make a bright display even during a poor summer. Water only when the plants show signs of wilting.

    For flowering under glass in late spring and summer, use 5 in. pots containing John Innes potting compost No. 1, setting five plants in each.

Propagation. Sow the seeds under glass in March, at a temperature of 18°C (64°F); prick out the seedlings into boxes of John Innes potting compost No. 1. If the plants are to be grown outdoors, harden them off in a cold frame before planting out in May.

    Alternatively, sow directly in the flowering site in April or May, just covering the seeds with soil; thin out the seedlings to the required distance.

Pests. APHIDS make plants sticky and sooty.

Diseases. DAMPING-OFF may cause seedlings to collapse at soil level.

Potato
Solanum tuberosum. Solanaceae

A tuberous-rooted perennial grown as an annual for its edible tubers. These are used throughout the year and are a staple source of starch.

The plant is half-hardy; spring frosts may damage the young foliage and retard growth until new foliage develops. The crop must be lifted and stored before autumn frosts. Sufficient supplies for yearly consumption can be raised in gardens, but potatoes require a great deal of space. In small gardens it is advisable to use a potato plot for early-maturing crops that are used when young.

VARIETIES

These are listed in three groups, according to time of maturing: first early, second early and main crop. The tubers may be round or kidney-shaped, the skin almost clear, flushed or eyed with red or purple. The flesh may be white or pale yellow, and the texture of the cooked flesh floury or waxy. Varieties vary greatly according to local conditions, and it is advisable to seek local opinion before deciding on a variety. Make sure, when purchasing tubers, that these are certified to be disease-free.

First-early varieties include the floury 'Arran Pilot', 'Home Guard' and 'Sutton's Foremost'.

'Ben Lomond' (floury) and 'Craig's Royal' (waxy) are good second-early varieties.

'Kerr's Pink' is a suitable variety for heavy soil and in areas with high rainfall; 'Pink Fir Apple' is an excellent salad potato with a pink skin and a firm, waxy, pale yellow flesh of nutty flavour; 'Red Craig's Royal' is a red-skinned variety, recommended for exhibitions.

For a main crop, grow the floury 'Arran Banner', 'King Edward' and 'Red King', or the prolific, waxy 'Majestic'.

Cultivation. Most types of soil are suitable for potato crops; even heavy and clay soils will give satisfactory results if a generous dressing of strawy manure is added during autumn. Dig all soils in late autumn or early winter, incorporating two buckets of well-rotted manure per sq. yd. Leave the ground rough to allow the frosts to break it up for spring planting. Just before planting, top-dress the bed with a general-purpose fertiliser at 6 oz. per sq. yd.

The plants are raised from small tubers, purchased in January. Start the tubers into growth in trays placed in a light, frost-proof place until they sprout. Keep two sprouts on each tuber at planting time, but rub off the remainder. It is less vital to sprout main-crop varieties as they have a long growing season.

Plant the sprouted tubers 4–5 in. deep, setting early and second-early varieties 12 in. apart in rows 24 in. apart; place main-crop varieties 15 in. apart in rows 2½ ft apart. In sheltered areas in the south and west, plant early and second-early varieties in March; in northern and exposed districts delay planting until mid-April. Have a supply of dry straw available to cover the young shoots during late frosts. Plant main-crop varieties at the end of April.

When the shoots are about 6 in. tall, draw up the soil to form 6 in. high sloping ridges on each side of the rows. Draw up a further inch of soil a month later and again three weeks later.

Particularly early crops may be obtained by planting sprouted tubers in cold frames during January or February. Cover the glass with straw, mats or sacking during frosty weather. Alternatively, set two sprouted tubers 3 in. deep in 10 or 12 in. pots of John Innes potting compost No. 3; start into growth in a greenhouse at a temperature of 4–7°C (39–45°F). Water sparingly at first, but as the foliage develops, increase the watering; raise the temperature to 10–13°C (50–55°F) and feed at intervals of 10–14 days with dilute liquid manure.

Harvesting and storing. Use forced crops, early and second-early varieties as soon as the tubers are large enough. Early potatoes should not be lifted until they are required, as they will continue to grow rapidly; they may double their weight in two weeks.

Lift the main crop in October and store for winter. Three weeks before harvesting, cut off and remove the haulms to reduce the risk of disease spores falling on the tubers as they are lifted. Prepare a clamp for storing potatoes as follows: take out a shallow 4 ft wide trench, line with straw, and arrange the tubers in a 3 ft high pile therein; cover the pile with 6 in. of straw, followed by 6 in. of soil. Push twists of straw through the top at 3 ft intervals along the clamp for ventilation.

Exhibition. Grow show potatoes in trenches, liberally dressed with stable manure in late autumn. Open up the trenches in March to a depth of 12 in. and add a 6 in. layer of equal parts (by volume) well-decayed manure and leaf-mould before replacing the soil. Plant the tubers as described under CULTIVATION.

Lift tubers for exhibition carefully, so as not to damage the skins; wash the tubers in tepid water with a soft sponge. Exhibit only tubers of uniform size, selecting them for quality rather than size; they should be shallow-eyed and free from any trace of scab.

Pests. APHIDS may infest seed potatoes and growing plants. Heavy infestations distort growth, and aphids also transmit virus diseases.

POTATO CYST EELWORM infests the roots and produces characteristic minute brown cysts. Plants growing in infested soils are severely checked; they often turn yellow, wilt and die.

SLUGS and WIREWORMS eat holes in tubers in the soil.

Diseases. COMMON SCAB may cause raised brown scabs with ragged edges on the tubers.

DRY ROT may affect seed tubers; diseased areas become shrivelled and sunken, and often bear white or blue pustules of fungal growth.

GANGRENE occurs on stored tubers and shows first as a slight depression which gradually enlarges until most of the tuber is decayed. Diseased areas bear minute black fruiting bodies of the fungus.

INTERNAL RUST SPOT shows as scattered brown marks in the flesh; it is only apparent when the tubers are cut open.

PHYSIOLOGICAL DISORDERS of various types may occur, but are usually due to an irregular moisture supply. Apparently sound tubers are hollow in the centre; the heel end of the tuber may become soft and rot.

POTATO BLACKLEG shows in early summer; the leaves turn yellow, and the shoots collapse, showing blackening of the stem-bases. Tubers already formed contain brown or grey slimy rot.

POTATO BLIGHT shows as brown blotches on the leaves which quickly turn black and rot.

Potato 'King Edward'

Potato 'Red King'

Tubers have a red-brown discoloration under the skin. Diseased areas are often entered by secondary bacteria which cause an evil-smelling SOFT ROT.

POWDERY SCAB shows on the tubers as uniform round and raised scabs which burst open to release a powdery mass of spores. Affected tubers may be malformed.

WART DISEASE shows as cauliflower-like out-growths near the eyes on the tubers which are often misshapen.

Potato-tree, Chilean: see *Solanum crispum*

Potentilla

Cinquefoil. *Rosaceae*

POTENTILLA NEPALENSIS HYBRID

A genus of about 500 species of hardy annuals and perennials, deciduous flowering shrubs and sub-shrubs. The annuals are of little garden value, but the perennials are suitable for borders or rock gardens where they make colourful displays from June to October. Most of the herbaceous perennials are hardy hybrids from the rarely cultivated species *P. atrosanguinea* or *P. nepalensis*.

Shrubby potentillas may be grown on sunny banks, in mixed or shrub borders, or in the case of the prostrate sub-shrubs, as ground cover. The flowers of all species appear in succession, and are generally saucer-shaped. They may be single or double and are usually borne in loose terminal and lateral clusters.

PERENNIAL SPECIES

P. chrysocraspeda: see *P. ternata*

P. nitida. S. Europe. Height 2–3 in.; spread up to 12 in. A tufted, mat-forming species suitable for a rock garden or as ground cover. It has silvery, silky, palmate leaves composed of three to five spathulate leaflets. The 1 in. wide flowers, which appear in July and August, are pale pink with crimson-pink centres. The species flowers sparingly even when grown in full sun.

Forms with larger and deeper-coloured flowers are occasionally available, including *P. n.* 'Rubra', with deep rose-pink flowers.

P. recta warrenii: see *P. warrenii*

P. tabernaemontani: see *P. verna*

P. ternata, syn. *P. chrysocraspeda*. N. America. Height 6–8 in.; planting distance 9 in. This species is equally suitable for a rock garden and for edging the front of a border. The tufted trifoliate leaves are bright green and covered with silky hairs. Shiny yellow flowers, $\frac{1}{2}$ in. across, appear in loose sprays from June to August. *P. t. aurantiaca* is a light orange variety.

P. verna, syn. *P. tabernaemontani* (spring cinque-foil). W. Europe, including Great Britain. Height 2–3 in.; spread up to 24 in. This evergreen mat-forming species has dark green digitate

leaves composed of five to seven obovate, toothed leaflets. The bright yellow flowers, $\frac{1}{2}$ in. across are borne on slender stems singly from the leaf axils. The main flowering season is in April and May, but a few flowers continue to appear until the autumn.

P. v. 'Nana' is a compact, less vigorous variety

P. warrenii, syn. *P. recta warrenii*, sometimes erroneously listed as *P. warrensii*. Europe. Height 18 in.; planting distance 15 in. An erect species with digitate, mid-green leaves. Bright yellow flowers, $\frac{1}{2}$ in. across, are borne singly from June to August. It is a short-lived species and needs to be replaced every three or four years.

P. warrensii: see *P. warrenii*

GARDEN HYBRIDS

The following hybrids from *P. atrosanguinea* have abundant strawberry-type, grey-green foliage. The loose flower sprays, 18–24 in. wide, are composed of single or double flowers which generally appear from June to September.

'Flamenco' (height and planting distance 24 in.), single, brilliant scarlet flowers; 'Gibson's Scarlet' (height 12 in.; planting distance 18 in.), semi-prostrate, with single bright red flowers; 'Glory of Nancy' (height and planting distance 18 in.), semi-double, crimson-maroon flowers from June to August. Named forms in rich scarlet colours, sometimes streaked with orange or yellow, are also available.

'Wm Rollison' (height and planting distance 18 in.), semi-double flame-orange; 'Yellow Queen' (height and planting distance 15 in.), silvery foliage and semi-double yellow flowers.

The species *P. nepalensis* has given rise to several hybrids. These have coarsely toothed deep green leaves; the sprays of single flowers are more erect and widely branching than the hybrids from *P. atrosanguinea*. Flowering, from June to August, is so profuse that the plants often exhaust themselves after a few years.

'Miss Willmott' (height 24 in.; planting distance 15 in.) has cherry-pink flowers with deeper pink centres; and 'Roxana' (height 24 in.; planting distance 15 in.) has pink, orange and brown-red flowers.

SHRUBBY SPECIES

P. arbuscula, syn. *P. fruticosa* 'Arbuscula'. Himalayas, N. China. Height 24 in.; spread 5 ft. The pinnately lobed, pale to mid-green leaves are coated with bronze hairs. Rich yellow flowers, about 1 in. across, are borne in loose clusters from June to October.

POTENTILLA ARBUSCULA

P. fruticosa. Northern Hemisphere. Height and spread 4–5 ft. A compact shrub with pinnately lobed, pale to mid-green leaves, sometimes so deeply cut as to appear composed of several leaflets. Buttercup-yellow flowers, 1 in. across, are produced singly or in twos and threes from May to August.

Potentilla nitida

Potentilla verna

Potentilla 'Gibson's Scarlet'

Numerous named varieties, flowering from June to October, include: 'Farreri' (height 4 ft; spread 3 ft), with finely dissected foliage and bright yellow flowers.

'Katherine Dykes' (height 4 ft; spread 5 ft), with deeply lobed leaves and primrose-yellow flowers; 'Mandschurica' (height 12 in.; spread 3 ft), mat-forming with silver-grey foliage on purple stems, and pure white flowers.

'Tangerine' (height 24 in.; spread 5 ft), with scarlet buds opening to tangerine-orange and becoming bright yellow in full sun; 'Vilmoriniana' (height 4 ft; spread 3 ft), with silvery foliage on upright branches profusely covered with ivory-white flowers.

POTENTILLA FRUTICOSA

P. glabra. N. China. Height and spread 24 in. or more. This erect shrub with smooth red stems bears pale to mid-green, pinnately lobed leaves. The solitary pure white flowers, about 1 in. across, are freely produced from June to October.

Cultivation of perennial species. Plant during suitable weather from October to March, in ordinary, well-drained garden soil and in full sun. Hybrids of *P. atrosanguinea* and *P. ternata* are long-lived and benefit from an annual mulch, in March, of decayed manure or peat. Water freely in dry weather.

The short-lived hybrids of *P. nepalensis*, and *P. warrenii*, should be cut back after flowering. Replant or replace every three or four years. Most other species and varieties die back naturally.

Cultivation of shrubby species. These species and varieties give best results when grown in light, well-drained soil and in full sun. They will tolerate partial shade, but flowering is generally then less prolific. Plant during suitable weather from October to March.

Propagation of perennial species. Divide and replant long-lived varieties in October or March.

Short-lived varieties and the species do not divide easily and are best raised from seeds or cuttings. Sow seeds in pans or boxes of John Innes seed compost in a cold frame, in March or April; when the seedlings are large enough to handle prick them off into boxes, later transferring to a nursery bed. Transplant to permanent positions in October. Seedlings of hybrids do not come entirely true to type.

Alternatively, take 2–3 in. long basal cuttings in April; insert in equal parts (by volume) peat and sand in a cold frame. When rooted, line the cuttings out in nursery rows, and transplant to permanent positions in September.

Propagation of shrubby species. Sow seeds in March and treat as described for perennial species. Named varieties seldom come true.

Alternatively, take 3 in. cuttings of half-ripe lateral shoots, with a heel, in September or October. Insert the cuttings in equal parts (by volume) peat and sand in a cold frame; in May,

line the rooted cuttings out in a nursery bed and grow on until October of the following year.

Pruning of shrubby species. No regular pruning is required, but the shrubs can be kept bushy and vigorous by the removal at ground level of weak or old stems. After flowering remove the tips of the dead flowering shoots.

Pests and diseases. Generally trouble-free.

Poterium canadense: see *Sanguisorba canadensis*

Poterium hakusanensis: see *Sanguisorba hakusanensis*

Poterium tenuifolium: see *Sanguisorba tenuifolia*

× **Potinara**
Orchidaceae

× POTINARA

A group of quadrigeneric orchid hybrids between *Brassavola, Cattleya, Laelia* and *Sophronitis.* In habit, arrangement of foliage and flowers these hybrids are similar to *Cattleya.* The flowering period extends from September or October to March.

See also ORCHIDS.

Several named forms are available and include: 'Bunty', a cross between × *Potinara* Red Friar and × *Sophrolaeliocattleya* Anzac, having 4–5 in. wide flowers with deep bright red petals and sepals and a darker coloured lip.

'Medea', an outstanding hybrid between × *Brassolaeliocattleya* Beatrice and × *Sophrolaeliocattleya* Cleopatra, has 5 in. wide, deep red-purple flowers with a lip of more intense colour, yellow in the throat. They have thick overlapping petals and wide sepals.

'Sunrise', a hybrid between × *Brassolaeliocattleya* Crusader and × *Sophrolaeliocattleya* Prince Hirohito, with 3–5 in. wide flowers; these are rich purple with a dark purple lip.

Cultivation, propagation, pests and diseases. See entry under CATTLEYA.

Primrose: see *Primula vulgaris*
Primrose, Cape: see Streptocarpus
Primrose, drumstick: see *Primula denticulata*
Primrose, fairy: see *Primula malacoides*
Primrose, Japanese: see *Primula japonica*

Primula
Primulaceae

A genus of about 500 species of deciduous and wintergreen, hardy and half-hardy perennials, widely distributed throughout the northern temperate zone and the mountains further south. A

Potentilla 'Glory of Nancy'

Potentilla fruticosa

× *Potinara* 'Bunty'

Primula obconica

Primula gracilipes

Primula × kewensis

Primula malacoides

few species are found south of the Equator. Among the many species in cultivation there are plants suitable for cool greenhouses, alpine houses, rock gardens, herbaceous borders, for waterside planting and for spring bedding.

In general the flowers are primrose-like, occasionally bell-shaped.

INDOOR SPECIES

The following species require greenhouse treatment and a minimim winter temperature of 7°C (45°F); they may also be grown as pot plants in the home.

P. × kewensis. Height 15 in. A perennial hybrid, originating at Kew. The light green leaves are spathulate, toothed, and covered with a waxy white farina (powder). Fragrant yellow flowers, $\frac{3}{4}$ in. across, are borne in whorls on the upright stems from December to April. The variety 'Red Gold' has bright green foliage that is almost free of farina.

PRIMULA MALACOIDES

P. malacoides (fairy primrose). China. Height 12–18 in. A perennial species, usually grown as an annual. The hairy leaves are pale green and ovate with rounded teeth. Slender stems carry whorls of star-like flowers, $\frac{1}{2}$ in. across, ranging from pale lilac-purple through red to white. They open from late December to April. Numerous named varieties are listed and fine mixtures are available. Recommended separate colour varieties, all with fragrant flowers, include: 'Fire Chief', brick-red; 'Jubilee', cherry-red; 'Lilac

Queen', soft lilac-purple; 'Rose Bouquet', carmine-red; 'Snow Queen', pure white; and 'Snow Storm', double, pure white.

PRIMULA OBCONICA

P. obconica. China. Height 9–15 in. This perennial species is usually grown as an annual. The light green ovate leaves are slightly hairy and can cause a painful allergic reaction on sensitive skins. Clusters of 1 in. wide pink, red, lilac or blue-purple flowers, sometimes with wavy-edged petals, are carried from December to May.

Several varieties are listed; these are chiefly the giant or large-flowered strains with blooms up to 2 in. across. Recommended varieties are: 'Caerulea', clear purple-blue; 'Fasbender Red', large deep red; 'Giant White', pure white; 'Salmon King', salmon-red; and 'Wyaston Wonder', rich deep crimson.

PRIMULA SINENSIS

P. sinensis. China. Height 10 in. This perennial species is usually grown as an annual. The bright mid-green hairy leaves are broad and ovate, forming an erect rosette. Thick stems carry two or three whorls of flowers, each 1–1½ in. across, from December to March.

There are numerous varieties, usually listed under Fimbriata, with fringed and cut petals: 'Dazzler', vivid orange-scarlet; 'Empress Mixed', in an outstanding colour range; 'Royal Blue', deep purple-blue. Other colours include lilac, rose, salmon, white and orange.

OUTDOOR SPECIES

The following species and varieties are hardy perennial plants. Alpine primulas require a humus-rich well-drained soil and are suitable for rock gardens or alpine houses. Border primulas require more moisture, and should be grown where the soil does not dry out or where they can be watered as necessary; they are ideal for bog gardens and waterside planting.

ALPINE PRIMULAS

P. allionii. Maritime Alps. Height 2 in.; spread 6 in. This species forms a hummock of sticky, spathulate, mid-green leaves. These may be completely hidden by the flowers, which are about 1 in. across, and are carried one or two to a stem in March and April. They vary from purple and rose-red to white.

Winter moisture may damage the leaves of this species and it is better grown in an alpine house, wedged between pieces of rock and in gritty soil with some lime and humus added.

P. altaica: see *P. amoena*

P. amoena. Europe, probably of garden origin. Height 8 in.; spread 4 in. This name covers a range of primrose-like plants which are often classified as *P. altaica*. The pale to mid-green leaves are irregularly crenate and spathulate in shape. Pink flowers, about 1 in. across and carried in umbels, open in April and May. Various named forms are available, in different shades of pink.

P. auricula. European Alps. Height and spread 6 in. This variable species forms clusters of pale to slightly grey-green ovate to obovate leaves which, in some forms, are covered in farina. Yellow or purple flowers, about ¾ in. across, are carried in umbels from March to May.

This species has been developed in cultivation to produce show auriculas in many colours: 'Old Yellow Dusty Miller' and 'Red Dusty Miller' are widely grown. Other popular varieties include 'Blue Fire', blue; 'Gold of Ophir', yellow; 'The Mikado', dark red; and 'Willowbrook', yellow.

PRIMULA AURICULA

P. × 'Bileckii'. Height 2 in.; spread 6 in. This hybrid forms a neat tuft of dark green toothed leaves. In May, 1 in. wide deep rose flowers appear just above the foliage. This plant does best in soil containing peat or leaf-mould with plenty of stone chippings; ideally it should be grown in a trough or in an alpine house.

P. clarkei. Kashmir. Height 2 in.; spread 6 in. A dainty species with round or oblong pale green leaves. The ¾ in. wide, bright rose-pink flowers

appear while the leaves are still unfolding in spring. Grow in well-drained soil, in semi-shade.

P. denticulata: see BORDER PRIMULAS

P. edgeworthii. W. Himalayas. Height 3–4 in.; spread 9 in. This species was formerly known as *P. winteri*. The grey-green spathulate to triangular ovate leaves are well covered in farina and have wavy dentate margins. The flowers, about ¾ in. across, are pale lavender, each with a yellow eye. They appear from January onwards and are carried in dense umbels.

Although slightly variable in colour the plant is particularly valuable for its early flowers.

P. farinosa. Europe, N. Asia. Height 4–6 in.; spread 6 in. This species has powdered silvery obovate leaves. The erect stems each bear an umbel of yellow-eyed rose-lilac flowers, ⅓–½ in. across, in March and April. It is variable and not reliably long-lived, but it makes an attractive plant for a small rock garden, scree or a trough, in soil enriched with peat or leaf-mould.

P. frondosa. Balkans. Height 4 in.; spread 6 in. A rosette-forming species with powdered grey-green obovate leaves. It produces stems with umbels of 10–30 rose-lilac flowers, each about ½ in. across, in April. It thrives in any lightly shaded moist position.

P. × 'Garryarde': see *P. juliae*

P. gracilipes. Sikkim. Height 3 in.; spread 9–12 in. This species makes a compact tuft of rosettes with wavy, finely toothed, mid-green leaves. The 1 in. wide flowers are lavender-pink with orange-yellow eyes; they open in April.

P. juliae. Caucasus. Height 3 in.; spread 12 in. This species forms a flat mat of creeping stems with mid-green rounded leaves that are cordate at the base. The ¾ in. wide red-purple flowers, with a yellow eye, appear from March to May.

Numerous named hybrids have been raised from crosses between this species and others. *P. × pruhoniciana*, syn. *P. × juliana*, with obovate mid-green leaves, is one of the better known; its variety 'Wanda' bears a profusion of bright claret flowers, often in mid-winter. The popular hybrid strain, *P. × 'Garryarde'*, with purple or bronze flushed leaves, is represented mainly by 'Guinevere', soft pink and 'Victory', purple.

P. × juliana: see *P. juliae*

P. marginata. Maritime and Cottian Alps. Height 4 in.; spread 6–9 in. A species usually with ovate-oblong leaves that are grey-green, dusted with farina, and silver edged. Umbels of up to 20 fragrant lavender-blue flowers, each ¾–1 in. across, are borne in April and May. 'Linda Pope' has larger flowers of a deep lavender-blue.

P. minima. Mountains of Europe. Height 2 in.; spread 6 in. A rosette-forming species with blunt-tipped, sharply toothed, mid-green leaves. The rose-pink flowers are 1 in. across and have deeply indented petals. They are borne one or two to a stem in April and May. This plant is best grown in a trough, a scree or a crevice, with plenty of leaf-mould or peat added to the soil.

P. nutans. Yunnan, Szechwan. Height up to 12 in.; spread 9–12 in. An attractive species with hairy, grey-green, lanceolate leaves. Scented flower heads of soft lavender-violet bells, ¾ in. across, are borne in June. This species requires a well-drained neutral soil, rich in humus.

P. × pruhoniciana: see *P. juliae*

Primula allionii

Primula auricula

Primula farinosa

Primula vialii

Primula denticulata

Primula florindae

Primula helodoxa

P. × pubescens. Height 4 in.; spread 6 in. This name is given to a group of hybrids between *P. auricula* and *P. rubra*, with obovate mid-green leaves; the flowers, which are carried in umbels, appear in April or May. 'Argus' is compact and produces purple flowers with white centres; 'Faldonside' has crimson flowers; 'Mrs J. Wilson' bears a profusion of rich lilac-purple flowers.

They are excellent plants for an alpine house, grown in 6 in. pans of John Innes potting compost No. 1 and repotted annually in September.

Outdoors they should be planted in gritty well-drained soil, enriched with leaf-mould.

P. reidii. N.W. Himalayas. Height 4 in.; spread 6 in. This species has softly hairy, primrose-like, pale green leaves. It is distinct from other primulas in that, the fragrant ivory-white flower heads each consists of three to ten semi-pendent bell-shaped flowers; these are ¾ in. across and appear in May.

The variety 'Williamsii' is taller, and the soft blue flowers are more fragrant.

PRIMULA ROSEA

P. rosea. N.W. Himalayas. Height 6 in.; spread 6–8 in. A compact, tuft-forming species. The mid-green, toothed, obovate leaves are not fully developed when the intense rose-pink umbels appear in March and April; each umbel bears 4–12 flowers, ¾ in. wide. For best results, grow this plant in boggy soil. The species is easily raised from seeds, but the plants vary. The variety 'Delight', syn. 'Visser de Geer', is more robust with larger, brilliant pink flowers; 'Grandiflora' is a larger-flowered, deeper pink variety.

P. rubra. Central Alps, Pyrenees. Height 2–4 in.; spread 6 in. A rosette-forming species with hairy, ovate to obovate, mid-green leaves. Numerous umbels of clear pink flowers, ¾–1 in. wide, are borne in March and April.

P. sieboldii. Japan. Height 6–9 in.; spread 12 in. This tufted hairy species has pale green ovate leaves with prominent rounded teeth. Umbels of rose-purple flowers, 1–1½ in. across, are produced in May and June. The species is also suitable for woodland planting.

Several garden varieties, of Japanese origin, are available; they range in colour through white, red and purple and the flowers may be cup-shaped or have deeply fringed petals.

PRIMULA VIALII

P. vialii. N.W. Yunnan, S.W. Szechwan. Height up to 12 in.; spread 9–12 in. A distinctive species with tufts of lanceolate, slightly farinose pale green leaves. Dense spikes, 3–5 in. long, of lavender-blue flowers appear in June and July; the flower buds and calyces are scarlet.

P. warshenewskiana. Afghanistan. Height 3 in.; spread 6 in. This early-flowering primula is similar to *P. rosea*, but somewhat smaller. It bears oblanceolate mid-green leaves and brilliant rose-red flowers, ¾ in. wide; these are produced on short stems in April. For best results, grow this species in a moist position.

P. winteri: see *P. edgeworthii*

BORDER PRIMULAS

Most of the following perennial species belong to the Candelabra group. These moisture-loving plants are characterised by having the flowers arranged in whorls up the stem.

P. acaulis: see *P. vulgaris*

P. aurantiaca. W. China. Height 12 in.; planting distance 9 in. Candelabra group. This species has narrowly obovate leaves that are mid-green and red-ribbed. Dark red stems bear yellow-orange flowers, ⅔ in. across, in June and July.

P. beesiana. Yunnan. Height 24 in.; planting distance 9–12 in. Candelabra group. A species with light green, oblong-obovate and rough-textured leaves. Lilac-purple, ¾ in. wide flowers, each with a yellow eye, appear in June and July.

P. bulleyana. W. China. Height 2–3 ft; planting distance 9–12 in. Candelabra group. The dark green leaves are oblong-obovate. Numerous stems bear light orange flowers, ⅔ in. across, from June to July.

P. burmanica. Burma. Height 2–3 ft; planting distance 9–12 in. Candelabra group. This species has mid-green oblanceolate leaves. The red-purple flowers, ¾ in. across, are produced from June to July.

PRIMULA DENTICULATA

P. denticulata (drumstick primrose). China, Himalayas. Height 12 in.; planting distance 9 in. This vigorous perennial, often grown as an annual or biennial, is suitable for spring bedding, for a rock garden and for waterside planting. The pale green farinose leaves are broad and slightly pointed, forming a compact rosette. Numerous small flowers are borne in dense globular heads, measuring 2–3 in. across, from March to May. The colours vary from pale lilac to deep purple, or rose to deep carmine.

'Alba' is a white form; 'Ruby' is rose-purple. Named varieties are available in several shades, including mixtures of blue, mauve and white.

P. florindae (giant cowslip). S.E. Tibet, China. Height up to 3 ft; planting distance 12–15 in. A species with mid-green ovate leaves that are toothed at the edges. Strong stems bear terminal umbels of fragrant bell-shaped flowers, ¾ in. across, on drooping stalks. They open during June and July and are usually pale yellow, but may also be in shades from light orange to blood-red. The species thrives in moist soil.

Primula marginata

Primula rosea

Primula vulgaris Pacific strain (Polyanthus)

Primula aurantiaca

Primula sieboldii

Primula juliae hybrid 'Wanda'

Primula pulverulenta

Primula secundiflora

Primula sikkimensis pudibunda

P. helodoxa. W. China, Burma. Height 2–3 ft; planting distance 9–10 in. Candelabra group. This species retains its shiny, light green, oblanceolate leaves throughout the winter. The tall stems bear whorls of bright golden-yellow flowers, ¾ in. across, during June and July.

P. japonica (Japanese primrose). Japan. Height 2–2½ ft; planting distance 9–12 in. Candelabra group. A somewhat short-lived waterside species with rosettes of pale green, oblong-obovate leaves. The stout stems carry several whorls of magenta-red flowers, each ¾ in. across, from May through to July.

'Miller's Crimson' is a selected form with bright red flowers; it comes fairly true from seeds; 'Postford White' has pure white flowers, each with a yellow eye; 'Rosea' is deep pink.

P. poissonii. China. Height 12–18 in.; planting distance 6–9 in. Candelabra group. The shiny oblong-obovate leaves are mid-green. Thin stems bear bright purple-red flowers, ¾ in. across, during June and July.

PRIMULA PULVERULENTA

P. pulverulenta. W. China. Height 2–3 ft; planting distance 9–12 in. Candelabra group. This species has pale green obovate or oblanceolate leaves. Several white farinose stems carry whorls of ¾ in. wide crimson flowers during June and July.

Recommended varieties include: 'Bartley Strain', pink with a deeper eye; 'Inverewe', with vivid orange-scarlet flowers, it can be propagated only by division; and 'Red Hugh', a variety, with brick-red flowers, that comes true from seeds.

PRIMULA SECUNDIFLORA

P. secundiflora. Yunnan. Height 18 in.; planting distance 9–12 in. An evergreen species with mid-green oblong-obovate leaves. Pendent bell-shaped flowers, clear wine-red and 1–¾ in. across, appear in July.

P. sikkimensis (Himalayan cowslip). Himalayas. Height 18 in.; planting distance 9–12 in. This species has pale green leaves that are oblanceolate and finely toothed. The pendent funnel-shaped flowers, pale yellow and fragrant, measure ¾–1 in. across; they appear in June and July. *P. s. hopeana* and *P. s. pudibunda* have larger, deeper yellow flowers.

P. vulgaris, syn. *P. acaulis* (primrose). Great Britain. Height 6 in.; planting distance 9 in. A dwarf compact species with a rosette of bright green corrugated leaves. Yellow flowers, 1 in. across, with deep yellow centres, are produced in March and April.

P. v. elatior: see POLYANTHUS

P. v. sub-species *heterochroma* has leaves that are white hairy beneath, and flowers of white yellow and, rarely, blue-purple; *P. v.* sub-species *sibthorpii* has pink or red flowers.

POLYANTHUS

These garden hybrids are thought to be derived from *P. vulgaris*; they are often listed as *P. v. elatior*, but more commonly under the popular name, polyanthus. Although chiefly grown out doors, they are also suitable for pot culture Flowers, up to 1½ in. across, are carried in large trusses on stout stems well above the leaves.

The Pacific strain has large early flowers in brilliant shades of blue, yellow, red, pink and white. Most seedsmen list one or more large flowered mixtures for outdoor culture, such as 'Giant Bouquet' or 'Goldlace', which has flowers with yellow-edged petals.

Several recently introduced varieties, such as 'Mother's Day' as well as the Pacific strain make excellent indoor pot plants, flowering from early January onwards. Particularly good for pot culture is the 'Biedermeier Strain'.

Cultivation of indoor species. Grow pot plants in 3½–4 in. or final 5–6 in. containers of John Innes potting compost No. 2. Once the flower stems start to lengthen, give regular weekly liquid feeds. In September or early October, move the plants into their final pots. For spring-flowering plants, a temperature of 10–13°C (50–55°F) is required. Keep the plants moist at all times.

P. obconica can be moved to larger pots and grown on for a second year, but it is better discarded after flowering.

Cultivation of alpine primulas. Special cultivation requirements have been included under the individual descriptions. In general, these plants do best in a well-drained gritty soil containing plenty of humus. Plant between September and March, in sun or partial shade.

In the alpine house, grow in John Innes potting compost No. 1, adding leaf-mould or extra gritty sand when necessary. Use 4–10 in. pans, according to the spread of the plant.

Cultivation of border primulas. These primulas thrive in any fertile garden soil that does not dry out in spring and summer. Plant between October and March, in full sun or partial shade. Break up the soil thoroughly before planting and incorporate peat or well-decayed manure and 4 oz of organic fertiliser per sq. yd. Keep the soil moist in dry weather, preferably by overhead spraying. Mulching with peat preserves moisture.

Plants to flower in winter and early spring indoors or under glass, should be potted in September. Set in 4–6 in. containers of John Innes potting compost No. 2 and place in a cold frame. Bring the plants indoors to a temperature of 7–10°C (45–50°F) at intervals from November onwards, to flower from January to April.

Propagation of indoor species. All primula seed germinate best when they are fresh, and are best sown as soon as ripe. *P. malacoides* and *P. obconica* can be sown as late as July for flowering in 3½–4 in. pots, but to obtain large plants seeds should be sown in February or March.

Sow the seeds in pots or pans of seed compost, on the surface or barely covering them. A temperature of about 16°C (61°F) is required for germination. Place the containers in polythene bags or cover with sheets of glass and keep in a shady position until germination has occurred.

Prick off the seedlings into boxes before moving them singly into 3½ in. pots of John Innes potting compost No. 2. Plunge outdoors in a shaded frame for the summer before transferring to 5–6 in. pots in early autumn.

Propagation of outdoor species. Most primulas can be divided after flowering and planted directly into their flowering positions. Division is particularly suitable for *P. clarkei, P. denticulata, P. juliae, P. rosea, P. florindae* and *P. japonica*.

Take 1–2 in. cuttings or small-rooted shoots of such dwarf, tufted or mat-forming species as *P. minima, P. marginata* and *P. auricula* from June to August. Set them in John Innes potting compost No. 1 in a cold frame and, when rooted, pot into 3 in. containers of the same compost. Plant out in flowering positions the following spring or autumn.

The remaining species can be increased successfully from seeds, although named varieties will not come true. Sow seeds as soon as ripe (usually from May to September), or immediately after purchasing, in boxes of seed compost in a cold frame. Cover the boxes with sheets of glass or polythene to preserve humidity; this is particularly important for the more moisture-loving border species. After germination keep the compost moist and the seedlings lightly shaded. One day of hot sun will shrivel primula seedlings beyond recovery.

Prick off the seedlings, when they are large enough to handle, into boxes of John Innes potting compost No. 1. Set the border and large-growing species in nursery rows outdoors, and pot up the dwarf species into 2–3½ in. pots of John Innes potting compost No. 1; plunge outdoors. Set the plants in their permanent positions in September or the following spring.

Pests. Primulas may be attacked by APHIDS which distort and cripple the flowering shoots.

CATERPILLARS feed on the leaves.

CUTWORMS and VINE WEEVILS may attack the root systems and cause collapse of the plants.

Diseases. Outdoors, primulas may be attacked by BROWN CORE. This causes the roots to rot back from the tips until only a small cluster of short roots is left. Infected plants wilt and are easily removed from the ground.

CROWN ROT, FOOT ROT and ROOT ROT can be due to secondary organisms, such as bacteria, and to several different fungi including RHIZOCTONIA and the BLACK ROOT ROT fungus. The tissues become black and rotten, the leaves are discoloured and the plants collapse.

Virus diseases, such as CUCUMBER MOSAIC and TOMATO SPOTTED WILT VIRUS, affect primulas, causing various symptoms: stunting of plants; chlorosis of leaves; browning of the veins of leaves, which subsequently die; inferior flowers with white flecks; mottling and distortion of leaves, which bear dark green blisters.

GREY MOULD causes rotting of tissues, both outdoors and under glass; the affected areas become covered with a grey fungal growth.

LEAF SPOT, due to one or more organisms, may develop on older plants, on the leaves of plants lacking in vigour, or on plants growing outside. It can also occur on younger leaves under glass. Small brown circular spots are formed.

RUST may show on the undersides of the leaves of *P. vulgaris*; the spore-bearing pustules are at first orange, then brown and finally almost black.

Prince's feather: see *Amaranthus hypochondriacus*

Privet: see Ligustrum

Privet, golden: see *Ligustrum ovalifolium*

Privet, Japanese: see *Ligustrum japonicum*

Prophet flower: see *Arnebia echioides*

Prunella

Self-heal. *Labiatae*

A genus of seven species of hardy, showy, perennial herbaceous plants. Those described are suitable for rock gardens, but as they are invasive they need to be kept within bounds.

P. grandiflora. Europe. Height 6 in.; spread 18 in. This species has ovate mid-green leaves. The purple-violet flowers are tubular with spreading lobes and ¾–1 in. long. They are arranged in 2–3 in. long dense terminal spikes and open from May to October.

P. webbiana. W. Europe. Height 9–12 in.; spread 15 in. or more. A similar plant to *P. grandiflora*, with shorter, broader leaves and more compact spikes of rose-purple flowers. In cultivation it is represented by several varieties: 'Alba', white; 'Loveliness', pale violet; 'Pink Loveliness', clear pink; and 'Rosea', rose-pink.

Cultivation. Plant in March in any ordinary, moderately moist soil in sun or partial shade.

Dead-head the plants regularly throughout summer to avoid the growth of self-sown seedlings which can be a nuisance.

Propagation. Divide the plants in September or March and replant direct in permanent positions.

Pests and diseases. Generally trouble-free.

Prunus

Rosaceae

A genus of 430 species of mainly deciduous trees and shrubs containing many of the most popular spring-flowering ornamentals. The majority are hardy and easy to grow in an open position in full sun. A number of species have rich autumn tints and a few have attractive fruits.

The ornamental species described have been divided into the following sections: almonds, peaches, plums, cherries and cherry laurels. The laurels are excellent evergreens, suitable for a shady position and for large hedges or screens.

Ornamental *Prunus* species bear cup or bowl-shaped flowers of five, usually rounded, petals which often open out flat.

ORNAMENTAL ALMONDS (deciduous)

P. × *amygdalo-persica* 'Pollardii'. Garden origin. Height and spread 20–25 ft. A vigorous hybrid between a peach and an almond with lanceolate

Primula vulgaris

Prunella webbiana 'Rosea'

Prunella webbiana 'Loveliness'

Prunus amygdalus
(unripe fruit)

Prunus tenella

Prunus triloba

Prunus persica 'Clara Meyer'

Prunus amygdalus

mid-green leaves. Almond-like rich pink flowers, 2 in. across, appear on the naked branches in March and April.

P. amygdalus, syn. *P. communis*, now correctly known as *P. dulcis* (common almond). N. Africa to W. Asia. Height and spread 18–25 ft. A vigorous tree with erect branches when young, and spreading later. The lanceolate leaves are mid-green; clear pink flowers, 1–2 in. across, cluster along the naked branches in March and April.

Available forms include: 'Alba', white flowers, and 'Rosea-plena', double pale pink flowers. The species is the cultivated almond; that and its forms are excellent ornamental trees, but rarely produce good-quality nuts in the British climate.

P. communis: see *P. amygdalus*

P. dulcis: see *P. amygdalus*

P. glandulosa. China. Height and spread 4–5 ft. A bushy shrub of neat habit with ovate-lanceolate, pointed, mid-green leaves. The slender shoots are covered in April with pink or white flowers, ½ in. wide. Forms include: 'Albo-plena', double white flowers in May; 'Sinensis', double bright pink flowers in April. Plant in a sheltered, sunny site.

P. nana: see *P. tenella*

P. tenella, syn. *P. nana*. S.E. Europe, W. Asia to E. Siberia. Height and spread 2–4 ft. A shrub with erect, willowy stems bearing oblong to obovate glossy bright green leaves that are pale green beneath. Bright pink flowers, $\frac{1}{2}$–$\frac{3}{4}$ in. across, cover the branches in April. Forms include: 'Fire Hill', possibly the best dwarf almond, with rose-

crimson flowers wreathing the stiff stems; *P. t. gessleriana* is a form with rich pink flowers. The species and both its forms are ideal shrubs for island beds or narrow borders. Plant in a well-drained position in full sun.

P. triloba, syn. *P. triloba multiplex*. Garden origin. Height and spread 10–15 ft. A shrub or small tree of dense and twiggy habit. The bright green leaves are coarsely toothed and sometimes three-lobed at the apex. Double rosette-like, clear pink flowers, up to 1 in. across, are carried in profusion along the slender branches at the end of March or in early April.

P. t. simplex, the wild form from China, has single pink flowers. Both forms may be grown on a single stem to form a small tree, or they may be trained fanwise against a sunny wall.

ORNAMENTAL PEACHES (deciduous)

P. davidiana. China. Height 25–30 ft; spread 10–15 ft. A small tree of erect habit, with lanceolate, long pointed, mid-green leaves. Single rose-coloured flowers, 1 in. across, open between January and March on the naked branches. 'Alba' has snow-white flowers. Both forms require a sheltered position; against a dark background the early flowers can be seen to their advantage.

P. persica (common peach). China. Height and spread 15–25 ft. Tree or large shrub of vigorous habit with lanceolate, tapering, mid-green leaves. Pale pink flowers, 1–1½ in. wide, open in early April. 'Cardinal', glowing red, semi-double flowers; 'Iceberg', free-flowering, with pure

Prunus 'Amanogawa'

Prunus avium 'Plena'

white, semi-double flowers; 'Clara Meyer', double bright pink flowers; 'Prince Charming', double rose-red flowers. Grow the species and its forms in full sun, in cold areas against a wall.

ORNAMENTAL PLUMS (deciduous)

P. × *blireiana.* Garden origin. Height 15–18 ft; spread 12–18 ft. This is a hybrid between *P. cerasifera* 'Atropurpurea' and *P. mume* 'Alphandii'. The ovate leaves are metallic coppery-purple. Double rose-pink flowers, 1–1½ in. across, clothe the slender branches in April.

P. cerasifera (cherry plum). Balkan Peninsula. Height and spread 20–25 ft. A bushy tree with a rounded head and green young shoots bearing ovate to obovate, mid-green leaves. White flowers, ¼–¾ in. across, crowd the twigs in February and March. Mature trees bear red or yellow cherry-shaped plums. The species is much used for hedging or screening.

'Atropurpurea', syn. 'Pissardii' has dark red young leaves, which turn deep purple, and flowers, pink in bud, opening to almost white; 'Nigra', black-purple leaves and pink flowers. Both these coloured-leaved forms may be used effectively for hedging, particularly in combination with the green-leaved type.

P. × *cistena.* Garden origin. Height and spread 4–5 ft. A hybrid between *P. cerasifera* 'Atropurpurea' and *P. pumila*. The small, rich red ovate leaves contrast with the white flowers, ½–¾ in. wide, as they appear in March and April. This shrub is excellent for a low hedge.

P. mume (Japanese apricot). Japan, China, Korea. Height and spread 15–25 ft. A small tree with green young stems and broadly-ovate to rounded, blunt-pointed, mid-green leaves. Pale pink flowers, ¾–1 in. across, cluster thickly along the slender branches in late winter or early spring; they are sometimes in full bloom by mid-February. 'Alphandii' has semi-double pink flowers; 'Beni-Shi-Don' has fragrant, rose-pink blooms; this is best given wall protection.

P. 'Pissardii': see *P. cerasifera* 'Atropurpurea'

P. spinosa (blackthorn, sloe). Europe, N. Africa to W. Asia. Height and spread 10–15 ft. A dense shrub or bushy tree bearing ovate to obovate dark green leaves. Masses of snow-white flowers, ½ in. across, smother the branches in March or early April. It is a familiar hedgerow shrub; the small damson-like fruits (sloes) are used in preserves, for wine making and for flavouring gin.

Varieties include: 'Plena', double white flowers, longer lasting than those of the type; 'Purpurea', rich purple foliage and white flowers; 'Rosea' (possibly a hybrid with *P. cerasifera*), bronze-purple leaves becoming green in summer, and clear salmon-pink flowers. These forms make attractive small trees or large shrubs and may also be used for hedging.

ORNAMENTAL CHERRIES (deciduous)

Unless otherwise noted, these trees have ovate to obovate leaves that are slender-pointed and toothed; they mature to mid-green. The flowers are often 1½–2½ in. across and are usually borne in dense clusters several inches long; they are single unless otherwise indicated.

P. 'Accolade'. Garden origin. Height 20–30 ft; spread 4–6 ft. A hybrid between *P. sargentii* and *P. subhirtella*. Semi-double rich pink flowers, 1–1½ in. across, are produced in great profusion during March and early April.

P. 'Amanogawa' (Japanese cherry). Garden origin. Height 20–25 ft; spread 6–8 ft. A tree of erect, columnar habit like a small Lombardy poplar. The young leaves are green-bronze. Semi-double, slightly fragrant, soft pink flowers, 1½–2 in. wide, are borne in dense clusters in late April or May. This is one of the most floriferous of the Japanese cherries and the most suitable where space is limited.

P. 'Asano' (Japanese cherry). Garden origin. Height 20–30 ft; spread 15–25 ft. A tree of upright habit; the young leaves are green-bronze. Double deep pink flowers, 1–1½ in. wide, are borne in dense clusters during late March and early April.

PRUNUS AVIUM

P. avium (gean, wild cherry). Europe, including Great Britain; W. Asia. Height 30–40 ft; spread 20–30 ft. A tree of vigorous, somewhat pyramidal habit, from which most of the cultivated sweet cherries are derived. The leaves may turn crimson in autumn. White cup-shaped

Prunus cerasifera 'Atropurpurea'

Prunus × *cistena*

Prunus spinosa (fruits)

Prunus 'Fudanzakura'

Prunus 'Kanzan'

Prunus 'Kiku-shidare Sakura'

Prunus padus 'Watereri'

flowers, up to 1½ in. wide, are borne in pendulous clusters, several inches long, and open with the leaves in April. 'Plena' has double white flowers; it is extremely floriferous.

P. 'Benifugen': see P. 'Daikoku'

P. *conradinae*. China. Height 25–30 ft; spread 15–20 ft. An early-flowering species whose fragrant white or pink flowers, ¾ in. wide, are produced in late February. It requires a sheltered position. P. c. 'Semiplena' has long-lasting, semi-double pink flowers.

P. 'Daikoku', syn. P. 'Benifugen' (Japanese cherry). Garden origin. Height 20–30 ft; spread 15–20 ft. A tree with strongly ascending branches and leaves that are yellow-green when young. The double flowers, up to 2 in. across, are purple-red in bud, opening to lilac-pink; they are carried in loose drooping clusters during late April or May.

P. 'Fudanzakura', syn. P. *serrulata* 'Semper-florens' (Japanese cherry). Garden origin. Height 15–20 ft; spread 10–15 ft. A round-headed tree with copper-red young leaves. The 1–1½ in. wide flowers, pink in bud, opening to white, appear in clusters at any time between November and April. The flowering branches are suitable for flower arrangements.

P. 'Fugenzo', syn. P. 'James H. Veitch' (Japanese cherry). Garden origin. Height and spread 25–30 ft. A flat-topped tree with copper-red young leaves. Double rose-pink flowers, 1½–2 in. across, are produced in drooping clusters along the branches in May. It resembles P. 'Kanzan', but is smaller and broader.

P. × 'Halle Jolivette'. Garden origin. Height and spread 15–20 ft. A hybrid between P. *subhirtella* and P. *yedoensis*. This is a graceful tree with willowy branches. Semi-double blush-white flowers, ¾–1 in. across, are borne profusely in April and May and continue over a long period. One of the most suitable ornamental cherries for a small garden.

P. × *hillieri*. Garden origin. Height and spread 25–30 ft. This broad-headed tree is a hybrid between P. *incisa* and P. *sargentii*. In April, the whole tree becomes a cloud of soft pink as the 1 in. wide flowers open. The leaves may turn rich crimson in autumn. 'Spire' is a variety of conical habit (height 20–25 ft; spread 8–10 ft), it is suitable for street planting or for a small garden.

P. 'Hisakura': see P. 'Kanzan'

P. 'Hokusai' (Japanese cherry). Garden origin. Height 20–25 ft; spread 25–35 ft. A vigorous wide-spreading tree with brown-bronze young leaves. Large clusters of semi-double pale pink flowers, 1½–2 in. wide, crowd the branches during the latter half of April. This is one of the best Japanese cherries for general planting.

P. 'Horinji' (Japanese cherry). Garden origin. Height 15–18 ft; spread 8–12 ft. An upright tree with ascending branches; the young leaves are green-bronze. Semi-double soft pink flowers, 1½ in. across, with purple-brown calyces are freely borne along the branches during the latter half of April or early May.

P. 'Ichiyo' (Japanese cherry). Garden origin. Height 20–25 ft; spread 18–20 ft. The leaves are bronze-green when young. Double shell-pink flowers, 1½ in. wide, with a fringed appearance are borne in long-stalked clusters during the latter half of April.

P. × *incam* 'Okame'. Garden origin. Height 20–25 ft; spread 18–25 ft. A hybrid between P. *campanulata* and P. *incisa*. Masses of small, carmine-rose flowers, ½–¾ in. across, open throughout March.

P. incisa (Fuji cherry). Japan. Height and spread 10–15 ft. This species is generally of shrubby habit, but it may be trained as a small tree. The leaves are sharply toothed. White flowers, $\frac{1}{2}$–$\frac{3}{4}$ in. wide and pink in bud, clothe the naked branches in March. The variety 'Praecox' flowers during late winter. Both forms make suitable specimen plants or attractive and unusual hedges.

P. 'James H. Veitch': see *P.* 'Fugenzo'

P. 'Jo-nioi' (Japanese cherry). Garden origin. Height 20–25 ft; spread 25–30 ft. A strong growing tree of spreading habit; the young leaves are pale golden-brown. White, sweetly scented flowers, 1–1$\frac{1}{2}$ in. across, wreathe the long branches in late May.

P. 'Kanzan' (Japanese cherry). Garden origin. Height 25–30 ft; spread 18–25 ft. A vigorous tree with stiff ascending branches and young coppery-red leaves. Double purple-pink flowers, 1$\frac{1}{2}$–2 in. wide, profusely cover the branches during the latter half of April. This is one of the most commonly grown ornamental cherries; it is sometimes incorrectly offered as *P.* 'Hisakura'.

P. 'Kiku-shidare Sakura' (Japanese cherry, Cheal's weeping cherry). Garden origin. Height and spread 15–20 ft. A tree with arching branches and pendulous branchlets. The young leaves are bronze-green. Double deep pink flowers, 1$\frac{1}{2}$ in. across, clothe the branches in March or April.

P. 'Kojima': see *P.* 'Shirotae'

P. × *kursar*. Garden origin. Height 20–30 ft; spread 15–25 ft. This hybrid between *P. kurilensis* and *P. sargentii* is a vigorous grower of upright habit. Rich clear pink flowers, $\frac{3}{4}$ in. wide, are borne in clusters in April.

P. 'Mikuruma-gaeshi' (Japanese cherry). Garden origin. Height 20–25 ft; spread 15–20 ft. The long ascending branches carry young bronze-green leaves. Blush-pink flowers, 1$\frac{1}{2}$–1$\frac{1}{4}$ in. wide and usually single, are borne in densely packed clusters in the latter half of April.

P. 'Ojochin', syn. *P. serrulata* 'Senriko' (Japanese cherry). Garden origin. Height 20–25 ft; spread 20–30 ft. A striking tree distinguished by its stout growth and large leaves; these are bronze-brown when young. Pale pink flowers, 2 in. across, are borne in numerous long-stalked clusters during the latter half of April.

P. padus (bird cherry). Europe, including Great Britain; N. Asia to Japan. Height 20–30 ft; spread 15–20 ft. Almond-scented white flowers, $\frac{1}{2}$ in. wide, are borne in slender 3–5 in. long racemes in May. In cultivation, the species is largely represented by 'Watereri', with freely borne racemes up to 8 in. long.

P. × 'Pandora'. Garden origin. Height 15–20 ft; spread 10–18 ft. A hybrid between *P. subhirtella rosea* and *P. yedoensis*; suitable for a small garden. Numerous soft pink blossoms, $\frac{3}{4}$–1 in. across, are borne in March.

P. × 'Pink Perfection'. Garden origin. Height and spread 20–25 ft. An upright growing hybrid between *P.* 'Shimidsu Sakura' and *P.* 'Kanzan'. The leaves are coppery-red when young. Bright rose-pink double flowers, 1$\frac{1}{2}$–2 in. across, are carried in long drooping clusters during the latter half of April.

P. sargentii. Japan, Korea. Height 25–30 ft; spread 18–25 ft. The young bronze-red leaves generally unfold in late March at the same time as

Prunus serrula (bark)

the clusters of clear pink flowers which are 1–1$\frac{1}{2}$ in. wide. This species is one of the first trees to change colour in the autumn, the leaves assuming orange and crimson tints.

P. serrula. W. China. Height 20–25 ft; spread 15–18 ft. The leaves are narrow and willow-like. Clusters of white flowers, $\frac{1}{4}$–$\frac{1}{3}$ in. in diameter, are produced in late April at the same time as the foliage and are hidden by it. This species is chiefly grown for its attractive bark, which peels in strips to reveal polished, red-brown new bark.

P. serrulata longipes: see *P.* 'Shimidsu Sakura'

P. serrulata 'Semperflorens': see *P.* 'Fudan-zakura'

P. serrulata 'Senriko': see *P.* 'Ojochin'

P. 'Shimidsu Sakura', syn. *P. serrulata longipes* (Japanese cherry). Garden origin. Height 10–15 ft; spread 15–25 ft. A flat-topped tree with wide-spreading branches. Fringed double flowers, 1$\frac{1}{2}$–2 in. across, pink-tinged in bud, opening to pure white, hang along the branches in long-stalked clusters during late April or May.

P. 'Shirofugen' (Japanese cherry). Garden origin. Height 20–30 ft; spread 25–35 ft. The young leaves are coppery. Double 1$\frac{1}{2}$–1$\frac{3}{4}$ in. wide flowers, pink in bud, opening to pure white and fading to purple-pink, appear in long-stalked clusters along the branches in May. This is one of the best Japanese cherries for general planting; it is strong-growing.

P. 'Shirotae', syn. *P.* 'Kojima' (Japanese cherry). Garden origin. Height 18–25 ft; spread 30–35 ft. A vigorous tree with a wide-spreading head of horizontal or drooping branches. The leaves are bronze-green when young. Single or semi-double fragrant snow-white flowers, 1$\frac{1}{2}$–1$\frac{3}{4}$ in. across, are borne in long drooping clusters during the latter half of April.

Prunus sargentii

Prunus sargentii (autumn foliage)

P. subhirtella. Japan. Height and spread 20–30 ft. Pale pink flowers, $\frac{1}{2}$–$\frac{2}{3}$ in. wide, profusely cover the branches in March and April.

Named forms include: 'Autumnalis' (autumn cherry), semi-double white flowers intermittently from November to March, ideal as cut flowers; 'Autumnalis Rosea' similar, but with pink flowers; 'Fukubana', rich rose-pink semi-double flowers in early spring.

'Pendula' (height 10–15 ft; spread 10–20 ft), pale pink flowers cover the slender drooping branches; 'Pendula Plena Rosea', semi-double rose-pink flowers; 'Pendula Rubra', deep rose flowers, carmine in bud.

P. 'Tai-haku' (Japanese cherry, great white cherry). Garden origin. Height 20–30 ft; spread 15–25 ft. The leaves are rich copper-red when young. Clusters of dazzling white flowers, 2–2$\frac{1}{2}$ in. across, contrast with the young leaves in April. This is a vigorous grower and one of the finest cherries for general planting.

Prunus 'Shirotae'

Prunus subhirtella

Prunus 'Taoyoma Zakura'

Prunus 'Tai-haku'

P. 'Taoyoma Zakura'. Garden origin. Height 20–25 ft; spread 15–20 ft. The young leaves are rich purple-brown. Semi-double, fragrant, shell-pink flowers, 1$\frac{1}{2}$–1$\frac{3}{4}$ in. wide, with purple-brown calyces, appear in clusters at the same time as the young leaves during the latter half of April.

P. 'Ukon' (Japanese cherry). Garden origin. Height 15–20 ft; spread 18–25 ft. The leaves are bronze-purple when young. The semi-double flowers, 1$\frac{3}{4}$–2 in. in diameter and cream to palest yellow tinged green, are freely borne during the latter half of April.

P. 'Umeniko'. Garden origin. Height 15–20 ft; spread 5–6 ft. A narrow tree with an upright head of branches. Pure white flowers, 1 in. across, are freely produced in clusters in April at the same time as the leaves. These often assume attractive autumn tints.

P. yedoensis (Yoshino cherry). Japan. Height 20–25 ft; spread 25–30 ft. A graceful tree with arching branches. Clusters of almond-scented blush-white flowers, 1–1$\frac{1}{2}$ in. across, are carried profusely during late March and early April.

Named forms include: 'Ivensii' (height 10–15 ft; spread 10–18 ft), wide-spreading branches and drooping branchlets with fragrant snow-white flowers; 'Moerheimii' (height 10–15 ft; spread 10–18 ft), weeping tree of wide-spreading habit, with pink flowers; 'Pendula' (height 10–15 ft; spread 10–18 ft), with branches that droop to the ground, and heavy clusters of single pale pink flowers, $\frac{3}{4}$ in. wide.

ORNAMENTAL CHERRY LAURELS (evergreen)

P. laurocerasus (cherry laurel, common laurel). E. Europe, Asia Minor. Height 15–20 ft; spread 20–30 ft. A vigorous shrub with oblong to obovate, leathery, pointed leaves that are shiny mid-green above, pale green beneath. White flowers are borne in axillary and terminal racemes, 3–5 in. long, in April. They are followed by small fruits which turn black. This is an outstanding species for hedging and screening; it is tolerant of shade.

Named forms include: 'Caucasica', of upright growth and with slender oblanceolate, dark green leaves; 'Latifolia', vigorous grower, with large glossy dark green leaves; 'Rotundifolia', a bushy form, most suitable for hedges; 'Schipkaensis', of low-spreading habit, with narrow lanceolate leaves; 'Zabeliana', similar to 'Schipkaensis', but almost prostrate, with lower horizontal branches, excellent for ground cover.

PRUNUS LAUROCERASUS

P. lusitanica (Portugal laurel). Spain, Portugal. Height and spread 15–20 ft. The pointed leaves are glossy dark green with red stalks. Cream, scented flowers are produced in slender, 6–8 in. long racemes in June. They are followed by small fruits which turn black. 'Variegata' is a slow-growing form with white-variegated leaves.

Cultivation. Most prunus are shallow-rooting and should not be planted too deeply, nor should the soil round them be cultivated too often or too deeply. This applies particularly to the ornamental cherries. Planting is best done in early autumn while the soil is still warm, but during mild weather winter planting can be continued until March.

The majority of prunus thrive in any ordinary, well-drained soil, preferably with a trace of lime, but most soils are suitable provided they are not too dry or waterlogged. For individual soil and aspect requirements see also descriptions of the species and varieties.

On exposed or windy sites, standard specimen trees require staking with stout supports until established. In country districts where hares are common the young stems of newly planted specimens should be protected with coils of chicken wire during winter.

Cherries with long spreading branches, such as 'Shimidsu Sakura' and 'Shirotae', should be supported with strong stakes to keep their branches clear of the ground in later years.

Hedges should be planted in October. For *P. cerasifera* and its forms. use 18–24 in. high plants and space at intervals of 24 in. *P. spinosa* should be planted when 12–18 in. high and at a distance of 15 in. The quick-growing *P. laurocerasus* and its forms are planted when 2–3 ft high and spaced at 2–3 ft. *P. lusitanica* is best planted when 18–24 in. high and at the same distance apart. After planting, remove the upper third of all shoots to promote bushy growth.

Screens of *P. cerasifera* should be planted in October, using 3–4 ft high plants and setting these at intervals of 5 ft.

Propagation. The species are best increased from seeds, but selected and named forms must be vegetatively propagated. Sow seeds outdoors immediately on gathering. Protect the fruits with nets while ripening on the trees. Seed-raised trees are generally longer-lived, though hybrids are likely to arise where different species grow and flower together.

Bud the Japanese cherries and other large-flowered hybrids in July or graft in March on to stock of *P. avium.*

Take heel cuttings, 3–4 in. long, in July of half-ripened shoots of the smaller-flowered species, such as *P. cerasifera, P. conradinae, P. incisa, P. spinosa* and *P. subhirtella.* Insert the cuttings in equal parts (by volume) peat and sand in a propagating case with a bottom temperature of 16–18°C (61–64°F); pot when rooted in 3 in. pots of John Innes potting compost No. 1, and overwinter in a cold frame. The following spring, line out in nursery rows and grow on for a further year or two before transplanting to permanent positions.

Take heel cuttings, 3–4 in. long, of *P. laurocerasus* and *P. lusitanica* in August or September and insert in equal parts (by volume) peat and sand in a cold frame. Treat the rooted cuttings as already described.

Remove and replant rooted suckers of *P. tenella* and its forms in early autumn. *P. glandulosa* and its forms, as well as *P. padus* and *P. cerasifera,* may be layered in early spring. Sever from the parent plants two years later.

Pruning. No regular pruning is required for ornamental almonds, but cut back the old flowering shoots of *P. glandulosa* and *P. triloba* to within two or three buds of the base immediately after flowering. This particularly applies to *P. triloba* when trained against a wall.

No pruning is needed for ornamental peaches. Pruning is generally not necessary for ornamental plums. Hedges of *P. × blireiana, P. × cistena, P. cerasifera* and its forms and *P. spinosa* and its forms may be clipped at any time during the year. If the hedges are grown for flowers, delay trimming until flowering is over, then prune back the old flowering shoots.

No regular pruning is required for ornamental cherries, but if it becomes necessary to remove a large branch, carry out the work in late summer. Hedges of *P. incisa* should be clipped immediately after flowering.

Prune cherry laurels hard back into the old wood of large, unsightly specimens in March or April. Hedges and screens should be trimmed with secateurs rather than hedging shears in March and April, or August.

Pests. During winter, BIRDS especially the bullfinches, sometimes eat the young buds and may severely limit the amount of blossom.

APHIDS, particularly cherry blackfly and mealy plum aphid, may infest leaves and young shoots.

CATERPILLARS may feed on the leaves.

Diseases. The ornamental species are sometimes subject to the same diseases and disorders as cherry, peach and plum, though seldom at the same time. These include BACTERIAL CANKER, CHLOROSIS, HONEY FUNGUS, PEACH LEAF CURL, SHOT HOLE and SILVER LEAF.

LEAF SPOT of *P. laurocerasus* shows as yellow spots which become purple and finally brown. The discoloured tissues fall away to leave large spherical or irregular holes.

POWDERY MILDEW shows as a white powdery coating on leaves and shoots of *P. laurocerasus.*

WITCHES' BROOMS show as dense masses of shoots; many twigs die, but others remain alive, and the brooms gradually increase in size.

Psalliota campestris: see Mushroom

Pseudotsuga

Douglas fir. *Pinaceae*

PSEUDOTSUGA MENZIESII

A genus of seven species of evergreen coniferous trees native to western N. America, China, Japan and Formosa. Only one species, with its variety, is in general cultivation in Great Britain. In sheltered sites it makes an excellent specimen tree; in more exposed areas, where the brittle crown may become thin, it is better planted in groups. It is fast-growing under good conditions and may increase annually by 24 in. or more.

See also CONIFERS.

P. menziesii, syn. *P. taxifolia.* S.W. United States. Height 30–75 ft; spread 15–20 ft. A hardy species, slender-spired for many years, but usually developing heavy branches and a flattened broad crown. Smooth and resin-blistered bark ages to dark brown; it becomes thick and corky with wide and deep tawny fissures. The buds are slender and spindle-shaped.

The dense, soft and sweetly aromatic foliage is composed of linear-oblong leaves, up to 2 in. long; they lie forward on the shoots and are rich dark green above with two silvery lines beneath. In less vigorous trees the needles are shorter and range through green to almost yellow. The female flowers are red and upright; they develop into downward-facing, soft, woody cones, up to 4 in. long, with three-pronged bracts extending from between the scales. The cones mature during their first season, but coning is rare until the tree is at least ten years old.

'Glauca'. Height 35 ft; spread 10 ft. This is more slow-growing than the species and more

Prunus 'Ukon'

Prunus yedoensis

Prunus lusitanica

suitable on dry and shallow soils. It has scaly, dull pewter-grey bark with black cracks; the leaves are blue-grey and the bracts of the cones bend back towards the base.

'Fletcheri'. Height and spread up to 24 in. A dwarf form of the species, developing into a rounded bush with glaucous leaves. Cones are rarely borne.

P. taxifolia: see *P. menziesii*

Cultivation. These conifers thrive in deep, fertile soil, well-drained but moisture-retentive. They grow particularly well in areas with high rainfall, although *P. menziesii* 'Glauca' tolerates drier and shallower soils with good drainage.

Plant in March using saplings up to 24 in. high, and set in an open sunny position.

Keep the root-run clear of weeds; in spring apply 2 oz. of general fertiliser per sq. yd.

Propagation. Sow seeds in March in open beds or in pans in a cold frame; prick out the seedlings, when large enough to handle, into a nursery bed. Grow on for two years before planting out in permanent positions.

Pruning. None is required except to reduce forked shoots to a single leader as soon as forking occurs. Branches may be removed at any time of year and as high as one-third of the height of the tree without adverse effect on growth.

Pests. ADELGIDS feed on stems and foliage and produce tufts of white waxy wool. Severe infestations may weaken young trees.

Diseases. GREY MOULD may be a troublesome disease on seedlings; it shows as a sparse web of grey fungal growth over the affected parts of the plant. When succulent shoots are attacked they collapse, wither and die.

Pseudotsuga menziesii (cones)

Pseudotsuga menziesii 'Fletcheri'

Pteris cretica

Pteris

Pteridaceae

A genus of 250 species of ferns. The species described are evergreen and are suitable for growing indoors and in cool greenhouses. *P. cretica* is widely grown commercially.

P. argyraea: see *P. quadriaurita*

P. biaurita quadriaurita: see *P. quadriaurita*

P. cretica (ribbon fern). S.W. Europe, Mediterranean islands, Iran, India, Japan. Height 12–18 in.; spread 9–15 in. The light green fronds are pinnate, with strap-shaped pinnae. In a cool greenhouse, spores often germinate in the pots of other plants.

P. c. 'Albolineata' has a white central band on each pinna. *P. c.* 'Wimsettii' is the group name for all the heavily crested varieties raised for the florists' trade.

P. ensiformis. Himalayas, Ceylon to Australia. Height 18 in.; spread 12 in. This species is a slender, deep green version of *P. cretica*, with more elongated pinnae. The variety most often grown, *P. e.* 'Victoriae', has slender, upright, fertile fronds, variegated with white, and smaller, more pendent barren fronds.

P. quadriaurita, syn. *P. biaurita quadriaurita.* Tropics. Height 1–2½ ft; spread 10 in.–2½ ft. The form usually cultivated is the strong-growing variety *P. q. argyraea*, syn. *P. biaurita argyraea*, which is now regarded as a separate species,

Pteris quadriaurita argyraea

P. argyraea. This has grey-green pinnate frond with broad, deeply lobed pinnae, each marked b a broad, central, pale green-white band.

P. tremula. New Zealand, Australia, Fiji. Heigh and spread 3–5 ft. The upper half of each soft bright green frond is bipinnate, the lower ha tripinnate. This handsome plant often seeds itsel freely in a cool greenhouse.

Cultivation. Grow all species in 5 or 6 in. pot containing a compost of equal parts (by volume leaf-mould or peat, loam and coarse sand. P cretica and *P. tremula* need a minimum temperature of 7°C (45°F), *P. quadriaurita argyraea* 10°C (50°F), and *P. ensiformis* 13°C (55°F). Shade variegated plants from bright sun, which stunt their growth. Water freely during the growing season, and for the rest of the year just sufficiently to keep the soil moist.

Propagation. Sow spores in March at a temperature of 13°C (55°F) (see entry under FERNS). Thi produces more numerous, better and faster growing plants than division.

Pests. The frond tissues may be invaded b LEAF-BLOTCH EELWORMS which make large blac marks on them.

Diseases. Generally trouble-free.

Pulmonaria

Lungwort. *Boraginaceae*

PULMONARIA SACCHARATA

A genus of ten species of hardy herbaceou perennials. They are low-growing plants suitabl for a rock garden or for ground cover in shade. I some species the green leaves are white-spotted

Pulmonaria saccharata

Pulmonaria officinalis

The flowers are usually pink on opening, turning violet or blue; some remain pink, however.

P. angustifolia, syn. *P. azurea* (blue cowslip). Central Europe. Height and planting distance 12 in. This species has unspotted, mid-green, lanceolate leaves. It produces sky-blue, broadly funnel-shaped flowers, about ¾ in. long, in April. 'Mawson's Variety' and 'Munstead Blue' have deeper blue flowers.

P. azurea: see *P. angustifolia*

P. officinalis (Jerusalem cowslip, spotted dog). Europe. Height and planting distance 12 in. The green, narrowly elliptic leaves are white-spotted. This species is the best known of the genus; it carries funnel-shaped purple-blue flowers, about ½ in. long, in April and May.

P. saccharata. Probably Italy. Height and planting distance 12 in. This species bears narrowly ovate leaves, strikingly spotted with silver-white. The funnel-shaped flowers, up to ¾ in. long, appear in March and April; they open pink and change to sky-blue.

Cultivation. Plant from October to March, in a shady position and in any ordinary garden soil. Keep the roots moist in the growing season by mulching with peat or by frequent watering.

Propagation. Divide and replant the roots in October or March. Seeds may be sown outdoors in April; they often produce inferior plants.

Pests. The leaves are eaten by SAWFLY larvae.

Diseases. Generally trouble-free.

Pulsatilla

Ranunculaceae

A genus of 30 species of hardy herbaceous perennials closely related to anemones, under which name they were formerly known and are sometimes still listed. They are suitable for growing on open parts of rock gardens and are long-lived once established. The foliage is generally hairy and fern-like and dies down in winter. The flowers are borne singly, each one subtended

by a ruff of narrow leaf segments often densely hairy. The leaves develop as the flowers fade.

P. alpina. Mountains of Europe, as far east as the Caucasus. Height 12 in.; spread 6 in. The ferny leaves are mid-green, deeply dissected into narrow segments. The hairy flower buds are blue or red-tinged and open in May and June into cup-shaped white flowers which flatten out to a width of 2–2½ in.

The form 'Sulphurea', syns. *P. sulphurea* and *Anemone sulphurea* (height 6–10 in.; spread 6 in.), has sulphur-yellow flowers which open from May until July. It varies considerably in height, depending on soil conditions.

P. sulphurea: see *P. alpina* 'Sulphurea'

P. vernalis. Mountains of Europe. Height and spread 6 in. A species which forms a prostrate tuft of deep green, hairy, pinnate leaves. Tawny, silky, hairy buds open to cup-shaped pearl-white flowers, about 2 in. across, in April and May.

P. vulgaris (pasque flower). Europe, including Great Britain. Height 12 in.; spread 15 in. This is a variable plant with several good colour forms. The mid-green foliage is fern-like and finely cut. Hairy flower buds open to cup-shaped flowers, 2–3 in. wide, in April and May.

The type has purple flowers. Varieties include 'Budapest', a variable plant, generally red-purple; 'Mrs Van der Elst', pale pink; and 'Rubra', red.

Cultivation. Plant in September in an open sunny position in any well-drained soil containing plenty of humus. In wet areas, protect the dormant flower buds of *P. vernalis* from excessive dampness in winter with panes of glass or with open cloches.

Propagation. Sow fresh seeds in July in boxes or pans of John Innes seed compost and place in a cold frame. Prick off the seedlings when they are large enough to handle. Overwinter them in a frame and pot into 3–3½ in. pots of John Innes potting compost No. 1 when the new leaves begin to show in spring. Water freely when the plants are in growth, and plant out in September of the year following sowing.

Pests and diseases. Generally trouble-free.

Pulmonaria angustifolia

Pulsatilla alpina 'Sulphurea'

Pulsatilla vulgaris

Pulsatilla vulgaris 'Budapest'

Pumpkin

Pumpkin 'Gold Summer Crookneck'

Punica granatum (flowers)

Punica granatum (fruits)

Pumpkins and squashes

Cucurbita maxima, C. moschata. Cucurbitaceae

PUMPKIN

These bushy and trailing half-hardy annuals, native to tropical America, are grown for their edible fruits. These ripen in summer or late autumn and have firm flesh similar to that of a vegetable marrow. They are used for the same culinary purposes as marrows. There is little practical distinction between pumpkins, squashes and edible gourds, and the terms are generally loosely applied. Pumpkins resemble marrows in growth habit and appearance, and bear similar, but less-prominently lobed, pale to mid-green, hairy, heart-shaped leaves and wide, bell-shaped, orange-yellow flowers.

VARIETIES

Reliable, small-fruited, summer varieties include the bush types 'Gold Summer Crookneck' and 'Prolific Straight Neck', and the trailing 'Noodle'. Large-fruited, winter-maturing bush varieties are 'Hundredweight', 'Large Yellow', 'Mammoth' and 'Turk's Cap'.

Cultivation. Pumpkins thrive in full sun in any fertile, well-drained and humus-rich soil that was well manured during winter.

Raise young plants in late April or early May by sowing one or two seeds in 3 in. containers of John Innes seed compost. Germinate at a temperature of 10°C (50°F), and harden off the young plants in a cold frame. Transplant to growing positions in early June, setting the seedlings at intervals of 3 ft.

Alternatively, sow seeds outdoors where the plants are to grow, from mid-April onwards; protect the seedlings with cloches until danger of frost is over.

Water freely during hot spells and apply a ½ in. deep mulch of compost, peat or lawn cuttings to preserve moisture.

Pinch out the growing tips of the main shoots of trailing varieties to encourage the production of laterals which bear most of the female flowers. It may be necessary to assist pollination by transferring pollen to the female flowers, distinguished by a bulbous ovary.

Varieties may be induced to bear larger fruits by heaping soil over the axils of fruit-bearing laterals. Further roots will then be produced to obtain more food and moisture from the soil.

Harvesting and storing. Cut small-fruited varieties as they mature during summer and use immediately. Large-fruited types should be left to mature on the plants until late autumn. Store fruits for winter use in a cool, frost-free shed.

Pests. Generally trouble-free.

Diseases. CUCUMBER MOSAIC VIRUS causes stunting of the plants; the foliage may be distorted and mottled with yellow. The fruits are mottled and covered with circular wart-like spots.

GREY MOULD attacks the flowers, causing the fruits to rot; the rotting tissues are covered with a grey velvety fungal growth.

POWDERY MILDEW shows as a white powder coating on leaves and stems.

Punica

Pomegranate. *Punicaceae*

A genus of two species of tender deciduous flowering shrubs or small trees. They are suitable for outdoor culture only in the mildest areas in the south and west; elsewhere they require greenhouse cultivation. Pomegranate fruits rarely ripen in the open, where they are chiefly grown for their attractive flowers.

PUNICA GRANATUM 'NANA'

P. granatum. Iran, Afghanistan. Height 8–10 ft, spread 5–8 ft. A slow-growing species with oblong, shiny, pale to mid-green leaves. Scarlet 1½–2 in. long, tubular flowers are borne singly or in clusters from June to September. The deep yellow or yellow-orange, red-flushed fruits have a leathery rind enclosing pulpy red flesh and numerous seeds. These edible fruits generally ripen only under greenhouse conditions, although in the warmer south fruits sometimes ripen in the open.

P. g. 'Nana', height and spread 3 ft or more, is a dwarf, twiggy form, somewhat hardier than the type species. It has narrower leaves and smaller flowers and fruits, and makes an excellent pot plant.

Cultivation. Plant in April or May in any ordinary, well-drained soil in full sun, choosing a site against a south-facing wall or a position with similar protection.

In the greenhouse, grow pomegranates in 9–12 in. pots or tubs of John Innes potting compost No. 2 or, preferably, planted out in the border. Maintain a minimum winter temperature of 5–7°C (41–45°F); to obtain edible fruit provide a temperature of 13–16°C (55–61°F) during late autumn. Water freely during the growing period, and keep the plants just moist in winter; ventilate the house freely at all times except during frosty and foggy weather.

Pot on every other year in March or April and give pot plants a weak liquid feed every 10–14 days from May to September.

Propagation. Sow seeds in March in pots of John Innes seed compost and place in a propagating frame at a temperature of 16°C (61°F). Prick out the seedlings into pans or boxes and later transfer them to 3 in. pots of John Innes potting compost No. 2. Pot on as required into 4–5 in. containers and overwinter the plants in a frost-free greenhouse or frame. Grow on for a further year in pots before setting the young plants out.

Alternatively, take 3 in. long cuttings of half-ripened lateral shoots with a heel, in late July; insert the cuttings in equal parts (by volume) peat and sand in a propagating frame at 16–18°C (61–64°F). Pot the rooted cuttings in 3 in. pots of John Innes potting compost No. 2, and overwinter them in a frost-free greenhouse. Grow on for a year in 4–5 in. pots, ready for planting out or potting on in April or May of the following year.

Pruning. None required.

Pests and diseases. Generally trouble-free.

Purple heart: see *Setcreasea purpurea*

Puschkinia

Liliaceae

A genus of small hardy bulbs which come from Asia Minor and countries eastwards to Afghanistan. There are two species, but only one is in general cultivation. The genus is closely related to *Chionodoxa* and *Scilla*. Puschkinias are suitable for planting outdoors in low grass, rock gardens or dwarf borders, or for growing as pot plants in a cool greenhouse or alpine house.

P. libanotica: see *P. scilloides*

P. scilloides, syns. *P. libanotica*, *P. sicula*, *Adamsia scilloides*, *Scilla sicula* (striped squill). W. Asia. Height 4–8 in.; planting distance 2–3 in. The leaves are strap-shaped and mid-green. Slender arching flower stems carry up to six pale blue, bell-shaped flowers, each ½ in. long and with darker blue stripes on the six petals. Flowering is from March to May.

P. sicula: see *P. scilloides*

Cultivation. A sunny or partially shaded position in any good garden soil suits these bulbs. Plant them 2 in. deep in October. Leave untouched unless the bulbs are wanted for propagation.

Indoors, set the bulbs, seven to eight in a 6 in. pan containing John Innes potting compost No. 1. Plant the bulbs in September or October for flowering the following March. Plunge the pots outdoors for six to eight weeks. Bring the pots in batches into a cool greenhouse from December onwards; when growth is apparent keep the compost moist at all times. After flowering, gradually withhold water. Repot and start into growth in September.

Propagation. Save the seeds when they ripen in June and sow at once in a frame or in boxes, using John Innes seed compost; just cover the seeds with compost and keep them moist at all times. After one year space out the seedlings into larger containers or plant them into a nursery row. Leave them for two or three years to reach flowering size, then lift in July and August and plant them at once in the permanent flowering site or in pots.

The bulbs produce offsets that can be lifted with the bulbs as the leaves die down. Dry them off in boxes in a shed or greenhouse; clean, divide and replant either at once, or in early autumn after storing in a cool shed.

Pests. The bulbs, stems and leaves may be eaten by SLUGS.

Diseases. Generally trouble-free.

Pyracantha

Firethorn. *Rosaceae*

PYRACANTHA COCCINEA

A genus of ten species of hardy evergreen flowering shrubs. They have spiny branches and bear bright berries, about ¼ in. across, that last from September until March. They are useful for growing as wall shrubs or as hedging plants, but when pruned to shape will not bear many berries.

P. angustifolia. China. Height up to 10 ft; spread 6–8 ft. This spreading shrub has narrow, oblong leaves which are mid-green above, grey and hairy beneath. Cream-coloured hawthorn-like flowers are borne in rounded clusters, 1½ in. or more across, during June and July. These are followed by flattened, globose, bright orange-yellow berries, ¼ in. wide.

P. atalantioides, syn. *P. gibbsii*. China. Height and spread 10–15 ft. This upright, fast-growing shrub has glossy deep green leaves. They are in various shapes, and may be oblong, elliptic or obovate. The white hawthorn-like flowers appear in flat, 2 in. wide clusters in June, followed by crimson berries. 'Aurea' has bright yellow berries.

P. coccinea. S. Europe, Asia Minor. Height and spread 10–15 ft. The narrowly obovate leaves of this species are pointed and mid-green. White hawthorn-like flowers, about ⅓ in. across, appear in 2 in. wide clusters in June, and are followed by bright red berries. 'Lalandei' has orange-red berries and broader leaves.

P. crenulata. China. Height 8–10 ft; spread 12–15 ft. This species is usually represented in cultivation by the form 'Rogersiana'. The mid-green leaves are narrowly obovate or oblanceolate. The white ¼ in. wide flowers open in June in clusters, 2 in. across, and are followed by bright, orange-red berries. The variety 'Flava' has bright yellow berries.

P. gibbsii: see *P. atalantioides*

P. × *watereri*. Reputedly a garden hybrid between *P. crenulata* 'Rogersiana' and *P. atalantioides*. This resembles a bushy, compact form of *P. crenulata* 'Rogersiana' and regularly each year produces abundant quantities of orange-scarlet berries in autumn.

Cultivation. Plant pot-grown plants between October and March in any fertile, well-drained garden soil, including chalky soil. They thrive in full sun or partial shade.

If grown as wall plants, provide trellis or wires for support. Tie in vigorous growths each year between July and September.

Set hedging plants 15–24 in. apart and prune back the current season's growths by half. Pinch out the growing points of young shoots when they reach 6–8 in., and repeat this process later in the year if necessary.

Propagation. Take 3–4 in. cuttings of the current year's shoots in July or August and insert them

Puschkinia scilloides

Pyracantha atalantioides (fruits)

Pyracantha coccinea 'Lalandei'

Pyracantha crenulata 'Rogersiana'

in equal parts (by volume) peat and sand in a propagating frame at a temperature of 16°C (61°F). When the cuttings have rooted, pot them singly into 3 in. pots of John Innes potting compost No. 1, and overwinter in a cold frame. Alternatively, take 4–6 in. hardwood cuttings in October and insert in a cold frame. Pot both types of cuttings in 4 in. pots the following April or May, and plunge the pots in an outdoor bed of soil or peat. Set the plants out in their permanent positions from October onwards.

To raise new plants from seeds, gather the berries when ripe in October and squash them to secure the seeds. Sow these in pans or boxes in October and place in a cold frame or greenhouse. When they are large enough to handle, prick off the seedlings into pans or boxes, later transferring them to 3 in. pots as described for cuttings. Plant out from the following October onwards.

Pruning. No pruning is necessary if the shrubs are grown as free-standing bushes. Trim surplus growth from wall plants between May and July, and shear established hedges to shape between May and July.

Pests. Stems and leaves may be infested with aphids, especially WOOLLY APHIDS, which produce conspicuous tufts of white wax on the growths.

SCALE INSECTS, particularly brown scale, infest stems and make the plants sticky and sooty.

Diseases. A blackening and shrivelling of flowers is caused by FIREBLIGHT; this also causes the progressive die-back of branches, bearing brown and withered leaves which do not fall.

PYRACANTHA SCAB shows as an olive-brown coating on the berries. The leaves may also be attacked and defoliation can occur.

Pyracantha crenulata 'Rogersiana Flava' (fruits)

Pyrethrum roseum 'Brenda'

Pyrethrum roseum 'Kelway's Glorious'

Pyrethrum
Compositae

A genus of 100 species of hardy herbaceous perennials. They have daisy-like flowers and are popular plants for a sunny border; they are excellent as cut flowers.

Botanically, these plants are classified as chrysanthemums, but most catalogues list them as pyrethrums.

P. corymbosum: see *Chrysanthemum corymbosum*

P. parthenium: see *Chrysanthemum parthenium*

PYRETHRUM ROSEUM

P. roseum, syn. *Chrysanthemum coccineum*. Caucasus. This species has been superseded by numerous hybrid varieties, all with bright green feathery foliage. Height up to 3 ft, planting distance 16–18 in. The flowers, 2–2½ in. across, may be single or double; they come in a wide range of colours and include the following:

Single: 'Avalanche', white; 'Ariel', salmon;

Pyrethrum roseum 'Eileen May Robinson'

'Brenda', cerise-pink; 'Bressingham Red', crimson-scarlet; 'Eileen May Robinson', clear pink; 'Evenglow', salmon; 'Kelway's Glorious', crimson-red; 'Silver Challenger', white.

Double: 'Carl Vogt', white; 'J. N. Twerdy', deep red; 'Lord Rosebery', red; 'Madeleine', clear pink; 'Mont Blanc', white; 'Princess Mary', deep pink; 'Prospero', salmon; 'Vanessa', pink, flushed gold; 'Venus', clear shell-pink.

P. uliginosum: see *Chrysanthemum uliginosum*

Cultivation. Plant pyrethrums in March in light, well-drained soil and in an open, sunny position. The plants require staking with short pea sticks in late April or early May.

Water freely during the growing season, and cut back all stems as soon as flowering is over; young plants may flower again in early autumn.

Propagation. Pyrethrums are best left undisturbed for three or four years, after which time they may be divided. Division is best carried out in March or in July after flowering when new basal growth has begun; old woody root portions should be discarded.

Seeds may be sown in March under glass at a temperature of 16°C (61°F), but the resulting seedlings seldom come true to type.

Pests and diseases. Generally trouble-free.

Pyrus communis: see Pear
Pyrus theifera: see *Malus hupehensis*
Quamash: see Camassia
Quamoclit pennata: see *Ipomoea quamoclit*
Queen of the meadows: see *Filipendula ulmaria*
Queen of the prairie: see *Filipendula rubra*
Queen's tears: see *Billbergia nutans*

Quercus
Oak. *Fagaceae*

A genus of 450 species of hardy and half-hardy evergreen and deciduous trees, and sometimes shrubs. The species described are mostly deciduous, hardy and long-lived trees, chiefly suitable in large gardens. The evergreen *Q. ilex* may be used for screens and windbreaks or for hedging in mild coastal areas.

The foliage, which varies considerably from species to species, sometimes assumes rich autumn colours. The female flowers are generally insignificant, green and bud-like; the male yellow flowers are borne in fluffy, slender catkins, when the leaves expand in late spring. The fruits are the well-known acorns, consisting of an ovoid nut held in a cup or saucer-like husk, sometimes with a mossy covering.

QUERCUS ROBUR

Q. borealis, syn. *Q. rubra* (red oak). E. United States and Canada. Height 25–30 ft; spread 15–20 ft. A hardy tree, erect when young but soon developing a large spreading head. The mid-green leaves resemble those of *Q. coccinea,* but are more broadly lobed; in autumn they turn from dull crimson to deep red-brown. The species is generally represented in cultivation by the larger form, *Q. b. maxima.*

Q. cerris (Turkey oak). S. Europe, Asia Minor. Height 25–35 ft; spread 15–20 ft. A hardy vigorous species with an ovoid head, spreading with age. The mid to deep green leaves are ovate or oblong, sharply lobed and slightly rough.

Q. coccinea (scarlet oak). S.E. Canada, E. United States. Height 25–30 ft; spread 10–15 ft. A hardy and fast-growing tree, narrow when young, but broadening as it matures. The ovate to obovate leaves have pointed, tooth-like lobes and are glossy mid-green, turning scarlet in autumn. 'Splendens' is an outstanding form with rich autumn colours.

Q. ilex (holm oak, evergreen oak). Mediterranean regions, S.W. Europe. Height 15–20 ft; spread 10–15 ft. This evergreen round-headed species, with corrugated bark, becomes pendulous with age. Although hardy, it is not recommended for very cold districts. The ovate-lanceolate, leathery leaves are dark glossy green above, grey beneath.

Q. pedunculata: see *Q. robur*

QUERCUS ROBUR 'FASTIGIATA'

Q. robur, syn. *Q. pedunculata* (common oak, English oak). Europe, including Great Britain; Caucasus, Asia Minor and N. Africa. Height 12–18 ft; spread 6–10 ft. This species is the familiar native oak. It is hardy and slow-growing, and eventually forms a large tree, usually with a broad rounded crown. The shortly-stalked mid to deep green leaves are obovate with rounded lobes. 'Fastigiata' is of columnar habit.

Q. rubra: see *Q. borealis*

Cultivation. Grow oak trees in any ordinary, well-drained garden soil; most trees develop a better shape in an open position in full sun, but they will tolerate partial shade. Plant *Q. ilex*

during late September or October, or in April and early May; the deciduous species can be planted at any time between October and March. Young plants up to 4 ft high need no support. During the first few years of growth an annual mulch of well-rotted manure, compost, peat or leaf-mould helps to establish the trees.

For hedges of *Q. ilex,* set the young plants at intervals of 24 in. After planting, remove the growing points to induce bushy growth.

Propagation. Oak seeds (acorns) are short-lived and must be sown within two months of gathering. Sow 2–3 in. apart in pots or deep boxes of seed compost in a cold frame. The following autumn, line out the seedlings in nursery rows and grow on for three or four years before planting in the permanent site.

Alternatively, sow the seeds directly in nursery rows, 3 in. apart, and thin out a year later. Seeds sown in the open, however, may be eaten by mice, squirrels or voles.

Selected forms may be grafted on to stocks of the type species in March.

Pruning. Remove lateral branches in February, when trees are two or three years old, to maintain a clean stem.

Trim established hedges of *Q. ilex* to shape annually in April; a further clipping may be necessary again in September.

Pests. CATERPILLARS of various species of moth and CHAFER BEETLES feed on the leaves and may cause defoliation.

Galls on leaves, stems, buds, inflorescences and roots are caused by GALL WASPS of different species; they seldom affect the health of established trees.

OAK PHYLLOXERA forms colonies on the undersides of leaves and may cause extensive discoloration and premature leaf fall.

Diseases. Neglected trees may be attacked by BRACKET FUNGI, which enter dead wood; rotting of the heartwood occurs, and later the large bracket-shaped fruiting bodies develop on the trunk or branches.

Many other fungi can cause CANKER and DIE-BACK; dead patches or cankers appear on shoots and, if girdling occurs, the shoots die back.

FROST DAMAGE may in severe winters injure young shoots of deciduous trees, and also damage the leaves of evergreen species. Cracking of the stems may occur.

HONEY FUNGUS may cause trees to die rapidly.

Malnutrition or an irregular supply of moisture can produce PHYSIOLOGICAL DISORDERS, even in established trees. The leaves become discoloured and fall prematurely, and die-back may occur, so that the tree becomes stag-headed.

POWDERY MILDEW shows on young soft leaves and shoots as a white, powdery deposit.

Quick: see *Crataegus monogyna*

Quince

Cydonia oblonga. Rosaceae

A hardy deciduous species, native to S. Europe and Asia, and closely related to *Chaenomeles* (ornamental quince). It is a branching tree or

Quercus borealis (autumn foliage)

Quercus robur (fruits or acorns)

Quince (flowers)

shrub, grown for its edible fruit and as a pear rootstock. The acid fruits are used for preserves.

The fruits generally ripen outdoors only in districts south of York. In the north, the trees may be grown against walls or fences and trained as fans or espaliers; however, this is not recommended practice as quinces do not respond to heavy pruning and training.

The quince (height 15 ft; spread 10 ft) is a self-fertile tree with crooked branches, especially when old, carrying ovate to elliptic leaves that are dark green above, grey beneath. The foliage often assumes bright yellow autumn tints. White or light rose-pink apple-blossom-like flowers, up to 2 in. across, are borne singly at the ends of short spurs in May. The flowers are followed by pear-shaped fruits, up to 4 in. long; these are golden-yellow when ripe and strongly aromatic.

Only two varieties, 'Portugal' and 'Vranja', are readily available.

QUINCE

Cultivation. Plant quinces during late October or November in a sunny, open position or against a sheltered wall or fence; they succeed in any ordinary garden soil, but thrive in loamy, moist soil and may be planted near water.

Gather the fruits in early October, before the threat of night frosts, and store in a cool, frost-proof place. Fruits will continue to ripen indoors after harvesting and generally last for six to eight weeks; they should be kept away from other fruits as these may become tainted with the pungent aroma of the quinces.

Propagation. In October or November, take hardwood cuttings, up to 12 in. long with a heel, of the current season's growths. Insert the cuttings in a nursery bed outdoors and grow on for two or three years before transplanting to permanent sites.

Long branches may be layered in September or October; they should have rooted sufficiently to be severed from the parent plant one year later and replanted.

Pruning. Thin out crowded branches during winter to preserve an open crown; wall-trained trees may be cut back at the same time to two or three buds of the previous season's growths.

Pests. BIRDS sometimes peck holes in ripe fruits, and cause rotting.

CODLING MOTH and APPLE SAWFLY larvae burrow into the core of the fruits.

APHIDS of various species infest young shoots, leaves and fruits; WOOLLY APHIDS may infest branches and twigs, covering them with conspicuous tufts of white waxy wool and initiating the growth of disfiguring galls.

CATERPILLARS of different species of moths may feed on leaves and young buds.

FRUIT TREE RED SPIDER MITES may attack the undersides of the leaves; in severe infestations these become bronzed, wither and die.

CAPSID BUGS pierce the tissues of young buds, fruits and leaves; the fruits are rendered inedible, and premature leaf-fall may occur.

Diseases. APPLE MILDEW, which shows as a white powdery deposit, may occur at bud-break; the disease spreads from the emerging growths to the foliage. Severely diseased leaves fall prematurely.

BROWN ROT causes rapid decay of fruits, which become covered with white, raised pustules of fungus spores.

Quince, flowering: see Chaenomeles
Quince, Japanese: see *Chaenomeles speciosa*
Quince, Maule's: see *Chaenomeles japonica*

Quince (fruits)

Radish 'Crimson French Breakfast'

Radish 'Scarlet Globe'

R

Radish

Raphanus sativus. Cruciferae

A hardy biennial grown as an annual for the edible roots, which are crisp, white-fleshed, pepper-flavoured and often red-skinned. Spring and summer varieties are usually eaten raw, but winter-growing, large-rooted radishes may be used raw or cooked like turnips.

Crops can be produced all year round, but the plants may bolt in summer. They are quick-maturing and suitable for catch crops.

VARIETIES

These may be round, long or ovoid. 'Red Forcing', a round variety, is one of the best for growing in frames or under cloches as an early crop. For general outdoor sowing from March onwards, the following types are recommended: 'Crimson French Breakfast', ovoid; 'Scarlet Globe', round; 'Sparkler', round, with red-and-white skin, crisp and tender with a sweet flavour. Mixed strains are also available for outdoor cropping; they provide a mixture of shapes and colours and mature at different times.

'China Rose' and the black-skinned 'Black Spanish' are large-rooted winter varieties.

Cultivation. Radishes should be grown quickly to produce tender roots. They require fertile, well-drained soil, enriched with well-rotted manure or peat.

Sow the seeds thinly in $\frac{1}{2}$ in. deep drills or by broadcasting. Thin the seedlings, if overcrowded, to prevent them making foliage rather than root growth. Keep the bed well watered, and pull the roots as soon as they are large nough; the texture is most tender and the flavour most delicate in young roots.

Make occasional sowings at three-week intervals. The first sowings can be made in cold frames or under cloches in January and February. Keep the plants well ventilated once they have germinated; but cover the glass with sacks or mats during frost. Start outdoor sowings in March. During summer, sow in a moist and cool position to prevent bolting.

Sow the large-rooted winter radishes from June to August in drills 9 in. apart, and thin the plants to intervals of 6 in. The roots may be left in the ground and lifted as required, or stored in boxes of sand in a cool, airy place.

Pests. Adults and larvae of the FLEA BEETLE tunnel into leaves of seedlings.

Diseases. Generally trouble-free, although COMMON SCAB may occur and show as sunken pitted scabs on the roots.

Ramonda

Gesneriaceae

RAMONDA MYCONII

A genus of four hardy rosette-forming evergreen species with attractive foliage and saucer-shaped flowers. These plants are suitable for north-facing positions on rock gardens.

R. myconii, syn. *R. pyrenaica.* Pyrenees. Height 4–6 in.; spread 9 in. The deeply toothed ovate leaves are deep green and hairy with a distinct red fringe. They form a flat rosette from which rise stems bearing lavender-blue flowers, each with a conspicuous cone of golden stamens. The flowers are 1–1½ in. wide and open in April and May.

'Alba' is a pure white form; 'Rosea' is a particularly good deep rose variety.

R. nathaliae. Bulgaria, Serbia. Height 4 in.; spread 9 in. The corrugated leaves are ovate and mid-green with a dense fringe of hairs. The 1½ in. wide flowers are lavender-blue with an orange eye; they appear in April and May.

R. pyrenaica: see *R. myconii*

R. serbica. Balkans. Height 4 in.; spread 9 in. This plant is similar in habit to *R. myconii*, but has slightly smaller leaf rosettes and lilac-blue flowers, 1 in. wide, with purple anthers.

Cultivation. Plant ramondas in March in well-drained, ordinary garden soil, setting them in north-facing vertical crevices on rock gardens or dry walls. If possible, enrich the soil with peat or leaf-mould. They may shrivel in summer drought but usually recover quickly if watered freely.

Propagation. Take leaf cuttings in June or July by pulling the leaves downwards to secure the dormant bud at its base. Insert the cuttings obliquely for one-third of their length, so that the bottom of the leaf is no more than 1 in. below the surface of the soil, in equal parts (by volume) peat

and sand in boxes or pans, and place in a cold frame. They will root in about six weeks, after which they should be potted singly in 3 in. containers of John Innes potting compost No. 1. Keep the young plants growing in the frame for a year before planting out in March.

Alternatively, sow seeds in pans of John Innes seed compost in September or March and place in a cold frame. If weather conditions are suitable the seeds may be stratified to aid germination. Prick off the seedlings, when large enough to handle, into boxes, subsequently potting them singly into 3 in. pots of John Innes potting compost No. 1. Plant out in permanent positions one year after sowing.

Pests. Leaves may be eaten by SLUGS.

Diseases. Generally trouble-free.

Ranunculus

Buttercup. *Ranunculaceae*

A genus of 400 species of annuals and herbaceous and tuberous-rooted perennials. Few of the species are of garden merit, but those described here are suitable for herbaceous borders, rock gardens or alpine houses; two species are aquatic plants. They are hardy plants with the exception of the tuberous-rooted *R. asiaticus* and its varieties. The flowers are bowl-shaped, often opening out almost flat when fully mature.

R. aconitifolius (fair maids of France). Europe. Height 24 in.; planting distance 12–18 in. The single-type form is seldom grown, but the double-flowered 'Flore-pleno' is a good border plant in moist soil and in sun or half-shade. The mid-green palmate leaves have deeply toothed lobes. Shining white flowers, about ½ in. across, are borne in profusion in May and June.

RANUNCULUS ACRIS 'FLORE-PLENO'

R. acris (common buttercup). Europe, including Great Britain. Height 2½ ft; planting distance 12–18 in. The single species is superseded by the double-flowered 'Flore-pleno'. This is a border plant with deeply cut and lobed, mid-green, palmate leaves. Bright yellow flowers, ½–¾ in. across, are borne from June to August.

RANUNCULUS AQUATILIS

R. aquatilis (common water crowfoot). N. Temperate Zones, including Great Britain. Water-depth 6–12 in.; stem length 24 in. or more;

Ramonda myconii

Ranunculus aconitifolius

Ranunculus asiaticus
(Semi-double mixed)

Ranunculus bulbosus
'Speciosus Plenus'

planting distance 9 in. This aquatic species can be invasive when well established. It produces slender flexible stems bearing both submerged and floating leaves. The submerged foliage is bright green and cut into thread-like segments; the floating leaves are glossy mid-green, orbicular and cleft into five toothed lobes. Pure white, $\frac{1}{2}$ in. wide flowers are borne above the water from April to July.

R. asiaticus. Orient. Height 12–15 in.; planting distance 6 in. This tuberous-rooted species is hardy only in mild districts; elsewhere it should be overwintered in a frost-free place.

Only the semi-double varieties with ovate, deeply cut mid-green leaves are in general cultivation. The flowers, up to 3 in. across, are long-lasting when cut. The most widely grown strains are in mixed colours ranging from red to yellow and white. In mild areas, the flowering period extends from May to June; plants set out in early spring flower from June to July.

R. bulbosus. Europe, Asia, North Africa. Height 12 in.; planting distance 18 in. The species itself is a troublesome weed, but the garden form 'Speciosus Plenus' is sometimes grown. Its dark green, deeply cut leaves are arranged in tufts. Branching stems, bearing fully double yellow flowers, 1–1$\frac{1}{2}$ in. across and with light green centres, appear in May and June.

R. calandrinioides. Morocco. Height and planting distance 4–6 in. This species is suitable for an alpine house. The long-stalked ovate-lanceolate leaves are smooth and grey-green with curled and waved margins. White flowers, flushed with pale pink and measuring about 2 in. across, appear during March and April in the open, from December to March under glass.

R. gouanii. Pyrenees. Height and planting distance 9–12 in. A tufted plant with rounded, deeply lobed, mid-green leaves. The golden-yellow semi-double flowers, 1–1$\frac{1}{2}$ in. across, resemble those of the globe-flower (*Trollius*); they open during May and June.

R. gramineus. S.W. Europe. Height and planting distance 12 in. A compact species with grey-green grassy leaves. Sprays of shining yellow flowers, about $\frac{3}{4}$ in. across, are borne on slender stems from May to July.

R. lingua (great spearwort). Europe, including Great Britain. Water-depth 4–12 in.; height 2–4 ft; planting distance 6–9 in. in garden pools, 12–18 in. in ponds and lakes. This aquatic perennial is narrow and erect in habit but quickly spreads by underground rhizomes to form large masses of growth. It makes a good marginal plant.

The thick hollow stems are copper-red in the early season, turning to mid-green, with long ovate leaves of deep blue-green. Submerged foliage persists throughout the winter. Flowers appear from June to August, borne terminally in loose sprays. They are 1–1$\frac{1}{2}$ in. across, and glistening golden-yellow. The form generally available is listed as *R. lingua* 'Grandiflora'.

Cultivation. Most of the species will grow in any ordinary garden soil, in sun or partial shade; *R. asiaticus* in soil enriched with well-decayed manure, compost or peat and in a sunny site. Grow *R. lingua* in soil that can be kept continuously wet or covered with water up to 6 in. deep; *R. aquatilis* requires 6–12 in. of water.

Ranunculus calandrinioides

Ranunculus gramineus

Ranunculus lingua

Plant during suitable weather between September and April; plant *R. asiaticus* in March or April, burying the dry roots about 2 in. deep with the claw-like roots downwards.

In the alpine house, pot young plants of *R. calandrinioides*, *R. gouanii* and *R. gramineus* between September and March, placing one to three in a 6–8 in. pan of John Innes potting compost No. 1. Repot or pot on every two years in March.

R. asiaticus may survive mild winters out of doors, but is best lifted when the leaves turn yellow. Dry the tubers in the sun and store for the winter in a cool but frost-free airy place until replanting in spring.

In small pools, both *R. aquatilis* and *R. lingua* generally require drastic thinning annually, in autumn or in spring.

Propagation. Divide and replant in October or March. The tuber clusters of *R. asiaticus* and its varieties can be separated and stored at lifting time in autumn.

Take 4–6 in. stem cuttings of *R. aquatilis* after flowering, and insert *in situ*.

R. calandrinioides and *R. gramineus* are usually raised from seeds. Sow in pans of seed compost during February or March in a cold frame, and prick out the seedlings into boxes when they are large enough to handle. Transfer the young plants to 3 in. pots of John Innes potting compost No. 1 and plunge outside or pot on. Plant out in permanent sites between October and March.

Pests and diseases. Generally trouble-free.

Raoulia
Compositae

RAOULIA LUTESCENS

A genus of 25 species of hardy and half-hardy evergreen perennial foliage plants suitable for ground cover on rock gardens or for growing in alpine houses. With the exception of *R. eximia* the species described are hardy in all but the most severe winters.

R. australis. New Zealand. Height $\frac{1}{2}$ in.; spread 12 in. This plant makes a prostrate silvery mat of ovate leaves that are no more than $\frac{1}{8}$ in. long. Insignificant star-like yellow flowers appear in April and May. The species is also suitable for growing in an alpine house.

R. eximia (vegetable sheep). New Zealand. Height up to 3 in.; spread 12 in. In its native habitat, where it grows much larger, this plant forms impressive silvery-white hummocks which, from a distance, look like recumbent sheep—hence its name. It has crowded rosettes of tiny, linear-spathulate, grey leaves and in cultivation is a plant for the alpine house. The minute red flowers are rarely produced.

R. glabra. New Zealand. Height $\frac{1}{4}-\frac{1}{2}$ in.; spread 12–18 in. This species forms an emerald-green carpet of minute ovate leaves and has tubular white flower heads which are $\frac{1}{4}$ in. across. These appear in May and June.

R. lutescens. New Zealand. Height $\frac{1}{2}$ in.; spread 12–18 in. This species makes a close grey-green mat of minute leaves which is dotted from April to June with tiny lemon-yellow flowers, each about $\frac{1}{8}$ in. across.

Cultivation. Outdoors, plant *R. australis*, *R. glabra* and *R. lutescens* during April in a sunny position and in ordinary, sharply drained soil.

In the alpine house, plant *R. australis* and *R. eximia* in April, in 4–6 in. pans of equal parts (by volume) John Innes potting compost No. 1 and grit. Repot every second or third year in April.

Propagation. Divide all species at any time between July and September and replant direct in permanent positions.

Alternatively, detach portions, about 1 in. across, from the edge of mature plants in April or May. Pot up in 3 in. pots of the growing mixture. Pot on or plant out the following April.

Pests and diseases. Generally trouble-free.

Rape: see Mustard and cress
Rape kale: see Kale
Raphanus sativus: see Radish

Raspberry

Rubus idaeus. Rosaceae

This hardy, deciduous cane fruit is native to most European countries from Spain to the Caucasus and including Iceland and Great Britain. Raspberries succeed in partial shade and flower after spring frosts. They do best in fertile, well-drained soil in positions sheltered from wind.

The varieties are divided into two groups, summer-fruiting (July and August) and autumn-fruiting (mid-September onwards). The fruits of the former are carried on shoots produced during the previous season; those of autumn-fruiting varieties on shoots produced the same season. Both types are susceptible to virus diseases, which cause stunted growth and reduced crops, but virus-free canes are available. The fruits are excellent for table use, preserving and freezing.

Raspberries grow 6–8 ft high, depending on the variety and conditions. They are generally trained on supporting wires.

RASPBERRY

'Lloyd George'. This vigorous summer-fruiting variety is a heavy cropper if healthy. It is prone to virus infection and the effects of this on growth and cropping are usually serious. The fruits are juicy, bright red, of good flavour and produced over a long season. They are excellent for desserts

and freezing. It may also be grown as an autumn-fruiting variety by cutting the canes to near ground level in February.

'Malling Jewel'. Although a vigorous grower, this summer-fruiting variety sometimes produces only a few new canes, particularly on poor soil. It is moderately resistant to grey mould. The berries are produced in early to mid-season and are sweet, medium red, of good flavour and suitable for table use and freezing.

'Malling Promise'. This widely grown summer-fruiting variety, which is tolerant of virus infection, is vigorous and sometimes produces excessive numbers of new canes. It is a heavy early cropper but the flavour of the large, medium red fruits is only fair.

'Norfolk Giant'. A tall, vigorous, summer-fruiting variety, the latest of this group to ripen. The juicy, acid fruits are of medium size and medium red in colour. They are good for preserving, including freezing.

'September'. An autumn-fruiting variety of American origin. It is only moderately vigorous and needs regular feeding and watering in summer. The berries are carried, from September to the onset of frost, on growths made during the summer. The fruits are of fair flavour and of medium size.

'Zeva'. An autumn-fruiting, vigorous and dwarf variety. The large, dark red juicy fruits are of excellent flavour, for table use and preserving.

Cultivation. Plant young raspberry canes in November. Ideally, they need a rich soil which is well-drained, but moisture-retentive. They will not thrive in dry or alkaline soils unless well supplied with organic matter, such as peat, compost or well-rotted manure.

Summer-fruiting raspberries flower in May and June. However, avoid planting in frost pockets if possible and in exposed positions where the fruiting laterals may be broken by wind. Choose a position in sun or partial shade. Eradicate perennial weeds before planting.

The canes can be tied into clumps to make them self-supporting, but are better supported with 12–13 gauge galvanised wires strained between 8 ft high wooden posts at the ends of the rows. Set the posts with 6 ft of their height above ground and fasten three wires at regular intervals between the posts. If the canes are to be tied into clumps, set them 18 in. apart in rows that are 18 in. apart. If more than two rows are grown, allow 4 ft between each pair of rows. Raspberries on wires should be planted 15–24 in. apart, depending on their vigour. For instance, plant 'September' canes 15 in. apart, 'Norfolk Giant' 24 in. apart. Allow at least 4 ft between rows, and tie the canes to wires as they grow, spacing the canes 3–4 in. apart.

Control annual weeds between the rows by shallow hoeing, avoiding damage to the roots.

Summer moisture is important, especially while the first fruits are ripening. Water during dry weather, to swell the fruits and to increase the length of the canes. In April, apply a mulch of compost, manure or peat to conserve moisture. Harvest the fruits regularly, as they soon spoil.

Feed with sulphate of potash at 1 oz. per sq. yd in winter, and with sulphate of ammonia at $\frac{1}{2}$ oz. per sq. yd, annually in March.

Raoulia eximia

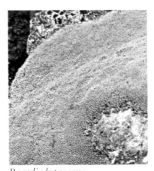

Raoulia lutescens

Raspberry 'Malling Jewel'

Propagation. Between November and March, but preferably during the autumn, lift and transplant young sucker shoots, retaining as much fibrous root as possible. Because of the risk of spreading virus diseases, propagate only from vigorous, healthy plants. Plant the young canes in their fruiting positions and cut each one back to a good bud about 9 in. above ground level.

Even after cutting back, raspberries may often bear fruit during their first season. This should be prevented, especially if the canes were planted late, by removing flowers as they appear.

Pruning. At the end of the first season of growth leave all strong canes at full length; cut out short weak ones. At the end of February each year, prune off the top of each cane of summer-fruiting varieties to just above the top wire.

The previous season's canes on established plants will produce laterals which carry the berries in summer. New shoots grow up from the ground, ready to crop the following year.

After fruiting, cut out the canes that have carried fruit. Thin out the new shoots to leave five or six strong ones to each parent plant; tie each cane to the supporting wires, spacing the canes 6–8 in. apart.

The plants will spread rapidly from the single cane first planted to form a continuous row, and will also go on growing into the space between the rows unless checked. Pull up unwanted canes while they are small so that there is a minimum of disturbance of the roots. Cutting off is less effective, as the cane will grow again.

Cut down autumn-fruiting varieties, such as 'September', right to ground level in February. This treatment will also induce 'Lloyd George' and 'Zeva' to fruit in the autumn.

Pests. RASPBERRY BEETLE maggots tunnel into the ripening fruits, making them inedible.

APHIDS infest young shoots and leaves, and transmit virus diseases.

Diseases. CANE BLIGHT causes the leaves on fruiting canes to wither during the summer. Infected canes become brittle and a dark area develops on them just above ground level. They snap off easily.

CANE SPOT develops on the canes in May or June and shows at first as small circular purple spots. They enlarge to become elliptic white blotches, about ¼ in. long, with a purple border. Later the spots split to form shallow pits or small cankers, giving the fruiting canes a rough and cracked appearance. In severe attacks, the tips of the canes may be killed. If infected, the leaves show small circular spots with white centres, and the fruits may become distorted.

CHLOROSIS shows on the leaves as a yellowing between the veins and the leaves may become almost white. The trouble is common on plants growing in soils that are too alkaline.

CROWN GALL may very occasionally occur at ground level, when a gall about the size of a walnut develops at the crown. It can also occur higher up the canes as numerous smaller galls.

GREY MOULD causes a rotting of the berries, and shows as a brown-grey fluffy growth.

HONEY FUNGUS causes rapid death of canes.

PHYSIOLOGICAL DISORDERS, due to unsuitable soil conditions, show as brown blotching or yellowing of the leaves, which may often fall prematurely; or they show as DIE-BACK of spurs or canes. Waterlogging destroys the canes.

RASPBERRY VIRUS DISEASES are due to many different viruses. The chief symptoms of these viruses are mottling or blotching of the leaves, which may be distorted, stunting of plants, poor cropping and, very occasionally, die-back.

SPUR BLIGHT shows first as dark purple blotches on the canes around the bases of the leaves. The patches increase in size and turn silvery; they are studded with black pin-point fruiting bodies of the fungus. Buds at the affected nodes die or, if shoots are produced in the following spring, they wither and die.

Rebutia

Cactaceae

A genus of about 50 species of greenhouse perennials. These globular cacti have small, closely set tubercles that are not always arranged in distinct ribs. Many species grow into clumps. The plants are grown for their brilliant flowers which are freely produced, several at a time, and last about a week, opening in the morning and closing in the evening. They are shortly trumpet-shaped, opening out flat.

The flowers are borne from areoles near the base of the plant, unlike other cactus flowers which are produced from the younger growth near the top.

See also CACTUS.

R. aureiflora. Argentina. Height and spread up to 2 in. The spherical or cylindrical plant body is dark green tinged with red. The ribs are spiral and divided into tubercles. The areoles bear 15–20 yellow-white central spines. Flowers appear in April and May; they are 2 in. in diameter and golden-yellow with a white throat. This species forms clumps.

R. deminuta. Argentina. Height and spread 3–4 in. A clump-forming species with globular stems, depressed at the tops. The stems are divided into 11–13 tuberculate ribs that are almost spirally arranged. The areoles bear 10–12 radial spines which are white with brown tips or completely brown. Deep orange flowers, up to ¾ in. in diameter, are produced from May to July.

R. kupperiana. Bolivia. Height up to 2 in.; spread 4 in. This species forms a clump of spherical red-green stems, each up to 3 in. in diameter. The areoles bear 12–16 white radial spines with copper-coloured tips, and one central spine. Red flowers, 1–1½ in. across, open from May to July.

R. marsoneri. Argentina. Height 2 in.; spread 4 in. The single dark green stem is globular, depressed at the crown. The areoles are on small tubercles and bear bristly hairs and 30–35 short spines, the lower ones white, the upper brown-red. Golden-yellow flowers, up to 1½ in. across, are borne in April or May.

R. pseudodeminuta. Argentina. Height and spread 3–4 in. The bright green globular stems of this clump-forming species are each 4–5 in. in diameter and depressed at the crown. The small areoles, borne on prominent tubercles, produce 11 radial spines and two or three central spines; all the spines are white, tipped with brown. The

Raspberry 'September'

Raspberry 'Zeva'

Rebutia marsoneri

flowers, which appear in May and June, are golden-yellow and over 1 in. across.

R. pygmaea. Bolivia, Argentina. Height 5 in.; spread 4 in. The ovoid plant body is olive-green to grey and grows from a thickened rootstock. The spirally arranged tubercles bear 9–11 radial spines, white at first, becoming grey. The 1 in. wide rose-purple flowers open in May and June.

R. senilis. Argentina. Height and spread up to 2 in. The pale green stem is spherical, about 4 in. in diameter, and depressed on top. The species is clump-forming. Tubercles are arranged spirally. Each areole bears 35–40 bristly white spines which almost conceal the plant body. Bright red flowers, ¾ in. across, appear from April to June.

R. spegazziniana. Argentina. Height up to 5 in.; spread 2½ in. The clumps consist of light green cylindrical stems up to 2 in. across and have tubercles arranged spirally. Each areole bears about 14 white radial spines pressed back against the stem, and two yellow, brown-tipped central spines. Dark red flowers, about 4 in. across, appear in May and June.

R. spinosissima. Argentina. Height 2½–3 in.; spread 2 in. Each of the pale green globular stems in this clump-forming species is about 2 in. across and slightly depressed at the top. The white hairy areoles on the spirally arranged, closely set tubercles bear numerous white radial spines and five or six thicker central spines that are yellow, tipped with brown. Pink flowers, up to 1½ in. in diameter, occur from June to August.

R. violaciflora. Argentina. Height up to 1½ in.; spread 3 in. The plant forms clumps of olive-green globular stems, each about 3 in. across and depressed at the top. Tubercles are arranged spirally. The areoles bear yellow-grey wool, 15 or more yellow-white radial spines, and between five and ten longer and thicker central spines that are white at first, becoming yellow. The lilac-rose flowers, borne in June, are about 1½ in. across.

R. xanthocarpa. Argentina. Height 1½ in.; spread 4–8 in. The plant forms clumps which consist of pale green stems, each up to 4 in. in diameter. They are covered with slender white spines up to ¼ in. long. The red flowers, ¾ in. across, appear from May to July.

Cultivation. Rebutias do best in a soil consisting of 4 parts loam, 3 parts leaf-mould and 2 parts sand (parts by volume), with 1 oz. bone-meal added to each 1 gal. bucket of soil. In March or April, set the plants in 4–6 in. pans in an airy position with maximum light and sun. Water whenever the soil becomes dry, except from the end of November until February. During this time they need only sufficient water to prevent shrinkage of the bodies. In winter, keep the plants at a temperature not lower than 5°C (41°F). Pot on at the beginning of the growing season if the plants have filled the pans with roots.

Propagation. Sow seeds in spring at a temperature of 21°C (70°F). Alternatively, detach offsets during summer and pot in the growing compost. As rebutias flower and seed freely, seedlings will often grow of their own accord round a plant.

Pests. Tufts of white wax are caused by MEALY BUGS. GLASSHOUSE RED SPIDER MITES may cause discoloration and produce a characteristic fine webbing over the plants.

Diseases. Generally trouble-free.

Rechsteineria
Gesneriaceae

A genus of 75 species of tender, tuberous-rooted herbaceous perennials. They are grown for their attractive tubular flowers and handsome foliage. They require greenhouse cultivation and, under the right conditions, the species described will flower from seeds in five to six months.

R. cardinalis. Brazil. Height 9–18 in.; spread 12 in. An attractive species covered with light purple hairs. The leaves are bright green and broadly ovate. The 2 in. long bright scarlet flowers, with a paler throat, are usually borne in flat, terminal clusters. By successive sowings, the species can be flowered all year round, but the main season is from June to August.

R. leucotricha. Brazil. Height and spread 9 in. or more. This species is densely covered with silvery hairs; the broadly ovate leaves, often borne in whorls, are bright silver-grey. The 2 in. long, salmon-red flowers are carried in clusters of three to five in the upper leaf axils from August to October.

Cultivation. Start the dormant tubers into growth by placing them in moist peat at a temperature of 21°C (70°F). When the young growths are 1–2 in. high, pot the tubers separately into 5 or 6 in. pots of John Innes potting compost No. 2 or a proprietary peat compost. Place the top of the tubers level with the surface of the compost.

Grow rechsteinerias in a shaded greenhouse at a minimum temperature of 16–18°C (61–64°F); feed the plants with a liquid manure at 10–14 day intervals from May to September. Water freely during the growing season.

After flowering, and as the leaves turn yellow, gradually cease watering. Remove dead flowers and leaves. Store the pots of tubers in a dry place at a minimum temperature of 12°C (54°F). Discard tubers more than three years old.

Propagation. Divide tubers with young growths in March prior to potting up, ensuring that each piece has two or three shoots. Pot the pieces separately into pots of the growing mixture.

Alternatively, take basal cuttings, 3 in. long, preferably with a sliver of the tuber attached, in April. Insert the cuttings in equal parts (by volume) peat and sand in a propagating case at a temperature of 18–21°C (64–70°F). When rooted, pot the cuttings singly into 3 in. containers of the growing compost.

Sow seeds thinly in February or March in pans or boxes of John Innes seed compost and germinate at a temperature of 21°C (70°F). When the seedlings are large enough to handle, prick off into boxes of the growing mixture, then singly into 3 in. pots.

Pests and diseases. Generally trouble-free.

Rebutia senilis

Rechsteineria cardinalis

Rechsteineria leucotricha

Rehmannia
Scrophulariaceae

A genus of ten species of half-hardy perennials. They are often treated as biennials, and are best grown in a cool greenhouse.

R. angulata (Chinese foxglove). China. Height in cultivation usually 18 in.; spread up to 12 in. The mid-green leaves of the basal rosette are up to 6 in. long, with deep lobes and toothed margins. The stem leaves are mid-green, smaller and shallowly lobed. Foxglove-like flowers, 2–2½ in. long and rosy-purple with a band of scarlet on the upper lip and orange dots on the lower lip, are borne from June to August.

This species is often confused with the similar *R. elata*, which may be offered in its place.

REHMANNIA ANGULATA

R. elata: see *R. angulata*

Cultivation. In mild districts, these plants may be grown outdoors in ordinary garden soil and in a sunny sheltered border. In the greenhouse, grow the plants in 6–8 in. pots containing John Innes potting compost No. 2 or 3. Overwinter the plants at a temperature of 7°C (45°F) and keep just moist. Increase watering from March and keep the atmosphere cool and airy; shade the plants lightly. They may be grown for a number of seasons, but are best discarded after two years; otherwise pot on and give a liquid feed at 10–14 day intervals from May to September.

Propagation. Sow seeds in March in pots or pans of seed compost at a temperature of 13–16°C (55–61°F). Prick out the seedlings into boxes, when large enough to handle, and then into 3 in. pots of John Innes potting compost No. 1. Move into 6–8 in. pots and stand them outdoors in a sheltered place. Take the plants into the greenhouse at the end of September.

Pests and diseases. Generally trouble-free.

Reinwardtia
Linaceae

REINWARDTIA TRIGYNA

A genus of only two species of tender evergreen flowering shrubs. The species in general cultivation is a handsome winter-flowering plant; it requires greenhouse cultivation.

R. trigyna, syn. *Linum trigynum*. Northern India.

Height and spread in cultivation 18–24 in. The elliptic pale green leaves are about 3 in. long. Funnel-shaped flowers, 1–1½ in. long, are borne either solitarily in the leaf axils or in a terminal cluster. They are bright yellow, and appear from October to March.

Cultivation. These plants may be grown as annual pot plants or, if large specimens are wanted, they may be potted on annually and finally planted out in the greenhouse border. Grow pot plants in 5–6 in. pots containing John Innes potting compost No. 2 or a proprietary peat mixture. A winter temperature of 13°C (55°F) is necessary to ensure that the flowers open, but the plants will survive at lower temperatures. In August, set the pot plants in an open frame exposed to the sun, so that the wood will ripen.

In the greenhouse, a humid atmosphere helps to establish young plants in their first pots. Thereafter, ventilate freely and keep the soil reasonably moist. Syringe the leaves frequently in warm weather; water freely from April to September, moderately at other times.

For larger plants, pot on annually in April for two or three years, after which the plants are best discarded. Feed all plants with liquid manure at weekly intervals from June to September.

Propagation. Take basal cuttings, 3 in. long, of strong young shoots from cut-back plants in April. Insert three or four cuttings in a 3 in. pot containing equal parts (by volume) peat and soil. Place the cuttings in a propagating case with a bottom heat of 13–16°C (55–61°F).

Pruning. Pinch out the plants two or three times during the first growing season to encourage bushy, compact growth. If they are to be grown on, cut the flowering shoots back to within 3 in. of the base after flowering.

Pests and diseases. Generally trouble-free.

Reseda
Mignonette. *Resedaceae*

RESEDA ODORATA

A genus of 60 species of annual and biennial herbaceous plants. The species described is a common cottage-garden plant, grown for the sweet scent of its flowers which attract bees. It is suitable for planting in annual borders, for cutting and as a late winter-flowering pot plant.

R. odorata. N. Africa. Height 1–2½ ft; planting distance 6–9 in. A hardy annual of upright branching habit. The leaves are mid-green, spathulate and smooth. The flowers, ¼ in. across, are carried in loose heads from June to October; each is composed of four to seven insignificant yellow-white petals and a tuft of orange-yellow stamens. Garden varieties include 'Goliath', which produces large spikes of red flowers, and 'Machet' with red-tinged flowers.

Rehmannia angulata

Reinwardtia trigyna

Reseda odorata 'Machet'

Cultivation. A fairly rich, well-drained and alkaline soil in a sunny position is best, although most well-cultivated garden soils give reasonable results. Add lime or old mortar to acid ground. Plants from a September sowing require cold-frame protection in the north.

For flowering under glass, grow three plants to a 5 in. container of John Innes potting compost No. 1. Pinch out the growing tips of young pot plants to encourage branching.

Propagation. Sow the seeds in the flowering site in March, April or September, just covering them with soil, and firm thoroughly. Thin out the seedlings to the required distance.

Alternatively, sow under glass in February or March at a temperature of 13°C (55°F). Prick out the seedlings into boxes when they are large enough to handle and harden off in a frame before planting out in May.

For winter-flowering pot plants, sow the seeds in 5–6 in. pots from July to September, thinning out the seedlings to leave three in each container.

Pests and diseases. Generally trouble-free.

Raphidophora: see Scindapsus
Raphidophora aurea: see *Scindapsus aureus*

Rheum

Ornamental rhubarb. *Polygonaceae*

A genus of 50 species of hardy herbaceous perennials, usually with a thick woody rootstock. The genus includes the edible rhubarb, and two other perennial species are in general cultivation. These are highly ornamental foliage plants, suitable as specimen perennials.

R. alexandrae. Szechwan, Tibet. Height 2⅓–3 ft; planting distance 24 in. The small rootstock forms a stout clump of fleshy roots producing glossy, mid-green, ovate leaves on short stalks. Erect flower spikes, 12–18 in. long, have overlapping, papery, cream bracts which resemble drooping tongues. The spikes appear in May.

R. palmatum. China. Height 5–8 ft; planting distance 3 ft. This species requires a good deal of space; the purple-red, deeply cut leaves are as large as those of the culinary rhubarb; the purple-red colour fades to green after flowering. Erect panicles, 2–3 ft long, clustered with deep pink or red bead-like flowers, appear in June.

R. rhaponticum: see Rhubarb

Cultivation. Plant from November to February in ordinary garden soil and in a sunny position. Rheums are easily grown plants, but flowering is more free in rich and moist soils. In summer, water freely during dry spells and give an occasional feed of liquid manure. The plants can be left undisturbed for several years. After flowering, cut the spikes down to ground level.

Propagation. Lift and divide old plants between November and February, ensuring that each division retains a dormant crown bud.

Seeds may be sown outdoors in March or April; prick out the seedlings when large enough to handle, grow on in a nursery bed and transplant to permanent positions in November of the following year.

Pests and diseases. Generally trouble-free.

Rhipsalidopsis

Cactaceae

A genus of only two species of greenhouse perennials. These epiphytic cacti are easily grown plants. The trumpet-shaped, often pendulous flowers occur singly at the ends of branches; each flower lasts three or four days. They are good plants for hanging baskets, and *R. rosea* may be grown as a house plant if kept on a sunny window-ledge.

See also CACTUS.

R. gaertneri, syn. *Schlumbergera gaertneri* (Easter cactus). Brazil. Height 18 in.; spread 3 ft. The jointed stems are spreading and pendulous. The fleshy joints are usually flat, though occasionally three to six-angled; they are dull green with purple, notched margins. Flowers and new joints grow from areoles on the tops of stems. The areoles bear short white wool and a few bristles. Bright red flowers, 2½ in. across, appear in March and April. *R. g. makoyana* has stiffer joints and numerous stiff bristles on the areoles. The joints lack the purple markings.

R. × graeseri. A hybrid between *R. gaertneri* and *R. rosea.* The flowers, in various shades of red, are similar to those of *R. rosea.*

R. rosea. Brazil. Height up to 6 in.; spread 9–12 in. A dwarf shrubby species. The freely branching stems are erect at first, but later become pendulous. The stems are composed of green-red joints, 1–2 in. long, usually flat but sometimes three, four or five-angled. Areoles on top of the stems bear short bristles. The widely expanded, slightly scented flowers are rose, pink or white. They are 2 in. across and are produced in May and June.

Cultivation. Rhipsalidopsis, except for *R. × graeseri*, are sometimes grafted on to *Pereskia aculeata*, but will grow well on their own roots. Plant in March or April in 4–5 in. pots in a soil composed of equal parts (by volume) leaf-mould, sand and fine gravel. Since their natural habitat is the forests of Brazil, the plants do best in a moist, warm position with some shade in summer. To provide the necessary humidity, syringe the plants twice daily during late spring and summer and, if kept in a greenhouse, damp down the staging on which they stand. Never allow the soil to dry out entirely, but take care to prevent saturation in the winter months.

After the plants have flowered, place them outside in partial shade to rest. In mid-September bring them inside and pot into larger pots, if necessary. During winter a minimum temperature of 13°C (55°F) is required.

Propagation. Take cuttings of the joints during summer. Let the cut surfaces heal for a few days. Insert in pots or a pan of coarse sand and peat in equal proportions. Place the cuttings under a bell-jar or in a closed frame or propagating case at a temperature of 16–18°C (61–64°F) until they are well rooted. Pot up in the growing mixture as already described.

Pests. Conspicuous tufts of white waxy wool on the plants are produced by MEALY BUGS.

Diseases. Generally trouble-free.

Rhodanthe manglesii: see *Helipterum manglesii*

Rheum alexandrae

Rheum palmatum

Rhipsalidopsis gaertneri

Rhipsalidopsis × graeseri

Rhododendron 'Naomi'

Rhododendron augustinii

RHODODENDRON
Ericaceae

A genus of at least 500 species of greenhouse and hardy, evergreen and deciduous trees and shrubs. It includes azaleas, formerly treated as a separate genus. These differ from other rhododendrons in the following ways:

Deciduous azaleas are the only deciduous rhododendrons that do not have scaly leaves. Evergreen azaleas are not true evergreens; the leaves that are formed in the spring on the lower parts of the shoots fall in autumn.

The following information, and that under the headings CULTIVATION, PROPAGATION, PRUNING, PESTS and DISEASES, applies to azaleas as well as to other rhododendrons unless otherwise stated.

The name rhododendron derives from the Greek *rhodon* (rose) and *dendron* (tree). The plants range from small creeping shrubs to trees 60 ft high. Taking the genus as a whole, most species are evergreen.

None of the species and hybrids described is truly tender: even cool-greenhouse rhododendrons, such as 'Fragrantissimum', can be grown in sheltered gardens south of London. However, many are sensitive to full sun and exposure to cold winds, and do best in woodland. In addition, those that flower before the end of April are unsuitable for low-lying gardens susceptible to spring frosts. Generally, the plants will not grow in limy soils.

The leaves are entire, and usually aggregated towards the end of each season's growth. The flowers are mainly terminal, occasionally lateral, and borne in clusters or singly. They are generally bell or funnel-shaped, but occasionally saucer-shaped or tubular. A few species are fragrant, some strongly so.

The flowers have a wide colour range: white, pink, lavender, violet, purple, yellow, crimson, scarlet and orange. The flowering season is exceptionally long; for instance, *R. mucronulatum* flowers from December onwards, but *R. auriculatum* does not flower until July or August. The young foliage of many species is especially attractive: examples are *R. concatenans* (blue-green), *R. williamsianum* (chocolate-bronze) and *R. mallotum* (rust-red and woolly).

Rhododendrons come mainly from Asia, notably the Himalayas, China, Tibet, India, Burma, and also from New Guinea. Several species, mostly azaleas, come from North America and Europe, and one tender species is native to Australia.

576

3–4 in. wide and 2 in. deep. This is one of the hardiest of the larger Chinese species and the parent of several excellent hybrids, including the Loderi group and 'Naomi'.

R. fulvum. China. Height 15–20 ft; spread 10–15 ft. This evergreen tree or shrub has ovate leaves that are up to 8 in. long. They are generally dark glossy green above (but occasionally dull matt green), and have their undersides covered with yellow-brown felt. The young shoots have a similar covering. There are up to 20 bell-shaped flowers, 1¾–2 in. across and 1½ in. long, in each compact cluster. They are white, tinged with pink and blotched with dark red, and bloom in March and April.

R. glaucophyllum. Himalayas. Height and spread 3–5 ft. An evergreen shrub with oblong leaves that are up to 3 in. long. These are mid-green above, blue-grey beneath. Rust-coloured scales cover the young leaves, growths and flower stalks. In May, each flower cluster bears five or six bell-shaped rose-red blossoms, ¾–1¼ in. wide and 1 in. long. The stems of old plants turn a glossy mahogany-brown. *R. g. luteiflorum* has butter-yellow flowers.

R. griersonianum. China. Height 8 ft; spread 8–12 ft. An evergreen shrub. It has lanceolate pale olive-green leaves, with down on the undersides. The buds have long, pointed scales. The trumpet-shaped flowers are a unique shade of geranium-scarlet. They are 3–4 in. wide and 2½–3½ in. long, and borne in clusters of 5–12 in June. The species is uncommon in gardens but is the parent of many crimson and scarlet hybrids, which usually inherit its distinctive buds. After a dull, wet summer the late growths sometimes fail to mature.

R. griffithianum, syn. *R. aucklandii.* Himalayas. Height up to 20 ft; spread 10–15 ft. The oblong-ovate leaves of this evergreen tree or shrub are up to 12 in. long, matt green above but with blue-grey undersides. Fragrant, white, bell-shaped flowers, sometimes tinged with pink, are borne in May in loose clusters of four to six; they are 5–6 in. across and 3 in. deep. This is the most magnificent and largest-blossomed of the white-flowered species and the parent of many fine hybrids. It is, however, suitable for growing only in mild areas.

R. haematodes. China. Height 3–4 ft; spread 6 ft or more. An evergreen shrub, of low, dense habit. The leathery obovate leaves are mid-green above; their undersides, and also the young shoots, are covered with orange-brown felt. There are six to ten funnel-shaped brilliant red flowers, 1½–2 in. wide and long, in each cluster. These appear in May. A most vividly coloured and hardy dwarf species.

R. hanceanum. China. Height and spread 3–4 ft. An evergreen shrub with lanceolate dark green leaves that are up to 4 in. long, scaly above and beneath. White to pale yellow funnel-shaped blossoms, ¾–1 in. across and long, appear in many-flowered clusters in March and April. *R. h. nanum*, which is only 18 in. high and is more free-flowering, is ideal for small gardens.

R. hippophaeoides. China. Height and spread 4–5 ft. An evergreen shrub which throws up suckers. The leaves are oblong or elliptic, grey-green and scaly. Deep mauve-blue, pale lilac-blue or pink flowers, ¾–1 in. across and shaped like wide funnels, appear in March and April. They form clusters of four to eight. This is one of the hardiest early-flowering species and useful for an early display of colour even in cold gardens.

R. hirsutum. Central Europe. Height and spread 3–4 ft. An evergreen shrub closely related in habit and flowering to *R. ferrugineum,* but the flowers, which are 1½–¾ in. across and ½ in. long, are a clearer pink and the leaves are edged with bristly hairs. This species will tolerate a limy soil.

R. impeditum. China. Height 6–18 in.; spread up to 24 in. An evergreen shrub. The close-set ovate leaves are about ½ in. long, grey-green and scaly. The flowers, 1 in. wide and ⅝ in. long, are borne in twos or threes in April and May. They are pale mauve to purple-blue and widely funnel-shaped. This free-flowering, fully hardy plant is ideal for small gardens; it is one of the best dwarf species.

R. imperator. Burma. Height 12 in.; spread up to 24 in. A low, spreading, evergreen shrub. The lanceolate or elliptic leaves are mid-green above, scaly and blue-grey on their undersides. Funnel-shaped mauve-pink flowers, 1½ in. wide and 1 in. deep, form singly or in pairs in May. This is an excellent species for a rock garden.

R. insigne. China. Height and spread 4–5 ft in the open, more in woodland. This evergreen shrub has elliptic leaves which are mid-green above but have glistening silver undersides. Bell-shaped flowers, 2 in. across and long, are borne in clusters of 15 or more in May and June. Each blossom is pale pink, with a deeper pink stripe down the centre of each lobe, and the throats are speckled dark red. An excellent medium-sized species for a small garden, with its striking foliage and hardy blossoms.

R. keleticum. Tibet. Height up to 12 in.; spread 3–4 ft. A dwarf evergreen shrub. The ovate mid-green leaves are ½ in. long, with scaly undersides. This free-flowering and fully hardy species bears funnel-shaped mauve-red blossoms, singly or in pairs, in June; they are 1½ in. across and 1 in. deep.

R. ledoides: see *R. trichostomum*

R. lepidostylum. China. Height 2–3 ft; spread 3–4 ft. An evergreen shrub with oblong leaves that are pale grey-green and bristly when mature, a bright verdigris when young. Green-yellow, broadly tubular flowers, 1 in. wide, are borne in June. They are hidden among the young growths.

R. leucaspis. Tibet. Height 12–24 in.; spread 2–3 ft. An evergreen shrub. It has ovate, leathery, blue-grey leaves, with scales underneath. The shallow, wavy-petalled flowers are 2 in. wide. They are borne one, two or three to a stem from February to April, and are white with brown anthers. This species is one of the most beautiful of the dwarfs, but the opening buds and flowers are often killed by frost. It is best grown in an unheated greenhouse.

R. lutescens. China, Tibet. Height up to 10 ft; spread 5–7 ft. A straggling evergreen shrub with lanceolate leaves which unfurl from a glossy bronze to a dull green. The widely funnel-shaped yellow flowers, 1–1½ in. across and sometimes tinged with green, are borne singly or in pairs from January to April. A beautiful, free-flowering species but susceptible to frost because of its early blossoming. It does best in light woodland.

Rhododendron haematodes

Rhododendron impeditum

Rhododendron lutescens

Rhododendron rubiginosum

Rhododendron racemosum

R. moupinense. China, Tibet. Height 2–5 ft; spread 3–4 ft. This evergreen shrub has rounded leaves that are mid-green and shiny above, paler and scaly beneath. The tubular white or pink flowers, 2 in. across and $1\frac{1}{2}$ in. long, are freckled with red. They appear in February and March, singly, in pairs or in threes.

R. mucronulatum. N.E. Asia. Height 6–8 ft; spread 4–5 ft. A deciduous shrub of sparse growth. The leaves are pale green and lanceolate. Widely funnel-shaped rose-purple flowers, $1\frac{3}{4}$ in. wide and long, are borne from December to February in clusters at the ends of the bare branches. The plant is fairly resistant to frost, despite its winter flowering. It does best in light woodland conditions.

R. neriiflorum. China. Height and spread 4–8 ft. An evergreen shrub that has oblong leaves with glaucous-white undersides. Scarlet bell-shaped flowers, $1\frac{1}{2}$–2 in. wide and deep, appear in March and April in clusters of 6–12. This is one of the most richly coloured species. It is best suited to woodland conditions in the south and west.

R. orbiculare. China. Height and spread 6–8 ft. An evergreen shrub, dense and almost spherical. The circular leaves are pale green above, blue-grey beneath. Bell-shaped flowers, 2–$2\frac{1}{2}$ in. across and deep, are borne in April and May in clusters of seven to ten; they are pink, sometimes tinged with purple. Fine habit and foliage but with less attractive flowers than other species.

R. oreodoxa. China. Height 12 ft; spread 8 ft. An evergreen small tree or shrub. It is almost identical to *R. fargesii*, differing only in its narrower, pointed leaves.

R. oreotrephes, syns. *R. artosquameum, R. exquisitum, R. timeteum.* China, Tibet. Height 6–8 ft; spread 4–6 ft. An evergreen shrub of erect habit. The ovate leaves have grey-green upper sides, smoky-blue and, scaly undersides. There are four to ten funnel-shaped flowers, $2\frac{1}{4}$ in. across and $1\frac{3}{4}$ in. deep, in each cluster; these are grey-lilac to rose-lilac and appear in April and May. A fine medium-sized species, well worth growing for its foliage.

R. pemakoense. Tibet. Height up to 24 in.; spread up to 3 ft. A small evergreen shrub which, in one form, throws up many suckers. The ovate to rounded leaves, up to $\frac{3}{4}$ in. long, are dark shining green above, blue-grey and scaly beneath. Funnel-shaped rose-mauve to purple flowers, $1\frac{1}{2}$ in. across and $1\frac{1}{4}$ in. long, are borne singly or in pairs in March and April. This is a free-flowering dwarf species, but susceptible to early frosts unless grown in a sheltered place.

R. ponticum. Spain, Portugal, Asia Minor. Height 12–20 ft; spread 20–35 ft. An evergreen tree or shrub. The leaves are oblong to lanceolate, dark green and glossy. Funnel-shaped flowers, $1\frac{3}{4}$–2 in. across and deep, appear in June in clusters of 10–15; they are purple, often tinged with pink. This species is naturalised in many parts of Britain and is sometimes a forestry weed in lime-free areas. It is useful for forming a large hedge or windbreak.

R. pseudoyanthinum, syn. *R. concinnum pseudoyanthinum.* China. Height 5–7 ft; spread 4–6 ft. An evergreen shrub, almost identical to *R. concinnum*, but its flowers are a deeper, richer shade of red-purple.

R. racemosum. China. Height 1–6 ft; spread 3–5 ft. An evergreen shrub. It has elliptic leaves that are glossy grey-green above, blue-grey and scaly beneath. The funnel-shaped flowers, 1 in. across and deep, form in both terminal and lateral clusters of three to six from March to May. They are in various shades of pink. A free-flowering and hardy species.

R. radicans. Tibet. Height 4 in.; spread 24 in. or more. A low, spreading, evergreen shrub, prostrate in habit and with tangled growth. The leaves, up to $\frac{1}{2}$ in. long, are dark and glossy above, scaly beneath. A single purple or mauve-pink funnel-shaped blossom, $\frac{3}{4}$ in. across and deep, is borne at the end of each stem in May. This species is one of the smallest rhododendrons and is suitable for a rock or heather garden.

R. radinum: see *R. trichostomum*

R. rubiginosum. China. Height 6–10 ft; spread 4–8 ft. An evergreen shrub. The elliptic, sharply pointed dull green leaves are scaly beneath. Funnel-shaped lilac-pink flowers, $1\frac{1}{2}$–2 in. wide and $1\frac{1}{4}$ in. deep, are borne from March to May in clusters of four to eight. This hardy, free-flowering plant is easy to grow and is perhaps the best medium-sized early-blossoming species for the average garden. It will tolerate lime.

R. russatum. China. Height and spread 2–4 ft. The scaly, ovate leaves of this evergreen shrub are up to $1\frac{1}{2}$ in. long and have orange-yellow undersides. Deep blue-purple funnel-shaped lowers appear in April and May, five to ten in a cluster. They are 1 in. across and $\frac{3}{4}$ in. long. This s a hardy, free-flowering, richly coloured species.

R. saluenense. China. Height 18–24 in.; spread 2–3 ft. An evergreen shrub with oblong or ovate leaves that are up to 1 in. long. They are dark glossy green and scaly, particularly on the undersides. Widely funnel-shaped flowers, $1\frac{1}{2}$–$1\frac{1}{4}$ in. across, in varying shades of purple with darker markings, are borne in twos or threes in April and May. Fully hardy; an attractive dwarf species.

R. sargentianum. China. Height and spread up to 24 in., but usually less. An aromatic, slow-growing evergreen shrub. The ovate leaves, up to $\frac{2}{3}$ in. long, are dark green above, paler and with small scales beneath. The shoots are also scaly. Primrose-yellow flowers form in May in tight clusters of 6–12; they are narrowly funnel-shaped to tubular, $\frac{1}{2}$ in. across and $\frac{1}{3}$–$\frac{1}{2}$ in. deep. This is a fine dwarf species, but flowers sparsely until mature.

R. scintillans. China. Height 2–3 ft; spread 2–4 ft. An evergreen shrub. The leathery, scaly leaves are up to $\frac{3}{4}$ in. long and oblong to lanceolate. They are mid-green above, grey beneath. Funnel-shaped lavender to violet flowers, $\frac{3}{4}$ in. across and $\frac{1}{2}$ in. long, appear in clusters of three to six in April. This species is one of the most distinctly blue-flowered rhododendrons.

R. sinogrande. China, Burma, Tibet. Height 30–50 ft; spread 15–20 ft. An evergreen tree with oblong or ovate leaves, normally 10–20 in. long and 6–12 in. wide. They are deep green above, silver beneath. The cream to canary-yellow bell-shaped flowers, sometimes with crimson stains in the throat, blossom in April in spherical clusters of 20–30; they are 2 in. wide and $2\frac{1}{2}$–3 in. long. As a foliage plant this is perhaps the most magnificent in the genus; leaves over 24 in. long are found in Cornwall and western Scotland. Although really suitable only for woodland gardens in the south-west and west, the species may succeed in sheltered, frost-free sites as far east as Surrey and Sussex.

R. souliei. China. Height 6–10 ft; spread 5–8 ft. An evergreen shrub. The leaves are rounded or kidney-shaped, blue-green when young but turning deep sea-green. Saucer-shaped, white to soft pink flowers, 2–3 in. across, blossom in May in loose clusters of five to eight. This attractive species is best grown in light woodland and flowers most prolifically in eastern England.

R. sphaeranthum: see **R. trichostomum.**

R. sutchuenense. China. Height and spread in cultivation up to 12 ft. An evergreen tree. The oblong-ovate leaves are 6–10 in. long and a deep glaucous-green. There are about ten bell-shaped flowers, 3 in. wide and long, in each cluster; these are rose-lilac, speckled with purple, and are borne in March. A fine example of the larger species but too early flowering to escape frost damage except in sheltered woodland.

R. tephropeplum. Burma, Tibet. Height up to 4 ft; spread about 3 ft. An evergreen shrub with oblong, leathery leaves that are dark green above, scaly and blue-grey on their undersides. Slender, bell-shaped magenta-pink flowers, $\frac{3}{4}$–$1\frac{1}{4}$ in. across and deep, appear in clusters of three to five in May. This is a free-flowering plant which needs protection from spring frosts.

R. thomsonii. Himalayas. Height 8 ft or more, spread 6 ft or more. A tall spreading evergreen shrub with broadly ovate to oblong leaves that are lustrous dark green above and blue-grey beneath. The bell-shaped flowers are blood-red with a waxy texture; they are $1\frac{1}{2}$ in. wide and $2\frac{1}{2}$ in. long, and open in clusters of five to eight during March and April.

RHODODENDRON THOMSONII

R. timeteum: see **R. oreotrephes**

R. trichostomum, syns. **R. ledoides, R. radinum, R. sphaeranthum.** China. Height 2–4 ft; spread 2–3 ft. An erect, evergreen shrub with narrow leaves that are grey-green above, yellow-green and scaly underneath. Tubular white to pink flowers, $\frac{1}{2}$ in. wide and $\frac{1}{4}$–$\frac{3}{4}$ in. deep, appear in May in spherical clusters of 12–20. This is one of the most free-flowering of the smaller species, but rather less hardy.

R. tsangpoense. Tibet. Height 12–24 in.; spread 2–3 ft. A dwarf evergreen shrub. The ovate leathery leaves are dull green above, blue-grey and slightly scaly underneath. Bell-shaped waxy flowers, ranging from pink to dull purple, appear in May in clusters of three to five; they are 1 in. across and deep.

R. t. pruniflorum, from Burma, bears greyish-purple blossoms in May. This is a fine variety, being free-flowering and hardy.

R. valentinianum. China. Height up to 18 in.; spread 2–3 ft. The ovate dark green leaves of this evergreen shrub are clad with stiff golden hairs above and scales underneath. The shoots are bristly. Bell to funnel-shaped light yellow flowers, 1 in. across and $1\frac{1}{2}$ in. deep, are borne in clusters of two to six in April. This is a slightly tender dwarf species which does best in sheltered gardens in the south and west.

R. wardii. China. Height up to 12 ft; spread 5–6 ft. An evergreen shrub with leaves ranging from round to ovate. They are smooth all over, dark green above, grey-blue beneath (the young leaves being bright blue-green). Saucer-shaped flowers, 2–$2\frac{1}{2}$ in. across, appear in clusters of 7–14 in May or early June; they are primrose to canary-yellow, sometimes blotched with crimson. This is one of the outstanding yellow-flowered species, but it is not as hardy as **R. campylocarpum.** It is closely related to **R. souliei.**

R. williamsianum. China. Height and spread 4–6 ft. An evergreen shrub, hemispherical in shape. The rounded or kidney-shaped leaves are a shining chocolate-bronze when unfurling, then change to dark green above, blue-grey beneath. Widely bell-shaped flowers, $2\frac{1}{4}$ in. across and $1\frac{1}{2}$–2 in. deep, appear in April. They are carried singly, in pairs or sometimes in a loose cluster of four. The flowers are red in the bud, fading to the softest pink. Its blossoms, foliage and habit make this one of the most handsome species, but it is susceptible to spring-frost damage.

Rhododendron thomsonii

Rhododendron wardii

Rhododendron williamsianum

Rhododendron yakushimanum

Rhododendron luteum

Rhododendron luteum
(autumn foliage)

Rhododendron schlippenbachii

R. xanthocodon. Tibet. Height in cultivation 6–8 ft; spread 5–7 ft. A small evergreen tree or a large shrub. The ovate, leathery leaves are pale olive-green above, blue-green and covered with scales underneath. The young shoots are clad in golden scales. Bell-shaped waxy flowers $1\frac{1}{4}$–$1\frac{1}{2}$ in. wide and deep, open in May in clusters of at least five. They are green in the bud, opening to soft yellow. This species is closely related to *R. concatenans* and *R. cinnabarinum.*

R. yakushimanum. Japan. Height 24 in.; spread 2–3 ft. An evergreen dome-shaped shrub with oblong to lanceolate leathery leaves, curving downwards at the edges. They are dark green above but covered beneath with thick fawn-coloured felt. The young shoots are clad in white wool. The broadly bell-shaped flowers, $1\frac{1}{2}$–$1\frac{3}{4}$ in. wide and long, appear in compact hemispherical clusters in May and June. They are pink in the bud, then fade to white. This species is now considered to be a variety of *R. metternichii.*

R. yunnanense. China. Height and spread 10–12 ft. A straggling evergreen shrub, semi-deciduous after hard winters. The dark green leaves are elliptic to lanceolate, rather brittle, and hairy on top. The funnel-shaped white or pale pink flowers are $1\frac{1}{2}$–2 in. wide and $\frac{3}{4}$–$1\frac{1}{4}$ in. long. They have red or brown spots and are borne in clusters of three to six in May or early June; sometimes the blossom bears a brown basal blotch. This free-flowering species may be tender in bud.

AZALEAS

R. albrechtii. Japan. Height 3–5 ft; spread 3 ft. A deciduous shrub with rounded leaves in whorls of five at the ends of twigs. They are mid-green above, paler beneath. The $1\frac{1}{2}$–2 in. wide flowers, appearing in April and May in clusters of three to five, are green-flecked mauve-pink, and their petals are lobed. This species is susceptible to spring frosts.

R. arborescens. N. America. Height 8–18 ft; spread 5–6 ft. A deciduous shrub. The obovate leaves are bright green above, grey and hairy beneath. White or pale pink, funnel-shaped, fragrant flowers, $1\frac{1}{2}$–2 in. wide and long, appear in clusters of six during June and July. A fully hardy species.

R. atlanticum. N. America. Height up to 3 ft; spread 4–5 ft. A deciduous, stoloniferous shrub with obovate grey leaves. Narrowly funnel-shaped flowers, 1–$1\frac{1}{2}$ in. across and 1 in. long, are borne in clusters of four to ten in April and May. They are white, tinged with pink, sticky on the outside and extremely fragrant.

R. calendulaceum. N. America. Height 4–10 ft; spread 4–5 ft. A deciduous shrub with oblong, mid-green leaves that are hairy beneath. They turn orange and crimson in autumn. Funnel-shaped orange-red or yellow flowers, 2 in. across and $1\frac{1}{2}$–2 in. long, appear in bunches of five to seven in May. This vivid azalea is the parent of striking orange and red hybrids.

R. flavum: see *R. luteum*

R. indicum. Japan. Height 3–6 ft; spread 3–4 ft. An evergreen shrub, which carries lanceolate leaves that are dark glossy green and bristly. The shoots, too, are bristly. Wide funnel-shaped, bright red or pink flowers, 2–$2\frac{1}{2}$ in. wide and $1\frac{1}{2}$ in. long, appear singly or in pairs in June. *R. i.* 'Balsaminaeflorum' is double, salmon-red.

R. kaempferi. Japan. Height and spread up to 5 ft. An almost deciduous shrub, with elliptic to ovate, dark green leaves. A few of the smaller leaves persist through the winter at the ends of shoots. The funnel-shaped flowers are orange, salmon-pink or brick-red, with darker speckles and appear in clusters of two to four in May (later in some varieties). They are $1\frac{1}{2}$–2 in. wide and 1–$1\frac{1}{2}$ in. long. This is a hardy, free-flowering species; it is a parent of the Kurume azaleas and other hybrids.

R. kiusianum, syn. *R. obtusum japonicum.* Japan. Height up to 3 ft; spread up to 5 ft. This almost deciduous shrub has ovate, glossy, dark green leaves. Flowers in various shades of pink or purple, with short 1–$1\frac{1}{2}$ in. wide tubes, are borne in clusters of three or four in early May. This is the chief parent of the Kurume azaleas.

R. luteum, syn. *R. flavum.* Europe, the Caucasus, Asia Minor. Height 6–10 ft; spread 4–6 ft. This is a deciduous shrub which throws up suckers. The oblong to lanceolate leaves are a light matt green, turning scarlet in autumn. Fragrant, tubular, rich yellow flowers, $1\frac{3}{4}$–2 in. wide and $\frac{1}{2}$–$\frac{3}{4}$ in. long, are borne in round trusses of 7–12 during May and June. This is a vigorous, free-flowering shrub, the parent of many hybrids.

R. mucronatum: see HYBRIDS, 11; 'Mucronatum'

R. mucronatum ripense: see *R. ripense*

R. obtusum amoenum: see HYBRIDS, 10; 'Amoena'

R. obtusum japonicum: see *R. kiusianum*

R. occidentale. N. America. Height up to 10 ft; spread 6–8 ft. A deciduous shrub with oblong to lanceolate soft green leaves. Fragrant funnel-shaped flowers, $1\frac{1}{2}$–3 in. across and $\frac{3}{4}$–1 in. long, are borne in June and July in clusters of 6–12; they are white, sometimes tinged with pink, with a yellow blotch. This species is fully hardy, free-flowering and the parent of several excellent hybrid varieties.

R. quinquefolium. Japan. Height and spread 3–5 ft. A deciduous shrub with rounded leaves in whorls of five; they are light green edged with mauve. Funnel-shaped white flowers, sometimes with green throats, appear singly or in pairs in April and May. They are $1\frac{1}{2}$–2 in. wide and 1 in. long. Both the foliage and the blossoms give this species a delicate appearance.

R. reticulatum, syn. *R. rhombicum.* Japan. Height up to 20 ft; spread 4–8 ft. A deciduous shrub. The rounded soft green leaves, which appear in twos or threes, are hairy when young. In autumn they turn orange and red. Widely funnel-shaped pink-purple flowers, $1\frac{1}{2}$–2 in. wide, are borne singly or in pairs in April.

R. rhombicum: see *R. reticulatum*

R. ripense, syn. *R. mucronatum ripense.* Japan. Height up to 3 ft; spread 5 ft. A semi-evergreen shrub with lanceolate to oblanceolate leaves which are bright green and slightly hairy. Funnel-shaped purple to lavender flowers, 2–3 in. wide and long, are produced in small clusters in early May.

R. schlippenbachii. Korea. Height 6–15 ft; spread 4–8 ft. The rounded mid-green leaves of this deciduous shrub are formed in whorls at the ends of stalks. In autumn they turn red and orange. Widely funnel-shaped to saucer-shaped flowers, $2\frac{1}{2}$–$3\frac{1}{4}$ in. wide and 1–$1\frac{1}{2}$ in. long, are

Rhododendron 'Damaris'

Rhododendron 'Blue Diamond'

Rhododendron 'Cilpinense'

Rhododendron 'Elizabeth'

RHODODENDRON

borne in clusters of three to six in April and May. They range from white to various shades of pink, speckled with dull red. This is a fine species, but susceptible to spring frost damage. It is best grown in light woodland.

R. simsii. China. Height and spread up to 5 ft. This half-hardy species and its numerous varieties are usually grown as pot plants and sold as 'Indian azaleas'. They are sometimes incorrectly listed under *R. indicum*, which is a distinct species. The dark green leaves are lanceolate or narrowly obovate and make a good foil for the bright flowers. The latter, which open in May if not forced, are widely funnel-shaped, 2–3 in. across and 1½ in. long, and borne in terminal clusters of two to five. The many varieties cover a wide colour range, including crimson, orange, magenta, salmon, pink and white. Double-flowered forms are also available.

R. vaseyi. N. America. Height 8–15 ft; spread 4–6 ft. A deciduous shrub with leaves that are ovate to lanceolate, slightly bristly and a bright pale green that changes to orange and red in autumn. Widely funnel-shaped pink flowers, 1½–2 in. across, appear in clusters of four to eight in April and May. A handsome and hardy species, this is a good substitute for *R. albrechtii* and *R. schlippenbachii* in cold gardens.

R. viscosum. N. America. Height 6–8 ft; spread 4–6 ft. A deciduous shrub. The leaves are obovate and light green, smooth above but with furry undersides. The tubular, fragrant, white or pink flowers, borne in July in clusters of six to ten, resemble those of the honeysuckle; they measure 1½–2 in. across and ¾–1 in. long. This is a fully hardy species.

HYBRIDS

The leaves of the following hybrids are oblong to elliptic, unless otherwise stated. Those of the evergreen groups are mid to deep green, those of the deciduous light green.

1. EVERGREEN RHODODENDRONS DERIVED MAINLY FROM ASIATIC SPECIES

The width of the flowers ranges from 1½–3 in., except where stated.

'A. Gilbert'. Height 8–15 ft; spread 6–10 ft. The funnel-shaped flowers are apricot in the bud, opening to primrose blotched with crimson in May and early June.

'Arthur Osborn'. Height and spread 3 ft or more. Rich ruby-red trumpet-shaped flowers are borne on long stalks from late June to August.

'Blue Diamond'. Height and spread 3–5 ft. Masses of widely funnel-shaped rich lavender-blue flowers appear in April. Although hardy, the flowers are sometimes damaged by frost.

'Bo-Peep'. Height 3–6 ft; spread 3–4 ft. Widely funnel-shaped primrose-yellow flowers, tinged with green, are borne in March. Fairly hardy despite its early flowering.

'Carmen'. Height 12–24 in.; spread 2–3 ft. Dark crimson bell-shaped flowers appear in May. They have a waxy texture.

'Chaste'. Height 8–15 ft; spread 6–12 ft Widely funnel-shaped primrose-yellow flowers are borne in April and May.

'Cilpinense'. Height and spread almost 3 ft. In March and April, bell-shaped white flowers, flushed and freckled with rose, are borne profusely. Hardy, despite its early flowering.

'Cowslip'. Height and spread 3–4 ft. Widely funnel-shaped primrose or ivory flowers, flushed with pink in the bud, open in April and May.

'Damaris'. Height 8–15 ft; spread 6–12 ft. Widely bell-shaped pale yellow flowers, with green throats, open in April. This is one of the finest of the hybrids; the leaves are a particularly rich green. The form 'Logan Damaris' has slightly deeper yellow flowers.

'Elizabeth'. Height 2–3 ft; spread 3–6 ft. Rich rose-crimson trumpet-shaped flowers are produced during April and May.

583

Rhododendron 'Humming Bird'

Rhododendron 'Fabia'

Rhododendron 'Lady Chamberlain'

Rhododendron 'Hawk'

Rhododendron Loderi

'Fabia'. Height 2–3 ft; spread 3–6 ft. Trumpet-shaped orange-salmon flowers are borne in June. A fully hardy and unusually coloured hybrid.

'Goldfort'. Height 8–12 ft; spread 6–8 ft. Pink buds open to widely funnel-shaped cream-yellow flowers, tinted with apricot. Flowers in profusion during April and May.

'Goldsworth Crimson'. Height 10–12 ft; spread 8–10 ft. Widely funnel-shaped clear crimson flowers are freely borne in April.

'Halcyone'. Height 8–10 ft; spread 6–8 ft. The widely funnel-shaped flowers, appearing in May, are deep rose in the bud, fading to pink or nearly white freckled with crimson.

'Hawk'. Height 8–10 ft; spread 6–8 ft. Widely bell-shaped lemon-yellow flowers, blotched crimson in the throat, are borne in May. The form 'Crest' is outstanding.

'Humming Bird'. Height 4 ft; spread 4–6 ft. Widely bell-shaped carmine-crimson flowers appear in late April and May. The petals have a waxy texture.

'Lady Bessborough'. Height 8–15 ft; spread 6–10 ft. Widely funnel-shaped flowers, pink in the bud and fading to cream-yellow, are produced in late May and early June. The variety 'Roberte' is pink with a darker basal blotch.

'Lady Chamberlain'. Height 6–8 ft; spread 4–5 ft. The flowers, borne in May and early June, are narrowly bell-shaped, drooping and waxy; they range from shades of sealing-wax red to orange-buff and apricot.

'Lady Rosebery'. Similar to 'Lady Chamberlain', but the flowers are a warm, rich pink.

'Letty Edwards'. Height and spread 8–12 ft. The flowers, produced in May, are pink in the bud, opening to soft yellow.

Loderi group. Height 20–25 ft; spread 15–20 ft. The funnel to trumpet-shaped flowers, appearing in May, are 5–6½ in. across, pale pink or white and richly fragrant.

Outstanding varieties are: 'King George', large, pink in the bud, fading to white with a pale green basal blotch; 'Pink Diamond', delicate pink; 'Sir Edmund', pink-white; 'Venus', pale pink.

'Marcia'. Height 8–10 ft; spread 6–8 ft. The flowers, borne in May, are widely funnel-shaped and lemon to primrose-yellow with a basal crimson blotch.

'May Day'. Height 3–5 ft; spread 4–6 ft. Brilliant scarlet funnel-shaped flowers in May.

'Naomi'. Height and spread 7–10 ft. Fragrant widely funnel-shaped flowers appear in May; they are 4 in. across, soft lilac-pink flushed with green-yellow, and freckled brown in the throat.

'Penjerrick Cream'. Height 15–20 ft; spread 10–15 ft. Widely bell-shaped flowers, 3–4 in. wide, are borne profusely in late April and May; they are primrose flushed with pink in the bud, opening to cream or ivory. The peeling, pink-brown bark is an added attraction in mature plants. In Cornwall and other mild areas this hybrid forms a small tree. 'Penjerrick Pink' is a variant with soft pink flowers.

Rhododendron 'Betty Wormald'

Rhododendron 'Britannia'

Rhododendron 'Mrs P. D. Williams'

Rhododendron 'May Day'

Rhododendron 'Praecox'

Rhododendron 'Pink Pearl'

Rhododendron 'Purple Splendour'

'Praecox'. Height and spread 4–6 ft. Abundant rose-purple flowers appear in February and March. Susceptible to frost.

'Russautinii'. Height 6–8 ft; spread 3–5 ft. Rich violet-blue flowers, which are widely funnel-shaped, are borne profusely in April. In cold gardens this is a good substitute for its parent *R. augustinii*; it is also more compact than the species plant.

'Snow Queen'. Height 15–20 ft; spread 10–15 ft. Widely trumpet-shaped pure white flowers appear in May, amidst dark green foliage.

'Temple Bells'. Height and spread 4–5 ft. Widely bell-shaped lilac-pink flowers open in late April and May.

'Vanessa'. Height 3–4 ft; spread 5–7 ft. The strawberry-pink flowers are trumpet-shaped or narrowly funnel-shaped and appear in mid-June. An outstanding late-flowering pink hybrid. 'Vanessa Pastel' has cream flowers tinged with shell-pink inside and stained scarlet outside.

2. HARDY EVERGREEN RHODODENDRONS FOR GENERAL PLANTING

The average height and spread are 10–15 ft—considerably more in moist, sheltered positions. Almost all flower from late May or early June to late June. All the flowers are widely funnel-shaped, except where stated, and measure 2–3 in. across.

'Bagshot Ruby', ruby-red, vigorous growth; 'Beauty of Littleworth', white, spotted with crimson, taller than average; 'Betty Wormald', lilac-pink with darker markings; 'Britannia', crimson-scarlet, bell-shaped, smaller and of slower growth than average.

'Cynthia', rose-crimson, vigorous growth; 'David', deep blood-red; 'Dawn's Delight', deep carmine in the bud opening to soft pink; 'Faggetter's Favourite', cream lilac-pink; 'Fastuosum Flore Pleno', lavender, semi-double.

'Goldsworth Orange', pale orange, height and spread only 5–6 ft; 'Goldsworth Yellow', apricot fading to pale yellow, the same size as 'Goldsworth Orange'; 'Gomer Waterer', pale lilac-rose fading to white; 'Lavender Girl', pale lavender, compact; 'Loder's White', mauve-pink fading to pink-edged white, mid-May.

'Marinus Koster', deep pink with lighter markings; 'Moser's Maroon', maroon-crimson, young growths copper-coloured; 'Mother of Pearl', pink ageing to pure white, a sport from 'Pink Pearl'; 'Mount Everest', white with a red or brown mark in the throat, fragrant, early May.

'Mrs A. T. de la Mare', white with a green throat, compact; 'Mrs G. W. Leak', light pink with a purple-brown blotch; 'Mrs C. E. Pearson', pale mauve with a brown blotch; 'Mrs A. M. Williams', deep red in the bud opening to rich rose-pink; 'Mrs P. D. Williams', ivory with a brown blotch.

'Pink Pearl', rose fading to paler pink, vigorous growth; 'Purple Splendour', deep purple with black markings; 'Sappho', white with a dark purple blotch, a straggly plant.

'Souvenir de Dr S. Endtz', deep pink, vigorous growth; 'Susan', lavender with darker markings, handsome foliage; 'Unique', pale cream-ochre tinged with yellow-pink, height and spread generally about 6–8 ft.

3. COOL-GREENHOUSE RHODODENDRONS

These plants do best under glass. Keep them in an unheated greenhouse, either all the year round or from October until all danger of frost is past. However, in sheltered Cornish gardens and in mild parts of Ireland and western Scotland they can be grown outdoors throughout the year.

Their average height and spread are 4–6 ft and they form rather straggly shrubs. Outside, they flower in late April and early May; under glass, a month or so earlier. All are fragrant, with funnel to bell-shaped flowers, 2–3 in. across.

'Fragrantissimum', white tinged with pink; 'Lady Alice Fitzwilliam', white with a yellow stain, the lobes of the petals tinged pink; 'Princess Alice', white, flushed with pink outside; 'Sesterianum', cream-white stained green-yellow.

4. AZALEODENDRONS

These are hybrids between azaleas and other species of rhododendron. They are deciduous or semi-evergreen, and fully hardy.

'Glory of Littleworth'. Height 4–6 ft; spread 4–5 ft. Funnel-shaped cream-yellow flowers, 2–3 in. wide and with an orange blotch, are borne in May.

5. GHENT AZALEAS

A group of hardy deciduous shrubs flowering from late May to mid-June. Their height and spread are usually 5–6 ft. The flowers are long-tubed, 2–2½ in. wide, and usually fragrant. They are less wide at the mouth than those of the other deciduous azalea hybrids but make a brilliant display. All these azaleas, except for the hybrid 'Daviesii', were raised from eastern N. American species and *R. luteum*.

'Bouquet de Flore', bright pink, deepening at the edges; 'Coccinea Speciosa', brilliant orange-scarlet; 'Corneille', cream tinged with rose, double; 'Daviesii', cream-white with orange-yellow blotches, buds buff-pink, fragrant.

'Hollandia', orange-yellow; 'Josephine Klinger', salmon-pink with a yellow blotch; 'Nancy Waterer', golden-yellow, more compact in growth than average.

'Narcissiflora', soft yellow, fragrant, double; 'Sang de Ghentbrugge', blood-red; 'Unique', orange-yellow, large flowers, tall growth.

6. MOLLIS AZALEAS

Most of these are hybrids between two rarely grown species of azalea, *R. japonicum* and *R. molle*; others are variously coloured forms of *R. japonicum*. Height 4–5 ft; spread often considerably more under good soil conditions—i.e. with adequate organic matter and summer moisture. Scentless funnel-shaped flowers, 2–2½ in. wide, appear in early May. The leaves are strap-shaped or lanceolate, rough and hairy, changing to brilliant orange and scarlet in autumn.

'Comte de Papadopoli', bright pink, shaded orange; 'Dr M. Oosthock', rich orange-scarlet; 'Hugo Koster', salmon-orange flushed with red.

'Lemonora', apricot-yellow flushed with pink, of compact habit; 'Mrs A. E. Endtz', deep rich yellow; 'W. E. Gumbleton', cream buff-yellow with orange markings.

7. RUSTICA HYBRIDS

These deciduous hardy azaleas are double Ghents crossed with *R. japonicum*. Height 6 ft; spread 8 ft. The fragrant flowers are 2½ in. across and are produced in late May and June.

'Byron', white flushed rose; 'Freya', cream-yellow tinted with salmon-orange.

8. OCCIDENTALE HYBRIDS

These are a group of azaleas derived from crossing the N. American *R. occidentale* with Mollis azaleas. Height 6–8 ft; spread 8–10 ft. The fragrant, delicately coloured flowers appear in late May and early June. They are funnel-shaped and 2–3 in. wide.

'Exquisita', cream flushed with pink, with a ray of orange; 'Graciosa', cream-pink with an orange-yellow basal blotch; 'Irene Koster', rose-pink, late-flowering.

9. KNAP HILL AND EXBURY HYBRIDS

These deciduous azaleas have come into prominence since 1945. Their parentage is mixed, consisting of all the species from which Ghent, Mollis and Occidentale hybrids have been bred. Height and spread are variable, both ranging from 3–6 ft.

The widely funnel-shaped flowers are usually a little larger than those of the Mollis hybrids and are borne in bigger trusses. They also open later, from mid-May to mid-June, after danger of frost is past. The young leaves are often tinted with bronze and attractively coloured in the autumn.

The number of named plants increases each year. Those listed are a selection of well-tested ones. Unnamed plants raised from seed (mixed or in one colour) are offered by some nurserymen. These are cheaper than, and sometimes almost as good as, the named plants.

'Balzac', deep orange-red with flame markings on the upper lobes; 'Basilisk', pale yellow with a deep orange blotch; 'Devon', blood-red, vivid autumn foliage; 'George Reynolds', deep butter-yellow with a darker blotch.

'Gibraltar', bright orange; 'Gog', orange-red, vigorous, fine autumn colour; 'Harvest Moon', pale yellow, not a strong grower; 'Homebush', rose-pink, semi-double, in tight trusses; 'Hotspur Orange', vivid orange-red, upper lobes orange-yellow.

'Kathleen', salmon-pink with an orange blotch; 'Persil', white with an orange blotch, one of the best of its colour; 'Satan', pure blood-red, vivid autumn foliage.

'Silver Slipper', white flushed pink with a yellow blotch; 'Strawberry Ice', translucent pink flushed deeper pink with a yellow blotch; 'White-throat', pure white, double, attractive autumn foliage.

10. KURUME HYBRIDS

These are evergreen azaleas with small glossy leaves, which were bred in Japan mainly from *R. kiusianum* and *R. kaempferi*. Most of these and the other evergreen azaleas in Section 11 are more tender than deciduous azaleas and need a position sheltered from cold wind and early-morning sun. The plants in both groups are generally 3–4 ft high and with a spread of up to 5 ft. The flowers are shallowly funnel-shaped, 1–1½ in. wide, and appear in April and May.

'Amoena', syn. *R. obtusum amoenum*, magenta-pink, hose-in-hose, larger growth than

Rhododendron 'Susan'

Rhododendron 'Coccinea Speciosa'

Rhododendron 'Daviesii'

Rhododendron 'Narcissiflora'

Rhododendron 'Dr M. Oosthoek'

Rhododendron 'Harvest Moon'

Rhododendron 'Glory of Littleworth'

Rhododendron 'Hugo Koster'

Rhododendron 'Irene Koster'

587

Rhododendron 'Homebush'

Rhododendron 'Hotspur Orange'

Rhododendron 'Hinodegiri'

Rhododendron 'Mme Auguste Haerens'

average, fully hardy and excellent as a specimen plant; 'Hinodegiri', rich carmine.

'Hinomayo', clear rich pink, taller than average and fully hardy, the best Kurume for general planting; 'Hoo', pale pink fading to white; 'Kirin', rose-pink; 'Kure-no-yuki', white, hose-in-hose flowers.

'Mme Auguste Haerens', semi-double waved petals, pale pink with a darker base; 'Princess Beatrix', semi-double, rich pink.

11. OTHER EVERGREEN HYBRID AZALEAS

A large, miscellaneous group, raised mainly in Europe and America. They need a position sheltered from cold winds and also from early-morning sun. Average height 3–4 ft; spread 4–5 ft. The 2–3 in. wide, funnel-shaped flowers are produced in May. The following is only a short selection from those obtainable.

'Addy Wery', dull orange-scarlet flowers, glossy leaves which are attractively tinted in winter; 'Betty', bright salmon-pink; 'Fedora', dark pink, taller growth than average; 'John Cairns', deep orange-red.

'Mucronatum', syn. *R. mucronatum*. Pure white flowers. More spreading growth than average. An outstanding azalea, with foliage resembling that of *R. ripense*.

'Noordtianum', similar to 'Mucronatum' but with slightly larger flowers, often flushed with mauve; 'Orange Beauty', soft orange, the colour fading quickly in sunny weather; 'Palestrina', white with a faint green stripe, fully hardy.

'Vuyk's Scarlet', deep vivid crimson, of dwarf habit; 'Willy', clear pink.

Cultivation. With a few exceptions, such as *R. hirsutum*, rhododendrons will not tolerate chalky or limy soil. The ideal is a well-drained sandy loam. Light soil can be enriched, and heavy soil lightened, with peat, hop manure or leaf-mould.

After chalk and lime, the worst enemies of rhododendrons are dryness at the roots, too much direct sunlight and cold, drying winds. They do best in sheltered, semi-shaded positions, but many of the species with small, scaly leaves, such as *R. impeditum* and *R. scintillans,* will thrive in full sun provided they are not allowed to dry out. Larger-leaved species require more shade than others and do best in gardens with plenty of trees or in light woodland, well sheltered from wind.

Most hardy hybrids tolerate sun, but their roots need to be mulched with strawy manure, half-rotted leaf-mould, bracken or peat. All rhododendrons flowering before the end of May must be planted where they are protected from early-morning sun, to avoid damage to flower buds and young growths caused by sudden thawing after frost. Do not plant near surface-rooting trees, such as elms, limes, poplars and sycamores, nor under trees with low branches.

Feed the plants each spring with 4–6 oz. of John Innes base fertiliser per sq. yd over an area equal to the spread of the plant.

Dead-head the plants with finger and thumb; secateurs can damage the shoots.

To grow *R. simsii* as a pot plant, plant it during October or November in a 6–10 in. pot, depending on the size of the plant. Use light, lime-free compost, proprietary peat composts being suitable provided no lime has been added. Alternatively, use equal parts (by volume) fibrous loam, leaf-mould, moss peat, and coarse sand.

Keep the plants in a cold frame or greenhouse until early December, but from then until the blooms open maintain a temperature of 13–16°C (55–61°F). Syringe the plants from above at least once a day until the flower buds show colour and are moved indoors, and maintain a humid atmosphere by damping between the pots and the floor. After flowering, return the plants to a frost-proof frame and harden them off during late April or May.

Plunge the plants in an outdoor bed or remove the frame lights completely from May to September, syringing overhead night and morning during hot, dry spells. Use lime-free (soft) water for both watering and syringing.

Propagation. The four main methods are by seeds, layering, grafting and cuttings.

The larger-leaved species are raised from seeds or by layering; hardy hybrids by grafting or cuttings; deciduous azaleas by grafting or layering; Kurume azaleas, alpine species and the half-hardy *R. simsii* by cuttings.

Sow the seeds thinly in February or March in pans of moist, finely sifted horticultural peat. Half-cover them with a sprinkling of silver sand either at sowing time or immediately after germination. Place the pans in a propagating frame heated to 13–16°C (55–61°F) and cover them with glass or asbestos sheeting until they germinate. Alternatively, delay sowing until late March or early April and place in pans in a shaded cold frame or unheated greenhouse.

Keep the seedlings well shaded and the compost surface moist. When they make their first two true leaves, prick them out 1 in. apart into pans or boxes containing a compost of 1 part sifted horticultural peat, 1 part leaf-mould, 1 part lime-free loam and 1 part coarse sand (parts by volume). If leaf-mould is not available use more peat and loam. Protect the seedlings from strong sun and keep the compost moist but not soggy. In summer the pans may be placed in shade in the open, but must be brought back under glass in autumn. The following April, plant out the seedlings in light, peaty soil in nursery beds or in cold frames.

Layering can be done at any time of the year. It requires young stems which are low enough for bending to ground level, enabling them to be covered with 2–3 in. of soil. Make a small lengthwise slit where the stem is to be buried; this hastens rooting. Anchor the stem with pegs and keep its end vertical by attaching it to a short stake. Sever the layer from the parent plant after two years, when it should be well rooted.

Hardy hybrids are usually saddle-grafted on *R. ponticum*; deciduous azaleas on *R. luteum*. Grafting is, however, not a very easy method of propagation for amateurs.

Cuttings may be taken from the young growths of those hardy species and hybrids that have small, scaly leaves. Take them from mid-July to late August (as late as December in the case of the very small-leaved species, e.g. *R. scintillans*) and root them in a cold frame or cold greenhouse, using a mixture of 2 parts fine sand and 1 part finely sifted horticultural peat (parts by volume). When well rooted pot them up in the compost recommended for pricked-out seedlings.

To propagate *R. simsii*, take 2–3 in. long half-ripe cuttings in June and insert them in equal parts (by volume) peat and sand with bottom heat of 16°C (61°F). When they are rooted, pot the cuttings into 2½ in. pots containing the rooting medium advised under CULTIVATION and grow on under frost-proof glass until the following April, then move them into 3½–4 in. pots. The cuttings are often erratic in rooting and frequently fail altogether. A mist unit gives the best results, and a hormone rooting compound is also helpful.

Rhododendrons are easy to transplant because of their compact root system. They can be moved in temperate weather at any time between September and April. Plant them firmly with the top of the root-ball level with, or slightly below, the surface of the bed. Mulch with peat or leaf-mould after planting, but never smother the root ball with heavy soil.

Pruning. Rhododendrons and azaleas do not need regular pruning. Spindly young plants may be lightly pruned or disbudded to make them bushy, and straggly older plants (with the exception of grafted ones, sickly ones and those with peeling bark) may be cut back hard in spring, if necessary to within 12 in. of the ground. If a rhododendron has outgrown its position it is better to move it than to prune it.

Pests. The most serious pest is RHODODENDRON LEAFHOPPER: by puncturing the buds and allowing spores to enter, it is the main cause of bud-blast disease (see DISEASES). Adult leafhoppers are bright green with conspicuous red stripes. They live on the leaves from July onwards. The females lay eggs in the bud scales from August to October.

RHODODENDRON BUGS also live on the leaves. They suck the sap and cause a mottling of the upper leaf surface; a rusty appearance develops on the underside of the leaves.

WHITEFLIES, particularly the azalea whitefly, infest the undersides of leaves. They suck sap and excrete honeydew, which encourages the growth of sooty moulds.

WEEVILS eat shallow, narrow notches out of leaf edges. CATERPILLARS of various species eat larger holes in leaf tissue.

Diseases. Young leaves and flower buds may be transformed into small swellings by AZALEA GALL. These are red or pale green at first, but soon receive a floury white coating of fungus spores. They eventually turn brown and shrivel.

CHLOROSIS turns the leaf yellow, except for the veins, which remain green. One or two applications of sequestrene compound will usually counteract the chlorotic symptoms, though only temporarily if the soil is alkaline.

FROST DAMAGE turns the flower buds brown; they become soft and rotten, and are easily removed. Leaves injured while in the bud or still small become distorted, but mature leaves show only purple spots. Severe frosts produce vertical cracks at the base of main stems or on smaller branches. DIE-BACK may also occur.

Rhododendron 'Princess Beatrix'

Rhododendron 'Palestrina'

HONEY FUNGUS quickly kills a shrub. The first symptoms are discoloured, drooping leaves, which do not fall.

Purple or brown LEAF SPOTS often appear on unhealthy shrubs; they are usually produced by different forms of fungi.

RHODODENDRON BUD-BLAST kills the buds. Black bristle-like heads of fungus spores appear in spring; the buds turn brown, black or silvery, but they do not rot and they remain firm.

RUST shows as orange-brown fungus spores on the undersides of leaves, whose upper surfaces become discoloured.

SILVER LEAF causes die-back of branches and sometimes whole shrubs. (Despite the name, the leaves do not turn silver.) Purple fruiting bodies of the fungus appear on the dead wood.

Rhodohypoxis
Hypoxidaceae

A genus of two species of perennial plants, with corm-like rhizomes. They thrive in moist, well-drained soil on rock gardens or in alpine houses. The only species in general cultivation is hardy outdoors in all but the most severe winters.

R. baurii. S. Africa. Height 3 in.; spread 4–6 in. This plant forms tufts of hairy, pale green, linear-lanceolate foliage and produces rose-red flowers from April to September. These have six petals which are arranged in threes, the inner three standing slightly higher than the outer. The whole flower is about 1 in. across. There are forms varying from white to dark rose.

Cultivation. Plant in September in a sunny position. Outdoors, grow them in lime-free moisture-retentive but well-drained soil. Give protection from excessive dampness in winter with raised panes of glass.

In the alpine house, set the plants in 4–6 in. pans of well-drained, lime-free compost. Water frequently and repot annually in September.

Propagation. Remove and replant the offset corms in September. They will generally flower the following year.

Pests and diseases. Generally trouble-free.

Rhoeo
Commelinaceae

RHOEO DISCOLOR

A genus containing only one species. This is an evergreen perennial grown for its foliage; it requires greenhouse cultivation.

R. discolor. Central America, W. Indies. Height and spread up to 12 in. This species, which is correctly named *R. spathacea*, forms in the young stages a rosette of semi-erect leaves up to 12 in.

Rhodohypoxis baurii

Rhoeo discolor

Rhoicissus rhomboidea

long. They are strap-shaped and fleshy, dark green on the upper sides, rich purple beneath.

With age the rosette extends into a short thick stem and lateral shoots are formed. Inconspicuous white flowers, which may be produced at any time, appear in boat-shaped purple bracts, about 2 in. long, from the leaf axils. 'Vittatum' has leaves with narrow longitudinal cream stripes.

R. spathacea: see *R. discolor*

Cultivation. Grow in 5–6 in. pots of John Innes potting compost No. 2 or in a proprietary peat mixture. During winter provide a minimum temperature of 7–10°C (45–50°F), and keep the plants moist. From March onwards provide a minimum temperature of 16–18°C (61–64°F) and water freely.

The plants require moderately shady conditions. Repot annually in April and give a weak liquid feed at fortnightly intervals from May to September. The plants are best discarded after two or three years' growth.

Propagation. In April, take cuttings, 3–4 in. long of basal shoots and insert singly in 3 in. pots containing equal parts (by volume) peat and sand. Root the cuttings at a temperature of 16–18°C (61–64°F). Pot on as necessary.

Alternatively, sow seeds in April or May in pots or pans of seed compost, at a temperature of 18–21°C (64–70°F). Pot the seedlings in 3 in. containers of John Innes potting compost No. 1 and pot on as necessary.

Pests and diseases. Generally trouble-free.

Rhoicissus
Vitidaceae

A genus of 12 species of tender evergreen climbing plants. One species is popular as an ornamental foliage plant for the greenhouse or a living-room.

R. rhomboidea. Natal. Height 4–6 ft in a pot, up to 20 ft in a greenhouse border. An evergreen climber of moderate growth which clings by means of tendrils. The dark green, shiny leaves are composed of three stalked leaflets that are boldly toothed and irregularly diamond-shaped. The young growths and immature leaves are covered with pale brown hairs.

'Jubilee' is a larger-leaved, more robust form.

Cultivation. Grow rhoicissus in 5–8 in. pots of John Innes potting compost No. 2 or in the greenhouse border. The plants need a winter temperature of 7–10°C (45–50°F) and do best without high temperatures in summer, when the greenhouse should be freely ventilated. Place in a well-lit position during winter, but provide light shade in summer.

They are easily grown house plants, as they are not harmed by gas or oil fumes and may be set in fairly shaded but not dark positions.

Pot on annually in April until the plants are in their final 8–9 in. pots, unless larger plants are required. Thereafter repot annually in April.

Give a weak liquid feed in the summer at fortnightly intervals from May to September. Keep the plants just moist during winter, and give only moderate quantities of water in spring and summer. Sponge the leaves occasionally.

Propagation. Take 3 in. long cuttings of lateral shoots in April or May. Insert in equal parts (by volume) peat and sand at a temperature of 16–18°C (61–64°F). Pot the rooted cuttings singly in 3 in. pots of John Innes potting compost No. 1 and pot on as necessary.

Alternatively, sections of a main stem, each containing at least two nodes, may be rooted in the same way as cuttings.

Pruning. Stop the plants two or three times during the first spring and summer to encourage bushy growth. If the plants grow too large, they may be cut back by two-thirds in March or April.

Pests. Generally trouble-free.

Diseases. A PHYSIOLOGICAL DISORDER results in brown or khaki-coloured blotches developing on the leaves, often at the tips.

Rhubarb

Rheum rhaponticum. Polygonaceae

RHUBARB

A hardy perennial grown for its edible red stems which are ready for use from February until mid-summer. The stems, which are used as culinary fruit, have a tart, acid flavour; the leaves contain a poison—oxalic acid.

VARIETIES

'Timperley Early' is an early-maturing thin-stemmed variety, suitable for forcing; 'Hawke's Champagne', with deep red stems, makes an excellent crop; 'The Sutton', a large, outstanding main-crop variety, seldom goes to seed; 'Victoria' is recommended for a seed-raised crop.

Cultivation. Rhubarb will grow in any ordinary garden soil. On a properly prepared bed and with regular attention, it will produce healthy stems over several years before needing division.

A few weeks before planting, dig the ground deeply and work in two buckets of well-rotted manure or compost per sq. yd and a liberal sprinkling of wood ash and bone-meal. Set purchased plants of small varieties, such as 'Timperley Early' and 'Hawke's Champagne', 2½ ft apart each way, but allow 3–4 ft each way between plants of large-growing varieties. Make sure that each root has at least one eye or bud. Plant the crowns firmly in March, with the top bud 2 in. below the soil surface.

Remove any flower stems that appear and keep the bed free of weeds. In early spring, apply a top dressing of general-purpose fertiliser. During the growing season give a dressing of nitrogenous fertiliser at the rate of 3 oz. per sq. yd, and when the season is over mulch the crowns with manure. Lift and divide the crowns every five to eight years.

Rhubarb may be raised from seeds, but the subsequent plants are often inferior, and it will be several years before stems can be pulled.

Sow seeds thinly in March in a seed bed, in 2 in. deep drills, 12 in. apart; when the seedlings show the first true leaf, thin to 9 in. apart. The following spring, set well-developed crowns in the permanent bed.

Forcing. Early crops can be obtained by covering a few crowns in December with a thick layer of straw or an open-ended barrel or box. Crowns that have been forced will give only a light yield the following year. Rhubarb may also be forced in a heated greenhouse at a temperature of 10–13°C (50–55°F). Lift the crowns after a frost and place in boxes of light soil, kept moist. Cover the boxes with black polythene to exclude light until the young shoots appear. Crowns used for greenhouse forcing are best discarded.

Harvesting. During the first season of growth do not pull any stems; in subsequent seasons pull three or four stems at a time from any one crown. Gather the stems by grasping low down on the crown and pulling outwards and twisting at the same time. Pull only fully grown stems and always leave at least three or four strong stems on each plant.

Pests. STEM AND BULB EELWORM may infest rhubarb, checking growth and causing rotting. Caterpillars of SWIFT MOTH tunnel into roots.

Diseases. CROWN ROT OF RHUBARB causes rotting of the terminal bud, followed by a soft brownish rotting of the pith, often with the formation of a cavity. Spindly side-shoots may develop but the leaves are dull in colour and may rot.

FROST DAMAGE in late spring turns the leaves brown, and the stalks become limp and rot.

HONEY FUNGUS may kill the plants; when the roots are cut open, white streaks of the fungus can be seen.

LEAF SPOT causes irregular brown spots on the leaves, and VIRUS DISEASES produce ring-spots and yellow flecks on the leaves.

Rhubarb, ornamental: see Rheum

Rhus

Sumach. Anacardiaceae

RHUS TYPHINA

A genus of 250 species of hardy deciduous shrubs and small trees which have brilliant autumn foliage after particularly good summers, and colourful clusters of fruits. The sap of some species may greatly irritate the skin. The smoke tree, frequently catalogued as *Rhus cotinus*, is botanically classified as *Cotinus coggygria*.

R. cotinoides: see *Cotinus americanus*

R. cotinus: see *Cotinus coggygria*

R. glabra (smooth sumach). E. United States. Height 5–9 ft; spread 5–6 ft. The smooth pinnate leaves are mid-green, with glaucous undersides, and turn brilliant red in September and October.

Rhubarb (forced)

Rhus typhina 'Laciniata' (autumn foliage)

Conical 4–6 in. long panicles of light red flowers open in July. These are dense and develop into striking clusters of deeper red seed vessels.

'Laciniata' has hairy, fern-like leaves with narrowly segmented leaflets which turn deep red and yellow in October.

R. trichocarpa. China, Korea, Japan. Height 15–20 ft; spread 8–12 ft. The mid-green pinnate leaves turn brilliant orange-scarlet in October and November. Inconspicuous flowers are borne in June in slender 3–6 in. long panicles, followed by pendulous clusters of spherical yellow fruits.

R. typhina (stag's horn sumach). Eastern N. America. Height 10–15 ft; spread 12–16 ft. The pinnate mid-green leaves grow up to 18 in. long on vigorous shoots if these are pruned to the ground in February each year. The foliage takes on shades of orange-red, yellow and purple from September onwards.

Minute, hairy, pale red flowers are borne in June or July in dense conical panicles up to 8 in. long and are followed by clusters of crimson fruits. This species is tolerant of atmospheric pollution. It differs from *R. glabra* in its densely hairy young shoots. 'Laciniata' has deeply cut mid-green leaflets which turn orange and yellow in October.

Cultivation. Plant between October and April in any ordinary garden soil in a sunny position.

Propagation. Take 4–5 in. cuttings of half-ripe shoots with a heel in July or August; insert the cuttings in sandy soil in a propagating frame, preferably with mist propagation, with a gentle bottom heat of 16–18°C (61–64°F). Pot up the rooted cuttings into 3 in. pots of John Innes potting compost No. 1 and overwinter them in a cold frame. Transfer to a nursery bed the following April, and finally plant out in their permanent positions in October.

Remove suckers from October onwards and plant in permanent positions.

Shoots layered in March or April will be ready for severing from the parent plant and planting out after one or two years.

Pruning. None is essential, but for an abundance of handsome foliage only, prune *R. glabra* and *R. typhina* to the ground between February and April each year.

Pests. Generally trouble-free.

Diseases. DIE-BACK of one or more branches may be caused by a PHYSIOLOGICAL DISORDER, due to unsuitable cultural conditions.

VERTICILLIUM WILT also causes die-back.

Rhyncospermum jasminoides: see *Trachelospermum jasminoides*

Ribes

Flowering currant. *Grossulariaceae* (formerly *Saxifragaceae*)

A genus of 150 species of half-hardy and hardy, evergreen and deciduous, flowering and fruiting shrubs. The genus includes the edible fruiting varieties of currants and gooseberry. The ornamental species described here are mainly grown for their pendent or erect flower racemes, which are composed of small fuchsia-like flowers.

Ribes aureum

Ribes sanguineum

Ribes speciosum

R. alpinum. N. and Central Europe. Height 3–6 ft; spread 3–4 ft. A hardy unisexual bushy shrub with deciduous twiggy stems bearing mid-green, coarsely toothed and broadly ovate leaves. Inconspicuous green-yellow flowers are borne in erect racemes, 1–1½ in. long, in April; they are followed by red globose berries when plants of both sexes are grown. This species is mainly used for hedging on poor soils and in shade.

R. aureum, syn. *R. tenuiflorum* (golden or buffalo currant). Western N. America. Height 6–8 ft; spread 4–5 ft. This hardy deciduous species is often, erroneously, listed as *R. odoratum*, a closely related species. The pale green leaves are coarsely toothed and turn yellow with an orange flush in October. Bright yellow, clove-scented, tubular flowers appear in 1–2 in. drooping racemes in April; they are followed by black globose fruits.

R. × gordonianum. Height 6–8 ft or more; spread 4–5 ft or more. A non-berrying, hardy, deciduous hybrid between *R. aureum* and *R. sanguineum*; it has glabrous mid-green leaves that are ovate and deeply lobed. Red flowers, yellow inside, are produced during April in pendulous racemes up to 20 in. long.

R. laurifolium. China. Height and spread up to 18 in. This is a hardy, evergreen, unisexual species suitable for an alpine house or a rock garden. The glabrous pale to mid-green leathery leaves are ovate. Green-yellow male flowers are borne in February or March in pendent racemes, 1½–2½ in. long. Female flowers occur in shorter, erect racemes; if the two sexes are grown together, purple-black ovoid fruits are set.

R. odoratum: see *R. aureum*

RIBES SANGUINEUM

R. sanguineum. Western N. America. Height 6–9 ft; spread 5–7 ft. A hardy deciduous species with roundly cordate, mid to deep green leaves with paler undersides. Deep rose-red flowers are borne from late March to May in 2–4 in. long pendent racemes. They are followed by globose blue-black berries in September and October.

Named varieties include: 'Brocklebankii', a smaller, slower-growing variety with golden-yellow foliage; 'King Edward VII', with small, deep crimson flowers; 'Pulborough Scarlet', with rich red flowers.

R. speciosum. California. Height 6–10 ft; spread 4–5 ft. This half-hardy deciduous species is one of the most showy of the ornamental currants; it requires the shelter of a warm wall in all but the mildest areas. The densely spined stems bear glabrous, deeply lobed, mid-green leaves that are ovate to obovate. Bright red flowers, 1–1½ in. long, are borne in clusters of three or four from April to June.

R. tenuiflorum: see *R. aureum*

Cultivation. Ribes thrive in any ordinary, well-drained garden soil, in sun or light shade. Plant during suitable weather from October to March. Top-dress annually with decayed manure or garden compost in April.

In the alpine house, grow *R. laurifolium* in 6–8 in. pots or pans of John Innes potting compost No. 2. Repot every second or third year in September or October.

For hedges of *R. alpinum*, set the young shrubs 12–15 in. apart; tip the shoots to within 6 in. of the ground after planting to induce bushy growth. Tip the resulting young shoots once or twice during summer, and thereafter shear hedges to shape once or twice annually between April and October.

Propagation. Take hardwood cuttings, 10–12 in. long, in October or November and insert in a nursery bed. They should be ready for planting out in their permanent flowering positions one year later.

Take 3–4 in. long cuttings of *R. laurifolium* in September and insert in equal parts (by volume) peat and sand in a cold frame. Pot the rooted cuttings in 3 in. containers of John Innes compost No. 1 and pot on as necessary or plant out.

Pruning. Cut out old wood at ground level, annually in May.

Pests. The leaves are sometimes infested by APHIDS, and discoloured blisters appear on the upper surfaces.

Diseases. Small brown spots on the leaves are caused by LEAF SPOT. These gradually coalesce until the whole leaf surface is covered; the leaves fall prematurely.

Ricinus

Castor oil plant. *Euphorbiaceae*

A genus of one tender shrubby species usually treated as a half-hardy annual. The plant is grown for its attractive foliage and is used in formal bedding schemes, as a conservatory pot plant, and in groups at the rear of borders.

RICINUS COMMUNIS

R. communis. Tropical Africa. Height 5 ft; planting distance 3 ft. A strong-growing, well-branched plant that can reach a height of 20 ft, but seldom exceeds 5 ft when grown as an annual. The mid-green palmate leaves, up to 12 in. across, are lobed and have serrated edges. Insignificant green flowers, which have no petals, are produced in 1 in. wide ovoid sprays in July. They are followed by round, spiny seed pods. Garden varieties listed include 'Cambodgensis', with black-purple stems and larger leaves; 'Gibsonii', a more compact variety with dark green stems and bronze foliage; 'Sanguineus', with red-purple foliage; and 'Zanzibarensis', producing leaves, 10 in. across, which have distinctive, light-coloured mid-ribs.

Cultivation. Grow in any well-cultivated soil, preferably enriched with organic matter, in a sunny site. Staking is advisable, especially for tall plants on exposed sites.

Grow pot plants under glass in final 8 in. pots containing John Innes potting compost No. 2.

Propagation. Sow the seeds under glass in February or March at a temperature of 21°C (70°F). Soaking for a day in water speeds germination. Move the seedlings to 5 in. pots and grow on at a temperature of 10°C (50°F); if the plants are to go outdoors, harden them off before planting out in late May or early June.

Pests and diseases. Generally trouble-free.

Robinia

False acacia. *Leguminosae*

ROBINIA PSEUDOACACIA

A genus of 20 species of hardy deciduous flowering trees and shrubs, with pea-like flowers, pinnate leaves and brittle stems that usually bear short spines at the nodes. They make excellent standard specimen trees, or they may be grown as wall shrubs.

R. hispida (rose acacia). S.E. United States. Height and spread 6–8 ft. The pinnate leaves are dark green on glandular bristly stems. Rose-pink flowers, 1–1¼ in. long, appear in May and June in pendent racemes. This species is suitable for training against a sunny wall.

R. kelseyi. S.E. United States. Height 8–10 ft; spread 8 ft. Smooth, pale-green, pinnate leaves are borne on prickly stems which have small spines at the leaf nodes. Bright rose flowers, ¾ in. long, appear in June in clusters of three to seven. This is a graceful tree when grown as a standard.

R. pseudoacacia (common or false acacia, black locust). E. United States. Height 30 ft or more; spread 10–15 ft. The light green leaflets are ovate, and the bark is deeply furrowed. Cream-white fragrant flowers are borne in June in pendulous racemes 4–7 in. long. This tree produces numerous thorny suckers; it tolerates atmospheric pollution and is frequently grown as a specimen tree in large parks.

'Frisia' has pinnate leaves which open golden-yellow in April and May and turn pale green-yellow in July; 'Inermis' (mop-head acacia), which seldom blossoms, has a compact, globular head of spineless branches.

Cultivation. Plant between October and March in any ordinary, well-drained garden soil in a reasonably sheltered, sunny position. Robinias will thrive in areas of low rainfall.

To train *R. hispida* against a wall, tie in the vigorous shoots to a wire or trellis support once or twice between July and September.

Propagation. Sow seeds in pans during March or April and place in a cold greenhouse or a cold

Ricinus communis (fruits)

Robinia hispida

Robinia pseudoacacia

frame. Prick off the seedlings into pans or boxes of John Innes potting compost No. 1, when they are large enough to handle, and subsequently plant out in a nursery bed. Grow on there for two or three years before planting out in their final positions between October and March.

Another method is to remove suckers between October and February and plant these in a nursery bed. Plant out rooted suckers in their permanent positions one or two years later, between October and March.

Pruning. Normally, no pruning is necessary.

To grow *R. kelseyi* as a standard, pinch out the tip of the leading shoot when it is 6 in. beyond the desired stem height. Remove all lateral shoots except the top four or five, and allow these to develop normally during the first year. The following February, shorten back these shoots by half or two-thirds their length. Prune to shape annually in the dormant period if the head is to be grown in a restricted form.

Pests. The stems may be infested with colonies of SCALE INSECTS.

Diseases. Generally trouble-free.

Robinia pseudoacacia 'Frisia'

Rodgersia pinnata

Rodgersia podophylla

Rochea

Crassulaceae

ROCHEA COCCINEA

A genus of four species of tender succulent plants with showy heads of carmine-red flowers. The following species is the only one in general cultivation, and is best grown in a cool greenhouse. It was formerly listed under *Crassula*.

R. coccinea. S. Africa. Height up to 15 in.; spread 9–12 in. The stems are thickly clothed with leathery, pointed, mid-green leaves arranged in four close ranks. Each fragrant bright carmine flower consists of a 1 in. long tube and five terminal petals forming a cross. The flowers are borne in terminal flattened clusters, 3–5 in. across, from July to September.

Cultivation. Grow rocheas in 5–6 in. pots of John Innes potting compost No. 2. Cool, airy conditions are essential, and the winter temperature need not exceed 5–7°C (40–45°F). Water moderately throughout the year, keeping the plants just moist during winter.

Give the plants full light, but shade them in summer if the greenhouse is likely to get overheated. Pot on annually in April to obtain larger plants; after two or three years the plants should be discarded. After the first year's growth, give a weak liquid feed at intervals of two or three weeks from May to August.

Propagation. Take cuttings, 3–4 in. long, of basal shoots from cut-back plants in April. The cut surfaces may be left to heal for a few days before inserting the cuttings in equal parts (by volume) peat and sand. Root the cuttings at a temperature

Rochea coccinea

of 13–16°C (55–61°F). Pot the rooted cutting singly in 3 in. containers of John Innes potting compost No. 1.

Pruning. Young plants should be stopped twice during summer to encourage the formation of basal growths. Cut down flowering shoots to about 4 in. from the base in February.

Pests and diseases. Generally trouble-free.

Rodgersia

Saxifragaceae

RODGERSIA PODOPHYLLA

A genus of six species of hardy herbaceous perennials, grown as border plants for their foliage as much as for their flowers. They are rhizomatous and usually take one or two years to become established. They are at their best in moist soil, sheltered from strong winds and sun.

R. aesculifolia. China. Height 3–6 ft; planting distance 2½ ft. A species with pinnate, glossy bronze foliage resembling the leaves of a giant horse-chestnut. Star-shaped white or pink flowers appear in plumes, 12–18 in. long, in July.

R. pinnata. China. Height 3–4 ft; planting distance 2½ ft. The pinnate deep green leaves are sometimes bronzed. Many-branched, 9–12 in. long panicles of starry flowers, ¼ in. across, rise above the foliage in July. The flowers range from white through pink to shades of red.

R. p. 'Superba' has bronze-purple leaves, and panicles, up to 21 in. long, of pink flowers.
R. podophylla. Japan. Height 3–4 ft; planting distance 2½ ft. The heavily netted, horse-chestnut-like leaves are mid-green. Sprays, 12–18 in. long, of pale buff flowers, are produced in June and July.

RODGERSIA TABULARIS

R. tabularis. China. Height 3 ft; planting distance 2½ ft. A species with bright green umbrella-shaped leaves, 1–3 ft across. Loose panicles, 6–9 in. long, of small cream-white flowers appear in July and August.
Cultivation. Plant the rhizomes in March or April in moist soil, preferably containing decayed vegetable matter. The crowns should be 1 in. below the surface. Planting positions should be in half shade and sheltered from strong winds. Water freely if the soil becomes dry during the growing season. Remove faded flowering stems.
Propagation. Divide and replant the slowly spreading rhizomes in March or April.

Sow seeds in March in boxes or pans of John Innes seed compost. Place the boxes in a cold frame and prick out the seedlings, when large enough to handle. Set out the young plants in a nursery bed when danger of frost is over, and plant out in permanent positions in March or April two years later.

Pests and diseases. Generally trouble-free.

Romneya

Tree poppy. *Papaveraceae*

ROMNEYA COULTERI

A genus of two species of herbaceous sub-shrubby perennials. These are attractive plants with poppy-like flowers, but are not always easy to establish. They are hardy only in the south and are not recommended for outdoor cultivation in the eastern parts of north England or in Scotland. They may prove troublesome in a herbaceous border, as they can be invasive and quickly spread by underground runners.
R. coulteri. California. Height 6–8 ft; planting distance 4–6 ft. A sub-shrubby border perennial with blue-green, broadly ovate, deeply lobed leaves. The white flowers, 4–5 in. across with golden stamens, appear from July to September.
R. trichocalyx. California. Height and planting distance 3 ft. A sub-shrubby species, smaller and

Romneya trichocalyx

more upright than *R. coulteri*, but similar in all other respects. The fragrant white flowers appear from June to September. This species may spread further, but less quickly than *R. coulteri*.
Cultivation. Romneyas resent root disturbance, and young pot-grown plants should be planted out with the soil ball intact. Once established they should not be disturbed. Set the plants in light, well-drained soil which has been previously prepared by digging deeply and incorporating plenty of peat or leaf-mould. Plant in April or May in a sheltered sunny position.

In late October cut the stems down to a few inches above ground level. From late October to March, especially for the first two years, cover the base of the plants with bracken, weathered ashes or peat.
Propagation. Sow seeds in February or March in pans of sandy seed compost and germinate at a temperature of 13–16°C (55–61°F). When large enough to handle, prick the seedlings into 3½ in. pots of a light sandy compost. Grow the young plants on at the same temperature until the roots are well through to the side of the pots; this will take three or four months. Overwinter in a cold frame and set out in permanent positions the following April.

Root-cuttings, 3 in. long, inserted in pots of sandy soil in February, will grow at a temperature of 13°C (55°F). The disturbance caused when taking the cuttings may damage the parent plants, and it is better to dig up and replant, in April or May, any suckers which appear some distance from the original crowns.

Romneya coulteri

Pests. Generally trouble-free.
Diseases. Yellowing of leaves and wilting of shoots is caused by a PHYSIOLOGICAL DISORDER due to unsuitable cultural conditions.

Rorippa nasturtium-aquaticum: see Watercress

595

ROSA

Rose. *Rosaceae*

Roses are found wild only in the Northern Hemisphere. They grow mainly in the temperate zone, although some species occur on mountains further south. Throughout the ages many different bush and climbing species developed, adapting themselves to temperature and soil conditions. Today botanists recognise about 250 distinct species, as well as many natural varieties.

The cultivation of the rose has been going on from very early times, but the use of the rose as a decoration in the garden and home was confined for many centuries to the wild species. Throughout the Middle Ages the rose was chiefly grown in monasteries for medicinal uses and religious ceremonies. Natural seedlings and mutants (sports) from the wild species gradually extended the range, and from the French rose (*Rosa gallica*), most prolific of the old parents, came the 'Apothecary's rose' or 'Red Rose of Lancaster' (*R. g. officinalis*) which in turn produced the well-known red-and-white mutant *R. g.* 'Versicolor'. Another significant natural development occurred in the scented Moss roses from *R. centifolia* in the 18th century.

Until the end of the 18th century the Gallicas, Centifolias, Damasks, Albas and Musks reigned supreme, the development of old European roses having been halted with the Moss rose.

Deliberate cross-pollination by hand was not practised until the early 19th century, when a new species reached Europe. This was the China rose, *R. chinensis*, and particularly its variety *semperflorens*, which has the quality rare among species roses of being what is loosely called perpetual, or more exactly remontant or recurrent, flowering off and on from May or June until November in western Europe.

Developments quickly began in France and England on slightly different lines, and in 1816 the first Hybrid perpetual appeared in the form of 'Rose du Roi'. This was a crimson, scented and double rose, more or less perpetual.

Another significant introduction in the early 19th century was the Bourbon rose, a natural hybrid found growing in the Île de Bourbon (now Réunion). This was a fusion of the China and Damask roses, giving continuity of bloom and rich scent, but of a much less sophisticated style than the modern Hybrid tea roses.

After the Bourbon rose came yet another to mingle its characteristics with other roses. This was *R. gigantea* which, when crossed with *R. chinensis*, resulted in *R. × odorata*, the Tea rose.

The next step in the evolution of the rose was the Hybrid tea. In 1867 the French nurseryman Guillot produced the celebrated 'La France'. This was a silvery-pink rose with a delicious scent and with the high-pointed centre and reflexed, rolled-edged petals which are associated today with the Hybrid tea. It was also hardy and fairly continuous-flowering. 'La France' is generally accepted to have been a cross between a Tea and a Hybrid perpetual.

It was not for another 17 years, however, that the Hybrid teas became recognised as a new race and they did not begin to displace the Hybrid perpetuals and the Tea roses until the 20th century.

The arrival of the double-flowered form of *R. foetida* in 1838, known as 'Persian Yellow', was of great significance in the history of the modern rose. Used initially as a pollen parent with the Pernetiana and Tea groups, it is the source of yellow and yellow-orange bi-colours.

The first of these new hybrids, sent out in 1900, was the orange 'Soleil d'Or', raised by Pernet-Ducher, after whom the new race was popularly called the Pernetiana roses. Since then the Pernet and the Tea roses have been completely absorbed by the Hybrid teas.

Further developments led to the modern Hybrid teas, and these, together with the Floribundas, have influenced the Modern shrub roses, the Climbers and even the Miniatures.

In the descriptions that follow, roses have been divided into several categories according to their characteristics: Species roses; Old roses (these are sub-divided into 13 groups according to their parentage); Hybrid teas; Floribundas; Modern shrub roses; Climbers and Ramblers; and Miniatures.

Rosa spinosissima altaica

597

Species roses

Included here are wild roses from various parts of the world, as well as natural and man-made crosses between two species. They are the ancestors of the modern roses, and deserve a place in all gardens. They are distinguished by often being resistant to pests and diseases. Basically a Species rose has a single flower of five petals only, but some double forms occur as sports even in the wild, and numerous double or semi-double flowers have been selected for garden cultivation.

The species described here are those generally available and of garden value. The hybrids of the species are mainly grouped in the section headed OLD ROSES, but the lines of demarcation between true species and hybrids are not always clear.

All Species roses, unless otherwise stated, are hardy and deciduous; they have pinnate leaves bearing ovate leaflets that vary in number and in colour from mid to pale green. Several species are outstanding for their freely borne, red hips.

R. × alba ('White Rose of York'). Height and spread 6 ft or more. This species is thought to be an ancient hybrid of *R. gallica* and *R. canina* or one of its forms. It is a handsome shrub with grey-green foliage; sweetly scented, single or semi-double white flowers, 2–3 in. across, are borne in small clusters in June. In autumn, oblong, bright red hips are prominently displayed. It has given rise to a distinct group among the Old roses with blooms ranging from semi-double to very full and from pure white to carnation-pink.

R. banksiae (Banks's rose). Central and W. China. Height 20 ft; spread 8–10 ft. A vigorous, somewhat tender climber, suitable for a south wall. This species and its forms should be pruned only lightly. It bears clusters of 1 in. wide, sweetly scented, double white flowers during May and June. Red, globose, small hips follow the flowers. *R. b. lutescens* is a single yellow form of the ancestral *R. b. normalis*; 'Lutea' has double yellow blooms; *R. b. normalis* is the original single white species.

R. brunonii, syn. *R. moschata nepalensis* (summer-flowering musk rose). Himalayas. Height 10–15 ft. This climbing species is often erroneously listed as *R. moschata*. Fragrant, white, 1–2 in. wide flowers are freely borne in large trusses during June and July. They are followed by small, globular, red-brown hips.

R. californica. W. United States. Height 6–7 ft; spread 4–6 ft. A shrub with carmine-pink flowers, 1½ in. wide, carried in clusters in June and July. Globose red hips are borne in autumn. The variety 'Plena' has sweetly scented double flowers and is more showy than the species.

R. canina (dog rose). Europe, including Great Britain. Height 6–8 ft; spread 4–6 ft. This is the wild briar commonly seen in hedgerows in southern England. The species and its numerous forms are widely used as rootstock for modern roses. The single flowers, borne solitarily or in small clusters in June, are white to pale pink and up to 2 in. across; they are followed by glossy, red, urn or egg-shaped hips. The varieties are chiefly of botanical interest.

'Andersonii' is an outstanding hybrid, with larger and deeper-coloured flowers.

R. centifolia (cabbage rose, Provence rose). Height and spread 3–5 ft. This is an ancient, sterile garden descendant of *R. gallica.* It bears 3 in. wide, double, deeply fragrant and flat-topped, pink blooms in June and July. The species is a parent of numerous sports, or mutants, which include the following:

'Bullata', with leaves crisped like lettuce; 'Cristata' ('Chapeau de Napoleon') with moss-like, resin-scented glands on the exposed edges of the sepals.

'Muscosa' (moss rose) has similar, resin-scented glands covering the sepals and sometimes the stalks and leaves as well; 'Alba Muscosa' ('White Bath') is a white sport of 'Muscosa'. 'Parvifolia' ('Burgundy Rose') is a miniature form with dainty rose-pink blooms 1 in. across; 'Pomponia' ('De Meaux'), is a dwarf mutation with light pink blooms; 'Variegata' has petals striped pink and white.

R. chinensis, syn. *R. indica* (China rose). Central China. This climbing, single-flowered species is not in cultivation. The China roses of gardens are derived from crosses of *R. chinensis* and other species. Height and spread 3–4 ft or more. These compact shrubs flower from early summer until the first frosts. Ovoid scarlet hips are prominent on some in autumn.

'Minima', syn. 'Roulettii' (height 12 in.), with single or double pink or rose-red flowers, 1 in. across, is the parent of the Miniature roses. 'Old Blush' has loose pink flowers 2–2½ in. across; 'Semperflorens', syn. 'Slater's Crimson' has smaller deep crimson blooms. 'Viridiflora' (green rose) has purple-green scales replacing the petals.

R. damascena (damask rose). W. Asia. Height and spread up to 6 ft. A shrub bearing grey-green foliage and double flowers, often with an incurved centre or green eye. The 3 in. wide blooms, borne in June and July, are fragrant, pink in bud and fading to almost white.

'Semperflorens' ('Four Seasons') is a sport that flowers again in autumn; 'Trigintipetala', with red-pink flowers, is cultivated for rose oil (attar) in S.E. Europe. 'Versicolor' ('York and Lancaster') has untidy, semi-double blooms; these are pink, white or bi-coloured.

R. ecae. Afghanistan. Height 5 ft; spread 4 ft. This well-branched prickly shrub has pliant red stems with tiny leaves. Vivid buttercup-yellow, single flowers, 1–1¼ in. across, are borne in May and June; the orange-scarlet hips are rarely produced. It thrives in sheltered areas.

R. farreri. N.W. China. In cultivation this species is represented by the variety *R. f. persetosa* (Threepenny-bit rose). Height 6 ft; spread 8–10 ft. This is an attractive bristly shrub with arching branches. Single pink flowers, up to 1½ in. across, are carried in great profusion during May and June. Small red ovoid hips ripen in early autumn.

R. × felicita. This garden hybrid between *R. sempervirens* and *R. chinensis* is better known as 'Félicité et Perpétue'. Height up to 10 ft. It is a vigorous, sprawling, semi-evergreen rambler with double white flowers, 1 in. across; these are freely produced in large clusters in June. 'Little White Pet' is a dwarf sport.

Rosa × alba

Rosa californica 'Plena'

Rosa ecae

Rosa canina 'Andersonii'

Rosa damascena

Rosa × highdownensis

R. filipes. W. China. Height 30–40 ft. This is a rampant climber with grey-green foliage and 1 in. wide, single white flowers, borne in large corymbs in June and July. It bears ovoid to globose red hips. 'Kiftsgate' is an extremely vigorous climber suitable for covering banks or trees (see CLIMBERS AND RAMBLERS).

R. foetida (Austrian briar). W. Asia. Height and spread 5 ft. A suckering shrub with conspicuous, solitary, buttercup-yellow flowers, 2–2½ in. wide. These appear in May and June and have a strong scent. All modern bright yellow and bi-colour roses originate from this species which was introduced by hybridisation through the Pernetianas in 1900.

R. f. bicolor (Austrian copper) has single orange flowers, the upper sides of the petals being scarlet, the lower sides yellow. 'Persiana' ('Persian Yellow') has double yellow blooms.

R. gallica ('French Rose', 'Provins Rose'). S. Europe, W. Asia. Height and spread 3 ft. This suckering shrub bears three or five large, dark green leaflets. Solitary, showy, purple-pink flowers, 2–3 in. across, appear in June; they are followed by round red hips 1 in. wide.

This species is the principal wild parent of the old shrub roses; it sports freely and crosses readily with most other species. Numerous varieties have been selected for their partly or fully double flowers. The colours range from pink to deep purple, flushed blue as the flowers fade; bi-coloured, striped and spotted varieties are also available.

'Officinalis', syn. 'Apothecary's Rose' or 'Red Rose of Lancaster', has large, loose, semi-double, light crimson flowers. 'Versicolor', syn. 'Rosa Mundi', is a semi-double sport of 'Officinalis'; it is the showiest of all the striped roses, having crimson flowers streaked with white.

R. gigantea. Burma, S.W. China. Height 30 ft. A vigorous but not reliably hardy species, suitable for a south wall. It bears 4–5 in. wide cream-white flowers during May and June and occasionally orange-yellow globose hips. It is a parent of the Tea and Hybrid tea roses through *R. × odorata.*

R. × harisonii, syn. 'Harison's Yellow'. Height 6 ft; spread 3–4 ft. This hybrid between *R. foetida* and *R. spinosissima* is a trouble-free, early-flowering shrub. It has clear yellow, semi-double flowers, 2½ in. across, in May.

R. × highdownensis. Height and spread 10 ft. A vigorous hybrid of *R. moyesii* and closely resembling it in foliage and flower. Single, soft-crimson flowers, 2–2½ in. across, with prominent yellow stamens, are freely produced in June. They are followed by a splendid autumn display of flask-shaped, glossy red hips.

R. hugonis. Central China. Height 9 ft; spread 6 ft. This well-branched species is particularly suitable as a specimen shrub. Solitary yellow flowers, 2–2½ in. across, are freely borne in May or even earlier. Dark red round hips appear in late summer.

R. indica: see *R. chinensis*

R. × kordesii. Germany. Height 8–10 ft. An artificial tetraploid climbing species derived from crossing *R. rugosa* and *R. luciae*; it was introduced in the mid-20th century. It is the parent of the repeat-flowering Kordesii ramblers.

Rosa foetida bicolor

Rosa gallica 'Versicolor'

Rosa × harisonii

Rosa hugonis

Rosa moyesii

Rosa pomifera (fruits)

Rosa primula

Rosa moyesii (fruits)

Rosa × paulii

The dark green foliage is usually attractively glossy. Semi-double, cup-shaped, pink flowers, 2–2½ in. across, are borne in loose clusters from June to September.

R. longicuspis. Assam. Height 20–25 ft. A vigorous climbing species, suitable for growing up a tree. It bears glossy, mid-green, deeply toothed leaves. Masses of single white flowers, up to 2 in. across, open from May to July.

R. luciae (memorial rose). E. Asia. Height up to 12 ft. A semi-evergreen climber with handsome, glossy foliage. Prominent trusses of single white flowers, ¾–1¼ in. wide, are borne in July and August. *R. l. wichuraiana,* syn. *R. wichuraiana,* has 1¾ in. wide flowers; it is of prostrate habit, ideal as ground cover on banks. This variety is the parent of the Wichuraiana ramblers.

R. moschata (autumn musk rose). Height up to 12 ft; spread 6–8 ft. A lax shrub bearing small clusters of single, white, musk-scented, 2 in. wide flowers from August to October. Species that flower in June and July are probably correctly *R. brunonii.*

R. moyesii. W. China. Height up to 12 ft; spread 10 ft. This handsome specimen shrub has red, slightly prickly branches with dark green foliage. The pink to vivid blood-red single flowers, 2 in. or more across, are borne singly in June. Flask-shaped, glossy red hips, 2–2½ in. long, are prominently displayed in autumn.

'Fred Streeter' and 'Geranium' both have blood-red flowers; 'Geranium' is of compact habit and with larger hips than the species; it is suitable for a small garden.

R. multiflora, syn. *R. polyantha* (Polyantha rose). China and Japan. Height and spread 15 ft. A vigorous, arching or sprawling shrub, a parent of the garden Polyantha roses and an important rootstock. Single white flowers, ¾ in. wide, are freely borne in large clusters during June and July. Small bright red and round hips are produced on the branches in autumn.

Varieties include: 'Carnea', double pink; 'Cathayensis', single pink; 'Goldfinch', semi-double, richly fragrant, peach-yellow; 'Nana', compact and dwarf; 'Platyphylla' ('Seven Sisters'), double flowers opening rich purple and fading through pink to mauve-white; 'Watsoniana', smaller flowers and narrow, crimped foliage like a Japanese maple.

R. × noisettiana ('Blush Noisette'). Height and spread 10 ft. This hybrid between *R. moschata* and *R. chinensis* is a lax shrub or climber. Profuse clusters of white flushed pink, double, fragrant flowers, up to 1½ in. across, appear from June to October.

R. × odorata (Tea rose). This hybrid shrub between *R. gigantea* and *R. chinensis* is somewhat tender. It bears solitary, near double, fragrant, cream-white flushed pink flowers, 2–3 in. wide, from June to September. It is one of the parents of the modern Tea and Hybrid tea roses.

R. × paulii. Height 4 ft; spread 15 ft. This hybrid between *R. rugosa* and *R. arvensis* is a low-growing, thicket-forming, prickly shrub. It roots as it spreads and is valuable for ground cover on banks and over tree stumps; it may also be trained as a climber. White fragrant flowers, 2½ in. across and with crinkled petals, are borne in clusters throughout summer. 'Rosea' is pink.

R. pimpinellifolia: see *R. spinosissima*

R. polyantha: see *R. multiflora*

R. pomifera, syn. *R. villosa* (apple rose). Height and spread 7 ft. This species closely resembles *R. canina* in habit. The grey-green foliage is resin-scented and the solitary flowers, up to 2½ in. across, are pale pink. Conspicuous, dark red, ovoid hips are densely covered with bristly hairs. 'Duplex' (Wolley-Dod's rose) is a double, red-purple garden hybrid.

R. primula. Turkestan to N. China. Height and spread 8 ft. An upright shrub with glabrous, double-toothed foliage that is aromatic when crushed. Pale yellow, fragrant, 1½ in. wide

Rosa rubrifolia

Rosa rugosa 'Plena'

Rosa rugosa 'Frau Dagmar Hastrup' (fruits)

flowers are borne singly in May; the scent is more heavy on warm evenings or after rain.

R. rubiginosa (sweetbriar or eglantine). Europe, including Great Britain. Height and spread 8 ft. This species is similar to *R. canina*, but the leaves are covered with glands that emit a sweet, pungent fragrance. Few-flowered clusters of bright-pink, 1½ in. wide, single flowers in June are followed by conspicuous orange-scarlet hips. It is particularly suitable for a dense hedge.

R. rubrifolia. Central and S. Europe. Height 7 ft; spread 5 ft. This species is related to *R. canina*, but has glaucous-purple stems and grey-purple leaves. The red-purple, 1½ in. wide, single flowers are borne in small clusters in June.

R. rugosa. E. Asia. Height 7 ft; spread 4 ft. A sturdy shrub with prickly, hairy branches and wrinkled foliage that is glossy above, downy beneath. The solitary, deep pink, heavily scented flowers, up to 3 in. across, appear in June and intermittently until autumn; they are succeeded by round orange-red hips in early autumn.

It is useful for hedging and for a wild garden, and has given rise to numerous named varieties and hybrids. 'Hollandica' is used as rootstock for standard roses, commonly sold as *R. rugosa*.

R. r. 'Alba', single white flowers; 'Plena' ('Roseraie de l'Hay'), large double, crimson-mauve flowers; *R. r.* 'Frau Dagmar Hastrup', single, delicate carnation-pink; *R. r.* 'Rubra', large single, magenta-purple; and *R. r.* 'Scabrosa', large single, rose-magenta flowers.

R. sericea. Himalayas, W. China. Height 9 ft; spread 4–5 ft. An erect shrub with leaves having 7–17 narrow leaflets. Four-petalled, 1–2 in. wide, cream-white, single flowers are carried in May. They are usually followed by small red or yellow pear-shaped hips. Varieties include *R. s. omeiensis*, with tapering hips; *R. s. polyphylla*, with numerous leaflets; and *R. s. pteracantha*, with thin, wing-like prickles, which glow mahogany-red on the young growths.

R. spinosissima, syn. *R. pimpinellifolia* (Scotch rose, burnet rose). Europe, including Great Britain; W. Asia. Height 1–3 ft; spread 2–4 ft. This is a low-growing, thicket-forming shrub. The prickly branches, densely covered with bristles, bear fern-like foliage. Solitary, cream-white flowers, 1–1½ in. across, appear in May and June; the hips are round and black-purple.

The species is variable, with numerous wild variants; some of these are in cultivation and known collectively as the Scotch roses (see OLD ROSES). They are selected for their taller habit and larger, often double flowers, ranging in colour from cream to pink. The bright-yellow Scotch roses are probably hybrids between this species and the rich yellow *R. foetida*.

R. s. altaica is a tall variety with larger, cream-yellow flowers; 'Andrewsii' has semi-double, cupped, pink flowers. *R. s. bicolor* 'Grahamstown' and 'Staffa' are similar to the species, but the cream-white flowers are splashed with pink. *R. s. hispida* has large sulphur-yellow blooms.

R. s. lutea and *R. s. lutea* 'Plena' have single and double yellow flowers respectively; 'Nana' has small, near-double, white flowers; and *R. s. rosea* has single pale pink flowers.

R. villosa: see *R. pomifera*

R. wichuraiana: see *R. luciae*

R. willmottiae. W. China. Height 6–9 ft; spread 9 ft. An arching shrub with purple branches; it is suitable as a specimen. Solitary rose-purple flowers, 1–1½ in. across, are produced in May and June.

R. xanthina. N. China, Korea. Height and spread 6 ft. This species is similar to *R. hugonis*, having brown stems with triangular prickles. Bright yellow, semi-double flowers, 1¾ in. across, are borne profusely in May and June. The wild species is the single-flowered *R. × spontanea*, which is represented in cultivation by 'Canary Bird' with clear yellow flowers.

Rosa willmottiae

Rosa xanthina 'Canary Bird'

Old roses

This section includes those deciduous shrubs that arose as sports or hybrids of the rose species and were much cultivated before the introduction of Hybrid tea roses. For ease of reference these shrub roses are here divided into 13 sub-sections, according to their parentage where known. A precise classification is difficult due to much inter-breeding; the descriptions also include a few varieties which are not correctly Old roses, but have the same characteristics.

Conversely, certain hybrids of the Musk and Scotch roses are included among the Modern shrub roses, to which they have a closer affinity.

These shrubs are valuable garden plants in shrubberies or as specimens. While the flowering season is generally shorter than that of the Modern shrub roses, the flowers are outstanding for their rich fragrance.

Several of the varieties listed have flowers described as quartered. This means that the flattened centre of each flower is composed of densely crowded petals, roughly arranged in four groups.

ALBAS These vigorous, erect shrubs all derive from *R. alba.* They are extremely hardy, having strong stems with few prickles. The pinnate leaves, composed of five or seven ovate, finely toothed leaflets, are generally grey-green. The clear white to pink flowers, up to 3 in. across, are sweetly scented and borne in profusion during late June and July. Alba roses thrive in most soils and under adverse conditions, and many are suitable for training against trelliswork or as espaliers. Recommended varieties include:

'Céleste', syn. *R. alba incarnata.* Height 6 ft; spread 4 ft. Semi-double, soft pink flowers.

'Félicité Parmentier'. Height 4 ft; spread 3 ft. Pale yellow buds open to blush-pink, fully double, rosette-like blooms.

'Königin von Dänemark'. Height 5 ft; spread 4 ft. Quartered, tightly packed, well-shaped blooms of pink deepening towards the centre.

'Maiden's Blush'. Height 5 ft; spread 4 ft. Exquisitely scented, blush-pink, full-petalled flowers with paler pink margins.

BOURBONS These hardy vigorous shrubs are descendants of *R. × odorata* and *R. damascena.* They are of open habit and generally bear bright to dark green glossy leaves composed of five ovate, slightly toothed leaflets. The densely petalled blooms are incurved, globular or cup-shaped, and richly scented. They measure 3 in. across; the season for these perpetually flowering shrubs begins in June and extends until the first autumn frosts.

The following are outstanding:

'Boule de Neige'. Height 6 ft; spread 4 ft. Crimson buds open to perfect, double white, deeply scented globular flowers.

'Bourbon Queen'. Height 6 ft; spread 5 ft. This is an old cottage favourite, flowering mainly in June. The graceful stems carry a profusion of crimped, double, cup-shaped flowers that are pink and magenta. It may reach 10 ft on a wall.

'Fantin Latour'. Height and spread 5 ft. Cup-shaped, warm pink, double flowers appear over a short period in mid-summer.

Rosa 'Céleste' (Alba)

Rosa 'Königin von Dänemark' (Alba)

Rosa 'Maiden's Blush' (Alba)

Rosa 'Fantin Latour' (Bourbon)

'La Reine Victoria'. Height 6 ft; spread 4 ft. Deep pink, intensely fragrant, double blooms appear over a long season. The shell-like petals are arranged in a circle, giving a cup-like effect.

'Mme Isaac Pereire'. Height 7 ft; spread 5 ft. This is perhaps the most fragrant of all roses. It has large, quartered, deep pink blooms, tightly packed with petals. Ideal for training over walls, pillars and fences where it may reach 15 ft.

'Mme Pierre Oger'. Height 6 ft; spread 3 ft. A double blush-pink sport of 'La Reine Victoria'.

'Souvenir de la Malmaison'. Height 4 ft; spread 3 ft. Full buds open to produce flat, flesh-pink quartered flowers. A climbing form is available which may reach a height of 10–15 ft with a spread of 8 ft. The flowers are larger, but produced less freely.

'Variegata di Bologna'. Height 8 ft; spread 5 ft. The thin stems of this variety need tying to supports. The globular blooms are quartered and deeply packed, and in contrasting stripes of white and deep crimson. It is prone to black spot.

'Zéphirine Drouhin': see CLIMBERS AND RAMBLERS

CABBAGE ROSES: see PROVENCE ROSES

DAMASKS A group of hardy shrub roses, originating from *R. damascena.* They are of lax and open habit, having bristly and thorny stems with small, rounded, downy grey-green leaves. The weak pedicels usually bear double 3 in. wide flowers in June and July. The fragrant flowers are borne in loose clusters that are generally short-lived. Most of these shrubs have long slender and hairy hips in late summer.

'Blush Damask'. Height and spread 6 ft. This dense shrub is ideal for hedging or a shrub border. It bears a profusion of nodding, short-lived blooms in June. The flowers are fully double, reflexing into a ball, and deep mauve-pink with paler edges to the petals.

'Celsiana'. Height 5 ft; spread 4 ft. A vigorous grower producing an abundance of loose, semi-double, bright pink flowers with conspicuous yellow stamens.

'Mme Hardy'. Height 6 ft; spread 5 ft. This variety is thought by some authorities to be a hybrid of *R. centifolia.* It has broad mid-green leaves, and bears large clusters of exquisitely formed, pure white flowers. These are faintly blush-tinted in bud, opening to flat, full quartered blooms with small green centres.

'Petite Lisette'. Height 3 ft; spread 24 in. A low-growing shrub with blush-pink rosetted flowers. The blooms are flat with folded petals and button eyes.

DWARF POLYANTHAS These hardy shrubs are the progeny of *R. multiflora* crossed with China tea and Noisette roses. They were selected for their dwarf habit and profusion of small blooms. The slender hairy stems bear mid-green downy leaves composed of seven to nine ovate leaflets. The pompon-shaped flowers, 1–2 in. across, open flat. They are produced in large clusters in June and July and usually again in September.

'Cécile Brunner'. Height and spread 24 in. The flowers are pale yellow shaded with rose-pink, darker in the centre. It needs a sunny position. This variety has produced a vigorous climbing sport which may grow to 10 ft high.

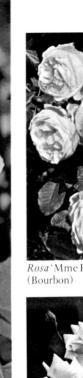

Rosa 'Mme Pierre Oger' (Bourbon)

Rosa 'Cécile Brunner' (Dwarf polyantha)

Rosa 'Boule de Neige' (Bourbon)

Rosa 'Mme Hardy' (Damask)

Rosa 'La Reine Victoria' (Bourbon)

Rosa 'Complicata' (Gallica)

Rosa 'Surpasse Tout' (Gallica)

Rosa 'Du Maître d'École' (Gallica)

Rosa 'Cardinal Richelieu' (Gallica)

ROSA GALLICA

'Paul Crampel'. Height and spread 24 in. Semi-double rosette-like flowers of orange-red.

'Perle d'Or'. Height and spread up to 3 ft. A robust shrub with rich yellow blooms borne in dense clusters.

GALLICAS This is the largest group of the Old shrub roses and closest in appearance to the wild *R. gallica*. They thrive on poor soil, but will not tolerate shade. They are hardy and compact shrubs with few thorns, and bear dark-green leaves of three or five pointed and toothed leaflets. The solitary flowers, varying in colour from pink to crimson and mauve, are borne in late June and July on stiff stems. They are double, richly scented and 2–3 in. across.

Outstanding varieties include the following, some of which are suitable for hedging.

'Belle de Crécy'. Height 4 ft; spread 3 ft. A variety of lax habit, usually needing support. It bears fragrant, fully double, purple-red blooms maturing to violet with a green button centre.

'Camaieux'. Height 3 ft; spread 24 in. An arching shrub with sage-green leaves; the semi-double flowers, with loose deep crimson-purple petals, are splashed and striped with white.

'Cardinal Richelieu'. Height and spread 4 ft. The fully double, pale pink blooms become deep violet-purple. A good hedging variety.

'Charles de Mills'. Height and spread 4 ft. Densely petalled, rich maroon flowers open flat; they shade to violet-purple. This makes a good dense hedge.

'Complicata'. Height 5 ft; spread 8 ft. A garden hybrid of *R. gallica*, with long arching shoots. It is suitable as a low climber or as a wide spreading specimen shrub. The single, brilliant pink flowers, 3–4 in. across, have a white centre; they are borne during June and July in small clusters along the entire length of the previous season's shoots.

'Duc de Guiche'. Height and spread 4 ft. Full double crimson flowers, splashed with purple and having green centres, open out flat. Excellent for hedging.

'Du Maître d'École'. Height and spread 8 ft. An arching variety bearing heavy, large double blooms that are magenta-pink, changing to lilac and mauve.

'Francofurtana'. Height and spread 3 ft. A vigorous grower, with rose-crimson, double, loose, cup-shaped flowers, fading to cerise pink. The blooms have little scent.

Rosa 'Belle de Crécy' (Gallica)

Rosa 'Buff Beauty' (Hybrid musk)

Rosa 'Charles de Mills' (Gallica)

Rosa 'Tuscany Superb' (Gallica)

Rosa 'Ballerina' (Hybrid musk)

'Old Velvet': see 'Tuscany'

'**Président de Sèze**'. Height 3½ ft; spread 4 ft. Double, rich maroon flowers, changing to purple. A good hedging variety.

'**Sissinghurst Castle**'. Height and spread 3 ft. Semi-double, maroon-purple blooms.

'**Surpasse Tout**'. Height and spread 4–5 ft. A vigorous grower with semi-double rose-crimson flowers. Suitable for hedging.

'**Tuscany**'. Height 4 ft; spread 3 ft. Small, semi-double flowers of rich purple, streaked with white on some of the inner petals, are freely borne. It is also known as 'Old Velvet'.

'**Tuscany Superb**'. Height 4 ft; spread 24 in. This is more vigorous than 'Tuscany' and has larger flowers and broader leaves. The double purple blooms open flat and lack the streaks.

HYBRID MUSKS These hardy, perpetually flowering shrub roses are derived from *R. moschata*. They are of lax, arching habit with sparsely prickly stems bearing five to seven ovate leaflets, dark green above, grey-green below. The 2 in. wide scented flowers are borne in large clusters from August until the first frosts. Colours include shades of pink, mauve-crimson, deep crimson-scarlet, soft yellow and pure white.

A few hybrid musks differing from the old types are included under MODERN SHRUB ROSES.

'**Ballerina**'. Height and spread 4 ft. Large sprays of pale pink flowers resembling apple-blossom.

'**Bonn**'. Height 5–6 ft; spread 4 ft. Clusters of slightly fragrant, orange-scarlet flowers.

'**Buff Beauty**'. Height and spread 6 ft. Double, full-petalled, tea-scented blooms of warm apricot are borne on dark green stems.

'**Cornelia**'. Height 5 ft; spread 7 ft. A variety with coppery-apricot, richly scented, double flowers borne in large trusses. It blooms almost continuously and is ideal for cutting.

'**Felicia**'. Height and spread 4½ ft. Clusters of silvery, salmon-pink and deeply fragrant double flowers are freely borne.

'**Pax**'. Height and spread 6 ft. This is the tallest shrub in the group and may reach 10 ft; it produces a continuous mass of semi-double, cream-white, sweetly scented flowers.

'**Penelope**'. Height and spread 5 ft. A vigorous variety with strong, branching shoots and broad, glossy foliage. It flowers freely and continuously, producing semi-double, musk-scented blooms of pink, flushed apricot, fading to pale yellow or cream-white.

HYBRID PERPETUALS These hardy roses were extremely popular in Victorian times, being descendants of the Portland, Bourbon and China roses and predecessors of the Hybrid teas, which have almost entirely displaced them. They are less perpetual than the modern Hybrid tea roses, but many are of great beauty, and a few are still in general cultivation. They are vigorous shrubs of upright habit and suitable for training against

Rosa 'Cornelia' (Hybrid musk)

Rosa 'Baroness Rothschild' (Hybrid perpetual)

Rosa 'Blanc Double de Coubert' (Hybrid rugosa)

Rosa 'Pink Grootendoorst' (Hybrid rugosa)

Rosa 'Sarah Van Fleet' (Hybrid rugosa)

walls. The mid to dark green leaves are composed of five ovate, toothed leaflets. Cabbage-like, rounded double flowers, 3–4 in. across, open flat. They are borne singly or in small clusters and appear from June to October.

'Baroness Rothschild'. Height up to 4 ft; spread 3 ft. An upright shrub with full, cupped flowers of rose-pink to white.

'Frau Karl Druschki'. Height 5 ft; spread 4 ft. This is a vigorous grower with pure white, double, scentless blooms, the buds tinted pink. If lightly pruned and the growths pinned down it flowers profusely. It makes a good standard.

'Général Jacqueminot'. Height 4 ft; spread 3 ft. Deep crimson, double, heavily fragrant and well-filled blooms.

'Mrs John Laing'. Height 5 ft; spread 3 ft. An upright grower with double, sweetly scented blooms of soft pink, borne on stiff stalks.

'Reine des Violettes'. Height 6 ft; spread 5 ft. Double mauve-purple flowers, opening flat, contrast well with the grey-tinged foliage. This variety should be pruned hard in February.

'Roger Lambelin'. Height 4 ft; spread 3 ft. Rich crimson-purple, velvety and fragrant double flowers, often with white margins to the petals.

HYBRID RUGOSAS Some of the best varieties of *R. rugosa* have been described under that species, and the following are hybrids of *R. rugosa* with other species or garden hybrids. The habit of these hardy shrubs varies, but most are vigorous, with prickly branches, bearing matt, mid-green leaves of five to seven leaflets. The shrubs are sometimes repeat-flowering and the flowers are generally heavily scented. They are

bowl-shaped, 3–4 in. wide, and open flat in small clusters during June and July and sporadically until September. Crimson-scarlet spherical, somewhat flattened hips, about 1 in. across, are displayed in autumn on fertile forms.

'Agnes'. Height 6 ft; spread 4 ft. This hybrid has fully double, pompon-shaped, rich yellow and fragrant flowers; these are borne in profusion.

'Blanc Double de Coubert'. Height up to 6 ft; spread 4 ft. A perpetually flowering hybrid with semi-double pure white flowers. Suitable as a hedging plant.

'F. J. Grootendoorst'. Height and spread 6 ft. Small double, crimson flowers with fringed petals are borne in clusters. 'Pink Grootendoorst' is a pink sport; neither has much scent.

'Sarah Van Fleet'. Height 8 ft; spread 5 ft. A sturdy, bushy, thorny shrub bearing an abundance of foliage. It is very free-flowering, producing masses of richly scented, semi-double, mallow-pink flowers until late summer.

'Schneezwerg' ('Snow Dwarf'). Height and spread 5 ft. This remontant-flowering hybrid produces flat and semi-double, snow-white, anemone-like blooms.

HYBRID SWEETBRIARS These shrubs, equally attractive in flower and fruit, are also known as Penzance Briars, having been raised by Lord Penzance at the end of the 19th century. They are hardy, vigorous shrubs bearing aromatic foliage composed of bright green leaves with five to seven leaflets. Hybrid sweetbriars are free-flowering shrubs, but often prone to mildew. The five-petalled, often semi-double saucer-shaped flowers, 1½ in. across, are richly scented

Rosa 'Nuits de Young' (Moss)

Rosa 'Mme de la Roche-Lambert' (Moss)

Rosa 'Salet' (Moss)

they are borne in abundance in small clusters during June and July. In autumn, the bushes are sometimes laden with shiny crimson-scarlet hips which often last well into winter. The following, which reach an average height and spread of 6 ft, are excellent for tall hedges.

'**Amy Robsart**'. Rich rose-pink, semi-double flowers.

'**Janet's Pride**'. Wide, almost single blooms that are bright cerise with a pale centre.

'**Lady Penzance**'. Single flowers with rich coppery-yellow tints.

'**Lord Penzance**'. This shrub bears buff flowers, flushed pink.

'**Meg Merrilees**'. Single, crimson flowers.

MOSS ROSES These hardy shrub roses are closely allied to the PROVENCE or CABBAGE ROSES, but differ in having the stems, branches and petioles densely covered with bristles; the backs and edges of the sepals are covered with resin-scented mossy glands. All Moss roses are sports of *R. centifolia* 'Muscosa' or hybrids derived from these sports. The deeply fragrant flowers, 3 in. across, are double or semi-double and borne singly or in groups of two or three in June and July. The shrubs range in size from dwarf varieties to tall pillar roses. The mossy glands are less prominent in the hybrids.

'**Alfred de Dalmas**': see 'Mousseline'

'**Capitaine John Ingram**'. Height 5 ft; spread 4 ft. A compact free-flowering bush with double, crimson-maroon, mottled flowers.

'**Comtesse de Murinais**'. Height 6 ft; spread 4 ft. A vigorous grower with blush-white flowers that later become pure white with a green eye.

'**Général Kléber**'. Height 5 ft; spread 4 ft. A vigorous shrub densely covered with moss. It has fully double blooms of earnation-pink.

'**Gloire de Mousseux**'. Height 4 ft; spread 3 ft. This sturdy shrub has light green leaves and full-petalled flowers, up to 5 in. across, lilac-pink fading to pale pink.

'**Henri Martin**'. Height 5 ft; spread 4 ft. A graceful shrub with dainty foliage scantily clad with moss. The semi-double flowers are vivid crimson with white midribs to the petals.

'**Mme de la Roche-Lambert**'. Height and spread 4 ft. This variety has brown moss on the stems; the semi-double vivid rose-purple flowers appear intermittently until autumn.

'**Mousseline**'. Height and spread 4 ft. This variety, which is sometimes listed as 'Alfred de Dalmas', makes a compact bush. The small flowers are full-petalled, and palest pink.

'**Nuits de Young**'. Height 5 ft; spread 3 ft. A slender wiry bush with dark moss. The velvety double flowers are deep maroon-purple, with prominent golden-yellow stamens.

'**Réné d'Anjou**'. Height 5 ft; spread 3 ft. A variety with bronze-coloured young leaves and brown-green moss. The soft pink, double flowers change to lilac-pink.

'**Salet**'. Height 4 ft; spread 3 ft. This variety flowers almost continuously during summer. The bright pink, full-petalled blooms, with few stamens, turn pale purple.

'**William Lobb**'. Height and spread 6 ft. This heavily mossed shrub is best trained up a pillar or wall. It produces large clusters of purple-magenta double flowers fading to lavender.

Rosa 'Henri Martin' (Moss)

Rosa 'Comte de Chambord'
(Portland)

Rosa 'Jacques Cartier'
(Portland)

Rosa 'Robert le Diable'
(Provence)

Rosa 'Stanwell Perpetual'
(Scotch)

Rosa 'Duc de Fitzjames' (Provence)

PORTLAND ROSES These are predecessors of
the Bourbons and Hybrid perpetuals and are
among the earliest surviving roses showing the
influence of *R. chinensis*. They are hardy, compact and often suckering shrubs bearing pale
green leaves of five to seven pointed leaflets. The
Damask-type flowers, 2–3 in. wide, are borne
singly or in small clusters. The main flowering is
in June and July, but flowers are produced
intermittently until the autumn.

'Comte de Chambord'. Height 4 ft; spread 3 ft.
An erect shrub which flowers almost continuously. The buds of rolled petals open to densely
filled flat flowers of rich pink with lilac tones;
they are heavily fragrant.

'Jacques Cartier'. Height 4 ft; spread 3 ft. This
vigorous grower flowers intermittently throughout summer. The full, quartered flowers are deep
pink with a green centre.

'Portland'. Height and spread 24 in. Semi-
double, cupped and bright crimson flowers open
in June and July and again in autumn.

PROVENCE or CABBAGE ROSES These hardy
shrub roses are all descended from *R. centifolia*,
but are generally of more compact habit. Most of
them need the support of stout stakes to prevent
the floppy branches from drooping. The thorny
stems bear pale to mid-green leaves with five to
seven ovate leaflets. The fragrant double flowers
measure about 2 in. across. They are borne in
clusters during June and July.

'Duc de Fitzjames'. Height 6 ft; spread 5 ft.
Clusters of semi-double, deep pink to purple
flowers, with green centres, fade to soft lilac.

'Petite de Hollande'. Height 4 ft; spread 3 ft.
This compact variety is suitable for a small
garden. It is a miniature form in all respects
with coarsely toothed leaves and pink flowers.

'Robert le Diable'. Height 4 ft; spread 3 ft. A
late-flowering variety with full-petalled, green-
centred flowers, deep pink to purple.

'Tour de Malakoff'. Height 6 ft; spread 5 ft. This
vigorous shrub is best trained as a pillar rose.
The large, loosely double flowers are predominantly purple-magenta on opening, later fading
to lavender and grey.

SCOTCH ROSES These hardy roses are vigorous suckering derivatives of *R. spinosissima*;
they spread quickly, particularly on light soils.
The branches bear straight bristles and small
pinnate leaves composed of 7–11 grey-green
leaflets. Saucer-shaped fragrant flowers, 1–1½ in.
across, are borne singly or in small clusters from
May to July.

The Scotch roses have produced several
shrub hybrids, such as 'Frühlingsgold' and
'Frühlingsmorgen' (see MODERN SHRUB ROSES).

'Falkland'. Height and spread 4 ft. Pale pink,
semi-double flowers, the base of the petals
tinted yellow.

'Stanwell Perpetual'. Height and spread 4 ft.
This is a hybrid between *R. spinosissima* and *R.
damascena*. It is a lax shrub with remontant,
flatly semi-double and fragrant flowers of blush-
pink fading to white.

'William III'. Height and spread 24 in. The
semi-double velvety flowers are brilliant maroon
with a pale lilac-tinted reverse to the petals.

Rosa 'Blue Moon' (Hybrid tea)

Rosa 'Bonsoir' (Hybrid tea)

Rosa 'Chicago Peace' (Hybrid tea)

Hybrid tea roses

These roses are the successors to the Hybrid perpetuals (see OLD ROSES). With their freely produced flowers and long flowering season from June to October, they are possibly the best-loved roses, equal in popularity with the Floribundas and the Modern shrub roses. They are excellent as cut flowers.

Hybrid tea roses thrive in sun or partial shade and in well-drained fertile soil, including acid; chalk soils should be enriched with well-rotted compost or manure. Most are prone to pests and diseases and must be protected against these.

They are hardy, deciduous shrubs with strong, sparsely or very prickly stems. The foliage, composed of seven ovate leaflets, is matt or glossy, mid to deep green and sometimes flushed with red, particularly when young. The flowers are generally double, although single forms exist; bowl-shaped flowers open from shapely conical buds, and measure 4–6 in. across. Some of the old varieties and a few of the more recent introductions are richly scented.

Several varieties, especially those with large, densely petalled blooms, are often damaged by heavy and prolonged rain, while others become full-blown and short-lived if exposed to continuous sun. Yellow varieties may fade in strong sun, but varieties such as 'Buccaneer', 'Diorama' and 'King's Ransom' preserve their colours.

Some rose growers maintain that Hybrid tea roses do best when confined to a bed of their

Rosa 'Diorama' (Hybrid tea)

Rosa 'Duke of Windsor' (Hybrid tea)

Rosa 'Brasilia' (Hybrid tea)

611

Rosa 'Eden Rose' (Hybrid tea)

Rosa 'Fragrant Cloud'
(Hybrid tea)

Rosa 'Elizabeth Harkness'
(Hybrid tea)

Rosa 'Gavotte' (Hybrid tea)

Rosa 'Ena Harkness' (Hybrid tea)

Rosa 'Ernest H. Morse'
(Hybrid tea)

Rosa 'Fred Gibson'
(Hybrid tea)

own, where border plants do not detract from their beauty. However, underplanting with bedding plants or ground cover, particularly under standards, makes a pleasing display.

Where several varieties are to be grown in the same bed, these should have the same degree of vigour. With annual hard pruning, most Hybrid teas grow to a height of 2–4 ft, but some, such as 'Josephine Bruce', of low and sprawling habit, seldom exceed 24 in.; and others, such as 'Sutter's Gold', may reach 5 ft or more. Vigorous growers, such as 'Peace', when only lightly pruned may easily reach a height of 6 ft. Planting distances vary according to vigour, but a good average is 24 in.

Where possible avoid planting these roses in sites exposed to the prevailing wind; standards, especially, are damaged by high winds. The positions should be open and away from high trees or walls.

Numerous named Hybrid tea roses include the following varieties:

'Alec's Red'. A rose of erect habit, with full-petalled, brilliant red, fragrant flowers.

'Birmingham Post'. The large flowers are pale pink with a deeper reverse to the petals.

'Blue Moon'. Silvery-lilac blooms which are fully petalled and fragrant. It is prone to rust.

'Bonsoir'. A rose with handsome, glossy dark green foliage. The fragrant, peach-pink flowers are damaged by prolonged rain.

'Brasilia'. A weather-resistant rose with light scarlet flowers, the petals being pale gold on the reverse. The shapely buds open to loose flowers.

'Brilliant'. A variety with fragrant, rich scarlet blooms freely produced. It is prone to mildew.

'Buccaneer'. A vigorous grower, resistant to rain and sun, and sometimes reaching 6 ft in height. The non-fading, rich yellow, slightly fragrant flowers are borne in clusters.

'Chicago Peace'. A sport of 'Peace' with large, full, phlox-pink blooms with a yellow base. Occasionally the flowers revert partly to the yellow parent.

'Colour Wonder'. A dwarf rose with slightly fragrant flowers that are orange-salmon, with deep yellow reverse and some fragrance. They are freely produced and composed of numerous small petals.

'Diorama'. A variety with large, high-pointed and fragrant flowers of apricot-yellow with a pink flush. They open quickly from the bud stage. This variety is prone to black spot.

'Duke of Windsor'. A rose with large, full flowers which are borne several together in clusters; they are bright orange and fragrant, but often of loose shape and easily damaged by heavy rain. It is prone to mildew.

'Eden Rose'. This fragrant variety opens quickly from well-shaped buds to reveal the deep pink petals with a lighter reverse. It requires only light pruning and is susceptible to mildew.

'Elizabeth Harkness'. An early-flowering rose with cream to buff, pink-tinged, fragrant flowers.

'Ena Harkness'. A rose with fragrant bright crimson-scarlet flowers of a velvety texture. The flower stems are weak, causing the blooms to droop, but this may be overcome by feeding.

'Ernest H. Morse'. A variety with rich turkey-red, well-shaped and fragrant flowers.

'Fragrant Cloud'. This is a variety in which the large, shapely flowers are dusky red in bud,

Rosa 'Gail Borden' (Hybrid tea)

Rosa 'Grand'mère Jenny' (Hybrid tea)

Rosa 'Guinevère' (Hybrid tea)

Rosa 'King's Ransom' (Hybrid tea)

Rosa 'Gold Crown' (Hybrid tea)

Rosa 'Grandpa Dickson' (Hybrid tea)

Rosa 'Josephine Bruce' (Hybrid tea)

Rosa 'Message' (Hybrid tea)

Rosa 'Mischief' (Hybrid tea)

Rosa 'My Choice' (Hybrid tea)

opening to coral-salmon, but fading as they age. Autumn flowers have an exceptionally strong fragrance. It is susceptible to black spot.

'Fred Gibson'. A vigorous rose with full flowers that are amber-yellow to apricot and are borne singly on long stems in the first flush and in clusters later.

'Gail Borden'. A variety with large, deep rose-pink blooms that have cream-yellow shading on the reverse; they are freely produced.

'Gavotte'. A vigorous grower of spreading habit. The large, silvery-pink flowers are freely produced, but often damaged by rain.

'Gold Crown'. Slightly fragrant deep yellow blooms, sometimes tinted red on the outer petals, are freely produced, particularly in the autumn. They are borne singly on tall, lanky growths and often develop with split centres.

'Golden Melody'. A rose that generally grows to a height of 2½ ft. The perfectly formed, richly scented flowers are cream with buff-yellow and pink shading. It is prone to mildew.

'Grand'mère Jenny'. This variety bears long-pointed buds that open to large fragrant blooms of peach-pink and honey-yellow. Susceptible to black spot.

'Grandpa Dickson'. This is a tall, upright grower with densely thorny stems. The large, full-petalled, cream-yellow flowers become pink-edged as they age.

'Guinevère'. A vigorous shrub, with full-petalled pink flowers, carried erect.

'Isabel de Ortiz'. A variety bearing large, well-shaped, deep pink flowers with a silver reverse.

'Josephine Bruce'. This is a spreading variety with faintly scented flowers that are deep

velvety crimson-scarlet, flushed with black. This rose should be pruned to inward-pointing eyes to prevent the stems flopping. It is prone to mildew; the blooms are damaged by rain.

'King's Ransom'. A rose with freely produced, erectly borne, fragrant and pure rich yellow flowers.

'Lady Sylvia'. This is a sport of 'Mme Butterfly'. The flowers are borne in almost Floribunda profusion and need disbudding to produce cut flowers. They are fragrant and light rose-pink, shading to pale apricot-yellow at the base.

'Message'. The freely borne white flowers, faintly tinged with green, are damaged by rain. Susceptible to mildew.

'Michèle Meilland'. This rose has well-shaped small flowers in a blend of pearly pink and amber, flushed salmon at the centre. The blooms, on wiry stems, are excellent for cutting.

'Mischief'. A well-branched rose with shapely coral-salmon and fragrant flowers, freely produced. It is susceptible to rust.

'Mme Butterfly'. This is a sport of 'Ophelia', which it resembles, but the fragrant flowers are pale pink with traces of apricot, shading to yellow at the base; they are borne profusely. Thrips may be troublesome.

'Mme Louis Laperrière'. This early and free-flowering rose produces well-formed, full-petalled and fragrant, deep crimson flowers.

'Mullard Jubilee'. This compact bushy variety bears large full flowers; they are pink, deeply fragrant and carried in clusters.

'My Choice'. This is a tall, branching grower. The high-centred, shapely and deeply fragrant blooms are pink with a pale yellow reverse.

Rosa 'Pink Favourite' (Hybrid tea)

Rosa 'Sutter's Gold' (Hybrid tea)

Rosa 'Peace' (Hybrid tea)

Rosa 'Peer Gynt' (Hybrid tea)

Rosa 'Super Star' (Hybrid tea)

Rosa 'Stella' (Hybrid tea)

Rosa 'Piccadilly' (Hybrid tea)

'National Trust'. An erect shrub bearing full-petalled, dark crimson flowers.

'Ophelia'. A variety reaching a height of $2\frac{1}{2}$ ft. The rather small, pointed buds on long stems open to fragrant, pale silvery-pink flowers, shading to yellow. The buds may be attacked by thrips in early summer.

'Pascali'. This is a tall upright grower with freely produced white flowers. These are easily damaged by rain.

'Peace'. This outstanding variety is a vigorous grower, tall and branching with dark green glossy foliage. The large, full blooms are pale yellow, sometimes deeper in autumn, with cerise-pink edges to the petals. It is generally best if only lightly pruned.

'Peer Gynt'. A compact rose with full, canary-yellow flowers.

'Piccadilly'. A tall-growing extremely reliable variety. The slightly fragrant flowers are moderately full, scarlet shaded yellow towards the base, with a pale yellow reverse.

'Pink Favourite'. This has large, well-formed blooms in shades of rose-pink.

'Prima Ballerina'. This vigorous, erect and slender shrub has heavily scented flowers which are deep pink and open quickly from the buds.

'Red Lion'. The full cerise-pink blooms are long-lasting and fragrant.

'Red Planet'. Slightly fragrant, crimson, full-petalled flowers are usually borne singly.

'Rose Gaujard'. This rose is a vigorous, tall-branching and disease-resistant grower. It is free-flowering with singly borne, pink flowers, with carmine veins and a silvery reverse.

'Royal Highness'. A blush-pink, scented and full-petalled rose. The flowers may be damaged by prolonged rain.

'Shot Silk'. A variety in which the flowers are richly fragrant, in shades of orange, carmine, pink and yellow. It grows to a height of 24 in.

'Stella'. This weather-resistant variety has large, full blooms. The centre of the flower is pale pink, surrounded by rose-pink outer petals.

'Summer Holiday'. A tall grower. The fragrant flowers are orange-red with a paler reverse.

'Super Star'. An outstanding variety which is tall and erect, with perfectly formed flowers that are brilliant light vermilion. It flowers freely, in autumn often producing the flowers in clusters.

'Sutter's Gold'. This upright, tall grower has pointed buds that open to well-shaped, fragrant flowers of orange, shaded red.

'Wendy Cussons'. A floriferous variety with fragrant, shapely blooms that are cerise, flushed scarlet; they are very fragrant. It is tall and well-branched.

Floribunda roses

The modern floribunda roses are basically derived from crosses between the DWARF POLYANTHA and early HYBRID TEA roses.

They are hardy deciduous shrubs with stems that are more branched than those of the Hybrid teas and are variably prickly with hooked thorns. The foliage is similar to that of Hybrid teas.

The flowers may be single, semi-double or fully double. They measure $2\frac{1}{2}$–$3\frac{1}{2}$ in. across when

Rosa 'Allgold' (Floribunda)

Rosa 'Anne Cocker'
(Floribunda)

Rosa 'City of Leeds' (Floribunda)

Rosa 'Charlotte Elizabeth'
(Floribunda)

Rosa 'Chinatown' (Floribunda)

Rosa 'Dearest' (Floribunda)

open and are borne in large terminal clusters during June and July and usually again in September and October. A few are fragrant.

Recent breeding achieved by crossing modern Hybrid tea with modern Floribunda roses has resulted in large-flowered Floribunda varieties. These, such as 'Pink Parfait' and 'Sea Pearl', are occasionally referred to as Grandifloras; they are difficult to classify as either Hybrid teas or Floribundas.

The cultivation is similar to that for Hybrid teas, but no disbudding is necessary. Pruning can be a little lighter, but after flowering the whole truss must be removed.

These roses may be grown in shrub borders, in mixed herbaceous borders or in beds of their own, underplanted with low-growing annuals or perennials. Unless otherwise stated the average height is 3 ft, and the spread 24 in.

ROSE (FLORIBUNDA)

'Allgold'. Height 2½ ft. This disease-resistant variety flowers throughout summer. The flowers are golden-yellow and do not fade in bright sun.

'Anna Wheatcroft'. Height 2½ ft. A vigorous, spreading shrub, with shapely buds that open to flat, light vermilion flowers.

'Anne Cocker'. Of upright and vigorous growth, with light vermilion flowers. These are fully double, on long stalks, and last well when cut.

'Arthur Bell'. A vigorous, upright grower with golden-yellow flowers that fade with age; they are scented and freely produced.

'Blessings'. This vigorous bushy shrub is a Grandiflora type. The fragrant coral-pink flowers are full and flat.

'Charlotte Elizabeth'. An upright grower with Hybrid-tea type flowers of deep rose-pink, tinged red; it is free flowering, but prone to black spot.

'Chinatown'. Height 4–5 ft, spread 3 ft. This is a vigorous-growing shrub of symmetrical habit. The full-blossomed, fragrant flowers, 4 in. across, are yellow with pink tints. If pruned only lightly it may grow to a height of 6 ft or more.

'Chorus Girl'. A bushy and compact variety, with moderately full vermilion-red flowers.

'Circus'. Height 2½ ft. A vigorous, branching and free-flowering shrub. It has fragrant, high-centred yellow flowers with pink and salmon shadings that deepen with age. Susceptible to black spot.

'City of Leeds'. This vigorous, free-flowering shrub has rich salmon flowers, moderately full and produced during most of the summer.

'Dainty Maid'. Height 4½ ft. A strong-growing variety, suitable for hedging. The deep pink single flowers have conspicuous golden stamens.

'Dearest'. A vigorous, branching shrub with abundant glossy dark green leaves. The full-petalled flowers are rose-salmon and borne in well-spaced trusses. They are fragrant and freely produced, but may be spoilt by heavy rain.

Rosa 'Dorothy Wheatcroft'
(Floribunda)

Rosa 'Evelyn Fison'
(Floribunda)

Rosa 'Goldgleam' (Floribunda)

Rosa 'Elizabeth of Glamis' (Floribunda)

Rosa 'Golden Jewel' (Floribunda)

Rosa 'Escapade' (Floribunda)

'Dorothy Wheatcroft'. Height 4 ft or more. This variety is suitable for the back of a herbaceous or shrub border, or for hedging. The flowers are bright red with deeper shading. It tends to become leggy and top-heavy.

'Elizabeth of Glamis'. Height 2½ ft. A compact shrub with semi-glossy dark green foliage. In spite of its name, this variety does not thrive in the north. The flowers are full and fragrant, light salmon with orange shadings.

'Escapade'. Height 2½ ft. The musk-scented, nearly single flowers are magenta-rose with a white centre, and are freely produced. A disease-resistant variety.

'Europeana'. Height 24 in. Large trusses of full, rosette-shaped, dark crimson flowers. Prone to mildew in the south.

'Evelyn Fison'. A vigorous shrub with semi-glossy, mid-green, leathery foliage. The slightly fragrant flowers are vivid red and scarlet.

'Faust'. Height 3½ ft. This vigorous shrub has leathery leaves and flowers of the Grandiflora type. They are golden-yellow with pink shading. Susceptible to mildew.

'Fred Loads': see under MODERN SHRUB ROSES

'Frensham'. Height 3 ft. An excellent variety for hedging, with an abundance of glossy mid-green foliage and deep scarlet-crimson flowers. Prone to mildew.

'Glengarry'. Height 2½ ft. A compact, bushy shrub of the Grandiflora type. The vermilion flowers are borne on short stems, singly or several together.

'Golden Jewel'. Height 24 in. A low-growing, spreading shrub, with golden-yellow full-petalled flowers.

'Goldgleam'. A weather-resistant variety with full, deep yellow flowers.

'Iceberg'. Height 5 ft. This variety is one of the most outstanding white roses. It is a vigorous,

branching and free-flowering shrub. The slightly fragrant flowers are small, but perfect in form. It is prone to black spot and mildew.

'Irish Mist'. Height 3–4 ft. A Grandiflora-type variety, with small trusses of orange-salmon Hybrid tea-like flowers.

'Isle of Man': see 'Manx Queen'

'Kim'. This compact and bushy rose is a dwarf variety, up to 2–2½ ft. It bears double canary-yellow flowers.

'King Arthur'. A Grandiflora variety bearing shapely salmon-pink flowers in trusses.

'Korona'. An upright, free-flowering grower with bright orange-scarlet, slightly fragrant flowers that fade to deep salmon. It sometimes has black markings on stems and foliage. Susceptible to black spot.

'Lilli Marlene'. An excellent, weather-resistant bedding rose, with abundant, bronze-tinted foliage. The scarlet-red, slightly fragrant flowers are produced in large trusses. Prone to mildew.

'Manx Queen'. Height 2½ ft. This is also known as 'Isle of Man'. It is a vigorous, branching grower with abundant, semi-glossy, dark green, leathery leaves. The flowers are rich gold with orange tips.

'Marlena'. A short, compact, branching shrub with double vermilion-red flowers.

'Masquerade'. Height 4 ft. This vigorous shrub bears large trusses of flowers that open yellow, mature to pink and gradually fade to deep red, giving a three-tone effect. It sets hips freely and these should be removed to ensure a second flush of flowers.

'Michelle'. Height 4–5 ft; spread 3–4 ft. An upright, vigorous variety bearing fragrant ivory-white flowers with a darker reverse.

'Molly McGredy'. A free-flowering Grandiflora-type variety with cherry-red flowers with silver reverse; they are borne on short individual stems.

Rosa 'Iceberg' (Floribunda)

Rosa 'Masquerade' (Floribunda)

Rosa 'Irish Mist' (Floribunda)

Rosa 'Ohlala' (Floribunda)

Rosa 'King Arthur' (Floribunda)

Rosa 'Lilli Marlene' (Floribunda)

'Moonraker'. Cream-white flowers that open flat; the colour deepens at the centre in the autumn flush. Resistant to weather damage.

'News'. Height $2\frac{1}{2}$ ft. A recent variety with wine-red buds that open to flat purple flowers with conspicuous golden stamens.

'Ohlala'. Height $3\frac{1}{2}$ ft. A vigorous, disease-resistant, branching shrub. It has scarlet-crimson flowers, fading towards the centre.

'Orangeade'. This branching, vigorous variety has semi-glossy, dark green, bronze-tinted leaves. The flowers are bright orange-vermilion and slightly fragrant. Susceptible to black spot.

'Orange Sensation'. A weather-resistant variety, with bright vermilion flowers shading to orange at the base; they are pleasantly fragrant.

'Orange Silk'. Height $2\frac{1}{2}$ ft. A good bedding variety of bushy, free-flowering habit. The flowers are orange-vermilion.

'Paddy McGredy'. Height 24 in. A Grandiflora-type rose with slightly fragrant flowers that are carmine with a lighter reverse. It flowers profusely in summer, less freely in autumn. Susceptible to mildew.

'Paprika'. An extremely free-flowering variety, of branching habit and with leathery, dark green glossy leaves. It produces an abundance of deep, luminous poppy-red flowers with a touch of purple in the centre.

'Pernille Poulsen'. Height 24 in. This shrub sometimes flowers as early as May. The fragrant pink blooms fade as they age.

'Picasso'. A bushy, compact variety with fairly full, rose-red and silver flowers, borne several together in small trusses.

'Pink Parfait'. A free-flowering Grandiflora-type shrub with pronounced Hybrid tea-like flowers; these are salmon-pink and ivory, opening flat to show the golden stamens.

Rosa 'Orangeade' (Floribunda)

Rosa 'Orange Sensation' (Floribunda)

Rosa 'Pink Parfait'
(Floribunda)

Rosa 'Queen Elizabeth'
(Floribunda)

Rosa 'Red Gold' (Floribunda)

Rosa 'Rosemary Rose' (Floribunda)   *Rosa* 'Pernille Poulsen' (Floribunda)

Rosa 'Scented Air' (Floribunda)

Rosa 'Violet Carson'
(Floribunda)

'Queen Elizabeth'. Height 6 ft or more. This disease-resistant Grandiflora variety is one of the most popular Floribundas; it is often classified and grown as a MODERN SHRUB. It is extremely vigorous, of erect habit, with long stems having few thorns. It is also suitable for hedging. The shapely, clear-pink flowers are slightly fragrant and excellent for cutting.

'Red Gold'. Height 2⅓ ft. A Grandiflora variety with golden-yellow flowers edged cherry-red.

'Rob Roy'. An upright and vigorous grower, with large trusses of bright scarlet-crimson Grandiflora flowers.

'Rosemary Rose'. A vigorous and branching variety with attractive bronze-tinted young foliage. The rosette-shaped, bright carmine blooms contrast well with the foliage. Prone to mildew.

'Scarlet Queen Elizabeth'. Height 4 ft. This shrub bears slightly fragrant flowers that are orange-scarlet and have a globular centre.

'Scented Air'. Height 4–5 ft. A vigorous, upright grower similar in habit to 'Queen Elizabeth'. The salmon-pink to red flowers are fragrant.

'Sea Pearl'. Height 3½ ft. A Grandiflora variety with typical Hybrid tea-type flowers, pale orange with a yellow reverse.

'Shepherdess'. A vigorous shrub with yellow flowers flushed pale salmon, of the Grandiflora-type variety.

'Shepherd's Delight'. Height 4 ft. This vigorous, branching shrub with dark green leathery foliage may be grown as a specimen plant and reach a height of 6 ft. The flowers, in a combination of flame, orange and yellow, are particularly fine in autumn. Susceptible to black spot.

'Tip Top'. Height 18 in. A free-flowering, compact shrub, ideal for edging or for a small garden. The well-formed, double, scented flowers are pink with salmon shading.

'Tombola'. A variety with flowers varying from deep salmon to carmine-pink, shaded gold; they are borne in large trusses.

'Travesti'. Multi-coloured flowers in shades of yellow and orange, flushed cherry-red with a yellow reverse; they deepen in colour as they mature.

'Vera Dalton'. This shrub is sometimes prone to black spot. The freely produced flowers are rose-pink and slightly fragrant.

'Violet Carson'. This Grandiflora variety bears soft peach-pink flowers with a silver reverse.

Modern shrub roses

These hardy deciduous shrubs are hybrids, chiefly between the SPECIES and OLD ROSES. They are of informal habit, reaching an average height and spread of 5 ft. They are suitable as specimen plants or among other shrubs, for hedging or, in the case of varieties of arching habit, for growing at the back of herbaceous borders.

The strong, variably thorny or bristly stems bear glossy pale to mid-green leaves composed of five to seven ovate and toothed leaflets. The flowers are 2–4 in. wide, single or semi-double and open out flat. A few varieties are slightly fragrant. They are generally repeat-flowering and borne either singly or in small clusters from June through to September.

Rosa 'Sea Pearl' (Floribunda)

Rosa 'Shepherdess' (Floribunda)   *Rosa* 'Frühlingsgold' (Modern shrub)

Rosa 'Constance Spry'
(Modern shrub)

Rosa 'Erfurt' (Modern shrub)

Shrub roses require only light pruning, although old, weak wood must occasionally be removed from the base. Some of the stronger Hybrid tea roses, such as 'Peace' and 'Eden Rose', and Floribunda roses, 'Queen Elizabeth', 'Iceberg' and 'Shepherd's Delight', may be similarly pruned to develop into shrubs.

'Constance Spry'. Height and spread 7 ft. Long arching sprays of single, clear rose-pink, fragrant flowers are produced in June and July.

'Erfurt'. Height 4–5 ft; spread 6 ft. The richly scented semi-double flowers are carmine with a pale lemon centre.

'Fred Loads'. Height 6–7 ft; spread 4–5 ft. This hybrid is sometimes listed as a Floribunda rose. It bears trusses of single, bright orange or vermilion flowers that are lightly scented.

'Fritz Nobis'. Height and spread 6 ft. A bushy shrub of arching habit. It bears a profusion of semi-double salmon-pink flowers which open out flat. These are clove-scented and appear in June and July only.

'Frühlingsgold'. Height and spread 7 ft. This outstanding hybrid flowers in May and early June only. The long arching stems are covered with large, semi-double, deeply fragrant flowers of sparkling pale gold.

'Frühlingsmorgen'. Height and spread 5–6 ft. Single flowers, of clear pink blended with yellow, appear in June and again in September. It has small, grey-green, matt leaves.

'Golden Chersonese'. Height and spread 4–5 ft. A thicket-forming shrub with dense foliage. The small, single, golden flowers are massed along the stems in May.

'Golden Wings'. Height and spread 5 ft. Single, large, pale gold and slightly scented flowers are borne in great profusion.

'Heidelberg'. Height and spread 6 ft. A vigorous shrub, bearing an abundance of large, bright red, full blooms in clusters.

'Iceberg'. This is described under FLORIBUNDAS; as a specimen plant it makes a handsome shrub.

'Joseph's Coat'. Height 6 ft; spread 3–4 ft. This is a moderately vigorous, branching rose. It may be grown as a shrub, but is more commonly seen as a CLIMBER or RAMBLER.

'Kassel'. Height and spread 6 ft. This perpetual-flowering variety is of loose but erect habit, and may be grown as a pillar rose. The large, profusely borne flowers are raspberry-red with a musk scent.

'Kathleen Ferrier'. Height and spread 8 ft. The clusters of carmine-pink, semi-double, deeply scented flowers are so large and heavy that the stems droop.

'Lavender Lassie'. Height 5 ft; spread 3–4 ft. Large clusters of lilac-pink, rosette-shaped and fragrant flowers with dense petals.

'Lichterlohe'. Height 5 ft; spread 24 in. A shrub with shiny, dark grey-green leaves. Velvety, scarlet-crimson, semi-double, scented flowers are borne in clusters.

'Marguerite Hilling'. Height and spread 7–8 ft. A sport of 'Nevada', similar in all respects, but with rose-pink flowers.

'Munster'. Height 5 ft; spread 3–4 ft. Double flowers of soft pale pink, shaded deeper pink.

'Nevada'. Height and spread 7–8 ft. An arching variety bearing the largest and most profuse

Rosa 'Fred Loads'
(Modern shrub)

Rosa 'Fritz Nobis'
(Modern shrub)

Rosa 'Golden Chersonese'
(Modern shrub)

Rosa 'Golden Wings'
(Modern shrub)

Rosa 'Frühlingsmorgen' (Modern shrub)

Rosa 'Margüerite Hilling' (Modern shrub)

Rosa 'Nevada' (Modern shrub)

Rosa 'Wilhelm' (Modern shrub)

owers (up to 5 in. across) of the perpetual-
owering Shrub roses. The arching stems are
eavily covered with large, ivory-white, single
owers, that are flushed pink in hot weather.
When fully open, the yellow stamens are promi-
ently revealed.

Nymphenburg'. Height and spread 7 ft. This
rching shrub flowers almost continuously. It
as small clusters of large, salmon-pink, gold-
nted Hybrid tea-type flowers that are richly
usk-scented. It is better grown as a climber
nd may as such reach a height of 10 ft or more.

Queen Elizabeth'. Described under FLORI-
UNDAS; it also makes a handsome large shrub
pruned only lightly.

Réveil Dijonnais'. Height up to 8 ft; spread 6 ft.
shrub of lax habit, suitable as a sturdy bush or
s a pillar rose. It bears showy, semi-double,
ightly scented, carmine-and-gold flowers.

Uncle Walter'. Height 7 ft, spread 3–4 ft. An
rect hybrid with full-petalled Hybrid tea-type
ark red flowers.

Wilhelm'. Height and spread 8 ft. A vigorous,
ree-flowering shrub. The crimson flowers are
emi-double, and appear in loose clusters.

Will Scarlet'. Height and spread 5–6 ft. A sport
f 'Wilhelm', with semi-double flowers that are
right scarlet, paler in the centre.

Climbers and ramblers

his group includes a vast range of ascending
nd scrambling roses, some of which are de-
cendants of the true climbing species, while
thers are mutants (or sports) of bush roses.

Those described are hardy and deciduous,
with glossy or matt mid-green leaves, often
nted red or bronze when young. The stems are
overed with hooked thorns.

ROSE (CLIMBER)

Several climbers, mainly those derived from
pecies roses, are exceptionally vigorous and are
uitable for growing up old trees and for cloth-
g house walls. They bear cream-white to
ellow, single and fragrant flowers, 2 in. or more
cross. These are carried in large clusters over a
hort period in June and July, occasionally with
maller flushes in the autumn.

The less-vigorous climbers, derived from the
Joisette roses and the Hybrid teas, are suitable
or more restricted areas, being ideal for growing
ver pillars, arbours, walls, pergolas, fences and
creens. The 3–5 in. wide flowers are basically of
Hybrid tea-type, single, semi-double or double;
ey are borne in small clusters from June
July and sometimes recurrently.

Ramblers, derived from *R. luciae*, are vigorus but supple-stemmed, and suitable for train-
g in confined areas over pergolas, arbours and
illars; they are less suitable than climbers for

walls as they are prone to mildew due to lack of
air circulation. They bear single, semi-double or
double, 2 in. wide flowers in large trusses during
June and July.

Plant all climbers and ramblers close to the
supports over which they are to grow.

ROSE (PILLAR)

For pergolas and fences, set the less-vigorous
climbers and the ramblers at intervals of 5–6 ft
and fan them out laterally as they develop. The
same distance applies when covering great expanses of walls.

In the subsequent descriptions each variety
is classified as follows:

    VC = vigorous climber
    C = climber
    R = rambler

'Albéric Barbier'. Height 25 ft. R. This hybrid
is a vigorous grower, ideal for an arch, pillar or
screen. It is yellow in bud, opening to large
massed clusters of very fragrant white blooms in
June and July.

'Albertine'. Height 18 ft. R. This hybrid is
suitable for an arch or pergola. It is vigorous,
producing thick growths with strong laterals.
The double blooms are a glowing copper-pink,
richly scented. This is a great favourite, but apt
to die back in some soils, and it is prone to
mildew. The petals do not drop, but turn brown.

'Alister Stella Gray'. Height 15 ft. C. This
climber flowers continuously, but often sparsely.
The fragrant Noisette-type double flowers open
from coiled apricot buds to quartered, buff
blooms in small sprays.

'Allen Chandler'. Height 15–30 ft. C. A vigorous, thick-stemmed climber suitable only for
large wall expanses. The semi-double, vivid,
dark-red Hybrid tea-type flowers, 3–4 in. across,
are borne recurrently.

'Bantry Bay'. Height 10 ft. C. This recurrently
flowering variety is suitable for a wall or pillar.
The bright pink, semi-double blooms have conspicuous yellow stamens.

'Blush Noisette': see *R. × noisettiana* under
SPECIES ROSES

'Bobbie James'. Height 25 ft. VC. Ideal as a tree
climber. Ivory-white, semi-double, musk-scented
flowers in large trusses in June and July.

'Caroline Testout'. Height up to 10 ft. C. A
climbing sport of the Hybrid tea bush-type with
masses of strongly scented, double, true rose-
pink flowers.

'Casino'. Height 10 ft. C. This repeat-flowering
variety is not fully hardy and is best grown on a
warm, sheltered wall. The Hybrid tea-type
flowers are yellow, shading to lemon.

'Cécile Brunner': see under DWARF POLYANTHAS

'Chaplin's Pink Climber'. Height 10–12 ft. C. A
vigorous grower ideal on a pergola or large arch.
The semi-double, bright pink flowers have conspicuous golden stamens.

Rosa 'Kassel' (Modern shrub)

Rosa 'Nymphenburg'
(Modern shrub)

Rosa 'Will Scarlet'
(Modern shrub)

Rosa 'Albertine' (Rambler)

Rosa 'Alister Stella Gray'
(Climber)

Rosa 'Chaplin's Pink Climber' (Climber)

Rosa 'Dorothy Perkins' (Rambler)

Rosa 'Golden Showers' (Climber)

Rosa 'Bantry Bay' (Climber)

Rosa 'Leverkusen' (Climber)

Rosa 'Maigold' (Climber)

Rosa 'Danse du Feu' (Climber)

Rosa 'Étoile de Hollande' (Climber)

'Crimson Glory'. Height 10–12 ft. C. A climbing sport of the Hybrid tea bush. The richly scented, full flowers are deep, velvety crimson. It is prone to mildew.

'Crimson Shower'. Height 9–10 ft. R. Suitable for growing over arches or as a weeping standard. It bears trusses of semi-double, crimson flowers from late July onwards.

'Cupid'. Height 12 ft. C. This variety is best grown against a south-facing wall. The nearly single peach-pink flowers are raspberry-scented.

'Danse du Feu'. Height 12 ft. C. Ideal for a wall or over a screen. The double flowers are orange-scarlet. Repeat-flowering.

'Dorothy Perkins'. Height 18 ft. R. Double blush-pink, rosette-shaped flowers are borne in large trusses. Prone to mildew.

'Easlea's Golden Rambler'. Height 8–10 ft. R. Richly fragrant, double flowers of deep yellow, shaded red in the bud. The handsome, glossy, dark green foliage is prone to mildew. Suitable for a pergola or as a pillar rose, but should be left unpruned for the first three or four years.

'Elegance'. Height 9 ft. C. A strong-growing variety which flowers in June and July and occasionally again in autumn. The full-petalled Hybrid tea-type flowers are clear yellow.

'Emily Gray'. Height 10 ft. R. A vigorous rambler with small, double, scented flowers of rich gold, in June and July or later. The glossy foliage is almost evergreen.

'Ena Harkness'. Height 10–12 ft. C. A climbing vigorous sport of the Hybrid tea rose of the same name. The bright crimson-scarlet, double fragrant flowers are borne throughout summer.

'Étoile de Hollande'. Height 10–12 ft. C. A climbing sport with loosely formed, double, deeply fragrant, dark red flowers.

'Excelsa', syn. 'Red Dorothy Perkins'. Height 1. ft. R. This rambler is similar to 'Dorothy Perkins', but with double crimson flowers.

'François Juranville'. Height 18 ft. C. The variety produces long, flexible stems, densely covered in June and July with double, deep fawn-pink flowers, sweetly scented.

'Gloire de Dijon'. Height 12–15 ft. C. An old variety of the Hybrid tea type; it is usually the first rose to flower if grown on a wall. The buff buds open in May to quartered double flowers of apricot and pink, with a strong scent.

'Golden Showers'. Height 8 ft. C. This hybrid essentially a pillar rose and is probably the best for that purpose. The pale gold, double, scented flowers are borne on long stems throughout summer and autumn. Susceptible to black spot.

'Guinée'. Height 8–10 ft. C. A strong climber best grown on a wall or tall screen. The dark velvety scarlet, black-shaded, double flowers are fragrant and borne almost continuously.

'Hamburger Phoenix'. Height 8–10 ft. C. A free-flowering and recurrent variety, with crimson, semi-double large flowers.

Rosa 'Mermaid' (Climber)

Rosa 'Mme Grégoire Staechelin' (Climber)

Rosa 'Mme Alfred Carrière' (Climber)

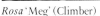
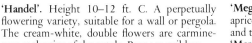

Rosa 'Meg' (Climber)

Rosa 'New Dawn' (Climber)

Rosa 'Parkdirektor Riggers' (Climber)

'Handel'. Height 10–12 ft. C. A perpetually flowering variety, suitable for a wall or pergola. The cream-white, double flowers are carmine-rose at the tips of the petals. Prone to mildew.

'High Noon'. Height 10 ft. C. A climber of erect habit, with semi-double, deep gold, scented flowers, produced continuously on long stems.

'Kathleen Harrop'. Height 7 ft. R. A pink sport of 'Zéphirine Drouhin', but less vigorous. It bears double or semi-double flowers.

'Kiftsgate'. Height 30–60 ft. VC. This variety of the species *R. filipes* is a true climber, suitable for growing up a birch or old apple tree. It is slow to become established, but bears enormous trusses of single, white, scented flowers.

'Lawrence Johnston'. Height 30 ft. VC. An extremely vigorous climber, best grown against a sheltered wall. The apricot buds open to bright canary, semi-double, sweetly scented flowers. These appear in June and again intermittently.

'Leverkusen'. Height 10–12 ft. C. A recurrently flowering variety, best grown on a wall or pillar. The pale yellow, semi-double blooms are produced in sprays on long stems.

'Maigold'. Height 11 ft. C. This sharply thorned climber is suitable for a wall or as an open shrub. The scented, bronze and yellow, double flowers are recurrent if dead-headed as they fade.

'May Queen'. Height 15 ft. R. This is a lax, vigorous rambler with abundant shiny leaves and masses of double pink flowers, flushed lilac.

'Meg'. Height 10–12 ft. C. Single pink and apricot flowers are produced in June and July and thereafter intermittently.

'Mermaid'. Height 25–30 ft. VC. This extremely vigorous, almost evergreen climber is suitable for a large expanse of wall; it does well on a north-facing wall, but needs protection from severe frosts. The single, scented, cream-yellow flowers, with amber stamens, are 5 in. wide.

'Mme Abel Chatenay'. Height 10–12 ft. C. A climbing vigorous sport of the Hybrid tea bush. It bears fragrant, pale pink, double quilled flowers in June and July.

'Mme Alfred Carrière'. Height 15–20 ft. C. A vigorous climber if grown in full sun. The white, faintly flushed pink, Noisette-type double flowers are richly fragrant; they are borne freely and recurrently.

'Mme Butterfly'. Height up to 10 ft. C. This upright climber is a sport of the Hybrid tea type. Sweetly fragrant, double flowers, pale pink tinted salmon, are freely borne in June.

'Mme Edouard Herriot'. Height up to 10 ft. C. A climbing sport of the Hybrid tea 'Daily Mail'; it is best grown on a pillar. Double or semi-double coral and flame-orange flowers are borne in June and July. Susceptible to black spot.

'Mme Grégoire Staechelin'. Height 15–20 ft. C. A vigorous climber for a north wall. Double flowers, coral shaded crimson and scented, are borne in profusion. Prone to mildew.

Rosa 'Paul's Scarlet Climber'
(Climber)

Rosa 'Pink Perpetue' (Climber)

Rosa 'Zéphirine Drouhin'
(Climber)

Rosa 'Schoolgirl' (Climber)

'**New Dawn**'. Height 9 ft. C. A moderately vigorous variety of bushy habit; it makes a good pillar rose or may be grown through a hedge. The sweetly scented, small double flowers are silvery-pink and borne almost continuously.

'**Nymphenburg**': see under MODERN SHRUB ROSES

'**Parkdirektor Riggers**'. Height 12–15 ft. C. A disease-resistant climber with abundant glossy dark green leaves. The blood-red, semi-double flowers are produced almost continuously.

'**Paul's Lemon Pillar**'. Height up to 18 ft. C. This variety will reach 18 ft only in a warm, sheltered position. The fragrant double flowers are pale lemon, turning ivory-white.

'**Paul's Scarlet Climber**'. Height up to 18 ft. C. An ideal pillar rose, also suitable against a sunny or even a north-facing wall. The scarlet, semi-double flowers are in clusters and appear in abundance during most of summer with a second, small show in September.

'**Pink Perpetue**'. Height 15 ft. C. A moderately vigorous variety, suitable for a pillar or an arch. The deep, two-toned pink, double flowers are borne in abundance in June and July and again in September.

'**Polyantha Grandiflora**'. Height 20 ft. R. This tree-climbing hybrid rambler, of uncertain origin, has the character of a wild species. Large trusses of small, single, white flowers with a heavy fruity scent appear in June and July.

'**Red Dorothy Perkins**': see 'Excelsa'

'**Rose-Marie Viaud**'. Height 15 ft. R. A rambler with almost thornless stems. The lilac-rose double flowers are borne in large trusses.

'**Rosy Mantle**'. Height 8–10 ft. C. This is suitable as a pillar rose or against a wall. Sweetly scented rose-pink flowers are freely borne.

'**Sander's White**'. Height 12–15 ft. R. A vigorous rambler, ideal for a large arch or screen. The white, double, scented flowers are produced in big trusses in great abundance in June and July.

'**Schoolgirl**'. Height 10–12 ft. C. A vigorous, disease-resistant climber, suitable for a wall or tall screen. The orange-apricot, sweetly fragrant, double flowers are borne continuously.

'**Shot Silk**'. Height 10–12 ft. C. This climbing sport of the Hybrid tea shrub bears double, fragrant, orange-salmon flowers.

'**Thelma**'. Height 9 ft. R. A nearly thornless variety, ideal for a pillar. The soft coral-pink, semi-double, fragrant flowers are borne in clusters over a long period.

'**Veilchenblau**'. Height 12 ft. R. This rambler is particularly suitable for growing over an arch. The mauve buds open to violet flowers with a pale centre, and fade to slate-grey. They are semi-double and fragrant, borne in large trusses.

'**Wedding Day**'. Height up to 30 ft. VC. An extremely vigorous tree climber, with yellow buds that open to deeply fragrant, almost single white flowers with prominent orange stamens.

'**Zéphirine Drouhin**'. Height 9 ft. C. This is a BOURBON climber with thornless stems bearing matt, pointed, light green foliage, tinted red. It is excellent for its continuity of bloom, but is prone to mildew. The bright carmine-pink, semi-double flowers have a rich fragrance. The autumn display is often superior to that of summer.

Rosa 'Baby Gold Star' (Miniature)

Rosa 'Baby Masquerade' (Miniature)

Rosa 'Eleanor' (Miniature)

Rosa 'Perla de Monserrat' (Miniature)

Miniature roses

This is a group of hardy deciduous small shrub-lets. The almost thornless branching stems bear mid-green foliage composed of five or seven ovate and toothed leaflets.

The semi-double or double flowers open flat from well-shaped buds and generally measure $\frac{3}{4}$–$1\frac{1}{2}$ in. across; they are borne in small clusters in June and July and are usually repeat-flowering. The yellow varieties are apt to fade in strong sun.

The true Miniatures derive from the dwarf semi-double China rose, *R. chinensis* 'Minima', known as 'Roulettii', introduced into Switzer-land by Dr Roulet. They have inherited the long flowering season and the beauty of form of the China rose. 'Roulettii' itself is still one of the most charming of the Miniatures. It has been crossed with Hybrid tea and Floribunda roses, whose characteristics are reproduced.

Miniatures should always be grown from cuttings, as those budded on to rootstocks soon lose their dwarf character; many varieties can be grown as small standards.

These roses have the same cultural require-ments as all other modern roses: a fertile soil, full sun, good drainage, systematic but light pruning and protection against pests and diseases. In the garden, miniature roses (average height 6–9 in.) are sometimes difficult to position advantageously, and are undoubtedly best grown in beds to themselves. Their attrac-tion will be more clearly appreciated if the beds are slightly raised, and the roses planted 6–10 in. apart. They are generally unsuited for grow-ing on rock gardens.

Miniature roses may be grown in deep window-boxes; they make handsome pot plants, set in 4–5 in. pots of John Innes potting compost No. 1 and repotted annually in February or March. The pots should be plunged outdoors during winter and top-dressed with peat. When in flower, they may be taken indoors for short spells. Long spells inside will cause the shoots to become drawn, followed by premature leaf-drop.

In the following descriptions, Miniatures of two groups occur: those that grow from 12–15 in. high and those that average about 9 in. Wherever possible it is best to keep the two groups separate.

A few climbing varieties are available. These make handsome specimens in small gardens and usually reach a height of 6 ft.

'Baby Crimson': see 'Perla de Alcanada'

'Baby Faurax'. Height 12–15 in. Fragrant, lavender-purple, semi-double flowers.

'Baby Gold Star'. Height 14 in. Semi-double, yellow flowers.

'Baby Masquerade'. Height 12–15 in. Flame and gold Floribunda-type double flowers. Suit-able as a standard.

'Cinderella'. Height 6–9 in. Double, shapely flowers of shell-pink shading to white at the edges. Suitable as a standard.

'Coralin'. Height 15 in. An outstanding Minia-ture, slightly large in all its parts. It makes a good standard. Coral flushed orange, semi-double flowers.

Rosa 'Cinderella' (Miniature)

Rosa 'Coralin' (Miniature)

Rosa 'Little Flirt' (Miniature)

Rosa 'Perla de Alcanada' (Miniature)

Rosa 'Pixie' (Miniature)

Rosa 'Rosina' (Miniature)

Rosa 'Roulettii' (Miniature)

Rosa 'Yellow Doll'
(Miniature)

'**Eleanor**'. Height 8–12 in. Double, deep pink flowers, shaded white at the base. Suitable as a standard.

'**Josephine Wheatcroft**': see 'Rosina'

'**Little Flirt**'. Height 12 in. Large, semi-double, red and yellow flowers.

'**Little Princess**': see 'Pixie'

'**Magic Wand**'. A climbing Miniature with bright red, white-centred, double flowers.

'**Maid Marion**', syn. 'Red Imp'. Height 8–10 in. The deep red flowers are full and rich in colour.

'**New Penny**'. Height 8 in. Semi-double flowers of blended salmon-pink and orange.

'**Peon**'. Height 4–6 in. This variety has deep crimson, white-centred, double flowers.

'**Perla de Alcanada**'. syn. 'Baby Crimson'. Height 10–12 in. The shapely buds open to semi-double carmine flowers.

'**Perla de Monserrat**'. Height 12–15 in. Coiled buds open to warm, rose-pink, double flowers with pale pink tips to the petals.

'**Pink Cameo**'. Possibly the most outstanding Miniature climber, bearing bright pink, perpetually flowering, double blooms. It may also be grown as a weeping standard.

'**Pixie**', syn. 'Little Princess'. Height 9 in. White, flushed pink, double flowers.

'**Pompon de Paris**'. A Miniature climber that may reach a height of 9 ft in good soil. It has dainty, rose-pink, pompon-like flowers.

'**Red Imp**': see 'Maid Marion'

'**Rosina**', syn. 'Josephine Wheatcroft'. Height 12–15 in. Perfect buds open to clear yellow double flowers.

'**Roulettii**'. Height 9–12 in. This is exquisite in bud, opening to clear rose-pink double flowers.

'**Showoff**'. This climbing Miniature has semi-double, buff flowers, flecked orange.

'**Yellow Doll**'. Height 10–12 in. Double yellow flowers turning ivory-white.

PROSTRATE ROSES

This is a small group of hardy deciduous roses which form mats or low hummocks. They make a dense cover and are useful on banks and over old tree stumps. The flowering season is short.

R. luciae wichuraiana. This is the parent of many of the rambler roses. It is prostrate, spreading to 10 ft and forming a dense carpet. It bears clusters of single, ivory-white and fragrant flowers, 1½–2 in. across, in August.

'**Max Graf**'. This hybrid between *R. rugosa* and *R. luciae* is a prostrate grower which quickly forms a dense ground cover. The 2–3 in. single flowers are rich pink; they are borne in clusters over a long period from late June onwards.

'**Raubritter**'. Height 3 ft; spread 6 ft. This forms a large, mounded hummock, with clusters of double, cup-shaped, fragrant flowers; they are bright pink and 2–3 in. wide. The flowering season lasts six weeks in July and August.

ROSE HEDGES

Several roses make excellent informal hedges, either on a boundary or to separate parts of a garden. As a boundary, avoid roses that will spread too quickly; plant at ordinary spacings and prune lightly to maintain shape.

The compact Floribundas are particularly good for hedging: 'Chinatown', 'Dainty Maid', 'Frensham', 'Iceberg', 'Masquerade' and 'Shepherd's Delight' are recommended.

Old shrub roses, especially the Hybrid musk are outstanding, although they spread widely 'Cornelia' and 'Penelope' are the most suitable Modern shrubs, such as 'Heidelberg', form dense and sturdy hedges; 'Queen Elizabeth' will eventually grow to a tall, leggy hedge.

Ramblers are sometimes recommended for hedging, but they require training against stakes and wires and are generally too untidy.

WEEPING STANDARDS

These are ramblers budded at the top of a 4–6 ft high stem of *R. canina* or *R. rugosa*. The trailing stems droop to the ground, like a floral skirt Weeping standards require support with stout stakes. An umbrella-shaped wire frame is usually fixed to the stake for the stems to be secured to so as to create a neat, shapely dome Very few varieties weep naturally, the best available being 'Crimson Shower', 'Excelsa' and 'Dorothy Perkins'. Suitable roses for training include: 'Albéric Barbier', 'Albertine' and 'Emily Gray' (described under CLIMBERS and RAMBLERS)

Prune weeping standards in the same way as when grown as Climbers and Ramblers; no flowers can be expected the first year.

Cultivation. Roses are adaptable to widely varying conditions, but certain basic provisions are essential. They require good drainage; roses will not thrive in waterlogged ground. They also need an open sunny position. A few tree-climbing roses do well in partial shade, but generally roses require as much light as possible. This may be in full sun, but some climbing roses will thrive on the north side of a house, with little direct sun but with ample light.

Although a free flow of air is advantageous windy situations may cause the roots to loosen the stems to break, and the heads of standards to snap off.

Roses require plenty of water; good soil cultivation will to some extent preserve water supplies below ground, but the plants should be watered if there is a dry period of a fortnight in spring or summer.

They thrive in any kind of soil except pure sand, solid chalk or the putty-like blue gault clay; even there they usually grow well after persistent cultivation. They are tolerant of lime but appear to be at their best in a soil that is slightly acid with a pH reading of 6·5.

With the exceptions of the Albas, Damasks Gallicas and some of the wild species, all roses require a rich soil. When this is not naturally present, organic or inorganic manures must be added. The ideal soil is a medium loam.

Prepare the planting site by marking out the bed, as long as required but not wider than about 5½ ft. Dig the bed and incorporate liberal quantities of well-rotted manure or compost; lighten heavy clay soil with half-rotted straw.

Dress the topsoil with plenty of peat mixed with hop manure and chopped-up turf. Fresh animal manure is harmful to the roots and should only be used in the bottom spit.

Whenever possible, prepare the planting bed at least a month in advance; August and September are good months for October and November planting. For single specimens, such as climbers or large shrub roses, the area to be prepared should be at least 4 ft by 4 ft.

Plant at any time from October to early April, during suitable weather. Mark the positions for each shrub with the appropriate spacings, which vary according to the type and variety of rose. The strong Hybrid teas and Floribundas need at least 24 in.; 'Eden Rose', 'Iceberg', 'Peace' and 'Prima Ballerina' 3 ft or more. Set all standards at intervals of 3 ft; shrub roses at 4–5 ft, and climbers and ramblers at 7 ft intervals.

These are general guide-lines. Roses of limited vigour can be planted more closely; 'Allgold' and 'Shot Silk' at 18 in. or less, 'Tiptop', 'Kim' and 'Marlena' at 15 in. or less and the Miniatures at 6–9 in.

Prepare a planting mixture consisting of a large handful of bone-meal to each 2 gallons of moist peat. Take out a 12 in. deep, fan-shaped hole, with the outer, curved perimeter towards the direction of the prevailing wind. Make the hole 4–5 in. deep at the narrow end of the fan and 8–9 in. deep at the extremity. Trim and shorten the roots, which on most roses, except standards, grow in the same direction.

Place the planting mixture in the hole to a depth of 2 in. and mix with the soil; set the rose in position with the union of the stock and scion (the crown) in the angle of the narrow end of the fan and just below the level of the soil. Spread out the roots well, and continue to add the planting mixture until the roots are covered, making sure that all gaps between the roots are filled. Add soil, and firm in the rose by treading. Level off if necessary, with more soil.

Roses that are planted in March can be pruned before planting.

Standard roses need a slightly different planting technique. The hole has to be more or less round and the tree must be planted at the right depth. Standards are often budded on to the stock of the wild *R. rugosa*, recognisable by the mass of small prickles on the stem, and should be planted not more than 3–4 in. deep. Standards on brier stock (*R. canina*) have fairly smooth stems; plant to about the same depth as bush roses.

Standards must be firmly staked and tied, the stakes being set in the planting hole first. Use durable stakes, such as oak, ash or chestnut, long enough to be buried about 15 in. and to reach the top of the flower stem. The portion of the stake below ground should first have been treated with a wood-preservative. After planting, tie stake and stem, at top and half-way, with strong, soft string or with plastic or rubber tree-ties. Protect the stem with a band of sacking, felt or rubber at any point where it rubs against the stake.

In windy, exposed positions, galvanised angle-iron posts may be used instead of wood. Plant each rose so that it faces away from the prevailing wind.

Climbers and Ramblers grown in restricted areas need tying to their supports of trelliswork, pergolas, arbours and pillars. Fasten the shoots in place as they grow to establish a framework.

Vigorous, tree-climbing varieties are usually self-supporting.

On established rose beds, ensure aeration by preventing the soil becoming compacted. Loosen firm soil gently with a garden fork and, when applying fertilisers in granular or powder form, work them into the soil, 1 in. deep, with the tips of the tines. Established rose beds should not be dug over with a spade.

If no other plants are grown in the rose beds, weeds can be kept down by applying a liquid weedkiller, based on paraquat. Alternatively, hoe just below the surface of the soil; on deep-rooted weeds, paint the leaves with a hormone-type weedkiller. These weedkillers must not be allowed to touch the rose foliage.

After pruning in spring, roses often develop two or more buds immediately below the pruning cut. These quickly become leafy shoots; on Hybrid teas and Floribundas these should be reduced to one while still small.

Most Hybrid teas also need disbudding or the removal of excess flower buds. Any group of buds clustering beneath the main terminal bud should be removed while the buds are still small.

All roses should be dead-headed as soon as the flowers have faded. Cut back as far as the first outward-pointing leaf; in the angle between leaf and stem a new bud will form. At the end of summer, dead-heading should be lighter so as not to encourage sappy young growths.

For the removal of suckers see PRUNING.

Mulching is beneficial to all roses as it fulfills several purposes: it conserves moisture; improves the physical condition of the soil; it is rendered down to plant food; and limits the germination of weed seeds. Many materials can be used, the best mulches being animal manure, compost, rotted leaf-mould, unrotted leaves, peat and lawn mowings.

All mulches should be applied while the soil is moist, and with the exception of animal manure and compost, a stimulant should be applied beneath the mulch. Peat has little nutritious value, and unrotted leaves and mowings take a certain amount of nitrogen from the soil as they rot. The most convenient stimulant is hop manure or mushroom compost.

Partially rotted cow or horse manure makes the best mulches, although unsightly and smelly at first. Apply in spring, soon after pruning; autumn applications result in the nitrogen being leached away by winter rains while the plants are mainly dormant.

Manure as a plant food need not be applied every year on good average soils; every two or three years is enough. On light soils, particularly sandy and chalky ones, however, annual dressings should be given.

Well-rotted compost has the same use as animal manure, and should be applied in spring.

Leaves, rotted or unrotted, make excellent mulches for conserving moisture, but do not become plant food until decomposed. Both forms are best applied in autumn.

Peat is valuable for retaining moisture and as a soil conditioner; it opens up clay soils when applied frequently. In appearance, peat is the most agreeable of all mulches, but it must be applied when thoroughly moist. Apply in autumn or spring, in a layer at least 2 in. deep.

Lawn mowings are useful for conserving moisture in summer, provided they contain no grass seeds or clippings from a lawn treated with a hormone weedkiller. The mowings generate

A young shrub or species rose with laterals and tips cut back

A newly planted Hybrid tea cut back to two or three buds

The stems of a young Floribunda are cut back to four buds

considerable heat and must be applied a little at a time and occasionally stirred with a fork.

Mulching, particularly with manure, provides a good food store for roses. Other forms of feeding, with organic or inorganic fertilisers, are also valuable, particularly as quick stimulants and to make good any deficiencies in the soil or the mulches. Feed at any time from late spring onwards, the most important time being early July, when the roses are in full bloom and preparing for making their next flush.

The organic fertilisers, available in liquid and powder forms, are mainly derived from fish refuse or seaweed; they are complete fertilisers, containing all the necessary chemical elements for plant health. They are easily applied in dilute liquid form and also act as a foliar feed.

Other useful organic fertilisers for roses are bone-meal and hoof-and-horn meal. These are slow-acting incomplete fertilisers, usually dug into the soil or pricked into the topsoil.

Wood ash has some manurial effect; it contains potash, which helps to ripen the stems and improve the flowers. Do not allow it to get wet before use, but spread it direct from the bonfire (after cooling) or store it under cover.

Several inorganic or chemical fertilisers are available; these are generally in powder or granular form, although a few are liquid. They are valuable as a quick tonic in July. Use only proprietary brands of complete fertilisers, preferably those made specifically for roses. Prick lightly into the soil or apply by watering-can.

Most soils benefit from a spring dressing of sulphate of potash, hoed in at 1 oz. per sq. yd.

Foliar feeds contain soluble salts that are absorbed through the stomata (or pores) of the leaves. Spray the solution on to the under-surfaces of the leaves. Such feeds act quickly and appear to be effective in countering any mineral deficiencies in the soil. Apply in early June and late July.

Propagation. Roses can be propagated by seeds, cuttings or by budding.

Only the species come true from seeds, and then only if hand-pollinated. They generally take two or three years to develop into flowering plants. Extract the seeds from the hips when ripe and sow thinly in pots or boxes of seed compost in October. Place in a cold frame. When the seedlings have developed two or three true leaves, set them straight out into nursery beds. Grow on for two years before planting out.

Seeds of mixed Floribunda-type roses are sometimes available under the name 'Polyantha Nana'; seed-raised plants will usually flower the first year, often on plants only 6 in. high.

Most roses can be successfully grown from cuttings, but this propagation method is more suitable for the true species and their hybrids, for the old shrub roses and for ramblers with one flush of bloom only. All but the strongest-growing Hybrid tea varieties are difficult to increase satisfactorily from cuttings, and the resultant plants generally lack vigour.

The advantage of raising roses from cuttings is that established plants are grown on their own roots and do not produce suckers. All shoots coming from below ground level will be of the cultivated variety and need not be removed.

Miniature roses should always be increased by cuttings.

Take 9–12 in. long cuttings, with a heel, of strong, non-flowering lateral shoots in August and September. Strip off all leaves except two or three at the top of each cutting and also remove the buds in the leaf axils.

Choose a sheltered, partially shaded place in the garden, not directly overhung by trees, and take out a V-shaped trench 6–8 in. deep. Fill the bottom inch with sharp horticultural sand, and after dipping the cuttings in a root-forming hormone powder, insert them, a few inches apart, in the sand. Firm the soil over the cuttings and water the foliage; if the weather is dry, water the whole trench thoroughly.

The cuttings will usually be ready to plant out in permanent positions the following autumn.

Take 2–4 in. heel cuttings of the Miniatures from July to October. Insert in equal parts (by volume) peat and sand in a cold frame. When rooted, pot the cuttings singly in 3 in. pots of John Innes potting compost No. 1; plunge outdoors the following May and grow on until transplanting to permanent sites in the autumn.

Alternatively, and this is the most commonly used method, propagate roses by budding. This is the process by which a growth bud of a desired variety (the scion) is inserted into the rootstock of a wild variety.

Various rootstocks are suitable. These can be grown from seeds, from cuttings or may be obtained from nurseries. On fertile soil, the most suitable rootstock is R. canina, the wild dog rose. Lateral stems from this species make good cuttings, and long, straight stems do well for standards. On light, sandy soils the thornless stock known as 'Polyantha Simplex' (a derivative of R. multiflora) is preferable, as are forms of R. rugosa. The latter are particularly good for standards, although they are less successful on limy soils.

Set the rootstocks out in November, about 18 in. apart, and in such a way that the short piece of stem between the roots and the green shoots is barely covered.

Budding is done in July and August when the stocks are in full leaf. Select strong, healthy scion stems that have just flowered. Such a stem is called the budwood and should be severed low down. Cut off and discard the soft top and all the leaves, leaving $\frac{1}{2}$ in. of the leaf stalks. If the budwood is in an ideal state, the thorns will snap off cleanly when lateral pressure from the thumb is applied.

Draw the soil away from the neck of the rootstock, and with a budding-knife make a T-shaped cut in the bark of the neck, close to or just below ground level. Make the horizontal cut $\frac{1}{2}$–$\frac{3}{4}$ in. long and the vertical one $1\frac{1}{2}$ in., and just deep enough to penetrate the bark. Prise open the bark on the vertical leg of the T with the back of the knife blade and open out with the tapered end of the budding-knife handle.

From the budwood slice out the buds, which are in the angle of the leaf axils. Insert the knife $\frac{1}{2}$ in. below the bud and draw it slantwise up the stem to a point about 1 in. above the bud.

The bud and the remaining leaf stalk is known as the shield. Generally, the percentage

PRUNING OF NEWLY PLANTED ROSES

A young Floribunda standard pruned as a bush rose

A newly planted rambler cut back to strong healthy buds

of successful budding is increased if the tiny sliver of wood just underneath the bud itself is removed. Gently slide the bud in position and push up firmly. Trim off the surplus bark of the bud, level with the flaps of the T incision. Bind the shield firmly to the stock with broad raffia that has been softened with water, or with plastic or latex budding tapes.

If, after about three weeks, the leaf stalk falls off when gently touched and the shield remains green, the budding is successful and the binding may be sliced through behind the bud, but not removed, to prevent constriction.

About the middle of February, sever all top growth of the rootstock 1 in. above the implanted bud of the scion. Leave the scions to grow on; in windy exposed sites they should be tied to 24 in. canes for the first season. Transplant the maiden shrubs to their permanent positions in early autumn.

Standard roses are budded in the same way, but the buds of the scion are put on in different positions. Use the same rootstocks as for bush roses, having selected one strong stem staked erect. Bud half-standards at about 3 ft; standards at 5 ft or less. After growing the stock for one year, sever the stem 6 in. above the required stem height in November, and allow a maximum of three shoots to develop at the top. The following June, bud each shoot near its base on the upper surfaces, as previously described. The following summer remove all growths just above the scion.

Pruning. To get the best results from roses of all types they should be pruned regularly and in the correct way. Certain general principles must be applied as follows: all cuts should be finished cleanly and be made immediately above a bud and as close as possible to it.

Dead or diseased wood should be removed immediately it is seen, whatever the time of year. Weak, damaged or crossing shoots should be removed entirely.

Always prune to an outward-pointing bud to allow light and air to reach the centre of the plant. The degree of severity of pruning is less important than maintaining an open bush.

Thick, vigorous healthy stems receive ample nourishment from the root system, and so are capable of supporting more new growths than are thin, weak ones. For this reason, weak stems should be pruned more severely to reduce the number of growths that they are required to maintain, and also to encourage the production of vigorous wood from low down in the plant.

Most roses produce their flowers on growths of the current year, but the true Ramblers, and many of the Species roses, Old roses and some of the Modern shrub roses flower on the previous year's growths. Pruning at the wrong time may result in the removal of some of the best flowering wood, and it is therefore necessary to know the group to which a rose belongs, before deciding when it should be pruned.

Roses that flower on the current season's growths can be pruned when the plants are completely dormant or just as growth is beginning in early spring. Roses that flower on the previous season's wood should be pruned as soon as flowering is over.

In mild areas, pruning may be done in autumn or early spring; in areas subject to hard frosts final pruning is best left until early spring. Pruning should not be attempted during a hard frost. Dormant pruning is recommended for mild areas and in sheltered gardens, such as those in large towns, where the warmth of buildings usually prevents very low temperatures. Remove dormant tissue after leaf-fall and while the plants are completely at rest, usually in November or December.

Tall-growing roses, such as the Floribunda 'Queen Elizabeth', may become loosened in the soil if planted in positions exposed to strong winds. The root systems may then be damaged by frost or drought, and stems may be broken or torn. This can be avoided by reducing the top growths by about one-third in early autumn; complete pruning in spring.

Early spring pruning is carried out from late February to early April, just as growth is beginning. It can safely be done over a period of several weeks, until the buds at the base of the plant have developed their first leaves.

Early spring pruning is recommended for most gardens; if the plants have been pruned while dormant, there is the risk of frost damage to the base of the plants. In the cold north-east, delay pruning until April.

During summer, remove faded flowers with a piece of stem back to a plump bud to ensure further flowering shoots. This is particularly important on Hybrid teas and Floribundas. Species roses, grown for their hips, should not be dead-headed.

PRUNING OF NEWLY PLANTED ROSES. All roses that have been planted in autumn or winter should be pruned early the first spring. If late planting is unavoidable, pruning can be done at the time of planting or delayed until development of the buds shows that active growth is commencing.

The initial pruning should always be severe, to establish a good framework of strong shoots from the base of the plant, and to reduce the strain on the root system, which will not be properly established at planting time.

Species and Shrub roses should have all weak and damaged wood removed and any laterals that have borne flowers the previous year. Remove soft tips back to firm wood on main growths.

After removing dead wood and weak or damaged shoots, Hybrid teas should be cut back to two or three buds from the base, and Floribundas to four or five buds.

Prune heads of newly planted standard roses as for Hybrid tea and Floribunda bushes, according to variety.

For Climbers and Ramblers, retain about 12–18 in. of the strongest growths and reduce the weaker ones to within 3–4 in. of the base. This initial pruning is particularly important for climbing roses in inducing the production of strong framework growths from low down in the plant.

PRUNING OF ESTABLISHED ROSES. Species and old shrub roses require little pruning except for the removal of soft tips and straggly growths. Neglected shrubs should have old weak growths removed at or near ground level. Spindly

PRUNING OF ESTABLISHED ROSES

An established Hybrid tea with shortened and cut-out stems

A Floribunda rose with weak and crossing branches cut out

lateral growths with poor flowers should be cut
back to the main stems.

On Hybrid tea bushes, remove entirely any
dead wood and all weak and damaged stems. For
bush and standard Hybrid tea roses, the purpose
for which they are grown has a bearing on the
amount of pruning they require. For garden
decoration, and to provide good flowers for
cutting, the strongest of the shoots retained
should be shortened to within four to six buds of
the base of the previous year's growth, the
weaker ones to two or four buds.

Only in exceptional cases should wood that is
more than one year old be cut into; this may be
done so as to encourage the production of fresh
growth from the base of an old plant.

Pruning should be rather more severe to
produce high quality and exhibition blooms.
This is done to limit the number of growths and
concentrate the energy of the plant into producing fewer flowers of perfect size and shape.

Floribunda, Polyantha and Hybrid polyantha roses. These are generally more vigorous
and free-flowering than Hybrid teas and the
pruning should consequently be less severe.
Shorten the strongest shoots to five or seven
buds from the base, and maintain the vigour of
the plants by cutting back the weaker shoots
severely. Except on vigorous varieties, light
pruning leads to the development of large,
weak-stemmed bushes with poor flowers.

Heads of established standards should be
pruned as for Hybrid tea and Floribunda bushes.

Climbing roses. Many of these are climbing
sports of bush Hybrid tea varieties, others are of
more complex parentage. Most flower on the
current season's growths and should be pruned
in early spring. Growths of three types will be
found on established plants: The main framework branches, which were trained out during
the early years to cover evenly the allotted space,
should be left as long as they retain their vigour.
The short lateral shoots, which bear flowers
during the current year, should be cut back to
two or three buds in spring.

A number of vigorous young growths appear,
usually from well up on the plant. These do not
flower in their first year, but are valuable for
extending the framework, and for replacing any
old branches which may have been damaged or
become exhausted. These young shoots should
be tied temporarily to their supports during the
autumn to prevent damage by gales or frost, and
trained into their permanent positions when the
rest of the plant is pruned in early spring. They
should not be cut back at all, except for the
removal of any damaged or soft tip growths.

Rambler roses. These differ from climbers in
having only one flowering period, usually completed by mid-August; they generally bear their
best flowers on the previous year's growths
which are produced annually from ground level.

As soon as flowering is over, cut the stems
that have flowered down to ground level, and tie
in the developing rods to replace them. If there
are not enough young growths to provide the
required cover, the best of the old shoots may be
retained for a second season and pruned by
cutting the laterals back to two or three buds
from their base.

PRUNING OF ESTABLISHED ROSES

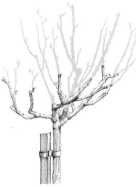

An established standard showing the main branches cut back

Lateral shoots of a climber cut
back to two or three buds

Weeping standards. These should be pruned in
the same way as Ramblers.

Most roses are propagated by budding on to a
stock which will provide a more vigorous root
system for the desired plant. Growths that
develop from one of these roots are suckers
which, if allowed to develop, will bear inferior
flowers, and may so sap the energy of the plant
that the desired variety will be swamped and so
weakened that it will cease flowering or even
die. Suckers may appear some distance away or
close to the bush, and can be recognised by their
differing stem or leaf colour and the shape and
quantity of their thorns.

A sucker should not be merely cut off at
ground level, since this will stimulate the
development of the dormant buds on the portion
of the stem below the surface. As soon as it is
large enough to handle, the sucker should be
pulled firmly away. It may be necessary to
scrape the soil carefully away and trace the
sucker back to the root. Wrench off cleanly.

Pests. Colonies of APHIDS infest stems, leaves
and flower buds, checking growth and making
the plants sooty and sticky.

Various CATERPILLARS eat leaves, stems and
flower buds. TORTRIX CATERPILLARS spin the
young leaves together with silk webbing.

LEAFHOPPERS feed on sap and cause a light
freckling on the upper surfaces of the leaves.

Larvae of various SAWFLIES damage the leaves.
One type rolls the leaves up tightly; another eats
away the surface tissues and exposes the veins.

CHAFER BEETLES, FROGHOPPERS and LEAF-
CUTTER BEES may also attack roses at times.

Diseases. Probably the most common is BLACK
SPOT. Distinct black or dark brown spots, up to $\frac{1}{2}$
in. in diameter, develop on the leaves; they may
be small and diffuse, or may increase in size
until large areas are discoloured. Affected leaves
turn yellow and drop, and in severe cases the
bush may be completely defoliated. The disease
overwinters on fallen leaves.

CROWN GALL may occur at ground level; a
gall about the size of a walnut develops at
the crown. It may also occur higher up on the
shoots, where numerous smaller galls appear.

Unsatisfactory cultural conditions can cause
DIE-BACK. Fungi, entering the plants through
dead wood, wounds and pruning cuts, result in
further die-back or a cankering and cracking of
the bark, particularly at ground level.

FROST DAMAGE shows as a purple or bronze
blotching of the leaves and stems, or the leaves
may curl. Shoots may die and are then often
attacked by grey mould fungus.

GREY MOULD may cause the flower buds to
turn brown and decay; affected tissues become
covered with a grey fluffy growth. In damp
weather blooms may also be attacked.

HONEY FUNGUS causes rapid death of bushes.

MINERAL DEFICIENCIES may cause discoloration
of leaves and poor growth. MAGNESIUM DE-
FICIENCY is particularly common, especially on
sandy soils and following heavy applications of
potash manures. Old leaves are affected first,
showing a yellow mottling and browning
between the veins.

POWDERY MILDEW forms a white coating on
the leaves, stems and flower buds. Climbers are

specially susceptible and the shoots and leaves
re often severely distorted. In winter, a grey
elty fungal growth can be seen on the stems.

RUST appears in spring as bright orange
atches, up to 1 in. long, on the stems and leaf
talks. In summer, the upper surfaces of the
eaves develop yellow spots with orange
owdery pustules on the undersides; these
radually turn black in the autumn. Leaf-drop or
ven death of the bush may occur.

SPRAY DAMAGE, due to the effects of hormone
veedkillers, shows as a distortion of the shoots
nd leaf stalks, which twist spirally; the leaves
re narrow and twisted, with parallel veining.

Roscoea

Zingiberaceae

ROSCOEA CAUTLEOIDES

 genus of 15 species of hardy herbaceous
erennials, all native to western Asia. They have
andsome, orchid-like flowers and are suitable
lants for rock gardens or the front of borders.

R. cautleoides. China. Height 18 in.; planting
distance 12 in. This bears lanceolate mid-green
eaves. The pale yellow flowers, 1½–2 in. long,
re carried in spikes in June and July.

R. humeana. N. China. Height 12 in.; planting
distance 15 in. Lanceolate and pointed bright
reen leaves sheath the short stems. The flowers
rotrude above the young foliage and carry two
o five, or more, violet-purple flowers, 2 in. long.
One petal is upright and the others curl
ownwards; flowering is in June and July.

Cultivation. Plant in March in any ordinary,
noisture-retentive soil, in sun or partial shade.
et the fleshy, dahlia-like roots 3–4 in. below soil
evel. New growth does not appear before May.

Propagation. Roscoeas are easily divided and
eplanted in March, as the crowns fall apart on
eing dug up. The plants resent root disturbance
nd propagation by seeds is preferable.

Sow seeds in a cold frame or greenhouse in
ugust or September; prick out the seedlings
vhen large enough to handle, and grow on
utdoors in a nursery bed for two seasons.

R. cautleoides may produce self-sown plants
 weeding is not too rigorous.

Pests and diseases. Generally trouble-free.

Rose: see Rosa
Rose, apple: see *Rosa pomifera*
Rose, Austrian briar: see *Rosa foetida*
Rose, Austrian copper: see *Rosa foetida bicolor*
Rose, autumn musk: see *Rosa moschata*
Rose, Bank's: see *Rosa banksiae*
Rose, blush noisette: see *Rosa × noisettiana*
Rose, burnet: see *Rosa spinosissima*
Rose, cabbage: see *Rosa centifolia*
Rose, china: see *Rosa chinensis*

Rose, Christmas: see *Helleborus niger*
Rose, damask: see *Rosa damascena*
Rose, dog: see *Rosa canina*
Rose, French: see *Rosa gallica*
Rose, green: see *Rosa chinensis* 'Viridiflora'
Rose, guelder: see *Viburnum opulus*
Rose, lenten: see *Helleborus orientalis*
Rose, memorial: see *Rosa luciae*
Rose, moss: see *Rosa centifolia*
Rose of Sharon: see *Hypericum calycinum*
Rose of York, white: see *Rosa × alba*
Rose, provence: see *Rosa centifolia*
Rose, rock: see Cistus and Helianthemum
Rose root: see *Sedum roseum*
Rose, Scotch: see *Rosa rubiginosa*
Rose, summer-flowering musk: see *Rosa brunonii*
Rose, sun: see Cistus
Rose, tea: see *Rosa × odorata*

Rosmarinus

Rosemary. *Labiatae*

A genus of three species of hardy and half-hardy
evergreen flowering shrubs. The flowers are
tubular, with a prominent lower lip, and are
borne in small axillary clusters. The linear-oblong
leaves are strongly aromatic and may be used,
fresh or dried, for flavouring meats, poultry and
fish. The shoots are distilled to make oil.

See also HERBS.

R. lavandulaceus, syn. *R. officinalis prostratus.* S.
Europe. Height 3–4 in.; spread 3–4 ft. A
mat-forming shrub which is half-hardy, surviving
outdoors only in sheltered sites in the south and
west; it is ideal growing at the foot of a sheltered
wall or trailing over a dry wall. The leaves are
mid to yellow-green; pale blue flowers, ½–¾ in.
long, appear from April to September.

'Severn Sea' is compact and less hardy than the
type species, with blue flowers on low-growing
arching branches.

R. officinalis. S. Europe, Asia Minor. Height 6–7
ft; spread 5–6 ft. An erect to spreading decorative
shrub, with mid to dark green leaves having
white undersides. Mauve ½–¾ in. long flowers
open in March or April and continue to appear
sporadically until September.

Varieties include: 'Albiflorus', syn. 'Albus',
white or very pale blue flowers; 'Erectus', syns.
'Fastigiatus' and 'Pyramidalis', of erect and
pyramidal habit; 'Jessop's Upright', a vigorous
and erect form with lighter mauve flowers.

R. o. prostratus: see *R. lavandulaceus.*

Cultivation. Grow in any ordinary, well-drained
garden soil, in a sunny position. Plant *R.
officinalis* and its varieties in March or April, *R.
lavandulaceus* in April or May.

Propagation. Take 4 in. cuttings of half-ripe
shoots in July or August and insert in equal parts
(by volume) peat and sand in a cold frame. Pot
the rooted cuttings in 3 in. containers of John
Innes potting compost No. 1 and overwinter in a
frost-free frame or greenhouse. Plant out in the
flowering site in May.

R. officinalis may also be increased from 6–9
in. cuttings of mature shoots planted directly in
permanent positions in September or March.

Roscoea cautleoides

Roscoea humeana

Rosmarinus officinalis

631

Rosmarinus lavandulaceus

Rubus cockburnianus
(in winter)

Rubus ulmifolius 'Bellidiflorus'

Rubus × tridel 'Benenden'

Pruning. Cut out any dead growths in March, and shorten long straggly shoots of *R. officinalis*. Old overgrown bushes may have all shoots cut back by half in April.

Pests and diseases. Generally trouble-free.

Rosemary: see Rosmarinus
Rowan: see *Sorbus aucuparia*
Rubber plant: see *Ficus elastica*

Rubus

Rosaceae

A genus of 250 species or, if the micro-species are counted, up to 3000 species of hardy, erect or scrambling evergreen and deciduous, usually prickly shrubs. Most species bear edible fruits, such as the raspberry and the blackberry. The genus also includes ornamental shrubs, grown for their winter stems, foliage or flowers.

RUBUS COCKBURNIANUS (IN WINTER)

R. cockburnianus, syn. *R. giraldianus*. N. and Central China. Height 7–9 ft; spread 5–6 ft. An ornamental deciduous species with slender-pointed, pinnate, mid-green leaves with pale undersides. Star-shaped purple flowers, $1\frac{3}{4}$ in. wide, appear in June. The erect stems, white tinged blue, are attractive in winter.
R. deliciosus. Colorado. Height 6–10 ft; spread 6–8 ft. This deciduous ornamental shrub has palmate, pale to mid-green, coarsely toothed leaves on thornless stems. Solitary white cup-shaped flowers open to flat, $1\frac{1}{2}$–2 in. wide blooms in May and June.
R. fruticosus: see Blackberry
R. giraldianus: see *R. cockburnianus*

Rubus phoenicolasius (fruits)

R. idaeus: see Raspberry
R. × loganobaccus: see Loganberry
R. odoratus. Eastern N. America. Height 6–8 ft; spread 4–5 ft. A deciduous vigorous shrub with velvety, vine-like leaves that are bright green and borne on thornless peeling stems. Fragrant bowl-shaped to flat, $1\frac{1}{2}$–2 in. wide, purple-rose flowers open between June and August. The species is grown for its ornamental value, although edible red fruits may be produced in August and September.

RUBUS PHOENICOLASIUS

R. phoenicolasius (Japanese wineberry). China and Japan. Height 6–8 ft; spread 8–10 ft. A deciduous species with bristly stems bearing mid-green leaves that are white beneath; they are composed of three or five coarsely toothed, ovate leaflets. The terminal pink inflorescences, 6–8 in. long, and the stems are covered with brilliant red hairs. Edible, rounded, scarlet berries, $\frac{3}{4}$ in. long, ripen in August; they are used in preserves and for table desserts.
R. × tridel 'Benenden'. Height 6–8 ft; spread 8–10 ft. A fast-growing deciduous ornamental hybrid between *R. deliciosus* and *R. trilobus*. The broadly ovate, pale to mid-green leaves are trilobed and borne on bristly twigs. In May glistening white saucer-shaped flowers, $1\frac{1}{2}$–2 in. across, and with masses of yellow stamens, are borne along arching stems. This hybrid does not produce fruits.
R. ulmifolius. Europe, including Great Britain. Height 3–4 ft; spread 5–6 ft. A semi-evergreen species forming an arching mound of tangled and prickly growths. The pinnate leaves are composed of three or five leaflets, deep green above, grey-green beneath. Pale purple-pink flowers which are cup-shaped and $\frac{3}{4}$ in. wide, are borne

from June to August in loose panicles 6 in. long. In cultivation, the species is represented by the sterile form 'Bellidiflorus' with fully double pompon-like rose-pink flowers.

Cultivation. Plant ornamental species between October and March in ordinary, well-drained garden soil, in sun or partial shade.

Plant shrubs, grown for their edible fruits, between October and March in fertile garden soil and in sun or partial shade. Set the plants in rows at intervals of 6 ft and train fanwise on wires, 12 in. apart, stretched between stout posts. Wineberries may also be trained against a sunny wall, securing the shoots with vine eyes.

Give fruiting species an annual dressing of 1 oz. sulphate of potash in winter and $\frac{1}{2}$ oz. sulphate of ammonia in March, both per sq. yd. Mulch in April with well-rotted manure or compost.

Propagation. Take 3–4 in. long semi-hardwood cuttings in August and September of all species except *R. ulmifolius*. Insert the cuttings in equal parts (by volume) peat and sand in a cold frame; the following April or May line the rooted cuttings out in nursery rows and transplant to permanent positions in October.

Alternatively, increase by division at any time from October to March.

Propagate *R. ulmifolius* by tip layering, pegging the shoots down in August. Sever and replant the new plants the following spring.

Pruning. After flowering, remove a proportion of the flowered shoots at ground level to keep the shrubs shapely.

The fruiting canes of *R. phoenicolasius* should be removed at ground level after fruiting, and the current season's basal shoots tied in on the wires as replacement shoots.

Pests. Generally trouble-free.

Diseases. Generally trouble-free, but the shrubs may occasionally be affected by the diseases that attack fruit-bearing rubus species.

CROWN GALL, GREY MOULD, RUBUS STUNT and RUST are the most common diseases.

Rudbeckia

Coneflower. *Compositae*

RUDBECKIA FULGIDA

A genus of 25 species of hardy annuals and herbaceous perennials. The following species are easily-grown, showy border plants and provide long-lasting cut flowers in late summer.

The vernacular name is derived from the cone-shaped centre of the daisy-like flowers.

R. bicolor. Texas. Height 24 in.; planting distance 12 in. An upright, branching annual having bristly stems and foliage. The leaves are oblong and mid-green. The flowers, 2 in. across, and yellow with a black central cone, are produced from July to August.

There are several garden varieties, including 'Kelvedon Star', deep gold-yellow with a mahogany zone and dark cone; and 'Superba' which has slightly larger flowers with maroon-backed petals.

R. fulgida, syns. *R. speciosa, R. newmanii.* S.E. United States. Height 2–3 ft; planting distance 18–24 in. A bushy perennial species which is rather variable. The leaves are mid-green, oblong or lanceolate. Yellow to orange flowers, $2\frac{1}{2}$ in. across, with purple-brown cones, are produced from July to September.

The true species is seldom grown, but the following varieties are recommended: 'Deamii', with 3–4 in. yellow flowers; 'Goldsturm' whose yellow flowers, up to 5 in. across, with dark brown cones, are produced into October; and 'Speciosa', with orange flowers, 3–4 in. across.

R. hirta (black-eyed susan). N. America. Height 1–3 ft; planting distance 12–18 in. A showy short-lived perennial of branching habit, usually grown as a hardy annual. The leaves are oblong to lanceolate, mid-green and, like the stems, covered with short bristles. The flowers, 3 in. across, have golden-yellow ray petals surrounding a deep brown-purple central cone. They are produced from August to October.

In addition to mixed hybrids, garden varieties include 'Golden Flame', 12 in., with golden-yellow, crimson-coned flowers; and 'Bambi', 12 in., with rich bronze, chestnut and gold flowers.

R. h. Tetra 'Gloriosa' (gloriosa daisy), height 2–3 ft, planting distance 24 in., is a tetraploid selection from *R. hirta.* This is a well-branched plant, excellent for annual and mixed borders and for cutting. The flowers, in shades of yellow and mahogany, including bi-colours, are up to 7 in. across; they appear from July to the first frosts.

'Double Gloriosa' has double or semi-double flowers in a similar colour range, most of the cone being replaced by the extra petals. There is also a yellow strain with an olive-green cone; it is known as 'Irish Eyes'.

R. laciniata. Canada, U.S.A. Height 6–7 ft; planting distance 24 in. The ovate, mid-green leaves of this perennial species are deeply cut or comprised of a number of leaflets. The flowers are yellow, 3–4 in. across and appear from August to September. There are several good garden varieties with similar-sized but double flowers in shades of yellow with green cones. They include:

'Golden Glow' (height 5–7 ft), lemon-yellow flowers from August to October; 'Goldquelle' (height 3 ft), deep yellow flowers.

R. newmanii: see *R. fulgida*

R. nitida. N. America. Height 6 ft; planting distance 24 in. This perennial species has been superseded by 'Herbstsonne', syn. 'Autumn Sun'. The mid-green leaves are deeply divided. Single yellow flowers, about 4 in. across, with a green cone, appear in August and September.

If the flowers are removed as soon as they fade, together with 12–24 in. of the stem, new flowering shoots will appear and continue to October. In rich, moist soil the variety may reach a height of up to 12 ft.

R. speciosa: see *R. fulgida*

R. subtomentosa. N. America. Height 3 ft; planting distance 18–24 in. This perennial species has ovate, mid-green leaves which are

Rudbeckia bicolor 'Superba'

Rudbeckia fulgida 'Goldsturm'

Rudbeckia hirta Tetra 'Double Gloriosa'

Rudbeckia hirta Tetra 'Irish Eyes'

finely covered with grey hairs. It bears yellow flowers, about 3 in. across, appearing from July to September. The deep brown centre is scarcely raised, and more button-like than cone-shaped.

Cultivation. Rudbeckias grow in any well-cultivated and well-drained garden soil. Choose an open and sunny site. All the described perennial species and varieties, together with the taller of the annual species, require staking in exposed positions.

Cut *R. hirta* back hard after its first flowering and give a liquid feed to produce a second flush of blooms. *R. hirta* Tetra 'Gloriosa' will flower in the second and third years if, in exposed cold gardens, the crowns are protected during the winter with a heap of sand, ashes or bracken.

Plant perennial species in October, March or April. On dry soils, mulch with peat or decayed manure early in spring, unless height restriction of the tall species or varieties is wanted. Dead-head regularly as the flowers fade and cut the stems down in November.

Propagation. Sow seeds of annual species in pots or pans of seed compost during March or April and place in a cold frame. Prick out the seedlings, when large enough to handle, and plant them out in the flowering site in May.

The perennials may also be raised from seeds, sown as for annuals; the seedlings should be transferred to nursery rows and grown on until October when they can be planted in the flowering site. These seedlings are variable and not true to type. It is better to divide and replant the roots between October and March.

Pests. Leaves, flowers and stems are eaten by SLUGS and SNAILS.

Diseases. Generally trouble-free.

Rudbeckia nitida 'Herbstsonne'

Ruellia macrantha

Ruscus aculeatus (fruits)

Rue: see Ruta
Rue, goat's: see Galega

Ruellia

Acanthaceae

RUELLIA PORTELLAE

A genus of five species of evergreen perennials and sub-shrubs. They all have attractive trumpet-shaped flowers, and some make good foliage plants. Those described here are tender and require greenhouse cultivation.

R. macrantha. Brazil. Height up to 3 ft; spread 24 in. An erect sub-shrub with lanceolate mid to dark green leaves about 6 in. long. Terminal clusters of rose-purple flowers appear from the upper leaf axils from January to April. Each flower is up to $3\frac{1}{2}$ in. long.

R. portellae. Brazil. Height and spread 9–12 in. A dome-shaped species with attractive foliage. The elliptic leaves, about 3 in. long, are deep green with a bronze sheen and silvery-grey veins on the upper surfaces; the undersides are entirely suffused with red-purple. The rose-pink flowers, $1\frac{1}{2}$ in. long, rise singly from the upper leaf axils from November to March or later.

Cultivation. Grow *R. portellae* in 4–6 in. pots, *R. macrantha* in 6–8 in. pots, of John Innes potting compost No. 2 or in a proprietary loamless compost. A winter temperature of 13–16°C (55–61°F) must be maintained to ensure flowering. Raise new plants every other year, as young plants produce better flowers than old ones.

Keep the plants moist at all times and give light shade in summer.

Repot established plants annually in September; during the second and subsequent season give a weak liquid feed at fortnightly intervals from October to June.

Propagation. Take 2–3 in. cuttings of basal shoots from cut-back plants in April or May. Insert four to six cuttings in a 4 in. pot containing equal parts (by volume) peat and sand and root at a temperature of 18–21°C (64–70°F). Pot the rooted cuttings singly in 3 in. containers of John Innes potting compost No. 2.

Pruning. Cut flowering shoots of *R. macrantha* hard back to 3 in. from the base as soon as flowering is over. *R. portellae* can be left unpruned, or the growths may be shortened by half after flowering. Pinch out young plants two or three times to promote bushy growth.

Pests and diseases. Generally trouble-free.

Rumex: see Sorrel
Runner bean: see Beans

Ruscus

Liliaceae

RUSCUS ACULEATUS

A genus of three species of hardy evergreen sub-shrubs, spreading by means of short rhizomes. The species are leafless; the apparent leaves are modified flattened stems (cladodes), which carry out the functions of a normal leaf. Male and female flowers are inconspicuous and are produced on separate plants. Handsome large red berries are borne in autumn on female plants, if groups of both sexes are planted together.

R. aculeatus (butcher's broom). Europe, including Great Britain. Height and spread 2–3 ft. This species is sometimes seen in shady woods and hedgerows in the south and west. The strong and erect green stems which branch in their upper parts are thickly covered with small, ovate, spine-tipped, dark green cladodes. Inconspicuous green flowers are borne on the surface of the cladodes in March and April; sealing-wax red berries as large as cherries are produced.

R. hypoglossum. Central, S. and E. Europe, Asia Minor. Height 12–18 in.; spread 2–3 ft. A spreading sub-shrub which forms large patches. The lanceolate mid-green cladodes are without sharp points. Yellow flowers are borne in April and May and are followed by small red berries, seldom freely produced. This species is an ideal woodland plant, tolerant of dense shade; it associates well with ferns and hellebores.

Cultivation. Plant these easily-grown shrubs in April. They thrive in any ordinary garden soil and do well on heavy clay or shallow chalk soil, in sun or dense shade. Plant in groups of three to five to contain both sexes.

Propagation. Lift, divide and replant large clumps during April.

Sow seeds when ripe, usually in September and October, in pans of John Innes seed compost placed in a cold frame, or sow in nursery beds outdoors. The seeds may take 18 months to germinate. When the seedlings are about 3 in. high, line them out in nursery rows and grow on for three years. Transplant to permanent positions in April.

Pruning. No pruning is required except the removal of dead wood in March or April.

Pests and diseases. Generally trouble-free.

Rush, bog: see Juncus
Rush, corkscrew: see *Juncus effusus* 'Spiralis'
Rush, Egyptian paper: see *Cyperus papyrus*

Ruta

Rue. *Rutaceae*

A genus of 60 species of hardy evergreen shrubs and sub-shrubs. The one species in general cultivation was formerly much used as a culinary herb; the leaves may be finely chopped and added sparingly to salads to impart a bitter flavour. It is now mainly grown as a decorative foliage plant in the herbaceous border, or as a low hedge.

R. graveolens. S. Europe. Height 2–3 ft; planting distance 18 in. A neat sub-shrub with ovate, deeply divided blue-green leaves that have an acridly aromatic odour. Stiff terminal clusters of sulphur-yellow, $\frac{1}{2}$ in. wide flowers with cupped petals are borne in June and July or later.

The variety 'Jackman's Blue' is a more compact form (height 18–24 in.; planting distance 15 in.), with brighter blue-grey foliage.

Cultivation. Plant from September to March in any ordinary well-drained soil and in a sunny position. Trim the plants back to old wood in April to preserve the bushy shape or to keep low-growing hedges from becoming leggy. In autumn, remove the dead flower clusters.

For hedges, set young pot-grown plants at intervals of 12–15 in. Pinch out the growing tips to induce bushy growth and thereafter trim annually in April.

For use in cooking, gather the sprigs fresh, or dry them and store in airtight containers.

Propagation. Sow seeds in March or April in pots or pans of John Innes seed compost and place in a cold frame. Prick off the seedlings into boxes of John Innes potting compost No. 1, and then into $3\frac{1}{2}$ in. pots. Plunge outdoors and set in permanent positions in September.

Alternatively, take cuttings, 3–4 in. long, of lateral shoots in August and insert in equal parts (by volume) peat and sand. Pot the rooted cuttings singly into 3–$3\frac{1}{2}$ in. pots of John Innes potting compost No. 1 and plunge in a cold frame. Plant out the following March.

Pests and diseases. Generally trouble-free.

Ruta graveolens
'Jackman's Blue'

Sage (variegated form)

S

Sage

Salvia officinalis. Labiatae

SAGE

This hardy, evergreen, aromatic, sub-shrub is used as a culinary herb.

S. Europe. Height 2 ft; planting distance 15 in. The strong four-sided stems, which become woody, carry stalked, ovate leaves that are grey-green and wrinkled. Small, tubular, violet-blue flowers, are borne in June and July.

Use the slightly bitter-tasting leaves, fresh or dried, with rich meat and poultry such as pork, duck and goose; sprinkle them on the meat before cooking or add them to stuffings. A variegated form is also available.

Cultivation. Plant in March or April in a sunny position in well-drained, light soil. Pinch off any flowers that appear, to encourage leaf growth. Sage is sometimes grown as an annual but, in any case, replace the plants after three or four years. They tend to become leggy and woody if not kept regularly trimmed.

Propagation. Sow seeds in pots or pans of seed compost, in a cold frame or greenhouse in March, or in open ground during April or May. Prick off the seedlings into a nursery bed, and later transfer them to their final positions, 15 in. apart.

Alternatively, take 3 in. heel cuttings in September and insert in equal parts (by volume) peat and sand in a cold frame. Pot the rooted cuttings singly in 3–4 in. pots of John Innes potting compost No. 1 and overwinter in the frame, nipping out the growing tips to induce bushy growth. Plant out in March or April.

Sagittaria latifolia

Saintpaulia ionantha 'Diana Double Pink'

Saintpaulia ionantha
'Rhapsody'

Harvesting and storing. Pick leaves at any time to use fresh; for drying, gather them just before the plants flower. Sage is difficult to dry well as the toughness of the leaves necessitates a long drying period which may destroy their colour and flavour. For drying methods see HERBS.

Pests. Young shoots are sometimes attacked by CAPSID BUGS, and the leaves may become distorted or develop small cracks and holes.

Diseases. In damp weather, GREY MOULD may attack young, soft shoots causing them to die back and become covered with a grey-white fungal growth on both leaves and stems.

POWDERY MILDEW shows as a white powdery coating on the leaves.

Sage, Jerusalem: see *Phlomis fruticosa*
Sage, white: see *Artemisia ludoviciana*

Sagittaria
Arrowhead. *Alismataceae*

SAGITTARIA SAGITTIFOLIA

A genus of 20 species of perennial aquatics, including hardy and tender species, grown as decorative marginal plants in outdoor and greenhouse pools and in aquaria. The two described are hardy and easy to grow. The common name refers to the arrow-shaped leaves of some species.

All species increase by underground runners, often so rapidly that the plants become a nuisance. Egg-shaped tubers are formed on the runners in late summer and remain attached during the winter.

S. japonica: see *S. sagittifolia leucopetala*
S. latifolia (duck potato). N. America. Water depth 4–18 in.; height 24 in.; planting distance 6–15 in. A fully hardy species, with light green ovate aerial leaves. Immature plants are often grown in aquaria. In July, the flower spike bears flattened, three-petalled, white flowers, $\frac{3}{4}$ in. wide, with green or yellow centres. Freely produced runners bear small winter tubers but young plants also persist in winter. These are completely submerged, with arching strap-shaped leaves that are dark green and semi-translucent.

S. sagittifolia (common arrowhead). Europe, including Great Britain. Water depth $\frac{1}{2}$–3 ft; height 1–2$\frac{1}{2}$ ft; planting distance 12–15 in. A hardy perennial plant found in ponds and slow-flowing streams. The underwater leaves, which occur only at the beginning of each season, are linear and pale green; the arrow-shaped surface leaves are light green, sometimes spotted with brown. Thick stems carry small whorled racemes of white flowers, $\frac{3}{4}$–1 in. across and tinted pink around the deep brown central boss of stamens. Flowering is in July and August. Freely produced runners bear winter tubers which are often blue-green in colour.

S. s. leucopetala (Japanese arrowhead) is a sub-species from S. and E. Asia, commonly sold as *S. japonica*. Water depth 6–12 in.; height 1$\frac{1}{2}$–2$\frac{1}{2}$ ft; planting distance 12–15 in. Thick succulent stems carry deep green arrow-shaped leaves which vary considerably in length and width. A fleshy flower stem emerges in July, terminating in a whorled raceme of pure white three-petalled flowers, each about 1 in. across with golden stamens.

The variety 'Flore Pleno' (double Japanese arrowhead) is similar to the sub-species but larger growing. It has paler leaves and a whorled raceme of fully double blossoms.

Cultivation. Grown as marginal plants in slow streams and ponds, sagittarias need fertile soil 6–8 in. deep covered by up to 18 in. of water. Plant in full sun. In early March or April push the dormant tubers 2–3 in. deep into soft mud, taking care not to damage the growing shoots.

For later plantings in June or July use young, small plants: large plants may be harmed by wind and sun.

Tall flower stems may require staking in exposed situations. Thin out the spreading plants as necessary during the growing season by uprooting unwanted plants.

Propagation. In June or July, remove and replant the smallest of the young plants arising around the parent growth.

Pests. Leaves and flowers may be infested with APHIDS, particularly water-lily aphids.

Diseases. Generally trouble-free.

St John's wort: see Hypericum

Saintpaulia
African violet. *Gesneriaceae*

SAINTPAULIA IONANTHA

A genus of 12 species of tender evergreen perennials, only one of which is in general cultivation. This free-flowering species and its varieties require greenhouse cultivation and are popular as house plants. They do well only if regular warmth can be maintained, and they are easily damaged by over-watering.

S. ionantha. Central Africa. Height 3–4 in.; spread 6–9 in. The mid to deep green heart-shaped leaves have a velvety texture. Single purple flowers, $\frac{3}{4}$–1$\frac{1}{2}$ in. across, are produced in small umbels throughout the year but most freely from June to October; they are somewhat violet-like, with expanded, rounded petals.

Varieties include: 'Blue Fairy Tale', deep blue; 'Diana Blue', rich velvety blue-purple; 'Diana Double Pink', semi-double, rose-purple; 'Diana Pink', pale rose-purple; 'Diana Red', red-purple; 'Grandiflora Pink', rose-pink; and 'Rhapsody', semi-double, deep purple-blue.

Saintpaulia ionantha 'Diana Pink'

Saintpaulia ionantha 'Diana Red'

Saintpaulia ionantha 'Diana Blue'

Cultivation. Saintpaulias do best in a compost of equal parts (by volume) lime-free loam, peat, sand and leaf-mould, or in a proprietary peat mixture. Grow the plants in 4–5 in. pots; keep the compost moist at all times but never let it become soggy. Keep water off the leaves to prevent them from becoming marked. A winter temperature of 13°C (55°F) is required.

Stand the pots in containers of moist peat, or in trays filled with pebbles, kept topped up with water. They may also be stood in polystyrene troughs. Place the plants in a light position, but shaded from direct sunlight.

Repot established plants every other year in April; give a weak liquid manure at intervals of 10–14 days from May to September.

Propagation. Take leaf cuttings with about 2 in. of stalk between June and September; insert the cuttings singly in 2½ in. pots of equal parts (by volume) peat and sand in a propagating frame at a temperature of 18–21°C (64–70°F). Pot on as the plantlets outgrow their containers.

Alternatively, sow seeds during March or April in pots or pans of equal parts (by volume) lime-free loam, peat and sand. Germinate at a temperature of 18–21°C (64–70°F). Prick out the seedlings, when large enough to handle, into pans or boxes, then singly into 3 in. pots of the growing compost. Pot on as necessary.

Pests. Infestations of TARSONEMID MITES on the growing points cause distortion and thickening of the leaves, and disrupt flowering.

EELWORMS may cause similar symptoms.

Diseases. Water left lying on the leaves results in a PHYSIOLOGICAL DISORDER that causes large yellow rings on the foliage.

TOMATO SPOTTED WILT VIRUS causes mottling on the leaves and streaking of flower colour; both leaves and flowers may be distorted.

Salix

Willow. *Salicaceae*

A genus of about 500 species of hardy deciduous trees and shrubs, which vary greatly in size. Some are decorative in winter, with coloured bark and slender drooping branches; others have fluffy, ovoid or cylindrical catkins, with male and female flowers on separate bushes. The male catkins are generally silky and silver-grey at first, but later turn yellow with pollen as the stamens expand. The female catkins are green and inconspicuous.

S. aegyptiaca, syn. *S. medemii.* Asia Minor. Height 10–12 ft; spread 8 ft. The slender-pointed, mid-green, downy leaves follow the yellow male catkins, which are up to 2 in. long and appear in January and February.

Salix alba 'Chermesina'

SALIX × CHRYSOCOMA

S. alba (white willow). Europe, N. Asia. Height 30–40 ft; spread 15–25 ft. Grey-green tapering leaves appear with the stalked catkins in May.

Salix apoda

Salix × boydii

Salix × chrysocoma

The green-yellow male catkins are up to 2 in. long. The young shoots of 'Chermesina', syn. 'Britzensis', are orange, making this tree particularly attractive in winter. The shoots of 'Vitellina' are yellow when young.

For *S. a.* 'Tristis' and *S. a.* 'Vitellina Pendula', see *S. × chrysocoma*.

S. apoda. Caucasus. Height 9–12 in.; spread 24 in. A gnarled, spreading or mat-forming shrublet, with mid-green ovate-lanceolate leaves. It is represented in cultivation mainly by the male form, which bears 1½–2 in. long erect silver-grey catkins in March. When mature, these are covered with pink and orange stamens.

S. babylonica (weeping willow). China. Height 20–25 ft; spread 20–30 ft. The slender lanceolate leaves are pale to mid-green on drooping brown branches. The 1 in. long male catkins are green-yellow. Although it is less commonly planted than *S. × chrysocoma*, it is less subject to canker. The leaves of the variety 'Annularis' are spirally curled.

S. × boydii. Height and spread 12 in. A single plant of this natural dwarf hybrid was found in Glen Fiagh, Scotland, in 1901. All the plants in cultivation have arisen from this original discovery. It is a slow-growing miniature tree with rounded, ovate leaves that are silver-grey, prominently veined and corrugated. Insignificant ovoid catkins, ½ in. long, appear in April.

S. × chrysocoma, syns. *S. alba* 'Tristis' and *S. a.* 'Vitellina Pendula'. Height and spread 20–25 ft. The slender lanceolate leaves are pale to mid-green, and borne on long, pendent yellow stems. The narrow, 1 in. long male catkins are yellow and appear in March and April. This spectacular weeping tree, which is a hybrid between *S. alba* 'Vitellina' and *S. babylonica*, makes a good specimen tree for a lawn.

SALIX DAPHNOIDES

S. daphnoides (violet willow). Europe, Siberia. Height 15–25 ft; spread about 15 ft. The lustrous mid-green leaves of this fast-growing tree are lanceolate. Yellow male catkins, up to 2 in. long, appear in March before the leaves. The purple-violet shoots are covered with a white bloom which is most attractive in winter.

S. elaeagnos, syn. *S. incana* (hoary willow). Central and S. Europe, Asia Minor. Height 10 ft or more; spread 8 ft or more. The long slender branches are covered with linear grey-green leaves. Yellow male catkins, 1–1½ in. long, appear in April. This distinctive bush is particularly attractive when grown beside water.

S. gracilistyla. Japan, Korea. Height 6–8 ft; spread 5–8 ft. When young, the grey-green lanceolate leaves are silvered with fine hairs. In March or April, the branches bear 2 in. long red and grey male catkins which turn yellow as the stamens expand.

S. incana: see *S. elaeagnos*

S. lanata (woolly willow). N. Europe, N. Asi Height 2–4 ft; spread 1–4 ft. This is a slow growing shrub suitable for rock gardens. Th rounded mid-green leaves are densely covered with a grey-white felt. The yellow catkins, whic appear in March and April, are stout and erect.

Salix lanata

S. matsudana. China, Korea. Height 20–30 ft spread 15–20 ft. The narrow-pointed leaves ar mid-green above, glaucous beneath, and borne o slender yellow branches. The green-yellow mal catkins, which appear in April, are about 1 ir long. 'Pendula' is similar in habit to *S. baby lonica*, but is a smaller weeping tree; 'Tortuosa' a slow-growing erect tree with twisted an contorted branches.

S. medemii: see *S. aegyptiaca*

S. repens (creeping willow). Europe, N.E. Asi Height 3–6 ft; spread 5–8 ft. The ovate o lanceolate grey-green leaves, which are covered with silvery silky hairs, become darker green b mid-summer but sometimes retain a hoar appearance. The leaves are borne on erect o ascending branches after the 1 in. long silver-gre male catkins appear in April or May. This plan grows as a dwarf shrub in dry or stony soils, but i taller and more luxuriant in a moist loam.

S. 'Wehrhahnii'. Switzerland. Height 4–5 ft spread 5–6 ft. This willow is now known to be variety of the rarely grown *S. hastata*. The ovat leaves are mid to grey-green. The bark is a dar purple-brown and the 1–1½ in. long male catkin which appear in April, are snow-white an resemble cotton wool.

Cultivation. Plant between October an February, preferably in moist soil in a sunr position. Most of the larger species are unsuitab for light, sandy soil unless the roots hav adequate moisture, as beside a pool.

Propagation. Take 9–15 in. long hardwoo cuttings between October and March and inser in moist soil in a nursery bed; plant out in th permanent positions a year later.

Pruning. Remove dead wood between Novembe and February. Willows grown for their coloure stems should be cut back annually in February within a few inches of ground level.

Pests. The leaves may be reduced to a skeleton o veins by CATERPILLARS and various beetle larva

GALL MITES stunt and distort young shoots, and SAWFLY larvae produce brightly coloured bean-shaped galls on the leaves.

APHIDS, particularly the willow stem aphid, infest the stems and produce large quantities of honey-dew, making the plants sticky and sooty.

SCALE INSECTS, especially willow scale, form encrusting colonies on the stems and shoots which, in severe infestations, look as if they have been whitewashed.

Diseases. Small black cankers on the shoots and small brown spots on the leaves are caused by ANTHRACNOSE OF WILLOW. The leaves are often distorted and fall prematurely.

BRACKET FUNGI may enter dead wood and cause rotting of the heartwood if the tree is neglected. Later, the large bracket-shaped fruiting bodies develop on the trunk or branches.

DIE-BACK and CANKER may be due to many fungi. Dead patches or cankers appear on shoots and, if girdling occurs, the shoots die back.

HONEY FUNGUS may kill the trees quickly.

Excessively wet or dry soil conditions may result in a PHYSIOLOGICAL DISORDER; the leaves become discoloured and shoots die back.

RUST, due to many different fungi, shows on the leaves as spore pustules which are at first orange and then brown.

Salpiglossis
Solanaceae

A genus of 18 annual, biennial and perennial herbaceous species. The one described is a half-hardy annual suitable for annual and mixed borders and for growing under glass in pots. The brightly coloured flowers can be cut and kept in water, although they are sticky to handle.

Salpiglossis sinuata

S. sinuata. Chile. Height 24 in.; planting distance 12 in. Slender branched stems carry narrow, light green leaves which have wavy edges. The funnel-shaped flowers, up to 2 in. long and 2 in. across the mouth, are multi-coloured in shades of crimson, scarlet, orange, yellow and lavender.

The petals have a velvety texture and many flowers are veined in deeper or contrasting colours. They are produced over a long period, from July to September.

Garden varieties include 'Grandiflora', 24 in., which bears compact heads of large flowers in a wide range of colours; and 'Splash', 24 in., an F$_1$ hybrid in mixed colours; it is compact and bears flowers in profusion.

Cultivation. Grow in a fairly rich soil in an open sunny site. On poor soil the F$_1$ hybrid does better than other varieties. Support the plants with twiggy sticks. Remove dead flower spikes to increase the size of flowers on the side-shoots.

Grow plants to flower under glass in 5 in. pots of John Innes potting compost No. 2.

Propagation. Sow the seeds under glass in February or March at a temperature of 18°C (64°F). Prick out the seedlings into boxes; harden outdoor plants off in a cold frame before planting out in May.

In mild areas the seeds may be sown directly in late April and May in the flowering site and the seedlings thinned to 9 in. apart. For winter flowering under glass, sow the seeds in September, and keep under glass at a temperature of 16–18°C (61–64°F).

Pests. Stems may be infested with APHIDS.

Diseases. Wilting of the leaves or complete collapse of the plants, often as they are about to flower, may occur as a result of FOOT ROT and ROOT ROT, due to a fungus.

Salsify
Tragopogon porrifolius. Compositae

A hardy biennial plant grown as an annual vegetable for its edible roots. This little-known plant is an easily grown winter vegetable with roots of a fleshy texture and oyster flavour. The roots are long, tapering and pale yellow, topped by narrow, grey-green leaves.

'Sandwich Island', a vigorous grower with large roots, is a popular variety.

Cultivation. Salsify does best in light, loamy soil, but will grow in all but extremely heavy soils. Prepare a bed by digging deeply a plot that was well manured the previous year. On recently manured soils, the roots may fork.

In April, sow seeds thinly in 1 in. deep drills spaced at 15-in. intervals; thin the seedlings until the plants are 9–10 in. apart. Hoe frequently. Keep the bed well watered, or the plants may run to seed.

Harvesting and storing. Roots will be ready for use from mid-October. They may be lifted and stored in boxes of sandy soil in a cool airy place, or left in the ground for lifting as required. Avoid damaging the stems or roots for storing, as they bleed.

Leave some roots in the bed until spring, when they will produce green, tender, flowering shoots known as chards. These may be blanched or left green; cut when they are 5–6 in. long, and cook as asparagus.

Pests. Generally trouble-free.

Diseases. WHITE BLISTER produces glistening white, blister-like pustules on the leaves.

Salix 'Wehrhahnii'

Salpiglossis sinuata 'Grandiflora' (mixed)

Salsify (foliage)

Salsify (roots)

Salvia horminum 'Blue Beard'

Salvia patens

Salvia splendens 'Blaze of Fire'

Salvia haematodes

Salvia

Labiatae

A genus of 700 species of hardy, half-hardy and tender annuals, perennials and mainly evergreen sub-shrubs. The species described are divided into half-hardy annuals, used for summer bedding or in annual and mixed borders, hardy and half-hardy perennials; and half-hardy sub-shrubs which generally require cool greenhouse treatment. The latter may also be grown against sheltered walls in the south and west.

The genus also includes the hardy sub-shrub *S. officinalis*, the culinary herb, SAGE.

The flowers are tubular and two-lipped, often hooded; they are borne in terminal racemes.

SALVIA HORMINUM

HALF-HARDY ANNUALS

S. horminum. S. Europe. Height 18 in.; planting distance 9 in. A true annual with erect branched stems carrying ovate mid-green leaves. The pale pink or purple flowers, $\frac{1}{2}$ in. long, appear from June to September. They are insignificant compared with the terminal tufts of coloured bracts, $1\frac{1}{2}$ in. long, in various colours. The flowers may be cut and dried for winter decoration.

Garden varieties include: 'Blue Beard', rich blue-purple bracts; 'Monarch Bouquet', a mixture containing white, rose, red, blue and purple bracts; 'Oxford Blue', broad blue bracts; and 'Pink Sundae', rose-carmine and red bracts.

S. patens. Mexico. Height 24 in.; planting distance 12 in. A perennial species, often grown as an annual, of erect and branching growth. The mid-green leaves are ovate and pointed. Clear blue flowers, 2 in. long, appear from August to September, widely spaced on the slender stems.

S. sclarea: see Clary

SALVIA SPLENDENS

S. splendens. Brazil. Height up to 15 in.; planting distance 9–15 in. A half-hardy perennial, usually grown as an annual. The bright green leaves are ovate with toothed edges. The clear scarlet flowers, $1\frac{1}{2}$–2 in. long, are surrounded by similarly coloured bracts, 1 in. long, and are densely packed in terminal spikes. They are borne from July until the first frosts.

There are a number of varieties, including 'Blaze of Fire' (height 10 in.), the most popular scarlet; 'Fireball' (height 15 in.), intense velvety scarlet, early-flowering; 'Purple Blaze' (height 12 in.), violet-purple to slate-coloured; and 'Salmon Pygmy' (height 9 in.), salmon-pink.

HARDY AND HALF-HARDY PERENNIALS

S. argentea. Mediterranean regions. Height and planting distance 15–18 in. A short-lived perennial, usually grown as a biennial, with rosettes of triangular-ovate leaves that are densely covered with silky, silvery-white hairs. White flowers, flushed with mauve and $1\frac{1}{2}$ in. long, are borne in panicles during July and August.

S. haematodes. Greece. Height up to 3 ft; planting distance 24 in. A short-lived, erect and branched plant. The basal leaves are slightly grey-green and broadly ovate with a corrugated surface. Purple flowers, 1 in. long, are borne in profusion from June to September.

SALVIA HAEMATODES

S. patens: see HALF-HARDY ANNUALS. This species may also be grown as a short-lived perennial in sheltered gardens in the south and west.
S. × superba: see *S. virgata nemorosa*
S. virgata nemorosa, syn. *S. × superba*. Garden origin. Height 24 in. or more; planting distance 18–24 in. A dense, clump-forming, erect plant with mid-green ovate-oblong leaves. The flowers are rich blue-purple, about ¾ in. long, and borne profusely from July to September.
HALF-HARDY SUB-SHRUBS
S. fulgens. Mexico. Height 2–3 ft; spread 18 in. This shrubby species bears somewhat hoary ovate leaves with rounded teeth, white and woolly beneath. Bright scarlet flowers, 1½–2 in. long, open from July to September.
S. neurepia. Mexico. Height 4–5 ft; spread 3–4 ft. The pale green ovate leaves have a sweetly aromatic fragrance when bruised. Carmine-red flowers, 1 in. long, open from July to October.
S. officinalis: see Sage
S. rutilans. Origin uncertain. Height and spread 24 in. or more. The pointed ovate leaves of this species are pale green and softly hairy; when crushed they have a pineapple-like fragrance. The ¾–1 in. long flowers are scarlet and carried in leafy racemes from June to September.
Cultivation of half-hardy annuals. Set out the young plants at the end of May, in ordinary, well-drained garden soil, in a sunny position. Pinch out the growing tips of young plants when 2–3 in. high, to encourage branching.
Cultivation of hardy and half-hardy perennials. Plant between October and March in any ordinary, well-drained garden soil, preferably enriched with well-rotted compost or manure. Choose a sunny position.
   S. haematodes may need staking with twiggy supports in exposed positions. Cut down all plants to ground level in November.
   Protect *S. argentea* against excessive winter wet with panes of glass or open-ended cloches.
Cultivation of half-hardy sub-shrubs. Grow these plants preferably in a greenhouse bed or border, or in 6–8 in. pots of John Innes potting compost No. 2 or 3. Water freely during the growing season; keep the compost just moist for the rest of the year. From May to September give a dilute liquid feed at seven to ten day intervals. Shade the glass lightly during the hottest months, and ventilate the greenhouse when the temperature exceeds 13°C (55°F). In winter, maintain a minimum temperature of 5–7°C (41–45°F).
   Pot on annually in March or April if large plants are required.

S. neurepia and *S. rutilans* may also be grown outdoors, at the foot of a sheltered and sunny wall in the south and west. Plant in late May, in any ordinary, well-drained soil. It may be necessary to protect the bases of the plants with a mulch of bracken, coarse sand or weathered ashes from November to March.
Propagation of half-hardy annuals. Sow seeds of all species in pots or pans of seed compost during February or March at a temperature of 18°C (64°F). Prick out the seedlings, when large enough to handle, into boxes, and harden off in a cold frame before planting out in May.
Propagation of hardy and half-hardy perennials. Divide and replant *S. × superba* at any time from September to March. *S. haematodes* can also be increased by division, but the rootstock is rather woody and the plant is short-lived. It is best raised from seeds, as is *S. patens* when grown as a perennial.
   Sow seeds in pots or pans of seed compost during April and place in a cold frame. When the seedlings are large enough to handle, prick them off into boxes and then into nursery rows. Plant *S. haematodes* in the flowering site at any time between October and March. Overwinter *S. patens* in a frame and plant out the following April or May.
   S. argentea can be propagated from its self-rooting lateral offshoots, which may be detached in April and replanted in the site.
Propagation of half-hardy sub-shrubs. Take 3 in. long cuttings of non-flowering lateral shoots, either from cut-back pot plants in April or May, or from mature plants in September. Insert the cuttings in equal parts (by volume) peat and sand in a propagating frame at a temperature of 13–16°C (55–61°F). When rooted, pot the cuttings singly into 3 in. containers of John Innes potting compost No. 2 and pot on as necessary. For outdoor planting, harden off the plants in a cold frame; plant out the following May.
Pruning. Pinch out the growing points of the greenhouse sub-shrubs two or three times during the growing season, especially in the case of pot-grown plants. In February, cut back all growths on pot plants to 4–6 in. from the base, and remove all frosted growths from plants grown outdoors.
Pests. A fine light mottling on the leaves of greenhouse plants is caused by GLASSHOUSE RED SPIDER MITES; a coarser mottling is caused by GLASSHOUSE LEAFHOPPERS.
Diseases. Yellowed foliage and stunted growth on young plants is due to a PHYSIOLOGICAL DISORDER, caused by too low temperatures.

Salvia neurepia

Sambucus

Elder. *Caprifoliaceae*

A genus of 40 species of hardy deciduous shrubs and small trees. The pinnate leaves, which in some varieties are golden, are divided into several narrowly lanceolate to ovate leaflets. The small, star-shaped flowers are white, or nearly so, and are followed by shiny black, red or blue fruits.
S. canadensis (American elder). N. America. Height 10–12 ft; spread 8–10 ft. A species with

Sambucus nigra (flowers)

mid-green leaves. The flowers appear in July in large flattened heads, 6–8 in. across, and are followed in September and October by round purple-black fruits. The variety 'Aurea' has golden-yellow foliage and cherry-red fruits. 'Maxima', syn. *S. pubens maxima*, has larger leaves and flower heads, 12–18 in. across.

S. nigra. Europe. Height and spread 12–15 ft. The pinnate leaves bear ovate, sharply toothed, mid-green leaflets. Cream-white flowers are borne in June in flattened umbels 4–6 in. across. These are followed in September by round shiny black berries. The young foliage of 'Aurea' becomes yellow-green; 'Aurea-variegata' has yellow-margined leaves; 'Laciniata' has finely cut fern-like leaves.

S. pubens maxima: see *S. canadensis* 'Maxima'

Sambucus nigra (fruits and autumn foliage)

Sambucus racemosa

Sanguinaria canadensis 'Flore Pleno'

SAMBUCUS RACEMOSA

S. racemosa. Europe, Asia Minor, N. China. Height and spread 8–10 ft. The mid-green leaves are slender-pointed and ovate. Yellow-white 1½–3 in. wide panicles of flowers appear in April and May, followed by scarlet berries in June and July. 'Plumosa Aurea' is slow-growing and has finely cut golden leaves.

Sambucus racemosa 'Plumosa Aurea'

Cultivation. Plant in any fertile garden soil between October and March, in sun or partial shade. The golden-leaved varieties colour earlier in a sunny situation, but retain their yellow-green colour longer in cool moist shade.

Propagation. Take 10–12 in. hardwood cuttings in October or November and insert them in a nursery bed. Grow on for a full year before planting the rooted cuttings out in permanent positions between October and March.

Alternatively, take 4–5 in. cuttings of half-ripe shoots with a heel in July or August and insert them in sandy soil in a cold frame. Plant out the rooted cuttings in a nursery bed during the following March or April and transfer to permanent positions the following October.

Pruning. For more brilliant colour from the young growth, although at the expense of flowers and berries, cut the stems back to within a few inches of ground level, during frost-free weather, between October and March.

Pests. Dense colonies of APHIDS may cause infestations on stems and leaves.

Diseases. In the spring, ARABIS MOSAIC VIRUS shows on the leaves as yellow bands along the veins. Symptoms fade during the summer but may reappear in the autumn.

Sanguinaria

Bloodroot. *Papaveraceae*

A genus of a single species. This is a hardy herbaceous perennial suitable for rock gardens. The common name is derived from the red sap that exudes from the fleshy roots.

S. canadensis. N. E. America. Height 6 in.; spread 12–15 in. The palmate, lobed, pale grey-green leaves develop quickly and die down by late summer. In April and May, single, white, cup-shaped flowers emerge from folded leaves, opening out flat to a width of 1–1½ in. The double form 'Flore Pleno' is more widely grown and flowers over a longer period than the type.

Cultivation. These plants grow best in well-drained soil containing leaf-mould or peat. They flourish under deciduous trees, but will also thrive in a sunny position. Plant sanguinarias as soon as the flowers have died, in May or June, or between October and March if the plants are purchased from a nursery.

Propagation. Divide the plants after flowering in May or June, and replant direct in final positions. Take care not to damage the roots.

Pests and diseases. Generally trouble-free.

Sanguisorba

Rosaceae

SANGUISORBA TENUIFOLIA

A genus of two or three species of hardy perennials which were formerly included in the genus *Poterium*. They are easily grown and are suitable for a border, in sun or half-shade. The cylindrical flower spikes with protruding stamens have the appearance of a bottle brush.

S. canadensis, syn. *Poterium canadense*. E. United States. Height 5 ft; planting distance 24 in. A species with pinnate pale green leaves. The white flower spikes are up to 6 in. long and are produced from August to October.

S. hakusanensis, syn. *S. obtusa*. Japan. Height 3–4 ft; planting distance 2½ ft. A species with pale green pinnate leaves, up to 18 in. long, which have blue-green undersides. Pink flower spikes, up to $3\frac{1}{2}$ in. long, are produced from June to August. The particularly long stamens give the spikes a fluffy appearance.

S. obtusa: see *S. hakusanensis*

S. tenuifolia, syn. *Poterium tenuifolium.* China. Height 4 ft; planting distance 24 in. This species is similar to *S. canadensis*, but the red flower spikes are smaller and appear in June and July.

Cultivation. Plant from October to March in sun or partial shade and in ordinary, moist soil, ideally by the waterside. Water abundantly during the growing season, and provide the plants with stout branching supports. Cut the stems down in November.

Propagation. Divide and replant the roots in March or April.

Sow seeds in March or April in pans of John Innes seed compost, and place in a cold frame. Prick out the seedlings, when large enough to handle, into boxes, and transfer the young plants to their flowering positions in October of the following year.

Pests and diseases. Generally trouble-free.

Sansevieria

Liliaceae

SANSEVIERIA TRIFASCIATA

A genus of 60 species of evergreen perennials. Two of the species are handsome foliage plants, suitable for cultivation in the home if a temperature of 16°C (61°F) can be maintained throughout the growing season.

S. hahnii. Tropical West Africa. Height 6 in. A rosette-forming species, with triangular-ovate leaves, about 4 in. long and $2\frac{1}{2}$ in. wide. These are dark green with grey and yellow transverse bands. There is a rare variegated form with two longitudinal yellow stripes near the margins.

S. trifasciata (mother-in-law's tongue). West Africa. Height 18 in. The erect, sword-like leaves are usually about 18 in. long in pot-grown specimens, but they may grow to a height of 4 ft. The leaves are dark green with mottled grey transverse bands. The form usually grown is the variety 'Laurentii', which has cream-yellow margins to the leaves.

Cultivation. Grow sansevierias in 5–6 in. pots of a proprietary loamless compost or in John Innes potting compost No. 2. As the plants have thick semi-succulent leaves they will tolerate periods of drought. They require a minimum winter temperature of 10°C (50°F), but will survive at 7°C (45°F) provided they are kept dry. From spring to autumn allow the plants to dry out completely between waterings.

Sansevierias are slow-growing, making only a few fresh leaves each year. Repotting is seldom required. They are best left undisturbed until the pots are packed with roots and leaves.

Sansevieria trifasciata 'Laurentii'

They can be placed in either a sunny or a shady position in summer, but the shade should never be heavy. Give the plants a weak feed of dilute liquid manure at monthly intervals from May to September.

Propagation. Increase *S. hahnii* and *S. trifasciata* by suckers or by leaf cuttings from May to August. Cut a leaf into sections, 3–4 in. long, and insert to half their depth in pots of equal parts (by volume) peat and sand; root at a temperature of 21°C (70°F). Pot on as necessary.

S. trifasciata 'Laurentii' can be propagated only from suckers. These are produced on underground stolons, and can be severed from the parent plant when two or three leaves have formed; pot up in the growing compost.

Pests. Generally trouble-free.

Diseases. A PHYSIOLOGICAL DISORDER results in brown blotches developing on the leaves. These may start at the tips and work downwards, or spread from the leaf margins.

Santolina

Cotton lavender. *Compositae*

SANTOLINA VIRENS

A genus of ten species of hardy evergreen dwarf shrubs with finely divided, aromatic foliage. They form attractive low mounds suitable for the front of a shrub border, or on rock gardens; they may also be grown as low hedges. Dainty tansy or button-like yellow flowers, $\frac{1}{2}-\frac{3}{4}$ in. across, are carried on long, slender and erect stalks.

S. chamaecyparissus, syn. *S. incana.* S. France. Height and spread 18–24 in. This species forms a

Sanguisorba canadensis

Sanguisorba hakusanensis

Sansevieria hahnii

Santolina chamaecyparissus (foliage)

dense mound. The silvery, woolly leaves are finely dissected and carried on white felted branches. Bright lemon-yellow flowers are borne during July.

S. c. corsica, syn. *S. incana*. Corsica and Sardinia. Height and spread 12–18 in. A dwarf compact variety, suitable for a rock garden. Bright lemon-yellow flowers appear in July.

S. incana: see *S. chamaecyparissus corsica*

S. neapolitana. Italy. Height and spread 2–2½ ft. This species also forms a mound of grey foliage, but the individual leaves are longer and more feathery than those of *S. chamaecyparissus*. Bright lemon-yellow flowers appear in July. 'Sulphurea' has pale yellow flowers.

S. virens. Origin uncertain. Height 24 in.; spread 3–4 ft. A species with green, thread-like leaves. Bright lemon-yellow flowers open in July.

Cultivation. These shrubs thrive in full sun and in any ordinary, well-drained soil. Plant in September and October or March and April. Remove the dead flower stems.

For hedges, set young plants 12–15 in. apart in spring; pinch out the growing points once or twice during the first years. Shear to shape at intervals throughout the summer.

Propagation. Take cuttings, 2–3 in. long, of half-ripened side-shoots from July to September; insert the cuttings in equal parts (by volume) peat and sand in a cold frame. The following April, pot the rooted cuttings in 3½ in. pots of John Innes potting compost No. 1; plunge outdoors and transplant to permanent positions in September.

Pruning. Old specimens become open and untidy in habit. Immediately after flowering, or in April, cut back hard into the old wood to encourage new growths from the base.

Pests and diseases. Generally trouble-free.

Santolina chamaecyparissus (flowers)

Santolina neapolitana

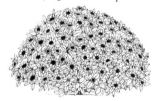

Sanvitalia procumbens

Sanvitalia

Creeping zinnia. *Compositae*

SANVITALIA PROCUMBENS

A genus of seven species of annual and perennial herbaceous plants. The hardy annual described is grown in borders, in hanging baskets and on rock gardens, as well as in pots to flower under glass.

S. procumbens. Mexico. Height 6 in.; spacing 3 in. A plant of prostrate habit with trailing stems. The mid-green leaves are ovate and pointed. Single daisy-like flowers, 1 in. across, appear in July. They are bright yellow with black centres. The variety 'Flore Pleno' has double flowers.

Cultivation. Grow in light, well-drained soil, enriched with peat, in an open, sunny position. Under glass grow the plants in 3½ in. pots of John Innes potting compost No. 1.

Propagation. Sow the seeds in the flowering site in September or March, just covering them with soil. Thin out the seedlings to 3 in. apart;

autumn-raised seedlings are best left unthinned until the spring. Plants to flower under glass can be sown indoors in March at a temperature of 13–16°C (55–61°F).

Pests and diseases. Generally trouble-free.

Saponaria

Caryophyllaceae

A genus of about 30 species of hardy and half-hardy annuals, biennials and perennials. The Latin name of the genus refers to the leaves of *S. officinalis*, which contain a sap having a soap-like action. The flowers are salver-shaped with a tubular corolla.

The following two annuals are suitable for annual and mixed borders, for rock gardens, edging paths and for cutting. The perennial species described, with their varieties, are easily grown although invasive; they make excellent plants for the wild garden.

S. × 'Bressingham'. Garden origin. Height 1½ in.; planting distance 6 in. This hardy perennial forms low hummocks of narrowly lanceolate, mid-green leaves with a covering of white hairs. Rich pink, white-eyed flowers, ½ in. across, with red-brown calyces, are profusely borne in May and June.

S. calabrica. Italy. Height and spacing 6 in. A hardy annual of compact growth, best planted in drifts to form a carpet. The smooth, light green leaves are narrowly lanceolate. Deep rose flowers, tubular and ½ in. across, are produced in great numbers from June to August.

SAPONARIA OCYMOIDES 'COMPACTA'

S. ocymoides. Alps and Jura Mountains. Height 3 in.; planting distance 12 in. A vigorous, prostrate, hardy herbaceous perennial with pale to mid-green, obovate to oblong-lanceolate leaves. Umbel-like heads of ½ in. wide, bright rose-pink flowers are borne in profusion from July to September. The variety 'Compacta' is slower-growing and more compact, forming a close darker green mat; 'Rubra Compacta' has rich carmine-pink flowers; 'Splendens' resembles the type species, but has darker pink flowers.

SAPONARIA OFFICINALIS

S. officinalis (soapwort). Europe, naturalised in Great Britain; temperate Asia. Height 1–3 ft; planting distance 24 in. This hardy perennial has

Saponaria ocymoides

Saponaria ocymoides
'Splendens'

Saponaria × 'Bressingham'

single pink flowers and pale-green elliptic to oblong-lanceolate leaves. In cultivation it has been superseded by double varieties: 'Alba-plena' has white flowers and 'Roseo-plena' pink. Both varieties produce 1–1½ in. wide flowers, rather like small shaggy carnations, in terminal clusters between late July and September.

S. vaccaria, syns. *Vaccaria segetalis, V. pyramidata.* Europe. Height up to 2½ ft; spacing 9 in. A hardy annual with smooth branching stems, popular for annual borders and for cutting; the pink form is often grown with the annual white *Gypsophila.* The light green leaves are smooth, narrow and lanceolate. Large sprays of deep pink star-like flowers, ½ in. across, are produced from June to August. There are several varieties listed, including 'Alba', white, and 'Pink Beauty', a free-flowering deep pink.

Cultivation. Grow in any fertile garden soil in sun or partial shade. The tall species require supporting with twiggy sticks. Cut back strong-growing plants after flowering to induce a second flush of blooms.

Plant the perennial species during suitable weather between October and March. Cut down to ground level in November. In autumn and winter cut round the plants with a spade, and fork out the spreading underground runners.

Propagation. For the annual species, sow the seeds in the flowering site in September or March and thin out the seedlings to the required spacing. Autumn-sown plants flower in May or June, March-sown plants in July or August.

For the perennial species, divide and replant the roots or remove underground runners and replant at any time between October and March. Seeds may be sown in March, but this is not recommended as the resulting seedlings are variable and seldom true to type.

Pests and diseases. Generally trouble-free.

Sarracenia

Sarraceniaceae

A genus of ten species of hardy and half-hardy stemless, evergreen and carnivorous herbaceous plants that are tufted and rosette-forming. In the wild, they grow in boggy areas throughout North and East America. They are most suitable for growing in pans in a cool greenhouse.

The pitcher-shaped leaves are variously coloured in attractive shades of red and purple; they contain a watery fluid in which insects are drowned and digested.

The bowl-shaped, pendulous flowers are composed of five prominent sepals, five petals and a conspicuous umbrella-shaped stigma to the ovary. They measure 2–4 in. across and are borne singly.

S. drummondii. N. America. Height 12–30 in.; spread 9 in. This half-hardy species is the most colourful of the genus. It has long, slender, erect pitchers, green on the lower parts, while the upper parts, including the pitcher lids, are white with rich purple veins. The yellow to red-purple flowers, 2–3 in. across, are borne during April and May.

S. flava. N. America. Height up to 24 in.; spread 9 in. A half-hardy species with long, erect pitchers that are yellow or yellow-green with a veining of crimson or purple in the throat. The flowers, which appear in April and May, are 3–4 in. across and yellow with a pungent odour.

S. purpurea. N. America, naturalised in Central Ireland. Height 9 in.; spread 12 in. This species, although hardier than the other two, will not survive winter outdoors except in mild areas. The purple and green semi-erect pitchers form a neat rosette. They are narrow and stem-like at the base, widening to about 2 in. towards the

Sarracenia flava (in flower)

top, then narrowing slightly at the mouth. The lids are green, with purple veins. In April it bears green-purple flowers, 2–3 in. across.

Cultivation. Plant sarracenias in February or March in 8–10 in. pans of equal parts (by volume) peat and chopped sphagnum, topped with living sphagnum moss. The compost should be kept permanently moist, and the pans are best stood in trays of water. Grow in a cool greenhouse that receives the maximum amount of light in winter, and where a temperature of 5°C (41°F) can be maintained. During summer, keep the atmosphere humid and spray the plants daily. Ventilate the house freely when the temperature exceeds 7°C (45°F).

Repot every second or third year, depending on vigour, in February or March.

Propagation. Sow seeds in March in small pans of the growing compost and germinate at a temperature of 13–16°C (55–61°F). Sprinkle the seeds thinly on top of the compost and water in. Prick off the seedlings, when they have three or four true leaves, into larger pans or singly into pots containing the growing compost.

Plants that have formed large, multiple crowns can be divided and replanted in March.

Pests and diseases. Generally trouble-free.

Sarracenia purpurea

Savin: see *Juniperus sabina*

Savory, winter

Saxifraga longifolia 'Tumbling Waters'

Savory

Satureja. Labiatae

SAVORY, SUMMER

These plants include summer savory, a hardy annual, and winter savory, a hardy, almost evergreen, dwarf perennial sub-shrub. Both are used as culinary herbs but, as the dried leaves of summer savory are generally preferred to the fresh leaves of winter savory, the latter is less widely grown.

Summer savory (*S. hortensis*). Europe. Height 12 in.; spacing 6–9 in. This plant is of bushy habit; it has hairy stems, square in section, that carry dark green, strongly aromatic, lanceolate leaves. Tiny tubular lilac flowers are borne from the leaf axils from July to September.

The leaves and young shoots have a strong, spicy flavour and should be used sparingly. They are used particularly with all kinds of beans, but may also be added to soups, meat, fish, egg and cheese dishes, stuffings and drinks. They are often used as an ingredient of *pot-pourri*.

Winter savory (*S. montana*). Europe, Asia. Height 12 in.; planting distance 9–12 in. This plant is compact and erect in habit, with woody, branching, square-sectioned stems. It carries small, grey-green, lanceolate leaves and, from July to October, tiny, rose-purple, tubular flowers which are borne from the upper leaf axils.

It is used as a culinary herb in winter with the same dishes as summer savory, but its flavour is much coarser.

Cultivation. Grow summer and winter savory in a sunny position in any fertile, well-drained soil. Winter savory becomes woody based; it should be replaced every two or three years.

Propagation. Sow seeds in April in shallow drills drawn 12 in. apart. When the seedlings are large enough to handle, thin them to 6–9 in. apart.

Winter savory can also be propagated by division in March and April and from 2 in. cuttings of lateral shoots taken in May. Insert the cuttings in equal parts (by volume) peat and sand in a cold frame; pot them singly in 3 in. pots of John Innes potting compost No. 1 when well rooted. Overwinter in the frame and plant out the following April.

For a winter supply of fresh shoots, sow a few seeds of summer savory in September to grow in pots in the greenhouse at a temperature of 7–10°C (45–50°F).

Harvesting and storing. Use fresh shoots when available. To dry summer savory for winter use, gather and dry the shoots in August as described in the entry under HERBS. They may also be deep-frozen.

Pests and diseases. Generally trouble-free.

Savoy cabbage: see Cabbage

Saxifraga

Saxifragaceae

A genus of 370 species of low-growing hardy and half-hardy annuals and perennials; most of the latter are evergreen. The genus is divided into 16 sections, but most of the cultivated saxifrages belong to four of them: *Euaizoonia*, *Dactyloides* (mossy), *Kabschia* and *Engleria*. The last two, which have similar appearances and requirements, are grouped together in this entry. Recommended plants in other sections are listed under MISCELLANEOUS. All are suitable for growing on rock gardens.

EUAIZOONIA SECTION. These saxifrages form large, silvery rosettes encrusted with lime. They grow in small groups, sometimes giving the plants a mat-like appearance, or singly. The relatively large star-shaped flowers are borne in graceful panicles. These saxifrages are especially suitable for growing in rock crevices.

S. aizoon, syn. *S. paniculata*. Mountains of Europe and N. America. Height and spread 12–15 in. The oblong to lanceolate leaves are silver-green; sprays of ½ in. wide, star-shaped, white flowers open in June. Varieties include:

S. a. baldensis from Mount Baldo in Italy. Height 4–6 in. This is the smallest saxifrage in the section; it has a compact dome of silver rosettes and white flowers. *S. a. lutea* (height 6–8 in.) has pale yellow flowers. *S. a. rosea* (height 6–10 in.) is a variety with deep green encrusted rosettes, and deep pink flowers.

S. × burnatii. Height 4–6 in.; spread 12 in. The silver-green rosette leaves are lanceolate to obovate. Red flower stems carry short panicles of ½ in. wide white flowers in June.

. *callosa*: see *S. lingulata*

. *cochlearis*. Maritime Alps. Height 8 in.; spread
–12 in. Leaves, similar to those of *S. × burnatii*,
orm silvery rosettes in humped masses. In June,
hese bear sparse sprays of $\frac{1}{3}$ in. wide milk-white
owers. *S. c. minor* (height 4 in.), is a miniature
ersion with compact silver hummocks.

. *cotyledon*. S.W. Alps north to Lapland and
celand. Height up to 24 in.; spread 12–15 in.
he short, strap-shaped, dark green leaves form
osettes that are lime-encrusted on the margins.
lume-like sprays, up to 24 in. long, of pure white
owers, each $\frac{1}{2}$ in. across, appear from June to
ugust. 'Southside Seedling', height 12 in.,
arries numerous white flowers, speckled with
ed spots, on arching sprays.

. *lingulata*, syn. *S. callosa*. W. Maritime Alps.
Height 12–18 in.; spread up to 12 in. The
osettes have oblong-lanceolate grey-green
aves. Arching panicles of white flowers, $\frac{1}{2}$ in.
cross, open in June and July.

. *longifolia*. Pyrenees. Height up to 18 in.;
pread 12 in. This is one of the largest species, but
ay grow for three or even five years before
roducing flowers. It usually dies after flowering.
he short leaves are strap-shaped and silver-
reen. White flowers, $\frac{1}{3}$ in. across and sometimes
potted with purple, are borne in large plume-like
anicles in June. 'Tumbling Waters' is a hybrid
erived from this species and *S. lingulata*.
t bears pyramidal panicles, 24 in. high, of glisten-
ng white flowers.

. *paniculata*: see *S. aizoon*

DACTYLOIDES SECTION. These saxifrages
erive their name from the moss-like appearance
f their dense hummocks of deeply divided
aves. Loose clusters of flowers, which are star or
aucer-shaped, are carried on wiry stems.

. *moschata*. Pyrenees to Caucasus. Height 1–3
n.; spread 12–18 in. Cushions of bright green
oliage produce yellow or white saucer-shaped
owers, $\frac{1}{2}$ in. across, in April or May. The species
s usually represented by a number of named
arieties. The following are recommended:

'Atropurpurea' is densely tufted with red
owers; 'Cloth of Gold' has yellow foliage which
etains its colour throughout the year; white
owers appear in May. It is best grown in partial
hade. 'Compacta' is a neat variety which forms
merald-green cushions and bears star-shaped
owers on 3 in. long stems.

Two hybrids derived from *S. moschata* are:
. × 'Peter Pan'. Height 3 in.; spread 12 in. This
nossy plant forms low hummocks of bright
reen leaves. The flowers are $\frac{1}{2}$ in. across with
lear pink reflexed petals. They open on crimson
tems in April or May.

. × 'Pixie'. Height 2 in.; spread 12–15 in.
his mossy hybrid is a compact dwarf plant with
nid-green foliage. The deep red flowers, which
ave reflexed petals, measure $\frac{1}{2}$ in. across and
ppear in April or May.

KABSCHIA AND ENGLERIA SECTIONS.
hese plants have grey-green or silver rosette
eaves with an encrustation of lime like the
uaizoonia saxifrages, but they are smaller and
row more densely in mats or hummocks. Unless
therwise stated, the flowers are saucer-shaped.
hough they are hardy, they are also excellent
lants for alpine houses.

Saxifraga cochlearis

S. × *apiculata*. Height 4 in.; spread 12–18 in.
Narrowly lanceolate, hoary green leaves are
packed into tight cushions. Yellow flowers, up to
$\frac{1}{2}$ in. wide, open in March or April. 'Alba' is a
white form.

S. × *borisii*. Height 3 in.; spread 12 in. A hybrid
with neat cushions composed of linear grey-
green leaves. Citron-yellow flowers, $\frac{3}{4}$ in. across,
open on red stems in March or April.

S. burseriana. Dolomites, E. Alps. Height 2 in.;
spread 12 in. This is the earliest and largest-
flowering of the Kabschias. It forms a dense flat
cushion of blue-grey lanceolate leaves and bears
pure white flowers, 1 in. or more across, on thin
red stems in February or March.

There are many selected forms: 'Brookside'
and 'Gloria' both have larger white flowers, the
latter variety on green stems; 'Major Lutea' has
large clear yellow flowers; 'Sulphurea' forms grey
cushions with pale yellow flowers.

S. × 'Cranbourne'. Height 1 in.; spread 9–12 in.
This is one of the finest of the Kabschias. It forms
domes of grey-green rosettes and bears almost
stemless clear pink flowers, $\frac{3}{4}$ in. wide, in March
and April.

S. diapensioides. European Alps. Height 2 in.;
spread 12 in. Linear grey-green leaves form a
hard, flat mat of small rosettes. Milk-white
flowers, up to $\frac{3}{4}$ in. wide, are borne in May and
June. 'Lutea' is a pale yellow form.

S. × 'Elizabethae'. Height 3 in.; spread 12 in.
This is another mat-forming species, with
wedge-shaped, dull green, spiny leaves. Light
yellow flowers, up to $\frac{3}{4}$ in. across, open on sticky
pink stems in March or April.

S. × 'Faldonside'. Height 3 in.; spread 12 in. This
long-established hybrid has linear silver-green
leaves. The 1 in. wide flowers are a vivid
butter-yellow, and open in March or April.

S. grisebachii. Mountains of Macedonia, Greece,
Albania. Height 6–9 in.; spread 9–12 in. Oblong
to lanceolate silver-green leaves form flat rosettes

Saxifraga burseriana

Saxifraga × 'Elizabethae'

that are heavily encrusted with lime. Bract-like leaves in the rosette centres turn crimson, then elongate to bear the inflated red calyces which hide the pink, ¼ in. wide, bell-shaped flowers. The flowering season is March to May. Stems and stem leaves are densely covered with crimson-red hairs. 'Wisley Variety' is more robust and sturdier and has more intensely coloured flowering stems, bracts and calyces.

S. × **haagii.** Height 3 in.; spread 9–12 in. This vigorous plant has linear dark green leaves. Clusters of rich yellow star-shaped flowers, ¾ in. across, are borne in March and April.

S. × **'Iris Prichard'.** Height 3 in.; spread 9–12 in. The leaves of this hybrid are wedge-shaped and grey-green. Buff-yellow flowers, ¾ in. wide, appear in March or April.

S. × **irvingii.** Height 1 in.; spread 12 in. Wedge-shaped grey-green leaves grow in a neat tuft. Stemless pink flowers, ¾ in. across, appear in March and April.

S. × **'Jenkinsae'.** Height 1 in.; spread 12 in. Wedge-shaped silver-green leaves form cushions which support a profusion of palest pink flowers, up to ¾ in. across, in March and April.

S. × **'Kellereri'.** Height 6 in.; spread 9–12 in. This is one of the first saxifrages to flower. The rosettes have grey-green wedge-shaped leaves. Soft pink flowers, ½ in. across, are produced in sprays from January to March.

S. × **kewensis.** Height 3–4 in.; spread 12 in. The grey-green rosette leaves are wedge-shaped with pointed tips. Sprays of pink flowers, ½ in. across, appear in February and March.

S. lilacina. W. Himalayas. Height 1 in.; spread 12 in. This plant forms a dense cushion of wedge-shaped mid-green leaves. Clear lavender-lilac flowers, ½–¾ in. across, appear in March or April. It grows best in lime-free soil.

S. × **'Riverslea'.** Height 2 in.; spread 12 in. A hybrid with closely tufted rosettes of wedge-shaped, silver-green leaves. Sprays of purple-red flowers, each ¾ in. across, are produced in March.

S. × **'Valerie Finnis'.** Height 1–1½ in.; spread 4 in. or more. This floriferous hybrid closely resembles its parent **S. burseriana.** Primrose-yellow flowers, ¾ in. across, open in March.

MISCELLANEOUS

S. × **'Bathoniensis'.** Height and spread 9 in. A vigorous hybrid, probably derived from **S. granulata** and a mossy variety, forming loose cushions of mid-green leaves. Branched stems bear crimson saucer-shaped flowers, 1–1¼ in. across, in April and May.

SAXIFRAGA FORTUNEI

S. fortunei. China, Japan. Height 12–18 in.; spread 12–15 in. This plant is too large for most rock gardens but it will flourish in cool, shady spots elsewhere in the garden. The deciduous leaves, which are orbicular, toothed and lobed, are deep green on the surface and red beneath.

Saxifraga grisebachii

Saxifraga × 'Jenkinsae'

Saxifraga × 'Valerie Finnis'

Saxifraga × *irvingii*

Saxifraga fortunei

Saxifraga oppositifolia 'Splendens'

The glistening white flowers are basically star-shaped, with one or more petals up to twice as long as the others. The normal width of the flowers is 1 in. They appear in October and November. Plant in April.

S. granulata (fair maids of France). Europe, including Great Britain. Height and spread 9 in. This deciduous plant has grey-green kidney-shaped leaves which die down in mid-summer. The pure white cup-shaped flowers, $\frac{3}{4}$ in. wide, open on leafy stems in April. This plant does best in a damp situation. 'Flore Pleno' has double white flowers, 1 in. across.

S. oppositifolia. N. Asia, N. America, Europe. Height 1 in.; spread 12–24 in. Wiry shoots form a creeping mat of slightly hoary wedge-shaped leaves. Terminal flowers, which are cup-shaped, are borne in March and April. They vary from white to purple and deep red-purple and are up to $\frac{1}{2}$ in. across. 'Alba', with white flowers, is not robust; it needs shade and soil containing peat or leaf-mould. 'Splendens', an easier plant to grow, bears larger purple-crimson flowers.

S. retusa. Pyrenees to Bulgaria. Height 1 in.; spread up to 12 in. This plant resembles *S. oppositifolia*, but is smaller and more congested and is suitable for a trough or scree garden. It has ovate mid to dark green leaves which are sometimes hoary. The rose-purple star-shaped flowers, $\frac{1}{3}$ in. across, are borne in April in clusters of two to five.

S. sarmentosa: see *S. stolonifera*

S. stolonifera, syn. *S. sarmentosa* (mother of thousands). Height 9–12 in.; spread 12 in. or more. A lightly tufted species, with numerous thread-like red stolons (runners), often several feet long, bearing young plants. The mid-green leaves are orbicular, with silvery veins above and red-flushed beneath. Loose racemes of starry, 1–1$\frac{1}{2}$ in. wide, pure white flowers, usually with one or two petals longer than the rest, open in July and August. 'Tricolor' is less vigorous and has leaves that are variegated with pale yellow and pink.

Although not reliably hardy, this species is useful for shady sites in the south and west. It is also often grown as a house plant.

SAXIFRAGA UMBROSA

S. umbrosa. Europe. Height 12 in.; spread 12–18 in. This species thrives in shade. The rosettes are slightly fleshy, with thick, mid to dark green, spathulate leaves. Masses of star-shaped pink flowers, $\frac{1}{4}$ in. across, are produced in 6 in. panicles in May. *S. u. primuloides*, a dwarf form, is less coarse than the type and has sprays of pink flowers. 'Elliott's Variety', which is even more compact, has deep rose flowers in 3–4 in. panicles. The form 'Variegata' has leaves irregularly splashed with yellow.

The original species is rare in cultivation, and plants sold under this name are *S. × urbicum*.

S. × urbicum (London pride). This hybrid between *S. umbrosa* and *S. spathularis* closely resembles *S. umbrosa*, but is more vigorous and with larger, darker green rosettes and taller flowering stems.

Cultivation. Saxifrages in the Euaizoonia section do best in sharply drained soil that contains lime and plenty of grit. They grow well in rock crevices. In sheltered districts in the south and west, they need a semi-shaded site facing east or west. Further north, they tolerate full sun.

Saxifrages belonging to the Dactyloides section prosper in any good soil, and grow best in a shaded site.

With the exception of *S. lilacina*, which requires a lime-free soil, plants in the Kabschia and Engleria sections require gritty soil, preferably chalky or with lime added. They must be shaded from the midday sun. These plants grow well in alpine houses in 6–8 in. pans containing 2 parts John Innes potting compost No. 1 and 1 part limestone chippings (parts by volume).

Plant saxifrages of all groups in September, October or March, except *S. fortunei*, which should be planted in April.

S. stolonifera may be grown as a house plant in a 5–6 in. pot or hanging basket containing John Innes potting compost No. 1 or 2. Repot every other year in April or raise young plants annually or every second year. A minimum winter temperature of 4°C (39°F) is required.

Propagation. All the saxifrages described, except *S. cotyledon* and *S. longifolia*, can be divided after flowering and replanted *in situ*.

However, the best method to increase the plants is to detach non-flowering rosettes in May or June and treat them as cuttings. Remove the lower leaves and insert the rosettes in a pan containing equal parts (by volume) peat and coarse sand and place in a cold frame. Soak the pan after inserting the rosettes, then water sparingly until the following April, when the plants should be watered more freely. Pot the plants individually in September, overwinter in a cold frame and plant out in September.

S. oppositifolia and *S. retusa* can be increased by means of soft tip cuttings taken between April and June. Insert them in equal parts (by volume) peat and sand. In the autumn, when they are rooted, transfer them to 2$\frac{1}{2}$ in. pots, overwinter them in a cold frame; plunge outdoors in April and grow on until planting out in September.

Pests. The roots of some saxifrages are attacked by WEEVIL GRUBS and ROOT APHIDS.

Diseases. Occasionally RUST shows on encrusted saxifrages as red-brown pustules.

Saxifraga × 'Bathoniensis'

Saxifraga stolonifera 'Tricolor'

Scabiosa atropurpurea 'Tom Thumb'

Scabiosa

Scabious, pincushion flower. *Dipsacaceae*

A genus of 100 species of annuals and herbaceous perennials. The two species described are suitable as bedding plants and for growing in mixed borders and herbaceous borders.

The daisy-like flowers are excellent for cutting; the overlapping ray-florets surround a large central disc with protruding styles. The dried seed heads may be used in flower arrangements.

S. atropurpurea (sweet scabious). S. Europe. Height 3 ft; spacing 9 in. A hardy annual which develops a compact rosette of narrow, mid-green, deeply lobed or cut leaves. The dark crimson flowers on slender stems measure 2 in. across. They are produced from July to September.

Numerous varieties are available, including mixtures and separate colours in dark purple, blue, cherry red, pink, lavender, salmon and white. Two of the most popular are 'Cockade Mixed', 3 ft, a large-flowered strain; and 'Tom Thumb', 18 in., a dwarf mixture.

SCABIOSA ATROPURPUREA

S. caucasica. Caucasus. Height 18–24 in.; planting distance 18 in. A hardy perennial which forms a low-growing cluster of mid-green, lanceolate leaves; the upper part of each leaf is cut into narrow segments. Almost leafless flower stems carry lavender-blue flowers, about 3 in. wide, from June to September.

The species has been superseded by several garden varieties, the most popular of which include: 'Bressingham White', white; 'Clive Greaves', rich mauve; 'Moonstone' (height 3 ft), light blue; 'Miss Willmott', white; 'Moerheim Blue', deep violet-blue; 'Penhill Blue' (3 ft), blue, shaded mauve.

Cultivation. Grow in any fertile, well-drained garden soil and in an open sunny site. Light staking may be necessary for the tall, large-flowering varieties, especially in wet weather. To induce continued flowering, cut the stems at the first joint as they finish flowering.

Autumn-sown annuals require cloche protection during the winter in all but the mildest areas.

Plant the perennial species in March or April. Cut the stems of these down to ground level in November.

Propagation. For the annual species, sow the seeds in the flowering site in September, March or April. Thin out the seedlings from the spring sowing as soon as they are large enough to handle, but leave the final spacing of autumn-sown plants until spring.

For the perennial species, take 2 in. long basal cuttings in March or April. Insert these in pots containing a mixture of equal parts (by volume) peat and sand, and place in a cold frame. When rooted, plant out in nursery rows and grow on before transferring to the flowering site at any time between September and March.

Alternatively, lift and divide established clumps every three or four years in March.

Pests. Young plants are often damaged by SLUGS and SNAILS.

Diseases. Collapse of the plants may be caused by ROOT ROT or sometimes BLACK ROOT ROT.

POWDERY MILDEW shows as a white powdery coating on the leaves.

Scabious: see Scabiosa

Schefflera
Araliaceae

SCHEFFLERA ACTINOPHYLLA

A genus of 200 species of evergreen tropical and sub-tropical trees and shrubs. The species described is a popular foliage plant and is suitable for cultivation in a greenhouse or as a house plant.

S. actinophylla. Polynesia. Height 6–8 ft; spread 2–3 ft. A slow-growing, single-stemmed species with glossy mid-green leaves. These are divided into a number of oblong to ovate leaflets, usually five in number but in young plants only three.

Cultivation. Grow scheffleras in 6–8 in. pots containing John Innes potting compost No. 2 or 3. They require a temperature of 10–13°C (50–55°F) and full light in winter. During spring and summer, give light shading. In the home, set the plants in a well-lit situation all year round, although they should not receive direct sunlight.

Keep the compost moist at all times and the atmosphere moderately humid.

Pot on young plants in April; once in their final pots, schefflera may be repotted every other year in April, or they may be potted on if large specimens are wanted. During the years when they are not being repotted give a liquid feed once a month from May to September.

Propagation. Sow seeds in February or March in pans of John Innes seed compost at a temperature of 21–24°C (70–75°F). Prick off the seedlings, when large enough to handle, singly into 2½ in. pots of John Innes potting compost No. 1. Pot on as necessary.

Pests and diseases. Generally trouble-free.

Schisandra
syn. **Schizandra**
Schisandraceae, syn. *Magnoliaceae*

SCHISANDRA RUBRIFLORA

A genus of 25 species of tender and hardy, deciduous and evergreen, woody flowering climbers. The species described here are hardy and deciduous plants, with twining stems. They may be grown on trelliswork, arbours and pergolas, but in cold districts are better planted against a south or west-facing wall.

The unisexual flowers are bowl-shaped and borne in few-flowered clusters from the leaf axils; they are occasionally followed by attractive fruits.

Scabiosa caucasica

Schefflera actinophylla

Schisandra rubriflora

S. glaucescens. Central China. Height 15 ft or more. This moderately vigorous climber has obovate leaves that are deep to mid-green above, somewhat glaucous beneath. Orange-red flowers, about 1 in. across, are produced in May and June, and may be followed by cylindrical, knobbly, scarlet fruits, 2–4 in. long.

S. grandiflora rubrifolia: see *S. rubriflora*

S. rubriflora, syn. *S. grandiflora rubrifolia.* China. Height 15 ft or more. A species of moderate growth, with obovate to obovate-lanceolate leaves, deep green above and paler beneath. Deep crimson flowers, about 1 in. across, appear in April and May. The fruits, when produced, resemble those of *S. glaucescens.*

Cultivation. Any ordinary, well-drained, but moisture-retentive soil is suitable. It should preferably be neutral to acid; apply a dressing of humus to excessively limy soils. Plant between September and April in a well-lit or partially shaded position, out of direct sun.

Top-dress the soil with leaf-mould or well-decayed compost in April. Wall-grown specimens may need watering during dry spells; provide strings or wires for support and tie in the young growths until they become established.

Propagation. Vegetative propagation is somewhat difficult, but 3–4 in. long cuttings of semi ripe wood can be taken during July or August; insert in equal parts (by volume) peat and sand in a propagating frame with a bottom heat of 15–18°C (59–64°F). Under mist, cuttings may be inserted from April to August, whenever suitable growths are available.

Pot the rooted cuttings singly into 3½–4 in. pots of 2 parts neutral or lime-free loam, 1 part peat and 1 part sand (parts by volume). Over-winter in a cold frame and plunge outside in March or April. Grow on, potting on into 4–5 in. pots when necessary, and plant out in permanent positions during autumn of the following year.

Layer long shoots in September; they will usually be ready to be severed from the parent and planted out one year later.

Seeds may be sown when ripe, usually in October; sow in pots or pans of seed compost and place in a cold frame. Prick off the seedlings, when large enough to handle, into 3–3½ in. pots and treat as described for cuttings.

Pruning. No regular pruning is required, but remove unwanted shoots and branches in January or February, to keep the plants shapely and within bounds.

Pests. Colonies of APHIDS may infest leaves and young growths.

Diseases. Generally trouble-free.

Schizandra: see Schisandra

Schizanthus

Butterfly flower. *Scrophulariaceae*

A genus of 15 species of annual plants. Those described are usually grown in pots in cool but frost-free greenhouses, but they are also suitable for annual borders and for cutting.

S. grandiflorus: see *S. pinnatus*

S. hybridus grandiflorus: see *S. pinnatus*

S. pinnatus, syns. *S. grandiflorus, S. hybridus grandiflorus.* Chile. Height 1½–4 ft; planting distance 12 in. A bushy plant with erect stems, excellent as a spring-flowering pot plant under glass. The pale green leaves are deeply divided and almost fern-like. The single, showy orchid-like flowers, 1½ in. across, are coloured rose, purple and yellow and attractively marked or spotted. Outdoors, the flowering period extends from June to October.

Numerous varieties are listed, including the popular 'Dwarf Bouquet', 12 in., a compact plant producing a mass of rose, crimson, salmon and amber to soft pink flowers; 'Pansy Flowered', 18 in., bears larger self-coloured flowers in a variety of colours.

SCHIZANTHUS PINNATUS

S. × wisetonensis. A garden hybrid of *S. pinnatus* and the rarely cultivated *S. grahami.* Height 18 in.; planting distance 12 in. A compact bushy plant with pale green, deeply cut, feathery leaves. The orchid-like flowers are up to 1½ in. across and in a wide range of rich colours, including rose, salmon-pink, crimson and combinations of these. Grown as a border plant, flowering is from June to October.

Cultivation. Outdoors, these plants require a light soil enriched with organic matter, and a sheltered sunny site. The most popular method of growing, however, is in pots under glass at a temperature of about 8°C (46°F), using John Innes potting compost No. 2 in the final 6–8 in. pots. Pinch out the growing tips of young plants when they are 3 in. high, and also the side-shoots when they reach the same length, to encourage bushy branch formation.

Thin twiggy supports are required, especially for the taller varieties. Pot on as necessary to make sure the plants do not become root bound, and water freely when growth increases.

Propagation. Sow the seeds under glass, just covering them with compost, in March for outdoor flowering and in August and September for growing in pots. Maintain a temperature of 16°C (61°F) until they germinate. For indoor plants, prick off the young seedlings into 3½ in. pots; for outdoor plants, prick out into boxes and harden off in a cold frame before planting out in flowering sites in May.

Alternatively, for outdoor plants sow directly in the flowering site in April and thin the seedlings to the required spacing.

Pests. Young plants may be infested by APHIDS, which check growth.

Diseases. The occurrence of CROWN, FOOT and ROOT ROT, due to several different fungi, may cause plants to collapse, particularly when they have been over-watered.

TOMATO SPOTTED WILT VIRUS causes severe wilting of the upper leaves, which become bronzed; infected plants soon die.

Schizanthus pinnatus

Schizanthus pinnatus 'Dwarf Bouquet'

Schizophragma

Hydrangeaceae

A genus of eight species of hardy, deciduous climbing plants, related to *Hydrangea*. The two species described are free-growing plants which attach themselves to a wall, pergola or tree trunk by aerial roots.

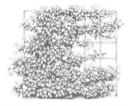

SCHIZOPHRAGMA HYDRANGEOIDES

S. hydrangeoides. Japan. In good conditions this species can reach a height of 20–30 ft. The plant is not commonly grown. The broad, cordate leaves are hairy and deeply serrated, and have distinctive red petioles; they are deep metallic green above, pale green and glaucous beneath. Large flat inflorescences, 10–12 in. across, are freely produced in July and August. The centres are formed of tiny cream-white flowers, surrounded by 1½ in. long, pale yellow bracts.

S. integrifolia. China. Height 15–20 ft. This is slightly less vigorous than *S. hydrangeoides* and has thicker and stiffer stems and different leaves. The latter are ovate-acuminate, and with either plain or only slightly serrated edges. They are bright green above, grey-green beneath, with hairy midribs and veins. Flowers are produced from mid-July to September in flat cymes 12 in. across. The small white flowers in the centre are ringed by 3½ in. long white bracts.

Cultivation. Plant in a rich, loamy, moisture-retentive soil, to which leaf-mould and peat have been added. Set out young plants from pots in semi-shaded positions during October or November, or in March or April. Place a mulch over the roots in spring. Train young growths until their aerial roots obtain a secure hold.

Propagation. Take 3–4 in. nodal cuttings from half-ripe growths and insert them in equal parts (by volume) peat and sand in a propagating frame, with bottom heat of 16°C (61°F), during July or August. Maintain a close atmosphere. Once they are rooted, grow the cuttings on in 3 in. pots in a frame. Finally, plunge the pots into an outdoor nursery bed until they are needed for planting out in their permanent positions.

Mature growths can be layered in October or November. They will root within a year.

Pruning. Remove old flower heads and other dead or unwanted growths from wall-trained plants in autumn.

Pests and diseases. Generally trouble-free.

Schizostylis

Iridaceae

A genus of two species of rhizomatous perennials, suitable for herbaceous and mixed borders or for pot culture under glass. They are good for

Schizophragma integrifolia

Schizostylis coccinea

Schizostylis coccinea 'Mrs Hegarty'

cutting. The species in cultivation is late-flowering and not fully hardy in exposed northern and eastern districts.

S. coccinea (kaffir lily). S. Africa. Height 2–3 ft; planting distance 9–12 in. A species with mid-green, flat and sword-like leaves. Six to ten bright scarlet, star-shaped flowers, about 1½ in. across, are produced on each stem in October and November; they are borne in spikes about 6–9 in. long, which extend as the flowers open.

The variety 'Major' has deep red flowers, larger than those of the type and on stronger stems; 'Mrs Hegarty' has clear pink flowers and is earlier-flowering; 'Viscountess Byng', with pale pink flowers, is more vigorous than the species.

SCHIZOSTYLIS COCCINEA

Cultivation. Plant in March in moist fertile soil, in a sheltered and sunny position. An annual mulch in April or May of peat or compost helps to retain moisture and encourages new growth. These plants are rampant and require division every two or three years. Water freely in summer and in dry weather. In winter, cut down any untidy growths and, in exposed sites, protect the roots with a layer of bracken or leaves.

For pot-grown plants under glass, set a cluster of rooted shoots in 6–8 in. containers of John Innes potting compost No. 2 in April. Plunge these in a bed outdoors or in a frame for the summer and keep moist. Apply a weak liquid feed at intervals of 14 days from June to October. In October bring the plants into a cool greenhouse with a temperature of 7–10°C (45–50°F) to prolong the flowering period to December or later. After flowering, place the pots in a cold frame until growth is restarted, or split up the clusters and plant in March in a sheltered border.

Propagation. Divide the clumps into clusters of five or six shoots and plant in permanent positions during March or April.

Pests. The roots of long-established plants may be attacked by SWIFT MOTH CATERPILLARS.

MILLEPEDES and other soil pests may damage the root systems.

Diseases. The leaves are frequently infected with BOTRYTIS which causes red-brown rust-like marks; it may also destroy the flower buds or lead to the collapse of the flower spikes.

Schlumbergera

Cactaceae

A genus of five species of greenhouse perennials. It now includes the genus *Zygocactus*. These stem succulents are free-flowering, bearing their single flowers at the end of branches. The narrowly trumpet-shaped flowers bend obliquely at the mouth. Each flower usually lasts for only three or four days.

These easily grown plants are epiphytic, and suitable for pots or hanging baskets. They can be grafted on to *Pereskia aculeata,* or grown on their own roots.

See also CACTUS.

S. × buckleyi (Christmas cactus). Garden hybrid. Height 6 in.; spread 9 in. The branching stems consist of flat joints, up to 2 in. long. The joints are mid-green, untoothed and with round indentations on the margins. Magenta or rose-coloured flowers, 2–3 in. long, are produced from December to February.

S. gaertneri: see *Rhipsalidopsis gaertneri*

S. russelliana. Brazil. Height up to 18 in.; spread 3 ft. The spreading brown branches are composed of oval or elongated joints, up to $1\frac{1}{2}$ in. long, with notches and bristles on their margins. Violet-pink flowers, $2\frac{1}{2}$ in. long, are freely borne from February to May.

Schlumbergera truncata

S. truncata (crab cactus). Brazil. Height 6–12 in.; spread 12–15 in. The jointed stems branch freely; they are bright green, turning red. The flat joints, 2–3 in. long, have two to four deeply incised notches on each side, the upper notches being more prominent than the lower. Flowers appear at any time from November to January. They are 2–3 in. long, pink to deep red; the lower petals are reflexed. There are several named varieties with flowers in shades of white, crimson, lilac, purple and blue.

Cultivation. Grow schlumbergeras in an open compost consisting of equal parts (by volume) loam, peat, leaf-mould and sand, with 1 oz. bone-meal to each 1 gal. bucket of soil. In March or April pot the plants in 5 in. pots and place in a semi-shaded position; provide good light and humidity during the growing season.

Damp down the greenhouse floor and staging, and syringe the plants regularly. When flower buds form, feed with weak liquid manure once a week. Do not allow the soil to dry out, or the flower buds will drop. The winter temperature should not be lower than 13°C (55°F). The plants may be stood outside in a position sheltered from bright sun, from June to the end of September. This ripens the new growths.

Propagation. Take cuttings of the joints during summer. Let the cut surfaces heal for a few days before inserting in a compost of equal parts (by volume) peat and sand. Keep the cuttings in a closed frame until rooted, when more air can be admitted gradually.

Pests. Infestations of MEALY BUGS produce conspicuous tufts of white waxy wool.

Diseases. A PHYSIOLOGICAL DISORDER due to incorrect watering causes discoloration or complete collapse of the top growths.

Schoenoplectus tabernaemontanus: see *Scirpus tabernaemontani*

Scilla
Liliaceae

The 80 species of bulbs in this genus are closely related to *Chionodoxa.* Several species which were formerly included in *Scilla* have now been classified in other genera, notably *Endymion,* the familiar English bluebell. The five or six species in general cultivation are dwarf, hardy bulbs with blue flowers. They are easy to grow and suitable for rock gardens, for flowering in short grass and for pots or bowls indoors. Their strap-shaped mid-green leaves are often glossy.

S. bifolia. Mountains of S. Europe and Asia Minor. Height 6–8 in.; planting distance 3 in. Two or more leaves break through the ground in late winter and early spring, then open out and allow the star-shaped flowers, which are $\frac{1}{2}$ in. across, to appear above them in March. The leaves remain short and hooded until the flowers fade, then lengthen. The flowers are variable in colour and number; there are seldom more than eight, and often fewer on each stem. Though generally deep blue, there are also less common pink and white forms.

S. campanulata: see *Endymion hispanicus*

S. festalis: see *Endymion nonscriptus*

S. hispanica: see *Endymion hispanicus*

S. monophylla. Spain, Portugal and Morocco. Height 8–12 in.; planting distance 4–5 in. The leaves are usually solitary. Bright blue bell-shaped flowers, $\frac{1}{3}$ in. long, are borne in loose racemes of 6–20 flowers in May and June.

S. nonscripta: see *Endymion nonscriptus*

S. nutans: see *Endymion nonscriptus*

S. peruviana (Cuban lily). Algeria, Italy and nearby islands. Height 9–12 in.; planting distance 6–8 in. The dense flower heads consist of up to 100 star-shaped blue flowers, each up to $\frac{3}{4}$ in. across, with long bracts beneath. Flowering is in May and June.

S. sibirica. Central and S. Russia. Height up to 6 in.; planting distance 3–4 in. The leaves appear first in early spring and the flower stems grow above them. Each bulb produces three or four stems, with from two to five brilliant blue bell-shaped flowers, $\frac{1}{2}$ in. long, on each stem in March. Plant at a distance from other blue flowers, which look dull by comparison.

Scilla bifolia

Scilla peruviana

Scilla sibirica 'Atrocoerulea'

Scilla tubergeniana

Scindapsus aureus

'Alba' is a white form; 'Atrocoerulea', syn. 'Spring Beauty', is a deeper blue and flowers earlier; *S. s. taurica* is a paler blue.

S. sicula: see *Puschkinia scilloides*

S. tubergeniana. Mountains of N. Iran. Height 3–4 in.; planting distance 3–4 in. This species is very like *S. sibirica,* but has paler blue, striped flowers and blooms earlier. It shows to advantage when planted among snowdrops and yellow winter aconites.

Cultivation. Any moist but well-drained soil will suit scilla bulbs. Plant the bulbs 2–3 in. deep in a sunny or partially shaded position as soon as they become available during late summer or early autumn.

Scatter the bulbs to approximately the spacings indicated and plant with a bulb trowel or dibber. No special care is needed thereafter.

For winter flowering indoors, see entry under BULBS, INDOOR.

Propagation. Seeds are not plentiful on these plants but some can generally be saved when they ripen in the early summer. Sow them in pans of John Innes seed compost in a cold frame or greenhouse. At the end of the second year, plant out the seedlings in nursery rows. If seeds are sown as soon as they are ripe, seedlings will reach flowering size in three to five years.

Offsets are not freely produced, but their presence on thriving plants is shown by the extra clusters of leaves. Offsets can be lifted as the leaves die down, then cleaned, divided and re-planted at once to flower a year or two later.

Pests. Bulbs in store may be infested by APHIDS, especially the tulip bulb aphid.

STEM and BULB EELWORMS may invade the tissues of bulbs, causing internal rotting.

Diseases. Yellow spots on both sides of the leaves, caused by RUST, produce powdery masses of dark brown fungus spores.

SMUT converts the anthers and, less frequently, the ovaries into masses of black, powdery, soot-like fungus spores.

Scindapsus

syn. Rhaphidophora. *Araceae*

A genus of 40 species of evergreen climbers. The genus is closely akin to *Philodendron,* but is native to S.E. Asia and the East Indies. One species is a popular foliage plant for cultivation in a greenhouse where it may reach a height of 20–30 ft; it is, however, more frequently grown as a house plant.

S. aureus, syn. *Rhaphidophora aurea.* Solomon Islands. Height 6 ft or more as a pot plant. A climbing species with aerial roots at the nodes. The juvenile leaves are ovate, pointed and about 4 in. long. They are bright green with yellow markings. Mature leaves are heart-shaped and up to 12 in. long. The form known as 'Golden Queen' has almost entirely yellow leaves. The variety 'Marble Queen' has leaves thickly dappled with white.

Portions of mature growths of this species are sometimes rooted and sold as 'Giant Leaf', but they soon revert to the juvenile form as they make further growth.

Cultivation. Grow scindapsus in 6–8 in. pots of John Innes potting compost No. 2 or in a proprietary peat mixture. Overwinter the plants at a temperature of 10–13°C (50–55°F); place in a well-lit position, particularly during winter, but out of direct sunlight in summer. Water sparingly during winter, and maintain an evenly moist compost for the rest of the year.

Train the plants up supports, ideally moss-covered stakes. Pot on every second or third year in April if large plants are wanted, otherwise repot. In the years when the plants are not repotted give a weak liquid feed once a month from May to September.

Propagation. Take cuttings of tip growths or basal shoots, 4 in. long, from May to July; insert in equal parts (by volume) peat and sand in a propagating case at a temperature of 21–24°C (70–75°F). Pot the rooted cuttings singly in 3–3½ in. containers of John Innes potting compost No. 1, and pot on as necessary.

Alternatively, take leaf-bud cuttings from May to June; cut into single-joint sections and root as described above.

Pruning. Large leggy plants may be cut back to half their size from May to July.

Pests and diseases. Generally trouble-free.

Scirpus

Bulrush. *Cyperaceae*

A genus of 300 species of hardy annual and perennial herbaceous plants which grow in marshy ground and in wet meadows. They resemble those of the genus *Juncus* (rush), having cylindrical stem-like leaves. The insignificant brown flowers are carried terminally in small tufts. Only a few species are suitable for garden cultivation, the others being too invasive or insufficiently attractive.

S. albescens: see *S. tabernaemontani* 'Albescens'

S. tabernaemontani. This species is now correctly known as *Schoenoplectus tabernaemontanus.*

The original type is seldom seen in cultivation, being represented by the following two varieties:

S. t. 'Albescens', syn. *S. albescens.* Origin unknown. Water depth up to 12 in.; height 5–6 ft; planting distance 12–18 in. This hardy perennial aquatic is a good marginal plant for ornamental pools. Cylindrical pithy stems, which are white with vertical green stripes, rise from a hard, creeping rhizome. The light green appearance fades to white after the first year. These stems are tough enough to withstand considerable wind and are long-lasting when cut for indoor flower arrangements.

S. t. 'Zebrinus', syns. *S. zebrinus, Juncus zebrinus* (zebra rush). Japan. Water depth up to 12 in.; height 2–4 ft; planting distance 9–15 in. A perennial herbaceous aquatic, which is hardy if wintered under water or covered with leaves. It grows best in the margin of a sheltered pool, forming compact clumps 6–12 in. across. The rather soft stems are banded in green and white like a porcupine quill, although they tend to become green all over as they age. Division and replanting in April or May maintains a good supply of the banded stems.

S. zebrinus: see *S. tabernaemontani* 'Zebrinus'

Cultivation. These plants thrive in rich loam in the margins of pools, ponds, lakes or streams. Plant the rhizomes, just covering them with soil, in April or early May in up to 12 in. of water. Cut down the old stems in late autumn. Lift, divide and replant *S. t.* 'Zebrinus' each spring, and cut out dark green stems regularly.

Propagation. Lift the plants in April and divide the rhizomes into pieces, each with growing buds or young stems already developing. Divide 'Zebrinus' into pieces 1–3 in. long, 'Albescens' into 4–6 in. lengths. Tough rhizomes may need cutting with secateurs. Plant the divisions as advised under CULTIVATION.

Pests and diseases. Generally trouble-free.

Scolopendrium: see Phyllitis

Scorzonera

Scorzonera hispanica. Compositae

A hardy little-known perennial vegetable grown for its edible roots. These are long and tapering, of dark purple-brown colour. A well-grown crop produces large, unforked and smooth-skinned roots; the attractive leaves are narrowly strap-shaped and glaucous-green. 'Giant Russian' is an outstanding variety.

Cultivation. Scorzoneras thrive in any fertile, well-drained garden soil, in sun or shade. Dig the ground in winter, mixing a liberal dressing of half-rotted manure in the bottom spit. Manure left in the top spit may cause the roots to become forked and fibrous. Alternatively, use ground that was manured for a previous crop.

Sow seeds in April or May in ½ in. deep drills, drawn 15 in. apart. Thin the seedlings until they are 8–12 in. apart.

Keep the bed free of weeds and the surface soil loose so that all available moisture reaches the roots; the plants are likely to run to seed if the roots become too dry.

Scorzonera (foliage)

Harvesting and storing. Roots are ready for use by October; lift them as they are required. Alternatively, lift the roots and store them in a clamp, or in boxes of moist sand or soil in a cool shed. Roots left in the ground will grow on and can be harvested the following autumn.

Pests. Generally trouble-free.

Diseases. WHITE BLISTER produces glistening white, blister-like pustules on the leaves.

Scrophularia

Scrophulariaceae

A genus of 312 species of annuals and herbaceous perennials and sub-shrubs. Some are weeds, and few are worthy of cultivation, but the following hardy perennial makes a good foliage plant.

S. aquatica. Europe. Height 2–3 ft; planting distance 18 in. The plant generally offered is *S. a.* 'Variegata'. It makes an outstanding specimen plant, with ovate toothed leaves, which are dark green and brightly variegated with cream. Insignificant maroon flowers are produced in July and August.

Cultivation. Plant from October to March in sun or half-shade and in any ordinary, moist soil. Pinch out the flower spikes as they appear. Cut down the stems in November.

Propagation. Divide and replant in March.

Pests. Larvae of the figwort WEEVIL may reduce the leaves to skeletons.

Diseases. Generally trouble-free.

Scutellaria

Labiatae

A genus of 300 species of hardy and tender perennial and evergreen shrubby plants. A few species, found in mountain regions in the

Scirpus tabernaemontani 'Zebrinus'

Scorzonera (roots)

Scrophularia aquatica 'Variegata'

tropics, require greenhouse cultivation, but of these only one is readily available. The other two species described are hardy, low-growing plants, ideal for rock gardens. The slender tubular flowers are two-lipped with a prominent hood, and borne in terminal racemes.

GREENHOUSE SPECIES

S. costaricana. Costa Rica. Height $1\frac{1}{2}$–$2\frac{1}{2}$ ft. An evergreen sub-shrubby species with pointed, ovate, dark green leaves borne on dark purple stems. The flowers appear in dense terminal racemes from June to September; they are 2–3 in. long, bright scarlet with a yellow throat.

HARDY SPECIES

S. alpina. Mountains of Europe to Central Asia. Height 9 in. or more; spread up to 18 in. A loose mat-forming species with procumbent stems turning up at the tips. The leaves are broadly ovate with rounded teeth, mid to hoary green. Purple flowers, 1–$1\frac{1}{2}$ in. long and with the lower lip sometimes coloured yellow, appear in August. 'Alba' is a pure white form.

S. indica. China and Japan. Height 6 in.; spread 6–12 in. A tufted species with semi-procumbent stems. The rounded to broadly ovate leaves with rounded teeth are mid-green and covered with fine white hairs. The 1 in. long flowers are blue-purple, and borne from June to September.

Cultivation of greenhouse species. Under glass, grow scutellarias in 5–6 in. pots of John Innes potting compost No. 2. Provide a winter temperature of 10–13°C (50–55°F), and keep the plants just moist in winter. Water freely during the growing season, and keep the plants in a well-lit position, out of direct sunlight. Lightly shade the glass from May to September and ventilate the house when the temperature exceeds 18°C (64°F). Provide a humid atmosphere in summer by frequent damping down.

Pot on in April; give a weak liquid feed at fortnightly intervals from May to September.

Cultivation of hardy species. Plant rock-garden scutellarias between September and March, in any ordinary, well-drained garden soil. They thrive in sun or partial shade.

Propagation of greenhouse species. Scutellarias are usually raised annually from cuttings, but may be kept for two years or more.

Take 3 in. long cuttings of non-flowering lateral shoots in March or April and insert in equal parts (by volume) peat and sand in a propagating case at a temperature of 18–21°C (64–70°F). When rooted, pot the cuttings singly in 3 in. containers of John Innes potting compost No. 2 and pot on as necessary.

Propagation of hardy species. Divide and replant direct in the flowering site during March.

Sow seeds during March or April, in pots or pans of seed compost in a cold frame or greenhouse. Prick off the seedlings into boxes and then into 3–$3\frac{1}{2}$ in. pots of John Innes potting compost No. 1. Plant out in September.

Pruning. Cut the plants back in February to within 3–4 in. of the base. Stop the main shoots of cuttings and young plants once or twice, to encourage a bushy habit.

Pests. Plants under glass may be infected by GLASSHOUSE RED SPIDER MITES; the leaves become mottled and may fall.

Diseases. Generally trouble-free.

Scutellaria costaricana

Scutellaria alpina 'Alba'

Scutellaria indica

Sea kale

Crambe maritima. Cruciferae

A hardy herbaceous perennial grown for its yearly crop of edible leaf-shoots which are blanched to produce tender, rhubarb-like, white stems, 8–9 in. long. The shoots are cut young when the leaves are barely developed and are a choice spring vegetable. Forcing extends the season from December to late spring.

VARIETIES

Few varieties are available; 'Lily White' is a heavy cropper with pure white and well-flavoured shoots.

Cultivation. Sea kale does best in a sandy loam containing plenty of lime, but most soils can be prepared to suit it. Dig the ground deeply in autumn, working in a large bucket of well-rotted manure or compost per sq. yd. Add plenty of sand and grit to heavy soils, and give a dressing of carbonate of lime at the rate of 2–3 oz. per sq. yd to all except limy soils. Leave the ground rough during winter, and in spring apply a top dressing of a general-purpose fertiliser at 4 oz. per sq. yd.

The quickest way to raise the plants is to buy well-developed root crowns. These can be planted at any time during winter or early spring, but preferably in March. Set them 24 in. apart each way and 2 in. below soil level.

The cheapest way to start a bed is to raise plants from seeds, but these take two or three years before they are strong enough to be forced, and they are variable in vigour.

Sow seeds in an outdoor seed bed during March or April, in 1 in. deep drills drawn 12 in. apart. The seeds germinate quickly and the plants make rapid progress. Keep the bed free of weeds. The following March or April transplant the one-year-old plants to their final quarters, setting them as described for purchased crowns.

Alternatively, sow seeds in small groups where the plants are to grow, at 24 in. intervals. Thin the seedlings to one at each station.

An inter-crop of salad onions, lettuces, radishes or cabbages can be grown in the bed before sea kale plants are old enough to be forced. During the non-cropping years, allow only one bud to develop on each plant.

Remove all flowering stems as soon as they appear. Water and feed the plants liberally; apply a mulch of strawy, decayed manure in early May, and in June add a top dressing of agricultural salt at 1 oz. per sq. yd.

Blanch mature plants after the leaves have withered in late October or November. Fork the ground over and cover batches of plants with large pots or boxes, packing manure or decaying leaves over them. The blanched shoots will be ready for cutting in spring.

Plants can be increased from root cuttings (thongs). When lifting plants for forcing, cut pencil-thick pieces of root, 5–6 in. long, and heel them in bundles in a cold frame for the winter. In spring, set the cuttings singly in their growing positions outdoors.

Forcing. Sea kale is readily forced to obtain crops by December. Forcing the plants in their beds does them little harm, and they can be

rced for six or seven successive years before
hey need replacing.

When the leaves have withered in autumn,
rotect the plants with pots and cover with
aves. This prevents the ground from freezing,
ut exposes the plants to cold. This is important
s it makes the plants respond quickly to the
varmth when forcing begins. After about a
nonth at low temperatures, 4–7°C (40–45°F),
emove the leaves and pack a 12 in. layer of
resh manure around and over the pots. Forcing
vill take six or seven weeks.

Forcing may also be done indoors: lift the
oots as they are required, pack them in soil,
eaf-mould or peat. Keep them in a dark place at
temperature of 7°C (45°F), raising this slowly
s forcing proceeds to 13°C (55°F).

Indoor forcing takes five or six weeks if
tarted in November, but gradually takes less;
y March sea kale can be forced in three weeks.
)o not attempt too hasty a forcing as this will
esult in thin, wiry shoots.

Harvesting. Cut the heads close to the base
vhen they are about 6 in. high. When all
lanched shoots have been gathered, discard
oots that were lifted for forcing indoors. Out-
oors, fork the ground around roots that have
ropped, and allow them to grow naturally for
ne remainder of the growing season.

ests. Generally trouble-free.

Diseases. CLUB ROOT may result in swollen and
istorted roots in soil with a low lime content.

VIOLET ROOT ROT produces a violet web of
ungal threads over the crown.

---

ea kale beet: see Spinach

Sedum

Crassulaceae

A large genus of 600 species of hardy, half-hardy
nd tender annuals and perennial, deciduous and
vergreen succulents. The one annual and the
ardy perennials described are suitable for grow-
ng in borders or on rock gardens and dry walls.
he remainder are mainly greenhouse plants,
lthough a few can be grown successfully as
ouse plants if kept on a sunny window-ledge.

See also CACTUS.

Sedums are grown for their attractive flowers,
orms, leaf shape and colour. The star-shaped
owers, in various shades of yellow, pink and
vhite, are borne in terminal panicles which are
ften flat-topped.

OUTDOOR SPECIES

S. acre (biting stonecrop). Europe, including
Great Britain; N. Africa; W. Asia. Height 1–2 in.;
pread 12 in. or more. A mat-forming evergreen
lpine species with mid to yellow-green foliage.
he overlapping leaves are bluntly conical in
hape. Yellow flowers, borne in flattened heads,
–1½ in. across, are freely produced during June
nd July.

The variety 'Aureum', syn. 'Variegatum', has
right, pale yellow shoot tips from March to June.

. aizoon. Japan, Siberia. Height 10–12 in.;
lanting distance 12 in. A perennial species of
ompact growth, with mid-green, shiny,

oblong-lanceolate leaves that are coarsely and
irregularly toothed. Flattened heads, 2–3 in.
across, of golden-yellow flowers appear in July.

The form *S. a. aurantiacum*, syn. *S. euphorbioides*, has brighter, orange-yellow flowers, and
the stems have a bronze hue.

S. album. Europe, including Great Britain; N.
Africa, W. Asia. Height 3–6 in.; spread 15 in. or
more. This mat-forming evergreen alpine plant is
similar in habit to *S. acre*, but has oblong
cylindrical leaves and pink stems. The white
flowers are profusely borne in loose clusters up to
3 in. across, in July.

S. × 'Autumn Joy'. Garden origin. Height 24 in.;
planting distance 18 in. This perennial is a hybrid
between garden forms of *S. spectabile* and *S.
telephium*, and one of the best border sedums.
The pale green leaves are obovate. The 4–8 in.
wide flower heads are pink on first opening in
September; later they deepen to orange-red and
finally, by late October, to orange-brown.

S. caeruleum. Mediterranean regions. Height
4–6 in.; spacing 6 in. An annual with ovate pale
green leaves; both the leaves and stems slowly
turn red when flowering commences. Clusters, 1
in. across, of pale blue flowers with white centres
appear in July. This species will self-seed if the
soil is left undisturbed.

Sedum cauticolum

S. cauticolum. Japan. Height 4–6 in.; spread 12
in. or more. A rather woody-based deciduous
species that forms a spreading tufted plant with
grey-green, broadly ovate leaves. Branched,
somewhat flattened heads, up to 4 in. across, of
crimson-cerise flowers are produced in August
and September.

S. dasyphyllum. S. Europe, N. Africa. Height
½ in.; spread 12 in. This hardy dwarf succulent
forms a dense mat of tiny blue-green ovate leaves.
Flat clusters, up to ½ in. across, of minute white
flowers appear in June.

S. euphorbioides: see *S. aizoon*

S. ewersii. W. Himalayas to Mongolia. Height
4–6 in.; spread 12–18 in. A species similar to *S.
cauticolum*, but with pink or pale purple flowers
in dense convex umbels.

Sea kale (in summer)

Sedum acre 'Aureum'

Sedum maximum
'Atropurpureum'

Sedum spathulifolium

Sedum spurium

Sedum morganianum

S. maximum. Europe. Height 1–3 ft; planting distance 15 in. The normal green species is seldom grown and has been superseded by 'Atropurpureum' (height 24 in.; planting distance 18 in.). This is an excellent border plant with dark purple stems. The purple leaves are broadly obovate and slightly toothed. Pink flower heads, 2–6 in. across, appear during September and October.

S. reflexum (stone orpine). Central and Western Europe, including Great Britain. Height 6–9 in.; spread 12 in. or more. This loose mat-forming or tufted evergreen alpine species has grey-green, linear-cylindrical leaves. Yellow flowers in 2–3 in. wide flattened heads open in July.

S. rhodiola: see *S. roseum*

SEDUM ROSEUM

S. roseum (rose root), syn. *S. rhodiola.* Cold and temperate zones of Northern Hemisphere. Height and planting distance 12–15 in. A perennial border species with rose-scented roots when dry. The glaucous-blue leaves are strap-shaped to obovate and are closely arranged along the thick stems. Heads, 3 in. across, of pale yellow flowers are produced in May and June.

S. × 'Ruby Glow'. Garden origin. Height 10 in.; spread 12 in. A perennial hybrid suitable for the front of a border. It has grey-blue ovate foliage; in July and August, 3–4 in. wide heads of bright rose-crimson flowers are produced.

S. spathulifolium. W. United States. Height 2–4 in.; spread 9 in. or more. This perennial is a low hummock or mat-forming evergreen species with crowded rosettes of grey-green spathulate leaves, often flushed red or purple. Flattened heads, about 2 in. wide, of bright yellow flowers appear in May and June.

The variety 'Purpureum' has leaves richly suffused with purple; 'Cappa Blanca' is entirely grey-white.

SEDUM SPECTABILE

S. spectabile. China. Height 12–18 in.; planting distance 18 in. This border perennial and its garden forms have broadly obovate white-green leaves in twos or threes at each node. Pink flower heads, 3–5 in. or more wide, and with a mauve tinge, appear from September to October. Several garden forms exist with brighter colours: 'Brilliant', deep rose; 'Carmen', bright carmine; 'Meteor', deep carmine-red.

S. spurium. Caucasus, N. Iran; naturalised in Great Britain. Height about 4 in.; spread 12 in. or

Sedum spectabile

more. A mat-forming perennial evergreen specie with broadly obovate, toothed, mid-green leave and red stems. Dense flattened heads, 2–3 in across, of rich pink flowers appear during Jul and August.

The form 'Album' has white flowers; 'Schon busser Blut' is deep red and often begins t flower in July.

S. telephium. Europe, including Great Britain Height 12–18 in.; planting distance 18 in. Thi perennial species is similar to *S. spectabile*, bu the leaves are rarely arranged in pairs. Red-purpl flower heads, 2–4 in. across, are produced i August and September. The species is seldor grown, being superseded by 'Munstead Dar Red', with dark red flower heads.

'Variegatum' (height 12 in.) is a variegate foliage variety; the leaves and stems are streake white and pink.

GREENHOUSE SPECIES

S. allantoides. Mexico. Height and spread up t 12 in. A half-hardy slow-growing succulent usually with prostrate stems and with glaucous grey, club-shaped leaves. Loose panicles, 4–5 in long, of green-white flowers are produced from May to June.

S. bellum. Mexico. Height 1 in.; spread up to 1 in. A tender, prostrate species with grey-gree ovate leaves. Flat 1–2 in. wide clusters of whit flowers appear during April and May.

S. brevifolium. S.W. Europe, Morocco. Heigh ½ in.; spread 12 in. A half-hardy, prostrat succulent which has tiny, ovate, white-gree leaves closely arranged round the stem Flattened clusters, ½–1 in. across, of white flower are borne in July.

S. dendroideum. Mexico. Height and spread u to 24 in. A half-hardy shrubby succulent. Th branches are bare except at the top, where eac bears a loose rosette of fleshy and rounded, shin light green leaves. Clusters, about 3 in. long, yellow flowers appear from March to May.

Plants in cultivation under this name, wit lanceolate, spathulate leaves, belong to the allie species *S. praeltum*.

S. lineare. Japan. Height 1 in.; spread 12 in. prostrate, half-hardy creeping plant. The narrov lanceolate, light green leaves are arranged i threes along the shoots. Clusters, 1½ in. across, of yellow flowers appear from May to July.

The variety 'Variegatum' has white-striped leaves and is suitable as a carpeting plant.

S. **morganianum** (beaver-tail, burro's tail). Mexico. This tender, prostrate species has stems 12–24 in. long, bearing fleshy, cylindrical, pale grey-green leaves densely arranged round the stems. The clusters, ¾–1½ in. across, of pale pink flowers are borne at the ends of the stems from June to September. It makes a good basket plant.

S. **pachyphyllum**. Mexico. Height up to 10 in.; spread 10–12 in. A tender, dwarf, succulent shrub, branched from the base. The fleshy, club-shaped leaves are blue-green, tipped red. Dense, flat clusters, 2–3 in. across, of yellow flowers appear in March and April.

S. **praeltum**: see S. *dendroideum*

S. **rubrotinctum**. Mexico. Height up to 8 in.; spread 8–12 in. A tender, shrubby species, branched from the base. It has thin shoots with fleshy, cylindrical, bright green leaves. The species does not usually flower in Great Britain. 'Aurora' is an attractive variety with grey-green leaves, tinged rose-red.

S. **sieboldii**. Japan. Height 2–3 in.; spread up to 15 in. The round, flat leaves of this half-hardy prostrate species are grey, edged with pink, notched in the margins, and loosely arranged in threes on the branches. Dense, flat clusters, 2–3 in. wide, of pink flowers appear in October. This species may be grown outdoors in mild areas.

The variety 'Medio-variegatum', which has leaves striped with white, is suitable for a hanging basket.

S. **treleasei**. Mexico. Height 12 in.; spread 6 in. A tender succulent shrub with blue-green, fleshy, ovate leaves. The rounded clusters of ½ in. wide, bright yellow flowers are borne at the ends of the branches in March and April.

S. **weinbergii**, syn. *Graptopetalum weinbergii*. Mexico. Height 8–12 in.; spread 12 in. This half-hardy succulent species has rosettes of fleshy, club-shaped leaves. These are glaucous, becoming red-amethyst in summer. White star-shaped flowers appear in 8 in. spikes in May and June. This shy-flowering species is useful for summer bedding.

Cultivation of outdoor species. Grow these hardy sedums in any ordinary, well-drained garden soil, in full sun. Most species are drought-resistant, but S. *maximum* and S. *telephium* need well-drained, moisture-retentive soil.

Plant all perennial species during suitable weather between October and April. After flowering, leave the dead stems on the plants until spring when they can easily be snapped off at the base.

Cultivation of greenhouse species. The succulents require soil that is not too rich or the leafy growth becomes rank and few flowers are produced. A mixture of 3 parts loam, 2 parts coarse sand or grit and 1 part peat or leaf-mould (parts by volume) is adequate. In March or April, set the plants in 4–6 in. pans in full light and sun, with ample ventilation except in cold weather. In winter the tender and half-hardy sedums require a minimum temperature of 5°C (41°F).

Propagation of outdoor species. Sow the seeds of the annual species, S. *caeruleum*, in the flowering

site during March or April, and thin out the seedlings to the appropriate spacing. In subsequent years this species usually reproduces itself from self-sown seedlings.

Sow seeds of perennial species in a cold frame in boxes of seed compost during March or April; named varieties do not come true from seeds. Prick off the seedlings, when they are large enough to handle, into boxes of John Innes potting compost No. 1, and then transfer to 3 in. pots. Plunge outside until October when the young plants can be set in the flowering site.

All perennial species are easily divided and replanted from October to March; even small pieces without roots will usually grow.

Stem cuttings, 1–3 in. long, taken from March to July and inserted in a nursery bed outdoors, will generally root easily.

Propagation of greenhouse species. Sow seeds during March or April on the surface of the seed compost, and germinate at a temperature of 15–18°C (59–64°F). When the seedlings are large enough to handle, prick them out into boxes or pans and later transfer singly to 3 in. pots of John Innes potting compost No. 1. Pot on the young plants as necessary.

Take 1–3 in. stem cuttings between April and September and insert them singly in 2–2½ in. pots of sand, first allowing the cut surfaces to heal for a few days. Treat the rooted cuttings as seedlings.

Large-leaved species, such as S. *morganianum* and S. *pachyphyllum*, may also be increased from leaf cuttings. Place the cuttings in boxes of sand, leaf face downwards, and keep the sand moist. When small plantlets appear, pot them individually in containers of the growing compost.

Prostrate species may be divided and replanted at any time except during winter.

Pests. Colonies of APHIDS may feed on stems and leaves and make the plants sticky and sooty.

MEALY BUGS often produce tufts of white waxy wool on the foliage of greenhouse specimens.

SLUGS eat leaves and stems and may check early growth.

Diseases. In over-wet soil conditions CROWN or ROOT ROT may occur.

Self-heal: see Prunella

Semiaquilegia adoxioides: see *Aquilegia ecalcarata*

Sempervivum
Houseleek. *Crassulaceae*

A genus of 25 species of hardy and half-hardy rosette-forming evergreen succulents. The species described are hardy plants, suitable for rock gardens, screes and dry walls; they may also be grown in pans in an alpine house.

The leaves are fleshy, ovate to elliptic in shape; they curve around each other to form close rosettes that are often tipped or flushed with red or purple. The flowers, which are carried in sprays, are generally star-like. In some species, such as S. *heuffelii* and S. *sobolifera*, the petals are fused, giving a bell-like appearance, and such species are now regarded by some botanists as belonging to a separate genus, *Jovibarba*.

Sedum rubrotinctum 'Aurora'

Sedum sieboldii 'Medio-variegatum'

Sempervivum arachnoideum

Sempervivum heuffelii

659

Sempervivum montanum

Sempervivum octopodes apetalum

Sempervivum tectorum

Sempervivum tectorum calcareum

The leaf rosettes are generally the main feature of the plants, but in some species, notably *S. arachnoideum*, the flowers are also attractive.

S. arachnoideum (cobweb houseleek). Mountains of Europe, Pyrenees. Height ½–1 in.; spread up to 12 in. Possibly the most popular species, with globular rosettes, 1–1½ in. across. The leaves are green, sometimes flushed red, and their tips are woven together with a white, cobweb-like mat of hairs. Bright rose-red flowers, ¾ in. across, appear on stems about 6 in. tall in June and July.

S. a. tomentosum is a form with somewhat larger rosettes, densely webbed. It is frequently listed as *S. a. laggeri*.

S. × 'Commander Hay': see *S. tectorum*

S. dolomiticum. Eastern Alps. Height 1 in.; spread 6–9 in. This species has bright green rosettes, 1½–2 in. across. The flowers, ¾ in. wide and borne on 6 in. high stems, are deep rose-red; they appear in June and July.

S. erythraeum. Bulgaria. Height 1–2 in.; spread 6–9 in. The rather flat rosettes of this species measure 2 in. across and are composed of grey-green leaves, overlaid with a faint purple sheen. Deep rose flowers, about 1 in. across, are borne on 6 in. stems in July.

The form 'Rila' has wider, green-tipped leaves which take on a red tint in summer.

S. × funckii. Garden origin. Height ½–1 in.; spread 6–9 in. The 1–1½ in. wide rosettes are bright green, sometimes tipped with purple; they are covered with fine, short white hairs. The 6–8 in. high stems carry rose-purple flowers, 1 in. across, in July.

S. heuffelii, syn. *Jovibarba heuffelii*. Mountains of S.E. Europe. Height 1–2 in.; spread 6–12 in. The rosettes are variable in size, generally 2–4 in. across. The leaves are mid-green or glaucous, sometimes tipped with brown; some forms are red-flushed. Yellow, bell-like flowers, about ½ in. across the mouth, open on stems 6–8 in. high from July to September.

S. montanum. Pyrenees, Alps, Corsica and Carpathians. Height 1 in.; spread 6–9 in. This species has dull green rosettes, 1–2 in. across. Pale red-purple flowers, ¾ in. wide, are borne on 6 in. stems from June to August. 'Burnatii' is a large form with pale green rosettes 2–4 in. across.

S. octopodes. S.W. Macedonia. Height ½–1 in.; spread 9 in. or more. The hairy rosettes of this species are 1 in. across, pale to mid-green, sometimes with dark maroon tips. New rosettes are produced on the ends of very long slender stolons. Yellow flowers, flushed with red at the base, are carried on 6 in. tall stems; they measure ¾ in. across and appear in June and July.

This plant is difficult to overwinter, but the variety *S. o. apetalum* is winter-hardy; this seldom produces its petal-less flowers.

S. soboliferum, syn. *Jovibarba soboliferum* (hen and chicken houseleek). Mountains of N. Europe. Height 1 in.; spread up to 12 in. A species with bright green leaves, sometimes flushed with red, that forms rosettes 2–3 in. across. Small, globular offsets are freely produced from the main rosettes, and quickly detach and root themselves. The flowers, similar to those of *S. heuffelii*, measure ⅔ in. across and appear in July.

S. tectorum (common houseleek). Pyrenees to S.E. Alps. Height 2–3 in.; spread up to 12 in. The rosettes, 2–6 in. wide, are composed of bright to mid-green leaves with maroon tips. Rose-purple 1–1¼ in. wide flowers are carried on 6–12 in. high stems in July.

S. t. calcareum is a form with smaller grey-green red-tipped rosettes; it seldom flowers. 'Commander Hay' is a popular hybrid with somewhat larger rosettes, coloured rich glossy purple-red with green tips.

Sempervivum tectorum 'Commander Hay'

Cultivation. Grow sempervivums in any ordinary, well-drained garden soil, in a sunny position. Plant from September to April.

In the alpine house, grow the plants in 8–10 in. pans of equal parts (by volume) John Innes potting compost No. 2 and grit or coarse sand. Repot every two or three years in April, or when the rosettes become congested.

Propagation. Offsets are freely produced; the rooted offsets may be removed and replanted in permanent positions during September, October, March or April.

Alternatively, sow seeds in March in boxes of seed compost in a cold frame. Prick off the seedlings, when large enough to handle, into pans and then into 3 in. pots of John Innes potting compost No. 1 or 2. Plant out in permanent sites from September onwards.

Pests. The rosettes, especially when newly planted, are often uprooted by BIRDS.

Diseases. Orange pustules on the leaves are caused by RUST; affected leaves become longer and thinner causing the rosettes to develop a more erect appearance.

Senecio

Compositae

A large genus of about 3000 species distributed throughout most parts of the world. It includes half-hardy and tender annuals and biennials, hardy herbaceous and tender succulent perennials as well as evergreen trees or shrubs. The evergreen shrubby species, which include climbers, are hardy, half-hardy or tender.

Most of the plants described have daisy-like flowers, often in shades of yellow; they are arranged in loose clusters. In the descriptions, the term planting distance is applied to border species which are usually planted in groups; spread applies to the eventual leaf spread of shrubby or prostrate plants.

ANNUAL SPECIES

These are half-hardy plants suitable for annual and mixed borders and as cut flowers. *S. cruentus* is the plant commonly known as *Cineraria* and widely grown as a winter-flowering pot plant.

S. arenarius. S. Africa. Height 18 in.; planting distance 9 in. A species with mid-green oblong leaves, often toothed and covered with sticky hairs. Loose flower clusters appear in July and August; they are pale purple with yellow centres and each $\frac{3}{4}$ in. across.

S. cineraria: see *S. maritima*

S. cruentus: see *Cineraria cruenta*

S. elegans. S. Africa. Height 18 in.; planting distance 6 in. This species is at its best when planted in bold groups. The leaves are dark green, oblong-ovate, usually deeply pinnately lobed like those of groundsel, and with a clammy feel. The purple flowers, 1 in. across, are carried in loose clusters in July and August.

Garden varieties listed are in a range of colours including white, pink, lavender and mauve; single and double forms are available.

SENECIO MARITIMA

S. maritima, syns. *S. cineraria*, *Cineraria maritima*. Mediterranean regions. Height 24 in.; planting distance 12 in. An almost hardy evergreen sub-shrub which, although it will survive most winters outdoors, is usually treated as a half-hardy annual. The leaves are oblong-ovate and deeply lobed; both leaves and stems are covered with white woolly hairs, giving the plant a felted texture and an attractive silvery appearance. The yellow flowers, 1 in. wide, are borne from July to September; they are a less attractive feature than the foliage.

Several varieties are listed, including 'Candicans', a uniform strain with deeply cut leaves; and 'Diamond', which has almost white, deeply divided leaves. 'Silver Dust' is densely white-felted, with dissected, fern-like leaves.

HERBACEOUS PERENNIAL SPECIES

Many of these hardy perennial senecios, such as groundsel and ragwort, are useless or a nuisance in gardens, but the following are suitable for borders. They are frequently confused with the genus *Ligularia* and some catalogues may list these species under that name.

S. clivorum: see *Ligularia clivorum*

S. hodgsonii: see *Ligularia hodgsonii*

S. maritima: see ANNUAL SPECIES

S. przewalskii: see *Ligularia przewalskii*

S. tanguticus. China. Height 5–7 ft; planting distance 3 ft. This is a rampant and invasive species which attains its full height only in moist soil. The mid to deep green ovate leaves are cut into oblong-toothed segments. Plume-shaped panicles, 6–12 in. long, of yellow flowers are carried in September.

SENECIO TANGUTICUS

SHRUBBY SPECIES

The following evergreen species are hardy in all but the coldest areas, and are particularly suitable for maritime gardens. They are notable for their silver-grey foliage which is used in flower arrangements. *S. greyi* and *S. laxifolius* make useful barrier hedges for windy seaside sites, forming dense, low-growing mounds. *S. monroi*, being slower-growing, is less suitable.

S. compactus. New Zealand. Height and spread 2–4 ft. A marginally hardy species, much resembling a dwarf spreading form of *S. monroi*, but with slightly larger leaves and flowers.

S. greyi. New Zealand. Height 3–4 ft; spread 4–6 ft. The plant listed under this name is almost invariably *S. laxifolius*. The true species has ovate mid-green leaves that are densely felted with grey-white hairs. Yellow flowers are borne in June and July in 6 in. long panicles terminating the branchlets.

S. laxifolius. New Zealand. Height 4 ft or more; spread 4–6 ft. Although often confused with *S. greyi*, this species is more reliably hardy. It has more lax growth and larger mid-green, white-felted leaves. Loose clusters of yellow flowers, 1 in. across, open in June and July.

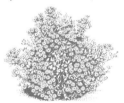

SENECIO LAXIFOLIUS

S. monroi. New Zealand. Height 4–6 ft; spread 2–4 ft. The oblong, wavy-edged leaves are mid to deep green with grey-white undersides. Bright yellow flowers, which open in July, are borne in 4–6 in. wide terminal clusters.

SUCCULENT SPECIES

Those described are greenhouse evergreens, chiefly grown for their attractive foliage. The insignificant groundsel-like flowers, $\frac{1}{2}$–1 in. long, are often arranged in loose clusters. The species may be classified under *Kleinia* and *Notonia*.

See also CACTUS.

S. citriformis. S. Africa. Height 4 in.; spread up to 12 in. A dwarf shrubby species with a tuft of fleshy stems, branching from a central rootstock. These are covered with succulent, almost sessile, spirally arranged leaves shaped like lemons. The blue-grey foliage is covered with a white waxy farina and has numerous vertical translucent lines. Yellow-white flowers are produced during December and January.

Senecio elegans

Senecio maritima 'Diamond'

Senecio maritima 'Silver Dust'

Senecio compactus

Senecio laxifolius

Senecio rowleyanus

S. haworthii, syn. *Kleinia tomentosa.* S. Africa. Height and spread up to 24 in. The stems of this species are solitary at first, but later branch from the base. The blue-grey leaves are cylindrical, tapering slightly at each end; like the stems they are completely covered with silver-white woolly hairs. Orange-yellow solitary flowers are sometimes borne in July.

S. herreianus, syn. *Kleinia herreiana.* S.W. Africa. Height 2–3 in.; spread 24 in. or more. A low, creeping plant with glaucous-green stems and leaves. The fleshy and globular leaves, resembling small grapes, are borne at intervals along the stems, and are marked with fine dark green lines. This species rarely flowers.

S. radicans, syn. *Kleinia radicans.* S. Africa. Height 3–4 in.; spread 24 in. A species with prostrate stems bearing numerous fat, almost spherical glaucous-green leaves. They resemble small grapes, and each leaf has a darker green stripe down the middle. Off-white, often solitary flowers may be produced on short stalks in December, but the species rarely flowers.

S. rowleyanus (string-of-beads). S.W. Africa. Height 2 in.; spread 2–3 ft. A mat-forming species with slender creeping stems which root freely. The glaucous-green leaves are globose or grape-shaped; each leaf has a vertical translucent band and a minute pointed tip. Solitary flowers appear on stalks, 2 in. long, from September to November. The white florets, with rich purple stigmas, are sweetly scented. This species is suitable as a carpeting or basket plant.

S. serpens, syn. *Kleinia repens.* S. Africa. Height 8–12 in.; spread 24 in. or more. An almost hardy, trailing and mat-forming species with a bright blue-white waxy sheen when grown in full sun. The fleshy stems bear spirally arranged, linear to lanceolate, glaucous-blue leaves. They are channelled above and form loose rosettes at the stem tips. White flowers appear in July and August.

Cultivation of annual species. Grow in any ordinary garden soil, in a sunny position, setting hardened-off plants out in May or when danger of frost is past. *S. arenarius* and *S. elegans* may need twiggy supports in exposed sites.

Cultivation of herbaceous perennial species. Any ordinary garden soil is suitable for these plants; *S. tanguticus* requires constant moisture and grows well by the waterside. A position in partial shade is preferable, although the perennials will thrive in sun provided the roots are kept moist and cool. Plant during suitable weather between October and April. Staking is only necessary in exposed, windy positions. Cut the plants down to ground level in November.

Lift and divide *S. tanguticus* every two or three years, in April or May; if this species is left undisturbed it can become invasive.

Cultivation of shrubby species. Plant between October and April in any ordinary, well-drained soil. All species do well in coastal areas, preferably in a sunny position, although they will tolerate light shade.

For hedges, space *S. greyi* and *S. laxifolius* 18 in. apart; pinch out the growing tips once or twice during the first year, to promote bushy growth.

Cultivation of succulent species. These require a sharply drained compost such as John Innes

potting compost No. 1. Pot the plants during March or April in 6–9 in. pans or 4–6 in. pots. Place in a sunny position and water freely during the growing season, and keep just moist for the rest of the year.

Stake erect species when necessary and, when they become too large, start them again from cuttings. The minimum winter temperature required is 10°C (50°F). Repot the plants at the beginning of the growing season if necessary.

Propagation of annual species. Sow seeds in pans or boxes of John Innes potting compost in February or March, at a temperature of 16°C (61°F). Prick out the seedlings into pots or boxes of John Innes potting compost No. 1 and harden them off in a cold frame before planting out in May. The seeds of *S. elegans* may also be sown directly in the flowering site during April, and the seedlings thinned to the appropriate spacing.

Propagation of herbaceous perennial species. Lift, divide and replant in April or May.

Propagation of shrubby species. In August or early September, take 3–4 in. cuttings of half-ripened lateral shoots and insert in equal parts (by volume) peat and sand in a cold frame. Set out the rooted cuttings in a nursery bed during April or May or place singly in 3½ in. pots of John Innes potting compost No. 1 and plunge outdoors. Plant out in their permanent positions from October onwards.

Propagation of succulent species. These are easily increased from stem cuttings taken in June or July. Let the cut surfaces heal for a few days before inserting them singly in 3 in. pots of equal parts (by volume) peat and coarse sand.

Clump-forming species may be divided and repotted from June to September.

Pruning. Remove faded flower stems and any damaged or straggly shoots of shrubby species, as they appear.

Hedges of *S. greyi* and *S. laxifolius* should not be clipped. Cut back old flowering stems to the first healthy leaf in autumn. Otherwise, merely remove straggly shoots.

Pests. All species may be infested by APHIDS which make plants sticky and check growth.

Annual and perennial species may be attacked by THRIPS which cause a fine light flecking and other discolorations on the flowers.

CHRYSANTHEMUM LEAF MINER maggots tunnel into the leaves of annual and perennial species.

In addition to aphids, greenhouse succulents may be infested by MEALY BUGS which produce conspicuous tufts of white waxy wool on leaves and stems. ROOT MEALY BUGS may attack the roots and check growth.

Diseases. Annual and perennial species may suffer from POWDERY MILDEW, which shows as a powdery white coating on the leaves.

RUST infects the annual *S. elegans* and shows on the leaves as orange spore-bearing pustules.

TOMATO SPOTTED WILT VIRUS affects annual and perennial species, and occasionally succulents. It produces severe mottling of the leaves, followed by brown streaks along the veins, particularly on the undersides. Affected plants are stunted, produce poor flowers and may die.

Shrubby species are generally trouble-free.

Sensitive plant: see *Mimosa pudica*

Sequoia

Taxodiaceae

SEQUOIA SEMPERVIRENS

A genus of two species of giant evergreen coniferous trees, native to western U.S.A. They are hardy, but grow best in areas of high rainfall. They are unsuitable for small gardens, but make outstanding single specimen trees in parks and large gardens.

See also CONIFERS.

S. gigantea, syn. *S. wellingtonia* (giant redwood). Sierra Nevada, California. Height 50 ft; spread 20 ft. This species is now classified as *Sequoia-dendron giganteum*. It is a vigorous and long-lived tree, widely grown throughout Great Britain. The crown is narrowly conic and pointed, or sometimes broadly conic with a narrowly domed top, and the lower branches grow downwards, sweeping upwards near the tips. The red-brown bark is fibrous, spongy and fissured. The shoots are clothed in short, stiff and curved awl-shaped leaves, dark green or grey, which are aromatic when crushed; old foliage often turns brown in July, giving a diseased appearance to the tree before falling. The cones, seldom borne before the tree is 30 years old, are ovoid, 2–3 in. long; they mature in their second year, turning pale brown and woody as they ripen. The cones are borne singly at the tips of short shoots, and are clustered all over the crown.

'Aureum' (height 25 ft; spread 15 ft) is a slow-growing variety with a more dense and upswept crown, with pale-gold new foliage. 'Pendulum' (height 20 ft; spread 2–4 ft) is a weeping variety of straight, narrow or arching habit with vertically downswept side-branches.

S. sempervirens (coast redwood). California and S.W. Oregon. Height 50 ft; spread 25 ft. A fast-growing species with a columnar tall crown that eventually becomes flat-topped. The upper branches are regular and horizontal, while the lower branches sweep down. The bark is orange or dark red-brown, thick and fibrous, in large criss-crossed ridges. Suckers arise at the base of some trees, and the species coppices readily.

The leaves are mid-green, linear-oblong; they are $\frac{1}{4}$ in. long, pointed and incurved on the main shoots; on lateral shoots they are up to 1 in. long, flat and narrow and dark green above with two white lines beneath. The globose cones, 1 in. across, have wrinkled, leathery scales. Small, yellow, drop-shaped male flowers appear at the tips of lateral shoots.

'Adpressa' has smaller leaves which are cream at first, then grey.

S. wellingtonia: see *S. gigantea*

Cultivation. These trees thrive in deep, moist, but well-drained soil in a sheltered position. *S. sempervirens* tolerates denser overhead shade than the other species, but grows faster in an open situation. Plant during suitable weather from November to March, using young plants 12–18 in. high. Taller plants will need staking unless the root system is established. Keep the ground moist and apply a deep mulch of leaf-mould in March or April in the early years after planting.

Propagation. Sow seeds in pans of John Innes seed compost in a cold frame in March. When the seedlings are 2–3 in. high, prick off into nursery rows outdoors or pot singly in $3\frac{1}{2}$ in. pots of John Innes potting compost No. 2 and plunge outdoors. Grow on for two years before planting out in permanent positions.

Alternatively, take 3–4 in. long tip cuttings of sucker shoots in September; insert the cuttings in equal parts (by volume) peat and sand in a cold frame. When rooted the following spring, line the cuttings out in nursery rows and grow on for one or two years.

Pruning. The leading shoot may be damaged after severe frosts, and natural recovery is variable. Wait until new growth has been made, by about early July, before selecting a new leader and cutting out competing shoots. Trees of *S. sempervirens* often regenerate from the base when destroyed by frost or fire. Normal forking is rare, but when it occurs the leader must be reduced to a single shoot.

Pests. Generally trouble-free.

Diseases. A common PHYSIOLOGICAL DISORDER, due to cold, dry winds, causes browning of the foliage in winter.

HONEY FUNGUS may kill the trees.

Sequoiadendron giganteum: see *Sequoia gigantea*

Sequoia gigantea (cones)

Sequoia sempervirens (cones)

Setcreasea

Commelinaceae

A genus of nine species of tender perennials, mainly grown for their decorative foliage. Those described are suitable as house plants.

S. purpurea (purple heart). Mexico. Height 12–15 in. This species forms tufts of erect, oblong-lanceolate, purple leaves, 6 in. long. During spring, it throws up branched purple stems, 12 in. high, which are crowned from May to December with a pair of boat-shaped purple bracts. These shelter a cluster of three-petalled, rose-purple, $1\frac{3}{4}$ in. wide flowers which open in succession.

S. striata. Southern U.S.A. Height 12 in. This spreading species is similar in appearance to the trailing *Tradescantia*. The dark green, downy, ovate leaves have ivory veins and are purple beneath. Insignificant white flowers, similar to but smaller than those of *S. purpurea*, are borne from May to October.

Cultivation. Grow setcreaseas in John Innes potting compost No. 2 or in a proprietary peat mixture. The plants require a winter temperature of 7°C (45°F) and will survive for short periods at slightly lower temperatures. Keep the plants just moist in winter, but water freely during the growing period. In summer, stand them in good light, but give slight shade on sunny days if the plants are kept in the greenhouse.

Setcreasea purpurea

Grow the plants in 4–5 in. pots and repot annually in April; usually setcreaseas are discarded after three years, but if large specimens are wanted they may be potted on into larger containers in April. Feed the plants with dilute liquid manure at fortnightly intervals from May to September.

Propagation. Take basal cuttings, 3–4 in. long, from May to August; insert in 3 in. pots of John Innes potting compost No. 1 at a temperature of 16–18°C (61–64°F). When well rooted, pot the cuttings on into 5 in. pots of John Innes potting compost No. 2.

Pruning. Remove old straggling flower stems of *S. purpurea* at the end of the growing season. No pruning is required for *S. striata*, but it may be stopped from time to time to encourage the production of side-growths.

Pests and diseases. Generally trouble-free.

Shadbush: see *Amelanchier canadensis*

Shallot

Allium ascalonicum. Alliaceae

A hardy bulbous plant used as a vegetable. The small, onion-flavoured bulbs, about 1 in. across, are produced in small clusters and are ideal for pickling. Slightly larger varieties are often used as a substitute for onions.

VARIETIES

'Red Dutch' and 'Yellow Dutch' are popular varieties; 'Hative de Niort' and its selected form 'The Aristocrat' have firm, smooth, round bulbs and are reliable exhibition varieties.

Cultivation. Shallots are best grown in an open sunny position and in fertile, well-drained soil that was manured for a previous crop. Work in a light dressing of a general fertiliser before planting during February or March. Set the bulbs 9 in. apart, in rows 15 in. apart, and in such a manner that the tips of the bulbs are level with the soil surface. Early planting, in February, is recommended, as stored bulbs begin to turn soft in spring.

Keep weeds down with a hoe, but take care not to disturb, damage or bury the bulbs. About the end of June, aid ripening by pulling the soil away from the base of the clumps of bulbs.

Harvesting and storing. As soon as the foliage turns yellow, about mid-July, lift the clumps of bulbs and lay them out to dry and ripen completely in the sun for a few days. Turn them daily while they are ripening. When completely dry, separate the bulbs and store in boxes placed in a dry, airy, cool but frost-free place.

Save some bulbs for planting the following year, ensuring that these are completely sound.

Pests. Maggots of the ONION FLY may tunnel into basal growths of seedlings and into maturing bulbs. This pest is generally most damaging on dry soils.

STEM AND BULB EELWORM feeds on leaf and bulb tissues, which become swollen and distorted, a condition often known as onion bloat.

Diseases. DOWNY MILDEW causes the leaves to turn grey before withering and drooping. In wet weather, they may show a purple coating.

A VIRUS DISEASE shows as yellow streaking o complete yellowing of the leaves which droop Diseased plants are stunted, and the leaves are crinkled and flat.

WHITE ROT causes the leaves to turn yellow the roots rot, and the bases of the bulbs become covered with a white fluffy fungal growth.

Shell-flower: see *Moluccella laevis*
Shoo-fly: see *Nicandra physaloides*
Shooting star: see Dodecatheon

Shortia

Diapensiaceae

A genus of eight or nine species of hardy evergreen perennials. The species described are suitable for cool, moist sites on rock gardens and can also be grown in alpine houses.

S. galacifolia. N. Carolina. Height 6 in.; spread 12–15 in. The pale green orbicular leaves have red tints on their shallowly toothed edges. White flowers, with five petals forming a shallow 1 in. long funnel, are borne during April and May.

S. soldanelloides. Japan. Height 4–5 in.; spread 9–12 in. This plant forms a glossy dark green mat of tough, ovate, toothed leaves on wiry stems. In exposed positions the leaves may bronze in autumn. The pendent, bell-shaped flowers are deep rose with fringed petals; they are ¾ in. long and appear in April and May.

S. uniflora. Japan. Height 4 in.; spread 12–15 in. The rounded leaves are pale green initially, some turning red in autumn and winter. Waxy pale pink flowers, 1½ in. across and broadly funnel-shaped with frilled edges, open in April or May.

S. u. grandiflora has deeply frilled, palest pink flowers.

Cultivation. Shortias grow best in peaty soil in partial shade. Plant in March or April. Remove faded flower stems.

For cultivation in the alpine house, grow shortias in 6–8 in. pans in a compost of equal parts (by volume) peat, leaf-mould, fibrous loam and sand. Keep the plants in a partially shaded position; after flowering move them to a shady open frame. Repot every other year.

Propagation. Divide the plants in June and replant direct in final positions.

Alternatively, take 1–1¼ in. cuttings of basal shoots in June or July and insert in equal parts (by volume) peat, leaf-mould and sand in a cold frame. Plant the rooted cuttings out in September; or pot them up in 3 in. pots of the growing mixture. Overwinter them in the frame and plant out in March or April.

Pests and diseases. Generally trouble-free.

Shrimp plant: see Beloperone

Sidalcea

Malvaceae

A genus of 25 species of hardy herbaceous perennials. They are easily grown border plants for a sunny position, but will not thrive in hot dry

Shallot 'The Aristocrat'

Shortia uniflora grandiflora

Sidalcea malvaeflora 'Rose Queen'

places or in full shade. In exposed positions they may be damaged or killed during severe winters.

S. *malvaeflora*. W. United States. Height 2½–4½ ft; planting distance 18–24 in. This species has mid-green lower leaves, which are round to kidney-shaped, and shallowly lobed, narrowly segmented stem leaves. Mallow-like, widely funnel-shaped flowers, in various shades of pink and about 2 in. across, are borne in a 9 in. spike at the top of the branched stems. The flowering period extends from June to September.

The species has been superseded by the following varieties (planting distance 15 in.): 'Croftway Red' (height 3 ft), rich deep red; 'Loveliness' (height 2½ ft), shell-pink; 'Mrs Alderson' (height 3 ft), clear pink flowers 2½ in. across; 'Oberon' (height 2½ ft), soft rose-pink; 'Puck' (height 24 in.), clear pink; 'Rose Queen' (height 2½ ft), rose-pink; 'William Smith' (height 3 ft), salmon-pink.

Cultivation. Plant in October or March in a sunny position in ordinary garden soil. The taller varieties may need staking with sticks or canes, and all should be cut down to 12 in. above ground

SIDALCEA MALVAEFLORA

level soon after flowering. This encourages the production of lateral flowering shoots.

Propagation. Lift, divide and replant in March, using healthy vigorous pieces from the outside of the clump and discarding the centre.

Seeds may be sown in boxes of John Innes seed compost in a cold frame in April, but named varieties do not come true from seed. Prick out the seedlings when large enough to handle, and grow the plantlets on in a nursery bed until they are set in their permanent positions in October.

Pests. Generally trouble-free.

Diseases. On the leaves, stems and fruits, RUST shows as raised, spore-bearing pustules, which are at first orange, but later turn brown. In severe cases shrivelling of leaves may occur.

Silene

Campion, catchfly. *Caryophyllaceae*

A genus of 500 species of annuals, biennials, perennial herbaceous plants and some sub-shrubs. Most of them are weeds, but some of the perennial species are suitable for rock gardens while the two annuals and the biennial described may be grown in mixed borders or used for bedding out.

The flowers are star or salver-shaped with tubular or inflated calyces and variably notched petals; they are carried in profusion from late spring until the end of summer.

ANNUAL SPECIES

S. *armeria*. S. Europe. Height 12–24 in.; spacing 6 in. A hardy species of upright habit. The erect stems carry elliptic grey-green leaves. Dense clusters of single flowers, ¾ in. across, are borne from May to September, depending on when the seeds are sown. They are purple, rose or white. The upper parts of the plant are sticky.

S. *coeli-rosa*, syns. *Lychnis coeli-rosa*, *Viscaria elegans* (rose of heaven, viscaria). Mediterranean areas. Height 18 in.; spacing 6 in. A hardy annual with oblong, grey-green leaves. The stems carry 1 in. wide, rose-purple flowers with white centres from June to August.

Several varieties are listed; they include: 'Candida', pure white, and 'Cardinalis', bright crimson. Oculata is a strain with dark-eyed flowers, and includes the following recommended selections: 'Blue Pearl', lavender-blue; 'Fire King', scarlet; and 'Rose Beauty', deep pink. 'Oculata Nana Compacta' is a strain of dwarf plants that seldom exceed 6 in.; 'Loyalty' is blue and 'Love', rose-carmine. Both strains are also obtainable as mixtures.

S. *compacta*, syn. *S. orientalis*. Asia Minor. Height 18 in.; planting distance 6 in. A hardy biennial that can also be grown as an annual. It has slender stems and smooth, elliptic, pointed, grey-green leaves. Bright pink flowers, 1 in. across, are carried in loose clusters from June to August or later.

S. *orientalis*: see *S. compacta*

S. *pendula*. Mediterranean regions. Height 6–9 in.; spacing 6 in. A striking, hardy plant of compact habit, the most widely grown of the annual species. The erect stems bear oblong, pointed, rather hairy mid-green leaves. Pale pink axillary flowers, ½ in. across, are carried in loose clusters from May to September, depending on when the seeds are sown.

Several garden varieties are listed, including 'Compacta Mixed', 6 in., with salmon-pink or crimson double flowers against a background of dark green foliage, excellent for edging paths and for rock gardens; and 'Triumph Mixed', 6 in., containing shades of pink, salmon and orange.

PERENNIAL SPECIES

S. *acaulis* (moss campion). N. Hemisphere, including Great Britain. Height 2 in.; spread 12–18 in. The narrow awl-shaped leaves are tightly packed into pale or mid-green mats. In May and June the plant bears vivid pink flowers, ½ in. across.

S. *maritima* (sea campion). Europe, including Great Britain; N. Africa. Height 6 in.; spread 12 in. This species has a woody rootstock from which appear numerous prostrate stems covered with lanceolate to ovate, grey-green leaves. White flowers, 1–1½ in. across, are borne in profusion from July to September.

In cultivation the species is represented by the double white variety 'Flore-pleno'.

S. *schafta*. Caucasus. Height 4–6 in.; spread 12 in. An easily grown species producing a spreading tuft of mid-green lanceolate leaves. Sprays of magenta-pink flowers, ¾ in. across, are borne from July to October.

Cultivation of all species. Grow silenes in any ordinary, well-drained garden soil and in a sunny or partially shaded position.

Plant perennial species at any time between September and March. These plants, once established, resent root disturbance.

Silene armeria

Silene coeli-rosa
Oculata (mixed)

Silene pendula

Silene acaulis

Propagation of annual species. Sow the seeds of *S. armeria* and *S. pendula* in the flowering site in September, March or April; thin out the seedlings to the required spacing. Autumn-sown plants flower in May and June; spring-sown plants from July to September.

To grow *S. compacta* as a biennial, sow outdoors in June or July. Prick off the seedlings and grow them on, 6 in. apart, in nursery rows, until September or October, when they can be planted in the flowering site.

For annual plants of this species, sow the seeds under glass in February or March at a temperature of 15°C (59°F). Prick off the seedlings into boxes and harden off in a cold frame before planting out in May.

Propagation of perennial species. Seeds of *S. acaulis* are rarely available. Take 1–1½ in. long cuttings of vigorous outer shoots in July and August. Insert in equal parts (by volume) peat and sand, singly or in groups of three or four, in a cold frame; when rooted pot the cuttings singly in 3 in. containers of John Innes potting compost No. 1. Overwinter in a cold frame and plant out in September of the following year.

Increase the double form of *S. maritima* from 2 in. cuttings of basal shoots in April; insert in equal parts (by volume) peat and sand in a cold frame. When rooted, pot the cuttings into 3 in. pots of John Innes potting compost No. 1 and plant out from September onwards.

Sow seeds of *S. schafta* in March in pots or pans of John Innes seed compost in a cold frame or greenhouse. Prick out the seedlings into boxes, then transfer them to 3 in. pots and plant out in September or October.

Pests and diseases. Generally trouble-free.

Silene maritima 'Flore-pleno'

Silene schafta

Silybum marianum

Silybum
Compositae

SILYBUM MARIANUM

A genus of two species of annual or biennial herbs. The species described, which is grown for its attractive foliage, is a striking plant for the back of a border and for wild gardens. It is not widely listed by seedsmen.

S. marianum (Our Lady's milk thistle, blessed thistle, holy thistle). Mediterranean regions. Height 4 ft; spacing 24 in. This hardy annual or biennial is a thistle-like plant. Glossy dark green, ovate and spiny lobed leaves, marbled with white veins, are carried in a flat rosette. Terminal heads of deep violet, faintly fragrant flowers, 2 in. across, appear from July to September.

Cultivation. Almost any soil will give satisfactory growth. An open sunny site is ideal.

Propagation. Sow the seeds in the flowering site, just covering them with soil. Sow in September or March if they are to be grown as annuals; in

May or June for biennials. Thin out the seedlings to the required spacing when they are large enough to handle.

Pests and diseases. Generally trouble-free.

Sinapis alba: see Mustard and cress

Sinningia
Gesneriaceae

A genus of 20 species of tender, tuberous-rooted flowering plants. The plants derived from *S. speciosa* are popularly known as gloxinias. The species described make handsome pot plants suitable for the greenhouse; they may be taken indoors when in flower. Given a night temperature of 18–21°C (64–70°F), the species can be brought to flower from seeds in five months.

The bell-shaped, velvety, foxglove-like flowers have short rounded lobes at the mouth.

S. eumorpha. Brazil. Height 6–8 in.; spread 9–10 in. A short-stemmed species with downy and glossy bronze-green ovate leaves. Pendent milky-white flowers, nearly 2 in. long and tinged with lilac and yellow in the throat, are freely produced from May or June to October.

Sinningia regina

S. regina. Brazil. Height 9 in.; spread 9–12 in. A species with short-stemmed, velvety, ovate-elliptic leaves that are white-veined, bronze-green above, deep red beneath. The pendent, violet-purple flowers, 2 in. long, are borne from May to July.

S. speciosa (gloxinia). Brazil. Height 9–10 in.; spread up to 12 in. This is the most popular species. It is almost stemless and bears large, oblong-ovate, dark green, fleshy, velvety leaves. Violet or purple flowers, 2–4 in. long, are borne profusely from May to August, or throughout the year by successive sowings.

The species is represented in cultivation by the large-flowered group, probably of hybrid origin, known as Fyfiana. These are the florists' gloxinias and range in colour from shades of red, pink and purple to white. Named varieties include: 'Emperor Frederick', scarlet with white edges; 'Emperor William', blue-purple with a white border to the petals; 'Mont Blanc', pure white, and 'Tiger Red', with deep red flowers having crimped petals. Most seed firms offer strains of mixed seeds, including double-flowered forms.

Cultivation. In February, place the dormant tubers in boxes of moist peat and start them into growth at a temperature of 21°C (70°F). When the young growths are 1–2 in. high, pot the tubers separately into 5–6 in. pots of John Innes potting compost No. 2 or a proprietary peat compost, placing the top of the tubers level with the surface of the compost.

Grow the plants on in a shaded greenhouse with a humid atmosphere and at a minimum temperature of 18°C (64°F). Feed the plants with a liquid manure, at seven to ten-day intervals, from the time the flower buds are visible until the last flower falls. Keep the plants moist throughout the growing period.

As the leaves turn yellow, gradually cease watering, remove dead flowers and leaves, and store the tubers in a dry place at 12–16°C (54–61°F). Discard tubers that are more than three years old.

Sinningias do particularly well when grown in plastic pots on a sand capillary bench.

Propagation. Sow seeds in February or March in pans or boxes containing John Innes seed compost. Germinate the seeds at a temperature of 21°C (70°F). When the second true leaves have developed, prick the seedlings separately into 2½ in. pots of the growing compost and, when established, lower the temperature to 18°C (64°F). Pot on as necessary. One-year-old plants will often produce flowers in late summer.

Divide the tubers in March. Cut them into pieces which each have one or two growing shoots, and seal the cuts with flowers of sulphur or powdered charcoal. Pot the pieces separately into 3 in. pots containing the growing mixture.

Alternatively, take 2–3 in. long basal shoots, with a sliver from the tubers, in March or early April. Insert the cuttings in equal parts (by volume) peat and sand in a propagating frame at a temperature of 21°C (70°F). Pot the rooted cuttings singly into 3 in. pots of the growing compost and grow on. They will reach flowering size in four to six months.

Leaf cuttings can be taken in June or July. With a sharp knife slash the veins on the under-side of the leaves just below the junction of the main veins. Place the leaves, cut side down-wards, on a mixture of equal parts (by volume) peat and sand in a propagating case at a temperature of 21°C (70°F). Small plants will develop and root from the cuts.

Pests. Generally trouble-free.

Diseases. FOOT and ROOT ROT, due to one or more fungi, show as blackening and rotting of the tissues at the base of the stem or the roots.

A PHYSIOLOGICAL DISORDER, due to incorrect watering, shows as yellow rings on the leaves.

TOMATO SPOTTED WILT VIRUS causes large thick brown rings on the leaves. These symptoms should not be confused with the physiological ring pattern.

Siphonosmanthus delavayi: see *Osmanthus delavayi*

Sisyrinchium
Iridaceae

A genus of 100 species of herbaceous perennials. Only a few species are available, and these are best grown in rock gardens.

The mid to grey-green leaves of the species described are linear to sword-shaped.

Sisyrinchium striatum

S. angustifolium, syn. *S. montanum crebrum* (blue-eyed grass). N. America, Ireland; natural-ised in Great Britain and New Zealand. Height 9–12 in.; planting distance 6–9 in. The hardy grass-like clumps carry star-shaped violet flowers, ½ in. across, from May to October.

S. bermudiana. E. United States, W. Ireland. Height 9–12 in.; planting distance 6–9 in. This hardy species is often confused with *S. angustifolium.* The erect, branched stems produce a succession of light-blue, star-shaped, ½ in. wide flowers with yellow bases in May and June.

S. brachypus. S. America. Height and planting distance 6 in. A hardy, tufted, iris-like plant with bright mid-green leaves. The sparsely branched, leaf-like stems bear a succession of bright yellow star-shaped flowers, ¾ in. across, from June to October.

S. douglasii: see *S. grandiflorum*

S. grandiflorum, syn. *S. douglasii.* N. America west of the Rockies. Height 8–10 in.; planting distance 3–6 in. A hardy plant with purple, bell-shaped flowers borne on erect stems. The flowers, up to 1 in. long, appear in March.

S. striatum. Andes. Height 12–18 in.; planting distance 6–12 in. An erect hardy plant with numerous star-shaped pale or cream-yellow flowers, ¾ in. across. These are carried on slender stems during June and July.

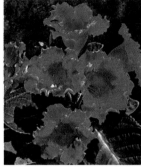

Sinningia speciosa 'Tiger Red'

Sisyrinchium brachypus

Sisyrinchium grandiflorum

Cultivation. Grow sisyrinchiums in a well-drained soil containing plenty of peat or leaf-mould, and in a sunny position.

Plant between September and March, in a site where the plants may remain undisturbed. Cut off dead flowering stems and leaves in autumn.

Propagation. Self-sown seedlings may occur if the surrounding soil is left undisturbed. Seeds may be sown in pans of seed compost in a cold frame, during September, October or March. Prick out the seedlings, when large enough to handle, into boxes and then into a nursery bed. Grow on for one year before planting in the final site.

Alternatively, established clumps may be divided and replanted in September or March.

Pests and diseases. Generally trouble-free.

Skimmia japonica (fruits)

Skimmia reevesiana 'Rubella'

Smilacina racemosa

Skimmia

Rutaceae

A genus of seven or eight species of hardy, evergreen, slow-growing shrubs. Male and female flowers are borne on separate plants in March and April. These are small and star-like and carried in dense ovoid, terminal panicles; they are followed by persistent berries. The young leaves may be damaged by severe frost unless given some protection by trees or taller shrubs. Skimmias tolerate atmospheric pollution.

S. × 'Foremanii'. Height and spread 3–4 ft. This hybrid is similar to *S. japonica.* It is a female form with dark green obovate leaves. The fragrant, cream-white flowers are borne in 2 in. long panicles. They are followed by brilliant red berries which persist throughout the winter.

S. fortunei: see *S. reevesiana*

SKIMMIA JAPONICA

S. japonica. Japan. Height 3–5 ft; spread 5–6 ft. The leaves are pale green, leathery and ovate-lanceolate. Cream-white fragrant flowers in 2–3 in. long panicles are followed by globular or shortly ovoid bright red berries which ripen in August and September. 'Fragrans' is a male form with strongly fragrant white flowers.

S. reevesiana, syn. *S. fortunei.* China. Height 1½–3 ft; spread 3–4 ft. The leaves of this compact shrub are narrowly lanceolate and mid to deep green. The cream-white flowers are arranged in crowded panicles, 2–3 in. long, and are followed by oval or obovoid crimson fruits which ripen in August. 'Rubella' is a male form with crimson flower buds.

Cultivation. Plant in September and October, or in March and April in any ordinary, well-drained garden soil in sun or partial shade. *S. reevesiana* does best in lime-free soil.

Propagation. In July or August take 3 in. heel cuttings of half-ripe lateral shoots and insert them in sandy soil in a cold frame. The following

April or May, plant out the rooted cuttings in a nursery bed and grow them on for two or three years before planting them out in their permanent positions in October or March.

Remove seeds from the ripe berries in September and sow them in pans of John Innes seed compost in a cold frame. When they are large enough to handle, prick off the seedlings into pans or boxes. Set them out in a nursery bed the following October or March and grow on for three or four years before planting out.

Pruning. None required.

Pests. Generally trouble-free.

Diseases. A whitening of the leaves may be caused by FROST DAMAGE.

A PHYSIOLOGICAL DISORDER which shows as yellowing of the leaves and die-back of the shoots is due to adverse cultural conditions.

Sloe: see *Prunus spinosa*

Smilacina

False Solomon's seal. *Liliaceae*

SMILACINA RACEMOSA

A genus of 25 species of hardy herbaceous perennials. They are woodland plants, and the two species in cultivation are best suited to moist and shady positions.

S. racemosa (false spikenard). N. America. Height 2½–3 ft; planting distance 18 in. The erect stems, rising from a rhizomatous rootstock, carry closely arranged, lanceolate, light green leaves. The arching, terminal flower spray is 4 in. long and is composed of densely packed, cream-white, scented flowers in May and June.

S. stellata (star-flowered lily of the valley). N. America. Height 18–24 in.; planting distance 12 in. The narrow pointed leaves are pale green. Arching flower stems carry sprays, 3–4 in. long, of white, star-shaped flowers in May and June.

Cultivation. Plant from October to March in deep, rich soil and in a partially shaded, moist position. The rhizomatous roots spread slowly and should not be disturbed for a few years after planting. In November, cut down to ground level.

Propagation. Lift and divide old plants in October.

Pests and diseases. Generally trouble-free.

Smilax: see Asparagus

Smithiantha

Gesneriaceae

A genus of eight tender species of rhizomatous, flowering herbaceous plants. In Great Britain they require greenhouse cultivation, and may be taken into the home when in flower.

The foxglove-like flowers are borne in handsome pyramidal panicles, in a wide range of pastel colours. Flowers can be obtained continuously from early summer well into winter if the tubers are started into growth at monthly intervals, from February to May.

SMITHIANTHA ZEBRINA

S. cinnabarina. Mexico. Height 18–24 in.; spread 12–18 in. The velvety, heart-shaped leaves are mid to dark green, flushed with red. Terminal clusters of pendulous flowers, 1½ in. long, are freely produced from June to December; they are scarlet with a red-spotted orange-yellow mouth and throat.

S. multiflora. Mexico. Height up to 3 ft; spread up to 18 in. The velvety, heart-shaped leaves, deep green above, paler beneath, are covered with long glandular hairs. Pale yellow-throated, pendent white flowers, 1½ in. long, are freely borne from June to October.

S. zebrina. Mexico. Height up to 3 ft; spread 12–18 in. The dark green, heart-shaped leaves are mottled with red-brown and covered with soft silky hairs. Nodding, 1½ in. long scarlet flowers, yellow in the throat, appear from June to October.

HYBRIDS AND VARIETIES A number of hybrids have been raised from crosses between *S. cinnabarina*, *S. zebrina* and other species. They resemble *S. cinnabarina* in form, but bear flowers in various shades of white, yellow, red, orange and pink, sometimes with purple markings. The following varieties are recommended: 'Abbey', peach-pink; 'Canary Bird', yellow, flushed with green; 'Elke', golden-orange, shaded with yellow within; 'Firebird', carmine-scarlet, with yellow scarlet-spotted throat; 'Santa Barbara', carrot-red, yellow within; and 'Swan Lake', cream-white, delicately flushed with salmon-pink.

Cultivation. Between February and May, start the rhizomes into growth in boxes of moist peat at a temperature of 21°C (70°F). When the growths are 1–2 in. high, pot them three to a 5 in. pot or five to a 7 in. pot of John Innes potting compost No. 2 or a proprietary peat compost at a slightly reduced temperature.

Rhizomes potted at monthly intervals from February to May will extend the flowering period. Grow the plants on at a temperature of 18–21°C (64–70°F); when flower buds appear, give the plants a feed of liquid manure at seven to ten-day intervals until the flowers fall. Keep the plants moist during the growing season, and shade the glass lightly from May to September.

The stems may need supporting with thin canes. Gradually cease watering when the plants stop flowering; remove dead flowers and leaves, and store the pots of rhizomes on their sides, in a dry place under the greenhouse staging, at a minimum winter temperature of 12°C (54°F).

Propagation. Divide the rhizomes into 2 in. sections at potting time between February and May, making sure that each has at least one strong shoot.

Take leaf cuttings in May or June. Shorten the leaf-stalks to ½ in. and insert in equal parts (by volume) peat and sand at a temperature of 21°C (70°F). When the plantlets, which develop at the base of the stalks, reach a height of 1½–2 in., pot them singly in 2½–3 in. pots of the growing compost. Pot on as necessary.

Pests and diseases. Generally trouble-free.

Smoke tree: see *Cotinus coggygria*
Snake-root, black: see *Cimicifuga racemosa*
Snake's head: see *Fritillaria meleagris*
Snakeweed: see *Polygonum bistorta*
Snapdragon: see Antirrhinum
Sneezewort: see *Achillea ptarmica*
Snowball bush: see *Viburnum opulus* 'Sterile'
Snowball, Japanese: see *Viburnum tomentosum* 'Plicatum'
Snowberry: see Symphoricarpos
Snowdrop: see Galanthus
Snowdrop, common: see *Galanthus nivalis*
Snowdrop tree: see Halesia
Snowflake: see Leucojum
Snowflake, summer: see *Leucojum aestivum*
Snow-in-summer: see *Cerastium biebersteinii*, *Cerastium tomentosum*; and *Helichrysum rosmarinifolium*
Snow on the mountain: see *Euphorbia marginata*
Snowy mespilus: see Amelanchier
Soapwort: see *Saponaria officinalis*

Solanum

Solanaceae

A genus of 1700 species of half-hardy and tender annuals and herbaceous perennials, and climbing evergreen shrubs and sub-shrubs. The genus includes ornamental plants and vegetables such as the egg plant (aubergine) and the tuberous-rooted potato. It also includes a number of weeds; only a few ornamental species are generally available.

The species *S. capsicastrum* is a popular house plant, grown principally for its attractive berries. The climbing or scrambling species are suitable for growing outdoors in mild sheltered areas or under glass.

SOLANUM CAPSICASTRUM

S. capsicastrum (winter cherry). Brazil. Height 12–18 in. A half-hardy evergreen sub-shrub of bushy habit, usually treated as an annual pot plant. It bears dark green lanceolate leaves. White, star-shaped, but insignificant flowers, ½ in. across, appear in June and July, and are followed in

Smithiantha 'Elke'

Smithiantha 'Firebird'

Solanum capsicastrum (fruits)

winter by dark green marble-like fruits, $\frac{1}{2}$–$\frac{3}{4}$ in. in diameter; these gradually turn yellow and then scarlet.

'Covent Garden' (height 12 in.) is a variety with bright red fruits.

SOLANUM CRISPUM

S. crispum (Chilean potato-tree). Chile. Height 15–20 ft. This bushy scrambling species is an almost hardy semi-evergreen plant, with ovate leaves that are dark green above, paler green beneath. The purple-blue star-shaped flowers, 1 in. wide, and with prominent yellow anthers, are produced in 3–6 in. wide corymbs from June to September.

'Autumnale', also known as 'Glasnevin Variety', is hardier than the species; it has flowers borne more freely over a longer period.
S. jasminoides (jasmine nightshade). Brazil. Height 10–15 ft. A slender evergreen species less hardy than *S. crispum* and with twining growths. The glossy pale green leaves are pinnately lobed. In good conditions the plant produces its branched cymes of star-shaped, $\frac{3}{4}$ in. wide flowers freely from July to October, or longer if there is no frost. The flowers are pale blue with conspicuous golden anthers.

The variety 'Album' has white flowers with yellow anthers.
S. tuberosum: see Potato
Cultivation. Grow *S. capsicastrum* in 5–6 in. pots of John Innes potting compost No. 2. Pinch out the growing tips when the shoots are 3 in. high to promote bushy growth. From June to September, the plants may be stood outside in a sunny sheltered position or in an open cold frame. When the flowers open, syringe the plants frequently with water to encourage the fruits to set and thereafter give a weak liquid feed at 14-day intervals from June until the fruits begin to ripen.

In September, bring the plants into a greenhouse or living-room and place in a well-lit position. Maintain a winter temperature of 10°C (50°F) and keep the plants just moist at all times.

If the plants are to be kept for a further year, cut back all growths by about one-third in March and pot on into 7 or 8 in. containers.

Grow *S. crispum* and *S. jasminoides* in any ordinary, well-drained garden soil, against a south or west-facing wall. Plant in April or May and secure the growths to trelliswork, wire or string supports. *S. crispum* needs tying in position at intervals throughout the summer; *S. jasminoides* is usually self-clinging, but may need occasional tying-in.

The climbing *S. jasminoides* may be grown in the greenhouse, in 8–10 in. pots of John Innes potting compost No. 2, or planted out in the border. Maintain a winter temperature of 5–7°C (41–45°F), and keep the plants just moist in winter. Water copiously during the growing season and ventilate freely.

Propagation. Sow seeds of *S. capsicastrum* in pots or pans of John Innes seed compost under glass during February or March; germinate at a temperature of 18°C (64°F). As soon as the seedlings are large enough to handle, prick them off into boxes of John Innes potting compost No. 2; later transfer them into 3$\frac{1}{2}$ in. pots and finally into 5–6 in. containers.

Take 3–4 in. long cuttings of side-shoots, in July or August, of climbing outdoor species; insert the cuttings in equal parts (by volume) peat and sand in a propagating frame with a temperature of 13–16°C (55–61°F). If a mist propagator is available, the cuttings can be taken whenever suitable growths are ready.

Pot the rooted cuttings in 3–3$\frac{1}{2}$ in. containers of John Innes potting compost No. 2 and overwinter them in a frost-free cold frame or greenhouse. Plant out in their permanent positions in May.
Pruning. In March or April, thin out weak growths of climbing species and cut back any main shoots damaged by frost or snow. To keep *S. crispum* within bounds, cut the previous season's shoots back to 6 in. in April.
Pests. Infestations of APHIDS on the shoots and leaves make the plants sticky and sooty.

GLASSHOUSE RED SPIDER MITES feed on the leaves of *S. capsicastrum*, producing a fine mottling of the upper surface, followed by bronzing of the foliage in severe infestations.
Diseases. In cold damp conditions, GREY MOULD may cause die-back of shoots; the affected tissues gradually become covered with a grey velvety fungal growth.

A PHYSIOLOGICAL DISORDER, due to unsuitable cultural conditions, shows as yellowing of the leaves which fall prematurely.

TOMATO SPOTTED WILT VIRUS shows as concentric rings all over the leaves. Browning sometimes occurs along the veins. Affected plants are generally stunted.

Soldanella

Primulaceae

A genus of 11 species of hardy perennial herbaceous plants. They are found in the mountains of Europe, and make good rock-garden plants. All have bell-shaped flowers with fringed petals; they appear in March and April.
S. alpina. E. Pyrenees, Alps, Apennines. Height 3 in.; spread 9 in. The deep green kidney-shaped leaves of this species make a slowly spreading mat. The lavender-purple flowers are $\frac{2}{3}$ in. long.
S. minima. S.E. Alps. Height 2 in.; spread 6 in. This ground-cover plant has orbicular, mid-green, shiny leaves. The lilac flowers are slightly narrower than those of *S. alpina*.
S. montana. N.E. Alps, W. Pyrenees. Height 6 in.; spread 12 in. This plant resembles *S. alpina* but is larger and more robust. It has orbicular deep green leaves. Bell-shaped lavender flowers, $\frac{2}{3}$ in. long, are borne on sturdy stems.
S. pindicola. Albania, N. Greece. Height 4–6 in.; spread 9–12 in. The orbicular leaves are mid-green above, paler beneath. The lavender-blue flowers are $\frac{2}{3}$ in. long.

Solanum crispum 'Autumnale'

Solanum jasminoides 'Album'

Soldanella alpina

S. pusilla. Alps, N.W. Apennines. Height 3 in.; spread 6 in. The dark green leaves are rounded and kidney-shaped. The pale lavender flowers, which are $\frac{1}{2}$ in. long, are usually borne singly.

S. villosa. Pyrenees. Height 4 in.; spread 12 in. The orbicular mid-green leaves are felted with tiny hairs. This species produces lavender-blue flowers shaded with deeper blue-purple, and measuring $\frac{2}{3}$ in. long.

Cultivation. All species require a well-drained soil in a sunny or partially shaded position. Add sharp grit round the clumps to help counteract winter dampness, and cover with panes of glass to keep off excessive winter rain. Plant in September and October or after flowering in May and June.

Propagation. Divide the plants in June and replant direct in final positions, or pot up the divisions in John Innes potting compost No. 1 with an extra part peat. Overwinter in a cold frame and plant out the following spring.

Alternatively, take cuttings of 1 in. long basal shoots in May or June and insert in 3 in. pots filled with a mixture of equal parts (by volume) loam, leaf-mould or peat, and grit. Place in a cold frame; water sparingly until the cuttings start to grow. Plant out the following year in September.

Pests. SLUGS attack young plants and may eat the flower buds.

Diseases. Generally trouble-free.

Soleirolia soleirolii: see *Helxine soleirolii*

Solidago

Golden rod. *Compositae*

SOLIDAGO CANADENSIS

A genus of 100 species of hardy herbaceous perennials. The following are suitable plants for herbaceous borders or rock gardens; the variously shaped plumes of tiny, yellow, clustered flowers are good for cutting.

Named varieties are preferable to the species. The plants are easy to grow, but are gross feeders and quickly exhaust the soil, unless divided and replanted regularly.

S. × arendsii: see GARDEN HYBRIDS

S. brachystachys. Height 6 in.; spread 12 in. This plant is considered by some authorities to be a variety of *S. virgaurea*. The leaves are lanceolate and mid-green. Tiny golden-yellow flowers, formed into plume-like clusters 4–6 in. long, appear in August and September.

S. canadensis. Eastern N. America, naturalised in Great Britain. Height 3–6 ft; spread 2$\frac{1}{2}$–3$\frac{1}{2}$ ft. A vigorous erect species with mid-green, sharply serrated, lanceolate leaves. Broad plumose heads of yellow flowers are borne from August to October. The following variety represents this species in general cultivation.

'Golden Wings' (height 6 ft; planting distance 2$\frac{1}{2}$ ft), broad panicles, up to 6 in. long, of deep yellow flowers in September.

S. × hybrida: see GARDEN HYBRIDS

GARDEN HYBRIDS

Height 1–7 ft; planting distance 12–15 in. for varieties up to 2$\frac{1}{2}$ ft high, 24 in. for taller varieties. The following varieties are primarily derived from *S. canadensis* and *S. virgaurea*, and are sometimes referred to under the names of *S. × hybrida* or *S. × arendsii*. They produce terminal plumes or horizontally spreading sprays of small, closely packed flowers between July and October. They are vigorous in growth and less invasive than the species.

'Golden Gates', height 3 ft, yellow-green foliage and soft feathery arching sprays about 12 in. long in September; 'Goldenmosa', height 2$\frac{1}{2}$–3 ft, yellow-green foliage and 6–9 in. sprays of fluffy flowers in late August; 'Golden Thumb', syn. 'Queenie', height 12 in., a rounded bushy plant with golden-yellow, 3–4 in. plumes in August and September; 'Golden Wings', height 5–6 ft, branching sprays 6–8 in. long of deep yellow flowers in August and September.

'Lemore', height 24 in., wide-branching, soft primrose-yellow, 8–12 in. long heads in September; 'Leraft', height 2$\frac{1}{2}$ ft, flat, bright golden-yellow sprays, 12 in. long, in August and September; 'Mimosa', height 4–5 ft, arching soft plumes, 6–9 in. long, of golden-yellow flowers in August and September; 'Peter Pan', syn. 'Goldstrahl', height 3 ft, erect and horizontally branching, bright yellow 12 in. long sprays produced in July and August.

Cultivation. Plant from October to March in sun or half-shade and in ordinary garden soil. The taller varieties require staking, but the stakes need be only half the height of the plants. Cut down all flower stems in October or November.

Propagation. Divide and replant the roots between October and March.

Pests. The leaves are spun together and eaten by the TORTRIX CATERPILLAR.

Diseases. A white powdery coating on leaves, stems and sometimes flowers is caused by POWDERY MILDEW.

Solomon's seal: see *Polygonatum × hybridum*
Solomon's seal, false: see Smilacina
Solomon's seal, giant: see *Polygonatum commutatum*

Sonerila

Melastomataceae

A genus of 175 species of tropical flowering perennials. Only one species is in general cultivation; it has decorative leaves and can be grown in closed containers or bottle gardens as well as in a warm greenhouse.

S. margaritacea. Java. Height 6 in. A low creeping plant with ovate-lanceolate leaves; they are up to 4 in. long, dark green and marked with silvery-white spots. The underside of the leaves is purple and the stems are reddish. Three-petalled rose-purple flowers are produced in 3 in. long panicles from May to September.

Soldanella montana

Solidago 'Goldenmosa'

Solidago 'Golden Thumb'

Sonerila margaritacea

Sophora japonica

Sophora microphylla

Sophora tetraptera

× *Sophrolaeliocattleya* Trizac

The variety *S. m. hendersonii* has leaves that are more heavily covered with small white spots; in *S. m. argentea* the spots are so numerous as to give a silver leaf marked with dark green.

Cultivation. Grow sonerilas in 4–5 in. pots of a proprietary peat compost. The plants require warm, shady and humid conditions; a winter temperature of 18°C (64°F) is necessary if the plants are to overwinter in good condition. They will survive for short periods at lower temperatures, but will usually be checked and suffer loss of leaves.

During winter, give enough water to prevent the plants drying out; in spring and summer, water more freely and provide a humid atmosphere. Do not allow strong sunlight to fall on the leaves, as this may cause them to shrivel.

Repot when necessary in April or May; give a light liquid feed at fortnightly intervals from May to September.

Propagation. Take basal cuttings, 2–3 in. long, from April to June; insert the cuttings in equal parts (by volume) peat and sand in a propagating case at a temperature of 16–18°C (61–64°F). When rooted, pot the cuttings in 3 in. pots of the growing compost and pot on as necessary.

Alternatively, sow seeds in pans of seed compost in April and germinate at a temperature of 21–24°C (70–75°F). Prick off the seedlings when large enough to handle, and treat as described for cuttings.

Pests and diseases. Generally trouble-free.

Sophora
Leguminosae

SOPHORA TETRAPTERA

A genus of 50 species of slow-growing hardy deciduous and tender evergreen trees and shrubs. Those described here are hardy and deciduous; they bear pendent racemes of flowers.

S. japonica (Japanese pagoda tree). China, Korea, Japan. Height 12–18 ft; spread 10–15 ft. The pinnate leaves of this species are mid-green. Cream-white pea-like flowers are borne in pendent racemes, 6–10 in. long, in September. The seeds, which follow the flowers only after a sunny summer, are encased in slender 2–3 in. long bean-like pods.

S. microphylla, syn. *S. tetraptera microphylla* (kowhai). New Zealand. Height 6–10 ft; spread 4–7 ft. A shrub, or sometimes a small tree, with slender zigzag branchlets and pinnate leaves. These are composed of 12 or more pairs of mid-green ovate-oblong leaflets. Pendent clusters of 1–1½ in. long, pea-shaped, yellow flowers with prominent helmet-like calyces are borne in April and May. They are followed by 6–8 in. long slender pods, resembling a string of four-winged beads.

S. tetraptera (kowhai, New Zealand laburnum). New Zealand. Height up to 20 ft; spread up to 10 ft. A large shrub or small tree, closely resembling *S. microphylla* but somewhat larger in all its parts and with fewer leaflets to each leaf.

S. t. microphylla: see *S. microphylla*.

Cultivation. Plant in March or April in any fertile well-drained garden soil in a sunny position, sheltered from north and east winds. Train the larger species on trelliswork against walls or fences. In cold areas, these shrubs are best grown in a cool greenhouse.

Propagation. Sow the seeds in March or April in a cold frame or greenhouse. When they are large enough to handle, prick off the seedlings into 3 in. pots of John Innes potting compost No. 1. Line out in nursery rows and grow on for two or three years before planting out in permanent positions any time from October to March.

Pruning. None required.

Pests and diseases. Generally trouble-free.

× Sophrolaeliocattleya
Orchidaceae

× SOPHROLAELIOCATTLEYA

A group of trigeneric orchid hybrids between *Cattleya, Laelia* and *Sophronitis*. They are similar in all respects to *Cattleya*; the flowering period extends from autumn to spring.

See also ORCHIDS.

The following are among the several named forms: Anzac, a hybrid between × *Sophrolaeliocattleya* Marathon and × *Laeliocattleya* Dominiana; it bears translucent deep red flowers, 4–5 in. wide.

'Jewel Box', a hybrid of *Cattleya aurantiaca* and × *Sophrolaeliocattleya* Anzac, has glowing red flowers, 3–4 in. across; three to five blooms are borne on each stem.

'Sunburst', a cross between × *Laeliocattleya* Sunburst and × *Sophrolaeliocattleya* Coccinea, bears 4–5 in. wide, brilliant yellow, heavy textured flowers.

Trizac, a cross between × *Sophrolaeliocattleya* Anzac and *Cattleya trinaei*, produces 4–5 in. wide flowers in shades of rose-purple and red; the petals are broad and waved.

Cultivation, propagation, pests and diseases. See entry under CATTLEYA.

Sophronitis
Orchidaceae

A genus of six species of epiphytic orchids, native to Brazil. These are dwarf evergreen plants with small single-leaved pseudobulbs arising at intervals along the creeping rhizome. The fleshy elliptic-ovate leaves are dark green. The erect flower stems arise from the base of the pseudobulb; each stem bears a single flower in various shades of red. The species described is the most widely grown and is used in hybridisation; it thrives in an intermediate greenhouse.

See also ORCHIDS.

SOPHRONITIS COCCINEA

S. coccinea, syn. *S. grandiflora*. Brazil. The 1 in. high pseudobulbs produce 1–1½ in. flowering stems. The brilliant scarlet flowers, up to 3½ in. across, open in autumn or winter. The variety 'Rosea' has rose-pink flowers.

S. grandiflora: see *S. coccinea*

Cultivation. Grow these orchids on fibre rafts, blocks of tree fern, or in 3–6 in. pots of 2 parts fine osmunda fibre and 1 part sphagnum moss (parts by volume). Shade the greenhouse between March and October, and ventilate throughout the year in mild weather. Water abundantly during the growing season, less frequently during the resting period from October to December; the compost should never be allowed to dry out.

Repot annually in March or April.

Propagation. Divide the rhizomes in March or April, ensuring that each section has at least one pseudobulb with a strong growing point. Pot up in the growing compost.

Pests. MEALY BUGS may attack the shoots.

Diseases. Generally trouble-free.

Sorbaria

Rosaceae

SORBARIA AITCHISONII

A genus of ten species of fast-growing, hardy, deciduous flowering shrubs with pinnate leaves. These species were formerly included in the genus *Spiraea*.

S. aitchisonii, syn. *Spiraea aitchisonii*. Afghanistan, Kashmir. Height 6–9 ft; spread 8–9 ft. The slender-pointed, ash-like leaves are mid-green on red stems. Minute white flowers appear in plume-like panicles, 18 in. long, during August and September.

S. arborea, syn. *Spiraea arborea*. China. Height and spread 8–15 ft. The slender-pointed deeply toothed leaflets are mid-green and ovate-lanceolate. Cream-white flowers appear in July and August in large plumes of pyramidal panicles that measure up to 12 in. in length.

Cultivation. Plant between October and March in ordinary, well-drained garden soil and in an open position, in sun or light shade.

Propagation. Remove rooted suckers at any time between October and March and grow them on in a nursery bed for one year before planting out in permanent positions.

Take 6 in. cuttings of ripe lateral shoots with a heel in July or August and insert them in a cold frame. Transfer them to a nursery bed during the following April or May and grow on for one or two years; plant out in permanent positions from October onwards.

Pruning. To restrict overall size and to produce larger leaves and flower heads, prune back to near ground level, annually in March. Flowers are borne on the current year's shoots.

Pests and diseases. Generally trouble-free.

Sorbus

Rosaceae

SORBUS AUCUPARIA

A genus of 100 species of hardy deciduous trees and shrubs which are easy to grow in most soils and situations. Many species and hybrids tolerate shade and atmospheric pollution. The hawthorn-like flowers are white or cream-white and are produced in flattened clusters in May or June. The berries, which vary in colour from white to yellow and from orange to pink and red, are often produced in great quantities. The leaves of many species turn yellow, orange, scarlet or red in autumn. With the exceptions of *S. aria* and *S. hybrida*, all species mentioned have pinnate leaves, with ovate leaflets.

S. americana nana: see *S. scopulina*

S. aria (common whitebeam). Europe. Height 15–20 ft; spread 10–15 ft. The ovate, toothed leaves are silver-white and downy when young. Later the upper surfaces become dark green and smooth, the undersides grey-white but remaining hairy. The leaves turn russet and gold in autumn. The flowers, which appear in May and June, are cream-white in flattened 4–5 in. panicles, like those of the hawthorn. Scarlet, globular fruits, ½ in. wide, are borne in large bunches and ripen in September. 'Decaisneana', syn. 'Majestica', is more robust and has larger leaves and fruits; 'Lutescens' has a more erect habit, and cream-white young foliage.

S. aucuparia (rowan, mountain ash). Europe, W. Asia. Height 15–25 ft; spread 8–12 ft. The leaves of this species are mid-green with grey undersides; they turn yellow and orange from October onwards. White flowers, borne in 4–6 in. wide heads, appear in May and June; they are followed by large bunches of globular orange-red berries, ⅓ in. across. These begin to ripen in August. The tree is short-lived in shallow alkaline soils.

Sophronitis coccinea

Sorbaria arborea

Sorbus aria (fruits)

Sorbus aucuparia (flowers)

Sorbus sargentiana (autumn foliage)

Sorbus aucuparia (fruits)

Sorbus hupehensis (fruits)

Varieties include: 'Asplenifolia', with deeply toothed and lobed fern-like leaves; 'Beissneri', of upright habit, with amber or orange bark and deeply divided yellow-green leaves; and 'Edulis', with larger leaves and larger, edible fruits.

S. cashmiriana. Kashmir. Height 10–15 ft; spread 6–8 ft. The leaves are mid-green with grey-green undersides. The 4 in. wide pendulous clusters of pale pink flowers appear in May. These are followed in August by glistening white or pink-tinged globular fruits, $\frac{1}{2}$ in. wide, which persist long after the leaves have fallen.

S. decora: see *S. scopulina*

S. hupehensis. Central and W. China. Height 15–20 ft; spread 9–12 ft. The leaves are composed of 13–17 blue-green leaflets which turn red or orange from October onwards. Clusters, 3 in. across, of white flowers appear in June. They are followed in August or September by bunches of white or pink berries.

S. hybrida. Scandinavia. Height 18–20 ft; spread 10–15 ft. The ovate leaves are divided at the base into two or three pairs of oblong mid-green leaflets with grey-felted undersides. Cream-white flowers in 4 in. wide heads appear in May and are followed in August and September by loose bunches of $\frac{1}{4}$ in. wide bright red fruits. 'Gibbsii' is a more compact form.

S. intermedia (Swedish whitebeam). N. Europe. Height 15–18 ft; spread 10–15 ft. The deeply lobed and toothed leaves of this dense rounded species are mid-green with grey, hairy undersides. The white flowers open in May in clusters up to 4 in. across. They are followed in August and September by fruits which are bright red, oval or oblong and $\frac{1}{2}$–1 in. long. This tree is tolerant of atmospheric pollution.

S. 'Joseph Rock'. Of uncertain origin, probably China. Height 15–18 ft; spread 6–8 ft. The sharply toothed leaves of this compact, upright tree have 11–15 glossy green leaflets which turn orange-red in August and September. Cream-coloured flowers appear in May in clusters up to 3 in. across. The pale yellow globular fruits, which ripen in August and September, are $\frac{1}{4}$ in. wide and are freely produced in dense bunches.

S. reducta. Burma, W. China. Height 12–24 in.; spread 12–18 in. The mid-green leaves of this small shrub have leaflets which are downy on the underside. The leaves turn red-purple from October onwards. White flowers, $\frac{1}{2}$ in. wide, appear in May or June in terminal clusters. The globular berries, $\frac{1}{4}$ in. across, ripen in August and September. They are rose-pink and often freely produced. This species is represented by suckering and non-suckering forms, the former producing a thicket of erect slender stems.

S. sargentiana. China. Height 10–18 ft; spread 8–12 ft. The leaves of this pyramidal tree have 7–11 mid-green leaflets with paler undersides. The bright red-brown winter buds, which are large and sticky, open into white flower clusters, 5–6 in. across, in May. The $\frac{1}{4}$ in. wide orange-red berries are borne in 6–9 in. wide flattened heads in September. The foliage is red in autumn.

S. scalaris. Japan. Height and spread 10–18 ft. The frond-like leaves have numerous, slender, glossy dark green leaflets. Dull white flowers appear in 4–5 in. wide clusters in May and June. Bright red fruits, $\frac{1}{4}$ in. wide, are borne in September in broad, densely packed bunches.

S. scopulina, syns. *S. decora, S. americana nana*. E. United States. Height 8–10 ft; spread 1–3 ft. This is a slow-growing columnar tree with closely packed fastigiate branches. The leaves are composed of 11–14 dark green leaflets. White 4–5 in. wide clusters of flowers open in May and June, followed by $\frac{1}{4}$ in. wide sealing-wax-red globular fruits. These are borne in 5–6 in. wide bunches and ripen in August and September.

S. vilmorinii. W. China. Height 8–12 ft; spread 5–8 ft. The fern-like leaves of this large shrub are mid-green and composed of 19–25 narrow ovate, toothed leaflets. White flowers open in June in loose clusters, 3 in. wide, and are followed by globose $\frac{1}{4}$ in. wide rose-red fruits which gradually change to white, flushed with pink. They ripen during September.

Cultivation. Plant in any ordinary, well-drained soil during suitable weather between October and March; a sunny or partially shaded position is equally suitable.

Propagation. Extract seeds from the berries in October and sow at once in John Innes seed compost in a cold frame. Prick out the seedlings into boxes and plant them out in nursery rows the following October. Grow on for three to five years before planting out in their final positions.

Pruning. None required.

Pests. Generally trouble-free.

Diseases. APPLE CANKER may cause severe cankers on these trees, sometimes killing large shoots.

FIREBLIGHT causes a blackening and shrivelling of flowers and a progressive die-back of branches bearing brown and withered leaves.

HONEY FUNGUS kills trees rapidly.

A PHYSIOLOGICAL DISORDER due to adverse soil conditions shows as discoloration of foliage followed by withering and premature leaf-fall.

RUST, which appears on *S. aucuparia* in Scotland, shows as orange horn-shaped structures borne in clusters on the leaves.

SILVER LEAF causes the die-back of shoots bearing leaves with a silvery tinge.

Sorrel
Rumex. Polygonaceae

The plants described here are hardy perennial herbs, used for flavouring and in cooking.

Sorrel (*R. acetosa*). Europe, including Great Britain. Height up to 18 in.; planting distance 9 in. This plant is the native common sorrel. The fleshy mid-green leaves are arrowhead-shaped and narrower than those of French sorrel. Red-green flowers are carried in narrow pyramidal panicles. The acid-tasting leaves are good for flavouring salads.

Sorrel, French (*R. scutatus*). Europe, Asia. Height 12–18 in.; planting distance 6 in. This is a slender, erect plant with triangular, mid to grey-green leaves. Tiny green to red flowers are borne in clustered spikes 6 in. long.

Add the acid-flavoured young leaves to salads, sandwiches and soups, cook them like spinach, or make a purée of them to serve with rich meats and fish.

SORREL

Cultivation. Sorrel succeeds on any well-drained, fertile soil in sun or partial shade. Pinch out the flowering stems as soon as they appear, to encourage the growth of new leaves.

Propagation. Divide established plants in March, April or September and replant direct in permanent positions.

Alternatively, sow seeds of both types in April in shallow drills drawn 18 in. apart. Thin the seedlings to 3 in. apart at first and finally to 6–9 in. distances.

Harvesting and storing. Use only the young leaves as these are the most tender and least bitter. They are best used fresh, but may be dried or deep-frozen. See entry under HERBS.

Pests and diseases. Generally trouble-free.

Sorrel, wood: see *Oxalis acetosella*
Southernwood: see *Artemisia abrotanum*
Spanish moss: see *Tillandsia usneoides*

Sparaxis
Iridaceae

The four or five species of this S. African genus grow from small corms; they are only half-hardy in most parts of Great Britain. Sparaxis are grown for the market on a small scale in Devon and Cornwall. Elsewhere, they are best grown in south-facing borders under walls or as pot plants under glass.

S. tricolor (harlequin flower). Height 12–18 in.; planting distance 4 in. The sparse, mid-green leaves are narrowly sword-shaped and grow to 12 in. high. Flat, open, six-petalled flowers, 1½–2 in. across, appear from May to June, several to a stem. They are multi-coloured in shades of red, yellow, purple and white, often with various colours on one flower. The many varieties raised from this species are usually bought as a mixture.

SPARAXIS TRICOLOR

Cultivation. Outdoors, sparaxis need well-drained, rich soil and a sheltered position in mild districts. Plant the corms 3–4 in. deep in November; earlier planting may induce risk of frost damage. For cutting, plant in rows 18–24 in. apart, with the corms spaced 4 in. apart. Keep weed-free during the growing season and lift as the leaves die down in July. Dry off in a warm shed or greenhouse and store in a dry, frost-free shed until planting time.

The same timing may be followed for pot-grown plants, although they can be planted earlier, in August or September, if housed in a frost-free greenhouse. Plant about six corms in a 5–6 in. pot of John Innes potting compost No. 2. Give the plants an initial soaking, then withhold water until they show leaves. Dry the plants off when the leaves start to turn yellow. Remove the offsets before repotting in August or September.

Propagation. Save seeds in July and sow during August or September, or the following March, in pots or boxes under glass at a temperature of 16°C (61°F). Prick off the seedlings into pots or boxes and grow them on in a frost-free frame or greenhouse for two or three years until the corms reach flowering size. Plant them in their outdoor flowering positions in the autumn when the leaves have died.

Offsets are produced from the flowering corms; if these are removed when repotting and replanted immediately, they may be grown on to reach flowering size in a year or two.

Pests and diseases. Generally trouble-free.

Sparmannia
Tiliaceae

A genus of seven species of tender evergreen flowering shrubs. Only one species is in general cultivation. It needs cool greenhouse treatment, and young specimens may also be grown as house plants.

S. africana (African hemp). S. Africa. Height 3 ft; spread 24 in. This species will flower when about 24 in. high; it is usually grown as a pot plant, but in a greenhouse border it may reach a height and

Sorrel, common

Sparaxis tricolor

Sparmannia africana

spread of 8 ft. The heart-shaped leaves are 6 in. or more long, bright green and covered with fine soft hairs.

Flowers appear in many-flowered umbels in May and June. Each flower is more than 1 in. wide and is white with a large boss of purple-tipped stamens in the centre. The stamens open outwards if the flowers are touched, or are blown by a gentle breeze.

SPARMANNIA AFRICANA

Cultivation. Grow sparmannias in 6 in. pots of John Innes potting compost No. 3 or plant out in the greenhouse border. Overwinter at a temperature of 7°C (45°F), and in winter give sufficient water to prevent the plants drying out; from April to October water copiously. The plants grow best in sun, but give light shade during the summer.

Ventilate freely during spring and summer to ensure that the atmosphere is not too humid.

In the home, the hairy leaves and stems are difficult to keep free of dust; stand the plants outside during rain in mild periods or syringe them frequently.

Sparmannias are vigorous growers; pot plants are usually discarded after one growing season, but if large specimens are wanted they should be potted on annually in March and April. Feed with liquid manure at intervals of seven days from May to September.

Propagation. Take 3–4 in. long cuttings of young growths from cut-back plants in April; insert the cuttings in equal parts (by volume) peat and sand and root at a temperature of 16°C (61°F). When rooted, pot the cuttings in 3–3½ in. pots of the growing compost and pot on as necessary.

Pruning. Plants grown in the greenhouse border should be kept within bounds by shortening all growths by half or two-thirds in March. Pot-grown plants should be cut back to about 6 in. of the base in March to provide young shoots for propagation purposes.

Pests. Generally trouble-free.

Diseases. A PHYSIOLOGICAL DISORDER produces yellow blotches on the leaves or causes them to become brown and papery; affected leaves fall prematurely.

Spartium

Spanish broom. *Leguminosae*

A genus of a single species. This hardy deciduous flowering shrub has rush-like green stems which give it an evergreen appearance. It grows best on sandy or alkaline soils and makes an excellent shrub for maritime gardens.

S. junceum. Mediterranean region, Canary Islands. Height 8–10 ft; spread 6–8 ft. The hoary mid-green leaves are narrowly ovate and soon fall

after reaching maturity. The golden-yellow, ¾ in. wide, pea-like flowers are fragrant, and appear from June to August in terminal racemes on the slender, almost leafless branches.

SPARTIUM JUNCEUM

Cultivation. Plant young pot-grown plants in September or October, March or April in an open sunny position in ordinary, well-drained soil.

Propagation. Sow seeds in March or April in pans or boxes of sandy soil in a cold frame. When the seedlings are large enough to handle, prick off singly into 4 in. pots of John Innes potting compost No. 1. Plant out in the permanent positions the following September or October.

Pruning. Remove dead flower heads to prevent seeding. Light trimming in autumn encourages earlier flowering.

Pests and diseases. Generally trouble-free.

Spathiphyllum

Araceae

SPATHIPHYLLUM WALLISII

A genus of 36 tropical evergreen perennials of which one species and a hybrid are popular greenhouse and house plants. They are related to *Anthurium*, but are more easily grown.

S. wallisii. Colombia. Height 9–12 in. A species with shiny, bright green, lanceolate leaves. The small flowers are arranged in a white, dense, column-like spike, 1½ in. long, arising from the base of a pure white, ovate, leaf-like spathe. The flowering period is from May to August.

S. × 'Mauna Loa'. Height 18–24 in. This hybrid is similar to *S. wallisii*, but with larger spathes and oblong-lanceolate leaves. It flowers freely in May; under warm conditions it usually produces flowers at intervals throughout the year.

Cultivation. Grow spathiphyllums in John Innes potting compost No. 2 or a proprietary loam-less compost. Final pot size for *S. wallisii* should be 4–5 in., for *S. × 'Mauna Loa'* 5–7 in. The plants need warm conditions, and although *S. wallisii* will survive at a winter temperature of 10°C (50°F), *S. × 'Mauna Loa'* requires 13°C (55°F). During spring and summer they will tolerate all the heat available.

Provide a humid atmosphere and syringe the leaves frequently. Water the plants freely when in full growth, but less frequently in winter, although they must be kept moist at all times. In

Spartium junceum

Spathiphyllum wallisii

Spathiphyllum × 'Mauna Loa'

the home, plunge the pots in a water-retentive substance such as peat. Give established plants a liquid feed at ten-day intervals from late March until the end of September and a weaker feed monthly for the rest of the year.

In summer, shade *S. wallisii*; *S.* × 'Mauna Loa' requires brighter conditions, especially in autumn. Admit as much light as possible during winter and, in the home, set the plants in a well-lit position. Repot annually in April.

Propagation. Divide the plants in April and pot up immediately in the growing compost. Keep the divisions shaded and moist until established.

Pests. Generally trouble-free.

Diseases. A PHYSIOLOGICAL DISORDER results in brown blotches on the leaves.

Spearwort, great: see *Ranunculus lingua*

Specularia

Campanulaceae

SPECULARIA SPECULUM-VENERIS

The ten species of annuals in this genus are now correctly included in *Legousia*. The one described is a hardy plant of erect bushy habit, suitable for mixed borders or wild gardens, for cutting or as an early spring-flowering pot plant.

S. speculum-veneris (Venus's looking glass). Europe. Height 12 in.; spacing 4 in. A showy plant with smooth, ovate, mid-green leaves. Saucer-shaped flowers, ¾ in. across, are produced in profusion from late June to September. They are violet-blue with white centres. The name 'Grandiflora' listed in some catalogues covers a strain with slightly larger flowers.

Cultivation. Grow in light, well-drained soil in either full sun or partial shade. Light staking may be required for plants which flower in early spring under glass. Plants from an autumn sowing need cloche protection in cold districts during the winter.

These September-sown plants will produce a second flush of flowers if the dead flower stems are removed after the first flush. Self-sown seedlings occur if the soil is left undisturbed.

For flowering under glass, grow the plants in John Innes potting compost No. 1, three to a 5 in. pot or five to a 6 in. pot.

Propagation. Sow the seeds in the flowering site in September, March or April, just covering them with soil. Thin out the seedlings to 4 in. apart.

For flowering under glass, pot September-raised seedlings as advised under CULTIVATION.

Pests and diseases. Generally trouble-free.

Speedwell: see *Veronica*
Spider flower: see *Cleome*
Spiderwort: see *Tradescantia virginiana*
Spikenard, false: see *Smilacina racemosa*

Spinach

Chenopodiaceae

These vegetables are grown for their edible and succulent ovate to triangular leaves. They include the annual summer and winter spinach (*Spinacia oleracea*), the annual New Zealand spinach (*Tetragonia expansa*) and the biennial spinach beet or perpetual spinach, also known as sea kale beet (*Beta vulgaris*).

The annual spinach is hardy and quick-growing; it may be used as a summer catch-crop between rows of beans and peas, cabbages and leeks. The dark green leaves may be harvested all year round if summer and winter crops are chosen to succeed each other.

'Long Standing Round' is a round-seeded summer variety: 'Greenmarket', 'Long Standing Prickly' and 'Winter Giant' are reliable, prickly seeded varieties.

New Zealand spinach, a native of Australasia, is similar to annual spinach, but with smaller leaves. It is a branching and spreading plant, 2–3 ft wide, with numerous dark green triangular leaves; it is half-hardy and will not survive autumn frosts.

Spinach beet or perpetual spinach is a hardy biennial plant. The mid to dark green broadly ovate leaves are similar in flavour to spinach; they are produced during summer and winter and withstand hot summers and cold winters better than annual spinach. Sea kale beet is a form of spinach beet with broad white stalks and midribs; it may be used as a substitute for sea kale. 'Rhubarb Beet' is a variety with red leaf stalks and midribs; it may also be grown as a decorative biennial in a border.

Cultivation of annual spinach. Summer spinach is best grown in deep, rich and moist soil. Prepare the bed by deep digging and by working in a bucket of decayed manure per sq. yd. Rake the ground level and apply a top dressing of fish manure at 4 oz. per sq. yd. The bed should preferably be in a partially shaded, cool position to prevent the plants running to seed.

Make the first sowing outdoors in early March in the south and late March in the north. Make successional sowings at two or three-week intervals until early July. Sow the seeds thinly in 1 in. deep drills drawn 12–15 in. apart.

Thin the seedlings as soon as they are large enough to handle, to encourage steady growth and to prevent premature running to seed in dry weather. Thin the plants to 6 in. apart at first and finally to 12 in. apart. The second thinnings will be large enough to use for cooking. Summer spinach will be ready for picking from May to October. Do not strip a plant of all its leaves, but gather the largest leaves as they are ready.

Winter spinach thrives on fertile, well-drained soil in a sheltered and sunny position. Prepare the ground as for summer spinach.

Make successional sowings from mid-July to late September as described for summer spinach. Growth is less vigorous and seedlings should be thinned at first to 3 in. apart, later to 6 in. From mid-November onwards, protect the plants with cloches or with thick layers of straw or bracken placed between the rows.

Specularia speculum-veneris 'Grandiflora'

Spinach 'Winter Giant'

Spinach, New Zealand

Winter spinach is usually ready for picking from mid-October onwards; gather the leaves as they become large enough. Do not strip the plants completely, or growth will cease.

Cultivation of New Zealand spinach. These plants succeed particularly well on light, well-drained soil in a sunny position.

For an early crop, sow seeds in pots or pans of seed compost during late March or early April and place in a greenhouse at a temperature of 13–16°C (55–61°F). As soon as the seedlings are large enough to handle, prick them out into boxes or singly into 3 in. pots of John Innes potting compost No. 1, and gradually harden off in a cold frame for planting out towards the end of May. For a main crop, sow seeds outdoors in early May, allowing 3 ft between rows and 18–24 in. between the plants.

Water frequently to encourage rapid growth, and pinch out the growing tips regularly to induce the production of leaf-bearing side-shoots. In five or six weeks the first leaves will be ready for picking as required; pick the leaves singly so that the shoots continue to grow.

Cultivation of spinach beet. These hardy biennials thrive on any ordinary, well-drained soil. Dress the soil liberally as advised for annual summer spinach to promote plenty of leaf growth. Sow seeds in April for plants to crop through summer and autumn, and in late July or early August for winter and spring crops. Sow thinly in ½ in. deep drills drawn 15 in. apart, and thin the seedlings to 8 in. apart. Keep the rows free of weeds and give occasional waterings during dry spells.

Pick the leaves, when large enough, with stalks attached and use immediately. Leaves left on the plants will slow down growth.

Pests. Leaves of annual spinach may be tunnelled into by MANGOLD FLY maggots; these cause blotch mines and check growth.

Germinating seeds of New Zealand spinach may be attacked by MILLEPEDES.

Spinach beet is generally trouble-free.

Diseases. The following diseases chiefly affect annual spinach and occasionally spinach beet. New Zealand spinach is generally trouble-free.

The disease known as spinach blight in annual spinach is caused by CUCUMBER MOSAIC VIRUS. It shows as a yellowing of the younger leaves which are thin and puckered. The leaf margins roll up, and the leaves gradually die.

DAMPING-OFF causes the collapse of seedlings.

DOWNY MILDEW shows on the leaves as yellow blotches; on the under-surfaces a greyish or violet-grey mould develops.

LEAF SPOT shows on the leaves as grey-brown sunken spots with well-defined brown or purple margins; the diseased tissues often fall away, leaving holes.

MAGNESIUM DEFICIENCY appears as pale areas between the leaf veins, followed by browning.

MANGANESE DEFICIENCY causes a trouble known as speckled yellows in which the leaves show yellow blotches between the veins; they have a tendency to roll inwards.

Spinach, sea kale beet

Spinach, 'Rhubarb Beet'

Spiraea × arguta

Spinacia oleracea: see Spinach
Spindle tree: see Euonymus
Spindle tree, common: see *Euonymus europaea*

Spiraea
Rosaceae

SPIRAEA JAPONICA

A genus of 100 species of hardy deciduous flowering shrubs with small, somewhat star-like flowers arranged in flattened or plume-shaped heads. They are at their best in open sunny positions in deep soil. All the species mentioned can be grown as flowering hedges.

S. aitchisonii: see *Sorbaria aitchisonii*
S. arborea: see *Sorbaria arborea*
S. × arguta (foam of May, bridal wreath). Height and spread 6–8 ft. A hybrid with narrow oblong-lanceolate leaves that are mid-green. The white flowers, on slender arching stems, appear profusely in late April or May in umbels up to 2 in. across.

Spiraea thunbergii

S. aruncus: see *Aruncus sylvester*
S. bullata. Japan. Height and spread 10–15 in. A compact shrub with rounded-ovate dark green leaves that have a puckered or corrugated texture. Crimson flowers are produced in freely borne flattened heads, 1½–2½ in. across, from July to September. This dwarf species is suitable for a large rock garden.
S. × bumalda. Height 3–4 ft; spread 4–5 ft. This plant is considered by some authorities to be a variety of *S. japonica*, by others to be a hybrid. It has sharply toothed lanceolate leaves that are mid-green. Bright crimson flowers in flat heads, 4–5 in. across, appear on erect stems in July and August. 'Anthony Waterer' has variegated cream and pink young foliage on some shoots.
S. digitata: see *Filipendula palmata*
S. discolor: see *Holodiscus discolor*
S. japonica. Japan. Height 3–5 ft; spread 4–6 ft. The sharply toothed lanceolate leaves are mid-green. In July and August, flattened 6 in. wide

eads of small pink flowers are borne on erect stems. The variety 'Anthony Waterer', sometimes attributed to this species, is described under S. × bumalda.

S. lobata: see *Filipendula rubra*
S. menziesii 'Triumphans'. Height 3–5 ft; spread 4–6 ft. The ovate toothed leaves are pale to mid-green. Dense 9 in. long panicles of deep rose flowers appear in July and August.
S. thunbergii. China, Japan. Height 5–6 ft; spread 6–8 ft. The lanceolate pale green leaves are borne on dense, slender, arching branchlets. White, 1 in. wide clusters of flowers appear before the leaves in March and April.
S. ulmaria: see *Filipendula ulmaria*
S. venusta: see *Filipendula rubra*
Cultivation. Plant between October and March in deep, fertile soil and in an open sunny position.

For hedging, plant shrubs 15–24 in. apart, depending on which species is grown, and cut back the previous season's growth to within 6 in. of ground level. Tip subsequent growths when they are 3–4 in. long, and thereafter shear over annually after flowering.
Propagation. In July or August, take 3–5 in. cuttings of half-ripe lateral shoots and insert them in sandy soil in a cold frame; set out in a nursery bed the following April. Grow on for one or two years before planting out.

Alternatively, take 8–12 in. hardwood cuttings in October and insert them in a nursery bed. They should have rooted and be ready for planting out the following October.

Divide the roots between October and March and replant direct in final positions.

Remove rooted suckers from *S. menziesii* 'Triumphans' and replant in permanent positions.
Pruning. For compact growth and large flower heads, prune *S.* × *bumalda* and *S. japonica* to within 3–4 in. of ground level in late February or early March.

Remove dead flower heads from *S. japonica*, *S.* × *bumalda* and *S. menziesii* 'Triumphans' and thin out all species occasionally, after flowering. Trim established hedges annually.
Pests. The leaves may be eaten by SAWFLY, and are often reduced to a mere skeleton of veins.
Diseases. Generally trouble-free.

Spleenwort: see Asplenium
Spleenwort, black: see *Asplenium adiantum-nigrum*
Spleenwort, green: see *Asplenium viride*
Spleenwort, maidenhair: see *Asplenium trichomanes*
Spotted dog: see *Pulmonaria officinalis*

Sprekelia
Amaryllidaceae

A genus of one species. This is a half-hardy bulb, closely related to *Hippeastrum*. It is a cool greenhouse plant, with attractive funnel-shaped crimson flowers.
S. formosissima, syn. *Amaryllis formosissima* (Jacobean lily). Mexico. Height 12–18 in. The few strap-shaped mid-green leaves grow as the flowers die. Flower stems appear in April and a

solitary flower, 4 in. across, opens on each stem from June onwards. The deep red flower has one broad upper petal flanked by two narrow, recurved ones, and three petals below.

SPREKELIA FORMOSISSIMA

Cultivation. Plant the bulbs singly in $3\frac{1}{2}$–4 in. pots or three to six together in larger containers. Use John Innes potting compost No. 3 and pot in August or early September, leaving the neck above soil level. Provide a temperature of 7–10°C (45–50°F). Do not water until the spring, then keep moist until the leaves begin to die in July or August. Give fortnightly weak liquid feeds from flowering time until the leaves die. Repot or pot on every two or three years, in September.
Propagation. Offsets removed at repotting time may be grown on, singly or in threes (according to size), in 3 in. pots. Repotted annually, and when large enough potted into 5 in. pots, they will flower in three or four years.
Pests. Conspicuous tufts of white waxy wool on the bases of leaves are caused by MEALY BUGS.
Diseases. Generally trouble-free.

Spring onion: see Onion
Spruce: see Picea
Spruce, black: see *Picea mariana*
Spruce, blue: see *Picea pungens* 'Glauca'
Spruce, Brewer's: see *Picea breweriana*
Spruce, Canadian: see *Picea glauca*
Spruce, Caucasian: see *Picea orientalis*
Spruce, Colorado: see *Picea pungens*
Spruce, Norway: see *Picea abies*
Spruce, oriental: see *Picea orientalis*
Spruce, Serbian: see *Picea omorika*
Spruce, Sitka: see *Picea sitchensis*
Spruce, West Himalayan: see *Picea smithiana*
Spruce, white: see *Picea glauca*
Squash: see Pumpkin
Squill, striped: see *Puschkinia scilloides*

Spiraea × *bumalda* 'Anthony Waterer'

Sprekelia formosissima

Stachys
Labiatae

A genus of 300 species of hardy and half-hardy annuals and herbaceous perennials with tubular, two-lipped flowers. The following perennials are easily grown plants for a border; they are hardy, but *S. lanata* may not survive in cold, wet or exposed districts.
S. betonica: see *S. officinalis*
S. lanata (lamb's tongue). Caucasus to Iran. Height 12–18 in.; planting distance 12 in. A half-hardy species of spreading habit. It is grown for its foliage, either at the front of a border, as ground cover, or as a summer bedding plant. The ovate mid-green leaves are densely covered with white silvery hairs which give it a woolly appearance. Spikes of purple flowers, $\frac{1}{4}$–$\frac{1}{2}$ in.

long, are borne in July. The leaves of *S. l.* 'Olympica' are a purer white and the flowers inclined to be pink; 'Silver Carpet' is a non-flowering variety.

STACHYS LANATA

S. macrantha, syns. *Betonica macrantha, B. grandiflora.* Caucasus. Height 1½–2½ ft; planting distance 12 in. A mat-forming species with hairy mid-green leaves that are triangularly ovate. Whorls of 1 in. long purple flowers are produced from May to July. *S. m.* 'Rosea' has rose flowers; *S. m.* 'Superba' is rich rose-purple; and *S. m.* 'Violacea' has violet flowers.

S. officinalis, syn. *S. betonica* (bishop's wort, wood betony). Europe. The species is a rather coarse plant which is superseded by the larger-flowered form, *S. o.* 'Grandiflora'. Height 6–12 in.; planting distance 12 in. This is a mat-forming plant with mid to dark green leaves, which are oblong to ovate with rounded teeth; it is suitable for the front of a border. A profusion of 9 in. long spikes of tubular magenta-purple flowers is carried in August and September.

STACHYS OFFICINALIS

S. spicata. Caucasus. Height and planting distance 18 in. A species of compact habit, with bright green, puckered and saw-edged, oblong-ovate leaves. Closely set, bright pink, lipped flowers are borne in erect 2–3 in. long spikes from June to August.

Cultivation. Plant between September and April in ordinary, well-drained garden soil, in sun or partial shade. Cut down in November.

Propagation. Divide and replant the roots between October and March or in April.

Pests and diseases. Generally trouble-free.

Stachyurus

Stachyuraceae

A genus of ten species of hardy deciduous flowering shrubs. The pendulous unopened racemes are conspicuous from October until the flowers open in spring.

S. chinensis. China. Height and spread 8–10 ft. This species has mid-green ovate leaves that are slender-pointed. The translucent yellow flowers, which appear before the leaves in March and April, are bell-shaped, ¼ in. long, and borne in slender 4 in. catkin-like racemes.

S. praecox. Japan. Height and spread 8–10 ft. A species with mid-green, ovate and slender pointed leaves. The pale yellow flowers with dull red calyces, which appear before the leaves from February to April, are ¼ in. or more across and borne in pendent racemes about 4 in. long.

STACHYURUS PRAECOX

Cultivation. Plant in any ordinary, well-drained garden soil, preferably enriched with leaf-mould, peat or compost, between October and March. Choose a sunny or partially shaded position, preferably sheltered from north and east winds.

Propagation. In July, take 4 in. heel cuttings and insert them in sandy soil in a propagating frame at a temperature of 16°C (61°F). Pot up the rooted cuttings in 3½ in. containers of John Innes potting compost No. 1 and overwinter them in a cold frame. Plant out in a nursery bed the following April and grow on there for two or three years before setting the plants out.

Sow seeds in October in a cold frame in John Innes seed compost. When the seedlings are large enough to handle, prick them off into pans or boxes, later transferring them to individual 3½ in. pots of John Innes potting compost No. 1. In sheltered areas, set them out in a nursery bed in April and plant out from October onwards. Elsewhere, pot on in 5 in. pots and grow on for a further year in a cold frame before planting them out from October onwards.

Shoots layered in March should be ready for severing within one or two years.

Pruning. None required.

Pests and diseases. Generally trouble-free.

Stanhopea

Orchidaceae

STANHOPEA WARDII

A genus of about 45 species of epiphytic evergreen orchids native to Mexico, Central America and the American tropics. The ovoid pseudobulbs are 2–3 in. high and bear a single stalked leaf rising from the apex of the bulb; the leaves are elliptic-ovate and mid to deep green. Each pseudobulb produces one strongly pendulous inflorescence which frequently forces its way down through the compost and appears out of the bottom of the basket.

The stem bears up to ten flowers with wide, reflexed petals and sepals. The lip is rigid and

Stachys lanata 'Silver Carpet'

Stachys macrantha

Stachyurus praecox

waxy with a pouch-shaped base, a usually heart-shaped mid-lobe and two curving horns where the base and mid-lobe join. The flowers last only a few days; they are strongly scented, sometimes unpleasantly so. These orchids require an intermediate or warm greenhouse.

See also ORCHIDS.

S. costaricensis. C. America. This species has ovoid, clustered pseudobulbs about 1½ in. high. From July to September each pseudobulb produces 5 in. long sheathed flower spikes with two flowers up to 5 in. wide. These have concave 3 in. long sepals that are buff-yellow with light red ring-spots. The buff-yellow petals are narrow with wavy margins and have small solid red spots; the lip has a pair of dark red patches at the base. Grow in a warm greenhouse.

S. eburnea, syn. *S. grandiflora*. Brazil. The pseudobulbs of this species are 1½ in. high. One or two flowers, each 4 in. across, are borne on stems 6–9 in. long from August to October. The long and narrow sepals and petals are ivory-white. The lip is narrow and lacks the usual long curving horns; it is ivory-white with a purple base. This species requires an intermediate greenhouse.

S. grandiflora: see *S. eburnea*.

S. oculata. Mexico. A species with 2 in. high pseudobulbs. The inflorescence, which appears from July to October, is more than 12 in. long, with three to ten fragrant, 4 in. wide flowers. These have light yellow sepals and petals with red spots. The lip is narrow, orange-yellow at the base with two or four large black spots; the tip is white with red or purple spots. This species thrives in an intermediate greenhouse.

S. wardii. Guatemala, Venezuela. The clustered 2 in. high pseudobulbs produce slender flowering stems at any time from July to November; they are 9–12 in. long and carry six to ten strongly scented flowers, 3–4 in. across. Petals and sepals are usually golden-yellow, spotted with purple; the deep yellow lip bears two circular, velvet-purple blotches. The colours are variable. Grow in an intermediate greenhouse.

Cultivation. Grow these orchids in hanging baskets containing a compost of equal parts (by volume) sphagnum moss and fibrous peat. Keep the atmosphere moist during the growing season from May to September, and ventilate night and day during mild weather; from October to March ventilate on sunny days only. Water freely during the growing season, but during the resting period give only enough water to prevent the pseudobulbs from drying out. Give an occasional feed of liquid manure from May to September. After growth is complete, allow a resting period. Lower the temperature by 2·5°C (5°F).

Repot every two or three years in summer.

Propagation. Divide the pseudobulbs in July or August, with a healthy growth to each section; pot up in the growing compost.

Pests and diseases. Generally trouble-free.

Stapelia
Carrion flower. *Asclepiadaceae*

A genus of 75 species of greenhouse perennials. Only a few species are obtainable in Britain, and although these are among the most difficult of succulents, their large, bizarre flowers make them worth a little effort.

The thickened stems are four-angled and coarsely toothed. The plants branch freely from the base and form dense clusters which spread outwards and, in the wild, die at the centre.

Five-petalled star-shaped flowers are produced from the base of the stems in late summer and early autumn. Although they are attractively coloured, they have an unpleasant smell of carrion which attracts the blowflies that pollinate the flowers.

In most species the flowers are preceded by large balloon-like buds and followed by long, horn-like seed pods. When these pods eventually burst, a mass of seeds, carried on long, delicate hairs that act as parachutes, is liberated.

See also CACTUS.

S. hirsuta. Cape Province. Height 9 in. The bronze-green stems are covered with short, soft hairs. The flowers, which are borne in August, are about 5 in. in diameter and yellow with brown markings. The surface of the petals is covered with brown-red hairs. This species is the least difficult to cultivate; it is a rapid grower and will soon fill a 6 in. pot.

S. pillansii. S. Africa. Height 6 in. A vigorous-growing plant with dark green, velvety-haired stems. The flowers, which appear in August, are about 6 in. across and deep purple-black, covered with dark hairs.

S. variegata. Cape Province. Height 4 in. This is the most commonly grown species. The grey-green stems are bare. Smooth-surfaced flowers, about 3 in. across are freely produced in August. They are pale yellow with brown markings and have a particularly unpleasant smell.

Cultivation. Stapelias need an open compost, consisting of equal parts (by volume) John Innes potting compost No. 2, and grit or sharp sand. Grow them in 4–6 in. pots. Keep the plants in a sunny position and water freely in summer. In winter, they should be kept in the warmest part of the greenhouse. Although they will usually survive a minimum winter temperature of 5°C (41°F), they are less likely to rot if maintained at 10°C (50°F). Do not allow the plants to dry out completely or the stems will shrivel badly; give them a little water on sunny days during winter. Repot each April. To obtain large specimens, pot on into bigger pots or pans.

Propagation. Sow seeds thinly in pans of John Innes seed compost or in equal parts (by volume) peat and sand, during March or April. At a temperature of 18–21°C (64–70°F), germination should take place within three or four days. Prick off the seedlings, when large enough to handle, individually into 2½ in. pots of the growing compost. Pot on as necessary.

Stapelias can also be propagated by breaking up the clump; rooted sections can often be split off. Individual stems can also be used as cuttings; dry them for about four days before potting. Use the same compost as for cultivation. The best time to take cuttings is from June to August.

Pests. Colonies of MEALY BUGS may infest plants, producing conspicuous tufts of white waxy wool.

ROOT MEALY BUGS check growth.

Diseases. Generally trouble-free.

Stanhopea wardii

Stapelia hirsuta

Stapelia variegata

Starfish: see Cryptanthus
Star of Bethlehem: see *Ornithogalum umbel-latum*
Star of the veldt: see *Dimorphotheca aurantiaca*
Statice: see Limonium
Stenolobium stans: see *Tecoma stans*

Stephanandra
Rosaceae

A genus of four species of hardy deciduous flowering shrubs. The graceful, tinted autumn foliage is much used in floral arrangements.

S. flexuosa: see *S. incisa*

S. incisa, syn. *S. flexuosa*. Japan, Korea. Height 5–7 ft; spread 4–6 ft. The ovate, deeply incised, lobed leaves, are mid-green, turning yellow in October. In June, clusters of tiny, green-white, star-shaped flowers open in crowded rounded panicles up to 3 in. across. The stems are brown during winter.

S. i. prostrata (height 1½–3 ft; spread 4 ft or more) is a low arching form, suitable for ground cover; the flowers are tinged with buff-pink.

STEPHANANDRA TANAKAE

S. tanakae. Japan. Height 5–7 ft; spread 6–7 ft. The broadly ovate, prominent and sharply toothed mid-green leaves turn deep yellow and orange from October onwards. The stems are bright green-brown. In June and July, dull white star-shaped flowers open in terminal panicles up to 4 in. long.

Cultivation. Plant from October to March in any ordinary, well-drained garden soil, in sun or in partial shade.

Propagation. Remove rooted suckers between October and March and either plant direct in permanent positions or, if they are small, grow on for a year in a nursery bed before planting out.

Alternatively, take 9–12 in. hardwood cuttings in October and set in a nursery bed. Grow the cuttings on for a year before planting out in permanent positions.

Pruning. Thin out old and decayed wood in February or March.

Pests and diseases. Generally trouble-free.

Stephanotis
Asclepiadaceae

A genus of five species of tender evergreen twining shrubs. The species described requires greenhouse cultivation; it is grown for its fragrant waxy flowers, and is much in demand by florists for buttonholes and bouquets.

S. floribunda. Madagascar. Height 10 ft or more. The leathery dark green leaves are broadly ovate-oblong and about 3 in. long. Heavily scented white waxy flowers are borne from May to October in axillary panicles of up to eight flowers. Each flower is about 1½ in. long and tubular with five spreading, ovate-oblong lobes.

STEPHANOTIS FLORIBUNDA

Cultivation. Grow stephanotis in John Innes potting compost No. 2, or in a proprietary peat compost. They can be grown in 5–6 in. or larger pots or in the greenhouse border. Train the shoots along strings and wire up to the ridge of the greenhouse and then horizontally along the roof; pot-grown plants should be trained over a cane framework. The plants will survive at a winter temperature of 10°C (50°F), but will do better if 13°C (55°F) can be maintained.

During winter, keep the plants just moist; from April until the end of October, the temperature should not fall below 18°C (64°F) for long, although it may rise higher. During this period, give the plants ample water and provide a humid atmosphere. Lightly shade the glass during summer, but allow full light at other times.

Pot on annually in April until the plants are in 8 or 9 in. pots; thereafter repot every three years in April. Give a fortnightly feed of liquid manure from May to September.

Propagation. Take cuttings, 4 in. long, of lateral non-flowering shoots from April to June; insert the cuttings in equal parts (by volume) peat and sand in a propagating case at a temperature of 18–21°C (64–70°F). When rooted, place the cuttings in 3 in. pots of the growing compost and pot on as necessary.

Pruning. Cut out all weak lateral growths at the end of February. If the plants are getting too large, cut them back at the same time by reducing lateral growths to 3 in. and shortening leading shoots by about half.

Pests. SCALE INSECTS, particularly hemispherical scale, form brown excrescences on leaves and stems and make the plants sticky.

MEALY BUGS produce conspicuous tufts of waxy wool on the leaves and stems.

ROOT MEALY BUGS infest the roots and check growth; in severe attacks, the leaves wilt and the plants die.

Diseases. BUD DROP results in the flower buds falling before opening.

A PHYSIOLOGICAL DISORDER causes the leaves to turn yellow and drop.

Sternbergia
Amaryllidaceae

The eight species of this hardy bulbous genus are found around the E. Mediterranean, and east to the Caucasus Mountains. Only three species are generally available, two of which flower in

Stephanandra tanakae
(autumn foliage)

Stephanotis floribunda

Sternbergia lutea

autumn; the other is spring-flowering. Looking somewhat like crocuses, the blooms differ in being borne on a true stem. Their mid to deep green leaves are strap-shaped.

S. clusiana, syn. *S. macrantha*. Asia Minor and countries eastwards. Height 6 in.; planting distance 6–9 in. Rich golden flowers, up to 4 in. long, appear from September to November. They have rounded, overlapping petals.

S. fischeriana. Caucasus. Height and planting distance 4–6 in. Bright yellow flowers, up to 2 in. long, appear in March and April.

S. lutea. E. Mediterranean, Iran. Height and planting distance 4–6 in. Shining yellow flowers, up to 2 in. long, open in September and October. The leaves appear with the flowers, but do not reach full length until spring. This plant is one of the contenders for the original Biblical lily of the field. *S. l. sicula* is a variety native to Sicily, with leaves and petals narrower than the species.

S. macrantha: see *S. clusiana*

Cultivation. Plant 4–6 in. deep during August or September in well-drained soil in a sunny position. Do not disturb unless the plants become crowded, in which case lift in August, divide and replant at once.

Propagation. Remove offsets from the bulbs when lifting and replant separately. They will flower in one or two years.

Pests. The flowers may sometimes be eaten by SLUGS. The bulbs may be disturbed by MICE.

Diseases. Generally trouble-free.

Stewartia: see Stuartia

Stipa

Feather grass. *Gramineae*

A genus of 300 species of hardy annual and perennial tufted grasses. The following species are perennials with handsome feathery plumes and linear leaves that are usually rolled into slender quills. They make good specimen plants for large lawns, and the plumes may be cut and dried for use in winter decorations.

S. barbata. Asia Minor. Height 24 in.; planting distance 18 in. This species forms a compact tuft of mid-green leaves. Slender, arching stems terminate in 12 in. long plumes of a light biscuit colour; they are borne from June to August.

S. calamagrostis. S. Europe. Height 3–4 ft; planting distance 24 in. A species with dense compact tufts of grey-green leaves from which the smooth stems arise. Silvery buff-violet plumes, 12 in. long, are produced from June to September.

S. gigantea. Spain. Height 3–4 ft; planting distance 24 in. A long-lived, near-evergreen species, forming dense clumps of grey-green leaves. Erect flower stems carry silvery purple-tinged plumes, 9–12 in. long and similar to those of pampas grass, in June and July.

S. pennata. Europe, Siberia. Height 2½ ft; planting distance 18 in. A species with narrow mid-green leaves. The erect flower stems have silvery-buff plumes, 9 in. or more in length, from June to August. The inflorescences of this species are particularly suitable for drying.

Cultivation. Plant in March or April in fertile, light soil and in full sun. For drying, cut the inflorescences when they are fully developed, usually in July.

Propagation. Divide and replant the roots in March or April.

Sow seeds in light soil outdoors in April. Transplant the seedlings to their flowering positions in May or June.

Pests and diseases. Generally trouble-free.

Stock, night-scented: see *Matthiola bicornis*
Stock, Virginian: see *Malcolmia maritima*
Stokes' aster: see *Stokesia*

Stokesia

Stokes' aster. *Compositae*

STOKESIA LAEVIS

A genus of one herbaceous perennial species, with lanceolate mid-green leaves. It is hardy, easily grown and long-flowering. The showy flowers resemble the China aster (*Callistephus*).

S. cyanea: see *S. laevis*

S. laevis, syn. *S. cyanea*. S.E. United States. Height 12–18 in.; planting distance 18 in. A variable border plant with white, blue, lilac or purple flowers. These are 1–3 in. across, with deeply notched florets, and appear from late July to October. 'Blue Star' carries sprays of light blue flowers, 3 in. across, from August to October.

Cultivation. Plant in April in sun or light shade and in light, well-drained soil; support the plants with twiggy pea-sticks. Cut down in November. The plants may be lifted in October to continue flowering under glass. Replant in April.

Propagation. Divide and replant in April.

Sow seeds in March in trays of John Innes seed compost; prick out the seedlings, when large enough to handle, into boxes containing John Innes potting compost No. 1. Plant out in nursery rows and transplant to permanent positions the following April. Plants raised from seeds seldom come true to type, but good colour forms may be produced.

Pests and diseases. Generally trouble-free.

Stone orpine: see *Sedum reflexum*
Stork's bill: see Erodium

Stranvaesia

Rosaceae

A genus of ten species of hardy evergreen flowering shrubs and small trees. The young leathery leaves are attractively tinted in spring and again in autumn. Only one species is generally found in cultivation.

Stipa calamagrostis

Stokesia laevis

S. davidiana. China. Height and spread 12–18 ft. The lanceolate leaves are dark green, some turning to shades of crimson from September onwards. White hawthorn-like flowers appear in June in 2–3 in. wide, flat heads and are followed by clusters of globular, ¼ in. wide, crimson berries which ripen in August and September. 'Flava' has yellow berries.

STRANVAESIA DAVIDIANA

Cultivation. Plant in October, March or April in any fertile, well-drained garden soil, in sun or partial shade.

Propagation. Sow seeds in October or November in seed compost in a cold frame. Prick off the seedlings into pans or boxes, later setting them out in a nursery bed. Grow on for two or three years before planting out in permanent positions in autumn or spring.

Take 3–4 in. cuttings of half-ripened lateral shoots with a heel in July, and insert them in equal parts (by volume) peat and sand in a propagating frame, preferably with gentle bottom heat of 16–18°C (61–64°F). Pot the rooted cuttings into 3 in. pots of John Innes potting compost No. 1 and grow on in a cold frame or greenhouse until the following April. Set out in a nursery bed to grow on for a further two years before planting out in permanent positions in October or March.

Pruning. None required.

Pests. Generally trouble-free.

Diseases. A blackening and shrivelling of the flowers and a progressive die-back of branches is caused by FIREBLIGHT. Such branches bear brown, withered leaves which do not fall.

Strawberry

Fragaria × ananassa. Rosaceae

STRAWBERRY

There are two main types of these herbaceous, low-growing perennial fruiting plants: those that carry a single crop of edible fruit in the summer and others, known as ever-bearing or perpetual, that crop at intervals from June to October.

Both types are derived from a hybrid race originated in the 18th century by crossing the two American species *Fragaria chiloensis* and *F. virginiana*. Forms of *F. vesca* from the European Alps are cultivated as Alpine strawberries; these are bushy plants without runners.

Under glass it is possible, but uneconomic, to produce strawberries all the year round. In practice, the season starts with fruits from plants forced under glass, followed by fruits that have been protected by cloches or frames. This is succeeded by outdoor summer-fruiting varieties and then the autumn-fruiting kinds, with the last of the crop ripened under glass.

Strawberries are easy to grow and give quick returns; they are excellent for table use, as preserves and for freezing. Certification schemes for trueness to type and the health of stocks have improved results greatly. However, virus diseases reduce vigour and cropping, and plants should be renewed after two or three crops. The ever-bearing varieties are not yet available as certified virus-free stock and should be isolated as far as possible from summer-fruiting strawberry varieties.

Most varieties, including those described, are self-fertile but need to be pollinated by insects. Forced crops have to be pollinated artificially.

'Baron Solemacher'. A vigorous, runnerless, alpine variety. Bright crimson, aromatic, fragrant fruits, held off the ground, ripen in summer and autumn. A heavy cropper.

'Cambridge Favourite'. Mid-season. Rounded, large, pink-red fruits. Fair flavour; sweet when fully ripe. A reliable and heavy-cropping variety.

'Cambridge Prizewinner'. First early. Large, firm, light scarlet fruits. Especially suitable for growing under cloches.

'Cambridge Rival'. Second early. Large crimson fruits with red flesh; the tips of the fruits are slow to ripen. Good flavour. Suitable for growing under cloches or for forcing.

'Cambridge Vigour'. Second early. Large, conical, glossy scarlet fruits with red-tinted flesh and a good, slightly acid flavour. Suitable for growing under cloches.

'Gento'. A perpetual variety that fruits from June to October. Large, round, crimson fruits with a good flavour. Berries are also carried on the runners while these are still attached to the parent plant.

'Grandee'. Early. The largest fruits in cultivation, scarlet-crimson, of good flavour, slightly less acid than 'Royal Sovereign'. In its second year it makes too much growth to be grown under cloches, but on good loamy soil may yield up to 3½ lb. per plant.

'Redgauntlet'. Mid-season. Large, scarlet-crimson fruits. Bred in Scotland and especially suited to northern conditions.

'Royal Sovereign'. Early mid-season. Large, wedge-shaped, scarlet fruits. A favourite garden variety on account of its flavour, but it is a comparatively poor cropper and is susceptible to virus diseases and botrytis. It may be forced.

'Sans Rivale'. A moderately vigorous, perpetual variety. Heavy-cropping, with long, conical, deep red fruits of fair flavour.

'Talisman'. Late mid-season. Conical, medium-sized, deep scarlet fruits. Excellent quality and flavour. Does not succeed on poor soil or in matted rows.

'Templar'. Mid-season. Large crimson fruits with a good flavour. Tends to make a large plant; fruit susceptible to rot. It is most successful in the north of England and in Scotland.

Stranvaesia davidiana

Strawberry 'Cambridge Vigour'

Cultivation. Strawberry plants grow best in soils rich in humus. Where humus is deficient, supply it in the form of well-rotted compost.

Although the flowers are susceptible to spring frosts and need protection with newspaper when frost threatens, strawberries are grown successfully over a wider area than most other fruits. Grow early crops in a sheltered, sunny border, main crops in an open sunny bed.

There are two ways of growing strawberries outdoors: as single plants with all runners removed, or in continuous rows which are formed by allowing the runners to root along the row. The former gives improved fruit size and is best in damp climates or for varieties particularly susceptible to grey mould. Matted rows give a heavier crop overall, but the berries are smaller.

In both cases, aim for a succession of fruits and allow for the regular replacement of beds after two or three crops. Use certified stock or select runners from healthy parent plants.

Late July is the time to plant strawberries that are to be forced or protected by cloches. They will crop the following year. Unprotected plants will fruit the following year if planted up to mid-August, or 21 months later if planted from October onwards. In cold areas and on heavy soils, where winter losses are more likely with young plants, planting in March will provide crops 15 months later.

There is a current trend towards growing strawberries as annuals, taking the first rooted runners in June and July. These plants produce large fruits of good quality the following year and are then discarded. This method reduces virus infection to a minimum, and generally avoids problems with weeds.

For growing without protection, set the plants 18 in. apart in rows $2\frac{1}{2}$ ft apart. If the plants are to be protected by cloches and frames, plant them 9–12 in. apart in single or double rows, according to the cover available. This spacing also applies to plants treated as annuals. Plant firmly, with the base of the central crown of the plant set level with the soil surface.

Watering is generally needed to help the plants become established in late summer, and also just before ripening to swell the fruits. If applied earlier than this it will increase the amount of foliage unnecessarily.

If the site has been well prepared before planting, using well-rotted compost or farmyard manure dug in at 10–20 lb. per sq. yd, there is no need for additional feeding. Otherwise, apply sulphate of ammonia in spring at $\frac{1}{2}$ oz. per sq. yd or give a complete fertiliser at 3–4 oz. per sq. yd.

Control weeds by shallow hoeing during the growing season; remove runners if the single-plant method is used.

Place any protection (cloches, polythene tunnels, etc.) in position early in February; attend to watering and pollination as necessary by spacing the cloches, removing the end covers or by lifting the polythene tunnels when pollinating insects are flying.

After the risk of frost has passed, provide some form of soil cover—straw, bituminised paper collars or polythene sheet—to prevent the berries becoming soiled before they ripen. This is essential for plants grown in the open.

Detach dessert fruits by nipping the stalks between the thumb and forefinger. Avoid touching the flesh, which bruises easily. For jam making, leave the calyx behind when pulling the fruits off. Remove and destroy damaged and diseased fruits as soon as they are noticed.

After harvesting is completed, cut off the leaves 4 in. above soil level and hoe off the remaining weeds.

Some varieties, such as 'Redgauntlet', sometimes give a second crop in the autumn. If possible, use cloches to encourage these late fruits to ripen.

Cultivation under glass. In late July and early August, plant pot-grown runners in 5 in. pots of John Innes potting compost No. 2, setting one plant at the side of each pot so that the fruits will hang clear of the rim.

Aim to get the plants well established, then allow the compost to dry out early in November and stand them outside. Bring the plants inside early in January and start them into growth again gradually, raising the temperature to 7–13°C (45–55°F) at night and giving more water as they respond with fresh growth. From about March, when the flowers open, until ripening of the fruits, raise the temperature to 24°C (75°F).

Hand-pollinate regularly with a camelhair brush, or the fruits will be imperfectly set and misshapen. Water carefully and give liquid feeds as the fruits swell. Thin the fruits to improve size. Forced plants are best discarded afterwards.

Cultivation in barrels. Barrels can be bought ready bored with 2 in. wide holes spaced 9 in. apart. Grow the plants in John Innes potting compost No. 3, or its equivalent, placing broken pots, bricks or stones on the base for drainage. Build up a central drainage core of the same material, retained by wire netting. Place a layer of turves, grass side down, on top of the drainage material, followed by the compost. Firm the compost as the barrel is filled and plant at the same time.

Discontinue the drainage core 6 in. below the top of the barrel; finish off at the top with compost and plant runners 9 in. apart on the surface. Water as necessary while the plants are growing; remove runners and feed before the start of the second season.

Propagation. Stocks are increased from runners which are produced freely by most varieties from June onwards (less freely by perpetual-fruiting varieties). Fasten the runners down into loose, cultivated soil, or into pots filled with John Innes potting compost No. 1.

Select plants for propagating purposes carefully, choosing healthy, disease-free specimens. Remove the flowers from these plants so that they will produce runners with increased vigour.

For alpine varieties such as 'Baron Solemacher', which do not form runners, sow seeds in autumn in boxes and place in a cold frame. Set the seedlings out in March or April. They will fruit from July to October of the following year.

Pests. BIRDS, SLUGS and STRAWBERRY BEETLES eat the ripening fruits.

APHIDS, EELWORMS and TARSONEMID MITES may infest plants, causing various leaf and flower distortions, and checking growth.

Strawberry 'Grandee'

Strawberry 'Sans Rivale'

GLASSHOUSE RED SPIDER MITES may be troublesome on protected crops.

Diseases. GREY MOULD rots the berries, which become covered with a brown-grey fluffy fungal growth.

LEAF SPOTS, due to various fungi, are often found on older leaves, or those of plants lacking in vigour. They show as small red or purple spots, which sometimes become grey or brown with red or purple margins.

PHYSIOLOGICAL DISORDERS, due to unsuitable soil conditions, show as large brown or yellow blotches on the leaves; waterlogging may cause plants to collapse. FROST DAMAGE causes the central portion of affected flowers to turn black; the petals remain white.

RED CORE, or Lanarkshire disease, infects the roots, turning them brown or black with a red core. Affected plants are stunted, bearing wilted leaves in late spring; fruiting is poor or non-existent. There is no effective cure, but the varieties 'Talisman', 'Cambridge Vigour' and 'Cambridge Rival' are resistant to the disease.

STRAWBERRY MILDEW causes the leaves to turn purple and curl upwards, exposing the undersides of the leaves, which have a grey appearance. Affected berries lose their shine.

STRAWBERRY VIRUS DISEASES cause a variety of symptoms, including the following:

YELLOW EDGE, in which the leaves show ill-defined yellow margins and the younger leaves are dwarfed; CRINKLE, which causes red or purple spots on the leaves, which become puckered; ARABIS MOSAIC VIRUS and other viruses, which cause distortion and mottling of the leaves. Another virus disease, which shows as flowers with green petals, prevents fruits from ripening and results in collapse of plants.

Strawberry tree: see Arbutus
Straw flower: see Helichrysum

Strelitzia reginae

Strelitzia

Musaceae

STRELITZIA REGINAE

A genus of five species of tender evergreen perennial plants requiring greenhouse cultivation. They have unique flower heads, shaped like a bird's head.

S. reginae (bird of paradise flower). S. Africa. Height 3–4 ft. This species forms a fan of large, ovate, mid-green, slightly glaucous, leathery leaves, borne on stalks about 18 in. long. The 6 in. long inflorescence is borne in April and May at the end of a stem about $3\frac{1}{2}$ ft long. It consists of a green, purple-flushed, boat-shaped, beaked bract, from which emerges a succession of long, keeled, orange and blue flowers; these stand erect to give a crest-like appearance.

Cultivation. Grow strelitzias in 8–12 in. pots of John Innes potting compost No. 3; the plants are more successfully grown in a greenhouse border. Maintain a temperature of 10°C (50°F) in winter, and keep the plants nearly dry. During spring and summer water freely, gradually decreasing the amount of water from September onwards. Light shading may be necessary during summer, but only sufficient to prevent scorching of the leaves. Ventilate the greenhouse freely when the temperature exceeds 18–21°C (64–70°F).

Pot on or repot every second year in March or after flowering; give a liquid feed at fortnightly intervals from May to September.

Propagation. Divide or detach single-rooted shoots at potting time or after flowering; pot up in the growing compost. The plants may also be raised from seeds sown in pans of seed compost in March or April at a temperature of 18–21°C (64–70°F). Prick off the seedlings, when large enough to handle, singly into 3 in. pots of John Innes potting compost No. 1; pot on into larger containers as necessary.

Pests. SCALE INSECTS of various species infest the leaves and make the plants sticky.

Diseases. A PHYSIOLOGICAL DISORDER causes brown blotches to develop on the leaves.

Streptocarpus

Cape primrose. *Gesneriaceae*

A genus of 100 species of evergreen, tufted or sub-shrubby tender plants, often with foxglove-like flowers. Some species are unique in having one leaf only throughout their lives. In Great Britain they need cool greenhouse cultivation.

STREPTOCARPUS DUNNII

S. dunnii. S. Africa. Height and spread of leaf up to 18 in. A species with only one large, downward-curving, hoary-green, wrinkled leaf, that is hairy and oblong-ovate. The rose or brick-red flowers, $1\frac{1}{2}$ in. long, are drooping and foxglove-like; they are borne in a rounded, branching, 9 in. long panicle. The flowering period is May and June.

S. holstii. E. Africa. Height and spread 18 in. An erect species with succulent branching stems having swollen joints. The opposite, deep green, ovate leaves are hairy with prominent veins on the undersurfaces. Blue-purple, violet-like flowers, $\frac{3}{4}$ in. across, with a white throat, are freely borne from June to September.

S. × hybridus. Garden origin. Height 9–12 in.; spread 9–15 in. This hybrid race is mainly derived from *S. rexii*. The tufted plants bear shortly strap-shaped, corrugated, hairy, mid-green leaves. Foxglove-like flowers, $1\frac{1}{2}$–$2\frac{1}{2}$ in. long, in shades of red, purple and white, are borne in small clusters from May to October.

Streptocarpus × hybridus
'Constant Nymph'

Named varieties include: 'Constant Nymph', satiny, blue-purple flowers with darker veins in the throat; 'Merton Blue', purple-blue with a white throat.

STREPTOCARPUS REXII

S. rexii. S. Africa. Height 9–12 in.; spread 9–15 in. A tufted species with a rosette of shortly strap-shaped, deep green, crinkled, hairy leaves. The blue or mauve foxglove-like flowers, 1½ in. long, are borne in May and June.

The species is represented in cultivation by the modern hybrids, which are frequently listed as *S.* × *hybridus*.

S. saxorum. E. Africa. Height 6–8 in.; spread up to 18 in. A spreading, semi-prostrate, sub-shrubby species with ovate, fleshy and hairy, dark to mid-green leaves. Pale mauve violet-like flowers, up to 1 in. across, are borne between April and October. This species grows well in a hanging basket.

S. wendlandii. S. Africa. Height 1½–2½ ft; spread 12–18 in. This is one of the most spectacular species in cultivation. It has a single, downward-curving, hairy leaf, deep green above and red-purple beneath. In May and June, 9–12 in. long rounded and branched panicles of violet-like blue-purple and white flowers arise from the base of the leaf.

Cultivation. Grow streptocarpus in 5–8 in. pots of John Innes potting compost No. 2 or a proprietary peat compost. From November to March provide a temperature of 10°C (50°F), and between April and October raise the temperature to 13°C (55°F). Water freely during the growing period and keep the plants just moist between November and March. Lightly shade the glass from April to September and ventilate the house freely during the hottest months. Give a weak liquid feed at 10–14 day intervals from May to September.

Pot on or repot tufted species annually in March. Single-leaf species are generally mono-carpic and should be discarded after flowering unless seeds are required.

Single-leaved plants should be stood on inverted pots to display the down-curving leaves and keep them free of the staging.

Periodically stake and tie bushy plants. *S. holstii* may need staking with cane supports; dead-head all plants after flowering unless seeds are required.

Propagation. Sow seeds in pots or pans of John Innes seed compost, at a temperature of 18°C (64°F). Seeds sown in January or February produce autumn-flowering plants; those sown in March or April do not flower until the summer of the following year.

When the seedlings are large enough to handle, prick them out into boxes and later singly into 3–3½ in. pots containing the growing compost; pot on as necessary.

Tufted species and varieties may be divided and replanted when repotting in March. Alternatively, between May and July propagate by small leaves or 3 in. long sections of large leaves. Insert in equal parts (by volume) peat and sand in a propagating case at a temperature of 18°C (64°F). When small plants have developed from the leaf sections, pot singly into 3 in. pots of the growing compost and pot on as necessary.

Increase *S. saxorum* by 3 in. long stem cuttings taken in April or May, and treat as advised for leaf cuttings.

Pruning. Trim sub-shrubby species lightly in February or March. Old straggly plants are best discarded and replaced by fresh stock.

Pests. APHIDS may infest young growths and make plants sticky.

Diseases. Generally trouble-free.

Streptosolen

Solanaceae

STREPTOSOLEN JAMESONII

A monotypic genus of one tender evergreen flowering shrub with showy masses of orange flowers. It requires cool greenhouse conditions.

S. jamesonii. Colombia. Height and spread 4–6 ft. A straggling shrub, best treated as a wall shrub. The ovate, soft mid-green leaves are up to 2 in. long. Terminal 4–8 in. long panicles of bright orange flowers are produced from May to July; the individual flowers are tubular with widely expanded mouths, and about ¾ in. wide.

Cultivation. Grow streptosolens in 5–7 in. pots or small tubs of John Innes potting compost No. 3, or plant them directly in a greenhouse border and tie the stems to supports or against the wall of a lean-to house. A winter temperature of 7°C (45°F), or slightly lower, is required; during summer, provide cool, airy conditions.

Give water sparingly in winter, freely during summer. The plants need full light in winter and only light shading in summer. Pot-grown plants can be stood outside in a sheltered site from June until the end of August.

Pot on annually in March or April and give a dilute liquid feed at fortnightly intervals from April to September.

Propagation. Take cuttings, 3 in. long, of lateral non-flowering shoots in March or April; insert the cuttings in equal parts (by volume) peat and sand in a propagating case with a temperature of 16–18°C (61–64°F). When rooted, pot the cuttings in 3 in. pots of John Innes potting compost No. 1 and pot on as necessary. Soon after the first potting, pinch out the growing tips of the young plants to promote bushy growth. Insert a single cane for support at the first stage; three canes will usually be required for additional support as the plants grow.

Streptocarpus × *hybridus* 'Merton Blue'

Streptocarpus saxorum

Streptosolen jamesonii

Stuartia pseudo-camellia
(winter bark)

Stuartia pseudo-camellia koreana

Stuartia sinensis (bark)

Stuartia sinensis (fruits)

Pruning. The plants are liable to grow leggy. Cut back old growths by one-third as soon as flowering is over. Alternatively, to provide cuttings for propagation, prune the plants back to 6 in. in February.

Pests. Generally trouble-free.

Diseases. TOMATO SPOTTED WILT VIRUS produces yellow rings or concentric circles on the leaves; some browning of the tissue may also occur.

String-of-beads: see *Senecio rowleyanus*

Struthiopteris germanica: see *Matteuccia struthiopteris*

Stuartia

syn. **Stewartia**. *Theaceae*

A genus of ten species of hardy deciduous flowering shrubs and small trees with single camellia-like blooms and colourful autumn foliage. The peeling bark is attractive in winter as are the glossy red seed capsules.

S. ovata, syn. *S. pentagyna*. S. United States. Height 8–15 ft; spread 6–10 ft. The mid-green ovate leaves of this slow-growing tree are downy beneath; they turn yellow in October. The cream-white saucer-shaped flowers, which open in July and August, are up to 4 in. wide with a central cluster of golden stamens.

S. pentagyna: see *S. ovata*

STUARTIA PSEUDO-CAMELLIA

S. pseudo-camellia. Japan. Height 15–20 ft; spread 10–15 ft. The mid-green ovate leaves turn yellow and red from October onwards. The cup-shaped single white flowers, which open in July and August, are 2 in. wide and have bright yellow anthers. *S. p-c. koreana* differs mainly in having broadly elliptic leaves, and flowers which open out flat.

S. sinensis. China. Height 15–20 ft; spread 10–15 ft. The bright green ovate leaves turn crimson in September and October. White, fragrant, saucer-shaped flowers, up to 2 in. wide, open in July and August.

Cultivation. These shrubs require a neutral to acid soil. Plant in March or April in well-drained peaty soil in partial shade. Leave the plants to grow undisturbed.

Propagation. Sow seeds in October in John Innes seed compost in a cold frame or greenhouse. Prick off the seedlings into 3 in. pots of John Innes potting compost No. 1 without lime, and set them out in a nursery bed the following October; grow on for at least three to five years before planting them out in permanent positions.

Take 3–4 in. cuttings of half-ripe lateral shoots with a heel in July or August and insert them in equal parts (by volume) peat and sand in a cold frame. Pot up the cuttings the following April or May and plant out in a nursery bed the following October. Thereafter, treat as seedlings.

Layers pegged down in September or October will not be ready for severing and planting out for at least two years.

Pruning. None required.

Pests and diseases. Generally trouble-free.

Sugar pea: see Pea, garden

Sumach: see Rhus

Sumach, smooth: see *Rhus glabra*

Sumach, stag's horn: see *Rhus typhina*

Sunflower: see *Helianthus annuus*

Sun plant: see *Portulaca grandiflora*

Swede

Brassica rutabaga. Cruciferae

A hardy biennial, grown as an annual winter vegetable for its large, swollen, yellow-fleshed roots. It is similar to the long-rooted turnip, but the roots, which have a milder flavour, take longer to mature and store better through winter and spring.

VARIETIES

Two selections, Purple Top and Bronze Top, are available. 'Western Perfection' is an outstanding Purple Top variety, specially selected to produce an almost neckless root even under exceptionally wet conditions. Bronze Top varieties are recommended for late crops because of their hard roots which store particularly well; 'Best of All' is a popular choice.

Cultivation. Swedes thrive in all fertile soils, except an acid one. This should be given a top dressing of carbonate of lime at 6 oz. per sq. yd. Grow swedes in ground that was well manured for a previous crop, never in freshly manured ground where the roots may fork and have an earthy flavour. Dig the bed over thoroughly before sowing and lightly rake in 3 oz. of fish manure per sq. yd.

Sow seeds in mid-May in the north, a month later in the south. Sow thinly in 1 in. deep drills, set 18 in. apart; thin the plants as they grow, spacing them finally at intervals of 12 in.

Harvesting and storing. Lift the roots as required from autumn until spring. Swedes may be left in the ground during winter, but it is advisable to lift and store a few in a clamp for use when the ground is frozen.

Pests. FLEA BEETLES, which chiefly occur in dry weather, eat small round holes in the leaves of seedlings and young plants.

Diseases. Grey or brown discoloured patches on the lower parts of the roots are caused by BORON DEFICIENCY.

CLUB ROOT causes the feeding roots to become swollen and distorted.

DAMPING-OFF results in the collapse of seedlings at soil level.

DOWNY MILDEW shows on seedlings as yellow blotches with mealy-white areas on the under-surfaces of leaves.

SOFT ROT, due to bacteria, occurs in store on damaged roots or where storage conditions are too damp. Affected roots are rapidly destroyed by a soft, watery rot.

SPLITTING of roots lengthwise is due to an irregular supply of moisture in the soil.

VIOLET ROOT ROT shows as a violet or purple web of threads over the lower part of the roots.

---

sweetbriar: see *Rosa rubiginosa*

Sweet corn
Zea mays. Gramineae

SWEET CORN

A half-hardy annual grass with stems up to 8 ft or more, bearing mid-green strap-shaped leaves. The plant, which is commonly known as maize, sweet corn, corn-on-the-cob or Indian corn, is grown for its edible grains arranged in large upright cobs, as well as for its ornamental foliage.

The female flowers, which are enclosed in a in. cigar-shaped sheath of closely overlapping leafy bracts, appear from the lower leaf axils in June and July. A silky tassel of thread-like styles emerges from the top end when the plants are ready for pollination.

The male flowers, borne on the same plant, appear in a loose plume-shaped panicle at the top of the stem. Pollen falls on to the female flowers by gravity or is carried by the wind.

CULINARY VARIETIES

Until recently, sweet corn was considered an unreliable crop in Great Britain. Suitable strains (height 4–5 ft) have now been developed, particularly by the John Innes Institute, and by various seed firms: 'Earliking' and 'John Innes Hybrid', syn. 'Canada Cross', are vigorous compact early-maturing growers with well-flavoured, freely produced cobs. 'Golden Bantam' is the hardiest variety, and can be planted out early; it gives a good crop of medium-sized rich and sweet cobs. 'Kelvedon Glory' is similar to 'Golden Bantam' and gives good cobs even in poor summers.

ORNAMENTAL VARIETIES

Several varieties have variegated foliage or coloured cobs; they may be used in summer bedding schemes as dot plants or to fill in gaps in herbaceous and mixed borders. They have the same cultural requirements as culinary varieties and should be grown in a sunny position protected from strong winds.

'Gracillima Variegata' (height 3 ft) is a slender, small-growing form with narrow white-striped leaves; 'Japonica' (height 4–5 ft) is shorter than the type species, with white-striped leaves; 'Quadricolor', syn. 'Gigantea Quadricolor', is a robust form with leaves variegated with white, pale yellow and pink.

The green-leaved variety 'Rainbow' is grown for its coloured cobs; these are composed of yellow, red, orange and blue-purple seeds in an irregularly patterned cob. The ripe, dried cobs can be used for winter decoration.

Cultivation. Sow seeds under glass in April for planting out in late May. Sow the seeds singly ½ in. deep in 3 in. pots of John Innes potting compost No. 1, at a temperature of 16–18°C (61–64°F). When the seedlings are 5–6 in. high, harden them off in a cold frame and plant out 18 in. apart in rows 18 in. apart. They are best planted in a number of short rows in a rectangular block to ensure good pollination.

Alternatively, sow seeds in the open in late May. Place the seeds in groups of three, ½ in. deep and 18 in. apart, later removing two plants from each group to leave the strongest. If cloches are available, seeds may be sown in early May.

An open sunny site is essential, and a soil that has been enriched with liberal amounts of well-rotted manure the previous autumn. Top-dress the bed with a general-purpose fertiliser at 2 oz. per sq. yd just before sowing or transplanting.

Hoe the ground regularly to keep down weeds, and water the plants copiously. The cobs are ready for picking about a month after the silky flower tassels appear, usually just as these begin to turn brown. Test the cobs for ripeness by pulling back the husks and pressing the seeds gently; if the cob is ready the milky content of the seed will squirt out. Pick and use the cobs as soon as they are ripe; if left too long on the plant the seeds become hard and starchy, and if stored after picking they lose their flavour and become tough. Freshly picked cobs may be deep-frozen.

Exhibition. Cobs selected for show purposes should be of uniform colour, cylindrical and well-set right up to the tip; the rows of seeds should be straight and undamaged.

Pests. BIRDS may damage the tips of cobs.

Diseases. Generally trouble-free.

Sweet galingale: see *Cyperus longus*
Sweet pea: see *Lathyrus odoratus*
Sweet pepper bush: see Clethra
Sweet rocket: see *Hesperis matronalis*
Sweet william: see *Dianthus barbatus*
Sword, flaming: see *Vriesea splendens*
Syagrus: see Cocos
Syagrus weddelliana: see *Cocos weddelliana*
Sycamore: see *Acer pseudoplatanus*

Symphoricarpos
Snowberry. *Caprifoliaceae*

SYMPHORICARPOS ALBUS

A genus of 18 species of hardy deciduous berry-bearing shrubs which are suitable for planting in shade. The generic name is sometimes spelt *Symphoricarpus*. These suckering shrubs bear large white or pink berries which are useful for autumn and winter floral arrangements. They may all be used for low hedging, 'White Hedger' being particularly suitable for this purpose.

Swede 'Best of All'

Sweet corn 'Kelvedon Glory'

Symphoricarpos albus 'Laevigatus' (fruits)

S. albus, syn. *S. racemosus*. N. America. Height 5–7 ft; spread 7–8 ft. The broadly ovate leaves are pale to mid-green with a grey cast. The small, pink, urn-shaped flowers appear from July to September in pendent 1 in. long clusters. They are followed by glistening white globose berries, up to $\frac{1}{2}$ in. in diameter, which persist from October to February. 'Laevigatus' has larger, pure white berries; 'White Hedger' has small white berries in erect trusses.

S. orbiculatus (coral berry or Indian currant). E. United States. Height 5–6 ft; spread 8–10 ft. A species with mid-green ovate to nearly round leaves. The pink flowers, which open from July to September, are urn-shaped and borne in pendent clusters $1\frac{1}{2}$ in. long. They are followed in October by pink or purple berries in clusters which persist until February.

S. racemosus: see *S. albus*

Cultivation. Plant between October and March in any ordinary, well-drained garden soil in sun or shade. For a hedge of 'White Hedger', set the young plants 15–18 in. apart, cutting them back to within 12 in. of ground level after planting. When subsequent growths reach 6 in., pinch out the growing points or shear off the tips to induce branch formation.

Propagation. Remove rooted suckers between October and February and either replant direct in permanent positions or, if they are small, set them out in a nursery bed for a year before planting out in final positions.

Take 8–10 in. hardwood cuttings between October and February and insert them in a nursery bed in the open. Grow on for a year before planting them out in their permanent positions between October and March.

Pruning. Thin out overgrown specimens and remove unwanted suckers occasionally between October and February. Trim established hedges to shape two or three times during summer.

Pests. Generally trouble-free.

Diseases. Large round brown spots on the leaves are caused by LEAF SPOT. The same fungus may cause die-back of shoots.

Symplocos paniculata (fruits)

Symphytum
Comfrey. *Boraginaceae*

A genus of 25 species of herbaceous perennial plants with fleshy roots. They are suitable for moist borders in sun or shade, or at the edges of streams and pools. The following species have lanceolate, rough, hairy, mid-green leaves, and carry bell-shaped or tubular, $\frac{1}{2}$–1 in. long flowers in branching cymose panicles.

S. caucasicum. Caucasus. Height up to 24 in.; planting distance 18 in. This species is suitable for a wild garden, where it will flourish in shady conditions. The drooping bell-shaped flowers are pink on opening, later changing to bright blue. They are freely produced from April to June.

S. grandiflorum. Caucasus. Height 8 in.; planting distance 15 in. A rapidly spreading species which affords good ground cover under trees and shrubs. Drooping, white, tubular flowers, which are short-lived, are produced in short terminal sprays during April and May.

S. orientale. Turkey. Height 24 in.; planting distance 15 in. A short-lived species which seeds itself freely. Erect, slightly branching flower stems, rising from a compact leafy rootstock, carry tubular white flowers in May and June.

S. rubrum. Armenia. Height 15 in.; planting distance 18 in. The dark green leaves are less coarse than those of other species. Sprays of deep red, tubular flowers are borne for several weeks from May to August.

SYMPHYTUM × UPLANDICUM

S. × uplandicum. E. Europe. Height and spread 3 ft or more. This hybrid was originally introduced as a fodder plant from Russia; it is naturalised in many parts of Britain. It is a robust, hairy plant with large, mid-green, lanceolate to ovate leaves on the winged stems. The $\frac{3}{4}$–1 in. long, tubular flowers are in various shades of blue-purple; they are borne in forked cymes in the upper leaf axils from June to August.

Cultivation. Plant in October and November or in March and April in ordinary garden soil, though *S. rubrum* does best in rich soil. Set the plants in a sunny or shaded position, *S. rubrum* preferably in moist semi-shade.

S. caucasicum occasionally requires staking. After flowering, cut back flower stems of all species to basal growth.

Propagation. Divide and replant the fleshy roots in October or March.

Pests and diseases. Generally trouble-free.

Symplocos
Symplocaceae

SYMPLOCOS PANICULATA

A genus of 350 species of hardy and tender trees and shrubs, several of which are attractive in flower or fruit. Only the following deciduous species is in general cultivation.

S. crataegoides: see *S. paniculata*

S. paniculata, syn. *S. crataegoides*. China, Japan, Himalayas. Height 6–8 ft; spread 4–6 ft. A hardy species with ovate, mid-green and slightly hairy leaves. Small, starry, fragrant white flowers appear in May in terminal clusters up to $2\frac{1}{2}$ in. long; globular bright blue berries, $\frac{1}{4}$ in. across are produced from September to November.

Cultivation. Plant between October and March in lime-free soil in a reasonably sheltered position. These shrubs do best in full sun.

ropagation. In July or August, take 3–4 in.
uttings of half-ripe lateral shoots with a heel and
nsert them in sandy soil in a cold frame. Set the
poted cuttings out in a nursery bed the following
pril, and grow on for two or three years before
lanting them out in permanent positions.
runing. None required.
ests and diseases. Generally trouble-free.

Syringa
Lilac. *Oleaceae*

. genus of 30 species of hardy, deciduous shrubs
nd small trees, popular for their late-spring
owers, which are often fragrant. All the species,
arieties and hybrids described have mid-green
:aves. They make handsome specimen shrubs,
r may be grown in shrub borders; bushy species
r varieties are recommended for planting as
iformal hedges or screens.

Syringas thrive in town gardens. Named
arieties of *S. vulgaris* produce numerous suckers
nless they are grafted on to stocks of *Ligustrum
valifolium* (privet).

SYRINGA VULGARIS

. × *chinensis* (Rouen lilac). Of garden origin.
Height 8–10 ft; spread 6 ft. This cross between
. *persica* and *S. vulgaris* is a dense, bushy shrub.
he ovate leaves taper to a point. Fragrant purple
owers are borne in broad, erect, pyramidal
anicles, 6–8 in. long, during May.

. × 'Fountain' resembles the Canadian hybrid
. × *prestoniae* in habit. It produces pale pink
owers in 6–9 in. long pyramidal panicles during
Aay and June.

. *josikaea* (Hungarian lilac). Hungary. Height
0 ft; spread 6–7 ft. A vigorous shrub with glossy
vate leaves. Deep violet flowers are borne in
rect pyramidal panicles, 4–8 in. long; they open
uring June.

. *microphylla*. China. Height and spread 4–5 ft.
\ slender-branched spreading shrub, ideal for
. large rock garden. The broadly ovate leaves are
owny. Fragrant lilac-coloured flowers appear in
void, erect panicles, 3–4 in. long, during June
nd again in September. 'Superba' (6–8 ft high)
roduces rose-pink flowers from May to October.

. *palibiniana*. Korea. Height and spread 5 ft. A
lense, compact, free-flowering shrub suitable for
. large rock garden. The leaves are broadly ovate.
avender-purple flowers appear in round,
unched panicles, 1–2 in. long, in mid-May.

. *persica* (Persian lilac). Iran to China. Height
–8 ft; spread 6–7 ft. A bushy, rounded shrub
vith lanceolate leaves that are often lobed.
'ragrant lilac-coloured flowers are borne in
nid-May in broad, erect, pyramidal panicles, 3–4
n. long. The variety 'Alba' has white flowers
nd more slender branches.

Syringa vulgaris 'Firmament'

S. reflexa. China. Height 10–12 ft; spread 8 ft.
This is a shrub of stiff habit with leaves that are
ovate-lanceolate and pointed. Fragrant, deep pink
flowers appear in June in drooping, cylindrical
panicles, 6–8 in. long.

S. sweginzowii. China. Height 10–12 ft; spread
8–10 ft. A graceful, open shrub with ovate to
lanceolate leaves. Fragrant, flesh-pink flowers are
produced in loose panicles, 6–8 in. long, during
May and June.

S. vulgaris (common lilac). E. Europe. Height
8–12 ft; spread 5–10 ft. A large, upright shrub or
small tree. The leaves are heart-shaped or ovate.
Fragrant, lilac-coloured flowers are borne in erect
pyramidal panicles, 6–10 in. long, during May
and June. There are single, double and semi-
double garden varieties. Among the best single-
flowered varieties are:

'Blue Hyacinth'. Fragrant flowers, mauve in
bud, opening to lavender-blue, are spaced out on
the panicles as in a single hyacinth. Open habit.
Early May.

'Candeur'. Large, scented flowers, cream in
bud, opening to white. Compact habit. Mid-May.

'Congo'. Scented flowers, dark red in bud
opening to rich pink. Compact habit. Free-
flowering. Mid-May.

'Esther Staley'. Fragrant flowers, red in bud,
opening to a pure pink without the usual mauve
tinge. Slender stems, erect habit and free-
flowering. Mid-May.

'Firmament'. Scented flowers, mauve-pink in
bud, opening to light lavender-blue. Compact
habit. Free-flowering. Early May.

'Marechal Foch'. Slightly scented, carmine-
pink flowers. Vigorous; open habit. Mid-May.

'Massena'. Fragrant, deep purple flowers.
Broad, spreading habit. Late May.

'Maud Notcutt'. The largest single, white-
flowered variety, with panicles borne well above
the foliage. Vigorous; erect habit. Mid-May.

Syringa palibiniana

Syringa vulgaris 'Candeur'

Syringa vulgaris 'Souvenir de Louis Späth'

Syringa vulgaris 'Vestale'

Syringa × *josiflexa* 'Bellicent'

Syringa × *prestoniae* 'Isabella'

'Primrose'. Slightly scented, cream-yellow flowers. Erect habit. Free-flowering. May.

'Souvenir de Louis Späth'. Scented, wine-red flowers. Vigorous; spreading habit. May.

'Vestale'. Fragrant, pure white flowers in long, loose panicles. Compact habit. Mid-May.

Syringa vulgaris 'Katherine Havemeyer'

Semi-double and double varieties include: 'Katherine Havemeyer' with double, strongly scented, purple-lavender flowers. Broad, open habit. Mid-May.

'Madame Antoine Buchner'. Semi-double, scented flowers, rose-pink in bud, opening to rose-mauve. Open habit. Mid-May.

'Michael Buchner'. Double, sweetly scented lavender flowers. Broad, open habit. Mid-May.

'Mrs Edward Harding'. Semi-double, scented red flowers. Open habit. One of the most outstanding reds. Late May.

'Paul Thirion'. Strongly scented flowers, carmine in bud, opening to rose-red. Vigorous; compact habit. Late May and early June.

'Souvenir de Alice Harding'. Double, heavily scented, alabaster-white flowers. Vigorous; erect habit. Late May and early June.

CANADIAN HYBRIDS These are a race of hardy, vigorous, fragrant, disease-free shrubs raised by Miss Isabella Preston of Ottawa.

S. × *josiflexa* 'Bellicent' is an outstanding form. Height 12–15 ft; spread 12 ft. A vigorous shrub with broadly ovate and pointed leaves. Rose-pink flowers are borne in May and June in semi-erect, slender, pyramidal panicles, 8–10 in. long.

S. × *prestoniae*. Height and spread up to 10 ft. The branches of this spreading shrub curve outwards, particularly when it is in bloom. It has ovate mid-green leaves and large, generally loose plume-like panicles of flowers which vary from pink to red-purple. Outstanding forms include:

'Elinor'. The flowers, dark purple-red in bud opening to pale lilac, are borne in semi-erect, slender, pyramidal panicles, 6–8 in. long, in May and June.

'Ethel M. Webster'. This is probably an S. × *prestoniae* type, but its parentage is in some doubt. It has panicles, 6–9 in. long, of delicate pink flowers in May and June.

'Isabella'. The purple-pink flowers are borne in semi-erect, slender, pyramidal panicles, 12 in. long, during May and June.

'Virgilia'. This shrub bears 9 in. long loose panicles of lilac-purple flowers in May and June.

Cultivation. Plant between October and November in sun or partial shade. These shrubs thrive in any fertile garden soil and need no attention once they are well rooted. However, they take one or two years to establish themselves after transplanting, and it is advisable to remove most of the flowers which appear during the first season.

For hedges and screens, set young plants at intervals of 6–10 ft depending on variety. No pinching or pruning is required.

Propagation. All the plants described can be raised from 3–4 in. long heel cuttings of half-ripe shoots. In the case of *S. vulgaris* varieties it is possible to obtain more uniform and vigorous plants by budding. Insert the heel cuttings in equal parts (by volume) peat and sand during July or August, either with mist propagation or in a propagating frame with bottom heat of 16°C (61°F). Soft-tip cuttings of the Canadian hybrids taken in May or June also root readily under the same conditions.

Pot all rooted cuttings individually into 4 in. pots of John Innes potting compost No. 2 the first year and grow on in a cold frame; plant them out in a nursery bed the following March. Grow on for two years or more before transplanting to flowering positions.

Bud *S. vulgaris* varieties in July on established stocks of *S. vulgaris* or common privet. Privet does not produce the vigorous spreading suckers which are the drawback of *S. vulgaris* stocks.

Pruning. Remove faded flowers and, from October onwards, thin out crossing and weak branches. Rejuvenate overgrown bushes by cutting them down during winter to 2–3 ft above ground level. Flowers will appear on the new growths after two or three years.

Remove all suckers as close as possible to the roots or main stem, from July onwards.

Pests. Tunnels in the leaf tissues may be eaten through by CATERPILLARS of LILAC LEAF MINER which produce disfiguring blotch mines. SCALE INSECTS, particularly willow scale, sometimes infest stems and, in severe infestations, these look as if they have been whitewashed.

Diseases. Due to the incompatibility of stock and scion, DIE-BACK of lilacs grafted on to privet rootstocks can occur. In extreme cases the whole top of the plant may become detached from the rootstock at the graft union.

FROST DAMAGE causes death of flowers and die-back of shoots. Affected tissues are frequently attacked by GREY MOULD, which shows as a grey-brown fungal growth. HONEY FUNGUS can kill plants.

LILAC BLIGHT causes small angular brown spots on the leaves, and young shoots blacken and wither away.

PHYSIOLOGICAL DISORDERS, due to adverse soil conditions, show as discoloration of foliage, premature leaf-fall, and die-back. The most common trouble occurs in mid-summer, when the leaves become brittle and curved; they show yellowing followed by brown blotching. This is associated with MAGNESIUM DEFFICIENCY.

SILVER LEAF can cause die-back of branches which then bear leaves with a silvery tinge.

Tacsonia mollissima : see *Passiflora mollissima*

Tagetes

Marigold. *Compositae*

TAGETES PATULA

A genus of 50 species of annual and perennial herbaceous plants. Several species and numerous garden varieties are widely grown in borders and bedding-out schemes. Both single and double-flowered forms are available. Single flowers are daisy-shaped, doubles somewhat carnation-like. They are excellent as cut flowers and last well in water. Bruised foliage emits a pungent smell.

T. erecta (African marigold). Mexico. Height 2–3 ft; planting distance 12–18 in. This half-hardy annual is a vigorous, erect, well-branched plant. It is excellent for mixed borders, for formal bedding and to grow for cutting. The deeply cut leaves are a glossy dark green and strongly scented. Lemon-yellow, broad-petalled, daisy-like flowers, 2 in. across, are produced from July to the first frosts.

There are numerous garden varieties. The introduction of the F_1 hybrids has greatly improved uniformity, vigour and flower size. Recommended tall varieties include the Climax series, F_1, $2\frac{1}{2}$ ft, with fully double, globular flowers 5 in. across, in mixed and in separate colours. 'Yellow Climax' is the best exhibition variety of the series; the other colours are golden-yellow, primrose and orange.

The Gold Coin series, F_1, 24 in., bear flowers up to 6 in. across on well-branched, compact plants. One of the best forms is 'Double Eagle', with frilled and ruffled golden-orange flowers.

The early and free-flowering 'Crackerjack', $2\frac{1}{2}$ ft, is one of the best general-purpose mixtures.

Recommended dwarf forms are: 'First Lady', F_1, 15 in., a neat and compact plant bearing a profusion of clear primrose-yellow flowers up to $3\frac{1}{2}$ in. across; and 'Spun Gold', 12 in., an early chrysanthemum-flowered type, with flowers 3 in. across.

T. lucida. Mexico. Height 18 in.; planting distance 12 in. A half-hardy perennial of bushy habit, usually grown as a half-hardy annual. The dark green leaves are smooth, lanceolate and toothed. Clusters of fragrant golden or orange-yellow flowers, $\frac{1}{2}$ in. across, open in August.

T. patula (French marigold). Mexico. Height and planting distance 12 in. This half-hardy annual, of compact and bushy habit, has dark green deeply cut and divided leaves. Brown-crimson or yellow single flowers, $1\frac{1}{2}$–2 in. across, are carried from June to the first frosts.

The many garden varieties listed include single and double forms and a range of compact plants. The following are recommended:

'Butterscotch', 8–10 in. high, compact, bearing single, mahogany flowers with golden-crested centres; 'Harmony', 9 in., single flowers with a central golden disc and collar of mahogany; 'Monarch Mixed', 9 in., compact, with double, ball-shaped flowers ranging from yellow to deep mahogany; 'Naughty Marietta', 12 in., single, rich golden-yellow flowers with a maroon blotch; Petite, 6 in., a strain containing a number of dwarf varieties, both single and double, in the full colour range; 'Spanish Brocade', 12 in., an early and free-flowering variety with double blooms, $2\frac{1}{2}$ in. across, in mahogany and gold; and 'Sunbeam' 6–9 in., single yellow flowers with crested centres.

T. signata : see *T. tenuifolia*

T. tenuifolia, syn. *T. signata.* Mexico. Height 24 in.; planting distance 12 in. A half-hardy annual with slender growths and finely divided, light green and sweet-smelling leaves. The yellow flowers, 1 in. across, open from July to September.

The varieties cultivated have arisen from *T. t. pumila,* a dwarf compact form. The two most commonly listed are 'Lemon Gem', 9 in., a clear lemon-yellow; and 'Golden Gem', 8 in., bright orange with a deep orange mark at the base of each ray floret.

Cultivation. These plants will grow in any well-cultivated site, even in poor, rather dry soils, but a moderately rich soil is ideal. Choose an open, sunny site. Dead-heading is not essential, but improves growth and flower size. The F_1 hybrids of *T. erecta* will flower earlier and for a longer period if restricted to eight hours of light per day for 30 days during the seedling stage.

Propagation. Sow the seeds under glass in March or April, just covering them with compost, at a temperature of 18°C (64°F). The seeds germinate rapidly; as soon as the seedlings are large enough to handle, prick them out into boxes and harden off in a cold frame. Plant out in late May.

Pests. Generally trouble-free.

Diseases. Plants may collapse due to FOOT ROT.

GREY MOULD may cause rotting of flower heads in wet weather, when they become covered with a grey velvety fungal growth.

Tamarisk : see Tamarix

Tamarix

Tamarisk. *Tamaricaceae*

A genus of 90 species of hardy deciduous flowering shrubs. These form useful windbreaks and informal hedges, particularly in coastal areas. They are not lime-tolerant.

Tagetes erecta 'First Lady'

Tagetes erecta 'Spun Gold'

Tagetes patula 'Butterscotch'

Tagetes patula 'Spanish Brocade'

T. hispida aestivalis: see *T. pentandra*

T. pentandra, syn. *T. hispida aestivalis*. S.E. Europe. Height and spread 12–15 ft. The overlapping awl-shaped leaves are pale to mid-green, sometimes with a grey glaucous cast. The 2–3 in. long feathery heads of tiny rose-pink flowers are borne on slender branches in August. 'Rubra' has deep rose-red flowers. The species and its variety can be grown as a hedge.

TAMARIX PENTANDRA

T. tetrandra. Mediterranean region, Caucasus. Height and spread 10–15 ft. The pale to mid-green leaves are awl-shaped. In May, bright pink flowers are borne freely in 1–2 in. long racemes on the previous year's growths.

Cultivation. Plant in any ordinary, well-drained garden soil in a sunny open position between October and March.

For a windbreak of *T. pentandra*, set the young plants 24 in. apart and cut back all branches to within 12 in. of ground level. Tip the resultant shoots when they are 6 in. long. Prune back the current season's growth of established wind-breaks and informal hedges annually to within 6 in. of the base, between October and February.

Propagation. Take 9–12 in. hardwood cuttings in October and insert them in sandy soil in an open nursery bed. Grow on for one year before planting them out in permanent positions.

Pruning. To keep the plants bushy, prune *T. pentandra* between October and February, *T. tetrandra* after flowering. In both cases remove from half to two-thirds of the previous season's growths.

Pests and diseases. Generally trouble-free.

Tanacetum
Compositae

TANACETUM HARADJANII

A genus of between 50 and 60 species of hardy perennial herbaceous plants. The one described, formerly included in *Chrysanthemum*, is a good rock garden or alpine-house plant.

T. corymbosum: see *Chrysanthemum corymbosum*

T. densum 'Amani': see *T. haradjanii*

T. haradjanii, syns. *T. densum* 'Amani', *Chrysanthemum haradjanii*. Anatolia. Height 6–8 in.; spread 12–15 in. The silver leaves are broadly lanceolate and deeply dissected, like the filigree foliage of carrot leaves. The groundsel-like

yellow flowers are only ⅛ in. across, but they are borne in dense clusters in August.

Cultivation. Tanacetums are completely hardy when grown in a gritty soil in full sun. Plant in March. Remove dead flower stems. In the alpine house, grow tanacetums in 6–8 in. pans of John Innes potting compost No. 1 and repot them in March every second or third year.

Propagation. Divide in March and replant direct in final positions.

Pests. Plants may be infested by APHIDS.

Diseases. Generally trouble-free.

Tangerine: see *Citrus reticulata*

Tarragon
Artemisia dracunculus. Compositae

TARRAGON

A hardy perennial plant also known as French tarragon. The leaves of this herb are used for flavouring.

Height 18–24 in.; planting distance 12–15 in. S. Europe. This strongly aromatic bushy plant has linear, mid to slightly grey-green leaves. In August it bears loose panicles of tiny green-white globular flowers which, in Great Britain, rarely open fully and do not produce viable seeds.

Use the leaves fresh or dried as *fines herbes*, in omelettes, *bouquet garni, sauce tartare*, and to flavour salads, vegetables, meat and fish. They have a strong, rather sweet taste somewhat reminiscent of mint. The fresh leaves are also used to make tarragon vinegar.

Cultivation. Plant in October or March in a sunny but sheltered position. Light, sharply drained soil is essential.

Established plants will grow for several years with little or no attention, but the flavour of the leaves generally deteriorates after two or three seasons. Tarragon may be grown as annuals and then require only a 12 in. spacing either way.

Encourage leaf growth by pinching out flowering stems as soon as they appear. To ensure a winter supply of fresh leaves, which have a better flavour than dried or frozen ones, lift a few plants in September; grow on in a cold frame.

Propagation. The rhizomes spread for a good distance round the plants. Sever these in March or April and replant 2–3 in. deep and 12 in. apart.

Alternatively, take 2–3 in. basal cuttings in April, insert them in sandy soil in a closed propagating frame at a temperature of 13–15°C (55–59°F). Pot the rooted cuttings in John Innes potting compost No. 1, grow them on for a few weeks in a cold frame, and then plant outdoors.

Harvesting and storing. Pick fresh leaves from mid-June to the end of September. Sprigs can be dried or deep-frozen. See entry under HERBS.

Pests and diseases. Generally trouble-free.

Tamarix tetrandra

Tanacetum haradjanii

Tarragon

Taxodium

Swamp or bald cypress. *Taxodiaceae*

TAXODIUM DISTICHUM

A genus of three species of deciduous coniferous trees. Only one species is in general cultivation in Great Britain; although hardy it grows best in sheltered southern areas with wet or permanently moist soil.

See also CONIFERS.

T. distichum. New Jersey to Florida and Texas. Height 35 ft; spread 15 ft. A long-lived hardy species of moderately slow growth and suitable as a specimen tree in large gardens or parks. The crown varies from tall-columnar to broadly conic and domed, and the branches are orange-brown and scaly with grey-green young shoots. The fibrous bark is pale red-brown, closely ridged with shallow, smooth fissures.

The linear leaves are bright yellow-green above with two grey lines beneath and are carried in two flattened ranks. The leaves and the secondary branchlets that bear them are shed in autumn. The foliage first turns fox-red and russet. Male and female flowers are borne together; in winter, the males are noticeable in prominent, 3–6 in. long, purple catkins, carried in groups of three at the tips of the shoots on trees over 30 ft high. The round green cones, 1 in. across, which ripen to mid-brown, are rarely seen.

Cultivation. These conifers thrive in fertile moist soil, but also grow well on poor gravel if moisture is always present round the roots. Choose a sheltered site in sun or partial shade; plant in April, using seedlings 2–3 ft high. No staking is needed. Plants less than 3 ft high require winter protection with bracken in frost-prone areas.

Propagation. Sow seeds in March or April in pans or boxes of John Innes seed compost in a cold frame. When the seedlings are 2–3 in. high, line out in nursery rows outdoors and grow on for two or three years. Plant out in permanent positions in April.

Pruning. None required except to reduce forked specimens to a single leading shoot as soon as forking occurs.

Pests and diseases. Generally trouble-free.

Taxus

Yew. *Taxaceae*

A genus of eight species of evergreen conifers occurring in Europe, Asia Minor, E. Asia and N. America. They are usually bushy or multi-stemmed trees, long-lived and sometimes of considerable girth. Male and female flowers are borne on separate trees.

The species described is hardy and tolerant of wind and drought. It makes a good boundary or background hedge and is also suitable for topiary work. All parts except the red flesh of the fruits are highly poisonous, and trees should never be planted near grazing land.

See also CONIFERS.

T. baccata (common yew). Europe, including Great Britain; N. Africa to Iran. Height and spread 15 ft. A broad, well-branched tree, slow-growing and almost indestructibly hardy. The branches are horizontal and covered with red and brown scaly bark. The linear-oblong leaves are dark green above, yellow-green beneath. Small, globular, pale yellow male flowers cluster along the undersides of the previous year's shoots; the female flowers are solitary, green and scarcely visible. They are followed by red, fleshy, cup-shaped fruits, $\frac{1}{3}$ in. long.

'Adpressa' is a bushy variety with slender branches and pendulous shoots bearing tiny ovate leaves on either side. The form 'Aurea' is slow-growing with luminous golden foliage.

'Dovastonii' (Westfelton yew) has a short central trunk and long, slightly ascending branches bearing curtains of hanging foliage and branchlets, 'Dovastonii Aurea' is a golden form; 'Fastigiata' (Irish yew) is a female form of erect growth and with dark green leaves spreading from round the shoots; it forms a dense columnar crown with a many-pointed top. Several male golden forms are in cultivation.

TAXUS BACCATA

Cultivation. Yews thrive on almost any garden soil: chalk, limestone or thin peat, in full sun or deep shade, and in any position except swampy sites. They are tolerant of exposure, drought and, to some extent, polluted air.

Plant during suitable weather from October to April using plants 12–24 in. high. No support or staking is required.

For hedges, use 15 in. high young plants, setting these at intervals of 15–18 in. The leading shoots may be pinched out to encourage bushy and branching growth.

Propagation. Sow seeds in October in pans or boxes of John Innes seed compost in a cold frame. When the seedlings are 2–3 in. high, line out in nursery rows outdoors and grow on for two or three years. Plant in permanent positions in March and April.

Named varieties do not breed true to type from seeds. Take 3–4 in. long cuttings of lateral shoots with a heel in September or October. Insert the cuttings in equal parts (by volume) peat and sand in a cold frame. When rooted, line the cuttings out in nursery rows and grow on for two years before transplanting to permanent sites.

Pruning. None is required except to clear clusters of sprouts or suckers from the trunk; this may be done at any time of year.

Pests. Colonies of SCALE INSECTS, especially yew scale, may encrust the stems.

Taxodium distichum (immature cones)

Taxodium distichum (autumn foliage)

Taxus baccata (fruits)

Taxus baccata 'Dovastonii Aurea'

Larvae of GALL MIDGES attack the ends of young shoots and produce conspicuous galls. MITES also infest buds and distort the foliage.

Diseases. HONEY FUNGUS frequently attacks yews, killing some of the roots. The tree itself is not necessarily killed.

A common PHYSIOLOGICAL DISORDER causes yellowing of the foliage due to waterlogging.

Tea tree: see *Leptospermum scoparium*

Tecoma stans

Tecoma

Bignoniaceae

TECOMA STANS

A genus of 16 species of evergreen flowering shrubs from the tropical parts of America. In Great Britain they need greenhouse treatment. The genus formerly included many species which are now classified in other genera, such as *Pandorea* and *Tecomaria*.

T. stans (yellow elder), syns. *Stenolobium stans, Bignonia stans*. W. Indies, Mexico to Peru. Height up to 12 ft; spread up to 9 ft. An erect shrub with pale to mid-green pinnate leaves, 6 in. long; the slender, pointed leaflets are lanceolate. The bright yellow flowers are funnel-shaped, 1½ in. long, and borne in 6–9 in. terminal panicles from June to August.

Cultivation. Grow tecomas preferably in the greenhouse border; they may also be grown in 8–10 in. pots or small tubs of John Innes potting compost No. 3. Provide a winter temperature of 7–10°C (45–50°F).

During winter, keep the plants just moist; give ample water while they are making new growths in spring and early summer, and water sparingly after flowering.

Tecophilaea cyanocrocus

To ensure the production of flowers the growths must ripen well, otherwise only vigorous leaf growth will result. Place the plants in a well-lit position; shading is not required, but ventilate the greenhouse freely during summer. Plants grown in the border should ideally be trained against the back wall of a lean-to house or up under the greenhouse roof.

Pot on when the new leaves begin to appear in March. Once the plants are in 8 in. pots, pot on every other year; give established plants a weak liquid feed, fortnightly from May to September.

Propagation. Take cuttings, 3–4 in. long, of lateral non-flowering shoots in March or April; insert the cuttings in equal parts (by volume) peat and sand in a propagating case at a temperature of 18–21°C (64–70°F). When rooted, pot the cuttings singly in 3 in. pots of John Innes potting compost No. 1 and pot on as necessary. Pinch out the growing tips when the plants are about 6 in. high, to promote bushy growth. Pinch out again before the plants are potted on.

Tellima grandiflora

Alternatively, sow seeds in pans of seed compost in April; germinate at a temperature of 18–21°C (64–70°F). Prick off the seedlings when large enough to handle, and treat the young plants as described for cuttings.

Pruning. When the plants become too large, cut back the current year's growths by half and shorten the laterals to about 3 in. in February.

Pests and diseases. Generally trouble-free.

Tecophilaea

Tecophilaeaceae

A genus of two species of S. American bulbous plants. The one described was introduced into Great Britain about 100 years ago, but even now is not widely grown or available. The genus was first assigned to the *Amaryllidaceae* family, but recently it has been assigned a family of its own, which includes five other allied genera. The plants described are only moderately hardy.

T. cyanocrocus (Chilean crocus). Chile. Height 3–5 in. A few linear, mid-green, slightly twisted leaves clasp the short stem. Deep blue crocus-like flowers, 1½ in long, appear in March and April, opening wide to show their pale throats.

T. c. leichtlinii has more white in the throat; *T. c. elegans* is a variety with narrower leaves and petals; the variety *T. c. violacea* is deep purple.

Cultivation. Needing long summer warmth to ripen the corms properly, these plants are not often successfully grown outdoors. They do best as pot plants in a cool greenhouse or alpine house at a minimum temperature of 7°C (45°F).

In October, plant up to seven bulbs 1–2 in. deep in a 5 in. pot, in reasonably moist John Innes potting compost No. 1. Do not water until the leaves appear, then water regularly until the leaves die in the early summer. Allow the plants to dry in the warmth of the greenhouse and do not repot unless additional leaves show that offsets have been produced.

Propagation. Well-grown plants usually produce a few cormlets. If these are present, knock the plants out of their pots in autumn, remove the cormlets and plant about 12 of them in a 5 in. pot of John Innes potting compost No. 1. They reach flowering size in three or four years.

If seeds are collected, sow these in pans in the autumn and leave the seedlings undisturbed for the same period as the cormlets; then space them out into pans or pots.

Pests and diseases. Generally trouble-free.

Tellima

Saxifragaceae

A genus containing a single species. This is a hardy evergreen perennial, chiefly grown for its foliage which makes good ground cover throughout the year. It does well in a shaded border or in a wild garden.

T. grandiflora. N. America. Height 18–24 in.; planting distance 18 in. The hairy, maple-like, bright green leaves are borne close to the ground. Erect flower spikes above the foliage carry numerous green-yellow bell-shaped flowers, $\frac{1}{2}$ in. long, from April to June. The variety *T. g.* 'Purpurea' has purple-bronze leaves.

Cultivation. Plant from September to March in ordinary garden soil. Tellimas are best grown in partial shade, but the plants are adaptable and will grow in sun, or in quite dry shade beneath trees. Cut off the flower spikes after flowering, unless seeds are required.

Propagation. Divide and replant between September and March when weather permits.

Seeds may be sown, in a cold frame or greenhouse, when ripe or in March; the purple-leaved form does not come true.

Pests and diseases. Generally trouble-free.

Tetragonia expansa: see Spinach, New Zealand
Tetragonolobus purpureus: see Asparagus pea

Teucrium

Labiatae

A genus of 300 species of hardy and half-hardy herbaceous perennials and evergreen shrubs and sub-shrubs. The species described are evergreen flowering shrubs and sub-shrubs, suitable for growing in an alpine house, on rock gardens in mild maritime areas or as wall shrubs inland.

The individual flowers are basically tubular, usually with a prominent lower lip and sometimes hooded. They are borne in terminal spikes or clusters.

T. aroanum. Greece. Height 4 in.; spread 12 in. A hardy compact sub-shrub, suitable for a rock garden, and with ovate silver-grey leaves. An abundant display of grey-blue flowers, $\frac{1}{2}-\frac{3}{4}$ in. long, appears in July and August.

T. chamaedrys (germander). Europe. Height 6–9 in.; spread 12–15 in. This hardy sub-shrubby alpine species has ovate leaves with rounded teeth; they are mid to deep green above, grey beneath. Spikes of flowers, each $\frac{3}{4}$ in. long, appear from July to September. They are mainly bright pink, but the lower lip of each flower may be spotted with red and white.

T. creticum: see *T. rosmarinifolium*

T. fruticans. S. Europe. Height 4–5 ft; spread 3–4 ft. A half-hardy shrub with ovate grey-green leaves that are aromatic when crushed. The pale lavender two-lipped flowers, $\frac{1}{4}-\frac{3}{4}$ in. long, are borne on white stems from June to September. 'Azureum' is a tender deep blue form.

T. pyrenaicum. S. Europe. Height 2–3 in.; spread 12–15 in. A hardy perennial rock-garden species with trailing stems. The orbicular leaves, with rounded teeth, are silver-green and slightly hairy. Tiny mauve and cream flowers are borne in dense terminal heads, 1 in. across, from June to August.

T. rosmarinifolium, syn. *T. creticum.* Crete. Height 3 in.; spread 9–12 in. This hardy sub-shrubby species has linear-oblong, white-haired leaves. The rose-purple flowers are each set in a white, woolly calyx; they are borne in branched racemes, about 2 in. across, from June to September.

Cultivation. Grow all species in a light, well-drained soil in a sunny position; low-growing species usually retain their compact habit better in poor soils. Plant rock-garden species from September to April; the half-hardy *T. fruticans* should be planted in May, preferably against a south or west-facing wall. The young shoots need tying to strings or wires for support.

In the alpine house, grow the plants in 6–8 in. pans of John Innes potting compost No. 1. Repot annually in March.

Propagation. Take half-ripened 2–3 in. cuttings of basal or lateral shoots of the sub-shrubs in May. Insert the cuttings in a cold frame in equal parts (by volume) peat and sand. When rooted, pot the cuttings singly in 3 in. containers of John Innes potting compost No. 1 and plunge outdoors until planting out the following March or April.

Increase *T. fruticans* by 3–4 in. heel cuttings of half-ripe lateral shoots taken in July or August. Insert the cuttings in equal parts (by volume) peat and sand in a propagating frame, with a temperature of 15°C (59°F). When rooted, place the cuttings singly in 3 in. pots of John Innes potting compost No. 1, and overwinter in a frost-free greenhouse or cold frame. Pot on into 4 in. pots in March and plant out in their permanent positions in May or June.

Pruning. None is required, but wall-grown specimens of *T. fruticans* should have frosted tips removed in April. At the same time shorten all growths by half to limit spread.

Pests and diseases. Generally trouble-free.

Thalictrum

Meadow-rue. *Ranunculaceae*

THALICTRUM AQUILEGIFOLIUM

A genus of 150 species of hardy herbaceous perennial plants. A few species are of garden value and are suitable for rock gardens or herbaceous borders. These plants are grown as much for their divided foliage, which often resembles maidenhair fern, as for their flowers.

T. adiantifolium. Europe. Height 3 ft; planting distance 18 in. This plant is now regarded as a form of *T. minus.* It is grown for its grey-green foliage composed of numerous small leaflets like those of maidenhair fern. The insignificant purple-green flowers appear in loose terminal panicles, 4–6 in. long, in July.

T. aquilegifolium. Europe, N. Asia. Height 2–3 ft; planting distance 12–18 in. The pinnate leaves are grey-blue and glossy. Open tufted panicles, 6–8 in. long, of fluffy mauve or purple flowers appear between May and early July.

Good varieties include: 'Album' (height 3 ft), white flowers; 'Dwarf Purple' (height 2$\frac{1}{2}$ ft), purple-mauve; 'Purpureum' (height 4 ft), light purple; 'Thundercloud', deep purple. The species and its varieties are good but short-flowering border plants.

T. delavayi: see *T. dipterocarpum*

Teucrium chamaedrys

Teucrium rosmarinifolium

Thalictrum aquilegifolium

Thalictrum dipterocarpum

T. dipterocarpum. W. China. Height 4—5 ft; planting distance 18 in. The leaves are mid-green and slightly glaucous. Loose sprays of minute mauve flowers with conspicuous yellow anthers are borne from June to August. There has been much confusion with the similar species *T. delavayi*; listed varieties of *T. dipterocarpum* may possibly be forms of *T. delavayi*.

'Album' is a white form; 'Hewitt's Double' has mauve double flowers.

T. flavum (yellow meadow-rue). Europe, including Great Britain. Height 4—5 ft; planting distance 18 in. This border plant has deep green leaves. Compact heads, about 6 in. across, of fluffy, soft yellow flowers are produced in July and August. The variety 'Glaucum' has grey-green glaucous leaves.

T. kiusianum. Japan. Height and planting distance 4—6 in. A tufted species with smooth, somewhat grey-green leaves, dissected into small lobed leaflets. Loose corymbs of $\frac{1}{3}$ in. wide, pale purple flowers, with prominent rose-purple stamens, appear in April and May.

T. minus: see *T. adiantifolium*

T. rocquebrunianum. Origin unknown. Height 4 ft; planting distance 24 in. The strong erect stems are purple-blue and bear glaucous, fern-like leaves. Loose, 6—8 in. long panicles of rose-lavender flowers with yellow stamens appear from June to August.

T. speciosissimum. Spain, Portugal, N.W. Africa. Height 3—5 ft; planting distance 24 in. The deeply divided foliage is blue-grey. Sprays, 6—9 in. long, of fluffy yellow flowers are borne in July and August.

Cultivation. Plant in March or April in sun or light shade. Any ordinary garden soil is suitable, but the plants thrive in rich and moist soil. Staking with stout sticks or canes is usually required and should be done, especially in moist soil, before the plants grow too tall. Cut down in November. Top-dress annually in March with decayed manure or peat.

Propagation. Divide and replant the roots in March or April. Divided plants are slow to become established; apart from the double forms, which are infertile, thalictrums are better propagated from seeds.

Sow seeds in pans of John Innes seed compost in March and place in a cold frame. Prick out the seedlings, when large enough to handle, and grow on in a nursery bed before planting out in permanent quarters the following March or April.

Pests and diseases. Generally trouble-free.

Thermopsis

Leguminosae

A genus of 30 species of hardy herbaceous perennials. They are easily grown plants, suitable for a herbaceous border, and resemble lupins.

T. fabacea: see *T. montana*

T. lanceolata: see *T. lupinoides*

T. lupinoides, syn. *T. lanceolata.* Siberia. Height 3 ft; planting distance 18 in. This species forms a stout, tough-rooted clump with trifoliate grey-green leaves. Clear yellow flowers are borne in 12 in. long spikes in May and June.

Thalictrum dipterocarpum 'Hewitt's Double'

Thalictrum speciosissimum

Thermopsis montana

T. montana, syn. *T. fabacea.* N. America. Height and planting distance 24 in. A species with creeping and spreading underground shoots, from which 6—8 in. long spikes of yellow pea-like flowers appear in May and June. The feathery leaves are glaucous green. An invasive plant which needs curbing by digging out the spreading roots.

THERMOPSIS MONTANA

Cultivation. Plant from October to April in ordinary well-drained soil and in a sunny position. After flowering, cut off the flower spikes to a few inches above ground; a second flowering may occur in early autumn.

Propagation. Divide and replant the roots in March or April; *T. lupinoides* resents root disturbance and may take several years to become re-established after division.

Sow seeds outdoors in April in a sunny position; prick out the seedlings when large enough to handle and grow on in a nursery bed. Transplant to permanent positions in October.

Pests and diseases. Generally trouble-free.

Thistle, blessed: see *Silybum marianum*
Thistle, cotton: see *Onopordum acanthium*
Thistle, globe: see Echinops
Thistle, holy: see *Silybum marianum*
Thistle, Our Lady's milk: see *Silybum marianum*
Thistle, Scotch: see *Onopordum acanthium*
Thorn, cockspur: see *Crataegus crus-galli*
Thorn, Glastonbury: see *Crataegus monogyna* 'Biflora'
Thorn, ornamental: see Crataegus
Thorn, 'Paul's Double Scarlet': see *Crataegus oxyacanthoides* 'Coccinea Plena'
Thousand mothers: see *Tolmiea menziesii*
Thrift: see Armeria

Thuja

Arbor-vitae. *Cupressaceae*

A genus of five hardy evergreen coniferous trees, native to China, Formosa, Japan and North America. With the exception of *T. plicata* these are small slow-growing trees. The crowns are usually densely conic or rounded irregular, with upright branches. The foliage is composed of flat scales closely clothing the shoots, the juvenile leaves being more spreading and pointed than adult leaves. Ovoid or urn-shaped cones, less than 1 in. long, are borne upright.

The slow-growing and dwarf foliage species and varieties described make handsome specimen trees for small gardens and are also suitable for rock gardens. The large species are suitable only for large gardens or for hedging.

See also CONIFERS.

T. lobbii: see *T. plicata*

T. occidentalis (white cedar). Eastern Canada and U.S.A. Height 25 ft; spread 15 ft. A slow-growing and short-lived tree with an open and often irregular crown. The flat scale-leaves are dull green above, yellow beneath; they have an apple-like scent when crushed. Curled sprays of foliage hang from short, upturned branches; the yellow cones, up to $\frac{1}{2}$ in long, are erect when young, later they become brown and pendulous.

'Globosa' (height and spread 2–3 ft) is of compact rounded habit with light, almost grey-green foliage in flat sprays; growth is dense, with much overlapping of the shoots.

'Lutea' is a robust tree, superior to the type; the foliage hangs in longer sprays, bright gold at the tips, shading to green in the dense crown; it is a distinctive specimen tree of moderate size. 'Spiralis' is a narrowly columnar form with rich dark green foliage.

'Umbraculifera' (height and spread up to 6 ft) is a strong-growing form with attractive blue-green foliage. 'Woodwardii' (height and spread 4 ft) is a vigorous form with rather coarse green foliage, open and stiffly held in vertical planes.

Dwarf varieties, forming globose or bun-shaped shrubs include 'Caespitosa' (height and spread 12 in.), a true miniature; 'Dumosa' (height 18 in.; spread 24 in.), a congested flattened bush with dense, irregular foliage and usually a few straight shoots appearing stiffly at the top of the plant.

'Ellwangeriana Aurea' (height up to 6 ft; spread 3 ft), a strong-growing conical form with mixed golden-yellow juvenile and adult foliage. 'Ericoides' (height and spread 4 ft), of broadly rounded habit with wholly juvenile foliage that is green in summer turning to walnut-brown in winter; it is easily damaged by snow.

'Hetz Pygmy' (height and spread 12 in.), a recommended miniature form; 'Rheingold' (height 3 ft; spread 24 in.), a slow-growing form with golden-yellow juvenile and adult leaves; the brightness of the foliage is seen at its best in winter sunshine.

THUJA ORIENTALIS

T. orientalis. N. and W. China. Height 15 ft; spread 10 ft. This species eventually becomes a gaunt tree, but when young forms an erect domed shrub. The foliage is held in vertical plates and is mid-green in summer, turning bronze in winter. The pale brown cones have six to eight scales, each terminating in a curved beak.

The species is valuable for the variety of dwarf and near-dwarf forms it has produced, many with attractive golden-yellow foliage in spring and early summer: 'Aurea Nana' (height 24 in.; spread 18 in.), an egg-shaped slow-growing bush; 'Conspicua', 'Elegantissima' and 'Semperaurescens' (height 8 ft; spread 3 ft or less) are taller-growing forms.

There is also a group of diminutive forms with juvenile or semi-juvenile foliage: 'Meldensis' (height up to 24 in.; spread 18 in.), an upright, oval bush with rough, dark green leaves; 'Rosedalis', often listed as 'Rosedalis Compacta', is similar, but has softer foliage that is green in summer, purple in winter and yellow in spring.

T. plicata, syn. *T. lobbii* (western red cedar). Western N. America. Height 55 ft; spread 20 ft. A long-lived and fast-growing tree, neat and narrowly conic when young. The light brown bark fissures into narrow strips which peel off; the bole is deeply fluted. Single trees on sheltered moist sites eventually develop huge low branches and broadly conic crowns. The species is also suitable for a dense hedge.

The flat, scale-like, pineapple-scented leaves are shiny rich mid-green above with narrow white marks beneath. Few-scaled, yellow-brown cones, about 1 in. long, are borne on mature trees.

THUJA PLICATA

'Aureovariegata', formerly known as 'Zebrina', is one of the best golden conifers; it forms a broad, conic tree with sprays of yellow-banded foliage. An even brighter form, nearly all white-yellow, is common in Ireland and has a more open crown.

Cultivation. These conifers are easily grown in any ordinary garden soil, but do best in a moist, deep soil and in a sheltered position in full sun. Plant during suitable weather from November to March, using plants under 24 in. high; these do not require support. Keep the site well watered and clear of competing weeds; apply a dressing of general fertiliser annually in spring.

For hedges, use plants 18 in. high and space at intervals of 18–24 in. The growing tips may be pinched out to promote bushy growth.

Propagation. The species are best raised from seeds, sown in February in pans of John Innes seed compost in a cold frame, or in March in open beds. When the seedlings are 2–3 in. high, prick off into nursery rows outdoors and grow on for two years before planting in permanent positions.

Named varieties must be increased from cuttings taken in September and October. Select 2–4 in. long tip cuttings and insert in equal parts (by volume) peat and sand in a cold frame. When rooted, line out the cuttings in nursery rows and grow on as described for seedlings.

Dwarf varieties are best potted in 3 in. containers of John Innes potting compost No. 1 and plunged outdoors. Grow on for one or two years before setting in permanent sites.

Pruning. None required.

Pests. Generally trouble-free.

Diseases. The less-common species are generally trouble-free. *T. plicata* is susceptible to attacks by HONEY FUNGUS, which infests and kills the roots.

A common PHYSIOLOGICAL DISORDER causes bronzing of the foliage in cold weather.

Thuja occidentalis 'Rheingold'

Thuja orientalis

Thuja plicata (cones)

Thujopsis
Cupressaceae

A genus containing only one species. This is an evergreen conifer, formerly included in *Thuja*, which it greatly resembles, but with more robust shoots and larger, scale-like leaves. It makes an excellent bushy specimen plant for a lawn.

See also CONIFERS.

THUJOPSIS DOLABRATA

T. dolabrata. Japan. The species is usually represented in cultivation by *T. d. australis*. Height 8–10 ft; spread 6–8 ft. This is a hardy slow-growing tree, single trunked and narrow or more usually a broadly conic thicket of small trunks. The large, flat, shiny leaves have a pattern of broad white marks beneath and are yellow or deep green above. The globose, pale brown cones are about 1 in. long, leathery, becoming woody, with a small spike on each scale.

T. d. 'Variegata' is a slower-growing, more bushy form with white or cream variegated shoots scattered among the branchlets.

Cultivation. This tree grows best in damp soil and in a sunny position, sheltered from north and east winds. Plant in April, using young trees 1–4 ft high. If the foliage turns yellow, apply a dressing of nitrogenous fertiliser in March, preferably in the form of dried blood or hoof and horn.

Propagation. Seeds and cuttings are both slow, but best results are obtained from cuttings. Select 3–4 in. long tip cuttings, preferably with a heel, in September and October; insert in equal parts (by volume) peat and sand in a cold frame. When rooted, line the cuttings out in nursery rows and grow on for three years before planting in permanent positions.

Pruning. The bushy form needs no pruning; a plant which shows signs of tree development can be encouraged to grow a single bole by the removal of lower branches in March or April.

Pests and diseases. Generally trouble-free.

Thunbergia
Acanthaceae

THUNBERGIA ALATA

A genus of 200 species of mainly annual and perennial climbers, but including a few erect herbaceous species. Those described here are tender flowering climbers that generally require greenhouse cultivation. They are grown for their handsome flowers, which are composed of a distinct tube expanding into five rounded, petal-like lobes at the mouth.

T. alata (black-eyed susan). South Africa. Height up to 10 ft. An annual twiner of moderate growth with ovate mid-green leaves. The 2 in. wide flowers have a dark purple tube and a flat orange-yellow corolla, with a chocolate-brown centre. They are borne singly from the leaf axils from June to September. In sheltered areas in the south and west, it may be grown outdoors.

T. gibsonii: see *T. gregorii*

Thunbergia grandiflora

T. grandiflora. N. India. Height 20 ft or more. A vigorous evergreen climber with ovate, mid-green leaves. Pale purple-blue flowers, 2–2½ in. across, are borne in terminal racemes from June to September.

T. gregorii. S. and E. Africa. Height 10 ft or more. This vigorous evergreen climber, often grown as an annual, is frequently listed as *T. gibsonii*. It has triangular-ovate mid to deep green leaves. Orange flowers, 1½ in. across, are borne singly from the leaf axils from June to September.

Cultivation. In the greenhouse, grow thunbergias preferably in the border, although *T. alata* and *T. gregorii* may also be grown in 6–8 in. pots of John Innes potting compost No. 2. Train these self-clinging climbers against strings or wires. Overwinter the evergreen perennial species at a temperature of 7–10°C (45–50°F).

During winter, keep the plants just moist, but water freely during the growing period; the plants require a well-lit position, but should be lightly shaded during the hottest summer months. Ventilate the house when the temperature exceeds 16°C (61°F).

Pot on or repot plants of *T. gregorii* annually in March or April. Give all species a weak liquid feed fortnightly from June to September.

In sheltered gardens, grow *T. alata* in ordinary, well-drained garden soil in a sunny, sheltered position against a wall or arbour.

Propagation. Sow seeds of *T. alata* and *T. gregorii* in pots or pans of seed compost in March. Germinate the seeds at a temperature of 16–18°C

Thujopsis dolabrata 'Variegata'

Thujopsis dolabrata (cones and underside of foliage)

Thunbergia alata

Thunbergia gregorii

(61–64°F), and prick out the seedlings into 3 in. pots of John Innes potting compost No. 2. Pot on as required.

Increase *T. grandiflora* by 4–6 in. stem sections taken in April or May; insert in equal parts (by volume) peat and sand at a temperature of 18–21°C (64–70°F). Pot the rooted cuttings as described for seedlings.

Pruning. Cut overgrown specimens of *T. gregorii* back to within 9 in. of the base in March. Mature plants of *T. grandiflora* may be thinned out and lateral growths reduced by half or more. Excessive pruning will inhibit flower production.

Pests and diseases. Generally trouble-free.

Thyme

Thymus. Labiatae

The plants described here are hardy, aromatic, evergreen dwarf shrubs, the shoots of which are used as culinary herbs for flavouring.

Common thyme, garden thyme (*T. vulgaris*). S. Europe. Height 4–8 in.; planting distance 9–12 in. The aromatic dark-green leaves are long and narrow. Clusters of tubular mauve flowers, $\frac{1}{3}$ in. long, appear from the leaf axils in June. The golden-leaved form, *T. v.* 'Aureus', may be grown both as a herb and for its ornamental foliage.

Thyme is used fresh or dried in *bouquets garnis* and in stuffings for rich meats, fish and in casseroles. The flavour is mild, a little sweet and slightly spicy. Commercially, thyme is used in soaps, in antiseptic preparations and in the liqueur Benedictine. Apart from its culinary uses, the plant also makes attractive ground cover; it may be grown as an edging plant, in crevices or on rock gardens.

Lemon thyme (*T. × citriodorus*). Height 12 in.; planting distance 9–12 in. This decorative hybrid is similar in appearance to common thyme, but has broader, lemon-scented leaves, and slightly larger flowers. Silver and gold-leaved varieties are often available.

Lemon thyme is used similarly to common thyme, and also in desserts and *pot-pourri*.

Lemon-scented thyme: see also *Thymus × citriodorus*

Wild thyme: see *Thymus serpyllum*

Cultivation. Thyme grows best in a sunny position in any well-drained garden soil. Replace the plants after three or four years, as they become thin and straggly.

Propagation. Established clumps may be divided and replanted in March or April.

Thyme can also be propagated from 2–3 in. cuttings of lateral shoots, taken with a heel in May or June. Insert the cuttings in equal parts (by volume) peat and sand in a cold frame. Pot the rooted cuttings singly in 3 in. containers of John Innes potting compost No. 1; plant out the following August and September.

Sow seeds of *T. vulgaris* in pans of John Innes seed compost in a cold frame during March and April. Prick off the seedlings, when large enough to handle, into 3 in. containers of John Innes potting compost No. 1. Plant out in September.

Harvesting and storing. Pick the shoots at any time for using fresh. They are best when newly picked, but they may be dried or deep-frozen. See entry under HERBS.

Pests and diseases. Generally trouble-free.

Thymus

Labiatae

THYMUS MEMBRANACEUS

A genus of between 300 and 400 species of hardy perennial herbaceous plants and sub-shrubs. Some are prostrate; others grow up to 12 in. tall. All the species described are aromatic and can be grown on rock gardens. The mat-forming species may also be treated as ground-cover plants or grown amongst dwarf bulbs.

See also Thyme for details of the culinary herbs *T. vulgaris* and *T. × citriodorus*.

T. carnosus: see *T. nitidus*

T. cilicicus. Asia Minor. Height 4–6 in.; spread 9 in. The leaves of this compact bushy species are linear and deep green. The tubular pale-pink flowers form dense terminal clusters, $\frac{1}{2}$ in. across, in June. These are subtended by purple bracts.

T. × citriodorus (lemon-scented thyme). Height 9–12 in.; spread 12–16 in. The mid-green lemon-scented leaves may be rhomboid, lanceolate or ovate. Pale lilac flowers, only $\frac{1}{5}$ in. long and ranged in small interrupted terminal clusters, open from June to August. The variety 'Aureus' has golden leaves, and 'Silver Queen' is variegated, though the foliage of both tends to revert to green.

T. doerfleri (more correctly classified now as *T. hirsutus doerfleri*, but this name seldom appears in catalogues). Balkans. Height up to 3 in.; spread 12–18 in. This is a mat-forming plant with linear grey-green leaves. The lilac-pink tubular flowers form hemispherical terminal clusters, $\frac{3}{5}$ in. wide, which open in June or July.

T. drucei: see *T. serpyllum*

T. herba-barona. Corsica. Height 3–5 in.; spread 12–15 in. This plant forms a caraway-scented mat with leaves that are ovate to lanceolate and dark green. The tubular and pale lilac flowers form terminal clusters, 3 in. long, in June.

T. hirsutus doerfleri: see *T. doerfleri*

T. membranaceus. Spain. Height 4–6 in.; spread 9 in. This is the most fragrant species of the genus. It has a densely branched twig-like habit, with leaves that are linear and hoary-green. Tubular pale lilac flowers are arranged in ovoid terminal clusters, $\frac{3}{4}$–1 in. long, which emerge from green-white bracts in July and August.

T. nitidus. Portugal. The plant commonly cultivated under this name is *T. carnosus*. Height 8 in.; spread 12 in. This species is suitable for the alpine house. The ovate leaves are mid to grey-green and grow in compact clumps. Tubular, bright lilac-pink flowers form oblong terminal clusters, up to $1\frac{1}{2}$ in. long, in May and June.

Thyme, common

Thyme, golden

Thymus serpyllum 'Coccineus'

T. serpyllum (wild thyme). The plants in cultivation under this name are now correctly called *T. drucei*. Europe, including Great Britain. Height 1–3 in.; spread 24 in. or more. The narrowly obovate and elliptic leaves are grey-green and sometimes hairy. The flowers, which vary from deep red through pink to white, appear in rounded terminal clusters, ½ in. across, from June to August.

The variety 'Albus' has white flowers and light green foliage; 'Annie Hall' is smaller, with pale pink flowers; 'Coccineus' has rich crimson flowers and dark green foliage; 'Lanuginosus' is grey-leaved and hairy, with lilac flowers.

T. vulgaris: see Thyme

Cultivation. Plant from October to March in an open, sunny position in any well-drained garden soil. Shear off the flower heads after flowering to maintain dense, healthy plants. In the alpine house grow *T. nitidus* in 6–8 in. pans of John Innes potting compost No. 1. Repot every other year.

Propagation. Divide in March, August or September and replant direct in final positions.

Take 2 in. heel cuttings in July of *T. cilicicus*, *T.* × *citriodorus*, *T. membranaceus* and *T. nitidus* and set in a well-ventilated cold frame in equal parts (by volume) peat and sand. Pot the rooted cuttings in 3 in. pots, ready for planting out a year later in October.

Pests and diseases. Generally trouble-free.

Tiarella cordifolia

Tiarella wherryi

Tibouchina semidecandra

Tiarella

Saxifragaceae

TIARELLA CORDIFOLIA

A genus of seven species of hardy, low-growing, mainly evergreen perennials suitable for rock gardens or as ground cover beneath trees and shrubs. They are closely allied to the genus *Heuchera*, bearing feathery spikes of white or pink-tinted star-shaped flowers.

T. cordifolia (foam flower). N. America. Height 6–12 in.; planting distance 12 in. This species is excellent for ground cover; the pale to mid-green, maple-like leaves on spreading surface runners form a dense carpet. Erect spikes, 6 in. high, of cream-white flowers appear in May and June.

T. polyphylla. China, Japan. Height 12–24 in.; planting distance 12 in. A clump-forming species of neat habit, with three-lobed, toothed, mid-green leaves. Racemes, 9 in. high, of white, pink-tinged flowers open from June to August.

T. trifoliata. N. America. Height up to 20 in.; planting distance 12 in. The mid-green leaves are trifoliate or ivy-shaped. Narrow panicles, up to 10 in. high, of nearly pure white flowers are freely produced from June to August.

T. wherryi. S.E. America. Height 6–14 in.; planting distance 12 in. A neat, tufted plant with ivy-shaped, pale green leaves which age to russet or brown in autumn. Erect, brown-stemmed feathery spikes, 10 in. high, of cream-white flowers appear in abundance from June to September or later.

Cultivation. Plant in October or in March or April in peaty or ordinary garden soil and in a cool shady position. The soil should never be too dry, although *T. trifoliata* and *T. polyphylla* are fairly adaptable. *T. cordifolia* requires moist but well-drained soil and is apt to die back if the ground dries out. Young outside growths may be replanted in September or October to fill in gaps.

The plants retain their foliage during winter.

Propagation. Divide and replant the roots of all species except *T. wherryi* in October or April.

T. wherryi, which does not divide easily, is best increased from seeds.

Sow seeds of *T. polyphylla*, *T. trifoliata* and *T. wherryi* in a cold frame in March. When the seedlings are large enough to handle, prick out in boxes and then into a nursery bed. Transplant to permanent quarters the following March.

Pests and diseases. Generally trouble-free.

Tibouchina

Melastomataceae

A genus of more than 200 species of evergreen or semi-evergreen tender shrubs, some of which are attractive in flower. One species is in general cultivation; it is suitable for greenhouse culture.

T. semidecandra. Brazil. Height and spread up to 15 ft. The true species is rarely seen; the one in cultivation is correctly named *T. urvilleana*. It forms a shrub bearing ovate, velvety, mid to deep green leaves; these are prominently veined and occasionally turn red in autumn. The flowers are produced in terminal panicles from July to November. Each flower is 3–4 in. across, saucer-shaped and a rich, satiny violet-purple.

TIBOUCHINA SEMIDECANDRA

T. urvilleana: see *T. semidecandra*

Cultivation. Grow tibouchinas in any good garden soil in the greenhouse border. They may also be grown in 5–7 in. pots of John Innes potting compost No. 3. The winter temperature required is 7°C (45°F). Young plants from the previous year's cuttings are slightly more tender and do better at a minimum temperature of 10°C (50°F). When growth has restarted, maintain as high a temperature as possible, but admit ample air whenever it exceeds 21°C (70°F).

Pot plants will require the support of one or three canes, depending on plant size. Border grown plants should be staked and are more effective trained as wall shrubs in a lean-to greenhouse or grown up under the roof.

Give the plants plenty of water when in growth and in flower, but keep them just moist in winter. If they can be started early into growth, by being given higher temperatures in February and March, they will start to flower earlier and will continue until late autumn. Place them in a well-lit position, although light shading may be necessary from mid-June to the end of August. Provide a humid atmosphere during spring and summer. The plants may be stood outdoors or planted in a border from the end of May; bring them back into the greenhouse before the first autumn frosts.

Pot-grown plants should be potted on annually in March until they are in their final pots. Give a weak liquid feed at 10–14 day intervals from May to September.

Propagation. Take cuttings, 4–5 in. long, of lateral non-flowering shoots in March and April; insert the cuttings in equal parts (by volume) peat and sand in a propagating case with a temperature of 18–21°C (64–70°F). When rooted, pot the cuttings in 3½ in. pots of John Innes potting compost No. 2. Pinch out the growing tips at the time of potting up and again when the lateral growths are 4–5 in. long.

Pruning. Cut flowering pot plants hard back at the end of February, or earlier if the plants have been started into growth. Shorten leading shoots by up to half and cut back lateral shoots to two pairs of leaves. Shrubs grown in the border should have the lateral growths cut back to two pairs of leaves in February.

Pests. Generally trouble-free.

Diseases. A PHYSIOLOGICAL DISORDER may lead to general discoloration of the foliage, and the leaves may fall prematurely.

Tidy tips: see *Layia elegans*
Tiger flower: see *Tigridia pavonia*

Tigridia

Iridaceae

A genus of 12 bulbous species from Mexico and South America, only one of which, a half-hardy plant, is in cultivation in Great Britain. The spectacular flowers, which blend the characteristics of tulips and irises, are brilliantly coloured. Each flower lasts only a day, but each stem produces from six to eight flowers in succession.

T. pavonia (tiger flower, peacock tiger flower). Mexico and Peru. Height 18–24 in.; planting distance 4 in. The mid-green lanceolate leaves are pleated. Yellow flowers, spotted with crimson-brown and up to 4 in. across, open on erect stems from July to September. They have three large petals, usually unspotted, with three small spotted petals between them, all spreading out from a spotted, cup-shaped base.

Named varieties include: 'Alba', white with carmine spots; 'Canariensis', yellow with red spots; 'Liliacea', red-purple variegated with white; 'Lutea', yellow; 'Red Giant', scarlet with yellow and red centre; 'Rubra', orange-red, and 'Speciosa', scarlet, both with yellow and red spotted centres.

Cultivation. Tigridias are useful for providing a late show among low-growing and earlier-flowering plants. Plant 3–4 in deep in rich

well-drained soil in April. They need all available sun and warmth, but must not be allowed to become dry. Lift before any serious frosts occur, dry the corms in the warmth of a greenhouse or heated shed and store in dry sand or peat until the following spring.

Propagation. In sheltered, south-facing borders, they may be left *in situ* for two or three years before lifting and dividing. One or more cormlets are produced annually. Planted and grown with the other corms, they will reach flowering size in a year or two.

Pests. Generally trouble-free.

Diseases. Corms suffering from STORAGE ROT, due to a BLUE MOULD, bear the buff-coloured or pink resting bodies of the fungus. Under moist conditions blue mould develops on the lesions, and the corms decay.

Tilia

Lime. *Tiliaceae*

TILIA × EUROPAEA

A genus of 50 species of hardy ornamental deciduous trees. Most are fast-growing, particularly when young. They make handsome specimen trees for large gardens and parks and are suitable for avenues. The flowers contain a sweet nectar and are much visited by bees. Some species are prone to severe attacks by aphids which cause large amounts of sticky exudations to fall on surrounding areas.

T. cordata (small-leaved lime). Europe, including Great Britain. Height 25–35 ft; spread 10–15 ft. The dark glossy green rounded leaves, which are sharply and finely toothed, have somewhat glaucous undersides. The small, bowl-shaped, fragrant, yellow-white flowers appear in July in 2–3 in. long pendulous cymes.

T. dasystyla: see *T. × euchlora*

T. × euchlora, syn. *T. dasystyla*. Origin uncertain. Height 25–35 ft; spread 10–15 ft. The broadly ovate leaves are shiny dark green on somewhat pendulous branches. This hybrid has largely superseded the common lime for street and park planting, as the leaves are not so prone to aphid infestation. Small yellow flowers are borne in drooping clusters, 1–1½ in. across, in July on 1–2 in. long stalks.

T. × europaea, syn. *T. vulgaris* (common lime). Height 30 ft; spread 10–15 ft. This vigorous hybrid between *T. cordata* and *T. platyphyllos* is subject to aphid infestations. The pointed, heart-shaped leaves are mid-green and smooth, with tufts of down on the undersides in the axils of the veins. Yellow-white flowers are borne in July, in pendulous cymes 2–3 in. long.

T. petiolaris (pendent silver lime). S.E. Europe. Height 20–25 ft; spread 10–15 ft. The rounded mid-green leaves are completely downy above,

Tigridia pavonia 'Alba' and 'Speciosa'

Tigridia pavonia 'Liliacea'

Tigridia pavonia 'Rubra'

Tilia × europaea

with slightly silvered, white-felted undersides. The slender branches are pendulous, forming a wide-spreading dome. Sweetly fragrant white flowers are produced in July and August in 2–3 in. long cymes.

T. platyphyllos (broad-leaved lime). Europe. Height 25–30 ft; spread 10–15 ft. The pale to mid-green leaves are broad and heart-shaped, with downy undersides. Yellow-white flowers are borne in 3–4 in. long pendent cymes in June and July. Mature trees of this species have semi-pendulous branchlets.

T. tomentosa (silver lime). S.E. Europe, W. Asia. Height 25–30 ft; spread 10–15 ft. The large rounded leaves are dark green, with silvery-white undersides. Dull white flowers appear from July to August in pendent cymes 2–3 in. long.

T. vulgaris: see *T. europaea*

Cultivation. Plant between October and March in any ordinary, moist but well-drained garden soil, in full sun or partial shade.

Propagation. Sow seeds in pans of John Innes seed compost in a cold frame during March. When the seedlings are large enough to handle, prick them off in pans or boxes of well-drained soil in a cold frame. Plant them out in a nursery bed the following October. Grow on for four years or more before setting the young plants out in their permanent positions, between October and March.

Shoots layered in September or October will usually be ready for severing and planting out two years later.

Pruning. Little pruning is necessary, other than removing sucker shoots from the base and bole.

Pests. Trees become sticky and sooty when the leaves are infested with APHIDS.

CATERPILLARS and various species of moth eat the leaves, and GALL MITES produce bright red 'nail' galls on the upper surfaces of the leaves.

Diseases. Several different fungi cause DIE-BACK and CANKER. Dead patches or cankers appear on shoots and if girdling occurs the shoots die back.

HONEY FUNGUS has been known to kill trees.

LEAF SPOT shows as brown spots with dark edges on the leaves and sometimes the leaf stalks and young shoots. Withering and premature defoliation may occur.

Tilia platyphyllos

Tillandsia lindeniana

Tillandsia usneoides

Tillandsia

Bromeliaceae

A genus of 500 species of tender evergreen perennials, some terrestrial, others epiphytic. These bromeliads are widely distributed throughout tropical and sub-tropical regions of North and South America.

Comparatively few species are in general cultivation; those described are interesting epiphytic plants, requiring warm greenhouse conditions and a high degree of humidity.

See also BROMELIADS.

T. cyanea. Ecuador. Height 9 in.; spread 12 in. An epiphytic species. The narrow leaf rosette is formed of spineless leaves, red-brown at the base and with brown vertical lines. The flower stem is robust and partially hidden. The inflorescence is elliptic, about 2 in. across and $3\frac{1}{2}$ in. high; it

consists of symmetrical overlapping bracts with blunt tips. The violet-blue three-petalled flowers, 2 in. across, emerge in ones or twos from the bracts. At flowering time the bracts assume pastel shades of rose to red, tinged with green.

TILLANDSIA LINDENIANA

T. lindeniana. Peru. Height 15–20 in.; spread 12–15 in. This is an epiphytic species with narrow linear leaves, dark green above, purple beneath. The flowers are borne in a short flattened spike, 6–8 in. long, on a stem up to 12 in. long. The inflorescence is composed of coral-pink or carmine bracts from which deep blue white-throated flowers emerge in succession, one or two at a time, during the summer months.

T. usneoides. South-eastern U.S.A. This species is the well-known Spanish moss that festoons trees in humid areas of southern North America. This pendulous epiphytic plant is composed of long, moss-like tufts of wiry stems and tiny, linear, scaly, grey leaves. Bright yellow-green, three-petalled flowers, $\frac{1}{3}$ in. across, are borne in the leaf axils at intervals throughout the summer.

Cultivation. Plant *T. cyanea* and *T. lindeniana* during March or April, in 4 in. pots containing equal parts (by volume) sand and leaf-mould or osmunda fibre. *T. usneoides* is completely epiphytic and needs no growing medium; attach pieces of the plant to twigs, wires or strings suspended in the greenhouse.

Water pot-grown species plentifully during the growing season; from late autumn throughout the winter, keep the compost just moist. A minimum winter temperature of 13°C (55°F) is required.

All species need a high degree of humidity; mist-spray the plants frequently from April to September, at least once a day in hot weather, and syringe *T. usneoides* daily. Shade the greenhouse during the hottest months.

Repot *T. cyanea* and *T. lindeniana* annually, in March or April.

Propagation. Detach the small offshoots produced by *T. cyanea* and *T. lindeniana*, and pot them singly in 3 in. pots of equal parts (by volume) peat and sand. Root at 16–21°C (61–70°F). Pot up in the growing mixture.

Remove a few shoots of *T. usneoides*, tie them together and attach to a new support.

Pests and diseases. Generally trouble-free.

Toadflax: see Linaria
Toadflax, ivy-leaved: see *Linaria cymbalaria*
Tobacco plant: see Nicotiana

Tolmiea

Saxifragaceae

A genus of one species. This hardy evergreen perennial is grown as a pot plant or outdoors as ground cover. It has the interesting habit of producing young plants on the leaves.

T. menziesii (pig-a-back plant, youth-on-age, thousand mothers). W. United States. Height up to 6 in.; spread up to 15 in. A tufted plant with short, creeping rhizomes and hairy, maple-like, mid-green leaves. In June, slender-branched, 18–24 in. high stems bear spires of green-white, red-flushed tubular flowers, each $\frac{1}{2}$ in. long, and with antennae-like growths at the petal tips.

Cultivation. Plant at any time between October and March in well-drained, humus-rich soil. Partial shade is ideal but the plants will grow in full sun. For pot culture, set the plants in 4–5 in. pots of John Innes potting compost No. 2.

Being hardy, tolmieas are particularly suitable for rooms that are seldom or never heated. Pot at any time between September and March and repot annually in March or April. Water freely during the growing period, and keep the plants just moist in winter. Feed once a month with a weak liquid manure from May to September.

Propagation. Detach leaves bearing well-developed plantlets and set them out either in seed trays, or singly in 3 in. pots, containing John Innes potting compost No. 1. Pot on as necessary when rooted.

Plants growing outside may have the leaves pegged down on to the soil, where they will root readily. Leaves often rest on the soil and root naturally without pegging. In both cases, when the young plants are well-rooted, lift and replant them direct in permanent positions.

Pests and diseases. Generally trouble-free.

Tomato

Lycopersicon esculentum. Solanaceae

TOMATO

A tender or half-hardy bushy or semi-procumbent annual, grown for its edible fruits which are used fresh in salads, cooked as a vegetable or made into chutneys. Under greenhouse conditions crops can be harvested at any time of year.

Tomatoes should be grown at a temperature that does not fall below 10°C (50°F), nor rise above 27°C (80°F). They should be given as much air and sun as possible and generally are best grown in heated greenhouses or under cold glass protection. In the south and west, outdoor cultivation is possible, but except during sunny, prolonged summers, a percentage of the fruits must be brought indoors for ripening.

VARIETIES

Numerous tall and dwarf varieties have been developed from the wild tomato. The fruits may be red, orange or yellow; large, medium-sized, or grape-like; unevenly grooved, plum-shaped, pear-shaped or globular.

Recent breeding work has extended the choice of suitable varieties. For early sowings in a heated greenhouse, the F_1 hybrids 'Euro-cross BB' and 'Kingley Cross' are recommended. Reliable main-crop varieties include 'Best of All' and 'Potentate'.

For sowings in an unheated greenhouse grow the heavy-cropping variety 'Moneymaker'; this lacks the flavour and fine texture of 'Ailsa Craig', 'Alicante', 'Early Market' and 'Sunrise'.

For outdoor crops, quick-maturing varieties such as the fine-flavoured 'Harbinger' and 'Leader' are recommended. For a heavy crop 'Moneymaker' may be successfully grown.

For small gardens, bush varieties such as 'Dwarf Gem' and 'The Amateur' are recommended. 'The Amateur' is particularly suitable for starting early under cloches. The prostrate or low hummock-forming 'Sub-arctic Delight' also provides a reliable crop of small round fruits.

Yellow-fruited varieties are often considered to have a sweeter and finer flavour. The rich yellow 'Golden Sunrise' and 'Sutton's Golden Queen' can be recommended.

Greenhouse cultivation. For indoor or outdoor cultivation, tomatoes are best raised from seeds. Sow the seeds $\frac{3}{4}$ in. apart each way in boxes of John Innes seed compost, and cover with sheets of glass or polythene.

Germinate the seeds at a temperature of 16°C (61°F); as soon as the young seedlings appear, remove the glass or polythene and put the boxes in the lightest part of the greenhouse or frame. When the seed leaves have opened fully, pot the seedlings singly into $3\frac{1}{2}$ in. pots of John Innes potting compost No. 2. Ventilate the house when the temperature exceeds 10°C (50°F). After about six weeks, harden off plants which are to be grown outdoors.

As the plants outgrow their pots, move them on to 6 in. pots and later into their final 12 in. pots, deep boxes or borders, under glass or in the open. Remove any side-shoots from all except bush varieties.

During winter and early spring, about 14 weeks are needed to bring greenhouse varieties from seed to readiness for their final quarters; a March sowing will yield fruit in four months or less under ideal conditions. An August or September sowing generally does not fruit in less than six months; to ensure winter supplies, sow seeds in the greenhouse during late July to produce plants ready for setting out in their final quarters by September.

In the greenhouse, grow tomatoes to maturity in John Innes potting compost No. 3 or in a mixture of 3 parts heavy loam, 1 part well-rotted dry manure or spent mushroom manure and 1 part coarse sand (parts by volume). If manure is unobtainable, it may be replaced by a complete tomato base-fertiliser. Add $1\frac{1}{2}$ oz. of lime per bushel of the growing mixture.

In the greenhouse border, set the plants at 15–24 in. intervals; the same border may be used for tomatoes for two or three years but thereafter the soil will be exhausted. Remove the top 18 in. of soil and replace with a new mixture. Pot-grown tomatoes are particularly suitable for ensuring a succession of fruits from early spring until the end of December.

Tolmiea menziesii

Tomato 'Ailsa Craig'

Tomato 'Alicante'

Support the plants with 6 ft high canes and tie in the stems loosely but securely as the plants grow. Continue to remove any side-shoots that appear, except on bush varieties, and cut off any leaves that turn yellow. Give the plants plenty of air throughout their growing season, and keep them well watered by thorough soakings when the soil begins to dry out.

When six or seven trusses of flowers have set, pinch out the growing tip of each plant. Assist pollination by increasing the temperature slightly, and by spraying the plants lightly at mid-day; alternatively, use a soft camel-hair brush to transfer pollen, or shake the flower trusses gently. After the fruit has set, apply a mulch of well-rotted manure round the plants or feed at seven to ten-day intervals with a liquid tomato fertiliser.

Ring culture is a recommended method for growing tomatoes in a greenhouse. In April, set the young plants in 10 in. wide bottomless containers, 8 in. deep, of John Innes potting compost No. 3. Place the containers on a bed of aggregate, of weathered ash or clinkers, or a mixture of 3 parts gravel and 1 part coarse vermiculite (parts by volume).

Tomatoes grown on the ring-culture system develop fibrous feeding roots in the containers, while the water-seeking roots grow into the aggregate, which must be kept permanently moist. As soon as the first flower truss has set, begin feeding the containers with a liquid fertiliser at intervals of three to four days.

Outdoor cultivation. Sow seeds in late March or in April as described under GREENHOUSE CULTIVATION. Transplant the seedlings or purchased sturdy plants, 8–10 in. high, to open ground during late May and early June. Crops will usually be ready from late August onwards. Select a warm, sheltered and sunny site, preferably near a south-facing wall or fence. Do not plant close to a hedge where the soil may dry out quickly in summer.

Prepare heavy soils in autumn and light soils in spring by incorporating a bucket of decayed manure or compost per sq. yd and leaving the bed in shallow ridges, 2½ ft apart. Set the plants on the ridges, 15 in. apart for cordons and 24 in. apart for bush varieties. During the first few nights, cover the plants with inverted pots. Give the plants a thorough watering before planting them out, but except during hot, dry weather, do not water again until they are established. Thereafter keep the plants well watered; a flower pot sunk into the soil beside each plant and frequently filled with water, ensures an adequate moisture supply. Stake each plant as soon as possible with a 4 ft stout stake and tie the plants in lightly but securely as they grow.

When the flower trusses have set, give a monthly liquid or granular feed or a foliar feed. Hand pollination is unnecessary.

Pinch out the lateral shoots of cordon types as they appear. In early August, nip out the growing tips to encourage more rapid swelling of the fruits; leaves may be removed to aid ripening during dull weather.

Gather the fruits as they ripen. Pick any trusses of green fruits that are just turning, when the cold weather begins, and place them in a drawer to ripen, preferably wrapped in wax paper or polythene sheeting.

Pests. On outdoor plants, the leaves may be eaten by CATERPILLARS, particularly those of the tomato moth, which tunnel into stems and fruit.

POTATO CYST EELWORM infests roots of plants grown in the open and causes stunted growth, yellow discoloration of the leaves and wilting.

APHIDS infest young shoots and leaves of plants grown under glass and outdoors; greenhouse plants are infested by GLASSHOUSE WHITEFLY and GLASSHOUSE RED SPIDER MITES.

Diseases. One or more of the following diseases may attack tomatoes grown under glass or in the open. BLOSSOM END ROT shows as circular brown or black patches on the fruits.

BLOTCHY RIPENING shows as hard green or yellow patches on the surface of the fruits.

DAMPING-OFF causes seedlings to collapse and rot at soil level.

FOOT and ROOT ROT can be caused by several fungi including RHIZOCTONIA and BLACK ROOT ROT fungus. The roots die and often show brown or black patches. The stem bases also become discoloured and may decay; the foliage turns yellow and withers, and diseased plants collapse.

GREENBACK shows as hard green or yellow patches on the fruit near the stalks.

GREY MOULD affects stems and leaves, causing them to rot; they become covered with a grey velvety fungal growth. The same fungus may also appear as pin-point spots with pale-coloured rings on green fruits; rotting seldom occurs.

LEAF MOULD shows as yellow blotches on the upper sides of the leaves; a purple-brown mould develops on the undersurfaces.

MAGNESIUM DEFICIENCY results in orange-yellow discoloration of the lower leaves, commencing between the veins.

POTATO BLIGHT FUNGUS, which usually only affects outdoor plants, produces brown blotches on leaves and stems, and later on the fruits, which rot.

SPRAY DAMAGE, due to the effects of hormone weedkillers, shows as a distortion of the stems and leaf stalks which twist spirally; the leaves become narrow, and show parallel veining.

STEM CANKER causes a darkening of the tissues at the base of the stems which shrink, causing plants to collapse.

TOBACCO MOSAIC and TOMATO SPOTTED WILT VIRUSES are two of the many TOMATO VIRUS DISEASES. They show as stunting of plants, mottling or blotching of the foliage, distortion of the leaves, and brown streaks on the stems.

Tomato 'Golden Sunrise'

Torenia fournieri

Torenia
Scrophulariaceae

A genus of 50 species of annual and perennial herbaceous plants. The one described is a half-hardy annual suitable for summer bedding and increasingly grown as a summer-flowering pot plant under glass.

T. fournieri (wishbone flower). Tropical Asia. Height 12 in.; planting distance 6–9 in. An attractive plant with pale green leaves that are narrow, pointed and marginally toothed. The tubular flowers, 1½ in. long, have deep violet-purple lips and lilac-purple throats marked with yellow; the petals have a velvety texture. The flowers are produced from July to September in such profusion that they almost hide the foliage. There are several named varieties available, including 'Alba'. 9 in., white.

TORENIA FOURNIERI

Cultivation. Outdoors, grow in moist garden soil in a sheltered and partially shaded site.

Grow pot plants in final 5 in. pots containing John Innes potting compost No. 2. Shade from strong sunlight.

Pinch out the growing tips of young plants, both outdoors and in pots, to encourage branching growth. Provide twiggy supports.

Propagation. Sow the seeds under glass in March at a temperature of 18°C (64°F), just covering them with compost. Prick off the seedlings into boxes or 3 in. pots. If the plants are to be grown outdoors, harden them off in a cold frame before planting out in late May or early June.

Pests and diseases. Generally trouble-free.

Touch-me-not, Himalayan: see *Impatiens roylei*

Trachelospermum

Apocynaceae

A genus of 30 species of evergreen climbing shrubs. The three species described are hardy in all but the coldest areas and spread even when young. They are of twining and self-clinging habit, suitable for covering walls and fences. The 1 in. wide, salviform, fragrant flowers are produced freely during July and August in slender cymes, 2–3 in. wide, at the ends of shoots.

TRACHELOSPERMUM ASIATICUM

T. asiaticum, syn. *T. divaricatum.* Japan, Korea. Height up to 15 ft. A plant of dense and compact habit, with dark green, leathery, narrowly ovate leaves. The cream-white flowers turn a deeper shade as they age.

T. divaricatum: see *T. asiaticum*

T. japonicum: see *T. majus*

T. jasminoïdes, syn. *Rhyncospermum jasminoïdes.* China. Height 10–12 ft. This is the most commonly grown wall climber in the genus. The slender growth is hairy when young. The leaves are dark green, leathery and ovate-lanceolate, the

flowers white. *T. j.* 'Variegatum' has leaves edged and mottled with cream-white.

T. majus, syn. *T. japonicum.* Japan. This vigorous climber reaches a height of at least 15–20 ft. It is hardier than the two other species described. In warm seasons its deep green ovate-oblong leaves turn brilliant red-bronze in autumn and winter. The flowers are pure white and only mildly fragrant. This species is ideal for covering a great expanse of wall.

Cultivation. Plant in late April or early May. The plants do best against a sheltered wall or fence with a south or west aspect and in light, well-drained, acid soil. Mix peat with the soil before planting. Insert twiggy sticks to give the young plants a start, training them in the early stages to establish a balanced framework.

Remove the faded inflorescences of all species after flowering.

Propagation. Take 3–4 in. nodal cuttings from side-shoots and insert them in sandy peat in a propagating frame during July or August. With a mist propagator, cuttings can be taken from April to September. Pot the rooted cuttings in 3 in. pots of John Innes potting compost No. 1. Overwinter in a cold frame and plant out in permanent positions the following spring.

Layer mature growths in October. They will be ready for severing a year later.

Pruning. Thin out vigorous shoots in March or April, if necessary, to restrict growth.

Pests. APHIDS may infest young growths.

Diseases. Generally trouble-free.

Trachycarpus
Chusan or fan palm. *Palmae*

TRACHYCARPUS FORTUNEI

A genus of eight species of evergreen palms with large fan-shaped leaves. They are slow-growing in the British Isles. Only one species is in general cultivation; this is hardy in all parts of the country with the exception of the north-east. It is chiefly grown as a specimen tree on sheltered lawns.

T. excelsa: see *T. fortunei*

T. fortunei, syns. *T. excelsa, Chamaerops excelsa.* China. Height 6–10 ft; spread 6 ft or more. Mid-green pleated leaves, about 3 ft wide, are borne on sharply toothed stalks up to 3 ft long. Small yellow flowers appear in May or June in dense panicles up to 24 in. long. Occasionally the flowers are followed by ½ in. wide, blue-black, globose fruits.

Cultivation. Plant in late April or May in ordinary, well-drained soil. Set in sun or light shade and sheltered from north and east winds.

Propagation. Remove basal suckers with two or three leaves in April or May. Pot them up in 6 in. pots of John Innes potting compost No. 1 and place in a frame or greenhouse with a minimum

Trachelospermum asiaticum

Trachycarpus fortunei

Tradescantia blossfeldiana 'Variegata'

Tradescantia fluminensis 'Quicksilver'

Tradescantia virginiana 'Isis'

Trifolium repens 'Purpurascens Quadriphyllum'

temperature of 10–13°C (50–55°F). Grow them on under glass for a year before hardening off and planting them out in May. Small suckers will require two years before planting out.

Sow seeds about 1 in. deep in sandy loam in a propagating frame, at a temperature of about 24°C (75°F) in March. Prick off the seedlings into 3 in. pots of John Innes potting compost No. 1, and grow on under glass at a temperature of 10°C (50°F) for two years; pot on successively as required. At the end of the second year, the young plants may be overwintered in a cold frame and grown on for two further years before finally being planted out in May.

Pruning. No pruning is necessary, other than to remove damaged leaves.

Pests and diseases. Generally trouble-free.

Tradescantia

Commelinaceae

A genus of 60 species of hardy and tender perennial flowering and foliage plants. The tender species described are popular as house plants. They are rarely sold under their specific names, but simply as tradescantias. Also described is one hardy species, easily grown and suitable for herbaceous borders.

Tradescantia flowers are three-petalled, basically triangular in outline; they are borne in terminal clusters.

GREENHOUSE SPECIES

T. albiflora (wandering jew). S. America. A foliage, mat-forming species suitable for a hanging basket, with broadly ovate, stemless leaves. In cultivation the species is generally represented by variegated forms. The most popular are variously striped with cream; 'Tricolor' has white and rose-purple stripes.

T. blossfeldiana. Argentina. This semi-erect species has oblong-elliptic leaves, dark green above and purple and hairy beneath. The fleshy stems are usually purple. Rose-purple, white-centred flowers, $\frac{1}{2}-\frac{3}{4}$ in. across, are borne in terminal clusters from March to July on mature plants. There is a variegated form, 'Variegata', striped with cream.

T. fluminensis, syn. *T. fluviatilis*. S. America. This species is similar to *T. albiflora*, but differs in having longer, elliptic-ovate leaves on short leaf stalks. In bright light the undersides of the leaves turn pale purple. There are several forms with yellow variegations; 'Quicksilver' is a robust variety profusely striped with silver.

T. fluviatilis: see *T. fluminensis*

T. purpurea: see *Zebrina purpusii*

HARDY SPECIES

T. × andersoniana: see *T. virginiana*

T. virginiana (trinity flower, spiderwort). N. America. Height 24 in.; planting distance 18 in. A hardy border plant with dull green, pointed, strap-shaped leaves. Flowers, 1–1½ in. across and varying from blue and purple to rose and white, are borne in small terminal umbels; they are freely produced from June to September.

Most, if not all, of the plants listed as garden varieties are hybrids which are now known collectively as *T. × andersoniana*. They include:

'Caerulea Plena', with light blue flowers; 'Blue Stone', deep blue; 'Isis', rich royal-purple; 'J. C. Weguelin', violet-blue; 'Osprey', white with fluffy blue centres; and 'Purple Dome', purple.

TRADESCANTIA VIRGINIANA

Cultivation of greenhouse species. As pot plants, tradescantias are easily grown in 4–6 in. pots, pans or hanging baskets containing John Innes potting compost No. 2 or a proprietary peat compost. Maintain a winter temperature of 7–10°C (45–50°F); keep the plants just moist.

During the growing period, water freely and keep the plants in a well-lit position, out of direct sunlight.

Repot annually in April and give a weak liquid feed at fortnightly intervals from May to September. The plants deteriorate quickly and are best discarded after two growing seasons.

Cultivation of hardy species. Plant from October to March in sun or partial shade and in ordinary, well-drained, but moisture-retentive garden soil. Staking with twiggy sticks may be necessary. Cut down in November.

Propagation of greenhouse species. Tip cuttings root easily even when placed in water. Insert three 2–3 in. cuttings in a 3 in. pot of John Innes potting compost No. 1, at a temperature of 16°C (61°F). Pot on the group as necessary. Cuttings are best taken from April to September.

Propagation of hardy species. Divide the plants every three or four years in March or April.

Seeds may be sown in March, but named varieties do not come true from seeds, and the seedlings are variable. Sow in pans of John Innes seed compost and germinate in a cold frame. Prick out the seedlings, when large enough to handle, into boxes and then into a nursery bed. Plant out in the flowering quarters in October.

Pruning. Pinch out the growing points of trailing species in the young stage to promote basal branching. Remove any pure green growths of the variegated forms as soon as they are noticed.

Pests. Outdoors, shoots may be eaten by SLUGS.

Diseases. Browning of the leaves is due to a PHYSIOLOGICAL DISORDER. The leaves shrivel and fall prematurely.

Tragopogon porrifolius: see Salsify

Trichosporum speciosum: see *Aeschynanthus speciosus*

Tricuspidaria lanceolata: see *Crinodendron hookerianum*

Trifolium

Leguminosae

A genus of 300 species of half-hardy and hardy annual and perennial plants. The perennial described is suitable for large rock gardens.

T. repens (white clover). Europe. Height 2–4 in.; spread 18–24 in. In cultivation this species is generally represented by the ornamental variety 'Purpurascens Quadriphyllum'. This clover has three to six green to purple leaflets to each leaf. The flowers are identical to those of the common white clover and open from June to September. The plant spreads vigorously by runners.

Cultivation. Plant from October to March in any reasonably well-drained garden soil in a sunny position. The leaf colour tends to become paler in a shaded site.

Propagation. Divide in March and plant out in permanent positions.

Pests. Generally trouble-free.

Diseases. A white mealy covering on the leaves and stems is caused by POWDERY MILDEW.

Trillium

Trilliaceae, syn. *Liliaceae*

This genus of 30 species of hardy rhizomatous herbaceous perennials was formerly included in the lily family. It has recently been re-classified, together with certain other genera, in a new family. *Trilliaceae.*

The species are distinguished by having all their parts, including leaves, sepals and petals, in groups of three. The ovate to obovate leaves vary from pale to mid-green, sometimes marbled with white or purple, and are borne in a single whorl at the top of each stem. The solitary flowers are composed of three ovate to lanceolate petals, erect or reflexed, with three pointed green sepals beneath. The flowering period extends from April to June.

The species in cultivation require moist positions beneath trees or in shady rock gardens or borders; they are most effective when grown in large clumps.

TRILLIUM GRANDIFLORUM

T. erectum. E. United States. Height and planting distance 12 in. A species with slightly nodding purple-red flowers, 1–1½ in. across; the petals are reflexed at the tips.

T. grandiflorum (wake robin). E. United States. Height 12–18 in.; planting distance 12 in. A clump-forming species bearing 2–3 in. wide flowers with slightly reflexed petals. The flowers, on short arching stems, are white on opening, then become flushed with rose-pink. Pink and double white varieties are sometimes available.

T. ovatum. W. United States. Height 8–10 in.; planting distance 9 in. This species carries 1½ in. wide flowers with petals similar to, but narrower than, those of *T. grandiflorum.* They change quickly from white to deep pink.

T. sessile. Central United States. Height 6–12 in.; planting distance 9–12 in. The leaves of this species are marbled grey and deep green. The stemless flowers, up to 3 in. long, have narrow, erect, pointed and slightly twisted petals. They range from red to maroon in colour and are faintly scented.

T. undulatum (painted wood-lily). Canada and U.S.A. Height 12 in.; planting distance 6–9 in. The flowers, 1–1½ in. across with spreading petals, are white with a purple zone at the base.

Cultivation. Grow trilliums in any moist but well-drained soil with plenty of humus incorporated. A partially shaded site or woodland conditions are ideal, but the plants tolerate sun if the soil is kept continuously moist. Plant the rhizomes as soon as they are available, in August or September, or at any time during suitable weather until March. Set the rhizomes 3–4 in. deep in groups.

Propagation. Lift and divide the rhizomatous roots after the foliage has died down in late summer, or at any time up to March. Ensure that each piece retains a growing point, and do not divide more than necessary, as the plants take time to become established after division.

Trilliums can also be raised from seeds, sown when ripe or as soon as purchased. Sow thinly in pots or pans of John Innes seed compost in a cold frame; they frequently take 18 months to germinate, sometimes as long as three years. At the end of the first growing season, lift and separate the tiny rhizomes, and pot them individually in 3 in. containers of John Innes potting compost No. 1. Keep the pots in a cold frame for one or two years before planting out. Plants raised from seeds may take up to six years to reach flowering size.

Pests. Young shoots and flower buds may be attacked by SLUGS.

Diseases. Generally trouble-free.

Trinity flower: see *Tradescantia virginiana*
Triteleia laxa: see *Brodiaea laxa*
Triteleia × tubergenii: see *Brodiaea × tubergenii*
Triteleia uniflora: see *Ipheion uniflorum*

Tritonia

Iridaceae

TRITONIA CROCATA

The 55 species of this genus of cormous plants come from tropical and southern Africa. Only two or three species are in general cultivation. They are closely related to *Freesia, Ixia, Sparaxis* and *Crocosmia,* with which they were once confused. Like these other genera, tritonias produce fans of narrow, sword-shaped, mid-green leaves which arise from small corms. Although some are hardy in a sunny position, all are best grown in a cool greenhouse to produce attractive flowers for cutting.

Trillium erectum

Trillium grandiflorum

Trillium ovatum

Trillium sessile

Tritonia crocata

Trollius × *hybridus*
'Lemon Queen'

Trollius pumilus

Tropaeolum majus
Gleam strain

T. aurea: see *Crocosmia aurea*

T. crocata. S. Africa. Height 12–18 in. Several shallow, cup-shaped, orange flowers, about 1½ in. wide, appear in two ranks at the top of the flower stem in May and June. Among named hybrids are: 'Isabella', yellow flushed with pink; 'Orange Delight', copper; 'Prince of Orange', rich orange; 'Princess Beatrix', deep orange; 'Rose-line', pale pink; and 'White Glory'.

T. hyalina. S. Africa. Height 12 in. Deep yellow flowers, 1½ in. wide and with six spreading spoon-shaped petals, are borne in May and June.

T. rosea. S. Africa. Height 18 in. Broadly funnel-shaped red flowers, 1 in. long, are borne in May and June.

Cultivation. In September, place five or six corms 2 in. deep in a 6 in. pot of well-dampened John Innes potting compost No. 2, spacing the corms evenly. Do not water until the leaves appear, unless the compost becomes dry. Maintain a winter temperature of 7–10°C (45–50°F).

The shoots may need supporting with small twiggy sticks or with thin canes and raffia unless the plants can be kept in full light all the time. Allow the temperature to rise as the days lengthen and the plants grow. After flowering, keep the plants well watered until the leaves begin to turn yellow, then allow the soil to dry out completely in the warmth of the greenhouse. Corms may be left in the pots for two years, but are best repotted annually in September.

Propagation. Separate the offsets from the larger corms when repotting, and grow these on to flower two or three years later.

Pests and diseases. Generally trouble-free.

Trollius

Globe flower. *Ranunculaceae*

A genus of 25 species of hardy herbaceous perennials. The globe-shaped flowers resemble large buttercups, and range from pale yellow to orange. The mid to deep green leaves are round to ovate and deeply cleft into toothed lobes. The plants are suitable for borders, or for growing at the margins of streams and ponds. Provided the roots are kept moist, the plants are easily grown in sun or light shade.

T. asiaticus. Siberia, Turkistan. Height 12–18 in.; planting distance 12 in. A species with dark yellow flowers, 1½–2 in. across, that appear in May and June.

T. europaeus: see *T.* × *hybridus*

T. × ***hybridus.*** Garden origin. Height 2–2½ ft; planting distance 18 in. These garden hybrids, which flower from May to June, are often listed as *T. europaeus*, but are thought to be crosses between that species and *T. chinensis*. Good varieties, with flowers up to 2¼ in. across, include: 'Canary Bird', pale yellow; 'Earliest of All', medium yellow; 'Golden Wonder', deep yellow; 'Goldquelle', golden-yellow; 'Lemon Queen', pale yellow; 'Orange Princess', orange-yellow; 'Prichard's Giant', strong-growing, medium yellow; 'Salamander', fiery orange.

T. ledebouri. E. Siberia. Height 2½ ft; planting distance 15 in. The open-petalled pale orange flowers, 2–2½ in. across, have prominent bright

yellow stamens and appear in June and July. The varieties 'Golden Queen' and 'Imperial Orange' both have deep orange flowers.

T. pumilus. N. India, W. China. Height 12 in. planting distance 9 in. This species is suitable for a rock garden. The shining yellow flowers, 1–1¼ in. across, appear in May and June.

Cultivation. Plant in October or April in ordinary garden soil. The plants do best in moist soil, and in sun or partial shade; during dry weather water freely. Cut the flower stems back to base after flowering to induce a second flush of blooms in late summer.

Propagation. Divide and replant the fibrous roots in September, October or April.

Sow seeds, as soon as ripe or from September to April, in boxes of John Innes seed compost in a cold frame. Old seeds may take more than a year to germinate. Prick out the seedlings in nursery rows when large enough to handle, and transplant to their flowering positions from October to April the following year.

Pests. Generally trouble-free.

Diseases. SMUT shows on leaves and stems as blister-like swellings which burst open to release a mass of powdery black spores.

Tropaeolum

Tropaeolaceae

A genus of 90 species of hardy annual and herbaceous perennial plants, mostly of climbing habit. The annual species described, including the familiar nasturtium, are suitable for growing in pots in greenhouses, in hanging baskets, and for covering trelliswork, fences and banks. The flowers last well when cut. The dwarf varieties are suitable for bedding, for edging paths and for rock gardens. The perennials include both climbing and prostrate species.

All species have shortly trumpet-shaped flowers, sometimes with petals of different sizes.

ANNUAL SPECIES

T. canariense: see *T. peregrinum*

T. lobbianum: see *T. peltophorum*

T. majus (nasturtium). S. America. Height 8 ft or more; planting distance 15 in. This annual of climbing and trailing habit is the most widely grown species. The mid-green leaves are smooth and circular with waved edges. Faintly scented yellow or orange flowers, 2 in. across and with a long spur, appear from June to September. When crushed, both leaves and stems have a pungent smell.

The numerous garden varieties include the Gleam strain (height 15 in.), which are bushy, vigorous plants with trailing stems 18 in. long. Recommended are 'Golden Gleam', with semi-double golden-yellow flowers; 'Indian Chief', with purple-tinted foliage and semi-double, scarlet flowers; and 'Orange Gleam', semi-double, bright orange flowers.

'Jewel Mixed', 12 in., is an early-flowering dwarf strain producing masses of semi-double flowers in a wide range of colours from yellow to salmon-pink, scarlet and crimson.

The Tom Thumb strain, 10 in., are dwarf and compact plants: 'King of Tom Thumbs' bears purple-tinted foliage and scarlet flowers; 'Golden King of Tom Thumbs' has deep yellow flowers.

T. peltophorum, syn. *T. lobbianum.* Colombia. Height 6 ft or more; planting distance 15 in. An annual of climbing habit, similar to *T. majus.* The mid-green leaves are round with waved margins and are carried on long stalks. The flowers, bright orange-scarlet, with a rounded upper petal and a clawed lower petal, are $\frac{1}{4}$ in. long and are produced from July to September.

T. peregrinum, syn. *T canariense* (canary creeper). Peru. This rapid climber can reach a height of 12 ft in one season; planting distance 3 ft. Although a short-lived perennial, it is usually grown as an annual. It will grow in shade but does best in a sunny and partially sheltered position on a wall, fence or dead tree. The habit is upright at first, then branching; there is no need to pinch out the growing points. It has blue-green peltate leaves with five lobes. Irregularly shaped yellow flowers, $\frac{3}{4}$–1 in. across and with green spurs, are freely borne from July to October.

Tropaeolum peregrinum

PERENNIAL SPECIES

T. polyphyllum. Chile, Argentina. Height 3–4 in.; spread 3–6 ft. A prostrate species with grey-green, lobed, palmate leaves. The yellow flowers, which are $\frac{1}{2}$ in. wide and open in June and July, are sometimes shaded with orange. Each bloom has a prominent spur up to $\frac{3}{4}$ in. long. The species is suitable for trailing over a dry wall.

TROPAEOLUM POLYPHYLLUM

T. speciosum (flame creeper). Chile. Height 10–15 ft; spread 2–3 ft. A deciduous perennial that dies down in the autumn. The narrow twining stems, with their mid-green, six-lobed leaves, form an attractive plant even before the flowers appear, and show to advantage when rambling over a shrub. The long-stalked, brilliant scarlet flowers are $1\frac{1}{2}$ in. across; they are composed of five rounded and waved petals that open out flat. They are borne singly on curling

stems from the leaf axils and provide a continuous display from July to September.

This species grows better in northern and western districts and in cool, moist areas in the south. It is not a plant for town gardens. The rootstock is a creeping rhizome.

T. tricolorum. Bolivia, Chile. Height about 4 ft; spread about 18 in. A slender, tuberous-rooted climber with mid-green palmate leaves divided into five to seven narrowly obovate lobes. The spurred and hooded flowers, $1\frac{1}{2}$–2 in. long, appear from May to July. The calyx is orange-scarlet tipped with dark purple, the petals are orange, and the spur varies from red to yellow with a blue-purple or greenish tip.

T. tuberosum. Peru, Bolivia. Height up to 10 ft; spread 3 ft. A vigorous climber with slightly glaucous, lobed, palmate leaves. Boldly spurred red and yellow flowers, $1\frac{1}{2}$ in. long, are borne on slender red stems from the upper leaf axils. The original species does not flower until September and is often cut down by frost, but the form offered as 'Early-flowering Variety' blooms from June to October.

Cultivation of annual species. Grow the annual species and varieties on a sunny site. *T. peregrinum* needs soil of average fertility; the others are better planted in poor soil, as rich, moist soil causes the leaves to develop excessively at the expense of flowers. In early May, set out plants raised under glass, and use twiggy sticks to support the young growths.

T. majus can also be grown as a summer-flowering pot plant in a 5–6 in. container of John Innes potting compost No. 2.

Cultivation of perennial species. Plant *T. polyphyllum*, *T. tricolorum* and *T. tuberosum* in sun or partial shade, in March or April, in any well-drained fertile soil. In cold districts, lift the tubers of *T. tricolorum* and *T. tuberosum* after the first frost. Store the tubers in a frost-free shed.

Set out *T. speciosum* plants in November or March. They need an acid or neutral soil with peat, leaf-mould and sand added. The main growths thrive in full sun, but the lower stems and roots require shade; the ideal planting position is the shady side of a low hedge, bush or wall. Plant the rhizomes horizontally and apply a top-dressing of well-rotted manure or compost each spring before growth begins. Insert twiggy sticks to give the young growths a start. Protect the base of the plants with a layer of leaves or bracken during winter.

Propagation of annual species. Sow the seeds $\frac{3}{4}$ in. deep in the flowering site in April, subsequently reducing the number of seedlings by thinning. In the case of *T. peregrinum*, sow two seeds where one plant is required. If both germinate, remove one of the seedlings.

For early flowering, or to provide plants for pots and hanging baskets, sow the seeds in February or March in pots or pans of John Innes seed compost, at a temperature of 13–16°C (55–61°F). When the seedlings are large enough to handle, pot them singly in 3 in. containers of John Innes potting compost No. 2 and pot on as required. If the plants are to grow outside, harden them off and plant out in April or May.

Propagation of perennial species. Divide the rootstocks of *T. polyphyllum* and *T. speciosum*

Tropaeolum polyphyllum

Tropaeolum speciosum

Tropaeolum tuberosum

in March, taking care to minimise damage to the roots, which grow to a depth of 6–9 in.

Tubers of *T. tricolorum* and *T. tuberosum* multiply in the same manner as those of the potato. They should be separated at lifting time or in spring when the tubers are replanted.

Pests. Stems and leaves may be infested by APHIDS, particularly the black bean aphid.

THRIPS and GLASSHOUSE RED SPIDER MITES may infest plants under glass.

Diseases. Several VIRUS DISEASES, including TOMATO SPOTTED WILT VIRUS, may cause small brown spots on the leaves, or mottling and distortion. Infected plants are stunted; they have few flowers or the flower colour may be broken.

Trumpet creeper: see Campsis

Tsuga

Hemlock. *Pinaceae*

A genus of ten species of evergreen conifers related to *Picea*, and native to N. America, the Himalayas and E. Asia. They have dense crowns of fine shoots, small linear-oblong leaves and ovoid cones. The species described are hardy and suitable as specimen trees or for hedging.

See also CONIFERS.

T. canadensis (Eastern hemlock). E. Canada and N.E. United States. Height 30 ft; spread 20 ft. A bushy, broad-crowned tree with rough-ridged, dark grey-brown bark. The hairy shoots arch slightly at the tips and bear dark green leaves; these partially cover the shoots and those along the centre are twisted so that the white-lined undersides are uppermost. The cones, which hang like droplets, are 1 in. long, green and purple, ripening to brown.

'Pendula' and 'Nana' (height 6 ft; spread 10 ft) are broad-headed bushes of pendulous branches which eventually rest on the ground; they are both usually listed as 'Pendula'.

The true 'Pendula' is a taller, less dense bush, drooping to the ground in several places.

TSUGA HETEROPHYLLA

T. heterophylla (Western hemlock). Western N. America. Height 60 ft; spread 15 ft. A shapely, slender, towering tree, regularly and narrowly conic with a long drooping leading shoot and dense foliage hanging from slightly ascending branches. On exposed sites, the crown becomes thin and growth is poor, but the shape is seldom affected. The bole is usually deeply fluted, with the dark brown bark furrowed into scaly ridges. It is excellent as a specimen tree and for hedging.

The white hairy shoots bear double ranks of parallel-sided leaves of mixed lengths, dark green above with two broad white bands below. Male yellow-green and crimson flowers are borne in globular clusters at the ends of small shoots. Female flowers appear singly at the ends of the larger shoots and develop into small, droplet-shaped cones. These are pale brown, 1 in. long, and open to reveal smoothly rounded woody scales. This species is self-fertile and numerous strong self-sown seedlings often occur.

T. mertensiana (mountain hemlock). Western N. America. Height 30 ft; spread 15 ft. Usually a slow-growing tree, highly attractive with its dense, pendulous, narrow spire of grey-blue leaves borne all round the shoots. The cylindrical and pendulous purple cones, pointed at each end, are almost 3 in. long. They cluster near the top of trees more than 20 years old. The dark red-brown bark is rough and scaly.

TSUGA MERTENSIANA

Cultivation. These conifers thrive in all soil types except those containing large amounts of lime; chalk overlaid with slightly acid sand will give adequate growth. They grow best in areas of heavy rainfall and in a partially shaded position, sheltered from drying east winds. Plant during suitable weather from October to early April. The young trees should be about 24 in. high and require no staking; *T. heterophylla*, in particular, should be planted in the young stage to avoid a check to growth. On thin soils or in dry areas, incorporate plenty of leaf-mould and compost.

For hedges of *T. heterophylla*, use 12–18 in. high plants, setting these at intervals of 18–24 in. The growing tips should be pinched out to promote bushy growth. Trim the leading shoots when 12 in. above the desired height to 12 in. below this height. This will encourage the formation of side-shoots that will soon form a solid hedge top.

Propagation. Sow seeds of the species in March or April in pans of John Innes seed compost in a cold frame. When the seedlings are 3 in. high, line out into nursery rows outdoors and grow on for one to three years, depending on the species, before planting in permanent positions.

Named varieties must be increased by cuttings taken in September. Select 1–3 in. long cuttings of lateral shoots with a heel; insert in equal parts (by volume) peat and sand in a cold frame. When rooted, pot singly in 3–3½ in. pots of John Innes potting compost No. 2 and plunge outdoors. Plant out after two or three years.

Pruning. Specimen trees require no pruning. Clip established hedges to shape annually in June or September.

Pests and diseases. Generally trouble-free.

Tsuga canadensis (cones)

Tsuga heterophylla (cones)

Tulipa 'Shakespeare' (Div. 12)

TULIPA
Tulip. *Liliaceae*

This genus of 100 species of hardy bulbs has been popular in Europe for over 300 years. Tulips were introduced from Turkey, where they had already long been prized, and brought to European gardens in the mid-16th century. They were an instant success, and less than 100 years later a tulip mania swept Holland and its neighbouring countries. Tulip bulbs were sold at ever-increasing prices.

Today in Holland, in certain areas of Britain, and in a few other countries, specialist growers cultivate hundreds of modern varieties. Meanwhile, over the centuries, plant collectors have continued to seek the original species in their native countries, ranging from Europe to the Himalayas, and particularly the Middle East.

Some of the first tulips to come from Turkey were cultivated forms or hybrids. This was not always realised by western botanists, who regarded them as true species. Nowadays these are classified as *Neo-tulipae,* examples being 'Acuminata', syn. 'Cornuta', and 'Marjolettii'.

Tulips are indispensable to planners of town parks and gardens, for they brighten beds and borders during April and May before the less-hardy summer bedding plants are in flower.

All tulips grow from rounded or ovoid bulbs, which have thin outer skins, and a pointed nose. Most carry one flower on an erect stem, but a few have two, three or even more flowers on each stem. The flowers are goblet-shaped, with six petals which vary from slender and pointed to broadly rounded; mature flowers tend to open out flat. One or two leaves grow at or near ground level, with two or three smaller ones up the stem. A few species, for example *T. tarda,* have a basal tuft of narrow leaves at flowering time.

Tulipa 'Pink Beauty' (Div. 1)

Nearly every form of tulip flowers well in the first year after planting: only a flooded garden or one of the serious pests or diseases can prevent this. After the first year, however, it requires care to induce some of the more difficult species, such as *T. pulchella* and *T. sylvestris,* to flower again.

Because they are produced commercially in vast numbers and in close rotation with other bulbs, tulips are vulnerable to diseases and attacks by pests. Constant attention by plant pathologists is needed to help growers and gardeners to combat these conditions.

Virus diseases, recognised as such only in the 1920's, have for centuries been responsible for colour breaks. Old flower paintings often show

Tulipa 'Keizerskroon' (Div. 1)

tulips with irregular, sharply defined splashes of contrasting colours (broken colours) which are characteristic of virus infection. These broken tulips, as they are called, were much in fashion and are still available (see DIVISIONS 9 and 10).

Tulips are particularly prone to producing mutations (sports) and the offsets will sometimes differ from their parents, giving rise to potential new varieties. Even so, most new tulips are raised from seeds. Some years ago the Royal General Dutch Bulb Growers' Society, with help from the Royal Horticultural Society, undertook to classify all known tulips in divisions. The list which originally had 23 divisions, has recently, in the light of further study, been reduced to 15 divisions. These are described here in their numerical order; the varieties mentioned are only a selection of those recommended.

Tulipa 'Electra' (Div. 2)

Tulipa 'Marechal Niel' (Div. 2)

Tulipa 'Peach Blossom' (Div. 2)

INDEX OF SPECIES, VARIETIES AND HYBRIDS

Tulipa 'Garden Party' (Div. 4)

Tulipa 'Schoonoord' (Div. 2)

Tulipa 'Athleet' (Div. 3)

'Red Riding Hood' (Div. 14)
'Rose Korneforos' (Div. 4)
'Scarlet Cardinal' (Div. 2)
'Scarlett O'Hara' (Div. 6)
'Schoonoord' (Div. 2)
'Shakespeare' (Div. 12)
'Smiling Queen' (Div. 8)
'Snowpeak' (Div. 6)
stellata (Div. 15)
'Stresa' (Div. 12)
'Sunshine' (Div. 10)
sylvestris (Div. 15)
tarda (Div. 15)
'The Bishop' (Div. 6)
'The First' (Div. 12)
'Triumphator' (Div. 2)
tubergeniana (Div. 15)
'Tubergen's Variety' (Div. 15, *T. praestans*)
turkestanica (Div. 15)
'Union Jack' (Div. 6)
'Van der Eerden' (Div. 3)
'Van der Neer' (Div. 1)
'Viridiflora' (Div. 8)
'Virtuoso' (Div. 4)
'White Parrot' (Div. 10)
'White Triumphator' (Div. 7)
'Wilhelm Kordes (Div. 2)
'William Pitt' (Div. 6)
wilsoniana (Div. 15)
'Yellow Dawn' (Div. 14)
'Zomerschoon' (Div. 9)
'Zwanenburg' (Div. 15, *T. praestans*)

DIVISION 1. Single Early

Height 6–15 in.; planting distance 4–6 in. These tulips flower outdoors in April or under glass in February. Their suitability for early forcing depends on the variety and on the treatment given by the growers between lifting and flowering. The lanceolate leaves sometimes have a grey cast and the flowers, 3–5 in. across, often have pointed buds that open out flat in full sun.

Varieties responding to early forcing, and which can also be grown outside, include: 'Brilliant Star', scarlet; 'Couleur Cardinal', orange-red; 'Diana', white; 'Pink Beauty', deep pink and white; 'Proserpine', carmine; 'Van der Neer', purple.

Varieties for later forcing or for early flowering outdoors include: 'Bellona', yellow; 'General de Wet', orange and gold; 'Keizerskroon', yellow and red; 'Pink Perfection', clear pink; and 'Prince of Austria', orange and scarlet.

DIVISION 2. Double Early

Height 12–15 in.; planting distance 6 in. The lanceolate leaves often have a grey cast. The double flowers, sometimes as large as 4 in. across, look rather like double paeonies. They open in April. This group has for many years been popular for early forcing and bedding.

The following varieties are all sports or mutants from the pink and white 'Murillo': 'David Teniers', violet-purple; 'Electra', pink-mauve; 'Madame Testout', rose-pink; 'Marechal Niel', shining yellow; Mr van der Hoef,

Tulipa 'Orange Wonder' (Div. 4)

Tulipa 'Golden Oxford' (Div. 5)

Tulipa 'Beauty of Apeldoorn' (Div. 5)

Tulipa 'Clara Butt' (Div. 6)

Tulipa 'La Tulipe Noire' (Div. 6)

Tulipa 'Jewel of Spring' (Div. 5)

Tulipa 'Charles Needham' (Div. 6)

Tulipa 'Scarlett O'Hara' (Div. 6)

Tulipa 'The Bishop' (Div. 6)

Tulipa 'Niphetos' (Div. 6)

Tulipa 'Union Jack' (Div. 6)

yellow; 'Orange Nassau'; 'Peach Blossom', deep pink; 'Scarlet Cardinal'; 'Schoonoord', white; 'Triumphator', deep pink; 'Wilhelm Kordes', orange and red.

DIVISION 3. Mendel

Height 15–20 in.; planting distance 6 in. The leaves are lanceolate, often with a glaucous tinge. Rounded flowers, 4–5 in. across, are carried on slender stems. Raised from crosses between single early and Darwin tulips, they flower outdoors in late April and early May. Varieties in this division include: 'Athleet', white; 'Krelage's Triumph', dark red with yellow edge; and 'Van der Eerden', red.

DIVISION 4. Triumph

Height up to 20 in.; planting distance 6–8 in. The leaves are lanceolate, sometimes with a glaucous tinge. Angular flowers, 4–5 in. across, are carried on sturdy stems. This group resulted from crossing single early with late-flowering varieties; they usually bloom in April. Varieties include: 'Dutch Princess', orange and gold; 'Edith Eddy', red with white edges; 'Garden Party', carmine-pink, white base and edging; 'Golden Eddy', a sport with yellow edges; 'Korneforos', red; 'Orange Korneforos'; 'Orange Wonder', bronze-orange, with scarlet shading; 'Pax', white; 'Rose Korneforos', rose-red; and 'Virtuoso', lilac-rose.

DIVISION 5. Darwin Hybrids

Height 2–2¼ ft; planting distance 6–8 in. Some of the largest-flowered and most brilliantly coloured tulips are in this group. They are the result of crossing Darwins with the species *T. fosteriana*. The lanceolate leaves are grey-green. Deep flowers, 7 in. across, open during April and May. Varieties include: 'Apeldoorn', rich red; 'Beauty of Apeldoorn', golden-orange within, with a black base and anthers, exterior flushed rose-red; 'Elizabeth Arden', rose-purple; 'Golden Oxford', pure yellow, showing narrow red margins with age; 'Gudoshnik', yellow, spotted red and flushed pink, base and anthers black; 'Holland's Glorie', scarlet, large; 'Jewel of Spring', sulphur-yellow, with a narrow red margin and a green-black base.

DIVISION 6. Darwin

Height 2–2½ ft; planting distance 6–8 in. The lanceolate leaves sometimes have a glaucous tinge. Rounded flowers, 4–5 in. across, appear in May. These are probably the most popular tulips for bedding. Varieties include: 'Bartigon', red; 'Bleu Aimable', lavender-mauve; 'Charles Needham', scarlet; 'Clara Butt', pink; 'Copland's Purple'; 'Heather Hill', lilac-purple with a white, blue-edged base; 'La Tulipe Noire', dark purple; 'Niphetos', pale yellow; 'Pink Supreme', deep pink; 'Queen of Bartigons', salmon-pink; 'Queen of Night', dark purple; 'Scarlett O'Hara', brilliant scarlet with a black and yellow base; 'Snowpeak', white; 'The Bishop', violet-purple; 'Union Jack', ivory-white flamed raspberry-red with a blue-edged white base; and 'William Pitt', red.

DIVISION 7. Lily-flowered

Height 18–24 in.; planting distance 6 in. The lanceolate leaves sometimes have a grey sheen.

Tulipa 'Dyanito' (Div. 7)

Tulipa 'Queen of Sheba' (Div. 7)

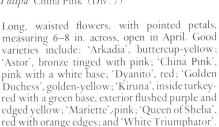

Tulipa 'China Pink' (Div. 7)

Tulipa 'Arkadia' (Div. 7)

Tulipa 'Artist' (Div. 8)

Long, waisted flowers, with pointed petals, measuring 6–8 in. across, open in April. Good varieties include: 'Arkadia', buttercup-yellow; 'Astor', bronze tinged with pink; 'China Pink', pink with a white base; 'Dyanito', red; 'Golden Duchess', golden-yellow; 'Kiruna', inside turkey-red with a green base, exterior flushed purple and edged yellow; 'Mariette', pink; 'Queen of Sheba', red with orange edges; and 'White Triumphator'.

DIVISION 8. Cottage

Height up to 3 ft; planting distance 6–8 in. The lanceolate leaves sometimes have a glaucous sheen. Ovoid or rounded flowers, 4–5 in. across, are carried on tall stiff stems in late April and early May. This old group, no longer much cultivated, includes: 'Artist', green and pink inside, purple and pink outside; 'Aster Nielsen', cream-yellow; 'Bacchus', dark violet-blue; 'Chappaqua', deep violet-rose; 'Dillenburg', deep orange; 'Golden Harvest', lemon-yellow, an early-flowering type; 'Grenadier', orange-scarlet; 'Groenland', syn. 'Greenland', green edged with pink; 'Henry Ford', cream-mushroom flecked crimson; 'Inglescombe Yellow'; 'Mirella', deep salmon-pink with a paler margin; 'Mrs John T. Scheepers', yellow; 'Palestrina', salmon-pink, exterior marked with green; 'President Hoover', orange-red; 'Princess Margaret Rose', yellow with orange edges; 'Smiling Queen', pink; and 'Viridiflora', green.

DIVISION 9. Rembrandt

These are broken Darwin tulips, similar except for the colour breaking to those described in Division 6. Varieties include: 'Absalon', coffee-brown and yellow; 'May Blossom', purple and cream; 'Zomerschoon', salmon-pink and cream.

DIVISION 10. Parrot

Height 18–24 in.; planting distance 6–8 in. The leaves are lanceolate, sometimes with a glaucous tinge. The flowers are often bicoloured and with twisted and irregularly fringed petals. Opening in April and May, they measure 8 in. or more across. Varieties include: 'Black Parrot', dark purple; 'Blue Parrot', mauve-blue; 'Fantasy', pink; 'Fire Bird', red sport of 'Fantasy'; 'Orange Parrot'; 'Red Parrot'; 'Sunshine', bright yellow; and 'White Parrot'.

DIVISION 11. Double Late

Height 18–24 in.; planting distance 6 in. Lanceolate leaves, often with a glaucous tinge. The showy flowers, 4 in. across and resembling double paeonies, usually appear in April. They remain for a long time in full bloom unless damaged by rain or wind. Varieties include: 'Blue Flag', light violet; 'Brilliant Fire', red and scented; 'Eros', white and scented; 'Gold Medal', deep yellow; 'Grand National', cream-yellow with gold centre; and 'Mount Tacoma', white.

DIVISION 12. Tulips mainly derived from the species *T. kaufmanniana*

Hybrids within this group have the same general characteristics as the parent plant. The long flowers are mostly in two colour shades. They include 'Cesar Franck', yellow and red; 'Fritz Kreisler', salmon-pink; 'Mendelssohn', cream and red; 'Johann Strauss', white, cream and red;

Tulipa 'Chappaqua' (Div. 8)

Tulipa 'Grenadier' (Div. 8)

Tulipa 'Groenland' (Div. 8)

Tulipa 'Smiling Queen' (Div. 8)

Tulipa 'Mrs John T. Scheepers'
(Div. 8)

Tulipa 'May Blossom' (Div. 9)

Tulipa 'Absalon' (Div. 9)

Tulipa 'Blue Parrot' (Div. 10)

Tulipa 'Red Parrot' (Div. 10)

Tulipa 'Sunshine' (Div. 10)

Tulipa 'Grand National'
(Div. 11)

'Shakespeare', salmon-red flushed scarlet, with golden-yellow base; 'Stresa', yellow within, blotched blood-red at base, exterior flushed red and margined yellow; and 'The First', carmine-red edged white, opening to ivory-white with a yellow base.

DIVISION 13. Tulips mainly derived from the species *T. fosteriana*

Most of the varieties are in varying intensities of red and have other characteristics similar to the parent species, but yellow predominates in a few varieties. Yellow varieties include 'Easter Parade'; red varieties include 'Cantata', 'Madame Lefeber', syn. 'Red Emperor', and 'Princeps'; 'Golden Eagle' is yellow and red; and 'Purissima' is cream-yellow.

DIVISION 14. Tulips mainly derived from the species *T. greigii*

All varieties have the maroon or purple-brown veined foliage of the parent plant, and flower in early April. They include 'Margaret Herbst', 'Oriental Beauty' and 'Red Riding Hood', all with red flowers; 'Pandour' and 'Yellow Dawn', both yellow and red; and 'Lamba', yellow and bronze-green.

DIVISION 15. Species

Over 30 species (including the *Neo-tulipae*) can be bought from specialist bulb growers and numerous varieties are offered every autumn. *T.* 'Acuminata', syn. *T.* 'Cornuta' (horned tulip). Height 18–24 in.; planting distance 4–5 in. The leaves are narrow and pale green. The 3 in. long flowers occur in red or yellow forms, with slender pointed petals; they appear in April. The common name refers to the twisted, pointed petals.

T. batalinii. Turkestan. Height 6 in.; planting distance 3 in. A plant with narrow light green leaves and 1½ in. long flowers with pointed cream-yellow petals. This species can be grown outdoors and will flower in April, but it does better in deep pots in a cool greenhouse and needs dry warmth during the resting period. A few bronze or pink-flushed varieties are offered for sale, usually hybrids with *T. linifolia*.

T. biflora. S. Russia and neighbouring countries. Height 6 in.; planting distance 3 in. The leaves are narrow and pale green; the stem bears from three to five flowers, each 1 in. long. They are white with yellow centres, opening to become pointed flat stars in March and April. This species will survive for many years in well-drained soil in a sunny position.

T. clusiana (lady tulip). Afghanistan and the N. Mediterranean shores. Height 9–12 in.; planting distance 3 in. The grey-green leaves are erect and exceptionally narrow. The white flowers, which have pointed petals and are 1–1½ in. long, are flushed with red; they are borne in April.

T. c. chrysantha is 6–8 in. high and has 1½ in. long yellow, flushed red flowers. The species, and its variety, is best grown in a sheltered sunny position in well-drained soil, where it will persist for a number of years.

T. 'Cornuta': see *T.* 'Acuminata'

T. dasystemon: see *T. tarda*

T. eichleri. Caucasus Mountains. Height 12 in.; planting distance 4–6 in. A sturdy species with grey-green, broad, basal leaves and rich red flowers, 4–5 in. across, borne on hairy stems in March and April. They have deep, pointed petals often with yellow, black-blotched margins. 'Excelsa' is a brilliant crimson variety.

T. fosteriana. Central Asia. Height 12–18 in.; planting distance 6 in. A variable species with

Tulipa 'Stresa' (Div. 12)

grey-green lanceolate leaves. Scarlet flowers, up to 9 in. across and with blunt-pointed petals, appear in April. This species was used to produce the Darwin hybrids listed in Division 13.

T. greigii. Turkestan and other parts of Central Asia. Height 9–12 in.; planting distance 6 in. The lanceolate grey-green leaves are veined or marbled with purple-brown and bronze. The blunt-pointed orange-scarlet flowers, 3 in. long, appear in early April. Listed in Division 14.

TULIPA KAUFMANNIANA

T. kaufmanniana (water-lily tulip). Turkestan. Height 4–10 in.; planting distance 6 in. A variable species with grey-green lanceolate leaves. The 3½ in. long white flowers, flushed with red and yellow on the outside, appear in March and April, the petals opening out to form a six-pointed star 4 in. or more across. Listed in Division 12.

T. linifolia. S. Russia. Height 6 in.; planting distance 3 in. This species has narrow grey-green leaves. The red flowers, opening in April and May, are 1½–2 in. long, with pointed petals.

T. 'Marjolettii'. S.E. France and N.W. Italy. Height 24 in.; planting distance 4 in. The leaves are lanceolate and grey-green; 2 in. long flowers, with pointed petals and yellow with red on the exterior, appear in May.

T. montana: see *T. wilsoniana*

T. 'Praecox'. S. France, N. Italy, W. Asia. Height 18 in.; planting distance 5–6 in. This plant has grey-green lanceolate leaves. It flowers in April; the red blooms, 2½ in. long and streaked with yellow inside, have blunt-pointed petals. It cannot be reproduced from seeds, but spreads by underground stolons.

T. praestans. Central Asia. Height 12–18 in.; planting distance 5–6 in. A species with two to five flowers on each stem, and broad grey-green leaves. The pure red 2 in. long flowers, with blunt petals, appear in March and April. Varieties include: 'Fusilier', 'Tubergen's Variety' and 'Zwanenburg', all in shades of red.

T. pulchella. S.W. Asia. Height 4–6 in.; planting distance 3 in. This species thrives in well-drained rock gardens. It has narrow, often red-margined leaves, and variable violet-red flowers with dark green-purple at their base. The flowers, deeply cup-shaped and 1¼ in. long, appear in March. *T. p. violacea* has a yellow base.

T. stellata. Himalayas. Height 8–10 in.; planting distance 3 in. The leaves are narrow and grey-green; the 1½ in. long white flowers, tinged with red and with a yellow base, have recurving pointed petals. They appear in April.

T. sylvestris. Europe, including Great Britain; W. Asia and N. Africa. Height 15 in.; planting distance 4 in. A species with grey-green narrow leaves and scented yellow flowers, 2 in. long, which have reflexed outer petals. Flowers are freely produced in April.

TULIPA TARDA

T. tarda, syn. *T. dasystemon.* Central Asia. Height 6 in.; planting distance 3 in. Numerous narrow mid-green leaves are borne in a rosette at flowering time. The flowers, as many as five on each stem, are borne in a tight terminal cluster. Each flower opens white, with a large bright yellow eye. They have pointed petals and are 1½ in. long. This species flowers in March; it can be grown in pots or in a well-drained border or rock garden.

T. tubergeniana. Central Asia. Height 12 in.; planting distance 4 in. The grey-green lanceolate leaves are borne some inches above the ground. The flowers appear in April; they are 3½–4 in. long, red with black blotches at the base and have wavy-edged petals.

T. turkestanica. Central Asia. Height 6–10 in.; planting distance 3–4 in. The leaves are narrow and grey-green. This species has up to nine pointed flowers on each stem. They are 1¼ in. long, white on the outside and cream within, and open in March.

T. wilsoniana, syn. *T. montana.* N. Iran. Height 8 in.; planting distance 3 in. The leaves are lanceolate and mid-green. The flowers, opening in April, are 2 in. long and have spoon-shaped petals. These are red with a black base.

Tulipa 'The First' (Div. 12)

Tulipa 'Purissima' (Div. 13)

Tulipa 'Red Riding Hood' (Div. 14)

Tulipa batalinii (Div. 15)

Tulipa clusiana chrysantha
(Div. 15)

Tulipa linifolia (Div. 15)

Tulipa praestans 'Fusilier'
(Div. 15)

Tulipa pulchella violacea
(Div. 15)

Cultivation. There are four methods of tulip cultivation. They can be forced for early indoor decoration from Christmas to Easter; grown as bedding plants or for cutting, to flower from late March to May; as perennials to provide splashes of colour on rock gardens and in borders each year; or in pots or pans in a cool greenhouse to flower during March and April.

For advice on forcing tulips for indoor decoration, see entry under BULBS, INDOOR.

To grow tulips as bedding and cutting plants, plant the bulbs in November; earlier planting may expose early growth to frost. Tulips thrive in an alkaline soil; apply 3–4 oz. of ground limestone per sq. yd. just before planting time if the soil is acid.

Tulip bulbs can be planted up to 12 in. deep in light soils, though 6 in. is more usual and makes it easier to lift the bulbs in summer. Do not plant deeper than 6 in. on heavy soils.

A few groups of bulbs planted in a border will provide enough cut flowers for the average household. If more are needed, plant the tulips in rows spaced 12–18 in. apart, with 4–5 in. between each bulb.

Plant bedding tulips 4–12 in. apart, depending on the effect wanted; for formal beds and borders, space the bulbs 4–6 in. apart, depending on bulb size, in rows or groups. Extra space can be allowed for informal plantings. Interplanting with other flowers, such as forget-me-nots or wallflowers, gives a more varied spring display.

Dead-head as the first petals fall, leaving the stems and leaves to feed the bulbs. Remove fallen petals, as they can harbour disease. Ideally, lift the bulbs when the leaves are turning yellow; however, if the beds are needed for summer plants the tulips can be lifted early, replanted in rows elsewhere and lifted again when the leaves have died down.

Place the plants in shallow boxes and store in a greenhouse or dry shed; remove the leaves when they and the stems are dry and brittle, together with the roots, old scales and soil.

When growing tulips as garden perennials, the smaller tulip species, such as *T. turkestanica* and *T. tarda,* can be planted in groups of 7–12 in rock gardens or borders.

Well-drained soil and a south-facing position sheltered from strong winds provide ideal conditions. Plant the bulbs 6 in. deep in November. After flowering, remove the leaves and stems as they die, keep the area free from coarse weeds, and leave the bulbs in the ground.

Some species, such as *T. kaufmanniana,* and their varieties, will ripen their bulbs in the soil and flower for many years and even increase. Those that gradually disappear, for example *T. biflora,* can be replaced as necessary. Others, such as *T. pulchella,* that fail if left in the ground, as well as especially valuable bulbs, should be lifted when the leaves turn yellow, and stored in the manner described for bedding tulips.

Greenhouse cultivation of tulips is concerned primarily with the smaller species, notably *T. pulchella,* which provide colour and interest in alpine houses or cold greenhouses. In October or November plant from five to seven bulbs 2 in. deep in a 5–6 in. pan containing John Innes potting compost No. 1.

Water the bulbs at planting time, then keep them moist until the leaves start to turn yellow after flowering. Also after flowering give three or four weekly feeds of liquid fertiliser until watering is stopped. Allow the compost to dry out for the resting period during summer.

Leave the pots undisturbed for two or three years unless they become filled with small bulbs, which can be detected by single leaves growing apart from any flower stem. Knock out the pots in early autumn, sort the bulbs and repot them separately. The young bulbs will reach flowering size in one to three years.

Propagation. Raising tulips from seeds is a slow, but interesting method. The species and their wild varieties come true from seeds, but seedlings from garden varieties are extremely variable.

Harvest the seeds in July and August by cutting off the seed pods as they turn yellow or just begin to split. Place the pods in shallow, paper-lined boxes and stand them in a warm dry place; the seeds will come out easily when dry. Within one or two weeks, sow the seeds thinly in pans or boxes of John Innes seed compost and place in an unheated frame or greenhouse.

The first small seedling leaves will die in the summer; when this happens leave the compost unwatered until the following February. The leaves will grow again and die during the second summer, after which the bulbs should be planted in drills outdoors during October, or spaced out in larger pots or pans. For outdoor nursery rows, choose a bed of good, well-drained soil, setting the bulbs 2 in. deep and 2 in. apart, in rows 6–8 in. apart. Lift and replant annually as for mature bulbs. Some species grown from seeds may flower in three or four years, but most species and varieties take five to seven years.

Propagation from the offset bulbs produced by all tulips is easier, and these are usually true to type. Colour sports may occur but they will not vary in size or shape and may be grown on as potential new varieties.

The offsets will be found either clustered at the base of the flower stems or on stolons or droppers growing outwards or downwards from the mature bulbs.

When lifting the bulbs, remove the offsets, separate them into large, medium and small sizes, and store at 16–18°C (61–64°F) in a dry place until planting time. Grading the bulbs facilitates planting them in batches at the right depth and spacing for each size. Plant the smallest 2 in. deep and the largest 6 in. deep, with twice the width of the bulbs between each.

The largest bulbs should flower the following season and the medium sizes the year after. The smallest may take over three years and are scarcely worth saving unless they come from valuable plants.

Pests. Tulip bulbs in store may be eaten by MICE; SLUGS may feed on the bulbs, stems and leaves of young plants. Slug damage occurs mainly below soil surface level and becomes apparent only when the stems emerge.

APHIDS of various species may infest young growths, both in store and outdoors.

STEM AND BULB EELWORMS sometimes cause malformation of stems and leaves and rotting of the bulb tissues.

Diseases. ARABIS MOSAIC VIRUS and CUCUMBER MOSAIC VIRUS are two of the several virus diseases that may affect tulips. The symptoms differ according to the virus present, one causing a breaking of the flower colour and another producing irregular white streaks along the leaves. Small brown spots and streaks on the leaves, and sometimes also on the stems and flowers, are produced by another virus, which usually kills affected plants.

BLUE MOULD may develop on injured bulbs, particularly in storage, or on bulbs affected by a physiological disorder.

GREY BULB ROT attacks the bulbs at the nose, which rots and becomes grey, preventing the shoots from getting above ground. The bulbs are soon destroyed, and small black resting bodies, developed on the rotting tissues, fall into the soil and may infect other bulbs the following season.

PHYSIOLOGICAL DISORDERS of several kinds occur as a result of unsuitable cultural conditions. BLINDNESS or withering of flowers before opening is due to planting bulbs in excessively dry soil. The latter can also lead to the development of long, elliptic growths, known as droppers, at the top of a bulb. Lifting too early and storing bulbs incorrectly can cause them to become hard and chalky; they may develop blue mould.

TULIP FIRE causes irregular scorched areas on the leaves and also small spots, which may occur on the flowers as well. Leaves and flowers decay in moist weather and may show a grey fungal growth. Small black resting bodies of the fungus are produced on the bulbs, which often rot.

Tupelo: see Nyssa

Turnip

Brassica rapa. Cruciferae

A half-hardy biennial grown as an annual vegetable for its swollen, fleshy, usually white, delicately mustard-flavoured roots. The tender leaves are also used as a winter green vegetable, and the young shoots may be blanched and used as a substitute for sea kale. Turnip crops can be harvested throughout most of the year, with proper cultivation and with the correct choice of varieties. These vegetables should be grown quickly and, except for winter-cropping varieties, may be used as a catch crop.

VARIETIES

There are globular, flattened and long-rooted types. 'Early Red Milan' and 'Early White Milan' are flat-rooted varieties suitable for an early crop. For summer crops, the globular 'Early Sixweeks' or 'Early Snowball' are recommended. For a winter crop, choose the globular 'Golden Ball' with particularly hard yellow roots that store well.

'Greentop White' is an excellent heavy-cropping variety grown for its leaves.

Cultivation. A friable, light loam suits turnips best, but any fertile soil rich in phosphates is suitable. Manure the soil liberally during winter, with well-rotted compost, being careful to bury the manure deeply or the roots may fork and have an earthy flavour. Give a top dressing of

carbonate of lime at the rate of 7 oz. per sq. yd on all but limy or chalky soils. Superphosphate and bone-meal are valuable additions to the soil, and should be applied prior to sowing.

Sow seeds in the open in mid-March for an early crop, choosing a south-facing plot; protect the plants with cloches if the weather turns cold. Later sowings can be made in less-sheltered positions; for summer supplies sow in April and again in May; for autumn and winter crops, sow in mid-July and in late August.

Sow seeds in $\frac{1}{2}$ in. deep drills drawn 12–15 in. apart; thin the seedlings as soon as they are large enough to handle and then again as they grow. Allow 6–9 in. between summer turnips and 12 in. between autumn and winter varieties. Give the young plants a thorough soaking once a week during prolonged dry weather.

Turnips grown for their leaves should be sown outdoors in September. No thinning is required; cut the foliage when this is about 8 in. high, generally eight to ten weeks after sowing.

Harvesting and storing. Use the summer turnips when young, pulling them as they are required. Leave winter turnips in the bed to be lifted as required, or lift all in November, cut off the foliage and store the roots in a clamp.

Pests. FLEA BEETLES, prevalent in dry weather, eat small round holes in the leaves of seedlings.

Diseases. Grey or brown patches on the lower half of the roots are due to BORON DEFICIENCY.

CLUB ROOT causes the feeding roots to become swollen and distorted.

DAMPING-OFF results in the collapse of seedlings at soil level.

DOWNY MILDEW may appear on the leaves of seedlings; it shows as yellow blotches with mealy white areas on the undersurfaces.

SOFT ROT, due to bacteria, occurs in store on damaged roots or where storage conditions are too damp. Affected roots are rapidly destroyed by a soft, watery rot.

SPLITTING of roots lengthwise is due to an irregular moisture supply in the soil.

VIOLET ROOT ROT shows as a violet web of fungal threads over the lower part of the roots.

Turnip cabbage: see Kohl rabi
Turnip-rooted celery: see Celeriac
Turtle-head: see Chelone
Twin flower: see Linnaea

Typha

Reedmace. *Typhaceae*

TYPHA MINIMA

A genus of up to 20 species of hardy perennial-herbaceous aquatics, commonly but incorrectly called bulrushes. They have long strap-shaped leaves and brown, cylindrical, mace-like flower

Tulipa sylvestris (Div. 15)

Tulipa tarda (Div. 15)

Tulipa turkestanica (Div. 15)

Turnip 'Golden Ball'

heads. These are marginal plants, mostly invasive and suitable only for large pools and lakes unless their roots are confined in a container. *T. minima*, however, is suitable for small garden pools. Typhas are easy to grow, but they do not form their characteristic flower heads freely until the growth is dense.

T. latifolia (great reedmace). Europe, including Great Britain. Water depth ½–4 ft; height 5–8 ft; planting distance 1–3 ft. A massive plant that forms large areas of foliage in lakes, even hiding the water completely. The abundant glaucous green leaves taper slightly. From June to August solid round flower stems appear which end in loose spikes of male flowers; just below these the female flowers are borne in plump, deep brown heads. Vigorous rhizomes are freely produced deep in the mud, making this an invasive plant that is difficult to eradicate.

Typha latifolia

Ulex europaeus 'Plenus'

Ulmus carpinifolia sarniensis 'Aurea'

T. minima (dwarf reedmace). Central and S.E. Europe. Water depth 2–9 in.; height 1½–2½ ft; planting distance 6–12 in. This small plant is hardy if covered with water in winter, but may be killed in cold areas if the short rhizomes are exposed. Dense clumps of foliage are formed by the light green grass-like leaves.

The flower heads, formed in June and July, are rounded to shortly ovate, 1–1¼ in. long, and carried on slender stems just above the leaves.

Cultivation. Grow in any rich loam. For *T. latifolia* the soil must be 6–12 in. deep, for *T. minima* 2–6 in. deep. Plant young growing shoots, with a short length of rhizome attached, in April or May, just covering the rhizome.

Propagation. Sever the rhizomes 1–3 in. back from growing shoots in April or May and set the severed portions in permanent positions.

Pests and diseases. Generally trouble-free.

UV

Ulex

Gorse, whin, furze. *Leguminosae*

A genus of 20 species of evergreen spiny flowering shrubs. The species described here are hardy and bear golden-yellow pea-like flowers which have a honeyed fragrance on warm days. The shrubs burn readily during a drought and should therefore not be planted near a house or the roadside.

ULEX EUROPAEUS

U. europaeus. W. Europe. Height and spread 5–8 ft. The leaves are scale-like and soon drop, revealing the intricately branched spiny, mid to dark green shoots. The ¾–1 in. long flowers are at their best from March to May, but continue to appear intermittently until late winter. 'Plenus' is a compact form with double yellow flowers.

Cultivation. Plant out pot-grown plants between October and March in poor or ordinary well-drained garden soil in full sun. Keep the soil ball intact to avoid root disturbance.

Propagation. In April, sow seeds at the rate of two to each 3½ in. pot of John Innes potting compost No. 1 in a cold frame or greenhouse. Thin out to one seedling later and plunge the pots in an outdoor nursery bed in June or July. Plant out from the following October onwards.

Take 3 in. cuttings of the current year's growths in August or September, and insert them in equal parts (by volume) peat and sand in a cold

frame. Overwinter the cuttings in the cold frame; pot into 4 in. pots of John Innes potting compost No. 1 in April or May and plant out in their permanent positions in September or October of the same year.

Pruning. Tall, leggy plants may be cut back to within 6 in. of ground level in March to induce new growth from the base.

Pests. Generally trouble-free.

Diseases. DIE-BACK may be caused by severe frost.

Ulmus

Elm. *Ulmaceae*

A genus of 45 species of hardy, deciduous, long-lived trees, suitable as specimen trees mainly in parks and large gardens. Green winged fruits develop as the leaves unfold.

U. campestris: see *U. procera*

U. carpinifolia (now correctly known as *U. minor*). Europe, N. Africa, W. Asia. Height 25–30 ft; spread 15–20 ft. This is a handsome but variable tree, with a rounded or oval head of branches which are often pendulous at the tips. The mid to deep green, coarsely toothed leaves are oblanceolate to sub-orbicular and turn chrome-yellow in November or December. The following varieties are more commonly seen:

U. c. 'Cornubiensis', syn. *U. stricta* (Cornish elm). S.W. England. Height 20–30 ft; spread 8–15 ft at the base. This tree has a conical shape, and glabrous leaves that are glossy mid to deep green and elliptic to obovate.

U. c. sarniensis, syns. *U. sarniensis*, *U. wheatleyi* (Wheatley or Jersey elm). W. Europe. Height 20–30 ft; spread 5–8 ft at the base. This tree has closely ascending branches and mid to deep green leaves. They are elliptic or obovate, glabrous and glossy above.

U. c. s. 'Aurea', syn. *U. c. wheatleyi aurea* (Dickson's golden elm) is a slow-growing variety with bright golden-yellow young foliage that fades to yellow-green by July.

U. c. wheatleyi aurea: see *U. c. sarniensis* 'Aurea'.

U. glabra, syn. *U. montana* (wych or Scots elm). N. Europe, including Great Britain. Height 20–30 ft; spread 10–18 ft. A species with an oval head. The ovate to obovate, toothed, mid-green leaves turn yellow in October.

'Camperdownii' has a dome-shaped head of branches; 'Exoniensis' is of erect, columnar habit; 'Pendula' (weeping wych elm) makes a flat-topped tree with stiffly pendulous branches and is suitable as a lawn specimen.

ULMUS GLABRA

U. × hollandica (Dutch elm). W. Europe. Height 25–35 ft; spread 10–18 ft. The leaves are obovate and dark shiny green. 'Vegeta' (Huntingdon elm) is a rather similar tree with lax branches and smooth bright green leaves.

U. minor: see *U. carpinifolia*

U. montana: see *U. glabra*

U. procera, syn. *U. campestris* (English elm). W. and S. Europe. Height 20–30 ft; spread 8–18 ft. This erect tree has mid to deep green leaves that are broadly ovate and turn deep yellow in autumn. 'Louis van Houttei' is a form with yellow leaves. 'Variegata' has leaves conspicuously blotched and margined with white.

U. sarniensis: see *U. carpinifolia sarniensis*

U. stricta: see *U. carpinifolia* 'Cornubiensis'

U. wheatleyi: see *U. carpinifolia sarniensis*

Cultivation. Grow elms in an open sunny position in any ordinary garden soil. Plant at any time between October and March.

Propagation. Remove suckers and grow them on in a nursery bed for at least two years. Plant out in final positions in October or November.

Peg down layers in September or October and leave them for one or two years before severing.

Bud weeping elm forms in July on to *U. glabra* stocks; or whip and tongue graft them in March.

Pruning. None necessary.

Pests. The leaves may be eaten by CATERPILLARS. Infestations by APHIDS distort the leaves, and GALL MITES produce blisters on the foliage. Elm bark BEETLES transmit DUTCH ELM DISEASE.

Diseases. Dead wood may be entered by BRACKET FUNGI, and heartwood may rot if the tree is neglected. Later, large bracket-shaped fruiting bodies develop on the trunk or branches.

DIE-BACK and CANKER may be due to any of several different fungi. Dead patches or cankers appear on shoots, and if girdling occurs the shoots die back. With CORAL SPOT, pink to red cushion-like pustules of spores develop towards the base of the dead wood.

DUTCH ELM DISEASE causes browning of leaves, which remain hanging in a withered condition on dead branches. Large branches may be killed, so that the tree takes on a 'stag-headed' appearance. Eventually the tree dies.

HONEY FUNGUS can kill trees rapidly.

Ursinia

Compositae

URSINIA ANETHOIDES

A genus of 80 species of annual and perennial herbaceous plants and shrubs. The species described are suitable for growing in mixed borders, for bedding out and for cutting, although the daisy-like flowers tend to close in the evening and to remain closed in dull conditions. Ursinias also make attractive pot plants.

U. anethoides. S. Africa. Height 18 in.; planting distance 12 in. A half-hardy perennial of bushy growth, invariably treated as an annual. This is the most widely grown species. The leaves are light green and finely divided. Daisy-like flowers, nearly 2 in. across, are produced from June to September. They are bright orange-yellow with a purple central disc.

Garden varieties include a mixture of hybrids that are more compact than the type; they are available in a range of orange shades. The variety 'Sunstar' has vivid orange-scarlet flowers, with a claret-coloured zone.

U. anthemoides. S. Africa. Height 12 in.; planting distance 9 in. A bushy half-hardy annual that is not widely listed by seedsmen. It is similar to *U. anethoides* except that the leaves are flatter and the undersides of the ray florets are purple.

U. cakilifolia. S. Africa. Height 12 in.; planting distance 4 in. This annual is somewhat hardier than the other species; it is not widely listed by seedsmen. The light green leaves are smooth and deeply cut. Bright orange-yellow flowers, 2 in. across, are produced from June to August.

U. pulchra: see *U. versicolor*

U. versicolor, syn. *U. pulchra.* S. Africa. Height 12 in.; planting distance 6 in. A half-hardy annual of bushy habit. The dark green leaves are scented and finely cut; the bright orange or yellow flowers have a purple zone. They are 2 in. across and produced from June to August.

Cultivation. For the best results, grow in sandy soil in a sunny site. The taller varieties require staking with twiggy supports. For flowering under glass from June onwards, grow the plants in John Innes potting compost No. 1.

Propagation. Sow the seeds under glass in March at a temperature of 15°C (59°F), just covering them with compost. Prick off the seedlings into boxes. If the plants are to be grown outdoors, harden them off in a cold frame before planting out in April or May. For pot culture, set three plants to a 5–6 in. pot.

Pests and diseases. Generally trouble-free.

Ulmus glabra (fruits and young leaves)

Ulmus procera

Ursinia anethoides

Vaccinium glaucoalbum

Vaccinium corymbosum

Vaccinium vitis-idaea

Valeriana phu 'Aurea'

Vaccaria segetalis: see *Saponaria vaccaria*

Vaccinium

Bilberry, blueberry, cranberry or whortleberry.
Ericaceae

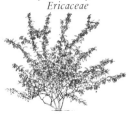

VACCINIUM CORYMBOSUM

A genus of about 400 species of tender, half-hardy and hardy deciduous and evergreen shrubs. They all bear edible fruits, used for desserts and in preserves, but several species are chiefly grown for their ornamental value. The deciduous species often assume brilliant autumn colours; the urn-shaped flowers are borne singly or in small clusters or racemes.

The young shoots of *V. glaucoalbum* may be damaged by late spring frosts.

V. corymbosum (swamp or high-bush blueberry). E. United States. Height 4–6 ft; spread 6–8 ft. A hardy deciduous species with ovate to elliptic mid-green leaves that are pointed and alternate; they turn brilliant red from September onwards. The white, pink-tinted flowers are borne in 2 in. long racemes during May and June. They are followed by $\frac{1}{3}$–$\frac{1}{2}$ in. wide, blue-black, globose berries, with a white waxy bloom; these ripen in August or September. Various named varieties are grown commercially for their fruits.

V. glaucoalbum. Himalayas. Height and spread 3–5 ft. An evergreen ornamental species with oblong-ovate leaves that are mid-green above, vivid blue-white beneath. White flowers, sometimes tinged pink, are borne in axillary racemes, 2–3 in. long, during May and June. The globose blue-black fruits are $\frac{1}{4}$–$\frac{1}{3}$ in. across.

V. myrtillus (bilberry, whortleberry). Europe, N. Africa. Height 6–18 in.; spread 12–18 in. The bright green ovate leaves of this deciduous hardy shrub turn dull purple and gold in October. Semi-translucent green-white flowers, flushed with pink and $\frac{1}{4}$ in. long, are borne singly in the leaf axils; they appear in May and are followed in July and August by blue-black fruits.

V. oxycoccus, syn. *Oxycoccus palustris* (cranberry). Mountains and moorland of the Northern Temperate Zone. Height 1–2 in.; spread up to 18 in. A hardy, prostrate, wiry-stemmed, evergreen shrub with dark green, oblong-ovate and pointed leaves. Nodding, $\frac{1}{3}$ in. wide, pale pink flowers are borne on thread-like erect stems in clusters of one to six. They open from June to August. Acid, globular or pear-shaped, red berries, $\frac{1}{3}$ in. across, are produced in August and September.

V. vitis-idaea (cowberry, mountain cranberry). Mountain ranges of the Northern Temperate Zone. Height up to 6 in.; spread up to 18 in. A hardy, semi-prostrate, evergreen species with dark green, glossy, obovate leaves. White or pale pink flowers are produced in 1 in. long racemes from the ends of the shoots during May and June.

They are followed by dark red, $\frac{1}{3}$ in. wide, globular berries that may persist well into winter.

Cultivation. Vacciniums thrive in moisture-retentive, peaty or lime-free soil in an open position. Plant between October and March in sun or partial shade. Once established, the shrubs can be sheared over in April to keep them bushy. Gather the berries when just ripe, usually in August, for preserving or pie-making.

Propagation. Long shoots may be layered and pegged down in September; they are usually ready for severing and replanting after one or two years. Plants may be divided between October and March and replanted in permanent positions.

Alternatively, in July, take 2–3 in. long cuttings of half-ripened shoots and insert in equal parts (by volume) peat and sand in a shaded cold frame. When rooted, pot the cuttings singly in 3 in. pots of 2 parts lime-free loam, 2 parts peat and 1 part coarse sand (parts by volume) and grow on in the frame. Set the young plants out in a nursery bed the following October and grow on for two or three years before planting out in permanent positions between October and March.

Sow seeds in October in a cold frame in 2 parts peat and 1 part sand (parts by volume). Prick off the seedlings, when large enough to handle, into pans or boxes, later placing them singly in 3 in. pots of the compost recommended for cuttings. Grow the seedlings on in an outside nursery bed for three years before planting out.

Pests and diseases. Generally trouble-free.

Valerian: see Centranthus

Valeriana

Valerianaceae

A genus of more than 200 species of hardy herbaceous perennials, sub-shrubs or shrubs. A number of species are weedy, and others are short-lived. The following species are suitable for rock gardens or borders.

V. arizonica. Arizona. Height 2–3 in.; planting distance 9 in. A dwarf, mat-forming species, with rounded to ovate, dark green leaves. Heads, 6 in. wide, of shell-pink flowers open in May and June.

V. phu. E. Europe, Caucasus. Height 2–3 ft; spread 18–24 in. An erect-growing species with oblong-ovate, mid-green basal leaves and deeply cut stem leaves. Tiny, white, tubular flowers are borne in dense panicles, up to 6 in. long, in August. The species is superseded by *V. p.* 'Aurea' which has bright yellow young foliage.

V. sambucifolia. Europe. Height 4–5 ft; planting distance 18 in. This species is suitable for the back of a border. The widely segmented leaves are dark green. The stems branch at the top into flattened heads, 4–6 in. across, of light pink flowers in June and July.

Cultivation. Plant from October to March in ordinary garden soil and in full sun. Staking with pea sticks in March is usually required for the taller species, especially if the plants are grown on moist soils or in exposed positions. Remove dead flower stems in October.

Propagation. Divide and replant the roots during suitable weather from October to March.

V. sambucifolia is also easily raised from seeds sown outdoors in April. Prick out the seedlings, when large enough to handle, into a nursery bed and transplant to flowering positions in October.
Pests and diseases. Generally trouble-free.

Valerianella locusta : see Corn salad
Valerian, Greek : see *Polemonium coeruleum*

Vallota

Scarborough lily. *Amaryllidaceae*

VALLOTA SPECIOSA

A South African bulb genus with only one species. This is not hardy and can be grown outdoors only in the extreme south-west, and in the Channel Islands. It does best as a pot plant in a cool greenhouse or on a sunny window ledge.
V. purpurea: see *V. speciosa*
V. speciosa, syn. *V. purpurea.* Height up to 24 in.; planting distance 12 in. The leaves are green, erect and strap-shaped. The flattened flower stem has up to ten bright scarlet flowers clustered at the top. The flowers, 3–4 in. long, are open, funnel-shaped and erect; they generally appear between July and September.
Cultivation. Using John Innes potting compost No. 1, start small bulbs in 3 in. pots; pot these on annually into larger pots. Plant large bulbs, 2–3 in. across, in 5–6 in. pots. In both cases plant during August or September, allowing the tips of the bulbs to protrude. Water regularly but avoid waterlogging the soil.

Leaves appear soon after planting, the single stem growing from each bulb somewhat later. If watered all the year round, the leaves will persist and new ones will grow before the old ones have died off. Remove each flower as it dies, and cut off the stem when it becomes yellow and limp.

Pot vallotas on to larger containers when the offset bulbs fill the pot.
Propagation. Remove the offsets, which are produced regularly at the bases of older bulbs, when repotting. Plant singly in 3 in. pots, using John Innes potting compost No. 1. The offsets will grow to flowering size in one to three years.
Pests. MEALY BUGS infest the base of leaves, causing conspicuous tufts of white waxy wool.
Diseases. A PHYSIOLOGICAL DISORDER due to poor growing conditions causes brown blotches or yellowing on the leaves.

Vanda

Orchidaceae

A genus of about 60 species of tropical evergreen epiphytic orchids, without pseudobulbs, from Asia. Both long and short-stemmed species occur; the mid-green or blue-green leaves are usually borne in two rows along the upright stems and are strap-shaped or almost cylindrical. The erect or pendulous flower stems arise from the leaf axils. Most species do best in warm conditions although some flower equally well in an intermediate house; good light is necessary for the proper development of flower colours.

See also ORCHIDS.

V. caerulea. N. India, Burma. The stems, which may reach a height of several feet, eventually become bare and leggy at the base; cut off the upper leafy portion just below the uppermost aerial roots, and repot. The stems bear several thick, strap-shaped, mid-green leaves. Each erect flower stem has up to 15 flowers 3½–4 in. across, from August to November. These have pale blue petals and sepals that are occasionally tessellated with a deeper shade of blue; the lip is deep blue-purple with blue-white side-lobes. There are several varieties ranging from white through pink to deep blue. Grow in a warm greenhouse.
V. teres. N. India, Burma. Height up to 10 ft. This species bears several dark green almost cylindrical leaves. From June to August, the flower stems each bear up to six flowers, 4 in. across, with white sepals and rose-magenta petals. The side-lobes of the lip are yellow-orange marked with red, and the mid-lobe is deep red-purple. Several colour varieties are in cultivation. Grow in a warm greenhouse.

VANDA TRICOLOR

V. tricolor. Indonesia. Height up to 7 ft. A robust species bearing thick, mid-green, strap-shaped leaves. The curving flower stems bear up to 12 2½ in. wide flowers from October to February. They have white or cream to pale mauve petals, and sepals that are heavily spotted with brown. The lip is basically the same colour, but the mid-lobe is deep rose. *V. t. suavis* is the form most usually grown; its flowers are sweetly scented. Grow in an intermediate or warm greenhouse.
Cultivation. Grow these orchids in pots, baskets or cylinders or on blocks of tree fern, in a compost of 2 parts osmunda fibre and 1 part sphagnum moss (parts by volume). Water freely from March to October, sparingly during the resting period from November to February. In the growing season give an occasional feed of liquid manure. Shade the house on sunny days from April to September and ventilate in hot weather.

Repot annually in March or April.
Propagation. Remove any side-shoots that have formed and pot into 4–5 in. pans of the growing compost in March or April.
Pests. Generally trouble-free.
Diseases. A fungus or a PHYSIOLOGICAL DISORDER may cause LEAF SPOT, which shows as brown or black spots on the leaves.

Vegetable sheep : see *Raoulia eximia*

Vallota speciosa

Vanda caerulea

Vanda tricolor suavis

× Venidio-arctotis

Compositae

A half-hardy hybrid genus raised in cultivation by crossing *Arctotis grandis* and *A. breviscapa* with *Venidium fastuosum*. The plants, which blend the characteristics of all three parents, form erect, well-branched specimens. They bear a profusion of 2½–3 in. wide daisy-like flowers from June to the first severe frosts. A number of forms are available.

VARIETIES

Height and spread 18 in. The following recommended varieties have oblong-lanceolate and lobed leaves, grey-green above, white-felted beneath: 'Aurora', chestnut-bronze; 'Bacchus', wine-purple; 'Champagne', ivory-white with a purple zone (a sport of 'Bacchus') 'China Rose', deep rose-pink; 'Mahogany', brown-crimson; 'Sunshine', buff-yellow, crimson zone; 'Tangerine', orange-yellow; 'Terra-cotta', rich brownred; 'Torch', deep bronze, crimson zone.

Cultivation. Grow venidio-arctotis in any well-drained garden soil, preferably enriched with decayed manure or compost. Plant out during May after the risk of frost is past. Choose a sunny or partially shaded position.

Propagation. Take 3–4 in. long cuttings of lateral shoots during August and September, removing any flower buds. Insert in equal parts (by volume) peat and sand in a propagating frame at a temperature of 13–16°C (55–61°F). When rooted, place the cuttings singly in 3 in. pots of John Innes potting compost No. 1, and overwinter at 4–7°C (39–45°F). Pot on into 4 in. pots in March and plant out in May.

Old plants may be lifted in October and overwintered in pots under glass, but they are less satisfactory than young plants.

Pests. Peach leaf APHIDS may attack the young shoots, distorting leaves and flower buds.

Diseases. Generally trouble-free.

× *Venidio-arctotis*
(mixed varieties)

Venidium fastuosum

Venidium

Compositae

VENIDIUM DECURRENS

A genus of 20–30 species of annual and perennial herbaceous plants. The species described are excellent for borders and for summer bedding; the large daisy-like flowers are good for cutting.

V. calendulaceum: see *V. decurrens*

V. decurrens, syn. *V. calendulaceum*. S. Africa. Height and planting distance 12 in. A half-hardy perennial, usually grown as an annual but not widely listed by seedsmen. The grey-green deeply lobed leaves form a rosette. Golden-yellow daisy-like flowers, with dark centres, appear from July to October. They are 2½ in. across.

V. fastuosum (monarch of the veldt). S. Africa. Height 24 in.; planting distance 12 in. This half-hardy annual is the best-known species. It has silver-white deeply lobed leaves which are rather woolly in texture. The flowers are 4 in. across and produced from June to October. Rich orange ray florets, purple-brown at the base, surround a black central disc. A strain with variously coloured flowers, ranging from white to lemon, is sold under the name 'Hybrida'.

V. hirsutum. S. Africa. Height 12 in.; planting distance 9 in. A half-hardy annual best grown as a greenhouse pot plant. The grey leaves are soft and deeply lobed. A profusion of vivid orange flowers, 2 in. across, with dark central discs, appears from June to September.

Cultivation. These plants grow reasonably well in any fertile soil, but light, well-drained soil enriched with organic matter is ideal. Choose a sunny site. Staking is generally required.

Move spring-flowering pot plants to their final 5–6 in. pots of John Innes potting compost No. 1 in October and maintain a minimum winter temperature of 8°C (46°F). Pot on summer-flowering plants to similar containers in May.

Propagation. Sow the seeds under glass at a temperature of 16°C (61°F), just covering them with compost. Sow in March or April for summer flowering outdoors or under glass, in August or September for early spring flowering under glass.

Prick out the seedlings into boxes or pots and harden off outdoor plants before setting them out in May. Alternatively, sow directly in the flowering site in May and thin out the seedlings to the required distances. These plants will be later in flowering.

Pests and diseases. Generally trouble-free.

Venus's looking glass: see *Specularia speculum*

Veratrum

Liliaceae

VERATRUM VIRIDE

A genus of 25 species of hardy herbaceous perennials with poisonous black rhizomes. The ribbed leaves are pleated; numerous tiny, star-shaped flowers are borne in plume-shaped panicles at the end of stiff, erect, leafy stems. The plants are suitable for growing in partly shaded herbaceous borders.

V. album. Europe, N. Africa, Siberia. Height 3–4 ft; planting distance 18 in. A species with light green oblong leaves. Dense sprays, about 12 in. long, of green-white flowers, appear in July.

V. nigrum. S. Europe, Siberia. Height 3–4 ft; planting distance 18 in. The mid to dark green leaves are oblong and narrow at the base. Narrow spikes, up to 3 ft long, and composed of densely packed black-purple flowers, appear in August.

Veratrum nigrum

viride. N. America. Height up to 7 ft; planting distance 2½ ft. This species bears mid-green leaves that are acute to ovate. Branching, 9–12 in. long sprays of yellow-green flowers open in July.

Cultivation. Plant in October or in March and April in moist, light soil and in a partly shaded position. Do not let the soil dry out in the growing season; if necessary, mulch with peat in May. Cut the stems down in November.

Propagation. Divide and replant the roots in October or in March and April.

Sow seeds when ripe, or not later than October, in pans of John Innes seed compost in a cold frame. Prick out the seedlings when large enough to handle; grow on in a nursery bed before setting in permanent sites. The plants take three or four years to reach flowering size.

Pests and diseases. Generally trouble-free.

Verbascum

Mullein. *Scrophulariaceae*

A genus of 300 species of hardy biennial and perennial herbaceous plants and sub-shrubs. For the most part they are stately plants, excellent for growing at the backs of borders, in groups on island beds, and for wild garden planting. The species described include two sub-shrubs and a hybrid variety that are suitable for rock gardens and alpine houses.

The flowers of these species are five-petalled and saucer-shaped, generally 1–1½ in. across, with a central boss of fluffy stamens. The large leaves are often thickly felted with white hairs.

ALPINE SPECIES

V. dumulosum. Asia Minor. Height and spread 6–12 in. A sub-shrubby species that produces tufts of grey-green and slightly woolly ovate leaves. Clear yellow flowers open on spikes 3–4 in. long in June and July.

VERBASCUM × 'LETITIA'

V. × 'Letitia'. Height up to 9 in.; spread up to 12 in. This compact twiggy bushlet is a hybrid of *V. dumulosum* and *V. spinosum*; it has lanceolate grey-green leaves. The flowers are clear yellow, opening on 3–4 in. spikes from June to August.

V. spinosum. Crete. Height and spread 9–12 in. This plant is a sub-shrub with wiry, woody, intricately arrayed branches bearing spiny grey-green leaves that are narrowly lanceolate and shallowly toothed. Yellow flowers are massed on 4 in. long spikes in June.

BORDER SPECIES

V. bombyciferum, syns. *V.* 'Broussa' or *V.* 'Brusa'. Asia Minor. Height 4–6 ft; planting distance 18–24 in. A biennial, rosette-forming species with pointed, ovate leaves covered with silvery hairs. The silvery branching stems are erect and densely covered with sulphur-yellow flowers, in 2–4 ft spikes in June and July.

V. 'Broussa': see *V. bombyciferum*
V. 'Brusa': see *V. bombyciferum*

VERBASCUM BOMBYCIFERUM

V. chaixii, syn. *V. vernale.* Central and southern Europe, to the Pyrenees. Height 3–5 ft; planting distance 18 in. A perennial species with tongue-shaped grey-green leaves covered with white woolly hairs. Yellow flowers with purple stamens are borne on slightly branching stems, 2–3 ft high, in July and August. 'Album' is white.

V. densiflorum: see *V. thapsiforme*

Verbascum hybridum 'C. L. Adams'

V. hybridum is a name often applied to hybrids from *V. phoeniceum* or to forms of that species. The following perennials (planting distance 12–15 in.) all flower from June to August, bearing 12–24 in. long spikes.

'C. L. Adams', height 6 ft, has spikes of deep yellow flowers with magenta stamens; the Cotswold range, which includes 'Cotswold Beauty', 'Cotswold Gem' and 'Cotswold Queen' (all 3–4 ft high), has biscuit-yellow spikes in shades of pink, maroon, purple or orange.

'Gainsborough', height 3–4 ft, has grey leaves and canary-yellow flower spikes; 'Golden Bush', height 24 in., is a natural hybrid with twiggy spikes of clustered yellow flowers with rose stamens; 'Harkness Hybrid', height 6 ft or more, bears spikes over 3 ft long of yellow flowers; 'Miss Willmott', height 6 ft, has white flowers. 'Mont Blanc' is similar to 'Gainsborough', but has white spikes; 'Pink Domino', height 3–4 ft, has deep rose-pink spikes.

V. longifolium. Southern Europe. Height 3–4 ft; planting distance 24 in. This perennial species has basal oblong-lanceolate leaves up to 24 in. long, and covered with white or yellow hairs. Golden-yellow flowers are borne in dense spikes, 18–24 in. long, from June to August.

Verbascum dumulosum

Verbascum × 'Letitia'

Verbascum chaixii

Verbascum hybridum
'Pink Domino'

Verbena × hybrida (mixed varieties)

Verbena × hybrida 'Amethyst'

Verbena peruviana

V. nigrum. Europe, including southern England. Height 2–3 ft; planting distance 12–15 in. A short-lived perennial with heart-shaped to ovate-oblong, grey-green, slightly downy leaves. Erect, slightly branching spikes, 18–24 in. long, of yellow flowers blotched red-brown, are produced from June to October.

V. olympicum. Turkey. Height 6–8 ft; planting distance 2–2½ ft. This is a long-lived rosette-forming perennial with grey-felted, broadly lanceolate leaves. Bright golden-yellow flowers are borne in imposing erect and branching spikes, 2–3 ft high, from June to September.

V. phlomoides. Southern Europe, Caucasus. Height 6 ft; planting distance 18 in. A monocarpic species chiefly suitable for a wild garden, where it frequently seeds itself. The oblong leaves are grey and woolly, as are the spikes. These are 2–3 ft long, and clustered yellow appear from May to September.

V. thapsiforme, syn. *V. densiflorum.* Europe, Balkans, Western Asia. Height 3½–4½ ft; planting distance 15–18 in. A short-lived perennial with a thin tap root and mid to dark green basal leaves arranged in a rosette. These are ovate or oblong, glabrous above and slightly hairy beneath. The branching flower spikes are up to 24 in. high and the flowers, with yellow stamens, vary in colour from near white to pink and purple shades; they appear from May to September.

V. thapsiforme, syn. *V. densiflorum.* Europe, Siberia. Height 4–5 ft; planting distance 24 in. A rosette-forming perennial with crinkly mid-green, oblong leaves. These and the stems are densely covered with yellow hairs. The tapering spikes, 2–3 ft high, of yellow flowers are produced from June to August.

V. thapsus. Great Britain. Height 3 ft; planting distance 12 in. A native biennial with clusters of oblong, marginally toothed leaves covered with white woolly hairs. Yellow flowers are borne in 12–18 in. long spikes from June to August.

V. vernale: see *V. chaixii*

Cultivation of alpine species. Plant dwarf verbascums in March or April, in any ordinary, well-drained garden soil and in a sunny site; they are ideal for dry walls or for screes. Cut off faded flower spikes just below the level of the lowest flower to encourage the growth of subsidiary spikes. *V. dumulosum* and *V. ×* 'Letitia' dislike winter dampness; protect the plants in winter with panes of glass.

In the alpine house, grow the plants in 6–8 in. pans of John Innes potting compost No. 1; repot annually in March.

Cultivation of border species. Grow verbascums in ordinary, well-drained garden soil and in full sun. Plant in October or in March or April. Tall plants may require staking in exposed positions, especially if the soil is very rich or moist. Remove faded flower spikes as described for alpines, and cut the plants down to ground level in November.

Propagation of alpine species. Take 2 in. heel cuttings between May and July and insert in equal parts (by volume) peat and sand in a cold frame. When they have rooted, which may take up to three months, pot the cuttings singly into 3 in. containers of John Innes potting compost No. 1. Overwinter in a cold frame and plant out the following March or April.

Propagation of border species. Increase the species by seeds sown during April in pans of John Innes seed compost and place in a cold frame. Prick out the seedlings 6 in. apart in nursery rows and grow them on, finally moving the plants to the flowering site in September.

The short-lived *V. phoeniceum* may be grown as an annual; sow the seeds under glass in February or March at a temperature of 13°C (55°F). Prick out the seedlings into boxes and harden them off before planting out in April.

Named varieties do not come true to type from seeds. Take 3 in. long root cuttings in February or March and insert them in equal parts (by volume) peat and sand in a cold frame. When the young plants show three or four leaves, line them out in nursery rows and grow on until September when they can be set in the flowering site.

Pests and diseases. Generally trouble-free.

Verbena

Verbenaceae

A genus of 250 species of annual and perennial herbaceous plants. The following species, and the garden hybrids in particular, are used extensively for annual summer bedding and in hanging baskets. They bear primrose-like fragrant flowers which are arranged in dense terminal clusters. Although strictly perennial, they are at their best in the first year when grown from seeds.

VERBENA BONARIENSIS

V. bonariensis. S. America. Height 4–5 ft; planting distance 24 in. A perennial border plant that flowers the first season from seeds if sown early. It can be overwintered outside in sheltered districts. The leaves are oblong and mid-green. Tall branched stems bearing rose-lavender flower heads, 2–3 in. across, are produced from June to October.

V. chamaedrifolia: see *V. peruviana*

V. hortensis: see *V. × hybrida*

VERBENA × HYBRIDA

V. × hybrida, syn. *V. hortensis.* Height 6–18 in.; planting distance 12 in. A race of beautiful hybrids producing bushy plants with leaves that are mid to dark green, ovate and serrated. Tight clusters of flowers, 3 in. or more across, open from June to the first frosts. Colours range from white, pink and red to blue and lilac.

The varieties are divided into two groups: *V. h.* 'Grandiflora' contains large-flowering plants, 12–15 in. high, including 'Ellen Willmott', bright salmon-pink with a white eye; 'Royal Bouquet Mixed'; and 'Mammoth Mixed'.

Plants in the second group, *V. h.* 'Compacta', are 9–12 in. high and more spreading; their branches can be pegged into the soil to provide dense cover. Recommended forms are: 'Sparkle Hybrids', a blend of bright and varied colours; 'Amethyst', mid-blue; and 'Blaze', crimson.

V. peruviana, syn. *V. chamaedrifolia*. South America. Height 3–4 in.; planting distance 12 in. A procumbent, half-hardy perennial with ovate-oblong, toothed mid-green leaves. Bright scarlet starry flowers, $\frac{2}{5}$ in. wide, are borne in short terminal spikes, usually in profusion. This plant is suitable for a sunny, sheltered rock garden, where it will sometimes survive the winter if given cloche protection.

V. rigida: see *V. venosa*

V. venosa, syn. *V. rigida*. Brazil and Argentina. Height 12–24 in.; planting distance 15 in. An attractive perennial that is almost hardy in mild areas. It is recommended for seaside planting. Erect stems carry ovate, marginally toothed, dark green leaves, and dense clusters of small purple flowers, each cluster 2 in. across. Flowering is from July to October. There is also an off-white variety, 'Alba'.

Cultivation. Grow in any fertile soil, adding manure or peat, in a sunny open border. Pinch out the leading shoot of each young plant to encourage bushy growth. For better ground cover, peg down lateral shoots in the soil as they grow. Water during long dry spells and give occasional liquid feeds. Dead-heading encourages a longer flowering period.

In mild areas and sheltered sites *V. bonariensis* and *V. venosa* can be overwintered outside; protect with a covering of bracken, ashes or coarse sand. Alternatively, lift the roots in October and store in boxes of soil in a frost-proof place, ready for division the following spring. Make sure the roots do not dry out.

Propagation. Sow the seeds under glass in January or March, just covering them with compost, at a temperature of 18–21°C (64–70°F). Germination is erratic and can take three or four weeks. Prick out the seedlings into boxes; harden them off in a cold frame before planting out in May.

V. bonariensis and *V. venosa* can also be propagated by root division in April. Alternatively, for a larger supply of new plants, place the roots in boxes under glass in March at a temperature of 10–13°C (50–55°F), and take the resulting young shoots as 2–3 in. cuttings. Insert these in a compost of equal parts (by volume) sand and peat in a frame. Plant out when well rooted.

Named varieties raised from seeds come true to type and colour, and vegetative propagation of *V. × hybrida* is rarely practised.

Pests. Young plants may have their growth checked by infestations of APHIDS and TARSONEMID MITES.

Diseases. Generally trouble-free.

Verbena, lemon-scented: see *Lippia citriodora*

Veronica

Speedwell. *Scrophulariaceae*

A genus of 300 species of half-hardy and hardy annual and perennial herbaceous plants. The hardy, small-growing perennials described are suitable for growing on rock gardens and dry walls. Taller varieties are better grown in herbaceous and mixed borders.

The saucer-shaped flowers, composed of a short tube and four irregularly sized petals, sometimes with darker veins, are borne solitarily or in terminal or lateral racemes.

The shrubby species, formerly included in this genus, are now classified as *Hebe*.

ALPINE SPECIES

V. cinerea. Asia Minor. Height 4 in.; spread 12–15 in. A prostrate, mat-forming species, suitable for ground cover on a rock garden. The narrowly lanceolate leaves are downy and grey-green. Axillary racemes, $1\frac{1}{2}$–2 in. long, of clear pink flowers are borne from June to August.

V. filiformis. Asia Minor. Height 1 in.; spread 3–4 ft or more. An invasive plant that rapidly forms a decorative ground cover. The mid-green leaves are orbicular. Solitary, $\frac{1}{3}$ in. wide, bright blue flowers are borne in profusion from the leaf axils from April to July.

V. gentianoides: SEE HERBACEOUS PERENNIALS

V. pectinata. Asia Minor, Syria. Height 3 in.; spread 12–15 in. This prostrate invasive plant bears ovate to obovate and toothed, grey-green leaves. Axillary racemes, 3–6 in. long, of deep blue flowers with a white eye, are borne in spires in May and June. 'Rosea' has pink flowers.

V. prostrata, syns. *V. teucrium prostrata, V. rupestris.* Europe, N. Asia. Height 3–8 in.; spread 12–18 in. A mat-forming species with ovate, toothed and mid-green leaves. The deep blue flowers appear in dense axillary racemes, 2–3 in. long, from May to July.

Varieties include: 'Pygmaea', similar to the type, but only 2 in. high; 'Rosea', with deep pink flowers; and 'Spode Blue', china-blue.

V. rupestris: see *V. prostrata*

V. satureioides. Dalmatia. Height 3 in.; spread 12–18 in. The oblong or obovate leaves of this species form glossy dark green mats. Axillary racemes, about 2 in. long, of dark blue, red-veined flowers, are borne from April to August.

V. teucrium. S. Europe, N. Asia. Height 9–15 in.; spread up to 24 in. This variable species forms loose hummocks of erect stems. The mid-green leaves are lanceolate to ovate, toothed, and sometimes lobed. Axillary racemes, 2–3 in. long, of sky-blue flowers, are borne at the tips of the stems from June to August.

V. t. prostrata: see *V. prostrata.*

In cultivation, the species is generally represented by named forms, such as 'Rosea' (height 6 in.), rose-pink, and 'Shirley Blue' (height 6–9 in.), deep blue. 'Trehane' (height 6–9 in.) has leaves flushed yellow, and pale blue flowers.

HERBACEOUS PERENNIAL SPECIES

V. exaltata. N. America. Height 4–5 ft; planting distance 18–24 in. A species with lanceolate mid-green leaves. Terminal racemes, 6–9 in. long, of soft pale blue flowers are borne during July and August.

Verbena venosa

Veronica filiformis

Veronica teucrium

Veronica longifolia

Veronica spicata 'Alba'

Veronica virginica

Viburnum × carlcephalum

Viburnum carlesii 'Aurora'

V. gentianoides. Caucasus. Height 9–15 in.; planting distance 9 in. A species suitable for the front of a border. It has glossy mid-green, ovate to lanceolate leaves, forming a cluster of basal rosettes. The terminal racemes, up to 6 in. long, of pale blue flowers are borne on 6–9 in. high stems in May and June.

'Variegata' has cream-white leaves.

VERONICA GENTIANOIDES

V. incana. Caucasus. Height 12–15 in.; planting distance 9 in. The bright silvery-grey leaves of this species are lanceolate and toothed. Small mid-blue flowers are produced in 6 in. long, terminal racemes from June to August.

'Wendy' is probably a hybrid between this species and *V. spicata*; it reaches a height of 18–24 in., and the flowers are pale blue.

V. longifolia. Central Europe, N. Asia. Height up to 4 ft; planting distance 18 in. This species bears oblong-lanceolate, mid to deep green toothed leaves in opposite pairs or in whorls of three. The terminal, dense racemes, about 6 in. long, of deep purple-blue flowers appear from June to August.

The variety 'Subsessilis' (height 3 ft) has branched racemes.

V. spicata. Europe, including Great Britain. Height 6–18 in.; planting distance 6–12 in. A variable species with oblong-lanceolate, toothed, mid-green leaves. Terminal, dense racemes, 3–6 in. long, of small flowers in various shades of blue, are borne from June to August.

Named varieties include 'Alba' (height 18 in.), white; 'Barcarolle' (height 12 in.), rose-pink; 'Crater Lake Blue' (height 15 in.), ultramarine-blue; and 'Pavane' (height 24 in.), grey-green foliage and deep pink flowers.

V. virginica, syn. *Veronicastrum virginica.* E. North America. Height 4–6 ft; planting distance 24 in. A distinct species with lanceolate, slender-pointed mid-green leaves in whorls of three to six. The terminal branched racemes, 8–10 in. long, of pale blue flowers are produced from July to September.

The form most frequently seen is 'Alba' with white flowers, often flushed pink in bud.

Cultivation of alpine species. Plant these veronicas in any ordinary, well-drained garden soil in a sunny position, from September to March. Remove the spikes of the erect-growing species and varieties after flowering.

Cultivation of herbaceous perennial species. Plant between October and April in ordinary garden soil, enriched with well-rotted manure; the soil should be well-drained, but moisture-retentive. Choose a site in full sun or partial shade. On exposed positions stake with twiggy supports. Cut the plants down to just above ground level in November, and divide every three years.

Propagation of alpine species. Divide and replant all species, except the invasive *V. cinerea* and *V. pectinata* in March or April.

All species can be increased from 2 in. cuttings of lateral shoots, taken in July or August. Insert in equal parts (by volume) peat and sand in a cold frame; when rooted, pot the cuttings singly into 3 in. containers of John Innes potting compost No. 1. Plant out in permanent positions the following March.

Propagation of herbaceous perennial species. Lift and divide the plants in March and April.

Pests. Generally trouble-free.

Diseases. POWDERY MILDEW occasionally attacks the foliage which becomes grey-white and slightly disfigured.

Veronicastrum virginica: see *Veronica virginica*

Viburnum
Caprifoliaceae

A genus of 200 species of deciduous and evergreen shrubs widely distributed in the temperate regions from North America to Japan. The majority are hardy and can be divided into those which flower in winter on the naked wood, those which flower with the leaves in spring and summer, and those which are grown for their decorative fruits in autumn. The flowers, which are borne in pendent clusters or flat corymbose heads, are usually tubular with five rounded spreading lobes; the tube is longer in the winter-flowering species than in those that flower in spring and summer.

V. betulifolium. China. Height and spread 8–12 ft. A deciduous species of bushy habit. The dark green toothed leaves are broadly ovate. The white flowers are borne in 2–4 in. wide corymbs in May and June and are followed by clusters of red currant-like berries in autumn. This species usually takes some years to berry.

V. × bodnantense. A deciduous hybrid between *V. fragrans* and *V. grandiflorum.* Height and spread 9–12 ft. The upright stiff growths carry dull green, ovate and toothed leaves; the young foliage is tinged with bronze. White flushed rose flowers are borne in clusters, 1–2 in. long, on the naked wood from December to February. This is one of the best, most frost-resistant winter-flowering shrubs. 'Dawn' is the form generally seen in cultivation.

V. × burkwoodii. China. Height up to 8 ft; spread 9–12 ft. This evergreen hybrid between *V. carlesii* and *V. utile* has dark green ovate leaves. The waxy, sweet-scented, white flowers are pink in bud; they are borne in flat 2½–3½ in. wide heads from March to May. 'Park Farm Hybrid' is of more spreading habit and has larger flowers.

V. × carlcephalum. Height up to 8 ft; spread 6–7 ft. A deciduous hybrid between *V. carlesii* and *V. macrocephalum,* with light green, broadly ovate leaves. The fragrant cream-white flowers are borne in broad heads, measuring 3–4 in. across, during April and May.

V. carlesii. Korea. Height and spread 4–5 ft. This deciduous species bears dull green, slightly hoary, broadly ovate leaves. The deeply fragrant, waxy white flowers are carried in convex 2–3 in. wide heads in April and May. Selected forms include: 'Aurora', red in bud, opening pale pink; 'Diana', of compact habit, red buds opening to apple-blossom pink.

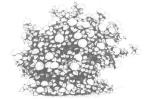

VIBURNUM CARLESII

V. davidii. China. Height 2–3 ft; spread 4–5 ft. This evergreen berrying species is suitable for ground cover. It has ovate, prominently veined, dark green leaves. The white flowers in flat heads, 2–3 in. across, appear in June and are followed by turquoise-blue berries if male and female plants are planted together.

V. dentatum. E. United States. Height 10 ft or more; spread 6–8 ft. An erect deciduous shrub with broadly ovate, coarsely toothed and prominently veined mid-green leaves that assume attractive autumn colours. Clusters, 2–3 in. wide, of white flowers appear in May and June. Blue-black ovoid fruits ripen in September.

V. farreri: see V. fragrans

V. fragrans, syn. V. farreri. N. China. Height and spread 9–12 ft. A deciduous winter-flowering species of upright habit. The bright green leaves are ovate, pointed and strongly toothed, bronze-tinted when young. Richly scented white, pink-tinged flowers are borne in pendent clusters, 1–1½ in. long, from November to February or March. 'Candidissimum' is a form with lighter green foliage lacking the bronze tinting, and pure white flowers opening from jade-green buds.

V. grandiflorum. Himalayas. Height up to 10 ft; spread up to 6 ft. An erect deciduous species, closely related to V. fragrans. The mid to deep green leaves are ovate-oblong and toothed. Flower clusters, up to 2 in. long, appear from December to April; the individual florets are larger and more strongly flushed with pink than those of V. fragrans.

V. × juddii. Height 6 ft; spread up to 8 ft. This deciduous hybrid between V. carlesii and V. bitchiuense has dark green ovate leaves. The sweet-scented flowers are white and pink; they appear in 2–3 in. wide heads in April and May.

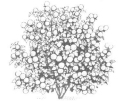

VIBURNUM OPULUS 'STERILE'

V. opulus (guelder rose). Europe, including Great Britain; N. Africa. Height up to 15 ft; spread 12–15 ft. A deciduous species of upright bushy habit. It has dark green, lobed, maple-like leaves. Flat heads, 2–3 in. across, of heavily scented white flowers, are surrounded by ¾ in. wide sterile bracts. The flowers are borne in May and June and are followed by translucent red, slightly ovoid berries in autumn.

Viburnum tomentosum 'Mariesii'

The following varieties are recommended: 'Compactum', free-berrying and up to 6 ft; 'Notcutt's Variety', large, brighter red berries; 'Sterile' (snowball bush), large round flower heads that open green and become snow-white; 'Xanthocarpum', one of the finest autumn-fruiting shrubs with rich yellow berries.

V. rhytidophyllum. China. Height 10–15 ft; spread 10–12 ft. An evergreen species with spreading self-layering branches. The lanceolate leaves are glossy deep green. Flat, white, 3–4 in. wide flower heads appear in May and June and are followed, when several plants are grown, by red ovoid berries which eventually turn black.

V. tinus (laurustinus). S.E. Europe. Height 7–10 ft; spread up to 7 ft. An evergreen species of bushy habit, with lanceolate to ovate, entire leaves that are mid to deep green. The white, pink-budded flowers are carried in flat heads, 2–4 in. across, at the ends of the shoots from November to May. Selected forms include: 'Eve Price', of denser habit with smaller leaves and pink flowers; 'French White', a good white; 'Variegatum', golden variegated leaves.

VIBURNUM TOMENTOSUM 'MARIESII'

V. tomentosum. China, Japan. Height 8–10 ft; spread 10–15 ft. This deciduous shrub has horizontal growths bearing dull green toothed, ovate leaves that taper to a point; they assume wine-red tints in autumn. The flat 3–4 in. wide heads are produced in May; the white fertile flowers are surrounded by sterile outer florets.

'Lanarth', more upright and with tiered growths; 'Mariesii', of tiered but spreading habit, with larger sterile florets; 'Plicatum' (Japanese snowball), larger leaves and round heads of long-lasting sterile flowers; and 'Rowallane', a dwarf form.

Viburnum dentatum (autumn foliage)

Viburnum grandiflorum

Viburnum opulus (fruits)

Cultivation. All viburnums thrive in any good moist garden soil, although the species described do not give good results on dry thin soils. Species grown for their decorative berries usually fruit better if planted in twos and threes. Early-flowering varieties should be planted in positions sheltered from cold north and east winds, and where early morning sun after spring frosts will not damage the young growths and flowers. All species are best grown in full sun. The evergreen species should be planted in September and October or from March to May; deciduous species from October to March.

Propagation. Take cuttings, 3–4 in. long, of lateral shoots with a heel in June or July or in September. Insert the cuttings in equal parts (by volume) peat and sand. Softwood cuttings taken in June and July require bottom heat, in a propagating case, of 16°C (61°F); cuttings taken in August and September can be rooted in a cold frame. Pot softwood cuttings when rooted in 3 in. pots of John Innes potting compost No. 1 and overwinter in a cold frame. The following April or May line out all cuttings in nursery rows outdoors and grow on for two or three years. Transplant the young plants to their permanent positions from September to March.

Alternatively, layer long shoots in September and sever about one year later.

Seeds may be sown when ripe (September or October) in pans of seed compost in a cold frame. Germination frequently takes 18 months, and subsequent growth of the seedlings is slow for the first year or two. Most species take four to six years to reach flowering size.

Pruning. Thin out old and damaged wood of evergreen species in early May. The deciduous species require no regular pruning, except to thin out overgrown shrubs and to remove dead wood after flowering. Prune winter-flowering species in April and summer-flowering shrubs in June.

Pests. Young leaves may be infested with APHIDS causing leaf curl, particularly on *V. carlesii*.

WHITEFLIES sometimes infest the undersides of leaves of *V. tinus* producing black scales, fringed with white wax.

Diseases. Dead shoots may have GREY MOULD which shows as grey velvety cushions of fungus spores. It usually follows FROST DAMAGE or other injury and can cause considerable DIE-BACK.

LEAF SPOT due to one or more fungi shows as pale or purple spots on the leaves; HONEY FUNGUS causes the rapid death of the shrubs.

A PHYSIOLOGICAL DISORDER causes the flower buds to wither without opening.

Vicia faba: see Beans (broad)

Vinca

Apocynaceae

A genus of seven species of deciduous and evergreen mat-forming shrubs, sub-shrubs and herbaceous perennials. One of the species, *V. rosea*, is tender and requires greenhouse cultivation; it may also be used for summer bedding in sheltered sites in the south and west. The other two species described are hardy and invasive

Viburnum tomentosum 'Plicatum'

Vinca rosea

Vinca major 'Elegantissima'

plants, suitable as evergreen ground cover in shrub and mixed borders or in wild gardens. The flowers are tubular with five angular or rounded petals opening out flat.

GREENHOUSE SPECIES

V. rosea. Tropics. Height 12–15 in.; outdoor planting distance 12 in. An erect, evergreen, tender sub-shrub, usually grown as an annual pot plant. The species is now correctly classified in the genus *Catharanthus*. It has oblong-ovate leaves that are glossy and mid to deep green. Rose-pink flowers, 1–1½ in. across, appear from April to October.

Several varieties are listed, including 'Little Pinkie' (height 9 in.), with rose-pink flowers held well above the foliage; and 'Little Bright Eye', bearing pure white flowers with deep rose-pink centres.

VINCA MAJOR

OUTDOOR SPECIES

V. major (greater periwinkle). Europe, including Great Britain. Height 6–12 in.; spread 3–4 ft. A spreading sub-shrub with ovate, glossy, mid to dark green leaves. Purple-blue flowers, 1–1¼ in. across, appear from April to June, sometimes with a second flush in September and October.

The variety 'Elegantissima' is slightly less vigorous and has variegated pale green and white leaves and pale purple-blue flowers.

V. minor (lesser periwinkle). Europe. Height 2–4 in.; spread 3–4 ft. The leaves of this spreading sub-shrub are elliptic to lanceolate and glossy dark green. The blue flowers, ¾–1 in. across, are borne from March to July, often continuing intermittently until October.

Varieties include: 'Alba', with white flowers; 'Albo-plena', double white flowers; 'Atro-purpurea', deep purple; 'Aureo-variegata', blue flowers and yellow variegated leaves; 'Azurea Flore-pleno', blue; 'Burgundy', wine-red; 'La Grave', deep blue-purple; and 'Multiplex', double plum-purple.

Cultivation of greenhouse species. Grow *V. rosea* in 5–6 in. pots of John Innes potting compost No. 2, potting young plants in March. Water established plants freely and give a dilute liquid feed at 10 to 14-day intervals from May to September. Ventilate the greenhouse freely when the temperature exceeds 18°C (64°F).

If grown as perennials, a minimum winter temperature of 13°C (55°F) ensures continuous growth and a long flowering season. The plants will survive the winter at a temperature of 7°C (45°F) if allowed a rest period; reduce the water supply in November, keeping the compost just moist until growth restarts in March. Repot or pot on annually in March, but plants are seldom worth keeping for more than two years.

Outdoors, set bedding plants in late May in any well-drained, fertile garden soil and in a sunny and sheltered position.

Cultivation of outdoor species. Grow these species and their varieties in a partially shaded position, in any ordinary, well-drained garden soil. Plant between September and March.

Propagation of greenhouse species. Sow seeds in pans or boxes of seed compost during March, at a temperature of 15–18°C (59–64°F). Prick off the seedlings, when large enough to handle, into boxes, then transfer to $3\frac{1}{2}$ in. pots of John Innes potting compost No. 1. Pinch out the growing tips once or twice to encourage bushy growth. Pot on as necessary, or harden off those for outdoor bedding in a cold frame before setting them out in late May or early June.

Plants can also be raised from 2–3 in. cuttings from plants that have been cut back in March. Take cuttings of greenhouse plants in April, of bedding plants in September. Insert the cuttings in equal parts (by volume) peat and sand in a propagating frame at a temperature of 15–18°C (59–64°F). Transfer the rooted cuttings to $3–3\frac{1}{2}$ in. containers of John Innes potting compost No. 1, pinching out the growing points as described for seedlings. Overwinter at a temperature of 10–13°C (50–55°F); pot on as necessary, or set out the bedding varieties in late May.

Propagation of outdoor species. Divide *V. major* and *V. minor* at any time from September to April and replant in the permanent sites.

The trailing stems of these species root from every node if they are in contact with the soil. Stem sections, 6 in. long, taken preferably in September, March or April and inserted obliquely in the flowering sites, quickly root.

Pests. Generally trouble-free.

Diseases. Stunting of *V. minor* may be caused by CUCUMBER MOSAIC VIRUS. The leaves show a yellow mottling; flowers have white streaks.

RUST occasionally attacks *V. major*, showing as pustules scattered thickly over the leaves and bearing brown, powdery masses of spores.

Vine: see Grape
Vine, cut-leaved: see *Vitis vinifera* 'Apiifolia'
Vine, cypress: see *Ipomoea quamoclit*
Vine, grape: see Vitis
Vine, Japanese crimson glory: see *Vitis coignetiae*
Vine, kangaroo: see *Cissus antarctica*
Vine, Kolomikta: see *Actinidia kolomikta*
Vine, parsley: see *Vitis vinifera* 'Apiifolia'
Vine, Russian: see *Polygonum baldschuanicum*
Vine, staff: see Celastrus
Vine, trumpet: see Campsis and *Lonicera sempervirens*

Viola

Pansy. *Violaceae*

A genus of 500 species of hardy annual and perennial herbaceous plants. The cultivated species are all perennials. *V.* × *wittrockiana*, the garden pansy, is one of the most popular of all garden plants and is used for bedding out and for edging paths; the hybrids produce a wide range of colourful flowers over a long period. The species with violet-like flowers are suitable for rock gardens and alpine houses.

The open flowers consist of five petals which in the pansy types are rounded, while violet petals are strap-shaped.

V. aetolica, previously *V. saxatilis aetolica*. E. Europe. Height 2 in.; spread 9–12 in. This species has tufts of mid-green leaves that are ovate with a wedge-shaped base. Pansy-like yellow flowers, $\frac{3}{4}$–1 in. across, open in May and June.

VIOLA BIFLORA

V. biflora. N. Hemisphere. Height 2–3 in.; spread 12 in. The kidney-shaped leaves are a bright fresh green. Vivid yellow violet-shaped flowers, $\frac{1}{2}$–$\frac{3}{4}$ in. across, open in April and May.

V. cornuta. Pyrenees. Height 4–12 in.; spread 12–15 in. The ovate to oval leaves, with rounded teeth, are mid-green. Deep lavender flowers, like large, angular violets, 1 in. wide and with a slender spur, open in June and July. 'Alba' is a white-flowered variety; 'Jersey Gem' is rich blue-purple with broader petals; 'Minor' (height 2 in.), makes a close mat of foliage with smaller lavender flowers.

VIOLA CORNUTA

V. cucullata. N.E. America. Height 3–6 in.; spread 12 in. The heart-shaped leaves are rounded and pale green. Violet-like flowers, $\frac{3}{4}$–1 in. across, varying from white to violet, with darker veining on the lower petals, open in May and June. 'Albiflora' (height 3 in.) has white flowers with violet veining.

V. gracilis. Asia Minor, Balkans. Height 4 in.; spread 12 in. The true species, rarely seen in cultivation, has broadly ovate mid-green leaves with rounded teeth. Deep purple pansy-shaped flowers, 1 in. across, open from April to June.

Varieties include 'Black Knight', purple-black; 'Major', with large, deep purple-blue flowers; 'Moonlight', clear primrose-yellow.

V. labradorica 'Purpurea'. Greenland, N. America. Height 4–5 in.; spread 12–15 in. The leaves, which are broadly ovate to orbicular, are mid-green suffused with purple. Violet-like mauve flowers, $\frac{3}{4}$ in. wide, appear in April or May.

V. odorata (sweet violet). Europe, including Great Britain; Asia, North Africa. Height 4–6 in.; spread 12 in. or more. This well-known species forms tufts of thick rhizomes and spreads by means of runners. The heart-shaped leaves are mid to dark green. Flowers, in shades of purple or white and $\frac{1}{2}$–$\frac{3}{4}$ in. wide, are borne from February to April, or sometimes in autumn.

Named colour forms include: 'Christmas',

Vinca minor

Viola biflora

Viola cornuta 'Jersey Gem'

Viola × *wittrockiana* 'Arkwright Ruby'

Viola odorata

Viola × wittrockiana
'Jackanapes'

Viola × wittrockiana
'Maggie Mott'

early-flowering, small white blooms with a green eye; 'Coeur d'Alsace', rich pink; 'Czar', deep violet-purple; 'Marie Louise', double mauve; 'Princess of Wales', rich violet flowers on long stems; 'Sulphurea', apricot-yellow, flushed violet-purple in bud.

V. saxatilis aetolica: see V. aetolica

VIOLA TRICOLOR

V. tricolor (heartsease). Europe, including Great Britain. Height 2–6 in.; spread 6–12 in. or more. The spreading stems carry ovate to lanceolate mid-green leaves with rounded teeth. The pansy-like flowers, $\frac{1}{2}$–$1\frac{1}{2}$ in. wide, vary from cream and yellow to dark blue and purple-black, or may be bicoloured. They are produced in profusion from May to September.

The numerous varieties bred from this species are described under V. × wittrockiana.

V. × wittrockiana (garden pansy), syns. V. tricolor hortensis, V. t. maxima. Height 6–9 in.; planting distance 9–12 in. A race of hybrids, largely derived from V. tricolor and basically similar but with larger flowers and more robust in growth. Flower sizes vary from 1 to 4 in. across.

In addition to summer-flowering plants, there are winter-flowering types which start to flower in late autumn in mild and protected sites and continue through the winter to spring. The summer-flowering hybrids are in bloom from May to September.

The following summer-flowering varieties are recommended: 'Arkwright Ruby', 6 in., with bright crimson fragrant flowers; 'Blue Heaven', 6 in., celestial-blue with a yellow eye; and 'Clear Crystals', 6 in., an early-flowering strain with

self-coloured flowers. This form is available either in single colours or as a mixture of golden-yellow, red, white, blue and violet. 'Jackanapes' (6 in.) is a dark blue-purple and yellow bicolor form.

Majestic Giants, F_1 (7 in.), is a strain with early flowers, 4 in. across, in a mixture of crimson, scarlet, purple, light blue, yellow and white.

Swiss Giants, 6 in., is one of the most popular strains, bearing attractively masked flowers with a velvety texture. These plants are slightly later flowering and are available as a mixture and in separate colours. The latter include 'Rhinegold', a deep golden-yellow, and 'Ullswater Blue'. 'Westland Giants', 6 in., one of the large-flowered varieties, is obtainable in a wide colour range.

The winter-flowering types are often sold as a mixture, but there are also separate varieties such as 'Celestial Queen', light blue; 'Helios', golden-yellow; and 'Ice King', white.

Also listed under V. × wittrockiana are the tufted pansies, partly derived from V. cornuta. These fully hardy perennials must be propagated vegetatively as they do not come true from seeds. They bear self-coloured, circular flowers from spring to autumn.

Among several named varieties the following are recommended: 'Admiration', dark purple-blue; 'Irish Molly', copper-yellow; 'Lily', lemon-yellow; 'Maggie Mott', light mauve; 'Norah Leigh', lavender-blue; 'Primrose Dame', primrose-yellow; and 'White Swan', pure white.

Cultivation. Plant violas in September, October, March or April. They will thrive in any fertile, moist, but well-drained soil in sun or partial shade. Remove the flowers as they fade to maintain a succession of blooms.

Violas can also be grown in alpine houses or cold greenhouses in pans 6–8 in. wide (depending on the size of the plant) containing John Innes potting compost No. 1. Repot annually in September or October.

Propagation. Sow seeds of V. tricolor and V. × wittrockiana in July or early August, either outdoors in a damp shaded site or in pans or boxes placed in a cold frame. Transplant the seedlings of those sown outdoors to stand 4 in. apart in a nursery bed until they are moved to the flowering site in September or October. Prick off the seedlings in the cold frame into 3 in. pots of John Innes potting compost No. 1; overwinter the young plants in the frame and plant out in the flowering sites in March or April.

Seeds of other species may be sown as described above, in March or July.

Seeds of V. tricolor may also be sown in the flowering site in March or April, thinning out the seedlings as necessary, or under glass between January and March at a temperature of 16°C (61°F). Prick off the greenhouse seedlings into boxes and harden the plants off in a cold frame before planting out in April.

All species can be propagated from 1–2 in. cuttings of non-flowering basal shoots taken in July and inserted in equal parts (by volume) peat and sand in a cold frame. Pot on into 3 in. pots of John Innes potting compost No. 1, when they are well rooted, and plant out at any time between September and March.

Pests. Generally trouble-free.

Diseases. Foliage may be infected by CUCUMBER MOSAIC VIRUS. The leaves often curl at the edges and are sometimes yellow mottled. The flowers are small and show white streaks.

LEAF SPOTS, due to any of several different fungi, may be irregular with a thin brown margin, or yellow with a dark green centre that frequently drops out, giving a shot-hole effect.

PANSY SICKNESS may be due to many different fungi. The leaves become yellow, and wilt; the roots, crowns and stem bases rot. Top growth collapses completely and can easily be lifted.

RUST may cause distortion of the stems, which swell and bear pustules producing yellow-orange spores; in late summer brown spores appear.

Violet, African: see Saintpaulia
Violet cress: see *Ionopsidium acaule*
Violet, damask: see *Hesperis matronalis*
Violet, dog's-tooth: see Erythronium
Violet, sweet: see *Viola odorata*
Virginia creeper: see Parthenocissus
Virginia creeper, Chinese: see *Parthenocissus henryana*
Virginia creeper, common: see *Parthenocissus inserta* and *P. quinquefolia*
Viscaria alpina: see *Lychnis alpina*
Viscaria elegans: see *Silene coeli-rosa*
Viscaria vulgaris: see *Lychnis viscaria*

Viscum

Mistletoe. *Loranthaceae*

VISCUM ALBUM

A genus of 60 or 70 species of hardy evergreen shrubs. They are parasitic and grow on a variety of trees, including apple, hawthorn, lime and poplar, but rarely on oaks or conifers. The inconspicuous male and female flowers are usually produced on separate plants, and both are required to form the white globose fruits.

V. album. Europe, N. Asia. Height indefinite; spread 1–3 ft. The obovate yellow-green leaves are borne in opposite pairs on repeatedly forking twigs. These form globular clusters up to 3 ft wide. Pale yellow-green flowers appear in stalkless, $\frac{1}{2}$ in. wide clusters from February to April, the female flowers being smaller than the male. The semi-translucent white fruits, which appear from September to January on the female plants, contain a sticky pulp surrounding the seeds.
Propagation. In February or March, press ripe berries into the bark crevices or beneath a sliced flap of bark, on the underside of a branch. Ideally, the tree should be of the same species on which the parent plant grew. The seeds may take two or three months to germinate; the plants seldom fruit before they are seven years old.
Pruning. None required.
Pests and diseases. Generally trouble-free.

Vitis

Grape vine. *Vitidaceae*

A genus of about 70 species of evergreen or deciduous climbing shrubs. They are particularly suitable for growing on pergolas and trees, but can also be grown on trellis or wires. They cling by means of tendrils. Though their natural habit is to grow straight up before branching, they can be encouraged to spread nearer the ground by cutting back at planting time.

Most species differ from the closely related genus *Parthenocissus* in the following ways: the bark on the stems peels; the leaves are undivided; and the flowers are borne in panicles, with their petals joined at the tips. All the species described are suitable for garden cultivation.

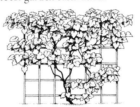

VITIS COIGNETIAE

V. amurensis (Amurland grape). Manchuria, China. Height up to 50 ft. This is a hardy, vigorous, deciduous vine with attractive red downy young growths. The leaves are dark green above, mid-green and downy beneath, and usually five-lobed. They turn rose-red, crimson and purple in autumn. Inconspicuous green-white flowers, in 3–4 in. long panicles, are produced during May.
V. coignetiae (Japanese crimson glory vine). Japan. Height up to 90 ft. This vigorous, hardy, deciduous species is the finest of all ornamental vines. It is best suited to growing on trees or over old buildings. The young stems have vertical ribs and are covered with a loose grey down. The thick, rounded, mid-green leaves are smooth above but covered with rust-red hairs beneath. They have a heart-shaped base, three or five pointed lobes, and are coarsely toothed. In autumn they turn yellow, orange-red and purple-crimson. Green flowers appear in May in panicles 3 in. long. They are followed by inedible black berries with a purple bloom.
V. davidii. China. Height 20–25 ft. This is a hardy, deciduous species for a pergola, or for rambling over a tree or large shrub. The young shoots have hook-shaped spines or bristles. The leaves are large and heart-shaped, tapering to a point. Bronze-green when young, they change to light green; finally, in autumn, they become rich crimson. Minute green flowers are produced during June and July in panicles 4–6 in. long. The edible black fruits have a pleasant flavour.
V. hederacea: see *Parthenocissus quinquefolia*
V. inconstans: see *Parthenocissus tricuspidata*
V. labrusca (fox grape). N. America. Height 15–20 ft. This is a vigorous, hardy but variable species. The leaves, some of which are entire and others three-lobed, are heart-shaped at the base. They are dark green above and covered beneath with rust-brown felt. Their brown-red autumn colouring is not as brilliant as that of the Asiatic species. Small green flowers appear during June

Viola × *wittrockiana* Swiss Giants (mixed)

Viola × *wittrockiana* 'Ullswater Blue'

Viscum album (fruits)

Vitis coignetiae (in autumn)

in panicles 2–4 in. long. In most seasons bunches of edible, thick-skinned, purple-black grapes with a musky aroma are produced.

V. odoratissima: see *V. riparia*

V. riparia, syns. *V. odoratissima, V. vulpina* (riverbank grape). N. America. Height up to 12 ft. This hardy, rambling species is grown chiefly for its luxuriant foliage and sweetly scented flowers. It has smooth stems and bright green, coarsely serrated leaves which are usually three-lobed. They are heart-shaped at the base and taper to a point. The foliage turns an attractive, though not brilliant, yellow-brown in autumn. Yellow-green fragrant flowers are produced during June in panicles up to 8 in. long. The small purple-black fruits have a dense blue-white bloom.

V. semicordata: see *Parthenocissus himalayana*

V. vinifera (grape vine, wine grape). Asia Minor, Caucasus. Height 20 ft. The many fruit-bearing varieties of this hardy, deciduous vine are grown for wine-making. Ornamental varieties include:

V. v. 'Apiifolia', syn. *V. v.* 'Laciniosa' (cut-leaved vine, parsley vine), with ovate dark green leaves, having three to five fringed lobes. Small green flowers are produced during June in panicles 3–4 in. long. The fruits are small and black, with a blue bloom. This is an attractive plant for an archway or pergola. *V. v.* 'Brandt' has palmate, lobed, mid to deep green leaves which colour crimson, pink and orange in autumn. Panicles, 3–4 in. long, of tiny green-white flowers appear in May and June; the globular fruits are red-purple. *V. v.* 'Purpurea' (Teinturier grape) bears claret-red foliage throughout the summer, turning rich purple in the autumn. The leaves are ovate to round, with three to five coarsely serrated lobes. Minute green flowers are borne during June in 3–4 in. long panicles. The oval, purple-black fruits have a blue bloom. See also GRAPE.

V. vitacea: see *Parthenocissus inserta*

V. vulpina: see *V. riparia*

Cultivation. A deeply cultivated, moist, loamy soil, enriched with manure or compost, is needed. Add lime if the soil is acid. Almost any position and aspect is suitable, though a south or west-facing site is needed if the fruits are to ripen for harvesting. Plant out the young vines from their pots or boxes in mild weather between November and March. Prune the growths to within 9–12 in. of the ground, and tie in the young growths.

Propagation. Sow the seeds during November in pans or boxes of seed compost placed in a cold frame or greenhouse.

With the exception of *V. coignetiae*, all the species described can also be propagated from cuttings. Take 4–5 in. heel cuttings from half-ripened growths in July or August and insert them individually in pots of sandy soil; root at a temperature of 13–16°C (55–61°F).

Pot rooted cuttings and pricked-out seedlings singly into 3 in. pots and grow them on in a cold frame or greenhouse. When they outgrow these pots, repot them in 5 in. pots and grow them on in a cold frame. When established, plunge the pots in a nursery bed before planting out and support the climbing growths with canes.

Hardwood cuttings, 10–12 in. long, can be taken in November; insert them in a sheltered border outdoors. Plant out when rooted.

Vitis vinifera 'Brandt' (autumn foliage and fruits)

Vriesea fenestralis

Vriesea splendens

Layer one-year-old growths of *V. coignetiae* in September or October. They will root in a year.

Pruning. Where space is restricted, thin out old growths and shorten young growths during the late summer.

Pests. SCALE INSECTS, especially brown scale, infest stems and make the foliage sticky and sooty.

MEALY BUGS also infest stems, petioles and leaves and produce conspicuous tufts of white waxy wool.

APHIDS may infest young growths.

GLASSHOUSE RED SPIDER MITES attack the leaves, causing a fine, light mottling, followed in severe infestations by bronzing, withering and death.

WEEVILS and CATERPILLARS feed on the leaves.

Diseases. Ornamental vines are not as susceptible to diseases and disorders as fruiting vines. They can, however, be affected by HONEY FUNGUS and by MAGNESIUM DEFICIENCY.

Vriesea

Bromeliaceae

A genus of 190 species and several hybrids of greenhouse ornamental perennials. They are terrestrial or epiphytic, and occur through Cuba and southern Mexico to northern Argentina and the West Indian and Caribbean Islands.

The evergreen leaves are smooth-edged and usually glossy. Colour may be plain green or with purple-red bases; they may be etched with purple-black hieroglyphics or be cross-banded with dark green lines. The leaves form perfect rosettes varying in size from a few inches to 6 ft in height and diameter. All have leaf reservoirs for retaining water.

The inflorescences vary greatly and may be slanting or horizontal. They may be candelabra-shaped or sword-like with the bracts neatly arranged in flattened parallel ranks. The tubular flowers are short-lived, but the bracts are long-lasting. Generally, plants with yellow flowers bloom by day and those with white flowers bloom at night.

See also BROMELIADS.

V. fenestralis. Brazil. Height 2½ ft. The spiral rosette consists of broad, recurving yellow-green leaves with a network of dark green veins, sometimes with purple circles on the undersides. The tubular sulphur-yellow flowers, 2½ in. long, are borne in a spike rising about 18 in. above the foliage. Flowering is in summer, but the plant is chiefly grown for the ornamental leaves.

V. hieroglyphica (king of bromeliads). Brazil. Height 24 in. The rosette is made up of broad, yellow-green leaves patterned with dark purple irregular hieroglyphics. The flowering stem reaches a height of about 2½ ft. The upper third is branched and carries pale green bracts and dull yellow tubular flowers, 2 in. long. Flowering usually occurs in spring.

V. splendens (flaming sword). Guyana. Height 18 in. The rosette is composed of slender dark green leaves with striking, purple-black cross-banding. The sword-shaped flowering stem is about 24 in. high, half of which comprises a spike of brilliant red bracts and yellow flowers, 2–3 in. long. Flowering is in late summer.

Cultivation. Plant in 4–5 in. pots in early spring in a compost of equal parts (by volume) sand and leaf-mould. Vrieseas require a shaded position, a constantly high humidity and a temperature of 18–21°C (64–70°F). Water freely from April to September, sparingly for the rest of the year. Repot every two or three years in March.

Propagation. Vrieseas may be increased from seeds, but seedlings take at least 10–15 years to reach flowering size.

Propagate by removing the rooted offshoots, which appear either between the leaves or at the base of the plant, when they are half the size of the parent plants. Leave the offshoots to dry for a few days, before potting up firmly in the same soil mixture as advised for full-grown plants.

Pests and diseases. Generally trouble-free.

× Vuylstekeara

Orchidaceae

This group of trigeneric orchid hybrids has been derived from *Cochlioda*, *Miltonia* and *Odontoglossum*. They are similar in appearance and cultural requirements to *Odontoglossum*, and flower from November to May.

See also ORCHIDS.

Several named forms are available and include the following: 'Estella Jewell', a cross between × *Vuylstekeara* Aspasia and *Miltonia* 'William Pitt', with 2½–3 in. wide flowers having rich plum-coloured petals and sepals and a broad crimson and white lip.

× VUYLSTEKEARA

Cambria, a hybrid between × *Vuylstekeara* Rubra and *Odontoglossum* Clonius. It includes 'Plush', with flowers of dark red sepals and petals; the white lip is blotched with red. Each flower is 3–4 in. across, and the lip 2 in. wide and high; each stem bears up to nine flowers in winter and spring.

'Edna', a hybrid between × *Miltonioda harwoodii* and × *Odontioda charlesworthii*; the flowers, 2–2½ in. across, have bright red sepals and petals and a pale orange lip.

Cultivation, propagation, pests and diseases. See entry for ODONTOGLOSSUM.

× *Vuylstekeara* Cambria 'Plush'

W,YZ

Wake robin: see *Trillium grandiflorum*
Wallflower: see Cheiranthus
Wallflower, Siberian: see *Cheiranthus × allionii*

Walnut

Juglans. Juglandaceae

WALNUT

A genus of 15 species of hardy deciduous trees, grown commercially for their valuable timber and edible nuts. They also make handsome specimen trees for parks and large gardens. Unisexual flowers are produced on the same tree; the tiny ovoid female flowers are borne in clusters of two or three; the male flowers are carried in numerous slender pendulous catkins. Edible nuts are produced on seed-raised trees after about 15 years of growth.

Common walnut (*Juglans regia*). E. Europe, N. Asia. Height 20–25 ft; spread 10–15 ft. This round-headed species may eventually reach a height of 100 ft, with a spread of more than 30 ft.

The bark of young trees is smooth and ash-grey; that of older trees is brown and fissured. The glossy, light to mid-green leaves are composed of several ovate leaflets. Flowers appear in May; the green female catkins are inconspicuous, but the yellow-green male catkins are 2–4 in. long. Mature trees bear ovoid, plum-shaped green fruits, 1½–2 in. wide, each of which contains a thick-shelled edible nut. This species is also valued for its fine timber.

Often male and female flowers do not mature at the same time and pollination is erratic; the following varieties, however, are recommended: 'Excelsior of Taynton', a vigorous tree with large conical nuts of good flavour; 'Leeds Castle', a large, vigorous tree with nuts that are especially good for pickling; 'Northdown Clawnut', a medium-sized tree with large, oblong nuts of good flavour.

Cultivation. Plant walnuts between October and March while they are young, as they do not transplant well. Any fertile, well-drained soil is suitable, in an open position protected from late spring frosts. Mulch with well-rotted manure annually in spring for the first few years until the trees are established.

For pickling, gather the nuts before they harden. Otherwise, gather nuts after they drop, remove the husk, clean the nuts carefully and dry in an airy room. Store in containers, between layers of sand or sprinkled with salt.

Walnut (male catkins)

Walnut (immature fruit)

Propagation. The species may be raised from seeds sown in October or November in nursery rows outdoors; grow on the seedlings for two or three years before setting in permanent sites.

Named varieties must be budded in April or May or grafted in March or July on to rootstocks of *Juglans regia.*

Pruning. No regular pruning is needed and should be generally avoided, as walnuts 'bleed' profusely when cut. April or August are the months to remove any dead or crossing branches.

Pests. Fruits are eaten by SQUIRRELS and BIRDS.

GALL MITES infest the leaves, causing blister-like pouches.

Diseases. Die-back of shoots is caused by FROST DAMAGE; the shoots are often entered by secondary fungi, which may cause further DIE-BACK.

HONEY FUNGUS rapidly kills trees.

Wandering jew: see *Tradescantia albiflora*
Wand flower: see Dierama

Watercress

Rorippa nasturtium-aquaticum, syn. *R. microphylla, Nasturtium officinale. Cruciferae*

A hardy perennial aquatic grown as a salad vegetable. It is native to Great Britain, and the young shoots are used fresh.

There are bronze-green and dark green types, the bronze-green being the hardier of the two.

Cultivation. For best results, watercress should be grown in running water. It may also be cultivated in shallow trenches kept permanently moist. In April or May, dig a trench 9 in. deep and 15 in. wide, incorporating a bucket of well-rotted manure or compost per sq. yd. Dibble in shoots, about 4 in. high, at intervals of 4–6 in. each way. Keep the plants moist at all times. In August, shear the plants to remove flowering stems and straggly growths.

Alternatively, broadcast seeds thinly in the trench in April, and thin the seedlings to 4–6 in. apart each way.

Harvesting. Beds planted in spring will produce crops for cutting from late autumn onwards.

Pests and diseases. Generally trouble-free.

Water-fir: see Metasequoia
Wattle: see Acacia

Weigela

Caprifoliaceae

A genus of 12 species of hardy deciduous shrubs formerly included in *Diervilla.* They are among the most popular summer-flowering shrubs, the species having largely been superseded by named garden varieties. They bear small, foxglove-like flowers in clusters on the previous season's wood during May and June.

W. florida, syn. *Diervilla florida.* China. Height and spread 6 ft. A wide-spreading bush with arching branches, and light green, ovate, finely wrinkled leaves that are prominently veined. The flowers, about 1 in. long, are carried in clusters at

Walnut (trunk)

Watercress

Weigela florida

Weigela florida 'Variegata'

the ends of short twigs along the branches; they are rose-pink outside, paler within.

'Foliis Purpureis' is slow-growing and more compact, with purple leaves and pink flowers; 'Variegata', of compact habit, has broad cream-white leaf margins and pale pink blooms; 'Venusta' has larger, brighter pink flowers.

WEIGELA FLORIDA

W. middendorffiana, syn. *Diervilla middendorffiana.* N. China, Japan. Height and spread 4 ft. A less robust species, requiring shelter and partial shade. The mid-green ovate-lanceolate leaves are wrinkled. Sulphur-yellow flowers, up to 1½ in. long, with orange markings on the lower lobes, are borne in small, terminal clusters during April and May.

HYBRIDS Height 5–6 ft; spread 5–8 ft. These are showy and free-flowering shrubs and are the results of crossing *W. florida* with other Asiatic species. They have ovate, slender-pointed, mid-green leaves, prominently veined and finely wrinkled. The flowers, generally 1–1¼ in. long, are borne in lateral clusters covering the branches in May and June.

Recommended forms include: 'Abel Carriere', with large, soft rose flowers; 'Bristol Ruby', ruby-red flowers; 'Candida', compact, with white flowers; 'Eva Rathke', slow-growing and compact, with bright red flowers; 'Fairy', with arching growths and soft rose-pink flowers.

'Looymansii Aurea', with golden-yellow foliage and pink flowers; 'Newport Red', dark red flowers; 'Styriaca', of arching growth, with red flower buds opening to pink.

Cultivation. Plant weigelas from October to March in any good, well-drained soil that does not dry out. They thrive in sun or partial shade and are excellent for planting on banks.

Propagation. Take cuttings, 3–4 in. long, of half-ripened, lateral, non-flowering shoots with a heel in June and July; insert in equal parts (by volume) peat and sand at a temperature of 16°C (61°F). Pot the rooted cuttings in 3 in. containers of John Innes potting compost No. 1 and overwinter in a cold frame. In April, line the cuttings out in nursery rows outdoors and grow on for one year before planting out.

Alternatively, take 10–12 in. long cuttings of strong shoots of the current season's growths in October. Insert the cuttings in an outdoor nursery bed and transplant to permanent positions the following autumn.

Pruning. Each year, remove one or two of the old stems on mature plants directly after flowering; cut the stems back to ground level.

Pests and diseases. Generally trouble-free.

× Wilsonara

Orchidaceae

× WILSONARA

A group of trigeneric orchid hybrids between *Cochlioda*, *Odontoglossum* and *Oncidium*. In growth habit and the arrangement of flowers and foliage these plants are similar to *Odontoglossum*. They flower from November to May.

See also ORCHIDS.

Several named forms, with flowers 2–2½ in. across, are in cultivation: 'Lyoth Gold', a hybrid between *Odontioda venusta* and *Oncidium claesii*, has dark red to orange self-coloured flowers.

'Tangerine', a cross between *Odontioda Yvonne* and *Oncidium macranthum*, bears flowers varying in colour from orange to yellow.

'Wendy', a hybrid of *Odontoglossum lambeanianum* and × *Oncidioda cooksoniae*, has vermilion-red flowers.

Cultivation, propagation, pests and diseases. See entry under ODONTOGLOSSUM.

Wistaria

syn. **Wisteria**. *Leguminosae*

A genus of ten species of hardy deciduous climbing shrubs. They are among the most beautiful of all climbing plants and are used to decorate walls, fences, arches, pergolas and trees. On walls and fences the twining growths need additional support. Cutting back when young encourages branching near the base.

Wistarias flower during May and June before the foliage is fully developed.

WISTARIA FLORIBUNDA

W. floribunda, syn. *W. multijuga* (Japanese wistaria). A vigorous species which often reaches a height of 30 ft when grown on trees or walls. The light to mid-green leaves are pinnate, each having 12–19 leaflets. Fragrant, violet-blue flowers are produced in drooping racemes, 10–12 in. long, from short side-growths. *W. f.* 'Alba' bears white flowers. *W. f.* 'Macrobotrys' produces lilac-blue and purple flowers in racemes up to 3 ft long. *W. f.* 'Rosea' is a distinctive variety, its pale pink or rosy flowers having purple wings. *W. f.* 'Violaceo-plena' is an unusual double-flowered variety with violet-blue blossoms.

W. × *formosa.* This handsome hybrid of American origin is a cross between *W. floribunda* and *W. sinensis*. Height 30 ft. The leaves each consist of 9–15 leaflets. These, and also the young shoots, are covered with a soft, silvery down. Light violet-pink flowers, all open at the same time, are borne in 10 in. long racemes.

W. multijuga: see *W. floribunda*

WISTARIA SINENSIS

W. sinensis (Chinese wistaria). China. Height up to 100 ft. This large species is the finest and most popular of the wistarias. The dark to mid-green leaves consist of up to 11 leaflets, which makes the species easily distinguishable from *W. floribunda*. Dense, 8–12 in. long racemes of fragrant mauve flowers are freely produced. *W. s.* 'Alba' has white flowers; *W. s.* 'Plena' has double mauve flowers.

W. venusta. Japan. Height up to 30 ft. This species has dark green leaves that are pinnate, consisting of 9–13 leaflets. They and the stems are covered with down. The fragrant flowers, borne in dense 4–6 in. long racemes, are white, with a yellow blotch at the base of the upright petals. *W. v.* 'Violacea' has violet flowers.

Weigela 'Bristol Ruby'

× *Wilsonara* 'Lyoth'

Wistaria sinensis

Wulfenia carinthiaca

Wulfenia orientalis

Yucca filamentosa

Yucca gloriosa

Cultivation. Wistarias grow freely in any soil that is not poor and thin. The ideal is a moist, rich, medium loam, but where this is not available prepare a planting site that will give plenty of room for root growth. The flower buds are susceptible to damage by late frosts or cold winds; they need the protection of a south or west-facing wall, particularly in positions where early-morning sun follows the frost. When the plant is grown on a tree, it does best in a partly sheltered position.

Plant out young pot-grown plants from October to March in temperate weather. Provide a permanent support and tie the growths to it until the twining stems can gain a firm hold.

Propagation. Graft scions from the previous year's wood on to *W. sinensis* roots in March. Place these in a propagating frame with a bottom heat of 16–18°C (61–64°F).

Take 3–4 in. heel or nodal cuttings from the base of current year's wood in August. Insert them in sandy peat, either in a propagating frame or with mist propagation, and ideally with bottom heat of 16°C (61°F).

Grow on grafted and rooted plants in 5–6 in. pots in a frame. Later, plunge them outdoors in a nursery bed until they are needed for planting in their permanent positions.

W. sinensis can be increased by layering during May. The layers will root within a year.

Wistarias can also be raised from seeds, although these plants may show poor spike formation and colour. Sow under glass in March or April at a temperature of 10–13°C (50–55°F). Pot the seedlings into 3 in. pots of John Innes potting compost No. 1 and stake. In June or July pot on into 5 in. containers and plunge into an outdoor nursery bed until ready for planting in permanent quarters.

Pruning. In February, cut back all growths to within two or three buds of the base of the previous year's growth. Where large specimens need to be controlled, cut the season's young growth back to within five or six buds of its base during July.

Pests. BIRDS attack the buds and flowers.

APHIDS may infest young growths.

GLASSHOUSE RED SPIDER MITES may damage the foliage, causing a fine mottling of the upper leaf surfaces.

THRIPS may also damage the foliage.

Diseases. BUD-DROP may occur, due to excessively dry soil or to cold night temperatures.

CHLOROSIS, due to very alkaline soil conditions, shows as a yellowing between the veins; the leaves may be almost white.

HONEY FUNGUS frequently kills plants.

LEAF SPOTS, due to one or more fungi, may show as brown or black spots on the leaves, but rarely cause leaf-fall.

A PHYSIOLOGICAL DISORDER may cause a discoloration of the foliage.

Wulfenia
Scrophulariaceae

A genus of three species of hardy perennial herbaceous plants. The tubular flowers, which appear in July, are the most attractive feature of the species described. These plants can be grown outdoors on rock gardens, but an alpine house is more suitable.

W. carinthiaca. Alps, Balkans. Height 8–9 in.; spread 12–15 in. The mid to dark green oblong-lanceolate leaves have rounded teeth. Erect flower stalks bear 2–4 in. long spikes of slender purple flowers in July and August.

W. orientalis. Taurus Mts, Asia Minor. Height 6 in.; spread 12–15 in. The shiny rosette leaves are oblanceolate, with rounded teeth; they have a fleshy texture and are mid to dark green with red margins. Bright lilac-blue flowers, 1 in. long, are set on loose spikes and open in May or June.

Cultivation. Plant wulfenias in well-drained soil enriched with peat or leaf-mould. Set the plants out in March or April. Choose a sunny or partially shaded position.

Alternatively, grow in an alpine house in 5–6 in. pots of John Innes potting compost No. 1. Give water regularly during the growing period, but keep the plants just moist during the winter. Repot annually in March.

Propagation. Sow seeds in pans or boxes in a cold greenhouse in March. Prick off the seedlings into pans or boxes, then pot into 3 in. pots of John Innes potting compost No. 1. Plunge them outside and plant out in September or October.

Pests and diseases. Generally trouble-free.

Yucca
Liliaceae

A genus of 40 species of hardy and tender evergreen shrubs and small trees. They are long-lived and thrive in seaside gardens, in poor sandy soil, flowering best during hot summers. The long, strap-shaped leaves are often spine-tipped. The species described are generally hardy in all but the coldest districts. There is a popular but erroneous belief that yuccas only flower every seven years and that the plants usually die after flowering.

Y. filamentosa (Adam's needle). S.E. United States. Height 2–2½ ft; spread 3–4 ft. A species with stiffly erect narrow leaves that are glaucous and mid-green. In July and August, cream-white, 2–3 in. long, bell-shaped flowers are borne in erect plume-like panicles which may be 3–6 ft high. This species flowers when two or three years old.

Y. gloriosa. S.E. United States. Height and spread 3–6 ft. This plant bears dense rosettes of erect deep green leaves at the top of a slow-growing woody trunk. Bell-shaped cream-white flowers, up to 3 in. long and tinged red on the outside, appear from September to November in dense erect panicles, 3–6 ft high. The species does not flower until it is about five years old.

YUCCA RECURVIFOLIA

Y. recurvifolia. S.E. United States. Height 3–6 ft; spread 6–7 ft. This species is similar to *Y. gloriosa,* but with narrower arching leaves. Bell-shaped cream-white flowers, 2–3 in. long, open from August to October in pyramidal panicles up to 6 ft high. This is the most frequently cultivated species in Great Britain. It seldom flowers before the woody trunk has reached a height of 3 ft.

Cultivation. Plant in April or October in any ordinary, well-drained garden soil, including poor, sandy soils, and in full sun.

Propagation. Remove rooted suckers in March or April and replant directly in permanent positions. Small suckers should be grown on in a nursery bed for one to three years before planting out.

Pruning. None required.

Pests. Generally trouble-free.

Diseases. LEAF SPOT shows on the foliage as large brown spots with grey centres.

Zantedeschia
Araceae

ZANTEDESCHIA AETHIOPICA

A genus of eight or nine species of rhizomatous, perennial, half-hardy and tender greenhouse plants. The flowers are borne on a spadix at the end of a long stem and surrounded by a large spathe. Forms of *Z. aethiopica* may be grown outdoors in mild districts.

Zantedeschia aethiopica

Z. aethiopica (arum lily). S. Africa. Height 1½–3 ft; planting distance 1–3 ft. A deciduous species, with mid to deep green, slightly glossy, arrow-shaped leaves. White spathes, 5–9 in. long, surrounding a conspicuous yellow spadix, are borne from March to June. 'Crowborough' is generally a hardier form.

Z. elliottiana. Transvaal. Height up to 2–3 ft; spread 18–24 in. A deciduous species bearing elongated heart-shaped, mid-green leaves with silvery, semi-transparent spots. Golden-yellow spathes, 4 in. long, appear in May and June.

Z. pentlandii. Transvaal. Height up to 24 in.; spread 15–18 in. The leaves of this deciduous species are mid-green and arrow-shaped. Spathes, 6 in. long and deep golden-yellow with dark purple basal blotches, are borne in June.

Z. rehmannii (pink arum). Transvaal. Height 12–15 in.; spread 9–12 in. A deciduous plant with lanceolate mid-green leaves, sometimes spotted with silvery-white flecks. The 3 in. long spathes, borne from April to June, range from pale pink to wine-red. White forms are also known.

Cultivation. Grow zantedeschias in 6–10 in. pots containing John Innes potting compost No. 2, or in a proprietary peat compost. Cover the rhizomes with 2–3 in. of soil and water immediately after planting in early spring. Keep the pots just moist until growth appears.

Z. *elliottiana* and Z. *pentlandii* need a winter temperature of 10–12°C (50–54°F); Z. *aethiopica* may also be grown at this temperature to obtain early flowers, but it will survive at 5°C (41°F). Z. *rehmannii* needs a winter temperature of 7–10°C (45–50°F).

Zantedeschia elliottiana

When growth appears, water moderately, gradually increasing the amount; when the plants are in full leaf, water copiously. Feed at weekly intervals from May to August with a liquid fertiliser. When flowering is over, gradually withhold water and give none to Z. *elliottiana*, Z. *pentlandii* and Z. *rehmannii* after mid-July.

Move Z. *aethiopica* outside in July and water sparingly until August; although evergreen, it should be treated as a deciduous plant and dried off. Bring it back into the greenhouse in late September and pot up in fresh soil.

This species may also be grown as a water plant, at the margins of a pool or in a herbaceous border. Grown as an aquatic in a water depth of 6–12 in., the species is hardy and will usually survive the winter in most districts. At a poolside and in a border cover the plants with a layer of weathered ashes, bracken or straw to protect them against frost.

After pot-grown plants have flowered, gradually withhold water until the leaves have turned yellow. Cease watering altogether and store the rhizomes in their pots under the greenhouse staging. Repot Z. *aethiopica* in October or November, the other species in January or February, and start into growth; the offsets may be grown on separately.

Propagation. Divide the rhizomes or take offsets when repotting is carried out. Pot Z. *rehmannii* rhizomes or offsets singly in 4 in. pots, or three to a 6 in. pot. Place those of other species singly in 6 in. pots of John Innes potting compost No. 1 or 2.

Pests. Generally trouble-free.

Diseases. CORM ROT OF ZANTEDESCHIA causes a wet soft rot of the corms; the disease spreads rapidly in heavy wet soils.

CUCUMBER MOSAIC VIRUS causes a light mottling of leaves with pronounced yellowing of the veins. TOMATO SPOTTED WILT VIRUS causes yellow-white spots, flecks and rings on the leaves. Flowers may be distorted or poor.

Zauschneria

Californian fuchsia. *Onagraceae*

ZAUSCHNERIA CALIFORNICA

A genus of four species of half-hardy sub-shrubby perennials. In the right positions they are long-lived plants, suitable for sheltered sites on large rock gardens or in herbaceous borders. They form bushy clumps, and bear racemes of tubular flowers with expanded mouths.

Z. *californica*. California, Mexico. Height 12–18 in.; planting distance 18–24 in. This species has lanceolate, grey-green, pointed leaves. Terminal sprays of 1–1¼ in. long bright red flowers appear from August to October.

Z. *c. latifolia* has broader, ovate leaves. Z. *c. microphylla*: see Z. *cana*.

Zantedeschia rehmannii

Zauschneria californica

Zebrina pendula

Z. *cana*, syn. Z. *californica microphylla*. Mexico. This plant is similar to Z. *californica*, but with linear grey leaves.

Cultivation. Plant in August or late April in light well-drained soil and in a warm, sunny position. Zauschnerias are best grown at the foot of a south-facing wall or in a sunny shrubbery. In winter, cover the plants with bracken or leaves in cold districts. Cut the plants down to just above ground level in March.

Propagation. Old plants may be separated and replanted in April, but division is not easy. New growths from below ground do not appear until late spring. Take cuttings of basal shoots when they are 2–3 in. long, usually during May. Insert in equal parts (by volume) peat and sand in a propagating frame at a temperature of 16–18°C (61–64°F). Pot the rooted cuttings singly into 3 in. containers of John Innes potting compost No. 1 and place in a cold frame. Plant in the flowering site in August or pot on into 4–5 in. pots and overwinter in a frame or greenhouse. Set out in permanent positions the following April or May.

Pests. APHIDS may attack young growths, distorting leaves and stems.

Diseases. Generally trouble-free.

Zea mays: see Sweet corn

Zebra rush: see *Scirpus tabernaemontani* 'Zebrinus'

Zebrina

Commelinaceae

ZEBRINA PENDULA

A genus of four species of trailing perennials, grown for their attractive foliage. Two of the species are popular house plants and will also do well in a greenhouse.

Z. *pendula*. Mexico. A trailing plant with ovate leaves up to 3 in. long. The upper leaf surfaces are mid-green with two silvery bands, while the undersides are suffused with purple. Three-petalled purple flowers, ½ in. wide, are borne in small clusters in boat-shaped bracts from June to September.

The variety 'Quadricolor' has the upper leaf surfaces striped with white and rose-purple; the undersides are purple. It is liable to lose these colours during the winter, but they will reappear as day length and light increase.

Z. *purpusii*, syn. *Tradescantia purpurea*. Mexico. This prostrate species is best grown as a hanging plant so that both sides of the attractive leaves can be seen. The ovate leaves are larger than those of Z. *pendula*, and are mid-green, flushed with purple on the upper surfaces and bright red-purple beneath. Bright rose-purple flowers, similar to those of Z. *pendula*, are borne in terminal clusters in October.

Zinnia elegans 'Envy'

Zinnia angustifolia Haageana 'Persian Carpet'

Cultivation. Grow zebrinas in 4–6 in. pots or pans or in 9 in. or larger hanging baskets containing a proprietary peat compost or John Innes potting compost No. 2. Maintain a winter temperature of 7–10°C (45–50°F), although the plants will survive for short periods at a temperature as low as 4°C (40°F).

Z. pendula 'Quadricolor' requires a temperature of 13°C (55°F). Keep all plants just moist in winter, but water freely in summer.

During summer, admit as much fresh air as possible. Zebrinas require a well-lit position, but out of direct sun. Lightly shade the greenhouse from May to September, and in the home keep the plants away from south-facing windows.

Repot or pot on annually in April and give a weak liquid feed at fortnightly intervals from May to September.

Propagation. Take tip cuttings, 3 in. long, from May to August; insert the cuttings in equal parts (by volume) peat and sand in a propagating case with a temperature of 16–18°C (61–64°F). When rooted, place the cuttings in 3 in. pots of John Innes potting compost No. 2 and pot on as necessary. Rooted cuttings may also be placed directly in a hanging container, six plants to a 9 in. basket.

Pruning. Remove any shoots that revert to green; pinch out the growing tips of young plants from time to time to promote bushy growth.

Pests. Generally trouble-free.

Diseases. A PHYSIOLOGICAL DISORDER causes the leaves to turn brown and fall prematurely.

Zinnia

Compositae

A genus of 20 species of annual and perennial herbaceous plants and sub-shrubs. The following are colourful plants for borders, for bedding out and for cutting. The daisy-like flowers are brightly coloured.

ZINNIA ELEGANS

Z. angustifolia, syns. *Z. haageana, Z. mexicana.* Mexico. Height 2–2½ ft; spacing 12 in. A half-hardy annual with upright stems and oblong, light green leaves lightly covered with bristly hairs. Bright orange single flowers, 1½ in. across, are produced from July to August. A form of this species, listed as *Z. a.* Haageana, has ray petals tipped red with a deeper orange base. A variety of this, 'Persian Carpet', 15 in., is compact and weather resistant, with small fully double flowers that are bicoloured in circular zones. It is available in a wide range of colours.

Z. elegans. Mexico. Height 2–2½ ft; spacing 12 in. This half-hardy annual is the most popular

Zinnia elegans 'Super Giants'

Zinnia elegans 'Double Gaillardia Flowered'

Zinnia elegans 'Giant Double Mixed'

Zinnia elegans 'Thumbelina'

Zygopetalum mackayi

species, being grown extensively in beds and borders as well as for cutting. The light to mid-green leaves are ovate and pointed. Coarse, upright stems carry showy purple flowers, 2½ in. across, from July to September. Several attractive varieties are available:

'Burpee Hybrids', 24 in., bear fully double flowers with wavy, quilled petals. The flowers resemble those of cactus dahlias. They are available in a wide colour range. Though usually sold as a mixture such as 'Super Giants', they can also be obtained in separate colour forms, such as 'Blaze', orange-scarlet.

The 'Gaillardia Flowered' strain, 18 in., has narrow-petalled flowers zoned or banded with maroon; 'Single Gaillardia Flowered' and 'Double Gaillardia Flowered' are available.

'Dahlia Flowered', 2½ ft, is the most widely grown strain with fully double, flat-petalled flowers in white, yellow, orange, scarlet, crimson, lavender and violet. These are available as a mixture, 'Giant Double Mixed', or in separate colours, such as 'Canary Bird', yellow; 'Orange King', 'Purity', white; 'Scarlet Flame' and 'Violet Queen'. This strain also includes the recently introduced 'Envy', 24 in., which is lime-green.

Varieties of similar form but with smaller flowers are found in the 'Pumila' strain, 15 in. These are free-flowering plants with rounded blooms that are ideal for cutting. Recommended selections are 'Pink Buttons', salmon-pink, and 'Red Riding Hood', scarlet. 'Early Wonder' bears fully double flowers in a mixture of colours.

'Lilliput', 10 in., is compact with pompon-like flowers. 'Thumbelina', 6 in., is an ultra-dwarf, early-flowering, semi-double form that does best in a sheltered position and should be spaced 6 in. apart. Both these varieties are sold as mixtures including white, yellow, pink, lavender, orange and scarlet.

Z. haageana: see *Z. angustifolia*
Z. mexicana: see *Z. angustifolia*

Cultivation. Zinnias will grow in any well-cultivated ground, but a rich, well-drained soil gives the best results. Choose a sunny and sheltered position. The large-flowered varieties are susceptible to damp conditions, and the blooms are easily damaged by heavy rain.

Pinch out the growing tips of young plants to encourage branching. Dead-heading improves subsequent flowering.

Propagation. Sow the seeds in March under glass at a temperature of 16–18°C (61–64°F). To avoid root disturbance, prick off the seedlings into 3 in. paper or peat pots, handling them gently. Harden the young plants off in a cold frame before planting out in May or June.

Alternatively, sow directly in the flowering site in May and thin out the seedlings to the required spacing. These plants will flower later.

Pests. Generally trouble-free.

Diseases. Plants may be affected by CUCUMBER MOSAIC VIRUS and TOMATO SPOTTED WILT VIRUS; these cause mottling of the leaves, which become distorted or may bear light coloured rings. Sometimes the flower crop is reduced; the blooms bear distorted and discoloured petals and the flower stalks are shortened.

DAMPING OFF and FOOT ROT may be due to RHIZOCTONIA or another fungus. Seedlings and

older plants collapse due to rotting of the roots and stem bases.

GREY MOULD can cause rotting of the flowers and also collapse of plants due to STEM ROT in wet weather. Affected tissues become covered with a grey, furry fungal growth.

SEEDLING BLIGHT shows on the leaves as red-brown spots with grey centres, and on the stems as brown, canker-like areas. Affected seedlings collapse and die.

Zinnia, creeping: see Sanvitalia
Zygocactus: see Schlumbergera

Zygopetalum

Orchidaceae

ZYGOPETALUM MACKAYI

A genus of 20 species of epiphytic evergreen orchids from Brazil, the Guianas, Venezuela and Colombia. These plants have ovoid pseudobulbs with two or more long, lanceolate, mid to deep green leaves that are carried terminally. The flower stems are erect and arise from the base of the pseudobulb. The flowers are usually green with purple spotting; the sepals form a short chin with the foot of the column, and the lip bears a crest. The species described is the one most frequently seen in cultivation; it thrives in an intermediate greenhouse.

See also ORCHIDS.

Z. mackayi. Brazil. The broad, ovoid pseudobulbs are 2–3 in. high. The flowering stems are 12–24 in. long, and from November to February carry five to seven fragrant flowers, each 2 in. across. These have spreading sepals and petals that are light yellow-green blotched with purple-brown. The broad lip is white with violet-purple streaks and spots and with a ridged crest.

Cultivation. Grow zygopetalums in wooden baskets or pans with plenty of crocks in the bottom. Use a compost of 2 parts fibrous peat to 1 part fibrous loam (parts by volume), with a little sphagnum moss and some sand added. In the greenhouse, maintain a minimum winter temperature of 13°C (55°F). Shade the plants from April to October and keep the atmosphere humid. Give plenty of water at all times; a resting period is not required. Ventilate the greenhouse from May to October, and on mild days from November to March. Feed occasionally with weak liquid manure from May to August.

Repot every two or three years in March or April. As these orchids resent root disturbance they should be divided only when overcrowding makes this necessary.

Propagation. Divide in March or April, ensuring a healthy pseudobulb in each section; pot up in the growing compost.

Pests and diseases. Generally trouble-free.

CONTENTS

PESTS AND DISEASES

The pests and diseases described here are those most commonly encountered on cultivated plants. No garden is likely to be attacked by all of them, and even serious infestations are often localised. However, plants that are known to be susceptible to pest and disease damage year after year should be regularly protected against serious injury. Soils that are known to harbour various destructive pests and diseases should be frequently cultivated, and seeds should be dressed with protective chemicals prior to sowing in the open.

A large number of insecticides and fungicides is available to the amateur gardener; these are sold under trade names and many, particularly the systemic insecticides, afford protection for several weeks. Plants should always be sprayed in dull, still weather; avoid spraying open flowers as this may kill pollinating insects. The manufacturers' instructions for use should always be carefully followed. In general, allow at least two weeks between the last spraying and harvesting of edible crops, except when using non-persistent insecticides such as malathion or derris, in which case a two-day interval is sufficient.

Some insecticides and fungicides are harmful to certain plants: in the greenhouse, azobenzene should not be used on gerbera, adiantum, pilea, roses, schizanthus and stephanotis, or on seedlings and young plants.

BHC is harmful to cucumbers, marrows, melons and other cucurbits, and also to hydrangeas, vines and young tomatoes. To avoid possible taint, this insecticide should not be used on fruits or vegetables nor as a seed-dressing on onion, leek, lettuce or radish seeds.

Chrysanthemums, calceolarias, cinerarias and ornamental prunus should not be sprayed with dimethoate; avoid using formothion on asters, begonias, cinerarias, chrysanthemums, gloxinias or zinnias.

Sulphur-shy varieties of apple, pear, plum, gooseberry or currants should not be sprayed with insecticides or fungicides containing sulphur. Malathion may harm the foliage and flowers of antirrhinums, crassulas, ferns, fuchsias, gerberas, petunias, pileas, sweet peas and zinnias.

Following recommendations by the Ministry of Agriculture, Fisheries and Food, the use of persistent organochlorine insecticides, such as DDT, is now being discouraged, particularly for edible crops. The organophosphorus insecticides, such as malathion, which break down rapidly on application, or the non-toxic chemicals, derris and pyrethrum, are suitable alternatives.

COMMON PESTS

Adelgids (*Adelgidae*)

These sap-sucking insects are related to aphids. They chiefly infest conifers and weaken the leaves and stems by extracting sap and by fouling the foliage with sticky honeydew that provides a medium for sooty moulds to grow on. Certain species also produce galls and other malformations on young growths. Adelgid colonies are conspicuous during summer when they produce coverings of white waxy wool which may prevent chemical control.

The spruce gall adelges (*Adelges viridis*) is an important pest of *Picea abies* (Christmas tree), producing disfiguring pineapple galls at the tips of young shoots. Other species attack larix (larch), pinus (pine), pseudotsuga (Douglas fir), abies (silver fir) and various species of picea. Protect seedlings and young trees by spraying with BHC or malathion in late spring and early summer.

Aphids (*Aphididae*)

Several names, such as greenfly, blackfly and blight, are applied to these common pests of cultivated plants. They feed on plant sap, thus distorting young growths; they produce unsightly galls on leaves and petioles, and foul stems and foliage with sticky honeydew that encourages sooty moulds. They also transmit virus diseases. Annuals, perennials, shrubs, fruits and vegetables are all liable to be attacked, and the pests are particularly troublesome on greenhouse plants.

Aphids reproduce rapidly under warm conditions, and many species have winged forms which migrate from plant to plant. Some species overwinter as eggs, laid on their winter host plants in autumn, and others breed continuously throughout the year. Particularly troublesome species include bean aphid (*Aphis fabae*); beech aphid (*Phyllaphis fagi*); cabbage aphid (*Brevicoryne brassicae*); cherry blackfly (*Myzus cerasi*); cypress aphid (*Cinara cupressi*); leaf-curling plum aphid (*Brachycaudus helichrysi*); mottled arum aphid (*Aulacorthum circumflexum*); orchid aphid (*Cerataphis orchidearum*); peach-potato aphid (*Myzus persicae*); spruce aphid (*Elatobium abietinum*); tulip bulb aphid (*Dysaphis tulipae*); water lily aphid (*Rhopalosiphum nymphaeae*); and willow stem aphid (*Tuberolachnus saligna*).

Infestations can be effectively controlled with insecticides. Aphid colonies that are fully exposed and readily accessible are easily killed by spraying with malathion or nicotine, but aphids in protected positions, such as in curled leaves or under waxy coverings, are best controlled with systemic insecticides such as dimethoate or formothion. On dormant fruit trees and bushes and on some deciduous ornamental plants, overwintering aphid eggs can be killed by spraying with tar-oil or DNOC/petroleum during winter.

See also ROOT APHIDS and WOOLLY APHID.

Apple sawfly (*Hoplocampa testudinea*)

The inconspicuous adult apple sawflies resemble small flying ants; they fly on to the apple trees in the spring and lay their eggs in the blossom. The newly hatched sawfly caterpillars tunnel under the skin of small fruits and later burrow into the core. When the fruits fall in June, the caterpillars leave them and remain in the soil until the spring.

Destruction of infested fruits and regular cultivation under trees reduce the numbers of overwintering caterpillars. Spray malathion or gamma-BHC thoroughly immediately after petal-fall to kill the young caterpillars before they enter the fruits.

Asparagus beetle (*Crioceris asparagi*)

Adult beetles and larvae feed on the young shoots and foliage of culinary asparagus from early June onwards; plants may be completely stripped by severe infestations. Spray or dust with derris or BHC as soon as the first damage is seen.

Bean seed fly (*Delia platura*)

The small, white, legless maggots eat into germinating seeds of beans, peas, sweet corn and other vegetable crops. Damage can be prevented by dressing the seeds with gamma-BHC/thiram before sowing.

Birds

A few species of birds are troublesome in gardens. Blackbirds and tits peck ripening apples and pears; bullfinches eat the young buds of plums, pears, gooseberries, ornamental cherries, forsythias and other shrubby plants during the winter months. Sparrows tear crocuses, polyanthus and other primulas apart. They also attack apple blossom and young shoots and the leaves of chrysanthemum, wistaria, carnations, and lettuce, pea and runner-bean seedlings. Wood pigeons may strip the leaves of brassica seedlings; they also eat fruits.

Various scaring devices such as scarecrows, bangers, glitter strips and recorded distress signals may be used to limit bird damage, and several chemical bird repellents are also available. However, none of these devices is fully effective, and persistent bird damage can only be overcome by protecting susceptible plants with netting or cages. Erect a fruit cage of wire-netting walls and a removable roof that can be taken off at blossom time to let pollinating insects in. Strong knotted plastic netting is also available.

Seedlings can be protected by temporary netting. or by criss-crossing black cotton over the plants.

Black currant gall mite
(Cecidophyopsis ribis)
This is the most serious pest of black currants; infested buds swell and fail to develop, a condition commonly known as big bud. The pests also transmit reversion virus (see DISEASES). The microscopic mites live within the leaf buds except for a brief period during April, May and June when they leave the old big buds and disperse in search of new buds. Control these mites by spraying with ½–1 per cent solution of lime-sulphur when the first flowers open, and repeat three weeks later.

Black-currant bushes, infected by reversion virus, cannot be cured. They should be destroyed and replaced with fresh healthy stock, preferably on a site well removed from any possible sources of mites from infested plants.

Box sucker *(Psylla buxi)*
Young box suckers feed on new shoots of buxus and produce cabbage-like clusters of malformed leaves. Repeated sprays of malathion, dimethoate or formothion usually check infestation.

Bryobia mites *(Bryobia* species)
These microscopic pests are closely related to red spider mites and are particularly troublesome on apples, gooseberries and hedera. They feed on the leaves which at first develop a light freckling on the upper surfaces and later bronze and wither. The eggs overwinter on the fruit trees and can be destroyed by thorough spraying with DNOC/petroleum in winter before the buds begin to swell. Sprays of dimethoate, formothion or malathion during the growing season are effective.

Bulb mite *(Rhizoglyphus echinopus)*
This small, pearly-white mite is common in soil and often invades rotting tissues of narcissus, tulip and hyacinth bulbs. It is generally a secondary pest, extending the damage caused by other pests, such as eelworms and insects, and bacterial and fungal diseases. Control measures should be taken against the primary injury.

Bulb scale mite *(Steneotarsonemus laticeps)*
This microscopic mite feeds and breeds inside narcissus and other bulbs; severe infestations cause rust-coloured streaks on flowers and foliage, and general stunting and distortion of leaves and flowers. The pest is particularly troublesome on forced bulbs, and chemical control is difficult. Immersion of the dormant bulbs in water maintained at a temperature of 43°C (110°F) for one and a half hours may eradicate infestations, otherwise infested bulbs should be destroyed.

Bumble bees *(Bombus* species)
These insects occasionally bite small holes in the corolla tubes or spurs of antirrhinum,

tropaeolum and other plants. Damage is seldom severe.

Cabbage root fly *(Erioischia brassicae)*
The small white maggots of this fly live in the soil and eat the roots of cabbages and other brassicas. Infested plants wilt, especially in dry weather. and young plants may be killed. The adult flies are active in April and May when they lay their eggs on or near plant stems at soil level. Three generations of adults develop during the summer and attacks may persist until mid-September.

In many areas this pest is now resistant to the organochlorine insecticides, such as gamma-BHC, that formerly gave good control. Trichlorphon, applied as a soil drench to established transplanted seedlings, is the only effective insecticide readily available.

Cabbage whitefly *(Aleyrodes proletella)*
This pest of cabbages and other brassicas is often first noticed when plants are disturbed, and the small adult whiteflies are seen to fly off the leaves. Whiteflies are often seen during winter, when most other insects are dormant. The young whitefly scales feed on the undersides of leaves, causing foliage discoloration and checking plant growth when present in large numbers. Thorough spraying with malathion generally checks infestations, but is necessary only if damage is severe.

Capsid bugs *(Capsidae)*
The common green capsid (*Lygocoris pabulinus*), the tarnished plant bug or bishop bug (*Lygus rugulipennis*) and the apple capsid (*Plesiocoris rugicollis*) all cause similar damage to herbaceous ornamental plants and certain fruit trees and bushes. These are sucking insects and both adults and nymphs feed on the sap of young growths, injecting a toxic saliva that kills plant tissues. Damaged leaves are tattered, puckered and distorted; buds and growing points may be killed, and developing fruits and flowers are often mis-shaped and discoloured. Capsid bugs move rapidly and have usually left the damaged plants long before the symptoms are apparent.

It is difficult to prevent damage, but spray applications of DNOC/petroleum in the winter to deciduous hosts, such as apples and currants, kill overwintering eggs. Summer infestations on ornamental plants may be reduced by thorough and frequent spraying with malathion or nicotine.

Some capsids overwinter in plant debris, and in leaf-litter in hedge bottoms. Good garden hygiene, and removal of plant debris, reduces the numbers of these pests carrying over from one season to the next.

Carnation fly *(Delia brunnescens)*
Maggots of this fly tunnel into the leaves and stems of carnations and pinks; infected shoots wilt and die. These pests are not easily eradicated once they have tunnelled into the plant tissues, but dusting or spraying with gamma-BHC in April and early May gives some control.

Carrot fly *(Psila rosae)*
The small, yellowish maggots of this fly feed on the roots of carrots, celery and parsnips. Young plants wilt and die, and the roots of older plants are spoilt by the extensive tunnels eaten out by the maggots.

The pest overwinters as pupae in the soil, and the adult flies emerge in early June. These lay their eggs in the soil near carrots and other host plants, and the maggots hatching from these feed on the roots for about a month. A second generation of adults often appears in August.

The numbers of overwintering pupae may be reduced by destroying all infested plants in the autumn, preferably by burning. Lift all edible roots before the winter. Prior to sowing, treat the seed with a seed-dressing containing gamma-BHC and, if necessary, water a trichlorphon solution into the soil around susceptible plants. Repeat twice at ten-day intervals. Apply the first treatment in mid-May on early carrots, in July on main crop.

Caterpillars *(Lepidoptera)*
These common garden pests are the larval stage of moths and butterflies, and more than 50 different species are pests of cultivated plants in Great Britain. Some species live in the soil and feed on roots, others tunnel into the stems, branches or fruit, but the majority feed on leaves.

Adult moths and butterflies, which are harmless in themselves, are active during spring and summer. They lay eggs on leaves and stems, or in the soil, and soon afterwards caterpillars hatch. They feed for about a month or, in some cases, for as long as a year before pupating either on the host plants, in the soil or on fences and buildings.

The most important caterpillar species are those that attack flowers, fruits or vegetables shortly before harvest. Tortrix caterpillars on carnations, codling moth on apples and cabbage moth on brassicas are in this category. Caterpillars of swift moths and winter moths feed on roots and leaves respectively, on a wider range of host plants.

Caterpillars are usually controlled by contact insecticides with some residual action. Such chemicals kill mainly by direct contact and are effective in destroying species that feed in exposed positions on leaves and shoots. Caterpillars feeding inside fruits and stems or in rolled leaves, and those living in the soil and other protected situations, are less easily eradicated. Apply insecticides to kill the young caterpillars before they gain the full protection of their feeding sites.

BHC, trichlorphon, malathion and derris are all effective against caterpillars; they may be applied as sprays, but dust formulations are also available for all except trichlorphon. Derris, malathion and trichlorphon are particularly recommended for edible crops as they are non-persistent; the produce may be harvested within two or three days of the last application.

In addition to chemical control, cultural measures such as regular cultivation, handpicking and destruction of caterpillars, cutting out or crushing egg-batches and grease-banding or sack-banding of trees may sometimes be effective.

See also CODLING MOTH, CUTWORMS, PEA MOTH, SWIFT MOTHS and TORTRIX CATERPILLARS.

Cats
These sometimes upset newly cultivated soil and may disturb seeds and young seedlings. Cats may be deterred by black cotton strung over newly sown areas or by the use of proprietary cat repellents.

Celery fly (*Phillophylla heraclei*)
The small, white, leaf-mining maggots of this fly burrow into leaf tissues of celery and parsnips and produce unsightly brown blotches. Severely infested leaves shrivel and die and plant growth is checked. The first attacks may occur in April, and the pests are present throughout the summer. Young plants are particularly susceptible to severe injury and should be protected by spraying with malathion, trichlorphon or dimethoate.

Chafer beetles (*Scarabaeidae*)
Adult chafers, such as the cockchafer (*Melolontha melolontha*), the summer chafer (*Amphimallon solstitialis*), rose chafer (*Cetonia aurata*) and also the garden chafer (*Phyllopertha horticola*), feed on leaves, flowers and fruits of various ornamental trees and shrubs. Damage from adult beetles is seldom severe, but the larvae, which live in the soil, can cause serious injury to roots, bulbs, tubers and stems of many ornamental plants. They may also damage lawns. The C-shaped larvae are fat and white, with a distinct brown head, a distended abdomen and three pairs of legs. They take two years to reach maturity.

Serious damage to foliage by adult chafers may be controlled by spraying with BHC. The larvae should be destroyed by treating infested soil with gamma-BHC dusts or sprays; their numbers may be reduced by frequent deep cultivation which will expose the grubs to birds and other predators.

Chrysanthemum eelworm (*Aphelenchoides ritzemabosi*)
This is one of the most serious pests of chrysanthemums and it will also damage China asters, calceolarias, paeonies and other ornamental plants. The microscopic eelworms penetrate leaf and stem tissues; infested leaves develop brown or black areas between the main veins, and severe infestations check growth and kill plants.

Eradication of established infestations is difficult. When possible, obtain healthy fresh stock of susceptible plants from reliable sources. The spread of eelworms can sometimes be contained by good garden hygiene and by keeping the foliage dry. This can be achieved under glass by ensuring adequate ventilation; outdoors, allow plenty of room between plants. There is no safe chemical treatment that will control eelworms in infested stocks, but hot-water treatment of dormant stools at 43°C (110°F) for 20–30 minutes may be effective. Otherwise dig up and burn infested stock.

Chrysanthemum leaf miner (*Phytomyza atricornis*)
Maggots of this small fly tunnel into chrysanthemum leaves, producing white, sinuous mines. Attacks may be continuous under glass, but only occur in late spring and summer outdoors. Cinerarias and other pot plants may also be attacked.

BHC or nicotine, applied as sprays or fumigants, kill adults and larvae; they must be applied as soon as the first signs of infestation are seen. One or two repeat applications at fortnightly intervals may be necessary if severe infestations develop.

Chrysanthemum stool miner (*Psila nigricornis*)
The light yellow maggots of this fly tunnel into chrysanthemum stools; severe infesta-tions inhibit the production of basal shoots for cuttings. The flies are active from May to September. Stools can be protected from infestation by watering them with a solution of BHC or dusting with BHC dust.

Codling moth (*Laspeyresia pomonella*)
Caterpillars of this small moth tunnel into ripening fruits and are the most common cause of maggoty apples. They are mainly pests of apples, but may also damage pears and other tree fruits. The young caterpillars enter the fruits, often through the eye end, and feed during July and August. They leave the infested fruits in late summer and over-winter in cocoons attached beneath loose bark, under tree ties and in similar situations.

Chemical control is difficult, especially on large trees, and to be effective must be carried out during the brief period between the eggs hatching and the young caterpillars gaining protection of the fruit. On manageable trees, spray with malathion about four weeks after blossoming has finished, and repeat three weeks later. Bands of sacking or corrugated cardboard tied around trunks and branches in mid-July will trap many caterpillars as they leave the fruits; remove and burn the bands in winter. Regular trapping of the caterpillars in this manner may reduce the number of codling moths after a few years.

Cutworms (*Noctuidae*)
These green or grey-brown fat caterpillars of various species of moth, especially those of the turnip moth (*Agrotis segetum*), the heart and dart (*Agrotis exclamationis*), and the large yellow underwing (*Noctua pronuba*), inhabit the upper layers of the soil. They are night feeders on the leaves and stems of herbaceous plants and various root vegetables. The stems are often eaten and severed at soil level, hence the common name applied to these caterpillars.

Thorough and frequent cultivation and good weed control usually reduce the numbers of cutworms in the soil. Dusts or sprays of BHC incorporated into the soil afford additional protection.

Earwigs (*Forficula auricularia*)
Both young and adult earwigs damage the blooms of chrysanthemums, clematis and dahlias, and may also feed on the leaves of these and other decorative plants. These pests feed at night, making ragged holes in petals and leaves.

Removal of dead leaves and other garden debris reduces the available resting sites; BHC or trichlorphon sprayed on and around infested plants kills both adult and young earwigs. Inverted flower pots, filled with straw, trap the earwigs and should be attended to daily.

Eelworms (*Nematoda*)
These are thin and transparent microscopic worms which resemble miniature eels. In spite of their minute size, they are serious pests of many herbaceous plants and vegetable crops. Eelworms live within the plant tissues and increase in numbers so rapidly that a single narcissus bulb, for example, may contain several million active eelworms. Infestations cause discolorations and deformities of the leaves and flowers, and affected plants usually die.

Chemical control of eelworms is difficult, and no effective compounds are available for amateur use. The only remedy is to destroy infested plants and avoid replanting susceptible hosts. Purchase healthy stock from reputable nurseries.

See also CHRYSANTHEMUM EELWORM, LEAF BLOTCH EELWORM, POTATO CYST EELWORM, ROOT KNOT EELWORM and STEM AND BULB EELWORM.

Flea beetles (*Phyllotreta* species)
Seedlings of many plants belonging to the *Cruciferae* family, such as turnips, swedes, cabbages and wallflowers, are damaged by adult flea beetles. These pests eat small circular holes in the seedlings and young leaves. They are particularly active on bright sunny days in April and May and severe attacks check the growth of young plants.

Good garden hygiene will reduce the number of beetles hibernating in debris and coarse vegetation. Derris or BHC, applied as a dust or spray, may be used to protect young seedlings. Seed dressings containing gamma-BHC also give effective protection in the early stages.

Froghoppers (*Cercopidae*)
Young froghoppers produce conspicuous masses of froth, commonly known as cuckoo spit, on the stems and leaves of lavender, chrysanthemums, roses and various other decorative plants. They feed on plant sap and distort young growth. These pests are effectively controlled by spraying forcefully with malathion, BHC or nicotine.

Fruit tree red spider mite (*Panonychus ulmi*)
These microscopic mites may cause considerable damage to the foliage of apples, plums and damsons. Related species cause similar damage on other fruits. See BRYOBIA MITES and GLASSHOUSE RED SPIDER MITES.

The mites infest the undersides of leaves and feed on the sap; severe infestations discolour the leaves, which bronze and fall prematurely. The mites breed continuously from early May until September, and over-winter on the trees as eggs laid in crevices on the bark of young branches and spurs.

Fruit tree red spider mite colonies are increased by the use of tar-oil winter washes and persistent insecticides. These chemicals kill off the natural predators, without affecting the mites. A winter wash of DNOC/petroleum, applied while the buds are still dormant, usually kills overwintering eggs. Thorough spraying with malathion, dimethoate or formothion after blossom fall prevents summer attacks. The use of the fungicide dinocap to control powdery mildew disease also gives some control of these mites.

Gall midges (*Cecidomyiidae*)
Adult gall midges are small flies, not more than $\frac{1}{10}$ in. long. The larvae are small, bright red, yellow or white maggots which feed on plant tissues. They often cause disfiguring galls on stems, leaves and flowers of many cultivated plants; severe infestations may check growth. The larvae are protected within the galls and are not easily reached by insecticides. The best control is obtained by spraying with a persistent insecticide, such as BHC, to kill the adult midges before they can lay their eggs in late spring or early summer.

Gall mites (*Eriophyidae*)

These tiny mites feed in or on plant tissues and stimulate the production of galls on leaves and buds. The mites are protected from contact with chemicals during most of the year, but may be exposed in spring when they migrate to new feeding sites. Thorough spraying with lime-sulphur in spring generally checks infestations.

See also BLACK CURRANT GALL MITE.

Gall wasps (*Cynipidae*)

The small larvae of these minute wasps live in plant tissues. They are the cause of the familiar apple, marble and spangle galls on quercus (oak). These galls do not harm established healthy trees and chemical control is generally unnecessary.

Gladiolus thrip (*Taeniothrips simplex*)

This is a serious pest of gladioli. The small, elongated thrips infest corms, foliage and flowers. Affected leaves and petals show a fine silvery flecking; severe infestations kill the foliage and prevent flowering. The thrips often overwinter on corms in store. Dust with gamma-BHC after lifting in autumn and again before planting.

Check infestations on growing plants by thorough spraying or dusting with BHC, malathion or nicotine as soon as the first symptoms are seen.

See also THRIPS.

Glasshouse leafhopper (*Zygina pallidifrons*)

The small pale yellow adult and immature leafhoppers feed on the undersides of leaves of many greenhouse plants. A coarse mottling shows on the upper surfaces of infested leaves, and the transparent cast skins of the young leafhoppers can often be seen adhering to the undersides of leaves.

Regular fumigation of the greenhouse with BHC or nicotine usually checks these pests; these insecticides may also be used as sprays.

Glasshouse red spider mites (*Tetranychus urticae*, etc.)

These small mites are serious pests of plants grown in greenhouses and in the home. Sometimes they also attack shrubs and herbaceous plants outdoors. Fuchsias, balsam, chrysanthemums, roses, peaches, vines, tomatoes and cucumbers grown in the greenhouse are particularly susceptible. The adult and immature mites feed and breed on the undersides of leaves, causing a fine light mottling of the upper surfaces. In severe infestations, this leads to extensive yellowing and bronzing, followed by leaf-fall. The withering leaves are often covered with a fine silk webbing. The mites cease breeding in the autumn, and female mites overwinter in crevices in brickwork and woodwork, in bamboo canes, stakes and plant ties.

Reduce the numbers of overwintering female mites by clearing out plant debris and by eliminating overwintering sites in late autumn and early winter. In the greenhouse, regular fumigation with azobenzene will prevent serious increases in mite populations. Thorough spraying with liquid derris extract, malathion, dimethoate or formothion will protect plants under glass and outdoors. The mites are likely to develop resistance to a given chemical if it is used too regularly, and control measures should be varied as

much as possible. Plants grown at high temperatures in dry, overcrowded conditions are often particularly susceptible to mite infestations; regular syringeing of infested plants with water may help to check the pests.

Glasshouse whitefly (*Trialeurodes vaporariorum*)

The undersides of leaves of many greenhouse plants, especially fuchsias, cinerarias, calceolarias and tomatoes, are often extensively infested by small, rounded scales. These are the immature stages of the glasshouse whitefly; they feed on plant sap and foul the plants with honeydew, a sticky excretion, which encourages the growth of sooty moulds. The small adult whiteflies, which resemble tiny, pure white moths, are usually present on infested plants and fly off if disturbed.

Frequent fumigation with BHC kills adult whiteflies, and BHC or malathion sprays applied to the undersides of infested leaves destroy the young whitefly scales. Dichlorvos resin strips suspended from the greenhouse roof often reduce infestation.

Gooseberry sawflies (*Nematus* species)

The caterpillars of various species of sawfly feed on the leaves of gooseberries and currants; they rapidly strip the bushes of almost all their foliage in severe attacks. The conspicuous, green, black-spotted caterpillars first appear in May, and damage may continue until September. The caterpillars often begin feeding in the centre of bushes, and infestation may not be noticed in time to prevent serious damage. At the first sign of injury, from May onwards, spray bushes with derris or malathion. Isolated attacks may be controlled by picking off the caterpillars by hand and destroying them.

Hares (*Lepus europaeus*)

These animals eat the bark off trees in severe winters, causing serious damage in nurseries and young plantations. They may also feed on ornamental plants and winter vegetables. Shooting is the only effective control measure, but valuable trees and plants can be protected with fencing, close-mesh netting or spiral strip tree protectors.

Holly leaf miner (*Phytomyza ilicis*)

The maggots of this small fly tunnel into ilex (holly) leaves, causing unsightly white blotches. Most hollies are attacked to some extent; they generally suffer little, but growth of young trees may be checked. If necessary, spray regularly with BHC from early June until October to reduce infestation.

Iris sawfly (*Rhadinoceraea micans*)

The bluish-grey caterpillars of this sawfly feed on the leaves of *Iris pseudacorus* and *I. laevigata* in June and July. Spraying or dusting with BHC or derris is effective, but if these plants are grown near ponds or streams, care must be taken to prevent these insecticides contaminating the water, as they are lethal to fish.

Leaf-blotch eelworm (*Aphelenchoides fragariae*, syn. *A. olesistus*)

This species is related to chrysanthemum eelworm, but attacks a different range of plants. It is particularly troublesome in the

greenhouse, on ferns, begonias, gloxinias, coleus and other foliage plants. It may also infest strawberries and other soft fruits outdoors. These minute worm-like pests invade the leaf tissues, causing brown or black blotches between the veins; they may also feed externally on buds and young growths, causing distortions.

There is no effective chemical treatment, and severely infested plants should be burnt to prevent the spread of infection.

See also CHRYSANTHEMUM EELWORM and EELWORMS.

Leaf-cutter bees (*Megachile* species)

These pests resemble small, hairy hive bees. The females cut semicircular pieces out of the leaves of roses, laburnum, ligustrum, syringa and other shrubby plants, and use these to construct thimble-shaped breeding cells. Damage is seldom severe, but continued attacks disfigure and weaken plants. There is no satisfactory chemical control, but the nests, in soil, decaying wood or old brickwork, should be located and destroyed.

Leafhoppers (*Cicadellidae*)

These small insects are related to aphids and, like them, feed on plant sap. They jump and fly off when disturbed, and may be found on many different plants, both under glass and outdoors. The young leafhoppers feed on the undersides of leaves and produce a light mottling of the upper surface; they also leave their cast skins attached to the leaves, which is a useful indication of their presence. Direct damage to plants is usually slight, but the pests may cause indirect damage by transmitting virus diseases. Control by spraying with malathion, BHC or derris.

See also GLASSHOUSE LEAFHOPPER and RHODODENDRON LEAFHOPPER.

Leaf miners

The larvae of various species of moths and flies mine or tunnel into the leaves of plants. Different species attack different hosts, and the form of the mine, which varies from a simple blotch mine to an extensive, sinuous, linear mine, is usually characteristic of the species. Maggots of the columbine leaf miners (*Phytomyza aquilegiae* and *P. minuscula*) cause serpentine mines on the foliage of aquilegia; caterpillars of the laburnum leaf miner (*Leucoptera laburnella*) produce spiral blotch mines on laburnum; and caterpillars of the lilac leaf miner (*Caloptilia syringella*) show their presence by simple blotch mines in the leaves of syringa and ligustrum.

Infestations by these pests do not always cause appreciable damage, and chemical control is generally unnecessary. When damage is persistent and severe, spray with BHC or nicotine as soon as the first mines are seen.

See also CARNATION FLY, CELERY FLY, CHRYSANTHEMUM LEAF MINER, HOLLY LEAF MINER, LILAC LEAF MINER and MANGOLD FLY.

Leatherjackets (*Tipulidae*)

The soft, but tough-skinned, fat, legless, greyish-brown grubs, known as leatherjackets, are the larvae of craneflies (daddy-long-legs). They live in the soil, feeding on the roots of plants; they are particularly troublesome in lawns, where they may kill whole patches of grass, and may also cause wilting and death of some ornamental plants and vegetables. Leatherjackets are particularly abundant in grassland, and tend to be most troublesome in newly cultivated ground.

The most effective chemical treatment is to incorporate persistent insecticides in the soil, but this is generally undesirable as the chemicals persist in the soil for longer than is necessary. It is preferable to reduce the numbers of leatherjackets by frequent and deep cultivation, so as to expose the grubs to birds, and the drying effects of wind and sun. On lawns, leatherjackets may be brought to the surface by soaking infested areas with water and covering with tarpaulin or black polythene sheets; the following morning the covers should be removed, and the leatherjackets may be swept up or left for the birds.

Lilac leaf miner (*Caloptilia syringella*)

The caterpillars of this species of moth burrow into syringa leaves; they also cause leaf-mine blotches on ligustrum. These pests are active from June onwards and may be controlled by thorough spraying with BHC or nicotine.

Lily beetle (*Lilioceris lilii*)

This pest is most troublesome in parts of Surrey and adjoining counties, although it also occurs elsewhere. The adult beetles are bright scarlet, with black heads and legs; the grubs are yellow. Both adults and larvae feed extensively on the leaves and other aerial parts of most lilies; they will also attack fritillaria, nomocharis and polygonatum.

Control is relatively easy, and a thorough application of malathion should eradicate these pests.

Mangold fly (*Pegomya betae*)

The maggots of this small fly tunnel into leaves of spinach and beetroot. Damaged leaves brown and wither, and severe infestations check plant growth.

Spray with dimethoate, formothion or trichlorphon as soon as the first symptoms are seen, usually from May onwards.

Mealy bugs (*Pseudococcidae*)

These are serious pests of many greenhouse plants. The adult females resemble small woodlice and are covered in a white mealy wax. Adults and immature stages usually live in colonies that are covered with conspicuous tufts of waxy wool. All stages feed on plant sap and excrete honeydew, which encourages the growth of sooty moulds on infested leaves and stems. Mealy bugs are mainly tropical and sub-tropical insects and thrive in heated greenhouses, where breeding may continue throughout the year.

Plants should be closely watched for the first signs of these pests; carefully examine the leaf axils and leaf bases in the crowns of plants, and similar protected situations. Thorough spraying with malathion usually checks small infestations; systemic insecticides such as dimethoate and formothion should be used against more persistent attacks. Treat infested small pot plants and house plants by painting one of these insecticides on to mealy-bug colonies with a fine paintbrush. Tar-oil may be used to eliminate colonies on dormant deciduous woody plants, such as vines; do not allow tar-oil to come into contact with non-woody stems.

See also ROOT MEALY BUGS.

Mice (*Mus musculus, Apodemus sylvaticus*)

These rodents may be troublesome in stores, where they eat into seed packets, devour bulbs and feed on fruit. Outdoors, they may dig up peas, beans and other seeds and eat bulbs. In store, conventional mousetraps are effective and proprietary poisons may be used to control severe infestations.

Millepedes (*Diplopoda*)

These worm-like creatures are often confused with centipedes; they can be distinguished by their speed of movement, which is slower than that of centipedes. Further, a millepede has two pairs of legs to each body segment, while a centipede has only one pair. Centipedes are generally beneficial, as they often prey on pests. Millepedes, which are often numerous in soil, leaf-litter and decaying plant tissues, damage plants by feeding on roots, tunnelling into bulbs and feeding on tubers and corms; they often extend injuries caused by diseases and by other pests, such as slugs.

Millepedes are difficult to control. Gamma-BHC dust incorporated in the soil protects seeds, bulbs and corms, but should only be used in severe infestations. The pests multiply particularly in damp soils with a high content of organic debris, and may be discouraged by deep cultivation.

Mites (*Acarina*)

These animals are more closely related to spiders and ticks than to insects. Adult mites can be distinguished by their four pairs of legs, while young mites have three pairs only.

Many mites are serious plant pests; they reproduce rapidly, and chemical control is difficult as they live in protected situations within buds, leaf tissues and cracks and crevices in bark. Many chemicals fail to kill mites, but do destroy the predators.

See also BLACK CURRANT GALL MITE, BRYOBIA MITES, BULB SCALE MITE, FRUIT TREE RED SPIDER MITE, GALL MITES, GLASSHOUSE RED SPIDER MITE, PEAR LEAF BLISTER MITE and TARSONEMID MITES.

Mushroom flies (*Sciaridae*)

The maggots of fungus gnats and other flies tunnel into the stalks and caps of mushrooms, rendering them inedible. The small adult flies, often present in large numbers, can be eradicated by fumigating with nicotine or spraying with nicotine or malathion. Control infestations of maggots by watering a spray-strength solution of nicotine into infested mushroom beds.

Mustard beetle (*Phaedon cochleariae*)

This adult metallic-blue beetle and the brown-yellow larvae both feed on leaves and stems of mustard and watercress, cabbages, swedes and turnips. The pests are active from May onwards, and damage is often particularly severe in August. Dusts or sprays of malathion generally give good control, but should not be used on watercress as streams and rivers may be contaminated. Raise the water level of the watercress beds so as to drown both larvae and adult beetles.

Narcissus flies (*Merodon equestris, Eumerus* species)

The maggots of the large narcissus fly (*Merodon equestris*) tunnel into bulbs and are serious pests of daffodils. Infested bulbs are usually killed, or they fail to flower, merely producing several narrow grass-like leaves. Damage can be detected at planting time as infested bulbs are soft; and a short, fat maggot will be found inside each bulb.

Small narcissus flies (*Eumerus* species) are found in a wider range of bulbs. The larvae are smaller than those of the large narcissus fly and several are usually present in each infested bulb. The small narcissus flies are secondary pests, often invading tissues that are already rotting from disease or from attack by other pests, such as eelworms.

There are no effective chemical control measures against these pests. Regular cultivation of the soil around bulbs after flowering will discourage the females from laying their eggs through the holes in the soil left as the foliage dies down. The flies are most active during warm, sunny spells in May and June, and the bulbs can be protected by keeping them covered with soil during this period. Dormant bulbs may be treated by immersing them for three hours in hot water maintained at 43–44°C (110–112°F).

Oak phylloxera (*Phylloxera quercus*)

These small, yellow insects, which are related to aphids, infest the undersides of oak leaves and feed on the sap. Infestation is often continuous during the summer and damaged leaves become blotchy and wither. Thorough spraying with dimethoate, formothion or malathion generally controls these pests on small trees.

Onion fly (*Delia antiqua*)

This is one of the most serious pests of onions, and also attacks shallots and leeks. Adult flies are active in May, and the females lay eggs on leaves and in the soil. The white, legless maggots hatching from the eggs tunnel into the plant tissues; the leaves yellow and wither, and stems and bulbs rot away. Young plants are particularly susceptible to injury, and attacks by successive generations of adult flies may continue until September.

Onion flies are attracted by the scent of crushed onion leaves; when possible avoid thinning crops in areas where this pest is prevalent. Trichlorphon is the only effective insecticide available; it should be watered into the soil in May and June.

Pea moth (*Laspeyresia nigricans*)

The caterpillars often found in pea pods are the larvae of this small moth, which is one of the most serious pests of culinary peas. Eggs are laid on the leaves in June, July and August, and the resulting pale yellow caterpillars quickly tunnel into the pods where they feed on the developing peas. Early sowings of peas for harvesting before mid-July are generally free from infestations, as are peas sown after mid-June.

Pea thrip (*Kakothrips robustus*)

Young and adult pea thrips are small, elongated insects that infest peas and broad beans in June and July, feeding on the leaves by scraping and sucking. Infestation results in a silver mottling of leaves and pods; severe attacks stunt plants and limit flowering and subsequent pod production. The plants should be carefully examined from June onwards and sprayed or dusted with nicotine or malathion as soon as the symptoms appear.

See also THRIPS.

Pear leaf blister mite (*Eriophyes pyri*)

This microscopic gall mite overwinters under bud scales. The mites emerge in early spring and burrow into the tissues of young pear leaves, where they form conspicuous pustules that are yellow at first, later turning dark brown. Extensive infestations of young trees may check growth and should be controlled by spraying with lime-sulphur at the end of March. Chemical control is generally unnecessary on established healthy trees.

Plum sawfly (*Hoplocampa flava*)

The caterpillars of this sawfly tunnel into young fruits, making conspicuous holes from which a sticky black substance exudes. Infested fruits drop prematurely, and severe infestations limit yields considerably. In areas where this pest is known to be troublesome, protect the fruits by spraying with dimethoate or formothion about a week after petal-fall.

Poplar beetle (*Melosoma populi*)

The larvae of this beetle resemble those of the ladybird. They feed on the leaf tissues of populus, leaving only a skeleton of veins; the adult beetles also feed on the foliage, eating irregular holes out of the leaves.

Chemical control is practicable only on small trees; spray with BHC in early spring or as soon as the first signs of attack are seen, and repeat if necessary.

Potato cyst eelworm (*Heterodera rostochiensis*)

This is a most serious pest of potatoes and also attacks tomatoes. These soil-borne pests hatch out from eggs, protected by tough brown cysts; the young eelworms invade root systems, checking plant growth. Severely infested plants collapse and die. Examination of infested root systems with a magnifying glass usually reveals the spherical yellow or brown cysts which are the enlarged bodies of female eelworms. The cysts, which each contain several hundred eggs, fall off the roots and lie dormant in the soil, often for several years. If potatoes or tomatoes are grown too frequently on the same site, the number of cysts in the soil will increase from year to year and will rapidly reach a damaging level.

There is no effective chemical control available to amateur gardeners. Avoid severe infestations by regular crop rotation; maincrop potatoes should not be grown on the same site more than once every five years. Early potatoes can be grown on the same site about twice every five years. Tomato crops should be similarly rotated or grown in sterile media.

Rabbits (*Oryctolagus cuniculus*)

Rabbits may graze on various herbaceous plants in winter and spring, causing a check to growth; they may also damage trees by eating the bark. In areas where the local rabbit population is high, the erection of rabbit-proof fences may be necessary; but it is usually sufficient to protect only plants that are particularly susceptible to damage. Young trees may be protected with spiral strips of tree protector wound around the trunks, and wire-netting may be used as a temporary screen to keep rabbits away from young herbaceous plants. Various chemical repellents are available and may prove effective.

Raspberry beetle (*Byturus tomentosus*)

The common grubs of this small, inconspicuous beetle tunnel into the developing fruits of raspberry, loganberry and blackberry, causing the fruits to be malformed and maggoty. For quality fruit, control measures with insecticides should be taken at the correct time, as the grubs must be destroyed before they enter the fruits. Spray raspberries and loganberries with malathion or derris as soon as flowering is over, and again when the first fruits begin to colour. Spray blackberries once, as soon as the first flowers open.

Rhododendron bug (*Stephanitis rhododendri*)

Both young and adult rhododendron bugs puncture the undersides of rhododendron leaves and feed on the sap. Severe infestations cause a fine light mottling of the upper surfaces and a rusty-brown or chocolate spotting of the undersides of the leaves. Infestations may be limited by cutting out and burning infested branches in May; in severe attacks spray with malathion or BHC two or three times at three-weekly intervals from mid-June onwards.

Rhododendron leafhopper (*Graphocephala coccinea*)

This is considered the most serious pest of rhododendrons in Great Britain. Through the lesions made in rhododendron buds by female leafhoppers inserting their eggs, the buds may be infected with the disease known as RHODODENDRON BUD BLAST.

The young leafhoppers are present on the leaves from May onwards, and the adults, which are dark green, with two bright red longitudinal stripes, mature in August and September. Thorough spraying with malathion two or three times in August and September may reduce leafhopper populations and thereby limit infection. The pests are, however, difficult to eradicate.

Root aphids (*Pemphigus* species)

Certain aphid species inhabit the soil, where they feed on roots and check growth. Infested plants often turn yellow and wilt. Root aphids are particularly troublesome on pot plants in greenhouses, but they also attack ornamental plants and lettuce grown outdoors. Control the pests by drenching infested root systems with spray-strength solutions of malathion or nicotine.

See also APHIDS and ROOT MEALY BUGS.

Root knot eelworm (*Meloidogyne* species)

These microscopic pests affect many greenhouse plants, especially pot plants. They are particularly troublesome on cucumbers and tomatoes grown under glass, and plants outdoors may sometimes be attacked. The eelworms invade the roots, which usually develop lumpy root galls. The whole root system may be affected and growth is checked. The leaves become discoloured; not all the plants are equally affected, and some plants may grow well despite moderate infestations.

There is no effective chemical control; newly acquired plants should be carefully examined for initial signs of the pests. Infestations may be checked by burning infested plants and sterilising contaminated pots and soil with formaldehyde.

Root mealy bugs (*Rhizoecus* species)

Some species of mealy bug infest the roots of pot plants grown under glass, upsetting the normal root function. Severely infested plants become discoloured and may wilt and die. Root mealy bugs are particularly troublesome on cacti and succulents, but drenching or washing infested roots in a spray-strength solution of malathion, formothion or nicotine usually gives good control.

See also MEALY BUGS and ROOT APHIDS.

Sawflies (*Tenthredinidae*)

Many different species of sawfly attack cultivated plants. The inconspicuous adults, which resemble flying ants, insert their eggs into plant tissues. The caterpillars that hatch from these eggs feed on the leaves. Most species feed on the leaf surfaces and are easily controlled by spraying with malathion or derris. Species that feed inside galls or plant tissues are protected from insecticides.

See also APPLE SAWFLY, GOOSEBERRY SAWFLY and PLUM SAWFLY.

Scale insects (*Coccidae*)

These small insects are generally most troublesome on greenhouse and house plants, but certain species attack ornamental shrubs and trees and fruit grown outdoors. Infestations are often first noticed when the leaves become sticky and sooty; close examination of stems and leaves may reveal the waxy brown, yellow or white scales that frequently form thick encrusting colonies. These scales are the female insects, which remain in the same position for most of their lives. Eggs are laid under the scales, and only the newly hatched young scales, commonly known as crawlers, move actively over plants and spread infestations.

The best control is obtained by spraying with malathion, nicotine, petroleum emulsion or a combined nicotine/petroleum emulsion spray when the crawlers are hatching. In heated greenhouses this can be at any time of year, but in the open and in unheated greenhouses infestations usually occur during the summer. Thorough spraying with a tar-oil winter wash in December or January gives good control of scales on deciduous trees and shrubs, including fruit.

Slugs (*Arion* species, *Agriolimax reticulatus*, etc.)

At least six different species of slug attack garden plants. They feed at night, eating holes in leaves, stems, buds and flowers above ground; below ground they damage roots, tubers, bulbs and corms. They hide under pots, seed boxes, stones and plant debris during the day, but the slime trails they leave indicate the extent of their nocturnal activities. Slugs are encouraged by mild, moist conditions and are most active in spring and autumn. They are generally abundant in soils with a high organic content and are favoured by mulching and by heavy applications of organic manures.

Metaldehyde may be applied as a solution sprayed or watered on to plants and soil, or as poisonous baits containing bran, bonemeal or similar materials. Metaldehyde is not always effective, and many slugs may recover from metaldehyde poisoning. They should be collected and destroyed while still stunned. Slug baits, based on the chemical methiocarb, kill slugs more effectively.

Snails (*Helix* species)

These affect plants in much the same way as SLUGS, but are generally less serious pests.

Squirrels (*Sciurus* species)

The naturalised North American grey squirrel (*Sciurus carolinensis*) is the most common species in Great Britain. It eats ripe fruits and damages shrubs and trees by eating buds and stripping off bark. Squirrels are most troublesome where gardens adjoin woodland, and the only effective control is by protecting valuable crops with netting.

Stem and bulb eelworm (*Ditylenchus dipsaci*)

This is one of the most serious EELWORM pests of cultivated plants. Narcissi are particularly susceptible, but severe damage may also be caused to onions and strawberries, phlox and tulips. A number of different biological races of *Ditylenchus* affect a wide range of host plants, including many weeds.

Stem and bulb eelworms are microscopic; they invade healthy plant tissues and multiply rapidly, causing infested plants to become soft, rotten and distorted. After the collapse of plants, the eelworms persist for some time in rotting tissues in the soil. Thereafter, they depend on the presence of suitable hosts.

Infested bulbs can be treated while dormant by immersion for three hours in hot water at a constant temperature of 43–44°C (110–112°F). This kills the eelworms without harming bulbs, but such treatment is generally impractical on a small scale. There are no safe chemical-control methods, and to prevent infestations, the amateur must rely on good garden hygiene, the purchase of healthy plants, and the proper rotation of susceptible crops. All infested plants should be dug up and burnt, and the affected site should be kept free of susceptible hosts for two or three years.

Strawberry beetles (*Pterostichus* species)

These active, shiny black ground beetles eat pieces out of ripening strawberries and may cause considerable loss of crop. The damage is easily confused with that caused by birds and slugs, but the beetles may be seen scuttling away from beneath affected fruit trusses.

Strawberry beetles are encouraged by weeds and by rank vegetation. There is no effective chemical control, but good garden hygiene should be sufficient.

Suckers (*Psyllidae*)

These pests are related to APHIDS, but differ in having a flattened body with large eyes and prominent wing buds. Young and adult suckers feed on plant sap, and foul infested plants with sticky excretions, which results in distortion of young growth. The apple sucker (*Psylla mali*) infests the blossom trusses of apples and causes symptoms that are sometimes mistaken for frost damage. It overwinters as eggs laid on the trees in autumn; these can be destroyed by applying a winter spray of tar-oil or DNOC/petroleum.

Pear suckers (*Psylla simulans*) cause similar injury to pears, but overwinter as adults and do not lay their eggs until mid-March. Spray with dimethoate, formothion or malathion shortly after petal-fall. This treatment may also be used against apple suckers, as an alternative to winter spraying.

See also BOX SUCKER.

Swift moths (*Hepialidae*)

The caterpillars of these moths live in the soil and can usually be seen when established herbaceous borders or weedy areas are dug over. They are 1–2 in. long, dirty white and with brown heads. They feed on the roots of many cultivated plants and on such weeds as docks and nettles. Good weed control and frequent cultivation discourages the pests; plants that are repeatedly attacked may be protected by working BHC dust into the surrounding soil.

See also CATERPILLARS.

Tarsonemid mites (*Tarsonemidae*)

These small mites feed and breed on young plant tissues, causing distortions, discolorations and superficial scarring. They are difficult to detect and to control as they live in protected situations within buds, at the bases of leaves or under the scales of bulbs. Strawberries, cyclamen, *Aster novi-belgii* (michaelmas daisies), begonia, narcissus, amaryllis and hippeastrum are particularly susceptible, but many other plants may be attacked. There are no effective chemicals available, but sulphur dust or lime-sulphur sprays will help to limit infestations. Hot-water treatment as for BULB SCALE MITE may be used on bulbs and strawberry runners.

Thrips (*Thysanoptera*)

These minute, elongated insects, commonly known as thunder flies, are often abundant in flowers and on leaves. They feed by piercing and sucking plant tissues, which results in silver mottling of affected leaves and petals. Severe infestations prevent normal flowering.

Thrips are easily controlled by dusting or spraying with malathion, applied as soon as the first symptoms are seen. Different species infest various plants, and gladioli, peas, privet and chrysanthemum are particularly susceptible to attacks.

See also GLADIOLUS THRIP and PEA THRIP.

Tortrix caterpillars (*Tortricidae*)

Tortricids differ from most other caterpillars in their habit of spinning silken webs, which are used to draw leaves, stems, fruits and flowers into a protective cover within which the caterpillars feed. Chemical control is difficult, but forceful spraying with trichlorphon may be effective.

The carnation tortrix (*Cacoecimorpha pronubana*) infests carnations and other plants under glass; various other species of tortrix attack fruits and ornamental plants growing in the open.

See also CATERPILLARS.

Wasps (*Vespidae*)

These insects are most troublesome in late summer and early autumn, when they eat into ripening fruits of apples, pears and plums. Usually they only enlarge the damage caused by birds. Wasps should be eradicated by locating and destroying the nests. About ⅓ pint of carbon tetrachloride, poured or injected into a nest, immobilises the adults almost instantaneously, and the nest can be dug out and destroyed soon after treatment. Nests are best treated after dusk, when most of the wasps are inside. An insecticide, such as derris, may also be used to poison nests, but it generally takes longer to act than carbon tetrachloride. Do not use carbon tetrachloride in a confined space, as the vapour is toxic.

Water-lily beetle (*Galerucella nymphaeae*)

Both the brown adult beetles and the fat black larvae eat holes in the upper surfaces of nymphaea leaves, which rot and disintegrate. The pests are most active from June to August. Nicotine sprays may be used to destroy the pests, but as this chemical may kill any fish in the water, it is safer to use non-chemical methods. Regular spraying with a strong jet of water, or submerging the foliage, will dislodge adult beetles and larvae, and the fish will eat them.

Weevils (*Curculionidae*)

Various species of weevil attack cultivated plants. The adults are small or medium-sized beetles, generally dark coloured and often with a prolonged snout. The larvae are white, legless grubs with a distinct head. Both adults and larvae feed on roots, tubers, corms, stems, leaves, flowers and fruits, but attacks are usually localised and damage is seldom severe.

The vine weevil (*Otiorhynchus sulcatus*) and the clay-coloured weevil (*Otiorhynchus singularis*) are the most troublesome as their larvae damage the roots of pot plants, such as cyclamen and begonia. Outdoors, the adults eat the leaves of rhododendrons and other ornamental plants and also damage strawberries and raspberries. They are generally nocturnal feeders, hiding in the soil or in plant debris during the day. Good garden hygiene may reduce the number of hiding places, and a persistent insecticide, such as BHC, applied as a dust or spray to foliage, soil or potting composts, gives good control.

Whiteflies (*Aleyrodidae*)

Adult whiteflies, or snowflies, resemble minute white moths, although they are more closely related to aphids and scale insects. Whitefly nymphs live on the undersides of leaves, where they feed on sap and excrete honeydew which makes the plants sticky and encourages sooty moulds. Spray with malathion, dimethoate or formothion as soon as young or adult whiteflies are seen.

See also CABBAGE WHITEFLY and GLASSHOUSE WHITEFLY.

Willow beetles (*Phyllodecta vitellinae*, etc.)

Adults and larvae of a number of species of these beetles feed on the leaves of salix (willow); severe infestations cause extensive defoliation. Thorough spraying with BHC adequately controls infestations on small trees; large, established trees generally withstand damage from these pests.

Wireworms (*Elateridae*)

These are the tough and horny larvae of click-beetles; they have a long, cylindrical, shiny yellow-brown body with three pairs of legs. They inhabit the soil, feeding on the roots of many different plants, and causing particularly severe injury to potato tubers, stems of lettuces, tomatoes and chrysanthemums. Large populations of wireworms are present in grassland, and severe infestations of garden plants may occur during the first few years on newly cultivated land. It is unusual for wireworms to persist for more than three or four years after land has been brought into general cultivation.

Insecticides such as gamma-BHC may be used to treat infested soil, but this chemical may taint edible crops. Reduce wireworm colonies by frequent and thorough cultivation of the soil, and treat seeds with an insecticide/fungicide seed-dressing before sowing in the open.

Woodlice (*Armadillium vulgare*)
These grey, hard-coated pests live in damp, shady places where they feed on organic debris; they are particularly troublesome in old greenhouses and frames. They feed at night and may cause serious damage to roots, stems and leaves of various plants, especially cucumbers, tomatoes and orchids. Spray or dust with BHC around the base of injured plants and on the hiding places.

Woolly aphid (*Eriosoma lanigerum*)
This species of aphid is a common pest of apple trees, and also attacks related ornamental trees and shrubs, such as malus, cotoneaster, crataegus and sorbus. The aphids infest twigs and branches; during summer the colonies are conspicuous, as they produce large protective tufts of white waxy wool. Continuous feeding on the same tree year after year results in the development of woody galls on the branches; serious deterioration and die-back may follow.

Chemical control is difficult, as the aphids overwinter in the protection of cracks and crevices in bark, and during summer they are protected by their waxy wool. A spray-strength solution of gamma-BHC or malathion, brushed into the colonies, is effective on cordon and dwarf pyramid trees. On a larger scale, spray thoroughly with malathion, dimethoate, formothion, gamma-BHC or gamma-BHC/menazon before bud-break and again after petal-fall.

DISEASES OF CULTIVATED PLANTS

Abutilon mosaic virus
Variegation of the foliage of several abutilon species is due to this virus which is transmitted by grafting. Severely diseased plants should be destroyed.

American gooseberry mildew (*Sphaerotheca mors-uvae*)
This POWDERY MILDEW disease is due to a fungus which produces a white powdery coating on leaves, shoots and fruits of gooseberries. It also attacks black currants late in the season, but the fruits are not affected. Badly diseased shoots become distorted at the tips and may die back; the fungus overwinters on the shoots and these should be cut out and burnt in late August or September. The disease is encouraged by stagnant air amongst the branches, and bushes should be pruned to allow circulation of air. Soft growth is more susceptible to attack, and heavy dressings of nitrogen should be avoided.

Spray with dinocap or lime-sulphur, except on yellow-fruited varieties which are generally sulphur-shy, or with washing soda ($\frac{1}{2}$ lb. to $2\frac{1}{2}$ gal. water) just before the flowers open, again as the fruit is setting and thereafter at fortnightly intervals.

On black currants, the disease may be contained by removing infected shoots in autumn; if it persists, spray with dinocap.

Anthracnose of cucumber (*Colletotrichum lagenarium*)
This fungus disease, which causes spotting and withering of the leaves and which also infects shoots and fruits, occurs on cucumbers, melons and vegetable marrows grown under glass. Strict hygiene must be observed to control the disease, and all affected leaves should be removed and burnt. At the end of the season, disinfect the greenhouse with cresylic acid or other steriland.

During the growing season, control by spraying with wettable or colloidal sulphur or dusting with sulphur. Reduce humidity in the greenhouse by careful ventilation.

Anthracnose of dwarf bean (*Colletotrichum lindemuthianum*)
A fairly common fungus disease, widely distributed in England and Wales where it is most severe on dwarf beans, and occasionally on runner beans, in cool, wet summers. Brown spots develop on leaves and stems; on the pods the spots are black-brown and sunken, often scattered all over the pod, and sometimes with an upper white crust. The fungus passes on to the seeds, the skin of which shows dark patches. The disease is seed-borne, but may also exist on debris in the soil. All diseased plants and seeds should be destroyed; do not grow beans in the same soil for several years.

Only disease-free seeds should be sown; if the disease appears and becomes serious, spray with captan, zineb or Bordeaux mixture at half strength before flowering.

Anthracnose of willow (*Marssonina salicicola*)
A fungus disease which may reach epidemic proportions in wet seasons and which is most prevalent in southern England. It is particularly troublesome on *Salix babylonica* and other weeping willows; badly infected trees may be almost leafless by August. Severe die-back follows.

The fungus is encouraged by mild, damp conditions; minute, whitish dots can be seen on infected areas. The initial infection arises from cankers from which spore masses are transmitted to the unfolding foliage.

Small trees should be sprayed with Bordeaux mixture or liquid copper fungicide as the leaves unfold; give at least two further applications during summer. Gather and burn fallen leaves, and cut out badly cankered shoots. Control may be difficult on large trees; feed with a general fertiliser of high nitrogen content to encourage vigour.

Apple canker (*Nectria galligena*)
This fungus disease is one of the most common and destructive diseases of apple trees; it may also affect pears, beech (fagus), ash (fraxinus), poplar (populus) and sorbus. The fungus enters through wounds, such as those caused by woolly aphids and APPLE SCAB fungus, and these troubles should be controlled. It may also enter through cracks and other small wounds. In summer, spores of the fungus are formed in white pustules on the sunken bark, and the spores are spread by wind. Small red bodies, which contain the winter-resting spores, later develop.

Small branches or spurs infected by canker can be cut out and burnt; on larger branches and main stems, the brown diseased areas should be cut out with a sharp knife until a clean white or green-white wound is left. Paint the wound with white-lead paint or grafting wax, or a proprietary canker paint. In severe attacks, spray the trees with Bordeaux mixture or liquid copper, after the fruit is picked, but before leaf-fall; again when half the leaves have fallen; and finally the following spring at bud-swelling stage.

Heavy, waterlogged soil may aggravate canker, especially on 'Cox's Orange Pippin'.

Apple mildew (*Podosphaera leucotricha*)
This POWDERY MILDEW disease is due to a fungus which produces a white powdery coating on leaves and shoots of apples, ornamental malus (crab apple), medlars, quinces and occasionally pears. The disease has a weakening effect, causing stunting of shoots on young trees and reduction of flowers and spurs in larger trees.

The fungus overwinters in the shoots and in bud scales; it spreads in spring by means of the white powdery spores to fresh young shoots. Where possible, remove and destroy badly infected shoots. Alternatively, spray with dinocap at pink-bud stage in late April or early May and repeat at 7–14 day intervals until mid-July. Lime-sulphur may also be applied, except to pears and sulphur-shy apple varieties, such as 'Lane's Prince Albert' and 'Newton Wonder'.

Apple scab (*Venturia inaequalis*)
A fungus disease which attacks only trees belonging to the genus *Malus*. It occurs annually in all districts, but varies in intensity and is most severe after a wet May. The fungus overwinters as small blister-like pimples on fallen leaves and on young shoots.

Some control can be achieved by gathering and burning fallen leaves, and by cutting out diseased shoots in winter. Complete control can be obtained by spraying with captan, at green-cluster, pink-bud, petal-fall and fruitlet stages. If necessary repeat applications at fortnightly intervals until mid-July.

Apricot die-back
A common disease on apricots which often results in the death of large branches. It may occur as a PHYSIOLOGICAL DISORDER if apricots are grown under unsuitable cultural conditions. Ensure that the soil is neither too wet nor too dry, and feed regularly with a general fertiliser as malnutrition may be the cause of the trouble. Die-back is occasionally caused by late spring frosts, but is more generally due to fungi entering the branches through a small wound. Cut out all dead wood, back to clean, living tissues, and paint the wounds with a protective paint.

Arabis mosaic virus
This virus has a wide host range, attacking bulbous, herbaceous and woody plants and causing serious trouble on fruit crops such as raspberries and strawberries, and on vegetables such as celery and horseradish. The virus is transmitted by a type of eelworm in the soil.

There is no effective chemical control, but

plants susceptible to infection should not be grown in soil harbouring the disease. The virus is seed-borne on some crops.

Armillaria: see HONEY FUNGUS

Ash canker (*Nectria galligena*, etc.)
The decayed areas caused by this disease vary from large erupting black cankers associated with extensive die-back of branches to insignificant warts on the bark surface. The disease is commonly caused by the APPLE CANKER fungus; it may also occur as a result of frost damage, or be due to a bacterium.

There is no effective chemical control; cut out badly infected shoots and cankered areas, and cover the wounds with a protective paint.

Aster wilt (*Verticillium vilmorinii*)
This form of VERTICILLIUM WILT only attacks species of aster, varieties of *A. novi-belgii* being most severely affected. Forms and varieties of *A. novae-angliae* are generally disease-free. The trouble is caused by a microscopic fungus that inhabits the root-stock. It emits a poison (toxin) which passes through the sap, killing leaf tissue.

Destroy infected plants, and propagate only from healthy stock which should be grown on a fresh site, as the disease is soil-borne. Rooted suckers of diseased plants should not be replanted, but cuttings can usually safely be taken from the top 1–2 in. of basal shoots.

Azalea gall (*Exobasidium vaccinii*)
Small-leaved rhododendrons, including pot-grown plants of *R. simsii* and Kurume azaleas, may be attacked by this fungus disease. It spreads by means of air or insect-borne spores which enter the plant tissues. The symptoms may not appear until several months after infection; leaves and flowers are replaced by fleshy galls, red or pale green at first, later producing a white floury coating of fungus spores.

Control the disease by cutting off and burning the galls before they turn white and begin to produce new spores. In the greenhouse, control spore-bearing insects. In severe attacks, spray with Bordeaux mixture or other fungicides, or zineb, before new leaves unfurl.

Bacterial canker (*Pseudomonas syringae, P. mors-prunorum*)
A serious disease of plums, also affecting cherries, peaches and ornamental prunus species. It is most troublesome on young trees, but may also attack established trees. The bacteria live on the leaves throughout summer and in autumn are washed down on the shoots. On plums and cherries, infections generally occur through leaf scars; wounds already cankered may become re-infected.

Control the disease by spraying the foliage thoroughly with Bordeaux mixture in mid-August, mid-September and mid-October. As infection of shoots occurs only in autumn and winter, pruning should be done during the summer months, and the wounds coated with a proprietary canker paint to prevent entry of the bacteria.

Bacterial canker of poplars (*Aplanobacterium populi*)
This bacterial disease shows first as a cream-coloured slime exuding from cracks in the wood of one-year-old shoots. The bacteria are spread by rain and may be transferred by insects from one tree to another; infections occur when the bacteria enter through leaf or bud-scale scars.

The subsequent cankers are unsightly, and there is no effective chemical control. Cut out badly infected shoots and cover the wounds with a protective paint; severely diseased trees should be destroyed entirely. All varieties of *Populus nigra* are disease resistant, but *P. balsamifera* and related species of balsam poplar are generally susceptible.

Basal rot
A disease which causes the rotting of bulbs such as lachenalia and lilium; it begins at the basal plate of the bulb and spreads upwards until the whole bulb is destroyed. The disease may be due to fungi such as FUSARIUM WILT or RHIZOCTONIA, but may also be caused by secondary fungi and bacteria which enter through dead or damaged tissues. In the early stages, diseased roots and tissues, or lily scales, may be cut out and the bulbs dusted with quintozene. Rake the same fungicide into the soil prior to planting. Destroy badly diseased bulbs.

Birch polypore (*Piptoporus betulinus*, syn. *Polyporus betulinus*)
A common bracket fungus which results in the die-back of birch trees. The grey-brown, horseshoe-shaped brackets are up to 6 in. across. The fungus enters only through dead wood, causing the rapid decay of wood after a branch has died.

Cut out all dead wood and coat wounds and pruning cuts with a protective paint to prevent the entry of this fungus. Mulch the trees regularly with well-decayed manure.

Bitter pit
This common disorder of apples may appear on half-grown fruits or in storage. The flesh is heavily marked with brown spots, but no rotting occurs. The disease, which may be of physiological origin, is more common in hot dry summers and appears to be connected with a shortage of water at critical times. Mulching with well-decayed compost or manure and watering before the soil dries out usually helps to prevent the trouble. Apply a complete and balanced fertiliser in spring and avoid excessive feeding with nitrogenous fertilisers. Young, vigorous trees are particularly susceptible to bitter pit, and only light pruning should be carried out in the initial stages.

The incidence of bitter pit can be reduced by spraying with calcium nitrate at the rate of 8 oz. to 5 gal. of water; apply in mid-June and repeat three times at intervals of three weeks.

Black leg
A disease that commonly destroys cuttings of pelargoniums, and may also occur on outdoor plants if diseased plants are bedded out, or planted in contaminated soil. The disease may be due to one or more fungi, and to bacteria; it is most troublesome on cold and wet soil. Prevent the trouble by good cultural treatment, strict greenhouse hygiene, and the use of sterilised compost.

Destroy severely diseased cuttings, although valuable plants may often be saved by removing the blackened base back to firm green tissue and re-inserting in fresh compost.

If the disease persists, check the water supply; if this comes from a tank or butt, it may be the cause of contamination. Purify by adding a pea-size lump of copper sulphate, or crystals of potassium permanganate until the water takes on a pale pink hue. Outdoors, do not grow pelargoniums in contaminated soil; if possible sterilise the site.

Black root rot (*Thielaviopsis basicola*)
This fungus is a frequent cause of rotting of roots and tissues at the crowns of all types of plants, outdoors and under glass. It cannot be identified with the naked eye, but its presence may be suspected if the rotting tissues are black. The fungus builds up in the soil when crops of the same type are grown in the same position year after year; rotation of crops will prevent this disease to a certain extent. Limited control can be obtained by watering infected plants at three-week intervals with a solution of captan.

Black spot (*Diplocarpon rosae*)
A rose disease which generally appears in mid-June on heavily pruned roses such as the Hybrid teas; symptoms may show in late April or early May on rose species and climbers which are only lightly pruned. The disease overwinters on the leaves and these should be burnt.

Control by spraying every two weeks with captan or maneb, giving the first application immediately after pruning. Apply a foliar feed, as the disease is worse on weak bushes.

Blight
A term loosely applied to describe troubles caused by pests and diseases. See also POTATO BLIGHT.

Blindness
Bulbous plants such as narcissi and tulips, particularly those grown in containers, may fail to flower, producing only leaves and sometimes flower buds which turn brown and wither. The usual cause is excessive dryness at the roots, or sometimes waterlogging. Contributory factors, especially with narcissi, are excessively high temperatures and a dry atmosphere just when the buds show above soil level.

Blossom end rot
This trouble shows as a circular brown patch on the skin at the blossom end of tomatoes. The patches enlarge and eventually penetrate into the flesh. Blossom end rot is due to drought at a critical stage in the development of the young fruits, and often only the fruits of one truss may be affected. Prevent the trouble by ensuring that the soil never dries out.

Blotchy ripening
A form of malnutrition on tomatoes under glass, due to deficiency of nitrogen or potash. Attacks are particularly severe when high temperatures occur, and adequate ventilation of the greenhouse usually prevents the symptoms from developing.

Blue mould (*Penicillium* species)
The massed fungus spores of this disease have a blue-green or green colour. Various species are found as secondary fungi on injured or dying tissues, and others may be troublesome on stored vegetables and on bulbs. Any plant

material in store should be examined at regular intervals, and diseased bulbs, corms and vegetables should be discarded. The fungi are encouraged by a moist atmosphere; storage conditions should be dry and fairly cool, and all plant material should be healthy when placed in store. Dust bulbs, but not vegetables, with quintozene prior to storing.

Boot-lace fungus: see HONEY FUNGUS

Boron deficiency

The edible roots of beetroots and swedes, subjected to this trouble, turn brown inside; similarly, brown cracks may appear across the stalks of celery. Correct the deficiency by applying 1 oz. of borax to every 20 sq. yds of soil; mix with light sand to ensure even distribution.

Botrytis

A name sometimes given to the disease GREY MOULD, caused by *Botrytis cinerea*. See CHOCOLATE SPOT, CORE ROT, LILY DISEASE, PAEONY WILT and TULIP FIRE.

Bracket fungi

These fungi produce shelf-like fruiting bodies, up to 12 in. across, on trunks and branches of trees. The spores enter only through dead or damaged tissues, and may cause rotting of the heartwood and die-back of the tree. The fruiting bodies may not appear until several months after infection; some species remain on the trunks, others disintegrate.

Small diseased branches should be removed; on the main trunk, the brackets and any rotting wood should be cut out, and all wounds coated with a protective paint. See BIRCH POLYPORE and SILVER LEAF.

Brown core (*Phytophthora primulae*)

This fungus disease can be particularly troublesome on *Primula vulgaris*, but may also affect other species of primula. Its presence should be suspected when primula plants collapse, especially if they have been growing on the same site for several years. Stunted roots, brown in the centre, indicate brown core. Destroy affected plants, and avoid growing in the site for several years.

Brown rot (*Sclerotinia* species)

A fungus disease that attacks apples, apricots, cherries, medlars, nectarines, peaches, pears, plums and quinces, and edible species of corylus (nuts). The disease occurs on injured fruits, which should be destroyed. Any mummified fruits should be removed in winter, and dead spurs and cankered branches cut out and burnt. Discourage wasps and birds which may peck and injure the fruits.

In store, the disease may spread if diseased and healthy fruits are in contact. Do not store bruised or damaged fruits, and examine for signs of the disease every two weeks.

Bud-drop

Dropping of buds prior to flowering is usually due to unsuitable cultural conditions. Too dry soil conditions at bud formation cause camellias, sweet peas and wistarias to lose their buds; these plants should be heavily mulched with decayed compost or manure and watered during dry periods.

In the greenhouse, extremes between day and night temperatures may cause gardenias to drop their buds.

Once the buds begin to fall, no chemical control is effective, and the trouble should be prevented by cultural treatment.

Callistephus wilt (*Fusarium oxysporum callistephi*)

This disease is a form of FUSARIUM WILT which attacks only species of callistephus. It is a common disease, with symptoms similar to FOOT ROT, but the fungus growths on the blackened parts of the stem are white or pink.

The disease is most troublesome on wet, badly drained soils; it is soil-borne, but may also spread from diseased to healthy plants by airborne spores. Infected plants should be destroyed, and annual asters should be grown on a different site. A number of wilt-resistant aster varieties are available and these should be grown in gardens where the disease has occurred.

Cane blight (*Leptosphaeria coniothyrium*)

A common fungus disease of raspberries in north-east England and Kent; it occasionally occurs elsewhere, the varieties 'Norfolk Giant' and 'Lloyd George' being susceptible. The fungus may also attack other rosaceous plants and is frequently found on dead rose shoots. It usually enters raspberry canes through cracks at soil level, and the soil may become contaminated.

Cut out all diseased canes at the base, below soil level. Spray new canes with a copper fungicide, such as Bordeaux mixture.

Cane spot (*Elsinoe veneta*)

This fungus disease is widely distributed, and attacks raspberries, loganberries and hybrid berries. Infection takes place from May to October, and summer spores spread the disease from infected to healthy canes. Infections in early summer are caused by over-wintered fungi. Badly spotted canes should be cut out and burnt to destroy the over-wintering spores, and the remaining canes should be sprayed with thiram, or 5 per cent lime-sulphur or liquid copper, at bud-burst, when the buds are about $\frac{1}{2}$ in. long. Repeat just before blossoming. Loganberries should not be sprayed with lime-sulphur; apply thiram or copper just prior to blossom-stage and again when the fruits have set.

Canker

A term applied to almost any kind of open wound on trees or shrubs, and occasionally on other types of plants. The limit of the canker is usually apparent by swollen bark, or by new tissue (callus) over the wound. See APPLE CANKER, BACTERIAL CANKER, PARSNIP CANKER and STEM CANKER.

Carnation ringspot (*Didymellina dianthi*)

A fungus disease of two strains, one of which attacks only *Dianthus barbatus* and the other *D. caryophyllus*. The trouble may be controlled to a certain extent by removing diseased leaves and spraying at regular intervals with Bordeaux mixture.

Carnation stem-rot and die-back (*Fusarium culmorum*)

This is caused by a common, soil-inhabiting fungus which enters the stems of dianthus through wounds. The same fungus may cause BASAL ROT of cuttings taken from diseased plants, or inserted in infected sand.

Control the disease by spraying stock plants with captan at 10–14 day intervals before and while taking cuttings.

Carnation virus diseases

A number of different viruses attack dianthus under glass, the principal ones being mottle, vein mottle, ringspot and etched ring viruses. Carnation vein mottle virus also affects *D. barbatus*; it is transmitted by aphids. These VIRUS DISEASES are frequently spread by propagating from diseased plants, and the troubles are best prevented by destroying all plants showing symptoms of virus infection. Always propagate from healthy plants, and purchase only stock which is known to be virus-free.

Celery heart rot (*Erwinia carotovora*)

This bacterial disease cannot usually be detected until the celery is lifted and found to have centres of a wet, slimy, brown rot, frequently extending up the stalks. The bacteria are thought to attack only through wounds such as those caused by careless cultivation or slugs, or severe frost injury.

Ensure good cultivation on well-drained soil and apply a balanced fertiliser; keep the plants carefully earthed up. Control slugs, and in cold districts give winter protection. Dusting with copper lime dust when earthing-up is a helpful precaution; change the site for celery every few years as the bacteria can build up in the soil.

Celery leaf spot (*Septoria apiicola*)

A seed-borne fungus disease of seedlings and mature plants of celery and celeriac. It may achieve serious proportions and, once present, spreads rapidly by means of spores, particularly in wet weather.

Use only healthy seeds, often listed as 'hot-water treated' or 'thiram treated' seeds. Spray seedlings and developing plants with Bordeaux mixture, liquid copper or zineb, and repeat as necessary. If the disease has been continuously troublesome, disinfect frames with 2 per cent formalin, and use sterilised compost for pricking out seedlings. Feed established plants with a complete fertiliser containing potash to avoid soft growth.

Chlorosis

This is a condition in which the green of a leaf is replaced by pale green, yellow or sometimes white; it may be caused by VIRUS DISEASES or MINERAL DEFICIENCIES. Plants on chalky soils are most often affected, and peach, wistaria, rhododendron and hydrangea are particularly susceptible. Chlorosis due to the alkalinity of the soil can be corrected by adding iron chelate at the rate recommended by the manufacturer, or fritted trace elements. Improve the acidity of the soil by digging in peat, and use only acid fertilisers. Chlorosis due to virus diseases cannot be remedied in this way, and severely infected plants should be destroyed.

Chocolate spot (*Botrytis fabae*, *B. cinerea*)

A fungus disease of broad beans, particularly common in humid weather, but seldom serious. Chocolate-coloured spots usually appear on the foliage in June or July, but may also show after frost in December or January on overwintered plants. Weak plants are more susceptible to attack; strong growth should be encouraged by liming and by feeding the soil with a potash fertiliser. Good drainage is essential, and seeds should be sown thinly; destroy infected debris. In severe attacks, spray with a copper fungicide soon after the foliage appears.

Chrysanthemum virus diseases

A number of different viruses may occur on chrysanthemums, outdoors and under glass, and the symptoms vary according to the virus responsible, the variety grown, cultural conditions and the season. Plants showing distortion of blooms, breaking or greening of the flower colour, or stunting or leaf mottling, should be destroyed as the viruses cannot be eliminated by chemical spraying. Many of the viruses are transmitted by pests such as aphids, and these should be controlled by suitable spraying.

Certain viruses have been eliminated from various stocks of chrysanthemums by heat therapy, and cuttings raised from such stocks are readily available. However, plants that are certified to be virus-free may later become re-infected.

Clematis wilt (*Ascochyta clematidina*)

Wilting or die-back of shoots of clematis, especially the *C. × jackmanii* types and other large-flowered garden varieties, is due to this fungus disease. It enters a plant low down on the stem, and first shows as the sudden wilting of the upper parts of a shoot, the youngest leaves wilting first, and the leaf stalks blackening where they join the blade.

Wilted clematis shoots never recover, but young, healthy shoots usually develop below the wilted area or even below soil level. Infected plants are rarely killed outright in one season. Cut out wilted shoots, back to clean, living tissues, and coat the wounds with a protective paint. Spray developing shoots in spring with a copper fungicide such as Bordeaux mixture.

Club root (*Plasmodiophora brassicae*)

This fungus disease attacks cruciferous plants, such as wallflowers, stocks, turnips and radishes, and is especially serious on brassicas. The disease is prevalent on acid, badly drained soils; drainage improvement helps to prevent the trouble. Control the disease by liming, using hydrated lime at 14 lb. to every 30 sq. yds; the beneficial effect may not be complete for 12–18 months.

Sprinkle 4 per cent calomel dust in the planting holes at the rate of 4 oz. to every 20 plants, or dip the roots of seedlings in a paste of 1 lb. of 4 per cent calomel dust to ⅓ pint of water plus a little clay. Use 4 per cent calomel dust on the seed bed, broadcast at 1½ oz. per sq. yd and raked in before making the drills, or sprinkled in the drills before sowing at 1 oz. per 5 ft run.

Cluster cup rust

A term applied to the cup-like structure formed at one stage by several RUST fungi. On caltha the fungus responsible is *Puccinia calthae*, and on aquilegia, *Puccinia recondita* sp. *agrostidis*; the disease is not serious, but severely infected plants are best destroyed.

Diseased anemones, infected by *Tranzschelia discolor*, should be burnt as the fungus is systemic within infected plants. The cluster cups will develop regularly each spring and the plants become distorted and fail to flower. The spores produced by the cluster cups on anemone infect prunus trees, especially plums, and rust develops.

Gooseberry cluster cup rust is due to the fungus *Puccinia caricina* var. *pringsheimiana*; infected leaves and shoots should be removed and burnt. If the disease is known to occur, spray the bushes annually, before flowering, with Bordeaux mixture or a similar copper fungicide. Do not mulch with sedge peat. The later stages of this rust develop on carex. Avoid growing the two types of plants close to each other. See also MINT RUST.

Collar rot

This disease, which affects greenhouse plants at or just above soil level, is due to one or more soil and water-borne organisms. The trouble is most common on badly drained soil and on over-watered plants. Early detection of the disease may help to save infected plants; remove all dead and decaying tissues and dust the infected areas with copper-lime dust or captan. Repot the plants in a lighter compost, and reduce watering.

Common scab (*Streptomyces scabies, S. tumuli*)

Potatoes, beetroots and radishes are affected by this disease, due to organisms closely related to bacteria. They are usually found in soils which lack organic matter, especially dry sandy or gravelly soils; liming of the soil immediately before sowing or planting is also likely to encourage the disease. The scabs which develop on the tubers or roots are superficial and do not render any of these inedible.

If the disease is troublesome, incorporate plenty of humus, such as mustard or green manure, and do not lime the soil. Sow disease-free seeds and grow resistant potato varieties, such as 'Arran Pilot', 'Maris Peer', 'Pentland Crown' and 'King Edward'. All debris should be burnt.

Coral spot (*Nectria cinnabarina*)

This fungus, which usually lives on dead twigs, may become parasitic if it enters living shoots and may cause the death of branches, or even large trees. Prevent the disease by cutting out and burning all dead wood, and coat the wounds with a protective paint. Shoots showing the disease should be pruned back 4–6 in. below the diseased area.

Core rot (*Botrytis gladiolorum*)

A fungus which causes storage rot of acidanthera, freesia and gladiolus corms. The fungus is encouraged by moist conditions, and corms should be stored in a dry atmosphere and at low temperatures. Dust the corms before storing with quintozene, or submerge them for one hour in a solution of captan, at the rate of 4 oz. of 50 per cent wettable powder to 1¼ gal. water.

Corky scab of cacti

This common trouble on certain cacti, such as epiphyllum and opuntia, shows as irregular rusty or corky spots where the outer layers of cells have been killed. The tissues beneath gradually die, and the patch becomes sunken. The trouble may be due to lack of light, combined with waterlogging or a too high humidity, but similar symptoms may also be caused by over-exposure to sunlight. Destroy badly affected plants.

Corm rot of zantedeschia (*Erwinia carotovora*)

A serious bacterial disease where zantedeschias are grown in large numbers under glass, and in wet soils. The plants wither and collapse, due to the rotting of the corms; these may show extensive brown areas, and roots coming from these areas are rotten. The corm lesions may be slight and remain dormant in storage, but when the corms are replanted the rot progresses rapidly. Flowering is curtailed or non-existent.

Badly infected plants should be destroyed; the soil should be sterilised and the house disinfected. Examine corms from storage; cut out any brown areas, and steep the corms in a 2 per cent formalin solution for two hours before planting.

Cox spot

The tan-coloured spots, frequently found on leaves of 'Cox's Orange Pippin' and less commonly on other apple varieties, are due to a PHYSIOLOGICAL DISORDER. It is often difficult to determine the exact cause, but the disorder occurs after drought. Mulch all apple trees and water thoroughly during dry periods. The trouble may also be partly due to MAGNESIUM DEFICIENCY.

Crinkle

This aphid-borne virus disease of strawberries may occur in two forms. In the mild form, yellow spots appear on the leaves; the centre of each spot may become red or purple, but the plants are not seriously affected. In the severe form, similar but more numerous spots appear, causing the leaves to pucker as the spots dry out and turn brown. The plants remain erect, but growth is retarded; the leaves are stunted, and little or no fruit is produced. The plants should be dug up and burnt. Prevent the disease by controlling the aphids (see PESTS).

Crown gall (*Agrobacterium tumefaciens*)

A bacterial disease occurring on many types of plants, including soft and top fruit, vegetables, shrubs and herbaceous plants. It is not a serious disease and is more likely to persist and spread in wet soils. The bacteria enter through wounds, and live and multiply in the outer layers of a gall; a chain of galls may develop along a root or shoot. The galls are hard or soft according to the host—soft on herbaceous stems, hard on woody plants. Infected plants may be slightly stunted, but galls are often not found unless the plant is dug up.

Avoid all injuries to roots, and prevent waterlogging by adequate drainage. Severely diseased plants should be destroyed, and new shrubs should have the roots dipped in a fungicide before planting.

Crown rot

A term applied to rotting of the tissues, at or just below ground level, on plants with a wide and flat crown. It is identical to COLLAR ROT.

Crown rot of rhubarb (*Pectobacterium rhaponticum*)

This is a common bacterial disease, encouraged by too wet soil conditions; it is seldom troublesome on well-drained soil. Burn infected plants, and site new ones in fresh ground. Avoid damage to the crowns as the soil-borne bacteria enter through wounds, often caused by eelworms or cultural treatment.

Cucumber mosaic virus

This is one of the most troublesome viruses, as it has a wide host range and is readily transmitted by aphids. It is frequently spread on pruning tools, and by handling diseased plants. Infected plants should be destroyed immediately the first symptoms are seen. This is particularly important for crops such as marrows, where all the plants may become diseased in a short time. Control aphids by suitable spraying.

Damping-off (*Pythium* species, *Rhizoctonia solani*, etc.)

A term used to describe attacks on seedlings by parasitic fungi which cause them to collapse and die. The various fungi may live as saprophytes on dead and decaying matter in the soil, and are only likely to attack the seedlings if these are overcrowded or growing in too wet conditions or in compacted soil. High temperatures also favour the disease. It can usually be prevented by correct sowing procedures and after-treatment of seedlings. Attacks may be checked by watering the seed boxes with Cheshunt compound, captan or zineb; captan and thiram seed dressings are also effective.

Dianthus leaf spots

Several fungi cause leaf spots on dianthus species; on *D. barbatus* and *D. caryophyllus*, one fungus causes pale round or oval spots surrounded by a purple border. Each spot bears minute black dots which are the spore-producing bodies. Another fungus of both species results in small, round, purple spots which gradually enlarge and coalesce, turning brown in the centre. Infected leaves become sickly and die off at the tips. Yet another fungal parasite of *D. barbatus* is common in Scotland, and occasionally affects *D. chinensis*. It produces large, white, circular spots which often spread over the entire leaf; minute black spores are dotted over the spots.

Control leaf spots by removing infected leaves and spraying plants with Bordeaux mixture or zineb. In severe cases two or three applications at two to three-week intervals may be necessary.

Die-back

This describes the death of young shoots of trees and shrubs, often followed by death of larger branches. In many cases die-back is due to PHYSIOLOGICAL DISORDERS, but it may also occur from frost damage, or be due to a parasitic fungus which has entered through a wound. GREY MOULD and CORAL SPOT fungi may result in die-back, as may APPLE CANKER and BACTERIAL CANKER.

Infected shoots should be cut back to clean, living tissue, and the wounds coated with a protective paint. If the trouble can be identified as due to a certain disease, the correct remedial treatment should be carried out; if no disease is found, cultural conditions need improving.

Downy mildew

This disease is caused by various fungi which all show characteristic white tufts or downy patches on leaves, generally on the undersurfaces. The fungal threads penetrate deeply into the plant tissues and later produce spores.

Resting spores are produced in the diseased tissues and are released into the soil.

Prevent the disease by good cultural conditions. Spray with zineb on all ornamental host plants; use Bordeaux mixture on brassicas and thiram on lettuces. In frames, sterilise the soil with formalin.

Dry rot (*Fusarium caeruleum*)

A common storage disease of potatoes, developing chiefly from January onwards and most troublesome on early-maturing varieties. The fungus is soil-borne and is present in all soils. Contamination occurs while the tubers are still in the ground, the fungus entering through eyes, breathing pores, scab wounds or abrasions. The disease is favoured by poor storage conditions and develops most rapidly at high humidity and at temperatures of 16°C (61°F). Store healthy tubers in a cool, but frost-proof, and dry place, and destroy all diseased tubers. Place seed tubers on sprouting trays; they may be dusted with tecnazene to prevent the disease, but as this dust inhibits sprouting, the tubers should be exposed to the air for at least a month before planting outdoors.

Dutch elm disease (*Ceratocystis ulmi*)

This fungus disease is spread by elm bark beetles which lay their eggs in weak or dying elm trees. The spores are spread to healthy trees when adult beetles fly up on the young shoots to feed. Spores enter through the wounds made by the beetles, and the fungus produces a toxin which causes die-back of the branches. The disease may kill a tree fairly quickly, or it may persist for several years, killing branches in succession. In some instances all the branches at the top die back, so that the tree becomes stag-headed.

There is no proven chemical treatment to control the disease, therefore all dead or badly damaged trees should be felled. In less severe attacks, remove all dead branches and burn diseased wood to destroy the fungus.

Eye rot (*Nectria galligena*)

A fungus disease that appears on apple and sometimes pear fruits at the eye end, from which the rot extends until the whole fruit is infected. Diseased fruits have a characteristic flattened appearance at the eye end and usually fall early.

The disease is caused by the APPLE CANKER fungus, and the control measures recommended for that disease should be carried out. Destroy all diseased fruits to prevent the fungus overwintering.

Fire

A term sometimes used to describe browning of foliage. See NARCISSUS FIRE, TULIP FIRE.

Fireblight (*Erwinia amylovora*)

This bacterial disease affects apples, pears and ornamental trees and shrubs belonging to the *Rosaceae* family, in particular crataegus and cotoneaster. It is chiefly confined to the southern half of England. The disease attacks only growing trees when the bacteria enter the nectaries in the flowers, turning them black. The infection spreads through spurs and twigs into the main branches, causing the leaves on infected shoots to turn brown. Cankers, which develop at the base of diseased tissues, remain dormant until the

spring; they become active at the same time as the first blossoms are opening.

Fireblight is a Notifiable Disease; if suspected, one is obliged by law to report to the local officer of the Ministry of Agriculture. Treatment usually involves cutting out the diseased wood to a point 2–4 ft below the infected areas.

Foot rot

A trouble of herbaceous plants which shows as a blackening and rotting at the base. It may be due to various fungi, including BLACK ROOT ROT and RHIZOCTONIA.

Foot rot can be controlled to a certain extent by good cultural methods and by using seed dressings of captan or thiram or by watering with captan, Cheshunt compound or zineb.

Several fungi produce spores which overwinter in debris in the soil; bedding plants such as asters, geraniums and petunias should be grown in sterilised soil if foot rot is known to be persistent. The same ruling applies to vegetables. In the greenhouse, treat the disease as recommended for BLACK LEG.

Frost damage

Apart from killing young leaves and shoots, frost damage can produce a variety of symptoms, including cracking of tree trunks, distortion or curling of leaves, the raising of the lower leaf epidermis, and blackening and browning of flower centres and buds. Damaged shoots should be cut out, after danger of frost is past, to prevent the entry of fungi.

Fusarium wilt

Several species of the fungus *Fusarium* cause wilting of plants, in particular dianthus, dwarf and runner beans, garden peas and lathyrus (sweet peas).

The fungi are soil-borne and build up in the soil, when the same type of plant is grown year after year in the same site. Crop rotation often prevents the trouble, and in severe outbreaks the soil should be sterilised. Destroy infected plants and propagate only from healthy stock.

See also CALLISTEPHUS WILT.

Galls

These are outgrowths which develop on leaves, stems, crowns and roots of plants, often causing considerable distortion. See CROWN GALL and LEAFY GALL.

Gangrene (*Phoma exigua* var. *foveata*)

A common storage disease of potato tubers. The fungus enters the tubers in the ground, through wounds. Poor storage conditions aggravate the trouble; careful handling and proper storage usually prevent the disease from developing. Burn rotting tubers.

Gladiolus dry rot (*Sclerotinia gladioli*)

This fungus, which causes dry rot of gladiolus, may also affect acidanthera, crocus and freesia corms, and has been found on imported corms of tritonia. The disease spreads to adjacent healthy plants, and more severe contamination of the soil occurs from diseased debris. Burn all diseased corms at lifting time; clean healthy corms and dust with quintozene or submerge them for one hour in a solution of captan ($\frac{1}{4}$ lb. of 50 per cent wettable powder to $1\frac{1}{4}$ gal. water). Store the dried corms in an airy but frost-free place at low temperatures. Rake quintozene into the soil prior to planting.

Gladiolus scab (*Pseudomonas marginata*)

A bacterial disease which overwinters in the soil. Diseased plants should be dug up and burnt, and healthy corms should be grown in a fresh site the following year. Treat the corms as advised for GLADIOLUS DRY ROT.

Gladiolus yellows (*Fusarium oxysporum gladioli*)

This soil-borne fungus disease of gladiolus and freesia enters plant tissues through the roots. The fungus is difficult to detect, as the symptoms appear within the corm tissues. There is no chemical control, and infected plants should be destroyed as soon as the first symptoms appear. Grow gladiolus on a fresh site each year.

Greenback

This PHYSIOLOGICAL DISORDER of tomatoes may be attributed to high greenhouse temperatures, to scorching of the fruits or to a shortage of potash. Prevent the trouble by applying adequate potash and by shading and ventilating the greenhouse. Tomato varieties resistant to greenback are available, and are listed as such.

Grey bulb rot (*Sclerotium tuliparum*)

Although most common on tulips and hyacinths, this fungus disease may also affect forced colchicum, crocus, fritillaria, gladiolus, iris, ixia, narcissus and *Scilla sibirica*. The black resting bodies of the fungus develop on rotting tissues and contaminate the soil, affecting susceptible host plants. Remove and destroy all diseased plants, together with some of the surrounding soil. Debris of diseased bulbs should also be burnt. Rake quintozene into the soil before planting, and dust the bulbs with quintozene. If possible, grow susceptible bulbs on a different site each year.

Grey mould (*Botrytis cinerea*)

This is possibly the most troublesome of all fungus diseases, as it can affect all types of plants, including weeds. Spores of the fungus are present in the air, and infection occurs through wounds and through dead and decaying tissues; it may also spread by contact.

Remove and burn infected parts; under glass, the fungus is encouraged by a still atmosphere. Good hygiene helps to prevent the trouble, but special control measures are necessary for certain plants:

Alpines, annual, biennial and herbaceous perennial plants: dust with captan or tecnazene, or spray the plants with captan, thiram or zineb.

Bulbs: remove diseased plants, dust the remainder of the clump with quintozene, and rake this fungicide into the soil before replanting.

Trees and shrubs: cut out infected tissues, and coat wounds with a protective paint.

Soft fruit: spray with dichlofluanid, captan or thiram, commencing as soon as the first flowers open, and repeat at ten-day intervals until just before the fruits ripen.

Vegetables: rake quintozene into the soil before planting out.

Under glass: fumigate or dust the greenhouse with tecnazene.

Gummosis of cucumber (*Cladosporium cucumerinum*)

A fungus disease which affects cucumbers, melons and vegetable marrows grown in frames and greenhouses. It is encouraged by wet, cool conditions, and can usually be prevented by adequate ventilation and heat.

Control the disease by spraying with zineb or captan, or by dusting with zineb; burn all diseased fruits. The greenhouse or frame should be disinfected before another crop is planted.

Hard rot (*Septoria gladioli*)

A fungus disease, chiefly of gladiolus, but also affecting acidanthera, crocus and freesia corms. Spores, produced by the small black fruiting bodies of the fungus, develop in diseased tissues, and in wet weather these spores spread rapidly. The fungus may overwinter on debris in the soil, and diseased plants should be destroyed. Prevent rotting of stored corms by treating these as advised for GLADIOLUS DRY ROT.

Heather die-back (*Phytophthora cinnamomi*)

This soil-borne fungus attacks the roots and collar parts of calluna and erica. Diseased plants should preferably be dug up and burnt, although they may be saved by spraying them regularly with a foliar feed. Gaps in heather beds should not be filled out unless the soil is changed. In severe outbreaks all plants should be removed, and the soil changed before fresh stock is planted.

Honey fungus (*Armillaria mellea*)

This is the most damaging of all soil-borne parasites, as it may attack almost any type of plant, including bulbs, herbaceous plants and vegetables. It is most commonly found on trees and shrubs. Ligustrum, rhododendrons and roses are susceptible.

The fungus produces honey-coloured toadstools which rarely spread the disease, as the spores infect only stumps and felled timber. The fungus usually lives as a saprophyte on dead wood, from where it passes through the roots and into the soil in the form of black, root-like structures (rhizomorphs). When the tips of these structures make contact with healthy roots they penetrate the fresh tissues. The fungal threads spread to the collar of the plant and can be seen as white fans beneath the bark.

Dead and dying plants should be removed, together with as many of the roots as possible. Change the soil before replanting or sterilise with creosote or a 2 per cent solution of formalin.

Ink disease (*Bipolaris iridis*)

Bulbous irises in particular are often affected by this fungus disease, which may also occur on lachenalia and tritonia. Black crusty patches on the outer scales of diseased bulbs contain the spores, which can spread through the soil. The foliage too may be attacked in a wet season.

Remove and burn all diseased bulbs. Burn off the foliage at the end of the season.

Internal rust spot

This disorder shows as brown spots and blotches in the flesh of potato tubers. The

cause of the trouble is unknown, but it may be due to unsuitable soil conditions. There are no chemical measures to prevent the disease, but careful cultivation in humus-rich soil and an adequate water supply is beneficial. 'King Edward' is generally resistant.

Iris mosaic virus

A virus disease that affects bulbous irises. It is spread by aphids and these should be controlled. Infected plants cannot be saved and must be destroyed.

Leaf mould (*Cladosporium fulvum*)

This is a common and often troublesome disease on tomatoes under glass. Spores of the fungus, produced on the lower leaf surfaces, overwinter on leaf debris and on the greenhouse structure. After a severe outbreak, the greenhouse should be disinfected. However, good cultural conditions and a maximum temperature of 21°C (70°F) usually prevent the trouble, and further precautions, such as spraying with zineb, maneb, nabam or copper fungicides, keep the disease in check.

Leaf rot (*Heteropatella valtellinensis*)

A common disease of dianthus, including garden pinks, and particularly active during winter. Remove and burn all diseased leaves; spray with a fungicide such as Bordeaux mixture and repeat if necessary.

Leaf spot

Numerous different fungi and some bacteria cause spots on leaves. Most of these diseases are specific to one type of host plant, and are unlikely to spread to other plants. They overwinter on leaf debris, but good garden hygiene and the removal of all leaves reduce the severity of attack. Various fungicides, such as captan, maneb and zineb, can be used to control leaf spot, and copper sprays such as Bordeaux mixture are also effective. Apply the fungicide after the removal of dead leaves, and give a further application a fortnight later. Trees susceptible to attacks should be sprayed in spring.

The fungi frequently attack only the leaves of plants lacking in vigour, and trouble may be prevented by correct feeding during the growing season.

Leafy gall (*Corynebacterium fascians*)

This bacterial disease may affect many types of plants. It is soil-borne, and the bacteria enter through wounds. Infected plants are not killed, but produce numerous abortive shoots, often fasciated and with thickened, distorted leaves. The disease is spread by propagating from diseased stocks, by infected implements and sometimes by seeds as with lathyrus and nasturtium.

There is no chemical control; infected plants should be destroyed.

Lettuce virus diseases

A number of viruses, including ARABIS MOSAIC and CUCUMBER MOSAIC VIRUSES, may affect lettuce. The seed-borne lettuce mosaic virus causes dwarfing of plants which bear crinkled and mottled leaves. Seeds certified to be virus-free are available.

Several of the viruses which affect lettuce are transmitted by organisms in the soil, and lettuces should, where possible, be grown on a fresh site annually. Other viruses are aphid-transmitted, and these pests should be controlled. Destroy diseased plants 'as soon as the first symptoms are seen.

Lilac blight (*Pseudomonas syringae*)
A bacterial disease which enters the leaves of syringa and spreads down into the shoots. Pockets of the bacteria form in the outer tissues, and remain viable for several years. Cut infected shoots back to healthy buds, and spray with Bordeaux mixture. Spray again the following spring.

Lily disease (*Botrytis elliptica*)
This serious fungal disease of lilium affects especially *L. candidum*, *L. regale* and *L. × testaceum*, but most species can be infected in the seedling stage. The fungus, which is most prevalent in wet seasons, attacks stems and leaves only, and it is unnecessary to destroy bulbs of infected plants.

Control the disease by spraying all plants with a copper fungicide, such as Bordeaux mixture or liquid copper, giving the first application soon after the leaves appear in spring. Repeat at fortnightly intervals until flowering and, during a wet season, spray again after flowering.

Magnesium deficiency
A lack of magnesium—one of the constituents of chlorophyll—shows as discoloration of the foliage. The leaves may have yellow bands between the veins, and brilliant orange, brown and red tints may also develop. Magnesium is likely to be deficient in light, acid soils, and also on other types of soils after heavy rain. An excess of potash in the soil makes magnesium unavailable to plants, and deficiency symptoms commonly develop on plants, such as tomatoes which have been fed with high-potash fertilisers.

Correct the trouble by spraying with a solution of magnesium sulphate (Epsom salts), at the rate of $\frac{1}{2}$ lb. to $2\frac{1}{2}$ gal. of water plus a spreader such as soft soap. Spray tomatoes as soon as the first symptoms are seen and thereafter regularly at seven to ten-day intervals. Fruit trees should be sprayed at petal-fall and thereafter two or three times at fortnightly intervals. Magnesium sulphate dust may also be raked into the soil at the rate of 1 oz. per sq. yd, but is easily leached out by rain.

Manganese deficiency
A lack of manganese is often found in sandy and alkaline soils, and frequently occurs with iron deficiency. The typical symptom is chlorosis, beginning on the older leaves, but in certain crops, such as garden peas, a well-characterised disease (marsh spot) shows as brown, circular patches and hollow seeds.

A trouble known as speckled yellows develops on beetroots and shows as red-brown speckling of the leaves. Manganese deficiency can be corrected by spraying plants with a solution of manganese sulphate (2 oz. to $2\frac{1}{2}$ gal. of water plus spreader) or by watering the soil with a solution of 10 oz. manganese sulphate to $6\frac{1}{4}$ gal. water. Iron chelate compounds and fritted trace elements containing manganese may also be used on alkaline soils.

Mildew: see DOWNY MILDEW and POWDERY MILDEW

Mineral deficiencies
All plants require a number of nutrient elements for healthy growth. Deficiency of nitrogen, phosphorus and potassium are unlikely to occur where general fertilisers are regularly applied, but neglected trees and shrubs often show varying symptoms. It may be difficult to determine which food material is lacking, as more than one may be deficient at the same time. Ensure that all plants receive the necessary food materials by applying correct fertilisers.

See also BORON DEFICIENCY, CHLOROSIS, MAGNESIUM DEFICIENCY, MANGANESE DEFICIENCY, POTASH DEFICIENCY and WHIPTAIL.

Mint rust (*Puccinia menthae*)
This fungus attacks various mentha species and may be serious on forced plants under glass. It also attacks savory. The first stage of the fungus appears in spring on the thickened and distorted shoots, and shows as CLUSTER CUP RUST bearing orange spores. These infect the leaves of healthy plants, as do the yellow summer spores. Black overwintering spores form on the leaves towards the end of the season; these germinate the following spring and produce yet another type of spore, which infects new rhizomes and stems. The fungus thereafter becomes systemic within all parts of an infected plant.

Establish a mint bed only from healthy rhizomes. Disease-free plants may be obtained by washing the cuttings in cold water and immersing them in water at a temperature of 41–46°C (105–115°F) for ten minutes; plunge in cold water before planting out. Although healthy when planted, such plants can become re-infected. Some control of the disease can be achieved by burning off the withered top growth of the mint bed in autumn or early winter.

Mosaic
A term used to describe certain symptoms caused by VIRUS DISEASES. This applies particularly to green leaves that show pale green mottling or spotting on a darker green background. Mosaic may also show as yellow mottling or blotching against the normal green background.

Mould
A term loosely used to describe any type of fungal growth on rotting plant tissues. See also BLUE MOULD, GREY MOULD and LEAF MOULD.

Mushroom diseases
Several fungal and bacterial diseases affect mushrooms, but are usually only serious on a commercial scale. Bacterial blotch, which causes mushrooms to become discoloured and sticky, is usually encouraged by high temperatures, by moist conditions and by inadequate ventilation.

Correct cultural treatment should prevent the trouble, but if it does occur, water with a sodium hypochlorite solution or chlorinated water. This treatment, as well as dusts or sprays of zineb or quintozene, will control certain other diseases of mushrooms.

The symptoms caused by the various diseases are similar, and expert advice should be sought before carrying out any corrective treatment. VIRUS DISEASES which also attack mushrooms can only be controlled by steam sterilising an infected bed.

Narcissus fire (*Sclerotinia polyblastis*)
This fungal disease is most troublesome in the West Country, and during wet seasons may cause considerable rotting of narcissus flowers. GREY MOULD spores develop on infected parts, and the disease is spread to the leaves. The fungus overwinters on debris, and spores cause infection the following spring.

Control this disease by destroying infected leaves to remove the overwintering stage. In the spring, plants showing infection should be removed, and the remainder sprayed, when 1 in. high, with thiram. Repeat at ten-day intervals until the flower buds emerge from the leaf sheaths.

Narcissus virus diseases
Several different virus diseases affect narcissus. Some, including ARABIS MOSAIC VIRUS, are transmitted by soil-borne eelworms; others, such as narcissus yellow stripe virus and CUCUMBER MOSAIC VIRUS, are spread by aphids. The symptoms vary greatly according to the viruses involved, the narcissus variety affected and the environmental conditions, and it is seldom possible to determine which virus is present.

All plants showing yellow striping and mottling of the foliage should be removed and burnt during spring.

Oedema
This common trouble may occur on the foliage of many types of plants, but is most frequently found on ivy-leaved pelargonium, camellia, succulent and semi-succulent plants. It is due to excess moisture in the soil and/or the atmosphere, and too high temperatures. The infected leaves should not be removed, and drier air and soil conditions will usually cause infected plants to recover.

In the greenhouse, provide adequate ventilation and keep the plants just moist; pot plants may benefit from being repotted in a lighter compost. Outdoors, lighten the soil by incorporating plenty of humus-rich material and improve drainage.

Oedema occasionally occurs as a reaction to chemical sprays of insecticide or fungicide —petroleum oil used to control fruit tree red spider mites may cause oedema on tomatoes. The damage can usually be rectified by discontinuing spraying.

Paeony wilt (*Botrytis paeoniae*)
This disease, also known as paeony blight, may be serious, particularly in wet seasons. It may cause considerable die-back of tree and herbaceous paeonies, the latter often being killed completely. The fungus forms at the stem bases of herbaceous plants and on or just below flower buds on tree paeonies; it shows as a dense GREY MOULD and spreads to form brown blotches on leaves of adjacent plants. Later in the season, small black resting bodies develop on infected tissues and germinate the following spring.

Cut out and burn all infected shoots; on herbaceous paeonies, cut back to well below ground level. Dust the crowns of plants with copper dust, and spray the plants with captan, thiram or zineb soon after the leaves appear. Repeat at fortnightly intervals until flower buds show, and again after flowering.

Pansy sickness
A fungus disease of violas showing symptoms similar to those of BLACK ROOT ROT and

RHIZOCTONIA. The soil-borne organisms enter the roots or stem tissues at ground level, causing these to rot, and infected plants collapse. Resting bodies are produced in the diseased tissues and remain viable for several years in debris in the soil. Violas are best grown on a different site each year.

Control the disease by watering seedlings and established plants with Cheshunt compound; repeat if necessary at weekly intervals. Sprinkle 4 per cent calomel dust in the holes before planting. Remove and destroy diseased plants, making sure that no roots are left in the soil.

Parsnip canker

Canker is the most troublesome and widespread disease of parsnips, causing various forms of rotting of the shoulder tissues during the autumn and winter. A number of fungi are responsible for canker, the most common showing as a superficial rot of the tissues. During the autumn the fungus also attacks the leaves which have small brown spots with green haloes. Another fungus causes a black rot of the roots, and small fruiting bodies of this fungus are often embedded in the rotting tissues. Yet another fungus results in rotting deep in the tissues at the crown and on the shank. Cankers that show as shallow orange lesions at the shoulder may be due to a PHYSIOLOGICAL DISORDER.

There are no effective control measures, but some reduction in the incidence of canker may be obtained by growing parsnips in deep, limy loam and by manuring with a balanced fertiliser. Crop rotation should be practised, and the seeds sown early, thinning the seedlings to about 3 in.

The variety 'Avonresister' is resistant to the fungus disease causing superficial rotting.

Peach leaf curl (*Taphrina deformans*)

A fungal disease common on almonds, apricots, nectarines, peaches and related ornamental prunus species. The fungus shows as masses of white spores on the surface of red swollen leaves. The spores may infect developing leaves during the growing season; others overwinter on the bud scales. The following spring, the overwintered spores germinate and enter the leaves inside the developing buds, so that the young leaves are already infected as they emerge.

Control the disease by spraying with lime-sulphur, or Bordeaux mixture, in January or February and again a fortnight later; spray again just before leaf-fall in autumn.

Peach mildew (*Sphaerotheca pannosa* var. *persicae*)

This POWDERY MILDEW disease is due to a fungus which forms a thick mealy coating on leaves, buds and fruits of peaches and nectarines. In severe cases growth is restricted. The fungus overwinters in the buds and as small, black fruiting bodies on the shoots. Spores are produced in spring from the fruiting bodies, and from the diseased leaves as they emerge.

Cut out all infected shoots well below the area of the disease. Spray with sulphur at the first sign of the disease; repeat at fortnightly intervals. Dryness at the roots encourages mildew, but this can be counteracted by mulching and careful watering. Wall-trained trees should be kept sufficiently away from the walls to ensure circulation of air.

Pear scab (*Venturia pirina*)

A fungus disease of pears that infrequently attacks eriobotrya. Pear scab occurs annually, but varies in intensity and is most severe after a wet May. The fungus overwinters on fallen leaves and on young shoots which show small blister-like pimples.

Partial control can be achieved by burning fallen leaves and by cutting out diseased shoots. Complete control is possible by spraying with captan at green-cluster, white-bud and petal-fall stages; repeat at fortnightly intervals if necessary until mid-July.

Petal blight (*Itersonilia perplexans*)

A serious disease on outdoor chrysanthemums in wet seasons, and under glass in too humid an atmosphere. It causes browning and subsequent death of petal tissue. It may also be troublesome on dahlias, cornflowers, anemones and globe artichokes. Vast numbers of fungus spores spread from the diseased petals; the fungus overwinters on chrysanthemum stools and on various weeds.

In the greenhouse, prevent the disease by maintaining adequate heat and ventilation. Spray or dust plants, outdoors and under glass, with zineb, just before the flower buds open and weekly as necessary.

Physiological disorders

For healthy plant growth certain factors are essential: water supply; mineral salts; atmosphere; temperature; and light. If any of these conditions are lacking, a physiological disorder may occur. The water supply must be continuous, although the amount required varies at different growth stages. Troubles occur when the water supply is deficient or irregular or in excess of the plants' normal requirements.

Mineral salts should be present in the soil in correct quantities and in an available form (see MINERAL DEFICIENCIES). If the atmosphere is too humid, OEDEMA occurs or fungal diseases may develop; a too dry atmosphere may cause poor growth and flower buds may drop. Temperatures either too high or too low produce various symptoms, described under the specific genera. Lack of light leads to thin, weak, colourless plants, and flowering may be reduced or cease.

Physiological disorders are often due to a combination of these factors and can only be corrected by improved growing conditions, such as feeding, mulching, watering or drainage, and spacing. Badly neglected plants may take several years to recover; sprays of foliar feeds, at ten-day intervals during the growing season, are beneficial.

Potassium deficiency

Potassium is one of the major requirements, and lack of it causes growth to become stunted and the leaves to turn dull blue-green. Browning occurs at the tips (tip-burn) or at leaf margins (rim-fire), or small brown spots may develop in irregular patches (scorch). Leaves of broad-leaved plants curl downwards towards the undersurfaces. Apples, pears and currants are particularly affected by lack of potassium.

In cases of slight deficiency, other troubles may develop more readily, such as CHOCOLATE SPOT and RUST on broad beans or the lack of flower production on herbaceous plants. Potassium is often deficient in light, peaty, or chalky soils, but is easily remedied by applying potassic fertilisers.

Potato blackleg (*Erwinia carotovora* var. *atroseptica*)

This bacterial disease appears on potatoes in June. It is a systemic disease, the bacteria infecting all parts of the plant, although one or two healthy stems may develop. Severely infected plants may die before tubers form, or they become infected as the bacteria pass along the underground stems. Some tubers are destroyed entirely while others may be only slightly infected when lifted. Infection of healthy tubers can occur at lifting time through direct contact with a diseased tuber.

Badly infected tubers decay in store; if slightly diseased tubers are planted, the infection will be present the following season. The disease does not spread from plant to plant, and there is little danger of the soil remaining contaminated unless numerous bacteria are present. Destroy infected plants and all rotten tubers. Ideally, purchase only certified seed potatoes.

Potato blight (*Phytophthora infestans*)

A serious fungal disease of potatoes, and occasionally tomatoes, with a number of different races. It may develop at any time between May and August, but is most prevalent during June and July, beginning in the west and spreading eastwards across the country. In dry weather the yellow-brown patches on the leaves turn brown and shrivel up, but in wet weather the fungus can be seen on the undersurfaces of the leaves as a mass of white fungal threads. The spores are spread by wind or are washed down into the soil, infecting healthy haulms and tubers near soil level. Severe rotting of haulms and tubers may occur in a wet season; infected tubers suffer from a dry rot, but the disease does not spread in store.

Bacteria often enter diseased tissues, causing a SOFT ROT which spreads to affect all stored tubers. The fungus overwinters in diseased potatoes, and blighted seed tubers should never be planted. Spray the plants at intervals of 10–14 days, particularly in a wet season, with maneb or zineb, or a copper fungicide such as Bordeaux mixture, giving the first application before the tops meet in the rows. Some varieties are certified resistant to most blights.

Powdery mildews

These numerous, closely related fungi produce a white powdery coating of spores on stems and leaves—often on both surfaces—and in some plants they also affect flowers and fruits. The short-lived spores, which produce the white powdery coating, are formed in spring and summer; they overwinter on the host plants in various ways. Some survive on the shoots as fungal threads which produce new spores in early spring; others overwinter within the buds of infected shoots, and emerging leaves will already be diseased. Yet other types of fungi produce fruiting bodies which overwinter on diseased tissues, and which give rise, the following spring, to different spores.

Some species of mildew attack a wide range of plants, while others are specific to a given host plant. The symptoms are similar and should be treated in the same way. Remove all diseased shoots in autumn to destroy the overwintering stage. During spring and summer, spray at fortnightly intervals with dinocap; on asters, spray with a copper fungicide, and on chrysanthemums and begonias, spray or dust with sulphur. In greenhouses, fumigate with dinocap.

Powdery mildew fungi are encouraged by humid atmospheres, and the greenhouse should be adequately ventilated. Plants are more susceptible if the soil is allowed to dry out, and mulching and watering in spring and summer discourage powdery mildews.

See also AMERICAN GOOSEBERRY MILDEW, APPLE MILDEW, PEACH MILDEW and STRAWBERRY MILDEW.

Powdery scab (*Spongospora subterranea*)

A disease, also known as corky scab of potatoes, which occasionally affects tomatoes and related plants. It is caused by a soil-inhabiting fungus, and tubers planted in infected soil are likely to become diseased. The raised scabs burst open to release a brown powder of spore masses. The disease may also transmit a VIRUS DISEASE, known as 'mop top'.

There is no chemical treatment for this disease, but crop rotation should be practised; destroy diseased tubers.

Pyracantha scab (*Fusicladium pyracanthae*)

This fungal disease shows as a thick, felt-like olive-brown or black coating on the leaves and berries of pyracantha; the spore masses resemble soot. The fungus overwinters in scabby lesions on the shoots, and all diseased shoots should be cut out. Control by spraying with captan at fortnightly intervals, beginning as soon as the disease is seen.

Raspberry virus diseases

These are grouped according to the manner in which viruses are spread.

Viruses spread by aphids: the several raspberry viruses differ according to variety, the virus involved and environmental conditions, but the symptoms are usually referred to as 'raspberry mosaic'. The most typical symptom is yellow blotching of the leaves, and occasional distortion. The varieties 'Lloyd George' and 'Malling Jewel' are the most susceptible.

Virus spread by leafhoppers: this virus, also known as 'rubus stunt', affects raspberries, but hybrid berries, blackberries and loganberries are also susceptible. The symptoms show as numerous dwarf and spindly shoots with a WITCHES' BROOM appearance.

Viruses spread by eelworms: different soil-borne viruses, including ARABIS MOSAIC VIRUS, may infect raspberries. The disease, known as 'raspberry yellow dwarf', is common in England, and particularly affects 'Malling Exploit'; infected plants produce only a few stunted canes with yellow-speckled leaves, and yield little or no fruit. 'Raspberry leaf curl' is common in eastern Scotland, but rare in England; infected plants are killed or produce a large proportion of distorted fruiting laterals. The following year these show conspicuous concentric rings of dark and light colours. 'Norfolk Giant' is most susceptible, and 'Malling Jewel' may show similar symptoms. 'Malling Promise' and 'Malling Exploit' merely show a diffuse yellow mottling of the leaves, while 'Lloyd George' is immune.

Viruses spread by other means: the trouble known as 'bushy dwarf disease' is a virus spread by seeds, which induces severe dwarfing in 'Lloyd George'. The virus can also be carried by plants of 'Norfolk Giant', which show no symptoms, and these two varieties should not be grown near each other. The diseases 'curly dwarf' and 'yellow blotch', most common in Scotland, attack chiefly the variety 'Lloyd George', but their method of spread is unknown.

There is no effective chemical control of these virus diseases, but the vectors—aphids, leafhoppers and eelworms—should be controlled with suitable pesticides. Infected plants should be destroyed as soon as the first symptoms are noticed. Purchase only canes certified to be free of virus, and plant preferably on a fresh site; it is advisable to grow resistant varieties.

Ray blight (*Mycosphaerella ligulicola*)

This fungal disease on the petals of greenhouse chrysanthemums spreads most rapidly under humid conditions when the temperature reaches 16 °C (61 °F). Some control can be achieved by reducing the humidity and by removing infected plants. Complete sterilisation or changing of the soil is the most effective measure.

Prevent outbreaks of the disease by spraying with captan or maneb at ten-day intervals after planting out. Apply at the rate of ¾ oz. of 50 per cent wettable powder to 2½ gal. water.

Reversion

The virus which causes this serious disease of black currants shows in early summer as leaves that are smaller and with fewer lobes than normally, on long, basal shoots. It is transmitted by BLACK CURRANT GALL MITE, and the most characteristic symptoms are produced on the flower buds which are hairless and bright magenta.

Diseased bushes will, over the years, cease to yield a good crop, but as this may be due to FROST DAMAGE, poor pollination or a deficiency of potassium, leaf and flower-bud symptoms should be verified before the disease can be determined. A certain measure of control can be obtained by spraying against the vector, but in severe outbreaks, all diseased bushes are best destroyed. Purchase stock certified as being virus-free.

Rhizoctonia (syn. *Corticium solani*)

A fungal disease of a wide range of plants, the symptoms depending on the host plant, and on the timing of infection. Seedlings may be attacked and are then damaged by DAMPING-OFF. On established plants COLLAR, CROWN, FOOT, ROOT and STEM ROTS usually develop after an attack of rhizoctonia, and the foliage becomes discoloured; plants may collapse completely. The disease may cause BASAL ROT of bulbs such as lilies.

The fungus is probably present in most soils, living on weed hosts or on humus; it exists as microscopic fungal threads and occasionally produces small black resting bodies which perpetuate the disease. It is usually only serious under poor cultural conditions and in unsterilised compost under glass. Use sterilised compost, and outdoors prevent serious damage by using seed dressings such as captan and thiram. On herbaceous plants, all rotting tissues and dead roots and those with brown patches should be removed, and the crowns dusted with

quintozene. Rake this fungicide into the soil before replanting.

Quintozene should not be used on cucumbers, marrows and melons.

Rhizome rot (*Erwinia carotovora*)

This bacterial SOFT ROT is a widespread disease of rhizomatous irises, particularly during wet seasons. The soil-inhabiting bacteria, which are encouraged by poor drainage, enter through wounds.

Prevent the disease by avoiding bruising of the rhizomes and dust with a dry copper dust such as Bordeaux powder. Kill slugs where these are known to be troublesome. All badly infected plants should be destroyed; on less severely diseased plants, the rotting parts may be cut out and the wounds dusted with copper.

Rhododendron bud blast (*Pycnostysanus azaleae*)

This disease, which is prevalent in southern England, may cause considerable damage to flower buds of evergreen rhododendron species and hybrids. The first symptoms appear between October and December, when infected buds turn grey or brown. The fungus is not apparent until the spring when it develops on diseased buds as black, bristle-like structures, each bearing a pin-head of fungus spores from which the disease spreads. The fungus enters only through wounds, and is thought to be transmitted by rhododendron leafhoppers.

Control the vectors (see rhododendron leafhopper in chapter on PESTS).

Root rot

Many symptoms, such as discoloration of foliage, premature leaf-fall, die-back of shoots or complete collapse of plants, are often due to rotten roots. Rotting may be caused by too wet or too dry soil conditions or by different fungal diseases, including BLACK ROOT ROT and RHIZOCTONIA. Such diseases are most likely to occur under poor cultural conditions, and seed dressings of captan or thiram may be beneficial.

Generally, there is no effective chemical control, as the plants are beyond saving by the time the symptoms appear. Watering with captan, Cheshunt compound or zineb may occasionally be successful. The fungicide nabam is effective in controlling root rot disease of chrysanthemums.

Herbaceous plants may be lifted and all rotting roots cut off before they are replanted in well-prepared soil on a different site. Rotation of vegetable crops and bedding plants usually checks the disease, which overwinters on debris and may build up colonies in the soil. In the greenhouse, the use of sterilised compost usually prevents root rot; if an outbreak does occur, infected seedlings should be destroyed.

Rotting

A term describing the breakdown of tissues. It is not always due to a disease, but frequently occurs as a result of secondary bacteria and fungi which enter through injured tissues.

Russeting

Roughening of the skin of apples, pears and other fruits. It is often a natural characteristic. It may also be a disease symptom caused by APPLE MILDEW, FROST DAMAGE, or by fungicides such as Bordeaux mixture or lime-sulphur used on lime-shy varieties.

Rust

In popular usage, this term is applied to brown or black spots on foliage, but a rust fungus is a plant parasite with a complex life cycle. There are five different spore forms in the complete life cycle of a rust fungus, as for example in mint rust. Some rust fungi have a short life cycle, the chrysanthemum rust forming only one type of spore.

Certain rusts spend their entire life on one type of host plant or on closely related plants, while others migrate from one host to a completely unrelated host. Spore stages may develop only on the areas of infection, but some rusts become systemic, the fungal threads spreading through a complete stem or whole plant. Rusts can be difficult to control; all diseased leaves should be burnt, particularly at the end of the season, to destroy the overwintering stages. If rust appears regularly on perennial plants, these are better destroyed as the fungus is probably systemic within all the tissues. Specific control measures are described here according to the host plants.

Vegetables and herbs: rusts are most troublesome on plants suffering from POTASSIUM DEFICIENCY; by correcting this trouble rust may not reappear. Control measures are usually not required, but severely diseased runner and dwarf beans may be dusted with sulphur. In autumn, burn to destroy the overwintering fungal stages.

Plants under glass: on chrysanthemums and carnations, rusts are encouraged by high humidity. Increase the ventilation, remove diseased leaves and destroy severely infected plants. Spray the plants with maneb, thiram or zineb at 10–14 day intervals. On pelargoniums, use thiram and zineb alternately at weekly intervals.

Annuals and perennials: remove and burn diseased leaves and spray with maneb, thiram or zineb at fortnightly intervals. Rust is more prevalent on plants grown under adverse conditions, but on *Dianthus barbatus* rust is most severe on soft lush growth, and these plants do best in soils not enriched with a nitrogenous fertiliser. Althaea is particularly susceptible to rust, and new plants should be raised every other year. Antirrhinum, too, is extremely rust-prone, but resistant varieties are now readily available, and are usually listed as such in catalogues.

Conifers: most of the rusts which affect conifers have a long life cycle; they have two different host plants. The rusts which affect abies have ferns as their alternate hosts; those which infect juniperus also attack sorbus, crataegus and certain other rosaceous plants; larix rusts infect populus and salix; a rust of picea completes its cycle on rhododendron, and a rust of pinus affects cineraria. The types of host plants should preferably not be grown in the vicinity of each other, particularly in the case of juniperus and sorbus. Rusts on the needles only, generally require no control measures, but branches with swellings and WITCHES' BROOMS should be cut out to a point 6 in. below the apparently diseased area. Similar symptoms may occur on other branches the following season.

Trees and shrubs, including fruit: on these hosts, rusts are only likely to be troublesome if the plants are suffering from

malnutrition or too dry soil conditions; these can be remedied by feeding, mulching and watering. Remove diseased leaves from small shrubs, such as buxus, mahonia, rhododendron and roses, and spray at fortnightly intervals with maneb, thiram or zineb. The fungus occasionally becomes systemic within shoots of species roses and appears annually in spring as bright orange patches on stems and leaf stalks; cut out and burn diseased shoots.

See also CLUSTER CUP RUST, MINT RUST and WHITE RUST.

Scab

A general term used to describe discoloured, brown or rough patches on the skin of fruits and vegetables.

Scald

A term applied to any skin injury of fruit caused by strong sun. In hot summers, apples may show sun scald as discoloured patches surrounded by a halo; plums may have red sunken patches. Most scalding occurs under glass, and tomatoes, grown too near the glass, often bear cream-white wrinkled patches. The flesh underneath may be undamaged, but affected fruits should be removed or they may be attacked by GREY MOULD.

Greenhouse grapes are extremely susceptible to scald, sunken areas developing on the shoulder of affected berries. Damping down the greenhouse should be carried out early in the day so that the moisture on the fruits can dry out before the sun becomes too strong. Give adequate ventilation.

Sclerotinia disease (*Sclerotinia sclerotiorum*)

This serious fungal disease affects a wide range of cultivated and weed plants. It usually produces a SOFT ROT of root crops in store, but may also cause rotting of herbaceous plants outdoors or under glass. The fungus shows on diseased tissues as a fluffy white mass which contains large black resting bodies; these overwinter in the soil or on decaying tissues.

Burn all rotting material and store only sound roots; good storage conditions are essential. Outdoors and under glass, infected plants should be destroyed; although the fungal threads are easily killed by soil sterilisation, the resting bodies remain.

Scorching

A term applied to the rapid discoloration and death of patches of the upper leaf tissues, affected areas becoming pale brown. Scorching, caused by cold drying winds, commonly occurs on young, soft foliage of acer and fagus. Plants outdoors and under glass may be scorched by hot sun, especially if they are lacking in vigour or if the soil is too dry. See also SCALD.

Little can be done to improve the condition of affected plants, but diseased leaves should be removed to prevent the entry of secondary fungi such as GREY MOULD. As new leaves develop, spray with a .foliar feed at 10–14 day intervals to encourage vigour. Outdoors, keep plants watered and mulched to conserve moisture.

Symptoms similar to scorching can occur as a result of a particular chemical insecticide. POTASSIUM DEFICIENCY occasionally causes a browning of the foliage on apples and pears which resembles scorching.

Seedling blight (*Alternaria zinniae*)

This seed-borne fungus disease of zinnias often spreads to healthy plants by means of spores produced on the diseased leaf and stem areas. Seeds which have been treated with a fungicidal seed dressing are sometimes offered; otherwise dust the seeds with captan prior to sowing. Protect seedlings in boxes by spraying with zineb or a copper-containing fungicide such as Bordeaux mixture. Once the disease has appeared, no chemical control is effective; destroy infected plants.

Shanking

This is a PHYSIOLOGICAL DISORDER of grapes due to the inadequate functioning of the root system and/or overcropping. Shrivelling of berries usually indicates that the vine is suffering from malnutrition or an irregular moisture supply; the trouble appears too late in the season to improve the condition of the berries, and most of them will be lost. Every effort should be made to determine the cause of the trouble, and may involve tracing the roots of old vines back to the active feeding roots. Carry out any necessary soil improvements before the next growing season.

Shothole

A term applied to holes in leaves caused by the falling away of dead tissues. The symptoms may be caused by leaf-spotting fungi, particularly on beet, horseradish and spinach, but may also be due to BACTERIAL CANKER.

Shothole of cherries, nectarines, peaches, plums and ornamental prunus species, is caused by a specific fungus disease. Considerable shotholing of the leaves occurs with a thin brown line around each hole. The fungus responsible is a weak parasite and is only likely to attack the foliage of trees lacking in vigour.

Control the disease by feeding annually, and by mulching and watering copiously in spring; small trees respond to foliar feeds. If the trouble occurs again the following season, spray at the first sign with a copper fungicide, using half-strength applications at intervals of 14–21 days during the summer months and one full strength just before leaf-fall.

Silver leaf (*Stereum purpureum*)

This fungal disease, common on plums and particularly on 'Victoria', may also cause dieback of branches or complete death of trees and shrubs. The fungus commonly lives as a saprophyte on dead wood; the air-borne spores can enter only through wounds. Fungal threads develop within the branch, and a toxin is produced which passes upwards in the sap. This poison causes air to develop just below the upper leaf surfaces, and the foliage of infected trees, with the exception of rhododendron, takes on a silvery appearance. In severe cases the leaves may become brown.

Die-back of shoots and branches eventually occurs, and fruiting bodies develop on the dead wood. These may be flat or bracket-shaped, overlapping each other like tiles; they are brown-purple, maturing to pale fawn or brown. The numerous spores spread the disease especially in damp weather.

Infected branches develop inner brown or purple stains. The presence of the disease can be ascertained by examining the cross-section of a cut branch, 1 in. across. If a stain is visible, the branch should be cut back to 6 in. below the point where the stain ceases. Coat the pruning cut with a fungicidal paint; by feeding and general care it is sometimes possible to save a tree once infected branches have been cut out.

Smuts (*Urocystis, Entyloma* species)
These plant parasites, some of which are seed-borne, live as fungal threads throughout affected plants, but the symptoms are not apparent until the black sooty spore masses are produced. Diseased plants are not killed and continue to grow normally, but new crops of spores are produced annually and spread to infect healthy plants.

Smut fungi are systemic within most infected plants, and these should be destroyed. On calendulas, the infection is restricted to the leaves; it can be controlled by burning infected leaves and spraying with a copper fungicide. Smut on phoenix can usually be controlled by cutting out and burning the infected leaf areas.

Spray healthy plants with a copper fungicide, such as Bordeaux mixture, and disinfect the frames or greenhouses.

Soft rot (*Erwinia carotovora*)
A bacterial disease of tissues which reduces them to a soft, mushy, evil-smelling rot. The bacteria enter through damaged tissues, and are most commonly found on plants which are grown too soft, or in badly drained soil. Bulbs and root vegetables stored in moist conditions are also susceptible.

Soft rot may also occur on forced bulbs if the tissues have been injured. Infected plants, bulbs and vegetables should be destroyed. Prevent the disease by suitable cultural methods and correct storage; injured tissue parts should be cut out before the bacteria can enter.

Splitting
This occurs on the skins of fruit and tomatoes and in root crops, such as carrots; it is due to an irregular supply of moisture. Once the trouble has appeared, no corrective treatment can be carried out, but splitting can be prevented by ensuring even growth and by mulching and watering.

Spray damage
Certain plants are susceptible to injury by insecticides and fungicides, some apple varieties and all yellow-fruited gooseberries being sulphur-shy. Copper fungicides may cause RUSSETING of apples, and SCORCHING of weak roses and rhododendrons. The fungicide dinocap often causes yellow streaks on the foliage of chrysanthemums and begonias. White-oil sprays may cause OEDEMA on tomatoes, and many insecticides are injurious to certain plants; it is essential to read the manufacturers' instructions on insecticides and fungicides before use.

Much damage results from the use of hormone-type weedkillers. Roses, tomatoes, cabbages and other brassicas are susceptible and show characteristic symptoms: the leaves become cup-shaped, the vein pattern in leaves becomes parallel, and the shoots show a spiral twisting. Accidental damage can occur by drift if a hormone weedkiller is used on a windy day. Plants may also be injured by the use of a badly rinsed watering can or spraying machine; special apparatus should be kept solely for the use of weedkillers. Do not use lawn mowings from a freshly treated lawn for mulching.

Plants injured by selective weedkillers usually grow out of the symptoms in due course, and crops such as tomatoes can safely be eaten. Brassica plants, however, are usually so severely injured that they fail to crop and should be discarded as soon as the trouble is recognised. Occasionally plants show symptoms of hormone damage after dressings of farmyard manure contaminated with an agricultural herbicide. It is advisable to check that no such weedkillers were used.

Spur blight (*Didymella applanata*)
This fungal disease of raspberries and loganberries infects the canes in June, but the first symptoms are seldom seen before August. Black pin-point fruiting bodies on discoloured patches on the canes produce spores which spread the disease to healthy plants; the fungus overwinters on the canes. Old infected canes should be thinned out immediately after fruiting, and superfluous young canes should be removed early. Spray the plants with Bordeaux mixture or liquid copper at bud-burst and again when the tips of the flowers show white. Alternatively, spray with captan at bud-burst stage only.

Stem canker (*Nectria cucurbitula,* etc.)
A fungal disease of picea which produces red fruiting bodies on dead bark. The fungus enters through wounds, usually following frost damage, and causes girdling and dieback of infected shoots. Cut out all dead shoots to clean living tissues, and coat the wounds with a fungicidal paint.

Stem rot
A term applied to rotting of stems due to a fungal disease. Various fungi may be responsible, but the most common cause is the GREY MOULD fungus. Stem rot is spread by fungus spores, and all diseased tissues should be cut out and burnt. Spray the plants with captan, thiram or zineb, or a copper fungicide such as Bordeaux mixture.

See also CARNATION STEM ROT and DIE-BACK.

Storage rots
Rotting generally occurs only on damaged bulbs, corms and vegetable crops or if these were already diseased when placed in store. All crops should be stored under cool, dry conditions; they should be examined periodically and any rotting material should be destroyed.

See also BLUE MOULD, SCLEROTINIA DISEASE and SOFT ROT.

Strawberry mildew (*Sphaerotheca macularis*)
This fungal disease of strawberries shows on the lower leaf surfaces and on fruits as a thin coating of floury white spores. The disease overwinters and new spores are produced the following spring.

Prevent the disease from overwintering by destroying old leaves at the end of the season. Dust affected plants with dinocap or sulphur, at intervals of seven to ten days after the fruits have been picked.

Strawberry virus diseases
A number of virus diseases infect strawberries; they are spread by different vectors and are arranged here accordingly.

Virus diseases spread by aphids: these pests spread the common diseases known as CRINKLE

and YELLOW EDGE. Control the spread of the diseases by spraying against aphids as advised in the chapter on PESTS.

Virus diseases spread by eelworms: the serious, soil-borne ARABIS MOSAIC VIRUS affects varieties to a differing degree. Generally, the leaves are distorted and mottled or blotched with yellow. 'Royal Sovereign' and 'Cambridge Favourite' become severely stunted. If the disease is serious, strawberries should not be grown on the same site again.

All infected plants produce diseased runners, and only healthy plants should be used for propagation. Destroy severely infected plants and replenish with stock certified to be virus-free.

Tar spot (*Rhytisma acerinum*)
A fungal disease, specific to acer, particularly *A. pseudoplatanus*. Black blotches of fruiting bodies develop on the leaves, and the fungus overwinters on fallen leaves to begin fresh infection the following year. Control the disease by burning all diseased leaves as they fall. Small trees may be sprayed in spring, as the leaves unfold, with a copper containing fungicide or captan.

Tobacco mosaic virus
There are various strains of this infectious virus, the most common strain causing TOMATO VIRUS DISEASES. Other strains may infect cacti and orchids, as well as herbaceous solanaceous plants. The various symptoms caused by this virus are described under the generic entries.

The disease survives in debris in soil, and infection may be spread through the roots. There is no effective chemical control, and all diseased plants and their roots should be destroyed. See also VIRUS DISEASES.

Tomato spotted wilt virus
This virus is transmitted by thrips to a wide range of plants. It generally shows as mosaic or mottling on the foliage, which may be distorted. The disease is most troublesome in the greenhouse, occurring on tomatoes and frequently on house plants, but it may also infect herbaceous plants outdoors.

All plants showing symptoms of virus infection should be destroyed immediately, and the thrips should be controlled. See section on PESTS.

Tomato virus diseases
Tomatoes are susceptible to a number of virus infections, spread by vectors such as aphids, thrips and eelworms. CUCUMBER MOSAIC VIRUS causes mottling with dark green areas on the foliage, and the young leaves are often reduced to half their width or to corkscrew-like tendrils, a trouble known as fern leaf. The symptoms resemble those caused by SPRAY DAMAGE.

Tomato aspermy virus causes plants to become bushy; the distorted foliage shows mottling or yellow spotting. The rare tomato black ring virus appears as small black rings on young leaves, and as dark streaks on petioles and stems; the leaves become black and shrivelled at the growing points and the plants die.

Young plants infected with TOMATO SPOTTED WILT VIRUS usually die; on established plants young leaves develop transparent veins and ring spots. Later, bronzing spreads over the leaf surfaces, the upper leaves curl downwards, and growth is checked. The fruits are pale, irregularly mottled or with distinct concentric rings. TOBACCO MOSAIC VIRUS is the common virus disease of tomatoes. Various strains of the virus cause different symptoms, such as mottling with dark and light green areas on the leaves. The trouble is less severe on young plants, which frequently yield a good crop if they are fed regularly. The aucuba mosaic strain shows as bright yellow spots and patches on leaves and fruits. Yet another strain causes brown marks on leaves and leaf stalks and brown stripes on the stems; the fruits are blotched with brown.

Potato virus X may infect tomatoes together with tobacco mosaic, and the developing fruits have raised brown markings.

All plants showing virus symptoms should be destroyed, making sure that no infectious debris remains in the soil; greenhouse pests should be controlled by spraying. Purchase only tomato seeds that are certified to be free of virus infection.

Tulip fire (Botrytis tulipae)
This serious fungal disease of tulips is encouraged by cold wet weather in early spring. The infection is often soil-borne, or may be spread by planting infected bulbs. The fungus shows on infected tissues as GREY MOULD. Small black resting bodies, which develop between the outer skin and the scales, overwinter in the soil.

Destroy all diseased plants, including the bulbs. Prevent the disease by spraying with thiram, maneb or zineb, commencing when the plants are 1–2 in. high; repeat at ten-day intervals until flowering. When lifting, destroy diseased bulbs and dust the remainder with quintozene; this fungicide should also be raked into the soil before replanting healthy bulbs in autumn.

Verticillium wilt (Verticillium species)
A disease caused by various species of the fungus, and affecting a wide range of host plants, including dianthus. It may also occur on some shrubs and trees. The fungus is soil-borne, existing on debris as fungal threads, or as resting bodies in the soil. The fungus infects young roots, but on established plants enters only through wounds. The fungal threads pass into the inner tissues, and a brown discoloration appears on the leaves and stems. Diseased plants wilt.

Diseased herbaceous plants should be dug up and burnt. On shrubs, usually only one or two branches are affected; the dead shoots should be cut back to living tissues, and the wounds coated with a fungicidal paint. Further die-back may occur in due course, but trees and shrubs are rarely killed.

Destroy diseased plants in the greenhouse, and if possible isolate the infected soil from adjacent healthy plants.

See also ASTER WILT.

Violet root rot (Helicobasidium purpureum)
This fungus, which attacks a wide range of host plants, including ornamental plants and fruit crops, is most troublesome on vegetables. It is particularly serious on asparagus. The fungus is soil-borne and attacks the underground parts of plants, which become covered with a violet or purple web of fungal threads. The resting bodies remain viable for a long time and produce further spores.

There is no chemical treatment, and all infected plants should be lifted and destroyed. Isolate the infected area by sinking pieces of

corrugated iron 12 in. deep. Asparagus should not be grown on the same site for several years thereafter.

Virus diseases
Viruses are microscopic particles, capable of causing disease in living cells; they can only enter plant tissues through wounds.

Viruses cause a number of different symptoms, such as colour changes in leaves, stems, flowers and tubers, distortion of organs, the development of outgrowths, killing of tissues, wilting and stunting of growth. One virus may cause different symptoms in one type of plant, while on the other hand similar symptoms may be caused by entirely different viruses. More than one virus may infect a plant at the same time, and different combinations of viruses cause different symptoms.

Viruses may be transmitted by handling plants, by vegetative propagation and grafting, and some viruses are seed-borne. Most viruses, however, are spread by vectors, such as aphids, eelworms, leafhoppers, mites, thrips and whiteflies. A few viruses are spread by soil-borne fungi.

There is no chemical treatment for virus-infected plants, and severely diseased plants should be destroyed. Only healthy plants should be used for propagation, and on purchasing new stock this should, where possible, be certified as free of viruses. Good garden hygiene and the control of vectors help to prevent virus diseases.

Wart disease (Synchytrium endobioticum)
A soil-borne fungal disease of potatoes, which survives in the soil as resting spores. These produce spores which infect the developing tubers and cause large warty outgrowths, particularly near the eyes. New resting spores are produced in the warts and pass into the soil as the tubers disintegrate.

This is a Notifiable Disease, and any occurrence of it must be reported to the Ministry of Agriculture. All new potato varieties are immune to the disease, but some of the older ones are not. All diseased tubers should be destroyed.

Whiptail
A disorder due to a deficiency of molybdenum. It affects broccoli and cauliflowers, causing distortion and a reduction of the leaf blade to the midrib, giving the leaves a tail-like appearance. Molybdenum is occasionally deficient in acid soils, but can easily be corrected by applying a solution of sodium molybdate; 1 oz. to 2 gal. water will treat 10 sq. yds of soil.

White blister (Albugo species)
This fungal disease affects several wild and cultivated plants belonging to the Cruciferae and Compositae families. The disease is more unsightly than crippling, showing as glistening white patches on the leaves. Fungal threads and resting bodies develop in infected leaves, and the spores overwinter in diseased debris. No control measures are necessary other than cutting off and burning diseased leaves.

White rot (Sclerotium cepivorum)
This fungus disease affects mainly salad onions and seedlings, but may also occur on maincrop onions, leeks, shallots and garlic. It is most troublesome in warm summers, and

if plants are grown too close together. The fungus overwinters in the soil as small black resting bodies, which the following year attack developing plants, covering them with masses of white threads. The fungus may remain viable in the soil for up to eight years, and onions should be grown on a new site every year. Otherwise, dust the seed drills with 4 per cent calomel dust, at the rate of 1 lb. to each 25 yds. Destroy affected plants.

White rust (Puccinia horiana)
A serious fungal disease of chrysanthemums, rarely encountered because of strict quarantine measures.

White rust is a Notifiable Disease, and any outbreak of it should be reported to the local Plant Health Inspector, or the Ministry of Agriculture. All diseased plants must be destroyed immediately.

Wilt
A term describing the collapse of shoots or whole plants. Wilting may be due to a number of causes, such as PHYSIOLOGICAL DISORDERS, FUSARIUM WILT and VERTICILLIUM WILT.

Winter killing
This trouble chiefly occurs on wallflowers. It may cause the death of plants, although sometimes only side-shoots die back. The GREY MOULD fungus is responsible following FROST DAMAGE. This trouble is most common on plants that have been grown too soft in soil containing too much nitrogen; late-planted specimens may suffer.

Prevent injury by dressing seed beds, boxes and planting sites with a complete fertiliser. Set out plants as early as possible so that they are fully established before winter.

Wire stem (Rhizoctonia solani)
This disease affects brassica and other seedlings. In young seedlings, it causes DAMPING-OFF, but later attacks show as a browning and shrinking at the stem bases which break off easily. The seedlings do not necessarily die, but may remain stunted. Prevent the trouble by raising seedlings in sterilised compost, or by raking quintozene into the soil before sowing in the open.

Witches' brooms (Taphrina species, etc.)
A term applied to the abnormal development of several shoots, all growing from one point and crowded together on infected branches of woody plants. The brooms are usually erect and can easily be seen among the larger branches. The disease is chiefly due to a fungus which may also affect the foliage and cause blistering of the leaves.

Treat the disease by cutting out infected branches to a point 6 in. below the broom; coat the wounds with a protective paint.

Yellow edge
This is an aphid-borne virus disease of strawberries and shows as yellow edges on young leaves. The leaves are abnormally small, and infected plants have a dwarfed and flattened appearance. The plants deteriorate and yield a small crop of worthless fruits.

The symptoms are most obvious in September, but can also be easily recognised in April. Several varieties, particularly 'Royal Sovereign', are highly susceptible. Destroy diseased plants and spray regularly to control aphids. See chapter on PESTS.

PLANTS FOR SPECIAL PURPOSES

The following categories are intended as a guide to plants suitable for growing in particular soils and/or aspects. The lists also group genera with outstanding features, such as foliage and fruits. By necessity, the categories do not include all the genera described in the Encyclopaedia, and not all species of a given genus can be considered suitable for a particular purpose. For detailed advice, the lists should be consulted in conjunction with the individual generic entries.

The footnotes on the following pages contain abbreviations additional to those under the group headings.

Annuals and biennials
H = hardy; H/h = half-hardy

Ageratum H/h	Centaurea H	Eschscholzia H	Lavatera H	Nemesia H/h	Sanvitalia H/h
Alyssum H	Chrysanthemum H	Godetia H	Limonium H, H/h	Nemophila H	Silene H
Anchusa H	Clarkia H	Gypsophila H	Linaria H, H/h	Nicotiana H/h	Tagetes H/h
Antirrhinum H, H/h	Convolvulus H, H/h	Helichrysum H, H/h	Linum H	Nigella H	Thunbergia H/h
Begonia H	Coreopsis H	Helipterum H, H/h	Lobelia H/h	Papaver H	Tropaeolum H, H/h
Brachycome H/h	Cosmos H/h	Iberis H	Malcolmia H	Phlox H/h	Ursinia H, H/h
Calandrinia H, H/h	Delphinium H/h	Impatiens H/h	Matthiola H, H/h	Platystemon H	Verbena H/h
Calendula H	Dianthus H/h	Ipomoea H/h	Mesembryan-	Reseda H, H/h	Viola H
Callistephus H/h	Eccremocarpus H/h	Lathyrus H, H/h	themum H/h	Salvia H/h	Zinnia H/h

Bulbs, corms and tubers for outdoor planting
N = for naturalising; V = spring-flowering; S = summer-flowering; A = autumn-flowering; W = winter-flowering

Acidanthera S	Chionodoxa N, W, V	Dahlia S	Galtonia S	Lilium N, S, A	Ranunculus S
Allium N, V, S	Colchicum N, A, V	Endymion N, V	Gladiolus S	Muscari N, V	Scilla N, W, V
Alstroemeria S	Crocosmia N, S	Eranthis N, W, V	Hyacinthus N, W, V	Narcissus N, V	Sparaxis V
Amaryllis A	Crocus N, W, V, A	Freesia S	Iris N, W, V, S	Nerine bowdenii A	Sternbergia A
Anemone N, V	Cyclamen N, W, V,	Fritillaria N, V	Ixia S	Ornithogalum N, V	Tulipa N, V
Begonia S	S, A	Galanthus N, W, V, A	Leucojum N, V, A, W	Pleione V	Zantedeschia S, A

Climbers and wall shrubs
N = north and east-facing walls; S = south and west-facing; * = self-clinging

Abelia S	Ceanothus S	Embothrium S	Jasminum N/S	Passiflora S	Trachelospermum N *
Abutilon S	Celastrus N	Fremontia S	Kerria N/S	Polygonum N/S	Tropaeolum N
Actinidia N	Clematis N	Garrya S	Lonicera N/S	Pyracantha N/S	Vitis S
Aristolochia S	Clerodendrum S	Hedera N/S *	Olearia S	Rosa S	Wistaria N/S
Campsis S *	Eccremocarpus S	Hibiscus S	Parthenocissus N *	Solanum S	

Greenhouse and house plants
C = greenhouse with no heating; Cl = cool greenhouse, min. 7–10°C (45–50°F); W = warm greenhouse, min. 13–16°C (55–61°F); H = house plant

Abutilon Cl	Aphelandra W, H	Caladium W	Chrysanthemum Cl, H	Cordyline C/Cl, H	Diplacus C/Cl
Achimenes W	Aporocactus W, H	Calanthe W, H	Cineraria Cl, H	Cotyledon Cl, H	Dipladenia Cl
Adiantum Cl/W, H	Ardisia Cl, H	Calathea W, H	Cirrhopetalum W	Crassula Cl, H	Dizygotheca W, H
Aechmea W, H	Aristolochia W	Calceolaria Cl, H	Cissus Cl, H	Crinum C, H	Dracaena W, H
Aërangis W	Asclepias W	Callistemon Cl	Citrus Cl, H	Crossandra W, H	Eccremocarpus C/Cl
Aërides W	Aspidistra Cl, H	Camellia C/Cl	Cleistocactus Cl, H	Cryptanthus W	Echeveria C/Cl, H
Aeschynanthus W	Asplenium Cl/W, H	Campanula Cl, H	Clerodendrum W	Cuphea Cl, H	Echinocactus Cl, H
Agave Cl, H	Astrophytum W, H	Canna W	Clianthus Cl	Cyclamen Cl, H	Echinocereus Cl, H
Aglaonema W, H	Begonia Cl/W, H	Capsicum Cl, H	Clivia W, H	Cymbidium Cl/W	Echinopsis Cl, H
Allamanda W	Beloperone Cl, H	Cassia Cl	Cocos W, H	Cyperus Cl, H	Eichhornia Cl
Aloe Cl, H	Bougainvillea Cl	Cattleya W	Codiaeum W, H	Datura Cl, H	Epidendrum Cl/W, H
Alstroemeria Cl	Bouvardia Cl, H	Celosia Cl, H	Coelogyne Cl/W	Davallia Cl, H	Epiphyllum Cl/W, H
Ananas W	Brodiaea Cl	Cereus Cl, H	Coleus W, H	Dendrobium Cl/W, H	Erica C/Cl, H
Angraecum W	Browallia Cl	Cestrum Cl	Columnea W	Dianthus C/Cl	Erythrina Cl
Anthurium W, H	Brunfelsia W	Chlorophytum Cl, H	Conophytum Cl, H	Dieffenbachia W, H	Euphorbia Cl, H

A = annual/biennial; Aq = aquatic plant; B = bulb, corm or tuber; C = climber or wall shrub;
E = evergreen; F = fern; G = greenhouse plant; M = marginal plant; P = perennial; S = shrub or sub-shrub; T = tree

Exacum Cl, H
× Fatshedera Cl, H
Faucaria Cl, H
Ferocactus Cl, H
Ficus W, H
Fittonia W, H
Freesia Cl
Fritillaria C
Fuchsia Cl, H
Gardenia W, H
Gasteria Cl, H
Gerbera Cl
Gloriosa Cl
Grevillea Cl
Guzmania W, H
Gynura W, H
Haemanthus Cl, H
Haworthia Cl, H
Hedera C, H
Hedychium Cl
Heliocereus Cl, H
Heliotropium Cl
Helxine C/Cl, H
Hibiscus Cl
Hippeastrum Cl, H

Howea W, H
Hoya Cl/W, H
Hydrangea Cl, H
Hymenocallis Cl, H
Impatiens Cl, H
Ipomoea W
Jacobinia Cl, H
Kalanchoe Cl, H
Kohleria Cl, H
Lachenalia Cl, H
Laelia W
Lampranthus Cl, H
Lantana Cl, H
Lapageria C/Cl
Leptospermum C/Cl
Leycesteria C
Lilium C/Cl
Limonium Cl
Lippia Cl
Lithops Cl, H
Lobivia Cl, H
Lophophora Cl, H
Luculia Cl
Lycaste W
Mammillaria Cl, H

Maranta W, H
Maurandia Cl
Maxillaria W
Mesembryanthemum Cl
Miltonia W
Mimosa Cl
Monstera W, H
Musa W
Neoregelia W, H
Nephrolepis W, H
Nerine Cl, H
Nerium Cl
Nidularium W, H
Notocactus Cl, H
× Odontioda W
× Odontocidium W
Odontoglossum W
× Odontonia W
Olearia C/Cl
Oncidium W
Opuntia Cl, H
Oxalis C/Cl
Pancratium Cl, H
Pandanus W, H

Paphiopedilum H
Parochetus C/Cl
Passiflora Cl/W
Pelargonium Cl, H
Peperomia W, H
Pereskia Cl
Peristrophe Cl, H
Phalaenopsis W
Philesia C/Cl
Philodendron W, H
Phoenix Cl, H
Phormium C/Cl
Pittosporum C/Cl
Platycerium W, H
Plectranthus Cl, H
Pleione C/Cl, H
Plumbago Cl
Polianthes Cl
Polygala Cl
× Potinara W
Pteris Cl, H
Punica C/Cl, H
Puschkinia Cl
Rebutia Cl, H
Rechsteineria W, H

Reinwardtia Cl
Rhipsalidopsis Cl, H
Rhodohypoxis Cl
Rhoeo W, H
Rhoicissus Cl, H
Ricinus Cl
Rochea Cl, H
Ruellia W
Saintpaulia W, H
Salpiglossis Cl
Sansevieria W, H
Sarracenia C/Cl
Saxifraga C/Cl, H
Schefflera Cl, H
Schizanthus Cl, H
Schlumbergera Cl, H
Scindapsus W, H
Scutellaria W
Sedum Cl, H
Senecio Cl
Setcreasea Cl/W, H
Sinningia W, H
Smithiantha Cl, H
Solanum Cl, H
Sonerila W

Sophronitis W
Sparaxis C/Cl
Sparmannia Cl, H
Spathiphyllum W, H
Sprekelia Cl, H
Stapelia W, H
Stephanotis W
Strelitzia Cl
Streptocarpus W, H
Streptosolen Cl
Tecoma Cl
Teucrium C/Cl
Thunbergia Cl
Tibouchina Cl, H
Tillandsia Cl/W, H
Torenia Cl, H
Tradescantia Cl/W, H
Tritonia Cl
Vanda W
Vriesea W, H
× Vuylstekeara W
× Wilsonara W
Zantedeschia Cl, H
Zebrina Cl/W, H
Zygopetalum W

Plants that require acid soil
*= suitable for peat beds or walls

Arctostaphylos S, T *
Calluna S *
Camellia S
Daboecia S *

Enkianthus S
Erica S *
Eucryphia S
Fothergilla S

Gaultheria S *
Gentiana P *
Heaths and heathers
Kalmia S

Lapageria C
Lilium B *
Lithospermum P *
Magnolia S, T

Menziesia S
Nomocharis B *
Nyssa T
Pernettya S *

Philesia S *
Phyllodoce S *
Rhododendron S *
Vaccinium S *

Plants that thrive in alkaline soil
(they also grow in all fertile soils)

Acantholimon P
Acanthus P
Acer T
Achillea P
Aesculus T
Aethionema S
Alchemilla P
Allium P, B
Althaea A, P
Alyssum A, P
Anaphalis P
Anchusa P
Anemone P, B
Anthemis P
Aquilegia P
Arabis P
Arctotis A
Armeria P
Artemisia P
Aster P
Astilbe P
Aubrieta P
Aucuba S
Bellis P
Bergenia P
Buddleia S
Buxus S
Campanula P
Carpinus T
Caryopteris S
Catananche P
Ceanothus S
Cedrus T
Centaurea P, A

Centranthus P
Ceratostigma S
Chaenomeles S
Chamaecyparis T, S
Cheiranthus P
Chicory P
Chimonanthus S
Chionodoxa B
Chrysanthemum A, P
Cistus S
Clarkia A
Clematis C, P
Colchicum B
Convallaria P
Convolvulus A, P, S
Coreopsis A, P
Cornus S
Cosmos A
Cotoneaster S
Crataegus S, T
Crocosmia B
Crocus B
× Cupressocyparis T
Cupressus T
Cyclamen B
Cytisus S
Dahlia P
Delphinium A, P
Deutzia S
Dianthus P
Dicentra P
Dimorphotheca A, P
Doronicum P
Echinops P

Echium A, P
Elaeagnus S
Endymion B
Eranthis B
Erigeron P
Erinus P
Eryngium P
Erysimum P
Escallonia S
Euonymus S
Euphorbia A, P, S
Fagus T
Filipendula P
Forsythia S
Fuchsia S
Gaillardia P
Galanthus B
Gazania P
Genista S
Geranium P
Geum P
Gladiolus B
Godetia A
Gypsophila A, P
Helenium P
Helianthemum S
Helianthus P
Helichrysum A, P, S
Helleborus P
Hemerocallis P
Hesperis P
Heuchera P
Hibiscus syriacus S
Hippophae S

Hosta P
Hyacinthus B
Hypericum P, S
Hyssopus S
Iberis A, P
Ilex S, T
Iris B, P
Jasminum S, C
Juniperus S
Kerria S
Kniphofia P
Laburnum T
Lathyrus A, P, C
Lavandula S
Lavatera A
Leucojum B
Libocedrus T
Ligustrum S
Lilium (some) B
Linaria A, P
Linum A, P
Lobelia A, P
Lonicera S, C
Lunaria A, P
Lupinus A, P, S
Lychnis A, P
Magnolia (some) S, T
Mahonia S
Malcolmia A
Malope A
Malus T
Matthiola A, P
Mesembryanthemum A, P

Muscari B
Myosotis A, P
Narcissus B
Nemesia A
Nemophila A
Nepeta P
Nigella A
Paeonia P
Papaver A, P
Parthenocissus C
Penstemon P, S
Petunia A
Philadelphus S
Phlox A, P
Physostegia P
Picea T
Pinus T
Polemonium P
Polygonatum P
Polygonum P, C
Potentilla P, S
Primula (some) P
Prunus T
Pulmonaria P
Pulsatilla P
Pyracantha S
Pyrethrum P
Ranunculus P
Rhus S
Ribes S
Rosmarinus S
Rudbeckia A, P
Salvia A, P, S
Sambucus S

Sanguisorba P
Santolina S
Saxifraga P
Scabiosa A, P
Scilla B
Sedum P
Sempervivum P
Sidalcea P
Silene A, P
Solidago P
Sorbus T
Spartium S
Spiraea S
Stachys P
Symphoricarpos S
Syringa S
Taxus S, T
Thalictrum P
Thuja S, T
Thymus S
Tilia T
Tradescantia P
Trollius P
Tulipa B
× Venidio-arctotis A
Verbascum A, P
Verbena A, P
Veronica P
Viburnum S
Vinca P
Viola A, P
Weigela S
Wistaria C
Zinnia A

A= annual/biennial; Aq= aquatic plant; B= bulb, corm or tuber; C= climber or wall shrub;
E= evergreen; F= fern; G= greenhouse plant; M= marginal plant; P= perennial; S= shrub or sub-shrub; T= tree

Plants with aromatic foliage

Artemisia S	Geranium P	Lippia S	Myrtus S. T	Perowskia S	Salvia S
Balm P	Hyssopus S	Marjoram P	Nepeta P	Populus T	Santolina S
Dictamnus P	Laurus S. T	Mentha P	Origanum P	Rosmarinus S	Tanacetum P
Eucalyptus T	Lavandula S	Monarda P	Pelargonium S. G	Sage S	Thyme S

Plants for bedding out
*= for spring display

Abutilon S	Campanula A, P	Dahlia P	Hyacinthus B *	Nemesia A	Ricinus A, S
Ageratum A	Canna A	Dianthus A, P	Impatiens A	Nicotiana A	Salpiglossis A
Alonsoa A	Celosia A	Diascia A	Kochia A	Nierembergia A	Salvia A
Alyssum A	Centaurea S	Dimorphotheca A	Lampranthus P	Onopordum A	Sanvitalia A
Anemone B *	Cheiranthus A *	Echeveria P	Lantana S	Papaver A	Scabiosa A
Antirrhinum A, P	Chlorophytum P	Echium A	Lathyrus A	Pelargonium S	Silene A, P
Arabis P *	Chrysanthemum A, P	Eucalyptus S	Limonium A. P	Penstemon P	Tagetes A
Arctotis A	Cineraria A	Felicia A	Linaria A	Perilla A	Torenia A
Aubrieta P *	Cleome A	Fuchsia S	Lobelia A	Petunia A	Tropaeolum A, P
Begonia B	Coleus P	Gazania P	Lupinus A	Phacelia A	Tulipa B *
Bellis A *	Collinsia A	Gilia A	Malope A	Phlox A	Ursinia A
Brachycome A	Cordyline S	Gladiolus B	Mentzelia A	Platystemon A	Venidium A
Browallia A	Cosmos A	Gomphrena A	Mirabilis A	Portulaca A	Verbena A
Calceolaria A	Crocus B *	Helichrysum A	Molucella A	Primula P *	Vinca P
Calendula A	Cuphea S	Heliotropium S	Myosotis A *	Rehmannia A	Viola A, P *
Callistephus A	Cynoglossum A	Helipterum A	Narcissus B *	Reseda A	Zinnia A

Plants for cut flowers
*= everlasting or suitable for drying

Achillea P *	Callistephus A	Digitalis A, P	Helichrysum A, P *	Monarda P	Silene A. P
Acidanthera B	Catananche A, P *	Doronicum P	Helipterum A *	Narcissus B	Solidago P *
Agapanthus P	Centaurea P *	Echinops P *	Heuchera P *	Nigella A *	Sparaxis B
Alstroemeria P	Cheiranthus P	Erigeron P	Iberis A	Oenothera P	Trollius P
Anaphalis P *	Chrysanthemum P	Eryngium P *	Iris B. P	Paeonia P	Tulipa B
Anemone P	Clarkia A	Gaillardia A, P	Lathyrus A	Phlox P	Valeriana P
Anthemis P	Coreopsis A, P	Geum P	Lilium B	Physostegia P	× Venidio-arctotis P
Antirrhinum A, P	Cortaderia P *	Gladiolus B	Limonium A, P *	Pyrethrum P	Verbascum A, P
Aquilegia P	Cosmos A	Godetia A	Lupinus P	Reseda A *	Verbena A, P *
Aster P	Dahlia A. P	Gypsophila A, P	Lychnis P	Rudbeckia P	Zantedeschia B
Astilbe P *	Delphinium A, P	Helenium P	Matthiola A	Scabiosa P	Zinnia A *
Calendula A	Dianthus A. P	Helianthus A. P	Molucella A *	Schizostylis P	

Plants for foliage effect

Autumn colour	Parthenocissus C	Euphorbia P	Sedum P	Thuja T. S/E	Ilex S/E
Acer T	Populus T	Salvia P	Sempervivum P	Thyme P/E	Iris P
Cercidiphyllum T	Quercus T	Santolina S	Tellima P		Lamium P
Cryptomeria T. S/E	Rhus S	Saxifraga P		**Variegated leaves**	Ligustrum S/E
Enkianthus S	Taxodium T	Sedum P	**Suffused yellow or**	Actinidia C	Mentha P
Erica S/E	Vitis C	Sempervivum P	**gold**	Ajuga P	Miscanthus P
Ginkgo T		Zauschneria P	Calluna S/E	Aucuba S/E	Pittosporum S/E
Hamamelis S	**Grey or silver-leaved**		Catalpa T	Cornus S	Sage S/E
Larix T	Alchemilla P	**Suffused red, purple**	Chamaecyparis T. S/E	Elaeagnus S/E	Scrophularia P
Liquidambar T	Artemisia P. S	**or copper**	Juniperus S/E	Euonymus S/E	Sedum P
Liriodendron T	Centaurea P. S	Ajuga P	Ligustrum S/E	Hebe S/E	Thyme P/E
Osmunda F	Cupressus T/E	Cotinus S	Robinia T	Hedera S, C	Ulmus T
Parrotia S. T	Eucalyptus T	Epimedium P	Sambucus S	Hosta P	Vinca S/E

Plants with fragrant flowers

Acidanthera B	Daphne S	Hamamelis S	Lathyrus A	Myrtus S	Robinia T
Angraecum P. G	Dendrobium P. G	Heliotropium S. G	Lavandula S	Narcissus B	Rosa S
Aponogeton P	Dianthus P	Hesperis P	Lilium B	Nicotiana A	Stephanotis C. G
Buddleia S	Erica S	Hoya C. G	Lonicera C	Philadelphus S	Syringa S
Cheiranthus A	Freesia B. G	Hyacinthus B	Magnolia S. T	Polianthes B	Verbena A
Chimonanthus S	Gardenia S. C	Iris B, P	Malcolmia A	Primula P	Viburnum S
Convallaria P	Genista S. G	Jasminum C	Matthiola A. P	Reseda A	Viola A. P

A= annual/biennial; Aq= aquatic plant; B= bulb, corm or tuber; C= climber or wall shrub;
E= evergreen; F= fern; G= greenhouse plant; M= marginal plant; P= perennial; S= shrub or sub-shrub; T= tree

Plants for ground cover
*= suitable for shade

Acaena P	Cotoneaster S	Helianthemum S	Mahonia S *	Pulmonaria P *	Thymus P
Ajuga P *	Dianthus P	Helxine P *	Oxalis P *	Saponaria P	Tiarella P *
Aubrieta P	Dryas P	Hosta P *	Pachysandra P *	Saxifraga P *	Tolmiea P *
Bergenia P *	Euonymus S *	Hypericum S *	Phlox P *	Sedum P	Vaccinium S
Brunnera P	Gaultheria S	Juniperus S	Polygonum P	Stachys P	Veronica P
Cornus P *	Geranium P *	Lamium P *	Potentilla P	Tellima P *	Vinca P *

Plants for hedges

Aucuba S/E	Crataegus S, T	Euonymus S/E	Ilex S, T/E	Prunus S, T/E	Santolina S/E
Berberis S/E	× Cupressocyparis	Fagus T	Lavandula S/E	Pyracantha S/E	Syringa S
Buxus S/E	T/E	Forsythia S	Ligustrum S/E	Quercus T/E	Tamarix S
Carpinus T	Deutzia S	Fuchsia S	Lonicera S/E	Ribes S	Taxus T/E
Chamaecyparis T/E	Elaeagnus S/E	Hippophae S	Olearia S/E	Rosa S	Thuja T/E
Cornus S	Escallonia S/E	Hypericum S	× Osmarea S/E	Rosmarinus S/E	Viburnum S/E

Plants for herbaceous borders
*= require staking

Acanthus P	Catananche P	Galega P	Linum P	Phormium P	Schizostylis P
Achillea P	Centaurea P	Galtonia P	Lobelia P	Phygelius P	Scrophularia P
Aconitum P	Centranthus P	Gentiana P *	Lupinus P	Physalis P	Sedum P
Agapanthus P	Chelone P	Geranium P *	Lychnis P	Physostegia P	Senecio P
Alchemilla P	Chrysanthemum P *	Geum P *	Lysimachia P	Phyteuma P	Sidalcea P
Allium B	Cimicifuga P	Glaucium P	Lythrum P	Phytolacca P	Silybum P
Alstroemeria P *	Clematis P *	Gypsophila P *	Macleaya P	Platycodon P *	Sisyrinchium P
Althaea P	Coreopsis P *	Helenium P	Malva P	Podophyllum P	Smilacina P
Anaphalis P	Crocosmia B	Helianthus P	Matthiola P	Polemonium P *	Solidago P *
Anchusa P *	Curtonus B	Heliopsis P *	Meconopsis P	Polygonatum P	Stachys P
Anemone P	Cynoglossum P *	Helipterum P	Mertensia P	Polygonum P *	Stipa P
Anthemis P *	Delphinium P *	Helleborus P	Mimulus P	Portulaca P	Stokesia P
Anthericum P	Dianthus P	Hemerocallis P	Miscanthus P	Potentilla P *	Symphytum P
Aquilegia P	Dicentra P	Hesperis P *	Monarda P	Primula P	Tellima P
Argemone P	Dictamnus P	Heuchera P	Morina P	Pulmonaria P	Thalictrum P
Armeria P	Dierama P	Hosta P	Myosotidium P	Pulsatilla P	Thermopsis P
Arnebia P	Digitalis P	Houttuynia P	Myosotis P	Pyrethrum P *	Tradescantia P
Artemisia P	Doronicum P	Incarvillea P	Narcissus B	Ranunculus P *	Trillium P
Asclepias P	Echinacea P	Inula P	Nepeta P	Rheum P	Trollius P
Aster P *	Echinops P	Iris P	Nicotiana P	Rodgersia P	Tulipa B
Astilbe P	Echium P *	Kniphofia P	Oenothera P	Romneya P	Valeriana P
Astrantia P	Eremurus P	Lamium P	Onopordum P	Roscoea P	Venidium P
Baptisia P	Erigeron P *	Lathyrus P	Paeonia P *	Rudbeckia P	Veratrum P
Bergenia P	Eryngium P *	Lavatera P	Papaver P *	Ruta P	Verbascum P
Brachycome P	Eupatorium P	Leucojum B	Pennisetum P	Salvia P *	Veronica P *
Brunnera P	Euphorbia P	Liatris P	Penstemon P *	Sanguisorba P	Wulfenia P
Caltha P	Filipendula P *	Lilium B	Phalaris P	Sanvitalia P	Zantedeschia P
Camassia B	Fritillaria P	Limonium P	Phlomis P	Saponaria P *	Zauschneria P
Campanula P *	Gaillardia P *	Linaria P	Phlox P *	Scabiosa P	Zinnia A

Plants with ornamental fruits
*= fleshy fruits; †= dry fruits

Arbutus T, S *	Celastrus C *	Hippophae S *	Malus T *	Ruscus S *	Taxus S, T *
Ardisia S *	Chaenomeles S *	Hypericum S † *	Physalis A, P † *	Skimmia S *	Tsuga T †
Aucuba S *	Cotoneaster S, T *	Ilex S, T *	Phytolacca P *	Solanum A *	Typha P †
Berberis S *	Crataegus S, T *	Lunaria A, P †	Pyracantha S *	Sorbus T *	Vaccinium S *
Capsicum A *	Gourds A *	Mahonia S *	Rosa S *	Symphoricarpos S *	Viburnum S *

Plants for pools or pool margins

Astilbe M	Hosta (some) M	Lythrum M	Osmunda M, Aq	Ranunculus M, Aq	Taxodium M, Aq
Caltha M	Iris (some) M, Aq	Matteuccia M	Polygonum M	Saggitaria M, Aq	Trollius M
Eichhornia Aq	Juncus M, Aq	Mimulus M	Pontederia P, Aq	Scirpus M, Aq	Typha M, Aq
Filipendula M	Lysimachia M	Nymphaea Aq	Primula P	Symphytum M	Zantedeschia M, Aq

A = annual/biennial; Aq = aquatic plant; B = bulb, corm or tuber; C = climber or wall shrub;
E = evergreen; F = fern; G = greenhouse plant; M = marginal plant; P = perennial; S = shrub or sub-shrub; T = tree

Plants for rock gardens

*= for scree and/or dry walls; †= suitable for the alpine house; §= suitable for paved areas

Acantholimon P † * §
Achillea P §
Aethionema P † * §
Alyssum P † * §
Androsace P † * §
Anemone P, B †
Aquilegia P †
Arabis P † * §
Arenaria P † * §
Armeria P † * §
Artemisia P † * §
Aubrieta P * §

Campanula P † §
Chamaecyparis (dwarf) S †
Cheiranthus P † §
Chionodoxa B † §
Chrysanthemum P † §
Corydalis P † *
Cotoneaster S * §
Crocus B † §
Cyananthus P † * §
Cyclamen B †
Cytisus S * §

Daphne S † * §
Dianthus P † * §
Erigeron P
Erodium P † §
Erysimum P † * §
Genista S † * §
Gentiana P † * §
Geranium P † §
Helianthemum S † * §
Hepatica P
Hyacinthus B
Hypericum S † * §

Iberis P † * §
Ionopsidium A † §
Iris B, P, † §
Juniperus S † * §
Leontopodium P † * §
Linaria P † * §
Lithospermum P † * §
Muscari B † §
Myosotis P † * §
Narcissus B † §
Oenothera P §

Oxalis P, B † §
Papaver P §
Penstemon P, S † * §
Phlox P † * §
Polygonum P §
Potentilla P, S † * §
Primula P † §
Pulsatilla P †
Ramonda P † *
Ranunculus P †
Rhododendron (dwarf) S † §

Salix (dwarf) S † * §
Saponaria P † * §
Saxifraga P † * §
Scilla B † §
Sedum P † * §
Sempervivum P † * §
Silene P † * §
Thymus P † * §
Tulipa B † §
Veronica P † * §
Viola P † §

Plants for seaside gardens

Acer T
Achillea P
Agapanthus P
Anemone P, B
Anthemis P
Antirrhinum A, P
Arbutus T
Arctotis A
Armeria P
Aster P
Aubrieta P
Buddleia A
Calluna S
Caryopteris S
Ceanothus S
Centaurea P

Chaenomeles S
Chamaecyparis T
Chionodoxa B
Chrysanthemum A, P
Colchicum B
Cordyline S, E
Coreopsis A, P
Cotoneaster S, T
Crocus B
× Cupressocyparis T
Cupressus T
Cyclamen B
Cytisus S
Dianthus P
Dimorphotheca A, P
Elaeagnus S

Erica S
Eryngium P
Escallonia S
Euonymus S
Euphorbia A, P, S
Forsythia S
Fuchsia S
Garrya S
Gazania P
Genista S
Geranium P
Griselinia S
Gypsophila P
Hebe S
Helianthemum S
Hippophae S

Hydrangea S
Hypericum S
Iberis A, P
Ilex S
Iris B, P
Juniperus S, T
Kniphofia P
Lathyrus A, P
Lavandula S
Ligustrum S
Limonium A
Linaria A, P
Linum A, P
Lobelia A, P
Lupinus arboreus S
Matthiola A

Mesembryanthemum A
Myosotis A
Narcissus B
Nepeta P
Olearia S
Papaver A, P
Penstemon A, P
Phacelia A
Phlomis P, S
Pinus T
Pittosporum S
Polygonum P, C
Potentilla S
Pyracantha S
Romneya P

Rosmarinus S
Rudbeckia P
Salvia A, P, S
Santolina S
Scilla B
Sedum A, P
Sempervivum P
Senecio S
Spartium S
Spiraea S
Stachys P
Tamarix S
Ulex S
× Venidio-arctotis P
Veronica P
Yucca S

Plants for shade

*= suitable for dry area

Anemone P *
Aquilegia P
Asperula P
Astilbe P
Athyrium F
Aucuba S
Bergenia P
Cimicifuga P

Convallaria P
Cyclamen B *
Digitalis A, P
Dryopteris F
Endymion B *
Epimedium P
Eranthis B
Erythronium B

× Fatshedera S
Fothergilla S
Galanthus B
Helleborus P
Heuchera P
Hosta P
Hypericum P, S *
Lamium P *

Lilium B
Mahonia S
Matteuccia F
Onoclea F
Oxalis P *
Pachysandra P
Podophyllum P
Polygonatum P

Polypodium F *
Polystichum F
Primula P
Pulmonaria P
Rhododendron S
Ruscus S *
Stuartia S, T
Symphoricarpos S

Tiarella P
Tolmiea P
Trillium P
Trollius P
Vaccinium S
Veratrum P
Vinca P *
Viola P

Plants for sunny dry banks

Acantholimon P
Achillea P
Alyssum P
Arabis P
Armeria P
Aubrieta P
Calandrinia A, P

Cerastium P
Cheiranthus P
Cistus S
Convolvulus P, S
Crocus B
Cytisus S
Dianthus P

Eryngium P
Eschscholzia A
Genista S
Gypsophila P
Helianthemum S
Hypericum S
Iberis A, P

Juniperus S
Linaria A, P
Linum A, P
Mesembryanthemum A, P
Nepeta P
Portulaca A

Rosmarinus S
Ruta S
Santolina S
Sedum P
Sempervivum P
Spartium S
Tamarix S

Thymus S
Tulipa B
Ulex S
Verbascum P
Weigela S
Yucca S
Zauschneria P

Trees and shrubs for small gardens

Acer T
Berberis S/E
Buxus S/E
Calluna S/E
Camellia S/E
Ceanothus S/E
Chaenomeles S
Choisya S/E

Cistus S/E
Cotoneaster S/E
Crataegus T
Cytisus S
Daphne S/E
Deutzia S
Erica S/E
Escallonia S/E

Euonymus S/E
Fuchsia S
Genista S
Grevillea S/E
Hebe S/E
Hydrangea S
Hypericum S/E
Ilex S, T/E

Juniperus S/E
Kerria S
Laburnum T
Lavandula S/E
Lonicera S/E
Magnolia S
Mahonia S/E
Malus T

Philadelphus S
Phlomis S/E
Potentilla S
Prunus T
Rhododendron S/E
Ribes S/E
Rosa S
Santolina S/E

Skimmia S/E
Sorbus S, T
Spiraea S
Symphoricarpos S
Symplocos S
Syringa S
Viburnum S/E
Weigela S

A= annual/biennial; Aq= aquatic plant; B= bulb, corm or tuber; C= climber or wall shrub; E= evergreen; F= fern; G= greenhouse plant; M= marginal plant; P= perennial; S= shrub or sub-shrub; T= tree

PROPAGATION

This branch of horticulture is concerned with the increase and reproduction of plants. The subject has been regarded with a certain amount of mystique but, in fact, the techniques described here are adaptations of the simple processes occurring in nature, and well within the scope of amateur gardeners.

There are two distinct types of propagation: by seeds (sexual propagation), and by vegetative methods (asexual propagation). Plants raised from seeds are entirely new and may differ from the parents, while vegetative propagation usually provides exact replicas of existing stock.

SEED PROPAGATION

Increasing by seed is the simplest and also the least expensive method of raising large numbers of plants. These small embryo plants, produced from the fertilisation of the female part of a flower (the ovules contained in the ovary) by pollen from the male section (anther), can be unpredictable in their form and habit. Sometimes ovary and anther occur on the same plant, in other cases on two separate plants growing in close proximity. In the process of fertilisation the characteristics of both parents are combined and reshuffled, and seedlings may show degrees of variability from their parents if these differ greatly. Plant breeders take advantage of this occurrence to raise new varieties, but often have to perform numerous crosses before a seedling of any value is produced.

Fortunately, most plants produce seeds which develop into plants of almost uniform appearance, and this is especially true of many of the annual flowers and vegetables. Such seed strains are said to be true to type and have arisen from natural self-fertilisation or by breeders always crossing plants with similar features. Any plant which differs from the parents—known as a rogue—is destroyed until the strain or variety is fixed.

Seed merchants are increasingly offering F_1 hybrid seeds which are the result of two pure-bred strains being crossed each time a given variety is required. F_1 plants show additional vigour and uniformity.

Most perennial plants can be propagated easily from seeds, but those with mixed ancestry do not come true. Examples are chrysanthemums, carnations, strawberries, black currants and most fruit trees which must be propagated by vegetative techniques. In addition, seed-raised plants of some shrubs and trees are slow-growing, or may take years to reach flowering or fruiting size.

Seeds vary immensely in shape and size, and these variations help to determine their cultural needs. They may be dust-like seeds, hard-coated, fleshy or oily; in addition they may be equipped with appendages, such as wings or hooks, which under natural conditions assist the distribution of the ripe seeds by wind or animals.

The life of a seed is its period of viability; some seeds, such as those of parsnip, are short-lived and usually die within a year; others, for example tomato seeds, remain viable for as long as 12 years. Modern methods of seed treatment and packing help to maintain seeds in the best possible condition over a long period.

A stored seed remains in a dormant stage until provided with certain external conditions. The small embryo plant does not commence active growth unless given adequate supplies of moisture, air and warmth. The correct timing, depth of sowing and the medium also help to ensure good germination. Once a seed has germinated, an adequate supply of food is required to maintain continuous growth. Each seed contains within itself a sufficient store of nutrients to feed the initial growth of the first shoot and, in some cases, for a short period afterwards.

Generally, seeds should be sown at a depth equal to their thickness, although the large seeds of peas and beans can safely be sown $1\frac{1}{2}$–2 in. deep. Small seeds need only a fine covering of the sowing medium. Light is sometimes an important factor in the germination of dust-like seeds, and these should be sown on the surface of the compost and covered with a pane of glass and paper.

TYPES OF SEEDS

The seeds of many plants have a thick, hard or fleshy covering which makes sowing difficult and prolongs germination. Commercially, seeds of such plants are stratified—that is, placed thickly in a moist medium to assist rotting of the pulp or softening of hard seed coats. A period of cold at this time may also help to break dormancy. The fruits are placed in a mixture of moistened peat and sand, and the pots stored outdoors, covered with chicken wire or a similar protection against birds and rodents. The period of stratification varies from 6 to 18 months, according to the hardness of the seed coat and known germination behaviour of the seeds. For example, most berberis species germinate in about three or four months, while those of davidia always take 18 months or more.

For the gardener concerned with raising only a few plants, stratification is generally unnecessary. It is easier to squeeze out the seeds from the pulp and sow them immediately. Some hard-coated seeds require a period of cold conditions to break their dormancy. Normally such conditions are provided by sowing the seeds in autumn outdoors, but where an autumn sowing is impracticable, the seeds may be placed in a mixture of equal parts (by volume) peat and sand in a glass container and kept in a domestic refrigerator at a temperature of 2–4°C (36–39°F) for six to eight weeks.

Tough or hard-coated seeds, such as those of sweet-pea varieties, may be nicked or scratched slightly before sowing to assist water uptake, thus hastening germination. Use a sharp knife or file, taking care to damage only the outermost casing.

Various seed composts are available, the best known being the John Innes seed and potting composts. The original seed compost, formulated by the John Innes Institute, consisted of 2 parts sterilised loam, 1 part peat and 1 part sand (parts by volume), with $1\frac{1}{2}$ oz. superphosphate and $\frac{3}{4}$ oz. ground chalk or limestone per bushel (the chalk being omitted for lime-hating plants). The formula was never patented, and the seed composts, selling under the name of John Innes, are not always made to the Institute's specifications.

Due to the difficulty of obtaining good loam, many firms are now offering alternatives to the John Innes composts, in the form of loamless mixtures of peat, sand, vermiculite and nutrients in suitable proportions. These composts give good results and have the advantage of being sterile, uniform, light, clean to handle and weed-free.

The keen amateur may make his own John Innes compost, the only difficulty being the sterilisation of the soil. A number of small electric sterilising units are on the market; alternatively, small amounts of soil may be sterilised in a domestic steamer. Do not fill the steamer more than 6 in. deep. Cool off rapidly after the soil surface has been maintained at 82°C (180°F) for ten minutes.

Seeds may be sown in various containers. Clay pots and wooden seed trays are being superseded by plastic containers; these look presentable, and the growth of plants is not impaired. In boxes deeper than $2\frac{1}{2}$ in. and pots larger than 4 in. in diameter, provide adequate basal drainage by placing a layer of crocks (small broken pieces of clay pot) about 1 in. deep at the bottom of the container. If crocks are not available, peat or coarse compost may be substituted. Lightly press the seed compost into the pot or tray, filling it to about $\frac{1}{2}$ in. below the rim. Level off the surface of the compost and firm.

SOWING SEEDS

Always sow seeds thinly. Very small seeds should be merely scattered on the surface; larger seeds should be covered to their depth with compost or sand shaken through a fine sieve. After sowing, water the surface with a fine spray or, preferably, place the container in shallow water until the compost has drawn up enough water to moisten it thoroughly. To conserve moisture, cover the pot or tray with a pane of glass, which must be wiped daily to remove condensation. The glass may be covered with newspaper, which prevents too high temperatures building up, and conserves moisture.

After sowing maintain, if possible, a temperature of 15–18°C (59–64°F). Germination of the more common annuals and perennials usually takes place within one to four weeks, depending on the species. After germination remove the paper and glass, and place the container in full light. Keep a watch for symptoms of damping-off; water with Cheshunt compound or a similar fungicide if there is any sign of fungal growth and sudden collapse of plants.

As soon as the seedlings are large enough to handle, which is usually when the first pair of leaves is fully expanded, they should be pricked off. This consists of lifting the seedlings carefully with the aid of a spatula or a wooden label, and planting at least 1½–2 in. apart in a seed tray containing a suitable compost. Handle the seedlings gently by the leaves, taking care not to pinch the stems. Using a blunt-pointed dibber, make planting holes large enough to accommodate the roots easily. Firm the surrounding compost, using the dibber and not the fingers.

Grow the pricked-off seedlings on in their trays at the temperature under which they were germinated. Gradually expose them to more air and light, finally placing the containers in a cold frame to be hardened off for planting outdoors. Half-hardy annuals may be planted out in their growing sites as soon as danger of night frost is past; seedlings of biennials and perennials may require to be potted up in 3–3½ in. pots of a potting compost and grown on until wanted for planting out. Alternatively, transplant the seedlings of biennials and perennials to an outdoor nursery bed and grow on for about six months before setting the plants in their flowering sites.

For outdoor sowing, the most important factor is the preparation of the ground. The soil must be dug in autumn, early enough to allow it to settle before the frosts. For vegetable crops, except root vegetables, enrich the soil with organic manure, preferably a strawy manure. Manure is also beneficial on flower beds, but may be replaced by peat, leaf-mould or well-decayed compost. In spring, firm the soil and rake it evenly to produce a fine tilth. Prior to sowing, rake in a general fertiliser, at 2 oz. per sq. yd.

Sow the seeds either broadcast or in drills. Vegetable seeds should be sown in drills spaced 6–24 in. apart, depending on the variety and its eventual height and spread. Mark the distances between the rows, and take the drills out with the corner of a draw hoe pulled against a taut garden line. Sow the seeds thinly and evenly in the drill, afterwards drawing the soil in place with the back of a rake. Firm the drill and rake lightly; watering is generally unnecessary, but during very dry weather the drills may be watered prior to sowing in order to hasten germination.

When the seedlings are growing strongly, they should, when necessary, be thinned to the required spacing.

Hardy perennials and biennials may also be sown in drills, but these are taken out in a nursery bed, for later transplanting to permanent planting positions.

Hardy annuals are generally sown in the flowering site. Prepare the soil as described for sowing in drills, and scatter or broadcast the seeds over the chosen area. Cover the seeds lightly with fine soil and rake gently; thin out the seedlings if necessary.

LAWNS

For lawns, the preparation of soil is extremely important. On poor and sandy soils, incorporate peat, leaf-mould or well-decayed manure at the time of digging. A firm, fine seed bed is essential, but over-consolidation of the soil by heavy rolling should be avoided. It is advisable to use a roller only on very light soils; otherwise the ground should be firmed by treading and levelled with a rake. Prior to sowing, rake in a balanced fertiliser, at 2 oz. per sq. yd.

Various types of grass-seed mixtures of different qualities are available. Choose a mixture suitable for the type of lawn required.

Sow the seeds from late March to May, or from August to early September, in quantities varying from 1–2 oz. per sq. yd, depending on the fineness of the seeds. The lighter rate is usually satisfactory in mixtures containing coarse grasses such as perennial rye grass. Most mixtures can be obtained treated with bird repellent.

Sowing is facilitated by dividing the mixture into two batches and carefully broadcasting it by hand, first walking lengthways up and down the site, then crossing from side to side with the second batch. Make sure that adequate seed is sown along the edges of the site. After sowing, lightly rake in the seed, preferably with a spring-tined rake; light rolling is optional. Germination takes place after 10–14 days.

VEGETATIVE PROPAGATION

There are several methods of vegetative propagation. Plants may be increased by cuttings, division, layering, budding and grafting. Certain types of growth, usually one year old or less, removed from a mature plant and placed in a suitable environment, will form roots. Young plants raised in this manner will be identical to their parents.

It has been suggested that continued vegetative propagation of plants leads to deterioration of the stock, possibly by the transmission of virus diseases. Heat therapy can be used to eliminate viruses from infected plants, but this is a difficult technique requiring the controlled conditions of a research station, and amateurs are advised to propagate only from healthy stock. Soft fruits such as black currants, raspberries and strawberries are particularly prone to virus diseases, and in these cases new stock should be regularly purchased and the old plants destroyed.

The Ministry of Agriculture operates certification schemes for many fruit plants and also for seed potatoes.

CUTTINGS

Increase of plants by cuttings is probably the most widely practised type of vegetative propagation. A leaf, bud, section of stem or root of a living plant is removed and treated in such a way that it becomes a new plant.

There are various types of cuttings, each with their own requirements, but certain general rules apply. For a cutting to strike, or take root, it must have adequate light, warmth and moisture. Except in special cases, very small cuttings should be avoided as they tend to exhaust their food reserves before roots can be formed. The rooting medium must be freely drained, yet capable of retaining sufficient moisture, and permit free passage of air. It must be free of diseases

SEED PROPAGATION

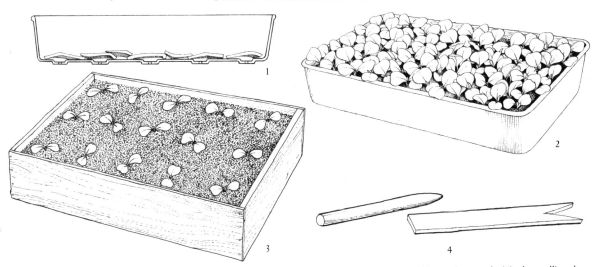

1. A layer of crocks is placed over the base of the seed box before filling with compost, to ensure adequate drainage. 2. Well-developed seedlings, showing the first pair of seed leaves, are ready for pricking out. 3. With the aid of a dibber and a spatula (4), the seedlings have been pricked out in a box of potting compost. Harden off the young plants in a cold frame before planting out

and pests. Loam should be sterilised. Many combinations and certain materials on their own make successful rooting mediums; John Innes seed composts are good, general-purpose media, or a general compost can be made up of equal parts (by volume) coarse sand and peat. The following mixtures (all parts by volume) are also recommended: 3 parts coarse sand to 1 part peat; equal parts coarse sand, peat and loam; coarse sand or Cornish grit, vermiculite, polystyrene granules, washed boiler ashes or sphagnum moss. The last four items may be used separately or in various proportions.

Some plants root easily if the cuttings are first stood in water; *Saintpaulia ionantha* and impatiens are examples. The resulting roots, however, are soft and are easily damaged unless potting is done carefully.

Cuttings generally root readily when taken at the correct time of year. If difficulty is encountered, various 'hormone' rooting media are available. These organic compounds, which hasten the formation of roots, may be purchased as liquid dips, or as dust preparations, and must be used according to the manufacturer's instructions. The dust compounds also often contain a fungicide which helps to limit basal rotting.

Apart from tender plants, most cuttings taken during the summer months will root in cold frames or unheated greenhouses. In the case of hardwood cuttings taken in autumn, a sheltered site in the open is all that is needed. Eye, bud and leaf cuttings, however, and cuttings of actively growing plants taken during the colder months, almost always require artificial heat. This can be provided in a greenhouse, but to preserve humidity the use of an enclosed frame or propagating case is recommended. A close, moist atmosphere diminishes transpiration, the process by which plants continually give off water vapour, and is therefore beneficial for any cuttings still in leaf. Shade the glass, keep the frame closed and occasionally syringe the cuttings with tepid water.

Depending on the plant material and species, temperatures of 13–18°C (55–64°F) are adequate, although in some cases higher values must be provided. Electrically heated propagating cases for the amateur are on the market. Good results can be obtained by using an unheated portable frame and siting it over hot-water pipes in a greenhouse. A wood and glass frame may be constructed fairly easily, or a glass fish tank makes a suitable alternative. Place a layer of crocks or similar drainage material at the bottom of the tank, cover with 4 in. of coarse sand, and place a sheet of glass over the top of the tank. Alternatively, place individual pots of cuttings in sealed polythene bags, and similarly cover trays completely with a polythene tent. All containers should be placed in warm positions but out of direct sun which might cause scorching. If direct sun is unavoidable, lightly shade the frame lights, using proprietary shading or single sheets of newspaper as a temporary measure.

Commercial growers and some amateurs root cuttings in a mist-propagation unit. This method, in addition to providing basal heat, automatically sprays a fine mist of water droplets over the cuttings, limiting transpiration and preventing them from drying out. Modern units are constructed so as to react to moisture conditions. Mist-propagating units of many sizes are on the

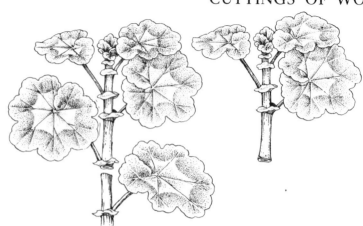

A softwood cutting of pelargonium. Sever the non-flowering shoot just below a node, and remove the lowest leaves before inserting the cutting in a propagating frame to root

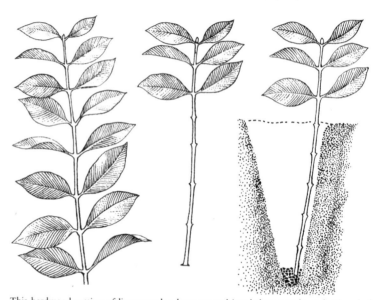

This hardwood cutting of ligustrum has been severed just below a node, and stripped of most of its leaves. The cutting is inserted in the open ground in a V-shaped trench with a layer of sand at the bottom to assist drainage. It will take about a year to root

market, but there may be installation difficulties in obtaining the correct water pressure; the initial outlay is also much higher than for a simple propagating frame.

Softwood cuttings. These are immature shoot tips and must be rooted under warm conditions in a frame, propagating case or suitable alternative. Chrysanthemums are invariably propagated by this type of cutting, and many perennials, sub-shrubs and house plants may be similarly increased.

Softwood cuttings can be taken throughout the year from plants grown under heated glass; on outdoor plants the young shoots are best removed during June and July. Selected cuttings should be firm but not hard; short, non-flowering side-shoots, 2–4 in. long, are ideal. Secateurs may be used to sever the chosen shoot, but the basal cut must be made cleanly and transversely with a sharp knife or razor blade, just below a bud (node), leaving

the bud intact. A nodal cutting is thought to root most easily, but in the case of clematis, the transverse cut can be made mid-way, internodally, between two pairs of nodes. Some cuttings may bleed when cut, but the flow of sap can be checked by immediately dipping the bases in powdered charcoal. Keep the cuttings in fresh condition by placing them in polythene bags or in a bucket covered with polythene until inserted.

The leaves on a cutting continue to manufacture food supplies and are therefore important for root formation. A few of the basal leaves may be removed to facilitate proper insertion, but further stripping of the foliage decreases the chances of successful rooting. If flowering shoots are used, the flowering tips or buds should be removed.

Some cuttings are easier to root if heel cuttings are taken. The shoots are cut or pulled from the main branch with a small

˙EMMED PLANTS

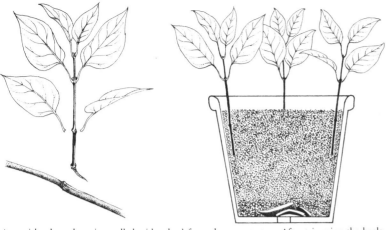

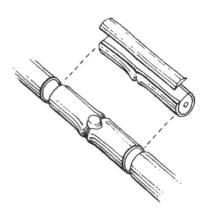

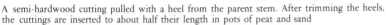

A semi-hardwood cutting pulled with a heel from the parent stem. After trimming the heels, the cuttings are inserted to about half their length in pots of peat and sand

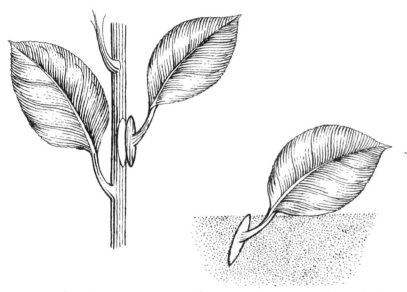

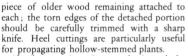

Leaf-bud cutting of *Camellia japonica*. This type of cutting, containing a small bud and with a leaf and a sliver of wood attached, should be scooped out of the parent stem. Insert the cutting in the rooting medium so that only the leaf shows on the surface

Eye cuttings may be used to propagate grapes. They should be taken during the dormant period, from leafless stem sections. Each cutting should contain a bud or eye. Remove the bark from opposite the eye and place the cutting, eye upwards, on the rooting compost. The cuttings should be set in a propagating frame with a temperature of 13–16°C (55–61°F). When strong roots have formed, pot the cuttings individually in 5 in. pots of John Innes compost No. 2

piece of older wood remaining attached to each; the torn edges of the detached portion should be carefully trimmed with a sharp knife. Heel cuttings are particularly useful for propagating hollow-stemmed plants.

If a 'hormone' rooting powder is used, the base of the cuttings should be dipped immediately after they are made. Using a dibber, insert the cuttings to one-third of their length, and 2–3 in. apart, in a bed of the selected rooting medium. Most cuttings will root ten days to a month after insertion, and should be potted up as soon as possible after this; otherwise, give applications of liquid feed until potting can be carried out. After removal from the propagating case, shade the cuttings from direct sunshine until strong roots are produced and the plants have become established.

It is possible to root cuttings singly or in groups in pots, rather than directly in the bed of a propagating case. The rooting medium may be replaced by a seed sowing compost, topped with ½ in. of sand. When the cuttings are inserted, the sand trickles into the dibber holes and provides good rooting conditions. Cuttings placed singly in pots establish themselves more readily, as they can easily be removed from the propagating frame for later planting out without any root disturbance.

Semi-hardwood cuttings. These are firmer than those of softwood, and less mature than hardwood cuttings. They are generally taken between July and September. In most cases no heating is required, and while some will root successfully in the open ground, a cold-frame cloche provides a more favourable environment. This type of cutting is particularly suitable for the increase of deciduous and evergreen shrubs, for heathers and many conifers.

Semi-hardwood cuttings generally take longer to root than softwood cuttings and consequently, since more food reserves are required, should be somewhat larger, about 4–6 in. long. Remove the soft tip of the cutting, which would soon wilt; sever the shoot cleanly just above a bud, and make the basal cut directly below a node, as for softwood cuttings, unless a heel cutting is required. Remove the leaves from the lower half of the cutting to make insertion easier. Conifer cuttings are usually prepared by pulling off small lateral shoots, 3–4 in. long, with a heel attached; a few of the lower leaves should be removed and the heel trimmed. Prepared cuttings may be dipped in 'hormone' rooting powder if desired.

Semi-hardwood cuttings should be inserted to about half or one-third their length in soil containing equal parts (by volume) peat and coarse sand. Keep the frame lights closed, and

LEAF CUTTINGS

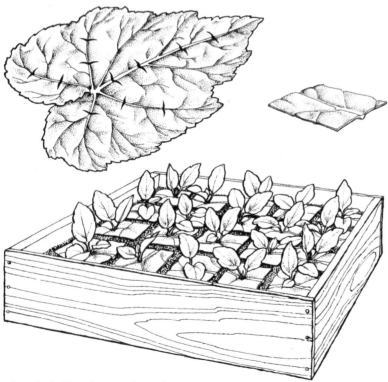

Leaf cuttings from a streptocarpus plant: a small leaf may be used as a single cutting, while a large leaf can be divided into sections. The cuttings are inserted vertically in the compost; small plantlets will develop from the base of the leaf

A large leaf of *Begonia rex* can be used to produce a number of new plantlets. Cut the main veins on the back of the leaf and place on the compost. Alternatively, cut the leaf into small squares and place, weighted down, on the rooting medium

lightly spray the bed at least once a day during warm spells. Shading of the glass may be necessary during very sunny periods. Soil warming may achieve a higher percentage strike or assist quicker rooting, especially of such shrubs as pyracantha and ceanothus, but is not essential. The following late spring, plant out rooted cuttings in nursery rows, leaving valuable frame space available for future crops. It is best to discard any unrooted specimens at this stage.

Some semi-hardwood cuttings may root outdoors, but only in very mild and humid areas, and generally the practice is not recommended. In such districts, follow the same procedure as recommended for hardwood cuttings.

Hardwood cuttings. These cuttings afford the simplest means of propagation, and are used to increase trees and shrubs. The cuttings are taken from October to March, while the plants are leafless and in a dormant state, and inserted in the open ground. Rooting is slow and may take up to 12 months, but there are fewer losses caused by excessive transpiration (loss of water).

The cuttings should be 6–15 in. long and trimmed beneath a node; some are preferably taken with a heel, so that the base of each shoot retains a small sliver of old wood. If the tip of the shoot is green or unripened it should be removed above a suitable bud.

Red and white currants and gooseberries are usually grown on a leg or short stem so that the branches are well clear of the ground. To produce a clear stem remove all buds except four or five at the top of the cutting. Gooseberry cuttings are best inserted before the leaves have dropped. Some propagators claim that retention of the lowest bud stimulates better root formation.

Insert hardwood cuttings in an outdoor bed. Choose a sheltered weed-free site and dig the soil at least a spit deep. Any well-drained and fertile garden soil is suitable; poor soils should be enriched with peat or well-decayed compost some time before the cuttings are inserted. Heavy soils may be loosened by incorporating coarse sand. Insert the cuttings to a depth of half to two-thirds their length, 3–6 in. apart and in rows 15–18 in. apart. Take out a V-shaped trench, the back wall being vertical, and place a layer, about 1 in. deep, of coarse sand in the bottom of the trench. This assists drainage and promotes aeration.

Insert the cuttings against the vertical wall, push back the soil from the opposite bank, and firm it thoroughly with the base of the heel. Firm planting is extremely important; cuttings loosened by frosts should be re-firmed immediately.

The cuttings should be left in the bed for a complete growing season before being lifted and transferred to the planting site; if very small, they may be grown on for a further year. Plants to be grown on legs should be replanted at a slightly shallower depth than the original cuttings.

Eye cuttings. These consist of small, ripened, leafless stem sections, each having only one bud. Transverse sloping cuts should be made $\frac{3}{4}$ in. above and below the bud, and a small strip of bark with a little wood should be removed from the side opposite the bud. Insert the cutting horizontally in the rooting medium, so that the eye just protrudes above the soil level; secure with small wire pegs if necessary. This method of propagation is

ROOT CUTTINGS

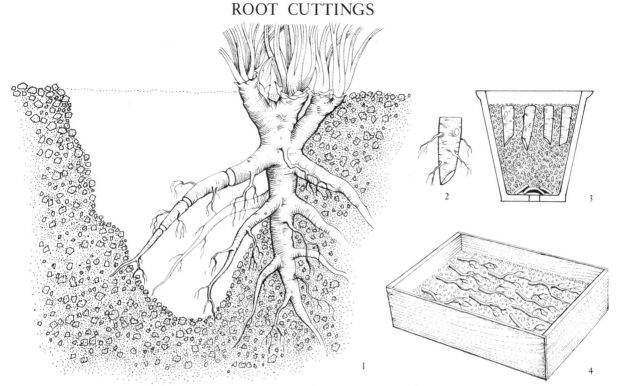

1. Root cuttings are taken from a plant in the open. 2. A section of thick root is prepared by making a horizontal cut at the top and a sloping cut at the base. 3. The cuttings are inserted, sloping edge downwards, in a pot of the rooting medium and just covered with a layer of sand. 4. Thin fibrous roots are placed horizontally in a box of rooting compost and lightly covered with sand

often used for grapes; the eyes are taken in February and rooted in a propagating frame at a temperature of 13–16°C (55–61°F).

This type of single-bud cutting may also be used to increase other plants, especially if propagating material is scarce. The cuttings are trimmed just above a bud with 1–1½ in. of stem below and inserted vertically in the rooting medium. Such cuttings are slow to become established. They are therefore best rooted in a greenhouse or frame at a temperature of 15–18°C (59–64°F).

Leaf-bud cuttings. These are forms of eye cuttings, taken during the summer while the plant is still in active growth. In addition to a bud, the stem section should also carry a leaf to supply nourishment to the developing roots. *Camellia japonica* is frequently propagated by this method.

The cutting may be a stem section, or a 'half-moon', containing bud and leaf, may be scooped out from the surface of the stem. Each cutting should be firmly inserted in the rooting medium, leaving only the leaf protruding, and rooted in a propagating case at a temperature of 15–18°C (59–64°F).

Leaf cuttings. A method of propagation used for greenhouse plants with thick and fleshy leaves, such as gloxinia, streptocarpus, peperomia, begonia and saintpaulia. A healthy mature leaf complete with stalk is removed from the parent plant and rooted in a compost of equal parts (by volume) peat and sand. Insert the stalk of the leaf so that the leaf itself is clear of the compost, and place in a propagating unit at a temperature of 16–18°C (61–64°F). Roots and shoots develop from the base of the leaf stalk.

Leaves more than 4 in. long, particularly of streptocarpus, may be cut into two or more horizontal sections. Each section above the basal piece should have its lower corners obliquely trimmed so that the central vein may be inserted into the compost.

Some plants, notably *Begonia rex*, may be encouraged to produce several plantlets from the same leaf. Cut the main veins at their junctions on the back of the leaf and press the severed leaf-stalk base in the compost so that the leaf rests on it. Weight the leaf down with small pebbles to ensure that all cuts are in contact with the compost. Plantlets will arise from the severed veins and can be potted individually when well rooted. Alternatively, the leaf may be cut into small squares or sections each with one or more strong veins.

Saintpaulias increase readily from leaf cuttings; if no propagating case is available, the cuttings may be induced to form roots by standing the stalks in small containers of water, keeping the leaf well clear. When sufficient roots have formed, pot singly in 3 in. pots of John Innes potting compost No. 1.

Some plants spontaneously produce small plantlets on their leaves. In some cases such as tolmiea and *Asplenium bulbiferum*, the leaves may be pegged down into the soil where the young plants will rapidly take root. Sever from the parent when the plantlets are growing strongly. Alternatively, the plantlets may be removed when well developed, and pricked off into containers of the growing compost, treated as seedlings and potted up.

Root cuttings. This method is used for propagating herbaceous perennials and shrubs with fleshy roots; most plants which produce suckers will also grow fairly easily from root cuttings. Root cuttings should never be taken from grafted plants, as only the understock will be increased.

Take these cuttings during the dormant period, in autumn or winter, preferably from lifted plants, although with skill and if only a small number are required, it is possible to remove sections of root from plants *in situ*.

The thickness of a root cutting varies from plant to plant. Cuttings of woody plants and herbaceous perennials with thick, fleshy roots should be ¼–½ in. in diameter and 2–6 in. long. Prepare the cuttings by making a horizontal cut at the top of the root and a sloping cut at the base. Insert the cuttings, sloping edge downwards, in an unheated frame, in the open ground or in pots or boxes, in a compost of equal parts (by volume) peat, coarse sand and loam. Cover the cuttings with ½ in. of sand; new roots will form and young shoots arise in spring. When the young plants are established they can be grown on in nursery rows until the autumn.

Certain plants, such as border phlox, with fibrous root systems also increase readily from root cuttings; these are thinner than cuttings from fleshy and woody plants and 3–4 in. long. Place the roots horizontally in trays of the rooting medium, and cover with a ½ in. layer of compost or sand.

Treatment of cuttings. With the exception of hardwood and most kinds of woody root cuttings, all cuttings require after-care. As soon as the cuttings are well rooted they should be potted up individually in John Innes potting compost No. 1. The first pot

PROPAGATION OF HERBACEO

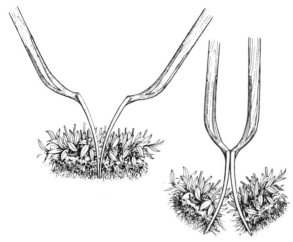

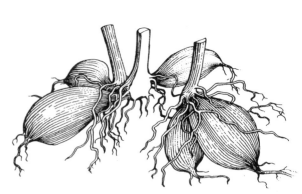

Division of the tough old crown of an established plant is made easier by using two garden forks. Insert these, back to back, in the centre and lever the clump apart; discard the centres

The swollen root tubers of dahlia do not bear buds. They are split by cutting upwards between the tubers in such a manner that each division contains a portion of the main stem

size is generally 3–3½ in., and in the beginning keep the young plants growing at the temperature under which they were rooted. Gradually expose the plants to the usually lower growing temperatures, and admit more light and air. Keep the compost just moist at all times. When the plants have filled their pots with roots, pot on into a larger size container of a richer potting compost. Thereafter treat the plants as recommended in the generic entries for established plants.

The various types of cuttings described here are those most commonly employed and are within the scope of the amateur gardener. The following definitions, although not strictly types of cuttings, are frequently met with in horticultural literature:

BASAL CUTTING. A non-flowering shoot taken from the base of a plant, at or just below ground level.

HEEL CUTTING. Usually a semi-hardwood or hardwood cutting retaining a small piece of the main stem or bark. Such cuttings may be pulled off, but are better removed with a knife and the ragged edges of the heel trimmed cleanly.

INTERNODAL CUTTING. Any stem cutting severed between the nodes or buds instead of just below a node.

IRISHMAN'S CUTTING. A colloquial term for a basal cutting which has already developed a few roots. It can be planted immediately.

NODAL CUTTING. A stem cutting that is severed immediately below a node.

PIPING. This term is applied exclusively to a stem cutting of carnations and pinks. It is taken by gripping the tip of a non-flowering shoot and pulling it firmly until it slides out of the pair of leaves just below.

STEM CUTTING. Applied to any type of cutting taken from a main branch or shoot as opposed to a leaf or root cutting.

TIP CUTTING. A cutting taken from the top growth of a non-flowering shoot.

DIVISION

This is the simplest method of vegetative propagation. Division is used to increase most perennials as well as shrubs of suckering habit. Plants which produce a crown or clump of shoots at, or just below, ground level may be lifted during the dormant period, readily divided into separate portions and replanted.

Apart from specifically increasing plants, division is also used to perpetuate existing stocks which deteriorate or become overcrowded after a few years. The old plants are lifted and split; old pieces should be discarded, and small portions from the outside replanted.

Division may be carried out at any time between October and April.

In the case of small, tufted herbaceous perennials, such as helenium, michaelmas daisies and rudbeckia, the clumps are teased apart by hand or with a small fork or trowel. Large, old crowns of plants may need to be levered apart with two garden forks back to back. Discard the older, woodier central parts and replant the outer portions. Generally, divisions for immediate replanting should include up to six buds or shoots. For a larger number of new plants, divide into smaller portions and grow on for a year in a nursery bed.

Plants, such as lupins and delphiniums, with tough woody crowns are less easily divided. Lift the plants in early spring, removing as much soil as possible; wash the crowns so that the growth buds are revealed. With a sharp knife cut the crown into divisions, each containing roots and buds.

Division of tuberous-rooted plants varies from genus to genus. Stem tubers, such as potato and some begonias, which are basically thickened stems, produce both buds and roots. They can be divided by cutting the tubers into pieces, each with at least one bud. New plants will be produced from the divisions. Root tubers, such as dahlias, are essentially swollen roots with food reserves. They do not bear buds and should be divided in such a manner that each portion retains a piece of the parent stem; cut upwards between the tubers with a sharp knife, shaving off a small section of stem with each portion.

Rhizomatous plants are divided by cutting the thickened underground stems into sections 2–3 in. long. Each section should have a few strong growths and should be taken from the outside, the old centres being discarded. Replant the sections at the same depth at which they were growing.

Certain woody and shrubby plants produce individual shoots or suckers at some distance from the parent plant. These suckering shoots allow quick and convenient means of propagation. After one or two growing seasons the suckers should have developed roots and may be severed with a sharp spade close to the parent plant, lifted carefully and replanted in a nursery bed or the permanent positions. Many trees and shrubs which have been grafted on to a rootstock of a different species or genus frequently produce suckers; these, however, can only be used to propagate new stock plants for grafting. Normally, they should be removed as soon as noticed.

Many bulbous and cormous plants undergo a process of natural division by forming offsets in the shape of bulbils or cormlets. Bulbs of, for example, narcissus and tulipa form offset bulbs beside the mature bulbs; at lifting time these offsets may be detached and grown on in nursery beds until they reach flowering size after a couple of years.

The corms of gladiolus shrivel up each year after having formed new corms as well as several small cormlets. In the autumn, detach the secondary corms and store under the same conditions as mature corms. The following spring, plant out the cormlets in a nursery bed and repeat the lifting and replanting cycle; they should reach flowering size after one or more years.

Hyacinths rarely produce new bulbs naturally, but may be induced to do so. During the latter part of the dormant season the bulbs are lifted and the basal portion of each scooped out. Place the bulbs in moist sand at a temperature of 18–19°C (64–66°F) and leave for a complete growing season. Considerable numbers of bulblets will be produced from the damaged surfaces and may be separated and grown on to flowering size.

Some species and hybrids of lilies produce small bulbils in the leaf axils. These may be gathered, in August and September, and set ½ in. deep and 2 in. apart in deep boxes of seed compost. The bulbils should reach flowering size after two or three years.

LAYERING

A method of vegetative propagation by which a stem or shoot of a plant is induced to form roots while being attached to the parent plant. Some plants, particularly pendulous

ANTS: DIVISION

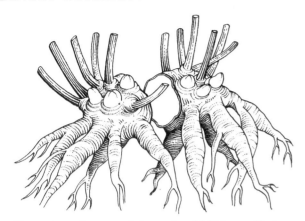

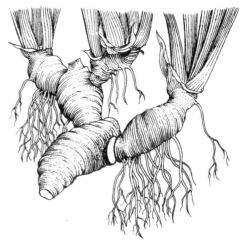

The tough woody crowns of plants such as delphiniums and lupins are difficult to sever. Use a sharp knife to split the lifted crowns into sections, each with a proportion of roots and growth buds

The thickened underground stems of rhizomatous plants are divided into pieces, 2–3 in. long, each with a few strong growths. Replant only the young outer sections, the centre being discarded

trees and shrubs such as *Forsythia suspensa* and *Salix × chrysocoma*, layer themselves naturally when stems touch the ground.

Most woody plants may be layered, and the method often succeeds where cuttings fail. Some herbaceous plants, notably carnations and pinks, will also respond to layering.

Shoots may be layered at any time of the year, but from September to November is the best time to layer shrubs. Dig the surrounding soil; enrich poor, thin soils with peat, and lighten heavy soils with coarse sand.

The chosen shoots should be healthy and vigorous, one or two years old. Bend the shoot down to soil level with the growing tip held upwards at a right angle to the soil. Insert the bent portion in the soil and secure in position with a U-shaped pin or stones. Cover with soil, firming thoroughly. The growing tip should be tied to a cane for support. Rooting is encouraged by wounding the bent section of shoot, either by removing a small sliver or a circlet of bark, or by making a shallow, oblique cut into the stem so that a small tongue opens when the shoot is bent. An application of a proprietary 'hormone' rooting powder to the wound is beneficial. Rooting is not rapid, but it should

be possible to sever connection with the parent after one to three years and to transplant the rooted section to its permanent position.

Transplanting is made easier by layering the shoots into pots or boxes buried in the soil, but care must be taken to prevent these shoots from drying out.

An extended method of layering (serpentine layering) may be employed on young pliable shoots of, for example, clematis. Choose an outer strong shoot and make slanting cuts, ½–1 in. long, close to a node at intervals along the stem. Bend the cut sections down into pots containing equal parts (by volume) peat and sand, sunk in the soil; secure the cut areas with bent wires. Shoots layered in June should have formed plantlets at the cut joints by early autumn. Sever the plants and pot up in John Innes potting compost No. 1; overwinter in a cold frame and plant out the following spring.

Border carnations are frequently layered. Choose healthy young side-shoots from the outside of the plant, slit the stems as already described, and peg down in the surrounding soil during July. Well-rooted plants are produced after two months.

Air layering. This is used where it is difficult to lower the branches of a plant down to soil level. Select healthy one or two-year-old shoots and wound the stems by slitting, 6–15 in. below the growing tip. Dust the wound with a 'hormone' rooting powder and keep the tongue open by packing it with sphagnum moss. Place an 8–10 in. length of polythene sleeving over the stem, and secure the lower end 3 in. below the wound, using adhesive tape or string. Pack the sleeving firmly with a thoroughly moistened rooting medium consisting of 2 parts sphagnum moss, 1 part peat and 1 part sand (parts by volume). Fill with compost to 2–3 in. above the wound, and secure the top of the sleeve firmly to the stem. The polythene must be completely airtight so that drying out will not occur.

Air layering is most successfully practised in March or April and is particularly recommended for ficus and magnolia. When the roots are visible through the polythene film the layered section may be removed and potted up in the growing compost. Harden off the plant in a propagating case.

Tip layering. The long, arching, woody stems of blackberry and loganberry will

INCREASE BY SUCKERS AND OFFSETS

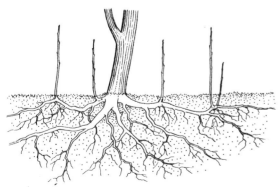

Strong-growing suckers, with well-developed root systems, are separated close to the parent plant, and replanted. Do not propagate suckers from grafted rootstocks

Small offset cormlets are formed at the base of a mature corm, bulbils at the side of a bulb. Such offsets can be removed at lifting time, and grown on in a nursery bed to reach flowering size

AIR LAYERING

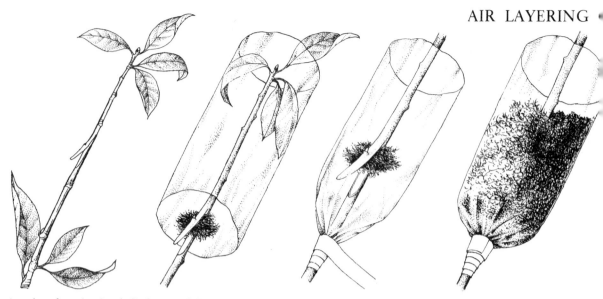

A section of stem is stripped of its leaves. A shallow cut, made upwards into the stem, is dusted with 'hormone' rooting powder, and packed with sphagnum moss. Polythene sleeving, placed over the cut section, is packed with moist rooting medium and bound

LAYERING OF BORD

A young vigorous shoot is selected from the side of the parent plant. The shoot is stripped of its lower pairs of leaves; a shallow oblique cut is made with a sharp knife, slicing upwards through the stem just below the top leaves and through the leaf node underneath. The cut should form a tongue that opens out and away from the parent plant. The tongue may be dusted with 'hormone' rooting powder

root where the tips touch the soil. During September, peg down the tips of healthy shoots into the surrounding soil, or into pots to make subsequent transplanting easier. The following April, the rooted tips may be severed from the parent plants and set out. **Runners.** The runners formed by healthy strawberry plants are a form of natural layering, and afford an easy means of propagation. In June, anchor the plantlets with pegs if the plants are grown in matted rows, and let them root into the soil, removing the remainder of the runners beyond the first plant. Alternatively, select the strongest plantlets and peg them down into pots, sunk to their rim in the soil, and containing John Innes potting compost No. 1. Water the pots frequently to aid root formation and remove all other runners as they form.

The plantlets should be separated from the parent plants in July or early August and planted out from their pots. If, for some reason, planting is delayed until the autumn, the young plants should not be allowed to crop the first season.

BUDDING AND GRAFTING
These are more complicated methods of vegetative propagation. They are practised on plants that do not come true from seeds or are difficult to increase by cuttings, division or layering. Most top fruits and a few shrubs, notably syringa, are grafted, while budding (a form of grafting) is generally confined to the propagation of roses, some fruits and ornamental cherries and crab apples.

Grafting consists of taking a portion of the variety to be increased (known as the scion) and uniting it with the chosen root system (known as the stock), so that the two become one living unit. The plant formed has the vigour of the stock while retaining the flowering or fruiting quality of the scion.

The scion may vary in size from a single bud (as in budding) to a shoot several inches long and bearing several buds. The stock usually consists of an established root system with a main stem to which the scion is joined, but occasionally, as with clematis and wistaria, the scion may be grafted on to a single portion of root and then planted.

Generally, grafting and budding take place in the open between March and April, or from July to September. The more difficult techniques, such as grafting on to roots or using scions which are in leaf, are best performed under glass and in a propagating

EMATIS

The packed polythene sleeve should be left intact until roots are visible

STRAWBERRY RUNNERS

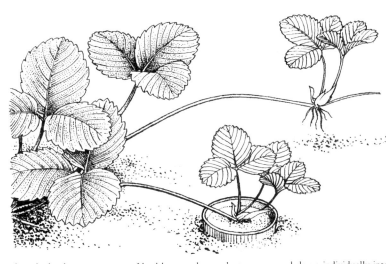

Selected plantlets on runners of healthy strawberry plants are pegged down individually into pots of John Innes potting compost No. 1. The pots are sunk to their rims in the soil

RNATIONS

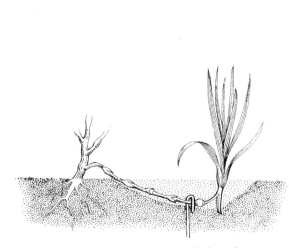

The side-shoot is bent down into the soil, with the cut kept open, and secured with a bent wire pin. The cutting should have rooted after six weeks and can then be severed from the parent

TIP LAYERING

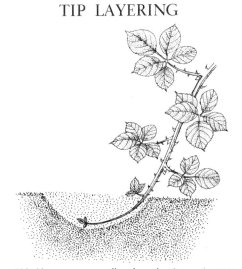

Stems of blackberry root naturally where the tips are in contact with the soil. In September, the tips can be pegged down with pins or held in place with stones until the following spring

frame. Grafting under glass is carried out during February or March, and the plants are invariably grown in pots.

Rootstocks vary from plant to plant. The essential requirement is that scion and rootstock be compatible so that the cambial layers of each will unite. In most cases they are of the same genus. Many tree and shrub varieties are grafted on to their common related species; clematis, ilex, rhododendron (including azalea) and syringa are such plants. Exceptions to this general rule include syringa, which may also be grafted on to ligustrum, cytisus which will unite with laburnum, and sorbus on to crataegus, but invariably the two genera involved are allied members of the same family.

In the case of top fruits and roses, much research has been done to evolve stocks which are healthy, vigorous and uniform, and which may themselves be easily increased by vegetative means. Examples include the Malling and Malling-Merton stocks for apples, designated variously by Roman numerals according to vigour. The 'M.IX' stock is used for cordons and dwarf pyramids suitable for restricted areas, and the 'M.XVI' is a suitable stock for large standard and orchard trees.

The Malling selections may also form stocks for ornamental crab apples, though usually unselected seedlings are used. Suitable stocks are also available for pears, plums, quinces, peaches and nectarines, and for ornamental prunus varieties. Rose rootstocks which are easily raised from either seeds or cuttings are also obtainable; *Rosa canina* (from seeds) and *Rosa multiflora* 'Simplex'

(from cuttings) are the stocks most frequently used.

These specially developed rootstocks are used primarily by professional gardeners and nurserymen, for whom grafting is a quick, convenient and economical way of propagating large numbers of varieties. For the amateur, grafting remains the most difficult of all propagating procedures. It is a highly specialised subject, and the following short descriptions only attempt to give a broad outline.

Budding. In this technique, a single bud is used as the scion. Budding is the easiest form of grafting; it is also a quick and economical method of increasing ornamental shrubs and trees such as roses and crab apples.

The chosen rootstock, either raised from seeds or cuttings or purchased from a

779

BUDDING

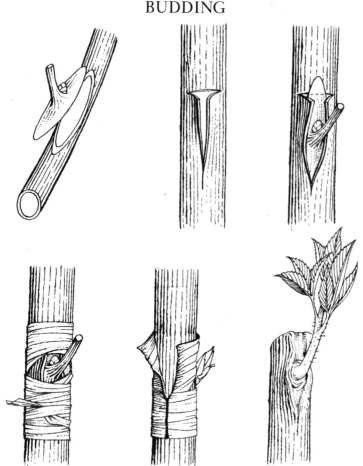

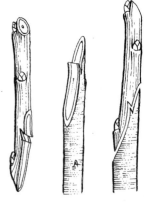

Whip and tongue grafting: small tongues are cut out from the oblique surfaces of scion and stock so as to interlock

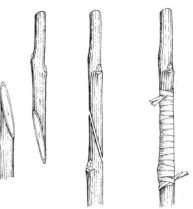

A scion bud is scooped out from the selected variety and inserted in a 'T'-shaped opening in the bark of the rootstock. Raffia is bound firmly round the union and loosened when growth is apparent. The stock is later cut down

In splice grafting, scion and stock are cut diagonally so that the two surfaces fit neatly together. Bind the union with raffia

nursery, should be planted and pruned to the desired height in autumn, and budding carried out the following July and August. Bush roses are budded into the stock at ground level while standards are budded at the desired height, generally 4–6 ft. For standards and half-standards, remove all shoots from the rootstock, with the exception of three or four evenly spread top branches, prior to budding.

Using a budding or sharp knife, make two cuts to form a 'T' in the bark of the stock where budding is to be performed. The top cut of the 'T' should be $\frac{1}{3}-\frac{1}{2}$ in. long, the vertical cut 1–1½ in. and both deep enough to just penetrate through the bark.

Cut out the scion buds from young, well-ripened shoots of the current season's growth of the chosen variety. Remove the soft growing tip of the shoot and all leaves, retaining ½ in. of leaf stalk beneath each bud. Begin the cut ½ in. below the first well-ripened bud and make a shallow-curved, slicing cut passing behind the bud and terminating it about ½ in. above the bud on the same side of the stem.

Hold the bud by the leaf stalk and insert the scion into the 'T'-shaped opening in the stock, using the spatula handle of the budding knife to open out the flaps of the bark. Push

the scion firmly into position and cut off the tail flush with the top of the 'T' incision. Bind the inserted scion firmly to the stock with raffia, covering all cut surfaces, but leaving the leaf stalk and bud protruding.

Signs of successful budding are usually apparent three or four weeks after insertion; the bud looks plump and green, and the leaf stalk drops off naturally. A failure shows as shrivelling of the bud, and the stalk remains attached. Loosen the ties four or five weeks after successful budding, by running a sharp knife down the back of the binding.

During early March cut down the rootstock with a sharp knife or secateurs to within ½ in. above the bud. Insert a cane close to the rootstock, and tie the new shoot to the cane. Any shoots arising from the rootstock should be removed.

Grafting. This method consist of joining a scion several inches long to a chosen rootstock, and is chiefly used to propagate fruit trees. Generally, grafting is done at the end of the dormant season, using scions from healthy, one-year-old woody shoots. Stock plants purchased from a nursery in autumn should be planted immediately in rich, well-drained soil and mulched with decayed compost or manure. The stocks will be ready for grafting the following spring. Rootstocks

from seed-raised plants require one or two complete growing seasons.

The scion shoots are selected during the winter and heeled in outdoors, preferably in a shady, north-facing border. The shoots will remain in a dormant condition until grafting takes place.

All graft unions should be bound with raffia or plastic tape and sealed with a proprietary grafting wax.

There are numerous methods of grafting, but basically the principles are identical. The following are those techniques most easily performed by the amateur gardener.

APPROACH GRAFTING. This is frequently used on varieties of camellia, magnolia and citrus trees, where other forms of grafts often do not take. Stock and scion are grown side by side, in separate pots. A shallow slicing wound is made on each stem to expose the cambium layers; the two wounded surfaces are fitted together and bound. After a couple of months, the top growth of the stock should be partially severed just above the union, and the scion partially severed from its roots just below the union. After a further month, severing of stock and scion may be completed.

BRIDGE GRAFTING. A form of tree surgery, whereby a damaged trunk or branch may be

~~GR~~AFTING METHODS

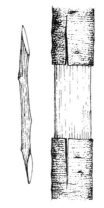
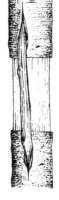

Approach grafting: a shallow slice of wood is removed from stock and scion, and the wounds bound. When the two have united, the top of the stock and the base of the scion are removed

Bridge grafting: vertical cuts are made in the bark above and below a damaged area of trunk. Scions, cut obliquely at each end, are inserted, cut surfaces inwards, to bridge the gap

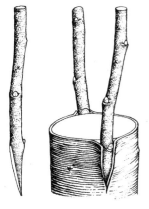

Crown grafting: scions, cut obliquely at the base, are inserted into vertical cuts in the bark of the stock so that the exposed inner surfaces touch. The union is sealed with wax

Saddle grafting: the top of the stock is sliced, with two oblique cuts, into a wedge. A corresponding wedge is cut from the base of the scion. The two are fitted together and bound

repaired. Scions of the same variety are used to bridge the gap between the two healthy areas of branch. Make a slanting cut, 1–2 in. long, at each end of the scions, and insert into incisions made above and below the wounded portion of bark. Tie the grafts with raffia or tape, and seal.

CROWN OR RIND GRAFTING. This is used to rejuvenate old fruit trees and consists of inserting several scions under the bark of the main stem or branches left after cutting back the tree. The scions are prepared by making sloping cuts about 1 in. long at one end and cut flush at the top, above a bud. Make 2 in. long, vertical cuts in the bark at the end of the stock, and push the scions down so that the two cut surfaces rest against each other. Bind and seal.

FRAMEWORKING. A method used to replace the top growth of the tree with a new variety. The main framework of the tree is retained, the side branchlets being pruned back. Scions of the chosen variety are grafted into the branches as stub grafts, side grafts or inverted 'L' grafts.

INVERTED 'L' GRAFTING. The scion is made as a pointed wedge, about 1 in. long. An oblique 'L' cut is made in the bark of the branch, forming a flap. The scion is inserted under the lifted flap so that the longer

surface lies against the exposed wood of the branch. The flap of bark and the scion are secured in position with a thin, flat-headed nail, and the surfaces sealed with wax.

SADDLE GRAFTING. Rhododendrons are often increased by this method. The top of the stock is cut on either side with two upward oblique strokes, producing a wedge-shaped point. A wedge is cut in the base of the scion so that it fits exactly over the stock; bind and seal the union.

SIDE CLEFT GRAFTING. A wedge-shaped, unequally sized scion is inserted into a cut in a main branch, at an angle of 20 degrees. Trim the bark behind the scion and seal the area with wax.

SPLICE GRAFTING. This simple technique may be used on broom, clematis and roses. Both stock and scion are sliced through diagonally, leaving each with an oblique surface. Fit the cut surfaces neatly together, and bind the join with raffia.

STUB GRAFTING. This differs from other frameworking techniques in that the scions are inserted into lateral branchlets. Trim the end of the scion to a wedge, one side shorter than the other. Make a downward incision in the lateral shoot as close as possible to the main branch, and gently bend out the lateral so that the cut opens slightly.

Insert the scion into the cut, longer side inwards; when the lateral is released it springs back to grip the scion in position. Trim off the remainder of the lateral above the scion, and seal all cut surfaces with grafting wax. No tying is necessary.

TOP WORKING. A form of framework graft whereby an old fruit-tree variety is replaced with another in the quickest possible time. The top growth of the old tree is sawn off and discarded, only the trunk, together with 2–3 ft of each of the main branches, being retained. Scions of the new variety are then grafted on to the ends of trunk and remaining branches, using crown or rind grafts.

On large trees it is advisable to leave one or two branches untrimmed, to draw the sap. These branches can be grafted with the new variety one or two years later; alternatively they may be removed entirely.

WHIP AND TONGUE GRAFTING. The most common method of grafting fruit and ornamental trees. The scion and stock are cut obliquely to produce slanting surfaces, each about 2 in. long. An upward slanting cut is made in each surface to produce a small tongue of wood; when the two surfaces are placed together the tongue is interlocked and holds the graft in place. Bind the union with raffia and seal with wax.

781

PRUNING

The operation of pruning consists of removing part or parts of mainly woody plants, trees and shrubs, including roses. The removal of stems, branches or roots is carried out in order to divert the energy of a plant so as to attain a certain purpose.

The correct time and the severity or lack of pruning are indicated under the generic descriptions. The following comments are the general principles applied to pruning.

The chief reasons for pruning are to keep a plant healthy, well balanced and evenly shaped, and also to encourage it to produce the maximum effect required from it. A plant is grown for its beauty of flower or foliage, for its quality of fruit, its brightly coloured stems or branches, characteristic shape or outline, or a combination of these.

Not all shrubs need regular annual pruning; many, especially when grown as single specimens, require only occasional light trimming to maintain shape, and this applies particularly to ornamental trees. The necessity for regular pruning can also be reduced by care and forethought at the time of planting, by ascertaining the eventual size and shape of the tree or shrub, and by allowing ample room for growth. Overcrowded trees and shrubs require drastic pruning each year to prevent them becoming weakened and mis-shapen as they compete for the available root space, light, food and water.

The health and vigour of a plant is maintained by correct pruning. It is important to remove all dead or damaged wood immediately it is noticed. The longer dead wood is allowed to remain on a plant, the greater is the risk of disease spores entering it, multiplying and eventually spreading to healthy tissue. In severe cases, extensive damage and even death of a whole plant may occur. Branches that cross or rub against one another are also a potential source of damage, and should be cut away before diseases can enter through the wounds.

Thin, weak growths are of little use, especially if they are produced in the centre of a bush, where they are starved of light and air. Well-ripened branches stand up better to severe weather and to disease. Consequently, the purpose of pruning should also be to keep the centre of a bush or shrub fairly open so as to allow light and air to circulate freely round the branches.

All pruning cuts should be made cleanly, leaving no ragged edges, torn bark, or bruising and crushing of the stems, as this results in the tissues dying. The pruning will heal (or callus) more rapidly if the cut is made nearly horizontally across a branch.

INITIAL PRUNING

In the initial stages, a young tree or shrub should be pruned fairly hard to train it into the desired shape. This involves the complete removal of weak shoots and cutting back of side-shoots to an outward-facing bud on one or, occasionally, two-year-old growths. As the buds are the only points from which further growth can develop along a stem, pruning cuts should be made as close as possible to a bud, the cut being begun on the side opposite to the bud and finished immediately above it.

PRUNING CUTS

The first three drawings show incorrect pruning cuts. They are too close to the bud, at the wrong angle or too far above the bud. The last cut is correct

After the framework of a tree or shrub has been established, pruning should be confined to maintaining shape by shortening, where necessary, one-year-old shoots back to a bud. Thin or unwanted shoots and dead or damaged shoots should be cut back flush with the main stem from which they arise. On no account should a short length of branch (snag) be left, as this will almost certainly die back. It may also produce unsightly clusters of short growths.

Pruning cuts, $\frac{1}{2}$–$\frac{3}{4}$ in. or more across, should have the edges pared cleanly with a sharp knife to assist callusing, and all large cuts should be painted with a fungicidal preservative such as a bitumastic paint.

Root pruning is chiefly practised on established fruit trees, and is aimed at restricting too-vigorous top growth at the expense of fruits. Most apple and pear varieties purchased from nurseries are grafted on to stocks of known performance and suitable for a given purpose, but as yet such rootstocks for plums and cherries are less readily available, and older, unfruitful trees may benefit from root pruning in October. A trench, about 18 in. deep and 9–18 in. wide, is taken out of the soil about 2–4 ft from the trunk, exposing the thick anchoring roots below the fibrous feeding roots. The feeding roots are severed on the far side of the trench; the thick roots are cut through at each side and the central portions removed. Refill the trench, being careful to avoid more damage than necessary to the feeding roots. After pruning the roots, the tree needs staking for at least 12 months to prevent wind-rocking. It is advisable to root-prune in two operations, cutting halfway round the trunk the first autumn and completing pruning the following October.

Pruning tools. Whatever tool is used for making the pruning cuts, it is essential that it should be of good quality.

The basic tool is the pruning knife. This is used for trimming the rough edges left by heavier tools, and for cutting back below any bruised or damaged tissue.

The pruning knife is generally designed with a curved handle, easily held in the hand, and a slightly curved blade. The resistance given by this curve as it is drawn across a branch enables a clean cut to be made.

Secateurs, which have an action rather like a pair of scissors, are commonly used for pruning shrubs, and good work can be

PRUNING TOOLS

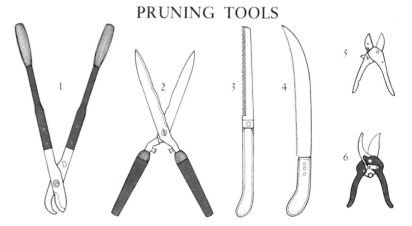

1. Long-handled secateurs (or pruners) for thick twigs and branchlets. 2. Shears for hedge cutting. 3 & 4. Pruning saws for cutting large branches. 5 & 6. Anvil secateurs and parrot-bill secateurs, mainly used for pruning twiggy shrubs and evergreen hedges

PRUNING OF ORNAMENTAL TREES AND

■ One-year-old stems

■ Old flowered stems removed in spring

Old flowered stems of hydrangea are left until the following March or April, to provide frost protection. In spring, they are cut back to base, leaving one-year-old stems to carry new growth

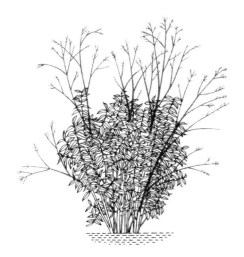

Buddleia davidii (above) flowers on the current season's shoots. Old wood is removed back to two or three joints in late winter or early spring, before new growth begins

Deutzia (left), like hydrangea, flowers on the previous season's wood. Old, twiggy, flowered stems are removed after flowering, either to ground level or back to healthy vigorous shoots

done with them even in unskilled hands. It is essential, however, that they should be kept sharp and in good condition, particular care being taken never to twist and wrench them when pruning, or to overstrain them by attempting large or hard branches.

Two basic types of secateurs are available. In the anvil secateur a straight-edged blade cuts on to a flat bar of softer metal, gripping the branch securely and making a clean cut. The parrot-bill secateur has one curved blade and a fixed bar against which the blade cuts. In both cases, best results will be achieved by making the cuts with the lower part of the blade rather than the tip.

For heavier work, that is for branches which the jaws of the secateurs will not hold comfortably or cut without straining, various types of shears are available. These are based on the same principles as secateurs, but the handles, 12–24 in. long, give greatly increased leverage and strength. Long-arm pruners—a secateur head fixed to a pole and worked by a lever connected to the blade by a strong wire—are particularly useful for reaching up into trees; they are only suitable for thick twigs and small branchlets.

A wide variety of pruning saws are used, all having a narrow blade tapering off to a point. They are essential for heavy work, but the cuts made are inevitably fairly rough and need careful trimming with a pruning knife afterwards. Straight-bladed saws may be single or double-edged, the latter having teeth of two degrees of coarseness, and requiring care in use.

For hedges, use short-handled shears; large-leaved evergreen hedges of such plants as the cherry laurels are better trimmed with secateurs. Several labour-saving mechanical trimmers are available.

Maintenance of tools. After use, wipe all pruning implements clean with an oily rag, and keep the working parts lubricated to prevent rust.

PRUNING OF ORNAMENTAL TREES AND SHRUBS

Pruning of these specimen plants is aimed at keeping the plants healthy and vigorous in order to maintain or improve their beauty of flower or foliage. Annual or occasional cutting back also controls or restricts their size.

Little pruning is generally required for evergreen trees and shrubs. Old and lanky shoots that spoil the appearance and outline of a shrub should be removed flush with the base in spring before growth starts, as should any damaged or diseased wood. Most flowering evergreens, particularly rhododendrons and heathers, should have the faded flower heads and stems removed; shoots may be shortened at the same time.

Deciduous trees and shrubs do not all require annual pruning, but those that do are divided into two groups: shrubs which flower on the previous season's wood, and shrubs which bear their flowers on shoots made during the current year. Before determining the correct time of pruning, it is essential to establish the growing and flowering habit of the shrub or tree.

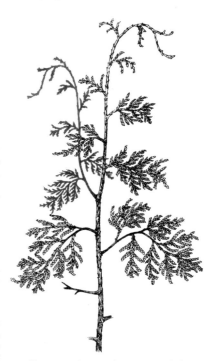

Leading stem of young chamaecyparis forking near the tip. In spring, the weaker of the two leading shoots is removed at the base

Shrubs in the first of these two groups generally flower at the same time as extension growth is being made, and pruning should be delayed until flowering is over. It is advisable to thin out the shrubs by removing several shoots entirely from ground level. In any case. many of the ornamental shrubs in this group tend to produce numerous twiggy growths unless old wood is regularly pruned out.

Shrubs which flower on shoots of the current year, such as *Buddleia davidii, Caryopteris* × *clandonensis* and *Spiraea japonica*, may be cut hard back in early spring before growth begins. Established plants should have the previous season's shoots pruned back to within a few buds of the base.

Young shrubs, whether evergreen or deciduous, seldom require pruning except for the removal of crossing branches or damaged shoot tips. Frosted and dead shoots should be cut back to healthy wood in spring. Young conifers may occasionally fork, in which case the weaker of the two leading shoots should be cut out at the base in March or April.

PRUNING OF CLIMBERS

Little pruning is needed for outdoor hardy climbers, except for the removal of dead wood and the thinning out of crowded shoots. Climbers trained over restricted areas and confined to an allotted wall space, on trellis supports and pergolas, usually require annual pruning. This is determined by the time of flowering. Climbers that flower on the previous season's wood usually bear their blooms from spring to early summer, while climbers in bloom from mid-summer onwards flower on current shoots.

PRUNING HEDGES

The upper half or two-thirds of the leading shoots are removed after planting young hedge plants. At the end of the first growing season, leaders and side shoots are again shortened by half. On two-year-old plants, all shoots are reduced by one-third

The former should be pruned after flowering by removing the flowered shoots at their base and by cutting out thin and crowded branches, leaving in their place young healthy laterals that will bear the following season's blooms.

Climbers flowering on the current season's wood should be pruned in February and early March. Remove all dead and damaged wood, thin out crowded shoots and, where necessary, shorten the growths back to a healthy, outward-facing bud.

Ornamental vines and other climbers grown for their foliage rather than their flowers may be cut back to shape and at the same time have dead or crowded shoots removed—during winter for deciduous climbers, and in early spring for evergreens. Certain variegated forms, particularly of ornamental vines, sometimes revert to green; such shoots should be removed entirely as soon as they are noticed.

PRUNING OF HEDGES

Although the cutting back of formal hedges and screens is technically a pruning method, this serves a different purpose from the pruning of ornamental shrubs. In the initial stages, a formal hedge is cut back quite severely to induce bushy growth and to train the hedge to the desired shape. Thereafter, hedges are trimmed once or several times a year, to keep them shapely.

Young formal hedges should be pruned after planting in early spring, by removing the upper half or two-thirds of the leading shoots to encourage vigorous side-branching. If young hedges are allowed to grow too quickly, without pruning, they rapidly grow lanky and bare at the base. Slow-growing hedging plants, particularly evergreens and most conifers, need less drastic pruning, and it is usually sufficient merely to tip the leaders. Repeat this initial training for one or

PRUNING CLIMBERS

Shoots removed after flowering

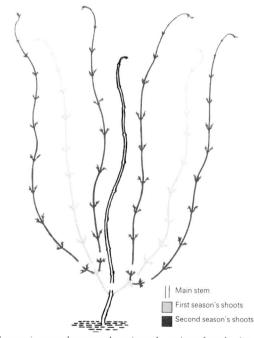

|| Main stem
▢ First season's shoots
◼ Second season's shoots

Clematis in the montana group flower on previous season's growths. After flowering, the shoots that carried blooms are removed. *Clematis* × *jackmanii*, however, flowers on the current season's wood. The

original stem is pruned to near base in early spring after planting. The following spring, the new shoots are pruned back to healthy buds from which new shoots will appear

GROWTH BUDS AND FRUITING SPURS

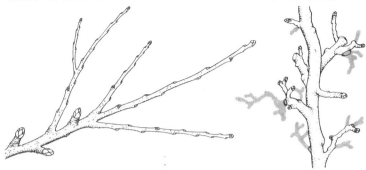

two winters until the desired height and shape of the hedge are reached.

Clip established hedges as growth demands by trimming lateral shoots and leaders with hedging shears or power-operated trimmers. Always clip from the base upwards, leaving the top of the hedge until last. Large-leaved evergreens, such as aucubas and cherry laurels, should be trimmed with secateurs to avoid damaging the leaves.

Dwarf hedges or edging plants, such as lavender and box, should be trimmed after flowering or in spring, and again once or twice during the summer.

Informal hedges should be cut hard back after planting, as with formal hedges, to encourage branching. Once established, little trimming is required and should be restricted to the thinning out of crowded shoots and the removal of spent flower heads. As with ornamental shrubs, timing depends on the growth habit: plants that flower on the current year's shoots should be pruned in spring, and plants that bear their flowers on shoots of the previous year should be cut back immediately after flowering. Use secateurs to prune informal hedges, although slow-growing plants, such as hebes and pyracanthas, may have untidy growths trimmed off with hedging shears in October or March.

PRUNING OF ROSES

This is described in detail under the generic entry for ROSA, both in regard to newly planted and established roses. These shrubs have a wide range of habit and form, and pruning instructions are given for each group.

In addition, the cutting of blooms and dead-heading are forms of summer pruning. It is less important to cut the flowers to an outward-facing bud as subsequent growth develops from the top of the plant. By regular dead-heading of faded flowers several flushes of blooms are generally assured on Hybrid tea and Floribunda roses, as well as on repeat-flowering Shrubs, Climbers and Ramblers. Cut the dead flower stems back to strong plump buds.

PRUNING OF FRUIT

The main purposes of fruit pruning are to assist in forming the desired tree shape in the early years, and later to keep the tree open and maintain the balance between growth and fruitfulness.

All types of fruit should be pruned annually when young, to form and maintain tree shape, and to remove badly placed shoots before they grow into branches. Winter pruning directs energy to the growth buds at the expense of fruit-forming buds, and should be kept to the minimum in the early years in order to regulate growth without delaying cropping unduly. Early fruiting may be encouraged by bending outwards and tying down shoots to open up trees; horizontal or pendulous shoots tend to produce more fruit buds. Subject to the influence of rootstock (in top fruits), soil and fruit variety, the object of pruning is to build up strongly branched, open trees that bear good regular crops.

Generally, pruning to encourage growth of top fruit, e.g. apples and pears, is carried out during frost-free weather in winter, between leaf-fall and bud-burst. Summer pruning is confined to trees grown in restricted form, such as cordons and espaliers. It is less stimulating to further growth and

An apple branchlet, showing one-year-old extension shoots. These bear small scale-like growth buds, and fruiting spurs with larger flower buds

Fruiting spurs on mature apple and pear trees are thinned out during winter, before bud-burst, to prevent too heavy fruit crops

also removes unwanted shoots. Established bush trees bearing stone fruits, such as plums, are also pruned, if necessary, in summer, because of risk of infection by silver leaf disease at other times.

All cuts should be made cleanly and just above the selected bud to speed healing. Cut young shoots just above a growth bud facing in the direction in which growth is required; large unwanted branches should be cut out flush with the trunk. Small cuts usually heal easily, but large cuts should be pared with a knife and painted.

Growth buds, which predominate on young trees, can be recognised as being pointed and closely pressed against the shoot. Unless they are at or near the ends of the growths of the previous year, or a pruning cut is made above them, they tend to stay dormant. Notching, by removing a small wedge of bark and wood just above a bud, can cause an otherwise dormant bud to grow. On the other hand, growth can be retarded by bud-nicking, which consists of making a deep incision just below a bud. Growth buds may change into fruit buds during the following summer or die out in time. Some fruits, such as pears, respond to hard pruning into old wood and, although no growth buds are visible, new shoots will usually be produced.

Fruit buds on the shoots increase as trees mature. They are often rounded and usually stand away from the shoot; in the season following their formation leaves and flowers are produced and short stems formed which become spurs. Certain varieties produce growths with fruit buds at their tips, for example 'Tydeman's Early' and 'Worcester Pearmain' apples, and 'Joséphine de Malines' pears. These varieties are known as tip-bearing, and growth is erratic unless these buds are removed. Pruning cuts made above fruit buds often result in unsatisfactory growth, but this treatment should be carried out on weak-growing trees.

Annual fruit pruning involves the shortening of lateral and leading shoots. A leader is the shoot at the end of each branch. If the tree or bush is growing strongly (18 in. or more of growth made in the previous year), the leading shoots require no pruning; upright leaders make more growth than horizontal ones. If a leading shoot is badly placed and not continuing the general line of the branch, it should be cut out in favour of a better-placed lateral.

The best laterals, or side-shoots, on young trees will later form the main branches. If left unpruned, fruit buds often form along part of the laterals, while pruning induces further growth.

Dead and diseased shoots and branches should be removed as they are noticed, as should crossing and congested stems, to allow light to all parts of the tree.

As mature trees make annual growth, the number of fruit buds increases. Some of these may need to be reduced, however, otherwise a heavy crop of small fruits can result. As trees get larger, less attention may be given to leaders and laterals, and pruning can be confined to the removal of complete branches and branchlets in November. Pruning should be completed before winter-washing.

Pruning of young trees (apple, pear, cherry and grape). These have usually been pruned at the nursery according to age and form of tree. Maiden trees (one-year-old), which have made a single main shoot in the season following budding or grafting, are cut back to the height from which the framework branches are required: 2–2½ ft for bush trees, 3½–4 ft for half-standards, and 6 ft for standards. Trees are often sold at two years or older, with the main branches already established.

After planting, the leaders of young trees should be cut back by one-third or a half, to a bud facing in the direction in which further growth is required. This leader-tipping should result in a doubling of the number of shoots during the following summer. In the second winter, more leader-tipping—removal of the top quarter of the shoots—can be done, more drastically if growth is poor. This should be done on the horizontal shoots to encourage growth; upright leaders, if they have grown by 24 in. or more, can be left unpruned. Continue to tip-prune all leaders until a good tree shape is established, after three or four years. Narrow angles between two shoots should be eliminated by removing one shoot completely, otherwise these may break away from each other under the weight of the crop.

Lateral shoots can be treated in one of the following manners while the basic shape of the tree is being built up: short laterals may be left unpruned to form fruit buds; long or badly placed shoots may be cut out completely. Alternatively, treat them as leaders by cutting out the branch beyond them and shortening the laterals as for leaders.

TRAINING YOUNG FRUIT TREES

Fruit trees are usually purchased ready trained, but the following diagrams show initial procedures for the most common growth forms. Dwarf pyramid: remove about 12 in. from the tip of the stem after planting. The following winter, cut out weak and crowded laterals and reduce the remainder by half. In subsequent seasons, summer prune the laterals back to three pairs of leaves. Cordon: no pruning is needed for maiden stems at planting time. In July, cut back all laterals by half, and in winter shorten back to two good buds. The following summer, cut laterals back to three pairs of leaves and sub-laterals to one pair of leaves. On espalier with the first tier, prune the leader in winter back to 18 in. and shorten the laterals. Repeat the following winter, pruning sub-laterals to 4–6 in. The next summer, prune laterals on tiers back to three leaves and sub-laterals to one leaf. Bush: cut back a maiden tree to 24 in., allowing the top four or five shoots to develop; in winter reduce these to 9 in. The next winter, cut leading shoots back to 12 in. and laterals to 6 in. Thereafter, remove one-third of leading growths and reduce laterals to 6 in. Fan-trained (peach): in April, cut back the maiden stem to 18 in. Select three or four of the resulting shoots, two of which should be opposite. Allow this pair to grow unrestricted; pinch back the other shoots at intervals during the summer. In April, cut out all growths above and below the selected pair and reduce this to 12 in. Allow three or four vigorous shoots on each to grow unrestricted and form the main branches.

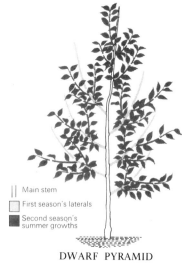

‖	Main stem
☐	First season's laterals
■	Second season's summer growths

DWARF PYRAMID

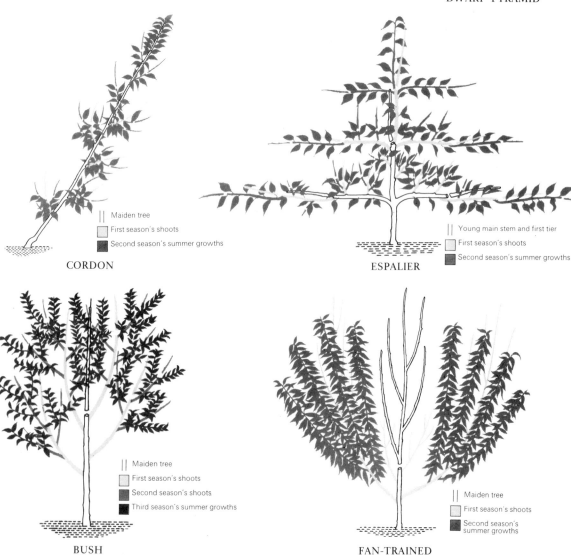

‖	Maiden tree
☐	First season's shoots
■	Second season's summer growths

CORDON

‖	Young main stem and first tier
☐	First season's shoots
■	Second season's summer growths

ESPALIER

‖	Maiden tree
☐	First season's shoots
■	Second season's shoots
■	Third season's summer growths

BUSH

‖	Maiden tree
☐	First season's shoots
■	Second season's summer growths

FAN-TRAINED

PRUNING PEACH

GRAPE

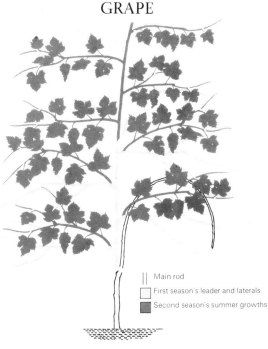

|| Two-year-old fruiting branch
☐ Leafing buds
■ Late summer growths

Standard replacement pruning: remove all leafing buds from one-year-old shoots, leaving one at the base and one at the apex

After planting, remove the soft unripened wood from the rod back to a plump bud. The following summer, cut back all laterals to 18 in., and in winter prune the same shoots back to two plump buds; remove soft growth from the leader. The next spring, select one strong shoot from the spurred-back laterals. These fruit-bearing shoots should be pinched back to one leaf beyond the fruits, and all subsequent laterals should also be pinched back to one leaf

|| Main rod
☐ First season's leader and laterals
■ Second season's summer growths

In subsequent winters, remove any badly placed or crossing laterals, and tip others from which growth is required. Otherwise leave the side-shoots unpruned to produce fruit buds. If branches are being pulled down by the weight of cropping, encourage replacement shoots.

Pears should be pruned like apples, but less heavily in the early years. Established trees of some pears, such as 'William's Bon Chrétien', tend to produce large-branched fruiting spurs which should be thinned out during late winter or prior to bud-burst, leaving three or four plump fruit buds.

Young plum trees should be pruned more lightly than apples. For the first two or three years, prune in early spring, cutting leaders back by about half on two-year-old trees, and by about a quarter on three-year-olds, to encourage branching growth. Remove completely any shoots forming narrow angles, and any short lateral shoots on the main stem. When the head of the tree is established, prune in summer from June onwards or immediately after harvesting. Keep the tree open by pruning out dead, broken, diseased and crossing branches and maintain growth by annual feeding. Summer-pruning cuts heal rapidly and are less likely to allow silver leaf fungus to enter through wounds.

Peach trees grown as bushes should be pruned in May. As growth starts, remove crossing shoots and tip shoots that have died, back to a healthy bud.

Acid cherry bush trees are treated like plums for the first three or four years. Thereafter they should be pruned after growth has commenced in spring, so as to produce vigorous young shoots which will crop the following year. This involves annual cutting into shoots two years old or more, and is necessary to prevent congested growth and poor fruit yield.

On newly planted grapes, rub out any misplaced laterals while they are still small and soft. When the laterals have reached a length of 24 in., during the following spring and summer, pinch out the tip of each lateral, and stop all sub-laterals at two leaves. Flower clusters that appear during this period should be removed. In the autumn, cut back the laterals to two buds, to form the basis of the fruiting spurs for the following season. Also remove the soft unripe tips of the leading rods. In spring, when the spur laterals begin to show immature flower-bud clusters, reduce these to one strong growth to each spur.

Pruning of young trees grown in restricted form (cordons, espaliers, etc.). In the first year or two after planting, these trained trees may need to be winter pruned to establish their framework. Thereafter, they should be pruned in summer to keep the plants to shape without encouraging too much growth. In order to maintain the restricted size, trained trees must be grafted on to dwarfing rootstocks, or on to semi-dwarf stock for trees grown on poor soil. Rich soil or a vigorous rootstock generally stimulates too much growth.

CORDONS OF APPLE AND PEAR. Trained trees require no pruning after planting. Summer prune from late July to September (mid-July in the case of pears) all established trees which are growing normally. Laterals should be cut back to three pairs, sub-laterals to one pair of leaves. Spread the pruning over several weeks and complete by mid-September; laterals that were pruned earlier and have produced more growths should have these shortened to one leaf.

When the leading shoots have grown so far that they fill the allotted space, prune them as laterals in May. As cordon trees age, spur systems become larger and should be thinned in winter if cropping is satisfactory, otherwise too much growth may result.

ESPALIERS OF APPLE AND PEAR. These trees are best bought ready trained. Each branch is a horizontal cordon and should be pruned

as such. Continue to train the leaders horizontally, shortening them by half each winter until the desired length is reached. Thereafter, treat all extension shoots as laterals; remove completely any excessively vigorous upright shoots. Avoid any winter pruning which will encourage stronger growth, especially from the upper tiers.

FANS OF PLUM, PEACH, NECTARINE AND ACID CHERRY. These trees are also best bought ready trained. Remove entirely shoots which grow out at the front and back of the fan. If necessary, balance the growth of different parts of the fan by raising (to stimulate) or lowering (to check) the branches temporarily. On three or four-year-old trees, new growth must be controlled or they will become crowded with unwanted shoots, which should either be rubbed out early in the season or, if space permits, tied into the framework as they grow. The tips should be pinched out when they have reached the desired length.

Usually the topmost bud is allowed to grow and extend the branch until the allotted space is filled. Lateral shoots are left at 3–4 in. intervals for acid cherry and plum, and at 6 in. for peach and nectarine; pinch out the remaining laterals. The chosen shoots are tied in as they grow and will usually crop the following year. During the year of fruiting, particularly for peach and nectarine, replacement shoots should be allowed to grow out, usually from near the base. Further laterals which develop may be left along the length of the shoot, but should be stopped at two or three leaves. All shoots that arise on fruiting stems should be pinched back to four to six leaves. After fruiting, the shoots that have carried the crop must be cut out, leaving the replacement shoots to be tied into the available space. Trained plums fruit on old as well as new wood and less attention need be given to the replacement shoots.

787

PRUNING LOGANBERRIES

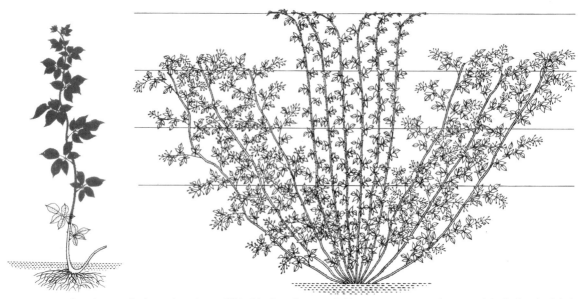

A young stem, taken from a tip layer, is pruned to 9 in. after planting

On established bushes. the outer fruiting stems are removed at ground level after the fruit is picked. Young central growths are trained in as replacement shoots

BLACK CURRANTS

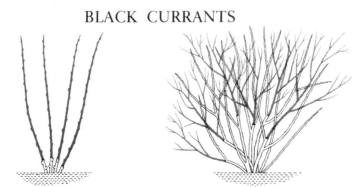

Young bushes are cut back to 3–4 in. above ground level, after planting in winter

A mature bush, showing the removal of poorly cropping three-year-old growths

FAN-TRAINED ESTABLISHED ACID CHERRIES should have old fruited wood removed in winter and new shoots trained in.

GRAPES. Cut all laterals back to two buds, in autumn. Remove any unripe growth from the tip of the rods, or cut these back to the top wire if ripened wood exceeds it. In subsequent years, treat the upper lateral as a fruiting spur.

NUT (COB-NUT, FILBERT, HAZEL NUT, WALNUT). Male catkins are produced on shoots of the previous season, female flowers and subsequent fruits on mature wood. After the catkins have shed their pollen in February, cut young shoots back by half. Remove entirely some of the oldest branches each year to keep the centre of the bush open. Short lateral shoots produced the previous year should be left unpruned.

Pruning of older trees. Annual pruning of mature trees is simply a modified form of the early treatment: take out dead, diseased and crossing shoots and branches, using a saw to cut first on the undersides of the

branches (undercutting) before finally sawing through from above. Between leaf-fall and bud-burst, thin out spur systems on apple and pear trees, to reduce the number of fruit buds to three or four on each spur, and to increase fruit size. The pruning of individual leaders and laterals is no longer practicable, but trim branches on trees lacking vigour. Remove old and weak shoots, and train in young healthy shoots.

Treat neglected trees similarly but spread over several winters, or pruning may result in the production of too much unwanted growth. The object is to improve vigour and cropping.

Pruning of neglected trained fruit trees. Rubbing out of unwanted shoots may have been neglected or an attempt made to control growth by severe winter pruning. This can be overcome by encouraging fruiting so that the energy of the tree is partly absorbed in the formation of fruits rather than growth buds. Remove badly placed shoots after growth has started in spring, and summer

prune crossing branches to admit light and air. For badly overgrown trees, spread the improvement of shape over several seasons. Vigorous shoots can be induced to form fruit buds by tying them down nearly horizontal in mid-summer.

Pruning of soft fruit (blackberry and hybrid berries, including loganberry). After planting, cut all shoots down to a bud about 9 in. above soil level to encourage the build-up of the root system. During the first summer, strong shoots will be produced and should be tied to the framework. At the end of the first season of growth, remove any weak shoots.

During the second season, growth made in the previous year will bear fruit. At the same time new shoots will be produced; at the end of the first cropping year and in subsequent years, the shoots which have fruited should be cut out and the new growths tied to the supporting framework for cropping the following summer.

The amount of fruited wood to be removed in the autumn. as soon as possible after fruiting has finished. depends on the amount and vigour of the new canes. If strong shoots arise from below ground level, the whole of each fruited cane can be removed; otherwise cut back to strong new shoots low down on the plant.

To reduce spread of cane diseases from old to new canes. keep the new growths separate from the old during the growing season by tying them in a bundle at the side of the framework. On exposed sites. after pruning. cut out the old shoots of loganberry, tie the bundle of new ones to the framework. but delay training them in until the spring.

BLACK CURRANTS. Cut all shoots down to 1–2 in. above soil level, preferably to an outward-pointing bud, after planting. This encourages growth to arise from below ground level. Strong shoots should be produced during the first season of growth; at the end of the

RASPBERRIES

Young canes are cut back to 6 in. above ground level. The following winter, the soft unripe tips of the new canes are removed

The following summer, cut down the canes to ground level after the fruit has been picked. Tie in the new shoots

RED AND WHITE CURRANTS

One-year-old bushes have the laterals cut back by half at planting time

On established bushes, summer-prune all sub-laterals to four to six leaves

growing period, weak shoots (less than 12 in. long) should be removed, leaving the rest full length to crop the following year. If, after the first year of growth, shoots less than 12 in. long have been produced, all the shoots should be cut hard down again.

During the second year after planting (or third year in the case of bushes cut down twice), the shoots of the previous year will flower and fruit, while more new growths are produced. After the first cropping year, a proportion of the shoots which have carried fruit should be pruned out, either to ground level or to a vigorous young shoot.

In subsequent years, pruning follows the same pattern of removing old shoots which have fruited and replacing them by young shoots. In time, the old shoots darken in colour, eventually becoming black, while the young shoots remain brown. Hard pruning while the bushes are young, combined with feeding and mulching, maintains a higher proportion of young, brown, fruitful shoots.

RED AND WHITE CURRANTS. These differ from black currants in their fruiting habits and are pruned by a different system. They are usually grown on a short leg 6–9 in. tall, and the lateral branches pruned to promote short fruiting laterals. Plants are sold as one or two-year-old bushes, and the branches should be cut back by about half their length to an outward-facing bud in winter. In subsequent winters, prune the leading shoots similarly and cut the laterals hard back to within two or three buds.

This method of pruning builds up a permanent framework of branches with fruit buds on spurs formed at the bases of the laterals. As the bushes get older, some branches should be cut out entirely and replaced by new shoots which should have their leaders and laterals pruned as already described. Keep the short length of stem below the branches clear of unwanted shoots by cutting them out completely in winter.

Cordons should be treated like individual shoots, removing during winter one-third of the length of the leaders until the available space has been filled. Thereafter prune each leader hard, like a lateral.

Summer pruning is possible with red and white currant bushes and is desirable on cordons to increase fruit buds and remove unwanted growths. From early July onwards, shorten the laterals to about five leaves.

GOOSEBERRY. The bushes should be pruned in winter, as recommended for red and white currants. Bushes are usually grown on a leg— a length of clear stem before the branches begin. Prune away any shoots which grow from below ground level to obstruct the leg. Where botrytis die-back of shoots is common, gooseberries can be grown like black currants with shoots that arise from below ground level.

For bushes grown on a leg, prune the leaders back by about half to an outward-facing bud except for spreading varieties which should be cut to an upward-facing bud. Cut laterals to 3–4 in. of their base. Remove weak laterals altogether so that those which are pruned are spaced 3–4 in. apart along the branches. Fruit size depends on the severity of lateral shortening and increased size will result from pruning the laterals harder. This applies particularly to cordon-trained gooseberries where laterals should be cut back to three buds.

Remove all dead, diseased, crossing and crowded branches so that picking is made easier. Old branches should be cut out entirely if the bush is becoming overgrown; replace by strong young shoots.

On older bushes, cut the leaders hard back by about two-thirds. Cordons should be pruned as individual branches during winter.

Summer prune cordons, and also bushes if desired, to encourage fruit-bud formation; remove the tips of laterals infected with American gooseberry mildew. Shorten all laterals to five leaves from the end of June.

RASPBERRY. Cut down the canes to 9 in. above ground level after planting. Remove all weak shoots at the end of the first growing season, but leave the remaining shoots to crop the following year. After cropping, cut out fruited shoots and tie in strong new growths to crop the following year. On established plants, reduce the number of canes by spacing them 6–8 in. apart. Check the spread of canes by pulling out unwanted shoots in summer when the bases become woody.

Autumn-fruiting raspberries such as 'September' should have all the shoots cut to ground level annually in February. Otherwise the canes will revert to summer fruiting.

GLOSSARY

Acaricide
A chemical spray or dust used for destroying parasitic spider mites.

Acid
Applied to soils with a pH content below 7·0. Most plants will grow on acid soil, and others, such as rhododendrons and many ericas, will not thrive in any other. As acid soil is deficient in lime, it precludes the successful cultivation of lime-loving plants, such as members of the brassica family, unless lime is added.

Acuminate
Applied to leaves and other plant organs that taper to a point.

Acute
Referring to a leaf, or petal that terminates in a sharp point.

Adventitious
A botanical term referring to the atypical origin of plant organs such as roots arising from a stem above ground.

Aeration
The loosening of soil by various mechanical means to allow a free passage of air.

Aerial roots
Applied to roots arising on stems above ground, as found on ivy and various orchids.

Alkaline
Applied to soils with a pH content above 7·0. Most plants, excepting those that thrive on an acid soil, e.g. rhododendrons and many heathers, do best on neutral or slightly alkaline soils.

Alpine
Botanically, a plant native to the alpine zone, defined as being between the upper limits of tree growth (the tree line) and the permanent snow line. Also loosely applied to any small plant suitable for growing on a rock garden.

Alternate
Applied to the arrangement of leaves on a stem; the single leaves are placed one above the other.

Annual
A plant that completes its life cycle from seed to seed within one growing season.

Anther
The functional part of a STAMEN which contains the pollen grains. It comprises two pollen sacs, or anther lobes, joined on a stalk.

Apex
The tip of a shoot or root from where growth is extended.

Aquatic
A plant that lives submerged in water, wholly or with leaves and flowers floating on the surface.

Areole
A curiously modified side shoot, unique to the *Cactaceae* family. It is usually a small cushion-like tubercle with woolly or barbed hairs and often with spines.

Aroid
Any plant belonging to the *Araceae* family, e.g. philodendron.

Awn
The bristle-like attachment to the seeds of some species of grass.

Axil, axillary
The angle between a leaf and stem, from which arise further growth or flower buds.

Beard
Usually applied to the growth of hairs along the upper surface of the petals of some irises.

Bedding plant
A hardy, half-hardy or tender annual, biennial or perennial used for temporary garden display.

Berry
A fleshy fruit, containing a number of seeds, which does not open, e.g. gooseberry, grape.

Biennial
A plant that requires two growing seasons to complete its life cycle, e.g. foxglove. Leaves are formed during the first year, flowers and seeds the following season.

Bigeneric
Referring to a hybrid plant derived from crossing two different genera, e.g. × *Osmarea*, 'a cross between *Osmanthus* and *Phillyrea*.

Bipinnate
Applied to a leaf that is divided into several segments which are again sub-divided. A mimosa leaf has two sets of leaflets.

Biternate
A term used to describe a leaf that is divided and sub-divided into units of three.

Blanching
The practice of excluding light from the stems and/or leaves of certain vegetable crops, such as celery and chicory. Blanching may be done by earthing up, or by covering the plants with paper collars or inverted flower pots.

Bleeding
The loss of sap from plant tissues after having been cut.

Bole
The clear trunk of a tree from ground level to the first branch.

Bolt(-ing)
Running to flower and seed prematurely. It is particularly applied to vegetables, such as lettuce and beetroot, and is often caused by a check to growth due to drought, or poor soil conditions.

Bonsai
A Japanese technique for creating dwarfed trees in small containers. Stunting is maintained artificially by severe root pruning and restriction, and by stem pruning.

Bottom heat
Heat applied from below, usually through electrically heated cables. It is used in frames and greenhouse beds for more efficient rooting of cuttings of half-hardy and tender plants.

Bract
A modified leaf. It may be scale-like and green or brown at the base of the flower stalk. Sometimes it is conspicuous and highly coloured as in *Euphorbia pulcherrima* (poinsettia).

Break
To grow out from an axillary bud, either naturally or artificially. The pinching out of the growing tips of a plant causes break buds to appear, thus promoting bushy growth. The rubbing out of break buds often induces better-quality flowers, as on chrysanthemums.

Broadcast
Applied to the sowing of seeds or application of fertilisers, by spreading evenly over a wide area and not confined to straight, shallow seed furrows.

Bud
A tightly condensed shoot usually protected by closely overlapping scales. Buds are a prominent feature of plants which rest during the winter, such as deciduous trees and shrubs and certain herbaceous perennials, e.g. paeonies.

Buds contain immature leaves and/or flowers, and are the means whereby a plant rapidly commences growth with the arrival of warm weather.

Buds vary greatly in size and shape and may be in shades of brown, green or purple, and hairy, sticky or waxy. In general, buds arise singly in the leaf axils, but occasionally in groups of three or more. Sometimes they may occur unnaturally on stem wounds directly from the bark.

Bulb
A bud-like storage organ, usually underground. It is composed of fleshy modified leaves or leaf bases closely wrapped around each other; in lilies it is made up of separate scale leaves. Unlike a CORM, a bulb always contains the young plant.

Bulbil
A small immature bulb, often formed at the base of mature bulbs or on stems above ground, as in certain species of lilies.

Cactus
A SUCCULENT plant belonging to the *Cactaceae* family.

Calcifuge
Literally, lime-hating. The term is applied to plants that will not thrive in limy soils, e.g. rhododendron, pieris and vaccinium.

Calyx
The outer protective part of a flower which consists of SEPALS fused together to form a bowl, funnel or tube-like structure.

Cambium
The actively growing tissue just beneath the bark of woody stems. This layer is responsible for the increase in tree girth.

Cane
A slender woody stem, often hollow or pithy in the centre. It is particularly applied to stems of raspberry, blackberry, loganberry and bamboo.

Capsule
A dry or barely fleshy fruit, usually containing loose seeds. These are shaken out by the wind or forcibly ejected by the capsule suddenly splitting when ripe.

Catch crop
The growing of a quick-maturing crop in between slower-maturing ones or in the gap between one crop maturing and another being planted. Crops of radishes or lettuce, for example, may be raised by the side of a celery trench.

Catkin
Applied to a flower spike, often pendulous, but sometimes erect, that is composed of prominent BRACTS. Each of these shelters one or more tiny stemless flowers, usually without petals and of one sex only.

Channelled
Applied to a narrow leaf whose up-curved margins form a channel.

Chimaera: see MUTANT

Chlorosis
The loss of, or poor production of, chlorophyll (the green colouring matter in plants), giving a bleached, yellow or white appearance to leaves. In extreme cases, browning and death of the tissues may follow. The usual cause of chlorosis is lack of essential minerals. Certain viruses may also be responsible.

Chromosome(s)
Minute bodies within the nucleus of a plant or animal cell that control the hereditary characters.

Cladode
A flattened, leaf-like stalk, performing the functions of a leaf. Also known as phyllode.

Clamp
A mound of soil and straw or bracken in which to store harvested root crops, such as potatoes, beet, carrots, swedes. A wide shallow trench is dug and lined with straw or bracken. After the leaves have been removed, the roots are piled on to this in a conical or roof-shaped heap, and covered with a layer of straw and soil from the trench. The soil covering must be firmed to a smooth sloping finish to divert excessive rain. Clamps larger than 6 × 4 × 4 ft wide will need aerating by inserting tufts of straw into the ridge at intervals of 4–6 ft.

Classification
The arrangement of plants (and all animate and inanimate organisms) into groups according to their natural—or assumed—affinities. Related plant species are grouped into genera and genera into families.

Cloche
Originally a bell-shaped glass cover, used in plant propagation or to protect early crops. Modern cloches are composed of separate panes of glass or plastic of varying sizes, and are primarily used for raising early crops in open ground.

Clone, clonal
A group of identical plants all obtained by vegetative propagation from a single individual parent plant.

Clove
Usually applied to one of the small sections that make up a shallot or garlic bulb.

Column
The flower organ formed by the fusion of female and male reproductive organs. It is mainly found in orchid flowers.

Compost
A term with two distinct meanings. It is applied to a mixture of loam, sand, peat, leaf-mould or other ingredients used for growing plants in pots or containers of all kinds. It also refers to a farmyard manure substitute obtained by carefully stacking together plant remains such as vegetable trimmings, non-seeding weed plants, straw and grass mowings. The decay of these materials can be hastened by the addition of chemicals until a sweet-smelling, brown and crumbly humus product has formed.

Compound
Used to describe leaves, flowers or fruits composed of two or more similar units. The pineapple fruit, for example, is the result of the fusion of a spike of small fruits; a daisy flower is a head of many tiny florets.

Cone
The fruit of a conifer, usually composed of a woody central stem and scales which bear and protect the seeds.

Conifer
A race of primitive trees and shrubs, usually evergreen, with needle-like or linear leaves. They generally bear their seeds in cones.

Contractile
Referring to roots on bulbs and corms that contract, thereby pulling the bulb deeper into the soil.

Cordate
A heart-shaped leaf or one with two rounded lobes at the base.

Cordon
Any plant restricted to a single main stem by controlled pruning. The term is applied to fruit trees. Double or triple cordons are plants restricted to two or three main stems.

Coriaceous
Tough or leathery, usually applied to leaves.

Corm
A plant storage organ, composed of a thickened stem-base, usually covered with a papery skin. At the top of the corm is a bud from which both shoots and new roots appear.

Corolla
The inner protective part of a flower consisting of wholly or partially fused petals. The corolla usually contrasts with the CALYX in being coloured.

Corona
Literally, a crown. Botanically the term refers to the trumpet or cup of such genera as *Narcissus* and *Hymenocallis*. In the latter, the cup is formed from the fusion of flattened stamen filaments, but in narcissus it is thought to have originated as an outgrowth of the petal segments.

Corymb
A flat-topped cluster of flowers, the stalks of which arise one above the other from a vertical stem or axis.

Cotyledon
The first seedling leaf or leaves to appear on germination and which were already formed in the seed. In some cases, e.g. broad bean, the seed leaves remain underground and the first shoot to appear bears true leaves. Seed leaves frequently differ in shape from true or adult leaves. The solitary seed leaves of onion and some lilies resemble blades of grass.

Colour break: see MUTANT

Crenate
With rounded teeth. The term usually refers to a leaf margin, but is occasionally applied to the margins of flattened or angled stems, as in the case of *Cissus cactiformis* and epiphyllum.

Crest
A comb-like tuft of hairs or soft bristles, found on petals, in particular on some iris species.

Crocks
Broken pieces of a clay flower pot, placed concave-side down over the drainage hole in a pot or container.

Crown
The basal part of a herbaceous perennial from which roots and shoots grow.

Curd
The dense mass of immature flower buds that forms the heads of cauliflower and broccoli.

Cutting: see chapter on PROPAGATION

Cyme
A domed, flattened or rounded cluster of flowers, usually with several arching branches radiating outwards.

Cymose

Damping down
Watering the floor and benches of a frame or greenhouse, usually in warm weather. This is done to create a humid atmosphere by evaporation.

Dead-heading
The removal of faded flowers to prevent seeding or to tidy the appearance of a plant.

Deciduous
Applied to a plant that loses its leaves at the end of the growing season. The term particularly refers to trees and shrubs.

Decumbent
Referring to a stem or a whole plant that is prostrate, but with the shoot tips ascending.

Dentate
Applied to a leaf that has tooth-like notches to the margins.

Dibber or dibble
A blunt-pointed stick or peg, usually of wood, used for making holes in the soil when transplanting seedlings.

Dicotyledon
All flowering plants are botanically classified into two main groups by the number of COTYLEDONS (seed leaves) present in the seed at maturity. Monocotyledons have one seed leaf, dicotyledons have two.

Digitate
A term used to describe a leaf that is composed of several radiating leaflets. These all grow from the top of the leaf stalk.

Dioecious
Referring to plants that have single-sexed (entirely male or female) flowers on separate plants. See also MONOECIOUS.

Diploid
Applied to a plant with cells containing the normal two sets of CHROMOSOMES.

Disc
The flattened or domed centre of a daisy flower, composed of numerous tiny tubular florets.

Dissected
Referring to a leaf or petal deeply cut into segments or lobes.

Distichous
Usually applied to leaves that are arranged in two flattened opposite ranks on the stem, and creating a fan-like effect.

Dormant
Applied to the resting period, normally autumn and winter, when a plant makes little or no extension growth.

Dorsal
A botanical term for the upright SEPAL at the back of some orchid flowers.

Dot plant
A plant, usually tall-growing, used as an isolated or specimen plant in a formal flower bed to emphasise contrast in height, colour and/or texture.

Drawn
Applied to plants that are growing too thickly, or in a poorly lighted place. They become long and thin and often pallid in colour.

Drill
A straight, usually shallow furrow in which seeds (usually vegetable) are sown outdoors.

Drupe
A single-seeded fruit composed of a fleshy outer covering surrounding a hard stony seed.

Earthing up
The practice of drawing up soil round plants to exclude light. Celery and chicory are earthed up to whiten the stems.

Elliptic
In the shape of an ellipse; generally applied to leaves, but also to sepals and petals.

Entire
Used to describe leaves or petals with smooth margins.

Epiphyte(s)
Plants which are adapted to live above the soil, usually adhering to tree branches or mossy rocks. Orchids and bromeliads provide the best examples, although many other plant families are epiphytic. Such plants are usually native to rain forests where a high humidity exists for all or much of the year. Epiphytes are not parasitic, gaining support only from their tree hosts. The roots that cling to the surface of a branch or rock may gain some nourishment from decayed plant remains in the crevices. Orchids also have thick spongy roots that hang free in the air and absorb atmospheric moisture and dissolved minerals.

Espalier
A type of trained tree, with a vertical trunk and one or more pairs of opposite horizontal branches, known as tiers, arranged at 12–15 in. intervals. Pears, apples and other top fruits are the only trees trained in this way.

Etiolate
Referring to abnormally long thin pallid growths caused by lack of sufficient light. Forced rhubarb is blanched or etiolated by deliberately excluding light.

Evergreen
Usually a tree or shrub, which bears foliage throughout the year.

Eye
An undeveloped or immature growth bud. The term is also applied to the centre of a flower, particularly when it is of a different and contrasting colour.

F₁ hybrid (first generation)
A term applied to a seed strain obtained by crossing two pure-bred, closely related selections or varieties. The resultant plants are usually of greater vigour.

Falcate
Curved like a sickle; generally referring to a leaf.

Falls
The pendulous outer petals, or perianth segments, of an iris.

Farina
Literally, flour. Certain plant organs, mainly leaves, stems and fruits, are sometimes covered with a white waxy powder.

Fasciation
An abnormal condition where a number of stems grow fused together side by side, forming a broad, flat, often ribbon-like stem. *Forsythia × intermedia* 'Spectabilis' often produces such growth. The term is also sometimes applied to any irregular fusion of stems, leaves or flowers.

Fastigiate
Referring to an erect, columnar habit of growth, particularly of trees and shrubs, e.g. Lombardy poplar and *Prunus* 'Amanogawa'.

Feathered
Relating to a maiden or young standard tree with lateral shoots on the main stem. These are left on for a year or two to help build a strong thick bole. When the trunk is established, the feathers must be removed.

Fertilisation
Basically, the fusion of a pollen-grain nucleus (male) with the undeveloped seed or ovule (female). It results in the formation of a mature seed.

Fertilisers: see MANURES AND FERTILISERS

Filament(s)
The stalk of a STAMEN which bears the two anther lobes.

Fimbriate
Applied to plant organs, such as bracts, stipules, sepals or petals with fringed margins. See also LACINIATE.

Flore-pleno
A term applied to flowers with an abnormally high number of petals, described as double or semi-double. Common examples occur in tulip, narcissus and carnation.

Floret
A small individual flower that forms part of a large head or cluster. In the daisy family (*Compositae*), each flower is a head of tiny, closely packed florets covering a central disc.

Flower
A plant organ composed of modified and highly specialised parts concerned with sexual reproduction. The essential parts are the female carpels or ovaries, which eventually bear the seeds, and the anthers which produce pollen or male sex cells. These are usually surrounded by an inner ring of coloured leaves known as petals and an outer ring of green protecting sepals. There are, however, a great many variations to this basic pattern. The great majority of plants bear flowers with both male and female organs (monoecious), while others have single-sexed flowers on separate plants (dioecious).

Petals and sepals are usually clearly differentiated in shape, size and colour, but sometimes, in for instance tulip, they are similar. Petals and sepals may be separate, as in a buttercup, or variously fused, as in the primrose and convolvulus. They may be entirely missing, as in hazel and poplar, or the petals may be missing (pachysandra and anemone). Occasionally, as in helleborus, the sepals act as petals and the petals are modified to secrete nectar (petaloid nectaries).

Forcing
The practice of hastening plants into flower or fruit before their natural time. This is chiefly applied to plants grown for indoor decoration during winter or for early crops of, for example, rhubarb and lettuce.

Friable
Referring to a crumbly soil that is easily worked and raked to a tilth.

Frond
A feathery leaf of a fern or palm.

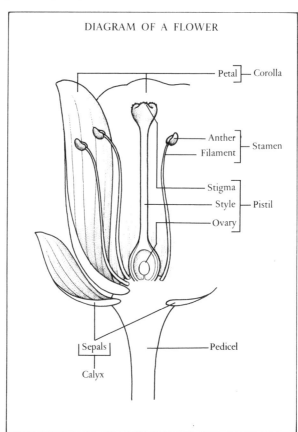

DIAGRAM OF A FLOWER

Petal — Corolla

Anther — Stamen
Filament

Stigma
Style — Pistil
Ovary

Sepals
Calyx

Pedicel

Fruit
Botanically, the mature ovary, bearing ripe seeds. The fruits may be dry pods or capsules, or they may be soft and fleshy.

Fruiting body
The reproductive organ of a fungus, e.g. mushrooms and toadstools and the pin-head-like structures on bread mould.

Fumigate
A method of killing pests and diseases under glass by using a volatile or inflammable insecticide, acaricide or fungicide. The practice is mainly restricted to smoke canisters or pellets which, when ignited, give off a dense smoke carrying the active ingredients to all parts of the greenhouse.

Fungicide
A substance used for killing fungal diseases. Fungicides are generally formulations of copper or sulphur, but other substances, including antibiotics, are being developed.

Gall
An abnormal outgrowth of plant tissue, e.g. marble gall and oak-apple on oak, pincushion gall on wild rose, bean gall on willow. Galls may occur on roots, stems, leaves and flowers and are primarily caused by insects or bacteria, sometimes fungi. Fungal galls, such as potato wart or club-root on brassicas (cabbage, cauliflower, etc.), can be severely damaging to the plant. In general, though, galls cause little harm other than a local check to growth.

Genus (pl. genera)
A category in the botanical classification of plants that identifies a group of allied species.

All the various types of birch, for example, are grouped under the genus *Betula*. See also SPECIES.

Germination
The first stage in the development of a plant from a seed.

Glabrous
Smooth or bare; referring to a part of a plant that is hairless.

Gland
A secretory organ or pore, usually small or minute, found on stems, leaves and flowers. The pores of *Saxifraga burseriana* secrete limy water, which on drying shows as encrusted whitened leaf margins. The glands of pinguiculas secrete a gummy liquid which traps insects.

Glaucous
Grey-blue; referring to leaves and stems covered with a grey or white waxy patina. *Euphorbia myrsinites* and sea kale are examples.

Globose
Globular or spherical; shaped like a ball.

Glochid
A small slender barbed hair, characteristic of many cacti.

Grafting
The uniting of a stem or bud of one plant on to the root of another to form a new individual. This method of propagation is usually applied to fruit trees and other plants that are difficult or slow to produce roots from cuttings. See also chapter on PROPAGATION.

Grex
A name applied to a group of plants, sometimes difficult to

TYPES OF TERMINAL FLOWER ARRANGEMENTS

Catkin

Corymb

Cyme

Panicle

Spike

Umbel

Plume

Raceme

Whorl

separate individually. They often arise from crossing two species or distinct varieties.

Ground cover

Of plants used to cover the soil, often between large plants such as trees and shrubs. They usually provide a dense weed-proof cover of ornamental foliage that requires little or no maintenance.

Haft

A term used to describe the narrowed, stalk-like base of petals, particularly the standards and falls of irises.

Half-hardy

This refers to two categories of tender plants grown in the open. It applies firstly to completely frost-tender species that can only be grown during the summer, e.g. begonia, canna, marrow, runner bean, French and African marigolds (tagetes).

Secondly, half-hardy also refers to shrubs and herbaceous perennials that will survive average winters outdoors. They must be sited in a sheltered position or grown in mild areas of the country (west and south), e.g. *Acacia decurrens dealbata*, various cistus species, *Fremontia californica* and *Lapageria rosea*.

Half-standard

A tree or shrub, usually with a single stem of 2½–4 ft before the head of branches.

Hardening off

The gradual acclimatisation of tender and half-hardy plants, grown under heated glass, to outside conditions. This is usually effected by placing the plants in a cold frame or greenhouse in late spring and gradually admitting more air until the lights of the frame are left off entirely.

Hardy

Referring to plants which survive frost in the open year by year, anywhere in Great Britain.

Haulm

The unproductive aerial part of a vegetable-crop plant, such as the leafy stems of potatoes and those of peas after harvesting the pods.

Haw

The fruits of crataegus species, in particular the native hawthorns, *C. oxyacanthoides* and *C. monogyna*.

Heel

The expanded base of old wood or stem on a side-shoot that is pulled or cut away from the main stem of a plant when preparing a heel cutting. Some cuttings root more readily when they have a heel attached. See chapter on PROPAGATION.

Hep: see HIP

Herbaceous

Any plant that does not form a persistent woody stem. Botanically, the term applies to annuals, biennials and perennials, but by common usage is chiefly associated with perennials which die down in autumn and reappear the following spring.

Heterophyllous

Applied to a plant that bears leaves of different shapes, such as the juvenile and adult leaves of various eucalyptus species and the spiny and spineless leaves of holly.

Hip or hep

The fleshy fruit of a rose.

Hoary

Usually applied to leaves or stems densely covered with white or pale grey, short hairs.

Hose-in-hose

An abnormal floral mutation in which the flowers appear to grow in pairs, one arising from the centre of the other. Primrose and polyanthus provide examples of hose-in-hose flowers.

Humus

The dark brown residue resulting from the final breakdown of dead vegetable matter. The term often describes partly decayed matter that is sweet-smelling, brown and crumbly, such as well-made compost or leaf-mould.

Hybrid

A plant derived from crossing any two distinct varieties, sub-species, species or, occasionally, genera. Such plants may either show a blending of characteristics from each parent or favour one more than the other.

Imbricate

Closely overlapping; usually referring to scale, bract or leaf arrangements. Good examples are the leafy shoots of *Araucaria araucana* (monkey puzzle), the rosettes of sempervivum (houseleek) and the tightly overlapping scales on winter buds of horse chestnut.

Incised

Referring to the margins of a leaf, stipule or bract that is deeply and sharply toothed or lobed.

Incurved

A term commonly applied to a particular type of chrysanthemum flower, the petals or florets of which curl inwards creating a ball-like bloom.

Inflorescence

That part of a plant which bears flowers. Inflorescences are classified, according to the floral arrangement, as spikes (lavender), racemes (hyacinth), panicles (gypsophila) or umbels (allium). See also CORYMB and CYME.

Inorganic

A chemical compound or fertiliser that does not contain carbon.

Insecticide

A substance used for killing injurious insects. A wide variety of chemicals are available, in liquid or powder form. They should always be used in accordance with the manufacturers' instructions.

Insectivorous

Applied to a carnivorous plant that traps insects, e.g. pinguicula (butterwort) and sarracenia (pitcher plant). Such plants often grow on poor soils; through the breakdown of the insect body, the plants absorb the necessary minerals and, in particular, the essential nitrogen.

Intercrop

A quick-maturing vegetable crop, e.g. radishes, grown between rows of slower-growing crops.

Internode

The length of stem between nodes (joints) or leaves.

Involucre

A ring of bracts, often closely overlapping, that is found beneath certain forms of inflorescences. Good examples are the basal sheathing leaves of a daisy or scabious flower, or the leaf-like bracts of astrantia and eranthis.

Joint: see NODE

Juvenile

Applied to plants which have a distinct early phase, when either the habit, leaf shape or some other character differs from those of adult specimens. Eucalyptus commonly bears juvenile and adult leaves; hedera (common ivy) produces juvenile climbing stems and palmate leaves as well as adult non-climbing stems with ovate or lanceolate leaves, and flowers.

Keel

The two lower petals of such leguminous plants as garden pea and lupin. The petals are pressed together laterally, creating the shape of a boat keel.

Labellum

The lip-like structure or lower petal of an orchid flower.

Laciniate

Fringed; used to describe leaves, bracts, stipules or petals with margins cut into numerous narrow segments.

Lanceolate

Shaped like the head of a lance. Applied to a narrow leaf, broadest at the base, tapering to a point and at least three times longer than it is broad.

Larva

The immature stage of certain insect families, such as butterflies, moths, sawflies and beetles. Larvae do not resemble the adults and are commonly known as caterpillars or grubs.

Lateral

A stem or shoot that branches off from a bud in the leaf axil of a larger stem.

Leaching

The removal of soluble minerals from the soil by water draining through.

Leader

The main stem (or stems) of a tree or shrub that extends the existing branch system.

Leaf-mould, leaf-soil

The partially decayed dead leaves which have broken down to a brown, flaky condition resembling peat. Oak and beech leaves are the most suitable materials, but all deciduous leaves can be turned into leaf-mould by composting methods. Like peat, leaf-mould is an important soil conditioner and maintains fertility. It may also be used instead of, or with, peat as a potting ingredient.

Lignotuber

The swollen base of a woody plant, as found on certain eucalyptus species. If top growth is killed, the base usually produces sucker shoots.

Lime

An important chemical (calcium) in horticulture. It may be used to neutralise acid soils. Some plants fail to grow satisfactorily in a soil containing excess amounts of lime as certain essential plant foods are rendered insoluble.

Linear

Referring to a narrow leaf, bract or petal, with parallel sides. It is at least 12 times as long as it is wide.

Loam

A reasonably fertile soil that is neither wet and sticky nor dry and sandy. It is moisture-retentive and contains a blend of clay, silt, sand and humus, rich in minerals.

Lobe

Applied to leaves, stipules, bracts or petals that are cleft into separate areas. They are still united to each other by part of the leaf surface, e.g. *Geranium endressii*.

INDIVIDUAL LEAF SHAPES

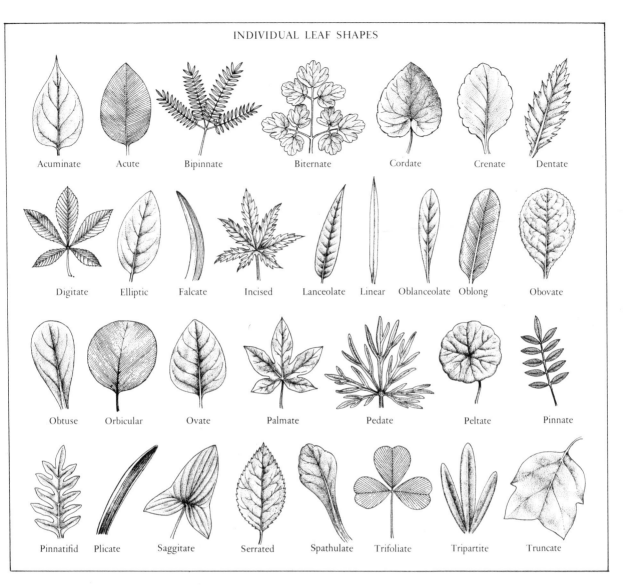

Acuminate Acute Bipinnate Biternate Cordate Crenate Dentate

Digitate Elliptic Falcate Incised Lanceolate Linear Oblanceolate Oblong Obovate

Obtuse Orbicular Ovate Palmate Pedate Peltate Pinnate

Pinnatifid Plicate Saggitate Serrated Spathulate Trifoliate Tripartite Truncate

BASIC ARRANGEMENTS OF INDIVIDUAL LEAVES

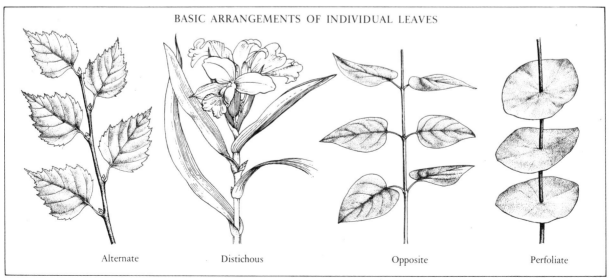

Alternate Distichous Opposite Perfoliate

Maiden

A nursery term for a young grafted tree still in the process of being trained. Particularly applied to one-year-old fruit trees.

Manures and fertilisers

Organic and inorganic substances added to the soil to increase its fertility. The former are derived from animal matter (excrement, bones, blood and hair) or dead plant remains. Inorganic manures are of mineral origin, either from natural sources or manufactured.

Bulky organic substances of animal origin (often mixed with straw, as in farmyard manure) are always known as manures. Bulky plant remains are known as compost. Both substances should be dug into the soil so that further bacterial action can break them down into humus and release plant foods. They may also be applied in a layer to the soil surface (see MULCH).

Inorganic substances and concentrated organic ones such as dried blood and bone-meal are known as fertilisers. These are best applied to the soil surface and raked in, so that their concentrated soluble fraction can be washed down by the rain. Water-soluble fertilisers, mainly of mineral or manufactured origin, are commercially available in concentrated dry or liquid form, as liquid feeds. They are relatively more expensive, but quicker acting than the dry or bulky manures and fertilisers and are mainly intended for short-term crops under glass, especially for plants grown in pots.

Dilute solutions of liquid feed may also be sprayed on to the foliage, where it is assimilated immediately and takes effect more rapidly than via the roots. Only recommended compounds sold as foliar feed should be used and applied strictly to the makers' instructions. These feeds greatly stimulate root action.

Green manuring is a term applied to the practice of digging or ploughing into the soil a crop of vigorous leafy plants sown for that purpose. The overall effect is equivalent to digging in compost or manure, but the soil cannot be used while the cover crop is growing and, ideally, for several months after it has been dug in. Plants used for green manuring include clover, mustard, rape and rye grass.

Manures and particularly fertilisers supply plants with essential nutrients, the main one being nitrogen, which promotes the growth of leaves and stems. Potash is essential for the production of plant tissues and the quality and colour in flowers and fruits. Phosphorus is a constituent of protoplasm and essential for the movement of food in the plant. A number of other minerals are needed for healthy growth, but only in small or minute quantities and are usually present in average, fertile garden soils. The most important ones are added to mixed or general fertilisers available commercially.

Marginal

A plant which requires a perpetually moist or wet soil and grows best at the edge of a pool.

Mentum

The chin-like projection at the base of the COLUMN in an orchid flower.

Microspecies

A group of plants so closely resembling each other that they are placed under one species heading. *Rubus fruticosus* (blackberry) is considered by some authorities to consist of several hundred microspecies.

Midrib

The large central vein of a leaf.

Mimicry

Referring to plants which resemble inanimate objects or each other. Certain succulent plants, such as lithops, resemble pebbles. Some orchids have insect-like flowers to induce pollen to be transferred by insect vectors.

Monocarpic

A term applied to a plant which dies after flowering and seeding. Annuals and biennials are true monocarpic plants, but the term is also applied to perennial plants which grow for a number of years before flowering profusely and then dying. *Saxifraga longifolia*, *Cardiocrinum giganteum* and *Agave americana* are examples of such perennials.

Monocotyledon

A group of flowering plants, typified by having only one seed leaf in each mature seed. See also COTYLEDON and DICOTYLEDON.

Monoecious

Applied to a plant that bears separate male and female flowers on the same plant, e.g. corylus (hazel nut) and juglans (walnut). See also DIOECIOUS.

Monotypic

A genus represented by one species only, such as *Morisia* and *Rhoeo*.

Moraine

The rocky or gravelly detritus terminating and bordering a glacier. Moraine beds may be created in a garden for growing high-altitude alpines, but unless an underground water supply in summer can be maintained, a SCREE bed is more suitable.

Moth

The mature stage of a caterpillar. Moths in themselves do not harm plants, but damage can be severe through the eggs which hatch into leaf-feeding caterpillars.

Mulch

A layer of organic matter, such as decayed manure, leaf-mould, compost, peat, straw or sawdust, spread on the soil surface around plants. A mulch conserves moisture, adds nutrients, suppresses weeds and protects fruits, such as strawberries, from mud splashing.

Mutant

An aberrant plant or part of a plant that arises spontaneously. The most common forms of mutants are variegated shoots or flowers of a different colour. These are popularly known as sports, or chimaeras. Mutant shoots may be propagated by cuttings and are the origin of many new varieties.

Naturalising

The growing of plants, particularly bulbs, in simulated natural environments, such as grass or in woodland conditions.

Nectar

A sweet liquid secreted by glands (or nectaries). These are usually found in flowers, but may also occur on stems and leaves. Floral nectar attracts insects that aid pollination.

Neutral

Applied to a soil that is neither acid nor alkaline, and with a pH content between 6·5 and 7.

Node

A stem joint, in some cases slightly swollen, from where leaves, buds and side-shoots arise.

Nymph

The immature stage of certain insect families, such as capsid bugs, leafhoppers and aphids. Nymphs resemble the adults but lack wings and sometimes mature colouring. See LARVA.

Oblanceolate

Reverse lance-shaped. Applied to a narrow leaf that is broadest towards the tip. See LANCEOLATE.

Oblong

Referring to a leaf, stipule or bract with parallel sides; it is three times longer than wide.

Oblong-orbiculate

Basically an oblong leaf, almost as long as it is wide and appearing almost round.

Oblong-ovate

Applied to an oblong leaf with sides that curve in at either end.

Obovate

Of an egg-shaped leaf having its broadest part at the tip.

Obtuse

Of a leaf or petal that is blunt or rounded.

Offset

A young plant that arises naturally, as on many sorts of bulbs, or on short lateral stems as in sempervivum (houseleek). Such plants are easily separated from the parents and form a ready means of propagation.

Opposite

The arrangement of leaves in alternate opposite pairs, as on ligustrum and syringa.

Orbicular

Applied to leaves or petals that are disc-shaped or almost so.

Organic

Applied to substances derived from the decay of living organisms, e.g. compost.

Ovate

Referring to leaves, stipules, bracts or petals that have an egg-shaped outline, broadest at the base.

Ovate-acuminate

An ovate leaf or petal terminating in a long slender point.

Ovate-cordate

Applied to an ovate leaf with a heart-shaped base.

Ovoid

Egg-shaped, usually applied to fruits or bulbs.

Oxygenator

A submerged aquatic plant, such as *Ranunculus aquatilis*, that releases oxygen to the water in a pool or artificial pond.

Palmate

Hand-shaped; basically a rounded leaf with deep triangular to finger-like lobes.

Pan

1. A layer of hard soil that sometimes forms as a result of frequent shallow mechanical cultivation to the same depth. 2. A layer of ironstone that forms at varying depths in certain types of sandy soil. It usually requires breaking up before cultivation can proceed. Panned, or panning, also refers to the surface of fine soil that has been beaten hard by heavy rain or watering. 3. A shallow clay or plastic pot used for raising seedlings or growing alpines.

Panicle

A large branched flower cluster, each with numerous individually stalked flowers.

Parasite

A plant which lives upon another, taking part or all of its nourishment from the host and not capable of an independent existence. *Viscum album* (mistletoe) is a partial parasite on several varieties of trees, taking water and minerals only from the hosts.

Peat

Organic matter, of relatively low mineral content, in an arrested state of partial decay, usually due to lack of oxygen under water-logged conditions. Common or moss peat is largely derived from sphagnum moss, and sedge peat from the roots of sedges and allied plants. They form in bogs and fens respectively. When worked into ordinary soil, peat breaks down, supplying humus and conditioning poor soils.

Peat wall

A raised bed or low terrace formed of peat blocks or bales filled with a peaty soil mixture. Such beds are ideal for gaultheria, cassiope, rhododendron and vaccinium, that require an acid spongy soil.

Pedate

Like a bird's foot; of a leaf form, similar to hand-shaped, but more deeply cleft.

Pedicel

The stalk of an individual flower; particularly applied to branched flower arrangements.

Peduncle

The stem that supports a flower arrangement.

Peltate

Usually disc-shaped leaf where the leaf stem is attached at the centre, e.g. *Tropaeolum majus*.

Perennial

Any plant that lives for an indefinite period. Usually applied to a non-woody plant.

Perfoliate

Applied to two opposite leaves that fuse together around the stem, as in the juvenile phase of certain eucalyptus species.

Perianth

A general term for sepals and petals, used when these organs are indistinguishable from each other. The combined sepals and petals of a tulip or hyacinth flower are known as perianths.

Petal

A modified leaf, usually coloured, which forms part of a flower. Petals protect and surround stamens and pistils and, when coloured, attract pollinating insects. Sometimes the petals are fused together; they are then known as the COROLLA.

Petaloid

Referring to floral organs that take on the form of petals. They are usually stamens, as in double paeonies and poppies, but may also be sepals, as in anemones, or even ovaries, e.g. *Ranunculus acris* 'Flore-pleno'.

Petiole

The stalk that attaches a leaf to the stem.

pH

The pH scale is a means of measuring the acid-alkaline balance of a soil. The neutral point on the pH scale is 7; a reading below this denotes an increase in soil acidity, above this an increase in alkalinity. A fairly simple colour soil-testing kit can be obtained from chemists and horticultural sundriesmen. By mixing an indicator liquid with a given volume of soil a clear-coloured liquid results on settling. This liquid is then compared with the chart marked into pH calibrations. Red (below pH 4·5) denotes very acid soil, green is neutral (6·5–7) and blue is alkaline (above 7·0).

Phylloclade

A short modified shoot having the shape and function of a leaf.

Phyllode : see CLADODE

Picotee

Referring to petals with a narrow marginal zone of contrasting colour. The term is particularly applied to a certain type of carnation.

Pinching out : see STOPPING

Pinna

The individual lobe or leaflet of a deeply divided leaf.

Pinnate

Applied to a leaf that is divided into several pairs of oppositely arranged leaflets. Fraxinus (ash) has pinnate leaves.

Pinnatifid

Similar to PINNATE, but the leaf is cut into lobes, not leaflets.

Pinnule

One of the individual leaflets of a BIPINNATE leaf.

Pistil

The complete female organ of a flower, comprising an ovary, stigma and style. The style may be short or sometimes non-existent.

Pistillate

Referring to flowers with female organs only.

Plicata

Applied to the flowers of bearded iris which are basically white or yellow, with a marginal stippled or feathered pattern of a contrasting colour.

Plicate

Folded back; referring to a leaf or petal with folded margins, such as the leaves of *Galanthus plicatus*.

Plumose

A description applied to a feathery, branched flower arrangement.

Plunge

To set a pot or any other plant container up to the rim in the soil or in a special bed of ashes, peat or sand. A practice mainly applied to pot-grown nursery plants to prevent them drying out rapidly and to protect the root systems of cuttings and plantlets against fluctuating temperatures while becoming established.

Pollard

A tree cut back hard to the main trunk and maintained in a bushy state by regular pruning at intervals of one to a few years.

Pollen

The male cells of a plant. They are contained in the anthers or pollen sacs.

Pollination

The transference of pollen grains on to the stigma of a flower. This may be effected naturally by gravity, wind or insects, or artificially by hand. See also FERTILISATION.

Pollinia

Pollen grains adhering together in a compact mass, and not contained in sacs. Unique to many orchid flowers.

Potting

Potting-up is the act of placing a plant and soil into the container in which it is to be grown temporarily or permanently. Potting-on is carried out when a plant gets too big for its container and further growth is required. The plant is knocked out of its pot and placed *en bloc* into a larger container and filled around with fresh compost. Re-potting is necessary to maintain the health of a plant kept in the same size container for several years. From time to time —usually no more than annually —a plant should be knocked out of its pot and the ball of soil and roots reduced enough to get it back into the same size container with sufficient room for fresh soil to be added.

Pricking off (out)

The first planting out of seedlings or small rooted cuttings. The resulting plantlets are later moved into larger pans or boxes, or set out into a nursery bed.

Procumbent

Prostrate; referring to plants with spreading, ground-hugging stems.

Propagation

The increase of plants, either by seed or vegetative means. See chapter on PROPAGATION.

Pruning

The controlled cutting back of a plant, particularly those with woody stems. It is carried out to restrict size, train to shape or to promote the formation of flower and/or fruit buds. See chapter on PRUNING.

Pseudobulb

A false bulb; the term is particular to orchids, where one or several joints of a stem become swollen with storage tissue and in some cases resemble a bulb.

Pubescent

Covered with short soft hairs.

Pupa

The transition phase between the larval and adult state of some insect groups. Pupae of moths and butterflies are legless and differ in appearance from larvae and adults. In moths, butterflies and beetles they are sometimes referred to as chrysalids.

Pyramid

A term applied to a trained tree or bush with a pyramidal outline, e.g. apples and pears. Also used of plant with a naturally conic habit.

Raceme

An unbranched flower arrangement. The individual flowers are stalked and spirally arranged, e.g. hyacinth.

Radical

Usually applied to the basal leaves of biennials or perennials. The leaves arise at, or near, soil level.

Recurved

Referring to leaves, branchlets or petals that curve back or arch.

Reflexed

Chiefly used of petals and leaves that are sharply bent or curved back on themselves.

Remontant

Flowering at intervals throughout the growing season, as in some roses.

Resting period

That period when a plant is either dormant or making little or no extension growth.

Reticulate

The fine branching network of veins clearly visible on a leaf or petal surface. Also used of the fine network of fibres surrounding some iris and crocus corms.

Rhizome

A horizontal creeping underground stem, which acts as a storage organ.

Rib

One of the main prominent veins of a leaf. Also applied to a ridge on stem or fruit.

Rogue

A term used for any atypical plant. Rogues may occur in a batch of seedlings or as mutants (sports) of a variety.

Root run

The approximate soil area occupied by the roots of a plant.

Rootstock

A propagation term for a plant upon which another is grafted. Flowering cherries are grafted on *Prunus avium* seedlings, and culinary apples are grafted on to stocks of known certain vigour to produce trees of a particular size. The term also applies to the crown and root system of herbaceous perennials and suckering shrubs.

Runner

A type of aerial stem which, on contact with moist soil, roots at the tip and forms a new plant. Blackberry and strawberry plants frequently root where they touch the soil.

Sagittate

Arrow-shaped. Applied to a lance-shaped leaf with two lobes projecting backwards.

Saprophyte

A plant which gains much, or all, of its nourishment from decayed organic matter. The bird's nest orchid is leafless, with yellow-brown stems, bracts and flowers.

Scale leaf

A non-foliage leaf which may be small and rudimentary, as on the subterranean stems of mint rhizomes. They may also be modified to perform special functions, as the protective winter bud scales of deciduous woody plants, or act as storage organs in lily bulbs.

Scandent

Ascending or loosely climbing, often by pushing long flexible stems up through other plants.

Scape

A leafless flowering stem; particularly used of bulbous plants such as scilla and bluebell, where all the leaves are basal.

Scion

A shoot or part of a shoot (bud) of one plant joined to a ROOTSTOCK of another. Scions and rootstocks are the means of propagating fruit trees by grafting, and roses by budding.

Scree

A heap or a slope of rocky detritus eroded from mountain-sides or cliffs. Various types of plants require similar conditions in the garden. A scree bed can be created by mixing coarse gravel or stone chippings with peat and soil.

Seedling

A young plant after germination, with a single unbranched stem. The term also applies to an older plant raised from seeds rather than by vegetative propagation.

Self-coloured

Applied to a flower of a single uniform colour.

Self-fertile

Applied to a plant, particularly a fruit tree, that does not need a pollinator to set fruits and seeds.

Self-sterile

Applied to fruit trees, particularly sweet cherries, that require a pollinator to produce fruits.

Sepal

One of the outermost whorl of modified leaves which compose a flower. It is usually green and protects the petals and sex organs. Sometimes sepals drop off when the flower expands, as in escholzia and papaver; in some cases they replace or function as petals, as in anemone and helleborus. When fused together, as in primrose, sepals are known as the CALYX.

Serrated

Like the teeth of a saw. Referring to the sharply cut indentations in the margin of a leaf.

Sessile

Stalkless; of a leaf or flower that arises straight from the stem.

Shrub

A branched perennial with persistent woody stems.

Single

Applied to a flower with the normal number of petals.

Spadix

Basically a fleshy flower spike with small flowers embedded in shallow pits. It is primarily found in the *Araceae* family, for example anthurium and zantedeschia, where it is surrounded and protected by a white or coloured bract. In some cases, the spadix terminates in a naked club or spindle-shaped organ which may heat up and give off a foetid smell that attracts pollinating insects.

Spathe

A modified leaf or large bract, sometimes coloured, which surrounds the flower spike of members of the *Araceae* family.

Spathulate

Spoon-shaped; applied to a leaf, bract or petal with a tapered base and an expanded tip.

Species

A unit of classification applied to an individual, or a group of closely allied plants, within a GENUS. Species have unique characters, which consistently breed true to type from seeds. The type species refers to the original plant collected and described.

Specimen plant

Any plant, but usually a tree or shrub, grown where it can be viewed from all angles.

Sphagnum (moss)

The generic name for bog mosses. They have unique water-holding, aerating and cleansing properties and are frequently used as a growing medium for orchids. In the partially decomposed state, sphagnum moss forms the main ingredient of moss peat.

Spike

An unbranched flower arrangement, the individual flowers are stalkless and spirally arranged.

Spine

A sharp, pointed, woody structure, derived from a modified branchlet, a stipule, leaf stalk or leaves, or from a flower stalk.

Spit

The depth to which soil is dug with a spade or fork, approximately 10–12 in.

Spore

A minute dust-like body composed of a single cell, by which lower plants, such as ferns, fungi and mosses, reproduce themselves. A spore gives rise to an intermediate generation upon which the sex organs are produced and these eventually produce plantlets.

Sport: see MUTANT

Spur

1. A short lateral branchlet of a tree (particularly on fruits such as apple and pear) which bears flower buds. 2. A tubular outgrowth of a sepal or petal that produces nectar.

Staking

The supporting of plants with stakes or canes. Usually required for top-heavy annuals or perennials. Some young trees and shrubs require staking during the early years, to prevent wind-rocking, until established.

Stamen

The complete male reproductive organ of a flower, comprising the filament, and two anther lobes which contain pollen grains.

Staminode

A non-functional, rudimentary male reproductive organ, sometimes similar to a narrow petal.

Standard

1. The upper petal of a pea flower and other members of the *Leguminosae* family. 2. One of the three erect petals of an iris flower. 3. A tree with a clear expanse of bare trunk before the head of branches.

Stellate

1. Starlike; usually applied to the flat, branched hairs found on leaves and stems of plants in the *Cruciferae* and related families. 2. A term sometimes used to describe a star-shaped flower.

Sterile

Applied to plants which seldom or never set seeds. Many double-flowered varieties are sterile, as the reproductive organs have become petals.

Stigma

The tip of the female reproductive organ. It secretes a sticky fluid when ready for pollination.

Stipule

One of the pair of leaf-like outgrowths at the base of a leaf stalk, e.g. in rose and potentilla.

Stolon

A prostrate creeping stem, rooting at the nodes, and giving rise to further stems or plantlets.

Stool

Usually applied to a tree or shrub maintained as a clump of young stems by annual pruning close to ground level. Stooling is carried out to provide young growths for propagation purposes; or maintain foliage effect, such as the juvenile stage of some eucalyptus, or the coloured winter stems of *Salix alba* 'Chermesina' and *Cornus alba* 'Siberica'. The term is also applied to crowns of herbaceous plants, for example chrysanthemum, which are lifted annually and used for propagation.

Stopping

The removal or pinching out of the growing point of a stem, to promote a branching habit and to induce formation of flower buds.

Strain

A particular selection of an existing variety or species that is always raised from seeds.

Strap-shaped

Loosely applied to a narrow leaf at least three times as long as it is wide, and with parallel sides.

Stratification

A method of breaking the dormancy of seeds borne in fleshy

fruits of many hardy plants. The seeds are exposed to a period of low temperature prior to sowing. The seeds are gathered as soon as fully ripe, bruised to assist the rotting of the flesh, and mixed or layered with sand, peat or friable soil in pots or boxes. The containers should be placed in a cold frame or plunged outside in a sheltered spot, and kept moist.

Strobilus
The flowers of a conifer, e.g. a pine, cedar and fir. Strobili consist of catkin-like male flower spikes. The females resemble mature cones in miniature.

Style
The stalk linking the ovary and stigma of a female flower. It may be curved or straight, long and slender, thick and short.

Sub-alpine
A plant native to mountain regions just below the alpine zone.

Sub-shrubby
Usually applied to a low-growing, soft-stemmed shrub with a woody base.

Succulent
Any plant with thick fleshy leaves or stems adapted to life under arid conditions. Cacti, with leafless stems swollen with water-storage tissue, are examples.

Sucker
A shoot which arises from below ground level, usually from the roots of a plant.

Synonym
An alternative plant name. Sometimes a plant has been named by more than one botanist or has been reclassified in the light of further knowledge. In such cases, the oldest, or most taxonomically accurate, name takes priority.

Tap root
The main anchoring root of a plant, particularly applied to trees.

Taxonomy
The botanical study of the CLASSIFICATION of plants.

Tender
Applied to any plant liable to frost damage.

Tendril
A modified stem or leaf that twines around supports and enables certain plants, such as sweet pea, grape and passion flower, to climb.

Tepal
The individual segment of a PERIANTH that cannot be clearly differentiated into a sepal or petal. Tulip is the best example.

Terete
A smooth stem, rounded in cross-section.

Terminal
Topmost; referring to the upper shoots, branches or flowers.

Ternate
In groups of three. Trillium has leaves and floral organs in groups of threes; and laburnum leaves have three leaflets.

Terrestrial
Growing in the soil. Applied to plants such as some bromeliads and orchids that are primarily EPIPHYTIC, but have become adapted to living in the soil.

Tessellated
Usually of petals with a distinct checkered pattern of a contrasting shade or colour.

Tetraploid
Applied to a plant with cells containing twice the normal number of CHROMOSOMES.

Tilth
The fine crumbly surface layer to the soil.

Tomentose
Densely covered with fine hairs.

Top dressing
The application of a layer of soil or compost, usually to plants in pots or in a confined space. An inch or two of the old soil is removed and replaced with fresh material. See also MULCH.

Transpiration
The continual water loss from leaf and stem surfaces. It varies greatly with the time of day and year.

Transplanting
Moving young plants from one place to another to allow them more room to develop.

Tree
A woody-stemmed plant with a clear trunk or bole before the head of branches.

Trench
A deeply dug strip of soil, often 2–3 ft deep. It is recommended for the cultivation of sweet peas, runner beans and other deep-rooting annual crops.

Trifoliate
Applied to a leaf that is divided into three leaflets.

Tripartite
Referring to leaves, sepals, petals or bracts cut into three lobes.

Triploid
A plant with three of the normal sets of CHROMOSOMES. Triploids usually arise from crosses between plants with the normal sets of chromosomes and those with twice the number; they are often sterile or partially so.

Truncate
Applied to leaves and other plant organs which end abruptly as though chopped off.

Trunk
The main stem of a tree from ground level to the first branch.

Truss
A popular term applied to a cluster of flowers or fruits.

Tuber
A thickened fleshy root (dahlia) or an underground stem (potato) which serves as a storage organ and as a means of surviving periods of cold or drought.

Tubercle
A wart-like swelling or pimple, particularly characteristic of cacti. They are usually crowned by woolly or barbed hairs, and spines. See AREOLE.

Tunic
Usually referring to the membranous or fibrous outer covering of some bulbs and corms, e.g. crocus and gladiolus.

Turk's-cap
Used to describe a flower that resembles an ancient Turk's cap, e.g. *Lilium martagon*. The petals are reflexed back so strongly as to form a full circle.

Umbel
A form of flower arrangement in which all the individual flower stalks arise from the same point. A compound umbel is an umbel of umbels.

Underplant
To surround and interplant larger plants with smaller ones. See also GROUND COVER.

Undulate
Referring to leaf, sepal or petal margins that are waved or crimped.

Unisexual
A flower of one sex only. See DIOECIOUS and MONOECIOUS.

Variegated
Applied to leaves (and sometimes petals) that are marked, spotted or otherwise decoratively patterned with a contrasting colour.

Vegetative
Relating to propagation by cuttings, division, layers or grafting, as distinct from propagation by seeds.

Ventilation
The creation of air movement by opening the ventilators of greenhouses and frame lights whenever the temperature exceeds that required for plant growth.

Viviparous
Producing plantlets without seeds, e.g. *Asplenium bulbiferum*, *Tolmiea menziesii* and *Lilium tigrinum*. These produce bulbils or small plants either on the leaves or the stems.

Weed
Basically, any plant growing spontaneously where it is not wanted. Usually the term is restricted to non-ornamental species of great vigour which swamp cultivated plants, unless they are removed.

Weeping
Applied to a tree or shrub of pendulous habit, either natural, as in some species of salix, or artificially induced as in weeping standard roses.

Whorl
Applied to the arrangement of leaves or flowers arising from one point like the spokes of a wheel.

Wild garden
An informal style of planting which endeavours to simulate nature. It is generally an area of open woodland, underplanted with flowering shrubs, bulbous, herbaceous and ground-cover plants. Provided adequate initial preparation is carried out and the right plants selected, this form of gardening requires the minimum of maintenance.

Xerophytic
Of a plant adapted to survive long dry periods, either by the formation of water-storage tissue as in leaf and stem SUCCULENTS, or by leaf and/or stem reduction (heathers, gorse, certain epiphytes and grasses).

PAPER, PRINTING AND BINDING BY
Butler & Tanner Ltd., Frome; Jarrold & Sons Ltd., Norwich; Schwitters Ltd., Zurich; Koninklijke Nederlandsche
Papierfabriek NV, Maastricht; C. Tinling & Co. Ltd., Prescot; Van Heek-Scholco Textielfabrieken NV, Almelo